EAGLE VALLEY LIBRARY DISTRICT
1 06 0003857691

The ENCYCLOPEDIA *of* CHRISTIANITY

Volume 4
P–Sh

The
of

Volume 4

editors

translator and English-language editor

statistical editor

William B. Eerdmans Publishing Company
Brill

ENCYCLOPEDIA CHRISTIANITY

P–Sh

Erwin Fahlbusch
Jan Milič Lochman†
John Mbiti
Jaroslav Pelikan
Lukas Vischer

Geoffrey W. Bromiley

David B. Barrett

Grand Rapids, Michigan / Cambridge, U.K.
Leiden / Boston

Originally published in German as
Evangelisches Kirchenlexikon, Dritte Auflage (Neufassung)

Published jointly 2005 by
Wm. B. Eerdmans Publishing Company
255 Jefferson Ave. S.E., Grand Rapids, Michigan 49503
www.eerdmans.com
and by
Koninklijke Brill NV
Leiden, the Netherlands
www.brill.nl

Printed in the United States of America

11 10 09 08 07 06 05 10 9 8 7 6 5 4 3 2 1

Library of Congress Cataloging-in-Publication Data

Evangelisches Kirchenlexikon. English.
The encyclopedia of Christianity / editors, Erwin Fahlbusch . . . [et al.]; translator and English-language editor, Geoffrey W. Bromiley; statistical editor, David B. Barrett; foreword, Jaroslav Pelikan.
p. cm.
Includes index.
Contents: v. 4. P–Sh.
ISBN-10: 0-8028-2416-1 (cloth: v. 4: alk. paper)
ISBN-13: 978-0-8028-2416-5
1. Christianity — Encyclopedias. I. Fahlbusch, Erwin.
II. Bromiley, Geoffrey William. III. Title.
BR95.E8913 2005
230′.003 — dc21 98-45953
CIP

Brill ISBN 90 04 14595 8

Contents

List of Entries

This list does not include headings that simply refer the reader to a cross-reference.

Introduction

This introduction provides a brief guide to the editorial conventions followed throughout the *Encyclopedia of Christianity,* as well as to the statistical information specially prepared for the *EC* by David Barrett.

ALPHABETIZATION

Articles are arranged alphabetically word by word (not letter by letter), with hyphens and apostrophes counted as continuing the single word; all commas are ignored. For example:

Antiochian Theology
Anti-Semitism, Anti-Judaism
. . .
Augsburg Confession
Augsburg, Peace of
. . .
Calvin, John
Calvinism
Calvin's Theology
. . .
Church Year
Churches of Christ

STATISTICS

The *EC* includes separate articles for each of the six major areas (formerly "continents") currently recognized by the United Nations (i.e., Africa, Asia, Europe, Latin America and the Caribbean, Northern America, and Oceania). It also presents separate articles for all independent countries of the world, omitting only those whose population, according to U.N. estimates for 1995, is less than 200,000 (e.g., Andorra, Nauru).

Accompanying each country article is a standard statistical box with the following format:

Argentina

	1960	*1980*	*2000*
Population (1,000s):	20,616	28,094	37,032
Annual growth rate (%):	1.55	1.51	1.19

Area: 2,780,400 sq. km. (1,073,518 sq. mi.)

A.D. *2000*

Population density: 13/sq. km. (34/sq. mi.)
Births / deaths: 1.90 / 0.78 per 100 population
Fertility rate: 2.44 per woman
Infant mortality rate: 20 per 1,000 live births
Life expectancy: 74.2 years (m: 70.6, f: 77.7)
Religious affiliation (%): Christians 92.9 (Roman Catholics 90.2, Protestants 5.9, indigenous 5.4, marginal 1.4, unaffiliated 1.1, other Christians 0.6), nonreligious 2.2, Muslims 2.0, Jews 1.5, other 1.4.

The demographic information in these boxes is taken from the *World Population Prospects: The 1996 Revision* (New York [United Nations], 1998). Depending on the presentation in U.N. tables, figures for 1960, 1980, and 2000 are either for that year alone or for a five-year period beginning with that year. In each case where the United Nations provides three estimates, the medium variant estimates are cited. Information on country area is taken from the *1996 Britannica Book of the Year* (Chicago, 1996). For countries like Argentina, where the birth rate minus the death rate (1.12 per 100 population) does not equal the annual growth rate (1.19), the difference is due to migration — in this case, *into* the country.

David Barrett, editor of the *World Christian Encyclopedia* (2d ed.; 2 vols.; New York, 2001) and senior researcher at the Center for the Study of Global Christianity, Gordon-Conwell Theological Seminary, South Hamilton, Massachusetts, has provided all the information on religious affiliation in the statistical boxes. In the first place, the boxes present the breakdown of overall religious affiliation for each country, using the following sixteen categories:

atheists — persons professing atheism, skepticism, or disbelief, including antireligious (opposed to all religion)

Baha'is — followers of the Baha'i World Faith, founded in the 19th century by Bahā' Allāh
Buddhists — followers of any of the branches of Buddhism; worldwide, 56 percent are Mahayana (northern), 38 percent Theravada (Hinayana, or southern), 6 percent Tantrayana (Lamaism)
Chinese folk religionists — followers of the traditional Chinese religion, which includes local deities, ancestor veneration, Confucian ethics, Taoism, divination, and some Buddhist elements
Christians — followers of Jesus Christ, either affiliated with churches or simply identifying themselves as such in censuses or polls
Confucianists — non-Chinese followers of Confucius and Confucianism, mostly Koreans in Korea
Hindus — followers of the main Hindu traditions; worldwide, 70 percent are Vaishnavas, 25 percent Saivas, 3 percent Saktas, 2 percent neo-Hindus and reform Hindus
Jews — adherents of Judaism
Muslims — followers of Islam; worldwide, 83 percent are Sunnites, 16 percent Shiites, 1 percent other schools
new religionists — followers of Asian 20th-century new religions, new religious movements, radical new crisis religions, and non-Christian syncretistic mass religions, all founded since 1800 and most since 1945
nonreligious — persons professing no religion, nonbelievers, agnostics, freethinkers, dereligionized secularists indifferent to all religion
Shintoists — Japanese who profess Shinto as their first or major religion
Sikhs — followers of the Sikh reform movement arising out of Hinduism
spiritists — non-Christian spiritists, spiritualists, thaumaturgists, medium-religionists
Taoists — followers of the religion developed from the Taoist philosophy and from folk religion and Buddhism
tribal religionists — primal or primitive religionists, animists, spirit-worshipers, shamanists, ancestor-venerators, polytheists, pantheists, traditionalists, local or tribal folk-religionists

The country boxes list each religious group that numbers at least 1.0 percent of the population of that county; any groups that number 0.9 percent or less of the population are grouped together under "other." Because of rounding, the totals of all the religious groups in a country may not equal 100.0 percent.

Second, for the category "Christians," the information in the boxes shows in parentheses the breakdown by ecclesiastical bloc, using the following seven categories:

Anglicans — persons in a church that is in fellowship with the archbishop of Canterbury, especially through its participation in the Lambeth Conference; Episcopalians
indigenous — Christians in denominations, churches, or movements who regard themselves as outside of mainline Anglican/Orthodox/Protestant/Roman Catholic Christianity; autonomous bodies independent of foreign origin or control (e.g., Independent Charismatic Churches [Braz.], house church movement [China], isolated radio believers [Saudi Arabia], Zion Christian Church [S.Af.], Vineyard Christian Fellowship [U.S.])
marginal — followers of para-Christian or quasi-Christian Western movements or deviations out of mainline Protestantism, not professing Christian doctrine according to the classic Trinitarian creeds (i.e., Apostles', Nicene) but often claiming a second or supplementary or ongoing source of divine revelation in addition to the Bible (e.g., Christian Scientists, Jehovah's Witnesses, Mormons, Unitarians)
Orthodox — Eastern (Chalcedonian), Oriental (Pre-Chalcedonian, Non-Chalcedonian, Monophysite), Nestorian (Assyrian), and nonhistorical Orthodox
Protestants — persons in churches that trace their origin or formulation to the 16th-century Reformation and thus typically emphasize justification by faith alone and the Bible as the supreme authority, including (1) churches in the Lutheran, Calvinistic, and Zwinglian traditions; and (2) other groups arising before, during, or after the Reformation (e.g., Waldenses, Bohemian Brethren, Baptists, Friends, Congregationalists, Methodists, Adventists, Pentecostals, Assemblies of God)
Roman Catholics — persons in a church that recognizes the pope, the bishop of Rome (with the associated hierarchy), as its spiritual head
unaffiliated — professing Christians not associated with any church

As with the different religions, so for the different types of Christians, any group that numbers at least 1.0 percent of the population of the country is listed. Any groups of Christians that number 0.9 percent or less of the population are included together under "other Christians." Because of rounding, the totals of all the individual Christian groups may not equal the total percentage of

Christians. Furthermore, where persons affiliate themselves with, or are claimed by, two Christian groups at once, the total of the percentages of the individual Christian groups in a country may exceed the countrywide percentage of Christians. This problem of double counting (evident, for example, in the Argentina box on p. x) is left unresolved in the *EC*.

Accompanying each major area article are three tables that list most of the information appearing in the individual country statistical boxes. The first table displays demographic information; the second, data on overall religious affiliation; the third, data on church affiliation. The religion tables list separately the 12 most popular religions worldwide (i.e., the above list of 16 minus Baha'is, Confucianists, Shintoists, and Taoists), with all the others accounted for under "Other." In the tables showing ecclesiastical breakdown, all Christians are counted in one of the seven categories (or, in cases of double counting, in more than one category). The tables of religion and of Christianity report country by country all adherents of a religious position or Christian grouping that total at least 0.1 percent of the population. In addition, all tables present totals for the major area as a whole, as well as for each region that U.N. statistics distinguish within the major area. (The tables accompanying "Africa," for example, show totals for the whole continent; for the regions of eastern, middle, northern, southern, and western Africa; and also for each country that has a separate article in the *EC*.) Finally, for purposes of comparison, relevant figures for the whole world appear as the top row of each major area table.

CROSS-REFERENCES

A variety of cross-references aid the reader in locating articles or specific sections of articles. One type appears as a main title, either (1) making clear where a subject is treated or (2) indicating the exact article title. For example:

(1) **Aid** → Christian Development Services; Development 1.4

Anathema → Confessions and Creeds

(2) **Ancient Church** → Early Church

Ancient Oriental Churches → Oriental Orthodox Churches

Other cross-references appear within the text of articles. Those referring to other sections of the present article have the form "(see 1)," "(see 3.2)."

Cross-references to other articles cited as such appear (3) within parentheses in the text, following a cross-reference arrow and using the exact spelling and capitalization of the article title, and (4) on a separate line after the text proper and before the bibliography. In both cases, multiple cross-references are separated by semicolons, and only a single, initial arrow is used. Items cross-referenced within the text of an article normally do not also appear following the text of the article.

(3) In the latter part of the 20th century some churches in the United States and Europe have tried to revive the right of church asylum for some refugees whom the government refused to recognize as political refugees (→ Sanctuary 3; Resistance, Right of, 2).

As such, dance rejects an antibiblical dualism (→ Anthropology 2.3 and 3.2; Soul).

The Roman Catholic Church reacted negatively, placing Beccaria's book on the Index (→ Censorship; Inquisition 2). Then in the 19th century F. D. E. Schleiermacher (1768-1834; → Schleiermacher's Theology) criticized theologically the theory of retribution.

(4) → Anglican Communion 4; Clergy and Laity; Consensus 4; Councils of the Church

→ Catholicism (Roman); Church 3.2; Lay Movements

→ Communities, Spiritual; Ethics 2; Monasticism 3.2.2; Property, esp. 3.2-3

Finally (5), cross-references also appear within the flow of the text, with an arrow appearing before a word or phrase that points clearly (but not necessarily exactly) to the title of another article. Specific sections referred to are indicated by section marks and numbers in parentheses. Normally (6), the exact name of an article is used if a specific section is cited.

(5) The extension of the problem to political matters makes it necessary to define the relations between the obedience of → faith (§3), → freedom (§2), and → reason.

In the controversy with the → Pelagians Augustine's main concern was to show that grace is not limited to external aids like the →

law (§§3.1-2) or the teaching and example of Christ.

Jewish → proselyte baptism incorporates the baptized not only into the religious fellowship but also into God's → covenant → people. This matter is relevant in the dialogue between Israel and the → church (§§1.4.1.3, 2.1, 5.5.3).

(6) ... the 19th-century → apocalyptic movement in the United States.

vs. ... the 19th-century apocalyptic movement (→ Apocalypticism 3) in the United States.

BIBLIOGRAPHIES

Within a bibliography (or separate section of a bibliography), entries are ordered first by author, then by title (disregarding an initial article in any language). Successive articles by the same author(s) are separated by semicolons.

In individual bibliographic entries, the names of series are included only if the title is omitted (typically only for biblical commentaries). For works appearing both in a non-English language and in English translation, normally only the English title is cited.

Consulting Editors

ULRICH BECKER *Education*
EUGENE L. BRAND *Liturgy; Worship*
FAITH E. BURGESS *Women's Studies/Issues*
CARSTEN COLPE *Religious Studies*
HANS-WERNER GENSICHEN† *Asia; Mission Studies*
MARTIN GRESCHAT *Biographies; Church History*
HEIMO HOFMEISTER *Philosophy*
HUBERTUS G. HUBBELING† *Philosophy*
ANASTASIOS KALLIS *Orthodoxy*
LEO LAEYENDECKER *Sociology*
EKKEHARD MÜHLENBERG *Church History*
HANS-JÜRGEN PRIEN *Latin America*
DIETRICH RITSCHL *Systematic Theology; Ethics*
JÜRGEN ROLOFF† *New Testament*
JOACHIM SCHARFENBERG† *Practical Theology; Psychology*
TRAUGOTT SCHÖFTHALER *Sociology*
RUDOLF SMEND *Old Testament*
ALBERT STEIN† *Law; Church Law*

Contributors

PAUL J. ACHTEMEIER, *Richmond, Va.*
Peter, Epistles of, 1

ROGER ALLEN, *Philadelphia*
Qur'ān

JOHN E. ALSUP, *Austin, Tex.*
Resurrection 1

URS ALTERMATT, *Fribourg, Switz.*
Popular Catholicism

PETER ANTES, *Hannover, Ger.*
Religion 1; Revelation 1

JAMES BARR, *Claremont, Calif.*
Scriptural Proof

HANS-MARTIN BARTH, *Marburg, Ger.*
Prayer 2-3

JOHN BARTON, *Oxford*
Prophet, Prophecy, 2

JOHN P. BEAL, *Washington, D.C.*
Pastoral Letters; Polity, Ecclesiastical, 2; Purgatory

ULRICH BECKER, *Hannover, Ger.*
School and Church

RONALD G. BECKMAN, *Westminster, Colo.*
Persons with Disabilities

HANS-KARL BECKMANN†, *Erlangen, Ger.*
Pedagogy

WOLFGANG BEINERT, *Regensburg, Ger.*
Relics; Rosary; Saints, Veneration of

GAETANO BENEDETTI, *Basel, Switz.*
Psychosis

REINHOLD BERNHARDT, *Basel, Switz.*
Providence; Regeneration; Reincarnation; Religion 2

OLOPH BEXELL, *Uppsala, Swed.*
Religious Orders and Congregations 4

WOLFGANG A. BIENERT, *Marburg, Ger.*
Patristics, Patrology
KARL-HEINRICH BIERITZ, *Rostock, Ger.*
Play; Rite 2
KLAUSPETER BLASER†, *Lausanne, Switz.*
Salvation 6-7
WERNER K. BLESSING, *Erlangen, Ger.*
Restoration
PETER BLICKLE, *Bern, Switz.*
Peasants' War
NILS E. BLOCH-HOELL†, *Oslo, Norw.*
Scandinavian Missions
OTTO BÖCHER, *Mainz, Ger.*
Prophet, Prophecy, 3
ALBERTO BONDOLFI, *Lausanne, Switz.*
Punishment 2
ROBERT BORNEMANN, *Philadelphia*
Palestine
MARTIN BRECHT, *Münster, Ger.*
Pietism
MICHAEL W. BRIERLEY, *Oxford*
Panentheism
CHARLES W. BROCKWELL JR., *Louisville, Ky.*
Sect
GEOFFREY W. BROMILEY, *Santa Barbara, Calif.*
Preaching 5; Promise and Fulfillment 5; Psychology 5; Religion, Legal Protection of; Rule of Faith 2
OLIVER BROWN, *Nescopeck, Pa.*
Prison Ministry
ROBERT F. BROWN, *Newark, Del.*
Philosophy 1-4; Philosophy of Nature; Positivism; Rationalism; Realism; Reason
AUGUST BUCK, *Marburg, Ger.*
Renaissance
CHRISTOPH BURCHARD, *Heidelberg, Ger.*
Sermon on the Mount
J. R. BURKHOLDER, *Goshen, Ind.*
Pacifism; Peace Movements
FREDERICK BURWICK, *Claremont, Calif.*
Romanticism
HUBERT CANCIK, *Tübingen, Ger.*
Roman Religion
JAMES H. CHARLESWORTH, *Princeton*
Pseudepigrapha
JEAN-MARIE CHARPENTIER, *Arles, Fr.*
Pluralism 2
JAMES M. CHILDS JR., *Columbus, Ohio*
Sexual Ethics 5
DAN-ILIE CIOBOTEA, *Celigny, Switz.*
Salvation 3
ALLAN HUGH COLE JR., *Austin, Tex.*
Pastoral Theology

CARSTEN COLPE, *Berlin*
Phenomenology of Religion; Polytheism; Quaternity; Religious Studies; Rite 1; Sacrifice 1
FRANK J. COPPA, *Brooklyn, N.Y.*
Pius IX; Pius XII
RICHARD CROSS, *Oxford*
Scotism
J. G. DAVIES†, *Birmingham, Eng.*
Pulpit; Religious Drama
RUSSELL H. DAVIS, *Charlottesville, Va.*
Pastoral Care of the Sick; Psychiatry; Psychoanalysis; Psychosis; Psychotherapy
KATHY L. DAWSON, *Decatur, Ga.*
Pastoral Care of Children
RALSTON DEFFENBAUGH, *Baltimore*
Refugees
GEORG DENZLER, *Bamberg, Ger.*
Papal States
FERDINAND DEXINGER†, *Vienna*
Samaritans
JÖRG DIERKEN, *Hamburg*
Rationalism
WALTER DIETRICH, *Bern, Switz.*
Righteousness, Justice, 1
BERND T. DRÖSSLER, *Erfurt, Ger.*
Scholium
MARGARITA DURÁN ESTRAGÓ, *Asunción, Para.*
Paraguay
DONALD F. DURNBAUGH, *Huntingdon, Pa.*
Philadelphian Society
HELGA EINSELE†, *Frankfurt*
Rehabilitation 1
UWE ENGFER, *Darmstadt, Ger.*
Service Society
CHRISTOPHER H. EVANS, *Rochester, N.Y.*
Rauschenbusch, Walter
TONY S. EVERETT, *Columbia, S.C.*
Pastoral Psychology
GEORG EVERS, *Aachen, Ger.*
Popular Religion 2
ERWIN FAHLBUSCH, *Montouliers, Fr.*
Piety; Polemics; Representation; Sacramentals; Salvation 0
D. WILLIAM FAUPEL, *Washington, D.C.*
Palmer, Phoebe Worrall
JOHN FIFE, *Tucson, Ariz.*
Sanctuary 3
BALTHASAR FISCHER†, *Trier, Ger.*
Sacred Heart of Jesus
MARTIN FORWARD, *Aurora, Ill.*
Paganism
HANS-JÜRGEN FRAAS, *Munich*
Religion, Personal Sense of

CHRISTOFER FREY, *Bochum, Ger.*
Probabilism; Quietism
MICHAELA VON FREYHOLD, *Bremen, Ger.*
Racism 1
ULRICH GÄBLER, *Basel, Switz.*
Revivals
ERICH GARHAMMER, *Würzburg, Ger.*
Priest, Priesthood, 3
KARL HEINZ GASSNER, *Cologne*
Salvation Army
ERICH GELDBACH, *Bochum, Ger.*
Plymouth Brethren
HANS-WERNER GENSICHEN†, *Heidelberg, Ger.*
Schweitzer, Albert
PETER GERLITZ, *Bremerhaven, Ger.*
Paradise; Priest, Priesthood, 1
JENNIFER N. GORHAM, *Wheaton, Ill.*
Sex Education
ANDREAS GRAESER, *Bern, Switz.*
Platonism
DAVID B. GREENE, *Raleigh, N.C.*
Pragmatism
LEONARD J. GREENSPOON, *Omaha, Nebr.*
Septuagint
CHRISTIAN GREMMELS, *Kassel, Ger.*
Religionless Christianity
HANS-JÜRGEN GRESCHAT, *Marburg, Ger.*
Rastafarians; Shamanism
DAVID RAY GRIFFIN, *Isla Vista, Calif.*
Process Philosophy; Process Theology
HEINER GROTE†, *Bensheim, Ger.*
Peter's Pence; Pontificals; Prelature, Personal; Promotor fidei; Secular Institutes
NICHOLAS W. GROVES, *Norwich, Eng.*
Paraments
JOACHIM GUHRT, *Bad Bentheim, Ger.*
Reformed Alliance; Reformed and Presbyterian Churches
T. JEREMY GUNN, *Reston, Va.*
Religious Liberty (Modern Period)
ROGER GUSTAVSSON, *Greencastle, Ind.*
Philosophy of Religion
KLAUS GUTH, *Bamberg, Ger.*
Pilgrimage
PETER HAENGER, *Basel, Switz.*
Senegal
FERDINAND HAHN, *Munich*
Sacrifice 3
HERBERT HANREICH, *Heidelberg, Ger.*
Pantheism; Relativism
ROBERT D. HAWKINS, *Columbia, S.C.*
Passion Music
ERIK M. HEEN, *Philadelphia*
Q
HERIBERT HEINEMANN, *Bochum, Ger.*
Pope, Papacy, 1.7
ANDREAS HEINZ, *Trier, Ger.*
Processions
LOTHAR HEISER, *Münster, Ger.*
Panagia
KLAUS HERBERS, *Erlangen, Ger.*
Santiago Cult
NORMAN A. HJELM, *Wynnewood, Pa.*
Pastor
JEANNE HOEFT, *Kansas City, Mo.*
Self
PAUL HOFFMANN, *Bamberg, Ger.*
Q
KARL HOLL, *Bremen, Ger.*
Pacifism
WALTER J. HOLLENWEGER, *Krattigen, Switz.*
Pentecostalism
HEINRICH HOLZE, *Rostock, Ger.*
Pelagianism
RICHARD L. VAN HOUTEN, *Grand Rapids*
Reformed Ecumenical Council
WOLFGANG HUBER, *Berlin*
Power 2
HANS HÜBNER, *Göttingen, Ger.*
Romans, Epistle to the
ARLAND J. HULTGREN, *St. Paul, Minn.*
Parable; Pastoral Epistles
ELIZABETH HUWILER, *Philadelphia*
Ruth, Book of
RAHEL JAEGGI, *Berlin*
Revolution
URS JAEGGI, *Berlin*
Revolution
WALTER JAESCHKE, *Berlin*
Secularism
BERND JANOWSKI, *Tübingen, Ger.*
Sacrifice 2
PAUL JENKINS, *Basel, Switz.*
Senegal
FRIEDRICH JOHANNSEN, *Hannover, Ger.*
Punishment 3
JACKIE DAVID JOHNS, *Cleveland, Tenn.*
Pentecostal Churches
STANTON L. JONES, *Wheaton, Ill.*
Sex Education
FRANK OTFRIED JULY, *Schwäbisch Hall, Ger.*
Philosophia perennis
ERIC JUNOD, *Lausanne, Switz.*
Protevangelium
OTTO KAISER, *Marburg, Ger.*
Proverbs, Book of
ANASTASIOS KALLIS, *Münster, Ger.*
Philocalia

Friedrich Wilhelm Kantzenbach, *Saarbrücken, Ger.*
Persecution of Christians 1-3
Roslyn A. Karaban, *Rochester, N.Y.*
Pastoral Care of the Dying
Martin Karrer, *Wuppertal, Ger.*
Parousia; Peter; Peter, Epistles of; Philemon, Epistle to; Philippians, Epistle to the; Revelation, Book of
Karol Karski, *Warsaw*
Poland
Arthur Kaufmann, *Munich*
Resistance, Right of, 1
Siegfried Keil, *Marburg, Ger.*
Sexual Ethics 1-4
Arthur L. Kennedy, *Washington, D.C.*
Roman Catholic Church
Thomas S. Kidd, *Waco, Tex.*
Puritans 3
Michael Kinnamon, *Webster Groves, Mo.*
Peace
Hans G. Kippenberg, *Bremen, Ger.*
Sacred and Profane 1
Hubert Kirchner, *Berlin*
Pope, Papacy, 1.6
Herbert Koch†, *Hannover, Ger.*
Prison Ministry
Robert Kolb, *St. Louis, Mo.*
Predestination
Karl König, *Göttingen, Ger.*
Psychotherapy
Martin Koschorke, *St. Blaise-la-Roche, Fr.*
Partnership
William Kostlevy, *Pasadena, Calif.*
Perfection
Thomas Koszinowski, *Pinneberg, Ger.*
Qatar
Manoj Kurian, *Geneva*
Public Health
Leo Laeyendecker, *Bunnik, Neth.*
Progress; Secularization 2
Stephen E. Lammers, *Easton, Pa.*
Reproduction Technology
Gary Land, *Berrien Springs, Mich.*
Sabbatarians
Peter Landau, *Munich*
Proprietary Church
Claus Leggewie, *Giessen, Ger.*
Populism
Falk Leichsenring, *Göttingen, Ger.*
Psychotherapy
José Manuel Leite, *Geneva*
Portugal
Reinhard Leuze, *Munich*
Pope, Papacy, 2
Wolfgang Lienemann, *Bern, Switz.*
Peace 2; Resistance, Right of, 2
Fairy von Lilienfeld, *Erlangen, Ger.*
Persecution of Christians 4.1
Carter Lindberg, *Northboro, Mass.*
Pietism
Günter Linnenbrink, *Hannover, Ger.*
Poverty 4-5
Wolfgang Lipp, *Würzburg, Ger.*
Power 1
Paul Löffler, *Lauenburg, Ger.*
Proselytism
Eduard Lohse, *Göttingen, Ger.*
Passover
Edward LeRoy Long Jr., *Wicomico, Va.*
Polity, Ecclesiastical, 1
Heather Looy, *Edmonton, Alta.*
Sexuality
David W. Lotz, *Naples, Fla., and New York*
Reformation
Gerd Lüdemann, *Göttingen, Ger.*
Primitive Christian Community
Ulrich Luz, *Bern, Switz.*
Righteousness, Justice, 2
Garry D. McClure, *Tucson, Ariz.*
Panama
Timothy A. McElwee, *North Manchester, Ind.*
Peace Education; Peace Research
Bruce D. Marshall, *Dallas*
Philosophy and Theology; Scholasticism
Paul Marshall, *Washington, D.C.*
Persecution of Christians 4.3
Robin Dale Mattison, *Philadelphia*
Passion, Accounts of the; Seafarers' Mission
Bernhard Maurer, *Freiburg, Ger.*
Reverence
John D'Arcy May, *Dublin, Ire.*
Papua New Guinea
Melanie A. May, *Rochester, N.Y.*
Prostitution; Sexism
Bartomeu Melià, *Asunción, Para.*
Reductions
Norbert Mette, *Münster, Ger.*
Practical Theology 3
John Meyendorff†, *Crestwood, N.Y.*
Palamism
Harding Meyer, *Kehl-Marlen, Ger.*
Reception, Ecumenical
Gregory Miller, *Canton, Ohio*
Reformers
Gerald F. Moede, *Waupaca, Wis.*
Pluralism 3

CONTRIBUTORS

JÁNOS MOLNÁR, *Cluj-Napoca, Rom.*
Romania
LEWIS S. MUDGE, *Berkeley, Calif.*
Pluralism
KARL-HEINZ ZUR MÜHLEN, *Meckenheim, Ger.*
Penitence 1
MICHAEL MUSTER, *Heidelberg, Ger.*
Patronage, Ecclesiastical
HERTA NAGL-DOCEKAL, *Vienna*
Philosophy 5; Philosophy of History
WOLF-DIETER NARR, *Berlin*
Pluralism 1
GERHARD WILHELM NEBE, *Heidelberg, Ger.*
Qumran
E. W. NICHOLSON, *Oxford*
Pentateuchal Research
FRIEDRICH NIEWÖHNER, *Wolfenbüttel, Ger.*
Philo-Semitism
KARL ERNST NIPKOW, *Tübingen, Ger.*
Religious Educational Theory 1
EDWARD NOORT, *Hamburg*
Philistines
BERND OBERDORFER, *Augsburg, Ger.*
Schleiermacher, Friedrich Daniel Ernst
MANFRED OEMING, *Heidelberg, Ger.*
Promise and Fulfillment 1-4
RUDOLFINE FREIIN VON OER, *Legden, Ger.*
Secularization 1
ERHARD OESER, *Vienna*
Philosophy of Science
RICHARD R. OSMER, *Princeton*
Practical Theology 2
RAINER OSSWALD, *Bayreuth, Ger.*
Saudi Arabia
KLAUS OTTE, *Frankfurt*
Sacred and Profane 2
GERT OTTO†, *Mainz, Ger.*
Preaching 1-4; Rhetoric 2
ALAN G. PADGETT, *St. Paul, Minn.*
Philosophy of Science; Science and Theology
DAMASKINOS PAPANDREOU, *Geneva*
Pan-Orthodox Conferences
PETER PARIS, *Princeton*
Racism 3
STEPHEN J. PATTERSON, *St. Louis, Mo.*
Parallels and Harmonies, Gospel
HENNING PAULSEN†, *Hamburg*
Parenesis
ALBRECHT PETERS†, *Ziegelhausen, Ger.*
Sanctification 3
CRAIG A. PHILLIPS, *Arlington, Va.*
Postmodernism
JOACHIM G. PIEPKE, *St. Augustin, Ger.*
People of God
HANS-CHRISTOPH PIPER†, *Hannover, Ger.*
Pastoral Care of the Sick 1
N. BARNEY PITYANA, *Pretoria, S.Af.*
Racism 2
PETER PLANK, *Würzburg, Ger.*
Patriarch, Patriarchate; Pentarchy
DIMITRY V. POSPIELOVSKY, *London, Ont.*
Russia; Russian Orthodox Church
HANS-JÜRGEN PRIEN, *Lübeck, Ger.*
Persecution of Christians 4.2; Peru
BRUNO PRIMETSHOFER, *Vienna*
Religious Foundation
MICHAEL PYE, *Marburg, Ger.*
Shinto
KONRAD RAISER, *Geneva*
Protestantism
GERALD D. W. RANDALL, *Norfolk, Eng.*
Paraments
ELIZABETH RAPLEY, *Ottawa, Ont.*
Religious Orders and Congregations 1
WALTER REBELL, *St-Blaise, Switz.*
Psychology 1-4
JOHN REES, *London*
Polity, Ecclesiastical, 3
JOHN D. REMPEL, *Elkhart, Ind.*
Peace Churches
JOHN REUMANN, *Philadelphia*
Righteousness, Justice, 1, 2; Salvation History
CYNTHIA L. RIGBY, *Austin, Tex.*
Resurrection 2
GERHARD RINGSHAUSEN, *Lüneberg, Ger.*
Salvation 5, 8
RONALD G. ROBERSON, C.S.P., *Washington, D.C.*
Religious Orders and Congregations 2
ROBERT B. ROBINSON, *Philadelphia*
Patriarchal Narrative; Primeval History (Genesis 1–11)
ANTJE ROGGENKAMP-KAUFMANN, *Göttingen, Ger.*
Pascal, Blaise
JAN ROHLS, *Munich*
Predestination
JÜRGEN ROLOFF†, *Erlangen, Ger.*
Paul; Pentecost; Salvation 1; Scribes
DIETRICH RÖSSLER, *Tübingen, Ger.*
Practical Theology 1
ENNO RUDOLPH, *Heidelberg, Ger.*
Philosophy of Nature
KURT RUDOLPH, *Marburg, Ger.*
Prayer 1; Sanctuary 1
HANS-JÜRGEN RUPPERT, *Bad Wildbad, Ger.*
Rosicrucians
EBERHARD RUPRECHT, *Seesen, Ger.*
Servant of the Lord

WILLIAM G. RUSCH, *New York*
Reception, Ecumenical
FAUSTIN RWAGACUZI†, *Butare, Rwanda*
Rwanda
ADELE MARIE RYAN, S.S.M., *Boston*
Religious Orders and Congregations 3
BJÖRN RYMAN, *Uppsala, Swed.*
Relief and Development Organizations; Scandinavian Missions
RISTO SAARINEN, *Helsinki, Fin.*
Porvoo Common Statement
ABDULAZIZ SACHEDINA, *Charlottesville, Va.*
Shia, Shiites
DOROTHEA SATTLER, *Münster, Ger.*
Sacrament
GERHARD SAUTER, *Bonn*
Reconciliation
BERNDT SCHALLER, *Göttingen, Ger.*
Pharisees; Sabbath; Sadducees
WOLFGANG SCHIEDER, *Cologne*
Popular Religion 1
JOHANNES SCHILLING, *Kiel, Ger.*
Pope, Papacy, 1.1–1.5
ANNEMARIE SCHIMMEL†, *Bonn*
Pakistan
MARGARETE SCHLÜTER, *Frankfurt*
Rabbi, Rabbinism
HANS SCHNEIDER, *Marburg, Ger.*
Reform Councils; Separatism
THADDEUS A. SCHNITKER, *Lingen, Ger.*
Psalms, Book of, 2; Serpent
GÜNTHER SCHNURR, *Heidelberg, Ger.*
Penitence 2
HEINZ SCHÖCH, *Munich*
Punishment 1
WALTER SCHÖPSDAU, *Bensheim, Ger.*
Penitence 3
WERNER SCHWARTZ, *Speyer, Ger.*
Responsibility
JOHANNES SCHWERDTFEGER, *Heidelberg, Ger.*
Peace 1
REINHOLD SEBOTT, *Frankfurt*
Pastoral Letters; Precepts of the Church
FRANK C. SENN, *Evanston, Ill.*
Requiem
KLAUS SEYBOLD, *Basel, Switz.*
Psalms, Book of, 1
LEONORE SIEGELE-WENSCHKEWITZ†, *Schmitten, Ger.*
Priest, Priesthood, 4
CHRISTIAN SIGRIST, *Münster, Ger.*
Pariahs
WERNER SIMON, *Mainz, Ger.*
Religious Educational Theory 2
T. VALENTINO SITOY JR., *Dumaguete City, Philip.*
Philippines
BALDWIN C. SJOLLEMA, *Geneva*
Program to Combat Racism
JAMES W. SKILLEN, *Annapolis, Md.*
Political Parties
NOTGER SLENCZKA, *Mainz, Ger.*
Reformation Principles; Sacramentality
T. RICHARD SNYDER, *Lincolnville, Maine*
Rehabilitation 2
RENATE SÖHNEN-THIEME, *Tübingen, Ger.*
Purana; Ramayana; Rig-Veda
WALTER SPARN, *Erlangen, Ger.*
Physicotheology
HERMANN SPIECKERMANN, *Göttingen, Ger.*
Semites
HANS SPITZECK, *St. Augustin, Ger.*
Poverty 1-3
MAX L. STACKHOUSE, *Princeton*
Political Theology; Politics; Public Theology
ALBERT STEIN†, *Brühl, Ger.*
Primate; Residence, Duty of; Seal of the Confessional
JÜRGEN STEIN, *Bremen, Ger.*
Paradox
PETER STEINACKER, *Darmstadt, Ger.*
Religion, Criticism of, 2
THOMAS STEININGER, *Darmstadt, Ger.*
Prejudice
HEINZ-GÜNTHER STOBBE, *Münster, Ger.*
Power 3
MARTIN STÖHR, *Bad Vilbel, Ger.*
Salvation 2
FRITZ STOLZ†, *Männedorf, Switz.*
Priest, Priesthood, 2; Prophet, Prophecy, 1; Sanctification 1; Sanctuary 2
HOWARD W. STONE, *Fort Worth, Tex.*
Pastoral Care
BERNHARD STRECK, *Leipzig*
Roma
GEORG STRECKER†, *Göttingen, Ger.*
Sanctification 2
THEODOR STROHM, *Heidelberg, Ger.*
Religious Socialism; Righteousness, Justice, 3
GERLINDE STROHMAIER-WIEDERANDERS, *Berlin*
Rome; Sacristy
MAX JOSEF SUDA, *Vienna*
Religion, Criticism of, 1
STEPHEN W. SYKES, *Durham, Eng.*
Proclamation; Revelation 2
LORINE TEVI, *Suva, Fiji*
Pacific Conference of Churches
WERNER THIEDE, *Neuhausen, Ger.*
Parapsychology

CONTRIBUTORS

Mark G. Toulouse, *Fort Worth, Tex.*
Restoration Movements

Sabine Udodesku, *Geneva*
Racism 2

Hans G. Ulrich, *Erlangen, Ger.*
Property

David A. Van Baak, *Grand Rapids*
Quantum Theory; Relativity Theory

Timo Veijola, *Helsinki, Fin.*
Samuel, Books of; Saul

Helmuth Vetter, *Vienna*
Phenomenology

Dankward Vollmer, *Sangerhausen, Ger.*
Roman Empire

Herbert Vorgrimler, *Altenberge, Ger.*
Rahner, Karl

Falk Wagner†, *Vienna*
Reason

Harald Wagner, *Recklinghausen, Ger.*
Salvation 4

Fritz Wallner, *Theresienfeld, Aus.*
Positivism

W. Reginald Ward, *Petersfield, Eng.*
Puritans 1-2

Duane F. Watson, *Canton, Ohio*
Rhetoric 1

Louis B. Weeks, *Richmond, Va.*
Reformed Tradition

Klaus Wegenast, *Bremgarten, Switz.*
Religious Instruction

Fritz West, *Marine on St. Croix, Minn.*
Readings, Scripture

Karl-Friedrich Wiggermann, *Münster, Ger.*
Prayer 4

Robert Wilken, *Washington, D.C.*
Patristics, Patrology

Jörg Winter, *Karlsruhe, Ger.*
Prelate

John Witte Jr., *Atlanta*
Religious Liberty (Foundations); Rights

David M. Wulff, *Providence, R.I.*
Psychology of Religion

Léon Wurmser, *Towson, Md.*
Shame

Walter E. Wyman Jr., *Walla Walla, Wash.*
Schleiermacher's Theology

Dietmar Wyrwa, *Bochum, Ger.*
Rule of Faith 1

Aron Zysow, *Cambridge, Mass.*
Shariʿa

Abbreviations

Abbreviations generally follow those given in the *Journal of Biblical Literature* "Instructions for Contributors." For those not listed there, the abbreviations in the second edition of S. M. Schwertner's *Internationales Abkürzungsverzeichnis für Theologie und Grenzgebiete* (Berlin, 1992) are used; for works of theology or related fields not listed in either source, new abbreviations have been formed.

Writings listed below under the section "Early Church Writings" include those of writers through Augustine.

BIBLICAL BOOKS, WITH THE APOCRYPHA

Gen.	Genesis
Exod.	Exodus
Lev.	Leviticus
Num.	Numbers
Deut.	Deuteronomy
Josh.	Joshua
Judg.	Judges
Ruth	Ruth
1-2 Sam.	1-2 Samuel
1-2 Kgs.	1-2 Kings
1-2-3-4 Kgdms.	1-2-3-4 Kingdoms
1-2 Chr.	1-2 Chronicles
Ezra	Ezra
Neh.	Nehemiah
Esth.	Esther
Job	Job
Ps.	Psalms
Prov.	Proverbs
Eccl.	Ecclesiastes
Cant.	Canticles / Song of Solomon / Song of Songs
Isa.	Isaiah
Jer.	Jeremiah
Lam.	Lamentations
Ezek.	Ezekiel
Dan.	Daniel
Hos.	Hosea
Joel	Joel
Amos	Amos
Obad.	Obadiah
Jonah	Jonah
Mic.	Micah
Nah.	Nahum
Hab.	Habakkuk
Zeph.	Zephaniah
Hag.	Haggai
Zech.	Zechariah
Mal.	Malachi
Add. Est.	Additions to Esther
Bar.	Baruch
Bel	Bel and the Dragon
1-2 Esdr.	1-2 Esdras
4 Ezra	4 Ezra
Jdt.	Judith
Ep. Jer.	Epistle of Jeremiah
1-2-3-4 Macc.	1-2-3-4 Maccabees
Pr. Azar.	Prayer of Azariah
Pr. Man.	Prayer of Manasseh
Sir.	Sirach / Ecclesiasticus / Wisdom of Jesus, Son of Sirach
Sus.	Susanna
Tob.	Tobit
Wis.	Wisdom of Solomon
Matt.	Matthew
Mark	Mark
Luke	Luke
John	John
Acts	Acts of the Apostles
Rom.	Romans
1-2 Cor.	1-2 Corinthians
Gal.	Galatians
Eph.	Ephesians
Phil.	Philippians
Col.	Colossians
1-2 Thess.	1-2 Thessalonians
1-2 Tim.	1-2 Timothy
Titus	Titus
Phlm.	Philemon

ABBREVIATIONS

Heb.	Hebrews	1-2-3 John	1-2-3 John
Jas.	James	Jude	Jude
1-2 Pet.	1-2 Peter	Rev.	Revelation

OLD TESTAMENT PSEUDEPIGRAPHA

2-3 Apoc. Bar.	Syriac, Greek *Apocalypse of Baruch*	*Jub.*	*Jubilees*
1-2-3 Enoch	Ethiopic, Slavonic, Hebrew *Enoch*	*T. Jud.*	*Testament of Judah*
		T. Lev.	*Testament of Levi*

EARLY CHURCH WRITINGS, WITH NAG HAMMADI TRACTATES

Act. Vercell.	*Actus Vercellenses*
Acts Phil.	*Acts of Philip*
Acts Thom.	*Acts of Thomas*
Apoc. Pet.	*Apocalypse of Peter*
Apos. Const.	*Apostolic Constitutions*
Athanasius	
Contra Arian.	*Apologia contra Arianas*
De incar.	*De incarnatione Dei Verbi*
Augustine	
Conf.	*Confessions*
De cat. rud.	*De catechizandis rudibus*
De civ. Dei	*De civitate Dei*
De cons. Evang.	*De consensu Evangelistarum*
De nat. et grat.	*De natura et gratia*
In Evang. Iohan.	*In Evangelium Iohannis Tractatus*
Barn.	*Barnabas*
1-2 Clem.	*1-2 Clement*
Clem. Hom.	*Clementine Homilies*
Clem. Recog.	*Clementine Recognitions*
Clement of Alexandria	
Strom.	*Stromateis*
Cyprian of Carthage	
Ad Quir.	*Ad Quirinum*
De eccl.	*De ecclesiae catholicae unitate*
Cyril of Jerusalem	
Cat.	*Catecheses*
Did.	*Didache*
Diogn.	*Diognetus*
Epiphanius	
De mens. et pond.	*De mensuribus et ponderibus*
Pan.	*Panarion*
Eusebius	
Ep. Carp.	*Epistula ad Carpianum*
Hist. eccl.	*Historia ecclesiastica*
Gos. Pet.	*Gospel of Peter*
Gos. Thom.	*Gospel of Thomas*
Herm. Man.	*Hermas, Mandate(s)*
Herm. Sim.	*Hermas, Similitude(s)*
Herm. Vis.	*Hermas, Vision(s)*
Hilary of Poitiers	
Coll. antiar.	*Collectanea antiariana parisina*
Hippolytus	
Comm. in Dan.	*Commentarium in Danielem*
De antichr.	*De antichristo*
Ign. [Ignatius]	
Eph.	*Letter to the Ephesians*
Magn.	*Letter to the Magnesians*
Phld.	*Letter to the Philadelphians*
Rom.	*Letter to the Romans*
Smyrn.	*Letter to the Smyrnaeans*
Trall.	*Letter to the Trallians*
Irenaeus	
Adv. haer.	*Adversus omnes haereses*
Jerome	
Contra Vigil.	*Contra Vigilantium*
De vir. ill.	*De viris illustribus*
Justin Martyr	
1-2 Apol.	*1-2 Apologia*
Dial.	*Dialogue with Trypho*
Mart. Pol.	*Martyrdom of Polycarp*
Origen	
C. Cels.	*Contra Celsum*
De orat.	*De oratione*
Pol. [Polycarp]	
Phil.	*Letter to the Philippians*
Ps.–Justin Martyr	
Coh. ad Graec.	*Cohortatio ad Graecos*
Tatian	
Orat.	*Oratio ad Graecos*
Tertullian	
Ad nat.	*Ad nationes*
Adv. Marc.	*Adversus Marcionem*
De paen.	*De paenitentia*
De praescr. haeret.	*De praescriptione haereticorum*
De pud.	*De pudicitia*
De spec.	*De spectaculis*

DEAD SEA SCROLLS AND RELATED TEXTS

(For listing of numbered texts, see the series *Discoveries in the Judaean Desert.*)

CD	Cairo (Genizah text of the) *Damascus (Document)*
1QapGen	*Genesis Apocryphon*
1QH	*Hôdāyōt (Thanksgiving Hymns)*
1QIsa	*Isaiah*
1QM	*Milḥāmāh (War Scroll)*
1QpHab	*Pesher on Habakkuk*
1QS	*Serek hayyaḥad (Rule of the Community, Manual of Discipline)*
1QSb	Appendix B *(Blessings)* to 1QS
3Q15	*Copper Scroll*
4QBeat	*Beatitudes*
4QFlor	*Florilegium* (or *Eschatological Midrashim*)
4QMMT	*Miqṣat Maʿaseh Torah*
4QSam[a, b, c]	First, second, or third copy of Samuel
4QTestim	*Testimonia* text
4QVisAmram[c]	Third copy of *Visions of Amram*
11QapocrPs	*Apocryphal Psalms*
11QPs[a]	First copy of Psalms

CLASSICAL TARGUMS AND RABBINIC WRITINGS

b.	Babylonian Talmud
m.	Mishnah
t.	Tosefta
y.	Jerusalem Talmud
B. Meṣ	*Baba Meṣiʿa*
Ber.	*Berakot*
Beṣa	*Beṣa (= Yom Ṭob)*
Gen. Rab.	*Genesis Rabbah*
Meg.	*Megilla*
Mek.	*Mekilta*
Midr. Gen. Rab.	*Midrash of Genesis Rabbah*
Midr. Ps.	*Midrash of Psalms*
Pesaḥ.	*Pesaḥim*
Pirqe R. El.	*Pirqe Rabbi Eliezer*
Šabb.	*Šabbat*
Sanh.	*Sanhedrin*
Šeb.	*Šebiʿit*
Sop.	*Soperim*
Tamid	*Tamid*
Tg. Yer. II	*Targum Yerušalmi II*
Yoma	*Yoma (= Kippurim)*

OTHER ANCIENT, MEDIEVAL, AND EARLY MODERN WRITINGS

Aeschylus	
Supp.	*Supplices*
Anselm	
Pros.	*Proslogium*
Aristotle	
Eth. Nic.	*Ethica Nicomachea*
Meta.	*Metaphysica*
Pol.	*Politica*
Rhet.	*Rhetorica*
CA	Confessio Augustana (Augsburg Confession)
CA Apol.	Apology of the Confessio Augustana
Calvin, J.	
Inst.	*Institutes of the Christian Religion*
Cassian	
Conf.	*Conferences*
Inst.	*Institutes*
Cicero	
De fin.	*De finibus*
De leg.	*De legibus*
De nat. deor.	*De natura deorum*
Formula of Concord	
Ep.	Epitome
SD	Solid Declaration
Herodotus	
Hist.	*History*
Homer	
Od.	*Odyssey*
Horace	
Sat.	*Satirae*
Hume, D.	
Inquiry	*An Inquiry concerning Human Understanding*
John of Damascus	
De fide orth.	*De fide orthodoxa*

ABBREVIATIONS

Josephus	
Ant.	*Jewish Antiquities*
J.W.	*Jewish War*
Juvenal	
Sat.	*Satirae*
Kant, I.	
Religion	*Religion within the Limits of Reason Alone*
Locke, J.	
Essay	*An Essay concerning Human Understanding*
Melanchthon, P.	
Treatise	*Treatise on the Power and Primacy of the Pope*
Peter Lombard	
Sent.	*Sentences*
Philo	
De Abr.	*De Abrahamo*
De Decal.	*De Decalogo*
De mut. nom.	*De mutatione nominum*
De spec. leg.	*De specialibus legibus*
De virt.	*De virtutibus*
Plato	
Grg.	*Gorgias*
Leg.	*Leges*
Phd.	*Phaedo*
Phdr.	*Phaedrus*
Plt.	*Politicus*
Rep.	*Republic*
Plotinus	
Enn.	*Enneades*
Schmalk. Art.	Schmalkaldic Articles
Suetonius	
Tib.	*Tiberius*
Tacitus	
Hist.	*Historiae*
Theodoret of Cyrrhus	
Haer. fab. comp.	*Haereticarum fabularum compendium*
Thomas Aquinas	
Summa theol.	*Summa theologiae*

MODERN PUBLICATIONS AND EDITIONS

AAS	*Acta apostolicae sedis*
AB	Anchor Bible
ABD	*Anchor Bible Dictionary*
AbNTC	Abingdon NT Commentaries
ACNT	Augsburg Commentary on the New Testament
AnBoll	*Analecta Bollandiana*
ANET	*Ancient Near Eastern Texts*
ANRW	*Aufstieg und Niedergang der römischen Welt*
Arabica	*Arabica. Revue d'études arabes*
ARelG	*Archiv für Religionsgeschichte*
ASR	*American Sociological Review*
ASV	American Standard Version
ATD	Das Alte Testament Deutsch
BC	Biblical Commentary (Edinburgh)
BDLG	*Blätter für deutsche Landesgeschichte*
BExC	Baker Exegetical Commentary
BGBR	*Beiträge zur Geschichte des Bistums Regensburg*
BibRev	*Bible Review*
BiSe	Biblical Seminar
BNTC	Black's New Testament Commentaries
BTZ	*Berliner theologische Zeitschrift*
CAH	*Cambridge Ancient History*
Cath(M)	*Catholica* (Münster)
CBC	Cambridge Bible Commentary
CBQ	*Catholic Biblical Quarterly*
CCen	*Christian Century*
CD	K. Barth, *Church Dogmatics*
CGG	*Christlicher Glaube in moderner Gesellschaft*
CGTC	Cambridge Greek Testament Commentaries
CH	*Church History*
CHLA	*Cambridge History of Latin America*
CIC	Codex Iuris Canonici
CivCatt	*Civiltà cattolica*
CKL	*Calwer Kirchenlexikon*
CleR	*Clergy Review*
CMind	*Catholic Mind*
Conc(D)	*Concilium* (German ed.)
ContCom	Continental Commentaries
CovQ	*Covenant Quarterly*
CPJ	*Corpus papyrorum Judaicarum*
CR.BS	*Currents in Research: Biblical Studies*
CRef	Corpus Reformatorum
CSEL	Corpus scriptorum ecclesiasticorum latinorum
CTM	*Concordia Theological Monthly*
DACL	*Dictionnaire d'archéologie chrétienne et de liturgie*
DBSup	*Dictionnaire de la Bible, Supplément*
DBWE	*Dietrich Bonhoeffer Works English* (Fortress Press)

DEM — *Dictionary of the Ecumenical Movement* (2d ed., 2002)
DH — Denzinger-Hünermann, *Enchiridion symbolorum* (37th ed., 1991)
DHI — *Dictionary of the History of Ideas*
Diak. — *Diakonia. Internationale Zeitschrift für die Praxis der Kirche*
Div. — *Divinitas. Pontificae Academiae Theologicae Romanae commentarii*
DJD — *Discoveries in the Judaean Desert*
DPC — *Dictionary of Pastoral Care*
DPCC — *Dictionary of Pastoral Care and Counseling*
DSp — *Dictionnaire de spiritualité, ascétique et mystique*
DTC — *Dictionnaire de théologie catholique*
ECC — Eerdmans Critical Commentary
EchtB — Echter Bibel
ECQ — *Eastern Churches Quarterly*
ECR — *Eastern Churches Review*
EcTr — *Ecumenical Trends*
EDNT — *Exegetical Dictionary of the New Testament*
EE.JEE — *Ethnologia Europaea. Journal of European Ethnology*
EI² — *Encyclopaedia of Islam* (new ed.)
EJ — *Encyclopedia of Judaism* (2000)
EK — *Evangelische Kommentare*
EKKNT — Evangelisch-katholischer Kommentar zum Neuen Testament
EKL — *Evangelisches Kirchenlexikon* (1st ed., 1956-59; 2d ed., 1962; 3d ed., 1986-97)
EkTh — *Ekklesia kai theologia*
EncPh — *Encyclopedia of Philosophy*
EncRel(E) — *The Encyclopedia of Religion* (ed. M. Eliade)
EncTheol — *Encyclopedia of Theology: The Concise* Sacramentum mundi
EpCom — Epworth Commentaries
ER — *Ecumenical Review*
ERE — *Encyclopaedia of Religion and Ethics*
EvT — *Evangelische Theologie*
ExpTim — *Expository Times*
FOTL — Forms of the Old Testament Literature
FPP — *Family Planning Perspectives*
FrS — *Franciscan Studies*
FS — *Franziskanische Studien*
FZPhTh — *Freiburger Zeitschrift für Philosophie und Theologie*
GAKGS — *Gesammelte Aufsätze zur Kulturgeschichte Spaniens*
GBL — *Das große Bibellexikon*
GDK — *Gottesdienst der Kirche. Handbuch der Liturgiewissenschaft*
GenSoc — *Gender and Society*
GGB — *Geschichtliche Grundbegriffe*
GOTR — *Greek Orthodox Theological Review*
HAT — Handbuch zum Alten Testament
HCL — Higher Christian Life
HDG — *Handbuch der Dogmengeschichte*
HFTh — *Handbuch der Fundamentaltheologie*
HKAT — Handkommentar zum Alten Testament
HKKR — *Handbuch des katholischen Kirchenrechts*
HLW(M) — *Handbuch der Liturgiewissenschaft* (ed. A.-G. Martimort)
HNT — Handbuch zum Neuen Testament
HPTh(B) — *Handbuch der praktischen Theologie* (Berlin)
HR/RH — *Historical Reflections/Réflexions historiques*
HrwG — *Handbuch religionswissenschaftlicher Grundbegriffe*
HS — Die Heilige Schrift des Alten Testaments
HTKAT — Herders theologischer Kommentar zum Alten Testament
HTKNT — Herders theologischer Kommentar zum Neuen Testament
HTR — *Harvard Theological Review*
HTTL — *Herders theologisches Taschenlexikon*
HUCA — *Hebrew Union College Annual*
HWP — *Historisches Wörterbuch der Philosophie*
HWR — *Historisches Wörterbuch der Rhetorik*
IBC — Interpretation: A Bible Commentary for Teaching and Preaching
IBMR — *International Bulletin of Missionary Research*
ICC — International Critical Commentary
IDBSup — Supplementary volume to the *Interpreter's Dictionary of the Bible*
IJPS — *International Journal of Peace Studies*
IJPsa — *International Journal of Psychoanalysis*
Interp. — Interpretation: A Commentary for Teaching and Preaching
IRM — *International Review of Missions*
ISBE — *International Standard Bible Encyclopedia* (rev. ed.)
ITC — International Theological Commentary
JAC — *Jahrbuch für Antike und Christentum*
JAOS — *Journal of the American Oriental Society*
JBC — Jerome Biblical Commentary
JBL — *Journal of Biblical Literature*
JCR — *Journal of Conflict Resolution*
JEH — *Journal of Ecclesiastical History*
JES — *Journal of Ecumenical Studies*
JETS — *Journal of the Evangelical Theological Society*
JHI — *Journal of the History of Ideas*
JL — *Jüdisches Lexikon*

JMF *Journal of Marriage and the Family*
JMLB *Jahrbuch des Martin-Luther-Bundes*
JPR *Journal of Peace Research*
JPsC *Journal of Psychology and Christianity*
JPsHS *Journal of Psychology and Human Sexuality*
JPsR *Journal of Psychiatric Research*
JPsT *Journal of Psychology and Theology*
JPSV Jewish Publication Society Version
JR *Journal of Religion*
JRS *Journal of Roman Studies*
JSCE *Journal of the Society of Christian Ethics*
JSHRZ *Jüdische Schriften aus hellenistisch-römischer Zeit*
JSJ *Journal for the Study of Judaism in the Persian, Hellenistic, and Roman Period*
JSNT *Journal for the Study of the New Testament*
JSSR *Journal for the Scientific Study of Religion*
JusEcc *Jus ecclesiasticum*
KEK Kritisch-exegetischer Kommentar über das Neue Testament
KHC Kurzer Hand-Commentar zum Alten Testament
KJV King James Version
KuD *Kerygma und Dogma*
KZG *Kirchliche Zeitgeschichte*
LÄ *Lexikon der Ägyptologie*
LAW *Lexikon der Alten Welt*
LBibNT I Libri Biblici. Nuovo Testamento
LCC Library of Christian Classics
LeDiv Lectio divina
Leit. *Leiturgia. Handbuch des evangelischen Gottesdienstes*
LM *Lutherische Monatshefte*
LMin *Liturgical Ministry*
LSs *Lebende Seelsorge*
LTK *Lexicon für Theologie und Kirche*
LuJ *Luther-Jahrbuch*
LW *Luther's Works*, "American Edition" (55 vols.; St. Louis and Philadelphia, 1955-76)
Mansi *Sacrorum conciliorum nova et amplissa collectio* (ed. J. D. Mansi et al.)
Mar. *Marianum. Ephemerides Mariologiae*
MECW Karl Marx and Friedrich Engels, *Collected Works*
MentRet *Mental Retardation*
MF.CJ *Marriage and Family: A Christian Journal*
MJTh *Marburger Jahrbuch Theologie*
MTZ *Münchener theologische Zeitschrift*
MuB *Mitteilungen und Beiträge der Forschungsstelle Judentum an der Theologischen Fakultät Leipzig*
MySal *Mysterium salutis*
NAC New American Commentary
NAKG *Nederlands archief voor kerkgeschiedenis*
NCBC New Century Bible Commentary
NCE *New Catholic Encyclopedia*
NClarB New Clarendon Bible
NEBrit *New Encyclopaedia Britannica*
NEchtB Neue Echter Bibel
NGDMM *New Grove Dictionary of Music and Musicians*
NHC *Nag Hammadi Codices*
NHE *Nouvelle histoire de l'église*
NIB New Interpreter's Bible
NIBC New International Biblical Commentary
NICNT New International Commentary on the New Testament
NICOT New International Commentary on the Old Testament
NIDOTTE *New International Dictionary of Old Testament Theology and Exegesis*
NIGTC New International Greek Testament Commentary
NIVApp NIV Application Commentary
NJBC *New Jerome Biblical Commentary*
NLH *New Literary History*
NovT *Novum Testamentum*
NRSV New Revised Standard Version
NSKAT Neuer Stuttgarter Kommentar, Altes Testament
NTD Das Neue Testament Deutsch
NTG New Testament Guides
NTS *New Testament Studies*
Numen *Numen: International Review for the History of Religions*
NZSTh *Neue Zeitschrift für systematische Theologie*
ODB *Oxford Dictionary of Byzantium*
ODCC *Oxford Dictionary of the Christian Church* (3d ed.)
ODJR *Oxford Dictionary of the Jewish Religion*
OEANE *Oxford Encyclopedia of Archaeology in the Near East*
OED *Oxford English Dictionary*
OEMIW *Oxford Encyclopedia of the Modern Islamic World*
OGIS *Orientis Graeci inscriptiones selectae*
OHPP *Oxford Handbook of Political Psychology*
OiC *One in Christ: A Catholic Ecumenical Review*
ÖL *Ökumene-Lexikon*
ÖR *Ökumenische Rundschau*
OR(E) *L'osservatore romano* (English ed.)

OrChr	*Oriens Christianus*
OS	*Ostkirchliche Studien*
ÖTBK	Ökumenischer Taschenbuchkommentar zum Neuen Testament
OTL	Old Testament Library
OTP	J. H. Charlesworth, *The Old Testament Pseudepigrapha*
OxyPap	*The Oxyrynchus Papyrus*
PaP	*Past and Present*
PAPS	*Proceedings of the American Philosophical Society*
PastPsy	*Pastoral Psychology*
PeCh	*Peace and Change*
PG	*Patrologia Graeca*
PKNT	Papyrologische Kommentare zum Neuen Testament
PL	*Patrologia Latina*
PNTC	Pillar New Testament Commentary
ProcC	Proclamation Commentaries
PTh	*Pastoraltheologie*
PThI	*Pastoraltheologische Informationen*
PuN	*Pietismus und Neuzeit*
PW	Pauly-Wissowa, *Real-Encyclopädie der classischen Altertumswissenschaft*
RAC	*Reallexikon für Antike und Christentum*
RB	*Revue biblique*
RDL	*Reallexikon der deutschen Literaturgeschichte*
REB	Revised English Bible
RelLife	*Religion in Life*
RelStSo	*Religion, State, and Society*
REPh	*Routledge Encyclopedia of Philosophy*
RevQ	*Revue de Qumran*
RGG	*Religion in Geschichte und Gegenwart*
RHPR	*Revue d'histoire et de philosophie religieuses*
RHR	*Revue de l'histoire des religions*
RKZ	*Reformierte Kirchenzeitung*
RöHM	*Römische historische Mitteilungen*
RoJKG	*Rottenburger Jahrbuch für Kirchengeschichte*
RSV	Revised Standard Version
RW	*Reformed World*
SJT	*Scottish Journal of Theology*
SKK.NT	Stuttgarter kleiner Kommentar. Neues Testament
SM	*Sacramentum mundi. Theologisches Lexikon für die Praxis*
SM(E)	*Sacramentum mundi* (English ed.)
SMTh	*Swedish Missiological Themes*
Sob.	*Sobornost'. The Journal of St. Alban and St. Sergius*
SocAn	*Sociological Analysis*
Spec.	*Speculum: A Journal of Mediaeval Studies*
StEv	*Studia evangelica*
StLi	*Studia liturgica*
Str-B	H. L Strack and P. Billerbeck, *Kommentar zum Neuen Testament aus Talmud und Midrasch*
StSpin	*Studia Spinozana*
StTh	*Studia theologica*
SZS	*Schweizerische Zeitschrift für Soziologie*
TDNT	*Theological Dictionary of the New Testament*
TDOT	*Theological Dictionary of the Old Testament*
Tem.	*Temenos. Studies in Comparative Religion*
TGA	*Theologie der Gegenwart in Auswahl*
THAT	*Theologisches Handwörterbuch zum Alten Testament*
THKNT	Theologischer Handkommentar zum Neuen Testament
ThSex	*Theology and Sexuality*
ThStKr	*Theologische Studien und Kritiken. Zeitschrift für das gesamte Gebiet der Theologie*
TLOT	*Theological Lexicon of the Old Testament*
TLZ	*Theologische Literaturzeitung*
TNTC	Tyndale New Testament Commentaries
TP	*Theologie und Philosophie*
TPINTC	Trinity Press International New Testament Commentaries
TRE	*Theologische Realenzyklopädie*
TToday	*Theology Today*
TUAT	*Texte aus der Umwelt des Alten Testaments*
TynBul	*Tyndale Bulletin*
TZ	*Theologische Zeitschrift*
UF	*Ugarit-Forschungen*
US	*Una Sancta. Rundbriefe für interkonfessionelle Begegnung*
USQR	*Union Seminary Quarterly Review*
VT	*Vetus Testamentum*
WA	M. Luther, *Werke. Kritische Gesamtausgabe* (Weimarer Ausgabe)
WA.DB	— Deutsche Bibel
WBC	Word Biblical Commentary
WCE	*World Christian Encyclopedia* (2d ed., 2 vols., 2001)
WDCE	*Westminster Dictionary of Christian Ethics*
WestBC	Westminster Bible Companion
WPKG	*Wissenschaft und Praxis in Kirche und Gesellschaft*
WThWB	*The Westminster Theological Wordbook of the Bible*
WzM	*Wege zum Menschen*

YLBI	*Year Book. Leo Baeck Institute of Jews from Germany*
ZAW	*Zeitschrift für die alttestamentliche Wissenschaft*
ZBK	Zürcher Bibelkommentar
ZBLG	*Zeitschrift für bayerische Landesgeschichte*
ZdZ	*Die Zeichen der Zeit*
ZE	*Zeitschrift für Ethnologie*
ZEvKR	*Zeitschrift für evangelisches Kirchenrecht*
ZKT	*Zeitschrift für katholische Theologie*
ZMR	*Zeitschrift für Missionswissenschaft und Religionswissenschaft*
ZNW	*Zeitschrift für die neutestamentliche Wissenschaft*
ZRGG	*Zeitschrift für Religions- und Geistesgeschichte*
ZRW	*Zeitschrift für Religionswissenschaft*
ZTK	*Zeitschrift für Theologie und Kirche*
ZZ	*Zwischen den Zeiten*

STATES AND PROVINCES

Ala.	Alabama
Alta.	Alberta
Ariz.	Arizona
Ark.	Arkansas
Calif.	California
Colo.	Colorado
Conn.	Connecticut
D.C.	District of Columbia
Del.	Delaware
Fla.	Florida
Ga.	Georgia
Ill.	Illinois
Ind.	Indiana
Ky.	Kentucky
La.	Louisiana
Mass.	Massachusetts
Md.	Maryland
Mich.	Michigan
Minn.	Minnesota
Miss.	Mississippi
Mo.	Missouri
Mont.	Montana
N.C.	North Carolina
Nebr.	Nebraska
N.H.	New Hampshire
N.J.	New Jersey
N.M.	New Mexico
N.Y.	New York
Okla.	Oklahoma
Ont.	Ontario
Oreg.	Oregon
Pa.	Pennsylvania
R.I.	Rhode Island
S.C.	South Carolina
Tenn.	Tennessee
Tex.	Texas
Va.	Virginia
Vt.	Vermont
Wash.	Washington
Wis.	Wisconsin

GENERAL

abr.	abridged
A.D.	*anno Domini,* in the year of the Lord
adj.	adjective
Akkad.	Akkadian
Arab.	Arabic
Aram.	Aramaic
art(s).	article(s)
aug.	augmented (by)
Aus.	Austria
Austral.	Australia
b.	born
B.C.	before Christ
bk(s).	book(s)
Braz.	Brazil
c.	*corpus articuli,* the body of the article (Thomas Aquinas)
ca.	circa
can(s).	canon(s)
cent(s).	century, centuries
cf.	*confer,* compare
chap(s).	chapter(s)
Chin.	Chinese
col(s).	column(s)
comp(s).	compiler(s), compiled (by)
corr.	corrected
C.R.	Costa Rica
D	Deuteronomic source
d.	died
diss.	dissertation

dist.	distinction
E	Elohistic source
ed(s).	edited (by), edition(s), editor(s)
e.g.	*exempli gratia,* for example
Egypt.	Egyptian
EKD	Evangelische Kirche in Deutschland
emp.	emperor
Eng.	England, English
ep.	*epistula(e),* letter(s)
esp.	especially
Est.	Estonian
est.	estimated, estimate
ET	English translation
et al.	*et alii,* and others
etc.	*et cetera,* and so forth
exp.	expanded
f	females
fem.	feminine
ff.	and following
Fin.	Finland
Finn.	Finnish
fl.	*floruit,* flourished
Fr.	France, French
frg(s).	fragment(s)
FS	Festschrift
ft.	foot, feet
G	*Grundlage* (see art. "Pentateuchal Research")
gen.	general
Ger.	Germany, German
Gk.	Greek
Heb.	Hebrew
Hung.	Hungary, Hungarian
ibid.	*ibidem,* in the same place
i.e.	*id est,* that is
in.	inch(es)
Ire.	Ireland
It.	Italy, Italian
J	Yahwist source
km.	kilometer(s)
κτλ.	κατὰ τὰ λοιπά, and so forth
L	material in Luke not found in Matthew or Mark
Lat.	Latin
Leb.	Lebanon
lit.	literal(ly)
LLat.	Late Latin
LXX	Septuagint
M	material in Matthew not found in Mark or Luke
m	males
m.	meter(s)
marg.	marginal reading
masc.	masculine
MEng.	Middle English
mi.	mile(s)
mm.	millimeter(s)
MS(S)	manuscript(s)
MT	Masoretic Text
n(n).	note(s)
n.d.	no date
NGO(s)	nongovernmental organization(s)
no(s).	number(s)
Norw.	Norway
NT	New Testament
N.Z.	New Zealand
OECD	Organization for Economic Cooperation and Development
OEng.	Old English
OFr.	Old French
orig.	original(ly)
OT	Old Testament
P	Priestly source
p(p).	page(s)
par.	parallel(s), parallel to
par(s).	paragraph(s)
Para.	Paraguay
patr.	patriarch
perf.	perfect
Pers.	Persian
Ph.D.	*philosophiae doctor,* doctor of philosophy
Philip.	Philippines
pl.	plural
pl(s).	plate(s)
Pol.	Poland, Polish
posth.	posthumously
prob.	probably
pt.	part
pub.	published, publication
Q	hypothetical source of material common to Matthew and Luke but not found in Mark
q(q).	question(s)
repr.	reprint(ed)
rev.	revised (by, in), revision
Rom.	Romania, Romanian
Russ.	Russian
S.Af.	South Africa
Sax.	Saxon
secy.	secretary
ser.	series
sess.	session(s)
sing.	singular
Skt.	Sanskrit
Slvn.	Slovene
sq.	square
St.	Saint
supp(s).	supplement(s), supplementary

ABBREVIATIONS

s.v.	*sub verbo,* under the word
Swed.	Sweden, Swedish
Switz.	Switzerland
Syr.	Syriac
trans.	translated by, translator(s), translation
Ugar.	Ugaritic
U.K.	United Kingdom
U.N.	United Nations
UNESCO	United Nations Educational, Scientific, and Cultural Organization
U.S.	United States
USSR	Union of Soviet Socialist Republics
v(v).	verse(s)
var.	variant (reading)
Vg	(Latin) Vulgate
vol(s).	volume(s)
vs.	versus
YMCA	Young Men's Christian Association
YWCA	Young Women's Christian Association
→	cross-reference to another article
*	passim [with Bible references]
§	section

The ENCYCLOPEDIA *of* CHRISTIANITY

Volume 4
P–Sh

P

Pacific Conference of Churches

1. Origin
2. Organization

1. Origin

The Pacific Conference of Churches (PCC), which grew out of a widely felt concern for cooperation among Pacific churches, was formally constituted in 1966 at the First Assembly, held at Lifou, Loyalty Islands, of New Caledonia. It describes itself as "a fellowship of churches which confess the Lord Jesus Christ as God and Savior according to the Scriptures and therefore seek to fulfill their common calling to the glory of the one God, Father, Son and Holy Spirit" (point 3 of the constitution).

The first interisland gatherings were youth conventions in the late 1950s. In 1959 the → International Missionary Council organized a conference (→ Missionary Conferences) of all churches and missions operating in the region. It took place in 1961 at Malua Theological College, Western Samoa, and led to the constitution of the PCC "as an organ of cooperation among the churches in the Pacific within the framework of the wider ecumenical movement."

2. Organization

The PCC holds a general assembly usually every five years, at which the general secretary and executive staff are elected. The most recent assembly was in 2002, in the Cook Islands. The general secretary is based at the head office in Suva, Fiji. In 2005 membership included ten → national councils of churches (in American Samoa, Federated States of Micronesia, Fiji, Kiribati, Niue, Papua New Guinea, Samoa, Solomon Islands, Tonga, and Vanuatu), as well as the Roman Catholic Bishops' Conference of Papua New Guinea and Solomon Islands and, representing the other nations and territories of Micronesia, Melanesia, and Polynesia, the Conferentia Episcopalis Pacifici (CEPAC, Episcopal Conference of the Pacific). The more than 20 member churches include the Anglican Dioceses of Polynesia and of Vanuatu, Congregational Christian Church in American Samoa and in Samoa, Cook Islands Christian Church, Evangelical Lutheran Church in Papua New Guinea, Free Wesleyan Church of Tonga, Methodist Church in Fiji and Rotuma and in Samoa, Nauru Congregational Church, Presbyterian Church of Vanuatu and of Aotearoa New Zealand, and United Church of Christ in Pohnpei and in the Marshall Islands.

In all its work and services the PCC emphasizes biblical and theological bases for the renewal of the church and society and for integral human → development, and it strives to equip the churches and people to face the ever-changing realities in the region. Its services have developed over the years, different programs being introduced according to the needs and issues of the moment. Of great concern are the issues of a nuclear-free and independent Pacific, → disarmament, → colonialism and neocolonialism, multinational corporations, environmental issues, and putting an end to drift-netting (→ Ecology; Environment). In addition, the PCC is responsible for the chaplaincy of the University of the South Pacific in Suva. It also has its own publishing house, Lotu Pasifika Productions. As a regional ecumenical body, the PCC has a working relationship with the → World Council of Churches in Geneva, in particular in the field of climate change. A joint meeting held in March 2004 in Kiribati issued the so-called Otin Taai Declaration, appealing to the industrialized countries to reduce their greenhouse gas emissions.

Bibliography: C. W. Forman, *The Voice of Many Waters: The Story of the Life and Ministry of the Pacific Conference of Churches in the Last Twenty-five Years* (Suva, Fiji, 1986).

Lorine Tevi

Pacific Islands → Oceania

Pacifism

1. Term and Usage
2. Christian Pacifism
   2.1. Christian Origins
   2.2. Pre-Reformation Pacifism
      2.2.1. Heretical groups
      2.2.2. Waldensians, Hussites, and Moravians
   2.3. Anabaptists and Mennonites
   2.4. Humanism and Anti-Trinitarians
   2.5. Quakers and Brethren
   2.6. Religious Pacifism in America
3. Modern Pacifism (1815-1945)
4. After World War II
5. Ethical Assessment

1. Term and Usage

The word "pacifism" came into use around 1900, apparently first in Europe, to describe a generalized attitude of opposition to → war. A more restricted sense found in early Christianity designates the absolute refusal to use force against persons (often called nonresistance, from Jesus' admonition in Matt. 5:39).

In contemporary usage, pacifism encompasses a wide range of antiwar and antiviolence views, often including the development of nonviolent strategies for social change. Earlier European use of the term embraced the unconditional pacifism of peace sects and → peace churches, as well as more political and philosophical varieties: the peace philosophy of Immanuel Kant (→ Kantianism), the democratic pacifism that accepted national wars of defense, the free-trade pacifism of British origin (→ Liberalism) that accepted wars to establish or restore free trade, radical Marxist revolutionary pacifism that opposed wars of imperialism (→ Marxism), and a pacifism grounded in the development of → international law. Under Anglo-American influence, pacifism came to include → conscientious objection to military service, as well as more radical forms of antiwar activism and civil disobedience. Thus a spectrum of pacifist views exists, from an absolutist personal ethic prohibiting all killing to more pragmatic plans for peaceful world order. Here we give central attention to pacifist issues in the story of the Christian church.

Ideas of nonviolence and ahimsa (Skt. *ahiṁsā*, "noninjury") emerged in ancient India centuries before the Christian era. Early → Hinduism, → Jainism, and → Buddhism prohibited the taking of human life, although this rule soon became an obligation only for members of monastic orders. Peter Brock, leading historian of pacifism, makes the case that the unconditional rejection of war in general, appearing first among the followers of Jesus in the first several centuries A.D., is exceptional among the great world religions.

2. Christian Pacifism

2.1. *Christian Origins*

Early Christian pacifism is grounded in the example and teachings of → Jesus, especially in the → Sermon on the Mount (Matt. 5:38-48). Christian practice up to the fourth century included rejection of the bearing of arms and military service, even at the cost of martyrdom (→ Early Church 2.1; Martyrs). No known Christian author from the first centuries approved of Christian participation in battle; citations advocating pacifism are found in → Tertullian, → Origen, Lactantius, and others, and in the testimonies of the martyrs Maximilian and Marcellus, who were executed for refusing to serve in the Roman army. Grounds for opposition to military service included fear of idolatry and the oath of loyalty to Caesar, as well as the basic objection to shedding blood on the battlefield.

Early Christian authors, however, did justify the government's use of the sword to punish evildoers and maintain order, beginning with the apostolic writings (Rom. 13:1-7; 1 Pet. 2:14). Only with the change that came with Constantine (306-37; → Church and State) did the church fundamentally break with pacifism. The dramatic shift from being a persecuted minority to citizenship under a Christian emperor changed the entire paradigm. Origen's claim that, instead of military might, it was the fervent prayer of Christians that held the empire together ("a special army of piety," *C. Cels.* 8.73) lost its power when by A.D. 416 only baptized Christians could serve in the army.

As Christianity became a state religion, Ambrose and → Augustine adapted the classic Roman code of conduct in warfare, infused with elements of biblical doctrine, to develop what has become known as the just (or justified) war theory. Inner attitudes were viewed as more important than actions; if one could avoid hatred, then killing as an expression of love became possible, it was argued. In the Middle Ages the pacifist ethic took a dualistic form (→ Dualism), applicable only to the monastic orders and the clergy.

2.2. *Pre-Reformation Pacifism*

2.2.1. *Heretical Groups*

Early pacifism lived on in the → Marcionites and in → Manichaeanism. It also appeared in the medieval → Cathari (first in the Bogomils of the late 11th cent.). The papal-initiated persecution and extirpation of the Albigenses (a sect of the Cathari) in southern France (12th to mid-13th cent.) exemplified the lengthy suffering endured by those European → heresies that advocated nonviolence, including rejection of the → death penalty and the refusal to take → oaths or hold secular office.

2.2.2. *Waldensians, Hussites, and Moravians*

As disciples of Jesus who practiced literal obedience to the commands of the Sermon on the Mount (→ Discipleship 2), the → Waldensians modeled their pacifism on Peter Waldo of Lyons (ca. 1170). After they had been driven into central Europe by → persecution, their pacifist convictions, along with similar elements in the theology of John → Wycliffe (ca. 1330-84) and his followers, appeared also among the early → Hussites, especially the Taborites. This group, however, in response to the threat of extinction by the Crown and the church and in expectation of the return of Christ, renounced their original espousal of nonviolence in favor of aggressive counterforce in the Hussite wars.

In controversy with militant Hussite → millenarianism, Peter Chelčický (ca. 1390-ca. 1460), influenced by his study of the Gospels, adopted an anarchist Christian philosophy of peace and rejected the → authority of the church, the existing social order, and all state use of force, whether in the death penalty or in war (→ Anarchy). One group of Chelčický's followers became the Unitas Fratrum, whose pacifist rigorism weakened over the years, initially with the more moderate majority led by Lukáš of Prague (d. 1528). Moravian refugees committed to the tradition of the Bohemian Brethren (Unitas Fratrum) found shelter at Herrnhut under Nicholas → Zinzendorf (1700-1760; → Pietism). When many of them later settled in the United States (→ Moravian Church) in the 18th century, they modified their pacifism and finally abandoned it altogether.

2.3. *Anabaptists and Mennonites*

The → Reformation brought a new wave of sectarian pacifism in the form of most → Anabaptist groups. A start came in Zurich in 1523/24 when in opposition to the aims of Ulrich → Zwingli (1484-1531; → Zwingli's Theology), an attempt was made by Conrad Grebel (ca. 1498-1526) and his followers simply to restore the apostolic church. Their effort was met with severe persecution but evoked a response elsewhere in Switzerland, Germany, Austria, and Moravia. The Schleitheim Confession (1527), rejecting the sword as "outside the perfection of Christ," grounds the Anabaptist doctrine of nonresistance in a church-world dualism of rigorous discipleship to Christ.

Balthasar Hubmaier (1485-1528) took the view, however, that secular office and armed resistance are legitimate, so that attitudes toward pacifism quickly brought division to the emerging Anabaptist movement. Very consistently, however, the followers of Jacob Hutter (d. 1536; → Hutterites) linked nonresistance to the sharing of goods and a highly organized communal lifestyle, which they clung to through all their persecutions and wanderings (→ Community of Goods). As Anabaptist teaching spread to the Netherlands and Westphalia, extremist apocalyptic expectations led to a violent theocratic regime in Münster under John of Leyden (1534-35).

Under the leadership of → Menno Simons (1496-1561), who strongly denounced the Münster episode, Anabaptists in the 1540s regrouped as peaceful believers, neither Catholic nor Protestant, who eventually became known as → Mennonites. Menno's views on holding political office were less rigorous than those of the earlier Swiss Brethren, but he taught a consistent nonresistance to lethal violence. By the late 16th century Dutch Mennonites had gained the right to substitute civilian service for the bearing of arms. With state tolerance, social acceptance, and growing prosperity, simple biblical faith and a disciplined nonresistant lifestyle came under threat.

Thoroughgoing pacifism was gradually abandoned by Mennonites in the Netherlands and Germany in the 19th century because of → acculturation, nationalism (→ Nation, Nationalism), and the egalitarianism of the draft. Nevertheless, some German-speaking Mennonites either continued their adherence to nonviolence in Alsace, Switzerland, West Prussia, and Galicia or evaded pressure by emigration to Russia (beginning in 1788). Mennonites in Russia established segregated agrarian colonies in which, up to the October Revolution of 1917, they were allowed to work in state forests instead of doing military service.

2.4. *Humanism and Anti-Trinitarians*

Contemporary with the Reformation, another variety of pacifism reflected Renaissance humanist influence (→ Humanism). Inspired by such diverse sources as the recovery of ancient philosophies and the newer optimism regarding the achievements of reason, humanist pacifists upheld a vision of human brotherhood transcending narrow nationalism and greed. Blending Christian and classical virtues, → Erasmus (1469?-1536) of Rotterdam moved beyond the accepted logic of the "just war." His pragmatic pacifism boldly condemned the territorial wars of Europe as wasteful, cruel, and foolish. He was the first in a long line of humanist pacifists that included Thomas More (1478-1535), Juan Luis Vives (1492-1540), Sebastian Franck (ca. 1499-ca. 1542), Duc de Sully (1560-1641), Émeric Crucé (ca. 1590-1648), William Penn (1644-1718), Abbé de Saint-Pierre (1658-1743), Immanuel Kant (1724-1804), and Jeremy Bentham (1748-1832). Kant's well-known dictum to "treat humanity never only as a means but always also as an end" seemed to rule out the violence of warfare.

The anti-Trinitarians (Socinians) who split off from Polish → Calvinism in the 16th century expressed near-Anabaptist views in their Racovian Catechism (1605). Sometimes known as Polish Brethren, they adopted pacifist convictions relative to the state, secular office, the death penalty, and war, which they often linked to social radicalism. By the early 17th century the more moderate position of Faustus Socinus (1539-1604) prevailed. As in the case of the pacifism of the Dutch Mennonites, the theory of Hugo Grotius (1583-1645) that a defensive war is justifiable did much to weaken Socinian pacifism (→ Unitarianism).

2.5. *Quakers and Brethren*

The Quakers (→ Friends, Society of), a significant historic peace church like the Mennonites, originated in British Puritanism (→ Puritans 2) about 1650. The church arose during the turmoil of Cromwellian England, a time of multiplying radical groups such as the Levellers, the Diggers, and the Fifth Monarchy Men. The founder of the Quakers, George Fox (1624-91), a charismatic proponent of the Inner Light, did not come immediately to his pacifist conviction, later expressed as living "in the virtue of that life and power that take away the occasion of all wars." As others such as Robert Barclay (1648-90) assumed leadership in the movement, their rejection of war and military service subjected them to severe pressure from the state. Yet in other matters like clothes and public office, they were quicker to adopt a more pragmatic attitude than Anabaptists and Mennonites, though still maintaining firm opposition to oath-taking.

In the 18th century, however, the Quakers' combination of nonviolence and pragmatism meant that they would sometimes provide substitutes for military service and accept the arming of ships, the holding of weapons, trading in weapons, and trading in war bonds. Later, Quakers in Britain and America played a vigorous role in the founding of peace societies (→ Peace Movements) and the campaign to end the slave trade (→ Slavery). The Quaker statesman John Bright (1811-89), a member of Parliament, opposed all of England's wars, arguing, however, not so much from Quaker beliefs as from pragmatic principles of sound public policy.

Originating around 1708 in the German Palatinate, the German Baptists known as Tunkers or Dunkers and later as the Church of the Brethren represented a merging of Pietist (→ Pietism) and Anabaptist influences under the leadership of Alexander Mack (1679-1735). An attractive vision of land and religious freedom in the New World brought them to Pennsylvania (1719-29), where the two Christopher Sauers, father and son, of Germantown, published articulate defenses of Brethren biblical pacifism.

2.6. *Religious Pacifism in America*

All three of the movements now known as the historic → peace churches (Quakers, Mennonites, and → Brethren) originated in Europe but increased in number in the New World. The Quakers, including William Penn, came first, in the 1650s. Then Mennonite migrations beginning in the 1680s were absorbed into the "Holy Experiment" of Penn's colony, which was established in 1681 and dedicated to religious tolerance. Moravians, German Baptists, and other German-speaking sects with inclinations toward pacifism also found refuge in Pennsylvania (i.e., "Penn's woods"). For more than seven decades (1682-1756), this colony provided a peaceful haven where no citizen was required to bear arms.

Quakers were able to rule in Pennsylvania by

making a moral distinction between war-making and the police functions of government; the latter were viewed positively, an approach at variance with Anabaptist rigidity. Penn himself drafted plans for peaceful international order that reflect more the vision of a pragmatic humanist statesman than that of sectarian pacifist purity. In mid-18th-century Pennsylvania, Quakers and Mennonites produced landmark testimonials on behalf of the absolutist pacifist → conscience.

3. Modern Pacifism (1815-1945)

Until the early 19th century virtually all pacifist thought in Europe and America was religious in origin. When nonsectarian peace societies were formed in England and the United States at the close of the Napoleonic Wars, the leaders were almost all from the churches. Their emphasis was → moral education rather than overtly political action, which is to be seen as part of a broad movement of humanitarian reform. Since their platforms included the abolition of slavery, however, almost all adherents to these movements other than absolute pacifists came to assert the just cause of the North in the American Civil War. Actual resisters to conscription in both North and South came largely from the pacifist sects.

Two outstanding global pacifist figures appeared before the turn of the century. Leo Tolstoy (1828-1910) was influenced by such sects of mid-19th-century Russia as the Doukhobors. His unique pacifism, summed up as "the law of love" found in the Sermon on the Mount, demanded the renunciation of possessions and implied virtual anarchy with regard to the role of state government. Tolstoy found followers not only in Russia but also in Europe, North America, and Japan. The only person to exert a similar global influence was Mohandas K. Gandhi (1869-1948), who recognized Tolstoy's influence, as well as that of the Bible itself, on his own theory and practice of civil disobedience, first in South Africa and then in India. Gandhi's developing philosophy, satyagraha, became a major inspiration for the spread of mass nonviolent action in the 20th century.

Although the outbreak of World War I pushed pacifist convictions to the margins of the church, conscientious objectors achieved grudging recognition in both Britain and America. A pledge to work against war made in 1914 between the German Lutheran Friedrich Siegmund-Schultze (1885-1969) and the English Quaker Henry Hodgkin (1877-1933) led to the founding of the → International Fellowship of Reconciliation (IFOR), which continues as the foremost global religious pacifist organization.

After the war French and German pacifists joined in criticizing the national polices that had resulted in conflict. New pacifist impulses surged in the years after the "war to end all wars," with the hopes of internationalists fixed on such efforts as the League of Nations. Historians of pacifism point to 1935 as a high-water mark for citizen involvement in peace activities. At the same time, Britain and America faced the rise of → fascism and Communism amid the pressures of economic depression. Religious pacifist leaders in 1930s Britain included George Lansbury, Muriel Lester, George MacLeod, Charles Raven, and Donald Soper. In America Sherwood Eddy, Harry Emerson Fosdick, Rufus Jones, Kirby Page, and John Haynes Holmes represented liberal Protestant pacifism in a variety of organizational settings.

As the situation in Europe worsened, some erstwhile pacifist voices began to consider coercive, even violent, strategies in the cause of economic and racial social justice, as they simultaneously debated the alternative political strategies of neutrality or internationalism. These cross-cutting tensions resulted in organizational divisions and shifts in leadership. Reinhold → Niebuhr (1892-1971) was the most prominent person to move from pacifist leadership in the IFOR to argue for the necessity of force in the face of evil and injustice.

The Japanese attack on U.S. forces at Pearl Harbor in 1941, coupled with the overwhelming threat of Adolf Hitler, resulted in a dramatic shift in American opinion. As the nation mobilized for war, only hard-core pacifists, along with the historic peace churches, expressed opposition to conscription. The percentage of conscientious objectors in both Britain and America, however, was higher in World War II than in World War I. Some were drafted into alternative service, and others went to prison as absolutist resisters.

4. After World War II

The nuclear bombing of Hiroshima and Nagasaki and the East-West confrontation that followed World War II resulted in a cold war strategy of nuclear terror that opened up discussion of war and peace on a hitherto unknown scale. Atomic scientists, appalled by the destructive potential of their achievements, spearheaded efforts calling for strict control of the new weaponry (→ Weapons). While internationalists pinned their postwar hopes on the → United Nations, fears of nuclear holocaust and skepticism regarding the effectiveness of the cold war policy of nuclear deterrence motivated the so-called nuclear pacifism movement. Mainline church leadership, as embodied in the → World Council of Churches, after 1983 combined a critique of war with a regard for creation as an irreplaceable resource entrusted to humanity.

From the 1930s onward, Abraham J. Muste (1885-1967) was the foremost American pacifist voice, providing until his death both organizational leadership and noteworthy political and ethical analysis. His lifework represents a creative combination of Christian theology with Gandhian sociopolitical strategy. Muste's influence among radical pacifist groups was extended to challenge racial segregation in the American South. The Baptist clergyman Martin Luther → King Jr. (1929-68) emerged as the leader of large-scale nonviolent campaigns in the → civil rights movement.

In the 1960s the massive mobilization in the United States against the Vietnam War involved millions of activists. Widespread protests — including public draft-card burnings, symbolic assaults on military installations, and other provocations — are perhaps best to be described as antiwar rather than pacifist, even though most actions were essentially nonviolent. Following the Indochina debacle, a threatened new deployment of nuclear missiles in Europe triggered the disarmament and nuclear freeze movements of the 1980s.

The 1983 American Catholic bishops' → pastoral letter "The Challenge of Peace," which strongly challenged the morality of nuclear war, epitomized the growth of pacifist awareness in the → Roman Catholic Church. Catholic pacifism had roots in Europe and was embodied in the United States by Dorothy Day (1897-1980) and the Catholic Worker movement, which was begun in 1933. It remained a tiny minority, however, until it raised a significant voice in the Vietnam era. John XXIII's encyclical *Pacem in terris* (1963), the Pax Christi movement, and the civil disobedience of the Berrigan brothers all stand as marks of the vitality and variety of Catholic pacifism.

With the collapse of the Soviet Union, other threats to world peace have kept issues of war and peace in the headlines. Pacifist voices at the turn of the 21st century, aware of the complexity of global relationships, now address many intertwined problems and crises such as the link between armaments and the military-industrial complex, the exporting of arms, the international armaments trade, the responsibility of the industrialized nations for the constant threat of famine in many parts of the → Third World (→ Dependence), widespread threats to the earth's → ecology, violations of human and civil → rights, and → racism and various other forms of oppression in many countries.

5. Ethical Assessment

The ethical problems of pacifism have been examined by Christian thinkers all the way from Augustine to Reinhold Niebuhr. Christians are taught to love both neighbor and enemy, but these obligations collide in situations where protecting the innocent demands harming, even killing, the aggressor. Thus the traditional ethic of justified warfare has separated the public responsibility of the soldier from the private duty to act only in → love. The absolute pacifist, however, holds that killing is always a denial of the way commanded by Jesus. It is better to suffer evil than to commit it.

Another way of posing the ethical dilemma is to place the principle of "do no harm" over against the intention "to do more good than evil," even if violence is deemed necessary. Thus the end justifies the means (teleogical vs. deontological → ethics). The historical survey above suggests that those with absolute pacifist convictions tended to hold on to their values in times of testing and crisis, while those more concerned with peaceful outcomes in the sociopolitical realm made pragmatic adjustments to the events of their times.

A possibility for transcending this dilemma appears with the 20th-century innovation provided by Gandhi, namely, nonviolent direct action strategies for confronting social evil without using the weapons of violence (→ Force, Violence, Nonviolence). As expressed by Martin Luther King Jr., "Christ furnished the spirit and motivation, while Gandhi furnished the method." The enduring pacifist impulse is more than merely opposition to war; it includes creative proposals toward a more just and peaceful social order.

Bibliography: P. Ackerman and J. DuVall, *A Force More Powerful: A Century of Nonviolent Conflict* (New York, 2000) • R. H. Bainton, *Christian Attitudes toward War and Peace* (Nashville, 1960) • P. Brock, *Pacifism in Europe to 1914* (Princeton, 1972); idem, *Pacifism in the United States, from the Colonial Era to the First World War* (Princeton, 1968); idem, *Twentieth Century Pacifism* (New York, 1970) • D. Brown, *Biblical Pacifism* (Nappanee, Ind., 2003) • M. Ceadek, *The Origins of War Prevention: The British Peace Movement and International Relations, 1730-1854* (Oxford, 1996); idem, *Pacifism in Britain, 1914-1945: The Defining of a Faith* (Oxford, 1980); idem, *Thinking about Peace and War* (Oxford, 1987) • C. Chatfield, *For Peace and Justice: Pacifism in America, 1914-1941* (Knoxville, Tenn., 1971) • C. DeBenedetti, *The Peace Reform in American History* (Bloomington, Ind., 1980) • H. Donat and K. Holl, eds., *Die Friedensbewegung. Organisierter*

Pazifismus in Deutschland, Österreich und in der Schweiz (Düsseldorf, 1983) • K. Holl, *Pazifismus in Deutschland* (Frankfurt, 1988) • H. Josephson, ed., *Biographical Dictionary of Modern Peace Leaders* (Westport, Conn., 1985) • P. Mayer, ed., *The Pacifist Conscience* (Chicago, 1967) • J. H. Yoder, *Nevertheless: The Varieties and Shortcomings of Religious Pacifism* (Scottdale, Pa., 1992).

J. R. Burkholder and Karl Holl

Paganism

1. Term

It is impossible to precisely define "paganism" or its related term "pagan." The LLat. *paganus* derives from *pagus,* "country district." Pagans, so we may deduce, practiced the → religion of the countryside. When town or city dwellers in the late → Roman Empire called someone a pagan, they were perhaps dismissively alluding to that person's beliefs and practices as those of yokels, which sophisticated urbanites had outgrown. Indeed, the terms "paganism" and "pagan" have come to convey entirely pejorative and imprecise judgments, generally from Christian perspectives: the assertion that some things or persons are non-Christian, in need of Christianizing, or even unrepentantly impervious to the Christian message. Consequently, the word "pagan" often takes on a moralizing overtone: a pagan can be defined as someone of little or no religion, even a → hedonist or → materialist, so that the impression is given of an immoral person.

In much later times, English-speaking Protestant → missionaries more often used the word "heathen," which denotes an uncivilized or irreligious person who has not come to faith in the God of the Christian Bible. The word derives from MEng. *heth* (whence our modern "heath"), meaning an area of wasteland. The implication is that such barbarous people as heathens live in wild places, which is similar to the implication of "pagan."

2. Historical Examples

The negative connotations of paganism can be clearly seen when we look at examples of how the term has been used to indicate or even shape hostile Christian attitudes to non-Christian groups. The triumph of Christianity in the Roman Empire, particularly after its patronage by Constantine (306-37) early in the fourth century and then its official status in 381, was at first mostly an urban phenomenon. Ancient polytheistic rites lingered in very rural areas (→ Polytheism). Although some people remained committed to the old gods and the ancient ways in urban centers of that time and place (there are even examples of the conversion of Christians to pagan rites), it became difficult to continue in that commitment. This tension is illustrated by the consequences of the protest of Quintus Aurelius Symmachus (ca. 345-ca. 402) when in 382 the statue of Liberty, which had been seen as a symbol of Rome's power since the days of Augustus, was removed on imperial orders from its altar in the senate house in order to appease Christian senators. Symmachus warned that → Roman religion was tied up with Roman law and that if one part of the heritage went, the other would surely soon follow. His complaint brought down the wrath of Ambrose (ca. 339-97), bishop of Milan. By threatening to withdraw the support of Christian leaders for imperial policies if the emperor tolerated pagan religion, Ambrose won the day. Nevertheless, Symmachus and others continued to practice their rites until 392, when an imperial law forbade visits to pagan temples and → sacrifices to the ancient gods.

No doubt the catastrophic events of the following century, such as the fall of Rome to the Goths in 410, led many to speculate that they were the result of abandoning the old cults. There was, however, no resurgence of pagan rites. Christianity actually flourished, not least because in those calamitous times its urban-based → bishops often stepped into the roles of secular leaders, presiding over such civic stability as was possible, and often persuading the conquerors to submit to Christian faith. In fact, Symmachus's warning failed to materialize precisely because Western Christian leaders upheld Roman → civil law as far as they could; they also incorporated much of it into → church law.

Western and central Europe thus slowly became mainly Christian. Several recent books refer to the Christianizing of Germanic and other tribes in the European "Dark Ages" as the conversion of the pagans. It could be argued that this term is objective and appropriate, on the grounds that such pagan groups were mainly "of the countryside," opposed to the civil, urban values of the late Roman Empire that Christianity preserved. In fact, "pagan" and "paganism" are mostly pejorative words, assuming (with some justification) that Christianity was a civilizing force among the barbarians.

Other references to these words by Christian writers, however, indicate just as clearly that they are imprecise and condemnatory terms. One example is the use of *paynim,* an Old French and Middle English form of the word "pagan." Christians especially used it to refer to Muslims in the High Middle Ages. Yet, ironically, Muslims were not country dwellers at all but originally desert people and then, at the time of this usage, inhabitants of great, urban-based civilizations in West Asia and North Africa and even in Europe itself, where they had a dominant presence in parts of the Iberian Peninsula from 711 to 1492 (→ Islam).

In the later Middle Ages, as the → popes grew more confident of their political power but were also aware of threats to their authority from a number of quarters, some made exclusive claims to the church's salvific role and to their own central importance within it. For example, during the Council of Florence in 1441, Eugenius IV (1431-47) promulgated the bull *Cantate Domino,* in which he asserted that "those not living within the Catholic Church, not only pagans, but also Jews and heretics and schismatics, cannot become participants in eternal life." Here the word "pagans" seems to be a dismissive and imprecise catchall for all those who do not fall within the other groups, yet are not members of the → Roman Catholic Church. The major group of people subsumed under this term at that time were Muslims.

Much later, Protestant missionaries employed the analogous word "heathen" to denote members of non-Christian religions. William Carey (1761-1834), for example, attempted to persuade opponents of the missionary challenge to its cause in a work entitled *An Enquiry into the Obligations of Christians to Use Means for the Conversion of the Heathens* (1792). Many of Carey's contemporaries also portrayed non-Christians as heathens.

Many Christians who use the language of paganism or heathenism are, at most, only vaguely alluding to its root meanings of "barbarous people" or "wild places." In fact, these expressions have proved handy though slippery terms to dismiss people of other religious persuasions as unreached by the God of the Bible. Nowadays, in most cases, it seems best to abandon their employment for the sake of precision and, arguably, of fairness and even of truth. So, if one means to denote a member of another world religion, a practitioner of local religious beliefs and practices, or someone in the → New Age movement, it is wise to use those terms, not "paganism" or "heathen." This usage would also have the merit of removing negative notions that "pagan/paganism" and "heathen" convey, forcing the observer to argue the case for his or her disapproval of whatever he or she is deeming pagan(ism) or heathen.

There has been one relatively recent case where the concept of paganism has been appropriated to describe ideas or movements that, in the minds of their proponents, are positive and important, not negative and outmoded. P. E. Schlund began using "paganism" in 1923 to refer to groups that supposedly adopted old Germanic customs. These groups did nothing of the sort. In fact, they built upon late 19th-century racism to idealize an Aryan myth that excluded, dehumanized, and even sought the extermination of others (e.g., Jews, "Negroes," Slavs).

3. Modern Paganism

One very important strand of paganism exists and even flourishes in the contemporary world. Numbers of people, overwhelmingly in the "developed" countries of the West, believe that ancient beliefs and practices survived the inroads of Christianity, especially in out-of-the-way places, and have been repossessing this heritage. Many describe their spiritual ways as modern paganism or neopaganism. They do not so much see themselves as direct descendants of the pagans of old but, rather, claim to have revived traditions that never quite died out.

3.1. *Characteristics*

The characteristics of modern pagans can be described under four broad headings, though there are many exceptions.

1. Modern pagans are a relatively recent phenomenon. Identifying themselves as such generally only after 1960, they are for the most part white, middle-class, college-educated, liberal in politics, and environmentally concerned; two-thirds of them are women. They typically affirm alternative sexualities, and many claim to have had magical experiences. It is impossible to determine how many modern pagans there are: some maintain that there are several million in the United States alone, but the eclectic nature of the groups makes such claims only guesses, and most religious minorities have a tendency to exaggerate their numbers.
2. Modern pagans distance themselves from New Age practices and Satanism but often embrace the title "witch" and practice modern → magic, aligning themselves with the powers of the earth. Since the earth is seen as a nurturing mother, it is often portrayed as a goddess. Indeed, many mod-

ern pagans believe "the goddess" to be the oldest repository of theistic worship.
3. In fact, modern pagans form an extraordinarily diverse group, including Goddess worshipers, shamans, Wiccans, Druids, → Unitarian Universalist pagans, and many more.
4. Within this diversity, certain common features emerge (including distinctive beliefs, though many modern pagans recoil from this word on the grounds that it impedes personal choice and implies the holding of divisive and unconvincing convictions). They include a view of divinity as → immanent rather than (or as well as) transcendent, the sacredness of all living things, the essential goodness of humans (though they may do evil), the affirmation of spiritual → autonomy, and celebration of "The Wheel of the Year." This wheel is a cycle of eight festivals based upon a solar calendar and also including key days based upon the phases of the moon.

Some have argued recently that paganism is a world religion, with a distinctive, if eclectic, theology. Its proponents point out that its spiritual perspective is found in such varieties as Indian, Chinese, and Japanese folk religion and in the faith of the world's "first peoples," as well as in Western neopaganism. It can be seen as the ancestral religion of all humanity, from which the major religions have evolved.

3.2. *Critique*

Attempts to define neopaganism as a world religion could be interpreted as part of a wider attempt to draw marginalized religious systems into the circle of "respectable" world religions. The most notable example has been that of Geoffrey Parrinder, who argues in *African Traditional Religion* (1954) that such religion should be classified as a world → religion. He lists four essential ingredients that define a distinct sub-Saharan religion that flourished before the coming of Muslims and Christians, and that still has many adherents (i.e., a supreme god, other gods, the ancestors, charms and amulets). Many now argue, however, that the diversity of African traditional religion is more significant than its supposedly essential ingredients. Moreover, the concept of religion has undergone much criticism in recent years and is now often depicted as more fluid, less boundaried, less adequate a description of families of faiths than has recently been held. Attempts to gain respectability for neopaganism by including it as one authentic religion among many others thus seem unconvincing and even misguided, because academic discussions about the nature and functions of religion have evolved.

Some critics of neopaganism have rejected its claim to be the ancestral religion of the whole of humanity. They argue that several of the characteristics of modern paganism, including its recent growth, the nature of its beliefs, and the socioeconomic and cultural makeup of its devotees, should cause one to make it, sociologically and religiously, a part of New Age beliefs, not a modern manifestation of an ancient spiritual way. Most neopagans would strenuously deny this view, yet to many outsiders they appear to have an extremely superficial, magpie-like attitude to the past, reviving customs that are imperfectly understood, wrenched out of the context of any living traditions, and made to serve the ends of contemporary privileged, Western, minority groups. On this view, it is unconvincing to compare neopaganism with folk religion or any customs that are found in the world's long-established religions.

Indeed, much of neopaganism looks like a revolt against Christian (and to some extent Jewish) patriarchy, its doctrines of → creation and redemption, and some of its traditional practices. Christians therefore find the beliefs and lifestyles of modern pagans to be unsettling, unacceptable, and sometimes even simply provocatively different. Some hold that, in a secular age that does not and cannot meet spiritual needs common to most people, the decline in church or synagogue attendance in many Western countries is bound to lead to the rise of ersatz religions that promise comfort while making few demands. A number falsely assert that modern pagans practice satanic worship and black magic.

Indeed, it may be wise of Christians to refrain from quick and easy criticisms of modern paganism. For in past times, although Christians have depreciated pagan customs, they have also "baptized" some of them into their own religion (e.g., placing → Christmas Day close to the winter solstice). Christians could have things to learn from, as well as condemn in, neopaganism. An approach based on → dialogue would seem to hold out more hope than one based on ready disparagement or confrontation.

Bibliography: H. Berger et al., eds., *Voices from the Pagan Census: A National Survey of Witches and Neo-Pagans in the United States* (Columbia, S.C., 2003) • D. Castille, *Du paganisme au christianisme* (Agnières, 2004) • R. Fletcher, *The Barbarian Conversion: From Paganism to Christianity* (New York, 1998) • M. Gardell, *Gods of the Blood: The Pagan Revival and White Separatism* (Durham, N.C., 2003) • J.-F. Lyotard, *Paganisme et postmodernité* (Paris, 1999) • S. Magliocco, *Witching Culture: Folklore and Neo-Paganism in*

America (Philadelphia, 2004) • M. York, *Pagan Theology: Paganism as a World Religion* (New York, 2003).

Martin Forward

Pakistan

	1960	1980	2000
Population (1,000s):	49,955	85,299	156,007
Annual growth rate (%):	2.69	3.42	2.59

Area: 879,811 sq. km. (339,697 sq. mi.)

A.D. 2000

Population density: 177/sq. km. (459/sq. mi.)
Births / deaths: 3.32 / 0.68 per 100 population
Fertility rate: 4.54 per woman
Infant mortality rate: 65 per 1,000 live births
Life expectancy: 66.1 years (m: 64.9, f: 67.4)
Religious affiliation (%): Muslims 96.2, Christians 2.3, Hindus 1.2, other 0.3.

1. History
2. Religion
   2.1. Islam
   2.2. Minority Religions
      2.2.1. General Situation
      2.2.2. Christianity
      2.2.3. Hinduism

Pakistan became an independent state on August 14, 1947. The idea of a Muslim area in the northwest of the subcontinent was first suggested and supported by Muhammad Iqbāl (1877-1938), the poet-philosopher of Indian Muslims, at the annual gathering of the All India Muslim League in Allahabad on December 30, 1930.

1. History

Muslims (→ Islam) came to India in 711 and took over the lower Indus Valley up to Multan (now southern Pakistan). By 800 a second wave came and, from Ghaznī in present-day Afghanistan, set up Muslim rule in northwest India. Bengal, in the east, was also under Muslim rule from the early 13th century, and from 1347 there were Muslim kingdoms in southwest India, the Deccan. The peak of Muslim dominion came under the Great Moguls (1526-1857), whose centers in Agra, Lahore, and Delhi astonished European visitors. Jesuit missionaries (→ Jesuits) reached India in 1594 under the Mogul ruler Akbar (1556-1605), but their early influence hardly extended beyond introducing religious pictures, which had an effect on Muslim art and → iconography. The Deccan saw relations between the kingdom of Bijapur and the Portuguese, who settled in Goa. The Mogul kingdom reached its broadest extent in 1687.

Many disasters overtook the Moguls in the 18th century, and the British East India Company, which had begun work in India in 1600, gradually took over more and more territory after the battle of Plassey (1757), which gave it access to the eastern part of the subcontinent (→ Colonialism). Toward the end of the 18th century the Mogul rulers of Delhi and the Shiite rulers of Awadh (modern-day Uttar Pradesh in northern India; → Shia, Shiites) were more or less under British control.

The main source of Muslim instruction, which was in religious institutions, was largely ended by British legislation. New financial regulations also made much of the population poorer. It thus is clear why Muslims disliked the new Christian → mission schools that rose up all over the land (→ Colonialism and Mission). Making English the official language (1835) was another factor in Muslim suppression, and the encouragement of regional languages helped to split the subcontinent. Some Muslim scholars did play a role in the new educational system, and Delhi College is a good example of Christian-Muslim cooperation (→ Islam and Christianity). On the whole, however, educated Muslims opposed the Christian educational policy. It was easier for Hindus, who had exchanged one rule for another, to go to British schools and to gain the knowledge needed for employment by the government.

The Muslims were blamed for an unsuccessful mutiny in 1857, at which point Britain took full political control except in the princely states. The Muslim reformer Sayyid Ahmad Khan (1817-98) accepted British rule for a time and tried to achieve understanding between Muslims and Christians. His (incomplete) commentary on the Bible was a first step in this direction, and the founding of the Anglo-Muslim College in Aligarh (1875) was a significant event. But he opposed Muslim participation in the Indian National Congress (1885), fearing that the Hindu majority would outvote the Muslim minority on all decisive issues.

The Muslims founded the Muslim League in 1906 as a representative party and as a forum for Indian Muslim separatism, though it was primarily allied to the upper classes and great landowners. With rising nationalist sentiments in India, tensions grew. Hindus and Muslims briefly joined forces in a common fight against Britain for Indian freedom, but the union did not last, and the founding of a state in which Muslims could live more autonomously seemed inevitable (→ Nation, Nationalism). Initially the problems caused by the scattering of Muslims across many parts of India were largely disregarded. M. A. Jinnah (1876-1948), an advocate of the Ismaili sect, championed the idea of Pakistan, a state for the Islamic-majority areas of India, which secured official approval at Lahore on March 23, 1940.

In 1947, after much difficult and not always fair negotiating, the new state of East and West Pakistan came into being, not as a friendly neighbor of India, as Iqbāl had hoped, but with much loss of blood and property. The new state organized itself with remarkable efficiency, with Jinnah as governor-general and Liaquat Ali Khan (1895-1951), Jinnah's right-hand man, as prime minister. But the death of Jinnah and the assassination in 1951 of his successor, Liaquat, created severe problems. Setting up a constitution was the hardest and most important, since it involved clashes over the meaning of an Islamic state. Pakistan was proclaimed an Islamic republic in 1956. When Ayub Khan (1907-74) took over in a coup in the fall of 1958, a period of military rule ensued, broken only by Zulfikar Ali Bhutto (1928-79, prime minister 1973-79) of the Pakistan People's Party (PPP), which had prevalent socialist ideas. In 1971 East Pakistan, 1,500 km. (930 mi.) away from West Pakistan, broke away after heavy fighting and became Bangladesh.

General Zia ul-Haqq seized power in Pakistan in a military coup in 1978, declared martial law, and postponed national elections. Zia instigated criminal investigations of the PPP leadership, which led to Bhutto's being convicted and sentenced to death for alleged conspiracy to murder a political opponent. He was executed in 1979. After the death of Zia ul-Haqq in a plane crash in 1988, Bhutto's daughter Benazir won elections but then in 1990 was dismissed on corruption charges. Polarization took place between the left-leaning PPP, founded by Z. A. Bhutto, and Jama'at-i-Islami, a strictly Islamic party formed in 1941.

Nawaz Sharif, of the Pakistan Muslim League, won elections in 1990 and became prime minister, but Benazir Bhutto returned to power after the elections of 1993. In 1996 she was again dismissed from her office on corruption charges, and elections in 1997 returned Sharif to the position of prime minister. He quickly amended the constitution to shore up the powers of the prime minister, but then in October 1999 he was removed by a bloodless coup led by army chief General Pervez Musharraf. Musharraf assumed the presidency in June 2001; the constitution, which had been suspended in 1999, was restored at the end of 2002.

Pakistan conducted nuclear tests in 1998 in response to India's tests earlier that year, and both countries faced U.S. sanctions as a result. After the terrorist attacks of September 11, 2001, however, the United States sought Pakistan as an ally and lifted sanctions. Pakistan was faced with international pressure to assist the United States against the Taliban regime in Afghanistan but also with domestic pressure from Islamic groups not to attack a Muslim ally. Despite domestic tensions, Musharraf did allow the U.S. military to use Pakistan's soil and air space for operations in Afghanistan. In December 2001 Pakistani-based militants attacked India's Parliament building, which severely strained the already tense relationship between the two states. In 2002 Musharraf began a government crackdown on these militant Islamic groups, outlawing them and attempting to suppress their activities.

Kashmir, a former princely state in the area of northeast Pakistan and northwest India, has been the focus of a hotly disputed territorial dispute between India and Pakistan. Violence flared in 1948, 1965, 1989, 1999, and again in 2001. A ceasefire was declared in 2003, and formal peace talks began in 2004.

2. Religion

2.1. *Islam*

Pakistan is an Islamic republic, with 97 percent of the population Muslim (2005). The Muslims are mostly Hanafite Sunnis (→ Sunna). The Jama'at-i-Islami is fundamentalistic, and the Barelwis (famous for their devotion to Muslim → saints) are closest to the Islam of the people. In 2005 it was estimated that three-quarters of the total population were Sunnis, and about 20 percent Shiites (most of them Twelvers), including many leading families. Some Sunnites have become Shiites because the Shiite law of inheritance is more favorable to women. Smaller groups are the Ismailis, both Khojas (under the Aga Khan; → Shia, Shiites, 5) and Bohras (or Bohoras), both of which are economically influential. A network of Sufi brotherhoods (→ Sufism) covers the land, and mystical leaders (→ Mysticism 1.2.8) make a strong impact, even in politics.

Between 1980 and 2000 some 4,000 people were killed in sectarian violence between Shiite and → Sunni groups. Extremist Islamic groups have been outlawed, but many still operate underground.

Members of the Ahmadi sect have also been victims of Muslim violence and discrimination. Although they themselves claim to be Muslims, yet because they deny the finality of the prophet Muhammad, the majority of Muslims reject them. In

1974 the Pakistani government officially declared Ahmadis to be non-Muslims.

Under blasphemy laws introduced in 1985, many Muslims, Ahmadis, and Christians have faced trial for blasphemy against Muhammad or defamation of the Qur'an. Since 1991 the → death penalty has been mandatory for convictions of blasphemy, although no one has yet been executed under this law. In a number of cases, however, defendants have died as a result of mob violence against them.

2.2. *Minority Religions*

2.2.1. *General Situation*

Although the laws of Pakistan grant some freedoms and protections to religious → minorities, in practice these guarantees have often been violated (→ Persecution of Christians 4.3.3). The formal incorporation of Islamic → Shari'a law in 1991 has added to the difficulties of Pakistan's non-Muslim minorities. For example, a non-Muslim's testimony in court is not given the same legal weight as that of a Muslim.

In 1985 a system of separate electorates was imposed, according to which citizens could cast votes only for candidates of their own religion. This arrangement, which greatly restricted the political influence of non-Muslims, was protested both by the minorities and by human → rights groups. The government restored the joint electorate system in 2002, and political representation is now geographically determined, although certain government seats are still reserved for religious minorities.

2.2.2. *Christianity*

Christians make up a small minority in Pakistan, slightly more than 2 percent of the population. They live mostly in Sind, the Punjab, and Peshawar in the Northwest Frontier Province. Many come from Hindu families of lower → castes and untouchables that converted under British rule. They are thus often of lower social status, despised, and with little chance of advancement, although some receive private help from the West. Some growth in the Christian population occurred when Christians from Goa, India, emigrated to Pakistan. → Conversions from Islam are rare and typically cause family problems.

By Islamic law Christians are *dhimmīy,* protected because they have a revealed Scripture (→ Islam 2). They have some freedom in education and may occupy any office except that of head of state. Christians' legal rights, however, are not always protected in practical experience.

Roman Catholics (→ Roman Catholic Church) make up slightly less than half of the Christian population. A → nuncio represents the Holy See in Islamabad. Roman Catholic bishops are at work, for example, in Karachi and the Punjab (Faisalabad). In 2003 there were 6 → bishops and 282 → priests for the 1.2 million Catholics in the country. In the past, the bishop in Karachi, joined by Christian and Muslim specialists, worked to develop a school syllabus that would do justice to the religious feelings and traditions of the various religions in Pakistan.

Roman Catholic orders (→ Religious Orders and Congregations 1) are present in Sind and the Punjab. There is a Jesuit center in Lahore where → Dominicans are also active. The Christian Study Center in Rawalpindi actively seeks to encourage Muslim-Christian → dialogue.

The Church of Pakistan, with over a million members, is by far the largest Protestant body in Pakistan. It was formed in 1970 through a → union of Anglican, Methodist, Lutheran, Presbyterian, and other Protestant denominations. A number of Adventist, Baptist, and Pentecostal groups have also begun work in Pakistan. Many of the Protestant churches belong to interdenominational organizations such as the → National Council of Churches in Pakistan, the Evangelical Fellowship of Pakistan, and the International Council of Christian Churches.

Christian presence has made itself felt in education. Many colleges founded under British rule continue almost unchanged. Z. A. Bhutto sought to nationalize schools and colleges in 1972, but since the mid-1980s some of these schools have been denationalized and returned to their original owners. Forman Christian College was returned to the Presbyterian Church (→ Reformed Churches) in 2003, and the Presbyterians also hope to recover Gordon College in Rawalpindi. Kinnaird College in Lahore has educated elite Muslim (and previously Hindu) girls for many years and continues to do so, since many leading families prefer to send their children to mission schools. In many cases the school's Christian character is not very pronounced, though the educators are Christian.

Christians have also taken the lead in medicine. The → Adventists' hospital in Karachi is very prominent, and doctors and nurses do sacrificial work in fighting leprosy and caring for victims of the disease (→ Medical Missions). Notwithstanding an increasing Islamization, official regard is given to Christian concerns. High statesmen are photographed attending Christian observances such as Christmas, though efforts to make → Easter a public holiday failed.

2.2.3. *Hinduism*

Hindus (→ Hinduism), who live primarily in Sind,

in Thar in the east, and in Las Bela in the west, are for the most part merchants or artisans. Hindu shrines such as Hinglaj in Makran can be freely visited. The cult of Kali is especially widespread among Sindhi Hindus.

→ Asian Theology; Iranian Religions

Bibliography: S. J. Burki, *Pakistan: Fifty Years of Nationhood* (3d ed.; Boulder, Colo., 1999) • S. P. Cohen, *The Idea of Pakistan* (Washington, D.C., 2004) • N. A. Jawed, *Islam's Political Culture: Religion and Politics in Predivided Pakistan* (Austin, Tex., 1999) • C. H. Kennedy and C. Baxter, eds., *Pakistan 2000* (Lanham, Md., 2000) • A. Schimmel, *Islam in India and Pakistan* (Leiden, 1982) • S. Syrjänen, *In Search of Meaning and Identity: Conversion to Christianity in Pakistani Muslim Culture* (Helsinki, 1984).

Annemarie Schimmel† and the Editors

Palamism

Palamism is the theological position associated with the name of Gregory Palamas (ca. 1296-1359), a Byzantine saint and archbishop of Thessalonica, affirming the experience of → *theōsis* (or "deification") and also a real distinction between the "essence" of → God (§6), which remains transcendent, and the "energies," or → grace, through which deification becomes accessible in Christ (→ Christology 3).

Before starting his activities as a theologian, Palamas was a Hesychast monk on Mount → Athos. He defended the Hesychasts, who claimed to have obtained the experience of a real vision of God (→ Visions) and were criticized by Barlaam (ca. 1290-ca. 1350), a Calabrian "philosopher." Barlaam was condemned by a council in Constantinople (1341). Other councils met successively in 1347 and 1351 to approve the position of Palamas on the distinction between essence and energies in God. This position was attacked by other Byzantine theologians, particularly Gregory Akindynos (ca. 1300-ca. 1349) and Nicephorus Gregoras (1295-1360) and later by the Thomists Demetrius Cydones (ca. 1324-ca. 1398) and his brother Prochorus Cydones (ca. 1330-ca. 1369).

Palamism was affirmed as Orthodox doctrine (→ Orthodox Christianity), and its position was included in the Synodikon, the annual liturgical proclamation of true doctrines on the first Sunday of Lent (→ Liturgical Books). Disciples of Palamas, particularly Patriarch Philotheus Kokkinos (in office 1354-55, 1364-76) and the lay theologian Nicholas Cabasilas (ca. 1322-ca. 1390), exercised wide influence in Byzantine society (→ Byzantium). The victory of Palamism also contributed to monastic and spiritual revival among Balkan Slavs and Russians (→ Slavic Mission).

→ Anthropology 3.3; Apophatic Theology; Monasticism; Starets

Bibliography: *Palamas's works: Gregoriou tou Palama Syngrammata* (Collected writings) (3 vols.; ed. P. Chrestou; Thessaloníki, 1962-70) further vols. planned • *The One Hundred and Fifty Chapters* (ed. R. E. Sinkewicz; Leiden, 1988) • *PG* 150-51 • *The Triads* [*in Defense of the Holy Hesychasts*] (ed. J. Meyendorff; New York, 1983).

Secondary works: G. Mantzaridis, *The Deification of Man: St. Gregory Palamas and the Orthodox Tradition* (Crestwood, N.Y., 1984) • J. Meyendorff, *St. Gregory Palamas and Orthodox Spirituality* (Crestwood, N.Y., 1974); idem, *A Study of G. Palamas* (London, 1964) • G. C. Papademetriou, *Maimonides and Palamas on God* (Brookline, Mass., 1994) • A. N. Williams, *The Ground of Union: Deification in Aquinas and Palamas* (New York, 1999).

John Meyendorff†

Paleography → History, Auxiliary Sciences to, 3

Palestine

	1960	*1980*	*2000*
Population (1,000s):	639	1,096	2,070
Annual growth rate (%):	2.54	3.02	3.93

Area: 6,242 sq. km. (2,410 sq. mi.)

A.D. 2000

Population density: 332/sq. km. (859/sq. mi.)
Births / deaths: 4.37 / 0.45 per 100 population
Fertility rate: 7.41 per woman
Infant mortality rate: 31 per 1,000 live births
Life expectancy: 69.3 years (m: 67.7, f: 70.8)
Religious affiliation (%): Muslims 70.5, Jews 12.6, Christians 11.0 (indigenous 6.1, Orthodox 2.8, Roman Catholics 1.6, other Christians 0.6), nonreligious 5.8, other 0.1.

Note: Figures include the West Bank, East Jerusalem, the Gaza Strip, and the Golan Heights.

1. Early and Middle Bronze Ages
2. The Iron Age
3. From Alexander to the Ottomans
4. World War I, Partition, and a Peace Process
5. The Christian Presence in Palestine

The name "Palestine" is commonly used to designate the ancient land of the Bible, the Holy Land — "from Dan to Beer-sheba." It is also the common name for the territory of the British mandate taken over by the United Nations in 1948 and held now by the Palestinian Authority and the State of → Israel (§2), with the Occupied Territories. Originally, however, its boundaries were not so definitely defined, and Palestine was not its name. To gain some perspective about this small, revered, and troubled spot, we consider it in its original, much larger geographic and historical setting.

1. Early and Middle Bronze Ages

The area usually called Palestine was not originally an entity in itself but simply part of the southern Levant, which goes northward along the coast of the Mediterranean Sea as far as the Orontes River and the ancient cities of Ugarit and Ebla, the northern limits of the ancient Canaanite world. The southern Levant was also the southern end of the so-called Fertile Crescent, which extends northwest from the Mesopotamian valley and southwest along the eastern coast of the Mediterranean Sea. It was the land bridge between Mesopotamia and Egypt, which is often called Syria-Palestine, or Syro-Palestine, a general geographic designation with no suggestion of political boundaries. Geographically, the southern Levant, Syria-Palestine, was the crossroads of the ancient Near East. "Thus Palestine and Syria became a middle ground between Mesopotamia and Egypt from both economic and political points of view. The mighty kingdoms on both sides of the Fertile Crescent considered this strip of land a thoroughfare; and both of them labored to impose their authority over it, mainly so as to control the trade routes passing through it and to use it as a bridgehead for defense or offense" (Y. Aharoni, 6).

Human habitation in the Levant is very ancient, known in the remains from Paleolithic times and later in the impressive Neolithic city of Jericho in the Jordan Valley, from about 7000 B.C. The Early Bronze Age (3300-2300 B.C.) was characterized by the rise of the first city-states: Ebla and Byblos (modern Jubayl, Leb.) in the north, and Tyre, Hazor, Megiddo, Gezer, Jerusalem, and Lachish in the south.

At the beginning of the Middle Bronze Age (2300-1550), a series of nomadic invasions, principally by the Amorites *(Amurru)*, Semitic-speaking peoples, brought great political changes in Mesopotamia. Moving westward and settling down, they established strong urban centers such as Mari. In Akkadian texts Syria-Palestine came to be known as the Land of the Amurru, and the Mediterranean as the Sea of Amurru.

During this time the Levant was generally under the control of Egypt, an early evidence of which is found in the story of Sinuhe, from the 20th century B.C. Sinuhe was an Egyptian officer who fled Egypt and took refuge in Retenu/Canaan, where his wandering took him as far north as Byblos and Qedem, and his exploits among the various groups of people inhabiting the land later won him honors in his native Egypt. There are also execration texts from the 20th to the 19th centuries that bear witness to Egypt as a dominant power, with their many references to towns and places in Syria-Palestine, such as Ashqelon, Jerusalem, Rehob, Byblos, Arqat, Tyre, and Beqa.

In the 16th century B.C., native Egyptian rule was interrupted by the Hyksos, a strong Semitic people. Known for their fortifications and great military power, they introduced the horse and chariot into warfare. They swept down from the north through the Levant and into Egypt, where they ruled during Dynasties 15-17, administering their empire from the Nile Delta.

Driving out the Hyksos, the native Egyptian rulers of the 18th and 19th Dynasties began a new era of expansion and empire building. Syria-Palestine became the scene of many passing armies and bloody battles. One of the earliest and most notable of these campaigns was led by the pharaoh Thutmose III (king 1504-1450 B.C.). His control over Canaan, however, was challenged by the Canaanite kings of Megiddo, Kadesh, Mitanni, and several other city-states. Leading his army by way of the sea (the Via Maris), Thutmose was halted at the Mount Carmel range in the north of what would become part of Isael some centuries later. On the other side of the Carmel range, in the Jezreel Valley, the Canaanite allies were waiting. The major pass through the mountain was protected by the fortress city of Megiddo. In an act of daring strategy Thutmose led his army through the pass, attacking the city directly and defeating the Canaanite forces. This was only the first of many military campaigns that Thutmose led through Syria-Palestine to enlarge Egyptian control.

The southern Levant would be the scene of many more confrontations between international powers. Amenhotep II (1450-1425 B.C.) led at least two campaigns through Canaan and to the north, even crossing the Orontes. Seti I (1318-1304) was active against groups in Canaan and confronted the Hittites at Kadesh in the far north of Syria-Palestine. Ramses II (1304-1237) led many campaigns through the area, his most famous achievement being a peace treaty concluded with the Hittites. His successor, Merneptah (1236-1223), claimed Egyptian control over all Syria-Palestine, and in a hymn of victory on a victory stela, he listed all the peoples and kingdoms he allegedly conquered. This stone is often called the Israel Stela because in the list of Canaanite cities and places, Israel is mentioned for the first time, significantly not as a settled people but simply as a group in the land.

2. The Iron Age

The beginning of the Iron Age (ca. 1200 B.C.) saw a new development: the emergence of local kingdoms in the Syria-Palestine area. In the north there were Phoenicia and Aram; to the south, Israel, soon divided as Ephraim and Judah; to the east and south, Ammon, Moab, and Edom; and to the west, Philistia, settled by a non-Semitic group related to the Sea Peoples, whose boundaries encompassed five major coastal cities: Gaza, Ashkelon, Ashdod, Ekron, and Gath.

This is the first occurrence of the name "Palestine," which is derived from the gentilic Philistine: Egypt. *pi-liš-ta,* Akkad. *pa-laš-tu* and *pi-liš-te,* Heb. *pělešet* (note *'ereṣ pělištîm,* "land of the Philistines"), Gk. *Palaistinē,* and Lat. *Palaestina.* In the ancient Egyptian and Akkadian inscriptions the name was used only to designate the Philistine territory, not including the territory of Israel and other adjacent kingdoms. For example, in a list Adad-nirari II (911-891 B.C.) writes of "Tyre, Sidon, Israel, Edom, Palestine, as far as the shore of the Great Sea of the Setting Sun" (*ANET* 281); Sargon II (721-705) speaks of "the rulers of Palestine, Judah, Edom, Moab, and those who live on islands" (*ANET* 287). The Hebrew Bible nowhere calls the nation Israel Palestine, but it lists Palestine as a kingdom among others as in Ps. 108:9-10 (NRSV 8-9, mentioning Ephraim, Judah, Moab, Edom, and Philistia; see also Ps. 87:4). Herodotus in the fifth century sees Palestine as part of Syria (*Hist.* 1.105; 7.89) but uses the name *pars pro toto* as meaning Palestine and everything east of it. The NT also does not use "Palestine" for the land of the Bible.

These small kingdoms at the crossroads of the Near East were always in the shadows of the great powers of the Nile and Mesopotamia. They were able to flourish when those powers were quiet or weak, but when the great powers were on the rise, the little nations of the Levant were at their mercy. So in the eighth century B.C. Assyria put down Aram and destroyed altogether the northern kingdom of Israel, leaving only Judah with its weak monarchy, and went on even to subject Egypt. In the seventh century Babylonia overcame Assyria and frustrated Egyptian ambitions for world power. In establishing its sovereignty over the strategic southern Levant, Babylon destroyed Jerusalem in 587, deported its leaders, and left Judea a province of Babylon. At the end of the same century, in 539 B.C., Persia became a great world empire under Cyrus the Great (558-529), and former small kingdoms still remained provinces. Later, Alexander the Great (356-323) defeated Persia and in 333 established the greatest empire yet in the Near East. The southern Levant — which Alexander called Coele-Syria (lit. "hollow Syria," for the Bekáa Valley), everything from the valley to the south — remained a strategic area for his ambitions.

3. From Alexander to the Ottomans

After Alexander's death the empire was divided among his generals, the eastern part of the empire going to Seleucus (king of Babylon, 312-281 B.C.) and Ptolemy (king of Egypt, 305-285). A long series of wars was fought between the Seleucids and Ptolemies, centering especially on securing the Levant. Judea, the southernmost part of the Levant, was caught in the middle. The Seleucids won out, but the Judeans rebelled against their oppressive rule and, under the Maccabees, gained a temporary freedom with the Hasmonaean monarchy, ending with the reign of Herod the Great (ruled 37-4 B.C.). This freedom actually ended earlier, however, in 73 B.C., when Pompey entered Jerusalem, and Judea became simply a province of Rome (→ Hellenism 2).

Little changed with the first Jewish revolt against Rome, in A.D. 66-70, except for the destruction of the temple. In 135, however, with the end of the second revolt and the short-lived rule of Bar-Kochba (132-35), the situation was drastically altered. The emperor Hadrian (117-38) leveled Jerusalem, redesigned it after the quarter fashion of a Roman camp, and renamed it Aelia Capitolina. A temple to Jupiter was erected over the site of the Jewish temple, and a forum in Hadrian's honor with a shrine to Aphrodite was built over the area venerated by Christians as the place of the crucifixion and resurrection. To remove all former associations, Hadrian renamed the province of Judea "Provincia Syria Palaestina," after one of Judea's most hated enemies. Moreover, Jews were prohibited entrance to → Jerusalem (§7.1) except on one day a year, and they were not allowed to live in proximity to the city.

This is the first time that the land of the Bible was called Palestine. Significantly, though, it was not just "Palaestina" but "Syria Palaestina," recalling its original unity with the southern Levant and Alexander's Coele-Syria. In subsequent years, during the fourth century of Byzantine rule, this broader understanding of the territory was underscored by the division of the land into three Palestines: *Palaestina Prima,* comprising Judea, Samaria, the coast, and Perea, with its capital at Caesarea; *Palaestina Secunda,* comprising Galilee, the Jezreel Valley, regions east of Galilee, and the western part of the Decapolis, with Scythopolis as the capital; and *Palaestina Tertia,* comprising the Negev, southern Transjordan (once Arabia), and most of the Sinai, with Petra as the capital.

With the rise of → Islam, Jerusalem became a holy site for Muslims, as important as Mecca. In 636 at the battle of Yarmūk, Syria-Palestine came under Arab rule, and a modus vivendi between Muslims and Christians was established. This stasis was disrupted by the → Crusades, which were inspired by the desire to rescue the Holy Land from the Muslims. The Crusaders succeeded in establishing the Latin Kingdom of Jerusalem in 1099, which lasted only until 1187, when Saladin's armies defeated the Crusaders and overran Jerusalem. Succeeding Crusades recaptured and lost control of Jerusalem until finally the last vestige of Crusader presence was removed in 1216 at the battle of Acre, and Muslim control was fully restored.

In 1215 the Mamluk Dynasty in Egypt extended its control over Syria-Palestine. In 1516 the Ottomans extended their rule over the whole of western Asia and maintained this sovereignty until the end of World War I. During this long period Palestine remained as a name, but its distinctiveness was lost in the changing administrative districts and policies of the Ottoman rulers. Tolerance was maintained toward Christian interests. Jews, too, were accepted, although they were relatively few in number, most of them settling in the Galilee.

4. World War I, Partition, and a Peace Process

Much changed in Palestine with World War I and the defeat of Germany and the end of the Ottoman Empire. In 1919 the present-day boundaries of Palestine were set. A system of mandates was established to replace the territories of the Turkish Empire, and at the San Remo Conference in April 1920, Palestine, including Jordan, was assigned to Great Britain. In 1922 the Council of the League of Nations approved separate administrations for Palestine and Jordan, while keeping it all under the British mandate.

Following World War I, immigration of Jews to Palestine greatly increased, encouraged by the Zionist movement and the Balfour Declaration of the British government in 1917, which favored the establishment of a Jewish state in Palestine. This development brought conflict between Palestinians and Jews, one that only increased with the influx of immigrants and refugees during Nazi persecution and World War II. In 1947 Great Britain decided to give up its mandate and hand Palestine over to the → United Nations.

The General Assembly of the United Nations adopted a plan, Resolution 181 (II), to partition Palestine into two states, Arab and Jewish. The British mandate was scheduled to end on May 15, 1948, but one day before, May 14, Israel proclaimed itself an independent Jewish state. War immediately broke out between the Palestinians, aided by sympathetic Arab states, and Israel. Israel prevailed, however, with its superior forces. Almost immediately, the State of Israel was recognized by the United States and the Soviet Union, and in 1949 it was admitted to membership in the United Nations. Wars in 1967 and 1973 further extended Israel's control and occupation of land. And thus were set the military and political realities in which Palestinians, Israelis, the Arab states, and Western nations are all involved in a continuing struggle for the establishment of a Palestinian state and general peace in the Middle East.

The way to achieving this goal has been slow and faltering. A forward step came in 1979 with the peace treaty brokered by the United States between Israel and Egypt, and with Israel's subsequent withdrawal from the Sinai in 1982. At the same time, this set of developments created unrest among the Arab nations and fostered continued hostility toward Israel. Civil war in Lebanon (1975-79) brought the intervention of Syria, whose troops and virtual control of Lebanon remained until April 2005. In the meantime, the Palestine Liberation Organization (PLO), now based in Lebanon after having been expelled from Jordan, continued its attacks against Israel, so much so that in 1982 Israel invaded Lebanon. Its troops did not leave the southern borders of Lebanon until 2000.

In 1994 Jordan signed a peace treaty with Israel. Another major step toward peace came in 1995 with the Oslo Interim Agreement, signed by the PLO and Israel, by which the Palestine National Authority (PNA) was created to be a negotiating body and the governing authority over parts of the West Bank. In 1996 Palestinians in the Gaza Strip and Palestinian-controlled areas elected Yasser Arafat (1929-2004) as chairman. Under the Oslo Agreement the PLO had agreed to end violence. Attacks continued, however, and Israel not only retaliated but continued to establish new settlements on the West Bank and in Gaza. The attempts by the United States to reach an agreement at the Camp David negotiations of July 2000 and in Washington in December went nowhere. In the same way, negotiations led by European and Egyptian leaders at Taba, Egypt, in January 2001 ended in failure.

A turning point, however, came in February 2002, when Crown Prince Abdullah of Saudi Arabia proposed that the Arab states end the war against Israel, that Israel in return withdraw from the Occupied Territories, and that satisfactory arrangements for Jerusalem and refugees be made. Arab states agreed to a modified form of the Saudi proposal. Subsequently the United States began consultations with representatives of the European Union, Russia, and the United Nations (they came to be known as the Middle East Quartet) to work out "a performance-based road map leading to a permanent two-state solution to the Israeli-Palestinian conflict." At this writing, with new leadership for the Palestinians and with Israel's withdrawal from Gaza, although unilateral, one can cautiously hope with the Quartet for "the fulfillment of the vision of two states, a safe and secure Israel and a sovereign, contiguous, democratic Palestine, living side by side in peace and security" (from "Joint Statement by the Quartet," March 1, 2005).

5. The Christian Presence in Palestine

→ Israel 3, "Christian Groups in Israel and Palestine"

Bibliography: Y. Aharoni, *The Land of the Bible: A Historical Geography* (2d ed.; London, 1979) • G. Ahlström, *The History of Ancient Palestine* (Minneapolis, 1993) • B. J. Bailey and J. M. Bailey, *Who Are the Christians in the Middle East?* (Grand Rapids, 2003) • O. Binst, ed., *The Levant: History and Archaeology in the Eastern Mediterranean* (Cologne, 2000) • G. R. Bugh and I. J. Bickerton, "Palestine," *NEBrit* (1998) 25.407-25 • A. Mazar, *Archaeology of the Land of the Bible, 10,000-586 B.C.E.* (New York, 1990) • J. B. Pritchard, ed., *The Times Atlas of the Bible* (London, 1987).

Robert Bornemann

Palmer, Phoebe Worrall

Phoebe Worrall Palmer (1807-74), an author, editor, social activist, evangelist, and lay theologian, was undoubtedly the most influential Methodist woman of the 19th century (→ Methodism). She is best known for her "Tuesday Meetings," "altar theology," and defense of women's right to → preach the gospel. For over a decade she acted as managing editor of the *Guide to Holiness,* whose circulation at the time of her death rivaled that of the most widely read Methodist periodicals. She wrote 18 books consisting of theology, poetry, and biography. During her evangelistic meetings and camp meeting engagements, she has been credited with leading over 25,000 people into the "higher Christian life."

Born the fourth of 16 children of Henry and Dorothea Worrall, an affluent Methodist family, Phoebe grew up on the lower west side of Manhattan. At the age of 20 she married Walter Clark Palmer, a New York City homeopathic physician. They had six children, three of whom died in infancy.

Phoebe's public life began in 1835, when along with her sister Sarah Lankford she began conducting a series of → Bible studies in the home that they and their husbands shared. Adopting the structure of John → Wesley's class meeting, the sessions consisted of Bible study, testimony, and → prayer. Proving to be more capable than her sister, Phoebe soon became the acknowledged leader of the group. The meetings drew people from all denominations and throughout North America and western Europe. Before long even → bishops, college presidents, and other church leaders came to sit at her feet, including the likes of Oberlin (Ohio) College luminaries Asa Mahan and Charles → Finney, prominent Quakers Hannah Whitall Smith and David B. Updergraff, Bowdoin (Maine) College professor Congregationalist Thomas C. Upham, and Nathan Bangs, editor of the *New York Christian Advocate.* This "Tuesday Meeting for the Promotion of Holiness" continued regularly in her home long after her death, until 1896.

The focal point of her teaching was Wesley's doctrine of Christian → perfection. Wesley believed that full → salvation not only resulted in the pardon of one's sins but also restored to the individual all that was lost in the fall. Otherwise, he reasoned, God's curse would be greater than his cure. His teaching, however, also involved human cooperation, for sometimes the individual must strive for a lifetime to achieve the sinless state of grace. In agitating for the centrality of this doctrine, Palmer sought to be faithful to her British mentor. In the context of American → pragmatism, however, she grew impatient with a doctrine that advocated a lifelong struggle. Seeking a shorter way, her approach became known as altar theology.

Palmer insisted that Christian perfection was an instantaneous experience. Regardless of the length of time that proceeded or the intensity of the struggle, there was a point when imperfect intention was made perfect. This happened, she maintained, when three conditions were met: full → consecration, → faith, and confession (→ Confession of Sins). She believed that Christ was both the sacrifice for sin and the altar upon which one's life could be laid in consecration. Claiming that "the altar sanctifieth the gift," she reasoned that through faith in Christ's atoning work on the cross, the Christian would experience release from self-will. By confessing publicly to this experience, a believer could maintain this state of → grace. Such a life would be characterized by a freedom from any inclination that did not spring from perfect → love. Palmer's understanding of Wesley's doctrine remained normative for the → Holiness movement well into the 20th century.

As Palmer's visibility and popularity grew, avenues beyond the Tuesday meeting became available to her. In 1839 she was instrumental in persuading her friend Timothy Merritt to publish *Guide to Holiness,* a periodical that propagated her views. She accepted invitations to speak at camp meetings, church conferences, evangelistic services, and other gatherings throughout North America. Enthusiastic responses to her calls for entire → sanctification in Canadian camp meetings during the summer of 1857, culminating in October in a revival in Hamilton, Ontario, were early manifestations of the 1857-58 → revival. With her husband she followed the spread of the revival to England in 1859, where she ministered to overflowing crowds in Europe for the next four years. Returning to North America at the end of the Civil War, Phoebe traveled throughout the Midwest and the western United States until 1871, when ill health forced her to return to her home, where she remained until her death, in 1874.

Palmer did not neglect the social dimensions of Wesley's doctrine of Christian perfection. She was an ardent supporter of overseas → missions, promoting efforts for health care (→ Medical Mission) and → education in those lands. On the home front she spearheaded efforts to establish the Five Points Mission, which cared for children in one of the poorest neighborhoods of New York City. She spoke out against → slavery, advocated just wages for domestic help, and took part in the emerging temperance movement.

Palmer's public visibility and the positions she took on controversial issues attracted critics. The bitterest attacks were directed at the fact that she was a woman speaking in a public forum. She responded by becoming part of the emerging woman's suffrage movement (→ Women's Movement). Her seminal work, *The Promise of the Father; or, A Neglected Specialty of the Last Days* (1859), argued on biblical grounds for an egalitarian → piety that affirmed women's rights to speak in religious assemblies and to share fully with men all other responsibilities in Christian work.

Bibliography: Primary sources: The Devotional Writings of Phoebe Palmer (ed. D. W. Dayton; New York, 1986; orig. pub., 1867) • *Phoebe Palmer: Selected Writings* (ed. T. C. Oden; New York, 1988) • *The Promise of the Father* (New York, 1985; orig. pub., 1859).

Secondary works: K. T. Long, "Consecrated Respectability: Phoebe Palmer and the Refinement of American Methodism," *Methodism and the Shaping of American Culture* (ed. N. O. Hatch and J. H. Wigger; Nashville, 2001) 281-308 • H. E. Raser, *Phoebe Palmer: Her Life and Thought* (Lewiston, N.Y., 1987) • C. E. White, *The Beauty of Holiness: Phoebe Palmer as Theologian, Revivalist, Feminist, and Humanitarian* (Grand Rapids, 1986).

D. William Faupel

Panagia

The title *panagia* (all holy), along with *theotokos* (God-bearer) and *aeiparthenos* (ever virgin), is a title of honor for Mary. The Greeks first used it in patristic hymns (→ Patristics) as synonymous with Mary, and in → iconography after the Iconoclastic Controversy it often replaces Mary. The → Acathistus hymn (6th cent.) lauds Mary as "the all holy chariot [*ochēma panagion*] of the One above the cherubim" (15th stanza).

The ascription rests on what the NT says about the virgin motherhood of Mary (→ Virgin Birth) and the angelic (→ Angel) saluting of Mary in Luke 1:28 as *kecharitōmenē* (perf.), "favored one" or "endued with grace" (ASV marg.). Unlike the → Roman Catholic Church in its → dogma of the immaculate conception (1854), → Orthodox Christianity extols Mary's holiness (→ Saints, Veneration of) in the → liturgy as a gift of the → Holy Spirit, yet without regarding her as free from original → sin. In her virginity Mary as the new Eve is an untainted image of God after the conception and birth. By her virtuous life in the Spirit, she became full of grace so that in the power of the Spirit she could be the mother of the divine Logos. The fullness of holiness will be hers when all is consummated (→ Transfiguration of the World). Hence the church presents the eucharistic offering for her (→ Eucharistic Prayer; Eucharistic Spirituality).

→ Mary, Devotion to; Mary in the New Testament

Bibliography: S. Brock, "Mary and the Eucharist," *Sob.* 2 (1979) 50-59 • G. Florovsky, "The Ever-Virgin Mother of God," *Collected Works* (vol. 3; Belmont, Mass., 1976) 171-88 • L. Heiser, *Maria in der Christus-Verkündigung des orthodoxen Kirchenjahres* (Trier, 1981) • A. Kallis, "'Erlösung der Tränen Evas.' Die Gottesgebärerin im Christusereignis," *Brennender, nicht verbrennender Dornbusch* (Münster, 1999) 222-41; idem, "Maria," *ÖL* (1983) 781-82 • P. Sherwood, "Byzantine Mariology," *ECQ* 14 (1962) 384-409 • K. Ware, "Mary Theotokos in the Orthodox Tradition," *Mar.* 52 (1990) 210-27.

Lothar Heiser

Panama

	1960	*1980*	*2000*
Population (1,000s):	1,126	1,950	2,856
Annual growth rate (%):	2.91	2.12	1.43

Area: 75,517 sq. km. (29,157 sq. mi.)

A.D. 2000

Population density: 38/sq. km. (98/sq. mi.)
Births / deaths: 2.03 / 0.51 per 100 population
Fertility rate: 2.42 per woman
Infant mortality rate: 19 per 1,000 live births
Life expectancy: 74.8 years (m: 72.6, f: 77.3)
Religious affiliation (%): Christians 88.2 (Roman Catholics 84.4, Protestants 13.7, indigenous 2.5, unaffiliated 2.0, marginal 1.8, other Christians 0.9), Muslims 4.4, nonreligious 2.4, Baha'is 1.3, other 3.7.

1. Historical and Social Context
2. Church and State
3. Roman Catholic Church
4. Other Christian Churches
5. Other Religious Groups
6. Ecumenical Developments

1. Historical and Social Context

The first signs of human settlement on the land mass now called Panama (whose indigenous name means "abundance of fish") are thought to be 10,000 years old. Panama's modern history began in 1501, when Spaniard Rodrigo de Bastidas sailed along its Caribbean coast. One year later Christopher Columbus visited the same coast. Not until 1513, however, when Vasco Núñez de Balboa hiked across the isthmus and became the first European to see the Pacific Ocean, did the geographic importance of Panama begin to be grasped. Panama became the mainland base and transshipment point for the Spanish conquest of the Americas. With so much gold and silver being transported from the Americas back to Spain, other European powers soon took note, and British, Dutch, and French buccaneers started looting Spanish ships. By the 1700s Spanish ships were sailing from the western ports of South America around Cape Horn to Spain in order to avoid the pirates who plundered the Caribbean shipping lanes. Panama went into decline (→ Colonialism).

In 1821 Panama declared its independence from Spain and joined with Venezuela, Ecuador, and Colombia to form Gran Colombia. When Venezuela and Ecuador separated from this union in 1830, Panama remained as a province of Colombia.

In the mid-1800s, when gold was discovered in California, thousands of passengers sailed from the east coast of North America to California via the Isthmus of Panama. To speed the passage of people and goods across the isthmus, an American company in 1855 completed an 80-km. (50-mi.) railroad.

In 1880 a French company started building a canal between the oceans. When that enterprise failed, the company tried to sell its construction rights to the American government. Colombia, however, refused to allow this transaction. In 1903 a group of foreign businessmen in Panama, with the backing of the United States, declared Panama to be an independent nation and, by force of arms, protected it from the Colombian military. These actions cleared the way for the U.S. construction of the interoceanic canal, which was completed in 1914.

American presence in Panama continued after the canal was built. It stationed troops in the Canal Zone — a band of land 8 km. (5 mi.) on each side of the waterway — for the protection of the canal and the many U.S. employees who operated and maintained the locks. The United States frequently intervened in Panama's political life to protect its assets and the neutrality of the canal. It also used its military presence in Panama to monitor and, from time to time, to intervene militarily in other countries of Central and South America.

In September 1977 President Omar Torrijos Herrera of Panama and President Jimmy Carter of the United States signed treaties granting Panama gradual control of the canal until full control would be assumed on January 1, 2000. The U.S. military bases would be gradually phased out during a 22-

year transition period. In 1989 the National Assembly of Panama named General Manuel Noriega, a former employee of the CIA and head of Panama's secret police, "maximum leader," and it declared that Panama was in a state of war with the United States. Within days, 24,000 U.S. troops seized control of Panama and captured Noriega.

On December 31, 1999, after 96 years of virtual control of the canal, the Canal Zone, and the nation of Panama, the United States handed over full control of the Panama Canal and the Canal Zone to the government of the Republic of Panama. During November 2003 Panama — now as an undivided republic — celebrated 100 years of national independence.

Panama's population is the most ethnically heterogeneous of all countries in Central America, with 72 percent mestizo/mulatto, 8 percent West Indians of African descent, 10 percent white (from Europe and the United States), and 10 percent Amerindian, East Indian, Chinese, and other Latins. About 51 percent of the people live in the commercial corridor connecting Colón (44,000), on the Caribbean side, with the capital, Panama City (1.2 million), on the Pacific side. While Panama's per capita income is one of the highest in Latin America, the distribution of wealth is unbalanced, as in many other countries of the region (→ Poverty).

2. Church and State

The constitution of Panama grants freedom of religion and worship for all faiths, with no limitation other than respect for Christian morality and public order (→ Church and State). Roman Catholicism is recognized as the faith of the majority (art. 34) and is taught in the public schools. Attendance, however, is not mandatory. All leadership positions above that of parish pastor in the Roman Catholic Church and in other faiths must be occupied by native-born Panamanians (art. 41).

3. Roman Catholic Church

The → Roman Catholic Church was first introduced into mainland America at the Isthmus of Panama in 1513, when Franciscan → missionaries arrived and formed part of the first American diocese, Santa Maria la Antigua del Darién. → Franciscans were followed by → Dominicans and → Jesuits (1582), then Capuchins and → Augustinians (1648).

Today, the Roman Catholic Church in Panama claims 2.4 million baptized, 180 parishes, 100 schools (with 8 percent of the national student population), 1 university, 2 seminaries, and various training centers for social programs, all served by 384 priests, 69 permanent deacons, 277 male religious, and 453 female religious. Church administration is divided among 1 metropolitan archdiocese, 5 dioceses, 1 vicariate apostolic (Darién), 1 territorial prelature (Bocas del Toro), and 1 papal nuncio.

Once a privileged pillar of colonial society, the Roman Catholic Church in recent years has chosen to support the just causes of the poor majorities in Latin America. Renewal movements promoting → worship, → ecumenism, social development, justice, → peace, and lay training for leadership and ministry are active and successful in Panama.

4. Other Christian Churches

Methodists were the first Protestants in Panama, arriving in 1815 from the Caribbean. Later, between 1855 and 1900, thousands of immigrants from the Caribbean area arrived, seeking employment with the construction companies building the railroad and, later, the canal. These immigrants were mostly black, English-speaking, and Protestant. The first Protestant church (Anglican) was built in Colón in 1860.

During the construction of the canal, various U.S. denominations became interested in Panama and started sending missionaries there. During the 1940s the majority of Protestants were black or white, English-speaking, and belonged to one of the historic mainline Protestant churches.

Today, however, the majority of Protestants are mestizo, Spanish-speaking, and belong to one of many → Pentecostal congregations. Pentecostals currently constitute just over half of the Panamanian Protestants, with evangelicals (non-Pentecostal) 27 percent, Adventists 16 percent, and Episcopalians (Anglicans) 7 percent. As a group, Panamanian Protestants are 69 percent mestizo, 17.5 percent black, 9.5 percent Amerindian, and 4 percent white. The Protestant churches operate schools, Bible institutes, camps, seminaries, translation projects, and bookstores, all of which tend to be closely tied to their supporting denominations.

5. Other Religious Groups

The largest marginal Christian groups in Panama are the Latter-day Saints (→ Mormons) and the → Jehovah's Witnesses. In addition, recent immigrations from Asia and the Middle East have increased the number of non-Christian religious groups in Panama. Since 1975 Egypt has sent Muslim (Sunni) missionaries to care for the Muslims in Panama (→ Islam). More than 4,500 converts have been won to the Japanese → new religion Soka Gakkai (→ Japan

5). The → Baha'i have established 97 centers and 1 temple. A significant number of indigenous people maintain traditional → animistic beliefs combined with some Christian beliefs and the practice of Roman Catholic rituals.

6. Ecumenical Developments

Building on the work of three previous organizations — the Panama Evangelical Alliance (Atlantic side), the Pacific Religious Workers' League (Pacific side), and the Archdiocesan Department of Ecumenism — many of Panama's churches and communities of faith presently participate in a successful ecumenical movement directed by the nongovernmental Comité Ecuménico de Panamá (COEPA, Ecumenical Committee of Panama), founded circa 1985. While previous organizations were founded in the 1940s to coordinate special worship services among different Protestant and/or Catholic groups, the new national ecumenical committee sponsors interreligious conferences, charitable projects, as well as joint liturgical celebrations. This committee of church leaders has also been invited to provide community oversight of the government, especially during times when public confidence is critical. Primary members of COEPA are the Roman Catholic Church, the Episcopal Church of Panama, the Calvary Baptist Church, the Evangelical Methodist Church of Panama, the → Methodist Church of the Caribbean and the Americas, and the Greek → Orthodox Church.

In 2001 COEPA joined with the Roman Catholic University of Santa Maria la Antigua (USMA) and the City of Knowledge Foundation to found the Institute of Ecumenism, Society, and Development (IESDE) on the grounds of the City of Knowledge (formerly Fort Clayton, a U.S. military base). The mission of the institute is to promote investigation of faith issues and dialogue between the churches and other communities of faith, and between them and the societies in which they live.

The ecumenical churches in Panama relate with other regional and international ecumenical organizations, such as the Ecumenical Program in Central America and the Caribbean (EPICA), the → Caribbean Conference of Churches (CCC), the → Lutheran World Federation, and the → World Council of Churches.

In addition to the hierarchical Roman Catholic Church and its organized institutions, there are a large number of Christian → base communities in Panama. The base community movement grew out of the realities of Latin America during the 1960s. In Panama this movement started in the San Miguelito parish, located in an economically poor community on the outskirts of Panama City, where the priests and religious workers developed a model of ministry with people in poverty that promoted human development, social change, and economic justice. This model of the base Christian community has been multiplied throughout Panama and reproduced in many countries of Latin America. It has also influenced the greater church in Latin America, as well as other faith communities in their service to others around the world.

Bibliography: D. B. Barrett, G. T. Kurian, and T. M. Johnson, *WCE* (2d ed.) 1.579-82 • E. L. Cleary, "Religion in the Central American Embroglio," *Repression, Resistance, and Democratic Transition in Central America* (ed. T. W. Walker and A. C. Armony; Wilmington, Del., 2000) 187-210 • M. Couniff, "Panama since 1903," *CHLA* 7.603-42 • C. Holland, *World Christianity: Central America and the Caribbean* (Monrovia, Calif., 1981) • J. Lindsay-Poland, *Emperors in the Jungle: The Hidden History of the U.S. in Panama* (Durham, N.C., 2003) • J. Major, "The Panama Canal Zone," *CHLA* 7.643-70 • S. M. Muschett Ibarra, "Church and Politics in Time of Crisis: Noriega's Panama" (Diss., University of Notre Dame, 1992).

Garry D. McClure

Panentheism

1. History of the Term
2. History of the Idea
3. Definition
   3.1. The Nature of Evil
   3.2. Metaphors of "in"
   3.3. Love and Mutuality
   3.4. Degree Christology
4. Potential

1. History of the Term

Panentheism — from Gk. *pan* (all), *en* (in), and *theos* (God) — is the doctrine that the cosmos exists within God, who in turn pervades, or is "in," the cosmos. Panentheism is commonly contrasted with *pantheism,* in which God is coterminous with, or identified with, and is not more than, the cosmos; and *classical theism,* in which God is portrayed as separate from the cosmos, either in the sense of not being affected by it or in the sense of being outside the cosmos and present within it only in such discrete instances as, for example, revealed scriptures, incarnation, and isolable interferences of a (holy) spirit. Classical → theism, panentheism, and → pantheism are basic types of the doctrine of → God and fundamental tools for analyzing *theism.*

While the word "pantheism" was apparently first coined in 1705 by the Irish → deist John Toland, the word "panentheism" seems to have been introduced by the German idealist Karl Christian Friedrich Krause (1781-1832) in his *Vorlesungen über die Grundwahrheiten der Wissenschaft* (1829). Closer comparative study remains to be done on the use of the word by Friedrich Jacobi (1743-1819) and Franz von Baader (1765-1841). The word seems to have been first used in English by W. R. Inge in his *Christian Mysticism* (1899) and was taken up by Roman Catholic modernists Friedrich von Hügel (1906) and George Tyrrell (1907), Anglican modernist Henry Major (1908), and another writer on → mysticism, Brigid Herman (1915).

The word was made widely known in America by the leading 20th-century exponent of the idea, Charles Hartshorne (1897-2000), the founding figure of process theism (a specific type of panentheism), particularly through his reader on the doctrine of God, *Philosophers Speak of God* (1953). The word was reintroduced to Britain by John Robinson (1919-83), whose *Exploration into God* (1967) developed the doctrinal suggestions of his controversial best-seller *Honest to God* (1963). Today the British panentheist par excellence is John Macquarrie (b. 1919), whose *In Search of Deity* (1984) is the classic British textbook on panentheism. Despite some reservations with the term (principally that its similarity to "pantheism" implies that the idea behind it is closer to pantheism than to classical theism), Macquarrie seems to have been content to use it increasingly in his later work.

The term "panentheism" is now self-applied by Jürgen Moltmann; → process theologians (e.g., David Pailin, Joseph Bracken, David Ray Griffin, and Daniel Dombrowski); a wide range of what might be called contextual theologians, such as "economic" → liberation theologians James Will and Leonardo Boff, → feminist theologians Sallie McFague and Carol Christ, and ecotheologians Matthew Fox and Jay McDaniel; and, most recently, theologians involved in the dialogue between science and religion (Arthur Peacocke and principally Philip Clayton; → Science and Theology).

2. History of the Idea

The origins of panentheism can be traced to Neoplatonism, with its emphasis on the emanation of the material from the immaterial, and hence the participation of the physical in the mental or spiritual. It is no coincidence that a number of 20th-century panentheists have written on Neoplatonists: Inge on Plotinus, Norman Pittenger on Erigena, Pailin on the Cambridge Platonists, and Clayton on Nicholas of Cusa. Full-blown panentheism, however, became possible in the wake of the → Enlightenment, when German → idealism began to predicate limitations on the divine and hence establish genuine reciprocity between God and the cosmos. Deist responses to the Enlightenment, on the one hand, and pantheist responses, on the other (chiefly that of B. Spinoza), seem to have encouraged others to formulate panentheist ideas.

F. D. E. → Schleiermacher, J. G. Fichte, Krause, G. W. F. Hegel, F. Schelling, F. C. Baur, G. Fechner, and O. Pfleiderer, as well as their slightly later counterparts in Britain John and Edward Caird and Andrew Seth Pringle-Pattison, can all be regarded as the first systematic panentheists; and → modernism, Paul → Tillich, and process thought can be viewed as the carriers of panentheism from the idealism to which they were indebted to liberal theologians such as Robinson in the second half of the 20th century. Contemporary → liberal theology can be regarded as the current purveyor of panentheism, standing in between the classical theism of neo-Thomism, some forms of Barthianism, and the movement of "radical orthodoxy," on the one hand, and the pantheism of nonrealism, on the other. In this respect, contemporary disputes with and within the church can often be diagnosed as conflicts between underlying, and frequently unarticulated, basic differences in the doctrine of God.

Besides Neoplatonic roots and idealist reaction to the Enlightenment, another equally significant component in the rise of panentheism has been mystical experience, with its readiness to see God and talk of union with God in and through the material world: Mechthild of Magdeburg, Meister → Eckhart, and → Julian of Norwich have all been acclaimed as panentheists. The witness that human religious experience at its deepest level is panentheistic in character parallels the impetus toward panentheism in idealist thought, in that both are reactions — one in terms of philosophy, the other in terms of spirituality — against the static resonances, inherent or perceived, of classical substance modes of thinking. Idealism and mysticism are respectively philosophical and spiritual attempts to adopt a relational rather than a substance → ontology.

Classical theism tends to conceive of God and the cosmos as substances, which makes it ever difficult to relate the two, since substances are essentially spatial and cannot overlap. Panentheism is the result of conceiving "being" in terms of relationship. Process theism is thus a type of panentheism, for "process" asserts that entities are (to use characteristically panentheistic language) inseparably interrelated, and thus that relatedness, rather than substance, is "of the essence."

3. Definition

The meaning of panentheism depends on how we understand the "in" of the cosmos being in God. Clayton has suggested that the "in" acts logically: the cosmos is included in God in the sense that we can show logically that the infinite must include the finite. The literal sense of "in" is spatiotemporal: the cosmos is in God in terms of space and time. This sense is effectively a metaphor, however, for saying that God has a spatiotemporal aspect, and that there is also more to God than space and time. If it is true, as many theologians hold, that all language about God is metaphoric (including such terms as "infinite" and "finite"), then the "in" needs to be explicated and judged according to the scriptural, philosophical, and moral criteria that are routinely involved in the interpretation of theological → metaphor and → symbol.

3.1. *The Nature of Evil*

Perhaps the first judgment to make in such interpretation concerns the nature of → evil, and whether the evil that is in the cosmos is in God, if the cosmos is in God. The determining factor here is whether evil is regarded as privative (i.e., as not existing in itself: as an absence of → good, albeit a gaping abyss). Many panentheists would regard evil in this way and therefore hold that the cosmos, but not its evil, is in God, since evil is a lack or deficiency. Other panentheists, such as Clayton, assign actual existence to evil and therefore suggest that the whole of the cosmos, with its mix of good and evil, exists within the divine. So John Robinson, for example, as he was dying, preached that God was "in" his cancer.

These two types of panentheism can correspond to the "weak" and "strong" panentheisms to which Gregory Peterson has alluded, where the former is God's presence in the cosmos, and the latter is God's identity with the cosmos: God could be present in the good of the cosmos; or the entire cosmos, evil as well as good, could be included in God. Certainly the understandings of evil as existent in itself or as privative color the resulting panentheisms in different tones. For panentheists who regard evil as privative, the cosmos can be characterized as fundamentally positive, because what exists is part of the goodness of God. For panentheists who credit evil with real presence, however, the moral character of the cosmos is more neutral.

The real presence of evil in the cosmos leads some classical theists (e.g., John Polkinghorne and Keith Ward) to resist panentheism and to hold instead to an eschatological or soteriological panentheism. This view asserts that whereas God is not yet in all, this is the situation that will transpire when God's work of salvation in the cosmos is completed at the end of time. So panentheism is not yet true but will eventually be so; in the meantime the classical model prevails.

3.2. *Metaphors of "in"*

Panentheists use two principal metaphors to illuminate the metaphor of "in." First, some panentheists talk of a sacramental universe. The cosmos being in God, God operates "in" and "through" the cosmos. These prepositions are not only language that is characteristic of panentheism; they are also characteristic of the language of → sacraments, as sacraments are physical things under, in, and through which God comes. The prepositions are intrinsic to both sacramentalism and panentheism, which refer to different aspects of the same reality. Thus, under panentheism, the cosmos or universe can be described as sacramental or itself a sacrament (Peacocke, and Christopher Knight): it is that through which God comes. In panentheism the sacraments are therefore not restricted to certain rites of the church; rather, the specific sacraments of the church are particular intensifications of the general sacramental principle — signs, symbols, and reminders that any and every thing has the potential and capacity to become a full vehicle of the divine.

Second, if the material (cosmos) is thought to be inextricably intertwined with the spiritual (God), then it has seemed natural to many (particularly process) panentheists to think of the relation of the cosmos to God as like that of a body to a person. The cosmos is thus described as God's body, and God as the embodied spirit or soul of the cosmos; part of God can be seen and touched, while part nevertheless exists "beyond." This metaphor safeguards the distinction of God and cosmos, as a body is distinct from a → person, yet does not, on a psychosomatic anthropology, allow their separation. The model also appropriately expresses a relationship of asymmetrical interdependence between God and cosmos: God and person are each dependent on cosmos and body, but not in the same way that cosmos and body are in turn dependent on them.

Peacocke and a number of other panentheists resist this metaphor because of its disanalogies. For example, body parts do not have conscious relations

Panentheism

with a person, unlike parts of the cosmos and God; persons do not have perfect knowledge of their body parts, unlike God's knowledge of the cosmos; and bodies are a "given" for persons in a way that the cosmos is not a given for God. Clayton, however, who has called the concept of divine embodiment the panentheistic analogy, has shown that it lies at the very root of the whole principle of → analogy. The analogy may be used, as long as the disanalogies are borne in mind.

3.3. *Love and Mutuality*

It has sometimes been asserted that Eastern → Orthodox Christianity is essentially panentheistic in perspective because of its doctrine of the divine energies pervasive in creation. Its reluctance, however, to predicate affectedness of the divine indicates that its theism is essentially classical. The decisive difference between classical theism and panentheism is the latter's insistence on mutuality, or interdependence, in the relationship between God and cosmos, so that God in some sense is affected by, and dependent on, the cosmos.

To put it another way, the difference between classical theism and panentheism lies in their respective conceptions of → love: classical theism views divine love as *agapē*, or benevolence, needing no love in return; panentheism regards the love of God as an inextricable mix (note again the characteristic language) of *agapē* and *erōs*, "gift-love" and "need-love," so that something of God's self is fulfilled in the act of loving — God "needs somebody to love" in order for the divine love to be complete.

Panentheists identify the effect on God of this mutuality, or reciprocal love, in two ways, the second logically dependent on the first, although a number of theologians resist the transition to the second. First, both the metaphor of divine embodiment and the nature of love imply that God suffers: the latter because it is in the nature of authentic love to suffer the response of the beloved, and the former because when a body suffers, the corresponding person suffers. These arguments, respectively the ontological and immanentist arguments for passibility (the doctrine that God suffers), stem from panentheistic presuppositions, and so panentheism entails passibility. There are other grounds for holding that God is passible, so panentheism does not lie behind every instance of passibility; but because of the connections between the two, passibility, in the course of its rise during the last century, has often led to panentheism. The recognized rise of passibility means that this theme is one of the most common when panentheism is discussed.

Second, if embodiment is an intrinsic feature of divinity, and if God and cosmos, although distinct from one another, cannot be entirely separate, then this interdependence leads panentheism to the unorthodox assertion that God needs the (or at least a) cosmos. Macquarrie believes that the language of necessity implies a coercive force external to God. He prefers to state that God freely creates, because on the Augustinian view of → freedom, to act freely is to act within the constraints of perfect love, and so to act within one's ultimate nature: freedom and necessity thus coincide. By Macquarrie's own admission, however, the language of freedom is susceptible to the misinterpretation that God could have acted otherwise. Given, therefore, that the language of freedom and the language of necessity are both open to misinterpretation, there does not seem to be any reason why the language of necessity may not be used, with the proviso that it does not mean that God is under some kind of external compulsion.

Clayton, like Macquarrie, resists the notion of a necessary divine dependence on the cosmos, subordinating, under the influence of Schelling, God's nature of love to God's freedom or will; God is therefore dependent on the cosmos only after a free choice to create. This conclusion follows because, for Clayton, a contingent world cannot exist of necessity. But it may be precisely that, through love, God needs a world that (by nature) is radically dependent on God. Some such association of necessity and dependence would therefore be entailed by the logic of God's love. If divine love qualifies necessity and contingency as qualities that distinguish between God and cosmos, then other qualities for distinguishing between their natures remain, namely, infinitude and finitude. Love demands that God and cosmos are each in some way dependent on, and necessary to, the other, but the difference in natures demands that they are not dependent on, and necessary to, the other in the same way. Panentheism can therefore hold that God is freely dependent on the cosmos, with no other option and without any outside force.

3.4. *Degree Christology*

One implication of panentheism for Christian theology that is not often noticed is that it requires a "degree Christology." A panentheistic model of God leads to a doctrine of Christ as different from other persons by degree rather than by kind. This is because, if God is somehow in the cosmos generally, then God's work in Christ needs to be related with some continuity to that cosmic work and not isolated from it; otherwise there is a dichotomy between God in Christ and the rest of the cosmos.

Because panentheism underlies such → Christology, the identification of a person's Christology as a degree Christology is evidence that they hold to a panentheistic doctrine of God. Degree Christology is explicitly claimed by Robinson and Macquarrie, and it is implied in the work of many others. Spirit, Logos, and Wisdom Christologies, for example, can often be in the degree mold. The panentheist who subscribed most explicitly to a degree Christology was Norman Pittenger, who first advocated the doctrine in 1939, gave it sustained treatment in an essay of 1956, and maintained the position in his two works on Christology, *The Word Incarnate* (1959) and *Christology Reconsidered* (1970).

4. Potential

Though classical theism has on occasion been caricatured by panentheists, just as panentheism has been so treated by classical theists, nevertheless the caricature of classical theism does tend to represent what the classical view has conveyed to the popular mind, and therefore the picture of God that people seem generally to have believed. Yet the contemporary → New Age movement (with its counterpart interest, within Christian faith, in Celtic → spirituality) is, like mysticism, testimony to the fact that panentheism expresses more accurately than classical theism the basic religious conviction of humanity. Christianity is therefore faced with the ironic situation of spiritual persons with panentheistic experiences or convictions (e.g., Marcus Borg) finding themselves in tension with their own inherited (classical theistic) images and forms of Christian faith. On this reading, the task of the Christian church is to offer panentheistic interpretations of divinity in order to establish for people of the 21st century the greater spiritual well-being that doctrinal integrity brings. The fewer problems raised by → theodicy for panentheism than for classical theism, and panentheism's own emphasis on (the divine) Spirit, (people's) spirits, and the connection between them (Geoffrey Lampe, Clayton) may be of potential here.

The spiritual potential of panentheism, however, does not lie simply in the realm of doctrinal integrity but in its interconnections with practical life. Panentheism has been deemed to respond more flexibly than varieties of classical theism to the concerns of feminist, lesbian and gay, ecological, and economic liberation theologies, as well as to the demands of → pastoral theology, the demands of → dialogue between science and religion, and the demands of dialogue between different faiths. For example, if the cosmos is God's body, then it demands respect; if the physical world is good, it should no longer be denigrated. Of the three basic types of the doctrine of God, panentheism accordingly has the most potential for fruitfully addressing issues of pressing political and social concern.

→ Feminist Theology; Liberation Theology; Process Philosophy

Bibliography: M. J. Borg, *The God We Never Knew: Beyond Dogmatic Religion to a More Authentic Contemporary Faith* (New York, 1997) • P. Clayton, *The Problem of God in Modern Thought* (Grand Rapids, 2000) • P. Clayton and A. R. Peacocke, eds., *In Whom We Live and Move and Have Our Being: Panentheistic Reflections on God's Presence in a Scientific World* (Grand Rapids, 2004) • D. R. Griffin, *Reenchantment without Supernaturalism: A Process Philosophy of Religion* (Ithaca, N.Y., 2001) • C. Hartshorne, *The Divine Relativity: A Social Conception of God* (2d ed.; New Haven, 1964) • C. Hartshorne and W. L. Reese, *Philosophers Speak of God* (Chicago, 1953) • J. B. McDaniel, *With Roots and Wings: Christianity in an Age of Ecology and Dialogue* (Maryknoll, N.Y., 1995) • J. Macquarrie, *In Search of Deity: An Essay in Dialectical Theism* (London, 1984) • J. D. Neil, *God in Everything: A Layman's Guide to the New Thinking* (Sussex, 1984) • D. A. Pailin, *Probing the Foundations: A Study in Theistic Reconstruction* (Kampen, 1994) • A. R. Peacocke, *Paths from Science towards God: The End of All Our Exploring* (Oxford, 2001) • G. R. Peterson, "Whither Panentheism?" *Zygon* 36 (2001) 395-405 • J. A. T. Robinson, *Exploration into God* (London, 1967).

Michael W. Brierley

Pan-Orthodox Conferences

The → Orthodox Church is planning a Pan-Orthodox → council of its 16 autocephalous and autonomous churches. This "Holy and Great Council," even in its preparatory stages, is an important historical event because all the preparations themselves involve Pan-Orthodox conferences. After a long process of alienation and isolation, the Orthodox churches, on the initiative of the → ecumenical patriarch (in encyclicals of 1902 and 1904), have seen the need to intensify their inter-Orthodox contacts and to study and solve together acute problems that urgently call for a Pan-Orthodox solution. The period of preparation features various conferences that represent a step-by-step approach to the council.

A Pan-Orthodox congress took place in Constantinople in 1923. This congress formulated the idea of a future council, and in 1930 a preparatory commission was set up in Vatopedi, on Mount → Athos. Political and internal ecclesiastical difficulties, however, constantly stood in the way of a council, and not until after World War II was the idea taken up again. In the 1950s Patriarch Athenagoras (1886-1972) called anew for a Pan-Orthodox gathering. The individual Orthodox churches accepted the invitation, and three Pan-Orthodox conferences at Rhodes followed (1961, 1963, 1964). They resolved unanimously to go ahead to a Holy and Great Council and in 1961 drew up a list of themes.

More significant by way of preparation, however, was the fourth Pan-Orthodox conference, at Chambésy, Switzerland, in 1968, which set up a secretariat to prepare for the council, formed an Inter-Orthodox Preparatory Commission (IOPC), involved all the churches in developing the agenda, and established inter-Orthodox commissions to initiate and carry on → ecumenical dialogue with other churches and denominations. This conference took up six themes from the Rhodes list and sent them to the local churches for study and for recommendations as to how the council should handle them. When the recommendations have been received and the secretariat has circulated the reports, the IOPC will meet to decide on the Pan-Orthodox approach to each of them. The Preconciliar Pan-Orthodox Conference (PPOC) has the task of studying the IOPC findings and drawing up a definitive response to each theme.

On the advice of IOPC I (Chambésy, 1971), but in keeping with the sense of God's people and Pan-Orthodox concerns, PPOC I (Chambésy, 1976) drew up a list of ten themes that will be the agenda of the Holy and Great Council:

1. the Orthodox → diaspora
2. → autocephaly and the way to proclaim it
3. → autonomy and the way to proclaim it
4. diptychs
5. the calendar question
6. impediments to marriage
7. the meaning and modern practice of → fasting
8. relations with the rest of the Christian world
9. the Orthodox Church and the ecumenical movement
10. Orthodox contributions to → peace, justice, → freedom, brotherhood, and → love among the nations and the removing of racial and other forms of discrimination (→ Racism).

PPOC II (Chambésy, 1982) dealt with themes 5-7. Its findings have no canonical validity, however, before the Holy and Great Council considers them. This conference also dealt with the tasks of IOPC II and PPOC III, setting the agenda for them.

PPOC III (Chambésy, 1986) dealt with themes 7 (again) and 8-10. After IOPC II (Chambésy, 1986) had worked out an Orthodox position on them, PPOC III settled on the final texts for unanimous presentation to the Holy and Great Council. It also approved of procedures and the agenda for PPOC IV. As soon as the local Orthodox churches are able to formulate their views concerning themes 1-4, especially the issue of the diaspora and the meaning of autocephaly, including the way of granting autocephalous status to a local church, then PPOC IV will meet. Following the work of this conference, the Holy and Great Council can be convened.

According to PPOC III the preconciliar Pan-Orthodox conferences are extraordinary assemblies of Orthodox churches that, in accordance with Orthodox practice, are composed of properly appointed delegates of the autocephalous and autonomous Orthodox local churches and that are preparing in concert for the Holy and Great Council. Contributing to this work of preparation are the journal *Synodica* (from 1976 onward in Greek and French), the preparatory secretariat, and the monthly *Episkepsis* (from 1970 onward in Greek and French).

→ Ecumenism, Ecumenical Movement; Oriental Orthodox Churches; Patriarch, Patriarchate

Bibliography: M. Aghiorgoussis, "Towards the Great and Holy Council: The First Pre-synodal Pan-Orthodox Conference in Geneva," *GOTR* 21 (1976) 423-28 • Damaskinos of Tranoupolis, "Towards the Great and Holy Council," *GOTR* 24 (1979) 99-116 • A. Jensen, *Die Zukunft der Orthodoxie. Konzilspläne und Kirchenstrukturen* (Zurich, 1986) • G. Tsetsis, "Pan-Orthodox Conferences," *DEM* (2d ed.) 878-79 • K. Ware, "Toward the Great Council?" *ECR* 4 (1972) 162-68.

Damaskinos Papandreou

Pantheism

1. Term
2. In the History of Philosophy
3. In the History of Theology
4. In World Religion

1. Term

"Pantheism" (from *pan,* "all," and *theos,* "god") is a term for the identity of God and the whole of reality. The English deist John Toland (1670-1722) first brought it into philosophical discussion in 1705. It then played a part in philosophical and theological controversies. Two important aspects are the notions that (1) all things are God, the divinizing of the world (panpsychism, acosmism, theopanism), and (2) God is all things, the secularizing of God (→ Idealism) and his consequent negation (→ Materialism; Monism; Naturalism). → Panentheism, which never truly established itself, stresses (1) but preserves God's transcendence by ruling out (2) and putting all things *in* God.

Pantheistic systems are directed chiefly against the idea of a personal Creator who transcends the world (→ Theism), but without wishing to abandon the claim of a → reason that can explain all being, including God. This combination of a criticism of → metaphysics and metaphysical premises explains the conflict with → theology.

→ Revelation, → creation out of nothing, and the personality of God are of little relevance for pantheism. From the time of W. Dilthey (1833-1911) pantheism has unquestionably been significant in the suppression of a theological view of things. With the introduction of the term, structurally analogous systems from the classical philosophical and theological tradition (esp. the pre-Socratics, → Stoicism, → Gnosticism, Neoplatonism, medieval → Aristotelianism, → mysticism, and the thought of G. Bruno) have in retrospect come to be regarded as pantheistic.

2. In the History of Philosophy

The philosophy of B. Spinoza (1632-77; → Spinozism), particularly its equation with pantheism and → atheism shortly after his death, was mainly responsible for the spread of pantheism. The offense in Spinoza's system lay in his attempt to overcome the → Cartesian → dualism of thought and being by making both of them the infinite attributes of a single divine substance. The resultant → immanence of God in being (nature) and thought made unnecessary the ideas of creation out of nothing and of a personal, transmundane God who can intervene arbitrarily in the course of the world. Nature and thought as the world's totality were themselves divine and perfectly ordered, and they could be rationally reconstructed.

F. H. Jacobi (1743-1819), in a communication to M. Mendelssohn (1729-86), reported that shortly before his death, G. E. Lessing (1729-81) had confessed to being a Spinozist, or pantheist. This report triggered the so-called pantheistic controversy in 1783. Jacobi, in criticism of Spinoza, argued that pantheism was the most consistent form of → rationalism or atheism. The only alternative was to make a leap of faith into a nonrational personalism. In defense of a religion of reason, Mendelssohn tried to describe Lessing as a purified or refined pantheist who accepted a God outside the world but not a world outside God. Asked by Mendelssohn to resolve the controversy, I. Kant (1724-1804; → Kantianism) replied that he saw in pantheism a precritical form of thinking that had not yet perceived the regulative function of God for reason.

This controversy caused the meaning of pantheism to shift. It was no longer the relationship between substance and God that came under the suspicion of pantheism but the philosophical thinking that equally recognizes both. The divinity of reason in the younger F. W. J. Schelling (1775-1854) and G. W. F. Hegel (1770-1831) associated both with Spinoza insofar as reason was seen to have a part, not in the actual personality of the → absolute, but in its process of self-relating in the sense of its informing within being. Adopting the arguments of Hegel and D. F. Strauss (1808-74) against a personal God, L. Feuerbach (1804-72) found in pantheism a logical forerunner of his own → anthropology, which he had "cleansed" of God and which he expounded solely in terms of the history of the species. His philosophy made clear the equating of pantheism and atheism.

With the increasing orientation to history in the 19th century, philosophical interest in pantheism waned. Yet in reaction to the developing → positivism of science, concepts deriving from J. W. von Goethe (1749-1832) and the Romantic philosophy of nature (→ Romanticism) found their way again into the study of nature. These cosmic and religious ideas (e.g., the unity of God and matter, or a higher "spiritual" order of nature) retained their vitality well into the 20th century.

3. In the History of Theology

In the 19th century, theological discussion of pantheism had its origin in the critical reaction to the philosophy of Spinoza and Hegel. C. H. Weisse (1801-66) equated Hegel's philosophy with → nihilism and atheism, which was typical of a theology that sharply rejected as pantheism any attempt to reconstruct the contents of faith with philosophical tools. → Philosophy and theology moved apart, "pantheism" became a term of reproach for any philosophy that was trying to comprehend all reality, and theological rivals were increasingly characterized by methodological self-awareness. When F. D. E. → Schleiermacher (1768-1834; → Schleiermacher's Theology) grounded religion in feeling, he added to the polarization, as did A. Ritschl (1822-89) and W. Herrmann (1846-1922) when they taught that we can know the existence of God only through the revelation in Christ (→ Christology 6).

The attempt of E. → Troeltsch (1865-1923) to

save the unity of religion and philosophy by making the belief in revelation historical and individual incurred the charge of a pantheism of history from R. Bultmann (1884-1976). Bultmann's own → demythologization (→ Existential Theology) involved a formulating of the sharpest possible antithesis to pantheism: We may know God neither in → nature nor in history. Equally radically, K. → Barth (1886-1968; → Dialectical Theology) rejected as pantheism any *necessary* link between God and the world: God is absolutely free in his relation to the world. Speculative pantheistic theologians took a different approach, following the example of Hegel and his philosophy of religion (W. Pannenberg, F. Wagner) or, especially in the United States, A. N. Whitehead (1861-1947), whose → process theology has been called the new pantheism.

4. In World Religion

Pantheistic elements may be seen in world religions that worship an impersonal deity, such as → Hinduism, → Taoism, → Islam, and the → cabala, also in atheistic → Buddhism. Quasi-religious forms of holistic thinking (→ New Age; Transcendental Meditation), often with an appeal to Eastern religions, take up pantheistic themes such as antidualism, the self-organization of matter, or a universal mind. They often quote the teachings of the Roman Catholic theologian P. Teilhard de Chardin (1881-1955), though at → Vatican I (1870) the → Roman Catholic Church officially condemned pantheism.

Bibliography: J. B. Cobb and D R. Griffin, *Process Theology* (Philadelphia, 1976) • R. L. Colie, "Spinoza and the Early English Deists," *JHI* 20 (1959) 23-46 • W. C. Dampier, *A History of Science and Its Relations with Philosophy and Religion* (4th ed.; Cambridge, 1948) • P. Harrison, *The Elements of Pantheism: Understanding the Divinity in Nature and the Universe* (Boston, 1999) • J. A. Lamm, *The Living God: Schleiermacher's Theological Appropriation of Spinoza* (University Park, Pa., 1996) • G. van der Leeuw, *Religion in Essence and Manifestation* (Princeton, 1986; orig. pub., 1933) • M. P. Levine, *Pantheism: A Non-theistic Concept of Deity* (London, 1994) • J. Rohls, *Theologie und Metaphysik. Der ontologische Gottesbeweis und seine Kritiker* (Gütersloh, 1987) • K. E. Yandell, "Pantheism," *REPh* 7.202-5.

Herbert Hanreich

Papal Blessing → Blessing 7

Papal Legate → Nuncio

Papal States

1. History
2. Criticism

1. History

The Papal States, or States of the Church (sing. in Ger. *Kirchenstaat,* Ital. *Lo Stato Pontificio* or *Lo Stato della Chiesa*), are the territories in central and southern Italy over which the → pope exercised temporal sovereignty. Private and public gifts of property from the fourth century onward formed the nucleus of the church holdings, known as the Patrimony of St. Peter. → Gregory I (590-604) reorganized and centralized these properties.

When Stephen II (752-57) appealed for help against the Lombards, the Frankish ruler Pepin (mayor 741-68), by the oath and donation of Quiercy (754), made St. → Peter and his vicar the holder of the duchy of → Rome, the Pentapolis (five cities from Rimini to Ancona on the Adriatic coast), Emilia, and the Byzantine exarchate of Ravenna. In return, the Frankish kings, given the title "patrician of the Romans" *(patricius Romanorum),* claimed certain rights of lordship in the Papal States. Charlemagne (768-814) confirmed the gifts of his father, Pepin, and added to them in southern Tuscany. Extensive additions came also from the childless Countess Matilda of Tuscany (d. 1115). Under → Innocent III (1198-1216) the Papal States reached their greatest extent in central Italy.

During the so-called Babylonian Captivity in France (1309-77), the popes founded a new Papal State in the territories of Avignon and Venaissin. For the Italian Papal States, which were in considerable decay, the papal legate Cardinal Gil Albornoz (ca. 1310-67) promulgated a legal code that initiated a new era and that remained in force until 1806.

The Papal States came temporarily to an end in the last decade of the 18th century, when French troops occupied part of them and declared the rest the Roman Republic. When Napoléon (1804-15) officially dissolved the Papal States in 1809, Pius VII (1800-1823) reacted by → excommunicating the "robber of the papal state." At the Peace of Paris (1814) and the Congress of Vienna (1815), Cardinal Ercole Consalvi (1757-1824) hailed the almost complete restoration of the Papal States as the one state under spiritual rule.

Risorgimento, the 19th-century movement for Italian unification, threatened the Papal States with unrest and revolt. When France withdrew its protective troops on the outbreak of the Franco-Prussian War in 1870, Italian soldiers entered the territory without opposition. In September 1870 they occupied the "holy city," Rome, officially declaring it to be the new capital of the kingdom of Italy the following year. → Pius IX (1846-78) protested against "the theft of the papal state" and rejected the favorable terms offered by the Italian government.

Only by the Lateran treaties of February 1929 (political and financial treaties and → concordat) did reconciliation take place between the Holy See and the Italian state. The Vatican ceded many of the guaranteed rights and privileges in the new concordat of June 3, 1985.

2. Criticism

Within the church there is criticism because a political holding like the Papal States conflicts with the principle of → Jesus that the church should not hold power or possessions, as well as with the understanding of the church at → Vatican II. The history of the Papal States shows how high a price many popes paid to earthly modes of thinking and action, and how greatly they neglected their true calling as preachers of the → gospel and shepherds of the → people of God.

→ Roman Catholic Church

Bibliography: P. Blet, *Histoire de la représentation diplomatique du Saint Siège des origines à l'aube du XIXe siècle* (Rome, 1982) • D. Buchel and V. Reinhard, ed., *Modell Rom? Der Kirchenstaat und Italien in der Frühen Neuzeit* (Cologne, 2003) • M. Caravale and A. Caracciolo, *Lo Stato Pontificio da Martino V a Pio IX* (Turin, 1978) • F. J. Coppa, *Cardinal Giacomo Antonelli and Papal Politics in European Affairs* (Albany, N.Y., 1990) • T. J. Dandelet, *Spanish Rome, 1500-1700* (New Haven, 2001) • I. Döllinger, *Kirche und Kirchen, Papstthum und Kirchenstaat* (Frankfurt, 1969; orig. pub., 1861) • V. Elm, *Die Revolution im Kirchenstaat. Ein Literaturbericht über die jüngere Forschung zur Vorgeschichte und Geschichte der Repubblica Romana (1798-1799)* (Frankfurt, 2002) • A. Esch, *Bonifaz IX. und der Kirchenstaat* (Tübingen, 1969) • H. Fuhrmann, *Quellen zur Entstehung des Kirchenstaates* (Göttingen, 1968) • H. Gross, *Rome in the Age of Enlightenment: The Post-Tridentine Syndrome and the Ancien Regime* (Cambridge, 1990) • T. Heydenreich, ed., *Pius IX. und der Kirchenstaat in den Jahren 1860-1870. Pio IX e lo Stato Pontificio degli anni 1860-1870. Ein deutsch-italienisches Kolloquium. Un convegno italo-tedesco* (Erlangen, 1995) • H. Jedin, K. S. Latourette, and J. Martin, *Atlas zur Kirchengeschichte* (Freiburg, 1970) pl. 33 • C. T. McIntire, *England against the Papacy, 1858-1861: Tories, Liberals, and the Overthrow of Papal Temporal Power during the Italian Risorgimento* (Cambridge, 1983) • S. Matsumoto-Best, *Britain and the Papacy in the Age of Revolution, 1846-1851* (Rochester, N.Y., 2003) • N. Miko, *Das Ende des Kirchenstaates* (4 vols.; Vienna, 1962-70) • T. F. X. Noble, *The Republic of St. Peter: The Birth of the Papal State, 680-825* (Philadelphia, 1984) • P. Partner, *The Lands of St. Peter: The Papal State in the Middle Ages and the Early Renaissance* (London, 1972); idem, *The Papal State under Martin V: The Administration and Government of the Temporal Power in the Early Fifteenth Century* (London, 1958) • P. Prodi, *The Papal Prince: One Body and Two Souls. The Papal Monarchy in Early Modern Europe* (Cambridge, 1987) • L. Scotoni, *I territori autonomi dello Stato Ecclesiastico nel Cinquecento* (Galatina, 1982).

Georg Denzler

Papalism → Pope, Papacy, 1.6

Papua New Guinea

	1960	*1980*	*2000*
Population (1,000s):	1,834	2,953	4,612
Annual growth rate (%):	2.24	2.18	2.15

Area: 462,840 sq. km. (178,704 sq. mi.)

A.D. 2000

Population density: 10/sq. km. (26/sq. mi.)
Births / deaths: 3.05 / 0.90 per 100 population
Fertility rate: 4.23 per woman
Infant mortality rate: 55 per 1,000 live births
Life expectancy: 59.9 years (m: 59.2, f: 60.7)
Religious affiliation (%): Christians 95.1 (Protestants 43.6, Roman Catholics 31.1, unaffiliated 10.2, indigenous 5.9, Anglicans 5.6, other Christians 0.5), tribal religionists 3.4, other 1.5.

1. Christian Missions and Churches
2. Ecumenical Cooperation
3. Church and State

With a population in 2003 estimated at over 5 million people, Papua New Guinea is by far the largest of the Pacific Island states. Since it gained its independence from Australia in 1975, the country's immense mineral wealth has led to both economic expansion and political upheavals, especially the attempted secession (1988-97) of the island of Bougainville.

1. Christian Missions and Churches

In the second half of the 19th century, Christian → missionaries were among the first Europeans to establish settlements on the coasts and islands and penetrate into the interior. They included Roman Catholic Missionaries of the Sacred Heart in the German territories of New Britain (1882) and the Bismarck Archipelago (1888), also in British Papua (1885); the Society of the Divine Word on the northwest coast of New Guinea (1895; → Catholic Missions); Lutherans of the Rhineland Mission in the same area (1887) and those of the Neuendettelsau Mission further to the east (1886; → German Missions); the London Missionary Society (LMS) in Papua (1871), followed by the Methodists in New Britain (1875), the Anglicans in eastern New Guinea (1891; → British Missions), and the Seventh-day Adventists (SDA) in Papua (1908) and New Guinea (1929).

The Lutheran missions formed the Evangelical Lutheran Church of New Guinea (now: Papua New Guinea, ELC-PNG) in 1956, with the exception of those of the Missouri Synod, which became the Gutnius Lutheran Church in the western highlands (1961; → Lutheran Churches). The Roman Catholic hierarchy was erected in 1966, and in 1968 the former LMS and the Methodists, together with some Presbyterians, formed the United Church of Papua New Guinea and the Solomon Islands. The Anglicans became an independent province in 1977.

The United Church is entirely indigenous, while the Roman Catholic clergy are still overwhelmingly expatriate. In 1960 the Anglican George Ambo was the first Melanesian to become a bishop. Leslie Boseto was made the first indigenous moderator of the United Church in 1972, and in the following year Zurewe Zurenuo became the first indigenous bishop of the ELC-PNG.

Statistics vary, but there are approximately 1.6 million Roman Catholics, 1.0 million adherents in the United Church, and 815,000 Evangelical and 95,000 Gutnius Lutherans. Other important groups include → Anglicans, SDA (→ Adventists), and Foursquare Gospel; also present in lesser numbers are members of Churches of Christ, Baptists, Church of the Nazarene, and the Union of Pentecostal Churches.

2. Ecumenical Cooperation

With the exception of the SDA, the major churches (including also one Baptist Union and the Salvation Army) cooperate in the Papua New Guinea Council of Churches (founded as the Melanesian Council of Churches in 1965, renamed 1991). Evangelicals formed the Evangelical Alliance in 1964, and the National Council of Pentecostal Churches was founded in 1979. Some churches belong to more than one of these organizations, and most cooperate with the larger churches in efforts such as media and health work, though they are reluctant to enter into serious → ecumenical dialogue, as the Catholics and Anglicans have done. Since 1956 the Summer Institute of Linguistics has tackled the daunting task of translating the Bible into the more than 800 languages of Papua New Guinea.

In 1970 Catholic missionary orders founded the Melanesian Institute, joined in 1974 by the Evangelical Lutherans, United Church, and the Anglicans. The institute offers orientation courses, carries out research projects, and publishes the respected journals *Catalyst* and *Point Series.* These churches have made significant contributions to development through schools and hospitals, → youth work and pastoral initiatives, alcohol and drug counseling (→ Substance Abuse), and rehabilitation of young criminals. The Lutheran rural development program Yangpela Didiman (young farmer), begun in 1973, is exemplary.

3. Church and State

Though predominantly Christian, Papua New Guinea has a secular constitution and is a lively parliamentary democracy. In the past the activities of fundamentalist sects caused problems, but now the increasing presence of → Islam, with significant numbers of converts and a mosque in the Port Moresby suburb of Hohola, is felt to be a threat to the nation's ethos, not least because Papua New Guinea shares a long land border with Indonesia, the world's largest Muslim country.

Bibliography: C. W. Forman, *The Island Churches of the South Pacific: Emergence in the Twentieth Century* (Maryknoll, N.Y., 1982); idem, *The Voice of Many Waters: The Story of the Life and Ministry of the Pacific Conference of Churches in the Last Twenty-five Years* (Suva, Fiji, 1986) • J. Garrett, *Footsteps in the Sea: Christianity in Oceania to World War II* (Geneva and Suva, 1992); idem, *To Live among the Stars: Christian Origins in Oceania* (Geneva and Suva, 1982); idem, *Where Nets Were Cast: Christianity in Oceania since World War II* (Geneva and Suva, 1997) • J. D. May, *Christus Initiator. Theologie im Pazifik* (Düsseldorf, 1990).

John D'Arcy May

Parable

1. General

The English word "parable" is derived from Gk. *parabolē,* and like its Greek antecedent its basic and primary meaning is "comparison." A parable is a figure of speech, such as a simile or a brief narrative, by which the speaker makes a comparison between some transcendent, mysterious, or otherwise puzzling reality and that which is familiar to common human experience.

The most widely known parables are those of → Jesus of Nazareth, which appear in the Gospels of the NT. But parables are also common in the literature of antiquity. Aristotle speaks of parables as illustrations that a teacher such as Socrates might use to confirm a point being made within a larger discourse (*Rhet.* 2.20). Figures of speech called parables appear in the works of Plato (e.g., *Grg.* 493-94; *Rep.* 6.487-89) and in the writings of certain Cynics and → Stoics (e.g., Epicurus, *Discourses* 1.14.15; 2.14.21-22).

Parables and parabolic sayings appear within the OT and other literatures of Jewish origin as well. The most well-known parable in the OT is the address of the prophet Nathan to King David after David had arranged for the death of Uriah and took Bathsheba as his wife (2 Sam. 12:1-4). The passage is not actually called a parable within the OT itself, nor are any other such stories that employ narration and partially resemble parables in content and function (e.g., 1 Kgs. 20:39-40; Isa. 5:1-7; 28:23-29). Parables appear also in rabbinic literature, illustrating the existence of parable telling in the ancient Jewish world. The degree to which the rabbinic parables antedate the rise of Christianity is debated. Most that remain are from the second and third centuries.

2. Jesus' Parables

2.1. Definition and Classification

The parables of Jesus are found in the → Synoptic gospels. (John 10:1-6 is sometimes considered one too, but it is usually regarded as a Christological discourse rather than a parable.) How many parables there are, and even what to include under the term "parable," has never been settled. The scholarly literature ranges from treating 53 units of gospel material as parables (A. Jülicher) to treating only 32 units as such (C. H. Dodd). What to include under the term "parable" is determined largely by how one defines the parables of Jesus. Generally it can be said that, in the case of Jesus' parables, a parable is a figure of speech in which a comparison is made between God's kingdom, actions, or expectations and something in this world, real or imagined. Under this broad definition, some three dozen units of gospel materials can be considered parables (see 2.2).

There are two main types of parables in the Gospels. Brief little parables called *similitudes* make comparisons without complete stories but by means of the words "the → kingdom of God is like" or "is as if." Analogies are made between their subjects and general and timeless observations. Included here are the parables of the seed growing secretly (Mark 4:26-29), the mustard seed (Mark 4:30-32 par. Matt. 13:31-32 and Luke 13:18-19), the leaven (Matt.13:33 par. Luke 13:20-21), the treasure in the field (Matt. 13:44), and the pearl of great price (Matt. 13:45-46). All of these have parallel versions in the *Gospel of Thomas* as well (*Gos. Thom.* 57, 20, 96, 109, and 76, respectively).

The other type of parables is *narrative parables,* in which the comparisons made include narration; these parables typically have a "once upon a time" quality about them and the particularity of stories set in the past. The majority and best known of Jesus' parables belong here, including the parables of the prodigal son (Luke 15:11-32), the unjust manager (Luke 16:1-8), the workers in the vineyard (Matt. 20:1-16), and the wise and foolish maidens (Matt. 25:1-13).

Included also among the narrative parables, but sometimes placed into a third category, are four parables found only in the Gospel of Luke that illustrate exemplary behavior: the parables of the Good Samaritan (10:25-37), the rich fool (12:16-21), the rich man and Lazarus (16:19-31), and the Pharisee and the tax collector (18:10-14). These four are often considered to be in a category by themselves, since their meanings are transparent (as models of behavior), and they simply call for application, whereas other narrative parables leave the hearer with enigmas to ponder.

Six narrative parables in the Synoptic gospels have parallels in the *Gospel of Thomas:* the sower (Mark 4:3-8 and par.; *Gos. Thom.* 9), the weeds in the wheat (Matt. 13:24-30; *Gos. Thom.* 57), the rich fool (Luke 12:16-21; *Gos. Thom.* 63), the great banquet (Luke 14:16-24; *Gos. Thom.* 64), the wicked tenants (Mark 12:1-12 and par.; *Gos. Thom.* 65), and the lost sheep (Matt. 18:12-14 and par.; *Gos. Thom.* 107). Moreover, that same gospel contains four additional parables not found in the Synoptics: the wise fisherman (*Gos. Thom.* 8), the disciples as little children (21), the woman with a jar (97), and the assassin (98). One parable, the lost sheep, appears also in the apocryphal *Gospel of Truth* (31-32).

2.2. *A List*

The parables of Jesus can be listed in several ways. Here they are listed according to their sources, based on the standard two-source theory of gospel origins. Although some interpreters would add to this list, these 37 units would appear in most lists.

Those that appear in the *Gospel of Mark* (a total of 5):

- the sower (4:3-8 par. Matt. 13:3-8 and Luke 8:5-8)
- the seed growing secretly (4:26-29)
- the mustard seed (4:30-32 par. Matt. 13:31-32 and Luke 13:18-19)
- the wicked tenants (12:1-12 par. Matt. 21:33-46 and Luke 20:9-19)
- the waiting slaves (13:34-37 par. Luke 12:35-38).

Those attributed to the → *Q source* (6):

- the Father's good gifts (Matt. 7:9-11 par. Luke 11:11-13)
- the wise and foolish builders (Matt. 7:24-27 par. Luke 6:47-49)
- the children in the marketplace (Matt. 11:16-19 par. Luke 7:31-35)
- the leaven (Matt. 13:33 par. Luke 13:20-21)
- the lost sheep (Matt. 18:12-14 par. Luke 15:4-7)
- the faithful and wise slave (Matt. 24:45-51 par. Luke 12:42-46).

Parables distinctive to the *Gospel of Matthew* (10):

- the weeds in the wheat (13:24-30)
- the treasure in the field (13:44)
- the pearl of great price (13:45-46)
- the dragnet (13:47-50)
- the unforgiving slave (18:23-35)
- the workers in the vineyard (20:1-16)
- the two sons (21:28-32)
- the wedding feast (22:1-14)
- the wise and foolish maidens (25:1-13)
- the talents (25:14-30).

Parables distinctive to the *Gospel of Luke* (16):

- the two debtors (7:41-43)
- the Good Samaritan (10:25-37)
- the friend at midnight (11:5-8)
- the rich fool (12:16-21)
- the barren fig tree (13:6-9)
- the great banquet (14:16-24)
- building a tower (14:28-30)
- the king going to war (14:31-33)
- the lost coin (15:8-10)
- the prodigal son (15:11-32)
- the unjust manager (16:1-8)
- the rich man and Lazarus (16:19-31)
- the slave at duty (17:7-10)
- the unjust judge (18:2-8)
- the Pharisee and the tax collector (18:10-14)
- the pounds (19:12-27).

2.3. *Features*

The parables of Jesus share a number of features with other parables of antiquity. But they also are distinctive in a number of ways.

2.3.1. *Direct Address*

Typically, Jesus addresses his hearers with such penetrating questions as "Which one of you?" (Luke 11:5; 14:28; 17:7; 15:4 par. Matt. 12:11), "What woman?" (Luke 15:8), "Is there anyone among you?" (Matt. 7:9 par. Luke 11:11), "What king?" (Luke 14:31), "Who among you?" (Luke 17:7), "Who then is the faithful and wise slave?" (Matt. 24:45 par. Luke 12:42), and "What do you think?" (Matt. 18:12; 21:28). Or he uses a simple indicative: "Everyone who hears . . ." (Matt. 7:26). Such opening phrases engage the hearers immediately, putting them on the spot and eliciting a response.

2.3.2. *Direct Messages*

The parables are not building blocks within a larger, longer argument that is to be concluded outside of the parables themselves, although an interpretive comment may be added at the end (e.g., Matt. 18:35; 25:13; Luke 16:8; 18:7). Rather, the parables themselves are bearers of the message of Jesus. In this respect the parables of Jesus differ from known rabbinic parables, which are typically used to interpret a biblical text or to make a point within a longer discussion of a topic at hand (→ Rabbi, Rabbinism). Jesus' manner of teaching by parables without recourse to biblical texts no doubt led to the saying that he taught "as one having authority, and not as the scribes" (Mark 1:22).

2.3.3. *Common Metaphors*

The → metaphors employed in the parables are drawn from everyday life in the world of Jesus and his hearers: men and women working; losing and finding; fathers and sons in strained and joyous relationships; kings, rich men, and slaves in stereotypical roles; domestic animals, seeds, plants, vineyards, leaven, and the like. There is very little previous knowledge that Jesus' hearers need beyond what is gained through common life experience.

2.3.4. *Surprise Endings*
In spite of their use of common metaphors, the best-known parables of Jesus do not portray human behavior in typical ways. The narrative leads the hearer along from the familiar to a surprising twist at the end. Within the parable of the workers in the vineyard (Matt. 20:1-16), for example, the "11th-hour workers" receive pay equal to that of those who worked all day. In the parable of the prodigal son (Luke 15:11-32), the father runs to meet his returning son, who has squandered all that had been given to him. And in the parable of the wedding feast (Matt. 22:1-14), the king orders that others, "both good and bad," be brought in as guests when the respectable persons first invited would not come. These surprises have a bearing on the message of the parables.

2.4. *Message*
Some of the parables of Jesus are theological; others are about human conduct. In actuality the two cannot be separated, but for discussion purposes the distinction is necessary.

2.4.1. *God*
The parables are thoroughly theological, but they do not describe God's attributes or discuss God's nature theoretically. What is characteristic, rather, is the sense of God's intimacy and familiarity through the use of striking but common metaphors — a father, king, shepherd, owner of a vineyard, or a woman who sweeps her house. The concreteness of the metaphors keeps the discussion from abstractions. What is striking is the way that these metaphors for God are put to work. The behavior of the protagonist is so often not typical, since the parables are about God, whose → love and → grace exceed normal expectations. Some outstanding examples are the parables of the workers in the vineyard (Matt. 20:1-16) and the prodigal son (Luke 15:11-32).

2.4.2. *Kingdom of God*
Frequently the parables are about the kingdom of God (or, in the language of the Gospel of Matthew, the kingdom of heaven). In such cases the kingdom itself can be the topic at hand, as in the similitudes, in which the growth of the kingdom (or reign) of God is affirmed as a certainty, as in the parables of the seed growing secretly (Mark 4:26-29), the mustard seed (4:30-32 and par.), and the leaven (Matt. 13:33 and par.). Or the joy of its discovery is illustrated, as in the parables of the treasure in the field (Matt. 13:44) and the pearl of great price (Matt. 13:45-46). In other cases a parable may begin with reference to the kingdom, but the story following is actually about the ways of → God in a more general sense.

2.4.3. *Conduct*
As indicated above, four of Jesus' parables teach exemplary behavior. Included in them are teachings concerning (respectively) neighborliness, not trusting in an increase in material resources to make life more meaningful, caring for the needy, and true → piety before God. But other teachings are provided as well, such as the need to extend → forgiveness (the unforgiving slave, Matt. 18:23-35), to use one's gifts (the talents, Matt. 25:14-30, and the pounds, Luke 19:12-27), to leave judgment up to God (the weeds in the wheat, Matt. 13:24-30), and to be faithful until the coming of Christ again (the faithful and wise slave, Matt. 24:45-51 and par.), even if it may be far in the distant future (the wise and foolish maidens, Matt. 25:1-13).

2.4.4. *Wisdom and Eschatology*
In regard to their teaching in general, the parables of Jesus capture, combine, and make use of two major Jewish traditions: → Wisdom and → eschatology. The hearer is to be wise and apply what is said (the Wisdom tradition), lest that person be cast out in the final judgment, which may be imminent (the eschatological tradition). Not all parables combine both traditions, but the two traditions are so interwoven among a sufficient number of the parables that such an interweaving can be considered characteristic of the teaching of Jesus.

2.5. *Interpretation*
From the first century into modern times, the allegorical method was used to interpret the parables of Jesus. By means of that method, meanings were assigned to virtually every detail narrated in a particular parable. This method appears already in the NT itself, as in the interpretations given there to the parables of the sower (Mark 4:13-20 and par.) and the weeds in the wheat (Matt. 13:37-43).

A decisive methodological break was made toward the end of the 19th century when A. Jülicher's two-volume work on the parables was published. He called for nonallegorical interpretation, insisting that the interpreter should seek to find and explicate the "one point" that a parable makes. While that view has been granted ever since Jülicher's work, the ancients cetainly did not distinguish as carefully as modern interpreters might between parable and → allegory, and the rich use of symbolism in the parables of Jesus is not to go unnoticed.

Major shifts were made in the 20th century. Particularly in the works of C. H. Dodd and J. Jeremias there was an attempt to recover the meaning of the parables within their ancient Palestinian setting and in the ministry of Jesus. Other interpreters have approached the parables in light of modern linguistic theories, including semiotics (D. Patte, B. Scott), psychological dynamics (R. Ford), and socioeconomic realities of the ancient world (W. Herzog). It has been recognized too that the parables can have multiple meanings (M. Tolbert). Then too, some seek to interpret the parables within the contexts of the particular gospels in which they appear (C. Carlston, J. Donahue, A. Hultgren, J. Lambrecht, E. Linnemann, B. Smith), an approach that recognizes that the parables reflect not only the preaching of Jesus but also that of the → early church, plus redaction by the gospel writers themselves.

Bibliography: C. Carlston, *The Parables of the Triple Tradition* (Philadelphia, 1975) • J. Crossan, *In Parables: The Challenge of the Historical Jesus* (2d ed.; Sonoma, Calif., 1992) • C. H. Dodd, *The Parables of the Kingdom* (rev. ed.; New York, 1961) • J. Donahue, *The Gospel in Parable: Metaphor, Narrative, and Theology in the Synoptic Gospels* (Philadelphia, 1988) • R. Ford, *The Parables of Jesus: Recovering the Art of Listening* (Minneapolis, 1997) • W. Herzog, *Parables as Subversive Speech: Jesus as Pedagogue of the Oppressed* (Louisville, Ky., 1994) • A. Hultgren, *The Parables of Jesus: A Commentary* (Grand Rapids, 2000) • J. Jeremias, *The Parables of Jesus* (2d ed.; Upper Saddle River, N.J., 1972) • A. Jülicher, *Die Gleichnisreden Jesu* (2d ed.; 2 vols.; Tübingen, 1899; repr., Darmstadt, 1963) • W. Kissinger, *The Parables of Jesus: A History of Interpretation and Bibliography* (Metuchen, N.J., 1979) • J. Lambrecht, *Once More Astonished: The Parables of Jesus* (New York, 1981) • E. Linnemann, *The Parables of Jesus: Introduction and Exposition* (London, 1966) • H. McArthur and R. Johnston, *They Also Taught in Parables: Rabbinic Parables from the First Centuries of the Christian Era* (Grand Rapids, 1990) • D. Patte, ed., *Semiology and Parables: Exploration of the Possibilities Offered by Structuralism for Exegesis* (Pittsburgh, 1976) • N. Perrin, *Jesus and the Language of the Kingdom: Symbol and Metaphor in NT Interpretation* (Philadelphia, 1976); idem, *Parable and Gospel* (Minneapolis, 2003) • B. Scott, *Hear Then the Parable: A Commentary on the Parables of Jesus* (Philadelphia, 1989) • B. Smith, *The Parables of the Synoptic Gospels* (Cambridge, 1937) • D. Stern, *Parables in Midrash* (Cambridge, Mass., 1991) • M. Tolbert, *Perspectives on the Parables: An Approach to Multiple Interpretations* (Philadelphia, 1979).

Arland J. Hultgren

Paradise

1. General
2. As Garden
3. As Island
4. As Mountain
5. Other Views
6. Features

1. General

Like → heaven and the → kingdom of God, paradise has a place among the great religious (and secular) → utopias of human history (→ Secularization). In the Old Iranian language Avestan *pairidaeza* referred to a walled area, a garden (also a zoo). Believers linked it to an eschatological → hope viewed as the inbreaking of the beyond into the here and now, of → time into eternity, and hence as an alternative to → suffering and → death (or → hell). It is a kind of counterworld, a cosmological prototype.

2. As Garden

The symbol of the garden was an apt one for this hope. The prototype for the Oriental expectation of paradise was the Sumerian myth of Enki and Ninhursag, which tells of Dilmun, the land of the blessed, where there is peace between humans and animals and where pain, suffering, and old age are unknown.

The garden motif is common in the → history of religion, especially in → mysticism. The → Qur'an speaks of "gardens of delight" (56:12), which are like oases with streams flowing with clear water, milk, wine, and honey, and there are fruits and food in abundance. The "garden of the [heavenly] light" (the meaning of "Ittō-en," a Japanese religion of that name founded in 1905) is a universal archetype. Greek → mythology has the Garden of Hesperides and the Elysian Fields with their glorious climate (Homer *Od.* 4.564-69). The Jōdo-Shinshū school of Japanese → Buddhism envisions the western paradise Sukhavati, the pure land of the Buddha Amitābha, or promises entry into paradisiacal nirvana by way of a stepwise meditative path. Garden art in India and Persia, with its abundance of flowers, fruits, and watercourses and symbolic topography, gives meaning to the symbol of paradise and offers the devout a foretaste of what awaits them.

3. As Island

The "islands of the blessed" are also a symbol of paradise. The place of perfection is far from the world of evil and darkness (hell), is hard to find, is located above or beneath the earth, participates in the deity, and is almost inaccessible. The Atlantis of Plato (427-347 B.C.) and the Celtic blessed isles are relevant here, as perhaps are also the South Sea paintings of P. Gauguin (1848-1903).

4. As Mountain

Holy mountains sometimes have a link with paradise because they offer a special symbol of closeness to heaven. The mythical Mount Meru of the Hindus was venerated as the center of the universe. The heavenly bodies circle around it, the gods live on it, and the rivers of paradise flow from it.

5. Other Views

Some ages are called paradisiacal, or → golden, ages. Thus Krita Yuga in Hindu mythology is the age of perfection because in it dharma, the fullness of right, order, and truth, is fully achieved. But this age ends, and in keeping with the law of periodicity, three ages follow that obscure dharma until finally all values are lost in Kali Yuga. Plato, too, had a cycle of eternal recurrence when he spoke of the reversal of ages and relations, of people becoming younger instead of older, and finally of a new human race emerging (*Plt.* 269C–271C). We may refer in this regard to periodic or cyclic ideas of paradise (→ Reincarnation).

6. Features

Features and characteristics of paradise are the same in all cultures — righteousness, → freedom, bliss, harmony, → peace between humans and → animals, empathy with → nature, knowing the languages of plants and animals, an end to all suffering and toil and especially death, a reversal of all things and values, the salvific age, and the dwelling place of the righteous.

→ Islam; Primeval History (Genesis 1–11)

Bibliography: B. Alster, "Dilmun, Bahrain, and the Alleged Paradise in Sumerian Myth and Literature," *Dilmun: New Studies in the Archaeology and Early History of Bahrain* (ed. D. Potts; Berlin, 1983) 39-74 • C. Auffarth, *Irdische Wege und himmlischer Lohn. Kreuzzug, Jerusalem und Fegefeuer in religionswissenschaftlicher Perspektive* (Göttingen, 2002) • C. Buck, *Paradise and Paradigm: Key Symbols in Persian Christianity and the Baha'i Faith* (Albany, N.Y.,1999) • E. Budge, trans., *The Paradise or Garden of the Holy Fathers* (New York, 1972) • M. Dessoir, *Vom Jenseits der Seele* (6th ed.; Stuttgart, 1931) • T. H. Fischer, "Indonesische Paradiesesmythen," *ZE* 64 (1932) 204-44 • R. H. Grützmacher, *Diesseits und Jenseits in der Geistesgeschichte der Menschheit* (Berlin, 1932) • J. Hick, *Death and Eternal Life* (Louisville, Ky., 1994) • J. Horovitz, *Das koranische Paradies* (Jerusalem, 1923) • G. Luttikhuizen, ed., *Paradise Interpreted: Representations of Biblical Paradise in Judaism and Christianity* (Leiden, 1999) • E. B. Moynihan, *Paradise as a Garden: In Persia and Mughal India* (New York, 1979) • H. B. Partin, "Paradise," *EncRel(E)* 2.184-89 • H. Ritter, *The Ocean of the Soul: Man, the World, and God in the Stories of Farīd al-Dīn ʿAṭṭār* (trans. J. O'Kane; Leiden, 2003; orig. pub., 1955) • A. Sadakata, *Buddhist Cosmology: Philosophy and Origins* (Tokyo, 1997) • F. Stolz, "Paradies," *TRE* 25.705-8; idem, "Paradiese und Gegenwelten," *ZRW* 1 (1993) 5-24 • G. Widengren, *The King and the Tree of Life in Ancient Near Eastern Religion* (Uppsala, 1951).

Peter Gerlitz

Paradox

1. Logic
2. Theology

1. Logic

A paradox in the broad sense is a startling statement that cannot be literally true. In the narrower logical sense it may be a formally correct statement but one that contradicts its premises (→ Antinomy). We find paradoxes in everyday speech ("Less is more"), as well as in academic disciplines like → theology (M. → Luther's *simul iustus et peccator,* "at once righteous and a sinner"). Paradoxes may open up very profitable discussions or humorously serve the cause of logical or rhetorical propaedeutic (→ Language 1; Logic; Rhetoric 1).

2. Theology

In the NT the word *paradoxos* expresses surprise at the → miracles of → Jesus (Luke 5:26). The church fathers, Scholastics (→ Scholasticism), and → Reformers tried as far as possible to resolve logical paradoxes rationally, for example, with regard to divine and human attributes. As in other religions → mysticism took them as a starting point on the road to inner vision.

After S. → Kierkegaard (1813-55) → theology in the 19th and 20th centuries adopted a new relation to paradoxes. It distinguished absolutely between → time and eternity but saw the two together in existence. Kierkegaard thought we should not leave "the narrow path of the paradox" (*Fear and Trembling* 3.127). In → dialectical theology every answer was a new question (K. → Barth's *Christliche Dogmatik,* 456). Strictly, paradox was here the only form of theological thinking (H. Schröer). K. Barth (1886-1968), P. → Tillich (1886-1965), K. Heim (1874-1958), R. Bultmann (1884-1976), and others viewed paradoxes in the faith as the basis of their theology. "All biblical and ecclesiastical assertions about the final → revelation have a paradoxical character" (Tillich, *Systematic Theology*, 1.150).

Bibliography: S. N. Dunning, *Kierkegaard's Dialectic of Inwardness* (Princeton, 1985) • G. W. Erickson and J. A. Fossa, *Dictionary of Paradox* (Lanham, Md., 1998) • I. L. Gotz, *Faith, Humor, and Paradox* (Westport, Conn., 2002) • P. Hughes and G. Brecht, *Vicious Circles and Infinity: A Panoply of Paradoxes* (Garden City, N.Y., 1975) • N. Rescher, *Paradoxes: Their Roots, Range, and Resolution* (Chicago, 2001) • H. Schröer, *Die Denkform der Paradoxalität als theologisches Problem* (Göttingen, 1960) • R. Sorensen, *A Brief History of the Paradox: Philosophy and the Labyrinths of the Mind* (New York, 2003) • P. Tillich, "Critical and Positive Paradox" (1923), *The Beginnings of Dialectic Theology* (ed. J. M. Robinson; Richmond, Va., 1968) 133-41; idem, *Systematic Theology* (3 vols.; Chicago, 1951-63).

Jürgen Stein

Paraguay

	1960	*1980*	*2000*
Population (1,000s):	1,842	3,114	5,496
Annual growth rate (%):	2.44	2.95	2.46

Area: 406,752 sq. km. (157,048 sq. mi.)

A.D. 2000

Population density: 14/sq. km. (35/sq. mi.)
Births / deaths: 2.96 / 0.51 per 100 population
Fertility rate: 3.84 per woman
Infant mortality rate: 37 per 1,000 live births
Life expectancy: 70.8 years (m: 68.6, f: 73.1)
Religious affiliation (%): Christians 97.7 (Roman Catholics 94.6, Protestants 3.7, unaffiliated 2.5, indigenous 1.3, other Christians 1.0), nonreligious 1.2, other 1.1.

1. General and Historical Account

Paraguay lies at the heart of Latin America. The river that gives it its name divides its territory into two natural regions, east and west. Over 97 percent of the people live in the east. Here is the capital Asunción, the 16th-century center of the Spanish conquistadores for the conquest and colonizing of the La Plata area (→ Colonialism). The west, the Chaco, covers 61 percent of the territory. The ground here is so dry that only 2.2 percent of the people can live in the area. In all, there are over 6.3 million inhabitants (2005 est.), of which 2 percent are Native Americans.

The history of Paraguay falls into three periods: the Guaraní period (6,000 B.C. to A.D. 1537), the colonial age (1537-1811), and the age of the republic (after 1811). In the third period we should note the liberal constitution of 1870, North American imperialism (after 1940), and the military dictatorship of Alfredo Stroessner (1954-89). Since the Colorado Party that supported Stroessner has remained in power, it is not clear whether his fall opened the door to genuine democracy.

Socially, Paraguay was permanently affected by two international wars. In the Triple Alliance War of 1865-70, Brazil, Argentina, and Uruguay opened up Paraguay to British trading interests by ushering in a liberal economic system. The Chaco War with → Bolivia (1932-35), with U.S. oil interests on the side of Bolivia and the British on the side of Paraguay, ended in victory for Paraguay. The first war put Paraguay under Brazilian political influence from 1874 to 1904 and under Argentinian-British influence from 1904 to 1939. U.S. influence crowded out that of Britain after 1940 and World War II.

2. Christian Churches

Christianity came to Paraguay in 1537 with the first conquistadores. Up to the end of the 19th century the → Roman Catholic Church was the only Christian presence, and it evangelized among natives, mestizos, mulattos, and Spaniards. Protestants have been present in Paraguay in any numbers only since the last decades of the 19th century.

2.1. *Roman Catholic Church*

With the founding of Asunción the first → missionaries came to Paraguay (→ Catholic Missions). They saw it as their task to give natives the → sacraments and, up to 1580, did systematic evangelization and set up → reductions (community settlements) under the supervision of the → Franciscans, later the → Jesuits. The diocese of Río de la Plata was formed in 1547, Asunción being the seat. The banning of the Jesuits in 1767 ended the most intensive work of evangelizing and teaching. The → Dominicans began educational work in 1779, granting diplomas, but only for a few years. Franciscan, Mercedarian, Dominican, and Jesuit convents had both schools for novitiates and grammar schools during the colonial period.

The republican era saw the end of royal → patronage in favor of a less tolerant state patronage (→ Church and State). After the Triple Alliance War the church was leaderless; its → bishops had been shot, and about 100 priests had died or were killed. The → religious orders returned after 1880, reorganized the church, and opened seminaries and schools. → Ideologies, → liberalism, and laicism eroded the Christian tradition among young people. Freemasonry (→ Masons) also gained followers, helped by the occupying powers from 1869 to 1876. The church replied to laicizing in schools by forming catechetical centers for the laity (→ Clergy and Laity) so as to propagate Christian teaching.

The military dictatorship gave the church recognition as a legal entity in 1963 (Law 863). It supported the church with state grants and privileges that the church gratefully accepted. The spirit of → Vatican II and especially Medellín (1968; → Latin American Councils 2.4), however, promoted the growth of → base communities and small fellowships. The related increase in social and political involvement showed itself particularly in the rural groups (Ligas Agrarias) of → Catholic Action, which questioned the structure of land tenure. After 1966 conflicts with the state authorities resulted. Although Roman → Catholicism is officially the state religion, the church has detached itself from the state, and in 1972 the archbishop of Asunción relinquished the place on the state council that the 1967 constitution had given him. The church's defense of human → rights and fight against social injustice have brought with them more vocations to the priesthood and an increase in the number of monks, nuns, and lay members.

The advent of democracy in 1989 coincided with the designation of Felipe Santiago Benítez as the archbishop of Asunción. Benítez replaced Ismael Rolón, who served as archbishop from 1970 to 1989. During his tenure, Rolón distinguished himself by his steady and determined posture against the abuses of the Stroessner dictatorship; moreover, even today as archbishop emeritus, Rolón continues to be an important figure in safeguarding human rights.

In 1990, during the bishopric of Benítez, *Sendero* (lit. "Pathway"), an official publication of the Episcopal Conference of Paraguay, was shut down. During the last decades of the Stroessner dictatorship, this weekly publication had maintained a clear defense against the violation of human rights. Archbishop Benítez devoted himself to the restoration of the permanent diaconate of married men and to the promotion of the laity, for whom he opened the Institute of Theology for Laity.

The Catholic Church publicly intervened during the "Paraguayan March" of March 1999, which marked the social unrest and protest that followed the assassination on March 23 of Paraguayan vice-president Luis Maria Argaña. On March 26 seven men were shot to death and hundreds were wounded during protests in Asunción. Two days later, more than 100,000 people swarmed the squares outside the Congress and the Presidential Palace in order to protest these shootings and to express support for a national-unity government led by González Macchi. The intervention of the church during the march occurred when Jesuit priest Pa'i (colloquial for "Father") Oliva rallied thousands of young people to a mass celebrated on the plaza directly in front of Congress, right when tanks were converging. Oliva, along with other church leaders, delivered a message of resistance to the enemies of democracy.

On July 14, 2002, Pastor Cuquejo succeeded Benítez as archbishop. During his tenure, Cuquejo celebrated the fourth century of the First Diocesan Synod of Asunción (1603-2003); the synod was the source of the first social texts of the Roman Catholic Church in the region encompassing Paraguay and Río de la Plata.

Because of the conservative character of the Roman Catholic Church in Paraguay, with the exception of two bishops (of the dioceses of San Pedro and of Concepción), no progressive priests have been elevated to a bishopric in recent years. One of these bishops, Fernando Lugo Méndez, gave strong support to the social struggle of Paraguay's underprivileged classes and as a result of political pressure was forced to resign his diocese in 2005. He remains a priest of the Congregation of the Divine Word.

2.2. *Other Churches*

2.2.1. The Evangelical Church of La Plata, which spreads over Argentina and Paraguay and is now a member of the → Lutheran World Federation, owes its origin to German immigrants who came to Paraguay in 1881 and founded agricultural colonies in the heart of the country (San Bernardino in 1881, Nueva Germania in 1887) and later in the southeast (e.g., Hohenau in 1900, formed by German Brazilians). In 1933 there were 24 settlements with German-speaking groups from Germany itself, Austria, Russia, and Switzerland. Of these about one-third were Roman Catholic, and the rest Lutheran and Reformed, with some German Mennonites coming from Russia (1926, 1930, 1947) to the Chaco.

The religious life of these non-Catholic German-speaking immigrants at first followed a familiar pattern. In 1893 the German consul in Asunción helped the Evangelical Church and School Community obtain a pastor and teacher from Berlin, and Nueva Germania, which formed the first church council in Paraguay in 1891, offered a secondary preaching station for the Asunción pastor. Other sites were also pastored from Asunción, so that no vital congregational life could develop before 1929, when Hohenau, Obligado, and Bellavista briefly had their own pastor. In 1954 Hohenau again had its own pastor. The congregation in the capital greatly influenced those in rural areas and developed a strong sense of responsibility for German → Protestantism in Paraguay. A German rather than Protestant identity was an obstacle, and it pulled many German Protestants in Paraguay into the morass of National Socialism (→ Fascism). An identity crisis resulted in 1945. Faced with an expansive educational policy on the part of Roman Catholics, the Asunción congregation began in 1963 to reflect on confessional identity and to develop a true confessional sense anchored in the larger church. In the 1970s it took the lead in ecumenical work for social reform and human rights (→ Oikoumene). In 2000 the church had 7,000 adherents.

Another Lutheran group in Paraguay has roots in the U.S. Lutheran Church–Missouri Synod. In 1995 it had 13 congregations and 3,800 adherents.

2.2.2. The origins of the → Anglican Church in Paraguay go back to 1888, when the South American Missionary Society began work among the Lengua Indians in the Chaco (→ British Missions). This mission does medical and educational work, has settlement projects, and builds up the churches. The Anglicans built a church for Spanish speakers in the capital in 1907. Evangelization is done today by the Colegio San Andrés, a high school for the children of wealthy Roman Catholics and qualified Anglicans. The church also finances primary schools and a mobile medical team for needy areas. In 2000 it had 36 congregations with 16,000 adherents.

2.2.3. From the United States the Disciples of Christ (9 congregations, 1,000 members; → Christian Church [Disciples of Christ]) came to Paraguay in 1918 and took up the work of the Episcopal → Methodist Church. They focus on schools and founded the International College in 1920. They also have two centers for free → rehabilitation and social work in Asunción and Coronel Oviedo. They offer medical and legal help to Indians (→ Medical Missions).

2.2.4. → Baptists began work in 1919/20 when missionaries of the Baptist Convention of Argentina came to Asunción at the request of Baptists who had settled there in 1912. The Evangelical Baptist Convention of Paraguay has been supported since 1945 by the Southern Baptist Convention of the United States. It opened the first Baptist hospital in South America in 1952/53, then a high school in Villa Morena, then a theological institute and other educational establishments. In 2000 the convention had 106 congregations scattered across Paraguay, with 19,000 adherents.

2.2.5. The largest Protestant group in Paraguay is the → Mennonites, who formed the Evangelical Mennonite Church in Paraguay in 1921. Another group, the Mennonite Brethren, constituted itself in 1930 (87 percent of its members are Lengua, Chulupi, or Guaraní). In 2000 they and ten other, smaller Mennonite groups in Paraguay had a total of 135 congregations, with 62,000 adherents. The best-known Mennonite colonies are Menno, Fernheim, Filadelpia, Neuland, Sommerfeld, and Bergtal in the Chaco. Between 1966 and 1980 Mennonite immigrants from Mexico and the United States founded eight colonies in the East. Ethnically, most of the congregations are German speaking. They have many schools and hospitals, do dairy work, and engage in Indian evangelization. They enjoy a special status in keeping with their beliefs, namely, exemption from military service (→ Conscientious Objection).

2.2.6. Among other groups we may note the Seventh-day → Adventists (first came in 1900; in 2000 they had 39 congregations and 14,000 members), the New Testament Missionary Union (1902, now with 20 congregations and 2,000 members), the → Salvation Army (1910, now with only a single congregation), and the New Tribes Mission, which since 1946, in close cooperation with the Department for Indian Affairs, has been active among several Indian tribes of the north (34 congregations, with 2,000 members).

After World War II the Pentecostal churches came to Paraguay, first the → Assemblies of God in 1945 (70 congregations, 37,000 members; → Assembleias de Deus no Brasil), who worked among Pentecostal immigrants from Eastern Europe and who formed a small national church in 1954, then the Church of God (Cleveland, Tenn.) in 1954 (146 congregations, 14,000 members), who also work among the Guaraní.

The largest non-Catholic Christian group in the country is El Pueblo de Dios (The People of God), a Paraguayan-based group started in 1963 by Leonar Paredes ("Brother José," 1898-1970). The theology of the group is basically Pentecostal, with some distinctive variations (→ Pentecostalism). Numbering

150,000 followers in 200 congregations, it has sent missionaries primarily to Brazil but also to Argentina, Uruguay, Colombia, and Italy.

2.2.7. Protestant churches, which in 1910 had a total of only 147 members and in 1929 only 3,000, experienced a 95 percent growth rate between 1980 and 1987, when they had 73,000 members. In 2000 the number of Protestants had risen to over 200,000.

3. Interchurch Relations

The churches cooperate domestically despite their differences. The Evangelical La Plata Church and the Disciples of Christ have a joint committee and friendship mission. Many churches support the Christian Union of Young Men (ASO), which sponsors cultural and sporting activities, and also work together in the Bible Society.

Before → Vatican II Roman Catholics and Protestants did little joint work. Conflict and mutual rejection marked their relations. But they now cooperate on programs like Alto Paraná Christian Aid (PAC) and the Itapua Churches Program, along with ASO and the → Bible Society.

4. Other Religious Groups

Marginal Christian groups in Paraguay include the Latter-day Saints (→ Mormons), who in 2000 had 40,000 members in 141 congregations, and the → Jehovah's Witnesses, with 10,000 members in 86 congregations. Other religious groups include Buddhists, → Baha'i, → Rosicrucians, and Spiritists. In 2000 also there were small numbers (fewer than 3,000 each) of Muslims and Jews.

5. Church and State

There is no → concordat between the Roman Catholic Church and the state, but the church benefits from special arrangements and privileges such as tax relief.

The restoration of obligatory Roman Catholic teaching in public schools created tensions with Protestant churches between 1945 and 1967. In 1967 a new constitution guaranteed freedom of religion. When the Evangelical La Plata Church and Disciples of Christ ran into new problems with the state, they asked the → World Council of Churches to send a delegation. It came and expressed solidarity with their work and their efforts on behalf of the poorest of the poor.

Bibliography: A. Brachettio, *Die Missionsarbeit der katholischen Kirke bei den Indianern in Paraguay* (Bonn, 1990) • W. E. Browning, *The River Plate Republics: A Survey of the Religious, Economic, and Social Conditions in Argentina, Paraguay, and Uruguay* (London, 1928) • R. A. Nickson, *Historical Dictionary of Paraguay* (2d ed.; Metuchen, N.J., 1993) • R. Plett, *El protestantismo en el Paraguay. Su aporte cultural, económico y espiritual* (Asunción, 1987) • F. J. Reiter, *They Built Utopia: The Jesuit Missions in Paraguay, 1610-1768* (Potomac, Md., 1995) • J. T. Shumaker, "Church Growth in Paraguay" (Thesis, Fuller Theological Seminary, 1972) • R. A. White, *Breaking Silence: The Case That Changed the Face of Human Rights* (Washington, D.C., 2004) on human rights in Paraguay, 1954-89.

Margarita Durán Estragó

Parallels and Harmonies, Gospel

1. Early Church
   1.1. Second Clement, Justin Martyr
   1.2. Tatian
   1.3. Ammonius, Eusebius
2. Middle Ages to the Enlightenment
3. Modern Period

A gospel harmony is a composite work that attempts to combine the various accounts of Jesus' life and ministry found in the canonical → Gospels — Matthew, Mark, Luke, and John — into one continuous narrative. The impulse to harmonize these texts derives, on the one hand, from the fact that they are not all the same and, on the other, from the conviction that the Gospels ought at least to be in substantive agreement (see Augustine's *De cons. evang.*). Early gospel harmonies attempted to create a single story from the four. In the modern era this practice, and the assumptions that warranted it, have largely been abandoned in favor of an approach that lays out the four gospels in parallel columns to facilitate comparison and critical study of the differences between them.

1. Early Church

1.1. *Second Clement, Justin Martyr*

The urge to harmonize two different gospel accounts is almost as old as the gospel texts themselves. Already in the early second century the author of *2 Clement* (→ Apostolic Fathers 2.3.2) can be seen to relate certain dominical sayings that seem to combine elements from both Matthew and Luke, and occasionally a noncanonical gospel source as well. Similarly, Justin Martyr (d. ca. 150) cites several dominical sayings in which elements of Matthew and Luke have been combined (H. Koester, 349-60, 365-74).

In neither case, however, does the author appear to have made direct use of these gospels themselves. Rather, the source of *2 Clement* was probably a series of dialogues in which sayings of Jesus from Matthew and Luke had already been incorporated and harmonized. Likewise, Justin also probably made use of a collection of logia in which sayings of Jesus drawn from Matthew and Luke had been harmonized and organized thematically (Koester, 360, 374-75). Whether the harmonization itself was undertaken consciously and according to a plan or scheme, or rather occurred piecemeal through the harmonizing proclivities of scribes working from memory in an environment of oral transmission of gospel texts once read but now inaccessible, is not known.

1.2. *Tatian*

The first conscious attempt to produce a harmony of the four distinct narratives of Matthew, Mark, Luke, and John was that of Tatian, who flourished in the middle of the second century. Tatian was a Syrian, probably from the region east of the Euphrates. At some point he wandered west to study philosophy and was ultimately converted to Christianity by reading the Jewish scriptures, probably the → Septuagint (*Orat.* 29). In Rome he became a student of Justin Martyr and a follower of Valentinus. After Justin's death he was → excommunicated, ostensibly for his Encratite and gnosticizing views (Irenaeus *Adv. haer.* 1.28.1; Epiphanius *Pan.* 46.1.8; → Gnosis, Gnosticism). Tatian returned to his home in the east, leaving behind but one extant work, his *Oratio ad Graecos*, an apologetic tract extolling the virtues of Christianity over against Hellenistic culture. He is best known, however, for his harmony of the Gospels, known as the Diatessaron, or "harmony of four parts."

The Diatessaron is one of the most challenging puzzles in early Christianity. Except for a small Greek fragment discovered at Dura in 1933, no actual copies of Tatian's Diatessaron appear to have survived antiquity. The text must be reconstructed based on the various witnesses that preserve it in part or that have in some way been influenced by it. Of these the most important is a commentary by Ephraem Syrus (d. 373) that survives in the original Syriac and in an Armenian translation (L. Leloir). This commentary preserves large fragments of Tatian's original harmony. Also important are an Arabic translation of the Diatessaron (A.-S. Marmardji); a Persian harmony of the gospels (G. Messina), which stands close to the Diatessaron; the Syriac versions of the Gospels, which hold many readings that appear to have been influenced by the Diatessaron (M. Black); and the many gospel quotations from the Syriac fathers (Ephrem, Aphrahat, Rabbula of Edessa, Ishoʿdad of Merv, etc.), which have been similarly influenced. Several Western witnesses to the Diatessaron are also of some importance, including Codex Fuldensis, a sixth-century Latin gospel harmony (E. Ranke), which seems to preserve many Diatessaronic readings, despite having been "Vulgatized" by a Latin scribe (T. Zahn, 300-303). This mysterious text was discovered by Victor, bishop of Capua (541-54), bearing the title "Diapente" (harmony of five parts) rather than Diatessaron, leaving scholars to speculate on what the fifth gospel text in this harmony might have been. Because of these difficulties, many questions about the Diatessaron remain in dispute, including its date and place of composition (Rome or Syria?), the original language of composition (Greek or Syriac?), the sources Tatian used (the four canonical gospels or a fifth as well?), and even the original title of the work.

Tatian's method was apparently to follow the basic path of Matthew, adding material from the other gospels to supplement it and creating a composite account where parallels exist. Sometimes he creates a piecemeal text, carefully combining exact details from each version of a story, while at other times he seems to take a broader approach, composing freely based on the parallel texts (W. L. Petersen, "Tatian's Diatessaron," 430). Speculation about Tatian's editorial hand includes charges of Encratism and a tendency to distance → Jesus from → Judaism, but the evidence for either is slim.

In the fifth century Theodoret, the orthodox bishop of Cyrrhus (423-ca. 460), found hundreds of copies of the Diatessaron still in use in the churches of Syria. He disapproved of the book because of its omission of Matthew's genealogy and certain other unnamed flaws aiming to disprove the descent of Jesus from "David according to the flesh" (*Haer. fab. comp.* 1.20) and so had them removed and replaced with copies of the four canonical gospels. But the Diatessaron continued to influence Syrian Christians for centuries to come. For example, the sixth-century Syrian-born hymn writer Romanos the Melodist included Diatessaronic passages in hymns composed for the court of Justinian in Constantinople (Petersen, "Tatian's Diatessaron," 412; also Petersen, *Diatessaron*). And in the West it continued to exercise influence in the many Latin harmonies and later medieval harmonies in Italian, Middle Dutch, Middle High German, Old Saxon, and Middle English (Petersen, "Tatian's Diatessaron," 413-19; D. Wünsch, "Evangelienharmonie," 628-29).

1.3. *Ammonius, Eusebius*

In the early third century Ammonius of Alexandria (d. 242) apparently produced a harmony somewhat comparable to that of Tatian, also following the lead of Matthew, and apparently also called Diatessaron (Eusebius *Ep. Carp.* 1). Unfortunately, it does not survive beyond a single reference in Eusebius's letter to Carpianus.

In this same letter Eusebius mentions his own alternative to this sort of harmony, the so-called Canons of Eusebius, a series of ten lists in which parallel texts from the Gospels are given for the purpose of facilitating comparison. First he lists things contained in all four gospels; then in only Matthew, Mark, and Luke; then in Matthew, Luke, and John; then in Matthew, Mark, and John; then Matthew and Luke; and so on through all the possible combinations, including things found only in one gospel. The lists were to be used as a kind of index of cross-references through which one could easily find any alternative versions to the passage one might be studying. It was probably the first "gospel parallels" composed explicitly for scholarly purposes.

2. Middle Ages to the Enlightenment

Popular gospel harmonies modeled on Tatian's Diatessaron continued to appear throughout the → Middle Ages, including the Liège Harmony in Middle Dutch (D. Plooij), the Pepysian Harmony in Middle English (M. Goates), and the Old Saxon poem *Heliand* (M. Scott). In the 15th century the reformer Johannes Gerson introduced his Monotessaron, a gospel harmony following the Johannine order, with harmonized versions of Synoptic pericopes inserted where he thought they might fit in the Johannine narrative (Wünsch, *Evangelienharmonien,* 15-20). Thereupon followed a spate of gospel harmonies, including those of Lucinius (1525), J. Beringer (1526), M. Alber (1532), A. Osiander (1537), Cornelius Jansen the Elder (1549), and M. Chemnitz.

The Chemnitz harmony, the *Harmonia evangelica,* finished and published after Chemnitz's death in 1586 by P. Leyser and J. Gerhard between 1593 and 1652, was the most ambitious effort of the genre. It too followed the Johannine order, adding harmonized versions of Synoptic pericopes where Chemnitz thought them appropriate. Chemnitz's aim was scholarly rather than popular. Each section thus begins with an explanation of the location of particular materials, followed by the parallel texts themselves, in Greek and Latin, and only then the harmonized version of the text, again with notes explaining the harmonization. Finally, he includes a commentary on the harmonized whole (Wünsch, "Evangelienharmonie," 633-34).

The popularity of gospel harmonies as a method for studying the life of Jesus continued for another century. With the coming of the → Enlightenment, however, as well as the newer tendency to contest the historicity of the gospel texts themselves, the scholarly effort that once was poured into a work like the *Harmonia evangelica* was channeled into more historical-critical reconstructions of the life of Jesus, like those of H. E. G. Paulus (1761-1851) and D. F. Strauss (1808-74). Likewise, works like *Vie de Jésus* (1863), by J.-E. Renan (1823-92), became heir to the popular harmonies like the *Heliand.*

3. Modern Period

In the modern period the comparative function once performed by the gospel harmonies was taken up by a new form — the gospel parallels, or synopsis. Here the attempt to harmonize the disparate texts is abandoned in favor of the desire to observe the differences between texts, thus better to assess their distinctive qualities. The most commonly used tool of this sort is Kurt Aland's *Synopsis Quattuor Evangeliorum* (from 1964), available in a variety of translations. In it the three Synoptic gospels are laid out in parallel columns, the order dictated by the hypothesis of Markan priority. The narrative integrity of Matthew and Luke is honored when they make major detours from the Markan text, and all Matthean and Lukan special material is included in its proper narrative context. Johannine parallels are also included where they occur. The result is a rather complex puzzle that facilitates comparison between the various versions of a particular pericope, but at the expense of any clear narrative sense for any one of the individual gospels.

This concern is addressed by Robert Funk's *New Gospel Parallels* (1985). In this work Funk presents each gospel consecutively in its entirety, first Matthew, then Mark, then Luke, each laid out as the lead text in the left-hand column of the page. Then, in vertical columns laid out to the right of the lead text, parallels from the other gospels are given, including parallels from John, the *Gospel of Thomas,* other noncanonical gospel literature, the letters of → Paul, the → church fathers, and various other sources for dominical sayings. A second volume follows the same format, now giving John the role of lead text, then Thomas, and various other noncanonical gospels. The result is a more expansive, but often repetitive, tool that allows one to sense the narrative structure of each text, as well as its sources.

Bibliography: K. Aland, *Synopsis Quattuor Evangeliorum* (15th ed.; Stuttgart, 2001) • M. Black, "The Palestinian Syriac Gospels and the Diatessaron," *OrChr* 36 (1939) 101-11 • R. W. Funk, ed., *New Gospel Parallels* (2 vols.; Philadelphia, 1985) • M. Goates, ed., *The Pepysian Harmony* (London, 1922) • H. Koester, *Ancient Christian Gospels: Their History and Development* (London, 1990) • C. H. Kraeling, *A Greek Fragment of Tatian's Diatessaron from Dura* (London, 1935) • L. Leloir, "Le commentaire d'Éphrem sur le Diatessaron. Quarante et un folios retrouvés," *RB* 94 (1987) 481-518; idem, ed., *Éphrem de Nisibe. Commentaire de l'Évangile concordant ou Diatessaron* (Paris, 1966); idem, ed., *Saint Éphrem. Commentaire de l'Évangile concordant. Texte syriaque* (Dublin, 1963); idem, ed., *Saint Éphrem. Commentaire de l'Évangile concordant. Version arménienne* (2 vols.; Louvain, 1953-54) • C. McCarthy, ed., *Saint Ephrem's Commentary on Tatian's Diatessaron: An English Translation* (Oxford, 1993) • A.-S. Marmardji, *Diatessaron de Tatien* (Beyrouth, 1935) • G. Messina, *Diatessaron persiano* (Vatican City, 1951) • W. L. Petersen, *The Diatessaron and Ephrem Syrus as Sources of Romanos the Melodist* (Louvain, 1985); idem, "Tatian's Diatessaron," *Ancient Christian Gospels,* Koester, 403-30 • D. Plooij et al., eds., *The Liège Diatessaron* (pts. 1-8; Amsterdam, 1929-70) • E. Ranke, ed., *Codex Fuldensis* (Marburg, 1868) • M. Scott, *The Heliand* (Chapel Hill, N.C., 1966) • D. Wünsch, "Evangelienharmonie," *TRE* 10.626-36; idem, *Evangelienharmonien im Reformationszeitalter. Ein Beitrag zur Geschichte der Leben-Jesu-Darstellungen* (Berlin, 1983) • T. Zahn, *Tatian's Diatessaron* (Erlangen, 1881).

Stephen J. Patterson

Paraments

1. Definition
2. On Altars
3. With Other Objects

1. Definition

1. Paraments (from Lat. *paro,* "prepare, furnish") are here defined as textile coverings and hangings for liturgical objects.

2. On Altars

The square early Christian → altars were covered with enveloping throwover cloths called palls. A linen cloth, the *palla corporalis,* was laid on top for the celebration of the liturgy, and the altar canopy was hung with veils on all four sides. Changes took place in the West from about 1200. Once the host was elevated, the veils were no longer used except during Lent (→ Fast), though the *Fastenvelum* (Lenten veil) survived in parts of southern Europe into the 20th century.

In northern Europe the pillars of the ciborium (canopy) remained, with riddels (curtains) between them on the north, south, and east sides, though the one on the east was sometimes replaced by a carved reredos (screen or partition wall) or retable (shelf). This style of altar is often, though mistakenly, called the English altar. Liturgical colors were introduced (→ Innocent III, *De sacro altaris mysterio*), and the altar was gradually lengthened. The silk pall became the antependium, or frontal; the linen pall covered the top of the table, and a small corporal, or communion cloth, was spread over it, on which the chalice and paten were placed. A superfrontal or dossal (ornamental cloth) sometimes hung above the altar in place of a reredos. The throwover cover (pall) enjoyed a revival during the 17th and 18th centuries and has found favor also in recent years.

2.1. Although the traditional colors are set out for guidance, the Roman Missal (1970) stipulates only that an altar should be covered by at least one cloth, whose shape, size, and ornamentation should be in keeping with the structure of the altar. However, the vestments of the altar, the chalice veil, and the burse (for storing the corporal) should match the vestments worn by the celebrant.

2.2. During the 19th-century Catholic revival in the Evangelical church and the Church of England (→ Anglican Communion; Book of Common Prayer), Wilhelm Löhe (1808-72) in Germany and the Tractarians and Ritualists in England revived the use of vestments and altar paraments (→ Oxford Movement). In 1865 Löhe wrote, "The sacrament is the substance or fullness, and all the paraments the outer covering; the richer our sacramental life, the more justified is our concern with paraments." As a result, much modern practice in both churches differs little from contemporary Roman Catholic usage. Liturgical colors are still used, but new colors and materials have been introduced, and a sense of suitable seasonal color is now often thought preferable to a rigid adherence to "correct" rules.

In → Reformed churches full sets of paraments are seldom used. In the (Presbyterian) Church of Scotland, for example, and in the English → free churches, the front of the Holy Table is usually left bare, and the top alone is covered with a white linen cloth.

2.3. In the Byzantine Rite (→ Orthodox Church) a square altar is still used. On each corner is placed a *hyphasma*, a piece of material embroidered with the name or symbol of an Evangelist. These are covered by a large white linen cloth *(katasarkion)*, on top of which is a silk cloth *(ependysis, endyton*, or *ephaplōma)*. The vessels are set out on a square linen cloth *(eilēton)* equivalent to the Western corporal. There are separate veils for chalice and paten, and a third that covers them both. Liturgical colors are optional (→ Eucharistic Ecclesiology).

3. With Other Objects

Further paraments used in the West include covers or falls for missal desk, reading desk, and → pulpit desk; rich pulpit cloths and cushions, once fashionable in Protestant churches, are rarely found today. In Orthodox churches the Holy Door in the center of the iconostasis is closed by a long curtain that is drawn aside during much of the liturgy but that is otherwise kept closed, except during → Easter week.

→ Church Year; Liturgical Vessels; Sacristy; Vestments

Bibliography: A. Fortescue, with J. B. O'Connell, *The Ceremonies of the Roman Rite Described* (12th ed.; London, 1962) • *Grundfragen evangelischer Paramentik* (Kassel, 1955) • F. W. Hopf, "W. Löhe als Zeuge des Altar-sakraments," *JMLB* 2 (1947) 69-78 • A. A. King, *The Rites of Eastern Christendom* (2 vols.; Rome, 1947-48) • W. Löhe, *Vom Schmuck der heiligen Orte* (ed. A. Rickert; Kassel, 1949; orig. pub., 1859) • *A New Dictionary of Liturgy and Worship* (London, 1986) articles on altar, altar hanging, ciborium, colours liturgical, corporal, frontal, pall, veil • C. E. Pocknee, *The Christian Altar* (London, 1963).

Gerald D. W. Randall, with
Nicholas W. Groves

Parapsychology

1. Concept

The term "parapsychology," which M. Dessoir (1867-1947) suggested in 1889, takes as the object of → psychology or its related disciplines certain phenomena that deviate from the normal life of the → soul. Alternative terms such as "scientific occultism" or "metapsychology" have been proposed, but "parapsychology" ultimately came into common use (supported by H. Driesch). The subjects of parapsychology include occult phenomena and other supersensory → experiences. Comparative studies of traditional and popular reports, along with research into spontaneous phenomena and experiments with persons who seem especially sensitive to such phenomena, make up the field.

Formally, parapsychology embraces two kinds of phenomena: (1) extrasensory perception, including telepathy, clairvoyance, and precognition (→ Divination); and (2) telekinesis or psychokinesis, the supersensory influencing of material processes or objects. For the most part, parapsychology takes both sets of phenomena to be proved but differs as to the criteria used in their scientific evaluation. In the meantime, fakes have long been associated with parapsychology. As far as the alternative between animist (i.e., anima in the sense of psyche, not the concept of → animism familiar from religious studies) and spiritist (→ Spiritism) hypotheses is concerned, scientific and theoretical considerations prompt parapsychology to prefer the former.

2. In History

The historical development of parapsychology ran parallel to the socially and historically influential spread of occultism. After some first critical studies of mesmerism (ca. 1778) and spiritism (ca. 1850), the founding of the Society for Psychical Research in London in 1882 brought recognition to parapsychology. But only in 1934 did it become part of the university curriculum in Durham and Utrecht. In 1953/54 chairs were set up in Utrecht and Freiburg; similar chairs exist in Britain and the United States.

Since the 1970s researchers have been discussing the various initiatives of "observational theories" inspired by quantum and system theory that consider the significance the observation of a given experiment might have for assessing results. Today parapsychology is carried out under scientific conditions in many countries, the Freiburg Institute being probably the best equipped in the world.

3. In Theology

From a theological perspective, parapsychology is assessed in many different ways and indeed is often simply dismissed altogether. General consensus holds that parapsychology might at most involve hidden dimensions of our own immanent sphere of → creation.

In the meantime, however, theological insights arising from a consideration of the → Trinity suggest that God is not to be understood simply as transcending the world entirely, suggesting further that theology might well engage in a more differentiated consideration of the results and questions of parapsychology from the perspective of pneumatologically considered "immanent transcendence."

→ Demons; Exorcism; Immortality; Magic; Theosophy

Bibliography: L. L. Adler and B. R. Mukherji, eds., *Spirit versus Scalpel: Traditional Healing and Modern Psychotherapy* (Westport, Conn., 1995) • H. Bender, ed., *Parapsychologie. Entwicklung, Ergebnisse, Probleme* (5th ed.; Darmstadt, 1980; orig. pub., 1966) • A. S. Berger and J. Berger, *The Encyclopedia of Parapsychology and Psychical Research* (New York, 1991) • R. Broughton, *Parapsychology: The Controversial Science* (New York, 1991) • H. Driesch, *Psychical Research: The Science of the Super-normal* (London, 1933) • E. Goode, *Paranormal Beliefs: A Sociological Introduction* (Prospect Heights, Ill., 2000) • P. Grim, ed., *Philosophy of Science and the Occult* (Albany, N.Y., 1990) • *Journal of Parapsychology* (1936-) • W. von Lucadou, *Psyche und Chaos. Neue Ergebnisse der Psychokinese-Forschung* (Freiburg, 1989); idem, *Psyche und Chaos. Theorien der Parapsychologie* (Frankfurt, 1995) • D. Radin, *The Conscious Universe: The Scientific Truth of Psychic Phenomena* (San Francisco, 1997) • W. Thiede, "Der neuzeitliche Okkultismus in theologischer Perspektive," *KuD* 33 (1987) 279-302; idem, "Parapsychologie und Theologie. Reflexion einer gemeinsamen Geschichte," *Grenzgebiete der Wissenschaft* 52 (2003) 57-81 • W. F. Williams, *Encyclopedia of Pseudoscience* (New York, 2000).

Werner Thiede

Parenesis

In the → primitive Christian community parenesis (from Gk. *paraineō,* "advise, urge") had the aim of giving ethical instruction to the post-Easter churches (→ Ethics). Presupposing → baptism, it linked basic theses to situational formulas. In its various forms parenesis was part of early Christian history and cannot be separated from it. We should also note the relation to the → Jesus tradition and its basic ethical directions (→ Sermon on the Mount).

Research based on the insights of M. Dibelius (1883-1947) traces primitive parenesis mainly to the Epistles (→ Literature, Biblical and Early Christian, 2). In orientation to the postbaptismal situation the texts, for all their differences, show that the great issue is the practice of → freedom in the Christian life. The variety of forms does not affect this thesis. We have → household rules (Col. 3:18–4:1; 1 Pet. 2:13–3:9), lists of → virtues and vices (Gal. 5:16-23), and proverbial sayings (in → Wisdom literature, also the Epistle of James).

Important parallels might be found in the ethics of late antiquity (Hellenistic → Judaism, economics, popular philosophy, and → Stoicism), which shows that Christian parenesis followed the traditions and modes of communication of the age. Differences, however, give the early church its own ethical and social profile. As regards the material heart of early Christian parenesis, the thesis of a Christianizing of popular Hellenistic philosophy will not suffice, nor can the study of religious history remove the features that give difficulty in the directions found in the Epistles.

A text like Phil. 4:8 (alongside 4:9) makes it clear that we cannot detach NT parenesis from its Christological base (→ Christology 1). We find proof of this connection in the prominence of the commandment of → love (§5; Rom. 12:9; 13:8-10; Col. 3:14; Eph. 5:2; 1 Pet. 1:22; 2:17; 4:8; Jas. 2:8). We may also point to the stress on "in the Lord" or "in Christ." The Christological aspect, which includes the eschatological (→ Eschatology 2), integrates rather than eliminates historical differentiation. In its centrality, though, it implies social orientation and activism, primarily in relation to the community, not to the outside world.

Integration into the context of the Epistles shows what the place and goal of parenesis are in church life. Its history raises a problem of → hermeneutics that is still with us. If we break the necessary bond between parenesis, freedom, and Christology and make the directions into absolute → norms, we fail to see the distinctive nature of parenesis in primitive Christianity.

→ Decalogue; Discipleship 1; Exegesis, Biblical; Hellenism; Jewish Theology; Torah

Bibliography: D. L. Balch, *Let Wives Be Submissive: The Domestic Code in 1 Peter* (Chico, Calif., 1981) • M. Gielen, *Tradition und Theologie neutestamentlicher Haustafelethik* (Frankfurt, 1990) • W. A. Meeks, *The Moral World of the First Christians* (Philadelphia, 1986) • K.-W. Niebuhr, *Gesetz und Paränese. Katechismusartige Weisungsreihen in der frühjüdischen Literatur* (Tübingen, 1987) • B. S. Rosner, ed., *Understanding Paul's Ethics: Twentieth-Century Approaches* (Grand Rapids, 1995) • W. Schrage, "The Formal Ethical Interpretation of Pauline Paraenesis" (1960), *Understanding Paul's Ethics,* ed. Rosner, 301-36 • S. Wibbing, *Die Tugend- und Lasterkataloge im Neuen Testament* (Berlin, 1959).

Henning Paulsen†

Pariahs

1. Term
2. In Independent India
3. Beyond India

1. Term

Pariahs (a simplified form of Tamil *paraiyar,* sing. *paraiyan,* "drummer") were originally the members of a → caste in South India (in Tamil Nadu and Kerala) made up of lower workers who earned their living as (at one time slave) farm laborers, though some also as drummers or handlers of animal carcasses. Their work, and especially their cutting of flesh, made them ritually unclean (U. von Ehrenfels; → Cultic Purity). Along the line of Sanskrit etymology the Abbé de Raynal (1713-96) at the end of the 18th century called them outcasts who were denied access to temples, markets, and wells. The term in its simplified form thus came to mean generally an outcast.

The *paraiyar,* however, were by no means the most despised caste, and they did have some ritual functions in important South Indian temples. Only as a result of a schematic use of the term by British authors and administrators did denial of sexual union, exclusion from important public spheres, and uncleanness come to be seen as characteristics of the Indian castes standing under the fourth varna (or grouping, the Sudra), whose members were stigmatized as untouchables. The British administration began classifying them "scheduled castes," to which it also added "scheduled tribes."

Mahatma Gandhi (1869-1948) condemned the doctrine of untouchability as a sinful deviation from true Indian religion. He tried to change the position of the pariahs by replacing their name with his term *harijan,* meaning "children of God."

2. In Independent India

After independence the Indian government made an effort to end discrimination, but periodic conflicts with higher castes resulted, and only privileged sections of the lower castes benefited. Most harijans are classified either as landless farm workers or as village artisans. In the cities they have such "dirty" jobs as cleaning streets and latrines.

In spite of → conversions Christian missions have not been able to effect much change for pariahs. Caste discrimination also continues in Muslim areas (→ Islam). The efforts of B. R. Ambedkar (1893-1956), an untouchable who became a lawyer and a government minister, to improve the situation of pariahs by conversion to → Buddhism also proved unsuccessful (→ India 4).

3. Beyond India

Following M. → Weber (1864-1920), we might define *pariah groups* more broadly as those living endogamously within a sociosymbiotic association; they are ritually distinct from the rest of their society and lack full legal rights. Weber also described *pariah peoples* as those who "form communities, acquire specific occupational traditions of handicrafts or of other arts, and cultivate a belief in their ethnic community. They live in a diaspora strictly segregated from all personal intercourse, except that of an unavoidable sort, and their situation is legally precarious. Yet, by virtue of their economic indispensability, they are tolerated, indeed frequently privileged, and they live interspersed in the political communities. The Jews are the most impressive historical example" (*Economy,* 933-34). Weber took the Indian term, then, and applied it to the Jews (*Judaism,* 3-4), though he pointed out that the Jews became a pariah caste in a noncaste milieu, whereas in India pariah castes found themselves in a hierarchy of castes (→ Judaism).

We must add to what Weber said by noting that already at an early time in the Near East there were castes, such as fishermen and some artisan groups (W. Dostal). Unlike other pariah groups, as Weber noted, the Jews promoted their pariah status by their own self-accepted ritual restrictions (→ Rite). Again, while Indian pariahs do not question their ranking, "the Jew anticipated his own personal salvation through a revolution of the existing social stratification to the advantage of his pariah people" (*Economy,* 494). Weber followed the thesis of F. → Nietzsche (1844-1900) that "the slave revolt in morality begins when *ressentiment* itself becomes creative and gives birth to values" (p. 36). Weber claimed that in the "theodicy of the disprivileged, the moralistic quest serves as a device for compensating a conscious or unconscious desire for vengeance" (Weber, *Economy,* 494).

As Weber saw it, Deutero-Isaiah, with its "glorification of sufferance, of ugliness, and of being despised" presents a message that is "plainly the glorification of the situation of the pariah people and its tarrying endurance" (*Judaism,* 375). This message is surprisingly similar to Protestant sermons: "All the elements of the utopian evangelical sermon 'resist no evil with force' are here at hand" (p. 376). Weber emphasized that a dualism of in-group and out-group morality (p. 343), exaggerated by exclusion, is an essential feature of pariah ethics and pariah capitalism, which is in negative contrast to the spirit of → capitalism. Though Weber personally abhorred → anti-Semitism, his thesis offered stereotypes that greatly influenced anti-Semitic propaganda and that were made worse by the stigmatizing connotations of the pariah concept. In criticism we may say that Jewish religion is inadequately perceived because of a nonhistorical projecting back of the situation of Judaism in medieval Europe.

The Jewish policy of National Socialism (→ Fascism) treated Jews consistently as a pariah people and thus mobilized the religious prejudices of the Christian tradition. The Jews were reconfessionalized, and medieval demarcations were reactivated. The forbidding of mixed marriages again made endogamy a matter of compulsion. The precarious legal situation became one of no legal standing at all, and physical extirpation was the direct consequence (→ Holocaust).

In general, the rise of pariah groups is the result of the concentration of → power and growing economic inequality. A religious overestimation of authority finds its counterpart in the demonizing of → marginalized groups.

→ Hinduism

Bibliography: Z. Bauman, *Wasted Lives: Modernity and Its Outcasts* (Oxford, 2003) • S. V. Desika Char, *Hinduism and Islam in India: Caste, Religion, and Society from Antiquity to Early Modern Times* (Princeton, 1997) • N. B. Dirks, *Castes of Mind: Colonialism and the Making of Modern India* (Princeton, 2001) • W. Dostal, "Pariagruppen in Vorderasien," *ZE* 89 (1964) 190-203 • L. Dudley-Jenkins, *Identity and Identification in India: Defining the Disadvantaged* (London, 2003) • U. von Ehrenfels, "Parayar in Indien," *ZE* 89 (1964) 180-89 • O. Mendelsohn, *The Untouchables: Subordination, Poverty, and the State in Modern India* (Cambridge, 1998) • W. Mühlmann, *Chiliasmus und Nativismus* (Berlin, 1961) • F. Nietzsche, *On the Genealogy of Morals* and *Ecce Homo* (New York, 1967) • Abbé de Raynal, *A philosophical and political history of the settlements and trade of the Europeans in the East and West Indies* (2d ed.; 6 vols.; London, 1798; orig. pub., 1770) • M. N. Srinivas, *Village, Caste, Gender, and Method: Essays in Indian Social Anthropology* (Delhi, 1998) • E. Thurston, with K. Rangachari, *Castes and Tribes of Southern India* (7 vols.; Madras, 1909) • M. Weber, *Ancient Judaism* (trans. H. H. Gerth and D. Martindale; Glencoe, Ill., 1952); idem, *Economy and Society: An Outline of Interpretive Sociology* (3 vols.; New York, 1968).

Christian Sigrist

Parousia

1. Concept
2. Greek Term
3. NT Development
4. Conclusion

1. Concept

Up to the end of the 19th century and even beyond, the parousia was mainly treated dogmatically in terms of the coming again of Christ to judge and to reign. The "again," however, cannot be traced back beyond the Constantinopolitan Creed (381); the → Apostles' Creed and the Nicene Creed (325; → Niceno-Constantinopolitan Creed) both simply have "come." What we have, then, is a systematizing at a later stage of statements about the earthly life of → Jesus and his expected coming as the exalted Son of Man (Mark 13:26; 14:62) and Lord (1 Thess. 2:19; 4:15).

J. Weiss (1863-1914) rejected this view and, on the basis of the NT term *parousia,* spoke simply of the arrival of the (Son of Man) Messiah, whom primitive Christianity, he thought, was still awaiting. As he saw it, later generations, definitively in John, transferred the attributes of majesty to the earthly Jesus (1900 ed.). A. → Schweitzer (1875-1965) went even further and argued that the history of Christianity rested essentially on the parousia not having taken place; there was a delay, and de-eschatologizing resulted (→ Eschatology 2 and 7.3).

The shift in thinking introduced by Weiss and Schweitzer greatly influenced 20th-century discussion (→ Eschatology 7). It moved the theme out of the sphere of dogmatics into that of exegetical history and also gave it a definite strangeness. The influential school of R. Bultmann (1884-1976; → Existential Theology) in particular styled a more specific understanding of the parousia as an apocalyptic scheme (→ Apocalyptic 3) but grounded the core of the → hope in God's saving act in Christ (→ Soteriology) so that, with → demythologizing of the apocalyptic worldview, that core might also be accessible through the experience of faith. Since the 1970s, however, the question has arisen whether the ministry of the earthly Jesus is even to be classified under apocalyptic. Important areas of scholarship have reduced the significance ascribed to the notion of parousia and to its delay.

2. Greek Term

The term "parousia" occurs in Hellenistically influenced thinking. It has no clear Hebrew equivalent in the LXX, and it does not occur in pre-NT apocalyptic writings. It derives from Gk. *pareimi*, "be present," and has the basic meaning "presence." Only secondarily does the meaning "coming to be present, arrival" develop, then "coming," especially in Hellenism for the appearing of a god or the visit of a high dignitary to a polis. By the end of the first century, we find the term used in Judaism for the one God.

Josephus (ca. 37-ca. 100) uses "parousia" for the theophany at → Sinai and also for God's almighty presence in history (*Ant.* 3.80, 202-3; 9.55; 18.284). *T. Jud.* 22:2 (hardly an interpolation) speaks of God's eschatological, saving appearance. In a reconstruction subsequent to its NT use, it applies in *2 Apoc. Bar.* 30:1 for the first time to the coming of the Messiah. The modern understanding of the term associates these motifs with the eschatological "day of the Lord."

3. NT Development

3.1. The oldest confession formulas of the NT speak of Christ's → death, → resurrection, and exaltation, but not of his parousia. We still do not find it in the hymns to Christ in Colossians 1, Ephesians 1, and John 1. It thus belongs to a special line of Christological development.

→ Paul is our first witness. As statements regarding his own parousia and that of others in his churches show (1 Cor. 16:17; 2 Cor. 7:6-7; Phil. 1:26, etc.), he is presupposing the basic meaning "presence" or "arrival." Except in a few cases (Phil. 2:12), Paul avoids any contrasting of the parousia of Christ with Christ's absence (1 Cor. 15:23; 1 Thess. 2:19; 3:13; 4:15; 5:23). The goal is that we may "be with the Lord forever" (1 Thess. 4:17).

In the parousia there is thus the basic tension of pressing on toward the definitive presence of Christ, who in virtue of the resurrection is not absent, but being with whom in the fullness of eschatology and epiphany is still awaited. Paul expects the parousia imminently and connects it in 1 Thessalonians 4 with the raising again of those who have already died. In further passages we have such themes as the overcoming of the powers and the (limited) lordship of the Son (1 Cor. 15:23-28), as well as, in a parallel expression, his judgment (1:7-8). The "day of the Lord" (= of God) becomes the "day of Christ" (or similar; Phil. 1:6, 10, etc.).

3.2. In 2 Thessalonians the parousia and believers' being gathered together to Christ are to come later (2:1-2). Over against the imminent expectations of enthusiasts, there is a development of epiphanic processions and apocalyptic ideas of the parousia (2:8-9; the adversary, the → antichrist, will have his own parousia). In Colossians and Ephesians there is less emphasis, and in the → Pastoral Epistles "epiphany" replaces "parousia."

In James parousia moves out of the Pauline circle with a reference to the Lord's imminent coming to judge (5:8-9). The author of Hebrews subsumes the notion of parousia under cultic considerations (9:28).

In the Johannine sphere we find parousia mentioned in 1 John 2:28. The author possibly corrects the Gospel of John, where judgment and → life (§1) are decided by Christ's presence (but cf. 14:2-3).

The older → Synoptic tradition does not use "parousia," though it looks ahead to the end and to Christ as the coming Son of Man (esp. Mark 13). But possibly already in → Q we find a discussion of the delay (see the so-called parables of the parousia in Matt. 24:32–25:46 and par., with emphasis on suddenness and vigilance). In Matthew the various lines converge. The parousia is linked in 24:3 to the end of the age (as is not yet done in 1 Thessalonians 4), and it is shown to be the parousia of the Son of Man in 24:27, 37, 39. It also involves the gathering together of the elect in v. 31. In contrast, Luke does not use the term. Here the period up to the (imminently?) expected end is the time for global witness (Acts 1:7-8). An equivalent to the parousia, perhaps, is seeing the glory of Jesus at death (7:55-56).

In 2 Pet. 3:3-13 the parousia of Jesus is linked to the day of the Lord, which will usher in a new heaven and a new earth (Isa. 65:17; 66:22; see also Rev. 21:1 after 14:14-16 and 19:11-16). The answer to the complaint made by opponents that the parousia is delayed is that time is relativized by the majesty of God, who grants us time for repentance (→ Penitence).

4. Conclusion

The above material shows that the subject is more complex than was thought at the beginning of the 20th century. The starting point is → Christology — more narrowly, the → hope of being with Christ at the last. Apocalyptic features fill out the picture, and the idea of Christ's eschatological coming to judge and to reign contributes to the church's development of its confession (→ Confession of Faith). The original imminent expectation shows how intense was the hope, and it can still emerge again, as at the → Reformation, also in the → free churches, → apostolic churches, and → Adventists, though without ever being constitutive. After much uncertainty, reflection on the parousia as the consummation of the way of Christ has now become strong again in some representatives of → systematic theology (e.g., J. Moltmann). Yet we cannot speak as yet of any broad integration of such shifting exegetical insights and the dogmatic tradition.

Bibliography: W. Eisele, *Ein unerschütterliches Reich. Die mittelplatonische Umformung des Parusiegedankens im Hebräerbrief* (Berlin, 2003) • K. Erlemann, *Naherwartung und Parusieverzögerung im Neuen Testament* (Tübingen, 1997) • T. F. Glasson, "Theophany and Parousia," *NTS* 34 (1988) 259-70 • E. Grässer, *Das Problem der Parusieverzögerung in den synoptischen Evangelien und in der Apostelgeschichte* (3d ed.; Berlin, 1977; orig. pub., 1957) • G. S. Holland, *The Tradition That You Received from Us: Second Thessalonians in the Pauline Tradition* (Tübingen, 1988) • E. Käsemann, "An Apologia for Primitive Christian Eschatology," *Essays on NT Themes* (Naperville, Ill., 1964) 169-95 • J. Moltmann, *The Way of Jesus Christ: Christology in Messianic Dimensions* (London, 1990) • J. Plevnik, *Paul and the Parousia* (Peabody, Mass., 1997) • W. Radl, *Ankunft des Herrn. Zur Bedeutung und Funktion der Parusieaussagen bei Paulus* (Frankfurt, 1981) • G. Sauter, *Einführung in die Eschatologie* (Darmstadt, 1995) • H. Schwarz, *Eschatology* (Grand Rapids, 2000) • A. Schweitzer, *The Quest of the Historical Jesus* (Minneapolis, 2001; orig. pub., 1906) • J. I. Snyder, *The Promise of His Coming: The Eschatology of Second Peter* (San Mateo, Calif., 1986) • A. C. Thiselton, "The Parousia in Modern Theology: Some Questions and Comments," *TynBul* 27 (1976) 27-53 • A. Vögtle, *Das Neue Testament und die Zukunft des Kosmos* (Düsseldorf, 1970) • D. F. Watson, ed., *The Intertexture of Apocalyptic Discourse in the NT* (Leiden, 2002) • J. Weiss, *Jesus' Proclamation of the Kingdom of God* (Philadelphia, 1971; orig. pub., 1892; 2d ed., 1900).

Martin Karrer

Particularism → Universalism and Particularism

Partnership

1. Definition
2. As a General Model of Relationship
3. As a Modern Form of Marriage Relationship
4. As a Modern Form of Male-Female Relationship
5. Levels of Partnership
6. Stability of Partnership
7. International Partnership

1. Definition

In a general sense partnership is a principle of → communication and cooperation, or a structured relationship between individuals or → organizations, that is based on a specific concept and that often unconsciously gives rise to a corresponding self-understanding, → behavior, and experience. We find partnership in many areas of life, commonly speaking of partnership in treaties, contracts, trade, professions, tariff agreements, tennis, dancing, and conversation. Churches and cities are also spoken of as partners.

2. As a General Model of Relationship

In the West the model of partnership applies to an appropriately modern answer to problems of communication and cooperation that result from differentiation and interdependence and to which complex and rapidly developing social systems are subject (→ Society). Three presuppositions of partnership are the recognition of differences among those participating, a minimal level of common interests or needs, and a readiness for communication or cooperation in a certain area.

In contrast to social orders that regulate social relations and dependencies predominantly hierarchically (→ Hierarchy), partnership rests on the idea of the equality of persons, namely, that they have equal worth and equal rights. Partners are of the same rank, and their rights are the same, unlike minorities, who must strive for equality (e.g., by → emancipation). Behind this idea we may easily see an → Enlightenment view (→ Anthropology 4) and → values such as → freedom, → equality, and fraternity.

Over against social orders that seek to institutionally guarantee the stability of social relations and to ensure social conduct that is regulated and predictable (→ Institution), individual → responsibility is to the fore in dealings between partners. The → persons or parties see to their own interests and agree on a course of conduct. → State and society form the setting that gives partnerships the needed security. In the background stands the ideal concept of a self-sufficent personality that can assert itself.

In relations between partners, then, clear agreements and conditions play an important part and ideally will be respected well before any problems arise. Nevertheless, all the partners will need to confidently subject the promotion of their own interests and the resolving of → conflicts to specific rules and to the principle of fairness. The idea of partnership as we now know it, along with the desire for cooperation, thus underlies the market principle of exchange (→ Economy). The same practical conditions apply to partnerships in the private sphere, though they may not always be known to those concerned, and disappointment will often result. Competition and rivalry are antitheses to partnership.

In the sphere of → politics, the use of the term "partnership," with its suggestion of equality in → power and → rights, regularly has the social function of masking relations of inequality and → dependence (→ Social Partnership).

3. As a Modern Form of Marriage Relationship

"Partnership" may be used specifically to describe the relation between husbands and wives, as also, in a parallel sense, relations within life partnerships of the same sex. On the one side partnership is an equivalent of → marriage, but on the other it stands in distinction from it. Marriage perpetuates a special model of relationship. A main feature is the indissolubility that confers stability in principle and that in a complementary division of sex roles ensures provision for the whole → family. This model found widespread acceptance so long as life in marriage was in practice much the same as life in the family, as was true in central Europe at least up to about 1900. But in areas where there are far fewer children in the family and a higher life expectancy, a smaller proportion of married life is spent with the family. In such cases family life is a relatively short stage of transition in a longer period of partnership, and this stage is much less significant in the individual → biography as a whole.

Today, then, in contrast to the traditional concept of marriage that is oriented to the family, the element of partnership is predominant. Strengthening this development is the fact that wives do not now depend so much on their husbands for support. Furthermore, sexual contacts (→ Sexuality) and the raising of children (→ Education) are less and less tied uniquely to marriage. Hence in some societies marriage has ceased to be so important as the → norm and exclusive model of a life shared by the sexes. Some societies now accept different forms of partnership, some of which were present before but not with complete social approval. Here marriage is one form, if still the most common. Partnership has become the supreme category.

4. As a Modern Form of Male-Female Relationship

"Partnership" describes not only a form of life but also the shape of a male-female relation on a basis of equality. In this process traditional ideas of marriage have found a place in the concept of modern partnership, just as ideals of partnership have influenced the modern concept of marriage. The longing for partnership is strong in both sexes, which the complex social background only strengthens.

The number of expectations and an idealizing of partnership exert heavy pressure. Yet the three principles of modern partnerships between man and woman — namely, that "no one be allowed to surrender himself or herself," that "in daily life each partner be able (in principle) to do anything that needs to be done," and that "each person constantly be developing himself or herself" — provide considerable latitude for individual elaboration and development, both for the individual partners themselves and for their children. In contrast to the world of → work and → vocation, such partnership ideally offers satisfaction, relaxation, and pleasure such as that other world cannot give. The concept of → love is changing, with the accent shifting from fidelity, care, and security to the giving of happiness and to depth of understanding. If living in partnership is successful, it can create extraordinary intimacy. Finding a balance between closeness and distance (i.e., the opportunity to be apart) is becoming a main problem in shaping lasting partnerships.

5. Levels of Partnership

In a partnership we may see three levels. *Partners as those in a life relationship* build up a common existence, follow vocational goals, create a home, and are together in → everyday life, on vacation, and at celebrations, finding satisfaction in successes, outside contacts, and → consumption. *Partners as parents* develop together with and over against the children, giving life to the children and finding continued life in them. *Partners as lovers* give and receive affection, love, attention, recognition, tenderness, and sexuality, finding satisfaction in intimacy. Each level has its own orientation and, as a rule, imposes lofty demands, which can lead to severe burdens and conflicts for the partners.

6. Stability of Partnership

Various typical conflicts threaten the stability of partnerships. Raising children poses a basically unresolved problem. After the birth of children wives often see little option but to adopt a traditional role and to fall back into dependence, thus forfeiting any equal opportunity to achieve personal goals. During the family phase the multitude of tasks will either have the above result or involve common parenting and often a neglect of the third level. The danger then is that the partner relationship will dry up and the partners will not later find themselves again. A model of relationship that stresses the satisfying of mutual needs and that depends on constantly renewing agreements about interests may indeed be shaped in many different ways, but it is also very fragile. If a proper balance between closeness and distance within the partnership is not found, the step to abandoning the partnership is not a big one. The practice or culture of partnership must be learned early.

Churches can help here by means of marriage and family counseling either within the → congregation or in special seminars, offering courses in the psychology of partnership and → pastoral psychology as an important branch of their → diakonia.

7. International Partnership

In non-Western cultures traditional ideas of sex relations still obtain, with a division of tasks and a mix of hierarchical and egalitarian relations. Yet thanks to television and movies the Western ideology of partnership is making an impact, especially in areas of urbanization (→ City) and industrialization (→ Industrial Society). Vast and increasing differences in power mean that the idea of partnership can hardly be a principle in shaping the relations between rich countries and poor. Here traditional principles such as that of sharing the earth in common are more relevant (→ Environmental Ethics).

Theologically, Christianity has undoubtedly contributed decisively to the developing of the concept of partnership, although it has not fully worked out its meaning or implications (though see J. Wiebering and → feminist theology).

Bibliography: J. Birtchell, *How Humans Relate: A New Interpersonal Theory* (Westport, Conn., 1993) • S. Duck, *Relating to Others* (2d ed.; Maidenhead, Berkshire, 1999) • I. Grau and H.-W. Bierhoff, eds., *Sozialpsychologie der Partnerschaft* (Berlin, 2003) • H. Herrmann, *Liebesbeziehungen–Lebensentwürfe. Eine Soziologie der Partnerschaft* (Münster, 2001) • M. Koschorke, "Ehe im Wandel. Auf dem Wege zur Partnership," *Zwischen Recht und Seelsorge* (ed. F. W. Lindemann; Berlin, 1990) 69-96 • D. Miell and R. Dallos, eds., *Social Interaction and Personal Relationships* (London, 1996) • J. Ridley, *Intimacy in Crisis: Men and Women in Crisis through the Life Cycle and How to Help* (London, 1999) • B. H. Spitzberg and W. R. Cupach, eds., *The Dark Side of Close Relationships* (Mahwah, N.J., 1998) • J. Wiebering, *Partnerschaftlich leben. Christliches Ethos im Alltag* (Berlin, 1985) • J. Willi, *Was hält Paare zusammen? Der Prozeß des Zusammenlebens* (Reinbek, 1991).

Martin Koschorke

Pascal, Blaise

Blaise Pascal (1623-62), a French mathematician, physicist, and lay theologian, was from a well-to-do family in Auvergne and spent most of his life in Paris. At the age of 16 he completed a well-respected treatise on conic sections, and in 1642 he invented a digital calculator. His father introduced him to the so-called Académie Mersenne, the circle around the Cartesian abbot Martin Mersenne. Pascal first came into contact with → Jansenists in Rouen between 1639 and 1647, and in 1647 he met René Descartes for the first time in Paris (→ Cartesianism). After his father died in 1651, Pascal's younger sister, Jacqueline, entered the convent Port-Royal in Paris against his will; Pascal himself undertook several journeys and generally sought contact with the courtly milieu.

This "mundane" life phase ended at the latest with a mystical → conversion experience on the night of November 23, 1654, which Pascal documented on single pieces of parchment and of paper known as his *mémorial.* Thenceforth Pascal led an ascetic life (including wearing a penitential belt; → Asceticism), occasionally withdrawing to Port-Royal-des-Champs, whose exponents his writings supported in their struggle against Sorbonne theologians. At the end of 1661 he signed a formulary condemning the doctrine of the Jansenists. He nonetheless continued to author treatises in mathematics and physics. And in early 1662, with the duke of Roannez, Pascal founded a company that for the first time provided public transportation in Paris. Pascal died on August 19, 1662, after receiving extreme unction (→ Anointing 2).

We know about Pascal's religious education largely by way of the biography written by his older sister, Gilberte Périer, who stylizes him as an ascetic Jansenist. It is doubtful that his contacts in 1646 with those affected by Jean Guillebert, a zealous pastor and preacher in Rouville (near Rouen), led to any initial meeting. Pascal's philosophical and spiritual works were not composed until after 1654.

Although Pascal's more strictly religious phase was doubtless anticipated by his tract "Conversion du pécheur" (On the conversion of the sinner, fall 1654), he documented his definitive conversion in the *mémorial,* which came to light only after his death. In his *Lettres provinciales* (Provincial letters), whose publication run reached more than 10,000 copies and that was placed on the Index in September 1657, Pascal defended the group around Antoine Arnauld and to that extent can be characterized as Jansenist, a view supported by the fact that Pascal continued his literary fight even after the bull of Alexander VII (1655-67) condemned Arnauld in the fall of 1656. At the same time, his letters and contemporaneously conceived *Écrits sur la grâce* (Writings on grace) suggest that ultimately Pascal was less concerned with the Jansenist understanding of → grace and its demand for rigorous severity than with his own hope in the triumph of truth in the quarreling church itself. Later writings — especially the *Prière pour demander à Dieu le bon usage des maladies* (A prayer to ask God to make good use of sickness, 1659) and the fragmentary *Pensées* (Thoughts, from 1657), originally planned as an apology of the Christian religion — no longer used the concepts of efficacious grace and sufficient grace that had played a role in the controversy surrounding the Jansenist understanding of grace. These writings also denied human free will (of Christians) with regard to the human relationship with God (→ Freedom). With respect to the "natural human being," they minimized the risk of "decision" by adducing the limitations of human reason and the necessity of choice.

During his work on *Pensées,* Pascal seems to have abandoned hope for any reconciliation between the quarreling parties in the church, as well as for any reconciliation between religion and the world in the larger sense. In this context, one can probably assume that Pascal underwent a "third conversion" (L. Goldmann). Pascal's writings now begin to concentrate more on portraying the → paradox of → faith, which suspends the analytic cognition of the *esprit de finesse* (spirit of finesse, i.e., intuition) within the religious vision of the *ordre du coeur* (order of the heart). The cognitive paradox (i.e., insight into the impossibility of discerning nothingness or the infinite) is now transferred to the paradox of faith, which is trust in a hidden God. Whereas early in his life Pascal shared his age's ideal of the scientifically thinking person, he later distanced himself from this understanding of the world, particularly from Descartes, whose cognitive principles he later criticized.

Bibliography: Primary sources: Oeuvres (14 vols.; ed. L. Brunschvicg and P. Boutroux; Paris, 1904-14; repr., 1965) with much supp. material • *Oeuvres complètes* (3 vols.; ed. J. Mesnard; Paris, 1964-91) • *Pensées* (trans. A. J. Krailsheimer; London, 1966) • *The Provincial Letters* (trans. A. J. Krailsheimer; Baltimore, 1967).

Secondary works: M. Bishop, *Pascal: The Life of a Genius* (New York, 1936) • F. Giesenberg, *Wahl und Entscheidung im Existentialismus sowie bei Platon, Aristoteles, Pascal, Descartes und Bergson* (Frankfurt, 1996) • L. Goldmann, *The Hidden God: A Study of Tragic Vision in the Pensées of Pascal and the Tragedies of Racine* (London, 1964) • L. Kolakowski, *God Owes Us Nothing: A Brief Remark on Pascal's Religion and on the Spirit of Jansenism* (Chicago, 1995) • R. Lockwood, *The Reader's Figure: Epideictic Rhetoric in Plato, Aristotle, Bossuet, Racine, and Pascal* (Geneva, 1996) • J. R. Maia Neto, *The Christianization of Pyrrhonism: Scepticism and Faith in Pascal, Kierkegaard, and Shestov* (Dordrecht, 1995) • R. J. Nelson, *Pascal: Adversary and Advocate* (Cambridge, Mass., 1981) • W. Schmidt-Biggemann, *Blaise Pascal* (Munich, 1999).

Antje Roggenkamp-Kaufmann

Passion, Accounts of the

1. "Passion" as a Term of the Church
2. The Reshaping of Traditions
3. Paul's Accounts
4. Mark's Account (11:1–15:47)
5. Matthew's Account (21:1–27:66)
6. Luke's Account (19:28–23:56)
7. John's Account (11:45–19:42)

1. "Passion" as a Term of the Church

The term "passion" has no connection with the modern English usage of "passion" as a strong, focused sexual emotion. Rather, its source (Lat. *passio,* "suffering, being acted upon") is connected with "passive" and "patient," conditions where one person is acted upon by another, for good or ill. For worshipers during → Holy Week, "passion" refers to the suffering caused to Jesus by others, from the time of his entry into → Jerusalem for the → Passover feast until his burial. It recalls Jesus' three predictions of the necessity of his suffering, death, and resurrection in the Synoptic gospels.

Beginning in the 13th century, 13 narratives chosen from more than one gospel became the fundamental passion material to be read or portrayed in liturgy, worship, art, music, and passion plays:

1. the triumphal entry into Jerusalem
2. the → foot washing
3. the Last Supper
4. the agony in the garden
5. the betrayal
6. the denial of Peter
7. Jesus before Pilate
8. the flagellation
9. the mocking of Jesus
10. the road to Calvary (including the crucifixion)
11. the deposition (taking down) from the cross

12. the lamentation
13. the entombment.

In the 14th century the traditions of the 14 → "stations of the cross" expanded the content of the passion of Holy Week beyond the material of the canonical gospels.

Today, worshipers still seek to experience these readings as if they were with Jesus in his passion. Three of these narrative units are regularly represented during Holy Week, with the worshipers acting as the crowd or the → disciples. They are Jesus' triumphal entry into Jerusalem, with the worshipers reading the crowd's parts and carrying palms in procession; Jesus' washing of the disciples' feet, with the worshipers washing one another's feet in response to Jesus' new commandment, "Love one another"; and the Last Supper during a Passover meal, with the worshipers receiving bread and wine in response to Jesus' command, "Do this in remembrance of me" (→ Eucharist 2). These last two are celebrated on Maundy (i.e., mandate, or commandment) Thursday.

This creation of a selective summary passion for the church has meant that units within the canonical gospels that do not focus on the suffering of Jesus or the giving of himself as the result of that suffering are remembered less well than the units in the church's passion as it is portrayed in worship, art, music, or passion plays or remembered differently than in the canonical gospels. Many Roman Catholics may incorrectly assume that the stations of the cross are a historically accurate part of the canonical gospels, and many Protestants may incorrectly assume that the foot washing and the institution of Holy Communion at the Last Supper are events portrayed in all the gospels.

In the process of developing the Holy Week passion, the church harmonized material not found in all the canonical gospels into one foundational story. On the one hand, the conflation created the impression that the church's passion represented a historical narrative of the life of Jesus by altering the timing of certain events, places, and characters. On the other hand, other events common to all the gospels were left out. For example, all the gospels report that after an entry into Jerusalem, Jesus challenged the religious authorities by overthrowing the tables of money changers in the temple, a proximate cause for the plot to arrest Jesus. All gospels report an account of an anointing of Jesus by a woman follower, with all but one (Luke) portraying the event as happening right before Passover. All report a number of women watching at the crucifixion, some of whom later appear at the tomb. Finally, the Holy Week passion readings sever the connections with the Gospels' accounts of Jesus' origin, teaching, miracles, and early dialogues with opponents, so that the individual values of each gospel are not distinct.

That worshipers remember the church's passion account more than that of the individual gospels is not surprising. The church's passion account is still effective for persuading people to develop or sustain a certain faith in Jesus. Necessarily, as the work of a medieval Christianity that had the full Bible in Latin and was now the religion of the dominant culture, it differed from the account of Jesus' last days in any one gospel. The church made additions and subtractions in the material out of their traditional beliefs about Jesus' suffering and also to make it useful for a church most of whose lay members could not read. However, none of the four canonical gospel writers or their communities had the experience of Christianity being the dominant religion of a culture, and none of the gospel writers had all four gospels. Their convictions and the concerns of their communities were different.

The changes in experience and beliefs over the centuries that necessitated a selective summary passion story for Holy Week do not represent a misuse of the tradition by the church. They simply continue a process of development within the tradition of Jesus' last days that began before the canonical gospels. As with the church's passion accounts, these traditions were altered to serve as a means for writers to nonliterate Christian assemblies to express their convictions about God and Jesus, evil and blessing, religious → authority, and the → vocation of Christian believers in the world. The gospel writers' convictions caused them to add other speeches, dialogues, and narratives that they valued and to remove or alter some of the events, places, and characters in the written accounts they received. Both Luke's and John's gospels articulate this need to their readers. Luke writes to his patron, Theophilus, that many people had already compiled narratives from the reports of eyewitnesses and ministers of the word, and that Luke would undertake the same so that Theophilus "may know the truth concerning the things about which [he has] been instructed" (Luke 1:4). John's gospel makes clear that it does not record every story about Jesus (John 20:30-31).

2. The Reshaping of Traditions

When writing his epistles (which preceded the four canonical gospels), the apostle → Paul also made changes in the Jesus traditions he had received. Between A.D. 38 and 48 Paul made two trips to Jerusalem to speak with the apostles Cephas (Peter) and James, each time staying long enough to receive complete details of the last days of Jesus (Gal. 1:18; 2:1). Yet Paul wrote letters with few spatial, temporal, or personal details about Jesus. His references to Jesus' obedience, crucifixion, and resurrection were written to be authoritative for → *Gentile* Christians, whose faith was largely shaped by his own conversion experiences as a former Pharisee and persecutor of the church who knew the Gentile world.

Mark's understanding of the purpose of Jesus' death and resurrection was not the same as Paul's understanding, although his gospel is as apocalyptic as Paul's writings are. The Gospels of Matthew and Luke added speeches, dialogues, and parables to Mark from a written sayings source unknown to Mark (the so-called → Q), while keeping Mark's overall narrative structure. They added infancy narratives and resurrection appearances that change the impression of the last days of Jesus. John's gospel shows evidence of having been written by several people over a period of time. The final form of the gospel has associations with Mark's outline and with Luke's long journey to Jerusalem, although the Q sayings source material has been replaced by the sayings tradition about Jesus from the sermons of the founder of the community, the "Beloved Disciple." This new material includes spiritual monologues by Jesus, controversy dialogues with religious leaders, crowd conflicts, miraculous signs, and prayers that were not part of the Synoptic tradition. After the founder's death, editors in the community added material that described the Beloved Disciple's relation to Jesus and to Peter.

To modern believers, the freedom of Paul and the gospel writers to change earlier traditions may look like license. This freedom shows how important it was for them to reshape preceding accounts in order to be persuasive in their own communities. Gospel writers changed narrative material in previous traditions to better support their own convictions about the nature of God's interaction with humans; the nature of evil and blessedness; the identity, authority, and purpose of the one who brings salvation from God; the ordering of religious authority; and the vocation believers are to have in the community and the world. Reed would be put to papyrus if these evangelists were convinced that their community did not know enough, was not competent enough, or was not willing enough to respond to the challenge of Jesus' life, death, and resurrection. Such uncertainty in early Christian communities might have arisen from those who lacked knowledge about the importance of Scripture for Gentile believers, were uncertain of how to speak before governors, were afraid in the face of → persecution, felt a threat to a community from its founder's death or from the fall of the Jerusalem temple to the Romans, or were in dispute with local synagogues about the law. If the persuasion of the gospel was successful, if it gave that specific community new information, new ability, and a strengthened will to continue being Christian, the narrative might then become authoritative for that community (→ Canon).

3. Paul's Accounts

The earliest references to Jesus' last days appear in Paul's letters. Paul records several features relating to those days:

1. a meal prior to Jesus' betrayal and impending death, with bread and wine as the elements of a new ritual concerning Jesus' body (1 Cor. 11:17-34)
2. Jesus' killing as accomplished by Jewish compatriots (1 Thess. 2:14-15) or his crucifixion by unnamed opponents (Rom. 6:6, 10; 1 Cor. 1:13, 23; 2:2; Gal. 2:19; 3:1; Phil. 2:1-11)
3. a legal scandal for Paul as a → Pharisee, connected with Jesus' death "on a tree" (Gal. 3:13)
4. Jesus' burial (1 Cor. 15:4)
5. the connection of Jesus' death with the Passover sacrifice (1 Cor. 5:7)
6. Scripture's accord with Jesus' death and → resurrection (§2) on the third day (1 Cor. 15:3-4)
7. a list of resurrection appearances, first to Peter, then to the → Twelve, then to more than 500 at once, then to James and all the → apostles, and finally to himself (1 Cor. 15:5-8)
8. Paul's certainty of Jesus' death and resurrection and the promise of his coming again (1 Cor. 15:22-28; 1 Thess. 1:10; → Parousia).

Paul had three basic convictions: that God was acting directly in situations in the present, beginning with raising Jesus; that God's acting again meant that the end times are near and therefore that all people need to be reached with the gospel of God's gracious action in raising Christ (→ Evangelism); and that the vocation of Gentile believers was to be types (imitators or examples) of Christ, sharing in his suffering and resurrection. Paul had confidence that Gentile believers could be good religious leaders by the power of an active God if they imitated the humility of Christ in their assembly, which he did not believe the Jerusalem apostles had done sufficiently (Gal. 2:1-14). The challenge to Paul was that the Gentiles he visited had many religions, not one God, and they did not believe in resurrection or the approaching end times. They did share Paul's value about imitation, but they believed in imitating the wise, not those foolish enough to be crucified (1 Cor. 1:20-25).

Paul focused his reporting of the story of Jesus on those portions that reinforced the effects of Christ's obedience and of God's resurrecting action on the Gentiles. He did not write about Jesus' origins except to say that Jesus was born of a woman, born under the law (Gal. 4:4). For example, in Phil. 2:1-11 Paul encourages the Philippians to imitate Christ's mind and behavior. Paul describes Christ's mind as producing his slavelike obedience to God, with its outcome of humble death on a cross. No details about Judaism or Jerusalem are mentioned. Since God has raised Christ, every knee in heaven and on earth, including Gentiles' knees, must bow to him. In 1 Thess. 2:14-15 Paul aims to persuade the Thessalonian Christians that the suffering that has come upon them at the hands of their Gentile compatriots is parallel to the suffering of Jewish Christians at the hands of Jewish compatriots and parallel to the killing of their Jewish Lord and the Jewish prophets by their coreligionists.

In 1 Cor. 11:17-34 Paul responds to abuses of the Lord's Supper by declaring that the Corinthians are mistaken to think that they participate in the Lord's Supper when they eat divided by social status. Such action demonstrates their failure to comprehend the intent of the act as Paul received it from the Lord. To participate worthily in the Lord's Supper, the Corinthian community must imitate the events of the Last Supper in light of the Lord's betrayal. Thanksgiving over bread and cup must be offered to God. Each time, the Lord's words offering his body and a new covenant to his followers need to be repeated. As often as the Corinthians eat the bread and drink the cup together, they proclaim the Lord's death until he comes again.

In Rom. 5:1-11 Paul asserts a reason for the crucifixion: Christ died for the ungodly and sinners so that believers would be reconciled by the death of God's Son. Paul labels the boastful performance of God's law as idolatrous, and he points to himself, a former Pharisee, as having been an example of such idolatry. This idolatry has been overcome by Christ Jesus' death as a criminal on the cross (see Rom. 7:1-5; Gal. 2:15-21), an event that makes it unnecessary for Gentile Christians to be circumcised and brought under the former covenant, which in Christ has been shown to be ineffective for salvation. Since God is acting again, believers must witness to and participate in the *present* revelations of God in Christ to everyone and not be strictly performing the past legal revelations given to Israel.

4. Mark's Account (11:1–15:47)

Here and in the following sections, we consider first the evident intention of the writer of the gospel as a whole, as a response to the apparent needs of the community receiving the writing. Second, we outline how the respective stories of Jesus' last days carry out each evangelist's convictions by reshaping an already received "last days" traditions.

4.1. Mark shared Paul's view that the new activity of God began with Christ, but Mark was convinced it was begun at Jesus' baptism by the → Holy Spirit and that God's new activity maintained continuity with previous → prophets, including John the Baptist (1:2-11). Mark believed the end times were near and that the response of individual believers to the resurrection should imitate Jesus' actions (13:3-6; 10:35-45). Mark also shared Paul's lack of confidence in the Jerusalem apostles as good group leaders for difficult times, but for different reasons. His largely Jewish Christian readers seem to be paralyzed by the Jerusalem temple being surrounded by Roman armies, a contemporary crisis that Mark inserted into Jesus' apocalyptic discourse (13:14-23). Mark's community may have first believed that the resurrection of Jesus would mean a quick and peaceful end to strife and the return of the Son of Man. Now they appear to be afraid for their lives and worried that God was not presently battling evil on behalf of believers. They had put their hope in the disciples in Jerusalem to see them through, but Mark had serious doubts about the ability of the apostles or of his own community to withstand coercion (14:27-31).

Mark's audience already knew times, places, and events relating to Jesus' last days, so Mark needed to work with those traditions in order to show, through Jesus' interactions with others, his beliefs about Jesus. Mark interwove some earlier written traditions of a miracle cycle and a controversy cycle to portray his conviction that illness, demon possession, and → sin were all equally bondage (1:21–3:30). Jesus, as the bearer of God's blessing from his baptism, breaks these bonds. Some of the religious authorities and the crowds who watch Jesus are astounded and call his actions a new teaching (1:21-28). The Gentile centurion, astonished by how Jesus died and by the temple curtain being torn in two, is convinced that Jesus was the Son of God (15:37, 39).

Jesus also engages in astounding actions that amaze and frighten the disciples, such as stilling the storm at sea and feeding the 5,000 (4:35-41; 6:30-

44). He makes every effort to help them realize that he is powerful over many forces, but not all, especially not over concentrations of faithlessness. He announces his suffering, death, and resurrection three times to the disciples (8:31-33; 9:30-32; 10:32-34). At the transfiguration the disciples even hear God directing them to listen to his Son (9:2-10). Despite all these astonishing public actions, the disciples are still confused and frightened. Such misunderstandings cause Jesus to sometimes caution the disciples and those healed to be silent so that no one will misconstrue his mission, even after the transfiguration (1:34, 44; 3:12; 5:43; 7:36; 8:26, 30; 9:9). Even in the face of the resurrection, not all bonds are broken. The last hope of the scattered disciples, the women at the tomb, flee without a word to anyone because they are afraid (16:1-8). Chronologically later endings from Luke's time soften this harshness (16:9-20) because they know that the resurrection has been proclaimed and many have believed.

Others who observe Jesus are astounded for ill, saying that forgiving sins is blasphemy and that Jesus works for Beelzebub (2:5-7; 3:20-27). Gerasene swineherds flee before a freed demoniac and possessed swine (5:1-20). In Jerusalem, those astounded for ill add their own astounding violence. Under the direction of the high priest, Jesus is arrested, spit on, blindfolded, struck, and beaten, and his death is called for by the religious authorities. Under Pilate and his soldiers, Jesus is condemned, flogged, dressed as a king, mocked and spit upon, stripped, and then crucified (14:43–15:37).

4.2. Mark's narrative of the last days of Jesus is a means by which he can share with his readers his convictions about the astounding actions of God in Jesus. As the earliest written gospel, Mark sets the pattern for the events of Jesus' last days for all the gospels by including the following incidents (11:1–16:8). Matthew, Luke, and John will make changes from this order:

1. entry into Jerusalem
2. cleansing of the temple
3. plot to destroy Jesus
4. questions about Jesus' authority from religious authorities and his parables in response
5. prediction to the disciples of the destruction of the temple and the coming of the end time
6. a gathering of followers with Jesus at a meal, near Jerusalem and right before the Passover, when a woman anoints him for burial, which angers some
7. Judas's hasty decision to betray Jesus, welcomed by religious authorities
8. arrangement for a Passover supper with the disciples
9. the Last Supper, in the presence of the betrayer, with bread and wine shared to represent Jesus' own body and blood and with Jesus' prediction of Peter's betrayal, which Peter protests
10. agonized prayer in the Garden of Gethsemane in which Jesus chooses → obedience to God over all, while the disciples sleep uncaring
11. arrest by religious authorities and the scattering of the disciples
12. investigations of blasphemy before Jewish religious authorities
13. confirmation of Jesus' identity to the Sanhedrin and Peter's denial of Jesus before a maid
14. abuse by religious authorities and their guards
15. investigations of sedition toward Rome by Pilate, the Roman authority
16. mocking and abuse of Jesus by soldiers
17. the crowd's choice of Barabbas, the preference of the religious authorities
18. a forced march toward Golgotha and crucifixion
19. crucifixion of Jesus with two bandits, with mockery by them, the crowd, and the religious authorities
20. Jesus' last cry to God, misunderstood as his calling for Elijah and being mocked for it
21. Jesus' death, marked by apocalyptic signs
22. the Gentile centurion being convinced that Jesus was God's Son
23. women followers watching from afar at the crucifixion
24. immediate burial and, after the Sabbath, a visit to the tomb by followers of Jesus
25. astounding events that announce the resurrection
26. the women not telling the disciples but running away afraid.

Mark uses the ordering of these 26 events to show that becoming Jesus' disciple means being obedient to God in all things, just as Jesus was. It is possible to imitate Jesus, but not if believers rely on the crowd's group wisdom or that of disciples, the Jewish religious authorities, or the → Roman Empire. The great crowds who welcomed Jesus to Jerusalem are easily swayed to kill him. The disciples continually misunderstand, seek each other's counsel, and scatter. The religious authorities continually object, consult one another, and determine to have Jesus killed. Pilate satisfies the crowd's desire for blood. When facing the religious authorities, Jesus answers that truly he is the Christ, the Son of the

Blessed, and that they will see the Son of Man at the right hand of power, words that are taken as blasphemy (14:61-64). When facing Pilate, a Gentile, Jesus does not expect to be understood and is taciturn. Only God has the power to rescue Jesus now.

Mark sees truly faithful believers as largely ordinary individuals whose behavior becomes intrepid and persistent when God through Jesus upsets their lives for good and they perceive they have everything to gain by abandoning their old way of life. Examples include blind Bartimaeus upsetting the crowd at Jericho (10:46-52), the woman who anoints Jesus for his burial upsetting those eating with Jesus, including Judas (14:3-9), and the young man at the tomb announcing the resurrection and causing fear in the women (16:4-8).

Mark's description of Jesus' last days provided a model for believers of proper faith and action in a time of severe distress. Mark was convinced that God was reliable and kept calling followers, but like Jesus, they would doubtless experience suffering, death, and resurrection. If disciples are courageous, choosing not to fear, knowing God will hear those who feel shamed and abandoned, the resurrection way will be cleared to Galilee (16:7), a place where God's power has already been received, and where those disciples will be empowered to tell the full story of Jesus as Mark has done in this gospel.

5. Matthew's Account (21:1–27:66)

5.1. Matthew created a gospel that is one of additions to Mark's gospel, with few subtractions. Matthew's convictions can be seen in the way he surrounded Mark's gospel with new material, front (infancy narratives, with new characters) and back (additional resurrection accounts, namely, appearances by Jesus to the women and the disciples). These additions express Matthew's valuation of divine patriarchal authority over human patriarchal authority, set up in terms of the primary kind of secular and religious authority in his day: the father–adult son relationship of authority and obedience.

Matthew believed that God is dramatically intervening in the present to save people for God from their present socioreligious structures, not to condemn them. Jesus was necessary as a God-begotten mediator in order for people to recognize God's new activity and conform their lives to God's goodness. Jesus' will was conformed to God's good will. Since God is acting again in the present as Father to Jesus and through him announcing that connection to all potential believers, the law will be fulfilled in some new and different ways. Believers will need to let their light shine before others so that, when they see the works the disciples do, they will give glory to the Father in heaven. If believers are not told about the goodness of God, they might return to an oppressive patriarchal pattern of human religious authority. Matthew opposes such an action because it would disenfranchise the Gentile Christians in the community and those who were not considered fully Jews according to the law.

From the contests over these issues in the gospel and the ultimate triumph of God's goodness in the resurrection-appearance additions Matthew made, it is apparent that Matthew wrote to a Christian assembly whose members had a strong heritage from Pharisaic Judaism and strong connections to the local synagogue. In their uncertainty of how to integrate that heritage with the continuing activity of God that they knew in Jesus' life, death, and resurrection, they were tempted to accept Pharisaic religious leadership and its view of the law. Matthew may have been impelled to write for this reason.

Matthew reshaped Mark's text by starting in a different place. He created his own version of the patriarchal genealogies of Genesis 5 and Ruth 4:18-22 and marked significant flaws in the tradition by pointing out who righted most of those flaws — Gentile women who were proactive for Israel's God, despite their marginal state (Tamar, Rahab, and Ruth, Matt. 1:3, 5). According to Matthew, however, the weight of wrongdoing of David's sin with the wife of Uriah and the deportation is such that, although Joseph was next in line to beget the → Messiah, it was God who rescued the lineage of David by begetting the Messiah through the Holy Spirit. Joseph, however, represents one of Matthew's prime values: conforming a believer's will to the abundant goodness of God. Despite what Joseph has learned before from the law of God about maintaining a pure marriage bed, since God chooses to do a new thing, Joseph will agree to its goodness. At the end of Matthew's gospel (28:18-20), Jesus proclaims to the disciples that he has received full authority from God as the permanent Son of the permanent Father. Now the Spirit will beget believers through baptism, and circumcision will be superseded. They will pray to God as Father, just as Jesus taught them (6:9-13).

The sayings source Q allowed Matthew to emphasize that Jesus fulfills Moses' public teaching role (chaps. 5–7), the prophetic role (by prophesying his own death and resurrection, 16:21-23; 17:22-23; 20:17-19), and David's kingly role (1:1-6). Matthew's conviction concerning the new relationship possible with God is signaled in the Beatitudes by Jesus' speaking to the disciples of "your Father in heaven" and by his descriptions of those who receive the kingdom as those who in difficulty know their need of the Father. They receive from the Father the inheritance of the kingdom and thus become sons (heirs) of God (5:3-15). Matthew emphasizes the public witness of Jesus and the Father by deleting five of Mark's references to Jesus' silencing others. Matthew uses another Q text to identify Jesus as the teacher of the church through Matthew's additions of → parables and discourse about church order (chap. 18).

Matthew is convinced that believers can do the will of God if they correctly perceive the goodness and fairness of the Father. If they do not perceive correctly, because of being misled by a wrong authority or by a history of doing the wrong thing, they will be certain that God is not active in the present and will be fearful of God's activity at the end time. → John the Baptist thus challenges the religious leaders, "Who warned you to flee from the wrath to come? Bear fruit worthy of repentance. Do not presume to say to yourselves, 'We have Abraham as our ancestor [lit. father]'" (3:7-9). Matthew is equally convinced that God has been active in the past through Scripture and that God is now active again in begetting Jesus and blessing and commissioning him (3:16-17). This activity of God is also seen in his appearances in → dreams to Joseph (1:20) and to Pilate's wife (27:19), in the guidance of the Gentile Magi by a star (2:1-12), in earthquakes and the appearance of saints in the city after the resurrection (27:51-53), and in the angel at the tomb (28:2-7).

5.2. Matthew's account of the "last days of Jesus" closely follows the account in Mark, since his convictions about obedience are similar. In one passage added to Mark's "last days," Judas repents of betraying Jesus before Jesus' death. The religious authorities reject Judas's witness to Jesus' innocence and buy a field to bury strangers in with the blood money they paid Judas (26:14-15; 27:3-10), thus fulfilling Jer. 32:6-15 and Zech. 11:12-13. However, more is at stake. Matthew has added a phrase to the saying over the cup at the Last Supper (26:20-29). Jesus' blood is shed to enact the forgiveness of sins, and now Judas has repented, but not the religious authorities.

Writing 15 years after Mark, Matthew has learned that the disciples, despite Peter's denial and the scattering of all the disciples, can be reliable religious authorities *if* they do not fall into the patterns exemplified by the Jewish authorities. To this end, → Peter is portrayed in two ways: first, as a model for → discipleship, when he identifies Christ as the → Son of the living God (16:16; → Christological Titles 3.3); second, as a false disciple, when he swears that God should forbid Jesus' death (16:21-23). The latter view leads him to his denial of Jesus in this gospel (26:31-35, 69-75). In Matthew's view, the women who come to the tomb do not flee. Instead, they function as loyal followers, receive the good news and a resurrection appearance from Jesus, and carry out their commission in a way the disciples should have done. Textually, these women parallel the women in the genealogy who righted a great wrong in extending the goodness of God by their own actions and persuading the disciples to accept this good news. By the time the resurrected Jesus meets with the disciples in Galilee, Peter has been sufficiently humbled by his denial, and the rest of the disciples by their scattering and the crucifixion, to finally recognize their need of God's fatherly goodness. Matthew's conviction about time shows in the last verse of the gospel: Jesus, who is "Emmanuel, which means 'God is with us'" (1:23), will be with the disciples until the end of the age (28:20). Unlike Mark, Matthew is convinced that the end time is a while away. Until then, the Christian assembly has Jesus' words and access to the Father through Jesus' teaching.

With his more positive portrait of the disciples and the repentance of Judas, Matthew's view of the religious leaders, especially the Pharisees, as announcing the law but not following it stands out more strongly. In Matthew's resurrection additions, the Jewish guards at the tomb see and hear the angel and report it but are bribed by the chief priests and elders to lie (28:11-15). Matthew's account thus features two sets of witnesses, one good (the women) and the other bad (the guards). While one might wish that Matthew meant to set up this positive and negative witness simply to be understood as antitype and type, competition with local synagogues makes that view unlikely. Post-Holocaust readers might prefer reading these verses as instruction regarding the kind of religious leaders they ought to be or ought not to be.

6. Luke's Account (19:28–23:56)

6.1. Luke created a gospel that, like Matthew's, worked from Mark's chronology, adding infancy and resurrection narratives, material from the sayings source Q, and from Luke's own source of parables and sayings. The result is quite different from Mark or Matthew, since Luke's goal is to provide a proper interpretation for events that his Gentile patron, Theophilus, already knows (see 1). Luke's efforts are focused on giving new knowledge so that Theophilus may properly interpret what he already has — God's law, the prophets, and the past accounts of Jesus' life, death, and resurrection, including his personal wealth — in light of the continuing activity of Jesus' spirit. Luke's goal is to teach hearers that inheriting eternal life means having a proper understanding of what the law means by commanding believers to → love God and → neighbor (10:25-28).

Luke believes that Jesus has already received all he needs in order to know how to interpret the actions of God both past and present, and how to proclaim them to others. He was conceived by God in Mary through the Holy Spirit (1:26-38). He was circumcised and, at the age of 12, taught in the temple (2:41-52); he was baptized as an adult (3:21-22), had a genealogy that went back to Adam, son of God (3:23-38), and was able to silence the → devil (4:13). He becomes for Luke the example of how believers are to love God and neighbor. In Luke's view, those in the religious hierarchy tend to know and keep the religious law about loving God, but they tend not to understand how to love their neighbors as themselves. Jesus uses the parable of the Samaritan to teach a religious lawyer about loving his neighbor as he does himself (10:25-37).

Those who lack training in the religious law — Mary and Martha (10:38-42) and the woman who washes Jesus' feet with her tears (7:36-50) — understand about loving neighbors but need to be taught about loving God, which they can learn from listening to Jesus. He teaches Martha about loving God when she believes her obligation to him is as neighbor. Jesus provides both groups with a new understanding of the portion of the law they are missing. With the proper understandings and Jesus' Spirit, believers can do as God would have them do and as Jesus did. In Luke's gospel, Mary, Martha, Anna, and Simeon already understand that God is acting again to bring the Messiah (1:26-56; 2:25-38). Zechariah is silenced until he adds God's present actions to his past understanding of Scripture (1:5-23, 57-79).

In Acts, Luke's second volume, Peter properly interprets prophecy to those assembled at Pentecost to explain why the disciples speak other tongues. Many repent and are saved (chap. 2). Philip draws near to the Ethiopian eunuch and teaches him the proper interpretation of the prophecy he is reading. The eunuch chooses to be baptized (8:26-40).

Writing his gospel after many other accounts, Luke felt no need to preserve Mark's messianic secret once Jesus set his face toward Jerusalem after the transfiguration. The disciples are to make clear to the Samaritans where he is going (9:51-53). Luke then departs from the Markan sequence for ten chapters, until 19:29. Luke takes the material from Q that Matthew used in the Sermon on the Mount, adds his own material, and provides a series of dialogues of Jesus with different audiences (disciples, Pharisees, crowds) about matters of wealth and faithfulness, such as the parable of the rich man and Lazarus (16:19-31). Mixed among Jesus' teachings to his disciples are healings of those whose social and physical conditions make it hard for them to worship God without fear of oppression (1:73-74; 8:51-55; 13:10-17; 14:1-6; 18:35–19:10).

6.2. Luke begins his account of Jesus' last days without the anointing at Bethany, having reshaped it and placed it earlier (before Jesus' going to Jerusalem) as Jesus' opportunity to instruct a wealthy, unthankful, and uncaring religious man with the example of a poor, sinful woman who is thankful and cares for Jesus (7:36-50). This transposition of the anointing in Bethany unit means that in Luke's gospel Jesus has not been anointed beforehand for burial. Nor is there a woman who knows more of what awaits Jesus than the disciples do and is honored for it. The Last Supper proceeds in a way similar to its treatment in Mark's account, although Jesus knows that Satan has demanded to have Peter, in the same way that he has already entered Judas (22:1-6, 31-34). All goes as God has planned. In the Garden of Gethsemane, Jesus is not in the agony portrayed in Matthew and Mark, since he knows the proper interpretation of things and events, yet he does ask whether he might be relieved of taking the cup of suffering (22:42). During the arrest, as in all the other gospels, the ear of the high priest's slave is cut off by one of Jesus' disciples, but only in Luke does Jesus heal the slave. Even in difficulty, Jesus loves his neighbor, even one with a low social status.

On the way to the cross, Jesus has the public support of many who weep (unlike in Mark, Matthew, or John), but he directs them to attend to the distress that will come upon them. They are in peril because they do not have the proper interpretation of the situation in front of them. On the cross Jesus no longer cries out to God in fear of abandonment but says, "Father, forgive them; for they do not know what they are doing" (23:34). Even as he dies, Jesus receives the confession of one thief, whom he assures will soon be with him in paradise (23:39-43). Luke repeats two images of this death scene when Stephen is stoned (Acts 7:54-60). Stephen sees Jesus standing at the right hand of God (paradise), and he begs Jesus not to hold this sin against the stoners (forgiveness).

Luke's added resurrection appearances also focus on the proper interpretation of Scripture and the situation one is facing. The women bringing spices to the tomb are enjoined to remember how Jesus interpreted the Scripture. By remembering, they believe (24:1-10). The two on the road to Emmaus do not believe, since they do not remember what Jesus told them. Jesus draws near to them and teaches them. They care for him and invite him to be host at their inn's table. In the breaking of bread, they recognize him and remember the meals they had shared and the prophecies he had made (24:13-35). The last unit in Luke's gospel describes the disciples rejoicing in the temple and praising God, a proper way to be thankful and an inversion of how Zechariah had conducted worship (1:8-9; 24:52-53).

Theophilus's vocation, if Luke persuades him, will be to draw near to others with a proper interpretation of the use of Scripture for Gentiles. He will also welcome others who draw near to him with a word from God. Theophilus will understand that the law has commanded him to love God and neighbor, with "neighbor" referring to the oppressed whom God has previously acted to save (including Jews, 1:46-55, 68-79; 2:29-32). He will use his wealth for the benefit of the oppressed, find courage and illumination in the Last Supper as the prime meal among many of Jesus' teaching meals, and be strengthened in all adversity by Jesus' Spirit, sent from the Father until the return of Jesus, now seen as far in the future.

7. John's Account (11:45–19:42)

7.1. John's gospel is a project of a Christian community that had a long, separate existence from the communities of the → Synoptic gospels. It had an embattled existence, as its view of Jesus as the provider of special and eternal knowledge to a small family of believers who thought of themselves as born again (Gk. "begotten") from above clashed with the orthopraxis of the local synagogue. By the time of the writing of this gospel in a final form, the synagogue and the Johannine community had bitterly split (6:66; 7:5, 13; 9:22). The effect on themselves of their vigorous defense was that, although they would employ the Gospels of Mark and Luke as a framework for their gospel, they were loath to ameliorate their view of Judaism or of the preexistent Jesus. Uncomfortably for modern believers, this gospel that contains the most spiritual of teachings is also the most earthly in its → anti-Semitism.

John's community believes that the → Word of God (§2.4), the Logos, being fully a part of God, was Life and Light in its preexistence. Sent into the world by God, the Word became flesh and was known as the Unique ("only," 1:14, 18 NRSV) Son of the Father, the sole mediator between the world and the Father. Jesus' vocation for those who receive him and believe in his name is to give them the power to become children of God after his resurrection (1:1-18).

In order for persons to receive such power from Jesus, several things are needed. First, like Nathanael, who is a student of Scripture under the fig tree, they must already be doing what is true in some partial way (1:47-48). Second, they must be willing to come to Jesus, the Light (3:19-21; 8:12), and have their whole lives exposed. In the gospel, two characters portray this second point as type and antitype: Nicodemus, who comes by night and does not understand what Jesus means about spiritual realities and who is not willing to have his failures as a teacher exposed (3:1-21), and the Samaritan woman at the well, who is willing to have her whole life exposed by Jesus and so learns that he is a prophet (4:1-42). Third, they must believe in Jesus' name as Unique Son and Light (1:4, 14). Fourth, they must believe in his testimony about earthly and heavenly things (1:49-52). Fifth, they need to experience the transformation of the Spirit so that they can see heavenly things (3:5-6; 14:17). Sixth, they must bear witness to others like the Samaritan woman's "Come and see!" (4:29). Finally, they will receive eternal life (20:31). John's community believes that evil is the opposite of these things listed above. This view is apparent in Jesus' charge to Nicodemus, who came by night (3:17-21), and in his charge to some traditional Jews who had believed in him (8:31-59). Both these incidents draw on traditions from the Beloved Disciple.

As the Word that has come down, Jesus is human, but his knowledge, will, and abilities come from his status as the heavenly Word. He chooses to lay down his life; it is not taken from him. He will pick it up again himself (10:17-18). Only in this gospel does God not raise Jesus; the Unique Son raises himself and ascends to the Father (3:13; 6:62; 20:17). His miracles are signs that point to his identity and, through him, back to the Father. They are not evidence of God's astounding power (as in Mark) or of God's compassion (as in Luke). Jesus' goal is to reveal earthly and heavenly things, with the result that in John dialogue with the Jewish religious authorities often ends badly as present tensions overwhelm past texts. John's community believes that the Jewish leaders have only an earthly, physical authority through their genealogy and relation to → Abraham (8:31-59). They are understood to be part of the world that opposes Jesus.

As in Luke's gospel, John's Jesus makes several trips to Jerusalem before the final Passover (2:13–3:21; 5; 7:10–11:16; 12:12-36). In each instance, he reinterprets a physical sign from a Jewish festival in terms of heavenly realities. In the same way, Jesus' feeding of the 5,000 from the Synoptic gospels becomes an address to the Jews that Jesus himself is manna, the bread of heaven, and that all must eat of him (6:22–7:1). He is also living water (4:14; 7:37-39), the Good Shepherd (10:11-16), the resurrection and the life (11:17-27), and the true vine (15:1-8). He is not, though, the broken bread of the Passover or the cup of wine poured out to represent suffering and death, as in the Synoptics.

7.2. John's gospel begins Jesus' last days near Jerusalem, and does so with deep irony. The chief priests and the Pharisees seek to stop Jesus because his signs will attract believers, which will anger the Romans (11:48). Caiaphas the high priest prophesies that Jesus will die for the nation in order to gather together the children of God, but he does so not of his own accord but through God and the Word, as the Prologue stated (1:1-4; 11:49-52). John follows Mark and Matthew in placing an anointing at Bethany before the Passover, but the participants are now Jesus' close believing friends, Lazarus, Mary, and Martha (12:1-8). Mary's anointing Jesus' feet prefigures Jesus' washing the disciples' feet and their washing each other's feet (13:1-20). The betrayer Judas, who steals from the community's purse (12:4-6), never repents as in Matthew; he is the one destined to be lost (17:12). After Jesus' triumphal entry, Greeks (Gentiles) for the first time wish to see him. In response, Jesus announces that his hour has now come (12:23). It did not come earlier (2:4), in rural Galilee at a wedding (a common image in the Synoptics for Jesus as the Bridegroom), but rather when the foreigners provide a new mission field for John's community, as it separates from the local synagogues.

There is no Last Supper or ritual of bread and wine in John's gospel, for the community believes that the Word cannot be broken. Previously, he had invited all to feed on him as the living bread of life, eating his eternal flesh and drinking his eternal blood, which are signs for what he reveals of the Father (6:25-59). The foot washing replaces the Eucharist as a means to bind the community together. All that is preserved of the meal is John's version of the betrayal, with Jesus handing a piece of bread to Judas to acknowledge that Judas is the one (13:21-30). Following Judas's departure, Jesus gives a new command to the disciples that they love one another. Four chapters of prayers from the material of the Beloved Disciple follow (14–17). Rather than the fear and agony of Jesus in Mark and Matthew, Jesus announces his departure to the Father (not his death) and promises that the Father will send the disciples a Counselor to sustain them in his absence (14:15-31). Having announced that he has overcome the world, Jesus begins to pray that he might be glorified by being lifted up on the cross. He has protected those entrusted to him, and now he prays that all those who believe through his disciples' witness may love as Jesus and the Father love. Then Jesus goes with the disciples to the garden to be arrested, retaining full authority as the Unique Son of God.

While the outline of Mark determines the order of events from arrest to burial in this gospel, Jesus' speeches continue to reaffirm his heavenly connection. When Jesus is dressed in royal purple robes and crown, John's community would read the irony in the abuse. He really is the King of the Jews and has overcome the world. His community knows that the writing above him — "King of the Jews" — is true. On the cross, with no apocalyptic signs around, Jesus knows that all is finished of his hour and gives up his spirit (19:30). John's community believes that a small family of believers was at the cross with Jesus, including his mother (19:25b-27). The community has omitted scenes with the thieves and centurion of other gospels, for it is Jesus as powerful Light and Life, not Jesus as suffering and dying Messiah, that overcomes the darkness of people's minds (1:5).

The resurrection appearances that John's community added function as two distinct conclusions to John's gospel. The chapter ending at 20:28-31 shows that Jesus blesses those who desire to believe in the future, such as the Greeks (12:20), but who cannot see the ascended Jesus. For them, the community compiled the witness of this gospel so that they can read the Word (John's gospel) and thus see Jesus in the writing and believe. As such, chapter 20 is an inversion and a response to the values expressed in the Prologue (1:1-18). Chapter 21 ends quite differently. Jesus' discussion with Peter about the Beloved Disciple (21:20-23), when (by the time this chapter was written) both have died and have received eternal life, indicates that Peter is being put forth as having some primacy in the community. It suggests that some leaders of the Johannine community are seeking association with other Jewish and Gentile Christians while still affirming the traditions of the Beloved Disciple as authoritative for themselves. The convictions of these leaders that their future lay with joining communities founded out of the Petrine traditions (i.e., those of Mark, Matthew, and Luke) perhaps led to adding this second conclusion to the gospel.

Bibliography: K. Aland, ed., *Synopsis of the Four Gospels: Completely Revised on the Basis of the Greek Text of the Nestle-Aland 26th Edition and the Greek NT 3rd Edition* (New York, 1982) English-only text; idem, ed., *Synopsis of the Four Gospels: Greek-English Edition of the Synopsis Quattuor Evangeliorum* (7th ed.; Stuttgart, 1984) • R. E. Brown, *The Community of the Beloved Disciple* (Mahwah, N.J., 1978); idem, *A Crucified Christ in Holy Week: Essays on the Four Gospel Passion Narratives* (Collegeville, Minn., 1986); idem, *The Death of the Messiah: From Gethsemane to the Grave; A Commentary on the Passion Narratives in the Four Gospels* (2 vols.; New York, 1994) • J. D. Crossan, *The Cross That Spoke: The Origins of the Passion Narrative* (San Francisco, 1988); idem, *Who Killed Jesus? Exposing the Roots of Anti-Semitism in the Gospel Story of the Death of Jesus* (San Francisco, 1995) • B. R. Gaventa and P. D. Miller, eds., *The Ending of Mark and the Ends of God: Essays in Memory of Donald Harrisville Juel* (Louisville, Ky., 2005) • J. P. Heil, *The Death and Resurrection of Jesus: A Narrative Critical Reading of Matthew 26–28* (Minneapolis, 1991); idem, *The Gospel of Mark as a Model for Action: A Reader-Response Commentary* (Mahwah, N.J., 1992) • W. H. Kelber, ed., *The Passion in Mark: Studies on Mark 14–16* (Philadelphia, 1976) • H. F. Knight, *Celebrating Holy Week in a Post-Holocaust World* (Louisville, Ky., 2005) • F. Matera, *Passion Narratives and Gospel Theologies: Interpreting the Synoptics through Their Passion Stories* (Mahwah, N.J., 1986) • J. Neyrey, *The Passion according to Luke: A Redaction Study of Luke's Soteriology* (Mahwah, N.J., 1985) • *NJBC* • J. Painter, R. A. Culpepper, and F. F. Segovia, *Word, Theology, and Community in John* (St. Louis, 2002) • D. Patte, *The Gospel according to Matthew: A Structural Commentary on Matthew's Faith* (3d ed.; Valley Forge, Pa., 1996); idem, *Paul's Faith and the Power of the Gospel* (Philadelphia, 1983); idem, *Structural Exegesis for NT Critics* (Valley Forge, Pa., 1996) • S. Ringe, *The Gospel of Luke* (St. Louis, 1995) • D. Senior, *The Passion Narrative according to Matthew: A Redactional Study* (Louvain, 1975) • M. A. Tolbert, *Sowing the Gospel: Mark's World in Literary-Historical Perspective* (Minneapolis, 1996).

Robin Dale Mattison

Passion Music

Musical settings of the → gospel passion narratives fulfill the liturgical demands of → Holy Week liturgies (→ Church Year; Liturgy). The earliest extant settings from the fifth century are not tour de force compositions but solo works consisting of "only a normal rendition of a special set of plain-song formulas" (E. Wienandt, 113). Such formulas assigned the lowest range to Christ's words, the mid-range to the evangelist (narrator), and the upper range to all other individuals or groups (*turba,* Lat. "crowd"). This convention has generally been observed ever since.

The earliest polyphonic settings date from mid-15th-century England. The addition of soloists and multiple choirs made possible dramatic contrasts, heightening already emotionally charged Scripture. Responsorial psalms made use of alternating soloists, small groups, and choirs while retaining Gregorian formulas (J. Walter, 1530). → Motet psalms set the entire gospel account, including the evangelist's role, for choir (L. Lechner, 1598; C. Demantius, 1631). Passions of the 16th and 17th century preserved the Gregorian narration with *turba* sections in contemporary, polyphonic style (W. Byrd, late 16th cent.; H. Schütz, 17th cent.). By the 16th century the biblical text was framed by an *exordium* and a *conclusio.*

The passion borrowed the recitative and dramatic solo writing of the oratorio. From the time of Schütz (1585-1672) to J. S. Bach (1685-1750), the passion became increasingly emotion-laden and dramatic, reflecting trends in → oratorio and opera (the passion oratorio and passion cantata), while Roman Catholic composers continued to write in *stile antico* because of a ban on instruments during Holy Week.

Compositions within the last century are reminiscent of the motet and responsorial passions (H. Distler and E. Pepping) or explore new compositional techniques (K. Penderecki).

→ Church Music

Bibliography: F. Blume et al., *Protestant Church Music: A History* (New York, 1974) • K. G. Fellerer, *The History of Catholic Church Music* (Baltimore, 1961) • K. von Fischer and W. Braun, "Passion," *NGDMM* 19.200-211 • A. T. Sharp, *Choral Music: A Research and Information Guide* (New York, 2002) • B. Smallman, *The Background of Passion Music* (2d ed.; London, 1970) • N. Strimple, *Choral Music in the Twentieth Century* (Portland, Oreg., 2002) • E. A. Wienandt, *Choral Music of the Church* (New York, 1965).

Robert D. Hawkins

Passion Plays → Oberammergau

Passover

1. Name
2. Origin
3. Development
4. In Christianity

1. Name

Exod. 12:13, 23, 27 relates the name of the Passover feast to the verb *pāsaḥ*, "pass over, spare." When → Yahweh saw the sign of blood on the houses of the Israelites, he would pass by and not cause the plague to strike them as it would the Egyptians. This comment seems to be a later explanation. Thus far, however, no clear etymological derivation has been found for the term. Originally, perhaps, the blood → rite was significant from the standpoint of protection against the power of the judgment, which ran up against the countervailing power of the blood (E. Otto). In Greek, *pascha* was always the rendering of the Aram. *pasḥâ*.

2. Origin

The Passover is often traced back to the nomadic period in Israel's history (→ Israel 1; Nomads). A blood rite would offer protection to family and flocks before they moved out to spring pastures. The blood of a slaughtered lamb was smeared on the lintel and doorposts, which was to ensure that no one would break in and do damage (L. Rost).

All the biblical accounts link the Passover to the exodus tradition (Exod. 12:21-22 J). This link to history fixed its meaning, and it came to be observed as a reminder of the liberation of Israel from Egypt. The judgment of Yahweh fell on the Egyptians (→ Wrath of God), but Israel was spared and divinely led to freedom. The feast makes it plain that the exodus had to be undertaken with haste (Exod. 12:11 P).

Although the feast was originally one for families and clans, the centralization of the cult tied it to the → temple at → Jerusalem (Deut. 16:1-7). Thus the Passover became a pilgrim feast (→ Pilgrimage). After the return from exile we also find celebration of the seven-day *maṣṣôt* (unleavened bread) feast (Deut. 16:8-12; Lev. 23:6-8). These feasts were so closely related that they might simply together be called the Passover. On the afternoon of Nisan 14 the lambs were slaughtered in the priestly forecourt of the temple, then prepared, and after sundown eaten in families or groups.

3. Development

3.1. After the destruction of the temple in A.D. 70, the Passover necessarily underwent change because there could be no more slaughtering of lambs. The → Mishnah fixed the basic features of the Passover liturgy (*Pesaḥ.* 10). During the feast four cups of wine are to be handed round and the Hallel Psalms (113-18) sung. The liturgy proper follows the second cup. The son asks how this night is distinguished from all other nights. The father then refers to the exodus to show why the Passover foods are different from those usually eaten. The celebration keeps alive recollection of that early deliverance but also looks ahead to the coming redemption (→ Soteriology). The God who brought his people out of slavery will finally grant them liberation. Along the same lines as the liturgy prescribed in the Mishnah is that of the Passover → Haggadah, which developed in the early Middle Ages and is still influential today.

3.2. Isolated groups in → Judaism have followed divergent Passover practices. Thus the → Qumran community used a solar calendar to prevent the Passover's falling on a → Sabbath and to ensure that the 14th of Nisan would always fall on a Tuesday.

The → Samaritans, who separated from the Jerusalem cultic community around the fourth century B.C., have maintained their own Passover rite in their small community, slaughtering their lambs and keeping the feast on Mount Gerizim (J. Jeremias).

The Ethiopian Falashas, a → marginal Jewish group, also have their own rite that goes back to the pre-Christian era.

4. In Christianity

→ Jesus was crucified in Jerusalem at the Passover season. It is disputed whether the Last Supper with his disciples was in the Passover context, as the → Synoptics indicate (→ Eucharist 2). In primitive Christianity Christ was called the Passover lamb that was sacrificed for us (1 Cor. 5:7). → Paul adds to this statement the admonition to cleanse out all the leaven during preparation for the Passover, for the church must not live "with the old yeast . . . of malice and evil" (v. 8).

Jewish Christian groups (→ Jewish Christians) have continued to observe the Passover but have given it a Christian interpretation. They relate Exodus 12 typologically to Christ (→ Typology). While the Jewish festival carries the expectation that the Messiah (→ Messianism) will come on Passover night, expectation of the → parousia is at the heart of the Christian celebration (note the Passover homily of Melito of Sardis). The so-called Quartodecimans remained loyal to Nisan 14 as the Passover day (B. Lohse), but the church as a whole broke free from this custom and chose the Sunday after the Passover as the day for → Easter.

→ Jewish Practices 2.2

Bibliography: P. F. Bradshaw and L. A. Hoffman, eds., *Passover and Easter: Origin and History to Modern Times* (Notre Dame, Ind., 1999); idem, eds., *Passover and Easter: The Symbolic Structuring of Sacred Seasons* (Notre Dame, Ind., 1999) • F. M Colautti, *Passover in the Works of Josephus* (Leiden, 2002) • T. H. Gaster, *Passover: Its History and Tradition* (London, 1958) • M. Harris, *Exodus and Exile: The Structure of Jewish Holidays* (Minneapolis, 1992) • J. Jeremias, "Πάσχα," *TDNT* 5.896-904; idem, *Die Passahfeier der Samaritaner* (Giessen, 1932) • H.-J. Kraus, *Gottesdienst in Israel* (2d ed.; Munich, 1962) • B. Lohse, *Das Passafest der Quartadecimaner* (Gütersloh, 1953) • E. Otto, "Fest und Feiertage II: Altes Testament," *TRE* 11.96-106; idem, "פָּסַח *pāsaḥ;* פֶּסַח *pesaḥ,*" *TDOT* 12.1-24 • E. Otto, G. Veltry, and T. Schramm, "Feste: Altes Testament / Judentem / Urchristentum," *RGG* (4th ed.) 3.87-93 • L. Rost, "Weidewechsel und altisraelitischer Festkalender" (1943), *Das kleine Credo und andere Studien zum Alten Testament* (Heidelberg, 1965) 101-12 • J. B. Segal, *The Hebrew Passover from the Earliest Times to* A.D. *70* (London, 1963) • O. Skarsaune, *In the Shadow of the Temple: Jewish Influences on Early Christianity* (Downers Grove, Ill., 2002) • J. A. Soggin, *Israel in the Biblical Period: Institutions, Festivals, Ceremonies, Rituals* (Edinburgh, 2001).

Eduard Lohse

Pastor

1. Term
2. Usage
3. Current Issues

1. Term

The term "pastor" is taken directly from Lat. *pastor,* "shepherd" (Gk. *poimēn*). In both the OT and NT, God is frequently described as a shepherd ("The Lord is my shepherd" [Ps. 23:1]; "For you were going astray like sheep, but now you have returned to the shepherd and guardian of your souls" [1 Pet. 2:25]). Similarly, the benediction in the Epistle to the Hebrews refers to "our Lord Jesus" as "the great shepherd of the sheep" (13:20). The Palestinian shepherd — and metaphorically, God and Christ — was responsible for his flock in the widest sense: he gathered the sheep together, led them to good pasture and into the sheepfold, and guarded them against wild beasts and thieves.

Thus Christ, himself the good shepherd who "lays down his life for his sheep" (John 10:11), could call his → apostles to ministry by summoning them, as he did → Peter, to tend and feed his sheep (John 21:15-17). In the NT church the image is carried further: the → elders of the church are admonished to "keep watch over yourselves and over all the flock, of which the Holy Spirit has made you overseers [*episkopous,* whence Eng. 'bishops'], to shepherd the church of God that he obtained with the blood of his own Son" (Acts 20:28). Similarly, Peter ("an elder myself") could write, "I exhort the elders among you to tend the flock of God that is in your charge, exercising the oversight [*episkopountes*] . . ." (1 Pet. 5:1-2). It is important to note that in the NT the ministerial function of shepherd *(poimēn)* is often paired with that of oversight *(episkopos).*

Furthermore, the collection of early Christian writings designated, since the 17th century, as the → Apostolic Fathers (§2.6) includes a work known as the *Shepherd* [i.e., Pastor] *of Hermas.* (It is to be noted that the Epistles to Timothy and Titus were not called → Pastoral Epistles until the 18th cent.) It is also significant that the *Regula pastoralis* (Pastoral rule) of Pope → Gregory the Great (590-604) was foundational to the medieval theory of the priest/minister as the pastoral ruler.

2. Usage

Certain terms applied in the NT to Christian ministry became the title of particular ordained offices (→ Ordination) — "priest" or → "elder" *(presbyteros),* → "deacon" *(diakonos),* and → "bishop" *(episkopos)* — but the term "pastor" did not. In common parlance, "pastor" is frequently used interchangeably with a number of other designations that have no particular theological or ecclesiological standing, such as "preacher" or "clergy."

"Pastor" is the title most commonly used in churches of the → Reformation, particularly in the Lutheran tradition (→ Lutheranism). In the Lutheran rite of ordination, however, the candidate is presented "for ordination to the holy ministry of Word and Sacrament." The title is, for this tradition, a matter of indifference. After stating that "the gospel bestows upon those who preside over the churches the commission to proclaim the gospel, forgive sins, and administer the sacraments," Philip → Melanchthon (1497-1560) wrote, "It is universally acknowledged, even by our opponents, that this power is shared by divine right by all who preside in the churches, whether they are called pastors, presbyters, or bishops" (*Treatise* [1537], §§61-62). At the start of the 21st century the following simple description of the role of pastor (from a clearly Protestant orientation) may be sufficient: "For the sake of good order, when the church gathers, some from among the 'priests' are to serve as 'priests' or 'servants of the servants of God.' These are called *pastors*" (W. H. Willimon, *Pastor: Theology,* 40).

In the → Roman Catholic Church today, the term "pastor" is increasingly used, without ecclesial specificity, to designate the senior → priest in a parish. Historically, Vatican I conferred on the pope the title "eternal pastor" in the dogmatic constitution *Pastor aeternus* (1870). In point of fact, each of the varying Christian traditions — Roman Catholic, Orthodox (→ Orthodox Christianity), Reformation Protestant, Radical Reformation (→ Anabaptists; Mennonites), Evangelical (→ Evangelical Movement), Pentecostal (→ Pentecostal Churches), African American (→ Black Churches), new churches of the Third World (→ Independent Churches) — has its own ideal view of the pastoral ministry, shaped by history, theology and ecclesiology, and current context. These traditions have varieties of systems, for example, for the placement of pastors. Ordination itself invariably requires, along with academic training, that candidates demonstrate a "personal call" to the → vocation of service (ministry) to the church. After acceptance of that call, however, placement in a parish or in some other ecclesiastical office is accomplished by varying methods, including a call voted by members of a → congregation and placement by governing or episcopal authorities without the participation of laity. Certain traditions, moreover, hold that a person is a pastor only in relation to a specific parish or congregation; most, however, hold that the office of pastor is given by the wider church, through ordination, as a permanent vocation.

In most, but not all, Christian traditions, the primary task of the pastor, classically phrased, is the preaching of the gospel and the celebration of the → sacraments. In certain traditions this task is augmented by giving to the pastor also the responsibility, with the authority, to lead and in some cases to govern the parish or congregation, as well as to function as counselor or educator. Ways have been designed in all traditions for the removal of pastors for cause, that is, the "unfrocking" of persons from the ordained ministry (→ Polity, Ecclesiastical).

The adjective "pastoral" is often used to describe various functions of those who are ordained: *pastoral ministry,* the service of ordained ministers in parishes or special ministries (e.g., → military chaplaincy or → prison ministry), as distinct from oversight, executive, or educational roles; *pastoral acts* such as → marriages and → funerals; and *pastoral care,* the task of ordained ministers in regard to "the care of souls" *(Seelsorge).* → Pastoral care has become an increasingly specialized aspect of ordained ministry, often requiring advanced training in disciplines such as → psychology and → counseling (→ Pastoral Care of Children; Pastoral Care of the Sick; Pastoral Care of the Dying). Such training now normally includes → Clinical Pastoral Education (CPE).

In addition, we have the nouns *pastoralia,* the classical branch of theology concerned with the regulation of the life and conduct of local parishes (→ Pastoral Theology 1.2), and *pastorate,* which designates the location and/or duration of pastoral service in a particular parish or congregation.

3. Current Issues

In the early and mid-1950s H. Richard Niebuhr (1894-1962) of Yale University, with the sponsorship of the Carnegie Corporation of New York, directed a major undertaking entitled "The Study of → Theological Education in the United States and Canada." The first report of that study, *The Purpose of the Church and Its Ministry* (1956), written by Niebuhr, described the ordained ministry as "the perplexed profession." Niebuhr pointed out that while the nature of pastoral ministry was relatively clear even through the tumultuous changes of the Middle Ages and the Reformation ("the preacher of the Word") and the periods of → Pietism and evangelicalism ("the minister as evangelist"), such precision was lost in the early decades of the 20th century. Niebuhr cited Mark May, who asked, "What is the function of the minister in the modern community? The answer is that it is undefined. There is no agreement among denominational authorities, local officials, seminaries, professors, prominent laymen, ministers or educators as to what it is or should be" (May, 2.385).

In 1981 Joseph Sittler of the University of Chicago famously described the same situation in an essay entitled "The Maceration of the Minister": "I sought for a less violent term to designate what I behold, but maceration was the only one sufficiently accurate. Among the meanings of the term listed in the dictionary is this grim one: *to chop up into small pieces.* That this is happening to thousands of ministers does not have to be argued or established; it needs only to be aggressively stated. The minister's time, focused sense of vocation, vision of his or her central task, mental life, and contemplative acreage — these are all under the chopper" (p. 57).

Niebuhr in his study proposed a vocational description of the office of the ministry as "pastoral director." Other definitions have been proposed, but unclarity as to the precise nature of the work of the ordained pastor remains.

Two additional factors seem necessary to address

if clarity is to be attained: First, the fruits of ecumenical studies and dialogues concerning the ministry (e.g., the → Faith and Order document *Baptism, Eucharist, and Ministry* [1982]) needs to be received (→ Reception, Ecumenical) in a way that gives theological and ecclesial specificity to the nature, status, and tasks of pastoral ministry. Not least, it is important to gain a renewed understanding of ordained ministry in relation to the sacrament of → baptism and the common calling of all baptized persons ("the priesthood of all believers"; → Priest, Priesthood, 4). Second, the growing discipline of "congregational studies" (a more current designation than *pastoralia*) needs to be rescued from a purely sociological or organizational orientation and invested with theological and ecclesial meaning. The role of the pastor, then, will be clearly related to the nature of all local expressions of church and ministry.

→ Episcopacy; Ministry, Ministerial Offices

Bibliography: D. L. Bartlett, *Ministry in the NT* (Minneapolis, 1993) • D. S. Browning, *A Fundamental Practical Theology: Descriptive and Strategic Proposals* (Minneapolis, 1991) • E. Farley, *Practicing Gospel: Unconventional Thoughts on the Church's Ministry* (Louisville, Ky., 2003) • J. F. Hopewell, *Congregation: Stories and Structures* (Philadelphia, 1987) • M. A. May, *The Education of American Ministers* (2 vols.; New York, 1934) • T. Nichol and M. Kolden, eds., *Called and Ordained: Lutheran Perspectives on the Office of the Ministry* (Minneapolis, 1900) • H. R. Niebuhr, *The Purpose of the Church and Its Ministry* (New York, 1956) • H. R. Niebuhr and D. D. Williams, eds., *The Ministry in Historical Perspectives* (New York, 1956) • J. H. Reumann, *Ministries Examined: Laity, Clergy, Women, and Bishops in a Time of Change* (Minneapolis, 1987) • J. A. Sittler, "The Maceration of the Minister," *Grace Notes and Other Fragments* (Philadelphia, 1981) 57-68 • W. H. Willimon, *Pastor: The Theology and Practice of Ordained Ministry* (Nashville, 2002); idem, ed., *Pastor: A Reader for Ordained Ministry* (Nashville, 2002) • World Council of Churches, *Baptism, Eucharist, and Ministry* (Geneva, 1982). See also the bibliographies in "Elder" and "Ministry, Ministerial Offices."

Norman A. Hjelm

Pastoral Care

1. Historical Perspective
2. Present Practice
3. Theology and Pastoral Care
4. The Verbal and Visible Word
5. Practical Considerations

1. Historical Perspective

"Pastoral care" is a broad, umbrella term for those tasks of → ministry that are part of *Seelsorge,* or care of the soul, the nurture and support of the → people of God. It involves such activities as visitation of the sick, comfort of the dying and bereaved, guidance for spiritual struggles, counseling for → depression or → anxiety, moral guidance, couple and family counseling, care for the lonely, and the like. The biblical image of the shepherd is the most common guiding metaphor for pastoral care, highlighting the shepherd's courage in guiding the flock and giving solicitous care to each of the sheep. The shepherd image has dominated our understanding of pastoral care from the time of the → early church.

Throughout the centuries other images have also influenced our conception of pastoral care. Alastair Campbell in *Rediscovering Pastoral Care* (1981) expands the understanding of pastoral care by speaking not only of the shepherd's courage but also of the "wounded healer" and the "wise fool." Other metaphors, images from Scripture, have also influenced the understanding of pastoral care. It is important not to allow one image of pastoral care to so dominate our imagination that all others are excluded, just as it is important to remember to rely upon all four functions of pastoral care described below.

In *Pastoral Care in Historical Perspective* (1964), William Clebsch and Charles Jaekle highlight four functions of pastoral care in the Christian tradition. Pastoral care can be understood historically to embrace the helping acts performed by representative Christians as they facilitate the healing, sustaining, guiding, and reconciling of troubled individuals. Clebsch and Jaekle found these four functions of pastoral care occurring throughout the history of the church. During any one epoch of church history, one of these tasks might overshadow the others, but all four have always been critical to the pastoral care offered in the church (pp. 32-66).

Healing is the pastoral function that "aims to overcome some impairment by restoring a person to wholeness and by leading him to advance beyond his previous condition." Historically, the function of → healing has been carried out through such acts as → anointing, → exorcism, prayers to the → saints, → pilgrimages to shrines, charismatic healing, and the mixing of medicinal potions.

Sustaining helps individuals to endure and rise above situations in which a restoration to their previous condition is unlikely. Church history records perseverance, consolation, and visitation of the sick and shut-ins as ways in which this function has been exercised.

The *guiding* function consists of "assisting perplexed persons to make confident choices . . . when such choices are viewed as affecting the present and future state of the soul." Throughout the centuries pastoral caregivers have used two basic forms of guidance. Inductive guidance leads the persons cared for to adopt a priori sets of values as the basis for making decisions. Eductive guidance (from "educe," i.e., "bring out") elicits criteria for decision making from people's own lives and values. Historically, pastoral guidance has been primarily inductive, at times involving such varied activities as moral guidance, advice-giving, spiritual direction, and listening.

The *reconciling* function seeks to reestablish broken relationships between persons, and between individuals and God. Historically, the function of → reconciliation has involved such activities as → forgiveness, discipline, penance (→ Penitence), confession (→ Confession of Sins), and absolution. In the contemporary church marriage and family care and counseling are centered in this function of pastoral care.

According to this understanding, pastoral care is the domain not only of the clergy but also of "representative Christians." Members of the congregation offer pastoral care for each other and also for persons outside the congregation. Visiting the sick, comforting the sorrowing, encouraging the downhearted, offering spiritual guidance, and addressing ethical issues is a task that many Christians share. There is, in effect, a pastorhood of all believers.

Clebsch and Jaekle conceive of the pastoral caregiver as a facilitator. The one giving care facilitates the healing, sustaining, guiding, or reconciling, but ultimately the → Holy Spirit moves when and where it will. Martin Luther (1483-1546) spoke of the minister as a fountain through which God's love and concern can flow. Pastoral caregivers do not control the movement of the Spirit or of God's love. They offer what they think to be the best, most reasoned care, but ultimately the Spirit moves in its own way.

In most cases, pastoral care addresses individuals or families in times of trouble. It offers its hand to the sick and dying. It responds to struggles in a marriage or in the family. It guides one who is wrestling with spiritual dryness or a barren prayer life. It cares for those who are anxious, depressed, or perplexed. But pastoral care does not only respond to difficulties. In the tradition of nurturing spiritual growth, the recipient's only "problem" may be a wish to deepen a relationship with God. Such care is not always individualistic. Many churches offer pastoral care through corporate education and growth programs (e.g., marriage enrichment), which help solid relationships to grow stronger.

Finally, pastoral care addresses difficulties that occur in the context of ultimate meanings and concerns. The underlying assumption is that every part of human life is of importance to God — not only the mountaintops but also the valleys and labyrinths of human existence. Even tragedy, conflict, disappointment, and failure are part of one's faith journey. Depression, for example, is not only a result of changes in one's biochemical tides but also at its base a spiritual struggle.

2. Present Practice

Pastoral care in the last hundred years has been greatly influenced by → psychology and the → social sciences. No other factor had such an effect as the gradual incorporation of psychology into the practice of pastoral care. In the 1920s Anton T. Boisen (1876-1965) was the first person of note to point to the benefit that psychology can have on shaping how we think about people and thus on the ministry of pastoral care.

The nondirective, or client-centered, method of → psychotherapy developed by Carl Rogers (1902-87) greatly influenced how pastoral care was taught in theological seminaries and carried out in the church. (Indeed, a study of major writers in pastoral counseling found more citations from Rogers than from any other psychologist or theologian [Stone, *Strategies*].) As a result of Rogers's influence, pastoral care gradually began to emphasize eductive guidance, with a secondary emphasis on the healing of the psyche. In the middle of the 20th century, with the rise of pastoral counseling as the queen of pastoral-care functions, eductive guidance for a time all but displaced the other three functions of sustaining, healing, and reconciling. E. B. Holifield suggests that this change actually occurred gradually over some three centuries, with the result that pastoral care shifted its focus from → salvation to some form of self-realization (→ Self).

Today, especially in the United States, three major approaches to pastoral care and counseling dominate the scene: the traditional method, emphasizing inductive guidance; the nondirective approach, emphasizing eductive guidance; and some form of a revised model that emphasizes all four functions.

Let us say that a husband and wife who are members of a very conservative church visit their → pas-

Pastoral Care

tor about a marriage problem. Using the traditional model of pastoral care, this pastor will typically read several verses of Scripture that instruct the man to be the head of the family and the wife to be submissive to her husband and then pray with them, thanking God that they know where to find the solution to their problem. Though somewhat extreme, this example illustrates the traditional approach to pastoral care that many have inherited from their youth.

The traditional method has its advantages. It is quick. It uses religious resources and builds on the community's residual acceptance of pastoral authority. It deals with the family system as a whole. It is action-oriented. Yet this method falls short because it offers little real consideration of a person's uniqueness, little learning from the positive benefits of modern psychology, and little opportunity for individuals to participate actively in the solutions to their problems.

In reaction to this traditional approach a new method of pastoral care came on the scene in the 1940s and 1950s. Relying mainly on Carl Rogers, with a nod to Sigmund Freud, it became known as the nondirective, or client-centered, approach. This method emphasized the structured 50-minute interview, the role of unconscious motivation in human → behavior, the childhood basis of most adult responses, and insight as the major goal of → counseling.

The nondirective approach came to the field of pastoral care like a breath of fresh air. It has many advantages. Pastors are trained to talk less and listen more to the pain of the people they encounter, which helps establish rapport and build a solid pastor-parishioner relationship. The negative connotations of ministerial authority long associated with the image of the dominant pastor are avoided.

Despite its obvious advantages over the earlier model, however, the nondirective approach also has its liabilities. It focuses almost exclusively on one form of pastoral care — eductive guidance, with its techniques of listening and uncovering and its emphasis on insight as the goal of pastoral care. Other disadvantages worth mentioning are a time-consuming focus on exploring past events, a fondness for the 50-minute hour as the (sometimes exclusive) setting for pastoral care, and a tendency to tailor care to individuals rather than to families or community systems.

A revised model made its appearance in 1966 with the publication of *Basic Types of Pastoral Care and Counseling,* by Howard Clinebell (b. 1922), one of the key works on pastoral care in the 20th century. Clinebell acknowledges the contributions of the nondirective model, but he also cautions that, allowed to stand alone, it will greatly limit the opportunities otherwise inherent in the office of pastor.

Clinebell's large body of work has gone a long way toward helping pastors return to the breadth of historic functions of pastoral care, and recent authors are lengthening the path he blazed. Yet, Clinebell's approach tends to focus more on counseling than on care and is still tied in large measure to eductive guidance. There is little impetus or direction for correlating the moral and theological tradition with the pastoral-care process, though it must be noted that Clinebell has been a major social-ethical voice in the field. The return to the theological roots of pastoral care toward the end of the last century did not abandon the knowledge and skills from psychology and psychotherapy but, rather, placed them alongside ministry's historical and scriptural resources for the care of souls.

3. Theology and Pastoral Care

In the 1970s and 1980s several authors expressed the concern that pastoral care, overly enamored with psychology, had lost contact with its roots. Don Browning, Charles Gerkin, James Lapsley, Thomas Oden, Howard Stone, and others argued that pastoral care had become so dependent upon its auxiliary discipline that it had veered off course and needed to return to its theological moorings. Along with the clear benefits that psychology has brought to modern society, to the church, and to ministers doing pastoral care, there was an attendant loss. In their actual care of persons, pastoral caregivers tended to ignore the basic foundations and full heritage of Christian care throughout the ages.

Caregivers had cut themselves off from the historical tradition of church and theology in at least two important respects: (1) pastoral care became identified so largely with pastoral counseling as to forget the larger meaning of care in its historically more encompassing aspects, and (2) it came to accept certain implied values and concepts of humanity embedded in secular mental health practice, thereby loosening its ties to Christian → theology. When pastoral care is faithful to its historical tradition, it is not theologically or morally neutral, as most psychotherapies claim to be, but seeks to help people grow in faithful Christian living. When it is not, it is virtually indistinguishable, in philosophy and in function, from modern psychotherapeutic practice.

One way to reclaim the theological heritage of pastoral care is to make a concerted effort to recon-

Pastoral Care

nect it to a theological understanding of ministry. Indeed, most denominations still think of ministry as the proclamation of the → Word and administration of the → sacraments. For many years after pastoral-care theory and practice began its dance with modern psychology, it had difficulty recognizing much of a relationship to ministry itself, and particularly to a ministry of Word and sacrament. Often it took fancy verbal footwork to portray pastoral care as any more central to the task of ministry than, say, coaching a volleyball team in the church gymnasium.

If the essence of pastoral care is conceived of as the proclamation of the Word (the Word that became flesh, lived among us, and died reconciling us with God), then caregiving that is truly pastoral needs to make this message known. The Word is not a frozen artifact of speech or marks on paper, nor is it an abstract philosophical concept or a pseudonym for reason. Rather, it is a living proclamation that can occur anew in countless specific situations. The Word is not an impersonal force in the universe but the One who shows personal interest in us and establishes a relationship with us. "If we return to the real significance of 'word,' implying as it does a relationship between speaker and hearer, then the word can become an event to the hearer, because it brings him into this relationship" (R. Bultmann, 218).

God addresses us in the Word; in the Word we encounter the One who is indeed with us. This meeting of God and person in the Word conveys a sense of call into a relationship. God as Word shows an intense interest in each person. The emphasis is not on a passive word as something that can be heard or read and then forgotten but on a living, active, vital occurrence. The Word enters our lives as a creative force, motivating, prompting, and enlivening. Through it we are brought into God's presence; we stand, as the → Reformers put it, "before God" *(coram Deo)*.

As in an intimate relationship we share deep feelings, secrets, hopes, and wishes, so the Word reveals God to us. Thus revelation is not only general, as in nature, or specific, as in written Scriptures, but also intensely personal, addressing every person as an individual possessed of personality, intuition, likes, dislikes, woes, and joys. We encounter God's revelation not only through the church's means of grace, but also through other people, art, drama, and literature, as well as our own thoughts and visions. Whenever God speaks, there is a new incarnation of the Word directed to us in, through, and by a human word. This word is God in personal relationship, as well as the message it brings, an intimate, personalized revelation.

Because of the character of Word as incarnational address, every human experience is potentially revelatory. No boundaries of → denomination, → dogma, or religious practice determine God's self-revelation through the Word. Neither does race, class, social standing, intelligence, educational level, gender, mental health or emotional stability, disposition, or temperament. God's Word can encounter us at any place, in any hour, through any event. Revelation occurs as the Word is embodied. God reveals God's self, as in Christ, in both spoken and visible form.

4. The Verbal and Visible Word

Augustine taught that "the Word comes to the element; and so there is a sacrament, that is, a sort of visible Word" (*In Evang. Iohan.* 80.3), a comment that has been interpreted and reinterpreted throughout the centuries. Although understandings of "the visible Word" have varied, one major theme has remained constant: when God speaks to us, the Word comes through some form of visible reality. In terms of the sacrament the Word of God is the water poured and the wafer broken (→ Sacrament). Augustine seems to suggest that liturgies and rites gain their efficacy from the Word, from God's communication with God's people. The elements in the sacrament are God's way of securing the Word in our sensory world and thus making it accessible to us.

While Augustine and most of his early interpreters contrasted visible word and invisible Word, the Reformers shifted the emphasis. They contrasted the visible with the verbal, spoken, or audible word, focusing on the distinction between hearing and the other senses. Augustine was reinterpreted to say that God speaks to us not only in linguistic symbols but also in images and signs that are seen, touched, tasted, smelled, and grasped — by any of the senses. The Reformation distinction between the verbal and the sensory ultimately can assist us in our clarification of the meaning of pastoral care as communication, or → proclamation, of the Word, because in every instance of effective communication some of the things transmitted are put in the form of sentences, whereas others are relayed to the senses in other ways through gestures, imagery, tone, taste, or tactile impression.

The *verbal Word* includes more than simply preaching; it also encompasses teaching, Scripture reading, and the written or spoken sharing of the gospel. Similarly, the *visible Word* includes more than simply administration of the sacraments; its meaning can be extended even to such things as an icon, the Brahms *Requiem*, a jazz mass, an embrace, time freely given to listen to another, a warm smile, a covered-dish meal brought to the bereaved, one's ministry of presence, and the sign of the cross. These too are all crucial ways in which God comes to us. The supreme instance of this visible Word is the → incarnation of Christ.

God as the Wholly Other is inaccessible to us; through the incarnation of the Word in gestures, rites, and other elements of the sensory sphere, the hidden is revealed and truth is spoken visibly in ways that we can apprehend. "The Father knows himself in Jesus' body that walked to the cross, and in the objects that are used and used up in the gospel-communication. That is, he knows them as visible words" (R. Jenson, 36). In his treatise *That These Words of Christ, "This Is My Body," etc., Still Stand Firm against the Fanatics* (1527), Luther likewise taught that God "sets before us no word or commandment without including with it something material and outward, and proffering it to us. To Abraham he gave the word, including with it his son Isaac [Gen. 15:4ff.]. To Saul he gave the word, including with it the slaying of the Amalekites [1 Sam. 15:2f.]. To Noah he gave the word, including with it the rainbow [Gen. 9:8ff.]. And so on. You find no word of God in the entire Scriptures in which something material and outward is not contained and presented" (*LW* 37.135-36).

God, however, is really present in both the verbal Word and the visible Word. The sacraments are not just signs derived from God; God is truly there. The sermon is not just words about God; it can become the Word of God. A pastor's care for the parents of a dying child is not just a sign of God's love; God is present in that care. God's desire is to communicate with God's people. "The whole world of creatures became a 'gratia externa,' an exteriorizing of grace, that is, grace itself in visible operation. Within this world-embracing manifestation of the Lord, the ministry of the Word and the rituals of the sacraments are only the glowing focus of the visible presence of → grace" (E. Schillebeeckx, 262).

5. Practical Considerations

In a day when people are bombarded with speech on every side, many of us have learned to ignore words as much as possible and even to mistrust the speaker. For this reason the visible Word is often so important at the beginning of a pastoral-care relationship; it can prepare receptive soil for the verbal message. As we approach a person in need of care, it is generally best to focus first on establishing a relationship of trust marked by → empathy and temporary suspension of judgment, functioning primarily out of the visible Word in a ministry of compassionate presence. In most cases to speak the Word of grace or of judgment prematurely will serve only to alienate the cared-for. But once a relationship has taken hold, the pastor no longer can be morally neutral. In fact, there will be times when the verbal Word must be spoken, either to convict of sin or to proclaim release through the Incarnate One.

Verbal expression of the Word in any care situation will be handled quite differently, depending on the distinctive personalities of both caregiver and cared-for, and on the their individual relationships with God. Such expression will emerge from a stance that involves expectant listening to and for the Word. It may gently nudge the person torn by guilt to look toward the source of reconciliation, perhaps as a question (e.g., Did Christ die on the cross for everyone except you?). Or it may involve bringing a message of hope and peace to a bereaved family in a way that goes beyond simply "being with" them. Or it could mean confronting a parishioner involved in some innocent-looking form of white-collar theft. In some cases, even, introduction of a spoken Word of God may be unnecessary.

Pastoral care remains today an essential endeavor of the church and of its ministry. Caring for the sick and dying, for those in crisis, and for persons seeking to strengthen their relationships to God in prayer is needed more than ever. Marital conflict, divorce, and family chaos abound and increase. Loss, personal and vocational struggles, and a host of complex moral choices face the people we serve. Pastoral care has benefited from the learnings and skills of psychological theory and practice; it has also benefited from the call back to its theological and historical moorings. The cure of souls has been a vital function of the church from its beginnings, is still, and will be in the ages yet to come.

Bibliography: A. T. Boisen, *Exploration of the Inner World* (New York, 1952) • D. Bonhoeffer, *Ethics* (Minneapolis, 2005); idem, *Life Together* (Minneapolis, 1996) • R. Bultmann, *Jesus and the Word* (New York, 1958) • A. V. Campbell, *Rediscovering Pastoral Care* (London, 1981) • W. A. Clebsch and C. R. Jaekle, *Pastoral Care in Historical Perspective* (New York, 1964) • H. Clinebell, *Basic Types of Pastoral Care and Counseling: Resources for the Ministry of Healing and Growth* (rev. ed.; Nashville, 1984) • J. Cobb, *Theology and Pastoral Care* (Philadelphia, 1977) • E. B. Holifield, *A History of Pastoral Care in America: From Salvation to Self-Realization* (Nashville, 1983) • R. W. Jenson, *Visible Words: The Interpretation and Practice of Christian Sacraments* (Philadelphia, 1978) • C. R. Rogers, *Client-*

Centered Therapy (Boston, 1951) • E. Schillebeeckx, "Revelation in Word and Deed," *The Word: Readings in Theology* (by K. Rahner et al.; New York, 1964) 255-72 • H. W. Stone, "Pastoral Care in the 1980s: A Call for Its Return to Christian Roots," *RelLife* 49 (1980) 349-59; idem, *Strategies for Brief Pastoral Counseling* (Minneapolis, 2001); idem, *Theological Context for Pastoral Caregiving* (New York, 1996) • E. Thurneysen, *A Theology of Pastoral Care* (Richmond, Va., 1962) • P. Tillich, "The Relevance of the Ministry in Our Time and Its Theological Foundation," *Making the Ministry Relevant* (ed. H. Hofmann; New York, 1960) 19-35.

Howard W. Stone

Pastoral Care of Children

This term "pastoral care of children" varies in meaning from one part of the world to another. Citizens of Great Britain and related countries would think of a concern for the well-being of pupils in a school setting, a holistic education that includes an eye to the child's whole life and affect, not just the skills learned in the classroom. Pastoral care of children in America shares some of the same goals as that of Great Britain, but the setting would be found mainly in churches, hospitals, or religious agencies. The structure for the pastoral care of children in the United States is more fluid and has a small but growing body of literature. Where the British definition is more proactive and curricular, the American literature supports a view of pastoral care in times of crisis. It has more of a religious or spiritual emphasis and is usually conducted by trained → clergy or laity rather than classroom teachers.

These two views of → pastoral care have in common their focus on the unique nature and needs of children (→ Childhood). Both draw heavily on developmental psychology in giving attention to the ways that children think, feel, and act. For instance, young children test their environment to ascertain whether or not it is trustworthy. Caregivers who are loving and consistent will help children learn to trust and to develop a healthy sense of mistrust toward things that might endanger them. Erik Erikson (1902-94), a psychosocial theorist, went further in stating that this sense of the trustworthy nature of their world allows children to embody the virtue of hope and is foundational to their belief in a trustworthy God, whom they cannot see.

Another example of the way that developmental psychology influences the pastoral care of children can be seen in the cognitive realm. School-age children are mainly concrete thinkers until the age of about 11 or 12, according to Jean Piaget (1896-1980). This fact comes across strongly in a crisis situation, when children typically have many questions about the physical details of accidents, illnesses, and death. For example, children may ask detailed questions about modes of death, the preparation of the body, the method of burial, and elements of the funeral service. A knowledgeable, supportive adult known to the grieving family can be helpful in answering these important questions of the child.

Growing out of the church's interest in developmental psychology has been the effort also to look at faith from a developmental perspective. This orientation is especially prominent in the work of James Fowler. Building on the work of Erikson, Piaget, and others, Fowler has stressed the importance of intuition, symbol, and story in how children approach the act of faith. In pastoral care this focus has translated into an increased emphasis in hearing worth in the child's faith story and listening for the ritual behaviors that will help them cope or process a sense of loss. Fowler also commends the work of Ana-Maria Rizzuto in understanding children's development of the representation of God in early childhood. Her work highlights the important linkage of children's caregivers to their emerging image of God. In caring for children who have lost contact with a parent or important adult, one must note that this experience also has great impact on their forming representations of God. Developmental psychology and its companion faith development are important to the pastoral-care process but are not the only body of knowledge that inspires pastoral care.

A growing body of literature in the United States is beginning to address the theology of childhood, for example, the work of Bonnie Miller-McLemore and Jerome Berryman. Where developmental psychology tends to emphasize the individual child, theologians are paying particular attention to historical and societal values and beliefs that have inspired particular ways of thinking and treating children. The emphasis is on looking at children in the context of the world and church of their time period. This approach allows for a similar exploration by practical theologians of the currents and beliefs influencing the family, church, and society of today. Growing out of this literature is a movement to recover spiritual practices that can nurture and sustain families as they face the challenges of life today.

For many years pastoral caregivers have addressed some of these challenges. Hospital and hospice chaplains have ministered to children dealing with illness and → death. They have noted the differing skills and approaches needed for children in acute situations and those with chronic or terminal illnesses. Knowing that children may express their → grief and → anxiety in ways other than words, these pastoral caregivers have become attuned to methods involving → play, music, drawing, puppetry, and storytelling as other means for ministering to children. Ascertaining children's interests and learning to speak their language and the language of their family is often the first step in a pastoral-care situation.

These same methods have been brought to bear on other childhood challenges that are prominent in society today. The rise in violence to and by children has prompted specific literature that views this phenomenon as a spiritual crisis (e.g., the writing of Donald Capps and Ronald Cram). The increase in international and domestic adoptions has prompted one pastoral theologian, Jeanne Stevenson-Moessner, to explore the pastoral and theological response to this issue. The educational emphasis on the individuality of the learner has prompted a growing interest in the challenges facing children with specific disabilities (→ Persons with Disabilities). While this literature is quite prevalent in schooling situations, churches are only beginning to address families who feel ostracized by the religious community as their children grow spiritually as well as physically.

Pastoral care of and with children continues to grow and change, much as humans do. For those who engage in this ministry, there will always be new challenges and new methods of care as diverse as the spiritual lives of the children with whom they interact.

Bibliography: J. Berryman, *The Complete Guide to Godly Play,* vol. 1, *How to Lead Godly Play Lessons* (Denver, 2002) • R. Best, P. Lang, and A. Lichtenberg, eds., *Caring for Children: International Perspectives on Pastoral Care and PSE* [Personal Social Education] (London, 1994) • D. Capps, *The Child's Song: The Religious Abuse of Children* (Louisville, Ky., 1995) • C. Corr, "What Do We Know about Grieving Children and Adolescents?" *Living with Grief: Children, Adolescents, and Loss* (ed. K. Doka; Washington, D.C., 2000) 21-32 • R. Cram, *Bullying: A Spiritual Crisis* (St. Louis, 2003) • K. Dawson, "When Does Faith Begin? Child Development in a Faith Perspective," *Children among Us: Foundations in Children's Ministries* (ed. C. Williams; Louisville, Ky., 2003) 25-50 • J. Fowler, "Strength for the Journey: Early Childhood Development in Selfhood and Faith," *Faith Development in Early Childhood* (ed. D. A. Blazer; Kansas City, Mo., 1989) 1-36 • D. Grossoehme, *The Pastoral Care of Children* (New York, 1999) • A. Lester, *Pastoral Care with Children in Crisis* (Philadelphia, 1985) • B. Miller-McLemore, *Let the Children Come: Reimagining Childhood from a Christian Perspective* (San Francisco, 2003) • J. Stevenson-Moessner, *The Spirit of Adoption: At Home in God's Family* (Louisville, Ky., 2003) • B. Webb-Mitchell, *God Plays Piano, Too: The Spiritual Lives of Disabled Children* (New York, 1993) • K. Yust, *Real Kids, Real Faith* (San Francisco, 2004).

Kathy L. Dawson

Pastoral Care of the Dying

1. Pastoral Care Redefined
2. Terminal Care
3. Significant Twentieth-Century Developments
4. Practical Issues

Pastoral care of the dying involves the care that representatives of communities of faith provide to those who are dying, which usually means those who have been diagnosed with a terminal illness. Certainly → death occurs on many levels (psychological, sociological, physical, and spiritual), and pastoral care of the dying could, for example, encompass those experiencing the death of a relationship through divorce. Here, though, we focus on persons who have knowledge (awareness) of having a life-threatening illness.

1. Pastoral Care Redefined

Pastoral care of the dying has changed in recent years as a consequence of several shifts in the broader understanding of pastoral care itself. Pastoral care has traditionally been defined as the cure or care of souls (Lat. *cura animarum*). Four functions, identified by W. A. Clebsch and C. R. Jaekle, have been associated with pastoral care: healing, sustaining, guiding, and reconciling. In the 1980s two more functions were added: nurturing (by Howard Clinebell) and liberating (by E. P. Wimberly).

"Representative Christian persons" (Clebsch and Jaekle, 4) (i.e., ordained → ministers and → priests) were the traditional providers of → pastoral care. Since the 1980s, however, a shift has occurred in the definition of pastoral care. It is now more commonly defined as the mutual care we give each other throughout life, grounded in our communities of faith. This shift to a broadening of who does the care reflects a shift to a "*communal contextual* paradigm for pastoral care" (J. Patton, 4) that emphasizes the whole community of faith as those responsible for providing pastoral care. The emergence of lay ministry, pastoral-care teams, and Stephen ministry (lay crisis care) reflects and contributes to this shift.

Another shift that has occurred in pastoral care is the reclaiming of the Judeo-Christian heritage. Pastoral care had become almost synonymous with *Christian* pastoral care. One final shift that broadens the understanding of pastoral care is to define pastoral care as care given in the context of communities of faith, Christian or otherwise. Pastoral care is now often defined more generally as *spiritual* care.

In the last two decades pastoral care has reclaimed its Jewish roots, broadened the definition of care, and shifted the understanding of who can and should provide this care.

2. Terminal Care

Having a life-threatening illness involves five phases. Pastoral caregiving occurs most often in the fifth phase but may be part of the other four. Phase 1 is the "prediagnostic phase," the time between the suspicion of a problem and the actual seeking of medical care and advice. Phase 2 is the "acute phase," the time of receiving a potentially terminal diagnosis. Phase 3 is the "chronic phase," a time when cures are sought. In phase 4, or the temporary "recovery phase," there is often a remission. In stage 5, the "terminal phase," the goal of treatment shifts from cure to comfort (K. J. Doka, 6-8). Many people in this terminal phase go on hospice care.

Hospices originated in medieval times and were places where people found food, shelter, and Christian care. The modern hospice movement began in 1879 with the opening of Our Lady's Hospice in Dublin, followed by St. Joseph's Hospice in London in 1905. More recently, Dr. Cicely Saunders, who opened St. Christopher's Hospice in London in 1967, is credited with revitalizing hospice care. The first U.S. hospice was opened in 1973 in New Haven, Connecticut.

Hospice is now considered to be more than a place, however; it is a philosophy and a process. Hospice care expands the concept of care to include not just the patient but the whole family as the unit of care. It focuses on quality of life versus quantity, care versus cure, and symptom management versus treatment of disease. Hospice care also uses an interdisciplinary, holistic approach.

3. Significant Twentieth-Century Developments

Hospice care and Elisabeth Kübler-Ross's book *On Death and Dying* (1969) are probably the two most influential influences in the 20th century on how we care for the dying. In her book Kubler-Ross identifies five stages of the process of dying: denial, anger, bargaining, depression, and acceptance. This analysis has been criticized in recent years as being too linear, but at the time, her work was groundbreaking. She was among the first to support telling the dying person of his or her impending death and openly to communicate about death with the dying person. Around this time other significant books emerged, including Cicely Saunders's *Care of the Dying* (1959), C. S. Lewis's *A Grief Observed* (1961), and Jean Charon's *Death and Western Thought* (1963) and *Death and Modern Man* (1964).

The first death-education program in the United States began in 1963 at the University of Minnesota under Robert Fulton. The 1960s also saw the growth of → Clinical Pastoral Education (CPE) training programs and the development of pastoral counseling programs and centers. The 1960s were a pivotal decade in shaping and changing how death and dying are viewed. Programs, courses, and books continued to emerge over the next four decades. In 1976, for instance, the Association for Death Education and Counseling was incorporated to provide workshops and certification procedures for death educators and counselors.

Many shifts in this field occurred in the United States and Europe throughout the entire 20th century. They include changing causes of death (from communicable diseases to degenerative diseases), changing mortality rates (longer life expectancies), changes in the place of death (from the setting of the home to the institution), changing societal structures (increased industrialization, urbanization, and multiculturalism), and changes in legal issues involving death, including the emergence of life-extending technologies, with accompanying ethical concerns and end-of-life directives such as do-not-resuscitate orders (DNRs), living wills, and health-care proxies, as well as right-to-die bills and laws. Finally, there have been significant shifts in attitudes toward death and dying, from accepting death as part of life (death-accepting) to seeing death as an unwanted enemy (death-defying) to relegating care for the dying to professionals and institutions (death-denying, or invisible death; T. A. Rando, *Grief*, 5).

4. Practical Issues

All the various changes mentioned here influence how pastoral care is provided today to those who are dying. We are most likely to provide this care in the terminal phase of a life-threatening illness, when the emphasis is on reminiscence for the dying person and the family and on ritual. This is also the time when those who are dying need to find meaning in their death and life. The pastoral caregiver, lay or ordained, is the one who provides spiritual care, through visitation, prayer, sacred Scripture, and the → sacraments.

The sacraments include the → Eucharist, → reconciliation, and → anointing of the sick. Depending on the religious tradition, some of these sacraments may be administered only by the ordained. The pastoral caregiver will help the dying person and his or her family deal with theological concerns such as the purpose of suffering, God's will, → forgiveness, reconciliation, → hope, → meaning, and concerns about the afterlife. To do so, pastoral caregivers need to be familiar with the resources, prayers, and rituals of their own religious tradition, as well as have some knowledge of other religious traditions.

In order to provide pastoral care, the caregiver will also need to have knowledge about the grieving and dying processes and the particular needs of the dying, which include control, dignity, self-worth, hope, love, letting go, and saying good-bye. The pastoral caregiver will need to be trained in listening skills such as → empathy, the ability to understand and communicate to dying persons that what they are saying is heard and understood from their own perspective. (See Karaban, 111-17, for a list of ten skills for ministering to the dying and bereaved.) The pastoral caregiver also needs to be aware of current trends in the field, including hospice care, medical-ethical issues, anticipatory → grief (predeath grief), disenfranchised grief (being denied the opportunity to grieve), and complicated grief (intense, long-term, unresolved grief). Most of all, pastoral caregivers need to be compassionate people of faith who are willing to walk the final journey with those who are dying.

In the → Middle Ages there were actual handbooks for pastors known as *Ars moriendi* (Art of dying) and *Speculum artis bene moriendi* (Mirror of the art of dying well), which told how to behave at a sickbed or deathbed. Today, there is no single such handbook, but one example of a guide is the Roman Catholic *Pastoral Care of the Sick* (1983), which aids the ordained pastoral minister in anointing, reconciliation, and the Viaticum (final Eucharist), as well as the lay pastoral minister in visitation, Scripture resources, and the Viaticum. There is today an abundance of resources on death, dying, and grieving, from both secular and pastoral perspectives, to help the pastoral caregiver, lay or ordained, provide good pastoral care to dying persons and their families. Today, the concept of pastoral care of the dying includes traditional prayers and rituals but also the ability to be present to the dying person, to help with the final tasks of life review and letting go, and to minister to the family during and after death.

→ Dying, Aid for the

Bibliography: M. Callanan and P. Kelley, *Final Gifts: Understanding the Special Awareness, Needs, and Communications of the Dying* (New York, 1992) • Catholic Church, *Pastoral Care of the Sick: Rites of Anointing and Viaticum* (Collegeville, Minn., 1983) • W. A. Clebsch and C. R. Jaekle, *Pastoral Care in Historical Perspective* (New York, 1964) • H. Clinebell, *Basic Types of Pastoral Care and Counseling* (rev. ed.; Nashville, 1984) • C. A. Corr, C. M. Nabe, and D. M. Corr, *Death and Dying, Life and Living* (3d ed.; Pacific Grove, Calif., 1999) • L. A. DeSpelder and A. L. Strickland, *The Last Dance: Encountering Death and Dying* (7th ed.; Mountain View, Calif., 2004) • K. J. Doka, with J. D. Davidson, eds., *Living with Grief: When Illness Is Prolonged* (Bristol, Pa., 1997) • G. Egan, *The Skilled Helper: A Problem-Management Approach to Helping* (Pacific Grove, Calif., 2002) • R. A. Karaban, *Complicated Losses, Difficult Deaths: A Practical Guide for Ministering to Grievers* (San Jose, Calif., 2000) • R. J. Kastenbaum, *Death, Society, and Human Experience* (8th ed.; Boston, 2004) • E. Kübler-Ross, *On Death and Dying* (New York, 1969) • J. Patton, *Pastoral Care in Context: An Introduction to Pastoral Care* (Louisville, Ky., 1993) • T. A. Rando, *Grief, Dying, and Death: Interventions for Caregivers* (Champaign, Ill., 1984); idem, ed., *Clinical Dimensions of Anticipatory Mourning: Theory and Practice in Working with the Dying, Their Loved Ones, and Their Caregivers* (Champaign, Ill., 2000) • J. Rupp, *Praying Our Goodbyes* (Notre Dame, Ind., 1988) • H. M. Spiro, M. G. M. Curnen, and L. P. Wandel, *Facing Death: Where Culture, Religion, and Medicine Meet* (New Haven, 1996) • E. P. Wimberly, *Pastoral Counseling and Spiritual Values: A Black Point of View* (Nashville, 1984).

Roslyn A. Karaban

Pastoral Care of the Sick

1. Biblical, Theological, Historical Contexts
2. In the Hospital: Pastors and Chaplains
3. Functions

1. Biblical, Theological, Historical Contexts

Care of the sick is an essential act of Christian kindness, with roots in the NT. To visit the sick is to minister to Christ himself — "I was sick and you took care of me" (Matt. 25:36). The sick are subject to social isolation and, at times, ostracism. Counter to this tendency are the hortatory injunctions for the sick to call for the → elders of the church and for the elders to → pray and to → anoint so that the sick may be saved and, if they have sinned, be forgiven (Jas. 5:14-16). Ministry to the sick is rooted in an understanding of Christian community as the body of Christ in which all members suffer when one does (1 Cor. 12:26). The → early church (e.g., Augustine) found that the motif of Christ the Physician set visitation of the sick at the heart of Christian care and action. Even → bishops should visit sick members of the church, since it is a great comfort for the sick to be visited by the leaders of the → priests (*Canons of St. Hippolytus* 24).

The biblical injunction to pray and to anoint the sick later became formalized in ritual and → sacrament. This ministry consisted in giving communion (→ Eucharist) with the reserved elements, anointing with oil, the → laying on of hands, and a formal prayer for strength for the sick. Later, in popular → piety, the sacrament of the sick came to mean the giving of "last rites," or "extreme unction." → Confession of sins would be made, and the promises of pardon given, so as to put right the sick person's relationship to God and neighbor.

After the → Reformation, the Protestant concentration on the → Word took precedence over ritual. The visitation of the sick might focus on → law and → grace. The sick would be encouraged to examine their → faith and to clarify whether there was a connection between their illness and sinfulness. Illness, then, might become an occasion for → conversion (§1) and the renewal of faith. Heinrich Bullinger (1504-75), successor to Ulrich Zwingli (1484-1531), urged pastors to visit the sick and help the dying "pass happily from this world" (J. T. McNeill, 196).

The → Enlightenment made its impact, especially upon Roman Catholic care of the sick, by initiating a program of training for priests in pastoral medicine. In such a framework C. Capellmann and W. Bergmann understood the sum of anatomical, physiological, hygienic, pathological, and therapeutic discussions, knowledge of which is necessary or useful in care of the sick.

In modern times, pastoral care of the sick involves not only the ministrations of → clergy but also the work of those involved in lay pastoral care (→ Lay Movements). Eucharistic ministers, in some traditions, take the reserved sacrament to those who are ill. Many churches and faith groups highly value lay ministry and provide formal training for those who wish to participate. A number of national training programs for lay ministers have evolved, such as the Stephen Ministries (begun in 1975 in St. Louis by Kenneth Haugk, a pastor and clinical psychologist). Whether or not lay ministers are formally recognized, studies show that lay ministry takes place — members reach out to one another during times of crisis, especially at times of illness and loss.

→ Pastoral Care

Bibliography: C. Capellmann and W. Bergmann, *Pastoralmedizin* (19th ed.; Paderborn, 1923) • H. Faber, *Pastoral Care in the Modern Hospital* (Philadelphia, 1971) • F. Lake, *Clinical Theology: A Theological and Psychological Basis to Clinical Pastoral Care* (abr. ed.; New York, 1987) • J. T. McNeill, *A History of the Cure of Souls* (New York, 1951) • K. R. Mitchell, *Hospital Chaplain* (Philadelphia, 1972) • H.-C. Piper, *Krankenhausseelsorge heute* (Berlin, 1985); idem, *Kranksein. Erleben und lernen* (6th ed.; Munich, 1999).

Hans-Christoph Piper† and Russell H. Davis

2. In the Hospital: Pastors and Chaplains

The pastoral care of the sick takes place in a variety of locations: in homes and in institutions for the sick such as hospitals, clinics, sanatoriums, and hospices, as well as on battlefields or, in the case of the homeless, in streets, shelters, and parks.

Christian hospitals seem to have emerged as early as the fourth century (Basil of Caesarea). The last 100 years have seen an enormous increase in the number of hospitals, and a huge increase in hospitals operating independently of faith-group sponsorship or affiliation.

Hospitals vary in complexity. Some are small community-based hospitals. Others serve as regional hospitals, while still others draw their patients from a national or international community. Hospitals vary considerably as to the types of accredited services offered. Some offer the latest and most expensive technologies; some are transplant centers or accredited level 1 trauma centers.

2.1. As the level of technology and sophistication rises, → pastor and patient may find that they are entering an unfamiliar and even alien world far beyond their level of knowledge and comprehension. Both may find themselves overwhelmed and intimidated by the severity of the illness or trauma, by the complicated decisions to be made about treatment alternatives, by difficult ethical decisions, as well as by the formidable foreign language of medicine and → technology, much of which is difficult to understand under any circumstances, but especially so in the midst of the anxiety of a life-threatening and life-altering crisis.

Because of all these factors, many denominations and faith groups recommend or require that parish ministers take at least one course of accredited → Clinical Pastoral Education (CPE) in order to become more comfortable in, and knowledgeable of, the hospital setting so as to be able to offer more competent pastoral care as healer, guide, sustainer, and reconciler (see 3). A decisive help in the ability to offer competent pastoral care to hospitalized patients has been given by the American pastoral movement associated with CPE. First offered in the United States in 1925, CPE reached Europe in the early 1960s and then spread rapidly. Today it exists around the globe, with strong footholds in Africa, Asia (e.g., Korea and Hong Kong), and some of the Pacific islands (esp. the Philippines).

Today, many churches expect that parish → clergy who give pastoral care in hospitals will have clinical training. Groups around the world that provide training also conduct research and have developed an extensive collection of literature on pastoral care of the sick published in a number of books and various journals, including *Journal of Pastoral Care* (1947-), *Journal of Religion and Health* (1961-), and *Journal of Healthcare Chaplaincy* (1987-). Writers and researchers have assembled a broad range of materials on the possibilities and limitations of pastoral care in a hospital. They have explored models of collaboration with physicians and other health care professionals who are called on to care for the sick, and they have investigated the attitudes of patients and their expectations of clergy during times of hospitalization. Perhaps most important, they have determined a set of skills necessary for effective ministry to those in distress.

Among these skills, two stand out — self-knowledge and empathic listening (→ Empathy). In giving pastoral care to the sick, it is helpful to see ourselves, in the phrase of Henri Nouwen (1932-96), as "wounded healers" who stand with, and not above, the patient. Who we are as persons and pastors, our strengths and weaknesses, our wounds and our partial healing, play an essential role in our capacity to engage in the second essential pastoral care skill: empathic listening.

2.2. In addition to the work of parish clergy who provide ministry to members of their respective parishes who are ill, other clergy work as professional hospital chaplains. Hospital chaplains are considered a part of specialized ministry, as are pastoral → counseling and a variety of chaplaincy ministries in other settings (military, prison, mental health, business and industry, hospice, and colleges and universities; → Military Chaplaincy). The COMISS Network (formed in 1979 as the Council on Ministry in Specialized Settings) is a forum for dialogue and action among five distinct pastoral care and counseling communities involving chaplains and pastoral counselors:

- professional certification organizations;
- professional accreditation organizations (of programs to train clergy on their way to becoming professional chaplains or pastoral counselors);
- religious endorsing bodies;
- professional pastoral care organizations (i.e., groups of chaplains or other pastoral care professionals); and
- chaplain and pastoral counselor employing organizations.

Hospital chaplains often work in a multifaith context. Their aim is to supplement, but not replace, the work of parish clergy. Hospital chaplains often help parish clergy negotiate the complex hospital system. Hospital chaplains are there to minister to patients and families who come from a distance, which may prohibit regular visits from clergy from their own church. Hospital chaplains are also ready to provide ministry to persons who do not have an active church affiliation. In addition to ministry to patients and families, hospital chaplains provide care and comfort to nurses, doctors, and hospital staff in the midst of difficult and stressful work. A moment of prayer during a crisis, a word of compassion after the → death of a patient to staff who also may grieve, a lighthearted word in difficult times — these and more are part of hospital ministry to staff. The chaplain may also provide memorial services for hospital employees who grieve the loss of a coworker.

Hospital ministry increasingly requires specialized knowledge. Chaplains often play a central role in hospital ethics committees and in clinical ethics consultations with patients and families, for which training in clinical and theological → ethics is quite helpful. Hospital chaplains often participate in critical incident stress management teams that work with hospital staff suffering stress beyond the ordinary stress of daily work in a high-intensity environment. Many chaplains receive training from a teacher certified by the International Critical Incident Stress Foundation, based on the model developed by Jeffrey T. Mitchell. Chaplains who minister to the sick also need to be well trained in crisis ministry and to be knowledgeable in areas of advance directives, organ donation, bereavement and grief, and family dynamics (→ Crisis Intervention). Chaplains develop their capacity for empathy by

Pastoral Care of the Sick

knowledge of the nature of specific illnesses and their impact on the person (L. E. Holst, R. Dayringer). Chaplains must have extensive multicultural competencies in order to work effectively with people in social locations different from their own.

Chaplains often walk in several worlds simultaneously — the worlds of medicine and of religion and spirituality, the worlds of the patients and of the institution. Each world has its own priorities, which can pull chaplains in conflicting directions (Holst). For example, since the institution may pay the chaplain, he or she may feel a tension between advocating for the patient's needs and job security.

Chaplains are bound by their code of ethics, by hospital policy, and by federal law to strict boundaries regarding patient confidentiality. Recent changes (2003) in the Health Insurance Portability and Accountability Act (HIPAA) in the United States, especially changes in its provisions regarding patient confidentiality, have led many hospitals to change radically the kind and amount of information provided to parish clergy. No longer can clergy receive a list of all patients who are members of their faith group. Patients must now authorize release of such information, which places the burden on patients and their families to notify their church or clergy when they are hospitalized. Informal observations of hospital chaplains suggest that a significant minority of church members do not want their church notified of hospitalization.

In November 2004 a historic agreement between several of the major → pastoral care and CPE organizations took place. Common standards for professional health care and hospital chaplains were adopted by six national organizations meeting simultaneously in Portland, Oregon: the American Association of Pastoral Counselors, the Association for Clinical Pastoral Education, the Association of Professional Chaplains, the Canadian Association for Professional Practice and Education, the National Association of Catholic Chaplains, and the National Association of Jewish Chaplains. The standards now define the education, training, and skills required for being certified as a professional chaplain, as agreed to by the six organizations, which represent more than 10,000 members. In addition, the six groups also agreed to common standards for pastoral educators in the CPE tradition, adopted a common code of professional ethics, and determined principles for processing ethical complaints against members.

3. Functions

Historically, according to W. A. Clebsch and C. Jaekle, Christian care of the sick has involved four pastoral functions: → healing, sustaining, guiding, and reconciling. Healing involves not only being restored to a condition of wholeness but also achieving a new level of spiritual insight and welfare. Through pastoral care, people increase in their ability to experience → health and sickness as filled with spiritual significance. Sustaining, where cure is not possible, helps a person in crisis endure what cannot otherwise be changed. Through compassion the sufferer is helped to move beyond resignation to affirmation; spiritual growth is achieved through a new attitude and through endurance of unwanted or harmful or dangerous circumstances.

The pastoral function of guiding aids persons who are perplexed or confused about ethical decisions to make confident choices. In modern times, educative guidance seeks to draw out the values and resources of the person making the decision rather than seeking to ensure compliance with the values of the person or religious institution offering help. The function of → reconciliation works to repair broken relationships between person and person, between person and religious community, and between person and God.

The means of achieving healing, sustaining, guiding, and reconciling have varied from time to time within the history of Christianity and from place to place. Healing, for example, has employed the ministrations of → prayer, → anointing with oil, → laying on of hands, application of herbs and medications, use of relics, speaking of words of → exorcism, offering of → vows to God, and → pilgrimages to shrines and holy places. Reconciliation is deeply connected to sacraments, rituals, and traditions of → forgiveness.

In modern times empathic listening and wise counsel, as informed by depth psychology and the behavioral sciences, have been added to the tools for healing, sustaining, guiding, and reconciling those who are ill. Whatever the means used, the choice of which pastoral function(s) to emphasize in a particular situation of illness will depend on the sensitivity and accuracy of the pastoral assessment of the spiritual needs of those being helped.

→ Human Dignity; Suffering

Bibliography: R. C. Cabot and R. L. Dicks, *The Art of Ministering to the Sick* (New York, 1951) • W. A. Clebsch and C. R. Jaekle, *Pastoral Care in Historical Perspective* (London, 1983) • R. Dayringer, ed., *Pastor and Patient: A Handbook for Clergy Who Visit the Sick* (London, 1982) • G. Fitchett, *Assessing Spiritual Needs: A Guide for Caregivers* (Minneapolis, 1993) • L. E. Holst, ed., *Hospital Ministry: The Role of the*

Chaplain Today (New York, 1985) • N. A. Kirkwood, *Pastoral Care in Hospitals* (Harrisburg, Pa., 1998) • J. B. McCall, *A Practical Guide to Hospital Ministry: Healing Ways* (New York, 2002) • T. C. Oden, *Care of Souls in the Classic Tradition* (Philadelphia, 1984) • *Pastoral Care of the Sick: Rites of Anointing and Viaticum* (Totowa, N.J., 1991) • P. Tillich, *The Meaning of Health: Essays in Existentialism, Psychoanalysis, and Religion* (Chicago, 1984) • L. VandeCreek, ed., *Spiritual Needs and Pastoral Services: Readings in Research* (Decatur, Ga., 1995) • L. VandeCreek and S. Mooney, eds., *Parish Nurses, Health Care Chaplains, and Community Clergy: Navigating the Maze of Professional Relationships* (New York, 2002).

Russell H. Davis

Pastoral Epistles

1. Origins
2. Church Order
   2.1. Presbyters
   2.2. Deacons
   2.3. Bishops
3. Theology
   3.1. God and Creation
   3.2. Christ
   3.3. Salvation
4. In History

1. Origins

The term "Pastoral Epistles" is applied to three letters within the Pauline corpus, namely, 1 Timothy, 2 Timothy, and Titus. The term is regarded as fitting, since these three offer instructions for pastoral oversight of congregations and specify the qualities and duties expected of church leaders. Paul Anton (1661-1730) is given credit for coining the term for the three letters, although → Thomas Aquinas (ca. 1225-74) had referred to 1 Timothy as "a pastoral rule" much earlier.

Each letter identifies its author as → Paul in the very first verse and then designates its recipient as either Timothy or Titus, each of whom has been entrusted by Paul with teaching and leading churches committed to their care. Nevertheless, serious reservations exist in modern scholarship concerning their actual authorship. Those reservations are based on five observations.

First, the Pastorals are not associated with the Pauline corpus in the earliest period. They were not listed by Marcion when he made a collection of the writings of Paul (ca. A.D. 150), and they were not included in the earliest known MS of Paul's letters ($\mathfrak{p}^{46}$, ca. 200). They are included, however, in the late second-century Muratorian → Canon, and they are considered Pauline in the works of → Irenaeus, Clement of Alexandria, and → Tertullian from that same era.

Second, the Pastorals differ in vocabulary and syntax from the other Pauline letters. Disregarding proper nouns, the Pastorals use 849 different words. Of this number, 306 (36 percent) are not found in the ten other letters attributed to Paul in the NT. And if one compares the vocabulary with only the "undisputed" letters of Paul (Romans, 1 and 2 Corinthians, Galatians, Philippians, 1 Thessalonians, and Philemon), the number of words not found increases to 326 (38 percent). In contrast, many (121, or 14 percent, of the 849) are found in the Apostolic Fathers and the apologists of the second century, causing some scholars to suggest that they were composed in the postapostolic period. Moreover, in addition to vocabulary, matters of composition are also distinctive. For example, to express the concept "with" the undisputed Pauline letters use the construction *syn* followed by a noun in the dative case 28 times, and also *meta* followed by a noun in the genitive case 37 times. In the Pastorals, however, only the latter construction appears (18 times). Other examples of writing-style differences can be given.

Third, important theological concepts known from the undisputed letters of Paul are missing in the Pastorals. These include the imminent → parousia of Christ (1 Cor. 15:51-52; 1 Thess. 4:15-18) and the familiar Pauline expression of the believer's living "in Christ" (Rom. 6:11; 8:1; 1 Cor. 1:30; 2 Cor. 5:17, etc.). Some concepts have different meanings. The term "faith" always means "the Christian faith" in the Pastorals (1 Tim. 1:2; 3:9, 13; 4:1; 2 Tim. 4:7; Titus 1:13, etc.) or a Christian virtue (1 Tim. 1:5, 19; 4:12; 6:11; 2 Tim. 2:22; Titus 2:2, etc.), whereas in the undisputed letters of Paul it more commonly has the meaning "trust," which is placed in God, Christ, or the gospel. Furthermore, ten times the Pastorals mention the important virtue *eusebeia* (1 Tim. 2:2; 3:16; 4:7, 8; 6:3, 5, 6, 11; 2 Tim. 3:5; Titus 1:1; NRSV "godliness," once "religion"), but this word never appears in the undisputed letters of Paul.

Fourth, the church order assumed as the norm in the Pastorals — with → bishops, presbyters (→ Elder), and → deacons — does not appear in the undisputed letters of Paul. It is more like church orders found in the writings of the → Apostolic Fathers than in the writings of Paul.

Finally, it is difficult to fit the Pastorals into the

career of the apostle Paul as we know it from other sources (Acts and the undisputed letters). In order to do so, one has to conclude that Paul was released from prison (as recorded in Acts), traveled to Spain, returned to Rome, wrote 1 Timothy and Titus while free, was arrested and imprisoned again in Rome, wrote 2 Timothy while in prison, and was subsequently executed. While not impossible, this sequence rests on a tradition known from the fourth century (Eusebius, *Hist. eccl.* 2.2), although that tradition could have originated from a reading of the Pastorals themselves.

Generally, scholars regard the origins of the Pastorals from four perspectives: (1) they are authentic (i.e., by Paul), in spite of the obvious difficulties; (2) they were dictated in the main by Paul but written up in their final form by a secretary who worked with considerable freedom; (3) they were written after the death of Paul but contain genuine fragments from him; (4) they are pseudonymous, impersonating Paul in a later situation. The last of these views has gained major support in international scholarship. According to this view, the letters were most likely composed at the end of the first century or at the beginning of the second by a writer devoted to Paul. The place of composition is uncertain but may have been → Ephesus or → Rome.

2. Church Order

The author of the Pastorals envisions a community ordered in rather explicit ways, more so than any other NT writer. Offices are mentioned into which persons are inducted (1 Tim. 3:10; 4:14; 5:22; 2 Tim. 1:6), and the persons so inducted are to be respected, as office bearers, for the sake of their work (1 Tim. 5:17). Three main offices are mentioned.

2.1. *Presbyters*

Presbyters (or "elders" in many English versions) are mentioned in two places (1 Tim. 5:17-19; Titus 1:5). Gk. *presbyteros* (the source of Eng. "priest") can refer simply to an older person in ordinary, secular Greek. In the Pastorals, however, it is the title for an office; age is not a consideration for being a presbyter, for in the Pastorals it is assumed that the incumbent will have children at home (Titus 1:6). The presbyters form a council (1 Tim. 4:14; Gk. *presbyterion,* "presbytery" or "council of elders"). These persons have a governing function, and some are engaged in → preaching and teaching (5:17).

2.2. *Deacons*

Deacons are mentioned once (1 Tim. 3:8-13). The Greek term for the office is *diakonos,* rendered "deacon" in some English versions but "servant" or "minister" in others. Their duties are not spelled out, but (as in later sources) they most likely served under the bishop in charitable work and temporal concerns.

2.3. *Bishops*

An officer called a bishop (Gk. *episkopos,* "overseer") is mentioned twice (1 Tim. 3:1-7; Titus 1:7-9). On the basis of reading all three Pastorals together, it appears that all ministry carried on in the community — both ministry of the Word and ministry of service — is under the supervision of the bishop. Nevertheless, disagreement exists among interpreters on the relationship between bishop and presbyter. Some have concluded that the two titles are equivalent (as perhaps in Acts 20:17, 28; 1 Pet. 5:1-2; and *1 Clem.* 44.4-5). The term "bishop," however, is always used in the singular in the Pastorals, while "presbyter" can be plural. On that basis, other interpreters have concluded that the bishop was the leading office bearer, who may or may not have arisen from the circle of presbyters (as Titus 1:5-9 can be taken to imply) and who provided primary oversight for a congregation or a cluster of congregations. The duties of the bishop are spelled out: (1) working with the presbyters and deacons, the bishop supervises the life of the community as though it were an extended household (1 Tim. 3:5), caring for all matters, whether spiritual, temporal, or organizational; (2) he combats false teaching and preserves what is sound (Titus 1:9); and (3) he devotes himself to sound teaching (1 Tim. 3:2; Titus 1:9) and preaching (1 Tim. 5:17).

Women carry on certain activities in the church (1 Tim. 3:11). Since they are referred to within a section concerning deacons (3:8-13), some interpreters have concluded that the term refers to women deacons (notice the mention of Phoebe in Rom. 16:1). But since the deacon is to be the "husband of one wife" (1 Tim. 3:12), the term probably refers solely to men. These women, however, may very well have been devoted to diaconal service, even if they did not bear the formal title. One group of women is clearly "enrolled" (on a roster) as a distinct group, the "widows" (1 Tim. 5:3-16). They are supported by the community (vv. 5, 16), and their primary responsibilities are prayer and charitable work (vv. 5, 10). In the second century the office of widow became formalized (Ign. *Smyrn.* 13.1; Pol. *Phil.* 4.3), if not already in the Pastorals themselves.

3. Theology

The Pastorals have often been read in light of the major undisputed letters of Paul, have been judged in light of them, and have been found less profound in their theology. Yet they have some distinctive theological concerns of importance.

3.1. *God and Creation*

Over against an early Gnostic form of Christianity that was apparently developing in his day (see 1 Tim. 6:20, "what is falsely called knowledge [*gnōsis*]"), which taught that there were two gods and that the present world was created by the lesser of those gods, the author of the Pastorals affirms that God the Father is one and that he not only has created all things but has created them good (1 Tim. 1:2; 2:5; 4:3-4; 2 Tim. 1:2; Titus 1:14-15), "gives life to all things" (1 Tim. 6:13), and "richly provides us with everything for our enjoyment" (6:17). Stress is placed on the goodness of → marriage and having children (1 Tim. 3:2-5; 5:10, 14; Titus 2:4), the legitimacy of secular authority (1 Tim. 2:1-2; Titus 3:1-2), the care of the elderly (1 Tim. 5:4), compassion for those in need (Titus 3:2, 8, 14), and courtesy toward all people (Titus 3:2). The love of wealth is to be avoided (1 Tim. 6:9-10; 2 Tim. 3:2). The way of life prescribed is one of good works (1 Tim. 2:10; 2 Tim. 2:21; 3:17; Titus 3:1), moderation (1 Tim. 6:8), and generosity (1 Tim. 6:17-18).

3.2. *Christ*

Four major → Christological titles appear in the Pastorals: "Christ," "Lord," "Savior," and "Mediator." The title "Son of God," used often in the undisputed letters of Paul, does not appear. The word "God" is applied to Christ once: Christians await their "blessed hope and the manifestation of the glory of our great God and Savior, Jesus Christ" (Titus 2:13). But more often a distinction is made between Christ and God (1 Tim. 1:1; 2:5-6; 5:21; 2 Tim. 4:1; Titus 1:4; 3:4-6). Perhaps the most that can be said is that God and Christ are intimately related, so much so that at his parousia Christ will bear the divine glory to complete the saving work of God, and in that sense he will be "God and Savior." Finally, the term "mediator" appears (1 Tim. 2:5) to refer not so much to Christ's nature as to his function in giving himself as a "ransom" for the salvation of humankind.

By these various titles the divine status of Christ is affirmed. There is an implicit affirmation of his preexistence and → incarnation (1 Tim. 3:16; 2 Tim. 1:9-10; Titus 2:11), even if it is not as obvious as in some other NT writers. Christ's true humanity is maintained (1 Tim. 2:5; 6:13; 2 Tim. 2:8), and his death is acknowledged (1 Tim. 2:6; 2 Tim. 2:11; Titus 2:14). He has been exalted to heaven and reigns in the present era (1 Tim. 3:16; 2 Tim. 1:10; 2:12). Finally, he will appear at the end of time (1 Tim. 6:14; 2 Tim. 4:8), when he will judge both the living and the dead (2 Tim. 1:18; 4:1, 8).

It is sometimes said that the → Christology of the Pastorals is one of "epiphany" (i.e., manifestation) — actually, two epiphanies, past and future. Jesus Christ has appeared once already as the earthly, visible manifestation of the grace, goodness, and lovingkindness of God (2 Tim. 1:9-10; Titus 2:11; 3:4), and he will appear at the end of time bearing the divine glory (Titus 2:13; cf. 1 Tim. 6:15-16).

3.3. *Salvation*

Humanity consists without exception of "sinners" whom Christ came to save (1 Tim. 1:15). The Pastorals, however, lack the profound Pauline concept of → sin as a power reigning over all persons apart from the saving work of God in Christ (Rom. 3:9; 5:12, 21; 7:14; Gal. 3:22). They speak instead of "sins" that people commit (1 Tim. 5:22, 24; 2 Tim. 3:6) as a result of serving the self and its passions (Titus 2:12; cf. 2 Tim. 3:2-5). The result is a life that leads away from eternal life and toward judgment and eternal death.

→ Salvation consists primarily of the divine rescue of persons from mortality — with its sins, ignorance, and unbelief — for life in the eternal and heavenly → kingdom of God (2 Tim. 1:10; 4:18). Christ came into the world and manifested there the grace and goodness of God. But even more, he gave himself as a ransom for all (1 Tim. 2:6), thereby bearing the divine judgment against sins for the benefit of others (Titus 2:14). Being raised from death, he "abolished death and brought life and imperishability to light" (2 Tim. 1:10), exposing it for all to see as a possibility for themselves. Finally, he will come to rescue his people and save them for his heavenly kingdom (2 Tim. 4:18). Meanwhile, the writer exhorts his readers to "take hold of eternal life" by accepting the gospel of Christ (1 Tim. 6:12, 19) and living the life characterized by "godliness" (1 Tim. 2:2; 4:7-8; 6:3-6, 11).

4. In History

The Pastorals have had an important role in Christian → theology, church life, and → liturgy. Their emphasis on the goodness of God, the → creation, and the ordering of the church has been significant over time, and echoes of their instructions on → baptism (Titus 3:5-7) and → prayer (1 Tim. 2:1-2) have been heard in books used for public worship.

But their impact on the church and society have also been experienced as a problem. The author of the Pastorals takes it for granted that some Christians are slaves (1 Tim. 6:1-2; Titus 2:9-10) and that some Christians are slave owners (1Tim. 6:2). He assumes that → slavery is to be preserved, and slaves and slave owners are exhorted to be respectful of one another. Moreover, the exhortation that women should keep silent in the church (1 Tim. 2:11) has, until modern times, had a lasting effect in regard to the role of women in the church. It does not likely reflect the views of Paul (1 Cor. 14:34-36 is commonly regarded as an interpolation, harmonizing Paul with the Pastorals), who speaks of women as prophets in the church (1 Cor. 11:5) and refers to one woman who is recognized as a deacon (Rom. 16:1) and to another who is an apostle (Rom. 16:7).

The Pastorals need not have the last word on all matters they take up. But their language and imagery concerning God and Christ, their strong affirmations of the divine will and actions for human redemption in Christ, and their passion for sound teaching and honorable living in the world have won their acceptance and their importance within the NT.

→ Ministry, Ministerial Offices

Bibliography: Commentaries: C. K. Barrett, *The Pastoral Epistles* (NClarB; Oxford, 1963) • J. Bassler, *First Timothy, Second Timothy, Titus* (AbNTC; Nashville, 1996) • M. Davies, *The Pastoral Epistles* (NTG; Sheffield, 1996) • M. Dibelius and H. Conzelmann, *The Pastoral Epistles* (Hermeneia; Philadelphia, 1972) • J. D. G. Dunn, "First and Second Timothy, Titus" (NIB 11; Nashville, 2000) 773-880 • A. T. Hanson, *The Pastoral Epistles* (NCBC; London, 1982) • A. Hultgren, *First–Second Timothy, Titus* (ACNT; Minneapolis, 1984) • L. Johnson, *The First and Second Letters to Timothy* (AB 35A; New York, 2001) • I. H. Marshall, *The Pastoral Epistles* (ICC; Edinburgh, 1999) • W. Mounce, *Pastoral Epistles* (WBC 46; Nashville, 2000) • T. Oden, *First and Second Timothy and Titus* (IBC; Louisville, 1989) • J. Quinn, *The Letter to Titus* (AB 35; New York, 1990) • J. Quinn and W. Wacker, *First and Second Letters to Timothy* (ECC; Grand Rapids, 1999).

Other works: L. Donelson, *Pseudepigraphy and Ethical Argument in the Pastoral Epistles* (Tübingen, 1986) • P. N. Harrison, *Paulines and Pastorals* (London, 1964); idem, *The Problem of the Pastoral Epistles* (London, 1921) • F. Young, *The Theology of the Pastoral Letters* (Cambridge, 1994).

Arland J. Hultgren

Pastoral Letters

Pastoral letters are official letters from pastors, and especially bishops, to all members of their church or diocese. Models are the NT letters of Paul and the other apostles, the letters of the postapostolic period, and the Easter letters of the Alexandrian bishops. For all Christian denominations, pastoral letters typically respond to concerns or problems within the community, exhorting the faithful to live according to the full implication of the gospel.

In the → Roman Catholic Church pastoral letters, or episcopal letters, are circular communications sent by a → bishop to the faithful in his → diocese. Charles Borromeo (1538-84), archbishop of Milan, introduced pastoral letters in a new form into Italy, and German bishops followed suit from around the middle of the 18th century.

Today Roman Catholic pastoral letters are regularly issued during fasts, for political elections, and in support of charities. The only reference to them in the 1983 → CIC is that such letters should be preserved in the parish archives (can. 535.4). They come, however, within the teaching and pastoral jurisdiction that is conferred upon bishops (375.1). Since the institution of bishops' conferences, which were set up for the first time in 1983 (CIC 447-59), the common pastoral letters of the bishops of a country have taken on significance.

The bishops' conference of the United States issued important and widely publicized pastoral letters on nuclear → war (*The Challenge of Peace: God's Promise and Our Response; a Pastoral Letter on War and Peace* [1983]) and on the demands of social justice on American economic institutions (*Economic Justice for All: Pastoral Letter on Catholic Social Teaching and the U.S. Economy* [1986]; → Economic Ethics). These letters were noteworthy not only for their themes and content but also for the process followed in drafting them. In both cases, the drafting committee held open hearings to solicit information and opinion from competent persons and published drafts of their document for approval. This process later broke down when the bishops attempted to draft a pastoral letter on the role of women in society and the church.

In his apostolic letter *Apostolos suos,* issued May 21, 1998, Pope John Paul II (1978-2005) significantly curtailed the authority of bishops' conferences to issue pastoral letters. Henceforth, bishops' conferences may issue pastoral letters involving doctrinal declarations only after a unanimous vote of the members of the conference or after the letter has received the *recognitio,* or endorsement, of the Holy See. This restriction on the freedom of bishops' conferences to issue pastoral letters can be expected to weaken the ability of such conferences to teach collegially.

Bibliography: John Paul II, "Apostolic Letter *Apostolos suos,* May 21, 1998," *AAS* 90 (1998) 641-58; Eng. trans.,

"The Theological and Juridical Nature of Episcopal Conferences," *Origins* 28/9 (July 30, 1998) 152-58 • G. K. Malone, "Pastoral Letters," *NCE* (1st ed.) 10.1077-78.

John P. Beal and Reinhold Sebott

Pastoral Psychology

Pastoral psychology may be described as a discipline that seeks to integrate religious beliefs and the practices of → ministry with psychological methods and insight regarding the human condition. Historically, the church has utilized available contemporary knowledge about the nature of human experience as a key source for practical ministry in community. For example, Arnobius of Sicca (3d-4th cent.) integrated ancient views of human nature with a theological understanding of faithful practice. Ambrose (ca. 339-97) described human relationships in his attempt to educate church leaders in practical methods of care for the poor. Gregory I (ca. 540-604) outlined specific ministry guidelines for parish → priests. Martin Luther (1483-1546) and Richard Baxter (1615-91) incorporated behavioral and theological insights in their sermons and pastoral letters. René Descartes (1596-1650) began to use insights from psychology to inform pastoral guidance in the care of souls.

By the beginning of the 20th century, → psychology and → psychiatry had become significant clinical disciplines for treating mental and behavioral disorders. During the first half of the century the training and supervision of ministers (particularly those who would specialize in → counseling and chaplaincy contexts) tended to be focused and evaluated within a psychological framework. Theological insights and perspectives often received little or even disparaging attention. By the 1950s an "antagonistic dissonance" had thus developed between those who interpreted their primary ministerial identity and practice within psychological models and those who understood their vocational praxis from a theological perspective. For some, the essential integrative lens was psychology; for others, it was → theology. One result of this tension was the desire to address growing differences and ambiguity with a more intentional and dialogic approach.

Around the middle of the 20th century the personal experience of Anton Boisen (1876-1965) as a psychiatric patient resulted in his more intentional study of the significance of emotional crises as opportunities both for religious growth and for the training of → pastors. This time period also witnessed the emergence of specific graduate-level training programs in pastoral psychology and pastoral-care psychology at Boston University School of Theology, Garrett Theological Seminary (Evanston, Ill.), and Southern Baptist Theological Seminary (Louisville, Ky.).

Another example of renewed integrative dialogue between ministry and psychology during the mid-20th century was the development of journals intended for professionals in the field. *Pastoral Psychology* (1950-2003) presented articles related to the methods of practical ministry. The *Journal of Psychology and Theology* (1973-) provides a forum for the sharing of integrative research. This renewed dialogue has led to the emergence of many additional courses in seminaries and graduate schools of theology.

Research methods and pastoral training models have developed in areas such as human development (Evelyn and James Whitehead, Paul Johnson), → grief work (Granger Westberg), mental illness (Kenneth Pargament et al., Stewart Govig), crisis intervention (David Switzer), global awareness (Larry Graham), pastoral diagnosis (Paul Pruyser, Nancy Ramsey), vocational assessment (Isabel Myers), → group dynamics (John Casteel), → family relationships (Edwin Friedman), and pastoral → counseling (Howard Clinebell Jr.).

Pastoral psychology continues to provide ministry practitioners with psychological methods and insights into human experience without usurping the distinct language, presuppositions, and framework that are at the center of religious faith. Pastoral psychology remains an integrative discipline for both research and the practice of ministry.

Bibliography: A. T. Boisen, *The Exploration of the Inner World: A Study of Mental Disorder and Religious Experience* (New York, 1936); idem, *Religion in Crisis and Custom: A Sociological and Psychological Study* (New York, 1955) • J. L. Casteel, ed., *The Creative Role of Interpersonal Groups in the Church Today* (New York, 1968) • H. J. Clinebell Jr., *Basic Types of Pastoral Care and Counseling: Resources for the Ministry of Healing and Growth* (Nashville, 1984) • E. H. Friedman, *Generation to Generation: Family Process in Church and Synagogue* (New York, 1985) • B. W. Gilbert, *The Pastoral Care of Depression: A Guidebook* (New York, 1998) • S. D. Govig, *In the Shadow of Our Steeples: Pastoral Presence for Families Coping with Mental Illness* (New York, 1999) • L. K. Graham, *Care of Persons, Care of Worlds: A Psychosystems Approach to Pastoral Care and Counseling* (Nashville, 1992) • G. L. Harbaugh, *Pastor as Person* (Minneapolis, 1984) • P. E. Johnson, *Psychol-*

ogy of Pastoral Care (Nashville, 1953) • I. B. Myers, with P. B. Myers, *Gifts Differing: Understanding Personality Type* (Palo Alto, Calif., 1995) • T. C. Oden, *Crisis Ministries* (New York, 1986) • K. I. Pargament, K. I. Maton, and R. E. Hess, eds., *Religion and Prevention in Mental Health: Research, Vision, and Action* (New York, 1992) • P. W. Pruyser, *The Minister as Diagnostician: Personal Problems in Pastoral Perspective* (Philadelphia, 1976) • N. J. Ramsey, *Pastoral Diagnosis: A Resource for Ministries of Care and Counseling* (Minneapolis, 1998) • D. C. Rogers, *Pastoral Care for Post-traumatic Stress Disorder: Healing the Shattered Soul* (New York, 2002) • D. K. Switzer, *The Minister as Crisis Counselor* (rev. ed.; Nashville, 1986) • G. E. Westberg, *Good Grief: A Constructive Approach to the Problem of Loss* (Minneapolis, 1997; orig. pub., 1962) • E. E. Whitehead and J. D. Whitehead, *Christian Life Patterns: The Psychological Challenges and Religious Invitations of Adult Life* (rev. ed.; New York, 1992).

Tony S. Everett

Pastoral Theology

1. Protestant Tradition
   1.1. Term
   1.2. Classical Period
   1.3. Modern Period
   1.4. Twentieth Century
      1.4.1. Broadening Focus
      1.4.2. Narrowing Focus
      1.4.3. Four Frameworks
   1.5. Contemporary Developments and Debates
2. Roman Catholic Tradition
   2.1. Term
   2.2. Modern Period to Vatican II
   2.3. After Vatican II

1. Protestant Tradition

1.1. *Term*

The phrase "pastoral theology" is imprecise; no single definition is universally accepted, particularly in Protestant traditions. Currently, it is understood principally in three related ways, but with different emphases: (1) a theology and practice of → pastoral care and → counseling; (2) an approach to → theology concerned with relating Christian faith claims to the broader world, giving particular attention to methods of pastoral reflection and practice; and (3) an academic discipline within theological education that attends to the foci cited in (1) and (2).

1.2. *Classical Period*

Taken from Lat. *pastoralis,* "of the shepherd," pastoral theology originally described the theology of Christian ministry broadly conceived and designated the work → pastors did in ministry. In this sense, all → clergy were pastoral theologians, and their practices were pastoral theology. In the late sixth century, sensing a need to guide pastoral practices in a more systematic way, Gregory the Great (ca. 540-604) published *Liber regulae pastoralis* (Book of pastoral rule, ca. 591). This ministry "manual," often translated into English as *Pastoral Care,* was similar in kind to an earlier tract by John Chrysostom (ca. 347-407) entitled *On the Priesthood* (368), which was concerned with guiding clergy in the "care of souls." Gregory's work gave rise to a body of literature *(pastoralia)* that increasingly became normative for clergy instruction and development.

The influence and use of this literature lasted through the medieval period and into the Protestant → Reformation, the latter marked by such classic works as Martin Bucer's (1491-1551) *On the True Cure of Souls* (1538) and Richard Baxter's (1615-91) *The Reformed Pastor* (1656). Some traditions continued using this literature even into the early 20th century. Along with naming the tasks and practices of ordained ministry, this body of literature (often designated "pastoral theology") offered principles and guidelines for ordained ministry and was concerned fundamentally with the personal and vocational formation and training of clergy. These understandings reigned until the → Enlightenment, when even more systematic and formal training of clergy increasingly became the norm and theological education began fragmenting into various areas of specialized study.

1.3. *Modern Period*

Specialization followed the rise and influence of the modern research → university in 16th-century Europe and was furthered in Protestant theological education by the efforts of Friedrich Schleiermacher (1768-1834) and his student Carl Immanuel Nitzsch (1787-1868) in early- to mid-19th-century Germany. The research university itself was becoming increasingly specialized. Attempting to secure theology's place in the university, these two men sought to "professionalize" theological education. They argued that like law and medicine, → theological education furthered the common good. Hence, like lawyers and physicians, clergy had to be trained in a specific knowledge base and set of skills, namely, those required for the leadership and practices of ministry. That training is what pastoral theology traditionally provided.

Pastoral theology thus came to describe both the education for, and practice of, clerical leadership and its tasks in a manner more formal, regularized, and "scientific" than ministry manuals alone could provide, though the manuals continued to be utilized. The tasks garnering the attention of pastoral theology included pastoral care (poimenics), instruction in the faith (→ catechesis), applying moral principles to life experiences (→ casuistry), and, in some circles, → preaching (homiletics), though Protestants typically treated preaching separately. Pastoral theology aimed to prepare the minister for attending to the four ancient pastoral functions required for "the cure of souls," namely, healing, sustaining, guiding, and reconciling (W. A. Clebsch and C. R. Jaekle, 32-66).

Rather than being scholarly or intellectual in its focus, however, pastoral theology was explicitly practice-oriented. It was grounded in the application to pastoral experience of various rules and techniques derived largely from more abstract theological principles and honed by experienced clergy. Hence, pastoral theology was applied systematic or dogmatic theology. In keeping with classical understandings, it often took the form of hints and directions for how clergy should carry out their duties in various situations, all the while guided by the doctrinal standards of the Christian faith and by the wisdom provided in the literature (i.e., the manuals) of pastoral theology.

Because of the influences of Schleiermacher and Nitzsch, by the mid-19th century some began to describe pastoral theology as a component of "practical" theology, which, along with "philosophical" and "historical" theology, named the primary areas or disciplines within theological education or what came to be called the theological encyclopedia. While Schleiermacher's and Nitzsch's influence was strong, → practical theology, like pastoral theology, came to have varied meanings; the former typically included the study of → ethics, along with many of the functions and tasks of pastoral leadership cited previously.

Some see Schleiermacher as having perpetuated the view that practical theology (including its component, pastoral theology) was reducible to applied principles and techniques of ministry, what Edward Farley has termed the "clerical paradigm," and also that Nitzsch made an attempt to correct this way of thinking. A close reading of Schleiermacher, however, reveals that he, like Nitzsch, resisted the notion of practical theology as being concerned simply with techniques or technical knowledge. Both men, in fact, claimed that practical theology was an autonomous theological discipline involving the acquisition and use of the minister's own "inner constitution," or *habitus,* "the truth and purity of a Christian disposition" (Schleiermacher, *Christian Caring,* 114), "rules of art," as opposed to "legalistic directives" (Schleiermacher, *Outline of Theology,* 25, 135). They claimed also that practical theology required "a convergence of all theoretical knowledge of Christianity that is becoming a church in order to establish a methodological consciousness for official practice" (Nitzsch, 34).

Hence, though Schleiermacher's legacy is the clerical paradigm, as Farley suggests, this is not what Schleiermacher himself envisioned and desired. He and Nitzsch sought to ground how pastors conceptualized their work in ministry, what that work entailed, and how it should be carried out in a manner more methodologically rich and intentional than in the classical understandings. Even so, this notion of pastoral theology as a part of practical theology, and as concerned merely with the training of clergy in the applied principles and techniques of ministry, prevailed in both Europe and North America until the early 20th century.

1.4. *Twentieth Century*

1.4.1. *Broadening Focus*

Throughout much of the 20th century, European thinking largely continued to follow the clerical paradigm, often substituting the term "pastoral studies" to denote a focus on the training of, and skills for, pastoral ministry and appealing largely to the principal of applied theology to describe pastoral theological method. In Great Britain and North America, however, and within a comparatively small group in continental Europe, by the mid-20th century pastoral theology tended to be viewed differently: more broadly in some ways, and more narrowly in others.

In the North American context, chiefly because of the influence of Anton T. Boisen (1876-1965), his student, Seward Hiltner (1909-84), and Wayne E. Oates (1917-99) and David E. Roberts (1911-55), it broadened to include critical reflection on both theory and practice. No longer was pastoral theology conceived simply as applied dogmatic or → systematic theology (theory) on the one hand, or merely as technical proficiency in ministry skills and wisdom (practice) on the other. Pastoral theology now gave much greater significance to the concrete lived experiences brought to pastors and, in Boisen's case, to chaplains and those serving in institutional ministries by persons with problems, conflicts, struggles, and needs.

Consistent with Schleiermacher's and Nitzsch's visions for practical theology a century earlier, pastoral theology came to include knowledge and perspectives gleaned from theory and practice brought together in an ongoing mutual, critical, dialectical, correlational, and hermeneutical relationship. The result was that while theological theory and doctrine may guide and shape pastoral practice and thus pastoral theology, as classical views held, critical reflection upon practice, including the uniqueness of concrete experience, is expected to play a central role in guiding and shaping theory and doctrine. Giving particular attention to pastoral encounters with human needs as the basis for discerning the relationship between the Christian faith and lived experience, pastoral theology in the mid-20th century drew increasingly on resources provided by → psychology, → psychotherapy and related clinical perspectives, other human sciences (esp. → anthropology [§§4-5], → sociology, and → critical theory), and hermeneutics. Pastoral theology appropriated critically the various perspectives offered by these disciplines in an attempt to "draw conclusions of a theological order from reflection on these observations" (Hiltner, 20).

1.4.2. *Narrowing Focus*

Simultaneously, however, especially in North America, pastoral theology channeled its broadened critical reflections more narrowly — almost entirely toward pastoral care and counseling. Pastoral theology also became more or less exclusively tied to Protestant → liberalism and its principal tenets, and it was influenced especially by the work of theologian Paul Tillich (1886-1965). Moreover, moving away from its classical focus on the concerns and practices of ministry more broadly conceived, pastoral theology tended by the mid-20th century to limit its concerns to experiences like bereavement, difficulties in relationships, crisis intervention and addictions; to understandings and concerns of identity development, personality, and personhood; and to clinical conditions like → depression and → anxiety.

The primary focus of pastoral theology thus became the individual → person, those in closest relationship to the individual, and eventually to the various systems, environments, or contexts in which the individual lived and related. Particularly influential figures in the second half of the 20th century in North America who represent the diverse understandings of, approaches to, and foci within, pastoral theology include Don S. Browning, Donald Capps, Howard Clinebell, James E. Dittes, Andrew D. Lester, Nancy J. Ramsay, Carroll Saussy, Charles W. Taylor, and Edward P. Wimberly; outside North America, we can mention Paul Ballard, Alastair Campbell, and Edward Thurneysen.

1.4.3. *Four Frameworks*

Various movements and disciplines closely related to, and often in conversation with, pastoral theology were either born or became more organized during this same period. Each tended, in various ways, to utilize theological and human scientific perspectives or conceptual frameworks for the concerns and tasks of pastoral care and counseling. Four are particularly noteworthy.

The first was *personalist care and counseling,* which grew out of philosophical personalism, as embraced especially by professors and students at Boston University. It is represented by Paul E. Johnson and Carroll Wise. It held that the individual person is the primary ontological category and unit of care, which includes the various components and constituents of personality, as well as the person's experiences, struggles, and needs. Wise in particular argued for human experience as the locus of theological experience, meaning that theological reflection must necessarily arise out of life as it is lived.

The second was *clinical theology,* a predominantly British phenomenon represented by Robert Lambourne and Frank Lake. The latter believed that care and counseling are necessarily "Christocentric," meaning that the adult → Jesus is the paradigm both of authentic personhood and of ideal pastoral care. As the pastoral caregiver or counselor engages in the process of correlating various understandings offered by faith, on the one hand, and, on the other, psychology and → psychiatry, faith and its precepts remain foundational and thus are the ultimate guide to, and shaper of, care and counseling.

The third was → *psychology of religion,* which remains a vital discipline, even though it is often disregarded by theological, religious studies, and the majority of psychology faculties because of its interdisciplinary methods and its largely critical stance toward both religion and psychology. That is, in applying the theories and methods of psychology, which tends to devalue the role of religion in human experience, precisely to the study of religion and theological beliefs, the psychology of religion simultaneously belongs to, and exists apart from, the established fields of religion, theology, and psychology. Influential representatives include Capps, Dittes, Diane Jonte-Pace, Paul Pruyser, Ann Belford Ulanov, and a Jesuit, W. W. Meissner.

The fourth, which also remains a vital movement, is → *Clinical Pastoral Education* (CPE). This approach began with Boisen's vision in 1925 and continues to focus on training pastoral caregivers by means of placing them in actual ministry situations in hospitals, prisons, and mental health clinics and having them reflect with peers and supervisors on their experiences. Particularly important is the development of critical self-awareness, along with a deepening understanding of the caring process itself. The CPE movement has been represented by Richard C. Cabot (also a pioneer in medical social work), Russell Dicks, and, more recently, Charles E. Hall Jr. and Charles V. Gerkin.

This narrowing of the focus of pastoral theology on pastoral care and counseling, including its related movements and disciplines, paralleled the pattern of increased specialization among theological disciplines that began in the 19th century, though the end result was quite different.

1.5. *Contemporary Developments and Debates*
Contemporary pastoral theology continues to be viewed primarily as the theology and practice of pastoral care and counseling, is still informed largely by Protestant liberalism, and is still centered chiefly on both "person-in-environment" transactions and a concern for concrete and contextual experience. Particularly influential figures, also diverse in their understandings of, approaches to, and foci within, pastoral theology, include some mentioned previously, as well as David W. Augsburger, Carrie Doehring, Robert C. Dykstra, Nancy J. Gorsuch, and Howard W. Stone; and outside North America, Riet Bons-Storm, Philip Culbertson, Valerie M. DeMarinis, Elaine Graham, and Stephen Pattison.

Contemporary pastoral theology, however, has broadened in at least two additional ways. First, because of the influences of Marxist, feminist, and liberationist thought, as well as critical social theories, some now conceive of pastoral theology as necessarily attending to more "public" concerns. These include the effects that various forms of abuse, oppression, and injustice have on both individual and corporate well-being. Continuing to bring the perspectives of theology and the human sciences into critical relationship through various methods of correlation and hermeneutics, pastoral theology thus envisioned draws heavily on the concept of praxis to underscore the view that once the insights of theory and practice in critical relationship are discovered, one must intentionally take action to enhance the public good in light of those insights. Pastoral theologians Pamela D. Couture, James Newton Poling, Christie Cozad Neuger, Bonnie J. Miller-McLemore, and Larry Kent Graham are representative of those increasingly interested in how pastoral theological reflection more broadly conceived, pastoral ministry, constructive theology, and particularly pastoral care and counseling are both influenced by and may influence not only the private or individual realms of daily life but also the ecclesial and political sectors in ways consistent with Christian precepts.

A second broadening, which is actually a move to reclaim the classical grounding of pastoral theology in theological principles and reflection, is also taking place. Central to this effort is the goal of reducing the predominant role the human sciences and cognate disciplines have had in shaping both the theories and methods of pastoral theology, so that pastoral theology is guided principally by theological precepts and perspectives that shape pastoral reflection and practice with respect to pastoral care and counseling and beyond. This current focus within pastoral theology is represented by yet another diverse group, including Deborah van Deusen Hunsinger and Daniel S. Schipani, who are influenced chiefly by neoorthodox and postliberal theologies, especially by Karl Barth; Andrew Purves, who is guided by both patristic emphases and Reformed orthodoxy; Michael Jinkins, who also works from Barthian and classically Reformed perspectives, and whose approach focuses largely on pastoral leadership and ecclesiology, thus demonstrating kinship with British understandings of pastoral theology; and Leonard M. Hummel, whose work is grounded particularly in Lutheran thought. Still a comparatively small movement, it has a growing set of voices, whose final impact on pastoral theology remains to be seen.

2. Roman Catholic Tradition

2.1. *Term*
Since → Vatican II the terms "pastoral theology" and "practical theology" have been used almost interchangeably by Roman Catholics. Strictly speaking, pastoral theology is an area or focus within the larger academic discipline of practical theology and attends to what is classically called poimenics, or pastoral care. Pastoral theology, however, is more commonly conceived in broader terms, denoting what poimenics along with all the branches of practical theology (catechetics, or → religious education, plus → moral theology and → social ethics, → liturgics, → missiology, and → canon law) seek to provide. According to Karl Rahner, the objective is engaging in theological reflection in order to discern how, in light of both the nature of the → church and concrete contextual circumstances, the church (clergy and laypersons) should engage in ministry, both within and beyond its walls.

2.2. *Modern Period to Vatican II*
From the late 18th century until the end of Vatican II in 1965, Catholic views of pastoral theology largely paralleled what has been described above as

occurring in Protestantism during the same era. That is, pastoral theology was concerned with the formal training and practices of → clergy and drew heavily on the guidance of *pastoralia,* as well as the collective wisdom and experiences of seasoned clergy within the tradition. Pastoral theology gave attention to poimenics, catechetics (esp. for children and converts), and casuistry, or applying moral and ethical principles to life situations — all of which matched the approach taken by Protestants. Also included, however, were training in the administration of the seven sacramental rites and numerous liturgies, canon law, and the overseeing of various transactions of parish life.

As was true in Protestantism, so pastoral theology in Roman Catholicism came to be seen essentially as applied theology, often taking the shape of directions for employing techniques of the practice of ministry derived from dogmatic precepts. Similarly, pastoral theology was focused exclusively on the ordained priesthood, provided little if any place for the participation of laypersons in the church's ministries, and fostered a restricted existence that attended more to parish membership and maintenance than to a mission to provide for broader and more public needs and concerns (R. A. Duffy).

2.3. *After Vatican II*

Pastoral theology broadened with the reforms of Vatican II to include what Rahner describes as "a theology of the Church in action and of action in the Church" (Rahner, 25). This change has produced several new foci and emphases. First, pastoral theology is no longer merely applied → dogmatics or technical knowledge but is praxis, the careful scrutiny of dogmatic precepts (theory) in light of concrete, real-life situations. While God is revealed in the church's doctrines and traditions, so too is God revealed in occasions of tangible ministry taking place in a myriad of contextualized settings both in the church and in the world. Pastoral theology thus seeks to understand as richly as possible the current state of affairs and contexts in which the church lives (what Rahner calls an ecclesial *existentiell*) for the purpose of discerning how the church must actualize itself in the world. In other words, pastoral theology involves reflection on praxis, which then shapes other types of theological reflection, namely fundamental and dogmatic theology. Both Latin American liberationist thinking, especially that of Gustavo Gutiérrez, Clodovis Boff, and Juan L. Segundo (→ Liberation Theology), and European → political theologies, particularly the work of Johann Baptist Metz, have informed and shaped this change in perspective.

Second, and related, increased attention has been given to the more public, ecumenical, and even transforming nature of the Christian faith and thus of pastoral theology. In North America David Tracy has been among the more influential proponents of this view.

Third, given the expanded place for the laity in Catholic thinking, no longer is pastoral theology solely the purview of the priesthood. Laypersons too are called to identify and utilize their own gifts for ministry and to contribute to the reflection and action of pastoral theology.

Fourth, given its focus on praxis, pastoral theology has enlarged the role of human scientific knowledge and resources in the theological enterprise. Appealing to methods of correlation, various hermeneutical relationships, and the methods of various critical theories, pastoral theology has become truly interdisciplinary, though typically a final appeal is made to how the findings of pastoral theology may be shaped by the perspectives and teachings of Roman Catholic tradition. Here too, David Tracy has been among the more influential voices, as have Thomas H. Groome, Dennis P. McCann, and Matthew Lamb in North America, and Johannes A. van der Ven in Europe and South Africa.

Though there has been a rapprochement between Protestant and Catholic understandings of pastoral (practical) theology, with respect to pastoral theology in the more narrow sense (i.e., as pastoral care), at least two Catholic emphases remain. One is the communal context of both thinking about and offering pastoral care; that is, the larger ecclesial community remains the locus of care, as opposed to a more "professionalized" setting like a counseling center. Second, care is still closely tied to the rituals and liturgies of Roman Catholic life and worship (→ Roman Catholic Church).

Bibliography: On 1.3: W. A. Clebsch and C. R. Jaekle, *Pastoral Care in Historical Perspective* (New York, 1964) • E. Farley, *Practicing Gospel: Unconventional Thoughts on the Church's Ministry* (Louisville, Ky., 2003); idem, *Theologia: The Fragmentation and Unity of Theological Education* (Minneapolis, 1983) • C. I. Nitzsch, *Praktische Theologie* (vol. 1; Bonn, 1847) • F. Schleiermacher, *Brief Outline of Theology as a Field of Study* (eds. of 1811 and 1830; Lewiston, N.Y., 1990); idem, *Christian Caring: Selections from Practical Theology* (Philadelphia, 1988).

On 1.4: P. Ballard, *Practical Theology in Action: Christian Thinking in the Service of Church and Society* (London, 1996) • P. Ballard, ed., *The Foundation of Pastoral Studies and Practical Theology* (Cardiff, 1986) •

A. T. Boisen, *The Exploration of the Inner World: A Study of Mental Disorder and Religious Experience* (New York, 1936) • D. S. Browning, *A Fundamental Practical Theology: Descriptive and Strategic Proposals* (Minneapolis, 1996); idem, *Religious Thought and the Modern Psychologies* (2d ed.; Minneapolis, 2004) • A. Campbell, *Rediscovering Pastoral Care* (2d ed.; London, 1987) • D. Capps, *Biblical Approaches to Pastoral Counseling* (Philadelphia, 1981); idem, *Living Stories: Pastoral Counseling in Congregational Context* (Minneapolis, 1998); idem, *Men, Religion, and Melancholia* (New Haven, 1997); idem, *Reframing: A New Method in Pastoral Care* (Minneapolis, 1990) • H. Clinebell, *Basic Types of Pastoral Care and Counseling: Resources for the Ministry of Healing and Growth* (rev. ed.; Nashville, 1984) • J. E. Dittes, *Driven by Hope: Men and Meaning* (Louisville, Ky., 1996); idem, *Pastoral Counseling: The Basics* (Louisville, Ky., 1999) • C. V. Gerkin, *The Living Human Document* (Nashville, 1984) • S. Hiltner, *Preface to Pastoral Theology* (Nashville, 1958) • P. E. Johnson, *Person and Counselor* (Nashville, 1967) • D. Jonte-Pace and W. B. Parsons, eds., *Religion and Psychology: Mapping the Terrain* (London, 2001) • F. Lake, *Clinical Theology* (London, 1966) • R. A. Lambourne, *Community, Church, and Healing* (London, 1963) • A. D. Lester, *Hope in Pastoral Care and Counseling* (Louisville, Ky., 1995) • W. W. Meissner, *Psychoanalysis and Religious Experience* (New Haven, 1984) • W. E. Oates, *The Christian Pastor* (3d ed.; Philadelphia, 1982); idem, *Pastoral Counseling* (Philadelphia, 1974) • P. W. Pruyser, *The Minister as Diagnostician* (Philadelphia, 1976) • N. J. Ramsay, ed., *Pastoral Care and Counseling: Redefining the Paradigms* (Nashville, 2004) • D. E. Roberts, *Psychotherapy and a Christian View of Man* (New York, 1950) • C. Saussy, *God Images and Self Esteem: Empowering Women in a Patriarchal Society* (Louisville, Ky., 1991) • C. W. Taylor, *The Skilled Pastor: Counseling as the Practice of Theology* (Minneapolis, 1991) • E. Thurneysen, *A Theology of Pastoral Care* (Richmond, Va., 1962) • A. B. Ulanov, *The Functioning Transcendent: A Study in Analytical Psychology* (Wilmette, Ill., 1996) • E. P. Wimberly, *Using Scripture in Pastoral Counseling* (Nashville, 1994) • C. A. Wise, *Pastoral Counseling* (New York, 1951).

On 1.5: D. W. Augsburger, *Hate-Work: Working through the Pain and Pleasures of Hate* (Louisville, Ky., 2004); idem, *Pastoral Counseling across Cultures* (Louisville, Ky., 1986) • R. Bons-Storm, *The Incredible Woman* (Nashville, 1996) • P. D. Couture, *Seeing Children, Seeing God: A Practical Theology of Children and Poverty* (Nashville, 2000) • P. L. Culbertson, *Caring for God's People* (Minneapolis, 2000) • V. M. DeMarinis, *Critical Caring: A Feminist Model for Pastoral Psychology* (Louisville, Ky., 1993) • C. Doehring, *Taking Care: Monitoring Power Dynamics and Relational Boundaries in Pastoral Care and Counseling* (Nashville, 1995) • R. C. Dykstra, *Counseling Troubled Youth* (Louisville, Ky., 1997); idem, *Discovering a Sermon: Personal Pastoral Preaching* (St. Louis, 2001) • N. J. Gorsuch, *Feminist Pastoral Care and Counseling* (Cleveland, 2001) • E. L. Graham, *Transforming Practice: Pastoral Theology in an Age of Uncertainty* (London, 1996) • L. K. Graham, *Care of Persons, Care of Worlds: A Psychosystems Approach to Pastoral Care and Counseling* (Nashville, 1992) • L. M. Hummell, *Clothed in Nothingness: Consolation for Suffering* (Minneapolis, 2003) • D. v. D. Hunsinger, *Theology and Pastoral Counseling: A New Interdisciplinary Approach* (Grand Rapids, 1995) • M. Jinkins, *Transformational Ministry: Church Leadership and the Way of the Cross* (Edinburgh, 2002) • M. Jinkins and D. B. Jinkins, *Power and Change in Parish Ministry: Reflections on the Cure of Souls* (Herndon, Va., 1991) • B. J. Miller-McLemore and B. Gill-Austern, *Feminist and Womanist Pastoral Theology* (Nashville, 1999) • C. C. Neuger, *Counseling Women* (Minneapolis, 2001) • J. N. Poling, *The Abuse of Power: A Theological Problem* (Nashville, 1991) • A. Purves, *Pastoral Theology in the Classical Tradition* (Louisville, Ky., 2001); idem, *Reconstructing Pastoral Theology: Christological Foundation* (Louisville, Ky., 2004) • N. J. Ramsay, *Pastoral Diagnosis: A Resource for Ministries of Care and Counseling* (Minneapolis, 1998) • D. S. Schipani, *The Way of Wisdom in Pastoral Counseling* (Elkhart, Ind., 2003) • H. W. Stone, *Brief Pastoral Counseling* (Minneapolis, 1994).

On 2: C. Boff, *Theology and Praxis: Epistemological Foundations* (Maryknoll, N.Y., 1987) • R. A. Duffy, *A Roman Catholic Theology of Pastoral Care* (Minneapolis, 1983) • R. D. Duggan, "Pastoral Care from a Roman Catholic Perspective," *Catholic Identity* (ed. J. H. Provost and K. Walf; Maryknoll, N.Y., 1994) 100-105 • G. R. Evans, ed., *A History of Pastoral Care* (London, 2000) • T. H. Groome, *Sharing Faith: A Comprehensive Approach to Religious Education and Pastoral Ministry* (New York, 1991) • G. Gutiérrez, *A Theology of Liberation* (rev. ed.; Maryknoll, N.Y., 1988; orig. pub., 1973) • R. L. Kinast, "How Pastoral Theology Functions," *TToday* 37 (1981) 425-38; idem, "Pastoral Theology–Roman Catholic," *DPCC* 873-74 • M. Lamb, *Solidarity with Victims: Toward a Theology of Social Transformation* (New York, 1982) • D. McCann and C. R. Strain, *Polity and Praxis: A Program for American Practical Theology* (Minneapolis, 1985) • J. B. Metz, *Faith in History and Society: Toward a Practical Fundamental Theology* (New York, 1980) • M. L. Poorman, *Interactional Morality: A Foundation for Moral Discernment in Catholic Pastoral Ministry* (Washington, D.C., 1993) • K. Rahner, *Theology of Pastoral Action* (New York,

1968) • J. L. SEGUNDO, *The Hidden Motives of Pastoral Action: Latin American Reflections* (Maryknoll, N.Y., 1978) • D. TRACY, *Blessed Rage for Order: The New Pluralism in Theology* (Chicago, 1996; orig. pub., 1975); idem, "The Foundations of Practical Theology," *Practical Theology: The Emerging Field in Theology, Church, and World* (ed. D. Browning; New York, 1983) 61-82 • J. A. VAN DER VEN, *Practical Theology: An Empirical Approach* (Kampen, 1993).

ALLAN HUGH COLE JR.

Patriarch, Patriarchate

1. Biblical Usage
2. Jewish History
3. Orthodox Church
4. Nestorian and Oriental Orthodox Churches
5. Roman Catholic Church
6. Eastern Catholic Churches
7. Czechoslovak Hussite Church

1. Biblical Usage

The LXX coined the Gk. word *patriarchēs*, which derives from *patria* (family, tribe). In the OT it may be used for any group leaders, but in the NT it refers specifically to → Abraham (Heb. 7:4), the 12 sons of → Jacob (Acts 7:8-9), and → David (2:29).

2. Jewish History

From the third century to the fifth, the *nasi* (prince), the head of the Tiberias Sanhedrin, was called *patriarchēs* in Greek documents. The office, which was a hereditary one in the family of the editor of the → Mishnah, Judah ha-Nasi (d. ca. 220), lasted until after 415 and was recognized and supported by the central Roman government as one of leadership for the Jewish people both within and outside → Palestine.

3. Orthodox Church

In the early days of the Christian → church, any → bishop (→ Ministry, Ministerial Offices) might be given the honorary title "patriarch" (→ Early Church), but from the middle of the fifth century, after the ending of the Jewish patriarchate, Greek usage reserved the title as a fixed hierarchical one for the bishops of the most important metropolitan churches, initially → Rome, → Alexandria, and → Antioch (Council of → Nicaea, can. 6; → Niceno-Constantinopolian Creed). Then Constantinople came to be ranked second (Council of → Chalcedon, can. 28; → Byzantium) and → Jerusalem fifth (→ Pentarchy).

In the high and late → Middle Ages, the chief bishops of Bulgaria (from the 10th cent. till 1118 and 1235-1393) and Serbia (1346-1459) adopted the title when their secular rulers were bold enough to call themselves czars with more or less clear claims to the imperial throne. An enhanced self-awareness also led to the adoption of the title by Georgian → catholicoses after 1012.

In spite of the loss of Serbian independence, the archbishops of Peć could still call themselves patriarchs between 1557 and 1766 through the good offices of the Turkish vizier Mehmed Paşa Sokollu (1505-79), who was of Serbian origin. Under the Hapsburgs the Serbian metropolitan of Sremski Karlovci also took the title from 1848 to 1913 by imperial decree.

In contrast, the establishment of the Moscow Patriarchate in 1589 by Ecumenical Patriarch Jeremias II Tranos (1572-79, 1580-84, 1587-95) was confirmed by two synods of the Orthodox patriarchs in Constantinople (1590 and 1593), which gave the new colleague, not the third place in the hierarchy of patriarchates that was sought, but the fifth place. Czar Peter the Great (1682-1725) left the office of patriarch unoccupied after 1700 and then in 1721 abolished it in favor of synodical government for the church (→ Synod). Only after the fall of the monarchy in 1917 could the Moscow Patriarchate be reestablished (→ Russian Orthodox Church).

As a result of Balkan restructuring in the 20th century, three new patriarchates were set up: in Serbia (1920), Romania (1925), and Bulgaria (1953).

4. Nestorian and Oriental Orthodox Churches

The → Nestorian church and the → Oriental Orthodox churches, which arose from the Christological controversies of the 5th century and did not accept the councils of → Ephesus (431) or Chalcedon (451), also use the title "patriarch." The → Coptic Orthodox Church and the → Syrian Orthodox Church use the title as heirs of the traditions of Alexandria and Antioch. The → Ethiopian Orthodox Church also adopted the title in 1959 when it achieved complete hierarchical independence from the Copts, as did the Eritrean Orthodox Church in 1998 when it became independent from the Ethiopian church. In the → Armenian Apostolic Church the bishops of Jerusalem and Constantinople have been called patriarchs since 1311 and 1461. The catholicoses of Echmiadzin and Cilicia rank higher; the former, as head of the whole church, combines both titles. From the 16th century onward, the heads of the non-Ephesian Nestorian church (also known as the Assyrian Church of the East or the East Syrian Church) have also combined the titles.

5. Roman Catholic Church

In the → Roman Catholic Church the title "patriarch" has never had any real significance. With the developing claim of the papacy to headship of the whole church, the original title "patriarch of the West" lost any authentic function, and in any case there could be no other real patriarchates in the sphere of Latin culture. Only the bishop of Aquileia traditionally held the title, though having in fact no more than metropolitan status. The ancient privilege of Aquileia was vested in the bishop of Grado up to 1751 and still lives on in the bishop of Venice.

When Isidore Mercator, the pseudonymous author of the ninth-century → False Decretals, sought to protect simple bishops against the powers of their metropolitans, he resorted to the stratagem of inventing the office of patriarchs or primates (Ps.-Anacletus, *PL* 130.73-76). But he had less success in this regard than with his emphasizing of central papal authority. The fiction did lead, however, to the setting up of primates and to the plan of Archbishop Adalbert of Bremen-Hamburg (1043-72) for a patriarch of the north.

More important than this development, however, was the influence of Western policies relative to the Eastern patriarchates, for the decretals taught the West to view patriarchs merely as ecclesiastical authorities midway between metropolitans and the → pope. The conquests made by the Crusaders (→ Crusades) made it possible to put this idea into practice as the invaders ousted the Orthodox patriarchs of Antioch in 1098, Jerusalem in 1099, and Constantinople in 1204. The Latin patriarchates that replaced them lasted only as long as the crusading states did. Afterward they were only titular, as the Latin patriarch of Alexandria had been from the very first (1219).

The Patriarchate of Jerusalem was revived in 1847 when the Holy City received a resident Roman Catholic bishop of the Latin Rite. Paul VI (1963-78) abolished the other three in 1964, along with the Patriarchate of the West Indies (i.e., of Spanish America), which from 1524 had been a purely titular one occupied mainly by the chief chaplain of the Spanish army.

The bishop of Lisbon took the title of patriarch in 1716 and still holds it, as does, since 1886, the archbishop of Goa and Daman, who is also patriarch of the East Indies. In the Roman Catholic Church of the Latin Rite, however, the title carries no real legal rights (1983 → CIC 438).

6. Eastern Catholic Churches

The situation differs in the Eastern Catholic patriarchates that arose through partial unions of Byzantine or Oriental Orthodox churches with the Roman see (→ Uniate Churches). For example, since 1182 the Maronite Catholic Church has had its own patriarchate within the Antioch tradition, as has the (West) Syrian Catholic Church from 1783. The Melkite Greek Catholic Church, following the Byzantine tradition, has been a patriarchate since 1740; the Coptic Catholic Church, following the Alexandrian tradition, since 1824 (renewed in 1895); and the Chaldean (East Syrian) Catholic Church, following the Chaldean tradition, from 1553, 1667, and 1830. The constitutions of these Uniate churches represent a compromise between autocephalous patriarchates (→ Autocephaly) and universal Roman primacy.

7. Czechoslovak Hussite Church

Nationalist circles in Czech Roman Catholicism had this sort of compromise in view from the end of the 19th century, aiming at a patriarch for their church. Their efforts resulted finally in the setting up of the Czechoslovak Hussite Church as a separate patriarchate in 1920.

→ Councils; Heresies and Schisms; Pan-Orthodox Conferences; United and Uniting Churches

Bibliography: On 1: K. Hutter, "Πατριά," *EDNT* 3.57-58. Also see "Πατριάρχης," ibid., 58.

On 2: L. I. Levine, "The Jewish Patriarch (Nasi) in Third Century Palestine," *ANRW* 2.19.2.649-88; idem, "The Patriarchate and the Ancient Synagogue," *Jews, Christians, and Polytheists in the Ancient Synagogue: Cultural Interaction during the Greco-Roman Period* (ed. S. Fine; New York, 1999) 87-100 • H. Mantel, *Studies in the History of the Sanhedrin* (Cambridge, Mass., 1961) 175-253 • G. Stemberger, *Jews and Christians in the Holy Land: Palestine in the Fourth Century* (Edinburgh, 2000; orig. pub., 1987) 230-68.

On 3 and 4: W. Baum and D. Winkler, *The Apostolic Churches of the East: A History of the Nestorian Church* (New York, 2003) • M. Burgess, *Lords Temporal and Lords Spiritual: A Chronological Checklist of the Popes, Patriarchs, Katholikoi, and Independent Archbishops and Metropolitans of the Autocephalous and Autonomous Monarchical Churches of the Christian East and West* (2d ed.; San Bernardino, Calif., 1995) • D. J. Geanakoplos, *A Short History of the Ecumenical Patriarchate of Constantinople (330-1990): "First among Equals" in the Eastern Orthodox Church* (2d ed.; Brookline, Mass., 1990) • B. Gudziak, *Crisis and Reform: The Kyivan Metropolitanate, the Patriarchate of*

Constantinople, and the Genesis of the Union of Brest (Cambridge, Mass., 1998) • H. Leclercq, "Patriarcat," *DACL* 13.2456-87 • J. Meyendorff, *The Orthodox Church: Its Past and Its Role in the World Today* (3d ed.; Crestwood, N.Y., 1981) • L. J. Patsavos, *Primacy and Conciliarity* (Brookline, Mass., 1995) • V. Pospischil, *Der Patriarch in der Serbisch-Orthodoxen Kirche* (Vienna, 1966) • J. Tawil, *The Patriarchate of Antioch throughout History* (Boston, 2001).

On 5: T. A. Kane, *The Jurisdiction of the Patriarchs of the Major Sees in Antiquity and in the Middle Ages* (Washington, D.C., 1949) • J. J. McGrath, "Patriarchate I: Historical Developments," *NCE* (2d ed.) 10.944-45.

On 6: P. Alappatt, *The Election of the Patriarch in the Eastern Catholic Canonical Tradition: A Historical-Juridical Study* (Rome, 1997) • C. Charon, *History of the Melkite Patriarchates (Alexandria, Antioch, Jerusalem), from the Sixth Century Monophysite Schism until the Present (1910)* (3 vols. in 4; Fairfax, Va., 1998-2001) • W. de Vries, *Rom und die Patriarchate des Ostens* (Freiburg, 1963).

On 7: L. Nemec, *Church and State in Czechoslovakia: Historically, Juridically, and Theologically Documented* (New York, 1955) • R. Urban, *Die Tschechoslowakische Hussitische Kirche* (Marburg, 1973).

Peter Plank

Patriarchal Narrative

1. History of Composition
   1.1. Gunkel
   1.2. Von Rad
   1.3. Challenges to the Hypothesis of Early Sources
   1.4. The Priestly Source
2. Final Form of the Narrative
   2.1. The First Generation: Abraham
   2.2. The Second Generation: Isaac
   2.3. The Third Generation: Jacob
   2.4. The Final Generation: Joseph

The patriarchal narrative (better, "ancestral narrative," since both women and men are thematically important) narrows the account of human interaction with God begun with → creation (→ Primeval History [Genesis 1–11]) to the story of the family of → Abraham and Sarah. At the beginning of the narrative (Gen. 12:1-3, 7), God's → promise to Abraham and Sarah of offspring, a land, protection, and blessings to themselves and to all nations through them establishes the scope of the narrative — a narrowly focused family history ultimately embracing all nations — and raises a crucial anticipation of fulfillment that animates the narrative. The ancestral narratives end with the promises only partially fulfilled with the blessings of the sons of → Jacob in Egypt. A new pharaoh who knows nothing of these ancestors will initiate the next stage in the story.

1. History of Composition

1.1. *Gunkel*

The stories now connected with one another in the ancestral narrative were originally independent legends recounted orally at gatherings of clan or tribe, stories of the exploits of ancestors that gave the present generation identity or of the appearance of a deity at a particular site to explain the holiness of the shrine erected there. As Hermann Gunkel (1862-1932) demonstrated at the beginning of the 20th century in his classic commentary on Genesis, the oral and legendary character of the origins of these stories explains some of the most obvious features of the individual stories: their colorful, unreflective, yet powerful character; the multiple designations for God, each originally associated with a different cultic site; the brevity of each independent legend and the intensity of focus within each episode.

At a slightly later stage some of these legends found use as explanations for the name of a particular spring or well or other significant site or as accounts of the origins of particular geological phenomena (such as the oddly human-shaped pillars of salt near the Dead Sea, Gen. 19:24-27) or social customs (e.g., the substitution of animal → sacrifice for human sacrifice, 22:1-14). Gunkel dated the earliest legends to the period before → Israel (§1) entered Canaan by observing that many of the places where the events in the legends were said to take place lay on the margins of Canaan, often to the south.

Other scholars compared customs mentioned in the stories with Mesopotamian parallels to arrive at very early dates for the events memorialized in the legends, as early as the first quarter of the second millennium. More recently, these dates have been seriously questioned. The Mesopotamian parallels now appear far less precise than originally suggested, and folklore studies have emphasized that oral traditions are seldom preserved much beyond 150 years, even in exclusively oral cultures. Precise dating is hampered by the paucity of unambiguous, concrete historical references in these local and familial traditions.

Quite obviously these originally independent legends came together and were finally written down to form a connected narrative, but the self-evident character of this observation does not make giving a coherent account of the process any less difficult. Gunkel assumed that the individual legends came together first as cycles of legends unified by association with a single figure such as Abraham or Jacob. These cycles were collected into written sources in a somewhat mechanical fashion, with inclusions of individual legends and other material by two distinct sets of anthologists, one designated *J* (Ger. *Jahwist,* Eng. Yahwist), and the other *E* (for Elohist), the designations corresponding to the characteristic name used for → God in each source. These sources were then combined into an extended JE account sometime late in the → monarchy (→ Pentateuchal Research).

The hypothesis of written sources accounts for a number of phenomena in the ancestral narrative. Gunkel noted rather negatively that the act of recording the legends often included the addition of more abstract and even pious observations that contrasted with the freshness of the oral forms. Combining the roughly parallel sources J and E resulted in duplications still evident in the text, such as the threefold repetition of the story of an ancestor, Abraham or Isaac, giving away his wife to a prominent man to secure protection for himself (Genesis 12, 20, and 26), or the dual form of the traditions about Hagar and Ishmael (chaps. 16 and 21). In addition, consistent patterns of variation in vocabulary found straightforward explanation in the notion that the different sources had different words for the same thing. Beyond the obvious distinction in the names for God, J called the patriarch Israel, while E continued to call him Jacob, even after the story of Jacob's name change at the Jabbok. Other distinguishing terminological differences are best seen in the Hebrew. Gunkel dated the production of these sources to the ninth century B.C. for J and the early eighth century for E, largely on the basis of the absence of perceptible prophetic influence on either source and a sense that many of the formulations in E appeared younger than corresponding elements in J.

1.2. *Von Rad*

In the generation after Gunkel, Gerhard von Rad (1901-71) both maintained the outline of Gunkel's reconstruction and refined it at one significant point. Gunkel had left the process by which the independent oral traditions came together into thematically connected narratives relatively unexplored. Von Rad argued that in the premonarchical period concise statements of the history of God's giving of a land to the → tribes of Israel had served as brief credos that were recited at the Feast of Weeks ceremony, in which all the tribes participated. These credos, now recorded in Deut. 6:21-22 and 26:5-11, provided an outline that drew the independent legends and cycles of legends together into a whole that was centered on a theology of the gift of land. The author of the J source appropriated this outline and the traditional material already associated with it, combining it with other traditional material (most important, the legal traditions about Mount Sinai) to produce the J source.

Von Rad's work indicated how, in the ancestral narrative, the very scattered and distinct legends about the ancestors could have come into association with each other. He further stressed the theological coherence of the assembled traditions and indicated the role that the Yahwist assigned to the ancestral period in the larger scope of the J source: the ancestors first received the promise of a land and laid the first tentative claims to the land of Canaan, a promise fulfilled only after the settlement in the land.

1.3. *Challenges to the Hypothesis of Early Sources*

Many scholars continue to subscribe to the broad outline of this account of the production of the written sources, but in recent times nearly every element in it has been challenged. Von Rad's short historical credos have come to be seen as late distillations of the narrative of Israel's history. The result of denying an early date to the credos has, oddly enough, not been to weaken the recognition of the theologically coherent nature of the narrative but to remove the single most comprehensive account of how that coherence came about.

Still more seriously, the very existence of an E source has been challenged from a number of different angles. Even in the classic formulations of the JE hypothesis, it was recognized that the amount of E material in the ancestral narrative, for instance, was relatively negligible compared with J — the sacrifice of Isaac in Genesis 22, one of the wife-sister stories (chap. 20) and one of the stories of Hagar and Ishmael (chap. 21), plus some additions to other J stories. The assumption was that J and E nearly overlapped in content and that the full contours of the E account had been displaced by parallel J stories at nearly all points where the two sources coincided. This assumption is hard to prove, and the fact remains that the amount of material attributable to E does not add up to a full documentary source. Other explanations for the duplications, differences in vocabulary and perspective, and simple contradictions that led to the hypothesis of two distinct sources have been offered.

Perhaps most dramatically, John Van Seters has

discovered in the historiographical works of Greek authors such as Herodotus (d. between 430 and 420 B.C.) the same sorts of duplications and inconsistencies in vocabulary and perspective used as criteria to distinguish the biblical sources (→ Historiography). Parallels to the biblical accounts are far from perfect, but if they and the late postexilic dating of the biblical sources, which bring the biblical accounts into historical proximity with the Greek works, are accepted, then the variants classically employed to distinguish E from J may be no more than standard historiographical practice in Israel as well.

On another front, H. H. Schmid and Rolf Rendtorff, working independently, employed a consistent history-of-tradition methodology to argue that there was no need to posit early sources in order to account for the variations in the text. The discrepancies and inconsistencies traditionally supposed to indicate separate sources could be adequately accounted for as unharmonized traditional features transmitted orally until a relatively late date. Both suggested that there was neither an E source nor a J source in the classic sense. The first written collection of the traditions was accomplished by → Deuteronomistic authors in the seventh century B.C.

The point here is not to adjudicate between currently competing models of interpretation. Many scholars are certainly not persuaded by the challenges to the classic source-critical hypothesis. The alternatives all have serious weaknesses and unanswered questions. Much more to the point is to recognize the implications of the lack of scholarly consensus on the crucial middle stages of the formation of the ancestral narrative. The text to be interpreted is unchanged, with its duplications, differences in terminology, and minor contradictions. At one time the source-critical hypothesis, with its blending together of J and E sources (and later the addition of P), was held to provide a generative explanation for these phenomena in the text. But the disarray in the field, the competition of internally coherent models, dates, and conceptualizations of the process of collection and fixation in writing of the text rob all of the models of much of their explanatory power.

1.4. *The Priestly Source*

A less skeptical conclusion is possible for the latest stages of the formation of the ancestral narrative. In the postexilic period an editor or editors combined the earlier documentary source JE (or J alone or some other equivalent document, depending on the reconstruction favored) with a more recent source designated *P* (Priestly) because of its interest in the careful organization of cultic practice, its close attention to the ritual calendar of rites, festivals, and sacrifices performed there, and its extensive system of laws and regulations, many of them directing proper worship practice at the temple. P material is easily recognized by characteristic vocabulary and style.

P contributed relatively modest amounts of material to the ancestral narrative — the renewed promise and → covenant of → circumcision in chap. 17, the purchase of the grave of Sarah in chap. 23, the five *tôlĕdôt* (generations, descendants) formulas (2:4; 5:1; 6:9; 10:1; 11:10, 27; 25:19), various genealogies, plus minor additions elsewhere — so that some scholars have questioned whether P constituted a full documentary source or was made up of various fragments exhibiting a priestly character. Resolving the matter is not particularly crucial in the ancestral narratives. Whether or not the priestly material combined with the earlier document constituted a full written source, it exhibited a chronological structure in its use of genealogies, *tôlĕdôt* formulas, and ages of the major characters, which was superimposed on the earlier source.

The editors who combined the documents did little to disturb the underlying sources, and little effort was expended to harmonize them. Some superficial conflicts result, such as the very advanced ages at which Sarah and Abraham produce a child or the specter of a 16-year-old Ishmael borne on his mother's shoulder. The broader effect of the combination is to embed the earlier narrative of the ancestors within a genealogical framework that at once preserves the narrow familial focus of the early legends and integrates the generations of the ancestors into a universal history that extends from creation to the establishment of proper temple worship in Israel. In the renewed promise and covenant of circumcision in Genesis 17, the promise of land takes on a subtly conditional character, and future generations are incorporated into the line of the promise through the legally articulated requirement to circumcise their sons. The editorial practice of combining unharmonized sources creates a work of great richness and often powerful ambiguity, as themes developed independently in the underlying sources interact with one another in the final narrative.

2. Final Form of the Narrative

The ancestral narratives proper begin with the defining promise to Abram and Sarai in Genesis 12. But that crucial episode and the narrative that unfolds from it are linked to the last act of the preceding primeval history in chaps. 1–11 by a minimal yet productive device, the linear genealogy stretching from Shem to Abram.

The genealogies of Genesis have a deep thematic significance. In the barest terms they chronicle the fulfillment of the command given at creation for humans to be fruitful and multiply. They serve further to depict the relatedness of peoples; nations are cousins, nephews, brothers. The genealogies make history into family history. And in the present case the linear genealogy, identifying only one individual in each generation, has decided thematic import. At the end of the story of tower of Babel, God prudentially scatters the people to prevent them from making common cause in still greater evil. The dispersion raises the question of God's continued interaction with the scattered people. Will there be myriad stories? The genealogy suggests a different tack.

God now focuses on a single line and ultimately a single pair, Abram and Sarai, whose introduction already suggests dramatic complications, an impending story. Sarai is barren. The linear genealogy for the moment leads to a fallow field.

2.1. *The First Generation: Abraham*

2.1.1. The opening of the ancestral narrative is abrupt. Without disclosing any motivations or reasons, God summons Abram and Sarai to leave their current home in the comforts of Haran and emigrate to Canaan. No motive is provided, but the silence allows inferences. God has not acted with human beings since the debacle at Babel. God is now stirring again but in an uncertain fashion, approaching obscure individuals, summoning them to a new land, a new story. The summons is accompanied by a far-reaching promise. God will make Abram and Sarai into a great nation, an assurance in some tension with Sarai's present barrenness. God will give them blessings and "make [their] name great" (12:2).

Again, we may hear in this word an unmistakable allusion to the tower of Babel story. The people built the tower in order to make a great name *for themselves.* They failed. Now God takes up the same task. Those who bless Abram and Sarai will be blessed, those who oppose them will themselves be cursed. Finally, in an intimation of God's broader intentions, God says that all the families of the earth will be blessed through this one pair (12:3). The land of Canaan is not mentioned. Once Abram and Sarai have left their "country and kindred" and arrived in Canaan, the land lying before them is added to the promise, distinct yet not separate (12:7).

This first encounter, this summons and promise, establishes the theme of the ancestral narrative. All the succeeding stories of the ancestors and beyond unfold from this one episode, so powerful is the thematic force of the promise. The stories display all the complexity of actual human stories; none is simply the pleasant and pious edifying tale of God's promise inevitably fulfilled.

The promise does not sponsor a → determinism of either personal destiny or history. For instance, Abraham's first act after arriving in the land now promised to his family is to leave it again, frightened by a famine. The movement toward fulfillment of the promise has left its tracks. In a truly bewildering decision he further imperils the promise by asking Sarai to tell possible suitors that she is his sister not his wife so that, as he imagines, they will not kill him to take her.

Much later, just after receiving a visitation from God announcing that the now long-awaited child will finally be born "in due season" (18:10, i.e., soon), Abraham repeats the incomprehensible decision to put his wife in the hands of another man. In both instances God intervenes to restore Sarai to Abram, with whom she must be if there is to be a great nation issuing from Abram. Also in both instances Abram and Sarai (now called Abraham and Sarah in the second story) receive gifts and compensation from penitent suitors who did nothing wrong, so that Abraham and Sarah prosper. This is an odd way to receive a → blessing.

Nothing Abraham does exhibits the slightest trust in the promise so recently and categorically given. His decisions are, to be kind, morally ambiguous. Yet the promise is fulfilled, Sarai defended, those who might derail the promise deterred, and Abram and Sarai's wealth increased. The story does not aim at the abstract point that the promise is unconditional and independent of human cooperation. In true narrative style action reveals character — here, God's → faithfulness to the promise. The character of the one who stands behind it is crucial in any account of the giving of a promise.

2.1.2. Other accounts of events involving Abraham and Sarah are also guided by the promise, although seldom explicitly. When Abraham mobilizes the men of his household against the five kings of the east in order to rescue his nephew Lot, little doubt about the outcome of the conflict can arise. As a near relative of Abraham and Sarah, Lot falls under the promise. Those who strike at Lot strike at Abraham as well. So Abraham and his servants overcome the far more powerful coalition of eastern kings, restoring Lot to his home and property and, incidentally, bringing blessing on Lot's neighbors, who have their goods and households returned. In one further turn on the blessing theme, Melchizedek, → priest of God Most High, blesses Abraham on his return home.

Abraham's intercession on behalf of the cities of

Sodom and Gomorrah is also closely related to the promise. Presumably out of respect for the promise, God reveals to Abraham God's intent to destroy the wicked cities of Sodom and Gomorrah. Abraham intercedes with the destroying angels and persuades them to spare the city if even ten righteous people can be found within its walls. As the sequel reveals, that condition cannot be met, but Abraham's bold intercession with God provides an instance of peoples being blessed by Abraham.

2.1.3. The stories of blessing and protection in the generation of Abraham and Sarah are important, but the driving element in this generation is the promise that Abraham and Sarah will produce a great nation. Here lies the tension that draws the story on. This promise is understood biologically; they will be the progenitors of an extensive people. But Sarah is barren. Her barrenness is a biological fact, but it is also a theological fact. God could at any time give her a child. God does not. Sarah passes the age of childbearing.

In nearly every encounter Abraham and Sarah continually cast up to God the failure to provide the child. God simply repeats the promise to its skeptical recipients. This pattern, which continually keeps the question of the child before us, dominates the story of Abraham and Sarah. The delay in the child's birth is inscrutable. It is not to allow the parents to demonstrate they are prepared or worthy or for their circumstances to become advantageous. The delay lies entirely hidden within God; only the promise itself is constantly reasserted.

At one point the plot thickens. Sarah offers Abraham her maid Hagar as a surrogate, so that Abraham may have an heir. In due course Hagar bears a son, Ishmael, to Abraham. His birth creates a counterpoint to the delayed expectation of fulfillment of the promise. Will this child be accepted by God? Abraham pleads that he may be (Gen. 17:18). But no. Ishmael receives a promise of his own because he is Abraham's son, but he is not the child God has promised. Very late, then, after all natural expectations or hopes of a child have been abandoned, God gives the child of the promise, Isaac, to Abraham and Sarah.

2.1.4. The fulfillment of the promise of a child dominates this first generation in the ancestral narrative. The promise of land is barely encountered. Abram's abandonment of Canaan during the famine is taken as a token of his failure to comprehend or trust the promise. Most of the stories concerning Abraham and Sarah take place in Canaan, but they hold no formal title to the land. They are sojourners, guests in the land.

Then late in this generation, following the death of Sarah, Abraham enters formal negotiations to purchase a small field and a cave near Machpelah in which to bury his wife. The purchase is concluded in good order, the first tenuous installment in the promise of the whole land.

2.1.5. The primary characters in this first generation are Abraham and Sarah, but the narratives are rich in secondary characters, all of whom are carefully related to the central pair. The heading for this section of the narrative is "These are the generations [*tôlĕdôt*] of Terah" (11:27), but the stories seldom even mention Terah; they focus intently on his son Abraham and Abraham's wife, Sarah. Other secondary characters are then carefully related to the Abrahamic line. Lot is Abraham's nephew, and so he receives protection within the promise to Abraham. Because of Lot's close relation to Abraham, there is interest of a slightly malicious order (Lot's sons are the result of an incestuous relationship with his two daughters) in the continuation of Lot's line. Ishmael is Abraham's son, so he receives a blessing and God's favor, and his genealogy is traced. The genealogical framework serves to relate all people to the central line of promise.

2.2. ***The Second Generation: Isaac***

In the next generation, the generation of Isaac, the initial concern is for the biological continuation of the line of Abraham. The full weight of that line is invested in a single individual, Isaac, and so it is remarkably vulnerable. The threat to the survival of the line now comes from an unfathomable quarter — from God. God tests Abraham by commanding him to sacrifice Isaac. Abraham immediately complies.

It must be said that this story is too deep for comprehension. Yet it may be recognized that the story of the binding of Isaac focuses intently on Abraham's character. The rubric "test" bestowed on the episode directs our focus to Abraham. In earlier stories the character of Abraham or Sarah had been more peripheral, as God's faithful character held center stage. The call to sacrifice on Mount Moriah explores Abraham's character, particularly his → obedience and → trust. Again the point of the story is not to say that the promise is contingent upon Abraham's character. That is far too abstract. The story explores Abraham's character in its own right, in relation to God.

Stories about the generation of Isaac are somewhat restricted in number, but they also revolve around promise. The first order is to secure an appropriate wife for Isaac. To that end a servant is dispatched to Abraham's family in Mesopotamia. The line of promise is very narrow. It still does not include Canaanite wives. The servant's quest is prospered by God, and Rebekah returns with the servant to continue the line of promise, soon bearing twin sons, whose tumultuous birth foreshadows the later story. In the womb the two fight with one another, at their birth Jacob seizes the heel of Esau and attempts to be born first, and Rebekah herself receives a vision that the older will serve the younger, a highly irregular relationship.

The birth of the twins secures the biological base of the continuation of the promise but opens the question of which child — or both? — will receive the promise. That question receives an unexpected and somewhat troubling answer in Rebekah and Jacob's deception of the aged Isaac. Isaac is intent on conveying the promise to his favorite, the firstborn Esau. Jacob impersonates Esau, successfully deceives Isaac, and usurps the blessing. When the hapless Esau finally appears, there is no more blessing to give except the inversion of what has already been given to Jacob.

Again the narrative does not offer general principles, as if the way to receive God's blessing were through deceit. But the continuation of the promise is thoroughly enmeshed in human contingency, even if the outcome of the episode is precisely what God had announced to Rebekah at the birth of her two sons.

2.3. *The Third Generation: Jacob*

The promise to Abraham, now unquestionably invested in Jacob, immediately comes under threat. Jacob's treachery infuriates Esau, who plots to kill him. Jacob flees, returning to the ancestral homeland for safety. But Mesopotamia is not Canaan, the only land where the promise can be fulfilled, and the promise remains under threat so long as Esau harbors his hatred. Still, the promise advances outside the land of Canaan.

Jacob marries once and then again, the trickster tricked by his father-in-law. His favored wife, Rachel, is barren, as Sarah was before her. Is a single child again to bear the promise, and must this child be born of Rachel? Jacob takes additional wives; they bear many children. Jacob prospers in ways that interweave his own cleverness and that of Rachel his wife with God's subtle boosting of the bearer of the promise.

Jacob and his family remain for many years in the household of Laban, his father-in-law in Mesopotamia, but the force of the promise is such that Jacob cannot remain permanently outside the land of Canaan. Before Jacob left Canaan, God assured Jacob that he would return (Gen. 28:15). In Laban's house that assurance is renewed (31:10-13). God's support is also practical. Jacob's experiments in selective breeding do not succeed by accident.

Still, at the end of his time away, Jacob's return is fraught with palpable danger to the promise. What certainty can there be that Esau's hatred has abated? Jacob therefore seeks to placate his brother with gifts that indicate obeisance or perhaps an effort to make restitution for what Jacob has despoiled from his brother. Seemingly, the gifts are unnecessary. Jacob finds Esau already perfectly reconciled to him.

2.4. *The Final Generation: Joseph*

At this point the story of the promise seems in equilibrium. Jacob and his wives have 12 sons, so that the threat of the line being extinguished is far less pressing than in the previous two generations. Jacob himself is a different character than formerly. At the river Jabbok, just before he meets Esau on his return, Jacob wrestles with an → angel and is transformed; his old name, Jacob, which looks back to the tumult of his birth, is replaced by the name "Israel," which looks forward to his relationship with God.

It is in fact not Jacob who disturbs the equilibrium of the narrative, at least not directly. His sons introduce the next tension into the story. One of the sons — Joseph, the firstborn of Rachel, Jacob's favored wife — has been pampered and spoiled by Jacob. In numerous ways he makes himself obnoxious to his brothers, carrying tales to his father, flaunting his father's gifts, regaling his brothers with accounts of his → dreams, in which they all bow down to him. The brothers understandably hate him, but that hatred presents a renewed threat to the promise. It is unclear at this point who is meant to receive the promise in this generation, whether all the brothers or just one. If all the brothers, then the hatred of the brothers for Joseph and their plan to act on it by killing him threatens the integrity of the 12-brother family. If only one is to receive it, then that one would be Joseph, and they propose to kill him. The promise is vulnerable.

That vulnerability soon becomes real. The brothers first think to kill Joseph but then substitute a plan to sell him into slavery in Egypt, out of sight, out of mind. The physical distance between Egypt and Canaan is emblematic of the distance between the brothers and of the tension introduced into the story by the enmity between the brothers. The promise is for Canaan, however, not Canaan and Egypt. Resolution of the tension is recounted in a tale that is often called a novella. Indeed, the twists in plot are worthy of a Fielding as Joseph moves toward a position where he has the power to bring about a resolution. But more properly the tale is a

Bildungsroman. Joseph's character must change and grow if he is to bring the conflict with his brothers to a conclusion that restores the integrity of the family. It is a mark of the high art of the story that nearly at the climax of the story, we are not certain that Joseph has grown enough to bring about that restoration. Has he lured all his brothers into Egypt only to gain revenge?

The climax is carefully contrived. All the brothers must be present, including Benjamin, who had played no part in selling Joseph into slavery. Joseph conspires to put this Benjamin, Joseph's successor as his father's favorite and presumably therefore no great favorite with his brothers, under threat. This time one of the brothers, Judah, volunteers to take Benjamin's place in prison. Immediately Joseph throws off his disguise and embraces his brothers. The integrity of the family is reconstituted. One brother has sacrificed himself for another. The generation after Jacob is intact. The promise can be passed to it.

The growth in Joseph's character and the uncanny twists in the plot that place Joseph in the throne room in Egypt when his brothers arrive are clearly the central developments in this section, but there is another. The brothers came to Egypt to secure food. Famine ravished Canaan, and they could not survive there. To soothe his brothers' fear and sense of guilt, Joseph protests to them that his presence in Egypt had a hidden purpose, however dastardly their actions in bringing it about had been. God had put him in Egypt to preserve his family in the famine.

The ancestral narrative thus ends as it began, with the giving of the promise. In this last ancestral generation the 12 sons receive individualized blessings from Jacob that look toward their development as the 12 tribes of Israel, the great nation God originally promised. The complete fulfillment of the promise to Abraham and Sarah lies ahead. The 12 brothers are in Egypt, not Canaan. Their claim on that promised land amounts to clear title to a few gravesites and wells. During 430 years in Egypt the numbers of the descendants of Abraham and Sarah will swell, but a king "who did not know Joseph" (Exod. 1:8) will enslave them. Complete fulfillment of the promise requires liberation of the people and return to the land, the ordering of the people by the → law given at Mount Sinai, and the establishment of proper worship of God, all stories yet to come. The ancestral narrative begins those stories, placing them all under the sign of the promise of God.

Bibliography: R. ALTER, *The Art of Biblical Narrative* (New York, 1981) • J. BLENKINSOPP, *The Pentateuch: An Introduction to the First Five Books of the Bible* (New York, 1992) • D. J. A. CLINES, *The Theme of the Pentateuch* (Sheffield, 1978) • H. GUNKEL, *Genesis* (Macon, Ga., 1997; Ger. ed., 1917) • G. VON RAD, *Genesis* (Philadelphia, 1972; Ger. pub., 1953) • R. RENDTORFF, *The Problem of the Process of Transmission in the Pentateuch* (Sheffield, 1990) • R. B. ROBINSON, "Literary Functions of the Genealogies in Genesis," *CBQ* 48 (1986) 595-608 • H. H. SCHMID, *Der sogenannte Jahwist. Beobachtungen und Fragen zur Pentateuchforschung* (Zurich, 1976) • H. SEEBASS, *Genesis,* vol. 2, *Vätergeschichte I (11,27–22,24)* (Neukirchen, 1977) • J. VAN SETERS, *In Search of History: Historiography in the Ancient World and the Origins of Biblical History* (New Haven, 1983).

ROBERT B. ROBINSON

Patristics, Patrology

1. Term
2. History
3. Ecumenical Significance

1. Term

Patristic theology came into use among Lutherans in the later 17th century (→ Orthodoxy 1) in an effort to provide evidence from early Christian tradition that the teaching of the → Reformers was in agreement with that of the → church fathers. Patristics, which was distinguished from both → biblical theology and → systematic theology, served to stress continuity between the → Reformation and the → early church.

The term "patrology" occurs for the first time in the title of a work by the Lutheran theologian Johann Gerhard (1582-1637): *Patrologia, sive de primitivae ecclesiae Christianae doctorum vita ac lucubrationibus* (Patrology; or, the life and writings of the teachers of the early Christian church, printed posthumously in Jena in 1653). Whereas the term formerly was synonymous with "patristics," it later came to refer more commonly to the serious historical and theological study of all early Christian writings, not only those that were part of the orthodox tradition.

With the rise of historical study in Protestant theology in the 18th and 19th centuries (→ Theology in the Nineteenth and Twentieth Centuries), patrology developed into the history of dogma (→ Dogma, History of) and eventually the history of Christian thought. Today the field has broadened to include the study of the life and teaching of the early church and the related religious, intellectual, and cultural history of late antiquity.

2. History

Jerome (ca. 345-420) wrote the first history of Christian literature, *De viris illustribus* (392), modeled on Suetonius's work of the same title. In more than half of the articles he depends on the church history of Eusebius of Caesarea (ca. 260-ca. 340). Later writers, including Gennadius of Marseilles (fl. 470), Isidor of Seville (ca. 560-636), and Ildefonsus of Toledo (ca. 607-67), followed Jerome's approach.

After the Christological controversies of the fifth century, citations of the church fathers (usually in excerpts), as well as of the decrees of synods and → councils, became a significant feature of all theological discussion and debate. This practice is most evident in the → *catenae* (chains) of extracts from earlier writings and the *florilegia* (gatherings of flowers) that preserved the church's exegetical and dogmatic tradition. A good example in the East is the *Sacra parallela* of John of Damascus (ca. 655-ca. 750). In the West collections of *Sententiae* (sentences) served in the → Middle Ages as the basis of theological discussion. The most famous were those of Peter Lombard (ca. 1100-1160).

The modern study of the church fathers began with the → Renaissance's return to original sources. From the end of the 15th century, editions were published by humanists, most notably Erasmus (1469?-1536) and Faber Stapulensis (ca. 1455-1536). In the 17th and 18th centuries the monks of Montfaucon, Ruinart, de la Rue, and others edited texts (→ Religious Orders and Congregations 1), which led to a blossoming of patristic study, especially in France. Many of these editions are still valued today. Beginning in the 18th century, Anglican scholarship also made a significant mark on patristic studies.

A new era was initiated in the 19th century by the Frenchman J.-P. Migne (1800-1875), who was the first to publish all the works of the church fathers according to the best available editions. His *Patrologia latina* appeared in 221 volumes (1844-64), and, with Latin translations, his *Patrologia graeca* in 161 volumes (1857-66). Five supplementary Latin volumes came out in 1958-75 (ed. A. Hamman). Though these editions do not meet modern standards for critical editions, scholars all over the world continue to depend on them because they are the most readily available for these sources.

The standard collections of modern editions of the church fathers are the following: for the Latin fathers, the *Corpus scriptorum ecclesiasticorum latinorum* (Vienna, 1866ff.); for the Greeks, *Die griechischen christlichen Schriftsteller der ersten drei Jahrhunderte* (Berlin, 1897ff.); for other writers, the *Corpus scriptorum Christianorum orientalium* (Rome [etc.], 1903ff.), with divisions for Arabic, Armenian, Coptic, Ethiopian, Georgian, and Syrian texts; and the *Patrologia orientalis* (Paris, 1907ff.) and *Patrologia Syriaca* (Paris, 1897-1926). At the time of World War II, French scholars began the publication of *Sources chrétiennes* (Paris, 1941ff.). At first this series contained only translations, but after the war Greek, Latin, and Syriac texts were published with French translations and notes.

The most complete collections of translations of early Christian literature in English are the still-valuable 19th-century editions: *The Ante-Nicene Christian Library* (Edinburgh, 1867-72) and *A Select Library of Nicene and Post-Nicene Fathers of the Christian Church* (Oxford, 1887-92; 2d ser., 1890-1900). In the 20th century the most extensive collections of translations into English are *Ancient Christian Writers* (Westminster, Md. [etc.], 1946ff.) and *The Fathers of the Church* (Washington, D.C., 1947ff.). Each of these series continues to publish new volumes.

There are two more limited series: *Oxford Early Christian Texts* (Oxford, 1971ff.), a bilingual edition with Greek or Latin texts and facing English translation, and *Sources of Early Christian Thought* (Philadelphia and Minneapolis, 1980-92), a series of nine paperbacks on particular theological and ecclesiological issues. A valuable new series is *The Early Church Fathers* (London, 1996ff.). Translations of some authors can be found in *Classics of Western Spirituality* (London, 1978ff.) and *Library of Christian Classics* (London, 1953-66). The Augustinians have begun to publish an English translation of all of Augustine's writings, *The Works of St. Augustine: A Translation for the Twenty-first Century* (Hyde Park, N.Y., 1990ff.). Some 30 volumes have already appeared, including 11 volumes of all of Augustine's sermons (including those recently discovered) and 6 volumes of his "Expositions of the Psalms," a homiletical commentary on all 150 psalms.

3. Ecumenical Significance

Today the study of patristics has profound influence on ecumenical relations, on theological thought, and on the spiritual lives of many Christians. All the communions within Christendom recognize that they share a common inheritance in the church's earliest teachers and in the ancient councils and creeds. The thought of the church fathers is a point of reference for many contemporary theologians, and the ancient spiritual classics are widely read in college courses.

Perhaps the most significant development in the last generation has been study of the exegetical writings of the church fathers and the role of the Scriptures in forming their thought. Many of the ancient commentaries on the books of the Bible are being translated for the first time into English (e.g., the series *The Church's Bible* [Grand Rapids, 2003ff.]), and new studies regularly appear devoted to the biblical interpretation of early Christian teachers. The church fathers lived in the world of the Bible, and through their writings modern readers have discovered anew the Bible as a book about Christ and the church and learned to read the Scriptures in light of the church's tradition of life, worship, and thought.

Bibliography: B. Altaner, *Patrology* (New York, 1960; trans. of 5th Ger. ed.) • O. Bardenhewer, *Patrology: The Lives and Works of the Fathers of the Church* (St. Louis, 1908) • E. Bury and B. Meunier, *Les pères de l'église au XVIIe siècle* (Paris, 1993) • F. Cayré, *Manual of Patrology and History of Theology* (2 vols.; Paris, 1936-40) • F. L. Cross, *The Early Christian Fathers* (London, 1960) • S. Döpp and W. Geerlings, eds., *Lexikon der antiken christlichen Literatur* (3d ed.; Freiburg, 2002) • L. Grane, A. Schindler, and M. Wriedt, eds., *Auctoritas Patrum* (Mainz, 1993) • P. J. Hamell, *Introduction to Patrology* (Cork, Ire., 1968) • A.-G. Hamman, *How to Read the Church Fathers* (New York, 1993) • J. A. McGuckin, *The Westminster Handbook to Patristic Theology* (Louisville, Ky., 2004) • J. Quasten, *Patrology* (4 vols.; Westminster, Md., 1950-86) • J. Tixeront, *A Handbook of Patrology* (St. Louis, 1946; based on 4th Fr. ed.).

Wolfgang A. Bienert and Robert Wilken

Patron Saints → Saints, Veneration of, 7

Patronage, Ecclesiastical

1. The term "patronage" covers the rights, privileges, and duties that by special law certain persons enjoy in relation to churches or ecclesiastical offices. One of the rights is that of presentation, that is, putting a name forward for an ecclesiastical appointment. Another right has to do with the control of endowments. An honorary position in the church is also a privilege. The most important duties are those that have to do with buildings and endowments. There are also patronage situations involving no obligations.

2. Patronage originated with the building and endowing of churches by feudal lords or ecclesiastical or secular corporations. At Lateran III in 1179 (→ Councils of the Church) Alexander III (1159-81) reached a compromise on this issue. Landlords would retain essential privileges, but → bishops alone would institute to office.

The → Lutheran Church and Anglicans retained patronage, but → Calvinism basically rejected it. Under the territorial system patronage came increasingly under state law (→ Church and State).

3. In the case of both Roman Catholics and Protestants, patronage may be material, personal, or corporate. In corporate patronage that of rulers occupies a special position.

4. The 1983 → CIC no longer mentions the right of patronage, but we find regulation of the nature and form of presentation in canons 158-63. The Roman Catholic Church is trying to abolish patronage, but canon 4 accepts it where it has not been revoked. From 1808, when F. D. E. → Schleiermacher (1768-1834; → Schleiermacher's Theology) drafted a church constitution, Protestantism has had an increasing desire to eliminate patronage. When state patronage ended in Germany in 1919, the church leaders sought to end patronage in general, and the right of presentation is now for the most part a cooperative right.

In Anglicanism (→ Anglican Communion) the situation has been much the same as among Roman Catholics, though with adjustments because of the merger of parishes. Patronage was a primary cause of the 1843 Scottish Disruption (the founding of the Free Church of Scotland), but its later abolition in the Church of Scotland helped toward substantial reunion in 1929.

→ Church Law

Bibliography: R. Chaput, "Patronage, Canon Law of," *NCE* (1st ed.) 10.1113 • C. Cross, ed., *Patronage and Recruitment in the Tudor and Early Stuart Church* (York, 1996) • G. W. Dameron, *Episcopal Power and Florentine Society, 1000-1320* (Cambridge, Mass., 1991) • B. Palmer, *Serving Two Masters: Parish Patronage in the Church of England since 1714* (Philadelphia, 2003) • P. Schoen, *Das evangelische Kirchenrecht in Preußen* (2 vols.; 2d ed.; Berlin, 1910) • E. Sperling, "Zur Rechtslage der Patronate," *ZEvKR* 21 (1976) 244-65 • A. K. Warren, *Anchorites and Their Patrons in Medieval England* (Berkeley, Calif., 1985).

Michael Muster

Paul

1. Sources

Paul is one of the best-known figures from the early days of Christianity and perhaps from all later antiquity. This knowledge derives from the nature of the sources. The NT → canon contains seven letters of Paul that are undoubtedly authentic. In the probable order of their composition, these are 1 Thessalonians, 1 and 2 Corinthians, Galatians, Romans, Philemon, and Philippians. The letters were public or official rather than private, for as we see from the greetings, Paul wrote them in the discharge of his office as an → apostle who had been called by Jesus Christ and as a church leader (Rom. 1:1; 1 Cor. 1:1, etc.). Nevertheless, the simple directness with which Paul addressed urgent problems in the churches, entered into conflict regarding them, and articulated his own feelings and experiences give the letters an intensely personal character. They show Paul to be a strong person, a theological thinker who expresses what he knows in extreme and uncompromising form, who in spite of his concern to make himself understood by the churches, passionately seeks dialogue with them, a pastor who astutely analyzes moods and situations with a view to finding the right word to speak to them, a church leader who in loving concern accepts solidarity with those entrusted to him yet will cheerfully enter into aggressive polemics with critics and opponents.

The second source, Acts, offers a secondhand picture of Paul, modified by the church, though one in which we may still detect in outline the specific features of Paul's theology. The significance of Acts is that it describes chronologically the work of Paul from his call in 9:1-22 to his imprisonment at Rome in 28:30-31. The stress is thus on his missionary activity (→ Mission 3). The information is incomplete and raises some historical problems, but it is of great historical value because it is largely drawn from personal traditions relative to Paul, church traditions (e.g., in → Antioch), and accounts of fellow workers.

2. History

2.1. *Chronology*

Reconstruction of a chronological biography of Paul rests on what we are told in the letters, supplemented by the information (critically evaluated) that we are given in Acts. The nature of the sources leaves us with some uncertainty. The reference to the apostolic council (→ Acts of the Apostles 8) in Gal. 1:15–2:1 provides us with a fixed point by means of which to arrange chronologically the different incidents in Paul's activity (i.e., a relative chronology). References to time later in Acts (19:8, 10; 20:3; 24:27; 28:30) and estimates of the length of journeys and periods of residence then enable us to put the ensuing events in a probable chronological order.

For absolute chronology we must rely primarily on the so-called Gallio inscription from the temple of Apollo at Delphi, on the basis of which we can date Paul's encounter with the Roman proconsul Gallio in Corinth (Acts 18:12-18) at early in A.D. 52. A second fixed date, though not wholly uncontested (e.g., by G. Lüdemann), is that of the expulsion of the Jews (Jewish-Christians?) from Rome under Emperor Claudius (see Acts 18:2), which according to Suetonius (*Vita Claudii* 25.4) took place in A.D. 49.

Recent research overwhelmingly supports a basic chronology for Paul as follows:

ca. 32/34	call in Damascus (Gal. 1:17)
ca. 35/36	first visit to Jerusalem (Gal. 1:18)
ca. 36/37	stay in Antioch (Acts 11:25-26)
46-47	mission to Cyprus and South Asia Minor ("1st missionary journey")
48	second visit to Jerusalem: the apostolic council (Gal. 2:1)
49	departure from Antioch (Acts 15:39-40)
49-50	independent mission to Asia Minor and Macedonia ("2d missionary journey")
50-52	first stay in Corinth (Acts 18)
50/51	*1 Thessalonians*
52-55	stay in Ephesus (Acts 19)
54	*Corinthian correspondence*
55	"collection" journey, to Ephesus, Troas, Macedonia, and Corinth (Acts 20)
55	*Galatians*
55/56	second stay in Corinth
56	*Romans*

56 arrival in Jerusalem with collection, imprisonment (Acts 20–21).
56-58 imprisonment in Caesarea (Acts 24–26)
58 transfer to Rome (Acts 27)
58 *Philippians; Philemon* (?)
58-60 stay in Rome (Acts 28:30) and martyrdom

Outlines deviating from the above generally try to accord more time for the independent mission in Asia Minor and in the Aegean region by dating that journey before the apostolic council (R. Jewett; Lüdemann). Doing so, however, actually creates more problems than it solves.

2.2. ***Background and Development***

2.2.1. *Before Conversion*

For the origin and career of the pre-Christian Paul, we are dependent on a few sparse references (1 Cor. 15:9; 2 Cor. 11:22; Gal. 1:13-14; Phil. 3:5-6; Rom. 9:3-4; Acts 21:39; 22:3). He was born and brought up in Cilician Tarsus, the son of a Jewish father who ranked as a Roman citizen. As a member of a Pharisaic family of the tribe of Benjamin, Paul likely studied in Jerusalem under Rabban Gamaliel I, a great contemporary scholar of the school of Hillel (Acts 22:3; 26:5). Paul trained to be a Pharisaic → scribe (→ Pharisees). Strongly rooted in the religious tradition of Judaism, he was also broadly receptive to Hellenistic culture and cosmopolitanism (→ Hellenism), as we see from his Hebrew-Greek double name "Saul" (Acts 9:4, 17; 22:7, etc.) and "Paul." Contrary to traditional beliefs, this name does not derive from his call, for when Acts begins to use it with his first missionary work (13:9), it is simply indicating that he was known by this name in the Greek-speaking churches.

Paul first made contact with followers of Jesus in Jerusalem in the form of the "Hellenists" (Acts 6:1), who spoke Greek and were critical of the → law. As a Pharisee, Paul was convinced that by being crucified, → Jesus had come under the → curse of the law (Deut. 21:23; see also Gal. 3:13). When the Hellenists then found Jesus to be the Messiah (→ Christological Titles 3) and end-time Consummator of Israel, it seemed to Paul that this conclusion was a blaspheming of the → Torah and good reason why he should make it his life's work passionately to unmask believers and expel them from Israel. It seems likely from Gal. 1:23 that he had at least some part in the measures taken by the Jerusalem Sanhedrin against the Hellenists, even if some edifying exaggeration is seen in Acts 8:3. In any case he had a major role in initiating persecution of the followers of Jesus in the Damascus → synagogue (Acts 9:1-2).

2.2.2. *After Conversion*

In Damascus or on his way there (Acts 9:3), Paul underwent a decisive change that governed both his life from that point onward and his theological thinking. Paul himself in 1 Cor. 15:8-11; Gal. 1:15-17; Phil. 3:1-11, as well as in the deutero-Pauline tradition (Eph. 3:1-7; 1 Tim. 1:12-17), called this experience his summoning to the service of the → gospel by the risen Christ, though in the stylized accounts in Acts 9:1-22; 22:3-21; 26:9-20 the elements of → conversion (§1) are more prominent. From the outset visions and auditions seemed to have played a part in the event. Yet Paul, looking back critically, differentiates both from subjective ecstatic-visionary experiences (see 2 Cor. 12:1-5) by interpreting the former as a divinely given historic → revelation whose content was the crucified Jesus as the "Son" who had been appointed the end-time Ruler by his resurrection from the dead (Gal. 1:16). The event had important implications for Paul's interrelated thinking and work.

As regards his thinking, the Damascus event brought total realignment. Hitherto the religious value system defined by the law had given his life meaning and security, but this support was now shattered (Phil. 3:7-11). Everything suggests that a prior → suffering under the law did not prepare the pre-Christian Paul psychologically for the crisis, since we are not to read Romans 7 autobiographically but as a typical depiction of the pre-Christian situation. The decisive point was that God himself had related → salvation, which Pharisaic Jews linked with the Torah, exclusively to the Crucified One, who had been raised from the dead. Jesus as the Christ thus took the place that had formerly been occupied by the Torah. Synthesis between the two was impossible, for the Torah had pronounced the sentence of death on Jesus (Gal. 3:13). God himself, however, acknowledged Jesus by the resurrection. The pre-Christian Paul had already seen that Jesus and the Torah excluded one another, and now for Paul as a Christian this antithesis became in a reverse sense a leading theme in his theology.

As regards his work, Paul described what happened in terms that echoed the way an OT prophet would describe his call (Gal. 1:15-16), and he even went further by seeing in it the last of the series of → resurrection appearances (1 Cor. 15:8), with a special commissioning and sending as its content. As the last to be "called to be an apostle of Christ Jesus" (1 Cor. 1:1 etc.), he seems to have inferred (1 Cor. 9:1) that he stood in a special, corresponding relation to → Peter as the first to be called (1 Cor. 15:5). The difference in their commissions was that

Peter was the apostle to the Jews, and Paul more particularly to the Gentiles (Gal. 2:7), now that the gospel had brought freedom from the law.

2.3. *Missionary Work*

Paul's missionary work stretched over two decades. It falls plainly into two phases separated by the apostolic council (A.D. 48). As we see from the Epistles, in the second phase Paul had already adopted his basic theological positions and was planning a broad missionary program. The first phase, according to the fewer references we have, was a period of clarification and development.

After a time of withdrawal in Arabia (Gal. 1:17), Paul made some initial attempts at missionary work in Damascus (2 Cor. 11:32-33). After a visit to Jerusalem during which he met Peter (Gal. 1:18), he spent some time in his home city of Tarsus. Then on the initiative of Barnabas he went to Syrian Antioch, where Hellenists from Jerusalem had founded what was at first a Jewish-Christian church (Acts 11:19-26; → Jewish Christians). This church was gradually being opened up to uncircumcised → Gentiles, and Paul himself probably contributed to the resultant loss of the Torah's influence. In the next step Paul, with Barnabas, was commissioned by the Antioch church to do missionary work in Cilicia (Gal. 1:21), Cyprus, and southern Asia Minor (Acts 13–14) on his so-called first missionary journey. This mission involved a deliberate reaching out beyond the limits of → Judaism, and its obvious success meant that these limits were passed as missionary churches with many Gentile Christians were founded.

This development made it imperative that a clarification be reached concerning whether uncircumcised believers who were not under the law could be members of the → church as the people of God. This clarification came at the apostolic council at Jerusalem (Gal. 2:1-10). There Paul and Barnabas as delegates from Antioch, despite opposition from radical Jewish Christians, secured the fundamental agreement of → James, the leader of the → primitive Christian community, and of Peter as well, for their Gentile mission and for the freedom of Gentile Christians from the law. Gentiles would rank as full members of the people of God on the basis solely of → faith in Christ and → baptism. Paul thus had a free hand to carry out his plan for a broad Gentile mission that would embrace all the inhabitants of the known world. To demonstrate the link between the Gentiles and Jerusalem as the ancient center of the people of God, he simply promised that he would take up a collection for the mother church (v. 10).

Jerusalem, however, had not fully clarified the question of the validity of the Torah, and conflicts resulted in Antioch that involved a breach of table fellowship between Jewish and Gentile Christians and an open confrontation between Paul and Peter (Gal. 2:11-14). Paul used the occasion to sever the tie to Antioch and to engage in mission on his own responsibility and in accordance with his own plan. A staff of freely chosen workers who were in agreement with his aims supported him.

A feature of the second phase of Paul's work that now opened was a decisive thrust to the west, first to Achaia, then to the capital, Rome, and finally, as a remoter goal, Spain (Rom. 15:24). This phase is usually said to contain the second and third missionary journeys, but the break suggested by Acts 18:21-22 was not a real one. The thrust through Asia Minor to the west was at first hampered by unforeseen events, so that there had to be a longer stay in Galatia, which resulted in the founding of churches there (Acts 16:6).

Moving to Macedonia (Acts 16:9-10), Paul used the strategy of founding churches in the central cities of provinces and districts, from which there could be missionary penetration into the interior, which he did at Philippi, Thessalonica, Corinth, and finally Ephesus. During a long stay in Ephesus he worked on the collection and planned a return visit to Antioch (Acts 18:22). His aim was to take the results of the collection to Jerusalem, along with representatives of the churches he had founded (Acts 20:4-6). In this way he hoped to give symbolic expression to the → unity of the church of Jews and Gentiles before undertaking the projected mission to Rome and Spain. But disaster struck. Pressured by the radical Jewish-Christian faction, which was now stronger, the mother church would not accept the Gentile-Christian offering, and Paul, accused of instigating religious revolt, was arrested by the Romans (Acts 21).

2.4. *Death*

After a long imprisonment in Caesarea Paul as a citizen appealed to the emperor (Acts 25:11) and was thus sent as a prisoner to → Rome (chap. 27). Acts closes with an account of his two years of imprisonment there (28:30-31). What happened next is unclear. One suggestion is that, according to hints in Acts 20:36-38 and 21:10-13, death rather than release followed. The important testimony of *1 Clem.* 5.7 suggests that Paul suffered a martyr's death in Rome (→ Martyrs).

3. Theology

We know Paul's theology only from the letters he wrote in the last years of his work, that is, when it was already developed. Although the basic features are always the same, various paradigms went into its evolution (thus the doctrine of → justification, with its legal vocabulary, is found only in Galatians and Romans), and there are detailed differences in individual passages — for example, on the law (Gal. 3:19-22; Romans 7), on → eschatology (1 Thess. 4:13-18; 1 Cor. 15:51-52; 2 Cor. 5:1-10), and on Israel (1 Thess. 2:14-16; Romans 9–11). The variety arises from the Epistles being strongly situational. Limits are thus set for any systematizing assessment.

Notwithstanding its originality, Paul's theology is strongly rooted in → tradition. Elements of Gentile missionary preaching and Hellenistic Jewish Christianity (e.g., Romans 1; 1 Thess. 1:9-10) combine in it with motifs from Jewish biblical scholarship (Galatians 3; Romans 4), → Wisdom literature, and → apocalyptic (1 Corinthians 15; 1 Thessalonians 4). In many quotations Paul shows familiarity with the kerygmatic (1 Cor. 11:23-25; 15:3b-5; Rom. 1:3-4) and liturgical (Phil. 2:5-11) traditions of primitive Christianity. → Stoic philosophy, → Gnostic mythology, and the piety of the → mystery religions no doubt had some influence; how much, though, is a matter of scholarly dispute.

3.1. *Paul and Jesus*

The weak part played by the Jesus tradition is striking. There are indications that Paul knew at least a collection of the sayings of Jesus, but in his letters he makes only incidental use of these sayings in indirect allusions, mainly in his ethical (e.g., Rom. 12:14, cf. Luke 6:28a; Rom. 13:7, cf. Mark 12:17; 1 Thess. 5:13b, cf. Mark 9:50) and eschatological (1 Thess. 4:15-17) teaching. The only instance of a direct quotation of a saying in the Synoptic tradition is in 1 Cor. 7:17-18 (cf. Mark 10:2-12 and par.). There are no references at all to narratives concerning Jesus.

Paul saw it as his missionary task, not to recall Jesus as messianic teacher in word and deed, but to proclaim the gospel as the message of God's present saving work in what happened to Jesus, especially in his crucifixion and resurrection (1 Cor. 15:1-5). He thus took his stand consistently on the new situation that the Jesus-event had created in → salvation history (2 Cor. 5:16-20). Accordingly, he called for a recognition in faith that the Crucified is the divinely appointed end-time Ruler of the world (Phil. 2:5-11).

All the same, Paul does not reduce the story of the pre-Easter Jesus merely to a formal statement about his human existence. The fact that the risen and ascended Lord is the same as the historic earthly Jesus is important for him, as he tries to show by sketching the basic story of Jesus. He who went to the → cross for our → sin lived a life of service for others (Rom. 15:3). The one who in execution of God's plan of salvation was sent into the world (Gal. 4:4) is the one who trod the path of → obedience to God, even unto death (Phil. 2:8).

3.2. *Christology*

At the heart of Paul's thinking is a strongly theocentric → Christology. God sent his Son into the world, the Son who was his before all time and from the very beginning, and who gave up this Son to death in order to demonstrate his → love for us — we who are hopelessly enslaved to the destructive forces of sin, death, and the law (Rom. 5:8). On this basis and with the OT understanding of → atonement in view, Paul further developed the soteriological teaching that we find already in the earliest Christological → kerygma (→ Soteriology), namely, that the death of Jesus is a vicarious death for sinners (Mark 14:24; 1 Cor. 11:24). Israel had always had the possibility of cultic expiation, but now in the last days God has gone further. He removed all restrictions and in the death of Jesus granted to all of us freedom from the power of sin and, with this freedom, access to fellowship with himself (Rom. 3:21-26). The cross is God's offer of reconciliation (Rom. 5:10; 2 Cor. 5:18), whose goal is our acceptance of it in faith.

For Paul God also defines his general relation to the world in the cross. In Jesus' dying on the cross in extreme shame and derision (Gal. 3:13), we see that God manifests himself in our world only in an act that runs contrary to all human ideas and expectations of greatness and power. This theology of the cross (→ Theologia crucis), which Paul develops especially in debate with the pneumatics of Corinth, expounds the supreme humiliation of God as an essential feature of his saving work, quite contrary to all human expectations (1 Cor. 1:17-18; Phil. 3:18).

3.3. *Justification*

Paul works out the anthropological implications of his Christology in his doctrine of justification, presented in Romans and Galatians. This doctrine had its basis in his own existential → experience, but he developed it in controversy with Judaizing Christians. It provided the theological reason for the antagonism between Christ and the law, which manifests itself in the fact that Christ, the one who brings end-time salvation, died on the cross accursed by the law, by Israel's Torah (Gal. 3:13). God's offer of salvation in the law cannot attain its goal because our human situation thwarts it. Instead of evoking joyful concurrence with the will of God, its demand provoked arrogant human resistance, the "flesh" (Rom. 8:3, 5), the result being that sin achieved dominance over the whole human race (Rom. 5:12,

21). In this situation the law, which was originally given for salvation, changes its character. It now proclaims God's unmet claim, subjects us to its judgment (Rom. 1:18; 3:20), and, as a disciplinarian, holds us fast in our sin (Gal. 3:23-24).

The saving change comes through Christ, who meets the claim of the law, diverts the curse, and opens up the salvation that the law could not give (Rom. 10:4). This salvation no longer has the structure of the salvation based on the law, which depends on human works. It is determined, rather, by the generous self-offering of God in Christ. We can appropriate it only in faith, which is a posture of grateful acceptance (Rom. 3:23-24; 9:32) and which stands in the sharpest possible antithesis to all human achievement. Renouncing self and all possibilities of their own, believers rely solely on God's creative power and love (Rom. 4:17).

3.4. *New Being*

Faith opens up access to the new being, which Paul defines centrally as a being "in Christ" (Rom. 8:1; Gal. 2:19-20). This concept is not a mystical self-identification with Christ (→ Mysticism). It means being historically governed by the way of Christ and his saving work. It finds concrete manifestation in the → sacraments. Thus → baptism signifies placing oneself under the salvation that Christ has procured and appropriating his victory over the destructive forces of sin and death (Rom. 6:1-11). It also means incorporation into the body of Christ (1 Cor. 12:13), the sphere of the historic manifestation of the new being in Christ (→ Church 2.1.4). By means of the → Eucharist the community experiences itself as the fellowship that is marked by the self-offering of Jesus for it (1 Cor. 10:16-17) and in which a new, free human interrelationship takes shape that leaves no place for → power or rule.

On the one hand, Paul emphatically states that the new being is the work of the → Holy Spirit, in whom God's end-time creative power bursts forth (Rom. 8:1, 11; 2 Cor. 3:6). On the other hand, he sharply draws the line against the type of enthusiasm that, with an appeal to the Spirit, claims that the consummation of salvation is here already. In opposition to that view he describes the present situation of Christians as one of tense existence between the "already" and the "not yet," between the fellowship with Christ that is already theirs in the Spirit and the ongoing threat of sin (1 Thess. 4:7; 5:4-5; Rom. 13:11-14). Faith still looks ahead in → hope to a bodily consummation that has yet to come (Rom. 4:18; 8:20-21). Only in the lowly form of the cross can we now see that which is to come (2 Cor. 12:9-10).

4. Influence

Paul's work quickly exerted widespread influence. The collecting and, in some cases (2 Corinthians, Philippians), editing of his letters provided the impulse. What probably amounted to a self-centered Pauline tradition had taken shape by A.D. 100 in the areas of his missionary work in Asia Minor, Greece, and also Rome. As some scholars see it, this tradition came to expression in the pseudepigraphic Pauline letters that they attribute to his disciples (2 Thessalonians, Colossians, Ephesians, and the Pastorals). On this view these letters contain the central theses and motifs and often exhibit direct literary dependence on the genuine Pauline letters but relate to new situations in the church.

In addition to Acts, we see the impact of Paul in 1 and 2 Peter, *1 Clement,* Ignatius, and Polycarp (→ Apostolic Fathers). The only hint of opposition is in Jewish-Christian circles (James and *Preaching of St. Peter*). Marcion (d. ca. 160; → Marcionites) advanced a first Pauline canon, but earlier scholars perhaps overestimated his influence upon the acceptance of Paul in the mainline church. The same qualification applies to the use of Paul by Gnostics, who adopted only specific motifs.

In the history of theology the orientation to Paul's doctrine of grace was important in → Augustine (354-430; → Augustine's Theology). Martin → Luther (1483-1546; → Luther's Theology) picked up on this theme with his revival of Paul's doctrine of justification by faith, which was determinative for the → Reformation. The influence of Paul reached a further climax in Karl → Barth's (1886-1968) theology of the Word of God (→ Dialectical Theology).

→New Testament Era, History of

Bibliography: C. K. Barrett, *On Paul: Aspects of His Life, Work, and Influence in the Early Church* (London, 2003) • J. Becker, *Paul: Apostle to the Gentiles* (Louisville, Ky., 1993) • G. Bornkamm, *Paul* (New York, 1971) • A. A. Das, *Paul and the Jews* (Peabody, Mass., 2003) • S. J. Hafemann, *Paul, Moses, and the History of Israel: The Letter/Spirit Contrast and the Argument from Scripture in 2 Corinthians 3* (Tübingen, 1995) • D. K. Harink, *Paul among the Postliberals: Pauline Thought beyond Christendom and Modernity* (Grand Rapids, 2003) • H. Hübner, *Law in Paul's Thought* (Edinburgh, 1984) • R. Jewett, *A Chronology of Paul's Life* (Philadelphia, 1979) • E. Käsemann, *Perspectives on Paul* (Philadelphia, 1971) • G. Kertelge, *"Rechtfertigung" bei Paulus* (2d ed.; Münster, 1971) • A. Lindemann, *Paulus im ältesten Christentum* (Tübingen, 1979) • G. Lüdemann, *Opposition to Paul in Jewish Christianity* (Minneapolis, 1989); idem, *Paul, Apostle to the*

Gentiles: Studies in Chronology (Philadelphia, 1984); idem, *Paul, the Founder of Christianity* (Amherst, N.Y., 2002) • C. N. Mount, *Pauline Christianity: Luke-Acts and the Legacy of Paul* (Leiden, 2002) • H. Räisänen, *Paul and the Law* (2d ed.; Tübingen, 1987) • B. I. Reicke, *Re-examining Paul's Letters: The History of the Pauline Correspondence* (ed. D. Moessner and I. Reicke; Harrisburg, Pa., 2001) • K. H. Rengstorf, ed., *Das Paulusbild in der neueren deutschen Forschung* (3d ed.; Darmstadt, 1982) • E. P. Sanders, *Paul, the Law, and the Jewish People* (Philadelphia, 1983) • W. Schmithals, *Die theologische Anthropologie des Paulus* (Stuttgart, 1980) • U. Schnelle, *Gerechtigkeit und Christusgegenwart* (2d ed.; Göttingen, 1986) • K. Stendahl, *Paul among Jews and Gentiles* (Philadelphia, 1976) • P. Stuhlmacher, *Revisiting Paul's Doctrine of Justification* (Downers Grove, Ill., 2001) • G. Theissen, *Psychological Aspects of Pauline Theology* (Philadelphia, 1987) • U. Wilckens, *Rechtfertigung als Freiheit* (Neukirchen, 1974).

Jürgen Roloff†

Peace

1. Sociology

1.1. *Problem of Definition*

The word "peace" has many meanings, making a comprehensive definition impossible. Definitions aim to make a word univocal and tend to stress one specific content. Peace might be a nonwarring state in national relations, an absence of violence (→ Force, Violence, Nonviolence), a state of actualized social justice (→ Righteousness, Justice, 3), a psychological factor in persons or their relations with others, a state of → law in a country or between countries, an organized world society, a rational relation between humanity and nature, or nonviolent relations between groups, organizations, or → religions. All these definitions bring into play a specific aspect but in so doing tend to neglect or suppress others. This insight is a warning that we should be open to other aspects in trying to define peace, taking into account their historical and cultural presuppositions and political feasibility.

1.2. *Western Ideas*

In the Greek and Hellenistic world, peace was bound up with the notion of the rational order of the *polis,* or city-state. Roman thinking connected it with legal relations that were regulated by treaties and established the just-war doctrine on this basis. Adopting the legal thinking of Rome, post-Constantinian Christian communities related peace *(pax)* to justice *(iustitia).* The just-war doctrine was set on a new basis, and a foundation was also laid for the development of → international law.

The modern European state bases domestic peace on a legal order that the state monopoly of power guarantees. In earlier monarchies, however, it left decisions regarding peace or war to kings. In opposition to this division, Immanuel Kant (1724-1804; → Kantianism) emphatically pointed out the mutual dependence between domestic order and international peace. Nevertheless, from this time onward the terms → "war" and "peace" came to be used almost exclusively for relations between → states. The rising middle class tried to connect peace with middle-class moral principles. These ideas anticipated a world order that would transcend national frontiers and guarantee peace, a notion that found organizational expression in the peace societies that were formed after 1815. With the development of nuclear → weapons, however, efforts to establish and safeguard peace by legal and moral principles ran up against the problem that they now had to incorporate science and → technology into schemes for the establishment and preservation of peace.

1.3. *Peace in the Nuclear Age*

Nuclear weapons have brought not only hitherto unimaginable forms of warfare but also a very precarious means of preventing it by terror. Nuclear terror rests on second-strike ability, that is, the ability to deliver an annihilating counterblow after an annihilating attack. But the stalemate persists only so long as each side is ready, and is believed to be ready, to actually use nuclear weapons. A destabilizing factor is the technological and psychological development of new weapons systems and the resultant arms race. The technological and psychological prevention of war by terror hampers political action on the part of the nuclear powers. It has finally shattered the doctrine of the just war. It also raises wholly new problems in international law.

1.4. *International Law*
International law developed out of just-war thinking. Restrictions that were adopted in the 18th and 19th centuries (e.g., in the Hague Convention of 1907) made possible a limitation of war in Europe. But limited peace corresponded to limited war. In the Kellogg-Briand Pact (1928) after World War I and in further efforts after World War II, international law has been used to try to prevent war and to establish peace by the creation of international organizations such as the League of Nations and the → United Nations. In light of the reality of nuclear threat, however, the only rational goal of peace politics and international law is the abolition of war as a political and legal institution.

1.5. *East-West and North-South Problems*
During the cold war the nuclear threat to peace manifested itself especially in the opposition between East and West. But since 1945 the disparity between North and South has also been a source of instability. Since the ending of the wars of liberation from → colonialism, this disparity has been marked less by direct military force than by structural violence (→ Peace Research). This concept (due to J. Galtung) refers to the potential for violence that is concealed in the political, economic, technological, and cultural structures that are dominated by the rich countries of the North, and that results in → dependence and increasing → poverty. The achievement of social justice is a presupposition for peace between North and South. A development of → Third World countries according to principles of social justice is made difficult, however, by the squandering of financial and material resources on armaments and on the extravagant demands of the affluence of the industrialized nations.

Since the end of the cold war, much attention has been focused on non-state-sponsored terrorism, including the use of hijacked airplanes as weapons in an attack on the United States (→ Power 1.6.3).

1.6. *Peace and Ecology*
Conflicts have erupted over control of natural resources, such as water and energy. How far exploitation of nature is a potential threat to peace has not yet been properly investigated (→ Ecology; Environment).

1.7. *Peace Efforts*
In efforts to establish and maintain peace, many different aspects call for consideration. Contradictory possibilities of action must be weighed against one another, and mutual recognition is required on the part of all those concerned.

So far with only partial success, efforts have been made to *limit armaments by making them purely defensive* or lessening their offensive capability. From this technological and strategic angle the final goal is → disarmament. Efforts of this kind are dependent on political conditions, on whether measures that promote confidence can defuse ideological differences, remove claims to hegemony, and balance power interests.

The promotion of peace by making efforts to *resolve tensions between states* is connected with the states' domestic stability and the degree of their historical and political experience. Peace can be lasting, therefore, only when it is maintained by many and not just organized by force by a few. The personal sphere, that of personal relations, is relevant in this regard. Experience in this sphere shows that even highly emotional conflicts can be settled peacefully in small groups. Here too, though, are the sources of human → aggression. → Peace education must begin at this level. Thus far it is unclear how far positive and negative experiences and influences in this microsphere have an impact on structures and changes in the political and social macrosphere.

The most logical counterstrategy to stability by terror, which has been called a state of organized lack of peace (D. Senghaas), is to *promote unilateral disarmament.* This choice is in keeping with the basic pacifist position (→ Pacifism). Close to unilateralism is the idea of nonviolent social defense (T. Ebert). Any concept that strives for step-by-step disarmament and the political conquest of war is called gradualism (A. Etzioni).

1.8. *International Organizations*
States are the most powerful actors in peace politics, but no longer the only ones. International organizations try to regulate conflicts, and social groups, nongovernmental organizations, and peace movements try to force peace policies on national and international players by appeals and direct action (→ Peace Movements). Efforts to secure agreement between all who work for peace in their debates about the way to disarmament, the overcoming of poverty and want, the securing of → freedom and human → rights, and the protection of nature would be themselves a demonstration of peace in a world in which peace and security can no longer be had at the expense of others.

Bibliography: T. Ebert, "Non-violent Resistance against Communist Regimes?" and "Organization in Civilian Defence," *Civilian Resistance as a National Defense: Non-violent Action against Aggression* (ed. A. Roberts; Harrisburg, Pa., 1968) 173-94, 255-73 • A. Etzioni, *The Hard Way to Peace: A New Strategy* (New York, 1962) • J. Fahey and R. Armstrong, eds., *A Peace Reader: Es-*

sential Readings on War, Justice, Non-violence and World Order* (New York, 1987) • J. Galtung, *There Are Alternatives! Four Roads to Peace and Security* (Nottingham, 1984) • W. Huber and J. Schwerdtfeger, eds., *Kirche zwischen Krieg und Frieden. Studien zur Geschichte des deutschen Protestantismus* (Stuttgart, 1976) • D. Senghaas, *Abschreckung und Frieden. Studien zur Kritik organisierter Friedlosigkeit* (Frankfurt, 1969).

Johannes Schwerdtfeger,
with Michael Kinnamon

2. Theology and Ethics

Discussion of the problems of peace in the light of theological → ethics helps orient us to conduct in terms of the biblical → revelation. Such discussion cannot simply deduce laws, values, or → norms from biblical statements but must examine the biblical testimonies for their significance in giving us actual direction both in the context of the biblical works themselves and in relation to the history of their exposition. As regards the biblical understanding of peace, we must ask about historical changes in that understanding and finally sketch the present state of ecumenical discussion.

2.1. *Biblical Understanding*

The Bible speaks about peace in very different situations, at very different times, and from very different angles. In spite of such variety, we may discern two basic features that define the testimony to it in both the OT and the NT. First, it is almost always set in an indissoluble relation to God and the human world. Second, peace is much more than the opposite and absence of → war or armed conflict; it is a total order of → salvation.

2.1.1. In the OT the word "shalom" denotes the state of salvation that God has planned for the world. In the cult it is promised to the people in the → blessing (Num. 6:26). People wish for and convey shalom (i.e., salvation and → happiness) to one another in greeting. The blessing of salvation does not have to do solely with a state of inner peace but also with the well-being of people, cattle, a city, or a nation. It may even be the shalom of armed conflict (2 Sam. 11:7).

The OT speaks of this peace against the background of experienced oppression, injustice, and strife. The king's political task of peace as it is described in Psalm 72 embraces not only the protection of the people against foreign foes but also the securing of justice for the poor and needy. Because the people of → Israel (§1) were liberated by God from slavery in Egypt, they were particularly sensitive to bondage, need, and violence. They had a strong sense of responsibility to God in these matters. When the right relation was broken and the divinely planned shalom lost, the people of Israel bore the guilt. Preexilic prophecy uncovered this guilt (Jer. 6:14; 8:11).

In the crisis of the exile the self-assertiveness of the power politics that trusted more in human → force than in divine direction came under the fire of prophetic criticism. In a time of great humiliation and profound conflict, the → prophets announced that Yahweh would still be faithful to his will for peace (Isaiah 40–48; Ezekiel 36–39). The hope was for a new world and a new messianic peace that God alone would initiate (→ Messianism) and that would reconcile people to one another and to nature, with the result that swords would be beaten into plowshares and spears into pruning hooks (Isa. 2:2-4; Mic. 4:1-4).

2.1.2. Like the OT (Isa. 9:6), the NT can predicate peace *(eirēnē)* of God, then of Christ. God is "the God of peace" (e.g., Rom. 15:33), and Christ is "our peace" (Eph. 2:14). Peace has a fixed place in greetings and blessings (e.g., the closing salutations in Paul's epistles). Above all, the Christmas song of praise in Luke 2:14, "Glory to God in the highest heaven, and on earth peace . . . ," proclaims the revelation of the longed-for messianic peace. The one who brings and protects this peace is God himself in the form of a child, a servant (Phil. 2:5-8). Essential features of the God who establishes peace are the vicarious acceptance of human guilt (Rom. 3:25-26) and God's own love of enemies (5:10). The Pauline writings develop this understanding of peace in two ways: peace is the epitome of the new relation between Creator and creature, and it is a mark of → reconciliation with others, especially between Jews and Gentiles (Eph. 2:13-14).

According to the witness of the NT, the messianic hope of peace in postexilic prophecy finds fulfillment in → Jesus Christ. God finally sealed his will for peace in Jesus of Nazareth, especially peace with his enemies. In their → discipleship the followers of Jesus, by word and deed, give testimony to the whole unredeemed world through their love of enemies (→ Enemy), which the → Sermon on the Mount proclaims. The disciples of the Messiah are lauded as peacemakers (Matt. 5:9; see also Rom. 14:19). In continuity with Israel, Christians expect a reign of eternal peace when there will be no more war or hostility.

2.2. *Historical Development*

Distinction must be made between peace as a divine gift of salvation and peace as a political, legal, and social task. Yet the two aspects cannot be separated.

Those who establish earthly → law and create peace correspond thereby to the heavenly gift and promise of peace. The tension between the two traditions that we note here has been with Christianity from the very first.

2.2.1. The peace of God is promised to Christianity, which has implications for its dealings with the problems of the surrounding world. From the outset, the biblical message of peace had to be set in relation to the political aspects of peace that obtained in antiquity. Thus people like Eusebius of Caesarea (ca. 260-ca. 340) could extol the political peace that prevailed under Augustus (27 B.C.–A.D. 14) because it ensured space for the proclamation of the gospel (*Hist. eccl.* 4.26.7). Yet, in view of the direction to love even enemies, early Christians for the most part would not serve in the army. Pagan philosophers like Celsus (fl. late 2d cent. A.D.) charged them with inconsistency and parasitism on this account. In reply, Origen (ca. 185-ca. 254) referred to the prayers that Christians offered for the emperor and his success.

2.2.2. Augustine (354-430) gave precision to the concept of peace (*De civ. Dei* 19). On the basis of his definition of the two cities — the city of God and the earthly city, or the city of the devil — he distinguished strictly between the this-worldly sphere, in which peace is safeguarded by → power and government and, in case of need, by a "just war," and the sphere of the transcendent, eschatological expectation of peace, which God alone will fulfill (→ Augustine's Theology). The two cities must be carefully differentiated, but in this age they permeate one another, even in the church, which is *corpus permixtum*, a mixed body. Who belongs to which will be evident only at the → last judgment (→ Eschatology). Although it is not within human power to establish God's eschatological peace, Christians have a duty to value and promote earthly peace as a supreme good (→ Religious Liberty [Foundations] 1; Progress 3).

2.2.3. On the basis of the distinction between divine and earthly peace, the Middle Ages tried to actualize Christian ideas of order in a world of powerful political antitheses. For many years peace and justice were the goal of political order. Law both served peace and expressed it. In the age of the Peace of God and the Peace of the Land (→ Feudalism; Crusades 3; Middle Ages 1.2.2), those who held secular and spiritual power were guardians of a peace that was designed to prevent widespread internecine warfare. This development reached a climax in 1495 at the Diet of Worms, which decreed a permanent Peace of the Land, the impact of which was still apparent in the Peace of Augsburg of 1555 (→ Augsburg, Peace of).

2.2.4. Although the Peace of God and the Peace of the Land were still separate, they came together in the idea of an empire *(imperium)* that would embrace all the West and indeed the whole inhabited globe. The supreme task of keeping the peace was committed in concert to the spiritual and secular powers, the pope and the emperor (→ Empire and Papacy).

Once the relation between the two was disturbed or disrupted by the claim of one side or the other to supremacy, however, the sacrally secured order of peace was threatened at the core. Against papal claims to supremacy (→ Pope, Papalism, 1.6), Dante Alighieri (1265-1321, in *De monarchia*), Pierre DuBois (ca. 1250-ca. 1320, *De recuperatione terre sacra*), and Marsilius of Padua (ca. 1280-ca. 1343, *Defensor pacis*) emphasized at the beginning of the 14th century that the safeguarding of political peace was a separate matter. In so doing, they anticipated modern motifs like that of a European federation and an international court of justice.

2.2.5. Martin Luther's (1483-1546) understanding of peace, which widely influenced the → Reformation, again linked the biblical witness to the traditions of social philosophy (→ Luther's Theology). In his → two-kingdoms doctrine, which derived from Augustine, Luther applied the differentiation of Aristotle and natural law between three states or hierarchies: → church, → economy, and → politics. What individual Christians do or refrain from doing in their own place integrates with what God is doing in the world (*The Bondage of the Will, LW* 33.241-45). In defining our special responsibility for keeping earthly peace as the supreme good on earth, Luther insisted that individual Christians should suffer wrong rather than defend themselves with force; as rulers, though, they must be ready, if need be, to protect others against aggression. Wars of faith or aggression were totally forbidden.

Because temporal peace is "the greatest of earthly goods, in which all other temporal goods are comprised" (*LW* 46.226), the task of preserving it is not committed to rulers alone but is a responsibility of all Christians in their respective places, for the people themselves must help and advise and rule. This insight influenced the → Anabaptists after the Münster disaster (1534/35), when they increasingly became the pacifist wing of the Reformation (→ Mennonites). Avoiding political office, these frequently persecuted minorities (esp. J. A. Comenius and the → Bohemian Brethren) committed themselves primarily to the nonviolent ethos of the Sermon on the Mount.

2.2.6. The division of Christianity in the West threatened the power of Christian truth to establish peace. In the religious wars (→ Thirty Years' War) truth became party propaganda. Thus the modern → state, to establish peace, had to ensure external order and neutralize the truth claims of conscience and faith (Thomas Hobbes). Rational → natural law was given the task of establishing peace without recourse to theology (Hugo Grotius). It is nevertheless plain that especially by the protection of → freedom of belief and conscience, the working out of human → rights, and the adoption of material criteria of justice, the impulses of a biblical ethos were still at work, even though the churches at first did not recognize them as such.

2.3. *Modern Discussion*

In modern → international law in Europe, war has ceased in large part to be a moral issue. Instead, it became a rational instrument by which to uphold national sovereignty. In the 18th and 19th centuries we thus see a bellicosity that was promoted especially by the war of liberation against Napoléon. But → peace movements and peace societies also arose at this time. The churches and Christians for the most part accepted nationalism and militarism. With few exceptions (e.g., D. Bonhoeffer and F. Siegmund-Schultze), they achieved a new understanding of peace only as a result of the experiences of World War II.

2.3.1. In view of the indiscriminatingly destructive power of modern → weapons and the global reach of weapon systems, the insight has gained ground in ecumenical Christianity since 1945 that weapons of mass destruction can no longer be justified as a means to protect law and peace. World peace has become an essential condition in a technological age (C. F. von Weizsäcker). Yet apart from the historic → peace churches, the churches have not yet seen their way to unanimously command → conscientious objection as an essential witness for their members. Though condemning the use of modern weapons, they accept them as a deterrent force, even though they realize that the credibility of the deterrent depends on a readiness to use them (see 1.3).

2.3.2 Most churches, including the → Roman Catholic Church, try to alleviate this moral dilemma of peace in a nuclear age by recognizing that military service and conscientious objection are both permissible decisions of conscience and by stating that the strategy of nuclear deterrence is an option that may still be accepted today. An important presupposition of this conditional consent to the keeping of peace by military force lies in the demand that the level of armaments should be reduced. Since this reduction has been slow to happen, in all churches voices are increasingly demanding that, not merely the use of nuclear and other modern weapons should be rejected, but also their development, production, and deployment. This position was officially taken by the → World Council of Churches at its Sixth Assembly, in Vancouver in 1983.

2.3.3. In *Gaudium et spes* (1965, the Pastoral Constitution on the Church in the Modern World), → Vatican II accorded recognition to those who refuse to use force in defense of their rights, limiting themselves to those means of defense that are at the disposal of the weak (§78, "Nature of Peace"). An impulse in the biblical tradition reemerges here according to which the peace of God that is promised especially to the poor, the weak, and the suffering ought to determine human action for peace today. Other churches have begun to insist that traditional Christian options for peacemaking, whether → pacifism or just war, are basically reactive. According to this view, Christians will not be effective peacemakers until they attempt proactively to change the conditions (e.g., → poverty) that contribute to conflict.

2.3.4. The ethos of a peace that is nonviolent is certainly not alien to non-Christian religions. The nonviolent path of M. Gandhi (1869-1948) might not be representative of all → Hinduism, but it shows that a sense of responsibility for peace that is grounded in religion is by no means a Christian monopoly. Peace is by no means served if we look at world religions solely from the limited standpoint of their peace ethic. But the threats to peace compel all religions to make the corresponding decisions in terms of the core of their beliefs.

→ Disarmament and Armament; Ecumenical Dialogue

Bibliography: R. H. Bainton, *Christian Attitudes toward War and Peace* (Nashville, 1983) • U. Duchrow, *Shalom: Biblical Perspectives on Creation, Justice, and Peace* (Geneva, 1989) • J. Gros and J. D. Rempel, eds., *The Fragmentation of the Church and Its Unity in Peacemaking* (Grand Rapids, 2001) • P. Lodberg, "Justice and Peace in a World of Chaos," *A History of the Ecumenical Movement,* vol. 3, *1968-2000* (ed. J. Briggs, M. Oduyoye, and G. Tsetsis; Geneva, 2004) 323-43 • M. E. Miller and B. N. Gingerich, eds., *The Church's Peace Witness* (Grand Rapids, 1994) • G. H. Stassen, ed., *Just Peacemaking* (Cleveland, 1998) • C. F. Weizsäcker, *Der bedrohte Friede. Politische Aufsätze, 1945-1981* (2d ed.; Munich, 1981) • W. Wink, ed., *Peace Is the Way: Writings on Nonviolence from the Fellowship of Reconciliation* (Maryknoll, N.Y., 2000).

Wolfgang Lienemann, with
Michael Kinnamon

Peace Churches

The → Anabaptists (whose descendants are → Mennonites, → Hutterites, and Amish), the Quakers (→ Friends, Society of), and the → Brethren (a movement originating in Germany in the late 17th cent., soon transplanted to Pennsylvania) are the historic peace churches (HPC). While each has a separate theological and historical identity, they share common impulses. Jesus' teaching of → love of enemies and his nonresistant death inspired these believers to do likewise because of their conviction that the Holy Spirit was at work in their lives no less than in the → early church.

The public and collective nature of their dissent brought on → persecution. Ironically, the longing that fueled these movements for "a peaceable kingdom" led apocalypticists like the Münsterites of the 16th century to turn to violence. The vast majority of these radicals, however, remained devoted to the experiment of living nonviolently in a violent world. Many retreated to rural enclaves for survival. Beginning in the 1680s, William Penn, Quaker governor of Pennsylvania, invited groups of all the HPC to settle in his commonwealth. For two generations a social order existed that tolerated all manner of dissent and that governed without a standing militia or capital punishment. All three churches developed "old orders" that preserved a rural, countercultural lifestyle, as well as moderate and progressive wings.

To the extent that such differences among and within denominations allow for generalizing, the following can be said concerning each of the pacifist traditions. The Anabaptist position is grounded in Jesus' teaching (supremely the → Sermon on the Mount) and death (willingly accepted suffering for others). For Mennonites, Hutterites, and Amish, believer's → baptism enacts the spiritual transformation that makes the way of the cross possible. The Quaker peace position relies on the immediacy of God's reign, which came in Jesus, in the present. Its appeal for people to live peaceably is based on the belief in "that of God in everyone." The Brethren position combines the Anabaptist teaching on the normativeness of Jesus' life for → discipleship with an emphasis on the direct experience of God's love as the source of nonviolence.

Through evangelistic and social mission beginning in the late 19th century, all three of the HPC spread beyond the North Atlantic world to Asia, Africa, and Latin America. In response to the carnage of World War I, all of them mounted large-scale relief efforts. The Quakers, moreover, were a benign background presence at the formation of the League of Nations in 1920. The HPC (with the → International Fellowship of Reconciliation) began their institutional cooperation in North America in the 1930s by together pressing for the right of → conscientious objection to military service in Canada and the United States and for negotiation as an alternative to violence in the resolution of the international conflicts of the day. After World War II they expanded relief work, engaged in microlevel development projects, and then pioneered in the field of conflict resolution.

At the beginning of the 21st century there is ferment in the HPC, especially in respect to the following aspects of the peace position: whether true peace is possible only through Christ, or whether it is a universal possibility; whether or not a socially engaged → pacifism and a stringent just-war position (starting with a presumption against war) can make common cause in what is called "just peacemaking"; and whether the North Atlantic articulation of the NT peace teaching is meaningful or valid for churches in non-Western cultures. In 2001 in Basel, Switzerland, and in 2004 in Nairobi, Kenya, agencies of the HPC sponsored consultations addressing these and other issues. Worldwide, Brethren churches total 500,000 adherents; Quakers, 300,000; and Mennonite-related churches, 1.5 million.

→ Force, Violence, Nonviolence

Bibliography: General: P. Brock, *Freedom from Violence: Sectarian Nonresistance from the Middle Ages to the Great War* (Toronto, 1991) • Continuation Committee of the Historic Peace Churches in Europe, *Peace is the Will of God* (Amsterdam, 1953) a pacifist appeal to the ecumenical movement • F. Enns et al., eds., *Seeking Cultures of Peace: A Peace Church Conversation* (Geneva, 2004) • J. Gros and J. Rempel, eds., *The Fragmentation of the Church and Its Unity in Peacemaking* (Grand Rapids, 2001) • D. Gwyn et al., eds., *A Declaration on Peace* (Scottdale, Pa., 1991) • Historic Peace Churches and the International Fellowship of Reconciliation, *The Christian and War* (N.p., 1970) a continuation with just-war theorists of the 1953 conversation • M. Miller and B. Gingerich, *The Church's Peace Witness* (Grand Rapids, 1994).

Brethren: D. Brown, *Biblical Pacifism* (Elgin, Ill., 1984) • V. Eller, *War and Peace from Genesis to Revelation* (Scottdale, Pa., 1981).

Quakers: American Friends Service Committee, *Speak Truth to Power* (N.p., 1955) • W. Penn, *No Cross, No Crown* (Richmond, Ind., 1981; orig. pub., 1669).

Mennonites: D. Friesen, *Christian Peacemaking and*

International Conflict (Scottdale, Pa., 1986) • J. Yoder, *The Politics of Jesus* (Grand Rapids, 1992).

John D. Rempel

Peace Education

1. Perspective and Origins
2. Emphases
3. Concerns
   3.1. International and Global Studies
   3.2. Bases of Peace
   3.3. Conflict Studies
4. Program Growth
5. Optimism

1. Perspective and Origins

Writing from the context of the civil strife and military rule of his Brazilian homeland in the 1960s, Paulo Freire suggested in his classic study *Pedagogy of the Oppressed* (1968) that theory without practice is verbalism, and practice without reflection is activism. Instead, he advocated the "radical interaction" between reflection and action and stressed that if one is sacrificed, the other suffers. Perhaps no more succinct and insightful summary can be found to illustrate the critically important integration of → peace movements, → peace research, and peace education.

Peace education in the United States can be traced to a 1914 school reform movement organized by the American School Peace League, directed by Fannie Fern Andrews (1867-1950). The Hague Appeal for Peace, arising from the Third Hague Peace Conference (May 1999), is committed to the goal of introducing peace education into school curricula, as well as community and family education, worldwide.

The majority of peace education programs, however, are located within colleges and university settings, where peace education is conducted under some version of the general heading "peace studies." Here it draws on a long and scholarly tradition that took root in the years between the two world wars and developed more substantially in the 1950s. A second major resurgence in the field took place, particularly in the United States, following the Vietnam War (1964-73).

2. Emphases

Although no common agreement exists regarding the proper definition of peace education, it is possible to propose a working definition. This lack of clarity arises partly because there are no tightly defined boundaries that adequately describe fundamental terms such as → "peace," → "war," or "justice." Nonetheless, most collegiate peace studies programs reveal some clear patterns of similarity and convergence in structure and purpose. At its essence, peace education contains at least the following four emphases: peace education is (1) multidisciplinary; (2) values oriented, or contains a clearly identifiable normative component; (3) committed to preventing overt as well as less visible forms of violence (→ Force, Violence, Nonviolence); and (4) dedicated to the creative and constructive transformation of human → conflict.

Within institutions of higher education, peace studies programs draw on a variety of academic disciplines, including many of the traditional humanities such as → philosophy and → religious studies, as well as the → social sciences, especially political science, sociology, economics, psychology, and history. In some instances, biology, physics, and other natural sciences are also part of the curriculum.

The → values orientation of peace education is often its most controversial characteristic and the source of much criticism. Much negative reaction arises simply because peace education challenges fundamental structures of the status quo. Opponents assert that peace education often lacks the requisite amounts of objectivity and neutrality. Proponents maintain that just as medical science is biased in favor of health, peace education is biased in favor of making peace through peaceful means. To carry the analogy further, just as a physician is commonly expected to provide an accurate diagnosis of an illness, a reasonable prognosis of future developments of the ailment, and a recommended course of action to cure the illness, so a peace educator is expected to accurately assess the causes of societal violence and occurrences of war, provide a description of potential consequences of the unrest and violence, and suggest appropriate means to peacefully transform the conflict at hand.

Regarding the focus on preventing violence, since the 1960s peace educators have drawn an important distinction between the concepts of *negative peace* (i.e., the absence of war) and *positive peace,* understood as the presence of life-affirming values and practices such as economic and social justice and environmental → stewardship. This dichotomy can also be understood by distinguishing between overt forms of violence (collective or individual) and what peace scholar Johan Galtung has termed *structural violence.* The latter occurs when people are placed at a disadvantage because of unjust political or economic systems and cultural traditions. To build a just and sustainable peace, we must not simply be against war but also be for something, namely, human well-being based on values such as justice and equality. In recent years, many peace educators have argued that effective peacemaking must integrate the pursuit of both negative and positive peace.

Within the field of peace education, conflict is increasingly understood as a common experience present in all relationships, and a positive source of change. Within some academic settings, the area of study known as conflict resolution functions as a relatively autonomous entity. Within many more contexts, conflict resolution (or, in the more contemporary expression, conflict transformation) is understood as a subfield within peace studies.

The term "conflict resolution" often implies, intentionally or not, that conflict is bad and therefore should be ended, preferably forever. It also generally assumes that conflict is a short-term phenomenon that can in fact be permanently resolved. The central question here is, How do we end something that is not desired? Proponents of conflict transformation do not encourage efforts to control or eliminate conflict. Rather, with an emphasis on restoring broken relationships, they recommend that disputants embrace conflict as a catalyst for change, accept the painful past, and embrace a potential shared future as a means of creatively and forthrightly dealing with the conflict at hand. The guiding question for conflict transformation is thus, How do we end something that is not desired, and together build something we do desire? (John Paul Lederach has been the most helpful in distinguishing conflict resolution and conflict transformation.)

3. Concerns

This intellectual core, based on the above characteristics, is applied to a wide variety of organizational plans within academe and society. At one time nuclear → weapons and U.S.-Soviet relations dominated most college peace studies programs. Today, peace studies programs around the world address an expansive array of concerns. A common model organizes these four constituent parts into three general categories: (1) international and global studies, (2) religious and philosophical bases of peace, and (3) interpersonal and intergroup conflict studies.

3.1. *International and Global Studies*

International and global studies typically begin with an examination of the etiology of war. Students consider, for example, whether war is caused primarily by greed, a violent human nature, the anarchic nature of the modern state system, imperialism, or the so-called clash of civilizations. From this initial discussion, other major topics within the subfield often include war prevention, ideology, international political economy, the role of diplomacy, international law and organization, human rights, weapons of mass destruction, disarmament and arms control, alternative security systems, global ecology, the quest for world order, and alternative futures. As the world grows increasingly interdependent and the responsibilities of global citizenship become more self-evident, many peace scholars have emphasized the critically important distinction between national interest and human interest.

3.2. *Bases of Peace*

Studies pertaining to the religious and philosophical bases of peace often center on the assumption that our relationship with → God (or the Divine, however conceived) cannot with integrity be separated from our relationship with other members of the human family. When such spiritual tenets are followed and the end goal of a peaceful world community is pursued, religious and philosophical norms can undergird effective peacemaking.

Recent scholarship, however, has concentrated on the role of religion in fomenting and exacerbating social and political conflict. Many have emphasized the disturbing pattern, evident in many contemporary cases of collective violence, of appropriating religious mandates and symbols in pursuit of political or economic goals. The rise of → fundamentalism has dominated a good deal of these debates. Even more critical to peace educators is the manner in which some fundamentalist leaders have advanced absolute truth claims, generated religious militancy, and declared holy war on those they have identified as enemies of their faith. Such rigid theologies of exclusivism and other patterns of corrupted religion that result in violence are often constructed on passionate declarations that the end justifies any means necessary.

Into such difficult settings, many have suggested, we must train and send forth religiously committed peacemakers able to effectively communicate and live out the most basic teachings of all religions, namely, a theology of inclusive → love. Blaise Pascal (1623-62) once observed, "People never do evil so completely and cheerfully as when they do it from religious conviction." Perhaps an antidote to this tendency is captured in Charles Kimball's simple but important assertion: "Experience makes plain that my experience of God, my human view of truth, does not begin to exhaust the possibilities" (p. 209).

Beyond these essential topics, other themes often included in this subfield include war and morality, the teachings of Mohandas Gandhi (1869-1948) and the spiritual bases of nonviolence, the just-war tradition, and schools of socioeconomic justice such as those based on → liberation theology or the writings of Martin Luther King Jr. (1929-68). Many peace education programs also grant consideration to the fact that during its first 300 years (i.e., before the conversion of Emperor Constantine), the Christian church was essentially pacifist (→ Pacifism). Historic peace-church traditions continue to emphasize that absolute pacifism holds the presupposition that a preferable alternative to warfare always exists and that such alternative courses of action are morally sound and conform most closely to the teachings of → Jesus.

3.3. *Conflict Studies*

The third subfield can perhaps be summarized through reference to the preamble of UNESCO's constitution: "War begins in the minds of men [and women]" (→ United Nations). This component of peace education has primarily evolved from psychological and biological studies devoted to investigating questions such as, Is the occurrence of war explained by innate human depravity and instinctive aggression?

The writings of Sigmund Freud (1856-1939), Konrad Lorenz (1903-89), Robert Ardrey (1908-80), and Margaret Mead (1901-78) are often key to these investigations. Many such studies conclude with an examination of the distinction between the indicative and the imperative, or what is sometimes referred to as the naturalistic fallacy: the mistaken belief that "is" implies "ought" — that is, that practice of a given behavior does not indicate that such behavior is good. Based on her distinguished career in anthropology, Mead is credited with advancing the insight that war is a human invention and not a biological necessity.

When scholars functioning within this subfield consider the influences of → group dynamics, they typically address the major themes of nationalism (→ Nation, Nationalism) and ethnocentrism; cross-cultural psychology and intercultural communications; ethnic, racial, and religious conflicts; and the role of mass communications (→ Mass Media) in the march toward war. The subfield also includes discussion of the above-noted distinction between the resolution and the transformation of conflicts. Such theories are often taught with practical applications in mind such as the training of third-party mediators and of experts skilled in the fields of conciliation, diplomacy, and intergroup negotiation. Louis Kriesberg has provided leadership in this field of study, much of which is captured in his affirmation that intergroup conflicts can be waged constructively.

4. Program Growth

Within higher education, peace studies programs have expanded rapidly. The first undergraduate program was established in 1948 at Manchester College (Indiana), a college of the Church of the Brethren, itself one of the historic peace churches. The 1970s brought major growth in peace studies programs within the United States and Europe, as well as the founding of the Consortium on Peace Research, Education, and Development (COPRED). Kenneth and Elise Boulding were instrumental in the creation of COPRED, self-described as a reflection/action association of institutions and individuals engaged in peace studies. It functioned as the North American affiliate of the International Peace Research Association.

The balance between reflection and action was a bit precarious throughout COPRED's 31-year existence. In 1987 a group of peace scholars who were active in COPRED but dissatisfied with the intellectual progress of the field formed the Peace Studies Association (PSA). Because many peace educators maintained memberships in both organizations, and because of the recognition of mutual interests and common goals in both organizations, in 2001 COPRED and PSA merged to form the Peace and Justice Studies Association. Based on COPRED's most recent *Global Directory of Peace Studies and Conflict Resolution Programs* (2000), there were 381 colleges and universities in 42 countries offering programs in peace studies, ranging from undergraduate degrees to master's and doctoral degrees.

Many of the original questions that were at the heart of peace education from the beginning continue to demand the attention of those committed to the goal of making peace through peaceful means. The field of study also continues to broaden. Many newly established programs now work closely with studies of women and gender, or with minority and ethnic studies; others include a more prominent emphasis on environmental protection.

5. Optimism

Despite the persistent critique of the legitimacy of peace education (see 1 above) and notwithstanding the daunting challenges of the 21st century, Freire's affirmation of the "radical interaction" between reflection and action and the promise of a more peaceful world order continue to inspire and motivate peace educators. Beliefs that prevent the creation of a more secure, just, and peaceful world are learned. Because they are learned and not part of human nature, such beliefs can change. Indeed, sweeping attitudinal change has been the driving force that has made progress possible throughout human history. It is therefore reasonable to hope that fundamental attitudes concerning human security will change and that a world with greater peace and justice will one day be achieved. Realizing this goal will require the concerted efforts of peace scholars and activists, the commitment of concerned policy makers, and the indomitable courage and conviction of an enlightened global citizenry.

Bibliography: R. H. BAINTON, *Christian Attitudes toward War and Peace: A Historical Survey and Critical Re-evaluation* (Nashville, 1960) • D. P. BARASH and C. P. WEBEL, *Peace and Conflict Studies* (Thousand Oaks, Calif., 2002) • E. BOULDING, *Building a Global Civic Culture: Education for an Interdependent World* (New York, 1988) • R. EISLER and R. MILLER, eds., *Educating for a Culture of Peace* (Portsmouth, N.H., 2004) • R. FALK, *On Human Governance: Toward a New Global Politics* (University Park, Pa., 1995) • P. FRIERE, *Pedagogy of the Oppressed* (New York, 1968) • I. M. HARRIS and M. L. MORRISON, *Peace Education* (2d ed.; Jefferson, N.C., 2003) • R. C. JOHANSEN, *The National Interest and the Human Interest: An Analysis of U.S. Foreign Policy* (Princeton, 1980) • C. KIMBALL, *When Religion Becomes Evil* (San Francisco, 2002) • J. P. LEDERACH, *Building Peace: Sustainable Reconciliation in Divided Societies* (Washington, D.C., 1997) • J. A. VASQUEZ, "Toward a Unified Strategy of Peace Education," *JCR* 20 (1976) 707-28 • M. WALZER, *Just and Unjust Wars: A Moral Argument, with Historical Illustrations* (New York, 1977) • S. ZEIGER, "Teaching Peace: Lessons from a Peace Studies Curriculum of the Progressive Era," *PeCh* 25 (2000) 52-69.

TIMOTHY A. MCELWEE

Peace Movements

1. Identification and Classification
2. Since 1815
3. Impact

1. Identification and Classification

Across the centuries of Christian history, the most consistent and enduring peace witness has been that of the so-called historic → peace churches: the → Anabaptists (existing today as → Mennonites, → Hutterites, and Amish), the Quakers, and the → Brethren. Here, however, attention is focused on other organized efforts to bring together persons opposed to war and violence, usually including the religiously motivated.

American peace historian Charles Chatfield has identified two general orientations among peace groups: (1) internationalists and (2) liberal or radical pacifists. The former advocate governmental policies establishing stability and order; the latter seek fundamental transformation of societies.

British scholar Nigel Young offers tools for classification of peace movements: by *traditions* (religious, internationalist, socialist, feminist, conservationist) and by *goals or objectives* (opposition to all → war or to a specific war, opposition to military conscription, opposition to arms races or to specific → weapons, advocacy for world order and nonviolent social change).

2. Since 1815

Organized peace societies emerged in the Anglo-American context in the early 19th century. Probably the first of its kind, the New York Peace Society was founded in 1815 by David Low Dodge (1774-1852), a Presbyterian layman. The London Peace Society was begun the next year. In 1828 William Ladd (1778-1841), a Unitarian minister, founded the first national group, the American Peace Society. As part of a larger wave of humanitarian reform in the next decades, emerging peace organizations embraced issues from international arbitration to personal → conscientious objection, with abolition of slavery a focal concern in the United States. Peace leaders espousing Christian views in the antebellum period included Noah Worcester (1758-1837), Adin Ballou (1803-90), William Lloyd Garrison (1805-79), and Elihu Burritt (1810-79).

As the United States moved toward civil war, divisions appeared between the absolute pacifists and those who advocated a just war (against → slavery), between those who accepted established processes of law and government and anarchists, between advocates of people's movements and hierarchical political organizers, between internationalists and isolationists. The positions advocated by these early voices represent the range of beliefs and values that continue to motivate and distinguish various peace groups.

Even as the American Civil War saw the decline of peace organizations, a series of international peace congresses in Europe (1843-50) were overshadowed by the Crimean War of 1853-56. By the end of the century, new initiatives such as the Hague Conferences (1899, 1907), proposed by Russia to reduce armaments, and the work of the Carnegie Endowment for International Peace (founded 1910) represented political and educational efforts by establishment leaders that gained the support of many liberal peace advocates.

The radical Christian → anarchism preached by Leo Tolstoy (1828-1910) was a major influence on Mohandas K. Gandhi (1869-1948) as he experimented with mass nonviolent action for social change, first in South Africa and then in his native India. In the United States an early 20th-century optimism was expressed in the growing movements for foreign → missions, church unity, and → peace, often combined with expansionist urges for a world order shaped in the American image.

But these hopes soon turned to despair as Europe was ravaged by war. From the crucible of World War I (1914-18) came such disparate groups as the Christian pacifist → International Fellowship of Reconciliation and the internationalist League of Nations Association. Christian concerns for peace and unity came to fruition in the 1925 Stockholm → Life and Work Conference, an achievement that merited its organizer, Swedish Lutheran archbishop Nathan Söderblom (1866-1931), the 1930 Nobel Peace Prize. A high point of the interwar period in Britain was a letter published in October 1934 by H. R. L. (Dick) Sheppard (1880-1937). This document launched the Peace Pledge Union, the peace group with the largest membership ever. Gandhi's nonviolent campaigns in India also gained worldwide attention during this period.

In America, as international → disarmament and world order plans became dominant issues in the 1920s and 1930s, many pacifists joined in promoting the World Court and the League of Nations. Pacifist leaders such as Jane Addams (1860-1935), Kirby Page (1890-1957), and Norman Thomas (1884-1968), recognizing social injustice as a basic root of war, advocated fundamental political and economic changes. But with the rise of → fascism in Europe, Reinhold → Niebuhr (1892-1971) was typical of many liberal pacifists who shifted to a justified-war stance. The swift rise and sudden fall of the Emergency Peace Campaign (1936-38) also exemplifies the competing tensions of the late 1930s between isolationism and interventionism.

The outbreak of war in Europe and the establishment of a military draft in the United States reduced the peace movement largely to convinced absolutists who applied for conscientious objector status (rather than military service) or were jailed. Yet during the war years the membership of the Fellowship of Reconciliation, led by A. J. Muste (1885-1967), nearly tripled. Committed to nonviolent social change, Muste and others extended Gandhian techniques to → civil rights campaigns, even in the midst of wartime. Conscientious objectors, although a tiny minority, were better understood and tolerated by the public in World War II (1939-45) than in the "Great War." Many of the objectors volunteered for European reconstruction after the war.

In the postwar period, as the world faced the reality of nuclear weaponry, atomic scientists took leadership in new efforts for peace. While internationalists energized support for the → United Nations, more radical activists went beyond educational and political strategies to organize mass public demonstrations and encourage symbolic acts of civil disobedience. Beginning in 1957, many peace groups joined in the National Committee for a Sane Nuclear Policy, or SANE, a coalition calling for a ban on nuclear testing. Parallel antinuclear movements gained large followings in Europe, such as the British Campaign for Nuclear Disarmament. Jean (1912-91) and Hildegard (b. 1930) Goss-Mayr, well-known Austrian Roman Catholic peace activists and philosophers, traveled widely in Europe and the Americas for the Fellowship of Reconciliation, teaching Gandhian nonviolence adapted for a largely Christian audience.

The escalation of America's war in Vietnam in the mid-1960s provoked massive counteractions. The antiwar movement embraced a wide range of constituencies — youth, labor, education, even military veterans — and strategies, from education and lobbying to huge demonstrations and civil disobedience such as draft-card burning. Brothers Daniel (b. 1921) and Philip (1923-2002) Berrigan, Roman Catholic activists, and William Sloane Coffin Jr. (b. 1924) appeared as leaders and indeed icons of the movement. Any attempt to understand this era, moving into the 1970s, is complicated by the interplay of assorted antiwar efforts with the emerging youth counterculture and consequent social upheaval. When civil rights leader Martin Luther → King Jr. (1929-68) spoke out forcefully against the Vietnam War in 1967, divisions surfaced among both his supporters and the general public. While in retrospect many thoughtful pacifists questioned the enduring impact of the more radical actions, it seems clear that the Vietnam era significantly reshaped American attitudes toward warfare.

The deployment of a new generation of missiles in Europe during Ronald Reagan's presidency (1981-89) was challenged by the nuclear freeze campaign, which sponsored a demonstration in New York City in June 1982 that drew nearly one million people, the largest peace rally in U.S. history.

Growing criticism of nuclear deterrence came from major church bodies in Europe and the United States; particularly significant was "The Challenge of Peace: God's Promise and Our Response" (1983), a pastoral letter of the American Roman Catholic bishops, a statement that for the first time ever approved absolute → pacifism as an option for Roman Catholic individuals. In the 1980s the → World Council of Churches launched a global multiyear program — "Justice, Peace, and the Integrity of Creation" — that extended into the 1990s.

With the collapse of the Soviet Union, the end of the cold war, and the acknowledged sole superpower status of the United States, peace activists at the dawn of the 21st century turned their attention to the complex Middle East situation and the dangers of nuclear proliferation, as well as to a critical evaluation of the conventional militarized reaction to the threats of global → terrorism. Worldwide demonstrations against the war in Iraq on February 15, 2003, involved an estimated ten million people, the largest single day of antiwar protest in human history.

3. Impact

The common element in these many movements has been the attempt to persuade people and governments to adopt more peaceable alternatives to existing policies. Strategies of the many peace movements cover a spectrum from education to dissent, protest, and active resistance. Recognizing that the focus of most peace activists is on foreign policy issues that are controlled by executive power and usually reflect the dominant culture, it is not surprising that peace movements have seldom achieved their objectives. Charles Chatfield has suggested that the long-term impact of the 20th-century peace coalitions, especially in the United States, has been to highlight nonviolent alternatives to war and to further the role of citizen activism in democratic decision-making.

→ Peace Education; Peace Research

Bibliography: C. Chatfield, *The American Peace Movement: Ideals and Activism* (New York, 1992); idem, *For Peace and Justice: Pacifism in America, 1914-1941* (Knoxville, Tenn., 1971) • C. Chatfield and P. van den Dungen, *Peace Movements and Political Cultures* (Knoxville, Tenn., 1988) • D. Cortright, *Peace Works: The Citizen's Role in Ending the Cold War* (Boulder, Colo., 1993) • C. DeBenedetti, *The Peace Reform in American History* (Bloomington, Ind., 1980) • R. Marchand, *The American Peace Movement and Social Reform, 1898-1918* (Princeton, 1972) • R. Taylor and N. Young, eds., *Campaigns for Peace: British Peace Movements in the Twentieth Century* (Manchester, 1987) • L. Wittner, *Rebels against War: The American Peace Movement, 1933-1983* (Philadelphia, 1984).

J. R. Burkholder

Peace of Augsburg → Augsburg, Peace of

Peace Research

1. Philosophy of War and Science of Peace
2. Academic and Governmental Initiatives
3. Negative and Positive Peace
4. Journals
5. Worldwide Human Solidarity

1. Philosophy of War and Science of Peace

War is often viewed as a failure of moral imagination and diplomatic ability. At least from the days of ancient Greece and the writings of Thucydides (d. ca. 400 B.C.) and Plato (427-347), humanity has sought to overcome the problem of war because of its profound impact on society. In the 16th and 17th centuries, based in part on suggestions by Niccolò Machiavelli (1469-1527) and Thomas Hobbes (1588-1679) that human beings are by nature predisposed to greed and violence, realists began to explain the existence of war and authoritarian political institutions as necessary countermeasures to these innately human tendencies (→ Force, Violence, Nonviolence).

Rejecting Hobbes's "war of all against all," John Locke (1632-1704) argued in favor of a natural social order based on conformity to divine law that was capable of achieving domestic and international harmony. Because Locke's philosophy of civil government is grounded in the consent of the governed, he retained the right of citizens to rebel against tyranny. In 1795 Immanuel Kant (1724-1804) suggested that world peace could be achieved only through an association of → democracies — an idea pursued by Woodrow Wilson (1856-1924) after World War I through his proposal for the League of Nations.

These and other theories of war prevention served as the basis of a science of → war. But only after the invention and first use of nuclear → weapons has there been a science of → peace, with its own presuppositions and strategies that go beyond the first beginnings of peace research in the → peace movements of the late 19th and 20th centuries. An important example of such peace research before World War II is seen in the efforts of Mohandas Gandhi (1869-1948) in the first recognized instance of nonviolent direct action: his satyagraha campaign in South Africa in 1907.

2. Academic and Governmental Initiatives

As Arthur Koestler noted, before 1945 we worried about individual deaths; after 1945 we worried about the death of humanity. In reaction to the unprecedented tragedies (or, as many have argued, the war crimes) of the atomic bombings of Hiroshima and Nagasaki, scientists gathered worldwide to issue public manifestos relating their work in pure science to political responsibility (esp. the Center for Advanced Study in the Behavioral Sciences Conference, 1954; Pugwash Conferences on Science and World Affairs, 1957; Declaration of Atomic Scientists, 1957; Union of German Scientists, from 1959). Building on the pioneering work of Bertrand Russell (1872-1970) and Albert Einstein (1879-1955), several prominent natural scientists launched peace research as an academic discipline. Some of them had been directly involved in the development of atomic weaponry; others were motivated primarily by the clarion call to professional responsibility issued by Russell and Einstein. Their aim was to transform the scientific methods that had produced enormously destructive capabilities into a new science capable of creating social systems to enhance global human security.

While → peace education is interdisciplinary by design, peace research is primarily based in the → social sciences. First came Pitirim Sorokin's writings in the 1920s, followed by the work of Quincy Wright and Lewis Richardson between the two world wars. These pioneering works were followed by the research of Kenneth Boulding, Anatol Rapoport, Herbert Kelman, Arthur Gladstone, Karl Deutsch, J. David Singer, and Johan Galtung.

In 1930 Theodore Lentz founded the Character Research Institute at Washington University in St. Louis, Missouri, a research endeavor that later became known as the Peace Research Laboratory. This was followed by the Institut Français de Polemologie (1945) in France, the Research Exchange on the Prevention of War (1952) and the Center for Research on Conflict Resolution (1957) in the United States, the International Peace Research Institute, Oslo (PRIO, 1959), in Norway, the Peace Research Institute (1959) in Canada, the Gandhi Peace Research Foundation (1959) in India, the Polemologisch Instituut (1962) in Holland, the Council on Peace Research in History (1963, now the Peace History Society) in the United States, the Peace Research Society International (1963), and, through state support, the Stockholm International Peace Research Institute (1966) in Sweden. These were the first scientific institutes devoted solely to the study of peace and → conflict.

In the 1950s, under the leadership of Greenville Clark, a visionary statesman, and Professor Louis B. Sohn, a highly respected theorist, the movement for *world peace through world law* (see Clark and Sohn's 1958 book by the same name) gained widespread respect, even notoriety, among world leaders. Emerging from the global tension of the cold war, Clark and Sohn's research proposed a significant revision of the U.N. Charter and emphasized the urgent need for creating international institutions capable of achieving general and complete → disarmament, global economic → development, and world peace through → international law. Many of these scholarly efforts, which were initially funded through an endowment by Greenville Clark, were subsequently underwritten by the Fund for Education concerning World Peace through World Law (later referred to as the World Law Fund, or WLF). The University Program of the WLF supported numerous educational efforts on the graduate and undergraduate levels, including consultancy, materials production, and teacher training in peace research and world order.

UNESCO, through its Social Science Division, is rightly credited with encouraging the internationalizing of peace research. Two important expressions of this effort are seen in the efforts of the Women's International League for Peace and Freedom, with pivotal leadership provided by Elise Boulding, and the founding of the International Peace Research Association (IPRA). In 1962 the former established the International Consultative Committee on Peace Research, and the latter was the outgrowth of a 1963 meeting convened by John Burton and Kenneth Boulding. The following year, under the leadership of Johan Galtung and Bert Roling, IPRA was established; its first general assembly was convened in 1965 in Groningen, Netherlands. Today IPRA is generally considered the most important international peace research organization.

The 1980s saw a dramatic increase in government-sponsored peace research institutes. New Zealand and Australia serve as excellent examples of this promising trend, as does the U.S. Institute for Peace, which was established by an act of Congress in 1984. Building on the tradition of the United Nations University, headquartered in Tokyo, which the General Assembly established in 1973 to serve as "an international community of scholars engaged in research, advanced training, and the dissemination of knowledge related to the pressing global problems of human survival, development, and welfare," the → United Nations in 1980 also created the University for Peace, in Costa Rica.

3. Negative and Positive Peace

A key debate within peace research centers on the concepts of *negative peace* (the absence of war and the study of the causes of war, including analysis of territorial rivalries, alliances, diplomacy, international law, and the implications of power politics) and the more contemporary emphasis on *positive peace* (defined as social, economic, and political systems based on values and structures that enhance human life and thereby minimize the occurrences of war and injustice). This new emphasis arose primarily out of a strengthened sense of solidarity with the poor and oppressed. The primary argument is that research focused narrowly on nuclear armaments, arms races, and the prevention of war tends to suggest that peace is present merely if organized state violence is absent.

When Galtung, who is credited with conceiving of the concept of positive peace, suggested in the late 1960s that more subtle forms of *structural violence* such as hunger or death through preventable disease are as deadly as the overt violence of warfare, peace research entered a new phase of development. Galtung pointed to the structural dimensions of unjust social conditions to underscore the manner in which such violence limits human potential because of economic or political injustice. Advocates for the pursuit of positive peace assert that societies that impair the well-being of their citizens by denying access to education, health care, political power, housing, employment, and other essentials, or that violate human → rights based on religion, ethnicity, or sexual orientation, are guilty of inflicting structural violence, which often leads to overt violence or warfare.

4. Journals

Three prominent peace research journals are especially worthy of note: *Journal of Conflict Resolution, Journal of Peace Research,* and *Peace and Change.* Under the leadership of Kenneth Boulding and Anatol Rapoport, the *Journal of Conflict Resolution: A Quarterly for Research Related to War and Peace* published its first issue in 1957 through the University of Michigan's Journalism Department. One of the fundamental goals of the journal is to stimulate research on the prevention of war.

The *Journal of Peace Research,* a publication of PRIO, was first published in 1966. Given that PRIO was founded under the leadership of Galtung, not surprisingly much of its emphasis centers on the arguments put forward by proponents of positive peace.

The journal *Peace and Change,* first published in 1972, is the creative enterprise of the Peace History Society (PHS). It was later cosponsored by the Consortium on Peace Research, Education, and Development (COPRED), the North American affiliate of IPRA. After COPRED merged with the Peace Studies Association in 2001 to form the Peace and Justice Studies Association (PJSA), *Peace and Change* became the joint publication of PHS and PJSA.

5. Worldwide Human Solidarity

Like → peace movements and → peace education, peace research reflects critically on the practical dimensions of public policies that affirm the validity of the threat and use of violence and armed conflict in pursuit of peace. At the center of this critique is an emphasis on → solidarity with the entire human species rather than a more narrow social identification based on, say, nationality, ethnicity, or class.

This assessment of the fundamental problems inherent in the war system often places peace researchers at odds with the status quo. In stark contrast to the famous statement by Winston Churchill that "the story of the human race is war," most peace researchers consider war to be a social invention that is neither desirable nor inevitable. The study and the pursuit of peace do not, however, ignore the inevitability or the importance of human conflict. Rather than denying or fearing conflict, it is viewed as a positive and naturally occurring catalyst for change. When viewed from this standpoint, conflict becomes an effective means of pursuing goals such as building restored relationships based on → trust, → forgiveness, and → reconciliation. Emphasis is placed on the search for peace through peaceful means and the creative transformation of unavoidable conflict.

At the global level, this perspective advocates the development of alternative security systems motivated by concern for the well-being of the world's people and based on a comprehensive international commitment to settle conflicts through nonviolent political or judicial processes to ensure that all peoples are protected against the use of violence. In place of the war system, which is grounded in the assumption that security can be obtained through the military prowess of governments, many contemporary peace researchers stress that the well-being of any nation or any people is inseparable from that of the rest of humanity. A global attitudinal shift of this magnitude, and the corresponding reduction in worldwide military spending, would in turn free up enormous resources that could be devoted to serving the needs of humanity through the pursuit of economic and social justice and ecological stewardship.

Bibliography: I. Abrams, "Memoirs of a Peace Historian," *PeCh* 30 (2005) 3-13 • C. F. Alger, "Challenges for Peace Researchers and Peace Builders in the Twenty-first Century: Education and Coordination of a Diversity of Actors in Applying What We Are Learning," *IJPS* 5 (2000) 1-13 • C. Chatfield, "International Peace Research: The Field Defined by Dissemination," *JPR* 16 (1979) 161-79 • C. G. Clark and L. B. Sohn, *World Peace through World Law* (2d ed.; Cambridge, Mass., 1962) • B. W. Cook, C. Chatfield, and S. Cooper, eds., *The Garland Library of War and Peace* (New York, 1971) • R. Eisler, *The Chalice and the Blade: Our History, Our Future* (New York, 1987) • J. Galtung, "Violence, Peace, and Peace Research," *JPR* 6 (1969) 167-91 • J. Galtung, C. G. Jacobsen, and K. F. Brand-Jacobsen, *Searching for Peace: The Road to Transcend* (2d ed.; London, 2002) • K. Kodama, *History of International Peace Research Association* (Tsu, Japan, 2004) • J. Pérez de Cuéllar and Y. S. Choue, eds., *World Encyclopedia of Peace* (2d ed.; 4 vols.; Dobbs Ferry, N.Y., 2000) • P. Wallenstein, ed., *Peace Research: Achievements and Challenges* (Boulder, Colo., 1988).

Timothy A. McElwee

Peasants' War

The Peasants' War (1524-25) is one of the outstanding events in German history. L. Ranke called it the greatest natural event of the German state. It was also a turning point in the historical process, according to K. → Marx and F. Engels. It has thus attracted the attention of many generations of students of history.

1. Course

After a first outbreak of fighting in Hegau (near the German Black Forest) in the summer of 1524, the → war began in earnest in January 1525 in Upper Swabia. Peasants from various estates and territories assembled by the thousands south of Ulm, by Lake Constance, and in the Algäu. In March 1525 two main writings appeared in the same area that voiced the peasants' concerns and were frequently reprinted: the Twelve Articles of the Peasants of Upper Swabia, and the Federal Order, the former a catalog of partly reforming and partly revolutionary demands, the latter a plan of political and military organization. The revolt spread from Upper Swabia, supported by 25 printings of the Twelve Articles, which were usually adopted as basic demands or only slightly modified. Unrest spread to Franconia and Württemberg in March and April, then reached the Black Forest, Alsace, the Palatinate, and some cities (esp. Frankfurt), and finally reached its peak in May and June 1525, spreading to Thuringia, Tyrol, and Salzburg.

During the conflict the peasants frequently looted and burned → monasteries and castles, often with support from cities (Württemberg, Tyrol, Salzburg). The middle and lower classes sometimes aided them in the imperial cities (Heilbronn, Rothenburg, Strasbourg), and some guilds came out in support for them (in Salzburg and Tyrol). The term "peasants" is thus rather misleading; "common people" might be more appropriate.

Despite spectacular successes (e.g., in forcing the Electorate of Mainz to accept the Twelve Articles), the movement soon ran into problems even where it was successful. Thus the "Peasants' Parliament" at Heilbronn planned an amalgamation of the insurgents, but counterattacks by the Swabian Alliance and imperial princes blocked it. In a few major battles in May and June the peasants suffered crushing defeat. Apart from an isolated conflict in Salzburg in the summer of 1526, the war was over. Contemporary estimates of casualties run to 100,000. As a rule, the peasants were disarmed (sometimes only temporarily), reparations were imposed to meet the costs, and the ringleaders were hanged.

2. Standard Interpretations

The Peasants' War stands at the point of intersection of many currents that are not fully described by such catchwords as "agrarian crisis," "early capitalism," "territorialism," "imperial reform," or "reformation." Rather, this variety only makes clear the difficulty of interpretation. The older interpretations that have kindled modern debate were those of G. Franz on the one side and the Marxist-Leninists (e.g., M. M. Smirin) on the other. Franz saw a struggle between the princely territorial state and the peasant community. The Peasants' War aimed to set aside the former in favor of the latter (and of the emperor). When it failed, the former triumphed, and for nearly the next three centuries the peasants were excluded from the life of the people.

To this predominantly political interpretation Marxist research, with its concept of early middle-class → revolution, opposed an alternative that gives prominence to economic and social developments. In the tradition of Engels, scholars in East Germany (A. Laube, M. Steinmetz, G. Vogler) linked the Peasant War and the → Reformation in a movement that reached its climax in 1525. This movement supposedly arose out of the contradictions of → feudalism (peasants and nobles) and out of developing → capitalism (mining and textiles). Objectively, according to the theory of the progress of social formations, it had to be a middle-class revolution, though only an early one, in view of the rudimentary stage of capitalist relations.

Using theological argumentation, Thomas → Müntzer (ca. 1489-1525) worked out a theory in keeping with events that carried further the attacks of M. → Luther on the church as a feudal superstructure, calling for a people's reformation.

3. New Perspectives

In the 1970s wrestling with → sociology and → Marxism, helped by better empirical research of recent decades into agrarian history, produced new interpretations, which we might sketch in terms of causes, goals, and results.

3.1. *Causes*

Corresponding to the comprehensive and principled nature of the Peasants' War, the causes are economic, social, political, legal, and religious. Demographic growth prior to the Peasants' War (D. Sabean), the reactivation of personal → rights to prevent migration to the cities, the restriction of common rights (e.g., through enclosures and the high price of wood), and the rapid rise in taxes (R. Endres) all created tensions in agriculture. This pressure had social repercussions inasmuch as the gap between rich and poor widened (swelling the lower classes in the villages), restrictions were imposed on marriage because of the small size of many states, and measures were taken to limit the autonomy of the villages. In contrast, the peasants had achieved a good deal of liberation in the later Middle Ages, with representation on some diets (e.g., Tyrol, Salzburg; see P. Blickle).

The Reformation sharpened these developments. As the → Reformers stressed "the gospel without human additions," or "the pure gospel," the peasants thought they were in a position to abandon the unjust old law, which could not resolve the conflicts, for what they called divine law. Assuming that they could draw this law from Holy Scripture, the peasants radicalized the ideas of U. → Zwingli (1484-1531) and M. → Bucer (1491-1551) regarding the practical relevance of the "pure → gospel." It was not by accident that the Peasants' War took place for the most part where it did.

3.2. *Goals*

Divine law was a starting point for the development of new constitutional models, which rested on the premise that the gospel is the parameter for secular orders. This assumption evoked the protest of Luther that a political structure may vary according to territorial conditions (H. Buszello).

Common to all the programs is that they make the rural and urban communities the basis of the national structure and that they want all political offices to be elective. Seen thus, they might be called revolutionary, and the Peasants' War might be called a revolution of the common people (Blickle). But it is debatable whether we may read the regional proposals as abstractly as this view demands. And it could well be argued that such aspirations are the ideas of intellectuals (B. Hubmaier, W. Hipler, et al.) and thus have little real validity.

3.3. *Results*

In spite of the military repression there were remarkable compromises and relaxations for the peasants in the Alpine areas and parts of Upper Germany, so that one cannot say that the Peasants' War was a total failure. The revolt of the common people greatly irritated the authorities, and the actions of the imperial diet (1526, 1529, 1530) are enough to show that they feared new outbreaks of unrest.

The significance of the war for the Reformation is debatable. In Upper Germany it seems that the older thesis that the Peasants' War ended the Reformation as a popular movement (Franz) still stands (J. Maurer). The opposite thesis, which argues from the progress of the Reformation in the northern German states (F. Lau), owes its strength more to the number of its supporters than to its plausibility.

It is incontestable that the Peasants' War was a landmark in at least the history of Germany because it gave intimation of the possibility of a political and social structure that was neither imperial nor territorial. Had it been successful, it would have given Germany a form of government akin to that of the Swiss Confederation.

Bibliography: P. Blickle, *From the Communal Reformation to the Revolution of the Common Man* (Leiden, 1998); idem, *The Revolution of 1525: The German Peas-*

ants' War from a New Perspective (Baltimore, 1981) • P. BURGARD, *Tagebuch einer Revolte. Ein städtischer Aufstand während des Bauernkriegs 1525* (Frankfurt, 1998) • H. BUSZELLO et al., eds., *Der deutsche Bauernkrieg* (Paderborn, 1984) • R. ENDRES, "Der Bauernkrieg in Franken," *BDLG* 109 (1973) 31-68 • G. FRANZ, *Der deutsche Bauernkrieg* (12th ed.; Darmstadt, 1984; orig. pub., 1933) • F. LAU, "Der Bauernkrieg und die angebliche Ende der lutherischen Reformation als spontaner Volksbewegung," *LuJ* 26 (1959) 109-34 • A. LAUBE, M. STEINMETZ, and G. VOGLER, *Illustrierte Geschichte der deutschen frühbürgerlichen Revolution* (Berlin, 1974) • G. MARON, "Bauernkrieg," *TRE* 5.319-38 • J. MAURER, *Prediger im Bauernkrieg* (Stuttgart, 1979) • D. SABEAN, *Landbesitz und Gesellschaft am Vorabend des Bauernkriegs* (Stuttgart, 1972) • T. SCOTT and B. SCRIBNER, eds., *The German Peasants' War: A History in Documents* (Atlantic Highlands, N.J., 1991) • M. M. SMIRIN, *Die Volksreformation des Thomas Münzer und der große Bauernkrieg* (2d ed.; Berlin, 1956) • J. M. STAYER, *German Peasants' War and the Anabaptist Community of Goods* (Montreal, 1991).

PETER BLICKLE

Pedagogy

1. Term
2. History
   2.1. Antiquity
   2.2. Middle Ages
   2.3. Reformation
   2.4. Baroque Period
   2.5. Enlightenment
   2.6. "German Movement"
3. Modern Academic Pedagogics
   3.1. Pedagogy as a Science
   3.2. Relation with Other Disciplines
   3.3. Comparative Pedagogics

1. Term

The term "pedagogics" goes back to Gk. *paideia,* which denotes the method and result of → education in both theory and practice. In modern usage emphasis lies on the relation between the practical and the theoretical.

2. History

Historically, a distinction has often been made between theory and practice, that is, the intellectual, social, and academic aspects and the practices in various fields and institutions. This distinction has also been relevant for the term "pedagogy."

2.1. *Antiquity*

In the West poets like Homer (9th/8th cent. B.C.) and Pindar (ca. 522-ca. 438) were the first to make pronouncements about pedagogics. Reflection on the subject came after 400 B.C., and various answers to the question of pedagogics were offered. The Sophists (→ Greek Philosophy) stressed the rhetorical and practical sides and worked out a doctrine of seven disciplines: three formal (grammar, → rhetoric, and → dialectic) and four material (arithmetic, geometry, astronomy, and music). These "seven liberal arts" became very important in higher education.

In contrast, Socrates (ca. 470-399 B.C.), Plato (427-347; → Platonism), and Aristotle (384-322; → Aristotelianism) stressed the importance of → philosophy and → science. Plato's Academy (387) became the prototype of all academies and schools of higher education. In his *Republic* and *Laws,* Plato for the first time systematized an ideal of education. Tensions were inevitable between the pedagogics of ancient philosophy and that of the world of Jewish and Christian faith. The latter emphasized that only the → grace of God, not the arts, can perfect us.

In ancient Rome pedagogics was oriented to the → state, but with a higher regard for the → family as an educational force. The ideal at this point was the good citizen (→ Bourgeois, Bourgeoisie), who would act ethically and think clearly. Theoreticians were Cicero (106-43 B.C.), who endeavored to fuse Roman individuality with the Greek spirit, and Quintilian (ca. A.D. 35-ca. 100), who, as a teacher of rhetoric, stressed both the importance of character building and the principles of didactics.

2.2. *Middle Ages*

→ Augustine (354-430; → Augustine's Theology) mediated between antiquity and the → Middle Ages. He integrated ancient *paideia* into Christian education. Along the same lines → Thomas Aquinas (ca. 1225-74; → Thomism) saw God as the only true teacher.

Education for → faith and → obedience dominated medieval pedagogics. The seven liberal arts brought intellectual unity to the period. Monastic, cathedral, and endowed schools, as well as the → universities (Bologna, founded in 1119; Paris, in 1200), were involved in pedagogics. Later, an aristocratic and episcopal culture developed in Italy and France. M. de Montaigne (1533-92), its representative, argued against book learning and advocated dealings with humanity and the world.

2.3. *Reformation*

M. Luther (1483-1546; → Luther's Theology), with his stress on the universal priesthood of all believers

(→ Priest, Priesthood, 4), gave pedagogics new tasks. People had to be educated for God with no intervening authority. This understanding meant the use of the mother tongue in the service of faith. Tensions between Christian faith and → culture are inevitable: though pedagogics was not meant to awaken faith directly, faith was thought to require the education and development of certain human abilities. → Luther's address "To the Councilmen of All Cities in Germany That They Establish and Maintain Christian Schools" (1524, *LW* 45.339-78) was a call to popular education, but it was not followed up. In both theory and practice great importance attached to P. → Melanchthon (1497-1560), known as the preceptor of Germany, who founded universities (e.g., Marburg in 1527, Jena in 1548) and academies that stressed Greek and Latin and classical literature. The first state academies (e.g., the princely foundations of Grimma, Meissen, and Schulpforte) were renowned later for their pedagogical work.

→ Calvinism first organized education in Geneva. With the spread of the Reformed faith in France, Scotland, Hungary, Holland, and England, Calvinist education followed. The Counter-Reformation (→ Catholic Reform and Counterreformation) adopted educational changes made under the aegis of the Reformation. The → Jesuits emphasized the humanities (→ Humanism) and built academies and universities. The Ursulines devoted themselves to educating girls, and the Piarists promoted popular education (→ Religious Orders and Congregations 1).

2.4. *Baroque Period*

The → baroque lifestyle, in the sense of a planned direction of life, affected pedagogics by combining → rationalism and theology as distinct from humanistic pedagogics. The most significant figure of the time was J. A. Comenius (1592-1670), the bishop of the → Bohemian Brethren expelled from Bohemia in 1627. For him a religious education was the heart of pedagogics. It drew on three sources of → experience: the world as God's handiwork, the divine impulse of humanity, and the → Word of God in the Bible. Along such lines he wrote textbooks that shaped practical pedagogics for over a hundred years (esp. *Gate of Tongues Unlocked* [1631] and *The Visible World in Pictures* [1658]). Even today his *Great Didactic* (1628-32) still makes an impact. Also relevant is his *Pampaedia; or, Universal Education* (first pub. only in 1960). His plan of schools for both sexes and all classes might be described as a religiously motivated plan of graded instruction.

From Holland Comenius exerted his main influence in Britain, Sweden, Hungary, and Transylvania. Spurred on by → Pietism, N. → Zinzendorf (1700-1760) revived the → Moravian Brethren (§3), who kept alive Comenius's Reformation views on education in many countries in Europe and elsewhere.

2.5. *Enlightenment*

The → Enlightenment arose in the 18th century but is still influential today. Its central principle is an unlimited confidence in human → reason. This thinking, along with a change in the role of the state, broadly affected pedagogics and education. In fact, we might think of the 18th century as a century of pedagogics (so F. I. von Niethammer) for many reasons. J.-J. Rousseau's (1712-78) *Émile* (1762) drew attention to the special nature of children, led to works being produced for them, and created a demand for "natural" education, which relied on the development of human abilities. The new movement of popular education led to compulsory schooling in parts of Europe (from 1763) and to the state's taking responsibility for the building of schools (1794; → School and Church). The increasing need for well-organized instruction was recognized, and a relative uniformity was achieved in the conditions of schooling and in the demands made upon schools. Pedagogics became a university discipline first at Halle in 1779, though a little later F. A. Wolf (1759-1824) switched attention to philology. The Enlightenment had a major impact on Austria, Bohemia, Denmark, and Switzerland.

2.6. *"German Movement"*

H. Nohl (1879-1960) described a "German movement" of pedagogics that had four phases: Sturm und Drang ("storm and stress," exalting nature and human individualism), → classicism, → Romanticism, and educational reform. According to Nohl, this movement put a high stress on the unity, primacy, individuality, and historicity of → life and made a great impact on pedagogics generally. J. H. Pestalozzi (1746-1827) represented the transition from the Enlightenment to the Sturm und Drang. He influenced pedagogical thinking and action mainly for popular education and oriented social pedagogics to the child, to a union of head, heart, and hand, and to a high estimation of individual development. His analysis of moral elements in education is of enduring value.

W. von Humboldt (1767-1835) was an important theorist and practical reformer at the university and secondary levels. F. D. E. → Schleiermacher (1768-1834; → Schleiermacher's Theology) and J. F. Herbart (1776-1841) were founders of pedagogics as a discipline. This discipline had to straddle philosophical and empirical elements (→ Empiricism), and it oscillated between the two poles.

Romanticism (esp. J. Paul, F. Fröbel) combated Enlightenment rationalism and, with Schleiermacher, stressed the thinking that involves weighing and deciding. In content the accent lay on addressing the child, on → play, and on cultivating the dispositions.

Educational reform came with international interaction and showed itself in many ways, for example, in the youth movement, the feminist movement, reform pedagogics, and vocational schools, each of which reflects a specific pedagogical approach. It effected a new understanding of the school as not merely a place of books and learning, as in the 19th century, and fostered new methods of education and instruction.

3. Modern Academic Pedagogics

To claim that pedagogics is scientific in nature is contestable. We read statements of this kind in academic and sociological circles, though here the debates take place on the basis of generally recognized presuppositions. In contrast, the debate about scientific status is much more profound in methodological conflicts within pedagogics itself. T. Litt's (1880-1962) judgment along these lines in the 1920s is still true today, namely, that the constitutive pedagogical question is how to help people develop their individual humanity through education and substantive encounter. In such an approach, educability and a person's inherent direction, pedagogical reference, goals, contents, and methods are central categories. The discipline of pedagogics must explain these elements and show how they relate to one another. Ultimately, these open questions concern education in a pluralist society. Under the claims of such a society, and for scientific reasons, various spheres (e.g., school pedagogy, → adult education, museums) and special themes (e.g., → play, → sex education) must be developed.

3.1. *Pedagogy as a Science*

A *scientific approach* to pedagogics long dominated, starting with Schleiermacher. The hermeneutical methodology of W. Dilthey (1833-1911; → Hermeneutics) constituted such an approach, especially if we include the insights from the pedagogical reform movement. Yet the term "scientific" is imprecise. It covers various methods, including the historico-systematic (Nohl, E. Weniger), hermeneutic-pragmatic (W. Flitner; → Pragmatism), phenomenological (O. Bollnow; → Phenomenology), and dialectical (Litt). Common to all of these methods is the emphasis on personal relations in education (→ Person) and therefore on a relative → autonomy. Development, historicity, and → responsibility count for more than practice. A leading conviction is that only such methods understand pedagogical activity and do justice to the complexity of the pedagogical field.

Today's *empirical emphasis* in the discipline of pedagogics had a forerunner in the experimental pedagogics of W. A. Lay (1862-1926) and E. Meumann (1862-1915). Its first important advocate was P. Petersen (1884-1952), but it received fuller recognition when H. Roth became a professor of pedagogics at Göttingen in 1961 and announced an empirical program in his inaugural address, something that led to the switch to realism. The empirical method involves an increasing development of experience-related methods.

With the profound changes in the late 1960s, representatives of pedagogics, especially on the scientific side, accepted the → *critical theory of the Frankfurt school.* Most influential was the critically constructive science of education advocated above all by W. Klafki (b. 1927). Methodologically, his approach seeks to combine hermeneutics, empiricism, and ideology. It calls itself critical because the criterion of pedagogics is → emancipation, that is, enabling children and young people to develop a growing self-determination, codetermination, and solidarity in every dimension of life. It calls itself constructive because it has a model of actively shaping practice by the participants.

Partly in debate with the above trend, and along the lines of P. Petersen and H. Roth (1906-83), so-called *realistic pedagogics* established itself after 1978. This pedagogics found its field of research and object of reflection mainly in contemporary social practice. It used the hermeneutical and (chiefly qualitatively) empirical methods, supplementing them with historical and comparative perspectives. The central goal was student development, to be accomplished by means of elaborating educational and instructional goals demanding decision in each situation. Pedagogics, in the realistic approach, was designed to offer aid in the concrete situation.

Following the "descriptive pedagogics" of A. Fischer (1880-1937) and R. Locher (1895-1978) and accepting critical rationalism (K. R. Popper, H. Albert), some scholars in the field developed a *critically rational science of education* that claimed to be fully scientific; it was concerned to develop a pedagogics that would be valid in every area of culture. In this scheme, philosophy of education would deal with the central questions of aims, while practical pedagogics would focus on the demands of practice.

Alongside these more open systems there were also closed ones, namely, systems that deduced pedagogics from prior philosophical or theological theses. Among these we may list the normative approaches of neo-Kantianism (A. Petzelt, M. Heitger), → Marxism (H.-J. Gamm), Roman Catholicism (H. Henz, F. März), and → anthroposophy (Waldorf School movement).

3.2. *Relation with Other Disciplines*

Pedagogics is often modeled as working in cooperation with related humanities. As such, theoretical problems (→ Philosophy of Science), contemporary trends, and ideologies are obstacles to full cooperation between the two. On this model, academic pedagogics is at home with → philosophy, → theology, and educational → psychology, whereas empirical pedagogics orients itself especially to general psychology and → sociology. Furthermore, critically constructive pedagogics emphasizes social science, and realistic pedagogics lays stress on the relation to theology, → ethics, and educational psychology.

Despite this relation to the humanities, pedagogics has typically ignored ethical and religious questions. Lately, however, an interest in → values and cultural issues has resurfaced. In general, however, the results achieved in neighboring disciplines have raised unsolved problems in pedagogy, in the relation between pedagogics and → anthropology.

3.3. *Comparative Pedagogics*

In the latter part of the 20th century, comparative pedagogics reflected comprehensively on methodological issues, analyzing and describing the structures and institutions of countries both East and West. Exact knowledge of the academic status of pedagogics in other lands was needed.

In the United States pedagogical research devotes itself especially to comparative education and to finding practical ways to improve schools (e.g., by measuring achievement and efficiency), but less to historical questions or goals. The emphases in the United Kingdom are much the same, the stress being on empirical studies of instruction and → action.

In France questions of pedagogics are dealt with largely within the sphere of sociology. In eastern Europe the collapse of Communism opened doors both materially and methodologically. We may note a return to Roman Catholic pedagogics, especially in Poland and the Czech Republic.

Britain, the United States, and Germany pioneered comparative pedagogics. Its spread to other countries was slow. At first there were attempts to analyze national systems of education, as in the joint Russian and British study of educational factors and traditions. Later came the problem-centered approach, that is, a study of special issues. A quantitative analysis of trends followed (by UNESCO and the OECD), along with an examination of comprehensive issues (B. Holmes, 1981).

In Great Britain the universities are supplemented by the work of the National Foundation for Educational Research. Eastern Europe had looked especially to the Soviet Union both for foundations (K. → Marx, A. S. Makarenko, N. K. Krupskaja) and also for goals (educating for collectives) and special questions (vocation). Comparisons of systems are relatively rare (but see O. Anweiler, W. Hörner and W. Schlott, and W. Mitter).

Bibliography: M. C. Alkin, ed., *Encyclopedia of Educational Research* (4 vols.; 6th ed.; New York, 1992) • O. Anweiler, ed., *Erziehungs- und Sozialisationsprobleme in der Sowjetunion, der DDR und Polen* (Hannover, 1978) • O. F. Bollnow, *Die Pädagogik der deutschen Romantik* (3d ed.; Stuttgart, 1977) • G. D. Borich, *Effective Teaching Methods* (3d ed.; Englewood Cliffs, N.J., 1996) • G. J. Clifford and J. W. Guthrie, *Ed School: A Brief for Professional Education* (Chicago, 1988) • J. A. Comenius, *Comenius's Pampaedia; or, Universal Education* (trans. A. M. O. Dobbie; Dover, Kent, 1986); idem, *The Great Didactic* (trans. M. W. Keatinge; New York, 1967); idem, *John Amos Comenius on Education* (New York, 1957) • D. M. Gollnick and P. C. Chinn, *Multicultural Education in a Pluralistic Society* (6th ed.; Upper Saddle River, N.J., 2002) • B. Holmes, G. H. Read, and N. Voskresenskaya, *Russian Education: Tradition and Transition* (New York, 1995) • W. Hörner, *Technische Bildung und Schule. Eine Problemanalyse im internationalen Vergleich* (Cologne, 1993) • W. Klafki, *Neue Studien zur Bildungstheorie und Didaktik* (5th ed.; Weinheim, 1996) • P. K. Kubow, *Comparative Education: Exploring Issues in International Context* (Upper Saddle River, N.J., 2003) • T. Litt, *"Führen" oder "wachsenlassen"* (13th ed.; Stuttgart, 1976; orig. pub., 1927) • W. Mitter, ed., *Pädagogik und Schule im Systemvergleich. Bildungsprobleme moderner Industriegesellschaften in Ost und West* (Freiburg, 1974) • H. Nohl, *Die pädagogische Bewegung in Deutschland und ihre Theorie* (11th ed.; Frankfurt, 1988; orig. pub., 1933) • H. A. Ozmon and S. M. Craver, *Philosophical Foundations of Education* (7th ed.; Upper Saddle River, N.J., 2003) • J. H. Pestalozzi, *How Gertrude Teaches Her Children: Pestalozzi's Educational Writings* (ed. D. N. Robinson; Washington, D.C., 1977) • L. Roth, ed., *Methoden erziehungswissenschaftlicher Forschung* (Stuttgart, 1978) • J. Schriewer and B. Holmes, eds., *Theories and Methods in Comparative Education* (Frankfurt, 1988) • E. Weniger, *Die Eigenständigkeit der Erziehung in*

Theorie und Praxis (Weinheim, 1952) • I. Westbury, S. Hopmann, and K. Riquarts, eds., *Teaching as a Reflective Practice: The German Didaktik Tradition* (Mahwah, N.J., 2000).

Hans-Karl Beckmann†

Pelagianism

1. Definition
2. Pelagius's Teaching
3. Two Phases of the Controversy
   3.1. 411-18
   3.2. 418-31
4. Semi-Pelagianism
5. Pelagianism in Church History

1. Definition

Pelagianism is an important theological trend that was an offshoot of a fourth-century ascetic movement (→ Asceticism 2). It takes its name from Pelagius (ca. 354-after 418), a British (Irish?) monk, who went to Rome in about 385.

2. Pelagius's Teaching

The → preaching of Pelagius had a practical ascetic thrust. He attacked a Christianity that had no results. With his demand that the whole → church should be holy, he gained numerous adherents among the clergy and nobility, among them Celestius (5th cent.).

In a commentary on Paul's epistles (406-9), Pelagius took issue with the → dualism of → Manichaeanism, which treated → evil as an independent principle and thus regarded → sin as a natural necessity. In opposition to this physical determinism he set his own doctrine of → freedom on the basis of God's gracious action. In line with the early → Augustine (354-430; → Augustine's Theology), Ambrosiaster, and → Origen (ca. 185-ca. 254; → Origenism), Pelagius first stressed the → grace of → creation. By this grace God has given us the ability, if we will, to avoid sin and to decide for the → good. Nevertheless, by the fall of → Adam reason has been darkened and the law of nature forgotten.

Pelagius did not deny the fundamental freedom of the will that is the basis of responsibility for our actions. But the power of sin manifests itself in the fact that committing sin has become a habit. Since we cannot overcome this habit in our own strength, God has shown us the grace of → revelation. By the → law of Moses he reminded the people of Israel (→ People of God) of the gift of reason that he gave at creation.

Israel, however, refused to render → obedience and turned aside from God. Hence God revealed to all of us the better righteousness of Christ, whose commands supplement those of Moses and the observing of which is urged upon us by the seriousness of coming judgment. By his life and teaching, Christ is an example of perfect obedience. All Christians can fulfill Christ's commands in their own lives and in this way bring to fulfillment God's will at creation. Sin, though, will not be completely overcome in this life, and thus God gives the grace of forgiveness, which is grounded in the death of Christ. We appropriate this grace in → baptism and receive it as → justification by faith.

3. Two Phases of the Controversy

3.1. *411-18*

These views resulted in controversy only when Pelagius and Celestius fled from the Goths and went from Rome to Carthage, where in the year 410 they came into collision with Augustine. Pelagius soon left Carthage for Jerusalem, but the problems of original sin and disagreeement over the possibility of sinless perfection resulted in a conflict between Celestius and Augustine that also reflected tensions between North Africa and Rome (→ Augustine's Theology 5). Celestius argued that Adam was created mortal. His sin affected him alone and not the race. Children at birth are in the same state as Adam was before the fall. We cannot speak of original sin, for sin is only a defect of will and not of → nature (§1.2). Infant baptism is not essential for the attainment of eternal life. Now Augustine too, in his *De libero arbitrio* (On free will, between 388 and 395), had taken the view that moral evil has its origin only in our free will. Pelagius could sometimes approvingly refer to this work.

In later writings, however, Augustine no longer developed his doctrine in terms of the grace of creation but began with the reconciliation that has been made in Christ (*Ad Simplicianum* [To Simplicianus, 396]; *De Spiritu et littera* [On the Spirit and the letter, 412]; *De fide et operibus* [On faith and works, 413]). His interest was in the relation between the grace of Christ and the human will. The grace of God precedes what we will and do. We cannot merit it, and it may even work in opposition to the human will. Augustine accused Celestius of weakening the significance of Christ's saving work by maintaining that even without grace, we can keep the commands of God. At a synod in Carthage in 411, Augustine secured the → excommunication of Celestius.

At the same time Pelagius in Palestine had to

ward off literary attacks by → Jerome (ca. 345-420). He successfully defended himself in his *Epistula ad Demetriadem* (413) and found broad support in the East, at the synods of Jerusalem and Diospolis (415). Even Pope Zosimus (417-18), to whom he dedicated his *Libellus fidei* (Brief statement of faith, 417), took his side. Only the violent protest of the North Africans and the fact that Emperor Honorius (395-423) in Ravenna favored Augustine in the dispute (*Sacrum rescriptum* [Sacred decree, 418]) changed the attitude of Rome. A further synod at Carthage (418) confirmed the condemnations that had already been pronounced. This step ended the first phase of the controversy. Pelagius had to leave Palestine, and he died shortly thereafter in Egypt.

In the West, however, the conflict continued, especially when Augustine in his doctrine of election (→ Predestination) advanced the extreme view that by God's eternal foreordination his grace saves only one portion of the race from perdition (*De praedestinatione sanctorum; De dono perseverantiae* [On the predestination of the saints; On the gift of perseverance, both 428/29]).

3.2. *418-31*

In the years that followed, Bishop Julian (ca. 386-454) of Eclanum, in Apulia in southeast Italy, became the advocate of Pelagianism. He strongly rejected original sin and predestination, charging that these doctrines had a Manichaean origin and accusing Augustine of undermining marriage with Augustine's view of the transmission of Adam's sin by concupiscence and conception. Julian was then deposed and fled to Constantinople, where he won the support of Nestorius (d. ca. 451). At the third ecumenical council, in → Ephesus in 431, both were declared heretics (→ Heresies and Schisms 2.2). This condemnation brought the second phase of the dispute to an end. Augustinianism had triumphed.

4. Semi-Pelagianism

Nevertheless, the predestinarianism of the later Augustine remained a matter of controversy. Objections were made against it especially in the → monasticism of southern Gaul, since it seemed to call into question the monastic striving for perfection. Augustine's fundamental authority was certainly recognized, but freedom as distinct from grace became the central point at issue.

John Cassian (ca. 360-after 430), abbot of Marseilles, attempted a compromise. He stressed the need for divine grace if we are to will and do anything, but he also claimed that God has regard to our good will, which is only weakened and not destroyed. Predestination simply rests on foreknowledge of what we will do and in no way restricts God's will to save (*Inst.* 12, *Conf.* 13).

Vincent of Lérins (d. before 450) set in opposition to Augustine's teaching the argument from tradition. A doctrine is heretical if it deviates from the tradition of the → church fathers, that is, from what has been believed always, everywhere, and by all. We must cling to the latter alone (*Commonitorium* [Memorandum, 434]).

It was in vain that Prosper, a monk of Marseilles and bishop of Aquitaine (ca. 390-ca. 463), supported Augustine's teaching against Cassian (*Contra Collatorem* [Against the contributor, 431/34]). Pope Celestine I (422-32) also gave his support, but even he could not prevent semi-Pelagianism (a term used for the first time in → Formula of Concord Ep. 2) from reigning supreme in southern Gaul for many decades. An example of this view appears in *De gratia Dei* (On the grace of God), which Bishop Faustus (d. ca. 490) of Riez in Gaul, former abbot of Lérins, wrote at the request of the Synod of Arles (470/71) in favor of a universalist interpretation of Christian election. Faustus argued that of our own will we can turn to God apart from prevenient grace.

Yet the tables turned again early in the sixth century. With support from Rome Caesarius, bishop of Arles (d. 542), secured the condemnation of semi-Pelagianism at the Synod of Orange (529). Under Boniface II (530-32) the conclusions of this synod received official recognition and came into the collections of canons (→ Corpus Iuris Canonici). Augustinianism thus became the basis of the doctrine of grace in the West.

5. Pelagianism in Church History

Pelagianism, however, has remained a fundamental question throughout church history. It appears in the age of the Carolingian renaissance (→ Middle Ages 1.2.2) when Gottschalk (ca. 804-ca. 869), a Fulda monk, took up the teaching of the later Augustine and taught double predestination in his sermons. At the instigation of Rabanus Maurus (ca. 780-856), the Synod of Mainz (848) condemned Gottschalk.

In → Scholasticism Pelagianism was regarded as synonymous with heretical teaching. We see this view in Thomas Bradwardine of Canterbury (ca. 1295-1349), who in his polemical work *De causa Dei contra Pelagium* (The cause of God against Pelagius) brought against the → nominalism of William of Ockham (ca. 1285-1347) the charge of Pelagianism.

At the time of the → Reformation the controversy broke out afresh in the dispute about free will between Martin → Luther (1483-1546; → Luther's

Theology 4.4) and → Erasmus (1469?-1536). The Lutheran confessional statements (→ Confession of Faith) aim the condemnation of Pelagianism against Roman → Catholicism and the radicals (CA 2, 18, et al.; → Anabaptists). In the Reformed Church criticism of the predestinarianism of John → Calvin (1509-64; → Calvin's Theology 2.3) early in the 17th century resulted in a violent controversy in which J. Arminius (1560-1609; → Arminianism) was accused of Pelagianism. It was left to the historians of the → Enlightenment to set aside the evaluation of Pelagianism as heretical.

C. W. F. Walch (1726-84) in his *History of Heresies* (11 vols., 1762-85) adopted an impartial position according to which there were misunderstandings and mistakes on both sides. He did not agree that Pelagianism should be regarded as a heresy. In the process, the question whether Augustine and Luther were theologically right was left unanswered.

→ Early Church; Patristics

Bibliography: Primary sources: Augustine, *Four Anti-Pelagian Writings* (Washington, D.C., 1992) • *Christianity in Late Antiquity, 300-450 c.e.: A Reader* (comp. A. S. Jardes and B. D. Ehrman; New York, 2004) • DH 221-31, 238-49, 267-68, 370-400 • R. F. Evans, *Four Letters of Pelagius* (New York, 1968) • *The Letters of Pelagius and His Followers* (ed. B. R. Rees; Woodbridge, Suffolk, 1991) • *Pelagius's Commentary on St. Paul's Epistle to the Romans* (trans. T. de Bruyn; Oxford, 1993) • *Pelagius's Expositions of Thirteen Epistles of St. Paul* (ed. A. Souter; 3 vols.; Cambridge, 1922-31).

Secondary works: G. Bonner, "Anti-Pelagian Works," *Augustine through the Ages: An Encyclopedia* (ed. A. D. Fitzgerald; Grand Rapids, 1999) 41-47; idem, *Augustine and Modern Research on Pelagianism* (Villanova, Pa., 1972); idem, *Church and Faith in the Patristic Tradition: Augustine, Pelagianism, and Early Christian Northumbria* (Brookfield, Vt., 1996) • R. F. Evans, *Pelagius: Inquiries and Reappraisals* (New York, 1968) • H. Holze, *Erfahrung und Theologie im frühen Mönchtum* (Göttingen, 1992) • G. Leff, *Bradwardine and the Pelagians: A Study of His "De causa Dei" and Its Opponents* (Cambridge, 1957) • B. R. Rees, *Pelagius: A Reluctant Heretic* (Woodbridge, Suffolk, 1988) • E. TeSelle, "Pelagius, Pelagianism," *Augustine through the Ages,* ed. Fitzgerald, 633-40 • C. W. F. Walch, *Entwurf einer vollständigen Historie der Ketzereien, Spaltungen und Religionsstreitigkeiten: bis auf die Zeiten der Reformation* (11 vols.; Leipzig, 1762-85) 4.519-846; 5.3-218 • R. H. Weaver, *Divine Grace and Human Agency: A Study of the Semi-Pelagian Controversy* (Macon, Ga., 1996) • O. Wermelinger, *Rom und Pelagius. Die theologische Position der römischen Bischöfe im pelagianischen Streit in den Jahren 411-432* (Stuttgart, 1975).

Heinrich Holze

Penitence

1. History
   1.1. Jesus and the Primitive Community
   1.2. Early Church
   1.3. Middle Ages
   1.4. Reformation
   1.5. Modern Period
2. Dogmatic and Ethical Aspects
   2.1. Concept
   2.2. Modern Teaching and Preaching
   2.3. Ethical Relevance
3. Roman Catholic Understanding and Practice
   3.1. Teaching
   3.2. Sacrament
   3.3. Structural Sin
   3.4. The Churches and Penitence

1. History

1.1. *Jesus and the Primitive Community*

→ John the Baptist summoned → Israel to repentance (Gk. *metanoia,* Matt. 3:8; Mark 1:4) in view of the eschatological judgment of the wrath of God (→ Last Judgment). Jesus in his teaching, however, issued a summons to penitence in the form of a saving intimation of the imminent rule of God (→ Kingdom of God) and the kindness of God that precedes his judgment. Both interpreted the present as a situation of eschatological decision (Luke 3:9, 11; 12:16b-20; 13:3-5; 16:1-7; → Eschatology). The call of Jesus to radical conversion, however, was primarily an invitation to enter into the → joy of God's approaching rule (Matt. 11:5; Luke 6:20; 14:16-24; 15:7).

The post-Easter community continued the summons to penitence as proclamation of the fulfilling of time and as invitation to faith in the → gospel (Mark 1:15). In demonstration of its eschatological holiness it was aware of empowerment for its office of binding and loosing, or forgiving and retaining sins (Matt. 16:18-19; 18:18; John 20:23). The same was true of → Paul (1 Cor. 5:1-5; 2 Cor. 2:5-11). Hebrews (6:4-6), the epistles of John, and Revelation also proclaimed the seriousness of the situation of eschatological decision and the related penitence (Rev. 2:2-5, 16, 21-23; 3:3, 18-19).

1.2. *Early Church*

In the postapostolic period the → early church stressed the eschatological holiness of the people of

God, basing it on the forgiveness of sins in → baptism. But faith in the mercy of God, which does not reject the sorrow of a penitent heart, had to recognize the possibility of penitence for the baptized unity as well (*1 Clem.* 7.5). The ensuing → confession of → sin was the presupposition of participation in the Eucharist (*Did.* 14.1). The related remorse was supported by → prayer, → fasting, and almsgiving. Hermas gave greater seriousness to penitence by allowing it only once (though with no time limitation) for grave sins like licentiousness, murder, or idolatry.

In the West the authority of the church's ministry to accept penitence was established in the third century in → Rome and North Africa against the rigorism of the Montanists and Novatianists. → Tertullian (d. ca. 225) at first accepted the possibility of a second repentance (*De paen.* 7.2), but after going over to → Montanism, he came to regard serious sins as beyond forgiveness (*De pud.* 5.4.14). He also put the power of the keys in the hands of bearers of the Spirit and not the church → hierarchy. Novatian in 251 would not receive back into the church those who lapsed in the Decian persecution, but → Cyprian (d. 258) did so, though tying the claim of confessors that they could forgive sins in cases of penitence to the ecclesiastical authority of the → bishop (→ Lapsi; Persecution of Christians 2). Readmission to the Eucharist took place in the form of public penitence *(poenitentia publica)* during → worship with → laying on of hands by the bishop and clergy after confession of sin to the congregation *(exomologesis)* and the attestation of remorse by appropriate acts.

→ Augustine (354-430) gave added depth to this form of penitence by stressing the virtue of penitence *(humilitas)* as one that embraces the whole of the Christian life. He still advocated public penitence but was also familiar with private reprimand. Since public penitence was so severe and humiliating and could take place only once, a semipublic penitence on one's deathbed became increasingly popular from the fifth century onward.

In the East penitence had more of a pastoral and pedagogic function in Clement of Alexandria (d. ca. 215) and → Origen (d. ca. 254). The issue in penitence was the → healing of → souls under the guidance of a bearer of the Spirit, that is, a monk. The practice of penitence recognized specific stages, such as weeping, hearing, kneeling, and standing. Then came reconciliation of the sinner and readmission to the Eucharist. In the Middle Ages the → Crusades led the East to adopt the Western sacrament of penance and, after 1274, the idea that there are seven sacraments.

1.3. *Middle Ages*

The early Middle Ages saw a shift of church practice by way of Irish and Anglo-Saxon churches, which had learned Eastern monastic practice from the Celtic church. Penitence became increasingly private *(poenitentia privata)* rather than public, and it was defined by Lateran IV (1215) and by theology as a → sacrament that is necessary to salvation for all Christians. Essentially there could now be a repetition of forgiveness in a secret action in which only an ordained → priest and the penitent sinner participated. Penitentials regulated casuistically the related penalties. By so-called redemptions and commutations (i.e., the substitution of acts for penances), the temporal penalties could be partially reduced. In the 11th century the → indulgence replaced these substitute acts. Public penitence became less and less common, persisting merely in the form of occasional *poenitentia solemnis,* a special penitence that the bishop alone could administer in particularly serious cases. At the heart of private penitence were confession of sins and absolution. Satisfaction was subordinate. After Lateran IV private confession became a duty once a year.

This new practice of penitence increasingly came to be defined by theological doctrines. In early → Scholasticism P. Abelard (1079-1142) taught that the sorrow that God pours into the heart brings remission of the guilt of sin and its eternal penalties. Satisfaction is self-evidently part of the process and is not to be replaced by an indulgence. Absolution simply declares the forgiveness that is grounded in repentance. Peter Lombard (d. 1160) taught that penance is a sacrament, and following → Jerome (d. 420) he described it as the second plank after shipwreck. God remits → guilt and eternal → punishment on the basis of sacramentally effected contrition of heart and auricular confession. Absolution has a declaratory function, and the satisfaction of works removes temporal penalties.

In High Scholasticism → Thomas Aquinas (ca. 1225-74) clarified undecided questions about the relation between contrition, confession, absolution, and satisfaction. Repentance, confession, and satisfaction are the matter of the sacrament, absolution is the form. As the disposition for receiving the sacrament, attrition (sorrow for sin arising from fear of punishment) is enough, but by the operation of the sacrament it becomes the complete contrition (sorrow for sin inspired by the love of God) that accompanies confession. Duns Scotus (ca. 1265-1308) laid special stress on sacramental absolution. By way of disposition it was enough not to put any obstacle in the way, that is, to be free of mortal sin. God himself changes attrition into contrition, which receives remission of guilt and of eternal penalties. Satisfaction that removes the temporal penalties is secondary. In late Scholasticism William of Ockham (d. 1347) and G. Biel (d. 1495) followed a similar line but emphasized our natural ability to achieve contrition. In absolution God pronounces remission of guilt and of eternal penalties in response.

In medieval → monasticism and the *devotio moderna,* the reconciliation of sinners was especially related to the inner → virtue of penitence. By the self-judgment of penitence monks can anticipate God's eschatological judgment (1 Cor. 11:31) and dispose themselves for the spiritual reception of divine charity and contemplation (e.g., → Bernard of Clairvaux). This experience does not rule out participation in the sacrament of penance, but it does not require it. Other critics of penance were J. → Wycliffe (d. 1384), John of Wesel (d. 1481), and Wessel Gansfort (ca. 1419-89), who all laid stress on inner penitence as the presupposition and place of the reception of grace. A perfect life before God replaced satisfaction and the indulgence that mitigates it.

1.4. *Reformation*

M. → Luther (1483-1546) at first inclined to view inner penitence along these lines when he stated in the first of the 95 Theses, "When our Lord and Master Jesus Christ said, 'Repent' [or 'Do penance'], he willed the entire life of believers to be one of repentance" (*LW* 31.25). True penitence springs from → faith and from → love of God. Not contrition but faith alone receives remission of all the guilt of sin and all its penalties, both eternal and temporal. No place remains for satisfaction, indulgences, merit, or → purgatory (→ Hell).

On the basis of this understanding Luther in 1517 and later came to a new theological view of the sacrament of penance. Its basis is the promise of divine forgiveness (Matt. 16:18-19; 18:18). The priest has no jurisdiction over this promise; he can only represent it. Luther retained the established, external word of absolution as a basis of faith and a weapon against → temptation. It was also the basis of private confession, which he accepted, though with no casuistic listing of sins (see also CA 11). Confession might also be made by one Christian to another.

Luther could initially call penance the third sacrament, but it really had no place alongside baptism, since it lacked a divinely appointed sign. The related promise of salvation coincides with the once-for-all baptismal promise, and penance for Luther was thus subordinate to baptism. It was no longer "the second plank after shipwreck" but a constant return to the baptismal promise (*LW* 36.58). As such, it was a constant turning away from the power and consequences of sin. Like faith, penitence springs from the → Word of God.

Hence Luther, and even more so P. → Melanchthon (1497-1560), emphasized against J. Agricola (1494-1566; → Antinomian Controversies) the role of the law in the awakening of penitence. For Luther, however, penitence was related to both → law and → gospel. For Melanchthon in CA 12 penitence, or repentance, is "to have contrition and sorrow, or terror about sin, and yet at the same time to believe in the gospel and absolution that sin is forgiven and grace is obtained through Christ." The fruit of penitence is personal change.

U. → Zwingli (1484-1531) after 1523 no longer accepted penance as a sacrament. Christians may have assurance of forgiveness of sins and penalties on the basis of divinely effected faith without any express word of absolution. In cooperation with the Zurich council Zwingli intensified penitential discipline, excluding from the Lord's Supper by the "little ban" those who caused public offense by their sins until they amended their lives.

J. → Calvin (1509-64) practiced a similar → church discipline. For him and other Reformed (including Anglicans), penitence was not a true sacrament (*Inst.* 4.19.15) but was above all the "turning of our life to God" (3.3.5). Along with forgiveness it constitutes the sum of the gospel (3.3.1). Calvin preferred public confession at worship to private confession but viewed it as spiritual counseling (3.4.6).

1.5. *Modern Period*

Modern → Protestantism has displayed an increasing tendency to restrict penitence to a specific act in the Christian life. The older Protestant → orthodoxy set it in the order of salvation and understood contrition and faith as specific acts effected by the grace of the Holy Spirit. In → Pietism P. J. Spener (1635-1705) understood penitence as Christian improvement and tried to keep penitence and the grace of baptism together, but in A. H. → Francke (1663-1727) interest focused on the penitential struggle of → conversion (§1) that precedes → regeneration. F. D. E. → Schleiermacher (1768-1834), W. Herrmann (1846-1922), and K. → Barth (1886-1968) were all concerned in different ways to understand penitence holistically as an actualizing of the Christologically understood constitution of the Christian life.

At the Council of → Trent (sess. 6, 14), the → Roman Catholic Church essentially endorsed the view of Thomas. Penitence was inwardly vitalized by the *Spiritual Exercises* (1548) of → Ignatius of Loyola (1491-1556).

The ecumenical world seeks to free penitence from confessional restriction and to focus afresh on the eschatological summons of Jesus to penitence in both its individual and its collective implications (see 3.3 and 3.4).

Bibliography: P. Anciaux, *The Sacrament of Penance* (London, 1962) • G. A. Anderson, "The Penitence Narrative in the Life of Adam and Eve," *Literature on Adam and Eve* (ed. G. Anderson et al.; Leiden, 2000) 3-42 • J. Becker and G. A. Benrath, "Buße IV-V," *TRE* 7.446-73 • H. von Campenhausen, *Ecclesiastical Authority and Spiritual Power in the Church of the First Three Centuries* (London, 1969) • J. Henderson, "Penitence and Penitents," *Piety and Charity in Late Medieval Florence* (Oxford, 1994) chap. 4 • L. Hödl, *Die Geschichte der scholastischen Literatur und der Theologie der Schlüsselgewalt* (Munich, 1960) • K. J. Lualdi and A. T. Thayer, eds., *Penitence in the Age of Reformations* (Aldershot, 2000) • B. Poschmann, *Penance and the Anointing of the Sick* (New York, 1964) • W. Schwab, *Entwicklung und Gestalt der Sakramententheologie bei Martin Luther* (Frankfurt, 1977) • Tertullian, *Treatise on Penance* (trans. W. P. Le Saint; Westminster, Md., 1959) • A. T. Thayer, *Penitence, Preaching, and the Coming of the Reformation* (Aldershot, 2002) • O. D. Watkins, *A History of Penance, Being a Study of the Authorities* (2 vols.; London, 1920).

Karl-Heinz zur Mühlen

2. Dogmatic and Ethical Aspects

2.1. *Concept*

At least from the beginning of the modern period, and still today, the understanding of penitence has been burdened with serious difficulties. On the one hand, it is viewed within the church as a central distinctive of Christian piety and theology. All denominations accept M. → Luther's basic principle that daily penitence is a feature of the Christian life, that the whole life of believers is therefore penitence (the first of the 95 Theses; see 1). This understanding is taken for granted in the → Orthodox Church and the churches of the Reformation. We see this attitude especially in → Pietism and similar movements and in those branches of the Reformation that practice → church discipline more strongly than the → Reformed churches do. But it is also true where there is a requirement that prior to Communion (→ Eucharist) at least once a year the sacrament of penance should be received, so that penitence is raised to the position of a minimal condition of being a Christian. The later legalistic misuse of this requirement was not intended by Lateran IV (1215).

On the other hand, in secular, legal, religious, and ecclesiastical use the term "penitence" has acquired a broad range of meanings in which the genuinely Christian element seems to be obscured if not totally eliminated. The original aspect of amendment or improvement also seems to have disappeared almost totally. The accent of punishment that is linked to the Latin *poenitentia* has pushed too much to the forefront, and with it the idea of active or passive satisfaction. The decisive element has become the suffering of punishment, or offering a substitute for it.

Only in the contrast between the penitent and the impenitent do we still catch a glimpse of the thought of amendment, of the ability and readiness for such change, though even here the aspect of accepting punishment is still predominant. Embedded in the concept are the attitude and awareness of being a miserable sinner, the penitential mien and garb. Melancholy and (self-)torture hold the field. Even in Christian circles we hear little of the joy of penitence (J. Schniewind), unless it be the perverted, tormented, and pretended joy of the righteous as they mortify the desires of Adam in the flesh, avoid worldly temptations, and assure themselves of their soul's salvation.

The seriousness of the "new → obedience," which is a natural part of the sincerity of living by justification by → grace alone, and therefore also of the changing and improvement of life, is primarily seen from the standpoint of achievement. It thus takes on the aspect of a rigoristic restriction that is hostile to life. Naturally these perversions of the seriousness of Christian penitence have been opposed not merely by modern critics of Christianity but within Christianity itself by those who set in contrast with them, as the model of full humanity, a more relaxed integrity and unashamed lack of constraint that foster love of life.

2.2. *Christian Teaching and Preaching*

Teaching on penitence must be soberly aware today that many mainline church members in secularized countries are slow to hear the message of penitence and that in their practical ethical conduct they are just as crippled and impenitent as the secularized, post-Christian pagans who are their neighbors. Yet it must be asserted with no theological compromise that as an authentic Christian concept, penitence can be made intelligible only in the context of a Christian understanding of → sin, → guilt, grace, → justification, and → sanctification.

Penitence is a reversal on the basis of a turning that is brought about by God's merciful turning to us. God's promise that he accepts those who are not acceptable (that he "justifies the ungodly," Rom. 4:5) uncovers the hostile and self-destructive intentionality and the self-enclosed situation of those who are against God. But it also bursts upon the ungodly and frees them from the bondage from which they cannot free themselves in their guilt. It also frees them *for* the corresponding action of those who are thus pardoned. It frees them to begin a better life, to pursue amendment. It frees them for renunciation of egotistically restricted modes of life, thought, and conduct, including egoisms of family, group, class, and nationality. It frees them for turning to God and to the world, which is loved by him, to the life of creation. It thus involves a radical change, amendment, reorientation, and renewal of the former life. It involves → conversion and → regeneration.

Penitence is thus a total reversal. It is a total act of person, heart, attitude, mind, emotion, feeling, will, behavior, and action. It affects the whole being. In its unconditional universality it is to be applied concretely to every situation. It is not to be regulated or limited either casuistically or more generally. Given the historicity of individual, interpersonal, and social life, it includes rather than excludes concrete occasions for penitential times or days, for reflection that stirs us up and admonishes us.

Penitence affects all dimensions of the reality of our cocreaturely life in every responsible relation. Over against the tendency to engage in individualistic shortcuts, we constantly need the call for change in matters of social responsibility, for the forsaking of suppression and exploitation and a throwaway consumer mentality (see 3.3). But penitence also involves the recognition and opposing of one-sided tendencies that afflict even justifiable programs. Social and ecological awareness may be overdue, but it should not lead to the neglect of individual and primary social problems (e.g., failure, loneliness, inefficiency, old age, death, guilt, withdrawal, betrayal, and despair).

2.3. *Ethical Relevance*

The ethical relevance of penitence is that Christian → ethics must be an ethics of penitence, of reorientation to a love of life, to an acceptance and promotion of existence as a gift, to the mitigating and, as far as possible, the healing of sorrow and suffering. Penitence is a reassertion of the loving will of the Creator God. It is thus an interrupting and forsaking of self-improvement strategies, programs, tendencies, and trends in social behavior, especially in the case of the attitudes and conduct of persons in places of responsibility. The Christian summons to penitence is an address to persons and a claim upon them. They are called upon to practice it and to train themselves in it.

Penitence and acts of penitence are free human decisions, often with severe inner conflicts and → temptations. Yet the penitent know that penitence is not their own achievement but a gift of divine grace, an impulse of the → Holy Spirit, who enlightens, vitalizes, comforts, and encourages. In life in the continually liberating power of the Spirit, there can be growth in penitence, in being "renewed more and more after God's image" (→ Heidelberg Catechism, q. 115).

Bibliography: H. P. Arendt, *Bußsakrament und Einzelbeichte* (Freiburg, 1981) • R. Lendi, *Die Wandelbarkeit der Buße* (Bern, 1983) • K. Lorenz, *Civilized Man's Eight Deadly Sins* (New York, 1974) • R. C. Mortimer, *The Origins of Private Penance in the Western Church* (Oxford, 1939) • J. Schniewind, *Die Freude der Buße* (Göttingen, 1956) • W. Schrage, *The Ethics of the NT* (Philadelphia, 1987) • K. Stadel, *Buße in Aufklärung und Gegenwart* (Paderborn, 1974) • W. Telfer, *The Forgiveness of Sins: An Essay in the History of Christian Doctrine and Practice* (Philadelphia, 1960) • W. Wickler, *The Biology of the Ten Commandments* (New York, 1972).

Günther Schnurr

3. Roman Catholic Understanding and Practice

3.1. *Teaching*

As acceptance of the → reconciliation that God gives, penitence is the basic movement of → faith in conversion to God and neighbor. For Roman Catholics it is also the special → virtue of contrition (DH 1713) and of readiness, by suffering, to make satisfaction for the penalties of sin that remain after forgiveness and to overcome the inclination to sin (DH 1676, 1690, 1693). The process of transformation by grace (which makes God's declaration of justification confirmatory, not based on Christ's righteousness) takes place in a life lived with the church and its sacraments, in the classic deeds of → prayer, renunciation, and love of neighbor, and in bearing the afflictions of life with Christ, whereby the treasure of redemption is increased (apostolic constitution "On Penance" [1966], 3b; apostolic letter *Salvifici doloris* [1984], §27). This salvific value distinguishes Christian penitence from immanent → asceticism (1983 Roman Bishops' Synod, *Instrumentum laboris*, §31).

The doctrine of the temporal punishment due for sin underlies → indulgences, with which the Roman Catholic Church "authoritatively dispenses and applies the treasury of the merits of Christ and the saints" (1983 CIC 992). Attempts to interpret indulgences as the infallible intercession of the church for penitents who are suffering the consequences of sin (K. → Rahner) have been officially rejected (apostolic constitution *Indulgentiarum doctrina* [1967], §8). In order to promote repentance and sacramental reconciliation during the → holy year 2000, Pope John Paul II (1978-2005) extended the occasions for obtaining an indulgence.

3.2. *Sacrament*

The specific connection between the divine gift of salvation and human conversion is articulated in the practice of the → church, which in analogy to Christ's threefold office has the duty of proclaiming, celebrating, and administering reconciliation. Regular liturgical elements (confession of sin, anamnesis of the sacrifice of Christ, the peace), nonsacramental penitential services, and times of penitence in the → church year give expression to → sin in its social as well as its individual dimension and open up individual penitence to social reorientation (see 3.3).

The sacrament of penance comprises contrition, full confession, satisfaction, and absolution (DH 1673-75). In Roman Catholic teaching it is the full form of reconciliation because it links the situation of individual conversion to the church as the means of salvation. To the extent that the church, in an absolute commitment of its being as the basic sacrament of → salvation, posits itself as present in situations of individual salvation and gives individuals a share in its own being by a final actualization of it (K. Rahner), penance is not a meritorious work but a self-fulfillment of the church, a celebration of reconciliation in which the believer and the priest engage together in the "liturgy of the constantly self-renewing church" (*Ordo paenitentiae* [1973], §11).

→ Vatican II stressed the ecclesial dimension of the sacrament of penance. Reconciliation with God follows at once reconciliation with the church, which was wounded by the sin of the baptized person and which as a mother goes on the way of penitence with the sinner (*Lumen gentium* 8, 11). In sacramental theology peace with the church is the sacramental sign of renewed fellowship with God. In indicative absolution by the minister, the deprecative pronouncement of God's forgiveness becomes real *(Ordo paenitentiae)*. Since absolution is a judicial act (DH 1709), the one who gives it needs a faculty of confession as well as the authority of ordination (1983 CIC 966).

Severe sins that disrupt fellowship with God and the church demand reception of penance with full personal → confession (DH 1707). Penance is not necessary for lesser sins but is recommended for perfecting the life of grace. Of the three forms of penance — individual; common, with individual confession and absolution; and common, with general absolution — the last is appointed only for emergency situations (danger of death or impossibility of confession for more than a month because of a shortage of priests) and is dependent for its efficacy on a readiness for future individual penance (1983 CIC 961-62). The intended restriction of general absolution is based on the fact that in emergency situations even the perfect contrition that includes the *votum sacramenti* (desire for the sacrament) requires the forgiveness of severe sins and disposes for reception of the → Eucharist (DH 1661).

Personal confession is a necessary part of the church's judicial and salvific action in penance (apostolic exhortation "Reconciliation and Penance" [1984], §31). With individual penance it defends the special right of the human soul against collectivism (encyclical *Redemptor hominis* [1979], §20). It also provides celibate ministers with the experience that is needed in the interests of realistic → pastoral care.

3.3. *Structural Sin*

The individualization of → guilt in confession contradicts the experience of the complexity of situations of guilt in family, society, and economic structures. The institution of penitence as exclusively administered by male priests can hardly address the reality of the life of women, whose experience of guilt is less oriented to the temptations of power than to that of the victim role, of compliance and apathy. Since structural injustice cannot be remedied by penance, there is a need for rites and strategies to arouse awareness of it, such as liturgies of complaint and conversion in the church and the quasi-religious ritual of protests and demonstrations in the world. But only by analogy can structures be called sinful, that is, to the extent that they arise out of sin and give occasion for it (see the International Theological Commission, "On Reconciliation and Repentance" [1982], A2.1-2; also "Reconciliation and Penance" [1984], §16).

Social conversion is the action of persons who participate in God's turning to the world, better expressing themselves in the Eucharist (Lima Declaration, "Eucharist," par. 20) than in penance. Radical → political theology, with its denial of a direct reference to God, rejects the possibility of forgiveness "from above" and views penitence as a social bearing of sin, and absolution by the wounded community (D. Sölle). Healing of memories and opening a path to the future are the aims of talks between victim and perpetrator and of truth commissions formed after the breakdown of unjust political systems (in central and eastern Europe in 1989, in

South Africa in 1990). Where sin is experienced under the threshold of the ethical as social misconduct, as in African communities that suffer under big business, Christian penitence should take the form of a converting and purifying of society. The dissolving of the traditional social structure indeed confronts the church with new challenges.

3.4. *The Churches and Penitence*

The church is a "sacrament of reconciliation" for the world ("Reconciliation and Penance," §11) only to the degree that as a "church of forgiven sinners" (Barmen, thesis 3), it itself lives by penitence and forgiveness. By the confession of guilt (e.g., the confession of guilt by the Evangelical Church of Germany in 1945; the sweeping apology for pardon made on March 12, 2000, by John Paul II for sins committed in the name of the Roman Catholic Church; an act of repentance for "the sin of racism" by the U.S. United Methodist General Conference on May 4, 2000), by dedication to reconciliation (e.g., Second European Ecumenical Assembly, in Graz in June 1997), and by the "option for the poor" (Third Latin American Bishops' Conference, Puebla, 1979), the churches offer model acts of social diakonia and conversion. Nevertheless, the insight that in social antagonism the churches can live out the universality of their task only by concretely taking sides (→ Liberation Theology) is opposed by established church structures (→ Volkskirche) and by a hierarchical → ecclesiology (Congregation for the Doctrine of the Faith, "Instruction on Certain Aspects of the 'Theology of Liberation'" [1984]).

The ecumenical movement links the divided churches in a spirit of "penitence for our divisions and our disobedience" (joint declaration of the Secretariate [now Pontifical Council] for Christian Unity and the WCC, 1984; → Ecumenism, Ecumenical Movement). Its goal is "reconciled diversity" (→ Unity). In view of the serious division between Israel and the church (→ Jewish-Christian Dialogue), the voluntary "dispossession" of Christological and ecclesiological views could count as a kind of penitence, even as it provokes the charge of subsuming the → cross under a natural theology of → salvation history.

Bibliography: J. D. Crichton, *The Ministry of Reconciliation: A Commentary on the Order of Penance* (London, 1974) • J. Dallen, "Penance, Sacrament of," *NCE* (2d ed.) 11.66-72; idem, *The Reconciling Community: The Rite of Penance* (Collegeville, Minn., 1991) • J. A. Favazza, *The Order of Penitents: Historical Roots and Pastoral Future* (Collegeville, Minn., 1988) • M. Greschat, ed., *Die Schuld der Kirche. Dokumente und Reflexionen zur Stuttgarter Schulderklärung vom 18./19. Oktober 1945* (Munich, 1982) • International Theological Commission, *Memory and Reconciliation: The Church and the Faults of the Past* (Rome, 1999) • John Paul II, *Reconciliation and Penance: Post-synodal Apostolic Exhortation* (Washington, D.C., 1984) • G. Nachtwei et al., *Buße* (= *Diak.* 32/3 [2001]) • L. M. Orsy, *The Evolving Church and the Sacrament of Penance* (Denville, N.J., 1978) • *Puebla and Beyond: Documentation and Commentary* (ed. J. Eagleson and P. Scharper; Maryknoll, N.Y., 1979) • K. Rahner, "Indulgences"; "Penance," *SM(E)* 3.123-29; 4.385-99 • D. Sölle, *Political Theology* (Philadelphia, 1974) • D. Tutu, *No Future without Forgiveness: A Personal Overview of South Africa's Truth and Reconciliation Commission* (London, 1999) • H. Vorgrimler, "Der Kampf des Christen mit der Sünde," *MySal* 5.349-461.

Walter Schöpsdau

Pentarchy

"Pentarchy" (lit. "the rule of five") denotes the widespread theory in the Greek East that the five → patriarchs of → Rome, Constantinople (→ Byzantium), → Alexandria, → Antioch, and → Jerusalem are jointly responsible for oversight of the church (→ Church Government). These patriarchs occupy the seats that were given a special preeminence by the ecumenical → councils of the fourth and fifth centuries.

The theory is first found in the laws of Emperor Justinian (527-65). It was given fuller theological development by the theologians of the eighth and ninth centuries who supported icons, and also by Ecumenical Patriarch Nicephorus I (758-828, esp. 806-15) and Theodore of Studios (759-826; → Icon). On this view the five patriarchs had the task of harmoniously preserving the apostolic inheritance and of acting as the five senses for the body (→ Bishop, Episcopate). The theory, however, was already to some extent anachronistic because the schisms of the fifth and sixth centuries (→ Heresies and Schisms) and the seventh-century Arab invasions had so greatly weakened the patriarchates of Alexandria, Antioch, and Jerusalem. All the same, the theory survived the East-West schism of 1054, though reshaped at times as a theory of tetrarchy (the five minus Rome).

With the rise of new autocephalous churches (→ Autocephaly), which in some cases have more adherents, the idea of numerical restriction is now outdated, but a higher ranking is still assigned to the older patriarchates. The theory does help to give some synodical structure to Orthodoxy as a whole.

Bibliography: P. O'Connell, *The Ecclesiology of St. Nicephorus I (758-828), Patriarch of Constantinople: Pentarchy and Primacy* (Rome, 1972) • B. Pheidas, *Ho thesmos tēs pentarchias tōn patriarchōn* (2 vols.; Athens, 1977) • A. Queenan, "The Pentarchy: Its Origin and Initial Development," *Diakonia* 2 (1967) 338-51 • N. van der Wal and B. H. Stolte, eds., *Collectio Tripartita: Justinian on Religious and Ecclesiastical Affairs* (Groningen, 1994).

Peter Plank

Pentateuchal Research

1. Sources
2. Oral Stage
3. Modern Views

1. Sources

Critical study in the 17th and 18th centuries identified three main criteria as the basis for analyzing the composition of the Pentateuch: (1) differences of style between narratives where such differences seem unwarranted by the subject matter, (2) alternation between the use of the divine names "Elohim" and → "Yahweh," and (3) duplicate narratives such as the → creation stories in Genesis 1–2. Three main theories were argued to account for these factors: the older *documentary theory,* according to which two main sources — the Elohist (E) and the Yahwist (J) — as well as other minor sources were combined; against this the *fragment theory,* that the Pentateuch was compiled from numerous literary fragments; and, in the early 19th century, the *supplementary theory,* according to which one main source, "an epos of the Hebrew theocracy," was editorially supplemented by further material of diverse origin. Of these theories the first, as revised and further elaborated throughout the 19th century, became the most widely accepted.

1.1. In 1853 H. Hupfeld (1796-1866) argued that E comprised two originally separate sources, E^1 and E^2. The distinctiveness of Deuteronomy (D) had earlier been emphasized, notably by W. M. L. De Wette (1780-1849). Thus by the middle of the 19th century four main sources had been identified in the order E^1 (later termed P, for Priestly Code), E^2 (later termed simply E), J, and D. In 1865 K. H. Graf (1815-69) argued that of these P was not the earliest but rather the latest.

Graf's conclusion was adopted by J. Wellhausen (1844-1918), who in a number of articles in 1876-77 brilliantly argued the results of this "newer documentary theory." J and E were dated to the ninth and eighth centuries respectively; the original core of Deuteronomy *(Urdeuteronomium),* which had been identified with Josiah's "book of the law" (2 Kings 22–23), to the seventh century; and the original P narrative to about 500 B.C. In the late preexilic period a redactor (the "Jehovist") combined J and E, a later editor combined JE with D, and a postexilic editor combined JED with P, P thus forming the framework of the completed Pentateuch.

1.2. Continuing analysis suggested further refinements, especially to J and E, which some now argued were the work of "schools" rather than of single authors. Others, however, rejected this conclusion but found evidence that J had incorporated an originally independent source, thus suggesting a five-source theory ("the newest documentary theory"). There was also critical dissent from major aspects of Wellhausen's conclusions. In particular, the postexilic dating of P was contested in favor of a preexilic origin. Some also questioned whether P had ever been an independent source rather than a Priestly editing of JED. Whether E, which is only fragmentarily preserved, had ever been an independent source was also disputed. These and other aspects of the documentary theory, including the criteria upon which it is based, have remained disputed until the present day.

2. Oral Stage

Source criticism limited itself largely to the documents and their authors without attempting an investigation of the history and transmission of the contents of these sources before the work of their authors. But from the late 19th century onward and under the influence of the → history-of-religions school, such an investigation was undertaken. The pioneer was H. Gunkel (1862-1932), who expounded and applied the new methods necessary for such research — *Gattungs-* or *Formgeschichte* (history of genre/form) and *Traditions-* or *Überlieferungsgeschichte* (history of tradition; → Exegesis, Biblical, 1.3). Gunkel's commentary on Genesis (1901) was particularly influential in attempting to trace the history of the patriarchal *Sagen* (legends, stories) from their oral origins and formation into *Sagenkränze* (cycles of *Sagen*) up to their appropriation by J and E, whom he regarded as collectors rather than as authors.

Gunkel's work stimulated a generation of form-critical and traditio-historical study of the Pentateuchal literature. Not until the studies by G. von Rad (1901-71) and especially M. Noth (1902-68),

Pentateuchal Research

however, was a more comprehensive investigation undertaken of the origin of the Pentateuch on the basis of the new methods.

2.1. In his monograph of 1938 von Rad attempted to trace the cultic *Sitz im Leben* of the *Landnahme* (occupation and settlement) tradition, briefly formulated in the ancient "creed" of Deut. 26:5b-9, and of the Sinai tradition (Exodus 19–24) in the premonarchical period. It was the Yahwist, dated by him to the Solomonic period, who, adopting the "creed" as his framework, expanded each of its main elements, incorporated into it the Sinai tradition, and prefaced all with an account of the → primeval history in Genesis 1–11. Against Gunkel, therefore, von Rad argued that the Yahwist was no mere collector but a creative author and theologian who gave the Pentateuch, or rather the Hexateuch, its definitive form.

Noth's main contribution, published in 1948, argued that a Pentateuchal *Grundlage* (G), or foundation, emerged in several stages during the period of the premonarchical Israelite amphictyony (→ Tribes of Israel) and especially at cultic assemblies at the central → sanctuaries. G's first stage was an elaboration of the exodus theme, with which the remaining themes were gradually combined in the following order: entry into the land, → promise to the ancestors, wilderness wandering, and finally the Sinai → covenant theme. Further "Auffüllung" (filling in) and "Verklammerungen" (connections) completed G. Both the Yahwist and the Elohist were dependent upon G, an assumption that accounts for the similarities between these sources. Moreover, since the main stages in the formation of the Pentateuch took place in the premonarchical period, there was less room for a creative contribution by the Yahwist than von Rad had maintained. The Elohist adhered closely to the plan of G, which, like E, contained no primeval history. The Yahwist, however, added a primeval history that was fundamental for his theology. While accepting that a tenth-century origin of J could not be ruled out, Noth expressed caution about such an early dating.

2.2. Though at first widely influential, the views of von Rad and Noth have in more recent years found much less support. The so-called creed of Deuteronomy 26, upon which von Rad placed so much importance, is now regarded as a Deuteronomic composition of no earlier than the seventh century B.C.; if so, it cannot have provided a basis for the work of the Yahwist at an earlier time. Von Rad's early dating of J has also been increasingly rejected.

In addition, integral to the research of both von Rad and Noth was the theory of an early Israelite amphictyony that, they believed, provided the historical and institutional context for the growth of the Pentateuchal traditions. But few today accept that there ever was such an amphictyony within which the alleged *Landnahme* and Sinai traditions or a supposed *Grundlage* could have been developed. Increasingly also Noth's notion of such a *Grundlage* has been regarded as too much of an abstraction.

3. Modern Views

Current Pentateuchal research is characterized by renewed controversy both about the methods employed hitherto and about the results achieved on their basis. In addition, various new theories about the origin of the Pentateuch have been argued. Most radical of all is that proposed by R. Rendtorff (1977), who argues that when form criticism is properly applied, it reveals that the major tradition-complexes of the Pentateuch first developed independently of each other. These "larger units" were (1) primeval history, (2) patriarchal history, (3) the bondage-exodus complex, (4) the complex of wilderness traditions, (5) the Sinai complex, and (6) settlement in the land. Only when each of these self-contained larger units had been completed were they combined to form the Pentateuch. Thus there never were J, E, and P narrative documents composed by individual authors and secondarily combined by editors.

Rendtorff concentrates on the → patriarchal history in Genesis 12–50, arguing that the various promises of God to Israel's ancestors here recorded (land, descendants, blessing, guidance) provide the key to the growth of this complex from smaller units into the larger unit that it now is. Furthermore, the striking absence of these promises, especially that of the land, from the exodus narratives is evidence that the latter developed independently of Genesis 12–50. E. Blum (1984) has similarly argued that Genesis 12–50 developed independently of the narrative of the exodus.

Various difficulties, however, render such a theory implausible. For example, the various promises upon which Rendtorff places crucial importance may themselves for the most part be secondary additions to the narratives. This assumption, too, would offer an explanation of their absence from the exodus narratives. If, however, such promises were an original part of Genesis 12–50, their presence would be strong evidence that this complex points beyond the end of Genesis to the remainder of the Pentateuch for the fulfillment of these promises. That is, a complex that so focused upon these promises, especially that of the land, and yet ended with Israel's ancestors in Egypt and thus far from the promised land, would be a torso.

It is equally improbable that, for example, the bondage-exodus and wilderness complexes were developed independently of one another. The latter not only presupposes the former; in several ways both complexes are closely interwoven, for example, by the presence in both of the "murmuring" tradition (Exod. 14:11-12; 15:22-27; 17:1-7), as well as by the climax of the exodus narrative (chap. 15) being also the first of Yahweh's actions on → Israel's behalf in the wilderness.

None of this critique is to question that each of the complexes identified by Rendtorff has its own themes and motifs. The separation of them that he proposes, however, is both forced and artificial.

3.1. Alternative theories have been proposed by, for example, J. Van Seters (1975, 1983) and R. N. Whybray (1987). On the basis of a study of the Abraham narratives, Van Seters argues that J and with it E, which in his view was never an independent document, emerged in three stages: two pre-Yahwistic stages, followed by the work of the Yahwist proper, which he dates to the exilic period. A postexilic editor added the P material, which never existed as an independent document, and some still later additions completed the process.

Whybray argues against this proposal that Genesis through Numbers, including the P material, was composed by a single author in the exilic period on the basis of many sources and as a sort of historical prologue to the Deuteronomistic G (see also the work of M. Rose, 1981). Whybray's work is notable for its rejection of the criteria upon which the documentary theory is based (see 1), and both he and Van Seters call in question the viability of penetrating behind the Pentateuchal literature to earlier alleged oral stages in the transmission of the literature and traditions.

3.2. Convincing arguments have been advanced, especially by H. H. Schmid (1976), against von Rad's Solomonic dating of the Yahwist. But it is questionable whether an exilic origin of J can be sustained, though it may contain some late additions from that period. For example, in sharp contrast to the known literature of the exilic period (Deuteronomistic G, Jeremiah, Ezekiel, Deutero-Isaiah), any hint of the catastrophe of the exile is absent from JE. It is also unlikely that an exilic writer would have composed or compiled the Jacob-Esau narrative (Genesis 27–33), at the conclusion of which Jacob, who represents Israel, bows before Esau, who represents Edom, Israel's most hated enemy after 586 B.C. (Gen. 33:1-11; cf. Psalm 137; Obadiah). In fact, there is little in JE that need be dated to the exilic period, and much that militates against such a dating; a preexilic origin of JE remains the more probable view.

3.3. The arguments of Rendtorff, Van Seters, Whybray, and others recently, especially Blum (1990), that the P material in the Pentateuch was never an independent source cannot be said to have added anything convincing to what some earlier scholars argued. For example, in spite of repeated attempts to argue that the P material in the flood story in Genesis 6–8 is only a Priestly redaction of an earlier J story, it remains probable that it derives from an originally independent P document that has secondarily combined with an existing J flood story (see J. E. Emerton, 1987 and 1988). Furthermore, in spite of repeated attempts to date P to the preexilic period, the majority opinion remains that, though it contains some ancient material, it derives from the postexilic period.

3.4. It is an obvious limitation of these new theories that they either are based upon the study of a relatively restricted portion of the Pentateuch or are stated in rather general terms. Quite apart from other difficulties, therefore, they lack the comprehensive treatment of the literature as a whole that the documentary theory offers. For this reason none of them succeeds in displacing that theory.

This is not to say that the documentary theory explains all the problems of the sources, their composition, origin, and redaction; it has never claimed to do so. In the final analysis it must be said that such is the complexity of the Pentateuchal literature and such the manifestly long process that went into its formation that it is unlikely that any theory will ever provide a solution to all of its problems. The documentary theory, however, remains the most coherent and plausible that has yet been argued.

3.5. It is another question, however, whether it is possible, as Gunkel and his followers believed, to penetrate with much success behind the literary sources J, E, and P. Here Van Seters and Whybray have rightly challenged the viability of form criticism to uncover the earliest stages of the literature and the traditions. While many parts of the Pentateuch have the imprint of oral tradition and the nature of folk literature, recent research in oral tradition has cast doubt on whether we can recover to any worthwhile extent the preliterary stages of its formation and transmission. It seems likely, therefore, that future traditio-historical research will yield more restricted results than was believed possible by scholars such as Noth and von Rad.

→ Torah

Bibliography: E. Blum, *Die Komposition der Vätergeschichte* (Neukirchen, 1984); idem, *Studien zur Komposition des Pentateuch* (Berlin, 1990) • J. A. Emerton, "An Examination of Some Attempts to Defend the Unity of the Flood Story in Genesis," *VT* 37 (1987) 401-20; 38 (1988) 1-21 • D. A. Knight, *Rediscovering the Traditions of Israel: The Development of the Traditio-historical Research of the OT* (rev. ed.; Cambridge, Mass., 1975) • H.-J. Kraus, *Geschichte der historisch-kritischen Erforschung des Alten Testaments* (3d ed.; Neukirchen, 1982) • J. L. Kugel, *The Bible as It Was* (Cambridge, Mass., 1997) • E. T. Mullen, *Ethnic Myths and Pentateuchal Foundations: A New Approach to the Formation of the Pentateuch* (Atlanta, 1997) • E. W. Nicholson, *The Pentateuch in the Twentieth Century: The Legacy of Julius Wellhausen* (Oxford, 1998) • M. Noth, *A History of Pentateuchal Traditions* (Chico, Calif., 1981) • G. von Rad, *The Problem of the Hexateuch, and Other Essays* (Edinburgh, 1966) • R. Rendtorff, *The Problem of the Process of Transmission in the Pentateuch* (Sheffield, 1990; orig. pub., 1977) • A. Rofé, *Introduction to the Composition of the Pentateuch* (Sheffield, 1999) • J. W. Rogerson, ed., *The Pentateuch* (Sheffield, 1996) • M. Rose, *Deuteronomist und Jahwist* (Zurich, 1981) • H. H. Schmid, "In Search of New Approaches in Pentateuchal Research," *Pentateuch,* ed. Rogerson, 24-32; idem, *Der sogenannte Jahwist. Beobachtungen und Fragen zur Pentateuchforschung* (Zurich, 1976) • R. J. Thompson, *Moses and the Law in a Century of Criticism since Graf* (Leiden, 1970) • J. Van Seters, *Abraham in History and Tradition* (New Haven, 1975); idem, *In Search of History: Historiography in the Ancient World and the Origins of Biblical History* (New Haven, 1983) • R. N. Whybray, *Introduction to the Pentateuch* (Grand Rapids, 1995); idem, *The Making of the Pentateuch* (Sheffield, 1987).

E. W. Nicholson

Pentecost

1. OT
2. Early Judaism
3. NT
4. Liturgical Development

Along with → Easter (deriving from → Passover), Pentecost is the only Jewish feast to have found a place in the Christian calendar. The term comes from Gk. *pentēkostē,* "50th [day]," which was used in Hellenistic Judaism (Tob. 2:1; 2 Macc. 12:32). The reference is to the festival on the 50th day after Passover.

1. OT

In the OT Pentecost is a → harvest festival at the end of the wheat harvest. The usual term for it is the Festival of Weeks (*ḥag* [*haš*] *šābuʿôt,* Exod. 34:22; Deut. 16:16, etc.), with reference to the seven weeks from the beginning of the harvest (Deut. 16:9-10). Already in Lev. 23:15-16 there is a fixed connection with the Passover, since 50 days, or seven Sabbaths plus a day, are to be counted from the Passover. The rite demanded the bringing of two loaves of leavened meal baked from the new wheat as offerings in the → sanctuary (Lev. 23:17-20; → Dietary Laws). Like the Passover and → Tabernacles, Pentecost was a pilgrim feast for all Israel, though in practice it was less important than the first two.

2. Early Judaism

In early Judaism the feast seems perhaps to have involved the transferring of an original agricultural festival into the sphere of → salvation history, in the course of which a change in pointing vowels made the "weeks" festival into an "oaths" festival (*ḥag haššĕbuʿôt*). In the late second century B.C. in Hasidean and priestly circles, the Book of Jubilees found the central meaning of the feast in the oaths that Israel had sworn in connection with the various divine covenants in its past history (*Jub.* 6:10-11). Pentecost was thus the feast of → covenant remembrance and covenant renewal (vv. 17-22).

The → Qumran community knew an annual feast of covenant renewal (1QS 1:8–2:18), probably at the end of the Festival of Weeks. A second step was taken in this direction when, only after A.D. 70, Pentecost became a day commemorating the giving of the law at → Sinai (with Exodus 19 as the reading).

3. NT

In the NT the only direct testimony to the festival appears in the Lukan account in Acts 2. It could well be that the immediate disciples of Jesus, after seeing him in Galilee (1 Cor. 15:5; Mark 16:7; → Resurrection), went up to Jerusalem for the pilgrimage feast following the Passover death and there made their witness to the people of Israel, having first participated in a manifestation of the Spirit of God. As the prophetic end-time promise of the Spirit that had been given to Israel was thus fulfilled (Joel 2:28-32; cf. Acts 2:17-21), the resurrection of Jesus was shown to be the dawn of the last age (→ Eschatology). At the same time, the disciples saw in their experience of the Spirit a renewal and confirmation of the commission that Christ had given them regarding Israel. As one might expect, the understanding of Pentecost as a feast of covenant renewal played a role in this connection. Thus the disciples saw it as their task in Jerusalem to proclaim the end-time renewal of God's covenant with his people.

Other traditions and interpretations, however, are also present in Acts 2. Thus the reception of the Spirit is depicted as a miracle of tongues and auditions, and the list of peoples in vv. 9-11 shows that the → mission is to be worldwide. Some scholars have theorized that the later practice of → glossolalia, unintelligible ecstatic speech, is here read back into the first days of the church (vv. 13, 15) as a manifestation of the Spirit.

Another point that has called for discussion is the separation of the → ascension and exaltation of Christ from the sending of the Spirit, which some see as at odds with the theological understanding (Eph. 4:8-10) and liturgical practice of primitive Christianity.

4. Liturgical Development

Liturgically, the Christian feast developed slowly (→ Liturgy 1.2) The NT offers no data, since 1 Cor. 16:8 and Acts 20:16 refer to the Jewish feast. Up to the fourth century Pentecost was a festival of the ascension and the sending of the Spirit after Easter. It came at the end of the 50-day feast that began at Easter. The development of a separate Ascension Day commemoration prompted by the Lukan dating meant that Pentecost itself became increasingly detached from Easter as a separate feast of the sending of the Spirit. Some more recent liturgies have tried to relate it once again more closely to Easter.

→ Holy Spirit; Jewish Practices 2

Bibliography: N. Adler, *Das erste christliche Pfingsfest* (Münster, 1938) • S. Brown, "Easter and Pentecost," *Worship* 46 (1972) 277-86 • M. Dömer, *Das Heil Gottes* (Cologne, 1978) • W. H. Harris, *The Descent of Christ: Ephesians 4:7-11 and Traditional Hebrew Imagery* (Leiden, 1996) • J. Kremer, *Pfingstbericht und Pfingstgeschehen* (Stuttgart, 1973) • G. Lohfink, *Die Himmelfahrt Jesu* (Munich, 1971) • I. H. Marshall, "The Significance of Pentecost," *SJT* 30 (1977) 347-69.

Jürgen Roloff†

Pentecostal Churches

1. Distinctive Characteristics
2. Origins
3. Early Groupings
   3.1. Holiness-Pentecostal Churches
   3.2. By Race
   3.3. By Theology
4. Early Twentieth-Century Developments
   4.1. Wesleyan Pentecostal Churches
   4.2. "Finished Work" Churches
   4.3. Oneness Churches
5. Later Twentieth-Century Developments
   5.1. Charismatic Movement
   5.2. Third Wave Movement
   5.3. Nondenominational Movement
   5.4. Indigenous Churches Movement
6. Summary and Projections

With a half billion adherents, Pentecostal/charismatic churches represent the second largest Christian tradition in the world today, second only to Roman Catholicism. The movement began in 1901, with origins in the 19th-century → Holiness movement. Pentecostal churches are often misunderstood because they defy categorization into the contemporary divisions of Christianity, whether based on theology, polity, or social standing. They may be Catholic or Protestant in tradition, Calvinistic or Arminian in theology, and episcopal, presbyterian, or congregational in → polity. Initially comprising largely the poor, their membership today spans the socioeconomic classes in numbers that are roughly proportionate to those of the general population.

1. Distinctive Characteristics

Regardless of their diversity in ecclesial identifiers, Pentecostal churches have common characteristics. They are primitivistic. Pentecostals share a belief that Christians of every generation should know God in the pattern of first-century believers; God desires to do now what he did then. Thus, the gifts and workings of the Spirit seen in the → Acts of the Apostles (§7) should be present today (→ Charisma; Primitive Christian Community).

Likewise, the Scriptures are for Pentecostals the verbally inspired, authoritative → Word of God. Unlike → fundamentalist Christians who emphasize the work of the → Holy Spirit in the creation of the text, Pentecostals approach the Bible as being continuously inspired by the Holy Spirit. The Bible carries the presence of God and serves as a central place for fellowship with him. Pentecostals are "people of the Book."

Pentecostals are also futuristic, interpreting the present in light of the imminent return of Christ (→ Parousia), seeing modern developments as rapidly progressing toward the fulfillment of all things. They reject aspects of modernity that are perceived to undermine the lordship of Christ over all of life (i.e., cultural shifts viewed as ethical deviations from scriptural norms and indicators of the "great falling away" before the return of Christ) while embracing others (e.g., technology as a divine gift for the proclamation of the gospel). → Pentecostalism may best be construed as a *paramodern* movement. Harvey Cox and others have portrayed Pentecostals as central figures in the rise of → postmodernity.

Similarly, Pentecostals share a theocentric worldview. God is at work in, through, and by all things. In both his → immanence and his transcendence, he is always personally present, desiring communion with his creation. Consequently, Pentecostals are more active than reflective. They have pragmatic tendencies that find expression in a missional ethos that values creative responsiveness to the leading of the Holy Spirit.

2. Origins

The Pentecostal movement may — but only with caution — be categorized through the historical trajectories that gave birth to it. It is generally recognized that the Azusa Street Revival in Los Angeles, California (1906-9), formed the hub and heart of the early movement (→ Revivals 2.1; Black Churches 2.1.3). As such, Pentecostal churches must be seen as having emerged from the 19th-century Holiness movement, and Azusa provides a critical lens for tracing and interpreting Pentecostal history. In this context early Pentecostal churches may be divided into three groups: preexisting denominations and congregations that came into the movement, denominations and congregations that were born out of Azusa, and groups that splintered off the earlier two.

It should not be overlooked that many expressions of the Pentecostal revival, with varying antecedents, erupted spontaneously around the world. Some existing churches, predominantly but not exclusively from the Holiness tradition, were swept into the revival. Fledgling denominations were incorporated in part or in whole into the movement. While the tendency of scholars has been to tie all Pentecostal churches to Azusa, many indigenous groups throughout the world have come rightfully to claim their own fountains of Pentecost. Some have little or no direct connection with the North American phenomenon. Pentecostalism may indeed have several mothers around the world.

It remains accurate to say, however, that the Azusa Street Revival served as the defining catalyst for Pentecostal churches throughout much of the world. The revival itself was led by William J. Seymour (1870-1922), a poorly educated African American from Centerville, Louisiana, who became the first apostle and lightning rod for the movement. Seymour's parents were former slaves who raised him as a Baptist. As a young man he moved to Indiana, Ohio, and Texas. At these junctures he transitioned from Baptist to the Methodist Episcopal Church (in Indianapolis), to the Holiness group known as the Church of God Reformation (in Cincinnati), under whose influence he experienced entire sanctification (→ Finney, Charles Grandison, 4) and came to anticipate a great outpouring of the Holy Spirit before the return of Christ.

Seymour was first introduced to the distinctive Pentecostal doctrine of baptism in the Holy Spirit with tongues (→ Glossolalia) as the initial evidence by his pastor, Lucy Farrow, in 1905 in Houston, Texas. Later that year her teacher, Charles Fox Parham (1873-1929), was in Houston, which led to Seymour's receiving further instruction. Parham is considered by many to be the father of Pentecostalism, being the first to formulate the essential tenets of the movement. In Topeka, Kansas, he had been a successful Holiness evangelist and pastor and operated a Bible school. Influenced by reports of xenolalia during a visit with Frank W. Sanford (1862-1948) in Shiloh, Maine, he returned to Kansas and formulated the doctrine of Spirit baptism accompanied by tongues, understanding tongues as a promised means of worldwide → evangelism. In 1901 Parham and some of his students had even experienced the "blessing," but with limited public notice. Parham's effectiveness as an evangelist increased after his Spirit baptism, leading to the expansion of his movement from Topeka, Kansas, to Houston in late 1905, where he met and taught Seymour.

Having accepted the doctrine of tongues as initial evidence but not having the experience himself, Seymour moved in 1906 to Los Angeles, where he preached the Pentecostal doctrine of baptism in the Holy Spirit. The experience of tongues, first by some of his congregants and soon by Seymour himself, led to bold street preaching and to the Azusa Street Revival.

The movement Seymour led (or, more accurately, moderated) was characterized by enthusiastic worship, glossolalia, and racial integration. This combination placed the group outside the acceptable norms of public opinion and made them a target of scorn. It did not help that the church was located in a rustic building that had variously served as a church, stable, and warehouse. Sermons and newspaper articles portrayed the revival as hysterical bedlam and racial miscegenation, with frequent speculations of immoral conduct. Participants were depicted as either insane or demon possessed. In contrast, joined by telegraph and by daily newspapers, Pentecostal publications spread news of the revival among spiritually hungry Christians scattered around the world. Conveniently located for both railroad and ocean travel, Los Angeles became a pilgrimage destination for thousands of seekers, the curious, and the scornful. Within months believers were carrying the message and the experiences of Azusa to all corners of the globe.

At the heart of the early Pentecostal movement was missionary zeal grounded in a fervent expectation of the imminent return of Christ. Participants saw themselves as recapitulating primitive Christianity in preparation for the final reign of Christ. Baptism in the Holy Spirit accompanied by the NT sign of speaking in tongues was understood as the promised "latter rain" (Joel 2:23 KJV) that would produce a great harvest of souls and conclude with the appearance of Jesus. Christian unity, especially between the races, was a common theme.

3. Early Groupings

When traced from Azusa, Pentecostal churches may be thought of as emerging in three waves: classical Pentecostals (1906 to the present), charismatic believers (1960 to the present; → Charismatic Movement), and neocharismatic believers, or the "third wave" (1980 to the present). Classical Pentecostals may further be divided according to a variety of classifications, including theological distinctiveness, racial divisions, and polity. They share a close link to Azusa, from which three central threads have been woven into the tapestry of their faith: (1) belief in divine → healing as a provision of the atoning work of Christ, (2) belief in a Spirit baptism subsequent to the new birth that empowers believers for Christian service, and (3) belief that speaking in tongues "as the Spirit gives utterance" is the initial evidence of Spirit baptism.

3.1. *Holiness-Pentecostal Churches*

One grouping of classical Pentecostals comprises the preexisting Holiness churches that adopted the Pentecostal message. They include the Church of God in Christ (COGIC), the Church of God (Cleveland, Tenn.) (COG-Cleveland), and the Pentecostal Holiness Church, later the International Pentecostal Holiness Church (IPHC; → Churches of God). Some of these churches attested to Pentecostal experiences before Azusa, but all credit Azusa with the doctrinal formulations of Spirit baptism and tongues as the initial evidence. Identification as Holiness churches remained important to each after adoption of the distinctive elements of Pentecostalism. Pentecost was viewed as the penultimate expression of their Holiness beliefs, the sign that the ultimate restoration of all things was imminent.

3.2. *By Race*

A second grouping of churches includes independent congregations that affiliated early in the movement, usually along racial lines. The first affiliation of Pentecostal congregations emerged in Los Angeles at the outbreak of the revival in 1906. The Pentecostal Assemblies of the World (PAW) was formed as a loose and racially integrated fellowship of churches that later joined the Oneness movement and eventually became predominantly a black denomination.

The foremost of the affiliations along racial lines was the formation of the General Council of the → Assemblies of God (AG) in April 1914. Early in the movement many white Pentecostal ministers were ordained by Charles H. Mason (1866-1961) of the COGIC. As cofounder of COGIC in 1897, Mason, an African American, was already a prominent figure in black Christianity when he traveled to Azusa and received his Spirit baptism in 1906. His testimony led to a split in the young denomination, with Mason's supporters reorganizing as a Pentecostal church in 1907. Organization of the AG may be attributed in part to theological differences with Mason (see 3.3), but it must also be recognized as racially motivated. The "open" invitation to attend the organizational meeting was conspicuously not circulated among African American congregations. The division, however, was amicably received by both sides. With few exceptions, racial unity was dropped as a core Pentecostal conviction. The division was highlighted when blacks were omitted from membership in the Pentecostal Fellowship of North America (PFNA) when it was organized in 1948.

3.3. *By Theology*

Theologically, classical Pentecostals fall into three main groups: Wesleyan Pentecostals, "finished work" Pentecostals, and Oneness Pentecostals. These distinctions arose very early. The first Pentecostals adhered to a soteriology that recognized three stages, or blessings, in Christ: → regeneration, → sanctification, and Spirit baptism (→ Glossolalia 5). The first major point of theological contention was over the Holiness doctrine of sanctification. William H. Durham (1873-1912), a prominent Pentecostal pastor in Chicago, initiated the controversy in 1910 when he began to criticize the Holiness doctrine. Soon other prominent leaders in the movement joined Durham in rejecting the Holiness teaching of entire sanctification as a second work of grace. They substituted an emphasis on the "finished work" of Calvary; sanctification was seen as a gradual appropriation of the atoning sacrifice of Jesus. The movement was sharply, and roughly equally, divided over this doctrine. The preexisting Holiness churches (COGIC, COG-Cleveland, and IPHC et al.) held fast to their Holiness roots. Many of the independent congregations that had come into the movement had backgrounds in the British Keswick Convention (→ Perfection 5.1; Fellowship Movement 3) and in Baptist churches. This latter group quickly embraced the new doctrine as more consistent with their heritage. When many of them came together to form the AG in 1914, the opening address by M. M. Pinson (1873-1953) was entitled "The Finished Work of Calvary."

The "Oneness," or "Jesus name," controversy provided the second theological conflict to divide the early Pentecostals. Influenced by the movement's radical commitment to be governed only by the NT, a group arose to challenge Trinitarian theology on the grounds that the word "Trinity" is not found in the Scriptures and that the doctrine usurps the biblical emphasis on the lordship and name of Jesus (→ Black Churches 2.2.3). The controversy can be traced to a camp meeting near Los Angeles in April 1913, when several participants agreed that baptism must be in the name of Jesus. Energetic evangelists and promotional periodicals carried the message around the world, challenging believers to be rebaptized in Jesus' name. A Oneness theology to support the baptismal formula quickly emerged, and the conflict was already present at the first General Council of the AG in 1914. The second council, in 1915, was called specifically to address the issue and resulted in an appeal for tolerance. The third council, in 1916, resulted in the formulation of the *Statement of Fundamental Truths* for the AG, designed primarily to disassociate itself from the Oneness doctrine and to "disfellowship" its adherents (→ Assemblies of God 1). This action resulted in the dismissal of 156 of the 585 ministers within the young fellowship.

Oneness Pentecostals quickly organized themselves as the General Assembly of Apostolic Assemblies (1916), followed by a merger with the PAW. This group initially attempted to maintain an emphasis on racial unity. By 1924, however, they had divided along racial lines. Recurring attempts to reconcile failed. The PAW emerged as the largest predominantly black group, although it has also included whites as prominent participants. The whites underwent numerous mergers and splits, with the United Pentecostal Church (UPC, formed in 1945) emerging as the dominant white representative of the movement.

4. Early Twentieth-Century Developments

By 1916 the primary divisions among classical Pentecostals in North America had been established: Wesleyan versus "finished work," black versus white, and Trinitarian versus Oneness. The Wesleyan Pentecostal churches are Trinitarian and trace their histories to the 19th-century Holiness movement, seeing the experience of sanctification as preparatory for Spirit baptism. Foremost among these in the United States have been the COGIC, COG-Cleveland, and the IPHC.

4.1. ***Wesleyan Pentecostal Churches***

The Church of God in Christ is the largest Pentecostal denomination in the United States. Guided for 55 years by C. H. Mason, its founding bishop, this group maintained a strong commitment to the original tenets of Azusa Street. Reluctantly accepting the racial division that had been thrust upon them, the church became the central expression of black Pentecostalism. Growth was modest until Mason appointed regional bishops in 1933, which led to phenomenal increases that were interrupted only by a split following Mason's death in 1961. The church has remained predominantly a U.S. church but does have congregations in 60 countries, many in Africa. In the latest figures available (1997), the church claimed eight million members.

Although the Church of God (Cleveland, Tenn.) began as an isolated Appalachian movement, its influence is widespread. First instituted in 1886 under the name "The Christian Union," it was founded upon the desire "to restore primitive Christianity and bring about the union of all denominations." The church experienced a revival in 1896 in Cherokee County, North Carolina, in which there were accounts of glossolalia and other charismata. In 1906 the name of the church was changed to "Church of God," and two years later, under the leadership of A. J. Tomlinson (1865-1943), it began to promote the doctrine of the baptism of the Holy Spirit, with tongues as the initial evidence. Throughout its history the church has been interracial in membership, but during the Jim Crow era (roughly 1876-1954), blacks were internally segregated with their own conventions and assemblies. Today the Church of God has a U.S. membership of approximately one million and a worldwide membership of seven million, with a presence in over 160 countries.

Another Pentecostal denomination that traces its origin to the Holiness movement is the International Pentecostal Holiness Church, which represents the merger of three groups in 1911 and 1915: the Fire-Baptized Holiness Church, the Holiness Church of North Carolina, and the Tabernacle Pentecostal Church. The denomination reports a U.S. membership of 222,900 and a worldwide membership of 1,288,260 (2003), not including affiliated churches.

These and most of the other smaller Wesleyan Pentecostal churches maintain modified Methodist or episcopal forms of polity, with local churches being subject to oversight and control by conferences and or → bishops. They are international bodies, with some form of ecclesial oversight of the whole.

4.2. ***"Finished Work" Churches***

The "finished work" stream of classical Pentecostals may be divided between the Trinitarians and the Oneness groups, with the Trinitarians forming the largest segment of classical Pentecostalism (→ Trinity). Of the Trinitarians, with a total membership of over 50 million, the AG represents the largest affiliation of classical Pentecostals in the world. The AG reports a membership of over 1.6 million and a constituency of 2.7 million in the U.S. (2003), placing them second behind COGIC. In the United States the AG presents itself as a "cooperative fellowship" instead of a denomination. They affirm the sovereignty of the local assembly, recognizing self-supporting congregations affiliated with the General Council as being fully autonomous (→ Congregationalism). Each national body of the AG is also self-governing, making the AG in essence a communion of affiliated churches known as the World Assemblies of God Fellowship. In September 1992 Pastor Cho Yonggi of Korea was elected as the chairman of the Executive Committee of the fellowship. Up to that time, the international leadership had rested solely in the control of the American leadership, but with the election of Pastor Yonggi, the leadership began to be shared for the first time.

The International Church of the Foursquare Gospel (ICFG), founded by Aimee Semple McPherson (1890-1944) in 1923, is another prominent group in the "finished work" stream of Pentecostal denominations. Beginning in the decade of the 1970s, several ICFG pastors and churches in the United States rose to prominence within evangelical Christianity, and denomination-wide growth followed. The group currently reports a worldwide membership in 141 countries of over 4 million (2003). "Foursquare" identifies the core doctrines of the group: Jesus Christ as the Savior, the Baptizer in the Holy Spirit, the Healer, and the Soon-Coming King. (The earliest Pentecostals preached a fivefold gospel of Jesus as these four, plus Jesus as the Sanctifier.) The ICFG differs from the AG in polity. ICFG churches are overseen by a → superintendent, with power to appoint pastors within his or her district.

Despite their differences, classical Trinitarian Pentecostals have forged relationships through associations and fellowships. The Pentecostal Fellowship of North America was founded as an all-white association of the Trinitarian denominations and churches. Throughout the turbulent years of the → civil rights era, the black and white branches of the movement drifted further apart until there was little if any contact between them except in storefronts and the tents of the healing evangelists. All of this segregation was reversed on October 18, 1994, in Memphis, Tennessee. On that date the PFNA disbanded, and the fully integrated Pentecostal/Charismatic Churches of North America (PCCNA) was formed. In what has been called the Memphis Miracle, representatives of the leading denominations publicly and emotionally repented and officially apologized for their → racism (→ Penitence). The new organization structured itself to ensure equitable representation of black and white leadership and the inclusion of others.

The Pentecostal World Fellowship (PWF) began in the 1940s with a commitment to hold triennial conferences for the purposes of promoting spiritual fellowship among Pentecostals and of demonstrating to the world the essential unity of Spirit-baptized believers. The conferences have always been worldwide in participation and highly influenced by European and South African Pentecostals, although dominated by representatives of the U.S.-based denominations. Recent years have seen a shift in name (from Pentecostal World Conference to PWF), a broadening of the mission, and a broadening of the leadership to include more Majority World representatives (→ Third World). Representatives of the North American Churches, however, remain disproportionately represented in the top leadership positions.

4.3. ***Oneness Churches***

The Oneness churches represent the third wing of classical Pentecostalism. This movement emerged in 1914 because of controversy within the Assemblies of God regarding traditional Trinitarian doctrine and baptismal practice. Oneness Pentecostalism represents a more modalistic view of God (→ Christology 2.1.2) and holds to a baptism in the name of Jesus rather than the triune formula of Matt. 28:19. In 1916 the Trinitarian/Oneness controversy resulted in the formation of the General Assembly of Apostolic Assemblies (GAAA). In 1918 this organization merged with the Pentecostal Assemblies of the World, with the new body taking the name of the PAW. Critical of the racial segregation of the AG and claiming faithfulness to the Azusa

Street Revival, this group attempted to maintain racial inclusiveness. With headquarters in Indianapolis, the PAW had a large African American constituency in the North and strong white representation in the South.

The PAW's view of racial harmony was difficult to maintain during the era of racial segregation in the United States. Southern segregation polices forced the church to hold its conventions in the North. Increasing in numerical strength, white Southerners objected to the difficulties of annual travel to the North and sought to restructure the organization. Failing to succeed, the whites withdrew in 1924. The PAW continues as an essentially black (but always integrated) Oneness group, with current membership of over 500,000. After years of struggle to unify, the whites eventually emerged as the United Pentecostal Church, with a current U.S. membership of approximately 500,000. Oneness Pentecostal denominations are located around the globe, with approximately 2.8 million constituents worldwide.

5. Later Twentieth-Century Developments

The Pentecostal movement during the second half of the 20th century was characterized by several major developments: the rise of the → charismatic movement and the so-called Third Wave churches (neo-Pentecostalism), the emergence of nondenominational Pentecostal and charismatic churches, and the explosive growth of indigenous churches within the Majority World. Each of these developments represents significant transformation not only of Pentecostalism but of Christianity as a whole. At the dawn of the 21st century the streams of classical Pentecostalism, Third Wave, charismatics, nondenominationals, and indigenous churches together represent over 500 million Christians throughout the world, with classical Pentecostals constituting less than half of that number.

5.1. *Charismatic Movement*

The charismatic movement is traced to the ministry of Dennis Bennett (1917-91), an Episcopal priest in Van Nuys, California. After publicly testifying to the experience of Spirit baptism and glossolalia, he was forced to leave his congregation. Bennett moved to an inner-city parish in Seattle, Washington, a parish that subsequently became a major center of charismatic spirituality in the United States.

The charismatic movement within mainline Protestantism is promoted by renewal movements within various denominations. These organizations promote charismatic spirituality by hosting conferences and publishing newsletters. Most mainline denominations have issued statements regarding the charismatic movement that, on the whole, are cautiously positive. Some denominations, however, such as the Lutheran Church–Missouri Synod, have developed statements in opposition to the charismatic movement.

The Roman Catholic charismatic movement exploded in the late 1960s. Duquesne University, Notre Dame University, and the University of Michigan became spiritual centers for this renewal movement. In particular, annual conferences at Notre Dame drew large crowds of people, reaching 30,000 by the mid-1970s. The charismatic renewal within Roman Catholicism is characterized by respect for tradition, coupled with varying interpretations of the baptism in the Holy Spirit. The dominant view is that the charisms (including tongues) are manifested as believers surrender to the inner working of the Holy Spirit, who was received at water baptism or confirmation.

Catholic and mainline charismatics share the Pentecostal belief in the continuation of the charismata in the life of the church. They see themselves as agencies of mission and renewal within their respective churches.

5.2. *Third Wave Movement*

"Third Wave" is used here to identify European- and American-based churches composed primarily of evangelical Christians who resist the labels "Pentecostal" or "charismatic." This movement, which arose in the 1980s, stresses the power of the Holy Spirit in prophetic and healing ministries. Third Wave churches reject the view that the baptism of the Holy Spirit is a second definite work of grace, holding instead to multiple fillings of the Spirit. They do not stress glossolalia. Rather, their worship is characterized by praise music, instructional sermons, and manifestations of the gifts of healing, prophecy, → exorcism, and others. The Vineyard churches have been at the forefront of this group. David Barrett estimates that there are now some 50 million believers worldwide who are part of this Third Wave of the movement.

5.3. *Nondenominational Movement*

The latter part of the 20th century also witnessed a rapid expansion in the numbers of nondenominational Pentecostal/charismatic churches in the United States and Europe. These churches hold in common a strong suspicion of denominational hierarchy and a belief in the freedom of the Spirit in worship. Their membership has come largely from classical Pentecostals who have tired of what they perceive to be ever-increasing denominational controls and from people who have left traditional denominations, perceiving their former churches as being too formal and closed to the power of the Holy Spirit. They may be seen as parallel to the first and second waves, integrating characteristics of each.

Nondenominational churches stress congregational autonomy but excel at networking for the purposes of fellowship and ordination benefits. Many of these fellowships are characterized by shared doctrinal beliefs, but they tend to reject using specific doctrines as a basis for membership. The movement is strongly influenced by the Word of Faith teachings of Kenneth Hagin (1917-2003). Hagin was a classical Pentecostal who merged a radical application of the "finished work" doctrine with a form of dualism to conclude that believers can actualize the realities of the atonement of Christ by their own words of faith when those words are verbalized as positive confessions of the promised realities. Kenneth Copeland (b. 1937), a protégé of Hagin, has replaced him as the central figure in the movement. The influence of the nondenominational movement can be seen around the globe.

5.4. *Indigenous Churches Movement*

Pentecostalism is truly a global movement. Its most rapid growth has been, and is, within the Majority World, where the statistics are staggering. In Africa close to one-half of all Christians are Pentecostal (over 126 million in 2000), be they Roman Catholic, Lutheran, or Baptist. In Latin America there are over 141 million adherents. It is estimated, for example, that 30 percent of the population of Guatemala is Pentecostal. Similarly in Asia, where there are over 135 million adherents, the movement is rapidly growing in countries such as South Korea, China, India, and Indonesia. Of the 50 churches of the world with over 50,000 members, all are outside of the United States, and most are Pentecostal/charismatic.

While there is a strong presence in all parts of the world of churches with ties to the Western Pentecostal churches, and while the PWF has been dominated by North Americans, most of Pentecostalism's growth has been fueled by indigenous churches. These churches fall into two groups: those that arose spontaneously at the beginning of the 20th century in reaction against the colonialism of Western Holiness missions, and those that were, or are, associated with Western Pentecostal/charismatic denominations. The latter are more influenced by the West but insist that their ethnic and cultural heritage is congruous with their faith and reject domination by others. Barrett estimated that in 2000 there were over 203 million indigenous neocharismatics in the world.

Indigenous churches are characterized by their ability to relate Pentecostal spirituality to local popular culture. With 85 million adherents in 2000, African indigenous churches (AICs; → Independent Churches) in particular offer expressions of Christianity quite different from those in Western models. Not upholding the same ethical mores as most Western Christians, they often face accusations of → syncretism. What cannot be denied is the increasing importance of indigenous forms of Pentecostalism in reshaping world Christianity in the 21st century.

Many indigenous churches have become missionary-sending churches. South Korea in particular has seen a great increase in the number of missionaries serving in other countries (over 10,000 in 2000). One Majority World denomination that has spread rapidly is The Universal Church of the Kingdom of God (Iglesia Universal del Reino de Dios), with headquarters in Brazil. Founded in 1977 by Edir Macedo (b. 1945), this group holds to many of the classical Pentecostal traits but emphasizes prosperity through a Word of Faith–type teaching, and it is less moralistic than other Latin American Pentecostals. The church maintains a strong centralized government, with Bishop Macedo closely monitoring all of the church's enterprises. Membership is currently estimated to be 6-10 million worldwide.

6. Summary and Projections

Pentecostalism in its various forms arose in a single century to become the second most influential Christian tradition in the world today. Incipient traits of the movement make it poised to become the dominant expression of Christianity in many parts of the world. In spite of its many divisions, Pentecostalism has retained an underlying drive toward Christian unity that promises to reshape → ecumenism. Although much of Pentecostalism retains a hostility toward other Christian traditions, several Pentecostal churches have taken ecumenical initiatives, even to the point of membership in the → World Council of Churches. The international Roman Catholic–Pentecostal bilateral dialogue has taken great strides toward theological understanding and ecclesial fellowship (→ Ecumenical Dialogue).

While there are also promising developments in racial reconciliation and recognition of the gifts of the Majority World participants, one challenge before Pentecostals is to enhance their own unity during an inevitable transition from First World to Third World leadership. This challenge is made difficult, not least by the prosperity and political alliances of the Western forms of the movement, which stand in stark contrast with those of the Majority World. Other challenges are being thrust upon the movement by its numerical success. How will it relate to Roman Catholicism in those areas of the world where masses of people are leaving the → Roman Catholic Church for Pentecostal expressions of the faith, threatening to unseat the historic church from its place of prominence? What will be the role of Pentecostals in the growing tensions between → Christianity and Islam? Pentecostals are at the forefront of world evangelization, yet they do not appear ready for an interfaith dialogue that might promote → tolerance between world religions.

→ Assembleias de Deus no Brasil; Protestantism 4.3

Bibliography: A. Anderson, *An Introduction to Pentecostalism: Global Charismatic Christianity* (New York, 2004) • D. B. Barrett, G. T. Kurian, and T. M. Johnson, *WCE* (2d ed.) • S. M. Burgess, ed., with E. M. van der Maas, *New International Dictionary of Pentecostal and Charismatic Movements* (Grand Rapids, 2000) • H. Cox, *Fire from Heaven: The Rise of Pentecostal Spirituality and the Reshaping of Religion in the Twenty-first Century* (Reading, Mass., 1995) • D. Dayton, *Theological Roots of Pentecostalism* (Peabody, Mass., 1991) • M. W. Dempster, B. D. Klaus, and D. Peterson, eds., *The Globalization of Pentecostalism: A Religion Made to Travel* (Oxford, 1999) • W. Faupel, *The Everlasting Gospel: The Significance of Eschatology in the Development of Pentecostal Thought* (Sheffield, 1996) • W. J. Hollenweger, *Pentecostalism: Origins and Developments Worldwide* (Peabody, Mass., 1997) • P. Jenkins, *The Next Christendom: The Coming of Global Christianity* (New York, 1998) • D. Martin, *Pentecostalism: The World Their Parish* (New York, 1998) • R. Shaull and W. Cesar, *Pentecostalism and the Future of the Christian Churches: Promises, Limitations, Challenges* (Grand Rapids, 2000) • V. Synan, *The Holiness-Pentecostal Tradition: Charismatic Movements in the Twentieth Century* (Grand Rapids, 1997); idem, ed., *The Century of the Holy Spirit: 100 Years of Pentecostal and Charismatic Renewal, 1901-2001* (Nashville, 2001) • G. Wacker, *Heaven Below: Early Pentecostals and American Culture* (Cambridge, Mass., 2001).

Jackie David Johns

Pentecostalism

1. Term
2. Historical Developments
   2.1. Roman Catholic and Holiness Roots
   2.2. Black and Oral Roots
   2.3. Types of Spirituality
   2.4. Organizational Evolution
   2.5. Worldwide Trends and Ecumenism
3. Evaluation
   3.1. Missiology
   3.2. Hermeneutics
   3.3. Pneumatology
   3.4. Wider Interactions

1. Term

The Pentecostal movement divides into three not always clearly distinct streams: (1) the so-called Pentecostal churches (our present theme), (2) the → charismatic movement, and (3) a new type of "nonwhite indigenous churches" (D. Barrett), also known rather loosely as → independent churches. All three streams flow from the same historical source.

According to Barrett and T. Johnson the movement embraces 570 million adherents (2004). More than half of these believers belong to the classic Pentecostal churches. We must handle the statistics with care, however, since it is often hard to differentiate between classic Pentecostal churches and independent churches, for example, those in India, Indonesia, Korea, Latin America, and Africa. Furthermore, the charismatic movement constantly produces new Pentecostal churches that are like the classic Pentecostal churches in structure and theology but for historical reasons do not figure in the statistics. The main thrust of the movement is in the → Third World (142 million believers in 1988, according to Barrett). Their growth, media presence, aggressive missionary work (→ Mission), beginnings of ecumenical cooperation (→ Ecumenism, Ecumenical Movement), and ecclesiastical, political, and theological significance now call for more than the modest theological investigation they have thus far received.

Western Pentecostals and evangelicals have sometimes used the above-mentioned statistics to try to prove their theological superiority, ignoring the fact that the main bulk of Pentecostals rejects Western missionaries. This rejection is often the very reason for growth. For Pentecostals in many countries, growth began only after Western missionaries left, for instance in China, where there are probably more Pentecostals than in the United States. These churches have integrated many of their pre-Christian rites into their pneumatology (→ Holy Spirit). In other words, they are syncretistic (as indeed all churches are, including the Western historic churches; see W. Hollenweger, *Pentecostalism,* 132-41).

2. Historical Developments

2.1. *Roman Catholic and Holiness Roots*

A history of the → Pentecostal churches must begin with the work of John → Wesley (1703-91), the founder of → Methodism (→ Methodist Churches), when he translated and edited some Roman Catholic devotional works for use by his lay preachers and argued from them that all Christians should have a second religious crisis experience that differs in time and content from that of conversion. He described this experience variously as "entire satisfaction" or "perfection in love." It was John William Fletcher (1729-85), Wesley's Swiss assistant and a former Calvinist, who replaced Wesley's terminology with "baptism in the Spirit" (L. W. Wood). Most histories of the movement start at this point and then go on to list the various developments and changes that Wesley's doctrine of perfection underwent in the American → Holiness movement (→ Perfectionism).

All early Holiness publications emphasize in their description of "the higher Christian life" not only a religious crisis experience (called holiness) but also its social and political fruits. For Charles → Finney, Thomas Upham, and other Holiness leaders, sanctification without these fruits was unthinkable. In fact, feminism, the antislavery movement, the anticapitalist movement, pacifism, and a worldwide peace-securing organization like the United Nations have their ideological roots, and partly also their organizational roots, in early Pentecostalism and in the Holiness movement. These facts, however, are obscured. Early Holiness and Pentecostal texts have been cruelly mutilated in order to present these movements as purely religious. All the more important is the integral reedition of these texts by D. Dayton. The theological explanation of these remarkable changes is seen in the shift from postmillennialism (Christ's return after the millennium) to premillennialism (Christ's return before the millennium; → Millenarianism).

A history of the movement that plays down the social aspect will tend to view the doctrine of the baptism of the Spirit individualistically (→ Individualism) and to stress the idea of the "initial sign," that is, speaking in tongues as a sign of the baptism (C. F. Parham; → Glossolalia). The → Assemblies of God and many, though not all, Pentecostal and charismatic groups take this view. They teach that all believers should have the Spirit's baptism, which normally the sign of speaking in tongues makes known. In this way the movement is defined as a religious fellowship whose members have a distinctive religious experience, which receives a specific theological evaluation (J. R. Goff). This interpretation is in keeping with the development of Pentecostal churches and the charismatic movement in Europe and America, where middle-class evangelical churches (→ Evangelical Movement) rapidly came into being. But an understanding of this type eliminates decisive elements that are responsible for the emergence and expansion of Pentecostalism in the Third World (see 2.2). In Western Pentecostalism the early down-to-earth spirituality is replaced by an effective fund-raising program, a growing clericalism, an almighty church bureaucracy, an ever-present media idolatry (e.g., Pat Robertson and his Christian Broadcasting Network), a conceptual theology of the Western type, and, in the United States, theological seminaries and universities.

The doctrine of the baptism of the Spirit has caused problems, for many members and even pastors have not in fact spoken in tongues. Furthermore, tongues may also be found outside the Pentecostal churches, such as in the charismatic movement, in the secular sphere (e.g., in some circles of jazz and the theater), and in non-Christian religions. The increasing number of Pentecostal academic theologians can no longer be satisfied with the explanation that machinations of the → devil are responsible for such parallels. The doctrine, then, has run up against opposition even within the Pentecostal churches (in Chile, Germany, Britain, the United States, and other places). Russell Spittler, a pastor of the American Assemblies of God and founder of the David du Plessis Center (1985) at Fuller Theological Seminary in Pasadena, California, can thus describe speaking in tongues as a human phenomenon: "If the doctrine of speaking in tongues as the initial physical evidence of the baptism of the Holy Spirit can be labeled the distinctive teaching of the Pentecostal churches, the belief that *distinguishes* the movement can only wrongly be thought of as describing the *essence* of Pentecostalism" ("Glossolalia," 340; see also P. Watt and W. Saayman, 330).

Speaking in tongues is seen in such circles as a gift of creation that we can make transparent for the → kingdom of God as we do with music or the eucharistic bread. It is a kind of nonverbal → prayer. If a whole congregation sings in tongues with no notes and in various harmonies, there is created a cathedral of sounds, a socio-acoustic → sanctuary, which expresses the presence of the Spirit in human sound (W. J. Samarin).

Nevertheless, most Pentecostals and charismatics do not accept this interpretation. As regards similar phenomena outside their churches (or at least outside Christianity), they view them as suspect (→

Occultism), as belonging to the domain of the prince of this world. A charismatic doctrine is developed that divides reality into natural and supernatural. The Christian charismata (→ Charisma) belong to the supernatural order, but so too do parapsychological phenomena (→ Parapsychology) outside Christianity, the difference being that the latter are demonic (see W. J. Hollenweger, *Geist und Materie*).

2.2. *Black and Oral Roots*

Focusing on the history of religious experiences, one can see Pentecostalism as an encounter between Roman Catholic and black → spirituality. The movement as a whole is the heir not just of the Holiness movement but also of the pre-Christian oral → culture and → religion of Africa (→ Afro-American Cults) that have been retained in black spirituality in the United States. These elements were handed down by black evangelists in the early days of Pentecostalism, among them composers and hymn writers, the most important being William Joseph Seymour (1870-1922), son of a slave. Seymour attended C. F. Parham's (1873-1929) Bible school and adopted Parham's definition of the baptism of the Spirit.

In the so-called Azusa Street Revival (Los Angeles, 1906), which most historians call the cradle of the Pentecostal movement, though without recognizing the theological import of this historical decision, Seymour brought many elements of black spirituality into the movement. For Seymour → Pentecost was not just a religious event but an experience that reconciled races, cultures, and social strata. In Los Angeles, at a time when such a thing was regarded as immoral and non-Christian, blacks and whites, as well as rich and poor, prayed together. Many later Pentecostal leaders received the baptism of the Spirit from Seymour by the laying on of hands, even though he was black. The most important features of the Azusa Street Revival were (1) oral liturgy; (2) → narrative theology; (3) maximum participation on the levels of thought, prayer, and decision; (4) scope for → dreams and → visions in public and private forms of prayer; and (5) a deeper understanding of the psychosomatic relation (→ Soul) as expressed especially in prayers for the sick but also in cultic → dance (I. McRobert, V. Synan).

The so-called independent churches of the Third World follow a similar structure. They arise and develop without any help from missionaries, Pentecostal or others. Their pre-Christian religious and social experiences (healing, prophecy, solidarity, etc.) are integrated into a biblical pneumatology. That orientation explains their dramatic growth in South Africa, West Africa, India, Indonesia, Korea, and Latin America (→ Assembleias de Deus no Brasil).

This fact poses almost insuperable difficulties for research. The movement is mostly portrayed as an American product with variations in different lands. But this view does not reckon with the fact that the movement has more members and is theologically more important outside the United States; that it has developed independently; that many Pentecostal churches belong to the → World Council of Churches; that they engage in intensive → dialogue with the Vatican (J. L. Sandidge), with the → World Alliance of Reformed Churches, and with the WCC (A. Bittlinger; → Ecumenical Dialogue); that in many places they work together with local councils of churches (→ National Councils of Churches); that they are evolving theologies, forms of piety, and political → ideologies that are in conflict with those of the West; and that recently they have made theological and political resistance felt among black Pentecostal churches in the United States and in Great Britain (R. Gerloff).

A further difficulty is that in Pentecostal churches more than others, a distinction must be made between the public and the true meaning of a confession (→ Confession of Faith). Black Pentecostalists who say "Hallelujah, I am saved!" are saying that they owe their physical, cultural, and spiritual life to the Lord of life and death. White charismatics or Pentecostalists saying the same words are saying that they have had a spiritual → experience that has given meaning and direction to their individual lives. Another point is that we have solid data only from a few countries. Research still must be done in important areas like Brazil, Chile, Peru, Mexico, the Caribbean, Indonesia, South Africa, West Africa, Great Britain, Italy, and other places. The Gemeinschaftsbewegung in Germany (→ Fellowship Movement) raises a special problem, for it originally welcomed the Pentecostal movement but then in the Berlin Declaration of 1909 said that it was inspired from below (→ Hell), rightly recognizing the black elements in the movement but unable to see them as charismata.

2.3. *Types of Spirituality*

We can divide Pentecostal churches into four different types of spirituality. Some view salvation as occurring in two steps: conversion and the baptism of the Spirit. The Assemblies of God and most European Pentecostal churches represent this group.

Second, other Pentecostal churches believe that salvation occurs in three steps: conversion, sanctification, and the baptism of the Spirit. The Church of God (Cleveland, Tenn.) and splits from it hold this view.

Third, there are so-called Oneness Pentecostal churches, which are most of the black Pentecostal churches in the United States and in Great Britain (→ Black Churches). Earlier this type was called Jesus-only Pentecostal because it regarded the original NT baptismal formula ("In the name of Jesus") as normative. More important, however, is its rejection of the traditional doctrine of the → Trinity. Pentecostals of this type could be considered modern Irvingites, for they view the Spirit of God as the power that permeates the whole cosmos. This is the only theological innovation of the Pentecostal churches, but it is a most important one (Gerloff).

Finally, we have Third World Pentecostal churches, which, out of their own pre-Christian traditions, develop → liturgies and narrative theologies that are methodologically comparable to primitive Christian literature before it took fixed written form. Especially with this fourth type, it is evident that to regard the Pentecostal churches as a variation on the churches of the → Reformation is an oversimplification that we can explain only by the fact that research has focused on the Pentecostal churches of the West and their evangelical conceptualization.

Even then, the thesis is a dubious one, for essential elements of Pentecostal piety have their roots in Roman Catholicism (see 2.1), a fact that was demonstrated long ago by Paul Fleisch and Nils Bloch-Hoell. Although Pentecostals are convinced that they belong to the Reformation tradition, a close scrutiny of their theology and spirituality reveals that Pentecostalism is to a great extent a form of → popular Catholicism, minus the juridical structure. This commonality explains their success in Catholic countries. An Italian, French, or Brazilian Catholic who becomes Pentecostal does not change his or her religion, only his organizational allegiance. Such a connection is seen in detail in the Pentecostal doctrine of → justification. In Pentecostal interpretation justification is not unconditional but depends on human cooperation with God, which is in essence the Roman Catholic understanding of justification. The doctrine of "free will" is accepted as a matter of course by Pentecostals. This issue was the very bone of contention between the Reformers and Roman Catholics in the 16th century (→ Predestination). That Pentecostals opt for "free will" is psychologically understandable, for people who have no say in earthly matters want at least to be able to decide on their eternal destination. Furthermore, Pentecostals distinguish in general between the natural and the supernatural world, which is a Thomistic approach (→ Thomism). At any rate, we perhaps do best to regard Pentecostal churches as a unique → denomination that has yet to position itself theologically.

2.4. *Organizational Evolution*

Much more important than characterizing the types of Pentecostal devotion is the organizational development of Pentecostal churches. These churches have gone through four phases over three or four generations. First we find the phase when they sought to be a movement of ecumenical renewal serving all the churches and only very loosely organized themselves. Then came the consolidation of local congregations apart from other churches, with an evangelical confession and piety. Next we find regional and national institutionalizing, with church buildings, Bible schools, pension funds, and → catechisms. Finally came ecumenical openness and academic theology, but also the splitting off of groups that wished to go back to the first phase.

This division into phases of development applies generally to the whole charismatic movement, which as yet, however, is only in the process of moving from the first phase to the second. Because of the proximity of Pentecostal to Catholic spirituality, the → Roman Catholic Church was successful in integrating the charismatic renewal into its structure, including Mariology, the veneration of saints, and the primacy of the pope. Presbyterian churches have had much more difficulty in accommodating charismatic spirituality into their ranks. A most interesting exception is the Presbyterian Church of Ghana (C. N. Omenyo).

2.5. *Worldwide Trends and Ecumenism*

In Europe the Pentecostal churches are strongest in Romania (200,000 members in 1,600 congregations). They are also strong in Hungary and the former → Soviet Union, where in some cases they managed to get along with the Communist regime but in others suffered bloody persecution. In Yugoslavia and Poland their pastors have for many years received university training. There are many Pentecostal churches also in western Europe (esp. Italy, France, and Scandinavia). In Holland, France, the United States, and the Third World we find the beginnings of ecumenism. By and large, the Pentecostal churches of the West are small in number compared to those in the Third World.

Conferences held at Zurich (1947), Paris (1949), London (1952), Stockholm (1955), Toronto (1958), Jerusalem (1961), Helsinki (1964), Rio de Janeiro (1967), Dallas (1970), Seoul (1973), London (1976), Vancouver (1979), Nairobi (1982), Zurich (1985), Singapore (1989), and Berlin (2003) were originally international gatherings to discuss disputed issues such as the baptism of the Spirit, healing and prayer, and international cooperation, but they gradually lost this character. Under the domination of Western Pentecostal churches and their mission churches, they became public-relations events with no legal or even pastoral authority. Hardly ever did a black South African receive an invitation to speak at the world conferences, although (or perhaps because) the many important black South African Pentecostal churches had produced significant theologians and opponents of apartheid (→ Racism) such as Frank Chikane, Pentecostal pastor and general secretary of the South African Council of Churches, as well as director-general in the South African Presidency (1999-present).

We see here the dilemma of the political orientation of the Pentecostal churches. Official conferences support conservative politics and theology. Western Pentecostal missionaries declared Nelson Mandela and his African National Council to be Communist, even though Pentecostals in South Africa voted him into power. Thus we find, on the one hand, support for dictators and police states (the police officer who tortured Chikane was a Pentecostal himself). On the other hand, we find those who fight for → peace and → justice and are ready to go to prison in the struggle. The problem is that, internationally, the latter have no public voice.

The most important decision at a world conference (1947) was that of publishing an international journal, *Pentecost* (1947-66). Appointed its one editor and publisher was Donald Gee (1891-1966), one of the most capable authors the Pentecostal churches have ever produced. During its short life this journal was full of news and sketches from all over the world and is still one of the best sources for study of the early history of the Pentecostal churches. Gee's editorials were famous, for in them he dealt with most of the important theological, political, ecumenical, missiological, and ethical problems of the Pentecostal churches in an astonishingly unconventional and critical way. No other Pentecostal writer has ever equaled Gee for brevity, precision, or openness.

Today the original critical function of the world conferences has been taken over by the conferences of the Society for Pentecostal Studies (held annually in the United States, with conference papers an important resource) and the European Pentecostal-Charismatic Research Conferences (first meeting in Louvain [1980/81], recent meetings in Prague [1997], Hamburg [1999], and Louvain [2001]; see also J. Jongeneel, *Experiences*). In particular, the new academically trained historians are investigating the roots of the movement, including black, ecumenical, and critical roots. They are discovering that many of their churches began as pacifist and ecumenical revival movements. In the United States in particular, study of the pioneers has revealed astonishingly clear criticism of the dependence of militarism on capitalism, a criticism that for many years was forgotten and even contested in the battle against the WCC. Conversations with the → Vatican, denominational unions, the universities, and the WCC, which had long been broken off, are now being renewed, a late fruit of the work of the two who blazed the trail ecumenically, David Du Plessis (1905-87) and Donald Gee.

3. Evaluation

The preceding discussion shows clearly that Pentecostal theology is in a transitional stage.

3.1. *Missiology*

The doyen of Pentecostal missiology, Melvin Hodges (1909-88), found the reason for the weakness of many mission churches in the treatment of converts as minors and the failure to grant independence to the churches vis-à-vis the missionaries, who forced American structures on them. He meant this analysis primarily to be a criticism of non-Pentecostal missionary societies. But Pentecostal societies have now become wealthy and are repeating the mistakes that Hodges earlier assailed. The theological → pluralism that results from mission is not being accepted and developed.

Theological recognition of independent churches deriving from Pentecostal missionary work would demand revision of Pentecostal biblical → exegesis, → dogmatics, → ethics, and missionary practice. Isolated instances of such revision may be seen, as in discussion of Oneness theology over against the doctrine of the Trinity, or of the "health and wealth" gospel over against the gospel for the poor, or of believers' baptism over against infant baptism (both are permissible), or of ultra-Protestant ecclesiology (→ Church 3.3-6) over against an ecclesiology that is in dialogue with the → Orthodox Church (see the Pentecostal M. Volf, a native of Croatia).

3.2. *Hermeneutics*

At all such points questions of → hermeneutics arise. What are the implications for a mature Pentecostal piety (J.-D. Plüss)? What is the exegetical principle? Why should some Pentecostals take the command to wash one another's feet literally but not other commands? How literally are we to take Paul on such issues as → slavery, the → ordination of women, or → homosexuality? Why do some Pentecostals have military chaplains (→ Military Chaplaincy), while others refuse military service (→ Conscientious Objection; War)? Why do some accept state support when others do not (→ Church Finances)? And the hardest question of all, why are there such different views on the baptism of the Spirit? (For a survey, see H. I. Lederle.)

3.3. *Pneumatology*

Pentecostal pneumatology is very weakly developed. Pentecostals indeed have an impressive practice of experience of the Spirit, but interpretations are usually in the categories of a Western *filioque* pneumatology (→ Niceno-Constantinopolitan Creed). Since the Spirit is seen mainly along the lines of → Christology, and since the standards of what is Christian are taken from the middle-class culture of the West, there is little openness in pneumatology to the phenomena of the Creator Spirit who was at work before the arrival of the missionaries. Theology has not yet been able to take this factor into account as regards missionary practice. (For an interesting introduction to a pneumatological theology of religion, see A. Young.)

The theological problems of the Pentecostal churches are those of Western churches in general. But learned societies for the study of the movement, which include many academically trained members, will, it is hoped, press on in their researches. Pentecostal journals show that promising ecumenical and scholarly work is being done in addition to official → apologetics.

3.4. *Wider Interactions*

Pentecostalism has come of age. This judgment is corroborated by its having becoming a subject of literature, from James Baldwin's *Go Tell It on the Mountain* (1953) to Per Olov Enquist's *Lewis resa* (Levi's journey, 2001). Some analysts interpret Pentecostalism as a form of modernism, even postmodernism, which perhaps explains the massive Pentecostalization of the historic churches. This development, in both its positive and its negative aspects, still awaits investigation.

Bibliography: Biblical study and theology: D. Christie-Murray, *Voices from the Gods: Speaking in Tongues* (London, 1978) • D. W. Dayton, *Theological Roots of Pentecostalism* (Peabody, Mass., 1991) • G. F. Fee, "Baptism in the Holy Spirit: The Issue of Separability and Subsequence," *Pneuma* 7/2 (1985) 87-99 • W. J. Hollenweger, *Geist und Materie* (Munich, 1988) • H. I. Lederle, *Treasures Old and New: Interpretations of "Spirit Baptism" in the Charismatic Renewal Movement* (Peabody, Mass., 1991) • J.-D. Plüss, *Therapeutic and Prophetic Narratives in Worship: A Hermeneutic Study of Testimonies and Visions. Their Potential Significance for Christian Worship and Secular Society* (Frankfurt, 1988) • W. J. Samarin, *Tongues of Men and Angels: The Religious Language of Pentecostalism* (New York, 1972) • R. Spittler, "Glossolalia," *Dictionary of Pentecostal and Charismatic Movements* (ed. S. M. Burgess et al.; Grand Rapids, 1988) 335-42 • M. Volf, *Work in the Spirit: Toward a Theology of Work* (Oxford, 1991) • M. Wenk, *Community-Forming Power: The Socio-ethical Role of the Spirit in Luke-Acts* (London, 2000).

Biographies: M. Bergunder, "From Pentecostal Healing Evangelist to Kalki Avatar: The Remarkable Life of Paulaseer Lawrie, alias Shree Lahari Krishna (1921-1989)–a Contribution to the Understanding of New Religious Movements," *Christians and Missionaries in India: Cross-Cultural Communication since 1500* (ed. R. E. Frykenberg; Grand Rapids, 2003) 357-75 • J. R. Goff, *Fields White unto Harvest: Charles F. Parham and the Missionary Origin of Pentecostalism* (Fayetteville, Ark., 1988) • W. J. Hollenweger, "Two Extraordinary Pentecostal Ecumenists: The Letters of Donald Gee and David J. Du Plessis," *ER* 52/3 (1998) 391-402 • C. van der Laan, *Sectarian against His Will: Gerritt Roelof Polman (1868-1932) and the Birth of Pentecostalism in the Netherlands* (Metuchen, N.J., 1991) • L. Price, *Theology out of Place: A Theological Biography of Walter J. Hollenweger* (London, 2002) • B. Rutherford, "From Prosecutor to Defender: An Intellectual History of David J. Du Plessis Drawn from Stories of His Testimony" (Diss., Fuller Theological Seminary, 2000).

Ecumenical dialogue: H. van Beek and R. Gerloff, eds., *Report of the Proceedings of the Consultation between the WCC and African and Afro-Caribbean Church Leaders in Britain* (Geneva, 1995) • A. Bittlinger, *Papst und Pfingstler. Der römisch-katholische/pfingstliche Dialog und seine ökumenische Relevanz* (Frankfurt, 1978); idem, ed., *The Church Is Charismatic: The World Council of Churches and Charismatic Renewal* (Geneva, 1981) • D. Cole, "Current Pentecostal/Ecumenical Tensions," *EcTr* 25 (1995) 1-16 • C. Dahling-Sander, K. M. Funkschmidt, and V. Mielke, eds., *Pfingstkirchen und Ökumene in Bewegung* (Frankfurt, 2001) • V.-M. Kärkkäinen, *Spiritus ubi vult spirat: Pneumatology in Roman Catholic–Pentecostal Dialogue (1972-1989)* (Helsinki, 1998) • C. Krust, "Pentecostal Churches and the Ecumenical Movement," *The Uppsala Report, 1968* (ed. N. Goodall; Geneva, 1968) 340ff. • C. M. Robeck, "The Assemblies of God and Ecumenical Cooperation: 1920-1965," *Pentecostalism in Context: Essays in Honor of William W. Menzies* (ed. S. Ma and R. Menzies; London, 1996) 107-50 • J. L. Sandidge, *Roman Catholic–Pentecostal Dialogue (1977-1982): A Study in Developing Ecumenism* (2 vols.; Frankfurt, 1987) • "Word and

Spirit, Church and World," *RW* 50/3 (2000) 128-56 (final report of Pentecostal-Reformed dialogue) • WORLD COUNCIL OF CHURCHES, *Consultation with Pentecostal Churches, Lima, Peru, 14-19 November 1994* (Geneva, 1996) • A. YOUNG, "'As the Spirit Gives Utterance': Pentecostal, Intra-Christian Ecumenism and the Wider Oikoumene," *IRM* 92 (2003) 299-311.

Histories and surveys: A. ANDERSON and W. J. HOLLENWEGER, eds., *Pentecostals after a Century: Global Perspectives on a Movement in Transition* (London, 1999) • N. BLOCH-HOELL, *Pinsebevegelsen* (Oslo, 1956; ET *The Pentecostal Movement: Its Origin, Development, and Distinctive Character* [London, 1964]) • B. C. CAMPOS, *De la reforma protestante a la pentecostalidad de la iglesia* (Quito, 1998) • H. COX, *Fire from Heaven: The Rise of Pentecostal Spirituality and the Reshaping of Religion in the Twenty-first Century* (Reading, Mass, 1993) • D. W. DAYTON, ed., HCL (50 reprints of Holiness and early Pentecostal publications) • P. FLEISCH, *Die moderne Gemeinschaftsbewegung in Deutschland,* vol. 2, pt. 2, *Die Pfingstbewegung in Deutschland* (Hannover, 1957) = HCL 18 • W. J. HOLLENWEGER, *Handbuch der Pfingstbewegung* (10 vols.; Geneva, 1965-67); idem, *Pentecostalism: Origins and Developments Worldwide* (Peabody, Mass., 1997); idem, *The Pentecostals* (3d ed.; Peabody, Mass., 1988) • D. MARTIN, *Pentecostalism: The World Their Parish* (Oxford, 1988) • S. PARSONS, *Ungodly Fear: Fundamentalist Christianity and the Abuse of Power* (Oxford, 1999) • K. POEWE, ed., *Charismatic Christianity as a Global Culture* (Columbia, S.C., 1994) • R. SHAULL and W. CESAR, *Pentecostalism and the Future of the Christian Churches: Promises, Limitations, Challenges* (Grand Rapids, 2000) • R. SPITTLER, "Are Pentecostals and Charismatics Fundamentalists? A Review of American Uses of These Categories," *Charismatic Christianity,* ed. Poewe, 103-16 • L. W. WOOD, *The Meaning of Pentecost in Early Methodism: Rediscovering John Fletcher as Wesley's Vindicator and Designated Successor* (Metuchen, N.J., 2002).

Mission: M. A. DEMPSTER, B. D. KLAUS, and D. PETERSEN, eds., *Called and Empowered: Global Mission in Pentecostal Perspective* (Peabody, Mass., 1981) • R. GERLOFF, ed., *Mission Is Crossing Frontiers: Essays in Honour of Bongani A. Mazibuko* (Pietermaritzburg, 2003) new look at black theologies • M. HODGES, *The Indigenous Church* (Springfield, Mo., 1953) • J. A. B. JONGENEEL, ed., *Pentecost, Mission, and Ecumenism: Essays on Intercultural Theology in Honor of Prof. Walter J. Hollenweger* (Frankfurt, 1992) • C. WÄHRER-OBLAU, "From Reverse Mission to Common Mission," *IRM* 89 (2000) 467-83.

Pentecostals regionally: A. ANDERSON, *African Reformation: African Initiated Christianity in the Twentieth Century* (Asmara, Eritrea, 2001); idem, *Zion and Pentecost: The Spirituality and Experience of Pentecostal and Zionist/Apostolic Churches in South Africa* (Pretoria, 2000) • A. ANDERSON and E. TANG, eds., *Asian and Pentecostal: The Charismatic Face of Christianity in Asia* (Oxford, 2004) • F. CHIKANE, *No Life of My Own: An Autobiography* (Maryknoll, N.Y., 1989); idem, *A Relevant Pentecostal Witness* (Chatsglan, S.Af., n.d.) • D. CHIQUETTE, "Latin American Pentecostalism and Western Postmodernism: Reflections on a Complex Relationship," *IRM* 92 (2003) 29-39 • A. CORTEN and R. MARSHALL-FRATANI, eds., *Between Babel and Pentecost: Transnational Pentecostalism in Africa and Latin America* (Bloomington, Ind., 2001) • R. GERLOFF, editorial, *IRM* 84 (2000) 276-77 (on Pentecostal immigrant churches in Europe); idem, *A Plea for British Black Theologies: The Black Church Movement in Britain and Its Transatlantic Cultural and Theological Interaction* (2 vols.; Frankfurt, 1992) • W. J. HOLLENWEGER, "Pentecostal Research in Europe: Problems, Promises, People," *EPTA Bulletin* 4/4 (1985) 124-53 • J. A. B. JONGENEEL, ed., *Experiences of the Spirit: Conference on Pentecostal and Charismatic Research in Europe* (Frankfurt, 1991) • E. K. LARBI, *Pentecostalism: The Eddies of Ghanaian Christianity* (Accra, 2001) • C. N. OMENYO, *Pentecost outside Pentecostalism: A Study of the Development of Charismatic Renewal in the Mainline Churches in Ghana* (Zoetermeer, 2002) • R. PFISTER, "Pentecostalism and Ecumenism in France: A Critical Examination of Seeming Antipodes," *Pfingstkirchen und Ökumene in Bewegung* (ed. C. Dahling-Sander et al.; Frankfurt, 2001) • I. PLUIM and E. KUYK, *Relations with Migrant Churches: Experiences and Perspectives* (Utrecht, 2002) • E. VILLAFAÑE, *The Liberating Spirit: Toward an Hispanic American Pentecostal Social Ethic* (Grand Rapids, 1993) • P. WATT and W. SAAYMAN, "South African Pentecostalism in Context: Symptoms of a Crisis," *Missionalia* 31/2 (2003) 318-33 • B.-W. YOO, *Korean Pentecostalism: Its History and Theology* (Frankfurt, 1988).

Reference works and bibliographies: D. B. BARRETT and T. M. JOHNSON, "Annual Statistical Table on Global Mission: 2004," *IBMR* 28 (2004) 24-25 • D. B. BARRETT, G. T. KURIAN, and T. M. JOHNSON, *WCE* (2d ed.) • S. M. BURGESS, G. B. MCGEE, and P. H. ALEXANDER, eds., *Dictionary of Pentecostal and Charismatic Movements* (Grand Rapids, 1988; rev. ed., 2002) • W. J. HOLLENWEGER, "Ein Forschungsbericht," *Die Pfingstkirchen. Selbstdarstellungen, Dokumente, Kommentare* (ed. W. J. Hollenweger; Stuttgart, 1971) 307-46 (the only polyglot and international bibliography) • C. E. JONES, *Black Holiness: A Guide to the Study of Black Participation in Wesleyan, Perfectionist, and Glossolalic Pentecostal Movements* (Metuchen, N.J., 1987); idem, *A Guide to the Study of the Holiness Movement* (2 vols.;

Metuchen, N.J., 1979); idem, *Perfectionist Persuasion: The Holiness Movement and American Methodism, 1867-1936* (Metuchen, N.J., 1974) • W. E. Mills, *Charismatic Religion in Modern Research: A Bibliography* (Macon, Ga., 1985); idem, *Glossolalia: A Bibliography* (New York, 1965).

Research centers: Centre for Pentecostal Studies (University of Birmingham, Eng.) contains the Harold W. Turner collection on nonwhite indigenous churches • Donald Gee Center (Mattersey, Eng.) contains much handwritten material • Flower Research Center (Springfield, Mo.) contains Assemblies of God archival records • Hollenweger Center for the Intercultural and Interdisciplinary Study of Pentecostal and Charismatic Movements (Free University of Amsterdam) contains Hollenweger's international library, correspondence, and archives.

Scholarly periodicals: Journal of Pentecostal Theology (London) • *Journal of the European Pentecostal Theological Association* (Nantwich, Eng., formerly *EPTA Bulletin*) • *Pneuma: The Journal of the Society for Pentecostal Studies* (Leiden).

Walter J. Hollenweger

People of God

1. The Bible
   1.1. OT
   1.2. NT
2. Church History
3. Systematic Theology

1. The Bible

1.1. *OT*

The OT uses several words for Israel as God's people:

> *gôy* (LXX *ethnos*), "people, foreigner";
> *ʿam* (LXX *laos*), "people, nation," also *ʿam YHWH*, "people of Yahweh";
> *mišpāḥâ* (LXX *dēmos*), "clan, family, people"; and
> *hāmôn* (LXX *ochlos*), "army, crowd, people."

Each one denotes a special relationship with God in human history.

From the time of → Abraham human actions have all been brought into relation with the divine will to save (→ Salvation 1). Abraham's obedience of faith had as its reward the → promise of extensive progeny, and this promise was the root of the idea of the people of God, who would bring salvation to all humanity (Gen. 12:1-3). The → covenant (§1.3.1) with Abraham established God's living relationship with his people. Their nomadic life made them a pilgrim people. God was the leader preceding them and their captain who overcame other peoples. → Yahweh ransomed his people in Egypt (Psalm 74) and also redeemed them (Exod. 15:13). At → Sinai the Lord called them "my treasured possession" (Exod. 19:5). He sanctified, elected, and protected them (Deut. 7:6).

The non-Israelite peoples became hostile Gentiles *(gôyîm, ethnē)*. With the conquest of the land and the building of cities, → Israel (§§1.2-3) finally became a people on their own account, with their own territory and government. By making the covenant (Deut. 26:16-19), God entered into an irrevocable and reciprocal relationship with Israel that is summed up by the prophetic saying "I will be your God, and you shall be my people" (Lev. 26:12; Jer. 7:23; also Jer. 30:22; Ezek. 36:28; → Prophet, Prophecy, 2). This declaration determined the history of Israel.

When the covenant was broken with the worship of Baal, Yahweh no longer recognized the people as his possession (Hos. 1:9, "you are not my people"). A remnant came back from the Babylonian captivity (→ Israel 1.7), and a new history with God began. God's faithfulness to his covenant led to the formation of a new people of God who would come to expression universally in the eschatological gathering of the nations (Isa. 2:2-4; 11:10; Zech. 2:11).

1.2. *NT*

The NT, following the LXX, adopted the OT usage. The peoples *(ethnē)* became the Gentiles. The word *ochlos* stresses the religious and social scorn to which the Jewish people of God was exposed by the elite. → Jesus shows that God is merciful to his people (Matt. 9:36; John 7:31). The poor with whom Jesus identifies himself are the people of God (Matt. 25:31-46; → Poverty 4). With their suffering, the poor are a visible sign of the saving presence of God.

The people of God now became the new community of believers in Christ (→ Congregation 1). These were a global people not tied genealogically to Israel (Rom. 4:16-17; Gal. 3:7, 29). They were "a people of his own" (Titus 2:14), "the Israel of God" (Gal. 6:16), "the circumcision" (Phil. 3:3), "God's temple" (1 Cor. 3:16), the church of Christ (Matt. 16:18), God's eschatological community (*qĕhal YHWH*, "assembly of Yahweh" / *ekklēsia tou theou*, "church of God"; → Church 2.1). In the power of the end-time gift of the Spirit, the people of God did miracles and proclaimed the → Easter message. Its members knew salvation. As the company of the elect and the body of Christ, it represented the totality of the church.

Israel, nevertheless, had not lost its promise as God's original people (Rom. 11:25-26). A remnant, chosen by → grace, belongs to the new people of God and dedicates itself to the work of salvation as God's covenant partner (2 Cor. 3:6; Heb. 9:15).

2. Church History

Delay of the → parousia changed the concept of the people of God. The people of God soon established themselves (→ Early Church 2) and spread out across the whole earth (→ Mission), including all classes and nationalities (→ Justin Martyr). They became a social entity like the barbarians, the Jews, and the Greeks (Aristides). Influenced by → Gnosticism, they were hypostatized as a supernatural, transcendent entity that began at → creation and that reflected cosmic reality (*1-2 Clement, Didache, Barnabas,* plus writings of Ignatius and Hermas). They showed loyalty to Rome so long as Rome did not demand emperor worship (→ Roman Empire 2).

Edicts by the emperors Constantine (313) and Theodosius (380) made Christianity a legal religion and gave its followers state support (→ Roman Empire 3). The people of God *(populus Dei)* became the Christian people *(populus Christianus).* They were identified geographically with the empire, and their civil rights were politically guaranteed. → Augustine's (354-430) *Civitas Dei* gave a theological basis to the fact that members of God's people were Roman citizens (→ Augustine's Theology 6).

The 11th-century Cluniac reforms (→ Cluny, Order of) brought a new distinction between the laity *(populus carnalis)* and the clergy *(populus spiritualis;* → Clergy and Laity). In contrast, the → lay movements of the 12th and 13th centuries (→ Middle Ages 1.3.4) stressed the fact that the congregation of the faithful is the people of God. This thought found expression in the movements of the poor *(pauperes Christi),* which were protests both inside and outside the church (e.g., by → Cathari, → Waldenses, Apostolici, Spirituals, and → Franciscans) and which sought renewal of the whole church.

The 16th-century → Reformers (esp. M. → Luther, U. → Zwingli, and J. → Calvin) gave concrete form to such protests and saw the → church (3.4 and 3.5), in its original form, as the people of God, which is the congregation of the faithful or communion of the saints.

On the Roman Catholic side → Vatican II (1962-65) identified the → church (§3.2) in the full sense as the people of God. Its dimension in → salvation history was developed, and confessional differences (→ Confession of Faith) were relativized ecumenically. Latin American → liberation theology and → Third World (§2) → contextual theology have made the concept of the people of God an ecclesiological model of historical responsibility (→ Base Community).

3. Systematic Theology

The people of God is the basis of the continuity of the chosen people of Israel, from whom salvation comes, with humanity and its history as a whole (→ Salvation History). Theologically, election shows that the people of God carry responsibility for salvation. It gives them the character of a sign in history (→ Church 5.5.3; Jewish-Christian Dialogue 6). It does not so much concern individual salvation or perdition of non-Christians (→ Theology of Religions). God's people are validated by → faith and → love. They achieve visibility sacramentally through → baptism and the → Eucharist. In this way individuals are incorporated into the body of Christ. The body of Christ and the people of God are one and the same thing.

The history of the people of God is that of the violence of the world power and the redeeming force of those who suffer (→ Power 3; Suffering 3). In them is displayed the impotence of humanity. They offer space to the saving grace of God. The story of the people of God concludes as humanity comes back to God in his → kingdom. Until then the → resurrection of Jesus Christ is humanity's radical → hope, against which we are to see both → life and → death, both joy and sorrow, both individual maturity and social order.

Bibliography: M. Barth, *The People of God* (Sheffield, 1983) • L. Boff, *Church, Charism, and Power* (New York, 1985); idem, *Ecclesiogenesis: The Base Communities Reinvent the Church* (Maryknoll, N.Y., 1986) • J. Comblin, *O Povo de Deus* (São Paulo, 2002) • H. F. Hamilton, *The People of God: An Inquiry into Christian Origins* (2 vols.; London, 1912) • F. Humphreys and T. A. Kinchen, *Laos: All the People of God* (New Orleans, 1984) • H. C. Kee, *Who Are the People of God? Early Christian Models of Community* (New Haven, 1995) • G. Lohfink and L. M. Maloney, *Does God Need the Church? Toward a Theology of the People of God* (Collegeville, Minn., 1999) • E. W. Nicholson, *God and His People: Covenant and Theology in the OT* (Oxford, 1986) • W. Pannenberg, *The Church* (Philadelphia, 1983) • G. von Rad, *OT Theology* (2 vols.; Louisville, Ky., 2001) • N. T. Wright, *The NT and the People of God* (Minneapolis, 1992).

Joachim G. Piepke

People's Church → Volkskirche

Perennial Philosophy → Philosophia perennis

Perfection

1. Term
2. Early Church
3. Middle Ages
4. Early Modern Church
5. Recent Expressions
   5.1. Nineteenth Century
   5.2. New Denominations
   5.3. Bonhoeffer

1. Term

The Christian notion of perfection has deep roots in the Hebrew Scriptures, where, as in Christian thought, it is closely linked to the holiness of → God. As used for God, "holiness" has reference to splendor or → glory, separation from the unholy or ritually defiled, and purity. In the classic texts from the → Torah, it describes both ritual purity (Leviticus) and ethical integrity. Unlike the current English definition, it does not mean "flawless." The actual Hebrew word for perfection *(tmm)* is generally defined as "complete, sound, sincere, perfect." It is not used for God but is employed to describe God's work, God's way, and God's → covenant (e.g., Deut. 32:4). In the Hebrew Scriptures *tmm* is often translated "blameless," and people are described as walking blamelessly or urged to do so (Gen. 6:9; 17:1; Deut. 18:13). A clear example of the perfectionist impulse in Judaism is the Rechabite tradition mentioned in Jeremiah 35.

In the NT Gk. *teleios,* commonly translated "perfection," implies completion, fulfillment, the attaining of a goal *(telos).* These words revolve around the concept of end or purpose. In the Gospel of Matthew the word commonly translated "perfect" implies "whole" or "undivided." By refusing to give up his possessions, the rich young ruler demonstrates that his loyalties to God remain divided, that he is not "perfect" (Matt. 19:21). In the → Sermon on the Mount (with *teleios* twice in Matt. 5:48), Jesus insists that undivided love of God means that we love even our enemies. In these two teachings of Jesus many advocates of Christian perfection in → monasticism and elsewhere have found justification for the devaluing of private → property and the rejection of → war.

2. Early Church

In the writings of the → apostolic fathers Ignatius (d. ca. 107), Polycarp (d. ca. 166), and Clement of Rome (d. 97), Christian perfection is understood as fulfilling the law of righteousness. One of the most important early Christian perfectionist impulses, → Montanism, emerged in rural Phrygia in Asia Minor in the late second century. Montanism was noted for ecstatic worship experiences (→ Ecstasy), a puritanical lifestyle (including the rejection of remarriage after the death of a spouse), women in leadership roles, and expectant → millenarianism. In fact, like many of the subsequent perfectionist movements that emerged among the underclasses, it combined millennialism, ecstatic worship, severe lifestyles, and a protofeminism. Its most important centers were on the fringes of the empire in Asia Minor and North Africa, where it attracted Tertullian (ca. 160-ca. 225), its most notable convert. He was drawn by its emphasis on continued revelation, millenarianism, and a strict lifestyle.

In cosmopolitan → Alexandria the impact of → Gnosticism and Hellenistic thought (→ Hellenism) led Clement of Alexandria (ca. 150-ca. 215) to see the Christian life as one of progressive growth from faith or simple trust in Christ to true knowledge as a higher Christian state. Unlike certain Gnostic groups, Clement strongly emphasized ethical behavior as a central feature of the Christian life. Drawing on Gnostic and → Stoic currents, and similar to a later mystical perfectionism, he did suggest that true knowledge led to complete disinterestedness and a passionless state in which the Christian contemplates God. Origen (ca. 185-ca. 254), Clement's successor, united the distinction between faith and knowledge and a passionless state of perfection with ascetic rigor (→ Asceticism). In Platonic fashion, perfection comes through victory over desire, especially sexual desire.

As Christianity moved toward cultural and social acceptability, the quest for perfection was reaffirmed, but now as a special calling for spiritual elites. In 270 Anthony (251?-356), in obedience to the words of Jesus to the rich young ruler, sold all his possessions and adopted a radically ascetic lifestyle. As time passed, Christian perfection became the near-exclusive property of monasticism, with its rejection of property, marriage, and war for those under monastic vows.

Among the most important representatives of monastic perfectionism are the → Cappadocian Fathers, especially Gregory of Nyssa (ca. 330-ca. 395), who drew deeply from the Alexandrian well. While perfection is freedom from bodily affections, it assumes, as Gregory affirmed, constant growth into the fullness of Christ. True perfection is in fact unlimited growth in → virtue. Especially significant in the history of perfectionism are the homilies traditionally attributed to Macarius of Egypt (fl. 4th cent.), commonly referred to as Pseudo-Macarius. Drawing on Alexandrian themes, Pseudo-Macarius defines perfectionism as a life of purity and virtue, including freedom from shameful passions, which is entered into through ecstatic experience.

In the thought of Augustine (354-430; → Augustine's Theology), the radical possibilities of perfection this side of death cease being a possibility. Perfection consists in the subjection of the passions to → reason. While the relative perfection of the monastic orders that rejected property, marriage, and warfare existed as a foretaste of the coming city of God, absolute perfection is not a possibility for ordinary Christians in a world where humanity remains enslaved to the passions, especially sexual passion. In his disputes with the ascetic radicalism of → Donatism, which argued for a pure clergy and a pure church, and Pelagius (ca. 354-after 418), who believed that faith without obedience is a fundamental betrayal of the gospel, Augustine posited a Christianity that affirmed the divine mission of the → Roman Empire and the necessity of warfare to defend that empire.

3. Middle Ages

While in the West the limited perfection of Augustine remained dominant, in the East the Alexandrian tradition continued to shape perfectionist impulses. At Constantinople Simeon the New Theologian (949-1022) continued to integrate Platonic and Christian thought in the manner of Origen and Gregory of Nyssa. Simeon united a deep commitment to the ascetic lifestyle and an emphasis on ecstatic experience. He insisted that there is a further significant experience following → conversion, the baptism of the Holy Spirit, with accompanying tears, in which a person becomes the special dwelling place of God.

Francis of Assisi (1181/82-1226) rediscovered the third-century message of Anthony that → poverty is the root of perfection. In a time of increased prosperity and Christian complacency, Francis inspired renewed dedication to apostolic poverty. After his death his disciples eventually divided with the majority, modifying the absolute poverty and simplicity of the primitive movement.

A small group known as the Spirituals fought all modifications of the absolute poverty prescribed by Francis in 1223. These → Franciscan Spirituals united the ascetic vision of Francis with the millennialism of Joachim of Fiore (d. 1202), who had predicted that history was on the cusp of a third dispensation, the age of the Spirit. In this age the spiritually sensitive would receive all spiritual gifts necessary for a life of perfection. While the Joachimite-inspired Spirituals were eventually declared heretical, the ideas of Joachim himself remained an unsettling force long after the waning of the Middle Ages.

Quite different were the perfectionist ideas of the → Cathari and one of their branches, the Albigenses, who united Gnostic ideas concerning the evil of matter with ascetic radicalism. Emerging in the south of France in the mid-12th century, Albigenses were divided between ethical elites, who rejected marriage and practiced extreme asceticism, and lay members, who were accused of rejecting all moral restraint while teaching that a final sacrament would free one's nonmaterial soul from enslavement to the material. The movement was brutally suppressed by Innocent III (1198-1216).

4. Early Modern Church

The → Reformers rejected monastic perfectionism. Drawing on Augustinian thought, they saw the church as a mixed company that served to reinforce the social order. → Marriage was seen as a positive state, apostolic poverty was shunned, and warfare was seen as essential for the social order. As in the age of Augustine, the call to perfection was relegated to sectarians, the → Anabaptists. In many cases they called for the creation of unspoiled Donatist-type churches, which often rejected war (as in the case of Conrad Grebel, Michael Sattler, and Menno Simons) and in some cases also the ownership of private property (e.g., the → Hutterites).

Even among Lutherans, perfectionist calls were not uncommon. The Pietist Philipp Jacob Spener (1633-1705) taught that the orthodox Lutheran emphasis on the impossibility of perfection encouraged moral laxity. For his part, Spener taught that Christians could rise to a state in which they did not sin intentionally; believers could achieve perfection of intention but not of knowledge.

Concurrent with → Pietism, Roman → Catholicism experienced its own resurgence of perfectionism outside of monasticism. Francis de Sales (1567-1622) insisted that the devout or perfect life was intended for all Christians. Standing in the tradition of Alexandria, de Sales taught that the perfect life is a life of → contemplation and resignation, not intellectual engagement or social radicalism. As developed by Miguel de Molinos (1628-96), Madame Jean Marie Guyon (1648-1717), and Francis Fénelon (1651-1715), this teaching, known as → quietism, saw the goal of the Christian life as one of death to self and disinterested love of God.

Among the most distinctive perfectionist movements in Christian history is Quakerism (→ Friends, Society of). While far less preoccupied with sin than contemporary or later Christians, George Fox (1624-91) preached emancipation from → sin in the here and now. As early as 1650 Fox dismissed the clergy of his day for excusing sin and imperfection. For Quakers the "inner light" was the living Christ of the Sermon on Mount, whose rejection of violence and social concern quickly evolved into subsequent calls for social and economic justice.

Impulses from Continental Pietism and quietism lay behind the great surge of perfectionism in 18th-century Britain. Particularly influential were the writings of Jeremy Taylor (1613-67) and William Law (1686-1761). For Taylor, the perfect (or, as he preferred, "devoted") life was one of undivided love or pure intention. Law saw the end of religion as union with God. Drawing on quietist currents, he saw self-denial as absolutely essential. In Jesus' parable of the pearl of great price, he found the key to unlock the door to perfection. It is a gift that requires that the recipient metaphorically pay the price. Like virtually all teachers of perfection since Anthony, Law laid great emphasis upon one's treatment of wealth as a crucial Christian test.

John Wesley (1703-91) united Taylor's emphasis on pure intention with Law's emphasis on → discipleship. Wesley drew on virtually every teacher of perfection, with words of praise even for Pelagius as he sought to locate the quest for holy life at the center of the Evangelical revival. Following Law, Wesley made the use of wealth a central emphasis. As did the apostle Paul, so Wesley saw marriage as a distraction that he urged his key preachers, male and female, to avoid. In the movement he led, Wesley's strong emphasis on the ethics of the Sermon of the Mount was supplemented by an experiential emphasis on a Pentecost-like experience as the normal gateway to the life of perfect love, or Christian perfection. This "Pentecostal" emphasis was especially true of his associates John Fletcher (1729-85), Mary Bosanquet Fletcher (1739-1815), William Carvosso (1750-1834), and Hester Ann Rogers (1756-94). In → Methodism debates concerning Christian perfection increasingly focused more on actually receiving full salvation than on the meaning of the experience.

5. Recent Expressions

5.1. *Nineteenth Century*

The teachings of John Fletcher and John Wesley found fertile soil in the optimistic climate of 19th-century North America. By the 1830s three distinct forms of Christian perfectionist teaching were vying for acceptance. On the Right, Methodist teachers of Christian perfection led by New York lay evangelist Phoebe Palmer (1807-74), drawing on Hester Ann Rogers, emphasized the experience of entire → consecration, laying one's all on the metaphorical altar.

This spiritual nonliteral perfectionism was challenged by the socially radical teachings emanating from western New York. Commonly known as Oberlin perfectionism and associated with the teachings of Oberlin College president Asa Mahan (1799-1889) and Oberlin faculty member and later president Charles G. Finney (1792-1875), Oberlin teachers taught that one could completely obey God. Deeply concerned with ethical implications of full salvation, Oberlin taught that → slavery was sin and became a pioneer in admitting female students.

More radical perfectionists questioned such social institutions as the church and the → family. Most notable (or notorious!) was the perfectionism of John Humphrey Noyes (1811-86), founder of the → Oneida Community, whose teachings on what he called complex marriage were misinterpreted to mean free love. Known as antinomian perfectionism, this teaching found variant expressions well into the 20th century.

Far to the right of Oneida are the so-called Keswick proponents of the higher life. Named for an English resort community where conventions for the higher Christian life have been held since 1875, Keswick emphasizes drawing on elements of quietism, practicing death to self, and suppressing the sinful nature. Its basic teaching is found in most standard evangelical → devotional literature.

In the years before the American Civil War, elements of Palmer-style Methodist perfectionism and Oberlin perfection found expression among Wesleyan Methodists, who in 1843 organized a denomination of antislavery Methodists known as the Wesleyan Methodist Connection. In 1860 B. T. Roberts (1823-93), a New York Methodist influenced by Palmer, organized the Free Methodist Church. An abolitionist and social reformer who strongly affirmed women in ministerial roles, Roberts was committed to an ascetic lifestyle that drew fire even from the socially conservative Phoebe Palmer. On the fringe of Free Methodism were advocates of marital purity or sexual abstinence within marriage. As with perfectionists of all ages, sexual purity was not infrequently linked with → pacifism, as in the teachings of E. E. Shelhamer (1869-1947), and at times even with the rejection of private property, as in the case of the Wisconsin-based Metropolitan Church Association.

5.2. *New Denominations*

By the 1880s new perfectionist churches were breaking away from traditional → denominations. The Church of God (Anderson, Ind.), organized in 1881 by D. S. Warner (1842-1925), and the → Salvation Army, organized in 1878 by William (1829-1912) and Catherine (1829-90) Booth, were two of the most significant new Holiness churches. While all Holiness bodies were deeply involved in missions and ministries among the poor, the Salvation Army made it a special emphasis of its mission (→ Holiness Movement).

As with Christian perfectionists in the early church, so in the 1890s a special millennial emphasis emerged. Its earliest advocates were David Updegraff (1830-94) and Seth C. Rees (1854-1933), Quaker champions of the experience of full salvation. Spreading among even Methodist advocates of perfection in the wake of the economic depression of the 1890s, it became the dominant emphasis of the movement by 1901. As with many of its precursors, including Montanism, early 20th-century perfectionists were frequently located among the socially and economically marginal and included a high percentage of women.

In spite of the loss of many Pentecostals in the wake of the Azusa Street Revival of 1906 (→ Pentecostalism), the movement continued to grow throughout the 20th century. New denominations continued to emerge, including the → Church of the Nazarene (1895), Korea Evangelical Holiness Church (1907), and Pilgrim Holiness Church (1922). Missionary-statesman E. Stanley Jones (1884-1973) was perhaps the greatest spokesperson for Christian perfection in the 20th century. Continuing the tradition of Anthony and the early church, he united pacifism with a skeptical attitude toward → capitalism. In the 1950s defections from the Church of the Nazarene, Wesleyan Methodists, and others resulted in the creation of a new family of denominations known as the Inter-Church Holiness Movement. Led by H. E. Schmul (1921-98), this group emphasized the rejection of popular entertainment and the adoption of a very strict lifestyle.

By the early 21st century, memberships of Holiness denominations worldwide stood at over 12 million. This figure does not include Pentecostals, many of whom understand themselves as being part of the Holiness tradition.

5.3. *Bonhoeffer*

In many ways the most significant perfectionist text of the 20th century was, ironically, by a German Lutheran — *The Cost of Discipleship* (1937), by Dietrich Bonhoeffer (1906-45), which contained many of the classic themes of perfectionist literature. As a study on the Sermon on the Mount, with support for pacifism, it emphasized the radical call to forsake all for the way of Jesus. In a time when perfection was frequently assumed to be the property of groups on the fringes, it emphasized its catholic dimension.

Bibliography: P. M. Bassett and W. M. Greathouse, *Exploring Christian Holiness,* vol. 2, *The Historical Development* (Kansas City, Mo., 1985) • S. M. Burgess, ed., *Reaching Beyond: Chapters in the History of Perfectionism* (Peabody, Mass., 1986) • M. E. Dieter, *The Holiness Revival of the Nineteenth Century* (Lanham, Md., 1996) • R. N. Flew, *The Idea of Perfection in Christian Theology: An Historical Study of the Christian Ideal for the Present Life* (London, 1934; repr., Oxford, 1968) • C. E. Jones, *Perfectionist Persuasion: The Holiness Movement in American Methodism* (Metuchen, N.J., 1974) • W. C. Kostlevy, with G.-A. Patzwald, *Historical Dictionary of the Holiness Movement* (Lanham, Md., 2001) • W. B. Pope, *A Compendium of Christian Theology* (3 vols.; New York, 1881) • W. Thornton Jr., *Radical Righteousness: Personal Ethics and the Development of the Holiness Movement* (Salem, Ohio, 1998).

William Kostlevy

Persecution of Christians

1. Term
   1.1. Significance
   1.2. Martyrdom and Mission
   1.3. Christians as Persecutors
2. Roman Empire
   2.1. Early Animus against Christians
   2.2. Roman Law
   2.3. Empirewide Persecution
   2.4. Figures
3. Middle Ages and Modern Times
   3.1. Disappearing Churches
   3.2. Persecution of Heretics
   3.3. French Revolution
4. Twentieth and Twenty-first Centuries
   4.1. The USSR and Eastern Europe
   4.2. Latin America
   4.3. The New Century

1. Term

The word "persecution" evokes a number of ideas, including opposition to the Christian shaping of society, hindrances to the exercise of the Christian religion, and the suppression and extirpation of people of Christian conviction. Similarly, there have been many events in Christian history in which Christians have suffered pressure of differing intensity and for different purposes. We cannot give a single definition of what may be recalled and recounted as persecution for the faith, for it covers the whole period from the → primitive Christian community right on to the present day. We must remember that what sounds like a very early phrase — "persecuted *for the faith*" — does not occur in the NT and that, on closer examination, it proves to be too limited. Matt. 5:10 has "persecuted for righteousness' sake," 5:11 "persecute you . . . on my account," and John 15:21 speaks of persecution "on account of my name."

1.1. *Significance*

Theologically, we must realize that persecutions in the strict sense are violent measures designed to overthrow the Christian religion, whether in institutional form or in the form of personal convictions. With their universal scope such measures take the form of laws, though popular movements have the same effect for those concerned. Experiences of the early Christians under the Roman Empire serve as both an example and a standard. Similar situations throughout history have kept those early experiences alive. In times of peace they provide examples of constancy for → preaching and → devotional literature. On occasion, Christian groups have even drawn persecution upon themselves in order to prove that they are the true church (e.g., → Donatists, → Anabaptists, and the → Confessing Church).

Martyrdom (→ Martyrs) could become an inalienable or at least an unforgettable component of the Christian self-understanding because it represented → discipleship of the Jesus of the passion — that is, taking up one's cross as he did. In → confession of the Christian faith in persecution, more was needed than simply the sincere courage to give one's life for one's own convictions (as those outside saw it, noting the Christian contempt for one's own life and failing to distinguish it from misguided fanaticism). What really had to be shown in confessing Christ over against all other claims to lordship was faith in the one Lord of death and life, to whom Christians were totally committed and to whom they surrendered themselves in martyrdom as in no other act. By persecuting believers on account of their being Christians, earthly powers showed themselves to be ungodly, for they wanted to triumph over human conviction by physical force and, in so doing, acted as though they were absolute. In their readiness for martyrdom Christians refrained from trying to refashion the world as the → kingdom of God, leaving the coming of his kingdom to God.

1.2. *Martyrdom and Mission*

There were many reasons and occasions for persecution. The material cause is that society demands a loyalty that Christians cannot give because of their faith. They reject its totality by direct or indirect resistance. They are thus regarded as revolutionaries, or in revolutionary societies as reactionaries, with antisocial leanings.

→ Mission and martyrdom are inseparable. Theologically, this connection is true not merely in terms of → Tertullian's famous statement that the blood of the martyrs is the seed of the church. This statement involves psychological and political calculation regarding the alleged, but by no means certain, power of martyrs to achieve → conversions.

The true point is that missionaries are witnesses to the lordship of Christ. This stance involves a crisis of truth for all the other powers on which people set their hearts. Missionaries, then, expose their convicting power, and themselves with it, to the dethroned powers. To proclaim witness to Christ in a world that is ruled by false gods is always to take into account the possibility that constancy to the faith will have to show itself in an act of confession and be sealed finally by death. In this way the missionary situation is comparable with that of persecution.

1.3. *Christians as Persecutors*

One should not overlook the fact that the Christian church itself has been responsible for persecution. It has brought persecution upon dissidents whom it has condemned as heretics (→ Heresies and Schisms; see 3.3), upon Jews, and upon → atheists. Persecution by Christians can occur only when the church thinks it should give political shape to the world and when it so identifies itself with the social or political order as to question the latter's autonomy (i.e., when the church regards itself and its form of faith as absolute).

2. Roman Empire

2.1. *Early Animus against Christians*

From the outset, Christianity involved persecution. Believers realized that they might suffer the same fate as their Lord and God — Jesus Christ, the Son of God. Their → faith had to be witness to Christ, and it was inspired by the hope that the proclamation of the risen Lord would spread among the nations until "every tongue should confess that Jesus Christ is Lord" (Phil. 2:11).

After the Christianizing of the empire by Constantine (306-37), the progress of Christianity came to be seen as a victory march with some obstacles that earlier, heroic warriors had overcome. In reality, however, it was an experience of the powerlessness of the human will against demonic powers that sought the destruction of Christianity. Confession of Christ claimed exclusiveness for the God of the Christian religion.

The Jews found in this new religious fellowship a blasphemous corruption of their own religious tradition, Jesus being set above and against → Moses and all the → prophets. The Romans judged that Christians had fallen victim to an obstinate superstition (Pliny the Younger). Christians rejected the ancestral gods, the polytheistic basis of the empire (→ Roman Religion), and, with their cult that had neither images nor sacrifices, the social structure intertwined with religion. They were filled with "hatred of the human race" (*odium humani generis,* Tacitus). The first generation of Christians suffered persecution at the hands of the Jewish religious leaders, with Stephen (d. A.D. 33 or 36) and James (d. 44) the earliest martyrs. These leaders were the ones who had brought Jesus to his death. In the empire Christians were at the mercy of mob feelings, since they enjoyed no protection from the authorities. They wrongly thought that they were universally persecuted, which was not really true until 249/50.

2.2. *Roman Law*

The legal reasons for bringing Christians to trial before the edict (250) of Decius (249-51), which required everyone to sacrifice, have been the subject of intense investigation. The few sources available (records and martyrology) provide no evidence against the assertion formulated by Tertullian (d. ca. 225) that simply being a Christian was an offense. Contrary to normal judicial practice, there was no need to prove a criminal act, and denial was enough to secure release.

Confirmation may be found in the description that the Roman legate Pliny gives of the proceedings in Bithynia (autumn 112) and in the rescript that the emperor Trajan (98-117) sent in reply to Pliny's question whether the latter had been taking the right course. The main points are that (1) there must be a complaint with the names of both accused and accusers; (2) there must be a trial, with execution as the penalty for confession of Christ; and (3) those who deny the charge must be released, but only after undergoing the test of making an offering to the Roman gods, swearing by the genius of the emperor, and cursing Christ. Repudiation of the emperor cult, lèse-majesté, contempt for law, and sacrilege were not relevant legal grounds according to the sources. These grounds are modern explanations that have been invented to vindicate Roman law in view of there being no analogies to the trials of Christians.

What about the attitude that seemed to show Christianity to be worthy of the death sentence? It was called a fanatical superstition that shook the foundations of society and the empire because it poured contempt on the ancestral gods (note the idea of *mos maiorum,* "ways of the ancestors," or "culture") as wicked → demons. Scholarly opposition (e.g., from Celsus [fl. late 2d cent.] and Porphyry [ca. 232-ca. 303]) also raised the thesis of revolutionary innovation, which would provide intellectual justification for the later imperial edicts of persecution issued by Valerian and the tetrarchy. On the whole, up to the middle of the third century the persecutions were only local outbreaks of mob violence against the strangeness of those who did not participate in the public life on which the state rested. Emperor Nero (54-68) exploited such feelings when he was accused of starting the great fire of Rome (64) and had to find a scapegoat.

2.3. *Empirewide Persecution*

To strengthen loyalty to the state, Decius in 250 passed an edict that demanded sacrifice from everybody. This ruling affected Christians in particular, and after years of peaceful growth it surprised them and led to devastating → apostasy. Valerian (253-60) then issued two edicts (257/58) that both profited the imperial treasury and damaged the church, involving enforced sacrifice for clergy on pain of death, prohibition of assembly, and confiscation of the property of churches and of Christians who belonged to the imperial aristocracy. These measures recognized that Christianity had taken institutional form and that persecution must extend to the institution if Christians were to be reintegrated into Roman society. The political and psychological strategy failed, not because Christianity could live without an institutional form, but because the bishops proved so steadfast. In 260 Gallienus (253-68) withdrew his father's edicts and restored the older legal position of no action against the churches, but also no recognition of the Christian religion.

The restorationism of the tetrarchy brought back the edicts of Valerian (leading to the so-called great persecution of 303-5 in the West, and of 303-11 in the East). Galerius finally recognized the futility of the enterprise, issuing the Edict of Toleration in 311. Since the measures had neither led Christians back to the Roman gods nor allowed them to worship their own God, he would no longer leave them bereft of religion but would grant them freedom to practice their religion. The Edict of Milan (313) under Constantine then marked the beginning of a comprehensive Christianizing of the Roman Empire.

2.4. *Figures*
The sources do not enable us to give any estimates of figures. It is certainly an exaggeration to say that in 300 there were 7 million Christians, one-tenth of the total population. But to lower the figure to one-twentieth is probably to put it too low, though it may be realistic for the city of → Rome in the middle of the third century.

Were there more than 1,000 martyrs? A Roman calendar of 354 lists 50 days commemorating martyrs, more than half of them from the first century. We must take into account the general legal uncertainty, the few that were publicly executed, especially in dramatic fashion in the arena, and, in contrast, the desire for identification with the persecuted. In the fourth century, and even before, this desire took the form of nostalgic edification, but it also served to keep alive the sense that discipleship of Christ means taking up the cross. The act of confession — "I am a Christian" — remained paradigmatic, faced as it was with the offer of pardon for denial.

3. Middle Ages and Modern Times
Listing persecution through the centuries serves as a reminder that Christian life is always lived on the frontier. Only the church can record the persecution as its own history, not as a history of either heroism or terror, but in humble commitment.

3.1. *Disappearing Churches*
It must be admitted as part of Christian history that outward circumstances such as political or religious pressure can cause churches to disappear (e.g., the destruction of church buildings or their conversion into → mosques). This pressure might take the form of direct persecution, but it was not decisive merely in the sense of physically exterminating Christians. The missionary churches of the East Syrian → Nestorians are an example, stretching as they did from Baghdad to the heart of Asia but fading out in the 14th century. So too were the churches of North Africa, all traces of which were lost in the Middle Ages.

In general, one cannot accuse → Islam of persecuting Christians, for by its religious law it tolerated Christians, though restricting their political freedom and lifestyle and forbidding missionary work. Yet when Islam became nationalistic, it led to the persecution of Christians, such as of the Armenian Christians in Turkey (an estimated 750,000 to 1.2 million dead between 1894 and 1916; → Armenian Apostolic Church) and the Nestorians, who still exist today but only as a tiny minority.

3.2. *Persecution of Heretics*
It must also be admitted that churches themselves have been agents of persecution. The → Inquisition and the → death penalty for heretics (legally established at the beginning of the 13th cent.) were medieval measures presupposing general belief in the supremacy of the spiritual arm, on which temporal well-being depended. Heresy rated as blasphemy and was punished as lèse-majesté (→ Beguines; Cathari; Hussites; Waldenses).

The age of the → Reformation adopted the same view and the same legal norm, first against the Lutheran heresy, then against the → Anabaptists in mainland Europe, then against the → Dissenters in England. The Protestant → Reformers found in blasphemy an act of revolt against authority, which is a divine order according to Romans 13. Doubts as to the validity of the death penalty when society suffers no material harm did not prevail. Persecution of heretics at this period did immeasurable damage to the relationship between the new denominations. The executions under Mary Tudor (1553-58), the St. Bartholomew's Eve massacre (1572; → Huguenots), the violence in the Netherlands — all these were events with long-range consequences (→ Catholic Reform and Counterreformation).

3.3. *French Revolution*
The French Revolution brought religious persecution to the church once again. When we study Voltaire (1694-1778) and J.-J. Rousseau (1712-78), it is not surprising that the Terror (1792-93) engulfed the clergy, both monks and priests (some 5,000 deportations and executions). Yet at the beginning many of the clergy joined the Third Estate and helped to prepare the way for revolutionary changes. The removal of privileges up to the Civil Constitution of the Clergy (1789 and 1790) might be regarded as a result of → Gallicanism to the degree that the church adjusted to the new order and placed the clergy, as public officials, under the supervision of the National Assembly.

This decision, however, meant a separation of the church from the papacy, and Pius VI (1775-99) responded with an unambiguous condemnation both of the Civil Constitution of the Clergy and of human and civil → rights. When the National Assembly decreed the Civil Constitution (1790), resistance developed that deportation for those who refused the oath could not overcome. Priests who would not take the oath came under not wholly unjustified suspicion of collaboration with foreign enemies of the revolution. Persecution increased and led to a wave of dechristianizing. The revolutionary charge that as enemies of the nation the clergy were enemies of humanity did not go away, even when the constitution granted liberty for the private exercise of religion. The revolution showed its own hostility to the church by persecuting it.

Bibliography: On 2: T. D. Barnes, "Legislation against the Christians," *JRS* 58 (1968) 32-50 • N. H. Baynes, "The Great Persecution," *CAH* 12.646-77 • H. von Campenhausen, *Die Idee des Martyriums in der alten Kirche* (2d ed.; Göttingen, 1964) • W. H. C. Frend, *Martyrdom and Persecution in the Early Church: A Study of a Conflict from the Maccabees to Donatus* (Oxford, 1965) • R. Freudenberger, *Das Verhalten der römischen Behörden gegen die Christen im 2. Jahrhundert* (2d ed.; Munich, 1969) • D. G. Kyle, *Spectacles of Death in Early Rome* (London, 1998) • I. Lesbaupin, *Blessed Are the Persecuted: Christian Life in the Roman Empire, A.D. 64-313* (Maryknoll, N.Y., 1987) • P. McKechnie, *The First Christian Centuries: Perspectives on the Early Church* (Downers Grove, Ill., 2001) chaps. 3, 6, 10 • G. de Sainte Croix, "Why Were the Early Christians Persecuted?" *PaP* 26 (1963) 6-38 • R. Selinger, *The Mid-Third-Century Persecutions of Decius and Valerian* (Frankfurt, 2002).

On 3: N. Aston, *Religion and Revolution in France, 1780-1804* (Washington, D.C., 2000) • G. Hamburger, *Verfolgte Christen. Berichte aus unserer Zeit* (3d ed.; Graz, 1979) • J. Lepsius, *Der Todesgang des armenischen Volkes* (Potsdam, 1919) • R. Reuss, *La constitution civile du clergé et la crise religieuse en Alsace* (2 vols.; Strasbourg, 1922).

Friedrich Wilhelm Kantzenbach

4. Twentieth and Twenty-first Centuries

Before considering the matter of the persecution of Christians in the 21st century, we review the experience of believers under Communism and in Latin America up through the 1980s.

4.1. ***The USSR and Eastern Europe***

4.1.1. On January 18, 1918, the Soviet government issued a decree separating the state from the church and the church from the schools. The church lost all its movable and immovable property, including all its hospitals and welfare institutions, and schools were nationalized. The Synod of the → Russian Orthodox Church (→ Orthodox Church) answered with an anathema. At once a spontaneous persecution began of the hierarchy and clergy, which was especially severe in villages on church land. Soviet historians stressed that it was a matter of overthrowing political opposition, but for Bolsheviks being a Christian was in fact the same as being a political opponent.

Actions against the church taken by the central government reached a climax in the period of widespread famine following the Civil War (1918-21). Patriarch Tikhon was imprisoned, then put under house arrest, under which he died in 1925. A new → patriarch could not be elected, and the → Synod could not meet. Most of the metropolitans or bishops were in prison or exile. The government attempted to subvert the church from within by means of a schismatic "living church" friendly to the regime, which failed because of the resistance of believers. Many open letters, the so-called testament of Patriarch Tikhon (which was put under Soviet censorship), and the declaration of solidarity with the Soviet regime of the acting patriarch Metropolitan Sergius (1927), which is still debated by believers, clarified the relation to the government along the lines of Romans 13. The state law of 1929, which brought together all previous laws concerning religion, allowed citizens to exercise a cult, forbade the church to engage in "religious propaganda" or religious instruction, and allowed "atheistic propaganda" (→ Atheism).

During the 1930s both clergy and laity were severely persecuted as a result of the collectivization of villages and the Stalinist "cleansing operations." During the 1920s "Western" Pietist congregations such as → Baptists, Pentecostals (→ Pentecostal Churches), and "Stundists" were still better off than the Russian Orthodox Church itself because their communal village organizations had gained them a measure of sympathy among the Soviets. During the 1930s, though, they too were severely persecuted.

The militant atheistic propaganda, however, was mitigated in 1941 at the beginning of the war, and the Russian Orthodox Church was again permitted to elect a patriarch. After a brief period of growth and development, a new round of oppression began in 1954 under Nikita Khrushchev (1953-64); lasting till about 1964, this persecution was especially inclined to use massive social and psychological pressure. Five of the eight seminaries that reopened after the war were closed again, and 7,000-8,000 churches were closed. The Russian Orthodox Church itself was forced to change its "statute" of 1945 such that priests were now employees instead of leaders of their own congregations.

A kind of modus vivendi settled in during the Leonid Brezhnev era (1964-82), granting a certain measure of freedom to the church. The Soviet government's Council for Religious Affairs controlled all its public utterances, as it also did those of the (rapidly increasing) Baptists. One group protesting against such governmental control split off from the latter and managed to escape the registration procedures required of all "cultic communities" by going underground. The state considered this group, as well as several other splinter groups that followed older rituals or simply split off from the Orthodox Church, as outlaw groups and thus as anti-Soviet.

4.1.2. Whereas churches in the Soviet Union lived completely from their own means, that is, from donations from believers themselves, this complete financial separation of → church and state was not fully carried out anywhere else in the socialist camp of Eastern Europe after World War II. In almost all these countries except the German Democratic Republic, the clergy received their basic salaries from the state (which could always be withheld). Otherwise the actual circumstances of the churches in these various countries differed considerably, depending on historic circumstances. Nowhere, however, were they able to develop unimpeded.

In Poland and the German Democratic Republic, the churches were able to maintain a relatively high level of activity throughout the various branches of church life. In Romania the churches received a measure of support from the various ethnic groups (the Romanians were typically Orthodox, the Hungarians Reformed, and Transylvania "Saxony" Lutheran), while in Hungary a certain balance obtained between state and church. In contrast, in Bulgaria and especially Czechoslovakia, every expression of church life and of the Christian faith was severely restricted.

Bibliography: T. Beeson, *Discretion and Valour: Religious Conditions in Russian and Eastern Europe* (London, 1982) • J. Chrysostomus, *Kirchengeschichte Rußlands der neuesten Zeit* (3 vols.; Munich, 1965-68) • W. C. Fletcher, *A Study in Survival: The Church in Russia, 1927-1943* (London, 1965) • R. Royal, *The Catholic Martyrs of the Twentieth Century: A Comprehensive World History* (New York, 2000).

Fairy von Lilienfeld

4.2. *Latin America*

Insofar as the Christian mission came to Latin America under the protection of Iberian weapons, there were never any persecutions in the strict sense. The first two martyrs — the → Dominicans Francisco de Córdoba and Juan Garcés — lost their lives in Pirítú, Venezuela, in 1515 during what was actually a peaceful mission attempt. They died not because the Indians rebelled against the proclamation but because after Gómez de Ribera landed there in violation of all previous agreements and forcefully enslaved the cacique and his wife and 17 other Indians, the Spanish government on Hispaniola did nothing to free them within the four-month deadline set by the Indians.

Peaceful missionaries also occasionally lost their lives when shamans incited rebellions against mission activities in still unconquered areas, as was the case, for example, with three Jesuit fathers in 1628 in the area of the Paraguay → reductions. At the same time, in Guayrá (Paraná), even though thousands of Guarani were organized into reductions, they were nonetheless forcefully enslaved by Paulista bandeirantes (slave traders from São Paulo). Significantly, Antonio de Montesinos, who as Dominican spokesman on Hispaniola took up the fight against Indian enslavement in 1511, was killed in Venezuela in 1540 by German Protestant lansquenets (i.e., mercenaries) under Nikolaus Federmann, for whom this Indian advocate — who was part of Charles V's Welsh expedition — had become a nuisance. Similarly, in 1550 Antonio de Valdivieso had been bishop of Nicaragua for only five years before being murdered by his own people because of his rigorous defense of Indians' human rights. It is striking that Rome has canonized none of these martyrs.

Christians fought against one another in many of the rebellions and revolutions in Latin America toward the end of the colonial period, particularly in the first quarter of the 19th century during the wars of independence. These affairs involved political rather than genuinely religious disputes, albeit political disputes sometimes masqueraded as religious ones (e.g., rule was defended as being "by God's grace"). The Christian social revolution in Mexico (1810-15), led by the pastors Miguel Hidalgo and José María Morelos, which ended with the execution of 125 priests, was the exception. Later 19th-century disputes between the anticlerical liberals and the Catholic Church, which resulted in the expulsion of bishops, the confiscation of church property, and the elimination of ecclesiastical privilege, ultimately represented sociopolitical power struggles. Only at the culmination of the Mexican revolution in the 1920s did anti-Catholic excesses result in murder, the destruction of churches, and the expulsion of priests and bishops in the spirit of what was in part a totalitarian doctrine of the state. The Marxist elements of this doctrine came to expression more in → atheism than in fundamental social and economic reforms on behalf of the impoverished masses.

The Catholic hierarchy entered into a test of wills with the Fidel Castro regime during the Cuban revolution (1950s) once its Marxist leanings became more apparent. The confrontation between church and state culminated with the U.S. bombardment of Havana on April 15, 1961, and two days thereafter in the Bay of Pigs invasion. In the aftermath 135 priests (largely from Franco Spain) were expelled, and church schools and the Catholic university were dispossessed. Even though there was no organized political fight against the church, the number of incidents increased as the crisis heightened. Christians were also occasionally subjected to legal discrimination. Ultimately, however, the state granted a measure of tolerance to the churches, even explicitly summoning nuns to remain in the country and to continue to provide their previous social services. Not even the papal nuncio, however, was able to stem their exodus.

With the increasing changes to socioeconomic and political consciousness, however, and prompted by positions taken by the church, by → liberation theology, and by → base communities since the 1960s, the following two decades witnessed military regimes engaging in the most widespread persecution of Christians in Latin American history. In the name of national security, the lives of some 1,500 victims were lost, from workers to bishops (most notably Bishop Enrique Angelleli in Argentina [1976] and Archbishop Oscar Romero in El Salvador [1980]), all of whom remained true to their faith despite threats of murder, prison, and → torture. They stayed true in their commitment to "integral liberation" by Jesus Christ, which includes liberation from → hunger and starvation, oppression, exploitation, and lack of legal recourse. By comparison, the expulsion of "undesirable" or "uncomfortable" priests by both right- and left-wing regimes is of less consequence.

Bibliography: M. Lange and R. Iblacker, eds., *Witnesses of Hope: The Persecution of Christians in Latin America* (Maryknoll, N.Y., 1981) • H.-J. Prien, *Die Geschichte des Christentums in Lateinamerika* (Göttingen, 1977; Span. ed., *La historia del cristianismo en América Latina* [Salamanca, 1985]).

Hans-Jürgen Prien

4.3. *The New Century*

At the beginning of the 21st century, most persecution of Christians is taking place in four settings: the remaining Communist countries; in South Asia, prompted by growing religious nationalism; the Islamic world; and Christian-on-Christian persecution.

4.3.1. The remaining Communist countries, or countries that still call themselves Communist, are China, Cuba, Laos, North Korea, and Vietnam (see 4.1; → Marxism and Christianity). To this list can be added post-Communist countries such as Turkmenistan and Uzbekistan, which are nominally post-Communist but in which the same regime has continued to hold power since the transition from the Soviet Union. In these countries, with the exception of North Korea, there may be relative freedom to worship in state-controlled religious bodies, but religious expression outside of these bodies is suppressed.

In China the → Roman Catholic Church includes both a body recognized by the government and one that maintains its allegiance with the → pope. The government regards the latter as illegal, since it recognizes an authority outside the country. Its → priests and → bishops have been imprisoned, while several hundred leaders of the Protestant underground church have also been jailed and sent to labor camps. In Vietnam the government has also violently repressed the rapidly growing churches among the tribal peoples; in Laos church leaders have been arrested. Turkmenistan and Uzbekistan also make it almost impossible for smaller Christian groups to register, which they then persecute as illegal. The situation in Cuba is similar, though the government often adjusts its policies when it can sense political gain by doing so. Reliable information on North Korea is hard to obtain, but it appears that almost every free Christian expression is forbidden and viciously repressed. Large numbers of Christians have been sent to labor camps.

4.3.2. South Asia has seen a resurgence of religious nationalism among Hindus and Buddhists in which country and state are identified with a religion (→ Hinduism; Buddhism). As a result, religious → minorities such as Christians have begun to be treated as second-class citizens and subjected to violent communal attack.

In India a growing number of states use anticonversion laws to target Christians, and the number of religiously motivated attacks, particularly on clergy and other religious workers, has risen to several hundred a year. In Nepal and Bhutan, Christians suffer discrimination and sometimes arrest. In Sri Lanka churches have suffered attacks, often led by more radical Buddhist monks. In Myanmar the military regime, lacking popular support and legitimacy, seeks to wrap itself in a cloak of Buddhism as part of its war against tribal minorities in the eastern part of the country, where Christians constitute a large proportion of the minorities. The regime's brutal attacks have destroyed whole villages, killed tens of thousands, and left hundreds of thousands of → refugees.

4.3.3. The greatest persecution takes place in the Muslim world at the hands of growing Islamic extremism. There are now intensifying attacks of three overlapping types on Christians from Morocco to the southern Philippines. The first is *direct → state persecution,* which is widespread in the Muslim world. Most starkly, in Saudi Arabia any non-

Islamic or dissident Islamic religious expression is forbidden. Christian meetings are outlawed, private worship services are raided by the *mutawa* (religious police), and their members are often imprisoned. The Saudis also enforce the Islamic legal provision requiring killing anyone who changes his or her religion from → Islam (→ Shari'a). In some other states of the Persian Gulf and in Mauritania, Sudan, Comoros, and Iran, this provision is part of the legal code. In many other places, such as Somalia, family members or vigilantes do the killing. In Sudan a major component of the civil war has been the effort by the Khartoum regime to impose its form of Islam on the largely Christian and → animist south. Two million people have died there of war-related causes. Christians in refugee camps have been denied food and water unless they convert, and there has widespread → slavery and forced → conversion.

In other countries, such as Iran and Pakistan, the threat also comes from *radical groups or mob violence,* with greater or lesser complicity by the government. Such violence, often prompted by radical Islamist leaders, occurs also in Egypt, where the → Coptic Church has been subject to church burnings and local massacres. It is widespread in northern and central Nigeria, where tens of thousands of people have died since 2000 in conflict over the introduction of Islamic law, and it is spreading in East Africa. In Pakistan in 1997 one Christian town, Shantinagar, was virtually razed to the ground by an attack of over 30,000 Muslims. In some cases, such as Indonesia, the government and major Muslim groups have opposed such attacks. In others, such as Egypt or Pakistan, local authorities have been complicit or quiescent.

There are also direct attacks by *radical Islamic terrorists* (→ Terrorism). In Algeria Islamist guerrillas opposed to the government have targeted, among others, Christians, especially priests, monks, and nuns. Similar situations exist also in the southern Philippines, Pakistan, Turkey, Egypt, Bangladesh, and Iraq. In Indonesia, long a place of relative toleration between Muslims, Christians, and other minorities, there has been an epidemic of bomb attacks on churches. In the eastern areas such as Maluku and Sulawesi, which have a majority of Christians, Islamist militias such as Laskar Jihad have massacred thousands of Christians and forcibly converted others.

4.3.4. Other instances do not fall into a clear pattern, but many are Christian-on-Christian persecution. In Eritrea all Protestants except the Evangelical Lutheran Church of Eritrea (→ Lutheran Churches) have been banned, and hundreds of independent Protestants have been arrested, many suffering → torture. In the Mexican state of Chiapas, local lay Catholic leaders, opposed by the church, have attacked Protestants. Other instances are of discrimination against minority Christian communities, especially in the Orthodox world, such as in Russia, Belarus, Greece, Armenia, and Ethiopia (→ Orthodox Church).

While it is impossible to total the individual Christians who suffer violent persecution, the Christian communities in the countries and areas where such persecution occurs number about 230 million. Several hundreds of millions more suffer from widespread discrimination. The persecution in the remaining Communist countries has remained relatively level over the last decade, although since the church is growing rapidly in many of these countries, the number of Christians affected has increased. Persecution in South Asia has been increasing, and with the continuing growth of extremist Islam, persecution in the Muslim world has been growing rapidly and, absent any major changes, is likely to keep on doing so.

→ Force, Violence, Nonviolence; Nation, Nationalism; Religious Liberty

Bibliography: D. B. Barrett, G. T. Kurian, and T. M. Johnson, *WCE* (2d ed.) • P. Jenkins, *The Next Christendom: The Rise of Global Christianity* (New York, 2002) • P. Marshall, *Their Blood Cries Out* (Nashville, 1997); idem, ed., *Religious Freedom in the World* (Nashville, 2000) • N. Shea, *In the Lion's Den* (Nashville, 1997). See also the U.S. State Department's annual *International Religious Freedom Report* and the U.N. annual *Report of the Special Rapporteur on Religious Intolerance.*

Paul Marshall

Person → Self

Persons with Disabilities

1. Terms and Statistics
2. Approaches to Caregiving
3. Opportunities for the Church

1. Terms and Statistics

Having a disability suggests being different or "standing out," being seen as not normal. One helpful step in defining "disability" is to distinguish it from "handicapped." According to the National Organization on Disability, "Disability is a permanent physical, sensory or intellectual impairment that substantially limits one or more of a person's major life activities, including reading, writing and other aspects of → education; holding a job; and managing various essential functions of life such as dressing, bathing and eating" (G. Thornburgh and A. R. Davie, 10). Disabilities may occur before birth, a few moments before death, or at any other time along the life continuum. Disabilities can result from disease, disorders, → war, accident, and other causes, such as defective genes.

A handicap is a barrier society places on the person with a disability. Architectural barriers can become a handicap to people with disabilities, denying accessibility to work, recreation, and needed services. Attitudes that are not welcoming and inclusive also become handicaps that deny participation to people with disabilities.

In 2005 nearly 60 million people living in the United States were classified as having disabilities. Considering the population as a whole, a 2003 study of demographics by the National Catholic Partnership on Disability indicated that 20 percent had one or more disabilities, and one-tenth of this group had severe disabilities. Of the total disability population, 58 percent had a physical disability, 9 percent had sensory disabilities, 4 percent were mentally retarded, 5 percent were classified as mentally ill, and the remaining 24 percent had assorted health problems that limited one or more of their daily living functions (p. 1).

According to U.N. figures, 10 percent of the world's population — that is, about 600 million people — are disabled. Of this number, 400 million live in developing countries, thus revealing a clear correlation between disabilities and → poverty.

2. Approaches to Caregiving

Historically, people with disabilities were "cared for" almost exclusively at home or in institutions. Frequently, this care and treatment was paternalistic, creating dependency on the part of people with disabilities. Hundreds of thousands of children and adults with developmental disabilities were institutionalized, many for their entire lives. The *medical model* that hospitals developed — typified by the question, What's wrong with the individual? — was applied to the treatment of people with disabilities in state-run institutions. → Churches and → religious orders also built institutions of → charity and provided much of the care. During the early years of the 20th century, these institutions grew in number and size. They were often seen by their critics as warehouses that brought abuse, neglect, and increased separation and isolation from society.

The late 1960s and the early 1970s saw a paradigm shift in the provision of services for people with disabilities. A social movement called *deinstitutionalization* began the effort of moving people with disabilities out of the institutions, back to their place and home of origin. The movement was led by care providers and parents of people with developmental disabilities and was based upon the principle of normalization.

The *normalization* theory, developed by Wolf Wolfensberger, a Canadian sociologist, proposed that people should live in the community's least restrictive and most "normal" setting possible if they were expected to behave "normally." The need is to change and "fix" society, not the people with disabilities. In a more person-centered approach, decisions must be made by the individual as often as possible, not by medical or rehabilitation professionals. As people with disabilities are integrated into community settings, they are invited and welcomed to participate in activities of the "normal" population.

The success of this movement is seen in the fact that of the 523,958 Medicaid developmental-disability recipients in the United States in 2002, about 80 percent received support through community residential facilities and other community-based services. Only 20 percent received support services institutionally, in nursing homes and various state and nonstate institutions (K. C. Lakin et al., 88-91).

A number of legislative acts aided the evolution of this independent living movement. Medicare and Medicaid were established through the passage of the Social Security amendments of 1965. These programs provide federally subsidized health care to people with disabilities and elderly Americans covered by the Social Security program. Passage of the Social Security amendments of 1972 created the Supplemental Security Income (SSI) program. The law relieves families of the financial responsibilities of caring for their adult children with disabilities. Passage of the Rehabilitation Act of 1973 marked the greatest achievement of the disability → rights movement. The act, particularly title 5, §504, confronted discrimination against people with disabilities and sparked the formation of "504 Workshops." The 1988 Fair Housing Amendments Act added people with disabilities to the groups protected by federal fair housing legislation.

The Americans with Disabilities Act of 1990 is the most sweeping disability rights legislation in history. It mandates that businesses with more than 15 employees make "reasonable accommodations" for people with disabilities and that public accommodations, such as restaurants and stores, make "reasonable modifications" to ensure access for people with disabilities and disabled workers. This act also mandates access in public transportation, communication, and other areas of public life.

3. Opportunities for the Church

The marginal person has not always prospered in society, historically experiencing deep-rooted → prejudice and discrimination. For example, Lev. 21:16-23 declares that people with certain disabilities were considered to be "blemished" and thus unqualified for priestly service. Early cultures, including ancient → Israel (§1), saw physical and mental defects as retribution for → sin or wrongdoing. Jesus rejected this theological perspective of retribution for sin as a cause for disability. When his disciples asked about a man born blind, wondering whose sin caused the condition, Jesus answered, "Neither this man nor his parents sinned; he was born blind so that God's works might be revealed in him" (John 9:3). The experience of what the apostle Paul calls bodily weakness helped him elaborate his profound "wisdom of the cross" (→ Theologia crucis). In 1 Corinthians 12 he speaks of the church as a body in which the members who "seem to be weaker are indispensable" (v. 22).

About half as many adults with disabilities as their neighbors without disabilities attend worship services in the United States (22 vs. 39 percent) on a given Sunday. A possible reason for their limited attendance is that one-third of those with significant disabilities report that their parish does little or nothing to facilitate their participation. Yet, eight in ten adults with disabilities say that their faith is very important to them.

→ Congregations that have been successful in being a welcoming fellowship to people with disabilities have long discovered that more is involved than having an architecturally accessible communion rail. An inclusive congregation requires an all-encompassing welcoming attitude; it recognizes, invites, and celebrates the many contributions people with disabilities make to the wholeness of the body of Christ. It is more than a condescending ministry *to* people with disabilities; it is an engaging ministry *with* them. It is practicing "people-first" language where people are treated first with dignity and respect, their disability coming second.

Institutionalization is sometimes justified (e.g., when persons who are mentally ill become prone to cause physical harm to themselves or others), but promoting independent living in community settings fosters self-worth, personal responsibility, and social integration. For the church it offers an evangelistic opportunity for wholeness. A church that is not inclusive of people with disabilities is incomplete and not yet the body of the crucified and risen Christ.

Bibliography: M. E. Bishop et al., *Religion and Disability* (Kansas City, Mo., 1995) • D. DeVries, "Creation, Handicappism, and the Community of Differing Abilities," *Reconstructing Christian Theology* (ed. R. S. Chopp and M. L. Taylor; Minneapolis, 1994) 124-40 • A. Fritzson and S. Kabue, *Interpreting Disability: A Church of All and for All* (Geneva, 2004) • G. A. Haugen, *Good News about Injustice* (Downers Grove, Ill., 1999) • K. C. Lakin et al., "Trends and Milestones," *MentRet* 42/1 (2004) 88-91 • National Catholic Partnership on Disability, *The Demographics of Disability* (Washington, D.C., 2003) • W. T. Reich, "Handicapped, Care of the," *WDCE* 258-60 • D. J. Simunson, *Where Is God in My Suffering?* (Minneapolis, 1983) • J. K. Struve, "The Church's Role in Health Care," *Lutheran Partners,* July/August 2003, 18-20 • G. Thornburgh and A. R. Davie, eds., *That All May Worship: An Interfaith Welcome to People with Disabilities* (Washington, D.C., 2000) • B. Webb-Mitchell, *Dancing with Disabilities: Opening the Church to All God's Children* (Cleveland, 1996) • W. Wolfensberger, *The Principle of Normalization in Human Services* (Toronto, 1972).

Ronald G. Beckman

Peru

	1960	*1980*	*2000*
Population (1,000s):	9,931	17,324	25,662
Annual growth rate (%):	2.88	2.36	1.60

Area: 1,285,216 sq. km. (496,225 sq. mi.)

A.D. 2000

Population density: 20/sq. km. (52/sq. mi.)
Births / deaths: 2.26 / 0.62 per 100 population
Fertility rate: 2.64 per woman
Infant mortality rate: 37 per 1,000 live births
Life expectancy: 69.8 years (m: 67.3, f: 72.4)
Religious affiliation (%): Christians 97.2 (Roman Catholics 92.0, Protestants 7.0, indigenous 1.8, marginal 1.8, other Christians 1.0), nonreligious 1.2, other 1.6.

1. Historical Conext

1.1. Peru is the heartland of one of the most important of the older American cultures, that of the Inca Empire, which stretched from modern Ecuador to Chile. The Inca language, Quechua, is still spoken by more than one-third of the people of Peru. The gruesome conquest, which began in 1532 under Francisco Pizarro (ca. 1475-1541), lasted until 1572, when the last Inca place of residence, Vilcambamba, was seized by the Spaniards and the Inca ruler, Tupac Amarú, was executed.

Isabel Flores de Oliva from Lima (1586-1617), who became known by her self-chosen nickname Rosa de Santa Maria, embodied the self-conscious identity of the Creoles that emerged in the 17th century to such a high degree that she was elevated to the status of the patroness of Lima and Peru long before she was canonized in 1671. Numerous churches and cities throughout the entire subcontinent are dedicated to Santa Rosa de Lima.

The name "Tupac Amarú" became a symbol of Indian resistance, which found its supreme expression in the revolt of 1780-81, the greatest of the colonial period, under the leadership of José Gabriel Condorcanqui (d. 1781), who styled himself Tupac Amarú II. In the days of the → revolutions for independence, Spanish troops made their last stand on the American mainland in Peru (1824). The constitution of 1856 finally ended all Indian tributes and Afro-American → slavery.

1.2. In recent decades the Peruvian government has featured a dreary record of autocratic rule by military and by dictator, all in the context of bloody guerrilla warfare and extreme → poverty. In 2003 an estimated 54 percent of the population was living below the poverty line.

A 12-year period of military rule from 1968 to 1980 "offered the lower-class majorities a real basis for their hope that at last a government would respond to their needs and aspirations. Under the banner of a → 'revolution' which was to be able to be 'neither Communist nor capitalist but Peruvian,' the military government in power proclaimed a series of reforms," expected since World War II, "with important implications for the average citizen." There was an emphasis on cooperatives that arose from "a combination of APRA [American Popular Revolutionary Alliance] → ideology and legislative initiatives, a new social mission perception of the Catholic church, and the long-standing myth (though with some basis in reality) of Peru's collective Indian tradition" (D. S. Palmer, 1, 3).

Under the neoliberal presidents Belaúnde Terry (1980-85) and Alán García Pérez (1985-90), foreign debt increased to over $20 billion, and hyperinflation (3,000 percent in 1990) accompanied the increase. During this period a leftist guerrilla group, Sendero Luminoso (Shining Path), became active. In response, presidents Terry and García consistently took control of the army. Massive human-rights violations occurred at the hands of both the guerrillas and the army. Also, peasant organizations were formed in the northern Andes for self-defense and administration, especially the Rondas Campesinas (lit. "peasants who make the rounds"). The *rondas* spread with astonishing rapidity in the late 1970s and early 1980s.

Under the chaotic and corrupt regime of García, a state of emergency developed, characterized by political violence, cocaine, corruption, disease, and misery. Amid the economic chaos, hyperinflation, failed economic policies in the administrative arm of government, corruption, drug trafficking, and guerrilla warfare, Alberto Fujimori (b. 1938), an agronomist and the son of Japanese immigrants, won election in 1990 with his movement Cambio 90 (Change 90), which took the motto "Honesty, Technology, Work" and promised to implement democracy. Instead, he dissolved the refractory Congress in 1992, dismissed 13 of 23 judges in the highest court, and in 1993 passed a new constitution tailored to him as president. Although the economy improved overall, Fujimori found himself forced to raise prices for basic necessities fourfold.

The Fujimori government rejected any cooperation with the Rondas Campesinas and other successful base organizations and jailed more than 100 *ronderos*. Nevertheless, Fujimori's public works and his many trips to the countryside meant also that the peasantry and the poor had gained a new place in the national society. It was no longer possible to govern in Peru by avoiding all reference to the poor majorities. "The rondas had helped force an unprecedented measure of accountability and representation from the bureaucrats and the politicians who were supposed to serve the populace and yet had not. The gains in the struggle for recognition and citizenship were fundamental and irreversible" (O. Starn, 272-73).

The regime of authoritarian president Fujimori brought an end to the Marxist-Maoist-inspired violence of the Shining Path through the arrest in September 1992 of Abimael Guzmán, its leader, and the dissolving of that group. The Fujimori dictatorship itself fell, however, when Fujimori fled to Japan in November 2000 after the systematic corruption of presidential adviser Vladimiro Montesino was publicly exposed in the fall of 2000. The Congress did not accept Fujimori's request to step down and instead declared the presidency vacant on the grounds of Fujimori's "chronic moral incapacity." The interim president established a truth commission to bring to light the truth about crimes of subversive terror and counterterror on the part of the regime.

In 2001 the truth commission investigating the crimes of guerrillas and the military presented its findings to President Alejandro Toledo, who was chosen to rule in free elections in 2001. The report indicates that in all likelihood the number of victims was nearly 70,000, including almost 10,000 missing persons. There were also tens of thousands of internal → refugees. Moreover, from 1992 to 2000 at least 22,000 innocent people were imprisoned under Fujimori. Even though racist contempt for Andean peasants repeatedly emerges from the commission's statements, and although 75 percent of the victims spoke indigenous languages as their mother tongue, the commission itself could not conclude that it was ultimately an ethnic conflict.

A year after entering office, President Toledo's popularity reached a low point. Although his efforts at democratization have generally been acknowledged, and although the army has largely been cleansed of collaborators of the former dictatorship, Toledo is accused of being out of touch with reality and of having broken his campaign promises. Although there is indeed economic growth, it has occurred primarily through a boom in mining that Fujimori had aggressively supported.

2. Religious Context

2.1. *Roman Catholicism*

Roman → Catholicism came to Peru as the religion of the conquerors. In the colonial period Peru had a viceroy and was the administrative headquarters for Spanish rule on the west coast of South America (→ Colonialism). Archbishop Toribio de Mogrovejo (1580-1606), later canonized, organized the church in Peru. At first an episcopal → Inquisition and then, from 1570, a tribunal of the Inquisition saw to it that violations of faith and morality were prosecuted, especially those committed by Jewish converts to Christianity, and that Protestants were banished. Provisional episcopal councils were established to watch over the Indians, and in the 17th century campaigns were undertaken to eradicate the worship of idols *(extirpación de idolatrías).*

After Peru achieved independence, the constitution of 1828 made Roman Catholicism the state religion, with corresponding protection for the church, a status enjoyed until eliminated by the constitution of 1979. In the reconstruction that followed the disruptive effects of the wars of independence, the church came under Roman influence up to the middle of the 19th century, and → Ultramontanism flourished with the help of clergy from Europe. Liberals, however, alienated themselves from the church, and after 1860 the church lost its intellectual leadership to → positivism in the form of English → empiricism, which reached its zenith in Peru from 1885 to 1915. In 1875 the Vatican recognized the Peruvian president's right of → patronage.

With assistance from conservative politicians the church stubbornly defended its colonial privileges. Only in 1869 did it lose control of cemeteries. In 1897 civil → marriage became legal for non–Roman Catholics. Divorce was legalized in 1930. The constitution had recognized → religious liberty in 1915, and individual freedom of religion was granted in 1933, but the church clung to its privilege of giving → religious instruction in the public schools. Bishops and clergy were paid by the state, and seminaries, schools, and hospitals received subsidies. In 1941 Roman Catholic instruction became compulsory in public and private schools and in prisons.

We can link this confirming of traditional church privileges to controversies regarding the identity of Peru in the years between the two world wars. The official church opposed the socialist-Indophile renewal movement advocated on the Marxist side (esp. by Luis E. Valcárel, José Carlos Mariátegui, and Víctor Raúl Haya de la Torre). It turned instead to the Peruvian Hispanophiles, who took the → fascism of B. Mussolini (1883-1945) and F. Franco (1892-1975) as a model and championed a corporative → state. The Roman Catholic University of Lima, founded in 1917, became the citadel of fascism, which promoted itself as the answer to → positivism, → capitalism, → democracy, and the → materialism that they promoted. In accordance with fascist thinking, and on the basis of a Peruvian identity deriving from the conquerors and the values of Spanish culture, the church built up its social work, especially among the Indians.

In 1927 a council at Lima (→ Latin American Councils) failed to recognize the plight of the proletariat and opposed → strikes as an expression of class thinking (→ Class and Social Stratum) and a threat to the order of society. In 1937 Pedro Pascual Farfán, who had become archbishop of Lima in 1933, stated without opposition that "poverty is the surest way to eternal felicity. Only the state that convinces the poor of the spiritual riches of poverty can solve social problems."

After 1945 the identity of Peru was sought in its mestizos. The church also did more social work among Indians. After 1958 it came out publicly for social justice and the reforming of society. From 1968, then, the → hierarchy lent its support to the great reforming projects of the leftist military regime.

The spirit of → Vatican II brought more religious liberty to Peru, so that separation of → church and state came with the 1979 constitution. According to article 50 of the present constitution (1993), "The government recognizes the Catholic Church as an important element in the historical, cultural, and moral formation of Peru and lends it its cooperation." In addition, "The government respects other → denominations and may establish forms of cooperation with them."

As early as 1968 the Ministry of Education of the military regime, in cooperation with the → Roman Catholic Church, the Concilio Nacional Evangélico del Perú (see 3), the Adventist Church, and the Jewish community developed an interconfessional curriculum for religion and introduced interconfessional religious instruction into the public schools.

The Catholic Church has repeatedly taken a critical public position regarding political, social, and economic developments, either at bishops' conferences or in regional groups of bishops (→ Latin American Councils 2.5). One particularly sensational event occurred on December 2, 1990, when *La República* published a manifesto in the daily newspaper composed by a group of theologians and pastoral workers associated with Gustavo Gutiérrez (→ Liberation Theology). By the time it was published, the manifesto had been signed by 1,002 priests and members of orders. It is much clearer than any of the explanations from the bishops' conferences and essentially constitutes an outcry of the disenfranchised, humiliated, marginalized majority of the Peruvian people. On the one hand, there is a concentration of wealth, tax evasion, money laundering, and access to luxury goods; on the other hand, 12 million Peruvians live in dire poverty, with minimum wage covering only 25 percent of the cost of supporting a family. → Racism and coerced military conscription continue.

2.2. *Protestantism*

A short period of religious toleration during the fight for independence made it possible for the British and Foreign Bible Society (→ Bible Societies), with the support of the liberator General San Martín, to send James Thomson (1788-1854) in 1822 to organize public schools along the lines of the Lancaster Society, whose agent he also was. In a translation that Roman Catholics also recognized, Thomson made the Bible a textbook in his schools. With the help of priests some 33 schools were founded that offered education to children of all social strata. But popular education stirred up the opposition of the great landowners, who were afraid that their workers might rise up against them.

Anglican work (→ Anglican Communion) began in Peru in 1849, but at first it was limited to the English colony and to seamen. More lasting Protestant missionary work among Peruvians began only in 1888, when the Italian Francisco G. Penzotti, a → Waldensian who was brought up in Uruguay, came to Callao with his family and the Bible colporteur J. B. Arancet of Uruguay. Under the aegis of the American Bible Society, Penzotti (who was active in Peru only 1888-91) not only sold Bibles from house to house but also did house → evangelism. Toward the end of his life Thomson had recognized that hopes for domestic Roman Catholic reform were destined to be disappointed, and he had thus urged that a missionary society for South America should be formed. Roman Catholic opposition brought Penzotti eight months in prison in 1890/91, but his imprisonment mobilized liberal forces on his behalf and led to a legal ruling that private religious encounters did not violate article 4 of the constitution. In spite of further hindrances under conservative regimes, the result was the beginning of Peruvian → Methodism (→ Methodist Churches) under Thomas Bond. The Iglesia Metodista Peruana, which engages in a good deal of educational work, had 24,000 affiliates in 2000.

In 1911 an → Adventist married couple, the Stahls, began working at an Indian school and pharmacy in Platería at the invitation of the Aymara Manuel Zúñiga. The bishop of Puno, Valentín Ampuero, responded in 1913 by inciting 200 Indians to vandalism in a bid to restore the absolute authority of the church and of the great landowners (→ Persecution of Christians 4.2). This action and similar incidents increased the efforts of the liberals and Protestant missionaries to establish religious toleration, and in 1915 they succeeded. Since then Adventist educational work among the Aymaras has developed strongly. In 2000 this church numbered 550,000 adherents, half of them Aymaras.

In 1896 independent Brethren missionaries began work in Lima, and in 1897 they joined forces with the Regions Beyond Missionary Union (RBMU), whose most important worker in the period from 1906 to 1952 was the Scottish Presbyterian John Ritchie. The labors of the RBMU and two other → faith missions, the Evangelical Union of South America (EUSA, from 1911) and the → Christian and Missionary Alliance (from 1933), resulted in the formation of what in 2000 was the second largest Protestant church in Peru, the Evangelical Church of Peru (300,000 members). This church is close to Holiness churches (→ Holiness Movement) such as the Wesleyans and → Nazarenes, which have been in Peru since 1903 and 1914 respectively. Smaller → Baptist missions started in 1927. There are also two small Presbyterian churches (→ Reformed and Presbyterian Churches). One was started by the Free Church of Scotland with the work of John A. Mackay (1916), who in 1917 founded the Anglo-Peruvian College, today Colegio San Andrés, the most prestigious Protestant school in Peru.

The strongest of the fast-growing → Pentecostal churches is the → Assemblies of God (→ Assembleias de Deus no Brasil), with 238,000 members in 2000. The Adventists, Baptists, RBMU, and EUSA practice adult → baptism by immersion, while the Holiness and Pentecostal church emphasize baptism with the Spirit.

Since 1921 the South American Indian Mission has been at work among Indians of the interior. After World War II the Wycliffe Bible Translators also focused on this field; in the 1970s they had 236 workers among 40 tribes. When anthropologists accused them of cultural alienation, however, the state placed restrictions on their work. Along with other churches a few European missionaries also work among the Indians, such as some from the Hermannsburg Mission (→ German Missions). Small independent Indian churches are mostly Pentecostal in orientation.

In 1961 non–Roman Catholic Christians numbered only 1 percent, but by 2000 the proportion had risen to over 10 percent. Protestants also make extensive use of radio, especially the Evangelical Alliance Mission (TEAM) and the Southern Baptists.

3. Interchurch Relations

The cooperation of the Protestant churches and missions began in 1916 with the founding of the Comité de Cooperación Misionera, from which the Alianza Evangélica del Perú developed. The imperative of emphasizing the unity of the churches and their national presence led in 1940 to the founding of the Concilio Nacional Evangélico del Perú (CONEP, National Evangelical Council of Peru), initially with eight member churches and church institutions. In 1999 virtually the entire spectrum of Protestantism, with 80 churches, associations, and missions, belonged to CONEP. Although the Methodists withdrew in 1966, claiming that it was too controlled by missions, they do work in other ecumenical institutions such as the association for theological education founded in 1965, in which ten seminaries participate. The Consejo Latinoamericano de Iglesias (CLAI, → Latin American Council of Churches) also began in Peru at the end of the 1970s. CONEP has occasionally made public statements concerning sociopolitical issues, reminding the state that it is God who charges the authorities with protecting and respecting the rights of citizens rather than curtailing those → rights.

The efforts at → ecumenical dialogue were sustained by the small Lutheran, Anglican, and Methodist churches, with the participation of other denominations. Such dialogue is hampered by the increasingly traditionalist and conservative membership in the Roman Catholic episcopate, a position evident, for example, in the planning paper for new evangelization initiated by the CELAM conference in Santo Domingo in 1992. This paper laments the growth of "various sects," since such growth constitutes a departure from the truth revealed by Christ, as well as a "serious problem for the cultural identity of our people." Here too the Catholic Church is asserting anew its own monopoly on Christian truth, attempting to secure that position with reference to a cultural identity that it itself shapes.

In 1999 Archbishop Cipriani demanded that the state implement a course for Catholic religion for the secondary-school diploma *(bachillerato).* He was reminded in an official declaration of CONEP that the church and state have been separate since 1979 and that one might at most adduce the 1968 model of interconfessional religious instruction.

4. Other Religious Groups

Other religious groups include some of Christian origin like → Mormons (320,000 affiliates in 2000) and → Jehovah's Witnesses (240,000), along with purely local groups of Peruvian origin such as the Evangelical Israelite Church of the New Covenant (280,000) and various indigenous Pentecostal groups (the two largest totaling 170,000).

Non-Christian groups number less than 2 percent of the population. The largest are tribal religionists, with adherents also of → Buddhism and of → Baha'i. The tiny Jewish community (→ Judaism) has been in conversation with the Christian churches.

→ Latin American Theology

Bibliography: Religion: F. Armas Asín, *Liberales, Protestantes y Masones. Modernidad y tolerancia religiosa. Perú siglo XIX* (Lima, 1998) • F. Armas Asín, ed., *La construcción de la iglesia en los Andes* (Lima, 1999) •

T. Hampe Martínez, *Santidad e identidad criolla. Estudio del proceso de canonización de Santa Rosa* (Cuzco, 1998); idem, *Santo oficio e historia colonial. Aproximación al Tribunal de la Inquisición de Lima (1570-1820)* (Lima, 1998) • J. L. Huys, *José de Acosta y el origen de la idea de misión. Perú siglo XVI* (Cuzco, 1997) • J. Klaiber, *The Catholic Church in Peru, 1821-1985* (Washington, D.C., 1992); idem, *Religion and Revolution in Peru, 1824-1976* (Notre Dame, Ind., 1977) • S. MacCormack, *Religion in the Andes: Vision and Imagination in Early Colonial Peru* (Princeton, 1991) • H.-J. Prien, *La historia del Cristianismo en América Latina* (Salamanca, 1985) • B. Schlegelberger, *Unsere Erde lebt. Zum Verhältnis von altandiner Religion und Christentum in den Hochanden Perus* (Immensee, 1992) • H. Urbano, ed., *La extirpación de la idolatría en el Perú (1621)* (by P. J. de Arriaga, S.J.; Cuzco, 1999).

Other topics: F. P. Bowser, *The African Slave in Colonial Peru* (Stanford, Calif., 1974) • O. Celestino and A. Meyers, *Las cofradías en el Perú. Región central* (Frankfurt, 1981) • A. F. Lowenthal, ed., *The Peruvian Experiment: Continuity and Change under Military Rule* (Princeton, 1975) • S. O'Phelan, *El Perú en el siglo XVIII. La era borbónica* (Lima, 1999) • D. S. Palmer, *Peru: The Authoritarian Tradition* (New York, 1980) • G. D. E. Philip, *The Rise and Fall of the Peruvian Military Radicals (1968-1976)* (London, 1978) • D. Poole and G. Rénique, *Peru: Time of Fear* (London, 1992) • O. Starn, *Nightwatch: The Politics of Protest in the Andes* (Durham, N.C., 1999) • O. Starn, C. I. Degregori, and R. Kirk, ed., *The Peru Reader* (London, 1995) • S. J. Stern, *Resistance, Rebellion, and Consciousness in the Andean Peasant World, Eighteenth to Twentieth Centuries* (Madison, Wis., 1987) • S. Strong, *Shining Path* (London, 1992) • D. P. Werlich, *Peru: A Short History* (Carbondale, Ill., 1978).

Hans-Jürgen Prien

Pessimism → Optimism and Pessimism

Peter

1. Before Easter
2. After Easter
3. In Tradition
4. The Papacy

1. Before Easter

The apostle Peter apparently came from a Greek-speaking family in Bethsaida. His original name, Simon, is a Greek form of Simeon. His brother Andrew, with whom he worked as a fisherman in Capernaum, had a purely Greek name. → Jesus called the brothers, who were at first attracted to → John the Baptist, at the beginning of his public ministry (Mark 1:16-18; John 1:35-42).

Peter had a leading position among the 12 disciples and was given a new name denoting his character (Mark 3:16 and par.). Derived from Aram. *kêpā'*, this name, research now indicates, does not signify a cliff but rather a stone or isolated rock; the Greek *petros* is its equivalent. The name carries some suggestion of preeminence (precious stone), as Roman Catholics stress, but also of outward appearance. The first Christian writings accept this ambivalence even after Matt. 16:18 (cf. John 1:42). In the conduct of Peter as a disciple, we see tension between a notable confession (Mark 8:27-30; John 6:67-69) and supreme denial (Mark 14:54, 66-72 and par.).

2. After Easter

Peter's work after Easter, based on an appearance of the resurrected Christ (1 Cor. 15:5), was important for his significance to the church. First among the 12 disciples and, along with John and James, a "pillar" (Gal. 2:9; see Jer. 1:18 on the concept of the community as the eschatological temple), Peter was a leader of the → primitive Christian community in Jerusalem.

Peter quickly began work as a missionary (Acts 1–12), and the apostolic council (Gal. 2:7-9) recognized his ministry to the circumcised. According to Gal. 2:14 he lived to a certain extent in Gentile fashion, which → Paul reminded him of when a controversy arose at Antioch regarding table fellowship between Gentile and Jewish Christians (Gal. 2:11-17). The 19th-century thesis that this incident led to a breach between Peter and Paul and that Peter was behind Paul's opponents all the way from Galatia to Corinth cannot be verified.

According to 1 Cor. 1:12-17 Peter had a wide influence as a charismatic figure in the early Christian community, although we cannot be sure that he actually served in Corinth. The indications seem to be that the missions of Peter and of Paul were to different groups in very different areas.

3. In Tradition

Early church recollections of Peter (though not supported by any primary sources) saw him as leaving → Jerusalem for unexplained reasons, then going to Syrian → Antioch, then losing touch with Paul as the latter engaged in his later → missionary work. In Antioch a play on words might have led to the understanding of the name "Petros" as "Petra" (large rock or cliff), that is, the rock on which the church is built. Matt. 16:17-19 gave currency to this understanding in wider church circles subsequent to what is recorded in Matt. 28:16-20. An important feature of the tradition is that it refers to the founding of the church, but with no successor to Peter in view.

According to tradition, the later ministry of Peter took him to → Rome, where he is said to have suffered martyrdom under Nero (54-68). Earlier records, however, especially *1 Clem.* 5.4, give this history only indirectly and thus offer no final certainty. The tomb of Peter, or *memoria*, is venerated under the present Basilica of St. Peter in Rome. Peter's death did not lessen his influence; John 21 evaluates him more positively than is done throughout chaps. 1–20.

The epistles that bear Peter's name rest on his authority and offer a more profound picture of him as a preacher in Greek, stressing his theological openness both by playing down → circumcision and the ritual side of the → law and by making favorable references to Paul (implicitly in 1 Peter, explicitly in 2 Pet. 3:15-16).

Throughout, Peter is an outstanding but isolated figure (see Ign. *Rom.* 4.3; *Smyrn.* 3.2). He is linked to no school in the narrower sense, nor is he depicted as the founder of the episcopate. Second-century writings ascribed to him hail him as the recipient of revelation, such as a vision of heaven and hell that underwent important development in the church *(Apoc. Pet.)*. He is also seen as one who accompanied the Lord *(Gos. Pet.)*. The *Kerygmata Petrou* (in a disputed reconstruction) set him in opposition to Paul (*Clem. Hom.* 2.16-17; 17.18-19). Toward the end of the second century such works no longer went uncontested in the church. (Serapion in Eusebius *Hist. eccl.* 6.12.3-6 wrongly relates *Gos. Pet.* to → Docetism. Possibly this association was in reaction to the increasing attribution of Peter to → Gnosticism, for which we have good evidence from the 2d to the 4th cent. in the → Nag Hammadi findings, especially a second *Apoc. Pet.;* see *NHC* 7.3, also 6.1 and 8.2.)

Artistic portraits of Peter began to appear in the third century (e.g., in the → house church in Dura-Europos). The typical depiction that prevailed throughout the Middle Ages had already emerged in the fourth century. The best-known feature, the → "keys of the kingdom," denotes the office of "binding" and "loosing" (Matt. 16:19). More rarely, and later, Peter is depicted as the supreme → pastor. Along similar lines, he is portrayed with Paul as the one to whom and through whom the law and revelation are given.

4. The Papacy

Writers in the third century (e.g., → Cyprian) began to claim that Peter had been → bishop of Rome and to use Matt. 16:17-19 as an extended reference to his successors in that office (→ Pope, Papacy). A high point of this view came with → Leo I (440-461). In contrast, → Gregory I (590-604) offered a very nuanced picture of Peter that allowed for mistakes and guilt. Gregory found no adherents to his view in subsequent histories of the papacy, although Roman Catholics today have rediscovered his approach.

Only in the Middle Ages did the theme of primacy appear. The most important feast from the 4th century onward has been that of Peter and Paul on June 29, which the → Reformation did not wholly reject. From the 17th century onward the papacy opposed the treatment of the two apostles as equals (DS 1999 and 3555). In the 19th century the Protestant Tübingen school postulated an opposition between Peter and Paul, a thesis that still has some influence. On exegetical grounds, however, the two are now commonly viewed as two poles or representatives of unity in primitive Christianity.

→ Apocrypha 2; Apostle, Apostolate; Passion, Accounts of the; Pentecost

Bibliography: R. E. Brown et al., eds., *Peter in the NT: A Collaborative Assessment by Protestant and Roman Catholic Scholars* (Minneapolis, 1973) • O. Cullmann, *Peter: Disciple, Apostle, Martyr* (Philadelphia, 1962) • P. Perkins, *Peter: Apostle for the Whole Church* (Columbia, S.C., 1994) • T. Smith, *Petrine Controversies in Early Christianity* (Tübingen, 1985).

Martin Karrer

Peter, Epistles of

1. First Peter
2. Second Peter

1. First Peter

The Epistle of 1 Peter is the earliest extant writing associating itself with → Peter. Because the ecclesiastical and cultural situation reflected in the letter suggests it was written during the period after A.D. 70, scholars since the 19th century have generally assumed deutero-Petrine authorship. F. C. Baur (1792-1860) viewed it as a mediation text between Jews and Pauline Christianity, though one 20th-century line of thought viewed it more as a deutero-Pauline writing. Recent scholars have uncovered several elements suggesting a more independent origin.

Although the address in 1:1-2 coincides with the Pauline mission to → Gentile Christians, it is formulated more according to the Jewish → diaspora letter and the Jewish understanding of election (note the triadic formula in v. 2).

This latter element acquires a more radical articulation in the basic theological exposition of 1:3–2:10. Those elected in faith in Christ now claim the → prophets (1:10-12) and Israel's royal priesthood (2:9, citing Exod. 19:6; 23:22; from the time of the Reformation, this was the key text supporting the notion of the priesthood of all believers; → Priest, Priesthood, 4). Ultimately, they receive God's compassion (2:10), according to Hos. 1:10; 2:1, 23. Unlike Romans (9–11), this epistle contains no reference to the existence of Israel alongside the church, reflecting the author's theological conviction that the reality of → Israel (§1) as the chosen people has been transferred without remainder to the church, now including both Jews and Gentiles. This understanding is confirmed by the use of terms for the Christian community once reserved for Israel in the OT, as the introductory verses make clear.

Next, 1 Pet. 2:11–4:19 provides an outline of political and → social ethics, presupposing that the elect in fact have the status of aliens in a threatening pagan environment that, in its own turn, presupposes institutions such as imperial authority and → slavery. The Christian readers are charged with acting in that environment in ways that accord with the fundamental mode of Christ's own actions. → Exegesis emphasizes a willingness to accommodate up to the point that such accommodation would compromise Christian belief and action; at that point there is a willingness to confront the culture (note the instruction to honor the emperor in 2:13-14, along with the reference to Rome as godless Babylon in 5:13).

The ethical circle is concluded in 5:1-11 with a reference to officeholders (→ elders, whom "Peter" joins) and to the congregational members' own behavior within the church, who cast their burden upon God (as in Ps. 55:22; 1 Pet. 5:8 evokes the striking image of the → devil as a prowling lion). The short section 5:12-14 concludes the letter.

It was once thought that 1 Peter is permeated by formulaic and hymnic material deriving especially from baptismal traditions. More recent research, however, has located those traditions more broadly within the larger Christian context. The passages 1 Pet. 1:18-21, 2:21b-24, and 3:18-19, 22 are of particular importance, the latter containing a sermon about Christ delivered to the "spirits in prison." Formulated in language that reflects → Enoch traditions *(1 Enoch)*, Christ announces final defeat to the forces that oppose God (3:22). While some have seen a connection between this sermon and 1 Pet. 4:6, the latter more likely refers to deceased humans, perhaps even deceased Christians, although the precise interpretation is disputed. This reference to Christ preaching to the dead has been a key text contributing to the church tradition of Christ's → descent into hell.

The strongest assessment of 1 Peter came from Martin → Luther (1483-1546), who found in it a summation of Christianity itself (*LW* 30.4, 143) and thus positioned it in his own translation ahead of the → Catholic Epistles (contradicting the Greek textual sequence).

Bibliography: Commentaries: P. Achtemeier (Hermeneia; Minneapolis, 1996) • J. Elliott (AB; New York, 2000) • L. Goppelt (Grand Rapids, 1993) • J. R. Michaels (WBC; Dallas, 1989).

Other works: W. Dalton, *Christ's Proclamation to the Spirits: A Study of 1 Peter 3:18–4:6* (2d ed.; Rome, 1989) • J. Elliott, *A Home for the Homeless: A Sociological Exegesis of 1 Peter, Its Situation and Strategy* (Philadelphia, 1981).

Martin Karrer and Paul J. Achtemeier

2. Second Peter

The Second Epistle of Peter refers to itself as Peter's second letter (3:1) and, according to 1:13-14, as his testament. The author is not identical to the author of 1 Peter. Differences that are stylistic (preference for rare Greek words and Atticisms) and theological (e.g., reference to Christ as *sōtēr,* "savior," and an emphasis on *eusebeia,* "godliness") reveal how much more directly he addresses Hellenistic religiosity. He considers the Christian community to be threatened by false doctrines. Earlier scholars regarded them as → Gnostic in origin, but today they are generally attributed to Christians who were intent on correcting the expectation of the → parousia and judgment in favor of more complete acculturation within → Hellenism and who were trying to loosen a rigorous understanding of Christian → ethics.

The author counters this group with traditional truth (2 Pet. 1:3-21), with polemic influenced by the letter of Jude (chap. 2; they strayed from "the way of righteousness" and turned back from "the holy commandment," v. 21), and with an apology for the parousia and judgment (3:1-16). The reference to world conflagration in 3:10, 12 betrays a point of view that since the discovery of 1QH 3:29-31 is no longer understood so exclusively from the perspective of → Stoicism, a point of view also leading systematically to the question of the annihilation of the world. The presuppositions of 2 Peter and Jude suggest that they were written in the later period of the primitive church (early 2nd cent.; R. Bauckham, 80-90, takes a different view).

Because the apostolic authorship of the letter was a matter of dispute even in the → early church itself, 2 Peter entered the → canon relatively late. Protestant criticism in the 20th century long viewed the letter as the most pronounced example of Hellenistic religiosity in the NT, and then as a classic document of so-called → early Catholicism. Roman Catholic exegesis tends only partially to follow these two criticisms. Actually, 2 Peter adduces for its argumentation the early → apostles (Peter, Paul, and others, in 1:1, 13-18; 3:2, 15-16) rather than a doctrinally authoritative contemporary office. Nor can such an office be interpolated into the textual exegesis of 1:19-21, which positively emphasizes the spiritual influence of prophecy.

As far as → Hellenism is concerned, 1:4, a verse of great significance especially for the → Orthodox Church, links the relatively new Christian striving to become "participants of the divine nature" with ethical impulses and an eschatological orientation, so that the search for → *theōsis* acquires more independent contours. The same applies to the continuation of → soteriology and God-Christology in 1:1 to the parousia → Christology in chap. 3. As a result, recent research understands 2 Peter more as a document of a struggle involving → contextual theology.

Bibliography: Commentaries: R. Bauckham (WBC; Waco, Tex., 1983) • M. Green (TNTC; Grand Rapids, 1968) • S. Kraftchick (AbNTC; Nashville, 2002) • D. Moo (NIVApp; Grand Rapids, 1996) • J. Nyrey (AB; New York, 1993).

Martin Karrer

Peter's Pence

Peter's Pence (Lat. *denarius Sancti Petri*) was an annual payment of devotion or recognition to the → pope, almost a quasi-tribute. It first arose in 8th-century England at the initiative of secular rulers. Later it spread to most of the countries under the papacy. The efforts of → Gregory VII (1073-85) and other popes to establish a feudal relation to the papacy on the basis of the → Donation of Constantine came to nothing (→ Feudalism). In the 16th century the practice of paying Peter's Pence fell into disuse, but it was revived in the 19th century when papal revenues from France, Italy, and Austria declined with the dissolution of the → Papal States.

Peter's Pence is now a payment that symbolizes the solidarity of Roman Catholic believers of all countries. It is usually collected in connection with the Feast of St. Peter and St. Paul (June 29). It is now a discretionary fund for the pope's use. The proceeds are published, listed by country, but no account is given of expenditures.

→ Catholicism (Roman)

Bibliography: R. E. Graham, "Breve storia dell'obolo di San Pietro," *CivCatt* 142 (1991) 231-42 • M. J. Hamilton, "Peter's Pence," *NCE* (2d ed.) 11.209-10 • W. E. Lunt, *Financial Relations of the Papacy with England* (2 vols.; Cambridge, Mass., 1939-62) 1.3-84; 2.1-53; idem, *Papal Revenues in the Middle Ages* (2 vols.; New York, 1934) 1.65-71; 2.55-81.

Heiner Grote†

Pharisees

1. Sources
2. History
3. Distinctives

Pharisees were members of one of the group movements that characterized early → Judaism (→ Essenes; Sadducees). The name, first found in Phil. 3:5 and based on Aram. *pĕrîšayyâ* (= Heb. *pĕrûšîm*, "separated ones"), might well have been first used by others to denote separatists, but the Pharisees themselves could also adopt it in the sense of holy or abstemious ones.

1. Sources

We have no reliable sources dating from the period before A.D. 70. For sources we are dependent on Josephus (ca. 37-ca. 100, *J.W.* and *Ant.*), primitive Christian writings (→ Paul, the Gospels, and Acts, which are in part anti-Pharisaic), and later rabbinic accounts (→ Mishnah; Talmud).

2. History

The origins of the Pharisaic movement are obscure. It is suspected that there are links to a "company of Hasideans . . . who offered themselves willingly for the law" (1 Macc. 2:42), which participated in the Maccabean revolt. We know little, however, about the spread or development of such a group.

We first find something tangible when under the → Hasmonaeans they opposed John Hyrcanus (135-104 B.C.) and Alexander Jannaeus (103-76). They then became a leading party under Salome Alexandra (76-67) and played a leading part in both the political and the religious life of Judaism in → Palestine, partly in opposition to ruling circles (e.g., → Herod the

Great) and partly as members of the Sanhedrin (Acts 5:34; 23:6). How far they might be found in the → diaspora is not clear. Even in Palestine their numbers were never very great (6,000, according to Josephus *Ant.* 17.42). Most of the members seem to have belonged to the urban middle class.

Under the Romans, and not counting the → Zealots, who split off from them, they adopted a moderate stance. They were the only party of Palestinian Judaism to survive the disaster of the first Jewish revolt, the destruction of the temple in A.D. 70, and the loss of political independence.

3. Distinctives

The Pharisees were organized in small groups, or *chaburoth.* They took as their standards the traditions and biblical expositions of their leading → scribes. Their eschatologically oriented goal was to actualize the people of God as "a priestly kingdom and a holy nation" (Exod. 19:6) by strict conduct ("most skillful in the exact explication of their laws," Josephus *J.W.* 2.162; Acts 22:3; 26:5) in accordance with biblical directions (e.g., keeping the → Sabbath and paying → tithes) and by the applying of laws for priests to the everyday life of the laity (Mark 7:1-4; Matt 23:25-26; → Cultic Purity). Pharisaic → piety, however, was not exclusively cultic but involved practical matters (see Matt. 6:1-18 on philanthropy, → prayer, and → fasting) and carried with it many religious concepts, such as the → hope of → resurrection (*J.W.* 2.163; Acts 23:6, 8).

With their lifestyle and beliefs the Pharisees not only gained recognition among their contemporaries, even though it might be critical as in the case of → Jesus, but also left their mark on the development of later rabbinic Judaism (→ Rabbi, Rabbinism). Even to this day their influence has helped to shape the general picture that Judaism presents.

→ New Testament Era, History of

Bibliography: D. B. Gowler, *Host, Guest, Enemy, and Friend: Portraits of the Pharisees in Luke and Acts* (New York, 1991) • R. W. Maqsood, *The Separated Ones: Jesus, the Pharisees, and Islam* (London, 1991) • J. Neusner, *From Politics to Piety: The Emergence of Pharisaic Judaism* (2d ed.; New York, 1979); idem, *The Rabbinic Traditions about the Pharisees before 70* (3 vols.; Leiden, 1971; repr., Atlanta, 1999) • A. J. Saldarini, *Pharisees, Scribes, and Sadducees in Palestinian Society* (Grand Rapids, 2001) • E. P. Sanders, *Judaism: Practice and Belief, 63 B.C.E.–66 C.E.* (Philadelphia, 1994) • P. Schäfer, "Der vorrabbinische Pharisäismus," *Paulus und das antike Judentum* (ed. M. Hengel and U. Heckel; Tübingen, 1991) 125-75 • E. Schürer, *The History of the Jewish People in the Age of Jesus Christ (175 B.C.–A.D. 135)* (3 vols.; ed. G. Vermes and F. Millar; Edinburgh, 1973-87) esp. 2.381-402 • D. R. Schwartz, "Josephus and Nicolaus on the Pharisees," *JSJ* 14 (1983) 157-71 • G. Stemberger, *Jewish Contemporaries of Jesus: Pharisees, Sadducees, Essenes* (Minneapolis, 1995).

Berndt Schaller

Phenomenology

1. Term
2. Husserl
3. Development

1. Term

The term "phenomenology" generally refers today to the philosophical trend or method that goes back to E. Husserl (1859-1938). In fact, however, the term was used in various connections long before Husserl. It was introduced by J. H. Lambert (1728-77), who in his *New Organon* raised the question whether the understanding has a capability for → truth. In pt. 4 he dealt with the issue whether appearance can influence the accuracy of human knowledge and called the related science phenomenology (the doctrine of appearance).

J. G. → Herder (1744-1803) and I. Kant (1724-1804; → Kantianism) adopted this usage, and G. W. F. Hegel (1770-1831; → Hegelianism) in his *Phenomenology of Mind* understood by "phenomenology" the doctrine of knowledge from appearance, a description of the path from natural awareness to absolute knowledge. Later the term became a rather loose one, but then F. Brentano (1838-1917) aimed at greater precision by using "descriptive phenomenology" as a term for descriptive psychology.

2. Husserl

Husserl followed up this usage by seeing in phenomenology, not descriptive psychology, but the basis of → psychology and indeed of all knowledge (→ Epistemology) and → logic, his maxim being that we must go back to "the object itself." A twofold claim was then made for phenomenology, first as the measure of all scholarship, then as an analysis of various approaches to phenomena (involving imagination, judgment, feeling, and willing) or as an analysis of the various modes of being of phenomena themselves. In ideas *noematic reflection* on the object corresponds to *noetic reflection* on the act. This correlation of act and object finds expression in the concept of intentionality (a term introduced by Brentano on the basis of a notion found in → Scholasticism), the main theme of phenomenology being that consciousness of an act is consciousness *of something*. Analyses bring to light many acts and many types of objects, and simplification produces a natural → everyday and scientific attitude.

A basic premise of phenomenological analysis is thus phenomenological reduction, or *epochē* (the suspension of judgment, a central concept of the skepticism of antiquity), the "bracketing" of "the general thesis of the natural world." Reduction as transcendental *epochē* discloses a new region of being, pure or transcendental awareness as the "phenomenological residuum" (→ Transcendental Philosophy). In this exposition of the innermost ego, even what is not proper to it receives ontic meaning by → analogy. Intentional exposition of alien → experience thus completes phenomenological-transcendental → idealism.

Later, *genetic phenomenology* supplements *transcendental phenomenology*. With his unfolding of the "world of life" as the unvarying basis of all the variable detailed forms of → culture, Husserl showed on the one hand that the crisis of modern science (→ Modern Period) derives from a forgetting of this basis, while on the other hand he traced back to a concealed subjectivity the historical achievements that confer meaning (→ Subjectivism and Objectivism). In this regard the task of the philosopher as a "functionary of humanity" is to bring true meaning to light in orientation to the *telos* of universal → reason (→ Teleology).

3. Development

The transcendental turn in Husserl distinguishes him from phenomenologists of the early Munich and Göttingen circle such as A. Pfänder (1870-1941) and M. Geiger (1880-1937), but also from other disciples. For M. Scheler (1874-1928) phenomenology meant making known the nexus of being in every objective sphere, not by going back to a transcendental ego but by intensive experience of the world itself. More than any other phenomenologist, Scheler dealt with individual fields of inquiry such as the → psychoanalysis of S. Freud (1856-1939).

M. Heidegger (1889-1976) brought against Husserl the criticism that he ignored the ontic meaning of the consciousness and of objectivity. Phenomenology had become the universal → ontology of existence; what is there is the common world that we must all appropriate for ourselves. In his *Being and Time* and then again in the later Heidegger, phenomenology was primarily a methodological concept. H. Rombach developed a structural understanding.

In France J.-P. Sartre (1905-80) worked out a phenomenology of → freedom, M. Merleau-Ponty (1908-61) made the body the center of a phenomenology of finitude and came close to → structuralism, Paul Ricoeur (1913-2005) represented a variant of hermeneutical phenemonology (→ Hermeneutics), and E. Lévinas began with Husserl and Heidegger but used Talmudic (→ Talmud) → piety in criticism of their identity thinking. In Czechoslovakia Jan Patočka (1907-77), who was a disciple of Husserl, founded the human → rights movement Charter 77 and thus became a pivotal figure in antitotalitarian → resistance.

Outside Europe disciples of Husserl helped to spread phenomenology, such as A. Schütz in the United States, who offered a phenomenological basis for → sociology. But criticism of the thinking of Husserl or Heidegger also played a part, for example, by Koichi Tsujimura in Japan, or the Korean Kah Kyung Cho, who has long taught in the United States.

As regards individual sciences, psychology has held a special position since Husserl, while there have been connections with the philosophy of → language since Husserl's contact with linguist R. Jakobson (1896-1982). Phenomenology brought liberation from → Cartesianism to → psychiatry and → psychotherapy (as in the various analyses of existence by L. Binswanger and M. Boss). In the United States the theme "phenomenological sociology" came into vogue in 1971. We also find a growing interest in → pedagogics.

→ Theology was influenced by Heidegger in two phases. R. Bultmann's (1884-1976) program of existential interpretation of the NT (→ Demythologizing; Existential Theology) owed much to *Being and Time*, while the hermeneutics of such men as H. Ott, E. Fuchs, and G. Ebeling built on the later Heidegger.

Bibliography: K. K. Cho, ed., *Philosophy and Science in Phenomenological Perspective* (Dordrecht, 1984) • U. Claesges et al., "Phänomenologie," *HWP* 7.486-505 • F. J. Crosson, "Phenomenology," *NCE* 11.230-34 • S. G. Crowell, *Husserl, Heidegger, and the Space of Meaning: Paths toward Transcendental Phenomenology* (Evanston, Ill., 2001) • L. Embree ed., *Encyclopedia of Phenomenology* (Dordrecht, 1997) • M. Heidegger, *The Phenomenology of Religious Life* (trans. M. Fritsch and J. A. Gosetti-Ferencei; Bloomington, Ind., 2004) • E. Husserl, *Logical Investigations* (2 vols.; trans. J. N. Findlay; London, 1970; orig. pub., 1900-1901) • P. Ricoeur, *A Key to Husserl's Ideas* (vol. 1; ed.

P. Vandevelde; Milwaukee, Wis., 1996) • H. Spiegelberg, *The Phenomenological Movement: A Historical Introduction* (3d ed.; The Hague, 1982) • D. Stewart and A. Mickunas, *Exploring Phenomenology: A Guide to the Field and Its Literature* (2d ed.; Athens, Ohio, 1990).

Helmuth Vetter

Phenomenology of Religion

1. Term and Beginnings
2. Religious Phenomena
3. Features of Religion
4. Tasks

1. Term and Beginnings

1.1. Between G. W. F. Hegel (1770-1831; → Hegelianism) and E. Husserl (1859-1938), "phenomenology" was a simple methodological term designed to indicate the fullest possible recording of facts and data. The phrase "phenomenology of religion" was used by P. D. Chantepie de la Saussaye (1848-1920) for the phenomenological part of his *Lehrbuch der Religionsgeschichte* (vol. 1; Freiburg, 1887; ET *Manual of the Science of Religion* [1891]). Others in later editions would speak of religious manifestations and ideas. Under this head Chantepie de la Saussaye brought together forces, powers, forms, and manifestations on the premise that the essential → religion that lies behind the shifting historical manifestations would then come to light. Further work went on along these lines, even when the original presupposition weakened or vanished. It did so either under the same title or by making the phenomenology of religion a discipline within → religious studies.

Interest in religion as a total phenomenon remained so dominant that for a long time the phenomena that were viewed as its components were particularized, especially in their historical and social contexts. For this reason the phenomenology of religion came to be accused of being a mere matter of cataloging. It can defend itself against this charge only if it repeats the phenomenological research that was done by Husserl, A. Pfänder (1870-1941), M. Scheler (1874-1928), M. Geiger (1880-1937), W. Schapp (1884-1965), H. Conrad-Martius (1888-1966), F. A. Grimme (1889-1963), and others, research that was often ignored or misunderstood.

1.2. Chantepie de la Saussaye was aware of his indebtedness to Hegel's *Lectures on the Philosophy of Religion* (1821, 1827, 1831), for these lectures brought to light the relation between the metaphysical, psychological, and historical sides of the problem of religion. He thus integrated his whole study of religion into the philosophy and history of religion. His concept of the nature of religion, replacing Hegel's "phenomenology of spirit" (1807), governed not merely his arrangement and evaluation of religious phenomena but also his explanation of phenomena as religious.

G. van der Leeuw (1890-1950) and M. Eliade (1907-86) in a Platonic way, and F. Heiler (1892-1967) in a Neoplatonic, and all three also in a Christian manner, wanted to make that which would otherwise escape us into something that can be the possibility or the consequence of faith. Van der Leeuw did not apply Husserl's "phenomenological reduction" to an analogue of the original phenomenon (i.e., relation to the object), as religious studies demanded, but focused on the "religious act" in the sense of Scheler, so that this act would be the presupposition for an "understanding" of the phenomenon (along the lines of → vitalism) and also of the existential religious attitude.

In a stereotyped way Eliade based that which is shown to us in religion on the holy, which is saturated with being and can suffer diminution only at the hands of history. Heiler regarded phenomena as peripheral, since they are sensory, institutional, and practical. We need to push on from them, by way of the world of ideas and experience, to their central divine reality. Neither practiced an epoche, or suspension of judgment. Van der Leeuw and K. Goldammer (b. 1916) did so, but in spite of their intention substituted erroneous themes — the former, that which lies behind phenomena; the latter, the historical relation that structures and evaluates. Goldammer in the process arrived at an essence of religious "forms" rather than religion.

In E. O. James (1888-1972) and G. Widengren (1907-96) we find a historical structure. Since the forms change, however, there is insufficient evaluation of what is existentially religious. D. Allen was the first to hit on the correct approach, using the standpoint of both the history of religion and phenomenology.

2. Religious Phenomena

Religious phenomena appear in the form of certain expressed or silent *feelings* (e.g., of trust, based on the father image, or of → anxiety), then as *ideas* (e.g., of God or the gods, of judgment, or of light and darkness), then as the *contents of belief* (e.g., → truth, redemption, or temptation), then as *actions* (e.g., → circumcision, rituals, attitudes in prayer). Finally, they appear all together in → *institutions.*

The implied interpretations also make religious phenomena (in more than one religion) out of *natural things,* such as meteorites, springs, or the flight of birds; *manufactured objects,* such as a bull-roarer, processional boats, or altars; or → *symbols,* such as the use of many arms to denote a plurality of powers, as in the case of the gods of India. The phenomena range from the simple (needing no more than two elements) to the complex (involving more than two, e.g., in the case of the so-called truce of God).

3. Features of Religion

For the religions each individual phenomenon is also a religious feature. Even in a complex religion a *simple phenomenon* is still a single feature (e.g., the menhir in Neolithic religion, the stone at Bethel in ancient → Israel, the meteorite at Pessinus in the Cybele-Attis mysteries, or the black stone in the Kaaba at Mecca; → Islam). A *complex phenomenon,* though made up of many elements, may still be a single feature (e.g., the laying down or outlawing of weapons, the protection of the weak, the designation of certain places or times as holy, ecclesiastical sanctions, the trend toward a theory of peace rather than just war). But it may also be seen as displaying many features, which then become *secondary features* of the religion concerned.

A symbol that is found in only one religion (e.g., nirvana in → Buddhism) or a symbol that stands for something specific (e.g., the seven-branched candelabra for → resurrection in the light of the Jewish law, or the → fish for the Son of God and Savior in Christianity) counts as a feature of only the one religion and not as an interreligious phenomenon. The phenomenology of religion must focus on religious phenomena and individual features of this kind. If one religion as a whole is studied as a phenomenon, then we have the typology of religions, not the phenomenology of religion.

4. Tasks

4.1. The first task of the phenomenology of religion is to name the phenomena. In the process of naming, however, we cannot naively assume that what is to be named is already existent. In some sense the naming must have a part in constituting the object, so that a dialectical relation exists between positing and naming. Naming, then, is a transcendental action in the sense of a Kantian schematizing (→ Kantianism).

The phenomenology of religion must test as well as catalog and classify phenomena, to see whether they are religious or not. We thus have here the presupposition for a second-stage epoche, namely, withholding judgment about whether the phenomenon is authentically or validly religious.

The phenomenology of religion knows no substitute religion. This fact makes it possible to discern the element of intentionality, that is, the direction in which our consciousness focuses on the uniqueness of the phenomenon (i.e., that which makes it what it is), which naturally also includes its historical embeddedness. Eidetic intuition can then lead us into awareness of the *logos* of a phenomenon (→ Phenomenology 2-3).

4.2. Understood in this way, the phenomenology of religion neither offers a basis for religion nor involves criticism of it (→ Religion, Criticism of). It neither relativizes → faith nor confirms it. Along with philosophical phenomenology and other relevant disciplines, it makes a contribution toward achieving the ideal of knowledge and reflection on matters of → anthropology and the history of culture by finding a place for religious phenomena, which are misunderstood but cannot be ignored.

→ Psychology of Religion

Biblography: D. Allen, "Phenomenology of Religion," *EncRel(E)* 11.272-85; idem, *Structure and Creativity in Religion* (The Hague, 1978) • A. Barbosa da Silva, *The Phenomenology of Religion as a Philosophical Problem* (Uppsala, 1982) • C. Colpe, "Religionstypen und Religionsklassen," *Selected Proceedings of the Sixteenth Congress of the International Association for the History of Religions* (Rome, 1994); idem, "The Science of Religion, the History of Religion, and the Phenomenology of Religion," *History, Historiography, and the History of Religions* (= *HR/RH* 20 [1994]) 403-12; idem, "Zur Neubegründung einer Phänomenologie der Religionen und der Religion," *Religionswissenschaft* (ed. P. L. Zinser; Berlin, 1988) 131-54 • M. Eliade, *Patterns in Comparative Religion* (New York, 1963) • G. D. Flood, *Beyond Phenomenology: Rethinking the Study of Religion* (London, 1999) • E. O. James, *Comparative Religion* (2d ed.; New York, 1961) • R. Kearney, *The God Who May Be: A Hermeneutics of Religion* (Bloomington, Ind., 2001) • S. D. Kunin, *Religion: The Modern Theories* (Baltimore, 2003) • G. van der Leeuw, *Religion in Essence and Manifestation* (2 vols.; Gloucester, Mass., 1967; orig. pub., 1933) • P. R. McKenzie, *The Christians: Their Practices and Beliefs. An Adaptation of Friedrich Heiler's "Phenomenology of Religion"* (Nashville, 1988) • O. Pettersson and H. Åkerberg, *Interpreting Religious Phenomena: Studies with Reference to the Phenomenology of Religion* (Stockholm, 1981) • J. W. Robbins, *Between Faith and Thought: An Essay on the Ontotheological Condition* (Charlottesville, Va., 2003) • M. Scheler, *On the Eternal in Man* (New York,

1961; orig. pub., 1921) • A. SHARMA, *To the Things Themselves: Essays on the Discourse and Practice of the Phenomenology of Religion* (Berlin, 2001) • G. WIDENGREN, *Religionsphänomenologie* (Berlin, 1969).

CARSTEN COLPE

Philadelphian Society

1. History
2. Beliefs

1. History

The Philadelphian Society was a dissenting movement in England in the late 17th and early 18th century, with adherents and patrons in the Netherlands and the Germanies. Its name derives from the Philadelphian church described in the Book of Revelation (3:7-13). In 1652 the Anglican clergyman John Pordage (1607-81) gathered a circle of seekers in Bradfield (Berks) to study the writings of Jakob Böhme (1575-1624; → Mysticism 2.5.2); they did not separate from the church (→ Anglican Communion). By 1674 Jane Leade (1624-1704), a widow, had become the leader of these Behmenists. Although she had little formal schooling, she won two former Oxford scholars, Dr. Francis Lee and Richard Roach, to her following, persuaded, as they were, that she had prophetic powers. Under their leadership the society took on more organized form, having at its height perhaps 100 members. They also assisted Leade in the further publication of her visionary works, which she had initiated in 1681.

A handsome gift from Baron von Knyphausen in 1694 allowed Leade's group to establish a center in London and to pursue further publication. After 1697 the society held many public meetings to popularize its beliefs and began the journal *Theosophical Transactions* (→ Theosophy). Beginning in 1698 many of Leade's works were published in Dutch and German translations in Amsterdam, eliciting considerable interest on the Continent. In 1703 the society sent a representative, Johann Dittmar, to the Netherlands and the German states to establish branches there; he claimed (not always accurately) over 100 German sympathizers within a short time. The Petersens — Johann Wilhelm (1649-1727) and Joanna Eleonora (1644-1724) — were the best known of the adherents. Heinrich Horche, Johann Heinrich Reitz, and Johann Friedrich Haug were other prominent Philadelphians, although they resisted organization, preferring an informal fellowship. Such circles developed in Württemberg, Hesse, Wittgenstein, and the Harz region. Johann Samuel Carl (1676?-1757) issued the *Geistliche Fama* (Spiritual report) in Wittgenstein to keep contact among them.

After Leade's death in 1704, Richard Roach gave leadership to the Philadelphian Society. When → Huguenot refugees called the French Prophets arrived in England three years later, the Philadelphians at first associated themselves with them, occasioning renewed public notice, albeit unfavorable in tone. Roach died in 1730, and the society faded from view.

With the recent wave of feminist interest in women as religious leaders has come more interest in Leade's writings. Her → visions are currently acclaimed by several alternative religions, especially by the House of David and its continuation, Mary's City of David (Benton Harbor, Mich.).

2. Beliefs

Basically pursuing a Behmenist theosophy, the Philadelphians incorporated Leade's chiliastic and adventist ideas (→ Millenarianism). The "Sardic" period of persecution of true believers, it maintained, was giving way to the Philadelphian church, a spiritual gathering of the reborn who receive the "Everlasting Gospel." Of particular interest was Leade's championing of universal restoration, the belief that a loving God would restore all humanity after death at some unknown time (→ Apocatastasis). As an autodidact, she never placed her visionary writings in systematic forms, content to allow them to stand as cosmic insights for the adept.

Bibliography: D. F. DURNBAUGH, "Jane Ward Leade and the Philadelphians," *The Pietist Theologians* (ed. C. Lindberg; Oxford, 2005) • B. J. GIBBONS, *Gender in Mystical and Occult Thought* (Cambridge, 1996) • S. M. GILBERT and S. GUBAR, eds., *Shakespeare's Sisters: Feminist Essays on Women Poets* (Bloomington, Ind., 1979) • P. McDOWELL, *The Women of Grub Street: Press, Politics, and Gender in the London Literary Marketplace, 1678-1730* (Oxford, 1998) • R. RUETHER and E. McLAUGHLIN, eds., *Women of Spirit: Female Leadership in the Jewish and Christian Traditions* (New York, 1979) • J. M. SPERLE, "God's Healing Angel: A Biography of Jane Ward Lead[e]" (Ph.D. diss., Kent State University, 1985) • N. THUNE, *The Behmenists and the Philadelphians* (Uppsala, 1948) • A. VERSLUIS, *Wisdom's Children: A Christian Esoteric Tradition* (Albany, N.Y., 1999) • D. P. WALKER, *The Decline of Hell: Seventeenth-Century Discussions of Eternal Torment* (Chicago, 1964).

DONALD F. DURNBAUGH

Philemon, Epistle to

The letter to Philemon was one of → Paul's prison letters, possibly written from Ephesus in 53-55. Though sent to an individual, it is not strictly private, for the recipient is called a coworker with a church in his house (vv. 1-2), and Paul writes in association with other fellow workers (1, 23-24). The letter consists chiefly of thanksgiving (4-7) and a petition on behalf of Onesimus (8-21).

Traditionally, expositors have found here a plea on behalf of a slave who had either misappropriated funds and run away or had not returned from a commission (an "example of Christian love" on Paul's part, as M. → Luther in WA.DB 7.292-93 and many others have called it). It should be noted, however, that the petition is limited to a remission of the debt without any thought to an elimination of the condition of enslavement itself (→ Slavery).

Some modern scholars see the picture rather differently. We are not expressly told in Philemon that Onesimus had been guilty of embezzlement or flight. It is more likely that Onesimus had left his master temporarily (as a vagrant, Lat. *erro*) or that he had been sent on an errand to Paul and been converted to Christ (vv. 10, 13) and that Paul had asked him to be a fellow worker. Paul's willingness to make financial restitution for this development (18-19) means that Paul was willing to intervene both charismatically and legally for Onesimus. The position of trust that Onesimus is to receive (15-16) relativizes his status as a slave. In this sense, although Paul does not overcome slavery in any fundamental fashion, he does considerably ease its conditions and in so doing also opens up the ancient church tradition of accepting slaves as officeholders in the early church (→ Ministry, Ministerial Offices).

Philemon also has significance for discussion of the → house church. Paul recognizes fellow workers in such a church but does not mention → bishops and → deacons. Hence the origin of these offices in house church ministries (see Phil. 1:1) remains uncertain.

Bibliography: Commentaries: P. Arzt-Grabner (PKNT; Göttingen, 2003) • M. Barth and H. Blanke (ECC; Grand Rapids, 2000) • J. D. G. Dunn (NIGTC; Grand Rapids, 1996) • J. A. Fitzmyer (AB 34C; New York, 2000) • J. Gnilka (HTKNT 10/4; Freiburg, 1982) • H. Hübner (HNT 12; Tübingen, 1997) • C. F. D. Moule (CGTC; Cambridge, 1957) • P. Stuhlmacher (EKKNT 18; 3d ed.; Neukirchen, 1989) • M. Wolter (ÖTBK 12; Gütersloh, 1993).

Other works: A. D. Callahan, *Embassy of Onesimus* (Valley Forge, Pa., 1997) • J. A. Harrill, "Using the Roman Jurists to Interpret Philemon," *ZNW* 90 (1999) 135-38 • P. Lampe, "Keine 'Sklavenflucht' des Onesimus," *ZNW* 76 (1985) 135-37 • W. Schenk, "Der Brief des Paulus an Philemon in der neueren Forschung (1945-1987)," *ANRW* 2.25.4.3439-95 • G. Schöllgen, "Hausgemeinden, οἶκος–Ekklesiologie und monarchischer Episkopat," *JAC* 31 (1988) 74-90 • C. S. de Vos, "Once a Slave, Always a Slave?" *JSNT* 82 (2001) 89-105 • S. C. Winter, "Paul's Letter to Philemon," *NTS* 33 (1987) 1-15.

Martin Karrer

Philippians, Epistle to the

1. General Features
2. Content
3. History of Reception and the Philippians Hymn

1. General Features

In about a.d. 48/50, and hardly before 40, → Paul founded the first Christian church in Europe in Philippi, which, since the decisive Roman battle of 42 b.c., bore the name "Colonia Julia Philippensis." In the Epistle to the Philippians Paul writes to this church in Greek, although most of the inscriptions from the city are in Latin; he also ignores its military history. The names in the epistle include only one in Latin ("Clement," 4:3). It seems, then, that most of the members did not belong to the city's upper Latin stratum. The names give no evidence of a Jewish core, and apart from Acts 16:13 we find little reference to a Jewish segment in the city. The church must have consisted for the most part of → Gentile Christians (→ Hellenism).

Paul was forced to leave Philippi very quickly (1 Thess. 2:2; see Acts 16:19-40). During his visit he can hardly have set up → bishops. He emphasizes them only in 1:1 (alongside → deacons), without telling us in what follows what the office actually entailed. It seems he did not have any great influence on the general development of the forms of → ministry.

Paul was perhaps alluding to another Philippian tradition in 3:20-21* when he stated that the church has its commonwealth and citizenship in → heaven, so that while integrated into its present situation, it was also distant from it. It resolves the resultant tension quite self-confidently. Even Paul's fellow worker Epaphroditus (named after Aphrodite) retained his pagan name.

2. Content

Though Paul's missionary visit was brief, a close relationship with the apostle was forged. The congregation supported him financially (4:15-16, see also 2 Cor. 11:9). One theory is that he wrote more than one letter to this church and that the present Philippians fused these epistles into one (see Pol. *Phil.* 3.2). In support of this theory it is argued that whereas the leading theme is joy in Christ, in 3:2 there is an abrupt switch to polemics. The dispute extends to 3:21. Individual references to this dispute appear in 4:1-9. A new section then begins in 4:10-20, including thanks for support, which might be linked up with the initial motif of joy. If three letters are discerned, we thus have

1. a letter of joy in 1:1–3:1,
2. a polemical letter against the emergent Judaizers in Philippi (rather than Jewish missionaries) in 3:2-21, and
3. a letter of thanks, or final section, in 4:10-20.

The hypothesis of various divisions, however, leaves unresolved the element of intermingling in 4:1-9, which runs counter to the sequential principle of ancient epistolary collections (→ Literature, Biblical and Early Christian, 2). Hence the notion that the letter represents an integral whole remains at least a possibility, either by way of a successive commitment to the written word corresponding to a changing situation, or — more plausibly — as a conscious structure. The arrangement in this case is as follows. Paul begins with thanksgiving and joy (though with shadows after 1:27). In chap. 3 he expresses his concern that the recipients should stand firm. He combines his themes in 4:1-9 and then in 4:10-20 (or 10-23) cites concrete reasons for returning to his main theme of joy.

Dating letter (3) becomes almost impossible if we split the letter. While the polemic in (2) would recall Galatians, (1) would allude to imprisonment and trial, whether in Ephesus (54/55), Caesarea, or Rome (ca. 60; quite conceivable). If we assume its unity, then (1) would provide the information concerning site and date.

In Philippians Paul combines the ancient rhetoric of friendship with that of consolation, developing all the while a striking Christology (see 3) and advocating joy in Christ, despite suffering. Commensurate with this situation is his attitude toward his own trial in 1:7-26. He makes the → gospel (§1.6), which is the charge against him, his defense. His course has been fixed by the Lord, even though it might mean his death. In 3:4-11 he thus looks back biographically to the great break that came in his life, when, with the knowledge of Christ, the → righteousness of God was revealed to him, a former → Pharisee.

3. History of Reception and the Philippians Hymn

The section 2:1-13 has had the greatest influence. Up to the 19th century it was thought to be Paul's own composition. The early church already was discussing vv. 6-7 in its Logos → Christology, but then it became less prominent in dogmatic history (→ Dogma, History of). V. 13 proved decisive in the → Pelagian controversy (DH 248-49, and then at the Council of → Trent, DH 1541).

Following Paul, the medieval and → Reformation ethics of humility (→ Discipleship 2) found a basis in 2:3, 7. M. → Luther (1483-1546; → Luther's Theology) also gave new Christological weight to v. 7. In its discussion of vv. 7, 9 the older → Protestantism developed its doctrine of the Christological states of humiliation and exaltation (→ Christology 2.2.4). The 19th-century Erlangen school pressed humiliation to the point of → kenosis.

The 20th century advanced the view that in 2:6-11 we have a pre-Pauline → hymn (an encomium) with two stanzas (vv. 6-8 humiliation, 9-11 exaltation). The more precise origin and interpretation are all subject to debate. The discussion has focused especially on whether in 2:11 Jesus is receiving the name (and thus also the majesty) of God in an unqualified fashion and whether 2:6 is referring to preexistence or to the earthly nature of Jesus. (For the phrase "form of God," cf. Gen. 1:27, and cf. Phil. 2:6bc with Gen. 3:5.) Again, are the humiliation and exaltation to be seen in terms of the form of God, or of → Jesus as eschatologically true man (→ Anthropology 2; Eschatology 2)? Soteriologically, it is to be noted that the discussion of Jesus' death in 2:8 does not include a "for," as is usual in Paul (→ Soteriology). Even so, various recent authors are once again ascribing the formulation of the text to Paul himself.

→ Jewish Christians; Righteousness 2.3

Bibliography: Commentaries: K. Barth (Richmond, Va., 1962) • M. Bockmuehl (BNTC 11; Peabody, Mass., 1998) • F. F. Bruce (NIBC; Peabody, Mass., 1989) • G. D. Fee (NICNT; Grand Rapids, 1995) • J. Gnilka (HTKNT 10/3; 3d ed.; Freiburg, 1980) • G. F. Hawthorne (WBC 43; Waco, Tex., 1983) • E. Lohmeyer (KEK 9; 4th ed.; Göttingen, 1964) • R. P. Martin (TNTC 11; Grand Rapids, 1987) • U. B. Müller (THKNT 11/1; Leipzig, 1993) • P. T. O'Brien (NIGTC; Grand Rapids, 1991) • W. Schenk (Stuttgart, 1984) • N. Walter (NTD 8/2; Göttingen, 1998).

Other works: J. Becker, *Paulus* (Tübingen, 1989) 322-50 • L. G. Bloomquist, *The Function of Suffering in Philippians* (Sheffield, 1993) • L. Bormann, *Philippi.*

Stadt und Christengemeinde zur Zeit des Paulus (Leiden, 1995) • R. BRUCKER, *"Christushymnen" oder "epideiktische Passagen"? Studien zum Stilwechsel im Neuen Testament und seiner Umwelt* (Göttingen, 1997) • J. A. FITZMYER, "The Aramaic Background of Philippians 2:6-11," *CBQ* 50 (1988) 470-83 • O. HOFIUS, *Der Christushymnus Phil 2,6-11* (Tübingen, 1976) • P. A. HOLLOWAY, *Consolation in Philippians* (Cambridge, 2001) • V. KOPERSKI, *The Knowledge of Christ Jesus My Lord: The High Christology of Philippians 3:7-11* (Kampen, 1996) • R. P. MARTIN, *Carmen Christi: Philippians 2:5-11 in Recent Interpretation and in the Setting of Early Christian Worship* (Grand Rapids, 1983) • R. P. MARTIN and B. J. DODD, eds., *Where Christology Began: Essays on Philippians 2* (Louisville, Ky., 1998) • P. PILHOFER, *Philippi* (2 vols.; Tübingen, 1995-2000) • J. T. REED, *A Discourse Analysis of Philippians: Method and Rhetoric in the Debate over Literary Integrity* (Sheffield, 1997) • M. RISSI, "Der Christushymnus in Phil 2,6-11," *ANRW* 2.25.4.3314-26 • U. SCHNELLE, *Paulus. Leben und Denken* (Berlin, 2003).

MARTIN KARRER

Philippines

	1960	*1980*	*2000*
Population (1,000s):	27,560	48,317	75,037
Annual growth rate (%):	3.01	2.47	1.80

Area: 300,076 sq. km. (115,860 sq. mi.)

A.D. 2000

Population density: 250/sq. km. (648/sq. mi.)
Births / deaths: 2.56 / 0.54 per 100 population
Fertility rate: 3.24 per woman
Infant mortality rate: 30 per 1,000 live births
Life expectancy: 69.8 years (m: 68.0, f: 71.7)
Religious affiliation (%): Christians 89.7 (Roman Catholics 83.1, indigenous 20.5, Protestants 4.4, unaffiliated 3.0, marginal 1.2, other Christians 0.2), Muslims 6.3, tribal religionists 2.7, other 1.3.

1. General Situation
2. Religious Situation
   2.1. Christianizing
   2.2. Protestant Churches
   2.3. Roman Catholic Church
   2.4. Social Role of the Churches
   2.5. Non-Christian Religions

1. General Situation

The Philippines are the northernmost island group of the Malaysian archipelago in Southeast Asia. They consist of over 7,000 islands, the two largest of which are Luzon in the north (with the capital, Manila) and Mindanao in the south. The 11 largest islands make up over 90 percent of the total land area.

The original inhabitants, the Negritos and the older Malaysians (Igorots, including the Kalinga and Bontoc), along with later Malaysians, converted to Islam and are now cultural → minorities. There are programs of development and protection on their behalf. Ethnic Chinese make up a small minority of about 2 percent. The later-arriving Malaysian majority consists of over 80 people groups, speaking as many languages. Since 1939 Filipino, which is based on Tagalog, has been promoted as the national language. English is also an official national language, spoken by a majority of Filipinos and used in government and higher education.

The first recorded European contact with the Philippines was made in 1521 by the Portuguese explorer Ferdinand Magellan (ca. 1480-1521). The Spaniards conquered the islands in 1565 and 1571 and integrated them into their colonial empire. Between 1565 and 1898 there were more than 100 revolts against Spanish rule. A nationalist movement arose at the end of the 19th century, and serious efforts were made to achieve independence after 1872. The writings of José Rizal (1861-96), among others, played a significant role in mobilizing the struggle for independence. In 1897 General Emilio Aguinaldo (1869-1964) was declared the president of a revolutionary government. The Spanish-American War of 1898 brought liberation from the Spaniards but transferred foreign rule into the hands of the United States, which had paid Spain $20 million to acquire the Philippines in the Treaty of Paris. The United States did not recognize Aguinaldo's government, and a costly guerrilla war ensued, lasting from 1899 to 1901.

In 1935 the Commonwealth of the Philippines, with Manuel Quezon as president, was established to prepare the country for political and economic independence after a ten-year transition period. World War II and the Japanese invasion intervened, but independence was finally granted in 1946, with a government patterned on that of the United States. Economic and military dependence on the United States continued, however; not until the 1960s did the Philippines break free economically. The last U.S. military forces departed the Philippines in 1992.

In 1965 Ferdinand Marcos (1917-89) was elected president. Marcos declared martial law in 1972, citing the threats of Communist rebellion and increasing lawlessness. Political parties were dissolved, and the press and justice system were tightly controlled, though with some liberalizing after 1981. Under Communist influence the National Democratic Front (NDF) organized opposition to the regime. This front included Christians for National Liberation (CNL). Its military organization, the New People's Army (NPA), brought some regions under its control. The assassination of opposition leader Benigno S. Aquino in 1983 led to mass demonstrations against the Marcos regime, which the → Roman Catholic Church joined in opposing. Fraudulent elections in 1986 sparked massive protests that resulted in the overthrow of the Marcos regime and came to be known as the People's Power movement. Corazon Aquino, widow of the slain opposition leader, came to power in 1986, and Marcos and his wife fled the country. A new constitution was approved under Aquino's government in February 1987. The new government, however, faced several coup attempts and could not establish the new order that it had promised, especially in land reform. The NPA continued its armed resistance, and conflict became sharper as anti-Communist defense groups were formed, the so-called Vigilantes, who were in part tolerated and in part supported at official levels. Many members of Christian → base communities and action groups were victims of these death squads.

New presidential elections were held in early 1992, won by the former defense minister General Fidel Ramos. His administration was marked by greater stability, progress on economic reforms, and efforts to reconcile with rebel groups. Joseph Estrada was elected president in 1998 but faced an impeachment trial on corruption charges in 2000. After widespread demonstrations following a breakdown of his trial, his vice-president, Gloria Macapagal-Arroyo, succeeded Estrada as president in January 2001 and then, in 2004, was elected to a six-year term of her own.

The Philippine government still faces threats from armed Communist insurgencies and from Muslim separatists in the south. The government has cracked down on the separatist group Abu Sayyaf, which gained notoriety in 2001 for the kidnapping and murder of foreigners. A semiautonomous Muslim region has been created in the south, and some steps toward reconciliation have been taken. Tensions remain, however, and there has been recurring violence.

The Asian financial crisis of 1998 affected the Philippines less severely than its neighbors. A significant factor was the high level of remittances (annually, $6-7 billion) received from its overseas workers.

In recent years serious natural disasters have struck the Philippines, including earthquakes, typhoons, and the eruption of Mount Pinatubo in June 1991, after it had lain dormant for centuries. These disasters caused many deaths and uprooted more than 250,000 people from their homes. The population has commonly interpreted these events as God's punishment for national moral failings.

2. Religious Situation

2.1. *Christianizing*

Christianity was brought to the Philippines by the Spaniards in the 16th century (→ Colonialism and Mission), in particular by the → Augustinians (1565), → Franciscans (1578), → Jesuits (1581), → Dominicans (1587), and Recollects (1606). The Spanish mission adopted the same practices as in Mexico (→ Mexico 2.1; Mission), and Mexican officials played a role in the administration of the Philippines. The 17th and 18th centuries brought protests and revolts against the corruption of the Spanish monks, and then in the 19th century, because of the loyalty of the religious orders to Spain, there were anticlerical and national independence movements that the national clergy joined. Thus the 1896-98 revolution was directed especially against the orders. The revolutionary government expelled the orders and confiscated their property. It appointed the priest Gregorio Aglipay (1860-1940), a member of Congress, as vicar-general.

After his → excommunication in 1902, Aglipay founded the Iglesia Filipina Independiente (Philippine Independence Church, PIC) in Manila, which had a nationalist orientation and to which a sizable minority of Roman Catholics belonged. Under American rule the replacement of Spanish bishops by Americans, Irish, Germans, and nationals weakened the original motive for the PIC schism. This development, along with the weight of tradition, strong kinship and social ties, and a favorable court settlement of Roman Catholic Church properties in 1906, enabled the church to recoup many of its 1902 losses; with its revival, PIC membership declined. Under the theological leadership of Isabelo de los Reyes (1864-1938), the PIC adopted → Unitarian doctrines, but after his death it returned to more orthodox Catholic teaching. In 1961 it allied itself with the Philippine Episcopal Church (PEC) in a mutual recognition of ministry and sacraments (intercommunion). It enjoys relations with many churches of the → Anglican Communion and with → Old Catholic churches. In 2000 it had 5.5 million members.

After the Spanish-American War Protestant missions began with the arrival of American Presbyterians and Methodists in 1899 (→ Methodist Churches), → Baptists and → Christian Missionary Alliance in 1900, Episcopalians, United Brethren, and Disciples of Christ in 1901, Congregationalists in 1902, and → Adventists in 1906 (→ North American Missions). Identified with the new American rule, Protestantism appealed to those seeking new values and a new place in society, drawing its first converts from the educated classes and upper middle classes. Strong nationalistic sentiments from 1900 to 1935 led to schisms from missionary-controlled churches. Two Methodist schisms produced the Iglesia Evangélica Metodista en las Islas Filipinas (1909) and the Philippine Methodist Church (1933). There were also minor schisms among the Presbyterians.

In 1913 Felix Manalo (1886-1963) founded an independent evangelical movement that resulted in the indigenous Iglesia ni Cristo (INC, Church of Christ). It claims to be the only true church and the only means to salvation, and it openly opposes both Roman Catholic and Protestant churches. It rejects traditional beliefs about the Trinity, the deity of Christ, and life after death. The church's hierarchy is highly authoritarian, and membership requirements, such as tithing and twice-weekly church attendance, are strictly enforced. Admission to church meetings is tightly controlled and forbidden to nonmembers. The INC instructs its members on how to vote and accordingly wields considerable political power. The INC has appealed to the lower socioeconomic classes and, through job-training programs, has been successful in raising the standard of living for its adherents. The church has experienced substantial growth and now has over 200 congregations in 67 countries outside the Philippines. The exact number of members is kept secret, but estimates range from 3 to 10 million worldwide, with perhaps 4 million members in the Philippines in 2000.

The → Mormons, who arrived in the Philippines in 1955, numbered 430,000 adherents in the year 2000; → Jehovah's Witnesses, in the country since 1912, numbered 400,000.

2.2. *Protestant Churches*

The early Protestant missionaries were imbued with a strong sense of unity and cooperation, which led to the Evangelical Alliance of 1901, then the National Christian Council in 1929, the Philippine Federation of Evangelical Churches in 1938, the Philippine Federation of Christian Churches in 1948, and the → National Council of Churches in the Philippines (NCCP) in 1963. The NCCP is a conciliar body that first included the PIC and PEC and then at a later stage the Philippine Lutheran Church and the → Salvation Army.

The first successful Protestant church → union was the United Evangelical Church of 1929, which brought together the Presbyterians, Congregationalists, and United Brethren. Inspired by this merger, the previous Presbyterian schisms united in 1931 to form the Iglesia Evangélica Unida de Cristo (UNIDA). In 1948 a larger merger, the United Church of Christ in the Philippines (UCCP), brought into one church the United Evangelical Church, the Philippine Methodist Church, and the Evangelical Church in the Philippines.

Before 1948 a few other Protestant denominations had entered the Philippines, such as the U.S. Lutheran Church–Missouri Synod, the Reformed Church in America (working mainly with the Chinese), the Assemblies of God, and the International Church of the Foursquare Gospel. With the closure of China to foreign missionary work in 1950, many new missionaries, mostly conservative evangelicals from America (esp. Baptists and Pentecostals), entered the country. In 1965 some of these workers formed the Philippine Council of Fundamental Evangelical Churches, while others who were not fundamentalists came together as the Philippine Council of Evangelical Churches (→ World Evangelical Alliance).

2.3. *Roman Catholic Church*

The Roman Catholic Church in the Philippines embraces well over 80 percent of the population, far more than the percentage of Catholics in any other Asian nation. It was at first heavily under Spanish influence but now takes many different and colorful forms. Within it → popular piety has sycretistic features (→ Syncretism). The constitution ratified in 1987, like its predecessors, separates → church and state but recognizes the cooperation of Roman Catholic → bishops. Thus elements of Roman Catholic social teaching (→ Social Ethics) have been adopted as state goals, including the sanctity of the family and protection for the unborn (art. 2). The church is guaranteed freedom from taxation and allowed to give religious instruction at public schools. → Opus Dei, which has set up a center for research and communications in Manila, is very influential.

As of 2003, in the 53 dioceses, 6 prelatures, and 8 apostolic vicariates, 63.7 million members are under the jurisdiction of 99 bishops. At work are 5,122 diocesan priests, 2,492 priests attached to orders, 627 brothers, and 11,044 sisters.

After 1965, parish priests, seminary students, members of orders (Jesuits), and the laity became socially involved in opposition to the conservative theological and social stance of the hierarchy. They helped to found unions of farmers and workers and centers of social action. In some dioceses base communities came to control church life. Emerging from the conflict with the bishops was the Mindanao Interfaith People's Conference, in which Christians work together with Muslims and tribal groups. Theological discussion goes hand in hand with social involvement. Struggles with the Marcos government and the sufferings of small farmers and slum dwellers stirred up reflection on a theology of conflict (M. R. Battung et al.). Filipino theology, however, has recourse to popular culture and Christology in opposition to a "wrongly understood inculturation" of European ideas (B. P. Beltran; → Christology 5).

In 1991 the Second Plenary Council of the Philippines showed that a learning process had begun among the bishops that would pay greater attention to the base communities. The council declared the need to become a church of the poor, emphasized the importance of becoming a true community of disciples, and committed itself to engage in renewed integral evangelization (→ Liberation Theology). In 2001 the Catholic Bishops' Conference of the Philippines convoked the National Pastoral Consultation on Church Renewal, which evaluated the progress made in the years since the 1991 council and called for greater implementation of, and renewed focus on, the council's recommendations.

Various charismatic renewal movements have appeared within the church, the largest of which has come to be known as El Shaddai. This movement is led by Mariano Velarde, a former businessman who is affectionately known by his followers as Brother Mike. El Shaddai, which has been called a Catholic prosperity movement, appeals to the lower classes, teaching that there are rewards for them on earth and not only in heaven. Velarde conducts weekly open-air gatherings in Manila, at which attendance can reach half a million or more. His following has been estimated to be as high as 8-10 million people (2004).

2.4. *Social Role of the Churches*

Initially, the early Protestant churches generally followed a threefold pattern of mission — evangelistic, educational, and medical — and presented a united voice in social issues (→ Medical Missions). With the rise of government health services and private hospitals, religious medical work became less important, but from the 1970s onward a new emphasis developed on social justice both in the NCCP churches and in the Roman Catholic Church. This involvement, which reached a high point in the People's Power movement of 1986, was dominated by Roman Catholics but also included Protestants. Both groups operate universities, schools, and radio stations, do medical work, are concerned for community development, have relief organizations, and are active in publishing.

To fight for women's rights and to combat the exploitation of women, in 1984 several Roman Catholic and Protestant women's organizations founded a joint society known as Gabriela. This society set up the Buklod Women's Center in Olongapo, near a former U.S. naval base, which counseled women on how to escape from → prostitution and offered skill training and help with child care. Other organizations that have been formed to help and protect women are the Coalition against Trafficking in Women and the Women's Education, Development, Productivity, and Research Organization.

In questions and problems of social justice, Roman Catholics and Protestants work together at many different levels. At several points conservative evangelicals also take part, though less so in social problems, since they generally focus their efforts on → evangelism (using radio and television) and church growth.

2.5. *Non-Christian Religions*

Muslims (→ Islam) constitute a sizable minority of over 4 million (2000), most of them living on Mindanao. Muslim armed resistance to the central government (Moro National Liberation Front, Moro Islamic Liberation Front, and other groups) has aroused international concern. For some years Christian groups have had an active concern for → dialogue with Muslims (→ Islam and Christianity).

There are some 2 million ethnoreligionists (animists, shamanists), predominantly among the tribal mountain dwellers. → Baha'i has grown steadily, with over 200,000 adherents in 2000.

Bibliography: G. H. Anderson, ed., *Studies in Philippine Church History* (Ithaca, N.Y., 1969) • M. R. Battung et al., eds., *Theologie des Kampfes. Christliche Nachfolgepraxis in den Philippinen* (Münster, 1989) • B. P. Beltran, *Philippinische Theologie* (Düsseldorf, 1988) • S. Burton, *Impossible Dream: The Marcoses, the Aquinos, and the Unfinished Revolution* (New York, 1989) • R. L. Deats, *Nationalism and Christianity in the Philippines* (Dallas, 1967) • K. M. Nadeau, *Liberation Theology in the Philippines: Faith in a Revolution* (Westport, Colo., 2002) • J. D. Rasul, *Agonies and Dreams: The Filipino Muslims and Other Minorities* (Quezon City, 2003) • S. Shirley, *Guided by God: The Legacy of the Catholic Church in Philippine Politics* (Singapore, 2004) • T. V. Sitoy Jr., *A History of Christianity in the Philippines* (Quezon City, 1985) • D. J. STEINBERG, *The Philippines: A Singular and a Plural Place* (Boulder, Colo., 2000) • M. YEGAR, *Between Integration and Secession: The Muslim Communities of the Southern Philippines, Southern Thailand, and Western Burma/ Myanmar* (Lanham, Md., 2002) • R. L. YOUNGBLOOD, *Marcos against the Church: Economic Development and Political Repression in the Philippines* (Ithaca, N.Y., 1990).

T. VALENTINO SITOY JR.

Philippism → Crypto-Calvinism

Philistines

The term "Philistines," which renders Heb. *pělištîm,* occurs 286 times in the OT, 152 of these in 1 Samuel. The LXX Hexateuch uses the corresponding words *phylistiim* (12 times) and *allophylos* (lit. "of another tribe," 269 times).

The Philistines were an important political and military force on the southern coastal plain of → Palestine from the beginning of the Iron Age (1150 B.C.) to the eighth-century Assyrian campaigns. They are undoubtedly to be equated with the *Plśt/ Prśt* of the Egyptian Medinet Habu texts. In the early days of the → monarchy they were Israel's most dangerous foes. Their military power destroyed → Saul, but → David managed to gain definitive mastery over them.

A reference in the Medinet Habu texts groups them with the sea peoples, who at the end of the Late Bronze Age profited from upheavals in the eastern Mediterranean and themselves contributed to them. They could have had a longer history of contacts with Palestine, even if the accounts of the sea and land battle of Ramses III (ca. 1184-1153 B.C.) in Medinet Habu are regarded as ideologically exaggerated. The Philistines came from Caphtor/Keftiu (Crete, see Jer. 47:4 and Amos 9:7, or perhaps Cyprus or Asia Minor).

Their Palestinian territory had the Wadi Gaza as its southern border, the Yarqon River its northern, and the sea its western, but no fixed border to the east (at the end of the Shephelah). Especially Gath (Tell es-Safi?), which formed the pentapolis with Gaza, Ashkelon, Ashdon, and Ekron (Tell Miqne), was often fought over. This league constituted the heartland. The city-states and their princes (*sěrānîm,* "lords") filled the vacuum left by Egypt and engaged in vigorous expansion.

Philistine culture was fairly fully integrated with that of Canaan. At the end of the late Bronze Age their luxury ceramics replaced imported ceramics. The anthropoid sarcophagi are no longer regarded as theirs. Tell Qasile (near ancient Joppa) was a new foundation of the Philistines. The background of their religion was Canaanite, their deities being Baal-zebub, Astarte (or Ashtart), and Dagon. Nothing is known for certain about their language.

Bibliography: J. F. BRUG, *A Literary and Archaeological Study of the Philistines* (Oxford, 1985) • T. DOTHAN, *Excavations at the Cemetery of Deir el Balaḥ* (Jerusalem, 1979); eadem, *The Philistines and Their Material Culture* (New Haven, 1982) • T. DOTHAN and M. DOTHAN, *People of the Sea: The Search for the Philistines* (New York, 1992) • C. S. EHRLICH, "'How the Mighty Are Fallen': The Philistines in Their Tenth-Century Context," *The Age of Solomon* (ed. L. K. Handy; Leiden, 1997) 179-201; idem, *The Philistines in Transition: A History from ca. 1000-730* B.C.E. (LEIDEN, 1996) • K. A. KITCHEN, "The Philistines," *Peoples of OT Times* (ed. D. Wiseman; Oxford, 1973) 53-79 • W. S. LASOR, "Philistines," *ISBE* 3.841-46 • A. MAZAR, *Excavations at Tell Qasile: The Philistine Sanctuary* (2 vols.; Jerusalem, 1980-85) • E. NOORT, *Die Seevölker in Palästina* (Kampen, 1994) • E. D. OREN, ed., *The Sea Peoples and Their World: A Reassessment* (Philadelphia, 2000) • J. STRANGE, *Caphtor, Keftiu: A New Investigation* (Leiden, 1980).

EDWARD NOORT

Philocalia

The word "Philocalia" (love [Gk. *philia*] of what is beautiful [*kalos*]), along with *kalokagathia* (the beautiful and the good), expresses the Greek ideal of a combination of the aesthetic and the ethical (→ Aesthetics; Ethics). It denotes love of, or striving for, the beautiful, → good, and noble. In the → Orthodox Church we find that the term is used more specifically for anthologies that have influenced Orthodox → theology and → spirituality.

1. The oldest Philocalia goes back to Basil of Caesarea (ca. 330-79) and his friend Gregory of Nazianzus (329/30-389/90), who compiled the *Ōrigenous philokalia* (Philocalia of Origen), an anthology of the writings of → Origen (ca. 185-ca. 254).

2. The main use of "Philocalia," however, is for the *Philokalia tōn hierōn nēptikōn* (Philocalia of the holy sober ones), which Bishop Macarius Notaras of Corinth (1731-1805) and the monk Nicodemus of the Holy Mountain ("The Hagiorite," ca. 1749-1809;

→ Athos) published in Venice in 1782. It is a comprehensive collection of ascetic-mystical and → Hesychastic texts from 38 Greek authors of the 4th to 14th centuries, offering either extracts or full works (→ Asceticism; Mysticism; Palamism) and dealing in particular with the Jesus Prayer. It helped to shape and inspire Orthodox spirituality from the 19th century onward.

This Philocalia made a particularly strong impact in the Old Church Slavonic translation, which was the work of the Startsy adherent Paisy Velichovsky (1722-94; → Starets), who had come to know the work while at Mount Athos. The first Old Church Slavonic edition of 1793, called *Dobrotoliubie,* was not exactly the same as the Greek. Bishop Theophan the Recluse (1815-94) published a Russian version in 1877-89. Literature testifies to the widespread influence of the work in Russia. Other redactions and independent Philocalic collections have also helped to give life to Orthodox spirituality.

3. The Patriarchal Institute for Patristic Studies in Thessaloníki initiated a new Philocalia when in 1978, in its patristic series (→ Church Fathers), it chose the title *Philokalia tōn nēptikōn kai askētikōn* (Philocalia of the sober ones and ascetics) for an announced 30-volume collection of Eastern ascetic writings, a work designed to bear witness to the mystical theology and spirituality of the Orthodox churches and to their identity.

The many new Philocalia anthologies of this type highlight a key feature of Orthodoxy (→ Orthodoxy Christianity) as it tries to spread more widely the traditional spiritual experience it has gained over the centuries and around the world.

Bibliography: On 1: Origen, *Sur les Écritures. Philocalie, 1-20* (trans. M. Harl; Paris, 1983); idem, *Sur le libre arbitre. Philocalie 21-27* (trans. É. Junod; Paris, 1976) • J. A. Robinson, ed., *The Philocalia of Origen* (Cambridge, 1893).

On 2: E. Kadloubovsky and G. E. H. Palmer, trans., *Writings from the Philokalia on Prayer of the Heart* (London, 1992) trans. from *Dobrotoliubie* • G. E. H. Palmer et al., trans., *The Philokalia: The Complete Text* (4 vols.; comp. St. Nikodimos of the Holy Mountain and St. Makarios of Corinth; London, 1979-95) • *Philokalia tōn hierōn nēptikōn* (Venice, 1782; 2d ed., Athens, 1893; 3d ed., 5 vols., Athens, 1957-63). For a summary of editions in other languages, see *DSp* 12.1343-48.

On 3: Philokalia tōn nēptikōn kai askētikōn (Thessaloníki, 1978ff.) 30 vols. planned.

Secondary works: R. Antoniadou, "Le thème du coeur dans la Philocalie," *Contacts* 34 (1982) 235-47, 323-37; 35 (1983) 71-74 • J. A. McGuckin, *Standing in God's Holy Fire: The Byzantine Tradition* (Maryknoll, N.Y., 2001) • M. Pirard, "Le Starez paisij Velickovskij (1722-1794). La tradition philologico-ascétique en Russie et en Europa orientale," *Messager de l'Exarchat du Patriarchat russe en Europe occidentale* 21 (1973) 35-57 • T. Spidlik, *The Spirituality of the Christian East: A Systematic Handbook* (Kalamazoo, Mich., 1986) • J. Touraille, *Le Christ dans la Philocalie* (Paris, 1995) • K. Ware, "Philocalie," *DSp* 12.1336-52.

Anastasios Kallis

Philology → History, Auxiliary Sciences to, 2

Philo-Semitism

1. Term
2. Jewish Evaluation
3. National Socialism
4. After 1945
5. Anglo-Saxon Use
6. Original Use

1. Term

In Germany the term "Philosemitismus" was originally a political rather than a theological one. It was coined with an anti-Semitic thrust in Berlin during the anti-Semitism controversy of 1880. H. von Treitschke (1834-96) used it for the first time in December 1880 when, in a debate in the Chamber of Deputies, he spoke of the "blind philo-Semitic zeal of the party of progress." T. Mommsen (1817-1903) had referred earlier to pro- and anti-Semitic attitudes and had spoken of "friends of the Jews" as opposed to anti-Semites. In January 1880 W. Ender had denounced non-Jewish Germans who had adopted so-called Jewish principles as Jewish fellow travelers. In June 1895 the first number of the journal *Im Deutschen Reich* referred to the division of the → political parties into the two groups of philo- and anti-Semites, the former taking the view that all citizens should be equal before the law and thus incurring the charge of being fellow travelers with the Jews. As late as 1912 the *Jüdische Rundschau* could complain of the aristocratic leaders of the Right being hostile to Jews and their associates.

In a second political sense the term ceased to be a term of denunciation hurled at the Left by the Right and became a term used in condemning the Right. The basis now was the statement of K. → Marx

(1818-83; → Marxism) in his "Zur Judenfrage" (1843; ET "On the Jewish Question") to the effect that "the bill of exchange is the real god of the Jew" (*MECW* 3.172). F. Mehring (1846-1919) could argue that since 1890 philo-Semitism had simply been a last ideological cloak for capitalist exploitation (→ Capitalism) that the socialist press had to fight (→ Socialism). He could speak equally of philo-Semitic capitalists and capitalist philo-Semites. Over against anti-Semitism he set "the brutalities of philo-Semitism," which are more a matter of deeds than of words. His struggle against middle-class philo-Semitism thus followed the line of revolutionary Marxism.

The term took on a third sense in the context of → Jewish missions. In 1884 J. F. A. de Le Roi described as philo-Semites those who, in the "destructive" conflict between Jews and Christians, promote a love that stops short of leading (Christian) truth on to victory. On his view philo-Semitism meant siding with the Jews against both anti-Semitism and Jewish missions for nonreligious reasons. In 1893 he set Treitschke and his desire to maintain the Christian character of Germany over against the philo-Semite Mommsen, who with his defense of the Jews did not even satisfy the Jews themselves.

A fourth use is found among thinkers who saw no Jewish question. In 1897 W. Rathenau (1867-1922) in *Höre Israel* stated that philo-Semites usually say there is no Jewish question. If Jews do harm, only a few are responsible. Let laws be passed or existing laws be strengthened to stop them. The exact reference in this case is not clear. J. G. → Herder (1744-1803) had formulated and fostered a view of this kind in his 1802 article "Bekehrung der Juden" (Conversion of the Jews). Though he did not use the term "philo-Semitism," we might perhaps regard him as the father of the type of philo-Semitism that sees no Jewish question.

This fourfold use shows that we cannot simply regard philo-Semitism as anti-anti-Semitism and why C. Brunner (1862-1937) in 1917 made a distinction at this point. Philo-Semites are always non-Jews, whereas anti-anti-Semites could include all members of the Verein zur Abwehr des Antisemitismus (Association in defense against anti-Semitism) of 1891-1933. Even F. → Nietzsche (1844-1900) could call himself an anti-anti-Semite in 1886; for this reason O. Weininger (1880-1903) in 1903 classified Nietzsche as a prominent philo-Semite along with G. E. Lessing (1729-81).

2. Jewish Evaluation

On the Jewish side J. Klatzkin (1882-1948) offered a critical evaluation of philo-Semitism. He contrasted it with anti-Semitism and concluded that both parties, accusers and liberal advocates alike, sought the destruction of Jewish existence as a people. Their only debate was about the best ways and means to weaken and kill Judaism. He thus proposed the founding of a league to combat philo-Semitism.

L. Feuchtwanger (1884-1958) was equally critical in 1927 in the *Jüdisches Lexikon* when he argued that, from the standpoint of Jewish politics, philo-Semitism had negative significance for all Jewish aspirations when seen in the light of its basic thinking.

3. National Socialism

Under National Socialism (→ Fascism) the term "philo-Semitism" was replaced by expressions like "love of Judaism," "parties friendly to the Jews," or "friends of the Jews," the last term, according to T. Fritsch, including such diverse figures as Mommsen, G. Dalmann, H. Laible, and H. Strack. But "friends of the Jews" now had political significance again, for all Social Democrats (→ Democracy) were seen as either Jews or friends of the Jews.

In 1942 in the Nazi organ *Weltkampf*, W. Grau wrote an article that is especially important for the modern sense of the term. In it he correctly spoke, not of anti-Semitism, but of anti-Judaism, and therefore not of philo-Semitism but of philo-Judaism. Dealing with the era before → emancipation, he had in mind the theological philo-Judaism of the 17th and 18th centuries, and he argued that we must differentiate this theologically based support of Christians for Jews from the political philo-Semitism of the 19th and 20th centuries.

4. After 1945

M. Friedrich has pointed out that after 1948 H.-J. Schoeps (1909-80) dealt with the same figures as Grau had adduced in 1942. He thus introduced the same phenomenon into academic discussion under the title "philo-Semitism." → Baroque, theologically motivated philo-Semitism was the theme of both. We can only conjecture why Schoeps then, in 1952, reverted to the political philo-Semitism of the days of the anti-Semitism controversy. Perhaps it was because other authors were thinking along these lines or because H. Blüher (1888-1955), who had been in debate with him on the issue since 1932, used "philo-Semitism" in a sense that is possible only if Judaism has no historical a priori and hence we cannot speak about it in either religious or historical terms. Schoeps vehemently refuted this view. His relating of philo-Semitism to theologically motivated movements in the 17th and early 18th centuries established itself in German research with only isolated dissent, such as from M. Sperber and L. Marcuse in 1969 and A. Bein in 1980.

5. Anglo-Saxon Use

C. Roth (1899-1970) introduced the term "philo-Semitism" to the Anglo-Saxon world when in his essay "England in Jewish History" (1949) he used the term with a reference to Schoeps's 1948 essay "Der Philosemitismus des 17. Jahrhunderts." In 1962 Roth included his own essay in a symposium but now with the new title "philo-Semitism in England." He thus gave currency to the term in England. As the history of philo-Semitism by A. Edelstein (1982) shows, the usage of Schoeps and Roth has now gained such a hold that the original meanings are completely forgotten.

6. Original Use

Despite the way, since 1948, the term "philo-Semitism" has come to be used for a certain friendliness to Judaism of some thinkers in the 17th century, it is still the case that the term was originally a political slogan in the anti-Semitism controversy. For this reason it is not listed separately in the "Index of Articles on Jewish Studies" (RAMBI) published by the Jewish National and University Library.

→ Jewish Philosophy; Jewish Practices; Jewish Theology; Judaism

Bibliography: J. van den Berg and G. E. van der Wall, eds., *Jewish-Christian Relations in the Seventeenth Century* (Dordrecht, 1988) • C. Brunner, *Der Judenhaß und die Juden* (Berlin, 1917; repr., 2001) • A. Edelstein, *An Unacknowledged Harmony: Philo-semitism and the Survival of European Jewry* (Westport, Conn., 1982) • L. Feuchtwanger, "Philosemitismus," *JL* 4/1.910-14 • M. Friedrich, *Zwischen Abwehr und Bekehrung. Die Stellung der deutschen evangelischen Theologie zum Judentum im 17. Jahrhundert* (Tübingen, 1989) • T. Fritsch, *Handbuch der Judenfrage* (12th ed.; Leipzig, 1933) • J. L. Horowitz, "Philosemitism and Anti-Semitism," *Midstream* 36 (1990) 17-22 • D. S. Katz, *Philo-Semitism and the Readmission of the Jews to England, 1603-1655* (Oxford, 1982) • J. Klatzkin, *Krisis und Entscheidung im Judentum. Die Probleme des modernen Judentums* (2d ed.; Berlin, 1921) • J. F. A. de Le Roi, *Die evangelische Christenheit und die Juden* (vol. 1; Berlin, 1884) • A. T. Levenson, *Between Philosemitism and Antisemitism: Defenses of Jews and Judaism in Germany, 1871-1932* (London, 2004) • I. Massey, *Philo-Semitism in Nineteenth-Century German Literature* (Tübingen, 2000) • F. Mehring, *Die Lessing-Legende. Zur Geschichte und Kritik des preußischen Despotismus und der klassischen Literatur* (Berlin, 1946; orig. pub., 1906; partial ET: *The Lessing Legend* [New York, 1938]) • C. Roth, *Essays and Portraits in Anglo-Jewish History* (Philadelphia, 1962) • W. D. Rubinstein and H. L. Rubinstein, *Philo-semitism: Admiration and Support in the English-Speaking World for Jews, 1840-1939* (New York, 1999) • H.-J. Schoeps, *Barocke Juden, Christen, Judenchristen* (Bern, 1965); idem, "Der Philosemitismus des 17. Jahrhunderts," *ZRGG* 1 (1948) 19-33, 162-67, 243-69, 327-34; idem, *Philosemitismus im Barock* (Tübingen, 1952) • F. Stern, *The Whitewashing of the Yellow Badge: Antisemitism and Philosemitism in Postwar Germany* (Oxford, 1992) • N. Valman and T. Kushner, eds., *Philosemitism, Antisemitism, and "the Jews": Perspectives from Antiquity to the Twentieth Century* (Burlington, Vt., 2004) • R. S. Wistrich, "Anti-Capitalism or Antisemitism? The Case of Franz Mehring," *YLBI* 23 (1977) 35-51 • M. Zimmermann, *Wilhelm Marr: The Patriarch of Anti-Semitism* (New York, 1986).

Friedrich Niewöhner

Philosophia perennis

Philosophia perennis, or "perennial philosophy," may be used in a very general, nonhistorical sense for philosophy as an ongoing conversation on the great themes that are dealt with by Western philosophy. In the history of philosophy, however, A. Steucho (1497-1548) introduced the term in an effort to equate *one* philosophy with revealed → religion (→ Revelation). The term then took on special significance in G. W. Leibniz (1646-1716), who was aware that each philosophy is timebound and who thus wished to show what were the common philosophical lines across the centuries.

The → neoscholastic philosophy of the 20th century used "philosophia perennis" in a more precise and specific sense for Platonic-Aristotelian philosophy (→ Aristotelianism; Platonism) in its relation to Thomistic thought (E. Przywara; → Thomism). The Vienna philosopher E. Heintel (1912-2000) stressed the broad field of perennial philosophy in distinction from the narrower fields of → positivism and → materialism.

→ Metaphysics; Ontology; Philosophy 1; Philosophy and Theology; Truth

Bibliography: C. L. Hancock, "Faith, Reason, and the Perennial Philosophy," *Faith and the Life of the Intellect* (ed. C. L. Hancock and B. Sweetman; Washington, D.C., 2003) • E. Heintel, *Die beiden Labyrinthe der Philosophie* (vol. 1; Vienna, 1968) • A. Huxley, *The Pe-*

rennial Philosophy (New York, 1945) • K. Jaspers, *The Perennial Scope of Philosophy* (New York, 1949) • F. J. Klauder, *A Philosophy Rooted in Love: The Dominant Themes in the Perennial Philosophy of St. Thomas Aquinas* (Lanham, Md., 1994) • L. Loemker, "Perennial Philosophy," *DHI* 3.457-63 • C. B. Schmitt, "Perennial Philosophy: From Agostino Steuco to Leibniz," *JHI* 27 (1966) 505-32 • A. Steucho, *De perenni Philosophia* (new introduction by C. B. Schmitt; New York, 1972).

Frank Otfried July

Philosophy

1. Introduction

In the *Republic* of Plato (427-347 B.C.) the ideal ruler excels at philosophy, or love of wisdom (Gk. *philosophia,* from *philein,* "to love," and *sophia,* "wisdom"). This love comprises knowledge of what is highest and best, as well as wisdom in living one's life well. Its enduring symbol is the owl associated with the goddess Athena. In the popular mind authentic philosophy is wisdom in living, more so than a highest knowledge.

Misconceptions and caricatures of philosophers and philosophy abound. Philosophers are held in awe yet said to be inept in everyday affairs, as in the story about Thales (6th cent. B.C.) falling into a well while strolling with his gaze on the heavens. Philosophy enjoys esteem as the noblest, most general knowledge, yet it supposedly has no practical use, as in the saying, "philosophy bakes no bread." In popular parlance a "philosophy" can be a sophisticated intellectual system, or just any person's half-baked opinions about things.

Philosophies can be classified by type (→ empiricism, → rationalism, → skepticism, etc.). Some get their labels from their originators (→ Aristotelianism, → Kantianism, → Marxism, etc.). The main account below proceeds by outlining the topics that philosophers most often address.

2. Western Philosophy

2.1. *Eras*

In the Homeric Age myth and legend were the principal means of transmitting → culture. Over time philosophy, history, and science gradually established themselves as ways of discovering truth by reasoning or empirical investigation. → Greek philosophy as rational inquiry into the actual nature of things began with the pre-Socratics (6th and 5th cents. B.C.). Their speculations sought to conceptualize the basic elements and processes of the cosmos, to account for the world as we experience it. Science as observation of → nature freed from assumptions of speculative cosmology arose several centuries later. Philosophy as wisdom for living had its roots in sayings attributed to the Seven Sages, who were contemporary with the pre-Socratics.

Plato was the first philosopher to discuss both strands — knowledge of reality and wisdom for living — extensively and as interconnected. His dialogues showcase teachings of his mentor, Socrates (ca. 470-399 B.C.), accompanied by Plato's own elaborations and innovations. His *Phaedo* and *Apology* are responsible for the heroic image of Socrates as the exemplary inquirer who faced trial and execution with the courage of his convictions intact, and who proclaimed that "the unexamined life is not worth living."

Plato's pupil Aristotle (384-322 B.C.) meticulously expounded his own views on the fundamental issues of being and knowledge, → ethics and → politics. Ultimately → Platonism and Aristotelianism towered over all others as the two ancient philosophies of greatest lasting influence. But philosophers directly after Aristotle headed in different directions, some to skepticism regarding the possibility of knowledge, some to Epicurean or Stoic prescriptions for how best to live, and some later on to the otherworldly vision of Neoplatonism.

Medieval philosophy gave major attention to the existence and nature of God and to God's relation to the world. Christian philosophers at first drew heavily upon Plato and then Aristotle to provide rational support for theology. → Jewish philosophy, epitomized by Moses Maimonides (1135-1204), and → Islamic philosophy, culminating with Ibn Rushd (1126-98), known to the West as Averroës (→ Islamic Philosophy 4.6), brought Aristotelianism into creative dialogue with their own religious traditions.

With its seeds in the → Renaissance, modern philosophy blossomed in the → Enlightenment of the 17th and 18th centuries. Philosophy reduced its ties to theology as new scientific theories and methods occupied its attention, along with innovative conceptions of social and political life. By making self-certainty the starting point for reflection, René Descartes (1596-1650) gave philosophy a "subjective turn" (→ Cartesianism). Epistemological issues moved to center stage in place of the once-dominant metaphysical systems of ancient and medieval thought.

Originally philosophy embraced many subjects that eventually split off as independent disciplines in their own right. Theophrastus (ca. 372-ca. 287 B.C.), a pupil of Aristotle, was an early natural scientist noted for his extensive botanical observations. In early modern times physical science began to free itself from metaphysical speculation by employing experimental methods and mathematical analysis. Even so, Isaac Newton (1642-1727) called his magnum opus *Mathematical Principles of Natural Philosophy* (1687), and amateur British naturalists long afterward dubbed their investigations "natural philosophy." Via 19th-century → positivism, → sociology broke away from the older, largely theoretical, forms of → social philosophy. → Psychology renounced philosophical speculations about mind and soul by transforming itself into an empirical and experimental science. At the same time, Darwinism liberated biology from the grip of biblical authority.

2.2. *Topics*

The many varieties and methodologies of the philosophies of the past few centuries cannot be described briefly. More feasible is a summary of the main topics on which philosophers work today.

2.2.1. *Logic*

→ Logic studies how reasoning processes arrive at reliable conclusions. Logic is a tool utilized in reasoning in general, not itself a source of substantive philosophical content. One of its modern branches, mathematical logic, overlaps with mathematics and computer science.

Deductive logic involves the formal relationships among the premises and the conclusion of an argument. Medieval logicians refined Aristotle's pioneering analysis of the different forms of syllogistic reasoning. In a valid argument form the conclusion follows of necessity from the logical relations of the premises to one another. A sound argument has a true conclusion because it has both a valid form and premises that are true. In modern logic prose arguments get translated into symbolic form and evaluated according to established rules, somewhat like the use of algebra in mathematics. Just as mathematicians devised non-Euclidian geometries, so modern logicians have devised alternative or many-valued logics that are not just of theoretical interest but have useful applications.

John Stuart Mill (1806-73) was the chief architect of *inductive logic*, the second major type. In it the reasoner observes a number of like instances and infers that other comparable instances not observed have the same features as those of the original set. An empirical method of generalizing from the known to the unknown, induction yields conclusions with degrees of probability, not the certainty of deduction. A method employed widely in social science research, it also underlies our ordinary beliefs about the world derived from repeated, everyday experiences. The difficulty lies in determining how many observations, and of what sort, warrant a general conclusion to which a specific probability can be assigned. Philosophers disagree about the appropriate algorithms for probabilistic inference.

Informal logic, of either a deductive or an inductive sort, evaluates arguments in their (sometimes incomplete) prose format in the media or in daily life rather than reducing them to symbolic form. The teaching of logic commonly subdivides into the informal logic of everyday discourse and the formal logic of explicitly structured reasoning, which lends itself to sophisticated analysis.

2.2.2. *Metaphysics and Epistemology*

→ Metaphysics is the theory or investigation of the nature of being or reality in general, and of the kinds of properties and relationships that beings have in themselves and with one another. It is often closely connected with → epistemology, which examines knowing, what it is possible to know, and how it occurs. This close relation of the two topics is not surprising, because a plausible account of being and beings hinges on our ability to know such objects, and an account of knowing can hardly be neutral with respect to the kinds of objects said to be knowable.

The theories of classical metaphysics typically deal with conceptual distinctions of appearance from reality, physical from nonphysical being, contingent from necessary being, created from eternal being, finitude from infinite being, as well as the phenomena of change and causation. Aristotle's *Metaphysics*, by its detailed analyses of the properties of beings and the kinds of causation, set the standard for many centuries thereafter. Much of classical metaphysics, whether it advocated rationalism, materialism, or some other theory, consisted of large-scale speculation and system-building. Most recent metaphysics disclaims large ambitions and more modestly tackles specific issues such as what is meant by the "identity" of two things with one another, or whether an entity is an enduring substance or just a localized, temporally changing process.

Modern epistemology comes in many varieties, but all must wrestle with the perennial challenges of distinguishing truth from error, reliable perception from illusion, conceptual thinking from the effects of sensation. Epistemology has affinities with logic, but it is increasingly impacted by results from empirical studies both of the brain and nervous system, and of language use. Some of the most interesting research interfaces with the philosophy of mind.

2.2.3. *Philosophy of Science*

In the late 19th century natural science dethroned speculative philosophy of nature as the way to interpret and explain the physical universe. The positivistic approach adopted by many philosophers became in the 20th century a → philosophy of science. Instead of hypothesizing about nature itself, it promoted scientific method as the reliable route to truth and took as its task analysis of the epistemic status of scientific hypotheses and accepted theories. Initially a *philosophy of physics,* it added a *philosophy of biology* and even a *philosophy of psychology.* Some philosophers take the philosophy of science to be the norm for epistemology generally and require other branches of philosophy to meet standards of scientific objectivity if they are to yield genuine knowledge.

2.2.4. *Philosophy of Mind*

The philosophy of mind captures the attention of many philosophers and others. Its studies of cognitive activity in conjunction with other disciplines involve more sophistication and scientific acumen than older-style philosophical debates about mind-brain relations. The ensemble of disciplines doing this work is called cognitive science. Philosophy of mind interacts with computer science studies of information processing and artificial intelligence. It overlaps with the *philosophy of → language* and → linguistics because language structure and use is basic to our cognitive activity. It draws upon physiological and cognitive psychology for its models of how thinking takes place.

2.2.5. *Ethics*

Ethics, or *moral philosophy,* concerns principles or rules for how we ought to behave. Most philosophers attribute some form of objective reality to ethical norms or at least take them to be binding apart from our subjective thoughts or feelings about them. Exceptions include moral → relativists such as Friedrich → Nietzsche (1844-1900), who treated all moral systems as human inventions, the atheistic existentialist Jean-Paul Sartre (1905-80), and those defending the metaethical view that assertions about the rightness or wrongness of actions do no more than evince the attitudes of those who make them. Religious believers who are philosophers often ground ethical norms in divine commands or revealed scriptures, although they may use reason to elucidate them. → *Metaethics* treats the ultimate foundations for systems of moral rules, their justification, rational or otherwise. Great ethical theories in the history of philosophy are, in the main, metaethical theories.

The term "morality" usually refers to a particular ethical system or to general behavior in conformity with its rules. *Applied ethics* makes applications of ethical theories to specific circumstances or areas of activity. While a particular application may enable confident decision-making, its moral adequacy finally rests on the validity of the metaethical assumptions behind it. Various specialties exist under the umbrella of applied ethics: *business* ethics, *medical* ethics, *professional* ethics, → *environmental* ethics, and others. Growing concern for *animal rights* conjoins both metaethical and applied dimensions.

2.2.6. *Aesthetics*

→ Aesthetics, or *philosophy of art,* reflects on the productions of the visual and performing arts and also of literature. In the past it dwelt primarily on such classical criteria for artistic excellence as symmetry in sculpture or catharsis and the resolution of conflict in drama. Because Plato and the medievals placed beauty among the transcendental qualities of being as such, some philosophers attributed aesthetic features to the world as a whole and even gave a place to aesthetic criteria in evaluating the adequacy or truth of metaphysical systems.

Most recent philosophers avoid making metaphysical claims for aesthetic properties. They endeavor to answer the question What is art? from an empirical or an analytic standpoint. One way judges how empirical properties of the object or performance elicit certain psychological responses from its audience. Another, seemingly circular, way is to declare art to be whatever critically acknowledged artists do and proclaim to be their art, whether it be an artifact produced, an activity performed, or even a "found" object displayed. Other interesting questions for aesthetics concern whether there is such a thing as truth and falsity in art (as there is in epistemology), and whether an indistinguishable copy or a forgery counts as art in the way that originals do.

2.2.7. *Philosophy of Religion*
→ Philosophy of religion applies rational criteria and methods of analysis to the beliefs and practices of religious communities. Historically it has been best equipped to deal with cognitive expressions of faith, namely, in the defense of religious beliefs or doctrines, the analysis of their meanings and implications, or their criticism and refutation. Philosophy of religion that employs the descriptive phenomenological method, however, is better suited to the study of religious practices because it classifies and interprets various religious types while suspending judgment as to their truth, consistency, or rationality. Some philosophers of religion are believers in a specific historic faith, some are agnostics or atheists, and a few develop a rational religious perspective of their own. Representative topics in classical philosophy of religion that are still widely discussed are the viability of proofs for God's existence (→ God, Arguments for the Existence of) and the challenges that natural and moral evils in the world present to belief in a good and powerful God (→ Theodicy).

2.2.8. *Philosophy of Human Nature*
The philosophy of human nature and existence is an important topic that has no widely used single name. As a standard part of traditional Roman Catholic thought, it was often called simply philosophy of man, which consisted of the characteristics of the human body and soul considered in relation to the creation and to God. Others refer to it as philosophical anthropology, though without tying it explicitly to the social science discipline of anthropology. Its issues include our biological constitution, mind, will, and emotions, all in relation to nature and, in religious contexts, to natural law and God. Humanistic philosophies and the varieties of → existentialism find their center of gravity here, as do other "philosophies of life" that focus on the conditions for happiness and the fulfillment of human potential.

2.2.9. *Social and Political Philosophy*
Social and political philosophy addresses the types and functions of social and political practices and institutions, often from a values perspective. It evaluates the strengths and weaknesses of competing political theories and their implementation (what for Aristotle was the study of different types of "constitutions"). Akin to ethics, it is distinct from the *philosophy of social science,* which studies the methods and theoretical structures employed by social scientists and which has affinity with the philosophy of science.

Occupying some of the same terrain as social and political philosophy but with its own angle of vision is the *philosophy of history,* which has two quite different strands. One gives close attention to the methods and criteria historians use for gathering and evaluating evidence about the past, inferring causal connections among particular events and establishing interpretations or generalizations with wider applicability to other historical circumstances. Some find these methods and criteria akin to those of the philosophy of science or argue that they ought to conform to that model of objectivity. The other strand is comfortable characterizing larger historical epochs or even finding pattern, meaning, or purpose in history taken as a whole. This second strand is open to challenge as a covert form of speculative metaphysics, a charge commonly leveled, for instance, against G. W. F. Hegel's lectures on the philosophy of history.

2.2.10. *Other*
Philosophers also explore a number of other topics. *Philosophy of law* examines not only the theoretical bases of legal systems but also specifics of their operation, such as criteria for evidence in a court of law and for suitable causal accounts of human behavior. It draws upon ethics, social and political philosophy, and epistemology, as does *philosophy of → education* in studying its own range of institutions, theories, and practices. The *philosophy of → technology* is quite different from the philosophy of science because its interests lie in the consequences of technological change, including consequences for our human self-understanding as individuals and as a species.

These main topic areas of philosophy can and do subdivide. For instance, within aesthetics some concentrate on philosophy of literature, or of film, or of music. There is also a *philosophy in popular culture* movement that defines itself not in terms of a particular methodology or traditional division of philosophy but by reference to an array of contemporary phenomena that philosophers can choose to examine in any manner they wish. In short, there are no limits to what philosophers can and do look into so long as it involves issues of reality, knowledge, or values.

3. Asian Philosophy

European students of Asian philosophies have classified them according to the historically dominant civilizations, Indian and Chinese, and these headings have persisted. Asians have been philosophizing for millennia and in more cultural settings than just these two. Asian philosophies are more diverse and sophisticated than most Westerners typically recognize; they deserve detailed attention that is not possible here. Because they often approach basic philosophical issues from different angles and assumptions than those of the West, it requires expertise in Asian languages and extensive knowledge of both Eastern and Western thought to bring about their mutual engagement in a worthwhile manner.

Much of philosophy in ancient India served to elucidate and debate about religious scriptures, about the Hindu, Jain, and Buddhist beliefs and practices based on them. Westerners thus at first took Indian philosophy to be simply religious philosophy and only slowly recognized the existence of metaphysical, epistemological, and logical systems that stand on their own rather than relying on religious assumptions.

The philosophies of → Confucianism and → Taoism in China seem religious more in the general attitudes toward life that they promote than in virtue of any explicit theological affirmations. Although accompanied by religious practices, as philosophies they fit more the mold of ethical systems with pronounced social implications and close attention to the interdependence of human life with the natural world.

Immensely varied Buddhist philosophies cut across Indian and Chinese cultures and, with them, spread to other Asian lands, interacting with indigenous religious practices of Bon in Tibet, → shamanism in Mongolia and Korea, and → Shinto in Japan.

In the modern world many philosophers from Asian lands employ the methods of Western philosophy, alongside colleagues who continue the influence of their own historic traditions.

4. Philosophies of Distinctive Groups

Socially marginalized groups, those whose perspectives and achievements the dominant cultural traditions neglected, have in recent times asserted themselves politically and intellectually. They affirm their group identities and individual dignity by means that include → ideology and philosophy. Historically oppressed peoples seek not only to understand and eliminate the causes of their exclusion but also to express in intellectual terms their distinctive contributions to human self-understanding and social justice.

Black philosophy, in North America often called *Afro-American philosophy,* has two themes. One expresses the experiences of the black minority in a white majority culture under slavery and ensuing racial discrimination. It includes the ideology and tactics of the struggle for social change, which ally it with liberation movements by people of color in South Africa and elsewhere in the world. Its second theme affirms that the cultures of sub-Saharan Africa, from which the ancestors of Western blacks came, created social institutions and practices highly conducive to human well-being; they are worthy of preservation and adoption, fostered by study of traditional *African philosophy.*

The experiences and struggles of women have given birth to *feminist philosophy* (see 5). Akin to other liberation movements, it has pushed hard and successfully for women's rights and opportunities in education, politics, business, law, religion, and all other areas of modern life. Feminist philosophers contend that women's experience, so long excluded from the attention of patriarchal institutions and of individual men, makes vital contributions to human self-understanding and to society generally. A more controversial view of some feminist thinkers is that women have a distinctive outlook with the potential to change the prevailing paradigms in mainstream areas of philosophy (epistemology, ethics, social philosophy), as well as those in other disciplines (theology, politics, law, medicine, science).

Other instances of philosophizing from the perspectives of a distinctive group include an emergent *Latin American philosophy,* which distinguishes itself from the history of philosophy in Spain, which is part of the European tradition. Native American worldviews expressed so far seem to center on traditional religious beliefs and practices, and on attitudes to the environment, rather than being cast in explicitly philosophical form. Whether the gay and lesbian movement (→ Homosexuality) will seek philosophical articulation as distinct from other expressions of group identity remains to be seen.

Bibliography: R. Audi, ed., *The Cambridge Dictionary of Philosophy* (Cambridge, 1999) • W. Chan, ed., *A Source Book in Chinese Philosophy* (Princeton, 1963) • F. Copleston, *A History of Philosophy* (9 vols.; New York, 1993; orig. pub., 1946) • E. Craig, ed., *Routledge Encyclopedia of Philosophy* (10 vols.; London, 1998) • A. Cudd and R. Andreasen, eds., *Feminist Theory: A Philosophical Anthology* (Oxford, 2004) • S. Dasgupta, *A History of Indian Philosophy* (5 vols.; Delhi, 1975) • P. Edwards, ed., *The Encyclopedia of Philosophy* (8 vols.; New York, 1967) • M. Fricker and J. Hornsby, eds., *The Cambridge Companion to Feminism in Philosophy* (Cambridge, 2000) • Y. Fung, *A Short History of Chinese Philosophy* (New York, 1948) • A. Garry and M. Pearsall, eds., *Women, Knowledge, and Reality: Explorations in Feminist Philosophy* (New York, 1996) •

T. Honderich, ed., *The Oxford Companion to Philosophy* (Oxford, 1995) • J. Mbiti, *African Religions and Philosophy* (2d ed.; Oxford, 1990) • E. Mendieta, ed., *Latin American Philosophy: Currents, Issues, Debates* (Bloomington, Ind., 2003) • S. Radhakrishnan and S. Moore, eds., *A Source Book in Indian Philosophy* (Princeton, 1967) • K. Wiredu, *Philosophy and an African Culture* (Cambridge, 1980) • G. Yancy, ed., *African-American Philosophers: Seventeen Conversations* (New York, 1998).

Robert F. Brown

5. Feminist Approaches

A complex discussion has developed in philosophy since the 1970s that goes by the name "feminist philosophy." This approach is not an additional partial sphere that can be smoothly integrated into the recognized canon of philosophical disciplines. Rather, it suggests using gender as a further analytic category that confronts every area of philosophy. For this reason there have arisen many subprojects that cover the gamut from feminist → ethics to feminist philosophies of law, society, and politics, as well as → aesthetics and → epistemology (A. Garry and M. Pearsall, H. Nagl-Docekal). The history of → logic, too, is reinterpreted from this angle (A. Nye). Another theme is the contribution made by women to philosophy.

Two general perspectives guide the various studies — the one critical, the other systematic.

5.1. The first critical question is how philosophy shared, and continues to share, in supporting the theoretical background of discrimination against women.

5.1.1. This question is put first to philosophical texts that do not seem to have any bearing on sexual discrimination. Many theories that are formulated in general language cannot claim to be gender neutral but instead show gender blindness. That is, a typical masculine outlook influenced them when they were coined.

The → Enlightenment philosophy of law might serve as an example. The term → "equality" suggests gender neutrality par excellence. But feminist philosophy brings to light the theoretical background, namely, a distinction between the public and the private spheres and the related division of labor by sex, which reserved the public domain for males and relegated women to the → family. This research makes it plain that women do not come under the law, which keeps the family as free as possible from encroachment by the state. Thus the reference may be very generally to the equal rights and duties of all citizens, but closer analysis shows that only male citizens (→ Bourgeois, Bourgeoisie) are in view. Thus human and civil → rights were originally seen only as male rights (H. Schröder).

5.1.2. Women are also put down in philosophical theories that expressly treat of gender relations (C. Klinger). There are, for example, the misogynous reflections of A. Schopenhauer (1788-1860) and F. → Nietzsche (1844-1900), or of O. Weininger (1880-1903), whose thesis that women are not part of the same species as men represents the culminating point of this denigration.

There is also the disparaging thesis of complementarity. A typical example of this idea appears in the tradition of thought that developed in the middle of the 18th century. In demarcation from the egalitarian conceptions of the early Enlightenment, J.-J. Rousseau (1712-78) advanced a dualistic picture that not only assigns the sexes to different spheres (as in the division of labor mentioned above) but also ascribes to them different character traits, portraying males as rational and independent, women as emotional and dependent. Numerous authors up to the middle of the 20th century adopted this polarization of character, including I. Kant (1724-1804), F. Schiller (1759-1805), J. G. Fichte (1762-1814), G. W. F. Hegel (1770-1831), and G. Simmel (1858-1918). We also find it in → psychoanalysis and → critical theory.

Two in some sense contradictory models of thought may be found in this tradition. Either the women's sphere is subordinated to that of men, or it is endowed with utopian qualities (→ Utopia) and forms a counterbalance to → modernity. The latter approach does not alter the underlying problems. As long as women do not enjoy participation in the relevant social processes of decision making and safeguards for their → autonomy, they have a dependent position (→ Dependence).

5.2. The true goal of feminist philosophy corresponds to the systematic perspective. The question that arises here is in part that of the means whereby philosophy can expose and challenge the subordination of women in its full compass, and in part that of rethinking the relation between the sexes so that asymmetrical structures may not perpetuate themselves. Various discussions have resulted. Feminist philosophy is clearly not a single line of thought with a claim to orthodoxy but, rather, a discourse that is not homogeneous.

At the heart of feminist philosophy are concepts of equal rights, as may be seen in many early Enlightenment authors, both men and women, in the period 1625-1750 (R. Baader), in John Stuart Mill (1806-73), in Harriet Taylor Mill (1807-58), in

Simone de Beauvoir (1908-86), and in the first phase of contemporary feminist philosophy in the context of the → women's movement that started in the late 1960s and early 1970s.

In the late 1970s, however, French authors (L. Irigaray, J. Kristeva, H. Cixous), inspired by psychoanalytic concepts and in debate with the theoreticians of → postmodernity, refocused discussion on the differences that characterize the feminine. A third phase then set in that is seeking to link the plausible motifs in both approaches. We find this development especially in feminist ethics, with its attempt to mediate between the universal and the contextual (see M. Hanen and K. Nielsen).

During the 1990s questions of philosophical anthropology moved into the foreground. Following the lead of constructivism, scholars questioned the distinction between "sex" and "gender," examining the extent to which physical differences that at first glance seem "natural" may in fact derive from societal norms. Are the two sexes of human beings ultimately the result of forced heterosexuality (J. Butler)? Objections to views of this sort generally adduce the notion of generativity and point out that sexual norms themselves have always presupposed bodies that are sexually differentiated.

→ Feminist Theology

Bibliography: R. Baader, *Dames des Lettres* (Stuttgart, 1986) • J. Butler, *Gender Trouble: Feminism and the Subversion of Identity* (New York, 1990) • A. Garry and M. Pearsall, eds., *Women, Knowledge, and Reality: Explorations in Feminist Philosophy* (Boston, 1989) • E. Gössmann, ed., *Archiv für philosophie- und theologiegeschichtliche Frauenforschung* (4 vols.; Munich, 1984-89) • M. Hanen and K. Nielsen, eds., *Science, Morality, and Feminist Theory* (Calgary, Alta., 1987) • M. Heinz, S. Doyé, and M. Nordmeyer, eds., *Feministische Philosophie. Bibliographie, 1970-1999* (3 vols.; Bielefeld, 1996-2002) • *Hypatia: A Journal of Feminist Philosophy* (Bloomington, Ind., 1983-) • A. M. Jaggar and I. M. Young, *A Companion to Feminist Philosophy* (Malden, Mass., 1998) • C. Klinger, "Woman–Landscape–Artwork: Alternative Realms or Patriarchal Reserves?" *Continental Philosophy in Feminist Perspective* (ed. H. Nagl-Docekal and C. Klinger; University Park, Pa., 2000) 147-74 • H. Nagl-Docekal, *Feminist Philosophy* (Boulder, Colo., 2004) • H. Nagl-Docekal and C. Klinger, eds., *Continental Philosophy in Feminist Perspective* (University Park, Pa., 2000) • A. Nye, *A Feminist Reading of the History of Logic* (New York, 1990) • H. Schröder, *Die Rechtlosigkeit der Frau im Rechtsstaat* (Frankfurt, 1979) • N. Tuana, ed., *Re-reading the Canon: Feminist Interpretations of Plato* (University Park, Pa., 1994) • M. E. Waithe, ed., *Ancient Women Philosophers, 600 B.C.–500 A.D.* (Dordrecht, 1987); eadem, ed., *Medieval, Renaissance, and Enlightenment Women Philosophers, A.D. 500-1600* (Dordrecht, 1989); eadem, ed., *Modern Women Philosophers, 1600-1900* (Dordrecht, 1991) • O. Weininger, *Geschlecht und Charakter* (Munich, 1997; orig. pub., 1903).

Herta Nagl-Docekal

Philosophy and Theology

1. NT Background
2. Early Christianity
3. Middle Ages and Reformation
4. Modernity
5. Theology and Analytic Philosophy

1. NT Background

In the NT one can discern at least two different attitudes toward → philosophy, both of which have ample echoes in later Christian tradition. On the one hand, by the cross of Christ God has brought to nothing the wisdom of this world (1 Cor. 1:17–2:5) and liberated the followers of Christ from captivity to the power of worldly philosophy (Col. 2:8-20; → Theologia crucis). On the other hand, → creation inherently displays the power and divinity of its maker, and God has written the requirements of the → law (§1) on every human heart, so that even those who have no part in the history of salvation can be held accountable for the knowledge of God and the conduct of their lives (Rom. 1:18-21; 2:6-16). The NT, moreover, evidently employs some ideas that were current in the philosophy of the time (perhaps most obviously the notion of the divine Logos in John 1), although the precise relationship between the NT text and any particular philosophical movement of the first and second centuries is very difficult to determine.

2. Early Christianity

In early Christian theology these two different attitudes toward philosophy became more explicit. Some thinkers, like Irenaeus (ca. 130-ca. 200) and Tertullian (ca. 160-ca. 225), see pagan philosophy primarily as a source of corruption and error and are correspondingly reserved about making theological use of pagan wisdom. Thus Irenaeus contrasts the clarity of the scriptural gospel, whose meaning and truth are openly available to the humblest believer, with the deliberately arcane speculations of → Gnostic heresy. Tertullian famously asks,

"What does Athens have to do with Jerusalem, the Academy with the Church?" (*De praescr. haeret.* 7.9), and is able to say — regarding the cross as the death of the incarnate God himself — "It can be believed, because it is foolish [*ineptum*]," just as the resurrection "is certain, because it is impossible" (*De carne Christi* 5.4). Yet both writers were well familiar with the philosophical views they criticized, and Tertullian in particular can be a lucid and subtle dialectician (→ Dialectic); he evidently prizes logical rigor even while he is wary of the metaphysics of Athens.

Others, such as Justin Martyr (ca. 100-ca. 165), Clement of Alexandria (ca. 150-ca. 215), and Origen (ca. 185-ca. 254), find in the philosophical claims of → Platonism and → Stoicism an intellectual challenge that Christianity must meet. Far from being a naive lower-class superstition, they argue, Christianity is the highest philosophy, which both embraces and surpasses the wisdom of the Platonists and the Stoics. The God of the Christians, Justin maintains, is the God worshiped by all rational persons (see *1 Apol.* 2 and 28), since according to the Christian gospel the Logos of God — the universal principle of → reason and → truth central to Stoic and Platonist philosophy — is fully incarnate and available to all (5 and 46). Christianity is thus the ultimate rational truth. The primal object of Christian belief is Christ, the very Logos and Wisdom of God, sought but only dimly perceived by pagan philosophy apart from his taking flesh. Clement and especially Origen elaborate this vision in considerable detail, articulating a rational understanding of the universe based in Christian Scripture, which includes layers of wisdom satisfying to both the simple and the sophisticated. Against the Platonist Celsus (fl. late 2d cent.), who argues that Christian claims like the → incarnation of the Word and the → resurrection of the body are irrational and unworthy of God, Origen develops perhaps the most substantial apologia for Christian belief in the ancient world *(C. Cels.)*, which aims to uphold these scriptural teachings while exhibiting their intelligibility and rational attraction (→ Apologists).

Later writers like Gregory of Nyssa (ca. 330-ca. 395) and Augustine (354-430) continued to borrow extensively from Neoplatonism (esp. from Plotinus, in Augustine's case). While conceptually Neoplatonist, sometimes deeply so, these theologians put Neoplatonist ideas to use in a way controlled by the most basic Christian convictions (not least in the wake of the extensive and philosophically involved disputes about the → Trinity in the 4th cent., and the resultant definitions of Trinitarian orthodoxy). The highest good is not simply beyond this world, untouched by space, time, and change, but is the cross of the incarnate Word, which persuasively displays the power and wisdom of God in ways that exceed every expectation of the Platonists (see Gregory of Nyssa's *Catechetical Oration*). "The books of the Platonists," Augustine gratefully acknowledges, contain many valuable truths, but apart from the Scriptures, which attest the humility of Christ the mediator, we would not be able "to see clearly what the difference is between presumption and confession, between those who see their goal without seeing how to get there and those who see the way which leads to that happy country" (*Conf.* 7.20). Early Christianity's engagement with → Greek philosophy aims on the whole at the Christianization of Platonism and its offshoots, and not, as has sometimes been thought, the reverse.

3. Middle Ages and Reformation

3.1. Two developments in particular mark the relationship between philosophy and theology in the Western Middle Ages: the development of → logic and the assimilation of Aristotle (→ Aristotelianism). The medieval → universities gave rise to a new sophistication in logic (and, correspondingly, much technical controversy among logicians) and in the application of logic and linguistic analysis to theological problems (esp. with Abelard [1079-1142] and his school in the 12th cent., and the school of Ockham [ca. 1285-1347] in the early 14th cent. and after). The introduction of the whole of Aristotle's philosophy in the Latin West during the course of the 12th and early 13th century generated a crisis for Christian theology, since many of Aristotle's ideas seem opposed to basic Christian teachings (such as creation in time and the → immortality of the individual soul), yet at the same time they look rationally compelling.

Medieval philosophers and theologians differed considerably over the extent to which the philosophy of Aristotle could be assimilated into a Christian view of the world. In the early 13th century the teaching of Aristotle (outside of his logical writings) was for a time forbidden at the University of Paris, and many theologians remained cautious about incorporating elements from his philosophy into their thinking (such as Bonaventure [ca. 1217-74], esp. later in his career). Others (such as Thomas Aquinas [ca. 1225-74]) drew much more extensively on Aristotle and thought the main elements in his teaching could, when rightly interpreted, be incorporated successfully into a comprehensive Christian theology. Still others, not among the theologians but among the philosophers on the arts faculties, were

Philosophy and Theology

full-blown Aristotelians (of an Averroistic stripe, like Siger de Brabant [ca. 1240-ca. 1284]), though they too remained generally convinced of the compatibility of Aristotle with Christian teaching. Later, Ockham and his followers turned rigorous logical analysis against Aristotelian realism in → metaphysics and → epistemology. The resulting → nominalism in philosophy considerably reduced, though it did not eliminate, the role of Aristotle in the theology of the late → Middle Ages.

While they often disagreed over particular philosophical issues and outcomes, and about the extent to which logic and the philosophy of Aristotle generated useful results in Christian theology, medieval philosophers and theologians virtually always agreed that no philosophical claim could be true that contradicted, whether expressly or by implication, the teaching of Christian faith given in Scripture and creed. The medievals were convinced, in other words, that philosophy can at best be the servant or handmaid *(ancilla)* of theology; they differed, not over the epistemically subordinate status of philosophy to theology, but over how useful the handmaid's ministrations might be to the queen of the sciences (→ Scholasticism).

3.2. The early Protestant → Reformers were often sharply critical of the corruptions, as they saw it, introduced into medieval theology by its assimilation of pagan philosophy. In holding this position, however, they simply retained the basic medieval view that philosophy is always subject to correction by Christian teaching. They sided, in effect, with those medieval theologians (such as Ockham) who thought that philosophy is finally of limited use in theology, though in Christological and eucharistic discussions the Reformers themselves could become overtly metaphysical (e.g., Martin Luther's [1483-1546] account of the modes in which a body can be present in a space in his *Confession concerning Christ's Supper* [1528]). The underlying continuity of outlook between the Middle Ages and the → Reformation on the ancillary character of philosophy allowed for the extensive reintroduction of Aristotelian logic and metaphysics in Protestant theology in the late 16th century, without generating widespread concern that the basic theological convictions of the Reformation had been forsaken (→ Protestantism).

4. Modernity

4.1. The characteristically modern relationship between theology and philosophy took shape in the 17th century, when philosophers on the Continent and in Britain deliberately began to reverse the ordering of the two that had obtained in the Middle Ages and Reformation. Whether in rationalist fashion (like René Descartes [1596-1650]) or in empiricist fashion (like John Locke [1632-1704]), philosophers now sought certainty independently of Christian teaching; more important, they argued that the certainties obtained by reason must judge the teachings of → religion. So Locke, for example, influentially distinguishes between truths according to reason, truths above reason, and truths contrary to reason (*Essay* 4.17.23). While there are surely truths that reason could not reach on its own (such as the resurrection of the dead), no claim against reason can possibly be regarded as true. Among the claims that purport to belong to divine revelation, reason must therefore judge which are genuinely possible and supported by relevant evidence, and which are impossible or groundless. Philosophy thus has the crucial task of discriminating between reasonable religious belief and irrational enthusiasm.

The distinction between truths of reason and truths above reason was often made in the Middle Ages, but now the epistemic priorities were reversed: reason itself judges which claims above reason are true, whereas for a medieval theologian like Aquinas, truths above reason, namely the central teachings of Christian faith, finally determine which among the claims of reason may be believed. While philosophers like Descartes and Locke retained a good deal of the substance of traditional Christian belief, philosophers later in the → Enlightenment, such as David Hume (1711-76) and Immanuel Kant (1724-1804), pushed the autonomy of philosophy much further than their 17th-century predecessors had. For these later writers Christianity and Christian theology turn out either to be quite devoid of any rational foundation (as with Hume) or to be the vehicle of a "rational meaning" (in Kant's phrase, *Religion,* p. 121) far different from — indeed, often opposed to — the manifest meaning embraced by traditional believers.

4.2. In modernity many theologians accept the Enlightenment reversal of epistemic priorities and turn to a dominant philosophy of their time in order to support the truth, or at least the intelligibility, of Christian statements (Schubert Ogden and Gordon Kaufman are recent examples). Lockean empiricism, various types of Kantianism, German idealism, and existentialism are among the chief philosophical movements from which theologians have sought guidance, but there are also many others. This approach gives rise to the recurrent worry that the philosophy upon which theologians rely will not support Christianity but undermine it, emptying Christian faith of any distinctive content.

4.3. Against this kind of submission to the philosophical claims of the Enlightenment, other theologians from the 18th century on basically reject modern philosophy. This approach can take the form of a broad antipathy to any use of philosophy in theology. But it can also appear as a vigorous critique of modern philosophy, arguing that modern thought has fallen into implausible and irrational conclusions (esp. in the loss of epistemological → realism, a genuine and intelligible contact of mind and world) because it has failed to grasp the insights of the premodern philosophical tradition. Neo-Thomism, which emerged in Roman Catholic thought in the mid-19th century, makes this kind of argument in an especially influential way (→ Thomism; Neoscholasticism). On this view Aquinas's revision and expansion of Aristotelianism is both rationally superior to the philosophical claims of the Enlightenment and an utterly necessary tool for the articulation of an intellectually adequate Christian theology (see, e.g., Joseph Kleutgen [1811-83] and Jacques Maritain [1882-1973]).

4.4. Unwilling to take either of these paths, a number of other theologians have developed an alternative strategy for coping with modern philosophy's assertion of its own autonomy. Neither philosophy nor theology is handmaid to the other. Instead, each operates on its own territory according to its own rules, and neither has any right to encroach on the territory of the other. Reducing one to the other is therefore impossible, and a relationship of noncompeting autonomy must obtain between them.

Friedrich Schleiermacher (1768-1834; → Schleiermacher's Theology) offers a rigorous and formative version of this approach. Philosophy (including the methods of history and natural science) is "the highest objective function of the human spirit," and religion is "the highest subjective function." At bottom, the human spirit cannot be at war with itself, so any conflict between philosophy and theology must be apparent rather than real, the result of a misunderstanding (*Christian Faith,* §28.3, also 30.2-3). This approach is especially prominent in Protestant theology after Kant, since it seems to allow a full embrace of modern philosophy without the sacrifice of any of the essential content of Christianity.

Such a strategy, however, has regularly proved to be unstable. Conflicts between theology and philosophy repeatedly arise and are resolved (if only implicitly) in favor of one or the other, rather than by leaving both entirely intact (i.e., by showing that the conflict was based on misunderstanding alone).

4.5. A fourth modern strategy for understanding the relationship between philosophy and theology is to reject the Enlightenment reversal of epistemic priorities between the two, while extensively adapting modern philosophies for Christian theological use. Blaise Pascal (1623-62), Jonathan Edwards (1703-58), John Henry Newman (1801-90), and Karl Barth (1886-1968) all exemplify this approach in various ways, the first three with considerable philosophical originality in their own right (as Schleiermacher also achieved, in the service of a different strategy). They maintain, in effect, the traditional priority of theology over philosophy (i.e., philosophy has the status of a handmaid), while being aggressively engaged with different types of modern philosophy (respectively, for the four names mentioned here, → Cartesian, Lockean, later empiricist, and idealist), rather than simply repudiating modern thought. For this approach a robust commitment to the central claims of Christian faith must reshape modern philosophy and incorporate it in a convincing way into a large-scale theological view of the world, rather than (as with the first strategy [see 4.2]) allowing modern philosophy to reduce and reshape the contents of Christian faith.

5. Theology and Analytic Philosophy

Although the analytic tradition came to dominate the philosophical world in the second half of the 20th century, especially in Britain and America, Christian theologians have been slow to become engaged with it. This hesitation may be due in part to the perception that → analytic philosophy is bound up with an atheistic and naturalistic view of the world, and also to the preoccupation of analytic philosophy with highly technical questions of logic and → language that may seem remote from the basic human concerns presumed to animate theology. Already in the 1950s, when logical positivism was still a potent force in the analytic tradition, some analytic → philosophers of religion attempted to address theological questions, especially of an epistemological sort (A. Flew and A. MacIntyre). Soon after, there were initial efforts to draw on the later philosophy of Ludwig Wittgenstein (1889-1951) to attack verificationist views of meaning and truth, which had made → positivism look like an unpromising tool for Christian theology. But these discussions attracted only limited interest on the part of theologians.

There followed, however, a generation of analytic philosophers intensely concerned about many of

Philosophy and Theology

the central issues of Christian theology and convinced that a wide range of traditional Christian convictions could be defended in a philosophically rigorous way. The rise of this "Christian philosophy" movement, primarily in America, can be traced most clearly to the publication of Alvin Plantinga's *God and Other Minds* in 1967. Plantinga argued that the existence of God is no less plausible than the existence of other minds, and since the latter is quite plausible indeed, belief in the existence of God is not nearly so unreasonable as analytic philosophers had generally been inclined to suppose. Subsequent Christian philosophy has been especially concerned with epistemological questions, and in particular with attacking evidentialist and foundationalist theories of knowledge — views (of the sort pioneered in one way by Locke, and in another way by Descartes) holding that Christian beliefs can be reasonable only if they are derived from some other beliefs that count as compelling evidence for them (A. Plantinga and N. Wolterstorff, also Plantinga's own later writings). But philosophers in this tradition have also taken up the existence and nature of God, the problem of evil (→ Theodicy), moral theory, and a number of topics often thought to be the special province of theology, such as the interpretation and authority of Scripture, Trinity, incarnation, and atonement.

Like one type of modern theology (see 4.5), these Christian philosophers have generally resisted the suggestion that the traditional teachings of Christianity must be rejected or revised in order for Christian belief to be philosophically respectable. At the same time — and here Christian philosophy has some kinship with the opposite strategy in modern theology (see 4.2) — these philosophers have typically sought to display the truth, or more often the plausibility, of Christian claims in terms any (analytic) philosopher should be able to accept, without making their arguments rely on any distinctively Christian beliefs. Perhaps as a result, this approach to the relationship between philosophy and Christian belief, while usually traditionalist in tone and conviction, is often revisionist in outcome (e.g., regarding divine and human action, where essentially Pelagian views are common; or regarding the Trinity, where some Christian philosophers [such as Richard Swinburne] hold a seemingly tritheistic position).

Since the 1980s some theologians have taken up various figures and arguments in the analytic tradition in a different way, adapting and revising them for theological use (along the lines of 4.5 above) in order to address a range of theological problems in new ways (e.g., George Lindbeck, Sarah Coakley, Bruce Marshall, Kathryn Tanner). But analytic philosophy has yet to find widespread recognition as a necessary conversation partner for Christian theology.

Bibliography: On 2 and 3: A. H. Armstrong, *Later Greek and Early Medieval Philosophy* (Cambridge, 1967) • A. H. Armstrong and R. A. Markus, *Christian Faith and Greek Philosophy* (London, 1964) • E. von Ivánka, *Plato Christianus: Übernahme und Umgestaltung des Platonismus durch die Väter* (2d ed.; Einsiedeln, 1990) • J. Marenbon, ed., *Medieval Philosophy* (London, 1998) • B. D. Marshall, "Faith and Reason Revisited: Aquinas and Luther on Deciding What Is True," *Thomist* 63/1 (1999) 1-48 • P. Vignaux, *Philosophy in the Middle Ages* (trans. E. C. Hall; London, 1959). See also the bibliography in "Scholasticism."

On 4: • K. Barth, *CD*, esp. III/2, III/3, and IV/3; idem, "Schicksal und Idee in der Theologie," *Theologische Fragen und Antworten* (Zollikon, 1957) 54-92 • J. Edwards, *Freedom of the Will* (1754; ed. P. Ramsey, New Haven, 1957); idem, *Religious Affections* (1746; ed. J. E. Smith, New Haven, 1959) • I. Kant, *Religion within the Boundaries of Mere Reason* (1793; ET Cambridge, 1996) • G. D. Kaufman, *In Face of Mystery: A Constructive Theology* (Cambridge, Mass., 1993) • J. Kleutgen, *Die Philosophie der Vorzeit* (2d ed.; 2 vols.; Innsbruck, 1878); idem, *Die Theologie der Vorzeit* (2d ed.; 5 vols.; Münster, 1867-74) • J. Locke, *An Essay concerning Human Understanding* (1690; Oxford, 1975) • J. Maritain, *Distinguish to Unite; or, The Degrees of Knowledge* (4th ed.; ET, Notre Dame, Ind., 1995) • J. H. Newman, *An Essay in Aid of a Grammar of Assent* (1870; Oxford, 1985) • S. M. Ogden, *On Theology* (San Francisco, 1986) • B. Pascal, *Pensées* (New York, 1966) • F. Schleiermacher, *The Christian Faith* (2d ed., 1831; ET, Edinburgh, 1928).

On 5: • W. P. Alston, *Perceiving God: The Epistemology of Religious Experience* (Ithaca, N.Y., 1991) • S. Coakley, *Powers and Submissions: Spirituality, Philosophy, and Gender* (Oxford, 2002) • A. Flew and A. MacIntyre, eds., *New Essays in Philosophical Theology* (London, 1955) • P. van Inwagen, *God, Knowledge, and Mystery: Essays in Philosophical Theology* (Ithaca, N.Y., 1995) • F. Kerr, *Theology after Wittgenstein* (Oxford, 1986) • G. Lindbeck, *The Nature of Doctrine* (Philadelphia, 1984) • B. D. Marshall, *Trinity and Truth* (Cambridge, 2000) • A. Plantinga, *God and Other Minds* (Ithaca, N.Y., 1967); idem, *Warranted Christian Belief* (New York, 2000) • A. Plantinga and N. Wolterstorff, eds., *Faith and Rationality* (Notre Dame, Ind., 1983) • P. Quinn and C. Taliaferro, *A Companion to the Philosophy of Religion* (Oxford, 1997) • R. Swinburne, *The Christian God* (Oxford, 1994); idem, *The Coherence of Theism* (2d ed.; Oxford, 1993);

idem, *Revelation: From Metaphor to Analogy* (Oxford, 1992) • K. E. Tanner, *God and Creation in Christian Theology* (Oxford, 1988) • N. Wolterstorff, *Divine Discourse: Philosophical Reflections on the Claim That God Speaks* (Cambridge, 1995).

Bruce D. Marshall

Philosophy of History

1. Antiquity and Christianity
2. Enlightenment
3. The Problem of Freedom
4. Modern Period

1. Antiquity and Christianity

The term "philosophy of history," which goes back to Voltaire (1756), coincides with the development of the philosophy of history in the true sense. The question of the nature of history is much older, but the concept had not been fully developed earlier. In antiquity Plato regarded Athens as the copy of an original lost Athens, which represented the cyclic view of history, with history being incorporated into → nature.

In contrast, the Judeo-Christian view of history was linear. From the standpoint of God's saving acts, human development was a single process with a beginning, middle, and end (→ Augustine: "Christ died but once for our sins," and "the ungodly merely walk about aimlessly in a circle," *De civ. Dei* 12.13). History, being seen here under the sign of → salvation history, has transcendent meaning (→ Immanence and Transcendence), for its goal is a consummation beyond history (→ Eschatology). In this view, however, world history has no relevance of its own. The political sphere is either suspect along the lines of → Augustine's theology, or it is part of God's plan of salvation (→ Theology of History), as in J.-B. Bossuet's universal history.

2. Enlightenment

The philosophy of history in the true sense began with the → Enlightenment. The question then was to find the immanent → meaning of history on the basis of → reason. The starting point was an explanation of the specific nature of humanity. Thus G. B. Vico (1668-1744), whose *Scienza nuova* (New science, 1725-44) was the first philosophy of history, centered on the social nature of the nations.

Before and during the French Revolution the concept of → progress became decisive. Human possession of reason implies a task that indicates also the goal of history, namely, to live together under the conditions of reason, that is, in → freedom. The attempt to expound and group all human history in terms of this goal was made by Voltaire (1694-1778), A.-R.-J. Turgot (1727-81), I. Iselin (1728-82), Condorcet (1743-94), H. Saint-Simon (1760-1825), and finally A. Comte (1798-1857), with his law of three stages. At this point philosophy of history merged into empirical sociology.

The philosophy of history of the Enlightenment was not primarily mechanistic. Freedom was to be increased by action, to which the philosophy of history itself would contribute. Thus J.-J. Rousseau (1712-78), though he did not adopt a model of linear progress, conceived of the philosophy of history as a program of education. As a critic of the Enlightenment, J. G. → Herder (1744-1803) demanded that the nations not be evaluated by their efforts on behalf of progress but, instead, be regarded in terms of their individual worth. He thus laid the foundations of → Romanticism and → historicism.

Noting the biologisms of Herder, I. Kant (1724-1804) developed the most differentiated philosophy of history (→ Kantianism). He began with the fact that we do not always act according to reason. Within and among nations, reason undoubtedly makes the institutionalizing of justice an unconditional moral → duty, but it in no way guarantees progress. In general, however, one may see progress, but it rests on the pragmatic balancing of antagonistic special interests. Since Kant it has been plain that only an uncritical philosophy of history can be in competition with eschatology.

3. The Problem of Freedom

The philosophy of history relates to a genuine problem, namely, that of the meaning of a practical commitment to freedom. In a comprehensive discussion of various cultures, G. W. F. Hegel (1770-1831) defined world history as the movement of the "world spirit" working out an awareness of its own being (→ Hegelianism). Insofar as the spirit is essentially freedom, world history is progress in the consciousness of freedom. Yet this progress is achieved under the cover of individual action, in what Hegel called the *List der Vernunft* (cunning of reason).

In his analysis of J. G. Fichte, F. von Schelling, and Hegel (→ Idealism), K. Löwith (1897-1973) argued that philosophy of history is a → secularization of Christian eschatology. In this regard he was also in opposition to K. → Marx (1818-83), who, in a reversal of Hegel's structural model of historical progress (→ Dialectic), found an economic basis for history and maintained a historical → materialism. The class struggles that result from the dialectic of the forces and relations of production will finally usher in the kingdom of freedom. Marx also adopted the idea that action must promote progress. In → Marxism, however, his philosophy of history was understood mechanistically. This position leads to the difficulty that freedom is inevitably negated if there is a law of history comparable to a law of nature.

4. Modern Period

Comparisons made in the 19th and 20th centuries between historical and organic → development (E. von Lasaulx, O. Spengler, A. Toynbee) resulted again in the problem of a cyclic view of history. A. Schopenhauer (1788-1860) initiated a radical flight from the philosophy of history. F. → Nietzsche (1844-1900) found in the concept of progress an idolatry of the factual. Historicism brought a formal philosophy of history to the fore. As a critique of historical reason, this position aimed to specify the foundations of historical scholarship (W. Windelband, H. Rickert, W. Dilthey, H.-G. Gadamer; → Hermeneutics). From the standpoint of modern philosophy of language (→ Analytic Philosophy), history is seen as a product of narrative construction (A. Danto).

In view of the political catastrophes of the 20th century, some thinkers understand the philosophical concept of progress as part of the "dialectics of the Enlightenment," rejecting it as one means of lending legitimacy to terror (T. W. Adorno, M. Horkheimer, W. Benjamin, H. Arendt). This criticism also informs the demands made by so-called postmodernism (M. Foucault, J.-F. Lyotard) to acknowledge the element of discontinuity and to replace the "great narrative" with a multiplicity of "smaller" histories that may well lack homogeneity. The philosophy of history is currently experiencing at least a partial rehabilitation in connection with cultural criticism.

→ Culture; Future; Historiography 3; Humanism; Worldview

Bibliography: S. Anderson-Gold, "Progress and Prophecy: The Case for a Cosmopolitan History," *Geschichtsphilosophie und Kulturkritik* (ed. J. Rohbeck and H. Nagl-Docekal; Darmstadt, 2003) 263-77 • E. Angehrn, *Geschichtsphilosophie* (Stuttgart, 1991) • G. W. F. Hegel, *The Philosophy of History* (New York, 1956; orig. pub., 1822-31) • J. G. Herder, *Ideen zur Philosophie der Geschichte der Menschheit* (Bodenheim, 1995; orig. pub., 1784-91) • M. Horkheimer and T. W. Adorno, *Dialectic of Enlightenment* (New York, 2000; orig. pub., 1947) • I. Kant, "Idea for a Universal History with Cosmopolitan Intent" (1784), *The Philosophy of Kant: Immanuel Kant's Moral and Political Writings* (ed. C. J. Friedrich; New York, 1949) 116-31 • K. Löwith, *Weltgeschichte und Heilsgeschehen. Die theologischen Voraussetzungen der Geschichtsphilosophie* (8th ed.; Stuttgart, 1990; orig. pub., 1953) • K. Marx and F. Engels, "Manifesto of the Communist Party" (1848), *MECW* 6.477-517 • J. Rohbeck and H. Nagl-Docekal, eds., *Geschichtsphilosophie und Kulturkritik* (Darmstadt, 2003) • Voltaire, *The Philosophy of History* (London, 1965; orig. pub., 1756).

Herta Nagl-Docekal

Philosophy of Language → Analytic Philosophy 2.3; Language 4-5; Linguistics 3

Philosophy of Life → Vitalism

Philosophy of Nature

1. Term and Concept

In a secular context → "nature" refers to "all that there is," all the matter and energy in the universe, all the objects and forces that can be studied by the physical sciences. A narrow and popular sense, as in "nature study," concerns mainly the plant and animal species, as well as the geology and meteorology, of earth's environments. Philosophy of nature in the broad sense involves theoretical consideration not only of the kinds of natural entities that exist but also their interconnections and functions or ways of acting, expressed in terms of general laws. It is not science as such but a more general understanding of the world as science depicts it and of the scientific methods used in doing so. Philosophy of nature will therefore be part of any systematic → philosophy or comprehensive → worldview.

Religions typically regard nature as accompanied by a supernatural realm of nonphysical beings or powers not normally accessible to scientific investigation and so not recognized as real or existent by science per se. → Theology and other religious expressions concern themselves with the supernatural not only for its own sake but also in its relation to the natural world. Thus they find philosophy of nature an inescapable topic, since they need to delineate boundaries between the two realms in human life and experience, and since interactions of the divine with nature via → creation, → providence, → miracles, and the like constitute central religious topics. Thus religious as well as secular worldviews have a vital interest in the philosophy of nature.

Non-Western thought certainly offers various philosophies of nature. Inclusion of them here, however, would take us too far afield. Hence the following is of necessity confined to the Western tradition.

2. Philosophies of Nature in Western Thought

2.1. *Ancient*

Ancient → Greek philosophy began with speculation about the being of nature. We have fragments of writings by Heraclitus, Parmenides, and other early thinkers compiled by later authors under the heading *peri physeōs,* "about nature." These early philosophers sought to grasp the origin and essence of nature as a whole, and then secondarily its internal processes. The first thorough and fairly systematic conception of nature in Western philosophy occurs in the *Physics* of Aristotle (384-322 B.C), taken together with his *On the Heavens,* his *On Generation and Corruption,* and *On the Soul.* No other ancient conception proved as influential as Aristotle's for the philosophy of nature in the subsequent medieval and early modern periods.

Aristotle's accomplishment presupposes a long history of thought about nature traceable back in part to the *Timaeus* of Plato (427-347 B.C.) and in part to pre-Socratic teachings. In addition to Plato, Aristotle's most important predecessors, whom he engaged constructively as well as critically, include the atomists Democritus (ca. 460-ca. 370) and Leucippus (5th cent. B.C.), and the Ionians Thales (6th cent. B.C.), Anaximander (610-546/45), and Anaximenes (d. ca. 528). Aristotle adopted from Empedocles (ca. 490-430) the doctrine of four elements (earth, air, fire, water) but added a fifth, the aether. In opposing atomism, Aristotle formulated four doctrines still relevant today, namely, a theory of the continuity of matter, his doctrine of the four causes (material, formal, efficient, final), his → teleology affirming an immanent purposiveness in nature as a whole as well as in its individual domains, and finally his definition of time as the measure of motion or change.

The chief concern of ancient Greek philosophy of nature in general and of its Aristotelian version in particular is the relation of the being of nature *(physis)* to being as such *(ousia),* and of both to the epitome of all being, namely, God, the ultimate end or goal of all lesser ends. The organic principle of purposiveness that orders the whole of nature provides the answer to this inquiry, just as for Aristotle's theology in the narrower sense does the doctrine of the prime mover. Aristotle made the doctrine of movement or change basic to his physics and so did away with the Parmenidean-Platonic subordination of becoming to being. This → Aristotelianism, conjoined to the → Stoic conception of reason *(logos)* as the formative principle in nature that underlies doctrines of → natural law, furnished the prevalent philosophy of nature in the medieval period.

2.2. *Medieval to Early Modern*

Although early medieval thinkers relied largely on Platonism for their philosophical tools, eventually a fuller Aristotelian corpus, transmitted by Syrian, Muslim, and Jewish scholars, came to the attention of Christian Europe. By the time of → Thomas Aquinas (ca. 1225-74), Aristotle's works in physics had become widely known. The commentaries of Aquinas on *Physics, On the Heavens,* and other treatises solidified the authority of Aristotelian philosophy of nature for scholastic thought, both in actual investigations of nature and in general theorizing about nature in philosophy and theology. For instance, Jean Buridan (ca. 1300-1358 or after), although replacing Aristotle's account of projectile motion with his own concept of "impetus," remained a defender of Aristotle in his general theories of time and → causality.

Despite emphatic opposition from Martin → Luther (1483-1546) and others, Aristotelianism held sway throughout the Reformation era. Its influence is evident in the *Loci communes* and Aristotle commentaries of the Lutheran theologian Philipp → Melanchthon (1497-1560), despite his modifications to Aristotelianism in his theology of → creation, as Aquinas before him had modified its cosmology. Above all, Aristotle's teleological mode of thinking (one also fundamental to Stoicism and Neoplatonism) binds medieval Aristotelian philosophy of nature to the cosmology of the → Reformers.

Galileo Galilei (1564-1642) and Johannes Kepler (1571-1630) shook this tradition to its foundations when, in continuity with → nominalism, they comprehended laws of nature on the model of mathematical formalism, which had the effect of pushing teleological thinking into the background. The Copernican revolution magnified this development because the planetary system of Nicolas Copernicus (1473-1543) no longer depicted earth as the center of the universe. But in employing the language of mathematics for understanding nature, neither Kepler nor Galileo wished to question the religious relationship between human beings and the creation. Instead, in the precision of nature's laws they saw even more clearly attested nature's provenance from a divine spirit.

With René Descartes (1596-1650) and Pierre Gassendi (1592-1655), we encounter a wholly mechanistic treatment of nature more pointedly dismissive of any teleological emphasis. They embraced gravity and planetary motion alike in a single mechanistic perspective, one fully in accord with the Cartesian concept of corporeal substance as *res extensa* (extended substance). For Descartes, substantiality is adequately defined by mathematical description of bodies as spatially extended magnitudes. He conceived the changes of state of bodies simply as owing to the action of other bodies on them by pressure or impact.

Quite different was the view of G. W. Leibniz (1646-1716), who made the basis of his entire doctrine of nature his conception of substances as bearing within themselves the powers of their matter and so founded the scientific discipline of dynamics. This conception, directed specifically against Cartesian mechanism, was of epochal significance in the history of the concept of energy. His formula for the conservation of energy $(E = m/2 \cdot v^2)$ still holds good today. Leibniz successfully revitalized organismic thinking and Aristotelian teleology, which, despite persistent criticism of Leibniz by Immanuel Kant (1724-1804), continued on and which both of them understood as in no way a substitute for the mechanistic approach but instead as supplementary to it.

2.3. *British Empiricism*

Unlike its Continental counterpart in the philosophy of nature, the British tradition displays a decidedly → utilitarian motivation. The originator of this orientation was Francis Bacon (1561-1626), who separated speculative natural philosophy, a theoretical approach that investigates causes, from operative natural philosophy, a practical concern for "production of effects." The theoretical approach divides in turn into a metaphysical branch for treating formal and final causes, and a physical branch for material and efficient causes, all in the Aristotelian sense. Focus on investigation of physical causes in their practical significance "for eliminating the deprivations of human life" *(ad sublevanda vitae humanae incommoda)* is Bacon's bequest to the ensuing philosophy of nature in Britain.

Thomas Hobbes (1588-1679) radicalized the Baconian approach by completely abandoning the teleological principle for explanation and, with it, the validity of final causation. For him, mechanism sufficed for all explanation of nature, even for the powers and causality of living things. Hobbes then carried his understanding of nature as monistic mechanism over to the sphere of practical philosophy, in particular, his political philosophy. Ontological → dualism à la Descartes or Kant was foreign to him. He envisaged the political state (the "Leviathan") on the model of a machine in which conflicting forces (analogous to interactive centripetal and centrifugal forces) must be centrally controlled to avert "war of everyone against everyone."

The idea of the → state as a mechanism of compulsion to which people sacrifice their individual → freedom, because it represents their only chance of preserving it collectively, greatly influenced Jean-Jacques Rousseau (1712-78) and others. This way of relating the "state of nature" to association in the political state, such that the latter offers the only possibility of securing a human existence worthy of the name, is the link between Hobbes and Rousseau. Neither used the idea of the "state of nature" as mirror and ethical norm for the political state, as did John Locke (1632-1704), for whom it played an essential role.

Similar to Hobbes and more consistently than Locke, David Hume (1711-76) gave radical expression to the Anglo-Saxon brand of critical → metaphysics in philosophy of nature generally and in → epistemology in particular. Hume took from Isaac Newton (1642-1727) the conviction that mathematics alone can give us certainty, and that only in a limited way. All other truths are to be tested in terms of their usefulness for practical life. In taking Locke's sensualism to an extreme ("There is nothing in the intellect that was not first in sense perception"), Hume championed the standpoint that even the principle of causality, as upheld by Bacon and in the interim given heightened value on the Continent by Leibniz, could not be a principle for knowledge of nature and so not a principle undergirding a science of nature. He took the deliberate risk of declaring as impossible not only metaphysics in general and speculative philosophy of nature in particular but even any science of nature at all.

Hume's influential → skepticism, embodying the most radical British position on philosophy of nature and scientific theory, lasted well beyond his own time. His theses prompted Kant to make a full-dress rebuttal, in his critical theory of an a priori knowledge said to function unconditionally and constitutively in our apprehension of natural laws.

Although Kant's transcendental philosophy ended for the time being the influence of British philosophy of nature on the Continent, the doctrines of Hume, Locke, and even Bacon continue to be influential in the English-speaking world and elsewhere right up to the present day.

2.4. *Kant and the Nineteenth Century*

Kant's theory of nature as set forth in his *Metaphysical Foundations of Natural Science* (1786) rests, like that of Leibniz, on a specific interpretation of the concept of force — in particular, on the reciprocal roles of attraction and repulsion as the two fundamental forces of nature. In this way Kant sought an epistemological legitimacy for the scientific progress of mechanism, above all Newtonian physics, and the reconciling of it with his own teleologically oriented theory of practical → reason.

Such a synthesis of philosophical and scientific thinking was unable to exert any decisive or lasting influence on the actual course of science. Instead, we should see it as philosophy's final attempt, from the standpoint of a general theory of science or a general theory of objective knowledge, to do justice to the unfettered development of natural science. This treatment of teleology and mechanism as complementary accounts was acceptable neither to those making further advances in science nor to the neo-Kantian philosophical tradition itself. As a result, German → idealism after Kant sought to surpass it rather than salvaging it.

F. W. J. Schelling (1775-1854) and G. W. F. Hegel (1770-1831) reproached Kant for implausibly abandoning all consideration of totality by his representation of truth only in terms of the antitheses of ideal and real, of reason and nature, of purpose and object. They made the most ambitious claims in the history of the philosophy of nature to prescribe for science its themes and methods. Schelling's philosophy of nature envisaged the real (physical) and ideal (cognitive, spiritual) domains as constituting a polarity within an all-embracing, intuitable, absolute identity, and then he construed contemporary scientific laws and discoveries in terms of his own philosophical concepts of mechanism and organism. Hegel sought to derive the truths of scientific knowledge of nature from his speculative concept of absolute knowledge, based in his *Logic.*

The collapse of this systematic endeavor of the early 19th century was apparent both in the increasing autonomy of the individual sciences vis-à-vis philosophy and in those philosophical currents that sought for their part to be compatible with the independence of science itself. Darwinism, in its philosophical adaptation by Friedrich → Nietzsche (1844-1900) and by its elimination of any dualism in explanations, called into question basic metaphysical and religious convictions every bit as much as did outright → materialism. Both Darwinism and materialism rid themselves of any hint of Cartesian subject-object dualism, and both contested the need to adopt principles of intelligibility not drawn from the empirical realm itself.

The philosophical orientation closest to the basic outlook of the evolutionary and materialist methods derives from the → positivism of Auguste Comte (1798-1857), which acknowledged empirically verifiable facts alone as pertinent to questions of → truth. With regard to both scientific theory and the history of science, this positivist approach in science has enjoyed convincing success right up to the present day.

2.5. *Twentieth Century*

Positivism in 20th-century philosophy of nature built on this successful approach. Leading examples include the epistemology and → philosophy of science of Ernst Mach (1838-1916), a forerunner of the Vienna Circle, and those of its leading members, including Moritz Schlick (1882-1936), Ludwig Wittgenstein (1889-1951) in his early work, and Rudolf Carnap (1891-1970). Noteworthy also is the methodological positivism of modern physics associated with Niels Bohr (1885-1962), as well as the work of Carl von Weizsäcker (b. 1912), Werner Heisenberg (1901-76), and other physicists.

Nevertheless, positivism by itself cannot do the whole job. The methods and results of modern science in such fields as genetic research and quantum physics call for philosophical examination of fundamental concepts involving the nature and origin of life in biology, as well as the standards for objectivity and knowledge in physics. Wide-ranging discussion of these and numerous other issues related to scientific theory, and to the interpretation and significance of research results, tends today to enlarge upon positivism's methods and achievements rather than undoing them. From the collapse of classical philosophy of nature, a new discipline was born to replace it, one now called philosophy of science.

One important exception to the positivist trend is the metaphysics of Alfred N. Whitehead (1861-1947). In *Process and Reality* (1929) he revamped Leibniz's theory of monads into a systematic account of an organic cosmos, the constituents of which are not substantial entities but processes of becoming, what he called "actual occasions," processes that develop organically rather than in a mechanical fashion compatible with materialist theories. He regarded nature as cosmic process that can be described empirically and expressed mathematically. Whitehead's renewal of systematic philosophy of nature, albeit one more compatible with the results of modern science, has been more influential in → process theology than in philosophy as such.

Growing environmental awareness and concern in the latter part of the 20th century, as a broadly based social and scientific movement, gave birth to a new kind of philosophy of nature. It focuses on human interdependence with the well-being of other species that share the planet. Not so speculative and anthropocentric as its predecessors, it emphasizes the intrinsic worth of other species apart from their utility for human purposes, and the cautious management of natural resources, both living and nonliving. It comprises the applied fields of conservation and environmental ethics, as well as theoretical reconsideration of humanity's place in, and attitudes toward, the natural world.

Bibliography: Primary sources: Aristotle, *The Complete Works of Aristotle* (2 vols.; ed. J. Barnes; Princeton, 1984) • F. Cornford, *Plato's Cosmology: The Timaeus of Plato, Translated with a Running Commentary* (New York, 1957) • G. Hegel, *Hegel's Philosophy of Nature* (3 vols.; ed. and trans. M. Petry; London, 1970) • W. Heisenberg, *Natural Law and the Structure of Matter* (London, 1970); idem, *Physics and Philosophy* (New York, 1959) • G. Kirk, J. Raven, and M. Schofield, *The Presocratic Philosophers* (2d ed.; Cambridge, 1983) • F. Schelling, *Ideas for a Philosophy of Nature* (trans. E. Harris and P. Heath; Cambridge, 1988) • C. Weizsäcker, *The Unity of Nature* (trans. F. Zucker; New York, 1980) • A. Whitehead, *The Concept of Nature* (Cambridge, 1920; repr., Ann Arbor, Mich., 1957); idem, *Process and Reality* (New York, 1929); idem, *Science and the Modern World* (New York, 1925).

Secondary works: E. Burt, *The Metaphysical Foundations of Modern Physical Science* (London, 1925) • E. Cassirer, *The Philosophy of the Enlightenment* (trans. F. Koelln and J. Pettigrove; Boston, 1951) • S. Cohen, *Aristotle on Nature and Incomplete Substance* (Cambridge, 1996) • D. Des Chene, *Physiologia: Natural Philosophy in Late Aristotelian and Cartesian Thought* (Ithaca, N.Y., 1996) • J. Edwards, *Substance, Force, and the Possibility of Knowledge: On Kant's Philosophy of Material Nature* (Berkeley, Calif., 2000) • S. Houlgate, ed., *Hegel and the Philosophy of Nature* (Albany, N.Y., 1998) • M. Jammer, *Concepts of Force: A Study in the Foundations of Dynamics* (Cambridge, Mass., 1957) • A. Koyré, *From the Closed World to the Infinite Universe* (New York, 1957) • A. Lovejoy, *The Great Chain of Being: A Study in the History of an Idea* (Cambridge, Mass., 1936) • E. McMullin, ed., *The Concept of Matter in Greek and Medieval Philosophy* (Notre Dame, Ind., 1965) • P. Mittelstaedt, *Philosophical Problems of Modern Physics* (Dordrecht, 1976) • J. Moore, *The Post-Darwinian Controversies: A Study of the Protestant Struggle to Come to Terms with Darwin in Great Britain and America, 1870-1900* (Cambridge, 1979) • N. Rescher, *Leibniz's Metaphysics of Nature: A Group of Essays* (Dordrecht, 1981) • E. Rudolph, *Zeit und Gott bei Aristoteles aus der Perspektive der protestantischen Wirkungsgeschichte* (Stuttgart, 1986) • E. Rudolph and I. Stamatescu, eds., *Philosophy, Mathematics, and Modern Physics: A Dialogue* (Berlin, 1994) • T. Torrance, *Reality and Scientific Theology* (Edinburgh, 1985) • S. Toulmin and J. Goodfield, *The Architecture of Matter* (New York, 1962); idem, *The Discovery of Time* (New York, 1965); idem, *The Fabric of the Heavens: The Development of Astronomy and Dynamics* (New York, 1961).

Enno Rudolph and Robert F. Brown

Philosophy of Religion

1. The Field

Philosophy of religion, a complex and broad field within → philosophy, has to do with such topics as religious → experience, religious language, the relations between religion and science, the relations between religion and history, and the bearing on one or another religious tradition of the aspects of philosophy that come under the headings of → metaphysics, → epistemology, and ethical theory (→ Ethics). In colleges and universities within the English-speaking world, the latter three directions of inquiry within general philosophy have mainly concentrated on the notion of → God that is common to the Jewish, Christian, and Islamic traditions, the notion often called → monotheism. It is not the object of the field as such to defend or endorse, or deplore or reject, claims representative of religious traditions, language, and experience; nor to promote or defend, or deplore or reject, such a doctrine as monotheism. The object of the field, as it is generally understood, is to study, analyze, and assess concepts and reasoning set out to justify belief and conduct importantly constitutive of one or another religious tradition. Particular participants in the discipline indeed have their own dispositions regarding the traditions mainly within their acquaintance, and such dispositions are likely to enter into their assessments of concepts and arguments.

The complexity of the discipline, in view of its history along with more recent developments, has been due not just to the many aspects of → religion. Since early in the 19th century and through the first years of the 21st, philosophy of religion has proceeded, in its literature, along at least four distinguishable lines. Beginning with G. W. F. Hegel (1770-1831), who perhaps coined the phrase "philosophy of religion," there first was a kind of broadly synthesizing inquiry to uncover, clarify, and set out the philosophical substance, the depth and breadth of concept, presumably underlying the life, practices, and overt figurative doctrines of a religious tradition. The principal example of this approach is Hegel's concept of the Absolute Spirit as it pertains to Christianity (→ Absolute, The). Under this heading would also come Ludwig Feuerbach's (1804-72) interpretation of the notion of God as a projection of human need and imagination or the more recent project of "demythologizing" elements of biblical narrative.

Second, there have been studies attending especially to religious experience, its types and formative concepts and symbols, and in what way or ways it can be thought to be a mode of cognition. Of note here are classic studies by William James (1842-1910) and Rudolph Otto (1869-1937), also such work as that of Paul Ricoeur (1913-2005) and studies under the heading → "phenomenology of religion," and recently William Alston's work on the epistemology of religious experience.

Third, the emergence in mid-20th-century philosophy of "the linguistic turn" has occasioned an interest among some philosophers of religion in the analysis of → language, mainly along two lines: (1) language types as they have important uses in the practices, rituals, and discourses of a religious tradition; and (2) the general matter of the role of language in religion, its enablements and its limitations.

And fourth, philosophers have published studies in a style suggestive of the craft of argument among the medieval scholastics and (for example) René Descartes (1596-1650) and G. W. Leibniz (1646-1716). These studies have consisted in analysis and assessment of the central concepts, propositions, and pertinent justifying arguments of a religious tradition, mainly as they are set down in writings. Within English-speaking settings this fourth kind of study has been especially to the fore, with much attention to refinements of concepts and arguments within the range of topics regarding monotheism.

2. Monotheism

It is useful to begin with the large topic of monotheism, both because of the above-mentioned prominence it has had in certain settings and because it provides a test case for the wider spread of studies in religious thought. Monotheism may be generally thought of as the doctrine that there exists an almighty, omniscient, and supremely good personal being and that this being is self-sufficient, infinite, and the creator of whatever else exists. Each of the predicates here has been the object of reflection and controversy, for about each of them it can be asked: what does it mean? What would we mean, for example, in supposing that God is the creator of whatever else exists? Does God make a world or worlds out of some primordial uncreated stuff? But this, it would be thought, contradicts the doctrine here. Should we think that God created a world or worlds out of nothing, perhaps by simply willing it or them to be? But does such a notion make any sense? Baruch Spinoza (1632-77) argued, in the first part of his great work *Ethics*, that it does not. We shall return to the matter of predicates below.

2.1. *Anselm, Aquinas, Scotus*

The tradition of thought about monotheism has included certain ways of reasoning about the existence of God (→ God, Arguments for the Existence of). These ways of reasoning have been viewed ambivalently as both "proofs" of the fundamental belief that the God of monotheism exists and ways by which, as it is said, faith seeks understanding of what is believed independently of any such proofs or arguments (as we may call them). For the latter view, what is in question in the arguments is not whether God exists but rather how, on the assumption that God exists, that existence is to be thought of in distinction from the sort of existence that characterizes created beings. The medieval thinkers, for their part, evidently thought of their arguments for God's existence mainly in the latter way. But they seem also to have had some interest in making clear how → reason on its own, independently of → revelation, could demonstrate that God exists.

The ways of reasoning in question here include arguments that were proposed and discussed by such medieval thinkers as → Anselm of Canterbury (1033-1109), → Thomas Aquinas (ca. 1225-74), and John Duns Scotus (ca. 1265-1308). In what is perhaps the most puzzling and intriguing of these arguments, Anselm suggested that we should start with the basic concept of God as that than which nothing greater can be conceived. But such a possible being, Anselm pointed out, has to exist: if it did not exist, it would be lacking the positive attribute of existence and therefore would not be a being than which nothing greater can be conceived. As it was often understood, it was an argument, later known as the ontological argument, *from* the sort of being God must be thought to have *to* God's existence. Whether existence as such is a positive attribute along with such attributes as being powerful, intelligent, all-knowing, and good came to be questioned by Immanuel Kant (1724-1804) and other philosophers, who for that or a similar reason rejected Anselm's argument.

Recent discussion of the argument, however, has attended to an aspect of it that its defenders have contended has greatly strengthened it. One of these defenders, Charles Hartshorne (1897-2000), noted that what was in question for Anselm was not existence as such but rather the modal status of that existence. Things other than God, we say, exist in such a way that it is possible that they not exist. They exist, as we might put it, contingently. But if God existed contingently, God would not be that than which nothing greater can be conceived: we could conceive something greater, something that exists in such a way that it is not possible that it not exist. Therefore God exists noncontingently, or necessarily. God has the positive attribute of necessary existence. But if God exists necessarily, then it follows, it is supposed, that God exists. In this "modal" form Anselm's argument for the existence of God has continued to be of interest to philosophers, some vigorously rejecting it, others affirming it.

Other arguments, usually called cosmological arguments, have depended on a principle of sufficient reason or cause. In a general form of such an argument, it may be noted that any given state, event, or entity that we observe has a cause consisting in some complex of states, events, or entities preceding it, that this in turn has a cause, and that such a series, so far as our reason (independently of faith informed by revelation) can tell, as Thomas Aquinas was willing to allow, might well extend back in time infinitely. Nonetheless, it may be supposed, the entire complex of such states, events, or entities — the universe, even if it is beginningless — must also have a cause, which is therefore a cause outside of the world's temporal series (→ Causality). There would therefore have to exist, proponents of this sort of argument conclude, a primary creating and sustaining cause of the universe. Aquinas set out such an argument from the causation of the things we observe, and also arguments of a similar pattern from motion (broadly considered) and from the contingency of everything in the world; and from these arguments he inferred the existence of a first uncaused cause, a prime unmoved mover, and a necessary being. A major part of his larger argument for God was to show that the first cause (or prime mover, or necessary being) must have the attributes the medievals supposed God to have: the attributes of pure actuality, utter simplicity and unity, immutability, and timelessness, as well as omniscience, omnipotence, and perfect goodness.

Scotus developed an elaborate version of the cosmological argument. But he also set out some elements of argument that tend toward an interesting variation of the modal argument, one that goes from the possibility of a necessary or uncreated cause to its existence. He argued that, as for anything that is the case or is not the case, for a necessary or uncreated cause of all else that exists not to exist there would have to be a reason. But such a reason could only be (1) a condition or ground implicit in the notion of a necessary or uncreated cause itself or else (2) something about other possible entities and conditions that would be sufficient to prevent a necessary or uncreated cause. The only possible condition or ground under (1) is that the idea of a necessary or uncreated cause contains or implies a contradiction. But the idea of such a being, so Scotus argues, is not self-contradictory. Could there be, as regards (2), a condition or ground sufficient to prevent the existence of a necessary or uncreated cause, something (in other words) more ultimate than it? Scotus thought the answer here, from the very notion of a necessary or uncreated cause, had clearly to be negative. Hence, there being no possible condition or ground for a necessary or uncreated cause not to exist, he concluded that such a cause exists. Scotus would suppose, of course, that the notion of a necessary or uncreated cause is partly what is to be meant by "God" and then would argue that there can exist only one such cause.

Both Scotus's argument from the possibility of God and the kind of causal arguments that Aquinas set out have been, in varying formulations, of continuing interest to philosophers even until recent times, with some of them seeing reason to reject or doubt them and others reason to suppose them defensible. Versions of these arguments turned up in

Spinoza's thought in support of his idea of God as identical with the universe considered to be a whole or system of a certain kind, multidimensioned and self-sufficient. He said that God was Nature or, in a special meaning of the word, "Substance" (→ Spinozism). Such arguments also appear in Leibniz's metaphysical papers and, with a good deal of cogent elaboration, in the writing of Samuel Clarke (1675-1729).

2.2. *Teleological Arguments*

The most commonsensical causal argument for the existence of God is the argument for an intelligent designer of the universe. It supposes that the universe in its order and intricacy, or particular lines of phenomena within it, could have been brought about only by such a great intelligence as the God of monotheism is defined to be. Critics of this way of arguing have noted that it is an argument by → analogy with the human case of a person designing and putting together a complex object, such as a watch. In his great literary-philosophical work *Dialogues concerning Natural Religion,* David Hume (1711-76) has his character Philo note that it is arbitrary to put the kind of analogy in question here ahead of any of the other, as he supposed, more plausible analogies, such as the way an animal or a plant comes into existence. Philo also pointed out that such an argument must fall well short of a justification for thinking of the divine designer as one being or as highly intelligent or as almighty. It might, for all we can infer in view of the world's manifest imperfections, Philo jauntily suggests, be a very youthful designer in one of his early and immature efforts or else a very elderly deity who has previously done better things.

The argument for a designer, however, has mutated into a broader form, one that would have us take into account not mainly singular instances of apparent design but intricacy and order in the physical world as a whole that make for its being intelligible, the possibility of evolutionary process, the emergence of organic forms, the possibility of thinking and moral creatures, and aspects of beauty — in short, all that the aesthetic, moral, and scientific parts of our experience reveal about the world (→ Evolution). With this broader range of considerations in view, so F. R. Tennant (1866-1957) in the second of the two volumes of his *Philosophical Theology* argued, the theistic outlook on the world seems more reasonable than the alternatives to it. This argument has the strength, or perhaps weakness, of informal probability and hence, it would be thought, weak conclusiveness. But then, Tennant would argue, this is the very sort of reasoning to which we commonly resort in justifying large-scale hypotheses in scientific work. Why shouldn't it, it can be asked, similarly suffice for the theist? More recently, Richard Swinburne, in his book *The Existence of God* (1979), has set out a probability argument similar to Tennant's but with attention to more recent probability theory.

There are also arguments regarding God as the necessary ground of morality. It would be thought that our claims about right and wrong or just and unjust do in fact have an aspect of objectivity about them that, it would be argued, cannot finally be accounted for in any other way than to suppose it is grounded in the nature or will of God.

3. Faith and Reason

We noted above a certain ambivalence about the earlier arguments regarding God's existence. Was it their purpose to demonstrate that God exists, or rather to make clear to faith's understanding something about the mode of God's existence? It continues to be part of debate concerning such arguments to inquire about their legitimate role in relation to the concrete life and faith of adherents to the theistic religious traditions. For the medieval philosophers the arguments for God's existence did not stand as fully conclusive and significant independently of revelation, and they are not properly thought of as preceding → faith or as necessary for faith. Later Christian thinkers who continued something of the tradition of the arguments did so with varying emphases on one or another of the different strains of argument and of their uses. Thinkers of the Lutheran and Reformed traditions, however, have often rejected altogether such → "natural theology," doing so for a theological reason. In their view, the practice of natural theology presumes a human capacity to come up with a knowledge of God solely by human reason and independently of the workings of divine → grace, something that is impossible, they would hold, in view of the disablements of human nature through → sin.

Some more recent philosopher-theologians, in taking note of what they find important in the traditional arguments, put aside their formal aspects as arguments and instead attend to fundamental apprehensions they think underlie the arguments. One such view, an "ontological approach," as Paul → Tillich (1886-1965) interprets it, recalls a theme as much from → Augustine as from Anselm. What Augustine had underscored was the unavoidability of → truth. He did so by noting that if we were to say there is no truth, then it would follow that it is true that there is no truth — and hence paradoxically there is truth. But then it is a short step to our apprehension of God. For, Tillich maintains, truth as such has a depth to it: in its depth or grounding, God is truth.

Another view, associated with Austin Farrer (1904-68), suggests a cosmological approach. By this view, we have something of a basic apprehension of God in clearly apprehending the contingency of any "finite" thing along with the entirety of the finite. The acute problem, on this understanding, concerns the difficulties of characterizing God. Farrer has explored this matter in much of its complexity in his *Finite and Infinite* and *Faith and Speculation.*

Considerations about the traditional arguments aside, some recent philosophers have maintained that religious faith can be shown to be rational in other ways. Of interest here are two lines of argument that in different ways find the basis of religious faith in experience. William Alston, following up on some of the cases to which William James attended, has argued that (1) our ordinary perceptions of physical objects may be put under as severe doubt as the doubt we might think to claim about the mystic's supposed apprehension of divine reality, but (2) we nonetheless, in the absence of good reasons to the contrary, reasonably take those ordinary perceptions to be trustworthy as perceptions of real things. Hence, Alston concludes, (3) it is likewise reasonable for the mystic himself or herself, and others of us by way of the mystic's testimony, to regard the mystic's experience as a veridical apprehension of God. Some philosophers, though they might concede that the mystic is apprehending something highly unusual, would wonder whether that something is identifiable as the God of the monotheistic traditions.

The second line of argument has less to do with extraordinary experiences and more with the day-to-day living with conviction on the part of ordinary sincere believers. To begin with, what should be made of the question, What does reasonable or justified belief that God exists consist in? What makes any belief that something is the case reasonable or justified? Does this belief, in order to be supposed reasonable or justified, have to be based on beliefs of a more basic sort that would constitute "evidence" for it? But then, it would be thought, we commonly take many of our beliefs, such as the belief that there exist other persons, to be reasonable or justified without our having to refer them to presumably more basic considerations. Why then, it would be asked, shouldn't the serious believer in one of the monotheistic faiths, one who feels deeply and intimately, as it seems to the believer, the presence of God in every hour and phase of daily life, take this belief to be reasonable without its having to be grounded on presumptively more basic beliefs? The view that would not allow this concession, as the philosophers who press these questions (esp. Alvin Plantinga and Nicholas Wolterstorff) would argue, presupposes a dubious notion of justified belief, one that divides beliefs into those that are basic (or underived from other beliefs) and those that are nonbasic (i.e., derived from other beliefs), and then contends that the believer's theistic belief can be neither a basic belief nor justifiably derived from basic beliefs.

At this point different philosophers who are sympathetic with the believer's experience and outlook are likely to offer two somewhat different replies to this skeptical approach. In common they would hold that the particular notion of justified belief, often referred to as classical foundationalism, is itself without any justification and indeed cannot, in the form above, be justified in its own terms. But some of these philosophers would allow that we can modify the model, retain something of the notion of "properly" basic beliefs, but then deny the claim that the believer's theistic belief cannot be properly basic, as basic as one's belief can be that there exist other persons, or that there is an external world, or that things physical will continue to behave in accordance with laws. Along with this line of argument, Plantinga has developed in much detail a theory of warranted belief and attempted to show how orthodox Christian beliefs satisfy the relevant criteria of warrant.

Other philosophers would take a somewhat different approach regarding the believer's theistic outlook. They would suppose that (1) there are in our set of convictions generally very capacious construing or interpreting belief-systems and that (2) the believer's belief that God exists must be taken as a part, doubtless an essential part, of such a broader system of belief. They would then argue that (3) a belief is reasonable provided that the belief-system of which it is an essential part is coherent within itself and coherent with other items that we commonly take to be knowledge, such as the findings and theories of the sciences, and provided also that it can be justified informally or by its "making sense" of the world and of human good and evil and by its capacity to generate cogent and plausible replies to objections. But they would hold that (4) a comprehensive theistic (or other religious) belief-system can be thought to meet the conditions in question and therefore is itself a reasonable system, one to which an assent is justified. This way of justification is how we would proceed, Basil Mitchell suggests, in justifying other large-scale convictions, such as our belief in democracy. But if the model makes sense in the case of belief in democracy, then why should it not be to the point for religious belief-systems that arguably meet the criteria?

It should be noted that the reference above to serious believers, whose experience, as it seems to them with their background, is one of deep and continuing presence of divinity, suggests a certain duality in the query about justified belief. It is the divide into the two considerations: (1) What makes it reasonable or justified for a person in his or her circumstances to assent to a certain belief about something's being the case? and (2) What makes the belief itself, what the person believes, reasonable or justified? Our account above has put the stress on (2). But discussions of what is often called "the ethics of belief" also involve (1). These matters of reasonable or justified belief have been developed and commented on extensively in different ways in the writings of such philosophers as John Hick, John E. Smith, Mitchell, Plantinga, and Wolterstorff.

4. Other Questions about Monotheism

The matter of justified belief is one of the main divisions of thought under the heading of monotheism. The other is a set of inquiries, such as the following:

- How is → evil to be accounted for if there exists an omnipotent (or, as some say, almighty), omniscient, supremely benevolent personal being?
- If God is omniscient and knows therefore what any of us will do at any future time, can it be supposed that we ever do anything freely?
- If God is eternal or somehow outside of time, how is it possible to think of God as acting, for example, as creating or sustaining the universe?
- What, more generally, is God's relation to time?
- What can be coherently meant in ascribing omnipotence to God? (likewise for all of God's presumed attributes)
- What metaphysics is implicit in the doctrines of the → Trinity and the → incarnation?

These topics are but a few of many.

The most profound, weighty, and ancient of the queries here is the first, the matter of evil. Philosophers since Hume have divided it into two distinct problems. The one is the old problem of the logical compatibility between the supposition of an almighty and supremely good deity on the one side and the facts in the world of appalling evils both of human doing and of nature's happenings on the other. It has become more difficult to claim this problem as definitively unsolvable. Such a conclusion would require a demonstration that an omnipotent and supremely benevolent person could not have had a good and sufficient reason for allowing the instances of evil in question, which proposition it seems difficult, and perhaps is impossible, to make good on. It need only be pointed out that God might have created the sort of universe we exist in at least in part as a domain allowing such finite agents as ourselves freely to become loving and just persons in accordance with a loving and just but noncoercive divine will. The → autonomy of human agency entails the risk of the great evils we in fact observe, such as injustice, oppression, and poverty. Such a universe also entails, as well as a natural order of intricate and vast fields and centers of energy, a nature, in the spaces of human and animal agency, behaving predictably or in accordance with laws that humans can discover and take account of. Such a setting, however, entails, under certain continuing conditions, such phenomena as earthquakes, hurricanes, and often what we call accidents. John Hick and earlier Austin Farrer have each developed theodicies in some variation of these considerations, Hick along the lines of an Irenaean view (from → Irenaeus, d. ca. A.D. 200), Farrer with a version of an Augustinian understanding (from Augustine, 354-430).

Marilyn McCord Adams has noted, however, that the problem of horrendous evils, as they afflict individual human beings (as with being a victim or a perpetrator in a Nazi death camp), remains intractable for traditional "generic and global" notions (as she calls them). In her view, the relevant question is: How might divine goodness be thought of in relation to a particular instance of evil, and this so as to find that such goodness somehow "defeats" the evil? What is needed, she argues, is a notion of transcendent good that as such is incommensurate with any degree or amount of other goods and could therefore in some way, as other goods cannot, defeat or overcome horrendous evil. Adams invokes distinctively Christian ideas here, such as the notion of God's participation in the human situation through Christ's passion and the possibility of the sort of presumably incommensurate good of a deeply sympathetic human participation in that divine act. Adams's argument needs only the possibility of a defeating good, which possibility, if it could be sketched out in some detail and shown in the concepts it entails to be coherent, would undercut the claim of contradiction between divine existence and horrendous evil.

As to the second problem of evil, it concerns what we can reasonably take to be likely about the world as we observe it. The antitheistic claim here is not for a clear logical incompatibility between God and evil. Instead, William Rowe has argued that the immense amount of appalling evils in the world make it unlikely that it is the creation of an almighty and supremely good personal deity. The considerations Farrer and Hick (and other philosophers) set out regarding the first problem would also weigh on our sense of likelihood or unlikelihood with the latter problem. In any case, this problem of evil remains a subject of lively dispute.

5. Words and Their Limits

Such inquiries about monotheism suppose that the belief in question is to be taken as possibly or actually true in a literal sense. But considerations concerning religious language entail complications that were well known among the medieval thinkers. Is God good or a person, does God know what God knows, in the same sense in which human beings are good or are persons and know what they know? It would be difficult, many philosophers say, to suppose that such a term as "know" or "person" applies to God in the same sense in which it pertains to human beings. Some philosophers think this also is the case with the term "good." It is fitting, they hold, to apply "good" to God, but the sense in which it pertains to God is related, as a kind of proportion, to the divine essence as the sense in which it pertains to human being is related to what is characteristic about human life and conduct. Since, as these philosophers hold, we have no access to the divine essence, we cannot know what the term "good" means as applied to God. A prominent doctrine from the medievals is that such predicates as "good," "wise," "know," and "act," as applied to God, are to be taken analogically rather than either univocally (as having the same sense) or equivocally (as having an altogether different sense) as compared with the senses the terms have as regards human beings. The notion of analogy here, which suggests the idea of similarity but is often taken instead as a matter of proportion (as above), is however a difficult and much discussed one.

In a broader reach of the matter of religious language, it has been often maintained that concepts and the words that express them — again, such concepts as "know," "cause," "essence," and "existence" as they turn up in philosophical theology are pertinent examples — are irrelevant to a worshiper's experiences of divinity and his or her need for talk about them. This view is to the effect that all such talk is fittingly offered only in → metaphor and → symbol. Of what use, then, are the abstractions of → theology? Some would say they are gratuitous, others that they serve in collating and ordering the metaphors and symbols of the primary level of practice and discourse, and yet others that they are the means, though not necessarily in their orthodox form, for translating or "demythologizing" the metaphors and symbols into an understanding of a basic human way of existing in the world, where the world, as it would be thought by some who have this general view, can no longer be understood as having a supernatural aspect. Tillich held that the term "being" in the proposition "God is being itself" is the one term that applies literally to divinity. All other terms, he supposed, can only be symbolic, which is to say that they only roughly or approximately "point to" or suggest aspects of divinity and divinity's relation to human life. Furthermore, Tillich denied that God is a being (as he was apt to put it) alongside other beings. God is rather, he said, "the infinite and inexhaustible ground of being" for any and all existing entities.

Toward the end of his *Tractatus Logicus-Philosophicus* (1921), Ludwig Wittgenstein (1889-1951), in a series of puzzling and haunting sentences, asserts that some of the most important concerns, such as those of ethics and the religious matter of the meaning of life and of the world, cannot, as he (and many others) would say, "be put into words." Only facts can have representation in words, and values as well as religious concerns transcend facts and do not enter into them. It does not follow that human beings cannot find their way through their deeper concerns. It is rather that they cannot do so by way of fact-representing language.

In a somewhat different way, Wittgenstein's later writing (and compilations of students' notes of his lectures) have been of interest to philosophers of religion and theologians in their efforts to clarify how religious and theological terms function and mean. In his *Lectures and Conversations on Aesthetics, Psychology, and Religious Belief*, for example, Wittgenstein works through several cases of "believing," as in believing there is a god or God, or believing in a last judgment. His initial point here is that "believing" in these cases is quite different from ordinary believing. As to ordinary believing, we ask for evidence. Regarding someone's believing there is a God or a last judgment, however, it would be absurd, Wittgenstein thinks, to inquire after evidences or proofs. Moreover, if someone believes firmly or strongly that there exists God or a last judgment, this firmness or strength has nothing to do with the strength of evidences or proofs but rather with the firmness of faith, the consistency with which the person "regulates" his or her life. This aspect of Wittgenstein's thought has been sympathetically considered by such thinkers as D. Z. Phillips, Paul Holmer, and Hilary Putnam.

6. Conclusion

As was asserted in §1, philosophy of religion takes as its subject matter such topics as religious experience, religious language, the relations between religion and science, the relations between religion and history, and the bearing on one or another religious tradition of the aspects of philosophy that come under the headings of metaphysics, epistemology, and ethical theory. This account has put to the fore what are but samples from among these topics, though they are important ones; and the samples have come from largely Christian sources or sources seriously affected by Christian ideas. An analogous account in relation, for example, to a Buddhist community and mode of thought would appeal to different — though perhaps not invariably altogether different — categories and arguments under the broad rubrics of metaphysics, epistemology, and ethical theory. As to ethics, the body of sayings and theory about the conduct of human life is at the heart of much thought in Buddhism, as is true also in the theistic traditions.

Of particular interest to Christian thought, for example, is Robert Adams's large-scale and intricately argued work *Finite and Infinite Goods* (1999), in which he sets out and defends the thesis that our considered designations of "good" in any of our worldly contexts must presuppose the notion, and reality, of a supreme → good. For Plato this good had been what he called "the Form of the Good," and in the Christian context it is God's own goodness. Within this framework Adams also works out a role for a theory that in recent times he and Philip Quinn have taken the lead in reviving, what has been called the "divine command" theory of ethical obligation.

Along with many others, Quinn and Adams represent a development of some notice in philosophy of religion during the latter half of the 20th century, that of philosophers thoroughly conversant with the queries and modes of formulation and argument in what has often been called → analytic philosophy and have written in that vein about topics in philosophy of religion. Central to the outlook of these philosophers is an interest in bringing a renewed clarity and rigor to the topics and arguments of the metaphysics of → theism. The influence of these philosophers within the discipline has been considerable and accounts for much about philosophy of religion as discussed here.

7. Problems

7.1. *Proper Orientation of the Field*

There remains a problem as to the proper orientation of philosophy of religion. It is usually said, as is noted above, that the object of philosophy of religion is not to try to persuade anyone, for example, of monotheism or of → atheism. Its object, rather, is to analyze and assess the reasons monotheists or atheists use to justify their views. It is, as is sometimes said, a "second-order inquiry," a discourse not itself religious about other discourse that in some way is religious. It is related to things religious as the philosophy of art is related to artistic activity, objects, and criticism. Hence it is thought by its more recent practitioners to be distinct from → apologetics and natural theology, distinct also therefore from thought and writing that rejects religious claims or practices, or that is atheistic.

What, then, about a philosopher's assessment of arguments in making a case for theism or atheism, or for a certain approach to one of the problems of evil? We can think here, for example, of Hartshorne's assessment, in several of his writings, of Anselm's modal argument for the existence of God, or Tillich's assessment of the ontological and cosmological "approaches" in his essay "Two Types of Philosophy of Religion," or any of the books and essays by our recent philosophers setting forth their → theodicies, or J. L. Mackie's (1917-81) defense of atheism in his *The Miracle of Theism*, or Hume's *Dialogues on Natural Religion* (or his essay "On Miracles"). These writings are good examples of philosophical analysis and assessment of religious ideas, of religious concepts, propositions, and arguments. They therefore presumably fall under philosophy of religion as a second-order activity. But in and with their being such, they are also examples of religious thought or philosophy: the assessments they set out, constructive and otherwise, of religious concepts and propositions and the primary arguments in which they appear support and in some cases establish substantive positions regarding religious perplexities. In this respect they are, so to say, "first-order" and presumably fall short of satisfying the rule of second-orderedness. We must leave unsettled this ambivalence about the discipline.

7.2. *Conflicting Ultimate Claims*

We have taken notice in the above that in principle the field is much broader than would be suggested by a concentration on the theistic traditions. For the sorts of philosophical studies that pertain to concepts and reasons within those traditions can also be worked out in ways that would be fitting for other traditions. Such studies have, for that matter, been on the scene in recent decades. A notable earlier comparative study was Ninian Smart's (1927-2001) *Reasons and Faiths* (1958), which concerned concepts and reasoning in → Buddhism and → Hinduism, as well as Christianity.

In this connection, both for philosophers of religion and for thinkers within the religious traditions, a certain obvious and troubling difficulty emerges. For how should we account for the many claims about the world and human destiny across the many religious traditions? Can we say they are all true? But they conflict. Some hold, as in the theistic traditions, that the ultimately real being is personal, while others, such as the Advaita-Vedanta school in Hinduism, think it to be impersonal.

These different ways of thinking about what is ultimate also entail different and incompatible ways of dealing with the limitations of human life, with evil, contingency, and death. Should we adopt a skepticism about all such claims? Should the members of a certain tradition (e.g., that of Christians who regularly affirm Christianity's traditional creeds) take themselves to be justified in asserting the exclusive truth of their tradition's claims? Are the members of *all* religious communities somehow justified in asserting the exclusive truth of their respective traditions' claims? What should we say that "justified" here entails? Are the claims about the ultimate and human destiny, across all of the traditions, to be thought of as symbolic enhancements for what at bottom have their real meanings in the particular ways of saying how best to order human life and live it out accordingly? Or, as the philosopher John Hick maintains, are the systems of claims of the different traditions with their varying symbols, doctrines, and customs but different ways of indirectly apprehending the same ultimately real? What seems reasonably clear from the continuing discussion of this difficult matter is that none of these approaches is immune from serious objection.

7.3. *Focus of the Field on Thought*

Some critics also wonder whether the field is too narrowly given over to the study of religious thought, of concepts and arguments, and of writings in which these appear. The name of the discipline, however, is philosophy of religion; and religion, as the presumed object of the discipline, it would be contended, involves more than thought.

In reply, it would first be noted that philosophical reflection on religion and religious traditions is not to be confused with any such other approach as the history, anthropology, sociology, or psychology of religions. Moreover, it might be said that the field, as currently in the main practiced, is observing an old dictum about philosophy itself, for it would not be a new thing to suppose that philosophy is precisely thought about *thought*.

Yet some practitioners of the field would agree with the reservation and would point to examples of philosophical reflection on such matters as ritual, prayer, and institutional structures. Such studies include those thought of as "phenomenological." We can anticipate that the future of the discipline will encompass a good many studies outside of the rubrics of the field as described above. We can also anticipate that those rubrics, in renewed guises, will continue to interest thinkers, scholars, and students.

Bibliography: M. M. Adams, *Horrendous Evils and the Goodness of God* (Ithaca, N.Y., 2000) • R. Adams, *The Virtue of Faith* (Oxford, 1987), esp. chap. 7, "A Modified Divine Command Theory of Ethical Wrongness," and chap. 10, "Moral Arguments for Theistic Belief" • W. Alston, *Divine Nature and Human Language* (Ithaca, N.Y., 1989); idem, *Perceiving God* (Ithaca, N.Y., 1991) • A. M. Farrer, *Faith and Speculation* (New York, 1967); idem, *Finite and Infinite* (London, 1943); idem, *Love Almighty and Ills Unlimited* (London, 1962) • R. Gale, *On the Nature and Existence of God* (Cambridge, 1991) • C. Hartshorne, *Anselm's Discovery: A Re-examination of the Ontological Proof for God's Existence* (La Salle, Ill., 1965) • J. Hick, *Disputed Questions in Theology and the Philosophy of Religion* (New Haven, 1993); idem, *Evil and the God of Love* (London, 1966); idem, *Philosophy of Religion* (3d ed.; Englewood Cliffs, N.J., 1983) • N. Kretzmann, *The Metaphysics of Theism* (Oxford, 1997) • J. L. Mackie, *The Miracle of Theism* (Oxford, 1982) • B. Mitchell, *The Justification of Religious Belief* (Oxford, 1973) • H. R. Niebuhr, *Radical Monotheism and Western Culture* (New York, 1960) • A. Plantinga, *God, Freedom, and Evil* (New York, 1974); idem, "Reason and Belief in God," *Faith and Rationality* (ed. A. Plantinga and N. Wolterstorff; Notre Dame, Ind., 1983) 16-93; idem, *Warranted Christian Belief* (Oxford, 2000) • P. Quinn and C. Taliaferro, eds., *A Companion to Philosophy of Religion* (Oxford, 1997) • J. Ross, *Philosophical Theology* (New York, 1969) • W. Rowe, *The Cosmological Argument* (Princeton, 1975); idem, "The Empirical Argument from Evil," *Rationality, Religious Belief, and Moral Commitment* (ed. R. Audi and W. J. Wainwright; Ithaca, N.Y., 1986) 227-47; idem, *Philosophy of Religion: An Introduction* (2d ed.; Belmont, Mass., 1993) • N. Smart, *Reasons and Faiths* (London, 1958) • J. Smith, *Experience and God*

(New York, 1968) • R. Swinburne, *The Existence of God* (Oxford, 1979) • P. Tillich, "Two Types of Philosophy of Religion" (1946), *Theology of Culture* (New York, 1959) 10-29 • N. Wolterstorff, "Can Belief in God Be Rational If It Has No Foundations?" *Faith and Rationality*, ed. Plantinga and Wolterstorff, 135-86.

Roger Gustavsson

Philosophy of Science

1. Historical Development
2. Modern Approaches
3. Scientific Methods

The philosophy of science studies the sciences, their methods, and their results, including a broad complex of questions relating to the analysis and reconstruction of scientific language, hypotheses, and theories, and the rationality and methodology of the natural and human sciences.

1. Historical Development

Historically, the philosophy of science reaches back to the beginnings of scientific knowledge in antiquity. Plato (427-347 B.C.) showed that knowledge can have different degrees of certainty. For him mathematics and → philosophy were rated first because they are grounded in universal principles (forms or ideas), from which all particular definitions and statements can be deduced. In contrast, Aristotle (384-322) introduced an empirical methodology and can thus be regarded as the founder of the inductive method, which he applied extensively in his scientific writings. During the late classical and medieval period, natural philosophy included what we would now distinguish as science and philosophy of science. Philosophy of science has thus been a central part of Western philosophy down through the ages.

While the Scholastics considered theology to be a science *(scientia)*, the distinction between natural philosophy and theology was important to the development of separate faculties in medieval universities such as Paris and Oxford (→ Scholasticism). This distinction allowed natural philosophy to develop its own methodology, which was empirical. Mathematics, especially geometry, was central to the development of natural philosophy in the late Middle Ages. Medieval natural philosophy, which was Aristotelian in tone, developed through commentaries on the scientific works of Aristotle, along with independent treatises on special topics.

Scientists of the early modern period, especially Nicholas Copernicus (1473-1543) and Galileo Galilei (1546-1642), continued to develop an independent natural philosophy that was mathematical, empirical, and soon became anti-Aristotelian, although not anti-Christian. The climax of this new methodology came in the work of Isaac Newton (1642-1727), but the spirit of this new approach was articulated earlier by the English lawyer and philosopher Francis Bacon (1561-1626). Bacon championed the new empirical, mathematical, and inductive approach, as over against the Aristotelian and Scholastic tradition. On the Continent, René Descartes (1596-1650) stands at the head of the more rationalist philosophy of science that developed there.

The British empirical tradition led to the skeptical philosophy of David Hume (1711-76), who questioned the validity of any knowledge (theological or scientific) beyond immediate experience other than conceptual truths (→ Empiricism). At the same time it also led to the "common sense" philosophy of Thomas Reid (1710-96) and the development of a natural theology that sought to demonstrate the existence and wisdom of God through reflection upon the world of science (→ Physicotheology).

Immanuel Kant (1724-1804) combined both the empirical and the rational approaches in a new and influential philosophy. His critical philosophy vindicated the rationality of science by limiting scientific knowledge to the world of appearances or phenomena. The basic principles of scientific method were located by Kant within the human mind, that is, in pure → reason or a priori → truth. Scientific knowledge is vindicated but limited to the world of → experience, and Kant was critical of any natural theology based upon science.

2. Modern Approaches

In the early 20th century the Vienna Circle identified philosophy with the logic of science, that is, with a logical analysis of the language used by science as the foundation for any meaningful utterance. According to this school of logical → positivism, associated largely with Rudolf Carnap (1891-1970), only verifiable sentences have meaning; the sentences of → ethics or → religion are therefore neither true nor false but meaningless.

This approach was contested at first. In his *Logic of Scientific Discovery* (1935), K. Popper (1902-94) pointed out that experience does not verify so much as falsify empirical theories. Falsification, then, is a restrictive criterion in both empirical science and metaphysics: meaningful theories must be falsifiable. Analytic philosophers soon applied this criterion to religious language, arguing that religion must somehow be falsifiable in order to be meaningful.

Ludwig Wittgenstein (1889-1951) represents a decisive break with the positivism of his own early work in his later philosophical development, especially his famous, posthumously published *Philosophical Investigations* (1953). Focusing on the actual working of ordinary language, Wittgenstein heralded a shift to the "grammar" of meaning grounded in life and practice rather than pure → logic.

Developing some of these ideas in a famous work devoted to the philosophy of science, *The Structure of Scientific Revolutions* (1962), Thomas S. Kuhn (1922-96) argued that science develops historically and socially, based upon "paradigms" that ground the methodologies and assumptions of a particular science. Changes in these paradigms, or "paradigm shifts," are not simply the result of pure logic and experiment but also include values and assumptions from a larger worldview. Since the work of Kuhn, philosophy of science has become closely allied with the history and sociology of science and the practice of working scientists. Postmodern philosophers of science question the unique rationality of science and its claims to discover facts about reality (realism) in an objective manner.

3. Scientific Methods

After Kuhn, philosophy of science has come to focus on the traditional and historical character of scientific rationality. Philosophy of science includes not only a study of physical sciences but also the human and social sciences. The social-scientific study of science itself has developed into interdisciplinary "science studies." Instead of the dream of a unified logic for all science, the many and various sciences instantiate differing rationalities that are appropriate for the areas they study and the communities of scholarship they represent. The notion that there is one right "scientific method" is rejected. This development allows room for some theologians and philosophers of religion to argue that Christian theology has its own legitimate rationality that cannot be reduced to that of the empirical sciences.

→ Science and Theology

Bibliography: G. Andersson, *Criticism and the History of Science* (Leiden, 1994) • L. Laudan, *Beyond Positivism and Relativism* (Boulder, Colo., 1996) • J. Losee, *Historical Introduction to the Philosophy of Science* (Oxford, 2001) • E. Oeser, *Wissenschaft und Information* (3 vols.; Oldenburg, 1976) • A. Padgett, *Science and the Study of God* (Grand Rapids, 2003) • W. Pannenberg, *Theology and the Philosophy of Science* (Philadelphia, 1976) • D. Ratzsch, *Science and Its Limits* (Downers Grove, Ill., 2000).

Alan G. Padgett and Erhard Oeser

Physicotheology

Physicotheology is theology that gathers evidences of purpose in nature. It arose in the early → Enlightenment as a form of the older European → natural theology. It made use of the same → allegorical interpretation of nature and of the same teleological proof of God (→ God, Arguments for the Existence of, 2.5), deducing the existence of an all-powerful and all-wise builder of the universe from its perfect, purposeful, and beautiful order.

1. Roots

1.1. ***Scientific***

Physicotheology was an important factor in the development of modern science. By demystifying nature in a pious fashion, it helped to make science widely acceptable. It represented a Christian → piety that established a correlation of → science and theology that has never been equaled. In opposition to the → atheism of its day, it had an → apologetic purpose (→ Deism; Pantheism).

Its primary aim, however, was to show that the world is God's → creation, a world for us humans, by means of what we can know about it scientifically, that is, by "the light of nature." Such was the intention of almost all scientists from N. Copernicus (1473-1543) to I. Newton (1642-1727), G. W. Leibniz (1646-1716), and L. Euler (1707-83). In the period from around 1650 and on into the 18th century, over 1,000 titles of edifying literature and poetry were published with physicotheological intention in the Protestant countries of Europe.

1.2. *Christian*

Appealing to Rom. 1:20 and → Augustine's → metaphor of the book of nature alongside Scripture (→ Augustine's Theology), physicotheology undertook to link Greek cosmogony (Plato's Demiurge; → Platonism) and Stoic anthropocentricity (Cicero's utility argument; → Stoicism) to the biblical belief in the Creator. It thus sought to follow Augustine (354-430) and → Thomas Aquinas (ca. 1225-74; → Thomism) in offering proof of the existence of God and his cosmically relevant attributes (power, wisdom, providence). But it also saw itself as a school devoted to praise of the Creator along the lines of Raymond of Sabunde (d. ca. 1436), Tridentine theology (R. → Bellarmine; → Trent, Council of), and Protestant theologians like J. Arndt, P. Gerhardt, and C. K. von Rosenroth.

2. Development

2.1. *Early Supporters*

Not by accident was the concept of physicotheology born in religiously, politically, and scientifically revolutionary England with W. Charleton (1617-1707), H. More (1614-87), S. Parker (1640-88), chemist R. Boyle (1627-91), botanist J. Ray (1627-1705), and theologian W. Derham (1657-1735), who popularized it. The Dutch zoologist J. Swammerdam (1637-80) and the physician B. van Nieuwentijt (1654-1718) were important authors.

In later 17th-century Germany human anatomy became a theme in natural theology. At Hamburg we might mention the polymath J. A. Fabricius (1668-1736), pastor F. C. Lesser (1692-1754), councillor B. H. Brockes (1680-1747), and theologian H. S. Reimarus (1694-1768). Reference might also be made to the physician A. von Haller (1708-77) and G. Gruner (1717-78) in Switzerland and to Archbishop F. de la Mothe-Fénelon (1651-1715) and Abbot N. A. Pluche (1688-1761) in France. Under pressure from atheistic materialism (J. O. de Lamettrie), however, as well as the criticism of optimism by French rationalists (esp. Voltaire), physicotheology soon lost its influence.

2.2. *Decline*

Even in the 18th century physicotheology was exhausting itself, not least through its journalistic success, which tempted it to take even the most mundane natural phenomena (grass, snowflakes, bees, frogs, grasshoppers, etc.) and, by minute and often dilettante analysis, to try to show how they promote the glory of God and human welfare. Plausibility depended not only on the observation of individual things and their structures and functions, including by the use of new instruments that gave an extra range to the senses, but also on the theoretical model of the machine, in which the regular constitutes the miraculous (with appeal made to Wis. 11:20, "you have arranged all things by measure and number and weight"). The effort depended also on empirical induction, in which the plenitude and beauty of natural things are affirmed as a reflection of the divine glory. The seeking of order is something that we still find today. The observation of nature, however, did not essentially mean anything more than traditional empiricism, and for this reason it was not as important as the theoretical construction.

Physicotheology also came into conflict with biblical natural history, which found no place for fossils in the mountains, unless resort was had to speculative explanations. The moral utilitarianism of physicotheology linked its fate to that of → theodicy, whose assertion of the harmony and → teleology of the world increasingly ran up against the experience of earthly evil.

Finally, D. Hume (1711-76) and I. Kant (1724-1804; → Kantianism) robbed physicotheology of its epistemological foundations. The teleological argument, though supposedly empirically based, is in fact an a priori cosmological argument, which in turn is a disguised ontological argument (→ Ontology), so that it lies outside the possibilities of human knowledge (*Critique of Pure Reason* B620-30, 648-58).

3. Evaluation

3.1. *Critique*

Because physicotheology reads more in the book of nature than the unaided senses can detect, it transgresses the ancient religious warning against theoretical curiosity. It can thus be the basis of a new quasi-divine self-awareness of human knowledge and can demand a deliberate attention to nature that an interest in mastering it requires (F. Bacon).

Physicotheology puts the book of nature on a par with that of → revelation, not as regards content but as regards certainty of knowledge. It thus makes scientists "priests of the Most High God in regard to the book of nature" (J. Kepler) and can even claim that its evidence is superior, since it is available not merely to those who are enlightened but to all rational beings.

Physicotheology also loosens the tie between God's creative work and his saving work by directly stressing the providence of God at the expense of Christian hamartiology (→ Sin). → Lutheranism found support for physicotheology in its opposition to the Calvinist doctrine of → predestination (regarded as deterministic), while → Calvinism offered support by its high religious estimation of the knowledge of nature, and → Puritanism especially by its → millenarian expectation that the new science would bring theoretical and practical → progress. At this point the perspectives of a theology of creation merged with those of a theology of salvation. Divine providence has not simply arranged the world for our profit but has so set it up that we may discern in it the divine plan of salvation and help to promote this plan by our knowledge and use of nature. Thus a pioneer of the new science could be viewed as a "Christian virtuoso" (so the title of a 1690 work by R. Boyle).

Physicotheology also reacted to the destruction of the Ptolemaic view of the universe by Copernicus and G. Bruno (1548-1600), but "cosmic nihilism" (W. Philipp) was already behind it. The shock of the "silence of endless spaces" (B. → Pascal) died down as the omnipresent God was found even in "the blessed void" (B. H. Brockes). In its own way, by a teleological interpretation of the physical world and its causal and mechanical interlinking, physicotheology helped to give humanity a central place in the cosmos. Human beings do stand on the margin of things, but appeal may be made to our rational nature. Thus even as → doxology, physicotheology shares the ambivalence of the anthropology of Enlightenment optimism.

3.2. *Influence*

In spite of its epistemological destruction, which found acceptance on the European mainland, though not in the natural theology of England and New England, physicotheology still had uncontested power to convince ordinary human reason (Kant). As J. W. Goethe noted, that which does not rank as proof may still carry force as feeling. Christian → pedagogics and → apologetics could still make use of physicotheology, then, until Darwin's theory of evolution (1859), which instrumentalized its teleology and robbed it of nature as a totality.

Only the 20th-century study of religion (→ Religious Studies) was able to recapture phenomenologically the emotional and religious significance of our human experience of nature. Roman Catholic theology still insists on the propaedeutic importance of the teleological proof of God, even if not in the form of demonstration. Protestant theology, however, has tended more and more aggressively to banish all physicotheology. The reason is not to be sought only in acceptance of the criticism of Kant but in the neological (→ Neology) reorientation of natural theology from external nature to the inner nature of pious experience, and then in the reconstruction of the doctrine of theological principles from the days of A. Ritschl (1822-89), which finally resulted in the complete loss of nature as a subject of theology no less than of science. We still might find approaches to natural theology (e.g., in A. Schlatter, K. Heim, W. Lütgert, and A. Titius), but they did not prevent an amusing but sharp rejection of physicotheology as an illegitimate theological enterprise (K. → Barth, *CD* III/1, 388-414).

3.3. *Relevance for Ecology*

A recent increase in interest in the era of the early Enlightenment in several different disciplines, including theology itself, has generated a commensurate increase in interest and research in physicotheology in connection with the shift from the age of → baroque to that of the Enlightenment. Although the results of this new research are only just now making an impact, ultimately one can expect them to throw considerable new light on the historical significance of physicotheology.

The present view of nature as our human → environment that is under threat from human culture has given the motif of physicotheology a new ecological urgency (→ Ecology). Along with occasional aesthetic and ethical revisions of Christian → piety and lifestyle, a new theology of nature demands that there be criticism of the presuppositions of early Enlightenment physicotheology that were so momentous in practice, namely, the logical order of nature, its usefulness for us, and the unlimited nature of its resources. When epistemologically clarified, however, the concept of nature that we find in physicotheology still offers the best starting point for harmonizing theology with natural science.

→ Philosophy of Nature

Bibliography: Classic works of physicotheology: R. Boyle, *A disquisition about the final causes of natural things* (1688) • B. H. Brockes, *Irdisches Vergnügen in Gott* (Earthly pleasure in God, 1721-48; repr., Stuttgart, 1999) • W. Charleton, *The darknes of atheism dispelled by the light of nature: A physico-theologicall treatise* (1652; repr., Bristol, 2002) • W. Derham, *Physico-theology; or, A Demonstration of the being and attributes of God from his works of creation* (1713; repr., New York, 1976) • J. A. Fabricius, *Hydro-Theologie* (Hamburg, 1730-34) • F. Fénelon, *Traité sur l'existence de Dieu* (Treatise on the existence of God, 1712; repr., Paris, 1990) • G. S. Gruner, *Die Eisgebirge des Schweizenlandes* (The glaciers of Switzerland, 3 vols., 1760) • A. von Haller, *Die Alpen* (Bern, 1729) • F. C. Lesser, *Insecto-theologia* (1738; ET *Insecto-theology; or, A demonstration of the being and perfections of God, from a consideration of the structure and economy of insects* [1799]) • H. More, *An antidote against atheism; or, An appeal to the naturall faculties of the minde of man* (1653; repr., Bristol, 1997) • B. VAN NIEUWENTIJT, *Het regt gebruik der werelt Beschouwingen* (The right use of contemplating the works of the Creator, 1715) • S. PARKER, *Tentamina physico-theologica de Deo* (Physicotheological examination of God, 1665) • N. A. PLUCHE, *Le spectacle de la nature* (8 vols. in 9, 1732-50; ET *Nature display'd, being discourses on natural history* [London, 1957-63]) • J. RAY, *The wisdom of God manifested in the works of creation* (1691; repr., New York, 1979) • H. S. REIMARUS, *Allgemeine Betrachtungen über die Triebe der Tiere* (General considerations on the instincts of animals, 1760; repr., 2 vols., Göttingen, 1982) • J. SWAMMERDAM, *Bybel der Natuur* (1737-38; ET *The Book of Nature* [New York, 1978]).

Other works: M. BÜTTNER and F. RICHTER, eds., *Physikotheologie im historischen Kontext* (6 vols.; Münster, 1995-97) • U. KROLZIG, "Physikotheologie," *TRE* 26.590-96 • R. H. VERMIJ, "The Beginnings of Physico-Theology: England, Holland, Germany," *Grenz-Überschreitungen* (FS M. Büttner; Bochum, 1993) 173-84 • C. ZELLE, "Sublimity in Early German Enlightenment: English Physicotheology and Its Influence on Barthold Hinrich Brockes' 'Irdisches Vergnügen in Gott,'" *State, Science, and Modernization in England from the Renaissance to the Modern Times* (ed. J. Klein; Hildesheim, 1994) 164-89.

WALTER SPARN

Pietism

1. Term, Movement, Time Span

Contemporary scholars characterize Continental Pietism, along with its sibling, Anglo-Saxon Puritanism, as the most significant movement of religious renewal in Protestantism since the → Reformation. Arising in the 17th century in the context of a perceived failure to realize the promise of the Reformation in terms of reforming and renewing Christian life as well as doctrine, Pietism pressed for the individualization and interiorization of religious life, developed new forms of personal → piety and social life that were often critical of the Zeitgeist, led to far-reaching reforms in theology and the churches, and left profound impressions on social and cultural life. The term "Pietist" was initially used in the 1670s for the followers of Philipp Jakob Spener (1635-1705), the so-called father of Pietism. In a letter of 1680 Spener refers to the term as a label of abuse and derision. The term came into wide use through a famous poem in 1689 by the Leipzig professor of rhetoric Joachim Feller (1628-91), a member of a local Pietist circle: "What is a Pietist? One who studies God's Word / and also leads a holy life according to it."

Pietism preceded and then both influenced and responded to the → Enlightenment. Pietism and the younger movement, the Enlightenment, ushered in a new period of Western Christianity that may be characterized by the imprecise concept → "modernity." Politically, this is the period from the Peace of Westphalia (1648), which concluded the → Thirty Years' War, the last major post-Reformation religious war, to the end of the old Holy Roman Empire (1806). Theologically and philosophically, classic Pietism is dated from Spener's *Pia desideria* (Pious desires, 1675), often regarded as the charter document of Pietism, to John → Wesley (1703-91), the founder of → Methodism, and Immanuel Kant's *Religion within the Limits of Reason Alone* (1793). The assigning of these temporal parameters to Pietism has not gone uncontested in scholarship.

Until well into the 19th century, Pietism was understood narrowly as the religious movement proceeding from Spener within the Lutheran Church and excluded → Zinzendorf and the → Moravians. A significant expansion of this understanding occurred through Albrecht Ritschl's major three-volume study *Geschichte des Pietismus* (1880-86). Ritschl presented Pietism in broad perspective as a renewal movement rooted in medieval mysticism that affected all the Protestant churches and included the Moravians and → separatism. He was highly critical of Pietism as a type of theology, seeing it as rooted in private religious experience and flight from the world, inimical to Reformation theology.

Other scholars, most notably Ernst → Troeltsch and Max → Weber, claimed that Pietism was theologically rooted in English Puritanism and Dutch Precisionism, describing it as an "innerworldly asceticism." Later scholars (e.g., Erich Beyreuther), however, viewed Pietism as a renewal and development of Reformation and post-Reformation theology. Recent scholarship lacks consensus concerning the definition and scope of Pietism. It has inspired polar evaluations as either a narrow-minded moralistic, biblicistic flight from the world or as the most significant Christian movement in modern times. Hence F. Ernst Stoeffler begins his *Rise of Evangelical Pietism* (1965) with the observation that Pietism is "one of the least understood movements in the history of Christianity."

More recent research on Pietism has tended to avoid the strictly alternative definitions of an ecclesiastical reform movement or a theological phenomenon and is more sensitive to the historical complexity of Pietism, with its diverse theologies, devotional orientations, and relations to society. There is a growing agreement in distinguishing (1) Pietism in a broad sense as a devotional movement going back to Johann Arndt (1555-1621) and expressing itself primarily in literary texts such as books of edification, spiritual poetry, and hymnody from (2) Pietism in a narrower sense expressing itself in religious renewal movements critical of orthodoxy and the early Enlightenment and forming independent groups and communities.

A major contemporary research issue concerns whether Pietism is a concept that reflects a particular period of history or an ahistorical typological concept. Johannes Wallmann, on the one hand, argues for the former, stating in numerous studies that Pietism in the proper sense of the term begins with Spener and extends into the 18th century because it was Spener who provided the distinctive characteristics of Pietism as a historical phenomenon, namely, the development of the conventicle movement, or the *ecclesiola in ecclesia* (a little church within the church); the chiliastic hope for "better times"; and a pronounced emphasis upon Bible reading and study.

Martin Brecht, on the other hand, argues for the latter, expanding the concept of Pietism to a transnational and transconfessional phenomenon beginning with the difficulties of the post-Reformation churches in bringing about a Christian life and society. According to Brecht, the scope of Pietism extends from Arndt into the 20th century and includes English Puritanism, the *nadere Reformatie* (further Reformation) in the Netherlands, the devotional movements in Germany, including Radical Pietism, as well as Zinzendorf and the Moravians. Furthermore, Methodism and the awakenings are seen as continuations of Pietism.

In light of the continuing controversies over the definition and scope of Pietism, Brecht and others recommend caution before making sweeping statements about Pietism. As it sees itself, and by its very nature, Pietism is still an important Protestant movement, even though it has undergone modifications in response to changing times. Though no one can deny its consistency, it is a complex phenomenon with certain internal tensions.

2. History

2.1. *Roots and Heritage*

In the 17th century → Protestantism clearly went through a crisis from the standpoint of piety. The state-church system (→ Church and State) and denominational conflicts contributed to the dissatisfaction of theologians, clergy, and middle-class laity with expressions of the Christian life. Reflecting the nascent scientific spirit of the age, a demand was made for verifiability and → experience. The use of anatomical imagery in the spiritual writings of the time expressed the efforts to probe beneath the surface and uncover hidden pathologies of the human heart in order to promote living faith and sanctification. The criticism of the mere appearance of godliness was epitomized in the statement of the radical Pietist Christian Hoburg (1607-75) that "justification is fiction, rebirth is fact." The radical traditions of the Reformation (esp. Carlstadt, Paracelsus, C. Schwenckfeld, and V. Weigel), → mysticism, and even the preparation of "spiritual exercises" by the → Jesuits were making a new impact. Reading of the related → devotional literature brought with it a new → individualism and threatened both ecclesiastical and denominational → unity.

2.2. *Seventeenth-Century Movements of Piety*

A devotional literature arose among the English → Puritans that focused on the practice of piety (e.g., L. Bayly's best-seller *The Practice of Piety*, R. Baxter's *Saints' Everlasting Rest*, J. Bunyan's *Pilgrim's Progress*), searching of one's → conscience, → meditation, and orientation to the hereafter (→ Immanence and Transcendence). Puritan devotional writings, translated into Dutch and German, became influential in the → Calvinism of the Netherlands and the → Lutheranism of Germany. The orthodox Calvinism of the Netherlands (→ Orthodoxy 2) called for "further Reformation," the reformation of life (W. Teelinck, G. Voetius, W. Amesius, J. van Lodenstein).

In Germany Arndt's *Four Books of True Christianity* (1605-10) and *Little Garden of Paradise Full of Christian Virtues* (1612) took up impulses from both the Radical Reformation and mysticism and applied them to the church. Arndt's work was the most successful of all Protestant devotional writings. His *True Christianity* went through some 300 republications and was also translated into the Scandinavian and Baltic languages, Czech, Dutch, English, French, Hungarian, Italian, Polish, Rhaeto-Romance, Russian, Turkish, and Yiddish. Missionaries in turn translated it into native languages. Some theological faculties (Rostock, Strasbourg, Jena), along with leading theologians such as J. V. Andreae, took up Arndt's call for more seriousness in church life, → church discipline, education, and theological training.

At the same time, efforts at domestic reform were accompanied by a radicalism that, fed by Arndt and Jakob Böhme (1575-1624), was sharply critical of the established churches' → confessions and the → church as institution (L. F. Gifftheil, C. Hoburg, J. Betke, and F. Breckling).

2.3. *Reformed and Lutheran Pietism in the Second Half of the Seventeenth Century*

The Netherlands witnessed the rise of the Labadists, a primitive Christian separatist movement (→ Heresies and Schisms) named after Jean de Labadie (1610-74), a former Jesuit who became a Calvinist pastor in Geneva and Middleburg. He set up → house churches in Amsterdam, Herford, and Altona. The German Reformed Pietism deriving from T. Undereyck (1635-93) remained within the church, as did the original Dutch group. G. Tersteegen (1697-1769) was one of the most important Protestant mystics.

Spener gave German Lutheran Pietism its essential shape. He was influenced by the Arndtian movement and Puritan devotional literature, as well as by his own academic training in pious Strasbourg orthodoxy. In 1666 Spener became senior pastor in Frankfurt am Main. At the urging of devout church members, he started to build up his *collegia pietatis* (schools of piety) in 1670. These were conventicles (→ Congregation) at which laity gathered in homes for → devotion and → edification. With them he created a form of fellowship that was highly significant for Pietism and that led to much criticism in the church at large. It seemed that he was setting up a church within the church. M. → Bucer (1491-1551; → Reformers 2.1.2) had already taken some steps in this direction in the 16th century, as had the separatists.

Spener himself was influenced by prior Lutheran and Reformed devotional movements. He set forth his program in *Pia desideria,* although in many ways he was simply summarizing earlier ideas. His basic hope was that the church would enjoy better times, which would also include → conversion of the Jews (→ Judaism; Jewish Mission). His views included an implied → millenarianism, which had lived on in the Puritans, Labadists, and outsiders in Germany. Such expectations became an integral part of Pietism. Concretely, Spener asked for intensive → Bible study (e.g., in the *collegia*), the practice of spiritual priesthood (→ Priest, Priesthood, 4), a reduction of → polemics, the training of theologians in piety, and edifying → preaching. Leading theologians gave the proposals a friendly reception but little more. Only when, to some extent under the influence of August Hermann → Francke (1663-1727), reforms in theological education were initiated at Leipzig in 1689, and at much the same time at Tübingen and Giessen, did the way open up for the success of Spener's reforms.

Pietism, though, threatened to discredit itself very quickly with its radical criticism of the church (→ Religion, Criticism of), its spiritualism, its perfectionism (→ Perfectionists), and its millenarianism. Spener himself, after a brief period as chief court preacher at Dresden, became provost in Berlin in 1691. He also became embroiled in a sharp controversy with Lutheran orthodoxy in which he was able to maintain to some degree the rightness of his cause.

2.4. *Halle Pietism*

Spener's Pietism gained widespread influence mainly through the next generation of theologians, the most important of whom was Francke. In 1687, during his student days, Francke experienced a sudden, life-shaping conversion after days of inner struggle that made him certain at the same time of God's existence and of his own rebirth. The importance of a sudden, datable, and one-time conversion — still alien to Spener — thus entered Pietism through Francke.

In 1692 Francke became a pastor and then professor at the newly founded University of Halle. For Francke the study of the Bible was the core of theology, requiring the reader to be reborn in order to recognize Christ as the kernel of Scripture. Halle itself became the most important center of Pietism, with a varied program of activities that extended from Russia to North America and from Scandinavia to India. These activities included theological training, an orphanage, educational work, → mission, a → Bible society, and care of the → diaspora. Halle Pietism also helped to stabilize the Prussian state, though never merging into it, through its emphasis upon industriousness, thrift, and obedience.

With its call for serious → penitence it influenced a whole generation of theologians.

Modern though Pietism was in many ways, conflict with the Enlightenment (C. Thomasius, C. Wolff) was unavoidable. Its belief in → revelation could not submit to the dictates of → reason, and its sense of → sin was incompatible with Enlightenment optimism regarding humanity. The confrontation with the Enlightenment in the universities finally ended with the defeat of Pietism after Francke's death in 1727.

2.5. *Radical Pietism*

The potentially disruptive force of the pietistic legacy showed itself in the fact that Pietists were constantly at odds with the church's confession and order (→ Church Orders) and that a small group of Spener's original Frankfurt followers actually separated from the church. Among them were the Petersens — Johann Wilhelm (1649-1727) and his wife, Johanna Eleonora (1644-1724) — who held distinctive views on millenarianism and → apocatastasis (→ Eschatology). In his work *Impartial History of the Church and Heretics* (1699), Gottfried Arnold (1666-1714), whose interest was in primitive Christianity as the norm for the true church, prepared the way for nondenominational accounts of history. J. K. Dippel (1673-1734) came close to the Enlightenment in his rejection of Christ's substitutionary suffering. The separatists found a home and opportunities for publishing in Isenburg-Büdingen and Sayn-Wittgenstein.

2.6. *Zinzendorf and the Moravians*

Count Nikolaus von Zinzendorf (1700-1760) was one of the most creative of 18th-century Pietists. Educated at Halle, he later toured the Netherlands and France, where he came to appreciate the "heart religion" of other confessional groups. In 1722 he accepted Protestant refugees from Moravia to his estate, where he formed the community of Herrnhut (lit. "[under] the Lord's watch"), which grew into an interdenominational renewal movement and mission church. The Moravian Brethren were for a long time among the most significant of Pietist groups, conducting missions throughout the world.

2.7. *Württemberg Pietism*

J. A. Bengel (1687-1752) gave Pietism in the territory of Württemberg its distinctive character. He developed the intentions of Spener and Francke in the form of a → biblical theology and built up a system of → salvation history *(Heilsgeschichte)* with end-time calculations. Bengel's theological contributions were in the areas of textual criticism of the Greek NT, biblical → exegesis, and the history of salvation.

Bengel's most important disciple was F. C. Oetinger (1702-82), who independently worked out a speculative *philosophia sacra* (→ Philosophy and Theology). The *collegia pietatis* received official approval in Württemberg in 1743. Pietism here was not so active socially as in Prussia, but its → biblicism had an influence that can still be detected today.

2.8. *Pietism beyond Germany*

To a large extent through Halle and the Herrnhut movement, Pietism spread beyond Germany. It reached as far as Scandinavia, the Baltic States, Hungary, Transylvania, Switzerland, Netherlands, Britain, and the North American colonies. In places it took distinctive forms, with the influence of Methodism (→ Methodist Churches) being especially important.

In Scandinavia one of the forerunners of the strong Danish and Norwegian Pietism was Erik Pontoppidan (1698-1764), bishop of Bergen, Norway, and then chancellor of the University of Copenhagen. His explanation of → Luther's Small Catechism, *Truth unto Godliness* (1737), influenced by Spener's extensive catechetical writing, was widely used in Denmark and Norway. Its English translation (1842) by Elling Eielsen (1804-83), an itinerant Norwegian-American Lutheran lay preacher who organized the first Norwegian Lutheran congregation (1843) and then synod (1846) in America, had great influence on Norwegian Lutherans in America. Inspired by A. H. Francke, Pontoppidan also strove to improve Norway's educational system.

Pontoppidan's writings, along with those of Arndt and H. Mueller (1631-75), a German theologian and author of devotional literature, influenced Hans Nielsen Hauge (1771-1824), a Norwegian lay preacher and revivalist who profoundly shaped church life in his country and then in America among Norwegian immigrants. Hauge, convinced that God had called him to awaken his "sleeping" countrymen, traveled throughout the country preaching and leading → revivals.

In Sweden the works of German Pietists, above all Arndt, had long been influential and, along with the influence of Zinzendorf and Moravianism, contributed to the great religious revivals of the 19th century. Influential Swedish figures were Lars Levi Laestadius (1800-1861), a Lutheran pastor also known for his botanical studies, and Carl Olaf Rosenius (1816-68), a lay preacher. Laestadius became a leader of the revival movement in Lapland and northern Finland (Laestadianism), and Rosenius edited the periodical *Mission Tidings* as well as the *Pietist* (1842-62). Influenced by Spener among others, his popular hymns permeated the revivals and were brought to America by immigrants. In Finland Paavo Ruotsalainen (1777-1852), a lay preacher, was for decades the spiritual father of "the awakened" in central Finland.

Immigrants to North America brought Pietism with them in their hearts and their luggage of devotional writings and Pietist → hymnals. A direct connection to German Pietism was through Henry Melchior Muhlenberg (1711-87), known as the patriarch of the Lutheran Church in America, whom Francke commissioned to serve congregations in America.

Pietism in America was and continues to be central not only in Methodism but in the Church of the Brethren. Missionaries to the so-called → Third World were strongly rooted in the Pietist tradition and thus inculcated characteristics typical of Pietism, such as a concentration on questions of eschatology, use of the Bible as the norm for religious life, emphasis upon religious experience, a tendency to emphasize → sanctification toward perfectionism, and the organizing of congregational life in small groups. These characteristics may also be seen in North American evangelicalism as expressed through John Wesley, George → Whitefield, Cotton Mather, and Jonathan → Edwards. Many British and American evangelicals not only were influenced by Continental Pietism but also corresponded with Francke and his son Gotthilf August Francke (1696-1769). Modern → Pentecostal churches and → charismatic movements also exhibit characteristics of historical Pietism.

2.9. *Post-Enlightenment Pietism*

Although Pietism is to be seen as a "modern" movement with its → subjectivism and its interest in experience, it opposed the → worldview and → ethics of the Enlightenment. Apart from mere opposition, however, in the later 18th century it also developed a critical self-awareness vis-à-vis the Enlightenment, for example, in the works of J. K. Lavater, J. G. Hamann, and P. M. Hahn. The Pietists' struggle against → dogmatism, "the religion of the head," and their emphasis upon "the religion of the heart," which fostered an ecumenism of experience, foreshadowed the Enlightenment. Indeed, some of the major figures of the Enlightenment — G. E. Lessing, I. Kant, F. Schiller, J. W. Goethe, and J. G. Fichte — came from Pietist backgrounds. Furthermore, the so-called father of → liberal theology, Friedrich → Schleiermacher (1768-1834), who was educated by the Moravians and referred to himself as "a Moravian of a higher order," grounded theology on the "feeling of absolute dependence."

The major leaders of Pietism would have recoiled from the Enlightenment reduction of theology to anthropology so pointedly expressed by Ludwig Feuerbach (1804-72). Yet it may be argued that the Pietist orientation to religious experience expressed in its emphasis upon → regeneration (a biological image) instead of → justification (a forensic image) prepared the ground for this development.

2.10. *Pietism in the Nineteenth and Twentieth Centuries*

It can hardly be contested that revivalism, though it took new forms, was a continuation of Pietism. In North America there were a series of awakenings along the eastern seaboard. George Whitefield (1714-70), ordained in the Church of England and a colleague of John and Charles Wesley, began a remarkable preaching tour in New England in 1740, which triggered the Great Awakening. The New England theologian and pastor Jonathan Edwards (1703-58) defended the revival and influenced generations of revivalists in calling for "new birth."

The Second Great Awakening, from about 1795 to about 1810, stimulated further revivals in the United States in the latter part of the 19th century. Awakenings also occurred in Great Britain and the Continent throughout the 19th century, which led to action and new dimensions in such spheres as missionary societies (→ Evangelical Missions), Bible societies, → diakonia (→ Inner Mission), and → youth work. The end of the 19th century witnessed the development of the → Fellowship Movement, as well as the → evangelical movement, which now largely represents the Pietist movement. The movement of spiritual renewal might be seen as its latest wave.

3. Evaluation

3.1. *Theology*

Theologically, Pietism is oriented to revelation, especially to the Bible (→ Canon). It does not neglect Bible exegesis but treats biblical criticism with reserve (→ Demythologization) and has a bent toward → fundamentalism. Direct → inspiration has played a role among various Pietists. The presuppositions of the Christian life are penitence, faith, conversion, and regeneration, which issue in renewal and sanctification. Eschatology takes concrete shape as an individual → hope (often chiliastic) or as hope in salvation history. Fellowship is defined either inside or outside the mainline church (→ Volkskirche). There are reservations regarding the church as an → institution, but they do not rule out participation in → church politics. Separation from the world can manifest itself in a rigorous ethical code

(→ Moralism), which sometimes leads to moral perfectionism.

3.2. *Social Aspects*

Pietism has found adherents in all social strata, including the middle class and the rural population. It has only a limited desire to mix in → politics. Except in its early stages, it has tended to opt for → conservatism, but it is the source of many significant social reforms in the areas of education, health, and welfare.

3.3. *Effects*

One of the effects of Pietism has been the cultivating of inwardness. With its acceptance of all devout Christians, Pietism has also helped to dismantle denominational barriers within Protestantism and has provided significant impulses to the development of the modern ecumenical movement (→ Ecumenism, Ecumenical Movement). Separation from the world has not prevented it from actively spreading abroad the → kingdom of God by missionary and diaconal work. Since it has done most Protestant missionary work, it originally had a vital impact on lifestyle and theology of the new Third World churches. Here perhaps was one of its greatest contributions to modern church history (→ Mission 3). As a vital movement, it still has a part to play in the development of Protestantism.

→ Modern Church History 1-2; Modern Period; Sect; Theology in the Nineteenth and Twentieth Centuries; World Evangelical Alliance

Bibliography: Historiography: D. Durnbaugh, "Pietism: A Millennial View from an American Perspective," *PuN* 28 (2002) 11-29 • M. Greschat, *Zur neueren Pietismusforschung* (Darmstadt, 1977) • H. Lehmann, "Engerer, weiterer und erweiterer Pietismusbegriff," *PuN* 29 (2003) 18-36 • M. Lienhard, "La piété comme objet d'étude de l'historiographie," *Frömmigkeit und Spiritualität. Auswirkungen der Reformation im 16. und 17. Jahrhundert* (ed. M. Arnold and R. Decot; Mainz, 2002) 7-14 • *Pietismus und Neuzeit. Ein Jahrbuch zur Geschichte des neueren Protestantismus* (Göttingen, 1974-) • M. Schmidt, "Epochen der Pietismusforschung," *Der Pietismus als Theologische Erscheinung. Gesammelte Studien des Geschichte des Pietismus* (Göttingen, 1984) 34-83 • H. Schneider, "Der radikale Pietismus in der neueren Forschung," *PuN* 8 (1982) 15-42; 9 (1983) 117-51 • J. Strom, "Problems and Promises of Pietism Research," *CH* 71 (2002) 536-54 • J. Wallmann, "L'état actuel de la recherché sur le piétisme," *Les piétismes à l'âge classique* (ed. A. Lagny; Villeneuve-d'Ascq, 2001) 31-55 • W. R. Ward, "Bibliographical Survey: German Pietism, 1670-1750," *JEH* 44 (1993) 476-505 • H. Weigelt, "Interpretations of Pietism in the Research of Contemporary German Historians," *CH* 39 (1970) 236-41.

Secondary literature (English): E. Benz, "Pietist and Puritan Sources of Early Protestant World Missions," *CH* 20 (1951) 28-55 • D. Brown, *Understanding Pietism* (Grand Rapids, 1978) • D. Brunner, *Halle Pietists in England* (Göttingen, 1993) • T. Campbell, *The Religion of the Heart: A Study of European Religious Life in the Seventeenth and Eighteenth Centuries* (Columbia, Ga., 1991) • P. Erb, ed., *The Pietists: Selected Writings* (New York, 1983) • K. Faull, ed., *Moravian Women's Memoirs: Their Related Lives, 1750-1820* (Syracuse, N.Y., 1997) • A. Freeman, *An Ecumenical Theology of the Heart: The Theology of Count Nicholas Ludwig von Zinzendorf* (Bethlehem, Pa., 1998) • M. Fulbrook, *Piety and Politics: Religion and the Rise of Absolutism in England, Württemberg, and Prussia* (Cambridge, 1983) • R. Gawthrop, *Pietism and the Making of Eighteenth-Century Prussia* (Cambridge, 1993) • E. Gritsch, *A History of Lutheranism* (Minneapolis, 2002) • H. Lehmann, "The Cultural Importance of the Pious Middle Classes in Seventeenth-Century Protestant Society," *Religion and Society in Early Modern Europe, 1500-1800* (ed. K. von Greyertz; London, 1984) 33-41 • C. Lindberg, *The Third Reformation? Charismatic Movements and the Lutheran Tradition* (Macon, Ga., 1983); idem, ed., *The Pietist Theologians* (Oxford, 2004) • R. Lovelace, *The American Pietism of Cotton Mather* (Grand Rapids, 1979) • R. Lundin and M. Noll, eds., *Voices from the Heart: Four Centuries of American Piety* (Grand Rapids, 1991) • E. McKenzie, *A Catalog of British Devotional and Religious Books in German Translation from the Reformation to 1750* (Berlin, 1997) • M. Noll, *America's God: From Jonathan Edwards to Abraham Lincoln* (New York, 2002) • K. J. Stein, *Philipp Jakob Spener: Pietist Patriarch* (Chicago, 1986) • E. Stoeffler, *German Pietism during the Eighteenth Century* (Leiden, 1973); idem, *The Rise of Evangelical Pietism* (Leiden, 1965); idem, ed., *Continental Pietism and Early American Christianity* (Grand Rapids, 1976) • J. Strom, *Orthodoxy and Reform: The Clergy in Seventeenth Century Rostock* (Tübingen, 1999) • P. Vogt, "The Attitude of Eighteenth Century German Pietism toward Jews and Judaism: A Case of Philo-Semitism?" *CovQ* 56 (November 1998) 18-32 • W. R. Ward, *The Protestant Evangelical Awakening* (Cambridge, 1992) • H. Yeide, *Studies in Classical Pietism: The Flowering of the Ecclesiola* (New York, 1997).

Secondary literature (German): T. Baumann, *Zwischen Weltveränderung und Weltflucht. Zum Wandel der pietistischen Utopie im 17. und 18. Jahrhundert* (Lahr, 1991) • E. Beyreuther, *Geschichte des Pietismus* (Stuttgart, 1978) • M. Brecht, "Pietismus," *TRE* 26.606-31; idem, "Probleme der Pietismusforschung,"

NAKG 76 (1996) 227-37; idem, "Zur Konzeption der Geschichte des Pietismus. Eine Entgegnung auf Johannes Wallmann," *PuN* 22 (1996) 226-29 • M. Brecht et al., eds., *Geschichte des Piestismus* (4 vols.; Göttingen, 1993-2004) • M. Jung, *Frauen des Pietismus. Zehn Porträts* (Gütersloh, 1998) • A. Langen, *Der Wortschatz des deutschen Pietismus* (Tübingen, 1968) • H. Lehmann, "Vorüberlegung zu einer Sozialgeschichte des Pietismus im 17./18. Jahrhundert," *PuN* 21 (1995) 69-83 • H. Lehmann et al., eds., *Jansenismus, Quietismus, Pietismus* (Göttingen, 2002) • D. Meyer and U. Sträter, eds., *Zur Rezeption mystischer Traditionen im Protestantismus des 16. bis 19. Jahrhunderts* (Cologne, 2002) • H.-J. Nieden and M. Nieden, eds., *Praxis pietatis. Beiträge zu Theologie und Frömmigkeit in der frühen Neuzeit* (Stuttgart, 1999) • A. Ritschl, *Geschichte des Pietismus* (3 vols.; Bonn, 1880-86) • P. Schicketanz, *Der Pietismus von 1675 bis 1800* (Leipzig, 2001) • M. Schmidt, *Pietismus* (Stuttgart, 1972) • U. Sträter, *Meditation und Kirchenreform in der lutherischen Kirche des 17. Jahrhunderts* (Tübingen, 1995); idem, ed., *Pietas in der Lutherischen Orthodoxie* (Wittenberg, 1998) • U. Sträter et al., *Studien zur Rezeption der englischen Erbauungsliteratur in Deutschland im 17. Jahrhundert* (Tübingen, 1987) • J. Wallmann, "Fehlstart. Zur Konzeption von Band 1 der neuen 'Geschichte des Pietismus,'" *PuN* 20 (1994) 218-35; idem, *Philipp Jakob Spener und die Anfänge des Pietismus* (Tübingen, 1986); idem, *Der Pietismus* (Göttingen, 1990); idem, *Theologie und Frömmigkeit im Zeitalter der Barock. Gesammelte Aufsätze* (Tübingen, 1995); idem, "Was ist Pietismus?" *PuN* 20 (1994) 11-27 • U. Witt, *Bekehrung, Bildung und Biographie. Frauen im Umkreis des Halleschen Pietismus* (Tübingen, 1996).

Martin Brecht, with Carter Lindberg

Piety

The word "piety" is a general one for a religious disposition and attitude ("inner religiosity," involving fear of God, godliness, zeal for God, etc.), and also for religious practice. It engages mind and will, as well as emotions, and expresses itself in a ("pious") lifestyle. It can refer not merely to individuals but also to the religious mentality that characterizes religious societies, whether → congregations or → religious orders. It may also denote the collective practices of larger population groups, as expressed in → pilgrimages, → processions, → eucharistic spirituality, and veneration of the → saints and of Mary (→ Mary, Devotion to). In everyday use the term can often be a disparaging one, such as when it is purely inward (a "pious soul") or a matter strictly of one's feelings ("piety of the heart"), when it seems rigidly fixed in externalities, or when the pious disposition is incompatible with what is done in other areas of life (e.g., sham holiness or hypocrisy).

The phenomenon of piety in its individual and collective forms is a matter of research in → theology, the study of → religion, → psychology, → sociology, history, and folklore. In the process, many views of piety arise; there is no precise definition.

Piety has become a central theme in Protestant theology. Today, however, the trend is to replace the word "piety" by → "spirituality," which is now common in ecumenical usage and academic discussion, as well as in much popular religiosity. (For a full discussion of this topic, see the article under this latter title.)

Erwin Fahlbusch

Pilgrim Fathers → Puritans 3

Pilgrimage

1. Religious Data
   1.1. Term
   1.2. OT
   1.3. Islam
2. Christian Pilgrimages
   2.1. History
   2.2. Theology

1. Religious Data

1.1. *Term*

A pilgrimage is a journey taken from one's home to a cultic site (→ Sanctuary), where one performs certain → rites (§1) and ceremonies before the cultic object. The → history of religion tells of many pilgrimages by individuals or groups, either at set times or by private resolve (e.g., in pledge of → vows). The thought behind these ritual actions is that at certain places God will come with power and → grace to those who seek him and trust in him, giving them special help (→ Experience 2; Revelation 1).

Many non-Christian religions (e.g., → Buddhism, → Hinduism, and, in → Tibetan religions, Lamaism) regard holy places as places of cleansing (→ Cultic Purity), illumination, and → healing. Theophanies are associated with springs, trees, stones, and other natural phenomena. Pilgrimages are also made to places that were of significance to founders of the religion or to other outstanding leaders, also to the graves of those who had special gifts and to the sites of miracle-working objects or images of the cult.

1.2. *OT*

Pilgrimages were common in → Israel and, at one point, became required. → Abraham made regular visits to selected holy places (Gen. 12:6-8; 13:3-4, 18). Bethel was a favorite pilgrimage goal for → Jacob (Gen. 28:18-22; 35:6; see also Judg. 20:18; 21:2). Shiloh, the location of the ark and the site of Samuel's calling, attracted pilgrims each autumn (1 Sam. 1:3, 21; 2:19).

From the days of → David, → Jerusalem was a central place of pilgrimage for → Judaism, the symbol of religious unity. Adult males would go up three times each year on the main festivals and present themselves to → Yahweh in Jerusalem (Deut. 16:16). Pilgrim songs were probably sung (Psalms 84; 120–34). From the standpoint of → eschatology the hill of Zion (in Jerusalem) became the goal of pilgrims from all nations that believed in the one God, Yahweh (Isa. 2:2-4; 60:3-16).

1.3. *Islam*

Islam requires that all free adult Muslims should make a pilgrimage to Mecca, the birthplace of Muḥammad (ca. 570-632). Once during their life believers should visit the sacred sites there (→ Islam 3.1). Medina, the place where Muḥammad worked and was buried, is the second most holy site. Here he founded the *ummah* (community, new nation) and was its first lawgiver.

2. Christian Pilgrimages

2.1. *History*

2.1.1. The → early church considered it a form of Christian → piety to visit the places where → Jesus had lived and worked in the Holy Land (→ Palestine), and also places associated with the → saints (including graves and → relics). This piety was rooted in the need to worship God at the holy place and in the belief that God was still at work through his → martyrs, → saints (§1.4), and their relics. Pilgrimages to the Holy Land and visits to places where God had appeared in the OT (e.g., Mamre), or to places associated with Mary, may be traced back to the days of Constantine (306-37). For reasons of safety, pilgrims often traveled in groups.

Beginning in the seventh century, Arabs menaced the sea passages, and Islamic princes made the journey by land difficult. The → Crusades were launched partly to make pilgrimages safe. The knights who took part in the First Crusade (1096-99) saw themselves as *milites Christi* (soldiers of Christ) engaged in a "pilgrimage" that would secure control of the holy places. Motivations included → penitence, the desire to make atonement, the goal of social liberation, the thirst for power, but also a desire to serve. A pilgrimage to Jerusalem, even when it was not under Christian control, was always of spiritual concern to Christians.

During the → Middle Ages pilgrimages were also started to → Rome and to Santiago de Compostela, Spain (→ Santiago Cult; Middle Ages 1.3.3). From the fourth century, pilgrims wished to see the graves of → apostles and → martyrs at Rome, but a concern for penitence and expiation drove them to Santiago, alleged burial place of the apostle James. In the late Middle Ages the ecclesiastical and secular structure found a place for penitential pilgrimages to Jerusalem, Rome, and Santiago. Pilgrims to these places could receive absolution from their → guilt, → indulgences from the temporal penalties of sin, and confirmation of their expiation.

2.1.2. Long-distance pilgrimages survived as a Protestant Christian custom as well, while short-distance pilgrimages to medieval reliquaries of the Lord (Aachen, Trier) and to graves of the saints or sites of the holy blood (e.g., Walldürn, Iphofen, Wilsnack) lost significance toward the end of the late Middle Ages.

Miracles and a widespread yearning for supernatural help and salvation confirmed anew the efficacious power of older Marian cultic sites and generated a new kind of pilgrimage movement, namely, popular Marian pilgrimages (→ Mary, Devotion to, 1.2.2). Preeminent examples of this development in the southern German sphere include → Altötting (1489), Andechs (after 1458), Einsiedeln (1466), and Mariazell (1494).

2.1.3. → Catholic reform and the → baroque period saw a new blossoming of Marian sites (→ Devotional Images). A pilgrimage culture developed with banners, standards, shields, shrines, and music on the way, and with pictures, votive gifts, souvenirs, and special architecture at the sites. These elements were confessionally oriented. Orders, sodalities, fraternities, and laymen *(Pilgerführer)* organized the pilgrimages.

The 19th and 20th centuries introduced a new type of Marian pilgrimage: mass pilgrimages, to places where there had been appearances of Mary, such as La Salette (1846) and → Lourdes (1858) in France, and → Fatima (1917) in Portugal. Modern transport is now used. → Processions form at the place of pilgrimage or at a nearby point. It is now reckoned that, either individually or in groups, several million pilgrims make their way annually to the various centers, both regional and international.

2.2. *Theology*

2.2.1. The roots of the Christian practice of pilgrimage are in the cult of → martyrs and in the veneration of saints and their relics. The concept of the communion of saints strengthened those who assembled at the graves of martyrs, confessors, and saints as they made their petitions by way of those who were already in the presence of God (→ Prayer 2). The communion of saints meant that by → baptism, both the living and the dead were members of the church, the fellowship of baptized saints. Holy men and women who had lived heroic lives were witnesses, models, and forerunners in the faith (see Heb. 12:1). To honor the saints was to honor God (→ Saints, Veneration of, 4).

Worship can be offered only to God, the Creator and Redeemer. Honoring saints, however, is an indirect way of honoring God's → grace to them. The theology of martyrdom was the basis of this concept. Mary deserved special honor (the *cultus hyperduliae,* or devotion that is "more than veneration"). The distinction between different kinds of worship was recognized by the Second Council of → Nicaea in 787 (DH 600) and endorsed by the Council of → Trent in 1563 (DH 1832). → Vatican II reiterated the same teaching (*Lumen gentium* 66).

2.2.2. The age of → polemics between the Reformers and Roman Catholics challenged the practice of pilgrimages, as well as the honoring of martyrs, Mary, and relics, and the associated indulgences. The Lutheran, Reformed, and → free churches still oppose the invocation of → saints (§5.3). To call upon them for protection, aid, or intercession is to question the mediatorship of Christ (→ Christology 2.4.2) and → justification (§2.2.2) by faith alone (→ Reformation Principles).

Roman Catholics, however, do not look at the matter from the standpoint of → soteriology and justification but view it ecclesiologically and anthropologically. Saints are members of the mystical body of the → church (§3.2). Through Christ its Head they participate in his mediatorship. As members of the church they may, through Christ, intercede for those who cry to them for help.

2.2.3. For Roman Catholics personal and liturgical prayer gives vitality to pilgrimages. The idea of the pilgrim → people of God on earth found expression in the Dogmatic Constitution on the Church accepted at Vatican II (chap. 7, "The Pilgrim Church"). The pilgrimage renaissance rests on the view that we are all "on the way."

New forms of individual, meditative praying and singing, with periods of silence but also constant movement, have now developed. The older and more spontaneous pilgrimage by foot has brought new fellowship to people as they have left their → everyday lives and set out with praying and singing, either individual or regulated. Pilgrimages demand persistent effort. They set the senses to work. Along with private, personal pilgrimages we now have church-directed mass pilgrimages that focus their participants' attention on → liturgy, sacramental practice (→ confession of sin and communion), spiritual direction, and individual religious action (→ Roman Catholic Church 5). Individual and congregational praying and singing play a big part, as do times of silence.

At the site of pilgrimage, circling, touching, and lustrations occur. Unity with Christ finds its ontic basis in baptism, but it comes to expression in time and space through common liturgical celebration and acts of individual devotion.

2.2.4. Mass pilgrimages are arranged to the great Marian centers. With processions honoring the saints, such pilgrimages in Latin America embody an emotional → popular religion that, through the splendor of the processions and acts of penitence on the way, enables people to forget everyday needs and offers them personal help, both present and future. In the poverty-stricken → Third World, regional pilgrimages symbolize the solidarity of the participants and help them both inwardly and outwardly.

Guided tours to the Holy Land and to other sites around the Mediterranean enable Protestants to visit the sites where Jesus and the first apostles worked and in this way serve some of the purposes of traditional pilgrimages.

Bibliography: Overview: S. M. Bhardwaj, *Pilgrimage in the Old and New World* (Berlin, 1994) • L. K. Davidson and M. Dunn-Wood, *Pilgrimage in the Middle Ages: A Research Guide* (New York, 1993) • K. Guth, "Die Wallfahrt–Ausdruck religiöser Volkskultur. Eine vergleichende phänomenologische Untersuchung," *EE.JEE* 16 (1986) 59-82 • G. Rinschede, *Pilgrimage in the United States* (Berlin, 1990) • G. Rinschede and S. Bhardwaj, eds., *Pilgrimage in World Religions* (Berlin, 1988) • J. Sumption, *Pilgrimage: An Image of Mediaeval Religion* (London, 1975) • G. Target, *Der grosse Atlas der heiligen Stätten. Die bekanntesten Pilgerreisen der Weltreligionen* (Munich, 2000) • V. Turner and E. Turner, *Image and Pilgrimage in Christian Culture: Anthropological Perspectives* (New York, 1995).

Historical: A. Angenendt, *Heilige und ihre Reliquien. Die Geschichte ihres Kultes vom frühen Christentum bis zur Gegenwart* (Munich, 1994) • P. Barret and J.-N. Gurgand, *Auf dem Weg nach Santiago. In den Spuren der Jakobspilger* (Darmstadt, 2001) • D. J. Birch,

Pilgrimage to Rome in the Middle Ages: Continuity and Change (Woodbridge, Suffolk, 1998) • R. C. Finucane, *Miracles and Pilgrims: Popular Beliefs in Medieval England* (Basingstoke, 1995) • R. Habermas, *Wallfahrt und Aufruhr. Zur Geschichte des Wunderglaubens in der frühen Neuzeit* (Frankfurt, 1991) • S. Hansen, *Die deutschen Wallfahrtsorte. Ein Kunst- und Kulturführer zu über 1000 Gnadenstätten* (Augsburg, 1991) • K. Herbers, *Spiritualität des Pilgerns. Kontinuität und Wandel* (Tübingen, 1993) • W. H. Swatos and L. Tomasi, *From Medieval Pilgrimage to Religious Tourism: The Social and Cultural Economics of Piety* (Westport, Conn., 2002) • J. E. Taylor, *Christians and the Holy Places: The Myth of Jewish-Christian Origins* (Oxford, 1993) • J. Wilkinson, *Jerusalem Pilgrimage, 1099-1185* (London, 1988).

Buddhism and Hinduism: H. Bakker, *The History of Sacred Places in India as Reflected in Traditional Literature: Papers on Pilgrimage in South Asia* (Leiden, 1990) • S. M. Bhardwaj, *Hindu Places of Pilgrimage in India: A Study in Cultural Geography* (Berkeley, Calif., 1973) • E. A. Morinis, *Pilgrimage in the Hindu Tradition: A Case Study of West Bengal* (Delhi, 1984) • H. W. Schumann, *Auf den Spuren des Buddha Gotama. Eine Pilgerfahrt zu den historischen Stätten* (Olten, 1992).

Islam: R. Dannin, *Black Pilgrimage to Islam* (Oxford, 2002) • I. R. Netton, *Golden Roads: Migration, Pilgrimage, and Travel in Mediaeval and Modern Islam* (Richmond, Eng., 1993) • F. E. Peters, *The Hajj: The Muslim Pilgrimage to Mecca and the Holy Places* (Princeton, 1994) • M. Wolfe, *The Hadjj: A Pilgrimage to Mecca* (London, 1994).

Klaus Guth

Pius IX

Giovanni Maria Mastai-Ferretti, born May 13, 1792, elected pope June 16, 1846, and died February 7, 1878, remains the longest-reigning → pope and one of the most controversial in the modern age. He was embroiled in the revolutionary events of 1848 and restoration of 1849; the Risorgimento and the unification of Italy; the Counter-Risorgimento, which pitted the papacy against the new Italian kingdom; and the → Kulturkampf in Bismarck's Germany, in which the liberals contrasted their "progressive culture" to the "medieval mentality" of the church. In the religious realm in 1854 he issued the proclamation of the immaculate conception of Mary (that she was born without original sin), convoked the First → Vatican Council (1869-70), which proclaimed papal → infallibility, fought to preserve the temporal as well as the spiritual power of the papacy, and waged war upon the "sinful" ideologies of the modern era. He, more than any other, molded the image of the → Roman Catholic Church before the Second Vatican Council (1962-65).

The youngest child of Count Girolamo Mastai-Ferretti, Giovanni Maria was born in Senigallia, outside Ancona. His early education was provided at home by his mother, but in 1803 he was sent to St. Michael's School in Volterra, Tuscany. Six years later Giovanni returned home following an epileptic seizure. At the end of 1815 he abandoned his plan to enter the Papal Noble Guard and decided upon the priesthood, enrolling in the Roman College. Provided a dispensation for his illness by Pius VII (1800-1823), he was ordained in 1819. His first assignment was at the Roman orphanage known as Tata Giovanni, where he remained until 1823. Despite the concerns of his mother, in 1823 Giovanni accompanied an apostolic delegation to Chile and Peru. Upon his return in 1825, Leo XII (1823-29) appointed him director of the Hospice of San Michele in Rome, and in 1827 archbishop of Spoleto, where he confronted the revolutionary events of 1831. In 1832 Gregory XVI (1831-46) made him bishop of Imola, and in 1840 named him to the college of → cardinals. Although staunchly traditionalist in religious matters, Mastai-Ferretti recognized the need for change in the → Papal States, proposing a moderate reformism in his "Thoughts on the Administration of the Papal States" (1845). Following the death of Gregory XVI, Mastai-Ferretti was elected pope, assuming the name Pius IX (It. Pio Nono).

Upon donning the tiara, the new pope, following the suggestions cataloged in the Memorandum of the Powers (France, Great Britain, Austria, Russia, and Prussia) of 1831, proposed a series of administrative, economic, and political innovations. Word of his reforms was facilitated by a new press law, which liberalized censorship and tolerated the expression of liberal and even nationalist sentiments. Liberals were delighted, but conservatives remained skeptical. Pius hoped that the creation of an Italian tariff league would coordinate economic activities and fulfill nationalist aspirations, while the creation of a Consulta, or consultative chamber, would satisfy liberal sentiments. These concessions provoked a clamor for more, including the creation of a civic guard and the granting of a constitution. Although the pope granted both, the Romans pressed him to enter the first war of Italian national liberation against Austria (→ Nation, Nationalism). His reluctance to do so, announced in an allocution in April 1848, provoked a revolution in Rome and his flight from the capital at the end of November 1848.

Only the intervention of the Catholic powers (France, Austria, Spain, and Naples) overturned Giuseppe Mazzini's republic and restored the pope's temporal power. Subsequently, France and England pressed him to introduce reforms, a call reinforced by liberals and nationalists, who appealed for concessions. Pius was little inclined to comply, recalling the fiasco of his earlier policy, but feared that pressure for reform would continue. In fact, the French president, Louis-Napoléon (after 1852 Emperor Napoléon III), pressed for the reestablishment of constitutional government in Rome. His foreign minister cataloged the reforms deemed essential for the preservation of the Papal States, including an amnesty, a law code patterned on that of France, abolition of the tribunal of the Holy Office, substantial modification of the privileges of ecclesiastical tribunals in civilian jurisdiction, and granting the Consulta a veto on financial issues. This agenda was rejected by the papal secretary of state, Cardinal Giacomo Antonelli, who reported that the Holy Father would make no concession that compromised his temporal power.

To prevent the passage of liberal reforms, Pius IX nominated a commission of conservative cardinals to govern in his absence. Dubbed the Red Triumvirate, their first decree annulled all that had transpired in the capital since November 16, 1848. Distressed by the diplomatic evasions of the pope, Louis-Napoléon in mid-August 1849 complained that the French Republic had not sent an army to snuff out Italian liberty but to regulate and preserve it, demanding political modernization in Rome. Nonetheless, Pius resisted a general amnesty, refused to base his laws on the Napoleonic Code, and opposed the rapid secularization of his administration, favoring a more conservative course. In September 1849 the pope revealed the institutions he sanctioned, providing for administrative autonomy and judicial reforms, a Council of State for administrative matters, and a Consulta for finances. Pius would concede no more. His characterization of the theory of nationalism as absurd and as criminal as that of → socialism put him at odds with the Italian national movement and with socialists at home and abroad. The pope's retreat from his earlier constitutionalism, his procrastination in returning to Rome, and the curia's intransigence on church-state issues antagonized the Piedmontese as well as the French.

Pius, for his part, distrusted Piedmont, charging that under the guise of reformism it restricted ecclesiastical control over education and undermined religion. The modernization wrought by the Siccardi Laws of March 1850 in the Kingdom of Piedmont/Sardinia abrogated the various forms of ecclesiastical jurisdiction enjoyed by the clergy, eliminated the church's ancient right of asylum, provided for the suppression of mortmain, and restricted the official observance of Catholic holidays, further arousing the pope. These measures only heightened Pius's suspicions of both progress and constitutional Piedmont. In contrast, he preserved cordial relations with the authoritarian Kingdom of Naples, which he left in April 1850 to return to Rome.

Back home, Pius turned his attention to religious matters, addressing the spiritual needs of the universal church, placing responsibility for the governance of his state in the hands of Antonelli, confirmed as secretary of state. Under Pio Nono's guidance the curia was transformed, and nonpriests and the more worldly clergy were systematically removed. Pius proceeded to condemn clergymen who had shown themselves receptive to liberal and modern ideas, including Vincenzo Gioberti for his work *The Modern Jesuit* (5 vols.; 1846-47) and Antonio Rosmini for his *The Five Wounds of the Church* (1848). Pius deplored the evils facing the church and society, citing the danger posed to the temporal power of the Holy See, deemed vital for the protection of its spiritual authority. He insisted that the successor of Peter, the Roman pontiff, holds a primacy over the entire world and is the vicar of Christ, head of the universal church and father and teacher of all Christians. Thus this pope exacted total obedience to the Holy See, requiring that national episcopacies execute whatever it teaches, determines, and decrees. Pio Nono's pronouncements proved to be precursors to the doctrine of papal infallibility.

While scientific socialists posited the initial triumph of economic → liberalism, followed by the inevitable collapse of → capitalism, Pius IX rejected both contentions. He opposed economic liberalism's enthronement of unrestrained freedom in quest of personal satisfaction. Instead, Pius relied on religion, focusing on the education and moral life of the rank and file of the clergy. In a series of encyclicals, he called upon the clergy to be trained in piety, virtue, and ecclesiastical spirit. He encouraged young seminarians to venture to Rome, reorganized the older national colleges and seminaries, and added to their number an American seminary, a Latin American college, a Polish seminary, as well as a new Irish college. Pius rewarded priests loyal to Rome, creating more *monsignori* in his pontificate than his predecessors had produced in the last two centuries. In 1850 he reestablished the → hierarchy in England, and that of the Netherlands in 1853.

During the course of his pontificate the church

erected new units of clerical administrative control, including apostolic vicarates and prefectures. At the same time the apostolic → nuncios, whose function had been largely diplomatic and political, representing the interests of the Papal States, increasingly served as intermediaries between the pope and → bishops in the governance of the church. He negotiated concordats with several states to protect traditional church interests, resisting all schemes to liberalize church-state relations. In 1850 the Madrid government approved an accord that pronounced Catholicism the religion of Spain, investing the clergy with broad powers and rights, including the supervision of education and settling matrimonial disputes without civil intervention. Talks were also opened with the Vienna government, which resulted in a → concordat (1855) that likewise made broad concessions to the church.

Religious scruples in 1858 led Pius to sanction the removal of a six-year-old Jewish boy, Edgardo Mortara, secretly baptized by a Christian domestic, from his parents in Bologna and to have him raised as a Christian, provoking a worldwide uproar that undermined the international status of the Rome government.

At Plombieres, in late July 1858, Napoléon III and Count Camillo Benso di Cavour of Piedmont planned for a war against Austria and for a diminution of the Papal States, which was deemed an anomaly in the modern world. The Mortara Affair, which widened the gap between the "medieval" papacy and the contemporary age, contributed to the outbreak of the Franco-Piedmontese war of 1859 against Austria, as well as the loss of the greater part of the Papal States, which was incorporated into the Kingdom of Italy in 1861. Pius refused to recognize this development. In June 1859 he excommunicated all those who provoked the action. Much of his opposition to reformism, constitutionalism, liberalism, and nationalism flowed from his suspicion of Piedmont-Sardinia, which he believed exploited these ideologies to undermine the papal temporal power and reorganize Italy under its banner. Consequently, the Risorgimento provoked the papal Counter-Risorgimento and contributed to Pio Nono's crusade against "modern civilization." In fact, some have suggested that papal centralization, culminating in the calling of the Vatican Council (1869-70) and the proclamation of infallibility, resulted from the weakening of the temporal power, provoking the Vatican's attempt to compensate by strengthening its spiritual control.

Undeniably, the war of Italian liberation and Sardinia's occupation of papal territory hardened the pope's heart against the Risorgimento. Convinced that a campaign was being waged against the papacy, in the decade between the restoration and the proclamation of the Italian kingdom in 1861, Pio Nono issued more than a dozen condemnations of Count di Cavour and his colleagues who worked to unite the peoples of Italy, rebuking every project that might be construed as approval of Piedmontese activity in papal territory. In March 1861 the pope noted that the adherents of "modern civilization" desired that he reconcile himself with progress and liberalism, while those who defended the rights of religion understood his need to preserve intact the "immovable and indestructible principles of eternal justice." He assailed modern doctrines that abandoned the quest for spiritual truth or that encouraged non-Catholic cults, invited the press to subvert the faith, and undermined the church. Rome's admonitions and → excommunications did not restrain Cavour, who in March 1861 proclaimed Rome the capital of the new kingdom.

On 15 September 1864 the Italian government concluded an accord (the September Convention) with the French Empire to regulate the Roman question without the pope's approval. Providing for a French withdrawal from the Eternal City within two years, the Italians promised not to attack the Patrimony of St. Peter and to prevent others from doing so from its territory. Distressed by the accord and other alleged abuses, the pontiff perceived the need for a forthright rejection of the prevailing values that generated the indifference to religion. This conviction led to the publication of the encyclical *Quanta cura* on December 8, 1864, to which was appended the → Syllabus of Errors, listing 80 errors drawn from previous papal documents and condemning various movements and beliefs, including the separation of → church and state. The encyclical reaffirmed the plenitude of papal authority and the absolute independence of the church vis-à-vis civil authority. Under ten headings the Syllabus of Errors condemned → pantheism, naturalism, → materialism, absolute as well as moderate → rationalism, and indifferentism, finding them incompatible with the Catholic faith. Socialism, communism, as well as liberal clerical associations, were all denounced. Likewise condemned were views limiting the temporal power of the pope. The critique of contemporary liberalism caused the greatest controversy, especially the condemnation of the 80th and final error, which was the call for the Roman pontiff to reconcile himself with progress, liberalism, and recent civilization. The pope clearly intended to continue his opposition to modern doctrines.

Pius envisioned convoking a → council to confront the problems burdening the church in an increasingly secular age, and on December 6, 1864, two days before issuing the Syllabus of Errors, he consulted the cardinals in → curia. Encouraged by their response, the pope hoped to have the council open shortly, but difficulties at home and abroad, including the Austro-Prussian War of 1866, followed by Giuseppe Garibaldi's incursion into the Papal States in 1867, delayed its opening until December 8, 1869. In an apostolic letter Pius cited the need to unmask the enemies of Christian society and free it from the grasp of "Satanic forces." The council issued a declaration of papal infallibility on July 18, 1870, the year the Italians seized Rome and ended the temporal power of the church. It specified that when the pontiff speaks ex cathedra, in discharge of his office as doctor of all Christians, he is endowed with the infallibility that the Redeemer bestowed upon his church.

Following the loss of Rome, Pius retreated into the → Vatican, declaring himself a prisoner therein, creating the "Roman Question," which was not resolved until 1929. Pio Nono's remaining years (1870-78), were marked by conflict with the Italians over the Roman Question, the anticlerical republic in France, the → Old Catholics, who refused to recognize papal infallibility, and with Bismarck's Germany over church-state relations, the Kulturkampf.

Pius IX, who commenced his pontificate as a prince determined to liberalize his state, ended it as a priest concerned with shielding the Roman Catholic Church from the perils of the modern age. Outraged by the unfortunate consequences of contemporary developments that restricted the temporal and spiritual power of the papacy, Pius assumed an intransigent stance in the religious and political realm, pursuing a policy of negation. Some claimed that his pontificate neglected the positive role the papacy and church might have assumed in mitigating the economic and social difficulties of the age, while ignoring the need to rehabilitate the diplomatic posture of the Holy See. Despite such criticism, the cause for his beatification was opened by → Pius XII in 1955, and he was beatified by John Paul II (1978-2005) in 2000.

Bibliography: Atti del sommo pontefice Pio IX, felicemente regnante (pt. 2; 2 vols.; Rome, 1857) • N. Blakiston, ed., *The Roman Question: Extracts from the Despatches of Odo Russell from Rome, 1858-1870* (London, 1962) • O. Chadwick, *A History of the Popes, 1830-1914* (Oxford, 1998) • F. Coppa, *Cardinal Giacomo Antonelli and Papal Politics in European Affairs* (Albany, N.Y., 1990); idem, *Pope Pius IX: Crusader in a Secular Age.* (Boston, 1979) • P. de Franciscis, ed., *Discorsi del sommo pontefice Pio IX pronunziati in Vaticano ai fedeli di Roma e dell'orbe dal principio della sua prigionia fino al presente* (3 vols.; Rome, 1872-78) • E. Hales, *Pio Nono: A Study in European Politics and Religion in the Nineteenth Century* (New York, 1954) • M. Giacomo, *Pio IX* (3 vols.; Vatican City, 1974-90) • F. Stock, ed., *Consular Relations between the United States and the Papal States: Instructions and Despatches* (Washington, D.C., 1945); idem, ed., *United States Ministers to the Papal States: Instructions and Despatches, 1848-1868* (Washington, D.C., 1933).

Frank J. Coppa

Pius XII

Eugenio Maria Giuseppe Giovanni Pacelli, born March 2, 1876, ordained a → priest April 2, 1899, elected → pope March 2, 1939, and died October 11, 1958, has emerged as the most controversial pope of the 20th century. Praised by some for his → asceticism and saintly persona, he has been denounced by others for his alleged silence during the → genocide of the Jews and Gypsies (→ Roma) during World War II. Like his 19th-century counterpart → Pius IX (1846-78), whose name he assumed upon donning the tiara, Pius XII was devoted to the Blessed Virgin Mary (BVM) and was certain of papal → infallibility. Pius IX unilaterally proclaimed the immaculate conception (1854) of the BVM, who was thus declared born free of the stain of original sin. Pius XII unilaterally proclaimed the doctrine of the assumption of the BVM — that she was taken into heaven, body and soul, after the completion of her earthly life. These doctrines were criticized by some Protestants. Even more, however, both popes were criticized for their political policies — the first for his lack of diplomacy and speaking too often and too publicly, the latter for being too diplomatic and not speaking forcefully enough in the face of evil. There is a general consensus that Pius XII confronted innumerable challenges during the course of his troubled pontificate, including the destructive World War II (1939-45), the abuses of the Nazi, Fascist, and Soviet regimes; the → Holocaust; and in the postwar period the spread of Communism, the cold war, and the threat of nuclear annihilation. Disagreement flows from conflicting assessments of his response to these challenges.

The fourth child of the lawyer Filippo Pacelli and Virginia Graziosi of the "black," or papal, aristocracy, his family had served the papacy since the early

19th century. Receiving his early education in the state primary schools, Eugenio completed his classical studies at the Visconti Institute and subsequently attended the Appolinare Institute of the Lateran University and the Gregorian University in Rome, earning degrees in law and theology. Displaying an early inclination toward diplomacy, he was appointed to the staff of the Papal Secretariat of State in 1901 and later assisted Cardinal Pietro Gasparri in drafting a new code of → canon law. He was also called upon to teach international law and diplomacy at the school for papal diplomats in Rome, and he published a number of legal studies. In 1914 he was named secretary of the Congregation for Extraordinary Affairs of the Secretariat of State. A supporter of Benedict XV (1914-22) in his stance of strict impartiality toward the belligerents of World War I and his attempts to mediate a peace (a policy Pacelli himself emulated during World War II), Pacelli was selected in 1917 by Benedict to serve as → nuncio in Bavaria and to advance his peace initiative to end the Great War. The Vatican's effort proved unsuccessful, but Pacelli remained in Munich. During the postwar Spartacist Rising there (1919), Communist intruders at one point burst into the nunciature, leaving an indelible impression on him and contributing to his enduring suspicion of Communism.

In 1920 Pacelli was appointed the first apostolic nuncio to the new German Republic, later moving his residence from Munich to Berlin (1925). In both places he sought to formalize a → concordat with the Weimar state that would regulate church-state relations and assure the pastoral position of the church in Protestant Germany. He proved unsuccessful but concluded agreements with the states of Bavaria (1924), Prussia (1929), and Baden (1932). His knowledge and love of Germany, as well as the recommendation of the outgoing secretary of state, Cardinal Pietro Gasparri, led Pius XI (1922-39) to name him to the college of → cardinals (1929), soon after appointing him the new secretary of state (1930). Five years later Pacelli was named papal chamberlain *(camerlengo)*, and thus administrator of the church during any interregnum. Pacelli complemented rather than mirrored Pius XI, who appointed him to these positions. While Pius XI often proved confrontational, Pacelli tended to be cautious. Nonetheless, both shared the conviction that Vatican interests could best be assured by concordats that aimed to preserve the church's freedom of action. In fact, Pacelli's brother Francesco helped Gasparri and Pius XI negotiate the Lateran Accords with fascist Italy in 1929, ending the "Roman Question" and restoring the principle of temporal power by creating an independent Vatican City. Eugenio, for his part, signed concordats with Austria (1933) and, in July of the same year, a controversial one with the Nazi regime.

Once secretary of state, Pacelli traveled widely, often by airplane, on papal missions to South America (1934), France (1935, 1937), the United States (1936), and Hungary (1937). Fluent in German and familiar with German affairs, he quickly emerged as the papacy's principal adviser on the Third Reich. Although Pacelli helped draft the anti-Nazi encyclical *Mit brennender Sorge* (With deep anxiety), March 14, 1937, in which Pius XI rejected the myths of race and blood, the secretary of state strove to prevent a break between the Vatican and Berlin. Thus in June 1938, when the pope commissioned the American Jesuit John La Farge to prepare an encyclical demonstrating the incompatibility of Catholicism and racism, Pacelli was not asked to participate, nor was he informed of the endeavor. Officials in the → curia, who favored a more diplomatic and less confrontational course toward Nazi Germany, delayed presenting the encyclical to Pius XI, who was dying, and very likely the ailing pope did not read it.

Following the death of Pius XI (February 9-10, 1939), Cardinal Pacelli was selected as his successor — the first Roman elected since Innocent XIII (1721-24), and the first secretary of state to immediately don the tiara since Clement IX (1667-69). Soon thereafter, Pius XI's projected encyclical *Humani generis unitas,* against → racism and → anti-Semitism, was returned to its Jesuit authors, revealing that the new pope sought to pursue a more diplomatic course.

Trained as a diplomat, Pius XII followed the cautious course paved by Leo XIII (1878-1903) and Benedict XV rather than the more confrontational one assumed by Pius IX, Pius X (1903-14), and Pius XI. Seeking to preserve the peace, Pius XII tried impartially, but unsuccessfully, to dissuade the European governments from waging a new → war. For this reason among others, when the Germans invaded Poland on September 1, 1939, Pius did not condemn their aggression. In his first encyclical, *Summi pontificatus* (On the limitations of the authority of the state), of October 20, 1939, Pius preserved his nonpartisan stance. Like Benedict XV, he insisted that the papal position was not one of neutrality, which he felt implied indifference, but impartiality. Nonetheless, Pius quietly informed the British government early in 1940 that a group of German generals were prepared to overturn the Nazi government if they could be assured an honorable peace, and he warned the Allies of the impending Nazi invasion of the Low Countries in May 1940.

In a series of Christmas broadcasts during the course of the conflict, Pius reiterated many of the themes announced by Benedict XV during World War I, invoking a new and less selfish world order. Impartial in his relations with the Axis and with the Allies, Pius did not directly challenge Nazi atrocities or those of the Soviet Union, refusing to sanction the Nazi invasion of the Communist state. In 1940 he welcomed Myron C. Taylor, President Franklin Roosevelt's personal representative to the Vatican, but did not heed the American's exhortations to condemn Nazi atrocities, referring instead more broadly to the evils of modern warfare. In his Christmas message of 1942 Pius revealed his sympathy for those "who without fault . . . sometimes only because of race or nationality, have been consigned to death or to a slow decline." Fearful of provoking reprisals, he refused to say more, lest direct public denunciations enrage the Hitler regime and provide a pretext for further brutality, while jeopardizing the future of the organized church. However, he was neither indifferent nor inactive. He established the Vatican Information Service to provide assistance to thousands of war → refugees and instructed the church to provide discreet aid to the Jews, which quietly saved many lives. Nonetheless, the pontiff was sharply criticized after the war for his "silence" in the face of the Holocaust, while having much to say on other subjects.

In his 1943 encyclical *Divino afflante Spiritu* (With the help of the divine Spirit), Pius XII sanctioned a limited use of historical criticism for biblical studies, and his *Mystici corporis* (Mystical body of Christ), of the same year, sought to promote a more positive relationship between the church and nonbelievers. His *Mediator Dei* (Mediator of God) of 1946 furthered liturgical reform.

Concerned about the safety of Rome, Pius sought to spare it from the scourge of war. When German forces occupied the city following Italy's surrender to the Allies in September 1943, Pius pleaded to have Rome proclaimed an open city, and he came to be known as *defensor civitatis* (defender of the city). During the occupation several thousand antifascist politicians and Jews found refuge in church properties. Less fortunate were 1,259 Romans rounded up in Jewish homes in Rome on October 16, 1943, a Sabbath. By quiet diplomacy the Vatican managed to secure the release of 252 of these persons who were either Aryan or of mixed marriages, but over a thousand Jews were transported to Auschwitz, where more than 800 were slaughtered.

As the war ground to an end, Pius opposed the unconditional surrender demanded by the Allies, fearing it would prolong the war and bring the Soviet Union and its Communist ideology into eastern and central Europe. The pope also had serious reservations about the Yalta Accords and the prominent role they envisioned for the Soviet Union in postwar Europe. His fears materialized as Soviet domination spread in eastern Europe, followed by the imprisonment of Cardinal Mindszenty of Hungary and Cardinal Wyszyński of Poland. To stem the Communist tide from inundating Italy and Germany, Pius endorsed the integration of postwar western Europe. For his part, Pius in 1949 issued a decree attacking the Soviet Union's → totalitarianism and authorizing the Holy Office to excommunicate Catholics who joined or collaborated with the Communists.

Fearful of a Communist takeover of Italy, Pius now had recourse to the independent Christian Democratic Party (CD), which he had earlier questioned, now encouraging the three million members of → Catholic Action groups to intervene in parliamentary politics in the Italian elections of 1948. Clerical intrusion in Italian public life reached another high point in the 1950s. In 1952 Luigi Gedda, president of Catholic Action, fearing that the Christian Democrats might lose the municipal elections in Rome, proposed a Christian Democratic coalition with the parties of the Right. This suggestion was rejected by Alcide De Gasperi, leader of the CD, but apparently the pope gave it his approval. Pius also stirred up resentment in the 1950s when he denounced the new ministry of French → worker-priests and censored the new theology emerging in France in his 1950 encyclical *Humani generis* (Of the human race). Others questioned his traditionalist stance on marital relations and → birth control, complaining also that his infallible declaration on the assumption of Mary undermined → ecumenism.

For many, Pius remained an enigma: pleasing conservatives and upsetting liberals by suppressing the worker-priests in France, but pleasing liberals and upsetting conservatives by taking steps to revise the liturgy and making evening masses possible. Likewise, there was a mixed reaction from the Left and the Right to his denunciation of atomic weaponry (→ Weapons), and also to his establishment in 1956 of the Latin American Episcopal Council. Finally, his emphasis on the importance of the laity in the church and the need to reform the curia dismayed some conservatives, who questioned his commitment to tradition. Liberals and conservatives wondered what he would have fostered had he convoked the church → council, which he had contemplated but did not call. With respect to the larger Christian community, he was not open to ecumenical contacts.

In church-state relations Pius continued to conclude concordats to assure the Vatican's pastoral and political ends, even with repressive regimes such as Franco's Spain (1953) and Trujillo's Dominican Republic (1954). However, he did not allow the postwar church, much less the Vatican, to become subordinate to such regimes, as exemplified by the → excommunication of Argentina's Juan Perón in 1955.

Pius XII's death, on October 11, 1958, marked an important transition for the church and its papacy, which was to embark on major reforms under John XXIII (1958-63) and the Second → Vatican Council (1962-65). In death, even more than during his life, controversy has surrounded Pius. Praised by world leaders and Jewish groups at his death for his actions during World War II on behalf of the persecuted, within a decade he was depicted by critics as indifferent to the genocide. Some of his defenders responded that raising an authoritative public voice on behalf of the persecuted would have made matters worse. Granted that his wartime public condemnations of racism and genocide were cloaked in generalities, most now concur that he was not totally silent or inactive, utilizing diplomacy to aid the persecuted. The debate continues whether a more forthright condemnation would have proved more effective in saving lives, even though it probably would have better assured his reputation. The move to beatify Pius XII at the end of the 20th century provoked a controversy that may have contributed to the Vatican decision to postpone such beatification, advancing instead the cause of the conservative Pius IX in 2000 in order to balance the legacy of the more liberal John XXIII.

Bibliography: P. Blet, *Pius XII and the Second World War: According to the Archives of the Vatican* (New York, 1999) • P. Blet, A. Martini, and B. Schneider, eds., *Actes et documents du Saint Siège relatifs à la Seconde Guerre Mondiale* (11 vols.; Vatican City, 1965-82) • O. Chadwick, *Britain and the Vatican during the Second World War* (Cambridge, 1986) • C. M. Cianfarra, *The War and the Vatican* (London, 1945) • S. Friedlander, *Pius XII and the Third Reich: A Documentation* (New York, 1966) • O. Halecki, *Pius XII: Pope of Peace* (New York, 1951) • R. Lieber, "Pius as I Knew Him," *CMind* 57 (1959) 292-304 • M. Phayer, *The Catholic Church and the Holocaust, 1930-1965* (Bloomington, Ind., 2000) • J. M. Sánchez, *Pius XII and the Holocaust: Understanding the Controversy* (Washington, D.C., 2002) • *Selected Documents of His Holiness, Pope Pius XII: 1939-1958* (Washington, D.C., n.d.) • D. Tardini, *Memories of Pius XII* (Westminster, Md., 1961) • *Wartime Correspondence between President Roosevelt and Pope Pius XII* (New York, 1947).

Frank J. Coppa

Platonism

1. Term
2. Plato's Philosophy
   2.1. Dialogues
   2.2. Main Theses
   2.3. Influence
3. Neoplatonism
4. Christian Platonism
5. Renaissance Platonism and Platonism Today

1. Term

The term "Platonism," coined in the mid-16th century, at first showed a bias in favor of Plato that is inappropriate for Christians. In this regard it reflects the corresponding construction in antiquity. The use of words like "Platonize" was meant instead to indicate critical reservations, though with recognition of what was really involved.

Today "Platonism" no longer implies any evaluation. It is used for the purpose of clarifying systematic or historical connections. Historically, it serves the purpose of showing that certain theses or opinions, such as the existential power of the beautiful, the preexistence of the → soul, and the priority of the intellectual or incorporeal over the sensory or corporeal, are part of the teaching of Plato (427-347 b.c.) and of giving information regarding their impact. Systematically, "Platonism" is used when, for example, it is desired to differentiate things like the existence of abstract constructs such as meanings, qualities, relations, classes, or numbers that express or reflect a specific philosophical approach from other competing theories. In this respect the question whether Plato himself ever advocated a thesis of the kind at issue is of no more than secondary interest. In principle it is enough to assume that a philosopher like Plato, in view of theses that he did espouse, would logically have had to plead for this or that thesis too.

2. Plato's Philosophy

Scholars today are divided as to whether to regard Plato as a philosopher who held a → philosophy in

Platonism

the sense of arguing for a system of set convictions or claims. Already in antiquity some thinkers viewed Plato as a skeptic (→ Skepticism) who had no certainty about anything, and the 20th century saw the thesis that Plato left everything in a dialectical fog or was interested only in fruitful educational situations. These latter views, however, are not the usual ones. Most scholars believe that Plato did have firm convictions that he argued for, and that readers should examine and critically evaluate his arguments.

The dispute itself poses a deep-seated problem. Apart from the letters, whose authenticity is disputed, Plato wrote only dialogues, in which he refers to the difficulties that all literary work involves in principle, especially when it is a matter of communicating philosophical → truth (*Phdr.* 275B–279C). In a philosophical excursus in his seventh letter, he points out how limited is the possibility of articulating philosophical insights (341B–344C). If, as some sources tell us, Plato gave lectures "On the Good," with contents different from those in the dialogues, going beyond them and making statements about the principles of all being (i.e., unity or unrestricted duality) that are hard to relate to the corresponding arguments in the dialogues, then the question must be asked how important the dialogues really are as compared to the unwritten teaching that we know only from indirectly transmitted theses and sketches.

Here again the views of scholars differ. Some regard the unwritten teaching as the core of Plato's philosophy and discount the dialogues, while others say that since we can reconstruct the unwritten teaching only from later sources, it is the least interesting part of his philosophy. The latter scholars can certainly insist that it was the dialogues and their reception that decisively promoted the development and discussion of philosophical questions.

2.1. *Dialogues*

The dialogues themselves represent a literary genre that fuses dramatic and mimetic elements with philosophical contents. They derive their vitality directly from recollection of the paradigmatic activities of Socrates (ca. 470-399 B.C.), who himself made no claims to knowledge but who punctured the claims of others. Little is known of the historical Socrates. Almost everything depends, then, on our picture of him from Plato's dialogues as the first philosopher whose opinions led to his death. Plato's dialogues have had an influence here more than that of any other writings and have helped decisively to bring about the depiction of Socrates as the quintessential philosopher that is so common today.

Only in the course of time were the 34 dialogues arranged and published in their present order. In part on the basis of speech and style, they have been divided into three groups. First, we have the early so-called *Socratic dialogues,* in which Socrates has the role only of criticizing and destroying the opinions of others.

Then we have the *middle dialogues,* in which positive theses increasingly emerge regarding the soul *(psychē),* the true nature of reality *(to ontōs on),* the ideas (sing. *idea* or *eidos*), and the relation of worldly things to eternal contents in the sphere of transcendental ideas. The dialogues reflect in part philosophical theories that were advocated in the school of Plato that was founded after 387 B.C. (the Academy, named after Akadēmos, a mythological Greek war hero). They also served as recruiting material for the school.

Finally, we have the *later dialogues,* which take up afresh many of the themes in the middle dialogues and to some extent challenge them. In relation especially to the dialogues *Theaetetus, Parmenides,* and *Sophista,* one might even speak of a self-critical Plato. Yet one may doubt whether he actually gave up any vital opinions. More natural is the assumption that in these and other dialogues he was dealing with questions regarding the meaning and implications of the central theses of the middle dialogues and trying to clear up problems of interpretation. Here again the dialogue form militates against any firm systematizing. As an author Plato sets a distance between himself and the thoughts that call for expression, and it is not always easy to distinguish what he really thinks from what he has others say.

2.2. *Main Theses*

2.2.1. In his youth Plato learned from Cratylus, a disciple of Heraclitus. He then came under the influence of Socrates. Heraclitus convinced Plato that the world of → experience is in constant flux and that thinking has nothing fixed on which to build. But Socrates taught him that the objects of knowledge must be capable of definition and that knowledge depends on the existence of things that do not change. This condition, though, is met only by entities of a special kind *(ousiai),* that is, constructs that, like Parmenides' being, are simple and indestructible and have self-identity.

Plato called such constructs ideas. *Idea* (or *eidos*) is etymologically related to Lat. *video* (see) and Ger. *wissen* (know) and thus has something of the sense of "visible form." Plato had in view that which shows itself to the eye of the intellect and that, once we recognize and grasp it, will guarantee certain knowledge of the things about which we speak or do not speak. Mathematics and its claim to exactness perhaps originally favored the notion that there are such things as intersubjective constructs accessible to us. Plato soon extended the sphere of ideas to aesthetic and ethical concepts (→ Aesthetics; Ethics). Thus the middle dialogues show how he handles the → good, the beautiful, the equal, the just, and so forth. They all function as ideal standards, as models *(paradeigma)*, as → norms of judgment, also as reliable points of reference for thought and knowledge.

The ideas, though, do more than give us the true meaning of such terms as "beautiful" or "just" and likewise do more than show us what the conceptual content or reliable object is of what we know intellectually. They obviously have also the task of explaining earthly things. In the middle dialogues they thus function as causes *(aitiai)*. It is through the beautiful that a beautiful thing is beautiful (*Phd.* 100B). A thing is what it is or becomes what it is because of the presence of the idea of the same name. Thus the doctrine of the ideas takes on an ontological function (→ Ontology).

Difficulties arise at this point. How can that which is immutable, invisible, and incorporeal influence things in the world? Plato had in mind here a special kind of relation that he called participation *(methexis)*. Such a concept, however, is not wholly clear. We simply shift the problem if we say that a thing is beautiful because an idea of beauty exists and the thing participates in it. Aristotle (384-322 B.C.; → Aristotelianism) criticized this theory as involving an empty → metaphor. This problem strengthened him in his own view that the form *(eidos, morphē)* is immanent and not transcendent.

2.2.2. Since the ideas function as prototypes and models, and since things that participate in these ideas simply copy these → archetypes *(archētypoi)* — as was said by Philo of Alexandria (b. 15-10 B.C., d. A.D. 45-50) and then by Plotinus (ca. 205-70), the founder of Neoplatonism — and can never be what the ideas are, Platonic philosophers naturally hold a corresponding view of reality. Only the ideas are real in the sense of what has true worth and is epistemologically reliable. The ideas are true being (*to ontōs on*, "the actually being," or *to alēthōs on*, "the truly being").

The present world in time and space has its own reality; in no sense is it simply a product of the → imagination. When seen from the standpoint of philosophical reflection, however, it has the status only of a world of shadows. The comparisons in the *Republic* are conclusive at this point. Most people gain their concepts from objects in the world. They thus fall victim to the mistake that reality is only what we can see and touch.

2.2.3. To reverse this view is the task of philosophy. Like the Pythagoreans, Plato was convinced that the soul is the true human self and that it will survive the process of bodily decay. He also assumed that in the hereafter the soul must answer for every failing. It is thus in our own best interests to live as far as possible with eternity in view and to direct our gaze to the primary constructs. This task is best performed corporately. Thus Plato projects an ideal state in his *Republic.*

This state will see to it that the life of each person is lived in the light of the validity of the ideas. Yet Plato is aware of natural inequalities. As all do not press on to a view of the ideas and hence to the knowledge that just government can alone legitimate (→ Righteousness, Justice), so gifted philosophers are not qualified for military service or other activities. Plato, then, envisions a state with different classes or social orders (philosopher-kings; warriors, or auxiliaries; and workers). This division will correspond essentially to the psychological aspects or to the cognitive achievements that the soul displays, which will be realized differently in different people (in the three classes primarily as reason, spirit, and desire). Political orders will thus reflect functions in the sphere of the soul. Since by definition ideas are accessible only to philosophers, those who belong to other strata must accept a destiny, the meaning of which they cannot perceive.

How serious Plato was regarding his educational program may be seen from the fact that art had no place in this state. Plato argued that art is essentially imitation *(mimēsis)*. Since artists simply copy things in the world, and these things themselves are only copies or imitations of ideal relations, art is remote from truth. It thus has a destabilizing impact on the human soul and necessarily works unfavorably on the moral life (*Rep.* bk. 10).

2.2.4. The truly cosmic dimension of Plato's view of reality finds expression in his account of the origin of the world in *Timaeus.* Whether he really believed the world had an origin is doubtful. It is more likely that he selected a familiar literary form of cosmogony for didactic reasons.

According to Plato, the Demiurge *(Dēmiourgos)*, a mythical cosmic builder who is characterized as good and free from envy, seeks to construct the best of all possible worlds, but in this project he does not enjoy complete freedom and hence is not omnipotent. Rather, he must use the material that is available to him in disordered elements. He must also follow a model that he has before him in the form of eternal ideas. Projecting the ideas into undifferentiated basic matter *(hypodochē)*, he transforms ideality into reality. The function of providing and preserving order is assigned to a world soul that structurally unites elements of ideal being with elements of mutable being.

Plato certainly did not have a personal God in view at this point. More likely the Demiurge symbolized the dynamic side of the idea of the good (*Rep.* bk. 6). The *Timaeus,* however, became a key dialogue for Christian thinking. It was probably on the basis of this dialogue that Christians first reinterpreted Plato's ideas as thoughts in the mind of God.

2.3. ***Influence***

2.3.1. Speusippus (410-339 B.C.) and Xenocrates (396-314) were Plato's immediate successors as heads of the Academy. They productively developed his speculative ideas and laid the foundation for his reception, thus opening up the way for Platonism.

Temporarily at least, however, speculative efforts seem to have flagged because other schools had arisen that were felt to be rivals, especially as they also claimed to be following Socrates. Thus the followers of Pyrrho of Elis (ca. 360-ca. 272) sought to achieve peace of soul by renouncing all claims to knowledge and by suspending judgment *(epochē).* Rivals also included the Epicureans, who — in contrast to Plato and Aristotle — taught a world of blind chance *(tychē)* and sought fulfillment and peace of soul in a life of pleasure (*hēdonē;* → Hedonism) on this side of all transcendent dimensions.

Most threatening of all was the competition of → Stoicism. Philosophers of this school espoused the view that the world is rationally organized, but they went much further here than Plato. For they thought that all reality is permeated by the Logos and must be understood as a tension of pneuma-structure *(tonikē kinēsis, pneuma).* To give effective plausibility to their idea of → reason in the world, the Stoics even advanced the idea of an unrestricted participation of matter *(hylē).* The Stoic worldview was thus totally materialistic (→ Materialism). It anticipated B. Spinoza's (1632-77) pantheistic view of reality (→ Pantheism; Spinozism). Among the special problems that this view of reality entailed was the question how there can be any meaningful place for → freedom and → autonomy vis-à-vis an all-determinative power.

2.3.2. We may thus understand, perhaps, why the philosophers of the Academy, first Arcesilaus (316/15-ca. 241 B.C.) and then Carneades (ca. 213-129), are primarily distinguished for launching critical attacks upon the Stoics and trying to involve them in self-contradictions. As the empiricist orientation was destroyed (→ Empiricism), the basis of larger claims to knowledge was shaken. In this way the philosophers of the Academy showed what they regarded as important in the work of Socrates. Whether they were still teaching Plato's philosophy, at least in the school, is not certain. This was a matter of debate in antiquity itself, and no decisive conclusion can be reached. In any case, the skeptical aspect of the Academy's work soon faded.

Philo of Larissa (d. 79 B.C.) seems to have lost interest in confronting Stoicism, and he weakened the theses of his school. Then Antiochos of Ascalon (d. ca. 68 B.C.), who was for many years his pupil, was more than ready to come to terms with the Stoics. When he took over the headship after Philo's death, the Academy again became a place of dogmatic philosophizing, though it is no longer possible to say today whether the Platonism that he advocated was really any different from Stoicism.

2.3.3. We see here the eclectic and syncretistic tendencies that are found also in the thinking of the Stoic Poseidonius (ca. 135-ca. 51 B.C.), who adopted Platonic and Aristotelian ideas and showed interest in the themes of *Timaeus.* We find similar receptivity in the Jewish philosopher Philo of Alexandria, who tried to set up a Platonic system on an OT basis, a system that in particular sees harmony between Genesis and the Platonic tradition. (Numenius in the second century A.D. drew on this connection when he depicted Plato as an Attic → Moses.)

Another force that gave new vigor to the speculative features in Plato's thinking was Neopythagoreanism, which regarded speculation on unity and plurality as a theological theme and paved the way for all Neoplatonic systems as regards the central understanding of the expositions of the nature of unity *(to hen)* in the second part of *Parmenides.* The one, which we can describe only by way of negations and which is "beyond what is" (see *Rep.* 508B), is now seen as the first deity. This conceptualizing of an absolute completes the theologizing of the ideal that in the systems of later Platonism may be seen in the express differentiating and ranking of a first, second, and third God, or in the differentiation between the one / the good, being / spirit *(nous),* and the soul *(psychē).* We find such distinctions, for example, in Numenius (fl. late 2d cent. A.D.), a Pythagorizing thinker and a representative of the so-called middle Platonism.

They were probably worked out further by the rather shadowy Ammonius Saccas (ca. 175-242), who was supposedly the teacher of Plotinus and who also had an → Origen as a student. Whether this was the Alexandrian Origen (ca. 185-ca. 254) is debated by scholars, as is the suggestion that Ammonius had two students of the same name.

3. Neoplatonism

3.1. The real founder of the movement that we call Neoplatonism, a term that took hold in the 19th century, was Plotinus, who came from Egypt and who must be regarded as an eminent religious thinker and an intellectual mystic (→ Mysticism 2). In one sketch after another, Plotinus formulated a reality that began with the one and, by way of the duality of thinking and what is thought, became the soul, finally taking shape as physical reality.

Plotinus was a monist (→ Monism) inasmuch as, unlike the representatives of Eastern religions, he did not see any real counterprinciple at work but had to explain the existence of → evil *(to kakon)* by a principle of derivation. He devoted special attention to the question how derivation occurs (→ Metaphysics) and how we are to evaluate the → absolute, relative to our concepts of consciousness, thinking, and striving. It will hardly surprise us, then, that in view of the limits in principle of all conceptual thinking, he could offer no definitive answer.

We find astonishing innovations in Plotinus, along with deviations from Plato when the differentiating of the three substantial realities *(hypostaseis)* necessitates a reevaluation of certain theorems. Thus the ideas in this system are thinking entities (*noerai ousiai,* see *Enn.* 5.9[5].8.2). The explanation of this thesis is that Plotinus located the ideas in the realm of the second hypostasis (spirit) but also took the Aristotelian view of the spirit as self-thinking *nous.* Since this spirit (see Aristotle *Meta.* 12.7) is not by definition different from its objects, the objects cannot be regarded as mere contents but themselves also must be thinking entities.

We find other interesting changes in the course of speculation on the true nature of the self. Plotinus tends to take the view that the core of the self is spirit and that it too is thus located in the second hypothesis. This means that the true self is not affected by the process of → incarnation, and if the self is *nous,* then an identification of the self as an idea is suggested. But then the question arises whether there are ideas of individuals. Plato had defined the idea as something that, along the lines of the later doctrine of universals (→ Nominalism; Scholasticism), would refer to more than one bearer and that, as meaning, stands opposed to general terms. This view seems to rule out any concept of ideas as individuals.

Such an approach was revived by Duns Scotus (ca. 1265-1308; → Scotism) at the opposite pole from → Thomas Aquinas (ca. 1225-74; → Thomism), for Scotus believed that one can solve the problem of individuation only on the premise of individual forms (*haeccitas,* or "this-ness"). For a Platonist who believes in transmigration, the final difficulty arises that successive individuals (e.g., Pythagoras, Socrates, Plato) would have to be related to one and the same individual form, but then the form itself could not logically be regarded any longer as an individual form.

In Neoplatonism more than in Plato himself, we have the thought that the ideal has a special kind of dynamic and that we must expound reality in terms of process *(proodos)* and regress *(epistrophē).* Proclus (410 or 412-85) gave this thesis a striking form in his "theological foundation" *(stoicheiōsis theologikē).*

3.2. Proclus systematized the thought of other Neoplatonists like Porphyry (ca. 232-ca. 303), the pupil of Plotinus and Iamblichus (ca. 250-ca. 330), and in so doing developed a kind of mathematical metaphysics. Justinian (emp. 527-65) closed the Platonic school in 529 as the last pagan institution. But for a long time Platonism had other centers, such as Alexandria, where commentaries were written on the works of Aristotle, and Gaza, though Christian thinking was dominant there.

4. Christian Platonism

Christian Platonism was developed by → Justin, who was martyred in about 165, Clement of Alexandria (ca. 150-ca. 215), Origen, and the → Cappadocians Basil of Caesarea (ca. 330-79), Gregory of Nazianzus (329/30-389/90), and Basil's brother Gregory of Nyssa (ca. 330-ca. 395). Neoplatonism also made headway in the Latin West as the thinking of Porphyry, and therefore of Plotinus, became known through the mediation of the orator Marius Victorinus (4th cent.) and → Augustine (354-430; → Augustine's Theology). Augustine, who saw a close link between Platonism and Christianity, adopted a view of Platonism that became influential in the → Middle Ages.

We might also mention Boethius (ca. 480-524), who made → Greek philosophy at home in the Latin world. By means of the translations and commentaries of Boethius, a basis was provided for what is known as the old → logic *(logica vetus),* that is, the logic that built on the propaedeutic writings of Aristotle and could be worked out only when the *Analytics* were known. Especially important and influential was Boethius's translation of Porphyry's introduction to Aristotle's work on the → categories, which formed the basis of medieval discussions of the status of general concepts.

Not least of all, these discussions were significant for theological reasons, for when the contents of

Christian faith needed to be elucidated in philosophical terms, the question soon arose how we are to think more precisely of the way that attributes exist and whether there are essences of the Platonic kind. Boethius's *Consolation of Philosophy*, which was widely read and commented upon in the Middle Ages, was very influential. This work developed many important thoughts, such as the distinction between → time and eternity, also problems relating to divine foreknowledge and human freedom. Through the work of the Christian author Chalcidius (4th cent.), Plato's *Timaeus* also attracted attention in the Middle Ages and was studied, for example, in the school of Chartres.

A truly independent speculative effort came only at the beginning of the Carolingian renaissance, especially with the work of John Scotus Erigena (ca. 810-ca. 877) *On the Division of Nature*. Erigena was one of the few scholars of the age who could read the Greek texts, and he also translated the work *On the Divine Names* by Pseudo-Dionysius. This Dionysius was thought to be the Areopagite whom Paul had converted in Athens with his speech on the unknown god (Acts 17:22-34). The work, however, shows dependence on Proclus, and hence its author cannot have been the Dionysius of Acts. The translation propagated the thoughts of Proclus in the Middle Ages. An important foundation was thus laid for reception into the Latin West of ideas from the Islamic world (→ Islam), such as the *Book on Causes*, which was translated from Arabic in the second half of the 12th century and was thought to be by Aristotle, though it actually came from Proclus. Aquinas recognized this fact and devoted an important and illuminating commentary to it.

The → Franciscans did most to foster the Platonic tradition in the Middle Ages, while → Dominicans developed the Aristotelian tradition. How strong the difference really was we need not discuss here. It is incontestable, however, that a Platonic orientation goes well with inwardness and strength of feeling, while Aristotelianism for the most part attracts rationalistic thinkers (→ Rationalism).

5. Renaissance Platonism and Platonism Today

5.1. Platonism enjoyed a true revival in the → Renaissance, when — thanks to the work of the so-called humanists, who devoted themselves to the humanities (i.e., poetry, → rhetoric, history, and moral philosophy; → Humanism) — the ancient texts were made more widely available. In 1438/39 the Byzantine philosopher Gemistus Plethon (ca. 1355-ca. 1452) won over the aristocrat Cosimo de Medici (1389-1464) for the idea of a Platonic academy in his villa in Florence, which had as its main head Marsilio Ficino (1433-99), who translated Plato and Plotinus into Latin. Pico della Mirandola (1463-94), supposedly the first scholar to try to understand works in the tradition of Judaism, and also a student of the → cabala, was one of the most important scholars attached to this school. Possibly under the influence of Nicholas of Cusa (1401-64), who worked in Upper Italy, a Christian Platonism thus arose in Florence that then spread to other parts of Europe.

5.2. The Romantic poet Novalis (1772-1801), one of J. G. Fichte's (1762-1814) first students at Jena in 1794, was fascinated by Neoplatonism. So was F. Hölderlin (1770-1843), who saw a problem in primal unity and division and thus pursued along other lines a question inherited from I. Kant (1724-1804; → Kantianism).

Even more so than Hölderlin, F. J. Schelling (1775-1854) in his extensive writings took up Neoplatonic thought. Like Fichte these two, along with G. W. F. Hegel (1770-1831; → Hegelianism), had had theological training. Schelling wrote a commentary on Plato's *Timaeus* and even felt his way into the world of thought of Giordano Bruno (1548-1600), who assimilated the thinking of Neoplatonism, perhaps more deeply than almost any other philosopher. Bruno was persecuted because of his pantheistic theses, being finally put to death at the stake. We may refer in this connection to Schelling's work on the → philosophy of nature (→ Romanticism) and to Hegel's discussion of estrangement in his Frankfurt period (ca. 1800).

5.3. Neoplatonism became even more important in Britain. The Cambridge Platonists took up the ideas of Plato and Plotinus. These men, including Ralph Cudworth (1617-88) and Henry More (1614-87), reacted against their → Puritan background and, unlike the great thinkers of their time René Descartes (1596-1650; → Cartesianism), Thomas Hobbes (1588-1679), and Spinoza, found a congenial orientation in Plato's metaphysics.

A century later Thomas Taylor (1758-1835) published many translations of Neoplatonic texts. His at times vehement anti-Christian polemics influenced the English Romantics William Blake (1757-1827), Samuel Coleridge (1772-1834), and Percy Shelley (1792-1822), who for their part reacted against the strong and in part misdirected influence of Isaac Newton (1642-1727). Coleridge and Shelley were able to read the texts in the original.

In his later poems the Irish poet William Butler Yeats (1865-1939) drew from the new rendering of Plotinus by Stephen MacKenna (1872-1934), which is still unrivaled for its linguistic and imaginative force and which must be regarded as an example of intellectual appropriation.

As regards a more strictly philosophical reception of Platonic thinking, we may refer to Maurice Blondel (1861-1949), Henri Bergson (1859-1941), and Alfred North Whitehead (1861-1947). Whitehead championed → process philosophy and, as a thinker, was especially fascinated by the subject matter dealt with in Plato's *Timaeus.* To him we owe the comment that European philosophy is simply a series of footnotes on Plato.

Bibliography: H. Dörrie, *Platonica Minora* (Munich, 1976) • M. J. Edwards, *Origen against Plato* (Aldershot, 2002) • R. Ferber, *Platos Idee des Guten* (2d ed.; St. Augustin, 1989); idem, *Die Unwissenheit des Philosophen, oder, Warum hat Plato die "ungeschriebene Lehre" nicht geschrieben?* (St. Augustin, 1991) • J. N. Findlay, *Plato and Platonism: An Introduction* (New York, 1978); idem, *Plato: The Written and Unwritten Doctrines* (London, 1974) • A. Graeser, *Hauptwerke der Philosophie. Antike* (Stuttgart, 1992); idem, *Die Philosophie der Antike,* vol. 2, *Sophistik, Sokratik, Plato und Aristoteles* (2d ed.; Munich, 1993); idem, *Philosophische Erkenntnis und begriffliche Darstellung* (Mainz, 1989) • G. J. P. O'Daly, *Platonism Pagan and Christian: Studies in Plotinus and Augustine* (Aldershot, 2001) • D. J. O'Meara, *The Structure of Being and the Search for the Good: Essays on Ancient and Early Medieval Platonism* (Aldershot, 1998).

Andreas Graeser

Play

1. Anthropological Sense
2. References in Practical Theology

1. Anthropological Sense

Play is a general phenomenon in both individual and social life. Yet no universally accepted definition of the term that would make it scientific has yet been found (H. Scheuerl).

From the days of I. Kant (1724-1804; → Kantianism), an essential feature of play has been the lack of any goals apart from itself (so W. Dilthey; → Hermeneutics 3.1.3.2; Vitalism 2). As involving a freedom from outward pressures (G. W. F. Hegel; → Hegelianism) or moral commitment (F. → Nietzsche; → Nihilism; Religion, Criticism of), this definition recurs in various transformed and expanded senses (H.-J. Roth). In F. Schiller (1759-1805; → Classicism) play forms the aesthetic dimension of human existence. We play only as we are fully human, and we are fully human only as we play. Play guarantees freedom, and it is successful only when we are free. It takes us out of the processes of nature (J. Huizinga; → Nature) and points us to an important role in becoming human (→ Anthropology).

A playful attitude is found among young → animals but is soon lost. It is a basic attitude for humans, however, throughout their entire lives (G. Bally). As compared with an animal relationship to the environment, it establishes an openness to the world (W. Pannenberg, with reference to M. Scheler, H. Plessner, A. Gehlen, A. Portmann, and F. J. J. Buytendijk; → Culture 4-5). It is thus the origin of the human power of decision, personal responsibility, and freedom of choice (H.-J. Roth; → Responsibility). Other writers recognize a related attitude among birds and mammals (G. Bally, I. Eibl-Eibesfeldt, J. S. Bruner, et al.).

Antonyms such as "seriousness," → "work," "reality," and → "life" fail to match the phenomenon in its fullness. Huizinga has mentioned an analogy between play and the cult, for in play there is an element of detachment such as we find elsewhere only in the sacral cult. Play represents a world of its own that disposes of its own place and time and follows its own rules in its vocabulary (Pannenberg, with reference to J. Sartre; → Existentialism). Agreement is needed with ourselves or with others in order to establish its reality and to begin a game or sport.

A definition of this kind is enough to cover all kinds of games, whether those of children, of sporting events, of chance, of love, or of society, along with aesthetic and sociocultural events, and the many games that adults play (E. Berne). But distinction must be made between play as warfare and as representation (Huizinga), and we must also take note of the difference between play as chance and as excitement (R. Caillois).

2. References in Practical Theology

2.1. Though little has been done to achieve a theology of play, it undoubtedly has a relevance in practical theology. It obviously plays a part in religious → socialization. J. Piaget (1896-1980) has convincingly shown how → identity forms in play. It involves direct detachment from the immediate environment and thus involves self-development (D. W. Winnicott). An adult can keep his or her identity, and continually regain it, only when there is the necessary room for play. The same applies to the lifelong reconstruction of religious identity, for this formation involves experience of a reality that is accessible only to symbolic (i.e., played out) understanding (→ Symbol).

2.2. A connection exists between play and the cult, ritual (→ Rite), or → liturgy. Huizinga suggests that in play cultic humanity actualizes the events represented afresh, in this way helping to keep in place the order of the world. Play and nonplay, the reality of the cult and the reality of the world, are related like two halves of a double-sided picture (R. Schaeffler). Reality is not represented or reflected in the cult but is basically upheld and renewed.

That Christian → worship (§7) can be suitably conceived of as play has been especially advocated by R. Guardini (1885-1968; → Person). He argues that playing is for God a work of art. Not accomplishing anything is the innermost essence of the liturgy. Materially, this understanding coincides with the distinction F. D. E. → Schleiermacher (1768-1834; → Schleiermacher's Theology; Liberal Theology 3) makes between active works that achieve an effect and representative works that remain the same. He too found in both liturgy and art a freedom from any goals and yet also a meaningful element.

2.3. Christian → pastoral care must deal with play in a very deep-seated way. Those who become involved in destructive relationships in families, groups, and partnerships — relations that bring illness to many people (→ Health and Illness) — need all the help they can get. More important than verbal statements or psychoanalytical techniques (→ Psychoanalysis), "countergames" will often be the remedy, opposing antitheses to destructive theses in the form of therapeutic intervention (E. Berne) and thus corresponding to the symptoms (P. Watzlawick).

2.4. The role of → Jesus' praxis according to the NT tradition is noteworthy in this respect (see, e.g., John 8:3-11, where Jesus initially avoids the implied "illusion of alternatives" inhering in his opponents' play, only to bring that play to an abrupt end in v. 7b by means of a paradoxical "symptom prescription"). We may see his → parables also as an attempt to depict the possible in and against the real (W. Harnisch) and thus to develop countergames in his hearers in which the possible reality of the kingdom of God will become a real possibility.

Christian → preaching that is pledged to this tradition can also be understood and developed as a countergame that describes, reflects, and develops the possible in and against the real, so that it too is play in the sense of a *theologia eventualis* (theology of the possible) that sets the attraction of the possible over against the power of the factual (J. Henkys).

Bibliography: On 1: G. Bally, *Vom Ursprung und von den Grenzen der Freiheit. Eine Deutung des Spiels bei Tier und Mensch* (Basel, 1945) • E. Berne, *Games People Play: The Psychology of Human Relationships* (New York, 1964) • J. S. Bruner, A. Jolly, and K. Sylva, eds., *Play: Its Role in Development and Evolution* (New York, 1976) • R. Caillois, *Man, Play, and Games* (Champaign, Ill., 2001) • I. Eible-Eibesfeldt, *Human Ethology* (New York, 1989) • C. Garvey, *Play* (exp. ed.; Cambridge, Mass., 1990) • J. Huizinga, *Homo Ludens: A Study of the Play Element in Culture* (New York, 1970) • W. Pannenberg, *Anthropology in Theological Perspective* (Philadelphia, 1985) • T. G. Power, *Play and Exploration in Children and Animals* (Mahwah, N.J., 2000) • H.-J. Roth, "Homo ludens," *EK* 25 (1992) 160-63 • J.-P. Sartre, *Being and Nothingness: An Essay on Phenomenological Ontology* (New York, 1956; orig. pub., 1943) • H. Scheuerl, *Das Spiel. Untersuchungen über sein Wesen, seine pädagogischen Möglichkeiten und Grenzen* (Basel, 1954) • B. Sutton-Smith, *The Ambiguity of Play* (Cambridge, Mass., 1997).

On 2: K.-H. Bieritz, "'Freiheit im Spiel.' Aspekte einer praktisch-theologischen Spieltheorie," *BTZ* 10 (1993) 164-74 • R. Guardini, *The Spirit of the Liturgy* (New York, 1998; orig. pub., 1922) • W. Harnish, *Die Gleichniserzählungen Jesu. Eine hermeneutische Einführung* (Göttingen, 1985) • J. Henkys, "Die praktische Theologie (Einführung)," *HPTh(B)* 1.11-56 • S. Keen *Apology for Wonder* (New York, 1969) • D. L. Miller, *Gods and Games: Toward a Theology of Play* (New York, 1970); idem, "The Kingdom of Play," *USQR* 25 (1970) 343-60 • J. Moltmann, *Theology of Play* (New York, 1972) • J. Piaget, *Play, Dreams, and Imitation in Childhood* (London, 1962) • H. Rahner, *Man at Play* (New York, 1967) • R. Schaeffler, "Der Kultus als Weltauslegung," *Kult in der säkularisierten Welt* (ed. B. Fischer et al.; Regensburg, 1974) • P. Watzlawick, *Die Möglichkeit des Andersseins. Zur Technik der therapeutischen Kommunikation* (5th ed.; Bern, 2002) • P. Watzlawick et al., *Pragmatics of Human Communication* (New York, 1967) • D. W. Winnicott, *Playing and Reality* (New York, 1971).

Karl-Heinrich Bieritz

Pluralism

1. Political and Social Aspects
2. Religious and Theological Aspects
   2.1. Its Many Facets
   2.2. Within the Church and Theology
   2.3. Opportunities and Limitations
   2.4. God, Revelation, Truth, and Paradox
3. Ecumenical Aspects

The word "pluralism" (from Lat. *pluralis*) refers to the presence, in any given setting, of a multiplicity of competing cultures, viewpoints, economic interests, religious perspectives, philosophical opinions, and the like. In such usages the word is a near synonym for "diversity." "Pluralism" can also mean the advocacy or defense of diversity as a matter of principle, as when pluralism is contrasted with terms such as "exclusivism" or "inclusivism" in regard to religious faiths other than one's own. In either sense, pluralism can take many forms: one may defend it in one sphere of life and be hostile to its presence in another. It follows that pluralism can be conceptualized in many different frames of reference. Pluralisms clearly differ in their import, depending on the contexts and horizons of meaning in question. Different formulations of this word's meaning may lend themselves either to upholding the social diversity to which it refers or to mounting attacks upon it. This article discusses pluralism in three contemporary spheres of life: the political and social (see 1), the religious and theological (see 2), and the ecumenical (see 3).

1. Political and Social Aspects

1.1. In a social or political sense, pluralism, as the opposite of → monism, refers to the fact of a multiplicity of interests in → society. Those who represent diverse interests in society commonly organize in groups, cooperating and competing with one another. Since in a pluralistic society there is no single or uniform interest, competition among interests produces varied results, which are then challenged by fresh competition. Such interaction among pluralistically organized interests presupposes a mobile, flexible, and open society. As the interests compete with one another, it is assumed that they do not exclude one another in principle. Some may achieve a majority at one time, others at another. Financial interests, which can be calculated, are the usual measures of competitive success. Interests that cannot be similarly calculated in the ebb and flow of pluralistic competition (e.g., religious interests; → Tolerance) tend to be marginalized or suppressed.

Pluralistic society is mainly a modern phenomenon (→ Modern Period; Modernity). It rests on the premise that in the → state individuals are free to organize (→ Organization) or assemble to promote or protect their interests. These political premises arose within modern mass society and developed gradually in the 19th and 20th centuries in central and western Europe, as well as in the Anglo-Saxon countries. Early → liberalism and → socialism put their stamp on these ideas.

Liberal → democracy is apparently the political form that best accommodates pluralism's many oscillating interest groups. In such democracies pluralism often expresses itself in the form of competing → political parties. The plurality of opinions and interests gives vitality to these parties, exerts pressure on them, and changes them.

1.2. Pluralism, however, can also take forms that threaten democratic institutions. At times when nations need to be united, the pluralism of competing groups and parties can be disruptive. The divisive activities of diverse interest groups can threaten to weaken common values or tear them apart.

Some complain that pluralism is found mainly in capitalist or otherwise restrictive polities where the range of viable viewpoints is limited by the nature of these societies. In such societies there is often a heavy concentration of upper-class, elitist, or behind-the-scenes → power in a few important arenas of influence, such as the → economy and the → mass media. For this reason, a corporative society is thought by many to be preferable. The decisive question for all democratic pluralism is how to give all citizens an equal opportunity to promote their interests.

Another objection to highly pluralistic societies is that they do not deal adequately with pressing issues such as those of → technology and dangers to the → environment. Trusting in the democratic process of working out conflicts of interest is no longer enough to meet the threats involved in these spheres and thus may invite a neglect of the future. These difficulties are not with the concept of pluralism as such, which allows for the discipline of democratic debate, but against its inadequate presuppositions and its inability in practice to deal with the problems that arise in contemporary societies.

Bibliography: M. Deveaux, *Cultural Pluralism and Dilemmas of Justice* (Ithaca, N.Y., 2000) • J. K. Galbraith, *American Capitalism: The Concept of Countervailing Power* (2d ed.; Oxford, 1980) • R. Kane, *Through the Moral Maze: Searching for Absolute Values in a Pluralistic World* (Armonk, N.Y., 1996) • R. Madsen and T. Strong, eds., *The Many and the One: Religious and Secular Perspectives on Ethical Pluralism in the Modern World* (Princeton, 2003) • J. D. Moon, *Constructing Community: Moral Pluralism and Tragic Conflicts* (Princeton, 1995) • W.-D. Narr, *Pluralistische Gesellschaft* (Hannover, 1969) • J. H. Olthuis, ed., *Towards an Ethics of Community: Negotiations of Difference in a Pluralist Society* (Waterloo, Ont., 2000) • I. M. Young, *Justice and the Politics of Difference* (Princeton, 1990).

Wolf-Dieter Narr, with Lewis S. Mudge

2. Religious and Theological Aspects

Both the condition of pluralism in its many forms and a wide range of attitudes toward it exist also in spheres of life beyond the social and the political. These spheres include the ethical, the cultural, the academic, and the religious or theological. The last-named sphere is particularly significant because of the nature of some religious or theological claims as either exclusive (rejecting all others) or inclusive (reaching out to others with themselves at the center).

2.1. *Its Many Facets*

With its many facets, the fact of pluralism affects → church and → theology relative to their position and claim in modern life and society. But pluralism within church and theology also impacts church life as such. Doctrinal pluralism challenges the idea of the → unity of → faith and of the church itself, as well as the notion of the unity of the human race. It allows for the existence of disparate theologies within single religious communities.

2.1.1. In pluralistically structured → industrial society the church is one sphere among others. → Politics, the → economy, → science, and → technology are other such spheres. The claims of other social spheres restrict the church's claim to the whole of life and therefore frustrate its desire for pervasive influence. Traditional ecclesiastical privileges come under criticism (→ Church and State), and the scientific character of theology and its position in the university are contested. Different positions and claims are forced to compromise within this web of rivalries and countervailing pressures.

Problems of → identity arise out of the interaction between ecclesiastical → institutions and other social → organizations, and also between secular and religious cultures, sometimes giving rise to the phenomenon of → civil religion. There is also competition between old and new religious fellowships with similar claims and intentions, between → worldviews that offer and assert rival outlooks, as well as between divergent understandings of existence that provide orientation and regulative → norms for living. The result is the opportunity to choose among alternatives. Examination and selection become imperative in the sector of religious → consumption.

Pluralism can make the communication of faith to others more difficult. What the church intends and does must functionally meet both individual and collective needs (→ Everyday Life 4). It is essential that the contents and standards of faith be made as plausible and useful as possible. The social process of forming opinions and balancing interests in the marketplace of religious ideas demands a readiness for → dialogue. But the churches' responses up to now seem to many to be dubious and inadequate in the sociocultural nexus of pluralistic society (→ Church 1.4.1.5).

2.1.2. Among the cultural, social, political, and economic factors in → Third World societies, the position and claim of Christian faith, burdened as it is with the weight of its → colonialist and missionary past, are limited by national cultures, → populism, nationalism (→ Nation, Nationalism), native → religions, and a host of different contextual experiences of life's relationships. This context gives pluralism a different dimension for church and theology.

In encounter with other religions and circumstances, the spectrum of alternative realities expands, and the array of problems for religious thought becomes more complex. Encounters with these things engender a greater awareness of the contingency of Christian → tradition, set the claim to validity and truth in question, call for a paradigm that accepts religious and cultural pluralism (→ Theology of Religions), and make interreligious relationships possible. Experience of a plural world underlines the need for a pluralistic theology of religion.

A pluralistic view of reality suggests a plurality of ways to religious truth, and thus to God. Religions then seem to be of equal rank. The claim to possess, and offer, the one valid way to → salvation no longer seems to be self-evident, even to believers. The Christian faith appears to be one among many historically and contextually limited religions. Coexistence demands peaceful cooperation, face to face with the global problems of humanity. The practice of interfaith communication seems to open doors toward growth in wisdom and toward greater knowledge of God and ourselves.

2.2. *Within the Church and Theology*

Pluralism is a powerful force within the church and theology.

2.2.1. The church's institutions are subject to the same organizational and bureaucratic tendencies (→ Bureaucracy 3) that accompany pluralism in other spheres. The → mass media naturally meet people's needs for information about religious questions. They thus take over, without being under church control, functions that have traditionally been part of the churches' pastoral task. Pluralism opens the way to dissonances and discords in the everyday experiences of church members (→ Everyday Life 3.4 and 4.1). Their individual → piety, their personal plans and values (→ Lifestyle), no longer find an anchor in the institutionalized church fellowship (→ Church 1.4.1.4).

→ Lay movements and the → counterculture give evidence of the emancipatory working of pluralism (→ Emancipation), as also does criticism of the church's structure (→ Hierarchy 2.3), its exercise of → power (§3), its beliefs, approaches, and norms (esp. in sexual ethics; → Norms 3), not to speak of its discussion of the ecclesiastical status and role of women. A secular understanding and sense of → freedom (§§1.2 and 2.7-9), together with various contextual conditions, produce diverse expressions of faith that collide with traditional formulas but claim at least as much justification as they (→ Base Communities; Church Growth).

2.2.2. The canonical NT writings offer us the highly varied forms of witness and reflection generated by primitive Christianity (→ Canon 2). Just for this reason, these writings can be read and interpreted in different ways (→ Exegesis, Biblical). The multiplicity of biblical theologies alone (→ Biblical Theology 1) demand this sort of flexibility. Articulating the authority of the Bible as such thus becomes a complex question. Along with the apostolic testimony as a central point of reference and unity, there are different experiences and views of reality in different contexts (plurality) that have, over time, influenced the reception and exposition of the biblical texts (→ Biblical Theology 2).

In the course of church history from its beginning in NT days, many Christian communities have differed in teaching, order, practice, and piety, but all have claimed churchly status, orthodoxy, and → catholicity, while delimiting themselves from → heresies and schisms (→ Confession of Faith 2). There have been many → sects and → denominations, all making claims for their distinctive expressions of faith and all insisting on their rights to exercise → religious liberty (→ Free Church) where the cultures around them permitted it. There is no room here to depict or discuss all the causes and impulses that gave rise to this Christian pluralism, the nature of interdenominational relations and conflicts, or the various marks of confessional and denominational identity (→ Church 2.2). Nevertheless, we must take note of the fact of such pluralism and point out that, despite ecumenical effort, it continues to increase.

The spectrum of communal faith-expressions is growing broader today because many of the various church bodies of the West are making efforts to exchange traditional practices for what is new and contemporary (→ Church 5.1), because global Christian movements have come into being outside the historical churches (→ Charismatic Movement; Pentecostalism; Transdenominational Movements), and because churches that have arisen in non-Western contexts (→ Third World 2) are breaking free from their missionary origins and developing their own cultural profiles. This is true also, to a limited degree, within the Roman Catholic Church. Some of these bodies are taking shape as national → Independent Churches (e.g., the → Kimbanguist Church).

Still, the witness of the early creeds to the "one church" and belief in the unchanging → truth of Jesus' message of → salvation (→ Church 1.1-3 and 5.4) has not been forgotten. Despite so-called nontheological factors (political and social circumstances, common interests, rational insights, etc.), the witness of faith calls for efforts to bring visibility to the God-given unity in the communion of the churches (→ Ecumenism, Ecumenical Movement; United and Uniting Churches). Unity in faith must assert itself in some way if pluralism is not to become Christianity's dominant social expression (→ Ecumenical Theology).

This situation requires that we tackle the theological problem of denominationalism (→ Confession of Faith 3) and the task of articulating the need for unity, as well as the theological conditions that must be fulfilled to make it possible. Indeed, it means clarifying the content of the truth that unites. In practice, we must confront the various claims to denominational identity (→ Confession of Faith 5) that, in the absence of consensus, may or may not permit → tolerance, that may display fundamentalist features (→ Fundamentalism), and that may include claims to uniqueness (→ Roman Catholic Church).

2.2.3. Corresponding to institutional pluralism is the pluralism of theologies resulting from historic debates about → revelation, faith, and salvation (→ Christology; God) promoted by the denominations in attempts to assert their legitimacy (→ Polemics). Histories of dogma and the comparative study of denominations provide us with materials in this regard.

Factors that tend to exacerbate theological pluralism today are the different methodologies of the different theological disciplines (→ Theology), the orientation of many theologians to contemporary secular studies and views of existence (→ Analytic Philosophy; Anthropology; Culture; Epistemology; Existentialism; God Is Dead Theology; Hermeneutics; Individualism; Philosophy; Philosophy of Religion; Philosophy of Science; Process Theology; Science and Theology; Subjectivism), and the growing independence of regional and contextual theologies (→ African Theology; Asian Theology; Biblical

Theology 2; Black Theology; Feminist Theology; Liberation Theology; Third World Theology).

2.3. *Opportunities and Limitations*

2.3.1. A mark of today's theological pluralism is that theological reflection is no longer entirely determined or limited by denominational affiliation. It reflects, perhaps even more, different experiential backgrounds. Pluralism today does not simply present us with alternatives along a discernible continuum. Positions are often disparate, and thus mutual communication is difficult.

Official Protestant and Roman Catholic surveys of pluralism often highlight the possibilities pluralism itself opens up. Pluralism gives space to the many gifts in the church, brings to light the limitations of human knowledge, relates the actual communicating of the faith to central contemporary problems, liberates theology from parochial traditions and outlooks, makes ecumenical breadth possible, and safeguards against overhasty condemnations of otherness in faith.

These studies also point to the limits of pluralism. All views cannot be equally right, individualism in principle is unjustifiable, and loss of content in basic matters must be resisted. "Jesus Christ the Lord of all life" must be the limiting criterion of a valid pluralism. The continuity of God's Word must be preserved across the centuries and continents. The ultimate basis of faith that is both one and many is the mystery of Christ, the mystery of the → Trinity (→ Incarnation). The witness of Scripture enables us to differentiate true pluralism from false pluralism, as it opens up access to the truth and is accepted in the confession of the believing and praying church. The church cannot silently acquiesce in transgressions of these boundaries. The Roman Catholic → teaching office (Magisterium) enforces its dogmatic definitions (→ Dogma), which may well be time-bound but still have ongoing relevance as the proper exposition of revelation. In opposition to ethical relativism, it recalls unchanging principles enshrined in the biblical witness. There is also an appeal to the general recognition of → human dignity that is the gift of God.

2.3.2. This balancing of opportunities and limits seems to do justice both to the contemporary phenomenon of pluralism in the church and theology and also to the need for unity. The cumulative buildup of insights and lifestyles that supplement and broaden the basic apostolic witness but leave its solid core untouched can meet the challenge of pluralism. The idea of "many in one" that makes communication and reconciliation possible facilitates the absorbing of pluralism into larger systems. Tension will still exist between the actual plurality and the sought-for unity, which is an unavoidable aspect of human history. But confident → hope in God's redeeming action can ascribe it to the provisional sphere of time.

If this problem can be pragmatically resolved, the result will justify the Christian claim to truth. It will correspond to the church's well-understood interest in positing meaning and offering orientation. The church does not bring to the question of pluralism a monistic view that offers a single outlook on the world. Nor does it make immutability a sign of truth and see stability as its guarantee. Not to grasp insights such as these is to have problems in interpreting traditional premises and axioms and to leave the meaning of pluralism an open theological question.

2.4. *God, Revelation, Truth, and Paradox*

Today's forms of pluralism in church and theology, rooted as they are in the crises of everyday life (→ Everyday Life 1.3), may be seen as deforming Christianity and dissipating its resources. But from another angle, they may be viewed as phenomena that indicate the churches' sharing in the reality of today's life, and hence as a profiling of incarnation itself and a following of its dynamic.

2.4.1. The diagnosis calls for therapy, and for a study of theological perceptions. But there does not seem to be much ground for therapeutic effort on the basis of what we know of theological and dogmatic approaches and their acting subjects.

In ideas of God, talk about God, and the witness of faith, immutability and unity relate to the deity or to reality as a whole. What is presented and believed may appeal to revelation or may be a product of imagination or projection. Either way, it eludes our direct grasp and cannot be reproduced in practice. The contents remain in the contexts of faith and its conceptualization, which as phenomena of human life simply bear witness to themselves and not to their ultimate referents (→ God). These phenomena are specific, and they are many. Under finite conditions they are always variable and unstable. They offer no adequate indications of the presence of something greater (universal, total) but only of the fact of dissatisfaction with this life as it is.

Revelation and truth involve contingency and complexity. Divine self-revelation and its truth are riveted to the original bearers and witnesses of revelation and to their time and place. In form and content they also involve many contingent features. This characteristic forbids differentiation between inner kernel and outer husk or reduction to what is essential and obligatory (→ Hermeneutics 2.3;

Kerygma). What we find, then, by way of more fundamental axioms implicit in contingent and complex experiences, can be received and allowed to work in other times and places only when the situation allows (→ Revelation 2). The effort to abstract what is revealed, to give it objectivity in regulative formulas and specific actions, and to provide it with organizational stability (e.g., rules of faith, sacraments, the church, tradition) has no criterion apart from a personal or collective confession and the experience of individuals or groups and fellowships. Error and → doubt cannot be excluded. In the same way, we cannot make an earlier reality present today without variable elements of exposition and situational reference (→ Hermeneutics 3.2). Thus revelation and truth are relational and necessarily combine with elements that weaken their claim to validity rather than strengthen it. (On the complex reality of the everyday as the place and problem of theology, → Everyday Life 3.)

2.4.2. A phenomenological survey of today's scene confirms the existence of crisis, change, upheaval, evolution, paradigm shift, and a growth in the complexity of the question of pluralism. What we see shows us how changeable the world is. Pluralism presupposes dissatisfaction with reality as it is, regards many directional decisions as possible, finds confirmation in the experience of history, and counts on continuing change. The following are implications for Christian thought and action.

Both theoretically and practically, faith under present conditions falls short of total truth (reality). It is situationally or contextually related and has no permanent place to stand. But in its relation to truth and situation, it can seek to be maximal as faith. It has to do so lest it ignore the people's feeling of dissatisfaction, underrate people's thirst for truth, and generally fail to measure up to the urgent needs of our global situation. The contextual pluralism that can consist of many positions alongside, with, or after one another nevertheless permits a pluralism of maximal expressions of Christian faith. The inevitable result will be discord, competition, and contradiction among the maximal positions. Degrees of → consensus are not ruled out, but these will be deficient and unserviceable if they select certain truths and maintain their immutability. At the same time, Christian faith must not be reduced to supposed generalities that are meant to be valid in any context.

Mutability and plurality make possible the comparison and interpretation of divergent positions, concepts, and phenomena. These conditions justify → doubt regarding the familiar and supposedly self-evident. They justify imagination to see that what is well known may be different from what we think it is, especially as reflected in the eyes of others. Such conditions allow theological pluralism to be received as a valid possibility in itself, and they allow it to form the basis of an ongoing dialogic process as a structural element in theology. (On ecclesiological pluralism and its implications, → Church 5.)

How, then, is an acceptable pluralism within theology to be theologically understood? Much depends on the horizons of meaning within which different understandings of pluralism, different pluralisms in the sense of different opinions about plurality itself, are formulated. Hence we have an eschatological question. Do we now accommodate a wide range of theological ideas, or even of distinct faiths, in the expectation that a plurality of irreconcilable visions of God will continue to exist at the end of history? That is, are we willing to give pluralism a finally normative status in our understanding of ultimate reality? Or can we only accommodate what seems now to be intractable pluralism in the confidence that this pluralism will be overcome when God is "all in all"? For a pluralism of irreconcilable meanings to be normative for the universe itself runs counter to our deepest assumptions. But the expectation of a final reconciliation of visions could tempt powerful religious authorities to believe that they have already anticipated its content, and therefore that they should do others the favor of imposing it on them.

Bibliography: H. U. von Balthasar, *Truth Is Symphonic: Aspects of Christian Pluralism* (San Francisco, 1987) • P. L. Berger, *The Heretical Imperative: Contemporary Possibilities of Religious Affirmation* (Garden City, N.Y., 1979) • E. M. Bounds, *Coming Together / Coming Apart: Religion, Community, and Modernity* (New York, 1997) • H. G. Coward, *Pluralism in the World Religious* (rev. ed.; Oxford, 2000) • P. Crowley, *In Ten Thousand Places: Dogma in a Pluralistic Church* (New York, 1997) • J. Dupuis, *Toward a Christian Theology of Religious Pluralism* (Maryknoll, N.Y., 1997) • E. Fahlbusch, *Einheit der Kirche. Eine kritische Betrachtung des ökumenischen Dialogs* (Munich, 1983) • D. R. Griffin, ed., *Deep Religious Pluralism* (Louisville, Ky., 2005) • R. Hutchison, *Religious Pluralism in America: The Contentious History of a Founding Ideal* (New Haven, 2003) • S. Kaplan, *Different Paths, Different Summits: A Model for Religious Pluralism* (Lanham, Md., 2002) • G. D. Kaufman, *God, Mystery, Diversity: Christian Theology in a Pluralistic World* (Minneapolis, 1996) • B. Lonergan, *Doctrinal Pluralism* (Milwaukee, Wis., 1971) • W. McClain, *Traveling Light: Christian

Perspectives on Pilgrimage and Pluralism (New York, 1981) • L. NEWBIGIN, *The Gospel in a Pluralist Society* (Grand Rapids, 1989) • K. RAHNER, "Pluralism in Theology and the Unity of the Creed in the Church," *Theological Investigations* (vol. 11; London, 1974) 3-24 • M. SUCHOCKI, *Divinity and Diversity: A Christian Affirmation of Religious Pluralism* (Nashville, 2003) • D. TRACY, *Plurality and Ambiguity: Hermeneutics, Religion, Hope* (New York, 1987) • R. WENTZ, *The Culture of Religious Pluralism* (Boulder, Colo., 1998) • A. WETHERILT, *That They May Be Many: Voices of Women, Echoes of God* (New York, 1984).

JEAN-MARIE CHARPENTIER, with LEWIS S. MUDGE

3. Ecumenical Aspects

The factors discussed above show why the 20th century, and now the 21st, have seen a new and more positive evaluation of pluralism. Scholars participating in → ecumenical dialogues have repeatedly reminded the churches that even in the biblical → canon several theological perspectives are to be found. At the 1963 World Conference on Faith and Order in Montreal (→ Ecumenism, Ecumenical Movement; Faith and Order Movement; World Council of Churches), for example, several addresses made clear that the NT canon provides the basis for a variety of → confessions of faith. There has also been ecumenical recognition, as indicated above, that theological positions are influenced by the culture and society in which they arise (→ Acculturation; Contextual Theology), and that place of origin does not determine the authenticity of a theological viewpoint. → Vatican II also extended the principle of legitimate diversity to differences in theological expression.

Does a plurality of legitimate theological viewpoints and approaches result in complete relativity of truth claims (→ Relativism)? If recent ecumenical discussion is any criterion, the answer to this question is no. Discernment of the limits to diversity was already underway in 1 John in the NT. In the discussion at Montreal referred to above, scholars recognized that the basic reason for striving to discover the *limits* to the diversity that is possible within unity is a need to distinguish, if that is possible, between → truth and error.

The question of the limits to diversity remains on the ecumenical agenda. Such discernment has already evolved, for example, in the all-but-universal declaration that apartheid is an unacceptable position for Christians (→ Racism). An unsuccessful effort to say the same of participation in warfare — that is, to say that today there can be no such thing as a just war — was made at the 1991 Assembly of the WCC at Canberra, but the discussion continues. It is notable that both these notions of limit to diversity turn on ethical, rather than dogmatic, questions. But this fact may in the end help to establish the view that all dogmatic questions are at the same time ethical in implication. The next era of ecumenical discussion will need to work further to establish the limits of pluralism along these, or other, lines.

Complicating the problem without doubt will be the fact that Christian ecumenism can no longer hold the question of its relation to other faiths, particularly the "Abrahamic" faiths, at the periphery of discussion (→ Jewish-Christian Dialogue). With many traditional ecumenical goals still unachieved and still needing devoted work, new questions of pluralism and diversity among the different faiths press themselves upon ecumenists.

Inseparable from these studies will be the determination of *how* the limits of acceptable diversity can be established. The → Holy Spirit's freedom to bring new insight into the church must be affirmed, but always in a way that all may be enriched in their understanding, not in a way that divides or splinters the body of Christ.

Bibliography: J. D. G. DUNN, *Unity and Diversity in the NT: An Inquiry into the Character of Earliest Christianity* (Philadelphia, 1977) • G. GASSMANN, ed., *Documentary History of Faith and Order, 1963-1993* (Geneva, 1993) • R. JEWETT, *Christian Tolerance: Paul's Message to the Modern Church* (Philadelphia, 1982) • M. KINNAMON, *Truth and Community: Diversity and Its Limits in the Ecumenical Movement* (Grand Rapids, 1988) • J. VAN LIN, *Shaking the Fundamentals: Religious Plurality and the Ecumenical Movement* (Amsterdam, 2002) • E. SCHLINK, "The Unity and Diversity of the Church," *What Unity Implies* (ed. R. Groscurth; Geneva, 1969) 33-51 • L. VISCHER, ed., *A Documentary History of the Faith and Order Movement, 1927-1963* (St. Louis, 1963) • W. A. VISSER 'T HOOFT, "Pluralism–Temptation or Opportunity?" *ER* 18 (1966) 129-49 • P. L. WICKERI, *The People of God among All God's Peoples: Frontiers in Christian Mission* (Hong Kong, 2000).

GERALD F. MOEDE, with LEWIS S. MUDGE

Plymouth Brethren

The Plymouth Brethren is a Christian body established in 1830 in Plymouth, England. The group traces it origin to John Nelson Darby (1800-1882), an Anglican clergyman who in 1828 joined a circle of eschatologically oriented Bible Christians in

Dublin and who left the Anglican Church in 1834 (→ Anglican Communion; Eschatology).

In debate with the Anglican Church and free-church groups in Switzerland, Darby developed the idea of the → apostasy of the → church and the impossibility of a restoration of the → primitive Christian community. He thought that the unity of the body of Christ lay outside all the → denominations and involved a rejection of everything hierarchical, institutional, liturgical, and sacramental. It would come to expression every Sunday in the breaking of bread at the Lord's Table, where "two or three" (Matt. 18:20) would gather together. By separation from the world and from all the churches — and if necessary from other assemblies of Plymouth Brethren — the bridal community of the end time, brought into being by the Spirit, would manifest itself up to the time of the imminent rapture (→ Apocalypticism 4.5; Latin American Theology 5.2).

Darby worked out a view of salvation history as a sequence of saving dispensations (→ Dispensationalism). As a schema of biblical exposition, this interpretation had a great influence on → fundamentalism and the → evangelical movement, and it underlies the *Scofield Reference Bible.*

Carl Brockhaus (1822-99) was a leader among the German Darbyites. His publishing house produced the Elberfeld Bible. Under the Third Reich many Darbyites and → Baptists formed the Federation of Evangelical Free-Church Congregations.

Because of sharp controversies in 1848 the Plymouth Brethren split into two parts, the "Exclusive Brethren" (following Darby, generally called Darbyites in Europe) and the "Open Brethren." Since then each part has undergone numerous schisms. Because of the lack of central organization, it is hard to estimate the number of Plymouth Brethren. In the year 2000 there were perhaps as many as one million worldwide.

Bibliography: Primary sources: J. N. Darby, *Collected Writings* (34 vols.; 2d ed.; Kingston-on-Thames, 1961-67); idem, *Letters of J. N. Darby* (3 vols.; Kingston-on-Thames, n.d.).

Secondary works: C. B. Bass, *Backgrounds to Dispensationalism: Its Historical Genesis and Ecclesiastical Implications* (Grand Rapids, 1960) • J. P. Callahan, *Primitivist Piety: The Ecclesiology of the Early Plymouth Brethren* (Lanham, Md., 1996) • G. Carter, "Irish Millennialism: The Irish Prophetic Movement and the Origins of the Plymouth Brethren," *Anglican Evangelicals: Protestant Secessions from the Via Media, c. 1800-1850* (Oxford, 2001) 195-248 • F. R. Coad, *A History of the Brethren Movement* (2d ed.; Exeter, 1976) • E. Geldbach, *Christliche Versammlung und Heilsgeschichte bei J. N. Darby* (3d ed.; Wuppertal, 1975) • G. Jordy, *Die Brüderbewegung in Deutschland* (3 vols., Wuppertal, 1979-86); idem, ed., *150 Jahre Brüderbewegung in Deutschland* (Dillenburg, 2003) • H. H. Rowdon, *The Origins of the Brethren, 1825-1850* (London, 1967) • T. P. Weber, *Living in the Shadow of the Second Coming: American Premillennialism, 1875-1982* (Grand Rapids, 1983).

Erich Geldbach

Pneumatology → Holy Spirit

Poland

	1960	*1980*	*2000*
Population (1,000s):	29,561	35,574	38,727
Annual growth rate (%):	1.27	0.90	0.14

Area: 312,685 sq. km. (120,728 sq. mi.)

A.D. 2000

Population density: 124/sq. km. (321/sq. mi.)
Births / deaths: 1.26 / 1.10 per 100 population
Fertility rate: 1.65 per woman
Infant mortality rate: 11 per 1,000 live births
Life expectancy: 72.0 years (m: 67.7, f: 76.5)
Religious affiliation (%): Christians 97.3 (Roman Catholics 93.1, Orthodox 2.2, other Christians 2.0), nonreligious 2.3, other 0.4.

1. Change

At the end of World War II, for the first time since the 14th century, Poland became a relatively united country again nationally and religiously (→ Nation, Nationalism). The ceding of eastern territories to the USSR reduced the number of Orthodox, who mostly belonged to Ukraine or Belarus by nationality. The extermination of millions of Jews in German concentration camps (→ Holocaust) had left only a remnant of adherents to → Judaism. The flight of Germans, most of them Protestant, reduced the size of → Protestantism by about 90 percent. In 2003 the population was 38.6 million (35 million in 1939). But now Poles are more than 95 percent of the total, compared to only 65 percent in 1939. The number of Roman Catholics has also jumped from some 70 percent to well over 90 percent.

2. Churches

2.1. *Roman Catholic Church*

In 2003 the → Roman Catholic Church numbered 34.4 million members in 40 → dioceses and 10,025 parishes, served by 28,300 → priests, 98 bishops, 17 archbishops, and 6 cardinals. (Here and below, religious statistics, valid for the year 2003, are taken from the 2004 *Polish Statistical Yearbook.*)

For academic theological training Poland has two Roman Catholic universities: Lublin and Warsaw (until 1999, an academy for Catholic theology), which also comprises several secular faculties; three so-called papal academies or faculties: in Kraków, Warsaw, and Wrocław (Breslau) (their legal status was regulated in 1989); and six theological faculties, all established after 1989, in the universities in Katowice, Olsztyn, Opole, Poznań, Toruń, and Szczecin. In all, there are about 20,000 students of theology (clergy and lay). The church owns 17,500 churches and → chapels.

The strength of the Roman Catholic Church of Poland lies in the nation's → faith (→ Religion, Personal Sense of). It finds expression in well-attended Sunday → worship and religious practices, especially → pilgrimages to the site of the Black Madonna (at the Jasna Góra Sanctuary in Częstochowa) and other shrines. In the closing days of the Communist regime it also manifested itself in so-called national masses. After the 1970s increasing demonstrations came to be linked to the election of the Polish Karol Wojtyła as Pope John Paul II (1978-2005) and to political crises. Under Communism the church enjoyed high moral → authority in both → society and the government. The bishops often spoke as representatives of the nation as well as of the church.

Nevertheless, there were weaknesses as regards individual faith and ethics. Reflection on the faith was minimal. Personal convictions were weakly developed and often diverged clearly from church beliefs. Ethically, moral → relativism was rife (→ Ethics; Moral Theology). Two-thirds of the members held liberal views on matters of sex before and outside marriage (→ Sexuality), divorce (→ Marriage and Divorce), → birth control, and → abortion (→ Liberalism). Clear deviations from official Catholic positions might also be seen in → social ethics, especially as regards work. It was not accidental that in June 1991 John Paul II made his fourth pilgrimage to Poland under the banner of the Ten Commandments (→ Decalogue). A further major problem is the high level of corruption encountered in Poland, in some cases even among the clergy.

2.2. *Orthodox Church*

The Polish Autocephalous Orthodox Church (509,700 members, 224 parishes, 6 dioceses, 300 priests; → Autocephaly) has good relations with all the other autocephalous → Orthodox churches. It shares the same → rites with them. It has six monasteries: three for men, and three for women. The convent at Grabarka, near Białystok, is especially well known as a place of pilgrimage.

2.3. *Uniates*

After 1989 the Catholic Church of the Ukrainian-Byzantine Rite (known as the → Uniate church) was again permitted an autonomous existence. During the Communist period state authorities severely restricted the activity of the Uniates, making their pastors and parishes subject to the authority of the Roman Catholic cardinal primate of Poland. Today the church is legally recognized as an autonomous structure. It has 82,000 members, with two bishops and two dioceses, 62 priests, and 136 parishes.

Another church associated with Rome is the small Armenian Church (8,000 believers).

2.4. *Historic Protestants*

Foreigners (esp. Germans, Swiss, Czechs) used to swell the ranks of the historic Protestant churches in Poland. A disproportionate number of these Protestants were leaders in the fields of science, economics, → politics, and → culture. After World War II only two such churches remain active, both typical churches of the → diaspora. One is the Evangelical Church of the Augsburg Confession in Poland (→ Lutheran Churches), with 79,000 members in 128 parishes. Staunchly Lutheran, it has strong churches in the south (Silesia). It is traditional in its religious life (→ Lutheranism), with a tinge of → pietism. Some 20 to 40 percent of the people attend Sunday services. There is no shortage of clergy, and women's → ordination is not allowed.

The other historic Protestant church is the Evangelical Reformed Church (→ Reformed and Presbyterian Churches), with 3,600 members in ten parishes. The tradition of the → Moravians still exerts some influence in this body. The laity accept much more responsibility for their church (→ Clergy and Laity). In 2003 the church ordained its first woman.

2.5. *Old Catholic Churches*

Poland has three → Old Catholic Churches: the Old Catholic → Mariavite Church in Poland (24,000 members, in 37 parishes, with 27 priests), the Catholic Mariavite Church (2,500 members, 24 parishes, 15 priests), and the Polish Catholic Church (22,000 members, 83 parishes, 102 priests). The work of the Polish National Catholic Church in America gave rise to the last of these groups in 1918. It broke away from the parent church in 1951 and joined the Utrecht Union of Old Catholic Churches.

2.6. *Free Churches and Marginal Groups*

In 1989 Poland had some 30 → free churches and religious groups with 55,000 members. In 2003 the most important were → Jehovah's Witnesses, which existed illegally in Poland for decades but gained recognition in 1989. Its 124,000 members make it the third largest religious group in the country. Other groups present are Pentecostals (20,500; → Pentecostal Churches), → Adventists (9,500), → Baptists (4,500 adult baptized members), and Methodists (4,400 members; → Methodist Churches).

After the political turn in 1989, about 100 new religious communities were registered, including free churches of Baptist and Darbyite origin, neopietist and evangelical churches, various charismatic (neo-Pentecostal) communities, healing movements, eschatological churches (Churches of God, Branham Movement), and apostolic churches (Neo-Apostolic Church, Mormons). It is extremely difficult to determine the actual number of adherents in all these groups.

3. Church Relations and Cooperation

3.1. *Polish Ecumenical Council*

Seven minority churches — the Christian Baptist Church, Evangelical Church of the Augsburg Confession, Evangelical Methodist Church, Evangelical Reformed Church, Old Catholic Mariavite Church, Polish [Old] Catholic Church, and Polish Autocephalous Orthodox Church — belong to the Polish Ecumenical Council (founded 1946; → National Councils of Churches). This body coordinates practical work such as interchurch aid and contacts abroad, though it has done little to bring the churches together theologically (→ Ecumenism, Ecumenical Movement).

The council also has ongoing contact with the church at large (→ World Council of Churches; Conference of European Churches). Cooperation with the German Evangelical Church (and, until 1990, also with the Federation of the Evangelical Churches in the German Democratic Republic) is designed to accomplish reconciliation between Poles and Germans.

3.2. *Roman Catholic Efforts*

In the Roman Catholic Church the Bishops' Commission for Ecumenical Questions carries responsibility for what is done ecumenically. Founded in 1966, it has sections for theology, pastoral care and liturgy, ecumenical contacts, and information.

Within the framework of the episcopate, teams have also been established since 1998 for bilateral contact and cooperation with Orthodox, Mariavites, Polish Catholics, Lutherans, and Adventists. The first ecumenical institute in Poland was established in 1983 at the Catholic University in Lublin. After the political turn two additional institutes were established in Kraków (1995) and Opole (2000).

3.3. *Steps of Cooperation*

The Polish Ecumenical Council and the Roman Catholic Church have been cooperating officially since 1974. Whereas such cooperation took place first within the framework of a joint commission, since 1998 this responsibility has fallen to the Dialogue Commission, formed from the Polish Bishops' Conference and the Polish Ecumenical Council. It coordinates events during the Week of Prayer for Christian Unity, initiates theological dialogue in various contexts, and much more. In January 1989 the Roman Catholic primate preached for the first time in a Protestant church in Warsaw, an event that had enormous psychological significance. During his fourth pilgrimage to Poland (June 1991), Pope John Paul II entered an Orthodox church (Białystok) and a Protestant church (Warsaw). In 2000 the Roman Catholic Church signed a declaration with the member churches of the Polish Ecumenical Council (with the exception of the Baptists) concerning mutual recognition of baptism.

As before, not only Protestants but even the Orthodox Church feel that the Roman Catholic Church discriminates against them in the question of → mixed marriages. Hence these churches are currently working toward a positive solution to this question both through a multilateral dialogue commission and through bilateral Catholic-Lutheran and Catholic-Orthodox commissions.

3.4. *Christian Theological Academy*

The interdenominational Christian Theological Academy was founded in 1954 as an offshoot of the work of the Faculty of Protestant Theology at Warsaw University. It has Orthodox, Old Catholic, and Protestant sections. It brings together students from over ten denominations who will be pastors and catechists in their churches. The wide-ranging lectures cover ecumenical themes (→ Dialogue; Ecumenical Theology). Ecumenical symposia are also held together with Roman Catholic theological seminaries.

4. Church and State

4.1. *Roman Catholic Church*

Political developments have controlled relations between → church and state. In 1945 the Council of Ministers invalidated the 1925 → concordat on the ground of interference by the Vatican during the war and occupation, contrary to the terms of the original agreement. In the so-called Stalinist era (1948-56; → Socialism) Roman Catholics came under → persecution (bishops, priests, and nuns imprisoned, the cardinal primate interned). After 1956 practical coexistence followed, but not without tensions (e.g., in 1966 when the church celebrated its one-thousandth anniversary in Poland). After 1970 the Communist Party (→ Marxism) decided to pursue a course of ongoing dialogue with the → hierarchy, and relations were resumed with the → Vatican. Papal visits in 1979, 1983, and 1987 further improved relations. Politically and socially the church became a stabilizing factor after 1980, and the state willingly accepted its role in this regard.

Decisive events came in 1989 when Parliament, still Communist, gave the church legal status and thus recognized its canonical structures (→ Codex Iuris Canonici), its institutions, its schools, and its → military chaplaincies (→ Religious Liberty). Full diplomatic relations with the Vatican were restored on July 17, 1989, after a 44-year hiatus.

After the political turn, the Roman Catholic Church tried to have the clause concerning the separation of church and state removed from the state constitution, arguing that as documented at a bishops' conference in 1991, the basic values providing the point of departure for the church's own mission complement in principle the goals the state itself is trying to realize. Pressure from the Catholic Bishops' Conference in 1990 also prompted the resumption of religious instruction in schools, even though such a decision violated both the constitutional separation of church and state and the church law of 1989, which designated instruction in religious questions to be an internal church matter. During the initial period, hardly any public event took place without the presence of a Catholic bishop or at least a priest.

In 1993, shortly before its own exit from power, the Solidarity regime signed a concordat with the Vatican. Both the manner in which this concordat came about and its content were criticized from various quarters in Poland. Minority churches objected that the signing introduced inequitable treatment of denominations. Serious concerns included especially the treatment of questions such as marriage, financial support, church schools, access to the mass media, social activities, the status of Catholic cemeteries, and much more. The post-Communist party came away victorious in the parliamentary elections in September 1993, whereas the rightist parties, which were closely allied with the church and the Catholic clergy, suffered enormous losses. This political defeat, with its additional confirmation in 1995 in the election of the post-Communist agnostic Alexander Kwasniewski as president, prompted the leadership of the Roman Catholic Church ultimately to distance itself from support of any political party.

In 1997, after four years in power, the post-Communists lost the parliamentary elections. To the great surprise of many, the Solidarity members who returned to power proposed a Protestant to be prime minister. Both public opinion at large and leading circles of the Roman Catholic Church were positively disposed when the Lutheran Jerzy Buzek took office, suggesting that Polish society is more tolerant than has often previously been supposed. Similarly, the ratification of the concordat in 1997 also failed to elicit the same emotions as four years earlier. Although the post-Communists have been in power again since 2001, no conflicts in the relationship between church and state have emerged.

4.2. *Minority Churches*

Many minority churches were granted legal recognition only after 1945, that is, by the Marxists. Article 70 of the constitution in effect from 1952 to 1997 guaranteed citizens freedom of conscience in religion and guaranteed all churches and religious associations freedom in the exercise of religion. In actual practice, however, the state interfered extensively in church matters for decades.

The parliamentary ratification of the law guaranteeing the freedom of conscience and religion on May 17, 1989, represented a new beginning in this respect and was supposed to function as a framework for non–Roman Catholic churches and religious associations in regulating their bilateral relationship with the state. During the 1990s several minority churches signed bilateral agreements with the state guaranteeing them the same latitude as enjoyed by the Roman Catholic Church as a result of the earlier concordat.

The equality of all churches and religious associations in Poland was confirmed in the new state constitution that the Polish parliament passed in 1997. Never before in their history have minority churches enjoyed the possibilities now available to them in the most varied spheres. They are able to elect their own leadership freely and through democratic procedures. They can cultivate contacts with their sister churches in foreign countries, as well as engage in ecumenical cooperation within Poland itself, without first having to ask for permission. They have free access to both television and radio, are permitted to engage freely in social welfare activities, establish various associations, publish periodicals and books, offer new forms of evangelization to broader groups within the population, and so on.

5. Non-Christian Groups

5.1. *Jews*

In World War II three million Polish Jews were murdered. Most of the survivors (ca. 170,000) decided to emigrate to Israel. After 1968 a state campaign against → Zionism (→ Anti-Semitism, Anti-Judaism) brought a new wave of emigration, and today only some 15,000 Jews are left. Those practicing their faith belong to the Fellowhship of Jewish Religious Congregations (1,230 members in 21 congregations). They are largely older citizens, though during recent years an increasing number of young Jews have come to embrace their faith. In 1989, after a 20-year hiatus, a rabbi began ministering in Poland.

5.2. *Muslims*

Muslims (→ Islam) came into Poland at the end of the 14th century. As descendants of the Tatars they traditionally lived in the northeast, which the USSR annexed in 1945. Muslims also formed small colonies in the former German areas.

The Muslim Religious Union of Poland, with some 5,100 members, six congregations, and five clergy, has recently experienced some revival. Three new mosques or houses of prayer have been built (Białystok, Gdańsk, Warsaw), and international contacts have been strengthened. Although several thousand Muslims from Arab countries settled in Poland after the political turn in 1989, their numbers have not yet been incorporated into the national statistics.

5.3. *Karaites*

In the same area as Muslims lived the Karaites, a Jewish → sect that rejected → tradition, the → Mishnah, and the → Talmud. After 1945 they all found themselves outside the new frontiers of Poland. Those resettling in Poland founded the Karaite Religious Fellowship, which has, however, no more than 150 members in three congregations.

5.4. *Others*

Newer religious communities include neopagan groups (practicing the religion of the ancient Slavs; → Paganism), Islamic associations and groups otherwise deriving from Islam (including → Baha'i), and associations of Buddhists (Theravada → Buddhism, Zen Buddhism) and those deriving from → Hinduism (the Yoga movement, Hare Krishna movement, Brahma Kumaris World Spiritual University). Altogether these various groups might have between 10,000 and 20,000 adherents.

→ Marxism and Christianity

Bibliography: D. B. Barrett, G. T. Kurian, and T. M. Johnson, *WCE* (2d ed.) 1.602-6 • F. Borggrefe, *Polens Protestanten zwischen rotem Bruder und schwarzer Schwester* (Kassel, 1983) • M. Buchowski, E. Conte, and C. Nagengast, eds., *Poland beyond Communism: "Transition" in Critical Perspective* (Fribourg, 2001) • M. Castle, *Democracy in Poland* (2d ed.; Boulder, Colo., 2002) • V. C. Chrypinski, "Church and Nationality in Postwar Poland," *Religion and Nationalism in Soviet and East European Politics* (rev. ed.; ed. P. Ramet; Durham, N.C., 1989) 241-63; idem, "The Roman Catholic Church in 1944-89 Poland," ibid., 117-41 • J. Moltmann and M. Stöhr, eds., *Begegnung mit Polen. Evangelische Kirchen und die Herausforderung durch Geschichte und Politik* (Munich, 1974) • C. Nagengast, *Reluctant Socialists, Rural Entrepreneurs: Class, Culture, and the Polish State* (Boulder, Colo., 1991) • A. Polonsky, ed., *Focusing on Aspects and Experiences of Religion* (London, 1998) • B. Szlachta, ed., *Polish Perspectives on Communism: An Anthology* (Lanham, Md., 2004).

Karol Karski

Polemics

Traditionally the term "polemics" has been used for theology after the Reformation that serves to uphold a confessional or denominational position (→ Ecumenical Theology 4). It can be used more broadly, however, for any militant → theology. It presupposes a basic confessional decision, inquires into specific dissent in theological discourse, and examines the points at issue. In the comparative study of → denominations its task is to examine denominational differences critically and to overcome them by argument. If a church is to proclaim its beliefs, polemics is indispensable to the recognition of what is truth and what is error or → heresy. The objection is made that it is difficult to set the boundary between the true church and the false, that a materially based hermeneutical difference separates the denominations (→ Hermeneutics), and that there is legitimate → pluralism in the working out of the Christian faith (→ Church 3).

In church history polemics has been characterized from the very first by debate about central questions of the Christian → faith (e.g., → Christology and → salvation) and by controversy regarding the church and its characterizing features (→ Heresies and Schisms; Church 3; Reformation). In the denominational struggles of the 16th and 17th centuries, polemics had the goal of defending one understanding of church against another. In contemporary → ecumenical dialogue it can serve to protect against all enthusiasm or resignation in the struggle for an appropriate view of the truth and reality of the → gospel in and above the denominations (K. G. Steck).

Bibliography: R. Kösters, "Zur Theorie der Kontroverstheologie. Wissenschaftlich-theoretische Reflexionen über Begriff, Gegenstand und Methode der Kontroverstheologie," *ZKT* 88 (1966) 121-62 • K. G. Steck, "Kontroverstheologie," *EKL* (1st ed.) 2.927-29.

Erwin Fahlbusch

Political Parties

1. Term
2. Historical Roots
3. Tasks
4. Problems of Structure and Function
5. Rapid Contemporary Changes
6. Christian Political Parties

1. Term

Political parties today are organizations that mobilize eligible persons to vote in legislative, executive, and sometimes even judicial elections for candidates approved or put forward by the parties. In most democratic countries these are mass parties, in the sense that they seek to mobilize large numbers of people to vote at election time. Increasingly in the West, however, and also in much of the rest of the world, the number of people who function actively as members of parties is very small. And in the United States, only about half of eligible voters turn out to vote in a national election.

Political parties are freely formed organizations; citizens are not required to join or participate in them. The word "party" (from Lat. *pars,* "part") refers to a "part" of the citizenry. In other words, parties have meaning as competitors among two or more of them. The idea of a "unity party," or a one-party system, in an authoritarian or totalitarian state is a contradiction in terms. The existence of two or more political parties in democratic societies is due to differences — sometimes fundamental differences — among citizens over the responsibility of government or over public policy priorities.

2. Historical Roots

Political groupings first began to take shape in England as an outcome of the struggle for constitutional limitation of the monarchy and the emergence of parliamentary government. Parties in 18th-century England, where there was a very limited franchise, amounted to little more than groupings around aristocratic leaders. In the 19th century, following the American and French Revolutions and along with the growth of representative government, notable leaders began to organize groups of citizens around common interests over against competitors. In Europe the first parties were "liberal," that is, organized to oppose monarchical and aristocratic privileges. In reaction, "conservative" parties were formed. As the industrial revolution developed, "socialist" parties — the first mass mobilization efforts — took shape.

The American Founding Fathers distrusted parties and feared the development of mass → democracy. Moreover, the new country had no aristocratic class, and the eventual party formation organized white, property-owning citizens around regional and largely economic interests and issues. Even after the Civil War and massive industrial expansion, all the important American parties operated within the same broadly → liberal ideology.

Not until nearly universal suffrage was established in democratic countries in the late 19th and early 20th centuries did the mass political party become dominant. The organizing of mass parties at the national level became necessary once people had a right to vote for their representatives. At this point the parties also became major organizations, with full-time paid staff members and career politicians. Yet in the United States, with its federal system, parties have always been organized chiefly as state organizations. National party organizations become important only every four years for the presidential elections. Still today, national party organizations in the United States have relatively little influence in choosing, approving, and controlling presidential candidates and the governing agendas of their members who win election to Congress.

Parties typically take shape around political →

ideologies (secular or religious, conservative, liberal, socialist, communist, etc.) or around interests (labor, business, race, environment). In the United States parties now depend on, or are tied to, diverse interest groups that typically have greater influence over political candidates than do the parties themselves.

3. Tasks

In countries that have strong parties, the parties accomplish a variety of tasks. They aggregate diverse interests, which helps to devise the parties' strategies and platforms for governing. On that basis party leaders help to recruit, educate, train, and discipline the candidates they will put forward to run for office. The parties must also work to organize members and mobilize voters at election time, which means communicating with the public at large to persuade eligible voters to vote for the party's candidates. In the United States and other countries with relatively weak parties, they largely concentrate on organizing candidates for elections and mobilizing voters through advertising campaigns.

In all cases, the aim of the political party is, through its candidates, to win power in government and thereby to have some say or control in governing. A party thus cannot succeed simply by articulating sound public goals or by educating citizens and politicians. Most parties must succeed in helping politicians win office, or they will be overtaken by more successful parties.

4. Problems of Structure and Function

Competing political parties are a feature of vital democratic countries. Yet in different ways they can become too closely intertwined or even identified with government, interest groups, and organizations like corporations or labor unions. In some European countries, particularly in the north, governments fund the parties, as illustrated by Germany and Finland. In the United States corporate interests and wealthy individuals typically fund parties or particular candidates. In order to gain an advantage for the political party they represent, legislators and executives may enact laws whose aim is more for political advantage than for the public good. This aspect of the parties in complex modern democratic systems is impossible to describe in a brief article such as this. The function of American political parties, for example, cannot be understood apart from the federal system, the authority of state legislatures to redraw electoral districts after the national census every ten years, strong federal bureaucracies, powerful interest groups, the short term of most legislative offices at state and federal levels, the rules of campaign financing, and the winner-takes-all, single-member electoral districts.

Two of the most significant factors in determining the structure and function of political parties are the system of representation (whether proportional or winner-takes-all) and the rules for financing campaigns. A system of proportional elections tends to encourage more than two parties, higher voter turnout, more disciplined party candidates and representatives, and political party influence that is greater than the influence of interest groups. A country with campaign financing controls that favor parties and voters over interest groups in the funding of election campaigns will tend to encourage legislative decisions focused more on the national interest and the common good than on interest-group brokering and regional bargaining.

5. Rapid Contemporary Changes

Throughout the world, many changes are taking place in the function of political parties. Many new democracies are democratic in name only, having weakly representative governments that are often rife with graft and corruption. The development of the European Union is affecting the function of political parties in the various European member states. With an increasing number of economic and social policies being decided at the EU level, domestic parties must show where they stand relative to the EU and not only relative to the policies of their own government. Moreover, there are now elections of representatives from each country to the European Parliament, which means that the domestic parties must coordinate relations with their Europe-wide counterparts in the European Parliament. In the United States political parties are less and less clearly identified by ideology and principles. In many wealthy countries, moreover, the → mass media, advertising, and the power of interest groups have more and more influence over electoral decisions and the functions of political parties.

6. Christian Political Parties

Parties identified as Christian Democratic arose in Europe and Latin America in the late 19th and early 20th centuries largely as a result of Roman Catholic reaction to the rise of liberal and socialist antagonism to the church following the French → Revolution. In Europe these parties played a decisive role in rebuilding Europe following World War II and in constructing the European Common Market.

Partly because of the growing → secularization of Europe and the rise of Latin American evangelical and Pentecostal movements, the old Christian Democratic parties have declined or lost their more distinctive Christian inspiration. Yet throughout most of the world beyond Europe, religions are growing in vitality and influencing → politics. What this trend might mean for religious party formation in the future remains to be seen.

Insofar as a political party's reason for being is its philosophy of life and government, there is no reason to judge that a self-described Christian party is inappropriate or unfitting for those holding Christian principles. But since several such parties might arise in the same country, along with parties of other ideological and religious persuasion, it is important that any such Christian party make clear its political principles and agenda and not use the arena of political competition to contend for a divinely ordained privilege to impose its view of life on all citizens simply because of its Christian claims. It is most important that such a party, in its policy arguments, articulate a Christian rationale for an open, democratic society, justice for all, equal public treatment of citizens of all faiths, and the priority of legal and peaceful settlement of disputes over violence and warfare (→ War).

→ Political Theology

Bibliography: D. J. Amy, *Real Choices/New Voices: The Case for Proportional Representation Elections in the United States* (2d ed.; New York, 2002) • A. Lijphart, *Patterns of Democracy: Government Forms and Performance in Thirty-six Countries* (New Haven, 1999) • L. S. Maisel and K. Z. Buckley, *Parties and Elections in America: The Electoral Process* (4th ed.; Lanham, Md., 2004) • G. B. Powell Jr., *Elections as Instruments of Democracy: Majoritarian and Proportional Visions* (New Haven, 2000).

James W. Skillen

Political Theology

1. Origins
2. Augustine through the Reformation
3. The Trend toward Statism
4. Recasting the Term: Schmitt and Bloch
5. Metz and Moltmann
6. New Turns in Political Theology

1. Origins

The tradition of political theology has its deepest Western philosophical roots in Plato (427-347 b.c.) and Aristotle (384-322), who influenced subsequent → Stoic thought (e.g., Varro [116-27] and Cicero [106-43]), where the concept is not clearly distinguished from → civil religion. Paralleling such philosophical roots, it has its deepest sociohistorical roots in ancient regimes that were dominated by either → hierarchy (ancient India) or → theocracy (ancient Israel).

The belief that either the priestly representative of the divine order of the universe or the Divine Will directly could and should govern the common life appeared in various combinations in the West. Many developments in early and medieval Europe, where priestly orders sometimes gained a fragile dominance over political authority, were not unlike the dominance of the Hindu Brahmanic caste. And when political authorities subordinated the clergy, it was not unlike ancient China, where the emperor of an epoch-making dynasty had a literati at his service who administered his will among the people and advised him in correct ritual behavior and in the "ways of heaven" according to classic sacred texts and the interpretation of cosmological signs. Both situations were highly stratified and authoritarian, with hierarchs (Gk. *hieros,* "sacred, priestly"), or religious leadership, basically dominant in one case and, in the other, a political ruler supported by clerics (Lat. *clericus,* "clergy," or other literate experts serving a bureaucracy).

In both cases, the political-military affairs and the religious or philosophical-ethical traditions were systematically intertwined, and together they sought to control all aspects of social life, from the top down — doing everything, of course, for "the good of all." This interlock was reinforced when, challenged by a rapidly expanding → Islam (with its jihadic conquests of the 8th and 9th cents.), the West felt it had to integrate religious and political power further to defeat a contending faith and force (via its Crusades of the 11th cent.). (A third primal center of social authority in almost all societies, the → family, is usually subordinated to such structures in complex societies and is tied to economic and subcultural status, as in hereditary caste, peasant-noble, or guild patterns of extended family identity.)

2. Augustine through the Reformation

In the West the concepts of political theology rooted in Greek and Roman philosophy influenced many intellectuals, including such church fathers as → Augustine (354-430), who used Stoic and Neoplatonic concepts selected and ordered by biblical themes in his formative *City of God.* Several hundred years later all of theology, including political theology, became more focused when → Thomas Aquinas (ca. 1225-74) wove Augustine and Aristotle into a fresh and comprehensive synthesis. Still later,

Political Theology

in Lutheran lands, Philipp → Melanchthon (1497-1560) drew together theocratic biblical ideas, reasserted by Martin → Luther (1483-1546), with Aristotelian-influenced nominalist ideas of science (→ Nominalism) and → ethics in another synthesis, shaping much of → Protestantism.

Many influential figures throughout this long history wrote on these matters and shaped both → theology and → politics and thus the West's legal history, as O. O'Donovan and J. L. O'Donovan have shown in their recent compendium *From Irenaeus to Grotius.* For more than a thousand years, Christian interpretations legitimated a "Constantinian" relationship of → church and state. This Constantinian pattern can be seen in the Austro-Hungarian Empire in central Europe, in the Roman Catholic royalty of Italy, Poland, Spain, and Ireland, and in the politically established churches of confessional Protestantism (→ Empire and Papacy). This pattern resulted in tendencies that were similar to those found in other key civilizations, except that the Christian theorists of political theology usually drew on Rom. 13:1-7 as the key legitimating biblical text (". . . there is no authority except from God, and those authorities that exist have been instituted by God . . .").

3. The Trend toward Statism

After the → Reformation, wars of religion were fought over which theology should be accepted, for theology was seen as the legitimating glue of → society and the indispensable spiritual architecture of governance, properly to be enforced. The conflicts were usually well mixed with questions of political status, control of fertile land and trade routes, and claims about the inheritance rights of noble families. A relative peace was established after the Peace of Westphalia (1648) stopped the fighting and assigned territorial boundaries. But it also established one side of the longer tradition by embracing the principle of → *cuius regio, eius religio,* or "whoever rules (may establish) his religion." This principle gave a monopoly to one or another branch of the faith within a specific territory, but it also demanded recognition internationally of a variety of faiths (within limits) and subordinated religion to a dominant political order. Each nation-state had its own confession, catechism, articles of faith, and book of worship. It also tended to make Christian theology part of its public cult.

Other developments reinforced this statist trend. N. Machiavelli (1469-1527), T. Hobbes (1588-1679), J.-J. Rousseau (1712-78), and the French Revolution, plus the great modern "masters of suspicion" — D. Hume (1711-76), L. Feuerbach (1804-72), K. → Marx (1818-83), F. Nietzsche (1844-1900), and the Russian Revolution — generated a great doubt as to whether politics needed religion at all. Backed by science, politics could become sufficient unto itself, intentionally controlling all aspects of the social system in ways that were thought to lead to plenty, peace, and harmony. These movements sought to secularize the political arena and to insist on a radical definition of sovereignty backed by postreligious "ideologies." On the one hand, they demanded a mass movement of populist sentiment; on the other, they dreamed of a national spirit embodied in a great leader, such as Napoléon (1769-1821), who would exemplify and consolidate the will of the people. Around these motifs grew a set of "secularized" political theologies linked to personality cults. Figures in the 20th century such as Mussolini, Hitler, Lenin, Stalin, and, on their heels, Mao, Papa Doc, Pol Pot, and a host of lesser tyrants, some still living, followed in this heritage.

4. Recasting the Term: Schmitt and Bloch

The modern revival and recasting of the term "political theology" came at the hands of two major figures — one who sought to return politics to its premodern meanings and one who sought to show how certain of the "modern" developments were in fact inheritors of the neglected radical wing of the classical heritage. Carl Schmitt (1888-1985) developed a theory of the state and law just after World War I on the basis of premodern traditionalism, which was quite critical of the → Enlightenment and any move toward parliamentary → democracy. Schmitt refocused the idea of sovereignty on the absolutist state — an idea that, coupled with → anti-Semitism, became important in the development of the National Socialist concept of the state under the control of a leader. His thought was theological in the sense that it regarded all legal concepts as secularized theological concepts and extolled Roman Catholicism as a paradigm of antidemocratic forms of life.

At about the same time, the radical philosopher of history Ernst Bloch (1885-1977) turned to the hypermodernist views of Marx and drew attention to another politically important strand of Christianity. He drew not only from Joachim of Fiore (ca. 1135-1202) but especially from Thomas → Müntzer (ca. 1489-1525), a militant theologian of the Reformation period who differed greatly from Luther and → Calvin and others. Bloch's heroes had an intensely historical view of the theological tradition, one that embodied the spirit of the Israelites' exodus from Egypt and that projected a utopian vision toward the future — a spirit and vision that cannot be fully defined but made real only by political struggle toward a new future. Bloch believed that Marx's "scientific theory of → revolution" was in fact a → secularization of theological motifs and that the workers' movements were a new messianic anticipation of a utopian historical possibility that promised a reversal of the unjust economic division of the classes. Bloch moved to East Germany after World War II to be a part of the new world he thought the proletarian socialist movements of → socialism and Communism could create, although his relationship with the government there was a troubled one.

5. Metz and Moltmann

In brief, the rebirth of political theology involved, on one hand, as with Schmitt, the divine promise of the use of coercive → force against enemies at the will of the sovereign as the defining characteristic of the regime (on the analogy of the law and omnipotence of God). On the other hand, as with Bloch, it involved the overturning of economic power as the primary social issue, involving revolutionary political actions of hope from below that would issue in a recovered communal harmony, a utopian vision of the future that is also a return to Eden. Both the Right and the Left offered political programs for finding a final solution to the crises of modernizing society. Political theology was divided against itself, and much of the European church withdrew into its own piety, creeds, and cultic liturgies, avoiding confrontation with either one. Neither wing believed what many others have argued: that the developments of "liberal democracy" in, for example, Holland, England, or the United States were driven by serious theological convictions or could issue in a viable vision of government.

After the defeat of the Nazis on the Right and the disenchantment with Communism on the Left during the cold war, direct dependence on Schmitt and Bloch declined, but the next generation of revisionist political theologians turned also to A. Gramsci (1891-1937), M. Blondel (1861-1949), and the Frankfurt school of → critical theory. They were led by the Roman Catholic theologian Johann Baptist Metz (b. 1928) and the Reformed theologian Jürgen Moltmann (b. 1926).

Metz and Moltmann reacted against tendencies to view the church as a pious public utility in which the faith is seen as a purely private matter, as several → existential theologians of that generation argued, or to view theology as a way of domesticating prophetic and apocalyptic accents to make them into a sweet promise of technological and material → progress by the use of instrumental → reason. In contrast, the Christian message, rightly understood and formulated, is a view that is constitutive of history in that it judges the structures of domination and → evil and demands the exercise of power by government for the common good. The positions of Metz and Moltmann had affinities to several forms of religious socialism, or "democratic socialism with a human face."

In this new form of political theology there is a modern rediscovery of → eschatology, a conviction that the God of the ultimate future has broken through into the present. It judges the old traditions and opens the prospect of a new world order. The advocates of this view appeal to Job, with his recognition of the tragic irrationalities of life and the problem of suffering. They also appeal to the → prophets, with their demand for → righteousness and social justice. And they see the → kingdom of God as a power of renewal within the struggles of history calling humanity to a new → discipleship marked by a personal willingness to take up the cross of participation and action. On these points, their rootage has been firmly in the Bible. The influences of Leonard Ragaz (1868-1945), Karl → Barth (1886-1968), Karl → Rahner (1904-84), Dietrich → Bonhoeffer (1906-45), and Helmut Gollwitzer (1908-93) were acknowledged, as was the memory of the → Social Gospel, the newer experiences of Vatican II and the → World Council of Churches, and the then-emerging themes of → liberation theology.

Perhaps the most distinctive theological feature of the views of Metz, Moltmann, and their followers has been their turning to a hermeneutical method. The interpretation of data, with sociohistorical and biblical-doctrinal input informing each other, involves an investigation of the power relations behind the data that recognizes that both interests and convictions are inevitably present in the interpretation, along with claims as to how these things really are. Even deeper, such interpretation seeks to discern what God is doing in the midst of the historical dynamics. Ethical and political overtones of the human understanding of life are never avoidable at this level.

In progressive circles of the Roman Catholic world, Metz has been highly respected. He developed the concept of political theology in this new way. He attached special importance also to the situation of theology after Auschwitz (→ Holocaust), the legacy of Jewish suppression in Christianity, and the dialogue with postmodern thinkers such as

Walter Benjamin (1892-1940) and Jürgen Habermas (b. 1929).

In many ways Moltmann has been central to the developments along this line in Reformed Protestantism. He depended heavily on the work of Bloch in his early writings, especially the latter's *Principle of Hope*, but he soon joined in the dialogues with the Frankfurt school, with advocates for human → rights, with representatives of the liberation movements (Latin, black, feminist, Dalit, minjung), and with activists of the environmental movements.

Both Metz and Moltmann have fed and drawn from the anticolonial movements that have overthrown the world dominance of European powers (→ Colonialism), establishing a host of independent nation-states around the world. It must be said, however, that they did not foresee that many of these new → nations would be marked by one-party regimes, with religion still playing the Erastian role of subservience to, and ideological support of, cultural identity and national interest.

The statist tendencies of this heritage were challenged in some ways by theological movements in Europe after the → Barmen Declaration (1934) of the → Confessing Church in Germany and the failures of the old East Germany, but it is also fair to say that much of the debate about political theology has remained Eurocentric and decidedly Germanic. Only some advocates of political theology were informed by American prodemocratic theologies, already mobilized during World War II by such voices as Reinhold → Niebuhr (1892-1971) and Paul → Tillich (1886-1965), as well as by ecumenically oriented American Roman Catholic leaders such as John Courtney Murray (1904-67), who were convinced that democracy and human rights are not, as earlier doctrine had claimed, purely secular or anti-Catholic. Still, like their American counterparts, Metz, Moltmann, and their followers came to see that these issues are implications of, or at least compatible with, other, deeper reaches of the Christian theological tradition that must be defended and extended within the church, as well as in the wider society.

The work of Metz and Moltmann signaled a form of political theology guided by the idea, not only that the pastor, believer, and theologian *may* address public matters, but that in fact they *must* do so, since the policies of every political order need critique, guidance, and transformation at the hands of theological-ethical insight. All the heirs of these developments, however, have remained committed to a rather centralized state, usually focused on an integrated and politically managed economic policy. Scott Paeth has recently argued, on this point, that the traditions of Europe and the crises of that continent at the hands of 20th-century → totalitarianism prompted such democratically oriented political theologians as Metz and Moltmann to be more statist in their presumptions than other aspects of their theology would suggest. A similar argument could be made for more recent progressive advocates of political theology, including Duncan Forrester in Scotland and the more conservative Oliver O'Donovan in England.

6. New Turns in Political Theology

In recent years the concerns forwarded by political theology have taken several new turns, usually in attempts to correct what is perceived to be its inherent statist tendencies. One direction not only seeks to raise the question of how to speak of theological matters in political discourse but also involves a quest for the political implications of doctrinal terms. Does it mean, for example, that to speak of the "Trinity," and not only of a monolithic God or of polytheistic gods, one should have an ordered → pluralism in political life, and neither a monolithic government nor a plethora of local autonomous units? And what does it mean to speak of the → kingdom of God in a world of democratic constitutions? And how do we think of Christ as Lord, as well as true prophet and true priest? These and other motifs are explored in the new *Blackwell Companion to Political Theology* (2004).

A second direction focuses on the internal life of the church and its faith. An influential → Anabaptist view is set forth by John Howard Yoder (1927-97), a neo-Pietistic view by Stanley Hauerwas, and a "radical orthodoxy" view by John Milbank, all of whom see themselves standing against a "modern liberal" politicized gospel of the West. They all hold that the church itself is the decisive "polis" of life, and that it is, and must, stand as an alternative community to the political world of nations and empires. Interestingly, they often ally themselves with philosophical motifs from Alasdair MacIntyre or Leo Strauss (1899-1973), who also oppose modern liberal thought and economics as well as politics.

And third, a number of advocates and new international centers of → "public theology" focus on the fact that it is a responsibility of the faith to form the sense of the → vocation of the laity in the various spheres of life to which they are called, and indeed to influence the shape of the many public institutions of civil society — for example, → technology, media, → economy, medicine, → education, and, of course, politics. This view seeks to extend the social-justice interests of political theology, but with a less statist focus, while avoiding the temptations to sectarianism that they perceive in the Anabaptist-pietistic-radical orthodoxy tendencies in the churches today. Furthermore, they are much more aware of the ways in which globalization is bringing a new, ambiguous set of public arenas that have minimal political integrity. The impact these new turns will have in modulating or superseding classical and modern forms of political theology remains to be seen.

Bibliography: E. Bloch, *The Principle of Hope* (Cambridge, Mass., 1995; orig. pub., 1946) • D. Forrester, *Christian Justice and Public Policy* (Cambridge, 1997) • S. Hauerwas, *After Christendom? How the Church Is to Behave if Freedom, Justice, and a Christian Nation Are Bad Ideas* (Nashville, 1991) • A. MacIntyre, *After Virtue: A Study in Moral Theology* (Notre Dame, Ind., 1984) • J. B. Metz, *A Passion for God: The Mystical-Political Dimensions of Christianity* (New York, 1998) • J. Milbank, *Theology and Social Theory* (Oxford, 1994) • J. Moltmann, *Theology of Hope* (New York, 1967) • O. O'Donovan, *The Desire of Nations: Rediscovering the Roots of Political Theology* (Cambridge, 1997) • O. O'Donovan and J. L. O'Donovan, eds., *From Irenaeus to Grotius: A Sourcebook of Christian Political Thought* (Grand Rapids, 1999) • S. Paeth, "From Church to the World: Civil Society, Public Theology, and the Theology of Jürgen Moltmann" (Diss., Princeton Theological Seminary, 2004) • C. Schmitt, *The Concept of the Political* (Chicago, 1996; orig. pub., 1932) • P. Scott and W. T. Cavanaugh, eds., *The Blackwell Companion to Political Theology* (Malden, Mass., 2004) • J. H. Yoder, *The Politics of Jesus* (Grand Rapids, 1994).

Max L. Stackhouse

Politics

1. Term
2. The Rise of Western Political Philosophy
3. The Role of the Priestly Class
4. Polity and Policy as the Human Exercise of Power
5. Twentieth-Century Violations of Just Law
6. Twenty-first-Century Challenges

1. Term

The term "politics" may be defined as the practical engagement in the formation of political structure (polity) by the use of political means (power) in order to accomplish political ends (purposes) by coordinated political actions (policies). Such engagement is necessary if a society is to survive and its members are to flourish. The term also applies to the study of these dynamics.

While politics is sometimes thought of only in regard to governments and the → bureaucracies established to carry out their policies, the dynamics are similar in all communities and associations. The difference is that governments are held to be the only set of institutions authorized to use coercive → force (through judicial, police, or military means) as a form of power to preserve its polity, advance or reform its purposes, and enforce its policies. In nongovernmental organizations, pressure and influence (social, economic, intellectual, religious, etc.) are decisive. → Political parties are nongovernmental organizations that undertake actions to gain power in government by building a constituency of involved citizens, usually by noncoercive means ("ballots, not bullets"), while revolutionary parties are willing to use violence. Both develop professional leaders who become experts in strategies and tactics.

Politics is necessary in human → society because groups consist of persons who do not always agree about who is to exercise leadership, in what way, for what ends; and because every complex society consists of many factions, interest groups, and organizations that have different needs and goals, all of which can be in conflict or be disrupted by crime or invasion unless some legitimated power provides for law, order, and defense. For this reason, religious and philosophical traditions of → ethics have acknowledged the duty to seek just rulers, fair polities, and broad guiding terms for the justifiable use of coercive force. (A classic distinction is *jus ad bellum,* which deals with the justifiable grounds for using coercive force at all, vs. *jus in bello,* the constraints on the use of those means in conflict situations.)

The term "politics" is derived from Gk. *polis,* "city, city-state," which developed to order and regulate the more civilized, settled societies that grew out of the cult, fortress, and trading centers of older amphictyonic leagues of tribes, usually led by warlords and heroic warriors. From early on it was a critical question whether some kind of royal chief, a council of representative elders, all free citizens, or some combination of these three should be dominant in determining the "affairs of state" *(ta politica)* in these cities. Plato's *Republic* and Aristotle's *Politics* became the historic classics that spoke to this new cultural form. Both presumed that all persons and institutions in society were to be subject to a unified polity whose policies would be the cultivation of virtue and the well-being of the whole.

2. The Rise of Western Political Philosophy

These roots of Western political philosophy were both adopted and modulated by Roman theories of the political order, especially those of Cicero, who in *De leg.* saw politics as a *res publica,* or public affair, something the "public" owned as a product of public philosophy, public debate, and public will — something forever threatened on the one side by tyranny and on the other by chaos, especially by forms of religion that misled the people.

These analyses were also recognized and modified by the Hebraic and Christian traditions, which argued on theological grounds for the independent sovereignty of the → family and, especially, of the community of faith *(synagōgē* or *ekklēsia),* over which the government could not rule (a key reason for the early → persecutions). The one represented a more primal institution than any political regime, and the other represented a "kingdom not of this world," but one that could and did judge and influence the moral fabric of worldly regimes because the true "natural law" *(lex naturalis),* as known by political philosophy, was held to be largely in accord with, even clarified and stabilized by, the "law of Moses" *(lex Mosaica)* and the "law of Christ" *(lex Christi)* known by theology, as one finds them in Philo or in → Augustine. In such views, it was argued that other institutions in society should have the right to pursue different ends than the regime, although all were to be governed by universal moral laws and ends knowable, in principle, by all.

There are only a limited number of basic known options when it comes to polity, each of which has found a home in one or another wing of the Western tradition, and each correlates with a dominant option found also in the world's great civilizations beyond the West. The option of a league of tribes was known not only to the Greeks but to the Hebrews and to a number of primal cultures around the world. The possibility of a single warlord rising to imperial rule and forming a dynasty with priestly scholar-advisers not only appeared in the Western Roman period under Constantine but was given ideal status in classical Confucian texts of East Asia and taken as normative by the gentlemen-literati of that tradition. They served as government officials, instructed the emperor in regard to right rituals, and exhorted the people to live in right relationships and according to the ancient → virtues.

3. The Role of the Priestly Class

The idea that a priestly class should rule over, and not merely be the intellectual servant of, a king was dominant not only in periods of Egyptian history and in those periods of the West when papal authority overrode that of local and regional princes (→ Empire and Papacy). It also was woven into the Indian system of hierarchy, in which the Brahmans were, as a priestly caste, held to be superior in status and authority over royal and warrior *(Kṣatriya)* castes, who were politically more powerful and who in turn were held to be superior to agriculturally productive and trading castes (→ Hinduism). These top two status groups were reversed in → Buddhism, which saw the king as the center of public authority, managing both political and economic matters, with royally sponsored orders of monks seeking spiritual purity viewed as "jewels in the crown" of a pious king. And in various movements in the West we have also seen the episodic rise of the theocratic ideal, much as it appears in Islamic history — rule by a representative prophetic figure who not only is thought to be guided by God and the founder of a new religion but also is the founder of a military-political regime (with the political side sometimes dominant, as the caliphate-Sunni wing, and sometimes the clerical-representative side dominant, as with the ayatollah-Shia wing).

In the West, however, the development of what became a quite powerful ecclesiastical order, in principle (if not always in fact) distinct from any particular political regime, took three distinct directions, each of which tended to ally it with one or another of these various polities. One was the *centralization and bureaucratization of the → clergy* by the formation of a → hierarchy under the → pope, a development that tended to ally the faith with strong emperors. The second was the *convening of conciliar and synodical gatherings,* in which the leaders of regional centers (→ bishops and → abbots) would come together to make policy and discern matters pertaining to the right ordering of the religious and common life, sometimes under papal leadership and sometimes opposing or even deposing it. This development tended to ally the faith with strong kings or princes, who governed regional political orders. And the third was the *development of popular movements and congregations among the people,* often in the great cities, deeply loyal to particular charismatic preachers and, as often, able to sway the policies of city magistrates with few loyalties to the church's distant hierarchy. In cultures where synods and congregations gained not only tolerance but the right to exist as independent associations, the legal base and the practical skills were in place for the formation of churches independent of papal authority and, eventually, of independent political movements that were able to contest the authority of pope and king, and even the representative character of the → councils.

When things began to go bad in a political regime, people would often turn to one or another of these three ecclesial models, using it as a pattern to challenge the legitimacy of the dominant authority and to mobilize sentiment for change in a particular direction. In fact the modern traditions of constitutional, representational → democracy derived much from this latter set of developments and drew on memories of the ancient ecclesial tradition of Greek democracy and of the republican traditions of old Rome. Both limited the power and authority of any king or emperor. Indeed, it is impossible to understand the political history of the West without reference to such religious developments, just as one cannot understand those of Africa, China, India, Southeast Asia, or the Arab Middle East without reference to other religions.

4. Polity and Policy as the Human Exercise of Power

In later European history, however, many tried to develop politics totally apart from any religious concerns. They did so by investigating political means and by making both polity and policy matters of the human exercise of power or will, rejecting the idea that there were either natural teleological moral ends or general theological principles that did or could govern politics. Thus, for example, Niccolò Machiavelli (1469-1527) shrewdly studied the mechanics of → power, its accumulation and exercise, and wrote a famous manual, *The Prince,* for guiding rulers on how to achieve and use power. He presumed the conflictual nature of society and the self-interested character of rulers and argued that assuring the peace of the city could enhance the ruler's power. Later, in a somewhat similar way, the realist Thomas Hobbes (1588-1679) argued that the will of the sovereign must define — indeed impose — the laws for the people to establish peace, for the people were otherwise doomed to fight each other over their divergent interests.

Meanwhile, many believers, finding politics dirty, violent, and hostile, focused their religion not on matters of polity or policy but on → piety alone, leaving the organization of society and of → religion itself to the prudence and interests of bishops or princes. In many cases rulers commissioned theologians to fashion national → creeds, → confessions, and → catechisms. These statements defined the official religion, the "glue" of the nation-state (as established by the ruler, esp. after the Peace of Westphalia in 1648). Few recognized that this development implied the possibility of the formation of a secular "civil religion," the articulation and worship of national values that reflected the cultural ideals of specific ethnic groups or the ideological interests of particular classes. Later, the critique of both → civil religion and of → Pietism prompted movements of → political theology — that is, overt attempts to draw on religious sources to reform polity and influence policy.

Yet, the focus on power and purpose formed an anti-idealist "political realism" that illumined a number of matters everywhere pertinent to politics. As a practice, politics is about the accumulation and strategic exercise of power for various purposes. But power is a complex concept that has many levels. It can mean the force of arms, either in the simple brutal sense of the strength of a fighter's muscles or in the more complex sense of disciplined troops armed with weaponry that they know how to use in a skilled and constrained way, as directed. Politics at some levels has indeed been known to rely on thugs, but in the sort of governance that generates genuine order and constructive policies, the latter is necessary. While humanist or religious groups have periodically sought to engage in politics in a noncoercive and nonviolent way, the realists will tell them that such strategies may work in certain circumstances and may be a morally superior tactic to oppose some forms of oppression, but that if they gain power, every law that they pass or policy they support will have to be enforced if it is to be real politics.

Still, gaining power is seldom easy. The hiring of troops, the buying of weaponry, and the training for skilled use all require organizational skills and financial resources that depend on other institutions in society besides government, whether a party grabs power by a → revolution or a coup d'état, inherits a crown, or wins an election. Even in a democracy, the defeat of an opposing candidate requires organizational skills and nonviolent weapons of conceptual and media "battles." Governments or parties may form their own schools and manufacture their own weapons, but they must get the funds for doing so from contributions or taxes of the people, and the people will not willingly make these offerings unless they are persuaded on other fronts. The two most important of these fronts are *legitimacy,* determined essentially by the legal traditions, and *authority,* determined essentially by the dominant religious or cultural traditions. The citizenry, the troops, the brains, and the contributors must have a sense that those running the political movement or government are legitimate and given to the kinds of moral principles and spiritual purposes they can respect; otherwise their support will begin to unravel. If these values are not perceived by the general public to be present, citizens will distrust leaders, troops will not follow orders, brains will organize opposition movements, money will dry up, and the recipe for a failed state is at hand, even if residues of the moral fabric of the common life are sufficiently present to enable the people to think about the reconstruction of a civil society with a viable government after the failure.

5. Twentieth-Century Violations of Just Law

Two massive attempts to form modern, complex civilizations on bases that (1) violated legitimate principles of just law and overthrew the spiritual sources of → authority and (2) intentionally sought to set forth other bases for the organization of the masses, the troops, the brains, and the money are what made the 20th century so short (1914-91) and so bloody. The neopaganism of the Nazi movement in Germany and the Axis it led, and the militant → secularism of the Communist movement in Russia and the bloc it led, became temporarily powerful. They defined the political agenda of the 20th century, fired the imagination of people seeking change from Latin America to China, and assessed every movement and policy in every part of the world as to whether it led toward or away from or against these possibilities.

The defeat of the one and the collapse of the other, both at the hands of constitutional democratic orders with capitalist economies, has prompted the attempt to recover the moral and spiritual bases of politics and has led to new conflicts about religion and public policy. Much of the world has reasserted or reformed old traditions — some quite militantly, to the chagrin of many influential intellectuals who are attempting to define a new, nonreligious, purely rational basis for political life.

6. Twenty-first-Century Challenges

A very complex situation confronts many societies and world politics in the still quite new 21st century, for the old systems of international order could not contain the militant threats — not the older sacred empires of East Asia or West Europe, or the subsequent "balances of power" that broke down in the world wars of the first half of the 20th century, or the "balance of terror" of the cold war, with its threat of nuclear annihilation, in the second half. The United States remains the only superpower, although a more united Europe, the growing political influence of China, a developing India, and a more fragmented and conflicted Arabic world all show signs of new energy.

All but Europe, however, are experiencing the growing influence of resurgent religion, which suggests the possibility of long-term and highly contested international politics. Indeed, some hold that the United States, by design or default or religious zeal, is overcoming its historic anti-imperial tradition and is establishing a new world empire, to the great consternation of many at home and abroad. The picture is complicated by the fact that something like a global civil society seems to be emerging, as evidenced by dynamic developments in economic life, → communication media, → technology, migration, → education, medicine, → ecology, and → international law. A new kind of "public" is being created, without an integrated political order but compromising the historic sovereignty of the nation-state system, including that of the United States.

The → United Nations appears to many to hold the promise of a more cooperative multilateral system that can point the way toward such an order, but it has not proved itself able to cope with the many local and regional conflicts that have arisen, or to aid cultures lacking the developed institutions and cultural resources that could largely determine their destiny. Many in the emerging global civilization are likely to have a very difficult time adjusting or making a significant contribution to the world situation.

In a sense, the decisive political issue of the foreseeable future is the question of what can guide the formation of the kind of global civil society that can move the left-out many toward wider development, viable civil societies, and responsible political participation in the new global environment without destroying the gains of the more developed societies, usually defined as constitutional democracy with human → rights and a legally ordered corporate/market → economy, deeply dependent on historical influences from the Protestant Christian tradition. Historically, no civilization has been able to be formed or long endure without a profound religious vision at its core, guiding the senses of authority and legitimacy. If this core is to be developed in the present context, it will surely require what some are today calling a → public theology to evaluate, critique, and embrace valid elements not only of political philosophy and practical wisdom but also of the historic religious traditions, the world's civil religions, and the concerns of modern political theology.

Many, however, do not focus on this large and

fateful question but on specific policy questions within the democratized nation-states. Overt religious motivation on policy questions has almost always been present, but often muted. Yet, some of the most intense debates in the United States and other developed nations, for example, have had much to do with the religious mobilization of popular opinion on → slavery and labor rights during industrialization, on the control of alcohol and pornography in the Victorian period, on the anti-Nazi and anti-Communist movements at the time of World War II and the cold war, and on civil rights for minorities soon thereafter — all led by "mainline Protestantism." Since the 1960s and 1970s, especially in the United States, a comparable mobilization has emerged with enormous energy and activity, now led by a new Roman Catholic and a growing evangelical activism, on issues sometimes identified with "cultural wars" — → birth control and → abortion, sexual permissiveness and use of drugs, → feminism and alternative family forms, stem-cell research, and faith-based approaches to welfare, poverty, and joblessness. Ironically, many who are concerned about global developments agree with mainline Protestantism on slavery, labor, and civil rights, but also agree with the neoconservatives on cultural issues. Politics is caught in the cross fire, with religious activists puzzled or angry that they have to cope with this expanded agenda.

Bibliography: J. D. Carlson and E. Owens, eds., *The Sacred and the Sovereign: Religion and International Politics* (Washington, D.C., 2003) • S. E. Finer, *The History of Government from the Earliest Times* (3 vols.; New York, 1998) • P. Jenkins, *The Next Christendom: The Rise of Global Christianity* (New York, 2002) • J. Keane, *Global Civil Society?* (New York, 2002) • O. O'Donovan and J. L. O'Donovan, eds., *From Irenaeus to Grotius: A Sourcebook of Christian Political Thought* (Grand Rapids, 1999) • D. Philpott, *Revolutions in Sovereignty: How Ideas Shaped Modern International Relations* (Princeton, 2001) • D. W. Shriver Jr., *An Ethic for Enemies: Forgiveness in Politics* (New York, 1995) • J. W. Skillen and R. M. McCarthy, eds., *Political Order and the Plural Structure of Society* (Atlanta, 1991) • M. L. Stackhouse, *Christ and the Dominions of Civilization* (Harrisburg, Pa., 2002) • M. Weber, "Politics as Vocation," *From Max Weber: Essays in Sociology* (ed. H. H. Gerth and C. W. Mills; New York, 1958) 77-128 • J. Witte Jr., ed., *Christianity and Democracy in Global Context* (Boulder, Colo., 1993) • S. S. Wolin, *Politics and Vision: Continuity and Innovation in Western Political Thought* (exp. ed.; Princeton, 2004).

Max L. Stackhouse

Polity, Ecclesiastical

Overview

The term "polity" refers to the ways any particular social organization or institution is governed, although it is most frequently used in connection with ecclesiastical bodies (→ Church Government). Governance involves both the authority to determine the standards of behavior that shall be controlling and the power to engender conformity to those standards. In voluntary associations, of which most contemporary churches are examples, polity may consist of stated rules, conformity to which is the condition of continued membership (→ Church Membership), but it may also function through strongly respected practices that shape behavior and determine how → authority is exercised. Polity can be especially important when disputes have to be settled.

The manner in which governance functions in ecclesiastical groups is affected by two factors: the polity of the group in question and the extent to which ecclesiastical authority is recognized by the political order of the state. In countries with an official establishment of religion, the authority of the → state is intertwined with that of the → church; in such cases jurisdiction may be ecclesiastical and civil at the same time. In countries with a separation of → church and state, the ecclesiastical jurisdiction is operative only insofar as members of a particular group acknowledge the authority of the church over their lives. But even in countries that honor the principle of separation of church and state, appeals are sometimes made to the civil court system to settle disputes or to redress injustices in the ecclesiastical sector, especially when parties are aggrieved.

1. Protestant

1.1. *The Connectional Role of Polity*

An important aspect of polity is the delineation of authority within any particular church body, which authority functions to hold the group together. Protestant → denominations achieve this function by a variety of structures, which run the gamut from episcopal governance (which finds unity in allegiance to → bishops), through presbyterian governance (which locates authority in groups composed of elected or designated → elders), to congregational governance (which places authority in local gatherings of believers that may or may not cooperate with each other). The polities of very few Protestant denominations in America constitute a pure form of just one of these patterns. Terms like "bishop" and "elder" are used in so many different ways that the identification of the polity in any denomination is a complex matter.

Episcopacy in Protestant groups varies considerably. The visibility of the bishop is probably greatest in the Episcopal Church in the United States, where it serves as the symbol of unity, but the decision-making power of the bishop is exercised only in conformity to the canons of the church, which are enacted by a General Convention, which acts by concurrent majorities of a House of Bishops and a House of Deputies of elected clergy and laity, or by conventions or "councils" of individual dioceses by concurring votes of clergy and elected lay representatives. Actions of bishops in each diocese are often made in consultation with a small standing committee of elected clergy and laity. The power of the bishop is probably greatest in Methodist polity (→ Methodism), particularly as regards the power to appoint clergy to particular charges. But the norms or standards that govern the denomination as a whole are determined by a legislative body called the General Conference, and matters of lesser import by the individual conferences (sometimes called jurisdictions). Methodist bishops themselves do not have the power of legislation but preside over the bodies that do.

In churches with presbyterian governance, the connectional function is located in corporate bodies (called presbyteries in the Presbyterian churches, classes in Reformed churches) that are composed of the ministers and an equal number of ordained lay elders delegated by all the churches in a given geographic area. These bodies have the power to determine ministerial standing and appointments, to supervise the actions of member churches (including the ownership and use of property), and to carry on mission activities as a corporate venture. The actions of presbyteries are subject to a constitution whose provisions are determined by actions of a churchwide legislative body (General Assembly or General Synod), actions that must be ratified by the majority of the presbyteries or classes in order to become official.

Congregational polities locate jurisdiction in the local community of believers. However, the freedom of the local congregations to determine policy differs from denomination to denomination. In Lutheran practice (Evangelical Lutheran Church in America), the assembly of a regional body called a → synod consists of representatives of local congregations authorized to exercise a high degree of supervisory control over the member congregations, with the synodical bishop acting primarily as administrative officer. Final authority rests in a churchwide assembly led by the denomination's presiding bishop. The autonomy of the local congregation is considerably greater in Baptist and Congregational polities, where the connectional function is carried out by conventions or associations (for Baptists) or synods (for others) that enunciate general policies that are more suggestive as guidance than coercive as laws. When individual congregations differ from the policies of the denomination as a whole, they do not lose their property or right to exist as churches. The connectional aspect of jurisdiction largely depends on the desire of individual congregations to be associated with the parent body (→ Congregationalism).

1.2. *The Disciplinary Function of Polity*

Ecclesiastical groups have various means for seeing that their members accept certain standards of belief and behavior. Most of them instruct potential members in the rudiments of their denomination's identity, instruction that is often minimal and perhaps even perfunctory. Certain questions are asked of those who seek membership, and they declare assent to certain → norms that characterize the faith and practice of the group in question. This ques-

Polity, Ecclesiastical

tioning is usually done on the parish level by sessions, consistories, boards of deacons, official boards, and other groups in the case of persons seeking to join as lay members. In some congregational polities, particularly those of → Baptists, the entire → congregation has sometimes inquired into the faith and practice of individuals seeking membership, but that function has now largely been designated to the governing board, acting on behalf of the congregation.

Joining a church involves accepting its jurisdiction (leaving a church is often called renouncing the jurisdiction). Accepting the jurisdiction implicitly involves certain obligations. Financial support is expected, and sometimes specified as a → tithe. Attendance at worship is also expected. A difference is made, though, between active (communicant) members and others on the basis of the frequency with which people attend services and their willingness to pledge support of their congregations. Most Protestant churches allow individuals to decide for themselves whether or not to partake of the sacrament of Holy Communion (→ Eucharist). The local governing boards of a parish or, in some cases, the → clergy may have the power to require members to abide by certain standards of support and conduct, but the day has passed in most denominations when the local imposition of ecclesiastical discipline carries any significant impact, particularly in countries that separate church and state.

In certain groups, however, local jurisdictional discipline still functions with a discernible impact. In the Church of Jesus Christ of Latter-day Saints (→ Mormons), for instance, the local official, who bears the title "bishop," can deny access to the temple and its ceremonial benefits to members of the local church (known as the ward) who fail to live up to certain expectations. In the Episcopal Church in the United States, as in some Lutheran churches, permission to partake of the Eucharist can be denied to people whose participation in the life of the congregation does not meet certain expectations. Among some → Mennonites, shunning is still practiced as a form of ecclesiastical discipline.

The clergy of many Protestant denominations are subject to a greater degree of disciplinary scrutiny than are the ordinary lay members. Most denominations require an annual accounting of the activities of their ordained members, and double standards are sometimes imposed that require behavior of ministers that is not required of laity. The matters involved differ, not only from group to group but from time to time, and have consisted of requirements such as refraining from smoking or the use of alcohol or explicitly avoiding sexually unacceptable → lifestyles. Moreover, connectional bodies that oversee the behavior of clergy frequently have constitutional provisions for trying cases according to strict procedural requirements. Such provisions frequently specify in considerable detail how judicial bodies shall be constituted, the rules of evidence they must follow, the rights of the accused, and the kind of, and limitations upon, sentences that may be imposed. Although disciplinary cases may be brought for strictly church-related offenses, ecclesiastical sanctions may be exerted against clergy who run afoul of civil laws. The supervision of, and constitutional protections of, clergy is less strictly prescribed in congregational polities, and the dismissal of clergy merely by the action of the local parish does occur.

1.3. *Matters of Dispute*

The exercise of discipline by an appropriate ecclesiastical court does not necessarily settle an issue. In many polities, particularly those with the highest degree of connectionalism, provision is made for appeal from decisions made by the body having initial jurisdiction. The constitutions of many denominations specify how the group before such appeals can be heard is to be constituted and how the deliberations are to proceed. The morphology of such provisions is most specific in denominations with the greatest degree of connectionalism and less clear in the case of polities in which the local body of believers is autonomous.

The civil courts become involved in ecclesiastical cases when aggrieved parties seek their help in obtaining the redress of grievances. If the judicial processes for discipline are clearly specified by the polity and have been followed, the civil courts are not likely to change the decisions made by the ecclesiastical process. In cases when it is less clear how matters of dispute are to be adjudicated and whether such provisions have been duly followed, civil courts may render an overriding judgment. Courts may remand a case to a church body if they determine there has been a miscarriage of procedure or a failure to exhaust the full remedies offered by the polity under which the case has arisen. Decisions in such cases may be influenced by taking into account customary practices, as well as statutory guidance.

Although civil courts hesitate to become involved in church controversies and are particularly hesitant to make decisions that would preempt the right of individual religious groups to exercise disciplinary functions according to the provisions of their polity, civil courts will assert their jurisdiction over matters or actions that affect the general welfare or are contrary to basic public policy. The cases in which civil jurisdiction will override ecclesiastical polity involve such matters as the protection of children from abuse and the protection of all persons from physical harm, including harm coming from denial of medical procedures that are commonly understood to be ordinary and necessary for the protection of life and well-being. Being a religious institution does not grant immunity from tort law or provide exemption from the requirement of civic obligations. Churches must conform to building codes, the provisions of legislation protecting public health and safety, and rules protecting the rights of employees and guests.

Bibliography: R. B. Couser, *Ministry and the American Legal System: A Guide for Clergy, Law Workers, and Congregations* (Minneapolis, 1993) • D. W. Hall and J. H. Hall, eds., *Paradigms in Polity* (Grand Rapids, 1994) • E. L. Long Jr., *Patterns of Polity: Varieties of Church Governance* (Cleveland, 2001) • F. S. Mead and S. S. Hill, *Handbook of Denominations in the United States* (11th ed.; rev. C. D. Atwood; Nashville, 2001) • R. L. Schenck, ed., *Constitutions of American Denominations* (3 vols.; Buffalo, N.Y., 1984).

Edward LeRoy Long Jr.

2. Roman Catholic

2.1. *Roman Catholic Church*

2.1.1. *A Communion of Churches*

The → Roman Catholic Church is a *koinōnia,* or communion, of 23 autonomous *(sui iuris)* churches united by their sharing a common profession of → faith, common sacraments, and common ecclesiastical governance under the primatial authority of the bishop of Rome. Although the Latin, or Roman Catholic, Church is the largest and best known of these churches, the Catholic communion also includes the Coptic, Ethiopian, Malankar, Maronite, Syrian, Albanian, Belorussian, Bulgarian, Georgian, Greek, Greek-Melkite, Hungarian, Italo-Albanian, Romanian, Russian, Ruthenian, Slovak, Ukrainian, Croatian, Chaldean, Malabar, and Armenian Catholic Churches. With the exception of the Maronite Church, all of these Eastern Catholic churches have counterparts in the Orthodox communion and are notably smaller than their Orthodox counterparts (→ Orthodox Church; Oriental Orthodox Churches).

All of the churches of the Catholic communion are organized and governed according to an episcopal polity, and each is divided into (usually) territorial particular churches or → dioceses (eparchies in the Eastern churches) presided over by bishops in hierarchical communion with the bishop of Rome. Although recent Catholic theology and → canon law have preferred to use the traditional language of → koinonia, or communion, rather than the more juridical language of an earlier era to delineate the key offices and structures of governance and their articulation, this somewhat irenic language does not mean that the hierarchical communion that maintains and fosters the unity of the Catholic Church is a vague sentiment or a benevolent attitude. This hierarchical communion is an organic reality that demands a juridical structure as well as charity (→ Church Government).

2.1.2. *A Visible Society*

The Roman Catholic Church holds that Christ established and sustains as a visible organization the community of faith, hope, and charity that is his mystical body. By analogy to the union of human and divine in the Incarnate Word, the church is understood to be one complex reality that is both a hierarchically structured institution and the mystical body of Christ, a visible society and a spiritual community. As a result of its insistence on the visible and societal dimension of the church, the Catholic Church has developed a rather elaborate legal system called canon law. This law delineates the rights and responsibilities of the two principal governance offices in Catholic polity: those of the Roman pontiff for the universal church (→ Pope, Papacy), and those of the diocesan → bishop for the particular, or local, churches.

2.2. *Twin Foci of Authority*

2.2.1. *Supreme Authority*

Supreme → authority in the Catholic Church rests in the bishop of Rome and in the *College of Bishops in communion with him.* In Catholic ecclesiology the bishop of Rome is understood to be the successor of → Peter, whom the Lord placed at the head of the apostles, and the College of Bishops is understood to succeed, not individually but as a collegial body, to the function of the → apostles. The College of Bishops, whose members are normally scattered throughout the world, occasionally gathers as a college at ecumenical → councils to exercise the supreme authority in the church with and under its head in a solemn way. Thus the doctrinal and disciplinary decisions of these councils are binding on the whole church. At other times the supreme authority is exercised by bishop of Rome as both Roman pontiff and head of the College of Bishops. Even when it is not gathered in an ecumenical council, however, the College of Bishops shares responsibility for the whole church. The bishops' relations, individually and jointly, with the Roman pontiff and with one another are to be governed by collegiality, and each bishop is to exhibit solicitude for the whole church, even though this solicitude entails no jurisdictional authority.

The *Roman pontiff* is the universal primate of the church and of the individual churches that it comprises. He is elected by the College of → Cardinals according to procedures detailed in canon law. Once he accepts legitimate election, the Roman pontiff assumes his office and cannot be removed, although he is free to resign. Since his is a primacy not merely of honor but also of jurisdiction, the Roman pontiff's authority in the church is supreme, full, immediate, and universal. As such, he enjoys supreme legislative, executive, and judicial power within the parameters set by divine law, both natural and positive. In practice, however, the Roman pontiff normally exercises his authority through the Roman → curia, the Vatican's bureaucratic complex of administrative agencies, tribunals, and offices that assist him in the governance of the universal church.

2.2.2. *Episcopal Authority in the Local Churches*

The primatial authority of the Roman pontiff is seen in Catholic polity as a force fostering the unity of the many local churches within the universal church and among themselves, not as an instrument for dominating the local churches or reducing them to the status of local branches of a vast multinational organization. Each particular or local church gathered under the presidency of a bishop in communion with the Roman pontiff and the rest of the College of Bishops is truly a church in which the one, holy, catholic, and apostolic church of Christ is present and manifest. Although bishops of particular churches either are directly appointed by the Roman pontiff or have their elections confirmed by him, they are not the vicars, delegates, or local representatives of the Roman pontiff but vicars of Christ. As authentic → pastors, they govern the local churches entrusted to their care with authority that is proper, ordinary, and immediate, although it is circumscribed by the boundaries of their territory and by other limitations imposed by the Roman pontiff for the good of the larger church and of the faithful. Diocesan bishops are, within the parameters established by canon law, the sole legislators and the chief executives and judges for their local churches, although they usually are assisted in their administrative and judicial functions by an episcopal curia. Just as the global church is composed of territorial subdivisions called dioceses or eparchies, so local churches are usually subdivided into territorial units called parishes, which are governed by pastors appointed or installed by the diocesan bishop.

2.3. *Tensions between the Universal Church and Particular Churches*

The rights and obligations of the Roman pontiff for the universal church and of diocesan bishops for their particular churches, the principal subaltern structures and agencies of papal and episcopal governance, and the articulation of these offices in the ordinary business of church governance are spelled out in canon law. In theory, the authority of the bishop in the particular church is not compromised but defended, upheld, and strengthened by the supreme power of the Roman pontiff; in practice, however, there have been tensions between the claims and prerogatives of the central papal and local episcopal authorities. In certain historical periods, strong assertions of episcopal authority have pushed the Roman pontiff into the background and occasionally threatened to fragment the church into a loose confederation of national churches. In other periods, the forces of centralization around the Roman pontiff have dwarfed the role of the local bishop and made him seem like a mere delegate of the Roman pontiff.

In the wake of the Second → Vatican Council, which came at the end of a period of Roman centralization, it was suggested that the principle of → subsidiarity could be used to delineate the relationships between the universal church and the particular churches, on the one hand, and the Roman pontiff and the local bishops, on the other. These suggestions, however, did not meet with unqualified acceptance. As a result, the long-standing tensions between the universal church and local churches and between primacy and episcopacy remain unresolved both in Catholic theology and in canon law.

2.4. *Intermediate Levels of Authority*

In the course of history, various intermediary structures of governance have emerged between the Roman pontiff and local bishops.

2.4.1. *Metropolitans or Archbishops*

Already in the patristic era, local churches clustered around the bishop of the major city of their region, developed a common discipline, and at local councils coordinated strategies for dealing with shared problems. These regional groupings became known as provinces, and the bishop of the metropolitan see the archbishop. While archbishops once had considerable authority to intervene in the governance of the dioceses of their province (their "suffragan" sees), this authority has waned with the waxing of the central authority of the Roman pontiff, until today archbishops have virtually no jurisdiction outside the territory of their own metropolitan sees. Canon law, however, still makes provision for provincial councils to develop common discipline and pastoral strategies for provinces, but such councils are rarely convoked today.

2.4.2. *Patriarchs*

Also during the patristic era, certain dominant sees, important for the foundation and spread of Christianity in their area, gained sway over the provinces of their area as patriarchal churches. The Council of → Chalcedon (451) recognized the patriarchal status of the churches of → Alexandria, → Antioch, Constantinople, → Jerusalem, and → Rome and their bishops as → patriarchs. Disagreements about primacy among these patriarchs and the scope of the autonomy of the several patriarchal churches contributed to the schism between the Roman Catholic and the Orthodox churches. While the Coptic, Maronite, Syrian, Chaldean, and Armenian Catholic Churches today have patriarchs, difficulties in harmonizing the traditional prerogatives of patriarchs with the primatial claims of the Roman pontiff remain a problem within the Catholic communion and an obstacle to reunion with the Orthodox churches.

2.4.3. *Primates*

As bishop of Rome, the Roman pontiff has long been recognized as the patriarch of the West. Consequently, additional patriarchal structures failed to develop in the Western church, even as the church expanded beyond the Mediterranean basin. Nevertheless, the bishops of leading sees of some traditionally Roman Catholic nations have been accorded the title → "primate." Although this title is largely honorary, primates have traditionally exercised some of the prerogatives of patriarchs. With or without the leadership of a primate, the bishops of particular nations have gathered periodically in plenary councils to coordinate discipline and pastoral practices for their countries. The three plenary councils of Baltimore during the 19th century (1852, 1866, 1884), for example, were particularly significant for providing the juridical framework for the growth of the Catholic Church in the United States. Canon law still makes provision for such plenary councils, although logistic problems in organizing and executing these councils and cumbersome regulations requiring approval of the Holy See for their convocation, agenda, and results have discouraged the use of plenary councils as a vehicle for governance.

2.4.4. *Episcopal Conferences*

Especially since the Second Vatican Council, the bishops of a nation have been gathered together in episcopal conferences. All bishops who perform a pastoral function in the territory of the conference are members. Although episcopal conferences are primarily designed to provide an opportunity for the discussion and coordination of pastoral activities within a particular nation, they also provide the bishops with a forum for exercising together their teaching office and possess some limited legislative competence, especially in approving translations of liturgical texts and proposing liturgical adaptation suitable to the customs of their regions. Although some had hoped that episcopal conferences would develop into genuine vehicles for episcopal collegiality and effective counterweights to the centripetal pull of centralization, the Holy See has moved in recent years to restrict rather narrowly the scope of the authority of conferences in the areas of teaching and governance (→ Latin American Council of Bishops).

2.5. *Church Property*

According to canon law, the Catholic Church itself, as well as each diocese and parish within it, is a moral or juridical person (i.e., an artificial person akin to a civil corporation, which is distinct from the persons or things that serve as its basis in reality), is established by the law by the mere fact of its establishment by competent authority, and enjoys the capacity for perpetual existence with its own rights and obligations, including the right to own and administer property. Other church-related institutions such as hospitals and colleges can be, but need not be, established as juridical persons independent of their sponsoring agency by the decree of competent authority. Temporal goods (e.g., real estate, buildings, financial instruments, personal property, and money) legitimately acquired by these juridical persons become "church property," not the property of the individual persons responsible for their acquisition and administration or of the persons for whose benefit this property was acquired and retained.

Each juridical person has a designated person charged with legal authority for the administration of its property — the bishop in the case of a diocese, and the pastor in the case of a parish. These legal representatives of dioceses and parishes are assisted by others. Diocesan bishops must, and pastors may, appoint finance officers to handle the day-to-day business of the juridical persons under their supervision. Moreover, both dioceses and parishes must have finance councils that assist bishops and pastors respectively in their administration of temporal goods and whose advice and occasionally consent are required for the transaction of more important business. Advice or consent from other individuals or groups may also be required prior to some decisions.

The financial administration by the legal representatives of juridical persons is supervised by their hierarchical superiors. Thus, bishops supervise the stewardship of pastors over the parishes entrusted to them, and the Holy See that of bishops over their dioceses. Canon law structures the exercise of this supervisory authority by requiring bishops and pastors to submit regular financial reports to their hierarchical superiors, by recognizing the right and duty of superiors to visit juridical persons subject to them and to correct irregularities in administration discovered in the course of → visitations, and by requiring that bishops and pastors receive permission of their hierarchical superiors before engaging in transactions that might jeopardize the financial situation of their diocese or parish. Nevertheless, this supervisory authority does not give hierarchical superiors an ownership interest in the property of the juridical person they supervise or the authority to interfere in its ordinary administration, except to correct gross negligence. Poor administration of temporal goods is, however, a recognized ground for the removal of a pastor.

2.6. *Dispute Resolution*

As a hierarchical church, the Roman Catholic Church has internal structures and procedures for resolving conflicts and disputes. Each diocese has its own tribunal or court with general jurisdiction over issues governed by → church law and an adequate legal staff. Decisions of diocesan tribunals can be appealed to the tribunal of the metropolitan or to another regularly designated appellate court and eventually to the Roman Rota, the highest court of the Roman curia for resolving appeals. The operation of these tribunals is governed by judicial procedural norms similar to those of the civil courts of continental European states. Since 1908 the jurisdiction of ordinary tribunals has been restricted to matters of private law and criminal. As a result, the vast majority of cases decided by ecclesiastical tribunals involve questions of the annulment of marriages.

Following the lead of countries whose legal systems had been shaped by the Napoleonic Code, the Catholic Church has exempted from the jurisdiction of its ordinary tribunals disputes arising from the exercise of administrative authorities in the church. These disputes can be resolved only by recourse to the hierarchical superior of the administrative official whose action gave rise to the dispute. For the resolution of disputes arising within a diocese from the administrative activity of pastors and other authorities subordinate to the bishop, recourse must be made to the diocesan bishop. Disputes arising from the actions of the bishop himself are resolved by recourse to the department of the Roman curia with competence over the subject matter of the dispute. Further recourse from the decisions of the department of the Roman curia is possible to the Apostolic Signatura, which functions as a supreme administrative tribunal and whose decisions admit of no further recourse. Although the procedures for this hierarchical or administrative recourse are loosely structured by canon law, the Roman Catholic Church lags behind most secular states in its administrative law and procedures.

2.7. *Church-State Relations*

Since the Roman Catholic Church considers itself to be a visible society autonomous from, and in some ways parallel to, the state, it claims freedom to organize itself and pursue its religious mission without interference from secular governments. Both historically and practically, this claim has been resisted to a greater or lesser extent by governments in whose territory the church is present. At times the church has vigorously resisted state encroachments; at other times it has muted its own claims and accommodated itself to peaceful coexistence with the state. Where possible, the church attempts to provide a forum for addressing its concerns by formalizing its relationship with states through diplomatic relations between the secular government and the Holy See. Where such relations exist, → nuncios or ambassadors of the Holy See represent the interests of the church to the government. Sometimes understandings between the church and state in areas of mutual interest and concern (e.g., → education, status of church property) are memorialized in the form of treaties or → concordats between the Holy See and the state. In the absence of concordats or formal diplomatic relations between the state and the Holy See, the church's dealings with the government are conducted by the local bishops.

To maintain its liberty, the church avails itself of privileges, exemptions, and immunities provided in the constitutional order of the state. Although the custom of maintaining diplomatic relations and entering concordats between the Holy See and secular states has been criticized by some within the church as an anachronism and as inappropriate Vatican meddling in local affairs, the supranational status that these practices give the Roman Catholic Church has, in practice, provided it with leverage in dealing with hostile regimes, giving local episcopates some insulation from political pressure.

Bibliography: Church documents: Codex Canonum Ecclesiarum Orientalium (1990) • Codex Iuris Canonici (1983) • CONGREGATION FOR THE DOCTRINE OF THE FAITH, *Some Aspects of the Church Understood as Communion* (Vatican City, 1992) • VATICAN I, *Pastor aeternus,* Dogmatic Constitution on the Church of Christ (1870) • VATICAN II, *Lumen gentium,* Dogmatic Constitution on the Church (1963).

Other works: J. AUER, *The Church: The Universal Sacrament of Salvation* (Washington, D.C., 1993) • A. DULLES, *Models of the Church* (New York, 1974) • J. D. FARIS, *The Eastern Catholic Churches: Constitution and Governance* (New York, 1992) • W. KASPER, *Theology and Church* (New York, 1989) • J-M. R. TILLARD, *Church of Churches: The Ecclesiology of Communion* (Collegeville, Minn., 1987).

JOHN P. BEAL

3. Anglican

3.1. *The Problem of Jurisdiction*

For most ecclesiastical bodies, "polity" imparts the notion of ordered "jurisdiction" over matters and relationships. "Jurisdiction" is, however, a problematic concept for Anglicans. Anglicanism derives its name from the Church of England, which in 1533 refused to acknowledge any longer the overriding jurisdiction of the bishop of Rome (→ Pope, Papacy), although it retained the corpus of Western → canon law, except insofar as it was incompatible with the sovereignty of the English Crown. Down to the present day, it has continued to draw heavily upon important insights from both Roman Catholic and Reformed traditions, holding them together in tension. In particular, it has retained the threefold order of ministry (→ deacons, → priests, and → bishops) as part of the one, holy, catholic, and apostolic → church, and it claims an unbroken succession of episcopal ministry, although its orders are not recognized by the Roman church. In many ways the jurisdictional basis of Anglicanism closely resembles that of the autocephalous Orthodox churches of the East (→ Orthodox Church).

The Church of England retains the jurisdictional structure established by the English Parliament in 1533, as a national church with the English sovereign as its supreme governor. It is not familiar with the concept of voluntary membership; all persons resident in England are its parishioners. They have certain legal rights in relation to its ministry, for example, to be married in their parish church or to be buried in its churchyards. In this regard, the Church of England continues to reflect Richard Hooker's (ca. 1554-1600) concept of the "Christian Commonwealth," with church and state as opposite sides of the same coin.

3.2. *The Global Communion*

Many of the above comments concerning the Church of England are not true of the other churches of the → Anglican Communion. Anglicanism has spread far beyond English shores, and there are now 43 churches worldwide that are in communion with the See of Canterbury. No Anglican churches outside England, not even those in Scotland, Wales, or Ireland, are "established by law" as the Church of England is; all others are voluntary-membership churches. But all Anglican churches, including the Church of England, now include elected representative structures that bring together bishops, clergy, and laity. These bodies are variously described as councils, conventions, or synods. As elsewhere in the → Reformed tradition, there is a far greater role than in the Roman or Orthodox traditions for the whole church to receive new developments, to give or withhold consent, and to express counsel to its bishops and archbishops. Anglicanism is often characterized as episcopally led and synodically governed.

Partly as a result of British colonial adventure and settlement from the early 17th century onward, and largely through the missionary movement of the 19th and 20th centuries (→ British Missions), Anglican patterns of church life have taken root in many diverse cultures worldwide. For jurisdictional reasons relating to the English Crown, episcopal succession for Anglicans in the United States came only after the American Revolution, and with the support of the archbishop of Canterbury through the Episcopal Church of Scotland. Changes in English law were needed to enable other bishops to be consecrated by the archbishop of Canterbury for the development of missionary dioceses in Africa, India, Canada, Australasia, and the Orient. English parliamentary legislation in 1841 provided for a joint Anglican-Lutheran bishop in Jerusalem. Since the mid-19th century, these missionary dioceses have gathered together into self-governing provinces, each with its own synodical structure and metropolitical jurisdiction, and new provinces emerged in increasing numbers during the later 20th century. There are now reckoned to be some 70 million Anglicans in the worldwide Anglican Communion.

3.3. *Instruments of Unity*

Despite its worldwide growth, however, there is no uniform system of polity or central jurisdiction in the Anglican Communion. Rather, it is a network of autonomous churches, in which each church has its own constitutional and legal provisions for its internal regulation and for mutual recognition of ministry and intercommunion of membership. In the absence, however, of any formal jurisdictional →

authority for the Anglican Communion as a whole, four "instruments of unity" have developed and are recognized by each of the constituent churches: the archbishop of Canterbury, the Lambeth Conferences of Anglican bishops, the Primates' Meetings of the episcopal heads of each province, and the Anglican Consultative Council (ACC), which includes bishops, priests, and laity from each province.

The archbishop of Canterbury is arguably the most important of these four instruments of unity, both historically and in terms of his personal involvement with individual provinces. He plays a pivotal role within the Communion, as the primus inter pares among the metropolitans of the Communion. It is he who convenes the Lambeth Conferences, which have met at roughly ten-year intervals since 1867, and he also convenes the Primates' Meetings, which meet as frequently as once per year "for leisurely thought, prayer, and deep consultation." The ACC is the nearest the Communion as whole comes to having an elected representative body, with laity and clergy as well as bishops or archbishops; it meets at three-year intervals and is serviced by a small secretariat that also provides administrative support for the Lambeth Conferences and the Primates' Meetings.

The issue of jurisdiction has been a matter of recurrent concern since the first Lambeth Conference was convened in 1867 by the archbishop of Canterbury in order to address doctrinal issues (→ Bishop, Episcopate, 3). Key bishops refused to attend on principle, and others attended only upon the condition that the conference was clearly understood as having no jurisdictional authority. Successive Lambeth Conferences, ACC meetings, commissions, and reports have affirmed this understanding, though equally emphasizing the obligations of mutual responsibility and interdependence among the churches of the Anglican Communion.

3.4. *"Bonds of Affection" and Growing Tensions* Anglicanism is, then, a global communion of churches held together not by any legal jurisdiction but rather, in the words of one of the ACC's reports, by "bonds of affection." It has a history of working flexibly and responsively, as what one bishop described as "a learning church as well as a teaching church." However, the absence of any central jurisdiction has meant that tensions may be difficult to resolve when controversial issues arise. In the mid-20th century the uniting of Anglican churches with Protestant missionary churches on the Indian subcontinent caused decades of agonizing over the nature of episcopal ministry (→ Church of South India). More recently, there have been tensions over the → ordination (§7.4) of women to the priesthood and to the episcopate, and over the recognition of same-sex relationships.

In some provinces, for example in the Church of England, formal steps have been taken to contain these tensions by the appointment of assistant bishops with a province-wide jurisdiction as "provincial episcopal visitors" (or "flying bishops"). Other provinces and dioceses have made similar arrangements more informally, for example, in New Zealand, where one bishop has particular responsibility for the Maori community throughout the province. In North America some disaffected congregations have purported to ally themselves, against the wishes of their own bishops, with bishops and archbishops from elsewhere in the Communion.

Just as the theological base of Anglicanism is diverse, drawing together Scripture, tradition, and reason in creative tension, so the hallmark of its polity is a dispersed jurisdictional authority, seeking to do justice to both its Catholic and its Reformed inheritance. It has been suggested that there may be some underlying *ius commune* in the Anglican Communion, a body of principles discernible through the diverse constitutional arrangements to be found in each of the provinces, and a resource to assist the instruments of unity in dealing with issues that impair the provinces' communion with each other. However that may be, in an era that values flexibility and networking above institution and hierarchy, Anglicanism's lack of any coercive central jurisdiction may yet prove to be more of a strength than a weakness.

→ Church Government; Porvoo Common Statement

Bibliography: H. S. Box, *The Principles of Canon Law* (Oxford, 1949) • *The Communion We Share: The Official Report of the Eleventh Meeting of the Anglican Consultative Council in Scotland 1999* (Harrisburg, Pa., 2000) • N. Doe, *Canon Law in the Anglican Communion: A Worldwide Perspective* (Oxford, 1998) • I. T. Douglas and Kwok P.-L., eds., *Beyond Colonial Anglicanism: The Anglican Communion in the Twenty-first Century* (New York, 2001) • G. R. Evans and J. R. Wright, eds., *The Anglican Tradition: A Handbook of Sources* (London, 1988) • U. T. Holmes III, *What Is Anglicanism?* (Wilton, Conn., 1982) • W. M. Jacob, *The Making of the Anglican Church Worldwide* (London, 1997) • Lambeth Commission on Communion, *The Windsor Report 2004* (London, 2004) • E. G. Moore and T. Briden, *Moore's Introduction to English Canon Law* (2d ed.; Oxford, 1985) • S. Neill, *Anglicanism* (4th ed.; London, 1977) • W. L. Sachs, *The Transformation of Anglicanism: From State Church to Global Communion* (Cambridge, 2002) • S. W. SYKES, *The Integrity of Anglicanism* (Oxford, 1978); idem, *Unashamed Anglicanism* (Nashville, 1995) • S. SYKES and J. BOOTY, eds., *The Study of Anglicanism* (London, 1988) • *The Virginia Report: The Report of the Inter-Anglican Theological and Doctrinal Commission* (Harrisburg, Pa., 1999).

JOHN REES

Polytheism

1. Term
2. Religious Studies

1. Term

From Thales, the Greeks believed that "all things are full of gods" (Aristotle, *De anima* 1.5, 411a8-9; → Aristotelianism). Only in concrete cases, however, did they call this idea polytheism (e.g., Aeschylus *Supp.* 424 mentions *polytheos hedra,* "seat of many gods," for an altar; → Greek Religion). Neither they nor other peoples made of polytheism an abstract concept. The Jews did so when, distancing themselves from polytheism, they criticized the lovers of *polytheïa* (Philo *De mut. nom.* 205). So too did Christians, for whom Orpheus taught the Greek *polytheotēs* (thus the ascription in Ps.–Justin Martyr *Coh. ad Graec.* 15.1). Jean Bodin (1530-96) imputed the latter term to the Neoplatonist Proclus (410 or 412-85; → Platonism), translating it *polythéisme.*

For various reasons the word was then accepted in such diverse fields as political theory, the study of antiquity, polemical theology (→ Polemics), travel narratives, criticism of religion, literature, and → philosophy. More recently the concept has been positively reassessed in connection with the critique of → reason (O. Marquard). This position, however, has in its own turn prompted a rejection of polytheism from those adducing the notion of → revelation in criticizing mythology from a theological perspective (J. Taubes). It is also used controversially as a cipher for the division of powers exercised by academic and political monopolies.

2. Religious Studies

Notwithstanding the various uses, "polytheism" is an apt term as a category in the study of religion (→ Religious Studies). It presupposes a right employment of the concept of → God (§1.2) and rejects numerical trifling with a multiplicity of nonhuman figures. Defined by it are interrelated actions that have gods as subjects, gods and humans as partners and recipients, and impersonal spheres of being as objects. A world order and specific intentions may be involved in a giving of meaning. There may be many different levels as human qualities are adopted that are thus given a transcendental basis, even as the gods themselves are seen anthropomorphically. This development takes place chiefly in myths. Here with 10 to 20 deities the structure of action and the involved picture of the world achieve coherence.

Smaller and more complex webs of meaning that result may be viewed as systems. There are positive correlations between them and the political and social orders of the peoples that have constructed the polytheism. If an overarching type of polytheism may be found, it may well go hand in hand with a specific social form such as an agrarian society or a centralized state, but there is no way to arrange such types in any sequence or evolution of supposed epochs in religious history.

→ Henotheism; Monotheism; Nature Religion

Bibliography: J. ASSMANN, *Egyptian Solar Religion in the New Kingdom: Re, Amun, and the Crisis of Polytheism* (London, 1995) • W. BURKERT, *Greek Religion* (Cambridge, Mass., 1985) chap. 5, "Polis and Polytheism" • G. DAVIES, ed., *Polytheistic Systems* (Edinburgh, 1989) • M. ELIADE, *The Sacred and the Profane: The Nature of Religion* (New York, 1959) • E. O. JAMES, *The Ancient Gods: The History and Diffusion of Religion in the Ancient Near East and the Eastern Mediterranean* (New York, 1960) • O. MARQUARD, "In Praise of Polytheism: On Monomythical and Polymythical Thinking," *Farewell to Matters of Principle: Philosophical Studies* (New York, 1989) chap. 5 • B. N. PORTER, *One God or Many? Concepts of Divinity in the Ancient World* (Chebeague, Maine, 2000) • M. S. SMITH, *The Origins of Biblical Monotheism: Israel's Polytheistic Background and the Ugaritic Texts* (New York, 2001) • J. TAUBES, "Zur Konjunktur des Polytheismus," *Mythos und Moderne* (ed. K. H. Bohrer; Frankfurt, 1983) 457-70 • R. J. Z. WERBLOWSKI, "Polytheism," *EncRel(E)* 11.435-39 • G. WIDENGREN, *Religionsphänomenologie* (Berlin, 1969) 93-129. See also the bibliographies in "Monotheism" and "Nature Religion" (esp. the items by D. Hume).

CARSTEN COLPE

Pontificals

In the → Roman Catholic Church pontificals (Lat. *pontificalia*) are official acts by the chief clergy at which → bishops, → cardinals, → abbots, or → prelates carry the pontifical insignia of miters and staffs (e.g., at High → Mass and confirmation; →

Initiation Rites). They include the → ordination of deacons, priests, and bishops; the → consecration of oil, altars, churches, and virgins; and certain → blessings, visitations, and solemn jurisdictional acts. In these cases there is a uniform worldwide liturgical order (→ Liturgical Books).

In the Roman Catholic Church and also in other denominations, "pontificals" refers as well to episcopal attire generally (→ Vestments).

Bibliography: Instruction "Ut sive sollicite," *AAS* 61 (1969) 334-40 • J.-C. Noonan, *The Church Visible: The Ceremonial Life and Protocol of the Roman Catholic Church* (New York, 1996) • *The Rites of the Catholic Church, as Revised by the Decree of the Second Vatican Ecumenical Council and Published by Authority of Pope Paul VI* (New York, 1976).

Heiner Grote†

Pope, Papacy

1. Historical Aspects

1.1. *General*

1.1.1. To present a history of the popes, church historians must pay particular attention to the distinction between specific historical situations and a presumed logical development (→ Philosophy of History). Are we to understand the papacy as a divine institution and its history as the entelechy of this nature? Or are we to deal with it as a historical phenomenon with a place in history that we cannot differentiate in principle from that of any other? Even if we adopt the second view, we still must see a certain logic in the development and assertion of the Roman claim to primacy.

1.1.2. The pope — → Gregory VII (1073-85) first reserved the title *papa* for the bishop of → Rome (*Dictatus papae* 11) — is "Bishop of Rome, Vicar of Jesus Christ, Successor of the Chief of the Apostles, Supreme Pontiff of the Universal Church, Patriarch of the West, Primate of Italy, Archbishop and Metropolitan of the Roman Province, Sovereign of the State of Vatican City" (*NCE* [2d ed.] 11.495). According to a doctrine that was defined at → Vatican I after a long and complex process of historical development, which was then adopted into the → Codex Iuris Canonici and later supplemented by the dogmatic constitution *Lumen gentium* of → Vatican II, the pope has primacy by divine right as the representative and guarantee of the church's unity; and as the supreme pastor of the church, he is also the → bishop of Rome. As the universal bishop, he has direct, lawful, supreme, full, and universal power of jurisdiction over the whole church and all individual churches (dogmatic constitution *Pastor aeternus* [1870], DH 3050-75; → Polity, Ecclesiastical).

The self-understanding and claim of the papacy, as well as the view of the surrounding spiritual and secular world, find expression in the many titles and descriptions. From the fifth and sixth centuries onward, the pope called himself the vicar of Peter. But then Eugene III (1145-53) raised this title to "vicar of Christ," and Innocent IV (1243-54) to "vicar of God." Special → vestments and insignia single out the pope. The high secular estimation of the papacy may be seen from the treating of papal → nuncios as doyens of the diplomatic corps (after 1815).

1.1.3. The papal term begins with election (see 1.7) and ends with death. In the → Middle Ages (§1) popes were often deposed. Celestine V (1294) possibly resigned of his own free will. John II (533-35) and John XII (955-64) were the first to change their names. From the time of Sergius IV (1009-12) this name-changing became the custom; Hadrian VI (1522-23) and Marcellus II (1555) were two 16th-century exceptions. The reasons for the choice of the papal name were often programmatic, as in the case of Sylvester II (999-1003), who sought favorable relations with the emperor such as Sylvester I (314-35) had experienced. Popes have usually adopted a motto (e.g., John Paul II: *totus tuus,* "totally yours" [i.e., the Virgin's]).

1.1.4. In support of the special position of the pope, the → Roman Catholic Church has appealed since the third century especially to Matt. 16:18-19, Luke 22:32, and John 21:15-23.

1.2. *Roman Empire*

1.2.1. The first pope was supposedly the → apostle → Peter, crucified at Rome in the persecution under Nero (64/67). His grave has been located under St. Peter's (→ Rome 3) but also on the Appian Way. The oldest sources are late and unclear, so that no final clarification is likely. It is probable enough that Peter did stay in Rome and die there.

Little is known of the Roman bishops of the first three centuries apart from their names (→ Roman Empire). The first sure fact is the transition from Calixtus I (217-22) to Urban I (222-30) in 222. The first precise date is that of the abdication of Pontian (230-35) on September 28, 235.

In its early days the Roman church did not have a monarchical bishop. Its awareness of being the church in the capital city of Rome, of its links to Peter and → Paul, of its → martyrs, and of its size and generosity came to expression in the first conflict about → Easter (§4), in which in about the year 190 Victor I (189-98) excommunicated the Quartodecimans (→ Heresies and Schisms). Rome first claimed primacy in practical questions rather than theological controversies. In the conflict with Carthage over → heretical baptism, Stephen I (254-57) demanded submission to the Roman custom; in so doing, he made the first appeal to the primacy of Peter (DH 111).

1.2.2. → Leo I (440-61) emphatically pressed home the claim earlier made by Siricius (384-99) and Innocent I (402-17) involving Roman primacy, universal jurisdiction, and Rome's position as guardian of the true faith. He saw in Peter and Paul the new and true patrons of Rome (instead of Romulus and Remus) and viewed the pope as Peter's vicar.

Gelasius I (492-96) distinguished between spiritual and secular power and placed the former above the latter (DH 347) — a key development for the West. Gradually the idea emerged that no one can judge the pope.

Gregory the Great (590-604), one of the original four Latin "doctors of the church," called himself "servant of the servants of God" in answer to the title "ecumenical patriarch" advanced at Constantinople. By means of his pastoral works, Gregory passed on the older theology, including the theology of → Augustine (354-430; → Augustine's Theology). The Middle Ages saw in him a model pope.

After Gregory the papacy took up charitable and administrative work in Roman Italy with new vigor. With his Anglo-Saxon mission (starting in 597; → Germanic Mission), the papacy moved into the Germanic world with considerable success. But even after Gregory's death Rome still depended on → Byzantium dogmatically and legally, though it was still viewed verbally as head of all the churches (607). Things changed only as the Arabs began to bring pressure on Constantinople.

1.2.3. The papal claim to doctrinal and jurisdictional primacy on the basis of exegetical and, increasingly, legal arguments was made in an empire in which emperors also claimed → authority in religious issues (esp. the Byzantine ruler Justinian I [527-65]) and could again and again force their will on popes, as in disputes with the other patriarchates (Jerusalem, Antioch, Alexandria), bishoprics (Carthage, Arles, etc.), and → synods. Rivalry with Constantinople as the New Rome (the imperial center after 330) was a basic fact in earlier papal history. Translation of the Bible (→ Bible Versions), formularies, and official histories helped to build up tradition and create unity.

In theological controversies Rome and its bishops were inferior in numbers and competence to Eastern theologians (→ Alexandrian Theology; Antiochian Theology; Early Church). In Christological disputes (→ Christology 2.2), which lasted well after the Council of → Chalcedon (451), Rome maintained the doctrine of the two natures. Then came the conflict about → images, which deepened alienation from Byzantium. Though claiming to be the final appeals court, Rome still had no central function in the church of the West. It could rely on the church in England, however, and its veneration of Peter as the heavenly gatekeeper (as decreed by the Synod of Whitby in 664).

1.3. *Middle Ages*

1.3.1. In papal history the boundary between antiquity and the Middle Ages is usually seen in the turning from Byzantium to the Franks (→ Germanic Mission 3). This switch was indeed an epochal turning point in European history (T. Schieffer). The work of Boniface (ca. 675-754) prepared the way by founding a church among the Franks linked to Rome. Around 700 there were four main powers: the papacy, Byzantium, the Lombards, and the Franks.

Pepin, mayor of the palace (741-68), was elected and anointed king of the Franks in 751 with the cooperation of Pope Zacharias (741-52), thus initiating the idea of a Christian king in the West. Then the spiritual alliance between Pepin and Stephen II (752-57), as well as the territorial promises of Pepin (the so-called Donation of Pepin), laid the foundations of the later → Papal States. In this connection the idea arose of the → Donation of Constantine as reported in the Pseudo-Isidorian Decretals (→ False Decretals). This donation gave the popes an imperial position in the West.

Charlemagne (768-814), the son of Pepin, held

the title *patricius Romanorum* (patrician of the Romans). Leo III (795-816) cemented the alliance with the Franks by crowning Charlemagne emperor on Christmas day 800. This act put the alliance between → empire and papacy on a new basis. Throughout the Middle Ages, however, the relation between the two was contested, with papal freedom constantly challenged by imperial policies.

1.3.2. The Pseudo-Isidorian Decretals enhanced the papal primacy, and Nicholas I (858-67) claimed supreme and direct authority for himself. But with this claim went the erosion of the church's episcopal and synodical structures. The decline of the Carolingians strengthened the popes only in appearance. Yet the idea gained ground that the popes could confer imperial dignity.

In the "dark century" of papal history, the popes held tenure only briefly and were dependent on the noble families of Rome and Italy. By setting up new archbishoprics (e.g., Magdeburg in 968, Gnesen in 1000, Gran in 1001) and dioceses (e.g., Bamberg in 1007), they gave new force to church organization in the mission fields of the East. The popes also claimed the right to elevate to sainthood with the canonizing of Ulrich of Augsburg in 993, and exclusively so from the time of Alexander III (1159-81). → Exemption of monasteries (→ Cluny etc.) forged stronger links with → monasticism.

Revival of the empire in 962 by Otto the Great (936-73) made the papacy dependent on Germany. As the spiritual and secular heads, pope and emperor were related to one another, and the Holy Roman Empire would be German until its final collapse. Under Emperor Otto III (983-1002) came the first German popes, Gregory V (996-99) and Sylvester II (999-1003). In 1046 at the synods of Sutri and Rome, Henry III (1039-56) had three rival popes deposed.

1.3.3. Under Leo IX (1048-54) reforming forces began work in Rome, a leader being Hildebrand, later Gregory VII. Canon law was collected (→ Corpus Iuris Canonici). Under the lead of canonists, especially Humbert of Silva Candida (d. 1061; → Canon Law 2), who championed enhanced primacy for Rome, the Roman church became the quintessence of the whole church, and the pope the center of ecclesiology. Borrowing from secular government, the papacy named the new administrative apparatus the *curia* from the early 12th century onward. It saw problems in → simony and the marriage of clergy and fought them.

In 1059 an election decree was passed that gave only cardinal bishops the right to vote (only → cardinals after 1179). After 1378 only a cardinal could be elected pope. The claim to primacy resulted in a breach with the East in 1054. The → Councils of Lyons (1274) and Florence (1439) attempted reconciliation but, with their strong emphasis on papal primacy (DH 861, 1307), could not succeed.

1.3.4. In the Investiture Controversy, which involved the personalities of Gregory VII and Emperor Henry IV (1056-1106) and the humiliation of Henry at Canossa in 1077, the pope advanced a fresh understanding of the Gelasian concept of two powers (see 1.2.2), making a hierocratic claim and demanding the freedom and supremacy of the church within the *corpus Christianum.* This claim damaged the sacral character of kingship. The Concordat of Worms in 1122 between Callistus II (1119-24) and Henry V (1106-25) ended the Investiture Controversy with a compromise separating temporalities and spiritualities.

Urban II (1088-99) initiated the → Crusades. His grant of plenary → indulgences made participation attractive as a religious enterprise. → Bernard of Clairvaux (1090-1153) wrote a work for Eugenius III summarizing papal qualities (*De consideratione* 5).

1.3.5. The age from → Innocent III (1198-1216) to Boniface VIII (1294-1303) was "the century of the papacy." Innocent reigned as vicar of Jesus Christ, successor of Peter, anointed of the Lord *(Christus Domini),* God of Pharaoh, and mediator between God and humanity (*PL* 217.658). He claimed to rule over both church and world. Like no other, he was able in almost every sphere to carry to success his grandiose and brilliant plans and conceptions. Lateran IV (1215; → Councils 3) demonstrated papal power and central church authority. It was a milestone on the way to giving Rome a full legal system. The process continued as Innocent's successors codified and promulgated new legal collections. Under Innocent the claim and reality of the papacy came uniquely to light.

At the same time a change came with his rule. The weakening of the empire and a vicious campaign against the imperial house entailed a new dependence on France. Unlike his successful forerunner Innocent, Boniface VIII could not make good his new and enhanced claim in the → bull *Unam sanctam* (1302, DH 870-75) — a claim that found expression in the insignia (statues and the papal tiara) and in the thesis that submission to the Roman pontiff is necessary for salvation, a formula adopted by → Thomas Aquinas (ca. 1225-74; → Thomism). A → holy year was proclaimed for the first time in 1300, with much success.

After the fall of Boniface secular rulers renewed the struggle for emancipation from Rome. Both nations and territorial churches took the place of the empire in opposing central authority.

1.3.6. The papacy suffered loss of both political and religious power with the exile in Avignon (1309-77), though the Spanish cardinal Gil Albornoz (d. 1367) was able to preserve the Papal States for the church.

In Avignon the pope was an absentee ruler living and ruling only in the papal palace. Dependence on France, dismantling of the curia and papal organization, increase in nepotism, enhancing of papal ceremonial (e.g., a new chapel for papal palace worship), and greater financial needs that oppressed the church led to growing alienation between the popes and many secular rulers, especially in Germany. With Louis IV the Bavarian (d. 1347) came the last great conflict between the empire and the papacy along with radical criticism of the papacy (Marsilius of Padua, William of Ockham, J. → Wycliffe, and later J. → Hus).

1.3.7. The Great Schism (1378-1417) promoted → conciliarism, which offered an escape from papal weakness. The Council of Constance (1414-18) overcame the schism (→ Heresies and Schisms 3) by deposing Gregory XII in Rome, Benedict XIII in Avignon, and John XXIII in Pisa and then appointing Martin V (1417-31). A conflict between papacy and councils ensued (→ Reform Councils) until the papacy regained its supremacy. The → Renaissance papacy promoted the arts and culture but neglected spiritual duties and responsibilities.

Julius II (1503-13) and Leo X (1513-21) were popes on the eve of the → Reformation. Lateran V (1512-17) condemned conciliarism and gave the papacy new authority and political security. Despite this outward success one may rightly regard the irregular situation of the papacy and curia as one of the presuppositions of the Reformation.

1.4. ***Reformation***

1.4.1. The Reformation contested the theological legitimacy of the papacy and put an end to its universal claim, which no longer applied in the East in any case. M. → Luther (1483-1546; → Luther's Theology) used his theological knowledge and pastoral sense, along with historical arguments, to refute the claim that the papacy held its position by divine right (see esp. *On the Papacy in Rome* [1520, *LW* 39.49-104]). He scoffed at any idea that the papacy is necessary to salvation and also criticized the admixing of spiritual and secular rule (→ Two Kingdoms Doctrine). After some hesitation he called the papacy the → antichrist and thus viewed himself as under command to attack it, which he did in many sharp works (e.g., the Schmalkaldic Articles [1537] and "Against the Roman Papacy, an Institution of the Devil" [1545, *LW* 41.257-376]). With his understanding of faith and the church, he was forced to contest the papal claim.

The Reformed (U. → Zwingli, J. → Calvin, J. → Knox, etc.), the Radicals (K. Grebel, → Menno Simons, etc.), and Henry VIII and the Anglican reformers (T. → Cranmer, N. Ridley, J. Hooper, M. Parker, etc.) shared Luther's opposition and threw off papal headship.

1.4.2. The reform of the Roman Catholic Church planned by Hadrian VI (1522-23) could be begun only by Paul III (1534-49; → Catholic Reform and Counterreformation 2.2). It took place in debate with the Reformation. At the Council of → Trent (1545-63), → Catholicism became the Roman Catholic confessional church. Stress fell on papal primacy, and centralism was enhanced, exemplified by the confirmation of the council's validity by the pope and the pledging of the clergy to the Tridentine Confession (DH 1862-70). Canon law and → liturgy were made uniform, the curia was tightened, and standing nuncios were appointed. The → Jesuits were now at the pope's disposal as an obedient counterreforming tool.

The idea of territorial church government, which was present from the early days of the Reformation and had its basis in the concept of state sovereignty, found expression in the Peace of Augsburg (1555) and the Peace of Westphalia (1648; → Augsburg, Peace of; Thirty Years' War), which were reverses for the papal claim. Even in Roman Catholic lands efforts were now made to check papal influence.

The papacy made its power felt in world mission with the constitution of the Congregation of Propaganda in 1622 (renamed the Congregation for the Evangelization of Peoples in 1988). From the middle of the 17th century, the popes focused their activity on the Papal States.

1.5. ***Modern Period***

1.5.1. → Gallicanism in France, Febronianism in the empire, and → Josephinism in Austria severely limited papal power. Among many less forceful popes Innocent XI (1676-89), who fought Louis XIV of France, and the learned Benedict XIV (1740-58) were exceptions. The → Enlightenment fostered antipapal thinking. Clement XIV (1769-74) had to suppress the Jesuits in 1773. Papal elections left the popes dependent on foreign powers.

1.5.2. The French → Revolution and its aftermath put the papacy in a new situation and deeply humiliated it. The Papal States were overrun and dissolved. Napoléon (1804-15) tried to subjugate the popes.

In Germany, however, → Romanticism brought new sympathy for the papacy. Antirevolutionary and authoritarian views of the papacy became widespread with the *Il trionfo della Santa Sede* (The triumph of the Holy See, 1799) of Bartolomeo Cappellari (= Gregory XVI [1831-46]), which discussed the sovereignty and → infallibility of the pope, and J. de Maistre's *Du Pape* (1819), which argued for the critical role in society of papal spiritual authority.

1.5.3. The long reign of → Pius IX (1846-78) saw inner consolidation and outer isolation. Pius concluded → concordats with many countries. The Papal States were diminished and finally abolished with the unification of Italy, Rome being captured on September 20, 1870. From the days of Lorenzo Valla (1407-57) the vision had always been present of a papacy focusing on its spiritual tasks and free from secular powers and responsibilities.

In 1854 Pius promulgated the dogma of the immaculate conception of Mary, that is, her complete freedom from original sin (DH 2800-2804; → Mariology 1.3.3; Mary, Devotion to). This act involved a new conception of the pope's teaching authority. In 1864 Pius issued his Syllabus, aimed against → pantheism, naturalism, → rationalism, and → socialism (DH 2901-80). After 1864 Pius prepared for an ecumenical council, the first since Trent. It convened on December 8, 1869. Its business was to give an authentic exposition of Trent and to define the nature of the church and the papacy.

Vatican I (1869-70) was important mainly because it promulgated papal infallibility and the definition of the universal episcopate of the pope. In a complex situation the church here tied its own hands in a way that many people of the day, including clergy and scholars, especially in the German-speaking world (e.g., I. von Döllinger [1799-1890]), regarded as fateful. In the end, however, all the bishops assented. It may well be right to see in this dogma no more than a fulfillment of what had been implied from the days of Leo the Great.

1.5.4. Leo XIII (1878-1903) was the most important pope between Benedict XIV (1740-58) and Pius XI (1922-39). He vigorously addressed intellectual and spiritual tasks. He ended the → Kulturkampf with Prussia. By opening the papal archives and giving access to the papal registers, he initiated a new era of research into papal history. With the → social encyclical *Rerum novarum* (DH 3265-71), he took up for the first time, though late and unsuccessfully, the acute question of labor.

Pius X (1903-14) pursued inner renewal (canon law reform and eucharistic adoration). But with his → Anti-Modernist Oath he showed how hard it was for his church to adjust to the realities of a secularized world (→ Secularism; Secularization). Legal separation of → church and state came in France in 1905 and Portugal in 1911, notwithstanding papal opposition in → encyclicals.

Benedict XV (1914-22) published the Codex Iuris Canonici (1917). His peace efforts in World War I did not succeed, but they did enhance the moral authority of the papacy.

Under Pius XI the Lateran Treaties (1929) with B. Mussolini solved the question of Rome, which had been up in the air since 1870; a small Vatican state was established. With his cardinal secretary and successor Eugenio Pacelli (1876-1958, → Pius XII from 1939), he concluded many concordats, some of which are still in force. Hotly contested was the concordat with A. Hitler in 1933. Did it secure the church's rights or sanction Hitler's Germany? National Socialism and Mussolini's → fascism presented a new challenge to the church. In 1950 Pius promulgated the dogma of the bodily assumption of Mary (→ Mariology 1.3.4), the climax of his teaching activity and the first use of papal infallibility.

John XXIII (1958-63) had an impact far beyond the confines of his own church. In his brief reign he nourished hopes of renewal (in part unjustified) with his summoning of → Vatican II (1962-65). This council modified the strict papalism of Vatican I in favor of the other bishops. John ended the limitation of the number of cardinals (imposed by Sixtus V) to 70 (modeled on Israel's elders, Exod. 24:1 etc.) and appointed more than 50 new cardinals. Renewal and → ecumenism were to be the signs of a new epoch.

John's successor, Paul VI (1963-78), closed the council. He wanted to leave room for new impulses but not to lose adherence to the church's tradition. He traveled widely, visiting the → United Nations and the → World Council of Churches. His encyclicals included *Populorum progressio* (1967, supporting involvement in the advocacy of human → rights) and *Humanae vitae* (1968, condemning abortion and artificial birth control). He recognized that his office, supposedly a sign of unity, was the greatest obstacle to it.

John Paul I (1978) reigned only 33 days; there was much speculation about his death.

In 1978, for the first time in 600 years (apart from the short pontificate of Hadrian VI [1522-23]), a non-Italian became pope, the Pole Karol Wojtyła (John Paul II). The new pope proved to be conservative and authoritarian, restoring preconciliar relations and restricting the freedom of liberation and university theologians (→ Conservatism 2; Liberation Theology). He traveled even more widely than his predecessor. In his encyclical *Centesimus annus* (1991) he revised *Rerum novarum*. He also set in train the formulating of a uniform Roman Catholic catechism, which Vatican I had been unable to produce.

→ Modern Church History 1; Theology in the Nineteenth and Twentieth Centuries

Bibliography: Reference works and general history: F. J. Coppa, *Encyclopedia of the Vatican and Papacy* (Westport, Conn., 1999) • E. Duffy, *Saints and Sinners: A History of the Popes* (New Haven, 2002) • H. Fuhrmann, *Von Petrus zu Johannes Paul II: Das Papsttum. Gestalt und Gestalten* (2d ed.; Munich, 1984) • M. Greschat, ed., *Das Papsttum* (2 vols.; Stuttgart, 1981) • J. Haller, *Das Papsttum. Idee und Wirklichkeit* (5 vols.; Basel, 1951-53) • J. N. D. Kelly, *The Oxford Dictionary of Popes* (Oxford, 1986) • G. Krüger, *The Papacy: The Idea and Its Exponents* (London, 1909) • H. Küng, *The Catholic Church: A Short History* (New York, 2003) • W. J. La Due, *The Chair of St. Peter: A History of the Papacy* (Maryknoll, N.Y., 1999) • P. Levillain, gen. ed., *The Papacy: An Encyclopedia* (3 vols.; New York, 2002) • L. von Pastor, *The History of the Popes, from the Close of the Middle Ages: Drawn from the Secret Archives of the Vatican and Other Original Sources* (40 vols.; London, 1891-1952; orig. pub., Freiburg, 1886-1933) • B. Schimmelpfennig, *The Papacy* (New York, 1992).

Early and medieval papacy: G. Barraclough, *The Medieval Papacy* (London, 1968) • *Book of Pontiffs (Liber Pontificalis)* (ed. R. Davis; Liverpool, 1989) • M. Borgolte, *Petrusnachfolge und Kaiserimitation. Die Grablegen der Päpste, ihre Genese und Traditionsbildung* (Göttingen, 1989) • E. Caspar, *Geschichte des Papsttums von den Anfängen bis zur Höhe der Weltherrschaft* (2 vols.; Tübingen, 1930-33); idem, *Das Papsttumn unter fränkischer Herrschaft* (Darmstadt, 1956) • F. Dvornik, *Byzantium and the Roman Primacy* (New York, 1976) • K. A. Fink, *Papsttum und Kirche im abendländischen Mittelalter* (Munich, 1981) • T. Frenz, *Papsturkunden des Mittelalters und der Neuzeit* (Stuttgart, 1986) • F. Gregorovius, *History of the City of Rome in the Middle Ages* (2 vols.; New York, 2000-2001; orig. pub., 1859-72) • G. B. Ladner, *Die Papstbildnisse des Altertums und des Mittelalters* (5 vols. in 3; Vatican City, 1941-84) • G. Tellenbach, *The Church in Western Europe from the Tenth to the Early Twelfth Century* (Cambridge, 1993); idem, *Church, State, and Christian Society at the Time of the Investiture Contest* (Oxford, 1959) • B. Tierney, *Origins of Papal Infallibility, 1150-1350* (Leiden, 1972) • W. Ullmann, *The Growth of Papal Government in the Middle Ages: A Study in the Ideological Relation of Clerical to Lay Power* (2d ed.; London, 1962); idem, *A Short History of the Papacy in the Middle Ages* (London, 2003) • H. Zimmermann, *Das Papsttum im Mittelalter* (Stuttgart, 1981).

Early modern and modern papacy: K. O. von Aretin, *The Papacy and the Modern World* (London, 1970) • E. Bizer, *Luther und der Papst* (Munich, 1958) • F. J. Coppa, *The Modern Papacy since 1789* (London, 1998) • S. H. Hendrix, *Luther and the Papacy: Stages in a Reformation Conflict* (Philadelphia, 1981) • F. Heyer, *The Catholic Church from 1648 to 1870* (London, 1969) • G. Maron, *Die römisch-katholische Kirche von 1870 bis 1970* (Göttingen, 1972) • G. Schwaiger, *Geschichte der Päpste im 20. Jahrhundert* (Munich, 1968); idem, *Papsttum und Päpste im 20. Jahrhundert. Von Leo XIII zu Johannes Paul II* (Munich, 1999) • A. D. Wright, *The Early Modern Papacy: From the Council of Trent to the French Revolution, 1564-1789* (New York, 2000).

Other works: Y. Congar, "Titel, welche für den Papst verwendet werden," *Conc(D)* 11 (1975) 538-44 • K. A. Fink, *Das vatikanische Archiv* (2d ed.; Rome, 1951) • B.-U. Hergemöller, *Die Geschichte der Papstnamen* (Münster, 1980) • R. Pesch, *Simon-Petrus. Geschichte und geschichtliche Bedeutung des ersten Jüngers Jesu Christi* (Stuttgart, 1980) • T. J. Reese, *Inside the Vatican: The Politics and Organization of the Catholic Church* (Cambridge, Mass., 1996).

Johannes Schilling

1.6. *Papalism*

The term "papalism" is mostly used in polemical contrast to → "episcopacy" or → "conciliarism." It denotes a principle of → church government that opponents say is too heavily weighted in favor of papal primacy.

The struggle for papal primacy both as a theological and canonical postulate and also as a maxim of papal church leadership even in secular affairs was an essential feature of church history in the West from the early Middle Ages onward (Nicholas I [858-67]). → Gregory VII (1073-85) made the claim that only the bishop of Rome may lawfully be called universal, that no one may dispute this claim, and that the → Roman Catholic Church has never erred nor will ever do so to all eternity (*Dictatus papae* [1075]; → Empire and Papacy).

At the height of papal power both politically and ecclesiastically, Boniface VIII (1294-1303) formulated as quasi dogma in *Unam sanctam* (1302) the postulate that subjection to the bishop of Rome is necessary for salvation (DH 875). In his tractate *De ecclesia sive summi pontificis potestate* (On the church and the supreme power of the pontiff), which underlay the bull, the canonist Giles of Rome (d. 1316) equated the church and the papacy, referring to "the pope, who can also be called the church" (§13). The Roman church had become the Roman curia, as Gerhoh of Reichersberg (d. 1169) had previously noted in criticism.

Against the efforts of the 15th-century → reform councils, which tried to use the collapse of the papacy and the church to enhance their own authority, John of Turrecremata (1388-1468) took a strong papalist line by finding in the pope the epitome of the supreme power of the church, which sums up within itself every lesser authority (*Summa de ecclesia* [1449], 2.83). Nonetheless, the bull *Pastor aeternus* (1516, DH 1445) of Leo X (1513-21) still failed to clarify the issue. The → Reformation added a fresh dimension to the problem. Only diplomacy could prevent a crisis following the Council of → Trent.

→ State churches (→ Gallicanism) tried to halt papal centralism, and new opposition arose at the theoretical level as well (from J. N. von Hontheim, the founder of Febronianism). The French → Revolution resulted in the deep humiliation of the papacy. Only the ensuing → restoration changed things.

Under the new conditions of the 19th century (→ Modern Church History 1), new thinking on the moral and spiritual authority of the pope and his jurisdictional supremacy and → infallibility (→ Ultramontanism) led to the development of an ecclesiological system that issued logically in the decrees of → Vatican I (1869-70) giving the pope "full and supreme power of jurisdiction over the whole church" (DH 3064) and stating that his official pronouncements on matters of faith and morals possess "infallibility." These pronouncements "are of themselves, and not by the consent of the church, irreformable" (DH 3074). Even though ultimate exaggeration was avoided, papalism finally achieved here a triumph that Vatican II could only in a very limited way reverse.

As far as what are essentially new initiatives toward a communio-ecclesiology are concerned, subsequent documents (e.g., the 1983 → CIC) and declarations of the teaching office concerning the relationship between the pope and bishops and particular churches expressly emphasize the unity of the episcopate *cum Petro et sub Petro* (with Peter and under Peter). On this view, the primacy of the bishop of Rome represents an essential element necessarily inhering within every particular church and determining its existence as a church (Congregation for the Doctrine of the Faith, *Communionis notio* 13). Similarly, the surprising offer of dialogue from John Paul II (1978-2005) in his → encyclical *Ut unum sint* (1995) concerning the form of implementation of this notion of primacy immediately ties such dialogue to the framework of traditional doctrinal development as the precondition commensurate with, and thus essential to, the will of Christ.

Bibliography: A. J. Black, *Monarchy and Community: Political Ideas in the Later Conciliar Controversy, 1430-1450* (Cambridge, 1970) • J. H. Burns and T. M. Izbicki, eds., *Conciliarism and Papalism* (Cambridge, 1997) • Congregation for the Doctrine of the Faith, *On Some Aspects of the Church Understood as Communion* (Vatican City, 1992) • C. M. D. Crowder, ed., *Unity, Heresy, and Reform, 1378-1460: The Conciliar Response to the Great Schism* (London, 1977) • H. Fries, "Wandel des Kirchenbilds und dogmengeschichtliche Entfaltung," *MySal* 4/1.223-85, esp. 240-72 • B. Tierney, *Foundations of the Conciliar Theory: The Contribution of the Medieval Canonists from Gratian to the Great Schism* (exp. ed.; Leiden, 1998).

Hubert Kirchner

1.7. *Papal Election*

→ Canon law governs the way in which the supreme jurisdictional officer in the → Roman Catholic Church is elected.

1.7.1. The election of the pope developed historically out of that of the bishop of → Rome. In the first century this bishop, like others, was chosen by the city clergy and neighboring bishops, with the participation of the people.

In his decree *In nomine Dei* (1059), Nicholas II (1059-61) laid down that only cardinal bishops had the right to elect. The decree *Licet de vitanda* (1179) of Alexander III (1159-81) made the whole college of → cardinals the electing body. Later decrees regulating the process (e.g., a two-thirds majority, election in conclave) all rest on Alexander's decision. In this context, the right of the college of cardinals to elect the pope has never been questioned. A consideration of its origins — that is, of the municipal Roman clergy who were actually entitled to vote (from titular churches and diaconates of the individual cardinals in Rome), as well as of the responsible neighboring bishops (titular bishoprics) — makes it clear why such questioning has never occurred.

In the 20th century papal legislation modified the process, including the apostolic → constitutions

Commissum nobis of Pius X (1903-14) in January 1904, *Vacantis Apostolicae Sedis* of → Pius XII (1939-58) in December 1945, and *Romano pontifici eligendo* of Paul VI (1963-78) in October 1975. Thus far, even for ecumenical reasons, expected changes (e.g., letting bishops' synods or the presidents of bishops' conferences take part) have not materialized.

1.7.2. According to 1983 → CIC 349, Roman Catholic cardinals "constitute a special College, whose prerogative it is to elect the Roman Pontiff in accordance with the norms of a special law." The 1917 CIC spoke only of the election (can. 219), but 1983 CIC 332.1 states that the pope acquires "full and supreme power in the Church when, together with episcopal consecration, he has been lawfully elected and has accepted the election." It is clearly implied that election does not mediate the papal office but simply creates the presupposition for its transfer.

The legal basis of papal election is the apostolic constitution "The Election of the Roman Pontiff" (1975) of Paul VI. Only cardinals not over 80 years of age may actively elect. All Christians may do so passively, irrespective of age, so long as they are not excluded by divine or church law. The election takes place "in conclave" (i.e., not publicly), at the latest 20 days after the pope's death. Two-thirds of the votes and one other (to counterbalance voting for oneself) are needed. After 13 unsuccessful ballots the cardinals may elect by an absolute majority plus one. If the one chosen is not a → bishop, the result is communicated to the people only after his consecration.

The latest contribution on this topic from the Vatican is the apostolic exhortation *Universi Dominici gregis*, "On the Vacancy of the Apostolic See and the Election of the Roman Pontiff" (1996) of John Paul II, which allows election by simple majority vote after a certain number of unsuccessful ballots and also addresses the need for heightened security against electronic surveillance.

Bibliography: F. J. Baumgartner, *Behind Locked Doors: A History of the Papal Elections* (New York, 2003) • F. A. Burkle-Young, *Papal Elections in the Age of Transition, 1878-1922* (Lanham, Md., 2000) • R. Metz, "Der Papst," *HKKR* 252-66 • W. M. Plöchl, "Papstwahl," *LTK* 8.60-63.

Heribert Heinemann

2. Systematic and Ecumenical Aspects

2.1. *Denominational Discussion*

The question of the papacy has now become an important one in ecumenical discussion (→ Oikoumene). Its place in doctrine differs considerably in the various → denominations. One approach, in view of growing agreement in controversial matters (→ Polemics), is to try to soften the sharpness of dissension on the point. Another approach is to see here a basic division that unmistakably shows how different the churches are from one another. Only a clarifying of the related issues can show how right either side is.

2.1.1. *Protestant and Roman Catholic Positions*

We must first ask whether the → institution of the papacy can be traced back to NT statements. This question is primarily a matter for NT → exegesis, but we must not underestimate the canonical and doctrinal implications.

Consensus exists that the papacy as → Vatican I and Vatican II defined it cannot possibly be said to derive directly from the NT. Said another way, the attempt to project back the developed papacy into the NT is doomed in advance to failure. But this fact, accepted by both Roman Catholic and Protestant scholars, can be judged in various ways as they leave the more solid ground of historical criticism and move on to theological evaluation, which unavoidably displays the confessional standpoint of each author. One side sees in the discrepancy the expression of a material difference between NT ideas of → ministry and the Roman view of the papacy, so that from the → Peter of the NT to the Peter of the Eternal City there is no path, but a qualitative leap must be made (E. Grässer). The other side integrates both into the dynamic of a historical development that produces new things in all denominations but without our having to see these new things as contradicting the common origin.

A possible middle position for Protestants might be that the NT does not a priori rule out the pope as the head of a united church so long as Roman Catholics for their part pledge themselves to testing and, if necessary, correcting the life and practice of the popes in light of what the NT has to say. Along such lines we may view the many statements by Roman Catholics dismissing the papacy as a historical phenomenon and replacing it by a Petrine ministry designed to play a leading role in achieving church → unity.

We must note, however, that thus far such suggestions have evoked no positive response from the historical papacy. On the contrary, efforts by the → Vatican to discipline Roman Catholic theologians threaten to make irrelevant efforts such as these to find an ecumenical basis for the papacy.

2.1.2. *Ecumenical Discussion*

Closely linked to the question of a NT basis is the question whether the papacy exists by divine right or only by human right. Roman Catholic → theology, appealing to Matt. 16:17-19, Luke 22:31-32, and John 21:15-23, opts for the first answer, Protestants at best only for the second. On this issue the → Reformers did not agree. M. → Luther (1483-1546; → Luther's Theology) in Schmalkaldic Articles 4 argued that the holy Christian church would do better without such a head. He saw no need for the office and demanded that the church remain without it. This thesis is more important than his historically conditioned equation of the pope with antichrist, with which Protestants would no longer agree. P. → Melanchthon (1497-1560) made a personal addition to the above confession (→ Confessions and Creeds 2) in which he could recognize the pope's supremacy over other bishops "by human right" (*Book of Concord,* 326). His *Treatise on the Power and Primacy of the Pope* (1537) sought to clarify this view.

The obvious disagreement is reflected in modern Protestant theology. Prominent German and Anglo-Saxon voices regard an office of leadership in the church as a whole as desirable, but others view the papacy as simply the climax of an alien confessional development and can only reject it.

Progress can be made in ecumenical discussion only when we overcome the basic alternatives of divine and human right. Many discussions between Roman Catholics and Protestants (→ Ecumenical Dialogue) have made this point clear and tried to forge ahead.

The so-called Malta Report (1972) of the Joint Lutheran–Roman Catholic Study Commission refers to the greater insight into the historicity of the church (→ Historiography), which, along with "a new understanding of its eschatological nature," must result in a rethinking of the concepts. No adequate distinction has yet been made between divine right and human right. We have divine right only in historically mediated forms. These forms not only are "the product of a sociological process of growth but, because of the pneumatic nature of the church, they can be experienced also as fruit of the spirit" (§31). It is difficult, however, to apply this basic insight concretely, for example, in assessing the papacy. If in §67 we read that a controverted issue between Roman Catholics and Lutherans is "whether the primacy of the pope is necessary for the church, or whether it represents only a fundamentally possible function," the alternatives have simply reappeared in another form.

The same applies to the document *Papal Primacy and the Universal Church,* which records Roman Catholic–Lutheran conversations in the United States in March 1974. This study also acknowledges that "the traditional sharp distinctions between divine and human institution are no longer useful." Yet the differences remain. Roman Catholics still insist that the papacy "is an institution in accordance with God's will." For Lutherans, however, "this is a secondary question" (§30). But Lutherans would no longer say that the papacy contradicts God's will as → sin or → evil does.

If appeal is made to the distinction made in the doctrine of election (→ Predestination) between God's antecedent and consequent will, one might say that given the plurality of denominations, the papacy is in keeping with the consequent will in the sense that God wills it for one denomination (i.e., the Roman Catholic). But one may not postulate or claim that it is anchored in the antecedent will, which would be true only if the papacy in its historical operation credibly represented the unity of all Christians.

2.1.3. *Perspectives*

If we evaluate the concept of God's will more carefully than has been done thus far, a way to overcome the unfruitful alternatives opens up. Roman Catholic theology should not only give up trying to offer a plain biblical basis for the papacy, since its own representatives admit that it cannot be done, but also give up attempting to forge an artificial link between the present papacy and biblical origins, a link that has no plausibility for other communions. An inquiry that ignores such exegetical and historical considerations need not limit itself to the possibility of a pragmatic basis for the supreme ministry of unity (H. Fries). Protestant arguments for such a ministry are always also theological arguments. They are theological inasmuch as → Reformation churches leave much more room for free judgment in the differentiating of church offices than does the Roman Catholic Church, whose fixed → hierarchy makes for much less flexibility, and whose premise does not enable it to strive after such flexibility.

On these presuppositions the arguments of some Protestant theologians for a supreme office of unity merit serious consideration. Two ideas in particular should be noted. First, the fact that humanity always feels itself to be one makes it necessary that there should be one representative voice for Christians. Along these lines the office of unity would have the task of expressing Christian → consensus in, for example, the ethical sphere (→ Ethics). We do not have in view empty formulas that command unanimous assent by saying nothing. At the same time, the evoking of dissent does not always mean that ethical directions are right, as we see from the many pronouncements on, for example, → sexual ethics

(→ Social Encyclicals). Second, the universal interrelation of churches can be shown most convincingly in a supreme ministry of unity. Such an interrelation could have prevented → Protestantism from making fatal alliances with national → states (→ Nation, Nationalism). Viewed in this way, an ecumenical papacy might serve the cause of the liberty of the church (J. Moltmann).

2.2. ***Supreme Office of Unity***

How far this kind of supreme office of unity can be linked to the present form of the papacy is a difficult question. It can be answered only as inquiry is made into established Roman Catholic definitions of the papacy.

2.2.1. *Jurisdictional Primacy*

First, we have what Vatican I said about primacy of → jurisdiction, that is, the granting to the papacy of full power over the whole church, not merely in doctrine and morals but also in discipline (DH 3059-64). Vatican II changed the ecclesiological emphasis but still upheld this principle in the *Nota praevia* (Preliminary note of explanation) to *Lumen gentium*, and even sharpened it, saying that "as Supreme Pastor of the Church, the Supreme Pontiff can always exercise his power at will, as his very office demands" (§4).

Internal Roman Catholic debate brings the problem into focus. K. → Rahner (1904-84) tried to show that not all church law is papal or episcopal. Beginning with valid church law such as that of papal elections, he postulated an essential church law that precedes all positive statutes. Roman Catholics should perhaps take more heed of his approach than they have done.

Non–Roman Catholics naturally find it impossible to accept jurisdictional primacy in its present form. P. C. Empie and T. A. Murphy's work *Papal Primacy and the Universal Church* makes it plain that the papacy must be renewed in the light of the principles of "legitimate diversity," "collegiality," and "subsidiarity" if non-Catholics are to see in it the supreme ministry of unity (chap. 1, "Common Statement," §§23-25). The principles demand clarification, however, if they are to avoid the suspicion of being empty formulas (W. Klausnitzer). The proposal that there should be "voluntary limitations by the pope of the exercise of his jurisdiction" (§27) moves in the right direction, but it is not yet clear how far an office will emerge that in using its → power does not "subvert Christian → freedom" (§28).

2.2.2. *Infallibility*

The dogma of papal → infallibility promulgated by Vatican I creates special difficulties. It argues that when the pope makes an ex cathedra pronouncement, his decision is "infallible" (DH 3074). Here again we do best to begin with internal Roman Catholic debate. H. Küng has shown that universal linguistic and hermeneutical considerations make it impossible to postulate infallible statements (→ Language; Hermeneutics). His discussions have been disciplined (→ Teaching Office 1) but not refuted. In principle a thesis may be true or false, but if it is to mean anything, it must be capable of proof in some form. A claim to infallibility cannot be a meaningful statement. To say "finally authoritative" instead of "infallible" (H. Fries) may ease the problem but hardly solves it.

The previously mentioned commission of U.S. Roman Catholic and Lutheran Theologians (see 2.1.2) addressed this question and provided a position on it in the document *Teaching Authority and Infallibility in the Church* (1980). The actual term "infallibility" has not in fact been much discussed as the real problem. Lutherans have even looked for equivalents in their own tradition (chap. 1, "Lutheran Reflections," §9). They accept "a ministry which has the responsibility of reformulating doctrine in fidelity to the Scripture when circumstances require" (§19).

We may accept this idea along the lines of what has been said above. But we must be clear that any Christian at any time may oppose these reformulations within the one church, and that the term "infallibility" rules out such opposition from the outset. Protestants do assent to the indefectibility of the church, namely, that it will remain in the truth as stated in John 16:13 (chap. 1, "Common Statement," §28). We must emphasize, however, that no church institution can be the absolute guarantee of this indefectibility. If the members of an American group say that they find it hard to "pinpoint exactly where or how we differ from each other on the question of infallibility" ("Lutheran Reflections," §16), this conclusion simply reflects the good climate of discussion and not the actual situation so far as the denominations are concerned.

2.2.3. *Perspectives*

It should be clear by now how hard it is for the churches to achieve unity in view of the above factors. The greater, then, is the merit of H. Fries and K. Rahner in asking how unity might be possible on these premises. Their eight theses are a notable step forward because they do not ask non–Roman Catholic churches to agree to Roman dogmas but are satisfied with what they call a realistic principle of faith: "Nothing may be rejected decisively and confessionally in one partner church which is binding dogma in another partner church" (thesis 2). Unhappily, Lutherans have not always sufficiently grasped how big a step this is (e.g., E. Herms).

Whether their proposals can offer a "real possibility" of unification may be doubted. Just as the Roman Catholic Church cannot give up its dogmas, so Protestant theology cannot give up the right to criticize them (→ Dogma, History of). This right, as practiced especially in the 19th century, rests on Luther's presentation of the freedom of Christian faith. That freedom enabled him to look critically at the NT and implied in principle the possibility of criticizing any articulation of faith, even the "fundamental truths of Christianity" adduced in thesis 1.

This criticism must go hand in hand with the duty of also saying positively what Christian → faith means today. The unavoidably entailed pluralism does not have to be viewed as a chaos that is far from God. Rather, it is a mark of the inner life of the church, which as a whole will never defect from the truth (John 16:13).

→ Apostle, Apostolate; Conciliarity; Councils of the Church; Ecumenism, Ecumenical Movement

Bibliography: Book of Concord: The Confessions of the Evangelical Lutheran Church (ed. R. Kolb and T. J. Wengert; Minneapolis, 2000) • P. C. Empie and T. A. Murphy, eds., *Papal Primacy and the Universal Church* (Minneapolis, 1974) • P. C. Empie, T. A. Murphy, and J. A. Burgess, eds., *Teaching Authority and Infallibility in the Church* (Minneapolis, 1980) • H. Fries, "Das Papsttum als ökumenische Frage," *Glaube und Kirche als Angebot* (Graz, 1976) 280-314 • H. Fries and K. Rahner, *Unity of the Churches–an Actual Possibility* (Philadelphia, 1985) • A. Hasler, *How the Pope Became Infallible: Pius IX and the Politics of Persuasion* (Garden City, N.Y., 1981) • E. Herms, *Einheit der Christen in der Gemeinschaft der Kirchen. Die ökumenische Bewegung der römischen Kirche im Lichte der reformatorischen Theologie: Antwort auf den Rahner-Plan* (Göttingen, 1984) • W. Klausnitzer, *Das Papstamt im Disput zwischen Lutheranern und Katholiken. Schwerpunkte von der Reformation bis zur Gegenwart* (Innsbruck, 1987) • H. Kung, *Infallibility? An Unresolved Enquiry* (exp. ed.; New York, 1994; orig. pub., 1970) • R. McClory, *Power and the Papacy: The People and Politics behind the Doctrine of Infallibility* (Liguori, Mo., 1997) • Pontifical Council for Interreligious Dialogue, *Interreligious Dialogue: The Official Teaching of the Catholic Church (1963-1995)* (ed. F. Gioia; Boston, 1997) • Pontifical Council for Promoting Christian Unity, *Directory for the Application of Principles and Norms on Ecumenism* (Vatican City, 1993) • K. Rahner, *Vorfragen zu einem ökumenischen Amtsverständnis* (Freiburg, 1974) • K. Rahner, ed., *Zum Problem Unfehlbarkeit. Antworten auf die Anfragen von Hans Küng* (Freiburg, 1971) • K. Schatz, *Papal Primacy: From Its Origins to the Present* (Collegeville, Minn., 1996) • B. Tierney, *Rights, Laws, and Infallibility in Medieval Thought* (Aldershot, 1997).

Reinhard Leuze

Popular Catholicism

1. Pre–Vatican II
2. The Ordinary Person
3. Outward Forms, Inner Dimensions
4. Social History

Within the → Roman Catholic Church the → popular religion of ordinary believers concerns the practice of rites and → customs in the life cycle and festivals in the → church year.

1. Pre–Vatican II

Before → Vatican II the faithful typically attended Sunday → mass, did penance and took communion at Easter, observed daily, weekly, and annual times of → devotion and → piety, and participated in festivals, → pilgrimages, and other events. Catholic piety covered the whole of life and found expression biographically at → baptism, First Communion, → confirmation, → marriage, and burial (→ Funeral; Initiation Rites 2). Being a Roman Catholic meant not only subscribing to the official faith but also belonging to a religious and social milieu (→ Catholicism [Roman] 1.2.1; 3).

2. The Ordinary Person

A basic question is whether "the people" (Ger. *Volk*), likewise "popular Catholicism" or "Catholicism of the people" (Ger. *Volkskatholizismus*), is a mere construct or a historical reality. For all the reservations one might have against notions associated with the word *Volk* — reservations that are certainly understandable in the German-speaking sphere — one must follow the lead of French historians in maintaining the term "popular Catholicism." Many people in middle-class circles link exotic features to this concept. Popular Catholicism seems to be synonymous with religious folklore and antiquated traditions, with a kind of hodgepodge of → superstition, → magic, and degenerative religious phenomena.

But a more generous view may be adopted. This form of Roman Catholicism is that of average Roman Catholics. In the forefront are not doctrinal and intellectual forms but religious life and practice as engaged in by ordinary people. → Faith and everyday piety take a simple form. They are not based on the complex structures of theologians or persons of the clergy. Unofficial practice counts, not the official norm. Popular religion is identical with the piety of ordinary people.

3. Outward Forms, Inner Dimensions

External manifestations are central, that is, the forms of → worship, the → sacraments, the work of clergy, priestly fraternities, congregations (→ Religious Orders and Congregations), and societies (→ Societies and Associations, Ecclesiastical; Roman Catholic Church 5). The various festivals of the church claim a prominent place. So do pilgrimages, veneration of the → saints, → Mariology (→ Mary, Devotion to), family devotions, → prayers, and → benedictions (→ Roman Catholic Church 3).

The outward forms should not cause us to neglect the inner dimensions, including doctrine (→ Dogma), → ethics (→ Moral Theology), sexual Puritanism (→ Sexuality), belief in → demons, and apocalyptic fears (→ Anxiety). The fears carry with them a religiously influenced view of → politics (§3.2) that may include → anti-Semitism, opposition to → socialism, and a distrust of the → Masons.

4. Social History

The → social history of everyday Roman Catholicism is less interested in the official dogmas and practices and more interested in what average believers make of them, either accepting them or ignoring them (→ Roman Catholic Church 7.4). In the religious lives of many, the saints play a larger part than does Jesus Christ. For this reason everyday Catholic piety is much less uniform and coherent than that of the educated elite. There is contradiction in what is everyday, since it is made up of various elements.

An important feature is that the forms of popular religious culture may run contrary to the → norms set down by the elite, though the model of popular religion is not a denial of the existence of the elite. The social history of → Catholicism (§2.4) offers many examples of the way in which the elite have integrated many elements of traditional popular religion into the system of intellectual religion. Often the forms of folk religion anticipate what the official church later sanctions.

If we try to view the antagonism between popular and elite Roman Catholic religion as an ideal type of dichotomy, we might analyze it as follows: popular religion is oral, spontaneous, and emotional; elite religion is literary, prescribed, and rational.

→ Everyday Life; Spirituality

Bibliography: U. Altermatt, *Katholizismus und Moderne. Zur Sozial- und Mentalitätsgeschichte der Schweizer Katholiken im 19. und 20. Jahrhundert* (Zurich, 1989); idem, ed., *Katholische Denk- und Lebenswelten. Beiträge zur Kultur- und Sozialgeschichte des Schweizer Katholizismus im 20. Jahrhundert* (Fribourg, 2003); idem, ed., *Moderne als Problem des Katholizismus* (Regensburg, 1995) • J. Baumgartner, ed., *Wiederentdeckung der Volksreligiosität* (Regensburg, 1979) • M. P. Carroll, *Irish Pilgrimage: Holy Wells and Popular Catholic Devotion* (Baltimore, 1999); idem, *Veiled Threats: The Logic of Popular Catholicism in Italy* (Baltimore, 1996) • J. P. Chinnici and A. Dries, eds., *Prayer and Practice in the American Catholic Community* (Maryknoll, N.Y., 2000) • G. Cholvy and Y.-M. Hilaire, *Histoire religieuse de la France contemporaine* (3 vols.; Toulouse, 1985-88) • C. Comoro and J. Sivalon, "The Marian Faith Healing Ministry: An African Expression of Popular Catholicism in Tanzania," *East African Expressions of Christianity* (ed. T. Spear and I. N. Kimambo; Oxford, 1999) 275-95 • O. O. Espin, "Mexican Religious Practices, Popular Catholicism, and the Development of Doctrine," *Horizons of the Sacred: Mexican Traditions in U.S. Catholicism* (ed. T. Matovina and G. Riebe-Estrella; Ithaca, N.Y., 2002) 139-52 • R. S. Goizueta, "Caminemos con Jesús: U.S. Hispanic Popular Catholicism," *Caminemos con Jesús: Toward a Hispanic/Latino Theology of Accompaniment* (Maryknoll, N.Y., 1995) 18-46 • D. M. Hammond, ed., *Theology and Lived Christianity* (Mystic, Conn., 2000) • A. Heller, T. Weber, and O. Wiebel-Fanderl, eds., *Religion und Alltag. Interdisziplinäre Beiträge zu einer Sozialgeschichte des Katholizismus in lebensgeschichtlichen Aufzeichnungen* (Vienna, 1990) • R. Kassimir, "The Politics of Popular Catholicism in Uganda," *East African Expressions of Christianity,* ed. Spear and Kimambo, 248-74 • B. Plongeron, ed., *La religion populaire dans l'occident chrétien. Approches historiques* (Paris, 1976).

Urs Altermatt

Popular Religion

1. Sociological Data

1.1. *History of the Term*

Historically, "popular religion" (a term coined in the late 18th cent.) has been distinguished from "popular piety." The → Enlightenment used "popular religion" for a form of Christianity that fell short of the demands of rational → religion (§2.2). Protestant theology, deriving from M. → Luther (1483-1546; → Luther's Theology), dismissed traditional late medieval forms of → piety as → superstitious. In the 19th century the → Kulturkampf, with its nationalism, anticlericalism, and anti-Romanism, denounced as forms of popular religion everything that was not culturally progressive. At the same time, what was allegedly superstition could also be transfigured into the people's "faith."

Students of religion protested against the confessionally motivated disparagement of popular religion (→ Confession of Faith). Protestant theologian P. Drews (1858-1912) suggested in 1901 that → pastoral theology should investigate popular religion. In the 1920s Roman Catholic theologian G. Schreiber (1882-1963) pleaded for an ecclesiastical rather than a religious study. A denominational concept replaced anticlericalism, though some of the 19th-century mythological overtones remained. Along the lines of M. → Weber (1864-1920), the phrase "religion of the masses" was used instead of "popular religion," and differentiation from the religion of the elite received prominence. Sociologically, an advantage of this terminology is that it does not connect mass religion solely with the church. The political, economic, and cultural context of religious ideas also must be taken into account.

1.2. *Religion of the Elite and of the Masses*

If a distinction is made between the → religion of the elite and that of the masses, their relationship must also be defined. It is unhistorical to think that they were always in opposition. Nor can we say historically that we have here two sociocultural systems that diverge in principle and that must be analyzed separately. From the early Middle Ages to the present, popular religion and official religion have always been in interaction, permeating and influencing one another. Periods of congruence alternate historically with periods of opposition. Times of extensive mass religion have yielded to more churchly religion, as when the 15th century gave way to the → Reformation, or → baroque piety to the → Enlightenment. The idea is untenable that the → secularization process is so strong in our present age that all the phenomena of popular religion will gradually vanish (→ Volkskirche). At many points we can see a link between the church's attempt at institutional validation and an increase in mass religion.

1.3. *Representatives*

An important sociological question concerns the representatives of popular religion (→ Social History). It is often thought that popular religious traditions are handed down orally, which, up to the time of the Reformation, was mostly true. Since then, however, Christianity in literature, with typical denominational distinctions, has also had an influence on the representatives of popular religious practices, especially with the spread of reading.

In Europe and elsewhere today popular religion is by no means restricted to the illiterate. The idea that only the laity and not the clergy (→ Clergy and Laity) practice popular religion is also false. Many of the clergy play prominent roles in popular religion, though the laity have helped to set the tone from below. It is surprising that when the older European social order collapsed around 1800, the 19th-century → Roman Catholic Church organized popular religion from above (→ Societies and Associations, Ecclesiastical).

1.4. *Forms*

We may distinguish three forms of popular religion. The first is that of the *veneration of saints,* which the Reformation helped to abolish from Protestant countries. It comes to expression in → church dedications, → images, and local → processions. → Pilgrimages also play a part. Besides numerous regional pilgrimages there are many worldwide pilgrimages, especially to Santiago de Compostela (→ Santiago Cult), → Rome, → Jerusalem, and → Lourdes. A distinction must be made between the older cult of saints (e.g., Barbara, the patron saint of miners; → Saints, Veneration of, 8) and the newer cults, such as the → Sacred Heart of Jesus (19th cent.) or the Joseph cult. → Mariology has an outstanding place in the popular religion of Roman Catholicism, as "secondary deity" is increasingly ascribed to the biblical Mary (F.-A. Isambert).

Religious festivals form a second sphere, including the feasts of the → church year and those connected with → initiation rites (§2) and other rites of passage. The church year moves from Christmas and New Year to the passion season with its plays and Easter Sunday, then finally the harvest festivals and Thanksgiving, and so back to → Christmas (→ Popular Catholicism). The various stages of life include → baptism, → confirmation, → marriage, and burial.

Third are *marginal religious practices* that lie outside the Christian realm. Among these we may mention the consulting of mediums (→ Divination), → astrology, and → healing practices. The 19th century also drew attention to what has been called a *vagierende Religiosität* (restless, or roaming, religiousness; T. Nipperdey). Everyday religion of a popular kind has increasingly claimed the attention of historical investigators.

→ Civil Religion; Everyday Life; Spirituality

Bibliography: K. von Greyerz, ed., *Religion and Society in Early Modern Europe, 1500-1800* (London, 1984) • D. Hempton, *The Religion of the People: Methodism and Popular Religion c. 1750-1900* (London, 1996) • F.-A. Isambert, *Les sens du sacré. Fête et religion populaire* (Paris, 1982) • T. Nipperdey, *Religion im Umbruch. Deutschland, 1870-1918* (Munich, 1988) • B. Plongeron, ed., *La religion populaire dans l'occident chrétien. Approches historiques* (Paris, 1976) • K. Rahner, C. Modehn, and M. Gopfert, eds., *Volksreligion, Religion des Volkes* (Stuttgart, 1979) • M. Scharfe, *Die Religion des Volkes. Kleine Kultur- und Sozialgeschichte des Pietismus* (Gütersloh, 1980) • W. Schieder, ed., *Religion und Gesellschaft im 19. Jahrhundert* (Stuttgart, 1993); idem, ed., *Volksreligiosität in der modernen Sozialgeschichte* (Göttingen, 1986) • S. Sharot, *A Comparative Sociology of World Religions: Virtuosos, Priests, and Popular Religion* (New York, 2001) • K. Thomas, *Religion and the Decline of Magic: Studies in Popular Beliefs in Sixteenth and Seventeenth Century England* (London, 1971) • L. Voye, "Popular Religion and Pilgrimages in Western Europe," *From Medieval Pilgrimage to Religious Tourism: The Social and Cultural Economics of Piety* (ed. W. H. Swatos Jr. and L. Tomasi; Westport, Conn., 2002) 115-36.

Wolfgang Schieder

2. Third World Data

2.1. *Popular Religion and Mission*

Popular religion is often a lesser form of official religion that expresses the longings, needs, → experiences, and → hopes of simple people in cultural and religious ways that do not measure up to the demands of the higher → culture. Phenomena like pilgrimages, the use of amulets (→ Superstition), the venerating of sacred times and places (→ Temple), exaggerated belief in → healings and → miracles, excessive veneration of the → saints, and the use of prayers such as novenas bring popular piety very close to superstition or to the forms of non-Christian religion (→ Religion, Personal Sense of).

Christian → mission has tried to deliver the peoples of Asia, Africa, and Latin America from → paganism and to suppress local rites of → initiation and marriage and burial. At first it made a serious effort to combat a syncretistic (→ Syncretism) admixing of different forms of piety and to enforce official forms of orthodox piety. But different → denominations took different paths. Roman Catholic missionaries would make concessions to popular religion and try to give traditional religious practices a Christian form. Protestant missions, with their often stricter principles, stressed the separation of official forms of piety from those of popular religion and also tried to avoid incorporating forms of popular religion into the newly established Christian communities.

2.2. *Asia*

In Asia popular religion has always rivaled the great Asian religions such as → Buddhism, → Hinduism, and → Islam. It has formed a basic component of cosmic religiosity within these metacosmic religions. Through adaptation and inculturation (→ Acculturation) Christianity in its mission sought to make headway in the higher religions, whether in relation to Sanskrit culture among the Brahmans or in relation to → Confucianism in China, Japan, or Korea. It held aloof from popular religion.

In more recent times, however, Christianity has made a greater effort to get to know popular religion, for example, the Dalit theology of India or the minjung theology of Korea. In the Philippines popular theology has come to play a large role with the veneration of the Santo Niño (Holy Child) and the Black Nazarene.

2.3. *Africa*

In Africa the Christian churches first proclaimed a radical break with popular religion. But neglect of important popular elements such as healing, → exorcism, and certain forms of → initiation led to the rise of → independent African churches. A stronger movement of acculturation has now resulted in the mainline churches taking popular religion more seriously, which helps to give meaning and to deal with the uncertainties of human existence. African forms of Christianity can become truly acculturated only when the positive elements in popular religion are adopted and integrated.

2.4. *Latin America*

In Latin America the struggle against popular religion began in the early days of Christian mission. The character of Indian popular religion changed with the coming of African slaves (→ Slavery).

Many mixed Afro-American forms arose (→ Afro-American Cults), such as Candomblé, → Umbanda, or → voodoo, which helped to integrate the poverty-stricken masses into an increasingly anonymous urban society. Many of the forms of popular religion in the Latin American → Pentecostal churches or evangelical groups support reactionary governments against → liberation theology in defense of the present social order.

2.5. *Theological Debates*

Theological debates about popular theology in churches of the → Third World (§2) have occupied theologians belonging to the → Ecumenical Association of Third World Theologians (EATWOT). Latin American liberation theologians first opposed popular religion in the tradition of Marxist criticism of religion as fatalistic escapism that could be used to uphold the status quo (→ Religion, Criticism of).

But intercontinental work within EATWOT led to the development of a different understanding. → Black theology in South Africa made it clear that popular religion can be a source of social change and can contribute to black liberation theology. The Latin American Bishops' Conference at Puebla (1979) gave positive support to popular religion (§§444-69, "Evangelization and the People's Religiosity"; → Latin American Councils 2.5). Furthermore, popular religion has increasingly gained in significance in Third World → feminist theology.

Bibliography: B. P. Beltran, *Philippinische Theologie in ihrem kulturellen und gesellschaftlichen Kontext* (Düsseldorf, 1988) • E. Dussel, "Popular Religion as Oppression and Liberation: Hypotheses on Its Past and Its Present in Latin America," *Popular Religion* (ed. N. Greinacher and N. Mette; Edinburgh, 1986) • V. Fabella, *Beyond Bonding: A Third World Woman's Theological Journey* (Manila, 1993) • S. Feuchtwang, *Popular Religion in China* (new ed.; Richmond, Eng., 2001) • J. L. González, *La religión popular en el Perú* (Cusco, Peru, 1987) • L. Maldonado, "Popular Religion: Its Dimensions, Levels, and Types," *Popular Religion,* ed. Greinacher and Mette, 3-11 • J. van Nieuwenhove and B. K. Goldewijk, eds., *Popular Religion, Liberation, and Contextual Theology* (Kampen, 1991) • S. Semporé, "Popular Religion in Africa: Benin as a Typical Instance," *Popular Religion,* ed. Greinacher and Mette, 44-51 • L. de Mello e Souza, *The Devil and the Land of the Holy Cross: Witchcraft, Slavery, and Popular Religion in Colonial Brazil* (Austin, Tex., 2003) • H. Ucko, *The People and the People of God: Minjung and Dalit Theology in Interaction with Jewish-Christian Dialogue* (Münster, 2002).

Georg Evers

Populism

The vague term "populism," which is used as a political slogan, has had a long career in → social history but is rarely defined very precisely. Deriving from Lat. *populus* (people), it denotes a → social movement from below, or political mobilization from above, which takes on force by harnessing the opposition of the (common) people to the established political elite or the political system. In the language and self-understanding of populist politicians, the "little people," a group not sociologically defined, confront those in power, by which they mean "out-of-touch" representatives or ruling castes (→ Class and Social Stratum). As populism sees it, office, wealth, and prestige merge into one another. Many → everyday populist theories include an element of conspiracy. Populism usually results in amorphous, thematically diffuse, weakly institutionalized, and ephemeral movements that have been on the fringe of society and now take center stage. In some cases these movements might organize themselves more permanently into parties and, as such, may achieve representation (→ Democracy).

Examples are the movements of agrarian socialism at the end of the 19th century in the midwest and south of the United States that protested against the modernization and infrastructure policies of the central government and the banks (→ Economy). In the movement of the Russian *narodniki* (sing. *narodnik,* "populist"), who in the latter half of the 19th century summoned intellectuals and farmers to unite against czarism and → capitalism, the dominant forces were left-wing anticapitalist and antiautocratic sentiments, radical democratic resistance motifs, social ideals, and deep resentment. Both these populist movements must be distinguished from the labor movement, which was oriented to industrial strife (→ Industrial Society), had a stronger urban character, and organized wage earners.

The 20th century saw the rise of populist movements in → Latin America in opposition to the effects of capitalism on the fringes of society. Under such charismatic figures as Juan Perón (1895-1974) and Getúlio Vargas (1883-1954), these efforts developed into great mass movements linked to factories. Between the wars → fascist parties in Europe adopted the motifs and forms of populism, including the ideal of a society that is without class or conflict and of a state-directed union of capital and labor for the general good. In the 1950s in France Pierre Poujade (1920-2003) led a movement (Poujadisme) of small shopkeepers and tradespeople that for a time managed to find a place in the party system of the Fourth Republic and to achieve parliamentary representation.

Populism occurs in many times and places in very different forms and under such various types of government as democracy, autocracy, and Third World postcolonial systems. It may have either a left-wing or a right-wing character. It is marked by the ambivalence of its social revolutionary, nationalistic, and right-wing authoritarian motifs. Common features are the hostility of the people to the elite, the general sense of being victimized by the process of modernization, a preference for charismatic leadership or for the leadership of average persons who rise up from among the common people, an emphasis on common values rather than interests (→ Values, Ethics of), a dislike of parties and organized lobbies, and distrust of structured public opinion. In general, populism has an antimodernist thrust. It questions the constant social division into separate systems and the rationalization and bureaucratization of government. The pathologies of the modern world (→ Modernity) always make populist movements attractive.

In the narrower sense populism is a manipulative technique that politicians use who are anchored firmly in the established system. They claim that they are overcoming the traditional divisions of left and right and uniting the people above the conflicts and cleavages of modern → society (e.g., cleavages between the center and the periphery, or conflicts between denominations and classes). Populist longings and calculations take up so-called people's parties into their programs and propaganda. Populist movements have chances to succeed when large groups, parties, and organizations are in a process of losing their collective identities and the political elite and systems are exposed to widespread dissatisfaction and doubts as to the efficiency or mandate of the regime. Populism responds to crises of representation in the parliamentary system and impediments to the alternation of ruling party and opposition or to generational change.

Populist politicians and parties increased in the 1980s. Obvious discontent (seen in lack of political interest or the failure to vote) and the tendency of citizens to focus on single issues or to champion special interests led to a diffuse repoliticizing in which populism gained force as a negative sanction in the political system. It combined this role with antiforeigner and nationalist moods (→ Racism 1; Nation, Nationalism) resulting from mass immigration in what has been called a national populism. In the former → Soviet Union populist movements, parties, and politicians also filled the vacuum created by the Communist crisis. There are overlappings with radicalism of the right, which can now break free from isolation with the help of populist techniques and themes. New socialist movements to protect the environment or to represent consumers also adopt and promote populist forces, as to do "antiparty parties."

→ Politics

Bibliography: H.-G. Betz and S. Immerfall, eds., *The New Politics of the Right: Neo-Populist Parties and Movements in Established Democracies* (New York, 1998) • H. Dubiel, ed., *Populismus und Aufklärung* (Frankfurt, 1986) • Y. Mény and Y. Surel, eds., *Democracies and the Populist Challenge* (New York, 2002) • H.-G. Soeffner, *The Order of Rituals: The Interpretation of Everyday Life* (New Brunswick, N.J., 1997) • G. B. Tindall, ed., *A Populist Reader: Selections from the Works of American Populist Leaders* (New York, 1966).

Claus Leggewie

Portugal

	1960	*1980*	*2000*
Population (1,000s):	8,826	9,766	9,788
Annual growth rate (%):	0.68	0.28	–0.08

Area: 92,135 sq. km. (35,574 sq. mi.)

A.D. 2000

Population density: 106/sq. km. (275/sq. mi.)
Births / deaths: 1.09 / 1.12 per 100 population
Fertility rate: 1.48 per woman
Infant mortality rate: 7 per 1,000 live births
Life expectancy: 76.3 years (m: 72.8, f: 79.8)
Religious affiliation (%): Christians 92.3 (Roman Catholics 90.9, Protestants 1.5, marginal 1.3, other Christians 1.3), nonreligious 5.3, atheists 1.1, other 1.3.

1. General Situation
2. Churches
3. Interchurch Relations
4. Church and State
5. Non-Christian Religions

1. General Situation

Portugal became a republic in 1910. Freedom of the press was promulgated, along with the right to strike and the separation of → church and state. Church property was confiscated, and the → religious orders (§1) were dissolved and banished. In 1926 a military regime was set up, and then, in 1932, António de

Oliveira Salazar (1889-1970) established a dictatorship. Portugal was then said to be a Catholic state (see 4), and democratic freedoms were abolished.

Salazar's retirement in 1968 plunged the country into crisis, made worse by the social immobility of the regime and the attempt to hold on to the colonies of Mozambique, Angola, and Guinea. Army opposition to the colonial wars and in favor of a political solution led to a military coup on April 25, 1974, accompanied by mass demonstrations. A mood of revolt in 1974/75 resulted in attempts at basic democracy, with landed estates being taken over and agrarian cooperatives established. By the end of 1975 all of Portugal's African colonies had been granted independence.

Portugal's economic crisis grew worse in 1975-85 as the trade and budget deficits mounted. In 1986 with its entry into the European Community (later the European Union), help from the other nations brought improvement and economic stabilization. The economy continued to improve with reforms that were undertaken to qualify Portugal for entry into the European Monetary Union, of which it was a founding member. Portugal has become an increasingly privatized, diversified, and service-based economy.

In July 1996 the Community of Portuguese-Speaking Countries (known by its Portuguese acronym, CPLP) was formed to foster cooperation among Portuguese-speaking peoples and governments. Members of this community are Angola, Brazil, Cape Verde, Guinea-Bissau, Mozambique, Portugal, São Tomé and Príncipe, and East Timor. In December 1999 Portugal handed over its last colony, Macao, to Chinese rule. The Azores and the Madeira Islands are autonomous regions of Portugal.

Portugal has seen a rise in immigration since the period of decolonization, reversing a long history of emigration. Immigrants have come primarily from the former African colonies, Brazil, and eastern Europe.

2. Churches

2.1. The → Roman Catholic Church (→ Church 3.2) has always been dominant in Portugal, predominantly in the north. Despite the high percentage of people claiming association with the church, only a fairly small minority are practicing members. A conservative → hierarchy supervises 17 → dioceses (2003). This hierarchy lost its privileges and much of its power after the 1974 revolution.

The religious life of the people contains many superstitious elements (→ Superstition; Religion, Personal Sense of). It is tied to the cult of Mary, whose center is → Fatima (→ Mariology; Mary, Devotion to). Modern → Catholicism in Portugal, though, still reflects an anticlericalism that arose during the 1910 republic. Despite efforts of the bishops' conference to unite Roman Catholics, there are many divisions.

The church operates the Universidade Católica Portuguesa at Lisbon (founded 1967). It owns the radio station Rádio Renascença (→ Christian Communication).

2.2. Protestant churches (→ Church 3.3, 3.6) form only a small → minority of less than 2 percent of the population. Many of them owe their origin to missions from abroad dating from the late 19th century. Many are dependent to some extent on foreign churches.

In the year 2000 the largest Protestant churches were the Universal Church of the Kingdom of God (UCKG, 120,000 adherents), Assemblies of God (75,000), the Manna Church (45,000), and Seventh-day Adventists (18,000). The UCKG, a neo-Pentecostal church founded in Brazil in 1977, first came to Portugal in 1989 and has experienced rapid growth. The Manna Church, founded in Lisbon in 1984 and also neo-Pentecostal, now exists in 19 other countries.

Other Protestant groups include the Christian Brethren and Congregation of Christ (with over 6,000 adherents each), and the Baptist and Lusitanian Churches (with over 5,000 adherents each). The Igreja Lusitana Católica Apostólica Evangélica was founded in 1871 by Roman Catholic → priests who left their church. It belongs to the Conselho Português de Igrejas Cristãs (COPIC; → National Councils of Churches), the → Conference of European Churches (CEC), the → World Council of Churches (WCC), and the → Anglican Communion.

The Methodist and Presbyterian churches also have a presence in Portugal. The first English missionary of the Igreja Evangélica Metodista Portuguesa (→ Methodist Churches) came to Porto in 1871. This church, which is integrated into the British Methodist churches, was at work originally only in northern and central Portugal but has now spread to the south. It belongs to COPIC and the CEC. The first church of Igreja Evangélica Presbiteriana de Portugal (→ Reformed and Presbyterian Churches) was founded by a Scottish missionary in 1845 on Madeira but was officially constituted only in 1947. It belongs to COPIC, the → World Alliance of Reformed Churches, the CEC, and the WCC.

2.3. Among other religious groups, note should be taken of → Jehovah's Witnesses, which has about

80,000 members in 650 congregations, and the → Mormons, with 40,000 members in 180 congregations.

3. Interchurch Relations

3.1. One interchurch organization is the Aliança Evangélica Portuguesa (→ World Evangelical Alliance), which was formed in 1935 to seek from the state universal freedom of conscience and → religious liberty (→ Rights) and to promote better relations among Protestants. Another is the Associação Cristã da Mocidade, founded at Porto in 1894. It now links → YMCA groups throughout Portugal and has contact with the World Alliance (United States) and the Comité Central (Switzerland). COPIC was founded in 1971 by the three synodical churches (Lusitanian, Methodist, Presbyterian) at Figueira da Foz to give a better manifestation of Christian unity; it maintains ties with the CEC and WCC.

The Sociedade Bíblica de Portugal started work in 1868 as an agency of the British and Foreign Bible Society (→ Bible Societies 4.1) for the distribution of Bibles in Portugal. It is now autonomous and works with all the churches. In 1993 the society, with collaboration by Roman Catholic and Protestant scholars, prepared a new translation of the Bible.

3.2. The fact that Roman Catholicism is so dominant and Protestantism so small makes ecumenical relations difficult. For a long time Rome did not accept the presence of other churches in Portugal, and many Protestants found their raison d'être in opposition to Rome. In the weak ecumenical dialogue we should note two dimensions: (1) relations between Rome and individual Protestant churches and (2) relations among members of COPIC and the Evangelical Alliance. The latter are trying to improve relations with Rome as well as with other Protestants. They meet on an informal and nonofficial level and work together on planning and carrying out various projects. In this regard stress should fall on the Centro Ecuménico Reconciliação, which has been hard at work in this area since the 1960s.

The bias of most Protestants toward → fundamentalism and the → conservatism of Roman Catholicism, which disregards in practice the results of → Vatican II and specifically the Decree on Ecumenism *(Unitatis redintegratio)*, block progress on the ecumenical front. At the diocesan and congregational levels there are ecumenical experiences, though they depend heavily on personal relations among those who bear responsibility for them (→ Local Ecumenism 2.1).

4. Church and State

Under the monarchy the Roman Catholic Church used its privileged status in the state. The resultant anticlericalism led to the ending of the orders, a break with the papacy, and separation of church and state. In 1926, under Salazar, the church began to win back its earlier place in → society, and in 1933 it succeeded with the constitution of the Estado Novo, which remained in force until 1976. This constitution granted religious freedom but called Catholicism the "traditional religion of the Portuguese nation," and it granted the Roman Catholic Church, notwithstanding separation of church and state, the status of a corporation under public law. The → Concordat and the Missionary Agreement of 1940 obligated the public schools to teach "Catholic religion and morality" and recognized church weddings according to canon law (→ Codex Iuris Canonici). In comparison, Protestant churches were barely tolerated (→ Tolerance) and had few rights. This situation changed fundamentally with the 1976 constitution and the later revisions, which have upheld separation and granted privileges to no religious organization.

5. Non-Christian Religions

Jews (→ Judaism) form a small but influential community in the Lisbon area. The first → synagogue after the → Inquisition was opened in 1813. In 2000 there were fewer than 1,000 Jews in Portugal. There are also some Marranos, secret Jews who were forced during the Inquisition to be baptized but maintained Jewish practices.

→ Islam founded a group in Lisbon in 1968, and with Arab help it has built a → mosque and cultural center in the heart of the city. Numbers rose with the loss of the colonies (esp. Mozambique and Guinea-Bissau) and an influx of Pakistanis. Estimates of the number of Muslims in Portugal in 2000 ranged from 25,000 to 50,000.

In 2000 there were also some 10,000 Hindus in Portugal (→ Hinduism), many coming from Goa, a former Portuguese colony on the west coast of India.

Bibliography: D. Alden, *The Making of an Enterprise: The Society of Jesus in Portugal, Its Empire, and Beyond, 1540-1750* (Stanford, Calif., 1996) • J. M. Anderson, *The History of Portugal* (Westport, Conn., 2000) • D. B. Barrett, G. T. Kurian, and T. M. Johnson, *WCE* (2d ed.) 1.607-11 • P. Blanshard, *Freedom and Catholic Power in Spain and Portugal: An American Interpretation* (Boston, 1962) • M. P. Cardoso, *História do Protestantismo em Portugal* (Figueira da Foz, 1985) • M. Kaplan, *The Portuguese: The Land and Its People*

(New York, 1992) • M. Oliveira, *História eclesiástica de Portugal* (Lisbon, 1968) • A. C. Pinto, ed., *Modern Portugal* (Palo Alto, Calif., 1998) • J. Saramago, *Journey to Portugal: In Pursuit of Portugal's History and Culture* (New York, 2000) • D. L. Wheeler, *Historical Dictionary of Portugal* (2d ed.; Lanham, Md., 2002).

José Manuel Leite

Porvoo Common Statement

1. Background
2. Issues
3. Developments
4. Questions

The Porvoo Common Statement (in the following: "Porvoo") is a theological text that serves as a foundation of church → unity between the British and Irish Anglican churches, on the one hand, and the Nordic and Baltic Lutheran churches, on the other. The text was completed in Porvoo, Finland, an old diocesan town near Helsinki, and was published in 1993. The participating churches approved it in their synods between 1994 and 1995. The Lutheran churches of Norway, Sweden, Finland, Estonia, and Lithuania have officially approved the text, whereas the Lutheran churches of Denmark and Latvia at this time have not, although they participated in the negotiations. The fellowship thus created is often referred to as the Porvoo communion. The last chapter of the Porvoo text contains "The Porvoo Declaration," a brief statement that the churches have issued together in which they acknowledge one another's doctrinal basis and ordained → ministries.

1. Background

The historical roots of Porvoo go back to discussions between the Church of England and the Church of Sweden in the late 19th and early 20th centuries. In 1920 and 1922 the Lambeth Conference and the bishops of the Church of Sweden approved intercommunion between the two churches. They also decided to participate in each other's episcopal → consecrations. → Bishops of the other church thus participated in such events in Uppsala 1920 and in Canterbury in 1927. Anglican theologians have traditionally appreciated the historical fact that episcopal succession continued in Sweden and Finland during and after the Lutheran → Reformation. In addition, the prominent role of Archbishop Nathan Söderblom of Sweden (1866-1931) in the emerging ecumenical movement created an atmosphere that facilitated Anglican-Lutheran agreements. According to Söderblom, the Lutheran Reformation in Sweden did not create a new church but was essentially a church improvement and a process of purification (*Together in Mission and Ministry*, 59).

During the 1930s similar arrangements were established between the Church of England and the Lutheran churches of Finland, Estonia, and Latvia. In Finland this agreement led to similar results as in Sweden, namely intercommunion, established in 1936, and since 1951, participation in episcopal consecrations. Because of the Communist takeover in Estonia and Latvia, similar exchanges were not possible in those countries before 1989. For the Estonian and Latvian Lutheran refugee communities during and after the Second World War, however, the Anglican recognition was of great pastoral encouragement (*Together in Mission and Ministry*, 56).

From the Anglican perspective, the historical and theological situation in Norway, Denmark, and Iceland was different from that in Sweden and Finland, since these three national churches had not preserved the historical succession of bishops. Nevertheless, these churches did have bishops, and their theological outlook was in all other respects very similar to that of Sweden and Finland. In negotiations between 1951 and 1956 it was agreed that although interconsecration of bishops between England and Norway, Denmark, and Iceland was inappropriate, mutual admission to Holy Communion could be recommended. In 1972, then, the Church of England authorized wider eucharistic hospitality to all baptized members of churches that confessed a Trinitarian theology.

Whereas the historical background of Porvoo can be found in these arrangements, its actual theology is shaped by the global ecumenical texts of the 1970s and 1980s. These include the Anglican-Lutheran dialogue documents, especially *The Niagara Report* (1988). Probably the most important background text, however, has been the → Faith and Order document *Baptism, Eucharist, Ministry* (1982). To a lesser extent, the bilateral Lutheran–Roman Catholic reports and the American Episcopal-Lutheran documents have contributed to the theological insights of Porvoo (→ Ecumenical Dialogue).

2. Issues

For the Church of England the basic ecumenical problem in negotiations with Nordic Lutherans was always the matter of the historic succession of bishops. Doctrinal orthodoxy in other matters was taken more or less for granted. For Lutherans, however, matters of church order have often remained secondary, whereas the substantive content of theological confession is seen as the primary ecumenical issue. The assumed Anglican lack of clarity concerning some distinctively Lutheran issues of doctrine — such as justification by grace through faith alone, the mutual relation of → law and gospel, and the real presence in the → Eucharist — has caused discussion among Lutherans. During the time of Lutheran → orthodoxy (§1) in the 17th and 18th centuries, Anglicanism was often considered to be a variant of → Calvinism and was therefore treated critically for the same reasons as Reformed theology was (T. Laine).

In the Porvoo document, this Lutheran interest can be seen in the doctrinal paragraphs that make explicit the common → confession of faith. For Lutherans, §32c is of special importance: "We share a common understanding of God's justifying → grace, i.e. that we are accounted righteous and are made righteous before God only by grace through faith." According to §32h the churches "believe that the body and blood of Christ are truly present." Although this formulation did not totally satisfy the most ardent Lutheran defenders of the "real presence," it was considered compatible with the Lutheran Augsburg Confession (O. Tjørhom, 62).

Such debates are not merely of historical interest; they may become ecumenically relevant when Porvoo is compared with Lutheran-Reformed agreements. Consider, for example, the → Leuenberg Agreement (in the following: Leuenberg) between continental European Lutheran and Reformed churches. Porvoo is surely different from Leuenberg insofar as → episcopacy is concerned. Since, however, Nordic Lutheranism has consistently viewed Anglicanism in the context of Calvinism, it is therefore important to see the elaborate explication of the Porvoo paragraphs speaking of the gospel (§32c), → baptism (§32g), and the Lord's Supper (§32h), matters that from the Lutheran perspective are constitutive for church unity. Not only Leuenberg but all Lutheran bilateral dialogues proceed from this constitutive primacy of "faith," which may leave "order" to a secondary role when church unity is discussed.

For Anglicans, however, the most difficult issue of Porvoo has been how a mutual understanding of episcopacy is to be reached. Following the insights of the *Niagara Report* and *Baptism, Eucharist, and Ministry*, Porvoo does not focus on bishops as such but on the ministry, or oversight (Gk. *episkopē*). This *episkopē* "is a requirement of the whole Church and its faithful exercise in the light of the Gospel is of fundamental importance to its life" (§42). Furthermore, "The ministry of oversight is exercised personally, collegially and communally" (§44). Because of this broad characterization of *episkopē*, Porvoo also embraces churches that have not preserved the historical succession of bishops but have nevertheless retained a ministry of oversight; in that sense they have retained apostolic succession. Historic episcopal succession is a "sign" (§§50-54) that makes the apostolic life of the church visible. But the sign alone does not "guarantee the fidelity of a church to every aspect of the apostolic faith, life and mission" (§51). On the basis of these insights, Porvoo affirms that "each church has maintained an orderly succession of episcopal ministry within the continuity of its pastoral life" (§56). Thus Anglicans can say, for example, that the Church of Norway has preserved the ministry of oversight and can use the sign of succession, even though its actual historical succession has not been similar to that of the church in Sweden, England, or Finland.

The Porvoo Common Statement, furthermore, concludes that "the time has come when all our churches can affirm together the value and use of the sign of the historic episcopal succession" (§57). In consequence, Lutherans can no longer continue their diverse practices, but they are committed to use the sign of episcopacy. The notion of sign thus enables the Anglicans to say that a true ministry of oversight has been preserved in all churches of the Porvoo communion. In parallel fashion, the Lutherans affirm the usefulness of historic episcopal succession and provide for it in their episcopal consecrations. Thus Anglicans have reinterpreted the past practices of Nordic churches to be compatible with the Anglican view of succession, and Lutherans are committed to understand their theology of episcopacy and its future in a manner compatible with Anglicanism.

3. Developments

Since 1993 member churches have been active in the implementation of Porvoo. Inasmuch as the geographic areas of these churches do not overlap, it is proper to ask what the practical significance of Porvoo has been. Many parish and diocesan contacts have been established. The exchange of priests and the creation of opportunities for pastoral service in another member church are among the achievements of Porvoo, as is the opportunity now available for laypeople to be full members of local congregations in other countries. A special challenge is the implementation of Porvoo in respect to national church laws. Scandinavian church laws are built on the presupposition of national citizenship, but to have parishioners who are not citizens of the country is now a legal option. The very concept of → church membership — based on baptism, eucharistic participation, or simple payment of church taxes — is also a matter that is regulated differently in Anglicanism and Lutheranism.

The Porvoo churches have organized church leaders' consultations (e.g., in Turku, Finland, in 1998, and in Tallinn, Estonia, in 2002) and theological conferences. A Web site (www.porvoochurches.org) provides information about events and developments in the member churches. At a Porvoo theological conference held in 2000 in Durham, England, it was recommended that the participating churches should develop means of mutual accountability by ensuring, for example, that "where a signatory church of the Porvoo Communion is in dialogue with churches outside the Communion, then other signatory churches within the Communion be invited to contribute to those consultations"; and "where a signatory church . . . intends to take an action which is likely to affect the boundaries of diversity within the Communion some structure of sharing information and concerns be established" (Durham 3.4, on the Porvoo Web site). These recommendations have to some extent been followed in the decision-making processes of the Porvoo churches, but the national structures of member churches sometimes do not leave much room for mutual accountability.

Porvoo has been highly successful as a model for the fostering of new Anglican-Lutheran communion agreements in other regions. Other unity agreements that are identical in outcome, although not necessarily in theological formulation, include the U.S. Lutheran-Episcopal agreement *Called to Common Mission* (1999) and the Waterloo Declaration (2001) in Canada between Anglicans and Lutherans. In Europe two other agreements have established intercommunion and a limited exchangeability of ministers: the Meissen Common Statement (1988), between the Church of England, the Evangelical Church in Germany (EKD), and a federation of evangelical churches in East Germany; and the Reuilly Common Statement (2001), between the British and Irish Anglican churches and the French Lutheran and Reformed churches. In Australia, Brazil, and some places in Africa, similar agreements are currently under discussion. Globally, the Anglican-Lutheran International Working Group monitors the situation and has reported on its developments (for all these agreements, see *Growth in Communion*).

4. Questions

The complex network of Porvoo-like regional agreements raises new questions. One deals with the issue of transitivity. For example, given that the Church of Sweden is in communion with the Church of England, can it be inferred that it is also in communion with other Anglican churches (→ Anglican Communion)? The text of Porvoo does not draw this conclusion, but the issue is indeed complex, not least since it was the worldwide Anglican Lambeth Conference that gave impetus to English-Swedish negotiations. Along the same lines, the Lutheran view of the constitutive importance of the theological foundations for interchurch agreements may lead to the conclusion that some transitivity between coherent and theologically sound bilateral agreements should be assumed. And similarly, a regional network might in the course of time grow organically into a global agreement. Although it has not yet happened, a "global Porvoo" is an option that needs to be considered in the future.

At the European level, Porvoo has also received some criticism, especially in Germany. The constitutive text of the Leuenberg Agreement is very different from Porvoo in its theological outlook. Leuenberg does not treat ordained ministry at all; rather, it establishes a basic consensus on → salvation and the → sacraments. This strategy is derived from the Lutheran and Reformed view that the content and foundation of "faith," not external "order," establish true unity among Christians. According to this view, the external manifestation of faith can often be regarded as a secondary and contingent dimension of Christian identity. From this Leuenberg perspective, an ecumenical text like Porvoo that focuses on external order and the visible signs of unity may become problematic (W. Hüffmeier and C. Podmore; I. U. Dalferth).

In view of the different theological strategies adopted in the two European agreements, it is important to notice that the Church of Norway and the Estonian Evangelical Lutheran Church are members of both Porvoo and Leuenberg. We should conclude that these churches regard the underlying theologies of the two agreements as being mutually compatible. Moreover, the Porvoo emphasis on the doctrine of ministry may be fruitful in ecumenical work with the → Roman Catholic Church and churches of the Orthodox family (→ Orthodox Church). At the same time, the Porvoo churches should continue to take seriously the Lutheran insistence on the primacy of the content of faith. For their part, Anglicans should realize that although Porvoo has been able to solve the issue of *episkopē*, the agreement as such does not offer any comprehensive ecclesiology.

Bibliography: I. U. Dalferth, *Auf dem Weg der Ökumene. Die Gemeinschaft evangelischer und anglikanischer Kirchen nach der Meissener Erklärung* (Leipzig, 2002) • *Growth in Communion: Report of the Anglican-Lutheran International Working Group, 2000-2002* (Geneva, 2003) • W. Hüffmeier and C. Podmore, eds., *Leuenberg, Meissen, and Porvoo* (Frankfurt, 1996) • T. Laine, "English Devotional Literature in Finland during the Swedish Era" (in Finnish, with English summary) (Diss., Helsinki, 2000) • *The Niagara Report: Report of the Anglican-Lutheran Consultation on Episcope* (Cincinnati, 1988) • O. Tjørhom, ed., *Apostolicity and Unity: Essays on the Porvoo Common Statement* (Grand Rapids, 2002) • *Together in Mission and Ministry: The Porvoo Common Statement, with Essays on Church and Ministry in Northern Europe* (London, 1993) • World Council of Churches, *Baptism, Eucharist, Ministry* (Geneva, 1982).

Risto Saarinen

Positivism

1. Nature and Origins
2. Nineteenth Century
3. Twentieth Century
   3.1. Natural Science and Philosophy
   3.2. Law, Religion, and Social Science

1. Nature and Origins

Positivism as an intellectual attitude emerged clearly in early 19th-century social theory. Henri de Saint-Simon (1760-1825), the founder of French → socialism, was the first to use the term. Auguste Comte (1798-1857), "the founding father of modern → sociology," developed positivism into a comprehensive → worldview that spread to other disciplines, in particular → philosophy and natural science.

The positivist outlook restricts the domain of knowledge to verifiable facts about the world (what is "posited," from Lat. *positus,* something "laid down" or "set firmly") that are accessible to human experience from observation and experiment — that is, from employing the scientific method. It rejects any speculation or → metaphysics that assumes the existence of unobservable, nonphysical, or nonnatural entities or forces lying outside the province of scientific investigation. It embraces not only empirical knowledge gained by the various social and natural sciences but also the study of general principles common to the theories and methodologies of those sciences. Precursors of positivism include Francis Bacon (1561-1626) and the subsequent British empiricists in philosophy, as well as others with high expectations for scientific and social progress stemming from the optimism of the → Enlightenment.

2. Nineteenth Century

Saint-Simon held that the traditional European social order rooted in medieval culture had been undercut by the rise of modern science and by progressive political movements. Outdated conceptual schemes derived from theology and metaphysics must give way to science, technocracy, and industrialism, with their correlative new forms of social organization. He coupled the economic and political theory of his utopian socialism with retention of a modernized religion as ethical teaching stripped of any theological underpinnings. In his *New Christianity* (1825) he promoted return to what he imagined was the socioeconomic perspective of the earliest Christian communities.

Comte confined possible knowledge to the sphere of observable physical objects. Science explains and predicts according to "laws of succession," not of causation (a metaphysical concept). All sciences are to be understood and pursued in this antimetaphysical manner. Each has some methods and laws peculiar to it; there is no hierarchy, with some sciences subordinate to, or derivative from, others. Comte described positive science as the third and final stage in the historical development of human intellect. In the first, or theological, stage our ancestors interpreted natural phenomena as the workings of supernatural beings. In the following metaphysical stage they construed phenomena conceptually with reference to abstract entities. Positive science sweeps all this away by focusing on the phenomena themselves and abandoning "final" explanations in terms of unobservable, presumably fictitious, factors.

Comte presented his comprehensive system in his six-volume *Cours de philosophie positive* (1830-42). To stress the scientific credentials of the new discipline of sociology, which he subdivided into "statics" (social organization) and "dynamics" (social development), he dubbed it "social physics." Comte confidently affirmed that social and intellectual progress is the essence of the history of civilization. His positivism not only rendered traditional religion obsolete but replaced it, for positivism itself assumed a pseudoreligious character by creating an annual calendar of secular saints (human benefactors) with their own chapels and festivals — a universal "religion of humanity," with Comte himself as its high priest.

British utilitarians welcomed the positivist inclusion of all the empirical disciplines under the umbrella of genuine science. Jeremy Bentham (1748-1832) aspired to make → ethics an exact science with a hedonic calculus for measuring the rightness or wrongness of actions by the pleasure or pain they produce. John Stuart Mill (1806-73) advanced scientific method with the principles of inductive reasoning explicated in his *System of Logic* (1843). Later he penned *Auguste Comte and Positivism* (1865), an appreciative study of the movement.

Others gravitated to positivism's emphasis on → progress and its potential for evolutionary social theory (→ Evolution). Herbert Spencer (1820-1903), famous for his "social Darwinism," contended that "survival of the fittest" is the natural outcome of competition in human history. His system of synthetic philosophy, spun out in many volumes on individual disciplines (biology, ethics, psychology, etc.), and his confidence in an inevitable social progress are clear echoes of Comte. Biologist Ernst Haeckel (1834-1919) wedded materialist and social-spiritual strains of positivism in a monistic philosophy that depicted the biological development of the individual (ontogeny) as retracing the developmental stages of the species (phylogeny).

At century's end a new form of positivism strongly influenced subsequent philosophy of science. Richard Avenarius (1843-96), the founder of this "empiriocriticism," excluded all metaphysical factors from knowing, thus reducing it to "pure experience," to "a natural concept of the world." Ernst Mach (1838-1916) proposed a "positivism of the senses," with more complex concept formation on the basis of its serving to meet our biological needs. For Mach, concise description by itself constitutes scientific explanation. His → epistemology paralleled the natural science of his era, with his denial of causality anticipating developments in modern physics and his strict sensualism setting him in opposition to the new atomic theory.

3. Twentieth Century

3.1. *Natural Science and Philosophy*

Members of the Vienna Circle, a working group of philosophers, mathematicians, and physical scientists, regarded Mach as a major forerunner. Moritz Schlick (1882-1936), its central figure, succeeded to Mach's academic chair in Vienna in 1922. Other key participants included Rudolf Carnap (1891-1970), Otto Neurath (1882-1944), Herbert Feigl (1902-88), Kurt Gödel (1906-78), and Viktor Kraft (1880-1975). About the same time a group with similar views coalesced in Berlin around Hans Reichenbach (1891-1953) and Carl Hempel (1905-97). The Vienna Circle called its philosophical method, so closely linked to natural science, "logical positivism." To distinguish it from its 19th-century predecessors, Carnap called it "neopositivism." Its horizons expanded when followers such as Ludwig Wittgenstein (1889-1951), whose *Tractatus Logico-Philosophicus* (1921) reflects the initial ethos of the Vienna Circle, turned to studies of → language as the bearer of logical relations and conceptual frameworks. This wider approach of Wittgenstein and others comprised more than just formal logic and natural scientific facts; taking broad account of experiential elements in knowing, it came to prefer the label "logical empiricism."

Two central themes arose from the wide-ranging discussions of the Vienna Circle. One, the verification principle, holds that the meaning of a statement is given by the method of its verification, thus by what it says about states of affairs in the world that are accessible to observation or experiment. The second theme concerns the demarcation of scientific from nonscientific (i.e., according to the verification principle, meaningless) statements. Both themes, disputed by others, as is usual with philosophical positions, were driving forces of intellectual progress within the Vienna Circle and beyond. For instance, they inspired Carnap to venture beyond positivism to a different type of philosophy of science, constructive → realism. Two other offshoots are the tolerance principle in → logic, which leaves open the choice of logical system to be employed, and the empiricists' inclusion of human action in their theories of description.

Karl Popper (1902-94) later replaced the verification principle with the falsification principle, which, instead of calling for direct confirmability as the criterion of meaningfulness, conforms to actual practices in science. Scientific hypotheses are most often tested by trying to disprove them, accepted ones having resisted all such efforts. The falsification principle takes the criterion of meaningfulness to be a statement's implicit specification of possible empirical conditions under which it could be tested and found to be false. As A. J. Ayer (1910-89) declared, any statement (esp. metaphysical, religious, ethical, or aesthetic) that fails to make an empirically testable claim is therefore meaningless, its putative truth of no consequence because it is compatible with any and every possible state of affairs.

When the Vienna Circle fell victim to the barbarity of Nazism, its members emigrated, most to the United States or Britain, where much of their influential work was done. There the methodology they brought emphasized detailed analysis of the logic of statements and the structure of language rather than metaphysical theory, and so it came to be known as → analytic philosophy. Wittgenstein, now in Britain, set forth in his lectures and in *Philosophical Investigations* (not published until 1953) an innovative philosophy of language that greatly influenced analytic philosophy. While analytic philosophy (rightly or wrongly) relegated some traditional topics to the dustbin of history, it also revitalized modern philosophy. Among its notable products are the linguistic studies of J. L. Austin (1911-60) and John Searle (b. 1932) and the mathematical logic of Bas Van Fraassen (b. 1941). W. V. Quine (1908-2000) used analytic tools to tackle classical issues with new methods and vigor. More recently, Richard Rorty (b. 1931) and others sought to transcend their roots in analytic philosophy by branching out to the use of other methods.

3.2. *Law, Religion, and Social Science*

Positivism in law holds that legal principles are not deducible from a philosophy of human nature or from a law supposedly manifest in the structure and operations of nature. Their origin and basis instead reside in the decisions and stipulations made by the societies in which they are promulgated. Thus laws are simply posited or given, not derivative from some other, nonlegal source (→ Law and Legal Theory). Legal positivism has roots perhaps traceable at least as far back as the distinction Hugo Grotius (1583-1645) drew between natural law *(ius naturale)* and the law of nations *(ius gentium)*, which is based on → consensus. Hans Kelsen (1881-1973) was one of the chief advocates of legal positivism in the 20th century. Its advantage is its ability to avoid thorny issues for natural law theory, such as how to get agreement on suitably specific concepts of human nature or of operations in the natural world. Its drawback is its inability to rule out authoritarian or obviously inhumane legal systems.

Positivism in religion most notably involves the theological conviction that the words of the Bible as such were directly revealed to its authors and, through them, to us. (Parallel views about other scriptures exist in Judaism, Islam, and some other religions.) Many pietists and all fundamentalists in Christianity adhere to some version of this conviction. Historically, it was the largely unchallenged view of mainstream → Judaism and Christianity up to the onset of historical-critical biblical studies in the late 18th century, and it remains today a dominant emphasis in much conservative religious opposition to the liberal theologies of the past two centuries.

Modern social sciences, though far more complex and methodologically sophisticated than the disciplines of Comte's day, are still a focus of energetic debates about positivism. In one major conflict Theodor Adorno (1903-69) and Jürgen Habermas (b. 1929), noted advocates of → critical theory, challenged the critical → rationalism, rooted in positivism, of Popper and Hans Albert (b. 1921). The dispute centered on whether there can be → truth in praxis and not just in factual matters, and whether any science can be value-free. Proponents of antipositivist perspectives typically regard positivism as a superficial and merely preliminary account of knowing and actuality. Marxists view it as a perpetuation of bourgeois → idealism. The term "positivistic" is often taken to indicate an uncritical reliance on modern science as a procedure for compiling data used for controlling the world in instrumental fashion. Max Horkheimer (1895-1973), in espousing the mediation of scientific knowledge by reflection and self-reflection, accused positivism of being a "philosophical technocracy."

Bibliography: Primary sources: A. Ayer, *Language, Truth, and Logic* (New York, 1952); idem, ed., *Logical Positivism* (Glencoe, Ill., 1959) • R. Carnap, *The Logical Structure of the World* (London, 1965) • A. Comte, *Auguste Comte and Positivism: The Essential Writings* (ed. G. Lenzer; New York, 1975); idem, *The Essential Comte, Selected from "Cours de philosophie positive"* (London, 1974; orig. pub., 1830-42); idem, *Introduction to Positive Philosophy* (ed. F. Ferré; Indianapolis, 1988) • H. Feigl and W. Sellars, eds., *Readings in Philosophical Analysis* (New York, 1949) • J. Habermas, *Knowledge and Human Interests* (Boston, 1971); idem, *On the Logic of the Social Sciences* (Cambridge, Mass., 1988; orig. pub., 1967) • M. Horkheimer, *Critique of Instrumental Reason* (New York, 1994) • H. Kelsen, *General Theory of Law and State* (New York, 1961) • E. Mach, *Knowledge and Error: Sketches on the Psychology of Enquiry* (Dordrecht, 1976; orig. pub., 1905) • J. Mill, *Auguste Comte and Positivism* (Ann Arbor, Mich., 1961; orig. pub., 1865); idem, *A System of Logic, Ratiocinative and Inductive* (London, 1884; orig. pub., 1843) • K. Popper, *The Logic of Scientific Discovery* (3d ed.; London, 1968) • W. Quine, *Ontological Relativity, and Other Essays* (New York, 1969) • H. Reichenbach, *The Rise of Scientific Philosophy* (Berkeley and Los Angeles, 1951) • H. Saint-Simon, *New Christianity* (London, 1834) • J. Searle, *Expression and Meaning: Studies in the Theory of Speech Acts* (Cambridge, 1979) • H. Spencer, *Essays: Scientific, Political, and Speculative* (New York, 1896); idem, *First Principles* (New York, 1958; orig. pub., 1862) • K. Taylor, trans., *Henri Saint-Simon (1760-1825): Selected Writings on Science, Indus-*

try, and Social Organization (London, 1975) • B. Van Fraassen, *Laws and Symmetry* (Oxford, 1989) • L. Wittgenstein, *Philosophical Investigations* (3d ed.; New York, 1958); idem, *Tractatus Logico-Philosophicus* (rev. ed.; London, 1961).

Secondary works: C. Cashdollar, *The Transformation of Theology, 1830-1890: Positivism and Protestant Thought in Britain and America* (Princeton, 1989) • V. Kraft, *The Vienna Circle* (New York, 1953) • J. Passmore, "Logical Positivism," *EncPh* 5.52-57 • W. Simon, *European Positivism in the Nineteenth Century* (Ithaca, N.Y., 1963) • F. Stadler, *The Vienna Circle: Studies in the Origins, Development, and Influence of Logical Empiricism* (Vienna, 2001) • F. Wallner, *Acht Vorlesungen über den Konstruktiven Realismus* (Vienna, 1990); idem, *Grenzen der Sprache und der Erkenntnis* (Vienna, 1983); idem, *Konstruktion der Realität* (Vienna, 1992) • A. Wernick, *Auguste Comte and the Religion of Humanity: The Post-theistic Program of French Social History* (Cambridge, 2001) • T. Wright, *The Religion of Humanity: The Impact of Comtean Positivism on Victorian Britain* (Cambridge, 1986).

Fritz Wallner and Robert F. Brown

Postmodernism

1. Terms

Attempts to define or delimit the meaning of the term "postmodernism" often falter in light of the lack of sufficient clarity concerning the scope and meaning of → "modernism." It is helpful, then, to distinguish between → "modernity" and "postmodernity," terms that refer to particular historical eras or periods, and "modernism" and "postmodernism," terms that are used to refer to particular theoretical or philosophical discourses. Because postmodernism is an heir to "modernism," as postmodernity is to modernity, it is important first to discuss "modernity" and "modernism."

1.1. *Modernity*

"Modern" → philosophy and → theology find their origins in the epistemological inquiries of René Descartes (1596-1650; → Cartesianism) and come to full bloom in the late 18th century with the → Enlightenment and its emphasis on the → autonomy of the human person. Immanuel Kant (1724-1804; → Kantianism) envisioned a new constitution of the self, free from all heteronomous influences, including → tradition and → dogma. This program of "enlightenment" *(Aufklärung)* was most clearly enunciated in Kant's essay "What Is Enlightenment?" (1784). Kant's choice of the word "enlightenment" was a self-conscious naming of an age, expressing a new hope of political and philosophical freedom from the constraints of past precedents, traditions, and ideals. Kant's slogan of enlightenment, *sapere aude* (dare to be wise), urged the newly announced modern subjects to think for themselves without the influence of heteronomous sources or traditions, particularly religious traditions. Modernity is thus founded on a suspicion, or even an open hostility, to religion *(religio)*.

In his metaphysics Kant searched for the limits of human → reason and its ability or inability to comprehend noumenal ideas, such as the transcendental concepts of truth, goodness, beauty, and the idea of God (→ Transcendentals). Kant asserted that the human subject itself constitutes the experience of the world around it; that is, every individual subject constructs his or her experience of the world by an innate set of universal transcendental categories fixed within the "mind" of that subject. The architectonics of Kant's overall tripartite project was to establish a → metaphysics, → ethics, and → aesthetics thoroughly grounded in human reason and rationality.

F. Schleiermacher (1768-1834; → Schleiermacher's Theology) initiated the theological response to the epistemological limits Kant placed on metaphysical, ethical, and aesthetic discourses. Schleiermacher was influenced by his own Pietist background and by the Romantic reaction to Kant's narrow focus on human reason as expressed in the works of F. Schlegel (1772-1829). Rejecting dogmatic theology in all its various forms, Schleiermacher found the origin of theological discourse within the "feeling" of the newly constituted modern human subject — more particularly, in the intuition or feeling that the modern subject can have of "absolute → dependence" on a higher cause, the cause being identified with God (→ Liberal Theology).

Modern theology after Kant was given its overall shape by the Kantian "turn to the subject," with the result that modern theological discourse after Kant focused not so much on doctrine (viewed with suspicion as a heteronomous influence) or on the objective being of God (as the source of → revelation that could not be derived from the experience of an individual human subject alone) but rather on the rational, emotive, and aesthetic activities of the human subject.

An emphasis on the activity of human reason and rationality is central to the philosophical discourses of modernity. Inherent also to the discourses of modernity is the organizing trope of → progress in scientific, technical, and industrial pursuits.

In the 19th century the discipline of → sociology emerged as a response to the crisis of modernity brought on by the rise of capitalist economies and life in modern urban cities (→ Capitalism; City). The breakdown of traditional societies, exemplified in modern urban life, led to social disintegration and a host of new social, economic, and political problems. Early sociologists such as Max Weber (1864-1920) sought to understand the crisis of modernity and at the same time hoped to find an antidote to social disintegration and fragmentation.

Weber noted the loss in modern society of traditions and religious explanations of the world. The "disenchantment of the modern world" is accompanied by the increase of often inhumane bureaucratic, scientific, and technological understandings of the world and accompanying practices that serve to further promote social fragmentation and the loss of human meaning and experience (→ Bureaucracy; Technology). This disenchantment destroyed the foundation of traditional → worldviews and, as Weber understood it, left no possibility for a rational grounding of → norms for human life in the modern world. All the human being can do now is choose between varying and competing norms that are irreparably torn free from what originally — in traditional, premodern society — gave them cogency and moral force.

This conclusion of Weber and others like him results in the → relativism found at the heart of both modernity and postmodernity. At the heart of the Enlightenment and its project of modernity one finds an instrumental rationality *(Zwecksrationalität)* that does not lead to human emancipation or freedom, the original promise of the Enlightenment, but rather to what Weber called an "iron cage" of bureaucratic rationality.

1.2. *Modernism*

Within the study of the arts, the term "modernism" refers to a European aesthetic movement of the early 20th century. (This movement is not to be confused with what is known as → modernism within Roman Catholic theology and history.) Modernist movements from 1880 to 1930 include symbolism, cubism, and → expressionism. Modernists include writers such as T. S. Eliot (1888-1965), E. Pound (1885-1972), J. Joyce (1882-1941), V. Woolf (1882-1941), F. Kafka (1883-1924), R. M. Rilke (1875-1926), and M. Proust (1871-1922). "High modernism" refers more particularly to the artistic movement and practices that flourished roughly between 1910 and 1930.

Modernism, like postmodernism, is not a term with a fixed meaning or set of artistic practices. Modernists for the most part rejected 19th-century forms of artistic expression, particularly realist expressions in word or image (→ Realism). Modernist artists often rejected the idea that there was a single objective reality or an integrated human subject. They explored the alienated or fragmented experience of persons in urban, technological, and industrial societies; they worked with an aesthetic self-consciousness continually reminding the reader/observer of the work of art, often by directing attention to the media itself in order to indicate that it was in fact a human creation. They also celebrated spontaneity, juxtaposing images and words in a montage of expression, creating a new unity by the placement of images, words, and perceptions.

In realist literature, for example, a story might be narrated from an objective or omniscient point of view, whereas in modernist literature the author might explore the perceptions of a character, moving from one event or sensation to another in no sequential order, that is, in a "stream of consciousness." The crisis of the individual modern subject, uprooted from traditional society and its religious traditions, is reflected everywhere in modernist art, as are a disappointment in the idea of progress and a fear of what industry and technology have unleashed into the world, particularly after the horrors of the First World War.

1.3. *Western Marxism and Modernism*

Following the failure of the revolution of 1848, Marxists in the West turned for the most part to aesthetics, seeing in works of art the expression of larger social issues, concerns, and the aporias of modern philosophy.

Western Marxists (→ Literary Criticism 6, 10), however, were not of one mind when it came to modernist forms of art. Some Marxist theorists, including G. Lukács (1885-1971), whose early philosophy was influenced by the sociological work of M. Weber and G. Simmel (1858-1918), wanted to return to earlier premodern, realist forms of art in which societal disintegration was not so fully expressed and in which the possibility of some societal wholeness or totality remained a possibility, even if only a distant one. Others like B. Brecht (1898-1956) celebrated the possibility that modernist art could be used in the service of social and political liberation from the oppression and repression seen at the heart of modern, industrial capitalist society.

The critical social theory of the Frankfurt School of Social Research (→ Critical Theory) arose out of an attempt to understand the rise of → fascism and the phenomenon of mass culture by a multidisciplinary method that employed elements of the Kantian critique of philosophical discourse and the Marxist analysis of society. The most prominent attack of this school on the project of modernity and its promised enlightenment was released by T. W. Adorno (1903-69) and M. Horkheimer (1895-1973). In their *Dialectic of Enlightenment* (Ger. ed., 1944; Eng. ed., 1986), they depict the Enlightenment project, centered on reason and progress, not as a liberating project, but rather as an oppressive, repressive, and even regressive one. Where liberation had been promised, only its opposite has been achieved. Adorno and Horkheimer indict instrumental reason and see in the horrors of fascism the logical end of the Enlightenment. The project of reason has ended in what Weber had predicted: the "iron cage" of modernity.

1.4. *Postmodernism*

The term "postmodernism" has no simple history or genealogy; its early usage was not uniform but rather haphazard, and at times widely divergent. The earliest references to postmodernism appear from the 1930s to the 1960s in discussions of literature and the visual arts. In the late 1960s and the early 1970s the term began to be used in the area of architectural → criticism. In the late 1970s and early 1980s, under the influence of French literary criticism and philosophy, postmodern theory became interwoven with poststructuralist discourses, particularly that of deconstruction. In the late 1980s postmodernism also became associated with antifoundationalist philosophical discourse, particularly within the field of → epistemology.

The word "postmodernism" first appeared in a 1934 anthology of Spanish and Spanish-American poetry from 1882 to 1932. In this book the editor, Federico de Onís (1885-1966), groups the work of selected poets into four historical periods: the transition from Romanticism to modernism (1882-96), the triumph of modernism (1896-1905), postmodernism (1905-14), and "ultramodernism" (1914-32).

In 1971 the journal *New Literary History* published an issue entitled *Modernism and Postmodernism: Inquiries, Reflections, and Speculations.* In this issue Ihab Hassan's essay "POSTmodernISM: A Paracritical Bibliography" identified a number of changes within modernism that "may be called postmodernism." Hassan specified a few leitmotifs within an emerging postmodern criticism: "the literary act in quest and question of itself; self-subversion or self-transcendence of forms; popular mutations; languages of silence" (p. 15).

Because any suggestion of newly emerging postmodern art forms involves first a description of what is meant by modernism, Hassan identified within modernism the "rubrics" of urbanism, technologism, dehumanization (including elitism, irony, and abstraction), primitivism, eroticism, antinomianism, and experimentalism, and in his description of these rubrics he cited representative authors or works of art. To each of these rubrics, Hassan also offered what he called "postmodernist notes," which are at best only suggestive, hoping to "open up alternatives to the Unimaginable." In many ways Hassan's view of postmodernism was shaped by the → countercultural movements of the 1960s and thus is to be seen as an emerging social and artistic avant-garde.

Although the term "postmodern" had previously been used in the 1960s by Nikolaus Pevsner (1902-83) and Philip Johnson (1906-2005), it entered the mainstream vocabulary of architectural criticism in 1970s. It appeared in Robert Venturi's critique of the modernist "international style" of Walter Gropius (1883-1969), Le Corbusier (1887-1965), and Ludwig Mies van der Rohe (1886-1969). The most influential architectural critic to define the meaning of "postmodernism" within the discipline was Charles Jencks. Jencks first analyzed the term in his essay "The Rise of Post-modern Architecture" (1975), refined its usage in *The Language of Post-modern Architecture* (1977), and again in *The New Paradigm in Architecture: The Language of Post-modernism* (2002). In these works he developed his concept of the "double-coding" of architectural structures, or the postmodern usage of a plurality of historical styles within one building.

By the mid-1980s postmodernism had become integrally connected with poststructuralist textual practices and → literary criticism (§10; → Language). Postmodern theory began to employ so many ideas and methods taken from French post-structuralism that postmodernism and poststructuralism were often understood to be synonymous, in spite of their obvious differences.

The most influential poststructuralist discourses

on the shape of emerging postmodern writings were the literary-critical work of Roland Barthes (1915-80), the decentering (or deconstructive) practices of Jacques Derrida (1930-2004), the genealogical criticism of Michel Foucault (1926-84), the psychoanalytic work of Jacques Lacan (1901-81), and the philosophical/sociological work of Jean-François Lyotard (1924-98). The critical methods employed by these French philosophers and critics for the most part were textual or linguistic, but their work served to bring the disciplines of philosophy and literary criticism closer together.

The articulation of a putative definition of postmodernism begins with the programmatic work of J.-F. Lyotard, *The Postmodern Condition: A Report on Knowledge* (1979). Lyotard defined the "postmodern" as an "incredulity towards metanarratives," the grand totalizing narratives of modernity that include "history" and "progress." (By extension, all formulations of totality come under a similar suspicion in postmodern thought.) Lyotard's postmodern rejection of the metanarratives of modernity paralleled the Kantian assault on metaphysics announced at the birth of so-called modernity.

Foucault focused attention on the relationship between → power and knowledge. His analysis of "discourses" and the "discursive formations" that emerged from them became one of the organizing principles of all subsequent postmodern thought, namely that every discourse is legitimized by a determinate set of power relationships that give that discourse its apparent authority or influence. Every theoretical or practical position, therefore, is an expression of a "will to power." All knowledge contains the ideological or political interests of the persons enunciating their either implicit or explicit desires, and therefore all knowledge is power.

Derrida sought to deconstruct the binary and hierarchical oppositions within the Western philosophical tradition, including, for example, presence/absence, speech/writing, mind/body, and inside/outside. The task of deconstruction is to show that such oppositions are not given or fixed but are rather constructions. Deconstructive criticism does not destroy the categories under investigation; it seeks, rather, to open up new possibilities for their use.

In his deconstructive analysis of language, Derrida severed the connection between the "signifier" (the word) and the "sign" (that to which the word was thought to refer), a connection that is central to structuralist accounts of how language functions in reference to → meaning or signification. When the connection between the → sign and signifier is sundered, Derrida argued, there is a dispersal of meaning; that is, there no longer is the possibility of arriving at a fixed meaning, but rather a multiplicity of meanings. To refer to this dispersal of meaning, Derrida employed the terms "différance" and "dissemination."

Derrida's deconstructive methods found particular resonance with literary critics, including P. de Man (1919-83), G. Hartman, H. Bloom, and H. Miller, who began to practice a distinctly American version of "deconstructive" criticism, influenced by the methods that Derrida had formulated in another context in response to French → structuralism. The postmodern practices of American "deconstruction" focus on a "close" reading of literary texts and on the indeterminacy and multiplicity of meanings in every text (→ Interpretation; Hermeneutics).

In *Anti-Oedipus: Capitalism and Schizophrenia* (1983) and in *A Thousand Plateaus: Capitalism and Schizophrenia* (1986), G. Deleuze (1925-95) and F. Guattari (1930-92) sought to undermine psychoanalytic theory and the practice of → psychoanalysis by unmasking their ideological foundations in Western capitalist societies. In so doing, they developed a new postmodern vocabulary both to describe the nature of subjectivity and to imagine new libidinal possibilities for it in multinational or global capitalist economies.

In the 1980s a more explicit link was forged in the area of epistemology between postmodern discourses and philosophy, particularly in the antifoundational philosophies of Richard Rorty and Gianni Vattimo. Rorty's *Philosophy and the Mirror of Nature* (1981) articulated a full assault from a postmodern perspective on Cartesian and Kantian views of epistemology. Rorty rejected the idea that knowledge is a form of representation, a mental mirroring of a world eternal to the mind, and the possibility of arriving at any objective philosophical standpoint. The task of philosophers, he argued, is "to help their readers, or society as a whole, break free from outworn vocabularies and attitudes, rather than to provide 'grounding' for the intuitions and customs of the present" (p. 12).

In place of the modernist need for strong rational foundations, Vattimo had proposed the concept of "weak thought" *(pensiero debole)*. Following F. Nietzsche, who argued that → truth is a conflict of interpretations, with no strong correspondence between a proposition and the thing to which it refers, Vattimo proposed a hermeneutics founded on rhetoric and aesthetics as a model for truth. Vattimo sees in modernism the endless cycle of attempts to introduce the ever new. Postmodernism, as he understands it, finally has broken the modern cycle of constant progress.

2. Critics of Postmodernism

The critical social theory of J. Habermas can be located within the larger tradition of the work begun by the members of the Frankfurt School of Social Research. Where Adorno and Horkheimer rejected the project of modernity, Habermas continues to search for a way to rescue the project of the Enlightenment with its promise of human emancipation and freedom from its own destructive tendencies and to provide a foundation for moral, ethical, and political choices (as they are seen after Weber). In the various formulations and reformulations of his philosophical work, Habermas has sought, in response to the relativism for modernity and postmodernity, to articulate "transcendental" or "quasi-transcendental" foundations for common human life that further the emancipation and liberation of all human persons. Many postmodernists greet with great suspicion the possibility of developing universal foundations for human action.

The most influential critics of postmodernism from within the aesthetic traditions of Western → Marxism are T. Eagleton and F. Jameson. Eagleton's *Illusions of Postmodernism* (1996) is a wry attack on the pretensions of postmodern theorists and postmodern theory itself. *After Theory* (2003) is his contribution to the question of what comes after postmodernism. In these two works Eagleton identified what he regards as the central defects or inconsistencies of postmodern theory. First, postmodernism is silent on the conditions of its own production. All knowledge is power, yet what configurations of power underlie postmodern theory itself? How is it able to pull the rug out from under every other theoretical position without having the rug pulled out from under itself? Second, Eagleton finds the cultural relativism and moral conventionalism of postmodern theory to be particularly unsatisfactory. With its rejection of all forms of essences and universal → categories, postmodern theory is also characterized by → cynicism and a determined localism. If, according to the relativist assumptions of postmodern theory, persons cannot decisively distinguish between right or wrong, or between good and evil, because every position is understood to be only an articulation of personal power and desire, then every person, or every particular cultural group, comes to be seen as a victim of someone else's exercise of power. Where Enlightenment universalism was exclusive in theory, the ethnic particularism so prevalent in postmodernism is exclusive not only in theory but also in practice. Finally, postmodern thought has no theory of political agency, with the result that it cannot decisively confront political movements like, for example, fascism. How can a postmodern theorist speak out on political issues with any moral force if all he or she can articulate is understood to be merely one more enunciation of a position of power, a relative position alongside many others?

In his essays and in *Postmodernism; or, The Cultural Logic of Late Capitalism* (1991), F. Jameson argued that postmodernism is a cultural manifestation of the "cultural logic of late-capitalism." His understanding of the nature of late-capitalism *(Spätkapitalismus)* is derived largely from the work of the economist E. Mandel (1923-95). Jameson maintained that postmodernism is correlative with the historical manifestation of global capitalism, or multinational capitalism, in much the same way that modernism was correlative with commodity capitalism. Jameson also argued that many of the key concepts of postmodernism, including, for example, the term "dissemination" (a word Derrida employed to refer to the dispersal of meaning in every word, every concept, and every text), are the symptoms of the effect of the experience of the subject, at once the consumer, living in late-capitalist economies.

In summary, postmodernism can be defined as a set of discourses, developed within multinational capitalist economies, that share a denial of the possibility of universal or rational principles, fixed meanings, or objective understandings of truth and transhistorical metanarratives such as history and progress. Postmodernism is wary of every truth claim, preferring truths, understood to be both partial and plural, in place of any notion of a single, univocal truth. Rather than talk, for example, about Christianity, postmodern theorists, always suspicious of underlying essences or overarching ideas that appear to be transhistorical or transcultural, would prefer to talk about Christianities, that is, the pluralities and diversities of Christian beliefs and practices that manifest themselves in divergent places and times. Postmodern discourses also can be playful, parodic, and eclectic, utilizing a pastiche of styles, images, and ideas.

The → anxiety so prevalent in modernist art and philosophy, particularly in the wake of World War I, was a result of the experience of having the foundations of the life that many had known eroded within modern, urban, and technological society. The rejection of foundations in postmodernist discourse, by contrast, was seen as an act of freedom and was celebrated as such.

The concept of postmodernism can be defined fully only in relation to modernism, the discourse that preceded it. Yet the exact relation of postmodernity to modernity remains an open question. Is postmodernity merely a continuation of modernity, albeit in a new light, or does it represent a radical break with all that came before it? Or are postmodern discourses, in their emphasis on the partial, the fragmented, and the multiple, as P. Lacoue-Labarthe and J.-L. Nancy have suggested, merely another manifestation of the Romantic rejection of the modern? Where some have seen a direct continuity and line of development beginning with the Enlightenment, through → Romanticism and modernism to postmodernism, others see only the radical discontinuity of postmodernism with all that precedes it. Others like F. Jameson understand postmodernism to be an expression of artistic, cultural, and philosophical concepts, ideas, and practices that correspond to the specific social, economic, and political conditions of a particular stage of late capitalism, namely, multinational or global capitalism.

3. Postmodern and Postliberal Challenges to Modern Liberal Christian Theology

3.1. ***The Neoorthodox Theology of Karl Barth***

In the 20th century the most important rejection of the historical relativism and subjective individualism of modern liberal theology was set forth by Karl Barth (1886-1968) in the second edition of his *Epistle to the Romans* (1922). Barth's → dialectical theology directly confronted the easy alliance of liberal theology and cultural Christianity, asserting in their place the radical dichotomy between God and the world. Barth and other so-called neoorthodox theologians, including Reinhold Niebuhr (1892-1971), stressed the radical transcendence of God and the brokenness and sinfulness of all human beings (→ Immanence and Transcendence).

In the exposition of his theology in *Church Dogmatics* (1936-69), Barth further developed — in direct contrast to the thought of F. Schleiermacher — a theology anchored not on the subjective expressions or feelings of the modern human subject but rather on the objective self-revelation of God to all human beings in Jesus Christ within the community of the church.

Barth's theology was a critique and rejection of modern, or liberal, theology. His theological method relied on a foundational metaphysics, particularly in his discussion of the being of God, and in his nonrelative use of epistemological truth claims. Although Barth's theology cannot be described as postmodern, his grounding of the faith within the community of the church provided the theological linchpin for future postmodern challenges to modern theology.

3.2. ***Postliberal Theology***

In his 1984 work *The Nature of Doctrine,* G. Lindbeck outlined the elements of what he calls "postliberal" theology. Although Lindbeck coined the term "postliberal," its theological method was shaped not only by Lindbeck but also by his colleagues at Yale P. Holmer (1916-2004) and H. Frei (1922-88). The key components of postliberal theology follow Holmer's understanding of the implications of the work of L. Wittgenstein (1889-1951) for theological discourse (→ Language 5; → Language and Theology 4.3.3), Frei's study of the role of narrative in theology (→ Narrative Theology), and Alasdair MacIntyre's rejection of the Enlightenment promise of a "universal rationality."

3.2.1. In *Philosophical Investigations* (1953, pub. posth.), Wittgenstein demonstrated how particular "language games" arise within particular communities, or "forms of life." Wittgenstein argued that the meaning of a word is expressed in its use within a particular form of life. Wittgenstein does not discuss theology per se in *Philosophical Investigations,* yet in two rather enigmatic sentences he points the way to an application of his work within contemporary theological discourse: "Essence is expressed by grammar" (§371) and "Grammar tells us what kind of object anything is (Theology as grammar)" (§373). Wittgenstein recognized that all thought and discourse are dependent on language. All descriptions or accounts of metaphysical or noumenal realities, therefore, are always already embedded in language; apart from language, both thought and expression about these realities are impossible. Because theology is a discourse that structures thoughts and expressions about God and other metaphysical concepts by means of language, Wittgenstein suggests that the discipline of theology provides a grammar that functions to control or regulate the usage of specific terminology or expressions within larger theological or metaphysical discourses.

3.2.2. In *The Grammar of Faith* (1978), Holmer argued that the human ability to speak meaningfully about God does not hinge on our ability to verify the existence of a being we might call God. Rather, the concept of God becomes meaningful as we learn to live in relation to that God within the community of faith. In his understanding that theology is first and foremost a product of the community of faith, that is, the church, Holmer, although critical of Barth's theology in other areas, thus united Wittgenstein's → analytic philosophy of language with Barth's understanding of theology as the task of the church. The church, therefore, can be described in Wittgensteinian terms as the "form of life" from which expressions of God and the revelation of that God in the person of Jesus Christ become uniquely meaningful.

3.2.3. In *The Nature of Doctrine* Lindbeck, following Wittgenstein and Holmer, suggested that just as grammar functions to regulate the usage of words within a particular language, so doctrine functions as a kind of grammar that regulates theological discourse within specific theological communities, or "forms of life." Lindbeck begins his exposition of "postliberal" theology by dividing the history of Christian theology into three paradigmatic periods: premodern theology, modern or liberal theology, and postliberal theology. According to Lindbeck, premodern theology before Kant was characterized by "cognitive propositionalism," that is, by a philosophy of language and a realist epistemology that saw a direct connection between human language and the being of God. When human beings spoke about God, they understood that they had the capacity to speak directly about noumenal things, including God's being and essence, and that through that language they could connect with the reality of God. Lindbeck's account of the inadequacy of cognitive-propositional theology echoes Richard Rorty's nonfoundational critique of realist metaphysics.

Second, modern or liberal theology, following Schleiermacher, was characterized by what Lindbeck calls the "experiential expressivist" paradigm, that is, a theology grounded on subjective human experience, including feeling and emotion.

Lindbeck's third paradigm, the postliberal, contained his critique *in nuce* of liberal theology. Lindbeck does not call this paradigm "postmodern," as he might have, but rather "postliberal," since the target of his criticism is more specifically the "liberal" theological method. Following Barth's emphasis on the community as the locus of theology and Wittgenstein's understanding of the integral connection between language and the forms of life in which language comes to life, Lindbeck called this paradigm the "cultural linguistic."

These three paradigms center respectively on reason, human experience, and the form (or forms) of life in which reason and human experience find their context and, so to speak, come to life. Human reason and religious experience, for Lindbeck and other postliberal theologians, make sense only within the context of the particular communities in which they arise and take shape.

The problem with the first two paradigms, for Lindbeck, is that they cannot account for the community, in which reason and experience are made possible. Both premodern and modern theology assume for the most part that reason and experience are transcultural and transhistorical, where in fact, Lindbeck argues, they make sense only within the particular cultural-linguistic forms of life from which they arise. In summary, postliberal theology is antifoundational in its rejection of "universal reason," radically historicist, and communitarian in its understanding that community (a cultural-linguistic form of life) is a prior condition for experience.

3.2.4. The philosophical ethics of Alasdair MacIntyre and the theological ethics of Stanley Hauerwas have also been shaped by postliberal theological assumptions. In *After Virtue* (1981) MacIntyre argued that modern ethics is in a state of "grave disorder" and that modern morality "is intelligible only as a set of fragmented survivals" from the Aristotelian tradition (pp. 3, 11, 257). Nietzsche, MacIntyre argued, is "the moral philosopher of the present age," an age immersed in the bureaucratic culture of the modernity that is essentially "Weberian" (p. 114). Nietzsche maintained that appeals to objectivity were in fact expressions of subjective will, expressions of the will to power of the person or persons making them, and therefore essentially irrationalist. In place of Nietzsche's account of ethics, in which human persons must be their own self-sufficient authority, MacIntyre proposed a return to the Aristotelian tradition, in which moral goods must be expounded in terms of "practice," "the narrative unity of a human life," and from within particular moral traditions and communities. The "grounds for the authority of laws and virtues," MacIntyre argued, "can only be discovered by entering into those relationships which constitute communities whose central bond is a shared vision of and understanding of goods" (p. 258). In *Whose Justice? Which Rationality?* (1988), MacIntyre maintained that every form of rationality is connected to a particular tradition, and therefore that universal reason, or rationality, is an impossibility.

Alasdair MacIntyre's nonfoundational retrieval of the Aristotelian tradition of virtue for philosophical ethics strongly influenced the development of Hauerwas's theological ethics within the Aristotelian and Thomist traditions (→ Aristotelianism; Thomism). Hauerwas, with MacIntyre, affirmed that the human being has no capacity to stand outside his or her own historical, social location so as to make purely rational ethical decisions. There is no universally objective place where human beings can stand outside of their own historical location and traditions. The locus of Hauerwas's ethics, therefore, is not rational decision-making from an alleged objective or universal standpoint. Rather, theological ethics takes its shape from the virtues that particular Christian communities or traditions embody in their corporate life and in which Christian character is formed. For Hauerwas, Christian virtues are shaped and Christian character is formed within the community of the → church. In the church, Christian character is formed by the narratives of God's loving and redemptive activity toward the people of Israel and in the person of → Jesus Christ. In his emphasis on the church as the proper locus of theology, Hauerwas continues a trajectory that runs from Barth through postliberal theology.

3.3. *Radical Orthodoxy*

The philosophical and theological roots of "radical orthodoxy" are found in the works of Plato, Aristotle, Augustine, Aquinas, and the 20th-century theologian Hans Urs von Balthasar (1905-88). The movement, which originated at Cambridge University in the 1990s, revolves for the most part around the work of three Anglican theologians: John Milbank, Catherine Pickstock, and Graham Ward. In 1999 all three contributed to and edited a volume of essays entitled *Radical Orthodoxy: A New Theology.* Where postliberal theology was formulated in response to liberal (modern) theology, radical orthodoxy arose in response to postmodernism. Radical orthodoxy uses the language of postmodernism and its theories to formulate a theoretical antidote, as it were, to the essential nihilism of modern and postmodern thought.

Milbank's *Theology and Social Theory: Beyond Secular Reason* (1990) provided the initial arguments for the later movement of "radical orthodoxy." In this book Milbank sought to deconstruct the notion of the secular as a realm autonomous from theology. The idea of the secular (from Lat. *saeculum,* "generation; the present world"), he argued, was originally employed as a theological concept to refer to the "present time" or the "current age." The secular was always already a theological term. In modernity the secular was understood to have nothing to do with the theological. According to Milbank, there is no "secular." If not, then all academic disciplines are distinctly theological, and theology thus has a central role to play within these disciplines.

Milbank asserts that Christians must seek to work out a nonviolent metaphysics of social interaction that can effectively replace the assumption that all relations within civil society are by definition antagonistic. This assumption of "foundational violence," common to modern and postmodern social theory, is most explicitly articulated in Nietzsche's notion of the will to power and in the poststructuralist social theory of Foucault. In place of the Nietzschean nihilism of modernity and postmodernity, Milbank and others seek to recover and develop a revived Augustinian Neoplatonic metaphysics in which all areas of life are ordered in God. In place of the nihilist assumption of unceasing conflict *between* identity and difference, radical orthodoxy offers the possibility of a harmonious identity *in* difference.

3.4. *Deconstructive Theology*

Mark Taylor was one of the first writers to apply the deconstructive methods developed by Jacques Derrida to the discipline of theology. His *Erring: A Postmodern A/theology* (1987) proposes the deconstruction of the Christian concept of God. The work is fundamentally Nietzschean in tone. If all that previously had been understood to be connected with God is now in the postmodern world emptied of God, then all discourses and all texts for which God was constitutive for their very meaning, lose their meaning. Without God there not only is no meaning in the world, the very idea of the self, whose self-constitution had been rooted in God, also loses its meaning and purpose. The task of the postmodern a/theologian is to mark the meaningless, purposeless, and "erring" wanderings of the self in a world without God and without meaning. Although the book at the time of its appearance offered a novel approach to theology, it did not have much of an influence on subsequent Christian theology.

4. What Comes after Postmodernism?

Although postmodern theory continues to exert its influence, in the period past its heyday (i.e., the late 1980s and 1990s), new movements in reaction to postmodernism have already emerged with a renewed philosophical — and theological — interest in ethics and metaphysics. In *The Ticklish Subject* (1999), Slavoj Žižek sought "to reassert the Cartesian subject," but from a post-Lacanian perspective. In this book he challenged both the postmodern denial of the subject as "discursive fiction, an effect of decentered textual mechanisms," and the postmodern replacement of the Cartesian subject with a multiplicity of subject positions. He also rejects the politics of postmodernism, particularly the postmodern preference for "identity politics" (i.e., "diverse forms of asserting one's particular subjectivity") in place of the project of "global social transformation" (p. 3).

In his philosophical work, Alain Badiou, who was trained as a mathematician, advocates a return to the politics of "truth." Badiou asserts the universality of truth but, at the same time, understands truth to be structured by coherence without objectivity. Truth for him can be attained only by going against the grain of the world and the established orthodoxies and approaches of philosophical thought. Guided by mathematics, Badiou rejects the distinction commonly made between analytic and Continental philosophy. He sees in the multiculturalism and ethical particularism of postmodern theory and practice a politics of ressentiment, in which the only way to legitimize one's claim is to present oneself as a victim. The postmodern emphasis on radical difference, he argues, is in fact a demand for radical sameness.

The return to traditions that predate postmodernism, exemplified, for example, in the philosophical works of Žižek and Badiou and in the theology of radical orthodoxy, can be understood as yet another instance of an eclectic postmodern retrieval of ideas or traditions from the past, or they can be viewed as new, yet to be named, positions that move beyond postmodernism itself. In any case, the overall shape of what comes "after postmodernism" (itself an oxymoron) is yet to be fully explored or developed.

Bibliography: On 1: T. W. Adorno and M. Horkheimer, *Dialectic of Enlightenment* (New York, 2000; orig. pub., 1944) • P. Anderson, *Considerations on Western Marxism* (London, 1979) • H. Bertens, *The Idea of the Postmodern: A History* (London, 1995); idem, *Literary Theory: The Basics* (London, 2001) • G. Deleuze and F. Guattari, *Anti-Oedipus: Capitalism and Schizophrenia* (Minneapolis, 1983); idem, *A Thousand Plateaus: Capitalism and Schizophrenia* (Minneapolis, 1986) • J. Derrida, *Dissemination* (Chicago, 1981); idem, *Margins of Philosophy* (Chicago, 1984); idem, *Of Grammatology* (Baltimore, 1976); idem, *Writing and Difference* (Chicago, 1978) • M. Foucault, *The Archaeology of Knowledge* (New York, 1972) • I. Hassan, "POSTmodernISM: A Paracritical Bibliography," *NLH* 3/1 (1971) 5-30 • C. Jencks, *The Language of Post-modern Architecture* (London, 1977; 2d ed., 1978; 3d ed.,1981); idem, *The New Paradigm in Architecture: The Language of Post-modernism* (New Haven, 2002); idem, "The Rise of Post-modern Architecture," *Architectural Association Quarterly* 4 (1975) 3-14 • P. Johnson, "On Style and the International Style: On Postmodernism; On Architecture," *Oppositions* 10 (1977) 15-19 • P. Lacoue-Labarthe and J.-L. Nancy, *The Literary Absolute: The Theory of Literature in German Romanticism* (Albany, N.Y., 1988; orig. pub., 1978) • E. Lunn, *Marxism and Modernism: An Historical Study of Lukács, Brecht, Benjamin, and Adorno* (Berkeley, Calif., 1982) • J.-F. Lyotard, *The Postmodern Condition: A Report on Knowledge* (Minneapolis, 1984; orig. pub., 1979) • D. Macey, ed., *The Penguin Dictionary of Critical Theory* (London, 2000) • F. de Onís, ed., *Antología de la poesía española e hispanoamericana (1882-1932)* (Madrid, 1934) • N. Pevsner, "The Return of Historicism" (1961), *Studies in Art, Architecture, and Design*, vol. 2, *Victorian and After* (London, 1968) 242-60 • R. Rorty, *Philosophy and the Mirror of Nature* (Princeton, 1981) • R. Rorty and G. Vattimo, *The Future of Religion* (ed. S. Zabala; New York, 2005) • R. Venturi, *Complexity and Contradiction in Architecture* (London, 1966) • R. Venturi, D. Brown, and S. Izenour, *Learning from Las Vegas: The Forgotten Symbolism of Architectural Form* (Cambridge, Mass., 1996) • M. Weber, "Science as a Vocation," *Max Weber: Essays in Sociology* (New York, 1974) 129-56.

On 2: T. Eagleton, *After Theory* (New York, 2003); idem, *The Illusions of Postmodernism* (Oxford, 1996) • F. Jameson, *Postmodernism; or, The Cultural Logic of Late Capitalism* (Durham, N.C., 1991) • E. Mandel, *Late Capitalism* (London, 1978).

On 3: K. Barth, *CD* (Edinburgh, 1936-69; orig. pub., 1932-67); idem, *The Epistle to the Romans* (2d ed.; London, 1933; orig. pub., 1922) • H. W. Frei, *The Eclipse of Biblical Narrative: A Study in Eighteenth- and Nineteenth-Century Hermeneutics* (New Haven, 1974) • S. Hauerwas, *Character and the Christian Life: A Study in Theological Ethics* (San Antonio, Tex., 1975); idem, *A Community of Character: Toward a Constructive Christian Social Ethic* (Notre Dame, Ind., 1981) • P. Holmer, *The Grammar of Faith* (San Francisco,1978); idem, "Wittgenstein: 'Saying' and 'Showing,'" *NZSTh* 22 (1980) 222-35 • G. A. Lindbeck, *The Church in a Postliberal Age* (Grand Rapids, 2002); idem, *The Nature of Doctrine: Religion and Theology in a Postliberal Age* (Philadelphia, 1984) • A. MacIntyre, *After Virtue* (Notre Dame, Ind., 1981; 2d ed., 1984); idem, *Whose Justice? Which Rationality?* (Notre Dame, Ind., 1988) • J. Milbank, *Theology and Social Theory: Beyond Secular Reason* (Oxford, 1990) • J. Milbank, G. Ward, and C. Pickstock, eds., *Radical Orthodoxy: A New Theology* (London, 1999) • C. Pickstock, *After Writing: On the Liturgical Consummation of Philosophy* (Oxford, 1997) • M. Taylor, *Erring: A Postmodern A/theology* (Chicago, 1987) • G. Ward, *Barth, Derrida, and the Language of Theology* (Cambridge, 1995); idem, *Cities of God* (London, 2000); idem, ed., *The Postmodern God: A Theological Reader* (Oxford, 1997) • L. Wittgen-

STEIN, *Philosophical Investigations* (3d ed.; Oxford, 2001; orig. pub., 1953).

On 4: A. BADIOU, *Saint Paul: The Foundation of Universalism* (Stanford, Calif., 2003) • P. HALLWARD, *Badiou: A Subject to Truth* (Minneapolis, 2003) • S. ŽIŽEK, *The Ticklish Subject: The Absent Centre of Political Ontology* (London, 1999).

CRAIG A. PHILLIPS

Poverty

1. A Global Phenomenon
   1.1. The Vicious Cycle
   1.2. Definition
   1.3. Measurement
2. Response
   2.1. United Nations
   2.2. Ecumenical Movement
3. Approaches of Theology
4. Biblical Teaching
5. Voluntary Poverty

1. A Global Phenomenon

Poverty represents a global mass phenomenon. According to consistent estimates of the World Bank, U.N. authorities, and nongovernmental organizations (NGOs), nearly half the world's population lives in poverty. In a world population of 6.1 billion people, 2.8 billion live either on the edge or beneath the minimum level of existence, and 1.2 billion — that is, one-fifth of all persons in the world — live in extreme poverty.

Poverty is generally understood as designating social circumstances that structurally exclude certain people or groups from access to the resources needed to conduct one's life (e.g., tillable fields, clean water, education, income through work). "Solidarity" is the social term that is antithetical to poverty. The "poor" are those who are unable to meet the basic human needs for existence. In biblical and theological understanding, the poor include those such as widows, orphans, and aliens who have slipped out of *ḥesed,* or the solidarity provided by the family. The poor are commended to God's protection because they still have a claim to justice (→ Righteousness, Justice). It is they to whom Christ and the → church pay special attention.

1.1. *The Vicious Cycle*

Poverty is particularly prevalent in developing countries. The primary reasons are economic and political, with factors involving climate, geography, religion, and culture playing a secondary role. As a pervasive and enduring phenomenon in the → Third World, poverty belies the presence of unresolved distribution problems of international proportions. Most developing countries lack the necessary personnel, finances, and technology to pursue sustainable economic and social development. Population increases then disrupt the delicate balance obtaining in the largely subsistence-level agrarian economies. The hungry rural population presses into the cities, which lack sufficient job opportunities. Zones of intense poverty characterize almost all larger cities in Africa, Asia, and Latin America.

Because of their high cost, the investments needed for satisfying elementary needs (e.g., → work, food, housing, → health care, and → education) are generally possible only to a limited extent in most developing countries. For many of these countries, the crisis of debt has contributed to a worsening of the situation insofar as such countries lack the economic capacity to service that debt. Moreover, in many developing countries sociopolitical conditions tend to provide privileges for the small minority that holds power while exacerbating the gulf between the impoverished → masses and the small upper class.

Escaping this vicious circle of poverty is possible only by implementing several different measures capable of addressing the extremely complex structure of this phenomenon. They involve the empowerment of the people — granting to the impoverished masses themselves the means to articulate and implement their own social, economic, and political interests. That is, civil structures within → society must develop, including strong labor unions and agricultural cooperatives, independent political parties, and NGOs. Such local or national measures must then be secured by global policies committed to long-term ecological and social viability, which make it possible for such countries to participate more equitably in international trade.

1.2. *Definition*

The definition of poverty is disputed. Economic definitions that understand poverty essentially as a lack of access to material goods are distinguished from sociocultural definitions (→ Economy; Economic Ethics). Conceptions of absolute and relative poverty can also be distinguished. Even into the 19th century, poverty was often understood as being self-incurred or as willed by God rather than as caused by any social factors. The emergence of a more powerful workers' movement and intensified discussion of social questions in industrial nations, however, led to an understanding of poverty as a mass phenomenon caused by economic processes best addressed by social policies implemented by the → state itself.

One presupposition for addressing poverty as a matter of social policy is to determine its parameters. Those people live in poverty who must live at a material level beneath the poverty line. This definition is based on an absolute understanding of poverty. A relative understanding of poverty describes conditions in which certain people feel disadvantaged in relation to other groups or feel they have been robbed of their rightful chance for → development. Relative definitions of poverty are able to consider subjective interpretations and the various levels of development within a society.

Social anthropology speaks about a *culture of poverty* when the standards and values of the poor are distinguished from those of the rest of society. One characterizing feature of such a culture of poverty is an excessive focus on the immediate and an incapacity to delay gratification. Other features include a lack of family planning, sexual activity at an early age, low self-esteem, and an absence of historical consciousness.

1.3. *Measurement*

In measuring poverty, one can distinguish monetary from nonmonetary methods, which examine how well various goods and various areas of life are serviced (e.g., for nourishment, whether there is a daily intake of 2,250 calories). It is the task of national social legislation to prevent poverty, and prevailing political understanding will be based on specific national parameters with regard to need. Administrative statistics of any given country will thus not recognize as impoverished those who receive social aid based on social legislation, since it is precisely the purpose of that social legislation to prevent people from falling beneath the poverty level in the first place. Hence for pragmatic reasons, comparative international studies frequently fix the poverty level at 50 percent of the average income of the country in question.

The World Bank generates statistics reflecting global poverty measured against income. An income of up to US$1 (according to 1985 prices) is understood as an expression of extreme poverty, whereas $2 per day designates the upper poverty level generally applied in countries with middle-income levels. In these dollar terms, 2.8 billion people live on less than $2 per day, and 1.2 billion on less than $1. Between 1987 and 1998 the percentage of the population in developing countries and countries in transformation that lives off less than $1 per day dropped from 28 to 24 percent. Because of population increases, the number of those living in extreme poverty hardly changed at all. There are, however, considerable regional deviations in this regard. Whereas the number of those living in extreme poverty decreased significantly in East Asia and less significantly in the Near East and northern Africa, in all other regions, including Europe and North America, that number increased during the same period. In 1998 about 70 percent of those living in extreme poverty lived in southern Asia and in sub-Saharan Africa.

2. Response

2.1. *United Nations*

In September 2000 a total of 198 countries accepted the Millennium Declaration of the → United Nations, which mutually obliges the signatories to engage in more pronounced global measures to eliminate extreme poverty and hunger, to improve health care, and to promote peace, human → rights, and ecological commitment. One goal is to decrease by half between 1990 and 2015 the number of those living in extreme poverty and similarly by half those suffering from hunger. The millennium goals also include measures to decrease debt, increase developmental aid, and expand trade and the transfer of technology to poorer countries.

2.2. *Ecumenical Movement*

Following the → World Council of Churches Assembly in Uppsala in 1968, which challenged churches to commit themselves unequivocally to solving developmental conflicts in the world, people began viewing church engagement on behalf of global justice as a touchstone of orthodox faith and credibility. Discussions with Latin American representatives of → liberation theology focused ecclesiologically on the concept of a church of the poor (→ Base Community). Taking up Reformed theological traditions, the WCC Commission on the Churches' Participation in Development demanded that the church itself be poor so that it might better identify with the poor. This identification of the church with the poor was to acquire the status of an additional *nota ecclesiae,* or mark of the church. Such thinking points to the unity of the Christian witness within the word and life of the church itself. In response to its own prophetic office, the church is to become engaged on behalf of the poor and oppressed.

The ecumenical movement understands the relationship between poverty and wealth as deriving from globalization and the increasingly inequitable distribution of income. Factors determining the parameters of wealth (the so-called greed line) have been defined, and programs against "mammon" suggested. As a way to globalize this solidarity, attempts have been made to establish a worldwide network of churches, the core of which will be the Ecumenical Advocacy Alliance, established in December 2000 at the invitation of the WCC. At the same time, churches have been charged with publishing a "World Church Report on Poverty and Wealth."

3. Approaches of Theology

Within → *systematic theology* critical discussion of poverty is generally taken as the object of → ethics — in particular, of → social ethics. → *Contextual theologies* take a different tack insofar as they develop God's solidarity with the poor as the heart of biblical faith. Poverty undermines the life bequeathed by God, the cause of poverty is injustice, and God is concerned especially with the poor.

Liberation theology speaks about God's option for the poor. According to Victorio Araya of Costa Rica, "For the 'third world' Christian there is no encounter with the Mystery of God the deliverer, God the lifegiver, without an efficacious decision to set out with God down the road to the liberating goals of history" (p. 152). More recent works from the Third World address the special status of women, street children, indigenous peoples, and ethnic → minorities. The characterizing feature of contextual theologies is that they engage "poverty" as a relational term in qualifying the relationship with God more closely.

In → *practical theology* poverty emerges as the field of action for welfare and social work, as well as internationally in church development services and in emergency aid in cases of catastrophe. The task of church development services is to overcome hunger and poverty. In pursuing this goal, it combines direct charitable engagement with sociostructural intervention. The WCC and the world denominational alliances mediate and in part coordinate the work of such developmental services within the Protestant churches. The WCC and, to an even greater degree, the Lutheran World Federation represent the churches before U.N. organizations and other international institutions.

→ Money; Property

Bibliography: V. Araya, *God of the Poor: The Mystery of God in Latin American Liberation Theology* (Maryknoll, N.Y., 1987) • W. F. Bello, *Dark Victory: The United States, Structural Adjustments, and Global Poverty* (London, 1994) • R. Dickinson, "Poverty," *DEM* (2d ed.) 916-19 • B. Geremek, *Poverty: A History* (Oxford, 1994) • G. Gutiérrez, *A Theology of Liberation: History, Politics, and Salvation* (Maryknoll, N.Y., 1973) • G. Linnenbrink, "Solidarity with the Poor: The Role of the Church in the Conflict over Development," *ER* 27 (1975) 270-75 • E. Øyen, S. M. Miller, and S. A. Samad, eds., *Poverty: A Global Review. Handbook on International Poverty Research* (Oslo, 1996) • J. de Santa Ana, *Towards a Church of the Poor* (Geneva, 1979) • Social Watch, *Report 2003: The Poor and the Market* (Montevideo, Uruguay, 2003) • M. Taylor, *Christianity, Poverty, and Wealth* (Geneva, 2003) • United Nations Development Programme, *Human Development Report 2003: Millennium Development Goals. A Compact among Nations to End Human Poverty* (New York, 2003) • World Bank, *World Development Report, 2000/2001: Attacking Poverty* (New York, 2000).

Hans Spitzeck

4. Biblical Teaching

The Bible offers different views and evaluations of poverty. The OT presents it as a state of need and does not regard it as an ideal. The poor rather than poverty are at the center of interest. Since the wealthy and powerful often harm and oppress the poor, the → prophets in particular become their advocates against the rich (e.g., Isa. 3:13-15; 10:1-2; Amos 2:6-7; 4:1; Jer. 5:26-28). They do so in the name of → Yahweh, the protector of the poor, who will help them to secure their rights.

The NT often states that the poor are nearer to God than the rich. The rich have come under the sway of mammon (Luke 16:19-31), or they are closed to the call to discipleship because of their riches (Mark 10:17-22 and par.). At issue here is more a special quality than material need as such. It is the attitude of the poor. They can hope for → salvation and deliverance from no one but God. This attitude is what makes them closer to God than the rich, who trust in themselves, in their own wealth and power.

5. Voluntary Poverty

Material poverty as a mass phenomenon is to be distinguished from the particular kind of poverty that individuals or groups accept voluntarily as a result of a religiously motivated decision (→ Asceticism; Religious Orders and Congregations). Such a decision presupposes that renunciation of material goods and a life based on a lack of material needs make possible a more intense form of → discipleship or religiosity. Voluntary poverty for religious reasons occurs not only in the Christian tradition but also in other religions (e.g., → Buddhism). In the Christian tradition an ascetic lifestyle is often a protest against a church and public that have come to embrace wealth, luxury, and ostentatious power.

This tradition of protest is also the basis for a theology of poverty (→ Base Communities; Liberation Theology; Political Theology) that understands poverty as → solidarity with the poor and as a protest also demanded of the church itself. "Only by rejecting poverty and by making itself poor in order to protest against it can the Church preach something that is uniquely its own: 'spiritual poverty,' that is, the openness of man and history to the future promised by God" (G. Gutiérrez, 301-2).

Bibliography: J. J. Bonk, *Missions and Money: Affluence as a Western Missionary Problem* (Maryknoll, N.Y., 1991) • G. Gutiérrez, *A Theology of Liberation: History, Politics, and Salvation* (Maryknoll, N.Y., 1973) • C. L. Mariz, *Coping with Poverty: Pentecostals and Christian Base Communities in Brazil* (Philadelphia, 1994) • J. de Santa Ana, *Good News to the Poor: The Challenge of the Poor in the History of the Church* (Maryknoll, N.Y., 1979).

Günter Linnenbrink

Power

1. Sociological Aspects

1.1. *Term*

Viewed from the perspective of its etymology (Lat. *posse, potestas*), power involves ability, possibility, and capacity. It is the potency inhering in all doing or making (→ Action Theory) and relates to motive and the use of means. Action is inconceivable without means, that is, the command of resources and potential. This statement applies equally to the natural, physical, cultural, symbolic, individual, and social aspects of action. In all these areas there is a tendency to extend the basis of power and to change it — "magically" enhanced — into the power to do everything. In a reverse fashion, any action that demonstrates power or an increase of power acquires (in the eyes of the public) a kind of radiating magical effect (such as that exhibited by those designated prophets, leaders, or "power women"; W. Lipp, "Magie").

1.2. *Definition*

Max → Weber (1864-1920) established a normative sociological definition of power (→ Sociology). As he saw it, power involves the opportunity to assert one's own will in a social context, even against opposition. It is not restricted to specific social spheres like → politics, religious life, or education. "Sociologically amorphous," it applies throughout society and is ubiquitous. There is economic as well as political power (→ Economy; Economic Ethics), judicial as well as executive and legislative power. Agencies, associations, and groups (e.g., "pressure groups"), as well as the people representing them, exert social power according to the respective social factors of each. At the same time, professionals, the "experts," may use and activate power at both functional and personal levels. And so typically do charismatics — whether strong personalities or light-footed charmers — by attracting or → manipulating others.

Such circles of power overlap. According to Weber, "rule" or "dominion" (e.g., in government) involves the opportunity to secure obedience for a specific command from specific people. It thus implies stable institutions and → hierarchies and well-anchored, unique patterns of → legitimation. In contrast, power remains many-layered, open-ended, and multipolar; it develops fluid features that overlap many different spheres.

1.3. *Organization*

By distinguishing between formal and informal power, organizational sociology has shown that power and government are not identical. Along with authorities that exert power formally (e.g., according to a "business plan"), there are usually groups that

Power

do so informally by developing special relations such as agreements with third parties, cliques, and media contacts. In this connection we find that leadership in → organizations may not be deducible strictly from a single point, namely, the hierarchical head. It may be twofold, involving officers and those in the ranks, or specialists and generalists, or functionaries and professionals. Again, it may be multiple. At least in nonmilitary organizations, such governance is practiced less according to Weber's model of "order and command" than it is to the model of a system. To direct an organization effectively requires that one eliminate or relativize strategies that rest on a (classic) mentality of there being "one best way." On the contrary, organizations typically face and solve problems using a process of "muddling through" (Lindblom; Lipp, "Börokratien"), which includes components that are adaptive, opportunistic, and hence suboptimal.

1.4. *Community*

The sociology of community offers similar insights. If we ask who in fact controls the destinies of communities, cities, or regions, we encounter the phenomenon that "power elites" (C. W. Mills) are not the same as the formal leadership, which they may infiltrate. In origin (whether class or estate), function, and clientele, their recruitment differs considerably. Reputation, influence, and the ability to make decisions correspond only approximately to regular institutional positions. They divide along the lines of specific, empirically quantifiable social networks (see E. O. Laumann and F. U. Pappi; R. Perruci and H. R. Potter). Those who seek power must find access to those who pull the switches — that is, to those who already have power (C. Schmitt, see also H. Popitz); similarly, they also must seek access to the networks.

1.5. *Politics*

In speaking of power, Weber stressed the reference to action. In this regard he also pointed out the relation to politics, maintaining that to engage in politics is to seek power. Power, though, refers not only to action — that is, the actions, means, and goals of politicians. It also fulfills emergent systemic functions. Systems, whether organizations, institutions, or societies as a whole, need power (T. Parsons, N. Luhmann). Power makes it possible to preserve achievements (e.g., acts of choice and productions of goods), keeping them from being nullified by routinization and allowing them to be continued in different forms for use in the future. Power appears both as the motor keeping this overall process running and as its key and currency, providing entry and access to it.

Perspectives of this kind imply two things. First, socially implemented power, the structure of power, and the distribution of power all involve circular and interrelated processes. They function as "reflexive mechanisms" (Luhmann), by which those who hold power — electors and elected, rulers and ruled, federated forces, central authorities, and so forth — intertwine with one another. Second, they involve a system that aims essentially at the enhancement of power. The processes of power do not engage in a neutral system of push and pull in the form of a "zero-sum game"; rather, in a cumulative fashion where they are engaged, they effect "gains," open up new sources, and reach out into other spheres of action.

1.6. *Modern Developments*

Power is not just a constituent part of elementary human action, nor is it — quasi-disembodied as it is — restricted to the regulation of merely abstract systems. It also involves processes with historical character and indeed emerges as a formative factor of history itself.

1.6.1. *Power Elites*

Michael Mann and others have articulated similar perspectives. Drawing from extensive comparative-historical research, Mann has shown that power does not represent something essentially one-sided, rigid, or inert; instead, it enters into changing alliances with changing actors in connection with ongoing economic, political, legal, and cultural agendas of the sort characterizing societies at large. Nor does power tend to grow merely quantitatively; it also acquires a new identity profile in the qualitative sense, establishing itself as a "power elite." Whereas power and the bearers of power generally emerge in a plurality, power elites strive for a hegemonic position against competitors, establishing themselves more securely in a hierarchical fashion. In such cases, the focal points of such processes can vary; insofar as they permeate one another dynamically in the historical process itself, they do not necessarily fulfill any discernible (e.g., teleological) pattern. Balanced solutions — for example, between the technocratic, administrative, and monetary exercise of power — seem to be more the norm; extreme variants include the more one-sided, uniform, and totalitarian constellations.

1.6.2. *Power and Violence*

One of the more interesting aspects of power has always been its relationship with violence or → force. Power and violence can be mutually sustaining or can even blend into each other. Formally, they stand in a continuum ranging from simple influence to conscious manipulation, on to the exercise of physical coercion. Even though they need not be either "good" or "bad" in and of themselves (C. J. Burckhardt), power and violence do convey these qualities within a concrete field of action and as such raise weighty political and ethical questions, both theoretically and practically. In an age of globalization in which societies are expanding to the point where we can speak of a global society, but also an age in which overarching cultural values are increasingly being dismantled, with a resulting loss of solidarity, it is becoming increasingly urgent to clarify this debate involving power and violence (U. Beck).

The enhancement of power and, concomitantly, the engagement of force or violence reach their historical apex when those who have (or are competing for) power manage to gain political control of force and are then able to engage it not only on behalf of their own interests but also on behalf of the commonwealth or community as such, enabling them to maintain law and order and an abiding peace. Max Weber understood this process (which in a concrete historical sense coincides with the emergence of the system of European states) basically as socially "rational." (In this context see also N. Elias, with his figure of the "royal mechanism," which marked the rise of the modern absolutistic state or, viewed from the opposite perspective, the demise of the magical-medieval, patrimonial, and → feudal form of rule.)

1.6.3. *Recent Polarization*

Things have shifted recently. On the one hand, increased functional networking has enabled the more highly developed "civilization" systems to grow closer together legally and politically; such developments, however, can in their own turn prompt what amounts to compulsive "cultural" countermovements — often along notorious lines of socioeconomic destitution — and return to fundamentalist positions, especially of the religious sort, and to epidemic social (self-)withdrawal and ultimately to violent, militant resistance.

This relational disunion results, on the one hand, in power-laden, dynamically open, and globally interconnected modes of life. On the other hand, it leads to forces that lag behind culturally, increasingly lose social power, and become focused on revolution or upheaval. This overall situation can be traced back to the history of the → Enlightenment, since it reflects certain characteristics originally associated with the French → Revolution: the "terror of progress," which the Jacobins enflamed, but also the "terror of reaction," which the former estates (those on the "losing end," as it were) actuated. Strengthened at different times by civil wars and by subsequent revolutions that transitioned into more permanent conditions, this constellation has ultimately persisted down into the present. Observers as early as Hannah Arendt (1955) anticipated a kind of concealed but disastrous "global civil war" (H. Kesting 1959) carried on by guerrillas lacking any concrete institutional support who would be fragmented and would engage in opportunistic → terrorism (see R. Koselleck, H. Lübbe).

If we take seriously the events in New York City on September 11, 2001, we recognize that terrorism — far from having reached a peak — will continue to have a major impact in our world. The more globalized, hence "civilized," societies seem to be, the more they will generate inconsistencies (esp. in the possession and distribution of common goods and cultural values) and, finally, violence.

The process unfolds contradictory perspectives. Whenever social elites — the makers and managers of "civilization" — abandon their basic charge to maintain law and order in society and shift over instead to pursue self-centered, laical, and secular styles of life, they will necessarily come into conflict with forces adhering to metaphysically grounded, fundamentalist "cultural" norms. From the latter, groups will arise and strategies develop that are prepared to contend against superior powers using the powerlessness of self-sacrifice, as has been exercised in the form of suicide bombing. Homeless and hopeless people who are deprived of, and who renounce, adequate uses of power stand over against those who combine and multiply power with the making of civilization itself.

The wars in which the opposing parties are engaged, as well as the forms, contents, and proportions of power they activate, acquire features of "asymmetry" (H. Münkler). The terms "culture" and "civilization" (see Lipp, "Kultur und Zivilisation") represent this antithesis and its accompanying implementations.

At one pole of this contrast, we renounce → weapons of mass destruction, which grow in their sophistication, anonymity, and scope. At the other pole, we stand against the desperate, maniacal, violent eruptions associated with variously interconnected conspiratorial networks, which rely on acts of terror such as the shocking phenomenon of the suicide bomber.

Bibliography: H. Arendt, *The Origins of Totalitarianism* (New York, 1955) • U. Beck, ed., *Perspektiven der Weltgesellschaft* (Frankfurt, 1998) • G. W. Domhoff, *The Power Elite and the State: How Policy Is Made in America* (New York, 1990) • G. W. Domhoff and T. R. Dye, eds., *Power Elites and Organizations* (Newbury Park, Calif., 1987) • N. Elias, *The Civilizing Process:*

Sociogenetic and Psychogenetic Investigations (rev. ed.; Oxford, 2000; orig. pub., 1939) • H. Kesting, *Geschichtsphilosophie und Weltbürgerkrieg* (Heidelberg, 1959) • R. Koselleck, *Futures Past: On the Semantics of Historical Time* (Cambridge, Mass., 1985) • R. M. Kramer, *Power and Influence in Organizations* (Thousand Oaks, Calif., 1999) • E. O. Laumann and F. U. Pappi, *Networks of Collective Action: A Perspective on Community Influence Systems* (New York, 1976) • C. G. Lindblom, "The Science of 'Muddling Through,'" *Public Administration Review* 19 (1959) 79-88 • W. Lipp, "Bürokratien und Kader, Parteien und Beteiligung–Grenzformen sozialer Steuerung," *Verwaltungsführung* (ed. A. Remer; Berlin, 1982) 232-68; idem, "Kultur und Zivilisation. Faktoren im Geschichtsprozess, mit Blick besonders auf Terror heute: Was ihn schürt und was er zerstört," *Festschrift für Eckart Pankoke* (Berlin, 2004); idem, "Magie, Macht und Gefahr. Zur Soziologie des Irrationalen" (1983), *Drama Kultur* (Berlin, 1994) 346-73 • H. Lübbe, ed., *Heilserwartung und Terror. Politische Religionen des 20. Jahrhunderts* (Düsseldorf, 1995) • N. Luhmann, *Funktionen und Folgen formaler Organisation* (5th ed.; Berlin, 1999; orig. pub., 1964); idem, *Macht* (Stuttgart, 1975; 3d ed., 2003; ET *Trust and Power* [Chichester, 1979]) • M. Mann, *The Sources of Social Power* (2 vols.; Cambridge, 1986-93) • C. W. Mills, *The Power Elite* (New York, 1956) • H. Münkler, *Die neuen Kriege* (Reinbek, 2003) • T. Parsons, "On the Concept of Political Power," *PAPS* 107 (1963) 232-62 • R. Perruci and H. R. Potter, eds., *Networks of Power: Organizational Actors at the National, Corporate, and Community Levels* (New York, 1989) • H. Popitz, *Phänomene der Macht* (2d ed.; Tübingen, 1999) • C. Schmitt, *Gespräch über die Macht und den Zugang zum Machthaber* (Berlin, 1994; orig. pub., 1954) • M. Weber, *Economy and Society: An Outline of Interpretive Sociology* (2 vols.; Berkeley, Calif., 1978; orig. pub., 1922).

Wolfgang Lipp

2. Theological Aspects

2.1. *Anthropological Definition*

Power is a basic concept in historical → anthropology, which studies human beings not merely in terms of natural endowment but also in terms of historical and social action. The initial insight is that → freedom and limitation, spontaneity and vulnerability, determine human existence in history. → Life is threatened and insecure, and therefore self-preservation is a duty. We differ from → animals inasmuch as we consciously take up this duty and strive just as earnestly to preserve life as to secure and give shape to freedom.

In this first approximation power is thus the ability to achieve the goal of self-preservation. In all its processes, however, we find in power a tendency to expand. This impulse is connected with the basic insecurity of life: we can never definitively eliminate the threats to human existence. Power thus tends to accumulate (C. F. von Weizsäcker).

2.2. *Political Theories*

Most theories of power deal with only a narrow sector of the phenomenon, namely, the sphere of political power (→ Politics). In so doing, they define power formally as sharing in the decision-making process (H. D. Lasswell and A. Kaplan), or they follow the definition of Max → Weber cited above in 1.2. Weber's definition relates solely to → conflicts of power. In a comprehensive study we must not neglect the buildup of power socially for the general good, namely, the use of power to promote → consensus rather than conflict.

Political power brings graphically before us the ambivalence of the phenomenon. On the one hand, power seems to be necessary for the sake of lasting peace and order within a society and between societies. On the other hand, it leads to misuse, excess, and tyranny. This ambivalence finds expression in differing evaluations. Some see it as a positive value (Lasswell and Kaplan), others as intrinsically evil (J. Burckhardt). Both evaluations evade the ambivalence, which is the key theme in theological reflection.

2.3. *Biblical Tradition*

In the biblical tradition terms for power relate primarily to God. The history of Israel begins with the experience of liberation from Egypt. The power of God meets the people in this experience (e.g., see Exod. 15:3-19). As the Lord of the → covenant (§1) with → Israel (§1) and the Lord of → creation, God shows himself to be the Almighty.

Human power is relative in contrast to this absolute power, which is true of our power over nature (Gen. 1:28), as well as of political power. Power can be legitimate only as used in the service of God and for the common good. Sinful rejection of God shows itself not least in transgression of the limits that are set for the human use of power (→ Sin). Prophetic criticism of the autonomous power of monarchy reflects this theme (→ Prophets, Prophecy, 2; Monarchy in Israel).

Already in the Hebrew Bible the power of God liberates rather than subjugates. His use of power, then, is not a contradiction but an expression of his → love. This *unity of power and love* is a basic NT theme. The impartial turning of God's love to us is an expression of his specifically divine power (note

Matt. 20:1-15). In the → incarnation of the Son and his path to impotent → suffering on the cross, we are thus to see an act of divine freedom and divine power (Phil. 2:5-11).

2.4. *Theological Tradition*

The theological tradition often ignored this unity of power and impotence in its discussion of the divine attribute of omnipotence. Instead, it presented the Almighty as an unrestricted Ruler and thus tried to trace all events in nature and history causally to his will.

In opposition to this approach, talk about God's omnipotence has been called a theological mistake (C. Hartshorne). This criticism has led to the insight that we can talk theologically about God's omnipotence only in terms of his power to restrict himself for love's sake. God shows his power, not by asserting himself against us, but by his act of turning precisely to the creature that rebels against him (W. Pannenberg).

2.5. *Tasks*

Here we also have a theological starting point for discussing the ways in which human power is misused. We must see power as a means rather than an end in itself. The few NT passages that deal directly with the phenomenon of political power underlie this view. We find recognition of the functions of the emperor and the authorities. God instituted them, and they are thus in keeping with his will. In this function of service they can claim the → obedience of their subjects (Rom. 13:1-7, see also Matt. 22:21).

Nevertheless, a provision of this recognition is that in the sphere of Christ's dominion, all relations of superiority and subjection have lost their validity (see Mark 10:43-44 and par.). This theology of power does not mean simply that power is demonic, that is, evil in itself. What it does involve is criticism of all *autonomy* of power. Since power can seduce us, controls are needed. Hence a theology of power has affinities to concepts of power-sharing and democratic participation (→ Democracy; State; State Ethics).

Since misuse of power may be measured by its failure to secure → human dignity or a successful society, we can institutionalize the critical testing of power as well as its use. This is a most important and inalienable task of the democratic constitutional state, but it can be done only if new institutionalizing of controls goes hand in hand with new forms of power, especially in the economic sphere. The present failure to control the power of multinational corporations brings this problem into clear focus.

2.6. *Church Tradition*

The relativizing of power in the biblical tradition did not always have an impact in the history of Christianity. When Christianity achieved recognition as the state religion of the Roman Empire in the fourth century, Romans 13 was often expounded as a demand for uncritical loyalty to the state. The Lutheran tradition also has included a widespread tendency to regard subjection to state power as an unquestionable duty. Opposing biblical traditions such as the depiction of the demonic perversion of political power in Revelation 13 or the statement of Peter that obedience to God takes precedence over all political loyalties (Acts 5:29) were pushed into the background. They lived on more strongly in the minority → free churches, especially the historic → peace churches, than in the mainline churches. An uncritical relation to political power contributed to the reluctance of many churches, especially in Europe, to support the development of constitutional states.

The manner of dealing with power in the church sharpened the problem. Church history offers many examples of the misuse of legitimate or usurped power. They include forced conversions, persecution of heretics, and the subtler forms of spiritual coercion and bureaucratic rule. The churches can credibly demand a responsible handling of power, and contribute to it, only if they learn in a convincing way to handle it fruitfully themselves. A free renunciation of power by either Christians or non-Christians can have great significance by way of example.

2.7. *Social Ethics*

An urgent need in the traditional mainline churches is that they should learn from the insights into power that are implicit in the Christian faith. Social developments in the 20th century led in many fields to a narrowing of differences in power, for example, between men and women, the generations, the European states and former colonies (→ Colonialism), and to some extent rulers and ruled (N. Elias). But new differences have also arisen. Human power over → nature has taken new forms that threaten humanity's control over its own destiny. The economic contrast between the industrialized states (→ Industrial Society) and the poverty-stricken → Third World (→ Poverty) has taken on new dimensions, and even within individual societies we find discrepancies in economic power.

In economic discussions of this new situation, we note different concepts. A messianic concept (→ Messianism) of political → ethics finds all power evil without distinction (Kim Yong-Bock, in J. Moltmann). Others ask whether power serves human life. To give a proper answer we need clarity on the decisive standards of a human use of power. In modern times universal human and civil → rights have been asserted as criteria of a responsible use of power, but this concept needs to be extended in two directions. First, the use of power must find a limit not merely in human rights but in the dignity of nonhuman nature. Second, it must be oriented not merely to the rights of those now living but also the → future of human life on earth.

Bibliography: H. Berkhof, *Christ and the Powers* (Scottdale, Pa., 1962) • J. Burckhardt, *Reflections on History* (Indianapolis, 1999; orig. pub., 1905) • E. Canetti, *Crowds and Power* (New York, 1981) • N. Elias, *The Germans: Power Struggles and the Development of Habitus in the Nineteenth and Twentieth Centuries* (Cambridge, 1996) • H. Greifenstein, ed., *Macht und Gewalt. Leitlinien lutherischer Theologie zur politischen Ethik heute* (Hamburg, 1978) • C. Hartshorne, *Omnipotence and Other Theological Mistakes* (Albany, N.Y., 1984) • R. Hauser, *Autorität und Macht. Die staatliche Autorität in der neueren protestantischen Ethik und in der katholischen Gesellschaftslehre* (Heidelberg, 1949) • W. Huber and H.-R. Reuter, *Friedensethik* (Stuttgart, 1990) • B. de Jouvenel, *On Power: Its Nature and the History of Its Growth* (New York, 1949) • A. Kenny, *Will, Freedom, and Power* (Oxford, 1975) • H. D. Lasswell and A. Kaplan, *Power and Society: A Framework for Political Inquiry* (New Haven, 1950) • J. M. Lochman, *Reich, Kraft und Herrlichkeit. Der Lebensbezug von Glauben und Bekennen* (Munich, 1981) • J. Moltmann, ed., *Minjung. Theologie des Volkes Gottes in Südkorea* (Neukirchen, 1984) • W. Pannenberg, *Systematic Theology* (vol. 1; Grand Rapids, 1991) • C. H. Powell, *The Biblical Concept of Power* (London, 1963) • B. Russell, *Power: A New Social Analysis* (London, 1938) • P. Tillich, *Love, Power, and Justice: Ontological Analyses and Ethical Applications* (New York, 1954) • M. Weber, *Economy and Society: An Outline of Interpretive Sociology* (2 vols.; Berkeley, Calif., 1978; orig. pub., 1922) • W. Weber, ed., *Macht, Dienst, Herrschaft in Kirche und Gesellschaft* (Freiburg, 1974) • C. F. von Weizsäcker, *The Politics of Peril: Economics, Society, and the Prevention of War* (New York, 1978).

Wolfgang Huber

3. Ecclesiological Aspects

3.1. *Theology and Power*

Theology finds it harder today than ever before to achieve a neutral or even a positive view of the phenomenon of power, which is mostly tied so tightly to experiences of domination, coercion, and violence (→ Force, Violence, Nonviolence). To seek, hold, and use power often seem in advance to be politically suspect and morally questionable, so that the power associated with offices in the church (→ Ministry, Ministerial Offices) is seldom described as such but is preferably called authority, which is more in line with NT usage.

3.2. *Use in Denominations*

This predominantly negative approach comes to light in analysis and discussion of the denominational problem. Thus in → ecumenical theology a transdenominational → consensus has developed whereby relations between the → denominations, especially those of an ecumenical nature, must have nothing whatever to do with the issue of power.

This idea, however, cannot be sustained either historically or systematically. Historically, we must say that the very process of forming a denomination, though it might ultimately have theological roots, cannot be understood apart from the arrangements made by the religious parties with the various social and political powers. Furthermore, for centuries power in the form of naked force decided between different theological trends, and this situation did not end because the contending parties achieved a better insight. Rather, only with the concentration of military force in the hands of the secularized national states (→ Secularization) and the development of neutral principles of → law were the denominations forced to settle their debates about the → truth with means other than that of physical force.

It is hardly surprising that even under changed political conditions, → polemics — a science of war and strife (so P. Tschackert) — long dominated the style of theological discussion. → Erasmus (1469?-1536), G. Calixtus (1586-1656), G. W. Leibniz (1646-1716), and mediating theologians (→ Mediating Theology) like P. → Melanchthon (1497-1560), M. → Bucer (1491-1551), and J. Gropper (1503-59) were unable to carry through to success their efforts at reunion, essentially because they lacked the necessary ecclesiastical and political power. Conversely, the 20th-century ecumenical movement could incisively alter the ecclesiastical and denominational situation because, for different reasons, it was and still is an important power factor (→ Ecumenism, Ecumenical Movement).

3.3. *Power, Law, Truth, and Love*

From a systematic standpoint we should note that denominations of the → modern period, diverging from the traditional view of → heresy, do not onesidedly stress a partial truth but at least claim to be representing the whole of the Christian faith. To the extent that they ultimately do so in different ways, they seem to be the result of a primal theological cleavage. Polemical differences or distinctions have thus had to work at a theological evaluation of power. They can develop this topic in the sphere of the doctrine of → God as they reflect on the description of God as Almighty in the creed, but they may also do so in the areas of theological → anthropology and especially of ecclesiology (→ Church 3). This systematic connection is clearest in the tradition of → Calvinism, which for this reason raises for us the material questions that we must consider in theological reflection on the phenomenon of power, namely, its relation to law, → righteousness, truth, and → love.

3.4. *Church Government*

The various denominational approaches have had their greatest historical impact in the sphere of → church government (→ Polity, Ecclesiastical). On a Roman Catholic view (→ Roman Catholic Church), we find a distinctive linking of the powers of consecration and jurisdiction. → Lutheranism and the → free churches, however, consistently broke free from this concept and radically secularized the legal regulation that was so closely tied to the problem of power and government, for example, in relation to the episcopal office, which was understood and exercised as a purely human ministry of leadership and oversight. Behind this desacramentalizing (→ Sacramentality) lay certain historical experiences with ecclesiastical power but also deeper theological, Christological, and anthropological considerations.

The reference to the passion (→ Suffering) and death of Jesus as a normative → revelation of the impotence of God often leads to a strong opposing of power to love, so that power and the striving for it seem per se to be a consequence and symptom of human sinfulness (→ Sin). The renunciation of power may thus be preached as the only true Christian attitude. As the example of Christian → pacifism shows, this conclusion has major implications for political ethics.

3.5. *Ecclesiological Implications*

The ecclesiological ramifications of a dogmatic and moral depreciation of power in principle are nicely illustrated by the distinction of R. Sohm (1841-1917; → Church Law) between the church as a legal fellowship and as a fellowship of love. This distinction rests on the idea that law is irrevocably bound up with the problem of its execution, that is, with force as a sanction, which is an element essentially alien to the church and in contradiction with it.

Exegetical findings are against this notion, for in both the OT and the NT we find legal statutes that carry the threat of → punishment for their nonobservance. God's love and righteousness thus do not basically rule out one another, and law can have a positive sense, even within the church as a fellowship of love. Consistent with this understanding was the development in the early church of a sacramental law that could even carry severe church penalties with it.

This spiritual understanding of church order and → church discipline has been retained in principle in the Calvinist, Anglican, Roman Catholic, and Orthodox traditions. The experiences of the → church struggle and the → Confessing Church nourished it afresh in the 20th century, when in the light of National Socialist aggression (→ Fascism), the autonomy and power of the ministry had to be reasserted and its secularization resisted. These experiences taught us anew that a theology that can no longer distinguish between a right use of power and its misuse not only delivers up the church to secular powers but increases and perpetuates the impotence of the victims of power in the political sphere.

3.6. *Tasks*

A relevant theology of power must refuse, then, to demonize power or to glorify impotence. Instead, it must develop criteria for the responsible handling of ecclesiastical, political, and social power (→ Responsibility). But it must do so ecumenically, for global threats to → life demand common action on the part of Christians and the churches. To be able to organize an effective counterforce to the self-destructive misuse of power on a worldwide scale and in the context of international → politics, the separated churches need ecumenical structures of consultation, decision, and action such as are sought in the conciliar process for justice, peace, and the integrity of creation.

3.7. *Ultimate Responsibility*

The general threat to humanity demands that theology not only take power seriously in an abstsract sense as a basic phenomenon of human existence but deal with it concretely as a core problem in the church's own life. It must do so, for example, in providing authoritative teaching in ecumenical societies (→ Teaching Office) or in sharing unequally divided resources in money and personnel. For the task of the church is to bear credible witness, in its own → proclamation, structure, and work, that all power comes from God and that it must serve his will to the benefit of creation.

Bibliography: H. Asmussen, *Über die Macht* (Stuttgart, 1960) • R. Guardini, *Power and Responsibility: A Course of Action for the New Age* (Chicago, 1961) •

P. Lengsfeld, "Macht als Faktor in ökumenischen Prozessen," *US* 28 (1973) 235-41 • K. Rahner, "The Theology of Power," *Theological Investigations* (vol. 4; Baltimore, 1966) 391-409 • H.-G. Stobbe, "Konflikte um Identität. Studie zur Bedeutung von Macht in interkonfessionellen Beziehungen und im ökumenischen Prozeß," *Ökumenische Theologie. Ein Arbeitsbuch* (ed. P. Lengsfeld; Stuttgart, 1980) 190-237 • P. Tillich, "Die Philosophie der Macht," *Gesammelte Werke* (14 vols.; Stuttgart, 1959-75) 9.205-32.

Heinz-Günther Stobbe

Practical Theology

1. Development in Protestant Germany

1.1. *Historical Development*

"Practical theology" is the term for a theological discipline that has church activities as its theme and that alongside biblical studies, church history, and → systematic theology forms an independent department of → theology on Protestant faculties. This understanding of practical theology and the organizing of → theological education developed in the 19th century and became the common rule in European → Protestantism. Roman Catholicism preferred the term → "pastoral theology" (→ Roman Catholic Church), which we often find in the English-speaking sphere.

1.1.1. *Term*

F. D. E. → Schleiermacher (1768-1834; → Schleiermacher's Theology) coined the term "practical theology" in its present sense. But the term itself is older. It derives from discussions in → Scholasticism regarding the question whether theology as a science is practical (Duns Scotus) or speculative (→ Thomas Aquinas). Protestant → orthodoxy adopted this distinction; D. Hollaz (1648-1713), for example, called theology an eminently practical discipline. → Pietism often described as practical theology the teaching it gave on the pious life (→ Piety) for both clergy and laity.

1.1.2. *Rise*

The → early church and the → Middle Ages had no specific practical theology, but they did have rules and handbooks for ministers from the very first, and the related literature might be regarded as leading up to practical theology. We can refer to the NT → Pastoral Epistles and then to → Chrysostom's work *On the Priesthood* (386) and the pastoral rules (*Liber regulae pastoralis* [591]) of Gregory the Great.

In the Middle Ages the poor training of clergy and the increasing importance of penance (→ Penitence) and other → sacraments gave rise to works that collected simple, practical instructions and that served as manuals. Things did not basically change with the → Reformation, and improvements came only slowly. We thus find similar handbooks for simple, uneducated clergy in the Reformation churches, such as *Pastor* (1524), by U. → Zwingli (1484-1531; → Zwingli's Theology), or *Pastorale Lutheri*, by C. Porta (1541-85). Pietism later took up the genre and developed it into pastoral theology. It focused on the minister as a → person and aimed at the cultivation of piety and then the enhancing of pastoral abilities (→ Ministry, Ministerial Offices). These goals still underlay 19th-century pastoral theology and kept open a place for it alongside practical theology. Of special importance in this regard were the pastoral theologies of C. Harms (1778-1855) in 1830-34 and C. Palmer (1811-75) in 1860.

Practical theology developed in the → modern period out of concern for the church's practical life and action as problems became evident in these areas. Practical theology became a theme of its own as the distinction came to be made between → religion as something for everyone and → theology as a preserve of the clergy. Religion was now the real theme of theology, and religion involved practical tasks and problems. This development had begun already in Pietism and found clear expression in the → Enlightenment (e.g., J. J. Spalding's work in 1772 on the usefulness and advancement of the pastoral office).

Neither Pietism nor the Enlightenment, however, set out a concept of theology that gave focus to these developments or offered any genuine solution to the problems. Since it was now clear that individual pastors alone could not do the work of the church, even though they bore a large measure of responsibility for it, the spread of Pietism and the theological Enlightenment did draw attention at least to practical questions of church life and pastoral work. Homiletical and catechetical matters thus began to receive treatment both basically and in detail, and a special literature emerged, as in the journal *Theologia pastoralis practica* (1737-59), edited by J. A. Steinmetz.

It was Schleiermacher who found a place for practical theology as a separate discipline in his theological system. In his *Kurze Darstellung des theologischen Studiums* (1811; ET *Brief Outline on the Study of Theology* [1966]), he placed it alongside historical and philosophical theology (→ Philosophy and Theology). Church leadership posed its tasks (§25). Unlike historical or philosophical theology, however, practical theology here was "a kind of artistic achievement, and thus requires an 'art doctrine,' or technology, which we designate by the term 'hermeneutics'" (§132). Technical disciplines rest on experience and consist of the resultant rules. Practical theology thus sets out "rules" (§265) for the solving of practical matters in every sphere of church leadership (→ Church Government), though the applying of these rules is an individual matter. As a craft, practical theology does not teach us how to see tasks correctly. It presupposes a correct understanding and then offers "correct procedures" for performing the tasks (§260).

1.1.3. *After Schleiermacher*

In his practical theology (1847-67) C. I. Nitzsch (1787-1868) criticized Schleiermacher's view and instead made practical theology a discipline of the same kind as historical or philosophical theology. Its task is to teach a correct understanding of the tasks. In order to understand the present and to act accordingly, it must arrive at a model concept of the → congregation (→ Primitive Christian Community), its life, and its pastoral activities (1.136ff., 2.129). The → church thus became a primary theme in practical theology. Nitzsch regarded all theology as *scientia ad praxin* (knowledge for practice), culminating as *scientia praxeos* (knowledge of practice, 1.5). Hence practical theology was not an appendix to theology but arose necessarily out of the very concept.

In the 19th century practical theology was first treated from a conceptual and disciplinary standpoint. Its relation to theology as a whole and its position within the encyclopedia were issues for P. K. Marheineke and T. A. Liebner. G. von Zezschwitz and others were interested in the way that its program arises out of the very nature of the church. Later attention focused on its history, with historical accounts being given of its individual fields (e.g., H. Hering's work on homiletics) or of practical theology as a whole (E. C. Achelis). Finally, toward the end of the century, attention shifted to the task of training, and issues regarding the practical work of pastors called for treatment (W. Otto). For all the differences in detail, the 19th century came to see that practical theology must always include homiletics, catechetics, and poimenics (i.e., pastoral theology). Equal attention was often paid to → liturgics and cybernetics, while → mission, the diaconate (→ Diakonia), and church law always had an accepted place.

The early 20th century took up the issue of practical education with more intensity. The training of ministers was now the essential goal (O. Baumgarten, "Praktische Theologie," *RGG* [1913] 4.1725-26). For the fulfillment of this task practical theology adopted new methods, themes, and disciplines such as the → psychology of religion, the → sociology of churches, or pedagogics, which might come to be seen as an all-embracing perspective (F. Niebergall). In the course of this development P. Drews (1858-1912) proposed that a distinction should be made between practical theology at the university, which would have a historical, psychological, and sociological focus, and practical theology at the seminary, which would consist of practical training (pp. 43ff., 54ff.).

In contrast, → dialectical theology sought once again to see practical theology in terms of theology. Like theology as a whole, practical theology should have its basis in the → Word of God. The proclamation of the Word of God is its true theme in every sphere (K. → Barth). Hence "practical theology" could no longer be a single term embracing every specific issue, and there could be no orientation to purely practical tasks and experiences. Yet this orientation and a concern to solve practical problems gave shape to practical theology in the later decades of the 20th century, and on this basis there has been a great expansion and intensification of fields. During recent years evidence suggests that some thinkers are again trying to establish a unified understanding of practical theology.

1.2. *Present Situation*

1.2.1. *Issues*

Practical theology is now a theological discipline that seeks to lay important foundations for pastoral work. In the territorial churches of Germany it has a regular place, being taught in the second phase of preacher training and having a place also in the further education of ministers. The central issues, however, have now shifted. Under the influence of dialectical theology other fields were oriented to homiletics, but from the end of the 1950s religious pedagogics came to the fore, along with the question regarding the legitimacy, basis, and goal of → religious education in the public schools (→ School and Church).

A decade later interest shifted to → pastoral care. In connection with the American pastoral-care movement (see 2), the practical tasks of helping people to live became the theme of instruction and found corresponding expression in the literature and in institutes for the training of those who offer pastoral care. With this development the danger arose that the relation of different fields to one another, and the importance of this relation, would be lost to view.

1.2.2. *Main Problems*

Themes and issues and discussions in practical theology have taken their own course. Thus in homiletics (→ Preaching) the important question of exposition has come to relate increasingly to hearers and the adapting of what is said to their situation (→ Rhetoric 2). In pedagogics the legitimacy of religious education in schools first came under discussion, but then, as in pedagogics in general, attention focused on curricula and their problems, and finally → religion and related questions of life and its stages (→ Biography, Biographical Research; Initiation Rites; Socialization) came to the fore. Pastoral care found a place for → psychoanalysis, → Clinical Pastoral Education, programs for the offering of psychological help, and → pastoral psychology, but also for discussion of psychological schools and trends and the legitimacy of psychologically oriented pastoral care in the church.

For all the differences in development in the various fields of practical theology, certain problems are common to all of them, which we might call the present-day problems of practical theology as a whole. First is the problem of the social and humane sciences and their relation to practical theology. Linked to this question is that of the goal of practical theology. Then there is the matter of practical theology's understanding of itself and of the sense in which it is to be viewed as a science. Finally, we note that the unity of practical theology and the relation of the fields to one another poses an essential question if practical theology as such is to be tenable at all.

Bibliography: Up till the early 20th century: E. C. Achelis, *Lehrbuch der praktischen Theologie* (3 vols.; Leipzig, 1890; 3d ed., 1911) • P. Drews, *Das Problem der praktischen Theologie* (Tübingen, 1910) • H. Hering, *Die Lehre von der Predigt* (Berlin, 1905) • T. A. Liebner, "Die praktische Theologie," *ThStKr* 16 (1843) 629-58; 17 (1844) 77-136 • P. K. Marheineke, *Entwurf der praktischen Theologie* (Berlin, 1837) • F. Niebergall, *Praktische Theologie* (2 vols.; Tübingen, 1918-19) • W. Otto, *Evangelische praktische Theologie* (Gotha, 1869-70) • M. Schian, *Grundriß der praktischen Theologie* (Giessen, 1922; 3d ed., 1934) • F. Schleiermacher, *Christian Caring: Selections from "Practical Theology"* (ed. J. O. Duke and H. Stone; Philadelphia, 1988; orig. pub., 1850) • G. von Zezschwitz, *System der praktischen Theologie* (3 vols.; Leipzig, 1876-78).

More recent works: C. Albrecht, *Bildung in der praktischen Theologie* (Tübingen, 2003); idem, *Historische Kulturwissenschaft neuzeitlicher Christentumspraxis* (Tübingen, 2000) • K. Barth, *CD* • V. Drehsen, *Neuzeitliche Konstitutionsbedingungen der praktischen Theologie* (2 vols.; Gütersloh, 1988); idem, *Wie religionsfähig ist die Volkskirche?* (Gütersloh, 1994) • G. Ebeling, *The Study of Theology* (Philadelphia, 1978) chap. 9, "Practical Theology" • W. Gräb, *Lebensgeschichte–Lebensentwürfe–Sinndeutungen* (2d ed.; Gütersloh, 2000) • W. Gräb and D. Korsch, *Selbsttätiger Glaube. Die Einheit der praktischen Theologie in der Rechtfertigungslehre* (Neukirchen, 1985) • C. Grethlein and M. Meyer-Blanck, *Geschichte der praktischen Theologie* (Leipzig, 1999) • A. Grözinger, *Praktische Theologie und Ästhetik* (2d ed.; Munich, 1991) • M. Josuttis, *Praxis des Evangeliums zwischen Politik und Religion. Grundprobleme der praktischen Theologie* (4th ed.; Munich, 1988) • H. Luther, *Religion und Alltag. Bausteine zu einer praktischen Theologie des Subjekts* (Stuttgart, 1992) • G. Otto, *Praktische Theologie* (2 vols.; Munich, 1986-88) • W. Pannenberg, *Theology and the Philosophy of Science* (Philadelphia, 1976) • R. Preul, *Luther und die praktische Theologie* (Marburg, 1989) • D. Rössler, *Grundriß der praktischen Theologie* (2d ed.; Berlin, 1994) • W. Steck, *Praktische Theologie* (Stuttgart, 2000) • E. Thurneysen, *A Theology of Pastoral Care* (Richmond, Va., 1962) • F. Wintzer et al., *Praktische Theologie* (5th ed.; Neukirchen, 1997). For more English-language works, see bibliography in §2 below.

Dietrich Rössler

2. Anglo-American Developments

The emergence of practical theology led to a number of international developments. While these ranged from the empirical theology of the Netherlands to the doctrinally based practical theology of South Africa, this section will focus on developments in the United States and the United Kingdom.

2.1. *Initial Reception*

Between 1830 and 1850 a steady stream of Americans studied at the universities of Halle and Berlin, where they encountered the encyclopedic approach to →

theology for the first time (→ Historicism). Over the second half of the 19th century, this approach gradually became dominant in American theological education and was accompanied by the appearance in English of books making use of this perspective (the W. Farrer translation of F. D. E. → Schleiermacher's *Kurze Darstellung* in 1850, G. R. Crooks and J. F. Hurst's *Theological Encyclopedia and Methodology on the Basis of Hagenbach* in 1884, and P. Schaff's *Theological Propaedeutic* in 1893). It was in the context of the encyclopedic approach that practical theology first appeared on the American scene.

Similar developments took place somewhat later in Scotland. It was not until 1924 that practical theology as a distinct subject was first taught at Edinburgh University (→ Theological Education). Bruce Nicol, minister of St. Margaret's Church and warden of the Pastoral Institute based there, began to offer courses in the university curriculum on a regular basis. Similar institutes soon were set up in other universities, and chairs in practical theology were established. This represented a unique development in the United Kingdom, for theological research and education in England continued to be structured along the lines of the classical curriculum, resisting the introduction of practical theology and the encyclopedic approach altogether.

It is important to point out that the initial reception of practical theology in the United States and Scotland was not based on the rich and complex program conceptualized by Schleiermacher (see 1.1.2; → Schleiermacher's Theology). Rather, it reflected the post-Schleiermacherian narrowing of practical theology to reflection on ministerial functions. It was viewed as the pragmatic branch of theology, mediating the insights of the other theological disciplines to church life. A "helps and hints" approach soon was dominant, focusing on a hodgepodge of ministerial techniques and advice (→ Pastor; Pastoral Sociology; Pastoral Theology).

2.2. *Transformations*

A number of developments led to the transformation of practical theology in the United States and Scotland during the first half of the 20th century. First, the pragmatic, clergy-oriented approach of practical theology proved untenable in the face of an increasingly secularized and institutionally differentiated social context (→ Secularization). Handing on advice about traditional roles was supplanted by critical reflection on the place of the → church in → society.

Second, the emergence of the social sciences afforded practical theology powerful tools with which to analyze the surrounding context. It also confronted it with a formidable methodological task: how to carry out an interdisciplinary → dialogue while maintaining its theological identity.

Third, professional education emerged as a viable alternative to classical education. Practical theology no longer could define itself in relation to the older "apprentice" model of education. Following the lead of social work, law, and business administration, it faced the task of providing a theoretical base for professionals who could think critically about practice.

Fourth, practical theology confronted the broader challenge being posed to the assumptions of the encyclopedic approach to knowledge, especially its view of practical → reason. Initially, the encyclopedia was based on a unified view of human rationality (→ Rationalism) and described philosophically the inner coherence of reason's findings as they emerged in science. Moreover, it reduced practical reason to the application of the findings of experimental or theoretical research. One of several challenges to this view of rationality was raised by philosophical → pragmatism in the United States. It argued that rationality is context-dependent and not subject to systematic integration on the basis of foundational metaphysical principles (→ Metaphysics). It also portrayed theory-building and critical reflection as grounded in and oriented toward the transformation of practice. Philosophical criticisms of the encyclopedic approach also were raised in the United Kingdom.

These challenges to the inherited, encyclopedic approach to practical theology began to make their impact felt during the first part of the 20th century and have continued to the present. In the United States the → pastoral care and counseling movement, as well as the religious education movement, exemplified attempts to form a more professional approach to ministry on the basis of a dialogue between theology and the social sciences. Similar interests can also be seen in the various pastoral studies programs emerging in the United Kingdom, which maintained a much better balance of sociological, political, and psychological emphases than did those in the United States.

These movements and programs led to new understandings of practical theology. In the United States Seward Hiltner distinguished between theological disciplines that are "logic centered" and those that are "operation centered," with the latter representing practical theology. Drawing on → process philosophy and pragmatism, Hiltner argued that practical theology's analysis of pastoral events can generate new theological insights that impact the findings of the logic-centered disciplines. In Scotland James Whyte and Duncan Forrester defined practical theology as the theology of practice, broadening its scope from pastoral occasions to reflection on patterned, replicable activity in any sphere of life. Robin Gill and Paul Ballard in somewhat different ways called attention to the tension between sustained theoretical research in practical theology and the kind of situational reflection necessary to the guidance of practice in the face of unique circumstances.

In spite of the differences in these definitions of practical theology, they reflect a consensus that began to emerge by the middle of the century. First, practical theology does not focus solely or even primarily on clergy functions or the church but, rather, on the world in relation to God. Second, practical theology must carry out its own research and engage in its own theory-construction. Third, much of practical theology's work is interdisciplinary, developing theological proposals that are enriched by a dialogue with the social sciences, the humanities, and other nontheological resources. Fourth, practical theology includes or supports the kind of situational reasoning that is inherent to critical practice.

2.3. *New Developments*

This consensus has given rise to a period of ferment in practical theology internationally. A number of emerging models can be identified that respond to the various facets of this consensus in different ways. Widely influential is what D. Tracy has called the revisionist model of practical theology found in the work of Don Browning. In this approach practical theology engages in a wide range of reflection, from an identification of guiding theological → metaphors and ethical (→ Ethics) principles to the formation of rules and roles that are appropriate to concrete contexts. The insights of theology and contemporary → culture are equal partners of an interdisciplinary method of mutually critical correlation.

Practical theologians influenced by feminist and liberation theologies have attempted to define practical theology in a manner that does not diminish the importance of → ideology-critique for every branch of theology (→ Religion, Criticism of). Practical theology has the unique task of providing concrete guidance to particular communities as they struggle to form liberating practices that can challenge forms of oppression (→ Dependence). P. Couture and R. Chopp advocate a method of critical praxis correlation in which interdisciplinary work is not primarily between academic disciplines but between movements struggling to embody emancipatory practices.

Still another approach to practical theology has begun to emerge from the renewed interest in K. → Barth (1886-1968; → Dialectical Theology) and L. Wittgenstein (1889-1951; → Language 5; Language and Theology 4.3.3) reflected in the writings of G. Lindbeck and S. Hauerwas. In R. Osmer's work, this approach has begun to lead to a recognition that practical reasoning follows different patterns in different communities. In the church this reasoning is shaped by the → dialectic between the Word, Scripture, and the language and practices of different cultural and historical contexts (→ Contextual Theology). Practical theology has the task of reflecting critically on the rhetorical modes by which the Word (→ Word of God) is given expression in various cultural contexts and formulating rules of art by which the church can give witness in its own time and place (→ Rhetoric 2).

Bibliography: D. Ackermann and R. Bons-Storm, eds., *Liberating Faith Practices: Feminist Practical Theology in Context* (Louvain, 1998) • P. Ballard, ed., *The Foundations of Pastoral Studies and Practical Theology* (Chippenham, Wiltshire, 1986) • P. Ballard and P. Couture, eds., *Globalization and Difference: Practical Theology in a World Context* (Cardiff, 1999) • D. Browning, *A Fundamental Practical Theology* (Minneapolis, 1991); idem, ed., *Practical Theology* (San Francisco 1983) • R. Chopp, *The Praxis of Suffering: An Interpretation of Liberation and Political Theologies* (Maryknoll, N.Y., 1986) • P. Couture, *Blessed Are the Poor? Women's Poverty, Family Policy, and Practical Theology* (Nashville, 1991) • D. B. Forrester, *Theology and Practice* (London, 1990); idem, *Truthful Action: Explorations in Practical Theology* (Edinburgh, 2000) • E. Graham, *Transforming Practice: Pastoral Theology in an Age of Uncertainty* (London, 1996) • G. Heitink, *Practical Theology: History, Theory, Action Domains* (Grand Rapids, 1999) • S. Hiltner, *Preface to Pastoral Theology* (Nashville, 1958) • R. R. Osmer, *A Teachable Spirit: Recovering the Teaching Office in the Church* (Louisville, Ky., 1990) • R. R. Osmer and F. Schweitzer, *Religious Education between Modernization and Globalization: New Perspectives on the United States and Germany* (Grand Rapids, 2003) • R. R. Osmer, F. Schweitzer, and J. W. Fowler, *Developing a Public Faith: New Directions in Practical Theology* (St. Louis, 2003) • B. Roebben and L. van der Tuin, eds., *Practical Theology and the Interpretation of Crossing Boundaries* (Münster, 2003) • P. Schaff, *Theological Propaedeutic* (2 vols.; New York, 1893) • J. Woodward and S. Pattison, eds., *The Blackwell Reader in Pastoral and Practical Theology* (Oxford, 2000).

Richard R. Osmer

3. Roman Catholicism

3.1. *Term*

Under the influence of the *Handbuch der Pastoraltheologie* (Handbook of pastoral theology, 1964-72), edited by F. X. Arnold, K. → Rahner, and others, an epochal work important even beyond the German-speaking sphere, "practical theology" and → "pastoral theology" have come to be used synonymously in Roman Catholic circles. Yet, properly speaking, "practical theology" is the more comprehensive term, denoting a department of theology made up of pastoral theology, religious pedagogics, catechetics, → liturgics, → church law, → missiology, and Roman Catholic social teaching (→ Social Ethics). It is this wider use that we shall now discuss.

3.2. *After Vatican II*

3.2.1. The *Handbuch*'s attempt to replace the classic disciplinary designation "pastoral theology" by "practical theology" programmatically belies the new understanding of this discipline as one with its own form and content alongside other theological disciplines rather than as a mere appendix dealing with application. This view developed before → Vatican II, but the council (→ Councils of the Church), with an orientation more pastoral than dogmatic, impressively confirmed it, not least of all by its momentous defining of the whole → people of God and not just the clergy as the subject of the church's ministry and of the orientation of this activity toward the salvation and welfare of all human beings. As in the *Handbuch,* practical theology is scientific, critical, and constructive reflection on the "self-fulfillment" of the → church under present conditions but also with a view to the future. Adequate methodological aids are used in this ministry of theological reflection.

3.2.2. The *Handbuch* triggered intensive discussion of practical theology's understanding of itself. It promoted fuller development of practical theology in many countries, notably Germany, Netherlands, Spain, Italy, and Canada. Criticism arose relative to the central concept of the church's self-fulfillment. A danger was seen that the church might thus be made the criterion of its own practice (→ Norms). The objection was also made that a serious misunderstanding might arise resulting in the replacement of the traditional centering on the clergy by ecclesiocentrism (→ Clergy and Laity). A further argument was that the *Handbuch* had failed to make its postulate convincing by an autonomous methodology of practical theology.

New approaches attempting corrections developed in the course of discussion (see the contributions in *Praktische Theologie heute,* ed. F. Klostermann and R. Zerfass). They include the normative orienting of church practice to the "historical" → Jesus (practical theology under the claim of the cause of Jesus, G. Biemer and P. Schiller, H. Schuster); a comprehensive structuring of practical theology rather than a compartmentalization after the manner of S. Hiltner (communicating, shepherding, organizing), with a model for the transforming of church practice (practical theology as a science of action, R. Zerfass); and concern to preserve or reform the practice of the church to meet the demands of the modern history of → Enlightenment and → freedom (practical theology as a critical theology of church practice in society, N. Greinacher). Stronger ecumenical cooperation in practical theology also began during this phase (→ Ecumenical Dialogue).

3.2.3. Vital impulses promoting fresh discussion regarding approaches to practical theology and its status have arisen from the following developments in the church and in theology:

1. in the context of → political theology (J. B. Metz), a greater emphasis on the practical historical and social implications, along with the shift to a postidealist paradigm (→ Idealism);
2. the impact of the theology and pastoral practice of liberation, which rigorously follows the above paradigm, especially in Latin America but also in other churches;
3. the emergence and impact of women in both theology and the church (H. Meyer-Wilmes et al.);
4. confrontation with the accelerating process of modernization (→ Postmodernity) and the related profound changes in life situations and states of awareness (including detraditionalizing, individualizing, and pluralizing);
5. the intensifying of the social and ecological threat in a global context and the perception of this problem as not just an ethical but also a theological challenge within the conciliar process for justice, → peace, and the integrity of → creation; and
6. pluralization in the religious sphere and the increasing fundamentalism in various religions — often arguing for the legitimacy of violence — as a reaction to modernity.

The four-volume pastoral theology of P. M. Zulehner (1989-90) is the most comprehensive and notable attempt, even if overstrongly oriented within the church, to relate pastoral awareness and action more forcefully to movements in church and society that are crucial for the → future. Better grounded theoretically, but worked out only in outline, are efforts to put Christian work, church work, and pastoral work in the framework of a theologically based theory of communication (H. Peukert) and to establish practical theology as an explicit theory of communicative action (Mette, *Theorie*). Along these lines and against the background of the → kingdom of God, contribution is made to transformed practice in dealing with individual and social crises, the focus being on the central question and not on contingent issues and the need to master them pastorally. In answer to the challenges of → liberation theology, practical theology conceived along such lines has given less prominence to the traditional coordinates of faith and unbelief and more prominence to the contrast between the God of life and the false god of death (→ Secularization). Along with this emphasis we find a new stress on prophetic and political diaconate in church work (B. Höfte; C. Floristán; H. Steinkamp; Mette, *Erkundungen;* → Diakonia).

The new Catholic *Handbuch Praktische Theologie* (Handbook of practical theology, 1999-2000) seeks to do justice to these developments, both conceptually and in specifics, by orienting this discipline toward the "praxis of human beings" and by understanding it contextually. The intent is to focus not on specific forms and areas of human behavior (e.g., church or religion) but instead more comprehensively on the praxis of each individual human being and of humanity in the larger sense, since Christian hope understands precisely these entities as being surrounded and sustained by the love of God, who seeks the salvation of all. In implementing and reflecting on this praxis, one must take seriously the stipulation that it take place not in some abstract fashion divorced from a specific locale but, rather, in a contextually bound fashion (see also D. McCann and C. R. Strain, C. Schneider-Harpprecht).

3.3. *Specific Questions and Problems*

3.3.1. It is generally recognized that, as a principled basis for action, practical theology needs an inductive procedure in accordance with the threefold schema of seeing, judging, and acting. Zulehner thus divides practical theology into kairology (apprehending the situation), criteriology (orientation to the task and goal), and praxeology (sketching models of action). When any one of these steps is made absolute, however, the result is respectively → empiricism, → fundamentalism, or → pragmatism. As a heuristic schema, this procedure needs closer methodological scrutiny (C. Boff).

3.3.2. A related issue is that of the link between practical theology and the social and humane sciences. The methods and insights of these sciences must unquestionably be used, but for methodological reasons we cannot treat them solely as auxiliary, advisory disciplines. At the same time, on different grounds, the interdisciplinary cooperation that is so often called for has not yet occurred. At most, practical theology has proved to be conformed to the interdisciplinary model as a social science as theoretical and methodological elements from the neighboring sciences have become constituent parts of theorizing in practical theology (Mette and Steinkamp; H. Haslinger).

3.3.3. The various forms of practical theology (social and analytical, critical and hermeneutical, practical and pastoral) call for different methodologies. In his *Practical Theology* J. A. van der Ven makes a clarifying contribution to a possible integrating of the various methodological approaches, showing how this integration could be tested in further studies. His great concern is to strengthen methodologically controlled empirical research in practical theology so as to achieve assured results regarding the practice on which it reflects and thus to be more effective in its applications. But to be able to see the importance and relevance of this study, we need a hermeneutical and communicative framework of reference (→ Communication; Hermeneutics). The cycle of research (development of problems and goals, induction, deduction, testing, evaluation) involves the relating of the two methodological approaches to one another and their merging.

3.3.4. The attempt to apply strict scientific criteria to practical theology constantly raises the question whether we do not have here a matter of wisdom *(sapientia)* rather than of science *(scientia)* as we seek to give orientation to those engaged in pastoral ministry. Practical theology must undoubtedly contribute to the development of active judgment (W. Fürst, *Praktisch-theologische Urteilskraft*). But along with other abilities in communication and spiritual life, an ability to critically clarify the given situation and thus to unlock new possibilities of action is essential (O. Fuchs).

3.3.5. Two tendencies have emerged from the continued development or revision of the theoretical understanding of practical theology (S. Knobloch). One is a deepening of the theoretical paradigm of action, following American pragmatism and the "linguistic turn" (M. Viau; → Linguistics 3.6-7). The other — and whether this tendency constitutes a complement or an alternative to the first is still an open question — is a more pronounced phenomenological and aesthetic foundation or orientation (Fürst, *Pastoralästhetik*). Both tendencies have had enduring consequences for methodology as well (e.g., a greater openness to semiotics).

3.3.6. A fresh departure in practical theology came with Vatican II and was stimulated by it. In view of the considerable tendencies toward church restoration, as well as the increasing crises in pastoral praxis (esp. because of an insufficient number of priests), this discipline in particular has the task of promoting church reform as a constant task, and of contributing to it.

→ Catholicism (Roman); Contextual Theology; Fundamental Theology; Moral Theology; Priest, Priesthood; Roman Catholic Church

Bibliography: F. X. Arnold, K. Rahner et al., eds., *Handbuch der Pastoraltheologie* (5 vols.; Freiburg, 1964-72) • K. Baumgartner and P. Scheuchenpflug, eds., *Lexikon der Pastoral* (2 vols.; Freiburg, 2002) • C. Boff, *Theology and Praxis: Epistemological Foundations* (Maryknoll, N.Y., 1987) • C. Floristán, *Teología práctica. Teoria y praxis de la acción pastoral* (4th ed.; Salamanca, 2002) • O. Fuchs, ed., *Theologie und Handeln* (Düsseldorf, 1984) • W. Fürst, *Praktisch-theologische Urteilskraft* (Zurich, 1986); idem, ed., *Pastoralästhetik. Die Kunst der Wahrnehmung und Gestaltung in Glaube und Kirche* (Freiburg, 2002) • H. Haslinger, ed., *Handbuch Praktische Theologie* (2 vols.; Mainz, 1999-2000) • B. Höfte, *Bekering en bevrijding* (Hilversum, 1990) • F. Klostermann and R. Zerfass, eds., *Praktische Theologie heute* (Munich, 1974) • S. Knobloch, *Was ist Praktische Theologie?* (Fribourg, 1995) • D. McCann and C. R. Strain, *Polity and Praxis: A Program for American Practical Theology* (Minneapolis, 1985) • N. Mette, *Praktisch-theologische Erkundungen* (Münster, 1998); idem, *Theorie der Praxis: Wissenschaftsgeschichtliche und methodologische Untersuchungen zur Theorie-Praxis-Problematik innerhalb der praktischen Theologie* (Düsseldorf, 1978) • N. Mette and H. Steinkamp, *Sozialwissenschaften und praktische Theologie* (Düsseldorf, 1983) • J. B. Metz, *Faith in History and Society: Toward a Practical Fundamental Theology* (New York, 1980) • H. Meyer-Wilmes, L. Troch, and R. Bons-Storm, eds., *Feminist Perspectives in Pastoral Theology* (Louvain, 1998) • H. Peukert, *Science, Action, and Fundamental Theology: Toward a Theology of Communicative Action* (Cambridge, Mass., 1984) • C. Schneider-Harpprecht, ed., *Praktische Theologie im Kontext Lateinamerikas* (Münster, 2003) • H. Steinkamp, *Solidarität und Parteilichkeit. Für eine neue Praxis in Kirche und Gemeinde* (Mainz, 1994) • J. A. van der Ven, *Practical Theology: An Empirical Approach* (Kampen, 1993) • M. Viau, *Practical Theology: A New Approach* (Leiden, 1999) • P. M. Zulehner, *Pastoraltheologie* (4 vols.; Düsseldorf, 1989-90).

Norbert Mette

Pragmatism

1. Origin
2. Development
3. Evaluation

1. Origin

American pragmatism arose as an effort to oppose both scientism and academic → philosophy by holding together the world of practical effects with the world of critical reasoning.

2. Development

The word "pragmatism" first appeared in an 1878 paper by Charles Sanders Peirce (1839-1914) of Cambridge, Massachusetts. Peirce asked about the practical conditions that make a term meaningful and then answered: A term's meaning is the operation one performs and the experiential results one learns to expect from such an operation. → "Truth" is the opinion that will be "ultimately agreed to by all who investigate." A term that has no pragmatic meaning is useless. Two terms that have the same pragmatic meaning are synonymous, no matter how different emotionally. Peirce saw implications for → theology. Because our idea of anything is our idea of its sensible effects, it is foolish for Roman Catholics and Protestants to think they disagree about the sacrament (→ Eucharist), since they agree about its sensible effects.

Peirce's friend Harvard professor William James (1842-1910) brought pragmatism to the world's attention. Unlike Peirce, he saw the possibility of truth in metaphysical statements (→ Metaphysics). Moving from Peirce's notion that our idea of anything is our idea of its effect, James held that all theories and beliefs are properly understood as "instruments, not answers to enigmas." Thus, religious and moral beliefs, no less than scientific ideas, "become true just insofar as they help us to get into satisfactory relation with other parts of our → experience." Both pragmatism and empiricism are devoted to facts, but pragmatism has none of the latter's materialistic bias.

John Dewey (1859-1952) of Columbia University, New York, focused pragmatism on social and ethical concerns (→ Society; Ethics). He applied Peirce's operational definition of meaning to value statements: Just as controlled observation gives the content of beliefs about the natural world, so observing the effects of behaviors and enjoyments can yield regulative moral standards (→ Norms). One need not either appeal to a priori eternal values or accept all enjoyments just because they happen to happen. A *satisfying* experience should be taken into account, but only as a possibility of values to be achieved; it can become an actual value — something *satisfactory* — only when its origins and effects are discovered. When such values become all-inclusive, allegiance to them is the true substance of a religious attitude (→ Religion, Personal Sense of; Value, Ethics of).

3. Evaluation

Critics were quick to note internal confusions in the pragmatists' theories of meaning and truth, but the vision of a path between → rationalism and → empiricism influenced thinkers as different as G. E. Moore (1873-1958) and Henri Bergson (1859-1941; → Vitalism). It was an important precursor to the verification theory of → meaning (§1). It led many Continental philosophers to see their work as a mode of inquiry, not the presentation of abstract ideas. It deeply affected the way Anglo-American philosophers read Ludwig Wittgenstein (1889-1951; → Analytic Philosophy).

The continuing appeal of the pragmatists' agenda can be seen in the energy with which recent American theology has elaborated an emphasis on praxis into a theology of liberation (→ Liberation Theology; North American Theology).

Bibliography: A. J. Ayer, *The Origins of Pragmatism* (San Francisco, 1968) • J. Dewey, *A Common Faith* (New Haven, 1934); idem, *Human Nature and Conduct* (New York, 1922) • M. Festenstein, *Pragmatism and Political Theory: From Dewey to Rorty* (Chicago, 1997) • W. B. Gallie, *Peirce and Pragmatism* (New York, 1966) • S. Hook, *The Metaphysics of Pragmatism* (New York, 1977) • W. James, *Essays in Radical Empiricism* (ed. R. B. Perry; New York, 1912); idem, *Pragmatism* (New York, 1907); idem, *The Will to Believe, and Other Essays* (New York, 1897) • H. O. Mounce, *The Two Pragmatisms: From Peirce to Rorty* (London, 1997) • C. S. Peirce, *Collected Papers* (ed. C. Hartshorne and P. Weiss; Cambridge, Mass., 1931-35) • S. Rosenbaum, ed., *Pragmatism and Religion: Classical Sources and Original Essays* (Urbana, Ill., 2003) • S. Rosenthal, *Pragmatism and Phenomenology: A Philosophic Encounter* (Amsterdam, 1980) • J. E. Smith, *Purpose and Thought: The Meaning of Pragmatism* (New Haven, 1978) • J. P. Soneson, *Pragmatism and Pluralism: John Dewey's Significance for Theology* (Minneapolis, 1993) • J. J. Stuhr, *Pragmatism, Postmodernism, and the Future of Philosophy* (New York, 2003) • M. White, *Pragmatism and the American Mind* (New York, 1973).

David B. Greene

Prague, Four Articles of → Hussites 2

Prayer

1. Religious Aspects
   - 1.1. General
   - 1.2. Terminology and Typology
   - 1.3. Content and Purpose
   - 1.4. Gestures and Means
   - 1.5. Times and Places
   - 1.6. Christian
2. Dogmatic Aspects
   - 2.1. Biblical Understanding
   - 2.2. Present Situation
   - 2.3. Theology of Prayer
   - 2.4. Ecumenical Perspectives
3. Pastoral Aspects
   - 3.1. Secular Crisis
   - 3.2. Basic Forms
   - 3.3. Traditional and New Forms
   - 3.4. Ecumenical Stimulus
   - 3.5. Sociological Insights
   - 3.6. Lifelong Learning
4. Liturgical Aspects
   - 4.1. Historical Basis
   - 4.2. Liturgical Development
   - 4.3. Theological Evaluation
   - 4.4. New Forms

1. Religious Aspects

1.1. *General*

The term "prayer" has to do with a central fact in the divine-human relation, at the root of which is asking. Etymologically, Eng. "prayer" (unlike Ger. *Gebet*) goes back to OFr. *preiere*, "act of asking" or "demand," and is akin to Lat. *precaria*, "a request." These and related terms are probably related also to OEng. *frignan*, "inquire" (cf. Old Sax. *fragon;* Old Ger. *pragan, frahen;* Ger. *fragen*), and introduced in connection with Christianization for an act of the church ritual.

The older theory that prayer developed out of magical sayings has now been abandoned. The boundaries between → magic and → religion are too fluid, and there is no historical proof of any such evolutionary development. Religious texts available to us point to a cultically anchored practice of prayer that was designed to keep alive and to express teleologically the contact between religious subjects and religious objects, whether one or many deities, spirits, heroes, ancestors, or the deceased. In prayer the worshipers, as part of a society or religious group, address a venerated Thou and thereby bear witness to contact with this Thou. It would be hard to find — or to imagine — a religion or religious community without prayer.

Prayer expresses an ongoing relation between two poles.

In form prayer is a special type of religious speech. Even when individual and free, it is strongly marked by tradition. Its style is dependent on literary topoi that make the literature of prayer a part of literary tradition and history. Often its forms, such as the → hymn, song, or saying, are among our oldest literary testimonies (e.g., the Gathas of Zoroaster or the Indian Vedas). The prayers of a religion usually say more about its nature and content than theological tractates or → confessions, for they embody its → piety. In singing or in recitative or rhythmic form, they are also musical testimonies. Music may accompany them. As an essential part of the cult or → worship, and governed by it, they are at the heart of a religion or religious tradition. In → Islam the Friday prayer *(ṣalāt al-jumʿa)* is what constitutes the official worshiping community.

1.2. *Terminology and Typology*

The language of prayer is very rich. Various verbs may be used for the act, which expresses dependence on the deity (crying, beseeching, imploring, demanding, singing, invoking, etc.). Praising and extolling divine acts are a fixed part of the literature of prayer, not merely by way of introduction, but as the main content, as in the hymn. But petition is predominant, with a varying stress on the demand for an answer. (The transition to magic is easiest here, though a purposeful prayer that counts on an answer does not have to be magical.) In some ancient popular religions (esp. among Indo-Europeans), the prayer of thanksgiving is less common, except as a form of praise. Complaints and prayers of → penitence are more common and came to be institutionalized in the form of ceremonies. The OT Psalms offer examples of most forms of prayer and show cross-connections with other Near Eastern materials (G. Widengren).

Correct formulation is mostly in the hands of specialists (→ priests, poets); typical in this regard is the ancient Vedic or Iranian hymn. Not merely in writing cultures but in unwritten religions, prayers belong to the sphere of guarded sacral tradition. Along with official prayers accompanying cultic acts are private prayers, which may follow a fixed form or may freely address personal concerns and feelings (as, respectively, the distinction between *ṣalāt* and *duʿā* in Islam). The attention of the venerated powers is often invoked by special cries or appeals (e.g., epiclesis). Henotheistic traits may play a part here as special significance is attached to the deity invoked (→ Henotheism). Expressing the basic significance of prayer is a special relation between a god (e.g., Asclepius, Greco-Roman god of medicine) and his or her worshipers. Gods can have names alluding to their inclination to hear (Isis was called Epikouros, Gk. "the one who hears") or may be represented with many eyes and ears (Egypt).

1.3. *Content and Purpose*

All that people desire from life finds a place in the literature of prayer. What are called earthly things are to the fore: health, long life, wealth, children, peace, victory in war, safety on journeys, protection from evils and death. This emphasis exists even in religions with more developed → ethics and theology, where spiritual values are more prominent, for to a large extent these areas do not affect popular belief (even in Christianity, esp. in its Roman Catholic form; → Popular Catholicism).

To disparage this side of the tradition and practice of prayer in terms of a dubious criterion oriented to → mysticism and theology (R. Otto, F. Heiler) is without justification from the standpoint of religious study and underestimates the practical character of faith and religion, which takes into account the actual needs of life and is relevant to them. Naturally, human desires and longings are especially reflected in prayer. This factor is the "prayer egoism" of O. Weinreich, and we see it also in litanies of dedication (e.g., Roman *devotio, dedicatio, consecratio,* and *evocatio,* all of which take form in prayer).

The philosophers of antiquity (Heraclitus, Plato, and Lucretius) took offense at this practice, as did the poets (Aristophanes), so that in Greek we find parodies of prayer and access to deity only by way of intellectual insight, especially when, as in → Stoicism, conformity to the unalterable cosmic order is the only true religious relationship. Nevertheless, here too we still find prayers, for example, that of Cleanthes (d. 232/231 B.C.).

1.4. *Gestures and Means*

Posture in prayer varies from religion to religion and cult to cult, often depending on the purpose and content. People pray standing, sitting, kneeling, or lying *(prostratio, proskynēsis).* Hands may be uplifted or folded. There may be beating the breast or touching the earth, idol, or → altar. The head may be covered (as the Romans did), kisses may be blown *(adoratio),* there may be hopping and dancing, and there may be circling around the altar to the right (Indo-Europeans) or with an inclination of the body to the right. In some religions (Judaism, Islam) special vestments are obligatory, in others sacral clothing (usually white) is worn. In Islam prayer must be made on a prayer rug.

A means of expression is the word (handed down

orally or in writing), which may be recited softly, in a murmur or loudly, with an outcry or silently. Prayer may be silent either out of → reverence or for the sake of an arcane discipline or → meditation; such prayer is common in mysticism. Since official prayers often accompany cultic ceremonies (e.g., sacrificial rites), the external attitude is governed by the latter. The assembly either participates directly or is represented by specialists (priests).

In Tibet participation is mechanical, by means of prayer flags and prayer wheels. Such practice does not necessarily rule out sincerity, since intention is required. In ancient Mesopotamia praying figures in temples expressed the community's ongoing intercession. Some Christian monks engage in constant prayer (→ Monasticism; Acoemetae), as do some ascetic schools in India.

1.5. ***Times and Places***

Since all cultic acts involve some prayer, prayer is linked to the festal calendar. In many religions the day begins (sunrise) and ends (sunset) with prayer, and there may also be midday, afternoon, and night prayer. → Judaism fixed on three times of daily prayer, and Islam on five (morning, midday, afternoon, evening, night).

The religious elite (monks, ascetics, priests, and teachers) do more praying — for example, in → Manichaeanism, which prescribed seven prayers for the elect and four for the laity. In Zoroastrianism (→ Iranian Religions 7) there are five times of prayer, and among the → Mandaeans there were mostly three (sometimes five). In Buddhist monasteries there is at least morning and evening prayer (e.g., in the Zen monasteries of Japan; → Buddhism). The lama spends the day in a round of prayer, meditation (→ Yoga), and instruction.

The primary places of prayer are holy places where cultic acts also take place (→ Temple; Church; Synagogue; Mosque; Monastery). Earlier, people prayed outside on hills, in sacred groves, near holy lakes, or in caves. The central → sanctuaries of some religions (as → Jerusalem, → Rome, Mecca, Medina, Karbala, Kyoto, Nara, etc.) are also special places of prayer for believers. These places sometimes fix the direction (Arab. *qiblah*) in which prayer is to be made, as Jerusalem does for Jews, and Mecca for Islam. The four points of the compass may also be significant in this regard. Rules about how and where to pray or not pray have helped to produce rules of ritual purity, enjoining, for example, washings and chastity (→ Cultic Purity).

1.6. ***Christian***

→ Jesus gave Christians a simple form of prayer (→ Lord's Prayer), as opposed to the "empty phrases" and "many words" of the Gentiles (Matt. 6:7). Later, however, the churches could not ignore the liturgical riches of Jews and Gentiles, and long litanies developed that are comparable to those of other religions (e.g., → Buddhism, → Hinduism, and Lamaism; see 2 and 3 below). There might be different theological evaluations of the content of prayer and of a phrase such as "in the name of . . . ," such as we find among believers and insiders, but all such elements are subject to generally recognized historical norms. The history of religion confirms that prayer has always been of great value and importance for the religious side of the human race.

→ Ecstasy; Spirituality

Bibliography: A. Carter, *The Prayer Tradition of Black People* (Valley Forge, Pa., 1976) • S. D. Gill, "Prayer," *EncRel(E)* 11.489-94 • F. Heiler, *Prayer: A Study in the History and Psychology of Religion* (Oxford, 1932; orig. pub., 1918) • P. R. McKenzie, *The Christians, Their Practices and Beliefs: An Adaptation of Friedrich Heiler's Phenomenology of Religion* (Nashville, 1988) chap. 9, "The Sacred Word 2: To the Deity" • J. Mbiti, *The Prayers of African Religion* (London, 1975) • F. Schwenn, *Gebet und Opfer. Studien zum griechischen Kultus* (Heidelberg, 1927) • "Prayer," *ERE* (1918) 10.154-214 (still the best and fullest overview, with examples) • E. von Severus, "Gebet I," *RAC* 8.1134-1258 • H. S. Versnel, *Faith, Hope, and Worship* (Leiden, 1981) esp. 1-64, "Religious Mentality in Ancient Prayer" • G. Widengren, *The Accadian and Hebrew Psalms of Lamentation as Religious Documents* (Uppsala, 1937); idem, *Religionsphänomenologie* (Berlin, 1969) chap. 9.

Kurt Rudolph

2. Dogmatic Aspects

"Prayer" is a term for the conscious → act in which individuals or a group shape their relation to what they find to be the ultimate basis and meaning of life. Religious criticism (→ Religion, Criticism of) and sociology have raised the question today whether prayer belongs only to a specific period in human development or to certain particular social or biographical situations. → Systematic theology thus has the task of considering and anchoring prayer afresh in the total context of Christian thought (H.-M. Barth, G. Ebeling).

2.1. ***Biblical Understanding***

Though the biblical understanding of prayer reflects many background influences, certain inalienable characteristics emerge.

2.1.1. In the OT prayer is as varied as life itself. There is no unified theoretical concept, but two basic types may be seen: complaint and petition on the one side, praise and thanksgiving on the other. These types articulate the two fundamental relations of believers to the reality around them, namely, resistance and submission. Prayer is not finally a pronouncedly religious act but a self-evident way of dealing with life.

At the same time, it is clear that prayer is always a reaction, a matter that the OT develops theologically. The initiative in prayer does not lie finally with the one who prays but with → Yahweh, who leads into situations that demand prayer. Thus prayer is first awareness, listening. We listen to God before calling upon him (e.g., Samuel hearing Yahweh's voice, 1 Samuel 3). Above all things, we must hear God's Word, or "hear" God. Israel's prayer presupposes the "Hear, O Israel" of Deut. 6:4. Hence the typical mode of prayer in Israel is not the adjuration linked to magical practices but the complaint, which then changes into praise even before there is any change in outward circumstances.

Because prayer is always an answer to what Yahweh says and does, its true place is in the community to which he speaks, which he has chosen, and to whom his → promise applies. The prayer of individuals is to be understood in the light of that of the congregation. This priority explains why the Psalms could become the prayer book of Christianity, as well as of countless numbers of individual believers.

2.1.2. The prayer of → Jesus shaped the NT understanding of prayer. In contrast to the usual Jewish practice of his day, Jesus spoke to God using the familiar, childlike, and confident address "Abba" (J. Jeremias). In simple trust Jesus lived out the prayers he prayed. He did so as the Son, one with the Father (note the so-called high-priestly prayer in John 17). Yet he also suffered the radical loneliness of a human being before God: "My God, my God, why have you forsaken me?" (Mark 15:34).

Christianity thus prays "in Jesus' name" (see John 16:23, 24, 26, etc.). Individual believers find power for prayer in him (see Luke 11:5-13). Jesus invites us to prayer and gives it its characteristic eschatological profile. The → Lord's Prayer came into the early church, and along with it the cry *Marana tha,* "Our Lord, come!" (1 Cor. 16:22).

The expectant prayer of sinners to God, the Father, and to Christ, who makes it possible, becomes the quintessence of Christian prayer. Prayer also acquires pneumatological components, for the Spirit actualizes the relation that is sought in prayer (1 Cor. 12:3; Rom. 8:26). Hence → Paul can even regard the Spirit as the subject of prayer (Gal. 4:6). Although Trinitarian dogma developed only later, Christian prayer is thus in the last resort Trinitarian: Prayer to the Father, through the Son, in the → Holy Spirit (→ Trinity). In this regard the address to God as "our Father" in the Lord's Prayer might be misleading, for prayer is now made to the whole Trinity.

2.2. *Present Situation*

The experience of unanswered prayer is not the main problem with prayer today. Recognizing that God "did not withhold his own Son" (Rom. 8:32), and having an assurance of the eschatological answering of all prayer, believers can always find sense in prayer (→ Theodicy). More difficult is dealing with the lack of motivation for prayer, with the absence of desire (*acedia,* "despair"; *siccitas,* "dryness") or with the sense of the irrelevance of prayer in a rationally ordered world. The arguments of religious criticism and sociology have their place here.

The objection, which goes back to antiquity, that prayer arises from wishful thinking and that for this reason it crops up especially in what seem to be hopeless situations was radicalized by Ludwig Feuerbach (1804-72) and Sigmund Freud (1856-1939), who argued that we may appropriately seek help only from ourselves and our fellows. For atheists (→ Atheism) prayer is self-evidently superfluous: no God, no prayer. Psychology gives prayer a relative place as an act of helpful regression, inner clarification, and psychological hygiene, but such an approach simply sharpens the crisis, although it also perhaps points to a solution (W. Bernet, D. Sölle). Discussion of the linguistic implications of prayer (V. Brümmer, R. Schaeffler) continues.

2.3. *Theology of Prayer*

A theology of prayer that tackles the present situation will first try to set aside misconceptions. These might arise in connection with the underlying doctrine of → God or with the anthropological presuppositions (→ Anthropology).

2.3.1. Every theology of prayer presupposes a doctrine of God. The definition of prayer as address to God (→ Augustine) or as the elevation or ascent of the mind toward God (Evagrius Ponticus) runs through the whole history of Christian prayer. On the first view, which reached an effective peak with a Christological focus on the Thou of Jesus in → Pietism, it is obvious that God is viewed somewhat anthropomorphically as a partner in conversation whose reactions are sought in prayer. If authentic biblical elements are combined here with theistic models, a view of prayer can easily result that is liable to attack by the critics of religion and that does not correspond to the Trinitarian basis of Christian prayer.

2.3.2. In some tension with this view is the mystical approach (→ Mysticism), which owes much to

Neoplatonic influences (→ Platonism) and in which the main concern is to pray, not for something, but for God himself. God's nearness might be thought of transpersonally, but God is "above all names" (as in the → apophatic theology of the East) and modes (Meister → Eckhart). → Contemplation or → meditation is the perfect form of prayer.

There is much in common here with what we find in other religions (see 1). The distinctively Christian features, though — the fact that Jesus Christ is constitutive — may be seen only in the background.

2.3.3. It is no wonder, then, that in modern discussion the central point is the recapturing of the Trinitarian dimension of Christian prayer, in which regard can be had to the creaturely presuppositions, the Christological foundation, and the pneumatological aspects. If God is triune, then the personal and transpersonal elements of prayer can be present alongside one another. Because the Spirit utters the "Abba" in believers, linking them with the prayer of Jesus and the sighing of unredeemed creation (Rom. 8:22), they know that they are shaped afresh by prayer. Prayer and work also cease to be rivals. Fighting in favor of the oppressed and contemplation join hands (→ Liberation Theology; Taizé Community).

In intercession believers achieve solidarity with those for whom they pray. Aware of the needs of others, they are also open to their own possibilities of taking on → responsibility for these needs. Both occur in trust in the Creator, the Redeemer, and the Consummator of the promised eschatological fulfillment. Prayer serves to glorify God by releasing those who pray and making them capable of action. In these two ways people come to themselves in prayer.

2.4. *Ecumenical Perspectives*

As a deeper understanding of prayer is sought, the ecumenical factor takes on particular significance (→ Ecumenism, Ecumenical Movement). The denominations have developed in distinctive and characteristic ways that which has emerged when prayer is viewed from a Trinitarian standpoint.

2.4.1. The → Roman Catholic Church has developed a particular understanding of prayer as a basic human act by creation. In keeping is the fact that it takes seriously such natural aids to prayer as places, times, and rules (see 3 and 4 below; → Hours, Canonical; Rosary). The strong feeling for liturgical prayer possibly has its roots here as well. What is called contemplative prayer takes up messages from the creaturely world and, in grateful acceptance of what is given, transforms them into praise of God.

2.4.2. The → Reformation had a particular concern for the grace wherein God calls sinners to himself and commands them to call upon him for Christ's sake. → Faith and prayer belong very closely together. For the → Reformers, then, prayer is primarily an answer to the → Word of God, to heard → preaching and the read word of Holy Scripture. The practice of meditation on the Word is consistent with this emphasis. The category of the individual also plays a stronger part as individuals take personal → responsibility for responding to the Word.

The Pietist prayer meeting gathers individuals together for prayer who bring their concerns to God extemporaneously rather than in liturgical forms. Such gatherings may also take up an active ministry or play a part in community life.

2.4.3. For Orthodox theology (→ Orthodox Church; Orthodox Christianity), prayer is a common dimension of the Christian life. On this view theologians are those who "know how to pray" (N. A. Nissiotis). The → worship and → spirituality of individuals are infused with a spirit of adoration. The prayer → piety of Orthodoxy may be seen especially in the practice of the so-called prayer of the heart, or Jesus Prayer.

2.4.4. The → charismatic movement, which has taken up many of the concerns of → Pentecostalism (→ Pentecostal Churches), draws attention to possible gaps in the theology and practice of prayer in the large denominations by engaging in prayer for → healing and by trying to take praying people seriously in their psychosomatic unity.

2.4.5. In the ecumenical sphere we find many views of prayer, some of which can be contradictory. Enthusiastic traits in the prayer practice of charismatics call for criticism, as do certain phenomena of alienation in Protestantism that result from activism. In Roman Catholic theology prayer to Mary (→ Mary, Devotion to; Mariology) and the → saints does not count as prayer in the true sense but as invocation. Protestantism, however, cannot make this kind of distinction.

Despite some difficulties, the Christian churches can clearly help one another to unfold the riches and depth of prayer "to God the Father through the Son in the Holy Spirit." In so doing, they can test what other religions have to offer and make fruitful the criticisms that come from sociologists and the critics of religion.

2.4.6. The prayer for peace in Assisi in 1986 initiated by John Paul II (1978-2005) raised the question whether members of different religions could pray collectively (in "interreligious prayer") or only alongside one another ("multireligious prayer").

Christian faith is confident that the triune God knows how to deal graciously with prayers that may go astray.

3. Pastoral Aspects

"To pray is human" (J. Sudbrack). If prayer is one of the essential expressions of Christian and even human life, we must pay special pastoral attention to it.

3.1. *Secular Crisis*

The crisis in prayer that may be seen in secular societies is to be regarded as a spiritual challenge. We must take it seriously from a pastoral standpoint inasmuch as an experience of God's absence and of the irrelevance of faith lies behind it. It is also to be understood within the context of an increasing inability to give linguistic expression to the relevant problems of life.

Existential yearning for → happiness and → meaning, which might lead to the formulating of prayers in a religious society, expresses itself today in the secular forms of wishes and hopes. These expressions need to be deciphered as rudimentary forms of Christian prayer associated with our human creatureliness (→ Hope).

On a Christian view prayer is a reply to the call of the triune God (see 2). We thus need to detect and create situations in which both religious and nonreligious people can be aware of this call. In this context Christian individuals and congregations will confess prayer and publicly accept theological responsibility for it.

3.2. *Basic Forms*

The basic forms of prayer as we find them especially in the Psalms and in both individual and congregational prayer are praise and thanksgiving, complaint, petition, and intercession. Protestantism is familiar with an extensive practice of spontaneous or free prayer in groups or congregational gatherings. Liturgical prayer, which makes use of the formulations of the Psalms and the Fathers and other set texts, characterizes especially Orthodox, Roman Catholic, and Anglican → worship (see 4; → Eucharistic Prayer; Hours, Canonical; Liturgy). In piety arising from the Reformation, praying with the hymnbook (H. Grass) plays an important part. In many cases a set prayer (e.g., the → Lord's Prayer) is an articulatory aid.

Encounter with non-Christian prayer and the practice of meditation has helped to discover and use forgotten treasures of the Christian tradition of prayer (e.g., silent prayer). Speaking in tongues (→ Glossolalia), which is important in the → charismatic movement, is usually regarded as an ecstatic phenomenon (→ Ecstasy) that is connected only indirectly with the understanding of prayer; already in the NT it is set under a caveat (1 Cor. 14:2-9). In contrast, the ecumenical world has paid renewed attention to the prayer of → healing (Jas. 5:13-15; → Pastoral Care of the Sick).

3.3. *Traditional and New Forms*

The renewal of Christian prayer involves tested forms first. A flexible and imaginative handling of tradition has produced new forms of table prayers (a table canon, the prayer breakfast, a minute of silence). Instead of daily times of prayer various weekends or other days may also be set aside for retreats or days of meditation (e.g., the ecumenical Week of Prayer for Christian Unity, week of prayer of the → World Evangelical Alliance, World Day of Prayer for Women's Ordination, and World Day of Prayer, initiated and carried out by women). Church conferences have also helped to revitalize the practice of prayer.

Dorothee Sölle's *Politisches Nachtgebet* (Political prayer night, from 1968) also offers a new model that protects against the misunderstanding of prayer as solely a private matter. The combination of information, meditation, and the beginnings of action shows that prayer and work belong indissolubly together. Prayer is increasingly coming to be felt as a dimension of life that brings inspiration and release to → everyday life.

3.4. *Ecumenical Stimulus*

The ecumenical movement can do much to promote the renewed practice of prayer. Many Christians have found forms of prayer fruitful that have no place in their own religious situation but that have for centuries been the means of intensive experiences elsewhere. By silent immersion in a detail of → creation, the "contemplative prayer" of Roman Catholics can give awareness of the Creator and one's own creatureliness. "Eternal adoration" is bound up with sacramental piety in the Roman Catholic world, and non–Roman Catholics can also achieve some sense of the mystery of an all-embracing fellowship of prayer. The → rosary, which repeats certain litany-like formulas, has been the source of much misunderstanding; it awaits rediscovery as a specifically Western form of meditation.

The practice of the Jesus Prayer in the Eastern churches, which is bound up with the process of breathing, involves the prayer "Lord Jesus Christ, Son of God, have mercy on me, a sinner" (with variations). It is gaining interest also in the churches of the West. In the prayer of the poor in the → Third World, a new spirituality is linked to → liberation and social action. Prayer processions and political demonstrations have been held, the two not necessarily opposed to each other (e.g., the *Montagsgebete*, which helped to dissolve the German Democratic Republic in 1989).

The contribution of Protestantism is free, spontaneous prayer in thankful response to the → Word of God and in a combination of → responsibility and → work (→ Vocation). Critical attention still needs to be paid, however, to the future form of Christian prayer. Speaking in tongues (see 3.2) is discussed theologically, as is, to a lesser extent, the charismatic prayer of healing. Prayer may mistakenly approximate to magical practices, such as we find in the encounter with non-Christian cults (→ Cargo Cult; Umbanda). Such approximation is to be avoided.

3.5. *Sociological Insights*

Insights from the social sciences, especially psychology and sociology, help to avoid false developments and processes of impoverishment. Prayer enables the clarification of difficult situations and the articulation of what is experienced, feared, or hoped for. It is a psychological release. It also integrates believers into the fellowship of the needy and of suppliants. It gives them new perspectives and equips them for action. Despite the suspicions of religious critics, prayer gives a stronger sense of reality.

Since a human being is a psychosomatic unity (→ Anthropology), prayer is not just an inward process. We also must take into account the external conditions. As it is harder to find a quiet place in modern dwellings (see Matt. 6:6), it is the more necessary for churches to provide places of quiet and prayer, and necessary for members to use them. From the same standpoint the gestures of prayer that Protestants tend to neglect (standing, kneeling, prostration, → sign of the cross, "body prayer") have a certain importance.

Prayer, however, is also part of a more comprehensive lifestyle that may be marked by other procedures (including → asceticism, → fasting, and silence) and a certain way of dealing with → time. Both theologically and sociologically, it is an impoverishment if prayer is merely private or does not go hand in hand with the corresponding conduct. By way of clarification, it helps to prepare the ground for responsible action.

3.6. *Lifelong Learning*

A special pastoral task arises from prayer involving a process of lifelong learning. The issue is not simply a matter of learning how to pray in a process of psychological development with parents, at preschool, or by means of → religious education. Even adult and mature Christians must realize that the practice of prayer can involve them in a process in which all their relationships and experiences are ripened and deepened. The traditional distinction of stages of prayer is theologically questionable, for God does not grant his presence in stages. Nevertheless, it is anthropologically helpful insofar as we can grow into an increasingly clear apprehension of the presence of God.

In this regard we must pay attention both to proclamation and to those who are themselves in a process of growth and progress. We must free ourselves from isolation in merely liturgical prayer. Prayer must be a theme of → preaching and must win back an honorable place in → pastoral care, for loss of prayer means loss in life itself.

→ Devotion, Devotions

Bibliography: On 2 (biblical and theological): V. Auvinen, *Jesus' Teaching on Prayer* (Åbo, 2003) • H.-M. Barth, *Wohin–woher mein Ruf? Zur Theologie des Bittgebets* (Munich, 1981) • K. Barth, *Prayer* (2d ed.; Philadelphia, 1985) • S. P. Becker, *Erkenntnis und Gebet. Die pneumatologische Grundstruktur von Karl Barths dogmatischer Arbeit* (Frankfurt, 1995) • R. Brandt, *The Spirit Helps Us to Pray: A Biblical Theology of Prayer* (Springfield, Mo., 1993) • O. Cullmann, *Prayer in the NT* (Minneapolis, 1995) • A. Cunningham, *Prayer: Personal and Liturgical* (Wilmington, Del., 1985) • G. Ebeling, "Reden zu Gott," *Dogmatik des christlichen Glaubens* (3 vols.; Tübingen, 1979) 1.192-244 • J. A. Jungmann, *Christian Prayer through the Centuries* (New York, 1978) • A. Kistenbrügge, *Das Gebet in der Dogmatik. Untersucht am Beispiel von Gerhard Ebelings "Dogmatik des christlichen Glaubens"* (Frankfurt, 2000) • R. Mössinger, *Zur Lehre des christlichen Gebets. Gedanken über ein vernachlässigtes Thema evangelischer Theologie* (Göttingen, 1986) • G. Müller, "Gebet VIII: Dogmatische Probleme gegenwärtiger Gebetstheologie," *TRE* 12.84-94 • F. MacNutt, *The Prayer That Heals: Praying for Healing in the Family* (London, 1988) • D. Z. Phillips, *The Concept of Prayer* (Oxford, 1981) • H. Reventlow, *Gebet im Alten Testament* (Stuttgart, 1986) • G. Wainwright, *Doxology: The Praise of God in Worship, Doctrine, and Life. A Systematic Theology* (New York, 1980) • M. Wriedt, "Gebet und Theologie. Skizzen zur Neubesinnung des Gebets im Kontext der systematisch-theologischen Theoriebildung," *FZPhTh* 31 (1984) 421-52.

On 2 (other themes): W. Bernet, *Gebet* (Stuttgart, 1970) • L. Boff, "De la espiritualidad de la liberación a la práctica de la liberación," *Espiritualidad y liberación en América Latina* (ed. E. Bonnin; San José, C.R., 1982) 49-58 • V. Brümmer, *What Are We Doing When We Pray? A Philosophical Inquiry* (London, 1984) •

V. Codina, "Learning to Pray together with the Poor: A Christian Necessity," *Learning to Pray* (ed. C. Floristán and C. Duquoc; Edinburgh, 1982) 3-7 • T. Dienberg, *Ihre Tränen sind wie Gebete. Das Gebet nach Auschwitz in Theologie und Literatur* (Würzburg, 1997) • S. Dietrich, *Das schweigende Gebet. Zur Grundlage des Verständnisses von schweigendem Gebet in ökumenischem Blickwinkel* (Leipzig, 2000) • D. N. Griffiths, *The Bibliography of the Book of Common Prayer, 1549-1999* (London, 2002) • R. M. Gross, ed., *Christians Talk about Buddhist Meditation, Buddhists Talk about Christian Prayer* (New York, 2003) • F. Heiler, *Prayer: A Study in the History and Psychology of Religion* (2d ed.; New York, 1958) • K. Hofmeister and L. Bauerochse, eds., *Viele Stimmen–eine Sprache. Beten in den Weltreligionen* (Würzburg, 2001) • *Interreligious Prayer* (= *Pro Dialogo/Current Dialogue,* Bulletin 98, no. 2 [1998]) • H. Luibl, *Des Fremden Sprachgestalt. Beobachtungen zum Bedeutungswandel des Gebets in der Geschichte der Neuzeit* (Tübingen, 1993) • G. Riedl, *Modell Assisi. Christliches Gebet und interreligiöser Dialog in heilsgeschichtlichem Kontext* (Berlin, 1998) • R. Schaeffler, *Das Gebet und das Argument. Zwei Weisen des Sprechens von Gott. Eine Einführung in die Theorie der religiösen Sprache* (Düsseldorf, 1989) • D. Sölle, "Gebet," *Atheistisch an Gott glauben. Beiträge zur Theologie* (Freiburg, 1968) 109-17.

On 3: H. U. von Balthasar, *Prayer* (London, 1961) • F. W. Bargheer, *Gebet und beten lernen. Die theologisch-anthropologischen Grundlagen und die lebensgeschichtliche Verarbeitung ihrer Krise* (Gütersloh, 1973) • R. Bohren, *Das Gebet* (vol. 1; Waltrop, 2003) • R. Deichgräber, *Wachsende Ringe. Die Bibel lehrt beten* (2d ed.; Göttingen, 1985) • C. Floristán and C. Duquoc, eds., *Learning to Pray* (Edinburgh, 1982) • M. Gibbard, *Prayer and Contemplation* (London, 1976) • W. Jäger and B. Grimm, *Der Himmel in dir. Einübung ins Körpergebet* (Munich, 2000) • M. el-Meskeen, *Orthodox Prayer Life: The Interior Way* (Crestwood, N.Y., 2003) • *The Philokalia: The Complete Text* (4 vols.; comp. St. Nikodimos of the Holy Mountain and St. Makarios of Corinth; trans. G. E. H. Palmer et al.; London, 1979-95) • A. Reiser and P. G. Schoenborn, eds., *Sehnsucht nach dem Fest der freien Menschen. Gebete aus Lateinamerika* (Wuppertal, 1982) • J. N. Ward, *The Use of Praying* (12th ed.; London, 1981) • K. Ware, *The Power of the Name: The Jesus Prayer in Orthodox Spirituality* (Oxford, 1986) • F. Winter, "Praktische Literatur zum Gebet in der Gemeinde," *TLZ* 110 (1985) 241-58 • J. Zink, *Wie wir beten können* (4th ed.; Stuttgart, 1995) • C. Zippert, *Leben mit Gebeten. Erfahrungen und Anregungen* (Gütersloh, 1978).

Hans-Martin Barth

4. Liturgical Aspects

4.1. *Historical Basis*

Liturgical prayer is oriented to the wealth found in the Psalms (note 1 Tim. 2:1; on its development, see O. Brodde, *EKL* [1st ed.] 1.1445-48). The most important liturgical prayers are collects, church intercessions, the → eucharistic prayers, introits, pulpit prayers, and special confessions of sin. Structurally, liturgical prayer has a place in → worship as prologue or response. The liturgical prayers of → occasional services are shaped by the understanding of the church or the sacraments, especially in → baptism, → confirmation (→ Initiation Rites), → marriage, → funerals, and other actions (→ ordination, → benediction, induction, → consecration). Prayer takes on special significance in the benedictions of the → Roman Catholic Church.

4.2. *Liturgical Development*

In the Roman Catholic tradition liturgical prayer and the development of → dogma enrich one another. As the prayer of the → church, liturgical prayer is ecclesiologically determined. More recently there has been stress on the communal character of worship (→ Liturgy 3; Mass).

In the tradition of the → Orthodox Church, the whole liturgical drama is cosmically oriented. The hymnal elements are repeated often (→ Hymn; Liturgy 2).

In the Reformation tradition emphasis on proclamation has reduced and accentuated liturgical prayers, worship being a holistic kerygmatic-euchological action (→ Liturgy 1). The → Lutheran churches retain some elements of the "purified Mass," but in the → Reformed churches, with their stress on preaching, a few long psalm-prayers predominate.

With its wealth of liturgical psalms the → Anglican Communion lies between the Lutherans and Roman Catholics. In the → free churches there are two traditions. The → Methodist churches have set prayers, but the → Baptists and → Pentecostal churches have no fixed liturgical forms of prayer, leaving a place for spontaneous testimonies and the prayers of the people. Liturgical development has been ecumenically rich and varied.

4.3. *Theological Evaluation*

Liturgical prayer qualifies worship. It is open to God and avoids human control. It gives God alone the glory (as distinct from conjuration). It is the most important form of religious release. It overcomes rubrical restriction and is always the prayer of the → congregation (using we-forms and the → acclamation → "Amen!"). All the baptized are euchologically competent. Liturgical prayer promotes private prayer. Hence there should be several times of silence in worship (at the beginning, during intercessions, and at the end), which themselves can be part of the liturgical structure.

A liturgy is defective when its prayers merely popularize individual theological views or when there are psychological, pedagogical, or moralistic pressures. The prayers of an interreligious day of prayer (e.g., the event in Assisi in 1986 hosted by John Paul II [1978-2005], attended by representatives of 15 religions) are not liturgical prayers.

4.4. *New Forms*

We constantly must work on liturgical prayer, either in preparation for worship or spontaneously. Models for new prayers are provided at church conferences and in → communities (meditative prayers). Sung forms and repeated acclamations (in harmony or unison) offer considerable variety. New forms also arise out of the revitalizing of old customs (e.g., the ecumenical prayer → stations of the cross). Local congregations can adopt new forms into their Sunday services.

New forms are important in group worship (in family services, children's services, youth services, and closed groups). Groups that work on the liturgy prior to worship can produce new forms, which can help give instruction in worship. Alternating forms are to be recommended.

Euchological education is needed, but is seldom included, as part of the church's educational program. Liturgical prayer should be the focus, but regular private prayer should also be included.

New forms find literary expression in many prayer books. They often are ecumenically oriented and have been translated into various languages.

→ Contemplation; Spirituality

Bibliography: R. Berger et al., *Gestalt des Gottesdienstes. Sprachliche und nichtsprachliche Ausdrucksformen* (Regensburg, 1987) • P. Evdokimov, *La prière de l'Église d'Orient* (Paris, 1985; orig. pub., 1966) • C. Jones, G. Wainwright, and E. Yarnold, eds., *The Study of Liturgy* (New York, 1978); idem, eds., *The Study of Spirituality* (London, 1986) • F. Kalb, *Grundriß der Liturgik* (2d ed.; Munich, 1982) • E. Lodi, ed., *Enchiridion euchologicum fontium liturgicorum* (Rome, 1979) ancient and medieval liturgical texts • A. G. Martimort, ed., *The Church at Prayer: An Introduction to the Liturgy* (4 vols.; Collegeville, Minn., 1986-88) • G. Wainwright, *The Praise of God in Worship, Doctrine, and Life: A Systematic Theology* (New York, 1984) • K.-F. Wiggermann, "Fürbitte. Ein Aspekt liturgischer Euchologie," *KuD* 50 (2004).

Karl-Friedrich Wiggermann

Preaching

1. Basis

We humans would not be what we are without → language (→ Anthropology). Our experience of ourselves and the world takes linguistic shape (H.-G. Gadamer). Here then is a necessary starting point for the discussion of preaching. We must relate theological reflection on preaching and its problems to this starting point.

From the days of antiquity → rhetoric has been the discipline that treats of our human faculty of language in relation to experience, and especially to public speaking (P. L. Oesterreich). We thus must relate preaching and the history and theology of preaching to rhetoric, even though other essential factors also enter in. The history of rhetoric and that of preaching and the theology of preaching are intertwined. Rhetorical studies have never contested this connection (W. Jens), but 20th-century theology sometimes minimized its significance.

2. Historical Perspective

We do not have any comprehensive history of preaching and the theology of preaching. In this context we can only mention some high points that are important as examples. With much else, the homiletical or rhetorical structures of the biblical tradition and of preaching in the first stages of the → early church will have to go undiscussed.

2.1. *Early Church*

The practice of → synagogue worship, contemporary forms like the Cynic-Stoic diatribe (→ Stoicism), and the kerygmatic missionary NT tradition (→ Kerygma; Mission) were determinative factors in the development of Christian preaching, along with prevailing social and political conditions. The multiplicity of these factors and the uncertainty of the early tradition make it hard to give an account of the origins.

By the time of → Origen (ca. 185-ca. 254; → Origenism), preaching was already a fixed part of worship, and it was normally based on a biblical passage. In the form of a homily, the text was sometimes expounded in its threefold sense: (1) natural and historical, (2) moral, and (3) mystical and speculative. By means of allegorizing, the statements of the text were applied to the lives of the hearers. Since the aim of preaching was the edification of the → congregation, exhortation took precedence over doctrine. Though Origen related his work to the structure of pagan philosophical studies, in his understanding of preaching he did not link it expressly to rhetoric. Perhaps, as we might say today, he was more oriented to problems than to his listeners. He wrote academic prose.

With the three great → Cappadocians — Basil of Caesarea (ca. 330-79), Gregory of Nazianzus (329/30-389/90), and Gregory of Nyssa (ca. 330-ca. 395) — preaching acquired a rhetorical quality. It was challenged to do so by the increasing pedagogical and apologetic demands placed upon it as Christianity spread and by the many different types of hearers now to be considered. Preachers could meet this challenge because they had rhetorical training, whether before → baptism or before they began to preach. Certainly the three Cappadocians had such training.

The contemporary Greek understanding of education not only was influenced by rhetoric but could not be detached from it. On this rhetorical basis fourth-century preaching reached a level that made it acceptable to the educated people of the day. At the same time, the situations in which it took place were now more varied. Church life involved more occasional opportunities in addition to the regular worship and apart from it, such as inductions to office, burials, and addresses relating to the veneration of → martyrs and → saints (→ Occasional Services). We thus find emerging the *logos panēgyrikos* (festival oration), similar to speeches given on secular occasions.

2.2. *Augustine*

In his *De doctrina Christiana* → Augustine (354-430; → Augustine's Theology) wrote a work of homiletics and hermeneutics that would be decisive for the → Middle Ages as a whole. Here we have the last rhetorical work of antiquity and the first of Christianity. Rhetoric was the main theme in book 4. In tandem with the *De oratore* of Cicero (106-43 B.C.), this work paved the way for the acceptance and development of rhetoric by Christian theologians and preachers. For Augustine rhetoric was a technique that might be either misused or put to good use. He viewed rhetoric instrumentally, so that, from the rhetorical standpoint, the question of truth did not arise. Augustine thus followed a line of rhetorical tradition set by Plato (427-347; → Platonism) rather than Aristotle (384-322; → Aristotelianism).

But the view held by Augustine was not totally instrumental. Orientation to Cicero and to the threefold rhetorical task of *docere, delectare, flectere* (teaching, pleasing, persuading) meant that decisions had to be made about content. From the standpoint of homiletical hermeneutics this perspective meant that the form of preaching must be in accord with the truth of → revelation. Preachers of the Word of God are seen also as its hearers. Their understanding grows out of their relation to the revealed Word. We have here a rhetorical theology that also relativizes the claims of rhetoric. In his own excellent summation, G. Mainberger maintains that Augustine's doctrine of Christianity, which at its core actually constitutes the theory of Christian preaching, places preachers in a broken relationship with rhetoric.

This position made an extraordinary impact. The instrumental thrust was stronger in later homiletics than the exceptions from it. Along with the greater strength of the instrumental components in general rhetorical history, this fact explains the frequently unfruitful relation between homiletics and rhetoric in the centuries that followed.

2.3. *Middle Ages*

In the Middle Ages (see esp. R. Cruel), Gregory the Great (ca. 540-604) also influenced the understanding of preaching with his *Regula pastoralis* (ca. 591). "Cure of souls" was his chief interest, and he supplemented Augustine's theory of preaching along such lines. If preaching is to be credible, there must be a unity of life, speech, and action in preachers. They must do justice to the different needs and dispositions and situations of their hearers. Though the theory of Augustine and the practice of Gregory were very influential, we still must recognize that the everyday standard of preaching was modest, and continuity could not be taken for granted.

A change came with Charlemagne (768-814). In 801 he passed a law enforcing regular preaching on

Sundays and feast days by → priests as well as → bishops. The central themes were to be the Creed and the → Lord's Prayer.

As the Middle Ages progressed, so did the rhetorical formalizing of homiletical theory (see D. Roth). We find examples in the works of William of Auvergne (d. 1249). In his *De rhetorica divina* William compared preachers to legal advocates. They represent believers before God and seek grace for them. In his *Ars praedicandi* William then set forth the six questions that are to be asked in homiletics: who? to whom? where? when? how? what? The preaching orders (→ Religious Orders and Congregations) brought new accents and impulses. In part the homily now became thematic. But this development meant detaching the homily from a pericope, as in Berthold von Regensburg (ca. 1220-72).

2.4. *Reformation*

The → Reformation involved a "language-event" of the first rank. Printing made duplication of the spoken word possible on a scale not previously dreamed of. But new forms and a new style were needed in consequence. We must relate Reformation preaching to this context. It is part of the whole movement of what H.-E. Bahr has called "Reformation mass communication," in which polemical works, tracts, and pamphlets also had a place. Finally, → humanism also influenced the Reformation and was related to it linguistically. It acted as a foil to Reformation preaching and homiletics.

P. → Melanchthon (1497-1560) wrote *De rhetorica libri tres* (Concerning rhetoric in three books, 1519) and *Elementorum rhetorices libri duo* (Elements of rhetoric in two books, 1531). His work offers a fine view of the relation between rhetoric and homiletics during this period. Rhetoric serves as a basis for any form of verbal → communication, including literature and its interpretation, addresses, or preaching, for it helps us to interpret sources and also to understand contemporary problems and to deal with them effectively in what we say (U. Schnell). For Melanchthon these two aspects were part of a single task.

M. → Luther (1483-1546; → Luther's Theology) did not leave behind any rhetorical study or system. What he had to say about preaching was incidental (see Clemen, vol. 7). The three essential elements in his theology, as they relate to preaching, were as follows: *preaching* depicts our being in grace by first depicting God's work for and in us, then the *saving acceptance* of this work by us in faith, and finally our *works* as we do them under the impact of the Word and faith (E. Herms). This theological account of Luther's view of preaching is in keeping with his homiletical rule that "nothing but Christ must be preached" *(nihil nisi Christus praedicandus)* or with his comment, "I preach the gospel of Christ, and with my bodily voice I bring Christ into your heart, so that you may form him within yourself" (*LW* 36.340).

It thus follows that preaching is the gospel for those who hear it. It is an exposition of Scripture, often fluid, not academically structured, giving centrality to what is seen as the main point of the text, following the movement of the text in the form of a movement toward the hearers. The hearers are an unconditional point of orientation for preaching, since they must be won over and convinced, but they are not the criterion of preaching. Stress also falls on relevance to the situation. Along traditional lines there is thus always a twofold task: teaching in a way that is clear to listeners' understanding, and exhorting in an address to the will. To be able to achieve these two ends preachers need dialectical training (→ Dialectic). Sermons must be humble, having no external adornment, with the Gospels as a model (though see E. Hirsch 1936 for a different emphasis).

The views of U. → Zwingli (1484-1531; → Zwingli's Theology) and J. → Calvin (1509-64; → Calvin's Theology) regarding preaching sermons did not perhaps have such a wide impact as those of Luther. They still call for notice, however, for both Reformers were notable preachers, and their sermons played a large role in their reforming work.

2.5. *To the Nineteenth Century*

In the post-Reformation period preaching and homiletics unmistakably underwent a certain flattening and formalizing. Rhetoric in the sense of systematizing such as we find in the Middle Ages (see G. Ueding and B. Steinbrink) was again determinative (for details, see A. Niebergall). The same was true in part of → Enlightenment preaching, though at that time there was so much variety that generalization is difficult (see W. Grünberg).

J. L. Mosheim (1694-1755), a gifted preacher and a critical representative of the early Enlightenment who stood midway between → orthodoxy and → Pietism (see M. Peters), is important in the history of theology. His posthumously published homiletics, which deals with rhetoric, and his sermons (*Heilige Reden* [Sacred discourses], 6 vols.), which strive after rhetorical perfection, give him the right to be called the creator of modern preaching.

In the 19th century, at a time when intellectual and social upheavals (→ Restoration) were reducing the influence of rhetoric and respect for it, a productive relation may be seen between a view of rhetoric that focused more on substance than on form and the contemporary understanding of preaching. Unquestionably, the most important treatment of the century was that of F. → Schleiermacher (1768-1834; → Schleiermacher's Theology). He was an influential preacher (see G. Otto, 1979, 1987), as well as a homiletical systematizer (see W. Gräb). The two go inseparably together.

Schleiermacher's systematic understanding involved three points. First, the verbal communication of religious feeling is vital to the possibility of the life of complex pious communities. Second, the actual form of religious address, the preaching, is secondary, but the goal — edification — is essential. In his *Christliche Sitte* (Christian ethics), Schleiermacher worked out this relationship in the context of his theory of depictive action, while in his *Praktische Theologie* (Practical theology), he offered explicit rules for preaching. Third, the modes of presentation in worship and preaching come within the province of art. We thus must have recourse to → aesthetics and rhetoric, which serve to achieve the goal of all theology, that is, "a united leadership of the Christian Church" (*Kurze Darstellung des theologisches Studiens* [Brief outline of theological study], §5). Theology and rhetoric belong inseparably together. From the standpoint of speech (see *Reden über die Religion* [Speeches on religion], 4), or edification, truth is truth only as *accepted* truth.

J. Bauer finely sums up this view of preaching, or of all public speaking, when he speaks of steady movement toward a final goal. The train of thought does not simply develop a given thesis but constantly brings forth new thoughts in → dialogue with the listeners. One antithesis or contradiction after another is cleared away, and speaker and hearers increasingly come closer to one another and to the truth.

3. Ecumenical Problems

We might sum up the problems of preaching from an ecumenical angle in terms of the following three perspectives.

3.1. *Orthodox Church*

In the → Orthodox Church preaching has its place within an understanding of → liturgy and worship. Worship as a whole mirrors the process of salvation history, and therefore the importance of preaching is naturally less. Preaching is typically not an exposition of pericopes in their bearing on everyday life. Its preferred themes come from the great festivals of the → church year, including those devoted to Mary (→ Mary, Devotion to) and the → saints and martyrs. Consulting the sermons of the → church fathers soon became the custom.

There has been little reflection on the task of preaching and little research into it. Nor are there many contacts with the doctrine of preaching found in other denominations. The Orthodox have little doctrine of their own in this regard. Great models play a primary role (see K. C. Felmy for the 19th cent.).

The preaching of the → Russian Orthodox Church both after the October Revolution of 1917 (examples are in K. Rose) and after the collapse of the Soviet Union in 1990-91 calls for investigation.

3.2. *Roman Catholic Church*

In the → Roman Catholic Church trends relative to the doctrine of preaching in the 20th century (historically, see J. B. Schneyer) show that apart from differences in terminology, many of the relevant questions and discussions run parallel to those on the Protestant side (for a succinct survey, see P. Wehrle). Though they overlap, we might differentiate four homiletical phases. First, we have preaching under the influence of the → liturgical movement of the 1920s and 1930s, that is, mystagogical preaching in interpretation of the liturgy. Then came kerygmatic preaching, still related to liturgy, but aware of the specific dimension of proclamation as distinct from academic theology (Wehrle). Third, we have preaching under the impact of biblical theology, which seeks to follow a clear path from text to sermon. From the middle of the 1960s the closeness to Protestant teaching was unmistakable. The next phase saw existential-hermeneutical preaching under the influence of R. Bultmann (1884-1976; → Existential Theology). This type of preaching was oriented to listeners both in its departures from the biblical tradition and in its constant existential structuring, irrespective of ages.

Surveying Roman Catholic homiletical discussion as a whole, we note its increasing approximation to the issues raised by empiricism and social anthropology, as in Protestant teaching. This course was easier for Roman Catholics to take, since the legacy of the → dialectical theology did not in their case impede access to anthropological discussion.

3.3. *American Protestantism*

In American Protestantism homiletical trends were not linked to denominations but to broader theological developments. Protestantism itself played the leading part (→ Modern Church History 2; North American Theology).

Dialectical theology in the form of neoorthodoxy reached the United States in the middle of the 1930s, and although it was less influential than in Germany, it brought renewal to preaching, to some extent in connection with a new → liberalism. According to David Buttrick, "At midcentury, the field of homiletics was dominated by famous preachers and standard texts. . . . The textbooks seemed to reflect a homiletic theory that derived from an odd mix of 19th-century Pietism, orthodox homiletic practice, and sometimes the rhetoric of Richard Whately" (p. 483).

Among other trends influencing preaching we might mention the ephemeral → God-is-dead theology, which raised anthropological, ethical, and sociological issues. From the late 1960s onward, homiletical and methodological questions came to the fore. F. Craddock pleaded for an inductive mode of preaching oriented to the experience of hearers. In the 1970s and 1980s the works of E. A. Steimle, M. J. Niedenthal, C. L. Rice, R. A. Jensen, and E. L. Lowry brought a narrative mode of preaching into the center of discussion (→ Narrative Theology). The same intentions may be noted in the tradition of black preaching (→ Black Theology), which especially Martin Luther → King Jr. (1929-68) brought to popular notice. African American culture showed its maturity here in a preaching oriented to mouth and ear.

From the 1980s onward, rhetorical interest became dominant in much homiletical discussion in the United States. D. Buttrick (1987) is an example of the waning of the influence of dialectical theology and a return to rhetorically pursued homiletics.

4. Modern Discussion

To understand the central issues in modern homiletical discussion, we must look first at the situation in the early 1920s.

4.1. *Diminished Interest in Rhetoric*

A primary feature of the 1920s was the general loss of concern for rhetoric as an instrument and even its disparaging. Theology, and homiletics in particular, had a hand in this change. After World War I dialectical and kerygmatic theology (E. Thurneysen, K. → Barth; → Theology in the Nineteenth and Twentieth Centuries 1) supported this trend by stressing the central importance of content (what is said rather than how it is said), the need for expository fidelity, and the indispensable ministry of the Holy Spirit. In this way theological sanction was given to a decreased interest in rhetoric. God himself must speak his own Word how and where and when he wills, though naturally preachers must work hard at their craft under the proper theological direction.

4.2. *Changes in Emphasis*

A shift came in homiletics, as in other fields such as → pastoral care and → religious education, at the end of the 1960s. Dialectical and kerygmatic theology lost some of its grip, and the dominance of exegesis was challenged. In the context of a general rhetorical revival associated especially with the name of Walter Jens, and against the background of an increasing study of communication, new emphases appeared ("new" only in terms of the immediate past, certainly not as compared to emphases of the past centuries). Two impulses might be distinguished that worked together in the period that followed.

Over against the homiletical primacy of exegesis, it was argued that preaching must be oriented both to the biblical text and to the hearers and their situation. This point had obvious implications for sermon preparation. E. Lange (1927-74) took the lead in this regard. The *Predigtstudien,* which he founded, and which came out from 1968 onward, offer an example of the changed approach, with later minor modifications.

Over against the antirhetorical sentiment of an earlier period, it was now claimed that rhetoric has basic importance in homiletics (M. Josuttis, G. Otto). The main feature of this approach, along with that of Lang's theses, is that rhetoric is to be viewed hermeneutically and not just instrumentally. In speech, and therefore in preaching, it was argued, form and content are inextricably intertwined, and thus we cannot ignore their relation to rhetoric. Rhetoric is not just concerned with the interchangeable adornment of content, nor is it simply a means of manipulating hearers. It involves a → conscience-based → responsibility on the part of speakers and preachers for what they say as a complex of form and content relating to given hearers. Putting preaching in the category of public speaking in general leaves untouched the factors of its specific content as God's Word, its subjection to the written Word, its required Christological centrality, and its relation to prayer and the ministry of the Holy Spirit. It is valid, however, on its own plane.

4.3. *Urgent Problems*

Two examples might be given of urgent problems in ongoing homiletical discussion.

4.3.1. *Liturgical Place of Preaching*

First, we have the problem of the liturgical place of preaching. What are the implications of the fact that preaching lies within the context of liturgical ritual (→ Rite 2; Worship)? Thus far there has been only sketchy discussion of this issue in studies of rhetoric and communication. The instructive empirical analyses of K.-F. Daiber and others offer no solution because, by intent, they simply depict the situation. A further difficulty that gives added urgency to the issue is that in some countries, especially in Europe, worship is finding less acceptance even within the church. It is not that people are leaving the church but that more and more of the members see no relevance of worship to them; it does not communicate. Is the same true of preaching as well? Or to what extent does the inability of worship to communicate affect preaching and destroy receptivity to it?

4.3.2. *Language of Preaching*

Then we have the problem of the language of preaching. To define more precisely what happens in preaching both for those who speak and for those who listen, the distinction between instrumental and "medial" language (J. Anderegg) may be helpful.

Everyday language, as an instrument for naming objects and things within a given reality, raises no problems (Anderegg). Here the "naming of reality" is not seen as an act of interpretation alongside which other acts of interpretation are possible. Thus what we call the world is fixed linguistically. In everyday life we do not note that this is so because we do not use speech to constitute things but to make confirmatory reference to what is already constituted. Language is simply an instrument to denote things (→ Language 1). By it we denote what is and make it available for use. Without this possibility we could not handle everyday life.

Medial language is different, even though the same linguistic symbols are used. Because the same symbols are used (→ Sign), we may not notice the difference from instrumental speech, but if we do not, agreement is not possible, and theological controversies and homiletical misunderstandings result. That which is said on the medial level is not an instrumental affirmation (or denial). What, then, is the characteristic of medial speech? It does not involve established meanings but an open question of meaning: What is really being said (or written)? The hearers or readers must find the → meaning, and it may be ambiguous.

If in instrumental speech the main concern is that what is said be unequivocal, in medial speech the decisive thing is openness that points beyond what may actually be stated. We find this kind of speech in fables or poems, in both prose and poetry, in myths, sagas, and → symbols, in → metaphors and → allegories. Religious speech is obviously medial speech inasmuch as it does not convey that which convention has established but something open, something that calls for interpretation, something that is thus ambivalent according to differing perspectives. Though we must use instrumental language in → everyday affairs, we are referred to something more if what is, is not to be all that is.

The language of preaching, on this view, thus must be largely, though not solely, medial language. This fact has implications for the understanding of preaching and for sermon preparation and homiletical instruction (see G. Otto, 1982, 1988). Preaching is not just objective exegesis or the giving of information. It takes a medial form because it triggers different interpretive processes according to the life histories and situations of the different hearers. From the rhetorical standpoint the homiletical task thus involves aesthetics (A. Grözinger). Preaching cannot be developed quasi-automatically out of exegesis alone, out of the perspective of a pericope. At the same time, the biblical tradition is the essential basis, and if the handling of the text and the situation of the hearers must be rhetorically more free and creative than simple exposition can be, the ultimate objectivity of the divine revelation must also be remembered, along with the fact that the Holy Spirit alone can finally speak the divinely intended Word to any hearer in any situation.

→ Practical Theology

Bibliography: General reference: Y. Brilioth, *A History of Preaching* (Philadelphia, 1965) • R. Jamison and J. Dyck, *Rhetorik, Topik, Argumentation. Bibliographie zur Redelehre und Rhetorikforschung im deutschsprachigen Raum, 1945-1979/80* (Stuttgart, 1983) • B. M. Kienzle and P. J. Walker, eds., *Women Preachers and Prophets through Two Millennia of Christianity* (Berkeley, Calif., 1998) • A. D. Litfin and H. W. Robinson, eds., *Recent Homiletical Thought: An Annotated Bibliography,* vol. 2, *1966-1979* (Grand Rapids, 1983) • H.-M. Müller, "Homiletik. Quellen," *TRE* 15.562-65 • P. L. Oesterreich, *Fundamentalrhetorik* (Hamburg, 1990) • H. O. Old, *The Reading and Preaching of the Scriptures in the Worship of the Christian Church* (4 vols.; Grand Rapids, 1998-2002) • W. Toohey and W. Thompson, eds., *Recent Homiletical Thought: A Bibliography,* vol. 1, *1935-1965* (Nashville, 1967) • W. H. Willimon and R. Lischer, eds., *Concise Encyclopedia of Preaching* (Louisville, Ky., 1995). See also the yearly biographies in *Rhetorik. Ein internationales Jahrbuch,* since vol. 3 (1983).

Early church through the Reformation: H.-E. Bahr, *Verkündigung als Information* (Hamburg, 1968) • L. Bolzoni, *The Web of Images: Vernacular Preaching from Its Origins to St. Bernardino of Siena* (Aldershot, 2004) • R. Bultmann, *Der Stil der paulinischen Predigt und die kynisch-stoische Diatribe* (Göttingen, 1910) • R. Cruel, *Geschichte der deutschen Predigt im Mittelalter* (Hildesheim, 1966; orig. pub., 1879) • M. B. Cunningham and P. Allen, eds., *Preacher and Audience: Studies in Early Christian and Byzantine Homiletics*

(Leiden, 1998) • C. H. DODD, *The Apostolic Preaching and Its Developments* (London, 1936; repr., 1963) • E. HERMS, "Das Evangelium für das Volk. Praxis und Theorie der Predigt bei Luther," *LuJ* 57 (1990) 19-56 • E. HIRSCH, *Das Alte Testament und die Predigt des Evangeliums* (Tübingen, 1936) • D. LITFIN, *St. Paul's Theology of Proclamation: 1 Corinthians 1–4 and Greco-Roman Rhetoric* (Cambridge, 1994) • B. MILEM, *The Unspoken Word: Negative Theology in Meister Eckhart's German Sermons* (Washington, D.C., 2002) • C. MUESSIG, ed., *Preacher, Sermon, and Audience in the Middle Ages* (Leiden, 2002) • S. M. OBERHELMAN, *Rhetoric and Homiletics in Fourth-Century Christian Literature: Prose Rhythm, Oratorical Style, and Preaching in the Works of Ambrose, Jerome, and Augustine* (Atlanta, 1991) • U. SCHNELL, *Die homiletische Theorie Philipp Melanchthons* (Berlin, 1969) • A. STEWART-SYKES, *From Prophecy to Preaching: A Search for the Origins of the Christian Homily* (Leiden, 2001) • A. T. THAYER, *Penitence, Preaching, and the Coming of the Reformation* (Aldershot, 2002) • P. WALTER, *Theologie aus dem Geist der Rhetorik. Zur Schriftauslegung des Erasmus von Rotterdam* (Mainz, 1991) • C. M. WATERS, *Angels and Earthly Creatures: Preaching, Performance, and Gender in the Later Middle Ages* (Philadelphia, 2004).

Reformation to the present: J. BAUER, *Schleiermacher als patriotischer Prediger* (Giessen, 1908) • O. CLEMEN, ed., *Luther's Werke in Auswahl* (7 vols.; Berlin, 1959-67) • D. DEVRIES, *Jesus Christ in the Preaching of Calvin and Schleiermacher* (Louisville, Ky., 1996) • W. GRÄB, *Predigt als Mitteilung des Glaubens. Studien zu einer prinzipiellen Homiletik in praktischer Absicht* (Gütersloh, 1988) • W. GRÜNBERG, *Homiletik und Rhetorik* (Gütersloh, 1973) • A. NIEBERGALL, "Die Geschichte der christlichen Predigt," *Leit.* 2.181-353 • G. OTTO, *Predigt als rhetorische Aufgabe. Homiletische Perspektiven* (Neukirchen, 1987); idem, *Von geistlicher Rede. Sieben rhetorische Profile* (Gütersloh, 1979) • C. H. E. SMITH, *The Art of Preaching: A Practical Survey of Preaching in the Church of England, 747-1939* (London, 1953) • L. TAYLOR, *Preachers and People in the Reformations and Early Modern Period* (Leiden, 2001) • G. UEDING and B. STEINBRINK, *Grundriß der Rhetorik. Geschichte–Technik–Methode* (3d ed.; Stuttgart, 1994; orig. pub., 1976).

Orthodox Church: K. C. FELMY, *Predigt im orthodoxen Rußland* (Göttingen, 1972) • I. LUNDE, *Verbal Celebrations: Kirill of Turov's Homiletic Rhetoric and Its Byzantine Sources* (Wiesbaden, 2001) • K. ROSE, *Predigt der russisch-orthodoxen Kirche* (Berlin, 1952).

Roman Catholic Church: B. DREHER et al., eds., *Handbuch der Verkündigung* (2 vols.; Freiburg, 1970) • R. HART, *Preacher as Risk Taker* (Collegeville, Minn., 2003) • P. JANOWIAK, *The Holy Preaching: The Sacramentality of the Word in the Liturgical Assembly* (Collegeville, Minn., 2000) • J. B. SCHNEYER, *Geschichte der katholischen Predigt* (Freiburg, 1968) • P. WEHRLE, "Zur Standortbestimmung der Predigt," *LSs* 28 (1977) 309-13.

American Protestantism: D. BUTTRICK, *Homiletic: Moves and Structures* (Philadelphia, 1987); idem, "Speaking between Times: Homiletics in a Postmodern World," *Theology and the Interhuman* (ed. R. R. Williams; Valley Forge, Pa., 1995) 147-59 • R. R. CAEMMERER, *Preaching for the Church* (St. Louis, 1959) • F. CRADDOCK, *Overhearing the Gospel* (Nashville, 1978); idem, *Preaching* (Nashville, 1985) • R. A. JENSEN, *Telling the Story* (Minneapolis, 1980) • C. J. LARUE, *The Heart of Black Preaching* (Louisville, Ky., 2000) • T. G. LONG, *Preaching and the Literary Forms of the Bible* (Philadelphia, 1989) • E. L. LOWRY, *The Homiletical Plot: The Sermon as Narrative Art Form* (Atlanta, 1980) • R. MOUNTFORD, *The Gendered Pulpit: Preaching in American Protestant Spaces* (Carbondale, Ill., 2003) • E. A. STEIMLE, M. J. NIEDENTHAL, and C. L. RICE, *Preaching the Story* (Philadelphia, 1980) • W. WILLIMON, *The Intrusive Word: Preaching to the Unbaptized* (Grand Rapids, 1994); idem, *Particular Speech: Preaching to the Baptized* (Grand Rapids, 1992).

Modern discussion: J. ANDEREGG, *Sprache und Verwandlung* (Göttingen, 1985) • K. BARTH, *Homiletics* (Louisville, Ky., 1991; orig. pub., 1966) • D. BONHOEFFER, *Worldly Preaching: Lectures on Homiletics* (rev. ed.; New York, 1991) • P. BUKOWSKI, *Predigt wahrnehmen* (3d ed.; Neukirchen, 1995) • D. BUTTRICK, *A Captive Voice: The Liberation of Preaching* (Louisville, Ky., 1994) • K.-F. DAIBER et al., *Predigen und Hören. Ergebnisse einer Gottesdienstbefragung* (3 vols.; Munich, 1980-91) • W. ENGEMANN, *Einführung in die Homiletik* (Tübingen, 2002); idem, *Semiotische Homiletik. Prämissen, Analysen, Konsequenzen* (Tübingen, 1993) • A. GRÖZINGER, *Praktische Theologie und Ästhetik* (2d ed.; Munich, 1991) • W. JENS, "Rhetorik," *RDL* 3.432-56 • R. W. KIRKLAND, *An Investigation of the Influence of the New Hermeneutic on Recent Preaching Theory* (Ann Arbor, Mich., 1988) • M. E. LYONS, "Homiletics and Rhetoric: Recognizing an Ancient Alliance," *Homiletic* 12 (1987) 1-4 • H. H. MITCHELL, *The Recovery of Preaching* (San Francisco, 1977) • J. P. MITCHELL, *Visually Speaking: Radio and the Renaissance of Preaching* (Louisville, Ky., 1999) • J. R. NIEMAN and T. G. ROGERS, *Preaching to Every Pew: Cross-Cultural Strategies* (Minneapolis, 2001) • G. OTTO, "Christliche Rhetorik I: Antike," *HWR* 2.197-205; idem, *Die Kunst, verantwortlich zu reden. Rhetorik, Ästhetik, Ethik* (Gütersloh, 1994); idem, *Praktische Theologie*, vol. 2, *Handlungsfelder der praktischen Theologie* (Munich, 1988); idem, *Wie entsteht eine*

Predigt? (Munich, 1982) • E. THURNEYSEN, *Das Wort Gottes und die Kirche* (Munich, 1971) • D. L. WILLIAMS, *The Relevance of Classical Rhetorical Canons for Evaluating Twentieth-Century Preaching* (Ann Arbor, Mich., 1988) • F. WINTZER, ed., *Predigt. Texte zum Verständnis und zur Praxis der Predigt in der Neuzeit* (Munich, 1989).

GERT OTTO†

5. Theology

5.1. *Gospel*

As human speaking, preaching is unquestionably a form of → rhetoric. It thus comes under the rules and criteria of rhetoric. Preachers who ignore this fact and fail to make use of the rhetorical resources available do so at their peril and in disservice to their task. At the same time — and this was the point of the theological and homiletical renewal initiated in the 1920s — from another and no less important angle, Christian preaching has always seen itself as a unique form of rhetoric. Although it must necessarily avail itself of what rhetoric can offer if it is to say what it has to say, the "what" of what it says must still be given equal and perhaps superior status alongside the "how." For the "what" of this human speech is a divine message, the good news of God's revealing and reconciling word and work in → Jesus Christ, the biblical → gospel. The "what" and the "how" do not have to be rivals or adversaries, yet each must be given its due. And in the last analysis, no excellence of the "how" can make up for the poverty or distortion or absence of the "what" or its replacement by another message made up of purely human opinions, analyses, teachings, hopes, rebukes, or exhortations.

News calls for a newsgiver, one who has received the news and has the task of passing it on to others, one who has been sent out with this task. "How are they to proclaim him unless they are sent?" asks → Paul (Rom. 10:15). Prerequisites of fruitful preaching thus include, along with knowledge of the "what" and commitment to it, an inner divine commission and constraint and an outer community calling (→ Vocation). Commitment to the message comes with this commissioning, constraint, and calling. Preachers who are thus sent cannot just say what they want to say or think or feel ought to be said. They cannot simply aim at making an impact of their own. The gospel is laid upon them, and woe to them if they do not preach it (see 1 Cor. 9:16). They are charged with this specific task in their preaching, namely, the proclaiming of this specific message in the full range of its content and the broad spectrum of its implications.

If commissioning means commitment to the gospel, it means also that preaching is a → ministry, a service. Paul in 1 Cor. 4:1-7 aptly speaks of this dimension in terms of → stewardship. Preachers are stewards of God, acting on his behalf. They are stewards to those to whom they speak, dispensing to them the things that God has for them. They are stewards of the mysteries of God, the uncovered truths of God's dealings with his human creatures in judgment and in grace. In this threefold ministry faithfulness is a primary requirement. Faithfulness indubitably means saying what has to be said with all the force and skill of which one is capable. Above all things, however, it means saying what God would have said, what the hearers need to hear from God, what the gospel has as its true content. Preaching can be true ministry only as gospel preaching.

5.2. *Word of God*

The distinctive message, commissioning, and ministry of preaching mean that preaching, though naturally and unavoidably taking human form, may be itself, at least in a subsidiary way, not just a human word but the → Word of God. In and through these human words God may and does speak his own Word. The message, commissioning, and ministry are all from God. This means that God himself has chosen to make his own voice heard through the voices of human preachers. Preachers dare not claim, however, that ipso facto all they say, no matter how eloquent or erudite, is what God says. They indeed recognize that, humanly speaking, the very idea is ludicrous, and any claim to it is foolish arrogance. Nevertheless, to speak the Word of God remains the preacher's first and final task. If it does not occur, then no matter how brilliant and impressive and instructive the preaching may be, it is a failure as Christian preaching.

Preaching can fulfill its first and final task as God's Word only if it relates clearly and consistently to the primary, eternal, incarnate, crucified, and risen Word of God, Jesus Christ, according to the normative witness that is borne to him by the secondary prophetic and apostolic Word, Holy Scripture. Whatever else, then, it may be or do, and however well or badly it may be crafted and delivered, preaching must always in some way present Jesus Christ if it is to be preaching at all. Accordingly, one can see posted in many Anglican pulpits, "Sir, we would see Jesus" (John 12:21 KJV). Or, as Paul said, "I decided to know nothing among you except Jesus Christ, and him crucified" (1 Cor. 2:2).

To be God's Word, preaching must always be Christological. But to be authentically Christological it must also be biblical. It need not be uniformly expository. It can and will also be directly → kerygmatic (announcing the good news), didactic (teaching what we should believe and do), hortatory (encouraging, admonishing, rebuking), or prophetic (applying the gospel to changing situations). What it says, however, must rest always on the primary biblical testimony to Christ and be in conformity with it if preaching is to be what it is meant to be, God's Word, God himself speaking to individuals, the → church, and the world by the words of those whom he has called and sent as ministers, witnesses, heralds, teachers, and stewards.

5.3. *Holy Spirit*

Authentic preaching points to the incarnate Word in consonance with the written Word. Yet these things alone are not what make it authentic preaching as God's own word. For only God himself can speak his own Word. If he has chosen to do so through preached words, the mere speaking of those words, for all the human qualities of rhetorical skill or faithfulness to the incarnate and written Word, cannot automatically guarantee that God himself actually speaks. God's speaking takes place only as the → Holy Spirit of God, "when and where he wills" (CA 5, Ger. text), makes use of the instrument that he has designed for the purpose and that is responsibly playing its part.

The divine speaking of the Spirit is sovereign. Preachers cannot command or control the Spirit. Good rhetoric may achieve impressive human results, intellectual, emotional, or volitional. Biblically and theologically informed addresses may serve useful human purposes of instruction and edification. Neither, however, can compel the Spirit to speak God's own Word or do God's work. Sometimes, indeed, the Word of God will sound forth through the simplest and least polished statements made by those who neither have the aptitude nor have had the training to preach with more depth or art. "The wind blows where it chooses" (John 3:8).

The sovereignty of the Spirit is the ultimate problem, as well as the ultimate promise, of Christian preaching. Nevertheless, the sovereignty of the Spirit is not caprice. If it involves divine choice that is beyond the preacher's comprehension, it also takes account of factors that are essential in preachers themselves. A first factor is the true divine calling and constraint. A second and related factor is genuine commitment to the ministry of the Word. A third, also related, is a profound sense of responsibility to the giver of the message, to the message itself, to its normative biblical formulation, and to those for whom it is meant. A fourth is humble recognition that there is no human sufficiency in this matter (2 Cor. 2:16; → Humility); "our competence is from God" (3:5), who can indeed overrule all that is inadequate and irrelevant and perhaps even erroneous and harmful in the human words, yet still speak effectively through what is good and sound and pertinent. A final factor is → prayer — the prayer of preachers, supported by that of believing → congregations, that the voice of preaching may indeed be the voice of the Spirit to people with their different needs for this life and for eternity, and that those who hear outwardly may have the inward ears to hear and the hearts and minds and wills to receive what God himself has for them.

Preachers can take nothing for granted. Yet, even beyond these five factors, they have cause to believe that they are still unprofitable servants (Luke 17:10). Nevertheless, the sovereignty of the Spirit will be the promise and not the problem of their preaching, so that it will achieve the ultimate and only authentic goal of presenting the eternal Word in the power of the eternal Spirit.

Bibliography: D. G. Buttrick, "The Use of the Bible in Preaching," NIB 3.188-99 • J. B. Green and M. Pasquarello, eds., *Narrative Reading, Narrative Preaching: Reuniting NT Interpretation and Proclamation* (Grand Rapids, 2003) • F. G. Honeycutt, *Preaching for Adult Conversion and Commitment: Invitation to a Life Transformed* (Nashville, 2003) • D. J. Lose, *Confessing Jesus Christ: Preaching in a Postmodern World* (Grand Rapids, 2003) • J. Piper, *The Supremacy of God in Preaching* (rev. ed.; Grand Rapids, 2004).

Geoffrey W. Bromiley

Precepts of the Church

1. Term
2. History
3. Purpose
4. Binding Character

1. Term

In the broader sense, the precepts of the church are all the doctrinal and disciplinary rulings of the → Roman Catholic Church other than those that formulate divine or natural → law. In the narrower sense, the reference is to five particular requirements: (1) attending → Mass on Sundays and holy days of obligation, (2) making → confession for sins at least once a year (→ Penitence), (3) taking Holy Communion (→ Eucharist) at least during the → Easter season, (4) keeping the feast days, and (5) observing the prescribed days of fasting and abstinence (*Catechism of the Catholic Church* [1994], §§2041-43).

2. History

These five precepts have been attested to from the year 1444. They received their present form in the → catechism of Peter Canisius (1554; → Catechism 3.1). Additional rulings, such as those relating to the church tax and to eucharistic sobriety, are also often called precepts of the church. The church as a whole has never officially adopted the → number five or any other number as delimiting the precepts of the church.

In many parts of the → Orthodox Church there have been similar "precepts of the church" from the time of the Orthodox confession of faith of Peter Mogila of Kiev (1638, first pub. 1645). For the Orthodox, however, the precepts do not have an obligatory character.

3. Purpose

Precepts of the church aim only indirectly at individual → sanctification (→ Perfection), but directly at the achievement of social order in the church (i.e., the common good). According to the classic definition of Thomas Aquinas (ca. 1225-74), law is a rational order that is adopted and promulgated by the standing authority for the attainment of the common good (*Summa theol.* I of II, q. 90, art. 4).

4. Binding Character

According to 1983 → CIC 11, church laws are binding on those who are baptized in, or received into, the Roman Catholic Church, who have "a sufficient use of reason," and who have reached their seventh year, unless express legal provision is made to the contrary. This definition does not obscure the fact that finally and properly, there can be only divine law in the church. What is usually called a human law, insofar as it is morally binding, is to be regarded as divine law made known by a human court.

→ Church Law

Bibliography: B. Häring, *Free and Faithful in Christ: Moral Theology for Clergy and Laity* (3 vols.; New York, 1978-81) • J. Listl, H. Müller, and H. Schmitz, eds., *HKKR*, 83-98 • W. Molinski, "Commandments of the Church," *SM(E)* 1.384-87.

Reinhold Sebott

Predestination

1. Antiquity
2. Middle Ages
3. The Reformation
4. Modern Period

1. Antiquity

The idea of predestination has its origin in the biblical concept of God's nature as Creator and Lord of all he has made, as well as that of God's work of election. In the OT this concept relates primarily to the people of Israel (→ People of God) as the subject of → salvation history, but it gradually becomes more particular and individual. A remnant is elect, or a single person. The NT continues this trend inasmuch as it no longer views empirical Israel as the subject of election but Israel only as the eschatological people of God (→ Eschatology), which is made up of those who have → faith in Christ. Since this faith itself has its origin in God, in → Paul and → John the idea of divine → grace culminates in the thought that God foreordains people to faith. Already in the OT and NT, without reconciliation, we find alongside one another the view that God is the cause of all things and the belief in human → freedom.

→ Gnostic writings and other ancient worldviews espoused a predestinarian → determinism, but for ethical reasons Greek theologians found it essential to uphold the free → responsibility of individuals (→ Ethics). They thus rejected the thesis of → Stoicism that God as → providence *(pronoia)* is the same as fate *(heimarmenē)*, and that as → reason immanent in → nature, he causally determines all that takes place. The defense of human freedom meant that → Justin Martyr (ca. 100-ca. 165), → Irenaeus (d. ca. 200), Clement of Alexandria (ca. 150-ca. 215), and → Origen (ca. 185-ca. 254) took the view that predestination *(prothesis)* as the foreordaining of reward or → punishment is determined by foreknowledge *(pronoia)* of the good or bad deeds of individuals. The presupposition of free individual responsibility meant that humans are not totally corrupted by → sin but still have the ability to do what is good.

Greek theology clung to this view, but in Latin theology, with the stronger emphasis on sin in → Augustine (354-430; → Augustine's Theology), the concept of unconditional predestination developed. Over against Pelagius (ca. 354-after 418), the assertion of unconditional → grace went hand in hand with that of our total inability to do what is good (→ Augustine's Theology 5; Pelagianism).

The voluntarist concept of God in the doctrine of predestination (→ Voluntarism), which replaced the Platonic view of God as the good (→ Platonism), determined the future course of the doctrine of → God in the West.

Protest against the teaching of Augustine came first from → monastic ranks, expressing an interest in the meritorious character of the ascetic life (→ Asceticism) and defending the freedom of the will. Thus the semi-Pelagianism of John Cassian (ca. 360-after 430) arose, which taught that even after the fall the human will is free to do what is good, albeit with the necessary assistance of divine grace. Faustus of Riez (d. ca. 490), in his defense of the freedom of the will at the semi-Pelagian Synod of Arles (455), condemned the Augustinian theses (1) that human effort is incompatible with divine grace, since sinners no longer have any will to do what is good, and (2) that Christ did not die for all, since God has predestined only some to salvation. In reply, the Synods of Orange (529) and Valence (ca. 529) stated that grace alone gives us the will to do what is good. The imparting of grace, however, is not anchored in predestination, and predestination to what is → evil is excluded, so that the defense of Augustine against semi-Pelagianism results in semi-Augustinianism.

2. Middle Ages

In the early → Middle Ages the debate about the Augustinian view of predestination broke out afresh in the Gottschalk case. Gottschalk of Orbais (ca. 804-ca. 869) claimed against Rabanus Maurus (ca. 780-856) that Augustine's doctrine of predestination necessarily implied that those whom God does not foreordain and elect to salvation are rejected from all eternity. Predestination is thus a double predestination *(gemina praedestinatio)* in the form of election and reprobation. Predestination is not grounded in divine foreseeing of human actions, for this view would be at odds with the divine immutability.

In → Scholasticism the central issue in the doctrine of predestination was still that of the relation between predestination and human freedom. The starting point was the linking of predestination to → reconciliation by → Anselm (1033-1109). On this view God from all eternity willed that there be a kingdom *(civitas)* in which a predetermined number of creatures would serve him. In place of the angels that were originally designated but fell, God created humans. Their fall made reconciliation necessary, on the basis of which God in grace can adopt a foreordained number of people into his kingdom.

In High Scholasticism we find various views regarding the relation between predestination and human freedom. For the → Franciscans Alexander of Hales (ca. 1185-1245) and Bonaventure (ca. 1217-74), predestination went hand in hand with divine foreknowledge in the sense that in terms of his ordered → power *(potentia ordinata)*, God grants salvation only to those who freely dispose themselves for the reception of grace and then win merits as the recipients of grace. But this relating of predestination to the divine foreseeing of human freedom at work does not occur in → Thomas Aquinas (ca. 1225-74; → Thomism), for whom God, the first cause behind all things, uses the human will as an instrumental cause. In this case the divine orienting of the will to the reception of grace means that predestination is independent of God's foreseeing the exercise of human freedom.

In later Scholasticism increased stress falls on both the idea of divine omnipotence and that of human freedom. J. Duns Scotus (ca. 1265-1308; → Scotism) taught that God in his absolute power might have predestined even Judas to salvation. If Judas did not experience salvation, it was in virtue of the ordered power by which God ties himself to the orders that he has himself set up. Thus God predestines to salvation only those who freely dispose themselves for grace. William of Ockham (ca. 1285-1347) did not link divine predestination to foreknowledge of our own free acts, since God's will is absolutely unconditional, yet → nominalism argued that sinners may freely prepare themselves for the receiving of grace, and in this way predestination is tied to human merits. Gregory of Rimini (ca. 1300-1358), Thomas Bradwardine (ca. 1295-1349), and John → Wycliffe (ca. 1330-84) called this teaching Pelagian. Adopting the view of Augustine, they espoused double predestination, so that the reception of grace is in no way decided by us in actualization of divine foreknowledge. Divine omnicausality thus takes precedence over human freedom.

3. The Reformation

Reformation theology links up with the revived Augustinianism of the later Middle Ages. If the → justification of sinners is grounded solely in divine grace, it must be traced back to divine foreordination to salvation. But all are not justified, and therefore predestination must be particular. Hence the → Reformation opposed the defense of human freedom by some → Renaissance → humanists. In the debate between → Erasmus (1469?-1536) and Martin → Luther (1483-1546; → Luther's Theology), Luther "asserted" (as he labeled his confessing his faith) that God, the Creator of all things, exercises responsibility for all that happens in his creation. The Reformer's *De servo arbitrio* (On the bondage of the will, 1525) is ultimately an expression of his theodical answer to the question of evil, his standing in awe and wonder without an answer before God, who determines all things yet holds human beings responsible for their sin (Rom. 11:33-36). On the way to that position, Luther taught that the fallen human will is bound under Satan's control, thus totally dependent on God's redemption in Christ for salvation. He distinguished the Hidden God, who governs all things and whose counsel dare not be probed, from the Revealed God, whose unconditional love for his chosen children is to be seen in Christ on the cross.

Some of Luther's contemporaries interpreted his position as double predestinarian, including Nikolaus von Amsdorf (1483-1565) and Johann Brenz (1499-1570). His Wittenberg colleague Philipp → Melanchthon (1497-1560) defended a strict single predestination view in his *Loci communes* (Common places, 1521), but under the impact of accusations of "Stoicism" and other factors, he came to a position that was founded upon the insistence that God was not the cause of evil, that human beings are fully responsible for their own sinfulness, and that paradoxically they are saved by grace through faith worked in their active wills by the Holy Spirit. Some of his students strove to assert this human integrity so strongly that they fell under accusation by other Lutherans of synergism because of their statements regarding the activity of the will in conversion, even though these statements included assertions of the necessity of the Holy Spirit's activity as primary. All Lutheran treatments of predestination and the will must be understood in the context of the distinction of → law and gospel, for predestination can be used, they argued, only as an expression of the gospel.

On the Reformed side U. → Zwingli (1484-1531; → Zwingli's Theology) anchored election and reprobation solely in the divine will, which is the cause of all things. But his thesis that the implementing of predestination is not tied to faith, so that morally qualified pagans might be elected to salvation, found no following. John → Calvin (1509-64; → Calvin's Theology) originally dealt with predestination within the doctrine of grace, but he finally integrated it into the doctrine of God and his eternal decree, whereby from all eternity he elected and rejected individuals in demonstration of his → glory in mercy and → righteousness. In time election is related to justification and → sanctification, so that good works that are the fruit of faith serve as marks of election.

The doctrine of predestination became a point of controversy between Lutherans and the Reformed. The Strasbourg Formula fashioned in 1563 by Cunmann Flinsbach (1527-71) and Johannes Marbach (1521-81) arose out of the latter's conflict with Jerome Zanchi (1516-90), who defended Calvin's doctrine of double predestination and the perseverance of the saints. This formula taught that God chooses his own unconditionally but that believers can fall from grace, thus preserving the ability to preach repentance (i.e., the proper distinction of law and gospel) to them. In the Formula of Concord (1577) Martin Chemnitz (1522-86) and Jakob Andreae (1528-90) built upon Cyriakus Spangenberg's (1528-1604) fresh formulation of the Lutheran understanding of God's unconditioned choice of those whom he would make believers through the means of grace. The Formula of Concord distinguishes God's foreknowledge of all things, even evil that he does not foreordain, from his predestination of believers and teaches both God's total responsibility for their salvation and sinners' total responsibility for their own damnation, again practicing the distinction of law and gospel.

Samuel Huber (ca. 1547-1624), professor at Wittenberg, defended a critique of Theodore → Beza's (1519-1605) doctrine of double predestinarian, asserting God's universal predestination, while holding that sinners can reject that predestining decision. He was opposed by his colleague Aegidius Hunnius (1550-1603), who taught that God predestines those who, as he foresees *(ex praevisa fidei),* will be brought to faith by the Holy Spirit. This view foreshadowed the development in later Lutheran orthodoxy of a synergistic position that taught predestination in view of faith *(intuitu fidei).*

Among the sharpest opponents of the double predestination of Calvinism were certain adherents of biblical → humanism. S. Castellio (1515-63) raised the objection that this view makes God the tyrannical author of sin. J. Arminius (1560-1609, → Arminianism), in debate with F. Gomarus (1563-1641), who held a supralapsarian position (i.e., before the fall God decreed the election or nonelection of each person), argued that we can think of predestination only as the general divine resolve to elect those who believe in Christ and who persevere in this faith. Predestination is thus conditioned by divine foreknowledge.

The Synod of Dort (1618-19) condemned the Arminian view, giving double predestination, though not in its supralapsarian form, confessional status (→ Confession of Faith). The infralapsarian version of predestination takes fallen humanity to be the object of predestination and in this way avoids giving the impression that God is the author of sin. Election is the divine resolve to graciously predestinate some fallen humans to salvation in Christ by means of →

faith, justification, sanctification, and perseverance. Rejection is the divine resolve to leave others in the misery that they deserve, to damn them because of their sins. The Helvetic Consensus Formula (accepted 1675; → Helvetic Confession) defended this view once again against the teaching of M. Amyraut (1596-1664), who held that we must distinguish between two divine decrees: a universal will to lead all who believe to salvation, and a particular will to grant faith only to some.

4. Modern Period

The predestinarian view of God found a place in counterreformation Roman Catholicism (→ Catholic Reform and Counterreformation) in the form of the Augustinianism of Cornelius Otto Jansen (1585-1638; → Jansenism), which fell under the criticism of the semi-Pelagian Luis de Molina (1535-1600; → Molinism). There is some affinity between the Jansenist view and that of early modern metaphysics (→ Modern Period). Adopting the philosophical approach of René Descartes (1596-1650; → Cartesianism), the occasionalism of A. Geulincx (1624-69) or N. Malebranche (1638-1715) assumes that we must think of God as the determinative cause of all things and that no kind of → causality can be ascribed to us. B. Spinoza (1632-77; → Spinozism) shared this view, equating God with the omnicausality immanent in nature.

The concept of predestination gradually changed in virtue of this link to the philosophical concept of omnicausality. Spinoza equated God's predestination with the universal laws of nature, so that all things take place by divine necessity. In this way the concept of predestination came to be much the same thing as Stoic → fatalism. G. W. Leibniz (1646-1716) tried to defend his own doctrine of preestablished harmony against both the fatalism of Spinoza and the double predestination of the Calvinists.

The real protest against the doctrine of predestination came with the → Enlightenment and Immanuel Kant (1724-1804; → Kantianism), who in the interests of morality defended the freedom of the will against divine omnicausality. The doctrine came under fresh consideration with modern efforts at union of the churches.

K. G. Bretschneider (1776-1848) set in opposition to what he regarded as the inconsistent Lutheran teaching the choice either to teach double predestination or to abandon predestination altogether. He himself favored the thesis that we can at least will the good without grace.

Friedrich → Schleiermacher (1768-1834; → Schleiermacher's Theology) defended unconditional predestination, but he also upheld the universality of grace, thus avoiding the particularism of the Calvinist doctrine of double predestination. He began with the Spinozist concept of divine omnicausality, which in his view corresponded to the feeling of absolute dependence. God is behind the whole cosmos, and for the sake of its completeness he has to set up in the human species both those who are receptive to grace and those who are not. But this distinction leads on to that between election and reprobation and is seen as just a phase in a development that will finally yield to universal reconciliation (→ Apocatastasis). Alexander Schweizer (1808-88) regarded this position as a consummation of the Reformed teaching.

In opposition to the Hegelians (→ Hegelianism), P. K. Marheineke (1780-1846) and W. Vatke (1806-82) stressed human freedom. Relative independence must be accorded to the human will, expressed in the fact that we may accept or reject universal divine grace and with it the good. If we accept, we fulfill our divine ordination to salvation. Salvation or perdition is thus allowed by God to be dependent on our own free choice.

Within North American Lutheranism a controversy broke out over predestination in the 1880s. C. F. W. Walther (1811-87) of the Missouri Synod defended the position he believed to be represented by the Formula of Concord; his former colleague Friedrich August Schmidt (1837-1928) and others interpreted it in light of the *intuitu fidei* position of later Lutheran orthodox theologians.

In the 20th century Karl → Barth (1886-1968; → Dialectical Theology) transformed the idea of double predestination in his doctrine of the election of grace. For him predestination was the election of all people in Jesus Christ (→ Christology 6), and it was thus viewed as the mystery of reconciliation (→ Soteriology). Inasmuch as Jesus Christ is both electing God and elect man, in him God takes up the cause of sinners and in their place bears the consequences of sin, so that his is the rejection, ours the election. This position simply relocates, however, the problem of the relation between divine election and human freedom, for if all are elect in Jesus Christ, it must be explained why some do not acknowledge their election in faith. If they do not, then in spite of being objectively elect, they are subjectively living the life of those rejected by God.

Bibliography: G. Adam, *Der Streit um die Prädestination im ausgehenden 16. Jahrhundert. Eine Untersuchung zu den Entwürfen vom Samuel Huber und Aegidius Hunnius* (Neukirchen, 1970) • K. Barth, *CD*

II/2 • J. S. Bray, *Theodore Beza's Doctrine of Predestination* (Nieuwkoop, 1975) • J. P. Burns, *The Development of Augustine's Doctrine of Operative Grace* (Paris, 1980) • J. Calvin, *Inst.* 3.21-24 • F. A. James III, *Peter Martyr Vermigli and Predestination: The Augustinian Inheritance of an Italian Reformer* (Oxford, 1998) • F. H. Klooster, *Calvin's Doctrine of Predestination* (Grand Rapids, 1977) • R. A. Muller, *Christ and the Decree: Christology and Predestination in Reformed Theology from Calvin to Perkins* (Durham, N.C., 1986) • K. Schwarzwäller, *Sibboleth. Die Interpretation von Luthers Schrift "De servo arbitrio" seit Theodosius Harnack. Ein systematisch-kritischer Überblick* (Munich, 1969); idem, *Theologia crucis. Luthers Lehre von Prädestination nach De servo arbitrio, 1525* (Munich, 1970) • R. Söderlund, *Ex praevisa fide. Zum Verständnis der Prädestinationslehre in der lutherischen Orthodoxie* (Hannover, 1983) • T. J. Wengert, *Human Freedom, Christian Righteousness: Philip Melanchthon's Exegetical Dispute with Erasmus of Rotterdam* (New York, 1998).

Jan Rohls and Robert Kolb

Preexistence → Christology 2.1.3

Prejudice

1. Term
2. Pathology
3. Approach

1. Term

Originally the word "prejudice," derived from Lat. *praeiudicium,* meant a preliminary judgment that might stand in need of revision. It was G. W. F. Hegel (1770-1831; → Hegelianism) who inaugurated the critique of the hitherto regnant philosophical conception of a reason that is free of prejudice. Sociology, → psychoanalysis, and → social psychology make it clear that from birth (→ Socialization) we identify with existing modes of thought and judgments in explanation of reality (→ Hermeneutics). The dialogic work of experience and reflection can offer a wider viewpoint from which to correct these prejudices, or prior opinions or judgments.

2. Pathology

Pathological prejudices remain, even though they can be shown to be false. They are not so much cognitive as emotional. They have an unconscious deep structure resting on social and individual factors in early parent-child relationships (→ Trust 1) and may in time achieve a destructive dynamic. Where the ego is weak, anything alien occasions responses such as → anxiety, hatred, envy, and scorn aimed at the self or significant others. Prejudice projects these feelings and impulses on others and in this way restrains them, combats them, and perhaps destroys them.

National Socialism (→ Fascism) displayed the deadly → power of prejudice in its hatred for the Jews (→ Anti-Semitism, Anti-Judaism). The defeat in World War I, with the resulting outward distress and inward disorientation, brought about social conditions that made the development of strong personality structures within families very difficult. National Socialist propaganda seized on the need for unburdening and, by an intensified hatred of the Jews (the "national curse"), offered the possibility of projecting onto the Jews all the anxieties of self-scorn and humiliation. The brutal procedures that followed resisted all corrective reflection and experience.

Prejudice has another aspect in religious → fundamentalism. In postmodern → society, which is fragmented, which lacks collective and individual identity-models (→ Identity), and which has seen the erosion of traditional religious certainties, fundamentalism seems to give many people a lasting shelter, even with its seemingly exorbitant demands. In a transcendent, superhistorical way it divides the → good from the → evil in its uncompromising outlook on both social and individual reality. Anxious, yet also aggressive, it defends itself and discriminates against such things as → modernism, historical criticism of the Bible (→ Exegesis, Biblical), the theory of → evolution, psychoanalysis, sociology, → psychology, and more enlightened → politics. To its advocates such things are snares of the devil. Anxiety seems to be the underlying experience. It is projected outward in what seems to be a successful way, though ultimately unsuccessful.

3. Approach

To recognize prejudice and combat it, one must be aware of both the cognitive and the emotional aspects. Pedagogy, theology, psychology, and politics must combine to create less anxious situations and to develop an understanding of how prejudice arises and functions. Sensitivity is needed to the inner compulsions that force people into projection and division. Only thus can we unmask prejudice and deal with it.

→ Xenophobia

Bibliography: T. W. Adorno et al., *The Authoritarian Personality* (New York, 1950) • G. W. Allport, *The Nature of Prejudice* (Cambridge, 1954) • D. Bar-Tal et al., *Stereotyping and Prejudice: Changing Conceptions* (New York, 1989) • C. Collingford, *Prejudice: From Individuality to Nationalism in Young People* (London, 2000) • J. Duckitt, "Prejudice and Intergroup Hostility," *OHPP* 559-600 • H. D. Fishbein, *Peer Prejudice and Discrimination: The Origins of Prejudice* (2d ed.; Mahwah, N.J., 2002) • W.-G. Jankowitz, *Philosophie und Vorurteil* (Meisenheim, 1975) • J. M. Jones, *Prejudice and Racism* (2d ed.; New York, 1997) • J. S. Legge, *Jews, Turks, and Other Strangers: The Roots of Prejudice in Modern Germany* (Madison, Wis., 2003) • M. S. Massa, *Anti-Catholicism in America: The Last Acceptable Prejudice* (New York, 2003) • B. Schäfer and B. Six, *Sozialpsychologie des Vorurteils* (Stuttgart, 1978) • A. Silbermann, *Alle Kreter lügen. Die Kunst, mit Vorurteilen zu leben* (Bergisch Gladbach, 1993) • H. Tajfel, *Human Groups and Social Categories: Studies in Social Psychology* (Cambridge, 1981).

Thomas Steininger

Prelate

"Prelate" (Ger. *Prälat*) is a legal term in the → Roman Catholic Church to describe all who hold leading offices of different ranking in the church, including honorary prelates without jurisdiction. The term derives from Lat. *praelatus,* a participle of *praefero,* here in the sense of giving preference or putting at the head.

In the regional churches of Baden and Württemberg, in southern Germany, the title "prelate" originally designated, not a specific church office, but membership in a regional diet, later the Parliament of a federal state. Currently, prelates in these churches are ministers with the tasks of → pastoral care, → counseling, and the ongoing education of vicars. Prelates support regional bishops in giving spiritual leadership to the → congregations. They act as consultants to the ruling council (Evangelischer Oberkirchenrat) but, in the interests of their pastoral tasks, are not integrated into the administrative structure. In Kurhessen-Waldeck, in central Germany, "prelate" refers to the permanent clerical deputy of the regional bishop.

On the national level, the title designates the council representative of the Evangelical Church in Germany (EKD) to the Federal Republic of Germany and to the European Union.

→ Ministry, Ministerial Offices; Offices; Religious Orders and Congregations

Bibliography: R. J. Murphy, "Prelate," *NCE* (2d ed.) 11.663 • A. Stein, *Evangelisches Kirchenrecht* (3d ed.; Neuwied, 2001).

Jörg Winter

Prelature, Personal

To meet the needs of → pastoral care and to achieve the most effective possible presence of the → Roman Catholic Church, → Vatican II took steps to establish "personal prelacies" (*Presbyterorum ordinis* 10), which would not primarily be territorial. In view are secular → priests and → deacons who are given special training and work with the laity, who in turn "can dedicate themselves to the apostolic work of a personal prelature by way of agreements made with the prelature" (1983 → CIC 296). The only institution thus far to have the rank of a personal prelature is → Opus Dei (granted in November 1982).

The relation of the personal prelature to the church, whether in the whole or in part, has not yet been clarified in detail.

Bibliography: J. E. Fox, *The Personal Prelature of the Second Vatican Council: An Historical Canonical Study* (Rome, 1987) • R. Ombres, "Opus Dei and Personal Prelatures," *CleR* 70 (1985) 292-95 • P. Rodríguez, *Particular Churches and Personal Prelatures: A Theological Study of a New Canonical Institution* (Dublin, 1986).

Heiner Grote†

Presbyter → Elder

Presbyterian Churches → Reformed and Presbyterian Churches

Priest, Priesthood

1. Religion
   1.1. Definition
   1.2. Personal Characteristics
   1.3. Priesthood
   1.4. Priestesses
   1.5. Hostility to Priests
2. OT
3. Roman Catholicism
   3.1. Biblical Data
   3.2. Historical Data
   3.3. Vatican II
   3.4. Ecumenical Conversations

1. Religion

1.1. Definition

No adequate definition of "priest" or of the → institution of the priesthood exists (→ Religious Studies). We cannot make generalized statements about the functions of the office and its social status, for they depend on each → culture-specific context. Yet structures of priestly action may be found in all religious systems, even in those in which priests in the strict sense are unknown (e.g., → Islam and Theravada → Buddhism).

Help in understanding the term may perhaps be found in the Babylonian term for priest, *ērib bīti* (i.e., one who may go into the temple; → Babylonian and Assyrian Religion), in the Egyptian term *ḥmw-ntr* (servant of God; → Egyptian Religion), in the Greek *hiereus* (one concerned with the holy; cf. Lat. *sacerdos*), and in the Roman *pontifex* (one who builds the bridge between gods and humans; → Roman Religion). On one level priests have the same tasks as male or female → shamans, who through → ecstasy and → magic forge links to deities and the spirits of the deceased. But they differ from shamans and other religious persons inasmuch as their ritual acts (→ Rite) are embedded in the cult as a whole, which involves regulation.

1.2. Personal Characteristics

The priestly dignity may be hereditary, as in Parsiism and the Vedic religion (the Brahman caste, into which one is born); it may be by election (by lot), as in the case of the vestal virgins in ancient Rome; or it may rest on → reincarnation, as in the Lamaism of Tibet (→ Tibetan Religions). Basic requirements in any case are that priests should have no physical or mental impairment, be free from moral aspersion, and be dedicated to → celibacy.

Personal blamelessness is a presupposition of cultic blamelessness. Observing rules of → cultic purity and → taboos, sexual abstinence, and dietary → asceticism (→ Fasting) precede induction into the office or → vocation and make possible access to the numen. → Consecration follows by → laying on of hands before the divine image (Egypt, Greece; → Greek Religion) or before the → congregation (ordination of monks in Buddhism). Sacramental succession must not be broken.

With their consecration, priests and priestesses become numinous persons. They wear cultic clothes and headgear, ornaments, and masks. They also have a divine name and are respectfully addressed as protectors of the god or singers of the god (e.g., of Amon). In this way they are distinguished from minor orders. To the outward symbols correspond sacred duties and supernatural, magical, mantic, and healing powers (granting authority and exclusivity).

The practical tasks of priests and priestesses are as varied as the various cultic-ritual, pastoral, and exorcist-therapeutic elements (→ Exorcism) in the different religious contexts. Common to all of them is the attempt to safeguard order or to restore lost harmony. What is done by priests on earth now is continued in the hereafter.

1.3. Priesthood

There is a → hierarchy of priests (e.g., the Fratres Arvales order in ancient Rome), and they are divided into → classes. Priest-kings function as mediators between the god and the → state. Examples include the *archōn basileus* in Athens, the *pontifex maximus* and *rex sacrorum* in → Rome, the Chinese emperor as the son of heaven (→ Confucianism), and the Dalai Lama as the embodiment of → theocracy. The whole sacerdotal order is under the → high priest.

In → Rigveda 1.1 Agni is installed as god-priest of the → sacrifice, as *hotṛ,* who establishes the four priestly groups. In ancient Egypt there were servants of the god, scholars, scribes of the book of the god, and reading priests. In ancient Rome the Collegium Pontificum included *flamines maiores,* who served the state gods, and *flamines minores,* who oversaw local cults (including rites of passage; cf. the Hindu *pūjā*), also the vestal virgins and the company of the augurs. In → Shinto the priesthood is led by the *saishu* of the great imperial shrine in Ise.

1.4. Priestesses

In almost all religions priestesses are equal to priests, although at times they seem to be better adapted as mediums than their male colleagues. They act as oracles and interpret oracles. They serve such supreme gods as Hathor, Amon, Zeus, and Athena. Even in a patriarchal → society like that of Japan, priestesses of the imperial house play a leading part at the imperial shrines. The numen they serve is not necessarily a female deity.

1.5. Hostility to Priests

Hostility to priests developed wherever a new → religion broke away from its original context in religious history. We see this response, for example, in the case of Islam, within which imams are simply leaders of the fellowship of prayer. → Jainism separated itself from the Brahman priesthood and set up an order of monks instead (→ Monasticism). We see the same phenomenon in early Buddhism and its break with the Brahman priests, who offered the sacrifices; it replaced the priest with the bhikku, a monk living in a monastic community (Skt. *sṅgha*) and taking over the priestly functions, including exorcism, burial rites, the interpretation of sacred scripture, and astrology (→ Buddhism 4).

→ History of Religion; Phenomenology of Religion

Bibliography: L. A. Babb, *The Divine Hierarchy: Popular Hinduism in Central India* (New York, 1975) • A. Bendlin et al., "Priesthoods in Mediterranean Religions," *Numen* 40 (1993) 82-94 • F. H. Cryer, *Divination in Ancient Israel and Its Near Eastern Environment* (Sheffield, 1994) • S. Dutt, *Buddhist Monks and Monasteries of India* (London, 1962) • A.-S. Fröhlich, *Priesterliche Aufgaben im sunnitischen Islam* (Hamburg, 1997) • C. J. Fuller, *Servants of the Goddess: The Priests of a South Indian Temple* (Cambridge, 1984) • F. Heiler, *Erscheinungsformen und Wesen der Religion* (Stuttgart, 1961) esp. 365-433 • W. Helck, "Priester, Priesterorganisation, Priestertitel," *LÄ* 4.1084-97 • E. O. James, *The Nature and Function of Priesthood* (London, 1955) • W. Klein, "Priester / Priestertum I.1: Religionsgeschichtlich," *TRE* 27.379-82 • G. Landtmann, *The Origin of Priesthood* (Ekenaes, Fin., 1905) • B. Lincoln, *Priests, Warriors, and Cattle* (Berkeley, Calif., 1981) • E. Neumann, "Priester," *HrwG* (1998) 4.342-44 • W. G. Oxtoby et al., "Priesthood," *EncRel(E)* 11.528-50 • W. Rahula, *The Heritage of the Bhikkhu* (New York, 1974) • J. Rüpke, *Die Religion der Römer* (Munich, 2001) • L. Sabourin, *Priesthood: A Comparative Study* (Leiden, 1973) • S. Sauneron, *The Priests of Ancient Egypt* (New York, 1960) • F. Staal, ed., *Agni: The Vedic Ritual of the Fire Altar* (2 vols.; Berkeley, Calif., 1983) • D. T. Suzuki, *The Training of the Zen Buddhist Monk* (New York, 1966) • M. Weber, *Ancient Judaism* (Glencoe, Ill., 1952) 169-93; idem, *The Religion of India: The Sociology of Hinduism and Buddhism* (New York, 1967) 33-44.

Peter Gerlitz

2. OT

2.1. Priestly mediation between God and his people took many forms in → Israel (§1). The more complex the cultural relations, the more clearly priestly tasks and functions were specialized.

In the early pastoral stage the clan → elders offered → sacrifice. Even then, there was nonspecific specializing. The early *kōhēn* was the guardian of the sanctuary and the giver of oracles (esp. by lot, using the Urim and Thummim). In this regard he resembled the ancient Arabian *kahin.*

The family of Eli watched over the → ark at Shiloh and served the oracle, for example, in time of war (1 Samuel 1–4). In the lawless days of the judges, priests also might serve idols (Judges 17). Scholars do not agree on how far the Levites, as a socially separate religious group, had strictly priestly functions at an early stage (→ Tribes of Israel).

2.2. Under the → monarchy, complex city cults were integrated along with the establishment of a state similar to the large Near Eastern states. → Jerusalem became the cultic center, and early cultic forms were set up there under the Zadokite priesthood. The king was head of the cult and the supreme priest (Ps. 110:1). He appointed priests to represent him and gave them an official status. With the division of the kingdom, similar structures might be found in both north and south. We find a hierarchical social → organization and a regulation of income from sacrifices. Other cults continued to exist along with the state cult.

The duties of priests in the stricter sense were to offer sacrifices on the people's behalf, to pass ritual judgments (*tôrâ,* deciding what is clean and unclean, or on the efficacy of a sacrifice; → Torah), and, through the use of lots, to serve the oracle. Ritual purity (→ Rite) was required for priestly ministry, which included being physically without blemish, purification, and avoidance of anything unclean (e.g., touching a corpse; → Cultic Purity).

Besides priests there were also → prophets. It is not always easy to differentiate their respective functions, for example, regarding the oracle of salvation.

2.3. Various new understandings of the priesthood emerged during the period of Israel's demise around the time of the exile. The Deuteronomic-Deuteronomistic restriction of the legitimate cult to Jerusalem envisioned the integration of the "rural priesthood" into the cult there (→ Pentateuchal Research). Ezekiel's fusion of priestly and prophetic impulses develops an understanding of future priestly responsibilities. The Priestly writing envisions a theocratic constitution of Israel dominated by priests (Aaron as Levite).

2.4. During the postexilic period a new priesthood established itself in Jerusalem at the rebuilt → temple, which in its own turn actualized certain exilic ideas (with occasional disputes concerning distinctions between various temple personnel: priests and Levites as lower orders). The understanding of the cult itself can be found in the ritual legislation of Leviticus and Numbers. The → Qumran community was founded by a branch of the Jerusalem priesthood.

Bibliography: A. Cody, *A History of OT Priesthood* (Rome, 1969) • W. Dommershausen, "כֹּהֵן *kōhēn* II-VIII," *TDOT* 7.66-75 • L. L. Grabbe, *Priests, Prophets, Diviners, Sages: A Socio-historical Study of Religious Specialists in Ancient Israel* (Valley Forge, Pa., 1995) • M. Haran, *Temples and Temple-Service in Ancient Israel* (Oxford, 1978) • R. D. Nelson, *Raising Up a Faithful Priest: Community and Priesthood in Biblical Theology* (Louisville, Ky., 1993).

Fritz Stolz†

3. Roman Catholicism

The derivation of the word "priest" from Gk. *presbyteros* (elder) would hardly suggest to us what debates there were in the → early church regarding the priestly office. To grasp the situation we also must take into account the use of *hiereus* (= Lat. *sacerdos*) in the OT and NT. This factor gave rise to later problems and deliberations on priests and their role.

3.1. *Biblical Data*

The NT uses *hiereus* both for the OT Levitical priesthood and for the Christian community as a whole. According to Hebrews, Christ himself is also, in a new way, the one eternal → high priest (9:11-12, 24-25; 10:10-11; 12:24-25). In him all prior priesthood came to fulfillment and was ended. For the author of Hebrews, Christ is the end of the priesthood and of the closely related cult.

But on another level the OT priesthood found fulfillment in the priesthood of all believers (see 4 below). We find the idea of a common priesthood of the baptized in 1 Pet. 2:5-10. The word *klēros* (whence Eng. "clergy"), which later came to be used for a special spiritual class in the → church, served to express the dignity of the whole community in 1 Pet. 5:3. Cultic language was used to denote a noncultic reality. This paradoxical use of → metaphor may be seen in other NT passages as well (e.g., Phil. 2:17; 4:18; Jas. 1:27).

In view of the exclusive use of *hiereus* for Christ and the comprehensive use for believers, it is understandable that the NT and the early church of the first centuries did not use this word, with its cultic connotations, for any specific group in the community.

3.2. *Historical Data*

3.2.1. The church faced new challenges in the third century, and new priestly terms were now developed for its leaders. This change came in both East and West and may be detected in the writings of the → church fathers (esp. Clement, → Origen, → Tertullian, → Cyprian, and Hippolytus) and in → ordination texts. In the theology of ministry in the period that followed, the → bishop was the true priest, and presbyters (→ Elder) were called priests only in a secondary sense.

As the church grew and parishes were formed, priests in practice came to have much the same tasks as bishops (e.g., officiating at → worship and → preaching). At the beginning of the sixth century we can see a reflection of this new development in the transfer of the term *sacerdos* to the presbyter and the absorbing of the latter description into the former. Presbyters came increasingly to focus on the → Eucharist, and their supreme power became that of consecrating the elements. Along these lines a new sacrificial priesthood emerged out of the original order of presbyters. Along with NT motifs the ordination rite now took over more and more features from the OT.

In definition of the priestly ministry, further distinctions gained in importance, for example, that between → clergy and laity, or between → sacred and profane (§2). Penance also underwent change (→ Penitence), and eucharistic discussion of → consecration intensified. These developments implied that priests were now mediators along with and over the community, and their ministry became predominantly liturgical and sacral. A result in the theology of the Middle Ages was a more precise definition of the → sacrament of orders.

3.2.2. The → Reformers gave new emphasis to the priesthood of all believers, opposed the sacrifice of the → Mass, rejected priest-centered absolution, and thus set less store by the cultic character of the office. The decisions of the Council of → Trent resisted these views, maintaining that the new → covenant involves a visible priesthood, that priesthood is conferred by ordination, and that an inalienable hierarchical structure of the → church is related to the priestly order (→ Hierarchy 2).

The rejection of the Reformers' objections, which were taken out of context, meant a treatment of the powers of the priesthood at the Eucharist and penance (→ Forgiveness) as essential and inalienable. But these features alone did not constitute the essence of priesthood.

After Trent the so-called Franciscan School (P. de Bérulle et al.) promoted Christological → spirituality and thus advanced an ascetic idea of the priesthood (→ Asceticism).

3.3. *Vatican II*

With → Vatican II a new phase in defining the priestly office began. Priority was given to the task of → proclamation in *Lumen gentium (LG)* 28 and *Presbyterorum ordinis (PO)* 4. The place of priests in the church was defined in terms of the whole fellowship (*LG* 1, 9-17). New attention was paid to the universal priesthood (10-11). The *munus triplex* (threefold → office) of Christ as prophet, priest, and king served as a framework (note references to this threefold office in *LG* 13, 21; *PO* 1; *Apostolicam actuositatem* 2, 10; *Unitatis redintegratio* 2; *Ad gentes* 15). All believers share in this office by → baptism and → confirmation (*LG* 31). This universal priesthood, however, still differs "essentially and not only in degree" from the official and hierarchical priesthood (10).

Vatican II opened the door again to a permanent diaconate, to which married men might be admitted. It was set up in June 1967 by the → motu proprio *Sacrum diaconatus ordinem* of Paul VI (1963-78). In the motu proprio *Ad pascendum* (1972) it was required that candidates for this office would first serve for a suitable time as → lectors and acolytes.

In the motu proprio *Ministeria quaedam* (1972) minor orders and the subdiaconate, which had given rise to problems, were reorganized. The → tonsure was abolished, and reception into the clergy, with a pledge of → celibacy and a responsibility to keep the → hours, came only with the diaconate. Lectors and acolytes were seen no longer in terms of orders but in terms of ministries, which were conferred upon them by liturgical institution.

In connection with the admission of women to the priesthood, which was burdening ecumenical relationships with the Anglican Church, Pope Paul VI wrote to Archbishop Coggan of Canterbury in November 1975 explaining the Roman Catholic position. He argued for the impossibility in principle of ordaining women (→ Ordination 7.4) by adducing the example of Christ, who chose only men to be apostles, and by referring to the consistent practice and doctrine of the church itself. He noted that the → Orthodox Church also adheres to this tradition. The declaration *Inter insigniores* (1976) of the Congregation for the Doctrine of the Faith develops this argument, declaring that because Christ's choice of men as apostles was a conscious one and did not derive from any sociological or cultural considerations, it was binding for the church. Because this document and its theological argumentation came under severe criticism, Pope John Paul II (1978-2005) issued the apostolic decree *Ordinatio sacerdotalis* in 1994, which declared the doctrine of the impossibility of priestly ordination for women to be definitive and obligated all believers to adhere to this decision.

3.4. *Ecumenical Conversations*

In ecumenical conversations (→ Ecumenical Dialogue) there have been notable agreements on the priestly ministry. A first breakthrough came with the Accra Text of 1974, which Roman Catholic theologians on the → Faith and Order Commission helped to produce (→ Ecumenism, Ecumenical Movement).

Discussion and revision of this document (esp. at the 1978 meeting of Faith and Order in Bangalore) made possible the agreed Lima Declaration *Baptism, Eucharist, and Ministry* (1982), which formulated important points of agreement and convergence on ministry, especially the thesis that all conversations on such matters as priesthood and ordination must begin with the church as a whole. The task of the church — its ministry of Word and sacrament in the reconciling of people to God — cannot in principle be restricted to specific individuals in the church. The Lima text states that all churches must take as their starting point "the calling of the whole people of God" ("Ministry," par. 6). How this universal priesthood of all the baptized can develop and take its place in the theology of ministry remains to be worked out. → Reception of the results of these ecumenical discussions is still an unresolved issue in the churches.

→ Roman Catholic Church

Bibliography: H.-M. Barth, *Einander Priester sein. Allgemeines Priestertum in ökumenischer Perspektive* (Göttingen, 1990) • Catholic Bishops of the United States, *Priests for a New Millennium* (Washington, D.C., 2000) • E. Drewermann, *Kleriker. Psychogramm eines Ideals* (8th ed.; Olten, 1990) • P. Eicher, ed., *Der Klerikerstreit. Die Auseinandersetzung um Eugen Drewermann* (2d ed.; Munich, 1990) • M. A. Fahey, ed., *Catholic Perspectives on "Baptism, Eucharist, and Ministry"* (Lanham, Md., 1986) • E. Garhammer, ed., *Unnütze Knechte? Priesterbild und Priesterbildung* (Regensburg, 1989) • G. Greshake, *Priester sein in dieser Zeit. Theologie–pastorale Praxis–Spiritualität* (Freiburg, 2000) • P. Hoffmann, ed., *Priesterkirche* (2d ed.; Düsseldorf, 1989) • K. Lehmann and W. Pannenberg, eds., *The Condemnations of the Reformation Era: Do They Still Divide?* (Minneapolis, 1990) esp. pt. 3, "The Sacraments," 71-145 • T. McGovern, *Priestly Identity: A Study in the Theology of Priesthood* (Dublin, 2002) • I. Raming, *Priesteramt der Frau. Geschenk Gottes für eine erneuerte Kirche* (Münster, 2002) • T. P. Rausch, *Priesthood Today: An Appraisal* (New York, 1992) • E. Schillebeeckx, *The Church with a Human Face: A New and Expanded Theology of Ministry* (New York, 1985) • S. K. Wood and M. Downey, eds., *Ordering the Baptismal Priesthood: Theologies of Lay and Ordained Ministry* (Collegeville, Minn., 2003) • World Council of Churches, *Baptism, Eu-*

charist, and Mininstry (Geneva, 1982) • P. M. ZULEHNER, *Priester im Modernisierungsstress. Forschungsbericht der Studie Priester 2000* (Ostfildern, 2001).

ERICH GARHAMMER

4. Priesthood of All Believers

4.1. *NT*

Believers in Christ in the NT community are all called to be priests, kings, and the holy people of God (1 Pet. 2:9; Rev. 1:6; 5:10; 20:6). This calling is based on the election and calling of → Israel (Exod. 19:6; Isa. 61:5-6). The NT reference to the royal priesthood shows how spiritualized the idea had become in contemporary → Judaism. The office was no longer seen as one that was concretely present. Hebrews uses the term "priest" to describe the saving work of Christ (chaps. 4–10). Christ alone is the high priest, sacrifice, and mediator for the community (→ Office of Christ).

The community itself is a royal priesthood because of its relation to the divine priest (Christ himself), and in expression of its spiritual life. Through → baptism and the gift of the → Holy Spirit, those who believe in Christ are called to priestly ministry and become spiritual *(pneumatikoi)*. They discharge their priestly ministry by proclaiming the → gospel (Rom. 15:16; → Mission), by intercession (1 Tim. 2:1-4), by mutual exhortation and encouragement (Col. 3:16; Gal. 6:1-2), and by works of love (1 Corinthians 13; Gal. 5:13-26). By thus dedicating themselves, they offer → sacrifices of praise and thanksgiving for their reconciliation to God. Neither cult nor ministry is the basis of the community of Christ but the Word and the Spirit, promised equally to all Christians as gifts of grace (→ Charisma).

4.2. *Middle Ages*

The → early church held fast to the idea of the priesthood of all the baptized. But with the distinction between ordained office bearers and "laity," the idea increasingly developed of a special priestly order (→ Clergy and Laity). In the medieval church two orders thus came into being: ordinary members of the church and an official hierarchical priesthood qualified by → ordination and enjoying special privileges (Decretum Gratiani, ca. 1140).

4.3. *Luther*

Trying to get back to the NT situation on the basis of 1 Corinthians 12 and Matt. 16:18-19 and 18:18, Martin → Luther (1483-1546), in his primary works from 1520 on, mentioned the priesthood of all believers as central to the Reformation understanding of the church (→ Church 3.4-6; Luther's Theology 3.2). Luther criticized the idea that the existence and future of the church depended on the ministry of priests. Instead, he made a plea for justifying faith (→ Justification 2), which is the work of Christ and which enables believers to be priests as they "pray for the world, that God would grant it faith" (WA 10/3.309.15-16).

Luther developed the doctrine of the priesthood of all believers in two directions: as criticism of the church, and as church reform. His view was antihierarchical as a basic challenge to the distinction between spiritual and secular, to the primacy of the → pope, and to the superior position of clergy (see *LW* 44.127-30). By the → grace of God all of us are brothers and sisters; "we have then altogether the same rights" (40.33). This insight conferred new dignity on the laity by seeing in priesthood a birthright of all believers.

Luther perceived seven priestly functions: → proclamation of the → Word of God, baptizing, blessing and administering the Lord's Supper (→ Eucharist), granting or withholding absolution (→ Penitence), offering the sacrifice of prayer and praise, interceding, and making doctrinal judgments. All people have a part, but the family is of special importance in this ministry. In it parents "make [their children] acquainted with the gospel" (*LW* 45.46), wives instruct servants, and midwives give emergency baptism (40.25). In the Reformation → church orders, the laity have roles in → worship, in giving catechetical instruction, and in helping the needy.

4.4. *Development in Protestant Churches*

The other → Reformers agreed with Luther on the matter of the priesthood of all believers but could still contend for a special office of public preaching (→ Ministry, Ministerial Offices, 3). All believers have the same spiritual status, but not all have the same ministry. The universal priesthood constitutes the community. The proclamation of the Word (→ Preaching) and the power of the → keys have been entrusted to it. It has the authority to call community members to take up this ministry for a period on behalf of all. Thus, as Luther also said, "A Christian assembly or congregation has the right and power to judge all teaching and to call, appoint, and dismiss teachers" (*LW* 39.301). With the organizing of territorial churches the importance of the universal priesthood waned. The office of public preaching came under theological direction. Preaching and administering the → sacraments were now privileges of → pastors, who were ordained to their office (→ Ordination).

As a Protestant principle, however, universal priesthood still had critical and renewing force in the history of the Protestant churches. We see this factor in Socinianism and → spiritualism, the → Pietism of P. J. Spener (1635-1705) and the → Inner Mission of J. H. Wichern (1808-81), the → Confessing Church at the time of the → church struggle, and numerous movements outside Germany that made more extensive use of the laity and disregarded or reduced the clergy-laity distinction. A → feminist theology can also make appeal to the universal priesthood in setting up a new relation between men and women in the church.

4.5. *Anglican Communion*

In the Anglican world some Anglo-Catholics (e.g., C. Gore) turned to the universal priesthood in justification of a sacerdotal ministry for clergy. The Anglican reformers, while retaining the title "priest" as a contraction of "presbyter," had banished sacerdotal intentions from the revised ordination services and sacerdotal functions from the liturgy, especially at eucharistic celebrations, where the altar had become the holy table and the only sacrifice was that of praise and thanksgiving. It was recognized, of course, that the whole people of God, according to the NT, has a sacerdotal ministry as itself a royal priesthood. The argument thus suggested itself that as a representative of the whole people, the priest may validly be called a *hiereus* or *sacerdos,* as well as a *presbyteros* — that is, that the word "priest" may be taken in its twofold English sense.

The fact remained, however, as Roman Catholicism was quick to respond, that Anglican priests were not ordained to a sacerdotal ministry. Especially they were not set apart to offer the sacrifice of the Mass, which in the Middle Ages had come to be seen as an essential (perhaps *the* essential) part of the presbyter's ministry (see the *Apostolicae curae* [1896] of Leo XIII, on the invalidity of Anglican orders).

4.6. *Ecumenical Aspects*

At the Council of → Trent the → Roman Catholic Church rejected the Reformation insight regarding the priesthood of all believers and insisted on the powers and privileges of the ordained priesthood (see 3.2). But → Vatican II evaluated the role of the laity afresh, though not abandoning the essential distinction between universal priesthood on the one side and an official, ordained, hierarchical priesthood on the other. It agreed that all believers in Christ participate in Christ's threefold office and therefore in the universal priesthood, so that in the context of the church's mission the laity have the task of → lay apostolate (see 3.3).

Over against this Roman Catholic view the → Orthodox Church brings its own specific understanding of the royal priesthood into the → ecumenical dialogue. Instead of the legal element in priesthood, the Orthodox stress the pneumatic element, which manifests itself in the liturgical event of worship and in the → teaching office that clergy and laity share.

The → Reformation view of the priesthood of all believers is still, however, a mark of differentiation in the → oikoumene. The acceptance or rejection of the ordination of women (→ Ordination 7.4) is for many a plain sign of this fact. (On ecumenical discussion of the relation between office and community, see → Ministry, Ministerial Offices, 5.)

Bibliography: Luther's views: "The Babylonian Captivity of the Church" (1520), *LW* 36.11-126 • "Concerning the Ministry" (1523), *LW* 40.3-44 • "Estate of Marriage" (1522), *LW* 45.11-49 • "On the Councils and the Church" (1539), *LW* 41.9-178 • "That a Christian Assembly or Congregation Has the Right and Power to Judge All Teaching" (1539), *LW* 39.301-14 • "To the Christian Nobility of the German Nation" (1520), *LW* 44.115-217.

Other works: H.-M. Barth, *Einander Priester sein. Allgemeines Priestertum in ökumenischer Perspektive* (Göttingen, 1990) • K. Blaser, *Calvins Lehre von den drei Amtern Christi* (Zurich, 1970) • C. C. Eastwood, *The Priesthood of All Believers* (London, 1960) • P. Neuner, *Der Laie und das Gottesvolk* (Frankfurt, 1988) • G. Scharffenorth, *Den Glauben ins Leben ziehen. Studien zu Luthers Theologie* (Munich, 1982) • B. Schultze, "Die byzantinisch-slawische Theologie über den Dienst der Laien in der Kirche," *OS* 5 (1956) 243-84 • A. Vanhoye, *OT Priests and the New Priest, according to the NT* (Petersham, Mass., 1986).

Leonore Siegele-Wenschkewitz†

Primate

In the → hierarchy of the → early church and the medieval church, "primate" refers to a → bishop of the Latin → Rite midway between a → patriarch and an → archbishop. The primate could summon councils and crown kings, and he had oversight over other bishops.

Today a primate, either by tradition or papal appointment, has only honorary rank (1983 → CIC 438). The archbishop of Salzburg was primate of Germany, and after 1945 the primate of Poland came to the fore as spokesperson for the church in dealings with the state. In the monastic world (→ Monasticism) the abbot primate has a similar position (→ Religious Orders and Congregations). Thus the abbot of Sant'Anselmo at Rome is abbot primate for the → Benedictines.

The archbishop of Canterbury (→ Anglican Communion) is "primate of all England," the archbishop of York, "primate of England." The *exarch* is the parallel of the primate in the → Orthodox Church, and the *primus* is the presiding bishop in the Scottish Episcopal Church.

Bibliography: P. Hofmeister, "Primas," *LTK* 8.760 • J. Listl, *HKKR* 329 • G. Moore, *Introduction to English Canon Law* (Oxford, 1967) 29 • J. Ratzinger, "Primat," *LTK* 8.762-63.

Albert Stein†

Primeval History (Genesis 1–11)

1. History of Composition
   1.1. J and P Sources
   1.2. Other Sources
   1.3. Redaction
2. Final Form
   2.1. Creation and Sin
   2.2. Genealogies
   2.3. The Flood
   2.4. The Tower of Babel
   2.5. Theme and Function

Biblical primeval history, Genesis 1–11, recounts the period beginning with God's → creation of the heavens and the earth and the forming of the first human beings through a series of largely dismal expressions of human sinfulness, and concluding with the dispersion of human beings over the face of the earth after the failed effort to construct a tower at Babel. The scale of the account is universal from the opening verse. Although many of the events recounted are quite commonplace, each one involves all of the human beings existing at the time of the event recounted. At the end, after the people have been scattered, the focus narrows to a single genealogical line that leads to the person of → Abraham, the progenitor of the family and nation that figure most centrally in the ensuing story (→ Patriarchal Narrative).

1. History of Composition

1.1. *J and P Sources*

It was precisely in the primeval history that scholars first observed and reconstructed two independent sources that had been secondarily combined into a single narrative. The Yahwistic source (or "J," from Ger. *Jahwist,* so-called because of its consistent use of the name "Yahweh" to designate God) was the earlier of the two, dating, it was most frequently asserted, from the period of the early to middle monarchy. The Priestly source ("P," named for the priestly interests of its author) was dated much later, usually in the fifth century B.C. (→ Pentateuchal Research).

More recent studies have questioned the dating of the sources and even the existence of P as a fully coherent source rather than a complex series of inclusions and editorial additions. The source hypothesis, though, has retained its vitality as a compositional explanation for the presence of repetitions, contradictions, and consistent variations in idiom and vocabulary in the text. The full utility of the source hypothesis and its necessary complexity can be gauged by comparing the creation story of Genesis 1:1–2:4a (P) with the story of the creation of the first humans in 2:4b–3:24 (J) and, yet again, by analyzing the story of the flood in chaps. 6–9 (J combined with P).

The written sources J and P (or the P material, if it did not achieve the status of a full source in the primeval history) exhibited distinct yet consistent thematic interests. J was dark, portraying a relentless pattern of human sinfulness stretching from the first → sin of → Adam and Eve to the shattering hubris of the tower-building at Babel. God responded to the sin with fitting → punishment yet in each instance mitigated the punishment so that, through God's mercy alone, life continued.

P was far more optimistic and expansive, embracing a narrative arc that began with God's establishment of the "very good" created order and culminating in the assurance of God's enduring presence among the people through the establishment of a legitimate cult at Mount Sinai. In the primeval history P acknowledged the existence of sin in the generation of the flood, but human sinfulness was met by God's → covenant never again to destroy the earth, sealed with the sign of the bow in the clouds.

1.2. *Other Sources*

The written sources J and P represent not the end of the process of the composition of the primeval history but more nearly its midpoint. There is a strong consensus among scholars that much of the material in this section arose outside of Israel itself, particularly in early Mesopotamian tradition. Mesopotamian origin is most clear in the narrative of Noah and the flood, in which details such as the sending out of the raven or dove in the aftermath of a world-encompassing flood are paralleled quite precisely in the Atrahasis and Gilgamesh epics. The antediluvian genealogies find close parallels in much earlier

Sumerian king lists. Attempts to trace the traditions in the P creation account of Genesis 1 to their origins in Mesopotamian myths, particularly the *Enuma elish,* have proved less successful. The location of the story of the tower in Babylon points to a Mesopotamian origin for this tradition. There is little evidence in the primeval history of Egyptian influence, but clearly Israel's developing primeval traditions were strongly influenced by the cognate traditions of its neighbors.

Other traditions, such as the creation of the first man and woman and their establishment in the garden, or the accounts of the first sin and first murder, presumably arose as oral traditions within → Israel (§1) or its direct precursors. In their oral form these legends of ancestors exhibited a strong etiological interest, the desire to explain current phenomena such as the enmity between human beings and snakes or the acute pain of childbirth by reference to primeval events. These traditions were originally recounted quite independently of each other at different locales throughout Israel. Their original independence and formation for purposes other than to constitute a single coherent narrative can explain many small discrepancies and shifts of emphasis still detectable in the sources. The nature of the process by which these legends drew together before being gathered into the sources remains somewhat obscure.

1.3. *Redaction*

Combining the written sources together into the final form of the primeval history involved redactional activity, much of which can be reconstructed only conjecturally. The J source was apparently combined with a largely parallel narrative source E (named for the consistent use of the name "Elohim" for God) to form JE, although there is little evidence that E contained an account of the primeval period. Subsequently, perhaps in the fifth century B.C., a Priestly redactor combined JE with the Priestly material to form a much larger work. Although P presumably used Priestly material as the frame for the new work, in the primeval history the theme of sin and God's response found in J was stronger than the Priestly frame itself. Nonetheless, the combination of material from the two sources altered the sense of the composite work in ways clearly discernible in the final form of the primeval history.

2. Final Form

2.1. *Creation and Sin*

The final form of the primeval history brings together the → optimism and universal scale of the original P account with the darker tones of J's emphasis on human sinfulness in a way that transforms both themes. J's account of the first human sin is tempered by a touching account of the creation of the first man from the dust and the first woman from his rib, which continues the positive view of humankind from the creation account in Genesis 1. The two accounts are subtly linked by the "these are the generations of the heavens and the earth" formula (2:4a). Human dignity in the Adam account is emphasized by the intimacy of the moment in which God breathes life into Adam, by God's solicitude in planting the garden to please Adam, and, most profoundly, by the command not to eat of the tree of the knowledge of good and evil with its accompanying threat of → death, a command that renders Adam a religiously serious person, one who could enter a relationship with God as deep as his life itself.

In the story of the first sin no effort is made to rationalize or explain the existence of sin. The serpent's insinuations strike at the relationship of trust with God and the proper attitude of obedience or respect, but ultimately the woman eats the fruit for the trivial reason that it looks good and the only slightly deeper motivation that it can render a person wise. The man eats because he is given the fruit. The real emphasis is on the effects of sin, the dissolution of natural relationships between man and woman (they are now ashamed in each other's presence) and with God (they hide), dissolutions further extended by the punishments meted out by God. Yet this first story, as the other stories of sin in the primeval history, ends with God's interventions to restore some approximation of the harmony that God had sought from the first moment of creation. God allows the man and woman to remain in each other's society by clothing them with more durable garments than they had concocted, and in an act that is anything but a punishment, God drives them from the garden and its tree of life so that the baleful effects of their sinful decisions will not expand without limit.

The pattern established in the primeval history, then, is of instances of human sinfulness that disrupt the existing harmony — as when Cain breaks the fraternal bond that should render Abel's murder unthinkable — followed by God's response. First there is punishment that acknowledges and responds to the nature of the sin (the earth that drank up Abel's blood will be cursed), and then God intervenes to set matters back on course, so much as is possible under the new circumstances created by the people's sin, by giving Cain a protective mark that allows human society to continue (4:10-15).

2.2. *Genealogies*
Interspersed through these narratives of sin and God's response are genealogies. Neither vestigial narratives nor mere antiquarian filler, the genealogies chronicle the relatively steady and uneventful fulfillment of the command to be fruitful and multiply. In this regard, at least, human beings follow the instructions of God and so complete the purposes of creation. At several points the genealogies directly intersect with the unfolding stories of human sin. Lamech's barbarous exultation in vengeance (4:23-24) breaks into the orderly genealogy to illustrate the force of sin even on the obligation to be fruitful and multiply. And at the flood human corruption brings to an end the genealogical line of all but a single family.

2.3. *The Flood*
The flood represents an important moment in the pattern of human sin and divine response. The near-universal extent of human corruption leads God to announce near-universal destruction, a reversal of creation back to the second day, when God separated the waters above from the waters below. Only the righteous Noah and his family are spared, as an act of justice or in hopes of beginning again with righteous seed. If the latter, then the strategy fails, for sin appears in the story of Noah, Ham, and his brothers (9:20-27).

After the flood sin continues, but equally important once again is God's response. Surveying the devastation after the flood, God explicitly recognizes that the inclination of human hearts is → evil from youth — sin is inveterate — yet God pledges never again to destroy all humanity through flood. God will interact with people as they truly are. The bow in the heavens attests God's intent.

2.4. *The Tower of Babel*
The final story in the primeval history is the tower of Babel. Once again it seems to follow the pattern of human sinfulness — in this case rooted in insecurity that feared scattering and in the hubris of a people that sought to make a name for itself. But this story is unusual. God does respond to the human actions, almost wistfully descending to see what they are about, but God's response in this case is not to punish, although the people are scattered and their tongues confused. The explicit purpose of God's intervention is not punishment but simply to thwart the spread of sin, much as when God drove Adam and Eve from the garden.

Once again we expect to find God seeking a way to reestablish basic harmony so that God's purposes, the filling of the earth and pleasant and virtuous interactions between people, can continue. But the primeval history ends at this point with an undivided genealogy, father to son, father to son, appropriate to this scattered people, a genealogy that leads in a single line to Terah and then to Abraham (11:24-26). God's intentions in God's responses to human action have not changed, but the mode of God's intervention has. Henceforth the story will trace God's interaction with a single-family line, not all of humanity at once.

2.5. *Theme and Function*
The primeval narrative in its final form is therefore dominated neither by a hopeless pessimism about the continuing spread of human sinfulness nor by the cosmic optimism rooted in God's powers of creation. It is, rather, a careful and realistic combination of the two tendencies. The power and depth of human sinfulness are forthrightly acknowledged. Each new sin in the primeval period creates dire new conditions, to which God responds. That response is always colored by God's high estimation of human value, an estimation enshrined in the creation of the cosmos and shown once again in the care of God's creation of Adam and Eve. That high valuation, explicable only through recognition of God's → love, remains unchanged through the ensuing stories, for which the primeval history serves as preparation.

Bibliography: J. Blenkinsopp, *The Pentateuch: An Introduction to the First Five Books of the Bible* (New York, 1992) • U. Cassuto, *A Commentary on the Book of Genesis* (Jerusalem, 1972) • D. J. A. Clines, *The Theme of the Pentateuch* (Sheffield, 1978) • T. E. Fretheim, *Creation, Fall, and Flood: Studies in Genesis 1–11* (Minneapolis, 1969) • H. Gunkel, *Genesis* (Macon, Ga., 1997; Ger. ed., 1917) • S. E. McEvenue, *The Narrative Style of the Priestly Writer* (Rome, 1971) • P. D. Miller, *Genesis 1–11: Studies in Structure and Theme* (Sheffield, 1978) • G. von Rad, *Genesis* (Philadelphia, 1972; Ger. ed., 1953) • H. Seebass, *Genesis,* vol. 1, *Urgeschichte (1,1–11,26)* (Neukirchen, 1996).

Robert B. Robinson

Primitive Christian Community

1. Sources
2. Expectation of the Parousia
3. Development
4. Self-Understanding
5. Gentile and Jewish Christians

1. Sources
The primitive Christian community was the main church of NT days. Its center was the first organized

group of adherents in Jerusalem (→ Disciples 2; New Testament Era, History of, 2.3 and 3). The most important non-NT source is the *Antiquities* of Flavius Josephus (ca. 37-ca. 100), specifically 20.200 and 18.63-64, if this so-called Testamentum Flavianum or parts of it are indeed authentic. Chronological data can also be picked up from some secular texts.

In the main, however, we must rely on NT sources in reconstructing the development and organization of the primitive Christian community, especially Acts (written ca. 90), which contains traditions of high value, even though some contexts are enhanced and events harmonized. The Pauline literature also contains some references (→ Paul), as do some passages in the → Synoptic gospels, which allow retrospective conclusions about the situation of the primitive community.

2. Expectation of the Parousia

The crucifixion of → Jesus (§3.2) was a decisive event that caused some of the disciples initially to leave Jerusalem. The → resurrection appearances, however, showed that God not only raised Jesus from the dead but identified him as the Messiah (Acts 2:32-36; → Christological Titles 3.1). The disciples gathered from these phenomena, which are probably to be understood as → visions, that Jerusalem would be the eschatological locus and center of God's final manifestation (→ Eschatology 2). Here they awaited the → parousia of Christ as the Messiah of God's coming kingdom and as King and Judge of Israel and all humanity (Acts 2:36; 3:20-21). In anticipation they received the pledge of the → Holy Spirit (§1.2; Acts 2:1-21), who also equipped them for mission.

Expectation of the Lord's return was an added incentive as the disciples sought to carry out the mission the Lord had laid upon them. The failure of the parousia to occur, however, dampened the initial enthusiasm, and the Jesus appearances ceased (see 1 Cor. 15:8). The idea of God's kingdom gradually lost its eschatological coloring, and the concept of the → church (§2.1.3) became more prominent.

3. Development

3.1. Community structures began developing. The "circle of 12" founded by Jesus (→ Twelve, The), which → Peter had reconstituted after Jesus' appearance (1 Cor. 15:5) in Galilee, was replaced by the so-called pillars, Peter, James, and John (cf. Mark 10:35-40). → James was executed by Agrippa I (before 44; → Herod, Herodians, 2.3), and another James, a brother of the Lord, replaced him (Gal. 1:18-19; 2:9). This James later became the main leader in Jerusalem (Acts 21:18; Gal. 2:11-12). After his martyrdom in A.D. 62, he was succeeded by Simon/Simeon, a cousin of Jesus (according to Hegesippus, quoted in Eusebius *Hist. eccl.* 3.32).

It is still debated whether the primitive Christian community fled to Pella in Transjordan before the Jewish War (66-70).

3.2. Jerusalem's varied geographic connections eventually attracted many kinds of members and influences into the primitive Christian community, including Hellenists (→ Hellenism 3), disciples of John (→ John the Baptist), Essenes (→ Qumran), and others with syncretistic and apocalyptic views (→ Apocalyptic 3). Greek-speaking Jews of the Hellenistic dispersion (→ Judaism 3.2) quickly became members. Such included the "group of seven," with Stephen at their head (Acts 6:1-7), a group within the early church that enjoyed more freedom from the → law (§2.2) and disparaged the temple cult and Jewish rules of purification (→ Cultic Purity). These attitudes brought them into collision with the Jewish community. Stephen was accused, condemned, and stoned to death (Acts 6–7). His followers (note the list of names in 6:5) escaped persecution by fleeing from Jerusalem (8:1). The law-abiding part of the church stayed in Jerusalem and probably continued to develop relatively undisturbed (see 12:1-17).

4. Self-Understanding

At first the primitive Christian community was part of the → synagogue fellowship and was not seeking to establish a new religious community. It saw itself as the righteous community, the remnant, the chosen core community of → Israel (§1.9). Its members referred to themselves as saints, brethren, the elect, and the poor. They worshiped Jesus as Messiah and Son of Man (→ Christology 1), the prophesied Son of David, the latter title already being a given for Paul (see Rom. 1:3). Jesus, who was initially the bearer of the notion of God's → kingdom, now became the content of the → proclamation. Now not only his teachings were preached but also the salvation-event revealed in him (→ Salvation 1.3).

The early cultic forms of the community helped to lead it away from Judaism. It read the OT as a pointer both to Jesus and to the end-time community (→ Church 2.1). Baptism became a specifically Christian rite of initiation given in the name of Jesus (Acts 2:38). Common meals in remembrance of Jesus (→ Eucharist 2) carried with them expectation of his return (Acts 2:42, 46; 4:32-37; 12:12; cf. Luke 22:16).

5. Gentile and Jewish Christians

5.1. The mission of the primitive community at first had an eschatological character. Itinerant preachers had already gone throughout Jewish territories in expectation of the end of the world (Matthew 10; Luke 10:1-24). At first there was no real thought of a Gentile mission (Matt. 10:5-6, 23), and the establishment of communities in the surrounding areas was probably not the result of planned missions. The scattered Stephen group (see 3.2), however, presumably founded new congregations with their preaching, for example, at Lydda, Joppa, Caesarea, Samaria, Damascus, and Antioch. The new freedom from the law opened the door to the Gentiles (Acts 8; 11:19-26). This development must have come about rather quickly, for on his conversion Paul already found a Christian community in Damascus.

It was presumably in Antioch, the first mixed Christian community, that the term "Christians" came into use, a word the Gentile political authorities then applied to the community (Acts 11:26). The Gentile church had no national boundaries and was free from the law, and in this regard it was not an organic continuation of the Jerusalem community. But it achieved recognition by the first disciples (Peter and John), and given Jerusalem's eschatological importance (Rom. 15:25-27), it still saw in Jerusalem the true center of the church,

5.2. Clarification of the relation of the Gentiles to the law was achieved by the so-called apostolic council (ca. A.D. 47, Acts 15:6-29; → Acts of the Apostles 8). The main issue was circumcision. After some hesitation the three pillars accepted Paul's Gentile mission (Gal. 2:6-9, cf. Acts 15:19-20). They urged Paul to arrange a collection for Jerusalem in his overseas congregations (Gal. 2:10).

An influential minority did not accept the compromise and engaged in anti-Pauline agitation in Galatia and perhaps also Philippi and Corinth. James was eventually won over by this group, which thereby came to predominate in the primitive community. The laboriously established unity between the Pauline congregations and the Jerusalem community was severed once and for all when the Pauline collection was rejected in Jerusalem, the likely scenario suggested by current scholarship.

An incident at Antioch — possibly before or even after the Jerusalem conference — sheds light on the controversy regarding the → law (§2.3). When delegates appeared from James, who was loyal to the law, Peter and Barnabas ceased to have table fellowship with Gentile Christians. They came under attack by Paul (Gal. 2:11-21), for whom there was in Christ neither Jew nor Greek, since all are one in him (Gal. 3:28). Paul himself, being a Jew, could follow the precepts of the law (Acts 21:23-26), but he saw no reason why Gentile Christians should be subject to its ceremonial and civil precepts.

The rapid expansion of Gentile Christianity and the destruction of Jerusalem in A.D. 70 changed the face of the primitive Christian community, which lost its importance. Some groups of anti-Pauline Jewish Christians, however, survived for several centuries in Transjordan.

→ Gentiles, Gentile Christianity; Jewish Christians

Bibliography: J. BECKER, *Christian Beginnings: Word and Community from Jesus to Post-apostolic Times* (Louisville, Ky., 1993) • H. CONZELMANN, *History of Primitive Christianity* (Nashville, 1973) • F. V. FILSON, *A NT History: The Story of the Emerging Church* (Philadelphia, 1964) • M. HENGEL, *Between Jesus and Paul: Studies in the Earliest History of Christianity* (Philadelphia, 1983) 1-29 • C. C. HILL, *Hellenists and Hebrews* (Minneapolis, 1992) • G. LÜDEMANN, *The Acts of the Apostles: What Really Happened in the Earliest Days of the Church* (Amherst, N.Y., 2005); idem, *Early Christianity according to the Traditions in Acts: A Commentary* (Minneapolis, 1989); idem, *Paul, Apostle to the Gentiles: Studies in Chronology* (Philadelphia, 1984); idem, *Primitive Christianity: A Survey of Recent Studies and Some New Proposals* (London, 2003) • W. A. MEEKS, *The First Urban Christians: The Social World of the Apostle Paul* (2d ed.; New Haven, 2003) • L. SCHENKE, *Die Urgemeinde. Geschichtliche und theologische Entwicklung* (Stuttgart, 1990) • W. SCHNEEMELCHER, *Das Urchristentum* (Stuttgart, 1981) • G. THEISSEN, *Social Reality and the Early Christians: Theology, Ethics, and the World of the NT* (Minneapolis, 1992) • J. WEISS, *Earliest Christianity: A History of the Period A.D. 30-150* (2 vols.; New York, 1959; orig. pub., 1914-17).

GERD LÜDEMANN

Prison Ministry

1. The term "prison ministry" describes the work of chaplains and ministers within the justice system. It also covers the work of volunteers who assist in this ministry and who often render service comparable to that of the minister or → deacon. The main forms of work are individual counseling (→ Pastoral Care), group discussions, and → worship. In view of the often miserable social conditions in prisons, the diaconal side is very important (→ Diakonia). Ministry to women prisoners, much of which is done by women ministers, often runs into special difficulties because the smaller numbers often means that they are housed indiscriminately, without regard to age, length of sentence, and so forth.

While prison chaplains personally lead worship and other religious activities, an important function of their role is also to act as the institutional advocate and guarantor of religious freedom. Prison chaplains ensure that the U.S. Constitution's guarantee of the freedom of religion (specified in the First Amendment) is translated into institutional policy and practice in a manner commensurate with the needs of institutional security. This guarantee means procuring religious materials and making arrangements for the practice of religions other than that which is espoused by the chaplain.

Those who work in this ministry may be supported by either the state or the church, often by mutual arrangement (→ Church and State). In some cases the tendency now is toward short-term ministry, which is linked to a theological understanding of the work and relates it more closely to the church. The proportion of chaplains to prisoners varies in different countries.

Most states give prison workers a special legal status that protects them against being forced to reveal anything disclosed to them in confidence. A conflict often arises between their passive role as the recipients of confidences and the active role they are expected to play on behalf of prisoners.

2. Theological discussion of this ministry must interpret the phenomenon that nowhere are church and state so closely related as in a prison, and yet precisely here they are especially distinct. Although closely related to the penal institution from an early date, prison workers are an entity apart, since their work finds its specific meaning in rights and duties corresponding to the constitutional provisions that prisoners have unhampered access to pastoral care, that is, to individual interviews with workers and to participation in all the services that the church provides in prison.

This ministry, then, manifests the difference in principle between the claims of the state and the claim of God manifested as God's gracious approach in Jesus Christ. Here is the specific theological basis of the ministry. Gospel proclamation in the doctrine of → justification means that prisoners cannot be regarded as sinners of a unique or an especially wicked type. We can say, though, that their special situation demands a special ministry. Tension can sometimes arise between this central theological position and the attitude of some of those engaged in voluntary prison ministry.

3. In the United States, more so than in Europe, the situation is strongly characterized by the rise of → criminality because of social conflicts, especially problems of race and minorities that are reflected in the prison population and that increase the potential for aggression in prisons. Most U.S. → denominations do prison work; that of the Society of → Friends and the Presbyterians has been particularly noteworthy.

Although in general the United States makes a strict separation between church and state, the state finances church work in state institutions, including prisons, and the Federal Bureau of Prisons appoints chaplains who have received ecclesiastical endorsements from their respective denominations. The bureau also requires two years of prior experience as a senior or sole pastor. → Clinical Pastoral Education is encouraged but not required. The upper age limit for entering the service is 37; as a rule, chaplains remain in the service until they retire, though they may move from one prison to another.

By its own claim, Prison Fellowship International is the most extensive criminal-justice ministry in the world. The first national organization was begun in the United States in 1976 by Charles W. Colson (b. 1931), who had served time in prison as a result of his involvement in the Watergate scandal centering on the U.S. White House, where he was a counsel to the president. Shortly before the time of his imprisonment, Colson was converted to Christianity, and then after his release he dedicated his life to prison ministry. Prison Fellowship International, now found in 108 countries, pursues an evangelical and largely lay volunteer ministry "working for the spiritual, moral, social, and physical well being of prisoners, ex-prisoners, their families, crime victims, and criminal justice officials."

4. There have been various developments in penal law and penal practice during the last decades. A corresponding need has developed for international contacts and for exchanges of experiences in prison ministry. To this end the International Prison Chaplains' Association was formed at Bossey, Switzerland, in 1985. This group, with headquarters now in Ottawa, Canada, holds consultations on relevant matters in cooperation with the → World Council of Churches and with the → Lutheran World Federation.

→ Guilt; Punishment; Rehabilitation

Bibliography: C. W. Colson, *Life Sentence* (Grand Rapids, 1999; orig. pub., 1979) • J. L. Esposito, *What Everyone Needs to Know about Islam* (New York, 2002) • M. Gonzalez-Wippler, *Santeria: The Religion* (St. Paul, Minn., 1994) • J. Hick, *A Christian Theology of Religions* (Louisville, Ky., 1995) • T. P. O'Connor and N. J. Pallone, eds., *Religion, the Community, and the Rehabilitation of Criminal Offenders* (New York, 2002) • J. Opata, *Spiritual and Religious Diversity in Prisons: Focusing on How Chaplaincy Assists in Prison Management* (Springfield, Ill., 2001) • J. Paper, *Offering Smoke: The Sacred Pipe and Native American Criminal Conduct* (Moscow, Idaho, 1988) • G. D. Walters, *The Criminal Lifestyle: Patterns of Serious Criminal Conduct* (Newbury Park, N.Y., 1990).

Herbert Koch†, with Oliver Brown

Probabilism

Probabilism is the casuistic view that, in disputed moral issues, any course may be followed that is "solidly" probable. It is an attempt to answer a question of normative → ethics, namely, should a moral norm that is of dubious validity to → reason be binding on those to whom it is given? Roman Catholic → moral theology debated this question in the early → modern period. The context of the battle of contending schools as to the right answer was penitential → casuistry, as well as spiritual direction. At issue was the individual moral conviction that takes a norm seriously in a given situation.

Moral theologians in the → Middle Ages had recommended *tutorism* (i.e., that we should advocate independence of a norm only if the argument against following it is the surer position). → Nominalism deviated from this position and appealed to probability: → freedom from a norm is to be preferred when the freedom is more probable (hence the name *probabiliorism*) than subjection to the norm. Individual subjection or freedom was here of greater account than an objective order.

Probabilism, which was advocated from the 16th century onward, relied on the rationally grounded probability of freedom from a norm that is not absolutely binding. In 1577 in his commentary on → Thomas Aquinas's *Summa theologiae* (I of II, q. 18, art. 6), Bartolomé de Medina (1528-80), a Dominican of the Salamanca school, argued that if an opinion is probable, it is lawful to follow it. The contrary opinion might be more probable, but freedom is of greater account. The → Jesuits and → Dominicans took this view, for which the → Jansenists charged the Jesuits with *laxism*. Such a charge is hardly justifiable on theoretical grounds alone, for probabilism was designed to oppose the laxity of giving greater supremacy to freedom.

By decisions of the Roman → teaching office (DH 2101-65, 2303), probabilism carried the day. Protestantism, however, viewed the controversy less in terms of the logic on which these decisions rested than in term of the attacks of B. → Pascal (1623-62) in his *Provincial Letters*, where he took up the issue of → grace and freedom in opposition to presumably lax Jesuit morality (5th letter). As Pascal saw it, → salvation depends on the grace of God, and Jesuits were truncating the importance of grace by upholding a lax morality.

Protestant ethics (→ Social ethics) never took up this kind of issue, but it can raise some important questions. First, concerning the relation between freedom and obligation as regards moral norms: Must freedom and moral norms oriented to one's neighbor be alternatives? Second, for everyday problems of moral evaluation: Does the norm fit the situation? Third, the social problem of nonapplication (i.e., the issue of laxism): How far does ethical advice go in meeting the demands of social → power and influence? Finally, the matter of "costly grace" (D. → Bonhoeffer) and the relevance of the implied obligation: Does it extend to specific norms only, or to our total situation?

As regards the once-dominant practice of probabilism, it must be conceded that no norm can be followed literally in every situation. There is need not only of the alternative of freedom but also of flexible adjustment both to the good of one's neighbor and to *equiprobabilism* (i.e., where certainty is not possible, any equally probable course may be followed). The problem of probabilism can teach us that we can never leave out → conscience. Precisely in a social situation the individual conscience is still present. Integrity in interrelation with others is the true answer to the problem posed by probabilism. An example may be found in the counsel of → Paul in Rom. 14:1–15:6 that we should forgo freedom when it harms the conscience of others.

Bibliography: C. A. J. Coady, "Probabilism," *Philosophy of Religion* (Notre Dame, Ind., 1997) 16-33 • F. J. Connell, "Probabilism," *NCE* (2d ed.) 11.727 • T. Deman, "Probabilisme," *DTC* 13.417-619 • B. de Medina, *Expositio in D. Thomae Aquinatis I/II* (Salamanca, 1577) • B. Pascal, *The Provincial Letters* (trans. A. J. Krailsheimer; Baltimore, 1967; orig. pub., 1657) • A. Schmitt, *Zur Geschichte des Probabilismus* (vol. 1; Innsbruck, 1904).

Christofer Frey

Process Philosophy

The term "process philosophy" can be understood in a broader or narrower sense. In the broader sense, all philosophical positions holding that process or becoming is more fundamental than unchanging being are examples of process philosophy. In an anthology entitled *Philosophers of Process* (1965, ed. D. Browning), Samuel Alexander, Henri Bergson, John Dewey, Charles Hartshorne, William James, Lloyd Morgan, Charles Peirce, and Alfred North Whitehead are all included. Longer lists of process philosophers would include Heraclitus, G. W. F. Hegel, and P. Teilhard de Chardin. Lists not limited to the Western philosophical tradition might be much longer, including at least Buddhist and Taoist philosophies. In the narrower sense, however, "process philosophy" has come to refer to the movement inaugurated by Whitehead (1861-1947) and extended by Hartshorne (1897-2000). Process philosophy in this narrower sense is the subject of this essay.

1. The Task of Philosophy

Whiteheadian process philosophy is based on the conviction that the central task of → philosophy is to construct a cosmology in which all intuitions well grounded in human → experience can be reconciled. Cosmologies were traditionally based on religious, ethical, and aesthetic, as well as scientific, experiences, but cosmology in the modern period has increasingly been based on science alone. Process philosophers find this modern cosmology, which Whitehead called "scientific materialism," inadequate to those human intuitions that are usually called aesthetic, ethical, and religious. They are also inadequate to various commonsense beliefs that we cannot help presupposing in practice, such as the belief that our thoughts and actions are not wholly determined by antecedent causes (→ Freedom). Rather than explaining away such beliefs, Whitehead argued, philosophers should take them as the ultimate criteria of adequacy (*Process and Reality* [henceforth *P/R*], 151). The worldview of scientific → materialism is also seen to be inadequate for science itself. Although this inadequacy is most obvious in biology and psychology, Whitehead emphasized that the problem exists even for physics (*Science,* 16, 35, 66, 73).

Part and parcel of philosophy's task is its role as "the critic of abstractions." Those thinkers who formulate the basic concepts of some specialized discipline, such as physics or theology, have a tendency to exaggerate. These concepts must therefore be reformulated before they can be integrated into a self-consistent cosmology (*Science,* 18, 59, 87, 142). Because the abstractions formulated by natural scientists have been dominant in recent times, the primary critical task now is "to challenge the half-truths constituting the scientific first principles" (*P/R,* 10). At the root of these half-truths is usually the "fallacy of misplaced concreteness," in which certain abstract features of a concrete individual (an actual entity) are equated with the concrete individual itself, as if it were nothing but this set of abstractions. A molecule, for example, is taken to be nothing but the bundle of attributes described by physicists and chemists. This fallacy lies behind scientific materialism, according to which everything, including human experience, is to be explained in terms of the locomotion of bits of matter devoid of spontaneity, internal process, and intrinsic value (*Science,* 17, 50-51, 131). Process philosophy's remedy for this fallacy involves reconceiving the world's basic units as processes.

2. Two Kinds of Process

Whitehead himself did not employ the term "process philosophy." Yet it is a good term for summarizing his position, because he said that "an actual entity is a process," emphasizing that "the reality is the process" (*P/R,* 41; *Science,* 72). Although all process philosophies in the broad sense could agree with these statements, it is the particular interpretation given to them by Whitehead that constitutes the distinctiveness of Whiteheadian process philosophy. Central to this interpretation is the idea that the actual units making up the universe are momentary "occasions of experience" that involve *two* kinds of process.

Partly through the influence of quantum physics, Whitehead conceived of the most fundamental units of the world — the most *fully* actual entities — not as enduring individuals but as momentary events. He called them, accordingly, actual *occasions.* Individuals that endure through time, such as electrons, molecules, and minds, are "temporally ordered societies" of these momentary occasions. All actual occasions are extended both spatially and temporally (*P/R,* 77). Their temporal extensiveness means that they cannot exist at an "instant," understood in the technical sense as a durationless slice of time. Just as it takes time for a musical note to exist, it takes time to be an actual entity. Each actual occasion constitutes, as Henri Bergson had suggested, a more or less brief duration — from perhaps less than a billionth of a second for a subatomic event to perhaps a tenth of a second for an event of human experience.

The idea that an actual entity is an actual occasion provides the basis for thinking of two kinds of process: a process *within* an actual occasion, called "concrescence" (because it involves moving from potentiality to concreteness), and a process *between* actual occasions, called "transition." These two kinds of process correlate with the two basic kinds of causation (→ Causality). Science-based philosophy in modern times has tended to speak exclusively of *efficient* causation, meaning the causal influence of one thing upon another. Causation in this sense refers to the transition from one actual occasion (or one group of actual occasions) to another actual occasion (or another group of actual occasions). But if this were the only kind of causation, all events in the world would be fully determined by antecedent events, which is the conclusion of most science-based philosophy. For Whiteheadian process philosophy, however, the second kind of process — the process within an actual entity in which it moves from potentiality to fully determinate concreteness — involves *final* causation, in the sense of self-determination.

Through this distinction between two kinds of process, Whitehead sought to fulfill what he called one of philosophy's central tasks, namely, "to exhibit final and efficient causes in their proper relation to each other" (*P/R,* 150, 84). Every actual occasion begins by receiving efficient causation from prior actual occasions; it then completes itself by exercising final causation, understood as self-determination; and then it exercises efficient causation upon subsequent occasions. The temporal process involves, in other words, a perpetual oscillation between these two kinds of process and hence between efficient and final causation. (The expression "perpetual oscillation" brings out Whitehead's point more clearly than his own expression "perpetual perishing," which has led to perpetual confusion!)

3. Panexperientialism and the Mind-Body Relation

As the doctrine that all actual entities are actual occasions shows, Whitehead rejected Cartesian dualism (→ Cartesianism), according to which there are two kinds of actual entities. Whiteheadian process philosophy is in this respect on the side of materialism, because they both affirm that, whereas the world consists of a plurality of actual entities, they are all of the same ontological type. But Whitehead's version of pluralistic monism avoids materialism's reductionistic conclusions. Whitehead's doctrine that each actual entity has an internal process of self-determination avoids, as we have seen, materialism's determinism.

This doctrine is in turn a dimension of the larger doctrine that every actual entity is an occasion of experience (*P/R,* 29, 167, 189). With this position, Whiteheadian process philosophy rejects the central feature of Cartesian dualism, namely, the difference between actual entities with experience (Cartesian "minds") and actual entities without experience (Cartesian "bodies"). Materialists also reject this distinction, but by denying the existence of minds (i.e., actual entities whose essence is experience). Materialism's way of overcoming dualism leads to the self-refuting idea that experience — including the conscious experience of the materialist philosopher articulating this doctrine — is a purely epiphenomenal by-product, being itself devoid of agency.

Whiteheadian process philosophy avoids both → dualism and materialism by rejecting the existence of "vacuous actualities," meaning things that are fully actual and yet wholly void of experience. This rejection is expressed positively by defining all actual occasions as occasions of experience. This doctrine means, with regard to the internal process of concrescence, that "process is the becoming of experience" (*P/R,* 166). This doctrine does not mean, however, that all actual entities are conscious. Unlike Descartes, Whitehead does not equate consciousness and experience but instead regards consciousness as a very high form of experience, which is attained by relatively few actual occasions.

Although "panpsychism" has been the customary name for philosophies of this sort, "panexperientialism" is a better term. One problem with the former term is that, being rooted in "psyche," it suggests experience that is too sophisticated to attribute to atoms or even living cells. Because of this same linguistic root, the term "panpsychism" also suggests that the ultimate units endure through time, rather than being momentary experiences.

The chief criticism of panpsychism, however, has been that it seems to entail that literally all things, including rocks and stars, are conscious. In relation to this criticism, the switch to the term "panexperientialism" would by itself help only a little because this term would still seem to entail that rocks and stars have experience of some sort, which is counterintuitive, even if that experience is not said to rise to the level of consciousness. In process philosophy's version of panexperientialism, however, the prefix "pan" does not refer to all things whatsoever but only to all genuine individuals. Animals, living cells, atoms, and even electrons enjoy a unified experience, but stars, rocks, and computers do not. A unified experience is attributed only to things whose behavior suggests self-determination and hence direction by a center of experience. This distinction is central to process philosophy's solution to the mind-body problem.

Panexperientialists, like materialists, consider insoluble the problem of dualistic interaction: How could mind and brain cells, understood as actualities of ontologically different types, interact? Materialism seeks to avoid this problem by its doctrine of "identism," according to which what we call "the mind" is somehow identical with the brain. There are not, therefore, two things that must interact. But materialists still face the problem — which some now admit to be insoluble — of how conscious experience could arise out of insentient neurons. Materialists also cannot do justice to freedom — to the assumption, which we all presuppose in practice, that our experience, rather than being totally determined by antecedent causes, is partly self-determining.

Whiteheadian process philosophy suggests, on the basis of its panexperientialism, a "nondualistic interactionism" that can avoid the problems of both dualism and materialism. It agrees with dualism that the mind and the brain are numerically distinct. That is, the mind is one thing, and the brain is another thing. More precisely, the mind is a temporally ordered society of very high-level occasions of experience. As such, the mind at any given moment is an individual with power to exercise self-determination. We need not consider our feeling of freedom — the feeling that we make real choices between alternative possibilities — to be an illusion.

But this numerical distinction between the mind and the brain does not mean an ontological dualism, which would make it impossible for our free decisions to affect our bodies. Panexperientialism allows for a nondualistic interactionism because each brain cell is also a temporally ordered society of occasions of (much lower-level) experience. This doctrine removes the main obstacle to understanding how our experiences could interact with our brain cells (D. Griffin, *Unsnarling the World-Knot*).

4. Perception and Prehension

Another distinctive feature of Whiteheadian process philosophy is its challenge to the "sensationalist" doctrine of perception, according to which all knowledge of the world beyond the mind comes through sensory perception. This doctrine rules out the possibility of genuine moral and religious experience. It has also made it impossible to explain how we have knowledge of mathematical and logical principles. It has also, insofar as philosophers have accepted Hume's analysis of the content of sensory perception, led to → solipsism and the denial that we have any perceptual experience of efficient causation. These and related problems led to Kant's → idealism, according to which such categories, being derived from a priori structures of the mind rather than from perception, could apply only to appearances, not to the actual world itself.

Whitehead avoided this counterintuitive conclusion by rejecting the sensationalist doctrine of perception. More fundamental than sensory perception is a nonsensory mode of perception called "prehension," which may or may not be conscious (*Science,* 41, 68-69). One example, which we call "memory," occurs when a present occasion of experience directly perceives occasions of experience in its own past. We do not see, hear, or touch our prior moments of experience, but we do perceive them. The doctrine that the mind is really a temporal society of distinct occasions of experience, each of which is an actual entity, helps us recognize that memory is simply a special form of perception.

Another instance of nonsensory perception, or prehension, is the mind's direct reception of influences from its brain. Sensory perception presupposes this nonsensory perception. For example, when I see a tree by means of my eyes, vast chains of causal transmissions are involved. There are the billions of photons that bring data from the tree to my eyes. Then there are the billions of firings in my optic nerves that transmit the data to my brain. But for me — my experience, my mind — to receive these data, my mind must prehend my brain cells. I do not see, touch, or hear my brain cells. But I do perceive the data that they have received from the external world. In this way, sensory perception presupposes nonsensory perception.

This direct prehension of other actualities is also called "perception in the mode of causal efficacy" because it provides the experiential basis, denied by Hume, for our idea of causation as real influence. In prehending the causal efficacy of prior actualities for our own experience, we are thereby directly aware of other actualities and the past. This mode of perception explains why no one in practice is afflicted by solipsism, let alone what George Santayana called "solipsism of the present moment."

5. Reconciling Science and Religion

As shown by the fact that the second book of Whitehead's metaphysical period was on religion (1926), he was very interested in using his philosophical position to show how science and → religion could be reconciled. He said, in fact, that the task through which philosophy "attains its chief importance" is that of fusing science and religion "into one rational scheme of thought" (*P/R,* 15).

Whitehead's doctrine of nonsensory perception is crucial to this task. The sensationalist doctrine of perception, by saying that all perception of things other than ourselves is rooted in our physical senses, had led modern thought to the denial that there can be any genuine religious experience, in the sense of a direct perception of a divine or holy Actuality. It has been widely argued, accordingly, that philosophy need not reconcile science-based knowledge with knowledge rooted in religious experience, simply because there is no knowledge of the latter sort. By replacing this sensationalist doctrine of perception with one in which nonsensory prehension is fundamental, process philosophy can regard religious experience as a source of important knowledge. It can do so, furthermore, without regarding religious experience as rooted in some special faculty or a priori category of the mind. It is rooted in the same mode of perception through which we know about causation, the past, mathematics, logical principles, and moral norms.

Whitehead's prehension-based doctrine of perception is simply one part of process philosophy's new version of naturalism, one intended to be adequate for religious as well as scientific purposes. The fact that there can be such a form of naturalism has been obscured by the tendency to equate naturalism with an atheistic, materialistic worldview. Naturalism in the most fundamental sense, however, is simply the rejection of supernaturalism understood as a position that allows the world's normal causal processes to be occasionally interrupted by a supernatural deity. Naturalism in this sense can be called naturalism$_{ns}$ (*ns* = *n*on-*s*upernaturalist). Naturalism in this generic or minimal sense is compatible with a religious, even a theistic, worldview. Because of contingent historical developments, however, when naturalism$_{ns}$ emerged in the 18th and 19th centuries, it came embodied in a worldview that can be called naturalism$_{sam}$ (*sam* = *s*ensationalist, *a*theist, and *m*aterialist). In process philosophy, however, naturalism$_{ns}$ is embodied in a worldview that can be called naturalism$_{ppp}$ (*ppp* = *p*rehensive doctrine of perception, *p*anentheistic doctrine of reality as a whole, and *p*anexperientialist doctrine of nature in general and the mind-body relation in particular; Griffin, *Reenchantment* and *Religion*).

Of these three dimensions of naturalism$_{ppp}$, it is the one not yet discussed, → panentheism, in which naturalism$_{ns}$ is especially embodied. Panentheism (the doctrine that the world is *in* God) differs from → pantheism ("the world is divine") in saying that God is distinct from the world and interacts with it, analogously to the way the mind interacts with its body. In distinguishing God from the world and saying that God acts in the world, process panentheism agrees with traditional → theism. It differs from the latter, however, by saying that it belongs to the very identity of God to be in relation to a world, in the sense of a realm of finite beings. Process philosophy's panentheism, in other words, rejects the doctrine of creatio ex nihilo, in which the *nihil* has been understood to mean "nothing" in the absolute sense, a complete lack of finite entities. The → creation of our world involved, instead, bringing about a new kind of order in the world, in the sense of the realm of finite beings (*P/R,* 95-96). So, although God has always existed in relation to *some* realm of finite actualities, our particular world — our "cosmic epoch" — is contingent.

This distinction leads to a different understanding of divine power. The doctrine of creatio ex nihilo, by making the very existence of finite actuality dependent on the divine will, said that the world's creatures have no inherent power. This doctrine provided the undergirding for a doctrine of absolute divine omnipotence, according to which events in the world can be totally determined by God. Although, according to this view, most events happen according to the world's normal causal principles, these principles, having been freely ordained, can be freely interrupted. In denying this doctrine of creatio ex nihilo, process philosophy says that finite actual entities have inherent power, which cannot be occasionally overruled. This inherent power, called "creativity," is the twofold power of every event, discussed above, to exert self-determination and then to exert efficient causation on other events. Although there is divine causation on every event, this divine causation is always a normal part of the world's causal processes, never an interruption thereof (Griffin, *Reenchantment*).

As stated earlier, the task of reconciling science and religion involves overcoming exaggerations from both sides. The main exaggerations from the side of science-based thought have been the sensationism, → atheism, and materialism of naturalism$_{sam}$. From the side of religion, the main exaggeration has been the doctrine of divine omnipotence undergirded by the idea of creatio ex nihilo. By rejecting this doctrine of divine power, process philosophy has overcome the theological exaggeration that put traditional theism into conflict with naturalism$_{ns}$, which is properly presupposed by the scientific community.

This same modification also overcomes the other main reason for the widespread rejection of traditional theism in intellectual circles: the problem of → evil. According to traditional theism, divine power is controlling power, which either controls all things or at least could do so. This doctrine implies that every event we consider evil, from the rape of a child to a genocidal → holocaust, was caused or at least allowed by God. Process theists agree with atheists that this implication of traditional theism has made a plausible → theodicy impossible. According to process philosophy's panentheism, by contrast, divine power is a persuasive, rather than coercive, controlling power (Whitehead, *Adventures*, 166-69; *P/R*, 190). This persuasive power is ultimately the most effective power there is. It has brought about our universe, which now includes beings with the power to ask philosophical questions. But although this divine power influences all events, it can unilaterally determine no event because the creatures have power of their own that cannot be overridden. The vast evils of our world do not, accordingly, contradict the goodness of its creator (Griffin, *Evil; God;* Hartshorne, *Omnipotence*).

6. Development and Influence

Although Whitehead was one of the first philosophers to be included in the Library of Living Philosophers series (P. Schilpp), his philosophy was largely ignored in the three decades subsequent to its articulation, partly because of the turn to antimetaphysical forms of philosophy. Another factor was that, even within circles still interested in developing a naturalistic cosmology, Whitehead's panexperientialism, naturalistic theism, and acceptance of nonsensory perception were felt to exceed the limits of a proper naturalism, which was largely equated with materialism. The most prominent advocate of Whiteheadian process philosophy in the following decades, furthermore, was Hartshorne, whose focus on the idea of God, while creating interest in theological faculties, reinforced suspicions in philosophical circles.

Around 1960, however, a spate of books on Whitehead's philosophy inaugurated a period of greater interest, the best being Victor Lowe's *Understanding Whitehead.* Soon there were several excellent collections of essays (I. Leclerc; G. Kline; Hartshorne, *Whitehead's Philosophy*) and monographs (E. Kraus) on Whitehead's philosophy. In 1971 the journal *Process Studies* was created for the purpose of furthering the study and development of process thinking, and in 1973 a new institution, the Center for Process Studies, was established in Claremont, California, for the purpose of promoting the exploration of the relevance of Whiteheadian process thought in the various disciplines. In 1991 a volume devoted to the philosophy of Hartshorne appeared in the Library of Living Philosophers series (L. E. Hahn).

For several decades the major influence of process philosophy was in philosophy of religion and theology (J. Cobb, *Natural Theology;* S. Ogden), and this influence has continued, with special attention being given to the relation between science and religion (I. Barbour, *Issues; Religion*). More recently, interest in the relevance of Whiteheadian process philosophy for science as such, especially physics, has greatly increased (T. Eastman and H. Keeton; M. Epperson). Other areas in which it has had growing influence include religious → pluralism (Cobb, *Beyond Dialogue;* M. Suchocki), ecological → ethics (Cobb, *Is It Too Late?* C. Birch), and the philosophy of → education (G. Allan).

→ Process Theology; Science and Theology

Bibliography: G. Allan, *Higher Education in the Making: Pragmatism, Whitehead, and the Canon* (Albany, N.Y., 2004) • I. Barbour, *Issues in Science and Religion* (Englewood Cliffs, N.J., 1996); idem, *Religion in an Age of Science* (San Francisco, 1990) • C. Birch, *Regaining Compassion for Humanity and Nature* (Kensington, Austral., 1993) • D. Browning, ed., *Philosophers of Process* (New York, 1965) • J. Cobb, *Beyond Dialogue: Toward a Mutual Transformation of Buddhism and Christianity* (Philadelphia, 1982); idem, *A Christian Natural Theology: Based on the Thought of Alfred North Whitehead* (Philadelphia, 1965); idem, *Is It Too Late? A Theology of Ecology* (Beverly Hills, Calif., 1972) • T. Eastman and H. Keeton, *Physics and Whitehead: Quantum, Process, and Experience* (Albany, N.Y., 2004) • M. Epperson, *Quantum Mechanics and the Philosophy of Alfred North Whitehead* (New York, 2004) • D. R. Griffin, *Evil Revisited: Responses and Reconsiderations* (Albany, N.Y., 1991); idem, *God, Power, and Evil: A Process Theodicy* (Philadelphia, 1976); idem, *Reenchantment without Supernaturalism: A Process Philosophy of Religion* (Ithaca, N.Y., 2001); idem, *Religion and Scientific Naturalism: Overcoming the Conflicts* (Albany, N.Y., 2000); idem, *Unsnarling the World-Knot: Consciousness, Freedom, and the Mind-Body Problem* (Los Angeles, 1998) • L. E. Hahn, ed., *The Philosophy of*

Charles Hartshorne (LaSalle, Ill., 1991) • C. Hartshorne, *Omnipotence and Other Theological Mistakes* (Albany, N.Y., 1984); idem, *Whitehead's Philosophy: Selected Essays, 1935-1970* (Lincoln, Nebr., 1972) • G. Kline, *Alfred North Whitehead: Essays on His Philosophy* (Englewood Cliffs, N.J., 1963) • E. Kraus, *The Metaphysics of Experience: A Companion to Whitehead's Process and Reality* (New York, 1979) • I. Leclerc, ed., *The Relevance of Whitehead: Philosophical Essays in Commemoration of the Centenary of the Birth of Alfred North Whitehead* (New York, 1961) • V. Lowe, *Understanding Whitehead* (Baltimore, 1962) • S. Ogden, *The Reality of God, and Other Essays* (New York, 1966) • P. Schilpp, ed., *The Philosophy of Alfred North Whitehead* (LaSalle, Ill., 1941) • M. Suchocki, *Divinity and Diversity: A Christian Affirmation of Religious Pluralism* (Nashville, 2003) • A. N. Whitehead, *Adventures of Ideas* (New York, 1967; orig. pub., 1933); idem, *Process and Reality* (corr. ed.; ed. D. Griffin and D. Sherburne; New York, 1978; orig. pub., 1929); idem, *Religion in the Making* (New York, 1996; orig. pub., 1926); idem, *Science and the Modern World* (New York, 1967; orig. pub., 1925).

David Ray Griffin

Process Theology

1. Whitehead and Hartshorne
2. Process Theology as Philosophical Theology
   - 2.1. Divine Dipolarity and Perfection
   - 2.2. Naturalistic Theism and the Problem of Evil
   - 2.3. Creation and Evolution
   - 2.4. Religious Pluralism
   - 2.5. Ecological and Feminist Theology
3. Process Theology as Distinctively Christian Theology
   - 3.1. God as Trinitarian
   - 3.2. Incarnational Christology
   - 3.3. Salvation

1. Whitehead and Hartshorne

Although the label "process theology" is sometimes used more broadly, it usually refers more specifically to the theological movement based primarily on the → "process philosophy" of Alfred North Whitehead (1861-1947) and Charles Hartshorne (1897-2000). Process theology in this more specific sense is in view here.

Whitehead, after having focused on mathematics and the → philosophy of nature in his native England, came in 1924 to Harvard University, where he began developing his metaphysical cosmology. In *Science and the Modern World* (1925), he argued that cosmology should be based on our aesthetic, ethical, and religious intuitions, as well as on science. He also argued that developments in science itself were pointing away from mechanistic → materialism toward an organismic → worldview. This new worldview led Whitehead, who had earlier been agnostic, to an affirmation, in order to explain the world's order, of the existence of God, understood as the "principle of limitation." In later books — especially *Religion in the Making* (1926), *Process and Reality* (1929), and *Adventures of Ideas* (1933) — Whitehead developed his idea of God far beyond this suggestion of an impersonal principle.

Hartshorne had developed his own philosophical theology before coming under Whitehead's influence as a postdoctoral research fellow at Harvard from 1925 to 1928, during which he served as Whitehead's assistant. But Hartshorne then adopted most of Whitehead's position, although he maintained his own emphases and even differed with Whitehead on some issues (L. Ford). Hartshorne has given special attention to the idea of God and to arguments for the existence of God, most thoroughly in *The Divine Relativity* (1948) and *Man's Vision of God* (1941), most popularly in *Omnipotence and Other Theological Mistakes* (1984). His overall theistic → metaphysics is expressed most comprehensively in *Reality as Social Process* (1953) and *Creative Synthesis and Philosophic Method* (1970).

Because of its employment of Whiteheadian-Hartshornean process philosophy, process theology is one of the few contemporary types of theology to be grounded in a metaphysical position in which → theism is defended philosophically and science and religion are included within the same scheme of thought. The basic ideas of Whiteheadian "process philosophy" are explained in the article of that title in this volume. Although some of these basic ideas, such as → "panentheism," are discussed here, others, such as "panexperientialism" and "prehensive perception," are simply presupposed in the present article, which summarizes some of the ways in which process theologians employ these basic ideas. We first consider process theology as a natural or philosophical theology (see 2), then as a specifically Christian theology (see 3).

2. Process Theology as Philosophical Theology

Insofar as process theology is an approach shared by theologians of several religious traditions, it is a *natural* theology in the sense of a *philosophical* theology, developing positions that can in principle be accepted by members of many religious traditions. Five of its dimensions are discussed in this section.

2.1. *Divine Dipolarity and Perfection*

One distinctive feature of process theology is its doctrine of divine dipolarity, which contrasts with traditional views of divine "simplicity." Process theology has, in fact, two dipolarities, one emphasized more by Whitehead, the other more by Hartshorne. Whitehead, who distinguished between the "primordial nature" and the "consequent nature" of God, thereby emphasized the distinction between God as influencing the world and God as influenced by the world. The primordial nature is God's influence on the world in terms of an appetitive envisagement of the primordial potentialities ("eternal objects") for finite realization. This is God as the divine Eros, who lures the world forward with a vision of novel possibilities. The consequent nature is God as affected by and responsive to the world.

The second dipolarity, emphasized by Hartshorne's distinction between God's "abstract essence" and "concrete states," is a distinction between God as unchanging and God as changing. God's abstract essence has most of the attributes given to God as a whole by classical theism — immutability, impassibility, eternity, and independence — leading Hartshorne to refer to his doctrine as neoclassical theism (Hartshorne, *Logic*). But this immutable essence is a mere abstraction from God. God as concrete is, for Hartshorne as for Whitehead, God as interacting creatively and responsively with the world.

Whereas classical theism, following → Greek philosophy, equates → perfection with completeness and therefore immutability, Hartshorne argues that we must think of God in terms of two kinds of perfection. God's abstract essence exemplifies the unchanging type of perfection. For example, to say that God is omniscient is to say that God always knows everything knowable; this abstract feature of God does not change. But God's concrete knowledge does change because, given the ultimate reality of process, new things are always happening and thereby becoming knowable. God's concrete states thereby exemplify the relative type of perfection, a perfection that can be surpassed. God in one moment is surpassable by no creature but only by God in a later moment. The same distinction can be made with regard to other attributes. For example, God at every moment loves all creatures perfectly, wishing them all well and feeling their experiences sympathetically — suffering with their pains, rejoicing with their joys. To say that God grows is not to affirm that God becomes wiser or more loving but only that, as new creatures arise and new experiences occur, the objects of the divine love have increased; in that sense the divine experience has been enriched.

2.2. *Naturalistic Theism and the Problem of Evil*

Process theism is a naturalistic theism. It is naturalistic, not in the sense of equating God with "nature" or otherwise denying distinct agency to God, but simply in the sense of rejecting supernaturalism, understood as the doctrine of a divine being that can interrupt the world's normal causal principles. This rejection is rooted in process theology's view of the relation of God to being itself, which it renames "creativity" to reflect the fact that that which all beings embody is not passive stuff but dynamic energy. → Creativity, more precisely, is each actuality's twofold power to exercise a modicum of self-determination (final causation) and then to exert influence (efficient causation) on future actualities. Traditional theism, with its (ontotheological) equation of God with being itself, said that this twofold power is essentially embodied in God alone. Because any power possessed by creatures was a gift, the normal causal patterns among creatures could be interrupted at any time. This position was fully enunciated only with the postbiblical development of the doctrine of → creation ex nihilo.

Process theologians return to the view, common to Plato, the Bible, and Christian thinkers before the end of the second century, that our universe was created by God's bringing a particular type of order out of chaos (C. Keller, *Face of the Deep*). For process theologians an essential implication of this idea is that creative power is essentially embodied in a world of finite actualities, as well as in the divine actuality. The divine power, accordingly, is necessarily persuasive; it could not be coercive in the sense of unilaterally determining what happens in the world. This view of the God-world relation thus reconciles theism with the scientific community's naturalistic assumption that no events, however extraordinary, involve violations of the world's basic causal principles (D. Griffin, *Two Great Truths*).

To emphasize the idea that the world is both intimately related to, and yet distinct from, God, process theologians sometimes, with Hartshorne, refer to their position as panentheism. This term, which means that *all (finite) things are in God,* signals process theism's difference from traditional theism's insistence that God could (and perhaps once upon a time did) exist all alone, without a world of finite actualities. The term "panentheism" emphasizes the idea that the existence of a world is internal to God — that it belongs to the very nature of God to be in relation to a world. What exists necessarily is not simply God but God-with-a-world. In contrast with pantheism, however, panentheism says that both God and the world have their own creativity, their own power, so that the evils in the world do not betoken → evil or even imperfection in God (Griffin, "Panentheism").

This view also provides the basis for a → theodicy that defends the perfect goodness of our creator without minimizing the evil of our world. The distinction between God and creativity provides, in fact, the basis for a robust doctrine of demonic evil, with the basic idea being that God's creation of human beings brought into existence a level of worldly creativity that not only could become diametrically opposed to the divine creativity but also could do so with sufficient power to threaten divine purposes (Griffin, *Evil*). This doctrine of the demonic is simply an extreme implication of the more general point: God's power is misconstrued if it is thought to be all-controlling power. Against traditional all-determining theism, affirmed by → Augustine, → Thomas Aquinas, Martin → Luther, and John → Calvin, process theologians deny that God determines everything that happens in the world. And against traditional free-will theologians, process theologians deny that God *could* control all events but refuses to prevent evil in order to leave room for human → freedom.

Process theologians say, instead, that the creation has its own creativity and hence its own inherent power. Also, in bringing forth more complex creatures, such as multicelled animals and especially human beings, God necessarily brought forth creatures with more creativity and hence more of the twofold power to exercise self-determination and causal influence on others. These higher creatures are, accordingly, necessarily more dangerous. Even God cannot have the greater good without the risk of the greater evil. Given this view of the God-world relation, the realization that our world is filled with horrendous evils need not lead to → atheism.

2.3. *Creation and Evolution*

The insistence that God does not have coercive, controlling power does not mean, however, that God does not act creatively and providentially in the world. God is the creator of our world. Both the novelty in and the directionality of the evolutionary process, through which our present world was created out of a chaotic state involving nothing but extremely trivial events, are explained through God's creative-providential activity.

One key to Whitehead's reconciliation of creation and → evolution is his rejection of the materialistic, mechanistic view of nature, according to which it is composed of bits of matter that can be affected only externally by other bits of matter. Rather, with his panexperientialism, he portrays the ultimate units of nature as experiential events, each of which "prehends" other events, taking influences from them into itself. Each unitary event prehends, thereby being internally constituted by, influences from everything in its environment. Given a panentheistic worldview, this environment includes not only other finite events but also the all-pervasive influence of God. This divine influence is the source of both the order and the ever-arising novelty in the world. Because different forms of novelty are relevant in different events, this divine influence is variable in content. But this variable divine influence does not contradict the idea that process theism is naturalistic because this divine influence, with its variableness, is a natural part of the normal causal processes of the world, never an interruption of them. The widespread assumption among evolutionists that naturalism requires atheism, or at least → deism, is shown to be untrue. Naturalism is fully compatible with panentheism.

From this perspective, there is no reason to accept the neo-Darwinian assumption that the evolutionary process must have proceeded without any cosmic directivity. Process theologians agree with the main Darwinian point that no species has been created ex nihilo. But they do not accept the much stronger claim that new species arise purely from the combined effect of random variations and natural selection, which amounts to the claim that the direction of the evolutionary process is explainable without appeal to any nonlocal influence. Given a naturalistic theism in which divine influence involves the suggestion of possible new forms of existence, which operate as "attractors," we can understand why evolution (evidently) proceeded by means of a series of leaps, rather than very tiny steps (as neo-Darwinism requires), and why the process has led, at least in some lines, to increasingly greater complexity, which produces increasingly richer forms of experience (Griffin, *Religion,* chap. 8).

2.4. *Religious Pluralism*

The distinction between God and creativity has also been employed by process theologians to develop a version of religious → pluralism that can regard theistic and nontheistic religious experiences as equally veridical. Theistic religious experience, which leads the experiencers to think of ultimate reality as a personal being who loves the world, is an experience of God. Nontheistic religious experience, insofar as it leads some Hindus to speak of "nirguna

Brahman" and some Buddhists to speak of "emptiness," is an experience of creativity. This position means giving up the old idea that there is only one ultimate reality. Process theologians speak, instead, of God as the *personal* ultimate and of creativity as the *impersonal* ultimate.

This more pluralistic view of ideas about ultimate reality is correlated with a more pluralistic idea of → salvation. Rather than holding, as do many pluralists, that the various religions promote basically the same kind of salvation, Whiteheadians argue that different religions promote different types of salvation, or different types of "wholeness" (J. Cobb, *Beyond Dialogue; Transforming Christianity;* M. Suchocki, *Divinity;* Griffin, *Deep*).

2.5. *Ecological and Feminist Theology*

One of the features of process theology that has made it especially attractive to many people in recent decades is that it provides the basis for a deeply ecological theology (→ Ecology). Given its panexperientialism, it rejects the traditional and early modern dualism between humanity and nature, which assigned intrinsic value only to human beings. According to process theology, all genuine individuals have intrinsic value, meaning value for themselves. God did not, anthropocentrists to the contrary, create "nature" simply as a backdrop for the divine-human drama, and certainly not for human plunder. God cherishes individuals of each kind for their own sakes. However, unlike egalitarian versions of deep ecology, process theology does not say that all individuals have the same degree of intrinsic value. A chimpanzee has more intrinsic value than a microbe, a human more than a chimpanzee. A basis is thereby provided for discriminating value judgments (C. Birch, *Regaining Compassion;* Cobb, *Is It Too Late?* Birch and Cobb; J. McDaniel).

In spite of its affirmation of a hierarchy of intrinsic values, however, process theology has a way of recognizing an element of truth in the egalitarian idea that all things have equal value. Besides intrinsic value, all things also have extrinsic value, a very important dimension of which is their value for sustaining the ecological system. And those things with the most intrinsic value generally have the least ecological value. So, when we consider the *total* value of each species, we can say that, roughly speaking, all things have equal value. Recognition of the hierarchy of intrinsic value therefore does not lead to the conclusion that species with less intrinsic value should be eliminated to make room for increased populations of those with greater intrinsic value. With its dual emphasis on intrinsic and extrinsic value, process theology reinforces respect and care both for individual animals (the respect that lies behind the humane society and the animal liberation movement) and for the ecological system as a whole (the respect that inspires deep ecologists and the earth liberation movement; Griffin, "Whitehead's Deeply Ecological Worldview").

Many features of process theology have made it attractive to feminist theologians. As illustrated by the writings of Catherine Keller, Nancy Howell, and Carol Christ, these features include process theology's emphasis on internal relations, its view that divine power is persuasive rather than coercive, and its conviction that the divine reality responds to and includes the world — all of which cuts against portraying the divine and the human in stereotypically masculine terms. The fact that process theology provides support for feminist concerns is arguably one of its most important features. Process theologian John Cobb, for example, has said that "culturally and intellectually, the most important movement of the twentieth century may prove to have been feminism" (Cobb, *Postmodernism,* 80). In any case, given the point of the prior paragraph, the form of feminism that process theology supports most strongly is ecofeminism (→ Feminist Theology).

3. Process Theology as Distinctively Christian Theology

To date, most, but not all, process theologians have been Christians. Although they typically spend much of their time on the philosophical doctrines of process theology, they also use those doctrines to deal with distinctively Christian themes. This side of Christian process theology will be illustrated with its treatment of trinitarianism (→ Trinity), → Christology, and salvation.

3.1. *God as Trinitarian*

The idea that God both affects the world and is responsive to the world is sometimes made in terms of a distinction between God's "creative love" and God's "responsive love" (Cobb and Griffin). With this distinction, we would have only a binitarian, not a trinitarian, doctrine. But process theology, besides distinguishing between God and creativity, also says that God is the primordial embodiment of creativity. We must distinguish, in other words, between creativity as embodied in God (divine creativity) and creativity as embodied in the world (creaturely creativity). The former differs from the latter by virtue of always being perfectly qualified by creative and responsive love. In other words, God's outgoing creativity is always aimed at promoting the greatest possible good for the creatures, while God's responsive creativity is always characterized by perfect compassion for the creatures. The divine threefoldness can hence be understood as consisting of divine creativity, creative love, and responsive love.

Besides suggesting such an "immanent" trinitarianism, according to which God is internally threefold, process theology also suggests an "economic" trinitarianism, according to which there is a threefoldness in the way in which God is manifest in the world. One economic trinity endorsed by process theologians focuses on God as creator, redeeming revealer, and sanctifier. According to the Nicene Creed, the divine reality that was incarnate in Jesus is as fully divine as the world's creator. The Council of Constantinople (381) extended this point to the Holy Spirit (→ Niceno-Constantinopolitan Creed). Christian process theologians can interpret these affirmations to mean that the way God as → Holy Spirit acts in relation to human experience generally — by persuasion — is the same way in which God acted in creating the world and in becoming revealingly incarnate in Jesus (Griffin, *Two Great Truths*).

3.2. *Incarnational Christology*

Having already discussed creation through persuasion, we will here discuss how God, working persuasively, could have been present in Jesus in a way that makes it appropriate for Christians to continue looking to him for their basic clue about the character of our creator.

Given process philosophy's understanding of causation and perception, this kind of → incarnation could have resulted from Jesus' experience of (his prehensions of) God's influence on him. Causation between two (experiencing) individuals does not involve an external relation, like the impact of one billiard ball on another, but involves an internal relation, in which the cause enters into the effect. Whitehead said that his philosophy "is mainly devoted to the task of making clear the notion of 'being present in another entity'" (*Process and Reality,* 50). In application to God, this point means that because God influences all events, God is present in all events. Whitehead even said that "the world lives by its incarnation of God in itself" (*Religion,* 156). Within this framework, then, there is no problem of understanding how God could have been incarnate in Jesus. The only question is how God could have been present in such a way as to make Jesus a decisive revelation of God.

Process theology can answer this question in terms of five points. First, God always presents initial aims toward the best possibilities open to the individual, given that individual's past history and present situation. These initial aims constitute prevenient → grace. Second, the best possibilities for different individuals can differ radically. For example, the best possibilities for a human being differ radically from the best possibilities for electrons or mice, and the best possibilities for a first-century Jew differed greatly from the best possibilities open to a Buddhist in India at the same time. The nature of the divine aims and therefore the prevenient grace for different individuals will thus differ radically. Third, the aims for some individuals will reflect the general divine aim more directly than the aims for other individuals. Fourth, assuming that the history of Israel, including especially the messages of the prophets, involved genuine revelation of the divine will, a devout person such as → Jesus, growing up in that tradition, would be well suited to receive divine aims highly reflective of the general aim of God for the world, especially the human world. Fifth, we can understand Jesus as one in whom God was incarnate in such a way that it is appropriate for us to apprehend Jesus as a decisive revelation of God's character, purpose, and mode of operation (Cobb, *Christ;* Cobb and Griffin).

3.3. *Salvation*

The good news proclaimed by Jesus evidently involved salvation in a threefold sense. His message revolved around the idea of a reign of God on earth, in which, as the prayer he taught his disciples said, God's will would be done on earth. This result would mean, among other things, that everyone would have their "daily bread." Jesus also referred to salvation in a life beyond bodily death. And Jesus presupposed, third, that our present life is everlastingly meaningful because it is known by God. Process theologians can affirm all three of these dimensions.

With regard to the third dimension, the doctrine of God's responsive love means that our present activities are received into God with compassion and remembered everlastingly. The threat of meaninglessness posed by modern atheism is hence overcome. All process theologians affirm salvation in this sense. Indeed, because some process theologians have, following Hartshorne, affirmed salvation only in this sense (S. Ogden), it is sometimes thought that this is the only sense in which process theologians affirm salvation.

But process philosophy, as Whitehead himself pointed out, allows for the possibility that the human soul can live on apart from the physical body. And some process theologians have, on the basis of this ontological possibility, combined with empirical evidence and faith in divine grace, affirmed the reality of a "resurrection of the soul" (Cobb, "Resurrection"). This affirmation can then provide the basis for hope for a process of → sanctification, in which God will gradually love the hell out of us (Griffin, *Parapsychology; Two Great Truths;* Suchocki, *End of Evil*).

Third, the idea of a reign of God on earth has also been developed from the process point of view. The next major evolutionary leap toward which the creative love of God is luring us is arguably global → democracy, in which the war system, with its inevitable imperialism and → terrorism, is replaced by democratic rule at the global level, through which the → rights and interests of all peoples would be protected and the common good promoted. Such a political reorganization would provide the most crucial necessary condition for a form of social-political-economic governance in which divine values of truth, justice, equality, compassion, peace, and ecological sustainability replace the demonic values in terms of which the planet has increasingly been ruled since the rise of the war system some 10,000 years ago (Griffin, "Moral Need"). Salvation in this sense makes a strong doctrine of the church important (B. Lee) and entails thinking of "process theology as → political theology" (Cobb, *Process Theology*).

Bibliography: C. Birch, *Regaining Compassion for Humanity and Nature* (Kensington, Austral., 1993) • C. Birch and J. Cobb, *The Liberation of Life: From the Cell to the Community* (Cambridge, 1981) • C. Christ, *Rebirth of the Goddess: Finding Meaning in Feminist Spirituality* (Reading, Mass., 1997); idem, *She Who Changes: Re-imagining the Divine in the World* (New York, 2003) • J. Cobb, *Beyond Dialogue: Toward a Mutual Transformation of Buddhism and Christianity* (Philadelphia, 1982); idem, *Christ in a Pluralistic Age* (Philadelphia, 1975); idem, *Is It Too Late? A Theology of Ecology* (Beverly Hills, Calif., 1972); idem, *Postmodernism and Public Policy: Reframing Religion, Culture, Education, Sexuality, Class, Race, Politics, and the Economy* (Albany, N.Y., 2002); idem, *Process Theology as Political Theology* (Philadelphia, 1982); idem, "The Resurrection of the Soul," *HTR* 80 (1987) 213-27; idem, *Transforming Christianity and the World: A Way beyond Absolutism and Relativism* (Maryknoll, N.Y., 1999) • J. Cobb and D. Griffin, *Process Theology: An Introductory Exposition* (Philadelphia, 1976) • L. Ford, ed., *Two Process Philosophers: Hartshorne's Encounter with Whitehead* (Tallahassee, Fla., 1973) • D. Griffin, *Evil Revisited: Responses and Reconsiderations* (Albany, N.Y., 1991); idem, "The Moral Need for Global Democracy," *Belonging Together: Faith and Politics in a Relational World* (ed. D. Sturm; Claremont, Calif., 2003); idem, "Panentheism: A Postmodern Revelation," *In Whom We Live and Move and Have Our Being: Panentheistic Reflections on God's Presence in a Scientific World* (ed. P. Clayton and A. Peacocke; Grand Rapids, 2004) 36-47; idem, *Parapsychology, Philosophy, and Spirituality: A Postmodern Exploration* (Albany, N.Y., 1997); idem, *Religion and Scientific Naturalism: Overcoming the Conflicts* (Albany, N.Y., 2000); idem, *Two Great Truths: A New Synthesis of Scientific Naturalism and Christian Faith* (Louisville, Ky., 2004); idem, "Whitehead's Deeply Ecological Worldview," *Worldviews and Ecology: Religion, Philosophy, and the Environment* (ed. M. E. Tucker and J. A. Grim; Maryknoll, N.Y., 1994) 190-206; idem, ed., *Deep Religious Pluralism* (Louisville, Ky., 2005) • C. Hartshorne, *The Divine Relativity: A Social Conception of God* (2d ed.; New Haven, 1964; orig. pub., 1948); idem, *The Logic of Perfection, and Other Essays in Neoclassical Metaphysics* (LaSalle, Ill., 1962) • N. Howell, *A Feminist Cosmology: Ecology, Solidarity, and Metaphysics* (New York, 2000) • C. Keller, *The Face of the Deep: A Theology of Becoming* (New York, 2002); idem, *From a Broken Web: Separation, Sexism, and Self* (Boston, 1986) • B. Lee, *The Becoming of the Church: A Process Theology of the Structure of Christian Experience* (New York, 1974) • J. McDaniel, *Of God and Pelicans: A Theology of Reverence for Life* (Louisville, Ky., 1989) • S. Ogden, *The Reality of God, and Other Essays* (New York, 1966) • M. Suchocki, *Divinity and Diversity: A Christian Affirmation of Religious Pluralism* (Nashville, 2003); idem, *The End of Evil: Process Eschatology in Historical Context* (New York, 1988) • A. N. Whitehead, *Process and Reality* (corr. ed.; ed. D. Griffin and D. Sherburne; New York, 1978; orig. pub., 1929); idem, *Religion in the Making* (New York, 1996; orig. pub., 1926).

David Ray Griffin

Processions

1. Term
2. Biblical Models
3. In Church History

1. Term

Taken from Lat. *procedo* (go forth), the word "procession" is used in the church for an orderly march of believers who give bodily expression to their prayerfulness by striding ahead, at times by leaps and bounds. The sense of fellowship and common fulfillment enhances the intensity of the act.

Processions that express in movement the human striving after God occur in all religions. With → prayer, song, and music, they lead into the presence of the deity and bring the deity into the life and working world of the faithful in order to avert evil and to seek → blessing. In → Hinduism huge, powerful divine carriages are a feature of processions. Circular processions seek to fence in specific areas as with a defensive ring.

2. Biblical Models

The biblical model of a procession is the march of Israel out of bondage to the land of promise (Exod. 40:36-38; Num. 9:17-18). King → David dancing before the ark (2 Sam. 6:14-15) has been used in justification of Christian processions of leaping and dancing (e.g., the annual dancing procession to the tomb of Willibrod in Echternach, Luxembourg). Nehemiah's processions set a protective ring around the city of God (Neh. 12:27-43). The → Synoptics portray the entry of Jesus into Jerusalem (Matt. 21:8-17 and par.) as a procession to the → temple. The religions of antiquity (→ Hellenistic-Roman Religion) found expression in many processions, including royal processions, triumphal processions, burial processions, and floral processions.

3. In Church History

3.1. The oldest form of Christian procession is the funeral procession. Beginning in the latter part of the fourth century, the bones of → martyrs were carried (or "translated") in festive processions (→ Relics). This tradition underlies the carrying of relics to put under the → altar at the Roman Catholic consecration of altars (optional after → Vatican II). In 312 it became possible to hold processions publicly in connection with new church buildings.

Baptismal candidates (→ Baptism) were led in procession to the → baptistery. Recalling these processions were the Carolingian processions on Sundays to sprinkle → holy water on the congregation. After Vatican II this practice became the introduction to the Sunday → Mass.

The celebration of the → Eucharist (§3.2) came to include a processional entry and a gospel procession with incense and lights (the "little entry" of the Byzantine liturgy). Then followed the processions with the offerings (the Byzantine "great entry") and the communion procession. Members of the congregation bring forth bread and wine (→ Justin Martyr *1 Apol.* 67). The general collection procession, which originated on Frankish soil, is now practiced with special solemnity on collection days for philanthropic causes.

In → Rome especially a procession is made to the → stations of the cross. On certain days (→ Church Year 2.2) commemorative processions are held. These began in → Jerusalem (see esp. the account by the Spanish nun Egeria of her pilgrimage in ca. 381-84). The procession of the mass of → light on the 40th day after the birth of Christ celebrates Christ as "a light to lighten the Gentiles" (Luke 2:32 KJV). On Palm Sunday it is customary to reenact the entry into Jerusalem with a procession. Originating in Jerusalem are the Good Friday processions to honor the crucifixion (along the Via Dolorosa) and the procession of light of the → Easter Vigil. Orthodox Christians play a special part in the burial procession on the evening of Good Friday. Both Eastern and Western Christians mark the resurrection by processions either overnight or in the early morning at Easter.

Eucharistic processions (→ Eucharistic Piety) are found only in the West. In Cologne from around 1270 the Host has been carried in the introductory procession of the Corpus Christi Mass, a model for one of the most spectacular of Roman Catholic processions.

3.2. The → Reformation discontinued many traditional processions but tolerated to some extent processions through the fields on the Rogation Days before Ascension Day (since 1559 in England; → Ascension of Christ). In place of the Roman Robigalia (public festival on April 25 in honor of Robigus, Roman god who protected crops from blight), processions had been started on April 25 (major litany), but they were discontinued in 1969. In their place we have the optional rogation processions (minor litany) that replaced pagan agricultural processions in the fifth century and were integrated into the Roman liturgy in about 800. The → Enlightenment contested the reviving of customary processions in the age of the baroque.

Some Anglican parishes hold processions around parish boundaries ("beating the bounds") in accordance with ancient custom, and introductory and closing processions and collection processions find a place in many Reformation churches. Processions are often headed by the → cross, representing the church's Head "going on before." Those who take part in processions see themselves as the → people of God on the march, and if the procession has the church as goal, the church represents the heavenly Jerusalem, at which Christians hope to arrive at the end of their pilgrimage. In some churches local bishops have jurisdiction over processions, especially when it is a matter of public eucharistic processions. Diocesan guidelines offer details as to participation and dignified procedure (1983 CIC 944). Processions of witness have now also become a common feature, often taking a transdenominational or ecumenical form.

→ Pilgrimage; Popular Catholicism; Popular Religion

Bibliography: T. BAILEY, *The Processions of Sarum and the Western Church* (Toronto, 1971) • A. BERGER, "Imperial and Ecclesiastical Processions in Constantinople," *Byzantine Constantinople* (ed. N. Necipoglu; Leiden, 2001) 73-88 • C. C. FLANIGAN, "The Moving Subject: Medieval Liturgical Processions in Semiotic and Cultural Perspective," *Moving Subjects: Processional Performance in the Middle Ages and the Renaissance* (ed. K. Ashley and W. Hüsken; Amsterdam, 2001) 35-52 • A. MARTIMORT, ed., *HLW(M)* 2.169-78 • H. B. MEYER et al., eds., *GDK* (2d ed.) 3.24-39 • B. I. MULLAHY, "Processions, Religious," *NCE* (2d ed.) 11.732-33 • M. RIGHETTI, *Manuale di storia liturgica* (3d ed.; Milan, 1964) 1.404-15 • S. TWYMAN, *Papal Ceremonial at Rome in the Twelfth Century* (London, 2002) • S. V. WEBSTER, *Art and Ritual in Golden-Age Spain: Sevillian Confraternities and the Processional Sculpture of Holy Week* (Princeton, 1998).

ANDREAS HEINZ

Proclamation

1. Term
2. Context
3. Event
4. Trinitarian Structure
5. The Church and Proclamation

1. Term

"Proclamation" is a general term signifying the activity of a herald (Gk. *kēryx*) or messenger (*angelos;* → Angel) in making public the content and meaning of what God has said or done for the → salvation of the world (→ Soteriology). It thus presupposes divine → revelation; in particular, proclamation is based upon the conviction that God is an agent in the world he has created (→ Creation 4; Salvation History). For example, in Hebrews 1–2 God is said to have spoken frequently in the past through the → prophets and through angels but has now spoken through his own Son (→ Jesus).

The NT uses a variety of nouns for the content of what is in origin God's own self-expression: *logos* (word), → *kērygma, euangelion* (gospel), *epangelia* (promise), or, in verbal form, *katangellō* (proclaim, → preach) and *euangelizomai* (preach the good news). There is no absolute distinction between proclamation and → preaching, though the latter tends to signify a particular event in the context of → worship when a biblical text is expounded. Proclamation is also closely related to witness *(martyria)* and confession (*homologia;* → Confession of Faith). It can refer primarily to the act of proclaiming, to the content of what is proclaimed, or to both act and content.

2. Context

Proclamation in the church occurs within the context that the content specifies; that is, it is an event within a comprehensive narrative of God's covenantal love for his people (→ Covenant). In the case of Israel, God, who has delivered his people from slavery in Egypt, gives them his → law (Exod. 20:2; 25:22; → Israel 1.2). For the new → people of God, the → gospel *(euangelion)* of God includes rules *(parangeliai)* to be handed on about how they are to live (1 Thess. 2:4; 4:2). The fact that a → church (§2.1) faithfully follows the → tradition becomes part of the story (1 Thess. 1:9; Rom. 1:8).

3. Event

The event of proclamation is communicative. As such, it invites analysis and reflection upon (1) the speaker(s), (2) the hearer(s), and (3) the message.

3.1. Although the biblical tradition makes the claim that God may speak directly with a given person, considerable attention is nonetheless paid to the possibility of false claims, and thus to the identity of those authorized to deliver the authentic message (→ Authority), or the gospel. → Paul, for example, claims to have been called by God to be an → apostle and set apart for the service of the gospel (Rom. 1:1, 5). In defending his credentials, Paul claims that his churches are the living evidence that God has empowered him to be a minister (*diakonos;* → Deacon, Deaconess) of the new covenant (2 Cor. 3:6). On this basis, despite being challenged and opposed, he is fully confident that he is acting as an ambassador on behalf of Christ, and that God is making the divine message clear through him (2 Cor. 5:20).

In the early churches, including those founded by Paul, conflict about the interpretation of the gospel, often exacerbated by personal rivalries, led to → heresy and schism (→ Church 2.1.5; Early Church 2.1). The growth of authorized offices, especially that of oversight (*episkopē;* → Episcopacy), was intended to safeguard the transmission of authentic tradition and the maintenance of unity in proclamation (→ Bishop, Episcopate, 1; Church 2.2.1; Early Church 2.2). The attempt to guarantee participation in the one true church led to the creation of a hierarchical structure (→ Hierarchy) for discipline and legal precision in the terms of doctrine (→ Rule of Faith) and the administration of the → sacraments.

Against such tendencies the churches of the →

Reformation reemphasized the supremacy of the → Word of God and the sufficiency of pure proclamation of that Word and right administration of the sacraments for the true unity of the church (CA 7; → Church 3.3.1, 3.4.1, 3.5.3; Ministry, Ministerial Offices, 1). Modern ecumenical discussion (→ Ecumenical Dialogue) continues to seek for a way of embodying the supremacy of God's self-expression in concrete structures serving the unity of the church and the coherence of its mission (→ Ecumenism, Ecumenical Movement, 2).

3.2. Proclamation is communication to a specific audience within a specific → culture or cultures. The experience of proclamation in the early centuries already illustrates the complexities of understanding and misunderstanding (→ Hermeneutics 2; Preaching 2). Letters of Paul to the Corinthian church, and possibly the letters of John, were designed to correct mistaken interpretations of earlier communications.

Although the gulf between the cultures of the NT world and those of subsequent centuries (→ New Testament Era, History of; Culture and Christianity) was frequently acknowledged, the European → Enlightenment introduced a heightened consciousness of this difference (→ Exegesis, Biblical, 2.1.5; Biblical Theology 1.2.2). Criticism of authority, whether of a clerical order or of a sacred text, led to attempts to formulate a distinction between the heart or essence of the gospel and what could be discarded as only of temporary value (→ Hermeneutics 2.3). This distinction brought the philosophical and cultural beliefs and assumptions of modern people into sharp focus as an element in the situation of proclamation (→ Biblical Theology 2.2; Modernity 2.3 and 4; Preaching 4).

The programmatic → demythologization of the gospel (R. Bultmann) and the adoption of existentialist forms of interpretation stimulated interest in hermeneutics (→ Existential Theology 2). Some speak of the way in which past and present are brought into relation to each other in the process of understanding as a "fusion of horizons" (H.-G. Gadamer; → Hermeneutics 3.2.2). All who hear proclamation bring with them a network of revisable expectations and assumptions, together with a pattern of behavior and belief, relevant in one way or another to assimilating or rejecting the content of the message in whole or in part.

It is therefore important to note that the content of proclamation is said from the first to be a mystery (Mark 4:11; 1 Cor. 2:7; 4:1; Eph. 1:9; 6:19; Col. 1:26; 4:3) and foolishness (1 Cor. 1:18; 3:19). Indeed, the whole character of the gospel is a reversal of expectation in the exaltation of the humble (Luke 1:52; Phil. 2:5-11); it is a stumbling block (Rom. 9:32; 1 Cor. 1:23; 1 Pet. 2:8). Pure conformity to human expectations is therefore not part of the claim of proclamation. → Tertullian's *Credo quia absurdum est* (I believe because it is absurd) and M. → Luther's exaltation of a theology of the cross (→ Theologia crucis) are authentic expressions of this contradiction. The task remains, however, of distinguishing between the authentic foolishness of the gospel and gratuitous irrationality.

3.3. Proclamation is a message with specific content, summarized as Christ, his person and his works (Phil. 1:15-18; Col. 1:28; → Christology), the "truth [*martyrion*] about God" (1 Cor. 2:1 REB). Proclamation is not, however, adequately understood as → information. Especially in the Gospel of John, the → truth is a living environment constituted by the fellowship of all believers, nourished and guided by the help of the → Holy Spirit. The Word of God is light, and believers walk in that light. Believers dwell in Christ, as branches in a vine. Proclamation is thus essentially relational, involving fellowship (→ *koinōnia*) with God and with one's Christian brothers and sisters, presupposing the fact of → reconciliation.

4. Trinitarian Structure

In Acts the Holy Spirit, who had come upon Jesus at the beginning of his ministry (Luke 4:18), is said to inspire the proclamation of the gospel (Acts 1:8; 2:17-18). Paul speaks of the Spirit as necessary to a proper discernment of "spiritual truths" (1 Cor. 2:13 REB). Proclamation therefore has a Trinitarian structure as God's own self-expression in Jesus Christ (→ Trinity), his Son, interpreted to humankind through the grace and power of the Holy Spirit. Theological hermeneutics is bound to take this factor into account, whatever role is assigned to human rationality and culture.

5. The Church and Proclamation

The life of the church founded upon the creative and redeeming Word of God is an embodiment within history of fellowship with God. Although Paul regards our bodies as "clay jars" containing the "treasure" of the gospel (2 Cor. 4:7), the mortal body ought still to reveal the life of Jesus (v. 11).

Similarly, the concrete life of the church itself may be held to be revelatory in → hope and anticipation of the *eschaton* (→ Eschatology). The way that Christians treat one another proclaims, or does not proclaim, the reconciled unity that → love inspires. The reconciliation of all things in Christ

(Eph. 1:10) involves a calling to "spare no effort to make fast with bonds of peace the unity which the Spirit gives" (Eph. 4:3 REB). The totality of the life of the church may therefore be seen as proclamation of the gospel, just as the celebration of the Lord's Supper (→ Eucharist) proclaims the death of the Lord and concretely manifests, or does not manifest, his body (1 Cor. 11:26-34). Obviously there is need for constant vigilance and criticism.

The discipline of → theology has been helpfully seen as offering the opportunity of holding the proclamation of the church true to the criterion of the Word of God, both in what the church says and in what it does (K. → Barth).

Bibliography: E. Achtemeier, *The OT and the Proclamation of the Gospel* (Philadelphia, 1973) • K. Barth, *CD* I/1; idem, *The Word of God and the Word of Man* (Gloucester, Mass., 1978; orig. pub., 1924) • J. Breck, *The Power of the Word in the Worshipping Church* (New York, 1986) • R. Bultmann, *Theology of the NT* (2 vols.; New York, 1959-60) • G. Delling, *Der Kreuzestod Jesu in der urchristlichen Verkündigung* (Göttingen, 1972) • D. C. Duling and N. Perrin, *The NT: Proclamation and Parenesis, Myth and History* (3d ed.; Fort Worth, Tex., 1994) • G. Ebeling, *Theology and Proclamation* (London, 1966) • M. Ellingsen, *The Integrity of Biblical Narrative: Story in Theology and Proclamation* (Minneapolis, 1990) • P. T. Forsyth, *Positive Preaching and the Modern Mind* (Grand Rapids, 1964; orig. pub., 1909) • F. Gogarten, *Die Verkündigung Jesu Christi. Grundlagen und Aufgabe* (Tübingen, 1965) • W. G. Jeanrod, *Theological Hermeneutics: Development and Significance* (Basingstoke, 1991) • J. W. Z. Kurewa, *Biblical Proclamation for Africa Today* (Nashville, 1995) • O. Kuss, *Auslegung und Verkündigung* (Regensburg, 1971) • B. C. Leslie, *Trinitarian Hermeneutics: The Hermeneutical Significance of Karl Barth's Doctrine of the Trinity* (New York, 1991) • A. D. Litfin, *St. Paul's Theology of Proclamation: 1 Corinthians 1–4 and Greco-Roman Rhetoric* (Cambridge, 1994) • A. E. McGrath, *Luther's Theology of the Cross: Martin Luther's Theological Breakthrough* (Oxford, 1990) • H. Rahner, *A Theology of Proclamation* (New York, 1968; orig. pub., 1939) • J. Ratzinger, *Dogma and Preaching* (Chicago, 1985; orig. pub., 1973) • C. F. Starkloff, *The Office of Proclamation* (Ottawa, 1969) • A. C. Thiselton, *New Horizons in Hermeneutics* (London, 1992) • E. Winkler, *Kommunikation und Verkündigung* (Berlin, 1977).

Stephen W. Sykes

Production, Productivity → Industrial Society

Profane → Sacred and Profane

Professio fidei Tridentina → Creed of Pius IV

Program to Combat Racism

1. Early History
2. Content and Implementation
3. Ecumenical Discussion

On scarcely no other matter in the ecumenical movement is there as strong a → consensus as now exists in the condemnation of → racism in all its forms. This antipathy may be seen in some 30 declarations that the movement has made, from the Stockholm → Life and Work conference in 1925 to the Uppsala Assembly of the → World Council of Churches (WCC) in 1968 and to all subsequent assemblies. These statements are not simply against racial discrimination itself but are united in making the broader point that racism is incompatible with the → gospel itself.

1. Early History

Under the influence of the → civil rights and black power movements in the United States and the intensified struggle for the liberation of racially oppressed peoples in southern Africa, the WCC sensed in the late 1960s the need for an active program that would go beyond mere declarations in active support of the struggle. Thus the Life and Work Conference at Geneva in 1966 emphatically drew attention to the relations between economic, political, and racial oppression, calling for radical structural change and open → solidarity with the oppressed. This conference prepared the ground for the 1968 Assembly of the WCC at Uppsala, Sweden, which charged the Central Committee to draw up an immediate plan of action for the WCC and its member churches in the fight against racism.

As a follow-up, the WCC held a study conference in 1969 at Notting Hill, London, that examined the nature, causes, and results of racism, especially white racism. Furthermore, it evaluated the theological and social foundations of existing church positions, with a view to proposing an ecumenical program of educational and practical action on the basis of the findings.

Later in 1969 after this preliminary work, the Central Committee held a heated and lively debate on a program against racism. Underlying the debate was the definition of racism given at Uppsala, which included, for example, ethnocentric pride in one's own racial group, preference for the special characteristics of this group, the conviction that these traits are fundamentally biological and will be transmitted to future generations, negative feelings toward other groups that do not have them, and the urge to discriminate against such groups, excluding them from full participation in the life of society. The definition offered by a group of experts at UNESCO was also used (→ United Nations; Prejudice). The WCC thus mandated a five-year Program to Combat Racism (PCR), which was extended in 1974. PCR activities continue to this day under the mandate of the WCC's Commission on Justice, Peace, and Creation.

2. Content and Implementation

PCR has consistently argued that racism is a global phenomenon that demands special attention today. Its mandate includes five major affirmations:

1. White racism in its many forms is by far the most dangerous element in the modern racial conflict.
2. Institutional racism as reflected in social, economic, and political power-structures must be challenged.
3. The battle against racism unavoidably means that the powerful must share social, economic, political, and cultural → power with the weak.
4. Strategies for the struggle against racism must be determined by regional conditions.
5. There is a need to analyze and correct the complicity of the churches in the perpetuation of racism.

To implement the PCR program the Special Fund to Combat Racism was set up to support organizations that either were established by oppressed racial groups or were formed to support the victims of racial discrimination; these organizations and groups were to have goals compatible with the general goals of the ecumenical movement. Through this special fund groups would find support in their struggle for economic, social, and political justice (→ Righteousness, Justice, 3). From 1970 to 2001 a total of more than $12 million was dispersed.

For more than two decades the focus of PCR work was southern Africa. PCR made important, but controversial, political decisions, for example, in calling for the withdrawal of all foreign investment from southern Africa, for the blocking of credit to the government of South Africa, and for the imposing of an arms embargo and other wide-reaching sanctions against South Africa. In consequence, the WCC ended its own business with any bank doing business with South Africa (→ Economic Ethics 3.4).

As changes began to come to South Africa, PCR was able to expand its efforts more globally. It has supported the struggles of indigenous peoples, notably, a land-rights consultation in 1989 in Darwin, Australia, which affirmed a wide range of → rights for indigenous peoples, including self-determination and control of their own territories. Through the initiative of PCR, the WCC, at its 1991 assembly in Canberra, issued a statement of commitment to indigenous peoples and to land rights, "Move beyond Words." PCR has also focused its attention on matters such as a program for racially abused women, on the plight of the oppressed Dalit people in India and the Ogoni people of Nigeria (→ Caste), on the resurgence and persistence of racism in Europe and North America, and on the issue of racism in → education and the → mass media.

3. Ecumenical Discussion

The PCR program has been one of the most controversial of all WCC initiatives. It found support among WCC member churches in all parts of the world, but many in Western churches sharply criticized its political decisions, especially the measures taken against South Africa, condemning them as politically one-sided. Criticisms of the WCC and of the PCR in particular were especially virulent in British and German media, most often with little reference to the facts. In the United States there were sharp attacks on the WCC at ten-year intervals in the *Reader's Digest* (1971, 1982, 1993), and during the cold war allegations were frequently made about a supposed connection between the ecumenical movement and Communist → Marxism.

In 1979 a process of deliberation about the participation of churches in the struggle against racism during future years was initiated by the WCC. That process culminated in 1980 with a world consultation at Noordwijkerhout, Netherlands, on the theme "The Churches Responding to Racism in the 1980s." The event concluded that it was the will of the churches to oppose every form of racism worldwide on different levels and to stand in solidarity with the oppressed. Only a few church bodies, however, heeded the call of this consultation to review their own racism — "in their own backyard."

Largely through PCR, the WCC has played a key role in drawing attention to and alleviating racial and ethnic oppression. One commentator has summarized these efforts: "The WCC reflects, to the extent that it is consistent with the ecumenical vision and its own objectives, the experiences of the victims and the oppressed. Also, by its actions of solidarity and prophetic statements, the Council has put its reputation as a moral arbiter in world affairs to the test." The WCC's consistent action against racism has managed to "isolate the ever-dwindling influence of the purveyors of racism and give courage and support to all Christians committed to the struggle against racism" (H. McCullum, 370).

→ Ecumenism, Ecumenical Movement

Bibliography: E. Adler et al., *A Small Beginning: An Assessment of the First Five Years of the Programme to Combat Racism* (Geneva, 1974) • A. van der Bent, ed., *World Council of Churches Statements and Actions on Racism, 1948-1985* (Geneva, 1986) • M. Conway, "Under Public Scrutiny," *A History of the Ecumenical Movement,* vol. 3, *1968-2000* (ed. J. Briggs, M. A. Oduyoye, and G. Tsetsis; Geneva, 2004) 433-58 • C. John, ed., *Human Rights and the Churches: New Challenges; A Compilation of Reports* (Geneva, 1998) • H. McCullum et al., "Racism and Ethnicity," *History of the Ecumenical Movement, 1968-2000,* ed. Briggs et al., 345-71 • Z. Mbali, *The Churches and Racism: A Black South African Perspective* (London, 1987) • B. Sjollema, "Programme to Combat Racism," *DEM* (2d ed.) 935-37 • T. Tschuy, *Ethnic Conflict and Religion: Challenge to the Churches* (Geneva, 1997) • P. Webb, ed., *The Long Struggle: The Involvement of the World Council of Churches in South Africa* (Geneva, 1994).

Baldwin C. Sjollema

Progress

1. Concept
2. Antiquity
3. Christian Tradition
4. Renaissance and Enlightenment
5. Criticism

1. Concept

The idea of progress implies a specific view and interpretation of history. One can regard history as either cyclic or linear. If it is cyclic, then after a longer or shorter period the historical process returns to its starting point. If it is linear, history goes further and further from its origin. In either case the process may be viewed either positively or negatively. The idea of progress is one of these four possible combinations, namely, the idea of a linear movement toward the good.

In the classic definition of J. B. Bury, the idea of progress means that civilization has progressed, is progressing, and will continue to progress in a desired direction. There are here three constitutive elements in progress. The social changes that it posits are (1) *ongoing,* that is, they will continue in the → future. They are (2) *cumulative,* for example, in → science, → technology, art, → religion, and → society as a whole. On the basis of clearly defined criteria, they may also be described as (3) *betterment.* Each of these elements raises empirical problems. Bury's view that progress in this sense is a modern concept is contested (e.g., by R. A. Nisbet), but it has not yet been refuted.

2. Antiquity

A cyclic view tended to be dominant in antiquity. It might relate to the cosmos as a whole or simply to → culture (→ Philosophy of History). According to the former, in which Babylonian and Indian influences were at work, the universe is constantly destroyed and re-created, as argued by Heraclitus, Plato (the cosmic year; → Platonism), and Stoicism (which spoke of *ekpyrōsis,* "[general] conflagration," after which the world would begin again). The latter view refers especially to changing political forms — thus Plato *(Republic),* Aristotle *(Politika),* and Polybius *(Historiae).*

Alongside these cyclic views the concept of primitivism (G. Boas) denotes an idea that the past was better than the present, which is possible on either a cyclic or a linear theory. This (chronological) primitivism may be found in the myth of the five ages in Hesiod (fl. ca. 800 B.C.; → Golden Age). There is also a cultural primitivism in which (as, e.g., the Cynics) a simple and natural lifestyle is extolled. Both forms have a critical purpose (→ Greek Philosophy).

Yet we also find indications of an ancient concept of progress, first in Xenophanes (ca. 570-ca. 478), who spoke of human beings seeking and finding what is better in the course of time, then in the myth of Prometheus, and most pregnantly in the *De rerum natura* (On the nature of things) of Lucretius (d. 55 B.C.), who spoke of a successive emergence of things in time. This concept related only to technical and scientific ability *(technē)* and did not imply any moral progress. Progress in the former might well bring instead moral regression.

3. Christian Tradition

The Judeo-Christian tradition offers a linear concept of → salvation history (creation, fall, redemption, consummation). It thus rejects cyclic thinking in principle (→ Theology of History); Christ died for sins only once (→ Augustine). Yet the ideas of antiquity infiltrated Christian thought. Redemption might be viewed as a once-for-all cycle with the restoration of the beginning at the end (→ Origen: the end is like the beginning), an idea that soon had to yield to the conviction that the end is better than the beginning (→ Tertullian: to reform for the better). The progress, however, is spiritual and cannot simply be transferred to secular society.

Overall, the linear view prevailed. It may be seen in → apocalyptic, which does not reckon with earthly progress. Eusebius of Caesarea (ca. 260-ca. 340) was the first to discuss this kind of progress (→ Historiography), followed by Ambrose (ca. 339-97). These two interpreted the blessings of the Pax Romana as a consequence of the coming of Christianity, from which they expected even greater benefits in the future.

This expectation perished with the fall of Rome (410), which led Augustine (354-430; → Augustine's Theology) to work out a Christian view of history in his *City of God.* Augustine understood history as a linear process relating to the destiny of two cities — the city of God *(civitas Dei)* and the terrestrial city *(civitas terrena).* Both these cities exist on earth as well as in eternity, but they are not identical with the → church and the → state. Augustine viewed their march spiritually as either toward God or away from him. That this march takes place in earthly history was of secondary importance for him, for the advance of the city of God cannot be equated with human progress. Like Lucretius, Augustine recognized human achievements in the technological and scientific spheres. These gains, however, were more than offset by evil in earthly life, and they counted for little from the standpoint of eternity. Augustine's view was dominant throughout the Middle Ages.

4. Renaissance and Enlightenment

The rediscovery of antiquity at the → Renaissance brought with it a brief revival of cyclic thinking (N. Machiavelli), but it soon gave way to the blossoming of the modern concept of progress, which imposed itself during the centuries that followed. While the Middle Ages had seen in history a process of aging and decay, the → modern period adopted a new interpretation that found in antiquity the youth of the race and in the present age its maturity.

In the 17th century the concept related only to knowledge and science (F. Bacon), but in the 18th century the conviction grew that a betterment of human life is possible thanks to science as people learn through → education (E. B. de Condillac, C.-A. Helvétius). During the French → Enlightenment Condorcet (1743-94) brought optimistic expectations for the future to their highest point when he found a limit to progress solely in the temporal limit set for the planet.

The Scottish and German philosophers of the Enlightenment were not so sure. The Scottish moralists (D. Hume, A. Smith, A. Ferguson) looked more on the dark side of things as they saw it concretely before them in the industrial revolution. Similarly, I. Kant (1724-1804; → Kantianism) could not believe that there is any permanent progress to the → good. We can find no sure plan in nature, though to understand history we have to act as if there were one. Nature necessarily brings forth fruits according to its essential being. Natural to us are → reason and → freedom, but they cannot be fully implemented in one human life. This implementation occurs only in history, which is thus a progressive actualizing of reason and freedom. We must be champions of both. For Kant, then, progress becomes an ethical summons to which we must be obedient in cases of doubt.

The experiences of the French → Revolution and the reactions that followed shattered Enlightenment optimism but did not result in a relativizing of the idea of progress. On the contrary, attempts were made to give it a firmer basis by seeing it as the product of external factors that were (relatively) independent of human folly. Progress thus took on an autonomous character. A. Comte (1798-1857) based it on an autonomous development of knowledge, H. Spencer (1820-1903) on a law of cosmic → evolution, G. W. F. Hegel (1770-1831) on the dialectical development of the spirit that comes to itself in the progressive sequence of nonrepeatable cycles (→ Dialectic), and K. → Marx (1818-83) on the automatic development of the means of production (→ Marxism).

In the 20th century P. Teilhard de Chardin (1881-1955) linked a law of cosmic evolution to an approach in terms of salvation history.

The modern concept of progress implies that social changes are linear, cumulative, and continuous. They are propelled by science and technology and entail an increasing → emancipation of the race from the dominion of nature, of social, political, and religious forces, and of evil impulses. This view is strongly ethnocentric, for it regards Western civilization as a climax and model.

The great success of this view cannot be divorced from the functions it has discharged and continues to discharge. Thus it can be used as a category to describe achievements that serve to improve the quality of life. It can also be used against others — both to justify the claims to power of social categories and Western peoples and to press these claims against them. Finally, as belief in progress, it can serve as an alternative view of life and the world modeled on Christian salvation history (K. Löwith).

5. Criticism

The concept of progress has always come under criticism. Even during the French Enlightenment there was a strongly pessimistic undercurrent that emerges in Voltaire (1694-1778), J. d'Alembert (1717-83), and especially J.-J. Rousseau (1712-78), who said in his *Émile* that everything crumbles in our hands. We find the same ambivalence and skepticism in A. de Tocqueville (1805-59) and J. C. Burckhardt (1818-97), who saw no way of achieving a valid accounting of losses and gains. Cyclic thinking came to expression in O. Spengler (1880-1936, *The Decline of the West*) and to some extent in A. Toynbee (1889-1975). → Historicism cannot in principle be reconciled with the idea of progress, and F. → Nietzsche (1844-1900) dismissed the idea as modern and therefore mistaken. He grounded → nihilism in the myth of eternal recurrence and denied that history bears any meaning.

Throughout the 20th century criticism of the idea of progress became stronger and focused on the basic elements. First, though it is possible to find linear and cumulative progress in science, technology, and economics, it is less clear in the social and political sector and hardly discernible in the fields of religion, morality, or art.

Second, continuity is doubtful, for even the movement that one may observe comes up against limits. Reserves will soon be depleted (→ Ecology; Energy), the → environment is being polluted, social frustrations are mounting (F. Hirsch), and → bureaucracy and centralization block the progress of democratic participation.

Finally, although improvements in human existence are unmistakable, they apply to only a limited portion of humanity, and no proper balance sheet of gains and losses is possible (Burckhardt).

Perhaps the most penetrating criticism focuses on the way in which scientific progress (→ Science and Theology) and economic → development have become autonomous and absolute. They no longer guarantee progress either individually or collectively; instead, they tend to hamper it (M. Horkheimer). The concept of progress is historically restricted and freighted. It is probably significant that the word "progress" is gradually disappearing and has been replaced, at least in political discourse, by terms such as (economic) "growth" and (scientific) "innovation." This change indicates not only a reduction of ambitions but also an accentuation of the recent one-sidedness of the concept. Perhaps a new orientation is desirable whereby an emphasis on progress gives way to one on → hope, a category not characterized by self-assurance and know-how.

→ Autonomy; Optimism and Pessimism; Time and Eternity; Worldview

Bibliography: G. E. Almond, M. Chodorow, and R. H. Pearce, eds., *Progress and Its Discontents* (Berkeley, Calif., 1982) • J. A. Bernstein, *Progress and the Quest for Meaning: A Philosophical and Historical Inquiry* (Rutherford, N.J., 1993) • G. Boas, "Primitivism," *DHI* 3.577-98 • J. B. Bury, *The Idea of Progress: An Inquiry into Its Growth and Origin* (New York, 1987; orig. pub., 1920) • E. R. Dodds, "Progress in Classical Antiquity," *DHI* 3.623-33 • F. Hirsch, *Social Limits to Growth* (London, 1977) • K. Löwith, *Weltgeschichte und Heilsgeschehen. Die theologischen Voraussetzungen der Geschichtsphilosophie* (8th ed.; Stuttgart, 1990; orig. pub., 1953) • L. Marx, *Progress: Fact or Illusion?* (Ann Arbor, Mich., 1996) • R. A. Nisbet, *History of the Idea of Progress* (New York, 1980) • R. J. Teggart, *The Idea of Progress: A Collection of Readings* (rev. ed.; Berkeley, Calif., 1949) • H. Vijverberg, *Historical Pessimism in the French Enlightenment* (Cambridge, Mass., 1958) • W. W. Wagar, *The Idea of Progress since the Renaissance* (New York, 1969).

Leo Laeyendecker

Proletariat → Marxism 1.3.1

Promise and Fulfillment

1. OT
2. NT
3. Church History
4. Dogmatics
5. Ethics

In their varied uses and functions, the words "promise" and "fulfillment" indicate a historical and theological category in which the → Word of God, a word of → salvation or judgment (→ Last Judgment), will assuredly achieve realization either in history or at the end of history.

1. OT

The OT uses these two terms hermeneutically in its structuring and theological interpreting of the history of → Israel. This history is neither contingent nor natural but under the direction of divine intervention and guidance (e.g., Gen. 50:20). In the Hexateuch (Genesis 12–Joshua 24, where the distribution of land is fulfilled in the occupation; → Pentateuchal Research 2.1), in the → Deuteronomistic histories, and in Chronicles, God's declaratory Word comes to fulfillment in bringing either weal or woe, though it does not happen all at once and may not be objectively perceptible (e.g., 1 Kgs. 13:2 and 2 Kgs. 23:16, 20). The assurance serves four functions:

1. it gives legitimacy (e.g., to the Davidic dynasty, 2 Samuel 7; to the temple, 1 Kgs. 8:24; and to genuine prophecy, Deut. 18:22);
2. it gives pastoral encouragement, through surveys of the past, in times of acute crisis (Jeremiah and Isaiah during the exile);
3. it gives hope for the future (Jer. 29:10; Dan. 12:9, 13); and
4. it gives a kind of proof of God's existence (Isa. 41:22-29; 44:7; 45:21, etc.) by assuring believers, through the fulfillment of past promises, that Yahweh is in full control (e.g., 2 Chr. 36:21-22; Dan. 9:2).

Historical criticism, however, has shown that most of the correspondences represent prophecies after the event *(vaticinia ex eventu)*, which seek to acknowledge the efficacy of the divine word retrospectively. That is, the thinking here is actually moving in a hermeneutical circle from → faith to faith.

Early → Judaism thought the schema most significant as an articulation of self-understanding, and groups like → Qumran (1QpHab) applied the prophetic tradition to their own situations.

2. NT

The NT adopted the same schema, using it as a hermeneutical key in interpreting the Hebrew Bible and in → Christology. It saw in Christ a primary fulfillment of the OT message (B. S. Childs). The birth of Christ (note the copious citations at the beginning of Matthew: 1:22-23; 2:5, 15, 17-18, 23; 4:14-16), his public ministry (John 12:38; 13:18; 15:25), and especially his passion (John 19:36-37) and → resurrection were all "in accordance with the scriptures" (1 Cor. 15:3-4; Luke 24:27, 32, 46-47; Mark 8:31 and par.; Luke 17:25). This conviction, though expressed in different ways, is a constant one throughout the NT.

Conversations with → Judaism raise problems. Did Christ really fulfill prophecy when he did not have the expected profile of the OT Messiah (cf. 2 Cor. 3:12-16)? Some NT scholars seriously question the NT proof from prophecy, arguing that what we find amounts to no more than antiquated → allegory and intellectually dishonest eisegesis. Against this view it may be claimed that here too a hermeneutical circle obtains. If no real connection may be established between promise and fulfillment, faith sees the promise opening itself up to fulfillment and vice versa.

There also remains the question of what has not yet been fulfilled. What about the prophecies of the coming of all peoples to Zion, the writing of God's law on their hearts in connection with worldwide military disarmament (Isaiah 2), and the reign of eternal peace even for the animal kingdom (chaps. 65–66)? Were such expectations really fulfilled by Christ, or are they the common hopes of all peoples — the church, Israel, and the Gentiles (see Romans 8; 9–11)?

3. Church History

From the early days of church history to the time of → liberation theology, the schema of promise and fulfillment has helped to show what historical place this or that group occupies as elements in the divine plan. Apocalyptic speculations and millennial expectations have been abundantly present in every age (→ Apocalyptic 3.4; Millenarianism).

4. Dogmatics

For a long period the terms "promise" and "fulfillment" played no great part in → dogmatics. Indeed, they were argued to have little constitutive theological relevance (see F. → Schleiermacher's *Christian Faith,* §12). Historical critics argued that the OT texts bore a completely different sense from that which the NT authors gave them (R. Bultmann). The danger existed that by relating the two terms, an objective → salvation history would be constructed (as in the early Pannenberg) in which everything has the character of promise and fulfillment (J. C. K. von Hofmann).

After 1960 a new orientation arose. Dialectical theology and existential interpretation had one-sidedly insisted that → salvation is now present in faith (see 2 Cor. 6:2-10; John 5:25), but now the dimension of the "not yet" came into prominence. K. → Rahner (1904-84) found in the future promised in Christ the prospective development of the whole personality. J. Moltmann viewed the Christ-event itself as a promise. G. Sauter saw in the future dimension of → eschatology a utopia of being. W. Pannenberg regarded the Christ-event as an anticipation of the *eschaton,* and the church and → sacraments as signs of future consummation, of the eternal future of God.

The → New Age movement has dubiously treated promise and fulfillment as a kind of soothsaying. Nostradamus, for example, allegedly predicted amazing facts, thus supposedly validating this orientation of life.

All → biblical theology and hermeneutics must wrestle intensively with this phenomenon. In → Jewish-Christian dialogue the ancient question has again become an urgent one. Did Christ really fulfill the OT promises? Are there promises yet to be fulfilled? Can we expect a common fulfillment (E. Zenger)?

Bibliography: J. Barr, *Old and New in Interpretation: A Study of the Two Testaments* (London, 1966) • R. Bultmann, "Weissagung und Erfüllung" (1950), *Glauben und Verstehen* (vol. 2; 5th ed.; Tübingen, 1968) 162-86 • B. S. Childs, *Biblical Theology of the Old and New Testaments* (London, 1992) • J. C. K. von Hofmann, *Weissagung und Erfüllung im Alten und im Neuen Testaments* (2 vols.; Nordlingen, 1841-44) • D. E. Holwerda, *Jesus and Israel: One Covenant or Two?* (Grand Rapids, 1995) • W. E. Kümmel, *Promise and Fulfillment: The Eschatological Message of Jesus* (2d ed.; London, 1961) • W. Kurz, "Promise and Fulfillment in Hellenistic Jewish Narratives and in Luke and Acts," *Jesus and the Heritage of Israel: Luke's Narrative Claim upon Israel's Legacy* (ed. D. P. Moessner; Harrisburg, Pa., 1999) 147-70 • J. Moltmann, *Theology of Hope* (New York, 1967) • W. Pannenberg, *Systematic Theology* (vol. 3; Grand Rapids, 1998) • K. Rahner, "The Hermeneutics of Eschatological Assertions," *Theological Investigations* (vol. 4; Baltimore, 1966) 323-46 • G. Sass, *Leben aus den Verheißungen. Traditionsgeschichtliche und biblisch-theologische Untersuchungen zur Rede von Gottes Verheißungen im Frühjudentum und beim Apostel Paulus* (Göttingen, 1995) • M. L. Strauss, *The Davidic Messiah in Luke-Acts: The Promise and Its Fulfillment in Luke's Christology* (Sheffield, 1995) • E. Würthwein, "Prophetisches Wort und Geschichte in der Königsbüchern," *Studien zum Deuteronomistischen Geschichtswerk* (Berlin, 1994) 80-92 • E. Zenger, *Das erste Testament. Die jüdische Bibel und die Christen* (Düsseldorf, 1991) • W. Zimmerli, "Promise and Fulfillment" (1952/53), *Essays on OT Hermeneutics* (ed. C. Westermann; Richmond, Va., 1966) 89-122.

Manfred Oeming

5. Ethics

The biblical testimony to God's faithfulness in the past, present, or future fulfillment of his promises has ethical implications for believers relative to their own promises. Even though the Bible does not specifically emphasize the principle involved, it makes it clear that Christians, too, must be no less faithful than God in standing by their → vows and promises. The kingdom of → truth excludes deliberate and persistent liars (Rev. 21:8; cf. John 8:44), and a particularly reprehensible form of lying is the making of false promises that there is little will or desire to keep, whether in the political, commercial, or social realms, in personal relations, or in dealings with God. It is better not to vow than to make a vow and then not fulfill it (Eccl. 5:4-5). Those who would dwell on God's "holy hill" must keep their promises, even though it proves hurtful to do so (Ps. 15:4). A faithful God expects → faithfulness in his servants.

Events, of course, are not under human control as they are under God's. It may be impossible to honor promises that are made in good faith. Paul had to tell the Corinthians that his projected plans to visit them had not proved practical. He contrasted human promises with the divine promises that are always Yes in Christ (2 Cor. 1:15-20). Human promises are subject to the "if the Lord wishes" condition of Jas. 4:13-15, being at the mercy of events and of decisions made by others that we cannot control. Christians, then, should rein in the promises they make, using restraint and circumspection in not promising too lightly or too lavishly. If they do, subject always to direct or indirect divine overruling, they too can achieve a match between promise and fulfillment.

→ Ethics; Righteousness, Justice

Geoffrey W. Bromiley

Promotor fidei

In the → Roman Catholic Church the promotor fidei (Lat. *promoter of the faith*) is the theologian who, as part of the Congregation for the Causes of Saints, presides over meetings that weigh evidence for beatification and canonization. In the 17th century the church tightened up its procedures in these matters, giving an official judicial role to the promotor fidei. His task originally was to oppose the arguments of the *postulator causae* (the one who was episcopally appointed to plead the case) and the *relatores* (those who reported back to the → curia). In popular parlance and in many works, he is called the devil's advocate.

The duty of the promotor fidei was to introduce unfavorable data and counterarguments into the proceedings, usually lengthy. He had to make a successful outcome difficult, doing everything possible to ensure that the future veneration of those newly beatified or canonized, and confidence in their intercession, would not be impaired by things either concealed or wrongly presented.

The apostolic constitution *Divinus perfectionis Magister* (1983) restructured the procedures for canonization (→ Saints, Veneration of, 5.2). It made the legal aspect of the office less prominent, stressing instead that the promotor fidei is to be a high-ranking theological examiner.

→ Catholicism (Roman); Polity, Ecclesiastical

Bibliography: P. Molinari, "Devil's Advocate," *NCE* (2d ed.) 4.705-6 • W. Schulz, *Das neue Selig- und Heiligsprechungsverfahren* (Paderborn, 1988).

Heiner Grote†

Proof from Scripture → Scriptural Proof

Property

1. Concept
2. Development
   2.1. Prior to Liberal Concept
   2.2. Liberal Concept
   2.3. Constitutional Protection and Ambivalent Results
   2.4. Marxist Socialism
3. Property in the Theological Tradition
   3.1. OT and NT
   3.2. Christian Ethics
   3.3. Theological Basis
4. Present Discussion
   4.1. Roman Catholic and Protestant Teaching
   4.2. Social and Ethical Problems
5. Future Tasks
   5.1. Relation to World Economic Order
   5.2. Ecumenical Discussion

1. Concept

"Property" is a basic concept in the ordering of human life in society to the extent that it is regulated and shaped in such a way that individuals, groups, and legal entities can own material goods or income-producing rights or goods. What counts as property in a → society cannot be put in a single definition. There have always been many forms of property characterized by different spheres (landed, personal, income-producing), different handling (use, misuse, control), and different legal forms (collective or private). We can say what property is only in terms of a framework that interrelates legal, economic, and political theories.

Politically and legally, the function and content of property have basically changed in modern economic society. Particularly important is the distinction between personal property that we can handle as we wish and is thus under our sovereign control, and property that produces income but that we do not materially control. Another distinction involves income that is ours by right but involves no ownership. The application of protection (to material ownership or income) is of great significance as regards the social implications (e.g., in the case of housing). In modern economic society the extension of property to various sources of income (e.g., state pensions or unemployment insurance) stands in need of clarification to the degree that viewing entitlements as property protects them. Decisive for the function and significance of property, then, is the question how far protection extends. By extension to all entitlements, protection has been adjusted to modern economic society. This adaptation leads in turn to conflicts between protected property and its just distribution, or fairness in possible participation in economic power where it is based on property.

2. Development

No single concept embraces the idea of property as it is understood in every society. The development in European culture was shaped by the understanding of property as the right of control in the tradition of Roman law.

2.1. *Prior to Liberal Concept*

In medieval → feudalism a modification took place, with use replacing control as the dominant concept of property. Medieval society was not organized simply in terms of property.

With the rise of middle-class society and the related market society (→ Bourgois, Bourgoisie; Capitalism), property came to have constitutive significance in social organization. In the liberal theories of property of the 17th century (H. Grotius, T. Hobbes, J. Locke), the reference was to the individual property that should enjoy protection in the → state. The official legal functions of property were reduced to the control ascribed to the individual. (Private) property thus became the constitutive factor for the middle-class subject and the state that protected it.

Such liberal views did not go unopposed. J.-J. Rousseau (1712-78) saw property as a legal institution and inviolable as such, but he criticized the view of property that was oriented to individual control.

2.2. *Liberal Concept*

The liberal concept suppressed approaches that viewed property as a legally mediated social order. We see this kind of conception already in →

Thomas Aquinas (ca. 1225-74) and in the ethics of the → Reformers. In contrast, the liberal concept emphasized the relation between the acquisition of property by individuals and its social protection or position. This idea was developed in 17th- and 18th-century approaches that established individual possession (→ Individualism) and constructed political theory on this basis, although in different ways. This theory, which was far-reaching in its consequences and which tied political participation to property, regarded the ordering of property as the basis of the social and especially the political order. It goes hand in hand with the transition to the middle-class constitutional state and the related economic order. Starting with individual property and individual control over it, this position solidified the connection between the economic and the political order.

In the Anglo-Saxon tradition of liberal → natural law, → freedom and property were viewed as equally valid (e.g., by J. Locke, who argued that a government was morally obliged to protect the life, liberty, and property of its citizens). In addition, there was a tendency (influential also in the United States) to mediate the one through the other. In that case the stress lay not merely on the protection of property from the attacks of others but on safeguarding its development. The idea that property is the basis and condition of freedom was a guiding one in the further development of the philosophical theory of property. In terms of an actualizing of personal freedom, this thought was mediated by speaking of an "outer sphere" of freedom, to which property belongs (G. W. F. Hegel).

2.3. *Constitutional Protection and Ambivalent Results*

As the protection of property became established in the ongoing course of constitutional history, it became quite obvious that this protection (based on an appeal to freedom) against the attacks of others might work to the disadvantage of the very people who were dependent on the property. Other ambivalent implications of the protection of property also had to be considered as time went on, especially the distinction between protection of property (also against the state) and the basing of social and political status on property. These problems arose largely out of the mediation between freedom and property as it was formulated in Hegel's philosophy of law.

Other theories of law and the conceptions of constitutional law stood in opposition to the liberal concept of property. Such theories did not refer the political order to the middle-class subjects (e.g., householders) constituted by property but sought to make the political order itself an institution. Property was here upheld in terms of "acquired rights," in distinction from property gained by labor or acquisition (F. J. Stahl).

2.4. *Marxist Socialism*

The liberal view of property remained valid under the banner of 19th-century industrialization, but property in the form of ownership of the means of (industrial) production gave rise to a new problem. K. → Marx (1818-83) and F. Engels (1820-95) took into account the increasing concentration of private ownership — based on capital — of the means of production (→ Marxism). As they saw it, this situation involved the expression of a basic contradiction between the work that individuals do for society and the private appropriation by others of the fruit of this work. Since there is no alternative to an individualistic view of property, it follows (so they thought) that a socializing of the means of production (→ Socialism) is the only way to resolve the conflict. This idea became a leading one insofar as ownership of the means of production is a specific means of (private or public) control.

Some early socialists (e.g., R. Owen, W. Weitling) were already moving beyond this way of looking at the problem, and late socialist theories followed suit. In particular, there were different views of the relation between property and the political order. → Religious socialism (H. Kutter, L. Ragaz, also P. → Tillich) focused attention more sharply on a religiously based social and property order, on a changed relation of persons to things, and on social legislation.

3. Property in the Theological Tradition

Reflection on the concept of property was more occasional in the theological tradition. Here property was not seen as an → institution that is basic to shared human life, even though it might seem to be a necessary element in this order. A change came when Christian → ethics adopted the liberal concept of property. Critically distinguished from this view was the understanding of property as an institution, which gave it a basis in the social legal order. Property thus had critical social significance, not merely for individuals, and its use became a theme of ethical discussion.

3.1. *OT and NT*

The origins of an understanding of property in biblical statements and the Christian tradition were decisive for achieving a view of property that would grasp its ethical significance, particularly in light of natural-law and liberal conceptions. The OT has no comprehensive view of property. The form of acquiring property and its relation to the owner came to linguistic expression in different ways. A most important point for its meaning is that terms for property could describe the relation between Yahweh and → Israel (Exod. 19:5; Ps. 135:4). The NT speaks similarly (Titus 2:14; 1 Pet. 2:9) as in its description of a perfect relationship to God (Eph. 1:14). → Dogmatics also views us as the property of Christ (→ Heidelberg Catechism, q. 34). Hence property cannot have constitutive significance for human life.

Another critical criterion arises out of the fact that in the OT Yahweh is the owner of the land and simply loans it to Israel (Lev. 25:23). On the OT view there is no unrestricted control over property, which serves as the basis of life itself. Its legal protection relates to this fact. Along these lines the commandment "you shall not steal" in the Decalogue (Exod. 20:15, also Deut. 5:19) protects property against aggression. The view that property is a basis of life that is divinely entrusted to us is important in Christian thinking. Property is not based on the measure of what we can appropriate to ourselves but on what is given to us in common as a basis of life. There is no special foundation for individual property.

In the OT and NT and also in the Christian doctrinal tradition, property is seen from two angles: (1) that of its relation to legal → justice, and (2) that of criticism of legal violations and of the social differences between the rich and the poor for which there is no legal justification. The ordering of property has no normative validity apart from law. We cannot speak of a recognition of property in principle without reference to this relation. Obviously human life together is regulated by property, and social conduct is shaped by it, but only in connection with law. From this angle the connection between property and philanthropy or even the Christian → community of goods is a theme in Christian ethics. Renouncing property is also a special feature of responsibility for it.

3.2. *Christian Ethics*

The renunciation of property was a leading theme in the detailed discussion of property in the → church fathers. Basically criticizing private property (e.g., the monastic ethics of Basil the Great), they thought that Christians should share possessions (John → Chrysostom), inasmuch as property is part of the world of the fall and may not be totally abolished. This did not mean the validation of existing property relations but a recognition that we need property to live. Only with this limitation may we hold property responsibly.

In developing an ethics of the responsible use of property, the leading thought is that of the relation to law (with a distinction between God's law and human law, esp. in → Augustine). Property is thus seen institutionally.

3.3. *Theological Basis*

In further theological discussion the social significance of property was still viewed in relation to law. Aquinas saw in it a legal institution (*Summa theol.* II of II, q. 66, art. 2, ad 1). His starting point was that all things belong to all people, and each person must be ready to share common goods as the need arises. This idea rests on natural law. In contrast, individual property has a secondary basis, though it is still part of the *ius gentium* (law of nations). Individual property includes the → duty of sharing what we do not use ourselves as alms. Thomas thus introduced his own emphasis over against the dominant medieval concept of control. Property is a legal order of shared human life.

Along similar lines M. → Luther (1483-1546) found a basis for property in the fact that apart from what we need to live, we need to have something to be able to give. But on a biblical basis a second aspect was now important. Renouncing property (as in monastic poverty; → Monasticism) comes into consideration as a mark of our eschatological status before God. For Luther, then, property does not underlie any far-reaching political concept or concept in social ethics. It is important, however, that for him the accent is on the social function of property. With reference to our eschatological status, the limited grounding of property is not merely relativized but ethicized. Property must be handled responsibly if we are to live together justly. Beyond this concern, property has no sustaining meaning (e.g., for human freedom). Reformation ethics thus stands in a critical relation to the further development of the understanding of a property along liberal middle-class lines, even as it contributed to the rise of middle-class society.

Recognition of the social function of property, which all the Reformers share (including U. → Zwingli and J. → Calvin), is one of the roots of capitalism to the extent that it does not rest on a striving for profit but on a responsible handling of property. (M. → Weber was right in his thesis regarding capitalism.) In a special way the attempts of the → Anabaptists at social reform bring to light the critical features of the Reformation view vis-à-vis the incipient middle-class social order.

4. Present Discussion

Present discussion — whether official, academic, or ecclesiastical — rests on the fact that elements of the liberal concept of property persist, even with legal restrictions and doubts as to its significance and scope. Solution to the tension between private property and the required social link is sought in the form of nationalization of the means of production and a broader distribution of property for a just sharing of economic goods and values. These approaches do not have to be mutually antithetical, for they deal with different problems: with an economic order that the order of property challenges, with problems of distribution within a given economic order, with changes in the control of economic power, and so forth. Related to these issues are the most diverse sociopolitical goals, which are determined by what "property," "defense of property," and "guarantee of property" mean and imply. The crucial question for ethics is whether the understanding of property can yield a feasible and comprehensive criterion for the solution of the various sociopolitical and socioeconomic problems. More broadly, what was and is the basic significance of property for modern economic society?

The questions are the more important inasmuch as individual property is guaranteed by law and legal decision. This guarantee applies especially to inherited property.

4.1. *Roman Catholic and Protestant Teaching*

In Roman Catholic social teaching (→ Social Ethics), discussion began at the end of the 19th century and focuses largely on the question of the legitimacy of private ownership of means of production. The → encyclicals of Leo XIII (1878-1903) and Pius XI (1922-39) reflect the connection between the legitimacy of private property and social obligation on the basis of liberal thinking in terms of natural law. A fundamental contribution to the solution of the social question is expected from widespread distribution of property, the sharing of common goods, and shared control, but no different economic order is envisioned.

In Protestantism the discussion that was renewed after World War II has moved in much the same direction. At times the emphasis is not so much on a legal order and a just sharing of goods as on the safeguarding of individual property. Thus property is viewed as a basic institution like → marriage, labor (→ Work), → vocation, the state, and the → church. The aim of social ethics is thus to bring the order of property more strictly into harmony with the national democratic order (→ Democracy). At times some limited aspects of the distribution of property and the control of economic power (e.g., codetermination) also come into consideration.

Roman Catholic and Protestant social ethics advance no large-scale theories, for example, of political economy. Thus the question remains how the order of property and the economic order relate to one another as regards the social obligation of ownership. The debatable point is whether social obligation can be better ensured by changing economic relations than by other ways of securing social justice. This issue was still pertinent in the 1960s. The one party stresses social justice, the other the safeguarding of individual → freedom as it relates to property. Social ethics has not yet developed an alternative in principle to the liberal concept of property, which we see from the memoranda of the German Evangelical Church and from Roman Catholic documents like the encyclical *Laborem exercens* (1981).

4.2. *Social and Ethical Problems*

A more recent question is whether the constitutional view of property is in keeping with the social and economic conditions of Western countries, since it has clearly failed to inquire into the breadth of the function of property (e.g., in the guaranteeing of social justice) or to ask how the social obligation of property can best be safeguarded. It has been asserted that we must uphold the distinction between ownership of the means of production and the use of individual property, so that the starting point cannot be a comprehensive concept of property. This view is in keeping with the development of welfare-state functions, which, largely independently, make the guarantees affecting the individual use of property (at least property that is any more than merely short-term consumer goods).

This basic development has been called a defunctionalizing of property (O. von Nell-Breuning; see also M. Honecker). It concerns both the social security of individuals and their freedom for development, and also some freedom of entrepreneurial enterprise. On this view property cannot guarantee this freedom because it has many economic and social ramifications and because freedom itself is restricted by social obligations and rights that are not based on property. This issue is seen as the decisive task in building up a social and legal state, which from the standpoint of social ethics has more far-reaching consequences for the relating of the economy and democracy than can be achieved merely by common ownership. The ensuring of income is more important than a broad distribution of property or sharing in productive capacity. In this connection the right to work is also preeminent.

An unsolved problem is that social and democratic functions do not do adequate justice to the public status of property relative to the common good, especially as concerns goods that cannot be increased or renewed but that are fundamental to life (the earth, raw materials, natural conditions; → Ecology; Energy). In particular, it is seen that a change is needed in the sphere of landed property that will take into account the growing urgency of the social obligation of owning it and will remove the intolerable contradictions between guaranteeing property and the common good. The understanding of property as an institution — which is expressed by giving to legislators the task of materially developing property, but also giving concrete form to its social obligations — can lead to further critical thinking along these lines.

5. Future Tasks

As regards development of the institution of property, the decisive point is how far it contributes to a solution of the problems of just distribution of the basic necessities of life, of making sure they are available for all, and of maintaining or improving the conditions of life for all. The status of ownership of goods that are important for human life (food, health, habitation) or those that underlie human life (soil, water, air, raw materials) is urgently in need of change. A regulated order is necessary that will permit the ethically responsible distribution and preservation of these goods and not leave them simply at the whim of market forces. The institution of property acquires here a new function that protects the goods themselves, and not merely control over them, in the general interest of all.

5.1. *Relation to World Economic Order*

Far-reaching and radical changes are required in the present economic system. Such changes must take account of (1) the differences in distribution, which are unavoidable under present economic conditions; (2) the progressive destruction and exploitation of raw materials (mostly used by industrialized nations) and natural resources; and (3) the growing → poverty of countries that are not integrated into the economic system of the industrial West (→ Third World). New models of a world economic order are thus being sought, especially models that aim, not at the (almost impossible) integration of poor countries into the systems of the wealthy industrialized nations, but at self-reliance. Achieving this goal will mean profound changes in the social structures of the poorer countries and their involvement with larger economic power structures, though without social assimilation to the industrialized states (→ Dependence; Development 1). These reforms will mean great changes relative to property, especially in agriculture, land ownership, and profits.

5.2. *Ecumenical Discussion*

Along with the task of making long-term changes in economic conditions, there is also an urgent need to share available goods and rights. In view of naturally caused unequal distribution (even between poor countries), models of sharing will have to be developed that give the poor a share in the wealth of others without any necessary return. In ecumenical discussion and studies (see the relevant section reports of the → World Council of Churches assemblies, beginning with Uppsala 1968), two main goals have been discerned: developing self-reliance, and finding models of sharing (esp. discussed at Vancouver 1983). As regards the latter, care must be taken not to expect changes merely from a new world economic order. Action by the churches is especially needed at this point.

The problems of the economic system can hardly be reduced to the problems of a changed economic order. Nevertheless, in the politics of raw materials and in land reform, changed relations in the actual control of property have far-reaching consequences. Such changes will have to presuppose corresponding reforms in the industrialized nations. Hence legislative work on the regulation of property is an urgent need.

→ Economic Ethics

Bibliography: M. Hengel, *Property and Riches in the Early Church: Aspects of a Social History of Early Christianity* (Philadelphia, 1974) • M. Honecker, *Konzept einer sozialethischen Theorie. Grundfragen evangelischer Sozialethik* (Tübingen, 1971) • G. Lantz, *Eigentumsrecht–ein Recht oder ein Unrecht? Eine kritische Beurteilung der ethischen Argumente für das Privateigentum bei Aristoteles, Thomas von Aquino, Grotius, Locke, Hegel, Marx und in den modernen katholischen Sozialenzykliken* (Uppsala, 1977) • P.-J. Proudhon, *What Is Property?* (Cambridge, 1994; orig. pub., 1840) • L. L. Rasmussen, *Earth Community, Earth Ethics* (Maryknoll, N.Y., 1996) • S. D. Ross, *The Gift of Property: Having the Good* (Albany, N.Y., 2001) • R. W. Rousseau, *Human Dignity and the Common Good: The Great Papal Social Encyclicals from Leo XIII to John Paul II* (Westport, Conn., 2002).

Hans G. Ulrich

Prophet, Prophecy

1. Religions
   1.1. Definition
   1.2. OT Background
   1.3. Iran
   1.4. Gnosticism

Prophet, Prophecy

1. Religions

1.1. *Definition*

In Greek the term *prophētēs* (prophet) refers to one engaged in public proclamation, as by oracles or poets. The word became significant when used to describe an OT phenomenon, as it came to denote the OT prophets in particular and then, by extension, similar NT figures, even though they were not specifically modeled on the OT prophets. The term then became a significant one in → Islam, but again with characteristic modifications. In the history of Christianity and Islam (→ History of Religion), the term has found constant use to describe such things as public proclamation, intimation of the future, and → ecstasy, whether in a favorable or an unfavorable sense (see 3.5).

In the → modern period the term has been generalized and applied to other cultural areas (→ Culture). Prophets in this broadened sense are no longer specifically religious figures but those who speak in a variety of contexts, according to phenomenological, psychological, or sociological criteria (→ Phenomenology; Psychology; Sociology). Prophets, then, speak variously by divine commission, at the command of an alien power, ecstatically, in an altered state of consciousness, or charismatically (→ Charisma), whether centrally or marginally. In all such instances we have an expanded use of the term. To gain a true understanding we need to look first at the OT prototype. Historically, prophecy belongs first to the Israelite-Judaic-Christian-Islamic context, to which phenomenological, psychological, and sociological factors must be related.

1.2. *OT Background*

The countries around OT Israel had technical means whereby to discern the will of the gods, such as by consulting entrails or oil on water. Inspirational knowledge played its part here (→ Inspiration). Individuals stepped forth in the name of this or that god and declared what the divine will was.

We find this activity in Mesopotamia, especially on the western edge, and most plainly in Mari (texts from the 18th-17th cents. B.C.). Prophecy (Akkad. *maḫḫûm*) here was controlled by the cult. The deity endowed officials (→ Priest, Priesthood, 1) and also private persons with messages for the king, including ritual demands, reproaches, and salvation oracles in times of → war. The Mari prophecy was strictly related to the cult and governed by it. It supported the monarchy but yet had much freedom to criticize it (in the priestly interest?).

Later, Assyria also offers strongly stylized examples of salvation oracles in times of war. In Egypt too we find directions in the name of deities, but the procedure is obscure in detail. Predictions after the event occur that apply to some royal successes, but texts of this kind rest on an actual → institution. Canaan also had a type of prophecy in which ecstasy played a part, but in every case it seems to have been specialized and under cultic control. In contrast, we find in the looser culture of the → nomads a more flexible type of prophecy that could give direction either by technical or by inspirational/charismatic means. In general the → organization of knowledge by → divination corresponds to a group's social organization, with greater division of labor making prophecy more specialized.

1.3. *Iran*

Zoroaster in the seventh century B.C. (dated, alternatively, in the 10th, 9th, 8th, or 6th/5th cents.) had a traditional role as a *zaotar*/priest who thrust the sacrificial offerings into the fire (→ Iranian Religions 6). Visions and auditions seem to have had a place in this role, but they took Zoroaster beyond the → tradition in opposition to bloody animal sacrifices and orgiastic cults. The new → preaching was not accepted, and therefore the prophets became an adversary as the contours of a new religious orientation emerged. In dialogue with the new (or newly emphasized) Ahura Mazda, an ethically dualistic concept developed that did not simply accept the world as it is but held critically aloof from it. In this regard there is some affinity between the religion of Zoroaster and that of → Israel (→ Dualism).

1.4. *Gnosticism*

It is debatable how far one may speak of prophecy in → Gnosticism, whose proponents were academic interpreters rather than prophets, even though we may trace links to primitive Christian enthusiasm.

Mani (→ Manichaeanism), at least, seems to have had some inspirational experiences.

1.5. *Islam*

We must see the prophecy of Muḥammad (ca. 570-632) in a twofold context. He was acquainted with the role of the older Arabic *kāhin,* an inspired figure whose activity ranged from magic to poetry. Muḥammad's forms of speech were at first taken from those of the *kāhin,* but he then increasingly moved in a different direction, plainly along the lines of prophecy in written religions, yet with a degree of independent individuality. He called figures from the OT and the NT "prophets," including some whom the OT and NT themselves did not describe as such. A prophet now was a witness to ongoing revelation within written religions. Muḥammad himself was the "seal of the prophets," the prophet who could not be excelled, the mediator of revelation.

Along with the prophets Muḥammad recognized "envoys" who were sent by God to Jews and Christians, and also to Arabs (notably the qur'anic prophets Hud and Salih), to confront them with the message of → monotheism. They experienced rejection, with the divine punishment coming on their audience as a consequence. Confessionally, Muḥammad himself is also called God's envoy, or messenger.

1.6. *Developments*

Although Islam regarded prophecy as coming to an end with Muḥammad, in fact inspirational processes might still be found in it, especially in → Sufism (→ Mysticism) and → Shia. The → qur'anic terms were not used, however, for the closing of revelation was not basically questioned. If claims were made by those thus inspired, possession of revelation could lead to persecution (such as the execution of the mystic al-Ḥallāj in 922). In some cases the concept of prophecy was eschatologized (e.g., in Mahdi expectation; → Eschatology). From time to time Mahdi might be equated with a living person. We find a similar development in Christianity, especially in mysticism or eschatological expectation (e.g., Joachim of Fiore; → Millenarianism 4; Franciscans 2).

Prophetic phenomena sometimes gave rise to religious movements that emanated from Islam. Thus we might refer to Babism in Iran from the middle of the 19th century. The founder, as *bāb* (gateway), styled himself Mahdi and claimed the dignity of Mahdi. This claim led to much political unrest and persecution, and today Babism has almost completely disappeared. From it, however, → Baha'i developed, whose founder also claimed the dignity of Mahdi, though the religion itself underwent change and adopted what are almost at times Enlightenment and modernist features. Finally, there is the Aḥmadīyah movement, which can no longer be called Islamic, in view of its founder's claim to revelation.

1.7. *Crisis Cultures*

Prophecy is very important in → crisis cults, which have been triggered by a movement toward modernization or by contacts between Western civilization and traditional cultures (→ Acculturation). Such situations call for a fresh interpretation or organization of the system of religious → symbols, which religiously inspired figures often undertake. In the 19th and 20th centuries, especially in the United States, we find upheavals of this type and the founding of separate → sects by their prophets (e.g., by → Adventists, → Jehovah's Witnesses, → Mormons, and fundamentalist groups; → Modern Church History 2). Problems of succession regularly arise after the founder's death, with problems of authority or new prophecies often leading to further splits. In other groups, especially in → Pentecostal churches, prophetic gifts are not a privilege of the founder alone but may be an experience of any member, so that control mechanisms must be found to preserve unity and authority.

In non-Western societies crisis cults manifest themselves, on the one hand, in a transforming and revitalizing, often an eschatologizing, of traditional symbol systems as prophets promise a quick salvation (perhaps, as in the so-called → cargo cults, in the form of increased material goods) or put themselves at the head of liberation movements. On the other hand, they show up in movements that adapt Christianity very strongly to traditional realities, so that the sending mission churches can no longer accept them as Christian (→ healing being of particular importance here). The two types often overlap. Individual movements may develop in many different ways, such as political movements or as traditional churches like the → Kimbanguist Church.

→ Charismatic Movement; Colonialism; Independent Churches; Messianism; New Religions

Bibliography: D. E. Aune, *Prophecy in Christianity and the Ancient Mediterranean World* (Grand Rapids, 1983) • W. J. Bergen, *Elijah and the End of Prophetism* (Sheffield, 1999) • W. Brueggeman, *Testimony to Otherwise: The Witness of Elijah and Elisha* (St. Louis, 2001) • C. Colpe, *Das Siegel der Propheten. Historische Beziehungen zwischen Judentum, Judenchristentum, Heidentum und frühem Islam* (Berlin, 1990) • H.-J. Greschat, *Westafrikanische Propheten* (Marburg, 1974) • J. K. Hadden and A. Shupe, eds., *Prophetic Religions and Politics* (New York, 1986) • I. M. Lewis, *Ecstatic Religion: A Study of Shamanism and Spirit Possession* (2d ed.; London, 1988) • J. C. de Moor, ed., *The Elusive Prophet: The Prophet as Historical Person, Literary Character, and Anonymous Artist* (Leiden, 2001) • N. I. Ndiokwere, *Prophecy and Revolution: The Role of Prophets in the Independent African Churches and in Biblical Tradition* (London, 1981) • E. Noort, *Untersuchungen zum Gottesbescheid in Mari. Die "Mariprophetie" in der alttestamentlichen Forschung* (Kevelaer, 1977) • A. Schimmel, *And Muhammad Is His Messenger: The Veneration of the Prophet in Islamic Piety* (Chapel Hill, N.C., 1985) • B. Sundkler, *Bantu Prophets in South Africa* (2d ed.; London, 1961).

Fritz Stolz

2. OT

2.1. *Term*

Gk. *prophētēs* (prophet) is the LXX translation of Heb. *nābî'*. The meaning and etymology of this word are debated. It may derive from Akkad. *nābi'um*, "one who calls" or "one who is called [by the gods]." For two reasons, however, etymology contributes little to the modern understanding of OT prophecy. First, the etymology was not known even in OT days, so that we have to reckon with a development that reaches much further back. Then in the immediate pre-Christian centuries *nābî'* came to denote in general a man of God of any kind, and in the plural form, *nĕbî'îm*, it came into use for the OT books that were not part of the → Pentateuch. (The *nĕbî'îm rišōnîm* [earlier prophets] encompass Joshua, Judges, Samuel, and Kings; the *nĕbî'îm 'aḥărônîm* [later prophets], Isaiah, Jeremiah, Ezekiel, and the Minor Prophets.)

By "prophets" today we understand not merely the *nābî'* but also the related "man of God" (*'îš 'ĕlōhîm*, e.g., 1 Kings 13 or 2 Kings 4) and the "seer" (*rō'eh* or *ḥōzeh*, e.g., 1 Sam. 9:9, Amos 7:12).

Biblical scholarship looks at prophecy phenomenologically rather than etymologically. In this regard prophecy in early Israel can be compared with that in the ancient Near East more broadly. In Mesopotamia especially there were ecstatic figures in the 2nd millennium b.c. who stood between the human world and the divine and who thus functioned as messengers of the gods and intercessors on behalf of humans. Most important in this regard are the Mari texts of the 17th century, in which ecstatics appear as prophets of woe (similar to the OT prophets). In the Deir ʿAllā texts (ca. 700 b.c.) we find the prophet or seer Balaam, to whom reference is made in Numbers 22–24. Here is important evidence that prophecy was not unique to → Israel but, like → Wisdom or the cult, was an international phenomenon.

2.2. *Stories*

According to the historical books of the OT, the first great prophets appeared in the early days of the monarchy (see 1 Samuel 9–10), though the OT also calls such figures as → Moses and Balaam and even → Abraham prophets in certain literary strata. The Books of Samuel and Kings contain many stories of the prophets. What is important here is that in many respects these stories differ considerably from the → "Deuteronomistic" understanding of the prophets, so that in most instances we must date them to a pre-Deuteronomistic period, that is, as preexilic — though doing so in no way necessarily means that they are historically authentic or derive from eyewitnesses. For example, the story of Balaam seems to have an international background and thus has little to tell us about the origins of prophecy in Israel.

In Samuel and Kings the prophets were not a homogeneous group. Some lived alone (→ Elijah, maybe also → Elisha), others in groups (e.g., the *bĕnê hannĕbî'îm*, "sons of [the] prophets" [KJV] or "company of [the] prophets" [NRSV], i.e., members of a prophetic group or guild). Some were outside the establishment (Elijah), others were in the king's service (1 Kings 22). Some seem to have had a cultic role alongside the → priests, others held aloof from the → cult.

Their messages also differed. Some like Nathan or Elijah could even criticize the king (2 Samuel 12; 1 Kings 21; → Monarchy in Israel); in contrast, even the great prophet Samuel could function as merely a local seer who did not primarily concern himself with matters of state but simply helped to find lost things (the asses of Saul's father, 1 Samuel 9). With Amos, the first writing prophet, the message then began to relate to the future of the people as a whole, and thus emerged what later generations would see as typical prophecy.

The prophets believed that they had access to the counsel *(sôd)* of → Yahweh (see 1 Kings 22). They could thus give the people reliable information about both present and future, and they interceded with Yahweh for the people. For this reason Abraham and Moses could also be seen as prophets (Gen. 20:7; Exod. 32:30-31; cf. Jer. 15:1).

2.3. *Writing Prophets*

The writing prophets made their appearance in the eighth century when Israel and Judah were in contact with the great empires (Assyria up to the 7th cent., then Babylon). They are called writing prophets because their prophecies were recorded in books, though whether they themselves wrote the books is contested, and even if they did, there is still debate about possible later additions.

Two burning issues typify the message of the writing prophets: the people's sins and Yahweh's punishment in the form of the conquest of the land by the Assyrians and Babylonians. The books themselves look ahead to restoration after the disaster, but some scholars suggest that in the case of Amos, Micah, and Isaiah, these salvation prophecies are later additions; not, however, in the case of Hosea and Jeremiah, where Yahweh first punishes his people but then makes them his own again (e.g., Hos. 1:10-11).

Another point of debate is whether the prophets, as the books indicate, did in fact see the possibility of a conversion that would avert the → wrath of God. R. Smend took the view that Amos was wholly negative, but conditional promises are found in Isaiah (1:10-20; 30:15). The sin that brings down judgment is, on the one hand, the cultic apostasy of the kings as they worship the gods of Canaan and Mesopotamia along with or instead of Yahweh (Hos. 2:1-13; Jer. 2:9-28) and, on the other hand, the social injustices for which the upper social classes are responsible as they afflict the poor, widows, and orphans (Amos 2:6-8; Isa. 5:8-23).

In the sixth-century exilic period the prophecies of disaster had been fulfilled, and now prophecy found a new voice that put judgment in the past and proclaimed a better future. We find the new message in Deutero-Isaiah and Ezekiel, who predicted the return of the exiled Israelites in Jerusalem and the rebuilding of the devastated city and the → temple. Yet even after the exile prophetic criticism of the people lived on (e.g., Zech. 7:8-14). For all their differences, the prophets agreed unanimously that the decisive element in Israel's history was not what the people might plan socially or politically but the Word of Yahweh, which would not return empty but accomplish what God pleased and do that for which he sent it (Isa. 55:11).

2.4. *Prophetic Speech*

The term "writing prophets" is a questionable one, for in the books themselves the oracles were originally oral rather than written. Even if the prophets wrote them down or had them written down (see, e.g., Jer. 36:4), they had their genesis in → preaching. Form criticism suggests that the prophets used fairly short and self-contained forms of speech, whose somewhat disorderly arrangement has resulted in the unevenness of the present texts. The three most important forms are as follows:

Accusations, in which the prophets censure the people for their sins (e.g., Isa. 1:21-23; Jer. 2:9-13; Hos. 4:1-2).

Threats, in which the prophets predict coming disasters (e.g., Hos. 12:1-2; Amos 2:13-16). Accusations and threats are often linked by "because" *(yaʿan ʾăšer)* or "therefore" *(lākēn),* as in 2 Kgs. 1:16 and Isa. 28:14-22.

Admonitions, in which prophets seek to bring home to the people their obligations to Yahweh (e.g., Isa. 1:16-17; Jer. 4:1-4; Amos 5:14-15). Since this type is not so frequent, one may conclude that in the main the prophets predicted disasters and gave reasons for them, not counting on the people's conversion. Nevertheless, an accusation might often be also an admonition. Those who had sinned should sin no more.

The prophets also used forms that are found in other types of writing.

Messenger formulas ("thus says the Lord," *kōh ʾāmar YHWH,* e.g., Amos 1:3, 6, 9, 11, 13) stand at the head of many oracles and define them as messages from God. This formula is typically prophetic, and yet it is of secular origin, with roots in the speeches of Near Eastern ambassadors (cf. 2 Kgs. 18:19).

Cries of woe ("woe" [RSV] or "ah!" [NRSV], *hôy*), as in Isa. 5:8, 11, 18, 20, 21, 22, had their origin in laments for the dead (1 Kgs. 13:30) but were adopted by the prophets as a sign that the people were already spiritually dead and would perish in the near future.

2.5. *Prophets and Other Groups (Cult, Wisdom, Deuteronomists)*

The great writing prophets and preclassical prophets like Elijah were independent of official circles in Israel, whether religious or political. Nevertheless, they had contacts with the → everyday life of the people in both kingdoms. Independent as they were, they were still members of a society in which there were no independent individuals in the modern sense. Three circles are especially important if we search for the "spiritual home" (H. W. Wolff) of the prophets.

2.5.1. First was the cult. The prophets no doubt took part in the cultic life of preexilic Israel, for some of the psalm oracles are best understood along such lines (e.g., Pss. 50:5; 54:6; 118:20), and others refer specifically to cultic participation (e.g., 2 Kgs. 23:2; Jer. 26:7, 11, 16). Amos 7:10-17 suggests that Amos was known to the → priest Amaziah as a cult prophet who ought to have functioned under priestly authority. At the same time, preexilic writing prophets seem also to have steered clear of the cult and even been in opposition to it (e.g., Isa. 1:12-17; Hos. 6:6; Amos 5:21-24). The relevant passages may sometimes suggest that their rejection of → sacrifices and feasts was ad hoc. Only those whose hands were not stained with the blood of the poor ought to offer sacrifices. But in some cases it seems to be a matter of principle, as in Amos 5:25 or Jer. 7:21-23. In that case the writing prophets can have had little to do with the cult.

After the exile the hostility between prophets and the cult was so completely at an end that Haggai and Zechariah could view the rebuilding of the temple as a prerequisite for divine → grace. See especially Hag. 1:1-11 and Zech. 8:9-13, where the prophets encourage the people to engage in the rebuilding.

2.5.2. Then we have Wisdom. According to Jer. 18:18 the three leading groups in Judah in the seventh century were priests, prophets, and the wise. Priests and prophets may have sometimes worked together, as did prophets and the wise. Modern biblical scholarship suggests that the writing prophets were strongly influenced by Wisdom, whether the more academic Wisdom of the royal court and officialdom or the popular Wisdom of small towns and villages. Worth noting in Amos is the "number Wisdom" of n and $n + 1$ (1:3, 6, 9, 11, 13; 2:1, 4, 6), as well as the series of sayings in 3:3-8. In Isaiah the parable of the farmer in 28:23-29 reminds us of Wisdom literature, and the ethical teaching in the woes of 5:8-25 and 10:1-4 reminds us of Proverbs 10–29. Several prophets compare the people to animals (e.g., Isa. 1:3; Jer. 2:23-24; cf. Prov. 30:15-31). The prophets censure those who are "wise in their own eyes," but they do not reject Wisdom as such.

Isaiah seems to have been a counselor to the king of Judah; if so, he must have had a Wisdom education. Amos reflects the popular wisdom of Tekoa (note the wise woman of Tekoa in 2 Samuel 14). Certainly there was no general conflict between the prophets and Wisdom (W. McKane).

2.5.3. Third, we have the Deuteronomists. Important themes in Deuteronomy and in the → Deuteronomistic history (Joshua through 2 Kings) appear also in the theology of the preexilic prophets, and prophets play an important role in these works. It is hardly to be doubted that there was a close connection between the Deuteronomistic school and the great prophets. We cannot say more about this relation in detail because we know too little about the preclassical prophets or the impact of the classical prophets on the works that are related to the Deuteronomistic school. The two-way influence makes investigation difficult. Jeremiah is crucial here, for although some scholars think the book underwent Deuteronomistic editing, the oracles that are indisputably authentic are closest to Deuteronomic theology.

2.6. *End of Prophecy*

After the exile Jerusalem and the temple were rebuilt, but there was no longer any truly independent Jewish state. Hence, prophecy could no longer find a place in the preexilic sense, in which it had been closely bound up with the monarchy, with → war and → peace, with resistance to enemies, and with capitulation to invaders. The peace that now held sway owed nothing to what the Jewish authorities either did or did not do.

In this new situation the prophets had less to say about the present and the sinful past that had caused it and more about the better future that the omnipotence of God would bring about. Instead of being politically and ethically informed commentators, the prophets increasingly became seers again, whose messages did not relate to the decisions and actions of king or people but more exclusively to the foreseeable purposes of Yahweh. Hence, prophecy gradually merged into → apocalyptic (e.g., Isaiah 24–27; Zechariah 9–14). Especially at the beginning of the Hellenistic age (end of the 4th cent.), the prophetic life was no longer an honorable one (see the association of prophets and the "unclean spirit" in Zech. 13:2-6).

The hope of renewed prophecy was not dead (Joel 2:28-29), but it would come only in the eschatological age (→ Eschatology 1). For the moment it was not a matter of vital interest. There thus arose among the rabbis the dogma of an age without prophets (R. Leivestad), which held that prophecy had ceased in the days of Ezra, so that no more remained of it than the echo (*bat qôl,* lit. "daughter of the voice").

The Judaism of the postexilic period had an understanding of prophecy as having ceased, which deviates considerably from the historical-critical view. According to the former, the prophets were preachers of repentance who were commissioned to teach the → Torah and had less to do with political and more general ethical issues. On this view of prophecy the eschatological elements were far less prominent than many scholars today now think. The conviction that the prophets were teachers of the Torah is still current in → Judaism, while in Christianity the eschatological interpretation prevails, the eschatological pronouncements being related to Jesus Christ. The historical-critical reinterpretation of the classic prophets has thus brought some new and revolutionary insights to both Judaism and Christianity.

Bibliography: J. Barton, *Oracles of God: Perceptions of Ancient Prophecy in Israel after the Exile* (New York, 1986) • J. Blenkinsopp, *A History of Prophecy in Israel* (rev. ed.; Louisville, Ky., 1996) • R. P. Carroll, *When Prophecy Failed: Cognitive Dissonance in the Prophetic Traditions of the OT* (New York, 1979) • P. R. Davies, *The Prophets: A Sheffield Reader* (Sheffield, 1996) • M. Nissinen, *Prophets and Prophecy in the Ancient Near East* (Atlanta, 2003) • D. L. Petersen, *Prophecy in Israel: Search for an Identity* (Philadelphia, 1987) • J. F. A. Sawyer, *Prophecy and the Biblical Prophets* (rev. ed.; Oxford, 1993) • R. R. Wilson, *Prophecy and Society in Ancient Israel* (Philadelphia, 1980).

John Barton

3. NT

3.1. *OT Prophets in the NT*

Continuity between the OT and the NT may be seen in the high regard for the OT prophets in the NT. The NT calls the Scriptures that were then to hand "the → law [*or* the law of Moses] and the prophets" (Matt. 5:17; 7:12; 11:13 par. Luke 16:16; Matt. 22:40; Luke 16:29, 31; John 1:45; Acts 13:15; 28:23; Rom. 3:21, etc.). By prophets who were impelled by the → Holy Spirit (§1), God spoke to the fathers (Acts 3:18, 21; Heb. 1:1; 2 Pet. 1:21). By their sufferings and death (Matt. 23:29-32, 35, 37 par. Luke 11:47-48, 50; 13:34; Acts 7:52), the OT prophets are linked to the Christian → martyrs (Rev. 6:9-11) and serve as models of Christian → suffering and → faith (Matt. 5:11-12 par. Luke 6:22-23; Heb. 11:36-38; Jas. 5:10).

Reference is made by name to Elijah, Elisha, Isaiah, Jeremiah, Daniel, Joel, and Jonah, also to Balaam; in addition, Moses, Samuel, and David, in keeping with the older Jewish view, are counted as prophets. Quotations also appear from Hosea, Amos, Micah, Habakkuk, and Zechariah as prophets. The prophets → Moses and → Elijah have special theological and typological significance (see Mark 9:2-8 and par.; Rom. 11:2; 2 Cor. 3:4-18; Jas. 5:17-18). → Jesus is a second Moses (Acts 3:22-23; 7:37; Rev. 11:6; 15:3), → John the Baptist, a second Elijah (Matt. 11:14; 17:10-13 par. Mark 9:11-13; Luke 1:17; Rev. 11:5-6; cf. John 1:21).

3.2. *John the Baptist and Jesus as Prophets*

In the NT both John the Baptist and Jesus are prophetic figures. The prophetic Spirit speaks through the parents of John (Luke 1:41-42, 67-79) and through the witnesses to the presentation of Jesus in the temple (Simeon in Luke 2:25-35 and Anna in vv. 36-38, a prophet according to v. 36). Though the Evangelists do not actually call John a prophet (John 1:21, 25, as they do Jesus; see Matt. 11:9 par. Luke 7:26), he probably understood himself as the new Elijah (see Mal. 3:1; 4:5-6; Sir. 48:10; Matt. 11:14; 17:10-13 par. Mark 9:11-13; Luke 1:17). He might be compared with a prophet of ancient Israel with respect to his life in the desert, his celibacy, his clothing, and his food (Mark 1:4, 6 and par.), and also with respect to his message of repentance and judgment (Matt. 3:7-12 par. Luke 3:7-9, 15-18), along with his ethical rigorism (Mark 6:18 and par.; Luke 3:10-14), his use of the prophetic sign (see, e.g., Ezek. 5:1-17; 24:1-14) of → baptism (Mark 1:4-5 and par.), and his violent death (Mark 6:17-29 and par.).

We find many indications that Jesus saw his task as a prophetic one, though, if he bore personal witness to this fact, it seems not to have found a clear place in post-Easter → Christology. Nevertheless, we still find in Mark 6:4 and par. and in John 4:44 proverbial descriptions of his prophetic destiny (see Matt. 23:37 par. Luke 13:34). In the parable in Mark 12:1-12 and par., Jesus as the last eschatological prophet (and Son of God) ranks himself among Israel's prophets and predicts his violent death, which, for example, Acts 7:52 and 1 Thess. 2:15-16 set alongside the killing of the Jewish prophets. Jesus' baptism, vision, and reception of the Spirit (Mark 1:9-11 and par.) might also be seen as a prophetic calling, and the 40 days in the wilderness (Mark 1:12-13; Matt. 4:1-11 par. Luke 4:1-13) and → celibacy might also be regarded as prophetic → asceticism. The preaching of Jesus contains both promises of salvation (Mark 10:29-30; Matt. 5:3-12 par. Luke 6:20-23; Matt. 13:16-17 par. Luke 10:23-24) and threats (Luke 6:24-26; Matt. 11:21-24 par. Luke 10:12-15, etc.).

Jesus had visions, auditions, and ecstatic experiences (Mark 1:10-11; Luke 10:18, 21; see also John 12:28). He knew hidden things (Mark 2:5, 8 and par.; Luke 7:39-50; cf. John 4:19) and the future (Mark 11:2; 14:13-16, 18, 27, 30 and par.). Like Israel's prophets he worked miracles (Mark 1:23-28 par. Luke 4:33-37; Mark 1:29-31 and par., etc.). He interpreted his healings and exorcisms as symbolic eschatological actions (Matt. 12:28 par. Luke 11:20); also symbolic were his choosing of the Twelve (Mark 3:14-19 and par.), his entry into Jerusalem (Mark 11:1-11 and par.), his cursing of the fig tree (Mark 11:12-14 and par.), his cleansing of the temple (Mark 11:15-19 and par.), his anointing in Bethany (Mark 14:3-9 and par.), and the Last Supper (Mark 14:22-25 and par.; cf. John 13:1-20).

Whereas the Gospels and Acts present John the Baptist clearly as a prophet (the new Elijah), thus showing him to be just a forerunner of Jesus (Mark 6:14-15 par. Luke 9:7-8; Acts 1:5; 11:16, etc.; cf. John

1:19-27), the tradition of Jesus as a prophet shows more ambivalence. If Jesus were a mere prophet, this title would not be appropriate to his dignity as Messiah and Son of God (see esp. Mark, → Q, and Paul; → Christological Titles). Yet we also find a prophetic Christology (F. Hahn, 352-406) that portrays Jesus as excelling the OT prophets in virtue of his → miracles (cf. Luke 7:11-17 with 1 Kgs. 17:17-24 or 2 Kgs. 4:18-37; Mark 6:32-44 and par. with 2 Kgs. 4:42-44). Contemporary confessions of the prophetic dignity of Jesus combine historical recollections and post-Easter Christological interpretation (Matt. 21:11, 46; Mark 6:15 par. Luke 9:8; Mark 8:28 and par.; Luke 7:16; 24:19; John 4:19; 9:17, etc.). Jesus as the new Moses (Acts 3:22-23 etc.) fulfills the prophecy of Deut. 18:15 (see also Matt. 5:1, 17-48).

3.3. *Prophetic Aspects of the Apostolate*

In their life and work and self-understanding, the → apostles, too, may often be compared to the prophets of the OT and Judaism. Mark 1:16-20 and par. reminds us of the calling of Elisha in 1 Kgs. 19:19-21 and of Amos in Amos 7:15. Paul's experience on the Damascus road (Acts 9:3-19 and par.; 1 Cor. 15:8-9; cf. Jer. 20:9 with 1 Cor. 9:16) is a prophetic calling by vision. The Q passages Matt. 23:34-35 par. Luke 11:49-51 and Matt. 23:37-39 par. Luke 13:34-35 include the Christian apostles among the Jewish prophets and view them as undergoing the same sufferings. The relation between the afflictions of Paul in 1 Cor. 4:11-13; 2 Cor. 6:4-10; 11:23-27 (see also 2 Cor. 4:7-10) and the list of prophetic sufferings in Heb. 11:36-38 is striking, and in 1 Thess. 2:15-16 Paul ranks the killing of Jesus and the persecution of his apostles ("us" in v. 15) with the Jewish killing of the prophets.

Like Peter (Acts 3:1-10; 9:32-35, 36-43), Paul heals the sick (Acts 16:16-18; 28:8-9) and raises the dead (Acts 20:9-12; see 1 Kgs. 17:21 and 2 Kgs. 4:34). We might well have symbolic actions in Mark 6:11 and par. and in Matt. 6:16-18 (see Ezek. 24:15-18), and perhaps there is something of the same in Paul's case in 1 Cor. 5:1-5 (cf. Mark 11:12-14 and par.). Neither the → Twelve nor Paul, however, are called prophets (though see Acts 13:1).

3.4. *Itinerant and Community Prophets*

In the NT we often find the gift of prophecy listed with other charisms and offices (→ Charisma 1). Itinerant prophets (see Matt. 10:41) like Agabus (Acts 11:27-28; 21:10-14) have the ability to see the future (11:28; 21:10-11) and act symbolically (21:11). The four unmarried daughters of Philip have the gift of prophecy (21:9). When prophets come to be linked to specific churches, such as Jerusalem (11:27-28; 15:32), Antioch (13:1-2, here with teachers), and Caesarea (21:8-9), it represented the beginning of an institutionalizing of the charism or office (i.e., there now are congregational prophets; see 13:1-3; 15:22-32).

Paul, who valued very highly the gift of prophetic speech (Rom. 12:6; 1 Cor. 12:10; 13:2), mentions prophets along with apostles and teachers (1 Cor. 12:28-29, cf. 14:6, also Rom. 12:6-8). Apostles and prophets are mentioned together in Eph. 2:20; 3:5; 4:11 (here also evangelists, pastors, and teachers). The church is built on the two ministries of apostles and prophets, now viewed as belonging to the past.

The one prophetic book in the NT is the Book of Revelation. The *angelus interpres* (interpreting messenger) speaks thus to its author: "I am a fellow servant with you and your comrades [brothers] the prophets" (Rev. 22:9; see also 19:10a). In alternating combinations we find servants (= prophets, see Isa. 20:3; Jer. 7:25; 25:4, etc.), prophets, saints, and apostles (Rev. 11:18; 16:6; 18:20, 24). These passages suggest a lofty prophetic sense; God reveals the future to the writer (1:1-3; cf. 10:7), who has visions and auditions (1:9-20; 4:1–22:17), from which he derives admonitions in the prophetic style (2:1–3:22). There is a visionary symbolic action in 18:21 (cf. Jer. 51:63-64). Yet "the testimony of Jesus is the spirit of prophecy" (19:10b), so that all church members, at least in principle, share in the prophetic Spirit (1:1; 7:3; 19:2, 5; 22:6b). Celibacy is a prophetic lifestyle on the part of the 144,000 (14:4).

Elsewhere also the distinction is fluid between itinerants who are called to be prophets and church members who are suddenly inspired. For Luke especially, the eschatological community is a prophetic community (Luke 12:12; Acts 2:1–4:13, 15-21 [see Joel 2:28-32]; 4:31; 19:6). Here ecstatic speech or speaking in tongues is a result of prophetic endowment. Paul, however, differentiates prophetic utterance from pneumatic → glossolalia, which is subordinate to prophetic utterance and needs to be supplemented by it (1 Corinthians 14). Speaking in tongues is a sign to unbelievers, but prophecy addresses believers (14:22; cf. Rom. 12:6). Paul assumes that there will be many prophets present at worship (1 Cor. 14:1, 5, 24, 29, 31, 39). Their task is to edify, encourage, console, and instruct church members (14:3, 31), but also to stir up the unbelieving and ignorant (vv. 24-25).

Undoubtedly, Christian prophets often presented their admonitions as words of the exalted Lord (see 1 Cor. 7:10; 9:14; 14:37; 1 Thess. 4:15-17). A statement like that in Acts 20:35b may also have such an origin (→ Agrapha), as also predictions and threats and admonitions in the Gospels that may lack any unequivocal (e.g., form-critical) accompanying criteria. The same approach applies to the "principles of sacred law" that E. Käsemann attributes to Paul (e.g., 1 Cor. 3:17; 14:38; 16:22).

3.5. *False Prophets*

Since prophetic utterance was subject to little control, the danger of heretical prophecy was present from the very first (→ Heresies and Schisms). The NT everywhere warns against false prophets (Matt. 7:15, 22-23; 24:11; 24:24-25 par. Mark 13:22; Luke 6:26; Acts 13:6; 2 Pet. 2:1; 1 John 4:1). Balaam was an OT prototype of the false prophet (2 Pet. 2:15-16; Jude 11; Rev. 2:14-15). The false prophetess in Thyatira is styled "Jezebel" (Rev. 2:20). The second beast of the devilish trinity of Revelation 12–13 (13:11-18), which corresponds to the Holy Spirit in the Trinity (cf. Rev. 13:15 [the gift of speech] with John 14:26; Rom. 8:26; 1 Cor. 2:13; Gal. 4:6, etc.) and perhaps relates to the propaganda for Roman emperor worship (→ Rite 1; Roman Empire), is also called the false prophet (Rev. 16:13; 19:20; 20:10).

3.6. *Early Church*

The → early church continued to hold the OT prophets in high esteem, since they had prophesied Jesus Christ and his church (*Barn.* 5.6; 6.2, 4; 11.1-11; 12.1-4, etc.; → Justin *1 Apol.* 31-35; *Dial.* 32, 68, 76, etc.). For → Jewish Christians Jesus was the prophet of Deut. 18:15 (*Clem. Recog.* 1.36.2; 39:1; 40.4; 43; *Clem. Hom.* 3.53.3, etc.). Church prophets were at first also highly regarded (*Did.* 10.7; 11.7-12; 13.1-7; Justin *Dial.* 82.1). In the middle of the second century Hermas still knew prophets who were filled with the Holy Spirit (*Man.* 11.8-9), but he did not style himself a prophet. The → apologist Melito of Sardis (d. ca. 190) respectfully called → Tertullian (ca. 160-ca. 225) a prophet (→ Jerome *De vir. ill.* 24).

Along with the demise of ecstatic and charismatic elements, prophets also gradually disappeared from the churches (see *Did.* 13.4). They were often discredited as false prophets, especially after the failure of → Montanism and its prophets (Eusebius, *Hist. eccl.* 5.16.4; 19.2; examples in G. Friedrich, 860-61). In the church's history false prophets often appealed to the Book of Revelation, which as a result has itself been disparaged at times (e.g., by M. → Luther in 1522). From the third century onward, teachers tended to replace prophets in the congregations (Hippolytus, *De antichr.* 31; Clement of Alexandria, *Strom.* 7.97.2).

Bibliography: D. E. Aune, *Prophecy in Early Christianity and the Ancient Mediterranean World* (Grand Rapids, 1983) • O. Böcher, "Johannes der Täufer," *TRE* 17.172-81 • M. E. Boring, *Sayings of the Risen Jesus: Christian Prophecy in the Synoptic Tradition* (Cambridge, 1982) • B. S. Childs, "Retrospective Reading of the OT Prophets," *ZAW* 108 (1996) 362-77 • J. D. G. Dunn, *Jesus and the Spirit: A Study of the Religious and Charismatic Experience of Jesus and the First Christians as Reflected in the NT* (Grand Rapids, 1997; orig. pub., 1975) • E. E. Ellis, *Prophecy and Hermeneutic in Early Christianity* (Tübingen, 1978) • T. L. Fenton, "Israelite Prophecy: Characteristics of the First Protest Movement," *The Elusive Prophet* (ed. J. C. de Moor; Leiden, 2001) 129-41 • C. Forbes, *Prophecy and Inspired Speech in Early Christianity and Its Hellenistic Environment* (Tübingen, 1995) • G. Friedrich, "Προφήτης κτλ. D: Prophets and Prophecies in the NT; E: Prophets in the Early Church," *TDNT* 6.828-61 • F. Hahn, *The Titles of Jesus in Christology: Their History in Early Christianity* (New York, 1969) • P. J. Harland, ed., *New Heaven and New Earth: Prophecy and the Millennium* (Leiden, 1999) • M. Hengel, *The Charismatic Leader and His Followers* (Edinburgh, 1996; orig. pub., 1968) • E. Käsemann, "Die Anfänge christlicher Theologie," *Exegetische Versuche und Besinnungen* (vol. 2; Göttingen, 1964) 82-104; idem, "Sätze heiligen Rechtes im Neuen Testament," ibid., 69-82 • W. G. Kümmel, *Promise and Fulfillment: The Eschatological Message of Jesus* (Naperville, Ill., 1957; orig. pub., 1945) • B. Peckham, *History and Prophecy: The Development of Late Judean Literary Traditions* (New York, 1993) • C. M. Robeck, *Prophecy in Carthage: Perpetua, Tertullian, and Cyprian* (Cleveland, 1992) • F. Schnider, "Προφήτης," *EDNT* 3.183-86 • E. Schweizer, *Church Order in the NT* (Naperville, Ill., 1961); idem, "Πνεῦμα κτλ. E: The NT," *TDNT* 6.396-451 • A. Stewart-Sykes, *From Prophecy to Preaching: A Search for the Origins of the Christian Homily* (Leiden, 2001).

Otto Böcher

Proprietary Church

According to the definition of U. Stutz (1895), a proprietary church is one in which a proprietor exercises control and spiritual leadership. Particularly in the West there have been such churches since the early Middle Ages. Stutz thought they derived from a Teutonic house-priesthood in proprietary temples. Yet they existed already in the fourth century on the great estates of the Roman nobility and as privately established district churches. Their origin lies in the economic development of lords of the manor (→ Feudalism). The original rights of → bishops regarding private churches were gradually reduced. Carolingian laws recognized the proprietary church but tried to guarantee that the proprietors provided proper support for the → clergy (Louis the Pious, in 818/19). In addition to churches and → chapels owned by the king, bishop, or baron, there were also proprietary cloisters.

The proprietary church often led to an oppressive dependence of the clergy on the lay ruler, an imbalance that Carolingian and post-Carolingian → synods tried to check. But the system did produce country churches and made possible the Christianizing of the rural population. Geographically, it covered Germany, France, Italy, England, and northeastern Spain. During the → Investiture Controversy the laity were put under obligation to hand back churches in the time of Urban II (1088-99). Gratian (d. 1145) considerably curtailed their right to churches. In 12th-century → canon law Rufinus of Bologna (fl. 1150-91), bishop of Assisi, developed the concept of → patronage and changed the proprietor into a patron. The influence of the proprietary church on later canon law has been exaggerated. We cannot, for example, derive institutions like the benefice or incorporation from it.

Bibliography: U.- R. Blumenthal, *The Investiture Controversy: Church and Monarchy from the Ninth to the Twelfth Century* (Philadelphia, 1988) • L. Scanlon, "The Friar's Tale: Chaucer's Critique of the Proprietary Church," *Narrative, Authority, and Power: The Medieval Exemplum and the Chaucerian Tradition* (Cambridge, 1994) 147-59 • U. Stutz, "The Proprietary Church as an Element of Mediaeval Germanic Ecclesiastical Law" (1895), *Mediaeval Germany, 911-1250: Essays by German Historians* (2 vols.; trans. G. Barraclough; Oxford, 1961) 2.35-70 • G. Tellenbach, *Church, State, and Christian Society at the Time of the Investiture Contest* (Oxford, 1959; orig. pub., 1940).

Peter Landau

Proselytism

Gk. *prosēlytos* was used by the LXX as the equivalent of Heb. *gēr*, which had the sense "immigrant" or "resident alien" but then came to take on the meaning "convert." Proselytism thus means originally the winning of converts to → Judaism. The sense does not have to be pejorative, for one of the seven in Acts 6:5-6 was a "proselyte" (Nicolaus, v. 5), and we read of "devout converts to Judaism [*prosēlytōn*]" at Antioch in Acts 13:43. For his part, Jesus could sharply criticize the proselytism of the → scribes and → Pharisees in Matt. 23:15, not in principle, but in terms of the results.

Along the lines of this criticism by Jesus, proselytism in the framework of ecumenical discussion began to be seen as a perverted form of Christian witness that uses secret or open manipulation, bribery, or force to bring about → conversions (§2). This problem of wrong methods has always been present where there has been organized → missionary activity, but only with the ecumenical movement has it been expressly linked to the term "proselytism" (→ Ecumenism, Ecumenical Movement). The → Orthodox Church has especially called for a rejection of proselytism in the sense of efforts by Protestants and Roman Catholics to win converts among its own members, for example, in the Middle East, Ethiopia, and India.

In 1961 the New Delhi Assembly of the World Council of Churches commended the document "Christian Witness, Proselytism, and Religious Liberty," which condemned proselytism but supported transdenominational witness and the right to move from one church body to another for reasons of conscience. In 1970 studies with the → Roman Catholic Church resulted in the publishing of a second document, "Common Witness and Proselytism." It was partially revised in 1981 and then in 1996 was updated as "The Challenge of Proselytism and the Calling to Common Witness." Ends and means now supplied the criteria for distinguishing between witness and proselytism. Witness is perverted when the end is stealing or division and when the means include force or enticement. As regards the rejection of proselytism according to these criteria, there is fairly general ecumenical → consensus, but tensions arise where there is competition or in majority-minority situations. In principle the same criteria apply to all missionary work, as the 1970 document states explicitly.

Bibliography: A. A. An-Na'um, ed., *Proselytization and Communal Self-Determination in Africa* (Maryknoll, N.Y., 1999) • "Christian Witness, Proselytism, and Religious Liberty in the Setting of the WCC," *Evanston to New Delhi* (Geneva, 1961) • T. M. Finn, *From Death to Rebirth: Ritual and Conversion in Antiquity* (New York, 1997) • M. Goodman, *Mission and Conversion: Proselytizing in the Religious History of the Roman Empire* (Oxford, 1994) • M. E. Marty and F. E. Greenspahn, eds., *Pushing the Faith: Proselytism and Civility in a Pluralistic World* (New York, 1988) • *Pluralism, Proselytism, and Nationalism in Eastern Europe* (= *JES* 36/1-2 [1999]) • J. Witte Jr. and M. Bourdeaux, eds., *Proselytism and Orthodoxy in Russia: The New War for Souls* (Maryknoll, N.Y., 1999) • J. Witte Jr. and R. C. Martin, eds., *Sharing the Book: Religious Perspectives on the Rights and Wrongs of Proselytism* (Maryknoll, N.Y., 1999).

Paul Löffler

Prostitution

Christian churches are today faced with an escalation of prostitution, a form of the exploitation of women that has many faces and is globally present. Traditionally, prostitution has been thought to be men buying the sexual services of an individual woman streetwalker, who may either be controlled by a pimp or have housing in a brothel. Streetwalkers have often been young women who have run away from home or abandoned women with no other means with which to support themselves or their children.

Prostitution and other forms of sexual violence have also long been present wherever there are soldiers and military bases. Rape and kidnapping and sexual slavery have accompanied armies for centuries. In the late 1930s, and throughout World War II, for example, the Japanese established an extensive system of "comfort stations" and tricked or recruited women, many young teenagers, to be prostitutes for the Japanese military. Only very recently have the comfort women overcome their sense of shame enough to speak out, fight for compensation, official acknowledgment of these war crimes, and apology. Today prostitution still flourishes around U.S. military bases in Europe, the United States, Korea, Okinawa, and elsewhere.

"Sex tourism" (→ Tourism) has also been tied to → war, for example, the American war in Vietnam. Bangkok became a center for R & R (rest and recuperation), so to speak. After the war, to keep the sex industry lucrative, the Thai government began to promote sex tourism. Numerous countries with prosperous economies, including Germany, the Netherlands, the United States, and later Japan, cooperated with the government of Thailand and also Korea, the Philippines, and elsewhere in Asia and organized tours especially designed to provide sex.

Child prostitution has escalated in consequence. In order to earn a living wage for their families, children from northern Thailand, for example, go south to Bangkok, where pimps wait for them in the train stations. These children are boys as well as girls. The HIV-AIDS epidemic has fueled the demand for children worldwide.

Finally, there is another face of the prostitution: in affluent societies, some middle-class women, whether students or homemakers or low-wage workers, occasionally enter prostitution to earn extra income.

Since the 1970s there has been a prostitutes' rights movement in the United States and in Europe that seeks to assert the personal agency of women who are "sex workers." These sex workers' movements not only resist the issues of illegality and of exploitative working conditions worldwide but also assert that practices of prostitution are not necessarily confirmation of male domination; these practices may themselves be acts of resistance and cultural subversion.

Most women, particularly feminists (→ Feminism), agree, however, that prostitution is tangled in deep-seated social and cultural attitudes and realities: an increasingly stratified economy that threatens the survival of more and more people (→ Economic Ethics), a disposable consumer economy that has commodified human beings as throwaways, a disregard for children that scholars have traced from late antiquity to the present, a profound ambivalence about → sexuality in the Christian tradition, and a double standard that enforces the control of women's sexuality and entitles men to satisfy hypermasculine sexual needs (→ Righteousness, Justice, 3.2.3).

The Christian church in the past has often been in the forefront both of judging prostitutes and of seeking to rehabilitate them, recalling → Mary Magdalene, who is regarded without convincing historical verification to be the penitent whore. The challenge before churches today is to engage the deep-seated economic, sociocultural, and theological affirmations (regarding sexuality, sin, grace, and incarnation) that unfortunately may allow and encourage the continued exploitation and violation of women and children through prostitution.

→ Force, Violence, Nonviolence, 2; Sexism

Bibliography: R. N. Brock and S. B. Thistlethwaite, *Casting Stones: Prostitution and Liberation in Asia and the United States* (Minneapolis, 1996) • E. Gateley, *I Hear a Seed Growing: God of the Forest, God of the Streets* (Trabuco Canyon, Calif., 1990) • M. E. Guider, *Daughters of Rahab: Prostitution and the Church of Liberation in Brazil* (Minneapolis, 1995) • G. Hicks, *The Comfort Women: Japan's Brutal Regime of Enforced Prostitution in the Second World War* (New York, 1995) • K. Kempadoo and J. Doezema, eds., *Global Sex Workers: Rights, Resistance, and Redefinition* (New York, 1998) • S. P. Sturdevant and B. Stolzfus, *Let the Good Times Roll: Prostitution and the U.S. Military in Asia* (New York, 1992).

Melanie A. May

Protestantism

1. Term and History of Meaning
2. Social Phenomenon
3. Dogmatic Elements

4. Global Protestantism
5. Ecumenicity

1. Term and History of Meaning

1.1. "Protestantism" is a general term for the form of Christianity that originated with the 16th-century → Reformation. It carries a specific reference to the "Protestatio" that the Evangelical princes presented at the Second Diet of Speyer in 1529. After that event the opponents of the Reformation called all its supporters Protestants, though the supporters themselves preferred the term "Evangelicals." In the 17th century the terms "Protestant religion" and "Protestant church" came into use as neutral secular descriptions of Reformation Christianity.

1.2. As a noun "Protestantism" took on its meaning only with the → Enlightenment and → Pietist criticism of the ecclesiastical and dogmatic system of Protestant → orthodoxy (§§1-2). For a long time the content was imprecise. From the middle of the 18th century onward, repeated efforts were made to define the nature and basic principles of Protestantism. Thus J. G. → Herder (1744-1803) found the principle of the Reformation in → freedom of → conscience. "Freedom is the foundation stone of all Protestant churches, as their very name indicates." This definition found pregnant and influential expression in G. W. F. Hegel (1770-1831; → Hegelianism), who found the distinctive principle of Protestantism in the rule that we should not be ready to recognize anything in the mind that is not justified by rational thought (1821). This formal definition of Protestantism as that which makes freedom possible could be expounded along both middle-class liberal (R. Rothe; → Liberalism) and national conservative (F. J. Stahl; → Conservatism) lines.

F. D. E. → Schleiermacher (1768-1834; → Schleiermacher's Theology) attempted a material definition. In the thesis at the head of §24 of his *Christian Faith* (1821-22), he stated that the difference between Protestantism and Roman Catholicism is that "the former makes the individual's relation to the church dependent on his relation to Christ, while the latter contrariwise makes the individual's relation to Christ dependent on his relation to the church." Schleiermacher's disciple and successor A. Twesten (1789-1876) introduced the idea of the two principles of Protestantism (1826), which became fixed when A. Ritschl (1822-89) adopted it in 1876. Holy Scripture was now the *formal principle*, and justification by faith the *material principle*. The interaction of the two principles gave validity to what has been the specifically Protestant freedom to use the methods of historical criticism in the exposition of Scripture (→ Exegesis, Biblical; Literature, Biblical and Early Christian, 2).

1.3. E. → Troeltsch (1865-1923) introduced an important distinction between the old Protestantism and the new (1906). He saw the old Protestantism of orthodoxy as part of the ecclesiastical culture of the → Middle Ages, but he regarded the new Protestantism as a religious expression of the modern world (→ Modernity) rooted in the → Enlightenment and the French → Revolution. Though subjected to much detailed criticism, this distinction has enjoyed general acceptance. → Culture Protestantism tried to answer the question it posed by thinking in terms of a Protestant shaping of the world. On this view the term "Protestantism" was a symbol of the fashioning of life in both church and world in accordance with the standards of Protestant truthfulness and freedom.

For a time the radical criticism of this liberal Protestant synthesis of Christianity and middle-class culture by → dialectical theology (K. → Barth) pushed the term "Protestantism" into the background and replaced it with an emphasis once again on the word "Evangelical." P. → Tillich (1886-1965) then gave a new turn to the question of the principle of Protestantism by distinguishing between the principle and the form or reality. The Protestant principle is grounded in the Reformation doctrine of our justification by grace alone. It comes to expression, however, as criticism and prophetic protest against any power structure that claims to be absolute, whether religious or secular. The Protestant form must constantly give practical historical expression to the criticism, showing itself to be the form of grace within secular reality.

2. Social Phenomenon

2.1. As the historical form of Reformation Christianity, Protestantism is a multifaceted phenomenon, as may be seen from the discussion of → denominational differences. The view has also gained force that Protestantism includes not only churches of the Lutheran (→ Luther's Theology), Calvinistic (→ Calvin's Theology), and Zwinglian (→ Zwingli's Theology) traditions but also such pre-Reformation groups as the → Waldenses and → Bohemian Brethren and such post-Reformation groups as the → Baptists, Congregationalists (→ Congregationalism), Independents (→ Dissenters 2.1), and Methodists (→ Methodist Churches), with the → Anglican Communion also confessedly Protestant, even if offering at some points a bridge to Roman Catholicism. We might also mention the → Pentecostal churches and the → charismatic movement. For all the differences within Protestantism, it is still possible to regard it as a third main form of Christianity alongside Roman Catholicism and → Orthodox Christianity.

2.2. Characterizing all forms of historic Protestantism is a close relation to middle-class society and culture. The crucial pioneer in social analysis of Protestantism was M. → Weber (1864-1920). In his famous study *The Protestant Ethic and the Spirit of Capitalism* (1905), Weber spoke of what he called an "ascetic Protestantism" that he found embodied in Calvinism, Puritanism (→ Puritans), → Pietism, and Methodism. He investigated the impact of this religious but secular asceticism on the rise of the spirit of economic rationalism that typifies modern → capitalism. Discussion of Weber's theses continues, but it was the merit of Weber to have demonstrated the specific role of Western, Anglo-Saxon Protestantism in giving shape to modern middle-class society and to have given the impetus to innumerable further studies (Troeltsch, R. H. Tawney, H. R. Niebuhr).

European Protestantism of the Lutheran tradition has been oriented to such orders of preservation as government, family, and vocation, with many related achievements in the educational, social, and political spheres. In contrast, Protestantism of the Western, Calvinist stamp has found its basic impulse in the calling of Christians in the world, by active sanctification and self-discipline, to contribute to the glorifying of God and to the constructing of an order that is in keeping with the command of God and his sovereign rule. Hence Western Protestantism very quickly became a pioneering fighter for a liberal order of → state and → society, even while German Protestantism was still immersed in conservative political thinking.

2.3. When the society of West Germany became democratic after World War II, the question of the social and political place of Protestantism arose afresh. E. Stammler tried to describe "the Protestant type," its feature being, he thought, "believing freedom." But increasing → secularization, loss of church membership, and ongoing denominational mixing would not let the question of the profile of Protestantism rest. On the basis of questioning, an attempt was made to fix the nature of "Protestant personality." It was supposedly characterized by expectations of living in an "open system" (G. Schmidtchen). Others (e.g., I. and W. Lukatis) doubted whether this analysis of denominational cultures was accurate. They noted greater differences of attitude between those without and those with church connections, regardless of their specific denominational allegiance.

The emergence of new religious movements (→ New Religions; Youth Religions) and also the increase of fundamentalist trends (→ Fundamentalism), especially within historic Protestantism, along with the postulated transition to → postmodernity, fed doubts as to whether there still is such a thing as traditional Protestant culture. Already in 1937 Tillich had predicted the end of the Protestant era. At any rate, the relation of Protestantism to the modern world came up afresh, whether answered along the lines of a new Culture Protestantism (T. Rendtorff et al.) or in terms of Protestantism as a religion of freedom in the midst of modern crises (J. Moltmann et al.)

3. Dogmatic Elements

3.1. Doctrinal as well as cultural diversity is a basic feature of Protestantism. The reason for this diversity is to be found in the fundamental conviction of Protestantism that the *ecclesia reformata* (reformed church) must also be *semper reformanda* (always reforming). Protestantism, then, lacks confidence in the institutional continuity of the church, the validity of a sacrosanct order, or the unchanging → truth of church doctrine (→ Dogma). It is marked instead by a positive relation to historical diversity (→ Pluralism).

Classic Protestantism before the Enlightenment tried to summarize the central teachings of Protestantism in confessions. For the Lutheran churches the → Augsburg Confession of 1530 became the normative confession (→ Confession of Faith). The Reformed churches, though, had several confessions, notably the → Heidelberg Catechism (1563) and the → Westminster Confession (1648), preceded by the First and Second Helvetic (1536, 1561 [published 1566]), Gallican (1559), Scottish (1560), and Belgic (1561) Confessions. Early attempts to overcome confessional differences either failed or were only regionally successful (→ Union). New attempts such as that made with the → Barmen Declaration of 1934 and the → Leuenberg Agreement of 1973 achieved an importance in much wider circles than the participating churches. For Protestantism, however, actual confessing has always been more important than written confessions.

3.2. The encounter of churches in the ecumenical movement brought the common dogmatic profile of Protestantism more clearly into view. Fundamental is the orientation of life and witness to the gospel of Jesus Christ, that is, the precedence given to the gospel over the church's teaching and order. All the efforts made by Protestantism to define itself and to achieve ecumenical understanding begin with an understanding of the gospel. It is a common Protestant teaching that Jesus Christ himself is the heart of the gospel. With an appeal to the Reformation confessions, it is believed that the message of → justification as "the message of the free grace of God" (Leuenberg Agreement) bears witness to a right understanding of the gospel in the sense of proclaiming the sole mediatorship of Jesus Christ.

The classic "alone" statements of the Reformation (→ Reformation Principles) still contribute to this understanding of the gospel: God accepts sinners (→ Sin) by *grace* alone *for Christ's sake* (→ Christology) and by → *faith* alone. Again, access to the gospel is by *Scripture* alone (→ Canon); Scripture is the → norm of all proclamation and also of all confession, which is the *norma normata* (standardized norm), in contrast to Scripture as the *norma normans* (standardizing norm). Here is the basis of Protestant freedom in face of the normative claim of church tradition.

3.3. The basic Protestant approach by way of the gospel of justification has far-reaching implications, especially as regards the understanding of the → church. The church is not itself a mediator of salvation. It is created by the Word and in this way relates to the gospel and has a part in communicating it. The church stands or falls with this "article." The most decisive and fully sufficient marks of the church are thus the right → proclamation of the gospel and the administration of the → sacraments in keeping with the gospel (CA 7).

The institutional continuity of church order and the authority of the → teaching office cannot guarantee that the church will still be the church; only the ministry of the → Holy Spirit of God can guarantee it, through the word of proclamation and the visible signs of the sacraments. It thus follows that the test of all church order is whether it serves to bear witness to the gospel. In Protestantism the validity of → ministries depends solely on whether there is commissioning to regular public proclamation of the gospel. All baptized Christians participate in this task (i.e., there is a priesthood of all believers; → Priest, Priesthood, 4).

3.4. The focusing of the question of → salvation solely on God's gracious work in the event of justification has helped to make Protestantism a religion of freedom in a very special way, a freedom that finds demonstration in its active shaping of the world (→ Ethics). A safeguard against uncritical affirmation of the modern sense of freedom is the specific linking of Christian freedom to the practice of → love of one's → neighbor along the lines of "communicative freedom" (W. Huber). The gospel is claim as well as promise. By its claim we experience "joyous liberation from the godless claims of this world to free and thankful service" (Barmen, thesis 2).

This statement shows us that the doctrine of justification must be constantly expounded afresh and not just presented as a traditional dogma. The correct relating of promise and claim, of → gospel and law, is still a matter of vigorous debate in modern Protestantism. Hence the distinction between the Protestant principle and the form and reality of Protestantism (Tillich) is still relevant. The Protestant concentration on the event of justification is, among other things, a critical standard. The strength of Protestantism lies in this basic critical orientation, but the same orientation is also the reason for its lack of unity in dogma and institutional structure.

4. Global Protestantism

4.1. The first three sections have focused on the classic profile of Protestantism as represented among the historic Reformation churches. A global look at Protestantism, however, leads to significant differentiations. According to recent statistics (D. B. Barrett and T. M. Johnson), there are approximately 2.1 billion Christians worldwide, of whom more than half are Roman Catholics and only 356 million (i.e., 17 percent) are Protestants. The large majority of Protestants, in particular among the churches of Lutheran and Methodist tradition, continue to be located in Europe and North America. However, while this concentration is very obvious for Lutherans (more than 80 percent), some two-thirds of Reformed/Presbyterian Christians live in the Southern Hemisphere.

The profile of Protestantism in North America has been influenced by the constitutional principles of the separation of → church and state and the guarantee of religious freedom. Gradually, the European Protestant tradition of established, or "folk," churches (→ Volkskirche) was transformed through the emergence of denominations, which became the predominant type of organization for North American Protestantism. Denominationalism presupposes the plurality and basic equality of Christian communities as voluntary organizations (→ Voluntarism).

Through intensive missionary activity, denominational Protestantism was transferred to Africa, Asia, and Latin America. Most of the newly emerging Anglo-Saxon denominations have their origin in an act of separation from one of the historic branches of Protestantism. They received their specific profile during one of the successive waves of pietistic or evangelical awakenings, which shifted the central emphasis in American Protestantism from the gospel of justification to the → assurance of personal salvation and the search for holiness of life.

4.2. The largest numbers of Protestant denominations represent a certain radicalization of the Western, Calvinist type of historic Protestantism with an emphasis on the freedom of God in God's action of salvation over against all traditions of sacramental mediation, the accent on active sanctification in order to glorify God, the strict grounding of faith and life in the biblical witness, and the valuation of the congregational principle over against all forms of ecclesial hierarchy. These characteristics are true in particular for the Baptist type of denominations, that is, the various Baptist conventions, Mennonites, Brethren, and many others. Numerically, they are concentrated in the United States, but with an expanding missionary presence in other regions, particularly in the South, but also in eastern Europe. Counting the total community, Baptists probably outnumber Lutherans, who otherwise remain the largest communion among historic Protestantism.

The other type is represented by the Methodist tradition, that is, the different Methodist churches, the Salvation Army, Holiness churches, the Church of the Nazarene, and others. At the center of the Methodist type of Protestantism, which has its historic roots in the Church of England and — through Moravian mediation — received strong influences from the Lutheran tradition, lies the search for personal sanctification through a life of prayer, self-discipline, and community. At the same time, Methodism has been characterized by a strong social commitment. Through intensive missionary activity churches of the Methodist tradition today are present throughout the world, but the United States has remained the heartland of Methodism, with about half of the worldwide Methodist community located there.

4.3. The Pentecostal awakening at the beginning of the 20th century has led to the formation of a rapidly growing number of new denominations, especially in Latin America and Africa (→ Independent Churches). While the Pentecostals have their roots in evangelical Protestantism, especially of the Methodist type and reinforced by strong influences of fundamentalism and a millenarian understanding of eschatology, they have outgrown their Protestant origins and today represent a new Christian "culture." According to recent estimates, Pentecostals meanwhile outnumber traditional Protestants and, with more than 500 million believers, have become the second largest grouping of global Christianity.

5. Ecumenicity

5.1. Although Protestantism is oriented to critical distinction rather than to synthesis, from the very outset it has faced the ecumenical question (→ Ecumenism, Ecumenical Movement). We see this tendency in the Reformation call for a truly ecumenical → council, which was still a factor right up to the time of Pietism. Even during the days of → Catholic reform and counterreformation and the religious wars (→ Thirty Years' War), the search for unity still went on, as in the appeal of G. Calixtus for → consensus on the basis of the first five centuries or in a concentration on basic articles. Concrete plans for union such as those of G. W. Leibniz or D. E. Jablonski did not achieve anything but found an echo in the ecumenical thrust of Pietism (A. H. → Francke, N. → Zinzendorf) and the overcoming of Protestant provincialism in the missionary movement (→ Mission).

5.2. The modern ecumenical movement arose within Protestantism. Both Protestantism and the ecumenical movement felt the impact of epochal 19th-century changes. Conservative Pietist and liberal cultural Protestant elements came typically close to one another in the origins of the ecumenical movement. They drifted apart only when crisis overtook the middle-class Protestant culture. The Protestant cast of the ecumenical movement was a prominent feature right up to the 1960s (in a kind of Christocentric universalism).

The active engagement of the → Roman Catholic Church in the ecumenical movement after → Vatican II and the strengthening of the Orthodox voice then changed the Protestant profile. This process was hastened by increasing polarization between critical liberal Protestantism and conservative evangelical Protestantism. The mainline Protestant churches entered into many bilateral and multilateral conversations, especially with Roman Catholics (→ Ecumenical Dialogue) in an effort to overcome antitheses that divide the churches.

At the same time, the critical prophetic principle of Protestantism came to life again beyond denominational boundaries in → liberation theology and → contextual theologies. Attempted here was a fresh appropriating of the gospel as the concrete, liberating, and converting → Word of God, not for the church alone, but for all humanity.

5.3. Recent developments in the ecumenical arena have once more sharpened the concern for the profile of Protestantism. In Europe and North America the historic Protestant churches have entered into relationships of full communion; the most notable example is the Fellowship of Protestant Churches in Europe (formerly Leuenberg Church Fellowship), with a membership of more than 100 Lutheran, Reformed/Presbyterian, United, Methodist, Waldensian, and Czech Brethren churches throughout Europe. In the United States conversations among Protestants have, after 40 years, led to the formation of the Churches of Christ Uniting. A breakthrough occurred in the dialogues with the Roman Catholic Church, concerning in particular the Lutheran churches, through the official agreement achieved in October 1999 in → *Joint Declaration on the Doctrine of Justification.*

The publication of the Vatican declaration *Dominus Iesus* in 2000, however, provoked sharp reactions among the historic Protestant churches and a strong reaffirmation of Protestant ecclesial identity. This concern for articulating the Protestant voice and profile within the wider ecumenical community of churches was strengthened in the context of dialogues with the Orthodox churches in the World Council of Churches and the publication of "The Report of the Special Commission on Orthodox Participation in the World Council of Churches" (*ER* 55 [January 2003]).

5.4. New reflection on the profile of Protestantism in the → oikoumene and in distinction from the Roman and Byzantine forms of Christianity demands that we overcome controversial formulations of the denominational problem (→ Denomination) and rediscover the mutual relations between the criteria of conformity to the gospel, sacramental catholicity, and epicletic orthodoxy. None of the great forms of worldwide Christianity has an exclusive claim to be labeled Evangelical, Catholic, or Orthodox. The task of Protestantism in the ecumenical world is to preserve its critical orientation to the form of life and doctrine that is in conformity with the gospel, and to do so for the sake of the integrity of the ecumenical movement. The question is primarily one of the modern form of Protestantism itself.

→ Baptists; Calvinism; Lutheranism; Methodism

Bibliography: On 1: K. Barth, *Protestant Theology in the Nineteenth Century: Its Background and History* (London, 1972) • H.-J. Birkner, *Protestantismus im Wandel* (Munich, 1971) • K. Heim, *The Nature of Protestantism* (Philadelphia, 1963; orig. pub., 1925) • H. J. Hillerbrand, ed., *Encyclopedia of Protestantism* (4 vols.; New York, 2004) • É. G. Léonard, *A History of Protestantism* (2 vols.; London, 1965-67) • M. E. Marty, *Protestantism* (London, 1972) • R. Prenter, *Der Protestantismus in unserer Zeit* (Stuttgart, 1959) • T. Rendtorff, *Theorie des Christentums. Historisch-theologische Studien zu seiner neuzeitlichen Verfassung* (Gütersloh, 1972) • P. Tillich, *The Protestant Era* (Chicago, 1957) • E. Troeltsch, *Protestantism and Progress: The Significance of Protestantism for the Rise of the Modern World* (Philadelphia, 1986; orig. pub., 1911).

On 2: J. Cohen, *Protestantism and Capitalism: The Mechanics of Influence* (New York, 2002) • W. Huber, *Protestantismus und Protest. Zum Verhältnis von Ethik und Politik* (Reinbek, 1987) • R. Mehl, *The Sociology of Protestantism* (Philadelphia, 1970) • J. Moltmann, ed., *Religion der Freiheit. Protestantismus in der Moderne* (Munich, 1990) • H. R. Niebuhr, *The Kingdom of God in America* (Chicago, 1937); idem, *The Social Sources of Denominationalism* (New York, 1929) • M. Weber, *The Protestant Ethic and the Spirit of Capitalism* (London, 1992; orig. pub., 1920).

On 4: R. H. Balmer and L. F. Winner, *Protestantism in America* (New York, 2002) • D. B. Barrett and T. M. Johnson, "Annual Statistical Table on Global Mission: 2004," *IBMR* 28 (2004) 24-25 • M. Marty, *The Protestant Voice in American Pluralism* (Athens, Ga., 2004); idem, ed., *Modern American Protestantism and Its World: Historical Articles on Protestantism in American Religious Life* (14 vols.; Munich, 1992-93) • W. R. Ward, *The Protestant Evangelical Awakening* (Cambridge, 1992).

On 5: E. Fahlbusch, *Kirchenkunde der Gegenwart* (Stuttgart, 1979) • E. Geldbach, *Ökumene in Gegensätzen* (Göttingen, 1987) • F. W. Kantzenbach, *Einheitsbestrebungen im Wandel der Kirchengeschichte* (Gütersloh, 1979) • K. Lehmann and W. Pannenberg, eds., *The Condemnations of the Reformation Era: Do They Still Divide?* (Minneapolis, 1990) • K. Raiser, *Ecumenism in Transition: A Paradigm Shift in the Ecumenical Movement?* (Geneva, 1991) • W. G. Rusch and D. F. Martensen, eds., *The Leuenberg Agreement and Lutheran-Reformed Relationships* (Minneapolis, 1989).

Konrad Raiser

Protevangelium

1. The term "Protevangelium" (first gospel) was coined in the 17th century but is not much used today. It describes an understanding of Gen. 3:15 in terms of → salvation history, according to which it is the kernel of gospel declaration. The enmity between the seed of the serpent and that of the woman will be decided in favor of the latter, which will suffer only a wound to the heel.

Three great lines of messianic exposition have arisen from this verse. The most common, which goes back to → Justin Martyr (d. ca. 165 B.C.), interprets the seed of the woman collectively. In the end, the human race will be triumphant over the → demon. Then already in → Irenaeus (d. ca. 200) we find a second line of understanding that adds a Christological element to the collective element (→ Christology). Christ, born of a woman (→ Mary in the New Testament), will be the victor. Finally in the 11th century Fulbert (ca. 960-1028) worked out a specifically Mariological exposition (→ Mariology 2). From Eve the line runs to the mother of the Savior (→ Soteriology), who conquers Satan. Later this third view was linked to the doctrine of the immaculate conception (→ Mariology 1.3.3). In virtue of her privileged position Mary can triumph along with the Son of God.

Contemporary exegetical work has forced Roman Catholic theologians to concede that the Mariological understanding can be based only on tradition. Often now the verse is taken more generally as a declaration of ongoing conflict, with no prediction of definitive victory.

2. "Protevangelium" has a second meaning as the modern title of an apocryphal infancy gospel, the Book of James (→ Apocrypha 2.1.5.1). Professing to be authored by James the brother of Jesus, this work dates from the second century and is primarily the story of Mary. G. Postel first gave it the title *Protevangelium Jacobi* in his Latin translation of 1552.

Bibliography: M. Fassler, "Mary's Nativity, Fulbert of Chartres, and the Stirps Jesse: Liturgical Innovation circa 1000 and Its Afterlife," *Spec.* 75/2 (2000) 389-434 • A. Feuillet, "La connexion de la révélation divine avec l'histoire du salut dans l'annonce prophétique du Sauveur messianique et de sa Mère. Le Protévangile, les oracles messianiques d'Isaïe et de Michée," *Div.* 32/2 (1988) 543-64; 32/3 (1988) 643-65 • R. F. Hock, *The Infancy Gospels of James and Thomas* (Santa Rosa, Calif., 1995) • R. A. Martin, "The Earliest Messianic Interpretation of Genesis 3:15," *JBL* 84 (1965) 425-27 • W. Vogels, "Der sogenannte 'Proto-Evangelium' (Gen. 3,15). Verschiedene Arten, den Text zu lesen," *TGA* 29 (1986) 195-203 • W. Witfall, "Genesis 3:15–a Protevangelium?" *CBQ* 36 (1974) 361-65.

Eric Junod

Proverbs, Book of

1. Description

The Book of Proverbs, together with the Books of Job and Ecclesiastes, belongs to the → Wisdom books of the Hebrew Bible. It thus belongs to a literary category that was widespread and greatly enjoyed in the ancient world because it transmitted the experience of past generations about the right ways of dealing with God and others. By means of its sayings and teachings, it promised a → life (§1) that would be long, happy, and successful.

Because Solomon traditionally ranked as the wisest king of → Israel (§1.4, 1 Kgs. 4:29-34 and 10:1-10), the Wisdom books up to the deuterocanonical Wisdom of Solomon and the Psalms of Solomon were ascribed to him (→ Apocrypha 1.3.12; Pseudepigrapha 1.1.8). Hence the final redactors of the Book of Proverbs also ascribed this book to Solomon, even though the Egyptianizing teaching in 22:17–24:22 and its addendum in 24:23-34 are described as "the sayings of the wise," chap. 30 as "the words of Agur son of Jakeh," and chap. 31 as "the words of King Lemuel of Massa, which his mother taught him" (REB).

The LXX dealt with the contradiction between the title in 1:1 (the proverbs ascribed to Solomon) by eliminating the titles in 30:1 and 31:1, putting 30:1-9 after 24:34, and inserting 31:10-31, the song of a good wife, behind 29:27. In this way it incorporated these texts into the sayings of the wise or the collection of Hezekiah in chaps. 25–29.

2. Structure

What has been said shows that Proverbs is a secondary composite work consisting of several originally independent collections of proverbs or teachings. It opens with fatherly instruction in chaps. 1–9, which contains a superscription and prologue in 1:1-7 that is simultaneously an introduction to the whole book. This section is followed by a Solomon collection in 10:1–22:16, then the so-called Egyptianizing teaching in 22:17–24:22 (34), the Hezekiah collection in 25:1–29:27, and finally the words of Agur in 30:1-14 (33) and of Lemuel in 31:1-9 (31), which in their own turn are compilations with multiple strata.

2.1. The *fatherly instruction* in 1:(1)8–9:18 consists of a consciously structured but multilayered composition of ten teachings, two admonitions, three warnings of Wisdom, personified as a woman, a recommendation of wisdom, and a warning against conduct that leads to ill-fortune and disaster. The first teaching begins with a warning against bad conduct in 1:8-19 and instruction by wisdom not to neglect its teaching (1:20-23). The second teaching, in 2:1-22, introduces four instructional themes. The pupils are to learn (1) that the fear of God is the sure way to achieve wisdom, (2) that it leads to right conduct toward others and to the avoidance of (3) evildoers and (4) strange women.

The teaching that follows develops these themes, culminating with the public invitation of wisdom to all who pass by. Here wisdom boasts of its eternal role as a companion of → Yahweh that will lead all its children to wisdom and to a long life that is pleasing to God (8:1-36). The end of this teaching comes with the dual-path scheme of the invitations of wisdom and folly, leading, on the one hand, to life and, on the other, to the underworld.

The self-boasting of wisdom in 8:22-31 seems to show dependence on Hellenistic Iris aretalogies. Hence some scholars believe that the determinative, final redaction of chaps. 1–9 and of the book as a whole dates to the third century B.C. Shortly thereafter chaps. 2–29 were likely subjected to editing that focused on the notion of righteousness, as particularly evident in 10:1–22:16 and 28–29. Wisdom is not a true hypostatization but a poetic personification commending the wisdom of the schools (H. M. Neher). Nevertheless, its development here and later in Sirach 24 decisively influenced the idea of the eternal Logos and its coming to humankind in the Prologue to John and the whole Logos Christology of the → early church (→ Christology 1.4 and 2.2.2).

2.2. The *Solomon collection* in 10:1–22:16 may be divided formally into 10:1–15:33 and 16:1–22:16. The first part deals with the contrast between the wise and the fool, or with the education of a wise son. The second part highlights themes of → righteousness and mercy. The focus on proverbs concerning Yahweh and the king in chap. 16 — and thus in the middle of chaps. 10–22 and of the book as a whole — suggests a systematic reworking. In its basic form, perhaps without the contrasting of the righteous and the wicked, the collection with an untainted ideal of the king must go back to the last third of the eighth century and is addressed to the educated upper class in the cities (→ Monarchy in Israel).

2.3. The *Egyptianizing teaching* in 22:17–24:22 is apparently dependent on the 12th-century teaching of Amenemope. Like its predecessor, it consists of 30 units, but since it is remote from the former's ideal of inward piety, it may have come from the middle years of the monarchy. The "sayings of the wise" appended in 24:23-34 probably date to the same period.

2.4. According to its superscription in 25:1, the *Hezekiah collection* in 25:1–29:27 represents a group of texts by Solomon allegedly collected by "the officials of King Hezekiah of Judah" (25:1). Scholars are still undecided whether this information is to be viewed as accurate or whether it was prompted by ideological considerations.

This collection consists of two sections, chaps. 25–27 and 28–29. Complex aphorisms and an increasing tendency to form groups, however, suggest that the first section dates to a later period than the Solomonic collections. The second section returns to two-part aphorisms reflecting a more inward → piety and presumably dates to the Persian period. Only through a thorough analysis of word fields (K. M. Heim) does the synthetic, antithetical, or comparative orientation of individual proverbs characterizing the overall composition of the collections emerge. In the same context, both direct and indirect allusions to Solomon's enormous wisdom also emerge at the transitional points of the overall, two-part collection (R. Scoralik).

2.5. The words of *Agur,* son of Jakeh, carry the name of an Arab ruler (30:1-9). Though divine wisdom is unattainable, it says, the Word of God is unchanging, and through → prayer it is possible to lead a life that is pleasing to God. This little composition can thus be given a Jewish interpretation. By way of the warning in v. 10, an anaphoric enumeration of evildoers follows in vv. 11-14, whose kinship with numerical sayings apparently attracted the collection of numerical sayings in vv. 15-33.

2.6. In 31:1-9 the words of *King Lemuel of Massa* that his mother taught him represent a doctrine of kingship in the special form of motherly admonition. The Aramaisms in v. 2 suggest a fairly late origin. Whether the teaching is Arabian or purely fictional is an open question. The warning in v. 3 not to spend one's strength on women opens the door to an alphabetic-acrostic extolling of the good wife in vv. 10-31 that has been added to the book as a thematically necessary conclusion.

3. Place in the Canon

Proverbs belongs to the third part of the Hebrew Bible (→ Canon 1), the so-called Writings. It appears between Psalms and Job, or between Job and the festival scrolls. In the LXX and the translations that follow it, including modern translations (→ Bible Versions), however, it appears between Psalms and Ecclesiastes, so that the three Solomonic books (including the Song of Songs) are grouped together.

4. Contents

The collections and teachings of Proverbs portray a simple morality reflecting a comfortably circumscribed background of agriculture, manual labor, and the royal court. Prudent conduct that fits in well with society will usually lead to success and recognition. The references to talking and silence (10:19; 18:21), to the righteous and the wicked (10:3; 28:1), and to wisdom and folly (10:1; 21:20) point to an ideal of wisdom as that of well-controlled and righteous persons. These teachings presuppose in principle that we are responsible for our own → happiness, though it is recognized that all success ultimately depends on God's will (16:9). The wise finally see in the → fear (§4) of Yahweh the beginning of all wisdom (1:7; 9:10). The monarchy forms the self-evident social framework for the preexilic collections (16:10-15; 20:26; 22:11; 25:2; 29:14).

In the Hezekiah collection we see signs of an early departure from the ideal of wisdom and its social reality, for example, in reserved criticism of the monarchy, which is not evident in earlier royal proverbs (cf. 25:4-5 with 16:10, and 29:14 with 16:12). We see, too, the start of a more inward-looking norm (e.g., 28:6). But the aphorisms contrasting the righteous with evildoers or the ungodly (11:21 and 16:5) still maintain the close connection between a person's action and that same person's actual fate as allotted by God. On this basis the latest collection of the fatherly instruction shows no hesitation in plainly warning young people against ill-advised behavior and company. Only in the words of Agur is there a small, but quickly closed, window to the skeptical attitude of Jewish Wisdom in the later Persian or early Hellenistic periods.

Bibliography: Commentaries: R. J. Clifford (OTL; Louisville, Ky., 1999) • E. F. Davis (WestBC; Louisville, Ky., 2000) • F. Delitzsch (BC; Edinburgh, 1873; repr., 1985) • K. A. Farmer (ITC; Grand Rapids, 1991) • M. V. Fox (AB; New York, 2000) chaps. 1–9 • D. A. Garrett (NAC; Nashville, 1993) • B. Gemser (HAT; 2d ed.; Tübingen, 1963) • W. McKane (OTL; Philadelphia, 1970; repr., 1985) • A. Meinhold (ZBK; Zurich, 1991) • R. E. Murphy (WBC; Nashville, 1998) • L. G. Perdue (Interpretation; Louisville, Ky., 2000) • H. Ringgren (ATD; Göttingen, 1962; 3d ed., 1981) • R. B. Scott (AB; New York, 1965) • C. H. Toy (ICC; Edinburgh, 1899; repr., 1970) • B. K. Waltke (NICOT; 2 vols.; Grand Rapids, 2004-5) • R. N. Whybray (CBC; Cambridge, 1972) • H. Wiesmann (HS; Bonn, 1923) • G. Wildeboer (KHC; Tübingen, 1897).

Other works: L. Boström, *The God of the Sages: The Portrayal of God in the Book of Proverbs* (Stockholm, 1990) • J. Hausmann, *Studien zum Menschenbild der Weisheit* (Tübingen, 1995) • K. M. Heim, *Like Grapes of Gold Set in Silver: An Interpretation of Proverbial Clusters in Proverbs 10:1–22:16* (Berlin, 2001) • C. Kayatz, *Studien zu Proverbien 1–9. Eine form- und motivgeschichtliche Untersuchung unter Einbeziehung ägyptischen Vergleichsmaterials* (Neukirchen, 1966) • B. Lang, *Die weisheitliche Lehrrede. Eine Untersuchung von Sprüche 1–7* (Stuttgart, 1972); idem, *Wisdom and the Book of Proverbs: A Hebrew Goddess Redefined* (New York, 1986) • D. G. Meade, *Pseudonymity and Canon: An Investigation into the Relationship of Authorship and Authority in Jewish and Earliest Christian Tradition* (Grand Rapids, 1987) • A. Müller, *Proverbien 1–9. Der Weisheit neue Kleider* (Berlin, 2000) • R. E. Murphy, *The Tree of Life: An Exploration of Biblical Wisdom Literature* (2d ed.; Grand Rapids, 1996) • M. Neher, *Wesen und Wirken der Weisheit in der Sapientia Salomonis* (Berlin, 2004) 18-153 • D. Römheld, *Wege der Weisheit. Die Lehren Amenemopes und Proverbien 22,17–24,22* (Berlin, 1989) • R. Scoralik, *Einzelspruch und Sammlung* (Berlin, 1995) • P. W. Skehan, *Studies in Israelite Poetry and Wisdom* (Washington, D.C., 1971) • U. Skladny, *Die älteren Sprüchesammlungen in Israel* (Göttingen, 1962) • S. Weeks, *Early Israelite Wisdom* (Oxford, 1994) • W. A. van der Weiden, *Le Livre des Proverbs. Notes philologiques* (Rome, 1970) • C. Westermann, *Roots of Wisdom: The Oldest Proverbs of Israel and Other Peoples* (Louisville, Ky., 1995).

Otto Kaiser

Providence

1. Source and History of the Idea
2. Modern Problems

1. Source and History of the Idea

1.1. The general human experience of contingency, with reference either to the fate of individuals or to the history of theistic beliefs (→ Theism), has always come up against the idea of a teleological action that sustains, accompanies, and guides the action of the gracious or judging → God. God is viewed as a personal ruler of both individual and universal history. This history is not subject to blind → chance, as in Epicureanism (→ Greek Philosophy 7.1), nor to the laws of nature, as in a mechanistic worldview following I. Newton's → philosophy of nature (§§5-6), nor to a historical determinism, as in dialectical → materialism (§5). Rather, it is under the control of God, who aims ultimately at salvation. Providence is not just foresight, nor is it merely passive "seeing" or "knowing." It thinks of God's overall relation to the world as one of active caring *(procuratio)*.

1.2. The thought of divine providence (Gk. *pronoia*, Lat. *providentia*) is not a biblical one. Its origin is Greek. We can find it in pre-Socratic cosmologies (Heraclitus, Anaxagoras, Diogenes of Apollonia; → Greek Philosophy 2). A divine cosmic reason *(logos, nous)* is here postulated as a power that steers and orders things (→ Teleology). The term occurs for the first time in Herodotus (*Hist.* 3.108.2).

→ Stoicism makes of the doctrine of *pronoia* a basic cosmological paradigm that pantheistically arranges all things harmoniously into a cosmic organism in accordance with divine law (→ Pantheism), so that in a rational way all things are directed to the → good. All events are absolutely necessary, though human → freedom is not ruled out.

1.3. Hellenistic → Judaism adopted this Greek tradition (Jdt. 13:11; Wis. 14:3; 17:2; Philo, *De virt.* 216), as did the Greek → church fathers (Clement of Rome, → Justin, → Irenaeus, Clement of Alexandria, → Origen), though always under the influence of the Israelite view of → God (§4). The subject of *pronoia* was no longer a rational cosmic principle but the personal Creator who sustained his → creation by his Word (Logos) and Spirit (Pneuma) and who led it on to its salvific consummation. Yet the Greek idea of an education *(paideia)* of the human race by God also played a significant role. There was less interest in cosmology and in the question of God's work in history and more concern about history (→ Theology of History). Providence now referred to God's work in history in his continuous salvific care for creation, for his → people, and for individuals (→ Salvation 1).

1.4. The NT does not speak of God's *pronoia*, but we find in it many points of contact with the later doctrine of providence. Many passages refer to God's concern for individuals, especially Matt. 6:25-34 and 10:29-31. The thought of → salvation history is also present, as in Luke's theology of history, with its "must" or "is necessary" (Gk. *dei*, e.g., Luke 9:22; 17:25; 21:9; 24:7, 44; Acts 3:21; 17:3; and note the divine counsel in Acts 2:23; 4:28; 20:27). We may also refer to → Paul in Romans 9–11 and 16:26 and to eschatological texts (→ Eschatology 2).

The two lines of individual providence and universal providence both have OT roots. After the exile God's work in history was given an individual reference in Jer. 1:5; Job 5:19-27; Prov. 16:9; Ps. 16:5-6, and many other references, yet it also covered salvation history as a whole, as in the → Deuteronomistic history.

1.5. → Augustine (354-430; → Augustine's Theology) fully developed these two trends in a way that would be normative for most of the theologians who followed him. God's hidden providence helps carnal people to grow into spiritual people, as seen in the *Confessions*, the story of his own life. It also conducts world history, including → evil, toward the goal of the → kingdom of God *(De civitate Dei)*.

Adopting the distinction between God's eternal plan of salvation and the divine dominion over the world, → Thomas Aquinas (ca. 1225-74; → Thomism) related providence exclusively to God's pretemporal foreordaining of all things (*Summa theol.* I, q. 22, art. 1). As that which God "foreordains" for the world, providence then largely coincides with → predestination, or the latter is even subordinated to it (ibid., q. 23, art. 1, c.).

1.6. The → Reformers, however, stressed the concrete acts of God in history. M. → Luther (1483-1546; → Luther's Theology) gave greater emphasis to God's cooperation with relatively autonomous human action, but J. → Calvin (1509-64; → Calvin's Theology) referred more to the omnipotent sovereignty of Almighty God, by which even raindrops are under his control. Yet Calvin, too, avoided a quasi-Stoic → fatalism that would subject human acts to an impersonal and ruthless nexus of omnicausality (*Inst.* 1.16.8). God is a gracious and caring God who sustains his creation and steers it toward the salvation that he has determined for it.

The older Protestant → orthodoxy (§§1-2) adopted the scholastic distinctions relative to providence, which may still be found in some modern systematics (K. → Barth, O. Weber, W. Pannenberg). For example, God's providence takes the three forms of sustaining *(conservatio)*, concurrence (or accompanying, *concursus*), and ruling *(gubernatio)*.

1.7. The philosophical and theological acceptance of a mathematical and scientific view of the world, as with G. W. Leibniz (1646-1716) and his doctrine of "preestablished harmony" (→ Organism 2.2; Predestination 4), led the → Enlightenment toward a doctrine of providence that was closer to Greek doctrines of the *logos* than to biblical belief in the reign of God. Providence was linked to a doctrine of → progress (§§3-4). God would bring rational perfection through cosmic events, leading to "the best of all possible worlds." The cosmos was like a clock that, once it has been set going, needs no further intervention by the clockmaker (→ Deism). An individualistic counterpart to this concept of providence in nature and history was the Pietistic belief that God personally directs each individual life (→ Pietism).

Against what he took to be a short-sighted belief in God's watching over and guiding individuals and their works, G. W. F. Hegel (1770-1831; → Hegelianism) again gave prominence to the global dimension (*Werke* 11.40). In his view cosmic reason, with an "absolute cunning" (8.420), directs all historical events to its own ends. With these ends in view, absolute necessity rules the progress of history.

2. Modern Problems

2.1. As so often in the past, so in the 20th century historical disasters plunged the understanding of providence and attempts to find global meaning in history into a profound crisis (C. Amery, *Das Ende der Vorsehung* [1972]; → Worldview). G. Benn (1886-1956) found in the world only a "preestablished disharmony" (*Werke* 2.167). The problem of → theodicy challenges belief in providence, especially in divine world dominion.

2.2. In his magnificent presentation of the doctrine of providence, K. Barth (1886-1968; → Dialectical Theology) perceived in God's sustaining and governing activity a consequence of his election and an implementation of his decree of predestination (*CD* III/3, 3). Barth was not thereby offering a global model that would explain the world or history. Rather, he was unfolding perspectives of faith that would enable us to see in creaturely occurrence a reflection of the history of the divine covenant that has its center in Christ (→ Covenant 3.2). In this connection he presupposed the problematic notion of the unrestricted power and omnicausality of an "acting" God. He had in some sense faced this question already in his discussion of divine omnipotence (*CD* II/1, 490-607).

2.3. A fresh approach to the doctrine of providence must clearly distinguish between God's foreseeing in his eternal counsel and what he can now do by his Spirit in conditions that are often adverse. If this distinction is made, it will be seen that God's working is not sovereign, and certainly not one of causal mechanical or final force. It is the working of one power among others, but always oriented to the eschatological goal of his kingdom (→ Kingdom of God 3.3). We are to see God's power in relational, rather than absolute, terms.

A pneumatological view of this kind does not in any way negate human → freedom. It also avoids the problem of theodicy. Prayer, too, makes sense (→ Prayer 2). It asks for knowledge of the divine foreseeing, and it also asks for the power of the Spirit and of → truth (§2) so that participation in the actualizing of that foreseeing might be possible.

Bibliography: R. Bernhardt, *Was heißt "Handeln Gottes"? Eine Rekonstruktion der Lehre von der Vorsehung Gottes* (Gütersloh, 1999) • L. J. van den Brom, *Divine Presence in the World: A Critical Analysis of the Notion of Divine Omnipresence* (Kampen, 1993) • P. Buehler, *Predestination et providence* (Geneva, 1999) • H. Davies, *The Vigilant God: Providence in the Thought of Augustine, Aquinas, Calvin, and Barth* (New York, 1992) • T. J. Gorringe, *God's Theater: A Theology of Providence* (London, 1991) • P. Gwynne, *Special Divine Action: Key Issues in the Contemporary Debate (1965-1995)* (Rome, 1999) • W. Härle and D. Lührmann, eds., *MJTh* 1 (1987) • P. Helm, *The Providence of God* (Downers Grove, Ill., 1994) • M. J. Langford, *Providence* (London, 1981) • J. Sanders, *The God Who Risks: A Theology of Providence* (Downers Grove, Ill., 1998) • E. Saxer, *Vorsehung und Verheißung Gottes. Vier theologische Modelle (Calvin, Schleiermacher, Barth, Sölle)* (Zurich, 1980) • L. Scheffczyk, "Schöpfung und Vorsehung," *HDG* 2/2a • A. von Scheliha, *Der Glaube an die göttliche Vorsehung. Eine religionssoziologische, geschichtsphilosophische und theologiegeschichtliche Untersuchung* (Stuttgart, 1999) • T. Schneider and L. Ullrich, eds., *Vorsehung und Handeln Gottes* (Freiburg, 1988) • R. Swinburne, *Providence and the Problem of Evil* (Oxford, 1998) • T. L. Tiessen, *Providence and Prayer: How Does God Work in the World?* (Downers Grove, Ill., 2000) • V. White, *The Fall of a Sparrow: A Concept of Special Divine Action* (Exeter, 1985) • M. Wiles, *God's Action in the World* (London, 1986).

Reinhold Bernhardt

Psalms, Book of

2.3. Revival in the Reformation
2.4. Liturgical Movements
2.5. Questions

1. OT

1.1. *Terms and Place in Canon*

The term "Psalms" or "Psalter" is used for the OT collection of 150 songs and prayers. It comes from the Greek OT (→ Bible Manuscripts and Editions; Bible Versions). The Codex Alexandrinus has *psaltērion,* which denotes a stringed instrument and is a rendering of Heb. *nēbel,* "lyre." What is meant, then, is a book of songs to be sung with a stringed instrument. In the Codex Vaticanus we find the title *psalmoi,* with the subtitle *biblos psalmōn* (book of psalms), a term appearing also in the NT (Luke 20:42; 24:44; Acts 1:20; 13:33). *Psalmos* corresponds to the Heb. *mizmôr,* "musical piece," or "song [with musical accompaniment]."

In the Hebrew tradition the book or scroll was not originally given a single title. Only in the noncanonical use (→ Canon) of the Jewish community did it come to be called *tĕhillîm* (Praises) or *sēper tĕhillīm* (Book of songs of praise, or Hymns). This usage involved an unusual collective plural. The term was reserved for the title, which designated the book as a whole as a group of praise songs or → hymns. In Ps. 72:20 we also find *tĕpillôt,* "prayers," for the portion that concludes here ("the prayers of David . . . are ended"). These titles represent an attempt to describe the collection in terms of its primary contents, though no single word really suffices. The term "Psalter" or "Psalms" fills the gap that other terms like "songs for the lyre," "praises" (Ger. *Preisungen,* Buber-Rosenzweig), or "hymns and prayers" are inadequate to fill.

The MT and LXX (followed by the Vg and some other versions) number the 150 separate texts in different ways. The LXX joins Psalms 9 and 10, and 114 and 115, then divides Psalms 116 and 147. The Psalms as a whole are a selection of early Israelite songs and prayers. There are a few other individual psalms scattered across the OT, for example, in Exodus 15, Deuteronomy 32 and 33, 1 Samuel 2, 2 Samuel 22 (= Psalm 18), Habakkuk 3, Jonah 2, and Isaiah 38.

The Psalms scroll 11QPs[a] from → Qumran contains an additional ten psalm texts. Some of these we knew (Psalm 151 LXX, Sirach 51, the Syriac Psalms), but others are new (Plea for Deliverance, col. 19; Apostrophe to Zion, col. 22; Hymn to the Creator, col. 26; David's Compositions, col. 27) and in part fragmentary. We must distinguish these texts from the Qumran collection 1QH (*Hôdāyōt,* Thanksgiving Hymns) and the *Psalms of Solomon,* which date from the middle of the first century B.C.

The Psalter forms the core of the third part of the Hebrew canon, the Writings *(kĕtûbîm).* Within the Writings they are often put first (Biblia Hebraica Stuttgartensia, though not in the Leningrad Codex or the Aleppo Codex, where the sequence is the Minor Prophets, Chronicles, Psalms, Job, and Proverbs). A special accent system in the MT for Psalms, Job, and Proverbs shows that they have a unique status. In the Greek Bible, Psalms opens the second part (together with Odes), the poetical books.

1.2. *Arrangement, Series, and Part Collections*

Some scholars today think that the complete Psalter did not find its way into the canon in the second century B.C. as a book of hymns and prayers for the second temple (once the common view), but rather as an edifying and devotional book for the laity (see N. Füglister, in J. Schreiner). Only a few of the chosen texts — for example, some individual hymns, the Hallel group (111–18), and hymns for special days (e.g., 92 for the Sabbath, 30 for the temple dedication festival) — were used in temple worship and the services of the synagogue. Yet even before its definitive canonization, the book was especially beloved, for example, at Qumran (31 MSS, including 11QPs[a]), by the Therapeutae in Egypt (according to Philo), in the first NT churches (the most quoted of all OT books in the NT), and in Pharisaic circles (see Psalm 1), which then saw to the acceptance of the book into the Hebrew canon (→ Primitive Christian Community; Pharisees).

The division of the Psalms into five books (1–41; 42–72; 73–89; 90–106; 107–50) is late and is not linked to the precanonical → Pentateuchal lectionary cycles but rather to older part-collections and their doxological endings (→ Doxology). The sequences reflect a process of development that we cannot wholly follow. Collections as to 2–72 (89), 1–119, and 1–150 suggest some of the stages. Strategic positions and structures seem to express editorial concepts.

Specific part-collections may be identified clearly (note the headings) and have their own character, origin, and history. Four David groups (2–41; 51–72; 108–10; 138–45) consist of individual prayers, as do probably the Korahite groups (42–49; 84–85; 87–88), which seem to be from the north, while the Asaph psalms (50; 73–83) are community prayers and songs. In 42–83 the more general term for God *'ĕlōhîm* replaces to a large extent the special name *YHWH* (→ Yahweh), and these psalms are thus called Elohistic. Materially, 93 and 95–99 go together as royal Yahweh hymns (with almost no superscriptions); 111–18 constitute the so-called Great Hallel; and 120–34, coming after the great poem 119, are ascent psalms or pilgrim psalms, concluded — like the final David collection 138–45 — by hymns (135–36 and 146–50). Psalms not part of a group include 86, 119, and 137 (G. H. Wilson). The various series, which in part interlock, are developed collections, but we know little about their origin. The David psalms come from Jerusalem, the Korah group perhaps from Dan, the Asaph group possibly from Bethel. A link to the guilds of temple singers mentioned in Chronicles in the postexilic → temple may be assumed.

1.3. *Authorship, Transmission, Use*

Each psalm has its own history, from its composition to its preservation in the canon. The final canonical form suggests a long process of transmission that might have included changes and additions. Parts were no doubt included first (e.g., 24; 108; 135), and in some cases the text was damaged (cf. 14 and 53; 49; 76, etc.). We have no general model whereby to understand the history of transmission. Some possibilities are as follows. *Individual prayers* like 3, 4, 5, and others derive as a rule from people in difficult circumstances, for example, suffering from sickness or under false accusation. They speak to God in prayer and seek his help. The written form is poetically stylized, since only the best possible manner of speech is suitable in prayer to God (see, e.g., 22; 42–43, etc.). Added is an assurance of hearing (22:24) or a promise of praise (13:6). A psalm of praise may also be added or included (22:25-31). A very good example of what takes place is 22 (see also 69).

Then we have *hymns,* which are either liturgical (100) or deal with theological themes that call for praise (e.g., → creation in 104). These texts seem to have been penned by skilled writers (see 45:1) and poets. They might nonetheless still be used in individual prayer (19, see vv. 11-14; 8, see vv. 2, 4), something attested by the so-called signatures or postscripts (104:31-35).

We also have *Wisdom songs* (→ Wisdom Literature), like the alphabetical texts, in which lines or sections begin acrostically with successive letters of the alphabet. These are scribal products, but for all their schematism they are astonishing works (e.g., 119, with its 176 lines, 8 for each letter, with virtually every line carrying a reference in some form to the → Word of God). Their aim is often that of practical devotional. They offer rosaries, as it were, stringing together mottoes and sentences for meditation.

Final verses of psalms suggest a use as prayers (25:22; 33:22; 145:21 according to 11QPs[a]).

The *royal YHWH hymns,* which used to be called coronation psalms (47, 93, 95–99), had a special role. They were no doubt part of the festal liturgy of the preexilic temple at Jerusalem. Of particular importance was the theologoumenon and confession *YHWH mlk,* "YHWH is king." Paradigmatically significant is 29. This psalm could well contain pre-Israelite material that has been worked over and made into a YHWH hymn depicting a theophany. It has left its mark on 96 and the Book of Revelation. Psalm 80 (apparently an exilic text with earlier elements from the northern kingdom), as well as 50, 81, 89, 91, and many others, may also be mentioned in the same connection.

Interesting from the standpoint of individual prayers is 40:7, where the psalmist says, "In the scroll of the book it is written of me." The reference is to a psalm of complaint in time of need that the one who has been delivered is placing in the sanctuary for general edification (v. 9). It perhaps remained there as a votive offering and record and then took shape as 40 (and perhaps 70) in the Davidic Psalter (= books 1 and 2?). But we see what seems to be an entirely different process in 45. Here is a song for a royal wedding written with the pen of a skilled writer such as a court poet (v. 1).

The textual individuality that is increasingly claiming the attention of research permits generalization only when psalms relate to the same circles (e.g., liturgies or prayers of those under accusation) or to similar circumstances or when they belong to the same group or part collection, as in the case of the pilgrim songs, the royal YHWH hymns, or the psalms of Asaph or of the Korahites. The liturgical and musical directions point to later use. Worth noting in this regard is the instruction in many psalms that they are texts (liturgical) to be used "with stringed instruments" (4, 6, 54–55, 61, 67, 76). Some texts, too, are for use as festal liturgies (30). Attempts to follow the history of transmission and of redaction are still being made.

Dating of the individual psalms is possible in only a few cases (e.g., 79 and 137). The royal psalms and cultic hymns are the oldest (2; 110 or 24; 29), coming from the preexilic time. Some exilic texts may be found in the Asaph group (50, 74, and 80). Many individual psalms could be postexilic. The majority of the individual psalms are probably postexilic, some only late in this period.

1.4. *Form and Style*

The three distinctives of Hebrew poetry are meter, parallelism, and assonance or alliteration. We find these features in many forms, but the same general laws usually apply. Various methods have been suggested to ascertain the *meter,* but with only approximate success. Meter is undoubtedly present, and depending on the literary type, the accentuating (word or accent based), alternating (syllable based), or stichometric (consonant counting) method seems to apply. As a rule, the rhythm is even and consistent but not fixed or schematic. Line organization often betrays clear structures (e.g., 13, 29, 111–12, etc.). The *māšāl* (proverb) meter is typical (e.g., 2, 78, 119), with its common 3-3 symmetry of words or accents (i.e., the two cola of each line, or couplet, with three stressed syllables each). Also typical are lines with 2-2 or 4-4 symmetry of words or accents (45, 93), asymmetrical 3-2 rhythm for dirges or laments (28, 42–43), and mixed and artistic forms, as in 13 (stepwise progression from long to short lines: four [or five] 5-stress cola, four 4-stress cola, two 3-stress cola, and two 2-stress cola), all figured according to the most common accentuation system. Most of the prayers take rhythmic form.

Parallelism symmetrically relates the two halves of a verse in their content, illuminating that content from two different perspectives in a kind of poetic multidimensionality. The parallelism does not have to be fixed. Strict synonymity is unusual. Examples are everywhere present (1:1, 2; 2:1-5; 22:1-31, etc.); we need not multiply them. Antithetic and synthetic parallelism occurs, as well as synonymous.

Less well-known are the *alliteration of consonants* and the *assonance of vowels* in the texts, yet this device is common and impressive. We have, for example, the *š* of *šālôm* repeated several times in 122:6, or an *i* assonance in 137:3. In 129:3 there are eight guttural syllables (involving the consonants *h, ḥ,* ʿ, and *r*) in describing "plowers" who "plowed on my back; they made their furrows long." In 29 three lines begin with *hābû* (ascribe!), seven with *qôl* (voice, giving this psalm the title "Psalm of the Seven Thunders"), also two lines with *YHWH.* Finally, we have the acrostic psalms with their alliterative forms (9–10, 25, 34, etc.).

The style of psalms is very varied. They range from simple prayers in everyday speech to complex rhythmic compositions. As a rule, the structures are plain to see. At times stanzas (strophes) may be indicated by refrains (42–43, 80). But we also find very complicated texts that defy analysis (50, 80). Psalms 13 and 57B have a steplike structure. Psalms 29 and 148 have the character of litanies. Not uncommon is the enframing of a psalm, as in 8, where v. 9 repeats v. 1. Many texts and liturgies are most complex (e.g., 22, 69; see W. G. E. Watson, L. Alonso-Schökel, and K. Seybold).

1.5. *Grouping and Classification*

Exposition has traditionally sought to group the psalms. Grouping has been by subject matter, analogous to the Davidic psalms. Thus we have the seven so-called penitential psalms (6, 32, 38, 51, 102, 130, 143), royal psalms (2, 18, 20, 21, etc.), enemy psalms (3 and many others), sickness psalms (6, 13, 38, etc.), psalms of trust (16, 23, etc.), malediction psalms (109, 137), Wisdom psalms (1, 19, 25, etc.), and so on.

H. Gunkel (1862-1932) suggested objective criteria whereby to subject the postulating of types to methodological control. In classification he noted a need to consider speech, situation *(Sitz im Leben),* and subject matter (*Introduction,* §1). His program initiated the establishing of types and their history. He himself distinguished hymns, Yahweh enthronement songs, communal complaint songs, royal psalms, individual complaint songs, individual thanksgiving songs, and smaller genres (sayings of blessing and curse, pilgrim song, victory song, thanksgiving song of Israel, legends, the Torah). He also found prophetic elements and Wisdom poetry in the psalms, as well as what he called mixtures, antiphonal poems, and liturgies (see Gunkel and J. Begrich). In Gunkel's view, the genres, mostly cultic, were models for individual texts primarily of spiritual or noncultic origin.

S. Mowinckel (1884-1965) related most of the texts as we now have them to the cult, and centrally to what he took to be the enthronement festival of Yahweh. Other scholars suggested other festivals, such as a covenant festival (A. Weiser) or royal Zion festival (H.-J. Kraus). Attention also focused on the prayers of those accused (H. Schmidt), on hymns (E. Crüsemann), and on other types. C. Westermann found only individual or collective complaint and praise, but with distinctions (i.e., complaints relating to God, enemies, and self, or praise in the form of record or description).

A switch has come in modern research to more emphasis on the individuality of the psalms, each being taken in and for itself, with more and more studies of individual psalms. At the same time, more attention is also paid to the traditional contexts (Wilson).

1.6. *Headings*

The headings and their significance have not yet been clearly understood. It seems they were added later and indicate subsequent classification or use. The commentaries should be consulted for details.

What the Hebrew means, for example, by the ascription to → David (73 times, 80 in the LXX), → Solomon, or → Moses is doubtful. The Heb. *lě* before the name does not have to mean that the person mentioned was the author, even when biographical details are also given, for it might have the significance, for example, "about David" or "for David," or it might be a kind of stamp denoting the collection. The term *lmnṣḥ* (to the leader [NRSV], for the leader [JPSV]), used 55 times in the MT, is also ambivalent.

Clearer are the indications of melody (22 etc.) and the special instructions for use (100, 102). Further classifications are provided by *šîr* (cultic song), *mizmôr* (song with instrumental accompaniment), *miktām* (inscription[?]), *tĕpillâ* (prayer), *tĕhillâ* (song of praise), and so forth. Differences between the LXX and Qumran show that the headings were not finally fixed when the canon was closed.

1.7. *Near Eastern Analogies*

Parallels and analogies to the Psalms have been found in the ancient Near East regarding both individual psalms and genres. (See the collections of texts listed below in the last section of the bibliography.) Sound methodology is demanded, however, if influence or dependence is to be asserted. Direct comparison is seldom possible.

1.8. *Relations to Cult, Wisdom, and Prophecy*

Much closer are the links to the great traditions of ancient Israel in the cult, wisdom, and prophecy. The psalms tell us little about any relation to the official → temple cult, priesthood (→ Priest, Priesthood, 2), or festal rituals. On the whole they seem to be more occasional devotional materials for the laity, with less connection to the → liturgy (except for the YHWH psalms). At times they keep a distance from the cult (and are perhaps postcultic).

Wisdom is present in various statements in the Wisdom psalms (1, 49, 73, 119, etc.).

As regards the → prophets (§2) there is little direct relation, but words of God are quoted (12, 50, 81), and prophetic forms of speech are used (82). More significant is the use of psalms or psalmlike poems in the prophetic tradition (Isaiah 12 etc.; Jeremiah 11; 15, etc.; Habakkuk 3; Jonah 2; Amos doxologies [4:13; 5:8-9; 9:5-6]; Nahum 1).

1.9. *Theology*

Psalms contains theological statements in such fullness and of such variety that we cannot summarize them adequately here. It is hardly possible to offer a theology of the Psalms either by picking out central themes, or by focusing on themes that seem to be central because they occur so frequently, or by assembling individual loci into a supposedly uniform doctrinal system. The different voices suggest that we should let each text present its own thoughts, that we should be content with the profile that the author has given to what is said.

Along these lines we have in the Psalms a discussion with many participants whose basic feature is the dialogic principle (M. Buber), made up of the twin components of praise and complaint, along with prayer. Here is a dialogic theology (C. Westermann), a socially critical theology (W. Brueggemann), at all events a → practical theology. It is sustained by the rich streams of tradition in ancient Israel that it inherits and filled out with living experiences that alternate between brokenness (31:12) and success (8:5). This is not a uniform theology but an active and dynamic theology that is forged in the process of rising up, falling, rising up again, and surviving.

The Psalms bear witness to a living faith. They offer us faith, speech, and logic. The theology is more implicit than explicit. → Theology understood as doctrine occurs mostly in the Wisdom psalms (119) or in hymns (104). Historical psalms (78, 105, 106) provide → narrative theology. Individual psalms (22, 23, etc.) give us theology in the form of a conceptual mastering of personal crises. The so-called gate liturgies (15, 24) state theology in the form of an ethical foundation. Nearly all the texts present theology as a linguistic appropriating of salvation. It is up to those who come after to use them as such.

Bibliography: Commentaries: P. Craigie, M. E. Tate, and L. C. Allen (WBC 19-21; Waco, Tex., 1983, and Dallas, 1990) • E. Gerstenberger (FOTL 14-15; Grand Rapids, 1988-2001) • H. Gunkel (HKAT; Göttingen, 1929; 5th ed., 1958) • F. L. Hossfeld and E. Zenger (HTKAT; Freiburg, 2000) Pss. 51–100 • F. L. Hossfeld and E. Zenger (NEchtB; 2 vols.; Würzburg, 1993-2002) vol. 1, Pss. 1–50; vol. 2, Pss. 51–100 • H.-J. Kraus (2 vols.; Minneapolis, 1988-89) • J. L. Mays (IBC; Louisville, Ky., 1994) • F. Nötscher (EchtB; Würzburg, 1947) • M. Oeming (NSKAT; Stuttgart, 2000) • H. Schmidt (HAT; Tübingen, 1934) • K. Seybold (HAT; Tübingen, 1996) • A. Weiser (OTL; Philadelphia, 1962).

Introductions: J. Day, *Psalms* (Sheffield, 1990) • H. Gunkel and J. Begrich, *Introduction to Psalms: The Genres of the Religious Lyric of Israel* (Macon, Ga., 1998; orig. pub., 1933) • K. Seybold, *Introducing the Psalms* (Edinburgh, 1990).

Monographs: L. Alonso-Schökel, *A Manual of Hebrew Poetics* (Rome, 1988) • W. Brueggemann, *The Message of the Psalms* (Minneapolis, 1984) • F. Crüsemann, *Studien zur Formgeschichte von Hymnus und Danklied in Israel* (Neukirchen, 1969) • P. W. Flint, *The Dead Sea Psalms Scrolls and the Book of Psalms* (Leiden, 1997) • E. Haag and F.-L. Hossfeld, eds., *Freude an der Weisung des Herrn. Beiträge zur Theologie der Psalmen* (Stuttgart, 1986) • B. Janowski, *Konfliktgespräche mit Gott. Eine Anthropologie der Psalmen* (Neukirchen, 2003) • O. Keel, *The Symbolism of the Biblical World: Ancient Near Eastern Iconography and the Book of Psalms* (Winona Lake, Ind., 1997) • H.-J. Kraus, *Theology of the Psalms* (Minneapolis, 1992) • M. Millard, *Die Komposition des Psalters* (Tübingen, 1994) • H. Graf Reventlow, *Gebet im Alten Testament* (Stuttgart, 1986) • J. Schreiner, ed., *Beiträge zur Psalmenforschung* (Würzburg, 1988) • K. Seybold, *Poetik der Psalmen* (Stuttgart, 2003) • H. Spieckermann, *Heilsgegenwart. Eine Theologie der Psalmen* (Göttingen, 1989) • F. Stolz, *Psalmen im nachkultischen Raum* (Zurich, 1983) • W. G. E. Watson, *Traditional Techniques in Classical Hebrew Verse* (Sheffield, 1994) • C. Westermann, *Praise and Lament in the Psalms* (Atlanta, 1981) • G. H. Wilson, *The Editing of the Hebrew Psalter* (Chico, Calif., 1985).

Texts from the contemporary world: J. Assmann, *Ägyptische Hymnen und Gebete* (Zurich, 1975) • W. Beyerlin, ed., *Near Eastern Religious Texts Relating to the OT* (Philadelphia, 1978) • A. Falkenstein and W. von Soden, *Sumerische und akkadische Hymnen und Gebete* (Zurich, 1953) • W. Mayer, *Untersuchungen zur Formensprache der babylonischen "Gebetsbeschwörungen"* (Rome, 1976) • W. H. P. Römer and K. Hecker, eds., *Lieder und Gebete,* 1, *TUAT* 2/5 • M.-J. Seux, *Hymnes et prières aux dieux de Babylonie et d'Assyrie* (Paris, 1976).

Klaus Seybold

2. Liturgical Use

2.1. *Assumptions*

Two assumptions underlie the use of the psalms in liturgy. The first is that "the Psalter is a body of liturgical poetry" (→ Book of Common Prayer, Episcopal Church [1979], 582) so that the choice, textual form, and musical settings must be subject to the demands of liturgy. The second is that from the days of the → early church, the Psalter has been interpreted Christologically (→ Christology), so that its use depends on the answer to the question whether and how Psalms speaks prophetically of the mission, death, and resurrection of → Jesus (and our own being taken up into these; see "Psalmus vox de Christo / Psalmus vox Ecclesiae ad Christum / Psalmus vox Christi ad Patrem," B. Fischer, 31).

2.2. *Decline*

The singing of psalms in the liturgy goes back to their liturgical use in early → Judaism. It became a fixed part of the Christian liturgy from the fourth century onward, finding a place both in the canonical → hours and in the → Eucharist.

2.2.1. As regards the canonical hours, there are two very different traditions in the use of psalms. At morning and evening services for the whole congregation in church, selected psalms were sung responsively. But → monasticism (from the time of the 4th-cent. Egyptian monks) had the psalms read in their biblical order without regard to the season, with silent → prayer after each psalm and a concluding collect offering a Christian interpretation. In modified form this system became the basis of the use of the psalms in the monastic hours, "Glory be to the Father" now being added at the end of either the psalms for the day or each individual psalm. With some exceptions this monastic use found its way into the canonical hours of churches in the West, the psalms being sung more or less in their canonical sequence.

2.2.2. From the end of the fifth century, psalms were sung in celebrations of the Eucharist, either in response or as accompaniment. Responsively, a psalm or part of a psalm was selected to respond to the preceding OT or NT lesson and to interpret it. It was sung by the cantor, the congregation answering. The singing and reflection were in such cases independent of any other action.

Soon the tunes began to be embellished, the texts were shortened, and no more than a few verses might be left. Psalms were also sung on entry, at the bringing of the gifts, and during communion; they were enframed by antiphons and accompanied the movements. From the eighth century onward the antiphon gradually came to the fore, and the psalm was reduced on entry to the first verse, disappearing completely at the offering and during communion.

2.3. *Revival in the Reformation*

In the 16th century little remained of psalmody. The same psalms were usually sung at the canonical hours (psalms for saints' days); at the Lord's Supper only one verse was sung on entry, and few were read or sung between the lections. In the Lutheran orders (→ Liturgical Books; Liturgy 1), strenuous efforts failed to preserve the canonical hours beyond the 17th century, and at the supper at most only the antiphon and one verse on entry remained.

At the same time, however, metrical psalms came into use in Reformation churches. M. → Luther took the lead here, but J. → Calvin played the most influential part, preparing a collection in Strasbourg, then in Geneva publishing the full metrical version prepared by C. Marot and T. → Beza. In England and Scotland the versions of T. Sternhold and J. Hopkins, W. Kethe, and others popularized metrical psalm singing, the familiar work by N. Tate and N. Brady following later in England. In many cases the desire to be as literal as possible worked against the poetic quality of these versions, but at their best, put to fine tunes (e.g., for Psalms 23, 24, or 100), the metrical psalms have made an important contribution to worship and devotion.

In the Church of England, and later in sister churches of the → Anglican Communion, Morning and Evening Prayer became substituted for the Eucharist as the main Sunday services, and in addition to metrical psalms the biblical psalms for the day were said or sung, chants (often impressive) being composed to accompany the words when sung. Selected psalms were appointed for the great festivals such as Christmas and Easter. No psalms were included in the communion service, since strict adherence to the rubrics would have this service follow Morning or Evening Prayer. The Venite (Psalm 95) became a regular part of Morning Prayer, and Psalms 67, 98, and 100 found optional use as canticles.

2.4. ***Liturgical Movements***

The → liturgical movements of the 19th and 20th centuries helped many churches to rediscover the liturgical value of the psalms. They encouraged congregations to make more use of morning and evening services with a modified version of psalms in sequence, or with fewer, specially selected psalms after the example of the early church. Making the Eucharist the main Sunday service also opened the door to a wider use of selected psalms in Roman Catholic, Old Catholic, and some Lutheran and Reformed churches with the interposition of a psalm between the lections and a restored entry psalm or communion psalm. In the Anglican world, however, elimination of Morning and Evening Prayer as main Sunday services greatly reduced the use of the psalms, the more so when churches do not include a psalm between the readings.

The growth of hymns and their use has also reduced the role of metrical psalms, though they still play an important part in many churches, especially of the Reformed tradition. Incidentally, selected psalms have also contributed to → occasional services (e.g., burials) in both their original and their metrical forms.

2.5. ***Questions***

Meaningful use of the psalms at worship depends on the answering of four main questions.

1. At canonical hours should a congregation say or sing all 150 psalms in sequence, or only a few selected psalms?
2. Can we expect congregations today to make use of psalms of malediction as the expression or content of their Christian faith?
3. Should a masculine word like "man" be used ("Blessed is the man who . . ."), or should a form be adopted that more obviously includes all church members ("Blessed are those who . . ."; → Liturgy 4)? A similar question arises regarding the use of masculine pronouns for God, that is, whether the church has any right to change or evade this usage.
4. How can the music adopted for singing the psalms do greater justice to the literary genre of the psalms used?

→ Church Music; Church Musicians; Hymnal

Bibliography: J. Dyer, "The Singing of Psalms in the Early Medieval Office," *Spec.* 64 (1989) 535-78 • B. Fischer, *Die Psalmen als Stimme der Kirche* (Trier, 1982) • H. A. Glass, *The Story of the Psalters: A History of the Metrical Versions of Great Britain and America from 1549 to 1885* (New York, 1972; orig. pub., 1888) • International Commission on English in the Liturgy, *The Psalter: A Faithful and Inclusive Rendering from the Hebrew into Contemporary English Poetry, Intended Primarily for Communal Song and Recitation* (Chicago, 1995) • M. Kunzler, *The Church's Liturgy* (New York, 2001) pt. 5 • A. Niebergall, "Agende," *TRE* 1.755-84; 2.1-91 • J. A. Smith et al., "Psalm," *NGDMM* (2001) 20.449-71 • C. Stuhlmueller, *The Spirituality of the Psalms* (Collegeville, Minn., 2002) • R. F. Taft, *The Liturgy of the Hours in East and West* (Collegeville, Minn., 1986).

Thaddeus A. Schnitker

Pseudepigrapha

1. OT Pseudepigrapha
   1.1. Apocalyptic Literature and Related Works
   1.2. Testaments
   1.3. Expansions of the OT and Legends
   1.4. Wisdom and Philosophical Literature
   1.5. Prayers, Psalms, and Odes
   1.6. Fragments of Lost Judeo-Hellenistic Works
   1.7. Addenda
   1.8. Conclusion
2. NT Pseudepigrapha and Apocrypha
   2.1. Definition and Background
   2.2. Gospels and Related Writings
   2.3. Acts
   2.4. Letters
   2.5. Apocalypses
   2.6. Others

The term "pseudepigrapha" literally means "falsely ascribed writings." It is a term given to a variety of ancient documents that are not part of either the Hebrew Bible (OT) or NT canon, nor are they included in what are called the OT → Apocrypha (deuterocanonical books). The convention of attributing such writings to someone other than their real author was common in antiquity. The attribution was generally for purposes of enhanced authority.

1. OT Pseudepigrapha

For at least two decades the technical term "Old Testament Pseudepigrapha" (OTP) has been recognized to denote about 66 writings that are related in content to the canon of the OT and especially to the OT Apocrypha, though some other documents should also now be included in this collection. (The OTP are translated into English in J. H. Charlesworth, *The OT Pseudepigrapha*, henceforth *OTP*.) The traditions preserved in the pseudepigrapha are often fascinating. For example, Jews before the burning of → Jerusalem in A.D. 70 imagined, among other things, that God rose from his throne and gave it to → Moses; that a stone once substituted for Jeremiah and even spoke; that the moon receives its light from the sun; and that the Egyptians, as well as the Babylonians, Greeks, and Romans, received their knowledge and wisdom from one of the patriarchs.

The pseudepigrapha often claim to have been written by biblical authors; hence, for example, the following titles: *Apocalypse of Adam, Apocalypse of Enoch, Testament of Abraham, More Psalms of David, Testament of Solomon, Martyrdom and Ascension of Isaiah,* and *Fourth Book of Ezra.* The OTP have mostly been preserved in the Christian tradition and in some cases are regarded by certain churches as part of the → canon (e.g., the → Ethiopian Orthodox Church includes *Jubilees* and *1 Enoch* in the canon). Some of the OTP, in Hebrew and Aramaic, and similar works have been found in the 11 → Qumran caves (the so-called Qumran pseudepigrapha). While rabbinic tradition tended to suppress pseudepigrapha after the destruction of the Temple in A.D. 70, the OTP are of great importance for understanding the history and theology of Second Temple → Judaism, as well as the origins of Christianity. The OTP also have significance for NT history, exegesis, and theology.

The OTP have been divided into the following categories: apocalyptic literature and related works; testaments; expansions of the OT and legends; Wisdom and philosophical literature; prayers, psalms, and odes; fragments of lost Judeo-Hellenistic works; and addenda. The OTP will be discussed under these genres, loosely defined, and then presented chronologically but tied to cycles of tradition (thus, e.g., the traditions that grew from the Enoch tradition will be presented together, and first).

1.1. *Apocalyptic Literature and Related Works*

In this category we may list the following 19 works.

1 (Ethiopic Apocalypse of) Enoch. This apocalypse is a collection of (perhaps five) Enoch "books" that are fully extant only in Ethiopic, with portions in the original Aramaic (found at Qumran) and in Greek, with fragments in Latin, Coptic, and Syriac. The oldest sections on the angels depend on Genesis 6 and date from approximately 300 B.C., and the latest portion, which refers to "that Son of Man" (→ Eschatology 1), probably took shape near the end of the first century B.C. The books of Enoch comprise 108 chapters. These apocalyptic compositions attributed to Enoch reveal the creative genius of the early Jews, their dependence on non-Jewish traditions, and their devotion to the → Torah. The documents were significantly influential in the Palestinian Jesus Movement; one section is quoted in Jude.

2 (Slavonic Apocalypse of) Enoch. 2 Enoch is fully preserved only in Old Slavonic. The work is not easy to date, but many scholars think it was composed sometime around A.D. 100. This Jewish work is an expansion of Gen. 5:21-32. The story begins with the life of Enoch ("a wise man and a great artisan") and continues to → Noah and the miraculous birth of Melchizedek. Christian glosses are evident. The major section is the translation of Enoch through the various heavens so he can see the future and teach morality to the saints when he returns to earth. In 73 chapters the author (and the editors) present a thoroughgoing → monotheism. In contrast to the authors of *1 Enoch*, the author has no interest in history.

3 (Hebrew Apocalypse of) Enoch. 3 Enoch, or *Sepher Hekalot* (Book of the Palaces), was composed and is preserved in Hebrew. It is a late composition with many early traditions; its final editing took place in the fifth or sixth century A.D. and helps trace the development of the Enoch cycle of texts. In 48 chapters the Jewish author claims to present an account by Rabbi Ishmael (early 2d cent. A.D.), who journeys to heaven and sees God's throne and chariot, obtains revelations from the archangel Metatron, and views the heavenly world.

Sibylline Oracles. This work comprises 14 books and fragments dating from the second century B.C. to the seventh century A.D., composed chronologically by Greeks, Romans, Jews, and Christians, with much later editing, all attributed to the Sibyl (or seer). This "old woman" passed on to her devotees words of wisdom that pertained to the present and the near future (cf. Virgil's *ultima aetas,* "final age"). The oracles often functioned as political propaganda. These epic verses are preserved in Greek and were composed almost exclusively in hexameters. According to Jewish traditions, Sibyl was the daughter or daughter-in-law of Noah. Book 3, though composite, was composed in the second century B.C. by a Jew in Egypt; it is dependent on Genesis. Book 4 is also composite, dating just after the time of Alexander the Great (356-323 B.C.), conceivably by a Jew, and edited by Jews at the end of the first century A.D., perhaps in Syria but most likely in the Jordan Valley (in Jewish baptist circles, because of the reference to baptism). Among other topics, the editor mentions the destruction of Jerusalem, the flight of Nero to Parthia, and the eruption of Vesuvius.

Treatise of Shem. This allegorical work is extant only in Syriac. It was most likely composed by a Jew just after the defeat of the Egyptian fleet at Actium in 31 B.C., probably in Alexandria. In 12 chapters the author describes the nature of each year according to the sign of the zodiac in which the year begins.

Apocryphon of Ezekiel. Composed by a Jew sometime between 50 B.C. and A.D. 50, this pseudepigraphon is extant in rabbinic Hebrew, Greek (cited by Epiphanius, *1 Clement,* and Clement of Alexandria), and Coptic. Hebrew or Greek is the original language. The work is divided into two chapters and five fragments. Some fragments are clearly edited by Christians. The most extensive fragment seeks to prove the → resurrection of the body and spirit (soul) together, both to receive reward or punishment together.

Apocalypse of Zephaniah. Perhaps 25 percent of this Jewish pseudepigraphon is preserved, and only in Coptic; there is a Greek quotation in the *Stromata* of Clement of Alexandria (ca. 150-ca. 215). The presumably Greek original was composed by a Jew sometime between 100 B.C. and A.D. 175, most likely in Egypt. In 12 chapters the Jewish author describes, in first-person narrative, a cosmic journey into the heavens and the coming judgment.

Fourth Book of Ezra. Along with *1 Enoch,* this document — specifically chaps. 3–14, called in Lat. MSS *4 Ezra* — is one of the most significant Jewish compositions from Early Judaism. These chapters were composed by a Jew in Semitic (most likely Hebrew) sometime in the latter decades of the first century A.D., and perhaps somewhere in ancient Palestine. Seven visions describe the future age and the coming of the → Messiah. The apocalypse is preserved primarily in Latin and Syriac, with major parts also in Arabic, Ethiopic, and Armenian, and there are fragments in Georgian, Coptic, and Greek (*OxyPap* 1010). The *Fourth Book of Ezra* is the full apocalypse, with the Christian expansions in chaps. 1–2 and 15–16. These additions to the Jewish core were written in the second or third century. One of the hallmarks of the Jewish apocalypse is the inscrutability of the "One and Only Creator." The document is pessimistic, a tone that the Christian additions try to shift.

Greek Apocalypse of Ezra. This apocalypse is in Greek and probably was composed in that language. In its present form the work is Christian. It could have been written during the first millennium, probably after A.D. 150. The chapters record a putative dialogue between the Lord and Ezra, the latter being able to argue with God (which shows a dependence on *4 Ezra*). Descriptions of punishment and the antichrist are significant.

Vision of Ezra. This Christian pseudepigraphon is closely related to the *Fourth Book of Ezra,* the *Greek Apocalypse of Ezra,* and the *Apocalypse of Sedrach.* Ezra is given a vision of "the judgments of the sinners" (v. 1). The document has 66 verses and is preserved in Latin, which is probably a translation of a Greek original. The original was composed sometime between the fourth and seventh centuries.

Questions of Ezra. This is a dialogue between Ezra and the Lord regarding the fate of human souls after death. It is preserved in Armenian in two recensions and was composed by a Christian who was influenced by early Jewish texts and traditions. Recension A has 40 verses, and Recension B 14 verses. The original language, date of composition, and provenance are not discernible.

Revelation of Ezra. This *kalandologion,* or document that describes the characteristics of a year according to which day of the week it begins on (cf. *Treatise of Shem*), must antedate the ninth century, since that is the date of the extant Lat. MS. The original language seems to have been Latin. It was composed by a Christian who refers to "the Lord's Day" (v. 1). The work has seven verses.

Apocalypse of Sedrach. This Christian composition of 16 chapters is extant only in one 15th-century Gk. MS. Sedrach preaches about love (chap. 1) and then is taken up into heaven by an angel to speak with God (2–16). The Jewish traditions it incorporates are ancient. The descriptions of the soul in chap. 10 are remarkable.

2 (Syriac Apocalypse of) Baruch. This apocalypse, extant in Syriac and Arabic, was composed by a Jew, perhaps in Hebrew, sometime around A.D. 100, perhaps in Palestine. It contains 87 chapters. In contrast to *4 Ezra,* this document is positive in tone; it places the blame for sin on the individual, not on Adam. The author exhorts obedience to Torah.

3 (Greek Apocalypse of) Baruch. This apocalypse

Pseudepigrapha

is preserved in Greek, perhaps its original language, and Old Slavonic. The work contains 17 chapters. It was composed either by a Jew in the second century A.D. and then edited by a Christian, or it was composed sometime later by a Christian using old Jewish traditions and perhaps writings. Baruch laments the destruction of Jerusalem and the temple. God sends an angel to guide him through the five heavens so that he may learn the mysteries. The author describes the phoenix bird (protector and mediator) and refers to the punishment of the → serpent who "eats earth like grass" (4:3). Origen may have known this document.

Apocalypse of Abraham. This apocalypse is extant only in Old Slavonic. It was composed by a Jew, probably in Hebrew, sometime after A.D. 70 and before 150, conceivably in Palestine. The work contains 32 chapters. The theme of the author is the election of Israel and its covenant with God. Jerusalem was destroyed (A.D. 70) because the Israelites had broken covenant with the Creator. A Christian editor added interpolations to the document.

Apocalypse of Adam. This document, extant only in Coptic, was composed sometime in the first or second century A.D., perhaps in Greek. In its present form it contains eight chapters and is → Gnostic, but the lost original may derive from Jewish baptist groups in ancient Palestine. The "secret knowledge" that Adam reveals to Seth concerns "the holy baptism" (8:17)

Apocalypse of Elijah. This document, preserved in Coptic and a Greek fragment, is not properly an apocalypse; it is shaped by prophetic traditions. The document was composed in Greek sometime before A.D. 400, most likely in Egypt. The extant work contains five chapters and is Christian but is based on Jewish traditions and most likely a Jewish document. The author is focused on the antichrist and the last days.

Apocalypse of Daniel. This Christian Byzantine apocalypse is extant only in Greek. It postdates the coronation of Charlemagne in Rome in 800 and was most likely composed in Greek. It may have been composed in Egypt or ancient Palestine. The extant 14 chapters preserve earlier traditions regarding the antichrist and the end of time.

1.2. *Testaments*

Nine OTP take the form of testaments.

Testaments of the Twelve Patriarchs. This document is preserved primarily in Greek and Armenian, and also in Old Slavonic. These Jewish testaments written before A.D. 70 and attributed to the sons of Jacob — notably to Levi (in Aramaic) and to Judah and Naphtali (both in Hebrew) — are different from the Greek testaments that bear these patriarchs' names. The pseudepigraphon labeled the *Testaments of the Twelve Patriarchs* is the center of controversy among scholars. A few experts claim that the document was composed by a Christian who inherited some (or a great deal) of Jewish traditions (M. de Jonge, H. F. D. Sparks). Most scholars, however, conclude that the author was a Jew who lived in the second or early first century B.C. (see *OTP, JSHRZ,* A. Dupont-Sommer and M. Philonenko, P. Sacchi). It is clear that the extant Greek text is Christian, and the Christian sections may not be limited to passages that are clearly interpolations easily removed. The categories "Jewish" and "Christian" are now less clear than they were decades ago. Each of the 12 sons of Jacob, as his last words, offers moral insights to his sons; sometimes the instruction is characterized by apocalyptic visions.

Testament of Job. This pseudepigraphon, which is similar to the *Testaments of the Twelve Patriarchs,* uses the OT Job to tell a story that has humor and one central message: endurance is a cardinal virtue. The text is divided into 53 chapters; it is extant in Greek and in Old Slavonic, and we have a Coptic fragment. It was composed, probably in Greek and perhaps in Egypt, near the end of the first century B.C. or in the early first century A.D.

Testament of the Three Patriarchs. The *Testament of Abraham,* then the *Testament of Isaac,* and finally the *Testament of Jacob* were written and then became part of a Jewish pseudepigraphon that originated perhaps around A.D. 100 in Egypt. In each testament Michael is sent to announce the imminent death of the patriarch. The three testaments, especially the latter two, also contain Christian elements that may be editorial additions.

Testament of Abraham. This testament is extant in Greek and was composed around A.D. 100 in Greek (both extant recensions derive from a Greek original), most likely by a Jew in Egypt. Recension A has 20 chapters, Recension B 14 chapters. The Torah and covenant are not significant in this document; the type of Judaism represented is cosmopolitan and universalistic (cf. also *2 Enoch* and *3 Baruch*).

Testament of Isaac. This testament is preserved in Arabic, Coptic, and Ethiopic. It is divided into nine chapters. As extant, the document helps to commemorate the deaths of → Abraham and → Isaac within the → Coptic Church.

Testament of Jacob. The pseudepigraphon is also preserved in Arabic, Coptic, and Ethiopic. It has eight chapters. The author has an angel inform Jacob (Israel) that Isaac "was a perfect sacrifice, acceptable to God" (2:13).

Pseudepigrapha

Testament of Moses. This document of 12 chapters has also been called the *Assumption of Moses;* it is extant only in one truncated Lat. MS (a palimpsest in Milan) and reached its present form in the first century A.D. (the text refers to the death of → Herod the Great [4 B.C.]). The document does not seem to have been authored by a Pharisee or an Essene; it may represent the → Hasidic movement. It is important for the study of Jewish views on martyrdom.

Testament of Solomon. This document is extant in Greek and was most likely composed by a Jew in Koine Greek, as was the NT. The work has 26 chapters and is a folktale about how → Solomon controlled the demons; it provides valuable insight into astrology, angelology, demonology, primitive medicine, and folkways. Its provenance is impossible to discern — it could have been composed in Egypt, Mesopotamia, Asia Minor, or ancient Palestine.

Testament of Adam. This document is extant in Syriac as well as in Greek, Arabic, Karshuni, Ethiopic, Georgian, and Armenian; it is composite. The original language is Syriac, and the sections that are Jewish may date from as early as the second century A.D. The final Christian edition took shape in the third century but may have additions that extend into the fifth century. Its provenance may be in Syria or Palestine. The *Horarium* (hours of the day and night) seems Jewish, and the prophecy may be Jewish, with some Christian editing (chaps. 1–3). The hierarchy is Christian (chap. 4). Before chap. 4 are the words "The End of the Testament of Our Father Adam."

1.3. *Expansions of the OT and Legends*

An additional 13 works present ancient expansions of one part or another of the OT.

Letter of Aristeas. This pseudepigraphon, composed in Greek by a Jew most likely in the second century B.C., perhaps in 170 and conceivably in Alexandria, is divided into 322 verses and is extant in Greek. The author has a keen knowledge of the Temple cult, which he describes, and Jewish customs. He defends the "divine" Torah and the superiority of Judaism over → Hellenism. He purports to be Aristeas, who writes to his brother Philocrates about the translation of the Hebrew Bible into Greek (the → Septuagint). He tells an apocryphal story that 72 scholars, 6 from each tribe of Israel, came from Jerusalem to Alexandria to accomplish what is declared to be a miraculous translation. The banquet celebrating this success involves questions addressed by the king to the translators.

Book of Jubilees. This document, also called "the little Genesis," is extant in Ethiopic and Syriac, along with Hebrew fragments found in the Qumran caves; there are also Greek and Latin fragments of the pseudepigraphon. It was composed in Hebrew by a Jew in Palestine in the second century B.C. In 50 chapters the author recounts the history of humans from Adam to Moses. He is a conservative Jew who, among other things, elevates the → Sabbath to such a degree that anyone who kindles a fire on the sacred day is worthy of death.

Martyrdom of Isaiah and Ascension of Isaiah. This document is extant in Ethiopic, and also in Latin, Old Slavonic, and Coptic; it is composite. Chaps. 1–5 are the *Martyrdom of Isaiah;* they include the *Testament of Hezekiah* (3:13–4:22). Chaps. 6–11 compose the *Vision of Isaiah.* The author of the *Martyrdom of Isaiah* was a Jew who wrote in Hebrew, probably in Palestine (he is anti-Samaritan) sometime about the middle of the second century B.C. He recounts how Isaiah was sawn in two on the order of Manasseh (11:41). The *Testament of Hezekiah* and the *Vision of Isaiah* are Christian and were most likely composed in Greek — the former about A.D. 100, and the latter sometime later; the three works were combined by the fourth century A.D.

Joseph and Aseneth. This author of this Hellenistic romance of 29 chapters is primarily interested in explaining why → Joseph (§1) could marry the daughter of an idolatrous Egyptian priest (Gen. 41:45). It is extant in Greek, its original language, and, because of its popularity, also in Syriac, Armenian, Latin, Modern Greek, and Romanian, and there are excerpts in the Ethiopian Synaxarion. It was composed in Egypt by a Jew sometime around A.D. 100 and certainly before 117, which marked the end of the Trajan revolt.

Life of Adam and Eve. This work, also called the *Apocalypse of Moses* in its Greek recension, is extant in Latin and Greek, as well as Armenian and Old Slavonic. The *Vita* (Life) is divided into 51 chapters, the *Apocalypse* into 43 chapters. The original pseudepigraphon was composed by a Jew, perhaps in Hebrew, sometime in the later first century A.D., most likely in Palestine. The author inherits two different traditions regarding paradise; the heavenly paradise is in the third heaven (as in *2 Enoch* 8). Pictorially clear is the book's description of the attempt of Eve and Seth to obtain the oil that flows from the tree of life to heal the dying (*Vita* 36–44).

Pseudo-Philo. This document, also called *Biblical Antiquities* (or *Liber Antiquitatum*), is extant in Latin and Medieval Hebrew. It was composed by a Jew probably a few decades before A.D. 70, most likely in Hebrew and in Palestine. In 65 chapters the author recounts biblical history from Adam to the death of Saul. A significant addition to the story is the "Lament of Seila" (chap. 40), Jephthah's daughter.

Lives of the Prophets. This document mentions the lives and often martyrdoms of many prophets. Those mentioned are the 3 major and 12 minor canonical prophets, as well as Daniel (who was considered a prophet by some early Jews). The prophets have miraculous powers, and for the first time we hear about some miracles not mentioned elsewhere. The composition is extant in Greek, which seems to be the original language, and the Syriac, Ethiopic, Latin, and Armenian versions all seem to derive from Gk. MSS. In 24 short chapters the author, most likely a Palestinian Jew, does not refer to demons but calls Satan "Beliar," who is the prince of evil and "the serpent" (12:13). Most scholars contend that this work is Jewish and antedates A.D. 100 *(OTP, JSHRZ);* other scholars conclude that it is a Christian composition (D. Satran). Most likely a Jewish core has been expanded by Christian scribes, who copied (and altered) the work. (Note, for example, 2:8: "This Jeremiah gave a sign to the priests of Egypt, that it was decreed that their idols would be shaken and collapse [through a savior, a child born of a virgin, in a manger].")

Ladder of Jacob. This pseudepigraphon is extant only in Old Slavonic. Most likely a Jew composed the work at the end of the first century A.D., conceivably in Greek. The work elaborates on Jacob's dream (Gen. 28:10-22) and features angels that ascend and descend (cf. John 1:51). The document is divided into seven chapters, of which the last is a separate composition about the birth and crucifixion of Christ.

4 Baruch. This document is also known as *Paraleipomena Jeremiou* (The things omitted from Jeremiah); the Ethiopic text has the title "The Rest of the Words of Baruch." This pseudepigraphon of nine chapters was most likely composed by a Jew sometime after A.D. 100 in a Semitic language, perhaps Hebrew, and in ancient Palestine. It has been edited by a Christian (esp. 9:20-21). Humor and folklore have shaped this work, which reports that Abimelech fell asleep for 66 years and that a stone, masquerading as Jeremiah, is itself stoned by the children of Israel.

Jannes and Jambres. The full text of this pseudepigraphon about two magicians in Pharaoh's court is lost. We possess references to the magicians, but not necessarily to the book, in the Cairo *Damascus Document,* in 2 Timothy, and in the *Testament of Solomon.* The first mention of a book about these persons is by Origen in the early decades of the third century A.D. Today we know of fragmentary texts in both Latin and Greek; it is evident that the book had more than one version. Although the document is Christian in its present form and may have been a Christian composition based on Jewish traditions, it is conceivable that a Jew composed the book in Greek in Egypt, perhaps Alexandria, in the first century A.D.; some scholars conclude that the Jewish work is even earlier and Hellenistic. The author is interested in astrology and necromancy.

History of the Rechabites. This apocryphon is preserved in Greek and Syriac, as well as in Ethiopic. One Syr. MS reports that the original Hebrew was translated into Greek and then into Syriac. As extant, the work is Christian and is divided into 18 chapters, although evidence of editing is clear; the Christian sections may be interpolations in an earlier Jewish document. This Jewish work may have appeared in the first century A.D. The author or editor claims that the Blessed Ones who live on a far-off island are the Rechabites who lived in Jerusalem during the time of Jeremiah (Jeremiah 35).

Eldad and Modad. The author of the *Shepherd of Hermas* refers to what is "written in the [book of] Eldad and Modad" (*Herm. Vis.* 2.3.4). The lost pseudepigraphon may be an expansion of Num. 11:26-29. Nothing can be discerned regarding this text other than that it must antedate the *Shepherd of Hermas,* which was composed in the second century A.D.

History of Joseph. This document is preserved in Greek and is an expansion of Genesis, especially chaps. 41–42. The author appears to be a Jew who composed the work in Greek in Egypt, long before the sixth century A.D., the date of the earliest papyrus. Parallels with *Joseph and Aseneth* and the *Testaments of the Twelve Patriarchs* indicate that the document may have been composed long before the sixth century. The author elevates Joseph above his status in the Bible, for example, calling him a king.

1.4. *Wisdom and Philosophical Literature*

Several OTP have the form of → Wisdom or philosophical literature.

Ahiqar. This non-Jewish and non-Christian work of 223 lines is included among the OTP because of its importance for understanding early Jewish thought, its popularity in antiquity, and its date. Its genre is similar to the Wisdom books in the OTP, and its author was imagined to be a Jew by some early Jews, including the author of Tobit. The earliest copy of the document was found in a Jewish colony in Egypt. The work was composed most likely in imperial Aramaic early in the sixth century B.C., perhaps in Syria.

3 Maccabees. This apocryphal work is preserved in Greek and is included within Codex Alexandrinus. It was composed by a Jew, most likely in Greek, in the early first century B.C. and perhaps in Egypt, most likely Alexandria. In this historical romance of seven chapters, the author writes "creative history" about Ptolemy IV Philopator (221-204 B.C.) to edify Jews, to declare that Jews are a special people, and to reveal that God is "the everlasting savior of Israel" (7:16).

4 Maccabees. This apocryphon is also preserved in Greek and was composed by a Jew in Greek during the century before the destruction of the Jerusalem Temple in A.D. 70. Its provenance is unclear, but assuming composition in a coastal town in the eastern Mediterranean helps explain the many metaphors of the sea. In 18 chapters this Jewish rhetorician, in first-person discourse perhaps under the influence of Plato, illustrates how reason masters all passions. The heroes he selected to celebrate this philosophical theme are Joseph, Moses, Jacob, and David. Nevertheless, a woman, the mother of the seven martyred sons, is really the champion of Judaism. The author sought to demonstrate that Greek "virtue" is best achieved by obedience to Torah.

Pseudo-Phocylides. Preserved in Greek and composed in that language by a Jew between 30 B.C. and A.D. 40, this pseudepigraphon celebrates the sixth-century Greek poet Phocylides, who is declared "the wisest of men." It was most likely composed in Alexandria. In 230 verses, this work shows little interest in theology; instead, the author is devoted to ethics and offers practical, generic maxims, concluding with the words, "These are the mysteries of righteousness."

The Sentences of the Syriac Menander. Preserved in Syriac in 474 lines, this pseudepigraphon is dedicated to the Athenian dramatist Menander (d. ca. 292 B.C), although he is unrelated to the text. The putative Jewish author compiles Wisdom sayings for practical living; in places he seems influenced by Sirach. The original language may have been Syriac, but the author may have translated Wisdom sayings that had circulated in Hebrew, Aramaic, or Greek. These sayings probably have different dates and take us back perhaps into the second or third centuries A.D., notably into Jewish circles in Egypt. The negative form of the → Golden Rule ("Everything that is hateful to you, you should not wish to do that to your neighbor" [250-51]) is similar to the famous saying attributed to Hillel (*b. Šabb.* 31a [cf. *Liber Graduum* and Aphrahat]) and to Tobit 4:15.

1.5. *Prayers, Psalms, and Odes*

Seven documents present prayers, psalms, or odes.

More Psalms of David. Five noncanonical psalms, as well as a fragment of a sixth, have been discovered and, in some collections, have been added to the Psalter. One is preserved in Greek, and three were found in the Qumran caves in Hebrew, and all in Syriac. These psalms were most likely composed in Hebrew by Jews during the fourth through second centuries B.C. The locus of their composition was probably Palestine.

Prayer of Manasseh. Extant in Greek and Syriac, this penitential prayer, pseudepigraphically attributed to Manasseh, the wicked king of Israel (687-642 B.C.), was composed in ancient Palestine in Hebrew or a Semitized Greek, probably within the century that antedates the destruction of the Jerusalem Temple in A.D. 70. The author was not a Christian (*pace* Fabricius, Migne, and Nau); he was a Jew who sought to supply in 15 verses Manasseh's prayer noted in 2 Chr. 33:12-13. The *Prayer of Manasseh* is a masterpiece that evokes the human need for divine forgiveness and compassion.

Psalms of Solomon. These 18 psalms pseudonymously attributed to Solomon are extant in Greek and Syriac. They were composed by a Jew, or by Jews, most likely in Hebrew in Jerusalem sometime near the middle of the first century B.C. The author knows about the death of the Roman general and statesman Pompey in 48 B.C. and looks forward to the coming of the Lord's Messiah.

Hellenistic Synagogal Prayers. These Jewish prayers are extant in Greek, which is probably the original language. Remnants of 16 of these synagogal prayers are preserved in the *Apostolic Constitutions,* which indicates that they must antedate 380 (the latter was written between 350 and 380). The prayers may have originated in Egypt, Syria, or elsewhere. They have been edited by a Christian, since the occasional Christian insertion often seems to replace a Jewish reference to Wisdom. The basically Jewish character of these prayers is evident, for prayers 2-7 parallel the "Seven Benedictions for Sabbaths and Festivals" chanted in synagogues. This document is important in that it demonstrates both the continuity between "Jews" and "Christians" and the direct borrowing of elements of synagogue worship by early Christians.

Prayer of Joseph. Only 164 words of this pseudepigraphon have survived. They are preserved in Greek in quotations by Origen (ca. 185-ca. 254), by Gregory of Nazianzus (329/30-389/90) and Basil the Great (ca. 330-79) in their compilation of Origen's writings known as the → Philocalia, and by Eusebius (ca. 260-ca. 340) in his *Praeparatio evangelica* (Preparation for the gospel), and in Latin by Procopius of Gaza (ca. 475-ca. 538). The name *Prayer of Joseph* appears in early lists of extracanonical works. The prayer was composed by a Jew in the first century A.D., perhaps in Egypt or Palestine. The author presents the unique claim that Jacob is the incarnation of the angel Israel.

Prayer of Jacob. This pseudepigraphon is extant in Greek, which is probably the original language. The extant fourth-century papyrus may preserve a document that dates from about the same time as the *Prayer of Joseph* and may derive from Egypt. The work has four invocations, three petitions, and one injunction. The author was a Jew who called on the "Lord God of the Hebrews" (v. 13).

Odes of Solomon. This impressive pseudepigraphic work attributed to Solomon is preserved in Syriac, with ode 11 also extant in Greek; five odes are also preserved in Coptic, and one verse is translated into Latin. The original collection of 42 odes was composed sometime between A.D. 20 and 125, the most likely date being around or shortly after 100. Since the author is a Jew converted to Christianity, some odes may have originally been Jewish, some Christian; some, furthermore, show the influence of an early → Gnosticism. The undeniable links between the *Odes of Solomon* and the Gospel of John have created heated debate among scholars, although it can be demonstrated that the *Odes* are neither clearly dependent on John nor John on them; perhaps they emanate from the same region or even community. The original language may have been Greek, but it most likely was Syriac. The author may have lived in Syria, but the provenience of a pseudepigraphon is almost always difficult to discern. The fundamental feature of the *Odes of Solomon* is joy in realizing that the long-awaited Messiah had finally been sent by God into the world.

1.6. *Fragments of Lost Judeo-Hellenistic Works*
All of the fragmentary works collected in the supplement to *OTP* 2 were composed in Greek, by Jews, and antedate Alexander Polyhistor (ca. 105-ca. 35 B.C.), who excerpted them in his work *On the Jews.* Alexander's work is lost and available only in excerpts made by Eusebius, Clement of Alexandria, and Pseudo-Justin (3d cent. A.D.). Pseudo-Eustathius also quotes from Ezekiel the Tragedian, and Josephus (ca. 37-ca. 100) cites Cleodemus Malchus and Pseudo-Hecataeus (see below). The extant fragments share an apologetic claim that the best Greek ideas were originally Jewish. For introductions and translations of the following authors and texts, see *OTP* 2.781-918.

Philo the Epic Poet. The six fragments of this work indicate that this Jew attempted to imitate the Alexandrian epics with their hexameter verses. He may have lived in Jerusalem but more likely in Alexandria. If the extant fragments are any indication, this Philo is interested in the famous water system of Jerusalem, mentioning a "fountain," perhaps the Gihon spring, and "another pool," conceivably the pools of Bethzatha.

Theodotus. This work's eight fragments disclose further evidence of Jewish interest in epic Greek poetry. The author could have been a Jew ("those in Shechem were impious") or a → Samaritan (he refers to Shechem as "a sacred town," which would have been inconceivable for a Jew after John Hyrcanus [ruled 135-104 B.C.] captured Shechem and burned the Samaritan temple in 129). Theodotus lived before Hyrcanus, since he knew Shechem "with a smooth wall," which archaeologically antedates 190 B.C. Theodotus shows dependence on Genesis 17, 27–33, and especially chap. 34. Among other points made by Theodotus is the necessity of circumcision: "the command remains unshaken, since God himself spoke it" (frg. 5).

Orphica. A Jew composed in hexameters a "testament of Orpheus," which purports to be Orpheus's esoteric teachings. The composition is preserved in short (36 lines) and long (45 lines) versions; it seems to date to shortly after the middle of the second century B.C. The author claims that "the Divine" can be seen only by the "Mind," yet Moses, "a certain unique man," saw the "ruler of mortal man" (God) because of his knowledge of astrology and astronomy.

Ezekiel the Tragedian. This "poet of Jewish tragedies," as Clement of Alexandria called him, wrote in iambic trimeter the *Exagōgē* (leading out), a tragic drama about the exodus from Egypt (he depends on the LXX of Exodus 1–15). The work seems to date from the beginning of the second century B.C.; the provenance may be Alexandria. Only 269 lines remain of this drama. One poignant passage describes a dream by Moses in which he sees a great throne on "Sinai's peak." God, described as "a man of noble mien" seated on a throne, offers it to Moses, handing him the scepter and the crown (lines 68-76).

Fragments of Pseudo-Greek Poets. Jews not only composed poetry in Greek, they also collected, edited, and reworked compostions by the famous Greek poets. Extant are lines — only fragments found in quotations by Clement of Alexandria, Eusebius, and Pseudo-Justin — attributed to Hesiod, Pythagoras, Aeschylus, Sophocles, Euripides, Philemon, Diphilus, and Menander. Aristobulus (3d-2d cent. B.C) quotes these spurious verses, so they antedate the middle of the second century B.C. Many of the fragments stress the oneness of God.

Aristobulus. In line with Jewish apologetics, Aristobulus, who may have lived in Alexandria, claimed that Plato and Pythagoras knew and borrowed from the Torah. Five fragments of this philosopher's compositions remain. Aristobulus is the first known exegete who employed → allegory. In this respect he was followed by those who used allegory as a rhetorical trope — Philodemus of Gadara (110-40 B.C.), Tryphon of Alexandria (1st cent. B.C.), and Cicero (106-43) — and by those who employed allegory in exegesis (esp. Philo, Plutarch, Paul, and Josephus).

Demetrius the Chronographer. Six fragments remain of a certain Demetrius, a Jew who was interested in the sacrifice of Isaac, the chronology of the patriarchs, and the genealogy of Moses and Zipporah; he also provided a synopsis of the events at Marah and Elim. He also explained that those who left Egypt during the exodus obtained their weapons from the drowned Egyptians (frg. 5). Demetrius may have lived in Alexandria.

Aristeas the Exegete. This Aristeas attempted to reconstruct the life of Job, who was formerly called Jobab, who becomes a descendant of Esau. Only one excerpt of Aristeas's oeuvre remains.

Eupolemus. Only five fragments of this Jewish historian's work remain. He composed a document that was probably known as *On the Kings in Judea.* He lived in Palestine about the middle of the second century B.C. The author may in fact be the famous Eupolemus, Judas Maccabeus's ambassador to Rome (1 Macc. 8:17; 2 Macc. 4:11), or related to him.

Pseudo-Eupolemus. Two quotations regarding Abraham in Eusebius's *Praeparatio evangelica* are attributed to an unknown author. The anonymous author is often dubbed Pseudo-Eupolemus, because he is not Eupolemus, although Alexander Polyhistor attributed one of the quotations to him. Now it appears that the first quotation should in fact be attributed to Eupolemus (*OTP* 2.874-76). One fragment salutes Abraham for teaching the Egyptian priests the sciences and astrology that was discovered by Enoch (who is also Atlas); the other traces Abraham's lineage back to the giants.

Cleodemus Malchus. Josephus and Eusebius are both dependent on Alexander Polyhistor for their citations of Cleodemus Malchus. This Jew, who lived perhaps in Carthage (he provides an African genealogy), was interested in Abraham's descendants through Keturah (Gen. 25:1-4). Abraham's sons Afera and Iafra fought with Hercules, who married Afera's daughter.

Artapanus. This Jewish author wrote a romance called *Judaica,* most likely near the end of the third century B.C. in Egypt. The three surviving references to his work feature Abraham, who taught astronomy to the Egyptians; Joseph, who was the consummate organizer and administrator in Egypt; and especially Moses, who was also Mousaeus, the teacher of Orpheus, as well as of Hermes.

Pseudo-Hecataeus. Some of the fragments collected under this name seemed authentic to Hecataeus of Abdera, who lived around 300 B.C. They are thus important for revealing how a non-Jew could at that time be so pro-Jewish, as were Clearchus, Megasthenes, and Theophrastus. One passage that seems authentic is a work attributed to Hecataeus called *On the Jews.* One section of that work claims that Alexander the Great honored the Jews; another section describes the Temple and reports that 120,000 Jews lived at the time in Jerusalem, obviously a hyperbole. At least two of these fragments may be inauthentic. Pseudo-Hecataeus seems to have composed *On Abraham and the Egyptians,* which argues that there is truly only one God. Little is known about Pseudo-Hecataeus's compositions (see test. 1 and frg. 2 in *OTP* 2.909, 911-12; also the mention of Hecataeus in *Letter of Aristeas* 31). Pseudo-Hecataeus may have been a Gentile who was philo-Judaic, but it is more likely that he was a Jew who lived in Egypt in the second century B.C.

1.7. *Addenda*

There are some early documents related to Judaism and perhaps composed by Jews but not included in the collections of OTP (*OTP, JSHRZ,* Dupont-Sommer and Philonenko, Sacchi, Sparks). Six of these are as follows:

Book of the Giants. This book was revered by the → Manichaeans, and selections from it are found in the *Midrash of Shemhazai and Azazel.* Moreover, fragments from the work were found in Qumran caves 1, 2, 4, and 6. It was composed in Aramaic by a Jew who was most likely in Palestine. It is an important witness to Jewish speculation during the period of the Second Temple. The *Book of the Giants* may have been influenced by the early sections of *1 Enoch,* and it aids in understanding *Pseudo-Eupolemus.*

Apocalypse of Elkesai. This apocalypse was composed by a Jew who may well have been influenced by NT documents or the traditions recorded therein. It dates from the first half of the second century A.D. The Elkesaites, who lived to the east of the Jordan River, considered this apocalypse to be divinely inspired.

Apocalypse of Pseudo-Methodius. Preserved in Greek, Latin, and Syriac, this document is very late. It seems to date from the seventh century A.D., but it preserves valuable early Jewish traditions. The work summarizes the history of humanity from Adam to the end of the world.

Pseudo-Philo: On Jonah (De Iona) and *On Samson (De Sampsone).* These documents are extant only in Armenian. They seem to be sermons preached in a synagogue of the → diaspora.

The Ethiopic History of Joseph. This work may be a candidate for inclusion in an expanded and updated edition of the *OTP.* While late and preserved only in Ethiopic, this document might help to better understand the transmission of Jewish traditions, the meaning of earlier Jewish statements concerning Joseph, and the shaping of pseudepigrapha primarily extant in Ethiopic.

Mani Codex. Finally, the apocryphal works excerpted by the compiler of this work are rather early. They seem to be Jewish and not influenced by Manichaeanism.

1.8. *Conclusion*

The OTP are exceedingly important for understanding (1) the texts of the OT, the Hebrew Bible; (2) insiders' views of the history from Alexander the Great to Hadrian (A.D. 117-38); (3) the theology and symbolism of Second Temple Judaism; (4) the historical, religious, and literary contexts of Jesus and the Palestinian Jesus Movement; (5) the concepts of inspiration, revelation, and canon; and (6) the context of the NT documents themselves. Thus, for example, it is imperative to read the Revelation of John, not only in light of the Gospel of John, but also in relation to other contemporary apocalypses, especially *1 Enoch* 37–71, *2 Enoch, 4 Ezra, 2 Baruch,* and the *Apocalypse of Abraham.*

In addition to the documents mentioned in this review of the OTP, one should be familiar with, read, and study the OT Apocrypha and the Qumran pseudepigrapha. The latter are pseudepigraphic documents known only from copies preserved in the 11 caves near → Qumran.

→ Jewish Christians

2. NT Pseudepigrapha and Apocrypha

2.1. *Definition and Background*

The NT pseudepigrapha and Apocrypha (NTPA) postdate almost all the documents collected in the corpus entitled "Old Testament Pseudepigrapha." It is wise at the outset to contrast the two collections.

The OTP are exceedingly important for understanding Second Temple Judaism. The Jewish compositions in the OTP provide windows for viewing the lives of early Jews in ancient Palestine and in other areas, especially Egypt. They inform us about how individuals and communities understood themselves, especially how they identified themselves by transmitting and interpreting Scripture, that is, the Hebrew Scriptures (the OT) and the Septuagint. These Jewish documents are fundamentally important for understanding the background and immediate context of Jesus and his earliest followers, as well as the authors of the documents in the NT. The Jewish OTP are earlier than, or contemporaneous with, the NT writings.

The NTPA postdate virtually all the documents in the NT. Almost all of the works in the NTPA date from the second half of the second century or later; they help us comprehend the contours of the Christian canon and the imaginations of early Christians. Again, we see how individuals and communities were achieving self-definition in a very hostile world.

The exceptions to the rule that the NTPA are always considerably later than the NT documents are three documents that preserve traditions that antedate A.D. 125. The *Gospel of Thomas* most likely preserves some sayings of Jesus that are authentic and without influence from the intracanonical gospels. The → *Protevangelium Jacobi* (or *Birth of Mary*), among other things, celebrates Mary's early life and is the fountainhead of → Mariology. The *Gospel of Peter* may contain some very early traditions about Jesus' → passion.

Some of the NTPA circulated anonymously, and others were composed pseudonymously. For example, the *Gospel of Thomas* is pseudepigraphically attributed, at the beginning and end, to Thomas. In assessing the attributions and titles of the works in the NTPA, it is necessary to realize that the intracanonical gospels may have originally circulated without attribution and were eventually pseudepigraphically attributed to apostles (Matthew and John) and perhaps to followers of Peter (Mark) and Paul (Luke). During the period before the fourth century, when Christianity became the religion of the → Roman Empire, and the time of the first council at → Nicaea (325), Christians often attributed their traditions and insights to the 12 apostles, to Paul, or to one of the prominent persons in the NT (esp. Mary and Mary Magdalene). Within Greek, Roman, Jewish, and Christian cultures, the art of pseudepigraphy was an accepted means of honoring traditions and great minds or persons. Obviously, the importance of a document was established when it was perceived to be ancient and associated with an admired human intellect like Phocylides, Pythagoras, Moses, Peter, Paul, James, or Clement.

Three insights and perceptions are essential to the study of the NTPA. First, → "heresy" did not al-

Pseudepigrapha

ways chronologically follow "orthodoxy." The use of terms like "heresy" and "orthodoxy" introduces anachronisms and misperceptions into the study of these apocryphal works. Scholars have also shown that such a term as "Jewish-Christianity" is problematic and misleading. Works often placed in this category were habitually read insensitively and categorized, imperceptibly, as heretical. Indeed, the category "Jewish-Christianity" often referred to works of great variety. The same judgment pertains to Gnosticism, since this term is often poorly defined; one should not be misled by the polemics against Gnostic writings found in the → church fathers.

Second, theological evaluation of the NT documents, the NTPA, and other related literatures should be informed by the recognition that the *Didache* (or *The Teaching of the Lord through the Twelve Apostles*) and the Apostles' Creed were once held to be compositions of Jesus' disciples. These two documents are clearly pseudepigraphic and postdate the first century A.D.

Third, the NTPA were composed during the period when the NT canon was open and not yet defined. Many early Christians and Christian communities believed that some works now found in the NTPA were as inspired and revelatory as what Christians throughout the world now deem the intracanonical works.

The NTPA should be read along with other writings contemporaneous to them. Among such similar collections of early Christian writings are the → Apostolic Fathers, the Nag Hammadi codices, and the ante-Nicene fathers (see also the *Hermetica*, or writings ascribed to Hermes Trismegistus).

The NTPA are categorized under the following genres: gospels, acts, letters, apocalypses, and others. These categories and genres are not definitive but suggestive. For example, the *Apocryphal Letter of James* could be categorized as a gospel (it includes parables about the kingdom of heaven) or as an apocalypse (it depicts the revelation of the ascended Jesus to James and Peter and from them to his disciples).

The NTPA include the *Christian Sibyllines*, although this work is usually categorized under the OTP (also note the Christian expansions of other OTP). Not to be included in the NTPA is the *Letter of Lentulus*, which is a medieval forgery. Many scholars have become convinced that the *Secret Gospel of Mark* may be modern. The latter two compositions have been incorrectly included in collections of the NTPA or in discussions of them.

Some collections of the NTPA include gospels that bear the names of arch-heretics, such as the Gospels of Cerinthus, Basilides, Marcion, Apelles, Bardesanes, and Mani. A good case can be made for including in the NTPA the Nag Hammadi *Gospel of Truth* (it is early and not marred by unattractive elements found in later Gnosticism).

The documents customarily included under these various categories are the following items, which here are simply listed.

2.2. *Gospels and Related Writings*

The Gospel according to the Hebrews
The Gospel according to the Nazarenes
The Gospel of the Egyptians
The Gospel of the Ebionites
The Traditions of Matthias
The Preaching of Peter
The Protevangelium Jacobi (Birth of Mary)
The Infancy Gospel of Thomas
The Arabic Infancy Gospel
The Gospel of the Twelve Apostles
Gospel of Pseudo-Matthew (Liber de Infantia Salvatoris)
The History of Joseph the Carpenter
Other infancy gospels
The Gospel of Thomas
The Gospel of Peter
The Gospel of Philip
The Gospel of Gamaliel
The Gospel (or *Questions*) *of Bartholomew*
The Book of the Resurrection of Jesus Christ by Bartholomew
Coptic narratives
The Gospel of Nicodemus
Pilate Narratives
The Narrative of Joseph of Arimathea
The Gospel of Judas
Lost gospels and fragments of gospels

2.3. *Acts*

The Acts of Andrew
The Acts of Barnabas
The Acts of James
The Acts of John
The Acts of Mark
The Acts of Paul
The Acts of Peter
The Acts of Philip
The Acts of Pilate
The Acts of Thomas
The Pseudo-Clementines
Other apocryphal acts

2.4. *Letters*

The Letters of Christ and Abgar
The Letter to the Laodiceans
The Letters of Paul and Seneca
The Letter of Paul to the Alexandrians
The Third Letter of Paul to the Corinthians

The Letter of the Apostles
The Apocryphal Letter of James
The Letter of Titus

2.5. ***Apocalypses***

The First Apocryphal Apocalypse of John
The Second Apocryphal Apocalypse of John
The Third Apocryphal Apocalypse of John
The Apocalypse of Paul
The Apocalypse of Peter
The Apocalypse of Stephen
The Apocalypse of Thomas
The Apocalypse of the Virgin
The Apocalypse of Zechariah
Other apocalypses

2.6. ***Others***

The Assumption of the Virgin
The Passing of Mary (Transitus Mariae)
Questions of Mary

→ Early Catholicism; Early Church; New Testament Era, History of

Bibliography: On 1: J. H. CHARLESWORTH, ed., *The OT Pseudepigrapha* (2 vols.; Garden City, N.Y., 1983-85) • L. DITOMMASCO, *A Bibliography of Pseudepigrapha Research, 1850-1999* (Sheffield, 2001) • A. DUPONT-SOMMER and M. PHILONENKO, eds., *La Bible. Écrits intertestamentaires* (Paris, 1987) • W. G. KÜMMEL and H. LICHTENBERGER, eds., *JSHRZ* (6 vols.; Gütersloh, 1973-) • P. SACCHI, *Apocrifi dell'Antico Testamento* (2 vols.; Turin, 1981-89) • H. F. D. SPARKS, ed., *The Apocryphal OT* (Oxford, 1984).

On 2: J. H. CHARLESWORTH, *The NT Apocrypha and Pseudepigrapha: A Guide to Publications, with Excursuses on Apocalypses* (Metuchen, N.J., 1987) includes many more documents than are usually categorized as works in the NTPA; idem, "Research on the NT Apocrypha and Pseudepigrapha," *ANRW* 2.25.5.3919-68 • J. K. ELLIOTT, ed., *The Apocryphal NT* (Oxford, 1993) • W. SCHNEEMELCHER, ed., *NT Apocrypha* (2 vols.; rev. ed.; Cambridge, 1991-92).

JAMES H. CHARLESWORTH

Pseudo-Isidorian Decretals → False Decretals

Psychiatry

1. Definitions
2. The Psychiatric Interview
3. Diagnosis
4. Psychiatric Treatment
5. Psychiatry and Theology

1. Definitions

Psychiatry is a branch of medicine that deals with the diagnosis, treatment, and prevention of mental, emotional, and behavioral disorders. Psychiatry developed as a new branch of medicine at the beginning of the 19th century. Since then, important steps have been taken and reforms made in the care of those who have mental disorders. Increasingly, psychiatry is being practiced by psychiatrists in the context of behavioral medicine, an interdisciplinary field concerned with the development, integration, and application of behavioral, psychosocial, and biomedical science to the prevention, diagnosis, treatment, and rehabilitation of persons with mental disorders (→ Persons with Disabilities).

A psychiatrist is a medical doctor who has completed four years of residency training in psychiatry after graduation from medical school. Specialization in a specific field of psychiatry — such as child and adolescent psychiatry, geriatric psychiatry, mood disorders, addiction or forensic psychiatry — requires additional training beyond the residency. Under licensing laws, psychiatrists are able to prescribe medication and order and interpret medical tests in order to diagnose and treat mental disorders.

2. The Psychiatric Interview

The psychiatric interview is a major tool for diagnosis. One of the purposes of the interview is to determine whether a mental disorder is present and, if so, what the correct diagnostic category is. The initial psychiatric interview determines the reason for the consultation and the presenting of problems or major complaints of the patient. The interview continues with gathering a complete personal, familial, and social history. Because symptoms of several mental disorders may be similar, the psychiatrist engages in differential diagnosis in order to arrive at an accurate assessment. The American Psychiatric Association's *Diagnostic and Statistical Manual of Mental Disorders* (4th ed., text rev.: DSM-IV-TR) provides guidelines for differential diagnosis.

As part of the diagnostic process of the psychiatric interview, the psychiatrist may conduct a mental status examination (MSE) and do a global assessment of functioning (GAF) inventory.

The MSE covers the following areas and observations of the patient: appearance, movement and behavior, affect, mood, speech, thought content, thought process, and cognition. The cognitive functions that are measured during the MSE include the person's sense of time, place, and personal identity; memory; speech; general intellectual level; mathematical ability; insight or judgment; and reasoning or problem-solving ability.

The GAF scale is a 100-point tool to rate the overall psychological, social, and occupational functioning of people over the age of 18 so as to assess their overall level of functioning in carrying out activities of daily life.

3. Diagnosis

Psychiatric diagnosis makes use of one of the two current, standard classifications: (1) the DSM-IV-TR and (2) the *International Classification of Diseases* (10th ed.: ICD-10), as developed by the World Health Organization and used extensively in Europe.

A psychiatric diagnosis utilizing DSM-IV-TR guidelines may have five axes. Axis 1 contains the diagnosed clinical disorder; it is what most people think of when they want to know the psychiatric diagnosis. Axis 2 contains any diagnosis of a personality disorder or mental retardation. Axis 3 contains the diagnosis of any known medical conditions. Axis 4 considers psychosocial and environmental problems: social, economic, educational, occupational, housing, health care, and legal. Axis 5 includes the results of the GAF.

4. Psychiatric Treatment

Psychotherapy may involve a discussion of problems that disrupt the patient's life. → Psychotherapy can help change thinking and patterns of emotions, relations, and behavior that perhaps contribute to mental suffering.

Medication can treat imbalances in brain chemistry, so that the patient can function normally and participate meaningfully in psychotherapy. Medications often used in psychiatric treatment are antidepressants, antipsychotics, mood regulators, and antianxiety drugs.

Electroconvulsive therapy (ECT) is a painless, safe, and effective treatment for major → depression and is especially useful for patients who do not respond positively to antidepressant medications, or for those who cannot take appropriate medications because of a medical condition or life-threatening suicidal intention.

Hospitalization for mental disorders may be desirable in severe cases in order to protect the patient during the acute phase of illness and to provide a behavioral-medicine treatment milieu conducive to recovery. Brief hospitalization may be especially important when a patient is actively suicidal, posing a threat of violence to others, or in need of detoxification where chemical abuse is part of the clinical picture.

5. Psychiatry and Theology

Relationships between the disciplines of psychiatry and theology have varied widely. In some cases there have been clashes of → ideologies. Some proponents of psychiatry have viewed religion as an inferior aspect of human behavior. They have considered religion unscientific and therefore untrue. They have also viewed it as comparable to an obsessional neurosis, and its beliefs as contributing to immaturity. Christian theology, in contrast, has at times vaunted itself as the queen of the sciences and viewed the scientific worldview of psychiatry as antithetical. Some religious leaders have encouraged their followers to have nothing to do with psychiatry, fearing that psychiatric treatment could destroy faith and lead to → atheism.

Practitioners of theology who work with people in crisis, though, have seen psychiatry and the behavioral sciences, however different their philosophical worldviews, as practical allies in the care of human psychological and spiritual distress (→ Science and Theology). Clinically trained clergy, pastoral counselors, and institutional chaplains, while abandoning neither their faith nor their theology, have combined knowledge of the psychiatric and psychotherapeutic disciplines with theological anthropology in order to render more effective care. Pioneers in this area were Anton Boisen (1876-1965), Wayne Oates (1917-99), and Seward Hiltner (1909-84), as well as the Program in Psychiatry and Religion at Union Theological Seminary (New York), founded by psychiatrist Earl A. Loomis. Since 1925 the number of clergy interested in the collaboration between psychiatry and religion has grown enormously. At the 1948 meetings of the American Psychiatric Association, 26 of the chaplains attending formed the Association of Mental Health Chaplains and elected their first president, J. Obert Kempson of South Carolina State Hospital in Columbia. By 1975 the group had grown to 500 mental health chaplains. Recently this group merged with the Association of Professional Chaplains.

In the last few years a growing number of psychiatrists (esp. J. K. Boehnlein and G. May) have begun to include interest in religion and → spirituality in their works, leading to what R. Shorto calls "a new science of the soul."

→ Healing; Health and Illness

Bibliography: American Psychiatric Association, *Diagnostic and Statistical Manual of Mental Disorders:*

DSM-IV-TR (4th ed., text rev.; Washington, D.C., 2000) • *Annals of Behavioral Medicine* (Mahwah, N.J.) periodical of the Society of Behavioral Medicine • D. Bhugra, ed., *Psychiatry and Religion: Context Consensus and Controversies* (London, 1997) • J. K. Boehnlein, *Psychiatry and Religion: The Convergence of Mind and Spirit* (Arlington, Va., 2000) • G. Collins and T. Culbertson, *Mental Illness and Psychiatric Treatment: A Guide for Pastoral Counselors* (New York, 2003) • M. F. Folstein et al., *Mini-Mental State Examination: Clinical Guide* (Lutz, Fla., 2002) • M. F. Folstein, S. E. Folstein, and P. R. McHugh, "Mini-Mental State: A Practical Method for Grading the State of Patients for the Clinician," *JPsR* 12 (1975) 189-98 • A. Francis, J. Clarkin, and S. Perry, *Differential Therapeutics in Psychiatry: The Art and Science of Treatment Selection* (New York, 1984) • W. B. Johnson and W. Johnson, *The Pastor's Guide to Psychological Disorders and Treatments* (New York, 2000) • E. Loomis, *The Self in Pilgrimage: New Insights in Psychiatry and Religion* (London, 1961) • R. A. MacKinnon and R. Michels, *The Psychiatric Interview in Clinical Practice* (Philadelphia, 1971) • R. A. MacKinnon and S. C. Yudofsky, *The Psychiatric Evaluation in Clinical Practice* (Philadelphia, 1986) • G. May, *Care of Mind, Care of Spirit* (San Francisco, 1992) • B. J. Saddock and V. A. Saddock, *Kaplan and Sadock's Comprehensive Textbook of Psychiatry* (8th ed.; Hagerstown, Md., 2004) • R. Shorto, *Saints and Madmen: How Pioneering Psychiatrists Are Creating a New Science of the Soul* (New York, 2000) • H. S. Sullivan, *The Psychiatric Interview* (ed. H. S. Perry and M. L. Gawel; New York, 1954) • A. Ulanov and B. Ulanov, *Religion and the Unconscious* (Philadelphia, 1975) • World Health Organization, *International Classification of Diseases: ICD-10* (10th ed.; Geneva, 1992).

Russell H. Davis

Psychoanalysis

1. Terms and Definitions

1.1. *Psychoanalysis*

Sigmund Freud (1856-1939), who developed a new paradigm of human psychological theory and created new methods of research, → psychotherapy, and analysis of culture, founded psychoanalysis. The theory of repression is the cornerstone of psychoanalysis and its most essential element (Freud, *Standard Edition of the Complete Psychological Works* [*SE*], vol. 14).

1.2. *Repression*

Repression is a defense against ego-dystonic unconscious mental activity. Repression makes an attempt to keep discordant, dynamic impulses and ideas out of conscious awareness. Repression is manifested as resistance — a struggle against reality, a resistance against accepting painful self-knowledge.

1.3. *Transference*

Transference appears in psychoanalytic treatment when the patient unconsciously responds to the analyst out of patterns of thought, emotion, and behavior that have their origin in childhood, especially in relation to the parents.

1.4. *Infantile Sexuality*

The theory of infantile → sexuality (*SE* 7) is complex but includes the understanding that the sexual drive does not first emerge in puberty. Rather, it exists from the beginning of life, in infancy. The sexual drive undergoes developmental progression through stages (oral, anal, latency) before its emergence as genitality. The sexual drive has a source (in the instincts and the zones), aims (to achieve bodily pleasure, actively or passively), and zones (oral, anal, genital).

1.5. *Dreams*

→ Dreams, "the royal road to the unconscious" (*SE* 4-5), allow unconscious ideas to be expressed metaphorically, and thus to escape the censorship of repression. Psychoanalytic dream interpretation is a method for understanding the wishes and desires expressed symbolically in dreams.

2. Development of Freud's Thought

Freud's thought developed over a period of more than 45 years, and the history of the evolution of psychoanalytic theory is complex (R. Fine) Early psychoanalysis, beginning in the mid-1890s, focused on methods of treatment (first catharsis, then free association) for hysterical neurosis. Freud developed a new theory shaped by findings emerging from his early psychoanalytic practice, findings concerning the nature of the dynamic unconscious. These discoveries, coming both from Freud's self-analysis and from his clinical work as a psychoanalyst, led him to a topographical model of the mind (*SE* 4-5) that posited the existence of regions of the mind: conscious, preconscious, and unconscious.

Freud distinguished between a descriptive unconscious (those ideas that are not in consciousness at the moment and therefore can be described as unconscious) and a dynamic unconscious. Ideas in the descriptive unconscious can be recalled at will. Ideas in the dynamic unconscious are impulsive desires held prisoner by the unconscious forces of repression and the resistance of the conscious self to disturbing self-knowledge.

2.1. *Libido Theory*

In the earliest psychoanalytic period, Freud's interest in the → libido was as a cause for → anxiety and anxiety → neurosis (dammed up libido, *SE* 4-5). With his publication of three essays on sexuality (*SE* 7), Freud introduced his theories of the libido and of infantile sexuality, which became cornerstones of psychoanalysis.

Freud began to explore the relationships between parent and child in light of the myth of Oedipus, which by 1910 became known as the Oedipus complex. The model for this complex was the classical story of Oedipus, who killed his own father and married, unknowingly, his mother. Freud came to believe that the Oedipus complex is a stage of psychosexual development that involves childhood feelings, in a boy, of competition with the father over the mother's affection and the wish for an exclusive relationship with the mother.

Later, when Freudian psychoanalytic theory had to defend itself against the competing views of Carl Gustav Jung (1875-1961) and Alfred Adler (1870-1937), Freud developed the theory of the inverted Oedipus complex, which he made the centerpiece of his theory of psychopathology (R. H. Davis).

2.2. *Metapsychology*

In the period between 1910 and 1920, Freud began to solidify his theories, writing a number of metapsychological papers on various aspects of psychoanalytic thought, many of which were answers to his opponents. By "metapsychology," Freud meant any psychology (and esp. psychoanalysis) that takes seriously the existence of a dynamic unconscious. The metapsychological papers addressed topics such as the nature of the unconscious, repression, dreams, instinctual vicissitudes, and the nature of the ego, especially in the states of mourning and in melancholia. Freud also published his *Introductory Lectures on Psycho-Analysis* (1916-17) to reach a more general audience. In them he made two assertions: first, that mental life is largely unconscious, with only a small part of our acts, desires, and thoughts being conscious; second, that sexual impulses, in both the narrower and the wider sense of the term, play an extremely large part in the causation of nervous and mental diseases.

2.3. *Theory of Aggression*

Only later in life did Freud move his focus from the sexual instincts to the aggressive drive (1920). The sexual instincts are ruled by the *pleasure principle,* which states that when instinctual desire arises, it creates tension (which the organism feels as unpleasurable); the instinct seeks release of tension, which brings pleasure. The sexual, or libidinal, instincts are the life instincts, inclined as they are toward procreation. Later, as Freud considered the aggressive drives, he came to see them as opposed to the life instinct and as leading to self-destruction, annihilation, and death. Hence, he named the aggressive drive the *death instinct.*

Freud came to these thoughts under the influence of a number of events: Adler's focus on → aggression, the outbreak of World War I, and personal loss in the Freud family. So it seems that Freud, in his consideration of two sets of psychological instincts in conflict, was also addressing larger philosophical issues as well: the nature of life and death, of war and peace, and of love and hate. Interestingly, Freud never called the death instinct *thanatos* (Gk. "death"), as have later authors.

2.4. *Structural Theory*

In addition to his topographical theory, Freud developed a structural model of the mind focused on the sense of what is me (ego), the sense of what is not-me (id), and the sense of what is over-me (superego, *SE* 19). Bruno Bettelheim (1982) has provided helpful insight concerning appropriate English translations of Freud's terms *Das Ich, Das Es,* and *Das Über-Ich.* Id, ego, and superego are often in conflictual relationships, much of which is unconscious. Freud used his structural theory to arrive at a new understanding of anxiety (*SE* 20) as a signal by the ego to avoid reexperiencing earlier trauma (→ Psychology 2).

2.5. *Religion and Culture*

Throughout his life Freud was extremely interested in → culture and → religion and turned his attention to both in a number of works. Freud used psychoanalytic theory and insight as a tool for analysis of civilization (*SE* 21), culture (*SE* 11), and religion (*SE* 21, 23).

For example, Freud described religion as an illusion (*SE* 11). In doing so, Freud made a play with words. He had a technical psychoanalytic definition of illusion that was different from the ordinary, everyday definition of illusion. By "illusion," Freud meant anything that was based on a wish and could represent that wish as fulfilled. Religion is based on the wish for an omnipotent parent to protect against the traumas of life; in religion that wish is represented as fulfilled in the monotheistic and benevolent God, who is the loving father of us all. At the same time, Freud took advantage of the common meaning of the word "illusion" as an erroneous mental representation. Yet Freud was open minded enough to allow publication of a rebuttal by Oskar Pfister (1873-1956), a Swiss pastor who was an advocate of psychoanalysis and a longtime friend of Freud's. Pfister's rebuttal (1928) argued that Freud's desire for a scientific future free of superstition and religion was itself a wish and thus, according to Freud's own definition, an illusion.

3. Beyond Freud

By 1910 Freud had begun to assemble a substantial following in Vienna, and regular meetings of the Vienna Psychoanalytic Society were held, the minutes being recorded by Otto Rank (1884-1939; see H. Nunberg). Freud and Jung, who was active in psychoanalytic circles, had formed a professional friendship, the pair traveling to the United States in 1909 for Freud's lectures at Clark University (Worcester, Mass.). Sometime after 1910, however, considerable dissension arose, leading to Jung's leaving the Freudian movement to develop what he called analytical psychology. Later others left as well, Adler and Rank of note. Adler's emphasis on the aggressive drive no doubt led Freud to develop a psychoanalytic theory of aggression. Otto Rank, after a stay in Paris, settled in the United States and was influential in bringing his version of → depth psychology to social work.

Within psychoanalysis proper, extensions in Freud's theory began to develop. Anna Freud (1895-1982), Freud's daughter, moved to London with her father and mother to escape the Nazi occupation of Austria, and probable internment or death. In London Anna worked with children, extending psychoanalytic ego psychology in respect to the mechanisms of defense. Erik Erikson (1902-94), a student of Anna Freud, extended the psychoanalytic understanding of human growth and development to the entire life cycle. Other notable psychoanalytic ego theorists were Heinz Hartmann (1894-1970) and David Rapaport (1911-60).

Other trends and schools include the object-relations theory developed in Great Britain by Melanie Klein (1882-1960) and D. W. Winnicott (1896-1971). This theory, a branch of psychoanalytic ego psychology, explores the inner world of object representations. Klein contributed greatly to the understanding of pre-oedipal development through her work with manic-depressive children. She extended psychoanalytic understandings of inner sadism to early childhood. Klein, seeing a parallel between dreams and children's play, began to analyze → play as well as dreams in her psychoanalytic work with children. Also at this time, the school of Jacques Lacan (1901-81) developed in France, emphasizing language in its real, symbolic, and imaginary forms.

Out of the study of the problem of → narcissism arose what has come to be called self-psychology (Heinz Kohut [1913-81], Otto Kernberg [b. 1928]) and the role of the self-object. At first, the developing child does not experience the mother as an independent object but, rather, as part of its own self. The mother, as a self-object, can be totally controlled, unlike the actual mother. When this childhood form of relating shows up in psychotherapy in transference, the therapist finds a patient who wishes to be mirrored, who has a desire to be reflected and recognized for greatness, and who is unable to tolerate differences. The patient, who forms an idealizing transference, has a need to see the therapist as an all-good ideal figure. Adult forms of self-objects may show up in idealized, rather than realistic, goals, values, groups, and life-partners.

4. Culture

Psychoanalysis, stemming both from Freud and his followers, has had an enormous influence on Western culture (M. Roth): on popular culture and on literature (E. Berman), literary criticism (M. Groden and M. Kreiswirth), and other arts, especially film (G. O. Gabbard) and film criticism (A. Kaplan). Psychoanalysis has had a significant impact on recent biblical → hermeneutics through the influence of Paul Ricoeur (1913-2005, K. Simms), as well as Jacques Lacan and French feminists such as Julia Kristeva (for the latter two, see M. Joy).

Bibliography: Freud's writings: The Standard Edition of the Complete Psychological Works of Sigmund Freud (24 vols.; ed. J. Strachey; London, 1953-66). See esp. the following: "Beyond the Pleasure Principle" (1920), 18.3-64 • "Civilization and Its Discontents" (1930), 21.57-146 • "The Ego and the Id" (1923), 19.3-66 • "The Future of an Illusion" (1927), 21.3-56 • "Inhibitions, Symptoms, and Anxiety" (1926), 20.77-172 • *The Interpretation of Dreams* (1900), 4–5 • *Introductory Lectures on Psycho-Analysis* (1916-17), 15–16 • "Leonardo da Vinci and a Memory of His Childhood" (1910), 11.59-137 • "Moses and Monotheism" (1939), 23.3-137

• "On the History of the Psycho-Analytic Movement" (1914), 14.3-66 • "Three Essays on the Theory of Sexuality" (1905), 7.125-45.

Other studies: A. Adler, *The Collected Clinical Works of Alfred Adler* (7 vols.; ed. H. T. Stein; Bellingham, Wash., 2003) • E. Berman, *Essential Papers on Literature and Psychoanalysis* (New York, 1992) • B. Bettelheim, *Freud and Man's Soul* (New York, 1982) • R. H. Davis, *Freud's Concept of Passivity* (Madison, Conn., 1993) • E. Erikson, *Identity and the Life Cycle* (New York, 1959) • R. Fine, *The Development of Freud's Thought: From the Beginnings (1886-1900) through Id Psychology (1900-1914) to Ego Psychology (1914-1939)* (Lanham, Md., 1973) • A. Freud, *The Ego and the Mechanisms of Defense in the Writings of Anna Freud* (vol. 2; Madison, Conn., 1990) • G. O. Gabbard, ed., *Psychoanalysis and Film* (London, 2001) • M. Groden and M. Kreiswirth, eds., *The Johns Hopkins Guide to Literary Theory and Criticism* (Baltimore, 1994) • H. Hartmann, *Ego Psychology and the Problem of Adaptation* (New York, 1964) • M. Joy et al., eds., *French Feminists on Religion: A Reader* (London, 1992) • C. G. Jung, *Collected Works of C. G. Jung* (20 vols.; New York and Princeton, 1953-92) • A. Kaplan, *Psychoanalysis and Cinema* (London, 1990) • O. Kernberg, *Borderline Conditions and Pathological Narcissism* (New York, 1974) • J. Klein, *The Writings of Melanie Klein* (4 vols.; New York, 1984) • H. Kohut, *The Analysis of the Self: A Systematic Approach to the Psychoanalytic Treatment of Narcissistic Personality Disorders* (New York, 1971) • H. Küng, *Freud and the Problem of God* (New Haven, 1979) • J. Lacan, *Ecrits: A Selection* (trans. B. Fink; New York, 2002) • H. Nunberg, ed., *Minutes of the Vienna Psychoanalytic Society* (4 vols.; New York, 1962-74) • O. Pfister, "The Illusion of a Future: A Friendly Disagreement with Prof. Sigmund Freud" (1928), *IJPsa* 74/3 (1993) 557-79 • P. Ricoeur, *Freud and Philosophy* (New Haven, 1988) • M. Roth, *Freud: Conflict and Culture; Essays on his Life, Work, and Legacy* (New York, 1998) • K. Simms, *Paul Ricoeur* (London 2003) • D. W. Winnicott, *Playing and Reality* (London, 1982).

Russell H. Davis

Psychology

1. Definition
2. History
3. Methods
4. Fields and Trends
5. Psychology and Theology

1. Definition

Psychology lies at the meeting point of the humane, social, and natural sciences, though with an increasing orientation to natural science. Phenomenological approaches to the world of the psyche (→ Phenomenology), which stem from the humanities branch of psychology, still call for notice and have indeed gained some new prominence in the form of → humanistic psychology. In spite of its preeminent orientation, then, psychology is not a pure natural science, and it never will be. For this reason we must resist the view that regards → behavior as the only object of psychological study (this alone being open to rigorous scientific investigation). Instead, justice must be done to writers who make both behavior and experience their theme.

The term "psychology" itself means the doctrine of the → soul. But in the philosophy, theology, and intellectual history of the West, the term "soul" is so heavily freighted that many psychologists who have a scientific ideal of knowledge can make nothing of it and refuse to use it. Nevertheless, it must be recognized that for many centuries psychology has been a discipline that has had the soul as its theme. Furthermore, the philosophical-theological psychology of the West has raised many questions that modern empirical psychology still must address.

2. History

The history of modern psychology began in the 19th century, and psychology today regards all previous handling of matters concerning the psyche as prehistory. If we find the revolution in treatment of the psyche as taking place in the 19th century, we have reason to agree with this assessment. Yet we must also recognize that much psychological knowledge was in fact acquired before modern psychology emerged.

Before the 19th century psychology was not an independent discipline. It formed part of → philosophy or → theology. The first great essays on the phenomenon of the soul came from Plato (427-347 B.C.; → Platonism) and Aristotle (384-322; → Aristotelianism), though already the pre-Socratics (e.g., Heraclitus [ca. 500 B.C.] and Democrites [ca. 460-ca. 370]) had written about the soul's substance and about organs as the centers of feeling (→ Greek Philosophy). But whereas Democrites regarded the mortal soul as having a material nature, for Plato it belongs to the realm of the ideas, to the nonmaterial world, and it lives in the body as in a prison. It also, however, is the organ or principle of the inner life, and it consists of three parts: the rational, or thought; the courageous, or will; and the impulsive, or desire. These three parts might be in conflict, and so it is vital that reason should be in control. In *Phaedrus* Plato dramatically described the soul's dynamics in terms of a charioteer who must direct two horses.

Aristotle's doctrine of the soul is less speculative and more rationalistic and empirical. He pursued psychology as an investigator of nature (see esp. his *On the Soul*), and the empirical parts of his teaching, which derive from his brilliant gift of observation, are still relevant today. Unlike Plato, who viewed the link between soul and body as ultimately an unfortunate one, Aristotle regarded this link as essential. For him the soul is the fundamental principle of the body, of everything that has life. Plants and animals, as well as humans, have souls. The vegetative soul of plants is still present in that of animals, which enjoy greater powers of orienting perception. Then the souls of plants and animals form part of the human soul, whose distinguishing feature is increased reason. Aristotle thus constructed a layered model of the soul that is still influential, having been adopted into what was not long ago a popular theory of personality (that of P. Lersch).

Christianity developed its view of the soul in close dependence on Plato and Aristotle. → Augustine (A.D. 354-430; → Augustine's Theology) and → Thomas Aquinas (ca. 1225-1274; → Thomism) were the most prominent Christian thinkers to elaborate a psychology. Augustine saw three parts to the soul: memory, understanding, and will. In his *Confessions,* which he put in the form of prayers, he pitilessly exposes his soul's life before God and offers detailed reasons for his actions. He thus became the founder of introspection.

A violent struggle broke out in → Scholasticism regarding the proper understanding of the soul. The victory went to the Aristotelian Aquinas, and his system became normative. Aquinas wrote extensive commentaries on the works of Aristotle, among them the work *On the Soul,* in relation to which he made a detailed analysis of knowledge and advanced a theory of the place and operation of the intellect, modifying Aristotle's view from a Christian angle. Aquinas stated that the rational soul *(anima rationalis),* the soul's supreme principle, enters the body 14 days after conception and is immortal. The nutritive soul *(anima vegetativa)* is in the body from birth.

A break with previous conceptions of the soul came with R. Descartes (1596-1650; → Cartesianism), who made a strict distinction between soul (or spirit) and body and viewed the body as a kind of machine to which the soul (or spirit) is not directly linked. The soul is no longer here, as in Aristotle, the principle of the life of the body but an independent sphere. Cooperation between soul and body occurs by way of the pineal gland.

The next most important advances in modern psychology were made by G. W. Leibniz and C. Wolff, on the one hand, and, on the other, by the 17th- and 18th-century British sensationalists and empiricists (J. Locke, G. Berkeley, D. Hume). In his monadology, borrowed from the psychology of antiquity, G. W. Leibniz (1646-1716) made a plea for the world of the psyche in opposition to the mechanical causal thinking of developing natural science. In C. Wolff (1679-1754) psychology became a discipline for investigating the general laws of thinking, conceiving, and desiring. The British thinkers rejected purely theoretical insights and thus prepared the way for an empirical methodology in psychology.

Psychology became wholly empirical in psychophysics (E. H. Weber, G. T. Fechner), in which an attempt was made to measure mathematically the relation between physical stimuli and experienced intensity. W. Wundt (1832-1920) then succeeded in institutionalizing psychology as a discipline in its own right, setting up a psychological laboratory in Leipzig in 1879. World War I brought a new departure in psychology and greatly strengthened it by applying its findings in constructing instruments of war (e.g., direction finders for artillery) and in the testing of soldiers. → Psychoanalysis had now emerged, and it too profited from the war as Sigmund Freud (1856-1939) and others found an important field of work in analyzing war → neuroses.

In America and Russia as well, scientific psychology had now come to the fore. On the Russian side we might mention I. P. Pavlov (1849-1936) and his research into conditioned reflexes (first published in 1904). On the American side the beginning of the 20th century brought behaviorism, a radical form of investigation of conduct that disregards all inner processes. Among the pioneers we might mention J. B. Watson (1878-1958).

Psychology has become a complex discipline with many different branches. It has attained great popularity, and both society and other disciplines, not least of all theology, have great expectations for it.

3. Methods

The most important methods in psychology are observation, experiment, field research, and testing. The resultant findings are evaluated with great mathematical precision. In this respect statistical procedures play an important role. Observation in psychology naturally differs from observation in everyday life. It is systematic and makes use of fixed rules and techniques. Introspection is no longer included among modern research methods, since its findings are too subjective.

The supreme method in psychology today is experiment. In structure, psychological experiments are like those in natural science. At universities psychology is very largely experimental psychology. Thus to measure stress, for example, participants in the experiment are exposed to various situations of stress, and measurements are taken. Field research is itself a kind of experiment. Data are assembled here from real life rather than from situations in the laboratory. The advantage is a greater closeness to life as it really is, but the price paid is the risk of greater distortion.

The many psychological tests may be roughly divided into achievement and personality tests. Intelligence tests belong to the achievement group but may be ranked separately. Achievement tests measure abilities or qualities like concentration or the faculty of observation. But this kind of test may also measure many different abilities (e.g., in assessing readiness for school). A common personality test, the thematic apperception test, involves showing pictures that can have many meanings to those taking the test and then asking them to make up stories about the pictures. The basic idea here is that aspects of personality will be projected into the scenes, with the invented stories revealing something about the self.

4. Fields and Trends

In modern psychology there are three great normative trends: cognitivism, depth psychology (→ Depth-Psychological Exegesis), and behaviorism. According to the first, we are essentially determined by insight and knowledge; in the second, by unconscious impulses and expectations; in the third, by the conditions of our environment (i.e., we are the product of our learning experiences). Subdisciplines and fields of work are methodologically related to these trends. Developmental psychology, for example, may be conducted from the standpoint of any one of them. Similarly, forensic psychologists may be pledged to any one of the three trends. But psychologists may also be eclectic according to the requirements of their particular case.

As regards subdisciplines, *general psychology* deals with perception, memory, thought, learning, motivation, and emotion. It studies what is most universally valid in experience and behavior. Unlike personality psychology, it does not take individual differences into account. Its task is to inquire into basic psychic processes and to advance theories, for example, regarding memory. *Developmental psychology* studies human experience and behavior from the standpoint of change. Thus it might investigate the successive stages of human life from early childhood to childhood, maturity, and old age, or the development of specific functions such as perception, thought, speech, or moral attitudes and religious orientation.

Personality psychology, which distinguishes between individuals, tries to embrace the totality of human personality. It has worked out trait theories, situationist theories, and interaction theories. In the first of these theories, qualities explain personality; in the second, situations clarify behavior as people react differently to them; and in the third, behavior is the result of interaction between situation and disposition. → *Social psychology* locates us in our social context, trying to understand us accordingly. "Social context," a wide-ranging term, includes the population as a whole but also the neighborhood, the family, the group, and other subgroupings. Social influences that are studied also include occupation, employment, and group norms.

These subdisciplines involve the work of university faculties. But there is also the vast field of *applied psychology,* which includes such branches of psychology as business, clinical, cultural, economic, environmental, forensic, industrial, leisure, media, military, pedagogical, and others. *Clinical psychology* is particularly important. At issue here is diagnosis and therapy for mental disorders. In the eyes of the general public, this kind of psychology is fundamental. Psychology of this kind unfortunately also offers leeway for many ill-trained practitioners, so that separating the wheat from the chaff in the therapy market is often difficult, especially as more than 300 forms of therapy have been distinguished (→ Psychotherapy).

Special note should be taken of the depth-psychology approaches of Freud, C. G. Jung (1875-1961), and A. Adler (1870-1937), which from the outset have had a therapeutic aim and are thus part of clinical psychology, but which also make statements about the personality as such, so that they offer personality psychology as well. In humanistic psychology we also find Rogerian psychology, linked to the name of Carl Rogers (1902-87). Experimental learning psychology has also produced behavior therapy, which does not try to find out the deeper reasons for psychological disorders but deals only with observed behavior — with considerable success, at least in the case of limited problems.

A psychotherapeutic approach can sometimes claim to be able to give comprehensive meaning to life. In this regard we find such slogans as "rebirth," "wholeness," "union with the cosmos," and "illumination." When these terms come into play, psychotherapy takes a religious turn and becomes a doctrine of salvation. Theologians cannot accept claims of this kind. They cannot allow psychology to become → soteriology. In their own → anthropology they must take into account the insights of psychology regarding human reality, but they must set them in a theological frame of reference. The same applies to the use of psychology in → pastoral care, on which much theological thinking and discussion are still required (→ Clinical Pastoral Education; Pastoral Theology).

Bibliography: Works in English: N. Block and G. Dworkin, eds., *The IQ Controversy* (London, 1977) • A. M. Colman, *A Dictionary of Psychology* (Oxford, 2001) • R. Corsini, ed., *Handbook of Innovative Therapy* (2d ed.; New York, 2001) • H. Gleitman, A. J. Fridlund, and D. Reisberg, *Psychology* (6th ed.; New York, 2004) • P. Gray, *Psychology* (4th ed.; New York, 2002) •B. R. Hergenhahn, *An Introduction to Theories of Learning* (Englewood Cliffs, N.J., 1976) • T. H. Leahey, *A History of Psychology* (Englewood Cliffs, N.J., 1980) • M. W. Matlin, *Psychology* (2d ed.; Fort Worth, Tex., 1995); idem, *The Psychology of Women* (5th ed.; Belmont, Calif., 2004) • T. Millon and R. D. Davis, *Personality Disorders and Modern Life* (2d ed.; Hoboken, N.J., 2004) • R. P. Philipchalk, *Psychology and Christianity* (Lanham, Md., 1987).

Works in German: M. Irle, *Lehrbuch der Sozialpsychologie* (Göttingen, 1975) • R. Oerter, L. Montada, et al., *Entwicklungspsychologie* (Munich, 1982) • W. Rebell, *Psychologisches Grundwissen für Theologen* (2d ed.; Munich, 1992) • P. Seidmann, *Tiefenpsychologie* (Stuttgart, 1982) • E. G. Wehner, ed., *Einführung in die empirische Psychologie* (Stuttgart, 1980) • P. R. Wellhöfer, *Grundstudium allgemeine Psychologie* (2d ed.; Stuttgart, 1990).

Walter Rebell

5. Psychology and Theology

Insofar as psychology and → theology have the human psyche (or even human behavior) as their common theme, they share a common interest and may profitably share their findings and concerns. Nevertheless a primary difference exists, for the psyche (→ Soul) is for psychology the chief object of study, but theology, in spite of some modern psychologizing trends, focuses first on God in his self-revelation and on the psyche only as it arises in relation to God as Creator, Reconciler, and Sanctifier. Serious tensions result where either psychologists or theologians fail to recognize the distinction.

Psychology, for example, unavoidably must deal with → God, but as a belief in God, a concept of God, even an illusion of God, not as the objective God who creates, reconciles, and sanctifies, and who has an eternal purpose for the human psyche. Conversely, the psyche for theology is specifically the creation of God, responsible to God, guilty before God, and deriving its true and final health only from God. Psychology as a specialized study can say many things about the psyche, offer analyses of its problems, and engage in helpful therapies that are all beyond the scope of theology. Theology in turn, as another specialized study of the psyche, knows things about the psyche and its problems, and has a remedy, that do not fall within the reach of psychology as such. Acceptance of the distinction can avert an adversarial relation.

All disciplines can and do embrace all others. Every discipline, then, tends to see every other in terms of itself. Extravagant claims may then be made that are harmful theoretically, and no less disastrous in practical application, when practitioners in one sphere invade the province that strictly belongs to another. Unhappily, this boundary-crossing often occurs between psychology and theology. Psychology and theology alike go beyond their terms of reference, and confusion and even conflicts arise in consequence. In contrast, psychology and theology may profitably complement each other when each focuses more strictly on its own specific discipline, tasks, and possibilities, and in so doing learns and profits from the other to the greater good of both individuals and society.

→ Science and Theology

Bibliography: M. R. McMinn and T. R. Phillips, eds., *Care for the Soul: Exploring the Intersection of Psychology and Theology* (Downers Grove, Ill., 2001) • G. R. Peterson, *Minding God: Theology and the Cognitive Sciences* (Minneapolis, 2003) • M. Stock, "Psychology (Classical)," *NCE* (2d ed.) 11.803-7.

Geoffrey W. Bromiley

Psychology of Religion

1. The Discipline and Its Projects
2. Describing Religious Experience and Expression
3. Explaining Religious Phenomena
   3.1. Biological Perspective
   3.2. Freudian Psychoanalysis

1. The Discipline and Its Projects

The psychology of religion consists of the systematic study and interpretation of → religion by means of the theories and methods of contemporary Western → psychology. "Religion" is most often understood to refer to individual experiences, attitudes, and conduct, but its referent is sometimes the diverse contents — images, doctrines, myths, rituals — of the historic religious traditions. Thus, broadly speaking, there are two variants of psychology of religion: one of religious persons, and another of religious content. Those who pursue a psychology of religious persons have tended historically to work within a single religious tradition, usually Protestant-Christian, often with a personal commitment to the tradition and little interest in interpreting its content psychologically. Those who favor a psychology of religious contents, in contrast, commonly seek to reinterpret such contents and trace out their origins, usually in terms of a particular psychological theory and sometimes in a comparative, cross-cultural framework (→ Religious Studies).

According to the "principle of the exclusion of the transcendent," laid out at the beginning of the 20th century by the Swiss psychologist Theodore Flournoy (1854-1921) and adopted since then by many others, psychologists of religion may neither affirm nor deny the reality of religious objects — that is, the reality of the transcendent as it is variously conceived and represented; this position is today called methodological → agnosticism. Thus, in their scholarly work, psychologists of religion are advised to remain religiously neutral, neither including the transcendent in their equations as they seek to understand religion nor drawing conclusions about the ontological status of the content of religious beliefs and experience. Ideally, they will also embrace an understanding of religion that adequately encompasses the world's religious traditions. However broad their focus, they should avoid imposing the categories of their own faith or → worldview.

Within the boundaries set by Flournoy's principle, psychologists of religion collectively pursue three different projects: (1) systematically describing religion, both as inner → experience and outer expression, with the goal of clarifying religion's essential characteristics and charting their development over the life course; (2) explaining the origins of religion, in history and in individual lives, thereby illuminating its fundamental nature; and (3) tracing out the consequences of religious ideas, attitudes, experiences, and practices, both in individual lives and in the larger world. Whereas the second task typically challenges the self-understandings of religious persons and traditions, the first and third undertakings are consonant with traditional religious attitudes and even have roots in the historic religious traditions themselves.

2. Describing Religious Experience and Expression

The initial task of describing religious experience is peculiarly difficult. Human experience is notoriously vague and elusive, and it is ultimately private, for no expression can adequately represent an experience to another. Religious experience in particular is exceptionally challenging, for beyond being extremely variable and typically vague, it refers to objects and events for which there is no adequate language and no adequate object — that is, no independently observable source of stimulation. Moreover, unlike many other forms of experience, it cannot readily be called forth on command, as in a laboratory setting. The descriptive study of religious experience has therefore had to rely heavily on first-person accounts of such experiences — either spontaneously written, as in a private journal or autobiography, or elicited from others by various means — while recognizing the difficulties and limitations of such descriptions. Some argue that it also requires researchers who are personally acquainted with such experience, or who at least possess an exceptional capacity for empathic understanding. This work has yielded generalized descriptions, as well as typologies of a variety of forms of religious experience and its expressions.

In his *Varieties of Religious Experience* (1902/1985), a classic contribution to the psychology of religion, William James (1842-1910) addressed all three of the tasks identified in this essay. The *Varieties,* though, is best known and most admired for its descriptive contributions. Ideally, says James, exploration of religious experience would be carried out by someone who knows it intimately from the inside. But as a professed outsider, James had to rely instead on insiders' written descriptions, which he assembled from a diversity of sources. On the basis of some 200 documents, especially ones written by the uncommon "experts" who live at the extremes, James identified two fundamental types: the healthy-minded and the sick soul. The congenitally happy, healthy-minded type sees everything in this world as good and looks to the divine with grateful admiration and a desire for union. The sick soul, in contrast, is struck by the precariousness of existence, the ubiquity of → suffering, and the ultimate nullification of life's values by → death; evil, including a painful discordancy felt deep within, seems to offer the essential clue to the world's meaning. The two types require different types of religion, James concludes, the sick soul finding its salvation only in → asceticism and → conversion.

Whereas James was widely admired for making accessible certain exceptional realms of experience, he was also criticized for his emphasis on pathological extremes. His student James Pratt (1875-1944), for example, argued that most of the positive fruits of → mysticism can be traced to the more commonplace mild forms, not the extreme types that fascinated James. Pratt also gave attention to topics overlooked by James, including the role of religious → symbols in the lives of ordinary people.

At about the same time in Europe, the so-called Dorpat school of religious psychology used "experimental introspection" to engage trained observers to report on their immediate responses to religious texts. From this painstaking work Karl Girgensohn (1875-1925), the founder of the school, concluded that the main structural elements of religious experience are *intuitive thinking*, which tends to be vague, unformulated, and more like feeling than thought; and *ego functions*, the cognitive evaluation of what has been intuited and the eventual taking of a stand in relation to it. Other early European contributors to the descriptive tradition include Rudolf Otto (1869-1937), famous for his analysis of the experience of the Holy as the *mysterium tremendum et fascinans*, and Friedrich Heiler (1892-1967), who developed an elaborate typology of → prayer, while also seeking to discern its essential core.

The descriptive approach continued to attract proponents in the second half of the 20th century, especially in Great Britain and Europe, and with greater attention to the religious experience of children. Increasingly, however, descriptive methods were used in conjunction with quantitative research. Most notable are adaptations of philosopher Walter Stace's (1886-1967) descriptions of the putatively universal elements of mystical experience. These features served Walter Pahnke (1931-71) as the core of his criteria for judging whether or not the entheogenic substance psilocybin, in combination with a religious disposition and a religious setting, facilitates experience akin to classical mystical experiences. Pahnke concluded that it did, and a 25-year follow-up study using the same criteria found that those who received psilocybin in the famous double-blind experiment had more vivid and detailed memories of their experiences, and viewed them as far more beneficial, than those who did not receive it. Stace's descriptions have similarly served Ralph Hood as the foundation for his "mysticism scale," which has proved serviceable in a variety of empirical studies investigating the correlates of mystical experience.

3. Explaining Religious Phenomena

The second project of the psychology of religion addresses the question, What are the origins or causes of the religious phenomena that have been described? With this task the psychologist departs most dramatically from the self-understanding of the religious individual. Whereas the latter is naturally disposed to invoke God or some other transcendent factor in accounting for his or her experience, the psychologist seeks to explain it in terms of a variety of mundane causes, ranging from early childhood experiences to ongoing brain states.

The fact that most psychologists exclude the transcendent from among the possible causes of religious phenomena reflects the stance of methodological agnosticism, along with the realization that to include the transcendent would risk transforming the psychology of religion into a sectarian undertaking — and a different one for each religious tradition. Some religious psychologists and psychiatrists have nevertheless formally distinguished true and false forms of possession and mysticism, the true forms assumed to involve transcendent factors and the false ones merely psychological causes. Most researchers, however, tacitly leave transcendent causes out of the equation, whatever their own personal religious views may be.

3.1. *Biological Perspective*

The range of possible explanations is as broad as psychology itself, although only a few perspectives in psychology have been extensively applied to religion. Perhaps the earliest is the biological perspective, which would include the temperamental differences that underlie James's two types. Whereas religion is often thought to be chiefly concerned with the fate of the human soul and is often antagonistic to bodily impulses, the body is in fact a pervasive presence in the religious traditions. We need only think of the diverse ways that the traditions appeal to the human senses, the bodily movements that are integral to religious rites, and the preoccupation with bodily attributes and states attributed to divine beings (→ Cultic Purity). Moreover, one does not have to look far to see the specific influences of the human upright posture and its expressive variations on the composition of these rituals and the construction of cosmologies.

Less obvious — and less easily demonstrated — are the neurophysiological processes that most certainly underlie all religious experiences. The development of increasingly sophisticated brain-scanning technology has today stimulated a growing interest in finding brain-state correlates of meditation, prayer, and other religion-associated states.

3.2. *Freudian Psychoanalysis*

Dynamic, or depth, psychologies, however, have been most thoroughly and systematically applied to religion. Sigmund Freud (1856-1939), the founder of → psychoanalysis, was himself interested in religion, which he associated foremost with the notion of a father-god and participation in minutely prescribed obligatory ritual. Such religious beliefs and practices, he argued, are rooted in the wishes and fears of childhood, especially those that constitute the Oedipus complex. The father-god that the religious devotee both loves and fears is, says Freud, none other than the omniscient and omnipotent father of infancy, now unconsciously projected into the cosmic realm. The sacred → rites that are compulsively carried out, along with religious ideas that may not be challenged without great risk, help to keep hidden the irrationality of religion's motives.

Theodore Reik (1880-1969), among others of Freud's orthodox followers, elaborated these themes in considerable detail, especially in regard to the Jewish tradition. Another close associate, Ernest Jones (1879-1958), turned the psychoanalytic lens toward certain Christian practices. Oskar Pfister (1873-1956), a Swiss Lutheran pastor, psychoanalyst, and lifelong friend of Freud, likewise applied psychoanalytic principles to the Christian tradition, but in this case, the goal was not simply a critique of religion. Rather, Pfister undertook to identify the neurotic traits that, over the centuries, have distorted the Christian tradition through hate, fanaticism, and cruelty. By means of his analysis Pfister sought to address the problem of religious fear in Christianity by restoring to the tradition Jesus' fundamental message of → love.

3.3. *Object Relations Theory*

As the psychoanalytic tradition evolved, so also did the dynamic accounts of religion. Most significant was British object relations theory, several of whose founders themselves wrote on the subject of religion. According to Harry Guntrip (1901-75), a psychotherapist who was a former congregational minister, religion, like psychotherapy, seeks to promote personal wholeness through satisfactory "object relations," a phrase referring to relationships with other persons. Religion, Guntrip says, provides a fundamental sense of connectedness to, and personal validation by, the universe, a connection that has it earliest roots in the positive infant-mother relationship. Religion thereby attracts those who are suffering from bad-object relations, signaled by a disposition to the conviction of sin and eventually the saving experiences of repentance and conversion. Given religion's attractiveness to neurotics, it inevitably becomes distorted by immature or neurotic trends, evident in hell-fire preaching and fanatical crusades. Guntrip urges religious educators to deepen their understanding of these dynamics, avoiding an emphasis on → dogma and prescribed rituals and fostering in their place genuine religious experience, which he says provides the largest scope for self-realization.

From the object-relations perspective of the pediatrician and psychoanalyst D. W. Winnicott (1896-1971), religion is a major repository of transitional phenomena — cultural forms and artifacts that, like the young child's teddy bear or cherished blanket, create an "illusory," intermediate area of experience that helps individuals to make the difficult and lifelong transition from immersion in utter subjectivity to full acceptance of reality. Thus Winnicott effectively rejects both Freud's reduction of religion to infantile wish-fulfillment and the religious fundamentalist's literalistic interpretation of religious texts and doctrines. Religious content is conceived, rather, as a construction of human longing that nonetheless reflects reality in vital ways.

Winnicott's understanding of religion was subsequently developed by the Dutch-born American clinical psychologist Paul Pruyser (1916-87), who explores more fully the intermediate, "illusionistic" world of creative imagination, emphasizing in particular its vulnerability to distortion in the religious traditions. On the one hand are *autistic* distortions, in the form of fantastic images of perfectly benign deities, horned devils, and apocalyptic visions of bloody retribution; on the other hand are *realistic* distortions, such as the doctrine of scriptural inerrancy and the viewpoint of → creationism, both of which, says Pruyser, strip illusionistic symbols of transcendence of their subtle nuances and mystery.

Winnicott's influence is likewise apparent in the work of the Boston psychoanalyst Ana-Maria Rizzuto, born and educated in Argentina, who offers clarifications of the complex development and dynamics of the individual God representation. As an illusory transitional phenomenon, the God repre-

Psychology of Religion

sentation ordinarily undergoes progressive development as the person matures, thereby becoming more adequate; but frequently it remains largely unchanged, gradually becoming anachronistic and irrelevant. Indeed, Rizzuto sees an individual's God representation — whether or not it is believed in — as a potential diagnostic indicator of overall psychic development.

3.4. *Analytical Psychology*

Whereas the psychoanalytic and object relations theorists assume that the unconscious roots of religion lie in the individual's own history, the Swiss psychiatrist C. G. Jung (1875-1961) posited deeper-lying origins in what he called the collective unconscious. These historically more remote layers of the psyche are said to retain sedimentations from the experiences of our ancestors, including the earliest forms of life. They dispose us, says Jung, to experience over and over again the types of persons, situations, and processes that recurred in our ancestors' lives and gradually formed → archetypes, the hypothetical building blocks of the collective unconscious. In addition to being a universal human structure filled with bipolar elements, the collective unconscious is a *process,* one that tends toward increasing differentiation and integration, or what Jung called individuation.

The end goal of the lifelong individuation process is represented in the unconscious by the archetype of the → Self, a state of balance and wholeness that is frequently expressed in such archetypal images as abstract geometric patterns featuring a circle or square, mythical objects such as the Holy Grail, powerful animals such as the elephant, layered blossoms such as the lotus, and deities or holy figures, including Christ and the Buddha. It is no coincidence, according to Jung, that so many archetypal images can be found in the religious traditions, for religion, he says, was historically the main facilitator of the individuation process. Thus he considered today's widespread loss of connection to religion to be a serious one indeed. A seeming friend of religion, Jung was accused by some critics of psychologizing it and thus undercutting the work of → metaphysics and theology.

3.5. *Other Explanatory Perspectives*

Still other explanatory perspectives have been brought to bear on religion, although none as prominently as the preceding ones. Akin to British object relations theory, for example, is the *self psychology* of Heinz Kohut (1913-81), who posited a second form of → libido, narcissistic libido, which undergoes development independent of Freud's object libido. According to Kohut, evolving narcissistic libido contributes to empathy, creativity, humor, wisdom, and — in relatively rare cases — cosmic narcissism, a self-transcending, quasi-religious state. Foreshortened development of narcissistic libido is said to underlie a variety of less lofty religious phenomena.

Likewise related to the psychoanalytic perspectives but influenced by ethology as well is the *attachment theory* of John Bowlby (1907-90), which has served some researchers as a framework for considering variations in relationship to God. → Social psychology has contributed *attribution theory,* which addresses how and why people explain various occurrences either naturalistically or religiously, as well as *role theory,* which, in the hands of the Swedish psychologist of religion Hjalmar Sundén (1908-93), conceives of religion as a process of role taking and subsequent transformations of perceptual experience.

4. Tracing Out the Consequences of Religion

The third major task of the psychology of religion is delineating the various consequences — what James called the fruits — of religion in individual lives and in society. While critical of institutional religion and the claims and conduct of some religious persons, James was nonetheless convinced that, taken as a whole, the fruits of religion vindicate it as a preserver of virtues essential to the welfare of the world. Empirical researchers a half century later, however, were more struck by the evidence of the fanaticism, intolerance, and persecution that James acknowledged as potential dispositions of certain religious minds. Again and again these researchers found that religious individuals were no more honest than nonreligious ones, no more generous to the needy, no more humanitarian; in some studies they were even less so. More disturbing, especially to psychologists who were themselves religious, were the findings that religiosity measures were consistently positively correlated with authoritarianism, ethnocentrism, dogmatism, social distance, intolerance of ambiguity, rigidity, and prejudice, especially against blacks and Jews.

Convinced that there was more to the story, especially by the finding that these positive correlations turn negative at high levels of religiosity, researchers came to distinguish two types of religious orientation: the intrinsic and the extrinsic. Those persons who are intrinsically religious conduct all aspects of their lives in accord with the religious ideals they embrace; the extrinsically oriented, in contrast, merely use religion when it is convenient, subordinating it to personal and social needs. Gordon Allport (1897-1967) and his students developed a questionnaire to measure these two orientations — the Allport-Ross Religious Orientation Scale — and they and others then set about to demonstrate that it is the extrinsically oriented, not the intrinsic types, who are responsible for the dark side of religion. Although research findings are not altogether consistent, they tend to support this hypothesis.

Unsatisfied by this work, C. Daniel Batson proposed a third religious outlook, the Quest orientation. Quest was intended to reintroduce aspects of Allport's notion of mature religiosity that Batson believed had been left out of the intrinsic scale: complexity, doubt, and tentativeness. According to Batson's view, persons high on intrinsic religiosity are chiefly motivated to think well of themselves and to appear virtuous in the eyes of others; only the quest types, he argued, are genuine in their humanitarianism. Through a series of quasi-experimental studies, Batson found support for this proposition; others have confirmed it as well. Like the intrinsic and extrinsic scales, however, the Quest scale has been the subject of much criticism, and other researchers have created alternative versions of it. The challenge of developing adequate measures of religiosity is ongoing, especially at a time when many people represent themselves as spiritual rather than religious (→ Religion, Personal Sense of).

Today the search for religion's consequences has shifted to an emphasis on mental health. Whereas James had considered a "psychopathic" temperament a virtual prerequisite for deep religious experience, contemporary researchers emphasize religion's potential for supporting positive personal and social adjustment. In searching for the mental-health correlates of religious commitment, investigators have found that fundamentalist religious values sometimes prove maladaptive, especially in the realm of → sexuality. When the Allport-Ross Religious Orientation scales were used, the predicted trends were generally confirmed: the intrinsic outlook was usually positively associated with mental health, and the extrinsic one, negatively. The Quest scale, less often used, has also yielded fewer significant results; if there is any relationship at all, it tends to be a very low but positive one with anxiety, depression, and other measures of personal distress. Tentativeness and → doubt, it seems, are not particularly salutary. The work of Kenneth Pargament and his associates has gone beyond the mere tracing out of such correlations to exploring how living religion becomes implicated — positively and negatively — in the complex coping process. While recognizing the dark side of religion, Pargament's coping model is a fundamentally positive one.

5. The Status of the Psychology of Religion Today
Virtually from its beginnings late in the 19th century, the psychology of religion has suffered a curious fate. On the one hand, it has attracted the active interest of some of the century's most prominent psychologists, as noted above. On the other hand, it has been — and continues to be — disdained by a majority of psychologists and is viewed with suspicion, if not hostility, by many scholars in religious studies as well. The result is that academic courses in the psychology of religion are relatively uncommon, offered chiefly at church-related institutions, and there are few graduate programs, most of them in Europe, in which one can pursue the subject matter. Nevertheless, books and journals — notably the *International Journal for the Psychology of Religion; Mental Health, Religion, and Culture;* and the *Archive for the Psychology of Religion/Archiv für Religionspsychologie* — continue to appear, and several organizations provide support for scholars in the field, including the International Association for the Psychology of Religion; Division 36, Psychology of Religion, of the American Psychological Association; and the Person, Culture, and Religion group of the American Academy of Religion.

Bibliography: C. D. Batson, P. Schoenrade, and W. L. Ventis, *Religion and the Individual: A Social Psychological Perspective* (New York, 1993) • J. A. Belzen and O. Wikström, eds., *Taking a Step Back: Assessments of the Psychology of Religion* (Uppsala, 1997) • R. W. Hood Jr., ed., *Handbook of Religious Experience* (Birmingham, Ala., 1995) • K. E. Hyde, *Religion in Childhood and Adolescence: A Comprehensive Review of the Research* (Birmingham, Ala., 1990) • W. James, *The Varieties of Religious Experience: A Study in Human Nature* (Cambridge, Mass., 1985; orig. ed., 1902) • K. I. Pargament, *The Psychology of Religion and Coping: Theory, Research, Practice* (New York, 1997) • J. B. Pratt, *The Religious Consciousness: A Psychological Study* (New York, 1920) • J. F. Schumaker, ed., *Religion and Mental Health* (New York, 1992) • B. Spilka, R. W. Hood Jr., B. Hunsberger, and R. Gorsuch, *The Psychology of Religion: An Empirical Approach* (3d ed.; New York, 2003) • D. M. Wulff, *Psychology of Religion: Classic and Contemporary* (New York, 1997).

David M. Wulff

Psychosis

1. Definitions
2. Changes in Understanding
3. Types of Psychotic Disorders
4. Etiology

5. Treatment
6. Creative Illness
7. Pastoral Care

1. Definitions

The term "psychosis" denotes a mental disorder characterized by gross impairment in reality testing as evidenced by delusions, hallucinations, markedly incoherent speech, or disorganized and agitated behavior. The patient is usually without apparent awareness of the incomprehensibility of his or her behavior. In the last 50 years, no universal agreement on the exact definition of psychosis has existed. The current definition of psychotic disorders in the fourth edition (text revision) of the American Psychiatric Association's *Diagnostic and Statistical Manual* (DSM-IV-TR) focuses on the presence of symptoms such as delusions and hallucinations. Earlier definitions of psychosis, for example in DSM-II and the ninth revision of the World Health Organization's *International Classification of Diseases* (1978) focused on the severity of functional impairment rather than on symptoms. The narrowest definition of psychosis is the presence of delusions or prominent hallucinations without insight into the pathological nature of such symptoms.

The classic symptoms of psychosis are commonly described as follows:

delusions: distortions in thought content such as erroneous beliefs that stem from a distortion of perceptions or experience

hallucinations: distortions in perception of any sensory modality (auditory, visual, gustatory, olfactory, or tactile) that occur when awake but not when awakening or falling asleep; most common are auditory hallucinations experienced as voices (Hallucinations may be a normal part of religious experience in certain contexts.)

disorganized speech: manifestions of a disorder of the thinking process such as loose associations (jumping from topic to topic), tangentialness (answers seem completely unrelated to the topic or questions), or complete incoherence ("word salad")

grossly disorganized behavior: examples are extreme unpredictability, sudden outbursts of aggression, highly inappropriate behavior (e.g., public masturbation), or marked deterioration in dress or appearance compared with earlier behavior

negative symptoms: affective flattening (immobile and unresponsive face), poverty of speech (brief, laconic, empty responses), the inability to initiate and persist in goal-directed activities, and anhedonia (difficulty in everyday life of experiencing pleasure in those things that formerly were a source of enjoyment).

2. Changes in Understanding

In the last 150 years views of mental illness, and especially of psychosis, have undergone a fundamental change in → psychiatry, as well as in theology. The change is due to the advent of humanistic and then scientific psychiatry, which has caused a shift in the cultural understanding of psychotic illness (→ Health and Illness). On the one side, the term has been secularized (→ Secularization) so that no personal → guilt is assigned to patients for their condition. Those who are diagnosed as suffering from psychosis or other severe mental disorders such as → depression, who might once have been considered possessed or witches and persecuted for socioreligious reasons, are now embraced in a bond of cohumanity with those who suffer.

On the other side, there has been a tendency to refer guilt to → society. Countless studies inspired by → psychoanalysis have used biographical reconstruction (→ Biography, Biographical Research) and psychodynamic models to show that society with its unending struggles for → power (§1), conflicts of interest, and → narcissism has in childhood, in the case of the psychotic, failed to provide the acceptance whose lack does at least play a part in the development of psychopathological disorders.

3. Types of Psychotic Disorders

Currently, the following disorders are classified as psychotic: schizophrenia, schizophreniform disorder, schizoaffective disorder, delusional disorder, brief psychotic disorder, shared psychotic disorder, psychotic disorder due to a general medical condition, substance-induced psychotic disorder, and psychotic disorder not otherwise specified (DSM-IV-TR).

Schizophrenia, as a diagnosis, requires two or more of the following symptoms lasting actively for at least one month, and with some signs persisting for six months: delusions, hallucinations, disorganized speech, grossly disorganized or catatonic behavior, and negative symptoms that restrict the range and intensity of emotional expression, the influence of thought and speech, and the ability to initiate goal-directed behavior.

4. Etiology

Specific causes of schizophrenia and other psychoses are unknown. Research suggests that a combination of physiological factors may predispose to schizophrenia, including immunological, biochemical, endocrinological, and neurophysiological, some of which may be genetic (M. H. Stone). In addition, psychological, developmental, and other environmental factors no doubt play a part.

5. Treatment

Treatment of psychotic disorders requires the services of a psychiatrist, who is likely to administer psychotropic medication. A short period of hospitalization in a psychiatric or behavioral medicine facility may be required in the acute phase of illness while the patient is being stabilized. Hospitals often employ multiple treatment modalities such as the extensive use of group therapies including socialization groups, → spirituality groups, and release planning groups, as well as milieu therapy in which the structure of the treatment center is intentional as part of the healing environment. Allied health professionals including psychiatric nurses, social workers, psychologists, and clinical chaplains often lead the treatment groups.

6. Creative Illness

In certain contexts hallucinations may be a normal part of religious experience (DSM-IV-TR). Henri Ellenberger would refer to such experiences as part of a "creative illness." Creative illness is found in various settings and among → shamans, mystics of various religions, certain philosophers, as well as creative writers and other artists. A creative illness follows a period of intense preoccupation with an idea, a search for a certain kind of truth. Creative illness takes many forms, both psychotic and nonpsychotic (including neurosis, depression, and psychosomatic afflictions). Whatever the symptoms, they are experienced as painful, even agonizing. The symptoms may improve, then worsen in alternating cycles — and may go on for months or years. The subject never loses the orientation of the dominating idea or preoccupation. The obsession is often compatible with the person's profession. The individual may appear to go on normally with profession and family but is deeply self-absorbed, suffering feelings of utter isolation, even if there is a mentor or guide. The subject emerges from the ordeal with a permanent transformation of personality and the conviction of having discovered a great truth or experienced a new spiritual world.

Ellenberger cites Carl Gustav Jung (1875-1961) and Sigmund Freud (1856-1939), among others, as examples of persons who experienced creative illness. Jung's illness was quasi-psychotic, Freud's more neurotic. Anton Boisen (1876-1965), who also suffered a creative illness, discovered his mission to start clinical pastoral training during his hospitalization as a psychiatric patient. After his release and recovery, Boisen became one of the founders of the → Clinical Pastoral Education movement. Boisen believed that some psychotic illnesses are spiritual quests gone astray.

How one discerns what is psychotic and needs psychiatric treatment, and what is a creative illness or a spiritual quest gone awry, is not clear. Jung and Boisen both availed themselves of the best psychiatric wisdom available at the time — Jung, a psychiatrist himself, through self-treatment, and Boisen through personal reflection and psychiatric consultation and hospitalization. Certainly the assessment of the degree of deterioration in functioning is an important undertaking in such discernment. The most prudent course seems to suggest that a creative illness be treated as both an illness in need of psychiatric intervention and a creative opportunity for personal transformation.

7. Pastoral Care

Clergy should not attempt to offer ongoing counseling to a person experiencing psychotic symptoms but should offer → pastoral care as an adjunct to making a referral to psychiatric treatment (→ Psychotherapy). Neither pastor nor congregation, however, should abandon a person suffering from a psychotic disorder because, during illness, the person is especially in need of continuing connection to a → community of faith (W. E. Oates, *Religious Care*). Chaplains specializing in behavioral medicine can help the pastor with role clarification and in understanding ways in which care may be best offered.

The → pastor, with the permission of the patient, should not hesitate to talk with the consulting psychiatrist for suggestions as to how best to be of help to the patient and the patient's family. If the family of the patient is part of the pastor's parish, they would themselves quite naturally need pastoral support and compassionate understanding. Sometimes families may blame themselves for what has gone wrong. Or they may be angry and rebuke the patient for lack of faith, which they mistakenly assume to be the cause of the psychotic disorder. If the patient is hospitalized and then discharged, the pastor should be thoughtful and intentional in helping reintegration into the congregation. Congregational members may need help in understanding, may be fearful of the person who is or has been ill, or may be tempted to shame or blame. In such cases, the pastor can be an agent of reconciliation (→ Pastoral Care of the Sick).

Bibliography: American Psychiatric Association, *Diagnostic and Statistical Manual of Mental Disorders: DSM-IV-TR* (4th ed., text rev.; Washington, D.C., 2000) • A. T. Boisen, *The Discovery of the Inner World: A Study of Mental Disorder and Religious Experience* (Philadelphia, 1936); idem, *Out of the Depths: An Autobiographical Study of Mental Disorder and Religious Experience* (New York, 1960) • H. Ellenberger, *The Discovery of the Unconscious: The History and Evolution of Dynamic Psychiatry* (New York, 1970) • G. Fitchett et al., "The Religious Needs and Resources of Psychiatric In-patients," *Journal of Nervous and Mental Disease* 185 (May 1997) 320-26 • J. Frosch, *The Psychotic Process* (New York, 1983) • C. G. Jung, *Memories, Dreams, Reflections* (New York, 1961) • W. E. Oates, *The Religious Care of the Psychiatric Patient* (Philadelphia, 1978); idem, *When Religion Gets Sick* (Philadelphia, 1970) • P. Schilder, *On Psychoses* (New York, 1978) • H. F. Searles, *The Nonhuman Environment in Normal Development and in Schizophrenia* (New York, 1960) • A. Siirala, *The Voice of Illness: A Study in Therapy and Prophecy* (2d ed.; New York, 1981) • M. H. Stone, *The Borderline Syndromes: Constitution, Personality, and Adaptation* (New York, 1980) • World Health Organization, *International Classification of Diseases: ICD-10* (10th rev.; Geneva, 1992).

Russell H. Davis and Gaetano Benedetti

Psychotherapy

1. Definition

Psychotherapy is the treatment of mental, emotional, and behavioral disorders using psychological methods designed to help the suffering person (→ Psychology 3-4). The term "psychotherapy" is broad, covering a wide range of psychotherapeutic procedures that aim to cure or mitigate problems in living by using psychological techniques. Psychotherapy per se does not include the use of psychotropic drugs or electroconvulsive therapy, although such modalities may be employed as an adjunct to psychotherapy. Although psychotherapeutic approaches to human problems have been prevalent throughout history, even in antiquity, the field has expanded enormously since the late 19th century, based on the pioneering work of Sigmund Freud (1856-1939).

2. Basis and Goals

All psychotherapy makes use of learning processes designed to encourage growth or change. Changing the basic cognitive, emotional, and behavioral patterns is designed to offset the deleterious effects of prior experiences, either removing the effects altogether or reducing them. Psychotherapies of different types may have different goals. Classic psychoanalysis, for example, seeks enhanced personality development, as well as reduction of symptoms. Other forms and methods simply seek to relieve symptoms. As a rule, brief or short-term therapies cannot effect any broad change of personality. Relieving symptoms is indeed a worthy goal and can improve the lives of patients significantly.

Usually people seeking psychotherapy have a diagnosable mental disorder of greater or lesser severity. (For classification, see the American Psychiatric Association's DSM-IV-TR.) Some, however, seek psychotherapy for personal growth and development or to solve difficult interpersonal relationships (→ Self).

3. Methods and Settings

The 20th century produced an enormous range of schools of psychotherapy, easily hundreds of different approaches, and far too many to list here. First, there are many analytically oriented approaches that are developments or offshoots of Freud and his followers and/or dissenters. Examples of approaches arising from Freud's work include → ego psychology (Anna Freud, Heinz Hartmann, and Erik Erikson), British object relations (Melanie Klein and Donald Winnicott), self psychology (Heinz Kohut and Otto Kernberg; → Psychology of Religion 3.5), and the French school (esp. Jacques Lacan; → Psychoanalysis). Examples of offshoots and dissenters from Freud are analytic therapies based on the work of Karen Horney, Alfred Adler, Carl Gustav Jung, Otto Rank, and Harry Stack Sullivan, to name a few.

Notable among the many other schools of psychotherapy are → behavior therapy, cognitive therapies (Aaron Beck), eye movement desensitization and reprocessing (EMDR, Francine Shapiro), family systems therapy (Ivan Boszormenyi-Nagy), → Gestalt therapy (Fritz Perls), interpersonal psychotherapy (Gerald Klerman), logotherapy (Viktor Frankl), neurolinguistic programming (NLP, John Grinder), person-centered psychotherapy (Carl Rogers), psychosynthesis (Roberto Assagioli), rational-emotive therapy (Albert Ellis), and transaction analysis (Eric Berne).

Methods include talking with a psychotherapist in a confidential setting, during which the therapist will use insights and techniques based on training and theory. Besides talking, many other techniques are used in psychotherapy, but the goal is always insight and change. Some of the other therapeutic modalities are art work, body work, dance movement, hypnosis, journaling, sandbox play, and creative writing, including poetry, psychodrama, and music. These other methods, which draw more on right-brain activity, may be an excellent supplement or alternative to left-brain insight therapies.

3.1. *Psychoanalysis*

Psychoanalysis is an intensive psychotherapeutic modality. Typically, the patient sees the psychoanalyst three to five times per week, a treatment schedule that may last many years. Psychoanalysis, founded by Freud, is designed to explore the deeper layers of personality and to work with thoughts, feelings, and ideas that have been repressed or are a part of a dynamic unconscious, which reveals itself in parapraxes (e.g., so-called Freudian slips), dreams, and mental symptoms. The treatment deals with many things, including the patient's unconscious transference onto the analyst of earlier relationships, especially parental and familial relationships. The goal is to bring the unconscious into consciousness. Because of psychological resistance, change is often not once and for all but a series of steps forward, then backward, then forward again. As a result, psychoanalysis is attentive to the need not simply to gain insight but to repeatedly work through old patterns.

Traditionally, the psychoanalyst is a medical doctor with a specialty in → psychiatry and with additional years of training as a psychoanalyst. The nonmedical psychoanalyst (called a lay analyst) normally practices a modified form of psychoanalysis called psychoanalytic psychotherapy. This latter approach, although using the same basic theories, involves certain modifications of psychoanalytic techniques; in addition, the frequency of analytic sessions may be less, as little as once per week.

3.2. *Group Psychotherapy*

Group psychotherapy, involving three or more people, is a means of psychotherapeutic change based on the premise that a great deal of human behavior and emotion is an adaptation to other people. The group's composition may be heterogeneous or homogeneous with regard to age, gender, or type of problem. The therapist may be directive or may allow the group members to set the agenda for conversation.

The → group acts as a field of social experimentation. It makes confrontations with dysfunctional modes of conduct easier, since they can be observed directly, whereas in individual therapy only the patient and an expert interact. In group therapy the patient's conduct is not restricted to so narrow a sphere, since interaction is with others, as well as with the therapist. The group becomes a microcosm of the outside world and its interpersonal relationships and problems. It can be a safe place to receive feedback on personal motivation and styles of interaction, as well as the impact of one's behavior on others. The group can be a place where small steps toward change and new behaviors can be tried out experimentally before trying them in other places such as work or home. If the group is peer led, it may consist of people with similar problems (as in Alcoholics Anonymous) and may utilize a specific plan for recovery such as the 12 steps.

3.3. *Family Therapy*

Family therapy, a form of group therapy, deals with family problems. By treating the entire family, and not just the person identified as the problem, family therapy works from a frame of reference that seeks to avoid making one person the scapegoat. The family therapist often views problems as dysfunctions in the family system rather than simply problems of an individual patient (→ Family 3).

3.4. *Couples Therapy*

Couples therapy, or marriage counseling, is a triadic form of psychotherapy focused on the relationship of the couple that present themselves for treatment. The couple may or may not be married but, regardless, see themselves as being involved in a committed relationship. Sometimes couples engaged to be married seek couples therapy to work out relationship difficulties prior to → marriage.

3.5. *Behavior Therapy*

Behavior therapy, also known as behavior modification, tries to treat human behavioral disorders through the reinforcement of acceptable behavior and the suppression of unacceptable behavior. Behavior modification has its theoretical roots in the work of Ivan Pavlov (1849-1936), a Russian physiologist famous for his observation of canine behavior.

He learned that dogs could be conditioned to respond to stimuli to which otherwise they would have remained unresponsive. B. F. Skinner (1904-90) extended the research of Pavlov and found that the use of positive reinforcement has greater effects on long-term changes in behavior than negative reinforcers such as → punishment.

In behavior therapy the scientific findings regarding classic and operant conditioning (behavioral modifiers) are applied to the therapeutic treatment of human beings. Behavioral therapy uses positive reinforcement incentives to change behaviors in residential communities set up as token economies. Good behaviors are rewarded with "tokens," which can be exchanged for desired privileges, such as a walk outside on a nice day or an extra dessert with a meal. Behavioral therapy also uses aversive conditioning to help people break unwanted habits and addictions. The unwanted habitual behavior is paired with an unpleasant stimuli.

Behavioral therapists also work with people who have phobias or anxieties that prevent them from living a full life. Through systematic desensitization, a stimulus that causes anxiety is paired with a pleasant sensation, or an anxious situation is met by taking tiny, manageable steps to facing, and eventually overcoming, the fear.

3.6. *Cognitive Therapy*

Cognitive therapy is especially used to treat mood disorders such as → depression and → anxiety, as well as to treat phobias. There are several different approaches to cognitive-behavioral therapy, including rational-emotive behavior therapy (Albert Ellis) and work with depression, as pioneered by Aaron Beck. In these approaches, thoughts are considered the cause of emotions, rather than the opposite.

The therapy consists in identifying irrational thoughts and replacing them with more constructive thoughts. For example, Beck believes that many forms of depression are due to what he calls learned helplessness, a form of distorted thinking. The job of the cognitive therapist is to help the patient replace thought patterns of helplessness with cognitions of empowerment. Cognitive therapy is not an overnight process. Old habits of thought do not die easily and may require months of concentrated efforts to replace destructive thought patterns.

3.7. *Pastoral Counseling*

Pastoral counseling is a form of specialized ministry conducted by clergy with specialized training in → counseling and psychotherapy. Pastoral counselors often practice at pastoral counseling centers that offer a wide variety of psychotherapeutic services that may include, depending on the resources of the center, individual psychotherapy, couples therapy, family therapy, child and adolescent therapy, and premarital counseling. Pastoral counselors may be certified by the American Association of Pastoral Counselors, which ensures a certain measure of quality control in regard to education, training, and practice, as well as adherence to a code of ethics. Pastoral counselors are trained to be sensitive to the religious ideas and practices of their clients.

3.8. *Other Methods*

Another procedure is hypnosis, which is not much used today, though it has had something of a revival in the United States in combination with systemic procedures (W. Erickson).

→ Autogenic training is common in German-speaking areas. It is a kind of self-hypnosis, teaching that physical processes such as muscle tone, breathing, and blood circulation are influenced by corresponding ideas. This is a symptomatic therapy that is indicated in the case of less serious functional disorders of the body.

4. Indications

Psychotherapy of one type or another is indicated in a wide variety of disorders: mental, emotional, relational, and behavioral. For → psychosis, psychiatric treatment is necessary. Psychotropic medications are usually essential, and at times blood levels need to be monitored. Psychotherapeutic treatment often plays an important part as well.

5. Chances and Possibilities of Healing

The forms of therapy mentioned above can all be helpful. About one-third of those treated will experience significant improvement, and one-third some improvement. The final one-third, however, will not be essentially helped. Sometimes supportive counseling helps in medical cases where help may be given but no medical cure is possible (arteriosclerosis, diabetes, cirrhosis of the liver, etc.).

For certain severe mental disorders, psychotherapy needs to be offered as a supplement to psychiatric treatment that offers appropriate medications or other forms of psychiatric treatment. Most forms of psychotherapy demand cooperation from patients. Thus the prognosis is poorer for disorders that harm the willingness to cooperate or the ability to take initiative. The question asked by Jesus, "Do you want to be made well?" (John 5:6), is relevant also to the psychotherapy patient. What patients learn and experience in therapy they must apply outside. Any problems they experience must be brought back to therapy. In psychoanalytically oriented therapy, causes for symptoms must be found; simply describing the symptoms to the psychotherapist is not enough.

6. Confidentiality

Psychotherapists must treat patient disclosures as confidential; they are required to do so by a code of → ethics (for those who are certified psychotherapists) and by law. There are, however, certain limits on confidentiality if the patient is revealing specific information about intentions to harm self or others. In some places, such as the United States, the psychotherapist may have a duty to warn others in cases where a patient has revealed a plan to kill another person.

Participants in group therapy may or may not be under obligations for confidentiality, since most groups work out their own ground rules regarding confidentiality and other matters. The sanctions for violating confidentiality by group members may be weak, usually amounting to nothing more than exclusion from the group.

7. Finances

Financing of therapy varies from place to place. Some countries have public financing for what is essential. Some health insurance plans provide mental health benefits. Some pastoral counseling centers offer what is known as a sliding scale, offering reduced fees for those unable to pay the full fee. Agreement about the cost of psychotherapy should take place before or during the first visit.

8. Pastoral Care

The pastor of a congregation often is unable to offer pastoral psychotherapy because of limits on training and knowledge or because of the limits of time and other duties. Since many people seek out their minister first during times of difficulty, the caring pastor will know the limits of his or her training and abilities and will have developed the art of the ministry of introduction (referral) to mental health professionals and psychotherapists. The pastor would do well to develop a list of mental health specialists of various kinds so as to be able to make an intelligent referral at the time of the pastoral consultation. The pastor should be fully supportive of the referral and should avoid the suggestion that the need for psychotherapeutic help is due to weak faith. The task of psychotherapeutic healing is difficult enough without the suggestion from church or pastor that there is a conflict between psychotherapy and religion.

The pastor might consider assuring parishioners seeking outside help that the church's commitment to them will continue and that a referral does not indicate abandonment or lack of interest. Rather, the intention is to expand, rather than diminish, the circle of care (→ Pastoral Care). The pastor, while continuing to be faithful to the pastoral care of the congregants, should resist the pressure some people may bring to rehash and critique each psychotherapeutic visit, thus using the pastor surreptitiously as a second psychotherapist.

→ Clinical Pastoral Education; Crisis Intervention; Narcissism; Pastoral Psychology

Bibliography: American Psychiatric Association, *Diagnostic and Statistical Manual of Mental Disorders: DSM-IV-TR* (4th ed., text rev.; Washington, D.C., 2000) • M. F. Basch, *Doing Psychotherapy* (New York, 1980) • I. Boszormenyi-Nagy, *Intensive Family Therapy: Theoretical and Practical Aspects* (New York, 1985) • J. Ehrenwald, ed., *The History of Psychotherapy: From Healing Magic to Encounter* (New York, 1976) • A. Francis, J. Clarkin, and S. Perry, *Differential Therapeutics in Psychiatry: The Art and Science of Treatment Selection* (New York, 1984) • W. Gaylin, *Talk Is Not Enough: How Psychotherapy Really Works* (Boston, 2000) • J. Grinder and R. Bandler, *Trance-Formations: Neuro-Linguistic Programming and the Structure of Hypnosis* (Moab, Utah, 1981) • C. G. Jung, *The Practice of Psychotherapy: Essays on the Psychology of the Transference and Other Subjects* (New York, 1954) • M. Klein, *The Psychoanalysis of Children* (London, 1932) • H. Kohut, *How Does Analysis Cure?* (Chicago, 1984) • J. H. Massermann, *Principles of Dynamic Psychiatry, Including an Integrative Approach to Abnormal and Clinical Psychology* (Philadelphia, 1946) • F. Perl et al., *Gestalt Therapy: Excitement and Growth in the Human Personality* (New York, 1951) • C. R. Rogers, *Counseling and Psychotherapy: Newer Concepts in Practice* (Cambridge, Mass., 1942) • A. Roth et al., *What Works for Whom? A Critical Review of Psychotherapy Research* (New York, 1996) • R. Schafer, *The Analytic Attitude* (New York, 1983) • F. Shapiro, *Eye Movement Desensitization and Reprocessing* (New York, 2001) • D. W. Winnicott, *Therapeutic Consultations in Child Psychiatry* (New York, 1971) • I. D. Yalom, *The Theory and Practice of Group Psychotherapy* (New York, 1975).

Russell H. Davis, Karl König,
and Falk Leichsenring

Public Health

2. Environment, Sanitation, and Demography
3. Reorientation
4. Relevance and Challenges

Public health is the science and art of promoting → health, preventing disease, and prolonging life through the organized efforts of society. Christianity has had a great influence on the evolution of public health from ancient to modern times. The role of Christianity and its practice of assisting in the implementation of public health strategies have been significant throughout history in most regions in the world.

1. Critical Christian Contributions

1.1. *Valuing All Humanity Equally*

The Judeo-Christian understanding that humankind is created in the image of God (Gen. 1:27) and that all are equally precious to God has contributed to valuing all individuals equally in health-care provision. This perspective has been further strengthened by the biblical imperative to relate to, and make a difference in, the lives of vulnerable persons and communities (Matt. 25:40). This value has been evident from the life of Jesus and his disciples throughout the centuries.

1.2. *Community Health*

The significant responses of Christians in serving whole communities in times of epidemics and health crises are obvious. Notable in history have been the responses to plague, leprosy, tuberculosis, smallpox, and, more recently, HIV-AIDS. Whether in the Byzantine monasteries of the Judean desert in the 4th and 5th centuries, sanitary cordons and quarantine stations in medieval Europe, leper colonies in Asia and Latin America in the 19th century, or hospices and home-based care services in Africa during the 20th century, the involvement of churches has contributed to, and continues to aid in, the control of epidemics and of the spread of ill health among communities (→ Medical Missions). Care continues to be mobilized for whole communities, valuing individuals, while seeing each person as part of the larger community. This care has been possible not only because of the churches' assistance to health care through church infrastructure but also because of the churches' contribution to the development and training of health professionals. Christianity provides the roots to vibrant volunteerism and a sense of calling and vocation to those involved in church-related health services.

Ethical practice in public health service provision is first documented in history in the OT. It was the fear of the Lord that motivated midwives in Egypt to disobey Pharaoh and not kill newborn Jewish males (Exod. 1:15-18). But through the centuries it was clear that providing "just care" was beyond merely disobeying unjust stipulations; it was, rather, the intentional provision of services to the most vulnerable and the empowerment of the → marginalized.

2. Environment, Sanitation, and Demography

The Bible clearly documents the importance that ancient communities gave to environmental and sanitation issues. The biblical traditions that have been built on these values contributed to the development of public health. The importance of cleanliness was always emphasized (Lev. 20:22-26; Prov. 30:11-12), yet the Bible's teachings consistently stressed that cleanliness and purity were matters of the heart and of one's conduct and therefore went deeper than merely the meticulous keeping of ceremonial rituals. Proper sanitary practices (e.g., Deut. 23:12-13) were stipulated to preserve and promote the health of communities. Purification of water so that it could be consumed has been documented (Exod. 15:22-27; 2 Kgs. 2:19-22). Instructions were given not to contaminate water sources for the benefit of the larger community. The fact that mildew within houses and clothing was considered a serious issue (Lev. 14:33-55) also shows the sensitivity of these ancient societies to issues of housing, ventilation, and cleanliness.

Epidemiology and statistics, which are critical contemporary sciences that equip the study and provision of public health, stem from a clear biblical tradition. Numbers 1 describes the taking of a census of the people of Israel. All males aged 20 and upward were counted under the leadership of Moses (v. 3). This tradition of meticulous documentation — including membership in the community, baptisms, and deaths — has been maintained in Christian communities through the centuries. These records provided the basis of pioneering works such as John Graunt's *Observations on the Bills of Mortality* (1662) and Johann Süssmilch's *Die Göttliche Ordnung* (The divine order, 1741), which analyzed the populations of parishes in order to establish mortality tables. These works set the basis of the development of both demographics and statistics.

3. Reorientation

For over 100 years since the 19th century, medical work provided a main focus for Christian missionary work, along with → evangelism and → education. As a result, by the 1960s thousands of Christian hospitals served the health-care needs of the developing world. With changing perceptions of health care in a rapidly developing world, however, the fact that more than 90 percent of the resources for the healing ministry was devoted to curative medicine was brought into question. Two Tübingen consultations, coorganized by the → World Council of Churches (WCC), the → Lutheran World Federation (LWF), and the German Institute for Medical Mission (DIFÄM) in 1964 and 1968, addressed many of these questions. These processes called for an integrated witness in which medical work would be correlated with social work (→ Social Services), nutrition, agriculture, and community development, a recognition that medical care is only one component of the diversity of disciplines necessary to promote and maintain health.

This conclusion led to the formation of the Christian Medical Commission (CMC) in 1968. The CMC, a unit of the WCC, assisted in the reorientation of the churches' health care toward a more comprehensive and community-oriented service. In consequence of CMC's close working relationship with the World Health Organization (WHO) in Geneva, its grassroots experience of the issues of community health was channeled to this international, intergovernmental body. Churches were able to make high-quality experiential and experimental contributions to a joint study process entitled "Alternative Approaches to Meeting Basic Health Needs of Populations in Developing Countries," undertaken by the WHO and the U.N. International Children's Emergency Fund (UNICEF).

The process of demystifying health care so that services could be tailored to the needs of the communities, with local populations being involved in the formulation of policy and the delivery of the system, led to the development of "primary health care." The philosophy of primary health care stressed an integrated approach of preventive, curative, and promotive health services both for the community and for the individual. This approach was adopted by the WHO in 1977, and it brought about a radical shift in the priorities of the WHO, with global implications in decentralizing health care and placing greater rights and responsibilities on people for managing their own health. The participation of the churches in the evolution of both the theory and the practice of primary health care has been a lasting contribution to public health.

In the 1970s Christian communities in developing countries began to train village health workers at the grassroots level. Equipped with essential drugs and simple methods, these workers have been able to treat most common diseases and to promote the use of clean water and better hygienic conditions. They facilitated the introduction of small health centers that offer low-cost in-patient care, as well as prenatal and early childhood health services. In these new decentralized health-care systems, many mission hospitals began to play the essential role of acting as intermediaries between local village health services and centralized, state-supported hospitals.

4. Relevance and Challenges

Many of the policies promoted by this new view of primary health care could not be effectively implemented by governments on a global basis. The recovery in the second half of the 1990s from the economic recession that had begun in the 1970s benefited only developed, and a few emerging, economies. The new millennium is showing increased levels of → poverty and greater inequalities between groups within regions and countries. The HIV-AIDS epidemic that is sweeping large parts of world, the resurgence of communicable diseases such as tuberculosis and malaria, complex natural disasters, ever-present violence and civil strife, and the displacement of populations have further compromised already stretched economies and limping health services. Political changes, the growth of populations, rapid and unplanned urbanization, and the degradation of the environment have also continued to challenge the ability of human societies to take care of their own health (→ Environmental Ethics).

In these situations the churches, which continue to be present throughout the developing world, maintain their focus on providing health care and services to remote, vulnerable, or impoverished communities, empowering them to take care of their own health. There are prominent challenges that certain conservative interpretations of Christianity place on key facets of public health such as reproductive health. Opposing ethical views regarding family planning and → birth control pose challenges to scientifically accepted norms of public health practice. It is therefore crucial for the different ecclesial traditions, disciplines, and service sectors to engage in creative dialogue. For the greater good of society there needs to be mutual challenge, which recognizes the integrity of the respective contributions to public health.

Bibliography: C. Benn and E. Senturias, "Health, Healing, and Wholeness in the Ecumenical Discussion," *IRM* 90 (2001) 7-25 • J. C. McGilvray, *The Quest for Health and Wholeness* (Tübingen, 1981) • G. Paterson, *The CMC Story* (= *Contact* [Geneva], no. 161/162

[1998]) • S. Sabbatani, "Health Service Organization during the Age of Pestilence," *Infez-Med* 11/4 (2003) 216-21 • J. Wilkinson, *Christian Healing and the Congregation* (Geneva, 1965).

Manoj Kurian

Public Theology

1. Term
2. Development of the Concept
3. Politics and Public Theology
4. Contributions of Roman Catholicism
5. The Emerging Global Civil Society
6. Christianity and Public Theology

1. Term

The term "public theology," of recent vintage, is often compared and contrasted with → "civil religion" and → "political theology." But each has a distinct genealogy, and each entails a particular set of assumptions and implications. Moreover, each of these differs from the Scriptures, confessions, and practices of various Christian traditions, even as each draws on them. The use of "public" is important, for it not only refers to public opinion as shaped by public worship, public schools, public health, public events, publicly held corporations, and so forth, all of which are related to, but distinct from, government.

The term also points to the creation of a new cross-cultural public that is broader than most of the world has previously imagined. Public life is no longer organized only by national identities, each with its own civil religion, nor only by political units, each with its own creed authorized by the state, although both remain. In this regard, public theology involves the current attempt to find a more inclusive, genuinely ecumenical, and catholic way of identifying a valid convictional and ethical framework on which to build the moral and spiritual architecture of an increasingly common life that will suffice for this global era.

2. Development of the Concept

The term "public theology" was first used in America by the well-known historian of religion Martin Marty (b. 1928). Initially, he wrote about the "public church," the attempts by religious bodies to influence political policy, or "public religion," which shared much with the concept "civil religion." He noticed that religious influence often becomes institutionalized in cultural convictions. But when writing on Reinhold → Niebuhr (1892-1971) and the development of "Christian realism" after the political-military struggles of World War II, he used the term "public theology" to identify the recognition of a new kind of issue, a contest between kinds of societies. The term was new, but it gained currency rather quickly, not because of its novelty or because the theological concerns to which it pointed were new, but because it seemed to capture one wide and deep, but widely neglected, strand of the classical theological tradition.

The idea is rooted in the interaction of biblical insight, philosophical analysis, and the ethical conviction that believers have the responsibility to engage in historical discernment and formation (or reformation) of the social order by giving it a new center, the church, and in and through that new center to have an effect on moral, familial, economic, political, cultural, and vocational life. Religious or social practices that are tempted to idolatry or arrogance could be brought under critique for distorting the fabric of the common life, as could forms of belief and behavior that could not offer normative guidance for the new forms of life in increasingly complex societies. The power of God's reign, it was believed, was working within and among the powers and principalities of the world, and it would harness and transform them so that they might contribute to the common good.

The deeper roots of this tradition had long presumed that theologians, clergy, and committed laity could and should draw on theological resources to teach, preach, and organize publicly to advance issues of truth, faith, and justice in society. They saw themselves as agents of Christ, the prophet, priest, and prince of peace, who had inaugurated the → kingdom of God that works within and among believers, in the church and throughout the fabric of civil society, often under the radar of political authority. The advocates of this view were convinced that they must take responsibility for the spiritual and moral architecture of the common life as the medieval church had done after the collapse of the → Roman Empire, as the → Reformers had done in the free cities of early modern Europe, and as the → Puritans and Pietists (→ Pietism) had done with regard to the formation of a society on the frontiers of America.

This tradition was interpreted in the age of industrialization in a way that honored those who — at the time of the → Social Gospel and later, in another way, the → civil rights movement — built not only the churches and the missionary societies, but also the schools and the hospitals, the industries and the unions, the stores and the banks, the railroads and steamships, the museums and the concert halls. The activists in these movements were creating a new kind of public world, one with many centers, many discrete pyramids of power, and many points of entry, with each sphere of human activity having its own basic logic and distinctive ethic, but with each also serving the whole society by building participatory and self-governing institutions, many of them voluntary associations, advocacy groups, "nongovernmental organizations," and a host of both nonprofit and profit-oriented corporations and foundations. This latter point is a matter of considerable contention, for some public theologians see the modern corporations as a decisive feature of the new sense of public life, while others see them as the primary corrupting force of civil society and call upon government to control them more extensively.

In any case, unlike the heritage of civil religion, public theology does not celebrate the solidarity of the social system and its → culture as it is. It critically evaluates that culture and selectively embraces some parts, while repudiating others. Furthermore, and unlike political theology, it neither seeks direct political power nor calls for radical transformation with a utopian vision enforced by governmental authority. It is reformist in style and intent more than it is conservative or revolutionary, and it takes this stand believing that this approach is the fruit of authentic → theology. Some things in life were and are created → good, and some were and are particularly subject to a fall into → evil.

Today, throughout those parts of the world that we used to call the → Third World, before the so-called Second World collapsed, it became recognized that that Third World lives also in the First World, and the First in the midst of the Third. Evangelical and Pentecostal movements in these contexts often induce lifestyle changes that alter the common life and indirectly even the political contours of a region, less by direct political agendas than by changing the fabric of the social interaction in families and communities and hence the institutions of civil society and the inherited culture. Efforts to develop "faith-based" social service agencies in America are rooted in the belief that this approach is a decisive means of creative social change and human service.

In light of this history, we can identify two main reasons for using the adjective "public." One is very simple: it is a modest protest against the dominant understandings of political theology and philosophy, which tend to use "public" only in regard to governmental programs. This protest is based on the conviction that the public is prior to the republic, that the fabric of civil society is, over time, prior to and determinative of governmental policy. Second, the core of society is inevitably the religious faith that is held among the people, assuming that it is a faith able to generate an articulate and effective theory of the organization of human social relations. Such a core is more determinative of, and normatively more important for, politics than politics is for society and religion.

3. Politics and Public Theology

→ Politics in human affairs makes great waves, like a hurricane or tsunami on the surface of the ocean, which has great and dramatic effects when it hits human habitats. These massive storms, however, seldom change the deeper tides, currents, or patterns of the ocean or of human civilization. At deeper levels, the ways in which the powers and principalities of life are ordered make a much greater difference over time, even determining what political storms get played out. Yet, public theology cannot be said to be antipolitical. Those who speak of public theology are well aware that arrangements for the building of police, military, judicial, educational, and infrastructural institutions (involving roads, bridges, harbors, etc.) are inevitably necessary and that all citizens must be willing to pay appropriate levels of taxes to do collectively what cannot be effectively done separately. And they are aware that principles developed in the theological tradition to guide choices about the just and unjust use of coercive force by legitimate authority are required to defend the civil society from violent disruption from within or invasion from without.

Politics, however, must be the limited and constrained servant of the other institutions of society, not their master. A people tutored to see both the reality of → sin and the prospect of an improved fabric of society will find ways to organize and constrain political institutions so that they do not seek to comprehend or dominate life. But there is a suspicion of antitheological political philosophies: if governments are not guided by an adequate public theology, mediated through the consciousness of the people, hopes for a utopian future can become apocalyptic in its destructiveness or imperial in its pretenses.

4. Contributions of Roman Catholicism

The idea that the faith can and should not only address believers in the faith community in ways that touch their souls but also empower the faithful to address the world in its wider structures and dynamics is often represented by certain themes in Roman

Catholic theology, both in its classic heritage and in its more recent developments. Such faith functions by developing the kind of realistic ethic that can form, assess, and reform, as needed, the institutions of civil society. The term "public theology" was not in currency, but the idea that key doctrines held and taught by the church can and should address "all people of good will" and are in principle understandable by all was routinely stated in official documents. Moreover, several notable Catholic thinkers who became public voices and unofficial representatives of theology in public discourse made a major mark. Jacques Maritain (1882-1973), for example, did much to advance the cause of human → rights during the drafting of the U.N. Universal Declaration of Human Rights, and John Courtney Murray (1904-67) defended the ethical validity of → democracy and → pluralism in ways that have gradually been accepted by much of the church.

This Catholic accent was cultivated further by a number of contemporary Roman Catholic thinkers such as theologian David Tracy, who has explicitly used the term "public theology" to identify the several publics that theology must address, including → church, → society, and the academy. He and others have drawn not only from the legacies of Maritain and Murray but from a close encounter with Protestant theology and with the widening scope of Catholic teachings in the → social encyclicals, from *Rerum novarum* (1891) on labor by Leo XIII, through *Quadragesimo anno* (1931) on the ideas of subsidiarity by Pius XI, to *Pacem in terris* (1963) by John XXIII, and perhaps most powerfully in *Centesimus annus* (1991) by John Paul II. Some of these documents have also addressed the role of economic and familial values in society. This reading of the tradition influenced Vatican statements to the → United Nations on → racism, human rights, pluralism, and the principle of → subsidiarity.

5. The Emerging Global Civil Society

Implicit in the view that various publics are emerging as dominating influences on the world scale is the prospect that a highly pluralistic global civil society may be emerging, what some believe could become the basis of a complex worldwide civilization. The most notable fact about this development is that it is happening without an integrated political order to guide it, although most scholarly treatments of this issue evidence a deep concern with extending the principles of freedom of religion, a pluralistic civil society, an open economic system, a legal system that defends human rights, and a limited state.

At the same time, twin perils are obviously afoot in the emerging global society: an apocalyptic fanaticism and a pretentious imperialism. To prevent the triumph of either, society needs to see how the various publics of an increasingly complex and worldwide civil society can be ordered into a differentiated, complex, and open system. This is an empirical and theoretical issue of great practical consequence: whether the various public spheres can preserve their distinctive character yet work together sufficiently to be a viable cluster of powers with moral authority that can be and should be prior to a regime.

To put the matter another way: public theology differs from political theology precisely in that public theology tends to adopt a social theory of politics, and political theology inclines to have a political view of society. Public theology is, oddly, like socialist theory in that it too sees the fabric of society as decisive for every area of the common life and determinative for the political regime. It differs from → socialism, however, in that it does not see class conflict as the fundamental characteristic of society — either in theory or in fact — and does not expect the state to control economic life by centralized planning and capitalization designed to abolish that conflict. This orientation contrasts also with that of political theology in that the latter tends to see politics, focused in populist movements supporting a centralized government, as the comprehending influence in society and the primary guarantor of viability. Politics, in this view, is dedicated to the accumulation, organization, and exercise of the kind of power that sees itself as responsible for the control and guidance of all the social institutions within a geographic territory. In this respect, political theology has tended to be closer to the way socialism actually worked.

A nonsocialist social theory of politics sees every political order as subject over time to the more primary powers in society, those spheres of life that embody moral and spiritual orientations and associations that are socially, ethically, and temporally prior to the formation of political orders. People's interests indeed play a role in each of the spheres of civil society; but public theology holds that these interests can be modulated and guided by religious and ethical conviction. In this view, political parties, regimes, and policies come and go. They are always necessary, but they are also always the by-product of religious, cultural, familial, economic, and professional traditions that are prior to government. Every government is, sooner or later, accountable to those traditions. Ideally, the political order itself becomes merely one of a series of spheres in the societal complex, having its own authority, just as the economy, academia, medicine, and the → family do. All of these spheres are in various ways subject to each other, while maintaining their own distinctive purposes, which ought not be invaded by the political order.

The most decisive long-term questions of the common life are thus how the prepolitical organizations of life are ordered in relation to the other sectors of life and, deeper still, what religious or ethical presumptions they seek to incarnate; these are the basic issues of public theology. For this reason, public theology has a preference for social theories of life and history that recognize how cultural, familial, economic, and intellectual traditions are shaped by religion. It then will seek to critically evaluate the comparative consequences of various kinds of world and civil religions in terms of the quality of civilization they generate or sustain.

6. Christianity and Public Theology

One key question, in view of these factors, is whether Christianity has anything special to offer as a public theology for a world in which a global civil society is being formed, albeit without a clear or centered political order. Does Christianity have normative models of how to order complex civil societies that reach beyond any single nation-state? There is a serious debate in contemporary social science as to whether a global civil society can be developed, and if so, what values will be at its core, as secular scholars such as John Keane and Mary Kaldor have debated without reference to religion. Scholars who reflect on the fragile civil societies of China and India are asking parallel questions. To mention these cross-cultural facts in the context of such questions about Christianity reveals a key assumption of public theology: it generally presumes that it is possible to discuss these matters on a cross-cultural and interreligious basis. Theology is a proper subject for public discourse.

The strongest arguments from a Christian theological perspective for this prospect draw on traditions that were engendered in critical times of transition, when it was necessary to reach out to perspectives other than those already at hand. A key historical example of this way of viewing matters is represented by the thought of Johannes Althusius (1557-1638), who understood society as a constructed fabric, a "consociation of consociations," a federation of "covenanted" communities under universal laws. Another, more recent, example is Abraham Kuyper (1837-1920), who developed a basic theory of the relative sovereignty of the "spheres" of life, a view that paralleled Ernst → Troeltsch's (1865-1923) "departments of life." In another way, the Gifford Lectures of 1948, by Emil Brunner (1889-1966), engaged these issues for Europe after the devastation of World War II and drew attention to the necessary reconstruction of the inner fabric of the several social systems that constitute society.

All of these public theological voices depended on the basic doctrine of the sovereignty of God, a doctrine that implies that all areas of life are under God and thus no earthly power can be sovereign over them all. Such doctrines raise the issue of how we should seek to order the relationship of these areas of life while keeping maximum freedom, under God, for each area, and while also working with other religions, cultures, and traditions, since they too share the basic capacity to discern the principles of right and wrong and live in societies also built on analogous spheres of social life, even if they have differing views of ultimate salvation.

In sum, then, public theology agrees with political theology against civil religion that the moral fabric of the common life is not simply the "bottom-up" sentiments or experiences of a particular community projected into the heavens in an act of cultural self-celebration. Rather, the moral fabric of the common life is a centripetal source of normative thought and life, rooted in revelatory insight. However, public theology sees this "top-down" reality as having implications, not in the first instance for the political order, but for personal convictions, the communities of faith, and the associations and patterns of life that they generate in an open society. These groupings will inevitably be plural and in contention but capable of moral ordering; the principles and purposes that order their interests do not stay in the religious community or in private associations. They work their way through the convictions of the people and the policies of the multiple institutions of civil society where the people live and work and play, which make up the primary public realm.

Indeed, public theology tends to hold that these conviction-incarnate centers in the lives of the public are, together, the most decisive core of life in civilization. With proper cultivation and development, they are refined as they work their way not from the bottom up, nor from the top down, but from the center out. They show up eventually in the formation of a limited political order that serves the people, protects their human rights, and allows the multiple institutions and spheres of a pluralistic society to flourish in an unavoidably sinful, but nevertheless morally and spiritually edified, community of communities.

Bibliography: V. E. Bacote, *The Spirit in Public Theology: Appropriating the Legacy of Abraham Kuyper* (Grand Rapids, 2005) • R. Benne, *The Paradoxical Vision: A Public Theology for the Twenty-first Century* (Minneapolis, 1995) • E. H. Breitenberg Jr., "To Tell the Truth: Will the Real Public Theology Please Stand Up?" *JSCE* 23/2 (2003) 55-96 • T. Brook and B. M. Frolic, eds., *Civil Society in China* (Armonk, N.Y., 1997) • E. Brunner, *Christianity and Civilization* (2 vols.; New York, 1948) • F. Carney, trans., *The Politics of Johannes Althusius* (Boston, 1964) • G. Das, *India Unbound: From Independence to the Global Information Age* (London, 2002) • M. Kaldor, *Global Civil Society: An Answer to War* (Cambridge, 2003) • J. Keane, *Global Civil Society?* (New York, 2002) • L. Lugo, ed., *Religion, Pluralism, and Public Life: Abraham Kuyper's Legacy for the Twenty-first Century* (Grand Rapids, 2000) • M. E. Marty, "Reinhold Niebuhr: Public Theology and the American Experience," *JR* 54 (1974) 332-59 • J. W. Skillen and R. M. McCarthy, eds., *Political Order and the Plural Structure of Society* (Atlanta, 1991) • M. L. Stackhouse, *Public Theology and Political Economy: Christian Stewardship in Modern Society* (Lanham, Md., 1991) • W. F. Storrar and A. R. Morton, eds., *Public Theology for the Twenty-first Century* (London, 2004) • D. Tracy, *The Analogical Imagination: Christian Theology and the Culture of Pluralism* (New York, 1981).

Max L. Stackhouse

Publishing → Christian Publishing

Puebla → Latin American Councils 2.5

Pulpit

The English word "pulpit" (Lat. *pulpitum,* "platform") recalls the desk for the reading of Scripture. German uses *Kanzel,* from Lat. *cancelli,* a tribunal's latticed screen. *Cancelli* were adopted in the early Christian basilica to demarcate the place of the clergy, and from there the sermon was delivered. The French term is *chaire,* which recalls the → bishop's *cathedra,* from whence he spoke until about A.D. 400.

Pulpits did not come into general use in parish churches until the 12th and 13th centuries; many fine wooden examples have survived from this era. The → Reformation emphasis on the Word and the Counter-Reformation stress on teaching (→ Catholic Reform and Counterreformation) brought pulpits into common use.

Protestants made the relation between pulpit and → altar a theological issue. Under the influence of Joseph Furttenbach (1591-1667) and Leonhard Christoph Sturm (1669-1719), Lutheran churches adopted the *Prinzipalstück,* that is, a single focus of altar, font, pulpit, and → organ. Neo-Gothic 19th-century churches often have a desk and pulpit on each side of the altar, while newly designed churches of the 20th century have a tendency to use a lectern for both Bible readings and sermon, with the abandonment of a large and lofty pulpit.

An interesting development in a few English churches was the three-decker pulpit with desk, lectern, and pulpit on different levels. To preserve the centrality of both pulpit and holy table, a Carlisle church in northern England used a movable pulpit that was routinely moved to a central position for the sermon and then moved back to the side.

→ Church Architecture

Bibliography: J. A. Jungmann, *The Mass of the Roman Rite* (2 vols.; New York, 1951-55) 1.391-461 • G. Langmaack, "Der gottesdienstliche Ort," *Leit.* 1.366-433 • W. M. Marshall, "Ambo," *NCE* (2d ed.) 1.334-36 • G. Randall, *Church Furnishing and Decoration in England and Wales* (London, 1980).

J. G. Davies†

Punishment

1. Legal Aspects

1.1. *Sanctions*

Legally, punishment is meant to right a wrong by inflicting something painful that brings to light public disapproval of the misconduct. Punishments are legal sanctions that are imposed by the courts when → guilt is proved. They may take different forms: imprisonment, fines, or a prohibition of travel. They may also include measures to guard against any further acts when a person is indicted for what is against the law but does not merit imprisonment (e.g., consignment to a psychiatric hospital). Further sanctions consist of warnings, suspended sentences, or confiscation. Special punishments apply to young people, who are often put under a (nonpenal) course of education or discipline.

We must also take into account the punishments that the church inflicts, which apply theoretically to all members of the community if they violate the elementary principles of Christian fellowship (→ Church Discipline). A biblical basis for the church's actions may be found in Matt. 16:18-19; 18:15-18; John 20:23; 1 Corinthians 5; 6:9-10; Gal. 5:19-21. The aim is to bring about a change of conduct in those affected. The punishment might take the form of exclusion from the → Eucharist or of taking away rights of membership such as the vote (→ Church Membership 5), but total exclusion from membership is inflicted only as a last resort. In fact, measures of this kind have little effect because offenders treat them with indifference. The → Roman Catholic Church has its own law involving either suspension or → excommunication and, in the case of clergy, removal from office and the loss of ministry or rights (1983 → CIC 1311-99). The aim in the former case is that of amendment, but in that of priests the punishment is that of expiation.

1.2. *Aims and Justification*

Various theories are advocated in justification of punishment. On the basis of a formulation of Protagoras (ca. 485-ca. 410 B.C.; → Greek Philosophy 3) handed down by Seneca (ca. 4 B.C.–A.D. 65), a distinction must be made between absolute and relative theories: *nemo prudens punit, quia peccatum est, sed ne peccetur* (a sensible person does not punish a man because he has sinned but in order to keep him from sin, *De ira* 1.19.7). On an absolute theory the punishment does not serve future aims but is *a fulfillment of justice.* In the form of the theory of retribution, such theories found their high point in the philosophy of German → idealism. Immanuel Kant (1724-1804; → Kantianism) in his *Metaphysik der Sitten* (Metaphysics of morals, 1797) sharply rejected utilitarian justifications of punishment (→ Utilitarianism) and demanded strict retribution according to a priori laws of righteousness. G. W. F. Hegel (1770-1831; → Hegelianism) in his *Grundlinien der Philosophie des Rechts* (Elements of the philosophy of right, 1821) called punishment a negation of the negation and therefore a removal of the transgression and a restoration of law.

A second form of an absolute theory, the law of punishment *as expiation,* stresses more strongly the individual → reconciliation of the evildoer with the legal society, or with the divine order against which he or she has offended, by personally bearing the guilt and accepting punishment. This view has been found not only in Christian social teachings but also in legal circles. A criticism is that it does not offer any metaphysical basis in theories of justice. It also neglects the individual malefactor and his or her social problems (→ Biography, Biographical Research).

In a relative theory, punishment serves *as a deterrence* against any future wrongdoing. For many years theories of general deterrence thought punishment would ward off potential criminals, but the reference today is more to the strengthening of fidelity to the law on the part of the population as a whole, and to the maintaining of confidence that the law will be upheld and applied. Where the theory of deterrence takes a more specific form, it serves especially to prevent any return to crime on the part of the individual malefactor. According to the "Marburg Program" (1882) of Franz von Liszt (1851-1919), the type of criminal and various views of criminality call for three approaches: amendment or → rehabilitation through education, protection of the public by imprisonment, and individual deterrence through threat of punishment.

A criticism of a general theory of deterrence is that it tends to get out of control and that it does not really deter. Most European students of jurisprudence and criminologists, although not in the United States and certain other countries, reject the → death penalty. Special deterrence is again open to question as a sanction if wrongdoers suffer from severe defects in socialization or from disturbances in personality. Doubts necessarily arise about the efficiency of rehabilitation, and the result is a crisis relating to the validity of punishment. In Germany, for example, questions have been raised regarding the dominant policy of special deterrence. The neoclassicism widespread in the United States has led to a revival of theories of retribution or general deterrence, with a great growth in prisons that is unusual in a democratic society. Abolition, or at least an end of imprisonment, suggests itself as an alternative. In practice it would be possible to decriminalize both lesser offenses and a minimum use of narcotics.

Many of the findings in research into criminal

sanctions, however, still support the modest efficacy of rehabilitation and the contribution of laws of punishment to a better keeping of the law by the population at large, even without any special severity. Theories that combine general and special deterrence now predominate, with the law of retribution in decline. Jurisprudence still maintains that punishment must take place in the sphere of guilt, so that even "from below" it cannot abandon the thought of a repayment of guilt (→ Law and Legal Theory).

1.3. *Types of Punishment Past and Present*
The law of revenge and clan feuding as the basis of punishment were largely replaced by expiatory punishments. The Peace of God in the 11th to the 15th centuries gave added strength to state law in place of private action (→ Peace 2.2.3; Middle Ages 1.2.2). At the beginning of the Middle Ages corporal punishment was still dominant. The 17th and 18th centuries regarded the beginning of modern imprisonment in Amsterdam (1596) as a move in the right direction.

With the rise of criminological study at the end of the 19th century, the insight gained ground that even imprisonment should be avoided because it has desocializing effects. Germany has seen considerable progress against imprisonment. It now has the lowest numbers in prison in Europe, though the criminals who are imprisoned serve longer terms.

1.4. *International Perspectives*
Internationally, the discussion is focused on the abolishment of capital punishment, which is rejected in many industrial nations for humanitarian reasons and for its ineffectiveness as a means of criminal policy, although the United States, Japan, and many Third World countries still maintain this form of punishment. Many countries have taken up the cause against long imprisonment, although at the end of the 20th century there were signs of retrenchment, not least in a country like Sweden, which has hitherto been marked by liberal policies in this regard. The Netherlands and Finland provide for imprisonment of only a few weeks, a "short sharp shock." Fines may also be used. Community service plays a part either as an independent sanction, as in France, Britain, and some states in the United States, or under direction. Restitution has gained ground, as in the compensation order in Britain, the Victim and Witness Protection Act (1982) in the United States, and the "active repentance" set up in Austria as a reason to waive punishment. The "contract treatment" advanced in Sweden and the United States is a voluntary action on the principle of therapy instead of punishment.

All these alternatives to traditional punishment face the danger of what is called "net widening," that is, the intensifying and extending of sanctions. Nations must meet the danger by legal limitations (consent, temporal limits, suitability) and by procedural guarantees.

→ Ethics; Freedom; Penitence; Responsibility; Rights

Bibliography: H. A. Bedau, ed., *The Death Penalty in America: Current Controversies* (New York, 1997) • J. W. Doig, ed., *Criminal Corrections: Ideals and Realities* (Lexington, Ky., 1983) • EKD, *Strafe, Tor zur Versöhnung? Eine Denkschrift der Evangelischen Kirche in Deutschland zum Strafvollzug* (Gütersloh, 1990) • L. M. Friedman, *Crime and Punishment in American History* (New York, 1993) • B. Galaway and J. Hudson, *Restorative Justice: International Perspectives* (Monsey, N.Y., 1996) • J. Gilligan and B. Lee, "Beyond the Prison Paradigm: From Provoking Violence to Preventing It by Creating 'Anti-Prisons' (Residential Colleges and Therapeutic Communities)," *Annals of the New York Academy of Science* 1036 (December 2004) 300-324 • L. Griffith, *The Fall of the Prison: Biblical Perspectives on Prison Abolition* (Grand Rapids, 1993) • G. Kaiser, *Kriminologie* (3d ed.; Heidelberg, 1996) • H. M. Kritzer, ed., *Legal Systems of the World: A Political, Social, and Historical Encyclopedia* (4 vols.; Santa Barbara, Calif., 2002) • J. J. Megivern, *The Death Penalty: An Historical and Theological Survey* (New York, 1997) • B.-D. Meier, *Strafrechtliche Sanktionen* (2d ed.; Berlin, 2001) • S. Nathanson, *An Eye for an Eye? The Morality of Punishing by Death* (Totowa, N.J., 1987) • A. R. Roberts, ed., *Critical Issues in Crime and Justice* (Thousand Oaks, Calif., 2003) • H. Schöch, *Empfehlen sich Änderungen und Ergänzungen bei den strafrechtlichen Sanktionen ohne Freiheitsentzug. Gutachten zum 59. Deutschen Juristentag* (Munich, 1992) • F. Streng, *Strafrechtliche Sanktionen* (2d ed.; Stuttgart, 2002) • United Nations, *The Eleventh United Nations Congress on Crime Prevention and Criminal Justice* (New York, 2005) • U.S. Department of Justice, *World Factbook of Criminal Justice Systems* (Washington, D.C.) http://www.ojp.usdoj.gov/bjs/abstract/wfcj.htm • D. van Zyl Smit and F. Dünkel, eds., *Imprisonment Today and Tomorrow: International Perspectives on Prisoners' Rights and Prison Conditions* (2d ed.; The Hague, 2001).

Heinz Schöch

2. Ethical and Theological Aspects

2.1. *Place in the System*
Punishment can arise at many points in theological → ethics. The Roman Catholic tradition of → moral theology (→ Ethics 4) distinguishes two types

of ethical and theological discourse, and punishment has a place in each. Medieval and scholastic ethics (→ Scholasticism) arranges and integrates its material into a list of virtues, and it deals with what it calls secular punishment in the doctrine of justice (→ Righteousness, Justice, 3.1.1). Taking up the problem of the validity of punishment, it fails to deal with social processes and → institutions in their complexity and their ethical relevance. On the other side, the achievement of justice is at the center of the discussion; here the danger of a theological glorifying of the institution that inflicts punishment is so much the less.

The danger of ideologizing (→ Ideology) is very great in post-Tridentine morality, which uses the → Decalogue as a basis (→ Moral Theology 1). Handbooks dealing with penance (→ Casuistry; Penitence) so directly objectify the will of God in individual commands that they unequivocally favor the idea that an authoritarian and capricious lawgiver takes the place of God. The usage is the same for divine judgment and human verdicts, and they often seem to be mechanically related.

At the same time and along parallel lines, the Protestant Lutheran → Reformation held to an abbreviated form of the → two-kingdoms doctrine. On this view the → state acts as the guardian of the divinely willed order and is thus justified in using its → power to punish as a means of upholding the law. Either view, when given confessional status, gives the state theological legitimacy and sees a relation between its authority and punishment that rests on a theonomous basis.

2.2. *Recent Criminological Research*

The results of more recent criminological research have radically criticized these naive assumptions on ideological grounds. Two of the approaches have figured in ethical discussion and have made a special impact relative to punishment.

2.2.1. The so-called *labeling theory* attempts to understand deviant behavior as an act that runs against historically real complexes of → norms. No behavior contains within itself the qualities of criminality, but acts and modes of conduct are in conformity or deviant insofar as they measure up to the norms of → society. For instance, shoplifting is not a form of behavior that carries within it any specific empirical qualities. Tying the act to the mental states of observers is the only way to embrace all the interactions that are involved between the actions and the law. If there is no such observation and interaction between the one who does the deed and the people around him, the behavior cannot be regarded as deviant. But the so-called labeling made by an outsider — and this is the originality of this labeling perspective — is not a one-dimensional process. The interrelation runs both ways. From the standpoint of the one who is labeled as deviant, the people can be called outsiders who make the rules, for the breaking of which he or she is found guilty (H. S. Becker).

Treating criminalization as a process of definition is of great heuristic significance for an understanding of the norms and administration of penal law. Distinctions between primary and secondary deviance can help to arrive at a nuanced understanding of criminality. Under labeling theory, criminologists treat primary deviance as a mode of conduct that is not oriented to existing and socially recognized norms. Secondary deviance, however, is conduct that follows up on primary deviance and runs up against social reactions. From this perspective, infliction of punishment does not itself mechanically lead to secondary deviance.

Many critics of this approach have objected to its extreme → relativism, claiming that it is impracticable. Despite the criticism, it may be argued ethically that only when the processes and rituals of stigmatizing are transformed into socially relevant modes of expiation is it possible that current talk of the rehabilitation of the criminal will have any genuine basis in reality.

2.2.2. In 1975 the French philosopher Michel Foucault (1926-84) wrote *Surveiller et punir. La naissance de prison* (ET *Discipline and Punish: The Birth of the Prison* [1979]), which might be read as depicting the great transitions in European systems of punishment — notably, the movement from the medieval system of corporal punishment to the modern system of imprisonment. A closer examination shows, however, that Foucault had another end in view. In the history of punishment he found that development was anchored, not in a change of thinking, but only in a change of the techniques used. He did not ascribe the processes and changes either to individuals or to classes seeking to achieve a specific goal. What he found were changes in techniques, in functional modes, that simply represented new forms of power. Power itself, the power to punish, is not the privilege of those who think they possess it but a kind of complex operation in which individuals participate. According to this view, changes in modes of punishment involve simply a historical interplay of the elements of knowledge and power.

Foucault divides the history of punishment into three phases: the period of torture during the prerevolutionary ancien régime, the epoch of just punishment under the reforming → Enlightenment, and finally the period of discipline during the 19th and 20th centuries. Each phase had its distinctive scenarios, agents, and goals.

The age of torture evidenced a technique of punishment that featured strict secrecy during the investigation process and an unconditional use of torture to evoke confession. There was a horrible logic in what was done. According to Foucault, we have here a ceremonial restoration of wounded sovereignty. No matter how hasty the public proceedings might be, they were a part of the great rituals of power that were here both obscured and renewed. The institution of the prison played a lesser role. It did not serve to punish but simply to keep delinquents under supervision who would later be subjected to the liturgy of torture (→ Inquisition).

The second period, that of Enlightenment reforms, no longer treated the body as the main point for the strategy of punishment. Though the reforms had humanization in view, Foucault held to a different understanding. By punishing and suppressing vice, the reformers aimed at strengthening a normative function that would embrace the whole of society. The form of punishment was no doubt less severe, but it was greater in universality and necessity, finding its anchor in the body of society as a whole.

The 19th century finally pointed out other features. A transition was now made to a universal discipline. This was defined as an art that did not aim at increasing the faculties of the human body but at the creation of a mechanism that would make the body more useful than it is. According to Foucault, the Panopticon of Jeremy Bentham (1748-1832) — a prison built radially so that a centrally placed guard can see all the prisoners — embodies the ideal of total discipline. Such a model prison anticipated today's total institution. In the latter each individual has a specified physical or psychological place. The plain and simple regularity of time and place, given by the architecture and the daily routine of a prison, aims at the total symbiosis of the bodies of prisoners and their work.

2.3. *Modern Ethical and Theological Thinking*
In antithesis, modern ethical and theological thinking stresses the Christian quality and suitability of ethical and theological arguments relating to punishment by the way in which they serve to reduce the power of the ideology of retribution and of state omnipotence.

If, however, we are fully to achieve such a result, various theological ideas concerning the sovereignty of → God (§7.2.4) call for fundamental revision. This does not mean that theologically motivated ethicists will enthusiastically and naively embrace the so-called rehabilitation or resocialization thesis (see 1). All pleading for resocialization must take into account, and stand by the dimension of, the → guilt and sinfulness of all human existence (→ Sin). In fact, the idea of resocialization has been called ethically neutral in most of the literature on punishment. If, however, we do not equate legal and ethical views of guilt, socializing measures are simply a technique of adjustment to existing society. Theological guilt, however, makes possible an understanding of (re-)socialization that in different ways affects all the people involved and makes them responsible, whether criminals, victims, or the society that observes and condemns. No free pardon goes along with the sin, for divine justice must not be too hastily confused with human justice.

Despite all the efforts of theological ethics to give a suitable interpretation of punishment, it is very hard to avoid scapegoating. Stigmatization always seems to be the quickest way to find oneself on the right side and to avoid asking too many questions. Giving up scapegoating and a definite and organized will for → reconciliation are always difficult. Christians realize that → reconciliation in the world has taken place once and for all. They need no more than their imagination to extend the exemplary practice of Jesus on the cross. Theological attempts to motivate and support penal reform should initiate interaction between criminals, justices, prison personnel, and the public. Realizing that they themselves are *simul iustus et peccator* (→ Justification 2.2.6), Christians ought to be able to treat criminals as → neighbors. They can do so if they avoid the unnecessary rituals of isolation and labeling either inside or outside the system of imprisonment.

Bibliography: G. Baum and H. Wells, *The Reconciliation of the Peoples: Challenge to the Churches* (Maryknoll, N.Y., 1997) • H. S. Becker, *Outsiders: Studies in the Sociology of Deviance* (new ed.; New York, 1997; orig. pub., 1963) • A. Bondolfi, *Pena e pena di morte* (Bologna, 1985) • M. Foucault, *Discipline and Punish: The Birth of the Prison* (2d ed.; New York, 1995; orig. pub., 1979) • H. L. A. Hart, *Punishment and Responsibility* (Oxford, 1968) • D. W. Shriver Jr., *An Ethic for Enemies: Forgiveness in Politics* (New York, 1995) • T. R. Snyder, *The Protestant Ethic and the Spirit of Punishment* (Grand Rapids, 2001) • W. Swartley, *The Love of Enemy and Nonretaliation in the NT* (Louisville, Ky., 1992) • M. Volf, *Exclusion and Embrace: A Theological Exploration of Identity, Otherness, and Reconciliation* (Nashville, 1996).

Alberto Bondolfi

3. Pedagogical Aspects

3.1. *Definition and Types of Corrective Punishment*

Punishment in the home or in schools uses some form of → suffering in pursuit of educational goals. When not carried to excess, it is not subject to criminal law. Affecting the → soul as well as the body, it uses measures that may deprive the person of privileges. Psychologically, bodily punishment runs the risk of wounding feelings of self-worth, even though it does not use violence. But so, too, does silence or other verbal withdrawals of love. The moderate conditioning of small children in order to safeguard them against dangers should not be regarded as punishment. At the heart of all pedagogical considerations is the relation between means and ends, which in turn depends on the basic understanding of education itself in a given → culture.

The culture or subculture will decide what measures might have a negative effect on a child's development. In school, for example, putting a child in a corner can be a real punishment only if the peer group finds it to be dishonoring. If it does not, the effect can be positive. A peer group can find real distinction in what a teacher regards as negative (see K. Lewin, "The Psychological Situation of Reward and Punishment," *A Dynamic Theory of Personality* [1935]). Appealing to parents also depends on the culture. Teachers stand in a special educational relation to their students. → Society (and the law) gives them certain powers relative to both order and education. The restriction imposed on teachers in some countries obviously reflects the changes that can take place in a culture's view of punishment.

3.2. *In History*

Excessive discipline ruled during the → Middle Ages and the early modern period (with typical appeal to the proverb "Spare the rod and spoil the child"). The 18th century, however, saw the ambivalence of existing forms of punishment and took steps to mitigate corporal punishment. August Hermann → Francke (1663-1727; → Pietism) certainly viewed punishment as necessary in principle because human nature tends to → evil and self-love, but at the same time he was sensitive to the different forms that punishment might take. J.-J. Rousseau (1712-78) was convinced that special forms of punishment, especially corporal, would corrupt the innate abilities of children, who are good by nature. Instead, he argued that we must teach children to experience the natural (including the negative) results of their actions. J. H. Pestalozzi (1746-1827; → Kindergarten 1.1) made trust between teacher and student the main point in his system, and on this basis he regarded punishment as meaningful and necessary. For Friedrich → Schleiermacher (1768-1834; → Schleiermacher's Theology), punishments were a sign of the imperfection of society.

The whipping of adults was ended in many areas during the 20th century, but not of children, though many reformers have pointed out the physical and emotional consequences and met with some success in their efforts both at the educational and the domestic level. In many countries the right of teachers to chastise students has been ended, and there is no law that gives any such right to parents, though on the basis of custom some moderate chastisement is usually allowed.

In a complex → industrial society with nuclear families, many of the tasks of → education are left to institutions like the preschool, school, or youth groups (→ Youth Work). This development has also brought a change relative to educational punishment. The parent-child relation is usually characterized by confidence, but such a relation must be earned in other situations. Since institutional and group norms determine the relation, measures used in punishment may easily be felt to be externally compulsive, which will render them educationally ineffective.

3.3. *Problems*

Discussion of suitable punishments has been taken for granted in classical discussions of pedagogy, but more recent treatment has cast doubt on punishment as a whole, and indeed on the whole use of force in education. In actual pedagogic debate, knowledge of the negative effect of punishment has led in many circles to avoidance of the term. Instead of "punishment" there is reference to "educational influence" or to "the keeping of order."

Putting the term "punishment" under a taboo has confronted many teachers with the fact that they have only limited options. They can simply add to students' knowledge but exert no personal influence. What is needed are teachers who can meet opposition and not avoid → conflicts. If conflicts are latent and no strategies exist to resolve them, forms of punishment that are often ritualized either at home or at school will result in a kind of emotional or spontaneous punishment, whose effects are often not discernible. To justify real punishment it is sometimes argued that children themselves wish to be punished, or even that under certain conditions corporal punishment can meet a child's feelings of → guilt and act as a check on → anxiety.

3.4. *Theological Considerations*

From the standpoint of theological → anthropology (§3), the dignity of a child (→ Human Dignity) rests on his or her divine likeness and related inalienable personhood (→ Self). Education on this basis seeks the development of a responsible subject (→ Responsibility) and involves modes of education that can be justified only if they accord with the child's self-responsibility at a given age and if teachers encourage the child to accept responsibility for conduct suitable to that age.

For an education in which punishment is not needed, an atmosphere of love and trust is crucial, as are a minimal level of rules and → dialogue about mutual needs and their limitations. On this view teachers must accept that theirs is a modest role. Even if they view punishment as a last resort in the case of students who are unsure of themselves, they must realize that all punishment is dysfunctional and deforming insofar as the aim of the educational process is the development of → autonomy and social competence.

→ Authority; Identity; Obedience; Socialization; Youth

Bibliography: J. H. Baron, "Corporal Punishment of Children in England and the United States: Current Issues," *Mount Sinai Journal of Medicine* 72/1 (2005) 45-46 • R. Dreikurs and P. Cassel, *Discipline without Tears* (rev. ed.; New York, 2004; orig. pub., 1972) on discipline in the schools • R. Dreikurs and L. Grey, *A Parent's Guide to Child Discipline* (rev. ed.; New York, 1970) • K. Lewin, *A Dynamic Theory of Personality* (New York, 1935) • W. K. Mohr and J. A. Anderson, "Reconsidering Punitive and Harsh Discipline," *Journal of School Nursing* 18/6 (2002) 346-52 • M. A. Straus, with D. A. Donnelly, *Beating the Devil out of Them: Corporal Punishment in American Families and Its Effects on Children* (New Brunswick, N.J., 2001).

Friedrich Johannsen

Purana

The Purana (Skt. *purāṇa,* "ancient"), strictly an ancient traditional history, is a literary form that the → Mahabharata, as an encyclopedia of traditional lore, carried forward into the post-Christian era. Along with the epics, Puranas are the most important literary source for → Hinduism.

By tradition the contents include the five areas of cosmology, the dying and rising again of the world, the genealogies of ancient gods and seers, the age of Manu (the first man), and the genealogies of kings (of the "moon race," from whom the heroes of the Mahabharata descend, and of the "sun race," to which Rama, the hero of the → Ramayana, belongs). In most Puranas we also find cosmography, that is, descriptions of the Indian worldview, with the rose-apple continent Jambudvīpa (in which Bhāratavarṣa = India is located) at the center, separated by oceans from the continents around it and from the layers of the heavenly worlds, the underworlds, and the hells. Common, too, are extolling of sacred sites (with the legends of their founding), their rituals, and their promises; legendary mythical cycles (→ Myth, Mythology), theological discussions of the supreme deity (which may vary in different Puranas), the story of Krishna, the avatars (incarnations) of Vishnu, legends relating to Siva and his consort, Parvati (also called Durga or Kali, as well as other names); and religious rules for everyday conduct, for important rites (e.g., expiation ceremonies and rites for ancestors, offerings, and the dead), and for the honoring of deities on special feast days.

Apart from imparting traditional knowledge, the Puranas have the aim of pointing out the ways of redemption *(mokṣa)* that are open to all (including women and low-caste persons) and that involve a good life, observance of ritual duties, visiting pilgrim sites (→ Pilgrimage), keeping feasts, and absorption into the being and acts of the supreme deity.

The Harivamsa seems to be the oldest work of the genre, an appendix to the Mahabharata that gives the genealogy of Hari (= Krishna) and the story of his youth. Other important Vishnuite Puranas are the relatively old Vishnu Puranas (ca. A.D. 500) and the Bhāgavata Puranas (ca. A.D. 1000), which in the celebrated tenth canto tells the story of Krishna's youth and especially his love game with the Gopis (the shepherdesses), and which has become a basic text of → Bhakti religion.

The Vāyu Puranas, Linga Puranas, and Kūrma Puranas are Sivaistic in orientation; the consort of Siva is honored in the Devībhāgavata Puranas.

Many Puranas have no specific religious orientation, for example, the Mārkaṇḍeya Puranas or the relatively late Brahma Puranas, which assemble bits of ancient traditions.

Bibliography: A. B. L. Awasthi, *Purana Index* (New Delhi, 1992) • K. Chakrabarti, *Religious Process: The Puranas and the Making of a Regional Tradition* (New Delhi, 2001) • W. Doniger, *Purāṇa perennis: Reciprocity and Transformation in Hindu and Jaina Texts* (Albany, N.Y., 1993) • P. Hacker, *Prahlada. Werden und Wandel einer Idealgestalt* (Mainz, 1959) • R. C. Hazra, *Studies in the Purānic Records on Hindu Rites and Customs* (2d ed.; Delhi, 1975; orig. pub., 1940) • R. Jarow, *Tales for the Dying: The Death Narrative of the*

Bhāgavata-Purāna (Albany, N.Y., 2003) • S. Parmeshwaranand, *Encyclopaedic Dictionary of Purānas* (New Delhi, 2001) • L. Rocher, *The Purānas* (Wiesbaden, 1986) • W. Ruben, *Krishna. Konkordanz und Kommentar der Motive seines Heldenlebens* (Istanbul, 1944) • R. Söhnen and P. Schreiner, *Brahmapurāna: Summary of Contents, with Index of Names and Motifs* (Wiesbaden, 1989) • *The Vishnu Purana: A System of Hindu Mythology and Tradition* (3d ed.; trans. H. H. Wilson; Calcutta, 1961).

Renate Söhnen-Thieme

Purgatory

1. Before the Reformation
2. Reformation and Council of Trent
3. New Developments in Roman Catholic Understanding

The term "purgatory" denotes the place and process of purging from the stains of postbaptismal → sin and suffering its remaining temporal penalties, occurring in the intermediate state between → death and → resurrection, or earth and heaven. The idea of purgatory emerged from reflection on the immemorial Christian custom of praying for the dead and particularly of offering the → Eucharist on behalf of the dead, especially on anniversaries of their deaths. This pious practice inevitably gave rise to the question: If the dead are already either in heaven and therefore no longer in need of prayers or doomed to hell and so beyond the reach of prayers, why do we pray for them? Prayers for the dead gave rise to the idea, already present in late Jewish piety, that there must be some intermediate but temporary state between → heaven and → hell, a state that eventually assumed the name "purgatory."

1. Before the Reformation

The idea of an intermediate state was given greater focus as the church addressed the problem posed by sin after baptism. → Baptism might bring full pardon and cleansing, but what about fresh offenses? An early rigorist view saw no hope for restoration, at least for mortal sin, and groups like the Novationists and → Donatists clung to this position when the → persecutions under Domitian (81-96) and Decius (249-51) brought large-scale → apostasy. Canonical, or sacramental, penance emerged as a once-in-a-lifetime opportunity for postbaptismal → conversion (§1), but it was often deferred until the end of life. Thus it did not relieve all the temporal consequences or stains of sin for those who deferred it until their deathbed, or who had not completed it before then. Nor did canonical penance provide a remedy for the enduring consequences of egoism manifested in daily sins. As a result, penitent offenders might be sure of heaven but not yet fit for it, further cleansing and penalties being needed before they could enter into the fullness of → salvation.

A basis for future purgation of this kind was found in passages like 2 Macc. 12:39-45, Matt. 12:31-37, and 1 Cor 3:11-15, to which Clement of Alexandria (ca. 150-ca. 215; Alexandrian Theology) alluded when speaking of the fiery purifying of deathbed penitents. With support from Augustine (354-430; Augustine's Theology) and Gregory the Great (590-604) in the Latin West, the doctrine of purgatory rapidly advanced, the more so as infant baptism increasingly became the norm and the Christian life had to be lived for longer postbaptismal periods. Obviously, apart from those dying in infancy, few could hope to live lives free even from some form of mortal sin or at least deeply rooted or habitual venial sins. With the passing of the age of persecutions and with it the prospect of certain salvation through martyrdom, it seemed obvious that most people died neither so totally good that they were prepared for heaven nor so completely evil that they deserved hell.

The sacrament of penance, which by the Middle Ages could be repeated, could offer → assurance of heaven in such cases; no matter how frequently repeated, however, sacramental penance could not eliminate the residual temporal penalties due for sins, which could be purged only by conversion and penitential works either in this world or in the next. For those who did not complete this penitential purgation in this life, purgatory was the place for this process in the next life. Its torments were luridly depicted in the Middle Ages as hardly less painful than those of hell, though of limited, if uncertain, duration.

A priority in medieval Christianity thus became the finding of means to escape or reduce the purgatorial stay, which all but the especially holy would have to experience. → Monasticism offered itself as a chief means, for observance of its counsels (rather than commands) of → poverty, chastity (→ Celibacy of the Clergy), and → obedience offered a way of radical conversion of life that might complete in this life or reduce for the next the required period of purgation. Thus not a few men and women of means retired to monasteries or "took the habit" in their later years to prepare for death by lives of penance. For nonmonastics, crusading, pilgrimages, almsgiving, and masses and prayers for the departed were alternative possibilities. The Councils of Lyons II (1274) and Florence (1439) affirmed the reality of purgation but did so in sober language, with little reference to its details.

Unfortunately, as a rather crass bookkeeping mentality crept into popular → piety and pastoral practice, indulgences came to play an important role as well. Through → indulgences the → pope could supposedly draw on the excess merits of Christ and the → saints (those who ended life with a credit balance) and cover some or all of a person's past offenses. Many of the abuses and financial scandals of the late Middle Ages resulted from these practices, not to speak of the associated distortions of Christian belief and piety.

In the East the → Orthodox Church did not go along with the West in elaboration of the doctrine of purgatory or the doctrinal and devotional distortions to which it gave rise. It resisted the concept of expiatory suffering and opposed any material or quasi-material understanding of purgatorial fire. Nevertheless, the Orthodox did not reject purgatory itself or the place and value of prayers for the dead.

2. Reformation and Council of Trent

The real revolt against purgatory came with the → Reformers, with their emphasis on the all-sufficiency of Christ's reconciling work, full → justification by → grace and by → faith, and consequent assurance of heaven without any need for intermediate purgation or expiation. The Reformers, indeed, found no basis for purgatory when they applied to it their scriptural rule, as can be seen from the condemnations in such statements as the Berne Theses (1528, no. 6), the Gallican Confession (1559, art. 24), and especially the Anglican Thirty-nine Articles (1571), which speaks of purgatory as "a fond [i.e., foolish] thing, vainly invented and grounded upon no warranty of Scripture, but rather repugnant to the Word of God" (art. 22). For doctrinal as well as devotional reasons, therefore, the Reformers scathingly condemned and ended the related abuses, especially indulgences, private masses, prayers for the dead, and a special ranking for saints in distinction from ordinary believers.

In contrast, the → Roman Catholic Church at the Council of → Trent (1545-63) stood by the doctrine of purgatory and its doctrinal and devotional implications. It initiated reforms to end obvious abuses and to revive a piety not so strongly oriented to finding relief from purgatory. Nevertheless, it retained penitential practices in general and sacramental penance in particular as important elements of ordinary Christian living and even enhanced their importance. It also insisted on a need in most cases for purgation and temporal satisfaction after death. It emphasized the value and necessity of prayers and masses for the dead. It maintained a distinction between saints, who go directly to heaven or who have already reached heaven after completion of their purgatory, and rank-and-file believers, who still must pass through purgatory.

3. New Developments in Roman Catholic Understanding

In the 20th century a gentler idea of salutary adjustments for heaven will often be found in place of cruder ideas of material fire, but purgatory itself continues to have an essential role in Roman Catholic teaching and practice. Stripped of some of the lurid imagery and the bookkeeping mentality that often obscured it in the past, the genuinely Catholic notion of purgatory is not Tertullian's (ca. 160-ca. 225) idea of an otherworldly concentration camp where the dead undergo more or less arbitrary torments. Rather, it is the necessary process of internal transformation in which the person is rendered capable of Christ, capable of God, and thus capable of unity with the whole communion of saints. The inner transformation called purgatory is rooted in an imperative that is at once anthropological and Christological.

Anthropologically, purgatory is a recognition that human sin is not merely an external violation of God's law but a manifestation of the sinful egoism deeply rooted in the human heart. While through faith God's grace in Christ immediately forgives the offense, it does not immediately eradicate the tentacles of egoism that gave rise to it. Receiving gratuitous divine mercy through faith does not exempt the believer from the need for inner transformation. Thus, in the Roman Catholic view, justification must be complemented by → sanctification. Purgatory is the continuation and completion of this process of sanctification after death. This purgation is not a replacement of grace by works but the painful process by which grace accomplishes its work precisely as grace.

While it is faith alone that saves, this fundamental orientation of faith is often buried under layers of, to use the Pauline expression frequently associated with purgatory in this tradition, "wood, hay, and straw" (1 Cor. 3:12). This accumulated debris needs to be purged, "burned away," before a person is capable of the fullness of what God has prepared for those who love him. "Encounter with the Lord *is* this transformation. It is the fire that burns away our dross and re-forms us to be vessels of eternal joy" (J. Ratzinger, 231). While the temptation to describe this transformation in terms of chronological time and physical torments is, and historically has been, difficult to resist, purgatory is what happens when flawed human lovers come face to face with infinite Love.

Although purgatory has only a superficial basis in Scripture, it is deeply rooted in Roman Catholic piety and imagination and in the Catholic sense of the church as a communion of saints that includes the living, the dead, and those yet to be born, and in which the dead and the living remain really present to, and exert an influence for good on, one another (→ Popular Catholicism). It is only when they are situated within this context that the Catholic practice of interceding on behalf of the dead — and of seeking the intercession of the saints, including the Virgin Mary — can be properly understood as something much more than morbid superstition. Since this Catholic sensibility is not readily articulated in the technical language of theology, it finds its best expression in the imaginations of poets (e.g., Dante Alighieri [1265-1321]) and visual artists (e.g., Hieronymus Bosch [ca. 1450-1516]).

Bibliography: R. K. Fenn, *The Persistence of Purgatory* (New York, 1995) • F. Fergusson, *Dante's Drama of the Mind: A Modern Reading of the Purgatorio* (Westport, Conn., 1981) • J. Le Goff, *The Birth of Purgatory* (Chicago, 1984) • A. Michel, "Purgatoire," *DTC* 1163-1320 • G. L. Muller, "Fegfeuer," *LTK* 1204-8 • "Purgatory," *ODCC* 1349-50 • K. Rahner, "Purgatory," *Theological Investigations* (vol. 19; London, 1984) 181-93 • J. Ratzinger, *Eschatology: Death and Eternal Life* (Washington, D.C., 1988).

John P. Beal

Puritans

1. Term
2. History
   2.1. Elizabeth
   2.2. James I
   2.3. Civil War
   2.4. Cromwell
   2.5. Restoration
   2.6. End of the Puritans
3. In Colonial America

1. Term

The terms "Puritan" and "Puritanism" were originally terms of abuse but were defined in 1646 by the Presbyterian John Geree (1601-49) as a moderate and middle way in religion: "The Old English Puritan was such an one that honoured God above all, and under God gave everyone his due. His first care was to serve God . . . making the word of God his rule in worship. He highly esteemed order in the house of God: but would not under colour of that submit to superstitious rites. . . . He reverenced authority within its sphere: but durst not under pretence of this subjection, worship God after the traditions of men. . . . He esteemed that manner of prayer best, where by the gift of God, expressions were varied according to present wants and occasions; yet he did not account set forms unlawful. . . . The Lord's day he esteemed a divine ordinance. . . . Just laws and commands he willingly obeyed . . . but such as were unjust he refused to observe . . . yet his refusal was modest and with submission to penalties."

Puritanism thus defined was not → Separatism, though both came from the same Calvinist stem (→ Calvinism). Its militancy as a movement varied according to the threat posed by the powers in church and state to its middle way. When, after 1660, politics destroyed the coherence of Puritanism, one of the traditions deriving from it — that identified with Richard Baxter (1615-91), Isaac Watts (1674-1748), and Philip Doddridge (1702-51) — persisted with the belief that it sought a middle way between Calvinism and → Arminianism, between human definitions of → orthodoxy (§2) and an anarchy of private judgment.

2. History

2.1. *Elizabeth*

The Elizabethan Puritan movement (Elizabeth I, 1558-1603) began nevertheless as a protest by English exiles returning to England against another middle way, the way between Rome and Geneva favored by the queen. Behind the Puritan desire to take the → Reformation further lay a common Protestant perception of the history of the true → church and a lively sense that "popery" constituted an international menace (→ Pope, Papacy). The desire to remove "popishe abuses yet remaining in the Englische Church" was particularly vigorous in those with an international outlook and firsthand experience of churches abroad.

Religious issues, even the question of → vestments, could have a political reference in the eyes of government and Puritan. Archbishop E. Grindal (d. 1583) was suspended from the primacy for refusing to suppress Puritan prophesyings in the south. In the north, where the government had a powerful → Catholicism to contend with, Puritan exercises were approved and did not come under serious attack till the 1630s. In the south, however, a movement capable of sustaining its own separate organization and a secret press seemed subversive, and Archbishops J. Whitgift (ca. 1532-1604) and R. Bancroft (1544-1610) sought to suppress it. The Puritans had powerful lay support (→ Clergy and Laity) in the country and at court, though their great lay patrons diminished notably in numbers after the 1590s.

By this date a movement that had begun by wishing to move the apparently transitory Elizabethan Settlement in a Protestant direction had been brought by the queen's obduracy to demand a fundamental reconstruction of the church. If royal obduracy evoked a Presbyterian movement, it also sharply limited what this movement could attain and gave time for a generation to grow up that was satisfied with the settlement they had inherited. From roughly 1590 to roughly 1620 the movement was in retreat, though its religious and pastoral appeal continued to attract, and lectureships, private chaplaincies, and donative cures provided a refuge for Puritan clergy.

2.2. *James I*

Under James I (1603-25) this cycle was repeated. In the Millenary Petition (1603) the new Calvinist king was skillfully lobbied in favor of moderate church reform. But, like Elizabeth, James resisted parliamentary interference in church affairs, and the bishops had no use for Puritan measures. Archbishop Robert Bancroft deprived about 90 ministers of their livings, but he encountered a good deal of lay resistance, and his successor, George Abbot (1611-33), was not inclined to push any policy with energy.

Stolid rather than violent opposition turned the Puritan movement inward to → preaching, to → theology, and, one of its most characteristic features, to the practical care of souls, what William Perkins (1558-1602) called "the science of living blessedly forever." Perkins's pupils included William Ames (1576-1633), who migrated to the Netherlands, and John Robinson (1576-1625), who founded → Congregationalism in Leyden and republished Perkins's → catechism there. Lewis Bayly (d. 1631) published his *Practice of Piety,* which reached a 25th edition by 1630 and was continually republished among European Protestants right into the age of → Pietism.

2.3. *Civil War*

In the 1620s this relative peace and latitudinarianism came to an end. War and economic recession drove the government forward just when Roman Catholic advance on the Continent was endangering the whole Protestant interest (→ Protestantism; Thirty Years' War), and from 1625 the government was led by Charles I (1625-49), who had a hypersensitive awareness of what was due to his honor, a politically influential Roman Catholic wife, and a new Arminian faction with which to work in the church.

A government of this sort, which cared little for its traditional brokers in the country, was bound to "politicize" and radicalize Puritanism, to thrust it into the company of opposition politicians and others bruised by Arminian innovations in the church. During the 1630s private conventicles multiplied, and both in the Netherlands and New England, there were numerous exiled Puritan ministers convinced of the advantages of a church order that was self-governing but not Separatist. By 1640 the Puritans were part of a virtually unanimous opposition to the policies of the Crown and remained deeply pledged to the parliamentary cause. When the Scots took up arms against England (1638), Charles could neither manage without Parliament nor cope with it. But rebellion in Ireland (1641) and parliamentary attempts to secure root-and-branch reform rallied those of conservative temper to his side and enabled him to commence a civil war (1642) that he should have won.

The Civil War and the need to purchase alliance with the Scots quickly converted the Puritan clergy and the propertied laity to Presbyterianism, despite the eclipse this system had suffered since the reign of Elizabeth. In 1641 Parliament had simply transferred the functions of bishops to lay commissioners; in 1643 the Scots were able to impose a full Presbyterian system, with the support of Puritan clergy who had no desire to exchange the tyranny of bishops for the tyranny of congregations. Yet appearances were deceptive. Baxter himself could say of the time as late as 1641: "I never thought what Presbytery or Independency were, nor ever spake with a man that seemed to know it."

Once the attempt was made to enforce Presbyterianism on the Scots pattern, there was a rapid growth of Independency, with a program of religious toleration and with New England support. A small but vital proportion of the best fighting force in the country, the New Model Army of Oliver Cromwell (1599-1658), proved to be assorted religious zealots who required the common platform of toleration, while Cromwell himself, whose denominational allegiance remains uncertain, had much sympathy with the → sects without committing himself to any one of them. Any prospect of creating a working Presbyterian establishment in England disappeared with the alliance of Charles I with the Scots in 1648 and their military defeat by Cromwell. Parliament itself seemed likely to go the way of king and presbytery as an army purge began a series of attempts to promote the reign of the saints.

2.4. *Cromwell*

Under Cromwell's personal rule a "public profession" (→ Confession of Faith) of the Christian religion remained, though no one was to be compelled to conform to it; Jews were to be permitted to settle in England for the first time since 1290 (→ Judaism), and Roman Catholics were treated relatively leniently. A religious establishment was to be supported by tithes until some less contentious provision could be made, and it was hoped to accommodate Independents and → Baptists within the nominal Presbyterian establishment. Puritans had long hoped to combine the gathered congregation with the religious establishment, but the attempt satisfied neither the religious zealots nor members of the general public. Cromwell, however, protected this system as he also protected the Reformed movement internationally in France, Switzerland, and Hungary.

2.5. *Restoration*

Immediately upon Cromwell's death the English Independents in the Savoy Conference (1661) confessed themselves one in theology with the Westminster Confession (→ Westminster Assembly and Confession) and with the Reformed tradition, though differing in church order. But without Cromwellian backing they had a bleak future; the Puritans who had always been mostly churchmen and not Separatists were, within two years of the restoration of Charles II (1660-85), to be ejected from the church and turned into persecuted Nonconformists (→ Dissenters).

When the Act of Uniformity (1662) required assent from all clergy, there were almost no advocates for a complete Scots system, though a few moderate Presbyterians might be found like Thomas Hall (1610-65), who was hot against unlicensed preachers and the sects, and Philip Henry (1631-95), who, though ejected from the church, would never become the pastor of a dissenting congregation. Richard Baxter led the right wing of the middle party, and John Owen (1616-83), who had become a convinced Independent, the left wing. Ecclesiologically the small number of Baptists were indistinguishable from the Independents. To the left again were individualists (→ Individualism), remnants of the sects, and the Quakers (→ Friends, Society of), who were both the fiercest critics of the Puritans and the embodiment of many old Puritan Separatist tendencies.

When toleration was achieved in 1689, each party had to be separately accommodated. In the 18th century, while the old Presbyterian cause was broken, the Quaker community was sidetracked, and the Independent and Baptist denominations were reconstructed by the influence of the Evangelical Revival. The old political Puritanism went underground and is to be traced only by the continuing publication of tracts of the "Good Old Cause"; it resurfaced at the time of the French → Revolution as radical Unitarianism.

2.6. *End of the Puritans*

In the third quarter of the 19th century, the defenders and the enemies of the established status of the Church of England tried to draw advantage from the experience of the Civil War, each asserting a continuity in English politics that was not really there. The belief that Puritanism played a key role in the development of English → capitalism has its advocates, but it ascribes too much force to Puritan ideas at a time, late in the 17th century, when they were palpably losing ground.

Puritanism as a fundamental historical influence stood its ground longest in American historiography, but it has proved impossible to write the history of the United States, or even of colonial America, around the history of New England. In the name of → pluralism, religious and racial, the attempt is now out of favor.

→ Anglican Communion; Church and State; Modern Church History 1-2

Bibliography: P. Collinson, *The Elizabethan Puritan Movement* (Berkeley, Calif., 1967) • C. Durston and J. Eales, eds., *The Culture of English Puritanism, 1560-1700* (Basingstoke, 1996) • N. H. Keeble and G. F. Nuttall, eds., *Calendar of the Correspondence of Richard Baxter* (2 vols.; Oxford, 1991-92) • W. Lamont, *Puritanism and the English Revolution* (3 vols.; Aldershot, 1991) • G. F. Nuttall, *Visible Saints: The Congregational Way, 1640-1660* (Oxford, 1957) • J. Spurr, *English Puritanism, 1603-1689* (Basingstoke, 1998) • D. Underdown, *Fire from Heaven: Life in an English Town in the Seventeenth Century* (New Haven, 1992) • M. R. Watts, *The Dissenters* (vol. 1; Oxford, 1978) • G. Yule, *Puritans in Politics: The Religious Legislation of the Long Parliament, 1640-1647* (Abingdon, 1981).

W. Reginald Ward

3. In Colonial America

The Puritan and Separatist exodus to colonial America began with the "Pilgrim Fathers," a group of about 90 Separatists who in 1620 left Holland on the *Mayflower* and settled at Plymouth in southeastern Massachusetts. William Bradford (1590-1657) became Plymouth's first governor elected under the Mayflower Compact, their governing document. Bradford's "History of Plymouth Plantation" (published in 1856) has become one of the most-studied texts of the period. In it Bradford describes the travails of the Separatist community in their quest for a pure church and society (→ Separatism).

As the English Puritans suffered under the → persecutions of Charles I (1625-49), some also decided to organize a colony in America. A group of Puritan merchants and lawyers, led by John Winthrop (1588-1649), secured a charter for the Massachusetts Bay Company and departed in 1630. On board the ship *Arabella* Winthrop delivered his famous "Model of Christian Charity" address, in which he asserted, "We shall be as a City upon a hill. The eyes of all people are upon us. So that if we shall deal falsely with our God . . . we shall be made a story and a by-word throughout the world." The Massachusetts Puritans established near-total political and religious control over the colony, which was ruled by a General Court. Winthrop served four terms as court-elected governor before his death.

Massachusetts was not the only Puritan colony founded in the new world in 1630; another was founded on Providence Island off the coast of Nicaragua. At the time, this colony seemed more promising to English Puritans than bleak and cold Massachusetts, but internal divisions debilitated the colony until it was overrun by the Spanish in 1641.

The New England Puritans spread quickly, founding the colonies of Connecticut (1636) and New Haven (1643) to serve particular theological camps. Massachusetts Bay colony remained the most powerful, however, and is the most studied. The Massachusetts Puritans set up a distinctive congregational system (→ Congregationalism). Individual churches governed themselves by elder rule, and they saw any ruling bodies above the local church as unbiblical (→ Church Government). Church attendance was legally required. Prospective church members had to demonstrate a reasonable hope that they were converted, a high standard that could keep membership numbers surprisingly low. Church members gained access to the Lord's Supper and could have their children baptized.

This system of → church membership worked fairly well until the 1650s, when many churches began to have large numbers of baptized nonmembers. The question arose whether these nonmembers could have their own children baptized. In 1662 a Massachusetts synod of ministers formally recommended the "Half-Way Covenant," meaning that churches should allow baptized adults who demonstrated godly behavior, but not conversion, to have their own children baptized (→ Baptism 3.1). The reform generated significant consternation among some who saw it as a corruption of biblical church practice, but by the end of the century the vast majority of Massachusetts churches had accepted the reform.

The Massachusetts Puritans demonstrated a remarkable degree of theological uniformity during the 17th century, but there were still many tensions within their ranks, as seen in the disputes over the Half-Way Covenant. Massachusetts authorities also periodically had to root out perceived heretics who jeopardized the purity of their Bible commonwealth (→ Heresies and Schisms). One of the first such troublemakers was Roger Williams, who arrived as a Puritan minister in 1631. Williams's ever-shifting theological opinions led him to the Separatists at Plymouth, where he began to sympathize with the plight of local Native Americans. The General Court became indignant at Williams's criticism of Massachusetts' treatment of Native Americans and his denunciations of the state authority of Massachusetts over the church, and they banished him from the colony in 1635. Williams and a few followers established a colony at Providence, Rhode Island, in 1636. For decades, however, he continued his public criticism of Massachusetts' persecution of → dissenters.

An episode that struck even closer to the heart of the Massachusetts church order, however, was the → Antinomian crisis of 1636-37. This controversy centered on minister John Cotton and his follower Anne Hutchinson. Hutchinson and her family had decided to follow Cotton to Massachusetts in 1634, and soon thereafter she began holding private meetings to discuss Cotton's sermons and various points of → theology. Cotton was the most vigorous preacher of "free grace" among the Massachusetts Puritans, denouncing any theological hint of the merits of good works. Hutchinson expressed the conviction that among the Boston ministers, only Cotton and her brother-in-law John Wheelwright were preaching the pure doctrine of → salvation by → grace. The General Court put a stop to this radical "free grace" movement by trying a number of its members, including Wheelwright and Hutchinson. The court seized upon Hutchinson's testimony that she had received spiritual insight by "immediate revelation" from God, a statement that smacked of Quakerism (→ Friends, Society of). The court denounced her as an antinomian, and Hutchinson and Wheelwright were banished by 1638. Cotton seems to have agreed to temper his doctrine enough to keep his position.

The seal of the Massachusetts Bay Company had featured an Indian saying, "Come over and help us," but relations with Native Americans proved to be even more troubling for the Puritans than their internal heretics. In general, the Puritans did little to evangelize their Native American neighbors, and instead spent much time at war with them. Cooperating with local Narragansett Indians, the Puritans in 1637 almost entirely wiped out the Pequot Indians because of land feuds. In the 1640s and 1650s the most famous Puritan → missionary, John Eliot, saw his greatest successes among the Indians, founding the model "praying town" for them at Natick, Massachusetts, in 1651. Eliot ruled Natick and other praying towns as a theocrat, mandating OT codes of morality for residents and demanding that they adopt English modes of civility. In 1675-76 King Philip's War, the most devastating of New England's Indian wars, put an end to most missionary efforts for almost a generation.

Puritanism in New England transformed into British dissenting → Protestantism after the Glorious Revolution of 1688, as New Englanders dropped their former hostility toward the monarchy and became committed to the success of Britain's ongoing wars with European Catholic powers and the preservation of the monarchy's Protestant succession. New England ministers regularly lamented how their colonies had sinfully fallen away from their original calling, but there is little convincing evidence that many people in the colonies had become significantly secular by the early 18th century. Nevertheless, calls for moral renewal transformed in the 1720s into prayers for a great revival of the churches, to be generated by a special outpouring of the → Holy Spirit. By the time of the Great Awakening (roughly 1740-45), Puritanism had ceased to exist as a specific movement in New England, but the spiritual intensity of emergent evangelicalism no doubt inherited much from its Puritan ancestry (→ Evangelical).

Bibliography: F. Bremer, *The Puritan Experiment: New England Society from Bradford to Edwards* (rev. ed.; Hanover, N.H., 1995) • D. Hall, *Worlds of Wonder, Days of Judgment: Popular Religious Belief in Early New England* (Cambridge, Mass., 1990) • A. Heimert and A. Delbanco, eds., *The Puritans in America: A Narrative Anthology* (Cambridge, Mass., 1985) • J. Knight, *Orthodoxies in Massachusetts: Rereading American Puritanism* (Cambridge, Mass., 1994) • P. Miller, *The New England Mind: From Colony to Province* (Cambridge, Mass., 1953); idem, *The New England Mind: The Seventeenth Century* (Cambridge, Mass., 1939) • H. Stout, *The New England Soul: Preaching and Religious Culture in Colonial New England* (New York, 1986).

Thomas S. Kidd

Purity → Cultic Purity

Q

Q

1. Investigation of the → Synoptic gospels in the 18th and 19th centuries produced a two-source theory according to which Matthew and Luke used not only Mark but also a collection of materials largely made up of sayings of → Jesus. For want of a better title, this collection has come to be called "Q," after Ger. *Quelle,* "source."

Synoptic comparison has made possible a hypothetical reconstruction of the wording and sequence of this nonextant collection. It is theorized that originally isolated sayings were grouped by themes in Q. The sequence of sayings, which we cannot localize in detail, may be detected in Luke. First there is the Baptist's preaching of judgment (3:7-9, 16-17), then the messianic temptation of Jesus (4:1-12), followed by his programmatic address (6:20-23, 27-37a, 38c, 41-49), the faith of the pagan centurion (7:1-10), John and Jesus (7:18-28, 31-35), the messengers of Jesus (10:2-16), the manifestation of the Son (10:21-22), prayer (11:2-4, 9-13), power over → demons (11:14-26), judgment on this generation (11:29-32), sayings against the → Pharisees and against the → scribes (11:39-52), confession in → persecution (12:2-10), sayings against anxiety and the heaping up of wealth (12:22-34), and finally the coming of the Son of Man (12:39-46; 17:22-37).

2. It is suggested that this special tradition came down through charismatic itinerant prophets and their followers in Palestine and Syria before the Jewish War of A.D. 66-70. Arranging the various stages is very difficult. The final redaction, it is thought, gives evidence of some distancing from → Israel. There might have been direct contacts between these circles and Matthew's community. Older research saw primarily in Q a parenetic supplementation of the → kerygma (→ Parenesis).

Modern research accords Q its own distinctive kerygmatic character. It presupposes proclamation of the message of the → kingdom of God after the death of Jesus, but in expectation of the imminent coming of the → apocalyptic Son of Man (→ Christological Titles 2), Jesus, the → prophet and messenger of → Wisdom, by whose message individual → salvation is decided (→ Eschatology). The death of Jesus as a prophet whom Israel rejected (not soteriologically interpreted) will be avenged at the approaching judgment. The group was apparently coming into increasing conflict with Jewish contemporaries.

In answer to the difficult social and economic situation, Jesus' promises of salvation to the poor and his demands for → love of enemies and mutual aid took on central significance. In charismatic → poverty and obvious defenselessness, his messengers (→ Twelve, The) went through the land to gather "sons of peace" and to proclaim to them the imminent coming of God's rule.

3. Since many scholars believe that Q represents early oral tradition, much of which stems from Jesus, Q became an important in the late 20th-century search for the historical Jesus. Based on the work of John Kloppenborg, many North American scholars came to believe that the oldest level of redaction in the hypothetical Q document represented Wisdom sayings and that apocalyptic sayings came in at some later point. Characterizations of Jesus based on such an analysis of Q tend to see him as a teacher of Wisdom rather than an apocalyptic or eschatological prophet.

In addition to its importance to the reconstruction of the historical Jesus, Q has also been at the center of a revisionist understanding of the origins of Christian → soteriology. The absence in Q of → passion and → resurrection traditions has been taken, by scholars such as Burton Mack, as an indication that at least some of the earliest followers of Jesus proclaimed a message of salvation through Wisdom that was not centered in these events. In this view the soteriology of Paul and the canonical gospels represents only one — and perhaps not the earliest — trajectory of Christian reflection on the meaning of Jesus' life and death.

→ Exegesis, Biblical, 2; Literature, Biblical and Early Christian, 2; New Testament Era, History of; Primitive Christian Community

Bibliography: R. A. Edwards, *A Theology of Q: Eschatology, Prophecy, and Wisdom* (Philadelphia, 1976) • P. Hoffmann, *Studien zur Theologie der Logienquelle* (3d ed.; Münster, 1982) • A. D. Jacobson, "Wisdom Christology in Q" (Diss., Claremont, Calif., 1978) • J. S. Kloppenborg, *The Formation of Q: Trajectories in Ancient Wisdom Collections* (Philadelphia, 1987) • B. L. Mack, *The Lost Gospel: The Book of Q and Christian Origins* (San Francisco, 1993); idem, *A Myth of Innocence: Mark and Christian Origins* (Minneapolis, 1988) • J. M. Robinson, "*LOGOI SOPHON:* On the Gattung of Q," *Trajectories through Early Christianity* (J. M. Robinson and H. Koester; Philadelphia, 1971) 71-113 • J. M. Robinson, P. Hoffmann, and J. S. Kloppenborg, eds., *The Critical Edition of Q* (Minneapolis, 2000); idem, eds., *The Sayings Gospel Q in Greek and English: With Parallels from the Gospels of Mark and Thomas* (Minneapolis, 2002) • S. Schulz, *Die Spruchquelle der Evangelisten* (Zurich, 1972).

Paul Hoffmann and
Eric M. Heen

Qatar

	1960	*1980*	*2000*
Population (1,000s):	45	229	599
Annual growth rate (%):	8.84	8.90	1.56

Area: 11,427 sq. km. (4,412 sq. mi.)

A.D. 2000

Population density: 52/sq. km. (136/sq. mi.)
Births / deaths: 1.84 / 0.44 per 100 population
Fertility rate: 3.44 per woman
Infant mortality rate: 14 per 1,000 live births
Life expectancy: 72.7 years (m: 71.0, f: 76.4)
Religious affiliation (%): Muslims 79.8, Christians 13.0 (Roman Catholics 6.7, indigenous 3.0, Anglicans 1.4, Protestants 1.0, other Christians 1.0), Hindus 2.7, nonreligious 2.3, Buddhists 2.0, other 0.2.

1. General Situation

The State of Qatar lies along the peninsula of the same name on the east coast of the Arabian Peninsula. East Arab Bedouin tribes began to settle there in the 18th century. Among them the Al Thani family played a leading role from the end of the 19th century. In 1872 the territory came under Ottoman rule with a Turkish garrison in Doha, the capital. When the Turks left at the beginning of World War I, Qatar became a British protectorate. By a treaty concluded in 1916, Britain took over responsibility for its defense and foreign policy (→ Colonialism).

1.1. Britain left the gulf in 1970, and Qatar achieved full independence in September 1971. By the provisional constitution of 1970 the emir is the executive, ruling through a cabinet that he appoints, which is made up mostly of members of the ruling family. An advisory council of 35 members nominated by the emir has had legislative power. Succession rests with the Al Thani family. The present ruler, Emir Hamad bin Khalifa Al Thani, ousted his father, Emir Khalifa bin Hamad Al Thani, in a bloodless coup in 1995.

In municipal elections held in March 1999, women participated for the first time as candidates and voters. In a 2003 referendum voters overwhelmingly approved a new constitution, which came into force in June 2004. This new constitution provides for a 45-member Advisory Council, of which two-thirds of the members are to be elected by the public, and the remaining one-third are to be appointed by the emir. The constitution also guarantees freedom of expression, assembly, and religion (→ Religious Liberty).

1.2. Qatar has been a member of the Gulf Cooperation Council since 1982. It also has recently been an ally of the United States, allowing U.S. and other foreign troops to deploy from its soil in military operations in the gulf.

The independent, pan-Arab satellite TV channel Al-Jazeera is funded by the emir of Qatar. Launched in 1996, it has become popular for its news coverage and controversial for its willingness to address sensitive topics (→ Mass Media).

1.3. Oil dominates the economy of Qatar. Development began in 1949 and had grown rapidly by 1984, when oil revenues became the basis of the prosperity of Qatar. Its population now enjoys one of the highest per capita incomes in the world. The natural gas reserves, also extremely important, were the third largest in the world in 2004. To broaden the economic base, a comprehensive program of industrializing was initiated with a petrochemical industry and steel works. The high revenues from oil have made possible a comprehensive program of social welfare, which is generally available, however, only to Qatari nationals.

Of the total population in 2000, only about one-fifth were native Qataris. The rest were guest workers, primarily Arabs (30 percent), Indians (18 percent), Pakistanis (18 percent), and Iranians (10 percent). The high number of foreign workers has led to social division between nationals, who have special rights, and underprivileged guest workers. Tensions have arisen because of these inequities. The government strictly controls foreign workers; for example, they normally are not allowed to bring their families.

2. Religious Situation

→ Islam took over in Qatar in A.D. 628. The emir and most of the citizens belong to the strict → sect of the Wahhabi, which spread from Saudi Arabia with the migration of Bedouin tribes from the southern Nejd. According to article 1 of the new constitution, Qatar's religion "is Islam, and → Shari'a law shall be a main source of its legislations." Only a small minority is Shiite (→ Shia, Shiites), principally the guest workers from Iran.

About the only Christians in Qatar are some among the Indians, Pakistanis, Egyptians, Filipinos, and Westerners who serve there as guest workers.

Bibliography: J. S. AL-ARAYED, *A Line in the Sea: The Qatar v. Bahrain Dispute in the World Court* (Berkeley, Calif., 2003) • D. B. BARRETT, G. T. KURIAN, and T. M. JOHNSON, *WCE* (2d ed.) 1.615-17 • EL-NAWAWY, *Al-Jazeera: How the Free Arab News Network Scooped the World and Changed the Middle East* (Cambridge, Mass., 2002) • Z. KURŞUN, *The Ottomans in Qatar: A History of the Anglo-Ottoman Conflicts in the Persian Gulf* (Istanbul, 2002) • P. VINE and P. CASEY, *The Heritage of Qatar* (London, 1992) • R. S. ZAHLAN, *The Making of the Modern Gulf States: Kuwait, Bahrain, Qatar, the United Arab Emirates, and Oman* (rev. ed.; Reading, Eng., 1998) 95-106.

THOMAS KOSZINOWSKI and THE EDITORS

Qoheleth → Ecclesiastes, Book of

Quakers → Friends, Society of

Quantum Theory

1. The Quantum Principle
2. Schrödinger's Wave Mechanics
3. Interpretations of Quantum Theory
4. Quantum Field Theory

"Quantum theory" is the term for a collection of physical theories about the behavior of matter, all of which are distinguished from previous Newtonian theory by their acceptance of discrete or discontinuous behavior of matter, and by their supplanting of Newtonian determinism in favor of a probabilistic description of material reality.

1. The Quantum Principle

The mechanical theory of mass, force, and motion ascribed to Isaac Newton (1642-1727) yields a picture of the world in which the physical variables describing an isolated system (such as position, velocity, momentum, angular momentum, and energy) can take on values varying continuously throughout some range. The most dramatic manifestation of alternative quantum-mechanical descriptions is that some of these variables, under some conditions, can take on only discrete, or "quantized," values, but not a whole continuum of values. Thus the angular momentum of a system can only take on values that are integral (or half-integral) multiples of $h/(2\pi)$, where h is Planck's Constant; similarly, the energy of such a system may take on values that (while not necessarily related by integral multiples) are nevertheless discrete and separate. One of the early successes of quantum-mechanical ideas was the derivation, by Niels Bohr (1885-1962), of the discrete set of "energy levels" allowed for the single electron bound to a proton to form a solitary hydrogen atom.

The manifestations of quantum mechanics are most dramatic in the microscopic regime, via the behavior of molecules, atoms, and nuclei, but macroscopic implications of the theories are also known. So far as is known, there is no upper limit to the size or complexity of systems to which quantum mechanics applies, although in most cases a quantum-mechanical description reduces to the more familiar Newtonian theory in the limit of macroscopic systems.

2. Schrödinger's Wave Mechanics

Max Planck (1858-1947) first introduced his constant to account for the observed properties of so-called blackbody radiation, but its most accessible implication is through the celebrated prediction by L. de Broglie (1892-1987) that any object possessing a momentum p will also be associated with a wave-like disturbance of wavelength $\lambda = h/p$. The deep nature of this "wave" is still in dispute, but such a relation led E. Schrödinger (1887-1961) to write his famous equation for wave mechanics, which assumes its simplest form in describing the nonrelativistic behavior of a single particle in a specified field of force.

One of the first successes of the Schrödinger equation was to permit concrete predictions for the behavior of atoms, either isolated or subjected to disturbances such as electric and magnetic fields, and such predictions have been tested in fine detail. The one-electron case of the hydrogen atom could be rederived using this theory, giving predictions consistent with Bohr's but going further; and (contrary to assertions sometimes still found in textbooks) the theory could also be applied to atoms and molecules involving many electrons, via techniques of numerical solution. An early success was the understanding of the relationships among all the chemical elements, as revealed in the structure of the periodic table.

The Schrödinger equation shed light on much more than atomic physics, however, and it still remains the starting point for descriptions of matter on all scales. The quite different fields of nuclear and solid-state physics are both illuminated by ideas from wave mechanics, and in both areas quantum mechanics remains an engineering tool for design and understanding. With the increasing demands of, and possibilities opened by, technological improvements, the scope of Schrödinger's mechanics continues to expand, and the wave properties it originally ascribed to objects such as electrons have been confirmed to exist for neutrons, for whole atoms, for diatomic molecules, and most recently for objects as large and complicated as the C_{70} molecule. There are even macroscopic manifestations of its predictions in multiparticle systems such as superfluid helium, superconductors, and, most recently, Bose-Einstein condensates.

3. Interpretations of Quantum Theory

The most radical attribute of wave mechanics has always been its probabilistic character (→ Probabilism). The Schrödinger "wave function" lies at the very boundary between determinism and probability, since the Schrödinger equation predicts that it evolves continuously and deterministically in time; but given the probability interpretation of M. Born (1882-1970), the wave function is held to predict not trajectories, orbits, or outcomes, but rather only the relative probability of possible outcomes. Quantum theory makes no statement about the causes of individual outcomes and leaves individual quantum events described only in statistical terms via their distributions. Thus there have always been questions about the nature of the wave function, and indeed about the scope or finality of quantum-mechanical descriptions.

Such concerns could formerly be relegated to → metaphysics, as being only questions of philosophical interpretation, but since the work of J. S. Bell (1928-90), they have been seen to lie at the heart of experimentally testable quantum phenomena. Bell's work led to experimental tests discriminating between orthodox quantum-mechanical predictions, on the one hand, and, on the other, the predictions of any and all "local realistic" theories of matter; and quantum mechanics has repeatedly passed tests of ever-increasing sophistication. The results also constitute evidence against "local → realism" and thereby give good evidence that the behavior of matter is either nonlocal or nonrealistic, in the technical sense.

Whatever else can be said about quantum mechanics, it is already more than clear that the successes of the theory have definitively undercut a view of the physical universe as deterministic in the Newtonian mechanical sense. The relevance of quantum mechanics to perennial philosophical and theological questions of mental determinism and human free will is still debated; some thinkers find in quantum mechanics room for a more "open" view of the future, while others find no comfort in the apparent replacement of iron determinism by blind chance (→ Freedom 1).

4. Quantum Field Theory

The Schrödinger equation is professedly nonrelativistic in character, and early developments by P. A. M. Dirac (1902-84) yielded an improved equation consistent with the requirements of Albert Einstein's (1879-1955) special theory of → relativity. The theory of Dirac led to immediate successes in the description of the electron's behavior, including most spectacularly the prediction of the existence of "antielectrons." Such objects were subsequently discovered and have since been called positrons; they represent the possibility of the existence of antimatter in general.

But the Dirac theory also takes note of the fact that a proper relativistic and quantum-mechanical description of particles must allow for the possibilities of the creation, and annihilation, of particles under certain conditions, and this line of thought has been followed to give "quantum field theories," in which "quantum fields" are the underlying realities, and material particles are merely their overt manifestations. An example of such a quantum field theory is quantum electrodynamics, the theory of electrons, positrons, and photons (the quanta of electromagnetic radiation). Despite the mathematical difficulties of this theory, it is possible to deduce from it exquisitely detailed predictions, and these predictions have been tested to fabulous accuracy and found to be correct.

Developments in quantum field theory have also included the so-called standard model of particle physics, which includes all known particles, and all known physical interactions except gravitation. The unification of gravitation with the other forces of physics remains a current research frontier, with "string theory" as the subject of the most effort; whatever string theory may yet do for our ideas of space, time, and matter, it remains a quantum-mechanical theory.

→ Science and Theology

Bibliography: J. S. Bell, *Speakable and Unspeakable in Quantum Mechanics* (Cambridge, 1987) • P. A. M. Dirac, *The Principles of Quantum Mechanics* (Oxford, 1958) • N. D. Mermin, *Boojums All the Way Through: Communicating Science in a Prosaic Age* (New York, 1990) • A. Pais, *Inward Bound: Of Matter and Forces in the Physical World* (Oxford, 1986).

David A. Van Baak

Quaternity

The → number four ranks high among the symbolically significant numbers (→ Symbol). In translations of → Monophysite arguments both for and against Apollinarius of Laodicea (d. ca. 390), theological Latin refers to *quaternitas* along with *trinitas.* "Two natures," it was argued, means "two sons," and hence we have a tetrad instead of a triad (→ Trinity).

In religious history the term "quaternity" denotes a fourfold structure. On the basis, for example, of the four points of → heaven, the four ages, the four sides of a square, the four temperaments, the four basic elements, and the four extremities of the body, we meet the number four more than any other. Thus in China we have the four quarters of the heavenly palace and of the earthly city; in India the four members of the cosmic Purusha corresponding to the Varna → castes; in → Buddhism the four noble truths of the "middle path," the agreed teachings of the 18 ancient sects, the proper life circumstances, and the stages of mystical absorption; in Iran Zurvan Akanarag as fourfold infinite space-time; in Judaism the tetragrammaton (→ Yahweh), the cherubim, the wheels and faces of Ezekiel, the horses and horns of Zechariah; in Greece the Pythagorean *tetraktys* (i.e., the sum of the first four numbers = 10); and in various cultures four world epochs and four mandala visions.

For C. G. Jung (1875-1961; → Psychoanalysis) quaternity was an archetype of the greatest universality and signified the entry, not of another masculine, but of a feminine element into the "inner God." As Sophia, this element was a personification of the anima in the subconscious and was linked to many new applications in Christianity, → Gnosis, and → alchemy.

In Trinitarian teaching the fear has sometimes been expressed that to speak of the one essence and the three persons of God is to think of God as a quaternity rather than a trinity.

→ Iranian Religions

Bibliography: R. L. Berner, *The Rule of Four: Four Essays on the Principle of Quaternity* (New York, 1996) • G. R. Elder, "Quaternity," *EncRel(E)* 12.133-34 • C. G. Jung, *The Collected Works of C. G. Jung,* vol. 11, *Psychology and Religion: West and East* (New York, 1958) esp. "Psychology and Religion" (1937-40), 3-105; "Transformation Symbolism in the Mass" (1954), 201-96; "Answer to Job" (1952), 355-470 • G. W. H. Lampe, *A Patristic Greek Lexicon* (Oxford, 1961) s.v. τετράς • A. Schimmel, *The Mystery of Numbers* (New York, 1993) • P. Wheatley, *The Pivot of the Four Quarters* (Chicago, 1971) • F. C. White, *On Schopenhauer's Fourfold Root of the Principle of Sufficient Reason* (Leiden, 1992).

Carsten Colpe

Quietism

"Quietism" is the term used for a mystically oriented, transdenominational movement in the 17th and 18th centuries (→ Mysticism 2). Two of its main features find expression in 18th-century Protestant poetry (→ Devotional Literature), namely, silence and simplicity, as in G. Tersteegen's "Gott ist gegenwärtig ... alles in uns schweige" (God is present, [let] everything in us be silent) and M. Claudius's "Laß uns einfältig werden" (Let us become simple). From the standpoint of social history quietism may be viewed as a form of → spiritualism and seen as individualistic (E. → Troeltsch). The community of J. de Labadie (1610-74), however, represented a strictly ascetic community (→ Sanctification 3).

The initiator of quietism was the Spanish priest M. de Molinos (1628-96), who based his spiritual life on the principle that by renouncing all activity (including → prayer), we may lose ourselves in God. In France Madame Guyon (1648-1717) advocated "disinterested love," and she in turn influenced F. Fénelon (1651-1715). P. Poiret (1646-1719) introduced this type of mysticism into the German-speaking world, and G. Arnold (1666-1714), A. H. → Francke (1663-1727), and Count N. → Zinzendorf (1700-1760; → Pietism) came under his influence.

Regarding quietism and its thinking, the question arises whether full surrender to God does not seek itself to be a kind of achievement. It must also be asked whether the → ethics of minimal participation in daily life does not involve withdrawal from active Christian citizenship.

The → Roman Catholic Church took a critical view of the teachings of quietism, and especially its antiecclesiastical tendencies. Innocent XI (1676-89) condemned the movement in the bull *Coelestis pastor* (1687), and its chief protagonists, Molinos, Guyon, and Fénelon, suffered under such repressive measures as imprisonment, temporary deposition, and forced recantation.

→ Contemplation; Devotion, Devotions; Meditation; Mystical Union; Unity

Bibliography: G. D. Balsama, "The Controversy over French Quietism during the Reign of Louis XIV: Doctrine and Politics, 1686-1700" (2 vols.; Ph.D. diss., Brown University, 1970) • M. De la Bedoyère, *The Archbishop and the Lady: The Story of Fénelon and Madame Guyon* (London, 1956) • F. Fénelon, *Oeuvres complètes* (10 vols.; Paris, 1848-52) • R. A. Knox, *Enthusiasm* (New York, 1950) • M. de Molinos, *Guía espiritual* (Madrid, 1977; orig. pub., 1675; ET *The Spiritual Guide Which Disentangles the Soul* [London, 1907]) • E. Troeltsch, *The Social Teaching of the Christian Churches* (London, 1949; orig. pub., 1912) 805-7 • M. Wieser, *Der sentimentale Mensch* (Gotha, 1924).

Christofer Frey

Qumran

1. General Data
   1.1. Texts
   1.2. Archaeology
   1.3. Paleography
   1.4. Library
   1.5 Historical Identification
   1.6. Faith and Life
2. Significance for the OT
3. Significance for Early Judaism
4. Significance for Early Christianity

1. General Data

Khirbet Qumran (KQ), or simply Qumran, is a location on the northwest shore of the Dead Sea at the Wadi Qumran, approximately 20 km. (12½ mi.) in a direct line east of → Jerusalem.

1.1. *Texts*

The Qumran texts broadly include the Dead Sea MSS, along with writings from Masada (A.D. 74), Naḥal Ḥever, Ṣe'elim, Mishmar, and Murabbaʿat (up to A.D. 132/35). More narrowly, the Qumran texts include the remains of about 750 various MSS (scrolls of leather, more rarely papyrus, in one case copper) that were found between 1947 and 1956 in 11 caves near Qumran and that use biblical and Mishnaic Hebrew, Aramaic, and, less frequently, Greek (exclusively so in the seventh cave, or 7Q). The Hebrew orthography includes both Palestinian-Square and Paleo-Hebrew scripts.

1.2. *Archaeology*

Archaeology suggests the following phases of building and settlement at KQ:

buildings with cisterns, 8th/7th cent. B.C.
rebuilt ca. 150/140
extended 110/100
destroyed by fire in 38 and by earthquake in 31
uninhabited up to 4 B.C., then partly rebuilt
destroyed by the Romans in A.D. 68
occupied as a military post by the Romans up to 74 or longer
occupied by Jewish rebels 132/35.

The cave MSS have been related to the KQ scriptorium and are dated before A.D. 68.

1.3. *Paleography*

Paleography has established a relative chronology for the scripts: Maccabean, Hasmonaean (150-30 B.C.), and Herodian (30 B.C. to A.D. 68). No text published thus far refers to the destruction of KQ in 68 or of Jerusalem in 70.

1.4. *Library*

The Qumran library does not contain records or documents of everyday life (apart from 3Q15, in Hebrew, and 6Q26; and perhaps 4Q342-48, 351-54, 356-61, in Aramaic), nor are the MSS autographs; they are copies. Linguistically, the Aramaic MSS are of different origin and seem to come from other library stocks. Some Hebrew MSS come from Qumran, others from Jerusalem or elsewhere in Palestine, being copied at Qumran.

Today some scholars regard KQ as purely a military post and do not connect the cave MSS with it. They theorize that the MSS were moved to the caves for safekeeping in A.D. 68, their true home being the temple library at Jerusalem.

1.5. *Historical Identification*

One can make historical deductions from CD (Damascus Document), 1QS (the Rule of the Community and related documents), 1QH (Thanksgiving Hymns), 4QMMT (*Miqsat Ma'aseh ha-Torah,* some Torah precepts), the commentaries *(pesharim),* and 4QTestim. Agreements of the texts with early accounts of the Essenes (by Pliny, Philo, Josephus, and Hippolytus) quickly led early scholars in the field to identify the people of Qumran with the Essenes. KQ in this view was one of many Essene communities, along with 'Ain Feshkha, 'Ain el-Ghuweir, and others scattered all the way from Palestine to Egypt. Qumran perhaps served as a remote study center for those wishing to withdraw from the world.

The origins of the Essenes go back to the "community of the new covenant in the land of Damascus" (CD 6:19 etc.). They were a predominantly lay organization with a special legal corpus (CD 9–16). The "Teacher of Righteousness" with his priestly followers, the "sons of Zadok," joined them later and gave them the new order of the *yaḥad* (i.e., community, 1QS 5–11). We learn more about the origins in 4QMMT. The Teacher, or already perhaps the earlier community (the "root of the planting," CD 1:7), writing in a letter to the political and religious (Hasmonaean) leadership in Jerusalem, says that the reason for their schism ("we have separated from the mass of the peo[ple]," 4QMMT C7)) lies in different practices of the Torah in matters of purification (→ Heresies and Schisms; Torah). The closeness of 4QMMT to a Zadokite understanding of the Torah raises the question of how far we are to see in Qumran a Sadducean splinter group.

Identification of the Teacher depends on who the opponent was to whom reference is made in the texts (the "wicked priest" or "man of lies"). It is perhaps best to see in him the → high priest of the period 159-153/150 B.C.

1.6. *Faith and Life*

The faith and life of Qumran aimed at seeking God in accordance with all the commands to which → Moses and the → prophets bear witness (1QS 1:1-5, 13-14). The time was thought to have come when the faithful "will be detached from anyone who has not withdrawn his path from all injustice" (1QS 9:20-21; 4Q258 8:5). As in Isa. 40:3, a way must now be prepared in the wilderness (1QS 9:19-20); this way was understood as → midrash of the Torah (8:15-16). → Exegesis of the Bible sheds light on the biblical laws and also brings new light to notice. The whole Torah is the key to understanding the present.

Life at Qumran was one of daily → asceticism (sacerdotal purity) marked by morning and evening → prayers and shared work, possessions, and meals. Individuals were seen as basically subject to divinely revealed law. Human creatureliness involves some measure of captivity to → sin (since the fall). God redeems human beings (who by themselves are weak), when helpless, purifies their perverted spirit, and integrates them into the family of the sons of heaven (1QH 11:19-22) among "those who know" (19:13-14). To some degree God's creative work is viewed as a double → predestination to good or evil acts (→ Anthropology 1-2; Creation).

According to 1QM a 40-year war against "the sons of darkness" under Belial will end with a victory for God and "the sons of light" under Michael. According to 1QS 4:18-23 evil will be destroyed by God in an appointed judgment, and God will then begin a new creation, the "glory of → Adam." In the end time a prophet (like Moses, Deut. 18:18) is expected, as also, based on Zech. 6:9-14, are two anointed ones: the priestly Messiah of Aaron, the true interpreter of the law (4QFlor 1-2 i 11; CD 7:18; cf. *T. Levi* 18), and the kingly Messiah of Israel (1QS 9:11; CD 12:23–13:1; 14:19; 20:1), who will deliver Israel (4QFlor 1-2 i 13; CD 7:20-21; 1QSb 5:20-28; cf. *T. Jud.* 24; → Apocalypticism 2-3; Eschatology 1-2; Messianism).

2. Significance for the OT

Some 250 MSS from Qumran are biblical texts, taken from all books except Esther and Nehemiah. In some cases Qumran is at least also a witness to the later MT. In others, its texts agree with the LXX and/or the Samaritan → Pentateuch, or else they differ from all traditions known thus far. In relation to the later textus receptus, the Bible of Qumran shows much textual freedom and often offers independent interpretation. Among the oldest MSS of the LXX are five copies of the Pentateuch, from Cave 4 (4Q119-22) and Cave 7 (7Q1), and the → Minor Prophets scroll from Naḥal Ḥever (*DJD* 8 [1990]). The Aramaic translations of Leviticus (4Q156), Job (4Q157; 11Q10), and Tobit (4Q196-99) are the oldest Targums (→ Bible Manuscripts and Editions).

3. Significance for Early Judaism

The Qumran texts are among the most important sources for understanding postbiblical Judaism, especially the theology of early Judaism from the 2d and 1st centuries B.C. to the 1st century A.D. Some texts go back to the 4th/3rd century B.C.; some derive from the cult and liturgy of the Jerusalem → temple; others give information on the history of the → Pharisees (separatists from the Hasidic community), the → Sadducees (4QMMT), and the Essenes (→ Jewish Theology; Judaism).

4. Significance for Early Christianity

The four larger Greek fragments from Cave 7 (7Q3-5, 8) are not parts of NT texts. Nowhere in the Qumran texts is there reference to → Jesus, to his brother → James, to → Paul, or to the → primitive Christian community. The MSS, however, give us information that leads to a better understanding of Jesus and the early church. We find linguistic similarities (e.g., cf. "the men of his favor" in 4QVisAmr[c] = 4Q545 4, 18 and 1QH 12:32-33 with Luke 2:14; 4QBeat with the Beatitudes; "Son of God" and "Son of the Most High" in 4Q246 [of Antiochus Epiphanes] with Luke 1:32, 35 [of Jesus]).

We also find similar concepts in the two settings. Dualism (e.g., "the three nets of Belial": "fornication, wealth, and the defilement of the temple" [CD 4:15-18; cf. 1QS 3:13–4:26] in Qumran and in 2 Cor. 6:14–7:1), and Satan is a cause of sickness (11QPs[a] 19:13-16 etc. and Luke 13:16 etc.). → Healing takes place through prayer and the → laying on of hands (1QapGen 20:21-29 and Acts 28:8) and through → exorcism (11QapocrPs and Mark 1:21-27 etc.).

→ Apocrypha; Cultic Meal; Cultic Purity; Pseudepigrapha; Sabbath

Bibliography: Qumran translations: M. G. ABEGG, P. W. FLINT, and E. ULRICH, *The Dead Sea Scrolls Bible: The Oldest Known Bible* (San Francisco, 1999) • F. GARCÍA MARTÍNEZ and E. J. C. TIGCHELAAR, eds., *The Dead Sea Scrolls Study Edition* (2 vols.; Grand Rapids, 2000) nonbiblical texts • D. W. PARRY and E. TOV, eds., *The Dead Sea Scrolls Reader* (6 vols.; Leiden, 2004-5) • M. O. WISE, M. G. ABEGG, and E. M. COOK, *The Dead Sea Scrolls: A New Translation* (San Francisco, 1996) nonbiblical texts.

Secondary works: J. J. COLLINS, *Apocalypticism in the Dead Sea Scrolls* (New York, 1997) • J. J. COLLINS and R. A. KUGLER, eds., *Religion in the Dead Sea Scrolls* (Grand Rapids, 2000) • F. M. CROSS, *The Ancient Library of Qumran* (3d ed.; Minneapolis, 1995) • C. A. EVANS, *Eschatology, Messianism, and the Dead Sea Scrolls* (Grand Rapids, 1997) • J. A. FITZMYER, *The Dead Sea Scrolls and Christian Origins* (Grand Rapids, 2000) • P. W. FLINT, *The Bible at Qumran: Text, Shape, and Interpretation* (Grand Rapids, 2001) • F. GARCÍA MARTÍNEZ and J. T. BARRERA, *People of the Dead Sea Scrolls* (Leiden, 1995) • M. HENZE, ed., *Biblical Interpretation at Qumran* (Grand Rapids, 2005) • J. MAGNESS, *The Archaeology of Qumran and the Dead Sea Scrolls* (Grand Rapids, 2002) • E. C. ULRICH, *The Dead Sea Scrolls and the Origins of the Bible* (Grand Rapids, 1999).

GERHARD WILHELM NEBE

Qur'ān

1. Etymology
2. Reception
3. Compilation
4. Language and Style
5. The Qur'ānic Message
6. The Impact of the Qur'ān

1. Etymology

Arab. *Qur'ān* (often previously transliterated "Koran") is a derivative of the verbal root *qr'*, with the general meaning "recite (orally)." The imperative of the same verb, *iqra'*, is generally acknowledged to be the opening of the first utterance revealed by God to the Prophet Muḥammad, in *sūrah* 96 (The Blood-Clot), v. 1, and is God's command to Muḥammad that he proclaim God's revelations. *Qur'ān* is thus best translated "recitation."

This etymology is of importance because it underlines both the oral origins of Islam's most authoritative source and the continuing function of oral recitation and of listening to the words and sounds of the Qur'ān within Islamic communities. The recording of the Qur'ān in textual form took place after Muḥammad's death, and the very process of transferring a memorized set of revelations to textual form had a profound effect on the development of the Arabic language, of a community of

Muslim faithful, and of hermeneutic methodology relating to the Qur'ān itself and other categories of text.

2. Reception

The contents of the Qur'ān are the revelations of God to his prophet Muḥammad (ca. 570-632). Tradition has it that the first revelation came to Muḥammad during a period of seclusion in a cave outside his native city of Mecca. At first he revealed the message of his revelations only to his first wife, Khadījah, and other close associates. Gradually, however, he was instructed to proclaim his message — one of warning concerning the consequences of → sin in this world, with examples of previous communities on whom God had wreaked vengeance — to the larger community of citizens of Mecca. At that time (late 6th cent.) the city was not only a major commercial center but also the site of the Kaaba (Arab. *ka'bah,* "cubic structure"), a renowned shrine to various deities and a place of → pilgrimage. It is thus hardly a surprise that the import of Muḥammad's message was initially not well received. As animosities worsened, he moved to the oasis of Yathrib to the northeast. (This move is the *hijrah* [emigration] of 622, which marks the beginning of the Islamic era.) The community of Yathrib thereafter developed into the city known as Madīnat al-nabī (City of the Prophet), or Medina.

At the time of Muḥammad's death in 632, the revelations of both the earlier Meccan period and the Medinan survived in the memories of Muḥammad's close companions and helpers within the small but expanding Muslim community. It was when a large number of these "carriers" *(ḥamalah)* of the Qur'ān were dying that it was deemed necessary to record the contents of Muḥammad's revelations in written form.

3. Compilation

While there are accounts of earlier compilations of Muḥammad's pronouncements, the Qur'ān in book form is the result of a recording process instigated by the third caliph, 'Uthmān ibn 'Affān (644-56), who expressed concern about the number of variants that, by the very nature of things, characterized the corporate memorization of a series of revelations spread over several decades.

The passages of revelation were recorded, tradition has it, from the memories of men and from a number of written fragments. The passages were categorized first as belonging to the "Meccan" (pre-*hijrah*) or "Medinan" (post-*hijrah*) period and then were gathered into sections, each of which was called a sūrah, with a title culled from a word or phrase found within the section. The 12th sūrah, for example, contains a version of the narrative of → Joseph (§1) and is called Sūrat Yūsuf; the 26th contains a reference to poets and is thus known as Sūrat al-Shu'arā' (sūrah of the poets). In addition to its title, each sūrah identifies the verses in it that belong to the Meccan and Medinan periods. The Qur'ān opens with the Sūrat al-Fātiḥah (sūrah of the opening), used as a prayer on numerous occasions in the life of a Muslim, but thereafter the 113 subsequent sūrahs are arranged according to length, starting with the longest, Sūrat al-Baqarah (sūrah of the cow), which contains 286 verses, and finishing with a number of very short sūrahs, all of which belong to the early Meccan period and are characterized by a very particular structure and diction. The 114th and final sūrah, for example, Sūrat al-Nās (sūrah of the people), contains six verses.

From the outset the Qur'ān, its message and cadences, were central to the life of every Muslim, and the reading of the text was an essential part of both corporate and individual acts of devotion. For that purpose the Qur'ān was also divided into 30 subdivisions, called *aḥzāb* (sing. *ḥizb*), so that, for example, the entire text could be read during the holy month of Ramadan and on significant communal or private occasions.

The Qur'ān was recorded in written form from memory, and it remains up till today an object of pride for Muslims to be able to memorize and cite the text of the Qur'ān. The memorization of the complete text has been a project undertaken in traditional Islamic schools (the *kuttāb*). The well-known autobiography of the Egyptian litterateur Ṭāhā Ḥusayn (1889-1973), translated into English as *An Egyptian Childhood* (1943), gives a clear indication of the pride that parents and community feel when a child becomes a hafiz (*ḥāfiẓ,* "one who remembers," i.e., a memorizer of the Qur'ān).

4. Language and Style

The Qur'ān is the word of God transmitted to his people through the mediation of a "messenger" *(rasūl),* whose function it was to relay the revelations to his contemporary listeners. God speaks in the first person, issuing commands ("recite," "tell") to Muḥammad the Prophet, who serves as the second-person addressee: "If my servants ask you about me, indeed I am near" (Sūrat al-Baqarah [2], v. 186). Third-person discourse is used both to depict the reactions of those who are listening to the message and, when appropriate, to narrate exemplary stories of earlier prophets and peoples. Thus, in addition to direct injunctions to Muḥammad to relay God's word, there are also passages that reflect the context of Muḥammad's revelations. In particular, the later sūrahs include passages that reflect the ways in which doctrinal issues would be raised within the emerging Muslim community. The usual formula is, "They will ask you concerning . . ." (e.g., the sacred month [ibid., v. 217], wine and gambling [v. 219], and menstruation [v. 222]), and the answer to each question is always prefaced with "Say . . ." (→ Islamic Philosophy).

The Qur'ān states clearly that it is "an Arabic Qur'ān" (Sūrat Yūsuf [12], v. 2) and goes on to note that every sacred revelation is presented to its people in their own language. The meaning of the utterances revealed to Muḥammad is *mubīn* (clear). From this notion there develops a major subfield of Islamic → hermeneutics and → criticism, the study of *bayān*, or "clarity of expression." With the expansion of the Muslim community far beyond its original linguistic and geographic boundaries, it became necessary to explore the meaning and ramifications of these central terms regarding the discourse of the Qur'ān.

As early philologists began the task of studying and preparing commentaries on the now canonical, written text, it emerged that the revelations were couched in a style and level of language that was characteristic of the Hejaz (Arab. Al-Ḥijāz) region of the Arabian Peninsula (within which lay the twin holy cities of Mecca and Medina) during the pre-Islamic period. This particular register was reserved for special occasions and was associated with the utterances of particular categories of public speakers. For that very reason, the text of the Qur'ān is very explicit at several points concerning the need to differentiate the function of Muḥammad as a → prophet (and thus revealer of God's word) from that of other users of this same style of recitation (named *saj*ʿ, usually translated "rhyming prose"), namely, soothsayers and poets *(shuʿarā')*.

When challenged by skeptics to illustrate his prophetic function by performing a → miracle, Muḥammad would always point to the Qur'ān. This was the "challenge" *(taḥaddī)*, as encountered, for example, in Sūrat al-Isrā' (sūrah of the night journey, 17), v. 88: "If mankind and jinn got together to produce the like of this Qur'ān, they would not produce its like." Continuing research on the Qur'ān led to the development of an enormous library of hermeneutical literature, including studies of problematic words and passages *(mushkil)* and an entire subfield of criticism devoted to the identification of its miraculous qualities (see 6).

5. The Qur'ānic Message

Central to the message of the Qur'ān is Allah, the absolute and single → God (§1). The statement of faith *(shahādah)* begins with the words: "There is no god but Allah" (Sūrat al-Ṣāffāt [sūrah of the rangers, 37], v. 35), and the sermon delivered by Joseph to his fellow prisoners poses the question: "Which is better: to have a number of different gods or God the One and All-powerful?" (Sūrat Yūsuf [12], v. 39). God is described in the Qur'ān with 99 epithets *(al-asmā' al-ḥusnā*, "beautiful names"); among many other attributes, he is merciful, sincere, knowing, great, and powerful. God has total power over humanity, and the charge of his message in the Qur'ān is to change human behavior in this world in order to be prepared for the next. As part of the process whereby the message is communicated, God offers → "signs" *(āyāt)* to illustrate his judgments, mercy and forgiveness, and punishments. The fate of ancient peoples is alluded to: ʿĀd and Thamūd are cited as two communities upon whom God wreaked vengeance for their idolatry and evil practices (Sūrat al-Aʿrāf [sūrah of the elevated places, 7], vv. 65-79). The deeds of the individual in this world will be weighed in the balance on the day of judgment; the choice is a stark one between a → paradise of eternal bliss — gardens with flowing streams — and Jahannam, a fiery → hell.

The opening sūrah of the Qur'ān expresses the choice before humans as being one between following "the straight path" *(al-sirāṭ al-mustaqīm)* and "going astray" *(ḍāllīn)*. Muḥammad's listeners are urged to believe in the one God and in his chosen prophet. The penalties for unbelief *(kufr)* and → apostasy are dire, as are those for people who make a pretense of their faith; their fate is the subject of some rather grim humor: "Give the hypocrites the good news: they will have a gruesome punishment" (Sūrat al-Nisā' [sūrah of the women, 4], v. 138).

The Qur'ān often resorts to the repertoire of homiletic and prophetic narratives that was presumably current in the Arabian Peninsula in the seventh century in order to provide exemplary stories of faith in adversity. Particularly during the period following the *hijrah* from Mecca to Medina, revelations refer to linkages between the revelations of the Qur'ān and those of previous scriptures: "the book he has revealed to his messenger, and the book he revealed before" (Sūrat al-Nisā' [4], v. 136). The status of Muḥammad as continuer and "seal" of the prophetic line *(khātam al-anbiyā')* is made explicit in a message specifically directed at "the people of the Book" (Jews and Christians): "Now our messenger has come to you, clarifying for you much from the Book that you have kept hidden" (Sūrat al-Mā'idah [sūrah of the table, 5], v. 15).

We have already seen the Qur'ān's inclusion of the entire narrative of Joseph (Sūrat Yūsuf [12]), but the lives and examples of many other exemplary figures are also mentioned. A short list would include → Noah, → Solomon, Lot, and → Jesus and → Mary (citations regarding whom are a particular feature of the decoration in the Dome of the Rock in Jerusalem). Notable in this regard is Sūrat al-Kahf (sūrah of the cave, 18), in that it contains not only the famous tale of the seven sleepers of Ephesus (vv. 9-20) but also an account of → Moses' testing at the hands of the mysterious figure of al-Khaḍir (vv. 60-98).

The incipient Muslim community in Medina in the period following the Prophet's emigration in 622 had heard the revelations that have been briefly summarized above, but inevitably there arose questions concerning details of faith and practice and challenges to specific statements and their implications. Of the five "pillars" *(arkān)* — statement of faith, → prayer, almsgiving, fasting, and pilgrimage — revelations now codify the nature of belief and religious practice for all but the pilgrimage. In response to questions from the community, guidance was provided concerning specific matters, including → marriage and divorce, inheritance, → dietary regulations, theft, gambling, distribution of spoils, and → usury. This list of topics, when coupled with references to "hypocrites" noted above, makes it clear that some of these revelations and the regulations that they impose are the consequence of particular incidents in the early life of the Muslim community in Medina. An especially notable example of this background occurs in Sūrat al-Nūr (sūrah of the light, 24), where a set of verses is clearly addressed to a group of people who have spread malicious gossip about 'Ā'ishah, one of the Prophet's later wives (vv. 11-20).

While these dicta in the Qur'ān itself serve as the basic source for the belief and conduct of Muslims and also as the primary authority in the establishment of the code of Islamic law (→ Shari'ah), the second most important source for matters of doctrine and practice is hadith (*ḥadīth,* "speech, report"). This categorized corpus of reports covers the acts and statements of the Prophet during his lifetime.

6. The Impact of the Qur'ān

The recording of the Qur'ān in written form was an event of major importance in that it stimulated the numerous scholarly endeavors that served as the foundation for what were to become the "Islamic sciences." That intellectual milieu also fostered a system of education whose impact was felt not only throughout the ever-expanding "domain of → Islam" *(dār al-Islām)* but also far beyond it. Initial studies of the Qur'ān needed to focus on the text itself: its language and syntactic structures (including such basics as the conventions of the alphabet) and the authenticity of the recorded segments. That focus led in turn to research on the genealogy of individuals and tribal groups and to the compilation of linguistic precedents, particularly in the form of an elaborate oral corpus of poetry from the pre-Islamic era. From the analysis of the Qur'ān's content emerged compilations of principles of belief, codifications of jurisprudence (→ Law and Legal Theory), and studies in theology. The urgent need to sift through the vast collection of hadith accounts of the Prophet's behavior and recorded statements led to the development of principles of textual analysis and criticism. The study of these and other subfields became the focus of a system of education whereby learning (the status of *'ālim,* "knowing, learned"; pl. *'ulamā',* "learned ones") became the path to religious authority as it was passed on from one generation to the next.

As methods of critical analysis were applied to various types of text, the unique nature of the Qur'ān itself, implicit in the challenge that had been posed by Muḥammad to replicate its qualities, was subsumed under the heading of "the Qur'ān's inimitability" *(i'jāz al-Qur'ān).* Several prominent figures in Arabic literature wrote texts in imitation of the Qur'ān's style; one of them is a poet renowned in history as "the would-be Prophet" (al-Mutanabbī [d. 965]) for doing so, while al-Bāqillānī (d. 1013) compares the stylistic and moral message of the Qur'ān and pre-Islamic poetry in order to prove the superiority of the former

The Qur'ān remains an indivisible part of the history of the Arabic language and its texts and of the peoples of the Islamic world. The advent of modern media means that the Qur'ān's presence in the oral dimension is even more powerful than heretofore: the daily interruptions of television programming in order to broadcast the five daily times of prayer, the availability in digitized form of the text and recorded versions of it, and the amplified sound of the *mu'adhdhin* (muezzin) summoning the faithful to prayer — to be heard in all Muslim communities — all testify to the continuing prevalence of the Qur'ān in the daily life of large segments of the world's population.

Bibliography: Selected English versions: A. J. Arberry, trans., *The Koran Interpreted* (London, 1955; New York, 1986) • N. J. Dawood, trans., *The Koran* (London,

1956) • M. M. PICKTHALL, trans., *The Glorious Koran* (London, 1976; orig. pub., 1938) • M. SELLS, trans., *Approaching the Qur'an: The Early Revelations* (Ashland, Oreg., 1999).

Selected studies: J. BURTON, *The Collection of the Qur'an* (Cambridge, 1977) • W. A. GRAHAM, *Beyond the Written Word: Oral Aspects of Scripture in the History of Religion* (Cambridge, 1987); idem, "Koran und Ḥadīṯ," *Orientalisches Mittelalter* (ed. W. Heinrichs; Wiesbaden, 1990) 166-85 • G. R. HAWTING and A.-K. A. SHAREEF, eds., *Approaches to the Qur'an* (London, 1993) • A. JEFFREY, *The Foreign Vocabulary of the Qur'an* (Vadodara, 1938) • K. NELSON, *The Art of Reciting the Qur'an* (Austin, Tex., 1985) • A. NEUWIRTH, *Studien zur Komposition der mekkanischen Suren* (Berlin, 1981) • A. RIPPON, *Approaches to the History of the Interpretation of the Qur'an* (Oxford, 1988) • M. SELLS, "Sound and Meaning in Sūrat al-Qāriʿa," *Arabica* 40 (1993) 403-30; idem, "Sound, Spirit, and Gender in Sūrat al-Qadr," *JAOS* 111/2 (1991) 239-59 • J. E. WANSBROUGH, *Qur'anic Studies: Sources and Methods of Scriptural Interpretation* (Oxford, 1977) • W. M. WATT, *Bell's Introduction to the Qur'an* (Edinburgh, 1970).

ROGER ALLEN

R

Rabbi, Rabbinism

1. Definition
2. History
   2.1. Second Temple Period to the Middle Ages
   2.2. Since Jewish Emancipation
3. Women Rabbis
4. Rabbinism

1. Definition

The term "rabbi" denotes a Jewish scholar and minister. The origin of the term is to be found in Heb. *rab* (master, great one). It seems originally to have been a form of address meaning "my master" or "my teacher" (see Matt. 23:7). In the second half of the first century A.D., it then became a title preceding the proper name. Rabbi Judah ha-Nasi (i.e., Judah the Patriarch, ca. 135-ca. 220) was simply known as the Rabbi. He was traditionally the redactor of the → Mishnah. Other patriarchs held the honorary title *rabban,* "our teacher," for example, Rabban Johanan ben Zakkai (d. ca. 80), one of the most important leaders after the destruction of the temple.

The title "rabbi" indicated that the one who bore it was a scholar who had studied the written and oral → Torah in the schools, who had also expounded and taught it, and who thus had the ability and the authority to hand down Halakic decisions (→ Halakah). This group of scholars (self-styled at first *ḥăkāmîm,* "wise ones, scholars," later *rabbānîm,* pl. of *rab*) was responsible for the so-called rabbinic literature, made up basically of the Mishnah, → Talmud, → Midrash, and Targums (→ Jewish Theology; Judaism 3.2).

2. History

2.1. *Second Temple Period to the Middle Ages*

2.1.1. The roots of the rabbinic class reach back into the period of the second temple, and especially to the → scribes *(sōpĕrîm),* who were trying to put study and application of the Torah at the center of → piety and daily life, also to a subset of the later → Pharisees, who accepted a cult-centered ideal of piety yet did not restrict it to the Aaronic priesthood but wanted to apply it to the whole population and hence to make all → Israel a holy people. After the destruction of the temple and the related ending of the cult, the two tendencies merged; at the center now stood the study and application of the Torah in → cultic purity. The rabbis who expounded the Torah now saw themselves as replacing priests, who had lost their functions, as guarantors of the fulfillment of the divine will as it is revealed in the Torah.

2.1.2. In the Talmudic period (ca. A.D. 70-640) and well into the Middle Ages (→ Judaism 3.3), the rabbis had no official position and discharged no official function in the → synagogue. Since it was frowned upon that the "crown of the Torah" should be exploited for personal profit, whether renown or livelihood (see *m. 'Abot* 4:5), rabbis did other work in agriculture or in trades (esp. as tanners, smiths, tailors, carpenters, cobblers, and laundrymen) or as scribes and judges. Their training involved a close teacher-student relation that had to be marked by high mutual respect. A pupil's honor had to be as dear to the teacher as his own (or that of his colleague), the honor of his colleague as dear as respect for his teacher, and respect for his teacher as dear as respect for heaven (i.e., God, *m. 'Abot* 4:12).

Instruction was not limited to actual teaching or common Torah-study in school but also involved lifestyle, commonly in a community dwelling. Here students, by serving their rabbi, would learn how to apply the Halakah in daily life and in this way find the right way of life (see Jesus' relation with his → disciples). This linking of theory and practice served as a guarantee of proper instruction. Disagreement among the teachers was explained by the increasing number of students, "who had insufficiently studied" (*b. Sanh.* 88b).

Originally the teacher-student relation did not come to any formal end, but soon we find the → ordination denoted by *semikah* (from Heb. *sāmak*, "lay [hands] on"), which gave authority to the ordained to teach independently and also to independently decide Halakic questions and discharge judicial functions, especially in relation to imposing and removing excommunication. The basis of ordination was found in the authorizing of → Joshua by → Moses (Num. 27:18, 23; Deut. 34:9). At first it was performed by → laying on of hands, later by a formula pronounced by the officiant (see *b. Sanh.* 5a). Later it was no longer to be simply an act involving teacher and student, however, but would require the consent of the patriarch or Sanhedrin. Since ordination was seen to be tied to the land of Israel, by way of distinction the Talmudic scholars of Babylon were called Rav. Ordination ceased with the decline of this center.

Over time the title "rabbi" lost its meaning as scholar and simply became a form of masculine address (= "mister"). With the strengthening of regional centers of Judaism in the Middle Ages, there were repeated attempts to revive Talmudic ordination, and despite the constant objection that it was neither necessary nor authorized, it became the practice in many countries. The titles conferred varied from time to time and from place to place. One that we find in medieval Germany was *morenu ha-Rav*, "our teacher, the master." The diploma signifying this achievement might be compared to those granted by universities to doctors (i.e., teachers). The term *manhig* (leader) was common especially in the 15th century, which points to the central position of the rabbi as a spiritual authority.

2.1.3. In the Middle Ages we find the same ideal of the scholar as one who will earn his keep in an independent calling, for example, as physician, goldsmith, winegrower, butcher, merchant, or moneylender (much liked because it gave enough time for study), later also publisher, printer, or private tutor. Then came compensation for the time spent in functions that more and more devolved on rabbis, for example, supervising the observance of → dietary laws or deciding personal matters (e.g., → marriage, divorce, levirate marriage, the status of widows when husbands were missing). These payments would later be the basis of contracts between congregations and rabbis whereby the independent scholar would become a congregational rabbi holding office along with other officeholders.

Institutionalizing did not involve all rabbis. Congregations either chose or appointed a rabbi as they had need, and other rabbis in the area had to respect the authority of this rabbi. Often the privileges and duties of such a rabbi were put in writing. The tasks, in addition to those already mentioned, included writing legal records, deciding issues of ritual, and giving Talmudic lectures, occasionally also (synagogue) sermons.

2.2. ***Since Jewish Emancipation***

Jewish emancipation during the 18th and 19th centuries brought a radical change in the tasks of rabbis, since the suspension of community autonomy eliminated the Jewish administration of law in civil matters. Even deciding ritual and marital questions was no longer a matter for individual rabbis but was now entrusted to central rabbinic courts. Rabbis instead had increased social and educational functions, for example, visiting the sick, conducting weddings and funerals, preparing young people for adulthood from the standpoint of religious law, including the related obligation to keep the commandments (Bar — and recently also Bat — Mitzvah, "son/daughter of the law"), and preaching frequently at worship services. In Reform Judaism rabbis often act also as leaders at (synagogue) worship.

For centuries training of rabbis followed essentially the model of the Talmudic era (see 2.1). The common study of teacher and pupil was determinative. The main subjects were the Babylonian Talmud and Halakic codices, including the growing number of commentaries. The more important the teacher, the more they had students from afar, who then spread abroad their fame and that of their yeshiva (school). This traditional pattern of students clustered around a teacher is still retained in ultraorthodox and Hasidic (→ Hasidism) circles.

As a result of the → Enlightenment and → emancipation, other movements in Judaism have not found the traditional way of learning adequate, and the state too has demanded that a fixed standard be met if rabbis are to be recognized. In the 19th century, then, colleges and seminaries for the training of rabbis on more academic lines were founded in western Europe and the United States. The curriculum in such institutions adds to Talmudic studies other areas of Jewish scholarship, for example, history, philosophy, religion, and literature, and is usually supplemented by university courses.

3. Women Rabbis

Although from biblical days there have always been women who have had a good grasp of Jewish law and its application (Deborah is a clear example), the ordaining of women as rabbis was not discussed before the 20th century. In 1903 Henrietta Szold (1860-1945) was allowed to study at the conservative Jewish Theological Seminary in New York, but only after agreeing not to seek ordination. The ordination of women as rabbis became an issue in Reform Judaism in the United States from 1921 onward, but not until 1972 was the first woman ordained (Sally Priesand, from Hebrew Union College at Cincinnati, the institutional center of Reform Judaism).

Regina Jonas, a graduate of the College for the Study of Judaism, in Berlin, was ordained by liberal rabbis in the 1930s, though not without opposition. Because of the extirpation of Jewish life in Germany under National Socialism (→ Holocaust), she had no one to succeed her as a woman rabbi until quite recently. In 1974 Sandy Eisenberg Sasso became the first woman to be ordained in Reconstructionism, a branch of Conservative Judaism. By the 1980s the Conservative movement had reached a Halakically defensible position favoring women's ordination. Orthodox Judaism, however, still maintained that the Halakah forbids the ordination of women, though even here voices may be heard rejecting this view and regarding women's ordination as both desirable and inevitable in the fairly near future.

4. Rabbinism

Rabbinism — a decisive strand that puts the oral tradition contained in rabbinic writings on a par with the written → Torah and that regards the resultant pattern of living as obligatory — has been a feature of Judaism for centuries. The first to radically reject and contest rabbinism were the medieval Karaites, who would accept only the Halakah that could be derived from the written Torah. Other movements set various other components alongside rabbinism, with its strong, though by no means exclusive, Halakic orientation, often in the form of the very same scholar. Thus Saʿadia ben Joseph (882-942, known as the Gaon [Excellency]) and Moses Maimonides (1135-1204) were both Halakists and religious philosophers (→ Jewish Philosophy 3), and Naḥmanides (ca. 1195-1270) was both a Halakist and a cabalist (→ Cabala). In contrast, some champions of rabbinism attacked philosophy, just as Maimonides steered clear of any kind of → mysticism.

In the Middle Ages German Hasidism featured the ethical and esoteric works of such rabbinic scholars as Judah ben Samuel (ca. 1150-1217, also known as Yehudah the Ḥasid [Pious]) and Eleazar ben Judah (ca. 1165-1238). In the 18th century, however, eastern European Hasidism, especially after its development as a popular mass movement focusing more on charismatic figures than Talmudic scholars, encountered such resolute rabbinic opponents as Elijah ben Solomon (1720-97, known as the Gaon [Excellency] of Vilna [later Vilnius]). The mystically messianic Sabbatianism of the 17th century and the 18th-century sect of the Frankists that followed it were downright antirabbinic, the result being a long feud with rabbis who were suspected of Sabbatian tendencies.

The Haskalah, or Jewish Enlightenment, which at first thought it possible in essentials to combine traditional Jewish (rabbinic) thought with more general ideas, as argued by Moses Mendelssohn (1729-86), had as a result the formation of many trends that differed in their commitment to traditional rabbinism. Some accepted it ([Neo-]Orthodoxy), others relativized it (Conservative Judaism), and some to a large extent rejected it (Reform Judaism). → Zionism arose in opposition to assimilation and partly in reaction to → anti-Semitism. It found both supporters and opponents in rabbinically shaped Orthodoxy, which in this regard does not differ greatly from other groups that are divided between acceptance and rejection.

→ Jewish Practices

Bibliography: R. Bonfil, *Rabbis and Jewish Communities in Renaissance Italy* (Oxford, 1990) • M. Breuer, "Die Stellung des Rabbinats in den rheinischen Judengemeinden des Mittelalters," *Köln und das rheinische Judentum* (ed. J. Bohnke-Kollwitz et al.; Cologne, 1984) 35-46 • I. Epstein, ed., *Hebrew-English Edition of the*

Babylonian Talmud (30 vols.; London, 1965-89) • W. S. Green, "Rabbi in Classical Judaism," *EJ* 3.1124-32 • A. J. Karp, *Jewish Continuity in America: Creative Survival in a Free Society* (Tuscaloosa, Ala., 1998) esp. pt. 2, "The American Rabbinate" • P. S. Nadell, *Women Who Would Be Rabbis: A History of Women's Ordination, 1889-1985* (Boston, 1998) • J. Neusner, *The Four Stages of Rabbinic Judaism* (London, 1999); idem, *Introduction to Rabbinic Literature* (New York, 1994) • J. L. Rubenstein, *The Culture of the Babylonian Talmud* (Baltimore, 2003) • P. Schäfer, *The History of the Jews in the Greco-Roman World* (rev. ed.; London, 2003) • S. Schwarzfuchs, *A Concise History of the Rabbinate* (Oxford, 1993).

Margarete Schlüter

Racism

1. Sociological Aspects

1.1. *Term and Types*

The term "racism" was coined around 1930 to define and criticize a doctrine holding that there are hereditary cultural and psychological differences between peoples that make those of Europe, especially Northwest Europe, biologically superior to all others. The inner distinctions of talent and character were believed to express themselves in external attributes such as skin color or the shape of the skull. This doctrine also included a belief that the superior peoples must keep their bloodlines "pure" and should not intermingle with other peoples, lest they lose their → power and → identity.

This doctrine itself became fashionable in the middle of the 19th century when attempts were made to explain all social differences biologically. It soon came to be refuted scientifically, as it was easy to demonstrate that the physical appearance of various peoples bears no relationship to their → cultures or abilities and that cultures are learned, not inherited. Furthermore, individual members of a people differ greatly in character and culture and often do not conform to what they themselves or others might regard as their desired or typical collective traits.

After the scientific refutation of the doctrine of racism and its ultimate moral condemnation after the → Holocaust, it became customary to speak of cultures rather than races, and those who argued for racist discrimination now insisted on the need for protecting their own culture from being overwhelmed by alien cultures. In this context, however, culture is spoken of as though it were an immutable totality common to all who belong by descent to a specific people. Against this misuse of the concept of culture for racist ends, it can be shown that the cultures of modern industrialized nations (→ Industrial Society) are not self-contained, static, homogeneous, or free from contradictions, nor are their practices necessarily restricted to those who share the same ancestors.

The neoracism that supposedly rests on culture does, however, display argumentative patterns similar to those of the biological racism that it has replaced. In northern Europe or the United States, it is directed against immigrants from southern Europe, Latin America, Asia, or Africa, whose cultures are allegedly incompatible with European civilization. It therefore makes sense to extend the term "racism" to cover all ideologies that view people, on the basis of their appearance or descent, as belonging to collectives with unchanging qualities, these qualities being positive in the case of one's own group, negative in the case of others. Modern racism does, however, rarely still take the form of a coherent → ideology or doctrine. More often it emerges instead in the form of public or private opinions and attitudes that are not embedded in any fixed interpretative context. Such opinions take their cue from existing power structures and social inequality. Racism is always directed against groups and people who are politically and often also economically weaker. It is thus linked to preexisting and deeply ingrained forms of social inequality. Whenever it is possible to diminish the real powerlessness of a social group that has been the object of racist discrimination, → prejudices against this group also become less pronounced. Racist prejudices, however, serve the function of legitimizing the ongoing unequal treatment of certain groups and peoples and have their staunchest defenders among those who benefit from these unjust power relationships.

An extended definition of racism that takes into account both its history and its present status might run as follows: racism is the refusal of equal human → rights and → human dignity to a certain group because it is considered to be biologically or culturally foreign. Racism may take various forms: an ideology or a doctrine, personal notions and prejudices, or the direct practice of discrimination and hostility against the group in question.

One may distinguish different types of racism according to the social institutions that exercise it:

- *state racism,* when the → state and its agencies exclude ethnic minorities from certain human and civil rights and social entitlements, directly or indirectly limit their opportunities, subject them to special and sometimes humiliating controls, and even put obstacles in their way to gain or to keep what they are legally entitled to;
- *economic racism,* when employers, insurance firms, credit agencies, landlords, and so forth intentionally or unintentionally discriminate against members of minorities (→ Economic Ethics);
- the *political-ideological racism* of some → political parties and associations that pursue specific demagogic social politics;
- *scientific racism,* when scholars try to justify racism;
- the *racism of public opinion,* which may be found in the → mass media and in statements of the regulars in their bars and pubs and the phrases that circulate at other informal gatherings;
- *everyday racism,* which involves a condescending, hostile, or discriminatory behavior toward foreigners; and
- *violent racism,* or the actions of groups that deliberately seek to insult and even injure members of ethnic minorities.

1.2. *Racism and Nation*

Racism is more than just the preferring of the company of one's own group and the avoidance of social intercourse with strangers. Such preferences may be found in all cultures and times. Racism is linked to modernity and two specifically European and North American achievements: the idea of the universality of the human race, and the idea of the nation-state (→ Nation, Nationalism).

In most premodern cultures it was more or less taken for granted that members of other cultures, whether friend or foe, were very different and therefore lived by different rules. Racists, however, arise from a background where the universality of human nature is taken for granted and then declare their own culture to be the standard against which all others ought to be judged, thus setting up a ranking scale and marking down foreign cultures as inferior. This type of thinking was particularly true in the case of colonial racism, when Europeans proclaimed that they were the most advanced expression of the human race, which gave them the right to despise and mistreat conquered peoples for allegedly failing to reach the highest level of human evolution (→ Colonialism). Racism is universalistic in its demand that members of minority cultures should adjust to the culture of the dominant majority, and it is particularistic by proclaiming that the members of the minority would — by nature — be unable and unwilling to do so and by denying them, in practice, the opportunity of integrating themselves.

Racism also relates to the project of the nation-state, which can be understood as the historical venture of bringing the members of a large and heterogeneous population together to imagine themselves as a homogeneous community, thus bringing state and people into close association. Wherever the nation began to be conceived as a community of descent and common bloodline, the followers of such a concept soon turned against alleged aliens in their midst, against other Europeans, but even more so against people of non-European ancestry.

The nation-state, which has thus provided a fertile ground for racism, has at the same time also provided the social space in which the lower classes (→ Class and Social Stratum), appealing to the sense of common nationality of those who controlled power and wealth, were finally able to enforce the class compromises that became the basis for the respect for universally defined human rights and civil liberties enshrined in various constitutions. In the 19th and early 20th centuries, human and civil rights were thus secured in many northern states, though only in the framework of the nation, so that it was still possible to disqualify nonnationals from the exercise of many of these rights.

1.3. *Sociopsychological Explanations*

Questionnaires show that racists often have had no negative personal experiences with those whom they dislike. Their knowledge of the behavior and culture of the minority in question is usually based on hearsay and rumors. Some admit to having aversions to the sight or the smell of the strangers, their very appearance causing → anxiety and → aggression. Others report that the contacts they have had with individual members of the minority were friendly, yet this experience did not change their general attitude toward the particular minority.

Racist reactions and attitudes are not rational responses but must be explained by → social psychology and by analyzing the way in which individuals experience their own status in → society. Because so many people have no sense of security and belonging and do not feel they can stand alone, they bolster their self-confidence by identifying with an imaginary collective and venting their anger about feelings of homelessness and isolation on those who allegedly do not belong. Many people learn very early to gain social recognition by overadjustment. Feeling the pressure of their conformity, they unconsciously project what they themselves would rather like to do on minorities who are allegedly lazy or violent or covetously taking advantage of the welfare system. During times of increased economic and social uncertainty, this tendency to project inner needs and aggressions on social minorities can be politically misused by demagogues. In western Europe "crisis racism" of this type is frequently introduced into debates on immigration policies, where openly racist arguments are sometimes expressed. Immigrants are then blamed for rising rates of unemployment, although, in reality, they usually suffer more from worsening economic conditions than do the members of the majority.

In all highly industrialized countries employment opportunities for people with lower qualifications have become scarce, which has led to increased → poverty among minorities and the deterioration of the residential areas in which they live. The police who must keep order under these circumstances are inclined to react with excessive violence, and racial unrest is the consequence, as has been the case in the United Kingdom and the United States. Today, racially disadvantaged minorities and groups may actually often suffer less from explicit prejudice against them than from the fact that their labor is no longer needed on the market and all ways of gaining a decent livelihood appear to be blocked.

Bibliography: T. W. Adorno et al., *The Authoritarian Personality* (New York, 1970) • D. Bell, *Faces at the Bottom of the Well: The Permanence of Racism* (New York, 1992) • R. Benedict, *Race and Racism* (London, 1983; orig. pub., 1942) • B. Carter, *Realism and Racism: Concepts of Race in Sociological Research* (London, 2000) • E. Cashmore, *The Logic of Racism* (London, 1986) • G. M. Fredrickson, *Racism: A Short History* (Princeton, 2002) • C. Guillaumin, *Racism, Sexism, Power, and Ideology* (London, 1995) • T. C. Holt, *The Problem of Race in the Twenty-first Century* (Cambridge, Mass., 2001) • J. Kovel, *White Racism: A Psychohistory* (New York, 1984; orig. pub., 1970) • R. Miles, *Racism after "Race Relations"* (London, 1993) • UNESCO, *Social Theories: Race and Colonialism* (Paris, 1980).

Michaela von Freyhold

2. Theological and Ecumenical Aspects

2.1. *Theological Reflection*

Racism has no rational basis or conceptual cogency. Its targets and victims find it incomprehensible. It consists simply of → prejudice. Though not rational, it can be understood in terms of underlying psychological factors, and its social effects can be seen and described. Consequently, a full understanding of racism must include psychosocial analysis (→ Social Psychology).

Although no cogent arguments can be made on behalf of racism, strenuous efforts have been made to justify it theologically. The aim is naturally to defend the status quo rather than to explain it. The defense seeks to find a moral foundation for what is already a social practice. When Christopher Columbus (1451-1506) discovered the New World, → conversion and Christianization were arguments used to justify the conquest, even though mission in this setting involved violent oppression. Ideas of racial superiority were also present. Some types of OT → exegesis and themes such as the chosen people and the exodus nourished and supported the racism of early missionaries. Nevertheless, some of them already had doubts about the theological justification of racism. Many indeed became defenders of native peoples against exploitation and oppression (→ Dependence).

A credible antiracist theology must realize that there are tensions in the Bible itself (e.g., between Israel and Gentiles, or between Jews and Christians). Theology and church history also offer numerous examples of those who were persecuted, banished, or put to death because they were different (→ Witchcraft). Any theology that tries to justify such injustices shows that it has already come to terms with the → ideology, → culture, and outlook of the dominant and oppressive part of the world. The resultant modes and models of theological thinking cannot but be alienating to those of nondominant cultures. The dominant-culture interpretations of the Christ-event ensure the spiritual hegemony of the guardians of the redemption story. They fix the boundaries of belief and control the ways and means of redemption (→ Hermeneutics). New ways of interpreting the Christian tradition must thus be considered, such as → demythologizing, → narrative theology, exegesis in terms of → social history, → liberation theology, → black theology, or → contextual theology. Consensus is also needed that Christians have the task not only of understanding injustice but also of eliminating it (→ Righteousness, Justice, 3).

These new beginnings in theology supply good

arguments for an emphasis on practice in the sense of a mutual linking and meaningful relating of reflection and action, which means that one of the fundamental dichotomies of the → Enlightenment must be overcome. John Paul II (1978-2005) bridged this → dualism in his encyclical *Centesimus annus* (1991), which commemorated the centennial of Leo XIII's (1878-1903) encyclical *Rerum novarum* (1891), when he said, "Today more than ever, the Church is aware that her social message will gain credibility more immediately from the *witness of actions* than as a result of its internal logic and consistency" (§57). For the ecumenical movement the fight against racism has been a summons to action and conflict.

2.2. *U.N. Statements*

Ecumenical social thinking often refers to the definition of the UNESCO committees of experts that met in 1967 and 1978. Essentially, this definition is to the effect that racism is the prejudiced conviction that physical qualities in themselves confer power and worth. An economic explanation of racism (→ Economy; Economic Ethics) relates it to the greed that led to → slavery and to the violent subjugation and exploitation of whole peoples in the interests of the colonial powers (→ Colonialism).

Resolution no. 3379 of the U.N. General Assembly on November 10, 1975, called → Zionism a form of racism, which triggered much discussion. It found in Zionism a movement that had overstepped the boundary between legitimate nationalism and racism (→ Nation, Nationalism), especially when the nationalism included violence (→ Force, Violence, Nonviolence), seizure of territory, discrimination, and all other forms of hegemony — in this case, to the hurt of Palestinians. This statement was quietly ignored in what the → United Nations said about → Israel (§2) and the Occupied Territories (→ Palestine 4). It was withdrawn in 1992 so as not to impede the Middle East peace talks then in progress.

2.3. *Engagement of the World Council of Churches*

In 1969 the Central Committee of the → World Council of Churches (WCC), meeting at Canterbury in England, labeled white racism the most comprehensive manifestation of racism. Racism, it argued, was an obvious product of colonialism, which brought with it the first encounters between peoples of different skin colors and cultures, as well as the seizure of property and resources so as to bring increased profits at home.

The World Missionary Conference at Edinburgh in 1910 (→ Missionary Conferences 2.1) pointed the way forward by putting the rights of native peoples and their treatment by colonial powers on the agenda (→ International Law). J. H. Oldham (1874-1969), general secretary of the → International Missionary Council (→ Ecumenism, Ecumenical Movement, 2.6.2), published his book *Christianity and the Race Problem* (1924) as a challenge to the churches. In the IMC conferences that followed, beginning at Jerusalem in 1928, the churches wrestled with the problem of world racism. The → Life and Work Conferences at Stockholm (1925) and Oxford (1937) also took up the topic.

All these conferences repudiated racism, though some underlying white paternalism in the repudiations still might be detected. Stockholm, for example, maintained that races are part of God's created order; for German delegates, differences were according to the will of God. It was argued that, although God's love is without respect of persons and all believers in Christ are one, we must accept the "orders" (i.e., people, → state, → family, race) and the related differences of gifts and tasks (Tambaram/Madras 1938; → Missionary Conferences 2.3). The German churches had already made the leap from this type of statement to the idea of a master race, with fateful consequences in the era of National Socialism (→ Fascism).

The WCC 1954 Evanston Assembly declared that "any form of segregation based on race, color or ethnic origin is contrary to the gospel and thus incompatible with the nature of Christ's church." It dealt in this way with the theme of theology and racism. The WCC general secretariat at Geneva then tackled the matter of racial and ethnic relations with a view to establishing good relations among races. Its first test would be the question of the attitude of the churches to apartheid in South Africa, a matter that divided South African member churches.

After Evanston, apartheid and its ideology became the great moral and theological issue for the ecumenical movement. W. A. → Visser 't Hooft (1900-1985), then general secretary of the WCC, reported on the dilemma posed by the support of the Dutch → Reformed churches in South Africa for apartheid. He claimed that the important thing is to make clear to a world in which there is tension that the tension has been overcome in Christ. The Evanston assembly urgently demanded that the churches reject all forms of racism and discrimination and work to end them in both church and society. To meet the objections of Dutch churches, Visser 't Hooft tells us in his *Memoirs* that he agreed to add to the final statement a recognition that achieving this goal would be very difficult for some member churches and that the ecumenical movement would offer these churches fraternal help and encouragement in overcoming the difficulties (chap. 34).

The Fourth Assembly of the WCC, at Uppsala in 1968, took an important step forward in opposition to racism by emphasizing the need "to embark on a vigorous campaign against racism" and to undertake "a crash program to guide the Council and the member churches" in this urgent matter. A consultation at Notting Hill (London) in 1969 brought together both racially oppressed persons and church leaders with a view to forming a coalition of the church with movements struggling for racial justice. Its report formed the basis for the mandate of the Central Committee at Canterbury, which in 1970 created the → Program to Combat Racism.

The Seventh Assembly of the WCC, at Canberra in 1991, maintained that "racism, one of the most dreadful of human sins, is incompatible with the gospel of Jesus Christ. It not only manifests itself in individual prejudices but is anchored in social structures and institutions. If members of one group seek domination over those of another, they are not really free but are the slaves of their own fears and search for power. On both sides oppression puts under tutelage" (Report Committee, §44). We see here the progress that had been made since 1948. Stress is put on racism as a structural phenomenon, as well as on the fact that it is sinful and evil and has no moral or theological justification.

2.4. *Roman Catholic, Lutheran, and Reformed Responses*

The papal commission Justice and Peace published an important statement on racism in 1989 under the title "Church and Racism: Towards a More Fraternal Society." As the title shows, this work had not yet attained the insight that racism must be seen in social structures. It rightly calls racism an individual → sin but fails to consider its collective and violent nature. In 1992, the 500th anniversary of Columbus's conquest, new theological interest arose in racism. In 1991 a summons to the bishops and missionaries in Panama had flung down the gauntlet by claiming that the church had justified and blessed the seizure of America, that the church was thus guilty of complicity with this terrible sin that had virtually destroyed the wealth of the Indians, and that a shadow had thus been cast over the gospel. This text called upon the churches to repent (→ Penitence) and to join in the fight against the → genocide of Indians in North and South America (→ Colonialism and Mission).

Once the churches had condemned racism as a sin, action was initiated against those who were held to be guilty of it. In 1977 the → Lutheran World Federation saw racism in terms of a → *status confessionis,* a denial of the gospel, with implications for communion between churches. In consequence, the membership of four white German-speaking → Lutheran churches in Namibia and South Africa was suspended in 1984 until they could publicly and unequivocally reject apartheid and thus end the split that racial issues were causing. After a period of intense pastoral consideration, this suspension was lifted in 1991.

In the same way the → World Alliance of Reformed Churches at its assembly in Ottawa in 1981 pronounced apartheid to be a → heresy and its theological justification a sin. For this reason it suspended the membership of the white Dutch Reformed Churches in South Africa two years later.

Bibliography: A. J. van der Bent, *World Council of Churches Statements and Actions on Racism, 1948-1985* (Geneva, 1986) • J. Cone, *God of the Oppressed* (Maryknoll, N.Y., 1997; orig. pub., 1970) • S. E. Davies and P. T. Hennessee, S.A., eds., *Ending Racism in the Church* (Cleveland, 1998) • J. W. De Gruchy, *The Church Struggle in South Africa* (2d ed.; Grand Rapids, 1986) • G. D. Kelsey, *Racism and the Christian Understanding of Man* (New York, 1965) • H. McCullum, "Racism and Ethnicity," *A History of the Ecumenical Movement,* vol. 3, *1968-2000* (ed. J. Briggs, M. Oduyoye, and G. Tsetsis; Geneva, 2004) 347-71 • J. H. Oldham, *Christianity and the Race Problem* (London, 1924) • S. Perkins and C. Rice, *Breaking Down Walls: A Model for Reconciliation in an Age of Racial Strife* (Downers Grove, Ill., 1993) • J. H. Schjørring, P. Kumari, and N. A. Hjelm, eds., *From Federation to Communion: The History of the Lutheran World Federation* (Minneapolis, 1995) • W. A. Visser 't Hooft, *Memoirs* (Geneva, 1987; orig. pub., 1973).

N. Barney Pityana and Sabine Udodesku

3. Case Studies

The history of both the United States and South Africa reveals two of the world's most prominent examples of the way racism was employed as a basic principle of political organization. The following will outline how that principle functioned to exclude African peoples from the → rights of citizenship in both the United States and South Africa. While both countries manifested racism toward their respective indigenous peoples, this discussion focuses only on the racial oppression of African peoples in those situations. Furthermore, this account assumes that the political principle of racism

Racism

was rooted in a philosophy that claimed the inherent superiority of European peoples over African peoples. In fact, African peoples were considered an inferior species.

3.1. *The United States*

Since the Constitution of the United States did not regard African slaves or their descendants as citizens — a viewpoint that was confirmed by the Supreme Court's decision in the 1857 *Dred Scott* case — the struggle to abolish slavery culminated in a bitter civil war. In 1863 President Abraham Lincoln issued the Emancipation Proclamation, which, along with the subsequent 13th, 14th, and 15th Amendments to the Constitution, gave the rights of citizenship to people of African descent for the first time, a right that was routinely violated during the period of Reconstruction (ca. 1865-77).

All the promises of → freedom were nullified by the Supreme Court's decision in the 1896 *Plesy v. Ferguson* judgment, which established the "separate but equal" doctrine that guided the nation's racial practices for the next half-century. It thus provided the constitutional foundation for the rise of numerous state laws supporting racial discrimination and segregation.

In May 1954 the Supreme Court reversed itself in the *Brown v. Board of Education* decision by striking down the separate-but-equal doctrine. That decision provided legal grounds that fueled the strategic endeavors of the nascent → civil rights movement under the leadership of Martin Luther → King Jr. (1929-68). After a momentous decade of struggle, the Civil Rights Act of 1964 and the Voting Rights Act of 1965 ended de jure racial discrimination and segregation throughout the nation. Yet, de facto racial inequalities in the economic and social spheres remain up to the present day (→ Economic Ethics). It is important to note, however, that the continuing struggle for racial justice assumes many forms that range along a continuum from the politics of accommodation to that of separation.

Throughout the nation's history many and varied defenses have been advanced in support of the unequal treatment of its African peoples. Scholarly defenses issued from such disparate disciplines as philosophy, theology, biology, psychology, and sociology; all of these have, for many generations, helped shape social policies on race and color. In the present day, scholars continue to measure the long-term impact of those policies on succeeding generations of African Americans. Others, however, have argued that the assertiveness of African Americans in effecting social change resulted in the restoration of personal dignity, moral resolve, and psychological well-being. Furthermore, gradual freedom from racial constraints has enabled African Americans to express their creative genius in the academy, professional sports, civil rights, religion, and the performing arts. Their many accomplishments in such fields have been globally recognized, which has had considerable effect in enhancing the self-image of African Americans both at home and abroad.

3.2. *South Africa*

The story of race relations in South Africa contains many similarities to those in the United States. The principal difference between the two, however, lies in the fact that the oppressive European population in South Africa was a minority one, while in the United States it was in the majority. Furthermore, in South Africa the struggle for domination occurred on two fronts. First, the English and Dutch settlers struggled against each other for domination over the indigenous population, a struggle that culminated in the Anglo-Boer War (1899-1902). Second, the English and Dutch joined forces in effectively denying black Africans, Asians, and the so-called colored peoples the rights of citizenship during most of the 20th century.

The year 1948 saw the birth of the most ideological period of racial separation, with the government enacting its infamous apartheid policy. Thereafter the international image of South Africa was characterized by the word "apartheid," that is, separateness. Though the basis for that action can be traced at least as far back as the Natives' Land Act of 1913 (amended many times for several decades thereafter) and the leadership of several premiers who were strong proponents of racial separation such as Louis Botha (1862-1919) and Jan Smuts (1870-1950), the policy will always be associated with the name of its major architect, H. F. Verwoerd (1901-66).

The tragic consequences of the apartheid policy were many and vast: the 1960 Sharpville massacre, the imprisonment of Nelson Mandela and many others, the infamous pass laws, the death by torture of thousands, and the impoverishment of hundreds of thousands in the squatters' areas of the townships and so-called homelands. Yet, the struggle for racial justice produced numerous good consequences, among which were a host of heroes and martyrs, three Nobel Peace Prize laureates, the Black Sash (previously the Women's Defence of the Constitution League, 1954), the Freedom Charter (1955), the Black Consciousness movement (late 1960s), the Soweto uprising (1976), the Kairos document (1985), the release of Nelson Mandela from prison (1990), the adoption of a new constitution (1993), and the historic 1994 democratic election, which,

Rahner, Karl

for the first time in the country's history, included all the people.

→ Black Churches

Bibliography: L. V. BALDWIN, *There Is a Balm in Gilead: The Cultural Roots of Martin Luther King, Jr.* (Minneapolis, 1991); idem, *To Make the Wounded Whole: The Cultural Legacy of Martin Luther King, Jr.* (Minneapolis, 1992) • T. R. H. DAVENPORT, *South Africa: A Modern History* (3d ed.; London, 1987) • J. W. DE GRUCHY, *The Church Struggle in South Africa* (2d ed.; Grand Rapids, 1986) • W. E. B. DUBOIS, *The Souls of Black Folk* (New York, 1989; orig. pub., 1903) • J. H. FRANKLIN, *From Slavery to Freedom: A History of American Negroes* (New York, 1964) • R. M. FRANKLIN, *Liberating Visions: Human Fulfillment and Social Justice in African-American Thought* (Minneapolis, 1990) • N. MANDELA, *Long Walk to Freedom: The Autobiography of Nelson Mandela* (Boston, 1994) • P. PARIS, *The Social Teachings of the Black Churches* (Philadelphia, 1985) • C. WEST, *Democracy Matters: Winning the Fight against Imperialism* (New York, 2004); idem, *Race Matters* (2d ed.; New York, 2001).

PETER PARIS

Radio → Mass Media

Rahner, Karl

Karl Joseph Erich Rahner (1904-84) was a Roman Catholic dogmatician, a philosopher of religion, and a → Jesuit. After completing the studies customary for the order in Feldkirch, Pullach, and Valkenburg (Netherlands), Rahner was directed to the study of philosophy and was able to participate in Martin Heidegger's exclusive seminar in 1934-36. After failing to gain his doctorate under the neoscholastic philosopher M. Honecker in Freiburg, Rahner earned his doctorate and inaugural doctorate *(Habilitation)* in theology in Innsbruck. After the National Socialist authorities interrupted his academic work through a *Gauverbot* (district prohibition, i.e., expulsion), he engaged in pastoral and lecturing activities. In 1949 Rahner became professor of → dogmatics and the history of → dogma in Innsbruck.

From 1961 John XXIII and the Viennese cardinal F. König assigned Rahner to help prepare → Vatican II. Although Rahner was under preliminary censorship by the Vatican in 1962-63, in 1964-65 he became an official and highly influential conciliar theologian. From 1962 to 1967 he succeeded Romano Guardini in Munich as professor of Christian worldview and religious philosophy. From 1967 to 1971 he was professor of dogmatics and the history of dogma in Münster. Through prolific publication and lecturing (as the editor of several lexica and with paperback book sales of over a million copies), Rahner exerted a previously unknown degree of theological influence. His international renown came to expression not least in his 15 honorary doctorates and in other distinguished awards (including member of the order *Pour le mérite,* one of Germany's highest civilian orders, and the Sigmund Freud Award for Scientific Prose from the German Academy of Language and Poetry in Darmstadt).

Influenced by J. Maréchal's understanding of I. Kant, Rahner in his works on religious philosophy tried to establish the conditions for the possibility of human beings discerning or perceiving God's → revelation. His major work in this field was *Geist in der Welt* (1939; ET *Spirit in the World* [1968]), with *Hörer des Wortes* (1941; ET *Hearers of the Word* [1969]) and *Grundkurs des christlichen Glaubens* (1976; ET *Foundations of Christian Faith* [1978]) also significant.

Rahner's theological works, collected in 16 volumes (*Schriften zur Theologie;* ET *Theological Investigations*), often take concrete problems as their point of departure in addressing (1) the transcendent-interior path of the divine mystery as God's offer of self-mediation and (2) the historic-concrete path of revelation through the word and incarnation of Jesus of Nazareth. The unity of these two paths under the primacy of God's anticipatory grace prompted Rahner to develop an optimistic understanding of → salvation for all human beings (→ Apocatastasis) and also an understanding of the strict unity of divine and human → love.

Rahner found the essential human religious act — the heart of the human capacity for → faith — in an affirmation of one's own essential human structure, that is, in the confident acceptance of one's own life. This understanding of a potentially "anonymous Christian being" (without any collective tendency!) has also provided a useful point of departure for developing a pluralistic theory of → religion.

Despite his considerable affirmation of concrete church existence, Rahner nonetheless did contribute to a certain relativization of the church and its institutions in drawing on impulses of → Ignatius of Loyola's nonelitist experience of God, even in daily life. The immediacy to God as experienced by the individual human being represented the ultimate ground for Rahner's reform suggestions (the right to share in decisions in the church, freedom of conscience and speech), including those that concerned ecumenical affairs. He considered it both possible and urgent that the churches that emerged from the → Reformation unite again with the → Roman Catholic Church.

Rahner's unremitting questions contributed to reflection on virtually all questions of dogma, and his views concerning → ethics, social doctrine, and the dialogue between theology and the natural sciences still remain relevant today. Finally, Rahner distinguished himself in the field of the history of dogma with studies on the history of → penitence and on the relationship between → nature and → grace.

Bibliography: Primary sources: Mission and Grace: Essays in Pastoral Theology (3 vols.; trans. C. Hastings; London, 1963-66) • *Sämtliche Werke* (ed. K. Lehmann et al.; Freiburg, 1995ff.) • *Theological Investigations* (23 vols.; trans. C. Ernst; Baltimore, 1961-92).

Secondary works: P. Burke, *Reinterpreting Rahner: A Critical Study of His Major Themes* (New York, 2002) • H. D. Egan, *Karl Rahner: The Mystic of Everyday Life* (New York, 1998) • P. Endean, *Karl Rahner and Ignatian Spirituality* (Oxford, 2001) • P. Imhoff and H. Biallowons, eds., *Faith in a Wintry Season: Conversations and Interviews with Karl Rahner in the Last Years of His Life* (New York, 1990); idem, eds., *Karl Rahner in Dialogue: Conversations and Interviews, 1965-1982* (New York, 1986) • T. W. Klein, *How Things Are in the World: Metaphysics and Theology in Wittgenstein and Rahner* (Milwaukee, Wis., 2003) • K. H. Neufeld, *Die Brüder Rahner* (Freiburg, 1994) • L. J. O'Donovan, ed., *A World of Grace: An Introduction to the Themes and Foundations of Karl Rahner's Theology* (New York, 1980) • H. Vorgrimler, *Understanding Karl Rahner: An Introduction to His Life and Thought* (New York, 1986).

Herbert Vorgrimler

Ramayana

The Ramayana (Skt. "vehicle *or* romance of Rama") is, with the → Mahabharata, one of the two great epics of ancient India. Tradition ascribes it to the poet Vālmīki. Written between the fourth century B.C. and the second century A.D., it contains some 40,000 couplets in Sanskrit, divided into seven books.

The older books (2-6) describe an important episode in the life of the king's son Rama. Because of an intrigue on the part of his stepmother, who wanted to see her own son crowned, he was banished for 14 years into the wilderness, where his wife, Sita, and his brother Laksmana followed him. Attempts after his father's death to bring him back as king failed because of his faithfulness to the word given by his father. During the exile his wife was captured by the → demon Ravana, but with the help of an allied army of monkeys (including the monkey-general Hanuman, who was later deified), Rama managed to take the demon city Lankā (later identified as Ceylon), to defeat Ravana, and to free Sita.

Book 1, which is later, tells of the hero's wonderful birth and youthful exploits. Book 7, even later, tells more about the opponent Ravana and describes Rama's ideal rule. Though a human hero in the earlier books, Rama, as the one who destroys → evil and demons, was later seen as an → incarnation of the god Vishnu and has thus become one of the most important figures in → Hinduism today. His history has been told in many popular languages. The 16th-century ancient Hindi version of Tulsīdās is important in → Bhakti Hinduism. The story is also widespread in Southeast Asia.

Rama's unconditional loyalty to a given promise (cf. Gandhi's satyagraha ideal of commitment to the → truth) and Sita's unchanging fidelity to her husband have become ethical models for Indians, while Rama's rule *(rāmrāj)* is viewed as the → kingdom of God on earth, for which we are to strive.

Bibliography: J. L. Brockington, *Righteous Rama: The Evolution of an Epic* (Delhi, 1985); idem, *The Sanskrit Epics* (Leiden, 1998) • P. Gaeffke, ed., *Tulsīdās: Rāmcaritmānas. Der heilige See der Taten Rāmas* (Stuttgart, 1975) • K. Jacobi, *Das Rāmāyana. Geschichte und Inhalt nebst Concordanz der gedruckten Recensionen* (Bonn, 1893; repr., Darmstadt, 1976) • G. Kam, *Ramayana in the Arts of Asia* (Singapore, 2000) • *The Ramayana of Valmiki* (trans. H. P. Shastri; 3d ed.; 3 vols.; London, 1976) • *The Rāmāyana of Vālmīki: An Epic of Ancient India* (7 vols.; trans. R. P. Goldman et al.; Princeton, 1984ff.) • R. Söhnen, *Untersuchungen zur Komposition von Reden und Gesprächen im Ramayana* (2 vols.; Reinbek, 1979).

Renate Söhnen-Thieme

Raskolniki → Old Believers; Russian Orthodox Church 4.1-3

Rastafarians

1. Background
2. Beliefs and Practices

1. Background

The Rastafarian movement is a → new religion from Jamaica, with adherents also in Britain, the United States, and Africa. Its name comes from Ras (Prince) Tafari (family name), the name of Haile Selassie (lit. "might of the Trinity," 1892-1975) of Ethiopia before he was crowned emperor in Addis Ababa in 1930, an event followed closely by the press in Jamaica. In 1928 he had assumed the title *negus* (king) and was hailed as a descendant of King → Solomon and as the Lion of Judah and King of Kings.

Earlier the renowned Jamaican Paul Bogle (ca. 1822-65), a black preacher and freedom fighter, and Marcus M. Garvey (1887-1940), a black Moses also from Jamaica who wished to take his people back to Africa, had predicted the coming of a black deliverer, a king from Ethiopia. Four visionaries — Leonard Howell, Joseph Hibbert, Archibald Dunkley, and Robert Hinds — had stated that Haile Selassie had revealed himself to them as the Messiah. The movement originated when their congregations joined forces in Kingston in 1934.

In 1935 Italy invaded Abyssinia, or Ethiopia. Jamaican newspapers extolled the courage of the resistance fighters. In 1966 Haile Selassie actually set foot in Jamaica, paying a state visit to Kingston.

For purposes of → mission, Rastafarians use reggae texts. One great singer was Bob Marley (1945-81), who won over many whites in the United States with his music. The reggae music of the Rastafarians is popular among blacks in Africa and Britain.

2. Beliefs and Practices

Rastafarians call themselves black Jews. Whites brought them into → slavery and misfortune, although the slaveholders had thought of themselves as orthodox, God-fearing, and devout. Marley sang of whites: "We're sick and tired of your kissing game," referring to the betrayal of blacks after the manner of Judas with a kiss. God, called Jah (Ps. 68:4 KJV, sometimes said to derive from "Jehovah"), is seen as the adversary of Satan, the ruler of Babylon.

Rastafarians express their relation to God in words, for words have power. God created the world with words, and by words it will be consummated. Rastafarians speak of themselves as "I and I," with the second "I" referring to God or to any other member, for the individual cannot stand alone.

"Babylon" stands for all → evil and oppression, "Zion" for the → good. Either Zion or Babylon is in the human heart. While Rastafarians live physically in Jamaica, their hearts are focused on Africa, or → salvation, which is seen in what they do or do not do. Over time, the → hope of a physical return to Ethiopia has diminished.

As black Jews, Rastafarians use the Jewish Bible, let their hair grow, and refrain from birth control. They shun politics, industry, and official positions as belonging to Babylon. They aim to live naturally and to eat only what grows in the earth. Marijuana *(ganja)* is sacred to them, since it is an aid to religious communication, but alcohol is forbidden (→ Substance Abuse).

→ Afro-American Cults

Bibliography: L. E. Barrett, *The Rastafarians* (Boston, 1997) • E. Cashmore, *Rastafari: Roots and Ideology* (Syracuse, N.Y., 1994); idem, *The Rastafarians* (London, 1984) • B. Chevannes, ed., *Rastafari and Other African-Caribbean Worldviews* (New Brunswick, N.J., 1998) • A. Hamid, *Ganja Complex: Rastafari and Marijuana* (Lanham, Md., 2002) • V. L. Jacobs, *Roots of Rastafari* (San Diego, Calif., 1985) • J. A. Johnson-Hill, *I-Sight: The World of Rastafari. An Interpretive Sociological Account of Rastafarian Ethics* (Evanston, Ill., 1995) • S. A. King, *Reggae, Rastafari, and the Rhetoric of Social Control* (Jackson, Miss., 2002) • O. Lake, *Rastafari Women: Subordination in the Midst of Liberation Theology* (Durham, N.C., 1998) • W. R. Lewis, *Soul Rebels: The Rastafari* (Prospect Heights, Ill., 1993) • R. M. Mulvaney, *Rastafari and Reggae: A Dictionary and Sourcebook* (New York, 1990) • N. S. Murrell, W. D. Spencer, and A. A. McFarlane, eds., *Chanting Down Babylon: The Rastafari Reader* (Philadelphia, 1998).

Hans-Jürgen Greschat

Rationalism

1. Term
2. In Philosophy
3. In Theology

1. Term

"Rationalism" and its cognates in European languages derived in the 17th century from Lat. *ratio,* "reckoning," also "reason," "plan," or "theory"; also "the faculty that calculates and plans." In religion the term designates standpoints based on reason that are critical of beliefs and practices relying on → authority and → revelation. More broadly, rationalism is any philosophical position affirming the ability of thinking, apart from sensory experience, to discover fundamental truths about the world or reality. The great rationalists in Western thought are Descartes, Spinoza, and Leibniz.

Rationalism

A common caricature is that rationalists are lost in abstract thought unconnected to the hard facts of experience and objective reality. Actually, not all historical examples of rationalism fit the model of purely a priori cognition. The disjunction between → reason and → experience is not as sharp as often assumed. Many treating knowledge and truth from the rationalist side engage in empirical investigations, just as empiricists cannot avoid dealing with the role of reason in their constructions of experience. In religion rationalism takes diverse forms and yields diverse conclusions.

2. In Philosophy

Some early philosophical views, such as Plato's theory of ideas, involve features of rationalism (→ Platonism). Normally, however, the term applies to modern philosophies that adopt an epistemological method anchored in self-aware human thinking not determined either by sense experience or by the ontological hierarchies of ancient philosophies.

Rationalism's first great proponent, René Descartes (1596-1650), subdivided created reality into the two distinct domains of "thinking substance" *(res cogitans)* and "extended substance" *(res extensa)*. The latter makes up the material universe, the former all nonphysical minds and their thoughts. Cartesian → dualism accounts for scientific knowledge by means of innate ideas grounded in geometric principles, such that deductive hypotheses govern experimental investigation of the physical world viewed in mechanistic terms. The clarity and distinctness of ideas as the mind entertains them is the touchstone of their truth. For Descartes, as for Plato before him, emotions arise from bodily states and should be controlled by our rational faculty. Cartesian dualism begets the persistent mind-body problem of how the two different kinds of substance can interact in us. Descartes's God is knowable by reason, namely, by the ontological proof (→ God, Arguments for the Existence of, 2.1), and serves to link the two domains as a whole, as their creator. Nicolas Malebranche (1638-1715), an extreme Cartesian, denied any causal connections among minds and bodies, declaring that God is the sole cause of every physical event, sensation, and thought, that God coordinates them all — a philosophy dubbed "occasionalism."

For Baruch Spinoza (1632-77) thought and extension are two of the infinite attributes of one infinite divine substance, the two that are accessible to human comprehension. His → monism of *Deus sive natura* (God or nature) is a → pantheism that affirms the kinship of human with divine reason, so that a rational grasp of things is possible for us; it rejects the Cartesian relegation of → nature to the status of mere mechanism devoid of soul or spirit. Spinoza's *Ethics* (published posthumously, 1677) teaches that all is necessity, nothing is contingent. Human blessedness is the intellectual love of God, the eternity and peace of realizing that one's mind is a participation in the infinite mind of God.

G. W. Leibniz (1646-1716) envisaged a world of myriad, distinct "monads" in which matter and motion are not mechanistic but are "the phenomena of percipient beings." Each monad is self-developing, not acted upon causally by the others. Yet each mirrors all the others from its perspective within the totality. Some monads are living, and some of these are minds. The others are not mere physical beings but are potentially alive, potentially minds. God is the master monad who creates the rest and coordinates their mutual development in the processes that constitute the history of the universe. Highly developed monads are free, rational beings. In his *Theodicy* (1710) Leibniz portrays God as considering all possible worlds (ensembles of monads) in advance, and with this foreknowledge choosing (being rationally obliged) to create only the ensemble that is "the best of all possible worlds." His philosophical vision captures the Enlightenment's confidence in reason's power to understand the world, with its expectations for scientific → progress. His successor, Christian Wolff (1679-1754), turned Leibniz's dynamic rationalism into a rigid deductive system that made an easy target for Immanuel Kant (1724-1804).

Pierre Bayle (1647-1706) launched skeptical attacks on religion and on supposedly self-evident rational truths, in articles in his *Historical and Critical Dictionary* (1695). These attacks provoked a response by Leibniz in his *Theodicy*, and they encouraged the British empiricists after Locke in their antimetaphysical tendencies. Thomas Hobbes (1588-1679) and John Locke (1632-1704), empiricists themselves, utilized conceptual arguments in their social and political works, inasmuch as social thought and action need a rational foundation. But they deemed nature to be the embodiment of rational structures discernible from sensory experience, not knowable a priori from thinking as such. Étienne de Condillac (1715-80) and others of the French *éclaircissement* made a corresponding turn from rationalism to sensualism, leading to the extreme → materialism of Baron d'Holbach (1723-89).

In Germany rationalism lived on in the religious philosophy of Moses Mendelssohn (1729-86) and the historical and critical essays of the dramatist-philosopher G. E. Lessing (1729-81), who allegedly on his deathbed declared himself to be a Spinozist. The famous "Spinoza controversy" between Mendelssohn and F. H. Jacobi (1743-1819) began in 1783 over the question whether Lessing was in fact a Spinozist. J. G. → Herder (1744-1803) upset Jacobi by endorsing Spinoza's pantheism, and his dialogue *God, Some Conversations* (1787) featured appreciative discussions of Spinoza and Leibniz on theological matters.

In his *Critique of Pure Reason* (1781), Kant tied rationalism to → empiricism, in that the activity of categorial synthesis based on the mind's spontaneity would be empty of content if deprived of the data of sensation. Kant calls knowing by the → categories "understanding" *(Verstand)*, an organizing of experience, in distinction from the illegitimate operation of reason *(Vernunft)* when it seeks to grasp abstract ideas in and of themselves. His moral philosophy in the *Critique of Practical Reason* (1788) relies, in contrast, on direct apprehension of the moral law, a universal, rationally given → norm in the structure of → morality itself. For Kant's idealist successors the burning issues were the justification for his way of distinguishing the rational and empirical spheres, and to what operations of thought, if any, it is appropriate. They declared that the operations and objects of reason are interconnected, that knowing in its various forms and its "other," the empirically given in which reason is manifest, ultimately develop from reason itself.

Other 19th-century positions, such as the later philosophy of F. W. J. Schelling (1775-1854), severed the idealist bond of reason and experience. Despite continuing influence of the Hegelians and the Marburg neo-Kantians, physical nature and human history increasingly became objects for exclusively empirical study. The older rationalism vanished, shoved aside by materialism and the new paradigms of → positivism. Also displacing it were the → voluntarism of Arthur Schopenhauer (1788-1860), the → vitalism of Henri Bergson (1859-1941), and the → nihilism of Friedrich → Nietzsche (1844-1900). Max → Weber (1864-1920) warned that rationalism in society and politics, dwelling on means-end calculations devoid of value considerations, locked institutions into the "iron cage" of bureaucratization.

The "critical rationalism" of Hans Albert (b. 1921) and Karl Popper (1902-94) in the 20th century was actually rooted in positivism. A more traditional strain survived with the American philosopher Brand Blanshard (1892-1987) as its leading figure. Postmodernists sometimes speak disparagingly of rationality as the motivation underlying sociopolitical institutions and forces that they opposed. But despite the limitations of rationalism as a school of modern philosophy, one can hardly avoid serious questions about the nature of reason and its essential place in human knowledge and life.

3. In Theology

Rationalism in theology typically holds that religious beliefs and practices should be confined to those aspects of religious tradition or revelation that are rationally comprehensible and (as is sometimes asserted) are discoverable by reason on its own. This standard excludes, for instance, → Thomas Aquinas (ca. 1225-74), who held reason and revelation to be compatible, since for him certain revealed truths (such as the → Trinity) surpass reason's ability to discover them or to understand them fully. Although the "Latin Averroists" went further in their contention that Aristotle has convincing arguments against the soul's → immortality and for the eternity of the world, they did not allow such arguments to trump Christian doctrines to the contrary, so even they are not theological rationalists in the proper sense.

The → Enlightenment gave birth to a robust religious rationalism in the 17th century. Herbert of Cherbury (1583-1648), known as the father of English → deism, set forth its basic convictions, all derived from natural or rational religion: there is one God, the creator, who is to be worshiped by moral and pious behavior and who bestows just rewards and punishments in this world and in the life after death. John Locke, in *The Reasonableness of Christianity* (1695) and other writings, distinguished → natural theology, which yields knowledge based on demonstrative arguments, from revealed theology, which yields beliefs only. The "reasonableness" of revealed theology depends on how convincing the evidence for it is in → miracles and fulfilled prophecy, although theology never entirely loses an aura of mystery. John Toland (1670-1722) went a step further in *Christianity Not Mysterious* (1696), excluding anything surpassing our rational powers. Matthew Tindal (1656-1733) held in *Christianity as Old as the Creation* (1730) that the Bible, properly understood, presents philosophical truths by other means, namely, by parables and wonders.

Deism on the continent of Europe especially sought to move beyond the divisive beliefs of Protestants and Catholics underlying the devastating → Thirty Years' War (1618-48) and earlier religious persecutions such as the martyrdom of John → Hus (1415) and the Spanish → Inquisition. French rationalists opposed traditional theology and clericalism more strongly than did the British. Voltaire (1694-1778), an unorthodox theist, attacked fanaticism and superstition in the church and denounced appeals to original sin and tests of faith as explanations for the disastrous Lisbon earthquake of 1755. In *Candide* his Dr. Pangloss is made to look ridiculous in defending the necessity of evil in this "best of all possible worlds."

The German *Aufklärung* was more conciliatory toward religion. Leibniz had harmonized reason with Christian revelation. For Wolff, historical revelation is the source of religious content, reason its competent expositor. The → neologists of the late 18th century proposed a theology dwelling on → ethics and practical life, one freed of authoritarian scriptural interpretation. But they were only moderate rationalists, for they challenged the controversial deism of H. S. Reimarus (1694-1768) as presented in Lessing's *Wolfenbüttel Fragments* (1774-78). Lessing attacked J. S. Semler (1725-91) and other liberal neologists, not on behalf of orthodoxy, but instead to clear the way for a more historically critical and rational theology. In *The Education of the Human Race* (1780) he declared that "revelation gives nothing to the human race that human reason could not come to on its own," that earlier times needed revelation but ultimately revealed truths were to be developed into (i.e., replaced in form by) truths of reason.

German theology wrestled with new historical-critical approaches to Scripture. Earlier, Spinoza's *Theological-Political Treatise* (published anonymously in 1670) had critically challenged orthodox views of the Hebrew Bible. Kant's *Religion within the Limits of Reason Alone* (1793) recast the biblical message to fit his rational moral philosophy, with emphasis on virtue, immortality, and the church as the moral kingdom of God. The moral teachings of → Jesus came to the fore; the supernatural receded as increasingly problematic. Theologian Friedrich → Schleiermacher (1768-1834), though not a rationalist himself, dispensed with the concept of miracle as a supernaturally caused event not conditioned by, or belonging to, the system of nature as such. H. E. G. Paulus (1761-1851) and others accounted for the miracle stories (of Jesus healing, walking on water, raising the dead, etc.) as misdescribing naturally explainable events or else as misperceptions by his disciples. Early chapters in Albert → Schweitzer's *Quest of the Historical Jesus* (1906; originally titled *From Reimarus to Wrede: A History of Research on the Life of Jesus*) recounted the bitter battle of theological rationalists with supernaturalist defenders of the tradition. Others sought a mediating position, a rational supernaturalism upholding both revealed content and its inherent reasonableness.

In America, deism strongly influenced the founding fathers George Washington, Thomas Jefferson, Benjamin Franklin, and Thomas Paine. The Unitarian-Universalist movement, with European antecedents in the anti-Trinitarianism of Michael Servetus and the Socinians, has rationalist affinities. An 1819 sermon in Boston by W. E. Channing (1780-1842) prompted the formation of the American Unitarian Association in 1825, which absorbed 125 liberal parishes breaking away from → Congregationalism. Originally a liberal Protestant rejection of the Trinity and the divinity of Christ, the movement came to comprise a wide range of free-thought stances on spiritual beliefs and practices. Ralph Waldo Emerson (1803-82), originally from a → Unitarian background, espoused a still more liberal credo in his → transcendentalism.

In the late 19th century other developments in European thought and culture pushed rationalism aside as the epitome of a lingering, superficial Enlightenment attitude leaning toward → atheism. The 20th-century → dialectical theology of Karl → Barth (1886-1968) and others, sometimes depicted as antireason, actually opposed not theological use of reason as a tool but reliance on metaphysical systems as normative frameworks for interpreting Scripture. The old-style rationalism largely has died out in recent theology. Its lasting heritage is widespread adoption of historical-critical methods in biblical studies, as well as suspicion of the cruder forms of supernaturalism still extant in popular culture and some types of theology.

→ Philosophy and Theology; Physicotheology; Theology in the Nineteenth and Twentieth Centuries

Bibliography: Primary sources: P. Bayle, *Selections from Bayle's Dictionary* (ed. E. Beller and M. Lee Jr.; Princeton, 1952) • R. Descartes, *Selected Philosophical Writings* (trans. J. Cottingham et al.; New York, 1988) • G. Herder, *God, Some Conversations* (trans. F. Burkhardt; Indianapolis, 1940) • I. Kant, *Critique of Pure Reason* (trans. P. Guyer and A. Wood; Cambridge, 1988); idem, *Religion within the Boundaries of Mere Reason, and Other Writings* (trans. A. Wood and G. DiGiovanni; Cambridge, 1998) • G. Leibniz, *Philosophical Papers and Letters* (trans. L. Loemker; Dordrecht, 1969); idem, *Theodicy* (trans. E. Huggard; Indianapolis, 1966) • G. Lessing, *Lessing's Theological Writings* (trans. H. Chadwick; London, 1956) • J. Locke, *The Reasonableness of Christianity* (ed. I. Ramsey; Stanford, Calif., 1958) • H. Reimarus, *Frag-*

ments (ed. C. Talbert; Philadelphia, 1970) • B. Spinoza, *Ethics* (trans. G. Parkinson; Oxford, 2000); idem, *Tractatus Theologico-politicus* (trans. S. Shirley; Leiden, 1989) • M. Tindal, *Christianity as Old as the Creation* (New York, 1978) • J. Toland, *Christianity Not Mysterious* (Stuttgart, 1978) • Voltaire, *Candide and Related Texts* (trans. D. Wooten; Indianapolis, 2000).

Secondary works: H. Allison, *Lessing and the Enlightenment* (Ann Arbor, Mich., 1966) • K. Aner, *Die Theologie der Lessingzeit* (Halle, 1929) • R. Brooks, *Voltaire and Leibniz* (Geneva, 1964) • E. Cassirer, *The Philosophy of the Enlightenment* (Boston, 1951) • R. Gennaro and C. Huenemann, *New Essays on the Rationalists* (New York, 1999) • E. Hirsch, *Geschichte der neuern evangelischen Theologie* (5 vols.; Gütersloh, 1949-54) • W. Lecky, *History of the Rise and Influence of the Spirit of Rationalism in Europe* (2 vols.; London, 1865) • H. Scholz, *Die Hauptschriften zum Pantheismusstreit zwischen Jacobi und Mendelssohn* (Berlin, 1916) • A. Schweitzer, *The Quest of the Historical Jesus* (trans. W. Montgomery; New York, 1961) • N. Torrey, *Voltaire and the English Deists* (New Haven, 1930) • E. Wilbur, *A History of Unitarianism* (2 vols.; Cambridge, Mass., 1945-52).

Jörg Dierken and Robert F. Brown

Rauschenbusch, Walter

Walter Rauschenbusch (1861-1918) was the best-known exponent of the → Social Gospel movement in North America. His formative theological writings reflected a distinctive synthesis of evangelical and liberal Protestantism that addressed systemically the social and economic problems of the late 19th and early 20th centuries. Rauschenbusch's theological writings helped define the Social Gospel movement at its point of greatest public influence in North America and played a major role in the subsequent development of theological → liberalism and Christian → social ethics.

Rauschenbusch was born in 1861 in Rochester, New York, the youngest child of August and Caroline Rauschenbusch. His father was a fifth-generation Lutheran clergyman from Germany who became a Baptist after emigrating to the United States in the 1840s. Spending his boyhood with his family in Rochester and in Germany, Rauschenbusch received a postsecondary diploma from a gymnasium in Gütersloh, Germany, in 1883. He earned a bachelor of arts degree from the University of Rochester in 1884 and a bachelor of divinity degree from Rochester Theological Seminary in 1886. From 1886 to 1897 Rauschenbusch served as the → pastor of the Second German Baptist Church in New York City. As the minister of this working-class German immigrant congregation in an impoverished neighborhood in the "Hell's Kitchen" section of Manhattan, he developed the major contours of his social and theological thought. Rauschenbusch was influenced by a wide range of religious and secular sources, including Christian socialism from the mid-19th-century Church of England, the liberal economic theories of Henry George and Richard Ely, and the writings of late 19th-century pioneers of American social Christianity, such as Washington Gladden, W. D. P. Bliss, and Josiah Strong.

In 1889 Rauschenbusch and a handful of supporters launched *For the Right,* a New York City newspaper reflecting "social Christianity." Although the paper soon folded, many of the themes articulated by Rauschenbusch in this phase of his ministry anticipated theological arguments that he developed in his later career. Rauschenbusch castigated traditional Christianity's exclusive insistence on personal salvation. He called for a modern interpretation of Christianity that could address the pressing social and economic problems of the late 19th century, focusing upon the church's imperative to support the economic → rights of the poor and working class. At the same time, Rauschenbusch's theology was strongly influenced by Baptist and Wesleyan → pietism, and his early and later writings frequently drew upon sources coming out of these traditions.

Rauschenbusch's ministry contributed to health problems that ultimately cost him most of his hearing. In 1891 his congregation granted him a sabbatical leave, and he spent nine months of rest and study in Germany. During this visit he absorbed the work of German liberal theologians such as Albrecht Ritschl and Adolf von Harnack. Although critical of the political → conservatism of most German theological liberals, their idealistic emphasis upon the → kingdom of God became central to all of Rauschenbusch's later writing. While in Germany he completed an extensive handwritten manuscript under the awkward working title "Christianity Revolutionary." This manuscript was published posthumously in 1968 under the revised title *The Righteousness of the Kingdom.*

In 1892 Rauschenbusch and a handful of East Coast Baptist ministers founded a caucus called The Brotherhood of the Kingdom. Through the 1890s and early 1900s the Brotherhood served as an ecumenical fellowship of Protestant clergy and a small number of laity that gave Rauschenbusch and other members a forum to address issues related to Christianity and social reform. Rauschenbusch delivered numerous public addresses and published several articles under Brotherhood auspices that served as the basis for much of his later pioneering work in social Christianity. In 1893 he married Pauline Rother, a Milwaukee schoolteacher and German-American immigrant. The couple had five children.

In 1897 Rauschenbusch accepted a faculty appointment at Rochester Theological Seminary in the school's German department, the same department that his father had headed between 1858 and 1888. With the seminary's mission being geared toward training German-immigrant Baptist pastors for ministry in the United States, Rauschenbusch taught practically every subject in the curriculum, including biblical studies, theology, and American history. In 1902 he became professor of church history in the seminary's English department and remained in this position until his death in 1918.

Between 1907 and 1917 Rauschenbusch wrote three books that established his reputation as the major exponent of the Social Gospel movement in North America. In 1907 he published his most influential work, *Christianity and the Social Crisis.* Combining a style that emphasized the dual themes of societal crisis and the opportunities afforded to contemporary humanity to engage in prophetic Christian social action, the book became one of the most influential works on American religion in the 20th century. Rauschenbusch's narrative incorporated the theological arguments of German liberal theologians such as Ritschl and Harnack with the biblical exegesis of prominent American liberal theologians such as Shailer Mathews and Francis Greenwood Peabody. Rauschenbusch argued that the primary significance of Jesus' teachings was not eschatological but rooted in the imperative to transform society. Rauschenbusch's persistent theme in *Christianity and the Social Crisis* was that Jesus' teachings on the kingdom of God needed to be directly applied to the socioeconomic problems of early 20th-century America. He viewed the kingdom doctrine as central to church history because it accentuated how the teachings of the OT prophets and Jesus' indictments against the prevailing sociopolitical structure of the first century formed the core of the church's message to contemporary society. As opposed to seeing Jesus' message in apocalyptic and otherworldly terms, Rauschenbusch argued that Christ's teachings on the kingdom represented a call to the church to create a just social order. In particular, Christians were summoned to work on behalf of the poor for economic justice and social equality. While the book gives an optimistic appraisal of the church's role in social reform, he cautioned that the goal of Christianity was to approximate a society of social and democratic equality, not to fully realize these goals in history.

Rauschenbusch's next two books expanded his theological arguments. In 1912 he published *Christianizing the Social Order,* which represented his most detailed discussion of how America could build a just economic and political order based upon the principles of a prophetic liberal Christianity. In 1917 he published *A Theology for the Social Gospel,* which represented Rauschenbusch's first and only effort to write a more systematic treatment of his key theological beliefs related to the doctrine of → God, → salvation, the nature of → evil, and, most especially, the kingdom of God. While this work received modest praise during Rauschenbusch's lifetime, it would be cited in later years as an important volume in the development of 20th-century theological liberalism. Rauschenbusch also published numerous articles and shorter books of a didactic and devotional nature, including *Unto Me* (1912), *Dare We Be Christians?* (1914), and *The Social Principles of Jesus* (1916), the last title published as a religious study guide for college students. A book of prayers entitled *Prayers of the Social Awakening* (1910) provides unique insight into the ways Rauschenbusch sought to integrate → spirituality and social action in his theology. The popularity of his writings was augmented by his appeal as a lecturer during the height of the Progressive Era in the United States between 1908 and 1917.

Rauschenbusch's popularity was affected negatively by World War I, beginning in 1914. Although never an absolute pacifist, he took a staunch antiwar position and argued in favor of American neutrality. His opposition to the → war, his efforts to defend the political motives of Germany, and his own German ancestry brought him heavy criticism from numerous religious and secular leaders in the United States, Canada, and Great Britain. He became associated with several antiwar organizations and lobbied American politicians and religious leaders to protect the civil liberties of German-Americans. Although Rauschenbusch tempered his criticism of the war after American entry in April 1917, he remained critical of a predominant sentiment within American Protestantism that tended to view the war as a righteous crusade.

In late 1917 Rauschenbusch fell ill to a series of ailments that remained undiagnosed until June 1918, when surgery revealed the presence of colon cancer. He died the next month in Rochester. His death has been viewed as marking a symbolic end of the Social Gospel movement in the United States. His teachings, nevertheless, remained very influential in American Protestantism in the decades following his death.

Commonly classified as an "evangelical liberal" because of the ways his thought balanced the themes of personal conversion and social justice, Rauschenbusch was highly critical of many late 19th-century evangelicals who emphasized premillennial views of the second coming of Christ. At the same time, he collaborated with Ira Sankey, the musical partner of the famed premillennial revivalist Dwight → Moody, in the publication in the 1890s of a two-volume German translation of Sankey's gospel hymns.

Rauschenbusch combined an eloquent literary style with a compelling theological message that addressed the urban-industrial context of Progressive Era America. Unlike many of the progressive idealists of the early Social Gospel, represented by clergy such as Washington Gladden, Rauschenbusch displayed a more vigorous engagement with numerous intellectual resources in the late 19th and early 20th century. While many of his writings reflected an irenic spirit toward the heritage of American evangelicalism, the intellectual heart of his theology came from the legacies of German, English, and American theological liberalism. Central to Rauschenbusch's theological outlook was his optimistic view of God's role in history that largely derived from German idealists like Ritschl and Harnack. Although Rauschenbusch remained confident that social progress would occur, it was not inevitable, and it would require great sacrifices on the part of individuals to achieve the permanent realization of a just society. His vision of Christian reform made generous use of late 19th-century democratic socialist ideals. Although he identified himself as a Christian socialist, his reform measures were largely predicated upon a model of liberal → capitalism. He advocated for extensive government regulation of business monopolies, although he rejected more radical measures of political → socialism.

On certain social issues Rauschenbusch fell on the conservative end of the spectrum compared with other Progressive Era reformers. While supportive of women's suffrage, he was ambivalent about women working outside of the home. Like most American Protestants of his generation, he tended to see women as the moral caretakers of society through their roles as wives and mothers.

Rauschenbusch's idealism was tempered by a belief in what he called the "superpersonal" nature of human evil, anticipating the arguments made by a later generation of American neoorthodox theologians. While Rauschenbusch rejected traditional Christian interpretations of the doctrine of original sin, he asserted that evil inevitably manifested itself collectively in modern → society. In many ways his arguments paralleled themes articulated by Reinhold → Niebuhr in his book *Moral Man and Immoral Society* (1932).

Rauschenbusch's insistence that Christianity's message was inherently social, requiring Christians to labor on behalf of the oppressed, had wide-ranging influence upon the future of North American Christianity. Even later neoorthodox critics of the Social Gospel movement conceded the importance of Rauschenbusch to the development of the church's social witness. In the 1950s Martin Luther → King Jr. cited Rauschenbusch's major influence upon his theological and social thought. Since the 1960s some exponents of → liberation theology, including Christians outside the context of North America and western Europe, have also claimed a theological debt to Rauschenbusch, as have segments of the evangelical community that embrace a more liberal political agenda. While many contemporary scholars have criticized the cultural and theological biases inherent within Rauschenbusch's thought, they continue to be inspired by his life and work.

Bibliography: Primary sources: Christianity and the Social Crisis (New York, 1907) • *Christianizing the Social Order* (New York, 1912) • *Dare We Be Christians?* (New York, 1914) • "The New Evangelism," *Independent* (New York) 56 (1904) 1055-61 • *Prayers of the Social Awakening* (Boston, 1910) • *The Righteousness of the Kingdom* (rev. ed.; Lewiston, N.Y., 1999; orig. pub., 1968) • *The Social Principles of Jesus* (New York, 1916) • *A Theology for the Social Gospel* (New York, 1917) • *Walter Rauschenbusch: Selected Writings* (ed. W. S. Hudson; New York, 1984). Rauschenbusch's family papers are housed in the American Baptist Samuel Colgate Historical Library, Rochester, New York.

Secondary works: H. Beckley, *Passion for Justice: Retrieving the Legacies of Walter Rauschenbusch, John A. Ryan, and Reinhold Niebuhr* (Louisville, Ky., 1992) • G. Dorrien, *The Making of American Liberal Theology* (vol. 2; Louisville, Ky., 2003) • C. Evans, *The Kingdom Is Always But Coming: A Life of Walter Rauschenbusch* (Grand Rapids, 2004) • P. Minus, *Walter Rauschenbusch: American Reformer* (New York, 1988) • D. Sharpe, *Walter Rauschenbusch* (New York, 1942) • D. Smucker, *The Origins of Walter Rauschenbusch's Ethics* (Montreal and Kingston, 1994).

Christopher H. Evans

Readings, Scripture

Readings, Scripture

Readings taken from the Bible are a constituent element of worship services in the Christian church. This article treats readings for Sunday → worship and feasts, touching only in passing upon those for weekdays, the sanctoral cycle (i.e., the cycle of saints days celebrated over the course of a calendar year; → Saints, Veneration of), and monastic communities. It has as its primary focus readings in the liturgical traditions of the West.

1. Background

1.1. *Terminology*

Synonyms remind us that "readings" refers in the church to passages selected for the purpose of being read aloud in public worship. The Greek liturgical terms *anagnōseis* and *anagnōsmata* mean "passages read aloud." The term *perikopē* — from Gk. *perikoptō,* "cut around, trim," and perhaps best translated "extract" — was used by the → early church, adopted by Lutherans in the 16th century, and has enjoyed wide use in the Western church since the Second → Vatican Council. The connotations of "lection" overlap these two. Originating in the Roman Catholic tradition, this term derives from Lat. *lectio/lectiones,* meaning variously a textual passage, a selection, and a reading. "Lesson," a usage peculiar to Protestants, places emphasis upon the catechetical function of readings.

The term "lectionary" (Ger. *Lektionar*) refers to readings organized into a system for use throughout the → church year. *Perikopenordnung,* which German Catholics use synonymously with *Lektionar,* is that and more for German Lutherans: a book containing annual series of pericopes, which are used both to form a lectionary and to serve as texts for → preaching.

1.2. *Function*

Readings of Scripture may serve a variety of functions, though their proclamation constitutes a single liturgical act. They may be selected to convert unbelievers or to teach believers. In times of disaster they may offer pastoral comfort, in face of injustice a prophetic word. Readings appropriate to feasts, like the infancy narratives at → Christmas, recall the moment in → salvation history being celebrated; spiritual formation is furthered by the repeated use of familiar passages. As an act of worship, readings offer praise to God; the use of historic lections joins a church to its tradition.

1.3. *Selection*

Scriptural passages are selected for worship between two poles: → canon and occasion (→ Occasional Services). On the one hand, there is the biblical canon, the integrity of the Bible as a whole, its subdivisions and books. The biblical canon may be honored by drawing readings from a certain section of the Bible (e.g., the OT, the Gospels, the NT writings), by assigning a particular book to a particular season, or by making canonical integrity a fundamental principle for selection.

In dialectical tension with the integrity of the canon stands the suitability of a passage for the occasion upon which it may be read. Readings may be selected to fulfill any of the functions noted above: pastoral care, teaching, or conversion by example. However, for much of the church, much of the time, occasion is understood seasonally. In this case the tension between canon and occasion is specifically that between canon and calendar; readings are chosen to suit the liturgical year. This tension is felt most intensively on feast days and during the seasonal cycles; it diminishes on Sundays whose seasonal character is less pronounced.

To accomplish these ends, readings are derived from Scripture in three ways. *Lectio continua* (continuous reading) proclaims the Bible or parts of it in toto. Selections are made so that each subsequent passage begins, without break, where the previous one leaves off. A second way is *lectio semicontinua* (Eng. "semicontinuous reading," Ger. *Bahnlesung*). Although this type is sometimes considered a variation of lectio continua, it is helpful to distinguish the two. As with lectio continua, this approach seeks to set forth the Bible or sections of it as a whole and to that end selects passages in order of their appearance in the canon. In contrast, however, lectio semicontinua does not require passages to follow immediately upon one another; verses may be left out between them. Finally, *lectio selecta* (selected reading) refers to a reading selected from the Bible for a particular occasion — a feast or a season, a funeral or another unexpected event. Here the meanings of the reading's biblical setting are subordinated to those that the text may provide for the occasion.

2. History

2.1. *Early Development*

While Scripture was publicly read in ancient Israel (Exod. 24:1-11; Nehemiah 8), historical evidence for the church's use of readings in worship leads back to the synagogue. In the second century A.D. the primary reading at → Sabbath prayer was the *qeri'at ha-Torah,* or the reading of the Torah. It was read lectio continua, over an annual cycle (in Babylon) or a triennial cycle (in Palestine). Originally, Torah readings were to have a minimum of 21 verses, while the maximum number was not fixed. Passages for festivals were chosen lectio selecta, appropriate to the day. Eventually all → Judaism settled upon set Torah selections, which were read over an annual cycle. A second reading followed, a passage from the prophetic writings, the haftarah, which on Sabbaths was read lectio selecta to suit the Torah reading and on feasts to accord with the day.

Lukan passages that refer to this ritual in the first-century synagogues visited by Jesus and his followers (Luke 4:16-21; Acts 13:14b-16, 27; 15:21) in no way contradict what we know of second-century practice. The repeated allusions to the "Law and the prophets" in the writings of Matthew, Luke, John, and Paul, along with "Moses and the prophets" in Luke, may allude to the two cycles of synagogue readings. Clear parallels to synagogue practice are also found later, in features of the liturgy of the Word celebrated in the fourth century. Both employ the pattern of a reading followed by a sermon; both use lectio continua and lectio selecta for selecting their readings; both celebrate a liturgical cycle based on the week (Sabbath and Sunday, respectively); both draw readings from subsections of Scripture.

For the reading of Scripture by the early church "on the day called Sunday," → Justin Martyr provides a direct description in about A.D. 150: "The memoirs of the apostles or [and?] the writings of the prophets are read as long as time permits. When the reader has finished, the president in a discourse urges and invites [us] to the imitation of these noble things" (*1 Apol.* 67). The parallels between synagogue and church practice provide a context for understanding this passage. It occurs at a weekly celebration of worship; it involves the reading of Scripture and a sermon. The phrase "as long as time permits" has a direct parallel in the contemporary synagogue, the length of whose readings had not yet been fixed. Finally, Justin mentions readings taken from different bodies of Scripture. While it is impossible to identify Justin's references precisely, specific parallels to the synagogue in this regard are found elsewhere. In the early third century → Tertullian (*De praescr. haeret.* 36) mentions readings from the Law, Prophets, Epistles, and Gospels (as a practice for Rome?), a pattern attested for Antioch in the fourth century (*Apos. Const.* 8.5). Later this pattern appears in lectionaries of Oriental churches (→ Nestorians; Syrian Orthodox Church). Whether or not the church appropriated synagogue practices without change, it clearly built upon its foundations.

It is important to bear in mind that "Scripture" for the early church was an amorphous entity; the process by which the canon came to be defined was slow and indeed influenced in part by the use of Scripture in worship. While Paul certainly urged that his letters be read in assembly (Col. 4:16; 1 Thess. 5:27), it took time for them to be regarded as Scripture. In contrast, some churches read writings in their worship that were eventually excluded from the canon, such as the *Apocalypse of Peter,* the writings of Hermas, and Clement of Rome's *Epistle to the Corinthians.* In 372, for example, the Council of Laodicea prepared a list of books held to be canonical and forbade the reading of noncanonical materials in worship. The process of canonization parallels the development of reading systems; both took definitive, though not final, form in the fourth century (→ Apocrypha; Pseudepigrapha).

2.2. ***Fourth-Century Patterns***

With the development of church structures after the Peace of Constantine (A.D. 313), basic patterns for readings become apparent. Above all, the liturgical year emerged to provide a new framework for the selection of readings. Previously the church made seasonal use of selected readings in the manner of the synagogue, that is, for feasts. Now the number of holy days multiplied; to → Easter were added Pentecost, Epiphany, and Christmas. Around these feasts, seasons began to develop, notably the seasonal cycle of Easter, for all of which readings had to be appointed. Not only were pericopes selected for certain days, but biblical books were assigned to particular seasons: Genesis and Proverbs to Lent, Job and Jonah to Holy Week, and the Acts of the Apostles and John to Easter.

At this time, however, we have evidence of specific readings only for feasts and seasons, leaving to conjecture what transpired on the other Sundays of the year. H. Old argues that Sundays of falling outside of the seasons were the occasion for lectio continua. Partial series of continuous readings in later lectionaries (Nestorian, Jacobite, Roman) may witness to this practice. Also the Fathers of the fourth and fifth centuries preached extended sermon series on biblical books (e.g., → Augustine on Psalms, → Chrysostom on Genesis; → Church Fathers). But we do not know for certain the setting of these sermons, whether they were given on Sundays or weekdays, addressed to a parochial congregation or to a monastic community (C. Vogel, 299-301). Others hold that lectio selecta soon became the pattern for all Sundays, including those falling outside of the seasons. Whatever system was used, the choice fell to the → bishop, who during seasons often followed the practice of influential church centers, notably Jerusalem, and at other times made his own selections.

In the fourth century ritual patterns become evident along with the calendrical. Liturgical traditions settled upon the number of readings and their sources. In the Greek and Latin churches a threefold pattern was accepted: a reading each from the OT, NT writings, and the Gospels. In East Syrian Christianity there were four readings: two from the OT and two from the NT. To this pattern West Syrian practice added a third OT reading, one taken from → Wisdom literature. While early Egyptian and Ethiopian liturgies may have followed Syrian patterns, they now customarily have four readings from the NT (from Pauline and Catholic Epistles, Acts, and the Gospels). Finally, rituals of reading become evident at this time. In the West they evolved to include an OT reading followed by a psalm, an epistle reading followed by an → acclamation, and a gospel selection.

2.3. *Medieval Form*

From the 5th to the 7th centuries Western lectionaries assumed the form they were to keep into the 20th century. In the first place, the church year took definitive shape, notably with the introduction of the season of Advent. With that development the second of the church year's two seasonal cycles took shape, and set readings were appointed. Second, the OT reading dropped out of both the Byzantine and Roman liturgies, probably in the 5th century. In the West the Milanese, Mozarabic, and (until the 11th cent.) Gallican liturgies retained an OT reading; in the East the Armenian, Nestorian, and Syrian Jacobite liturgies did likewise. Turning to the West, we see that readings — now only two in number, an "epistle" (= any nongospel NT reading) and a gospel — were appointed lectio selecta for the Sundays falling outside of the seasons. These developments did not happen systematically. The gospel and epistle cycles developed independently of one another and, when combined, were only rarely coordinated.

The Western medieval Sunday lectionary emerged in several forms. Originally the Bible, either as a whole or in parts, was used as a liturgical book. Readings were noted in the margins, either by marking where a pericope began and ended or by writing its incipit and explicit (i.e., the opening and closing words). However, as feasts and saint's days were added to the calendar and the number of readings multiplied accordingly, margins were increasingly unable to accommodate notations of this kind with ease. There then developed the capitulary *(capitularia),* a book used in conjunction with a biblical text listing readings by incipit and explicit. Finally, readings came to be incorporated in full in a variety of books: sacramentary, plenary missal, lectionary book, evangelary, and epistolary. The term *comes* or *liber com(m)icus,* originally applied to collections of full texts, came to refer to capitularies. These subsequent forms did not wholly supplant one another, however. While full texts become more common over time, all forms existed side by side until the 15th century, when, with the invention of movable type, complete texts could be inexpensively produced.

2.4. *Reformation Solutions*

Ironically, for the majority of Christian churches in the West, the → Reformation led to a restoration of the medieval eucharistic lectionary. Martin → Luther was highly critical of that lectionary, especially the epistle cycle, which he regarded as more law than gospel. Luther appreciated the value of Scripture being read in worship lectio continua. Aware, however, that few clergy were up to preaching in this manner, Luther reconciled himself to the continued use of the medieval lectionary, making only a few alterations, notably in the epistle cycle (*German Mass,* 1526; *LW* 53.51-90). On Sundays Luther used this lectionary, always preaching on the gospel texts; on weekdays he preached lectio continua.

Nonetheless the average worshiper experienced a revolutionary change. In the first place, the lections were read in German rather than Latin. Second, regular use of the Sunday lectionary was itself an innovation. By the eve of the Reformation the sanctoral cycle had grown to such an extent that readings for saint's days falling on Sundays largely replaced those of the eucharistic lectionary. Using evangelical criteria, Luther trimmed back the sanctoral cycle and feasts, allowing the medieval annual cycle of two readings, epistle and gospel, to stand alone. This compromise solution was not adopted by Lutheran churches in all regions, at least not immediately. The churches of Riga, Brandenburg-Nuremburg, and Poland chose to read Scripture lectio continua; the Swedish church only adopted lectio selecta with caution.

A similar pattern can be seen elsewhere. Like the Lutherans, the Anglicans curtailed the sanctoral cycle on evangelical grounds and employed the medieval lectionary. Since, however, Morning Prayer was the service normally held on Sunday morning in English parish churches, the eucharistic lectionary was used only when the Lord's Supper was celebrated, which was quarterly until the 19th century (→ Eucharist). Thus congregations typically heard the readings for the daily office, Morning and Evening Prayer, which worked through most of the OT once and most of the NT twice during the year and the whole Psalter once a month. The Tridentine reforms of the → Roman Catholic Church also curtailed the sanctoral cycle, though less severely, and made some minor changes in the cycle of readings.

The Reformed churches submitted readings in worship to a more thoroughgoing revision. Emulating the → church fathers, its leaders used lectio continua: M. → Bucer in Strasbourg, U. → Zwingli in Zurich, and later J. → Calvin in Geneva. Thence it spread throughout the Reformed wing of the Reformation as a whole. The intent was to provide evangelical instruction by preaching the Word of God rather than a festal lectionary, which snipped the Bible into "the epistles and gospels" to serve the liturgical year. So that "people may be better acquainted with the whole Body of the Scriptures," the Westminster Directory (1645) instructed Presbyterian ministers to employ lectio continua, reading all the canonical books in order, at least one chapter from each Testament at every Lord's Day service. Though not as common as it once was, this approach to scriptural selection or variations upon it are still used today by ministers in the Reformed tradition.

2.5. *Modern Developments*

Since the beginning of the 19th century the readings used in worship have been scrutinized, existing readings revised, and new systems devised. These many ventures addressed concerns about (1) clarifying the shape of the liturgical year and (2) appointing texts to articulate it; these texts had to (3) respect canonical integrity, (4) be appropriate for preaching, and (5) be understandable in worship. Examples include the lectionary of the Catholic Apostolic Church (1842), the *Perikopenordnung* of the Eisenach Church Conference (1896), and the lectionaries of the British Joint Liturgical Group (1967 and 1988). Out of these various efforts emerged the lectionary systems now in use.

European Lutherans built a new system on medieval foundations. Two goals were paramount: to maintain continuity with the medieval lectionary and to offer more pericopes for preaching. The approach was guided by the recognition that a passage of Scripture has a liturgical use quite distinct from its role as a preaching text. As liturgical texts, the readings of the medieval lectionary have molded European Christian consciousness over more than a millennium and currently join Lutherans to the historic Western lectionary tradition. Thus there is value in reading these texts, especially the Gospels, even when they are not preached, as they provide for the faithful a kind of scriptural anamnesis. In contrast, as a set of preaching texts, the medieval lectionary's annual cycle of two readings was wanting. While Pietists in the 18th century and reformers in the 19th criticized that lectionary, its actual revision spans the 20th century.

Using six annual cycles of readings, one of psalms, and a variety of auxiliary pericopes, the current *Perikopenbuch mit Lektionar* (1978, rev. 1985) offers both a lectionary of three readings and a variety of preaching texts. At the center of this system lies the traditional gospel reading; all readings appointed for any Sunday or occasion are chosen in consonance with it. The readings that the lectionary employs are the (lightly revised) traditional Gospels of series 1, the (extensively revised) Epistles in series 2, and an OT reading drawn from series 3-6. As to the six annual cycles of preaching texts, the Gospels and Epistles of the lectionary (series 1 and 2 respectively) provide those for the first two cycles. The annual cycles of preaching texts provided by series 3-6 are either the OT reading of the lectionary (whenever it occurs in these four series) or a substitute for one of the lectionary readings, whether OT, epistle, or gospel.

This approach offers both continuity and variety. As to continuity, all three readings of the lectionary are read intact on one half of the Sundays in the six-year cycle, and two of its readings plus a substitute on the remaining Sundays. Thus on every Sunday no fewer than two readings of the lectionary are read. As to homiletic choice, this system, with its six cycles of preaching texts and auxiliary pericopes, provides for Sundays and feasts, in all 859 preaching texts. It also allows for latitude in use. As an alternative to using all three readings, the *Perikopenbuch* allows for the traditional pattern of epistle and gospel; in practice, preachers use as few as one reading and as many as four (the three lectionary readings plus a preaching text).

In comparison, the lectionary that came out of the reforms of the Second Vatican Council diverged from the Western lectionary tradition. *Sacrosanctum concilium,* the Constitution on the Sacred Liturgy (1963), directed that "the treasures of the Bible are to be opened up more lavishly so that a richer fare may be provided for the faithful at the table of God's word" (§51). Promulgated in 1969, *Ordo lectionum missae* (OLM; Eng. terminology: The Roman Lectionary) is marked by a three-year cycle in which the Synoptic gospels are read in subsequent years: Matthew in year A (begun with Advent in years divisible by 3), Mark in year B, Luke in year C. Readings from John are found in all three years, especially in the seasons. Restoring the OT, the OLM appointed three readings for each Sunday: OT, epistle, and gospel. The year is divided into Sundays in the Seasons (i.e., the Christmas and Easter cycles) and Sundays of the Year, or Ordinary Time. The latter treat as one unit all Sundays other than the former, both those falling between Epiphany and Ash Wednesday and those coming after Pentecost until the end of the liturgical year.

The seasonal character of Sundays is indicated by assigning particular books of the Bible to particular seasons (Isaiah to Advent; the Gospel of John to Christmas, Lent, and Easter; Acts of the Apostles, the Catholic Epistles, and Revelation to Easter) and by aligning all three texts appointed. Especially notable is the initiatory understanding of Easter, whereby Lent is regarded as a period of baptismal preparation, Easter (and esp. the Easter Vigil) as the preeminent occasion for baptism, and Eastertide as a time for mystagogical catechesis. The Sundays of the Year are organized differently, using lectio semicontinua for both the epistle and the gospel texts (excluding those pericopes appointed in the seasons). As in the medieval lectionary, they constitute independent cycles of readings. The OT reading, however, was chosen to support the gospel selection, in a relationship commonly referred to as typological.

This lectionary system struck a chord beyond the Roman Catholic Church, especially among American Protestants. Within five years of its publication, in a spontaneous display of ecumenical agreement, the majority of American mainline denominations had adopted some version of it. Use of this lectionary over time, however, made apparent the need for adjustments. Small differences between the various versions in selection, nomenclature, and calendar were regarded as irritants to ecumenism. A truly common lectionary was desired. Additionally, the use of the OT in Ordinary Time was judged to offer an inadequate proclamation of Israel's covenantal witness.

The final product of this reevaluation, the *Revised Common Lectionary* (RCL, 1992), is properly understood as a lectionary resource from which churches can create a lectionary adapted to their own traditions and requirements. All churches using the RCL share a common calendar, nomenclature, and system for assigning readings to Sundays. Additionally, however, there are choices. The Feast of Transfiguration can be celebrated either on the last Sunday after Epiphany or (as in the OLM) on the second Sunday in Lent; also, churches may choose readings from the Apocrypha.

The most significant choice, however, involves the OT readings following Pentecost. To give the OT an independent voice, three new sets of readings were provided along with the typological. These series present major OT narratives using semicontinuous readings spanning most of the Sundays after Pentecost. In year A God's covenant with Israel is taken from the Octateuch (Genesis–Ruth), in year B the rise of the nation of Israel from the historical books, and in year C Israel's prophetic witness from the prophetic writings. Since the OT, epistle, and gospel readings of this option are selected as independent series, connections between them on any given Sunday are coincidental. A choice of OT readings after Pentecost is provided, along with other options, to render this revised lectionary appealing to preaching and eucharistic traditions alike.

The RCL has enjoyed widespread acceptance, first among Protestants in the English-speaking world, and now beyond it. The vast majority of the churches that have adopted this lectionary, even those with a eucharistic tradition, employ the semicontinuous readings after Pentecost. A few Reformed churches (Swiss, Reformed Church in America) recommend it for use only during the seasonal cycles. Despite interest in this lectionary shown by the U.S. Conference of Catholic Bishops, it has not received the Vatican approval necessary for use.

In Protestant churches where the responsibility for selecting Scripture falls to the minister, patterns of reading Scripture vary. While the RCL is commonly used in mainline churches of this kind, other approaches predominate in evangelical churches. They may select Scripture "topically" to suit the subject matter of the sermon. Such readings may be brief, perhaps no more than a verse. In other congregations, language and sermons are permeated with scriptural allusions but no specific passage of Scripture per se is read. Here scriptural authority is imparted by the Bible as a whole rather than through the formality of proclaiming particular passages of Scripture.

3. Theology

A key theological issue raised by readings in worship is the relationship of Scripture to → revelation. Unlike → Islam, which regards the → Qur'an to be a direct revelation of Allah to Muḥammad, Christianity draws a distinction between Scripture and revelation. Revelation is an act of God, Scripture the human witness to it. Christ is the Son of God, the Gospels the church's record of him. Both Protestants and Roman Catholics, however, regard Scripture used in worship to be (at least potentially) revelatory. The Catholic tradition locates this moment in the Gospel reading, which, being chosen by the church and carried by its liturgy, sounds the voice of Christ. In contrast, the Protestant tradition locates revelation in the proclamation of the Word. As Scripture is read in worship and interpreted by the sermon, persons can be addressed by God and called by Christ.

Bibliography: General: P. Bradshaw, "The Use of the Bible in the Liturgy: Some Historical Perspectives," *StLi* 22 (1992) 35-52 • H. Old, *The Reading and Preaching of the Scriptures in the Worship of the Christian Church,* vol. 1, *The Biblical Period;* vol. 2, *The Patristic Age;* vol. 3, *The Medieval Church;* vol. 4, *The Reformation Period* (Grand Rapids, 1998-2002).

Jewish: J. W. Aageson, "Early Jewish Lectionaries," *ABD* 4.270-71 • I. Elbogen, *Jewish Liturgy: A Comprehensive History* (Philadelphia and Jerusalem, 1993) 129-49 • J. Mann, *The Bible as Read and Preached in the Old Synagogue* (2 vols.; Cincinnati, 1940).

Early church: P. Cobb, "The Liturgy of the Word in the Early Church," *The Study of the Liturgy* (rev. ed.; ed. H. Jones, G. Wainwright, and E. Yarnold; New York, 1992) 219-29 • K. Junack, "Early Christian Lectionaries," *ABD* 4.271-73.

Eastern: G. Barrois, *Scripture Readings in Orthodox Worship* (Crestwood, N.Y, 1977) • W. J. Grisbrooke, "Word and Liturgy: The Eastern Orthodox Tradition," *StLi* 16, no. 3/4 (1986/87) 13-30 • R. Taft, "Lectionary," *ODB* 2.1201.

Western: R. Cabié, *The Eucharist* (new ed.; Collegeville, Minn., 1986) 59-66 • J. Jungmann, S.J., *The Mass of the Roman Rite* (vol. 1; New York, 1951) 391-455 • A. Nocent, O.S.B., "The Roman Lectionary for Mass," *Handbook for Liturgical Studies,* vol. 3, *The Eucharist* (Collegeville, Minn., 1986) 177-88 • C. Vogel, *Medieval Liturgy: An Introduction to the Sources* (rev. ed.; Washington, D.C., 1986) 291-355.

Reformation: W. K. L. Clarke, *Liturgy and Worship* (London, 1932) 296-301 • G. Kunze, "Die Lesungen," *Leit.* 2.87-179.

Modern: K.-H. Bieritz, "The Order of Readings and Sermon Texts for the German Lutheran Church," *StLi* 21 (1991) 37-51 • N. Bonneau, *The Sunday Lectionary* (Collegeville, Minn., 1998) • Joint Liturgical Group, *The Calendar and Lectionary: A Reconsideration* (London, 1967) • A. McArthur, *The Christian Year and Liturgical Reform* (London, 1958) • E. Nübold, *Entstehung und Bewertung der neuen Perikopenordnung des Römischen Ritus für die Meßfeier an Sonn- und Festtagen* (Paderborn, 1986) • *Perikopen–Gestalt und Wandel des gottesdienstlichen Bibelgebrauchs* (Hamburg, 1978) • F. Schulz, "Perikopen," *EKL* (3d ed.) 3.1123-30 • F. West, "An Annotated Bibliography on the Three-Year Lectionaries," *StLi* 23 (1993) 223-44; 24 (1994) 222-48; idem, "The German Lutheran and Roman Catholic Lectionaries: A Historical-Comparative Study," *LMin* 13 (2004) 181-90; idem, *Scripture and Memory* (Collegeville, Minn., 1997).

Fritz West

Real Presence → Eucharist 3.2.2

Realism

1. Term and Concept
2. In the History of Philosophy
3. Types

1. Term and Concept

Realism in philosophy affirms that the objects of our senses and concepts exist independently of our sensing and conceiving them, and that they possess the properties we experience them as having. Normally these are spatiotemporal properties of physical objects, but not everything called realism fits this profile. Varieties of antirealism include → idealism, phenomenalism, and critical perspectives lacking metaphysical commitment to any particular view of the nature of reality.

Other disciplines use the term "realism" in ways paralleling its philosophical meaning. Literary realism depicts characters and situations in a straightforward, unvarnished manner, including the harsher aspects of life. Realism in art presents likenesses of objects and scenes as they naturally appear to the senses. Realism in → politics pursues specific practical or material goals rather than general ethical or ideological aims. Realism in Christian → theology refers primarily to the Roman Catholic doctrine of transubstantiation, namely, transformation of the actual eucharistic elements, though not their accidental, sensory features, into the body and blood of Christ. The Lutheran doctrine affirms a "real presence" of Christ "in, with, and under" the sacramental elements.

We find the clearest instances of philosophical

realism in 20th-century Western thought. Although some Asian philosophies, such as India's Cārvāka (materialism) and naturalistic forms of → Confucianism in China, share some features with Western realism, they do not have enough in common to be considered here.

2. In the History of Philosophy

For Plato (427-347 B.C.; → Platonism) the objects of knowledge, the eternal ideas, are neither in space and time nor accessible to bodily senses, for they have a perfect, nonphysical being independent of the rational soul's thinking of them. Early medieval "realists" espoused Platonic → epistemology in opposition to the nominalists, for whom universal terms expressed in concepts are just names, not extramental realities. This metaphysical doctrine of "Platonic realism" is not realism in the modern sense. For Aristotle (384-322), whom → Thomas Aquinas (ca. 1225-74) embraced in the 13th century as a moderate realist, concepts have their origin in sense experience of physical objects. The concepts, however, are abstract mental constructs from general features of multiple sensory experiences of certain sorts and not direct apprehension of individual objects as such, so this position is more aptly termed "conceptualism."

René Descartes (1596-1650) held that our clear and distinct ideas, including ideas of physical things and their interactions, adequately reflect the natures of their objects. His position is not standard realism, however, for it relies on proof of God's existence and the conviction that God is not a deceiver, in order to assure the correspondence of our ideas to their objects. The critical philosophy of Immanuel Kant (1724-1804; → Kantianism) undermined realism by construing known objects as constructs made up both from contents given in sense experience and from categories furnished by the understanding, with the result that the "things in themselves" that presumably produce our sensations are inaccessible and unknowable.

The empiricist John Locke (1632-1704) propounded a type of realism proper. For him our thinking is about ideas we acquire from sense experience and reflection on it. The idea of something is a complex mental object composed of simpler ideas produced in the mind by properties of the external object impacting the sense organs. The sensations or simpler ideas represent to the mind the properties or primary qualities of the thing. So in Locke's "indirect" or "representative" realism, sensations mediate the mind's encounter with, and knowledge of, the external world of objects.

3. Types

Modern realism emerged clearly in the rejection of idealism in the late 19th and early 20th century. The growing influence of → positivism reinforced confidence that the methods of observation and experimentation in physical science yield direct, perceptual knowledge of the objects and forces of the natural world. *Scientific realism* uses the abstract language of mathematics to express physical laws and processes, as did Galileo and Newton in earlier centuries. Nevertheless, it holds that things are much as they present themselves in our experience, that scientific theories and explanations are directly about actual features of the world. Atomic theory in chemistry, along with experimental results and theoretical advances in physics, underscores the difference between how things appear to the senses at the macro level and how they actually are at the micro level, but this discrepancy does not require abandonment of realism.

The relevant watershed event in philosophy as such was the 1903 essay "Refutation of Idealism," by G. E. Moore (1873-1958). Its main targets were the contention of Bishop Berkeley (1685-1753) that "to be is to be perceived" and the Hegelian idealism of F. H. Bradley (1846-1924), for whom all relations among things are ultimately internal aspects of a single, spiritual reality. For Moore, introspection shows that awareness of our sensations is distinct from the things of which they are sensations, hence those objects exist independently of our sensing them. Moore had difficulty showing exactly how the objects themselves are related to the sensory data of which we are aware. Still, for most English-speaking philosophers his essay discredited idealism and opened the door for realism to flourish.

Most of the philosophical forms of realism can be classified as either *direct* realism or *indirect* (or *representative*) realism. Both face the problem of distinguishing veridical experiences of external objects from illusions or hallucinations, for the claim to knowledge of external objects depends upon showing what does and does not count as constituting it.

Direct realism attacks idealism and phenomenalism for treating the mind's objects in cognition as states or contents of consciousness. No internal objects or intermediaries occupy a place between knowing itself and what exists apart from the knower. *Naive realism* is allegedly the stance of the ordinary person, who takes everything at face value. Its philosophical form, a subtler affirmation that objects are just what we take their experienced properties to be, traces its lineage back to the Scottish "commonsense" philosophy of Thomas Reid (1710-96) and was attractive to the Oxford linguistic analysis movement of the 20th century.

Direct realists deny that the mind experiences something within itself that is a likeness of the external object's properties, something mental that consciousness is aware of. Instead, the mind simply adopts a distinctive way of apprehending the object. Advocates of the *adverbial theory*, for instance, say, "I see the object greenly," not "I have a green experience in my mind that reproduces a green property of the object." Direct realists typically explain illusions as having perceptual features that can be distinguished from veridical experiences, or else as being the sort of sensory mental images that veridical experience lacks.

According to indirect or representative realism we are conscious of effects produced in our minds by external objects that convey likenesses of the properties of external objects. Indirect realists call these effects impressions, sensations, or sense data. Scientific, causal accounts of the nervous system's nature and operations fit better with indirect realism. Its drawback is the difficulty of showing convincingly that consciousness actually experiences external objects — what it intends to show — and not just contents of consciousness itself. A recent philosophical debate highlighted the issue by posing the question, How do I know I am not just a brain kept alive in a vat, artificially stimulated rather than having sensory experiences of actual external objects? Indirect realism says that illusions mimic impressions of real objects but are distinguishable in that they do not change, as do perceptions of actual things from variations in lighting, angle of vision, and the like.

Critical realism, a modification of direct realism, concedes that a mental state mediates between consciousness and the external object. But it seeks to distinguish known objects from a mediating mental state more convincingly than indirect realism does. One way is a version of → materialism called *physical realism*. Biological systems of the body interact with the external world to produce effects in the brain that present configurations of known objects. Nonmaterialist critical realists speak instead of "character-complexes" that present to consciousness characteristics of external objects. They propose sophisticated analyses of perception that challenge the assumptions of representative realism as to how objects produce impressions (Locke's simpler ideas) in the mind.

Metaphysical realism, the general view that objects of knowledge have being independent of the mind and genuine extramental relations with one another, is a broader use of the term. While recent philosophers who adopt it usually limit its scope to spatiotemporal objects, the concept itself can include Plato's theory of ideas. *Moral realism* is the metaethical affirmation that ethics is objective, that moral properties are intrinsic to beings and circumstances themselves, apart from the subjective beliefs or attitudes we may hold about them.

Bibliography: W. Alston, *A Realist Conception of Truth* (Ithaca, N.Y., 1996); idem, ed., *Realism and Antirealism* (Ithaca, N.Y., 2002) • D. Armstrong, *Universals and Scientific Realism* (Cambridge, 1978) • J. Austin, *Sense and Sensibilia* (London, 1962) • M. Devitt, *Realism and Truth* (2d ed.; Oxford, 1991) • R. Hirst, "Realism," *EncPh* 7.77-83 • G. Moore, *Philosophical Papers* (London, 1959) • I. Niiniluoto, *Critical Scientific Realism* (Oxford, 1999) • J. Passmore, *A Hundred Years of Philosophy* (London, 1957) • H. Putnam, *Realism and Reason* (Cambridge, 1983) • R. Sellars, *The Philosophy of Physical Realism* (New York, 1932) • E. Sosa and E. Villanueva, eds., *Realism and Relativism* (Boston, 2002) • W. Werkmeister, *A History of Philosophical Ideas in America* (New York, 1949).

Robert F. Brown

Reason

1. Term and Issues

The term "reason" derives from Lat. *ratio*. Earlier in history Gk. *nous* and *logos* expressed some of the same meanings. Reason is usually said to be an intellectual or mental ability or faculty, one distinguished from other psychological or bodily powers or activities of will, emotion, and sensation. Philosophers work with diverse concepts of reason and use the term in different ways.

A number of issues arise in considering the nature, operations, and limitations of human reason. Is it a theoretical faculty, an ability to grasp the natures of things, to understand the world? Is it an ability to envisage possibilities, with links to → imagination? Is reason intuitive, a mental "beholding of truth," or does it calculate by means of specifiable rules as in a mathematical proof? Does reason have the practical orientation of skill in accomplishing things, of intelligence applied to everyday life? How does reason relate to nonrational experiencing and acting, to sensation, emotion, and will? Does reason function differently in science, law (→ Law and Legal Theory), → philosophy, → theology, the arts, and interpersonal relations? Are there limits to what reason can know, owing either to the nature of the human mind itself or to the nature of its objects? Is reason unique to humanity, or do other species or devices with artificial intelligence reason too? Are there superhuman beings (deities, angels, extraterrestrials) that reason, and if so, how might our rationality compare with theirs?

2. In Western Thought

2.1. *Ancient to Early Modern*

Most ancients and medievals made a basic epistemological distinction between sense perception and conceptual thinking. Plato (427-347 B.C.; → Platonism) and Aristotle (384-322; → Aristotelianism) tied it to the psychological distinction between conceptual thought and will. Plato separated knowing *(nous, noēsis)* directed to the true being of the ideas from sense perception *(aisthēsis)* of physical things and the imprecise and unreliable belief or opinion *(doxa)* arising from it. His parallel, tripartite distinction opposed willing in accord with reason *(logistikon)* both to impulses and affections of bodily senses and to willing by the spirited aspect of the soul.

Aristotle took a similar approach by segregating the knowing of theoretical reason from the striving of will in practical life, in ethics and politics. Unlike Plato, however, Aristotle said that rational knowing occurs in conjunction with sense perception, for the properties of reason's objects have their actual, extramental existence only in the objects of sense experience, from which the mind abstracts them to construct its concepts. In addition to this passive or receptive reason *(nous pathētikos)*, Aristotle also recognized a purely active reason *(nous poiētikos)*, exemplified metaphysically and theologically in his unmoved mover absorbed in eternal thinking of itself.

Medieval philosophers drew upon the ancient views of reason found in Plato and Aristotle, as well as in the Neoplatonists and → Stoics, adding refinements in light of their theological concerns. But it does not suffice just to distinguish and relate reason and sense experience as these ancient formulations do. Exactly how intuitive reason *(nous* or *intellectus)*, the purely intellectual vision *(theōria)* of the ideas of what is eternal and divine, differs from the discursive thinking of understanding *(dianoia)* remained unresolved until Kant.

Rationalists of the 17th and 18th centuries held that reason acquires knowledge independently of the senses. For René Descartes (1596-1650; → Cartesianism) minds are a different kind of substance from bodies that sense or are sensed, and thinking substance or reason discovers → truth from its ideas that are clear and distinct. Baruch Spinoza (1632-77; → Spinozism) portrayed rational thought as human beings' participation in the mind of God, as our route to grasping all things physical and metaphysical that our minds are capable of knowing. G. W. Leibniz (1646-1716) conceived of God as a creator bound by rational norms, and human beings as independent minds capable of knowing the created world's rational structures. Empiricists dissented, treating reason not as a mental faculty in its own right but as a habitual way of organizing and interpreting sense experiences in configurations or sequences according to their similarity or spatiotemporal contiguity.

2.2. *Kant and Afterward*

In his *Critique of Pure Reason* (1781), Immanuel Kant (1724-1804; → Kantianism) distinguished particular and general senses of reason. More generally, Ger. *Vernunft* and its correlative *Verstand* indicate our abilities to grasp truth, form judgments, and engage in ordinary reasoning processes. In a particular or special sense, however, Kant distinguished knowledge gained by the understanding *(Verstand)* from thinking by reason *(Vernunft)*. Empirically conditioned knowing by the understanding organizes the phenomena of sensory intuition into objects in accordance with the mind's categorial structures. Reason as a "faculty of principles" directs itself not to sense experience but rather to the understanding as such. Reason thinks the very concepts that the understanding utilizes in its knowing, thinking them in an unconditioned way, not in their application to the data of sense experience. By working purely theoretically, by combining and extending the pure categories of the understanding beyond their legitimate use, reason creates the false problem of how what is unconditioned relates to the conditioned objects actually known by the understanding.

Kant showed how reason treats the unconditioned according to logical relationships taken from the categories used by the understanding. Reason specifies it in three transcendental ideas that have no sensory or empirical content, namely, the ideas of the self or I, of the world as a whole, and of God. Reason thus begets the three speculative endeavors of psychology, cosmology, and theology. Properly understood, the three furnish reason with no knowable objects, just regulative principles for organizing our knowledge of the sensible objects that the understanding can know. That is why, for instance, traditional proofs for God's existence that treat God as an object knowable by theoretical reason cannot work (→ God, Arguments for the Existence of). In this way Kant cleared the ground for an autonomous domain of practical reason in which → God, → freedom, and → immortality are not knowable objects but instead postulates linked to our awareness of the moral law and the conditions of its fulfillment. This move made possible a "metaphysics of morals" independent of the role of reason in → epistemology.

The Kantian treatment of reason set the main agenda for the German → idealists, who dissented from it in various ways. Most notable is G. W. F. Hegel (1770-1831; → Hegelianism), who accepted in principle the *Verstand-Vernunft* distinction and the Kantian criticism of those who regard God as a knowable supernatural being existing alongside the world. Yet he did not dismiss pure reason as simply transcendental thinking by an illegitimate extension of rational principles. For Hegel reason constitutes the very structure of reality, of → absolute spirit and its temporal self-development in nature and history, and of our self-reflective thinking that comprehends this rational structure in its dialectical unfolding. Hegel's *Logic* (1812-16) is the exposition of this absolute reason that is the very substance and spirit of being itself and of our comprehension of it.

Shifting views of history and language challenged a priori accounts of reason. In his studies of the "human sciences" *(Geisteswissenschaften)*, Wilhelm Dilthey (1833-1911) presented a "critique of historical reason." He historicized the knowing subject, reducing it to the psychologically describable facts of consciousness of an individual concretely situated in life and experience. Yet to describe reason as historically relative presupposes that reason has an ahistorical aspect too, a constant of our inner life, though one manifest only under diverse empirical-psychological conditions, of which different cultural forms are variants expressible in a typology of worldviews. The historicity of reason includes a linguistic dimension already explored in Kant's day by his critics J. G. Hamann (1730-88), J. G. → Herder (1744-1803), and F. H. Jacobi (1743-1819). If we learn to reason in learning a language, as some linguists and others affirm, then reasoning processes may differ depending on the language learned and the cultural rationality embedded in its structures. → Analytic philosophers of the 20th century dwelt on how thinking, language use, and their settings in varied "forms of life" are interdependent, and they adopted views of the nature of reason accordingly.

C. S. Peirce (1839-1914), an early exponent of → pragmatism, emphasized how theory connects to practice, knowing to doing. His system of semiotic rationality treats our use of signs or symbols for grasping, and communicating about, features of our experienced world. Peirce's successors among the pragmatists said that knowing or reason is not mainly for representing the truth about things but is for facilitating action. We engage ourselves with our natural and social environments in goal-directed endeavors. Reasoning that matters is reasoning that makes this engagement possible and effective. The "instrumental reason" advocated by John Dewey (1859-1952) stressed prediction and control in scientific and social contexts, far removed from Kant's theoretical reason as an epistemic faculty.

2.3. *Critics of Rationality*

→ Empiricism offers one way to criticize the high value placed on reason. Empiricism does not disparage reason as such, but it holds a modest view of the actual nature of reason and of its function in knowing, namely, that reason does not discover truth but instead just organizes — by reliance on custom, habits of mind, inductive thinking, and the like — the information we receive from perception by the bodily senses. A different kind of criticism denies that reason is, or should be, the primary determiner of our thought and action. → Psychoanalysis contends that much of our thought and behavior is in fact caused not by reasoning but by contents of the unconscious mind. → Existentialism, in contrast, asserts that self-conscious free will and not rationality is the central feature of a human being, and that passions and emotions play a legitimate part in the choosing of our lives. The most severe criticism, however, attacks rationality in principle as itself the direct cause of societal problems. This destructive critique goes far beyond mere recognition that rational norms are conditioned by historical factors and the vagaries of → language.

Friedrich → Nietzsche (1844-1900) insisted on the historically conditioned status of reason, arguing that our confidence in the rationality of language is undercut by the wide range of word meanings and interpretations in practice and in thrall to the weakness of finite thinking. Nietzsche's criticism prepared the way for an enlightened reason that seeks to be reflective and self-critical. Theodor Adorno (1903-69) and Max Horkheimer (1895-1973) turned this criticism into a critique of the instrumental reason that is purpose-driven and guided by the principle of its own self-preservation and advancement. Its technological mastery of external nature presupposes human self-mastery. Inner nature and the external world, individual and society, all fall prey to a single constraint, to total control by instrumental reason. Pursuit of instrumental reasoning in this resolute fashion presupposes detachment from personal considerations that fall outside the scope of its concerns.

The deconstruction movement challenged assumptions about even limited kinds of reason by attacking reason-centered and subject-centered thinking in order to speak, as does Jacques Derrida (1930-2004), of multiple meanings, irreducible differences, and sheer otherness. Its criticism of rationality culminated in the "archaeology of knowledge" project of Michel Foucault (1926-84), which so reduces all forms of theoretical and practical rationality to the "will to power" that deconstruction seems unable to differentiate knowledge from power, order from terror. But just as reasoning is presupposed by an ability to identify what is irrational facticity, so we must be rational in order to be able to distinguish reason from irrationality. To relinquish reason in order to serve mere terroristic power would require the immediate, abstract annihilation of all claims to rationality, including even rationality of the most pluralistic or fragmentary sort.

3. Reason and Religious Faith

Although the ways that → faith and reason are distinct yet related can be examined from the side of either faith or reason, we must rely on rational insight and discourse to recognize and state the issue itself. The Christian faith affirms its dependence on given facts authenticated by the authority of canonical scriptures and church tradition. In the modern world an independent, enlightened reason is critical of professions of faith on such a basis, for they risk speaking simply from an authoritarian or a supernaturalist standpoint. The gulf between faith and reason, viewed from the side of reason, is mitigated to a degree when we turn from confessional theology to the concerns of → practical theology, in which the knowledge and techniques of the → social sciences play a part, or when we characterize faith in terms of those language games or speech-act theories that assign it to an autonomous, noncognitive domain of human experience (→ Linguistics).

How theology handles the faith-reason issue hinges on whether, and to what extent, reason contributes to the content affirmed by faith, or alternatively, whether reason is seen merely as a technical or formal tool for presenting and explicating a content that is given by Scripture and tradition and ultimately based on → revelation. Roman Catholic dogmatic theology employs a model of harmony between faith and reason according to which our knowledge of God stemming from the natural light of human reason is supplemented and enhanced by a supernatural revelation that is itself not contrary to reason. Thus reason illuminated by faith, and faith clarified by reason, are in no conflict but are even mutually supportive.

The Protestant → Reformers, and some later Protestants who endorsed the Kantian critique of reason, unilaterally stressed the positivity of biblical revelation by insisting on the autonomy of the articles of faith, with reason relegated to the task of reflection on the theological given. In this limited role reason is simply a formal instrument and not a source of religious truth. So views of reason held by Protestant thinkers can change in accord with the philosophical currents of the time. Also, without necessarily returning explicitly to a Roman Catholic perspective, some liberal Protestants regard reason as an independent source of religious truth. The nonsectarian deists ranked a commonsense version of reason above revelation, or they interpreted revelation strictly in accord with their rational assumptions.

Despite their differing assessments of the faith-reason relationship, Roman Catholic and mainstream Protestant theologians agree that a believer's stance on the issue should be taken up within the faith and not from outside or as beholden to any particular philosophical or scientific account of rationality. Nor should it short-circuit the gap between faith and reason by postulating a perspectivally neutral unity of the two. Consequently, an explanation of religious faith that presents it in a rationally understandable form must utilize a reason that does not simply coincide with faith, a circumstance that highlights the bounded character of faith itself.

Bibliography: T. Adorno, *Negative Dialectics* (New York, 1973) • H. Albert, *Treatise on Critical Reason* (Princeton, 1985) • J. Bermudez and A. Miller, eds., *Reason and Nature: Essays in the Theory of Rationality* (Oxford, 2002) • B. Blanshard, *Reason and Analysis* (London, 1962); idem, *Reason and Belief* (New Haven, 1975) • I. Dalferth, *Theology and Philosophy* (Oxford, 1988) • J. Dewey, *Logic, the Theory of Inquiry* (New York, 1938) • W. Dilthey, *Introduction to the Human Sciences* (Princeton, 1989) • M. Foucault, *The Archaeology of Knowledge* (London, 1972) • J. Habermas, *Knowledge and Human Interests* (Boston, 1971); idem,

The Philosophical Discourse of Modernity: Twelve Lectures (Cambridge, Mass., 1987) • G. W. F. Hegel, *Hegel's Science of Logic* (trans. A. Miller; London, 1969) • M. Horkheimer, *Critique of Instrumental Reason: Lectures and Essays since the End of World War II* (New York, 1994) • M. Horkheimer and T. Adorno, *Dialectic of Enlightenment: Philosophical Fragments* (Stanford, Calif., 2002) • I. Kant, *Critique of Pure Reason* (trans. P. Guyer and A. Wood; Cambridge, 1988) • W. Pannenberg, *Basic Questions in Theology: Collected Essays* (2 vols.; Philadelphia, 1970-71) • C. Peirce, *The Essential Peirce: Selected Philosophical Writings* (2 vols.; ed. N. Houser and C. Kloesel; Bloomington, Ind., 1992-98) • F. Wagner, *Was ist Theologie? Studien zu ihrem Begriff und Thema in der Neuzeit* (Gütersloh, 1989) • W. Walsh, *Reason and Experience* (Oxford, 1947).

Falk Wagner† and Robert F. Brown

Reception, Ecumenical

1. Term and Usage

The English word "reception" traces its meaning back to Lat. *recipio,* which can be translated "receive, accept, allow." With these several meanings it can include the notion of receiving or accepting externally from something or someone *other.*

"Reception" has become a technical term in several different areas. In legal history it denotes the process by which Roman law was adopted in the German lands during the 13th through 15th centuries. In → literary criticism of the late 20th century, "reception" has been employed to explore the relationship of the reader to a text. In the study of → philosophy the term describes an intellectual or cultural exchange, a meaning highlighted by the German philosopher Hans-Georg Gadamer (1900-2002).

2. Classical Reception

2.1. *Biblical Usage*

"Reception" also has had a long history of use in → theology. In biblical scholarship the idea has been used to portray a number of actions: → creation receives its being from God; God's → revelation is received by human beings; Israel receives God's → covenant; Christ receives his mission from the Father; the church as a community of faith receives life from Christ, its Lord; and the church receives the gift of the Spirit. In contemporary biblical scholarship, "reception" has been viewed as an invaluable biblical concept, often present without the corresponding Greek words *lambanō* or *dechomai,* or the Latin terms *recipio* or *receptio.*

2.2. *Early Church*

During the pre-Constantinian era in church history, "reception" described a process by which the decisions of local and regional → synods were made part of the life of, and were shared between, various local churches. The → early church in fact perceived itself as a fellowship *(koinōnia)* of local churches participating in a lively process of giving and taking from one another. This process was considered something more than juridical action. It included the entire community in a spiritual process that involved more than simply accepting passively the conciliar decisions of other churches. The → canon of Scripture itself was received in this manner, as attested in the Muratorian Canon (ca. 190). Scripture, → liturgy, local laws and customs, → church discipline, the remembrance of certain → saints, the content of → preaching, and → catechesis were all part of this ongoing, spiritual process.

With the emperor Constantine (306-37) a new factor appeared in the reception process. Decisions of ecumenical → councils (e.g., Nicaea in 325, Constantinople in 381, Ephesus in 431) acquired the status of imperial law, and the force of the → Roman Empire was placed behind them. At the same time there are examples where such councils failed to be received by the greater church (e.g., the Synod of Ephesus in 433) or received only partial acceptance (the Council of → Chalcedon in 451). Either "reception" or "nonreception" were possibilities. Even in the Constantinian and post-Constantinian periods reception was a process in which the laity, monks, and church leaders, as well as government leaders, took active roles. Between the fourth and the eighth centuries two factors were of preeminent importance in the reception process: the "consensus of antiquity" and the "consensus of universality."

2.3. *Middle Ages*

In the medieval period, the Western church grew more → hierarchical. This ecclesiological development militated against seeing the church as a fellowship of local churches. Rather, it was viewed as a universal corporation under the bishop of Rome. There was also a distinction between the teaching and learning church. "Reception" came to be understood as acceptance of papal decretals in the courts and in canon law. This understanding is evident especially in the writings of Honorius III (1216-27) and Boniface VIII (1294-1303). *Recipio* in such contexts now meant "recognize, approve, sanction."

These developments did not occur in the East, where at least in theory a vital link was always maintained between reception and the active participation of all the faithful, and where there was a tendency against the codification of "reception" in legal categories. Eastern Orthodoxy has tended to see reception in the context of its total ecclesiology (→ Orthodox Christianity). "Reception" includes agreement with the faith of the undivided church throughout the centuries. It is the fruit of the charismatic work of the → Holy Spirit. The → Orthodox churches have seen reception as a dialectic between the laity and the clergy. This position has brought about some tension in Orthodox theology between, on the one hand, the view that an ecumenical synod or council is the highest authority and, on the other hand, the view that a synod's decisions can become valid only when they are accepted by the whole church. In any case, there is agreement that reception is never a general plebiscite but that it has its origin in the action of the Spirit, who dwells in the church, supports it, and will maintain it in truth.

2.4. *Protestant Reformation and After*

In the 16th-century → Reformation of the Western church, the process of reception was conspicuous. The → Reformers engaged the issue of receiving the doctrinal decisions of the early church, as well as their own confessional documents that arose in the context of the Reformation debates. In these discussions the issue of reception was not based upon the approval of a church magisterium but on the question of whether these 16th-century confessions were faithful witnesses and interpreters of the Scriptures. The reception by Lutherans in 1580 of the Book of Concord is a clear example of this unfolding process. But similar processes can also be identified in the Reformed and Anglican traditions with the acceptance of their own confessions and the → Book of Common Prayer (from 1549). In most cases these processes were not immediate but involved trial, error, and testing over many years. At the same time, Roman Catholics engaged in the reception of their own Council of → Trent (1545-63).

Behind all these events one can observe different concepts of → authority and its basis, all of which influenced reception. For Roman Catholics reception was largely a matter of the binding acceptance of decisions of an infallible papal teaching office or of councils approved by the pope. Generally for the Orthodox and the Protestant traditions, including Anglicanism, acceptance of conciliar decisions or of confessional and liturgical documents was seen to rest on agreement with the teaching of Scripture.

"Reception" in the sense described to this point has been referred to as *classical reception*. It concerns a process within individual churches. This process was never only a juridical event, and never the mere acceptance of theological texts from church councils. It was a process of interpretation and reinterpretation, a lively engagement of the church drawing from resources of its past to meet present circumstances. Certainly in the patristic church it included a willingness of one church to receive from another. Only in the latter half of the 20th century did scholarly interest in this idea of classical reception revive.

3. Second Vatican Council

The Second → Vatican Council (1962-65) changed this situation in three ways. First, Roman Catholic thought and practice had to reengage in the process of the reception of a council of the church. Second, other Christians needed to reflect on what the Roman Catholic reception of this council would mean for their relationship to the → Roman Catholic Church. Third, the council brought interconfessional → dialogue to the fore in ecumenical work as a means of overcoming church-dividing differences. Between the 1960s and the 1970s, attention focused again on "classical reception," or reception of a council.

4. Recent Practice

By the 1980s a shift was taking place from classical reception to a new form: *ecumenical reception*. Causing this change was a rapid multiplication of theological and ecclesiological dialogues on both international and national levels. These dialogues involved the Roman Catholic Church and other churches in official, representative conversations designed to identify, and then perhaps resolve, century-old differences. These dialogues in many cases pushed their sponsoring churches into ecumenical reception. This new form of reception is an ongoing process by which a church, seen to be under the guidance of the Spirit, makes the results of a bilateral or multilateral dialogue a part of its faith and life. A church does so because it sees the results of such a dialogue to be in conformity with the teachings of Christ, the apostolic community, and its own tradition.

Ecumenical reception has proved challenging for all churches. It has raised questions about the continuity of individual churches with the past, about the identification of appropriate organs within these bodies for reception, and about how ecumenical reception is even possible within an incomplete or broken eucharistic community.

Nevertheless, there are several cases of ecumenical reception, at least at the level of official formal action. More notable examples include the following, with the date of the final draft of each document indicated in the parenthesis:

→ Leuenberg Agreement (1973), between Lutheran and Reformed in Europe;
Meissen Agreement (1988), between the Church of England and the Evangelical Church in Germany;
→ Porvoo Common Statement (1993), between Anglicans and Lutherans in the Nordic and Baltic countries;
Formula of Agreement (1997), between the Evangelical Lutheran Church in America (ELCA), the Presbyterian Church (U.S.A.), the Reformed Church in America, and the United Church of Christ;
Called to Common Mission (1999), between the Episcopal Church, U.S.A., and the ELCA;
Following Our Shepherd to Full Communion (1999), between the ELCA and the Moravian Church in the United States; and
→ Joint Declaration on the Doctrine of Justification (1999), between the churches of the → Lutheran World Federation and the Roman Catholic Church.

In all these cases the ongoing process of a reception that influences the life and thought of the churches and makes greater fellowship possible continues at uneven paces. There are always possibilities of a "nonreception" (a refusal to accept ecumenical proposals) or a "de-reception" (the rejection of something earlier received within a tradition or in the ecumenical movement). Much of the future of the modern ecumenical movement will depend on ecumenical reception, understood as a gift of God's Spirit to the church.

→ Ecumenism, Ecumenical Movement

Bibliography: A. Birmelé, "La réception comme exigence oecuménique," *Communion et réunion. Mélanges Jean Marie Roger Tillard* (ed. G. R. Evans and M. Gourgues; Louvain, 1995) 75-94 • Y. Congar, "Reception as an Ecclesiological Reality," *Election and Consensus in the Church* (ed. G. Alberigo and A. Weiler; New York, 1972) 43-68 • G. Gassman, "Rezeption im ökumenischen Kontext," *ÖR* 26 (1977) 314-27 • H. Goertz, *Dialog und Rezeption* (Hannover, 2002) • A. Grillmeier, "Konzil und Rezeption," *TP* 45 (1970) 321-52 • G. Routhier, *La réception d'un concile* (Paris, 1993) • W. G. Rusch, *Reception: An Ecumenical Opportunity* (Philadelphia, 1988) • O. Rush, *The Reception of Doctrine* (Rome, 1997) • J. Zizioulas, "The Theological Problem of 'Reception,'" *OiC* 21 (1985) 137-93.

Harding Meyer and William G. Rusch

Reconciliation

1. Term
2. Meaning
3. History of Theology
4. New Interpretations
5. Shift of Meaning

1. Term

The term "reconciliation" has been an important one in Christian theology, although it is used sparingly in the NT. It is most prominent in 2 Cor. 5:18-21. God has restored to himself the relationship with the world that human transgressions had irretrievably broken. Reconciliation really involves a new creation, in which a person "is in Christ" (2 Cor. 5:17; → New Self). God accomplished this new creation by redeeming the world "in Christ."

Reconciliation is the same as atonement, which strictly means "at-one-ment." But atonement has come to have a narrower use, for it points to the expiation that, offered on behalf of sins, leads to reconciliation. Reconciliation has found a much broader use. For example, in → social ethics it can denote the making of peace between classes, races, and nations.

2. Meaning

"Reconciliation" is a complex term theologically. Three fields of meaning may be discerned. Cultically (→ Worship), God offers the possibility of approaching him through → sacrifices, which indicate the guilt of those who have forfeited their right to life but which also redeem them from the death they have deserved (→ Atonement 1). Legally, reconciliation restores a right relationship (→ Law and Legal Theory). Socially, it purges → guilt and its consequences, puts an end to → conflict, and makes undiminished coexistence possible.

Reconciliation is a basic principle in the divine action in which → God declares himself by actively relating himself to us as the one who is "for us." Jesus Christ is the name of this divine "one who is for us" (→ Christology). Christ is the Reconciler, manifesting God's reconciliation in his life and death, which also show us how unreconciled and unreconcilable we are. God had to act by taking our human guilt upon himself and thus taking it away. The guilty are required to accept what God has done, and Paul even entreats them to do so (2 Cor. 5:20). Reconciliation, then, is God's unfathomable and unconditional approach toward us. In the relation thereby established, we can live only by → forgiveness and as we impart forgiveness. By refusing forgiveness to others, we jeopardize our own right to it (see the parable in Matt. 18:23-35).

3. History of Theology

Theology in the East (→ Orthodox Christianity) stressed human deification (→ Theosis) as the aim of God's action in redeeming us from → sin and → death. Western theology focused more on the process of reconciliation, on what God did once and for all, and on behalf of all, in his dealings with us in Christ. Opinions differ on the way this event is to be viewed, on the new humanity that was created, and on its human implications.

→ Anselm of Canterbury (1033-1109) adopted a predominantly cultic and legal understanding. By his sacrificial death Jesus Christ restored a legal relationship with God that our sin had destroyed. As true God and true man, he alone could make the satisfaction that was demanded by the holiness of God that we had infringed. This truth was the reason for the incarnation *(Cur Deus homo).* P. Abelard (1079-1142) found in reconciliation a work of overflowing → love (§5) that came upon us and brought divine righteousness to us. God's love kindles our responsive love and thus flows out in expanding form.

The → Reformers made it quite clear that divine reconciliation is not linked to human merit, whether this merit precedes or follows it. Reconciliation was exclusively a work of Christ's priestly "office," as emphasized especially by J. → Calvin (1509-64; → Calvin's Theology).

4. New Interpretations

Theologians in the → modern period have asked whether we need to link reconciliation to God's action for us in and by Jesus Christ. Did reconciliation really need the sacrifice of Christ? Does not this approach imply an image of God that is not compatible with the divine love that Christ revealed? This objection occurs, for example, in → feminist theology, which also radicalizes the traditional view of sin. Does not a vicarious act limit our own responsibility? (D. Sölle).

We avert, or at least reduce, these problems if we view reconciliation as a divine change of mind on our behalf that draws us to God and makes us ready to bring ourselves into conformity with his purposes. F. D. E. → Schleiermacher (1768-1834; → Schleiermacher's Theology) saw in reconciliation a gradual overcoming of the consciousness of sin by acceptance of divine grace. A. Ritschl (1822-89) stressed the priority of the love of God over his wrath. Emphasizing reconciliation also prevents us from viewing God only objectively.

In contrast, M. Kähler (1835-1912) pointed to the fact that the mission of Jesus Christ, in total obedience to God, culminated in reconciliation. K. → Barth (1886-1968; → Dialectical Theology) expounded reconciliation as God's incessant movement to us and our movement to God by way of the crucifixion.

Reconciliation was a key philosophical concept for G. W. F. Hegel (1770-1831; → Hegelianism). It put to an end the division between God and the world. Divine love revealed itself in Jesus Christ, who embodied divine-human unity. Reconciliation thus made possible the dialectical uniting of opposites (→ Dialectic). Under the influence of F. W. J. Schelling (1775-1854; → Idealism 8), reconciliation was seen as an overcoming of alienation, for example, between essential being and historical existence (P. → Tillich [1886-1965]; → Existential Theology 3.1). → Process philosophy and → process theology do not separate divine and human action but see them cooperating in an evolutionary dynamic.

5. Shift of Meaning

Today the church and theology often equate reconciliation with the resolution of conflicts and the making of → peace. In the background stands the need for international trust, for understanding when political and social antitheses arise, and for the restoration of a shattered harmony with the → environment ("reconciliation with nature"). Striving for reconciliation brings to light the causes of conflict. An unconditional readiness for reconciliation is not enough, as, for example, the South African Kairos Document (1985) noted. Reconciliation demands that racial discrimination be ended and that political equality and social justice be restored.

This shift of meaning that equates reconciliation with the ending of strife and the making of peace at different levels expresses a deep-seated change of consciousness that has developed over the last 200 years and especially in more recent decades. Reconciliation now must take place between opposing individuals, groups, and peoples. Reconciliation between God and the world puts an end to a disrupted relationship and evokes responsive action in us. We see this principle at work in theology. The reconciliation of the world with God is a peacemaking measure that is a model and spur for human efforts to create or restore peaceful relationships. The question is open whether human attempts at reconciliation will always bear reference to the preceding divine reconciliation.

In → ethics reconciliation has to do with social relations. Reconciliation comes about when moves are made to change hardened relations, something that can take place only if there is hope for change. In the political reorganization of South Africa and in other conflicts (e.g., Northern Ireland), "reconciliation" is used as a catchword for a new political and social beginning. Reconciliation overcomes tensions and functions as a healing power by eliminating the historical causes of conflict so that good relations can be restored. Reconciliation comes to mean the same thing as political understanding in trying to establish a new order based on truth, justice, and human rights. In law we must ask whether reconciliation can help reestablish a criminal's distorted social relationships in a way that makes possible a socially responsible life in the future.

Bibliography: K. Barth, *CD* IV, *The Doctrine of Reconciliation* • N. Biggar, ed., *Burying the Past: Making Peace and Doing Justice after Civil Conflict* (Washington, D.C., 2003) • D. Bloomfield, T. Barnes, and L. Huyse, eds., *Reconciliation after Violent Conflict* (Stockholm, 2003) • H. R. Botman and R. M. Petersen, eds., *To Remember and to Heal: Theological and Psychological Reflections on Truth and Reconciliation* (Cape Town, 1996) • D. Bronkhorst, *Truth and Reconciliation: Obstacles and Opportunities for Human Rights* (Amsterdam, 1995) • J. W. De Gruchy, *Reconciliation: Restoring Justice* (Minneapolis, 2002) • B. Frost, *Struggling to Forgive: Nelson Mandela and South Africa's Search for Reconciliation* (London, 1998) • C. E. Gunton, ed., *The Theology of Reconciliation* (London, 2003) • T. Herr, *Versöhnung statt Konflikt* (Paderborn, 1991) • G. Hummel, *Sehnsucht der unversöhnten Welt. Zu einer Theologie der universalen Versöhnung* (Darmstadt, 1993) • E. Käsemann, "Some Thoughts on the Theme 'The Doctrine of Reconciliation in the NT,'" *The Future of Our Religious Past* (ed. J. M. Robinson; New York, 1971) 49-64 • J. M. Lochman, *Reconciliation and Liberation: Challenging a One-Dimensional View of Salvation* (Philadelphia, 1980) • A. Ritschl, *A Critical History of the Christian Doctrine of Justification and Reconciliation* (trans. J. S. Black; Edinburgh, 1872) • G. Sauter, ed., *"Versöhnung" als Thema der Theologie* (Gütersloh, 1997) arts. from Anselm to the present • D. Sölle, *Christ the Representative: An Essay in Theology after the "Death of God"* (London, 1967) • C. W. du Toit, ed., *Confession and Reconciliation: A Challenge to the Churches in South Africa* (Pretoria, 1998) • G. Wenz, *Geschichte der Versöhnungslehre in der evangelischen Theologie der Neuzeit* (2 vols.; Munich, 1984-86) • D. L. Wheeler, *A Relational View of the Atonement* (New York, 1989) • V. White, *Atonement and Incarnation* (Cambridge, 1991).

Gerhard Sauter

Redemption → Salvation; Soteriology

Reductions

1. Caribbean and Central America
2. South America

1. Caribbean and Central America

As early as 1503 a law was passed for the gathering of → Indians in Latin America into settlements called reductions, with the aim of introducing them to a "political and human life" as the precondition of their true Christianizing. A Spanish edict of 1578 describes the purpose as follows: "In order that, as the rational beings they are, they may be able to be truly Christian and political, it is essential that they be gathered and brought into settlements and not live scattered lives on the mountains and in forests."

We may distinguish three phases in the history of reductions. The first attempts were made on the Antilles (1503-30), where the conquerors used the reductions to keep a watch on the Indians and to impose forced labor on them. Then reductions were set up on the mainland (1530-48), especially in New Spain (including the area of modern Mexico and the rest of Central America). A moderate policy and the promise of freedom from → slavery allowed the → Franciscans to collect the Indians into reductions in Guatemala from 1540 to 1553. In laying out the settlements, a checkerboard pattern was adopted with a central square. The third phase came in Paraguay after 1548 and closed with the → Jesuits (1609-1768). So as not to expose Indians to the bad example of the Spaniards and to protect them against the abuses of the conquistadores, the Jesuits put their reductions under the direct leadership and responsibility of the members of the order and Indian leaders, and they separated the Indians spatially from the Spaniards.

2. South America

The Franciscans had founded the first reduction in Paraguay in 1580. A group of Jesuits who arrived in 1609 from Peru adopted the same method. Two factors contributed to the success of the reductions. First, the Indians' socioeconomic and cultural structures were maintained to some extent. Second, the Jesuits, with their faith, educational methods, and technical processes, were able to combine civil → development with agrarian production (crops and cattle), with surpluses (e.g., in hides, fur, wool, and tobacco) being available for regional trading. → Literacy was encouraged in the Guarani language, and there were important literary developments. → Baroque architecture, sculpture, and music were successfully introduced, and by 1687 there were 30 Guarani settlements. In 1743 their combined population was 141,182.

Systematic colonial assaults (→ Colonialism) inflicted damage on the reductions in Paraguay. The most devastating came from São Paulo between 1628 and 1641 and from the Spanish-Portuguese army in the so-called Guarani War of 1753-56. An inexorable process of disintegration began with the expulsion of the Jesuit order in 1767.

Almost everywhere in the Americas where there were simple agricultural communities (→ Society 2), reductions were fairly successful, but attempts to reproduce them among hunters and gatherers failed (→ Nomads). → Missionaries found their best chances for Christianizing in the reductions, but colonial society was not ready to accept the conditions they demanded in pursuit of this policy.

→ Colonialism and Mission

Bibliography: S. Abou, *The Jesuit "Republic" of the Guaranís (1609-1768) and Its Heritage* (New York, 1997) • P. Borges, *Métodos misionales en la cristianización de América, siglo XVI* (Madrid, 1960) • P. Caraman, *The Lost Paradise: The Jesuit Republic in South America* (New York, 1976) • G. Furlong, *Misiones y sus pueblos de guaraníes* (Buenos Aires, 1962) • B. A. Ganson, *The Guaraní under Spanish Rule in the Río de la Plata* (Stanford, Calif., 2003) • R. Konetzke, *Colección de documentos para la historia de la formación social de Hispanoamerica, 1493-1810* (5 vols.; Madrid, 1953-62) • C. J. McNaspy, *Lost Cities of Paraguay: Art and Architecture of the Jesuit Reductions, 1607-1767* (Chicago, 1982) • B. Melià, *El Guaraní, conquistado y reducido* (4th ed.; Asunción, 1997) • H.-J. Prien, *Die Geschichte des Christentums in Lateinamerika* (Göttingen, 1977).

Bartomeu Melià

Reform Councils

1. Term and Prior History
2. Fifteenth-Century Reform Councils
   - 2.1. Pisa
   - 2.2. Constance
   - 2.3. Basel
3. Results

1. Term and Prior History

The term "reform councils" in the broad sense refers to all → councils that dealt with the matter of reform in the church and that made reforming decisions. In the narrow sense it refers to the 15th-century councils of Pisa, Constance, Pavia-Siena, and Basel, which viewed it as their chief aim to reform the → church "in head and members."

All through the → Middle Ages church reform had been linked to councils and synods. Already in the Merovingian age reforming synods had sought to restore the law of God and the church's order. In the 11th century the reforming papacy, beginning with Leo IX (1048-54; → Pope, Papacy, 1.3.3), preferred to use councils to institute reforming measures against → simony and lay → investiture and in favor of → celibacy. As papal power increased, papal synods (→ Councils of the Church 3) commanded greater respect. → Innocent III (1198-1216) linked his efforts to reform the church to the summoning of Lateran IV (1215), which had as its aim the reform of the whole church. Church reform was also an issue at Lyons II (1274) and Vienne (1311-12). The latter had the stated aim of correcting and reforming the church. The treatise on councils and church reform that William Durandus the Younger (d. 1330), bishop of Mende, prepared for the council (*Tractatus de modo concilii generalis celebrandi*, "On the mode of observing a general council," 1309) helped to make an even closer link between church reform and the idea of councils. It popularized the slogan "in head and members" and called for a periodic holding of councils.

2. Fifteenth-Century Reform Councils

The main reason for the summoning of the 15th-century reform councils was the Great Schism (→ Heresies and Schisms 3), which began in 1378 when rival popes in Rome and Avignon, with their supporting bodies (obedientiaries), confronted one another, and → conciliarism seemed to be the only way out of the impasse. Numerous reforming tractates tied councils and church reform closely to one another, arguing that church reform in general, as well as the ending of the schism, could come only by a council that would limit papal power and prevent its misuse.

2.1. *Pisa*

The Council of Pisa (1409), which was summoned by the cardinals of both obedientiaries, failed to restore → unity to the church. Both parties asserted their claims. When the two popes were declared deposed, the election of Alexander V (1409-10) simply set up a third group and heightened the confusion.

2.2. *Constance*

The ending of the schism was achieved at the Council of Constance (1414-18), which met as a result of cooperation between Emperor Sigismund (1410-37) and the strongest of the popes, John XXIII (1410-15), who led the Pisan obedientiaries. Besides healing the schism, this council made dealing with current heresies and reforming the church its main business. Reflecting university structures and political relations, it organized itself into "nations" (German, French, English, Italian, and later Spanish), each of which (just like the college of cardinals) had one vote. When John XXIII took flight, Sigismund held the council together. By the decree *Haec sancta* (1415), the council solemnly declared its supremacy over the papacy in matters of church unity, faith, and church reform, and on this basis it argued that it could deal with the rival popes. By Sigismund's skillful diplomacy the supporters of the three popes, who were deposed, were won over for the council. The schism was thus brought to an end.

The council also asserted its supremacy by definitively deciding doctrinal matters that had not been resolved when there had been no clear papal authority. It condemned posthumously the teachings of J. → Wycliffe (ca. 1330-84), and it tried, condemned, and burned J. → Hus (ca. 1372-1415; → Hussites) as a heretic. It tackled reform "in head and members," but in this field, in spite of lengthy discussions, it could achieve no solid results under the shadow of the politics of schism. The many proposals for the renewal of religious life found no acceptance. In order to carry out reform, however, and to maintain a kind of constitutional control, it was resolved that there should be periodic councils (in 5 years, then in 7 years, and then every 10 years, according to the decree *Frequens* [1417]).

Rivalry between the papacy and the council was already emerging when after the election of Martin V (1417-31) by a special procedure, the new pope snatched the reforming initiative out of the hands of the council by means of so-called → concordats with the various nations. Struggles between the newly strengthened papacy and the militant conciliarists broke out at the Council of Pisa-Siena (1423-24), which was held after a five-year interval but quickly dissolved, and which postponed any further efforts at reform.

2.3. *Basel*

The Council of Basel (1431-49) was the model of a reform council. It addressed the extirpation of heresy and peacemaking among rulers, but its main task was church reform. From the very outset, however, tense relations with the new pope, Eugenius IV (1431-47), overshadowed the deliberations. A first and hasty attempt of the pope to dissolve the council and to summon a new one at Bologna (1431) failed. Basel, which repeatedly confirmed the decree *Haec sancta,* followed radical conciliarism and made itself the church's supreme administrative and judicial court, setting up its own mechanism for the purpose, deciding disputed issues, and controlling appointments and depositions. One of the council's successes was the agreement it made with Hussites in the Prague Compactata of 1433.

Though overburdened with its tasks, the council made some important reforming decisions, for example, the arranging of regular provincial and diocesan synods, the measures taken against clergy concubinage, the prohibition of too easy use of the interdict (→ Church Discipline 1), and directions for a more appropriate celebration of → worship and the → hours. It also resolved to strictly limit the powers of the papacy and the → curia, forbade appeals from the council to the papacy, reduced the revenues of the curia, made new decisions about papal elections (→ Pope, Papacy, 1.7), and reduced the college of cardinals to 24 members.

The conflict with Eugenius IV came to a head in 1438 when, against the will of the majority, the pope moved the council to Ferrara, then to Florence (1439), then Rome (1443), where it became a papal general council. The group meeting in Basel continued as a rump council, made the council's superiority over the pope a → dogma (1439), declared Eugenius deposed as a heretical pope, and elected Duke Amadeus of Savoy as the new pope (Felix V [1439-49]). France and Germany stayed neutral in the conflict but gave statutory force to some of the reforms (e.g., the Pragmatic Sanctions of Bourges in 1438, which limited papal authority over the church in France, and the Mainz Acceptation of 1439, which had a similar effect in Germany).

Basel, however, could not stand up to Eugenius when he successfully (albeit not permanently) achieved reunion with the Greeks (1439), Armenians (1439), and Copts and Jacobites (1442; → Oriental Orthodox Churches). Eugenius and his successor, Nicholas V (1447-55), gradually won over the most important powers, as with the (German) Princes' Concordat of 1447 and the Vienna Concordat of 1448. Under pressure from Emperor Frederick III (1440-93), the rump Basel Council moved to Lausanne, and it dissolved in 1449 when Felix V abdicated.

3. Results

Though a strengthened papacy won the victory over the reform councils, they had considerable consequences. The European powers profited from the struggle, greatly expanding their areas of influence in church affairs. The link between councils and reform remained strong in the 15th century. Many appeals to a general council, which Pius II (1458-64) in his bull *Execrabilis* (1460; → Bulls and Briefs) condemned as an intolerable abuse, show that conciliarism was not dead. Theological writings and works of → canon law tell the same tale. The popes might ignore the decree *Frequens*, but an attempt was made to revive the Basel Council in 1482, and France and opposition cardinals held a conciliarist conventicle at Pisa in 1511. The papal council held in response in 1512-17, Lateran V, did nothing to solve the urgent problems demanding reform.

The failure of reform councils and church reform in the 15th century forms a background to the → Reformation and to → Catholic reform in the 16th century.

Bibliography: Primary sources: W. Brandmüller, *Das Konzil von Pavia-Siena, 1423-1424*, vol. 2, *Quellen* (Münster, 1974) • H. Finke et al., eds., *Acta Concilii Constantiensis* (4 vols.; Münster, 1896-1928) • J. Haller et al., eds., *Concilium Basiliense. Studien und Quellen zur Geschichte des Konzils von Basel* (8 vols.; Basel, 1896-1936) • H. von der Hardt, ed., *Magnum Oecumenicum Constantiense Concilium* (6 vols.; Frankfurt/Leipzig, 1696-1700) • G. Hofmann et al., eds., *Concilium Fiorentinum. Documenta et scriptores* (7 vols.; Rome, 1940-58) • *Mansi* 26-28 • J. Miethke and L. Weinrich, eds., *Quellen zur Kirchenreform im Zeitalter der Grossen Konzilien des 15. Jahrhunderts* (2 vols.; Darmstadt, 1995) • N. P. Tanner, ed., *Decrees of the Ecumenical Councils* (2 vols.; London, 1990) esp. 1.403-591

Secondary works: G. Alberigo, ed., *Christian Unity: The Council of Ferrara-Florence, 1438/39–1989* (Louvain, 1991) • R. Bäumer, ed., *Von Konstanz nach Trient. Beiträge zur Geschichte der Kirche von den Reformkonzilien bis zum Tridentinum* (Munich, 1972) • C. M. Bellitto, *The General Councils: A History of the Twenty-one Church Councils from Nicaea to Vatican II* (New York, 2002) • W. Brandmüller, *Das Konzil von Konstanz* (vol. 1; Paderborn, 1991); idem, *Das Konzil von Pavia-Siena, 1423-1424* (vol. 1; rev. ed.; Paderborn, 2002) • C. M. D. Crowder, *Unity, Heresy, and Reform, 1378-1460: The Conciliar Response to the Great Schism* (New York, 1977) • A. Franzen and W. Müller, eds., *Das Konzil von Konstanz. Beiträge zu seiner Geschichte und Theologie* (Freiburg, 1964) • J. Gill, *The Council of Florence* (Cambridge, 1959); idem, *Konstanz–Basel–Florenz* (Mainz, 1968) • H. Jedin, *A History of the Council of Trent* (3 vols.; London, 1957-61) • L. R. Loomis, *The Council of Constance: The Unification of the Church* (New York, 1961) • H. Müller, *Die Franzosen, Frankreich und das Basler Konzil (1431-1449)* (2 vols.; Paderborn, 1990) • J. W. Stieber, *Pope Eugenius IV, the Council of Basel, and the Secular and Ecclesiastical Authorities in the Empire: The Conflict over Supreme Authority and Power in the Church* (Leiden, 1978) • P. H. Stump, *The Reforms of the Council of Constance, 1414-1418* (Leiden, 1994) • J. Wohlmuth, *Verständigung in der Kirche. Untersucht an der Sprache des Konzils von Basel* (Mainz, 1983).

Hans Schneider

Reformation

1. Term

In contemporary historiography "Reformation" is a specialized (but not exclusive) designation for the complex series of ecclesiastical, theological, political, and academic events that led, in 16th-century Europe, to the emergence and establishment of Protestant churches ("confessions"), with their distinctive patterns of belief and practice.

The present article will principally use this understanding of the term. The term also refers to a wide variety of religious protests and proposals for reform (of church and society, of theology, and of life) that did not invariably lead to institutionalization, to incorporation in particular → church orders and governmental statutes. Today, moreover, historians routinely speak of "Roman Catholic Reformation" and the "Counter-Reformation." The former term serves to identify significant movements of renewal within the Roman church that emerged before the onset of "Protestant reform" or appeared concurrently with it. The latter term, first used in the 17th century to designate efforts by ruling authorities to restore their territories to the Roman obedience, now refers mainly to specific actions directed against the Protestant Reformation by a rejuvenated and newly militant Roman Catholicism, following upon the sweeping institutional reforms and doctrinal consolidation effected by the Council of → Trent (1545-63; → Catholic Reform and Counterreformation).

It bears noting, however, that throughout the 16th century itself, especially during its first half, "reformation" was a broad and fluid term, not yet narrowed to the churchly sphere or to any particular religious tradition or to the designation of a temporal period. This general idea of reformation included connotations of change/transformation, renewal/rebirth, restoration/reparation, correction/improvement, and it was operative equally in the personal-individual, ecclesiastical, sociopolitical, legal, and academic arenas.

2. Pre-Reformation Movements

Significant efforts at ecclesiastical reform occurred throughout the later → Middle Ages (§1.4), especially in response to decay in monastic institutions (→ Monasticism 5). A primary motive was that of reform by returning to the strictness of the original rule of a monastic founder, notably that of → Benedict of Nursia (ca. 480-ca. 547). This impulse is evident, for example, in the large family of monasteries affiliated with the reforming Benedictine abbey of → Cluny (founded 910), and in the establishment of the even larger → Cistercian order (Cîteaux, founded 1098) which sought to follow the Rule of Benedict to the last letter and which dominated the 12th century as Cluny had the 11th. The ideals of Cluny, moreover, inspired the so-called Gregorian reformation (→ Gregory VII [1073-85]), which aimed to liberate the papacy and ecclesiastical hierarchy from control by secular authorities (→ Investiture Controversy).

The 12th century also witnessed the rise of the "apostolic life" *(vita apostolica)* movement among clerics and laypeople (both women and men alike), who sought a return to the primitive church and to the voluntary → poverty (§5) of Christ and his apostles. This call to apostolic poverty resounded throughout the later Middle Ages and informed the creation of the → Franciscan, → Dominican, and other mendicant orders, as well as inspiring the → Waldensians and the groups of religious women known as → Beguines.

In the course of the 14th century two phenomena — one known as German → mysticism (under Dominican guidance), the other as the New Devotion (*Devotio moderna,* originating in the Netherlands with the Sisters and Brothers of the Common Life) — shared the conviction that the regeneration of church and society required personal religious renewal: a religion of true inwardness rather than of mere conformity to outward rites and ceremonies. Both movements sought direct personal contact with God, the former through the mystical union of the soul with God, the latter through a practice of the presence of God that did not involve actual mystical experience.

During its long residence at Avignon (1309-77) on the river Rhone, the papacy elicited severe criticism and opposition, both religious and political, owing to its extravagant expenditures and oppressive taxation (→ Empire and Papacy 5). One such outspoken critic was the Oxford theologian John → Wycliffe (ca. 1330-84), who demanded a return to the poverty of the primitive church, declared the papacy to be of human origin and its financial system unchristian, stressed the → authority of Holy Scripture over that of popes and scholastic doctors, and rejected the dogma of transubstantiation as defined at the Fourth Lateran Council (1215). His growing radicalism cost him the support of the English nobility and Crown, but his teachings lived on among his followers, the "Lollards." Wycliffe's writings, studied by Bohemian and Moravian students at Oxford, had a powerful influence on Jan → Hus (ca. 1372-1415), the heir and principal leader of a native Czech tradition of religious reform, and on the → Hussites, who elevated Scripture to supreme authority and demanded unfettered preaching of God's Word, the return of the eucharistic cup to the laity, apostolic poverty, and a strict clerical and lay life.

The Great Schism of 1378-1417, with two rival popes after 1378 and three after 1409, divided Latin Christendom into competing "obediences" and brought the papacy to its nadir in popular esteem (→ Pope, Papacy, 1.3). The result was → conciliarism, which aimed to replace the absolute papal monarchy with the representative authority of a general church council and to effect a "reformation of the head as well as of the members," that is, a comprehensive reform of the church from the top down in matters of both morality and administration (but not of doctrine). To this end → reform councils were held from 1414 to 1449. That of Constance (1414-18) succeeded in ending the schism, but the papacy that emerged from the "conciliar experiment" largely evaded the envisioned reforms and again became absolutist in its claims.

In reality, however, ever since the end of the Great Schism, the papacy — in order to secure its political independence in Italy and to meet its exigent and escalating financial needs — was obliged to grant the secular powers extensive control over church affairs in their respective territories (chiefly France, England, and Spain). Germany, nonetheless, remained under the weight of papal taxation. From 1456 onward the empire assembled its formal complaints about the papacy in the *Gravamina nationis germanicae* (Grievances of the German nation), while anticlericalism became rife in reaction against clerical abuse of office, avarice, and loose living.

Of signal import was the reforming humanist movement. Originating in Italy in the 14th century, → humanism (*studia humanitatis,* the study of the humane, or liberal, arts) took root north of the Alps in the later 15th century, where it gave rise to what has been labeled Christian, or biblical, humanism (to identify its animating concerns). Under the slogan *ad fontes* (back to the sources), the northern humanists — preeminently Desiderius → Erasmus (1469?-1536) — devoted themselves to the study of the Bible and → church fathers, as well as the Greek and Latin classics. Out of this union of "sacred letters" and "humane letters," they fashioned a variety of programs for reform of church and society, including a reorientation of popular piety (in favor of "Christian simplicity") and of theological education. Since they were strenuous critics of → Scholasticism, they put philology, rhetoric, history, poetry, and moral philosophy in the place of Aristotelian logic (dialectic) and metaphysics. They developed a new → hermeneutics that required competence in biblical Hebrew and Greek, replaced medieval allegorical exegesis with a literal-historical interpretation of Scripture, and thereby promoted text-criticism and fresh translations of the Bible into the vernacular (→ Bible Versions 3-4).

By 1500, then, calls (and plans) for reform and renewal were well-nigh universal in Christian Europe. The old slogan of "reform in head and members" still captivated the popular imagination, albeit with the added proviso that ecclesiastical reform would now likely have to come "from below," given the moral failings and intransigence of Renaissance popes and prelates. This idea of a total reformation also stirred the larger social and political scene, where eschatological and apocalyptic expectations of a dawning Golden Age, a millennial kingdom of peace and justice, fed popular discontent with the status quo. In such a context, accordingly, *reformatio* might well entail revolution, not simply remedy and restitution.

3. The Protestant Reformation

3.1. *Message and Doctrine*

The Protestant Reformation, viewed in its totality, did not promulgate a single, unified message, nor did the evangelical movement emanate from a single center such as Wittenberg. Still, both the message and the movement were inseparably bound up with the career of the erstwhile Augustinian friar Martin → Luther (1483-1546), the century's most published author, who largely shaped the course of reform until 1523/24 and whose formative influence, whether direct or indirect, continued long thereafter.

The Reformation message, in its incipient form and basic themes (→ Luther's Theology), arose out of Luther's experiences with late medieval theology and piety and his intensive study of the church fathers (principally → Augustine) and of Scripture, aided by the hermeneutics of biblical humanism. During the course of his early lectures (1513-18) as professor of Bible at Wittenberg University, Luther came to regard God's righteousness (Ps. 31:1; Rom. 1:16-17) no longer as God's punitive justice that categorically condemns the unjust but rather as the very righteousness of Christ that God freely imputes and imparts to sinful human beings who are united with Christ by faith alone. One is thus "justified," or made right with God, both now and at the last judgment, solely by God's unconditional grace or mercy, not because God (in the language of late medieval theology) grants his justifying grace to those persons who "do their moral best."

Luther's exegetical insight, as articulated in his developing theology of → justification (§2.2) and its correlates, banished all thought of religious achievements by which to elicit God's favor and then, empowered by such → grace (§4), to earn eternal → salvation (§5) as a just reward. It thus robbed of their meritorious value such things as → indulgences, mandatory times of → fasting, invocation of the → saints and veneration of their relics, religious → processions and → pilgrimages, private masses, and the monastic life. → Assurance of salvation might now be had solely through → faith (trust) in the gospel's unqualified promise of acceptance before God for Christ's sake alone (→ Reformation Principles). Foundational to both the Reformation movement and message, therefore, was the insistent call — issued by Luther and the early → Reformers — for free proclamation of the "pure Word of God," namely the prophetic and apostolic gospel as attested in the Scriptures, without recourse to medieval authorities (scholastic teachings, papal pronouncements, conciliar decrees) or, in general, to "human traditions."

Opposed as it was to Scholasticism, Reformation theology contested the strong influence of → Aristotelianism in "divine matters." And then, after 1518 and beginning at Wittenberg, the universities and schools were reformed, with emphasis on study of the biblical and classical languages, history, and literature (poetry). The supreme authority of sacred Scripture — as the source of all binding doctrine and the judge of all the church's teachers and teachings — underlay the whole movement and challenged the authoritative claims of the papacy. Anticlerical criticism found a place, and the doctrine of the priesthood of all believers (→ Priest, Priesthood, 4) gave this critique added depth, while at the same time contesting the divine right of the hierarchy. When Luther burned collections of → canon law on December 10, 1520, he thereby declared existing → church law to be invalid.

The evangelical message thus proclaimed freedom from the pressure for religious achievement, from religious insecurity over sin, death, and final judgment, from mandatory clerical → celibacy and other papal laws, from monastic → vows, and from exactions that were due to clerical greed for power and money. It questioned the exercise of secular power by the clergy and pointed the way to a life of love for God and neighbor originating in gratitude to God for salvation freely bestowed (with good works now viewed as spontaneous "fruits of faith"). This message also kindled widespread hopes of liberation from the inequities and injustices of the current ordering of society and thereby gave rise to sociopolitical conflicts or intensified existing ones (e.g., between peasants and landlords, between burghers and oligarchic town councils).

For Luther, medieval efforts at reform had simply aimed at amendment of life (morals), whereas he reformed doctrine, doing so on the basis of Scripture. Like the humanists, among whom he found his earliest cadre of supporters, he went back to the "sources," in this case the Bible. He agreed with them, too, in demanding the removal of "medieval accretions." But he did not seek a restoration of the → primitive Christian community, nor did he expect change only from an apocalyptic event. He regarded himself instead as the instrument of a reformation that God himself was accomplishing, to be completed only at the end of time with the final conquest of sin, death, and the devil. Only rarely did Luther himself use the word "reformation."

3.2. *Propagation*

Reformation teaching was propagated by many and diverse media: sermons, lectures and disputations, letters, treatises, pamphlets (most with illustrations) and broadsides (single-leaf woodcuts), vernacular translations of Scripture and vernacular liturgies, catechisms, hymns and ballads, poems and plays. The authors of such works included numerous educated laymen (and some women), as well as members of the clergy. Printing on paper by movable type, a technological innovation of the 1450s, played a central role as a relatively cheap means of communication, effectively creating a new forum of public opinion. Pamphlets, often carried by merchants along with their wares and by itinerant students, facilitated the rapid spread of ideas and information. Pamphlets could be read aloud to the illiterate, and their contents were widely discussed at such gathering places as markets, town squares, inns, and mills. Also most influential were preachers: reforming clerics who often occupied endowed pulpits in the leading towns and cities and who, like Luther, were university trained and often former mendicant friars.

The first impact was to end such acts of medieval piety as the purchase of indulgences, pilgrimages to shrines, and the veneration of saints, images, and relics. Individuals soon began to break the laws of fasting, to leave monasteries, to stop endowing masses for the dead, and to break vows of priestly celibacy. The → Mass then came to be read in the vernacular, and contrary to the conciliar decree of 1415, the cup was given to the laity at Communion. Reformation preaching, in short, unleashed a Reformation movement that can be called evangelical, inasmuch as the emphasis shifted from demands for an internal reform of the Roman church (correction of abuses) to the setting up of non-Roman ecclesial communities founded on the gospel, the "pure Word." This shift is understandable in light of the determined opposition to Reformation teaching and preaching on the part of popes, the Roman curia, and local prelates. Preachers and their hearers began to think in terms of the right, and even the duty, to resist if efforts were made to suppress the movement.

3.3. *Introduction*

During the early 1520s the evangelical movement was launched "from below" by popular response to the reformers' spoken and written (and sung) message. It could and did take hold and spread without the immediate sufferance or support of rulers — often, indeed, in direct opposition to their decrees. Still, the creation and perpetuation of new (non-Roman) churches in particular territories were usually dependent on favorable government action. At the outset this response might involve only toleration of the Reformers' preaching and publications in the name of maintaining public peace and unity. In some cases a territorial lord or city council might promote reform by appointing an evangelical minister, frequently under strong congregational or communal pressure. In the ensuing conflict over what constituted "right doctrine," the authorities might make Scripture the norm for all preaching and teaching or stage public disputations and then declare victory for the Reformers.

The cities were from the outset of prime importance as lively centers of communication. As early as 1524-25 citizens could force their councils — frequently transforming them in the process — to introduce and promote evangelical religion. The German "free" imperial cities (which owed allegiance to the emperor alone) were especially influential in this regard. Of 65 such cities, more than 50 officially accepted the Reformation, at least for a time, during the 16th century.

The first phase of the movement in the early and mid-1520s was often attended by outbreaks of iconoclasm, the destruction of religious images (→ Reformers 3.2). This phase, which ordinarily included the dissolution of monasteries and the ending of clerical celibacy, culminated by the late 1520s in the setting up of an evangelical order of worship, centered on the sermon, with the distribution of the cup to the laity and the elimination of any thought of the Eucharist as a propitiatory sacrifice offered to God by a priest on behalf of the living and the dead. In the process the Roman church lost its doctrinal and juridical authority in many regions, while the influence of secular government in ecclesiastical matters correspondingly increased. Princes and magistrates, to be sure, had long claimed and exercised supervision of church institutions and personnel in their lands; now, however, they were uniquely positioned to define a new religious orthodoxy and to legally enforce it.

3.4. *Establishment*

The Reformation's actual establishment, accordingly, required that it be enshrined in law — in civic ordinances and princely mandates and parliamentary decrees, as well as in territorial church orders ("constitutions") regulating such matters as the form and number of services, the ministerial offices (e.g., pastor, preacher, deacon, cantor, teacher; → Episcopacy 4), parochial finances, and care of the poor. Institutionalization thus brought with it the evolution of a new religious culture. Clerics lost their traditional exemptions from civic duties and from trial in secular courts. The old ecclesiastical (episcopal) courts were replaced by courts and consistories composed of lay, as well as clerical, representatives; they also assumed responsibility for matters of marriage and communal discipline. Proceeds from the dissolution of monastic properties were used to finance the local churches' work, to found schools and hospitals, to provide for poor relief by funding a communal treasury or "common chest," and, not least, to bring personal enrichment to rulers and various opportunists.

The establishment and enforcement of reform in the territories regularly came through → visitations, with teams usually composed of jurists and theologians, who sought to determine whether ministerial incumbents were able to perform their duties in an evangelical congregation and whether the laity had sufficient grasp of evangelical tenets. One principal response to perceived deficiencies was the preparation of → catechisms (§2), which also served for the spiritual and moral formation of young people by inculcating the "fear of the Lord" and proper respect for all duly constituted authorities (esp. parents and rulers).

Some evangelically minded persons rejected incorporation in the territorial churches and tried to set up independent communities of the "Elect Friends of God's Word" (e.g., Thomas → Müntzer; → Reformers 3.3), of those uniquely illumined and instructed by the interior witness of the → Holy Spirit (→ Spiritualism), or of "true believers" opting for a Christian communal life marked by adult baptism and use of the ban (→ excommunication) for disciplinary purposes (→ Anabaptists; Free Church). Luther viewed such people as enthusiasts *(Schwärmer)*, or fanatics; today they are referred to as radical reformers, as distinct from the "magisterial reformers," who, like Luther, carried out reform in cooperation with the governing authorities.

Since the German emperor, Charles V (1519-56), wanted to help the papacy suppress the evangelical movement, the imperial estates (electors, nobles, cities) had to decide whether to support the emperor or to protect the Reformation and secure it politically. In this way diets, → confessions of faith, and political-military alliances came to play a large role in promoting and safeguarding the Reformation, not only in Germany but also in other countries and internationally.

3.5. *Revolution?*

Some historians (mainly earlier generations of Marxists) have endeavored to identify a specific → class or social stratum as the principal agent or "motor" of the Reformation. Was the latter, then, a sociopolitical and economically motivated revolution (with religion functioning as its rationalization)? This thesis must be denied if it means that the Reformation effected a general overthrow of a dominant social class (e.g., urban patricians or landed magnates) by another class (e.g., upwardly mobile artisans or rebellious peasants). The Reformation, in fact, appealed to members of all social and economic strata.

To be sure, both the cities and the countryside were rife with social tensions, often overt conflicts, and the evangelical message was quickly invoked in support of demands for fundamental changes in the old order of things. The great German → Peasants' War of 1524-25 was in part inspired by a direct linkage between sociopolitical and economic grievances (e.g., concerning serfdom and tithes) and evangelical principles (e.g., the liberty of Christians and the community's right to elect its own pastors; → Religious Liberty [Foundations] 3-4). In some cases, moreover, political support for the Reformation created a virtual Protestant state within an existing Roman Catholic state (as happened in France) or led to rebellion against a Roman Catholic regime and its replacement by a new Protestant one (as happened in the northern Netherlands, i.e., the Dutch Republic).

The only general revolution occasioned by the Reformation, however, was in the sphere of religious practices, institutions, and ideas, all of which, as indicated above, were radically changed by the evangelical movement and its introduction and establishment in many European lands.

4. Course

4.1. *Germany*

4.1.1. *Development of the Message*

On October 31, 1517, Luther posted his 95 theses, in Latin, for academic disputation on true → penitence and against the traffic in indulgences. Soon published in German, the theses found remarkably widespread popular acclaim, but they also aroused the determined opposition of the Dominicans and the curia. Luther thus felt compelled to give proper shape to his theology. He quickly won support among his Wittenberg students and colleagues, also at large by means of his Heidelberg (1518) and Leipzig (1519) Disputations and his many pamphlets. In 1520 he published path-breaking treatises basic to a new ethics *(On Good Works);* to ecclesiastical, educational, and social reform through the agency of lay authorities *(To the Christian Nobility of the German Nation concerning the Reform of the Christian Estate);* to a new doctrine of the → sacraments *(The Babylonian Captivity of the Church);* and to the Christian life in general *(The Freedom of a Christian)*. Since Leo X (1513-21) sought the support of Luther's prince, Elector Frederick III the Wise (1486-1525), for papal policy in the impending imperial election (June 1519), it was not until June 15, 1520, that Luther came under threat of excommunication, which followed on January 3, 1521.

4.1.2. *Start of the Movement*

The evangelical movement may be said to have begun when Luther and his followers were placed under the imperial ban by the Edict of Worms (May 8, 1521). The movement's adherents included all those who identified themselves with Luther's cause or, more broadly, with the cause of evangelical reform in opposition to "Romanists" and "papists." While Luther was hidden at the Wartburg castle (early May 1521 to early March 1522), spontaneous outbreaks took place in various locales, marked by flights from monasteries, priestly marriages, destruction of images, and the giving of the cup to the laity.

In Wittenberg Luther's colleague Andreas Bodenstein of Carlstadt (or Karlstadt, ca. 1480-1541) tried to set up a new church order, based on "biblical law," by civic decree. He also pursued the criticism of Scholasticism to the point of advocating the dissolution of universities and schools, with reliance solely on immediate deliverances of the Holy Spirit. Already at this juncture, then, fissures were becoming evident within the reform party itself (which was never a homogeneous group). In 1521 Thomas Müntzer (ca. 1489-1525) called for the restitution of the apostolic church (the postapostolic church having become a harlot) and for participation in a divinely conducted apocalyptic conflict that would issue in the renewal of Christianity. In 1525 he assumed a leadership role in the Peasants' War, believing that with peasant help God would destroy the wicked. Luther steered clear of these developments on the ground that reformation must come by the Word and not by force. The purpose of new church orders is not to prescribe a new religion but to give a renewed → piety appropriate form. Against appeal to the "inner Word" of the Spirit (i.e., to visionary experiences and special revelations granted to the elect), Luther argued that God has bound himself to his "outward," or public, Word disclosed in Scripture.

When Erasmus at last gave way to papal pressure and attacked Luther in 1524, contending for the freedom of the human will in the matter of salvation, Luther in his *Bondage of the Will* (1525) stressed the depth of the will's servitude to → sin in its relation to God. This break with Erasmus did not entail a break with humanism as such, for by 1522 the majority of younger humanists (under age 40) had already embraced the evangelical cause.

Charles V could enforce the Worms edict in his own hereditary lands but not over the whole empire. His power was frequently limited, since, from 1521 to 1556, he was engaged in five wars with France for hegemony in Italy and, in the process, was often at odds with the pope as the ruler of the → Papal States. Repeatedly, too, he had to seek the aid of the evangelical estates against the Turks. Hence the evangelical movement was able to proceed apace and gain strength in many areas of the empire.

The movement, however, was further differentiated in the later 1520s by a bitter controversy over the → Eucharist, or Lord's Supper. Luther and his Wittenberg associates adhered to the traditional and, as they judged, the NT doctrine that the body and blood of Christ are physically present in the consecrated elements of bread and wine and are distributed to all who commune, including the ungodly. By contrast, Ulrich → Zwingli of Zurich (1484-1531; see 4.2) and his Swiss and South German adherents maintained that since Christ's body is now in heaven, at God's right hand, his presence in the sacrament can be only a spiritual one, granted only to believers. The supper, therefore, is a memorial of Christ's atoning death on the cross, not (as the Lutherans taught) an actual communication of his body there broken and his blood there shed for the forgiveness of sins. This great controversy failed of resolution throughout the Reformation era and prevented the creation of a united Protestant front vis-à-vis Roman Catholicism.

4.1.3. *Founding of Churches*

The formation of evangelical churches began in about 1525. Whereas Frederick the Wise tolerated the Reformation, his brother and successor, John the Constant (1525-32), vigorously promoted it. At his urging Luther's *German Mass* (1526) was introduced in Wittenberg. At the Diet of Speyer in 1526 all the estates agreed that the Edict of Worms could not be enforced on a national basis and unanimously resolved so to comport themselves "as they hoped and trusted to answer for it before God and his imperial majesty." The evangelical princes and cities speedily interpreted these actions as a legal warrant for ordering their ecclesiastical constitutions as they saw fit. Visitations in electoral Saxony and Hesse organized the new church in 1526-29. Cities such as Nuremberg (1525) and Brunswick (1529) accepted the Reformation. Important aids were Luther's two catechisms (1529), revised editions of his hymnbook (→ Hymnal 1.1) and prayer book (also in 1529), and his complete German Bible (1534).

4.1.4. *Emergence of "Protestantism"*

The terms "Protestant" and "Protestantism" derive not from religious or theological considerations as such (hence their limited usefulness), but from the politics of the German Empire during the 1520s. At the Second Diet of Speyer in 1529, Archduke Ferdinand of Austria (deputy of Charles, 1521-58), representing his absent brother Charles, the emperor, won from the majority a decision to rescind the unanimous recess of 1526, to enforce the Edict of Worms, and to end all religious innovations. On April 19 five evangelical territories and 14 cities entered a protestation, declaring that in matters of God's honor and the soul's salvation, each must stand and give an account alone before God: an important decision for freedom of conscience. (The Latin verb *protestari* does not mean "oppose" but "profess, bear witness openly.") Henceforth the evangelical estates came to be called "those who have protested." This designation should not be construed to mean that these first "protestants" were thereby repudiating Catholic Christianity. To the contrary, they considered themselves "good Catholics" intent upon rescuing the church's true catholicity from the papacy's deformations of the biblical gospel. Hence they rejected any unqualified equation of "Catholic" with "Roman" or "papal."

At the Diet of Augsburg in 1530 four South German imperial cities submitted their Tetrapolitan Confession, while the Wittenbergers presented the → Augsburg Confession, chiefly the work of Philipp → Melanchthon (1497-1560), who asserted the catholicity of "our churches" on the basis of Scripture, the church fathers, and the creeds of the ancient church. In 1531, after Charles V judged this confession refuted, the evangelical estates (five princely territories and 11 cities) formed the Schmalkaldic League for defensive purposes (→ Lutheranism 2.1). Under its protection the Protestants won important new accessions. Charles, however, was later victorious in the so-called Schmalkaldic War of 1546-47, and at the Diet of Augsburg in 1548 he imposed the "Augsburg Interim," which involved many concessions to Rome (→ Ecumenism, Ecumenical Movement, 2.3). But under Duke Moritz of Saxony (1541-53), who in 1546 had sided with the emperor (for which he was awarded the electoral dignity), a Protestant uprising succeeded (1552). In 1555 the Peace of Augsburg recognized the situation by putting Roman Catholics and Lutherans (adherents of the Augsburg Confession; → Augsburg, Peace of) on equal legal footing in the empire, thereby endorsing the principle, as it was later called, of → *cuius regio, eius religio*, "whose [the] reign, his [the] religion."

4.2. *Switzerland*

The foremost leader of the early Reformation in the Swiss Confederation (comprising 13 cantons) was Zwingli. Trained in the classics at Bern and in theology, philosophy, and humanist studies at the universities of Vienna and Basel, he first served as a parish priest at Glarus (1506-16) and until late 1518 as a chaplain at the famous pilgrimage shrine of Einsiedeln. During these years he attained proficiency in the biblical languages, studied the church fathers, and absorbed the writings of Erasmus — above all, the latter's 1516 edition of the Greek NT. In January 1519, by now a serious biblical humanist and influential preacher, Zwingli became people's priest in the Great Minster in Zurich. He immediately began a verse-by-verse exposition of the entire NT in his preaching, abandoning the traditional lectionary and any recourse to medieval authorities, thereby giving proof of his conviction that only the Bible, evangelically interpreted, is binding on Christians. His intense sense of spiritual mission was awakened by a near-fatal experience of the bubonic plague in 1519. By 1521 he was also making careful study of Luther's writings as published at Basel from 1517 onward, although he consistently denied dependence on Luther for his acceptance of the evangelical position.

By 1522 Zwingli was attacking such "man-made" Roman practices as indulgences, pilgrimages, the cult of the saints, mandatory clerical celibacy, and monastic vows. In March 1522 a small group of Zurich citizens broke the Lenten fast by eating sausages, citing Zwingli's assertion of *sola Scriptura* as justification, and Zwingli now preached and published in defense of such "Christian liberty." Two public disputations ordered by the city council in 1523, with Scripture as the norm, established Zwingli's leadership when his reformist teachings and those of his pastoral associates prevailed. In 1524 the magistrates ordered the removal of images from the churches and, in 1524-25, closed the monasteries. During Holy Week in 1525 the Latin Mass was replaced by Zwingli's simple German Communion service: a solemn commemoration and contemplation of the mystery of humankind's redemption at Calvary in which the faithful bring Christ to the supper, since he is not bodily present in the supper. In 1525 Zwingli also inaugurated what he called *Prophezei* (prophecy) for the training of theological students and the retraining of the clergy. It involved rigorous daily Bible study based on the Latin (Vg), Hebrew, and Greek texts.

By the end of 1523 some of Zwingli's most ardent supporters in Zurich had now come to regard him as a false prophet because he waited on dilatory secular authorities to effect reforms plainly mandated by God's Word, such as the immediate abolition of images and of the Mass. Under the lead, among others, of Conrad Grebel (ca. 1498-1526) and Felix Mantz (ca. 1500-1527), this group held up the ideal of a "true church" composed of believers who display genuine conviction of sin, penitence, and amendment of life, to be followed by adult baptism in full consciousness of faith. In mid-January 1525, after a public disputation, the city council dismissed the group's objections to infant baptism as unfounded and enjoined conformity. On January 21, however, a small band of these → "Anabaptists" (a prejudicial title) carried out the first "rebaptisms" in Zurich; shortly thereafter, in the nearby village of Zollikon, they did the same, this time accompanied by household Communions. Persecution — banishment, imprisonment, executions — did not prevent, but actually promoted, the movement's rapid spread throughout various areas of Switzerland, Austria, Germany, the Netherlands, and eastern Europe (e.g., Moravia, Poland; → Persecution of Christians 1.3).

In 1529 the old Swiss rural cantons of Uri, Schwyz, Unterwalden, and Zug, along with Lucerne, allied with Hapsburg Austria in defense of traditional beliefs. A full-scale armed confrontation — the battle of Kappel, on October 11, 1531 — brought defeat to Zurich and death to Zwingli. With military help from Bern and the religious leadership of Heinrich Bullinger (1504-75), the Reformation went on as before at Zurich, albeit more peacefully. A prolific writer and preacher, Bullinger exercised an international influence through his voluminous correspondence and his Second → Helvetic Confession (1566), a comprehensive statement of the Reformed faith (as distinct from the Lutheran; see below) that was adopted by Reformed churches in Switzerland (except Basel), Germany, France, Scotland, Poland, and Hungary.

The city of Basel, an important center of printing, notably of works by Erasmus and Luther, found a reformer in the distinguished humanist Johannes Oecolampadius (1482-1531), who taught biblical → exegesis at the university from 1523 onward, became a friend and supporter of Zwingli, and in 1529, backed by popular demands, secured the council's approval of the Reformation (abolition of the Mass and the issuance of a new church ordinance). In 1534 the council adopted the → Basel Confession, based on a formulation of faith prepared by Oecolampadius before his death.

Other cantons that opted for the Reformation included Schaffhausen and Glarus, but the principal victory for the cause came at Bern, the largest of the Swiss city-states. Its chief reformer, the town preacher Berchtold Haller (1492-1536), was greatly influenced by Zwingli, who took the lead and triumphed in a disputation ordered by the Bernese authorities in early January 1528, on the basis of ten theses prepared mainly by Haller. Bern, which officially became Protestant in February 1528, sponsored reform in other areas, especially through the work of a fiery French orator, Guillaume Farel (1489-1565), who in 1532 began preaching in Geneva, which was not a canton but an ecclesiastical state. In 1536 the Genevans, with military support from Bern, achieved independence from their prince-bishop and from the Catholic duke of neighboring Savoy. In May 1536 a general assembly of citizens resolved henceforth "to live in this holy evangelical law and Word of God" and to abolish "all masses and other papal ceremonies and abuses, images, and idols." In July of that same year Farel constrained a young French acquaintance, John → Calvin (1509-64), who was passing through the city, to accept a call to church work in Geneva, first as an expositor of Scripture and later as a pastor.

Calvin, university-trained in law and largely self-taught in theology, had been associated with leading French humanists in his student days, and along the lines of biblical humanism he had learned the evangelical faith from his study of the Bible in its original languages, from the church fathers, and also from Luther's works. In 1538, when he and Farel failed to secure approval from the city council for their new church order and when they refused to obey government directives, they were expelled from Geneva. Calvin found a post at Strasbourg ministering to a congregation of French exiles, and there he enjoyed the friendship of the eminent reformer Martin → Bucer (1491-1551). Already in 1536 Calvin — a superb stylist in both French and Latin — had published the first edition of his *Institutes of the Christian Religion,* designed as an introduction to the faith in six chapters; in 1539 he brought out a second, enlarged edition of what would be his foundational and most influential work, especially in its final Latin edition of 1559, which numbered 80 chapters (→ Calvin's Theology 1).

In 1541 the Geneva council persuaded Calvin to return to the city (Farel was now at Neuchâtel), and he promptly secured the adoption of his new constitution for the Geneva church, the *Ecclesiastical Ordinances,* a work of seminal importance for all "Calvinist" churches. He also prepared a new catechism and introduced a → liturgy based on that used in Strasbourg. The *Ordinances* held that Christ has instituted four ministerial offices: pastor, teacher or doctor, elder, and deacon. They further provided for a consistory, or church tribunal, composed of the pastors and elders, to exercise strict communal discipline. Not until 1555, however, and only after a prolonged and bitter struggle, did Calvin's insistence on the consistory's right to excommunicate the unrepentant prevail, and only then did he and his supporters, now including many refugees fleeing persecution in France and elsewhere, win full control of the city.

Calvin had a strong concern for doctrinal unity and uniformity. He tolerated differences of opinion in nonessentials, but not on such cardinal teachings as the → Trinity. Thus he endorsed the → death penalty for the Spanish humanist and physician Michael Servetus (ca. 1511-53), who denied the orthodox doctrine of the Trinity and the validity of infant baptism, who was already under a death sentence imposed by a French court, who rather inexplicably came to Geneva in 1553, and whose trial before the Genevan magistrates led to his execution by burning that same year. Calvin also labored on behalf of Christian unity. In 1540-41 he participated in several Protestant-Catholic "reunion" dialogues sponsored in Germany by Charles V, during the course of which he came to know Melanchthon and other German reformers. In 1549 he and Bullinger achieved concord on the Eucharist and related matters in the important Consensus Tigurinus, or Zurich Agreement, with the result that one could now speak of a common "Reformed" Protestantism, in contrast to which Lutheranism came to be identified as "Evangelical" (→ Confessions and Creeds 3.2). In 1566, as already noted, the Swiss Reformed, apart from Basel, united under Bullinger's Second Helvetic Confession.

Calvin believed and hoped that the Zurich Agreement would be a first step toward agreement in doctrine among all the Protestant churches. He also deemed his eucharistic teaching much closer to Luther's than to Zwingli's in that he regarded the sacramental bread and wine as "efficacious signs" of the true presence of Christ's body and blood, transported from heaven by the power of the Holy Spirit to all who communed in faith, albeit not to the unworthy or unfaithful. Hence Christ's body and blood were really given "with" the elements but were not "in and under" them, as the Lutherans taught, and so were not orally received by all, the ungodly to their condemnation (→ Eucharist 3.3). During the 1550s Calvin's doctrine met with vehement opposition from Joachim Westphal (ca. 1510-74), the Lutheran superintendent in Hamburg, whose polemical tracts and Calvin's no less polemical replies opened a controversy that deepened the antithesis between the two confessions (→ Crypto-Calvinism).

Calvin's crowning achievement was the founding, in 1559, of the Geneva Academy under the rectorship of Theodore → Beza (1519-1605), who was soon to succeed Calvin as the city's head pastor. Primarily devoted to → theological education, the Academy dispatched hundreds of ministers to — and trained students from — Reformed churches throughout Europe, with special concern for the French congregations. Comparable training centers were eventually established in France (Saumur and Sedan), Germany (Heidelberg and Herborn), and the Netherlands (Leiden). Some historians have come to speak of the Second Reformation, namely, the emergence of international → Calvinism as the most dynamic form of → Protestantism during the last half of the century. During these same years, by contrast, Lutheran expansion was retarded by a series of divisive theological controversies, centered in Germany, that were not resolved until the promulgation of the → Formula of Concord in 1577.

4.3. ***France***

In 1521 the leading French biblical humanist, Jacques Lefèvre d'Étaples (Faber Stapulensis, ca. 1455-1536) and his followers (including G. Farel) joined Lefèvre's former student Guillaume Briçonnet (1470-1534), the reform-minded bishop of Meaux. The Meaux group was attracted by Luther's writings, which were available in Paris by 1519, and enjoyed the patronage and protection of Margaret of Navarre (1492-1549), the sister of King Francis I (1515-47) and herself a religious poet of note. In late 1523, however, Briçonnet repressed evangelical preaching in his diocese — Farel now left for Switzerland — and by 1525 the entire circle broke up. Already in 1521 the Theological Faculty of Paris had denounced Luther's teaching and, after 1527, persecuted followers of both Luther and Erasmus. Strenuous opposition to the spread of new doctrines also came from the Parlement of Paris, France's supreme court of justice, which forbade the sale and possession of Luther's books.

The king's attitude toward reform vacillated, depending on his fortunes in war with Charles V and his foreign-policy concerns. Initially a patron of Renaissance humanism and supportive of the Meaux group, Francis would not tolerate any teaching or actions that threatened public order. In 1533, during his absence, an evangelical sermon by Nicholas Cop (ca. 1501-40), delivered as his rectoral address at the University of Paris, caused such an outcry that Cop and his friend John Calvin, the address's wrongly suspected author, were forced to flee France. In 1534, after placards (broadsheets printed in Switzerland) attacking the Mass in violent language were simultaneously posted in Paris and other cities, Francis endorsed a systematic persecution of suspected heretics, which intensified during the last years of his reign and continued unabated under his son and successor, Henry II (1547-59).

Although such persecution ended the first, or "Lutheran," phase of the French Reformation, it was during these very years that Reformed churches were being established throughout France at the instigation of Calvin and Geneva, from where publications (including French editions of the *Institutes*) and pastors were sent in increasing numbers to their embattled coreligionists. By the close of the 1550s the remarkable growth of these churches appeared to be irrepressible. In 1559, meeting secretly at Paris, they held their first national synod. It adopted 40 articles of faith, Genevan in origin and later known as the Gallican Confession, which also provided for a → church discipline inspired by the Genevan consistorial model. Estimates suggest that by the early 1560s as much as 10 percent of the total population of France, between 1.5 and 2 million people, were Reformed Protestants, or → Huguenots, as they came to be known, organized in more than 1,200 congregations chiefly located in the towns and cities of southern France. The majority of Huguenots were from the artisan and professional classes, but the party's imposing political strength resided in its numerous accessions from the aristocracy, including some of the highest nobles of the realm. Among the converts were many noblewomen, notably Jeanne d'Albret (1528-72), queen of Navarre (from 1562), a devoted Calvinist and mother of Henry of Navarre (1553-1610), later King Henry IV (from 1589).

In 1560 Catherine de Medici (1519-89) became regent for her ten-year-old son, Charles IX (1560-74). She was initially intent upon reconciling Catholics and Protestants, who were now preparing themselves for armed conflict. Civil war, the Wars of Religion, broke out in April 1562, sparked by the killing and wounding, by retainers of the Catholic duke of Guise, of many Protestant worshipers legally gathered in the small town of Vassy in Champagne. The cycle of violence, repeated eight times, lasted until 1598, with periods of pacification that accorded limited rights of assembly and worship to the Huguenots. Catholics were angered by repeated Protestant attacks on sacred images ("idols") and their clerical custodians, as well as by disruptions of the Mass and of religious processions. Protestant sentiment was especially outraged by the so-called St. Bartholomew's Day Massacre, which began in Paris on August 24, 1572, during a time of truce. Emboldened by the court-ordered assassination of the Huguenot leader Gaspard de Coligny (1519-72), admiral of France, and of other Protestant nobles, fanatical mobs in Paris and other French cities killed thousands of Huguenots over a period of weeks, while many others sought refuge in Switzerland, Germany, and England.

Hostilities did not end until 1598, nine years after the then leader of the French Protestants, Henry of Navarre, succeeded to the throne as Henry IV. In order to secure a durable peace, he converted to Roman Catholicism in 1593 and gradually won the allegiance of the country. He did not, however, forget his former coreligionists. The Edict of Nantes (1598) granted a significant measure of religious freedom and civil rights to the Huguenots, including the right to exist without being regarded legally as heretics. They were also granted many "secure places," or strategic strongholds (towns, cities, castles), as a surety against further troubles. In 1685, however, the edict was revoked by Louis XIV (1643-1715), and the Huguenots again became a persecuted, martyr church (→ France 3.1).

4.4. *The Netherlands*

The rapid spread of the evangelical movement in the Low Countries, comprising 17 provinces, was in part due to the preaching of Luther's fellow Augustinians in Antwerp and elsewhere, as well as to the continuing influence of an Erasmian biblical humanism. Although the University of Louvain had already condemned Luther's teachings in 1519 and possession of his books had in 1521 been proscribed under penalty of death by Emperor Charles V, more than 60 of his writings were published in Antwerp and Leiden between 1520 and 1540. His works found a cordial reception in the small clandestine groups devoted to → prayer and → Bible study that formed in many towns and cities of the Netherlands during the 1520s. Non-Lutheran reformist thinking also emerged. In about 1520 Cornelis Hoen (d. 1524), a humanist lawyer in The Hague, composed an *Epistola* that advanced a symbolic interpretation of the Eucharist, which was subsequently welcomed by Zwingli, who published Hoen's "letter" in 1525, a momentous development that ultimately divided the Protestant ranks.

Charles V resolutely opposed adherents of the Reformation in his Burgundian lands, as evidenced by the burning in 1523, at Brussels, of Luther's fellow Augustinian friars Hendrik Vos and Jan van Esschen — Europe's first Protestant martyrs. Between 1523 and 1566 some 1,300 "heretics" were executed in the Low Countries under Charles V and his son Philip II. A majority of the victims were Anabaptists, whose ranks began to swell in the early 1530s, especially in the northern provinces of Friesland, Holland, and Zeeland. Their main source of inspiration at this time was the itinerant lay preacher Melchior Hoffman (ca. 1500-ca. 1543), who in 1530 came from Strasbourg to Emden in East Friesland, where he carried out many rebaptisms and proclaimed the imminent return of Christ (→ Parousia) and the last judgment, to be marked by the attendant destruction of the godless.

In 1534-35 several thousand Anabaptists under the leadership of two Dutch "Melchiorites" — Jan Mathys (d. 1534) of Haarlem and Jan Bokelson (d. 1536) of Leiden — attempted to establish and enforce a millennial kingdom, their "New Jerusalem," in the nearby city of Münster in Westphalia, Germany, where local Anabaptists had gained political control. Following the abysmal failure of this venture, which ended in military defeat by combined Catholic and Lutheran forces, the sorely persecuted and scattered Anabaptists in the Netherlands were reconstituted by the lay reformer David Joris (ca. 1501-56) and, most importantly, by the former priest → Menno Simons (1496-1561). The pacifist → Mennonites increased considerably in number throughout the second half of the 16th century. The debacle at Münster, however, long led many persons, not least the ruling authorities, to equate Anabaptism with sociopolitical radicalism and revolution.

As of the mid-1540s Reformed (i.e., Calvinist) communities began to take shape in the southern Netherlands: in West Flanders, in various Walloon (French-speaking) provinces, and especially in the mercantile city of Antwerp in Brabant. Reformed preaching attracted not only artisans and low-wage workers but also merchant families and the intelligentsia. Severe persecution, which came in waves, led to the formation of refugee churches in England (London and Sandwich), in East Friesland (Emden), and in Germany (Frankfurt and the Palatinate). These churches in exile supplied their home churches — those still "under the cross" — with ministers and publications, including Bible translations, psalters, and catechisms (e.g., the important → Heidelberg Catechism of 1563; → House Church). The earliest Reformed confession in the Low Countries appeared in 1561; its primary author was Guido (Guy) de Brès (1522-67), a Calvinist minister from the south. This "Belgic Confession" mirrored the French Gallican Confession of 1559, emphasizing church discipline and a presbyterian polity but, unlike its French counterpart, sharply distancing itself from Anabaptism (→ Confessions and Creeds 3.2).

In 1566, inspired both by popular revulsion against the Spanish regime's relentless persecution of dissidents and especially by open-air Calvinist preaching in Flanders and Brabant, outbreaks of iconoclasm occurred throughout the Netherlands. From this year, the *annus mirabilis* (wonder year) in Reformed reckoning, also dates the incipient organization of Reformed churches in the northern provinces, notably Holland and Zeeland. In 1571 the Synod of Emden defined the future of Dutch Protestantism by accepting a doctrinal standard based on the Belgic Confession and the Heidelberg and Geneva Catechisms. Meantime, in the mid-1560s, leadership of the Protestant cause had been assumed by William of Nassau (1533-84), prince of Orange, the greatest of the Netherlands magnates. Born a Lutheran, then for a time a Roman Catholic, he became a Calvinist in 1573 and, ultimately, the hero of Dutch independence, which was not secured until 1609 under his son Maurice of Nassau (1567-1625). Decades of intermittent civil and religious warfare — the Revolt of the Netherlands, from 1572 — resulted in the establishment of the Reformed church in the seven northern provinces (i.e., the Dutch Republic). The ten southern provinces, modern Belgium, were saved for Spain and Catholicism largely by the military and diplomatic skills of Alessandro Farnese (1545-92), duke of Parma, who became governor-general of the Netherlands in 1578.

In the Dutch Republic citizenship did not as such confer membership in the Reformed church. In the early 1600s perhaps only 10 to 20 percent of the population were full, or "communicant," members, which required clerical scrutiny and acceptance of discipline. The especially numerous Anabaptists and the Lutherans held status as tolerated non-Calvinist churches. Although Roman Catholic worship was prohibited, magistrates often chose not to enforce the anti-Catholic laws. In the southern provinces Protestantism was officially banned, and freedom of conscience was not recognized.

4.5. *England*

In England numerous cells of Lollards kept alive Wycliffe's demands for reform. Also influential was a Bible-centered humanism of the sort advocated by John Colet (ca. 1467-1519), dean of St. Paul's in London, who in a famous 1512 sermon to the Convocation of clergy censured their "worldly living." He was joined in his critique of ecclesiastical abuses by his friends Erasmus and Thomas More (1478-1535). As early as 1519-20 merchants were bringing Luther's works into England, and his new doctrines were inspiring younger university scholars at Oxford and, especially, Cambridge. One such scholar was William Tyndale (1494?-1536), who resolved to translate the Bible into English. Failing to win support at home, he worked in exile on the Continent, publishing the first edition of his NT at Worms in 1525, which was much indebted to Luther's 1522 German version. By 1526 copies of this translation were streaming into England.

Official opposition, however, was strong. In 1521 King Henry VIII (1509-47) wrote a learned treatise against Luther, earning for himself the title *fidei defensor* (defender of the faith) from Leo X. Persecution of reformers ensued under directives from Thomas Wolsey (ca. 1474-1530), cardinal archbishop of York, papal legate, and lord chancellor of England (1515-29), whose own avarice, opulence, and licentiousness added to anticlerical sentiment. Persecution intensified under More as chancellor (1529-32). His own humanist leanings did not restrain an intransigent intolerance of suspected "Lutheran" heretics.

The situation changed dramatically in the early 1530s when Henry — angered by the refusal of Clement VII (1523-34) to nullify his 1509 marriage to Catherine of Aragon (d. 1536), which had produced no male heir — carried out a total break with the papacy through acts of the so-called Reformation Parliament (1529-36). By the Act of Supremacy (1534) Henry and his successors were declared "the only supreme head in earth of the Church of England" (→ Reformers 3.5). The principal architect of this revolution in church and state was Thomas Cromwell (ca. 1485-1540), the king's chief minister since 1532 and, from 1535, his vice-regent and vicar-general for ecclesiastical affairs. During the years 1536-40 some 800 monasteries were dissolved in England and Wales, and their lands secularized. In 1533 Thomas → Cranmer (1489-1556), the newly consecrated archbishop of Canterbury, annulled Henry's first marriage and confirmed his new marriage to Anne Boleyn (d. 1536).

As far as circumstances allowed, both Cromwell and Cranmer actively promoted the Protestant cause, above all through the production and official sanction of vernacular Bibles, notably the Great Bible of 1539, the masterwork of Miles Coverdale (1488?-1569), who made full use of Tyndale's previously banned translations. The ever-willful Henry, however, reasserted his Catholic orthodoxy, except in matters of papal authority, through the Six Articles Act, passed by Parliament in 1539, which upheld a strict doctrine of transubstantiation, rejected lay communion in both bread and wine, and forbade clerical marriage.

With the accession of the boy-king Edward VI (1547-53), the Reformation made rapid headway, at least as regards legislation and official statements of faith and practice (→ Reformed Tradition 3.6). Edward was Henry's son by his third marriage, to Jane Seymour (d. 1537), and he began his reign under the protectorship of his uncle, Edward Seymour (d. 1552), soon to be duke of Somerset, who was the leader of the Protestant party in the privy council and at court. In 1549 Parliament authorized the universal use of a → Book of Common Prayer in English (First Prayer Book, largely the work of Cranmer and showing Lutheran influence), which preserved many details of traditional worship while eliminating what was deemed unevangelical. An Ordinal, embodying Reformation views of ministry, followed in 1550. Cranmer's Second Prayer Book of 1552 brought a more radical liturgical reform, especially in eucharistic theology, which harmonized largely with the teaching of Calvin. In 1553 the young king authorized Cranmer's Forty-two Articles of Religion; they were decidedly more Swiss Protestant in tone than even the revised prayer book.

These developments reflected the influence of a number of eminent Protestant refugees from the Continent, among them the Italians Peter Martyr Vermigli (1499-1562) and Bernardino Ochino (1487-1564), the Polish reformer John Laski (or John à Lasco, 1499-1560), and, most notably, Martin Bucer of Strasbourg. Many practical reforms were also enacted, including the allowance of clerical marriage, the appointment of special preachers to bring the new order to the people, the provision for better catechetical instruction, the removal of images from the churches, and the dissolution of the chantries.

England's next monarch, Mary Tudor (1553-58), daughter of Catherine of Aragon and cousin of Charles V, devoted herself to retarding and reversing the Protestantization of her realm. She repealed all reform legislation passed by her father and brother, made a firm alliance with Catholic Spain by marriage to her cousin Philip II (1556-98), forced hundreds of clerical reformers and their lay supporters into exile on the Continent, and initiated a grisly persecution at home. Among the nearly 300 persons burned at the stake during her reign, most of them from the working classes, were three former bishops: Hugh Latimer (ca. 1485-1555) of Worcester, Nicholas Ridley (ca. 1500-1555) of London, and Archbishop Cranmer himself. Given the brevity of Mary's reign, however, and the fact that she died childless, these countermeasures proved abortive, and the burnings, on a scale unprecedented in English history, deeply revolted popular sentiment and thereby advanced the Protestant cause in the nation at large.

It thus remained for Elizabeth I (1558-1603), daughter of Anne Boleyn, to consolidate the Reformation with the so-called Elizabethan Settlement, so that by the 1580s England had become a predominantly Protestant nation (→ Episcopacy 3; Puritans 2.1). In 1559 Parliament confirmed Elizabeth as "supreme governor" of the Anglican Church in temporal affairs, thus reasserting her father's original break with Rome. The immediately ensuing Act of Uniformity restored the Second Prayer Book of 1552, with minor changes, and also restored legislation for the church that Mary had repealed. Cranmer's doctrinal formulary of 1553 was readopted by Convocation in 1563; in its final and somewhat revised form, as the Thirty-nine Articles, it was approved by both Convocation and Parliament in 1571. Meantime, leading positions in the church were filled by returning Marian exiles, though many of them favored a more comprehensive reform akin to that of the Swiss-Calvinist Reformed churches on the Continent. While the settlement was thus accomplished in relatively short order, it was also soon threatened from two sides: from that of Rome, the pope having excommunicated Elizabeth in 1570 and urged her subjects to depose her; and, with even more explosive potential, from the side of those zealous reformers who wished to purge the church's public worship and ministry of every vestige of "popery" and who came to be pejoratively labeled "Puritans."

4.6. *Scotland*

Lutheran teachings gained considerable support in Scotland during the reign of the Stuart king James V (1513-42), owing in part to widespread dissatisfaction with the church's wealth and fiscal exactions. Most prominent among the early evangelical preachers were the Lutheran Patrick Hamilton (d. 1528) and the Zwinglian George Wishart (d. 1546), both of whom were burned for heresy. A stand for Protestantism was made by Wishart's supporters at St. Andrews castle in 1546-47, with John → Knox (ca. 1513-72) as their preacher, but the venture failed with the castle's capture by French troops. Knox, after imprisonment for 19 months as a French galley slave, made his way to England in 1549 and, in 1554, to Geneva.

Under Mary of Guise as regent (from 1554) for her young daughter Mary Stuart, Queen of Scots (1542-67), French influence was paramount, and movements of reform were held in check. Protestant sentiment developed strongly in the cities and among the nobility, however, fueled in part by nationalist yearnings for liberation from the French yoke. In 1557 a group of Protestant nobles — the so-called Lords of the Congregation — entered into a covenant to "establish the most blessed Word of God and his congregation." The years 1558-60 proved to be of decisive import for the nascent Scottish Reformation, marked by Mary Stuart's marriage in 1558 to the French heir, soon to be Francis II (1559-60), Knox's return to Scotland in 1559, financial and military aid from Elizabethan England in early 1560, followed by the death of Mary of Guise in June of that same year and culminating in the withdrawal of French troops in July and victory for the Protestant side.

In August 1560 the Scottish "Reformation Parliament" adopted as the creed of the realm a Calvinist confession of faith prepared by Knox and five associates; it then proceeded to abolish papal jurisdiction and to forbid celebration of the Mass. Public worship was soon regulated by a Book of Common Order (1564), sometimes mistakenly called Knox's Liturgy, modeled on that of Calvin's Geneva. In 1560 Knox and his colleagues also composed a First Book of Discipline, calling for an ecclesiastical polity along Calvinist lines, an improved educational system, and provisions for poor relief. Though not officially sanctioned, the book laid the foundations of → church government by the "kirk session," or "eldership" (minister, elders, deacons), while also allowing for regional → "superintendents," including some willing bishops, to exercise oversight in stated places.

A Second Book of Discipline, in 1578, put forward a polity that was more consistently presbyterian, vesting jurisdiction in the local eldership ("session"), a district meeting of ministers, → elders, and doctors ("presbytery"), a provincial gathering of churches ("synod"), and a "General Assembly" of the national church. An important contributor to the latter book was the educational reformer Andrew Melville (1545-1622), at the time principal of Glasgow University. Concerted efforts by the Stuart kings of Scotland and England to retain bishops and an Anglican-style liturgy long prevented final settlement for Scotland. Hence it was not until 1690, following the deposition of James VII (James II of England) and the accession of William and Mary, that presbyterianism became Scotland's legally established form of church government.

4.7. *The Nordic Countries*

Ever since the Union of Kalmar in 1397, Denmark, Norway, and Sweden had been dynastically united under the Danish throne. The Reformation in Scandinavia, which was largely effected "from above" by royal decree and official acts of church and state, was also shaped by struggles for national independence and by the eventual dissolution of the Kalmar Union in 1523, when Sweden withdrew.

4.7.1. *Denmark*

A precondition of the Reformation in Denmark was a biblical humanism and reform Catholicism represented, most prominently, by the Carmelite provincial Paul Helie (ca. 1480-ca. 1534), who initially welcomed Luther's church criticisms and Christocentric piety but who came to abhor his break with Rome. Another such humanist, Christian Pedersen (ca. 1480-1554), eventually converted to Lutheranism and in 1529 published a Danish translation of the

NT and, later, of the entire Bible. King Christian II (1513-23) supported humanistic ideas and some Lutheran reforms, but in 1523 he was forced into exile by the bishops and nobles. Under his uncle and successor Frederick I (1523-33), permission was given (in 1526-27) for the free preaching of the gospel and for clerical marriage. An evangelical movement soon developed in the market towns and cities, led by the popular preacher Hans Tausen (1494-1561), a former monk and former Wittenberg student who was active in Viborg and Copenhagen and who later (1541) became the bishop of Ribe in Jutland.

The Lutheran Reformation was officially implemented in 1536-37 by King Christian III (1534-59), the eldest son of Frederick I and the victor in a civil war that ravaged Denmark from 1534 to 1536. In 1537 Johannes Bugenhagen (1485-1558), having come from Wittenberg at Christian's invitation, crowned the king in Copenhagen, prepared a new church ordinance (in Latin), and consecrated seven new Lutheran bishops (superintendents). One of these was the Wittenberg-trained Peder Palladius (1503-60), who, as the first evangelical bishop of Zealand (Copenhagen), exercised much influence on the next generation of Lutheran clergy in both Denmark and Norway. The Danish Reformation was promoted by many vernacular publications, including a translation of Luther's Small Catechism (1537), a church order (1539), a hymnbook (1544), the whole Bible (1550, based on the earlier work of C. Pedersen), and a liturgical manual (1556, by Palladius).

4.7.2. *Norway*

The Reformation in Norway produced no outstanding leader and long lacked significant popular support. Norway was an independent kingdom but was under the Danish king by the terms of the Kalmar Union. In the early 1530s the primate of the Norwegian Catholic church, Archbishop Olav Engelbrektssøn of Trondheim (ca. 1480-1538), endeavored to secure national independence by supporting the claims to the Danish throne of the exiled Christian II, a nominal Lutheran who had returned to Roman Catholicism. The attempt failed when Christian III proved victorious in the Danish civil war. In 1536 Norway formally became a Danish province, and the Roman church's rule there ended. The Danish (Lutheran) church ordinance of 1537 was now imposed by royal decree. Because the king used the Reformation to promote the Danish language and culture, he met with opposition from the people, although the clergy largely complied. Not until 1607, under Christian IV (1588-1648), did Norway receive its own church ordinance.

4.7.3. *Iceland*

Merchants, fishermen, and returning students brought the Reformation message to Iceland, then under Danish rule (→ Iceland 1). Young assistants to Ögmundur Pálsson, bishop of Skalholt (1521-40), joined in study of the Bible and evangelical writings under the direction of Gissur Einarsson (1508-48) and Oddur Gottkálksson (1500-1556), both of whom had studied abroad and had adopted Lutheran doctrine. The latter secretly translated the NT into Icelandic and, in 1540, had it printed in Denmark. In 1538 Iceland's two Roman Catholic bishops, Pálsson and Jón Arason of Hólar (1524-50), rejected the Danish church order of 1537 that Christian III sought to impose. Einarsson, however, whom the king appointed bishop of Skalholt in 1540, worked on behalf of the evangelical cause in his diocese. After Einarsson's death in 1548, Arason vainly tried to suppress the Reformation by force, which led to his execution in 1550. In 1552 the Hólar diocese also submitted to Christian III and accepted the Danish church ordinance. The newly established Lutheran church had a Bible in Icelandic in 1584, a hymnal in 1589, and a service book in 1594. These publications and many others issued from the printing press of Gudbrandur Thorláksson (ca. 1541-1627), who became bishop of Hólar in 1571 and whose educational labors laid the foundations of Iceland's religious culture.

4.7.4. *Sweden*

In Sweden Gustav Trolle (d. 1535), archbishop of Uppsala and himself a Dane, supported Christian II of Denmark in efforts to retain the Kalmar Union and Danish hegemony. A war of independence, however, put Gustav Vasa (1496-1560) on the throne in 1523, thus bringing the union to an end. Vasa aimed to set up a more centralized government with control over church property. He was aided by his chancellor Laurentius Andreae (ca. 1482-1552), archdeacon in Strängnäs, who sought to develop an independent national church. Andreae cooperated with Sweden's outstanding reformer, Olaus Petri (1493-1552), who had studied at Wittenberg and who is often called the Martin Luther of Sweden. Merchants brought Luther's works to Sweden, and an evangelical movement started in Stockholm, where Petri was preaching from 1524 onward. In 1526 he published his Swedish translation of the NT. At the Diet of Västerås in 1527 the king won assent to state control of "unnecessary" church property. The "pure Word of God" was now to be clearly preached everywhere, and the clergy was made subject to civil law. A reform-oriented national church thus came into being under Vasa's protection, vacillating though he was in church politics, and both preaching and worship became evangelical. Petri published a liturgical manual in 1529 and, in 1531, his Swedish Mass. The first Swedish translation of the entire Bible appeared in 1541, a joint work of Olaus Petri and his younger brother Laurentius (1499-1573), who had also studied at Wittenberg. After a serious rebellion in southern Sweden in 1542, inspired in part by Roman Catholic traditionalists, the 1544 Diet of Västerås proclaimed Sweden an evangelical kingdom, albeit without a formal confession of faith, and proscribed such Roman practices as the cult of the saints, → requiem masses, and pilgrimages.

Meantime, in 1531, Laurentius Petri had become the first evangelical archbishop of Uppsala. Because he was consecrated by the Roman Catholic bishop of Västerås, Petrus Magni, the historic episcopate ("apostolic succession") was preserved in Sweden. During his long tenure in office Laurentius effected the consolidation of Lutheranism. He published a book of sermons in 1555 and a hymnbook in 1567. In 1561 he drafted a church ordinance that was not adopted into law until 1571, after Erik XIV (1560-68), Vasa's son, had been deposed for tolerating Calvinists. John III (1568-92), Erik's younger brother, favored Roman Catholic reform and for several years allowed Jesuits to operate a secret theological school in Stockholm. His son and successor, Sigismund III (1592-99), an ardent Roman Catholic who was already king of Poland (1587-1632), planned to restore Catholicism to Sweden. In 1593, however, a national synod of clergy and laity, meeting at Uppsala, reinstated the Lutheran church ordinance of 1571 and, for the first time, required subscription to the Augsburg Confession of 1530 as the realm's doctrinal standard.

4.7.5. *Finland*

In Finland, under Swedish rule and legislation, native Finnish leaders sponsored the Reformation and at the same time promoted the Finnish language and culture. Reformist (Lutheran) ideas were abroad in Turku (Swed. Åbo) from as early as 1523. Its highly respected bishop, Martin Skytte (1528-50), a Dominican friar and biblical humanist of an Erasmian sort, was open to the new views and supported young Finns in their studies at Wittenberg. One of these was Mikael Agricola (1509-57), the so-called Finnish Luther and Finland's true reformer, who studied in Wittenberg from 1536 to 1539. Upon his return he served as the bishop's assistant and principal of the cathedral school, becoming Skytte's successor in 1550, though not appointed as bishop by Gustav Vasa until 1554.

Agricola is justly styled the father of written Finnish. His vernacular publications included a lengthy prayer book in 1544, the NT in 1548, a church manual and Mass in 1549 (based on the Swedish texts of Olaus Petri), and parts of the OT in 1551/52. In his many writings, as in his pastoral labors, he showed himself to be a conservative reformer, preserving all that he considered evangelical in medieval piety and little given to polemic against the Roman church. When a second bishopric was founded by Vasa at Vyborg (Swed. Viborg, Finn. Viipuri) in 1554, presumably to reduce the power of the bishop of Turku, it was entrusted to Paavali Juusten (d. 1575), who had studied at Wittenberg from 1543 to 1546 and who has been ranked as the Finnish Melanchthon.

4.8. *The Baltic Countries*

The course of the Reformation in the Baltic lands of Livonia and Lithuania was influenced by the cities belonging to the Hanseatic League, by the higher nobility, by the Baltic branches of the Teutonic Order, and, as a result of the Livonian War of 1558-82, by Muscovy (Russia), Denmark, Sweden, and Poland-Lithuania. (In 1569 the Union of Lublin joined the grand duchy of Lithuania and the kingdom of Poland in a confederation, with one king and one Diet.)

4.8.1. *Livonia (Latvia and Estonia)*

In Livonia, then comprising Latvia and Estonia, the Reformation began in, and spread from, the Hanseatic towns of Riga, Reval (Est. Tallinn), and Dorpat (Tartu). The beginning came in 1521, in Riga, Latvia, with the preaching of Andreas Knopken (1468-1539), a former student and associate of Johannes Bugenhagen at the school in Treptow, Pomerania (→ Latvia 2). Knopken soon had broad popular support, as well as that of the town council, whose two leading members pursued epistolary relations with Luther in 1522-23. In 1527 Johann Briesmann (1488-1549) came from Königsberg in Prussia to help implement reform. His evangelical order of service, published in 1530, was used in both Riga and Reval for many years. Reformation preaching began in Reval, Estonia, in 1523, and in 1524 Johannes Lange (d. 1531) was elected the town's chief pastor. The council approved a Lutheran church ordinance in 1525. In Dorpat, Estonia, Hermann Marstow (d. 1555), who had been appointed evangelical preacher by popular demand, was expelled by the Livonian archbishop in 1524 and could not resume his work there until 1529. These three cities adopted a common church order in 1533, thus consolidating the Lutheran Reformation.

By 1554, when the Livonian Diet proclaimed freedom to preach the gospel everywhere, the Reformation had largely prevailed throughout the whole country, at least on an official level. On a popular level, the religious needs of the different ethnic-linguistic groups were met by sermons, worship services, and publications in Lettish, Estonian, and German. The Reformation's spread to the countryside was furthered by Gotthard Kettler (1517-87), who in 1561 resigned as master of the Livonian branch of the Teutonic Order, became duke of Courland (or Kurland) as a vassal of the Polish king, and proceeded to establish a Lutheran territorial church. In 1558 the czar of Muscovite Russia, Ivan IV "the Terrible" (1547-84), invaded Livonia with such devastating effect that the country disintegrated and became partitioned among the neighboring and "protecting" states of Sweden, Denmark, and Poland-Lithuania. In southern Estonia, under Polish rule since 1582, Roman Catholicism was officially restored by King Stephen Báthory (1575-86) and was inculcated at large by the Jesuit mission centered in Dorpat. In 1625, however, Livonia came almost entirely under Swedish control, and Lutheranism remained the principal confession in both Estonia and Latvia.

4.8.2. *Lithuania*

The Reformation came to the grand duchy of Lithuania in the later 1520s and the 1530s, when the territory became a refuge for Lutherans undergoing persecution in Poland by King Sigismund I (1506-48). Also important were a widespread popular dissatisfaction with the vast wealth of the Roman church and increasing contacts with Reformation centers in Germany and Switzerland. Lutheran congregations were to be found in western Lithuania, near the Baltic Sea, as well as in the major towns of Vilnius (Russ. Vilno) and Kaunas (Kovno). The first book in the Lithuanian language, a Lutheran catechism, was published in 1547, followed by a hymnal in 1570 and a lectionary in 1579. During the 1550s Reformed Protestantism came to the fore, as also in Poland. Nicholas Radziwill (1515-65), a Lithuanian magnate and grand chancellor of Poland-Lithuania, openly espoused Calvinism in 1553, set up a Reformed congregation in Vilnius, and financed a Polish Bible that was published at Brest in 1563. By century's end there were some 200 Reformed congregations in the grand duchy, all joined in the Lithuanian Evangelical Reformed church, which had been established in 1557. Lutheranism continued in the relatively few congregations serving Germans. There was also a small number of congregations of the Church of the Lithuanian Brethren, who held → anti-Trinitarian and antipedobaptist views. Owing to the Counter-Reformation and the labors of the → Jesuits (from 1569), Roman Catholicism again became dominant in Lithuania by the mid-17th century.

4.9. *Eastern Europe*

4.9.1. *Prussia*

When the duchy of Prussia was established in 1525, the evangelical movement was already flourishing there. The grand master of the Teutonic Order, Albert of Brandenburg-Ansbach (1490-1568), cultivated relations with Luther from 1521 onward. In 1523 the Wittenberg theologian Johann Briesmann began preaching the "pure Word" in Königsberg. One of his converts was George von Polentz, bishop of Samland (1518-59), who publicly embraced the new faith on Christmas Day, 1523. A year later Prussia's other prelate, Erhard von Queiss, bishop of Pomesia (1523-29), did the same. In April 1525 Albert dissolved the Teutonic Order and transformed Prussia into a secular hereditary duchy under Polish suzerainty. A Lutheran church ordinance was then approved, with a hymnal following in 1526. Sermons and writings employed Lithuanian and Polish as well as Prussian. Duke Albert made his state a center of Lutheranism with the founding of the University of Königsberg — "the Wittenberg of the East" — in 1544.

4.9.2. *Poland*

In 1466, following a series of military defeats, the Teutonic Order ceded parts of western Prussia to the Polish crown. It was here, in the Germanized Hanseatic cities of Royal (or West) Prussia, that the Reformation first emerged in Poland. As early as 1518 and throughout the 1520s the evangelical message was proclaimed in Danzig (Pol. Gdańsk), Elbing (Elbląg), and Thorn (Toruń), and Lutheran ministers were appointed to parish churches. In 1525 an uprising of the Danzig civic commune led to a reconstituting of the city council, the abolition of Roman practices and jurisdiction, and armed intervention by King Sigismund I. Although the king, in 1520, forbade the importation of Lutheran writings and later, in1526, threatened the death penalty for apostasy from Catholicism, his repressive measures did not stop the spread of Lutheranism. Luther's works circulated at an early date in the university at Cracow (Kraków), and from 1530 Lutheran books in Polish were disseminated from Königsberg in Ducal (or East) Prussia.

After 1548, under the tolerant rule of Sigismund II (1548-72), Calvinism spread rapidly among the Polish and Lithuanian nobles, both the middling nobility and the great landed magnates. They were attracted by the governing role that

Swiss-Calvinistic presbyterianism accorded lay elders; they also favored it as a patriotic alternative to "German" Lutheranism. The most famous organizer of the Polish Calvinist churches, of which there were some 200 by century's end, was John Laski, who from 1556 worked in his birthland after spending many years abroad in service of the Protestant cause.

The religious spectrum in Poland was further altered, after 1548, by the arrival of thousands of → Bohemian Brethren fleeing persecution in their homeland, who now found protection and support among the Polish nobility. Beginning in the 1550s, moreover, anti-Trinitarians ("Arians") put down roots in various Calvinistic communities. In 1565 they broke with the Major Reformed church and set up their own Minor Reformed church, the Polish Brethren. Their leader was Fausto Sozzini (Faustus Socinus, 1539-1604), and their center was Raków, where their best-known statement of belief (the Racovian Catechism) was first issued in 1605 (→ Pacifism 2.4).

The confessional fragmentation of mainline Polish Protestantism prompted several attempts to achieve consensus. In 1555 the Calvinists and the Bohemian Brethren formed a union at Koźminek. In 1570, at Sandomierz (Russ. Sandomir), they were joined by the Lutherans in a compact of mutual recognition. This Consensus Sendomiriensis aimed to protect Protestants against Roman Catholic repression and to counter anti-Trinitarian (Unitarian, Socinian) heterodoxy. The zenith of Polish Protestantism came in 1573 with the Warsaw Confederacy, an alliance of nobles that forbade the king and the nobility to punish anyone on account of religion and thus laid the basis for a general religious toleration. However, with the (re)conversion of the great nobles to Catholicism, which had begun in 1569, the old faith was effectively restored to Poland during the reign of Sigismund III and under the aggressive lead of Stanislaus Cardinal Hosius (1505-79), bishop of Ermeland (Pol. Warmia) from 1551, and Piótr Skarga (1536-1612), Jesuit court chaplain and powerful preacher.

4.10. Bohemia, Moravia, and Silesia

The three crown lands of Bohemia, Moravia, and Silesia had indirectly been part of the German Empire, but in the later 15th century they came under the kings of Hungary. Then, in 1526, they became subject to the Hapsburg rulers and their increasingly anti-Reformation policies.

4.10.1. *Bohemia*

Already in the 15th century, as a result of the Hussite revolution of 1419-36, the kingdom of Bohemia centered on Prague had a non-Roman established church, namely that of the Utraquists, so named because of their insistence on lay communion in both bread and wine (*sub utraque specie*, "under each kind"; → Hussites 1). Many Utraquists saw in Luther a disciple of Jan Hus, who had been executed at Constance in 1415. Czech translations of Luther's works began to come out in 1520. After 1524 the conservative Old Utraquists had only loose ties to Luther, but by 1540 the quasi-Lutheran New Utraquists, who were especially influenced by Melanchthon, were in the ascendancy. Yet another Hussite party, heirs of the radical Taborites, was that of the Unitas Fratrum, or Unity of the Brethren, who also made contacts with Luther and Wittenberg. Lacking official recognition and legal prerogatives, these "Bohemian Brethren" were eventually banned, in 1546-47, by King Ferdinand I (1526-64, Holy Roman Emperor from 1558). Many of them sought refuge in Poland, although they also maintained themselves in Bohemia and, especially, in Moravia.

During the 1520s and 1530s Luther's message had spread with great rapidity in Germanized northern and western Bohemia — in the mining towns and noble estates bordering Saxony. Evangelical preachers were appointed, church ordinances introduced, and schools established. Lutheranism's regional center was Joachimsthal (Czech Jáchymov), where Johannes Mathesius (d. 1565), Luther's table companion and first biographer, served as rector of its distinguished Latin school and later as pastor. In time Lutheran leadership came to the fore among the kingdom's non-Catholic parliamentary estates. In 1575 Lutherans, New Utraquists, and Brethren adopted a common Confessio Bohemica, or Bohemian Confession, based on the Augsburg Confession but also showing Calvinist influence.

4.10.2. *Moravia*

In the margravate of Moravia, as in the neighboring Bohemian kingdom, the faith of the majority of Czechs was Utraquism, while a minority joined the Bohemian Brethren. Again in Moravia as in Bohemia, those towns with sizable German populations early embraced Luther's teachings, and most German-speaking churches eventually became Lutheran. Beginning in about 1550, however, Calvinist doctrine proved increasingly attractive to the nobles and clergy of the Moravian Unity of the Brethren, several of whose leaders advocated a formal union with Calvinist churches. Earlier, from the mid-1520s, Anabaptism also took root in Moravia, which became a haven for thousands of refugees from Switzerland, South Germany, Upper Austria, and the Tyrol. The tolerant and semiautonomous Moravian nobles, such as the lords of Liechtenstein, protected and even joined the burgeoning Anabaptist communities, whose leaders included Balthasar Hubmaier (1485-1528), at Nikolsburg (Czech Mikulov) from 1526, and Jacob Hutter (ca. 1500-1536), who from 1529 organized and stabilized the often contentious Anabaptist groups. Both men were burned at the stake by the Hapsburg regime of Ferdinand I (→ Moravian Church 1).

4.10.3. *Silesia*

The Reformation came early to the various duchies of Silesia and its capital city, Breslau, where Luther's works began to be printed in 1519. In 1523 the Breslau council appointed Johann Hess (1490-1547) pastor of one of the city's two main churches, and in 1525 it appointed Ambrose Moibanus (1494-1554) to the other. Both men, of humanist orientation, held advanced degrees from Wittenberg and carried out reforms in consultation with Luther and Melanchthon. Strong supporters and defenders of Lutheranism were Frederick II (1499-1547), duke of Liegnitz, and George "the Pious" (1484-1543), margrave of Brandenburg-Ansbach (and brother of Duke Albert of Prussia). In 1523 George purchased the Silesian duchy of Jägerndorf (Czech Krnov), which became a center of evangelical efforts. Here and in his other Silesian holdings, George appointed Lutheran ministers and introduced the church order of Brandenburg-Nuremberg.

By the late 16th century Silesia was predominantly Protestant, but its Roman Catholic diocesan organization remained intact, and the Counter-Reformation took effect during and after the → Thirty Years' War (1618-48). In both Bohemia and Moravia, however, Protestantism was largely eradicated by 1628, during the war's early stages.

4.11. ***Hungary***

In Hungary King Louis II (1516-26) and the Diet vainly attempted with threats of punishment (1523, 1525) to combat the writings of Luther and his supporters, including a group of humanists at the court in Buda whom even Queen Mary tended to favor. The disastrous defeat of the Hungarian army by the Ottoman Turks at Mohács, in 1526, led to the election of two rival kings as successors to Louis, who had fallen in battle, along with seven of the kingdom's bishops and many of its leading magnates: John Zápolya (1526-40) of Transylvania and Ferdinand I (1526-64) of Hapsburg (crowned king of Hungary in 1527). No less consequential was the realm's triple division into an Ottoman region in central Hungary, which the Turks controlled by 1541; a Hapsburg region (so-called Royal Hungary) in western and Upper (or northern) Hungary (Slovakia); and an eastern Hungary and Transylvania under Zápolya and his successors. A divided kingdom with rival rulers and Turkish control of its heartland, as well as a sorely weakened Roman Catholic hierarchy, proved favorable for the spread and staying power of Protestantism (→ Hungary 1-2).

During the 1530s and 1540s Lutheran doctrines, which itinerant preachers had already broadcast in the 1520s, were adopted by the cities of Upper Hungary and the towns of Spĭs (Ger. Zips) County, whose inhabitants were in the main German and Slovak. Under Leonhard Stöckel (1510-60), who had studied at Wittenberg (one of more than 1,000 Hungarians who did so during the century), the royal city of Bardejov (Bartfeld) became a Lutheran bastion, with a school of such wide influence that Stöckel came to be called the preceptor of Hungary. He also drafted the first Hungarian Protestant confession of faith, the Confessio Pentapolitana (Five-City Confession), based on the Augsburg Confession and adopted in 1549 by the five royal cities of Upper Hungary. Two other Upper Hungarian confessions, likewise based on Augsburg, were eventually adopted: the Confessio Montana (1559) of the region's seven mining towns and the Confessio Scepusiana (1569) of the towns of Spĭs County.

The evangelical movement came to Transylvania (Hung. Erdélyi, Ger. Siebenbürgen) already in 1519 and made rapid headway among the urban Germans ("Saxons"), whose centers included Braşov (Ger. Kronstadt), Sibiu (Hermannstadt), and Sighişoara (Schässburg). The region's leading Lutheran reformer was Johannes Honter (1498-1549), a humanist, printer, and school reformer who from 1533 worked in his native Braşov, becoming city pastor in 1544. After introducing an evangelical liturgy and church order in 1543, he prepared a new church ordinance for all the Transylvanian Lutherans, which was adopted at a synod in Sibiu in 1547.

The majority of the early reformers in Hungary were quite eclectic in their theological views, often combining an Erasmian-type humanism with the new teachings emanating from Wittenberg. One such notable figure was Matthias Biró Dévai (ca. 1500-1545), a Magyar from Transylvania and former Franciscan who made three visits to Wittenberg, where he was well regarded. A popular, twice imprisoned, and much traveled preacher who worked in Buda, Košice (Ger. Kaschau, in Slovakia), Debrecen, and on the estates of various nobles, Dévai has been styled the Hungarian Luther. In fact he owed more to Melanchthon's theology, and in the early 1540s he was attacked, by Stöckel, among others, for his spiritualizing interpretation of the Lord's Supper, which also evoked Luther's displeasure.

After 1550 Reformed Protestantism established itself among the Hungarian-speaking (Magyar) nobles and burghers in eastern Hungary and Transylvania, in northeastern Upper Hungary, and in central (Turkish) Hungary. Although labeled Calvinistic, this Protestantism was broadly Swiss or Helvetic, initially owing more to Zurich and Bullinger than to Geneva and Calvin and his successor, Beza. A founder and principal leader of the Hungarian Reformed church was Péter Somogyi Melius (also Juhász, ca. 1536-72), who from 1558 worked at Debrecen in eastern Hungary and made this city a citadel of Reformed theology. In 1559 he prepared the first Protestant confession in Magyar, on the Lord's Supper. He also translated Calvin's catechism into Magyar and produced a vernacular church ordinance, order of worship, and hymnbook. In 1562, when the predominantly Reformed residents of Debrecen were under pressure from the bishop of Eger to return to Roman Catholicism, Melius prepared the Confessio Catholica, or Catholic Confession, which served Hungarian-speaking Protestants as a foundational statement of faith. In 1567 he convened a synod of Reformed leaders at Debrecen that adopted the Catholic Confession, in both Latin and Hungarian versions, and that consolidated the Reformed church organization on the basis of Bullinger's Second Helvetic Confession (1566).

These several confessions, which corresponded to the developing confessionalization of Hungarian Lutheranism, also enabled the Reformed congregations to distance themselves from the anti-Trinitarians who appeared in their midst, especially in eastern Hungary and Transylvania, where they had the support of King János Zsigmond Zápolya (1540-71), who eventually became one of them. In 1568 the → Unitarians formally separated from the Reformed community; after the king's death their influence in Transylvania waned, although it continued in Turkish Hungary.

Meanwhile, in 1557, the Transylvanian Diet of Torda (Ger. Thorenburg) officially recognized Roman Catholicism, Lutheranism, and Calvinism as "approved religions." In 1571 this recognition was also extended to the Unitarians. Transylvania thus became the first European territory to grant religious liberty. Not until the first half of the 17th century, however, and only then by the armed resistance of three anti-Hapsburg Calvinist nobles from Transylvania, did Reformed and Lutherans achieve legal recognition, and the right of independent organization, in the Hungarian kingdom as a whole. To this day the Reformed church in Hungary remains one of Europe's most substantial.

4.12. ***Slovenia and Croatia***

Royal (Hapsburg) Hungary, in its southwestern reaches, also included most of Croatia and Slovenia with their South Slavic population. Moreover, large sections of the population in the Inner Austrian provinces of Styria, Carinthia, and Carniola were Slovene-speaking.

As early as 1527 a circle of reformers was active at Laibach (Slvn. Ljubljana) in Carniola (Ger. Krain). They were joined by the cathedral canon Primus Truber (1508-86), who began evangelical preaching in about 1531. Although initially influenced by the Zurich Reformation, he became more strongly inclined to Lutheranism when he had to flee persecution in 1547 and took refuge in Nuremberg. In 1550 Truber laid the foundation of a written Slovenian language with a grammar and catechism. He then published the Slovenian NT in installments between 1557 and 1577. By authorization of the estates he founded an evangelical church in the duchy of Krain, serving as its first superintendent from 1561 and issuing a Slovenian church ordinance for it in 1564. A complete Bible in Slovenian was published at Wittenberg in 1584, the work of Truber's associate Jurij Dalmatin (ca. 1547-89).

The Reformation reached the Croats from Krain and Hungary, in part through the labors of the Hungarian Lutheran preacher Michael Sztárai (1520-75), who from 1544 until 1564 served in Turkish-occupied territory and by 1551 had organized some 120 congregations in southern Hungary.

Beginning in 1560 Count Hans Ungnad von Sonegg (1493-1564), formerly head of the government in Styria, promoted the Reformation among the South Slavs by establishing a printing house at Urach in Württemberg (Germany), near Tübingen. Here, under Truber's sponsorship, a Croatian translation of the NT was published in 1563. Here, too, selections from the Bible and many Reformation pamphlets were issued in Slovenian, Croatian, and Italian, using the Glagolitic, Cyrillic, and Latin alphabets as needed. Although Protestantism in the Hapsburg-dominated South Slavic lands was short-lived, the publications of Truber, Dalmatin, and the Ungnad press were of long-lasting import for the development of Slovenian and Croatian literature and intellectual life.

4.13. ***Italy***

While the Italian peninsula witnessed a lively and widespread popular interest in Reformation teachings during the 1520s and 1530s, prompted by moral criticism of the Roman curia and corrupt clerics, no sustained movement for an independent Protestant church ever developed. The Roman → Inquisition, created by Paul III (1534-49) in 1542, saw to it that Protestantism, after midcentury, was increasingly confined to isolated individuals or to small clandestine groups of dissidents, ever subject to discovery and persecution.

Lutheran ideas and books came to the Venetian mainland state at an early date, carried by merchants and itinerant preachers. A significant number of Protestants, mainly Lutherans and Calvinists, inhabited the Venetian state during the 1540s and 1550s. There was also a somewhat smaller number of Anabaptists, whose teachings came to exhibit anti-Trinitarian viewpoints. A synod of some 60 Anabaptist leaders met at Venice in 1550 to resolve their doctrinal differences. In 1530 Antonio Brucioli (ca. 1495-1566), a Florentine exile of Protestant leaning, published at Venice a vernacular NT, followed by a complete Bible in Italian in 1532. The Bible that came to be most commonly used by Italian Protestants was that of Giovanni Diodati (1576-1649), a native of Geneva, where his version was first published in 1607.

Groups of evangelical humanists and reform-minded clerics gathered at Naples under the Spanish humanist Juan de Valdés (ca. 1500-1541), and at Ferrara under Duchess Renée d'Este (Renée of France, 1510-74), whom Calvin visited in 1536 and with whom he carried on a lifelong correspondence. Circles of evangelicals also formed in Modena and Lucca, the two Italian cities where Reformation ideas were perhaps most strongly promulgated; Lucca later supplied a high percentage of the Italian emigrants to Geneva. The Valdésian circle at Naples, which began meeting in 1535-36, included many well-known participants. Among them were the celebrated religious poet Vittoria Colonna (1490-1547); the humanist poet Marcantonio Flaminio (1498-1550); the papal secretary Pietro Carnesecchi (1508-67); Peter Martyr Vermigli, Augustinian abbot in Naples, later prior in Lucca; and Bernardino Ochino, at that time the foremost preacher in Italy and vicar-general of the Capuchin order from 1538 to 1541. Under threat of arrest by the Inquisition, Vermigli and Ochino fled Italy together in 1542, leading to their service as Protestant reformers in England, Switzerland, and various lands of northern Europe. Another prominent convert was Pier Paolo Vergerio (1498-1565), papal diplomat and bishop of Capodistria, near Trieste, who left Italy and the Roman church in 1549 — the first Italian bishop to "apostasize" to Protestantism.

Perhaps the finest fruit of the Italian Reformation was the treatise *Beneficio di Christo*, published anonymously at Venice in 1543, composed by the Benedictine monk Benedetto da Mantua (Benedict of Mantua, dates unknown, who may have belonged to Valdés's circle), and revised by the poet Flaminio. The book extols the benefits of Christ's expiatory death on the cross, teaches justification by faith alone, and shows the influence of Luther, Melanchthon, Calvin, and Valdés.

4.14. ***Spain***

Protestantism in Spain, more so than in any other European territory, was always an exotic growth, confined to but a few small groups of evangelicals who were increasingly subject to persecution by the Spanish Inquisition. Created in 1480 by the joint sovereigns Ferdinand of Aragon (d. 1516) and Isabella of Castile (d. 1504), whose marriage in 1469 laid the foundation of the modern Spanish state, the Inquisition remained under direct royal control. It became especially active against suspected heresy from about 1530 and still more vigilant following the accession of Philip II in 1556.

Merchants, soldiers, and royal officials stationed in Germany brought Luther's works to Spain at an early date, though by 1521 the reading of his books was specifically forbidden under threat of severe penalties. Lutheran ideas, however, flowed into the much larger and more powerful current of reform deriving from the biblical humanism of the new University of Alcalá (opened 1508) and, more especially, from the critical humanism of Erasmus that Spain's intellectual elite so enthusiastically welcomed. Also important was an indigenous movement of the so-called Alumbrados, or "enlightened ones," namely those who claimed a unique illumination by the Holy Spirit and who thus stressed a quasi-mystical "interior" piety. All these strands of thought are evident in the work of Juan de Valdés, who left Spain for Italy in about 1531. During the 1520s the Alumbrados of Seville were particular targets of the Inquisition. By the close of the 1530s heterodox Erasmian humanism had been either eradicated or driven underground by the Inquisition.

As of midcentury two communities of evangelicals, or "Lutherans" (a generic designation for all suspected heretics), had formed in Valladolid and Seville. That at Valladolid numbered some 55 members, over half of whom were executed by the Inquisition in 1559. The Seville group, numbering perhaps twice that in Valladolid and showing some Calvinist influence, was centered at the monastery of San Isidro del Campo (St. Isidore). It too was broken up by the Inquisition in the late 1550s. Its leading members included Constantino Ponce de la Fuente (1502-59), preacher at the Seville cathedral, who died in prison while awaiting sentence; Cassiodoro de Reina (ca. 1520-94), who fled to Geneva in 1557; and Cipriano de Valera (ca. 1532-ca. 1603), who in 1558 also fled to Geneva. The latter two fugitive monks from San Isidro, who became devoted workers for the Protestant cause in northern Europe, were especially intent upon translating the Bible into Spanish, not least because the Inquisition (in 1551, again in 1559) had proscribed vernacular Bibles. The first complete translation of the Bible, including the Apocrypha, into Spanish (Castilian) was the work of Reina, published at Basel in 1569 and reissued at Frankfurt in 1602, with revisions by Valera. Reina's NT was dependent on the earlier translation (1556, at Geneva) of Juan Pérez de Pineda (ca. 1500-1568), another exiled member of the conventicle in Seville.

By 1560, then, the brief history of Spanish Protestantism had come to an end. Spain, with its militant yet also reformist Catholicism, had become the center from which radiated the Roman Catholic Reformation and Counter-Reformation.

5. Impact

The most evident and the longest-lasting effect of the Reformation was the sundering of Western (Latin) Christendom into diverse and competing confessions or ecclesiastical systems (Lutheran, Reformed, Anglican, and now including Roman Catholicism), as well as organized communities of Nonconformists. This heretofore unprecedented religious → pluralism, as compared with the "universal" church of the Middle Ages, had other consequences as well: several devastating wars between Protestants and Catholics, although religion was but one of many contributing causes, and the development of territorial states on the basis of confessional identity and uniformity as the glue that holds a society together (so-called confessionalization). In time, however, it became clear that religious pluralism required a significant degree of religious toleration, not least because the Reformation message itself, notably in its radical form, declared that while states might control body and property, they had no jurisdiction over the individual conscience, answerable to God alone. (Herein lay the seeds for the eventual separation of → church and state.)

Moreover, the Reformation insistence on "Scripture alone" — a devoted Christian must be able to read and understand the Bible — made lay literacy and education, at all levels of society, a priority. Likewise, marriage and the → family (§2.4), as the training ground of Christian faith and life and thus the prototype of the church, were elevated in importance. So, too, the realm of secular → work, not the contemplative life of the monk and mystic, was accorded signal value, freed now of all taint of sinfulness and inferiority and lauded as contributing both to God's honor and to societal well-being.

Although historians are no longer inclined to identify the Reformation as the dividing line between medieval and modern times (Martin Luther, for example, was in many respects a quite medieval man), several of these developments are rightly seen as preconditions of → modernity.

Bibliography: General: T. A. Brady Jr., H. A. Oberman, and J. D. Tracy, eds., *Handbook of European History, 1400-1600* (2 vols.; Grand Rapids, 1996) • E. Cameron, *The European Reformation* (Oxford, 1991) • P. Collinson, *The Reformation: A History* (New York, 2004) • A. G. Dickens and J. Tonkin, *The Reformation in Historical Thought* (Cambridge, Mass., 1985) • S. L. Greenslade, ed., *The Cambridge History of the Bible,* vol. 3, *The West from the Reformation to the Present Day* (Cambridge, 1963) • H. J. Hillerbrand, ed., *The Oxford Encyclopedia of the Reformation* (4 vols.; New York, 1996) • C. Lindberg, *The European Reformations* (Oxford, 1996) • D. MacCulloch, *The Reformation* (New York, 2003) • A. E. McGrath, *The Intellectual Origins of the European Reformation* (Oxford, 1987) • H. A. Oberman, *The Dawn of the Reformation: Essays in Late Medieval and Early Reformation Thought* (Edinburgh, 1986) • S. Ozment, *The Age of Reform, 1250-1550* (New Haven, 1980); idem, *Protestants: The Birth of a Revolution* (New York, 1992) • J. Pelikan, *The Christian Tradition,* vol. 4, *Reformation of Church and Dogma, 1300-1700* (Chicago, 1984) • L. W. Spitz, *The Protestant Reformation, 1517-1559* (New York, 1985) • J. D. Tracy, *Europe's Reformations, 1450-1650* (Lanham, Md., 1999) • G. H. Williams, *The Radical Reformation* (3d ed.; Kirksville, Mo., 1992).

Pre-Reformation movements: P. A. Dykema and H. A. Oberman, eds., *Anticlericalism in Late Medieval and Early Modern Europe* (Leiden, 1993) • T. Fudge, *The Magnificent Ride: The First Reformation in Hussite Bohemia* (Brookfield, Vt., 1998) • A. Hudson, *The Premature Reformation: Wycliffite Texts and Lollard History* (Oxford, 1988) • F. Oakley, *The Western Church in the Later Middle Ages* (Ithaca, N.Y., 1979) • H. A. Oberman, ed., *Forerunners of the Reformation: The Shape of Late Medieval Thought* (New York, 1966) • H. A. Oberman and C. Trinkaus, eds., *The Pursuit of Holiness in Late Medieval and Renaissance Religion* (Leiden, 1974) • R. W. Southern, *Western Society and the Church in the Middle Ages* (Baltimore, 1970) • L. W.

SPITZ, *The Religious Renaissance of the German Humanists* (Cambridge, Mass., 1963) • G. STRAUSS, ed., *Manifestations of Discontent in Germany on the Eve of the Reformation* (Bloomington, Ind., 1971); idem, ed., *Pre-Reformation Germany* (New York, 1972).

Regions, general: T. A. BRADY JR., H. A. OBERMAN, and J. D. TRACY, eds., *Handbook of European History, 1400-1600,* vol. 2, *Visions, Programs, and Outcomes* (Grand Rapids, 1996) • O. CHADWICK, *The Early Reformation on the Continent* (Oxford, 1991) • G. R. ELTON, ed., *The New Cambridge Modern History,* vol. 2, *The Reformation, 1520-1559* (2d ed.; Cambridge, 1990) • A. PETTEGREE, ed., *The Early Reformation in Europe* (Cambridge, 1992); idem, ed., *The Reformation World* (London, 2000) • A. PETTEGREE, A. DUKE, and G. LEWIS, eds., *Calvinism in Europe, 1540-1620* (Cambridge, 1994) • M. PRESTWICH, ed., *International Calvinism, 1541-1715* (Oxford, 1985) • B. SCRIBNER, R. PORTER, and M. TEICH, eds., *The Reformation in National Context* (Cambridge, 1994).

Regions, particular: C. F. BLACK, *Early Modern Italy: A Social History* (London, 2001) • P. COLLINSON, *The Religion of Protestants: The Church in English Society, 1559-1625* (Oxford, 1982) • I. B. COWAN, *The Scottish Reformation: Church and Society in Sixteenth-Century Scotland* (London, 1982) • A. G. DICKENS, *The English Reformation* (2d ed.; University Park, Pa., 1991) • C. S. DIXON, ed., *The German Reformation: The Essential Readings* (Oxford, 1999) • G. DONALDSON, *The Scottish Reformation* (repr. ed.; Cambridge, 1979) • E. DUFFY, *The Stripping of the Altars: Traditional Religion in England, c. 1400-c. 1580* (New Haven, 1992) • A. DUKE, *Reformation and Revolt in the Low Countries* (London, 1990) • G. R. ELTON, *Reform and Reformation: England, 1509-1558* (Cambridge, Mass., 1977) • M. GREENGRASS, *The French Reformation* (Oxford, 1987) • O. P. GRELL, ed., *The Scandinavian Reformation: From Evangelical Movement to Institutionalization of Reform* (Cambridge, 1995) • R. PO-CHIA HSIA, ed., *The German People and the Reformation* (Ithaca, N.Y., 1988) • G. KINDER, *Spanish Protestants and Reformers in the Sixteenth Century* (London, 1983) • R. M. KINGDON, *Geneva and the Coming of the Wars of Religion in France, 1555-1563* (Geneva, 1956); idem, *Geneva and the Consolidation of the French Protestant Movement, 1564-1572* (Geneva, 1967) • R. J. KNECHT, *The French Wars of Religion, 1559-1598* (London, 1989) • K. MAAG, ed., *The Reformation in Eastern and Central Europe* (Aldershot, 1997) • D. MACCULLOCH, *The Later Reformation in England, 1547-1603* (Basingstoke, 1990) • G. MURDOCK, *Calvinism on the Frontier, 1600-1660: International Calvinism and the Reformed Church in Hungary and Transylvania* (Oxford, 2000) • A. PETTEGREE, *Emden and the Dutch Revolt: Exile and the Development of Reformed Protestantism* (Oxford, 1992) • H. RAWLINGS, *Church, Religion, and Society in Early Modern Spain* (Basingstoke, 2002) • R. W. SCRIBNER, *The German Reformation* (Atlantic Highlands, N.J., 1986); idem, *Popular Culture and Popular Movements in Reformation Germany* (London, 1987) • M. TODD, *The Culture of Protestantism in Early Modern Scotland* (New Haven, 2002) • M. E. WELTI, *Kleine Geschichte der italienischen Reformation* (Gütersloh, 1985).

Topics and themes: P. BLICKLE, *The Revolution of 1525: The German Peasants' War from a New Perspective* (Baltimore, 1981) • J. EDWARDS, *The Spanish Inquisition* (Stroud, 1999) • M. U. EDWARDS JR., *Printing, Propaganda, and Martin Luther* (Berkeley, Calif., 1994) • C. M. N. EIRE, *War against the Idols: The Reformation of Worship from Erasmus to Calvin* (Cambridge, 1986) • H.-J. GOERTZ, *The Anabaptists* (London, 1996) • B. S. GREGORY, *Salvation at Stake: Christian Martyrdom in Early Modern Europe* (Cambridge, Mass., 1999) • O. GRELL and B. SCRIBNER, eds., *Tolerance and Intolerance in the European Reformation* (Cambridge, 1996) • S. KARANT-NUNN, *The Reformation of Ritual: An Interpretation of Early Modern Germany* (London, 1997) • C. KRAHN, *Dutch Anabaptism: Origin, Life, and Thought, 1450-1600* (2d ed.; Scottdale, Pa., 1981) • C. LINDBERG, *Beyond Charity: Reformation Initiatives for the Poor* (Minneapolis, 1993) • S. OZMENT, *When Fathers Ruled: Family Life in Reformation Europe* (Cambridge, Mass., 1983) • P. ROREM, *Calvin and Bullinger on the Lord's Supper* (Nottingham, 1989) • H. SCHILLING, *Religion, Political Culture, and the Emergence of Early Modern Society* (London, 1992) • R. W. SCRIBNER, *For the Sake of Simple Folk: Popular Propaganda for the German Reformation* (Cambridge, 1981) • G. STRAUSS, *Luther's House of Learning: Indoctrination of the Young in the German Reformation* (Baltimore, 1978) • L. P. WANDEL, *Voracious Idols and Violent Hands: Iconoclasm in Reformation Zurich, Strasbourg, and Basel* (Cambridge, 1995) • M. E. WIESNER, *Women and Gender in Early Modern Europe* (2d ed.; Cambridge, 2000) • M. E. WIESNER-HANKS, *Christianity and Sexuality in the Early Modern World: Regulating Desire, Reforming Practice* (London, 2000).

DAVID W. LOTZ

Reformation Principles

1. By the term "Reformation principles" the → Formula of Concord and Protestant → orthodoxy (§1) understand negatively slanted formulations of the doctrine of → justification, above all *sola fide,* "by faith alone," on the basis of Martin Luther's (1483-1546) rendering of Romans 3:28 (see *LW*

35.187ff.; → Faith 3.5.3). This exclusion of works as a ground of justification does not mean the isolating of faith but singles out justifying faith because it receives the → righteousness of Christ that is given by → grace alone. The formula thus has the implication of *solus Christus* (Christ alone) and *sola gratia* (grace alone), as we see from the *Examen* of M. Chemnitz (1522-86), the *Theologia* of J. A. Quenstedt (1617-88), the Second → Helvetic Confession (1566, art. 15), and the → Heidelberg Catechism (1563, qq. 60-61). Not excluded, of course, are the works that follow justification (Formula of Concord, SD 3.41ff.; → Sanctification), as is argued in response to traditionalist objections. Nor are the Word (→ Preaching) and → sacraments excluded as means of justification (note Quenstedt's reply to Calvin *Inst.* 4.14.14, also Consensus Tigurinus [1549] 11-13, 15, where there is a tendency to play off the Reformation principles against the means). We might also describe as negative Reformation principles brief summaries of the law and as positive Reformation principles brief summaries of the gospel (→ Law and Gospel).

Another Reformation principle is *sola Scriptura,* Scripture alone, which excludes human → tradition and → reason as sources and norms of true doctrine, or subjects them to Scripture alone as "the only guiding principle" (Book of Concord [1580], title page), the one binding authority *(norma normans non normata),* and then to the church's biblically consonant → confessions *(normae normatae).*

2. From the beginning of the 19th century, justification by faith alone and Scripture alone as the supreme authority came to be called the "material" and "formal" principles of the → Reformation or of → Protestantism. A. D. C. Twesten (1789-1876; *Vorlesung* §20.273ff.) introduced this form of expression, and it was much debated by A. Ritschl (1822-89), I. A. Dorner (1809-84), and C. Stange (1870-1959; → Theology in the Nineteenth and Twentieth Centuries). In this case the principles refer to the basic or essential laws that underlie and control the various doctrinal decisions of Reformation Christianity.

Bibliography: M. Chemnitz, *Examen Concilii Tridentini* (Berlin, 1861; orig. pub., 1578) • W. H. T. Dau, "The Heritage of Lutheranism," *What Lutherans Are Thinking* (ed. E. C. Fendt; Columbus, Ohio, 1947) 9-25 • I. A. Dorner, "Das Prinzip unserer Kirche nach dem inneren Verhältnis des materialen und formalen Seite derselben zueinander," *Gesammelte Schriften* (Berlin, 1883) 48-152 • A. C. Piepkorn, "Suggested Principles for a Hermeneutics of the Lutheran Symbols," *CTM* 29 (1958) 1-24 • R. D. Preuss, *The Theology of Post-Reformation Lutheranism* (2 vols.; St. Louis, 1970-72) • J. A. Quenstedt, *Theologia Didactico-Polemica sive Systema Theologiae* (Leipzig, 1702) • A. Ritschl, "Über die beiden Prinzipien des Protestantismus" (1876), *Gesammelte Aufsätze* (Freiburg, 1893) 234-47 • H. Sasse, *Here We Stand: Nature and Character of the Lutheran Faith* (New York, 1938; repr., Minneapolis, 1946) • C. Stange, "A. Ritschls Urteil über die beiden Prinzipien des Protestantismus," *ThStKr* 70 (1897) 599-621 • A. D. C. Twesten, *Vorlesung über die Dogmatik der evangelisch-lutherischen Kirche* (vol. 1; Hamburg, 1834).

Notger Slenczka

Reformed Alliance

The Reformierter Bund, or Reformed Alliance, was founded at Marburg, Germany, in 1884 as a free association of churches, congregations, and individuals. The first statutes stated its aim as the preserving and promoting of the Reformed church in doctrine, → worship, and constitution. The main thrust of its work initially was to foster theological literature and education, for example, by means of study centers at Halle, Erlangen, and Göttingen, and later through a school of theology at Elberfeld (1928). After World War I it increasingly assumed more and more of the tasks of an alliance of churches instead of pursuing a single aim.

The → church struggle hastened this development. A crucial event was the holding of the First Free Reformed Synod of Barmen-Gemarke on January 3/4, 1934, which adopted the "Erklärung über das rechte Verständnis der reformatorischen Bekenntnisse in der DEK" (Declaration on the true understanding of the Reformed confessions in the German Evangelical Church), drafted by Karl → Barth. The main assembly approved the statement the next day; in so doing, it clearly took the course that was being followed by the → Confessing Church (→ Barmen Declaration).

The preservation of the Reformed Alliance in the church struggle was helpful when reconstruction came after 1945. The new moderator after the war was W. Niesel (1946-73). The 1946 assembly deplored the tendency to split the Evangelische Kirche in Deutschland (EKD, Evangelical Church in Germany) into confessional blocks. The Reformed Alliance never sought to be a counterpart to the United Evangelical Lutheran Church of Germany. In its 1971 Theses it called upon the EKD to uphold →

unity in plurality and pledged itself to advocate confessional openness and not uniformity. From the outset it helped to achieve the → Leuenberg Agreement (1973), and it contributed to the doctrinal conversations that followed (→ Ecumenical Dialogue). Earlier, it participated in the → Arnoldshain Conference (1957) and its findings. It has belonged to the → World Alliance of Reformed Churches since 1892.

The alliance holds a general assembly every two years and has an executive committee of 24 members. In 1970 it defined itself as a free association of churches, congregations, societies, and individuals that accept the Reformed confession and wish to serve the alliance. Although strictly an association, the Reformed Alliance has the role of a body representing the Reformed churches within the family of Protestants in Germany (the EKD).

In its constitution the Reformed Alliance has described a threefold task: (1) to work for a common direction among churches of Reformed origin and responsibility, (2) to seek links with Reformed churches abroad and to contribute to the work of the World Alliance and the ecumenical movement, and (3) to foster relations with Protestant churches and to cooperate with them in common tasks and agencies. In 1999 it included four Reformed church families in Germany, as well as approximately 400 congregations and 600 individual members.

The Reformed Alliance holds a theological conference every two years in pursuit of its aims. It also arranges regional conferences of → pastors, → elders, and church members. It offers guidance for confirmation classes in the → Heidelberg Catechism and publishes a service book with prayers for use at worship. Two of its publications have found wide acceptance: *Das Bekenntnis zu Jesus Christus und die Friedensverantwortung der Kirche* (Confession of Jesus Christ and the church's responsibility for peace, 1982), which makes the question of peace in an age of → weapons of mass destruction a matter of confession (→ Status confessionis) and which is a summons and invitation to concrete obedience on the part of the community of faith, and *Wir und die Juden — Israel und die Kirche* (We and the Jews — Israel and the church, 1990), adopted by the General Assembly after intensive preliminary work involving Jews and Dutch theologians (→ Jewish-Christian Dialogue).

→ Ecumenism, Ecumenical Movement; Reformed and Presbyterian Churches

Bibliography: J.-J. Bauswein and L. Vischer, eds., *The Reformed Family Worldwide* (Grand Rapids, 1999) 183 • J. Guhrt, ed., *Hundert Jahre Reformierter Bund. Beiträge zur Geschichte und Gegenwart* (Bad Bentheim, 1984).

Joachim Guhrt

Reformed and Presbyterian Churches

1. Term and Origins
2. Distinctive Doctrines
   2.1. Word of God
   2.2. Election
   2.3. Law of God
   2.4. Church
   2.5. Model of Ministry
   2.6. Church Discipline
   2.7. Relation to the State
3. Confession
4. Range
   4.1. Europe
   4.2. North America
   4.3. Latin America
   4.4. Asia
   4.5. Oceania
   4.6. Africa
5. Unity and Diversity

1. Term and Origins

The adjective "reformed" refers first to what the Reformation was seeking to accomplish: *ecclesia reformata et semper reformanda,* that is, the church reformed and always self-reforming. Later, usually beginning with capitals, it came into use for those churches reformed according to the Word of God that received official recognition in the empire by the 1648 Peace of Westphalia. In the English-speaking world churches of this kind have come to be known for the most part as Presbyterian because they rejected → episcopalianism in favor of presbyterianism.

The origins of the Reformed churches are to be sought in the city reformations in Switzerland and then in southern Germany. U. → Zwingli (1484-1531; → Zwingli's Theology) in Zurich, M. → Bucer (1491-1551) in Strasbourg, J. Oecolampadius (1482-1531) in Basel, and B. Haller (1492-1536) and others in Bern (→ Reformers) sought reform without the aid of princes and had the vision of a new civic order based on the spirit of the rediscovered gospel. Along with → justification they laid more stress on → sanctification, which would involve not only individual life but also social and political structures.

The first Protestant community arose in Zurich

under Zwingli (→ Reformation 2.2), whose theology, in spite of its orientation to Scripture and its affinity to that of M. → Luther (→ Luther's Theology), had distinctive features deriving from → humanism and the study of → Augustine (354-430; → Augustine's Theology). As people's priest at the Old Minster in Zurich, Zwingli faced directly the questions of practical life and sought to answer them. The actual Reformation broke out in 1522 over the question of obligatory fasting, a practical issue. The first public disputation, in January 1523, advanced the movement, and the city council, which arranged the event, took over leadership of the church. In the disputation Zwingli defended his Sixty-seven Articles, which he then justified in a comprehensive exposition and defense. The disputation ended with the city's recognition of Zwingli's message. After a second disputation, in October 1523, the council decided to terminate the veneration of → saints, radically change → worship, abolish images from the churches, end monasticism, set up marriage courts replacing the bishop's jurisdiction in such matters, and introduce Zwingli's form of the → Eucharist.

The confessional division between Lutherans and Reformed began in 1525 over the issue of Christ's real presence in the Supper. The Marburg Colloquy (1529) could not bridge the deep gulf between Luther and Zwingli, despite the zealous efforts of Bucer to act as mediator. When Zwingli died in 1531, H. Bullinger (1504-75) replaced him as chief pastor. By Bullinger's writings, especially the popular *Hausbuch,* which enjoyed wide sales in many lands, by his letters to almost all European countries, and by his work on the Second Helvetic Confession (1566), Zwinglianism in its later form achieved great influence.

The continuation of the Reformation in French-speaking western Switzerland, however, had Bern as its center after 1531, and then Geneva. G. Farel (1489-1565) preached in Geneva in 1532 and was influential in getting J. → Calvin (1509-64) to stay there. Geneva soon welcomed many who were exiled for their faith, and as a result of Calvin's work, it became an international center of → Protestantism. Calvin's *Institutes* (1536, final ed., 1559) made a lasting impact as the first systematic account of Reformation teaching. At the Genevan Academy students from all over Europe were present, and they carried the Reformation back to their own countries (e.g., J. → Knox to Scotland). The church order that Calvin drafted, *Ecclesiastical Ordinances* (1541), which he largely adopted from Strasbourg, became a model for self-governing churches free from state interference. → Calvinism was of great help to Reformed and Presbyterian churches, which in the second half of the 16th century were struggling against hostile secular authorities and needed to safeguard themselves in matters of church order.

2. Distinctive Doctrines

We find many different confessions and doctrinal traditions among the Reformed and Presbyterian churches. Certain features, however, are common to all of them.

2.1. *Word of God*

Holy Scripture as witness to revelation is viewed as the → Word of God. It shows its divine character and efficacy in the testimony of the Holy Spirit, not by historical verification. The OT and NT writings are not ranked qualitatively by any hermeneutical principle of selection (such as → law and gospel; → Hermeneutics). The doctrine of the unity of Scripture, to which the unity of the → covenant corresponds, rules out in principle any theological → anti-Semitism. In biblical preaching, "the very Word of God is proclaimed" (Second Helvetic Confession 1).

Christ himself is present in true → proclamation, as he is in the → sacraments when rightly administered. The sacraments are linked to the Word as visible signs and seals of the proclamation of → grace. The church, created by the Word, is oriented to its proclamation as a gathered congregation. The → liturgy is to be simple, includes no sacerdotal actions, and does not have set forms for every age and place. The prohibition of images (Exodus 20) means that there must be no visual representations of God or Christ; the focus, rather, is on a ministry of → preaching.

2.2. *Election*

Election in Christ is the ontic basis of the church and of → faith. To be a Christian is to be elect. → Salvation does not depend on our human disposition or goodwill. The consistent exclusion of → synergism, however, does not exclude responsible action, for election places us in a fellowship of faith and obedience with Christ. For all its defects the church is safe in the faithfulness of God (thus the doctrine of perseverance). Hence the churches always have the courage and strength to go on, even in difficult situations and under persecution. The more far-reaching doctrine of double → predestination, including reprobation, is less important and is not to be seen as an essential principle of Reformed theology.

2.3. *Law of God*

The → law of God, which we find not merely in the → Decalogue but throughout the OT and NT, is re-

Reformed and Presbyterian Churches

garded not merely as a court that judges and condemns sinners but also as a standard for the life of faith, for which Christ has freed sinners by his redeeming work. It is a rule of gratitude in its use by the regenerate. With justification God's right is established, and the goal is sanctification.

Law and gospel are not antagonistic entities. One may thus speak of the law of → freedom and the demands of the gospel. Calvin viewed the law as the form of the gospel. Instead of the usual word order "law and gospel," K. → Barth could teach us to say "gospel and law." The point here is that doing God's law presupposes hearing of the gospel. It is the work of the gospel to produce Christian action. When it has this basis, → ethics is not just the motivational ethics of the noble-minded individual (→ Motive, Ethics of), nor does it seek to set up definitively binding → norms (as in legalism).

Ethical action in the political sphere has a part, for there are no autonomous spheres of life outside the claim of God. K. Barth (1886-1968; → Dialectical Theology) provided new impulses for political action with his analogy between the community of Christ and the civil community.

2.4. *Church*

The → church (§3.5) embraces the whole people of God in both the OT and the NT, the church of every time and all places. It is the body of Christ, its Head and Subject, who gathers, protects, and upholds it by his Word and Spirit. The Reformed and Presbyterian churches, along the lines of the → Apostles' Creed, → Niceno-Constantinopolitan Creed, and → Athanasian Creed, lay claim to catholicity, which they demonstrate by their ecumenical orientation (→ Ecumenism, Ecumenical Movement).

Their → unity and oneness in faith derive from Christ the Head. The different Reformed and Presbyterian churches are seen as manifold manifestations of the one true church, which is grounded in Christ. Catholicity thus includes pluriformity. The unity is Christological and pneumatological (→ Christology; Holy Spirit), the achievement of which does not have to mean uniformity. Nor do the unity and universality of the church reside in any special office.

2.5. *Model of Ministry*

The model of ministry, which goes back to Calvin, still obtains today in Reformed and Presbyterian churches, although with modifications (→ Ministry, Ministerial Offices, 1.2). Through the operation of the Holy Spirit, all believers, who take part in the universal priesthood, have a part in Christ's threefold office as prophet, priest, and king (→ Office of Christ). As regards ministers, the threefold office finds its counterpart in the offices of the pastor (the minister of the Word), the → elder, and the → deacon, whom the congregation calls by election. The offices do not represent the church or take the place of the Head. Ministers of all three types share in leadership of the church as the church council or presbytery.

Each congregation is in the full sense the church. Together, churches make up the synod. The synod is a gathering of ministers and officeholders to regulate matters of common concern. The presbyterial-synodal church government is not a product of democracy but is grounded in a Christological-pneumatological ecclesiology, and it expresses the spiritual fellowship of the congregations. Many churches of other denominations have adopted this constitution in past decades, though more in the sense of parliamentary representation of the people, without direct reference to the confession. As a model of power, this type of order has played its part in the development of modern → democracy, especially in the New England states (→ Modern Church History 2), where church institutions preceded secular institutions. With their own form of organization Reformed and Presbyterian churches have been able to protect their independence and freedom vis-à-vis state influence, especially where they are in a minority or in non-Christian countries.

2.6. *Church Discipline*

→ Church discipline, often misunderstood as moral tutelage, has as its goal the framing of an evangelical lifestyle and the relating of worship to → everyday life. According to the rule of Matt. 18:15-19, mutual brotherly or sisterly admonition comes first. Exclusion from communion is rare today. Nor is discipline regarded now as a mark of the church. It was always related to proclamation of the Word and administration of the sacraments.

2.7. *Relation to the State*

The orientation of the Reformed and Presbyterian churches in their relation to the state (→ Church and State) is toward the → two-kingdoms doctrine, the distinction between God's ecclesiastical rule and his civil rule. Yet this distinction does not mean separation, for by the public proclamation of his Word, Christ sets forth his claim to sovereignty over the whole world.

The church has a prophetic office as watchman. Reformed and Presbyterian churches have thus spoken out on issues of → peace, justice, human → rights, and → racism. The relation to the world in the comprehensive sense that includes → culture, → politics, the → economy, and → society is one neither of withdrawal nor of domination. The church's task is to openly proclaim God's will to save and to bear witness to it by a visible obedience of faith.

3. Confession

The Reformed and Presbyterian churches have published some 60 classic confessional statements. As particular confessions, these documents bear witness to Holy Scripture in specific situations. They do not claim to lay down doctrinal norms of permanent validity. Some even contain clauses allowing that they should be revised if better instruction is given by Scripture, as we see from the Bern Synod of 1532 or the Scots Confession (preface) of 1560. Relative validity rules out confessionalism, though confessionalist tendencies will always be apparent. It also makes possible union with other churches.

The unity of the church does not rest on doctrinal uniformity, which is often demanded and promoted in the interests of the authorities (as in the case of the state ideology Pancasila in Indonesia or of the union forced on Protestant churches by imperial → fascism in Japan in 1941). It is a vital unity in Christ. Of particular importance are the Second Helvetic Confession in Switzerland, Austria, and Hungary; the Westminster in the Anglo-Saxon sphere (→ Westminster Assembly and Confession); and the → Heidelberg Catechism in almost all European countries.

The Reformed and Presbyterian churches have never had a common confession or a universally binding collection of confessions such as → Lutheranism has in the → Formula of Concord (1577) and Book of Concord (1580). When the → World Alliance of Reformed Churches discussed the question of a common Reformed confession in 1925, the idea was rejected after Karl Barth pointed emphatically to the Reformed view that the confessions are relative and specific.

New confessions have now emerged in churches in Africa and Asia that do not go back directly to the European Reformation and that see themselves threatened as minority churches if they do not give an account of their faith in their own particular cultural and sociopolitical context. As they take up traditional confessional statements and reformulate them, they are doing something that began with the Barmen Declaration of 1934. The titles they adopt — for example, Confession regarding the United Church of Christ in Japan during the Second World War (1967), Common Understanding of the Christian Faith (of Indonesian churches, 1984), Living Faith (Presbyterian Church in Canada, 1984), Song of Hope (in Vischer, 222-27), and Basis of Union (Church of South India, 1941; Ghana Church Union Committee, 1965; Uniting Church of Australia, 1979; and United Reformed Church in the U.K., 1981) — show not merely how much variety there is in content and style but also that the statements are made as a concrete act relating to a specific situation.

Twice a *status confessionis* has been declared, both in 1982: by the World Alliance of Reformed Churches on racism in South Africa, and by the Reformed Alliance in Germany on nuclear, biological, and chemical → weapons. In both cases the basic confession of Jesus Christ was related to specific situations. Only superficially might it be objected that moral judgments are deciding the confessional content. The basic insight is that if an ethical question (e.g., apartheid) has become the expression of a fixed → ideology and if one's position on that question involves an implicit affirmation or denial of the gospel, then the church is summoned to confess the truth of God concretely and publicly, even as regards its ethical content.

4. Range

Spread across the globe, Reformed churches in 2003 included more than 75 million persons. Most Reformed churches, along with the united churches, belong to the World Alliance of Reformed Churches. Of the 39 members of the → Reformed Ecumenical Council (founded 1946), more than half belong also to the World Alliance.

Figures in the subsections below, taken from *The Reformed Family Worldwide* (1999, ed. J.-J. Bauswein and L. Vischer), show the total membership of the respective churches. The English names of the various churches also come from this volume.

4.1. *Europe*

In Germany there are two autonomous Reformed churches: the Church of Lippe (219,000 members, with a Lutheran classis) and the Evangelical Reformed Church (204,000, constituted in 1989 by a union of the churches of the Northwest and Bavaria). There also are some 200 congregations of Reformed confession that took part in the 19th-century → Union. The first Reformed territorial church was in the Palatinate, where a church order and the Heidelberg Catechism were adopted in 1563. A union church was established there in 1818, and unions also arose in Nassau (1817) and in Baden (1821). Reformed churches could retain their own confessional position in the old Prussian Union (Rhineland, Westphalia, Saxony, and Brandenburg), and there is a strong Reformed element in Anhalt. Free Reformed churches were mostly founded by exiles, for example, Huguenots, Walloons, and Dutch. In the 1830s, when theological liberalism gained a foothold (→ Theology in the Nineteenth and Twentieth Centuries), the small Evangelical Old Reformed Church, with congregations in East Friesland and Bentheim, was a product of a movement of return to the Reformation confession. Many efforts in the 19th and 20th centuries to set up a Reformed church in Germany failed because, according to their self-understanding, the churches did not want to be confessionalist. Altogether, there are about 2 million Reformed in Germany. The → Reformed Alliance was founded at Marburg in 1884, and though it has no function of leadership, it represents the Reformed churches in the Evangelical Church in Germany.

In France, where the first synod adopted the Gallican Confession in 1559, the Reformed Church of France has 182,000 members in small, widely scattered congregations. Two smaller churches are the conservative Reformed Church of Alsace and Lorraine (33,000) and the National Union of Independent Reformed Evangelical Churches of France (11,000). The work of the Paris Mission (→ French Missions) has given rise to French-speaking Reformed churches in Africa and Oceania.

In the Netherlands the Reformed Church was earlier predominant and had a strong cultural influence up to recently. In 1892 the Reformed Churches in the Netherlands (Gereformeerde Kerken in Nederland, today 727,500 members) broke away from the original Netherlands Reformed Church (Nederlandse Hervormde Kerk, 2.3 million). There are also several smaller churches, many representing a particular ethnic group. The total Reformed membership is 3.4 million. In May 2004 the process of church unification known as Samen op Weg (Together on the way) brought into church union the two largest Reformed churches and the Evangelical Lutheran Church in the Kingdom of the → Netherlands (§2.4).

In Hungary the Reformed Church was the spiritual center of resistance to the Hapsburg counterreformation (→ Catholic Reform and Counterreformation). Though Presbyterian, this church has bishops, not in terms of the apostolic succession, but as presidents. Along with the church in Hungary (1.6 million members), there are Reformed churches of Hungarian nationality in Romania (725,000), Carpatho-Ukraine (130,000), Slovakia (120,000), and the former Yugoslavia (17,000). In the former Czechoslovakia the Evangelical Church of the → Moravian Brethren came into being in 1918 as the evangelical churches of the Augsburg and Helvetic Confessions united and adopted the Moravian tradition. Today in the Czech Republic and in Slovakia, the two parts of this church together have 155,000 members.

In Switzerland the Reformed churches are independent cantonal churches. In 1920 they joined forces, along with some smaller bodies, to form the Federation of Swiss Protestant Churches, with 2.8 million members. These churches are pledged to the witness of Holy Scripture and thus resist confessionalism. The churches have different relations to the authorities in each canton, some being closely tied to them as territorial churches, others being completely independent.

The Church of Scotland claims 1.2 million members, a decline from the numbers in recent years. Its main confession is the Westminster (1647). In the 1929 Declaratory Articles it sets forth its independence of secular authorities and lays claim to self-government. Many Presbyterian churches in Asia and Africa derive from its missionary work. In England Presbyterians and Congregationalists (→ Congregationalism) came together in 1972 to form the United Reformed Church; in 1980 the Reformed Association of Churches of Christ also joined the union (103,000 members in all). Among the churches of this union, elders represent the Presbyterian tradition, gathered congregations the Congregational.

Ireland has a strong Presbyterian Church (308,000 members). We also find small but vital Reformed Churches in Belgium (40,000), Austria (Helvetic Confession, 14,000), Lithuania (11,000), and Spain (10,000), with smaller bodies in Denmark, Greece, Luxembourg, Poland, and Portugal.

4.2. *North America*

In North America settlers from Europe (mainly Scottish, English, Dutch, French, German, and Hungarian) formed several Reformed churches. The largest bodies in the United States are the Presbyterian Church (USA) (3 million members), which was formed in 1983 from a merger of the United Presbyterian Church in the USA with the Presbyterian Church in the United States, which had separated in 1861 over the issue of → slavery; United Church of Christ (1.9 million), the product of a union in 1957 of Presbyterians, Congregationalists, → Baptists, and Methodists (→ Methodist Churches); Reformed Church in America (313,000), formed by Dutch immigrants in 1628; Christian Reformed Church in North America (279,000), formed in 1857 by Dutch immigrants in the U.S. Midwest who ten years earlier had separated from the national Reformed church in the Netherlands; Presbyterian Church in America (278,000), arising in 1973 from a separation of conservative members out of the

Presbyterian Church in the United States; Evangelical Covenant Church (93,000), with Swedish Lutheran roots; and Cumberland Presbyterian Church (88,000), formed in 1810 as the result of a revival movement in Kentucky and Tennessee.

In Canada the United Church of Canada (3.1 million) brought together Presbyterians, Methodists, and Congregationalists in 1925. At the time, about 30 percent of the membership of the Presbyterian Church in Canada did not join the union; today they number 237,000. The third largest Reformed Canadian group is the Christian Reformed Church in North America (Canadian Branch) (82,000), whose numbers were increased especially by Dutch immigrants after World War II.

Many Reformed churches in Latin America, Asia, and Africa have come into being through the missionary work of these various bodies (→ North American Missions).

4.3. *Latin America*

In Mexico the National Presbyterian Church has 1.2 million members; five other Reformed churches have a total of 33,000.

Brazil is home to several Reformed churches, the largest being the Presbyterian Church of Brazil (480,000), founded in 1859 by U.S. missionary A. G. Simonton; Independent Presbyterian Church of Brazil (100,000), founded in 1903 as a schism from the former church; Renewed Presbyterian Church (57,000), formed in 1975 with roots in the Pentecostal movement; Union of Congregational Churches of Brazil (50,000), founded in 1855 by Scottish medical missionary R. R. Kalley; and Evangelical Congregational Churches of Brazil (42,000), started in 1942 by Congregationalist missionaries from Argentina.

In Argentina the two largest Reformed bodies are the Evangelical Church of the River Plate (45,000), founded in 1843 by German and Swiss immigrants, and the Evangelical Congregational Church (20,000). The Presbyterian Church in Trinidad and Tobago (40,000) is the fruit of mission work of the United Church of Canada.

Smaller Reformed churches exist in Chile, Colombia, Guatemala, Guyana, Jamaica, Uruguay, and Venezuela (→ Latin America and the Caribbean).

4.4. *Asia*

Indonesia and South Korea each have important Reformed churches. Indonesian Protestantism is rooted in various European traditions, so that there are many different churches, many belonging to a specific island or region. Of the several dozen Reformed churches, 18 have a membership exceeding 100,000. The largest are the Christian Evangelical Church in Timor (850,000 members), begun in 1947 and benefiting especially from → the revivals of 1966-69 and the influence of the → charismatic movement; Evangelical Christian Church in Irian Jaya (650,000), which arose from the work of two German missionaries who began their labors in 1855 on behalf of a → Dutch mission; Christian Evangelical Church in Minahasa (633,000), another product of Dutch mission; and Protestant Church in the Moluccas (454,000), autonomous since 1935.

South Korea, where Protestant missionaries first appeared only in the 19th century, today has almost 100 distinct Reformed churches, many the result of a series of schisms. Many Reformed churches are large, very active in spiritual discipline and prayer, as well as sending missionaries to other countries, and overall growth has been steady, if not phenomenal. The five largest churches are the Presbyterian Church of Korea (PCK) (HapDong, 2.2 million members), the original united church from which so many others arose; PCK (TongHap, 2.1 million), a branch of the church that is open to → ecumenism and that, since 1995, has ordained women; PCK (HapDongBoSu II, 669,000), a very conservative church that opposes both the → World Council of Churches and the → International Council of Christian Churches; Korean Presbyterian Church (GaeHyuk I, 634,000); and PCK (HapDongJeongTong, 611,000).

The Presbyterian Church of India (798,000), the largest denominational body in Northeast India, arose from the work of Welsh missionaries who arrived in 1841.

The Presbyterian Church in Taiwan (222,000 members), hampered by state laws regarding religion, emphatically espouses → religious liberty and human rights and has issued statements about the latter and Chinese nationalism.

In Japan in 1941 the government pressured Protestant denominations to unite, which resulted in the United Church of Christ in Japan (Kyodan). This church continues as the largest Protestant body in Japan (205,000 members). In 1951 the Church of Christ in Japan (13,000), the result of missionary work from 1872 by North American Presbyterians and Reformed, left the enforced union. Since 1967 it has made repeated statements against the new nationalism (esp. regarding the Yasukuni shrine).

Strong Presbyterian and Reformed churches joined the united churches in North India (1.25 million), Pakistan (400,000), and Thailand (69,000).

Smaller Presbyterian churches exist in Lebanon and Myanmar.

4.5. *Oceania*

The Uniting Church in Australia (inaugurated 1977, with 1.4 million members in 1999) includes Presbyterians, along with Congregationalists and Methodists. Presbyterians who did not join are now mainly in the Presbyterian Church of Australia (70,000), which over the years has become more conservative in its positions. In New Zealand the Presbyterian Church of Aotearoa New Zealand (541,000) experienced rapid growth in the 1950s and 1960s through the New Life Movement and an active Sunday school program.

Small Reformed churches exist on American Samoa, Kiribati, Marshall Islands, and Vanuatu.

4.6. *Africa*

Reformed churches are strong in South Africa. Besides three Dutch Reformed churches that trace their roots to 1652 and the original Dutch settlers — the Nederduitse Gereformeerde Kerk (1.3 million members), Nederduitsch Hervormde Kerk van Afrika (130,000), and Gereformeerde Kerke in Suid-Afrika (114,000) — the largest body is the Uniting Reformed Church in Southern Africa (1.2 million). This group resulted from the merger in 1994 of churches that pursued missionary work along color lines. The Presbyterian Church of Africa (927,000) is a black church founded in 1898 by a group of six black ministers. We also have the United Congregational Church of Southern Africa (278,000) and several other smaller Presbyterian and Congregationalist churches. All told, Reformed churches in South Africa number 4.2 million believers.

Reformed and Presbyterian churches are thriving in many other African countries. Their increase in membership over the past decades, which in some cases has been remarkable, reflects the surging growth of Christianity throughout Africa during the 20th century. We thus have, in *Angola,* the Evangelical Congregational Church in Angola (250,000) and Evangelical Reformed Church of Angola (100,000); in *Burkina Faso,* three smaller Reformed churches with a total membership of 131,000; in *Cameroon,* Evangelical Church of Cameroon (1.2 million), Presbyterian Church of Cameroon (600,000), Presbyterian Church in Cameroon (300,000), Orthodox Presbyterian Church of Cameroon (100,000); in *Congo (Brazzaville),* Evangelical Church of the Congo (135,000); in *Democratic Republic of the Congo,* Presbyterian Community in the Congo (1.25 million); in *Egypt,* Evangelical Church–Synod of the Nile (300,000); in *Ethiopia,* Ethiopian Evangelical Church Mekane Yesus (2.1 million), a thriving united church with synods and presbyteries that reflect its original Lutheran and Presbyterian roots (the latter, now accounting for about one-quarter of the total membership); in *Ghana,* Presbyterian Church of Ghana (444,000) and Evangelical Presbyterian Church, Ghana (143,000); and in *Ivory Coast,* Evangelical Protestant Church of the Christian and Missionary Alliance (250,000).

In *Kenya* we have the Presbyterian Church of East Africa (3 million) and Reformed Church of East Africa (110,000); in *Lesotho,* Lesotho Evangelical Church (211,000); in *Madagascar,* Church of Jesus Christ in Madagascar (2.5 million), the product of a 1968 union of three churches, and Tranozozoro Atranobiriky (100,000), which emerged in 1893 from a dispute between a local pastor and missionaries of the London Missionary Society; in *Malawi,* Church of Central African Presbyterian (General Synod) (769,000); in *Mozambique,* Presbyterian Church of Mozambique (100,000); in *Nigeria,* Evangelical Church of West Africa (2.2 million), Evangelical Reformed Church of Christ (1.5 million), Church of Christ in Nigeria (1 million), Church of Christ in the Sudan among the Tiv (900,000), Reformed Church of Christ in Nigeria (500,000), Christian Reformed Church of Nigeria (160,000), Brethren Church of Nigeria (150,000), Presbyterian Church of Nigeria (124,000); in *Rwanda,* Presbyterian Church in Rwanda (120,000); in *Sudan,* Presbyterian Church of the Sudan (450,000); in *Togo,* Evangelical Presbyterian Church of Togo (300,000); in *Zambia,* United Church of Zambia (1 million), which arose from a union of four churches in 1965, and Reformed Church in Zambia (500,000); and in *Zimbabwe,* seven smaller Reformed churches, with a total membership of 190,000.

There is a strong, but smaller, Reformed presence also in Botswana, Gabon, Namibia, and Uganda.

5. Unity and Diversity

Reformed ecclesiology, which bases unity neither on a superior → teaching office nor on a single representative, has favored considerable splitting, so that we often find more than one Reformed or Presbyterian church in the same country. This development has given rise to doctrinal controversies, the carrying of different traditions to churches in other lands by mission or immigration, the influence of revival movements, different approaches to political and social issues, and racial segregation in some cases. Nevertheless, an open ecclesiology that does not fall within confessional categories alone means that increasingly the Reformed churches have been able to unite with others such as the Congregationalists and Disciples of Christ and also the Anglicans and Lutherans in Pakistan and North India.

The manifestly unbiblical segregation that the white Reformed churches practiced in South Africa on the pretext of respecting differences of language and culture as a structural principle triggered intensive rethinking of the nature and task of the church among nonwhites. This debate led to the Belhar Confession of 1982, which acted as a catalyst in nonwhite churches toward the formation of the United Reforming Church in Southern Africa, which has no racial barriers.

Bibliography: K. Barth, *Church and State* (London, 1939); idem, "The Desirability and Possibility of a Universal Reformed Creed" (1925), *Theology and Church* (trans. L. P. Smith; New York, 1962) 112-35 • J.-J. Bauswein and L. Vischer, eds., *The Reformed Family Worldwide* (Grand Rapids, 1999) • R. Benedetto, D. L. Guder, and D. McKim, eds., *Historical Dictionary of Reformed Churches* (Lanham, Md., 1999) • G. D. Cloete and D. J. Smit, eds., *A Moment of Truth: The Confession of the Dutch Reformed Mission Church* (Grand Rapids, 1984) • P. Coertzen, *Church and Order: A Reformed Perspective* (Louvain, 1998) • E. Fahlbusch, *Kirchenkunde der Gegenwart* (Stuttgart, 1979) esp. "Unionskirchen," 255-62 • J. F. G. Goeters, "Die Situation der Reformierten im 19. Jahrhundert und die Entstehung der Reformierten Landeskirche Hannovers und des Reformierten Bundes. Vielfalt und Einheitsstreben unter den deutschen Reformierten," *RKZ* 5 (1983) 130-33; 6 (1983) 158-61 • *Handbook of Member Churches, World Alliance of Reformed Churches* (Geneva, 1989) • H. Heppe, *Reformed Dogmatics* (ed. E. Bizer; trans. G. T. Thomson; London, 1950) • T. Kuperus, *State, Civil Society, and Apartheid in South Africa: An Examination of the Dutch Reformed Church-State Relations* (New York, 1999) • G. W. Locher, *Die Zwinglische Reformation im Rahmen der europäischen Kirchengeschichte* (Göttingen, 1979) • A. E. McGrath, *A Life of John Calvin: A Study in the Shaping of Western Culture* (Oxford, 1990) • D. McKim, ed., *Encyclopaedia of the Reformed Faith* (Louisville, Ky., 1992) • G. Murdock, *Calvinism on the Frontier, 1600-1660: International Calvinism and the Reformed Church in Hungary and Transylvania* (Oxford, 2000) • J. Rohls, *Reformed Confessions: Theology from Zurich to Barmen* (Louisville, Ky., 1998) • D. Schellong, "Barmen II und die Grundlegung der Ethik," *Parrhesia* (FS K. Barth; Zurich, 1966) 491-521; idem, *Das evangelische Gesetz in der Auslegung Calvins* (Munich, 1968) • H. Schilling, ed., *Die reformierte Konfessionalisierung in Deutschland. Das Problem der "Zweiten Reformation"* (Gütersloh, 1986) • M. F. Swart, *The Call of Africa: The Reformed Church in American Mission in Sub-Sahara, 1948-1998* (Grand Rapids, 1998) • L. Vischer, ed., *Reformed Witness Today: A Collection of Confessions and Statements of Faith Issued by Reformed Churches* (Bern, 1982).

Joachim Guhrt

Reformed Ecumenical Council

The Reformed Ecumenical Council (REC) in 2004 comprised 38 Reformed and Presbyterian denominations in 25 countries, with approximately 12 million believers in all. The REC began in 1946 as the Reformed Ecumenical Synod, an international body that grew to some 30 members over the next couple of decades. It appointed its first permanent staff in 1963, giving it more permanence and visibility. In 1988 it adopted its current name.

Members of the REC agree to the basis and purpose of the council, as found in its constitution. The REC bases itself on the "Holy Scriptures of the Old and New Testaments, which bear witness of Jesus Christ, Savior and Lord, who is the foundation of the Church." Secondarily, the basis mentions a "subordinate standard founded on the Scriptures," which is "the Reformed faith as a body of truth articulated in the Gallican Confession, the Belgic Confession, the → Heidelberg Catechism, the Second → Helvetic Confession, the Thirty-nine Articles, the Canons of Dort, and the → Westminster Confession."

Adherence to the Reformed confessions is a distinguishing mark of the REC, although it does not specify how its members must deal with the confessions. In this way, its history is different from other Reformed ecumenical bodies, such as the → World Alliance of Reformed Churches (WARC). In its early history, most REC members refused to join the WARC, viewing WARC membership as an unacceptable compromise with some of its more liberal members. Today, though, more than half of the REC members are also members of the WARC. The REC and the WARC have had regular conversations since 1998 about areas where they might cooperate. The REC has joined the Reformed team in the Reformed-Pentecostal dialogue (→ Ecumenical Dialogue) and has placed a member on the Mission in Unity board, both of which are initiatives of the WARC.

In other ecumenical relations the REC general secretary participates in the annual Conference of Secretaries of → Christian World Communions. It is an affiliate member of the Council for World Missions and Evangelism. It sends and receives delegates from other communions at international assemblies.

For its members, the REC meets about every four years in an international assembly (scheduled in 2005 for Utrecht, Netherlands). Between assemblies an executive committee governs the council, and a small secretariat manages its business. The secretariat publishes a monthly newsletter, the *REC News Ex-*

change, in English, Spanish, and Indonesian. It also publishes the quarterly journal *REC Focus,* which carries discussion of issues within the work of its four permanent commissions: Human Relations, Theological Education and Interchange, Mission and Diakonia, and Youth and Christian Nurture.

The REC secretariat helps the smaller, emerging seminaries associated with its members through the Library and Textbook Program, enabling them to develop a solid core of resources for learning. The Leadership Development Network works to link church-nominated students and schools so its members can train leaders in the most efficient way for their most critical ministries (→ Theological Education).

The REC speaks out where its members suffer hardship or discrimination and has supported specific → peace processes that affect its members. Since 1996 the council has addressed the issue of religious → pluralism. The relationship of REC members to their governments is important, and the council provides a forum where members consult and compare their experiences. The economic development of the communities where members are found is an important concern. In 1999 the REC urged its members to join in the Jubilee 2000 campaign for the forgiveness of international debt (→ Economic Ethics). The council has a long history of a witness in South Africa and frequently discusses ethnocentrism and → racism. Other issues for council discussion have included → sexuality and the → family, human → rights, → hermeneutics and → ethics, and stewardship of the → environment.

→ Reformed and Presbyterian Churches

Bibliography: J.-J. Bauswein and L. Vischer, eds., *The Reformed Family Worldwide: A Survey of Reformed Churches, Theological Schools, and International Organizations* (Grand Rapids, 1999) • H. Zwaanstra, *Catholicity and Secession: A Study of Ecumenicity in the Christian Reformed Church* (Grand Rapids, 1991).

Richard L. van Houten

Reformed Tradition

1. Terms
2. Development of Reformed Churches
3. Reformed Christians in Britain
4. Reformed Christians in America
   4.1. Early Settlers
   4.2. Through the War of Independence
   4.3. Growth and Division
   4.4. Twentieth Century
5. Global Mission among Reformed Christians
6. Reformed Churches Today

1. Terms

All Christians share more in worldview and theology than they differ among themselves in distinctive beliefs. All Protestants and Catholics in the Western tradition rely, for example, on the theology of Augustine (354-430; → Augustine's Theology). In general use, the term "reformed" refers to all the portions of Western Catholicism that emerged in → Protestantism during the European → Reformation of the 16th century, frequently termed the triumph of Augustine's doctrine of → grace over his doctrine of → church. More particularly, Reformed Christianity represented and represents a middle way in evangelical Protestantism between, on the one hand, moderately reforming Lutheran and → Anglican communions and, on the other, the → Anabaptists and radical believers (esp. Mennonite and Amish). Reformed work and worship sought and seeks to balance deference to scriptural authority with discerning and constructive engagement with contemporary life. Since Martin Luther (1483-1546) and John Wesley (1703-91), for example, were "reformers," on occasion the communions that followed them are known as reformed. But more particularly, "Reformed" applies to the Christian leadership of John Calvin (1509-64), Ulrich Zwingli (1484-1531), Martin Bucer (1491-1561), and John Knox (ca. 1513-72) and to the Protestant communions that follow their theological perspectives.

The term "Presbyterian" arose in the 17th century among English-speaking Reformed Christians who sought to follow Scripture in → church government, providing for shared leadership between → clergy and laity, and among local, regional, and national governing bodies. They based their position regarding polity on Acts 15, which speaks of the gathering of the → elders (Gk. *presbyteroi*), and they also noted that Moses relied on shared leadership. The one church universal, they believed, appeared in different governing bodies according to geography and political boundaries. Presbyterians thus distinguished themselves from Congregationalists, who gave primary authority, also biblically based (e.g., on Jesus' word in Matt. 18:20 about two or three being *gathered*), to local judicatories. Congregationalists also eschewed bishops, such as those in the Anglican Church, in much of → Lutheranism, and in some eastern European Reformed communions.

Reformed communions understand that change is necessary and desirable, frequently citing the motto *ecclesia reformata, semper reformanda,* "the church reformed, always reforming" (or "always being reformed"). At the core of Reformed faith and practice is the confidence that the Holy Spirit inspires true believers to see in Scripture a blueprint for worship and work, a coherent pattern that the early church perceived and later Roman Catholics corrupted. But especially at first they also believed that they could transform human society so it could conform to the mandates of Scripture. The law of God, received as providing punishment for sinners and a call to repentance by the church, was also seen by Calvin and subsequent Reformed Christians as a guide for faithful living. Thus the → Sabbath, the → tithe, and other selected elements of OT law were reinterpreted to become explicit parts of the Christian lifestyle. Accordingly, the Sabbath laws were seen as applying in some measure to Sunday, and the tithe was seen as applying for the most part to monetary income.

2. Development of Reformed Churches

For the origins of the Reformed tradition, many point to the work of Jan Hus (ca. 1372-1415) in Bohemia, who sought moral and eucharistic reform based on Scripture, that of John Wycliffe (ca. 1330-84) in Britain, the preaching of Girolamo Savonarola (1452-98) in Italy, and the → humanism of Desiderius Erasmus (1469?-1536) in Holland. But most acknowledge Luther's successful reform movement in Germany as providing the basis for that of Zwingli in southern Germany and Switzerland. As Reformed churches sprang up in the nascent states, almost every one gathered leaders to write a → confession of faith or catechism. The Helvetic (1536, 1566), Heidelberg (1563), French (1559, 1571), and Belgic (1561) statements were among the early ones. The emphasis of Luther and Zwingli on God's work in providing grace, the work of Jesus Christ on the cross, and the quickening of belief through the Holy Spirit — all, they asserted, central in the Bible — became pivotal doctrines among Reformed Protestants.

Calvin refined and systematized these and attendant doctrines — that God alone was sovereign, that human beings were so flawed that righteousness could not be attained by mere effort, that God's grace alone provided redemption, and that the death and resurrection of Jesus Christ alone were sufficient for this redemption. Calvin offered insights from Scripture in lectures and commentaries on most books of the Bible, and his several editions of *The Institutes of the Christian Religion* (from 1536 to 1559) presented a Reformed worldview that influenced Christian leaders from many parts of Europe (→ Huguenots; Reformers 3.2.1; Religious Liberty [Foundations] 4).

Calvin, deeply immersed in French humanism, followed the biblical texts closely. He saw → baptism and → Eucharist both exercised in the life of → Jesus and required by Scripture for believers. He also considered → church discipline to be virtually a mark of the church. The theology of Calvin was characterized by attention to God's grace at every point from creation onward, and consequently he focused on human gratitude as the appropriate Christian response in life and worship. The Academy at Geneva provided instruction for leaders in reform throughout Europe. In the Lord's Supper, a major matter of contention among Christians of his time, Calvin did not view Roman Catholic theology, which spoke of the elements changing into the body and blood of Christ by transubstantiation, as accurately reflecting biblical teaching, but also he saw the Eucharist as more than an act of remembering the sacrifice of Jesus on the cross, as Zwingli was commonly seen to profess. Calvin, with other influential contemporaries like Martin Bucer of Strasbourg and Thomas Cranmer (1489-1556) in England, perceived a middle way, a "real presence of Christ" in the sacrament, but, in contrast to Luther, a "spiritual presence" rather than a corporeal one. And Calvin thought people could make progress in Christian living toward deeper faith and more righteousness, though only Jesus Christ offered perfect faith and life. John → Calvin's theology was so determinative of later Reformed thought that many call the Reformed "Calvinists." Most in Reformed communions, however, do not want the insights of any one person so honored and typically call themselves "Reformed."

Calvin concluded his *Institutes* with the Latin inscription *Sola Deo gloria,* "To God alone be the glory." In many ways this phrase characterizes Reformed Christianity. Other Reformed have voiced a three-part motto: "by Scripture alone, by faith alone, by grace alone" (→ Reformation Principles).

In various forms of Reformed → Orthodoxy (§2) the deep → piety and sophisticated ethic of Calvin were reduced in subsequent theology, much as the many-hued thought of Luther was reduced soon after his death. Orthodoxy focused on propositions that seemed to make sense according to the Bible and human logic. Differences concerning the sequence of God's activity and human activity in → salvation and damnation — frequently described as the → order (or economy) of salvation — gave countless parties platforms for argumentation and debate. Biblical authority could be employed on almost every side of each argument. Did God save

Reformed Tradition

people before the creation of time? Did a person have assurance of salvation? By God's grace how much could a person approach → perfection in this life or in the world to come?

Among the Dutch, a major synod at Dort (1618-19) sought to formulate essential Reformed teachings, naming total depravity, unconditional election, limited atonement, irresistible grace, and the perseverance of the saints as those essentials. For many Reformed, even today, these five doctrines summarize the major tenets of the faith. Approximately three decades later, in 1647, British Calvinists wrote the Westminster Standards.

Increasingly a "covenant theology" came to characterize Reformed thought. A "covenant of works," as voiced in God's commands at Sinai, especially in the Ten Commandments, had been replaced with a "covenant of grace" in the life, death, and resurrection of Jesus, as had been stressed by Calvin, Heinrich Bullinger (1504-75), and Theodore Beza (1519-1605).

3. Reformed Christians in Britain

The history of English-speaking Reformed Christians is here given at greater length than can be afforded the equally complex histories of communions in other parts of the Reformed world. In the British Isles Thomas Cranmer was deeply influenced by Calvin and Bullinger. In his role as guardian for Edward VI (1547-53), Cranmer oversaw the composition of the Anglican → Book of Common Prayer (1549, 1552), in which elements of Reformed theology and worship were prominent. After the death of Mary Tudor (1553-58), Elizabeth I (1558-1603) authorized the issuing of the Thirty-nine Articles (1563, 1571), which carried over much Reformed practice and theology into the Church of England. Already the Scots had received Protestantism through the teaching and martyrdom of Patrick Hamilton (ca. 1504-28), and the English encouraged Reformed thought in the struggle to wrest Scotland from France. John Knox, much influenced by the reforms he witnessed in Calvin's Geneva, helped consolidate Reformed Presbyterianism. His *First Blast of the Trumpet against the Monstrous Regiment of Women* (1558) sought the overthrow of Roman Catholic hegemony. Under Elizabeth I the Scots gained a measure of independence to develop the (Reformed) Church of Scotland, and they issued the Scottish Confession in 1560. Election of ministers by their congregations, education for everyone, and care for the poor marked their social agenda. The National Covenant of 1638 ultimately pledged Scotland to Presbyterianism.

Meanwhile in England, Elizabeth I and James I (1603-25) tried to achieve a balance within the Church of England: in pursuit of a comprehensive national church they promoted a Catholic-oriented Anglicanism but also allowed for considerable Reformed theology and practice. James I authorized an English translation of the Bible, the "King James Version," for which Reformed Christians, despite an earlier preference for the Geneva Bible, a pace-setting translation from the 1560s, soon adopted. The KJV continues to enjoy a large place in many Reformed churches. When Charles I (1625-49) tried to restore High Church Anglicanism, Scots and English, Presbyterians and Congregationalists arose to lead Parliament in calling the → Westminster Assembly of 1643, even as civil war was raging. From that assembly of divines, primarily Presbyterian, came Reformed documents that have guided most English-speaking Reformed ever since: the Directory of Public Worship, Westminster Confession of Faith, and Westminster Larger and Shorter Catechisms. The Church of Scotland adopted these standards, but under radical Congregationalist Oliver Cromwell (1599-1658), the English failed to ratify them.

With the restoration in 1660 of the Stuart monarch Charles II (1660-85), Reformed Christianity receded in England as an Anglican Catholicism prevailed, and even briefly under James II (1685-88), there was a definite move toward Rome. With James in exile the Glorious Revolution of 1688 made William and Mary sovereigns, and Britain came to combine the established Church of England and the constitutional monarchy with Reformed politics and social practice. The monarchs and Parliament provided rights for Protestant dissenters, however, and the Presbyterian Church of Scotland was made that kingdom's established church. Congregationalists and Presbyterians in England, or → Dissenters, began to cooperate constructively.

As a strategy for governing Ireland and taming Roman Catholic dissent there, James I had relocated many Scots to Ulster Plantation, the northern portion of the island. The Presbyterianism of the immigrants clashed with the religion of most of the settled Irish. At the start of the English Civil War, Irish Catholics attacked some of the newcomers, and to protect them the Scots sent troops with Presbyterian chaplains in 1641. From these chaplains came the first Scotch-Irish presbytery. With the restoration of Charles II, Presbyterians were forced to endure discrimination, and many began leaving for the New World, where Congregationalist dissidents and Anglicans had already established patterns of relative toleration, or at least had taken steps toward less oppression.

As the Church of England made a measure of peace with Reformed Christians following the revolution of 1688, Reformed identity became less discernible in the established Church of England and more obvious in the separate denominations. Especially with the → Oxford Movement of the 19th century, a movement toward Catholic worship and theology, earlier strains of English Puritanism within the Church of England receded. These earlier English Puritans (Anglican, Presbyterian, and Congregational) all upheld Reformed teaching, though differing in practice.

In contemporary Britain, the Presbyterian Church in Ireland, the Presbyterian Church of Scotland, and the Presbyterian Church of Wales continue as significant denominations. The United Reformed Church in England was formed from the merger of Presbyterian and Congregationalist churches in 1972. Various smaller denominations — the Reformed Presbyterian Churches of Scotland and of Ireland, the Free Presbyterian Church of Scotland, and others — maintain separate identities, sometimes fiercely. Over the last century, Puritan and Reformed elements have been ably promoted by figures like the Anglican J. I. Packer and the Congregationalist David Martyn Lloyd-Jones, as well as by publishers like the Banner of Truth Trust.

4. Reformed Christians in America

4.1. *Early Settlers*

The presence of Reformed Christians in the American colonies began to be felt after unsuccessful attempts to settle in Brazil (1557) and in Florida (1562). There were subsequent permanent settlements of Pilgrims and → Puritans in New England, and many Low Church Anglican settlers and some Germans were also to be identified as Reformed. Their number included Dutch in New Amsterdam, Huguenot refugees from France, and Welsh immigrants. What had begun in Europe as an international movement now constituted a patchwork of ethnic colonies and enclaves of dissenters, which ultimately formed the dominant tradition of Protestant theology in North America. The Pilgrims in Massachusetts had fled England for Holland, and then to America, expecting some degree of parish autonomy and the right to elect ministers without bishops supervising them. The more numerous Puritans frequently still held office and property in England, but they too sought freedom from Charles I, Archbishop William Laud (1573-1645), and other state and church officials, most of whom they perceived as being Arminian in theology.

By 1648 the Puritans of Massachusetts Bay and Connecticut had established the Cambridge Platform, a statement based on the religious experience of the members, who "owned the covenant." According to the platform, councils and synods have an advisory role but no legal authority in local church government.

Reformed Puritans, including Roger Williams (ca. 1603-83) and Anne Hutchinson (1591-1643), rebelled against the rigidity of the Puritan establishment. Their reading of Scripture led them to champion believer's baptism, direct promptings of the Spirit unmediated by the divines, and other departures from the "New England Way." Early Baptist congregations in Rhode Island and some mid-Atlantic colonies and some other dissenters' groups were thus English Reformed but not Puritan.

Gradually the few numbers of those "owning the covenant" led New England Reformed to institute the "Half-Way Covenant" (1662), which permitted the baptized children of believers to have their own children baptized if they affirmed that the covenant had been a part of their parents' witness (→ Baptism 3.1).

Jonathan Edwards (1703-58), arguably the most influential and profound American theologian to date, reinvigorated the classic Reformed doctrines and reinterpreted them for his day. He also helped lead a → revival in the 1740s that stretched to most colonies and connected with parallel movements in Britain. This "Great Awakening" involved Dutch Calvinists in New York, many Puritan "New Light" believers in New England, nascent Methodist dissenters from strict Anglicanism, and even some Low Church, or evangelical, Anglicans — all finding ways to reconcile experiences of Christian → conversion and doctrines of → predestination.

Meanwhile in the middle colonies, Presbyterianism began to flourish. Increasing numbers of Puritans also came to appreciate connectional government as the Presbyterians exercised it. Francis Makemie (1658-1708), an Ulster Plantation Scot merchant and slave owner, settled on the eastern shore of Virginia, where he helped organize Presbyterian congregations in the 1680s and 1690s; he later did the same on the eastern shore of Maryland and in Barbados. By 1706 Presbyterians counted sufficient believers and churches to organize a presbytery, and in 1716 they organized a synod comprising three presbyteries, with congregations in Maryland, Delaware, New Jersey, and New York.

4.2. *Through the War of Independence*

Some American Reformed Christians, both Congregationalists and Presbyterians, came to emphasize doctrinal orthodoxy, while others sought in their common practice to live more under direct scriptural authority. Presbyterians in the colonies split in 1741 between those affirming the revivals as a work of the Holy Spirit (the "New Sides") and those opposed to "religious enthusiasm" as dishonoring of God (the "Old Sides"). Historians have discerned among American Reformed then and subsequently two emphases — "head" and "heart." Many later movements, such as the revivalism of the 19th century, the missionary movement, and evangelical pietism, might be seen as heavily experiential, or "heart." Others, such as 19th-century "subscriptionism" (the attempt to make all ministers subscribe to essential tenets of Calvinism), the Unitarian controversies, and → fundamentalism, have mostly involved belief, or "head."

Most but not all of the Reformed wanted separation from Britain, so much so that George III (1760-1820) termed the Revolution of 1776 the "Presbyterian War." John Witherspoon (1723-94), a Scottish Presbyterian who in 1768 came to preside at the College of New Jersey (later Princeton University), sided with Congregationalist John Adams and others from New England to sign the Declaration of Independence. Reformed in North and South Carolina, as well as many in the Valley of Virginia and in New Jersey, were also among the stalwarts for independence.

Victory and independence in America did not at first affect the establishment of Congregational churches in Massachusetts, Connecticut, and other New England states. But where Presbyterians were present, religious disestablishment led to the formation of "denominations," separate church bodies that were self-governing and self-supporting. Gradually this denominationalism prevailed throughout the country, with Massachusetts in 1833 being the final state to cease governmental support of its Congregational church. The Presbyterian Church in the United States of America (PCUSA) was organized in 1788 and pledged loyalty to the new U.S. president, George Washington. Many Scots and Scotch-Irish Americans were unwilling to join this body, and they established the Associate Reformed Church. Numerous other independent synods and presbyteries became Reformed denominations in the early national period. In 1801 Congregational and Presbyterian leaders agreed on the "Plan of Union," according to which neither would encroach where the other had churches, pastors could move from one communion to the other, and the two groups would collaborate in missions to the unsettled West and in efforts for transforming society.

4.3. *Growth and Division*

On the frontier, in Kentucky and Tennessee especially, the "Great Revival" occurred at the turn of the 19th century. Thousands converted, frequently to become Presbyterian. Others, though, led by Presbyterian ministers Barton Stone (1772-1844) and Alexander Campbell (1788-1866) and others, soon separated to form the → Christian Church, which attempted to embrace all of Protestantism by using the Bible only and no creeds. The Christian Churches and Disciples of Christ finally emerged from this movement. This → "Restorationist" family of churches retains elements of Reformed Christianity, without the latter's propensity to construct confessions of faith.

When Presbyterians, because of growth largely from revival movements, found themselves unable to secure the services of ordained pastors, they began to ordain men from among their number, first as catechists and then as pastors. The PCUSA forbade what they termed "irregular appointments," and in 1810 the Cumberland Presbyterian Church was formed in protest. It considered portions of the Westminster Standards of 1647 irrelevant, and it advocated on-the-job apprenticeship for the training of pastors rather than graduate education.

There was collaboration, however, among the Reformed groups, including other evangelical Protestants, in movements to distribute the Bible, provide → missionaries for the unchurched frontier and other parts of the world, seek African colonies for the resettlement of freed slaves (→ Slavery), open → Sunday schools for the poor, establish colleges and seminaries for the training of pastors and other church leaders (→ Religious Educational Theory), and ameliorate the general condition of America's poor. During the early decades of the 19th century, African American slaves were frequently part of Presbyterian congregations to which their masters belonged, and gradually congregations composed of free blacks began to emerge in the PCUSA, as they did elsewhere in Protestantism.

Meanwhile among the Congregationalists, there were frequent differences in doctrine and emphases, based on variant readings of the Bible and made possible by the semi-autonomy of local congregations. → Universalists came to believe that God would redeem all, not just those who profess Jesus Christ. Free-will Baptists departed from two traditional elements in → Calvinism, infant baptism and predestination. And Unitarians, from their understanding of the Bible and from English strains of

Reformed Tradition

free thought (→ Freethinkers), stressed the oneness of God over what they regarded as the postbiblical development of the doctrine of the → Trinity. In 1825 a separate organization of Unitarians was formed in New England, drawing many Congregationalists into its congregations and seeming to dilute the Reformed nature of many who remained.

After the Civil War, Congregationalists reasserted an evangelical Christian identity, establishing in 1871 the National Council of Congregationalist Churches and between 1850 and 1890 founding several new theological seminaries across the country. Within the denomination severe differences of opinion resulted in the → Social Gospel on the one side and conservative Reformed orthodoxy on the other, although most congregations seem to have walked a middle road of "progressive orthodoxy," a term popularized by Horace Bushnell (1802-76).

Before the Civil War, portions of the PCUSA (the "Old School") gradually came to reject partnership with Congregationalists based on the 1801 Plan of Union, especially as the abolitionist movement and agitation to send freed slaves back to Africa became stronger. This group also objected to theological compromises among the Reformed that they considered a lessening of the authority of the Westminster Standards. In 1836-38 they separated from the "New School" Assembly, which favored abolition, "new measures" in revivals, and ecumenical efforts among Protestants.

Though in the late 1830s these two schools of Presbyterians were of equal size, by the time of the Civil War the rapid growth of the southern Presbyterian wing, the strength of Princeton Seminary in the north and Union Seminary in Virginia, and the clarity of its denominational vision helped the Old School outpace the New School. Interestingly, Old School Presbyterians borrowed quickly the new measures offered by New Schoolers and their Congregationalist colleagues. Over time, Charles Finney (1792-1875) and his revival successes bridged many of these differences in theology.

One major force in establishing the strength of the Old School was Charles Hodge (1797-1878), a pious and irenic professor at Princeton Seminary from 1822 to 1878. In his many writings, especially *Systematic Theology* (1873), nuanced Reformed theology sometimes gave way to what John T. McNeill terms "studied avoidance of novelty." Hodge's son, A. A. Hodge, and B. B. Warfield, who succeeded the younger Hodge at the seminary, provided additional support for a "Princeton theology" that repudiated what it termed modernism in favor of covenant theology and Calvinism.

The Civil War split the Presbyterians North and South, with most Old School state synods joining to form the Presbyterian Church in the Confederate States of America. After the war Old and New School denominations in the North reunited to form again the PCUSA, while Old School Southerners united with border synods not part of the PCUSA to form the Presbyterian Church in the United States (PCUS).

Frequently PCUSA and Congregational missionaries assisted African Americans who were already Presbyterian, so that during Reconstruction black churches grew up among slaves and free blacks in the North and South. As black, self-governing congregations grew, along with schools, colleges, and then seminaries, more African Americans affiliated with Reformed Christianity. During the latter half of the 19th century, Congregational and Presbyterian "domestic" missionaries from the United States also worked among the Native American, Spanish-speaking American, and emerging Asian American populations, and their numbers increased.

Meanwhile, significant Scots, German, Dutch, and other European immigrations of Reformed heritage led to several other growing denominations: the Reformed Church in America, a mix of earlier congregations from New York and New Jersey, with newer waves of Dutch Reformed in Michigan and Iowa especially; the Christian Reformed Church, Dutch Calvinists less ready to adapt thoroughly to American pluralism; the United Presbyterian Church of North America (UPCNA), formed originally from Scots covenanters and others in their villages; and the Evangelical and Reformed Synods of German Protestants from the Palatinate and other German-speaking areas, who settled heavily in the Midwest and did not join the PCUSA. Some Hungarian Reformed, or at least Hungarian-speaking congregations, were formed, as were some congregations where Czech, French, or Italian was spoken.

Reformed Christians of every stripe, as also → Methodists, → Baptists, and others were doing, established colleges to train leaders and generally to educate their members for American life. At the turn of the 20th century a majority of college graduates in America came from such church-related schools. Theological seminaries, orphanages, retirement homes, camps, conference centers, hospitals, settlement houses, chapels, and a host of other institutions were created and sustained to support Reformed belief and practice in the various denominations.

4.4. *Twentieth Century*

In the early 20th century, as modern culture and urbanization brought increasingly secular learning, and especially following the rise of Darwinism and of biblical scholarship that approached texts critically, many Christians developed a set of "fundamentals," seeking to rid the church of those who deviated toward → "modernism." Thus was born the term "fundamentalism." Heresy trials occurred in several Protestant denominations, including both the PCUSA and the PCUS. In Reformed circles the five fundamentals were biblical inerrancy, the → virgin birth of Jesus, the → resurrection of the body, a satisfaction theory of the → atonement, and the literalness of Jesus' → miracles as recorded in the Bible. Other Protestants included among the fundamentals the second coming of Jesus (→ Parousia) but excluded the atonement article. Successive PCUSA General Assemblies struggled to determine whether to demand explicit affirmation of these essentials. Interestingly, they neglected such stalwart Reformed doctrines as the sovereignty of God, the twofold nature of the → incarnation (human/divine), the total depravity of humanity, and the quickening work of the → Holy Spirit. In 1906, in the midst of these controversies, Cumberland Presbyterians voted to reunite with the PCUSA, and the more liberal half of that group did so. Perhaps the reunited Cumberland Presbyterians tipped the balance toward a somewhat more liberal answer to these contentious theological issues.

Presbyterians uncomfortable with the failure to require affirmation of the fundamentals formed other denominations, as for example the Orthodox and Bible Presbyterian churches. Southern Presbyterians, who did not fight similar battles in General Assemblies at that time, nevertheless held to biblical inerrancy for the most part and to a "spiritual" view of the church as a body focusing on explicit biblical teaching and not taking positions on matters of → politics.

Around World War II a flurry of changes occurred. Professors at mainline Reformed seminaries and pastors of major congregations, who had for the most part been suspicious of higher-critical methods of interpreting Scripture, holding rather to traditional, confession-oriented theology, began to teach and preach using methods of → biblical theology that took seriously the historical-critical approach to Scripture championed by German and British scholars. The theology of Karl Barth (1886-1968), Emil Brunner (1889-1966), and Suzanne de Diétrich (1891-1981), among others, offered a "neoorthodoxy" that both countered the → liberal theology that some had espoused (although others had rejected) and the conservative theology that did not confront and seek to transform culture. → Christian education, → pastoral care, and pastoral → counseling came into seminary curricula, employing insights from depth psychology, sociology, and a host of other social sciences.

At the same time, the burgeoning modern ecumenical movement drew Reformed churches into its orbit. Several significant organic unions took place: in 1931 between the Congregational and the Congregational Christian Churches, which had been part of the Christian movement emerging from the Great Revival; in 1957 between the Congregational Church formed in 1931 and the Evangelical and Reformed Church of German background, forming the United Church of Christ (UCC); and in 1958 between the PCUSA and the United Presbyterian Church of North America, which formed the United Presbyterian Church in the U.S.A. (UPCUSA). And in 1983 the UPCUSA and the PCUS merged to form the Presbyterian Church (U.S.A.), or PC(USA). These merged denominations and their antecedent bodies were instrumental in the formation of the → World Council of Churches in 1948 and the → National Council of the Churches of Christ in the U.S.A. in 1950 (→ Ecumenism, Ecumenical Movement).

As the 20th century proceeded, campaigns for → civil rights for American racial and ethnic minorities and for women drew Reformed Christians into new areas of witness and work. African Americans had long belonged in most Reformed denominations, but new emphases on the inclusion of their clergy and laity as leaders led some white resisters to withdraw from active membership. New denominations, such as the Presbyterian Church in America (PCA), formed in 1973, resisted forced integration and also championed more traditional interpretations of historic Reformed theology.

The ordination of women began for both Congregationalists and Presbyterians in the 19th century, although it was not until after World War II that women in significant numbers began to study for the ministry. Women are now present at all levels of leadership in the UCC and the PC(USA). The PCA, along with other small Presbyterian bodies in the United States, continues to reject the ordination of women.

5. Global Mission among Reformed Christians

As membership rose from the Civil War onward, Reformed Christians from America cooperated with Reformed from other countries to establish missions throughout the world. These new missions followed in the train of earlier mission efforts involving Reformed believers, notably the London

Missionary Society (1795; → British Missions 1), the Basel Mission (1815; → German Missions 1), and the Paris Mission (1822; → French Missions). This work by Americans took place largely where European colonies existed and access to indigenous populations was afforded. Thousands of missionaries went to Africa, Latin America, and Asia, even to places where long-standing Christian communities already existed (e.g., Coptic Christians in Egypt and Ethiopia, and Mar Thoma Christians in India). Euramerican missionaries built the same kinds of educational and social welfare institutions that had been developed in their homelands. In some places, such as Indonesia and South Africa, Dutch and English colonial structures supported Reformed Christianity. More frequently, as in the Congo, Kenya, Ghana, and India, colonial authorities allowed evangelical Protestants to open missions because they could ameliorate the impoverished conditions of the people. China, a special case, was only partially opened, but great energy and resources were devoted to work there because of the huge population and the perception that the country offered fertile ground for mission.

Korea was special because it had been subjugated by other countries with non-Christian religions, especially by Japan during the first half of 20th century. Reformed Christianity in Korea moved almost immediately to become self-supporting, self-governing, and self-propagating, by mutual decision of the missionaries and the early Korean leaders, many of whom died for their faith. Reformed Christians in South Korea may now be the most numerous in the world, ranking ahead of the Reformed presence in the United States, Indonesia, and South Africa.

In Ghana and other parts of West Africa, Reformed Christian churches are reevaluating, in light of Scripture, the wisdom of mission emphases, ways of worship, and personal ethics. Many have reintroduced traditional African music in worship, permitted tribal authorities to become members and officers in churches, and engaged in service activities with Muslims and adherents of indigenous religions as partners. Missiological questions are among the most important and most debated in Reformed Christianity.

6. Reformed Churches Today

A bewildering array of denominations — more than a hundred in the United States alone — either consider themselves Reformed or find Reformed Christianity in their active tradition. In a tradition that sees itself in constant reformation in the light of Scripture, it is impossible to determine how many of these denominations continue to teach and believe all the historic tenets of Reformed Christianity. Nor can accurate numbers be offered concerning the numbers of Reformed Christians worldwide. In the Netherlands, for example, about four million people are members of six major bodies of Reformed Christians, but millions more depend on these churches for spiritual guidance and for rite-of-life ceremonies. In South Korea more than six million Christians belong to four major Presbyterian denominations, and more than one million other Koreans and others in many parts of the world are affiliated with those denominations through their mission outreach. In South Africa, Dutch Reformed and Presbyterians from England and Scotland all have had significant impact on the nation, and currently more than a dozen denominations comprising several million members see themselves as Reformed Christians.

In many areas of the world, churches now independent that began as missions of particular denominations have not perceived Euramerican history and theological traditions as extremely important, so Reformed, Presbyterian, and Congregational churches have merged with those of Methodist, Baptist, Anglican, and other backgrounds. Most of the leaders in these churches see themselves as Christian in theology and both connectional and congregational in polity. A good example is the → Church of South India, which began with the union of two Reformed bodies, then united with Anglicans and Methodists to form the present denomination (→ Union; United and Uniting Churches). Others whose names reflect such wider allegiances today include the China Christian Council, Christian Church in East Timor, Church of North India, East Java Christian Church, Evangelical Church of Iran, Evangelical Church of the Republic of Niger, Protestant Church of Algeria, and Protestant Church of Senegal. Other, sometimes newer churches reflect more of their Reformed identity in their names and missions: Presbyterian Church in Cameroon, Presbyterian Church of Brazil, Presbyterian Church of East Africa (headquarters in Kenya), Presbyterian Church of India, Presbytery of Liberia in West Africa, Reformed Church in Zambia, Reformed Church in Zimbabwe, Reformed Presbyterian Church of Ecuador, and United Evangelical Church of Ecuador. Most of these bodies are members of → the World Alliance of Reformed Churches, a federation that traces its own roots back to 1875.

→ Reformed and Presbyterian Churches

Bibliography: W. M. ALSTON JR. and M. WELKER, eds., *Reformed Theology: Identity and Ecumenicity* (Grand Rapids, 2003) • J.-J. BAUSWEIN and L. VISCHER, eds., *The Reformed Family Worldwide* (Grand Rapids, 1999) • J. W. COAKLEY, ed., *Concord Makes Strength: Essays in Reformed Ecumenism* (Grand Rapids, 2002) • M. J. COALTER, J. M. MULDER, and L. B. WEEKS, eds., *The Presbyterian Presence* (7 vols.; Louisville, Ky., 1990-94) • B. A. GERRISH, *Grace and Gratitude: The Eucharistic Theology of John Calvin* (Minneapolis, 1993); idem, ed., *Reformed Theology for the Third Christian Millennium* (Louisville, Ky., 2003) • D. K. MCKIM, ed., *Encyclopedia of the Reformed Faith* (Louisville, Ky., 1992); idem, ed., *The Westminster Handbook to Reformed Theology* (Louisville, Ky., 2001) • J. T. MCNEILL, *The History and Character of Protestantism* (Oxford, 1960) • J. L. STOTTS and J. D. DOUGLASS, eds., *To Confess the Faith Today* (Louisville, Ky., 1989) • D. WILLIS and M. WELKER, eds., *Toward the Future of Reformed Theology: Tasks, Topics, Traditions* (Grand Rapids, 1999).

LOUIS B. WEEKS

Reformers

1. Term

The term "Reformers" refers specifically to the 16th-century theologians and churchmen who were associated with the beginnings of → Protestantism. As commonly used, this group includes first-generation leaders such as Martin → Luther (1483-1546), John → Calvin (1509-64), Thomas → Cranmer (1489-1556), and → Menno Simons (1496-1561) and extends (at most) to their immediate successors, such as Theodor → Beza (1519-1605) in Geneva and the authors of the Lutheran → Formula of Concord (1577). In traditional Protestant periodization, the "age of the Reformers" ends with these second-generation Reformers and is followed by the "age of confessionalization."

There are difficulties with this definition of "Reformer." There have always been reformers in the church (including 16th-cent. reformers among those loyal to the → Roman Catholic Church; → Catholic Reform and Counterreformation), so the limitation of this term to these men is a particularly Protestant valuation that contains within it a specific theology of church history. The fact that late-medieval critics of the church — such as John Wycliffe (ca. 1330-84) and Jan → Hus (ca. 1372-1415) — are sometimes included in the list of Reformers or "pre-Reformers" does not negate the Protestant orientation of the term, for these medieval reformers generally are described thus only in relation to Luther and the Protestants. A second difficulty is that although these men shared much in common, the group identification as Reformers should not mask the deep divisions among them that led to the fragmentation of Protestantism and the development of the various Protestant confessions (→ Anabaptists; Calvinism; Lutheranism).

Despite these definitional difficulties, however, the term can serve as a helpful category for a specific group of Christian leaders at an important juncture in the history of the church.

2. Characteristics

Although there is considerable biographical variety among the Reformers (→ Biography, Biographical Research), they shared many characteristics. The majority came from the urban middle class; only a few were peasants or nobles by birth. They formed an educational elite, most being educated in grammar schools and universities. Many were ordained as → priests and/or belonged to monastic orders (→ Monasticism). Most had studied → theology, which was unusual for clergy in the later → Middle Ages. Some, like Luther, were trained in the scholastic tradition, but the → Reformation in general cannot be understood as simply a development from either → Scholasticism or the → nominalism that opposed it. → Humanism in general, and → Erasmus (1469?-1536) in particular, influenced almost all the Reformers, and many were members of learned humanist sodalities.

Although Luther must not be seen as the sole font of the Reformation (→ Luther Research), across Europe Reformers of all theological convictions were influenced or spurred to action by Luther's theological writings and biblical commentaries (→ Bible Exegesis 2.1.4). Luther also made a personal impact on many Reformers as a teacher or colleague (e.g., Thomas → Müntzer [ca. 1489-1525], Andreas Bodenstein von Karlstadt [ca. 1480-1541], Nicholas Amsdorf [1483-1565], John Bugenhagen [1485-1558], and Philipp → Melanchthon [1497-1560]) or by personal encounter, for example, at the Heidelberg and Leipzig Disputations (e.g., Martin → Bucer [1491-1551] and John Brenz [1499-1570]), persuading many to opt for the Reformation movement.

There was general agreement among the Reformers on the central theological theme of justifying → faith as the gift of God's → grace *(sola fide, sola gratia),* although there were clear differences in emphasis, especially regarding the relation of → justification to → sanctification. The same general agreement applied to the recognition of the Bible as the primary criterion of truth *(sola Scriptura)* against what they considered to be the accretions of erroneous tradition (→ Reformation Principles).

In addition to these two essential theological themes, the Reformers in general also rejected several doctrines and practices of the Roman church, including transubstantiation, → purgatory, the authority of the → pope, monasticism, and clerical → celibacy. Although most Reformers upheld traditional Christian doctrine such as the Trinitarian and Christological rulings of the → ecumenical councils and original → sin, they shared a sense of restoring the church to earlier, purer forms, as modeled by the → early church and the → church fathers. Often the Reformers' sense of their own place in history was shaped by their belief that they were standing on the threshold of a global historical upheaval in which the kingdom of Christ would replace the kingdom of the dominant anti-Christian papacy.

3. Groups

Although the Reformers agreed on many essentials, theological differences soon splintered incipient Protestantism. These differences, in combination with the impact of different geographic areas, national languages, social and political contexts, and (not least) personalities, created a kaleidoscope of belief and practice among the Reformers. Beginning in the Reformation but not culminating until the period following it, these variations were unified into distinct communities and national-confessional churches. For this reason one should be careful not to draw too sharply the boundaries of groups of Reformers during the Reformation.

With this caution in mind, however, the most helpful categorization of Reformers has traditionally been to divide them into four main branches: Lutheran, Reformed, Radical, and Anglican. Geographic and political context plays a particularly important role in the major subdivisions among these branches. Because of the complexity and variety of reform in eastern Europe, the activities of Reformers in Bohemia, Hungary, and Poland are treated here in a separate section.

3.1. *Lutheran*

The most important early Reformers in the Lutheran tradition were closely connected to the university at Wittenberg. Professors like Luther, Melanchthon, Bugenhagen, Amsdorf, and Justus Jonas (1493-1555) made an impact on the rising generation of Reformation pastors and helped to give shape to the new ecclesiastical and educational system in Saxony by → visitations and → church orders. Many of them also promoted the Reformation in the cities and territories of northwest Germany and Scandinavia or held important offices — for example, Amsdorf as → bishop of Naumburg or Jonas as → superintendent at Halle. They also gave counsel to Reformation-minded princes and kings, sometimes by extensive correspondence throughout Europe. The need for educated Protestant ministers meant that university professors of theology were particularly important. This was true not only at Wittenberg but also, for example, in the universities of Marburg, Heidelberg, and Tübingen.

3.1.1. *Luther and Melanchthon*

Although it is important not to elevate Luther (→ Luther's Theology) to be the standard against which all of the Reformers are measured, in every essential area his unique spiritual insights and doctrinal positions were foundational for this group of Reformers. Luther had a similarly significant role in his relationship to secular authority. As seen specifically in his Invocavit sermons following the Wittenberg disturbances of 1522, Luther advocated an orderly, moderate reform that utilized the support of the prince of Saxony. Because Luther and his colleagues worked in conjunction with and through secular lords to implement reform, they are often referred to as magisterial Reformers, or as examples of the "princely" type of reform.

Melanchthon comes after Luther as the chief representative of this group of Reformers. A relative of the Hebraist John Reuchlin (1455-1522), Melanchthon quickly became known as a philologist and Greek scholar and was called to be professor of Greek literature at Wittenberg in 1518. In his inaugural address, "On the Reform of Studies," he called for a return to the sources and courses in Hebrew and Greek. He was soon won over for Luther and the Reformation cause. His *Loci communes* (Common Places, 1521, 1535, 1543/44, 1559) is the most influential systematic expression of the Lutheran Reformers. He also composed the chief creed of the Lutheran Reformers, the → Augsburg Confession (1530, variata 1540). As the author of philological, philosophical, and historical studies, he helped to decisively link Protestant education to humanism and was given the honorary title *Praeceptor Germaniae* (Teacher of the Germans). He was by nature a bridge-builder among the Reformers.

Melanchthon's different emphases in regard to the human role in justification and his willingness to compromise with Calvinists (concerning → Christology and the Eucharist; → Cryto-Calvinism) and with the imperial government (concerning the Leipzig Interim, a plan for ecclesiastical compromise between Catholics and Lutherans) brought him into violent collision with the → Gnesio-Lutherans centered on Matthias Flacius (1520-75), who claimed to be more faithful to Luther's original teachings. This controversy precipitated the last of the Lutheran Reformers' major statements of faith, the Formula of Concord. This document, drawn up by a number of theologians, including Martin Chemnitz (1522-86) and Jakob Andreae (1528-90), represents the conclusion of the initial period of the Lutheran Reformation.

3.1.2. *In Scandinavia*

Lutheranism spread to Scandinavia in the 1520s through German merchant communities resident in Scandinavian towns. Throughout the region Protestantism was aided by recent political changes that established new monarchies in Sweden/Finland and Denmark/Norway. The combined regional weakness of the Roman Catholic Church (all three Scandinavian archbishoprics were vacant on the eve of the Reformation) and desperate financial need inclined the new monarchs, Gustav I Vasa of Sweden (d. 1560) and Frederik I of Denmark (d. 1533), to appropriate church lands and identify with Lutheranism.

Early success was greatest in the Duchy of Schleswig-Holstein, where the preaching of Wittenberg-trained Hermann Tast in 1522 received the support of Duke Christian (1503-59), later King Christian III. The reform became official policy with his victory in civil war (1536). The church orders of 1537 and following were written under the supervision of Luther's Wittenberg colleague Bugenhagen. In all respects the personal support of Christian III was essential for the success of reform in Denmark, making it a clear example of "princely" Lutheran reform.

Although Vasa, the new Swedish king, was never a committed Protestant, his weak political position and his confiscation of church lands allowed the gradual development of Lutheran influences. Not until the Uppsala Assembly of 1593, however, was doctrinal stability achieved and the triumph of Lutheranism secured.

3.2. *Reformed*

The origin of this group of Reformers is traditionally traced to early eucharistic controversies that splintered the early Reformers in the mid-1520s. The representative figure among the early Reformed was Ulrich Zwingli (1484-1531) of Zurich. Zwingli was a humanistically trained preacher who reached the conviction of the Scriptures as being the sole source of authority for faith and practice independently from, and contemporaneously with, Luther (→ Zwingli's Theology).

Zwingli was careful to publicly demonstrate his independence from Luther, particularly concerning his understanding of the Lord's Supper. Zwingli, utilizing Renaissance humanist hermeneutics, argued that the elements of the Eucharist symbolized, rather than contained, the true body and blood of Christ. For Luther, this was no minor theological matter but represented a decisive break with his understanding both of → salvation and of the appropriate interpretation of Scripture. The attempt by Protestant-minded princes to develop a common Reformed creed failed as a result of a face-to-face dialogue at the Colloquy of Marburg in 1529 over both Luther's and Zwingli's intransigence on this point. The theological embodiment of this early Swiss reform was the → Basel Confession (1534), a Zwinglian-style formula based on the work of John Oecolampadius (1482-1531) and Oswald Myconius (1488-1552).

After Zwingli's battlefield death in 1531 defending Zurich's Protestant confession, Heinrich Bullinger (1504-75) was recognized as the leader of Zurich Protestantism. His Second → Helvetic Confession (1566) was the most thorough of all Reformed statements of faith and found approval in Reformed churches in Switzerland, Hungary, Poland, Scotland, and France. Bullinger's work is noted for both its comprehensiveness and its repeated references to the church fathers and the ecumenical creeds.

By the 1550s, however, John Calvin in Geneva came to be regarded as the preeminent leader among the south German and Swiss Reformers. Under Calvin's leadership (→ Calvin's Theology), the Reformed theologians abandoned Zwingli's purely symbolic understanding of the Eucharist in favor of the doctrine of the spiritual presence of Christ in the elements. They nevertheless maintained a clear distinction from the Lutherans on many points, including their understanding of the use of the law after salvation, the adoption of a more presbyterian rather than episcopal ecclesiastical government, and a thoroughgoing iconoclasm. These Reformers were particularly prominent in several of the Swiss cantons, the Rhineland, and some southern German towns.

Although the preceding describes the primary characteristics of this group of Reformers, there was in reality considerable variation among them. They all had to work closely with the city magistrates, without whom no church reform could have been successful. For this reason these Reformers are often considered to represent an "urban" or "city council" form of the Reformation distinct from the "princely" form typical of Lutheranism. In addition to Zwingli and Calvin, this group also includes Bucer and Wolfgang Capito (1478-1541) of Strasbourg, Bullinger and Theodor Bibliander (ca. 1504-64) of Zurich, William Farel (1489-1565) and Beza of Geneva, Oecolampadius of Basel, Casper Megander (1495-1545) of Bern, Girolamo Zanchi (1516-90) of Heidelberg, and Ambrosius Blarer (1492-1564) of Constance. Most of these Reformers were in personal contact with one another and mutually influenced one another.

No longer like the clergy of the Middle Ages did these Reformers represent the church as an → institution; they were the ecclesiastical representatives of a → city as a political and social unit. At times through marriage they made alliances with the councilors and became part of the city elite. Reformers of this type were often the ministers and preachers of especially important city churches. In their theology they took account of the civic context and stressed both the visible side of the church and the elements in church life that were tied to the community. → Church discipline was also highly important for them.

It was not until the second generation of Reformed theologians (esp. Beza and Peter Martyr Vermigli [1499-1562]) that a strong articulation of double predestination became a defining characteristic. By the 1550s Heidelberg had become an important center of Reformed theology, and it was a group of university theologians there, including Zacharius Ursinus (1534-83), Thomas Erastus (1524-83), and Zanchi, who drew up the most widely recognized statement of the Reformed tradition, the → Heidelberg Confession (1563).

3.2.1. *French Reformers*

The representative leaders of French Protestantism, Farel and Pierre Viret (1511-71), were products to some degree of the religious humanism associated with Bishop G. Briçonnet (1470-1534) of Meaux and Faber Stapulensis (also known as Lefèvre d'Étaples, ca. 1455-1536). Because of the close connection of the French Reformers to Geneva, they can be considered broadly under the heading of Reformed, although they are commonly referred to as → Huguenots. Calvin, himself a native of Noyon, France, had the greatest influence both doctrinally and ecclesiastically in the early days of the French Reformation movement. At a later stage Philippe de Mornay (1549-1623) emerged as a powerful Huguenot leader. He was a counselor for Henry of Navarre, helped draft the Edict of Nantes (1598), and founded the academy at Saumur.

The French Reformers were strongly shaped by the distinct political culture in which they worked. From the beginning they struggled against a centralized monarchy that was generally hostile to Protestantism. After the death of Henry II in 1559, this hostility erupted into civil war. Unlike the situation in the free imperial cities or the independent Swiss cantons, that of the French Reformation leaders was continuously precarious. In the earlier stages of the Reformation in France, noble supporters such as Margaret of Navarre (1492-1549) and Gaspard de Coligny (1519-72) gave credibility to the Reformed theology of Calvin and Beza.

In response to violent → persecution, however, and in particular the St. Bartholomew's Day Massacre (1572), the French Reformation took on distinctive characteristics. These included a strong devotion to singing the Psalms set in metrical French (by Clement Marot [ca. 1497-1544]) and in the development of theories of → resistance to tyrannical monarchs (as in the anonymous *Political Discourses* of 1578 and the writings of Mornay). In the final analysis the most important French Reformers may very well have been the hundreds of little-known Geneva-trained → pastors who faithfully but covertly ministered to their scattered flocks.

3.2.2. *Scottish Reformers*

St. Andrews and Aberdeen were early Reformation centers where Luther had some influence and where humanistically oriented Greek studies began. The two prominent Reformers of the first period were Patrick Hamilton (ca. 1504-28) and George Wishart (ca. 1513-46). Both had aristocratic connections and had to flee the country for some years. Both suffered martyrdom, the former for more Lutheran beliefs, the latter for more Reformed (→ Martyrs).

In his last years Wishart gained a follower in → John Knox (ca. 1513-72). Knox, a former priest educated at St. Andrews, was strongly influenced by his experience of exile to Geneva, a place he called the best "school for Christ" since the days of the apostles. It should be noted, however, that the Reformed theology that Knox imbibed was that shaped by the experience of the Huguenots with their theories of resistance and their attempt for national rather than local urban reform. Knox was a leader of the so-called Lords of the Congregation, who pursued an anti-French policy and affected the Reformation. A powerful preacher and strongly Reformed in theology, Knox instituted a Genevan-style ministry, simplified worship, provided sound education and strong discipline, and helped to draft the Scots Confession (1560).

Andrew Melville (1545-1622), perhaps the leading second-generation Scottish Reformer, had a distinguished academic career as a student at Geneva and principal at Glasgow and St. Andrews, but he made his name chiefly by securing adoption of the Second Book of Discipline in 1582. Although conflict with James VI eventually resulted in his exile to Leiden, his scholarship and leadership helped to solidify the dominance of Reformed theology and presbyterian ecclesiology in Scotland.

3.2.3. *Dutch Reformers*

Reform activity began early in the Netherlands and was met with staunch opposition by the administration of Holy Roman Emperor Charles V (1519-56). Two Augustinian monks were burned at the stake in 1523 for their Lutheran views, and many others suffered martyrdom thereafter. During the 1530s the Radical Reformation gained adherents, first in its apocalyptic form as preached by Melchior Hoffmann (ca. 1500-ca. 1543) and the Münster radicals, and then in its pacifist form as preached by Menno Simons. By the 1540s Reformed theology was assuming the dominant Protestant position.

The key individual in this process was Guido de Brès (Guy de Bray, 1522-67), the primary author of the Belgic Confession (1561). This statement of faith unified Reformed believers in the Netherlands and facilitated an alliance between Calvinism and Dutch nationalism.

Under the leadership of William of Orange (1533-84), the northern seven provinces of the Hapsburg Netherlands fought a religiopolitical war of independence that ultimately resulted in the formation of the United Provinces. Although Reformed theology was dominant, William of Orange intentionally had worked during the war against the Spanish to permit a greater degree of religious toleration than was characteristic for the era. This attitude, along with the failure to approve a uniform church order (1591), gave Lutherans, Radicals, and even Catholics the opportunity to hold their own religious services in the Dutch Republic.

3.3. *Radical*

The diverse group of Reformers categorized under the rubric "Radical" possessed certain distinctive features that marked them off from both Lutherans and Reformed. Reformers such as Karlstadt, Müntzer, Konrad Grebel (ca. 1498-1526), and Felix Mantz (ca. 1500-1527) of Zurich, Balthasar Hubmaier of Waldshut (1485-1528), as well as Hans Hut (ca. 1490-1527), Michael Sattler (1490?-1527), and Menno Simons, were advocates of radical changes in doctrine, practice, and society. Anticlerical motifs and actions played an important role among them, and they minimized or even dispensed with → sacraments. Because they did not work with or through secular overlords, as Reformers they are often contrasted with the "magisterial" reform of Luther, Calvin, and others. Radical Reformers as single figures or as leaders of communities were scattered across all of Europe but were most prominent in Switzerland, the Rhine Valley, Poland, and the Austrian Hapsburg lands. Many promoted adult believer's baptism and are known by the then-derisive term "Anabaptist" (lit. "rebaptizer").

Typology among such a diverse group is difficult, but in addition to the Anabaptists, the Radical Reformers may be said to have included also Spiritualists and Unitarians/Rationalists, although there is considerable overlap among the three subdivisions. Anabaptists advocated a voluntary, called-out church with a strong tendency toward biblical primitivism and communal understandings of the Christian life. The refusal of many of them to allow their infants to be baptized was viewed by other Protestants and Roman Catholics alike to be a shocking and execrable rupturing of the Christian social order. Political motifs were also prominent among them, including calls for social equality, the abolition of the → tithe, and the refusal to swear → oaths.

These Reformers included lay figures of lesser academic attainments and in some cases without higher education (Hut, Hoffmann). They strongly supported the belief in the priesthood of all true believers (→ Priest, Priesthood, 4) and eliminated the distinction between → clergy and laity. Often persecuted, they distanced themselves from mainline Reformation theology and what they called its new papists. They avoided the use of Latin in their writings, and with a focus on the ethical demands of Jesus and a readiness to suffer, they established their own style of fellowship separate from the national churches. Many preached a strongly apocalyptic message and expected the imminent establishment of Christ's kingdom.

Representative of the early violent and chiliastic radicals was Müntzer, who as a priest at Zwickau had contacts with Luther. Forced out of Zwickau to Bohemia, he expressed his apocalyptic expectations in the Prague Manifesto of 1521, with its passion theology oriented to the living voice of God in the depth of the soul (→ Mysticism). He then became pastor at Allstedt (1523), where he instituted liturgical reforms and demanded radical changes from the Saxon government in view of impending judgment. Coming under pressure from Luther and the authorities, he left Allstedt and formed a movement of social protest at Mühlhausen (→ Social Movements). When the → Peasants' War started in the north (1525), Müntzer took to arms but was captured at Frankenhausen and executed. His defeat, and that of similar chiliastic outbreaks such as the proclamation of the → kingdom of God at Münster (1536) and its subsequent violent collapse, cleared the way for the more peaceful radicals. Gradually the → pacifism of Sattler, as articulated in the Schleitheim Confession (1527), and of Menno Simons of Friesland (→ Mennonites) became the norm, as did also a strict discipline enforced by the ban.

Spiritualists among the Radical Reformers such as Sebastian Franck (ca. 1499-ca. 1542) and Caspar Schwenckfeld (1490-1561) rejected most outward forms of religious expression in favor of a mystical inward → piety and advocated religious toleration.

In most cases the Unitarian/Rationalist Reformers began in more orthodox branches of Protestantism and believed themselves simply to be completing the work of reform begun by Luther, but they came to reject the → Nicene Creed (and later ones) as the result of a radical biblical primitivism. These Reformers, including for example Laelius Socinus (Lelio Sozzini, 1525-62) and his nephew Faustus Socinus (Fausto Sozzini, 1539-1604), found fertile ground for activity in less politically centralized eastern Europe, especially Transylvania, Lithuania, and Poland. The most successful denominational development occurred in Poland, where, under the leadership of Faustus Socinus, Unitarians possessed an officially recognized creed — the Racovian Catechism (1605) — and a significant number of churches.

3.4. *Reformers in Eastern Europe*

Because of its unique development and extensive ecclesiastical diversity, eastern Europe is best treated separately in discussing Reformers. In the early modern period, the lands of Hungary, Bohemia, and Poland formed the core of a distinctive eastern European political order. Here nobles formed an important political counterweight to the Crown and possessed considerable local autonomy. This political dynamic played an essential role in shaping reform in this area.

In the 1530s and 1540s, particularly among the Utraquist successors of Jan Hus (→ Hussites), Lutheran reform began to gain large numbers of adherents in Bohemia, Moravia, Silesia, and the German-speaking communities of Hungary and Transylvania. Less centralized political control throughout the region meant that local nobles and town councils often had a considerable degree of independence in their religious policies. After the Peasants' War (1524-25), some of these nobles offered settlement opportunities to Anabaptist groups who were fleeing persecution in western Europe. Hut and Hubmaier arrived in Moravia in 1526. Particularly important is Jacob Hutter (d. ca. 1536), who, after Hubmaier's execution in 1528, attempted to unite the Anabaptists around principles of a pure, separatist community of believers, the abolition of private property, and collective economic activity (→ Hutterites). From the 1560s, however, the influence of the Calvinist Reformers began to be ascendant, although the Reformed theology in this part of Europe was always more eclectic and included Lutheran and Zwinglian elements.

By 1600 the majority of parishes in eastern Europe were Protestant, with Hungary a particular Calvinist stronghold as a result of the work of Szegedi Kis István (1505-72) and Melius Juhász Péter (ca. 1536-72), whose Reformed formula was the first confessional document in Magyar (1559). Under Melius's leadership the Reformed community in Hungary also produced translations of Calvin's → catechism, a Reformed order of worship, a hymnbook, and a vernacular Bible.

In Poland Reformed theology gained ground rapidly in the 1550s, in part as a result of a nationalist desire to demarcate "Lutheran" Germany from Poland. The most important Reformer among the Calvinists was John Laski (1499-1560), who coordinated the development of Polish Calvinism from Cracow in an effort to organize Polish Protestantism into a national church along Genevan lines.

Protestantism in eastern Europe was always, however, significantly dependent upon the support of local princes. In Poland a league of Protestant nobles was crushed by the Catholic king, and counterreformation followed quickly and bloodlessly. In Bohemia and Hungary Protestantism was enmeshed with an anti-Hapsburg political agenda. As a result, its followers became vulnerable to accusations of disloyalty and even of pro-Turkish sympathies. The military defeat of Protestant forces at the Battle of White Mountain (1620), outside Prague, began the rapid re-Catholization of the area, although Protestant churches maintained a position of strength in Ottoman territory and Transylvania until the later 1600s.

3.5. *Anglican*

The Anglican Reformation is unique in that its initial impulse was due to the dynastic concerns of Henry VIII (1509-47) and his desire to marry Anne Boleyn (1507?-36), not to any theological motive. Although Henry VIII did remove the Church of England from papal authority (by the Act of Supremacy, 1534) and dissolved the → monasteries of the kingdom, in many respects the Anglican Church remained Catholic. During the reign of the young Edward VI (1547-53), however, the spectrum of Protestant influences gained prominence, especially through supportive university scholars and members of the higher clergy. These foreign influences built upon the significant popular impulse called Lollardism, a movement that had reached out to the lowest social orders since the 1300s. The Lollard emphasis on lay preaching and Scripture in the vernacular had much in common with Protestantism. Thus the Anglican Reformation can be said to have occurred through a unique combination of monarchical fiat, academic reflection, and popular religiosity.

The best known of the Anglican Reformers — Cranmer, Hugh Latimer (ca. 1485-1555), William Tyndale (1494?-1536), and Nicholas Ridley (ca. 1500-1555) — all attended either Oxford or Cambridge. The twin influences of biblical humanism and Luther resulted in an early focus on Scripture and justification. Tyndale was inspired by Erasmus's NT work (→ Bible Manuscripts and Editions 3) and his call for translations but then learned principles of translation and teaching on justification by faith from Luther. The Anglicans did not accept Luther's eucharistic teaching and moved toward a Reformed view that later gained wide acceptance and found liturgical and confessional expression under Cranmer and Ridley. They followed the Lutheran pattern, however, in → church and state relations, liturgical revision, and episcopal polity. The Anglicans engaged in the usual practical reforms, for example, ending of private masses, the approval of clerical marriage, reduction of liturgical ceremony, and the use of the vernacular. The new order of service, the → Book of Common Prayer (largely the work of Cranmer), expressed these changes and served as the central unifying point in Anglicanism.

Ridley was in many ways a typical Anglican Reformer. He studied at Cambridge (1518), learned scholastic theology at the Sorbonne, did intensive study of Greek back at Cambridge, then moved to an episcopal career as bishop of Rochester and then London (1550). Ridley gave centrality to Scripture and justification, but by 1545 he became convinced that medieval eucharistic teaching was an innovation and adopted a Reformed view. He participated in preparing the 1549 and 1552 Book of Common Prayer and helped to bring Reformed sacramental teaching into the liturgy and articles. He worked vigorously for practical reform and sought to divert as much as possible of chantry endowments to schools and hospitals.

During the reign of Mary Tudor (1553-58) Protestant practices were actively suppressed, and several Anglican Reformers were executed, including Ridley, Latimer, and Cranmer. Others fled the kingdom or were exiled. Many of these went to Geneva, where they were profoundly influenced by Reformed theology.

Upon their return with the ascension of Elizabeth I (1558-1603), churchmen such as Thomas Cartwright (1535-1603) and Walter Travers (ca. 1548-1635) pressed for a more thoroughgoing reform along the lines of Geneva. Eventually these impulses would result in the movement known as → Puritanism. Considerable inspiration to fortitude was given them by *Acts and Monuments of Matters Happening in the Church* (1563), by John Foxe (1516-87) — popularly known as Foxe's Book of Martyrs — which glorified the deaths of the first-generation Protestants as martyrs. Some churchmen, such as Robert Browne (ca. 1550-1633) in *Reformation without Tarrying for Any* (1582), went so far as to advocated separation from the Church of England. Officially, however, the Elizabethan Settlement of 1559 sanctioned a moderate reform of worship (the so-called via media, or "middle way") that permitted a variety of theological understandings. The settlement had its most important theological supporter in Richard Hooker (ca. 1554-1600), whose work on → natural law was a foundational influence on John Locke and English political theory in general.

4. Conclusion

The age of confessionalization that followed the work of the second generation of Reformers was a time of continued theological and ecclesiastical refinement of the central positions outlined here. Although the Counterreformation almost completely eliminated Protestantism from eastern Europe and

France, elsewhere the work of the Reformers was thoroughly established. A new period can be said to have begun, however, in the fact that no radical doctrinal or ecclesiastical changes were advocated. Rather, the work of these theologians and churchmen was primarily directed toward the systematization and implementation of the insights of the Reformers, a truly remarkable group of 16th-century leaders.

Bibliography: General: T. A. BRADY JR., H. A. OBERMAN, and J. D. TRACY, eds., *Handbook of European History, 1400-1600* (2 vols.; Grand Rapids, 1996) • E. CAMERON, *The European Reformation* (Oxford, 1991) • R. L. DEMOLEN, ed., *Leaders of the Reformation* (Selinsgrove, Pa., 1984) • G. R. ELTON, ed., *The Reformation, 1520-1559* (2d ed.; Cambridge, 1990) • T. GEORGE, *Theology of the Reformers* (Nashville, 1988) • B. A. GERRISH, *Reformers in Profile: Advocates of Reform, 1300-1600* (Philadelphia, 1967) • C. LINDBERG, ed., *The European Reformations Sourcebook* (Oxford, 1996) • D. MACCULLOCH, *The Reformation: A History* (New York, 2003) • S. E. OZMENT, *The Age of Reform, 1250-1550* (New Haven, 1980); idem, *Protestants: The Birth of a Revolution* (New York, 1992) • A. PETTEGREE, ed., *The Early Reformation in Europe* (Cambridge, 1992); idem, ed., *The Reformation World* (London, 2000) • D. C. STEINMETZ, *Reformers in the Wings* (2d ed.; Oxford, 2001) • J. D. TRACY, *Europe's Reformations, 1450-1650* (Lanham, Md., 1999).

Lutheran: M. BRECHT, *Martin Luther,* vol. 1, *His Road to Reformation, 1483-1521;* vol. 2, *Shaping and Defining the Reformation, 1521-1532;* vol. 3, *The Preservation of the Church, 1532-1546* (Minneapolis, 1985-93) • S. DIXON, *The Reformation in Germany* (Oxford, 2002) • G. EBELING, *Luther: An Introduction to His Thought* (Philadelphia, 1970) • O. P. GRELL, ed., *The Scandinavian Reformation: From Evangelical Movement to Institutionalisation of Reform* (Cambridge, 1994) • B. LOHSE, *Martin Luther's Theology: Its Historical and Systematic Development* (Minneapolis, 1999) • H. A. OBERMAN, *Luther: Man between God and the Devil* (New Haven, 1989) • R. W. SCRIBNER, *The German Reformation* (Atlantic Highlands, N.J., 1986).

Reformed: W. J. BOUWSMA, *John Calvin: A Sixteenth-Century Portrait* (Oxford, 1988) • B. B. DIEFENDORF, *Beneath the Cross: Catholics and Huguenots in Sixteenth-Century Paris* (Oxford, 1991) • U. GÄBLER, *Huldrych Zwingli: His Life and Work* (Philadelphia, 1986) • M. GREENGLASS, *The French Reformation* (Oxford, 1987) • G. MURDOCK, *Calvinism on the Frontier, 1600-1660: International Calvinism and the Reformed Church in Hungary and Transylvania* (Oxford, 2000) • A. PETTEGREE, A. DUKE, and G. LEWIS, eds., *Calvinism in Europe, 1540-1620* (Cambridge, 1994) • G. R. POTTER, *Zwingli* (Cambridge, 1976) • M. PRESTWICH, ed., *International Calvinism, 1541-1715* (Oxford, 1985) • M. TODD, *The Culture of Protestantism in Early Modern Scotland* (New Haven, 2002) • F. WENDEL, *Calvin: The Origins and Development of His Religious Thought* (New York, 1963).

Radical: A. FRIESEN, *Thomas Muentzer, a Destroyer of the Godless: The Making of a Sixteenth-Century Religious Revolutionary* (Berkeley, Calif., 1990) • H.-J. GOERTZ, ed., *Profiles of Radical Reformers: Biographical Sketches from Thomas Müntzer to Paracelsus* (Scottdale, Pa., 1982) • K. MAAG, ed., *The Reformation in Eastern and Central Europe* (Aldershot, 1997) • R. E. MCLAUGHLIN, *Caspar Schwenckfeld, Reluctant Radical: His Life to 1540* (New Haven, 1986) • J. M. STAYER, *The German Peasants' War and the Anabaptist Community of Goods* (Montreal, 1991) • G. H. WILLIAMS, *The Radical Reformation* (3d ed.; Kirksville, Mo., 1992).

Anglican: A. G. DICKENS, *The English Reformation* (2d ed.; Philadelphia, 1991) • S. DORAN and C. DURSTON, *Princes, Pastors, and People: The Church and Religion in England, 1500-1700* (2d ed.; London, 2003) • E. DUFFY, *The Stripping of the Altars: Traditional Religion in England, c. 1400-1580* (2d ed.; New Haven, 2005) • C. HAIGH, *English Reformations: Religion, Politics, and Society under the Tudors* (Oxford, 1993) • D. M. LOADES, *Revolution in Religion: The English Reformation, 1530-1570* (Cardiff, 1992) • D. MACCULLOCH, *The Later Reformation in England, 1547-1603* (2d ed.; Basingstoke, 2001); idem, *Thomas Cranmer: A Life* (New Haven, 1996) • R. O'DAY, *The Debate on the English Reformation* (London, 1986) • J. J. SCARISBRICK, *The Reformation and the English People* (Oxford, 1984).

GREGORY MILLER

Refugees

1. History and Definition
2. Present Situation
3. Response of Churches

The church is well acquainted with the plight of refugees. The Holy Family fled to Egypt to escape the persecution of Herod (Matt. 2:13-23). Athanasius (ca. 297-373) was exiled from his diocese of Alexandria to live in far-off northern Gaul. John Calvin (1509-64) was forced to flee France, finding a home in Geneva. Cardinal József Mindszenty (1892-1975) was sheltered in the American embassy in Budapest for 15 years during the Communist era. And the Bible throughout calls on God's people to show hospi-

Refugees

tality to the stranger: "When an alien resides with you in your land, you shall not oppress the alien. The alien who resides with you shall be to you as the citizen among you; you shall love the alien as yourself, for you were aliens in the land of Egypt" (Lev. 19:33-34); "do not neglect to show hospitality to strangers" (Heb. 13:2; → Marginalized Groups).

1. History and Definition

The plight of refugees has evoked a special humanitarian response from the international community. After World War I the Norwegian explorer Fridtjof Nansen (1861-1930) was designated League of Nations High Commissioner for Refugees and given the authority to issue identity documents ("Nansen passports") to stateless persons displaced during the war.

At the end of World War II, millions of "displaced persons" found themselves uprooted by the → war, having lost their possessions as well as their home countries. The occupying powers, with support from many charitable and religious groups, set about providing assistance and new homes for the displaced and created new institutions to better carry out this work. The Office of the United Nations High Commissioner for Refugees (UNHCR) was established in 1950; the next year, under U.N. auspices, the Convention relating to the Status of Refugees was adopted. This convention, together with its 1967 Protocol, still sets the framework for the international protection and care for refugees. Today the UNHCR is one of the largest and most highly respected of the U.N. agencies.

Under → international law, a refugee is defined as a person who is outside of his or her country and who is unable or unwilling to return to it because of "well-founded fear of being persecuted for reasons of race, religion, nationality, [or] membership of a particular social group or political opinion" (1951 Convention, art. 1.A.2). Note that this definition does not include persons who have had to flee for reasons such as → poverty, economic dislocation, or environmental change. The broader term "forced migrants" has been coined to incorporate such persons as well as refugees.

For much of the cold war period, support for refugees was politicized. Western countries gladly offered refuge for people fleeing Communist regimes, notably after the Hungarian uprising of 1956 and the crushing of the Czechoslovakian Prague Spring in 1968. An enormous resettlement effort took place after the fall of Saigon, Viet Nam, in 1975; since then, the United States alone has taken in more than a million refugees from Southeast Asia. Those fleeing from comparable persecution at the hands of non-Communist regimes often had more difficulty finding safety. This came to a head in the 1980s when hundreds of thousands of refugees fleeing death squads and civil war in El Salvador and Guatemala were denied → asylum in the United States. Many churches and individual Christians responded by offering informal and extralegal "sanctuary" in their communities (→ Sanctuary 3). The matter was resolved in the early 1990s when the United States took measures to depoliticize its system for granting political asylum.

In Africa and in Latin America more generous regimes of refugee protection arose. In some African nations (such as in Malawi, with Mozambicans), the welcome was so generous that as many as a tenth of the total population were refugees. As wars and civil strife have been resolved, most of those refugees have been able to return home. Meanwhile, in the Middle East the Palestinian refugees are addressed outside of the U.N. Refugee Convention through UNRWA, the U.N. Relief and Works Agency for Palestinian Refugees in the Near East. A durable solution has yet to be found. After three generations, the four million Palestinians (in the Gaza Strip, the West Bank, Jordan, Lebanon, and Syria) remain the world's largest refugee population (→ Palestine).

2. Present Situation

As of the end of 2003 the U.S. Committee for Refugees and Immigrants (USCRI, a nongovernmental organization that produces the annual *World Refugee Survey*) estimated that there were 11.9 million refugees in the world. In addition, USCRI estimated that there were at least 25.8 million "internally displaced persons" (IDPs) — persons who have also fled persecution who would fit the refugee definition except that they are still within their country. The number of refugees and IDPs rises and falls depending on the conflicts and human → rights violations within the world and the success or failure to resolve them.

The international care for refugees involves both protection and the search for "durable solutions." Refugee protection includes the granting of refuge or asylum to a person fleeing persecution, as well as the granting of certain rights so that the refugee may live in safety and dignity. It also includes the prohibition of expulsion or return *(refoulement)* of a refugee to a territory where his or her life or freedom would be threatened. Three durable solutions are sought for refugees: (1) repatriation to the country of origin (after the situation has changed so that it is possible to return in safety and dignity), (2) local integration in the country of first asylum, and (3) resettlement in a third country.

In their flight, refugees have often had to leave everything behind and face hunger, thirst, lack of shelter, and disease. Such problems are particularly acute for women and children, who typically make up at least three-quarters of refugee populations. Through host countries, the UNHCR, and their partners, emergency care is sought for the urgent survival needs of refugees. Thereafter, attention is paid to getting refugees back on their feet and the search for durable solutions.

In many ways the world community has responded compassionately and effectively to refugee needs. Large amounts of material assistance are mobilized quickly when a new refugee crisis arises, and fewer lives are lost now than would have been the case a generation ago. Of the three durable solutions, repatriation has been the one most successfully used. In recent years there have been massive and successful repatriations to countries as diverse as Afghanistan, Sierra Leone, Mozambique, and Guatemala. In the first decade of the 21st century, there are millions fewer refugees than there were ten years earlier.

With the other two durable solutions, however, the picture is not so bright. At most, only 1 percent of the world's refugees are resettled in a given year, and then to only a few countries (notably, the United States, Canada, Australia, and the Nordics). As for local integration in the country of refuge, few nations are willing to allow refugees the exercise of their internationally accepted refugee rights such as engaging in economic activity, moving about freely, accessing → education, and reuniting with family. This failure, combined with the protracted nature of many refugee situations (USCRI reckons that 7 million out of the world's 11.9 million refugees have been displaced for more than ten years), has led to the coining of the term "refugee warehousing." All too often, refugees are kept alive but are trapped in a kind of limbo, not accorded their full human rights and not allowed the opportunity to build a new life. And in Western Europe and North America, the system of political asylum is under threat as refugees come more and more to be confused and lumped together with economic migrants.

3. Response of Churches

Churches and church-based agencies have a centuries-long tradition of caring involvement with refugees at the local, national, and international levels. Large faith-based agencies such as Caritas International, the → World Council of Churches, the → Lutheran World Federation, and World Vision work in partnership with UNHCR and host countries to provide emergency relief and longer-term care for refugees. In response to the biblical mandate to welcome the stranger (Matt. 25:35), national and local churches and church agencies help implement the durable solutions of repatriation, local integration, and resettlement.

→ United Nations

Bibliography: E. G. Ferris, *Beyond Borders: Refugees, Migrants, and Human Rights in the Post–Cold War Period* (Geneva, 1993) • A. C. Helton, *The Price of Indifference: Refugees and Humanitarian Action in the New Century* (New York, 2002) • M. E. Marty, *When Faiths Collide* (Oxford, 2005) • J. H. Schjørring, P. Kumari, and N. A. Hjelm, eds., *From Federation to Communion: The History of the Lutheran World Federation* (Minneapolis, 1997) • U.N. High Commissioner for Refugees, *The State of the World's Refugees: In Search of Solutions* (New York, 1995); idem, *The State of the World's Refugees: Fifty Years of Humanitarian Action* (New York, 2000) • U.S. Committee for Refugees and Immigrants, *World Refugee Survey 2004* (Washington, D.C., 2004). See also the UNHCR and USCRI Web sites: www.unhcr.ch and www.refugees.org • D. W. Wilbanks, *Re-creating America: The Ethics of U.S. Immigration and Refugee Policy in a Christian Perspective* (Nashville, 1996). See also the UNHCR and USCRI Web sites: www.unhcr.ch and www.refugees.org.

Ralston Deffenbaugh

Regeneration

1. NT
2. History
3. Systematics

1. NT

1.1. According to the → history-of-religions school, the NT references to regeneration derived from the Hellenistic → mystery religions, whose adherents thought that present → salvation could be achieved by cultic participation in the death and regeneration of the deity (the myth of the dying god). The NT understanding of regeneration, however, differs from that of the mystery religions. For the latter, regeneration represented a magical, ritual transforming of human nature by the inflowing of divine power at dedication. In the NT, however, regeneration denotes the incorporation of believers into newness of life in Christ (→ New Self), which is the work of God through his → Word and his Spirit.

The new life cannot be regarded as an inalienable possession of salvation. It rests on the reality of eschatological resurrection (→ Eschatology 2), which has now been actualized proleptically. It is both a gift and a task. It must show ethical results.

The term "regeneration" is Hellenistic, but its NT use is set in the context of Jewish eschatology, which derived from the → prophets and was shaped by → apocalyptic (§2). In the background is the hope of a new end-time creation.

1.2. → Paul does not normally use the term "regeneration." Nevertheless, the thought of a new creation *(kainē ktisis)* was central for him. By receiving the message of Christ through the Spirit, believers share in Christ's death and resurrection (→ Holy Spirit 1.2.3). The "old self" dies (Rom. 6:6). The new is incorporated into Christ's body (note the Adam typology in 1 Cor. 15:22). It undergoes a total existential renewal (2 Cor. 5:17). → Baptism (Rom. 6:4), the "water of rebirth" (Titus 3:5), is a sacramental depiction.

Similar to Paul in content, but more hortatory in mode, are the references to regeneration in 1 Pet. 1:3, 23. Peter gives to this threatened community the eschatological hope of an imperishable salvation on the basis of the resurrection of Jesus imparted by the Word of God and appropriated by baptism. Similar uses are found in 1 Pet. 2:2 and in Jas. 1:18.

John's writings make an even fuller metaphoric use of the ideas of divine procreation and new birth. The new birth is "of God" (John 1:13; 1 John 2:29; 3:9; 4:7; 5:1, 4, 18), or "from above" (John 3:3, 7, *gennēthēnai anōthen,* which can also mean "born anew"). Indeed, John almost exclusively uses this terminology in describing Christians as the children of God (1:12-13). Regeneration becomes a central concept of standing in Christ (A. von Harnack).

2. History

2.1. In primitive Christianity baptism was regarded as the goal and consequence of regeneration. Both materially and chronologically, it thus followed regeneration (as in Paul and 1 Peter). But already in John (and Titus 3:5) baptism can be seen as the place of generation "by water and Spirit." Early church theologians could even put baptism first, as they found in it a washing away of → sins and the conferring of the power of → immortality.

Neglect of Paul meant that regeneration came to be viewed as the function of a sacramental event (→ Sacrament) in which the → grace of God impacted our human nature. This sacramental understanding became predominant in patristic and medieval theology, and the concept of regeneration was pushed into the background by other soteriological motifs. In → mysticism, however, the birth of God in the human soul was seen as the trigger to a momentary (though not permanent) regeneration affecting only the soul, not the total person.

2.2. The → Reformers recaptured some of the Pauline understanding of regeneration (note J. → Calvin's use of *vivificatio* and *mortificatio* in *Inst.* 3.3.3, 8, 20). For them regeneration was not an isolated act on the mystical way but was a creative renewal of all life inseparably bound up with → justification. It was justification experienced individually and appropriated by faith alone. The Reformers were concerned to clarify and systematize the relation between God's gracious address and the existential achievement.

This concern lay behind the controversy with A. Osiander (from 1549) relative to the interpretation of M. → Luther's (1483-1546) doctrine of justification. A forensic exposition meant that a later act of → sanctification had to follow, which could be called regeneration (P. → Melanchthon). But regeneration might easily be equated with justification (M. Flacius). Finally, regeneration might be viewed as an awakening to → faith that precedes justification and that reaches its goal in sanctification (A. Calovius, J. A. Quenstedt). The systems of Protestant → orthodoxy constructed various orders of salvation, all of which found a place for regeneration (→ Order of Salvation 2.1).

2.3. → Pietism and → Methodism viewed regeneration as an effective, Spirit-induced transformation that involved awakening to faith, justification, and the creation of a new self. At the center stood, not justification from without, but the spiritual perfecting of the individual regenerated person, enjoying the assurance of awakening and the fruits of sanctification. The individualistic devotion of the Pietists focused on the personal experience of regeneration and ran into the danger of not seeing that social and political structures and institutions also have relevance relative to salvation.

F. D. E. → Schleiermacher's (1768-1834) doctrine of regeneration (*Christian Faith,* §§127-32), however, regarded the relation to the community as constitutive (→ Schleiermacher's Theology). Regeneration, as a personal change brought about by union with Christ, also means incorporation into the church's fellowship with Christ, in which Christians share in Christ's God-consciousness. Regeneration is the basis and commencement of a new life; sanctification is its continuation. Regeneration includes justification (forgiveness of sins, the positing of a new self-consciousness by adoption as God's children) and → conversion (§1, a turning from sin through penitence and faith). Individual regeneration is linked to there being "only one eternal and universal decree justifying men for Christ's sake" (§109.3). The regeneration of the race materially precedes that of individuals, but that of individuals displays the universal dynamic of the Spirit's work of renewal.

P. → Tillich (1886-1965) put regeneration ("participation in the New Being") before justification ("acceptance of the New Being") and sanctification ("transformation by the New Being"; *Systematic Theology* 2.176-80). Regeneration in this instance is not primarily individual renewing but "the objective reality of the New Being," which in Christ has broken in, "the state of having been drawn into the new reality manifest in Jesus as the Christ" (p. 177).

2.4. Today the doctrine of regeneration plays a central part in the ministry of the → free churches, which find in faith a personal, Spirit-effected renewing of life. In these churches 16th-century → Anabaptism, 17th- and 18th-century Pietism and Methodism, 19th-century → revivalism, and 20th-century → charismatic movements have all made their impact. Regeneration may be linked sacramentally to baptism, as in the → Apostolic churches (§2); it may be viewed nonsacramentally as a regeneration by faith, as by the → Baptists; or it may be seen as endowment with the Spirit, as in the → Pentecostal churches.

3. Systematics

Regeneration is an excellent → metaphor for God's sovereign action through his Word and his Spirit by which he grants the participation in the eschatological reality of the resurrection, which radically changes the orientation and meaning of → life. The reference to regeneration expresses an important aspect of the Christian hope of salvation. The danger is that it will cease to be treated as a metaphor or → analogy and be given a static objectivity, being equated either with the single act of conversion (the Pietist reduction) or with baptism (the sacramental reduction). If individualized and interiorized in this way, it can easily lose both its universal historical dimension and its orientation (stressed esp. in Matt. 19:28, "the renewal of all things") to the new, end-time creation of heaven and earth that we still await. This orientation is one of the most important advantages of the Christian model of regeneration as compared with the doctrines of → reincarnation that other religions and philosophies espouse.

→ Immortality

Bibliography: ER 19/3 (1967) special issue on conversion • W. G. McLoughlin, *Revivals, Awakenings, and Reform* (Chicago, 1978) • O. H. Pesch, *Frei sein aus Gnade. Theologische Anthropologie* (Freiburg, 1983) • O. H. Pesch and A. Peters, *Einführung in die Lehre von Gnade und Rechtfertigung* (Darmstadt, 1981) • S. M. Powell and M. E. Lodahl, eds., *Embodied Holiness: Toward a Corporate Theology of Spiritual Growth* (Downers Grove, Ill., 1999) • W. T. Purkiser, P. M. Bassett, and W. M. Greathouse, *Exploring Christian Holiness* (2 vols.; Kansas City, Mo., 1983-85) • P. Toon, *Born Again: A Biblical and Theological Study of Regeneration* (Grand Rapids, 1987).

Reinhold Bernhardt

Regula fidei → Rule of Faith

Rehabilitation

1. Term and General Survey
2. Restorative Justice

1. Term and General Survey

The term "rehabilitation," for which "resocialization" is often used as a synonym, is a central one in social work (→ Social Services); it refers to the reincorporating of those who have been guilty of misconduct into → society and its → norms and → values. In the process it is often overlooked that values and norms are also socially conditioned and mediated and that there may also be social causes for individual misconduct.

Legally, resocialization describes the goal of remedial punishment. The point here is that prisoners are viewed as suffering from severe problems socially and that bringing them back into free social life is the aim of their treatment in prison. Rehabilitation is thus a form of → socialization, the process by which individuals make their own the norms, values, orientation, and modes of conduct of the group to which they belong. If this is the aim of → punishment, then concepts such as retribution, deterrence, and repayment are no longer relevant (→ Guilt).

On this view the focus is no longer on the misdeed but on the one who did it. Physical punishment and capital sentences would thus be replaced by correction, as for the idle, vagrants, and youthful thieves at Amsterdam (for the first time) in 1596. For their own good, these persons were forced with a "hard hand" to work. A more liberal practice replaced the hard hand in the 19th century, a change based theoretically on the dignity of the autonomous individual (→ Autonomy; Enlightenment; Human Dignity). When it was discovered that severe psychological damage was often being done through the punishments exacted, movements of reform resulted.

At the end of the 19th century Franz von Liszt (1851-1919) proposed that instead of retribution there should be an understanding (if compulsory) treatment aiming at amendment and reintegration (special prevention). G. Radbruch (1878-1949) then spoke in terms of educational punishment (→ Resistance, Right of, 1.1). In contrast, rehabilitation stresses the social relations of offenders, recognizing that there can be no reincorporation into society if these relations are ignored. Consistent with this approach is the principle of the social → state, which presupposes the view that even prisoners, who have basic human → rights, have a claim to legal protection. These principles promote rehabilitation by demanding suitable treatment, support for personality development (→ Self), and social integration by the formation of work habits, education, and social training. In the process the help of religious and humanitarian groups is desirable, especially at the time of release (→ Prison Ministry). Such aid has usually been available.

A common theme of discussion today is whether resocialization, even for the protection of society itself, would not in most cases be better achieved by measures that do not involve incarceration and the taking away of social liberties. Fines and probation are means that may increasingly be used to this end.

Bibliography: A. Bandura, *Social Learning Theory* (Englewood Cliffs, N.J., 1977) • G. A. Bernfeld, D. P. Farrington, and A. W. Leschied, eds., *Offender Rehabilitation in Practice: Implementing and Evaluating Effective Programs* (New York, 2001) • E. Lask, G. Radbruch, and J. Dabin, *The Legal Philosophies of Lask, Radbruch, and Dabin* (trans. K. Wilk; Cambridge, Mass., 1950) • S. Maruna and R. Immarigeon, eds., *After Crime and Punishment: Pathways to Offender Reintegration* (Portland, Oreg., 2004) • T. P. O'Connor and N. J. Pallone, eds., *Religion, the Community, and the Rehabilitation of Criminal Offenders* (New York, 2002) • G. Radbruch, "Der Erziehungsgedanke im Strafwesen," *Der Mensch im Recht* (Göttingen, 1957) 50-62.

Helga Einsele†

2. Restorative Justice

One of the most interesting new developments with respect to rehabilitative efforts is the spread of "restorative justice" approaches. Restorative justice, with its roots in Aboriginal practice and philosophy, has gained international recognition and momentum in the latter part of the 20th century. Three principles are central to this approach: the injustice of crime is viewed as primarily a violation of persons (victims, the community, and the offender) and of relationships among them (→ Self) and only secondarily of the → state and the law; justice seeks to repair the harm rather than to punish (→ Punishment); and justice is best carried out by collaboration among all stakeholders — victims, community, and offender — and not just by criminal justice professionals.

This approach takes many forms, including community resolution teams, family conferencing, victim-offender mediation, sentencing circles, and others. The majority of cases have so far dealt with juvenile crimes, although adult crime is increasingly being handled in this manner. Criticisms of this approach have been raised by victims who perceive restorative justice as "offender driven" and who argue that it fails to recognize that "healing" may not always be possible.

→ Forgiveness; Prison Ministry

Bibliography: J. Consedine, *Restorative Justice: Healing the Effects of Crime* (2d ed.; Lyttleton, N.Z., 1995) • B. Galaway and J. Hudson, eds., *Restorative Justice: International Perspectives* (Monsey, N.Y., 1996) • P. McCold, *Restorative Justice: An Annotated Bibliography* (Monsey, N.Y., 1997) • T. R. Snyder, *The Protestant Ethic and the Spirit of Punishment* (Grand Rapids, 2001) • H. Zehr, *Changing Lenses: A New Focus for Crime and Justice* (Scottsdale, Pa., 1990); idem, *The Little Book of Restorative Justice* (Intercourse, Pa., 2002).

T. Richard Snyder

Reign of God → Kingdom of God

Reincarnation

1. Term
2. History of Religion

1. Term

The term "reincarnation" refers to doctrines of transmigration, which speak of the passage of the soul after death into another body (i.e., metempsychosis) or the migration of different souls into one body (metensomatosis). Transmigration may take place in the present world or in some future world.

What is reincarnated may be the personal → self or the spirit of the ancestors.

2. History of Religion

2.1. From the very beginning of religious history, belief in reincarnation found a place in many religions. It was part of the cult of ancestors among the Egyptians, the Germans, and the Celts (→ Ancestor Worship; Egyptian Religion), who believed that the dead would find reincarnation among their successors. We still find the same belief in central Australia and West Africa.

Among the Hindus (→ Hinduism) the doctrine of samsara refers to the successive transmigrations of souls *(jīva)*. This belief is closely linked to the doctrine of → karma, which holds that what was done in the past, in this or previous lives, measured by the law of cosmic dharma (i.e., duty), will determine one's state in the future life. The goal is to break free from the "cycle of reincarnation" and hence from the world as the place of suffering and uncertainty.

→ Buddhism contests the existence of a soul that survives → death. The stream of conscious life that feeds on karma leads on to a new being.

The Greek Pythagoreans and Orphics (→ Greek Philosophy), followed by Plato (427-347; → Platonism), believed that an immortal soul *(psychē)* is imprisoned in the human body and the material world. The soul is seeking redemption from all carnal desires by way of a chain of animal and human metensomatoses that has as its goal "the philosophical life," marked particularly by a vision of pure ideas.

2.2. The theologians of the → early church condemned the doctrine of reincarnation (although → Origen did speak of the preexistence and ensomatosis of the soul; → Origenism 2.3), but it reemerged at the time of the → Renaissance and was part of the esoteric teaching of the → Rosicrucians and the Freemasons (→ Masons). It also found new life among the German classical and → Romantic writers (esp. G. E. Lessing, J. G. → Herder, J. Goethe, B. Kleist, and Novalis). From these writers it passed over into → anthroposophy.

These sources, along with encounter with Eastern religions, have given it a place in the so-called → new religions of our time (→ New Age; Theosophy). In these instances it is viewed positively, offering opportunity for both individual and collective development.

2.3. Belief in reincarnation involves a cyclic view that differs from that of Judeo-Christian faith, with its concept of the historical uniqueness of → life and its → hope of physical → resurrection after death. Nevertheless, in some places belief in reincarnation holds a considerable attraction also for Christians. In a European poll reported in 1986, over 20 percent of those canvassed accepted it (R. Friedli, 20-26). One reason for this attraction is that the belief offers an explanation of existing inequalities, of the contingency of fate (→ Happiness), and of innocent → suffering, thus leaving no scope for the issue of → theodicy. It also demands → reverence for all the creatures in which the soul might find a temporary home. Furthermore, it can be a powerful impulse toward ethical action, even if ultimately one's own interests lie behind this action.

Bibliography: M. von Brück, *The Unity of Reality: God, God-Experience, and Meditation in the Hindu-Christian Dialogue* (New York, 1991) 212-34 • S. Davis, ed., *Death and Afterlife* (New York, 1989) • M. Eliade, *Rites and Symbols of Initiation: The Mysteries of Birth and Rebirth* (New York, 1965) • R. Friedli, *Zwischen Himmel und Hölle. Die Reinkarnation* (Freiburg, 1986) • G. Greshake, *Gottes Heil–Glück des Menschen* (Freiburg, 1983) 226-44; idem, *Tod, und dann? Ende, Reinkarnation, Auferstehung. Der Streit der Hoffnungen* (2d ed.; Freiburg, 1990) • H. Häring and J. B. Metz, eds., *Reincarnation or Resurrection?* (Edinburgh, 1993) • R. Hummel, *Reinkarnation. Der Glaube an die Wiedergeburt* (2d ed.; Freiburg, 1989) • H. Küng, *Eternal Life? Life after Death as a Medical, Philosophical, and Theological Problem* (Garden City, N.Y., 1984) 59-65 • H. Küng et al., *Christianity and the World Religions: Paths of Dialogue with Islam, Hinduism, and Buddhism* (Garden City, N.Y., 1986) 230-40 • G. MacGregor, *Reincarnation in Christianity: A New Vision of the Role of Rebirth in Christian Thought* (Wheaton, Ill., 1978) • J. Moltmann, *The Spirit of Life: A Universal Affirmation* (Minneapolis, 2001) chap. 7, "The Rebirth to Life" • L. Näreaho, *Rebirth and Personal Identity: A Philosophical Study on Indian Themes* (Helsinki, 2002) • L. Scheffczyk, *Die Reinkarnationslehre in der altchristlichen Literatur* (Munich, 1985) • C. Schönborn, *From Death to Life: The Christian Journey* (San Francisco, 1995) • I. Stevenson, *Where Reincarnation and Biology Intersect* (Westport, Conn., 1997).

Reinhold Bernhardt

Relativism

1. Epistemological
2. Normative-Ethical
3. Criticism
4. In Theology

The term "relativism" came into vogue with the increasing importance of → historicism at the end of the 19th century. It reflects insight into the fact that our theoretical and practical dealings with the world are conditioned historically, culturally, socially, economically, politically, and anthropologically. Relativism, then, contests the view that we have objective and universally valid criteria by which to say that our theoretical knowledge or moral action is true or right. True knowledge, action, or even being, it claims, cannot be absolutely regarded as the expression of a universal idea or as deriving from pure → reason, as taught in the system of G. W. F. Hegel (1770-1831; → Hegelianism). Rather, they are relative to mutable cultural and historical factors. Relativism is extremely critical of → metaphysics. We find several different forms of relativism.

1. Epistemological

Epistemological relativism states that everything we know is relative to the knowing subject, so that in principle there can be no self-existent, objective, and generally accessible reality (→ Subjectivism and Objectivism).

1.1. This epistemological relativism may take a critical form. In this case it doubts whether we can adopt any unchanging and absolute standpoint as regards knowledge — whether, then, we can know true being. Relativism of this kind dates from antiquity (esp. the Sophists and other skeptics; → Greek Philosophy). In opposition to the understanding of → truth in → Platonism and → Aristotelianism, which posited agreement of thought with what is assumed to be true, this approach led to a gradual detaching of the criterion of truth from being, and for this reason any systems with this tendency (such as → nominalism, → Cartesianism, or → empiricism) might be called relativistic.

Nevertheless, up to the 20th century these same philosophical systems sought to find a criterion of truth in the subject instead. This orientation to the subject, in a transcendental transformation, is plainest in I. Kant (1724-1804; → Kantianism; Transcendentalism). Objectivity here simply guarantees the way in which objects are present in the human consciousness.

The further historicizing of both the subject and the "objective" world, which Hegel began and W. Dilthey (1833-1911) and F. → Nietzsche (1844-1900) continued, finally did away with any possible categories of congruence. A → hermeneutics that modestly does not make epistemological claims does not now try to explain the "world" metaphysically but seeks instead to grasp the actual world of being and knowledge without reference to any objective criterion.

1.2. *Linguistic relativism* opposes the idea that → language is an instrument of knowledge mirroring the objective world. Language, it says, constantly develops, so that the words used cannot carry any fixed and unequivocal meaning. Rather, the logical structure and sociocultural development of language can form and construct only some specific reality. On this point widely divergent writers like W. von Humboldt (1767-1835), L. Wittgenstein (1889-1951), and B. L. Whorf (1897-1941) all agree.

1.3. *Scientific relativism*, advocated especially by P. Duhem (1861-1916), T. Kuhn (1922-96), and P. Feyerabend (1924-94), opposes the assumption that we can know objective facts and data by using some "true" method to investigate them. The scientific community, whose paradigms are subject to historical change, itself defines what may be accepted as an "objective" interpretation of these facts and theories. In this sense, then, "objectivity" does not correspond to any metaparadigmatic reality but is always only the result of the historical development of theory.

2. Normative-Ethical

Normative-ethical relativism states that all moral and ethical norms are relative to a given → culture and history. There are no values or norms that are intrinsically valid for all subjects and cultures.

2.1. *Cultural relativism* takes the view that accepted moral norms and values are all culture related and might be rejected in some other culture. Individuals are normatively bound only by what their own culture demands. As we see most clearly in M. J. Herskovits (1895-1963), we must thus reject the ethnocentric thesis that interculturally valid norms exist and must show → tolerance for alien norms.

2.2. *(Meta-)ethical relativism* argues that we cannot decide rationally which of many possibly contradictory moral principles to prefer (→ Ethics; Metaethics). Behind this view stands the point that Kant was already making and that M. → Weber (1864-1920) regarded as basic, namely, that imperatives have their own validity and are not to be derived from indicatives. Relativist positions such as decisionism (C. Schmitt), legal positivism (H. Kelsen; → Law and Legal Theory), and American → pragmatism (W. James, R. Rorty) largely appeal to Weber.

3. Criticism

The ultimate insight of any relativism that understands itself as a scientific theory — namely, that ultimate insights are not possible — is self-contradictory as an epistemological theory insofar as that which it asserts is negated in the assertion itself (→ Logic). The normative implications — for example, as regards the relation between tolerance and intolerance or the ethically limited validity of → human dignity (Herskovits; → Minorities) — are questionable for similar reasons.

4. In Theology

The theological discussion of relativism at the beginning of the 20th century, which E. → Troeltsch (1865-1923) closely linked to the issue of philosophical historicism and to the attempt to mediate between this position and dogmatism, involved the question whether "history can lead to any result that can serve as a basis for → faith" (R. Bultmann [1884-1976]). If it can, then we must assume that there is in all of us the basis of the possibility of the knowledge of God and faith, as Hegel and F. D. E. → Schleiermacher taught (1768-1834; → Schleiermacher's Theology) with reference to a religious a priori.

→ Dialectical theology, however, vehemently rejected this position as one that "confused revelation and history" (E. Brunner). "We can attain to God only as we let go of everything relative" (Brunner). If we do not, then → theology falls prey to the destructive forces of historical and psychological relativism (K. → Barth). Here we see the tasks, but also the difficulties, that confront Christian theology. On the one side, recourse to God is a constitutive basis for the possibility of speaking about him. On the other hand, all we say about God and all dogmatic systems are relative because they are still a matter of finite human knowledge and are subject to the impact of the linguistic, cultural, and intellectual context. We may speak about what is → absolute, but we can do so only in a finite and historically mediated way.

Bibliography: N. Behnegar, *Leo Strauss, Max Weber, and the Scientific Study of Politics* (Chicago, 2003) esp. chaps. 1-2 • R. Boudon, "Should We Believe in Relativism?" *Wege der Vernunft* (Tübingen, 1991) 113-29 • E. Brunner, *Erlebnis, Erkenntnis und Glaube* (Tübingen, 1921) • R. Bultmann, "Liberal Theology and the Latest Theological Movement," *Faith and Understanding* (vol. 1; New York, 1969) 28-52 • P. E. Devine, *Relativism, Nihilism, and God* (Notre Dame, Ind., 1989) • W. Dilthey, *The Formation of the Historical World in the Human Sciences* (Princeton, 2002; orig. pub., 1910) • R. P. Farrell, *Feyerabend and Scientific Values: Tightrope-Walking Rationality* (Dordrecht, 2003) • N. Goodman, *Ways of Worldmaking* (Indianapolis, 1978) • M. J. Herskovits, *Cultural Relativism* (New York, 1973) • S. Lukes, *Liberals and Cannibals: The Implications of Diversity* (London, 2003) • J. W. Meiland and M. Krausz, eds., *Relativism, Cognitive and Moral* (Notre Dame, Ind., 1982) • T. Rendtorff, "Religion 'nach' der Aufklärung," *Religion als Problem der Aufklärung* (ed. T. Rendtorff; Göttingen, 1980) 185-201 • R. Rorty, *Contingency, Irony, and Solidarity* (Cambridge, 1989) • H. Siegel, *Relativism Refuted: A Critique of Contemporary Epistemological Relativism* (Dordrecht, 1987) • E. Troeltsch, *Der Historismus und seine Probleme* (Tübingen, 1922) • M. Weber, "'Objectivity' in Social Science and Social Policy" (1904), *Readings in the Philosophy of Social Science* (ed. M. Martin and L. C. McIntyre; Cambridge, Mass., 1994) 535-46.

Herbert Hanreich

Relativity Theory

1. Galilean Relativity
2. Special Theory of Relativity
3. General Theory of Relativity
4. Cosmological Implications

The theories of relativity arise from the study of the motion of objects in space and time, particularly from the fact that such motion may be viewed by observers who themselves might be in a state of motion. The result of this study has been three related and far-reaching theories, which provide the deepest picture yet of the nature of physical space and time.

1. Galilean Relativity

Galileo Galilei (1564-1642) was the first to state the "principle of relativity," which asserts that the state of rest and any state of uniform translational motion are indistinguishable for an experimenter lacking reference to external observations. He offered this principle as a defeater for the claim that the motion of the earth on its axis, and around the sun, would give rise to obvious perceptible consequences. In a very appealing and convincing thought experiment, he wrote, "Shut yourself up with some friend in the main cabin below decks on some large ship, and have with you there some flies, butterflies, and other small flying animals. Have a large bowl of water with some fish in it; hang up a bottle that empties drop by drop into a wide vessel beneath it. With the ship standing still, observe carefully how the little animals fly with equal speed to all sides of the cabin. The fish swim

Relativity Theory

indifferently in all directions; the drops fall into the vessel beneath; and, in throwing something to your friend, you need throw it no more strongly in one direction than another, the distances being equal; jumping with your feet together, you pass equal spaces in every direction. When you have observed all these things carefully (though there is no doubt that when the ship is standing still everything must happen in this way), have the ship proceed with any speed you like, so long as the motion is uniform and not fluctuating this way and that. You will not discover the least change in all the effects named, nor could you tell from any of them whether the ship was moving or standing still" (pp. 186-87).

This principle of the "relativity of motion" has come to be generally accepted, even though it is not philosophically obvious a priori, since the parallel instance of uniform rotational motion is certainly detectable (via obvious "centrifugal" effects), even for an experimenter in an environment closed off from external references. The Galilean principle of relativity is incorporated into Newtonian mechanics via Newton's first law of motion, and nothing in experimental physics or in the later theories of relativity associated with the name of Albert Einstein (1879-1955) has arisen to contradict it.

2. Special Theory of Relativity

J. C. Maxwell's (1831-79) electromagnetic theory of light, which appears to predict an absolute (rather than a relative) speed for light, would nevertheless seem to be in conflict with the relativity principle. This tension was resolved in 1905 by Einstein's special theory of relativity, which preserves the Galilean relativity principle and all the successes of Maxwell's theory of light, at the cost of revising Newtonian views of the nature of space and time. In particular, Einstein's theory controverts the view of time implicit in Newton's axiom that "absolute, true, and mathematical time, of itself, and from its own nature, flows equably without relation to anything external," substituting for it the view that for each uniformly moving observer there is a particular set of time-and-space coordinates, differing from the coordinates assigned by another observer in relative motion, but equally legitimate as a basis for the study of physics.

The special theory of relativity might be counterintuitive, but its concrete predictions have been abundantly verified. One of the first confirmations of the theory came from its retrospective explanation of the negative results of the Michelson-Morley experiment of 1888, which had failed to find any evidence of the motion of the earth relative to the "luminiferous ether" previously postulated. The theory also led, via the famous relation $E = mc^2$, to the confirmation of the interconvertibility of mass and energy. The theory's predictions for the behavior of objects moving at speeds comparable to that of light have also passed all experimental tests. The most famous of these predictions is the so-called twin paradox, which states that persons who separate from each other at equal age may reunite to find themselves of differing ages if during their separation they have been traveling on different journeys. This prediction has been confirmed not only for elementary particles, which age more slowly when moving at nearly the speed of light, but also for macroscopic objects as ordinary as atomic clocks, whose high accuracy permits the differential-aging effect to be detected using ordinary aircraft speeds.

It is often thought that the special theory implies that "everything is relative," but this is assuredly not its prediction. So far from having anything to say about moral → relativism, the theory's implications lie within physics and center on those features of objective reality that are observer-independent. For example, while the time ordering of two events occurring at distinct points in space may be observer-dependent, the special theory of relativity nevertheless does preserve all cause-and-effect relationships, asserting that if event E is the cause of result R (and thus precedes it in time) according to one observer's viewpoint, then the cause will also precede the effect according to any other (moving) observer's timescale (→ Causality).

3. General Theory of Relativity

The special theory of relativity has been extended to cover cases of accelerated, as well as uniform, relative motion, and it leads to a relativistic mechanics that supplants Newtonian mechanics (though the relativistic theory reduces, as it must for consistency, to the Newtonian theory in cases of motions with speeds small compared to the speed of light).

But there remains the separate question of Newtonian gravitational theory, which was famously corrected by Einstein's general theory of relativity. This is not only a theory of space and time (consistent with special relativity) but also a theory of matter and the gravitational effects it produces. It is not the only theory of gravitation consistent, in the proper limiting cases, with Newtonian gravitation and with special relativity, but it is the simplest and most elegant of such theories to survive contact with experimental tests. The characteristic interpretation of the general theory is that it predicts that space-time is curved (in a precisely defined mathematical sense) in the vicinity of massive objects, and that the effects ascribed in a Newtonian outlook to gravitational forces can be reinterpreted as due to the motion of bodies through this curved space-time. Another prediction of the theory is that gravitational influences are propagated through space not instantaneously but at the same universal limiting speed that light itself exhibits. Under the proper conditions, variations in the character of space-time called gravitational waves are predicted to be able to propagate, and indirect confirmation of their actual existence and of their ability to carry energy has indeed been obtained.

Independent of such a "curved space-time" interpretation, the general theory of relativity also makes other concrete experimental predictions, and several kinds of these predictions have been extensively and precisely tested by terrestrial and solar-system experiments and observations. The special and general theories of relativity have come to have even industrial significance, in that widely used satellite-based position-finding systems such as the Global Positioning System depend, in an engineering sense, on the use of Einstein's theories for their correct design and operation.

4. Cosmological Implications

The general theory of relativity is also the basis of modern cosmological theories and is incorporated into the description of the universe's present expansion and past state of high density. The validity of general relativity, together with observed features of the present universe, allow one to infer that there is a "singularity" in the past history of the universe, which entails the existence of only a finite duration of past physical time. This feature is captured in "big bang" theories of the formation of space, time, and matter in the universe, which are thus curiously consistent with the theological position of → creation ex nihilo.

The general theory of relativity, combined with astrophysical theories of stellar development, predicts that a possible destiny of massive stars is to evolve into black holes, and there is good, though still indirect, evidence of their existence in our galaxy. General relativity is also involved in the interpretation of the massive object at the center of our galaxy, almost certainly a very massive black hole. Finally, general relativity is also part of the basis for understanding the long-term future of the physical universe. The present understanding is that the universe on the largest scale is represented by a flat space-time, destined to expand indefinitely into the distant future. The theological connections, if any, of this outlook to → eschatology are still unclear.

→ Science and Theology

Bibliography: G. Galilei, *Dialogue concerning the Two Chief World Systems–Ptolemaic and Copernican* (2d ed.; Berkeley and Los Angeles, 1967; orig., 1632) • N. D. Mermin, *Space and Time in Special Relativity* (New York, 1968) • C. W. Misner, K. S. Thorne, and J. A. Wheeler, *Gravitation* (San Francisco, 1973) • H. C. Ohanian, *Gravitation and Spacetime* (New York, 1976) • C. M. Will, *Was Einstein Right? Putting General Relativity to the Test* (New York, 1986).

David A. Van Baak

Relics

1. Christian History
2. Church Regulations
3. Motives
4. Piety

In religion relics (Gk. *leipsana,* Lat. *reliquiae*) are artifacts that are related to deceased saints and that are venerated as a result. First we have bodily parts, then objects they touched, such as portions of silk or cloth *(brandea)* or mantles *(palliola),* then things connected with their graves (*eulogia, hagiasmata,* e.g., dust from the grave). We find veneration of relics in → Egyptian and → Greek religion, as well as in → Buddhism and → Islam.

1. Christian History

In the Christian world the development and understanding of relics was closely linked to the veneration of → saints. At first this practice was connected with the graves of → martyrs, from which they might exert power. Churches thus placed value on their corpses (*Mart. Pol.* 18.2) and, from the early third century, attributed → healing power to them (*Acts Thom.* 170). Since areas that had few martyrs wanted a share in this power, the bodies in the East were shared, or "translated," from one place to another (from 354 onward), and in the West the custom developed of putting cloths on the graves to give them a share in the power (6th cent.). A search for forgotten martyrs' graves also began in all the relevant regions.

As veneration of relics became more intense, it came under private patronage. Helena (ca. 255-ca. 330), Charlemagne (768-814), and the → Crusaders did much to foster it. Abuses were unavoidable, as for example, in magical understanding (the seeking of → miracles; → Magic), quantitative thinking (which led to collections of relics from the 4th cent.), absurdities (Mary's milk), and also thefts, deceptions, trading, and even war. Legislators (Codex Theodosianus 9.17.7) and theologians (Vigilantius in the 5th cent., Claudius of Turin in the 8th, Guibert of Nogent in the 11th, and Nicholas of Cusa in the 15th) opposed such abuses.

Pioneers of the → Reformation (J. → Wycliffe and J. → Hus) and the → Reformers rejected the veneration of relics. The great collection of Frederick the Wise (1486-1525) started the debate about indulgences; later M. → Luther found the veneration of relics incompatible with the omnipotence of God (Schmalk. Art. 2, Large Catechism on the 3rd commandment). J. → Calvin (1509-64) criticized the idolatrous tendencies in this veneration (*Treatise on Relics* [1543], CRef 6.405-52; → Calvin's Theology). Nevertheless, even though frauds were unmasked and relics were disposed of, for example, with the suppression of monasteries, relics might still be found in some Protestant churches, as at Nuremberg.

The clericalizing of the → liturgy strongly enhanced the veneration of relics in baroque Roman → Catholicism, and new developments included clothed skeletal figures and pyramids of relics. But even in this sphere the → Enlightenment brought some sobriety and skepticism, so that relics no longer have a major role.

2. Church Regulations

Church authorities have had much occasion to take up the issue of relics and their veneration. They have stressed their legitimacy (Nicaea II [787], can. 7; Martin V, bull *Inter cunctas* [1418], DH 1269; → Trent [1563], DH 1822; → Vatican II, *Sacrosanctum concilium* [1963] 111), guarded against misunderstandings (Lateran IV [1215], DH 818; Trent, DH 1825), and made determinations that were theological (Nicaea II, DH 601; John XV, encyclical *Cum conventus esset* [993], DH 675) or liturgical (Nicaea II, N. P. Tanner, 1.137) in nature. The 1983 → CIC forbids in principle the selling or permanent transferring of relics or the placing of relics within the → altar (cans. 1190.1-2, 1237.2). The Congregation for the Causes of Saints (→ Curia) has supervision in this field.

3. Motives

For motivation in the veneration of relics, we should look at universal human piety, which may be seen also in the Jewish honoring of the dead and the Greek hero cult. Theologically important is the idea of the holiness of the body, which is destined for → resurrection, and the concept of the communion of saints, which reaches beyond death (→ Jerome *Contra Vigil.;* Cyril of Jerusalem *Cat.* 18.16, etc.). Biblical support has been sought in texts such as Acts 5:15 and 19:12. → Popular religion hoped for protection against misfortune by palpable means (see the Greek phylacteries). Roman Catholic theology stresses the way that the relic points to the holy person (→ Symbol) and then beyond this person to God (*cultus relativus,* "relative honoring"), not being in itself an object of veneration (*cultus absolutus,* "absolute honoring").

4. Piety

The veneration of relics strongly influenced piety in general from the 4th and 5th centuries onward, and it also helped greatly to promote → pilgrimages. Relics attracted large bodies of pilgrims in the Middle Ages, especially to → Rome, Aachen, Trier, Maastricht, and Canterbury. They made an impact, too, on art (reliquaries from the days of Charlemagne, Romanesque and Gothic shrines, relic tablets, relic ostensories from the 13th cent.; → Christian Art) and on sacral architecture. (From early Christian memoria, rooms adjacent to graves, there developed cultic rooms above the graves of saints, e.g., at Salonae in 315; basilicas with → crypts, e.g., 6th-cent. Rome; and after the introduction of translations, city basilicas.) From the 4th century onward, relics were placed under altars in the West or, in the East, on the *antiminsion* (lit. "instead of a table"), the portable altar.

→ Middle Ages; Sacred and Profane

Bibliography: A. Angenendt, *Heilige und Reliquien. Die Geschichte ihres Kultes von frühen Christentum bis zur Gegenwart* (2d ed.; Munich, 1997) • W. Beinert and F. Schüssler Fiorenza, eds., *Handbook of Catholic Theology* (New York, 1995) • J. Bentley, *Restless Bones: The Story of Relics* (London, 1985) • P. Brown, *The Cult of the Saints: Its Rise and Function in Latin Christianity* (Chicago, 1982) • F. W. Deichmann, "Märtyrerbasilika, Martyrion, Memoria und Altargrab," *RöHM* 77 (1970) 144-69 • C. L. Diedrichs, *Vom Glauben zum Sehen. Die Sichtbarkeit der Reliquie im Reliquiar* (Berlin, 2001) • J. Dillenberger, *Images and Relics: Theological Perceptions and Visual Images in Sixteenth-Century Europe* (New York, 1999) • N. Herrmann-Mascard, *Les reliques des saints. Formation coutumière d'un droit* (Paris, 1975) • B. Kötting, *Ecclesia peregrinans. Das Gottesvolk unterwegs* (2 vols.; Münster, 1988); idem, *Peregrinatio religiosa. Wallfahrten in der Antike und das Pilgerwesen in der*

Relief and Development Organizations

alten Kirche (Münster, 1950) • A. LEGNER, *Reliquien in Kunst und Kult* (Darmstadt, 1995); idem, *Reliquien. Verehrung und Verklärung* (Cologne, 1989) • H. S. STONE, *St. Augustine's Bones: A Microhistory* (Amherst, Mass., 2002) • N. P. TANNER, ed., *Decrees of the Ecumenical Councils* (2 vols.; London, 1990) • E. THUNØ, *Image and Relic: Mediating the Sacred in Early Medieval Rome* (Rome, 2002) • K. TRAINOR, *Relics, Ritual, and Representation in Buddhism: Rematerializing the Sri Lankan Theravāda Tradition* (Cambridge, 1997).

WOLFGANG BEINERT

Relief and Development Organizations

1. The Christian Tradition of Service
2. World Wars and Reconstruction
   - 2.1. Before World War II
   - 2.2. World War II and the Ecumenical Movement
   - 2.3. Rebuilding
   - 2.4. British Efforts
   - 2.5. Later Work
3. Third World
   - 3.1. Biafra, 1968
   - 3.2. Sahel, 1973
   - 3.3. Ethiopia, 1984
4. Political Involvement, Advocacy

Relief and development organizations (RDOs) of Christian origin belong to the 20th century. As humanity during that century lived through violence, oppression, and → wars in a magnitude never before experienced, a Christian response was to organize relief and development organizations. Secular, government, and nongovernmental organizations (NGOs) also grew at an escalating pace in the middle of the 20th century as a response to disasters, wars, and oppression. One of the foremost tasks of the → United Nations has been to set up specialized agencies for human needs generally, like the U.N. High Commissioner for Refugees, or for specific needs in disaster or war-torn areas. In areas of conflict Christian RDOs often relate to U.N. agencies in solving the task of giving relief to people in need, regardless of nationality, race, gender, or creed. In this effort, the need of suffering human beings, not a political agenda, stands at the center.

1. The Christian Tradition of Service

Love for one's neighbor is a central teaching of the NT. Jesus himself was the Good Samaritan, who could not pass a downtrodden stranger without giving relief and paying for his recovery. This parable (Luke 10:25-37) and many like it are often used as a theological motivation for Christian RDOs. The motive of agape as God's eternal → love for humans is one theological foundation for church-related development organizations. The sharing of bread among the first Christians in Acts 4:32-37 is, similarly, another theme for many campaigns by churches in rich countries for sharing food in order to eradicate hunger. Paul organized relief for the Christian community in Jerusalem by calling for continuous giving: "I do not mean that there should be relief for others and pressure on you [Corinthians], but it is a question of a fair balance between your present abundance and their need, so that their abundance may be for your need, in order that there may be a fair balance" (2 Cor. 8:13-14).

From the question of Cain, "Am I my brother's keeper?" (Gen. 4:9), and throughout the Bible, many events, passages, and reflections have been used to motivate support for RDOs. There are three types of such references, depending of the profile of the organization: immediate *relief* of human need, long-term sustainable → *development*, and *political advocacy* to change unjust structures.

Present-day Christian RDOs stand in a long tradition of practical caregiving. From the earliest days of the church, congregations and church bodies developed institutions for taking care of the sick, the poor, orphans, and the elderly (→ Community of Goods). In the → Middle Ages many religious orders in the → Roman Catholic Church committed themselves to these tasks. On the Protestant side these tasks were shared by church and state as the European nation-states evolved.

In the 19th century, largely as an outgrowth of → revival movements, organizations for → inner mission and diaconal work evolved in northern Europe and North America. The newly discovered biblical expression → *diakonia* became a catchword, particularly in Lutheran and Reformed churches. In the middle of the 20th century, starting in Protestant Germany, the term "international diakonia" was used frequently. This phrase caught on in the → World Council of Churches (WCC) as expressive of one of the tasks of the churches in the globalization process; other tasks named have been *liturgia*, *koinonia*, and *kerygma*. Diakonia has become central to the self-understanding of many Protestant and Orthodox churches, and the role of international diakonia has taken a privileged place in their lives.

If diakonia is one inspiration for RDOs, another unmistakable inspiration has been the mission organizations of the churches. In the colonial era → missionaries were the first ones to bring education (in the Western sense), medical care and hospitals (→ Medical Missions), as well as the Christian message itself. Well into the 20th century, mission organizations took pride in being the first modern development agencies in many countries. Many of the Protestant missionary organizations were part of the → International Missionary Council (IMC), which became part of the WCC in 1961. From the 1950s on, as the European and North American RDOs became more and more involved in emergency aid in Africa and Asia, there developed between them both cooperation and competition, a reality that has given rise to many studies on the subject. One such debate started in 1972 with a letter from Christians in Ethiopia to members of the → Lutheran World Federation (LWF), "Proclamation and Human Development." In the Christian tradition RDOs have gained inspiration from the diakonia and the mission of the church, and the ecumenical movement has been instrumental in amalgamating these concerns (→ Ecumenism, Ecumenical Movement)

2. World Wars and Reconstruction

2.1. *Before World War II*

Red Cross societies were the major relief organizations before World War II. Through this Christian symbol they were supported by many Christians and churches. Their main task, however, was the treatment of victims of war.

Christian relief organizations existed before World War II, but they were small in scope and often depended on a charismatic entrepreneur. The traditional → peace churches, especially the Quakers and the → Mennonites, formed voluntary aid groups such as the American → Friends Service Committe and the Mennonite Central Committee, which after World War I developed into well-functioning relief organizations in times of both peace and war.

One of the oldest relief organizations of the traditional churches is the Danish group Folkekirkens Nødhjælp, in English called DanChurchAid. Its initiator in 1922, Alfred T. Jørgensen (1874-1953), offered assistance to evangelical Lutheran minority churches in eastern Europe that were suffering discrimination in the nationalism arising in the new countries as a result of the peace agreements after World War I. This initiative was linked to the Lutheran World Convention, in which several American Lutheran churches participated, spearheaded by John A. Morehead (1867-1936). Because of meager resources during the Great Depression, however, relief organizations during this period were typically very short-lived.

In 1922, under the leadership of Adolf Keller (1872-1963), Swiss and American churches founded the European Central Bureau for Inter-Church Aid (Europäische Zentralbüro). This organization had an ecumenical agenda and, although small-scale, served as a prototype for the ecumenical relief organizations created after 1945.

Many private initiatives of Christian origin developed into relief organizations, and several dedicated individuals tried to move mountains through their empathy and zeal. Some of these initiatives were church related and were merged into other organizations; others faded away. An outstanding example is Albert Schweitzer (1875-1965), doctor in three disciplines and renowned organist. On the basis of his theology of "reverence for life," he built up an important hospital in Lambaréné in present-day Gabon; through his writings and personal example he personified Christian peace and development ideals long before they were institutionally established.

2.2. *World War II and the Ecumenical Movement*

World War II had a devastating effect on most parts of Europe, including its churches and parishes. The period between the world wars had seen the birth of the modern ecumenical movement. Peace had been one of its aims, although most of its efforts had been in vain. Even before its formation in 1948, the World Council of Churches had established its provisional center in Geneva, and under the leadership of W. A. Visser 't Hooft (1900-1985), secret relations were established with resistance groups in Germany, Holland, and Norway, and channels were kept open to New York, London, and Sweden.

On the basis of this ecumenical network and its contacts with the anti-Nazi resistance, postwar rehabilitation efforts started quickly, with support from the Allied powers. Politically, this response was possible because the ecumenical movement had maintained contacts with anti-Nazi personalities during the war, a fact that was known to John Foster Dulles (1888-1959) and Allen Dulles (1893-1969), prominent Protestant brothers from the United States who had been stationed in Switzerland during the war and who subsequently became leaders in their government.

2.3. *Rebuilding*

The U.S. mainline churches were by far the largest contributors to church-related rehabilitation work in postwar Europe. This effort was much facilitated (not least theologically) by the Stuttgart Declara-

Relief and Development Organizations

tion, a confession of guilt by German church representatives in October 1945. Even in September of that year, however, relief efforts in Germany itself had started to mushroom.

The agency Evangelisches Hilfswerk had started its work to relieve people from hunger and disease, as well as to provide a new start in life for the 12 million → refugees and displaced persons of German origin. The initiator and first director of this effort was Eugen Gerstenmaier (1906-86), who was part of one of the resistance groups and who had been arrested after the attempt on Hitler's life on July 20, 1944. His energetic administrative ability helped this organization expand quickly, as he recruited an extremely competent staff of young Germans who at that time had no other employment. Foreign resources came from neutral Sweden and Switzerland, as well as from the victorious United States and Britain. Raw materials were also imported from these countries to start industrial enterprises such as printing and clothing.

A combination of self-help, educated people, good organization, and resources from the outside made the German economic miracle possible, even within the churches. From 1948 the political developments west of the Iron Curtain, together with Marshall Plan aid, contributed to this miracle. (The fast pace of reconstruction in Europe set the political tone for development aid in → Third World countries in the 1960s. Through large new Marshall Plan aid packages, it was thought that rapid development would take place. This idea proved to be a misconception.)

One of the largest relief organizations created in this postwar period was the Church World Service of the American Federal Council of Churches, and subsequently of the → National Council of the Churches of Christ in the U.S.A. Lutheran World Relief, formed by a majority of the U.S. Lutheran churches, collected large sums for rehabilitating European churches (by 1949, it had raised $25 million). This aid also benefited eastern European countries, which gradually became Communist-ruled "people's democracies." After 1948, however, aid to these eastern churches was severely restricted.

In all, approximately 80 percent of the funds for church-related aid during the postwar period came from the United States. One significant person in this endeavor was Sylvester Michelfelder (1889-1951), who in 1945-46 first headed the ecumenical office of postwar reconstruction in Geneva, even as he was instrumental in establishing the LWF, of which he became the first general secretary (1947-51). Under his leadership the relief and refugee services of these organizations became the motors of the WCC, LWF, and other international church organizations.

2.4. *British Efforts*

The British churches started their relief efforts to their enemy, the Germans, as soon as the unconditional surrender ending World War II was signed in May 1945. George Bell (1883-1958), the bishop of Chichester, was the leading ecumenical spokesperson in Britain. He had had close links to Dietrich Bonhoeffer (1906-45) and other German theologians of the → Confessing Church before and during the war. As a man of peace and reconciliation, but also one who resisted totalitarian ideologies, he was one of the initiators of the first acts of → solidarity of the British churches. Already in May 1945 a collection was made in Anglican parishes for the reconstruction of the churches in Germany, the recent enemy state.

This collection and the rehabilitation work that took place in the British zone in northwestern Germany gave rise to Christian Aid, the ecumenical relief and development organization affiliated with the British Council of Churches. Ever since 1945 an annual fund-raising campaign with visits to homes has taken place under the auspices of Christian Aid. Hundreds of millions of pounds have been raised this way for relief and rehabilitation in other parts of the globe.

2.5. *Later Work*

In the 1950s the established relief organizations continued their support to needy churches in Europe, but this work gradually faded away as the welfare of Europeans improved. Emergency aid was rendered at disasters, such as the flooding in Holland in 1953 and the frequent earthquakes in Mediterranean countries. By far the greatest mobilization occurred after the Hungarian uprising in the fall of 1956 was suppressed by Soviet armor. The feeling of despair and the anti-Communist sentiments of those days contributed to the large amount of aid given to Hungarian refugees.

Another area of aid to refugees was in Palestine after the establishment of the State of Israel in May 1948. In August the American colony in eastern Jerusalem cabled reports about the plight of the Palestinian refugees to Amsterdam and the founding General Assembly of the WCC. Quakers and Mennonites were treating the wounded in Palestine, and an international Christian committee was quickly formed. From this spontaneous appeal relief work was organized, later renamed the Department of Service to Palestinian Refugees, directly under WCC. This relief effort to displaced Palestinians in

Jordan, Gaza, Galilee, Lebanon, and eastern Jerusalem took place in a most explosive political environment. This first spontaneous relief to human need found it necessary later to advocate for human → rights for the refugees. The issue of peace clearly became most important, and the relief organizations had to position themselves in relation to it. There, on biblical soil, justice and reconciliation have long been preached and prophesied, yet injustice and hatred still influence the lives of ordinary people. In this atmosphere the task that aid organizations perform is difficult, and they encounter many obstacles. Dialogue between people of different monotheistic religions and different political standpoints also became part of the agenda for the development organizations, particularly in the latter decades of the 20th century.

The LWF had similar experiences in the Middle East, particularly when in 1950 the organization took responsibility for the Augusta Victoria complex on Jerusalem's Mount of Olives. Since then, Augusta Victoria has served as a hospital for Palestinian refugees in the area. Its finances have come from contributions from church development organizations and the U.N. Relief and Works Agency. No one could have foreseen that this service would continue for more than half a century.

In the 1950s the LWF's refugee work in Jordan made it the third largest employer in the country. Other RDOs came to the Middle East immediately after the conflict started and have remained since. They are not the foremost actors in the enduring Israel-Palestine drama, but they are important not only for sustaining people in need but also for providing information, → dialogue, and → reconciliation.

3. Third World

In the 1950s, as the reconstruction of Europe seemed to be successfully completed and the initial aid to Palestinians was still considered temporary, the question of "foreign aid," or development assistance in its technical sense, appeared on the international agenda. South Korea, India, and Pakistan in Asia attracted attention as the cold war grew colder. For the rich countries there was new attention on Africa as the decolonization process took place, culminating about 1960. Governments started to set aside money for → development — that is, economic and technical assistance — in what were then called underdeveloped countries. During the presidency of John F. Kennedy (1961-63), as much as 0.6 percent of the U.S. gross national product (GNP) was devoted to foreign aid, including its newly established Peace Corps. The United States was then in the lead.

At that time the United Nations challenged all industrialized countries to appropriate 0.7 percent of their GNP to unrestricted foreign assistance. Since the 1970s a few countries have for a number of years appropriated up to 1.0 percent of their GNP to development assistance, most consistently the Netherlands, Denmark, Norway, and Sweden, four small Protestant nations with mixed economies and progressive social welfare policies. They have tended to support countries that strive for equality for all its citizens. Since the end of the cold war, U.S. international assistance has dwindled to less than 0.2 percent of its GNP.

The peak period of attention to the Third World for church-related development organizations was from 1965 to 1985. This was a period of economic growth and positive developments in many poor countries, when education efforts and health care reached major parts of the population. Diseases such as smallpox were eradicated, polio was diminished, and leprosy decreased. After 1985, however, HIV/AIDS emerged and began to take a heavy toll, particularly in sub-Saharan Africa, where, in the absence of any countermeasures, the crisis grew out of proportion. U.N. estimates as of December 2004 show 39.4 million people worldwide living with HIV.

From 1982 the international debt crisis severely weakened governments and most programs of public welfare and education in impoverished Third World countries. As the lending of money increased to governments after the oil crisis of 1974 (the so-called petro dollars), many expanding economies of the nations of Africa, Asia, and Latin America found themselves in a debt trap from which there was no way out other than to follow the structural adjustment programs of the International Monetary Fund and the World Bank, which people felt to be harsh and unfair. Not for 15-20 years did these organizations change course, but by that time the development landscape looked different. The RDOs were among the first to protest against these harsh measures, as they saw the positive effects of the development programs evaporate.

Emergency aid during the period 1965-85 gave enormous publicity to the RDOs. Reports on emergency operations in Bangladesh, India, and Cambodia in Asia, as well as the Biafran War in Nigeria (1967-69), the drought in the Sahel, south of the Sahara (1973), and the drought in Ethiopia and the Horn of Africa (1984), brought fund-raising to proportions almost unheard of. Through mass media and the activity of development organizations, a great deal of compassion was channeled to the victims of these emergencies. In the aftermath of many of these crises, however, we have also seen "compassion fatigue."

In analyzing the causes of these emergencies and the role of politics in them, as well as the misuse of land and water resources, the complexities of the various emergencies have become evident. Three examples are given here of relief and development emergencies during this period and the churches' response to them: civil war in Biafra (1968), drought and desertification in the Sahel (1973), and dictatorship and forced resettlement in Ethiopia (1984).

3.1. ***Biafra, 1968***

The Biafran civil war started in 1967 when Igbos, the Christian majority in the oil-rich eastern region of Nigeria, declared themselves independent. This move followed a slaughter of 30,000 Igbos in northern Nigeria carried out by Muslim Hausa. Great Britain and the Soviet Union supported the federal government against Biafra. The Biafrans soon were without supplies, and the people, particularly the children, were at the point of starvation; their leaders, however, continued to fight. Relief agencies were at a loss how to deal with this large emergency. Several rescue attempts were made by Norwegian Church Aid and its leader, Elias Hauge.

In August 1968 Captain Carl Gustaf von Rosen (1909-77), flying 50-100 feet above sea level in a DC-7 loaded with food supplies, made a daring flight from the island of São Tomé into Biafra, landing on a road at Uli just before sunset. This flight began an airlift of food supplies to the starving Biafrans, as von Rosen's Swedish crew continued these flights. Next day, in support of the airlift, three Scandinavian church agencies formed Nordchurchaid. They were soon joined by 40 American and European Protestant and Catholic relief agencies, all of which cooperated in forming Joint Church Aid, an ecumenical venture that eventually sponsored 5,300 flights in this airlift. It was the single largest ecumenical relief operation, and the largest one to date in Africa. Sadly, it was followed by many more over the following decades, as wars of attrition became a favorite way to deal with internal conflicts.

The image of a starving African child on prime-time TV etched itself into the minds of affluent viewers. The response was to donate to relief agencies, which experienced a peak in fund-raising. Approximately $100 million was raised and used in the 15-month Biafra airlift. The relief organizations received favorable attention for their bravery and risk-taking, especially since attempts at a political solution failed miserably. Two million civilians died in this conflict, and 13 pilots are buried close to the airstrip at Uli.

The world at large became acquainted with relief organizations whose white pilots flew in food to helpless Africans. During the war many churches and missionaries had been able to continue their work in hospitals and with agricultural projects inside Biafra, but airlifts became synonymous with relief. Power-hungry African politicians refused to negotiate, and wars of attrition against their own population became common in Sudan, Somalia, Ethiopia-Eritrea, Liberia, Sierra Leone, and Rwanda. In these situations relief organizations drew from their experience in Biafra. Additionally, peace education on a grassroots level became important, as did programs of reeducation for former soldiers who had made their living in armed conflict. RDOs came to view the conversion of soldiers into farmers as a major part of their task.

3.2. ***Sahel, 1973***

Another staggering African disaster was the drought of the Sahel in 1973, which struck the countries south of the Sahara. Regions that were used to having 200-300 mm. (8-12 in.) of rain a year suddenly received virtually none. Agriculture and grazing failed, traditional herds perished, and people starved in ten countries from the Horn of Africa in the east to Mauritania in the west. Relief supplies from agricultural surpluses in Europe and North America were shipped overseas, transported on inadequate local roads, and distributed at high cost. This type of aid eventually reached millions of people, even as it often required them to travel to distribution points, where they passively settled.

Most Christian relief organizations participated in this effort in cooperation with African partner churches. In Ethiopia it was again the pilot Carl Gustaf von Rosen who developed the technique of "food bombing" from small airplanes to mountainous areas that could not be reached by trucks, another example of an avant-garde technique first used by church agencies and later developed by U.N. organizations.

Causes of the drought were studied carefully, and it was concluded that overgrazing on the borders of the Sahara was one major cause for the expansion of the desert southward; overpopulation of humans and cattle made the topsoil blow away and the groundwater diminish. Soil and water, the foundations for life, disappeared. Since biblical times a nomadic way of herding sheep and cattle had been maintained as a lifestyle, for example, by the Tuaregs, or "blue people," but recurring droughts made nomadic life impossible as livestock demanded more water and land for grazing. The people had to flock to the cities and were cut off from their traditional family life.

To meet this new situation, development organizations set up many projects: planting trees to ward off the spread of the desert, conscientizing people concerning the importance of environmental protection and saving the meager water resources, water and soil conservation, small-scale agricultural projects, and "agroforestry," which became a catchword. Churches in Africa, both Protestant and Roman Catholic, set up internal development departments, receiving support and expertise from northern partners. Many of these departments were successful in achieving their aims, particularly those that stayed small in scale and had devoted and enthusiastic leaders. Resistance came to this development, however, from the agricultural policies adopted by their own African governments, especially as these policies were supported by the rich northern countries (mainly the United States and Europe), whose agricultural subsidies paid for the export of surpluses to these countries. African agriculture thus could never compete with that of the northern countries, not even at home. Receiving these surpluses, African governments had a kind of monopoly that enabled them to pay African farmers less than a fair price for their products, effectively forcing African farmers to stop producing.

In the new century these issues continue to involve the development organizations. Merely to bring relief or establish sound development projects has not been enough, however; advocacy to change governmental policies is now part of the development agenda.

3.3. *Ethiopia, 1984*

Ethiopia and Eritrea were badly affected by the drought of 1973, leading to political and social revolutions. Ethiopian emperor Haile Selassie was deposed in September 1974, and he died in prison one year later. At first the Marxist military regime that replaced the emperor enjoyed popularity, for the people blamed the emperor for the starvation. As scientific → socialism was established by a murderous one-party dictatorship, however, Ethiopians experienced a long period of wars with neighboring countries, civil war, forced migration, ill-planned land reforms, confiscation of property, and persecution of "foreign religions" (esp. Lutheran and Pentecostal).

These horrors culminated in 1983-84, when another drought hit the country, said to be the 50th such drought since the 13th century. The death toll was immense, in part as a result of political inertia in the country. Church development organizations were on the alert in 1983, but their efforts fell far short of what was needed. The Ethiopian government denied that starvation existed in its country, and for one year the U.S. and British governments refused to send supplies because the nation was ruled by Communists. The limited efforts by ecumenical agencies in 1983 received hardly any notice, even though they made serious commitments to aid the Ethiopians and the Eritreans through their church partners.

In October 1984 a film clip showing starving Ethiopians in a landscape devastated by drought appeared on 425 television channels throughout the world. This one event created a storm of outrage, resulting in political action and concrete acts of compassion. From that time on, the TV medium set the agenda, forcing politicians to promise immediate sending of relief, particularly from the United States and United Kingdom, where such commitments had earlier been refused. The emergency aid was late in coming, however, and a million people died in this holocaust. Millions more were starving, and the Ethiopian government had not even said a word. In November 1983 church agencies set aside $100 million for an emergency operation, forming the group Churches Drought Action in Africa (CDAA), which involved all relief organizations connected to the WCC, the LWF, and the Roman Catholic agency Caritas International.

In subsequent years the money raised and spent by CDAA multiplied, since not only Ethiopians were starving, but every third African. This aid program from combined church organizations was one of the largest ever undertaken. In Ethiopia it managed to overcome stubborn government obstacles. The 50 million Ethiopians had only a few paved roads, and the expansive mountainous country could not be reached by trucks. People who had already been displaced walked to the roads in the hope of receiving some food. The northern parts of Tigray, Wollo, and Eritrea were experiencing civil war, and the harvest had failed almost completely. The churches managed to have cease-fire lines drawn, and food supplies were distributed under the most difficult situations.

This emergency occurred when the northern cold war was coldest and the U.N. system could not function satisfactorily; at that time the relief organizations were far ahead of governments and the United Nations. Because of their preparedness the relief organizations were able to operate in a country where little functioned under a revolutionary one-party state. Thanks to the local churches and their committed leaders, an even worse catastrophe was avoided. As the Ethiopian government fell in 1991 and as Eritrea became independent, the political problems in one of Africa's oldest kingdoms changed.

This Ethiopian emergency, which has in large measure continued until the present, was one of the worst of the latter part of the 20th century. The emergency has shown how well functioning the church relief network has become, but perhaps the most important lesson from this emergency is that the disaster was political as much as it was natural. The politics of aid has become a problem urgently needing solution.

4. Political Involvement, Advocacy

"The world sets the agenda" is a slogan sometimes used to describe the unexpected activities of RDOs. Wars, famines, natural disasters, and dictatorial regimes are some of the common problems calling for the intervention of relief organizations. From their own experience the RDOs have found it necessary to become advocates of the voiceless poor and of victims of war and oppression. This role has sometimes led to political controversy at high levels. Some have argued that it is the duty of the relief organizations to speak out against injustices, even if that should lead to their being expelled from the countries in which they work. Others have stated that it is important for RDOs to continue to work in places of tension, using only diplomatic channels to address politically sensitive issues. Some of the RDOs have transformed themselves into advocacy groups, lobbying for fair trade, for cancellation of debt, against agricultural subsidies, and other issues.

Most RDOs try to maintain a holistic approach, incorporating advocacy in their tasks of bringing relief and furthering development. Church organizations find support in the Bible for these various standpoints. Some prefer to emphasize the OT prophetic tradition, including the prophetic message of → Jesus. Others stress a theology of creation, along with Martin Luther's call to every person to fulfill his or her → vocation. Without question, the pace of globalization and the use of modern → communications have led to new forms of networking in action, with calls for social justice against the structures supported by the wealthy nations of the North.

One such successful network was the anti-apartheid movement, which supported liberation in all countries of southern Africa. Another was Jubilee 2000, a campaign for the eradication of the burden of international debt borne by Third World countries.

In some cases church organizations linked to the Lausanne Committee for World Evangelization, as well as to the growing Pentecostal movement in Africa and Latin America, have criticized RDOs for being too political. Such groups have created their own church-supported RDOs, which tend to do little work in political advocacy. One major such relief and development group is World Vision International, which in 2003 offered material, emotional, social, and spiritual support to 100 million people in 99 countries.

Traditional church RDOs, especially in Europe, have since around 1970 received substantial grants from their governments and from the European Union for emergency and development aid. Some church-related agencies actually receive more money for their work from governments than they receive from their churches or from private donations. For these governments and the EU this support is a sign of appreciation for the effectiveness of NGOs and church-related organizations in difficult circumstances when governments cannot act. Government grants are increasingly also awarded to RDOs for long-term projects. Politically, it seems appropriate to grant a greater share of official development funding to NGOs, although this practice has been far more common in Europe than in the United States.

While the churches of the United States after World War II were by far the largest contributors in all categories of aid and reconstruction, their place has been overtaken since 1970 by the German and Nordic churches. The German agency Evangelisches Hilfswerk transformed itself to a large diaconal institution, mainly for overseas aid. Brot für die Welt (Bread for the World), a fund-raising campaign during Advent 1959, was so successful that it still continues as an institution. A similar campaign in Roman Catholic parishes under the name of Misereor has made German Catholics a strong contributor to relief and development work, particularly through the Caritas International network. Since 1962 the German government has allotted large sums to both Protestant and Catholic relief organizations.

At the start of the new millennium, most RDOs stressed the importance of local participation and gender awareness in all externally financed projects and programs. In the age of globalization the poorest countries of the world and pockets of → poverty in rich countries remain outside the material benefits of globalization. Their own human resources are their best asset; to develop them in a holistic manner is a challenge for all. Church-related RDOs will definitely have a future in the 21st century, particularly since the Christian presence seems to be stronger in the poor countries of Africa, Asia, and Latin America than in affluent North America and Europe. The ways RDOs operate, however, will certainly continue to change as much as they have in the period since World War II.

Bibliography: J. W. Bachman, *Together in Hope: Fifty Years of Lutheran World Relief* (Minneapolis, 1995) • A. Chepkwony, *The Role of Non-governmental Organizations in Development* (Uppsala, 1987) • R. Dickinson, *Poor, Yet Making Many Rich* (Geneva, 1983) • C. Elliott, *The Development Debate* (London, 1971) • H.-W. Hessler, *Five Aspects of Development Work: An Analysis Based on Three Projects in Asia, Africa, and Latin America* (Geneva, 1979) • J. Lissner, *The Politics of Altruism: A Study of the Political Behaviour of Voluntary Development Agencies* (Geneva, 1977) • K. Poser, ed., *Diakonia 2000: Called to Be Neighbours; Official Report, WCC World Consultation, Inter-Church Aid, Refugee, and World Service, Larnaca, 1986* (Geneva, 1987) • *Proclamation and Human Development: Document from a Lutheran World Federation Consultation, Nairobi, Kenya, October 21-25, 1974* (Geneva, 1977) • E. H. Robertson, *Unshakeable Friend: George Bell and the German Churches* (London, 1995) • B. Ryman, "The Influence of the Kreisau Group in Shaping Swedish Inter-Church Aid," *KZG* 12 (1999) 389-403; idem, *Lutherhjälpen: The First Fifty Years. The History of Church of Sweden Aid, 1947-1997* (= *SMTh* 85, no. 2 [1997]) • J. H. Schjørring, P. Kumari, and N. A. Hjelm, eds., *From Federation to Communion: The History of the Lutheran World Federation* (Minneapolis, 1997) • P. Selby, *Grace and Mortgage: The Language of Faith and the Debt of the World* (London, 1997) • K. Slack, *Hope in the Desert: The Churches' United Response to Human Need, 1944-1984* (Geneva, 1986) • R. W. Solberg, *As between Brothers: The Story of Lutheran Response to World Need* (Minneapolis, 1957); idem, *Miracle in Ethiopia: A Partnership Response to Famine* (New York, 1991) • M. H. Taylor, *Not Angels but Agencies: The Ecumenical Response to Poverty* (Geneva, 1995) • T. J. White, "Diakonia," *DEM* (2d ed.) 305-10.

Björn Ryman

Religion

1. Study of Religion

1.1. *Term*

In modern usage the term "religion" is a master concept primarily in the description of ideas, attitudes, and actions vis-à-vis the reality that we accept and call forces or → power, spirits or → demons, gods or God, the holy or the → absolute, or simply transcendence. This reality is supremely important for us, meriting respect and in most cases worship (E. Feil, 29). Defining the term intellectually in this way shows plainly how related it is to time and space. The questions naturally arise whether this definition applies to academic inquiry into the phenomenon in earlier times and other → cultures (see 1.2), what it implies for the treating of religion as a subject of research (see 1.3), and how far a typology will help us to a better understanding of the relevant material (see 1.4).

1.2. *Religion and Culture*

It is now customary to call Christianity, including early and medieval Christianity (→ Middle Ages 1), a religion. The question is seldom put whether this usage coincides with the way Christianity saw itself in earlier days. Feil has shown that the usual terms then were *fides, secta,* and *lex,* not *religio.* The etymological explanations of antiquity — from *relegere,* the scrupulous observance of rules (Cicero), or from *religati,* our obligation to God (Lactantius) — do not shed much light on the development of the modern understanding. The only obvious point is that each author explains the term along the lines of his or her own understanding of religion.

This tendency is even more true when we turn from Latin to Greek or to equivalents in non-Christian cultures. Inductive studies (C. Baladier) show that in all cultures, and not only the West, the general definition is almost always rooted in a specific religion and its understanding (J. Waardenburg, 251). Thus the definition in a Christian context is largely influenced by Christian theological premises and has, for its part, so strongly influenced the criticism of religion (→ Religion, Criticism of) that the critical conclusions have been carried over into accounts of other religions. Research into religion has the task today of overcoming this contextual bias if it is to meet the demands of a systematic study of religion (→ Religious Studies).

1.3. *Research*

Research into religion today can no longer take the path of F. Heiler (chap. A, §§II-IV) and simply list the various cultural aspects (i.e., objects, places, and times). It must accept the impossibility of achieving a general definition of religion (Waardenburg, 26). Without absolutizing, it must propose many different questions, engaging in historical, comparative, contextual, and hermeneutical research. It cannot say that religions are "simply" historical entities (→ Historicism), or complexes of alien phenomena (religious phenomenologism), or socially relevant constructs (in → legitimation of specific social relations), or intellectual constructs, as in idealizing, mystifying, and gnosticizing theories (Waardenburg, 41)

1.4. *Typology*

The wealth of material makes categorizing and typologizing impossible. In this regard H. Biezais has shown that scholars choose their own criteria of selection, so that the criteria are subjective, even though they may be tested and hence academically responsible. If, for example, we make religions with founders a type, this group would include Buddhism and Christianity, but Buddhism would drop out if we speak instead of prophetic religion or religion of → revelation.

Categories applying to religions generally might be one-God religions on the one hand (→ Monotheism; Henotheism) and many-gods religions on the other (→ Polytheism), or those that group religions by geographic distribution of their adherents, for example, whether they are global or tribal. Reference might be made to individuals or groups within religions (e.g., → priests, laity, saints, mystics), to generations or to novelties (→ Youth Religions; New Religions), or finally to sacred times and places. From a systematic standpoint some grounds for division (e.g., "primitive religions") are questionable because they involve prejudices or value judgments that can no longer be defended today. The study of religion clearly now regards itself as primarily a humane discipline, and it thus views research into religion as a contribution to cultural studies.

→ Phenomenology of Religion; Sociology of Religion

Bibliography: P. Antes, "'Religion' einmal anders," *Tem.* 14 (1978) 184-97 • W. E. Arnal, "Definition," *Guide to the Study of Religion* (ed. W. Braun and R. T. McCutcheon; London, 2000) 21-34 • C. Baladier, ed., *Le grand atlas des religions* (Paris, 1988) • U. Bianchi, ed., *The Notion of "Religion" in Comparative Research* (Rome, 1994) • H. Biezais, "Die typologische Methode in der religionsgeschichtlichen Forschung," *Tem.* 17 (1981) 5-26 • W. Braun, "Religion," *Guide,* ed. Braun and McCutcheon, 3-18 • E. Feil, *Religio. Die Geschichte eines neuzeitlichen Grundbegriffs vom Frühchristentum bis zu Reformation* (Göttingen, 1986) • F. Heiler, *Erscheinungsformen und Wesen der Religion* (Stuttgart, 1961; 2d ed., 1979) • P. R. McKenzie, *The Christians, Their Practices and Beliefs: An Adaptation of Friedrich Heiler's Phenomenology of Religion* (Nashville, 1988) • J. G. Platvoet and A. L. Molendijk, eds., *The Pragmatics of Defining Religion: Contexts, Concepts, and Contests* (Leiden, 1999) • J. Z. Smith, "Religion, Religions, Religious," *Cultural Terms for Religious Studies* (ed. M. C. Taylor; Chicago, 1998) 269-84 • V. Turner, "Religion (in Primitive Culture)," *NCE* (2d ed.) 12.64-69 • J. Waardenburg, *Religionen und Religion. Systematische Einführung in die Religionswissenschaft* (Berlin, 1986).

Peter Antes

2. Theological Factors

2.1. *Universality and Anthropology*

In its original Stoic-Roman usage (→ Stoicism), "religion" meant veneration of God and all that went with it, for example, justice and virtue (Cicero). The term retained this orientation to attitude and conduct rather than faith, even when adopted in Christian theology (Lactantius, → Augustine) and on into the late → Middle Ages.

A decisive universalizing and anthropologizing came with the → Renaissance. Nicholas of Cusa (1401-64) saw in *religio* a universal disposition in virtue of which all peoples in some way worship God or the gods (*una religio in rituum varietate,* "one religion in a variety of rites"). This shift of meaning was completed at the → Enlightenment. "Religion" then came to be used for all historical religions and also for the anthropological religious bent that in all of us genetically and normatively precedes the specific religions. On this view, all empirical religions derive from a core of universal and eternally valid truths, that is, from the "natural religion" that is innate to our rational nature (→ Reason).

The concept thus broke free from the context of a theology of → revelation, now split into warring confessional factions (→ Confession of Faith), and became a general normative concept subsuming all empirical forms of worship but also making criticism of them possible. The term could now cover all known religious traditions throughout the world, and the various traditions in turn could be objectified as self-enclosed belief systems that are outwardly delimited and isolated from their cultural background (→ Culture).

Three levels of meaning resulted from this universalizing. First, "religion" in the singular became a philosophically normative ideal type, the essential core of religion as such. Second, "religions" in the plural became an empirically descriptive collective term for the world religions. Third, "religion" became a subjective term for a religious attitude and religious practice.

2.2. *Historicism and Subjectivity*

Works by J. G. → Herder (1744-1803, *Von Religion, Lehrmeinungen und Gebräuchen* [On religion, opinions, and customs, 1798]) and F. D. E. → Schleiermacher (1768-1834, *Reden über die Religion* [1799; ET *On Religion: Speeches to Its Cultured Despisers* (1988)]; → Schleiermacher's Theology) criticized the nonhistorical character of the Enlightenment concept of a pure rational religion. With the principle that religion exists only in the religions, they gave the decisive impulse toward a historicizing of the understanding of religion. Nevertheless, they too, like the Enlightenment theologians, sought a general essential core of religion in all religions.

Schleiermacher found this core in the autonomous sphere of feeling, an affective receptivity to the universal dimension of being, which is not at all the same as → metaphysics and morals, as thought and action. We are aware of this sphere when we realize that we owe our own existence to God. This awareness, which relates to the ground of being, finds expression in empirical religion. The derivation of all positive religion from a power of the human consciousness gave religion its own autonomy, but at the cost of subjectivizing its core. In this historicized but also subjectivized form, the concept of religion became in the 19th century a basic concept in the constructing of theological theory.

Integrating Christianity into a general understanding of religion resulted in apologetic attempts to establish its superiority. To this end a model of evolutionary stages emerged that typologized religions and arranged them in a → hierarchy of values ranging from primitive nature religions to the intellectual, personal (→ Person), and ethical (→ Ethics) higher religions, at the head of which was the Christian religion. E. → Troeltsch was the last important advocate of this view in his *Die Absolutheit des Christentums und die Religionsgeschichte* (1902; ET *The Absoluteness of Christianity and the History of Religions* [1971]). This Eurocentric sense of superiority reflected the colonial claims to mastery that an imperialist age was making before World War I.

2.3. *Rejection of the Term*

Karl → Barth (1886-1968) contested the integrating of the message of Christ into a general theory of religion that is dependent on a subjective experience of transcendence. In this battle he threw out religion completely as a central theological concept (*CD* §17). Religion, reduced to subjective religiosity (→ Religion, Personal Sense of), seemed to him to be the epitome of all our human efforts, in a desire for → autonomy (→ Anthropology 3-4), to set up a true relationship with God in our own power. It seemed to him to be a striving for self-justification before God and therefore to be unbelief (→ Faith). Over against it Barth set the revelation of God in Christ, which God alone can give, which is always beyond our control, and which has chosen the intrinsically sinful Christian religion as true religion (→ Sin; Dialectical Theology).

D. → Bonhoeffer (1906-45) went a step further and envisioned the end of religion in a secularized world that has come of age, that is, the dawning of a new "religionless" era (*Letters and Papers from Prison* [1951]; → Secularism). For him "religion" meant a metaphysics and inwardness that were the product of European culture (→ European Theology [Modern Period]), that triggered a movement of flight from the this-worldly reality of life on earth to an otherworldly sphere above, and that was thus opposed to the claiming of the world by the sovereignty of Christ (→ Religionless Christianity).

2.4. *Theological Rehabilitation of Concept and Reality*

The general turning toward the empirical social sciences at the end of the 1960s rekindled interest in religious structures and functions (N. Luhmann, *Funktion der Religion* [1977]). From the perspective of social function an emphasis developed on the involvement of religion in its sociocultural context, in contrast to typically 19th-century attempts to treat religion independently.

In the late 20th century there was also a widespread rebound of religion. → Islam, → Hinduism, and → Buddhism all strengthened their missionary work, even in the European and American cultural sphere; → new religions emerged; and Christianity continued its global advance. To deal with these developments Protestant theology needed to return, theologically and hermeneutically, to the reality that the concept of religion has in view. This concern found important expression in the study *Religionen, Religiosität und christlicher Glaube* (Religions, religiosity, and Christian faith, 1991), prepared by the United Evangelical Lutheran Church of Germany (VELKD).

2.5. *Roman Catholic Developments*

Roman Catholic theology has maintained a more constant understanding of religion than Protestant theology. The sense of the mutual penetration of → nature and supernature (the *analogia entis,* "analogy of being [between the two realms]"), the sacramental understanding of reality (→ Sacrament), and the incarnational view of → grace all make possible the interpretation of Christianity as a religion in which the divine and the human merge. Religion is here the social form of revelation. This interrelating of religion and revelation finds expression in Latin American → liberation theology. In the practical demonstration of life in → solidarity, divine → truth is set free, which then goes to work to change reality (→ Roman Catholic Church).

→ Vatican II made an epochal breakthrough in the evaluation of non-Christian religions when it stated in 1965 that "the Catholic Church rejects nothing that is true and holy in these religions" (*Nostra aetate* 2). Karl → Rahner (1904-84) paved the way here with his doctrine of anonymous Christianity and his treatment of religions as valid ways of salvation (*Theological Investigations* 5.115-34).

2.6. *Anglo-American Theology*

Anglo-American theology, like Roman Catholic, has typically not seen a problem in the relation between religion and Christianity, due largely to the way in which it related the → philosophy of religion and the empirical study of religion to theology. With its more empirical, historical, and practical orientation, this theology always felt itself obliged to relate its theoretical concepts to religious experience and hence to the material unearthed by the study of religion. In this climate that was so favorable to empirical research, important initiatives were taken in the United States like the Chicago school of religious studies (J. Wach, M. Eliade), the Center for the Study of World Religions at Harvard University (W. C. Smith), and the many departments of religion at secular universities.

P. → Tillich (1886-1965) helped to stimulate discussion of the concerns of → dialectical theology in the context of → North American theology. He traced historical religion back to the brokenness of human existence and subjugated it to "absolute religion," in which the reality of the new being manifests itself. That which is of ultimate concern to us transcends and relativizes all religious forms, which reach out to it and seek to control it. "Religion," then, represents both demonic human attempts at self-redemption and the uncontrollable coming of the unconditioned to our → salvation (*Systematic Theology* 1.211-35; 2.78-96; 3.138-61, 162-243).

2.7. *Theology of Religion*

The more we see how varied religion is, the more we need to reflect theologically on the concept and reality of religion and religions. It seems that we urgently need a theology of religion that is open to → dialogue in reflection on the hermeneutics of how we understand religion and interreligious encounters.

→ Theology in the Nineteenth and Twentieth Centuries; Theology of Religions

Bibliography: H.-M. Barth, *Dogmatik. Evangelischer Glaube im Kontext der Weltreligionen* (Gütersloh, 2001) • R. Bernhardt, *Der Absolutheitsanspruch des Christentums* (2d ed.; Gütersloh, 1993) • D. Cohn-Sherbok, ed., *Interfaith Theology: A Reader* (Oxford, 2003) • M. Eliade, ed., *EncRel(E)* • C. Elsas, ed., *Religion* (Munich, 1975) • H. Halbfas, *Religion* (Stuttgart, 1976) • J. Hick, *An Interpretation of Religion: Human Responses to the Transcendent* (New Haven, 1989) • P. Koslowski, ed., *Die religiöse Dimension der Gesellschaft. Religion und ihre Theorien* (Tübingen, 1985) • H. Lübbe, *Religion nach der Aufklärung* (2d ed.; Graz, 1990) • G. Mensching, *Die Religion* (Stuttgart, 1959) • K. Nishitani, *Religion and Nothingness* (Berkeley, Calif., 1982) • W. Oelmüller, ed., *Kolloquium Religion und Philosophie,* vol. 1, *Wiederkehr von Religion?* (Paderborn, 1984) • W. Oelmüller et al., eds., *Diskurs. Religion* (2d ed.; Paderborn, 1982) • C. Olson, ed., *Theory and Method in the Study of Religion* (Belmont, Calif., 2003) • C. H. Ratschow, *Die Religionen* (Gütersloh, 1979) • N. Smart, *Worldviews: Crosscultural Explorations of Human Beliefs* (3d ed.; Upper Saddle River, N.J., 2000) • N. Smart and S. Konstantine, *Christian Systematic Theology in a World Context* (Minneapolis, 1991) • W. C. Smith, *The Meaning and End of Religion* (New York, 1963) • H. Timm, *Das ästhetische Jahrzehnt. Zur Postmodernisierung der Religion* (Gütersloh, 1990) • F. Wagner, *Was ist Religion?* (Gütersloh, 1986) • K. Ward, *Religion and Community* (Oxford, 2000); idem, *Religion and Creation* (Oxford, 1996); idem, *Religion and Human Nature* (Oxford, 1998); idem, *Religion and Revelation: A Theology of Revelation in the World's Religions* (Oxford, 1994).

Reinhold Bernhardt

Religion, Criticism of

1. In Philosophy
   1.1. Basic Problem
   1.2. Issues
      1.2.1. Anthropomorphism
      1.2.2. Theism
      1.2.3. Miracles
      1.2.4. Support of the Religious Establishment
      1.2.5. Existence of Evil

1. In Philosophy

1.1. *Basic Problem*

Insofar as thinking is part of faith, a critical and questioning element is involved in faith as well as an interpretive element. This form of criticism of religion is immanent or intrinsic, involving distinction between inalienable contents and those that are less central. We find examples in → Wisdom literature, for example, Job and Ecclesiastes in → Judaism or the → Upanishads in → Hinduism, then in the → Enlightenment, with its interest in the philosophy of religion (e.g., G. Berkeley, G. E. Lessing, I. Kant), then in the modern → philosophy of religion.

External criticism, in contrast, holds aloof from religion altogether. We might think here of the broad stream of modern philosophical criticism of religion represented by P. Bayle, J. O. de La Mettrie, D. Hume, P. H. Holbach, L. Feuerbach, K. → Marx, F. → Nietzsche, S. Freud, J.-P. Sartre, B. Russell, and others (→ Modern Period). Whether the criticism is internal or external is not always easy to decide. To which category do thinkers belong when the social nature of religion is a matter of indifference to them, or when they advocate a philosophical faith, as K. Jaspers does?

We must also distinguish between positive and negative criticism. Positive criticism of religion gives an existing religion a new dynamic, as in the case of the affirmative reinterpretation of ancient Chinese religion by Confucius (551-479 B.C.), which ultimately produced the new religion of → Confucianism, or the criticism sponsored by the internally critical representatives of the Enlightenment, who initiated the philosophical religious thinking and Protestant theology of → idealism (J. G. Fichte, F. Schelling, G. W. F. Hegel, F. D. E. → Schleiermacher, et al.).

Negative criticism of religion seeks to eliminate religion. Thus the OT prophets sought to stamp out Canaanite religion, and atheistic criticism (→ Atheism) has the extermination of religion as its goal. External criticism is commonly negative.

1.2. *Issues*

1.2.1. *Anthropomorphism*

Criticism of religion notes with astonishment and derision that all-too-human conditions obtain in the otherworldly sphere, from which religion receives its → revelations. → Yahweh walks in the garden in the cool of the day (Gen. 3:8). The gods of Olympia are the victims of greed and conflict, and so forth. Human forms and attitudes in the world of the divine are an offense to the criticism of religion. It loves to cite the argument of Xenophanes (ca. 570-ca. 478 B.C.) that if cattle or horses or lions had hands, they would make gods in the shape of cattle, horses, or lions (frg. 15; → Greek Philosophy).

In a refinement of the same charge, L. Feuerbach (1804-72), probably the most influential of modern critics of religion, claimed that God is the most obvious personification of human nature, the law of what it thinks and does (*The Essence of Christianity* [1841]). To be sure, this criticism implies a revolutionary vew of the divine and of theology. Xenophanes understood the divine as the *apeiron* (i.e., the infinite or unlimited), Feuerbach as the human nature.

1.2.2. *Theism*

Criticism of religion also complains about the notion of a personal God. How can we say that an absolutely superior principle is both totally different from us and yet like us in the sense of being personal? I. Kant (1724-1804) wanted to find a place for God as a moral postulate, theoretically not provable yet still irrefutable, but for speculative reason this was still no more than an infallible ideal (*Critique of Pure Reason*, B669; → Kantianism). This form of the criticism of religion might involve rejection of the proofs of God (→ God, Arguments for the Existence of), → atheism, or → agnosticism, but also → pantheism or → mysticism, even in cases within a theological framework.

1.2.3. *Miracles*

With an appeal to scientific observation of → nature, criticism of religion attacks miracle stories. D. Hume (1711-76) set the pattern here with his assault upon the support found for the resurrection of Jesus in the eyewitness account of his disciples. He did not think he could accept the resurrection of Elizabeth I of England, even if physicians and courtiers bore witness to it (*Inquiry*, "On Miracles," 2.24).

1.2.4. *Support of the Religious Establishment*

Criticism of religion often points out that from antiquity to the industrial age, religion has commonly given its support to government. K. Marx (1818-83; → Marxism and Christianity 2) for this reason did not view religion as an independent system but as a secondary system disguising middle-class interests — in short, as an → ideology.

S. Freud (1856-1939; → Psychoanalysis) was

more concerned about the psychological background, arguing that sons had killed a primal father and then out of a sense of guilt had installed him as an omnipotent deity (see his work on Moses and monotheistic religion). In this way religion prepares the human psyche to accept established social structures of government (→ Psychology of Religion).

1.2.5. *Existence of Evil*

The Book of Job, which deals with the question of what since Leibniz we are used to calling → theodicy, is sometimes seen as an example of the immanent criticism of religion in the form of a poetic dialogue. Epicurus (341-270 B.C.) briefly stated the problem as a logical dilemma involving four possibilities. God is

1. willing to take away evils but is unable to do so,
2. able but unwilling, or
3. neither willing nor able, or
4. both willing and able.

If (1) is true, then God is feeble, which is not in accordance with the character of God; if (2), he is malicious, which is equally at variance with God; if (3), he is both malicious and feeble, and therefore not God; and if (4), which alone is suitable to God, from what source then are evils? or why does he not remove them? (cited in Lactantius, *De ira Dei*, 13).

G. W. Leibniz (1646-1716) in his *Essais de théodicée* (1710) tried to justify God. But faced with the Lisbon earthquake of 1755 and the 60,000-90,000 people it left dead, Voltaire (1694-1778) wrote his *Candide* in reply (1759), in which he ironically rejected theodicy.

1.3. *Summary*

Criticism of religion often initiates the renewal of the religion it criticizes. The development of theology from the days of the early → apologists would have been unthinkable without this type of philosophical → criticism. Criticism of religion becomes radical when it argues that the basis of religion, whether viewed as God, revelation, redemption (→ Soteriology), or enlightenment, cannot stand at the bar of human reason. Atheistic criticism has no time for ongoing preoccupation with what is of "ultimate concern" (P. → Tillich).

Criticism of religion, however, cannot break free from religion. Not only do religions still have their adherents, but criticism of religion must also postulate religion in order to destroy it. Indeed, it must admit its importance if it is not to say that it is wasting its own time. Religion is always on trial but always threatens to put criticism of religion itself on trial and to overthrow it.

Against the background of atheism F. Nietzsche (1844-1900) in his *Gay Science* has his madman who proclaims the death of God cry out and draw the consequences of this death: "Are we not plunging continually? And backward, sideward, forward, in all directions? Is there still any up or down? Are we not straying as through an infinite nothing?" (no. 125). There are, then, only two possibilities for the most radical criticism of religion. It must either show what is the meaning of what is "meaningless" in the religion that it criticizes, or it must be silent, and then religion will have the last word. This is the dilemma of L. Wittgenstein (1889-1951) at the end of his *Tractatus logico-philosophicus* (nos. 6.52–7).

Bibliography: G. Fraser, *Redeeming Nietzsche: On the Piety of Unbelief* (London, 2002) • N. R. Goldberg, *The End of God* (Ottawa, 1982) • H. Gollwitzer, *The Christian Faith and the Marxist Criticism of Religion* (Edinburgh, 1970) • E. Heinrich, *Religionskritik in der Neuzeit. Hume, Feuerbach, Nietzsche* (Freiburg, 2001) • H.-J. Kraus, *Theologische Religionskritik* (Neukirchen, 1982) • H. Küng, *Freud and the Problem of God* (New Haven, 1990) • T. La Rocca, *La critica marxista delle religione* (Bologna, 1985) • R. Mugerauer, *Symboltheorie und Religionskritik* (Marburg, 2003) • G. Piller, *Von der Kritik der Vernunft zur Kritik der Religion. Kant, Feuerbach, Freud* (Regensburg, 2002) • J. S. Preus, *Explaining Religion: Criticism and Theory from Bodin to Freud* (New Haven, 1991) • G. L. Reece, *Irony and Religious Belief* (Tübingen, 2002) • M. J. Suda, "Religion und Atheismus im Verhältnis von Identität und Widerspruch in der Gedankenwelt der Linkshegelianer," *Hegel-Jahrbuch 1979* (ed. R. W. Beyer; Cologne, 1980) 324-32 • J. Thrower, *Marxist-Leninist "Scientific Atheism" and the Study of Religion and Atheism in the USSR* (Berlin, 1983) • M. Weinrich, ed., *Religionskritik in der Neuzeit. Philosophische, soziologische und psychologische Texte* (Gütersloh, 1985).

Max Josef Suda

2. In Theology

Theological criticism of religion arises out of the central nexus of a religious community and, either from outside (→ Religions) or from within it, addresses the understanding of its own development. We find this kind of criticism of religion in the four spheres of → polytheism, → monotheism, the religions, and → civil religion. It has a place, too, in discussions with analytic philosophy.

2.1. *Polytheism*

Polytheistic religions often reject exclusive monotheism as barbarism. Even though many religions might coexist, criticism may still find a place in the striving to assert the superiority of one deity over others in a holy war (→ Hinduism; Monolatry; Tribal Religions).

2.2. *Monotheism*

2.2.1. The prophets of Israel (→ Prophet, Prophecy, 2) gave the → Decalogue the sharp edge of exclusive monotheism. They scorned gods and idols as the work of human hands or as nonexistent (Hos. 13:2-3; Isa. 41:29; 44:18-20). Politically, they thus ruled out any genetic link between the king and God (Ps. 146:3; → Monarchy in Israel).

Early Christianity (→ Primitive Christian Community) took over this monotheism without question as a legacy from → Israel and the religion of → Jesus. → Paul (Rom. 1:19-23; Gal. 4:8) and Luke (Acts 17:22-31), however, tried to show that the Jewish God is the God of all people. They thus found God concealed in other religions. The theology of the → early church took up this line of thinking when it made use of → philosophy as a means of expression for faith (e.g., → Justin Martyr's use of the Stoic phrase *logos spermatikos*, "seed-logos" or "seminal Word"; → Philosophy and Theology). Christianity, it was argued, succeeds the religions.

This view still prevails, even though it might also be claimed that the religions offer a demonic perversion of the true worship of God. G. W. F. Hegel could argue in the 19th century that Christianity as the absolute religion replaces all others, even if, like others, it rests on a religious a priori. Yet it might be only the highest point in the history of religion thus far and not necessarily the consummation (E. → Troeltsch).

2.2.2. M. → Luther (1483-1546; → Luther's Theology) made a decisive contribution by basing the critical potential of Christian faith on the distinction between → law and gospel. The religions think that with our own strength we can attain to forgiveness of sins and eternal life (*LW* 34.314). In so doing, however, they become the law that is beyond our powers. The only real basis for forgiveness of sins and for reconciliation between God and the world is to be found in the cross (→ Theologia crucis) and resurrection of Jesus Christ, which we receive in → faith.

The → Enlightenment turned the argument of succeeding religions against Christianity. Natural religion will be the successor of historical religion.

F. D. E. → Schleiermacher (1768-1834; → Schleiermacher's Theology) reclaimed the field for theological criticism of religion. In reply to the Enlightenment he showed that "natural religion" is a construct. But criticism of religion can no longer appeal to exclusive → revelation because all religion rests on revelation (*Christian Faith*, §10 postscript). This is the premise of such varied critics of religion as W. Pannenberg (criticism of religion as a function of the religions in the debate concerning reality) and C. H. Ratschow (criticism of religion as a factor in Christianity's understanding of itself).

2.2.3. A different model of inclusive theological criticism of religion may be found in the theology of the → Roman Catholic Church, which took new paths after triumphing over → modernism. → Vatican I essentially saw in atheistic criticism of religion a historical intellectual result of "the Protestant heresy," put it under anathema, and condemned it as intellectual and moral decadence (*HFTh* 1.110ff.). → Vatican II, however, sought to understand it as a critical reaction against religion, including the Christian religion (*Gaudium et spes* 19). An attempt was thus made to deal with it, as in critical dialogue with other religions (→ Theology of Religions), by conceding that all people who do not know the gospel through no fault of their own but who are sincere in the search for God may attain to eternal → salvation (*Lumen gentium* 16). Because Christ died for all, → grace is invisibly at work in all who are of goodwill, and they are moving on to the resurrection (*Gaudium et spes* 22).

This line of argument bears features of K. → Rahner's (1904-84) theory of "anonymous Christians," which ascribes a nonthematic knowledge of God to everyone. The history of religion as explication of this knowledge is evolving toward salvation in Christ. Jesus Christ is the criterion of all-inclusive criticism of religion.

2.3. *The Religions*

The positions of K. → Barth (1886-1968), P. → Tillich (1886-1965), and D. → Bonhoeffer (1906-45) offer examples of a criticism of religion arising out of problems with one's own religion. Barth's exclusive understanding of revelation meant that he criticized religion fundamentally as unbelief (*CD* I/2, §17.2), for in it we make our own gods. Barth extends the critical aspect of S. → Kierkegaard's "infinitely qualitative distinction between God and humanity" to every form of religion. Natural theology falls under the same criticism. Later Barth found "lights" in the religions, but they all receive their light from Jesus Christ, who alone is the Light of God (IV/3, 96; → Dialectical Theology).

The critical aspect of Tillich's concept of religion is that in its concrete form as religion, the state of being grasped by an ultimate concern seeks self-redemption and thus falls under divine judgment (→ Existential Theology).

Bonhoeffer saw religion merely as clothing for Christianity. Hence the criticism of religion in → secularism (§4) provided Christianity in the future with an opportunity to cast off its religious clothing, to interpret its basic texts in nonreligious terms, and to experience transcendence through → discipleship of Jesus in his "being for others" (→ Religionless Christianity).

The → God-is-dead theology oriented itself to F. → Nietzsche (1844-1900) in its criticism of religion. The God of theism, it thought, must be criticized as an obstacle to the development of human → freedom.

→ Buddhism argues similarly that the gods belong to the world that perishes. We must therefore throw off religious rites and regulations as fetters on the path of salvation.

2.4. *Civil Religion*

Criticism of civil religion culminates in two charges: first, that something conditioned (the → state, race, basic beliefs, etc.) replaces the unconditioned; second, that civil religion is only affirmative and has no prophetic or messianic component.

2.5. *Analytic Philosophy*

The criticism of religion in → analytic philosophy accuses religion of semantic meaninglessness. The main target is → metaphysics rather than religion (R. Carnap). Whether the texts of religion and theology correspond to any reality outside them is something we cannot decide rationally. Thus the question has no meaning.

Theological criticism of religion cannot be equated simply with existentializing, which sees only a subjective and not an objective point of reference for faith (R. Bultmann; → Existential Theology), nor with the reduction to practice, as in the transformation of theology of "language games" (L. Wittgenstein; → Language). Faith with its relation to the world, its intellectual development, and its eschatological criticism would then have no place. Theological criticism of religion must show instead that positing universal criteria for meaning and meaninglessness is itself religious rather than rational, that it is enough to demonstrate some probability for a meaningful faith in God (R. Swinburne), and that theological criticism of religion may well compete with other structures of meaning, with other religions, and with agnostic philosophies (→ Agnosticism), having its own critical point, which is both rational and transrational.

Bibliography: K. Barth, *CD;* idem, *The Epistle to the Romans* (London, 1953) • D. Bonhoeffer, *Letters and Papers from Prison* (ed. E. Bethge; New York, 1971) • W. Pannenberg, *Systematic Theology* (vol. 1; Grand Rapids, 1991) • C. H. Ratschow, *Die Religionen* (Gütersloh, 1979) • F. Schleiermacher, *On Religion: Speeches to Its Cultured Despisers* (New York, 1988; orig. pub., 1799) 5th speech, "The Religions" • R. Swinburne, *The Existence of God* (rev. ed.; Oxford, 1991) • G. Theissen, *A Critical Faith: A Case for Religion* (Philadelphia, 1979) • P. Tillich, *Christianity and the Encounter of the World Religions* (New York, 1963) • E. Troeltsch, *The Absoluteness of Christianity and the History of Religions* (Richmond, Va., 1971) • VELKD [United Evangelical Lutheran Church of Germany], *Religionen, Religiosität und christlicher Glaube* (Gütersloh, 1991) • H. Zirker, *Religionskritik* (Düsseldorf, 1982).

Peter Steinacker

Religion, Legal Protection of

In the → Middle Ages and → Reformation and post-Reformation eras, most European states had strict laws against blasphemy and attacks on religion, whether verbal or physical, though enforcement might vary, as, for example, when the Reformers staged their assaults on the papal church. Even modern states that are religiously neutral (→ Church and State) may prohibit some attacks on religion, confessions, and worldviews when these actions might come under the rubric of disturbing the peace. A constitution like that of the United States guarantees the free exercise of religion. In addition, some religious bodies have their own laws limiting criticism, at least on the part of their own members. Thus the 1983 → CIC has a section on offenses against religion (bk. 6, pt. 2, titles 1-2), and Muslim fundamentalists are prepared to call for the death penalty in the case of attacks on → Islam, not without the support of some Islamic governments.

At one time European countries also gave legal protection to specific confessions by means of acts of uniformity, as we see from the system sponsored by the Peace of Augsburg in 1555 (→ Augsburg, Peace of) or the Elizabethan Settlement in 1559. While refugee congregations might enjoy special exemptions, dissent under these arrangements became a punishable offense and could incur very severe penalties if sedition was also suspected, as, for example, in the case of some Roman Catholics involved in plots to replace Elizabeth Tudor by Mary Stuart. Some Muslim countries still adhere to this policy, tolerating foreign groups and minority churches of long standing but treating any defection from Islam as a punishable offense. Indeed, even in the 20th century Roman Catholics in Latin America and Orthodox Catholics in countries like Greece still sought to restrict the work of other Christian churches by law, and after the fall of Communism in Mongolia Buddhists sought to make it a Buddhist state. For the most part in the West, however, although some communions may still enjoy certain privileges, legal protection against dissent has ended, and all bodies have the same legally protected rights of → liberty of conscience, of teaching and preaching, and of practice (→ Toleration).

Nevertheless, legal protection in the sense of → religious liberty has its limits, even in lands that offer the widest freedom. Thus if churches or religious bodies were to promote human sacrifice, they would run up against ordinary criminal law. In the West polygamy also cannot claim legal protection on religious grounds, and the psychological pressures exerted by sects may also be in conflict with compelling public interest. Insofar as church activities include matters like education, child care, and public health, they also come under the relevant regulations. The same applies to building programs, and especially to commercial and financial dealings. Furthermore, one religion or religious group may not claim the free exercise of religion as sanction for violent attacks on the adherents of other groups who advocate opposing but legally recognized positions or practices such as abortion.

The general right of freedom of speech that is legally or constitutionally guaranteed can pose a problem for religions and their members by robbing them of protection against offensive statements or virulent or scathing verbal attacks except insofar as they might be able to appeal to laws against libel. Oddly, although the movement of so-called political correctness discourages and at some levels (e.g., universities) even punishes forms of speech that especially minorities find offensive, Christians seem not to enjoy much if any protection under this heading from their insensitive fellows. Happily, perhaps, they are driven again to find their true security and strength, not in legal protection or the social conscience, but in the promise of special blessedness for those who are reviled (Matt. 5:11).

→ Persecution of Christians; Suffering

Bibliography: H. J. Berman, "Religious Freedom and the Challenge of the Modern State," *Faith and Order: The Reconciliation of Law and Religion* (Atlanta, 1993) chap. 9 • G. D. Nokes, *A History of the Crime of Blasphemy* (London, 1928) • W. A. R. Shadid and P. S. van Koningsveld, eds., *Religious Freedom and the Neutrality of the State: The Position of Islam in the European Union* (Louvain, 2002).

Geoffrey W. Bromiley

Religion, Personal Sense of

1. General Concept
2. Theories of Origin
3. Forms of Expression

1. General Concept

Whereas the relationship between the individual and God or the gods in → tribal religion is determined by participation in group-specific rituals (→ Rite), individual relationships with God become possible in the so-called high religions. Hence the personal sense of religion in the narrower sense (American usage refers more frequently to → "spirituality"; P. B. Vaill, 177-88) is associated with modern → subjectivity. Against the backdrop of the separation of society and religion and the resulting → pluralism of religions and confessions, this modern subjectivity is consciously or unconsciously inclined to take the initiative itself in determining and shaping its relationship with God. It does so within (and recently also outside of) the parameters of the religion already existing within a given sociocultural context.

Globalization and an increasing privatization of one's personal orientation toward the world and system of values have resulted in a "vagabond" or "patchwork" sense of personal spirituality as an expression of → postmodernism. Such spirituality is characterized by multiple changes in religious orientation prompted by various life situations or stages (different choices, inclination to experiment), but also by an accompanying loss of commitment or by a general indifference toward religious questions as such and a lack of familiarity with religious traditions in the larger sense. Such inclinations, however, are often enough accompanied — at least during certain stages in a person's life — by an insistence on at least external participation in socially transmitted rituals such as → baptism, → confirmation, → marriage, and → funerals. Participation in these events can be prompted by a sense of tradition, by a feeling of social obligation at least to appear religious, or by remants of a person's frequently unconscious ties to an archaic-magical → piety.

Modern religious theory distinguishes between substantive and functional → religion. The first sense defines religion as belief in God, gods, or a higher being. Reference to the *homo religiosus* can mean a certain understanding of the world or one particular type of human being among others, for example, in the sense articulated by E. Spranger (1882-1963). Given this understanding of substantive religion, many people today would not qualify as having a "personal sense of religion."

In the second sense, religion is understood in the sociological sense as the praxis of dealing with contingencies (N. Luhmann et al.). As such, it is understood as one aspect of human existence in the larger sense, namely, the aspect of self-transcendence. In this sense, every attempt to interpret life, to bestow meaning on life, or to derive meaning from it is an expression of religion. On this view, human beings must of necessity be designated as religious, though doing so empties the notion of religion of any specific content.

If, however, one insists on the right to call oneself religious or nonreligious, one will have to take a middle path, namely, that of understanding religion as the individual development of a person's relationship with the transcendent ground of being (in F. → Schleiermacher's words, the "whence" of one's existence). Also, however, one can do without religion insofar as one derives personal meaning from strictly immanent considerations.

→ Dialectical theology (K. → Barth) criticized the personal sense of religion as being theologically questionable because of its focus on psychological inwardness, and it accordingly completely neglected both this personal sense as well as the → psychology of religion in the larger sense. Nonetheless, as the interior psychological shaping of a person's faith, the personal sense of religion remains both theologically and psychologically relevant.

2. Theories of Origin

The various theories of personal spirituality are shaped by the personality theories on which they are based. Derivation from a specific disposition (whether ontological, biological, or genetic) of the idea of God is no longer persuasive. Instead, personal spirituality is thought to be grounded structurally in the essence of human existence as such (which includes self-transcendence, the need for → meaning and for cognitive and emotional harmony, the need to come to terms with the experience of disparity with regard to finitude, → guilt, and so on). In terms of content, however, it is shaped by social and historical factors. An immediate experience of the numinous (R. Otto) — as an experience of boundaries (dealing with contingency), as a key experience (J. T. Ramsey: "disclosure"), as an experience of being overwhelmed by the unpredictable element within nature or within interpersonal relationships or art or other areas — is interpreted in terms of the corresponding referential framework within the given cultural milieu and thereby becomes a religious experience. These experiences come to expression in texts, various lifestyle forms, community rituals, → symbols, and so on, becoming thereby part of the cultural heritage that is transmitted within the framework of ongoing → socialization by participation in the life of the family or religious community (→ Congregation).

In the cognitive terms of the school of J. Piaget, the personal sense of religion develops within "reflexive operations" in which people express or articulate their relationship with the ultimate (F. Oser, P. Gmünder, and U. Fritsche; a more complex view is offered by J. Fowler). Attribution theory (B. Spilka, L. A. Kirkpatrick, J. A. van der Ven) understands religion as the human attempt to ascribe a religious dimension to certain events under certain circumstances (religious knowledge, the church sphere, failure of rational explanations). Following the lead of → psychoanalysis, some view personal spirituality in connection with the oedipal dispute with the father (S. Freud) or, more recently (and under the influence of H. Kohut's and others' theory of the → self as, among other things, "formed narcissism"), with the severance of a child's early ties to its mother (A.-M. Rizzuto et al.). The developmental theory of E. H. Erikson maintains that religious symbols help us deal with identity conflicts.

3. Forms of Expression

Understanding personal spirituality as a constitutive element and an expression of one's personality requires that we also describe it as a commensurately complex phenomenon with various dimensions (U. Boos-Nünning, following C. Y. Glock). Given these intimate mutual relationships, one can also expect it to come to expression in forms that may be specific to a given personality (between → mysticism and → fetishism), to a certain developmental stage or age (magical, moralizing, etc.), or to a given individual or culture or even group. Such forms can include a withdrawal from the world, mystical communion with God, cultic rituals, systematic reflection, ethical engagement that seeks to shape the world, though also pathological phenomena prompted by various personality characteristics (compulsive ritualism or → moralism, depressive antipathy toward life, rigid → fundamentalism inimicable to ambivalence), and finally various forms that are either personal (→ Judaism, Christianity, → Islam) or apersonal (→ Hinduism, → theosophy). At least in the Western world, apersonal mystical-esoteric piety tends to become alienated from Christianity and to seek out especially religious elements from the Far East.

Current issues in scholarship include gender-specific personal spirituality, interreligious dialogue, and (given the influence of fundamentalist thinking, especially in specific Islamic groups) the influence of religious ideas on politics and on attempts to shape the world, as well as the relationship between → faith, → ideology, and delusion.

Bibliography: N. Ammermann, *Religiosität und Kontingenzbewältigung* (Münster, 2000) • W. S. Bainbridge, *The Sociology of Religious Movements* (New York, 1997) • U. Boos-Nünning, *Dimensionen der Religiosität* (Munich, 1972) • A. Dörr, *Religiosität und psychische Gesundheit* (Hamburg, 2001) • J. Fowler, *Stages of Faith: The Psychology of Human Development and the Quest for Meaning* (New York, 1981) • H.-J. Fraas, *Die Religiosität des Menschen* (Göttingen, 1990) • A. Huth, *Flucht in die Gewissheit. Fundamentalismus und Moderne* (Munich, 1995) • L. C. Moffitt, *Religiosity: A Propensity of the Human Phenotype* (Commack, N.Y., 1997) • F. Oser, P. Gmünder, and U. Fritsche, "Stufen des religiösen Urteils," *WzM* 3 (1980) 386-98 • A.-M. Rizzuto, *The Birth of the Living God: A Psychoanalytic Study* (Chicago, 1979) • B. Spilka, P. Shaver, and L. A. Kirkpatrick, "General Attribution Theory for the Psychology of Religion," *JSSR* 24 (1985) 1-20 • P. B. Vaill, *Learning as a Way of Being* (San Francisco, 1996) • J. A. van der Ven, "Theologische und lerntheoretische Bedingungen der Glaubenserfahrung," *Religiöse Erziehung und Glaubensentwicklung* (ed. H.-J. Fraas and H.-G. Heimbrock; Göttingen, 1986) 39-62 • A. Vergote, *The Religious Man: A Psychological Study of Religious Attitudes* (Dayton, Ohio, 1969).

Hans-Jürgen Fraas

Religionless Christianity

1. Background
2. Understanding of Religion
3. Nonreligious Interpretation
4. Impact

1. Background

Many attempts have been made since the → Enlightenment to differentiate essential Christianity from (1) the → church and from (2) religion. Regarding the former, R. Rothe in 1862 raised the question whether, if Christ were again to come among us incognito, many of those who cannot accept the church's confession would not feel attracted to him and be unwilling to forsake him, whereas many of those in the church would pass him by without recognizing him (E. Klinger, 165). If Christianity and the church are not identical, then one can conceive of a Christianity outside the church, an "unconscious Christianity" (Rothe, M. Rade) or "anonymous Christianity" (K. → Rahner).

Regarding the latter, Christianity has always been in fact a form of → religion. But it might one day become clear that this religious a priori does not really exist, that it is only "a historically conditioned and transient form of human self-expression" (D. → Bonhoeffer, 280). The fact that Christianity and religion are not identical raises unavoidably the theological question of how we are "'religionless-secular' Christians" (280).

2. Understanding of Religion

Religion is influenced by → metaphysics, inwardness, partiality, and a corresponding view of God (E. Bethge, *Dietrich Bonhoeffer*, 871-79; E. Feil, 152-66; K. Bartl, 169-98). It thus belongs to an epoch that is ending, so → Bonhoeffer thought, with the development of → autonomy and "humanity's coming of age" (→ Adulthood). Sharpened by W. Dilthey (1833-1911; → Hermeneutics), historical criticism of religion (Feil, 167-77; Bartl, 200-209) was related by Bonhoeffer to the tradition of K. → Barth and its systematic criticism of religion. As Barth said in his commentary on Romans, religion is not "the presupposition or condition of our positive relation to God" (p. 102). It is not the condition of salvation, stated Bonhoeffer (281), especially in his poem "Christen und Heiden" (Christians and pagans, 348-49).

3. Nonreligious Interpretation

Bonhoeffer's "open and unfinished discussion" of religion rests on the diagnosis that "people as they are now simply cannot be religious any more"; his prognosis was that "we are moving towards a completely religionless time" (279). The theological implication is that we must move on to a nonreligious interpretation of biblical concepts. G. Ebeling expounded this thesis hermeneutically as a call to theological reflection on → proclamation, and G. Sauter expounded it dogmatically (→ Dogmatics) as a call to reflection on the subject matter of → theology (see P. H. A. Neumann, 249).

4. Impact

Bonhoeffer's ideas about religionless Christianity were widely circulated in what was at times a one-sided and popularized form. J. A. T. Robinson took them up in the United Kingdom in his *Honest to God* (1963), as did Harvey Cox in the United States in his *Secular City* (1965). The → "God is dead" theology also spread them. When not misunderstood as demanding the elimination of → preaching, → worship, and the cult, they have been criticized as ill considered and fragmentary, and as a theological sanctioning of the positivism of the development of culture (G. Krause). Nevertheless, as a symbol of the fact that it is "only by living completely in this world that one learns to have faith" (Bonhoeffer, 369), and regardless of ongoing reevaluations of religion and the various religions, they still have a future.

→ Atheism; God, Arguments for the Existence of; Natural Theology; Philosophy of Religion; Secularization; Theism; Theology in the Nineteenth and Twentieth Centuries

Bibliography: K. Barth, *Der Römerbrief* (2d ed.; Munich, 1922) • K. Bartl, *Theologie und Säkularität. Die theologischen Ansätze Friedrich Gogartens und Dietrich Bonhoeffers zur Analyse und Reflexion der säkularisierten Welt* (Frankfurt, 1990) • E. Bethge, "Bonhoeffer's Christology and His 'Religionless Christianity,'" *Bonhoeffer in a World Come of Age* (comp. P. Vorkink; Philadelphia, 1968) 46-72; idem, *Dietrich Bonhoeffer: A Biography* (rev. ed.; Minneapolis, 2000) • D. Bonhoeffer, *Letters and Papers from Prison* (ed. E. Bethge; New York, 1971) • P. M. van Buren, "Bonhoeffer's Paradox: Living with God without God," *Bonhoeffer*, comp. Vorkink, 1-24 • E. Feil, *The Theology of Dietrich Bonhoeffer* (Philadelphia, 1985) • E. Feil, ed., *Internationale Bibliographie zu Dietrich Bonhoeffer = International Bibliography on Dietrich Bonhoeffer* (Gütersloh, 1998); idem, ed., *Streitfall "Religion." Diskussionen zur Bestimmung und Abgrenzung des Religionsbegriffs* (Munich, 2000) • C. Gremmels and I. Tödt, eds., *Die Präsenz des verdrängten Gottes. Glaube, Religionslosigkeit und Weltverantwortung nach Dietrich Bonhoeffer* (Munich, 1987) • E. Klinger, ed., *Christentum innerhalb und außerhalb der Kirche* (Freiburg, 1976) • W. Krötke, *Gottes Kommen und menschliches Verhalten. Aufsätze und Vorträge zum Problem des theologischen Verständnisses von "Religion" und "Religionslosigkeit"* (Stuttgart, 1984) • P. L. Lehmann, "Faith and Worldliness in Bonhoeffer's Thought," *Bonhoeffer*, comp. Vorkink, 25-45 • G. L. Müller, *Für andere da. Christus, Kirche, Gott in Bonhoeffers Sicht der mündig gewordenen Welt* (Paderborn, 1980) • P. H. A. Neumann, ed., *"Religionsloses Christentum" und "nicht-religiöse Interpretation" bei Dietrich Bonhoeffer* (Darmstadt, 1990) • R. K. Wüstenberg, *A Theology of Life: Dietrich Bonhoeffer's Religionless Christianity* (Grand Rapids, 1998).

Christian Gremmels

Religious Drama

1. Origin
2. Development
3. Rejection by the Reformers
4. Modern Revival

1. Origin

Without question, drama in its origins was religious. In classical Greece theaters were built within the leading sanctuaries because the performances were deemed religious events. Indeed it was its connection with pagan deities that led the church to be so hostile to the stage. According to → Tertullian (d. ca. 225), "The entire apparatus of the shows is based upon idolatry" (*De spec.* 4), as well as promoting profligacy and immodesty. Not surprisingly, actors wanting to be baptized had to give up their profession.

2. Development

2.1. This negative attitude to plays persisted for many centuries, although dramatic elements were incorporated into the → Eucharist when, with the conversion of Constantine, it became a public spectacle. This process, which culminated in the creation of Christian plays, was advanced when the → Mass was interpreted as itself a drama. The pioneer of this exegesis was Amalarius of Metz (ca. 780-ca. 850), who expounded every detail in dramatic terms. Thus the opening prayer of the canon was held to be parallel to Jesus' prayer in Gethsemane, and the commixture showed forth the reunion of his soul and body at the → resurrection.

2.2. The bridge that ultimately led from ritual to drama, according to most scholars, was the *Quem quaeritis* (Whom do you seek), which was probably composed in northern France or the Rhineland in the 9th century. This was a dialogue with actions representing the visit of the three women to the tomb on Easter morning and the angelic message that the Lord is risen. In the 11th century liturgical drama took a further step forward with the production of Christmas plays, all modeled on the *Quem quaeritis*. In the course of time a whole series of episodes, including complex resurrection plays, were developed, yet these plays were not regarded as separate entities but parts of one cycle that covered the entire → church year.

At some point before the middle of the 12th century, this liturgical drama divided into two branches. The first moved in the direction of complex Latin plays, preserving ceremonial features and a ritual dramatic structure. The second issued in vernacular plays, such as the Anglo-Norman *Mystère d'Adam*, which is entirely representational and independent of the → liturgy, deriving from other sources. The subjects of all the mystery plays were taken from the Bible, but there were also morality plays, which recounted the lives of → saints or conveyed some moral lesson.

3. Rejection by the Reformers

Sponsored by the medieval craft guilds, the plays were acted sometimes in churches, sometimes on wagons drawn through the streets. Indeed the economic decline of the guilds in the 16th century, together with the suppression of the monasteries, which had frequently provided patronage, has been held responsible for the cessation of these dramatic performances. However, the principal cause is rather to be found in the attitude of the → Reformers. Insofar as they considered the mysteries to include false doctrine and idolatrous practices, they were hostile to their performance. Martin → Luther (1483-1546) allowed the life of Christ to be played in schools, but it was not to include the passion. Philipp → Melanchthon (1497-1560) objected to religious drama in general, and the Genevan Calvinists regarded it as an abomination.

Performances ceased. Thus the Freiburg Whitsun play was staged for the last time in 1523, and after 1575 the Chester cycle was no longer repeated. It was not that most Protestants were opposed to religious plays per se — they did use them for propaganda against Roman → Catholicism — but the outcome of their rejection of the medieval examples was their virtual termination. This ban also applied to areas still faithful to the papacy.

There were survivals, for example, in the Tyrol in the 17th century and in Spain in the 18th, while the → Oberammergau play continues to this day, but they were subjected to greater control and often discouraged. Thus St. Charles Borromeo (1538-84) regarded them as inappropriate and liable to provide Protestants with grounds for scoffing. Yet the value of drama for teaching purposes was recognized by the → Jesuits, whose plays were shown worldwide.

4. Modern Revival

Luther had resisted passion plays because he did not think anyone could properly represent Christ. This attitude, coupled with emphasis on the sacredness of the Bible, remained unchallenged until the onset of biblical criticism (→ Exegesis, Biblical) and the advance of science in the 19th century.

At the same time, an antiquarian interest led to revivals. In 1901 *Everyman* was staged in London; it was seen by Max Reinhardt (1873-1943), who induced Hugo von Hofmannsthal (1874-1929) to join in a German version that became an annual event at Salzburg. In France, Paul Claudel (1868-1955) was writing religious plays, to be followed by T. S. Eliot (1888-1965) in England. In 1951 the Chester cycle, a well-preserved series of 24 plays from creation to the last judgment, was revived and is now performed every five years.

Radio and television also made their contribution. Drama for education was developed, and the popularity of religious themes has been strikingly illustrated by musicals such as *Jesus Christ Superstar* and *Godspell* (both first appearing in 1971). Religious plays have reentered church buildings and become a normal feature of Christian life in many circles as a dramatic means of preaching the gospel and stressing important theological and ethical matters.

→ Dance; Popular Religion

Bibliography: C. Davidson, C. J. Gianakaris, and J. H. Stroupe, *The Drama of the Middle Ages* (New York, 1982) • H. C. Gardiner, *Mysteries' End: An Investigation of the Last Days of the Medieval Religious Stage* (New Haven, 1946) • W. Lipphardt, ed., *Lateinische Osterfeiern und Osterspiele* (9 vols.; Berlin, 1975-90) • L. R. Muir, *The Biblical Drama of Medieval Europe* (Cambridge, 1995) • J. A. Parente, *Religious Drama and the Humanist Tradition: Christian Theater in Germany and in the Netherlands, 1500-1680* (Leiden, 1987) • M. J. Rudwin, *A Historical and Bibliographical Survey of the German Religious Drama* (Pittsburgh, 1924).

J. G. Davies†

Religious Educational Theory

1. Protestant
   1.1. Unity and Basis
   1.2. As an Academic Discipline
2. Roman Catholic
   2.1. Historical Development
   2.2. As a Discipline within Practical Theology

Religious educational theory can conveniently be divided into two parts, Protestant and Roman Catholic. Although nothing at the theoretical level makes this distinction necessary, it is helpful because of the markedly different settings of these two streams of Christianity.

1. Protestant

The Protestant → Reformation, because of its effect of producing difference and diversity within Christianity, created a new context for religious education. As a result, religious education became a focus of theoretical discussion.

The concept of religious education embraces primarily the tasks, presuppositions, processes, and results of planned religious instruction. However, it also covers unplanned, religiously relevant → socialization in → culture and → society, with special reference to influences on the other aspects of life by religious fellowships. In some countries programs of religious education exist at national schools (→ School and Church), and therefore there is special training for those who teach it. This training may go hand in hand with that of ministers both at college and university, though courses may also be offered at special colleges for the training of church workers. Research and teaching also take into account → adult education as the churches offer it both congregationally and in society at large.

1.1. *Unity and Basis*

1.1.1. Scholarship on religious education thus raises the question of its unity. What binds together all that is done in the field in both school and congregation, → church and state? What is the overarching goal that gives religious education its inner coherence? The prevailing historical answer depends on whether what is done is church related and regarded as part of the discipline of practical theology or whether it is related to general religious developments and regarded as part of educational theory and nontheological religious studies.

1.1.2. The church's responsibility in this field gives religious education its unity (K. E. Nipkow 1990). This unity holds, even when we distinguish between → confirmation instruction and religious education in day schools, for which the state may also bear responsibility. This view of religious education is in keeping with the comprehensive thinking of → Reformers such as M. Luther (1483-1546) and educators such as J. A. Comenius (1592-1670; see esp. his *Pampaedia; or, Universal Education*) and A. H. → Francke (1663-1727; *Der Große Aufsatz*, on educational reform), who sought to renew the church and society through education. The unity of religious education draws from the church's original responsibility, namely, its universal duty to teach (*didaskō*, Matt. 28:20).

Not all would agree that religious education is a theological discipline. In the → modern period in Europe, Christianity was increasingly understood in personal, cultural, or social terms, with no special orientation to the church. This view made religious education superfluous as a church responsibility. In the 18th century classical thinkers such as J.-J. Rousseau (1712-78) and J. H. Pestalozzi (1746-1827) and philanthropists such as C. G. Salzmann (1744-1811) viewed the tasks of religious education as simply a part of general secular → education, something outside the church's jurisdiction. In fact, they thought that this approach might avoid what the church of the day advanced as its own dogmatic understanding of Christianity through its own church-based special religious education.

Similarly in the 19th century the educational school of J. F. Herbart (1776-1841) viewed religious education in terms of the development of the religious and moral person, not something within the church's jurisdiction. Educational and cultural theories played increasingly greater roles in setting the tasks of general religious education outside the church's purview. F. D. E. → Schleiermacher (1768-1834; → Schleiermacher's Theology) could thus relate religious education to the two disciplines of education (pedagogics) and → practical theology (see Nipkow and F. Schweitzer). In the 20th century, however, religious education was increasingly relegated to the margins of educational theory or general teaching theory, or pedagogics.

Religious education, however, has not entirely disappeared from scholarly discussion or as an identifiable practice. As religion takes different forms and as religious education becomes part of plural and open multireligious societies (→ Pluralism), it assumes different academic and theoretical bases. In the United States, for example, it comes under the rubric of religious studies. In Britain, which is increasingly multicultural and multireligious, it comes under the concept of religious phenomenology (N. Smart), where world religions are given prominence. Sweden, in reaction against its church-state tradition, has developed something called objective religious education. In Germany religious education for a short time came partly under the rubric of critical theory, with its critical glance at religiously mediated and grounded modes of conduct (G. Otto, in K. Wegenast, 1.364).

1.1.3. The above-mentioned theoretical approaches that try to ground religious education in separation from church and theology all have their weaknesses. Yet, tying religious education too closely to the church and its theology also has its weakness, bringing the threat of a narrow clerical, denominational, or dogmatic understanding. On the one hand, such a relationship affects the whole → theology; on the other, it does not provide adequate criteria for the actual practice of religious education.

One might wish to overcome these difficulties with the aid of a conglomeration of disciplines, in the first place religious studies, together with theology, pedagogics, and sociology/psychology (G. Otto, in Wegenast, 1.360). However, the constructive interplay of these empirical-analytic and hermeneutical disciplines, both theological and nontheological, still does not provide religious education with its required normative basis (→ Norms). What can provide such an integrating basis?

Three conclusions suggest themselves. First, religious education can show itself to be an academic discipline only if it engages in express and self-critical discussion of its own basis and principles. Second, it can do so properly only if it can present a historical understanding of its own origins and development. Third, to do so it must always have a definite historical position, even when it has a supposedly supratemporal and universally valid concept of religion as its foundation (note J. Hick and P. F. Knitter on the analogous problems of constructing a pluralist → theology of religions, L. Swidler on constructing a universal theology of religion; → Pluralism). In the German-speaking European countries (Germany, Austria, Switzerland), the majority of Protestant academic religious educators follow the three guidelines just mentioned, maintaining a Protestant theological identity.

1.2. *As an Academic Discipline*

1.2.1. Religious education in the modern sense arose in the 18th century in the era of the → Enlightenment, even though it was only later that a specialized discipline evolved (esp. through F. Niebergall [1866-1932] and O. Eberhard [1875-1966]). Like practical theology, religious education as a whole is a historical answer to the shattering of traditional claims to validity that used to be taken for granted and to the forsaking of traditional Christian paths. As it developed, religious education brought to light distinctions within Christianity itself between its ecclesiastical, personal, and social manifestations (D. Rössler). But its presuppositions reached much further back.

These roots included the development of individualism within Christianity itself. The individual mystical → piety of the later → Middle Ages (→ Mysticism 2), the Reformation's protest against the church as a hierarchically structured and authoritarian body for the mediating of salvation (drawing on the idea of the priesthood of all believers; → Priest, Priesthood, 4), and finally the emphasis on the personal practice of piety (→ Pietism) were three very important shifts toward → individualism in the history of Christian religious expression. They carried with them the thought of the direct relation of the individual to God, anchoring religious assurance in subjective → experience. As Christian truth became the victim of competing and warring → confessions, and as a sense arose that Christianity is simply one religion among others, the Enlightenment pressed this development further. Religious subjects, using the test of their own natural and rational powers, now became the standard by which to evaluate the truth of religion.

The appeal of religion was certainly not merely to the individual's experience but to those elements in the Christian tradition that were generally persuasive (e.g., the person and ethics of → Jesus) and that in a time of crisis made it possible to pass on the Christian heritage with some plausibility. In the Protestant world, religious education generally developed under the lead of personal and cultural Christianity, and it did so in a way that even in church circles could no longer ignore personal → responsibility. The question of the goal of religious education might still be materially answered in different ways or brought again into relation to the church, but religious education now had to accept the formal and principal criteria of religious → freedom, independence, and → adulthood that Schleiermacher had sought to make binding for the ecclesiastical and theological context (see his *Speeches on Religion,* 3d speech). Religious education had now to meet the demands that were made upon the church and theology as a whole.

A second and accompanying condition of modern religious education was the discovery of the fact of human → development (§§2-3). Children (→ Child) are not little adults. They develop in many ways, including religiously, especially in their understanding of faith. Even advocates of catechetics, which during the Enlightenment had become a university discipline, could not overlook this fact (see C. Palmer in the 19th cent. and, in the 20th cent., G. Bohne, M. von Tiling et al., sponsors of a newly argued proclamation-oriented educational practice). Religious education today is probing more deeply into this side of the task, with inquiries into the problems (Schweitzer) and empirical studies of the cognitive-structural aspects of the development of faith over the course of one's life (J. W. Fowler, F. Oser; → Biography). These inquiries complement previously accepted investigations, from the standpoint of → psychoanalysis and → social psychology (E. H. Erikson), into → identity formation.

When note is taken concerning the criterion of understanding in the process of learning, then the structure of education and instruction changes. It moves beyond an expository communication of "pure" doctrine in teaching of the → catechism by way of recitation, learning by heart, and repetition. Furthermore, → Pietism (P. J. Spener) had already advocated an integrative process that was aiming at personal appropriation and application. The → Enlightenment then related what was taught to natural everyday experiences, to the ability to make rational judgments, and to the supernatural truths of faith along the lines of the Socratic method. For religious education, Schleiermacher brought the idea of → dialogue (§1) into the theory of teaching.

1.2.2. As a result, the discipline of religious education began to take shape at the Enlightenment. A theologically based religious education viewed itself as a discipline that not only incorporated pedagogical insights but also was fundamentally committed to the pedagogical ethos, especially when, even on theological grounds, it had to accept advocacy for both children and adults. Nevertheless, even today this view of religious education is not yet prevalent.

In part, this situation had to do with a view of Protestant Christianity itself. The 19th century saw a determinative struggle between newer views of → Protestantism and a conservative countermovement in the church and theology (→ Conservatism 2). In ecclesiastical catechetics the latter movement championed → catechesis along the lines of mediating theology, or a positive theology of → revelation (→ Positivism), or at any rate in orientation to the doctrinal content of the church's confession. In the early 20th century this historically important polarization led in many places to a programmatic demand for the separation of catechizing from religious education. As a result, the reasons became very different for placing religious instruction in day schools versus its place in churches. The rationale for the latter was more for doctrinal teaching; for the former it depended more heavily on → psychology and the → history of religion. In the schools religious education was partly developing into religious studies (R. Kabisch; Niebergall; see Wegenast, 1.54).

1.2.3. In Germany, from the end of World War I to the 1950s (see, among others, E. Thurneysen, G. Bohne, T. Heckel, M. Rang, O. Hammelsbeck, and H. Kittel), there was sharp theological criticism of what was seen as a profoundly questionable Protestant → liberal theology in the age of → Culture Protestantism by advocates of → dialectical theology and neo-Lutheranism. The very term "religious education" was now avoided or was viewed as the pedagogical aspect of a wholly theological discipline. As a result, it often was viewed merely as the pedagogical aspect of a theological discipline. In fact, this view obscured the three basic issues facing religious education (see 1.1.3), which must see itself as a distinct, self-critical academic discipline facing its own historical origins and recognizing its historical situation. Despite sometimes perceiving itself as merely teaching past doctrines, religious education nevertheless also continues to develop as a project of post-Enlightenment theology (Schweitzer).

In that vein, since the 1960s, the theological task of expounding the biblical tradition historically has increasingly found acceptance in religious education as well. Understanding is now coming to be seen as entering into the tradition on one's own responsibility (M. Stallmann in Wegenast, 1.336). This is accomplished in the context of interpretive instruction, with the religious teacher as interpreter, under the conditions of unbelief (H. Stock) and with the use of historical-critical exegesis (K. Wegenast, U. Becker, W. Dignath, et al.).

At the same time, the waning power of the → family and congregation to help the younger generation develop a living adult faith affects all previous ideas. This decline means increased and perhaps exaggerated expectations of what can be done institutionally. Religious education is now often called upon to transmit the message of faith to young students by way of religious experiences (Kabisch, Eberhard), of religious encounter and decision (G. Bohne), by bringing them face-to-face with questionable or contested situations (M. Rang). The idea of opening the door to religious experience is now a leading category in Protestant and Roman Catholic religious education (G. Lämmermann), notwithstanding the known limitations in how much can be taught or learned. The hope of helping younger Christians toward religious certainty by all-encompassing experience-related paths has brought religious education into severe tension with the Enlightenment's critical emphasis on the task of exposition.

The most important basic problem for religious education is that of unity or integrality. This issue can be put more sharply as the question of the meaning and form of religious education as a whole. Religious instruction in day schools stands permanently under the need for justification, and religious education in general faces the question of its constitution (see 1.1.2). To come back full circle, we outlined in the first section the context in which to answer this question, namely, that of → ecumenism and the faith dialogue between religions. Religious education in this sense serves as a touchstone of the material and contemporary relevance of what the church and its theology are doing.

Bibliography: N. C. Everist, *The Church as Learning Community: A Comprehensive Guide to Christian Education* (Nashville, 2002) • J. W. Fowler, K. E. Nipkow, and F. Schweitzer, eds., *Stages of Faith and Religious Development: Implications for Church, Education, and Society* (New York, 1991) • M. Grimmitt, *Religious Education and Human Development* (Great Wakering, Essex, 1987) • T. H. Groome, *Sharing Faith: A Comprehensive Approach to Religious Education and Pastoral Ministry. The Way of Shared Praxis* (San Francisco, 1991) • M. Harris and G. Moran, *Reshaping Religious Education: Conversations on Contemporary Practice* (Louisville, Ky., 1998) • W. G. Jeanrond and L. S. Cahill, *Religious Education of Boys and Girls* (London, 2002) • H.-C. Kang, *Contemporary Philosophical Issues in Christian Education* (Seoul, 2003) • H.-S. Kim, *Christian Education for Postconventionality: Modernization, Trinitarian Ethics, and Christian Identity* (Seoul, 2002) • H. Kittel, *Evangelische Religionspädagogik* (Berlin, 1970) • G. Lämmermann, *Grundriß der Religionsdidaktik* (Stuttgart, 1991) • E. Nicholson, ed., *A Century of Theological and Religious Studies in Britain* (Oxford, 2003) • K. E. Nipkow, *Bildung als Lebensbegleitung und Erneuerung. Kirchliche Bildungsverantwortung in Gemeinde, Schule und Gesellschaft* (Gütersloh, 1990); *Bildung in einer pluralen Welt* (2 vols.; Gütersloh, 1998); idem, *Grundfragen der Religionspädagogik* (3 vols.; Gütersloh, 1975-82; vols. 1-2, 4th ed., 1990; vol. 3, 3d ed., 1992) • K. E. Nipkow and F. Schweitzer, eds., *Religionspädagogik. Texte zur evangelischen Erziehungs- und Bildungsverantwortung seit der Reformation*, vol. 1, *Von Luther bis Schleiermacher* (Munich, 1991) • R. R. Osmer, *A Teachable Spirit: Recovering the Teaching Office in the Church* (Louisville, Ky., 1990) • R. R. Osmer and F. Schweitzer, *Religious Education between Modernization and Globalization: New Perspectives on the United States and Germany* (Grand Rapids, 2003) • R. W. Pazmiño, *God Our Teacher: Theological Basics in Christian Education* (Grand Rapids, 2002) • D. Rössler, *Grundriß der Praktischen Theologie* (2d ed.; Berlin, 1994) • F. Schweitzer, "Religionspädagogik als Projekt von Theologie nach der Aufklärung. Eine Skizze," *PThI* 12 (1992) 211-22 • J. L. Seymour, ed., *Mapping Christian Education: Approaches to Congregational Learning* (Nashville, 1997) • J. L. Seymour and D. E. Miller, eds., *Contemporary Approaches to Christian Education* (Nashville, 1982) • K. Wegenast, ed., *Religionspädagogik*, vol. 1, *Der evangelische Weg;* vol. 2, *Der katholische Weg* (Darmstadt, 1981-83) • B. Wilkerson, ed., *Multicultural Religious Education* (Birmingham, Ala., 1997).

Karl Ernst Nipkow

2. Roman Catholic

Religious education in the Roman Catholic context has remained closely connected to the church. Also in this context, however, there has been a scholarly focus on the character, content, practice, and goals of religious education.

2.1. *Historical Development*

After the Council of → Trent (1545-63), catechizing resumed for both children and adults. Later, when education became compulsory, catechetical → religious instruction also found a place in day schools. Both forms of religious education were oriented to the doctrinal and ethical teaching set forth in the → catechism. The instruction given in biblical history was functionally related to this teaching. Academic reflection on → catechesis, as part of → pastoral care, was institutionalized in the form of what has come to be called catechetics, a department of → pastoral theology (1774).

In 1831 J. B. Hirscher (1788-1865) presented a comprehensive outline of a biblically based catechetics related to → salvation history. He suggested that catechesis has in view the living practice of a → faith that is at work in → love, the actualizing of the → kingdom of God in the lives of individuals and communities. Psychologically, it must take account of the receptivity of the learners according to age (→ Biography; Biographical Research); pedagogically, it must both instruct and educate (→ School and Church).

From the middle of the 19th century, however, the approach of neoscholastic catechesis and catechetics became dominant, which set a lower didactic and pedagogical horizon. In keeping with the understanding of → revelation as the authoritative imparting of a knowledge of supernatural truths, and of faith as an obedient acceptance of these things as true, this catechetical model featured an authoritative rehearsal of doctrines. The goal was to gain a knowledge of the faith, and the main forms of instruction were analysis of the text and memorization (→ Vatican Council I and II 1).

Without challenging the theological approach of → neoscholasticism, the reforming catechesis of the first third of the 20th century (the so-called Munich and Vienna methodology movement; the catechetical congress at Vienna in 1912 and at Munich in 1928) helped to promote contemporary → pedagogics. (Important elements were the formal stages of the Herbartians, mediated by O. Willmann, as well as the so-called work school [*Arbeitsschule*] and the pedagogics of experience and values.) The goal was to improve the learning process psychologically and didactically, giving training in the religious and moral life and preparing for living in the world. Religious instruction would now also include issues of general education, with the goal of developing understanding, disposition, and will.

J. Göttler (1874-1935) put forth an "outline of contemporary catechesis" (1923) in the form of religious and moral pedagogics, or a comprehensive theory of religious education (not merely instruction). He placed it within the context of a Christian science of education that had theology as a norm in its basic anthropological, axiological, and teleological assumptions (→ Anthropology; Axiom; Teleology). On this view religious education became the central chapter in a pedagogics of culture and values linked to a specific → worldview.

The traditional Roman Catholic exposition of the relation between → grace and → nature (i.e., nature as a presupposition of grace, not set aside but perfected by grace) provided the theological justification for this harmonious interrelating of faith and education. Interpretation of this axiom led by way of analogy to an understanding of the natural human work of education and God's gracious saving work as complementary. A mixing of soteriological and pedagogical categories, questionable both theologically and pedagogically, resulted in a quasi-sacramental overestimation of education on the one side and, on the other, what we could call a distorting pedagogizing of the gracious act of God.

From the middle of the 1930s, in the context of proclamation theology (J. A. Jungmann), a kerygmatic catechesis developed that remained dominant until the 1960s. Involved here was a turning aside from religious pedagogics and a turning back to a definitely theological catechesis. Catechesis was now seen as part of the church's work of → proclamation. As proclamation of the saving message of the dawning of the kingdom of God with the coming of Jesus Christ, it aimed at the response of faith and was in the service of faith. The material, kerygmatic renewal (→ Kerygma) put the emphasis on salvation history and Christology and thus led to a focus on content. Methodologically, the Munich stages were usually taken into account with a fresh kerygmatic interpretation.

The process of social modernization (→ Modernity) hastened the change in the sociocultural presuppositions of religious → education. The resultant procedural changes (shaped by the crisis in catechetical instruction and the rediscovery of the congregation as the place to learn the faith) brought a search for new approaches to both theory and practice. They were given their profile by (1) the broad reception and integration of insights, methods, and questions from the discipline of education and the humane and social sciences, and by (2) approaches to a theology oriented to experience and context (→ Vatican Council I and II 2; Contextual Theology). The goal was religious communication that would lead to Christian → truth and practice; the context was the posing of religiously relevant questions of → meaning against the background of actual human life (correlation didactics; → Experience; Liberation Theology). The three-volume *Handbuch der Religionspädagogik* (Handbook of religious education, 1973-75, ed. E. Feifel et al.), which involved ecumenical cooperation, developed what became the normative approach to a theory of religious education that was based on both theology and experience.

2.2. *As a Discipline within Practical Theology* Religious education is a separate discipline within → practical theology. As a science, its subject matter covers religious education as a whole. It does so against the background of Christian faith and in the context of the educationally relevant sociocultural learning process. It thus needs both a theological and a pedagogical basis. Being the theory of practice, it works within the sphere of both theory and practice and unites empirical-analytic, teleological-normative, and practical considerations in setting its goals. The differentiating and interrelating of religious education and catechesis occur in different ways. As a rule, both are seen to be aspects of the discipline. Catechesis relates to learning processes that, in the context of the church's work of proclamation, aim at introducing students to faith and the fellowship of faith.

Religious education relates to faith in the form of the Christian religion. → Religion here is meant in the sense of an anthropological possibility that is part of human nature, that of living in fellowship with a ground of being that both transcends and relativizes the finitude of human existence (existential religion; → Religion, Personal Sense of). As such, religion is sociologically and culturally mediated, and it thus stands always related to the reality of specific historical religions. The social process of modernization has altered the social form of the Christian religion. Institutional religion, the culturally mediated model of religion, and the religion of individual life have moved apart and are now mutually affecting one another in ways that mean great tension for religious education.

Faith and education are separate, but each refers to the other. The relation between theological and pedagogical reflection that is normative for religious education can thus no longer be developed according to a hierarchical or an analogical model, but instead according to a dialogic model (→ Hierarchy; Analogy; Dialogue). Vatican II stressed the "autonomy of earthly affairs" on the basis of a theology of creation (*Gaudium et spes* 36, also 59). We must shape these realities responsibly, respecting the autonomy of created → reason, which is valid in each sphere. One of these realities is that of education. To that extent we cannot derive pedagogical norms from the theological norms of meaning.

Faith describes a background of meaning and motivation for educational work. It integrates autonomously developed pedagogical programs into a content of meaning that transcends them and at the same time criticizes them from this standpoint for their anthropological defects and distortions. It gives perspective, urgency, and composure to pedagogical involvement. Faith is not a product of the work of education, but it comes in the context of the process of human teaching and learning. There are helpful learning processes both in and with a view to faith (J. Werbick), and educational work can helpfully accompany, stimulate, and support this kind of learning.

→ Development; Ecumenical Learning; Roman Catholic Church; Socialization

Bibliography: K. Barker, *Religious Education, Catechesis, and Freedom* (Birmingham, Ala., 1981) • G. Bitter, R. Englert, G. Miller, and K. E. Nipkow, eds., *Neues Handbuch religionspädagogischer Grundbegriffe* (Munich, 2002) • E. Feifel, R. Leuenberger, G. Stachel, and K. Wegenast, eds., *Handbuch der Religionspädagogik* (3 vols.; Zurich, 1973-75) • J. Göttler, *Religions- und Moralpädagogik* (Münster, 1923) • T. H. Groome and H. D. Horell, eds., *Horizons and Hopes: The Future of Religious Education* (Mahwah, N.J., 2003) • J. B. Hirscher, *Katechetik* (Tübingen, 1831) • T. C. Hunt, E. A. Joseph, and R. J. Nuzzi, eds., *Handbook of Research on Catholic Education* (Westport, Conn., 2001) • J. A. Jungmann, *Handing on the Faith: A Manual of Catechetics* (Freiburg, 1959) • N. Mette and F. Rickers, *Lexikon der Religionspädagogik* (2 vols.; Neukirchen, 2001) • G. Moran, *Religious Education as a Second Language* (Birmingham, Ala., 1989); idem, *Religious Education Development* (Minneapolis, 1983) • D. O'Brien, *The Idea of a Catholic University* (Chicago, 2002) • J. A. van der Ven, *Education for Reflective Ministry* (Louvain, 1998) • K. Wegenast, ed., *Religionspädagogik,* vol. 2, *Der katholische Weg* (Darmstadt, 1983) • J. Werbick, *Glaubenlernen aus Erfahrung* (Munich, 1989).

Werner Simon

Religious Foundation

The term "religious foundation" (Ger. *Stift*) refers to a college of clergy (canons and prebendaries) who are responsible for choral services (→ Choir; Prayer) and who are supported by an endowment. In a → diocese the chapter of the cathedral church is counselor of the → bishop and, according to the relevant law, may have the right to elect the bishop. In the later Middle Ages the → monasteries of the older orders (→ Benedictines; Cistercians) partially took over the organization of these foundations, with the abbey (→ Abbot, Abbess) being or becoming the foundation, and the monks members of it. Aristocratic women's foundations consisted of fellowships of mostly unmarried women who in many cases lived in secularized convents and had only a distant religious character.

Bibliography: K. Dexter, *"A Good Quire of Voices": The Provision of Choral Music at St George's Chapel, Windsor Castle, and Eton College, c. 1640-1733* (Aldershot, 2002) • I. Gampl, *Adelige Damenstifte* (Vienna, 1960) • J. Hirnsperger, "Stift," *LTK* (3d ed.) 9.1001-2.

Bruno Primetshofer

Religious Instruction

1. Historical Data
2. Social and Legal Data
3. Conceptional and Didactic Factors

1. Historical Data

Religious instruction in schools occurred first in the Latin and native-language schools of the 16th century. It centered on the → catechism, doctrine, and their biblical basis. J. A. Comenius (1592-1670), → Pietism, and the → Enlightenment regarded Holy Scripture as the → alpha and omega in all schools.

We see this value in the German tradition, for example. H. J. Hübner's (1668-1731) *Zweymal zwey und funfzig auserlesene Biblische Historien* (Twice 52 selected biblical stories, 1713/14), A. H. → Francke's (1663-1727) *Kurtzer und einfältiger Unterricht* (Short and simple instruction, 1702), and C. G. Salzmann's (1744-1811) *Über die wirksamsten Mittel, Kindern Religion beizubringen* (On the most effective means of teaching religion to children, 1809) all address this point in various ways. The Pietists had in view a life of piety, whereas the Enlightenment envisioned a knowledge of religious truths. The Enlightenment replaced the prevailing method of memorization by rational and orderly teaching that would inculcate true concepts. The individuality of the children was also taken into account at this point.

In general, the 18th century saw the beginning of

a historical study of the Bible and a retreat from confessionalism in religious education. J. F. Herbart (1776-1841) initiated methodological reflection. T. Ziller (1817-82) divided religious education into formal stages. In 1854 Prussia supported religious education in schools for moral and political reasons. In countries like England the churches took the lead in promoting popular education in church schools, which naturally found a place for religious education in the curriculum.

Impulses from → Reformation → pedagogics and → liberal theology governed religious education at the beginning of the 20th century. In this tradition it was argued that → religion can be taught and that, moreover, religion is at the heart of all the education that children may claim (R. Kabisch). The goal of education emerging from these impulses was inner religious experience. Christianity, the school, and education were regarded as inseparable, even in secular schools (→ Secularization), if only because Jesus had given high spiritual rank to childlike religion (F. Niebergall). But it was necessary to strike out on new paths in the spirit of modern theology (O. Baumgarten) if these impulses where to be realized in religious instruction.

Conservatives such as O. Eberhard (1875-1966) spoke of education for life and society. In Germany the Weimar constitution (1919) marked a change away from liberal theology's emphasis on inner religious experience by recognizing the place of religious education for political reasons, although leaving participation optional. In this regard England, when incorporating church schools into a public system, had already made it legal for children to withdraw from classes in religious instruction for reasons of conscience. In Germany the influence of state governments could also hamper schools in discharging their responsibility for religious education (→ Church and State).

→ Dialectical theology attempted to solve the problem of the relation between education for inner religious experience and that for life and society by offering a theological definition of religious instruction. Thus G. Bohne (1895-1977) in *Das Wort Gottes und der Unterricht* (The Word of God and instruction, 1929) defined religious education as the confrontation of the student with the whole seriousness of decision that Christian faith involves. But pedagogically this approach left many things unclear. The discussion that followed, led by such thinkers as O. Koepp, M. Doerne, M. von Tiling, and G. Merz, ended in 1933 before achieving any enlightening theological and pedagogical understanding of religious education. After 1945 H. Kittel (1902-84), O. Hammelsbeck (1899-1975), M. Rang (1900-1988), Bohne, and others attempted to describe the churchly character of religious education, but the churches had a different view of churchmanship from such authors. Part of the problem was the continuing lack of clarity concerning the aim of religious instruction.

Various countries developed different approaches in this regard. During World War II Britain took steps to bring back a form of religious instruction into all public schools, with enhanced training for teachers at universities and training colleges. In spite of its promise and location (in post-high-school education), the program suffered increasingly from diffuseness of subject matter and a failure on the part of many schools to take the discipline seriously. The United States moved in the opposite direction by banning all direct religious instruction from public schools on the basis of the constitutional separation of church and state, with a consequent flight of many students to private schools that would still provide religious instruction. The German authorities cooperated with the churches in setting up programs and in training teachers, but among Protestants religious education suffered from failures in practice and problems relating to the place of religious education in educational politics.

In all of these developments, an underlying hermeneutical question arose. The problem was to develop an understanding of the biblical texts that would be consonant with the modern sense of truth and reality, while shedding light on the stubborn issue of the function of religious education in the modern world. After 1950 religious educators such as M. Stallmann, H. Stock, G. Otto, and K. Wegenast tried to find a new paradigm for religious instruction that would preserve what had been learned from dialectical theology but would also do justice to the conditions of secular society and to students living in these conditions. In countries where religious pluralism has increasingly become the rule, the possibility of providing a generally acceptable form of religious education in public schools, but one that also has depth and focus, was obviously fading, and it thus seemed best to many to leave religious education to the churches and to private schools that have a specific religious orientation or connection.

2. Social and Legal Data

Western societies have become industrialized and competitive (→ Industrial Society), with little regard for what is economically irrelevant. The pluralistic outlook (→ Pluralism) knows no uniformity of religious adherence and has no set educational programs or norms. Different countries, then, have tried in different ways to relate popular education to religion in such a way as both to allow for the undoubted cultural and educational importance of religion and yet to preserve the neutrality of the state and the right of conscience in matters of faith.

In the multifaith societies of Great Britain and Sweden, for example, religious education now utilizes the approach known as the → phenomenology of religion. In parts of Switzerland, and also in Bremen, Germany, supradenominational Christian religious instruction is offered, the responsibility resting solely on the school. In the Netherlands and in other Swiss cantons, religious education designed and financed by the churches is available. France, except in Alsace and Lorraine, offers no religious education in public schools. The same is true in the public schools of the United States except insofar as the Bible, for example, might be treated as literature or Christianity and other religions play a part in history. The former socialist lands of eastern Europe also banished religious instruction from the schools, but moves were soon afoot to bring back at least the moral teachings of religion. In Roman Catholic countries such as Italy and Belgium, church-commissioned → priests and laity (→ Clergy and Laity) provide state-financed teaching in Roman Catholicism. In Germany and Austria lawgivers tried to reconcile the neutrality of the state with the recognition that a secular state rests on presuppositions that it cannot itself guarantee (→ Modern Period 4-5). Religious groups are thus allowed to expound these presuppositions but without impinging on the rights of other groups. What is not clear in these various strategies is how religious instruction relates to the general task of education or how schools think of themselves. Only in private schools that have definite religious connections does the conviction hold that religious instruction is a basic and inalienable constituent of education as such.

Another issue that surfaced during the 20th century was that of the possibility of ecumenical religious instruction (→ Ecumenical Learning). As the German Evangelical Church has noted, religious instruction needs to be related to the witness and service of the Christian community. The historical nature of the Bible and the creeds also poses a need for exposition of the tradition in which teachers must carry the responsibility and in which there must also be a readiness for open → dialogue with other denominations and those without traditional religious convictions. The synod of German Roman Catholic bishops took a similar line in 1974, but the Vatican (J. Ratzinger) and many experts in church law appeal to the unchanging dogmatic position of the → Roman Catholic Church. The religious education that this church commissions, directs, and supervises is thus pledged to that position.

3. Conceptional and Didactic Factors

Various writers on religious instruction have had to take account of the new pluralist situation after 1945, and also of a new generation of students.

M. Stallmann (1903-80) was quick to see the signs of the times. Building on general pedagogical theory, he realized that religious instruction could no longer be church proclamation with the function of ideological criticism relative to the worldviews espoused in other disciplines (→ Ideology). It now had to be the place for the teaching of tradition with due regard for theological scholarship. According to Stallmann, religious instruction received its purpose from the questionability of human existence as a whole (→ Existential Theology). In its teaching of the tradition it had to confront possible ways of understanding ourselves and the world. The changing outlook on the function of education meant much reorientation. Academic reorientation (T. Wilhelm, *Theorie der Schule* [Theory of the school, Stuttgart, 1967]) caused religious instruction to take new measures from theology and general pedagogics, to enter into dialogue on curriculum theory, and to inquire into the function of the discipline relative to the life situations of the students and how they are to cope with them.

In the 1970s education came under the impact of → critical theory and the setting of global aims for academic work; both developments had an impact on the understanding of religious instruction (S. Vierzig, G. Otto, D. Stoodt; → Adulthood). Religious instruction, it was argued, must now shed critical light on religion and facilitate religious → socialization, for example, with the help of biblical texts. There was a thrust toward setting fixed → values and → norms again as the basis of education. This approach also had implications for religious instruction, since it could result in a new denominational emphasis and a new stress on especially Christian content (J. Ratzinger, G. Sauter). Those who in the face of rapid changes in education pleaded for a simple orientation to church standards must remember that a ghetto situation in religious instruction is of no help to anyone.

In fact, religious instruction now stands in a free relation to the → church (A. Feige). Clearly, only a living community with visible models of communal and individual life (→ Lifestyle) can be a suitable basis for religious instruction, but those at work in education do not see themselves first as church members but as adult partners of the church with their own task, in company with the students, of communicating the → tradition and → experience critically and from many angles. For the church this situation means broad openness to its tradition but also the ability to engage in dialogue in an ecumenical and multireligious context (K. E. Nipkow). In encounter with the didactics of W. Klafki, students, who for many years were of interest only in terms of their learning capacities, have now become a central theme for religious instruction (Loch, Wegenast). What is the importance of religious instruction for them? How can their experiences be relevant in posing problems, setting themes, and designing courses? What is the significance for religious instruction of their cognitive, moral, and religious development (Nipkow, F. Schweitzer, J. W. Fowler et al.)?

For a time after 1945 theology had only limited importance relative to religious instruction. This situation changed with the discovery of the hermeneutical task (Stallmann, Otto; → Hermeneutics). With the help of R. Bultmann's (1884-1976; → Demythologizing) existential interpretations, the biblical texts entered into a dialogic relation with modern views of existence in the search for an understanding of the world and humanity. We find examples of this kind of work on the texts in Stock, Wegenast, W. Dignath, and others.

It then emerged that too little attention was paid to the reality of the students and that many students seemed to question the relevance of religious instruction. Then social ethics rather than academic → exegesis became the main focus in religious instruction (→ Ethics; Moral Education). With pedagogics this focus would offer help in dealing with the problems of youth. But in this problem-oriented religious instruction (H. B. Kaufmann), the function of the Bible was unclear. So-called total forms of biblical exposition increasingly played a part. We see this approach in symbol-didactics (P. Biehl, H. Halbfas), which seeks to explain religious → symbols in such a way as to make it plain how faith enables us to combine new experiences with old. In this context we may mention the efforts of I. Baldermann to read biblical texts experientially with students.

When we seek to embrace the relevant factors in → society, school, church, students, and scholarship, Christian religious instruction has didactically two centers: the Christian religion in its ecclesiastical, public, and private manifestations (Biehl), and student problems of orientation and identity in the modern world (→ Development 2-3; Everyday Life). Nipkow lists four basic tasks that he considers important for all the church's teaching, including religious instruction. It must (1) give practical help in finding and securing the self (→ Ego Psychology), (2) foster critical and diaconal social responsibility, (3) promote religion that is critical of self and the church, and (4) develop conciliar responsibility ecumenically and dialogically.

These tasks are helpful in defining goals, choosing contents, and shaping religious instruction that will serve the needs of students. A crucial point is that all decisions in and for religious instruction should be made only on the basis of questions of content and recipient, with due regard for the context of the students. Various didactic options are available in this respect. We might refer to Otto's view that religious instruction should reflect the relation between religion and society with no denominational strings, or the conception of religious instruction as instruction in the faith that explains the church's faith (G. Ringhausen et al.), or the understanding of religious instruction as the invitation to a common search that deals objectively and critically with faith, the church, and religion, both past and present, in the context of students and school.

On closer examination only the last option does justice to the tasks and themes listed. This type of religious instruction might help students, offer the church a striking model of an alternative form of life in society, and show the modern relevance of Christianity. It might also be the place where values and norms and problems of → meaning and → hope are discussed against student backgrounds, and thus show what Christianity can offer that is relevant to life today. A school that does not wish merely to teach values and techniques that are of economic value but wants to help the rising generation to a critical appreciation of its basic rights, including → religious liberty, can hardly be willing to reject giving religious instruction of some such kind as this.

Bibliography: On 1-2: G. Adam and R. Lachmann, "Begründung des schulischen Religionsunterrichts," *Religionspädagogisches Kompendium* (ed. G. Adam and R. Lachmann; 6th ed.; Göttingen, 2003) 121-37 • P. C. Bloth, *Religion in den Schulen Preußens* (Heidelberg, 1968) • H. W. Burgess, *Models of Religious Education: Theory and Practice in Historical and Contemporary Perspective* (Nappanee, Ind., 2001) • S. A. Curtis, *Educating the Faithful: Religion, Schooling, and Society in Nineteenth-Century France* (Dekalb, Ill., 2000) • R. Dross, *Religion und Verkündigung* (Hamburg,

1964) • E. S. Gibbs, ed., *A Reader in Christian Education: Foundations and Basic Perspectives* (Grand Rapids, 1992) • E. C. Helmreich, *Religious Education in German Schools: An Historical Approach* (Cambridge, 1959) • K. E. Nipkow and F. Schweitzer, eds., *Religionspädagogik* (3 vols.; Gütersloh, 1991-94) • H. Schröer and D. Zillessen, eds., *Klassiker der Religionspädagogik* (Frankfurt, 1989) • D. Stoodt, *Arbeitsbuch zur Geschichte des evangelischen Religionsunterrichts in Deutschland* (Münster, 1985) • K. Wegenast, ed., *Religionspädagogik* (2 vols.; Darmstadt, 1981-83).

On 3: G. Bitter, R. Englert, G. Miller, and K. E. Nipkow, eds., *Neues Handbuch religionspädagogischer Grundbegriffe* (2 vols.; Munich, 1986) • A. Bucher and K. H. Reich, eds., *Entwicklung von Religiosität* (Fribourg, 1989) • E. Feifel, R. Leuenberger, G. Stachel, and K. Wegenast, eds., *Handbuch der Religionspädagogik* (vols. 1-2; Zurich, 1973-74) • A. Feige and K. E. Nipkow, *Religionslehrer sein heute* (Münster, 1988) • N. T. Foltz, ed., *Handbook of Planning in Religious Education* (Birmingham, Ala., 1998) • J. W. Fowler, K. E. Nipkow, and F. Schweitzer, eds., *Stages of Faith and Religious Development: Implications for Church, Education, and Society* (New York, 1991) • M. Grimmitt, *What Can I Do in Religious Education?* (2d ed.; Great Wakering, Essex, 1978) • T. H. Groome, *Christian Religious Education: Sharing Our Story and Vision* (San Francisco, 1980) • M. Harris, *Teaching and Religious Imagination* (San Francisco, 1987) • G. Lämmermann, *Grundriß der Religionsdidaktik* (2d ed.; Stuttgart, 1998) • K. Langer, *Warum noch Religionsunterricht?* (Gütersloh, 1989) • J. M. Lee, ed., *The Religious Education We Need: Toward the Renewal of Christian Education* (Mishawaka, Ind., 1977) • N. Mette and F. Rickers, eds., *Lexikon der Religionspädagogik* (2 vols.; Neukirchen, 2001) • K. E. Nipkow, *Bildung als Lebensbegleitung und Erneuerung* (2d ed.; Gütersloh, 1992); idem, *God, Human Nature, and Education for Peace: New Approaches to Moral and Religious Maturity* (Aldershot, 2003); idem, *Grundfragen der Religionspädagogik* (3 vols.; Gütersloh, 1975-82) • J. Ratzinger, *Die Krise der Katechese und ihre Überwindung* (Einsiedeln, 1983) • H. Schmidt, *Religionsdidaktik* (2 vols.; Stuttgart, 1982-84) • J. L. Seymour and D. E. Miller, eds., *Contemporary Approaches to Christian Education* (Nashville, 1982) • K. Wegenast, *Glaube, Schule, Wirklichkeit. Beiträge zur Theorie und Praxis des Religionsunterrichts* (Gütersloh, 1970); idem, "Religionspädagogik," *TRE* 28.699-730; idem, ed., *Religionsunterricht–wohin?* (Gütersloh, 1971) • J. H. Westerhoff III, *Will Our Children Have Faith?* (New York, 1976).

Klaus Wegenast

Religious Liberty (Foundations)

Overview

In its most basic sense, religious liberty is the → freedom of individuals and groups to make their own determinations about religious beliefs and to act upon those beliefs peaceably without incurring civil or criminal liabilities. More fully conceived, religious liberty embraces a number of fundamental principles of individual liberty — freedom of conscience, freedom of association, speech, worship, and exercise, equal protection and treatment under the law (→ Law and Legal Theory), freedom from religious discrimination, freedom of religious and moral education of children, and more. It also involves a number of fundamental principles of corporate liberty — freedom of religious groups to define their own doctrine and liturgy, to organize their own polity and leadership, to hold and use corporate property, to establish institutions of worship, education, charity, and outreach, to maintain contact with coreligionists at home and abroad, to set standards of admission, participation, and discipline for their members and leaders, and more.

The Western Christian tradition came to this full understanding of religious liberty only after many centuries of hard and cruel experience. Much of the ancient, medieval, and early modern history of Christianity was preoccupied with carving out the liberty of the church vis-à-vis the multiple tribal, imperial, royal, ducal, feudal, manorial, urban, and other rulers that composed the → state. In early modern and modern times, new emphasis was placed on the religious liberty of individuals in expression both of new → Enlightenment postulates and of reformed Christian insights. This article focuses on the foundations, the slow evolution of religious liberty in the Christian West through early modern times. The following article takes up the story of religious liberty in the West and beyond in the → modern period.

1. The First Millennium

In the first three centuries of its existence, the Christian church was largely isolated from official Roman society. It received virtually no support from the Roman political authorities and virtually no protection against periodic oppression by them. Christians refused to acknowledge the divinity of the emperor, as required by Roman law, or to swear the oaths or to join the pagan rituals necessary for participation in Roman civic, political, or military life (→ Roman Religion).

Early Christians taught obedience to the authorities but only up to the limits of Christian conscience, following Christ's call to "render . . . unto Caesar the things which are Caesar's, and unto God the things that are God's" (Matt. 22:21 KJV). They also sought to expand their faith and reform society, following Christ's call for them to "make disciples of all nations, . . . teaching them to obey everything that I have commanded you" (Matt. 28:19-20). Both this nonconformity and this agitation for reform by Christians brought reprisal from the Roman authorities. Even before the infamous reign of Emperor Nero (54-68), the Roman authorities began to repress Christians, departing from Rome's usual policy of indifferently tolerating all faiths that remained politically subservient and religiously sequestered. By the end of the first century, Rome declared Christianity to be an illicit religion and Christians to be guilty of treason unless they recanted their faith. Imperial edicts outlawed Christian worship, charity, and education and instituted intermittent waves of brutal → persecution (§2) against Christians.

With the → conversion of the Emperor Constantine (306-37) in 312, Christians came to enjoy an ample measure of religious toleration under Roman law. The imperial Edict of Milan (313) for the first time guaranteed to Christians, alongside adherents of all other faiths, "a public and free liberty to practice their religion or cult" (Lactantius, 71-73). The Edict of Milan also recognized the rights of Christian groups to property and places of worship and the right to restitution of properties confiscated in earlier times of persecution. Even in Constantine's reign, however, and increasingly thereafter, the Roman emperors moved from a policy of open religious toleration of all to one of increasing preference for and control of Trinitarian Christianity. An imperial edict of 380 sealed this shift in policy and for the first time legally established Trinitarian Christianity as the official religion of the → Roman Empire and declared all other faiths heretical.

This formal legal establishment of Trinitarian Christianity brought the church under both the support and the control of Roman political authorities. On the one hand, Christian → clergy were given special military protection, legal privileges, and financial support to spread the faith, to educate the young, to care for the poor, and to build new churches, monasteries, schools, and charities. Heretics, pagans, and Jews, in turn, were subject to severe repression and legal disability, which Christian bishops sometimes led at the behest of the emperor. On the other hand, the Roman emperors declared themselves to be the supreme rulers of both civil and religious affairs in the empire. The Roman emperors and their delegates convoked and presided over the major church → councils, appointed and removed bishops and other clergy, and chartered and administered churches and monasteries. Numerous imperial laws regulated the internal activities of the church, the lives of its clerics and monks, the acquisition and disposition of church property, and the definition of church doctrine and liturgy. The great compilations of Roman law — the *Theodosian Code* (438) and the *Corpus iuris civilis* (529-33) and *Novels* (ca. 565) — were filled with new laws that governed the doctrine, liturgy, polity, and property of the church.

This radical new form of church-state relations drew to itself a variety of new Christian political theories. The most famous theory was developed by Augustine, bishop of Hippo (354-430), who saw in this new arrangement not a betrayal of apostolic ideals of separation of the church from pagan society but a better way of understanding the spiritual and temporal dimensions and powers of the earthly life. In his *City of God* (413-27), Augustine contrasted the city of God with the city of man, which coexist on this earth. The city of God consists of all those who are predestined to salvation, bound by the love of God, and devoted to a life of Christian piety, morality, and worship led by the Christian clergy. The city of man consists of all the things of this sinful world, as well as the political and social institutions that God had created to maintain a modicum of order and peace on earth. Augustine sometimes depicted this dualism as two walled cities separated from each other, but his more dominant teaching was that, in the Christianized Roman Empire, these two cities overlapped in responsibility and membership. Christians would remain dual citizens until these two cities were fully and finally separated on the return of Christ and at the last judgment. A Christian remained bound by the sinful habits of the world, even if he or she aspired to the greater purity of the gospel. A Christian remained subject to the power of both cities, even if he or she aspired to be a citizen of the city of God alone. If the rulers of the city of man favored Christians, rather than persecuting them, so much the better.

It was crucial, however, that the spiritual and

Religious Liberty (Foundations)

temporal powers that prevailed in these two cities remain separate in their core functions. Even though Christianity became the one established religion of the Roman Empire, patronized and protected by the political authorities, Augustine and other → church fathers insisted that political authorities not intrude upon core spiritual functions. All magistrates, even the Roman emperors, were not ordained clergy but laity. They had no power to administer the → sacraments or to mete out religious discipline. They were bound by the teachings of the Bible, the decrees of the ecumenical councils, and the traditions of their predecessors. They also had to accept the church's instruction, judgment, and spiritual discipline. Thus, for example, Ambrose, bishop of Milan (ca. 339-97), excommunicated the powerful emperor Theodosius (379-95) for massacring the people of Thessalonica and readmitted him to communion only after he had done public penance for his immoral act. Pope Gelasius (492-96) put the matter famously in 494 in a letter rebuking the emperor Anastasius (491-518): "There are, indeed, most august Emperor, two powers by which the world is chiefly ruled: the sacred authority of the Popes and the royal power. Of these the priestly power is the more important, because it has to render account for kings of men themselves at [the last judgment]. For you know, our clement son, that although you have the chief place in dignity over the human race, yet you must submit yourself faithfully to those who have charge of Divine things, and look to them for the means of your salvation" (S. Z. Ehler and J. B. Morrall, 10-11). This "two powers" passage became a locus classicus for many later theories of a basic separation between pope and emperor, → clergy and laity, *regnum* and *sacerdotium* (→ Empire and Papacy; Church and State).

This system of tempered imperial or royal rule within the church largely continued in the West after the fall of the Roman Empire in the fifth century to various Germanic tribes. Before their conversion, many of the pagan tribal rulers were considered to be divine and were the cult, as well as the military, leaders of their people. Upon their → conversion to Christianity, they lost their divinity yet continued as sacral rulers of the church within their territories. They found in Christianity an important source of → authority in their efforts to extend their rule over the diverse peoples that made up their regimes. The clergy not only supported the Germanic Christian kings in the suppression of → tribal religions but also looked upon such leaders as the Frankish emperor Charlemagne (768-814) and the Anglo-Saxon king Alfred (871-99) as their spiritual leaders. Those Germanic rulers who converted to Christianity, in turn, supported the clergy in their struggle against → heresies and gave them military protection, political patronage, and material support. Feudal lords within these Germanic domains further patronized the church by donating lands and other properties to the church in return for the power to appoint and control the → priests, → abbots, and abbesses who occupied these lands.

2. The Papal Revolution

This model of church-state relations was turned upside down after 1050. In the name of "freedom of the church" *(libertas ecclesiae)*, Pope Gregory VII (1073-85) and his successors threw off their political and feudal patrons, declaring the Catholic Church itself to be an independent and superior legal and political authority of Western Christendom. In his revolutionary manifesto *The Dictates of the Pope* (1075), Gregory VII proclaimed that emperors and kings had no authority over the church, or over its clergy and polity. Only the → pope, he declared, had authority to ordain, discipline, depose, and reinstate → bishops, to convoke and control church councils, and to establish and administer abbeys and bishoprics. Only the pope had authority "to enact new laws according to the needs of the time" that were binding on all. Only the papal court was "the court of the whole of Christendom," open and available to all Christians. The pope "may depose emperors," and "the pope is the only one whose feet are to be kissed by all princes" (O. O'Donovan and J. L. O'Donovan, 242). Such a bold proclamation did not go unchallenged. For more than three generations thereafter, a good deal of Europe was locked in bitter religious and civil war, with the papacy and its supporters ultimately prevailing.

In the course of the 12th and 13th centuries, the → Roman Catholic Church made good on many of Gregory's claims. The pope and his clergy now claimed more than a spiritual and sacramental power over the church's affairs; they claimed a vast new jurisdiction, an authority to proclaim and enforce law, literally "to speak the law" *(ius dicere)* for Christendom. They claimed exclusive personal jurisdiction over clerics, pilgrims, students, heretics, Jews, and Muslims. They claimed subject-matter jurisdiction over doctrine, liturgy, patronage, education, charity, inheritance, marriage, oaths, oral promises, and moral crimes. And they claimed concurrent jurisdiction with state authorities over secular subjects that required the church's special forms of Christian equity. A vast torrent of new → church law, called → canon law, issued by popes, bishops, and church councils, came to govern Western Christendom. A vast network of church courts, headquartered in the papal court, enforced these laws throughout the West. In the period from about 1150 to 1350, the Roman Catholic Church ironically became "the first modern state" in the West (H. J. Berman, 113). The church's canon law became the first modern → international law.

This late medieval system of → church government and law was grounded in part in a new theory of the two swords that supplanted the tradition Gelasian formula of two powers. The two-swords theory taught that the pope is the vicar of Christ on earth, in whom Christ vested his whole → authority. This authority was symbolized in the "two swords" discussed in the Bible (Luke 22:38), a spiritual sword and a temporal sword. Christ had metaphorically handed these two swords to the highest being in the human world — the pope, the vicar of Christ. The pope and lower clergy wielded the spiritual sword, in part by establishing, through canon law, rules for the governance of all Christendom. The clergy, however, were too holy to wield the temporal sword. They thus delegated this temporal sword to those authorities below the spiritual realm — emperors, kings, dukes, and their civil retinues, who held their swords "of" and "for" the church. These civil magistrates were to promulgate and enforce civil laws in a manner consistent with canon law. Under this two-swords theory, civil law was by its nature inferior to canon law; civil jurisdiction was subordinate to ecclesiastical jurisdiction. The state answered to the church.

The church further predicated these jurisdictional claims on Christ's famous delegation of the → keys to Peter (Matt. 16:19) — a key of knowledge to discern God's word and will, and a key of power to implement and enforce that word and will by law. And the church predicated its more specific subject-matter jurisdiction on its traditional authority over the form and function of the Christian sacraments. By the 15th century the church had gathered whole systems of law around the seven sacraments of → baptism, → Eucharist, penance (→ Penitence), orders (→ Ordination), extreme unction (→ Anointing 2), → confirmation, and → marriage.

The medieval church's law, canon law, was based in part on the concept of individual and corporate → rights (*ius*, pl. *iura*). Canon law defined the rights of the clergy to their liturgical offices and ecclesiastical benefices, their exemptions from civil taxes and duties, and their immunities from civil prosecution and compulsory testimony. It defined the rights of ecclesiastical organizations like parishes, → monasteries, charities, and guilds to form and dissolve, to accept and reject members, to establish order and discipline, to acquire, use, and alienate property. It defined the rights of church councils and synods to participate in the election and discipline of bishops, abbots, and other clergy. It defined the rights of the laity to worship, evangelize, maintain religious symbols, participate in the sacraments, travel on religious → pilgrimages, and educate their children. It defined the rights of the poor, widows, and needy to seek solace, succor, and sanctuary within the church. A good deal of the rich latticework of medieval canon law was cast, substantively and procedurally, in the form and language of rights.

To be sure, such rights were not unguided by → duties. Nor were they available to all parties. Only the Roman Catholic faithful — notoriously not Jews, Muslims, or heretics — had full rights protection, and their rights were to be exercised with appropriate ecclesiastical and sacramental constraints. But the basic medieval rights formulations of exemptions, immunities, privileges, and benefits, as well as the free-exercise rights of religious worship, travel, speech, and education, have persisted, with ever greater inclusivity, to this day.

In the course of the 14th century and thereafter, this intricate system of religious rights, and of church-state relations, began to break down. Strong monarchs began to increase their control over the church, and clerical authority began to wane — in part because of widespread corruption and compromise, even at the highest levels of church government. In 1309 the papal seat was moved from Rome to Avignon, where it came under increasing constraint and control by the kings of France. In 1377 the pope returned to Rome, only to have a rival pope appointed the next year in Avignon, claiming the same prerogatives as his Roman rival. In 1415 yet a third pope was appointed in Pavia, compounding the already widespread confusion and dissent within the church hierarchy.

In response, in 1414 the German emperor Sigismund (1410-37) convoked at Constance the first of a series of great church councils that declared their authority over church polity and canon law, despite papal disapproval (→ Reform Councils). In the Pragmatic Sanction of Bourges (1438) and again in the Concordat of Bologna (1516), French kings banned various papal taxes, limited appeals to Rome, required French bishops to be elected by French church councils called by the king, subjected the clergy in France to royal discipline, and increased royal control over church property. In Germany strong princes and city councils began to pass what they called "legal reformations" that placed limits on church property and taxation, disciplined wayward clergy, and curtailed the jurisdiction of church courts over crime, family, inheritance, and contracts. In the 15th century Spanish monarchs subordinated the ecclesiastical courts in Spain to the civil courts and assumed exclusive political and legal control, through the Spanish Inquisition, over the prosecution and execution of heretics, Jews, and Muslims.

3. The Protestant Reformation

In retrospect, such developments could be seen as storm signals that announced the coming of the Protestant → Reformation. The Reformation — inaugurated by Martin Luther's (1483-1546) posting of the Ninety-five Theses in 1517 and burning of the books of canon law in 1520 — began as a call for religious freedom. Luther, John Calvin (1509-64), Thomas Cranmer (1489-1556), Menno Simons (1496-1561), and other 16th-century reformers all began their movements with a call for freedom of the individual conscience from intrusive canon laws and clerical controls, freedom of political officials from ecclesiastical power and privileges, freedom of the local clergy from central papal rule and oppressive princely controls. "Freedom of the Christian!" became the rallying cry of the early Reformation. It drove theologians and jurists, clergy and laity, princes and peasants alike to denounce canon laws and ecclesiastical authorities with unprecedented alacrity and to urge radical constitutional reforms. The reforms that they eventually instituted, however, often simply reestablished new forms of Christian faith, now again under civil control.

The Protestant Reformation broke the unity of Western Christendom and eventually laid the foundations for the modern Western system of religious → pluralism. The Lutheran Reformation *territorialized* the faith. Luther replaced the two-swords theory of the papal revolution with a new → two-kingdoms theory. The "hidden" church of the heavenly kingdom, Luther argued, is a perfect community of saints, where all stand equal in dignity before God, all enjoy perfect Christian liberty, and all govern their affairs in accordance with the gospel. The "visible" church of this earthly kingdom, however, embraces saints and sinners alike. Its members still stand directly before God and still enjoy liberty of conscience, including the liberty to leave the visible church itself. But unlike the hidden church, the visible church needs both the gospel and human laws to govern its members' relationships with God and with fellow believers. The clergy must administer the gospel, but the magistrate must administer the law. For the magistrate is God's vice-regent, called to appropriate and apply God's law in all aspects of earthly life.

This Lutheran understanding of the role of the magistrate in religious affairs, predicated in part on precedents of Roman law, was cast into enduring constitutional form. The Peace of Augsburg (1555; → Augsburg, Peace of) established the principle of → *cuius regio, eius religio* (whose region, his religion) for much of Germany and surrounding polities. Under this principle, princes, dukes, or city councils were authorized to establish by civil law the appropriate forms of religious doctrine, liturgy, charity, and education for their polities — with religious dissenters granted the right to worship privately in their homes or to emigrate peaceably from the polity. This new constitutional policy rendered Germany, with more than 350 distinct polities, a veritable honeycomb of religious pluralism.

The Anglican Reformation *nationalized* the faith. When the papacy denied him an annulment from his marriage with Catherine of Aragon, King Henry VIII (1509-47) ultimately severed all ties between the church in England and the pope. The Act of Succession (1534), which denied papal authority over marriage and divorce, granted Henry his annulment. Succeeding acts effectively divested the Roman Catholic Church of all its remaining jurisdiction and banned tithes, annates, and appeals to Rome, dissolved the monasteries and guilds, and confiscated massive holdings of church property in England. The Supremacy Act (1534) declared the monarch to be "the only Supreme Head in Earth of the Church of England called *Anglicana Ecclesia*" (C. Stephenson and F. G. Marcham, 311-12). The church *in* England had become the Church *of* England.

As spiritual and temporal heads of the Church of England, Henry VIII and his successors, through their parliaments, established a uniform liturgy, doctrine, and administration of the sacraments, issued the → Book of Common Prayer (1559) and the Thirty-nine Articles of Religion (1571), and ordered the preparation of the Authorized Version of the Bible (1611) in English translation, which came to be known as the King James Version. The Crown and Parliament also claimed jurisdiction over poor relief, education, marriage, and other activities that had previously been carried on under Catholic Church auspices and had been subject to canon law. Communicant status in the Church of England was rendered a condition for citizenship in the Commonwealth of England. Contraventions of royal religious policy were punishable both as heresy and as

Religious Liberty (Foundations)

treason. Roman Catholics and dissenting Protestants were subjected to severe repression, and many of them were martyred.

The Anabaptist Reformation *communalized* the faith by introducing what Paul had called a "dividing wall" (Eph. 2:14) between the redeemed realm of religion and the fallen realm of the world. → Anabaptist religious communities were ascetically withdrawn from the world into small, self-sufficient, intensely democratic communities. These ascetic religious communities were governed internally by biblical principles of → discipleship, simplicity, charity, and hospitality. When such communities grew too large or too divided, they colonized themselves, Anabaptist communities eventually spreading from Russia to Ireland to the furthest frontiers of North America — under such variant denominational labels as Amish, Hutterites, Mennonites, and Baptists.

The Calvinist Reformation *congregationalized* the faith by introducing rule by a democratically elected consistory of → pastors, → elders, and → deacons. During John Calvin's tenure in Geneva from 1541 to 1564, the Geneva consistory was still an appointed body and exercised wide legal authority within the city and surrounding rural areas. By the later 16th century, however, Calvinist consistories in many communities became elected representative bodies with jurisdiction only within their congregations. These consistories featured separation between the offices of preaching, discipline, and charity, and a fluid, dialogic form of religious polity and policing was developed, centering on collective worship, the congregational meeting, and the regular election of church officers. This flexible form of ecclesiastical polity rendered the Calvinist Reformed churches and communities mobile and adaptable. They eventually spread throughout Europe under such labels as Scottish Presbyterians, English Puritans, Dutch Pietists, French Huguenots, and various Reformed groups.

The Protestant Reformation broke not only the unity of Western Christendom but also the primacy of corporate Christianity. Protestants gave new emphasis to the role of the individual believer in the economy of salvation and the individual rights that should attach thereto. The Protestant Reformation did not invent or discover the individual or the concept of individual rights; there were ample precedents for this in Greek, Roman, patristic, and medieval sources. But the 16th-century Protestant Reformers, more than most of their Roman Catholic contemporaries, gave new emphasis to the (religious) rights and liberties of the individual in both religious and civil law (→ Individualism).

The Anabaptist doctrine of adult baptism gave new emphasis to a voluntarist understanding of religion. The adult individual was called to make a conscientious choice to accept the faith through adult baptism — metaphorically, to scale the wall of separation between the fallen world and the realm of religion in order to come within the perfection of Christ. Later free-church followers converted this cardinal image into a powerful platform of liberty of conscience and free exercise of religion — not only for Christians but eventually for all peaceable believers.

The Calvinist and Lutheran branches of the Reformation laid the basis for an even more expansive theory and law of (religious) rights. Classic Protestant theology teaches that a person is both saint and sinner, *simul iustus et peccator.* On the one hand, a person is created in the image of God and justified by faith in God. The person is called to a distinct vocation, which stands equal in dignity and sanctity to all others. The person is prophet, priest, and king and responsible to exhort, minister, and rule in the community. Every person, therefore, stands equal before God and before his or her neighbor (→ Equality). Every person is vested with a natural liberty to live, to believe, to serve God and neighbor. Every person is entitled to the vernacular Scripture, to education, to work in a vocation. On the other hand, people are sinful and prone to evil and egoism. They need the restraint of the law to deter them from evil and to drive them to repentance. They need the association of others to exhort, minister, and rule them with law and with love. Every person, therefore, is inherently a communal creature, a member of a family, a church, a political community.

Protestant groups in Europe and America cast these theological doctrines into democratic forms designed to protect religious rights. Protestant doctrines of the person (→ Self) and → society were cast into democratic social forms. Since all persons stand equal before God, they must stand equal before God's political agents in the state. Since God has vested all persons with natural liberties of life and belief, the state must ensure them of similar civil liberties. Since God has called all persons to be prophets, priests, and kings, the state must protect their freedoms to speak, to preach, and to rule in the community. Since God has created persons as social creatures, the state must promote and protect a plurality of social institutions, particularly the church and the family.

Protestant doctrines of → sin were cast into democratic political forms. The political office must be protected against the sinfulness of the political official. Political power, like ecclesiastical power, must be distributed among self-checking executive, legislative, and judicial branches (→ Politics). Officials must be elected to limited terms of office. Laws must be clearly codified, and discretion closely guarded. If officials abuse their office, they must be disobeyed; if they persist in their abuse, they must be removed, even if by force. Such views would eventually have a monumental influence on the theories of inalienable rights and political revolution in early modern Europe and 18th-century America.

4. Religious Establishment versus Religious Freedom

The Reformation's splintering of Western Christendom into competing religious polities — each with its own preferred forms and norms of religious governance — was a recipe for religious warfare and persecution and for corresponding movements toward religious freedom.

In the 1570s, for example, the Spanish monarch Philip II (1556-98), who was also Lord of the Netherlands, ordered a bloody inquisition against the growing population of Dutch Protestants, ultimately killing thousands and confiscating huge portions of private and church → property. This action sparked the revolt of seven northern provinces on the strength of Calvinist principles of → revolution. Presaging American developments two centuries later, the Dutch revolutionaries established a confederate government in 1579 by the Union of Utrecht, which included a provision that "each person must enjoy freedom of religion, and no one may be persecuted or questioned about his religion." The confederacy led the revolutionary war against the Spanish monarch. In 1581 the confederacy issued a declaration of independence, invoking "the law of nature" and the "ancient rights, privileges, and liberties" of the people in justification of its revolutionary actions (W. G. Grewe, 2.82ff.). When the war was settled, each of the seven Dutch provinces instituted its own constitution. These provincial constitutions embraced some of the day's most benign forms of religious toleration and helped to render the Netherlands a haven for religious dissenters from throughout Europe — and a common point of departure for American colonists, from the *Mayflower* Pilgrims of 1620 onward.

In the opening decades of the 17th century, much of northern Europe was locked in bitter religious warfare between and among Catholic and Protestant forces (→ Thirty Years' War). This religious warfare finally ended with the Peace of Westphalia (1648). Confirming and extending the principles of the 1555 Peace of Augsburg, this new treaty authorized each ruler to establish by civil law either → Catholicism, → Lutheranism, or → Calvinism in his territory. Dissenting religious groups, though denied the right to worship publicly, were granted special privileges to assemble and to worship privately and to educate their children in their own faith, eventually in their own private religious schools (→ Religious Instruction). The spiritual jurisdiction of canon law and papal authority over clergy and church property were guaranteed for Catholic territories. But canon law was barred from use in the Protestant territories, and Catholic clerics and groups were divested of any remaining privileges of forum, tax exemption, and other civil immunities.

While this policy of balancing religious establishment with religious toleration proved effective in securing peace for a good deal of Europe for the remainder of the 17th century, it did not ultimately constrain France and England. In France the monarchy gradually abandoned its earlier policies of religious toleration — particularly as they had been set out in the Edict of Nantes (1598), which had granted modest toleration to Calvinist and other Protestant nonconformists. Supported by the antipapalism of the revived Gallican party and by the new theories of absolute monarchy expounded by Jean Bodin (1530-96) and others on the strength of Roman law precedents, the French monarchs consolidated their control over a national Catholic church. The French monarchy sharply curtailed remaining papal power over church property, ecclesiastical courts, and clerical nomination. Louis XIV (1643-1715) passed more than 100 acts against Catholic and Protestant dissenters, confining their freedoms and imposing crushing taxes upon them. Finally, in the Edict of Fontainebleau (1685), Louis XIV ordered all Protestant churches and schools destroyed, proscribed all liturgies and theologies that deviated from officially sanctioned → Gallicanism, and banished all dissenting clerics from France. Protestants fled from France by the tens of thousands, many making their way to Belgium, the Netherlands, Switzerland, England, and Germany — and eventually to distant colonies in North America and southern Africa.

Similarly, in early 17th-century England, Kings James I (1603-25) and Charles I (1625-49) and their Parliaments established a series of increasingly repressive laws against the few remaining Catholics and the growing numbers of Protestant → dissenters in England. As official and unofficial persecution mounted in the 1620s and 1630s, tens of thousands

Religious Liberty (Foundations)

of → Puritans, Anabaptists, Lutherans, and other "sectaries," as English law called them, poured out of England to make their way to the Continent, and often from there to North America. When the English monarchy persisted in its abuse, the remaining Puritans led a revolutionary struggle against the English Crown. The revolutionaries ultimately deposed and executed Charles I. Furthermore, they outlawed the establishment of the Church of England and granted toleration to all Protestants — though not to Catholics or Jews. This experiment was short-lived. In 1660 royal rule was restored, Anglicanism was reestablished, and dissenters were again repressed. But when the dissenters again rose up in revolt and threatened a new civil war, Parliament ultimately passed the Toleration Act of 1689, which guaranteed freedom of association and worship to all Protestants dissenting from the Church of England. Many of the remaining legal restrictions on the civil and political liberties of Protestants fell into desuetude in the following decades. Catholicism and Judaism, however, continued to be formally proscribed by criminal law until the Catholic and Jewish Emancipation Acts of 1829 and 1833.

This checkerboard of rival religious and political groups in early modern Europe was projected in part onto the New World. European powers, eager to extend their political and religious regimes, issued charters and privileges to colonial companies that would establish themselves in the New World under the rule of the distant mother country and mother church. Thus Spanish and Portuguese Catholic rulers from the early 16th century onward extended their regimes through much of Latin America, the Caribbean, Mexico, and modern-day Florida (→ Colonialism and Mission). From the later 16th century onward, → Jesuits and other missionaries made frequent forays into the American frontier, reaching north to the Carolinas and Virginia, and more successfully west to modern-day Alabama, Louisiana, New Mexico, and California. French Catholics sent colonists to Quebec and the Canadian Maritimes, many of whom migrated south into New England. By the 18th century, numerous Catholic families from Quebec had also settled in New York and Pennsylvania, and hundreds more had moved down the midwest corridor and the Mississippi River to Louisiana and westward. Dutch Protestant authorities chartered companies of Dutch Calvinists to New York (called New Amsterdam) and parts of New Jersey and Pennsylvania. These companies, though only modestly successful, were amply bolstered in the 18th century by new waves of Calvinist colonists from the German Palatinate, as well as by French → Huguenots. Swedish Lutheran monarchs sponsored scattered colonial companies to Delaware and eventually into Maryland, Pennsylvania, and New York as well.

The most prominent colonizers of all, however, were the British, who established colonial companies all along the Atlantic seaboard — from the north in Ontario and the Canadian Maritimes to the southern colonies of Virginia, the Carolinas, and Georgia. Among the earliest and most influential colonies was Virginia, which was founded as an Anglican stronghold. The British eventually assumed formal control of the Middle and New England colonies as well. The royal charters of all these colonies confirmed the rule of English laws and liberties, including its ecclesiastical laws. By the time of the American Revolution of 1776, there were Anglican churches in every American colony, and every American colony was formally under the jurisdiction of the bishop of London and the archbishop of Canterbury.

Colonial America was not only a frontier for European establishments but also a haven for European dissenters, many of whom introduced their own experiments in religious liberty. Both the Plymouth Colony of 1620 and the Massachusetts Bay Colony of 1629 were founded by Puritan dissenters from the Church of England and eventually became havens for Calvinist refugees from throughout Europe, though for few others until well into the 18th century. Providence Plantation was established in 1636 as "a lively experiment [for] full liberty in religious concernments," in the words of its founder, Roger Williams (ca. 1603-83). The colony's policies of protecting "liberty of conscience" and "the free exercise and enjoyment of all their civil and religious rights" eventually attracted Anabaptists and other Christian dissenters from Europe and other North American colonies (J. Witte 2005, 16).

Maryland was founded by the Catholic leader Lord Baltimore (Cecilius Calvert [1605-75]) in 1633 as an experiment in Roman Catholic and Protestant coexistence. Its famous Act of 1649 guaranteed free-exercise rights for all Christians and protected against religious coercion. Though ultimately frustrated by persistent Catholic-Protestant rivalries and slowly eclipsed by the new Anglican establishment policies of the 1660s onward, the Maryland experiment provided ample inspiration during the constitutional debates of the next century. Equally inspirational was the "holy experiment" in religious liberty instituted in Pennsylvania in 1681 by Quaker leader William Penn (1644-1718).

By the 18th century the concept of religious liberty was at once very old and very new. For a nation like America to contemplate the disestablishment of religion altogether and to grant religious liberty to all without obstruction was, indeed, a novel exercise. But legal precedents for such an experiment lay closely at hand in the constitutional example of 16th-century Holland and more distantly in the imperial edicts of 4th-century Rome. And firm legal principles to implement this experiment — liberty of conscience, freedom of religious exercise, separation of religious and political authorities, guarantees of religious group rights, and the like — were readily at hand in Catholic canon law, Protestant civil law, and European peace treaties alike. But as American founder James Madison (1751-1836) put it: "It remained for North America to bring the great & interesting subject to a fair, & finally, to a decisive test" (Witte 2005, 17). The ultimate success of the American experiment in religious liberty provided an important inspiration, if not prototype, for the expansion of religious liberty in the West and well beyond.

Bibliography: H. J. Berman, *Law and Revolution: The Formation of the Western Legal Tradition* (Cambridge, Mass., 1983) • S. H. Cobb, *The Rise of Religious Liberty in America: A History* (New York, 1902) • S. Z. Ehler and J. B. Morrall, eds., *Church and State through the Centuries: A Collection of Historic Documents, with Commentaries* (Westminster, Md., 1954) • W. G. Grewe, *Fontes historiae iuris gentium = Quellen zur Geschichte des Völkerrechts* (3 vols.; Berlin, 1988-95) • Lactantius, *De mortibus persecutorum* (ca. 315) (Oxford, 1984) Eng. and Lat. • J. Lecler, *Toleration and the Reformation* (2 vols.; New York, 1960) • K. G. Morrison, *Tradition and Authority in the Western Church, 300-1140* (Princeton, 1969) • J. T. Noonan Jr. and E. M. Gaffney, *Religious Freedom: History, Cases, and Other Materials on the Interaction of Religion and Government* (2d ed.; New York, 2001) • O. O'Donovan and J. L. O'Donovan, eds., *From Irenaeus to Grotius: A Sourcebook in Christian Political Thought, 100-1625* (Grand Rapids, 1999) • C. Stephenson and F. G. Marcham, eds., *Sources of English Constitutional History: A Selection of Documents from A.D. 600 to the Present* (rev. ed.; New York, 1972) • G. Tellenbach, *Church, State, and Christian Society at the Time of the Investiture Conflict* (Oxford, 1940; repr., Toronto, 1991) • B. Tierney, *The Crisis of Church and State, 1050-1300* (Englewood Cliffs, N.J., 1964) • K. Voigt, *Staat und Kirche von Konstantin dem Grossen bis zum Ende der Karlingerzeit* (Stuttgart, 1936) • R. L. Wilken, *Christians as the Romans Saw Them* (New Haven, 1984) • J. O. Witte Jr., *Law and Protestantism: The Legal Teachings of the Lutheran Reformation* (Cambridge, 2002); idem, *Religion and the American Constitutional Experiment* (2d ed.; Boulder, Colo., 2005).

John Witte Jr.

Religious Liberty (Modern Period)

1. A Modern Consensus
2. The Church-State Consensus of 1750
3. 1750-1800: Breakdown of the 1750 Consensus
   3.1. The Enlightenment
   3.2. Reforms of the "Enlightened Absolutists"
   3.3. American Experiments
   3.4. The French Revolution
4. 1800-1940: Trends toward Religious Freedom
   4.1. Conflict between Church and State
   4.2. Incremental Political Compromise and Reform
5. The International Situation before World War II
6. Twentieth Century: From Genocide to International Norms
   6.1. International Commitments
   6.2. Roman Catholic Involvement
   6.3. National Constitutions
   6.4. Elaborating and Questioning the Modern Consensus
7. Continuing Challenges for Religious Freedom

1. A Modern Consensus

By the beginning of the 21st century, a broad consensus had emerged internationally among most human → rights scholars and advocates, religious leaders, international organizations, and the majority of political officials that religious liberty and → tolerance should be described as positive values. The rhetoric supporting religious liberty is now so pervasive that even those governments that do not respect it in theory or practice rarely repudiate it explicitly. Rather than rejecting the rhetoric of religious freedom, those who do not support it in practice typically argue that they are actually promoting it in ways that are consistent with their countries' needs as understood through their unique histories, religious traditions, and cultures. Thus the rhetoric of religious freedom and tolerance generally prevails, even where the practice does not.

However self-evident and widespread the rhetoric favoring religious freedom and tolerance might be at the beginning of the 21st century, it nevertheless achieved such acceptance relatively recently. Indeed, these notions may be said to have become

Religious Liberty (Modern Period)

widespread only after the 1940s, and only in conjunction with the development of the modern human rights system that began with the Universal Declaration of Human Rights in 1948. Even in the United States, a country that prides itself on respecting religious freedom, federal constitutional protection for the rights of freedom of religion for individuals arguably may be said to have begun only in the 1940s, during the same decade in which the international consensus was first articulated. As the following discussion will show (see 3.3.4), the U.S. Supreme Court did not hand down its first modern decision that enshrined freedom of religion as a fundamental right until 1943, in *West Virginia State Board of Education v. Barnette.* And it was not until the decisions of *Cantwell v. Connecticut* (1940) and *Everson v. Illinois* (1947) that the religion clauses of the First Amendment were found to apply to the individual states.

2. The Church-State Consensus of 1750

Just as it may be said that there had emerged a widespread (though certainly not universal) consensus regarding the positive values of religious freedom and tolerance by the beginning of the 21st century, so it may similarly be observed that there was a general consensus, particularly in the Western world, that *opposed* religious freedom and tolerance 250 years earlier. An illustrative example of this "consensus" worldview that existed before 1750 can be seen in an exchange between Roger Williams (ca. 1603-83) and Samuel Rutherford (ca. 1600-61). In 1644 Williams, who was trained as a Puritan clergyman in England, had just returned to London from Rhode Island, where he was attempting to establish a political system that would support religious freedoms that were unavailable in the colony of Massachusetts. In that year he published *Bloody Tenent of Persecution,* which is now considered one of the early great classics supporting tolerance and religious freedom.

Rutherford, a Scottish Presbyterian, attacked Williams in a then-famous work entitled *A Free Disputation against Pretended Liberty of Conscience* (1649). For Rutherford, whose beliefs rested on a strict interpretation of the Bible, tolerance and → freedom of conscience were dangerous ideas that threatened to destroy the unity of religion and the → state. Truth, for Rutherford, needed to be determined by properly trained and anointed religious and political authorities who had been chosen by God and who acted under the authority of God to ensure the unity of society. From Rutherford's perspective, Williams was foolish to suggest that individuals should be permitted to make their own decisions about religion. If Roger Williams's general position may loosely be suggested as articulating what has become the 21st-century consensus, so Samuel Rutherford's beliefs may loosely be said to have articulated a general consensus that largely existed in the West prior to 1750.

One of the awkward logical difficulties for Rutherford, who argued that there can be only one true religion, was that he was writing not only for a Presbyterian audience in Scotland, where the Presbyterian Church was the established church, but also for an Anglican audience in England, where the Church of England was established. Thus the core of his argument, that there is "one faith, one baptism, and but one Religion," was already flatly contradicted in his two target audiences, which were ruled at that time by one British king, who headed two different religions within his realm. (The monarch of England and Scotland was then "supreme governor" of both the Church of England and the Presbyterian Church of Scotland.) Rutherford, who certainly was not prepared to abandon his own Presbyterianism in favor of the logic of his own one-religion argument, seems to have been oblivious to the fundamental inconsistency of his supposedly biblically based argument.

On the opposite side of the English Channel, the famous French Catholic prelate Jacques-Bénigne Bossuet (1627-1704) made arguments similar to those of Rutherford, but this time on behalf of Roman Catholicism in Louis XIV's (1643-1715) France. Bossuet, who is remembered for being one of the principal proponents of the doctrine of royal absolutism, praised Roman Catholicism because it was "the most intolerant of religions." Tolerance and religious freedom were not desiderata but were revolutionary notions that threatened to undermine the unity of society and the unity of true religion. He believed that those who opposed tolerance were performing a benefit to religion by defending political authority and a unified society. But as in Rutherford's argument, there was an awkward difficulty within Bossuet's position. Though he argued in favor of the unity of the → Roman Catholic Church, he also advocated → Gallicanism, according to which the king of France, and not the → pope in Rome, has ultimate responsibility for religious matters in France, including the appointment of the clergy. Thus the political and social realities that Bossuet and Rutherford accepted conflicted with their own one-true-religion arguments. Although these viewpoints ultimately would lose their influence during the next 300 years, they nevertheless prevailed widely throughout Europe in the mid-18th century.

It can reasonably be said that as late as 1750, European political, intellectual, and religious elites generally shared a consensus view regarding the proper relationship between church and state. (Terminologically, → "church and state" was characteristic of the 18th cent., signifying the relation of the state to a particular Christian denomination; "religion and the state," a more pluralistic term, is more typically used in the 21st cent.) It was commonly assumed that the monarch bore the responsibility of deciding which religions were acceptable and which were not, and that the laws of the state could prohibit deviant religions, prosecute blasphemy, and compel the payment of tithes and attendance at church. It was widely believed that religious dissent was closely allied to treason and that religious dissenters were disloyal to the state. Although some individuals who lived before this time would have disagreed sharply with many of these assumptions, including Roger Williams, John Locke (1632-1704), and Pierre Bayle (1647-1706), they were unusual exceptions and frequently were believed to be dangerous eccentrics or radicals who typically had fled their homelands and wrote anonymously in order to avoid persecution.

The following assumptions regarding the proper relationship of church and state were widely held by the political and intellectual elites in Europe and America in 1750:

Religion is necessary for the good order of → society. Religion was understood to be part of the glue that held society together, providing moral discipline for the potentially unruly masses. Religion provided valuable moral instruction as well as otherworldly incentives to regulate and improve behavior in this world.

The functions of church and state should be closely connected. Although there were many disputes about the relative primacy of church and state, as well as about their respective roles, it was nevertheless generally believed that the political sovereign (typically the monarch) ruled by divine right. These monarchs typically assumed the authority to appoint the high religious officials within their kingdoms. The Catholic monarchs of France and Spain insisted on having final control over the naming of the clergy. Peter the Great (1682-1725) of Russia made the Holy Synod of the → Russian Orthodox Church (§4.2) a department of his state administration. Political authorities also were often understood to have authority to determine religious doctrine. With convocation, the English Parliament determined the theological doctrine of the Church of England, which itself was governed by the monarch. In some Protestant states, as well as the → Papal States, the head of state was also the head of the church. This arrangement had been true in England since the execution of Thomas More (1478-1535) by Henry VIII in the 16th century, and a similar arrangement existed in the Islamic Ottoman Empire as well.

State religions (or confessions) should be established in political territories (→ State Churches). In 1750 Catholicism was the state religion in Spain (and its territories in America), Portugal, France (and Quebec), Poland, the Hapsburg Empire, and many of the smaller states and principalities that lay within the borders of what is now Germany and Italy. Anglicanism as an established religion (→ Anglican Communion) existed in England, but also in some American colonies, such as Virginia. → Lutheranism as a state religion prevailed in the Nordic lands, Estonia, and the non-Catholic German principalities. → Calvinism was the state religion in Geneva, and Presbyterianism (→ Reformed Tradition) was the state religion in Scotland. Eastern Orthodoxy (→ Orthodox Church), in its different national forms, was the state religion in many Slavic countries, and → Sunni Islam dominated in areas under the control of the Ottoman Empire. Even the lightly populated colonies of Massachusetts and Connecticut had established → Congregationalism as their "standing order." (Some important, albeit limited, exceptions to this general rule included the Dutch Republic, some Swiss cantons, and the colonies of Rhode Island and Pennsylvania.)

The head of state should be an adherent of the state religion. Even if the ruler was not the head of the church, as in Catholic countries that recognized the Roman papacy, the ruler was necessarily a baptized member of the church. Protestants ruled over Protestant lands, and Catholics ruled over Catholic lands. The German-born Catherine II of Russia (1762-96) converted to Russian Orthodoxy upon becoming empress.

The church and the state should be visible in each other's domains. The highest religious authority within a state typically was responsible for crowning the political ruler, and the political ruler typically appointed the principal religious officials. The principal religious building in the kingdom had a throne or seat designated for the political ruler. Royal palaces almost always included royal chapels. The state provided funds for religious activities, including the building and operating of churches and monasteries.

The state religion and its institutions should have

responsibility for many of the important social and civic functions of society. The established religion typically was responsible for performing marriages, keeping official records of births and deaths, and operating schools, hospitals, orphanages, and workhouses for the poor.

There is a deep correlation between national identity and religious identity. The official religion was not simply a collection of beliefs and rituals, nor was it a series of theological positions on disputed issues. Rather, the religion was connected to the deepest cultural roots of the society. The most famous religious monuments in a country were entwined with the history and culture of the country: the cathedrals at Reims, Chartres, and Canterbury; → pilgrimage churches such as Santiago de Compostela (→ Santiago Cult 3); the Kiev-Perchersk Lavra in Ukraine; the Jvari church in Mtskheta, Georgia; and Jasna Góra (and the Black Madonna) in Poland. The sites were, and still are, tied not only to the history of a religious → denomination (§§2-3) but to the political and cultural history of the nation and people. Although the terms "national" and "identity" came into currency only in the 19th and 20th centuries, respectively, the core assumption already existed that there was a close link between (what we now call) nationality (or ethnicity) and religion. Thus, to be Polish, Croatian, Spanish, Italian, Austrian, or French was widely understood to be tantamount to being Catholic. To be English was to be Anglican; to be a Turk was to be a Muslim; to be Greek, Russian, Georgian, Ukrainian, or Moldovan was to be Orthodox; to be Swedish was to be Lutheran.

For a citizen to openly reject the state religion is, to some extent, a mark of disloyalty to the state. Before 1750 disloyalty to the state religion was often seen not simply as blasphemous but as treasonous. To be a Roman Catholic in Henry VIII's England was not a matter of individual conscience; it was an affiliation that raised questions about one's loyalty to the king. Although by 1750 the worst excesses of the 16th and 17th centuries had abated, there remained a widespread belief that nonadherence to the state religion at a minimum disqualified a person from holding public office and at worst was an act of treason. The English Act of Toleration of 1689, a milestone in its day, did not extend general civil rights to religious minorities but simply allowed some → dissenters to worship. (Even the ability to worship did not extend to Catholics and → Unitarians.) Laws and practices forbidding religious dissenters from holding political office were widespread, even in the American colonies, where Catholics often were disenfranchised or barred from holding political office. Accordingly, it was seen as permissible to expel from the political territory those groups whose religion did not correspond to the national religion. The most obvious group that had repeatedly been expelled was the Jews, but Muslims had been expelled from Spain, and Protestants and Catholics also had suffered expulsions and forced migrations. Whereas in reality minority religions were most likely (at least when left alone) to be harmless, many nevertheless saw them as dangerous fifth columns and as deeply threatening to the state. (Echoes of such attitudes toward minority religions continue to be observed, even in the 21st cent.)

3. 1750-1800: Breakdown of the 1750 Consensus

For the majority of elites in 1750, who accepted the general consensus described above, the modern rhetoric of religious freedom would have sounded incomprehensible, absurd, and dangerous. How, then, did the viewpoint that dominated Europe and the Americas in 1750 regarding church and state come to be replaced by the consensus worldview favoring religious freedom in the 21st century? The history of the change is long and complicated, and it did not proceed in a linear, progressive, or steady direction. Each country had its own particular path, and there were almost as many steps backward as there were forward. Nevertheless, in 1750, with the qualified exception of the Netherlands, no major European state had accepted arguments like those advocated by Roger Williams and the proponents of religious freedom, freedom of → conscience, and tolerance. But between 1750 and 1800 the prevailing consensus regarding church and state began to collapse. Although it certainly cannot be said that complete religious liberty came to be supported widely by the public during the second half of the century, the idea was transformed in perception from one held only by eccentrics and refugees to one that in some places became very fashionable among the elites and was even embodied in laws (though not necessarily in practice).

Four of the most significant developments between 1750 and 1800 that undermined the 1750 consensus were the → Enlightenment, the reforms of the "enlightened absolutists," the so-called American experiments, and the French Revolution.

3.1. *The Enlightenment*

The most famous, fashionable, and influential European intellectual during the 18th century was Voltaire (né François Marie Arouet, 1694-1778). In 1728 Voltaire published *La Henriade,* a defense of religious toleration, followed in 1734 by *Philosophi-*

cal Letters, which helped ensure his fame throughout Europe. Numerous related publications later appeared, including his *Treatise on Tolerance* (1763). He cultivated supporters within the French aristocracy, most notably the Marquise du Châtelet (1706-49) and the Marquise de Pompadour (1721-64). Although Voltaire had high patrons, he also developed many enemies. With the death of the Marquise du Châtelet, Voltaire left France for the court of Frederick II (1740-86) of Prussia and spent much of the remainder of his life in self-imposed exile.

Several of Voltaire's writings attacked superstitions, condemned the excesses of the Roman Catholic Church, and promoted religious tolerance. His publications influenced a generation of writers who continued his attacks on formal religion and who promoted greater freedom of conscience (→ Religion, Criticism of). It is always difficult to assess objectively the influence that intellectuals, even those as famous as Voltaire, actually have on society, mores, and public opinion. He (and others) nevertheless did influence some people who could make a difference: the "enlightened absolutists."

Other important writers during the 18th century became famous for their criticisms of intolerance. Gotthold Lessing (1729-81), for example, wrote *The Jews* (1749) and *Nathan the Wise* (1779) in an attempt to undermine the → anti-Semitism that was widely and unfortunately shared, even by such illustrious figures as Voltaire himself. John Toland (1670-1722), an Irishman, similarly published a pamphlet entitled *Reasons for Naturalizing the Jews* (1714).

3.2. *Reforms of the "Enlightened Absolutists"*

The 18th century witnessed monarchs who, like Louis XIV, sought to embody absolute power and divine right over their states and subjects. But three of these absolute monarchs — Frederick II of Prussia, Joseph II of Austria (Holy Roman emp. 1765-90), and Catherine II of Russia — have nevertheless been described by historians as being "enlightened absolutists" because they used their powers to foster dramatic legal, political, and social reforms. These monarchs also introduced innovations involving religious freedom that broke sharply with the consensus that had prevailed prior to 1750.

In 1752 Frederick issued his *Political Testament*, which broke dramatically with the consensus described above in declaring: "Catholics, Lutherans, Reformed, Jews and other Christian sects live in this state, and live together in peace. If the sovereign, actuated by a mistaken zeal, declares himself for one religion or another, parties spring up, heated disputes ensue, little by little persecutions will commence and, in the end, the religion persecuted will leave the fatherland, and millions of subjects will enrich our neighbors by their skill and industry. It is of no concern in politics whether the ruler has a religion or whether he has none. All religions, if one examines them, are founded on superstitious systems, more or less absurd. It is impossible for a man of good sense, who dissects their contents, not to see their error; but these prejudices, these errors and mysteries, were made for men, and one must know enough to respect the public and not to outrage its faith, whatever religion be involved" (G. L. Mosse et al., 112). These words break completely with the arguments of Bossuet and Rutherford, not only by separating the religion of the monarch from the religion of the realm, but by openly challenging the legitimacy of → religion itself.

Joseph II of Austria, who reigned jointly with his mother, Maria Theresa (1740-80), until her death, first gained control over the dominant Catholic Church in a way similar both to other autocrats and to revolutionaries (→ Josephinism). He seized church property, closed seminaries, monasteries, and convents, and forbade direct communication between the clergy and the pope. In 1781 he issued *Toleration Patent*, which announced that Orthodox, Calvinists, and Lutherans could freely worship without official harassment. The minorities also were permitted to found their own churches, schools, and hospitals, and significantly, they were no longer denied entry into government service. While Joseph II did not permit Jews the same religious freedoms as Christians, he allowed them to worship (albeit in private), lessened official harassment, and reduced their taxes.

Catherine II of Russia, a German princess who married Czar Peter III (1762), grandson of Peter the Great, became empress following the murder of her husband. An avid reader of Enlightenment literature, including Voltaire's works, she instituted many wide-ranging reforms in Russia, including an early but ultimately unsuccessful abolition of serfdom. In 1763 she issued a *Manifesto* declaring that all foreigners coming to Russia could have "free and unrestricted practice of their religion according to the precepts and usage of their church." They would also be allowed, within some constraints, to build their own churches. They were nevertheless forbidden from attempting to convert Russians from Orthodoxy. Although the *Manifesto* of Catherine falls far short of the *Political Testament* of Frederick, it nevertheless presumed that different religious beliefs could cohabit without undermining the security of the state or the authority of the sovereign.

Religious Liberty (Modern Period)

3.3. *American Experiments*
Some of the Western world's first attempts at political experiments with more modern notions of religious freedom took place in North America. Before 1750 the colonies of Rhode Island and Pennsylvania had already conducted some limited experiments with more modern notions of religious freedom, and other colonies, including Roman Catholic Maryland during a brief period, attempted to provide some forms of openness to a variety of religious beliefs. Within America four important political developments in the second half of the century undermined the consensus of 1750: the Quebec Act of 1774, the constitutional experiments of the individual American states, the Virginia Statute of Religious freedom (1786), and the U.S. Constitution (in effect in 1789) and its First Amendment (in force in 1791).

3.3.1. As a result of the French and Indian Wars (1754-63), France lost Quebec and its other North American holdings within the territory of what is modern-day Canada. The French-speaking Catholic inhabitants of Quebec nevertheless remained, and England was forced to decide how best to govern its new Catholic subjects. The Treaty of Paris (1763), by which England acquired Quebec, obligated the English to respect the religious rights of Catholics in their new domains. England initially attempted to impose its system on the newly conquered inhabitants (or force them to emigrate), just as it had done when France was forced to cede Newfoundland, Acadia, and Hudson Bay under the Peace of Utrecht (1713). This time, however, English officials in Quebec ultimately convinced Parliament to adopt a different approach in the Quebec Act of 1774, which permitted the continuation of French law and allowed Roman Catholicism to operate relatively openly and freely. In addition, if Catholics pledged loyalty toward the king, they would be permitted to hold government offices, which sharply differed from law and policy in England.

The innovations of the Quebec Act of 1774, however sensible they might seem from a modern perspective, not only failed to satisfy the French Canadians but also provoked an exceedingly hostile reaction from American colonists to the south, who decried it for allegedly establishing Catholicism in Quebec. Rather than applaud the law for furthering religious freedom, most American revolutionaries denounced it as an "intolerable act" that promoted the papacy and "established" Catholicism.

Although in many ways the Quebec Act failed to accomplish its desired goal of pacifying French Canadians, it constituted an important, albeit modest, step toward legalizing → Catholicism within English law. It also may well have had the effect of fostering sufficient loyalty from the French population that they sided with the English during the American Revolution and ultimately rebuffed an attempted invasion of Quebec City by an American army in 1775.

3.3.2. The revolutionary period between 1774 and 1783 in the 13 American colonies south of Quebec also furthered the legal and social transformations regarding freedom of religion. As relations with the mother country deteriorated, provoked in part by the Quebec Act, colonists of different religions began to overlook their religious differences and joined together in a common political effort to separate themselves from England. George Washington (1732-99) was a member of the established Anglican Church (which later declared its own independence from the mother church). The revolutionary leaders John Adams (1735-1826), Samuel Adams (1722-1803), and John Hancock (1737-93) were Massachusetts Congregationalists. Catholics in Maryland, notably Charles Carroll (1737-1832), also joined the revolutionary cause. Revolutionaries placed priority not on religious adherence but on loyalty to a political concept of freedom that united rather than divided religious groups. It is indeed ironic that the revolutionary fervor that was stoked in part by the Quebec Act's tolerance of Catholicism in 1774 subsequently promoted religious tolerance for Catholics among those who had originally been offended.

Several of the state constitutions that were drafted during the revolutionary years added modest provisions enhancing religious freedom and removing political disabilities on religious dissenters. (Anti-Catholicism, however, remained prevalent in many quarters of the United States well into the 20th cent.)

3.3.3. In 1786 the Virginia legislature enacted the Statute for Religious Freedom, which may be described as the first fully modern law to support broadly religious freedom. The legislative history leading up to its adoption began inauspiciously enough with a bill introduced by Patrick Henry (1736-99) that sought to provide state financial support "for teachers of the Christian religion." Although it initially appeared that the Henry bill would be adopted, James Madison (1751-1836), then a member of the Virginia legislature, criticized the bill in a famous 1785 publication entitled *A Memorial and Remonstrance against Religious Assessments*. This short piece, which helped turn the tide against the Henry bill, was one of the earliest modern articulations of the ideology of religious freedom and the separation of church and state. In it Madison made 15 separate, albeit interrelated, arguments regarding religious freedom that effectively rejected not only each element of the consensus of 1750 described above but also articulated all of the elements that would become part of the modern consensus about religious freedom (see 6.4).

In brief, Madison argued that the state prospers not by ensuring uniformity of religion or by funding the majority religion but by guaranteeing freedom of conscience. Similarly, religion itself prospers best when it relies not on support from the state but on the support of its adherents. Moreover, political officials as such have no special knowledge, competence, or authority to legislate regarding religious matters, and they act illegitimately whenever they involve themselves in deciding issues of religious doctrine. After the *Memorial and Remonstrance* helped turn the tide against Henry's proposal, Madison took the next step and reintroduced a bill on religious liberty that had first been written by Thomas Jefferson (1743-1826) in 1777 but had since languished. Thus Jefferson's original draft, as amended, became the Virginia Statute on Religious liberty in 1786.

The Virginia Statute, as adopted, declares that political authorities as such have no competence in religious matters and that when they enact laws in the religious domain, they turn both themselves and the people into hypocrites. The statute provides that "no man shall be compelled to frequent or support any religious worship, place, or ministry whatsoever, nor shall be enforced, restrained, molested, or burthened in his body or goods, nor shall otherwise suffer, on account of his religious opinions or belief; but that all men shall be free to profess, and by argument to maintain, their opinions in matters of religion, and that the same shall in no wise diminish, enlarge, or affect their civil capacities."

3.3.4. In 1787, the year after the adoption of the Virginia Statute for Religious Freedom, the Constitutional Convention in Philadelphia, again with the significant influence of James Madison, adopted the Constitution of the United States, which became the world's first modern constitution and is now the world's oldest extant written constitution. Although the famous First Amendment, drafted in 1789, contains the Constitution's most cited provisions pertaining to religion, article 6 of the original Constitution, within the 18th-century context, was perhaps of greater immediate practical significance. This article provides that "no religious test shall ever be required as a qualification to any office or public trust under the United States." This wording effectively severed the connection between loyalty to a religion and loyalty to the state.

The First Amendment added the important provisions that "Congress shall make no law respecting an establishment of religion, or prohibiting the free exercise thereof. . . ." Scores of books and hundreds of court decisions have been written arguing and explaining the meaning of these 16 words. Until the 1940s, however, they were generally understood to apply only to the U.S. federal government. The first ten words, the Establishment Clause, is generally understood to prohibit government financial support for, or endorsement of, particular religions. The second part, the Free-Exercise Clause, has generally been understood to allow freedom of religious activities.

Americans might be inclined to think of the importance of the religion clauses as lying fallow until the courts began to interpret and apply them in concrete cases in the late 19th century, and as providing little positive support for religious freedom until the mid-20th century. While from one perspective this view is correct, it overlooks how the original underlying constitutional ideology and assumptions regarding religion constituted a significant break from the consensus of 1750. The Constitution rejected, at least from a federal perspective, several important elements of that consensus, including the notions that the unity of the state demanded unity of religion, that the sovereign could demand adherence to the sovereign's religion, and that rights and privileges of citizens could be altered based upon religious affiliation. (It should be recognized that some of the individual states did have laws that discriminated on the basis of religion and that personal and social discrimination existed within the federal government, despite the constitutional prohibitions.)

3.4. ***The French Revolution***

In France the revolutionary decade from 1789 to 1799 saw a number of dramatic, and often conflicting, actions that affected the development of religious freedom. In order to understand the effect of the → Revolution, we first must consider two important underlying factors. First, the Roman Catholic Church in France had a powerful influence over society as a result of its financial wealth, political influence, and intellectual dominance, including its effective dominance in education. Second, France had a long tradition of Gallicanism, whereby the monarch used his political power to control religion. Thus the church and state each sought to influence the other in order to enhance its own power and prestige.

In the heady first days of the Revolution of 1789, the National Assembly promulgated the Declaration of the Rights of Man and of the Citizen, which included the important declaration that "no one may be disturbed on the basis of opinions, including religious opinions, provided that the manifestations do not interfere with the public order established by law." This declaration, though it has not had an uninterrupted life in French law, has been one of the most rhetorically influential declarations of religious freedom since the time it was adopted. It was later incorporated into the French Constitution of 1958 and thus has constitutional status in France today.

Although the 1789 declaration speaks of the liberty of conscience advocated by the Enlightenment philosophes, the practices followed in France during the years following its promulgation resemble more typically the Gallican approach to religion, where the state involved itself deeply in religious affairs in order to enhance perceived state interests. Many of the actions taken during the following ten years did not emphasize formal religious freedom per se but were instead state attacks on the power, wealth, and influence of the Roman Catholic Church. During the decade some important steps were taken that promoted religious freedom, including the emancipation of the Jews in 1791, but others were vindictive assaults on religious power. Though the Gallican measures taken during the different phases of the Revolution may have been intended less to promote freedom than to undermine the Catholic Church, they had the significant effect of undermining the consensus of 1750 by rejecting the once-sacred notion of the unity of church and state.

By the end of the 18th century, the principal arguments in support of religious freedom had been articulated fully by philosophers, theologians, and political analysts, including the arguments based upon the natural rights of the individual, the God-given right of conscience, the incompetence of the state to determine religious doctrines, and the view that religious freedom would enhance rather than undermine the power and wealth of society. In addition to these philosophical arguments, numerous laws and political measures had been undertaken in states ranging from the autocratic to the democratic to the revolutionary. While it would be incorrect to imagine that a new consensus had emerged by 1800, it certainly can be said that the 50 years between 1750 and 1800 demolished the old consensus.

4. 1800-1940: Trends toward Religious Freedom

After 1800 religious minorities and others were increasingly emboldened to change national laws and practices that interfered with freedom of religion. Although each state within western Europe and northern America pursued a different path regarding freedom of religion, two basic trends emerged within states between 1800 and World War II (1939-45). The first may be described as one of hostile conflict between church and state, particularly in countries with large and powerful Roman Catholic constituencies. The second trend was that of incremental political → compromise and reform, which gradually extended religious liberty to groups considered to be dissenters. Although these two general trends can be identified, it should be emphasized that there were many variations within them. Reformers were active in countries that principally pursued a conflictual approach, and conflict often lay close to the surface (and sometimes erupted) in states that generally followed the reformist trend.

4.1. *Conflict between Church and State*

Since the 16th-century → Reformation, Catholics and Protestants typically thought of each other not as coreligionists in the body of Christ but as fierce opponents in a struggle to assume the mantle of the true church. For more than 200 years they had fought against each other and imagined the other to be a bitter enemy. Each had seen the worst in the other and had minimized its own shortcomings. Until 1965, when the Second → Vatican Council issued *Dignitatis humanae,* the Declaration on Religious Liberty (see 6.2), the Roman Catholic Church as an institution was officially opposed to religious freedom.

During the 19th century, as European states were undergoing the upheavals of social and political revolution and witnessing the rise of nationalism, → democracy, religious freedom, industrialism, science (particularly Darwinism), and efforts to establish public education, the Vatican issued numerous → encyclicals and papal letters in reaction to these developments. For example, in the encyclical *Mirari vos* (1832), one of the most famous statements of opposition to the modern trends, Gregory XVI (1831-46) proclaimed his opposition to liberty of conscience, the separation of church and state, and democratic rule. The encyclical decried the "absurd and erroneous proposition which claims that liberty of conscience must be maintained for everyone. It spreads ruin in sacred and civil affairs, though some repeat over and over again with the greatest impudence that some advantage accrues to religion from it" (§14). This language, which echoes the consensus of 1750, insists that "certain teachings are being spread among the common people in writings which attack the trust and submission due to princes; the torches of treason are being lit everywhere. . . . Therefore both divine and human laws cry out against those who strive by treason and sedition to drive the people from confidence in their princes and force them from their government" (§17). It predicted that civil unhappiness would be created if the church were to be separated from the state, because such an arrangement would "break the mutual concord between temporal authority and the priesthood. It is certain that that concord which always was favorable and beneficial for the sacred and the civil order is feared by the shameless lovers of liberty" (§20). Thus liberty, free conscience, freedom of religion, and democracy were all anathema.

Pius IX (1846-78), who began his papacy as a reformer, ultimately returned to his predecessor's condemnation of emerging democratic forms of government and of liberty of conscience in *Quanta cura* (1864) and in the famous *Syllabus errorum* (→ Syllabus of Errors, 1865). In addition, he articulated other dogmas that seemed to non-Catholics to distance Catholic teachings even further from other Christian traditions. Two of the most important were the teaching that Mary's immaculate conception paralleled Jesus' miraculous birth, as announced in *Ineffabilis Deus* (1854; → Mariology 1.3), and the First Dogmatic Constitution on the Church of Christ (1870; → Infallibility 3), which asserted that the → pope was incapable of error when speaking ex cathedra and that the Roman Catholic Church had primacy over all other churches. Regardless of whether these teachings were sound Catholic doctrine, they certainly helped convince non-Catholics that the church was opposed both to religious liberty and to all other forms of Christianity.

With both imagined fears and sober readings of papal pronouncements, both Protestants and secularists, suspicious of Catholic intentions, believed that this powerful church constituted a dangerous threat. In several countries, most notably France, Germany, Italy, and Spain, this lingering suspicion of Catholicism, combined with official Catholic denunciations of Protestants and → modernism, led to ferocious conflicts.

4.1.1. The archetypal conflict took place in France, where the anti-Catholic Revolution of 1789-99 was followed by a Napoleonic interregnum that once again subjected Catholicism to Gallicanism until the Bourbon → restoration (§4.1) was complete in 1815. But the restoration that followed unwisely attempted to raise Catholicism to the position that it had held before the Revolution. This restoration in turn provoked a counterreaction, followed by efforts to reestablish Catholicism. Thus in 19th-century France, as regime followed regime, the religious and antireligious passions did not exhaust each other but continually fed the fears of the other.

When virulently anti-Catholic leaders of the Third Republic finally came to power in the 1880s, the lingering hostilities and conflicts overflowed in a series of laws and actions that sought to control Catholic influence in a way that, although less bloody than the Revolution, nevertheless was hostile. By the end of the 1880s, Catholic control over education had largely ended. Between 1901 and 1907 a series of laws sought to permanently end Catholic dominance and bring much of its former influence under the control of the state.

The conflicts continued through World War II, when Catholic reactionaries aligned themselves with the regime of Maréchal Philippe Pétain, which acceded to Nazi demands. Each step of this conflict provoked counterreactions, with the unity of church and state seeming less and less a reality and more and more a fantasy.

4.1.2. In Germany and Italy, each of which began the 19th century as disjointed principalities and territories, the quest for political unification conflicted with perceived Catholic interests. Ultimately a battle developed between the leaders of unification and the Roman Catholic Church, including Otto von Bismarck (1815-98) and William I (king of Prussia 1861-88, German emp. 1871-88) in Germany's → Kulturkampf, and in Italy's Risorgimento, led by King Victor Emmanuel II (1861-78), Giuseppe Garibaldi (1807-82), and Count Camillo Benso Cavour (1810-61).

4.1.3. Spain, which had effectively been unified politically since the late 15th century, similarly experienced the conflicts between Catholics and anti-Catholics both in the 19th century and during the Second Spanish Republic and the Civil War of the 1930s. Both left-wing Spanish Republicans and the various Catholic elements that united as the Confederación Española de Derechas Autónomas (Spanish Confederation of Autonomous Rightist Groups) had no difficulty justifying their own excesses as a necessary response to the excesses of their opponents. Regardless of the merits of the positions of the opponents, and regardless of the arguments that they might articulate, the battles exposed the reality that a regime with a unified church and state operating harmoniously was no longer possible. To the extent that there would be a unification of church and state — as in Spain until the 1970s — it could be achieved only through repressive measures imposed by a dictatorial regime.

4.1.4. Many of the countries that experienced the conflicts between those who sought to keep church and state unified and their opponents nevertheless attained something of a truce. In these cases the consensus of 1750 was undermined less by a wise recognition that society needed to be tolerant to different points of view than from exhaustion caused by bitter struggles. In Germany Bismarck's Kulturkampf has largely faded into historical memory. In France the church-state conflict has left wounds that can be reopened by the slightest of provocations. In Italy an uneasy truce continues to prevail in a society that remains overwhelmingly and symbolically Catholic, but where the political and moral authority of the Vatican is frequently ignored. By 1940 the rightists in Spain had violently suppressed the Republicans, and the consensus of 1750 reemerged as an official orthodoxy under the dictatorial regime of Francisco Franco (1936-75). It was not until the mid-1970s, with the death of Franco and the accession of Juan Carlos to the throne, that Spain fully abandoned the ideology of 1750 and began to follow a path of compromise and reform.

4.2. *Incremental Political Compromise and Reform*

Not all countries followed the path of open hostility between a church that largely refused to reform and a society that increasingly was willing to seek power through conflict and often violence. Two revealing and illustrative examples are those of Belgium and Great Britain.

4.2.1. Following the defeat of Napoléon and the decisions of the Congress of Vienna in 1815, Belgium and Netherlands were united under the Dutch king William I (1815-40). The largely Catholic population of Belgium resented having a Protestant king. The French Revolution of 1830, which ousted the last Bourbon king, Charles X (1824-30), inspired the Belgians to oust the Dutch from Brussels.

Though the political and social circumstances were entirely different from those of the American Revolution of the 18th century, the Belgians of different religious and political positions similarly chose to unite in favor of independence, overlooking their religious differences. This approach of compromise in order to achieve other goals led to the adoption of the Belgian Constitution of 1831, which arguably is the first constitution to articulate rights of religious freedom in what has now become the fully modern style. Belgium's later Constitution of 1994 preserved the text of the four articles pertaining to rights of religious freedom from the 1831 constitution, and thus it may be said that the compromise from the first third of the 19th century has largely prevailed for almost 200 years.

4.2.2. From the 16th century, England had experienced violent conflicts related to claims of religious freedom. The first was that between the Church of England and Catholic dissenters. The second major conflict occurred during the 17th-century English civil wars between the Puritans and the Church of England (though they nevertheless were able to unite against the Irish Catholics, their common foe). These violent conflicts left bitter memories on all sides and deep suspicions by the majority Protestants that Roman Catholicism was not simply a different religious belief system but a treasonous threat to the state. As it entered the 19th century, England easily could have followed the path of open and violent conflict, though it ultimately adopted a policy of reform. Over the opposition of traditionalists, reformers between 1828 and 1832 enacted several highly unpopular measures that nevertheless had the long-term effect of diffusing what might later have become explosive.

The first of the 19th-century reforms came with the 1828 repeal of the Test and Corporation Acts for dissenting Protestants, thereby allowing them to become members of Parliament. In 1829 and 1832 highly controversial Catholic Emancipation Acts were adopted that legalized Catholicism and allowed it to establish charitable enterprises. The Religious Disabilities Act of 1846 subsequently extended basic rights to Jews.

5. The International Situation before World War II

Some of the earliest written legal guarantees for freedom of religion came in the form of treaties in which states obligated themselves to protect religious groups that existed within their realms or spheres of influence. Some of these treaties predated 1750: the Capitulation of 1535 (subsequently renewed), which gave France responsibility for protecting Christians in Palestine, and a secret clause in the 1625 marriage treaty between England and France (involving Charles I and Henrietta Maria) promising to suspend English penal laws against Catholics.

As mentioned above, freedom of religion was also one of the components of the Treaty of Paris (1763), in which England agreed to protect the rights of Catholics living in newly acquired Quebec. Other such examples include the decisions of the Congress of Vienna (1814-15), which extended rights to Catholics in Belgium and Savoy; a protocol to a treaty in 1830 pertaining to Greece that was signed by England, France, and Russia requiring the new Greek state to allow public offices to be held by people regardless of their religion; the Treaty of

Paris (1856), guaranteeing rights to Christians living in parts of the Ottoman Empire; the Treaty of London (1864), extending and renewing provisions of the 1830 protocol with Greece; the Treaty of Berlin (1878), which provided guarantees to religious minorities in the Balkans; and the Treaty of Constantinople (1914), providing for religious freedom for Muslims.

Following World War I, a series of multilateral treaties commonly known as the minority treaties were signed that guaranteed the rights of → minorities living in the Balkans and central Europe. The most famous of these agreements pertained to Poland, whose treaty became the model for those pertaining to Romania, Serbia-Croatia-Slovenia, Czechoslovakia, and Greece. Although these minority treaties were not designed to protect religious freedom per se, they did attempt to protect minorities whose identity often was defined or shaped by their religion. In addition, several states (including the Baltic countries, Albania, and Iraq) were required to make declarations that they would protect religious minorities as a condition of being admitted into the League of Nations. It is generally conceded that these treaties were a failure, although they have had lingering influence on some international lawyers and human rights activists, who admire their approach to group, rather than individual, rights.

6. Twentieth Century: From Genocide to International Norms

Although the consensus of 1750 regarding church and state had broken down by 1800, the new consensus regarding religious freedom (see 1) did not emerge until after World War II. This new consensus, whose antecedents had at least been articulated by 1800, is now embodied internationally in human rights commitments, as well as domestically in national constitutions and laws.

6.1. *International Commitments*

The single most dramatic development regarding religious freedom in the last hundred years has been its incorporation in international human rights commitments. Following the recognition of the failure of the interwar minority treaties, and in response to the revulsion felt against the Nazi → Holocaust of the Jews and the lesser but appalling wholesale persecution of Roma, Sinti, and Jehovah's Witnesses, the international community, largely through the → United Nations, began to negotiate and prepare agreements that would protect human rights.

Two of the earliest embodiments of the new concern were drafted in 1948: the Universal Declaration of Human Rights and the International Convention on the Prevention and Punishment of the Crime of → Genocide. Article 18 of the Universal Declaration states, "Everyone has the right to freedom of thought, conscience and religion; this right includes the freedom to change his religion or belief, and freedom, either alone or in community with others and in public or private, to manifest his religion or belief in teaching, practice, worship and observance" (→ Religion, Legal Protection of). This international standard goes beyond religious freedom to include protections for matters of conscience as well. It also includes the right to change one's religion, an issue that has since become more controversial in light of the opposition of several Islamic states to allowing Muslims to convert to other religions. The international standard was further enforced in the International Covenant on Civil and Political Rights (1966), which is legally binding on its signatories rather than being merely declaratory. More than 150 countries have ratified the International Covenant, whose article 18 on religion closely resembles that of the Universal Declaration.

The last fully international document to have been promulgated in this area was the 1981 Declaration on the Elimination of All Forms of Intolerance Based on Religion or Belief. This declaration is the most extensive international instrument on religious liberty, though it is not formally a treaty and does not have the status of → international law.

In addition to these three documents, several other multinational conventions, treaties, and instruments have incorporated these standards. They have been taken particularly seriously by the European Court of Human Rights, which judges cases under the European Convention of Human Rights, and by the Organization for Security and Cooperation in Europe.

6.2. *Roman Catholic Involvement*

Perhaps the second most dramatic development of the new consensus regarding religious freedom in the last hundred years has been the → Vatican II document *Dignitatis humanae* (1965). In sharp contrast to the 19th-century encyclicals *Mirari vos* and *Quanta cura* (see 4.1), the 1965 declaration states: "The human person has a right to religious freedom. This freedom means that all men are to be immune from coercion on the part of individuals or of social groups and of any human power, in such wise that no one is to be forced to act in a manner contrary to his own beliefs, whether privately or publicly, whether alone or in association with others, within due limits" (§2). The Roman Catholic Church, long a staunch supporter of the old consen-

Religious Liberty (Modern Period)

sus of 1750, has clearly now joined the new consensus favoring religious freedom.

6.3. National Constitutions

The vast majority of the world's current constitutions were adopted following World War II. Although there are exceptions, the overwhelming majority of them contain protections for religious freedom that either follow the language of the international instruments or adopt earlier articulations of religious freedom from prior constitutions, as in Belgium, France, and Germany. The most obvious exceptions to the post–World War II consensus regarding religious freedom are either in countries that have retained vestiges of earlier state religions, as in Great Britain and Norway, or in those that declare that → Islam is the religion of the state. Some formerly Communist countries with large Orthodox populations have shown a limited tendency to revert to pre-Communist times, when the → Orthodox churches had more influence.

6.4. Elaborating and Questioning the Modern Consensus

Beyond the rhetorical acceptance of freedom of religion generally (see 1), there is now a broadly shared consensus among Western governments and human rights activists and scholars that religious freedom includes such minimal basic liberties as the right of individuals to join and leave religious communities, to express religious opinions, to manifest their religion openly and publicly (provided that the manifestations do not disrupt the public order), and to adhere to their religion without suffering political or civil sanctions (such as losing the right to vote or to participate in government). There also is a broadly shared consensus among human rights scholars and activists that the state should not favor one religion to the exclusion of others and that religious groups should be treated neutrally, equally, and without discrimination.

Although it can be said that these points of consensus are widely shared by those actively involved in promoting human rights, there nevertheless remain many disagreements about how the general understandings should actually be applied in practice. There also are sharply different understandings about what religion is — that is, whether it should be seen as something akin to a belief system that individuals should be free to adopt, change, or renounce; or whether it is like an unchosen but deep-seated identity, similar to ethnicity, gender, mother tongue, or family. The different conceptions of religion as either a *belief system* that is governed by individual choice or an *identity community* into which one is born is often the source of profound misunderstanding, not least in respect to matters of → mission and → proselytism. Whereas some missionaries might understand religious freedom as supporting their efforts to help people make a free choice about accepting the true religion, the community being proselytized may see the missionaries as violating religious freedom through their efforts to undermine a community's deeply felt ethnic and religious identity. In this regard it is important to note that conceiving of religious freedom as a right belonging in large part to individuals is a relatively modern, and perhaps even Western, notion that is not fully accepted in the world today.

7. Continuing Challenges for Religious Freedom

Although it may be said that a new consensus favoring freedom of religion and belief has replaced the consensus of 1750 regarding the role of church and state (or now, "religion and the state"), it should not be imagined that states, jurists, and scholars understand the terms of this consensus in a uniform way. As is always the case, some hypocritically accept the consensus rhetorically while denying it in practice. Some nations that profess to accept religious freedom deny even basic rights of worship to believers. Many states continue to discriminate in favor of majority or traditional religions and against newer or unusual religions. Despite the oft-repeated ideal of treating religious groups and believers "neutrally" or "equally," discrimination occurs in virtually every state, with the real questions being the degree to which they discriminate and the groups that are targeted for unfavorable treatment.

During the 21st century four significant issues are likely to challenge the practical realization of the new consensus on religious freedom:

First, the *increasing religious → pluralism* within societies will bring both social and legal challenges to countries. As new religious groups demand equal treatment in societies, legal institutions and societal → prejudices will respond unevenly and often in a discriminatory manner.

Second, *increasing irreligion* within societies will create challenges for governments and religious institutions. Though many now argue that the old theories of the → secularization of the world were wrong, it nevertheless should be recognized that many components of society are becoming increasingly irreligious, which can become a source of conflict. Those favoring either irreligion or secularism will be increasingly unlikely to support state policies favoring financing of religious institutions; in turn, some societies in which religion is strong are likely to react against nonbelievers in their midst.

Third, *increasing pressures on governments by extremist religious movements* (whether Islamic, Hindu, Christian, or other) will prompt increasing countermeasures by governments that oppose such trends (→ Fundamentalism). These competing pressures may have an effect not only on the rights of extremist groups themselves but also on those who may incorrectly be identified as extremist. Such conflicts have already erupted into violence, as with the Hindu nationalist Bharatiya Janata Party (BJP) in India; Jewish extremists, who murdered Muslim worshipers at the Tomb of the Patriarchs in Hebron (1994) and assassinated Yitzhak Rabin (1995); and Islamist groups such as al-Qaeda.

Finally, there is a *significant likelihood of internal changes in states remaining under Communist rule* (including Cuba, China, Vietnam, North Korea, and Laos). These changes will occur as an earlier generation of leaders is replaced, as in China and Cuba, or as they undertake dramatic economic reforms, as in China and Vietnam. Pressures for liberalization of religious practices in such countries will likely continue. The results of these conflicts and challenges may lead to a further deepening of the consensus, or they might possibly undermine it.

Bibliography: P. Halsall, ed., *Internet Modern History Sourcebook: Enlightenment* (Fordham University) http://www.fordham.edu/halsall/mod/modsbook10.html; idem, ed., *Enlightened Despots* (Fordham University) http://www.fordham.edu/halsall/mod/modsbook11.html • H. A. F. Kamen, *The Rise of Religious Toleration* (New York, 1967) • N. Lerner, *Religious Beliefs and International Human Rights* (Maryknoll, N.Y., 2000) • J. F. Maclear, *Church and State in the Modern Age: A Documentary History* (New York, 1995) • M. D. Miller, *Religious Liberty and International Law in Europe* (Cambridge, 1997) • G. L. Mosse et al., eds., *Europe in Review* (Chicago, 1957) • M. D. Peterson and R. C. Vaughan, eds., *The Virginia Statute for Religious Freedom: Its Evolution and Consequences in American History* (Cambridge, 1988) • J. Witte, *Religion and the American Constitutional Experiment* (2d ed.; Boulder, Colo., 2005) • P. Zagorin, *How the Idea of Religious Toleration Came to the West* (Princeton, 2003).

T. Jeremy Gunn

Religious Orders and Congregations

Christian monasticism — the withdrawal of believers from other church members for the sake of prayer and ascetic devotion — is known from almost the earliest days of Christianity. In the Roman Catholic tradition, this practice led to the development and spread of an enormous variety of religious orders and congregations, many of which focused ultimately on vocations other than monastic (e.g., charity, education, mission, and social justice). Although not organizing its monastic life as the Roman Catholic Church did, the Orthodox Church nonetheless continued to develop its monastic traditions (see 2). In branches of Christianity that went their separate ways at the time of the Reformation, religious orders and congregations have survived, albeit in chastened form. The latter groups are represented here by the Anglican Communion (see 3) and the Church of Sweden (see 4).

1. Roman Catholic

1.1. *Definitions*

The word "order" derives from Lat. *ordo,* "rank, class, arrangement." The term *monasticus ordo* meant, in the early Middle Ages, the monastic way of life. It did not then convey any sense of organization or central direction. In time it came to signify a family of communities, joined together by one of four rules (Benedictine, Augustinian, Basilian, or Franciscan) and sharing a set discipline. A religious order is distinguished by the solemn vows of → poverty, chastity (→ Celibacy of the Clergy), and → obedience that its members take. It is the original form of religious association within the → Roman Catholic Church.

A "congregation" is (1) a subgroup of a religious order, communities also observing the rule and taking solemn → vows but sharing a discrete internal organization (e.g., the Benedictine congregation of Saint-Maur), or (2) a completely separate organization living under its own constitutions and taking only simple vows (e.g., the Sisters of St. Joseph).

Since 1983 the Roman Catholic Code of → Canon Law no longer distinguishes between orders and congregations. Instead, religious communities are divided into three categories: (1) religious institutes, whose members take public vows and live in community; (2) → secular institutes, whose members take public vows but generally live "in the world"; and (3) societies of apostolic life, whose members take private vows and live in community.

1.2. *The Evolution of Orders*

Christian → monasticism existed for centuries before religious orders appeared. The orders evolved gradually as a means of spreading the rule, ensuring monastic discipline, and protecting communities from outside interference.

1.2.1. *Early Monastic Groupings*

The first Christian monks, the Desert Fathers, lived solitary lives as hermits. (The word "monk" derives from Gk. *monos,* "single, alone.") Yet even they, following the lead of their patriarch, St. Anthony of Egypt (251?-356), gathered together occasionally for counsel and instruction. Then in 315, after living some years as a hermit, Pachomius (ca. 290-346) brought together other hermits into a community, giving it a rule and adding obedience to the vows of poverty and chastity. His creation, a cenobitic community offering a shared monastic life less rigorous than that of the hermit, was so popular that by the time of his death, thousands of monks were living in communities under his rule. ("Cenobite" derives from Gk. *koinobios,* "living in a community.")

The monasticism that spread through Italy and into continental Europe took with it the Pachomian Rule but not its organization. The typical → monastery of the sixth century numbered 12-15 monks. It was freestanding; it depended on a local patron, and its → abbot was answerable to no superior ecclesiastical authority, short of instances of grave culpability. It was for such a community that the rule of Benedict of Nursia (ca. 480-ca. 547) was written (ca. 535-45). Through the following centuries, this rule became the single binding force for hundreds of autonomous communities, male and female, across western Europe.

The Carolingians looked for greater cohesion. Charlemagne's son Louis the Pious (778-840) attempted to enforce a more uniform observance among the many monasteries of the empire, summoning their abbots to gatherings at Aachen in 816, 817, and 818 to receive directives from his protégé, the reforming abbot Benedict of Aniane (ca. 750-821). But the project collapsed, just as the Carolingian Empire itself collapsed. The turbulent conditions of feudal Europe made such a level of organization impracticable.

1.2.2. *Medieval Monastic Orders*

The development of religious orders as known today began with the foundation of the monastery of → Cluny in 909, under the Benedictine Rule and with the privilege of depending directly on the Holy See. This privilege, of little consequence at first, became more significant as the papacy gathered strength. It protected the abbey from interference by any local power and allowed it to develop a widespread spiritual preeminence. After 994, under its fourth abbot, Odilo (961/62-1048), Cluny transformed its spiritual preeminence into actual suzerainty, requiring every monastery that it founded or reformed to become its direct dependent. By the 12th century the Cluniac monastic empire numbered between 1,000 and 2,000 houses of monks, plus a number of nunneries, all recognizing the abbot of Cluny as their immediate superior and feudal overlord.

In time a reaction developed. Groups of monks broke away, seeking a simpler, more austere form of life in imitation of the early Desert Fathers. Most of these eremitic communities (i.e., communities of hermits) took shape in Italy (e.g., Vallombrosa, Camaldoli, Fonte Avellana), and some of them developed into orders. The most successful was the Grande Chartreuse, founded in Dauphiné in 1084 by Bruno of Rheims (ca. 1032-1101), which combined solitude with a measure of community life. Together with its offshoots, this new "Carthusian" order experienced a modest growth and gained lasting respect across Europe as the only order that, through the centuries, could claim never to have been reformed (because "never deformed"!).

The most influential reform of the 12th century

Religious Orders and Congregations

was that of Cîteaux, another breakaway from traditional Benedictinism. In their first half-century (1098-1153) these "white monks" (→ Cistercians) founded or aggregated 339 abbeys across Europe. They owed their success to three factors: their return to a simple observance of the Benedictine Rule, the charisma of their great champion, Bernard of Clairvaux (1090-1153), and the genius of their organization. Two innovative institutions — that of yearly → visitation (whereby the abbots of founding abbeys became responsible for visiting and correcting their daughter abbeys) and that of the General Chapter (the gathering of the abbots at Cîteaux to legislate for the collective) — allowed for expansion without loss of discipline. The Cistercian order was the first true religious order of western Europe. Its form of organization, after being adopted by several other monastic groups, was mandated for the rest by the Fourth Lateran Council (1215). Many Benedictine monasteries ignored this command, however, and retained their traditional autonomy.

Cistercian nuns soon appeared, a haphazard and not too welcome addition to the order. Women, often relatives of the monks, gathered in houses close to the monasteries, adopting observances that might or might not conform to the rule. In 1213 the Cistercian General Chapter decided to incorporate into the order only those communities that submitted to strict clausura (i.e., complete enclosure); then in 1228, pointing to the problems that the guidance of women caused the brothers, it forbade the incorporation of any more houses. Whether subject to the monks or to their bishops, however, the number of Cistercian nunneries continued to grow, reaching 900 by the middle of the 13th century. Like their brothers they became a model for others. In 1298 Boniface VIII (1294-1303) decreed that all professed nuns must follow them in accepting perpetual clausura.

1.2.3. *New Formations*

The → Middle Ages saw the development of new religious orders because society itself was evolving, creating new needs and demands.

1.2.3.1. *Military and hospitaller orders.* Special military and hospitaller orders appeared in the 12th century, a time of growing confrontation between Christians and Muslims. They served three purposes: caring for pilgrims, defending the holy places, and ransoming Christian captives. The Order of St. John of Jerusalem (later the Order of Malta) was created around the year 1100 to operate a hospital for pilgrims in Jerusalem. In 1137 it took on a military role. The Order of the Temple, or Templars (or Knights Templar), started around 1118 as a handful of knights charged with the protection of pilgrims traveling through the Holy Land. In 1128 they asked for, and received, recognition from the church as a full religious order, adding to the three monastic vows a fourth: never to surrender in battle. By necessity both orders departed from the standard monastic pattern, creating quasi-military bodies that were divided into provinces but held together by all-powerful grand masters.

Their model was soon copied by a number of smaller military orders, mostly in Spain, where the war against the Moors was of paramount concern. They were immensely popular through two centuries, but their attraction faded after the loss of Acre to the Saracens (1291). The Templars were destroyed in 1307, but several of the other orders continued into modern times, maintaining their vocation as hospitallers (i.e., caregivers to the sick) after their military justification had vanished. Some of them allowed the creation of female communities that, in keeping with knightly traditions, accepted only women of proven nobility.

The Teutonic Knights (approved by Celestine III in 1191) later moved from the Holy Land to eastern Europe, where they waged a long war against the non-Christian populations and carved out a huge territory of control. At the → Reformation Albert of Prussia (1490-1568), then the grand master, converted to → Protestantism and was secularized, becoming the first Hohenzollern duke of Prussia.

1.2.3.2. *Canons regular.* The 11th and 12th centuries were the golden age of monasticism. Much of Christian life was penetrated by its spirit, which can explain the development of the many institutions of canons regular. Chapters of canons (i.e., clerks dedicated to the service of the cathedrals) had existed since the fourth century. "Secular" canons did not share a common life. They enjoyed generous endowments and lived privately, acting as assistants to the bishops and, in the Middle Ages, electing them. Now some canons, seeking greater → perfection, redefined their pastoral vocation in monastic terms; hence their adoption of the title "regular." The rule that they adopted was that ascribed to Augustine (354-430), preferable to the Benedictine Rule because it left room for adaptation. Many chapters joined together in congregations, following the example of Cluny or Cîteaux.

The most successful of these organizations was the Order of Prémontré, founded in 1120 by St. Norbert (ca. 1080-1134). Heavily influenced by the Cistercians, Norbert adopted their institutions of visitation and General Chapter, taking the organization a step further by subdividing the order into provinces *(circaries)*, which enabled the central authority to maintain control of the members as they spread further afield. He founded double monasteries, which did not endure, and nunneries, which did. He also created an order for the laity, an institution later adopted by the friars.

By the 13th century the canons regular, including the Premonstratensians, had opened 2,000 houses across Europe and the Middle East. In their success we see the beginning of a valuation of the apostolic life *(vita apostolica)* by a society still dominated by monastic ideals.

1.2.3.3. *Mendicant orders.* By the late 12th century, demographic changes in western Europe — above all the growth of urban centers — were creating a challenge for the church: a more demanding, more informed laity on the one hand, a deficient and negligent secular clergy on the other. With the friars (also called mendicants, because they begged for their living), a new kind of order appeared, dedicated specifically to the evangelization of the people. The Order of Friars Minor, founded by Francis of Assisi (1181/82-1226), received official standing as a religious order with its own rule in 1223.

The Order of Preachers, under the Augustinian Rule, was confirmed in 1228. Its founder, Dominic of Caleruega (ca. 1172-1221), gave it a constitution that divided the body into provinces, each with its own administration and chapter, all bound together by a central administration and General Chapter. A second characteristic of the Order of Preachers was its rejection of the monarchical conception of power. All brothers were equal; all positions in the order were elective. The model was adopted by other mendicant orders, including the Carmelites, the → Augustinians, and the Servites.

All friars abandoned several key monastic practices: the chanting of Divine Office, the obligation of stability, the corporate ownership of → property. Instead, they emphasized → preaching, learning, and an exemplary life of poverty. Whereas the monastic vocation demanded retreat from the world, the mendicant vocation was for involvement and the saving of souls.

Each of the mendicant brotherhoods soon developed its own "second order" for women. Since the wandering life was incompatible with clausura, however, the new nuns were enclosed and subjected to various versions of the Benedictine and Augustinian Rules, while remaining under the guidance of the brothers. Only Clare of Assisi (1193/94-1253) won a significant concession from the pope: the "privilege of poverty," which allowed for a new rule, under which her sisters were able to live without an assured income. In 1263 the Poor Clares (Cordelières) were joined by the Rich Clares (Urbanistes), who were dispensed from this privilege, while otherwise following the same rule. In the 14th century a reform undertaken by Colette of Corbie (1381-1447) led to the creation of another group of Franciscan nuns, the Colettines.

Besides Clare and Colette, the mendicant orders produced many great women for the church, including the Dominican tertiary Catherine of Siena (1347-80) and the Carmelite Teresa of Ávila (1515-82), whose reforms turned her order into a powerhouse of sanctity in the 16th century.

In recognition of the need, and the potential, of the laity, the founders also instituted "third orders," confraternities of men and women committed to living piously and charitably without renouncing the world. From 1221, when the first → tertiaries received a rule from Francis, they became an important force in the Christianizing of society. A number of active religious communities were founded by members of third orders.

1.3. ***Reform Movements***

1.3.1. *Late Medieval Reforms*

The orders experienced gradual decline over the following centuries. The monks suffered first, victims of their own wealth, from constant tampering by outside powers attracted by that wealth (much of it received *in commendam*, that is, the diversion of top positions in monasteries, along with their revenues, to outsiders), and of their inability to compete with the friars in the fields of learning and evangelization. But by mid-14th century the friars, too, were losing public esteem, by reason of their perceived worldliness. In context it must be remembered that the church itself was in disarray, first with the exile of the papacy in Avignon (1309-77), then with the Great Schism (1378-1417).

During the years 1300-1500 there were some significant efforts of monastic reform. In Italy the monastery of Mount Olivet became, in 1344, the founder of a small congregation of observant → Benedictines (Olivetans). A larger congregation was initiated at Santa Giustina in 1419. It owed its success to an innovative constitution in which supreme authority was vested in the annual General Chapter, thus stripping authority away from the local abbot, who too often was an outsider holding his position *in commendam*. Its version of reform spread throughout Italy and into Castile, where it inspired the congregation of Valladolid. In 1504, after it reached the ancient abbey of Monte Cassino, it took the title "Cassinese Congregation," which it still bears.

Religious Orders and Congregations

A characteristic of the Italian reform movements was their return to primitive Benedictine observance. They inspired similar movements on the other side of the Alps. In 1412 an Austrian, Nicholas Seyringer (ca. 1360-1425), entered the reformed monastery of Subiaco; in 1418, when Nicholas returned to Germany, Martin V (1417-31) authorized him to reform the monasteries of Austria and Bavaria according to the Subiacan customs. Melk, on the Lower Danube, became the first of 32 monasteries to be thus reformed. A parallel reform with strong Cluniac influences originated in the Bavarian abbey of Kastl. Neither of these movements led to the creation of a congregation. But a third reform, initiated in 1433 in the abbey of Bursfeld, did. By the end of the 15th century, over 150 communities, male and female, were living under its constitutions.

These and other reform movements were, however, little more than bright spots in a generally dark picture. In spite of urgings by → popes and → bishops, most Benedictine and Cistercian houses remained untouched.

For the friars, also, wealth and worldliness were stubborn problems. In addition, both the major orders suffered ruptures, the → Dominicans as a result of the Great Schism, the → Franciscans because of internal differences over the question of poverty.

In 1378 the election of two popes, one Roman (Urban VI), the other French (Clement VII), split the Dominicans, with inevitable consequences for good order. The pro-Roman master general began a movement for renewal that continued through the 15th century. Without confronting the existing unreformed institutions, he encouraged the growth of small observant communities that, once they were strong enough, formed "congregations" that bypassed their provincial superiors and answered directly to the master general. These congregations, in their search for a more spiritual life, are seen as having downgraded the order's intellectual standards, but they enabled the Dominican order to flourish throughout the 15th century.

The Franciscans experienced numerous turbulences. A long-lasting quarrel over the order's commitment to poverty (which brought 72 so-called Spirituals to trial before the → Inquisition) led in 1373 to a rift between the status-quo "Conventuals" and the reforming "Observants." The reform was led by Bernardino of Siena (1380-1444), who himself founded 300 convents of Observant friars. Only in 1517 did the movement receive papal recognition, with the bull *Ite vos.* Shortly thereafter, in 1529, the Capuchins appeared, a breakaway group that received papal approval and became one of the great preaching orders of the Counter-Reformation (→ Catholic Reform and Counterreformation).

1.3.2. *The Protestant Reformation*

Spiritually weak, burdened down by wealth and worldliness, the monks of western Europe provided easy targets for the → Reformers. To the argument of Martin Luther (1483-1546) and others after him that monasticism had no place in Christian life, the monks had no convincing rebuttal. Many monks, nuns, and friars joined the Reformers; many simply faded into secular life. Where there was resistance, local activists took a hand, with acts of force and iconoclasm that Luther himself condemned but could not stop. Wherever the → Reformation took hold, the monasteries succumbed. Within a few decades the monastic population of Europe was cut in half.

1.3.3. *Orders of the Catholic Reformation*

The Council of → Trent (1545-63) was ambivalent about monasticism. Since its plan for reform was centered on the bishops and the parish clergy, there was even some thought that the monastic orders should be suppressed altogether. In the end, it considered monasticism briefly and legislated conservatively, mandating a minimum age for entrants, a year of novitiate, and a reestablishment of the common life. Monasteries that were exempt from episcopal control were ordered to adopt the congregational system of governance (visitation and General Chapters). All professed nuns were to be enclosed.

Though the council itself envisaged no innovation, innovation was in fact already underway. In Italy the Theatines (1524), the Barnabites (1531), and the Somaschi (1532) were the first of a new type of religious: clerks regular, men bound by simple vows, committed to methodical prayer and living in community, while otherwise giving priority to the apostolate and to charitable works.

At the same time and in the same mold there appeared the Society of Jesus, the → Jesuits, created by Ignatius Loyola (1491-1556) and a small group of companions and approved in 1540 by Paul III (1534-49). It has been called the last word in the evolution of the religious order. In its constitutions the religious life as practiced in monasteries was almost completely transformed: the cycle of prayer and Divine Office within a cloister was exchanged for a life of mission wherever it was required. Their special vow of obedience to the pope made its members the perfect instrument for the reforming papacy. Their total submission to their head, or general — who, once elected, exercised unchallenged power for life — turned them into a highly centralized, highly mobile force. The military comparisons that are often made are not inappropriate.

Italy also saw experimentation among religious women. Most successful were the Ursulines of Brescia, who, under the guidance of Angela Merici (1474-1540), a Franciscan tertiary, succeeded in living without clausura, performing charitable works, and catechizing children. Paul III approved their constitutions in 1544.

At the outset none of these new congregations was intended to fight → heresy. Their avowed purpose was to care for and Christianize their own people and, in the case of the Jesuits, to go on mission to the Holy Land. The future of these orders, however, and of the many institutes of active life that followed them, and indeed of the reformed monastic orders, lay in counterreformation activity and in the Catholic renewal that followed.

1.3.3.1. *Restored monasticism.* The hermits of Mount Carmel, who came from the Holy Land to Europe in the 13th century, had been recognized as an order of mendicants in 1235. Together with other friars, they experienced decline in the 14th century, which repeated efforts at reform were unable to reverse. Reform, when it came, was the work of a Carmelite nun, Teresa of Ávila. In 1562 she introduced the primitive rule to a small community of sisters, and in 1567 she received permission to extend her reform to other nunneries. Later she began, against considerable resistance, to found reformed convents for men. Before she died in 1582, she had founded 17 houses of nuns and 15 of brothers. In 1593 the → Discalced Carmelites separated from the original order. ("Discalced" refers to wearing sandals, a practice that conformed to the ancient rule, which had long been abandoned; it was part of a return to a more penitential lifestyle. The word now came into use to distinguish the reformed from the unreformed Carmelites.)

Teresa insisted that the contemplative life could be a source of apostolic fervor, a contention borne out when, in 1604, five Carmelite nuns went to France, a country still recovering from its religious wars. Their appearance clearly forwarded Catholic renewal. In 40 years they opened 55 houses. In 1606 Carmelite nuns went to Brussels and from there expanded throughout the Spanish Netherlands and into Poland and central Europe.

Reform came only gradually to the ancient abbeys because the practice of *commendam* hindered change. An important step was taken in Lorraine with the establishment in 1600 of the Benedictine congregation of Saint-Vanne, based on the Cassinese model. By joining in a congregation, the monks were able to dismantle the system of *commendam* and take reform into their own hands. In 1618 an offshoot of Saint-Vanne became the French congregation of Saint-Maur, which 60 years later numbered 178 houses. In addition to an austere life, Saint-Maur encouraged scholarship, its most distinguished member being the great writer Jean Mabillon (1632-1707).

The needs of the period led many Benedictine monks to include an element of action in their contemplative lives, as teachers or preachers. For reformed Benedictine nuns, in contrast, the choice was often for an intensified prayer life of reparation and intercession. The congregation of Calvary (1617) and the union of monasteries of Perpetual Adoration of the Blessed Sacrament (1641) are examples.

The French Cistercians also made efforts at reform. In 1577 Jean de la Barrière (1544-1600) established a severe regime in his abbey of Feuillant. In 1592 the Feuillants, their excesses moderated by papal command, became an independent congregation of monks and nuns that lasted until the French Revolution. The main body of the Cistercian order, however, spent almost 50 years in a bitter internecine quarrel between proponents of "strict" and of "common" observance. One of the protagonists was Abbot Armand-Jean de Rancé (1626-1700), founder of the reformed community of la Trappe (1664). His austere interpretation of the rule, much criticized in his lifetime, would become the accepted version in the 19th century, when the first Cistercians to reestablish in France were Trappists.

A famous reform, that of Port-Royal under Angélique Arnauld (1591-1661), was obstructed by her Cistercian superiors and safeguarded only when the abbey was removed from their jurisdiction (→ Jansenism). Unlike monks, nuns were forbidden to organize into congregations with General Chapters; their ability to reform or innovate thus depended on their canonical superiors (usually bishops).

1.3.3.2. *Apostolic congregations.* The Reformation had exposed glaring deficiencies in Catholic preaching and catechetics. The machinery barely existed, however, to correct the problems: the secular clergy was still poorly educated, and there were as yet few diocesan seminaries. The new congregations, principally the Jesuits and the Capuchins, were the first to answer to the need. In time they were joined by associations of priests: the Fathers of Christian Doctrine (Milan, 1560; Avignon, 1592), the priests of the Oratory of Divine Love (Rome, 1575; Paris, 1611), the Lazarists (Paris, 1625), and the Sulpicians (Paris, 1642). Some of these associations were bound by solemn or simple vows, some by no vows at all. Their defining characteristic was their commitment to evangelization.

It was soon recognized that preaching must be reinforced by religious instruction. When Ignatius died in 1556, the Jesuits were running 35 colleges; two centuries later, that number had grown to 800. Besides educating young men (increasingly, elite young men), the colleges served as bases from which the fathers could reach the laity by preaching and by the organization of sodalities, or religious guilds. They were also an excellent source of recruits. The only serious competition to the Jesuits in Catholic Europe came from the Oratorians and the Fathers of Christian Doctrine, who also established colleges.

One of the great discoveries of the 17th century was the importance of basic instruction in religion, which at first took the form of catechizing (→ Religious Instruction). Groups of children were brought together to hear and recite formulas incorporating the articles of faith. The inadequacy of such instruction for otherwise unformed minds soon became apparent, however, and the rush to open primary schools began. In Catholic Europe this movement created an opportunity for religious women to enter the apostolate. While boys' schools remained, for the most part, the work of parish-based schoolmasters, there was no corresponding arrangement for girls. Several teaching women's congregations appeared. The Daughters of Notre-Dame (Bordeaux, 1607) were, from the start, cloistered nuns. The French Ursulines (Avignon, 1597) and the Canonesses of the Congregation of Notre-Dame (Mattaincourt, 1598) began as *congréganistes,* uncloistered and bound only by simple vows. They were soon constrained to accept claustration and solemn vows. They were all allowed to operate day schools out of the cloister, however, which enabled them to develop their teaching profession and establish their usefulness to society.

The most daring of female initiatives was that of Mary Ward (1585-1645), who in 1609 founded the Institute of the Blessed Virgin "to read, write and sew for the honor of God." She hoped that her community of "English Ladies" would become a female counterpart to the Jesuits — uncloistered, free to travel, and responsible to the pope alone. The reaction against what was seen as her presumption was so powerful, however, that it reached the papacy, and in 1628 her institute was suppressed. It was rehabilitated in the 18th century.

Rome's strictures against women entering the apostolate loosened within a few years. By mid-17th century, numbers of female congregations were in existence, the difference being that their members, while living in community, avoided the characteristics of a religious order (i.e., solemn vows, distinctive habit, and clausura). While many of these secular congregations operated under diocesan control, some achieved a degree of independence previously denied to religious women. This important advance was the work of Vincent de Paul (1581-1660) and Louise de Marillac (1591-1660), the founders of the Daughters of Charity. Their company of women became so successful and politically influential that in 1655 it was granted partial exemption from diocesan control, with central direction by a superior general. Although this arrangement did not receive official papal endorsement until 1900, it was by that time common practice in a number of other women's congregations.

Only after several unsuccessful attempts was a congregation of schoolmasters formed: the institute of the Brothers of Christian Schools (popularly, "Christian Brothers"), founded in 1688 by Jean-Baptiste de La Salle (1651-1719) and approved in 1720 by Clement XI (1700-1721). The expansion of the Christian Brothers, solid before the French Revolution, became spectacular in the 19th century.

1.3.3.3. *Charitable congregations.* Service to the poor had been always been a Christian ideal. The monasteries had practiced hospitality at their gates, and numbers of small brotherhoods and sisterhoods had served the indigent sick in hospitals and leprosaria. The military orders continued the hospitaller function. The Order of the Most Holy Trinity (approved 1198) and that of the Brothers of St. John of God (approved 1571) served in numerous hospitals up to, and then again after, the French Revolution. Nuns also worked as hospitallers, usually under the Augustinian Rule. The most famous of these, the Augustines of the Hôtel-Dieu of Paris, served that hospital continuously from its foundation in 1210 until their expulsion in 1907.

In the 17th century numerous other female congregations entered the nursing profession. Some of them were also cloistered nuns, linked for life to their own institutions. But more, like the Daughters of Charity and the Sisters of St. Joseph (1651), were secular sisters bound by simple vows, working on contract, and ready to nurse or teach or perform social services as the need arose. Whereas the cloistered communities were located in urban centers, these sisters were free to work in either town or country, in communities small or large. In time they came to dominate the fields of nursing and social service (→ Relief and Development Organizations).

1.4. ***Crisis, Regeneration, and Decline***

1.4.1. *The Ancien Régime and the Orders*

By the mid-18th century, religious orders and congregations covered the face of Catholic Europe:

Religious Orders and Congregations

some 15,000 houses of men, 10,000 of women. They outnumbered the secular clergy. They enjoyed a near monopoly in secondary education, and the lion's share of primary education, both male and female. They were the chief purveyors of health care and social services. In many regions they served in parishes.

Collectively, the orders were extremely rich, holding as much as 10 percent of the land surface, enjoying huge rights and economic privileges and, sometimes, considerable political power. Where they did not hold sway, however, was in the realm of ideas. The principles on which they were founded were inimical to the → Enlightenment. Under continuous attack from the philosophes, monasticism as an institution lost much of its public esteem. For this reason, when the state authorities decided to dismantle it, they met with little resistance.

In 1750 the Society of Jesus numbered 20,000 members in Europe, with 2,000 more in the Americas and Asia. In the following years it was evicted from one country after another, until in 1773 Clement XIV (1769-74), under pressure, decreed its suppression. The power that the Jesuits had amassed and the allegiance that they were seen to owe to their general and to the pope ran counter to the policies of the centralizing states, and these factors are usually given as the reason why they were so rudely manhandled by princes who, in other respects, were loyal Catholics. The Society of Jesus disappeared from Europe until 1814, when it was reconstituted by Pius VII (1800-1823).

In France the Crown began interfering with religious life in 1732. The Commission des Secours was created to investigate the state of the country's 2,000 women's communities, with a view to assisting some and closing others. At first it was intended to inspect men's communities as well, but this step was considered too politically dangerous for the times. By 1766, however, the Commission des Réguliers was ready to do exactly that. The former commission closed some 250 convents and downsized many more; the latter closed 458 and devised detailed rules for the rest.

These two French commissions set precedents for the more aggressive action of the Austrian monarchy known as Josephism. In 1782 Emperor Joseph II (1780-90) established a program that resulted, finally, in the dissolution of 700 monasteries — a third of the total in the empire — and the diversion of their goods to a program of parish renewal. The evicted monks were given the chance to join the parish clergy; otherwise they, together with almost all nuns, were given pensions.

1.4.2. *The French Revolution and the Orders*
The legislators of the French → Revolution decided to take this restrictive policy a step further by banning solemn vows altogether and by turning the monasteries' property over to the nation. Originally they planned to allow pensions and limited rights of tenure for the dispossessed religious, but the subsequent souring of relations between → church and state, a consequence of the enactment of the Civil Constitution of the Clergy (1790), resulted in a total rupture. In an increasingly anticlerical climate, the religious orders came to be seen as hotbeds of *incivisme* (lack of patriotism). In September/October 1792 all religious communities were closed down and their members evicted. Then, within a few months, France's wartime successes enabled it to export its dechristianization. The revolution's antimonastic policies followed the French armies through Europe, so that wherever they were victorious, there was a wholesale suppression of monasteries.

1.4.3. *Napoleonic Europe*
Napoléon continued the process. Between 1796, when he first entered Italy, and 1814, when his empire collapsed, almost every monastery in Europe disappeared. Frequently the local powers cooperated in the dissolutions in exchange for a share of the spoils. The Treaty of Lunéville (1801), which gave the left bank of the Rhine to France, compensated the German princes by allowing them to absorb monastic lands. By 1812 some 400 German monasteries had been suppressed. As king of Spain, Joseph Bonaparte (1768-1844) ordered the abolition of all male orders. In 1812 the new government allowed for their restoration, while severely limiting their numbers. (In 1815 this restrictive policy was reversed, and the monks were all welcomed back, only to be evicted altogether in 1835.)

Thus the years 1789-1815 saw a dramatic collapse in the monastic population of Europe. There was, however, one outcome beneficial to the orders: a diaspora (the first of several) that led to the establishment of communities in new parts of the world. For example, the 90 Trappists who fled France in 1790 became 700 by 1827, living in houses in England, Belgium, Piedmont, Spain, Germany, and Canada. Benedictine refugees from France and Belgium founded the English abbeys of Downside and Ampleforth.

Some secular congregations had a less disastrous experience. Many jurisdictions, recognizing their usefulness, exempted them from suppression. Elsewhere, where they had been banished, they were eventually allowed to return. After the signing of the

→ Concordat (1801), the French government reinstated the Lazarists, the Christian Brothers, the Daughters of Charity, the Dames de Saint-Maur, and other institutes of active life. These congregations henceforth had the advantage over the old monastic orders.

1.4.4. *Nineteenth- and Twentieth-Century Expansion*

In 1773 in Europe there were more than 300,000 members of the regular clergy (i.e., men living under a rule); by 1825 the number had shrunk to fewer than 70,000. Nuns, fewer in number to begin with, underwent a similar decline. Recuperation was slow. By the 1850s, however, a dramatic trend was evident. The old orders were back, though greatly outnumbered by new communities. Only a small fraction of monks and nuns were now contemplatives. The Trappists, the Carthusians, and various communities of contemplative nuns reclaimed their former way of life. The Benedictine abbeys of Solesmes (France, 1833), Subiaco (Italy, 1851), and Beuron (Germany, 1863), with the congregations they created, returned to primitive observance of the rule. But many Benedictine communities adopted a pastoral, and sometimes missionary, purpose. From 1846 Swiss and German Benedictine monks and nuns served the German-speaking immigrant populations of America. From 1834 to 1883 English Benedictine monks directed the dioceses of Australia.

But the great expansion came in the new "apostolic" congregations. Worldwide, over 600 were created in the 19th century alone. Some clerical congregations, such as the Oblates of Mary Immaculate (1816) and the White Fathers of Africa (1868), had a clear missionary purpose from the start (→ Catholic Missions). The Salesians (1859) dedicated themselves to school teaching. In 1900 they numbered 3,526; by 1965 they had multiplied to 22,383. Lay teaching congregations, such as the Christian Brothers, restored in 1802, and the Marist Brothers (1817) also knew strong growth.

Though the men's congregations enjoyed a century of unprecedented expansion, more than trebling their numbers between 1875 and 1965, they were eclipsed by the even more phenomenal expansion of women's congregations. Before the French Revolution there had always been more men than women in religious life; the situation was now reversed. In France, for instance, the number of nuns grew during the 19th century from 13,000 to 130,000; in Ireland, the 120 nuns of 1800 became 8,000 by 1900; in the United States, the 1,344 sisters of 1850 became 40,340 by 1900. Similar expansions took place across the Roman Catholic world. By 1970 the number of women in religious congregations was nearing a million. Most of the congregations that these women entered shared certain characteristics: they were created in the 19th century, they were designed for a specific activity (teaching, nursing, social welfare, missionary service), and they were modeled on one or another of the older traditions. Thus in the United States in 1809, Elizabeth Bayley Seton (1774-1821), having come to know the sisters of St. Vincent de Paul while she was in France, used their example to found a community that later grew into the American congregation of Sisters of Charity, some 10,000 strong. In the same way, hundreds of women's congregations were created to serve in the active life while adopting the Franciscan or the Dominican charism. While many of the new congregations remained within diocesan boundaries, others, such as the Religious of the → Sacred Heart (1826) and the Sisters of Mercy (1831), developed a worldwide membership.

In spite of widespread anticlericalism and occasional outright → persecution by the state (e.g., the → Kulturkampf in Germany, 1875-85; in France, the Law of Separation of Church and State, 1905), the congregations continued to thrive. In particular, nuns came to play a central role in an expanding network of Catholic schools, charitable institutions, and parishes.

The first suggestions of decline appeared in the mid-20th century. Serious questions began to be raised about the quality of religious life and its relevance in the modern world. In 1950 Pius XII (1939-58) summoned the heads of congregations to a meeting in Rome to consider how they could adapt their institutions to the changing times. Men and women in religion thus had to face the challenge of *aggiornamento* some years before the calling of → Vatican Council II. For the most part, though, the challenge was not immediately embraced.

1.5. ***Global Expansion (16th-20th Centuries)***

For five centuries, Catholic Europe occupied itself with the evangelization of the rest of the world. The greater part of this undertaking always fell to the religious orders.

1.5.1. *The Americas*

Franciscan, Dominican, and Augustinian friars arrived in the Americas with the conquistadores and began their own conquest of the indigenous cultures. They were joined by the Jesuits, whose most famous missions, the Paraguayan → reductions, begun in 1609, came in the 18th century to be seen as a challenge to Portuguese power and led to the downfall of their society.

Religious Orders and Congregations

Throughout the colonial years in Latin America, the religious orders continued to bear the responsibility of evangelizing and caring for the native people. With the coming of independence, they found themselves caught in church-state battles that lasted through the 19th century and into the 20th. Furthermore, as a result of serious social problems, internal divisions arose, with social progressives espousing ideas that alarmed and angered conservatives. This polarization increased with time until, in the 1960s, some members of religious orders became prominent in the movement associated with → liberation theology. Some of them paid for their social activism with their lives.

In Canada the Jesuits' attempt at a Paraguayan-style reduction of the Huron nation, commenced in 1634, failed within a few years; their influence on the colony of New France, though, was more permanent. After the conquest of 1759, they, together with the Sulpicians and the Recollets, were expelled. They returned, followed by other regulars, in 1842. Meanwhile the communities of hospital sisters and teaching nuns (Ursulines, sisters of the Congregation of Notre Dame), pioneers from the 17th century, succeeded in remaining at their posts, to be reinforced in the 19th century by incoming congregations from France. Quebec was a bastion of Catholicism within Canada; later, communities of Irish immigrants became especially strong in Ontario.

In the United States the Catholic presence was initially very slight but was much increased by heavy immigration, predominantly from Ireland and Germany. Between 1815 and 1850 the number of Roman Catholic church members increased from 150,000 to 1.7 million. The religious orders followed the people, often for the purpose of serving their countrymen in their own language. By midcentury there were 50 male and 160 female communities, working in churches, colleges, schools, and mission posts. From that time on, outnumbering the secular clergy by as much as five to one, they provided the underpinning for Catholic life across the United States.

The religious communities of North America shared the European experience: strong growth until the 1960s, followed by decline, with an aging membership. This pattern has continued into the 21st century.

1.5.2. *Asia*

As in the New World, so in Asia the Roman Catholic explorers were followed almost at once by → missionaries: Jesuits, Franciscans, and Dominicans. In India, Japan, China, and Indochina, there was considerable initial success, much of it due to the perceptiveness of the Jesuits Francis Xavier (1506-52), Matteo Ricci (1552-1610), and Alessandro Valignano (1539-1606), who recognized the need to respect local customs and rituals.

In China, however, internal quarreling, which culminated in the 18th century in the Chinese Rites Controversy, undermined the missionaries' efforts. There and in other countries, the growing hostility of the local powers led in time to the expulsion of the missionaries and the destruction of many convert communities. The most complete debacle had already taken place in Japan, which by the end of the 17th century had completely closed itself off to foreigners. Though reduced, the Asian missions struggled on, until in the 18th century the suppression of the Jesuits, followed by the revolutionary crisis in Europe, dried up the flow of missionaries. As the 19th century opened, apart from a vibrant Catholic presence in the Philippines, there was little to show for the efforts of the religious orders in the Far East.

This situation changed at midcentury, as the European nations began to exercise power, either directly or through diplomacy, across Asia. Among the concessions that they extracted in their treaties with local authorities was freedom of religion. This freedom, in fact, translated into protection by the imperial powers of the missionaries. Armed with these safeguards, missionaries flooded in, bringing with them their traditional institutions (schools, hospitals, colleges, orphanages). Frequently, the religious orders were given full control of the dioceses. They were able to report good progress. The price of this success, though, was a too-close identification with their protectors. For many of them, the interests of religion came to be conflated with the interests of their own home countries.

The pioneering missionaries of the 17th century had recognized the importance of respecting the local cultures; the missionaries of the modern era were not so sensitive. It took Benedict XV (1914-22), in his 1919 apostolic letter *Maximum illud*, and other popes after him to effect plans for the training of native clergy. In 1926, when six Chinese bishops were consecrated in Rome, it became clear that the future belonged to such a clergy. By 1939 Asian bishops had taken over 48 former missionary territories. Since then, the churches of Asia have been increasingly repatriated. Communist persecution in China, North Korea, and Vietnam has seriously damaged, but not altogether extinguished, the Christian community.

Where they have been free to develop, religious communities, some Western, some local in origin, have done well. One of the most famous of 20th-century congregations is that of the Missionaries of Charity (1950). Though founded by an Albanian, Mother Teresa (1910-97), and now active in many parts of the world, it truly belongs to India.

1.5.3. *Africa*

Before the 19th century, missionary effort in Africa had been small-scale and unrewarding. As in Asia, the major expansion took place only after the European powers guaranteed the freedom of the missionaries (1876); also as in Asia, evangelization tended to follow the flag. The renewal of religious fervor in the home countries and widespread public interest in this newly opened continent gave rise to a flood of missionary vocations. Several congregations were created specifically for Africa, including the Sisters of St. Joseph of Cluny (1800), the Holy Ghost Fathers (1848), the Scheutt Fathers (1862), the Mill Hill Missionaries (1866), and the White Fathers (1868). Other orders were not slow to enter the arena. As European influence in Africa expanded, so did the missionary field. In 1850 there had been 2 apostolic vicariates in sub-Saharan Africa; in 1900 there were 61.

The African missionaries, however, like the Asian, lived with the conflict of loyalties between homeland and mission country, which made them, in a sense, forever strangers. In the 1920s this problem began to receive critical attention from thinkers within the church. After World War II the self-examination was overtaken by a tide of nationalism (→ Nation, Nationalism), as African countries gained independence. Increasingly, the foreign missionaries gave way to a local clergy. When Vatican II opened, there were 36 African bishops in attendance, and the number has grown steadily since then. Indeed, the decline in the numbers of religious in the developed countries has been offset by an increase in the number of religious in other parts of the world. The religious congregations, both those of European origin and those created locally, have seen a steady influx of African men and women, to the degree that some of them now come to work in the First World, as once the First World came to them.

1.6. ***Vatican II and After***

The challenge that Pius XII had thrown down in 1950 was repeated by Vatican Council II. With *Perfectae caritatis* (1965), the Decree on the Appropriate Renewal of the Religious Life, the religious orders were asked to examine themselves in the light of the present world, to renew their fidelity to the charism of their founders, and to adapt their practices, wherever possible, to modern needs. This self-examination began in earnest in 1967, as the institutes met in special chapters to discuss their constitutions. The following years saw considerable unrest, with many in the rank and file of the congregations questioning the purpose of the consecrated life and, especially, the meaning of the vow of obedience. This uncertainty helped to create a crisis within some communities, leading to a shrinkage in numbers as more people left the religious life and fewer entered it. By 1979, with the situation stabilizing, John Paul II (1978-2005) proclaimed that the time for experimentation was over. By 1987 almost all institutes had presented their updated constitutions. Nevertheless, the decline in their membership, at least in North America and Europe, continued.

In recent years, as a result of renewal in the church, new forms of association have appeared. In the first place there are ill-defined movements that can group together thousands of adherents espousing a given form of → spirituality without taking vows or living in community (e.g., the so-called charismatic renewal and the Cursillo movements). In addition to their spiritual focus, many of these movements have a dedication to a particular cause, such as social justice or the promotion of world → peace. The church has been slow to recognize such movements, given their fluid and changing nature. Over the last few years, however, some have received formal recognition, with approved statutes for their central body.

There are also "associations of the faithful." Some of these are purely voluntary, without ecclesiastical recognition. Some are recognized as "private" associations, carrying out their activities on behalf of their members; others are approved as "public" associations, carrying out their apostolate in the name of the church itself. If an association grows and shows signs of stability, it may become a society. In North America there are at present 700 new associations in various stages of formation. Because of the number and variety of associations, there is a risk of polarization, and church authorities are slow to grant recognition. But the very fact of the involvement of so many Christians in these new movements and associations is a sign of hope for the future.

For almost 2,000 years, monasticism has been a powerful force in the development of Christian spirituality and culture. In the Western church, the development of orders and congregations has endowed that force with discipline and efficiency. Present-day society, in whatever part of the world those orders and congregations penetrated, bears their imprint.

Bibliography: General: E. Dufourcq, *Les aventurières de Dieu* (Paris, 1993) • R. Hostie, *Vie et mort des ordres religieux* (Paris, 1972) • P. King, *Western Monasticism* (Kalamazoo, Mich., 1999) • D. Knowles, *Christian Monasticism* (New York, 1979); idem, *From Pachomius to Ignatius: A Study in the Constitutional History of the Religious Orders* (Oxford, 1966) • G. Le Bras, ed., *Les ordres religieux. La vie et l'art* (2 vols.; Paris, 1979-80) • J. McNamara, *Sisters in Arms: Catholic Nuns through Two Millennia* (Cambridge, Mass., 1996) • L. Rogier et al., *Nouvelle histoire de l'église* (5 vols.; Paris, 1963) • B. de Vaulx, *History of the Missions* (London, 1961).

Medieval: B. Bolton, *The Medieval Reformation* (Baltimore, 1983) • P. Johnson, *Equal in Monastic Profession: Religious Women in Medieval France* (Chicago, 1991) • E. Makowski, *Canon Law and Cloistered Women: Periculoso and Its Commentators, 1298-1545* (Washington, D.C., 1997) • M. Parisse, *Les nonnes au Moyen Age* (Le Puy, 1983).

Early modern: D. Beales, *Prosperity and Plunder: European Monasteries in the Age of Revolution, 1650-1815* (Cambridge, 2003) • J. Boussoulade, *Moniales et hospitalières dans la tourmente révolutionnaire* (Paris, 1962) • B. Diefendorf, *From Penitence to Charity* (New York, 2004) • R. Po-chia Hsia, *The World of Catholic Renewal, 1540-1770* (Cambridge, 1998) • C. Langlois, *Le catholicisme au féminin* (Paris, 1984) • A. L. Martin, *The Jesuit Mind* (Ithaca, N.Y., 1988) • J. O'Malley, *The First Jesuits* (Cambridge, Mass., 1993) • E. Rapley, *The Dévotes: Women and Church in Seventeenth-Century France* (Montreal, 1990) • L. Rogier, "Le siècle des lumières et la révolution," *NHE* 4/1.9-233.

Modern: G. Bertier de Sauvigny, "La restauration (1800-1848)," *NHE* 4/2.265-468 • J. Bruls, "Des missions aux jeunes églises," *NHE* 5/4.421-79 • P. Day, *A Dictionary of Religious Orders* (London, 2001) • M. Dumont, *Les religieuses sont-elles féministes?* (Montreal, 1995) • E. Kolmer, *Religious Women in the United States* (Wilmington, Del., 1984) • R. Latourelle, *Vatican II: Assessments and Perspectives* (New York, 1989) • F. Pike, "Le catholicisme en Amérique latine," *NHE* 5/3.353-417.

Elizabeth Rapley

2. Orthodox

The Eastern churches did not experience the proliferation of religious orders that took place in the West, nor did they see the development of similar apostolic or mission-oriented communities. → Monasticism based on ancient models, however, has continued to flourish and plays a decisive role in the development of the → spirituality, → theology, and → worship of these churches.

2.1. *Forms*

Eastern monasticism is based on the concept of the monk or nun as *monachos,* which refers to the person as being alone, withdrawn from the world and its pleasures, in order to engage in ascetic practices leading to greater holiness of life. This monastic vocation has taken three basic forms, all of which can be traced back to fourth-century Egypt. First there are the hermits, who generally take up residence alone in solitary places, living in huts or caves. The great exemplar of this "eremitic" or "anchoritic" style was St. Anthony of Egypt (251?-356), who spent 20 years in solitude in the Egyptian desert.

The second form of Eastern monasticism is "cenobitic," in which monks or nuns choose to live together in community, following a rule and worshiping together, led by a hegumen (→ Abbot, Abbess). Pachomius (ca. 290-346) is considered to be the founder of cenobitic monasticism; his rule was later developed by Basil the Great (ca. 330-79), who advocated a strong social role for cenobitic communities, including the staffing of orphanages, hospitals, and similar institutions.

The third form is semi-eremitic life, which combines elements of the first two. In this case monks or nuns live together in more loosely structured groupings of small communities called sketes, under the guidance of a charismatic elder. These small communities often form a kind of monastic village, all of whose inhabitants gather on Sundays and feast days to attend services in the central church.

In the Christian East all these forms of monasticism are considered ways of living out a radical Christian spirituality, an eschatological realization of one's baptismal promises. As such, monks and nuns are taken simply to be exemplary Christians who are aware of their sinfulness and thirst for → salvation like all the baptized. Indeed, the great majority of monastics in the East are not ordained.

Each monastic community is self-standing and under the pastoral care of the local → bishop, except for the larger or more prestigious "stavropegic" monasteries, which come directly under the jurisdiction of the → patriarch. Because married men can be ordained to the priesthood but bishops must be celibate, most of the bishops in the Eastern churches are taken from the monasteries.

2.2. *Branches*

Monasticism has flourished at various times in all of the Eastern churches, but its development has taken different courses, depending on the historical circumstances of each one.

2.2.1. There was a strong monastic tradition in the Assyrian (→ Nestorian) Church of the East in the early centuries, and it was the monks who spearheaded strong missionary thrusts into central Asia and other regions far from the church's Mesopotamian homeland. But with the church's steady decline after the Mongol invasions, cenobitic monasticism eventually vanished, and the only remnant today is a few individuals who take a personal vow of → celibacy.

2.2.2. Each of the → Oriental Orthodox Churches has its own monastic traditions that survive to the present day. The strongest of these is found in the → Coptic Orthodox Church in Egypt, which has witnessed an extraordinary flourishing of monasticism in recent years. There are now 12 monasteries with close to 600 monks, and 6 convents with about 300 nuns. The monasteries have become centers of → pilgrimage and spiritual renewal for the Coptic laity around the country.

In the → Armenian Church monasticism once played a vital role, especially in the field of → education, but today only three significant monastic communities remain. They are associated with the church's administrative centers in Echmiadzin, Armenia, in Jerusalem, and in Antelias, Lebanon.

The ancient → Ethiopian Orthodox monastic tradition divided into two streams in the 14th century, one more strict than the other, and today there are many thousands of monks and nuns often living in inaccessible regions around the country.

Several ancient Syriac Orthodox monasteries survive with small communities in the Tur Abdin region in the Mardin Province of southeast Turkey. New establishments have been formed in the West (→ Syrian Orthodox Church).

2.2.3. Monasticism in the much larger Eastern (Byzantine) → Orthodox Church is also very strong. It appeared in and around Constantinople in about 382 under the patronage of John Chrysostom (ca. 347-407), then patriarch of the city. It expanded in the imperial capital, especially during the reign of Justinian (527-65). By the ninth century there were hundreds of monasteries scattered around the city. During the same century Theodore of Studios (759-826) adapted the rule of Basil to the new conditions and crystallized what has become the standard type of Orthodox cenobitic monasticism.

By the 11th century, however, the center of Orthodox male monasticism shifted from Constantinople to Mount → Athos, a 35-mile-long peninsula in what is now northern Greece that even today is inhabited exclusively by monks. At the beginning of the 20th century there were over 6,000 monks living on Athos. A steady decline in numbers followed, bottoming out in 1971, when only 1,145 remained. Since then there has been a modest revival with the arrival of a number of young monks; today it is estimated that about 1,500 monks live in the peninsula's 20 major monasteries or in smaller dependencies and hermitages. Of the 20 monasteries 17 are Greek; the other three are Serbian, Bulgarian, and Russian.

In modern Greece monasticism is greatly respected for the role it played in the preservation of Greek culture during the long centuries of Ottoman rule. But the establishment of an internationally recognized Greek state in 1833 ironically proved catastrophic for Greek monasticism, for the new government closed 412 of the 563 existing monasteries in the country and allowed only 4 women's communities to remain open. This event triggered a lengthy period of decline. In recent years many of the monks have left their monasteries (including the well-known ones situated atop rock towers at Meteora) to take up residence on Mount Athos. According to official 2004 statistics there were 1,041 monks in the Church of Greece and 2,500 nuns. These figures do not include Mount Athos, Crete, or the Dodecanese Islands, which come under the jurisdiction of the Patriarchate of Constantinople.

2.2.4. Orthodox monasticism had its greatest flowering to the northeast of Constantinople, in Russia. After the Mongol destruction of Kievan Rus' in the 13th century, monastic life shifted to the solitude of the vast northern forests of Russia. The main figure in this revival was Sergius of Radonezh (ca. 1314-92; → Russian Orthodox Church 2.2), who founded the Holy Trinity Monastery north of Moscow, based on the Studite rule. An area of deep forest to the north of Moscow became known as the Northern Thebaid because of the large number of monasteries in the region. (Thebaid is an Egyptian desert that from the 4th cent. A.D. was home to thousands of monks and nuns.)

In the 18th century there was a strong revival of the characteristically Russian practice of *starchestvo,* the revelation of one's inner life to a → starets, or spiritual father, centered at the Optina Monastery, near St. Petersburg. The monks would reveal their thoughts to the starets daily, but countless pilgrims would also come to a starets for an occasional word of guidance. The 19th century saw a true golden age of monasticism in Russia. By 1914, on the eve of the Bolshevik revolution, there were 550 men's monasteries, with 11,845 monks and 9,485 novices, and 475 women's communities, with 17,283 nuns and 56,016 novices.

The Communist regime in Russia unleashed a decades-long ferocious → persecution (§4.1) of monasticism as one aspect of its general antireligious policies. As a result, by 1985 there were fewer than 1,500 monks and nuns, most of them elderly, remaining in a handful of monasteries. Since the end of Communism in 1991, however, monasticism has experienced an unprecedented resurgence, even though there are still far fewer monastics now than in 1914. Many monasteries have been returned to the church, though in many cases there are still not enough monks or nuns to inhabit them, and enormous financial resources are needed to restore them from their often crumbling state. In 2004 the Russian Orthodox Church had 620 monasteries, including 298 male monasteries and 322 convents, as well as 38 hermitages.

2.2.5. Monasticism has survived only with difficulty in the Eastern Catholic churches, most of which derive from groups of Orthodox who have come into full unity with the Roman Catholic Church while preserving the majority of their ancient Eastern traditions (→ Uniate Churches). While most of these churches have a few monastic communities, most religious belong to new apostolic orders based on Latin models that were founded after their union with Rome.

Bibliography: S. Bolshakoff, *Russian Mystics* (Kalamazoo, Mich., 1980) • D. J. Chitty, *The Desert a City: An Introduction to the Study of Egyptian and Palestinian Monasticism under the Christian Empire* (Crestwood, N.Y., 1966) • E. G. Farrugia, ed., *Devotion to Life: The Cost of Full Religious Commitment; Proceedings of the Second Encounter of Monks East and West, Malta, 16-20 February 1994* (Msida, Malta, 1994) • A. Golitzin, ed., *The Living Witness of the Holy Mountain: Contemporary Voices from Mount Athos* (South Canaan, Pa., 1999) • S. Joanta, *Romania: Its Hesychastic Tradition and Culture* (Wildwood, Calif., 1992) • O. Meinardus, *Monks and Monasteries of the Egyptian Deserts* (Cairo, 1989) • M. B. Pennington, ed., *One Yet Two: Monastic Tradition, East and West* (Kalamazoo, Mich., 1976) • "The Place of the Monastic Life within the Witness of the Church Today," *Orthodox Visions of Ecumenism* (ed. G. Limouris; Geneva, 1994) 74-78.

Ronald G. Roberson, C.S.P.

3. Anglican

3.1. *Statistics*

The → Anglican Communion began in England and spread by means of colonization, migration, and → missionary work. Accordingly, in the opening years of the 21st century one finds Anglican religious orders not only in the British Isles but far beyond as well, notably in Africa, Asia, Australasia and the Pacific, Europe, North America, and the Caribbean. There are approximately 2,400 religious in the Anglican Communion. Of this number, just over 900 are men, and nearly 1,500 are women. The three geographic regions with the greatest concentration of Anglican religious are Australasia and the Pacific (820), Europe (750), and Africa (400).

Globally, there are about 100 different Anglican religious orders. A few are quite small, with only two or three members. As of 2004 the Melanesian Brotherhood, founded in the 1920s and based in the Solomon Islands, is the largest, with 320 members and 261 novices. Religious orders with sufficient members often establish branch houses both in their country of origin and in other lands.

3.2. *History*

Anglican religious, in conjunction with their sisters and brothers in the → Orthodox and → Roman Catholic churches, see themselves as part of a movement that began in the earliest years of Christianity with the consecrated virgins and widows and the desert hermits. It is a way of life, however, that is not limited to the Christian faith.

Although religious communities were numerous within the pre-Reformation English church, amid the conflicts of the → Reformation they were abolished. Despite the dissolution of the religious orders, however, their values, way of life, and good works were never totally eradicated from the corporate memory of the English people. For 300 years the values and practices of the ancient religious houses were manifested in various ways: in parish life, ordered by the → Book of Common Prayer, with its regular pattern of Divine Service; in hospices, almshouses, university colleges, and communal family life such as that established in 1636 by the Ferrar family at Little Gidding, in Huntingdonshire.

In the 1830s and 1840s the Church of England began to recover its historical perspective, recapturing its Catholic theology and ecclesiology. At the same time, many pressing social needs among the citizens called for response. The desire to meet those needs led some people to work vigorously toward the restoration of the religious life in the English church. When, on June 12, 1841, Marian Rebecca Hughes (1817-1912) made religious vows of → poverty (§5), → celibacy, and → obedience, she became the first woman in the Church of England to take such vows since the Reformation. In 1849 she because the first superior of the Society of the Holy and Undivided Trinity, at Oxford. Other orders for women soon came into being, all of which combined an active life of ministry among the poor and needy with a life of → prayer and → worship. The first Anglican religious community for men, the Society of St. John the Evangelist, was founded in 1866 at Oxford, and other men's communities were subsequently established in England.

In the United States the first indigenous community for women was the Community of St. Mary, founded in 1865 in Peekskill, New York; the first for men was the Order of the Holy Cross, founded in 1881 in West Park, New York. In Canada the Sisterhood of St. John the Divine was founded in 1884 in Ontario, and in Australia the Community of the Holy Name was begun in 1886 in Melbourne.

In the 20th century, new communities continued to be founded, although at a slower pace. These newer communities are to be found throughout the Anglican Communion, especially in developing nations, even as some of the older communities in the United Kingdom and the United States have dwindled in membership or even died out.

The 19th-century restoration and subsequent growth of Anglican religious orders was not without difficulties. Many Church of England → bishops were suspicious of the religious orders and their founders, doubting their loyalty to the established church and presuming many to have "papist" leanings. In turn, the religious were often mistrustful of the bishops, worried that they might wish to suppress or control their lives. In time, however, this mutual mistrust was largely dispelled. Religious orders, by the good works and dedicated lives of their members, won over the trust of people and prelates, achieving recognition by the institutional church while yet maintaining a cherished degree of independence from overbearing ecclesiastical control.

3.3. *Organization*

In 1935 the Church of England set up the Archbishops' Advisory Council on the Relations of Bishops and Religious Communities, thereby providing official approval of religious life within the church. Parallel organizations exist in several provinces in Africa, as well as in Australasia, Canada, and the Episcopal Church in the United States. In the Church of England and the Anglican Church of Canada, religious have official representation in General Synods.

Every religious order recognized by the church has a "bishop visitor or protector," whose duty it is to assure the wider church that the members of the order, while self-governing, are faithful to their rule and statutes. The bishop visitor or protector is also available to give advice when called upon and acts as arbitrator in the event of serious dispute. This person is chosen by the members of the order, usually for a term of years, and does not need to be the bishop of the diocese in which the community is located.

By the midpoint of the 20th century, Anglican religious orders had established a pattern of meetings that enabled interchange between them through regular gatherings of the leaders of the communities and frequent conferences for the members. Representatives of Anglican religious communities are also involved in ecumenical consultations of religious. They have found that the unifying reality of living the vowed life in community is a powerful bridge and bond between different communions.

3.4. *Orientation*

Within Anglican religious life one can identify features of the well-known orders of the Roman Catholic Church, especially the → Benedictines, → Franciscans, Carmelites, and → Cistercians. Other Anglican orders take the inspiration for their rule from the communities founded by Francis de Sales (1567-1622) and Vincent de Paul (1581-1660).

Religious life in Anglicanism shares with monastic life in general the desire to seek God alone; to find God in prayer, worship, and study; to share a communal life; and to serve others by apostolic works. The majority of Anglican religious live what has been called the "mixed life," signifying that the centrality of prayer (both personal private prayer and common prayer in → Eucharist and Office) issues in good works often outside the walls of one's religious house.

In the 19th century Anglican sisters accompanied Florence Nightingale (1820-1910) to her nursing ministry during the Crimean War (1853-56), nursed the poor in their homes, and ministered in urban slums. In 1999 and 2000 members of two men's communities and two women's communities played an important role as peacemakers in the Solomon Islands, a ministry that cost the lives of seven of the brothers. After the attack on the World Trade Center in New York City on September 11, 2001, Anglican religious ministered day after day at Ground Zero. Anglicanism, however, also includes communities that are strictly contemplative and semicloistered, whose chief work is prayer. Most communities offer space for guests to come for retreat and spiritual refreshment, an aspect of the ministry of religious houses that has grown dramatically in recent times.

While the majority of Anglican communities are single-sex, a few are made up of both men and women. Some communities offer the opportunity to those who feel so called to live the eremitic life while remaining in the membership of their religious family. Anglicanism also provides for those who do not feel drawn to life in community but who wish to be vowed to celibacy and to live a consecrated life as "solitaries" under the authority and guidance of a bishop.

Anglican religious understand themselves as called by God to live out their → baptism in a particular and intense way. The vows of poverty, celibate chastity, and obedience, as well as the Benedictine alternative of conversion of life and stability, are directly related and are founded upon the vows of holy baptism: to live in a right and holy relationship with God, with other people, and with possessions afforded by the world.

Bibliography: P. F. Anson, *The Call of the Cloister: Religious Communities and Kindred Bodies in the Anglican Communion* (rev. ed.; London, 1964) • P. Dunstan, ed., *Anglican Religious Communities Year Book, 2004/2005* (Norwich, 2003) • M. Hill, *The Religious Order: A Study of Virtuoso Religion and Its Legitimation in the Nineteenth-Century Church of England* (London, 1973).

Adele Marie Ryan, S.S.M.

4. Church of Sweden

At the start of the 21st century the Church of Sweden, an evangelical Lutheran church, includes a number of orders and congregations, both female and male. Their background is largely the High Church movement that developed in the 1910s and 1920s.

4.1. ***History***

During the → Middle Ages there were approximately 50 religious congregations and communities in Sweden. At the time of the → Reformation, at the initiation of King Gustav Vasa (1496-1650) and other Lutheran leaders, these communities were closed, the last one being the great cloister of the Sisters of St. Birgitta at Vadstena, closed by Parliament in 1595. The so-called Edict of Toleration of 1781 allowed Roman Catholics to return to Sweden, but the establishment of religious orders was expressly forbidden. In 1866 the Sisters of Elizabeth were invited by the Catholic apostolic vicar to come to Sweden in order to work among the poor and sick. This open community, which was not regarded as being a religious order, attracted many followers.

Inspired by workers from the diaconate in Kaiserswerth, Germany, and also by the continental Roman Catholic Sisters of Mercy, the Inner Mission of the Church of Sweden in 1851 established a diaconal institution in Stockholm that called unmarried women to a sacrificial life in community *(vita communis)*, based on a theologically grounded rule. Ersta, that community, still exists and until the middle of the 20th century continued to maintain a communal life with its sisters, or deaconesses, directly related to the motherhouse. This character, however, has now been completely lost.

According to the Law of Religious Freedom of 1951, religious orders may be established in Sweden with governmental permission, but no minors may be admitted to membership. In 1958 the government gave permission for the establishment in southern Sweden of a Carmelite congregation that practiced clausura, the separation of at least a portion of a community's religious house to the exclusion of those of the opposite sex.

4.2. ***Development***

The *Societas Sanctae Birgittae* (SSB) was established in 1920 as a tertiary order (i.e., an order of men and women who live in the world on the basis of common promises) whose members practiced a → spirituality tracing back to St. Bridget of Sweden (ca. 1303-73). SSB is a living and active fellowship of prayer in the high liturgical tradition. In 2004 it had approximately 140 male and female members, who were led by a "confessor"; its annual General Chapter meets in Vadstena. This group has good contact, but no formal relationship, with the Roman Catholic Bridgettine nuns and monks; it also has a strong international network of supporters.

At approximately the same time and with a similar structure, the *Sodalitium Confessionis Apostolicae* (SCA) was founded by clergy in southern Sweden. Its intention was to provide a spiritual safeguard against → liberal and rationalistic theology. The SCA today also has laymen and laywomen among its members. Inspired principally by these two fellowships, a number of religious orders based on a variety of rules have been founded within the Church of Sweden.

It is customary to identify as the starting point of this development an event on Pentecost 1954, when the influential High Church leader Gunnar Rosendal (1897-1988), vicar in Osby in southern Sweden, received the → vows of Marianne Nordström (b. 1925). She had lived for a time as a novice in the Benedictine Order of the Holy Paraclete (OHP) at St. Hilda's Priory, Whitby, England. The founder and superior of that order, Margaret Cope (1886-1961), had visited the general chapter of SSB in Vadstena in 1948 in order to lecture on Anglican religious life. There were plans at Whitby to establish a daughter community in Sweden, but they did not materialize, since neither the archbishop nor the Council of Bishops of the Church of Sweden was able to give the community the sanction in church law that the leadership of the British order desired. In this context and by taking her vows individually, Marianne Nordström established what is now known as the *Sisters of the Holy Spirit*. In the heated debate that followed her vows, it was questioned whether Rosendal had overstepped his authority as a priest in the Church of Sweden. He was called before the Cathedral Chapter in Lund and given a public admonition. The Sisters of the Holy Spirit have had a number of novices, and today it numbers three sisters. Its cloister is within a parish near Uppsala that has received considerable attention as a place of asylum for refugees (→ Sanctuary 3). The constitution of this order is a contemporary interpretation of the rule of St. Benedict (ca. 480–ca. 547).

Arising quite directly from the SCA is the *Sisters of Mary, the Mother of Jesus* (JMMS), founded in 1957 by Magda Wollter (1895-1968), who in 1939 took the initiative of founding a women's branch of SCA. In 1960 she took lifetime vows before Bishop Gustaf Aulén (1879-1977). JMMS strove for a contemplative life in accordance with the Benedictine Rule, with certain emphases taken from the → Cistercians. In 1946 Wollter, without public formalities, had established a community of sisters in Malmö that practiced the discipline of silence. In 1969 the JMMS moved to a location near Kristianstad, also in southern Sweden. In 1983 the entire sisterhood converted to the → Roman Catholic Church, becoming a congregation of the Benedictine Rule. In 1991 they dedicated a new cloister, Mariavall, in the southern Swedish province of Skåne, where today there are 17 nuns.

In 1956 a number of clergy invited James A. Fenwick (b. 1918) to Sweden. He was a member of the Society of St. Francis, established in 1931, in Cerne Abbas, Dorset, England. Father Hugh resided in Uppsala in 1959 and 1960, during which time the *Brotherhood of the Holy Cross* (HKB) was founded. HKB maintained its first community from 1965 to 1971 in Barkarö, near the cathedral city of Västerås. Barkarö became a focal point for young clergy, and in the 1970s the community played a leading role in the development of a High Church vision for pastoral and parish renewal. When the order's new cloister in Östanbäck was dedicated in 1975 and four monks took their solemn vows, a private citizen placed charges against the order for failing to follow the governmental regulations for religious life that had been mandated in 1951. This issue was taken to the highest authorities, with the result that in 1977 these regulations were overturned.

In 1966 Arthur Kreinheder (1905-89), an American, became an overseas member of HKB. He was active in the United States as a member of the Lutheran Church–Missouri Synod, although in 1956 he had been ordained in the Church of Sweden. In 1958 he, together with three additional brothers, formed the *Congregation of the Servants of Christ* (CSC) at St. Augustine's House in Oxford, Michigan. While Kreinheder was still living, CSC was regarded as a community within HKB. Kreinheder inspired many of the brothers who entered HKB to work for corporate reunion between evangelicals and Roman Catholics, forming in the United States the League for Evangelical-Catholic Reunion. In 1965 the League for Christian Unity was established in Sweden with the goal of bringing about reunion between the Evangelical Lutheran Church of Sweden and the Roman Catholic Church, based on a previously formulated statement of common faith. This ecumenical commitment became part of HKB spirituality, not least through its superior at the time.

The *Benedictine cloister in Östanbäck* today has ten monks. It is affiliated with a Roman Catholic cloister in the Netherlands and lives in an international fellowship of → Benedictine tradition and spirituality. The order's superior is regularly invited, along with Anglican Benedictine abbots, to participate in congresses of Benedictine abbots in Rome.

With a totally different background and tradition of piety, the *Congregation of the Daughters of Mary of the Evangelical Way of Mary* is an order established by Swedish and Danish women that in 2004 had 26 sisters in houses in Sweden, Denmark, and Finland. Its founder was Gunvor Norrman (1903-85), who became known as Sister Paulina Mariadotter (Daughter of Mary). Norrman was a member of the → Oxford Movement (Moral Rearmament), and in a 1938 conversion experience she felt a call from Christ to work, with others, for the salvation of unmarried women. As a result of a similar experience in 1943, she felt called to help German prostitutes who had been sent to war fronts. When the character of → Moral Rearmament changed after World War II, Norrman and others left. In a visionary experience of the Virgin Mary in 1949, she became convinced that she was "a servant of the Lord's Mother" called to lead women on "the evangelical way of Mary." Nine women committed themselves to follow her, forming a community similar to a religious order. A decision to work in Germany was decisive for the community's development and was first put into effect when from 1954 to 1964 Paulina Mariadotter and a number of sisters lived in Trier. There she came in contact with the Roman Catholic Sisters of St. Joseph and also encountered Marian → mysticism (→ Mary, Devotion to). In 1958 the sisters received confirmation of their community through a churchly act "consecration to service," performed "privately" by Lutherans who had nevertheless informed the local bishop. In

1960 clausura was adopted, along with the communalization of property; in 1963 it created a "Rule of Life," which was subsequently reworked, reaching its present form in 1989. In 1970 a new community was established in Vadstena, and in 1988 it converted to Roman Catholicism. This community took on Benedictine characteristics but remains in fellowship with the Daughters of Mary throughout the Nordic lands.

When the motherhouse system was dropped by the Diaconal Institute of the Church of Sweden, several deaconesses felt called to establish a community with a diaconal vocation. In Stockholm in 1968 they formed the *Sisters of St. Mary Magdalene.* This community has no direct model, although it feels a kinship with the Little Sisters of Jesus, inspired by Charles de Foucauld (1858-1916).

In 1971 two Lutheran men, a Swede and an American, became Franciscan novices in England. In 1973 in the area of Göteborg, they established, in the → Franciscan tradition, the *Brotherhood of St. Francis,* and sometime later a companion *Sisterhood of St. Francis* was formed. In 1983 members of the Brotherhood converted to the Roman Catholic Church, and in 1988 the community became affiliated with the Third Order Regular of St. Francis of Penance. The Sisterhood has remained in the Church of Sweden.

4.3. *Role*

Orders and congregations in the Church of Sweden do not have a canonically regulated status, but over the course of time all of the orders have chosen a → bishop as "visitator." In 1990 the Council of Bishops of the Church of Sweden expressly sanctioned these orders and congregations, stating that their life "in binding fellowship is an authentic form of life and a living testimony in an evangelical church. To offer life in giving service, praise, and prayer is a calling for everyone baptized into Christ. Persons who together seek to fulfill this calling under the guidance of a common rule can with God's grace serve as models in obedience and faith." The bishops desire to develop and maintain contacts of fellowship with the orders. At the same time, however, the orders stand in a critical relation to the Church of Sweden, in which they are regarded as High Church and as standing outside both the church organization and, since the separation of the church from the state (2000; → Church and State), the strong organizational structure of the parliamentary political parties.

Bibliography: O. Bexell, *Sveriges kyrkohistoria,* vol. 7, *Folkväckelsens och kyrkoförnyelsens tid* (Stockholm, 2003) • S.-E. Brodd, *Evangeliskt klosterliv i Sverige* (Stockholm, 1972) • G. Inger, "Klosterförbudet i Sverige och dess upphävande," *Statsvetenskaplig tidskrift* (Stockholm) 65 (1962) 133-73 • B. Laghé, *Den evangeliska Mariavägen till enhet. En studie av Paulina Mariadotters spiritualitet* (Skellefteå, 2004) Eng. summary: "The Evangelical Way of Mary to Unity: A Study of Paulina Mariadotter's Spirituality" • G. Rosendal, *Kyrka och ordensliv* (Kallinge, 1954) • Y. M. Werner, ed., *Nuns and Sisters in Nordic Countries after the Reformation: A Female Counter-culture in Modern Society* (Uppsala, 2004).

Oloph Bexell

Religious Socialism

1. Beginnings
2. Nineteenth Century
3. Blumhardt and Kutter
4. Ragaz
5. After 1918
6. After 1945
7. Developments in the United States and France
8. Effects

1. Beginnings

Like → socialism in general, religious socialism is a political and social movement that sought to replace the existing order by a new and more just social order. Triggered by the drastic social effects of the industrial revolution (→ Industrial Society) but largely irrelevant after World War II, it involved the idea that the Christian faith has crucial relevance for the carrying out of political, economic, and social tasks (→ Politics; Economy; Society). Rooted in the older Christian traditions of the → Middle Ages and the left wing of the → Reformation, it was directly stimulated by the so-called early socialists, especially C. Fourier (1772-1837), R. Owen (1771-1858), and C. H. Saint-Simon (1760-1825).

Roman Catholics who followed Saint-Simon took up his idea of a new brotherhood, finding in it the core of the → gospel. P. J. B. Buchez (1796-1865) thus saw in socialism an implication of Christianity when it is rightly understood, that is, of *charité chrétienne.* F. Huet (1814-69) presented this meaning of Christian socialism in his book *Le règne social du christianisme (The social reign of Christianity, 1833).* On his pilgrimage from → Ultramontanism to → revolution, the priest H. F. R. Lamennais (1782-1854) proclaimed the gospel of the sovereignty of the people (*Paroles d'un croyant* [Words of a believer, 1834]), which would put an end to the modern → slavery of industrial workers. This strong position of Lamennais meant a break with the church. He made an emphatic call for a general sharing of goods in his *Livre du peuple* (Book of the people, 1838). In Germany W. Weitling (1808-71) linked his communistic ideas to the sharing of goods in the → primitive Christian community (*Die Menschheit, wie sie ist und wie sie sein sollte* [Humanity, what it is and how it should be, 1838]).

After 1848 the establishment of workers' unions, which had been undertaken by Buchez since 1831, became a main part of the program of English Christian socialism, represented by J. M. Ludlow (1821-1911), F. D. Maurice (1805-72), and C. Kingsley (1819-75). This group founded a short-lived periodical *Politics for the People,* in which they lamented the egoism and greed of capitalists (→ Capitalism), which plunged the majority of people into misery. The aspirations of workers could well go hand in hand with those of Christians, who believed in the earthly relevance of the → kingdom of God. Widespread moral renewal could be a profitable first step. In Britain Christian socialism greatly influenced the labor movement, and through its work in the fields of education, housing, and health, it also had an impact on community life as a whole. Though not directly the heirs of Maurice and like-minded socialists, many later labor leaders at the level of both party and government had strong Christian roots.

2. Nineteenth Century

The 19th century gives evidence of a close link between socialist ideas and Protestant Christianity. Thus J. H. Wichern (1808-81) believed the development of the → Inner Mission in 1848 to be in harmony with religious socialism. Even Otto von Bismarck (1815-98) could tell the Reichstag that his social laws were practical Christianity at work legislatively, though he played off his state socialism against the socialist movement.

Socialism was associated with social reform or reformation, while the revolutionary social movement of Weitling, and later of K. → Marx (1818-83; → Marxism) and his followers, came to be called Communism. The concern of religious socialism within Protestantism was to understand the deeper aims of socialism, and even of revolutionary Communism, as Christian tasks. Central here was the establishing of positive links between the → church and the workers. Various options for alliances and programs thus arose.

3. Blumhardt and Kutter

The real beginning of religious socialism in the strict sense is usually traced to Christoph Blumhardt (1842-1919), who lived in full expectation of the coming of God's kingdom and saw in social democracy a special sign of divine judgment and promise. As the son of Johann Christoph Blumhardt (1805-80), a pastor and mission founder renowned for miraculous healings, Christoph sought at Möttlingen and Bad Boll to espouse the cause of justice and in this way to show himself to be both Christian and progressive (→ Progress). He found messianic meaning in the socialist → hope, his commitment being, not to the party, but to the yearning for a new age. What alone counted for him was the will of Jesus that the world be overturned. He was a member of the Social Democratic Party from 1899 onward and from 1900 to 1906 represented Göppingen in the Württemberg Diet.

In Switzerland the Zurich pastor H. Kutter (1863-1931) took up Blumhardt's ideas. Kutter had served at Vinelz on the Bielersee from 1887 to 1898 and was then at the Neumünster in Zurich from 1899 to 1926. In his prophetic book *Sie müssen! Ein offenes Wort an die christliche Gesellschaft* (They must! A frank word to Christian society, 1903), Kutter saw divine necessity in the rise of social democracy. Social Democrats were doing what God had demanded of his witnesses from the very first. Could God not be with them when their sole concern was for the poor and enslaved? Nothing showed up the ungodliness of Christians more starkly than their opposing social democracy. The living God might not be with Christendom, but he was at work among Social Democrats. Although Kutter found in socialism a divine thrust toward world change, he regarded party membership as a betrayal of the gospel. The Christian contribution, he insisted, must be a new → preaching and nothing else.

4. Ragaz

A movement of religious socialism was underway by 1906. It was triggered by a lecture of L. Ragaz (1868-1945) entitled "Das Evangelium und der soziale Kampf der Gegenwart" (The gospel and the present social struggle). While Kutter had understood socialism more as a judgment on the church and middle-class → society, Ragaz saw in it the promise of a new world order in which all reality would come under the rule of God and share in his redemption. As a result of his initiative, groups of socialists formed in the Swiss churches. Ragaz called socialism the midwife of religious hope. What it sought, however, needed the powers of the kingdom of God for its achievement. His concern was not with a new party or church but with the world as a whole. One of his main thrusts was against the Bolshevist belief in force and the decision of the Swiss Social Democrats to join the Third International, or Communist International (founded 1919). It was largely due to Ragaz and his friends that the latter never carried out this decision. In 1921 Ragaz gave up his professorship and devoted himself to bringing workers together in the Zurich district of Aussersihl.

From 1910 others abroad — for example, T. Fallot, E.-J. Gonuelle, W. Monod, C. Gide, P. Passy, and W. → Rauschenbusch — joined forces with Kutter and Ragaz. The Swiss religious socialists took the lead in arranging an international congress for social Christianity at Basel in September 1914. Unfortunately, world war intervened.

5. After 1918

Religious socialism enjoyed its true, although brief, blossoming after 1918. In 1919 the Volkskirchenbund evangelischer Sozialisten (People's church federation of Protestant socialists) was formed in Baden, and similar groups arose in the Palatinate, Württemberg, Bavaria, and Thuringia. Their aim was to bring to bear all the vital forces of Protestant Christianity on social problems and to make the church a living community of religious socialism. To do so, it was argued, the church must take up the cause of the oppressed and, although not joining any party, serve the socialist ideal.

Much more strongly political were the goals of G. Dehn (1882-1970) and B. Göring (1898-1949) and the two groups that they founded in Berlin in 1919. These groups came together as the Bund religiöser Sozialisten (Union of religious socialists) in December 1919, whose concern was to see the principle of brotherhood worked out in the just transformation of political relations both at home and abroad. In 1922 this body joined forces with the Vereinigung der Freunde für Religion und Völkerfrieden (Organization of friends for religion and international peace), which concentrated on religious educational work among the proletariat. A circle that had been founded at Cologne in 1919 also belonged to this group. The final grouping at Meersburg in 1924 was the Arbeitsgemeinschaft (changed in 1926 to Bund) der Religiösen Sozialisten Deutschlands (Working group [*later* Federation] of German religious socialists), under the leadership of G. Wünsch, E. Eckert, and E. Fuchs, who saw affinity between the social analysis of Marxism and Christian social ethics.

Closely allied to religious socialism was the circle around P. → Tillich (1886-1965), who advocated an ethical socialism (→ Ethics; Social Ethics). In 1933, shortly after the publication of Tillich's *Die sozialistische Entscheidung* (The socialist decision), an attack on National Socialist → ideology, he was expelled from Germany (→ Fascism). Along with Tillich C. Mennicke, E. Heimann, A. Rüstow, A. Wolfers, and A. Loewe belonged to the so-called Berlin Circle. As Tillich saw it, the goal of religious socialism is theonomy, in which intellectual and social forms are filled with the content of the unconditioned. The great *kairos* in the coming of Jesus must be experienced afresh in relative and specific *kairoi,* for example, the labor movement.

6. After 1945

After the collapse of National Socialism the movement of religious socialism was reconstituted in the form of the Bund der religiösen Sozialisten Deutschlands, Gemeinschaft für Christentum und Sozialismus (Alliance of religious socialists in Germany, society for Christianity and socialism), with headquarters in Frankfurt. The Internationaler Bund der Religiösen Sozialisten (International alliance of religious socialists), with headquarters in Bentveld, Holland, embraces groups from European countries, the United States, and Japan.

7. Developments in the United States and France

Parallel to the Protestant movement of religious socialism was the American → Social Gospel movement, which made an impact from the closing years of the 19th century to the 1920s. Under the leadership especially of W. Gladden (1836-1918), R. T. Ely (1854-1943), and W. Rauschenbusch (1861-1918), this movement tried to bring the reforming power of the gospel to bear especially on the problems caused by urbanization and industrialization.

In France after 1945 → worker-priests made it their aim to achieve → solidarity with workers and the labor movement and to bring their priestly ministry into harmony with socialist goals (→ Priest, Priesthood, 3).

8. Effects

On the whole, religious socialism was marginal as a movement after 1945. Nevertheless, its basic ideas underlay many ecclesiastical and theological efforts and new ventures in the field of social politics. This orientation appears in the program that the resistance against A. Hitler (1889-1945) had set out for the future (e.g., the Kreisauer Kreis), and it was true later of the founding phase of the Christlich-Demokratische Union (the Cologne principles of the Aalen program), with its confession of Christian socialism, and especially of the new beginning of social democracy in the Godesberg Program. Thus we find the concept of a social and political → diaconate (e.g., H. D. Wendland, A. Rich), the concern for dialogue between → Marxism and Christianity (e.g., H. Gollwitzer, J. Hromádka), interest in the path that the church should take in the former East Germany (e.g., H. Falke, A. Schönherr), and the penetration of → liberation theology into the ecumenical movement (e.g., R. Schaull, L. Boff; → Ecumenism, Ecumenical Movement).

→ Atheism; Christians for Socialism; Modern Church History 1; Social Movements; Socialism; Theology in the Nineteenth and Twentieth Centuries

Bibliography: P. d'Alroy, *The Christian Socialist Revival, 1877-1914: Religion, Class, and Social Conscience in Late-Victorian England* (Princeton, 1968) • F. M. Balzer, *Klassengegensätze in der Kirche. Erwin Eckert und der Bund der Religiösen Sozialisten* (Cologne, 1973) • W. Deresch, *Predigt und Agitation der religiösen Sozialisten* (Hamburg, 1971); idem, ed., *Der Glaube der religiösen Sozialisten* (Hamburg, 1972) • R. T. Handy, ed., *The Social Gospel in America, 1870-1920* (New York, 1966) • C. H. Hopkins, *The Rise of the Social Gospel in American Protestantism, 1865-1915* (New Haven, 1961) • E. R. Norman, *The Victorian Christian Socialists* (Cambridge, 1987) • A. Pfeirrer, ed., *Religiöse Sozialisten* (Freiburg, 1976) • K. T. Pongo, *Expectation as Fulfillment: A Study in Paul Tillich's Theory of Justice* (Lanham, Md., 1996) • L. Ragaz, *Signs of the Kingdom: A Ragaz Reader* (ed. P. Bock; Grand Rapids, 1984) • M. A. Stenger and R. H. Stone, "Religious Socialism and Liberation Theology," *Dialogues of Paul Tillich* (Macon, Ga., 2002) chap. 10 • M. Stöhr, ed., *Theologische Ansätze im religiösen Sozialismus* (Frankfurt, 1983) • T. Strohm, *Kirche und demokratischer Sozialismus. Studien zur Theorie und Praxis politischer Kommunikation* (Munich, 1968) • P. Tillich, *Political Expectation* (New York, 1971) • A. R. Vidler, *Prophecy and Papacy: A Study of Lamennais, the Church, and the Revolution* (New York, 1954); idem, *Witness to the Light: F. D. Maurice's Message for To-day* (New York, 1948) • S. Wehowsky, *Religiöse Interpretation politischer Erfahrung. Eberhard Arnold und die Neuwerkbewegung als Exponenten des religiösen Sozialismus zur Zeit der Weimarer Republik* (Göttingen, 1980).

Theodor Strohm

Religious Studies

1. Term

The → prophets of Israel with their criticism of Canaanite worship, as well as the philosophers of antiquity with their attacks on Greek → myths, held aloof from what we now call → religion, an attitude that is essential in the study of religion. The same applies to Islamic geographers, Christian missionaries, European explorers, and students of mythology from the days of the → Enlightenment, also of comparative linguistics from the days of → Romanticism, especially when new knowledge was brought to light.

The whole complex of what might be called religion in the form of a *secta, lex, latria, fides,* or *superstitio,* along with the associated *cultus, ritus,* or *ceremoniae,* first became the object of the discipline named religious studies at the hands of the Göttingen circle influenced by J. G. → Herder (1744-1803) and including F. Stäudlin (1761-1826), I. Berger (1773-1803), C. Meiners (1747-1810), and C. W. Flügge (1773-1827). Another term for the discipline was the → history of religion. No attempt was made at this time to make a distinction from comparative theology. The first to do so was F. Max Müller (1823-1900) with his *Introduction to the Science of Religion,* published in and for Oxford in 1873. The translation of this work into German helped to give religious studies a place as an academic discipline with varied relations to specialized disciplines and subdisciplines. Individual scholars, educational interests, and administrative presuppositions have a large influence on the discipline in actual practice.

2. Subject and Definition

Religious studies deals with religion(s) as a collective empirical entity. Religion may consist of emotions, ideas, statements, actions, and → institutions, all with considerable intermixing. The academic interest may be in a comparison of constant features or in the history of transformations, but the two approaches are complementary.

Scholars in religious studies must cooperate with those in history and in cultural and social studies, especially → anthropology, → psychology, → sociology, philology, → linguistics, art, and literature. Because of the need for dates and textual data and surveys, religious studies is materially dependent on these other disciplines, but it is methodologically autonomous inasmuch as they have developed their own criteria by which to identify their themes. In this regard it uses a universal or higher-stage epoche that enables it to avoid the question whether its statements are metaphysically or theologically true or false. Hence it does not employ such terms as "superstition." Its approach in this respect has given rise to comparative religious studies and to a universal → history of religion. The focus on emotions and ideas links it to the → psychology of religion, that on actions and institutions to the → sociology of religion. Since all departments of the university deal with phenomena, there is a place likewise for the → phenomenology of religion. The psychology, sociology, and historical phenomenology of religion are separate disciplines when the treatment is diachronous rather than synchronous.

3. Philosophy of Religion

Religious studies is not the same thing as a constructive philosophy of religion that in dialogue with the → perennial philosophy attains to a qualified concept of religion that in turn enriches philosophy. It is not the same thing as a philosophical interpretation of the theological tradition or "philosophical theology." Yet it may be or become an → analytic philosophy that begins with given religions and especially with their theses. It then must show why it can use the term "god" only as a predicate (e.g., Zeus is a god) and not as a proper name in the way that theology does (e.g., God is the Father of Jesus Christ). Also it becomes an analytic philosophy of religion whose underlying logic can then compel it to call their evaluations correct or mistaken rather than true or false.

4. Religious Studies and Theology

Religious studies is methodologically autonomous in relation to → theology, but it is materially independent as well. It is not a preparatory or auxiliary theological discipline. Nevertheless, we abuse its function as one that is critical of → ideology if we make religious studies hostile to theology. It then becomes a cryptotheology or a substitute theology.

Religious studies cannot accept a division of labor that would reserve, for example, → Judaism and Christianity for theology and leave to religious studies all the other religions, no longer to be called foreign (foreign though they might seem to be). Judaism and Christianity can also be studied from the standpoint of religion and their theology integrated into the history of religion.

Again, theology itself can engage in a study of religions (→ Theology of Religions) and pursue religious studies in relation to the tasks of → missiology and ecumenical and interreligious → dialogue. Religious studies of this kind can perhaps see many things more sharply, but finally it must differ from religious studies in general inasmuch as it does not engage in any transcendental reduction of → faith or unbelief to a pure act of consciousness. Rather, it distinguishes between true and false religion, even though ready to take the latter in full seriousness and to accept it as it is. Religious studies that thus operates with potential truth judgments does not indeed have the same interests, goals, or methods as theology does, but it shares with it the criterion and phenomenon of religion and therefore a common subject-matter, for it does not doubt that absolute dependence, ultimate concern, that which is of unconditional relevance, or whatever else makes up the essence of religion really stands in relation to the Wholly Other or the Holy and not simply, as is possible in the world of objects, to money or party or similar "powers."

When, however, theology and religious studies that regards true-false evaluations as mistaken deal with common themes such as the biblical proclamations of faith, testimonies to revelation, and statements about salvation, theology can derive from them only a normative compendium for confessional construction. In contrast, religious studies views them as predicates for conceptual construction.

Bibliography: L. E. CADY and D. BROWN, eds., *Religious Studies and the University: Conflicting Maps, Changing Terrain* (Albany, N.Y., 2002) • W. H. CAPPS, *Religious Studies: The Making of a Discipline* (Minneapolis, 1995) • C. COLPE, *Theologie, Ideologie, Religionswissenschaft. Demonstrationen ihrer Unterscheidung* (Munich, 1980) • M. ELIADE, ed., *EncRel(E)* • C. ELSAS, comp., *Religion. Ein Jahrhundert theologischer, philosophischer, soziologischer und psychologischer Interpretationsansätze* (Munich, 1975) • T. FITZGERALD, *The Ideology of Religious Studies* (New York, 2000) • H.-J. GRESCHAT, *Was ist Religionswissenschaft?* (Stuttgart, 1988) • D. G. HART, *The University Gets Religion: Religious Studies in American Higher Education* (Baltimore, 1999) • L. HONKO, ed., *Science of Religion: Studies in Methodology* (The Hague, 1979) • K. K. KLOSTERMAIER and L. W. HURTADO, eds., *Religious Studies: Issues, Prospects, and Proposals* (Atlanta, 1991) • W. TYLOCH, *Current Progress in the Methodology of the Science of Religions* (Warsaw, 1984) • J. WAARDENBURG, *Religionen und Religion. Systematische Einführung in die Religionswissenschaft* (Berlin, 1986); idem, ed., *Classical Approaches to the Study of Religion* (2 vols.; The Hague, 1973-74).

CARSTEN COLPE

Remonstrants → Arminianism

Renaissance

1. Term and Problem
2. Research after Burckhardt
3. Socioeconomic Context
4. Relation to Antiquity
5. Literature and Art
6. Philosophy and Science
7. Religion
8. Reception of the Italian Renaissance in Europe

1. Term and Problem

The idea of Renaissance, or rebirth, has its roots in the longing for youthful renewal that comes when the present grows old and shows a need for reform. In the Christian tradition we find → regeneration in the NT with respect to → baptism and the → Eucharist (→ Sacrament). In Italy in the 12th and 13th centuries, this sacramental idea of renewal in the Spirit inspired a living hope of → salvation such as we find especially in Joachim of Fiore (ca. 1135-1202) and his prophesying of the dawn of the age of the → Holy Spirit (→ Eschatology). Cola di Rienzo (1313-54) thought he could combine this theme with a renewing of → Rome. As he found useful things for the present in his reading of ancient texts, he adopted the principle that would relate the Renaissance to antiquity.

With the → secularization of the idea and its application to poetry, the Renaissance became the key concept in epochal understanding of the self. The synonymous concept of the → resurrection of a poet of antiquity emerges first in a poem in which Benvenuto Campesani (d. 1323) celebrated the discovery of a manuscript of Catullus (d. ca. 54 B.C.). Giovanni Boccaccio (1313-75), relating the birth of a new poetry to the recovery of the authors of antiquity, hailed it with the prophecy of the sibyl in the Fourth Eclogue of Virgil (70-19 B.C.), and other authors followed him in thus celebrating the Renaissance as a new → golden age.

With reference to Giotto's (ca. 1267-1337) art and its faithfulness to reality, Boccaccio extended the idea of Renaissance to painting as well, and later other arts and sciences came to be included in what Matteo Palmieri called the *rinascere l'arti perdute* (revival of lost arts). Finally, N. Machiavelli (1469-1527) declared that Italy was summoned to infuse new life into *all* dead things; Renaissance was its historical mission.

To the extent that the age of Renaissance saw itself as a new age, it stressed its opposition to the immediate past, which it considered a time of darkness between antiquity and the present, against which the light of the Renaissance shone all the more brightly. Out of this conception arose what is still the common division of history into antiquity, the → Middle Ages, and the → modern period (→ Historiography).

Giorgio Vasari (1511-74) found this structure in the development of Western art when in 1550 he distinguished three periods: *maniera antica* (the way of antiquity), which reached the height of perfection; *maniera vecchia* (the old way), the decline in art from the Byzantines to the barbarian Goths; and *maniera moderna* (the modern way), the rebirth of art, reaching perfection again especially in Michelangelo. The *rinàscita,* or rebirth of art, beginning in the middle of the 13th century, preceded the third stage. What was meant was a return to both → nature and antiquity. Artists should learn from antiquity how to imitate nature and perfect it. At much the same time we find in Pierre Belon (1517-64) the term "Renaissance" used for the first time in 1553 in the sense of a rebirth of the *bonnes disciplines* that are now emerging out of a deep sleep of ignorance into the light, just as plants in springtime develop new powers under the warm rays of the sun.

Confident of its powers, the Renaissance increasingly took a positive view of whether or not it could match antiquity and create new things unknown to antiquity. The Renaissance was already raising what would be the issue in the famous dispute between the ancient and the modern (or *querelle des anciens et des modernes;* → Modernity). Even at the risk of relativizing the absolute → authority of antiquity, the view obtained that the Renaissance was beginning a new epoch characterized by intellectual → progress over the past. From this angle J. d'Alembert (1717-83) would later see in the Renaissance a necessary preparatory stage for the → Enlightenment, which would cause the → light kindled by the Renaissance to shine all the brighter.

→ Romanticism rehabilitated the Middle Ages and condemned the ostensibly pagan Renaissance as a threat to the Christian values of Western culture. Then the French historian J. Michelet (1798-1874), under the influence of G. W. F. Hegel (1770-1831; → Hegelianism), studied the Renaissance for the first time as a historical epoch (*Histoire de France* [vol. 7, 1855]; → Philosophy of History) in which modern thinking came to birth with the "discovery" of the world and of humankind. In this epoch human beings found themselves again. To be sure, Michelet restricted the Renaissance to the 16th century and failed to see what a leading role Italy had played.

Only with Jacob Burckhardt's (1818-97) *Kultur*

der Renaissance in Italien (1860), which underlies modern Renaissance research, did it become plain that Italy was the cradle of the Renaissance. The close link between the folk spirit of Italy and the rediscovery of antiquity gave rise to the predominantly aesthetically oriented culture of the Renaissance as an expression of the independently developing modern individual (→ Aesthetics; Individualism; Person). Standing at the gateway to the modern age, Renaissance culture is the model closest akin to our own culture and still exerts an influence.

2. Research after Burckhardt

We may arrange research after Burckhardt in three phases: assimilation of the new Renaissance view, then criticism, then the development of a fresh understanding on the basis of a revision of Burckhardt and with the help of wider knowledge of the sources and new inquiries. After prolonged, often polemical debate there is now general acceptance of the Renaissance as an epochal term (for the period 1300-1600) and acceptance of what were in part its contradictory tendencies.

Modern studies are above all interdisciplinary, with the various disciplines following their own methodologies. They range from the history of → theology to natural science. In this way there is some assurance that we will increasingly see the Renaissance in its complex totality.

3. Socioeconomic Context

The political, social, and economic development of the Italian city-states, especially Florence since the high Middle Ages, created a favorable climate in which the middle class could bear the main responsibility for Renaissance culture. With the emergence of the → money economy of early → capitalism, the middle class began to free itself from traditional lifestyles and views. The wealth it acquired offered a welcome means of personal development and the cultivating of cultural interests. Thanks to a lay education that resulted from addressing practical needs, the middle class was open to literary pursuits. Merchant writers were typical of the society of Florence in the 14th and 15th centuries (C. Bec), and humanistic ideas were appearing in their works (→ Humanism). These ideas were being discussed in middle-class circles that were interested in this new education. In their delight in the beauty of art, wealthy citizens commissioned works of art, had fine buildings erected in their cities, and collected the works of antiquity.

Only in the late 15th and early 16th century, when the court replaced the city as the social basis of Renaissance culture, did the more extensive and grand system of patronage develop. Thenceforth the courtly culture shaped Renaissance culture, which in the 16th century spread from Italy to other European lands.

4. Relation to Antiquity

The reawakening of antiquity was only one aspect of the general intellectual and historical change triggered by the Renaissance. The change involved a new relation to antiquity wherein the ancient authors took on new life, rather than so much a sudden increase in knowledge of these authors. To give them present-day relevance was a primary concern of the humanists, who, starting with Petrarch (1304-74), felt related to them as to living partners in dialogue. From the end of the 13th century, humanists in their enthusiasm for antiquity began scouring monastery libraries for forgotten works of ancient writers and copying and collecting them. Thanks to numerous finds, Latin literature became almost as well known by the middle of the 15th century as it is today. Also, many Greek works were imported from the East as knowledge of Greek spread (→ Greek Language).

Although antiquity was the primary authority and normative model, the creative achievements of the time did not seek merely a repristination of the models of antiquity but their creative appropriation, their assimilation to the new consciousness. It would be pointless, argued Poggio Bracciolini (1380-1459), to gather the fruits of a reading of ancient authors without applying them to our own lives, as though one were to assemble wood and stones and mortar but never build a house.

5. Literature and Art

In no area of the intellectual activity of the Renaissance was the principle of following ancient models *(imitatio)* taken more seriously than in literature. In literary theory and practice the Latin and Greek classical authors listed in catalogs played a central role. To illustrate what was meant by an eclectic imitation that would still leave a modern writer a certain stylistic independence, use was made of a bee analogy taken from Lucius Annaeus Seneca the Younger (ca. 4 B.C.–A.D. 65). As bees gather nectar from various flowers but then make something new out of it (i.e., honey), so authors should make something new on the basis of their literary models. In contrast to the freedom that this approach allowed, Ciceronianism permitted no deviation from the stylistic model.

The main literary language of the Renaissance up

to the 16th century was Latin, as far as the works of humanists and those influenced by them were concerned. But gradually popular works in vernacular languages began to appear that adopted a Latin style and Latin genres; the content of these works largely coincided with that of humanism and also presupposed commensurately educated readers. Since it was held that → rhetoric and writing can both be taught, many theoretical treatises were composed in both Latin and the vernacular dealing not only with a normative literary canon but also with both the rules and the nature of literature.

As Renaissance art developed in Italy, it diverged in two ways from the art of the Middle Ages. It was more naturalistic (→ Naturalism), and it was more akin to the art of antiquity. These features both passed into the classical style of the High Renaissance at the turn of the 16th century, and this style then spread across the Alps. With enhanced self-awareness and humanistic training, artists both reflected on their work (L. B. Alberti and Leonardo da Vinci) and achieved recognition by → society in virtue of their achievements.

5.1. In practice European Renaissance literature followed the Italian school. Petrarch and Boccaccio pointed the way. With his Latin works the former was the father of humanist literature in Europe. Petrarch's *Canzoniere* (the usual name for his poems), which drew inspiration from his beloved Laura, influenced European lyric poetry right up to the days of → baroque. Boccaccio's *Decameron* (prob. 1348-53) set the style for the modern short story. Then L. Ariosto (1474-1533) with his *Orlando furioso* (1516) revived the chivalrous novel of the Middle Ages in the Renaissance spirit, so also T. Tasso (1544-95) with his *Gerusalemme liberata* (1581) and M. de Cervantes (1547-1616) with his *Don Quixote* (1605-15). In G. B. Guarini's (1538-1612) *Pastor fido* (1590), the Italian pastoral acquired European renown.

In productive interaction with Italian influences, Renaissance literature flourished in other European countries as well. In addition to *Don Quixote* we might mention, in France, F. Rabelais's (ca. 1483-1553) gigantic narrative output, the *Essais* (from 1572) of M. de Montaigne (1533-92), and the mystical verse of Fray Luis de León (1527-91); then in Portugal, the epic *Os Lusíadas* (1572), extolling Portugese voyages of discovery, by L. de Camões (1524/25-80); and in England, T. More's (1478-1535) *Utopia* (1516) and E. Spenser's (1552/53-99) *Faerie Queene* (1590).

5.2. Related to the same epochal self-understanding were works in the plastic arts, architecture, and music that blossomed in a revival of the culture of antiquity. A Renaissance style developed in Florence during the first half of the 15th century and then spread to the rest of Europe. One feature of this style was a realism deriving from lively new interest in the visible world. We also find more secular themes.

With the use of perspective Masaccio (1401-28) learned to present three-dimensional space on a two-dimensional surface. Donatello (1386-1466), the greatest sculptor of the early Renaissance, sought exact fidelity to nature in sculptures depicting people both active and suffering. F. Brunelleschi (1377-1446) pioneered a new architecture with the Florentine cathedral dome, which symbolizes the city.

Leonardo da Vinci (1452-1519) introduced the High Renaissance with his *Last Supper* (1495-97), in which he idealistically enhances realism. The center of the High Renaissance was Rome, where Raphael (1483-1520) and Michelangelo (1475-1564) were active. The former in his human portrayals created a lofty ideal of the beautiful and gave spiritual life to the classical form. The latter was a painter and sculptor of genius. Also in his great later works — the frescoes, for example, in the Sistine Chapel, and his later marble statues — Michelangelo moved on to new forms of expression that inaugurated the baroque.

5.3. In the Middle Ages music was closely related to mathematics (→ Theology and Music), but in the Renaissance, with an appeal to antiquity (esp. Plutarch), music was brought closer to poetry. In the process it was subordinated to the text. The ideal, that is, was to preserve word accentuation in the simple form of monody (G. Zarlino). The Académie de Poésie et de Musique, founded in 1570 by J.-A. de Baïf (1532-89), cultivated music that accommodated itself to verse that followed ancient meters. The efforts of the Florentine Camerata in the late 16th century to revive Greek music (V. Galilei, father of Galileo) produced the first melodramas (text by O. Rinuccini, music by J. Peri), which fused elements from the medieval miracle play and Greek tragedy. Here we have the forerunners of opera, which ushered in a new era in the history of the theater.

6. Philosophy and Science

Though → Scholasticism lived on, modern → philosophy had its origins in the Renaissance. Anthropological (→ Anthropology) and cosmological questions were raised afresh and answered with a reference back to antiquity, primarily to a revived → Platonism or → Aristotelianism, though also in dialogue with → Stoicism, the Epicureans (→ Hedonism) and → Skepticism. The result was a philosophy that followed the general secular path and increasingly broke loose from the church. The roots lay in humanist moral philosophy insofar as this discipline, resting on reflection on manifestations of the human, drew up rules of right conduct that would take into account not only individual instruction but also society and the → state. We find new approaches not merely in → ethics but also in → logic, → metaphysics, and the → philosophy of nature. On the basis of rhetoric an attempt was made to replace the Aristotelian organon with a new and real, rather than formal, logic (L. Valla, J. Agricola, P. Ramus, and M. Nizzoli).

Breaking away from the theological metaphysics of the Middle Ages, Nicholas of Cusa (1401-64), M. Ficino (1433-99), C. de Bovelles (1472?-1553), and G. Bruno (1548-1600) sketched out a new type of metaphysics. Cusa conceived of God as developing in a temporally and spatially infinite universe, the macrocosm, which is most perfectly reflected in the human microcosm. The other thinkers mentioned here took up this view and added other features.

New thinking in the philosophy of nature paved the way for modern science. It increasingly sought access to nature by way of → experience that could be verified by experiment and tested by mathematics (Leonardo da Vinci). The legacy of antiquity acted as a catalyst in the reviving of mathematics, astronomy, practical technical arts, botany, and mineralogy. N. Copernicus (1473-1543) appealed to the Pythagoreans in support of his heliocentric system. At every point new advances in thinking show how decisive the Renaissance was in the development of modern philosophy and science (S. Otto).

7. Religion

It hardly needs demonstration today that the turning back of the Renaissance to antiquity did not involve opposition to the Christian religion or the → church. Nevertheless, we do see a basic change in the attitude toward Christianity inasmuch as it was now seen more as a subjective frame of mind (→ Religion, Personal Sense of) rather than as objective → proclamation (→ Subjectivism and Objectivism). The center of theological interest shifted from dogmatic speculation (→ Dogmatics) to discussion of the Christian life. Leaders in this shift were the Christian humanists from Petrarch to D. → Erasmus (1469?-1536), who sought a synthesis of Christian teaching and the wisdom of antiquity and who believed that in this regard they had forerunners in the → church fathers.

When the Christian humanists accused medieval theologians of culpably neglecting study of the Fathers, it was only one element in their general criticism of Scholasticism — more specifically, of later Scholasticism (→ Nominalism; Middle Ages 2), which it censured for its inclination to engage in sterile games with subtle distinctions and absurd conclusions. The accompanying externalizing of → piety into a matter of commandments, ceremonies, and → rites — a development commensurate with the formalism of late Scholasticism — also came under their judgment. They themselves sought a spiritualizing of religious relations with less importance attached to the outward forms of the cult (→ Spiritualism; Worship).

This criticism of the existing state of the Christian religion arose out of a desire to revive Christian teaching in its earlier form. As in the secular sphere the Renaissance tried to purge the ancient authors of all later distortions, so here its aim was a new edition of the Bible according to current philological and historical criteria. The most important achievement in the biblical philology of humanism was Erasmus's edition of the Greek NT, which he published in 1516 on the basis of L. Valla's (1407-57) *Adnotationes ad Novum Testamentum* (written in the 1450s but not printed until 1505; → Bible Manuscripts and Editions 3). It was through reading the unadulterated Bible, primarily the NT, the most important source of humanist theology, that the personal piety of the humanists was nurtured, for whom the church was far less important as a mediator between God and humankind or as an institution of salvation. In the Gospels they found the teaching that we need to live a life that is pleasing to God, especially in the → Sermon on the Mount, whose commandments found their most perfect fulfillment in the life of the one who issued them. This life is our supreme model, which calls for our imitation (→ Discipleship). Christian humanism culminated in imitation of Christ the teacher of life (→ Christology).

With its unbounded trust in the goodness of human nature and its reshaping of religion as ethics, Christian humanism came into diametrical opposition to the teaching of the → Reformation. Its work on the Bible and its censuring of late medieval abuses (e.g., the influence of Erasmus on U. → Zwingli or W. Tyndale and that of J. Colet on the early English reformers) no doubt opened the door to the Reformation, but we nonetheless have here two totally different pictures of our human situation. On the one hand, we see a stress on human dignity and a confidence in human ability; on the other, a sense of human impotence before God (→

Justification 2; Luther's Theology; Sin). Optimism that we can be masters of our destiny ran up against pessimism in the estimating of human possibilities (→ Optimism and Pessimism). The Renaissance and humanism contained many influential Christian elements, but at their heart they were building up a secular culture. The Reformation, in contrast, made our relation to God the center.

8. Reception of the Italian Renaissance in Europe

The influence of the Italian Renaissance on Europe rested on the intellectual hegemony of Italy in the 15th and 16th centuries. It was helped by the emergence of printing from the middle of the 15th century, which made possible a rapid dissemination of new ideas. Reception varied from country to country in accordance with different national traditions and changing socioeconomic conditions. Wherever reception involved the productive assimilation of what was foreign to the cultural legacy (→ Acculturation), original works resulted. Although conflict about beliefs challenged the cultural unity of Europe, the intellectual legacy of the Renaissance in European culture lives on in the modern era insofar as its own beginnings are found in the Italian Renaissance, whose claims to innovation were justified by its cultural achievements.

Bibliography: H. Baron, *The Crisis of the Early Italian Renaissance* (Princeton, 1966); idem, *In Search of Florentine Civic Humanism: Essays on the Transition from Medieval to Modern Thought* (Princeton, 1988) • C. Bec, *Les marchands écrivains. Affaires et humanisme à Florence, 1375-1434* (Paris, 1967) • J. Brotton, *The Renaissance Bazaar: From the Silk Road to Michelangelo* (Oxford, 2002) • A. Brown, *The Renaissance* (2d ed.; London, 1999) • A. Buck, *Humanismus. Seine europäische Entwicklung in Dokumenten und Darstellungen* (Freiburg, 1987); idem, *Die Rezeption der Antike in den romanischen Literaturen der Renaissance* (Berlin, 1976); idem, ed., *Renaissance, Reformation. Gegensätze und Gemeinsamkeiten* (Wiesbaden, 1984); idem, ed., *Zu Begriff und Problem der Renaissance* (Darmstadt, 1969) • J. Burckhardt, *The Civilization of the Renaissance in Italy* (New York, 2002; orig. pub., 1860) • P. Burke, *The Renaissance* (2d ed.; Basingstoke, 1997); idem, *Tradition and Innovation in Renaissance Italy: A Sociological Approach* (London, 1974) • R. De Maio, *Donna e Rinascimento* (rev. ed.; Naples, 1995) • W. K. Ferguson, *The Renaissance in Historical Thought: Five Centuries of Interpretation* (Boston, 1948) • E. Garin, *La cultura filosofica del Rinascimento italiano* (Milan, 1994); idem, *Italian Humanism: Philosophy and Civic Life in the Renaissance* (Oxford, 1966) • H. A. E. van Gelder, *The Two Reformations in the Sixteenth Century* (The Hague, 1961) • D. Hay, *The Italian Renaissance and Its Historical Background* (2d ed.; London, 1977) • L. H. Heydenreich and A. Chastel, *Italienische Renaissance* (4 vols.; Munich, 1965-75) • P. O. Kristeller, *Renaissance Thought and Its Sources* (New York, 1979) • A. von Martin, *Sociology of the Renaissance* (New York, 1963) • S. Otto, ed., *Geschichte der Philosophie in Text und Darstellung*, vol. 3, *Renaissance und frühe Neuzeit* (Stuttgart, 1994) • E. Panofsky, *Renaissance and Renascences in Western Art* (2 vols.; 2d ed.; Stockholm, 1965) • *Il Rinascimento. Interpretazioni e problemi* (FS E. Garin; Rome, 1983) • B. Thompson, *Humanists and Reformers: A History of the Renaissance and Reformation* (Grand Rapids, 1996) • C. Trinkaus, *In Our Image and Likeness: Humanity and Divinity in Italian Humanist Thought* (2 vols.; Chicago, 1970); idem, *The Scope of Renaissance Humanism* (Ann Arbor, Mich., 1983).

August Buck

Repentance → Penitence

Representation

1. Legal
2. Sociological
3. Theological

1. Legal

The term "representation" denotes acting on behalf of another based on legal stipulation, private statutes, or plenipotentiary arrangements. The legal representative (e.g., parent, guardian, trustee) acts in the name of the other within defined legal limits. It makes no difference whether willingness to do so is expressly stated or arises naturally out of the circumstances. The essential point is that the representative, in the absence of the one represented, acts alone but does so legally in the name of the other and not in his or her own name.

2. Sociological

Sociologically (also politically), representation means more generally the representing of some members of a social unit by others in such a way that what is done is ascribed to all of them. In a representative → democracy the ones elected by the people to represent them govern in the name of the people. Those selected carry out the political will of those whom they represent, who are absent but who still participate in this way.

The term "collective representation" (F. Durkheim) may be used for → symbols such as banners, crosses, concepts, slogans, or language in general that expresses and represents the common ideas, opinions, experiences, or interests of a collective — that is, a group, organization, or society. What they represent usually more or less transcends any single personal experience and has its own reality, with emotional and cognitive significance for members of the collective.

3. Theological

Ecclesiastically and theologically, representation has a wider meaning in the Roman Catholic Church. What is to be represented is not viewed simply as absent or as transferred to or replaced by a representative figure. The object of representation is an ongoing and present, perhaps invisible, operation to which visible form is to be given. At issue here is the function of the church in its sacramental presentation of the divine work of salvation (→ Church 3.2; Sacraments; Sacramentality). The church has the saving commission to give visible expression both to fellowship with God (Christ) and to the fellowship of believers as the body of Christ and the people of God. A twofold representation is thus demanded of it.

The hierarchical organs take up this two-dimensional task (*Lumen gentium* 25-29; 1983 → CIC 375-80). The → bishop represents Christ by taking his place, acting in his name, symbolizing fellowship with God in the bishop's own person, and giving visibility to Christ's presence. He also offers representation of the body of Christ (ecclesial representation) by building up the fellowship of believers through proclamation of the faith and the sacraments and by leading it as a pastor, though he can do so only because and insofar as he, as Christ's representative, is conformed to the Head of the body of Christ. This twofold representation takes place especially impressively in the celebration of the → Eucharist (§3.2). The bishop or his delegate, the → priest, "in the person of Christ . . . effects the eucharistic sacrifice and offers it to God in the name of all the people" (*Lumen gentium* 10.2). By his ministry "the spiritual sacrifice of the faithful is completed in unity with the sacrifice of Christ the only mediator" (*Presbyterorum ordinis* 2.4).

→ Roman Catholic Church 2.2, 3.1, 6.3

Bibliography: "The Constitution on the Sacred Liturgy," *Vatican Council II* (ed. A. Flannery; Grand Rapids, 1975) 1-36 • É. Durkheim, "Individual and Collective Representation," *Sociology and Philosophy* (trans. D. F. Pocock; Glencoe, Ill., 1953) 1-34 • G. Leibholz, *Das Wesen der Representation und der Gestaltswandel der Demokratie im 20. Jahrhundert* (3d ed.; Berlin, 1966) • J. Mansbridge, "What Does a Representative Do?" *Citizenship in Diverse Societies* (ed. W. Kymlicka and W. Norman; Oxford, 2000) 99-123 • P. E. Persson, *Repraesentatio Christi. Der Amtsbegriff in der neueren römisch-katholischen Theologie* (Göttingen, 1966) • M. S. Williams, "The Uneasy Alliance of Group Representation and Deliberative Democracy," *Citizenship in Diverse Societies*, ed. Kymlicka and Norman, 124-54.

Erwin Fahlbusch

Reproduction Technology

Overview

Reproduction technology (RT) is not a single technology but a series of technologies that can be used in order to bring about the birth of a desired child or the birth of a child with (at least some) desired characteristics. These characteristics may be sought for their own sake or in order to avoid illness for the child or to assist another already living human being. Reproduction technology accomplishes these goals by various means that are used to (1) assist women in becoming pregnant, (2) assist women who cannot become pregnant in having a child genetically related to them through surrogate mothers, (3) create embryos and inform the couples about the future child's genetic makeup as well as implanting the then-selected embryos, and (4) inform parents about the condition of the fetus during an actual pregnancy. In the future new forms of these technologies may assist couples in the creation of offspring genetically identical with one of the parents through cloning.

Because of the ways in which these technologies can be used in conjunction with one another and because the possibilities are expanding so rapidly, we find that relatively little attention is being paid to their long-term human consequences. Also we should note that the very idea of reproduction technology itself is contested. For some Christian critics, the term brings pregnancy and childbirth into the realm of production, wrongfully removing them from the realm of procreation.

The field of RT has been the object of a good deal of reflection by Christians on how these technologies ought to be used and not used (→ Medical Ethics). It also has been the subject of controversy in many Western societies, especially when it is argued that public funds should be used in order to assist those who wish to avail themselves of these technologies. RT supporters celebrate the freedom these technologies bring to women who might otherwise be unable to have their own genetically related children (→ Feminism; Women's Movement). RT critics worry about what the technology does to our understanding of → marriage and procreation. Here we consider a limited number of these technologies and Christian responses to them.

1. Fertility Assistance

Much of the current theological discussion of reproduction technologies focuses upon in vitro fertilization (IVF). This procedure involves the manipulation of human gametes outside the womb and the implantation of the resulting embryo in the womb. Even before IVF, however, there was controversy about another form of fertility assistance, artificial insemination (AI), whether from the husband's (AIH) or from a donor's sperm (AID). For some Christian critics of AI, the objections were straightforward: sexual intercourse has at least two purposes — the unity of the couple and the creation of new life — and these purposes should not be separated (→ Sexual Ethics). Artificial insemination, unless done using AIH and unless done in conjunction with sexual intercourse between the couple, divides these two purposes too sharply. Indeed, when using AID, the genetic link between the child and the parents is deliberately broken.

Artificial insemination makes surrogate motherhood a possibility. Surrogate mothers carry a child not necessarily genetically related to them through pregnancy. The practice developed to assist women who could not bring a pregnancy to term. The surrogate mother is supposed to return the child to the parents when the pregnancy is completed. In some cases, however, the gestational mother wishes to keep the child, which makes surrogate motherhood particularly controversial.

In vitro fertilization continues the separation of acts of sexual intercourse from procreation itself. Critics who have rejected AI thus reject IVF. Supporters of the use of IVF and of AI within marriage point out that the preceding claims that these practices separate the unitive and procreative purposes of marriage depend upon an analysis that begins with a focus upon each and every act of sexual intercourse instead of the fuller context in which acts of sexual intercourse are taking place. These critics affirm that the unitive and procreative aspects of sexual intercourse are indeed kept together once we consider the marriage as a whole. Focusing upon individual acts, so the commentators claim, distorts the setting within which IVF and AI most often take place.

A central issue here is the place of fertility in a good human life. Some commentators argue that what is at stake is one's sense of participation in the world. Infertility may be the occasion of a profound spiritual crisis for the couple that suffers from infertility, a crisis that few Christian communities address at that level.

Another important set of considerations at this point centers on how infertility is to be classified. It does not neatly fit the usual medical model of an illness (→ Health and Illness). Having children is perceived to be a choice of the couple, and there are other ways in which they might have children, including adoption. According to commentators who take this perspective, infertility should not be treated primarily as a medical problem. Persons do not *need* to have children; they *choose* to have them. Indeed, secular defenders of all forms of RT celebrate it precisely for this reason. RT gives a couple choices that they did not have before, first, with respect to fertility itself and, second, with respect to the children who will come into existence as a result of using these technologies.

For those who adhere to the classic understanding of marriage, infertility may be accepted, or one can point to the Christian appropriation of adoption and present it as one way of responding to infertility. That classic understanding of marriage and adoption has been challenged, not on its own terms, but because of the ways in which adoption is put forward as a response to infertility. Commentators point out that there are many children who are without parents and are vulnerable, but the causes of their vulnerability need to be addressed directly instead of simply denying resources for reproductive technologies. Furthermore, the call to adopt is often applied selectively, to the infertile, rather than to the entire Christian community.

In addition to the role the Christian community might play in addressing the infertile couple, the question still remains about what role medicine might play in this issue. If the goal of medicine is to relieve important sources of → suffering that are due to deficiencies of the body, infertility often is classified as a malady to be remedied, since some infertility is related to disease.

If the goal of medicine is more limited, however, then society perhaps has no obligation to use the resources of medical science to relieve the suffering brought about by infertility. This line of argument is important for those societies that provide basic medical treatment to all their citizens (i.e., most of the industrialized world). Should the resources be used for infertility treatment(s) when they might be spent elsewhere? If the resources were spent elsewhere, many poor would not be able to seek infertility treatment because the cost is so prohibitive (→ Poverty).

Even if one decides that it is a legitimate goal of medicine to try to relieve infertility, important questions remain. For example, the success of IVF is not high; furthermore, it is expensive. If public funds are used to support IVF, a further question involves the limits of that support. Specifically, how many cycles of this treatment should be given, when each cycle might cost between $5,000 and $10,000?

But the difficulties do not end there. When successful, IVF can lead to pregnancies with more than one fetus, which sometimes put both the mother and the children at risk. One of the ironies of modern reproductive medicine is that it has led to an increase in high-risk multiple births. Sometimes the effects of these multiple births continue throughout the lives of the children.

The reason for this increased risk is simple. IVF involves the implantation of one or more embryos in the woman. Chances of success (i.e., of a pregnancy) are enhanced if more rather than fewer embryos are implanted. If a pregnancy results, however, there is a chance of multiple children. The number of embryos implanted is regulated in some societies in order to limit the risks to mother and children if the implantation procedure is successful. Note that limiting the publicly funded support for the number of cycles of infertility treatments, however, puts pressure upon physicians to implant more embryos, rather than fewer, in order to maximize the chances of success. In societies where the number of embryos implanted is not regulated, it is often routine to offer selective fetal reduction when there are a high number of children for the particular pregnancy. For those opposed to → abortion, selective fetal reduction is morally not an option.

2. Prevention of Defects, Selection of Desired Characteristics

In vitro fertilization was controversial enough when the only issue was the desire to bring children to those who could not otherwise have their own genetically related progeny. When this → technology is coupled with the desire to have children of a particular sex, in order to prevent sex-linked disease, or to have children not at risk for a given genetically linked disease, then even more controversy ensues. IVF thus makes possible another layer of complexity in the process of reproduction.

As a result of advances in genetic testing of embryos, it is possible to inspect the embryo before it is implanted in the woman. This step opens the door for parents to decide whether they will accept or reject the embryo, which is the special worry of some Roman Catholic critics of these procedures. The Vatican's instruction *Donum vitae* (1987) observes that there is a necessary connection between the acceptance of some embryos and the rejection, and destruction, of others. Given that official Roman Catholic teaching presents the embryo as deserving all the protections of a fully developed human being, such destruction is morally reprehensible. IVF has set the stage for the potential destruction. IVF is thus to be rejected not simply because it separates the love of the couple from the activity of procreation but also because of the practices that have developed surrounding the embryos created by the process.

These genetic testing technologies clearly turn the embryo into an object that can be manipulated. If the embryo meets the standards set by its creators, then it can be implanted or saved for future attempts at pregnancy. If it does not meet these standards, then it may be discarded. The standards become ever more rigorous with the development of increasingly sophisticated testing technologies. Furthermore, pressures are increasing to make the testing of the embryo and then the fetus the norm and not the exception. This trend is apparent in the development of fetal testing in the last decade, so that in many parts of the industrial world the fetus is routinely tested and the results given to the mother for her decision about what should be done. Testing for the embryo before it is implanted will doubtless become more and more sophisticated with advances in genetic testing technology. But the difficulties do not end there.

Some observers note that society has moved from a stance of preventing disease or the possibility of disease for the future child to a view that it is permissible to seek children with certain characteristics so that the children might succeed or meet other parental purposes. This attitude threatens the traditional Christian practice of hospitality toward all children. Instead, children increasingly become desired to the extent that they have the characteristics their parents decide they should have. In this scenario a child becomes less a gift and more a commodity.

For those whose central value is → freedom, the control is to be celebrated. For those who are concerned about our attitude toward ourselves as expressed toward how we act toward our children, our willingness to try to control them is worrying.

An example of the use of this technology that may involve prevention of disease or simply meeting parental desires is sex selection. Embryos and fetuses can be tested for their sex. Some diseases are sex linked and, in order to minimize the risk of the disease, all embryos of a certain sex may be discarded. In the case of fetuses, they may be aborted.

Sex selection, however, does not take place solely to prevent disease. It can and does occur because of cultural norms. It is now possible for parents to seek out RT in order to ensure that a child is of a particular sex. If this technology involves testing of the embryo, it is completed before a pregnancy begins and thus eliminates the necessity of an abortion should the embryo turn out to be of the undesired sex. The moral problems with this and associated practices remain.

The moral difficulty turns on the objectification of the embryo, for it is not being treated like a human being, with all the protections human beings are due (→ Rights). Rather, it is viewed as something at the disposal of its creators, to be used or abandoned as they see fit. This underlying attitude toward the embryo is the source of much concern in some quarters.

Critics of the direction of this technology point out that instead of respect for the embryo, we have developed ever more opportunities for the manipulation of the embryo. For example, when IVF was first considered, it was usual to recommend that embryos should not be created for experimental purposes. Today, proponents of embryonic stem-cell research argue that the best way forward is to create embryos for the purposes of research.

3. Benefits to Other Children

One of the newer and more controversial uses of reproductive technologies involves the creation of children with specific genetic characteristics that will be lifesaving for children who need those characteristics. The process usually involves genetic testing of an embryo in order to determine that the embryo has the desired characteristics. If it does, it is implanted. Once the child with the desired characteristics is born, those characteristics can be transferred to an existent child, usually through a bone marrow transplant. Testing thus has not only expanded its reach from existing human beings, back through fetuses in the womb, and back further to eight-cell embryos. It has also expanded its focus so that embryos will be retained or discarded not simply because their genetic characteristics will be desired for the embryo being tested but because the embryo has characteristics that will be helpful to others after it is born (→ Eugenics; Genetic Counseling).

4. Societal Backdrop

One of the disappointing features of the current discussion of reproductive technology is the lack of sustained attention to the social conditions that make it more likely that couples will wish to use these technologies. Women are encouraged to put off childbearing in order to further their careers, yet it is known that age and infertility are positively correlated. Also, the increased incidence of sexually transmitted diseases, with their side effects of infertility, again increases the desire for the use of RT. While the latter matter might be approached through more education and through encouraging changes in sexual mores, the former would involve changing employment practices and career expectations that are deeply ingrained in our modern world. For example, ovarian transplants, originally developed in order to give women who suffer cancers early in life a chance to have children after chemotherapy, are now discussed as a way that any woman, regardless of medical circumstances, can put off having children until later in life in order to pursue a career.

In the view of some, even if one wishes to begin with freedom as the highest good, women are less free if they cannot begin their reproductive lives at an earlier age instead of being servants of the market. Feminist critics divide on this point: some argue that the freedoms gained by this technology outweigh the losses; others think that women are being subordinated, subtly to be sure, through these pressures generated by postindustrial capitalism.

Bibliography: Congregation for the Doctrine of the Faith, "Instruction on Respect for Human Life in Its Origin and on the Dignity of Procreation: Replies to Certain Questions of the Day *(Donum Vitae)* (February 22, 1987)," *Gift of Life: Catholic Scholars Respond to the Vatican Instruction* (ed. E. D. Pellegrino, J. C. Harvey, and J. P. Langan; Washington, D.C., 1990) • Health Council of the Netherlands, Committee on *In vitro* Fertilization, *IVF-Related Research* (Rijswijk, 1998) • J. F. Kilner, P. C. Cunningham, and W. D. Hager, eds., *The Reproduction Revolution: A Christian Appraisal of Sexuality, Reproductive Technologies, and the Family* (Grand Rapids, 2000) • P. Lauritzen, *Pursuing Parenthood: Ethical Issues in Assisted Reproduction* (Bloomington, Ind., 1993) • O. O'Donovan, *Begotten or Made?* (Oxford, 1984) • T. Peters, *For the Love of Children: Genetic Technology and the Future of the Family* (Louisville, Ky., 1996) • Pontifical Academy for Life, *Final Communiqué on "The Dignity of Human Procreation and Reproductive Technologies. Anthropological and Ethical Aspects"* (Rome, 2004) • President's Council on Bioethics, *Beyond Therapy: Biotechnology and the Pursuit of Perfection* (Washington, D.C., 2003) • M. A. Ryan, *Ethics and Economics of Assisted Reproduction: The Cost of Longing* (Washington, D.C., 2001) • T. A. Shannon and L. S. Cahill, *Religion and Artificial Reproduction: An Inquiry into the Vatican "Instruction on Respect for Human Life in Its Origin and on the Dignity of Human Reproduction"* (New York, 1988) • M. Warnock, *A Question of Life: The Warnock Report on Human Fertilisation and Embryology* (Oxford, 1985) • B. Waters, *Reproductive Technology: Towards a Theology of Procreative Stewardship* (Cleveland, Ohio, 2001).

Stephen E. Lammers

Requiem

1. Term and Form

1.1. *Term*

"Requiem" is the → Roman Catholic Mass for the dead. The name derives from the introit for the → Mass, "Requiem aeternum dona eis, Domine, et lux perpetua luceat eis" (Eternal rest grant to them, O Lord, and let perpetual light shine on them; cf. 2 Esdr. 2:34-35). The Requiem Mass may be used as a → funeral service before burial or as a memorial service after burial.

1.2. *Origin*

The origin of the Requiem Mass can be traced to the early Christian practice of celebrating the → Eucharist on the mensa (Lat. "table") over the grave of the deceased on the third day after burial. Commemorations on the 7th and 30th days were also known in the fourth century. There is no evidence of the Eucharist being celebrated as part of the burial rites of the deceased before the seventh century. The development of using the Mass as a funeral service was influenced by the monastic practice of bringing the body of the deceased monk into the monastery chapel for the saying of a mass before burial.

1.3. *As Votive Mass*

The Requiem is a votive mass, that is, a mass offered for special intentions. The intention of the Requiem is to commend the soul of the departed to God. During the Middle Ages requiems were paid for by relatives or friends of the deceased to hasten the passage of the soul from → purgatory to → paradise.

1.4. *Form*

The Requiem is not different in form from other masses. It was distinguished by the insertion of a *memento* (memorial) of the dead and a suitable *Hanc igitur* (Graciously accept . . .) in the canon of the Mass. Special prayers for the dead are already included in the Verona (Leonine) Sacramentary and in the older Gelasian Sacramentary. As a weekday votive mass, the Gloria in Excelsis and the Credo were omitted. The sequence hymn *Dies irae* (Day of wrath) first appeared at the end of the 12th century as a sequence for the first Sunday in Advent. It did not become an official sequence for the Requiem until the reform of the Roman Missal in 1570, although it was used earlier. The Alleluia was suppressed in the Requiem Mass because of its solemn character. It is a → liturgy more conscious of → sin and → death, and of the soul's destiny in purgatory, than of the promise of the → resurrection of the body and the hope of eternal → life, except in the anthems *In paradisum* and *Chorus angelorum.*

1.5. *Roman Catholic Liturgy of Death*

The Constitution on the Sacred Liturgy of the Second → Vatican Council emphasized the paschal character of Christian death (→ Easter). The Requiem in the 1969 *Ordo Exequiarum* (Order of funeral rites) restores the Alleluia and suppresses the *Dies irae.* The readings and prayers express the hope of sharing in Christ's resurrection, and the absolution of the corpse is transformed into a final farewell of the deceased. The 1970 Roman Missal contains a wide selection of Scripture readings in the lectionary and five prefaces for Christian death in the sacramentary (→ Readings, Scripture).

2. Practices

2.1. *Orthodox*

There is no tradition of celebrating the Eucharist at funerals in the Eastern churches (→ Orthodox

Church). The Byzantine funeral service centers on the funeral blessing with its troparia, the Beatitudes, Scripture readings, and the final leave-taking. In the Byzantine Rite the dead may be commemorated at the liturgy on the 9th and 40th days after death and on the anniversary of the departure.

2.2. *Reformation*

The → Reformation rejected the Requiem Mass on theological grounds because of its association with purgatory and its character as a votive mass. The 1549 → Book of Common Prayer provided for a Funeral Communion Service, but it was abolished in 1552, although it was restored in the 1560 Latin version of the prayer book. Medieval burial rites were replaced with simple orders. Lutheran and Anglican revisions retained the form of the Office of the Dead from the monastic breviaries with its psalms and traditional texts, such as the *In media vita* (In the midst of life [we are in death]). The Reformed arranged for services to comfort the bereaved after the burial.

Generally in the Reformation tradition, funeral services were the burial services conducted at the place of interment. Memorial services held in the church building after burial were for the comfort of the deceased and to honor the memory of the faithful departed.

2.3. *Recent Revisions*

Revisions of Protestant rites in recent times have been influenced by the reforms of the Second Vatican Council. The paschal emphasis is more prominent in new Protestant funeral services. The Office of the Dead has been abandoned in favor of a Liturgy of the Word. The possibility of a funeral Eucharist is provided in North American Lutheran, Episcopal/Anglican, and United Methodist worship books.

3. Musical Settings

3.1. *Notable Requiems*

There have been notable musical settings of the Requiem Mass by G. Palestrina, W. A. Mozart (incomplete), A. Dvořák, G. Fauré, and M. Duruflé that are suitable for liturgical use (→ Church Music), although today they are typically performed as concert pieces. The expansive symphonic and operatic settings by H. Berlioz and G. Verdi are suitable only to the concert hall. A typical concert requiem includes the following sections: (1) Requiem aeternum, (2) Kyrie eleison, (3) Dies irae, (4) Domine Jesu Christe, (5) Sanctus, (6) Lux aeterna, and (7) Libera me, Domine.

3.2. *Nonliturgical Settings*

Not all musical works that are called requiems follow the Latin text. J. Brahms's *Ein deutsches Requiem* (1868) has seven sections using texts from the German Bible; in Protestant fashion, it is more concerned for the comfort of the living than the fate of the deceased. F. Delius's *Requiem* (1914-16) is a setting of passages from F. → Nietzsche's writings and has a pagan character. P. Hindemith's *Requiem* (1946) is a setting of a poem by Walt Whitman. B. Britten's *War Requiem* (1961), which intersperses the Latin texts with the war poems of World War I victim Wilfred Owen, is intended to evoke a sense of outrage.

→ Hymn; Hymnody; Mass, Music for the, 8; Oratorio; Rite 2; Theology and Music

Bibliography: A. Cornides and R. Snow, "Requiem Mass," *NCE* (2d ed.) 12.134-36 • J. A. Jungmann, *The Mass of the Roman Rite* (New York, 1951) 219, 295, 488 • T. Karp, F. Fitch, and B. Smallman, "Requiem Mass," *NGDMM* (2d ed.) 21.203-8 • G. Rowell, *The Liturgy of Christian Burial* (London, 1977) • R. Rutherford, *The Death of a Christian: The Rite of Funerals* (New York, 1980) 27-29, 56-59.

Frank C. Senn

Rescue Mission → Inner Mission

Residence, Duty of

The duty of residence is that imposed by → church law upon the holders of ecclesiastical offices, which stipulates that they should reside in the place where they minister (the clergy in manses or vicarages) and leave this place only on some task or on leave or with permission of some kind. The duty of residence came into → canon law in the → Middle Ages because of the scandals associated with pluralism, simony, and nonresidence. It was given greater emphasis at the Council of → Trent.

Today the 1983 → CIC lays down the rules for the various ministers, while Protestant churches may have similar regulations and limitations of exceptions. Other callings do not usually have any such restrictions, and this special duty for pastors is one that congregations usually greatly appreciate. In Roman Catholic → pastoral theology a reason is found in the need for the priest always to be ready to offer sacramental ministry (→ Sacrament) to the sick. The desire that Protestant ministers be always easy to reach has to do with both congregational and pastoral tasks.

It is often argued today that the expectations of the → congregation can be met by well-organized pastoral practice, so that pastoral claims need not impinge upon the private life of ministers' families. The duty of residence is properly understood, but also limited, in terms of the basic explanation that the pastor's ministry should have visibility in and for the people. Thus the duty of residence does not have to be in conflict with the proper use of modern office technology or with → dispensations in special cases. In England, for example, the grouping of parishes under a single pastor, or a pastoral team, has made it impossible for a pastor to be resident in every parish, but modern means of transport can still provide ready availability.

→ Ministry, Ministerial Offices

Bibliography: K. Hungar, "Pfarrer–ein freier Beruf?" *LM* 23 (1984) 10-12 • "Residence," *ODCC* 1387.

Albert Stein†

Resistance, Right of

1. Legal Considerations
   1.1. States That Employ Unlawful Means
   1.2. States Based on the Rule of Law
2. Theological-Ethical Considerations
   2.1. Theological Premises
   2.2. Exemplary Conflicts
   2.3. Civil Disobedience

1. Legal Considerations

1.1. *States That Employ Unlawful Means*

The classic understanding of the right of resistance was developed in connection with the problem of tyrannicide in antiquity by Aristotle (384-322 B.C.; → Aristotelianism) and Cicero (106-43), in connection with medieval Christian → natural law by → Thomas Aquinas (ca. 1225-74; → Thomism), and during the → Reformation by M. → Luther (1483-1546; → Luther's Theology) and P. → Melanchthon (1497-1560; → Reformers 2.1.1). The key issue is that such resistance may direct itself against a state that employs unlawful means (e.g., tyranny, dictatorship). Accordingly, the right to resistance is generally understood as the right of citizens to defend themselves against state power being imposed by illegal means, the goal of such resistance being to reestablish whichever laws have been violated; by contrast, → revolutions aim to topple the old order and establish a new one. In the broader sense, one speaks of the right of resistance on behalf of a constitution when such resistance directs itself against individuals or groups that are threatening the constitution.

Depending on the situation, such resistance can be passive (involving the refusal to obey) or active, nonviolent or violent. Amid the circumstances in Germany on July 20, 1944, for example, the assassination of A. Hitler might have helped reestablish the lawful order (→ Modern Church History 1.4.3). The resistance movement around M. Luther → King Jr. (1929-68; → Modern Church History 2.7; Black Churches 1.6) was nonviolent but certainly active.

According to natural law, every morally justifiable resistance is also legally legitimate. This equating of law and morality, however, fails to recognize the independence of jurisprudence and its function with regard to peace (the securing of justice).

The rejection of the perspective of natural law does not necessarily lead to the adoption of the positivist perspective (→ Law and Legal Theory 1), according to which law and morality are completely different and resistance can be justified morally but not legally. This understanding is similarly unsatisfactory insofar as it views every act of state violence, even the most criminal, as lawful and thus as beyond the reach of resistance.

The increasingly popular "third solution" adopts G. Radbruch's (1878-1949) understanding of the invalidity of "lawful injustice." On this view, one must basically adhere to positive, or statutory, law for the sake of securing the law and justice itself, even if in individual cases it leads to unjust consequences. Resistance is in this case inadmissible. If, however, positive law is intolerably incompatible with → righteousness and justice, then it acquires the status of nonlaw (the so-called argument of injustice); against this sort of injustice, resistance is fundamentally justified, even in the legal sense.

If resistance against injustice on the part of the state is to be legally justified, however, numerous other presuppositions must also be fulfilled, including especially the following. Such resistance must involve an act of social self-defense against an authority whose unlawful behavior is, so to speak, written all over its face, particularly in the case of violations of property and human → rights. Here resistance is considered only subsidiarily, that is, as a last resort. The means employed must also be commensurate with the envisioned goal. Although there should be some prospect for success, failed resistance can also certainly possess its own moral value (e.g., the July 1944 assassination attempt against Hitler; the Kreisau Circle, a clandestine intellectual and political salon in Nazi Germany hosted and led by conspirator Count Helmuth von Moltke; White Rose, a student resistance group in Nazi Germany led by Hans and Sophie Scholl). Those actually engaged in the resistance must also be capable of understanding and assessing the attendant circumstances. And finally, resistance may be engaged only on behalf of justice itself.

Because of the experiences with the National Socialist dictatorship (→ Fascism 3), attempts have been made in the Federal Republic of Germany, especially in connection with emergency laws, to "positivize" the right of resistance in the federal constitution (art. 20.4) and in several state constitutions (those of Berlin, Bremen, Hesse, Saxony, and Saxony-Anhalt) according to the model of the French declaration of human and citizen rights in 1789. Such attempts at establishing a positive framework for the implementation of rights that can in fact obtain only in an overriding (suprapositive) fashion, however, are bound to fail; in such cases, a system of laws is in fact trying to institutionalize a system-external capacity for control in what is really a system-internal fashion. Such regulations possess a mostly symbolic character insofar as their intention is to underscore the intention of the → state to follow the principle of law and justice.

1.2. *States Based on the Rule of Law*

After World War II it was especially in the United States that a doctrine of civil disobedience was developed in a state based on the rule of law, the model for this doctrine being M. Gandhi (1869-1948), who in turn was influenced by H. D. Thoreau (1817-62). From these beginnings, this doctrine then made its way — largely in the form articulated by J. Rawls (1921-2002) — to other Western countries.

Civil disobedience involves the special case of resistance against violations of justice by an authorized state power in what is otherwise a just society (a parliamentary → democracy). Here one must apply the Radbruch formula discussed above in maintaining that if such civil disobedience — which must be nonviolent — directs itself against valid but deficient acts of the state, then it is illegal, and those engaging such resistance must accept the prescribed sanctions. If resistance involves a refusal to obey unjust laws (→ Obedience), however, then it is legal and may not prompt sanctions. It is according to such distinctions that, to take but one example, one is to judge blockade sit-ins before munitions depots or nuclear plants.

Bibliography: S. H. BENNETT, *Radical Pacifism: The War Resisters League and Gandhian Nonviolence in America, 1915-1963* (Syracuse, N.Y., 2003) • D. BÖTTCHER, *Ungehorsam oder Widerstand? Zum Fortleben des mittelalterlichen Widerstandsrechts in der Reformationszeit* (Munich, 1991) • M. K. GANDHI, *Non-violent Resistance* (Ahmadabad, 1951; repr., New York, 1961) • A. KAUFMANN, *Vom Ungehorsam gegen die Obrigkeit. Aspekte des Widerstandsrechts von der antiken Tyrannis bis zum Unrechtsstaat unserer Zeit, vom leidenden Gehorsam bis zum zivilen Ungehorsam im modernen Rechtsstaat* (Heidelberg, 1991) • M. L. KING JR., *The Trumpet of Conscience* (New York, 1968) • S. LYND and A. LYND, eds., *Non-violence in America: A Documentary History* (Maryknoll, N.Y., 1995) • A. OPEL and D. POMPPER, eds., *Representing Resistance: Media, Civil Disobedience, and the Global Justice Movement* (Westport, Conn., 2003) • G. RADBRUCH, "The Concept of Law," *German Essays on Science in the Twentieth Century* (ed. W. Schirmacher; New York, 1996) 271-77; idem, *The Legal Philosophies of Lask, Radbruch, and Dabin* (trans. K. Wilk; Cambridge, Mass., 1950) • J. RAWLS, *A Theory of Justice* (Cambridge, Mass., 1971) • K. REMELE, *Ziviler Ungehorsam. Eine Untersuchung aus der Sicht christlicher Sozialethik* (Munich, 1992) • E. SCHNIEDER, *Ziviler Ungehorsam in der anglo-amerikanischen Rechtswissenschaft* (Frankfurt, 1993) • M. B. STEGER, *Gandhi's Dilemma: Nonviolent Principles and Nationalist Power* (New York, 2000) • H. D. THOREAU, *Walden; or, Life in the Woods; and, "On the Duty of Civil Disobedience"* (New York, 1999).

ARTHUR KAUFMANN

2. Theological-Ethical Considerations

2.1. *Theological Premises*

Loyalty conflicts and questions of the right or obligation of resistance are certainly no strangers to religion, although the models employed in justifying different positions vary widely. Here one cannot draw on any general understanding of the right of resistance in Jewish or Christian traditions.

2.1.1. Resistance in the name of → Yahweh, who takes the part of victims of unlawfulness, abuse of power, and → force or violence, plays a central role in the Bible and has been called one of the most important sources of justice (F. Crüsemann). Early Christianity, rather than developing a doctrine of the right of resistance, emphasized instead → obedience for the sake of → conscience. Resisting authority meant resisting one of God's ordinances (Rom. 13:1-7). The → Sermon on the Mount (Matt. 5:39) and → Paul (Rom. 12:21) both inculcate the fundamental duty to counter evil with active nonviolence rather than to resist it directly. One may refuse to follow human laws if the latter coerce a person to disobey God (Acts 5:29) and violate the voice of conscience (thus rejection of the imperial cult of the → Roman Empire; → Early Church 2.1; Martyrs). By contrast, the NT says nothing about a minority engaging in active resistance in a Gentile environment.

2.1.2. A completely different situation arises when political rulers who themselves belong to the church violate the law, resort to tyranny, or intentionally and grievously violate the principles of justice. According to the classic doctrine of resistance developed in the High Middle Ages (→ Empire and Papacy 4; Asylum 3; Slavery 1.3), resistance is permitted when unlawful intrusions into the freedom of the church *(libertas ecclesiae)* occur or when worldly rule is perverted into tyranny (→ Force, Violence, Nonviolence, 1.1.1). Around 1160 John of Salisbury (ca. 1115-80) insisted that killing a tyrant not only was permitted but was right and appropriate (*Policraticus* 3.15).

Resistance against attacks on the freedom of the church can easily be justified on the basis of biblical traditions such as Acts 5:29. By contrast, resistance for the sake of reestablishing a legal order violated by a ruler is frequently justified both philosophically and from the perspective of jurisprudence (→ Law and Legal Theory). → Thomas Aquinas (ca. 1225-74) considers resistance justified when tyrants seek their own benefit rather than the common welfare (*Summa theol.* II of II, q. 42 art. 2; see also Aristotle *Pol.* 3). The criteria here, which resemble those for conducting a just → war (§4.1), have lost none of their capacity for providing a point of orientation up to the present, even if their actual application — for example, in connection with the positively disposed Indian policies of Spanish colonial ethics (J. Höffner; → Inquisition) — repeatedly fail in the face of actual power relationships (→ Sublimis Deus). As part of feudal law (→ Feudalism), the right of resistance was restricted to the estates.

M. → Luther (1483-1546) did not initially consider resistance to the emperor to be justified and was thus hesitant to support political alliances in defense of the → Reformation. Not until 1530 did he acknowledge the duty to resist as a commandment of worldly law, which in its own turn was part of the "care of religion" *(cura religionis)* of the princes (see E. Wolgast; H. Scheible). The Peace of Augsburg (1555; → Augsburg, Peace of) defused the potential conflict inhering within this understanding, although Luther still entertained the possibility of an apocalyptic tyrant — a "slayer of souls" — whom one would have to resist. Luther's experiences in the German → Peasants' War prompted him to accept the right of resistance, but only for the estates; individuals should submit to the law applicable to all persons rather than decide their own cause (→ Luther's Theology 4.2).

J. → Calvin (1509-64) was at least equally vehement in emphasizing obedience to existing authorities (*Inst.* 4.20). In extreme situations one might hope that a hero such as Samson in the OT would appear as the executor of the divine will in addressing intolerable circumstances. By contrast, all possibility of a class right of resistance recedes entirely, and for subjects without office it was in any case not even a consideration (→ Calvin's Theology 3.7). Thinking particularly of France, Calvin hoped to persuade the authorities to sanction his pure doctrine, whereas he warned Protestants themselves against engaging in arbitrary acts of violence even in crises and advised them instead to obey and have patience. U. → Zwingli (1484-1531) affirmed violent resistance in exceptional situations (→ Zwingli's Theology 2.8).

It was only the subsequent confessional disputes in France (→ Huguenots), Scotland, and England (→ Dissenters; United Kingdom 1.3-4) that prompted a new understanding of the limits of the power of the state under the presupposition of antagonistic religious parties (→ Persecution of Christians 3.3; Catholic Reform and Counterreformation 2.2). After the massacre of Huguenots in Paris on St. Bartholomew's Day (1572), the Protestant monarchomachians (T. → Beza, F. Hotman, P. du Plessis-Mornay, H. Languet, J. → Knox, J. Milton, and others) articulated a legal legitimation of resistance encompassing a wider group of subjects in which the estate of the *magistratus inferiores* also had an important role to play and in which a just minority might under certain circumstances be authorized to engage in resistance. Even Roman Catholic monarchomachians such as J. de Mariana (1536-1624) adopted this position. The more radical understanding of such ideas presupposes a divinely ordained right to → revolution (§2).

Following the establishment of absolutist states and principalities in Europe (→ Modern Period 2), the right of resistance was discussed especially in nontheological contexts, for example, in connection with → natural law (§2.3) during the early modern period and in connection with → state ethics (L. Feuerbach, J. G. Fichte, I. Kant, B. de Spinoza, among others). The impetus to secularize political discussion, though, was certainly also evident in the Calvinism of the 16th and early 17th centuries (L. Danaeus, J. Althusius, B. Keckermann; see F. Goedeking).

2.2. ***Exemplary Conflicts***

2.2.1. Insofar as Christians understand all law and justice as being ultimately grounded in God's own order (Rom. 13:1), every serious violation of justice and → righteousness (§2.3) challenges their understanding of the obedience of faith. Demands for obedience to various political ideologies during the 20th century — often imposed by totalitarian rulers — repeatedly prompted the renewed theological justification of the right of resistance, for example, in the struggle against the National Socialist state and its abuse of power (→ Fascism 3-5; Church Struggle).

In Norway, Bishop E. Berggrav (1884-1959) strengthened the resistance of his fellow Norwegians against the German occupiers with a secretly but widely distributed speech "When the Driver Is out of His Mind: Luther on the Duty of Disobedience" (1941; *LW* 44.94-95). In his Gifford Lectures of 1937/38 K. → Barth (1886-1968) recalled the First Scottish Confession (1560; → Confessions and Creeds 3), written by J. Knox (ca. 1513-72), making the point that one cannot from the outset simply ignore the possible consequences of violent resistance.

Although the → Confessing Church in Germany had considerable difficulties with precisely such questions, in his speech "Die Kirche vor der Judenfrage" (The church and the Jewish question, April 1933), D. → Bonhoeffer (1906-45) maintained that a state that deprives a group of its citizens of their rights and interferes with the free → proclamation of the church has engaged in an act of self-negation, forcing the church itself into a → *status confessionis* and prompting it to "leap into the spokes of the wheel itself." Very few others, however, followed Bonhoeffer's path into conspiracy and active resistance.

2.2.2. This situation has often been compared with the broad deprivation of the rights of the nonwhite majority through apartheid legislation in South Africa, and models such as Bonhoeffer exercised considerable influence on the spiritual and intellectual orientation of resistance against apartheid. Strikingly, in hindsight one can see that quite different confessional traditions joined forces in lending legitimacy to resistance in South Africa, the unified perception of grievous violation of elementary human and civil → rights ultimately leading to the view that such a system was irreconcilable with God's will (→ Social Ethics 4). That is, the modern understanding of human rights — with its universal practical insistence on the right to protect people against the arbitrary use of power and against deprivation and violence — includes a theological element that also obligates the Christian community within the parameters of its own ethos.

2.2.3. One disputed issue has been the question whether (and, if so, the extent to which) the elementary duty to engage in resistance, a duty deriving from inalienable human rights, could and should have been maintained in the face of the circumstances surrounding the modern Communist dictatorships. Although the exercise of power in → socialism could not be qualified appropriately simply by reference to the older concept of tyranny, there is little doubt that it scorned the standards required of any state that rules by just laws. At the same time, however, because the exercise of political power in industrial societies can no longer simply be ascribed to certain persons as the responsible parties, perhaps the old right of resistance has now reached the limits of its capacity to establish standards for its own orientation.

2.3. *Civil Disobedience*

In a state based on the rule of law, resistance against state ordinances and laws should be sustained by a fundamental moral willingness to obey the law and to acknowledge legal state institutions and procedures. Demonstrations and boycotts against the construction of nuclear plants and against the stationing of additional nuclear weapons (→ Weapons; Disarmament and Armament), like the granting of church asylum (→ Asylum 4; Refugees 5), represent symbolic actions that, in the name of the capacity to improve laws, are intended to draw public attention to dangerous developments without calling the rule of law as such into question. Those who violate valid laws for the sake of bringing justified criticism to public attention must as a rule also be prepared to submit to lawful → punishment (§1), which is why one should refer in such cases to civil disobedience in the form of active nonviolence. Civil courage is the lesser manifestation of the greater right of resistance.

→ Liberation Theology; Two Kingdoms Doctrine

Bibliography: K. Barth, *The Knowledge of God and the Service of God according to the Teaching of the Reformation, Recalling the Scottish Confession of 1560* (London, 1955) the 1937/38 Gifford Lectures • E. Berggrav, "When the Driver Is out of His Mind: Luther on the Duty of Disobedience," *Man and State* (Philadelphia, 1951) 300-319 • D. Bonhoeffer, "The Church and the Jewish Question," *DBWE* 12, *Berlin 1933* (Minneapolis, forthcoming) • J. Childress, *Moral Responsibility in Conflicts: Essays on Nonviolence, War, and Conscience* (Baton Rouge, La., 1982) • F. Crüsemann, *Der Widerstand gegen das Königtum* (Neukirchen, 1978) • J. Dugard, *Human Rights and the South African Legal Order* (Princeton, 1978) • F. Goedeking, "Die 'Politik' des Lambertus Danaeus, Johannes Althusius und Bartholomäus Keckermann" (Diss., Heidelberg, 1977) • J. HÖFFNER, *Kolonialismus und Evangelium. Spanische Kolonialethik im Goldenen Zeitalter* (2d ed.; Trier, 1969) • C. LIENEMANN-PERRIN, *Die politische Verantwortung der Kirchen in Südkorea und Südafrika* (Munich, 1992) • C. LIENEMANN-PERRIN and W. LIENEMANN, eds., *Political Legitimacy in South Africa* (Heidelberg, 1988) • H. SCHEIBLE, ed., *Das Widerstandsrecht als Problem der deutschen Protestanten, 1523-1546* (Gütersloh, 1969) • E. WOLGAST, *Die Religionsfrage als Problem des Widerstandsrecht im 16. Jahrhundert* (Heidelberg, 1980).

WOLFGANG LIENEMANN

Resocialization → Rehabilitation

Responsibility

1. Term
2. Scripture and Theology
3. Ethics of Motive and Ethics of Responsibility
4. Philosophy and Sociology
5. A Responsible Society
6. Open Questions

1. Term

Responsibility has to do with relations. It speaks of the account we must give for our actions; we are answerable for them. Originally, in law, it meant responsibility to a judge. Have we fulfilled our duties? Have we observed generally acknowledged precepts? In theology we are responsible both to God as the Judge of the world and also to others and to our own → conscience. → Education will prepare people to accept responsibility by showing them the relevant → norms, equipping them with powers of decision, and giving them some understanding of the resultant consequences. In certain cases, though, it must be asked whether some people can be responsible for their actions.

The concept of responsibility offers the possibility of an open relationship to normative traditions according to different views of the world and ways of grasping a situation. It has thus become a key term in contemporary → ethics.

2. Scripture and Theology

2.1. The word "responsibility" is rarely used in Scripture, but implicitly it underlies all the ethical principles of both the OT and the NT. We find the concept already in the → Decalogue and the legal precepts of the → Book of the Covenant (Exodus 20–23), which enjoin care for the weak (aliens, slaves, widows, orphans, the poor). This ethical norm reflects → Israel's own experience. God had cared for it, liberated it, and watched over it in its history. The → prophets developed the theme, reminding the people that they were under obligation to help those in need. Ethical conduct of this kind would show what the relation to God and faith meant when put into practice.

In the NT → Jesus exemplified responsibility in both his teaching (e.g., the parable of the Good Samaritan, Luke 10) and his work. The early Christians took him as a model. In the → pareneses of the Epistles (e.g., 1 Corinthians 8), → Paul asked the strong members of the community to take responsibility for caring for the weak. James defined pure religion as caring for orphans and widows in their distress (Jas. 1:27); a true faith will show itself in a concern for brothers and sisters who are without clothes or daily food (2:15-17).

2.2. The motif of responsibility recurs constantly in theological history. For example, it is related to arguments for the orders of creation (→ Two Kingdoms Doctrine). Medieval theology adopted the theme from → Augustine (354-430; → Augustine's Theology). We find it in → Thomas Aquinas (ca. 1225-74; → Thomism). The → Reformers regarded it as the duty of the civil powers to maintain law and order so that the → proclamation of the gospel might not be hampered. Similarly, it was the duty of subjects to assist their rulers by preserving order.

Certain radicals had seen it as their responsibility to set up a community in which goods would be shared (cf. Acts 2:44-45; 4:34-35; 6:1). The Reformers rejected this experiment. Nevertheless, they still maintained that "every man ought, of such things as he possesses, liberally to give alms to the poor, according to his ability" (Thirty-nine Articles 38). Christians of every denomination have willingly and generously tried to live up to this responsibility.

3. Ethics of Motive and Ethics of Responsibility

Modern ethical discussion began when M. → Weber (1864-1920) in his "Politik als Beruf" (1919) tried to distinguish between the ethics of → motive *(Gesinnungsethik)* and the ethics of responsibility *(Verantwortungsethik)*. He discerned here two incompatible ethical orientations. The ethics of (neo-)Kantianism emphasizes duty and hierarchically ordered → values (→ Kantianism). Christian ethics, based on the → Sermon on the Mount, stresses motivation. Motivation, purpose, the agreement of moral duty and innermost conviction — these are what counts when we ask whether an action is ethically justified or not. We may disregard the consequences. Responsibility ethics, however, follows a different model. It takes into account the foreseeable ramifications of actions or decisions and judges them accordingly. Even morally dubious or dangerous means may be adopted if the end in view is good.

Weber's view of responsibility ethics is in danger of evading issues of motive, of being out of touch with reality, of losing itself in a utopian world (→ Utopia), and even of justifying → totalitarianism. Judgment and responsibility are certainly needed in practicable political ethics, but Weber reduces ethics to a rational consideration of consequences, which becomes his only basis of evaluation. He does bring many value orientations to bear upon each situation now that religious systems are no longer important, but he evades the real meaning of value when he replaces the necessity of objective discourse by subjective decisionism. By focusing his moral argument solely on the consequences, he avoids subjecting individual actions to normative ethical arguments, thus making them autonomous.

4. Philosophy and Sociology

After World War I → dialectical theology (F. Gogarten), I-Thou philosophy (M. Buber; → Jewish Philosophy 6), and → existentialism (M. Heidegger) made accountability a central point in → anthropology. Responsibility thus became a fundamental ethical category. W. Schulz regarded → freedom and responsibility (to neighbors and to history) as determinative ethical values on both nearer and more distant levels.

The experience of enormous technological → progress and its threat to the → future led H. Jonas (1903-93) to ask whether we can accept responsibility for every imaginable development. If human power becomes a threat to life on the earth, ethics must surely consider what the future consequences will be of the things we do today. Jonas attacks a utopian optimism of progress (→ Utopia 5.2) with its expectation that "true humanity" will finally emerge. Instead, he advocates a nonutopian ethics of responsibility that will guarantee the future continuation of humanity, even in its brokenness.

In connection with the investigation of risk, → sociology has more recently considered the inflationary use of the term "responsibility" and raised the question of the conditions under which responsibility can be ascribed to individuals or → organizations for events and their implications in an unforeseeable world. It distinguishes the ethical problem, that of the moral self-responsibility of individuals, from the legal problem, that of liability, and also from the organizational problem, that of the responsibility of officials. It attempts to articulate standardized models that accommodate these different categories.

5. A Responsible Society

At assemblies at Amsterdam in 1948 and Evanston in 1954, the → World Council of Churches (→ Ecumenism, Ecumenical Movement) formulated the goal of a responsible society that would seek a just social order in which responsible individuals would seek the good of → society, and society that of individuals, and in this way give evidence of their responsibility both to others and to God. The concept (due primarily to J. H. Oldham) involved universally accepted principles of human → rights, participatory structures, and democratic organization.

This view was challenged by the → theology of revolution (World Conference on Church and Society, Geneva, 1966) but found development in the discussion of a just, participatory, and sustainable society (World Conference on Faith, Science, and the Future, Boston, 1979). What resulted was a conciliar process of justice, peace, and the integrity of creation (→ Ecology; Peace Research 4; Salvation 7.2; War 5.2). Raising tabooed political and economic issues, sharing models of action, and offering perspectives of → meaning and → hope, the ecumenical world has tried to take seriously its responsibility for society economically, politically, and ecologically.

6. Open Questions

Theological ethics has shown that there is responsibility both *for* causes and persons and also *before* courts. Relationship with God is found to be the basis of freedom and involvement in relations with others (→ Social Ethics). The modern → pluralism of ethical orientation means a dialogic and reflexive understanding of responsibility as consideration is given to the freedom of others. An ambivalence of the ethics of responsibility is hard to avoid. The strong must see to the needs of the weak, humans caring for animals, parents for children, the healthy for the sick. The goal is not the overthrow of hierarchical structures but the responsible use of → power, as, for example, in the dealings of → industrial societies with the → Third World. → Liberation theology has taken up some of the insights of an ethics of responsibility. We now must consider the way in which our present actions will affect both those to whom they relate and also the future of → life on this earth.

Bibliography: K.-O. Apel, *Diskurs und Verantwortung. Das Problem des Übergangs zur postkonventionellen Moral* (3d ed.; Frankfurt, 1997) • H. Arendt, *Responsibility and Judgment* (New York, 2003) • M. Honecker, *Einführung in die theologische Ethik* (Berlin, 1990) • H. Jonas, *The Imperative of Responsibility: In Search of an Ethics for the Technological Age* (Chicago, 1984) • F.-X. Kaufmann, *Der Ruf nach Verantwortung. Risiko und Ethik in einer unüberschaubaren Welt* (Freiburg, 1992) • N. Luhmann, *Risk: A Sociological Theory* (New York, 1993) • H. Morris, ed., *Freedom and Responsibility: Readings in Philosophy and Law* (Stanford, Calif., 1961) • R. Niebuhr, *An Interpretation of Christian Ethics* (New York, 1955) • J. H. Oldham, "A Responsible Society," *Man's Disorder and God's Design,* vol. 3, *The Church and the Disorder of Society* (New York, 1948) 120-54 • G. Picht, *Wahrheit, Vernunft, Verantwortung* (Stuttgart, 1969) • W. Schulz, *Philosophie in der veränderten Welt* (6th ed.; Stuttgart, 1993) • W. Schweiker, *Responsibility and Christian Ethics* (Cambridge, 1995) • M. Weber, "The Profession and Vocation of Politics," *Weber: Political Writings* (ed. P. Lassman and R. Speirs; Cambridge, 1994) 309-69 • E. Würthwein and O. Merk, eds., *Verantwortung* (Stuttgart, 1982).

Werner Schwartz

Restoration

1. Term and Concept

The term "restoration" comes from Lat. *restauro,* "restore, rebuild, renew." In the early → modern period in Europe, "restoration" was normally used, as in classical Latin, for external reparation in the sense of keeping in repair or improving, especially buildings. But occasionally even in the 17th century, and then increasingly in the 19th, it took on the sense of cultural, intellectual, or religious renewal or restoration. England in the 17th century also gave the term political significance.

Around 1800 "restoration" underwent significant expansion of usage, for as a term for the whole epoch from 1815 to 1830 or 1848, it became both a universal historical category and a political slogan. What it now denoted was the reestablishing of an earlier political and social state that had been either naturally or divinely ordained. Theologically, the age of → Catholic reform and Counterreformation could also be understood as an epoch of restoration.

2. The English Restoration

The Restoration of 1660 was an important event in the life of both the English nation and the church, with ramifications for Scotland as well. The Royalist defeat in the Civil War and the execution of Charles I in 1649 had brought the monarchy to an end and overthrown the established → Anglican Church. The → Puritans, especially in the form of Independency, ruled supreme under Lord Protector Oliver Cromwell (1599-1658). The unsuccessful attempt of the Scots to put Charles II back on the throne in 1651 resulted in the loss of national independence for Scotland, though its form of church government remained presbyterian. The death of Cromwell in 1658, however, created a vacuum that, it was realized, only a restoration of the monarchy could fill.

With the Restoration, Charles II (1660-85) reassumed the throne, and the Church of England was restored to its position as the national church. Charles had promised liberty for "tender consciences," but when efforts at reconciliation between Anglicans and Puritans at the Savoy Conference (1661) failed, the Act of Uniformity (1662) enforced the Book of Common Prayer, and the so-called Clarendon Code (four statutes passed 1661-65) suppressed or restricted dissent. The Scots regained national independence and set up a combined episcopal and presbyterian system of church government, but this move ran into heavy opposition from the Covenanters and collapsed when the Scottish bishops refused allegiance to William and Mary in 1689.

3. Reaction to Revolution

At the turn of the 19th century, reaction to the excesses of the French Revolution (1789) led to a sharp revulsion against the principle of → revolution in European thought on the grounds that it brought people into radical conflict with the given order. Where → progress was not seen as the law of history but a cyclic view prevailed (to the effect that when order is disrupted, it must be restored), the Christian tradition was set over against the ideas of 1789, which represented the culmination of the → Enlightenment view of the individual and society. Restoration in this sense thus derived from reaction to revolution. To the direct or indirect heirs of revolution, restoration thus seemed to be mere reaction in the sense of regression, two concepts that liberals saw as identical (→ Liberalism 1-2).

At first, however, the idea of restoration was by no means unequivocal. The Swiss K. L. von Haller (1768-1854), whose six-volume work *Restauration der Staatswissenschaft* (Restoration of political philosophy) systematized the concept, looked for a conservative → utopia, which would mean a return to the feudal patrimonial state beyond absolutism (→ Conservatism 1.2.2-3). For F. Gentz (1764-1832), who set the pace in literature, restoration had the pragmatic aim of warding off a fresh revolution. J. von Görres (1776-1848) regarded restoration as the common cause of legitimists and liberals. In France, too, where revolution had struck hardest and there was thus the most thinking about restoration, expression was given in various ways to the idea of some sort of Christian state. L. de Bonald (1754-1840) and J. de Maistre (1753-1821) even argued for the supremacy of the → pope over the king, but F. de Chateaubriand (1768-1848) sought a synthesis of royalism and parliamentarianism.

The collapse of belief in reason and of the theories of → natural law and social contract, which had resulted in the dominance of J.-J. Rousseau's (1712-78) ideas and profoundly shaken Europe (→ Modern Church History 1.2.2), opened the door to a new order of legitimacy (→ Legitimation), → authority, and stability. This development was simply the temporary convergence of a comprehensive movement of forces that had not come fully into their own in the 18th century (E. Troeltsch). It also found expression in late → Romanticism, which, especially in the case of F. Schlegel (1772-1829), supported restoration.

4. Political

Politically, the principles of restoration offered guidelines when the hegemony of revolutionary France perished with Napoléon (1804-15) and a new order had to be set up on the Continent. To establish a lasting rule of law and → peace after the manner of the prerevolutionary public law in Europe (*ius publicum Europaeum;* → International Law), the victorious powers agreed on wide-scale restitution. They restored dethroned dynasties, national and constitutional structures, and the central European federation. They used preventive and repressive measures to obviate upheaval. As the Holy Alliance (1815), they resorted both to domestic controls and to international supervision, including direct intervention.

The peace system set up by the Congress of Vienna (1814/15) was at the heart of European restoration. A simple return to the ancien régime was not possible, for it was seen that the new relations resulting from new laws or from the treaties that Napoléon had concluded could not be set aside. Legitimacy and legality overlapped in such a way that compromises varying from state to state could alone promise pacification and stability. Prince Metternich (1773-1859) at first even wanted to retain a Napoleonic dynasty. Since the new order ran up against vital forces that were revolutionary, reforming, Bonapartist, and nationalistic, it contained latent conflicts from the very outset. Conservative solidarity was also subject to the interests of the various powers, so that liberal and national movements gained added strength.

4.1. *France*

France and Germany, which had known the most turmoil, were the main theaters of restoration. In France the return of the Bourbons and the divine right of kings went hand in hand with constitutionalism and ongoing Napoleonic reforms. This remarkably open form of restoration, which sought to reconcile the old regime, revolution, and empire, was distorted by the governments of Louis XVIII (1814-15, 1815-24) and Charles X (1824-30). It lost authority to such a degree both among ultraconservatives in the nobility and the church and among liberals in the middle class that the 1830 revolution effectively ended restoration. Nevertheless, the bourgeois monarchy of Louis-Philippe (1830-48) preserved some prerevolutionary elements amid → liberalism, republicanism, and Bonapartism.

4.2. *Germany*

In the German federation restoration meant the Metternich system. P. Gentz and A. Müller were its propagandists. Though sanctioning many reforms, it was conservative. It set the states that had survived the storm in a new organization that was part of the so-called concert of Europe, which saw itself as a bulwark against revolution. Southern Germany alone found a place for constitutional government, though it was restricted after 1830.

The state absolutism of Prussia and Austria was dominant, despite rising unrest. Domestic policies of restoration brought unity, for after becoming conservative in 1819, Prussia followed the lead of Metternich, and after 1840 Frederick William IV

Restoration

(1840-61) deliberately espoused Romantic legitimism and the idea of a Christian state (proposed by the brothers von Gerlach and by F. J. Stahl). In the 1830s, however, the initiative passed to the opposition and a latent crisis developed, so that the principles of restoration, though dominant up to 1848, were on the defensive (→ Modern Church History 1.3).

4.3. *Britain*

Britain, too, saw a swing to conservative policies in the period immediately after 1815. In foreign policy under Foreign Secretary George Canning (1770-1827), it helped to stop any possible intervention on behalf of Spanish rule in South America, calling on the New World to "redress the balance of the Old," as Canning aptly put it. In this regard restoration had already lost its hold in the 1820s.

4.4. *Russia*

The situation differed greatly in → Russia (§1), perhaps the country where restoration was taken most seriously and entrenched itself most strongly. In Russia restoration meant simply a rapid restoration of the state as it was before the disruption caused by Napoléon's onslaught and defeat. Despite growing disaffection, repressive policies continued in place throughout the century. Only timid and tardy concessions were made, which were not enough to avert the final revolutionary explosion of 1917, with shattering consequences for both church and state (→ Russian Orthodox Church).

5. Social

Socially, restoration was promoted by the powers and favored by the spirit of the times after a long period of upheaval. It came at once under pressure, however, for it was out of touch with social development, especially in politics and the incipient industry. The dynamic of the middle class, which was economically expanding and liberally and nationally inclined, along with unrest among the lower orders (→ Social Movements), undermined its validity. Fearing revolution, governments fought shy of reforms, relied on censorship and the police, and became reactionary. By preserving order both at home and abroad, they did offer lasting peace, civil calm, and outward stability.

The age of restoration, though, had two faces. These might be halcyon days (so L. von Ranke), but serious social opposition was developing. Over against the harmonious Biedermeier culture stood ossification, suppression, and resistance.

6. Ecclesiastical

As regards the churches, the restoration won them over intellectually, for the forces of revolution had attacked them as props of the old order (→ Secularization). Restoration publicly valued → piety and promoted the revitalizing of churches, which had been weakened both inwardly and outwardly during the 18th century, making this task a duty of the state (→ Church and State).

6.1. *Roman Catholic Church*

The → Roman Catholic Church was the most visibly useful tool of restoration. The → Papal States were revived, new bishops were appointed to fill seats long vacant, and concordats were drawn up safeguarding the rights of the church in many countries (esp. through the efforts of Cardinal E. Consalvi; → Concordat 2.1). While moral religion had been politically favored in the age of reform, the rapidly growing number of advocates of theological and pastoral renewal (→ Modern Church History 1.3.1) now had the state and much of the public behind them.

Institutionally, this climate led to the reviving of old → religious orders (§1) and the founding of new ones (→ Jesuits 3; Pope, Papacy, 1.6). A more inward-looking type of → priest now offered → pastoral care, long-suppressed → popular religion found new opportunities, and the churches had more impact on educational and social issues (→ Diakonia 4.3; Inner Mission; Societies and Associations, Ecclesiastical). The effects of → rationalism and → secularism receded rapidly, as unusual support from without furthered the work of the church within.

Yet there was no simple restoration of → baroque Catholicism, for many of the changes brought about by the Enlightenment and the state in about 1800 lived on, including new diocesan boundaries more closely aligned with the states, simpler liturgical forms, and internal debate regarding what attitude to take toward the world (in France, esp. toward revolution). In general the spirit of restoration brought → Catholicism into profound philosophical tension with the age, made it dependent on the state, and opposed it to sharper liberal attacks, especially when → Ultramontanist centralization and mobilization began.

6.2. *German Protestant Churches*

Restoration tied the German Protestant churches and their territorial governments more tightly to the state. The territorial churches developed hand in hand with the new political structures from the beginning of the 19th century and were pressured politically and theologically toward → union. Both institutionally and intellectually, the churches came into conformity with the state. Only in western Germany did synodical forms find some place.

The religious renewal developed largely in regional → revival movements side by side with the church. Partly pietistic, partly mystical, and partly in touch with like-minded Roman Catholic groups, these movements resisted pulpit rationalism in favor of a very personal and vital piety that often gave attention also to social needs.

6.3. *Theology*

At the same time, theology received a powerful impulse for renewal from the romantically based aesthetic and humanistic → idealism of F. D. E. Schleiermacher (1768-1834; → Schleiermacher's Theology). These forces brought changes to the church in the 1830s. Lutheran neoorthodoxy was normative in this regard (esp. that of E. W. Hengstenberg), which, with its confessional and authoritarian emphases, upset not a few congregations (→ Theology in the Nineteenth and Twentieth Centuries 1.1). The conservative → worldview of this movement was so closely akin to political restoration that it found much favor as a factor for order under the slogan "throne and altar."

This emphasis, however, did not take hold everywhere. In many territorial churches rationalism held its own, and there was liberal and national resistance to restoration that later supported the 1848 revolution. Notwithstanding these and new denominational differences, the churches responded to social issues with new efforts, which long helped give religion a more positive image.

6.4. *British Churches*

In Britain, too, restoration forged something of a link between political conservatism and the church, so that church and Tory became the British equivalent of throne and altar. In the post-1815 period Parliament was even ready to make a grant to the established church for the building of new churches to meet growing needs in the cities. To some extent the churches could also be relied upon to help stem the rising demand for political and industrial reform and for measures to combat the poverty caused by postwar dislocation and industrial invention.

In Britain, though, the churches did not wholly support restoration, nor was there the same political commitment to it. The free churches moved over to the side of the reform with the development of the so-called Nonconformist conscience, and even Anglicans, though they might be politically conservative, sponsored much reforming legislation (e.g., the Factory Acts) under Evangelical impulses, playing also a leading role in the furtherance of popular education.

Anglo-Catholicism no doubt favored restoration theologically and liturgically, but it began as a protest against state interference with the church and devoted much of its energy to work among the urban poor. Indeed, the combined efforts of Evangelicals and Anglo-Catholics meant that the Church of England itself had thriving churches in artisan and slum areas, as well as among the nobility and the middle class. By the middle of the 19th century, in spite of the crushing of movements like Chartism, restoration had little significance on the British scene, either politically or religiously.

Bibliography: G. de Bertier de Sauvigny, *The Bourbon Restoration* (Philadelphia, 1967) • R Dufraisse, ed., *Revolution und Gegenrevolution, 1789-1830. Zur geistigen Auseinandersetzung in Frankreich und Deutschland* (Munich, 1991) • T. S. Hamerow, *Restoration, Revolution, Reaction: Economics and Politics in Germany, 1815-1871* (Princeton, 1958) • R. A. Kann, *The Problem of Restoration: The Problem of Comparative Political History* (Berkeley, Calif., 1968) • N. H. Keeble, *The Restoration: England in the 1660s* (Malden, Mass., 2002) • F.-L. Kroll, *Friedrich Wilhelm IV und das Staatsdenken der deutschen Romantik* (Berlin, 1990) • D. Laven and L. Riall, eds., *Napoleon's Legacy: Problems of Government in Restoration Europe* (Oxford, 2000) • H. Maier, *Revolution and Church: The Early History of Christian Democracy, 1789-1901* (Notre Dame, Ind., 1969) • F. Sengle, *Biedermeierzeit. Deutsche Literatur im Spannungsfeld zwischen Restauration und Revolution, 1815-1848* (3 vols.; Stuttgart, 1971-80) • J. Spurr, *The Restoration Church of England, 1646-1689* (New Haven, 1991) • J. H. Stewart, *The Restoration Era in France, 1814-1830* (Princeton, 1968) • E. Troeltsch, "Die Restaurationsepoche am Anfang des 19. Jahrhunderts," *Gesammelte Schriften* (Tübingen, 1925; repr., 1966) 587-614 • C. Wall, ed., *A Concise Companion to the Restoration and Eighteenth Century* (Malden, Mass., 2005).

Werner K. Blessing

Restoration Movements

1. In Great Britain
   1.1. Glas and Sandeman
   1.2. The Haldane Brothers
2. In the United States
   2.1. Disciples of Christ
      2.1.1. Stone
      2.1.2. The Campbells
      2.1.3. Beliefs
      2.1.4. Divisions
   2.2. Landmark Baptists
   2.3. Mormons
   2.4. Assessment

1. In Great Britain

In the days since the Protestant → Reformation began in Europe, many individuals and groups have laid claim to capturing the essence of → primitive Christianity. This emphasis on the primitive church, sometimes called primitivism, sometimes called the desire for restitution, but mostly referred to in literature as the hope for a "restoration" of ancient Christianity, took root in emerging Protestant soil. Michael Servetus (ca. 1511-53), for example, put to death by John Calvin, published a book on the need to restore Christianity because of its 4th-century alignment with Rome. This "restorationist" idea had considerable strength in the 16th-century church and, according to George H. Williams, constituted one of the marks of the Radical Reformation, as compared with the main lines of the Magisterial Reformation. Most of these groups, many Anabaptist in nature and stressing believer's baptism, believed they were building their churches according to the patterns established in the NT (→ Reformers 3.3).

During the 17th century few restoration movements outside of Anabaptism possessed much influence or demonstrated significant staying power. In England, according to an analysis provided by R. T. Hughes and C. L. Allen, restorationism showed up in the 16th century when a combination of Reformed theology and Christian → humanism met the covenant theology of William Tyndale (1494?-1536). These three sources fed a growing concern for restoration within the developing Puritanism. The concern surfaced through Puritan interest in restoring ancient Christian writings to prominence and promoting the moral virtues associated with Christian antiquity. Throughout the late 16th and early 17th centuries, Puritan dissent in England featured a strong desire to reproduce the life of the early church on English soil (→ Dissenters).

1.1. *Glas and Sandeman*

During the 18th century in both Scotland and England, several small movements emerged from traditional church circles with a commitment to restore the purity of early Christianity to churches in their own locations. John Glas (1695-1773), a Presbyterian minister, led one of the more important efforts in Scotland. Glas, like earlier → Anabaptists, opposed any kind of connection between → church and state. He also sought doctrinal freedom from synods, believing that the church should look to the NT, rather than church authorities, for its doctrine and structure. With these commitments, Glas broke with the Church of Scotland in 1728 and began to develop a sustained effort to restore apostolic Christianity. His son-in-law, Robert Sandeman (1718-71), joined him in the effort and quickly surpassed him in both notoriety and significance.

Sandeman's theological work became known in England because of his published attacks on the theology associated with James Hervey (1714-58). Hervey, who received early tutoring by John Wesley (1703-91), remained a → Calvinist, even as he assumed a role in the English Evangelical Revival. In response to Hervey's emphasis on the necessity of God's "special act of enabling grace" for salvation, Sandeman stressed that → salvation occurs when human beings respond to the evidence found in testimonies about Christ's work; salvation results when a rational human being believes in Christ. But Sandeman's → Arminian tendencies possessed a Calvinist twist: he believed that a person's ability to believe or not believe the evidence is predetermined by God's sovereign decisions concerning who is elected to salvation and who is not. Hervey's and Sandeman's theological arguments about salvation continued to be published in England into the early 19th century, well after their deaths.

The Glasite, or Sandemanian, churches, probably never more than 30 congregations across Great Britain and a few others in New England, stressed weekly observance of the Lord's Supper, scriptural names for their churches (mostly "Church of Christ"), a plurality of elders within each congregation, and a refusal to use "Sabbath" in reference to → Sunday. Congregations in the movement divided with one another over baptism after some in Scotland adopted immersion of believers as a practice, and questions arose related to who should administer the Lord's Supper. A few of these congregations still remain in both England and the United States, though congregations in America, where Sandeman settled in 1764 (in Portsmouth, N.H.), had difficulty surviving their loyalist commitments during the Revolutionary War.

1.2. *The Haldane Brothers*

Another early group in Scotland dedicated to the idea of restoration emerged when two wealthy brothers, Robert (1764-1842) and James Alexander (1768-1851) Haldane, broke from the Church of Scotland in 1799. For years, the brothers had worked within the church to promote the evangelical themes commonly associated with Reformed Protestantism. But their desire to create new forms of both individual and congregational association, and their apparent lack of interest in existing forms among Presbyterians, led to tensions within the church. In 1799 they established their first independent congregation in Edinburgh and later also a number of congregations in Great Britain and a few in America (→ Reformed Tradition).

The Haldanes emphasized a common evangelical witness. They disliked denominational divisions, though they did not necessarily make theological calls for the unity of the church. Instead, they sought to build Christian churches and Sunday schools dependent only on the NT witness. They made the Bible central to their work, underscored congregational independence, and eventually practiced weekly Lord's Supper and believer's immersion. All these efforts resulted from their attempt to be faithful to their vision of the restoration of the apostolic church. Like other church movements with restorationist tendencies, congregations associated with the Haldanes divided over different interpretations of early church practices, particularly over the shift to → baptism by immersion and questions associated with whether one elder or a plurality of → elders should govern congregational life.

Both the brothers wrote regularly about theological matters. Robert remained a committed Calvinist loyal to expressions found in the → Westminster Confession ratified at Edinburgh in 1647, emphasizing that the Bible explicitly taught a doctrine of election emphasizing divine sovereignty over salvation. James rejected the authority of the Westminster Confession, preferring to place authority only in the Bible, but he remained committed to the theology associated with the confession. The brothers, especially after 1799, regularly spoke of the dangers associated with establishment. Haldane churches never really constituted a clearly defined sect, since all congregations remained fully autonomous and the movement itself never developed a cohesion strong enough to overcome that autonomy.

2. In the United States

As Hughes and Allen have documented in their work on Protestant primitivism in America, early New England Puritans carried on the primordial concern found among their English counterparts. Used in England as a tool to foment dissent, restorationism in the hands of Puritans in New England became the basis for the established church in the Massachusetts Bay Colony. The 17th century, first in England and later in the colonies, witnessed the dawning of the → Enlightenment, where modern and reasonable religion replaced the Puritan concern for → orthodoxy rooted in Christian antiquity. For many Enlightenment thinkers, however, primordial appeals to antiquity remained, appeals now being made instead to nature, to original creation, or to "nature's God." Such appeals are prominent features in the writings of Thomas Jefferson (1743-1826) and Thomas Paine (1737-1809) as they sought to root human → rights in the created order itself.

By the early 19th century in America, the American revolutionary period had helped to spawn new emphases associated with Christian millennialism, which coexisted with so-called primordial themes. The coming of the millennium, theologians argued, would include a restoration of the primordium, for which the new nation seemed the perfect setting. Shortly after the American Revolution, fervor associated with both millennium and primordium produced a number of new progeny (→ Millenarianism). Restorationism in America found its most productive home among such offspring, especially among the Disciples of Christ.

2.1. *Disciples of Christ*

Disciples trace their roots to the work of four founders: Barton Stone (1772-1844), Thomas (1763-1854) and Alexander (1788-1866) Campbell, and Walter Scott (1796-1861). Of the four, only Barton Stone was born in America (→ Christian Church [Disciples of Christ]).

2.1.1. *Stone*

In 1801, while ministering at a Presbyterian congregation in Kentucky, Barton Stone helped to sponsor the Cane Ridge Revival, which historians estimate attracted between 10,000 and 30,000 people. Such camp meetings provoked controversy among the Presbyterians, and Stone withdrew and formed, with a few others, a small group of congregations that took the name "Christian." These churches began multiplying in North Carolina, Kentucky, Ohio, and southern Virginia.

2.1.2. *The Campbells*

Thomas Campbell and his son Alexander, Scottish-Irish Presbyterians, arrived in America in 1807 and 1809 respectively. Thomas served with the Presbyterians until authorities in 1808 rebuked him for serving the Lord's Supper to Christians not associated with his brand of Presbyterianism. By 1809 he had formed the Christian Association of Washington, Pennsylvania, an independent group of Christians resolved to restore original Christianity in Pennsylvania. Within the year, his family joined him, and Alexander, then 21, quickly assumed a leadership role. The group adopted the name "Disciples." By 1830, with the help of evangelist Walter Scott, who had arrived from Scotland in 1818, the movement grew rapidly in Ohio, Pennsylvania, and western Virginia.

Thomas and Alexander Campbell, who provided the intellectual leadership for the group, were deeply influenced by the Scottish Enlightenment. They preferred reason to enthusiasm, affirmed the developments of science, and tended to emphasize church polity and structure more than inner spiritual life. Yet they expressed confidence that a proper return of the church to its primordial patterns would help create the context for the onset of the millennium, as is evidenced in the title Alexander chose for his long-running journal, *Millennial Harbinger* (1830-70).

2.1.3. *Beliefs*

When these four former Presbyterians assumed leadership roles in this new indigenous American movement, they stressed the authority of Scripture. Each believed that the Bible contained a road map Christians could follow in order to establish both the structure and the practices associated with the ancient church. They understood the Bible, and especially the NT, as a "constitution" for the church. In addition, they preached that all Christians had the right to approach the Bible for themselves. No one needed church authorities, creeds, or church confessions to dictate proper meaning. They believed the Bible's meaning to be clear for all those who read it with a reasonable and open mind.

Shortly after the birth of a daughter in 1812, Alexander Campbell examined the Bible to determine whether she ought to be baptized. His study of the Bible led him to affirm believers' baptism as the only proper Christian baptism. This belief led to a brief affiliation between → Baptists and Disciples (1815-30). Controversy marked the relationship, however, as Campbell and other early Disciples attempted to convince Baptists to give up their denominational name and ways in order to unite around the practices of primitive Christianity. By 1830 Disciples were no longer welcome in Baptist circles.

The Disciples' solitary existence did not last long. During the 1820s Campbell's Disciples ("Campbellites") and Stone's Christians had discovered one another. In 1832 they reached a formal union that led to a movement connecting churches and about 22,000 members across a fairly wide region spanning eight states (Pennsylvania to Missouri, Tennessee to Virginia).

The early Disciples' commitment to reforming American Christianity along the lines of the ancient church depended especially on the passages of the Bible connected to a "thus saith the Lord." These, they believed, were clear scriptural propositions binding on all Christians and churches. In addition, they highlighted "approved precedents" in Scripture, NT descriptions of the practices of early congregations and Christians, which they believed to be equally authoritative. Their dismissal of denominational traditions, together with their emphasis on both the propositional truth and approved precedents found in the Bible, led to the development of several distinctive emphases within Disciples church life. Throughout the 19th century these Christians emphasized → baptism by immersion of all believers, preached that Christians could approach the Bible for themselves (→ Bible Study), highlighted the importance of lay leadership in the church (→ Lay Movements), celebrated the Lord's Supper together every Sunday, believed that history would culminate both in a restored church and the eschatological triumph of God's redemption, and stressed the unity of all Christians who would proclaim Christ without dependence on denominations, creeds, or confessions.

2.1.4. *Divisions*

After the Civil War some Disciples modified their approach to the Bible. Beginning in the 1880s, some Disciples scholars became familiar with the historicocritical method as it was developing in Germany. As Disciples embraced this approach to the Bible, some began to question the historical reliability of the Gospels and stressed instead the effect of the culture of biblical times on the content of the Bible itself. For such Disciples the propositions and practices of the Bible no longer possessed the authority so easily affirmed by earlier generations. These Disciples emphasized the historical development of the church and were no longer able to affirm a golden age of the church that needed to be restored.

These kinds of shifts in Disciples' commitments led to two divisions within the movement. In some ways, these divisions tragically illustrate an irony associated with the life of Disciples, who are best known for their historic commitment to the unity of the church. They have been active in the mainline ecumenical movement both in America (in the → National Council of the Churches of Christ in the U.S.A.) and worldwide (in the → World Council of Churches). In 1906 the → Churches of Christ (at the time comprising 160,000 members, who remained committed to the original vision to restore primitive Christianity) claimed a separate identity. After this first split, disagreements about baptism, biblical interpretation, and the structure of missionary societies continued to plague Disciples during the first half of the 20th century.

Then in the late 1960s, as Disciples restructured their church life yet again, they lost close to one-third of their more conservative congregations. These Christians left the Disciples (currently around 700,000 members) and formed the Christian

Churches and Churches of Christ (currently with 1.3 million members). In 2005 only the Churches of Christ, the largest (numbering 2 million members) of the three groups claiming historical association with the earliest Disciples of Christ, continued to speak of restoring primitive Christianity.

2.2. ***Landmark Baptists***

The commitment to restorationist aims also found other homes in American religion during the 19th century. A small but influential movement among Baptists during the 1840s stressed a very rigid form of restorationism. James R. Graves (1820-93), founder of the Landmark Baptist movement, most clearly represents the trend among Baptists to use restorationism as a way to meet threats posed by Christian competition on the American frontier. The name of the movement came from Prov. 22:28, "Remove not the ancient landmark, which thy fathers have set" (KJV). For Graves and other Landmarkists, Baptists abandoned the "ancient landmark" when they recognized non-Baptist churches as if they were true churches (→ Separatism).

Graves's leadership emerged during the late 1840s in Nashville, Tennessee. While working in an editorial office of a denominational journal (the *Baptist*), Graves became involved in a heated controversy over Christian baptism. He believed that only Baptist congregations performed proper Christian baptism and thus that only Baptist baptism was true baptism. In the next few years Graves developed a series of resolutions declaring the nature of the true church. Since Baptists were organized on the pattern of the earliest churches and depended upon the Bible to define the nature of the church, only Baptist churches were "gospel churches," and only Baptists were truly Christian. Two other Baptist preachers, James M. Pendleton (1811-91) and Amos C. Dayton (1811-65), who were associated with the Southern Baptist Convention (formed in 1845), adopted these views and helped Graves spread them throughout the Southwest.

James Graves's Christian world was easily divided: either become a member of the true church, the Baptist church defined in a very particular way, or miss out altogether on Christianity and its benefits. Shortly after the turn of the 20th century, the Landmark movement became situated largely in two splinter Baptist groups: the American Baptist Association and the Baptist Missionary Association of America, each having about 250,000 members.

2.3. ***Mormons***

During the 19th century, restorationism also surfaced in yet another indigenous American religious movement — Mormonism. When in 1830 Joseph Smith (1805-44) founded the Church of Christ, which became the Church of Jesus Christ of Latter-day Saints, he also combined primordial concerns with millennial expectations. Like Disciples, → Mormons emphasized the importance of restoring ancient practices. Unlike Disciples, however, who looked to the Bible, and particularly the NT, as their only reliable guide, Mormons emphasized the prophetic standing of Joseph Smith himself and the authority of the *Book of Mormon,* reproduced for contemporary history through Smith's prophetic vision and translation.

Mormons believe that the original *Book of Mormon* existed on golden plates buried by ancient American Christians. In the 1820s God reached into contemporary history and connected Joseph Smith with the primordial past. Through God's anointing of Joseph Smith, God once again had personally created the true Church of Jesus Christ on earth. The restored church was created whole and immediately, directly by the hands of God. Mormons understand themselves as stewards of the restored church until the millennium should come. Membership in 2005 numbers approximately 12 million worldwide, in 120 countries and territories.

2.4. *Assessment*

The restorationist impulse, as it operated through these three movements in 19th-century America, served as a powerful check against arbitrary hierarchies and authoritarian appeals to tradition. It trumpeted → religious liberty in the face of the existing institutional manifestations of religion. Yet for Disciples, Landmark Baptists, and Mormons alike, as individuals or groups within these movements became certain of their own identification with the primitive church or confident of their own success in capturing the ancient practices and beliefs, self-righteous behavior emerged. Some became so confident that primordial patterns had been restored that they attempted to limit the freedom of those who disagreed with them or sought to force fellow Christians to accept ancient practices as they understood them. At such points endeavors seeking to uncover and restore the ideals of the primitive church, at the heart of restorationism, were ironically replaced by modern-day efforts (in effect, crass denominational efforts) to dictate the marks of the true church.

Bibliography: Primitivism: R. T. Hughes and C. L. Allen, *Illusions of Innocence: Protestant Primitivism in America, 1630-1875* (Chicago, 1988) • G. H. Williams, *The Radical Reformation* (Philadelphia, 1962).

Glas, Sandeman, and the Haldanes: J. T. HORNSBY, "John Glas: A Study of the Origins, Development, and Influence of the Glasite Movement" (Diss., Edinburgh, 1936) • D. W. LOVEGROVE, "Unity and Separation: Contrasting Elements in the Thought and Practice of Robert and James Alexander Haldane," *The Stone-Campbell Movement: An International Religious Tradition* (ed. M. W. Casey and D. A. Foster; Knoxville, Tenn., 2002) 520-43 • L. MCMILLON, "The Quest for the Apostolic Church: A Study of Scottish Origins of American Restorationism" (Diss., Waco, Tex., 1972) • W. WALKER, "The Sandemanians of New England," *Annual Report of the American Historical Association, 1901* (Washington, D.C., 1902) 131-62.

Disciples of Christ: M. W. CASEY and D. A. FOSTER, eds., *The Stone-Campbell Movement: An International Religious Tradition* (Knoxville, Tenn., 2002) • D. A. FOSTER, P. M. BLOWERS, A. L. DUNNAVANT, and D. N. WILLIAMS, eds., *The Encyclopedia of the Stone-Campbell Movement* (Grand Rapids, 2004) • W. E. GARRISON and A. T. DEGROOT, *The Disciples of Christ: A History* (St. Louis, 1948) • R. T. HUGHES, *Reviving the Ancient Faith: The Story of Churches of Christ in America* (Grand Rapids, 1996) • L. G. MCALLISTER and W. E. TUCKER, *Journey in Faith: A History of the Christian Church (Disciples of Christ)* (St. Louis, 1975) • M. G. TOULOUSE, *Joined in Discipleship: The Shaping of Contemporary Disciples Identity* (rev. ed.; St. Louis, 1997); idem, *Walter Scott: A Nineteenth-Century Evangelical* (St. Louis, 1999) • H. E. WEBB, *In Search of Christian Unity: A History of the Restoration Movement* (Cincinnati, 1990) • D. N. WILLIAMS, *Barton Stone: A Spiritual Biography* (St. Louis, 2000); idem, ed., *Disciples and American Culture, 1880-1989: A Case Study of a Mainstream Denomination* (Grand Rapids, 1991).

Landmark Baptists: J. E. TULL, *A History of Southern Baptist Landmarkism in the Light of Historical Baptist Ecclesiology* (New York, 1980).

Mormons: L. J. ARRINGTON, *Brigham Young: American Moses* (New York, 1985) • L. J. ARRINGTON and D. BITTON, eds., *The Mormon Experience: A History of the Latter-day Saints* (New York, 1992) • R. BUSHMAN, *Joseph Smith and the Beginnings of Mormonism* (Urbana, Ill., 1984) • J. SHIPPS, *Mormonism: The Story of a New Religious Movement* (Urbana, Ill., 1985).

MARK G. TOULOUSE

Resurrection

1. NT

The NT documents agree in affirming Jesus' resurrection from the dead. They announce not the extension of his earthly life (*Wiederbelebung,* resuscitation) but his entry upon a new, glorified existence, a new creation (1 Cor. 15:12-58; Phil. 3:21, et al.). In one sense, this affirmation was not any easier to accept and to proclaim then than it is today. And yet it was and remains at the heart of the Christian faith theologically and at the beginning of the church's emergence historically (see L. Goppelt, *Theology*). The earliest of our extant writings literarily (ca. A.D. 50), 1 Thessalonians, contains both the recollection of missionary preaching regarding Jesus' resurrection (1:9-10) and a theological development of its consequences for → faith and → hope (4:13-18).

This pivotal location of the resurrection at the heart of Christian faith notwithstanding, the reality to which the word "resurrection" points has been and remains to this day the subject of impassioned debate. In contrast to the crucifixion of Jesus, the factuality of which is debated by no one, even if the significance is, the resurrection of Jesus remains outside the historically accessible and demonstrable data of his life and ministry. These data and the resurrection do have in common, however, that their significance cannot be concluded apart from theological reflection and proclamation, the media through which they have been passed on from faith to faith, generation to generation.

Consultation with the enormous bibliography over the resurrection will make immediately clear that the contours of the debate exceed the NT exegetical discussion (demonstrated below; see 2). Yet, the latter is a crucial, if complex, starting point. The NT texts themselves demonstrate a profound variety that defies pat reductions and easy harmonizations of their witness. The goal of this study is a brief but methodologically discriminating delineation of the history of research, a concise differentiation of text types and genres, and a frank discussion of the issues and interpretive options.

1.1. *History of Research*

In the history of research one historical/systematic-theological line of questioning has dominated, by and large, the investigation of resurrection traditions in the NT: did Jesus really rise from the dead, and if so, how did it happen? The most learned attempt at a reconstruction of the events of Easter morning was undertaken by Hans von Campenhausen in his 1952 work *Der Ablauf der Osterereignisse und das leere Grab* (The course of the Easter events and the empty tomb); its contribution, however, focused on the historically empty grave. This matter of the historicity of the Easter-event itself is, to be sure, of critical significance and must be addressed with all candor. The issue has become: when does one raise that question, and how does one lay the foundation for advancing it at all methodologically so that the maximum potential for a satisfactory answer may be achieved?

Based on its influence upon subsequent reflection and writing, a singularly most influential publication on the resurrection narratives in this generation was a monograph by Hans Grass, *Ostergeschehen und Osterberichte* (Easter event and Easter accounts, 4th ed., 1970). Grass was able to grant qualified acceptance to the "did it happen" question, but he was uncompromisingly opposed to the claim "that it happened" as the Easter stories tell it. Like Rudolf Bultmann, Grass contended that these accounts do more to shroud and obscure than to clarify and illuminate what actually happened at Easter. On the principle "longer is later, shorter is earlier," the brief kerygma and confessional statements on resurrection and a constructed shape to → primitive Christianity became the places to begin.

Skepticism over against the resurrection appearance stories of the gospel tradition has had a long and complex history. Though that history is not entirely identifiable with the work methods of the → history-of-religion school, it is certainly associated with it and its popular but vaguely defined and loosely applied notions of → "myth" (see 1.4.2) and "legend" at the turn of the 20th century. These labels have had such a prejudicial effect on modern NT discussion that an unbiased critical study of the resurrection narratives in the Gospels has been by and large impossible or of little interest. The impasse has been costly for church and university alike. Beginning with the historicity question and acceptance of the primacy of briefer traditions has been methodologically responsible for far-reaching resentments and misunderstandings; they have impaired the ability to listen afresh to the gospel texts.

Hence, a lesson to be learned from a review of the history of research is that in fairness to the NT itself, it is incumbent to suspend temporarily the historicity question and acceptance of the "briefer earlier, longer later" maxim so that the texts may be heard and examined in their own contexts and functions. With perspective on these, then, the investigation of the historicity question can be joined with integrity and understanding.

1.2. *Texts*

It becomes quite crucial how one looks at the texts bearing witness to resurrection traditions. To be sure, all NT texts (esp. the Gospels) are resurrection texts, since they have all been influenced to one degree or another by a postresurrection perspective, resurrection faith, and the earliest form of proclamation. In a strict sense, however, the following general breakdown by genre points up the variety of resurrection texts per se:

1. First is the so-called → *kerygma tradition,* that is, the brief, credo-like statements of affirmation that Jesus rose from the dead (and appeared): for example, 1 Cor. 15:3b-7 or 1 Thess. 1:9b-10.
2. Related to the first tradition but incorporated into narrative materials of apostolic → preaching (§2.1) is the *summary tradition,* for whose preservation Luke was largely responsible: for example, Acts 2, 3, 5, 10, and 13.
3. Also found in Acts but representing a distinct grouping is the *heavenly radiance tradition* associated with the resurrection encounter of Saul of Tarsus on the road to Damascus: Acts 9, 22, and 26.
4. In the Gospels the *empty-tomb tradition* is found with some variations in both the Synoptic and Johannine gospels: Matt. 28:1-8; Mark 16:1-8; Luke 24:1-12, 22-24; John 20:1-13.
5. Also to be found in these resources and their cousins, the so-called extracanonical gospels, is the *appearance-story tradition* (delineation below). Finally, and in close connection with this tradition, some gospels contain references drawn from an *ascension tradition.*

1.3. *Issues and Options*

The delineation of text and genre types leads to the recognition that the resurrection traditions were varied and represented separate voices witnessing in concert to the Easter message. For the earlier hearers/readers the achievement of the Evangelists, for example, was all the more noteworthy as they recognized that these formerly disparate traditions had been woven together into a pointed theological confession (see, e.g., the complex weave of the kerygma and the empty-tomb traditions in Mark 16:6-7). At stake, moreover, in genre differentiation is an awareness that while one is attentive to the final redactional achievements of the gospel writers in combining traditions, it would be a mistake to think for one moment that they themselves were historically the source of the traditions.

History-of-tradition analysis seeks to move behind the redactional wall, so to speak, to the earliest Christian beginnings, the times and settings from which these traditions take their birth. They enjoyed a life before literary inclusion in the Gospels, functioning in particular *Sitze im Leben* and in their sometimes literary, but mostly oral, contexts of debate, oration, storytelling, preaching, teaching, and so forth. One of the most fascinating questions of contemporary NT research remains: how are we to understand the forms and unique statement-intention of these traditions on the other side of that "wall" before redactional appropriation? It is, to be sure, no great distance to the temporarily suspended historicity question; in terms of historical antecedents one may ask: where and how did they take their inception? And did eyewitness accounts (of something) give rise to the resurrection traditions?

The textual locus of debate for this line of questioning has been the postresurrection appearance stories of the gospel tradition. In seeking to trace the origin and development of resurrection traditions, they offer themselves as the groups of texts that purport to recount the encounters between the resurrected Jesus and his followers. No one is described as actually witnessing the resurrection itself in the Gospels; the confession "God raised Jesus from the dead" remains here as elsewhere a *deduction* from the postresurrection appearances and hence their critical location in theological reflection. The empty-tomb tradition(s) was connected very early to the appearance tradition; only in this connection did they speak a clear resurrection witness. The question of the origin and development of these appearance stories is too complex to be rehearsed here (see J. Alsup), but in summary the following points may be made.

1.3.1. It is not possible to trace a relationship of dependence, as Martin Dibelius once tried, from the very early short-form kerygmatic statements (see 1.2) to the larger and ostensibly later, physically materialistic statements of the gospel appearance stories. The latter cannot be described as late paradigms or illustrations for early Christian preachers. The appearance stories circulated independently of, and complementary to, the kerygma tradition.

1.3.2. Furthermore, it is not possible to reduce the resurrection of Jesus to the pat history of an idea that was appropriated from the OT and transferred to the destiny of an individual (see C. F. Evans; for a fascinating perspective on resurrection in the context of → Judaism, however, see also the learned and provocative P. Lapide). While NT resurrection texts emerged, generally speaking, within the context of the first-century world of Hellenistic Judaism (→ Hellenism), and while both OT (prophetic) texts and extrabiblical accounts can be adduced that proffer the hopes of Israel for a day of resurrection in the future, the specific antecedents of the resurrection appearance stories of the Gospels are not traceable to the general concept of resurrection in that world (see 1.3.6-7 and 1.4 below).

1.3.3. A careful history-of-tradition analysis points to Matt. 28:16-20, Luke 24:13-35 and 36-49, John 20:14-18 and 19-29, and John 21:1-14 as the primary sources comprising the postresurrection appearance stories of the gospel tradition.

1.3.4. A rigorous comparative study of traditional versus redactional form elements shows that at the redactional level there was a literary expansion of certain motifs, such as the theft hypothesis (Matt. 27:64; 28:2, 15), proof of physical body (Luke 24:36-43), and concentration of doubt on one paradigmatic disciple (John 20:24-29); yet we discover a striking similarity of motif and theme pattern at the traditional level. This similarity strongly suggests that originally they were held together by a common world of thought and expression, that they shared a vital conceptual shape that can be described by the technical literary and sociological term *Gattung*, or "genre."

1.3.5. A résumé of the constitutive elements of this *Gattung*/genre would be:

- The human participants in the encounter are in a crisis as the result of Jesus' death.
- Jesus appears, coming upon the scene unexpectedly and at his initiative.
- He is seen but not recognized. There is doubt.
- He addresses the participants, and a verbal exchange ensues.
- They then recognize him as Lord, the Jesus of their former experience. Doubt is overcome.
- The appearance culminates in a sending/commissioning or going out of the participants and a departure of the Appearing One.

1.3.6. That this *Gattung*/genre was without precedent in the milieu of primitive Christianity cannot be claimed. Formal parallels do exist in the Hellenistic world of the period in the stories of "divine men," the so-called *theoi andres,* such as Apollonius of Tyana (fl. 1st cent. A.D.), Romulus, and others. Internal differences in substance and statement-intention, however, do prohibit linking the two in a direct, analogous sense. Both formal and substantive parallels do exist, nevertheless, in the OT theophany stories in which God appears in human form (e.g., Genesis 18, Judges 6 and 13, etc.).

1.3.7. The conclusion appears compelling that the postresurrection appearance-story tradition was formulated from its inception in direct reliance upon this OT theophany tradition and probably in conversation with the Hellenistic "divine man" tradition in order to give it a particular theological form of expression and precise direction of statement. "Myth" and "legend" are too diffuse and imprecise to serve as useful categories here (see 1.4.2)

1.4. *History, Faith, and Eschatological Existence* Form-critical and history-of-tradition categories have made possible the recognition of the variety of NT traditions witnessing to the resurrection and the focus on the origin and development question of one of the neglected, major streams. Those categories have also enhanced the ability to trace its shape as *Gattung*/genre back to the earliest period; the theophanic/declarative pattern of this OT tradition was apparently not a variable. It is there as a constant for all of the traditional-level sources. This determination of form must have been deliberate in order for it to have been the constant for this tradition. That conscious decision by the formulators of the tradition must be taken most seriously if one is to be interpretively honest.

Another consequence of form determination, however, is that something had to have been made to conform to the pattern; the variety within motif and theme expression makes it impossible that the pattern was self-generating, the construct of widespread collusion. Even where possible indicators of an eyewitness account of personal experience can be postulated (see B. Gerhardsson), they have been relegated to a subordinate role in the *Gattung*/genre. The genre enabled a reality that was without parallel to come to conceptual shape and expression in the mode of a pious approximation drawn from the biblical world of the encounter. The genre spoke uniformly as a word of witness within a stream of theological consciousness and invited the response of faith. Hence, the categories of form and tradition do not preclude the historicity question, but neither can they assist in its demonstration. The great "what," therefore, remains the object of faith and not the datum (in the conventional sense) of historical inquiry.

1.4.1. In the interest of finding meaning in the "idea of resurrection," some recent attempts at interpretation have enlisted a contemporary preference for the philosophical language of → symbol and → metaphor (e.g., the concluding way of promise for the compendious work of Pheme Perkins); others (e.g., Gerd Lüdemann and Gerd Theissen), seeking to press the historicity issue, have relied on sociological and psychological categories as a means of reshaping theological ones. Disenchanted with traditional theological interpretation, yet determined to expose the origins of the resurrection accounts, Lüdemann, for example, proposes a reading of historical probability mediated by behavioral assessments; disappointment, guilt, and denial "illuminated by eternity" most likely prompted — in this view — the "visions experienced" by → Paul and → Peter as primary "witnesses" of resurrection. The ripple effect of this recourse to a popular former hermeneutical path of the subjective/objective visions (Grass et al.) of (para)psychology with modern-day twists has spawned an international debate of considerable consequence (see H. Verweyen; also, most recently, the expansive N. T. Wright). What remains for further exploration are understandings of faith and destiny that exceed personal existential preferences and encompass God's relationship to history. (See the theologically pregnant horizons in 1 Cor. 15:20-28 as well as the provocative exploration of the → descent-into-hell tradition of Easter Saturday by A. Lewis.)

1.4.2. The resurrection of Jesus is believed, is proclaimed, and is believed again in the *oikos* (household) of faith, the church. As the Pauline Epistles affirm, its belief and proclamation rest on the foundation of the hope of resurrection for all who are tethered to the resurrected-appearing One in faith. It is this One who declares to those with ears to hear that it really happened, that God raised Jesus from the dead, and that God shall raise many faithful witnesses at the end of the age. (See G. Sloyan for a nuanced understanding of "myth" and history within the context of apocalyptic; see also 1.3.2 above.)

What exists between the declaration regarding Jesus' destiny and the promise regarding that of the believer is a way of being, seeing, and behaving that is related substantively to the tradition-level themes and motifs of the appearance-story *Gattung*/genre (see 1.3.5); resurrection broadcasts something new, namely, eschatological existence in the midst of the old, fading existence. Similarly, Leonhard Goppelt comments on 1 Peter: "Living in society a life that comes from the resurrection means eschatological existence within the context of history" (*Commentary*, p. 67).

1.4.3. The motifs of the resurrection-appearance story lend themselves to the ongoing dialogue over the foundation of eschatological existence. The fundamental crisis of Christian existence is that the old existence is a crucified one; into that crisis the Resurrected One enters at his own initiative to bring a new reality to life. The constant dilemma is mortal eyesight, the (theologically) mysterious inability to perceive and recognize the presence of the new reality. In the encounter with the eschatological reality, a life-conversation of great consequence ensues; little by little — or in the momentary flash — the voice of address is heard, the new creature taking on the shape of the Crucified/Resurrected One is recognized, and people of faith are led to confess anew Jesus as Lord. Finally, this recognition grows into the understanding that one has been taken into the service of that eschatological existence. The God of resurrection sends people out marked by a new direction to follow the One who goes before.

Bibliography: J. Alsup, *The Post-Resurrection Appearance Stories of the Gospel Tradition: A History-of-Tradition Analysis, with Text-Synopsis* (Stuttgart, 1975) • H. C. C. Cavallin, *Life after Death: Paul's Argument for the Resurrection of the Dead in I Cor. 15* (Lund, 1974) • C. F. Evans, *Resurrection and the NT* (London, 1970) • B. Gerhardsson, "Evidence for Christ's Resurrection according to Paul: 1 Cor. 15:1-11," *Neotestamentica et Philonica* (ed. D. E. Aune et al.; Leiden, 2003) 73-91 • L. Goppelt, *A Commentary on 1 Peter* (ed. F. Hahn; trans. and aug. J. Alsup; Grand Rapids, 1993); idem, *Theology of the NT* (vol. 1; Grand Rapids, 1981) • P. Lapide, *The Resurrection of Jesus: A Jewish Perspective* (Minneapolis, 1982) • A. Lewis, *Between Cross and Resurrection: A Theology of Holy Saturday* (Grand Rapids, 2001) • G. Lüdemann, *The Resurrection of Jesus: History, Experience, Theology* (Minneapolis, 1995) • G. Lüdemann, with A. Özen, *What Really Happened to Jesus? A Historical Approach to the Resurrection* (Louisville, Ky., 1996) • P. Perkins, *Resurrection: NT Witness and Contemporary Reflection* (New York, 1984) • G. Sloyan, "'Come, Lord Jesus': The View of the Post-resurrection Community," *Who Do People Say I Am?* (ed. F. A. Eigo; Villanova, Pa., 1980) 91-121 • G. Theissen, *Psychological Aspects of Pauline Theology* (Philadelphia, 1987); idem, *The Shadow of the Galilean: The Quest of the Historical Jesus in Narrative Form* (Philadelphia, 1987; repr., London, 2001) • H. Verweyen, ed., *Osterglaube ohne Auferstehung? Diskussion mit Gerd Lüdemann* (2d ed.; Freiburg, 1995) • N. T. Wright, *The Resurrection of the Son of God* (Minneapolis, 2003).

John E. Alsup

2. Theology

The Christian church has, from its inception, proclaimed belief in the resurrection. The → Apostles' Creed bears witness both to the resurrection of Jesus Christ and, correlatively, to the resurrection of the saints (the church). "On the third day [Jesus Christ] rose again from the dead," reads the second article; "he ascended into heaven, and sitteth on the right hand of God the Father Almighty." While explicit mention of "bodily" resurrection is not made, the reference here to Christ's sitting at the side of the Father implies that the resurrection is in some real sense physical, as well as spiritual. "I believe in the resurrection of the body," reads the third article, affirming resurrection as both integral to the Holy Spirit's work and consistent with the existence of the "communion of saints," who forgive each others' sins and look forward to the "life everlasting." Again, resurrection is not depicted as something abstract, esoteric, or triumphalistic, but as that which is the concrete inheritance of the → people of God (e.g., Rom. 8:12-30).

These creedal confessions naturally provoke questions for Christian believers as people of "faith seeking understanding" (→ Anselm). How, we might ask, are we to understand "bodily resurrection," wondering about different interpretative approaches and struggling with the matter of the historicity of the resurrection event. We may also want to explore the relationship between Jesus Christ's resurrection and other elements of his life. In what sense, if any, does the resurrection override or reframe the incarnational event, and to what degree is it in continuity with Jesus' prior life and ministry? Particularly salient, in this regard, is the matter of the relationship of resurrection to the passion and the cross. Even if we know better than to reduce the meaning of the resurrection to a happy ending of a painful story, how do we avoid construing it in a triumphalistic way that minimizes, by comparison, the significance of God's suffering with us? Furthermore, how do we live as "resurrection people" of → hope who boldly proclaim victory over death while at the same time grieving, and entering deeply into, the → suffering of the world?

2.1. *Meanings of the Resurrection*

In the context of the Christian tradition, "the resurrection of the body" is understood to differ, fundamentally, from both "resuscitation" and "the → immortality of the soul." Hence, in Christian confession we do not claim that the bodies we have had on earth will one day be reanimated; neither is it the case that our souls will endure even when our bodies are no more. Rather, to confess the bodily resurrection is to take seriously the reality of → death, creaturely mortality, and the end of our existence. It is to believe that we will one day be made anew, ex nihilo — in a glorified state that is simultaneously, in some way, in continuity with who we are now, in our earthly existence. As Paul puts this "mystery," we will all be transformed; what is perishable will put on imperishability, but our mortal bodies will serve as "seeds" from which will come our spiritual bodies (see 1 Cor. 15:35-58).

Traditionally, resurrection is understood both as the remedy to death and as the promise of new life. Commonly, Christian theologians have viewed death as being in some sense problematic. While theologians do not all agree that death is a consequence of the fall, there is consensus that the suffering, pain, and loneliness often associated with our mortality runs counter to God's creative intentions. Resurrection, in relation to the human predicament, is God's promise to us that we have not been abandoned, despite appearances to the contrary. It is God's assurance that the suffering we experience in our mortal existence is not the end of the story. In the final analysis, the workings of God's sovereign plan will be evident: death will no longer have any "sting" (1 Cor. 15:55-56), and every tear will be wiped from our eyes by the one who makes "all things new" (Rev. 21:4-5). In and through the death and resurrection of Jesus Christ, in fact, we see not only that suffering and death *will be* conquered but that death *is* conquered. Thus, those who have been baptized into the Savior's life, death, and resurrection need not be overtaken with dismay in the face of their mortality, knowing that "neither death, nor life . . . nor anything else in all creation, will be able to separate us from the love of God in Jesus Christ our Lord" (Rom. 8:38-39).

Resurrection is also understood as a → symbol for the new life that comes with one's identification with the Resurrected One. "In Christ, there is a new creation," writes Paul; "everything old has passed away; see, everything has become new!" (2 Cor. 5:17). The new life is typically characterized by changed behavior. No longer does → sin have dominion; to live in light of the resurrection is not to be drawn to sin but to engage in works of → love. Those who are resurrected in Christ have died to sin and are living as partners with him in the ministry of → reconciliation (v. 18). In remembering Jesus Christ's resurrection, we hear him instructing us, as his disciples, to "go and meet him in Jerusalem," where we will be involved in the continuing work of the → kingdom (E. Schüssler Fiorenza).

Insistent that the resurrection impacts our lives in the here and now, many contemporary theologians make an even more explicit link between resurrection and political liberation (see, e.g., Gustavo Gutiérrez, Leonardo Boff, James Evans, Delores Williams; → Liberation Theology). To proclaim the resurrection is to confess not only that we are free from bondage to personal sin but also that we are no longer controlled by systemic or corporate sin. To be resurrected with Christ, then, is to be made "captives" who have been "released" from the hunger, nakedness, abuse, and oppression perpetrated by those who disempower others in order to gain power for themselves (Luke 4:18). In contrast to living in captivity, to be resurrected is to live in peace, with daily bread provided, as those who are known and treated as brothers and sisters of the Resurrected One.

The resurrection, finally, reminds us that we live a sacred existence as those who have been "raised with Christ" and whose lives are therefore "hidden with Christ in God" (Col. 3:1-4). Participating in the life of the One who entered into existence with us and raised us up, we are told, "Set your minds on things that are above" (v. 2), living today as members of the kingdom for which we watch and work.

2.2. *Resurrection and Empirical Verifiability*
It is often noted that since → modernity, it is difficult to believe in the notion of resurrection in anything other than a spiritual sense. This is, in part, because the modern embrace of the empirical method discourages exceptions to the rule that human beings do not come back to life after having been dead for three days. The explanation that God violated the natural order of things by accomplishing a supernatural act is not acceptable to many modern theologians, not only because it runs counter to scientific sensibilities, but also because it disrespects the consistent, steadfast character of God (→ Miracle; Science and Theology). As some contemporary theologians ask, Would not the committal of such supernatural acts violate the created order itself, which God both created and identified as good? Austin Farrar argues (with these concerns in mind) that resurrection is not a supernatural event that confounds the natural order but is, in reality, consistent with the order of things as God has ordained them. Miracles such as healing and resurrection, Farrar argues, should be understood as "enhancements of the creature" that are built into the fabric of our created — and creative — ontologies. We do not consider the healing of cut fingers supernatural; resurrection, though much more dramatic, is not something utterly alien to our everyday experience.

Other theologians of the modern period take a more existential tack, attempting to articulate the essential place of resurrection in the Christian confession of faith, at the same time acknowledging the scientific impossibility of dead men coming back to life. Friedrich → Schleiermacher understands Christ's resurrection to be a manifestation of his "fully actualized God-consciousness," believing that it serves as a vehicle of hope for all Christian believers, and even for all human individuals. In confessing the reality of Christ's resurrection, according to Schleiermacher, we simultaneously recognize that we are not destined to live out our lives as those alienated from God and one another, but as those who will one day live in "fellowship with the Redeemer" and in "fellowship with the blessed" (§161; → Schleiermacher's Theology 2.2.5). Rudolf Bultmann, following in this tradition, is known for his conviction that one could preach Christ crucified on Easter morning while at the same time acknowledging that he did not, historically, rise from the dead. "If the event of Easter Day is in any sense an historical event additional to the event of the cross," Bultmann argued, "it is nothing else than the rise of faith in the risen Lord... The resurrection itself is not an event of past history. All that historical criticism can establish is the fact that the first disciples came to believe in the resurrection" (p. 42; → Demythologizing). For both Schleiermacher and Bultmann, hope in the resurrection is grounded kerygmatically, not historically. In and through the church's proclamation "Jesus Christ is risen," Christian believers are freed from the existential predicament to participate in new life.

Understanding modern notions of empirical verifiability and historicity to be of significant value in the shaping of theological claims, some contemporary theologians hold that those from the Bultmann school of thinking have gone too far in divorcing the resurrection of Jesus Christ from → historiography. Wolfhart Pannenberg, for example, currently leads in discussions of how historical and empirical findings must come into play in exploring faith claims, including our confessions about resurrection. "The Easter appearances are not to be explained from the Easter faith of the disciples; rather, conversely, the Easter faith of the disciples is to be explained from the appearances," Pannenberg argues (p. 96). In these words one might hear echoes of Paul's assertion that, if Christ is not raised from the dead, "we are of all people most to be pitied" (1 Cor. 15:19).

Karl → Barth and other theologians have tried to bear witness to the truth of the resurrection while being respectful of, but not confined by, modern sensibilities. In other words, instead of arguing for or against the empirical viability of bodily resurrection, Barth and others attempt to redirect their audiences to the person of the risen Lord himself. Barth points out that the gospel accounts themselves spend little time discussing the "miraculous character" of the resurrection events (see 1); rather, they attest "Jesus Himself . . . [and] the miraculous consequence of the divine act of His awakening from the dead as it took place for Him and therefore for them" (p. 148). While it is crucial, according to Barth, to recognize that the resurrection is a historical event, we must simultaneously acknowledge that it is like no other event in history and cannot be empirically verified. More important than fixating on the details of "what happened" is to meet the Resurrected One, who, in his resurrection, has exalted us to participation in the very life of God (→ Dialectical Theology).

2.3. *Resurrection and Incarnation*

Theologically speaking, the resurrection of Jesus Christ must be understood in continuity with the → incarnation. To understand the resurrection as in any way overpowering, negating, or rendering temporary the confession that "the Word became flesh" (John 1:14) would be to compromise on the reality that God is with us in this world; it would be to risk Christological → Docetism. Gregory of Nazianzus's formative insight "That which is not assumed is not saved" reminds us, along these lines, of the significance of Jesus Christ's *bodily* resurrection. The resurrected Jesus Christ did not leave behind this world, these bodies, and creaturely existence, even as he triumphed over sin and death. On the contrary, he demonstrated, in his embodied, resurrected state, that all that he was as a human being — as the one born of the Virgin Mary, who suffered under Pontius Pilate — is taken into the very life of the triune God. The bodily resurrection affirms not only that death is not the end of the story but that we have not been abandoned by Emmanuel, who is still with us, even in the context of our creaturely existence and sufferings.

Christ's ongoing participation in our existence makes the relationship between our resurrection and his all the more apparent. The One who emptied himself, becoming obedient even unto death on the cross, is the same One whom the Father has also highly exalted (Phil. 2:6-11). The Resurrected is the Crucified, and the Crucified is the Resurrected. When we look to the Christ who rose from the dead, we identify with him by virtue of his shared participation in the existence that we know; he promises us that through this identification he will exalt us to participation in a new existence.

2.4. *Resurrection and the Cross*

Similarly, then, the cross is not left behind in the event of the resurrection. As Martin → Luther insisted in the Reformation, ours is not a *theologia gloriae* (theology of glory) but a → *theologia crucis* (theology of the cross). Four centuries later Dietrich → Bonhoeffer insisted that all Christological triumphalism be avoided, for "only a suffering God can help" (p. 361). Recent theological works, including a unique study by Alan Lewis on the significance of Holy Saturday, explore what it means for us soteriologically to recognize that the one who rose for us first entered fully into the abyss of death. Stunned by the "foolish wisdom . . . of the God who elects to be located on a cross and in a tomb," we gain the assurance that there is nowhere we can go that we are without God (p. 195; see Psalm 139).

Reflecting on resurrection in light of the cross, Jürgen Moltmann has, in the last four decades, ably explained that to think of the resurrection as laying aside the cross would be to give up our hope that God is with us in the midst of suffering. In the moment of suffering itself, resurrection is meaningless if it is extrapolated from the cross. Moltmann explains that he came to think of resurrection in relationship to the cross when he was, from 1945 to 1948, a prisoner of war (after six months of serving as a soldier in the German army, he had surrendered to the British). Reading the Bible in the context of living in the prison camps, Moltmann came to realize that the transforming power of the resurrection is grounded in the fact that the Resurrected One is the Crucified One — the one who has not abandoned us, the one who understands our need. To look at the cross apart from the resurrection leads to hopelessness, for it leaves us merely with a suffering companion, and not with a Savior. But to look to the resurrection apart from the cross equally leads to hopelessness, for it leads to the depiction of Jesus Christ as a kind of superhero, rather than as the God who is truly with us in our moment of need.

2.5. *Resurrection and Christian Hope*

The resurrection is traditionally associated with the doctrine of → eschatology, or "last things." Since the publication of Moltmann's *Theology of Hope* (1967), however, eschatology has been more consciously identified with life in the present, as well as with the character of the life to come. Consequently, theologians have been thinking, in recent decades, about the impact of resurrection on Christian hope in the here and now. The primary reason for the shift of emphasis, as recommended by Moltmann, is that a futuristically oriented eschatology (including the doctrine of resurrection) is unable to address the theological and spiritual needs of a post-Holocaust world. As theologians such as J. B. Metz and Sharon Welch point out, eschatologies that paint a futuristic picture of a better world are too often used as an excuse to avoid addressing the needs of the present moment. Instead of waiting around for God to inaugurate a better future, they argue, we need to realize that what we do today will determine the shape of tomorrow.

To confess the resurrection is not to look past the realities of this place and time precisely because, as we have argued, the Resurrected One, in whom our hope is grounded, is also the one who entered into existence with us and died on the cross. But to say that this world is included in resurrection hope is not to say that this world is, finally, all that there is. While Metz and Welch are right to remind us that what we do today has an impact on the shape of tomorrow, it is crucial that we add — from the standpoint of our Christian confession — that what we do neither determines nor impedes, in the final analysis, the coming of God's kingdom. Whenever we confess the resurrection of Jesus Christ and our bodily resurrections to follow, we are simultaneously bearing witness to the sovereignty of God. The God who resurrects the dead is the God who promises us that all tears will one day be wiped away, regardless of our sinfulness, our stellar record of service, or our ambivalence toward helping those in need.

But the certainty of our resurrections, founded in the reality of the resurrection of Jesus Christ, is no excuse for passivity on our part. Indeed, to live in Christian hope in the resurrection, knowing that the future lies in the hands of God, frees us to engage in works of love for the sake of those whom we serve, rather than with the burden of ushering in the kingdom ourselves. Furthermore, to live with the realization that the resurrection reality is God's certain promise is not only to live in hope for what is to come but is to experience deep anguish for that which is not yet evident. "Thy kingdom come!" we pray, impatiently yearning for the fullness of God's presence. "Thy will be done," we add, again remembering our commitment to service. Inevitably, then, to live as resurrection people is to live in the tension between grief and hope, believing so strongly in the promise of the not yet that we are overcome by our desire for its presence in the here and now.

Bibliography: K. Barth, *CD* IV/2 • L. Boff, *Jesus Christ Liberator: A Critical Christology for Our Time* (Maryknoll, N.Y., 1978) • D. Bonhoeffer, *Letters and Papers from Prison* (New York, 1997) • R. Bultmann et al., *Kerygma and Myth* (New York, 1961) • J. Calvin, *Institutes of the Christian Religion* (2 vols.; Philadelphia, 1960) • J. Evans, *We Have Been Believers: An African*

American Systematic Theology (Minneapolis, 1992) • A. Farrar, *Faith and Speculation: An Essay in Philosophical Theology* (Edinburgh, 1988) • G. Gutiérrez, *A Theology of Liberation* (Maryknoll, N.Y., 1973) • A. E. Lewis, *Between Cross and Resurrection: A Theology of Holy Saturday* (Grand Rapids, 2001) • M. Luther, "The Heidelberg Disputation" (1518), *LW* 31.35-70 • J. B. Metz, *Faith in History and Society: Toward a Practical Fundamental Society* (New York, 1980) • D. L. Migliore, *Faith Seeking Understanding: An Introduction to Christian Theology* (Grand Rapids, 2004) • J. Moltmann, *Theology of Hope: On the Ground and Implications of a Christian Eschatology* (New York, 1967) • W. Pannenberg, *Jesus, God and Man* (Philadelphia, 1977) • F. Schleiermacher, *The Christian Faith* (Edinburgh, 1986) • E. Schüssler Fiorenza, *Jesus: Miriam's Child, Sophia's Prophet; Critical Issues in Feminist Christology* (New York, 1994) • S. D. Welch, *A Feminist Ethic of Risk* (Minneapolis, 1990) • D. Williams, *Sisters in the Wilderness: The Challenge of Womanist God-Talk* (Maryknoll, N.Y., 1993).

Cynthia L. Rigby

Return of Christ → Parousia

Revelation

1. Religious Aspects

1.1. *Judeo-Christian Source*

As a technical term in religious usage, "revelation" comes from the Judeo-Christian tradition, more narrowly, from Christian theology. Its adoption as an academic term has brought with it a material expansion of meaning, the aim being to discover and systematically describe essential elements of biblical religion as they might appear in nonbiblical religious traditions. The legitimacy of this procedure has been variously evaluated according to the definition of the term and the reliability of the process relative to the self-statements of the religions described, that is, whether or not these religions consider themselves to be religions of revelation, or whether it is enough for → religious studies to show that they rest on revelation.

The success of transferring the concept to nonbiblical religions depends decisively on the understanding of revelation that is proposed. Those who find in → religions only an expression of the human search for God, or who, like K. → Barth (1886-1968), contrast them with the biblical revelation, as many do, cannot use the term for nonbiblical religions. But those who find revelation also in this sphere adopt a definition that is not strictly Christian but can apply effectively to other cultures as well.

1.2. *Features*

To speak of revelation implies that certain individuals or social groups claim insights that as such, or as regards their mediation, do not arise in the same way as those deriving from natural ways of knowing (→ Epistemology). Instead, with a binding claim, they are manifestations of something supernatural or numinous, which is traced back to a personal author (God, gods, goddesses, or spirits), or in some cases to impersonal forces like mana (→ Immanence and Transcendence; Sacred and Profane).

There are thus many explanations of (1) the *origin* or *author* of revelation, who brings us into contact with the Wholly Other or the numinous, or of (2) the *means* or *instruments* that give the insights, for example, natural signs such as stars, animals, plants, stones, also cultic sites and special times, or phenomena like → dreams, → visions, → ecstasy, or communications in words or sacred books. Differences exist regarding (3) the *content*, by which the existence or will of a deity, the divine presence in protection or punishment, divine direction for human conduct, and the specific tasks that we must undertake are communicated to us. The variety of these possibilities corresponds to (4) the variety of potential *recipients* or *addressees* of revelation, for example, medicine men, → priests, → prophets, mediators, kings, shamans (→ Shamanism), soothsayers, and so forth. Finally, reference must be made to (5) the *effect on the recipients*, in which we note specific religious differences, including a sense of divine mission, oracles, → inspiration, or → incarnation.

1.3. *Non-Christian Religions*

T. P. van Baaren, J. Deninger, and others regard these five areas as features of revelation that make it possible for us to speak of revelation in nonbiblical traditions without adopting C.-M. Edsman's general verdict that revelation is part of the self-understanding of every religion. From the standpoint of the → phenomenology of religion, we can thus regard as revelation many of the religious utterances of → nature religions and of antiquity that are traced back to hierophanies (M. Eliade).

This conclusion applies to → *Jainism* and to many forms of → *Buddhism*, especially that of the Mahayana schools. F. Heiler (1892-1967) even found a revelation in the teaching of *Confucius* (→ Confucianism), though "heaven" does not speak here but appears only in the inflexible course of nature.

There is a kind of claim to revelation in classical → *Hinduism*, with its distinction between religious tradition in sruti (Skt. *śruti*, "what is heard") and in smriti (*smṛti*, "what is remembered"). The former embraces the religious knowledge (Veda) that was heard of old by seers and that is thus traced back to a divine rather than a human origin. But in smriti too there are texts that count as revelation, for example, the → Bhagavad Gita. Since the 19th century Hinduism has further developed this idea of revelation and in various ways has given it the form of a universal conception (Heiler).

A true claim to revelation may be seen in *Zoroaster* (→ Iranian Religions 6-7), though many questions regarding Zoroaster's life and work are still open. → *Manichaeanism* and → *Islam* both lay specific claim to revelation. Both are a continuation of biblical revelation and regard themselves as its completion. For this reason Islamic theology calls → Judaism, Christianity, and → Islam (§1) the heavenly religions, that is, religions of revelation.

Many newer religions such as *Sikhism* (→ Sikhs) and → *Baha'i*, as well as some of the so-called → *new religions* in Japan and elsewhere, make a claim to revelation.

→ God; Messianism; Mysticism; Theogony; Theosophy; Youth Religions

Bibliography: T. P. van Baaren, "Voorstellingen van openbaring phaenomenologisch beschouwd" (Conceptions of revelation phenomenologically considered) (Diss., Utrecht, 1951) • J. Cornaroff and J. L. Cornaroff, *Of Revelation and Revolution* (Chicago, 1991) • J. Deninger, "Revelation," *EncRel(E)* 12.356-63 • C.-M. Edsman, "Offenbarung I: Religionsgeschichtlich," *RGG* (3d ed.) 4.1597-99 • M. Eliade, *A History of Religious Ideas* (3 vols.; Chicago, 1978-85) • F. Heiler, *Erscheinungsformen und Wesen der Religion* (Stuttgart, 1961; 2d ed., 1979) 486-99 • J. P. Mackey, "Revelation, Religion, and Theology," *The Critique of Theological Reason* (Cambridge, 2000) chap. 6 • K. Ward, *Religion and Revelation: A Theology of Revelation in the World's Religions* (Oxford, 1994).

Peter Antes

2. Theological Aspects

2.1. *Origin of the Term*

The term "revelation" may refer either to the act of revealing *(revelatio)* or to the things that have been revealed *(revelata)*. Christianity is commonly, but not universally, held to be a "revealed religion" in both senses, both by its own theologians and by philosophical analysts, and revelation is a technical theological concept that has played a very large role in, especially, scholastic theology, both Catholic and Protestant. Here it has been taught that the content of revelation is → truths communicated by God to human beings by means beyond the ordinary course of nature. This strongly didactic concept of revelation has given rise in modern → theology to strenuous debate. Revelation has proved to be one of the most controversial and complex of theological concepts, for a variety of reasons.

2.2. *Causes of Complexity*

2.2.1. *Narrative Character of God's Agency*

A necessary condition for speaking of Christianity as a revealed religion is the affirmation that God is an agent. Only if God is active in the universe may he be identified as the origin or author of revelation; conversely, if God's agency is denied or subject to reductive interpretation, then the concept of revelation becomes redundant.

The Hebrew scriptures use many different verbs to express the divine activity of revealing: *gālâ* ("uncover, unveil," e.g., of an intention, 1 Sam. 9:15, or of God himself, Gen. 35:7), *yāda*ʿ ("proclaim, make known," e.g., in speech, Exod. 25:22, or in the action of bringing Israel out of Egypt, Exod. 20:9), *nāgad* ("report, communicate," e.g., God's own name, Gen. 32:29, or his plan, 41:25), and *ʾāmar* ("say, speak," e.g., a self-revelatory word, such as, "I am the Lord, the God of Abraham your father and the God of Isaac," Gen. 28:13), and *dibber* ("speak," e.g., "the Lord God has spoken," Amos 3:8).

In each of these examples an event within an overarching narrative involves other agents. At its most general, that narrative may be spoken of as the call of Israel to be in a covenantal relationship with God (→ Covenant 1). The reality of who God is, and thus of his will and purpose in → creation and human history, structures the narrative as narrative. Revelation has thus two inseparable meanings. On the one hand, it is unveiling of the *theme* of the narrative as a whole (what God intends to achieve in creation and human history). On the other hand, it is the *context* of any discrete act or intervention within any particular set of events, including the event by which the theme of the narrative is disclosed.

Fundamental, however, to the biblical tradition is the denial that God is an agent like any human agent in a narrative. There is accordingly an interpretative tension within the narrative mode. Of any proposition of the form "God did *x*," there must be a correlative denial, "God did not do *x*." What eventually came to be called → apophatic, or → negative, theology (Dionysius the Pseudo-Areopagite, early 6th cent.) insists that God is not any of the things that he is called in cataphatic, or positive, theology. Thus all knowledge of God is necessarily provisional and partial.

2.2.2. *Human Ignorance and Fallibility*

Correlative to the very concept of revelation is that of human ignorance and fallibility. The narratives of the Hebrew scriptures display the wickedness of which human beings are capable, but also God's ability to bring → good out of → evil. Duplicity and deviousness are human characteristics, as are folly, boastful ignorance, and blindness of heart. What God makes clear, therefore, is revealed especially to the humble and teachable (Ps. 25:8-9).

Although Christian theology has always affirmed the limitations of what human beings may know for themselves in their natural condition, there are major disagreements about the exact consequences of human ignorance and fallibility. The reason for these differences in theologies of revelation is that the precise boundary between human knowledge and ignorance is quite uncertain, especially in moral questions (→ Ethics), and therefore the human appropriation of the relationship with revelation varies in different accounts.

2.2.3. *Faith and Responsibility*

Biblical narratives depict human beings as responding to events of revelation in a variety of ways corresponding to the variety of instruments or means of revelation. Both → obedience and disobedience are possible; revelation therefore requires a human response and incurs guilt if that response is inappropriate. Especially in early Christian theology faith in God became central and was considered to have characterized the response of → Abraham to God's revelation of his purposes (Gal. 3:6; Heb. 11:8-10). Similarly, faithlessness was judged severely as a culpable fault, since enough knowledge of God was publicly evident (i.e., revealed) to make an appropriate moral response possible (Rom. 1:19-32; → Natural Theology). Neither of these two cases involves faith in what for the rest of the NT is crucial, namely, the teaching, deeds, → suffering, and → resurrection of Jesus Christ (→ Christology). Revelation is therefore a single term designating a plurality of objects and contents of faith and → responsibility.

2.3. *Apocalyptic and Revelation*

The NT was composed within the period during which what is known as the apocalyptic movement was important in → Judaism (3d cent. B.C. to end of 1st cent. A.D.; → New Testament Era, History of). The Greek word *apokalypsis* is used in this regard to express the disclosure of supernatural persons or secrets, frequently including eschatological revelations, but by no means confined to them. What is distinctive about the literature containing this kind of material is its claim that the revelation proceeds directly from God; it is not the result of interpretation of the Hebrew scriptures, nor is it the product of human reasoning or observation (→ Reason). Apocalyptic expresses a speculative interest about → heaven, → hell, and human destiny, also the world process, that is not satisfied by the results of → exegesis. Gaps in our knowledge are filled up by direct divine disclosures, based indeed on the Scriptures, but going beyond them. Apocalyptic writers are sometimes rebuked for their willingness to pry into things beyond their reach (Sir. 3:21).

Early Christianity (→ Primitive Christian Community) might best be described as an eschatological teaching based on apocalyptic means. There are specific revelations, concealed from the learned but made known by the Son of God (→ Christological Titles) to whomsoever he chooses (Matt. 11:25-27). There are "secrets of the → kingdom of heaven" that only a few can understand (Matt. 13:10-15).

In the Johannine interpretation of this teaching, revelation is not an intellectual communication of truth to be received mentally. Rather, Jesus brings a new divine reality and presence, changing the believer from flesh to spirit. The communication of the Holy Spirit creates a new human being (John 20:22; → New Self).

If specific contents of mysteries are revealed (→ Mystery Religions), so too is the total theme of the narrative in which these discrete acts of revelation take place. The new theme is *redemption through Christ* (→ Soteriology). The NT describes this event as a final speech-act, completing the sequence begun "in many and various ways" in the → prophets of the old covenant (Heb. 1:1-3). It is a → gospel revealing "the mystery that has been hidden throughout the ages and generations but has now been revealed to his saints" (Col. 1:26; cf. Eph. 3:1-13). And because the denouement lies in the → future, there is an eschatological revealing of Jesus Christ that is inseparable from the gospel (2 Thess. 1:7; 2:8) and in which believers will be finally redeemed (Rom. 8:18-25). One may say that the plurality of revelations acquires a Christological focus.

This speech-act is intelligible in the light of the narrative character of God's agency. The gospel as a whole is a manifestation of the → righteousness of God at work (Rom. 1:17; cf. 16:25-27). It is a → word of God, personally embodied, and thus visible, audible, and tangible (1 John 1:1-4) — a life-giving gospel. Ignatius (ca. 35-ca. 107) could summarize it in the following sentence: "God revealed himself through his Son Jesus Christ, who is his Word, which proceeds from silence" (*Magn.* 8.2).

2.4. ***Revelation and Authority***

Apocalyptic is by definition authoritative (→ Authority). But because it is communicated in words, it is subject to interpretation and misunderstanding. The status of the gospel as revealed is inseparable from the development of means of authoritative interpretation. Although the intention of apocalyptic is to fill the gaps and uncertainties of human reasoning, it cannot do so without either a continuous series of revelations or a process of authoritative interpretation. The evidence indicates that the early Christians were conscious of this problem. → Paul distinguished between his own (less authoritative) opinions and a "command of the Lord" (1 Cor. 7:25, on the unmarried). There were difficulties with those who claimed to disclose new mysteries in the Spirit (chap. 14; → Ecstasy). There were continuing problems about the status and interpretation of the cultic and moral laws of the Hebrew scriptures (Galatians). Christian → discipleship could come in forms that made plausible but specious claims to authenticity, and careful discrimination was called for (1 John 4:1-6). In addition, there were plainly many speculative or philosophical questions on which Christian revelation simply had nothing to say; to fill up the gaps with other teachings required considerable vigilance, since other teachings sometimes involved wholly alien assumptions and attitudes (Col. 2:8).

The early Christian churches (→ Early Church) thus found themselves with a series of urgent problems to solve if the authority of the original claims for revelation was to be preserved. Three processes may be observed. The first was the objectification of the contents of the original revelation as a sacred tradition ("what has been entrusted to you," 1 Tim. 6:20). The second was the development of an authoritative class of officeholders with the specific task and spiritual endowment to make the necessary decisions (2 Tim. 1:6; → Ministry, Ministerial Offices). The third was the passage through a series of classic conflicts in which the scope and range of claims for supplementary revelations were defined in principle.

The churches' encounter with → Gnostic teachings of various kinds during the second century determined the lines on which revelation was to be treated in future theology. The Gnostic claim for further esoteric knowledge (→ Esotericism) was sufficiently plausible to attract Christian adherents. But the extravagance of some forms of Gnosticism provided the necessary provocation for the drawing of sharp boundaries between authentic and inauthentic traditions and teachers (→ Irenaeus). A limited collection of scriptures was given the status as → canon; a specific line of teachers (→ bishops tracing their descent from the → apostles) was to be followed, subject to the usual moral criteria; an articulated rule gave the gist of Christian teaching in essential outline. Speculation outside the Scriptures was held to be hazardous and needed special spiritual gifts if it was to be undertaken at all.

The process might be described as a battle for organizational stability against the inherent factors making for variety, instability, and conflict. Just as the appeals for unity to be found in the NT are intelligible only against a background of real disunity and threatened disintegration, so the theological tradition that sees "revelation" as a stable datum can be interpreted only in the context of factors making for complexity and controversy. The history of the theological interpretation of the concept demonstrates that "revelation" is a conceptual construct with an essentially contested and contestable meaning. Christian history has known of two major families or trends of construal: the institutional-sacramental (→ Institution; Sacrament) and the personal-experiential (→ Experience); the purpose of both is to give greater stability to the idea and content of revelation.

2.5. ***Institutional-Sacramental Model***

Through the developmental process of routinization (M. → Weber), the later patristic and medieval church acquired an institutional form sufficient to ensure adequate coherence and stability of leadership (→ Patristics; Middle Ages 1). Part of the cost of institutionalization lay in the suppression of the history of theological variety and the acute simplification of the account of early Christian history. But the Scriptures themselves provide ample evidence of the charismatic and sectarian origins of the Christian movement and continually provoked further charismatic outbreaks (→ Charismatic Movement;

Sect), some of which involved splits from the church (e.g., → Montanism), while others (e.g., → monasticism) were contained within the church, though with difficulty.

The constant pressure of the practical problems requiring resolution gave rise to a demand for clear boundaries between the sphere of revelation and that of error or wickedness. Sociologically, this demand resulted in the search for, and → legitimation of, a finally authoritative decision-making structure, and the maximum precision possible in the language of revelation. Thus the conceptual context of revelation came to be emphasized rather than its theme, and the doctrine of the → church became the foundation upon which all other doctrines were built. The church is the salvation-guaranteeing outcome of the whole work of God. It alone possesses the means of salvation, whose administration can be precisely identified by the fulfillment of legally specifiable conditions. Through its divinely assisted and authorized officers, it infallibly (→ Infallibility) declares the content of the truths of revelation, including truths about God, Jesus Christ, the church, and the sacraments. Thus → dogmas that the church proposes as revealed are "truths which have come down to us from heaven" (the antimodernist decree *Lamentabili,* July 3, 1907; → Catholicism [Roman]; Roman Catholic Church; Transcendental Theology).

On this account, it is not necessarily denied that these truths are personal and give rise to experiences of salvation. But the experiential is the realm of uncertainty, individualism, and the possibility of error, and it must accordingly be subordinated to the objectivity of institution and sacrament.

2.6. *Personal-Experiential Model*

The person-involving character of the narrative of salvation, especially that of Jesus Christ, the focus of revelation, constitutes an alternative way of reducing the contested content of revelation. On this model the foundation of Christian faith and life can lie only in personal participation in Christ, who is himself the Savior. Here the theme of the narrative of salvation takes precedence over the particular contents, or truths, of revelation. Since what is revealed is said to be a person, the only appropriate mode of response is that of personal encounter, especially in the experience of forgiveness through the atoning death of Christ, and in new life in the Holy Spirit. Revelation does not primarily consist, therefore, of truths communicated to rational beings by a belief-worthy authority; it constitutes a pathway through a series of personal, self-authenticating experiences.

This model appeals strongly to the preinstitutional, charismatic elements of the NT, and to its frequent references to transactions in the "heart" of the believer. Because the heart is the seat of faithlessness, its conversion and remaking is therefore crucial to the actuality of revelation. It is God alone who has access to the secrets of the heart (Acts 1:24; 15:8); it is God alone who opens the heart (Acts 16:14), where he lets his light shine (2 Cor. 4:6), pouring in his love (Rom. 5:5). In the heart Christ may dwell (Eph. 3:17), through faith and in love.

It is not necessarily denied that there is or should be an institution to sustain and support these experiences, or that doctrines may not need to be expressed with as much clarity as possible. But the institutional is the realm of → power, → money, and status, which subvert fundamental Christian attitudes and virtues and thus must be rigorously subordinated to the realm of the personal. Sacramental objectivity and precision, moreover, are said to tend toward legalism and → magic; sacraments are better understood as external reminders of an interior transformation than as guaranteed instruments of it.

2.7. *Criticism*

Although these trends are not mutually exclusive, at the → Reformation they were formulated in mutually antagonistic ways. Modern theology inherits the moral mistrust of all claims for revelation that lead to, and justify, gross hostility, persecution, and warfare (→ War; Theology in the Nineteenth and Twentieth Centuries).

The NT itself is critical of specious claims for revelation and demands that the "spirits" be tested (1 John 4:1-6). Here the criteria are said to be dogmatic (does the "spirit" confess Jesus in the flesh?), institutional (do the "prophets" belong to "us"?), and experiential (do they continue in love?). But there are also unarticulated rational criteria whose extent and relevance are necessarily controversial, since they bear upon human ignorance and fallibility. Clearly, there is a considerable body of reliable knowledge about the world that is apparently independent of what is said to be revealed.

The attempt to achieve harmony between revelation and human rationality implies an integration of the concept of truth within a Christological framework. But repeatedly, and most notably at the → Enlightenment, the articulation of universal criteria of rationality has led to criticism of revelation itself (J. G. Fichte). Where mathematics was used as the paradigm of all knowledge (R. Descartes), the program of integration broke down, and revelation was accommodated, if at all, only as a restatement in mythical form of truths already accessible rationally (E. Herbert of Cherbury; → Myth, Mythology, 1), or as a special source of exceptional information

(J. Locke), or a form of practical reason (I. Kant). Major efforts were made to reintegrate revelation with reason in reconstructed theories of the nature of human beings as inherently oriented toward God (F. D. E. → Schleiermacher) or as part of a spiritual-rational world process (G. W. F. Hegel). All these attempts remained controversial in → Protestantism and were wholly rejected by Roman Catholic theologians until the 20th century.

The most massive modern attempt to reassert a Christological (→ eschatological) framework for all knowledge was that of Karl → Barth (1886-1968; → Dialectical Theology), who interpreted reality in the light of the incarnate, crucified, and risen Christ. Similarly, → liberation theology attempted to set the whole of revelation within the perspective of praxis, based upon a critical appraisal of → ideology. A history of the modern understanding of revelation would amount to a history of modern theology, illustrating the complexity and variety of the connotations of the term.

It is evident that to use the term "revelation" either of the theme or of the context of Christian theology provides no protection against critical inquiry into the truth of what is said to be revealed. Revelation is not a supernaturally guaranteed premise for theology but a disputed part of theology itself.

→ Analogy; Augustine's Theology; Calvin's Theology; God, Arguments for the Existence of; Inspiration; Law and Gospel; Luther's Theology; Philosophy; Philosophy and Theology; Religion; Theology of History; Thomism

Bibliography: J. Baillie, *The Idea of Revelation in Recent Thought* (London, 1956) • K. Barth, *Offenbarung, Kirche und Theologie,* (Munich, 1934) • D. Brown, *Tradition and Imagination: Revelation and Change* (Oxford, 1999) • E. Brunner, *Reason and Revelation: The Christian Doctrine of Faith and Knowledge* (London, 1947) • B. S. Childs, *Biblical Theology of the Old and New Testaments: Theological Reflection on the Christian Bible* (Minneapolis, 1993) • Y. Congar, *Tradition and Traditions* (New York, 1966) • A. Dulles, *Models of Revelation* (New York, 1983) • G. Ebeling, *The Word of God and Tradition* (Philadelphia, 1968) • E. Farley and P. C. Hodgson, "Scripture and Tradition," *Christian Theology: An Introduction to Its Traditions and Tasks* (2d ed.; ed. P. C. Hodgson and R. H. King; Philadelphia, 1985) 61-87 • H. W. Frei, *The Eclipse of Biblical Narrative: A Study in Eighteenth- and Nineteenth-Century Hermeneutics* (New Haven, 1974) • D. Kelsey, *Uses of Scripture in Modern Theology* (Philadelphia, 1975) • H. de Lubac, *The Sources of Revelation* (New York, 1968) • H. R. Niebuhr, *Meaning and Revelation* (New York, 1941) • W. Pannenberg, R. Rendtorff, T. Rendtorff, and U. Wilckens, *Revelation as History* (New York, 1968) • P. Ricoeur, *Essays on Biblical Interpretation* (Philadelphia, 1980) • N. Schiffers, K. Rahner, and H. Fries, "Revelation," *EncTheol* 1453-73 • E. Schillebeeckx, *Revelation and Theology* (New York, 1967) • R. F. Thiemann, *Revelation and Theology: The Gospel as Narrated Promise* (Notre Dame, Ind., 1985) • P. Tillich, *Systematic Theology* (vol. 1; New York, 1953) • K. Ward, *Religion and Revelation: A Theology of Revelation in the World's Religions* (Oxford, 1994).

Stephen W. Sykes

Revelation, Book of

1. Genre and Place in Religious History
2. Historical Locus
3. Contents
4. Theological Emphases
5. Influence

1. Genre and Place in Religious History

As the Book of Revelation itself says in 1:1-2, 9-11, it is a → "revelation" *(apokalypsis)* of → Jesus Christ that is meant for Christians and is given through "John." Though being an epistolary work in dialogue with the churches of Asia Minor (1:4, 11), it has predominantly the features of ancient → apocalyptic.

The → early church used the term "apocalypse" for other Christian texts and for Jewish texts that were received by Christians, for example, the Syriac *Apocalypse of Baruch.* Finally, the Book of Revelation appeared as the primary representative of a Jewish-Christian apocalyptic genre. The genre itself, however, is nonetheless difficult to define. What is actually involved is more a broader religiohistorical field of reference.

In Pauline communities, which the Book of Revelation is in fact addressing, according to its own salutation in 1:4, 11, such apocalyptic inclinations are only partially in evidence; the result is that the Book of Revelation's contact with Paulinism is a critical one. Its relationship with Johannine literature (as evidenced by motifs such as the water of life in 21:6 etc.) and to pre-Gnostic developments still awaits clarification. (Several different Gnostic writings call themselves apocalypses.)

2. Historical Locus

The historical locus of Revelation explains its rootage in various fields. The text refers to isolated experiences of martyrdom (2:13, also 18:24), from which the author concludes that a great persecution is imminent (one that, in the opinion of contemporary critics, he overstates). At the same time, the proud → Judaism of Asia Minor is attacking the reliability of Jesus as Savior (polemically reflected in 2:9; 3:9, etc.). In some places Christian behavior is no longer satisfying strict demands (3:2, 15). Finally, in the Nicolaitans and in the group around a woman "prophet" in Thyatira, an enthusiastic (pre-Gnostic?) trend has emerged that is interested in profound knowledge but not in separation from modes of conduct of the surrounding pagan world (2:14-15, 20-21, 24).

All these factors call into question the thesis that Christians in fact represent the unrestricted dominion of God (1:9 and elsewhere). The Christian sense of present salvation, a sense already widespread in Asia Minor and reflected in Rev. 1:5b, 6a (note the theological development from Colossians and Ephesians), enters into a serious crisis. Hence, Revelation is a comprehensive attempt, by means of an authoritative revelation of Jesus Christ, to refute Gnostic knowledge-revelations, to chastise the ethically careless, and to interpret external pressures, with the help of apocalyptic traditions, as a final assault of Satan that is bound to fail (→ Antichrist).

The anti-Roman thrust of the antithesis in chaps. 13 and 17 suggests a date very late in the reign of Domitian (81-96), who had a temple in → Ephesus and who claimed the title "our lord and god," which is deliberately reserved for God in 4:11. One must note, however, that some scholars also advocate early datings to the later period of Nero (54-68) and late datings to the time of Trajan (98-117). Things get even more complicated if, as some authors suspect, the basic text of the Book of Revelation was actually a Jewish writing (from the Jewish War of 66-70) that then underwent Christian redaction.

3. Contents

Revelation has a rhetorically skillful line of argument. After the introduction, 1:9–3:22 as *prothesis* describes the tension between oppression and faith in God's lordship (→ Kingdom of God) in circular letters to seven cities. The way to victory over the tension is also shown. God is establishing his lordship with Jesus, in which all Christians have a part insofar as they defeat ungodly forces.

In 4:1–11:19, the *probatio*, we have positive proof. The lordship of God and of Jesus may be seen in the throne room (chaps. 4–5; 7:9-17) and in divine acts in the world: in plagues (6; 8–9), in the prophetic preaching of repentance (11:1-14), and in the sealing of salvation (7:1-8). Theophany provides visible proof (6:14-17; 11:19).

Next comes the *refutatio* in 12:1–19:10. The revolt of ungodly powers, basically described in chap. 12 and limited to earth, is met. The → gospel, which demands the acknowledgment of God, has here the aspect of judgment (14:6-7; → Last Judgment) in the form of plagues (15–16) and finally in the fall of Babylon (17–18), which stands for → Rome.

With 19:6 comes a new affirmation of the lordship of God that is both to judgment (19:11–20:15) and to salvation (21:1–22:5). The conclusion (22:6-21) stresses the nearness of the consummation of salvation by God and by Jesus as it is anticipated in the → Eucharist (22:17, 20).

4. Theological Emphases

The point of Revelation is the struggle for the present and the future of the saving lordship of God in the face of the current afflictions. The basis of this lordship, which is already in place, takes material precedence: as Creator, God is Lord (chap. 4; → Creation); and Jesus, the mighty Lamb that was slain for us, controls history (5:1–6:1 etc.). The visions of future events in 6:1–22:5 prove this control. They disclose an → eschatology that is oriented to the present and that does not take into account long periods of church history or world history.

Consistent with this theme is the radical nature of the → anthropology — according to 1:5 (cf. 18:4), Christians are released from their past sins — and also of the → ethics, which with its readiness for suffering and social and economic criticism stresses distinction from the world (13:9-10; 18, etc.). The integration of the vision of the Lamb and the throne room in 4–5 responds to Jewish questioning of the saving worth of Jesus. The exclusively historical → dualism of 12–16 contradicts possible beginnings of a pre-Gnostic cosmological dualism among opponents. The Satanizing of universal earthly → power in 13 rejects the claims of state power to divinity (much more critically than in Romans 13; → Emperor Worship). Finally, description of the heavenly Jerusalem in 21:1–22:5 outlines an ecclesiological model.

5. Influence

In virtue of its claim to be revelation, the Book of Revelation was at first readily received, but then it fell under criticism because of its inclination toward → millenarianism. John's authorship was disputed, and the canonizing of the work came only hesitantly (→ Canon 2).

The evocative power of its images made a great

impact, as in the critical visions of → Hildegard of Bingen (1098-1179) and Karl Kraus (1874-1936). Although questionable exegetically, an interpretation in terms of church and world history was much favored. Martin → Luther (1483-1546), for example, in his preface to Revelation found in it an attack on the Roman church.

The work also exerted a great influence on → Christian art, especially in depicting the majesty of God (chaps. 4–5), the saints (5; 7), the four horsemen, war, and distress (6:1-8), the woman (12:1-2), and world judgment (20; → Iconography). Important cycles in book illustration have come from Albrecht Dürer (1471-1528), Jean Duvet (1485-1561), and moderns like Herbert Böckl (1894-1966); see also the Bamberg Apocalypse (ca. 1020). Although citations in music and film have reduced the theological points, they have turned the Book of Revelation into an object of modern popular culture.

→ Apocalyptic; New Testament Era, History of; Theology of History

Bibliography: Commentaries: D. E. Aune (WBC 52A-C; 3 vols.; Dallas, 1997-98) • G. K. Beale (NIGTC; Grand Rapids, 1999) • W. Bousset (KEK; 6th ed.; Göttingen, 1906; repr., 1966) • R. H. Mounce (NICNT; rev. ed.; Grand Rapids, 1998) • U. B. Müller (ÖTBK; Gütersloh, 1984) • P. Prigent, *Commentary on the Apocalypse of St. John* (Tübingen, 2001) • J. Roloff (ContCom; Minneapolis, 1993) • C. Rowland (EpCom; London, 1993) • E. Schüssler Fiorenza (ProcC; Minneapolis, 1991) • L. L. Thompson (AbNTC; Nashville, 1998).

Other works: M. Barker, *The Revelation of Jesus Christ: Which God Gave to Him . . .* (Edinburgh, 2000) • R. Bauckham, *The Climax of Prophecy: Studies on the Book of Revelation* (Edinburgh, 1993); idem, *The Theology of the Book of Revelation* (Cambridge, 1993) • O. Böcher, *Die Johannesapokalypse* (4th ed.; Darmstadt, 1998) • A. Y. Collins, *The Combat Myth in the Book of Revelation* (Missoula, Mont., 1976) • J. M. Court, *The Book of Revelation and the Johannine Apocalyptic Tradition* (Sheffield, 2000) • S. J. Friesen, *Imperial Cults and the Apocalypse of John: Reading Revelation in the Ruins* (Oxford, 2001) • T. Holtz, *Die Christologie der Apokalypse des Johannes* (Berlin, 1962) • J. N. Kraybill, *Imperial Cult and Commerce in John's Apocalypse* (Sheffield, 1996) • G. Kretschmar, *Die Offenbarung des Johannes. Die Geschichte ihrer Auslegung im I. Jahrhundert* (Stuttgart, 1985) • F. Lücke, *Versuch einer vollständigen Einleitung in die Offenbarung des Johannes und in die apokalyptische Litteratur überhaupt* (2 vols.; 2d ed.; Bonn, 1848-52) • G. Maier, *Die Johannesoffenbarung und die Kirche* (Tübingen, 1981) • J. W. Marshall, *Parables of War: Reading John's Jewish Apocalypse* (Waterloo, Ont., 2001) • F. van der Meer, *Die Visionen des Johannes in der europäischen Kunst* (Freiburg, 1978) • S. Moyise, ed., *Studies in the Book of Revelation* (Edinburgh, 2001) • E. Schüssler Fiorenza, *The Book of Revelation: Justice and Judgement* (Philadelphia, 1984) • T. B. Slater, *Christ and Community: A Socio-historical Study of the Christology of Revelation* (Sheffield, 1999) • L. T. Stuckenbruck, *Angel Veneration and Christology: A Study in Early Judaism and in the Christology of the Apocalypse of John* (Tübingen, 1995) • J.-W. Taeger, "Offenbarung 1.1-3. Johanneische Autorisierung einer Aufklärungsschrift," *NTS* 49 (2003) 176-92 • L. L. Thompson, *The Book of Revelation: Apocalypse and Empire* (New York, 1990) • R. Zimmermann, *Geschlechtermetaphorik und Gottesverhältnis. Traditionsgeschichte und Theologie eines Bildfeldes in Urchristentum und antiker Umwelt* (Tübingen, 2001).

Martin Karrer

Reverence

In Gk. *aidōs* and Lat. *reverentia,* reverence is regard, respect, veneration, awe. It signifies being gripped by the revered object and restrained by awe. The original idea is that of astonishment and stillness in the presence of the divine. It is a basic religious experience, the substratum of all such experience (F. Heiler). It is also the basis of the moral consciousness (E. Brunner). It rests on direct feeling (not a natural disposition) but is also a historically conditioned attitude. It forms part of our humanity (→ Anthropology) and is also one of the foundations of → culture. As an awareness of → life in its religious and cosmic connections, it integrates emotion and will, and constitutes a → virtue.

In the Bible reverence for God — the fear of the Lord — is a reflection of the perception of God and the beginning of knowledge, wisdom, and → sanctification. It protects faith against false security but is overcome in trust in God's → love. Christian reverence involves worship of God (expressed succinctly in *soli Deo gloria,* "to God alone be the glory"), is related to → devotion, and finds expression in → prayer (→ Lord's Prayer). It leads to a recognition of → human dignity and a valuing of all life as God's → creation. It also entails a respectful relation to → nature and the symbols of faith. Part of it is tension between approach and distance, but it contains no ambivalence. The sense of distance bound up with the limitation of one's own experience rules out the arrogance that appropriates to oneself the honor that is due to God. Without a relationship to God and to a being that is felt to be worthwhile, → fear can come (as wrong fear of God, of other people, of → death, and of important or terrible events).

Reverence should not be exploited as a means of repression or of preserving the status quo. But we must also reject the rationalistic Enlightenment demand to eliminate (in science and in the way we seek to influence human behavior) all awe or reservation before the intimate sphere in human life, as we similarly must reject its popularization (→ Mass Media) and a ruthless destruction of the rights of nonhuman creatures (→ Ecology). Reverence does not derive from a renunciation of knowledge. It is a principle of knowledge and enhances our understanding of reality. Only as the Logos impels us to reverence do we see reality's dimension of depth. Reverence is no bar to curiosity so long as it does not tempt us to destroy the inner distance to objects and therefore our inner peace. When medieval theology asked for a restriction of curiosity, it was not thinking of knowledge as such but of the mystery of → God. God is no mere object but reality, and faith discloses itself only in life and only to those who know they do not know (*docta ignorantia,* "learned ignorance").

J. W. Goethe (1749-1832), borrowing from the pseudo-Pythagorean *Golden Sayings,* distinguished reverence for what is over us, for what is like us, and for what is under us. From these three forms springs the supreme reverence for the self. The three also develop out of the latter, so that we achieve the highest of which we are capable (*Wilhelm Meisters Wanderjahre,* 2.1). The harmony of the three is the basis of true religion. As Goethe saw it, education in reverence is the task of all authentic religion.

Faced with the impossibility of deriving a meaningful ethics from contemplation of the world, A. → Schweitzer (1875-1965) tried to base ethics on an inner obligation to life. He described reverence for life as a decisive motive for action rather than a passive mood. K. → Barth (1886-1968) and E. Brunner (1889-1966) criticized this mystical approach and taught the reverence for God's will and creation that is demanded in God's command. H. Jonas (1903-93) drew attention to the dangers in technological civilization (which he saw as an "initial negative") and demanded positively an ethics of → responsibility. We must relearn reverence and awe to protect humanity against the mistakes of → power.

→ Experience 2; Humility; Sacred and Profane

Bibliography: K. Barth, *CD* III/4 • J. Bentley, *Albert Schweitzer: The Enigma* (New York, 1992) • O. F. Bollnow, *Die Ehrfurcht* (2d ed.; Frankfurt, 1958) • E. Brunner, *The Divine Imperative* (Philadelphia, 1947; orig. pub., 1932) • R. Guardini, *The Virtues: On Forms of Moral Life* (Chicago, 1967) • H. Jonas, *The Imperative of Responsibility: In Search of an Ethics for the Technological Age* (Chicago, 1984) • M. Meyer and K. Bergel, *Reverence for Life: The Ethics of Albert Schweitzer for the Twenty-first Century* (Syracuse, N.Y., 2002) • H. A. Oberman, *Contra vanam curiositatem. Ein Kapitel der Theologie zwischen Seelenwinkel und Weltall* (Zurich, 1974) • M. Scheler, *Vom Umsturz der Werte* (5th ed.; Bern, 1972; orig. pub., 1919) • A. Schütze, *Von der dreifachen Ehrfurcht* (Stuttgart, 1973) • A. Schweitzer, *Civilization and Ethics* (3d ed.; London, 1946; orig. pub., 1924) • W. Trillhaas, *Ethik* (3d ed.; Berlin, 1970).

Bernhard Maurer

Revivals

1. Definition

The term "revivals" is a general one used to describe the movements of awakening that covered all the Protestant territories of Europe and North America in the 18th and 19th centuries. The term remains popular, especially in those parts of the Protestant world under American influence. Revivals are seen as counteracting Christian decline, both spiritual and social, and, by special evangelistic and organizational means (→ Evangelism), as renewing → church and → society on a biblical and reformative basis.

To portray revivals as a whole is very difficult. Quite apart from the lack of preparatory critical work, the movements cannot easily be distinguished from preceding, contemporary, and subsequent developments. Especially fluid are the boundaries with → Pietism, → Methodism, → Romanticism, → idealism, → restoration, and confessionalism, as well as with the → fellowship, → holiness, Pentecostal (→ Pentecostalism), and → charismatic movements. There are also regional distinctions, a special point being that the developments in the English-speaking lands differ both chronologically and materially from those on the European mainland. In these circumstances the use of the term "revivals" must be regarded as no more than a necessary historiographical device.

2. History

2.1. *North America*

When the highly educated Jonathan Edwards (1703-58) preached against a weakening of the traditional Calvinist doctrine of → justification in his church at Northampton, Massachusetts, it triggered an awakening. Beginning in 1734 and later receiving the help of the itinerant English preacher George Whitefield (1714-70), it spread across all the colonies that were under Reformed influence. In his assessment of the revivals Edwards took a very cautious view both of the human ability to turn to God and of his own part in these events. He found in revivals, rather, the work of the → Holy Spirit. Despite this skepticism, however, Edwards became a chief witness for the theory and practice of revival. This stirring, or First Great Awakening, may be seen as the correction of a development within → Calvinism; the Second Great Awakening (roughly 1790-1835) was directed to those who were outside the church in both urban and rural areas.

In contrast to Edwards, Charles Grandison Finney (1792-1875) abandoned traditional → Reformation positions and totally subordinated the content of his → preaching to the goal of → conversion. He accompanied his preaching with measures that would promote conversions: evangelistic weeks, public gatherings to discuss the problems of individual faith, the altar call, the mourners' bench ("anxious seat"), music, lay participation, and pastoral follow-up. With the introduction of these so-called new measures, Finney initiated the popular evangelism of modern times.

In the 1830s social problems also began to be tackled. There was an attack on → slavery and also on drunkenness (→ Substance Abuse), paralleling movements for abolition and temperance. The piety of American revivalism had a democratic and anti-intellectual trait that went hand-in-hand with a rationalizing of conversion and awakening, so that the legacy of the → Enlightenment was preserved rather than contested. The second half of the 19th century brought a new wave of awakenings that came to be associated with the name of Dwight L. Moody (1837-99), who worked especially among the → masses in the growing cities. Revivalism in North America continued into the 20th and 21st centuries through persons such as Billy Sunday (1863-1935) and Billy Graham (b. 1918).

The outbreak of Pentecostalism associated with the 1906 Azusa Street mission in Los Angeles represented a strong revival with mostly Methodist and Holiness origins. That revival shared many features with a mass popular movement in the Welsh churches during 1904-5 and with significant movements of renewal and church expansion that took place during the same years around Pyongyang, Korea, and the Mukti Mission of Pandita Ramabai (1858-1922) in India. In turn, the newer Pentecostal movements, which have spread throughout the world, have been active promoters of revival, not least in the United States. Throughout the 20th century and into the 21st, many evangelical and fundamentalist churches in America continue to feature revival emphases, especially in Baptist and independent Bible churches, where regular revival meetings are sometimes scheduled on an annual basis. During the last century revivals also occurred regularly at conservative Protestant colleges and, from the 1960s, in some Catholic institutions associated with the charismatic movement.

With Graham, the descriptive word "revival" gave way to "crusade." With Graham, moreover, a highly sophisticated use of modern → mass media communication technology has become instrumental in evangelistic work. Furthermore, it is to be acknowledged that American "revival movements" have in a clear sense merged with other predominantly conservative theological, ecclesiastical, sociological, and political movements to give shape to many expressions of an increasingly strong and diverse American → evangelical movement. The theological and, especially, sociopolitical significance of this movement is increasingly important in American public and private life. It must also be noted that, in the North American context, revival movements have played a significant and abiding role in the development of both Afro-American and Pentecostal churches. The judgment of W. W. Sweet, who had a section "Revivalism on the Wane" in his *Revivalism in America* (1944), was clearly in error.

2.2. *Great Britain*

Howel Harris (1714-73) and Daniel Rowland (1713-90) started evangelistic work in Wales in the 1730s. The Anglican theologian John Wesley (1703-91) had his "Aldersgate experience" in May 1738, which gave him his preaching commission. Wesley knew both the life and teaching of the → Moravians of Herrnhut and the writings of Jonathan Edwards. In a setting of rational Christianity and social inaction, he linked his message of justification by faith to a summons to → love of → neighbor. With his brother Charles (1707-88) and George Whitefield,

John Wesley preached tirelessly throughout Great Britain. His aim was to renew the Church of England from within (→ Anglican Communion), but a break became inevitable in 1795.

In various parts of England Anglican ministers like William Grimshaw (1708-63), John William Fletcher (1729-85), John Newton (1725-1807), and William Romaine (1714-95), in spite of initial opposition, experienced revivals in their parishes that gave rise to a powerful Evangelical movement within the church. Various groups came together to form the London Missionary Society in 1795, the first interdenominational missionary society, and then to set up the Religious Tract Society (1799) and the British and Foreign Bible Society (1804), each of which had an impact on the European mainland.

Revivals affected the highest ranks of society (e.g., the so-called Clapham Sect; → Lay Movements 1.4), which made possible the attempt to remedy social ills by legislative action. William Wilberforce (1759-1833) set an example with his campaign to abolish the slave trade (1807) and then → slavery itself (1833), and others tackled a whole series of other problems, especially Lord Ashley (1801-85, the Seventh Earl of Shaftesbury), with his labor for factory workers, the mentally ill, those in the garment industry, and boy chimney sweeps. From the middle of the 19th century, American visitors brought a new impulse — Finney with his new measures of revivalism (1849-51, 1859-60), and Moody with campaigns in industrial cities (1873-75, 1881-84). In both England and Wales, however, revivals still drew their main strength from the churches and parachurch movements.

In Scotland → Methodism made little headway, in view of the area's strong Calvinist orientation. The opposition of the laymen Robert (1764-1842) and James Alexander (1768-1851) Haldane to the established church led in 1799 to the founding of a Congregationalist church in Edinburgh (→ Congregationalism). The roots of this movement lay in commonsense philosophy, as well as in the Calvinist traditions. Rationalist tendencies (e.g., in extended proofs of the truth of the Christian revelation) thus combined with revivalist piety.

The same trends appeared also in North America, which in turn influenced Finney. Since Robert Haldane traveled extensively in Europe, it is not surprising that we find a similar combination in other Calvinist churches, for example, Geneva and France, as well as North America (→ Restoration Movements 1.2).

The Haldanes prepared the ground for the work of Thomas Chalmers (1780-1847) in Glasgow, who was converted in 1811 under the influence of Wilberforce and who was well known not only as a university professor but also for his parish organization. He tried to meet the needs of the city's poor by a strict system of self-help and parish support based on a rural model (→ Poverty). All social, pastoral, and educational tasks were to be discharged under the church's leadership. Though this program of re-Christianizing the masses was not a total success, it influenced similar efforts elsewhere, for example, in Germany.

Attaining a leading position in the church, Chalmers opposed the growing interference of the state through the patronage system in Scotland, and this stance led to the Disruption of 1843, when Chalmers and over 470 (out of 1,203) ministers left the Established Church of Scotland and founded the Free Church of Scotland (→ Free Church). With its ecumenical orientation, this church had a hand in founding the Evangelical Alliance in 1846 (→ World Evangelical Alliance). As in England and Wales, and also Northern Ireland, so in Scotland revivals marked the middle of the 19th century, especially in the Highlands, and strong evangelistic work continued into the 20th century.

2.3. *Switzerland and France*

An awakening in Geneva was made possible by the survival of Moravian traditions. A group of younger theologians led by Ami Bost (1790-1874) criticized the rationalistically inclined Reformed church, accusing it of denying its heritage. A visit by Robert Haldane resulted in the founding of free congregations after 1817. The Evangelical Society of Geneva, founded in 1831, took up the work of evangelization and → education. To produce trained leaders, a theological school was set up within the Evangelical Society in 1832 (→ Theological Education), at which Jean-Henri Merle d'Aubigné (1794-1872) and Louis Gaussen (1790-1863) taught. The separated churches joined together in the Église Libre in 1849. This revival in Geneva affected the neighboring cantons of Vaud (where a free church was founded in 1845) and Bern (where an evangelical society was established in 1831). Through the evangelizing work of César Malan (1787-1864), the revival also spread to France, Belgium, Netherlands, and Great Britain.

Adolphe Monod (1802-56) inspired the French awakening. He had studied in Geneva and experienced conversion in 1827 under the influence of the Scot Thomas Erskine (1788-1870). Called the same year to Lyons as a pastor, Monod advocated a Christian lifestyle and a return to biblical and Christocentric preaching. With some hesitation he founded an evangelical congregation in 1832 but maintained links to the national church as a professor in Montauban (from 1836) and Paris (from 1847). While he focused on a preaching ministry, his brother Frédéric Monod (1794-1863) united the separated French congregations into a single body on an orthodox Reformation basis (1849). Revivals in northern France, especially in Paris, were under direct British influence, for immediately after the Napoleonic era stimulation came from Britain to set up tract, Bible, and missionary societies (1818-22). In the French-speaking areas there was less involvement in social issues, the main thrust being toward a restoration of traditional Calvinist positions.

2.4. *Netherlands*

Behind the Dutch awakening stands the work of the Dutch branches of the German Christian Association (Deutsche Christentumsgesellschaft), founded in Basel in 1780, and the Netherlands Missionary Society (Nederlandsch Zendelingsgenootschap), founded in 1797 on the English model. From around 1820 we may note three main centers of revival. Under the influence of the Romantic and patriotic poet and historian Willem Bilderdijk (1759-1831), the very gifted Isaäc da Costa (1798-1860) was converted from → Judaism to Christianity. He confronted the thinking of the Enlightenment in his *Bezwaren tegen de geest der eeuw* (Objections against the spirit of the century, 1823), a much-noted treatise that challenged the spirit of the times. Through → Bible study groups in Amsterdam and popular writings, he then proclaimed a personal Christianity, idealizing the country's Calvinist past. An expectation of Christ's return (→ Parousia) played an important role in his work.

Guillaume Groen van Prinsterer (1801-76), who, under the influence of Merle d'Aubigné, took an active role in politics, shared da Costa's basic antirevolutionary outlook and took practical steps to establish Reformation and Calvinist principles in state, church, school, and society. He stood at the beginning of the movement toward a Christian party in the Netherlands.

Otto Gerhard Heldring (1804-76), a friend of da Costa and Groen, devoted himself to social work, such as the battle against intemperance and → prostitution. He took the lead in setting up the first Dutch deaconess house (1842) after the model of Kaiserswerth (→ Religious Orders and Congregations 4.1). This awakening set the climate for groups committed to the Calvinist confession to leave the established church in order to set up independent churches. First was the Afscheiding (lit. "separation"), in 1834; then, in 1886, came the Doleantie ("grieving"; → Netherlands 2.1). In 1892 some 700 of these separated congregations united as the Gereformeerde Kerken in Nederland.

2.5. *Germany*

Toward the end of the 18th century various individuals opposed rationalistic trends in Germany and, partly under the influence of older Pietist traditions, sought to uphold the biblical and Reformation heritage. Johann Georg Hamann (1730-88), Johann Heinrich Jung-Stilling (1740-1817), Johann Friedrich Oberlin (1740-1826), and Johann Kaspar Lavater (1741-1801) were all able to form loose groups of supporters.

The → diaspora work of the Moravians formed a supraregional network to gather believers together, as did the work of the German Christian Association, preparing the way for true revivals both spiritually and organizationally. A decisive push came from England not to retreat in face of the movement away from the church but to contest it. When Karl Friedrich Adolf Steinkopf (1773-1859), one-time secretary of the German Christian Association, visited the German Savoy congregation in London in 1801, he became an intermediary between British and German revival movements. Encouraged by the groups in England, he used his former contacts with members and friends of the German Christian Association to set up a tract society (1802), the Württemberg Bible Institute (1812), the Basel Mission (1815), and various → inner mission movements. We have here a spectrum of organized Christian involvement such as the older Pietism never knew. These activities mark the beginning of a blossoming of Christian → societies and organizations, though the regionally splintered nature of German Protestantism meant that they seldom covered any wide area. In Germany, then, the revivals were strongly marked by regional differences.

The Bavaria revival had an expressly ecumenical character, for Roman Catholic clergy like Johann Michael Sailer (1751-1832) and Martin Boos (1762-1825) kindled awakenings that, from 1806, spread into Upper Austria. The Erlangen theologian Christian Krafft (1784-1845) worked among students and stressed allegiance to Scripture and the Reformation → confessions. Although he was Reformed, Krafft helped in this way to create a strongly Lutheran tradition at Erlangen.

In Württemberg we see best the continuity between the older Pietism and revivalism. There the varied manifestations of revivals range from activities in the German Christian Association and the Basel Mission, by way of fruitful institutional work (e.g., by Christian Heinrich Zeller [1779-1860] in

Beuggen) and the core Lutheran preaching of Ludwig Hofacker (1798-1828), to eschatologically oriented groups that decided to emigrate to Russia and America. Although Pietism took a new lease on life in Württemberg in the first half of the 19th century, revivals made hardly any impact at all on Baden or Hesse.

Stimulation from Netherlands and Britain, however, influenced a Reformed type of revival in the Lower Rhine and from there in Siegerland, Wuppertal, and Minden-Ravensberg. Lay preachers like Tillman Siebel (1804-75) played the main part in Siegerland. In Wuppertal, then in process of industrialization, two outstanding Reformed theologians were at work: Gottfried Daniel Krummacher (1774-1837) and Hermann Friedrich Kohlbrügge (1803-75). The revivalist spiritual leader in Minden-Ravensberg, Johann Heinrich Volkening (1796-1877), was deeply rooted in the piety of the Moravians. In the territorial church he implemented things learned from them.

Except for Hamburg, the German cities were behind those of Britain in responding to the pressures of urbanization (→ City). The revivalist Johann Wilhelm Rautenberg (1791-1865) set up a → Sunday school in Hamburg in 1825. Then, under his influence, Johann Hinrich Wichern (1808-81) opened the Rauhe Haus (1833), which channeled his boundless practical and theoretical energies in helping the → Inner Mission. Adalbert Graf von der Recke-Volmerstein (1791-1878) had already founded an orphanage in Düsseltal in 1822. Also in Hamburg Amalie Sieveking (1794-1859) founded the Weiblicher Verein für Armen- und Krankenpflege (Female association for the care of the poor and sick) in 1832. Across the border of Schleswig-Holstein, Claus Harms (1778-1855) preached strongly against → rationalism, opposed the Prussian → Union, and thus prepared the way for neo-Lutheranism (→ Lutheranism).

In Berlin Johann Evangelista Gossner (1773-1858) engaged in all the activities typical of revival. Along with preaching and writing, he organized diaconal work (→ Diakonia) and overseas → mission (→ German Missions). The socially involved Baron Hans Ernst von Kottwitz (1757-1843), with his revivalist lay theology, attracted supporters in the palace and also among church people and theological students. Pomerania was greatly influenced from Berlin. Adolf von Thadden (1796-1882) helped to gather a group of pastors open to revival that met regularly after 1829. Revival took a Lutheran turn also in Saxony, where the Dresden (later Leipzig) Mission was founded in 1836, and in Silesia, where the Old Lutheran Free Church was founded under the leadership of Gottfried Scheibel (1783-1843), Henrik Steffens (1773-1845), and Eduard Huschke (1801-86). This church maintained contact with revival circles in Berlin.

The changes of the post-Napoleonic period formed the setting for revival in Germany. Though there were various influences, it moved ecclesiastically and theologically in the direction of confessionalism, and politically and socially in that of → conservatism. Unlike its broad effect in Britain and the United States, this orientation limited its impact in Germany, steering it mainly into the territorial churches. Yet it expressed elements and motifs that later found more general recognition, especially the concern for mission, the higher regard for the laity and lower classes, and an awareness that the work of the → church of Jesus Christ cannot be restricted to what the → congregation does when it gathers for → worship.

2.6. *The Nordic Lands*

In Sweden influences from British and Moravian traditions led to the founding of a → Bible society (1815) and a missionary society (1835). The Stockholm city missioner Carl Olof Rosenius (1816-68) directed revivals into confessional Lutheran channels, though holding somewhat aloof from the established church. In Norway the influential lay preacher Hans Nielsen Hauge (1771-1824) tried deliberately to work within the established church, though he encountered a good deal of official opposition. In Denmark the movement of reform and renewal launched by Nikolas Frederik Severin Grundtvig (1783-1872) aimed at the population as a whole in an indissoluble interrelating of church and people (→ Denmark 1.2.3). In Finland revivals developed in two ways as a movement of repentance within the church (→ Penitence). The itinerant preacher Paavo Ruotsalainen (1777-1852) put judgment in the forefront, but Henrik Renquist (1789-1866) stressed prayer, from which alone salvation can come.

→ Devotional Literature; Theology of Revivals

Bibliography: E. Beyreuther, *Die Erweckungsbewegung* (2d ed.; Göttingen, 1977) • E. L. Blumhofer and R. Balmer, eds., *Modern Christian Revivals* (Urbana, Ill., 1993) • R. Carwardine, *Transatlantic Revivalism: Popular Evangelicalism in Britain and America, 1790-1865* (Westport, Conn., 1978) • M. Crawford, *Seasons of Grace: New England's Revival Tradition in Its British Context* (New York, 1991) • U. Gäbler, *"Auferstehungszeit." Erweckungsprediger des 19. Jahrhunderts* (Munich, 1991) • R. T. Jones, *Faith and the Crisis of a Nation:*

Wales, 1890-1914 (ed. R. Pope; Cardiff, 2004) • M. J. McClymond, ed., *Embodying the Spirit: New Perspectives on North American Revivalism* (Baltimore, 2004); idem, ed., *Encyclopedia of Religious Revivals in America* (Westport, Conn., 2005) • W. G. McLoughlin, *Modern Revivalism: Charles Grandison Finney to Billy Graham* (New York, 1959); idem, *Revivals, Awakenings, and Reform* (Chicago, 1978) • M. A. Noll, *The Rise of Evangelicalism: The Age of Edwards, Whitefield, and the Wesleys* (Downers Grove, Ill., 2003) • T. L. Smith, *Revivalism and Social Reform in Mid-Nineteenth-Century America* (Nashville, 1957) • W. W. Sweet, *Revivalism in America: Its Origin, Growth, and Decline* (New York, 1944).

Ulrich Gäbler

Revolution

1. Term
2. Historical Development
3. Theories
   3.1. Socialist Theory
   3.2. Various Theories and Controversies
4. Contradictory Twentieth-Century Revolutions
5. The Church and Revolution

1. Term

"Revolution" refers to basic upheaval, radical break, profound change, and new beginning. We must differentiate between a narrower and a broader use. "Revolution" might signify a rapid overthrow by → force, a revolt after the manner of civil war, the overturning of social, economic, and political relations. Or it might denote a longer process of structural change or development as in the case of the industrial or technological revolution. As an overextended slogan (boldly employed even in commercial advertising), the term has become a catchphrase for innovation and developmental upheaval in the larger sense.

"Revolution" is a specifically modern term that has been brought into use to give legitimacy to comprehensive changes in the general interest (R. Koselleck). Such changes are therefore distinguished from revolts, rebellions, riots, or civil wars. In distinction from revolution in the sense of a return to the traditional, a modern defense of revolution is that it ushers in a new age, the kind of change that forms the basis of a new world order.

2. Historical Development

2.1. The medieval order found no place for the idea of basic upheaval, either intellectually or from a practical standpoint (→ Middle Ages). If the existing order owes its validity to its being part of a comprehensive divine order, then phenomena like revolt and rebellion naturally seem to be due to self-seeking, personally motivated opposition to the forces of order. They are thus to be rejected as ungodly and illegitimate. A right of → resistance exists only for the sake of restoring order when wicked people have disrupted it. This right is a constitutional means of maintaining order, not destroying it.

Nevertheless, the Middle Ages did have some pioneering sponsors of ideas of revolutionary renewal. We find essays in this direction in the chiliastic → eschatology of Joachim of Fiore (ca. 1135-1202; → Millenarianism) and the spiritualist-ascetic mass movements of the 14th and 15th centuries (→ Anabaptists).

2.2. Equating the → Reformation with, for example, M. → Luther's (1483-1546; → Luther's Theology) establishment of a church imposes limits on the expectations that, in the mood of the age, were linked to *reformatio* as renewal of the Christian community. The concept of reformation meant upheavals and movements of change coupled with revolutionary end-time hopes. At the time of the Reformation, then, popular "orgiastic revolutionary thinking" could develop (K. Griewank). In the Peasants' War, which T. → Müntzer (ca. 1489-1525) supported in opposition to Luther, we find elements of the modern concept of revolution: a mass movement, overthrow of the social and political systems, and a basis and validity in an idea (appeal to the original → authority of divine → revelation; → Reformers). Nevertheless, expectation of divine intervention to reestablish order (after the medieval manner of thinking) meant that there was no precise goal.

2.3. Just as a sense of revolution emerged only slowly, so the concept only gradually assumed its modern signification. As originally used in astronomy, "revolution" had to do with the movement of the heavenly bodies; in this area it meant turning around or turning back. Only in the 17th and 18th centuries did the term increasingly come into political use for constitutional or governmental change. As an "astropolitical" term (E. Rosenstock-Huessy) the word contained the thought of regularity. In keeping was the understanding of revolution as the restoration of legitimate order. We find this idea in the so-called Glorious Revolution in England in 1688, the event that led to the applying of the term to events in political history. For here the deposing of James II in favor of William and Mary, accomplished with a minimum of bloodshed, reestablished the constitutional order that the monarch had been seeking to overturn.

The 18th-century American Revolution might be understood to a large extent along similar lines. It certainly involved a radical break by force, the birth of a new republican nation, and many new and progressive ideas, but fundamentally it was a struggle for traditional rights that George III was increasingly overriding. In this case something new emerged out of the reestablishing of the old, so that we have here a transitional usage.

2.4. The French Revolution, which has been called "the zenith of revolutions" (Rosenstock-Huessy), was the first revolution to involve the self-understanding that revolution means a break with the traditional order and the establishment of a new one. The participants saw themselves as emphatically revolutionary. At first there was a measure of going back with the summoning of the Three Estates, but by September 22, 1792, the decision to introduce a new calendar expressed a sense of a completely new beginning in world history, with the revolution as an actualizing of the rational → natural law of the → Enlightenment (J. Habermas) and of human and civil → rights.

We find the new meaning of the term in the famous exchange between Louis XVI (1774-92) and Count Liancourt (1747-1827):

> Louis: *C'est une révolte?* (Is this a revolt?)
> Liancourt: *Non, sire, c'est une révolution.* (No, sire, it's a revolution.)

This usage shows that validity was now being given to the event as a necessary political upheaval, as lasting change in distinction from fruitless revolts, as something that was inevitable. The course of the French Revolution gave the term its modern sense. Thus the revolutionary masses took part (the storming of the Bastille), force was used as a means, and events moved at a quickening pace. We also find the Romantic aspects, the enthusiasm of revolution that believes it can resolve all contradictions, storm the center of power, and create new totalities (→ Romanticism).

2.5. As concerns the concept and the theoretical understanding, the most important consequence was the linking of revolution to → progress as advance to a higher stage of human society in the sense of universally progressive → emancipation. In this sense "revolution" became a "collective singular" (Koselleck) and, as such, a principle of world history. From this standpoint the term functioned as a term that confers validity and offers self-understanding. It means the achievement of "natural" rights in a supratemporal order. It entails the sovereignty of the people and the nation (M. Kossock) and therefore self-mastery.

3. Theories

This self-understanding of revolution in the modern sense initiated reflection on the event and attempts to come to terms with it. Theories of revolution thus became a factor in revolutions.

3.1. *Socialist Theory*

3.1.1. The Marxist theory of revolution involves the two components of an overthrow of power structures by force and long-term structural change. Revolution is a qualitative leap in historical economic development. The proletarian revolution envisioned by K. → Marx (1818-83) would be in the common interest, with the vast majority achieving a classless society no longer under the influence of minority interests. Revolution here is both social and political. In opposition to the ruling class it overturns economically based power relations. The subject of this revolution is the proletariat, a term linked to ideas of emancipation and progress, with an appeal to history.

Yet on this view the new social order is not free or unconnected. It is the result of a process of economic development presupposed in the Marxist philosophy of history. It is thus formed in the womb of the old society. The increasing contradiction between the forces of production and the relations of production, between social production and private ownership, is what will lead to the revolutionary reversal. Conditions must become ripe for revolution. The industrial revolution must reach a high stage, the world economy must develop, and the subject of revolution must be present, namely, the proletariat, which with the advanced concentration of capital comes into confrontation with the small class of private owners. There must be an economic crisis, though some Marxists disagree (→ Marxism).

3.1.2. Is revolution the result of human action, the → freedom to create something new, or is it simply the outworking of a quasi-law of natural development that is independent of human action, will, and awareness? Analysis of the material basis of revolutions in distinction from the → voluntarism of early socialists and utopian anarchists threatens to fall victim to historical determinism. On this view the revolutionary is simply a mindless agent. P. L. Lafargue (1842-1911) expressed this fatalistic understanding when he saw in Communists no more than spokespersons for economic phenomena. Clearly we have here an increasing departure from

Revolution

the idea of revolution as a means of social change such as we find also in discussions of reform.

Reformists like E. Bernstein desired a gradual and peaceful transition to socialism, not a dramatic upheaval. This change would come about by democratic participation and the implementation of reforms.

3.1.3. In contrast, V. I. Lenin (1870-1924), leader of the Russian Revolution of 1917, insisted on the need for a revolutionary dissolving of the → state and a seizure of power by the proletariat. Revolution needs resolute action by revolutionaries. The proletariat will not develop a revolutionary sense merely as the mechanical product of its situation as a class. This avant-garde model of revolution involved mass mobilization under the central leadership of a Communist party that would replace the trade-unionist idea of the proletariat with a revolutionary idea. As an advanced class the proletariat would make an alliance with the peasants, who, in the industrially less developed relations of Czarist Russia, formed the majority of the population. The Russian Revolution ran counter, then, to a central Marxist theorem, namely, the need for advanced industrial development.

3.1.4. The 1949 Chinese Revolution also faced a feudal society with a backward peasantry. Mao Zedong (1893-1976) thus developed the theory of the division of the world into rich and poor countries, so that the peasant masses of the Third World (→ Dependence) rather than the metropolitan industrial workers were destined to be the true subjects of revolution. This theory was the basis of the influence of Maoism outside of China and his role in Third World revolutionary movements. Determinative in these revolutions were anticolonial strivings for national independence and social revolution. Western theoreticians spoke in this regard of "revolutions of development."

3.1.5. When the antiauthoritarian New Left (ca. 1968) used the term "revolution," it laid more stress on social and cultural change, the need for self-determination and a new sensitivity as both the presupposition and the goal. These needs are allegedly material, ethical, and rational. H. Marcuse (1898-1979) thought that marginal groups outside society could best escape the pressure to conform and thus had the most revolutionary potential.

3.2. *Various Theories and Controversies*

3.2.1. In distinction from those who found here the classic features of revolution, H. Arendt (1906-75) criticized the prejudiced assertion — one emerging with the French Revolution — that the social question is the true core of all revolutions. She maintained that pushing this aspect to the fore destroyed the political side and freedom. Here the concept of necessity as an unchanging organic life process allegedly began to dominate → politics. Herewith both the concept and the goal of revolution changed. The happiness of the people rather than freedom became the goal. The consequence was that this necessity, namely, the urgent distress of the people, unleashed the terror and destroyed the revolution. Arendt favorably compared the American Revolution to the French as a revolution of freedom and as a revolution with a political goal.

3.2.2. E. Rosenstock-Huessy (1888-1973) found in revolutions the principle of movement that gives meaning to history. He defined a revolution as a total upheaval that seeks once and for all to bring a new principle into world history, as a crisis, a process of fusion that puts all the ideas, characteristics, and customs of the people in a white heat. He could thus speak of new people being fashioned by revolution. V. Pareto (1848-1923) had a more sober definition. Revolution for him was the ongoing replacing of the elite. Whether revolutionary change was necessarily tied to the use of force is constantly under discussion.

4. Contradictory Twentieth-Century Revolutions

4.1. The debatable term "conservative revolution" covers many intellectual and political trends, groups, and movements that helped to make up the political climate of the Weimar Republic and that together prepared the ground for National Socialism (→ Fascism). As they themselves saw it, the true point here was counterrevolutionary resistance to the ideas of 1789. Romantically and antirationalistically (→ Irrationalism), they opposed → modernity as a whole: the → Enlightenment, the principles of → equality and → reason, the idea of progress, and that of emancipation. They propagated the idea of human and cosmic immutability and recurrence.

The opposition to the idea of progress shows how paradoxical it was to link → conservatism and revolution. Conservative revolution meant being both conservative and yet also revolutionary in fighting against the status quo that was influenced by ideas of progress and emancipation. Revolution in this sense was a "bloodletting," a cutting away of growths that are a hindrance to life, the shattering of a restrictive form (A. Mohler). In this regard force and conflict assume metaphysical significance (→ Metaphysics) and have a value of their own.

4.2. National Socialism used for itself such terms as "uprising," "awakening," and "resurrection," but it could also call itself a national revolution, a people's revolution, conservative and reactionary, not conforming to any one theory of revolution, inherently contradictory, yet carrying the emotional appeal of the slogan "revolution of the people" (H. Freyer). In discussions of this view, which applies equally to other fascist coups d'état, the polemical sense of the term as an "ideological party slogan" (Koselleck) is plain. If we define revolution as an emancipatory overthrow of existing socioeconomic power relations *(Lexikon des Sozialismus)*, then there must be an orientation to the values of freedom and equality, and we cannot call fascist seizures of power revolutions.

E. Nolte, for example, tries to avoid this normative meaning by speaking of an empirical revolution, which as a profound change could include National Socialism and Italian fascism, along with the Russian Revolution. Beginning with the basic industrial revolution, which underlies all political movements in the 20th century, he could group all these different phenomena together as revolutions, as totalitarian attempts to deal with the social tensions resulting from the basic revolution.

K. D. Bracher called the 20th century the age of contradictory revolutions. We cannot use for its upheavals the classic definition of revolution oriented to the French Revolution. Under the concept of totalitarianism we can see in revolutions of both the Left and the Right new forms of seizing power.

4.3. It may be questioned whether we are right to use the term "revolution" for a modern phenomenon like the so-called Islamic Revolution (→ Islam). The 1979 revolution in Iran undoubtedly meant basic social, political, and cultural change. But as a restoration of older theocratic → traditions, this revolution did nothing progressive or new. At first it did overthrow the shah's regime with the help of the overwhelming mass of the people and was thus a political and social, not just a religious and fundamentalist, revolution (→ Fundamentalism). But then it set up an Islamic → theocracy.

Modern fundamentalist movements give evidence of the conflict between tradition and modernization. Thus the Islamic Revolution opposes Western values and Western models of history and progress.

4.4. The question is still open whether we should use the term "revolution" for the so-called peaceful revolution that came to Eastern Europe and resulted in the disintegration of the → Soviet Union. Was not this simply an economic collapse, an implosion independent of human action? Habermas refers to it as a "catch-up" revolution in which democratic civil rights were implemented.

The French historian of revolutions F. Furet finds in this collapse implications for our understanding of revolution and of history as a whole. For him the breaking apart of the USSR was the end of a cycle during which the French Revolution was cultivated as the privileged form of historical change. The end of revolutions involves an "amputation" of our understanding of the world because, along with revolutions, history with a capital *H*, namely, the secularized form of the religious concept of → salvation, is now also dead.

5. The Church and Revolution

5.1. The position of J. von Stahl (1802-61), a 19th-century counterrevolutionary theoretician, exemplifies the understanding of the → church as a conservative and antirevolutionary force. He saw in the French Revolution the extreme antithesis of Christianity. His systematic understanding made him view revolution as the basing of the whole public order on human will rather than on divine ordinance and governance. It was thus an impermissible emancipation of human beings, a destruction of the divinely ordained order.

This view underlies the largely antirevolutionary stance of the Protestant churches, as well as of the → Roman Catholic Church. It held sway in Germany up to the Weimar Republic and partly explains the official church response to National Socialism, which ranged from open support to passive acceptance. The → Darmstadt Declaration of the → Confessing Church reflects this experience when it states, "We have denied the right of revolution but tolerated and welcomed the development of absolute dictatorship."

5.2. On the basis of such insights some in the churches now take a different view of revolution. Against the background of the social situation and the partly revolutionary conditions in developing countries that increasingly confront Roman Catholics in particular, the 1960s initiated discussion of a → theology of revolution (R. Shaull) or the necessity of a Christian ethics of change.

→ Capitalism; Democracy; Marxism and Christianity; Philosophy of History; Political Theology; Social Ethics; Social Movements; Socialism

Bibliography: H. Arendt, *On Revolution* (New York, 1963) • J. Baechler, *Revolution* (New York, 1978) • C. Brinton, *The Anatomy of Revolution* (rev. ed., New York, 1965; orig. pub., 1938) • C. Freeman and F. Louçã, *As Time Goes By: From the Industrial Revolutions to the Information Revolution* (Oxford, 2001) • F. Furet, *The Passing of an Illusion: The Idea of Commu-*

nism in the Twentieth Century (Chicago, 1999) • F. Furet and E. Nolte, *Fascism and Communism* (Lincoln, Nebr., 2001) • J. P. Greene, *Understanding the American Revolution: Issues and Actors* (Charlottesville, Va., 1995) • K. Griewank, *Der neuzeitliche Revolutionsbegriff* (3d ed.; Frankfurt, 1992; orig. pub., 1955) • R. Koselleck, "How European Was the Revolution of 1848/49?" *1848–a European Revolution? International Ideas and National Memories of 1848* (ed. A. Körner; New York, 2000) 209-22; idem, "Revolution," *GGB* 5.653-788 • A. Mohler, *Die konservative Revolution in Deutschland, 1918-1932* (5th ed.; Graz, 1999; orig. pub., 1950) • R. H. T. O'Kane, *Paths to Democracy: Revolution and Totalitarianism* (London, 2004) • E. Rosenstock-Huessy, *Die europäischen Revolutionen und der Charakter der Nationen* (3d ed.; Stuttgart, 1961); idem, *Out of Revolution: Autobiography of Western Man* (New York, 1938) • T. Skocpol, *States and Social Revolutions: A Comparative Analysis of France, Russia, and China* (Cambridge, 1979).

Urs Jaeggi and Rahel Jaeggi

Rhetoric

1. History of the Rhetoric and the Bible

1.1. *History of Rhetoric*

Corax of Sicily is credited with having conceptualized and systematized rhetoric in 476 B.C. Its introduction to Greece is attributed to Tisias, a student of Corax. Gorgias, an ambassador from Sicily, is thought to have presented rhetoric to Athens in 427 B.C. and to have stayed and founded a school of rhetoric. Rhetoric was further systematized quickly in response to the judicial and political needs of democratic society in Greece. At this time the Sophists added rhetoric to the educational curriculum as practical preparation for civic life in the Greek city-state. Isocrates (436-338), a student of Gorgias, founded a professional school in the 390s that blended the Sophists' rhetorical techniques with professional practice, and he devised a rhetorical approach to literature. His school provided a model for subsequent secondary education in the Greco-Roman world.

Philosophy rejected the pragmatic approach of the Sophists (→ Greek Philosophy; Pragmatism). Socrates (ca. 470-399 B.C.) and Plato (427-347; → Platonism) taught that → dialectic (obtaining the → truth through question and answer) should be distinguished from rhetoric, for rhetoric seeks to persuade but not necessarily to obtain truth and knowledge. Aristotle (384-322; → Aristotelianism) appeased this animosity between the rhetors and philosophers, arguing that dialectic and rhetoric both deal with knowledge — the former philosophical, the latter political. This debate resurfaced in the second century B.C. as part of the Greek philosophers' disdain for the Roman preference for rhetoric over philosophy.

As indicated in the writings of the first Roman rhetorician, Cato the Elder (234-149 B.C.), the Romans borrowed Greek rhetoric in the late third century B.C. As in Greece, rhetoric was common to the judicial and political systems, constituted the core of secondary education, and heavily influenced literary composition. The writings of the greatest Roman orator, Cicero (106-43 B.C.), give us the main picture of oratory and rhetoric in the Roman republic. With the empire, Augustan Rome replaced Greece as the center of rhetorical study. However, the accompanying decline of debate in government in the Senate and Assembly diminished the role of rhetoric in → politics, a role replaced in part by declamation (public rhetorical exercises).

Ancient rhetoric identified three forms of oratory: judicial, deliberative, and epideictic. The judicial concerns accusation and defense and was employed mainly in the law court. Deliberative rhetoric involves persuading and dissuading regarding the expediency of a course of action, particularly in the political arena. The epideictic type is the rhetoric of praise and blame, and of public ceremonies such as festivals and funerals.

The practice of rhetoric was discussed under the five categories of invention, arrangement, style, memory, and delivery. Invention entails devising arguments from ethos (moral character), pathos (emotion), and logos (inductive and deductive reasoning) to support or refute propositions. Arrangement is the persuasive ordering of the proofs and parts of the speech. Style is the felicitous choice of words, figures of speech, and thought to further meet the needs of invention. Memory and delivery are the practical aspects of executing the speech.

Arrangement, which was most carefully described for judicial rhetoric, consisted of six major parts:

1. *exordium,* or introduction, striving for attention and goodwill;
2. *narratio,* describing the background of the cause;
3. *propositio,* setting forth the propositions to be developed;
4. *probatio,* or the main body, confirming the propositions through argumentation;
5. *refutatio,* disproving the propositions of the opposition; and
6. *peroratio,* or conclusion, summarizing the argumentation and appealing to the audience's emotion.

After the *probatio* the NT often has situational exhortation consisting of some general and some specific admonitions (→ Parenesis). Deliberative and epideictic rhetoric use a simplified version of this pattern.

1.2. *Rhetoric and the NT*

The NT is a product of its Hellenistic environment. The NT texts are composed in large measure according to the principles of Greco-Roman rhetoric that systematized widely used rhetorical conventions, many of which had permeated Jewish oral and literary culture or had been devised independently in that culture. These principles are outlined in extant *progymnasmata* (schoolbook exercises) and rhetorical handbooks by Aristotle *(Rhetorica),* Cicero *(De oratore, De inventione),* and Quintilian (A.D. ca. 35-ca. 100, *Institutio oratoria*), among others.

The role of Greco-Roman rhetoric in the NT has been known from apostolic times (→ Early Church) but has received a very uneven emphasis in subsequent interpretation. Understanding the NT rhetorically was common during the → Reformation, an outstanding example being the commentaries of Philipp → Melanchthon (1497-1560; → Reformers). German scholarship in the 19th century produced the first systematic works on biblical rhetoric, particularly analysis of genre and style (such as figures of speech and thought). The declining role of rhetoric in 20th-century Western education, however, narrowed analysis of the NT to merely stylistic considerations.

Since the 1970s there has been a renewed interest in the rhetoric of the Bible, the NT in particular. Studies have appeared that thoroughly investigate all of the NT texts according to the interaction of invention, arrangement, and style. Although it is debated whether the biblical writers were formally educated in rhetoric or consciously used rhetorical conventions, all NT books as a whole, or in their constituent parts, provide classic models of rhetorical composition. NT books attest to a wide variety of rhetorical skill among their authors, ranging from mere acquaintance with oral and written rhetorical forms gleaned from their use in daily communication, to experience of trained public oratory, and to studied rhetorical composition learned in secondary school. For example, the author of James has acquaintance with rhetorical forms for the elaboration of themes and arguments in 2:1–3:12 that can be attributed to daily conversation and observation of trained orators. Paul's letters exhibit formal study in rhetoric, especially in passages like 2 Corinthians 10–13, where a sophisticated mix of boasting, comparison, irony, and other rhetorical techniques is found.

Rhetorical analysis of the Gospels indicates that the sayings of → Jesus were orally transmitted and written down according to patterns dictated in the *progymnasmata* for the elaboration of a *chreia* (broadly, "necessary or useful thing"; pl. *chreiai*). A chreia is a saying, portrayal of an action, or both that is credited to a person or group and helpful for living. Chreiai were common to discussions of philosophy and biography and were often extensively elaborated using rationales, contraries, → analogies, examples, citation of authorities, exhortations, and conclusions. Simple and elaborated chreiai form basic units of the gospel accounts of the words and deeds of Jesus and the 12 apostles. An example of a simple chreia of Jesus is contained in Mark 1:14-15: "Now after John was arrested, Jesus came to Galilee, proclaiming the good news of God, and saying, 'The time is fulfilled, and the kingdom of God has come near; repent, and believe in the good news.'" An elaborated chreia is found in Mark 9:38-40.

All the letters unquestionably attributed to → Paul have received extensive rhetorical analysis (Romans, 1 and 2 Corinthians, Galatians, Philippians, 1 Thessalonians, and Philemon). Paul made considerable use of rhetorical conventions of invention, arrangement, and style in meeting the needs of his churches. For example, Galatians has been extensively examined and is currently understood as deliberative rhetoric intended to persuade the Galatians to adhere more firmly to Paul's → gospel and to dissuade them from embracing an opposing gospel. H. Betz has outlined Galatians as epistolary prescript (1:1-5), *exordium* (1:6-11), *narratio* (1:12–2:14), *propositio* (2:15-21), *probatio* (3:1–4:31), *exhortatio* (5:1–6:10), and epistolary postscript (6:11-18).

The Book of Revelation uses Jewish and other images and symbols to create an alternative symbolic world. The rhetoric provides the recipient churches with meaning as they struggle with being members of the kingdom of God, yet persecuted by an empire that challenges the lordship of Christ with its demand for emperor worship. The images and symbols create meaning and channel emotion in an attempt to persuade the recipients to hold firm to their allegiance to Christ. This symbolic world gives meaning to their persecution and possible death for that allegiance.

As regards the OT, it mostly predates the Hellenistic era, in which rhetoric became highly conceptualized, but still shares literary forms, genres, stylistic devices, and rhetorical techniques common to antiquity. Because of its high degree of conceptualization, Greco-Roman rhetoric partially informs OT interpretation.

1.3. ***Biblical Interpretation and Rhetoric***

Rhetorical analysis has many implications for biblical interpretation. Recognition of the role of the chreia in the Jesus tradition and the Gospels has once more raised the issue of the relationship between the historical Jesus and the Jesus of the Gospels. The encapsulation of the sayings and deeds of Jesus in chreia form, either by Jesus himself or by his initial audience, provided parameters for their transmission. The first Christians and the gospel writers, however, also shared in a culture that elaborated and modified chreiai in ways that were not strictly historical to meet the needs of oral and written discourse.

Knowledge of the rhetorical tools and approaches available to the biblical writers to address their situations provides many insights. Literary forms had rhetorical functions, so that identifying the literary forms within a NT work illuminates their purpose in the larger work. Also, observing the selections that the biblical writers make among rhetorical types and options in invention and arrangement clarifies their purposes in writing. For example, knowing that Paul is using judicial rhetoric indicates that he feels the need to defend himself against charges made against him. Having determined the intricacies of the authors' approaches to their audiences, rhetorical criticism illumines the situation that evoked the writings. In this sense rhetorical criticism is a welcome supplement to historical criticism and social-scientific study of the NT (→ Exegesis, Biblical). It also demonstrates that the power of the NT texts resides in part in the utilization of persuasive language that effectively speaks to the needs of the audiences.

→ Hermeneutics; Language; Literature, Biblical and Early Christian, 1-2; New Testament Era, History of

Bibliography: R. D. Andersen Jr., *Ancient Rhetorical Theory and Paul* (rev. ed.; Louvain, 1999) • H. D. Betz, *Galatians: A Commentary on Paul's Letter to the Churches in Galatia* (Philadelphia, 1979) • C. C. Black, *The Rhetoric of the Gospel: Theological Artistry in the Gospels and Acts* (St. Louis, 2001) • G. A. Kennedy, *The Art of Persuasion in Greece* (Princeton, 1963); idem, *The Art of Rhetoric in the Roman World: 300 B.C.–A.D. 300* (Princeton, 1972); idem, *NT Interpretation through Rhetorical Criticism* (Chapel Hill, N.C., 1984) • B. Mack, *Rhetoric and the NT* (Minneapolis, 1989) • D. F. Watson, *Rhetorical Criticism of the NT: A Bibliographic Survey* (Leiden, 2005).

Duane F. Watson

2. Practice and Theology

2.1. ***Definition***

As the art of speaking well, rhetoric reflects on the efficacy and persuasiveness of speaking or writing, the suitability of its form, and, in content, its ethical basis and its aptness for the situation and hearers or readers. This view of rhetoric goes back to the tradition of antiquity, especially in its Aristotelian form (M. H. Wörner; → Aristotelianism; Greek Philosophy). It rules out a purely formal understanding, which would be neither relevant nor responsible in → practical theology (as against U. von den Steinen; on the history of this connection, see W. Jens, "Rhetorik"; G. Ueding and B. Steinbrink).

2.2. ***Rhetoric and Homiletics***

It is well to consider the significance of rhetoric for homiletics in the broadest sense, including different pertinent situations in addition to that of → preaching, for example, the media. Up to the 19th century, homiletics was not thinkable except in dialogue with rhetoric, just as the dialogue of rhetoric with homiletics calls for notice in the history of rhetoric. But then, especially under the influence of → dialectical theology, the two parted company, and in general rhetoric came to be disdained.

A change came at the end of the 1960s and the beginning of the 1970s as rhetoric experienced a renaissance in Germany (Jens, *Rede*) and dialogue resumed between homiletics and rhetoric (M. Josuttis, *Rhetorik;* G. Otto, *Predigt*). Inasmuch as preaching addresses hearers in a given situation and is governed by the speaker's desire to be understood and to convince, it calls for rhetorical reflection. Such reflection is important in sermon preparation (Otto, *Wie entsteht*), in delivering sermons, and in analyzing them according to the principles of rhetorical study (H. F. Plett). Josuttis has offered an illuminating definition of the relation between rhetoric, homiletics, and theology.

2.3. *Rhetoric and Practical Theology*
Homiletics is not the only field in which rhetoric is relevant. Speech is a constitutive dimension of everything with which practical theology is concerned. Handling speech makes necessary a broad approach in practical theology that must cover many different areas. Academically, rhetoric has always been the place to develop this area, a relation that is being neglected in modern scholarly and theological history (→ Modern Period). We need to return to the original breadth of the horizon of rhetorical thinking, for in the tradition of rhetoric we find all the basic questions of modern studies in linguistics, interpretation, → communication, and → hermeneutics. Some examples will quickly show how important rhetorical discussions are in the most varied of fields in practical theology.

2.3.1. For many reasons, rhetoric is relevant to all *teaching and learning processes,* regardless of the situation. First, a basic didactic principle belongs to the sphere of rhetoric. Teaching seeks to impart something that by way of conviction or new insight will motivate change in knowledge, opinion, judgment, or conduct. Then historically, schools and teaching have always been linked to rhetoric (J. Dolch). Finally, even to the present time speech is the medium of teaching (→ Religious Educational Theory; School and Church).

2.3.2. → *Pastoral care and* → *counseling* both involve language. Conversation is their basic form (J. Scharfenberg, *Pastoral Care*), and thus we have a fundamental speech situation. In → psychology and → psychoanalysis much attention is paid to this fact (B. Boothe). There is an obvious application in → pastoral psychology and the use of → symbols (Scharfenberg, *Einführung*).

2.3.3. → *Worship* is a complex nexus of communication that features speech along with other things, whether in set forms (→ Liturgy) or free. Yet obviously here, in analyzing and drawing up worship, rhetoric is not the only approach. Semiotic (→ Sign) and linguistic approaches are also important (R. Volp).

In preaching and other areas of practical theology, speech is not something abstract but is related to acts. Words are never mere words. Those who speak them do things even as they speak, and they trigger acts among those who hear them (H. Luther, with bibliography of speech-act theory; → Action Theory).

In general we must avoid the misconception that rhetoric is a global discipline that dominates all others. The horizon of rhetorical thinking is significant, yet it has no claim to monopoly. If reflection on practical theology is to correspond to the complex reality, it must adopt different approaches and methods, in various combinations.

2.4. *Evaluation*
To take the constitutive importance of rhetoric seriously has two implications. First, we must set aside the tradition the carves up preaching, worship, pastoral care, and education into relatively independent disciplines (Otto, *Grundlegung; Handlungsfelder*). Then we must see that rhetoric is important not only for an understanding of practical theology but for an understanding of theology in general. A theology that takes rhetoric seriously must be dialogic theology (→ Dialogue), not the kind of "dogmatic" theology (→ Dogmatics) that authoritatively lays down what is valid once and for all.

Bibliography: J. M. Atwell, *Rhetoric Reclaimed: Aristotle and the Liberal Arts Tradition* (Ithaca, N.Y., 1998) • R. Barilli, *Rhetoric* (Minneapolis, 1989) • B. Boothe, "Psychoanalyse als Verständnisprozeß," *WzM* 42 (1990) 335-47 • D. Buttrick, *Homiletic: Moves and Structures* (Philadelphia, 1987) • J. Dolch, *Lehrplan des Abendlandes* (Ratingen, 1959; 3d ed., 1971) • E. Garver, *Aristotle's Rhetoric: An Art of Character* (Chicago, 1994) • J. Jasinski, *Sourcebook on Rhetoric: Key Concepts in Contemporary Rhetorical Studies* (Thousand Oaks, Calif., 2001) • W. Jens, "Rhetorik," *RDL* 3.433-56; idem, *Von deutscher Rede* (Munich, 1969; 4th ed., 1985) • M. Josuttis, *Rhetorik und Theologie in der Predigtarbeit. Homiletische Studien* (Munich, 1985) • L. Keck, "Toward a Theology of Rhetoric/Preaching," *Practical Theology* (ed. D. S. Browning; San Francisco, 1983) 126-47 • H. Luther, "Predigt als Handlung," *ZTK* 80 (1983) 223-43 • G. Otto, *Grundlegung der praktischen Theologie* (Munich, 1986); idem, *Handlungsfelder der praktischen Theologie* (Munich, 1988); idem, *Predigt als rhetorische Aufgabe* (Neukirchen, 1987); idem, *Wie entsteht eine Predigt?* (Munich, 1982) • H. F. Plett, *Textwissenschaft und Textanalyse. Semiotik, Linguistik, Rhetorik* (2d ed.; Heidelberg, 1979) • W. A. Rebhorn, *The Emperor of Men's Minds: Literature and the Renaissance Discourse of Rhetoric* (Ithaca, N.Y., 1995) • J. Scharfenberg, *Einführung in die Pastoralpsychologie* (2d ed.; Göttingen, 1990); idem, *Pastoral Care as Dialogue* (Philadelphia, 1987) • U. von den Steinen, "Rhetorik–Instrument oder Fundament christlicher Rede?" *EvT* 39 (1979) 101-27 • G. Ueding and B. Steinbrink, *Grundriß der Rhetorik* (3d ed.; Stuttgart, 1994) • R. Volp, ed., *Zeichen. Semiotik in Theologie und Gottesdienst* (Munich, 1982) • M. H. Wörner, *Das Ethische in der Rhetorik des Aristoteles* (Freiburg, 1990) • H. Yunis, *Taming Democracy: Models of Political Rhetoric in Classical Athens* (Ithaca, N.Y., 1996).

Gert Otto†

Righteousness, Justice

1. OT

1.1. ***Term***

The Heb. root *ṣdq* is as comprehensive in meaning as the Eng. "right(eous)," Ger. *(ge)recht,* Gk. *nomos,* or Lat. *ius* (→ Law). It embraces, besides the narrower legal sense of justice, judgment, and standard for what is right (Ger. *Gericht, Rechts-norm*), the wider ethicosocial sphere of wholesome and salutary relationships. The masc. *ṣedeq* denotes a state of beneficently ordered relationships between people or between people and God; the fem. *ṣĕdāqâ* refers to conduct that corresponds to this state or promotes it; the verb *ṣdq* describes the related action, and the adj. *ṣaddîq* characterizes those who perform it. The root occurs altogether 523 times and is always positive. The sense of distributive justice and certainly that of punitive justice lie far afield. Terms like "faithfulness," "truth," "goodness," and "peace" form the larger semantic field.

1.2. ***God's Righteousness***

God's righteousness is universal in scope (Ps. 96:13). God directs his royal council in righteousness; "righteousness and justice" support his throne (Ps. 9:7-8; 89:14-16). In Mesopotamia and Egypt, gods of righteousness uphold the throne (→ Egyptian Religion). In pre-Israelite → Jerusalem a god Ṣedeq was worshiped, with whom → Yahweh seems to be equated (Ps. 17:1, *YHWH ṣedeq;* cf. 4:1). Here the religion of Israel plainly took up common Near Eastern views — not to its detriment. The righteous God is the supreme court of appeal for Israelites who are unjustly accused (Ps. 35:24, 28), the helper for everyone who is upright against unjustified attacks (throughout the Psalms). In case of doubt, one must rely on God and not on earthly protectors (Zeph. 3:5; Jer. 9:23-24).

God's righteousness has less to do with a diffuse, neutral "world order" than with the concrete rectification of unjust relationships. The same applies in the political-national realm. In righteousness God helps his oppressed people to liberation and victory (Ps. 129:4; Judg. 5:11; Isa. 42:6). Righteously he creates for them → blessing (Ps. 24:5) and the fruitfulness of the land (Ps. 65:9-13; Joel 2:23-27). Indeed, in righteousness God gives them his good → Torah (Ps. 119:137-38; Deut. 4:8) and enables them to execute righteousness (Ps. 99:4; Isa. 33:5).

1.3. ***Human Righteousness***

1.3.1. *Human* righteousness corresponds to divine, or ought to do so. At the top, the king is to exercise it (→ Monarchy in Israel). If he rules righteously, his reign is a bad time for the perverse and flatterers (Prov. 22:5; 16:12-13), but those who do righteousness receive their due (Ps. 45:4; 72:7 MT), the weak are protected (Jer. 22:15; Ps. 72:1-4; Prov. 31:9), and the land flourishes (2 Sam. 8:15; 1 Kgs. 10:9). A king of this kind experiences God's righteous acts (Ps. 18:20, 24). If, however, there is too wide a gap between ideal and reality, criticism and conflicts ensue (Jer. 22:3; 2 Sam. 15:4; see also Dan. 4:27).

1.3.2. The → *society,* too, is under the norm of righteousness. The legal sphere must be clearly and truly in accord with what is right (Exod. 23:6-8; Lev. 19:15; Deut. 25:1), economic dealings must be honorable and honest (Lev. 19:36; Deut. 25:15; Ezek. 45:10), and community life must show humanity and solidarity (Hos. 10:12; Psalm 15). The cultic community likes to define itself as a company of "the upright" or "the righteous" (Ps. 33:1; 118:20) and hopes for God's beneficent righteousness (Prov. 8:18; Isa. 3:10-11). But what if righteousness is lacking in Israel? The → prophets speak repeatedly to this problem and dispute, therefore, any claim to divine aid (Isa. 5:7; 48:18-19; 59:14; Jer. 3:11; Ezek. 16:51-52; Amos 5:7).

1.3.3. *Individuals* in Israel likewise seek to live in righteousness. This means working steadily (Gen. 30:33; Prov. 10:16), remaining modest (Prov. 16:8), not deceiving (Prov. 12:20; 24:28; 26:19) or lying (Prov. 13:5), being generous to an → enemy (1 Sam.

24:18), thinking and acting with social responsibility (Ezek. 33:14-20; Ps. 112:9; Job 29:14), and caring for family and for domestic animals (Gen. 38:26; Prov. 12:10). Naturally, too, it means being loyal to the religion of the ancestors (Ezek. 18:5-29). People of this kind may expect God and others to show them righteousness (Ps. 7:8; Prov. 24:23-25) and the blessing of God to enfold them (Prov. 10:25; Job 27:16-17; cf. 42:10-12).

Yet this happy picture of reciprocal righteousness is not without problems. Is it possible for anyone to be perfectly righteous (Job 4:17; 15:14; Ps. 143:2)? Even if it is, does it really pay, either with others (Amos 2:6; Isa. 5:23) or with God (Jer. 12:1; Job 9:15, 20; Eccl. 7:15-16)?

1.3.4. Plagued by self-doubts, prophetic criticism, and painful experiences, Israel achieved the insight that righteousness can be given to us only by God (Ps. 99:4; Isa. 61:11), imputed (Gen. 15:6; Ps. 106:31), without any merits on our part (Ps. 143:1-2). Righteous action is certainly expected of the justified unrighteous; mere → piety is not enough (Amos 5:4; Prov. 21:3). In particular, the *prophets* realize that only a basic renewal of individuals and their relationships can bring true righteousness (Isa. 1:26; 60:17; Jer. 31:23). In the messianic kingdom perfect righteousness will obtain (Isa. 11:4-5; Jer. 23:5-6). → Apocalyptic longs for this righteousness, but without losing sight of the ethical aspect.

In this twofold sense the people of → *Qumran* call themselves "sons of righteousness" (1QS 3:20, 22, etc.).

1.4. ***Righteousness in Early Judaism***

The twofold character of righteousness as divine gift and as human action was not lost in intertestamental and rabbinic → Judaism. The → LXX could use *dikaiosynē* (righteousness) and *eleos* (mercy) for Heb. *ṣdq(h),* with both a divine and a human reference (Ps. 87:13 [NRSV 88:12], "saving help"; Isa. 5:7; 56:1, "what is right" and "deliverance"). Heb. *ḥsd* (act of faithfulness and love) could at times be translated *dikaiosynē* (Gen. 19:19, with a divine reference; Gen. 21:23, with a human).

In the synagogue, too, God's righteousness remains his beneficence. In *y. Šeb.* 4 35c 31 and in the → midrash on Ps. 22:32, it is his earlier saving action. The so-called *Psalms of Solomon* (1st cent. B.C.) show that, alongside this traditional view (e.g., 8:33-34), another enters in, namely, righteousness as divine judgment (e.g., 8:26-31), which, it is true, is expressly "justified" (8:26, *dikaioō* in a doxological sense; 8.23, "God was proven right in his condemnation of the nations of the earth," *OTP* 2.660). The → rabbis see that God's mercy (the rendering of the *ṣĕdāqâ* of Gen. 18:19 in Gen. Rab. 49; see Str-B 3.196) far outweighs his punitive righteousness.

Human righteousness, too, means doing good and not merely, as is often thought, in the sense of almsgiving. This special sense is often present, but where the LXX translates *ṣĕdāqâ* by *eleēmosynē,* the latter has a broader meaning (e.g., Deut. 6:25; Isa. 1:27). And when Hillel, on the basis of Isa. 32:17, equates *ṣĕdāqâ* with knowledge of Torah and possession of wisdom, he can scarcely have only almsgiving in view.

At times the rabbis consider the question of this-worldly and otherworldly reward for the doing of righteousness. This association has led Christians to accuse them of teaching a righteousness of reward and achievement, in contrast to Paul's righteousness of → grace (§1.2). But the charge is hardly a just one. In early Judaism we look in vain for developed *do-ut-des* thinking (i.e., "I give in order that you may give," a principle found in → Roman religion and in Gk. *philia,* "friendship"). Human righteousness does not earn divine righteousness but derives from it (see E. P. Sanders, 419-28; → Justification 1.4). As for Christians → sanctification follows justification, so for Judaism election demands the doing of what is right. Believers do righteousness in order to help fill out the space that God's righteousness has opened for sound relations to God and to others. Thus grace always remains great and is never cheap.

Bibliography: W. Dietrich, "Der rote Faden im Alten Testament," *EvT* 49 (1989) 232-50 • F.-L. Hossfeld, "Gedanken zum alttestamentlichen Vorfeld paulinischen Rechtfertigungslehre," *Worum geht es in der Rechtfertigungslehre?* (ed. T. Soeding; Freiburg, 1999) 13-26 • K. Koch, "צדק *ṣdq* to be communally faithful, beneficial," *TLOT* 2.1046-62 • E. Otto, "Gerechtigkeit," *RGG* (4th ed.) 3.702-4 • G. von Rad, *OT Theology* (2 vols.; Louisville, Ky., 2001) 1.370-83 • D. J. Reimer, "צדק," *NIDOTTE* 3.744-69 • H. G. Reventlow and Y. Hoffman, eds., *Justice and Righteousness: Biblical Themes and Their Influence* (Sheffield, 1992) • R. A. Rosenberg, "The God Ṣedeq," *HUCA* 36 (1965) 161-77 • E. P. Sanders, *Paul and Palestinian Judaism: A Comparison of Patterns of Religion* (Philadelphia, 1977) • H. H. Schmid, "Creation, Righteousness, and Salvation," *Creation in the OT* (ed. B. W. Anderson; Philadelphia, 1984) 102-17; idem, *Gerechtigkeit als Weltordnung* (Tübingen, 1968) • J. J. Scullion, "Righteousness (OT)," *ABD* 5.724-36 • H. Spieckermann, "Gerechtigkeit Gottes," *RGG* (4th ed.) 3.718-20. See also the bibliography in "Justification 1."

Walter Dietrich, with John Reumann

Righteousness, Justice

2. NT

2.1. *NT Linguistic Usage*

The NT use of *dikaiosynē* (righteousness) and *dikaios* (righteous) is rooted in that of the → LXX and indirectly in that of the OT and → Judaism: "righteousness" is a term that expresses the relation of individuals and the community (→ Church 2.1.1) to God. God's own righteous action (1 John 1:9: the forgiveness of sins; Rom. 3:25-26: the sacrificial death of Christ; Rev. 16:5-7; Acts 17:31: God's righteous judgment) is the norm, basis, and goal of human action. As an answer to God's righteousness, human righteousness is the practice of God's (commanded) righteousness (Jas. 1:20). The Greek distinction between righteousness relative to others and → piety relative to God, the conception of righteousness in terms of *isotēs* (equity; see Col. 4:1, "fairly"), and its treatment as a → virtue (see Phil. 4:8) make only a marginal impact. The OT rootage may be seen especially in the numerous OT quotations and the many passages in which the devout people of the OT and devout Jews are called righteous (Matt. 1:19; 13:17; 23:29, 35; Luke 2:25; 2 Pet. 2:7; etc.).

2.2. *Jesus*

In respect to content, one might sum up the proclamation and work of → Jesus as a "new righteousness" (P. Stuhlmacher, *Gerechtigkeit Gottes,* 237-58). God establishes a new relation to Israel by showing mercy to the poor, to women, to marginal people, and to sinners, independently of their own righteousness (Mark 2:17). Linguistically, however, Jesus seems never, or hardly ever, to have expressed this relation by means of the term *ṣdq* (see 1.1). The NT's new assessments indeed interpret the work of Jesus, but they connect linguistically in different ways, not with Jesus, but with Jewish linguistic use.

Consider three examples of this usage. First, Jesus can be understood Christologically as the Righteous One; here primitive Christianity seems to be linking up with Jewish expectations of the Messiah as "the Righteous One" (Acts 3:14; 7:52). Second, since the death of Jesus can be regarded as the suffering of the Righteous One (Wis. 2:10-22), Luke, through the centurion at the foot of the cross, can extol Jesus as righteous, the hoped-for reaction of spectators to Christian martyrdom (Luke 23:47 NRSV marg.). Third, the death of Jesus, in keeping with Jewish concepts of the vicarious death of the righteous and of → martyrs (e.g., 2 Macc. 7:37-38; 4 Maccabees), can be interpreted as the death of the righteous for the unrighteous (1 Pet. 3:18; 2 Cor. 5:21). In all these statements, the work of Jesus is the material, but not the linguistic, presupposition.

As regards the proclamation of Jesus, Luke especially stresses the "new righteousness." The justified tax-gatherer (Luke 18:14) is contrasted with the → Pharisees, who represent those who try to justify themselves (16:15; cf. 10:29). Paul's doctrine of → justification seems decisive here. It is for Luke not a peculiarity of Paul but the general teaching of the church (see Acts 15:8-11) and the message of Jesus.

2.3. *Paul*

2.3.1. *Justification and Baptism*

The presupposition of Paul's doctrine of justification was that the early communities understood → baptism as anticipation of God's end-time judgment and therefore as a real making righteous (1 Cor. 6:11). Even before → Paul, baptism went hand in hand with the interpretation of the death of Jesus as the basis of justification (Rom. 3:25-26 and 1 Cor. 1:30 possibly interpret baptism) and probably also with exhortation of the baptized to righteousness (Eph. 4:22-24; 5:8-9; see also Rom. 6:12-23). The Pauline doctrine, then, is not a new construct; it is rooted in the church's understanding of baptism. There are analogies in Jewish statements about righteousness, for example, at → Qumran (see 1QS 11:12-14) or in 4 Ezra (see 8:36, 48-49).

The Christian communities grounded God's unconditional work of → grace, which Jewish texts also could describe by *ṣĕdāqôt* of God (Judg. 5:11, triumphs, saving acts, righteousnesses of Yahweh; 1 Sam. 12:7; J. J. Scullion, 734F) in the vicarious death of Jesus, and they saw it as actualized in baptism. Paul's contribution is that in Romans he brings the phrase "righteousness of God" strongly to the forefront (Rom. 1:17; 3:5, 26, etc.) and thus accentuates the theocentric aspect and links God's deity to his work of justification. Pauline, too, is the relating of what is said about justification in antithesis to the → law, which Paul worked out on the basis of his decisive encounter with Christ on the Damascus road and subsequently.

2.3.2. *Recent Issues*

Righteousness/justification has been among topics at issue in recent Pauline studies, not least with regard to what have come to be regarded as caricatures of early Judaism (see 1.4 above; → Jewish-Christian Dialogue 1; Justification 1.2). E. P. Sanders stressed the pattern of "covenantal nomism" in Palestinian Judaism and distinguished "getting into" the covenantal relationship with God (by national election, → circumcision, but not "works of the law") from "staying in" (by doing God's righteous will). Not justification but "eschatological participation" is central in Paul.

Particularly intertwined has been reevaluation of

→ law (§2.3; e.g., by A. A. Das, W. D. Davies, J. D. G. Dunn, K. Kuula, H. Räisänen, and L. Thurén; see S. Westerholm, *Israel's Law*) and of → faith (§2.3; e.g., by C. J. H. Wright), especially the meaning of *pistis Christou* (Rom. 3:22, 26; Gal. 2:16). Traditionally, this phrase has been rendered "faith in Christ" (NRSV), but periodically it has been taken as "the faith of Christ" (i.e., how Jesus trusted or showed → faithfulness, NRSV marg.; so, among others, R. B. Hays, *Faith of Jesus Christ;* contrast Dunn, "Once More").

All this constitutes the "new perspective" in Pauline studies (Dunn), often posed against "the 'Lutheran' Paul." But there is criticism of aspects of Sanders's work in the "post-Sanders era" (D. A. Carson et al.; F. Thielman; Stuhlmacher, *Revisiting Paul's Doctrine;* Westerholm, *Perspectives;* on *pistis,* see R. B. Matlock).

2.4. *Matthew*

Differently from Paul, Matthew uses the term *dikaiosynē* to stress the ethical demand of Jesus rather than the saving significance of his death. Matthew brings to the fore the ethical implications of the → kingdom of God: Seek first God's righteousness (6:33). Righteousness is everywhere the essence of God's salutary will, which it is the community's task to do. Righteousness also emphasizes the continuity of the demand of Jesus with that of → John the Baptist (see 21:32) and Judaism. This righteousness is not to be totally different from that of the Pharisees and → scribes but is to be "exceed" theirs (5:20), on the basis of → love. Jesus lived it out completely in his own life (see 3:15).

Matthew, then, expresses God's saving action, not by the term "righteousness (of God)," but by the story of Jesus, within which the demand for righteousness is proclaimed. Some, however, see 6:33, "[God's] righteousness," as a gift, like the kingdom; 5:6 as soteriological promise in a setting of → salvation history (3:15; 21:32). Several passages (e.g., 5:10, 20; 6:1, 3) present the imperatives (*ABD* 5:754-56; Reumann, 265) in an "imperatival indicative" approach (G. Strecker).

Bibliography: D. Aune, ed., *Rereading Paul Together: Roman Catholics and Protestants Discuss Pauline Theology* (Grand Rapids, 2005) • R. Bultmann, *Theology of the NT* (2 vols.; New York, 1951-55) §§28-31 • D. A. Carson, P. T. O'Brien, and M. A. Seifrid, eds., *Justification and Variegated Nomism,* vol. 1, *The Complexities of Second Temple Judaism* (Grand Rapids, 2001) • A. Dihle, "Gerechtigkeit," *RAC* 10.233-360 • J. D. G. Dunn, "Once More, pistis christou," *Pauline Theology,* vol. 4, *Looking Back, Pressing On* (ed. E. E. Johnson and D. M. Hay; Atlanta, 1997) 67-81 • R. B. Hays, *The Faith of Jesus Christ: The Narrative Substructure of Galatians 3:1–4:11* (2d ed.; Grand Rapids, 2002) • K. Kertelge, "Rechtfertigung II: Neues Testament," *TRE* 28.286-307 • W. Klaiber, "Gerechtigkeit I.2: Neues Testament," "Gerechtigkeit Gottes III: Neues Testament," *RGG* (4th ed.) 3.704-5, 720-21 • D. Lührmann, "Gerechtigkeit III: Neues Testament," *TRE* 12.414-20 • R. B. Matlock, "'Even the Demons Believe': Paul and *pistis Christou,*" *CBQ* 64 (2002) 300-318 • B. Przybylski, *Righteousness in Matthew and His World of Thought* (Cambridge, 1980) • J. Reumann, "Just, Justice, Justification, Righteous, Righteousness," *WThWB* 262-71 • E. P. Sanders, *Paul and Palestinian Judaism: A Comparison of Patterns of Religion* (Philadelphia, 1977) • J. J. Scullion, "Righteousness (OT)," *ABD* 5.724-36 • M. A. Seifrid, *Christ, Our Righteousness: Paul's Theology of Justification* (Downers Grove, Ill., 2000); idem, *Justification by Faith: The Origin and Development of a Central Pauline Theme* (Leiden, 1992) • G. Strecker, *Der Weg der Gerechtigkeit. Untersuchungen zur Theologie des Matthäus* (Göttingen, 1962) • P. Stuhlmacher, *Gerechtigkeit Gottes bei Paulus* (Göttingen, 1965); idem, *Revisiting Paul's Doctrine of Justification: A Challenge to the New Perspective* (Downers Grove, Ill., 2001) • F. Thielman, *From Plight to Solution: A Jewish Framework for Understanding Paul's View of the Law in Galatians and Romans* (Leiden, 1989) • S. Westerholm, *Israel's Law and the Church's Faith: Paul and His Recent Interpreters* (Grand Rapids, 1988); idem, *Perspectives Old and New on Paul: The "Lutheran" Paul and His Critics* (Grand Rapids, 2004) • J. A. Ziesler, *The Meaning of Righteousness in Paul: A Linguistic and Theological Enquiry* (Cambridge, 1972).

Ulrich Luz and John Reumann

3. Dogma and Ethics

3.1. *Divine Righteousness*

3.1.1. *Early Church and Middle Ages*

The great breadth and fullness of the biblical concept of the righteousness of God was soon lost in the history of theology. In Gnostic-dualistic fashion Marcion (d. ca. 160) sharply contrasted the OT God and his wrathful righteousness with the NT God of love (→ Marcionites). The → Apostolic Fathers, thinking in a Hellenistic context, understood righteousness predominantly in ethical terms. In contrast, the Greek and Latin → church fathers gave new force to the expression "righteousness of God." This was seen first as God's own righteousness and might express faithfulness to his promise (Ambrosiaster) or retributive righteousness. In the latter sense it became a term for God's judicial action, along Aristotelian lines denoting his distributive righteousness, whereby he reacts to human conduct with reward or punishment (e.g., Tertullian). According to this view, God's righteousness stands in antithesis to his → grace, though it may also include grace inasmuch as it is fitting for God to accept sinners that flee to him (Ambrosiaster).

At the time the righteousness of God was also seen as the gift of a righteous walk before him (e.g., Theodore of Mopsuestia). More deeply along these lines Augustine (354-430) linked the righteousness of God to his grace and defined it as the righteousness that in grace he gives to the ungodly to make them righteous (→ Augustine's Theology).

The age that followed preserved this insight but also stressed God's own righteousness, thus posing the medieval problem of reconciling God's righteousness and his grace. In Anselm (1033-1109) we have a strongly juridical attempt to define the connection in such a way that God's mercy is thought of as originating in his righteousness (*Pros.* 9-11). The righteousness of God means both his truth and honor and also the action in which he is true to himself. In the satisfaction linked to the incarnation of God, God is justified and his honor is restored, along with the order of creation that → sin had disrupted.

Abelard (1079-1142) took a different path from Anselm, starting with the → love of God that is poured into us by the → sacraments and that awakens a response of love in us. Since this responsive love is also something we are responsible for, God's distributive righteousness relates to the degree of our own active love.

In Peter Lombard (ca. 1100-1160) and finally Thomas Aquinas (ca. 1225-74), the various strands of tradition come together. Expounding Rom. 1:17 in his *Commentary on Romans,* Thomas views God's righteousness first in Aristotelian fashion as judicial righteousness, then as God's faithfulness to his promise (Ambrosiaster), and finally as the gift whereby God justifies us (Augustine). These disparate elements are not reconciled, and thus there is tension in the understanding of divine righteousness (→ Thomism; Scholasticism).

3.1.2. *Protestant Tradition*

Martin Luther's (1483-1546) reforming discovery lay in the perception that the → gospel rather than the → law is the locus of divine righteousness. In contrast to the philosophical view of God's righteousness as formal or active, Luther understood it as the gift of God, the passive righteousness "with which merciful God justifies us by faith" (*LW* 34.337). Though linguistically Luther stressed primarily the character of God's righteousness as gift, his view went beyond a defining of God's righteousness as "the righteousness that avails for God" (WA.DB 7.31). God's righteousness is not a quality that God enjoys alone. It is his creative and saving action and also a mark of the fellowship that he initiates with us by this action. The granting of righteousness is set against the background of the → last judgment. In his Word, God pardons sinners by imputing to them, not their sin, but the righteousness of Christ. There is thus an anticipatory intimation of God's end-time verdict, which as the verdict of God is also the imparting of new being. The → sanctification that takes on reality in human life and work is to be understood as life in the operational sphere of God's righteousness (W. Joest; → Luther's Theology).

Philipp Melanchthon (1497-1560) did not bring out as well as Luther did the factor of union with Christ, and he thus understood the righteousness of faith forensically. In the judgment of God we are declared righteous on the basis of Christ's satisfaction, and this step is followed by renewal of life but does not properly include it.

John Calvin (1509-64) also stressed the forensic character of justification, distinguishing along these lines between declaring righteous, which is the basis of assurance of faith, and human renewing. But he also treated the righteousness of God that is manifest in Christ as the honor of God (*Inst.* 3.13.2) and the creative power of God (2.16.3), which are brought to light in the imparting of righteousness (3.13.1; → Calvin's Theology).

Whereas for Protestant → orthodoxy (§1) the righteousness of God was again defined scholastically as a quality in the sense of proportional righteousness, the → Enlightenment sought to demonstrate the righteousness of God in the face of evil in the world (→ Theodicy). F. D. E. Schleiermacher (1768-1834), unlike the Reformers, listed righteousness among the divine attributes that relate to the sense of sin and thus defined it as penal righteousness (*Christian Faith,* §84).

A. Ritschl (1822-89), in contrast, interpreted the righteousness of God in terms of love as the very essence of God. Rejecting the satisfaction theory, he linked righteousness to grace and defined it as the consistency of God's leading to salvation (*Unterricht in der christlichen Religion,* 13-14).

In their own distinctive ways G. Gloege (1901-70) and K. Barth (1886-1968) set forth the universal and historical character of divine righteousness. Gloege expounded righteousness as grace for the world, defining it as the movement of God's mercy that embraces the world in order to subject it to his righteousness. Barth characterized God's righteousness as a perfection of his love (*CD* II/1, 375-77). Righteousness is a form of love precisely as retributive righteousness inasmuch as it passes judgment on human sin in the Son and therefore as → reconciliation. From this standpoint Barth saw that "the task of the doctrine of → justification is to demonstrate the righteousness of God which overrules in the reconciling grace of God" (IV/1, 518). Putting into effect his covenant will and his right as Creator, God's grace is vindicated in the justification of sinners, and therefore God himself is justified.

3.1.3. *Roman Catholic Tradition*

For the Council of → Trent justification is identical with our inner healing. The efficacious cause of justification is God's graciousness, the meritorious cause is Christ's passion, and the single essential cause is God's righteousness, that is, the righteousness by which he makes us righteous (DH 1528-30). To maintain personal encounter between God and us, our own righteousness is differentiated from that of God or of Christ, but the relation between the two can be seen as one of → analogy, so that God's righteousness is reflected in ours.

The Roman Catholic tradition regards God's righteousness as basically a moral quality of the will of God to give to each his own. The only norm of this righteousness is the agreement of God's will and work with his own being. The various forms of righteousness may be found by analogy in God. *Judicial* righteousness is appropriate for God inasmuch as by natural and moral law he orients creatures to the common good. *Retributive* righteousness is fitting for God insofar as he rewards → good and punishes → evil. For the sake of God's dignity the punishment that hands over sinners cannot be merely a means of betterment (B. Sattler, G. Hermes). Yet it must not be pressed to the point where God's righteousness implies a demand for full satisfaction (Anselm, H. de Tournely, F. X. Dieringer).

K. Rahner (1904-84) tried to show that the real point of Roman Catholic teaching is that the righteousness of God, by which we are made righteous and thus participate in God's righteousness as his essential holiness, is the effect of his merciful grace. In its own turn, this grace is to be called "righteous" because it makes us into those for whom his love is also essentially and efficaciously righteous.

3.1.4. *Orthodox Tradition*

Orthodox theology (→ Orthodox Christianity) defines righteousness as a dynamic quality or energy of God that has its basis in the equality of the Trinitarian persons, manifests itself in the creation of the world, and aims at the participation of creatures in the divine blessedness, the restoration of the full equipoise of creation, and therewith the leading back of the world to righteousness. The mercy and righteousness of God are related, which safeguards both God's freedom (which is not caprice) and the dignity of the created world and human efforts. Full correspondence between divine and human righteousness is already achieved in Christ, who unites deity and humanity. Our union with Christ means participation in his righteousness as both God and man. Our striving for inner righteousness entails a concern for outer righteousness, though this goal remains subordinate to righteousness in the spiritual order.

3.1.5. *Dogmatic Significance*

The righteousness of God is a central dogmatic concept. It leads us into the profundities of the idea of → God and expounds the → salvation that he provides for us from the standpoint of the end-time consummation of the world. The righteousness of God revealed in the gospel denotes the creative and regulative action of God in which he acts according to his nature as love and the relation that he established with us at → creation, showing himself to be faithful and thus justifying himself by pronouncing unrighteous sinners to be righteous and in this way asserting his right to his creatures. Righteousness, then, is *an expression of the love of God.* The reference to God's self-justification is the theological answer to the problem of theodicy.

God's judging is to be seen as a function of his love, as an action in which, with an orientation to his right, he gains the victory over unrighteousness. Our justification by God involves a verdict in which he imputes to sinners the alien righteousness of Christ, anticipates their pardon at the last judgment, and already effects in them the new creation. Those who are justified in → faith are freed from the compulsion of → sin and set in a new → obedience, through which they have a part in the establishment of God's rule in the world.

With this comprehensive and dynamic understanding of divine righteousness, consensus on the doctrine of justification is possible in the → dialogue between evangelicals and Roman Catholics (Malta Report, 1972), and there are points of convergence with the cosmically oriented Orthodox doctrine of redemption. A lively question in the ecumenical movement is that of the relation between the righteousness of God and human → rights or social justice (Treysa Conference, 1950; → Ecumenism, Ecumenical Movement).

3.2. *Human Righteousness*

3.2.1. *Ethics*

Righteousness is at the heart of both theological and philosophical → ethics. It is bound up with the → responsibility of believers, which is based on the eschatological Christ-event and with which they bear witness to the gospel in the world. Here is the source of their advocacy of life, → freedom, righteousness, → peace, and → joy — that is, the positive qualities that mark salvation in the → kingdom of God (Rom. 14:17). Representing these gifts of salvation in the world means opening up access to a responsible life (D. Bonhoeffer).

Righteousness was defined as a general → virtue in Greek ethics. Aristotle (384-322 B.C.) found in it the epitome of all ethical virtues, the perfect exercising of virtues to others (*Eth. Nic.* 5.5). In a more precise sense it is distributive righteousness and equalizing righteousness. Later, in harmony with Roman traditions, righteousness was defined as the virtue "according to each his own."

Characteristic of the medieval tradition was the synthesizing of various strands. Following Augustine and Aristotle, Thomas Aquinas found in righteousness the principle of a world order in which all things, both visible and invisible, both mortal and immortal, are related in a precise way and in an orderly beauty. All sensory striving and all conscious willing relate to something good. Thus "natural law" is a transcription of "eternal law" in the human → soul, reason, and heart. In → natural law the rational creature has a part intellectually in the law of the world. In human law human beings make specific rules for specific cases. Righteousness or justice stands alongside wisdom, courage, and temperance as a cardinal virtue. It is indeed the most basic of these virtues. Without righteous people there is no righteousness in society.

3.2.2. *The Reformers and Their Descendants*

The → Reformers, especially Luther, rejected an understanding of righteousness that integrated it into a given teleological order detached from the will of God (→ Teleology). No cause prescribes measures for the will of God. God himself both is and gives the rule for all things. "For it is not because he is or was obliged so to will that what he wills is right, but on the contrary, because he himself so wills, therefore what happens must be right" (*LW* 33.181). Luther contrasted divine righteousness with human righteousness, which under the requirement of the law arises out of human works, that is, which human beings acquire as a quality by righteous action. At this point Luther abandoned the understanding of righteousness found in Thomas and late Scholasticism, and even more so the understanding in the ethics of antiquity, in Aristotle, for whom "righteousness follows upon actions and originates in them. But according to God, righteousness precedes works, and thus works are the result of righteousness" (*Lectures on Romans* [1515/16, *LW* 25.512]). Our own righteousness, then, springs from an alien righteousness, and it expresses itself in self-denial, love, and a humble fear of God. But this Christ-righteousness is accompanied, not by a private Christian morality, but by a righteousness that works publicly, that instructs, that rights wrongs, and that punishes sinners. For Luther the righteousness of God that corrects and judges is decisive: "The good law and Spirit must regulate all law on the left hand, that is, outwardly in the world" (WA 17/2.94.17). Judging by corrective clemency in individual cases becomes the decisive criterion of all human justice. In content Luther adduces the → Golden Rule and the second table of the → Decalogue. Here is the "common, divine, and natural law which even the heathen, Turks, and Jews have to keep if there is to be any peace or order in the world" (*LW* 46.27).

For Calvin, too, "God's will is . . . the highest rule of righteousness" (*Inst.* 3.23.2). He found here the source of law; ethics is Decalogue ethics. The Decalogue is an authentic interpretation of natural law, which has no metaphysical basis. Law is thus an element in covenant theology (→ Covenant 3), and the concept of the covenant is an element in judicial order.

Only gradually were the productive impulses of the Reformation worked out in Protestant ethics. Samuel Pufendorf (1632-94), following Hugo Grotius (1583-1645), regarded justice as a formative principle of life in this world. We relate to it, not as a rational idea, but as a contingent creation of the divine will. Pufendorf had some original criteria of justice that helped to prepare the ground for later declarations of universal human rights. Human dignity is embedded in sociality as a regulative principle. The moral freedom that constitutes human dignity leads on to natural → equality and then to natural freedom before the law. Justice as a matter of state law demands the promotion of → humanity and of individual → happiness in rights, life, freedom, and honor, with protection against injustice and sickness.

Along these lines I. Kant (1724-1804) laid down the cardinal ethical principle that people should always be regarded as ends and never as means (→ Kantianism). He viewed justice as a supreme principle based on → reason as a sense of the unrestricted nature of human activity. The outcome of justice is a contract with which free, equal, independent people establish laws to which they subject themselves. The Golden Rule is universalized as the → categorical imperative; it contains the unconditional command of practical reason, which is legislative.

In debate with Kant and → utilitarianism, John Rawls (1921-2002) later laid down two necessary basic rules for just conduct in a fictional primal situation: the same rights and duties for all, and permission of inequalities only for the good of all, especially those who are badly placed (*A Theory of Justice,* §40). Rawls was trying in this way to link a priori moral law to an empirically universal form of justice.

3.2.3. *Modern Concerns*

A modern concern is to counteract the decay of the Western idea of justice (E. Brunner). The thesis that we cannot know true right has led to → relativism, while the assertion of the unrestricted validity of positive law has resulted in → positivism. The way was thus prepared for the principle of totalitarianism in real → nihilism. Already in 1866 the emergence of the idea that "might is right" led conservatives like Ludwig von Gerlach to protest against Bismarck that justice is the true foundation of kingdoms. The resistance to Hitler drew strength from this principle. The credo of legal positivism dissolved the link between positive law and the criterion of justice. The positivist decomposition of humanity also left citizens helpless against totalitarianism, barbarity, and technology.

Such experiences highlighted the urgent need for reflection on a higher right, and denominational differences became less important. Thus Brunner (1889-1966) in his work on justice appealed to the doctrine of the *imago Dei,* thereby seeking to redefine the Aristotelian and Stoic doctrine of natural law on the basis of the order of creation and with totally new content. Justice is here a virtue and an objective world order in which it is a matter of social relations and the distribution of property. Love and justice go together; love transcends and permeates justice.

Brunner joined hands with Roman Catholics in a concern to systematize natural law. He deduced special forms of justice from justice in general. Legal relations between individuals, he claimed, stand under the claim of *communicative* justice. The legal relations of individuals to society stand under *distributive* justice. Those of society to individuals stand under *legal* justice, which may be *vindicative* justice in cases of disobedience. Linking natural law to evolutionism (→ Evolution), Roman Catholic social teaching (→ Social Ethics) can interpret social justice as the formative principle of social dynamics (F. Kleiber). In principle this point has been argued as a result of → Vatican II (see *Iustitia in mundo* [1971] of the Synod of Bishops).

Protestant theology (e.g., of K. Barth) has also radically evaluated the relationship between justification, justice, and law, and the responsibility of the Christian community to establish justice in the civil community. Justice in the → state is here viewed as a parable of the kingdom of God, which the church proclaims. Justice is understood as part of the historic process of God's covenant with human beings. This perspective leads to concrete advocacy of human rights, a constitutional state, and an "optimum of social justice."

Along more ontological lines Paul Tillich (1886-1965) worked out the relation between love, power, and justice (1960). → Power is a reality posited with the race and related to God's essential power. Justice arises out of the human encounter and becomes actual as a claim or demand for justice, taking shape as either proportional or creative justice. Power and justice achieve authenticity only through the dynamic of love, by which justice as an outward form receives its sustaining content.

The theoretical debate continues. Some (e.g., N. Luhmann) give priority to law and distrust an overpositive ideal of justice, but others contend that in rational discourse some ethical principles of law can win consensus. There is an unmistakable tendency toward constitutional positivism. Thus the Bonn Basic Law claims higher validity than the Weimar constitution did, for it states that "inviolable and inalienable human rights" are "the basis of every community, of peace, and of justice in the world" (art. 1.2). Fundamental ideas of justice and humanity play a significant role in the administration of justice. It may be seen here that unless there is agreement in the legal world and linkage with such other nontemporal principles as peace, humanity, equality, and freedom, justice will also be weakened.

Justice as a criterion for the international and social economic order governs the work of the Pontifical Council for Justice and Peace, which was instituted in 1967. In its thinking on a responsible society, the → World Council of Churches lays down the rule that it must be "just, participatory, and sustainable." At Vancouver in 1983 it called for "justice, peace, and the integrity of all creation." Social justice and the international economic order has been a theme for Protestant-Catholic study. Roman Catholic bishops in the United States have demanded economic justice for all, with the several dozen million people in view who live below minimum standards. The Church of England study *Faith in the City* (1983) focused on the same criterion of justice.

Ethically, the category of justice is now being strongly presented and universally applied, for example, with reference to creation or the generations. It has been put in the service of an ethics of responsibility that relates to God's universal ministry to the world and gives concrete shape to our responsibility to God, to others, and to the creaturely world as a whole.

→ Law and Legal Theory

Bibliography: B. A. Ackerman, *Social Justice in the Liberal State* (New Haven, 1980) • B. M. Barry, *Theories of Justice* (Berkeley, Calif., 1989) • K. Barth, *CD* II/1 (1957); IV/1 (1956); idem, *Church and State* (London, 1939) • H. Bedford-Strohm, *Vorrang für die Armen. Auf dem Weg zu einer theologischen Theorie der Gerechtigkeit* (Gütersloh, 1993) • E. Brunner, *Justice and the Social Order* (London, 1945) • G. Del Vecchio, *Justice: An Historical and Philosophical Essay* (Edinburgh, 1952) • J. Ellul, *The Theological Foundation of Law* (New York, 1969) • D. B. Forrester, *Christian Justice and Public Policy* (Cambridge, 1997) • G. Gloege, *Gnade für die Welt. Kritik und Krise des Luthertums* (Göttingen, 1964) • L. E. Goodman, *On Justice: An Essay on Jewish Philosophy* (New Haven, 1991) • R. D. Hatch and W. R.Copeland, eds., *Issues of Justice: Social Sources and Religious Meanings* (Macon, Ga., 1988) • T. P. Jackson, *The Priority of Love: Christian Charity and Social Justice* (Princeton, 2003) • K. Kipnis and D. T. Meyers, eds., *Economic Justice: Private Rights and Public Responsibilities* (Totowa, N.J., 1985) • R. Niebuhr, *Love and Justice* (1957) • J. Rawls, *A Theory of Justice* (Oxford, 1972) • J. H. Reiman, *Justice and Modern Moral Philosophy* (New Haven, 1990) • D. Staniloae, *Orthodoxe Dogmatik* (vol. 1; Gütersloh, 1985) • P. Tillich, *Love, Power, and Justice: Ontological Analyses and Ethical Applications* (London, 1960) • M. Walzer, *Spheres of Justice: A Defense of Pluralism and Equality* (New York, 1983).

Theodor Strohm

Rights

1. Term and Distinctions
2. Classical Formulations
3. Medieval Formulations
4. Protestant Reformation
5. Enlightenment
6. Modern Age

1. Term and Distinctions

The term "rights" today is so commonplace that it is in danger of becoming cliché. Rights talk has become a dominant mode of political, legal, and moral discourse in the West, and rights protections and violations have become increasingly important issues in international relations and diplomacy. Most nation-states now have detailed bills or recitations of rights in their constitutions, statutes, and cases. The → United Nations and various other groups of nation-states have detailed catalogs of rights set out in treaties, declarations, conventions, and covenants. Many Christian denominations and ecumenical groups, alongside other religious groups, have their own declarations and statements on rights as well. Thousands of governmental, intergovernmental, and nongovernmental organizations are now dedicated to the defense of rights around the world, including a large number of Christian and other religious lobbying and litigation groups.

Various classes of rights are commonly distinguished, including the following:

1. public or constitutional rights (those that operate vis-à-vis the state) and private or personal rights (those that operate vis-à-vis other private parties);
2. human rights (those that inhere in a human qua human) and civil rights (those that inhere in citizens or civil subjects);
3. natural rights (those that are based on → natural law or human nature) and positive rights (those that are based in the positive law of the state);
4. individual rights and the rights of associations or groups (whether private, like businesses or churches, or public, like municipalities or political parties); and
5. unalienable or nonderogable rights (those that cannot be given or taken away) and alienable or derogable rights (those that can be voluntarily given away or can be taken away under specified legal conditions).

Increasingly today, distinctions are also drawn among the discrete claims of particular parties and groups that have historically not received adequate rights protection — women, children, workers, migrants, minorities, prisoners, captives, indigenous peoples, religious parties, the mentally and physically handicapped, and more. And distinctions are also increasingly drawn among "first generation" civil and political rights, "second generation" social, cultural, and economic rights, and "third generation" rights to peace, environmental protection, and orderly development.

Different types of legal claims and jural relationships are inherent in these classifications of rights. Some scholars distinguish rights (something that triggers a correlative duty in others) from privileges (something that no one has a right to interfere with). Others distinguish active rights (the power or capacity to do or assert something oneself) and passive rights (the entitlement or claim to be given or allowed something by someone or something else). Others distinguish rights or privileges (claims or entitlements to something) from liberties or immunities (freedoms or protections from interference). This latter distinction is also sometimes rendered as positive → freedom (the right to do something) versus negative freedom (the right to be left alone).

In all these foregoing formulations, the term "right" and its equivalents are being used in a "subjective sense" — what is called a subjective right. The right is vested in a subject (whether an individual, group, or entity), and the subject can have that right vindicated before an appropriate authority when the right is threatened or violated. This subjective sense of right is quite different from right in an "objective sense" — what is called an objective right. "Objective right" (or "rightness") means that something is the objectively right thing or action in the circumstances. Objective right obtains when something is rightly ordered, is just, is considered to be right when judged against some objective or external standard. "Right" is here being used as an adjective, not as a noun. It is what is correct or proper — "due and meet," as the Book of Common Prayer put it.

These subjective and objective senses of right can cohere, even overlap. One can say that "a victim of theft has a right to have his or her property restored" or that "it is right for a victim of theft to have his or her property restored." Knowing nothing else, these are parallel statements. But if the victim is a ruthless tycoon and the thief a starving child, the parallel is harder to draw: even though the subject (tycoon) has a right, it might not be objectively right to respect or enforce it. Sometimes the subjective and objective senses of right are more clearly dissociated. Even if it is objectively right for someone to perform an action, it does not always mean the beneficiary of that action has a subjective right to its performance. Though it might be right for you to give alms to the poor, a poor person has no right to receive alms from you. Though it is right for a parishioner to give tithes to the church, a church has no right to receive tithes from that parishioner.

This basic tension between the subjective and objective senses of the English term "right" has parallels in other languages. Ger. *Recht,* Fr. *droit,* It. *diritto,* and Lat. *ius* all can be used in both subjective and objective senses — and sometimes in other senses as well. And just like English, each of these languages has developed its own terms for privileges, immunities, powers, capacities, freedoms, liberties, and more, which are used to sort out various types of rights.

These linguistic tensions and tangles of our rights talk today are products of a two-millennium-long evolution in the West. The intellectual history of Western rights talk is still very much a work in progress, with scholars still discovering and earnestly disputing the basic roots and routes of the development of rights concepts and structures. What follows is a brief sampling of some of the highlights of this still highly contested story.

2. Classical Formulations

The Roman jurists of the first centuries after Christ used the ancient Latin term *ius* to identify right in both its objective and subjective senses. (*Ius* also meant law or legal order more generally.) The objective sense of *ius* — to be in proper order, to perform what is right and required, to give to each his or her due *(ius suum cuique tribuere)* — dominated their texts. But these Roman law texts also sometimes used *ius* subjectively, in the sense of a person "having a right" *(ius habere).* Many of the subjective rights recognized at Roman law involved → property: the right to own or co-own property, the right to possess, lease, or use property, the right to build or prevent building on land, the right to gain access to water, the right to be free from interference or invasion of one's property, the right or capacity to alienate property, the right to bury one's dead, and more. Several texts dealt with personal rights: the rights of testators and heirs, the rights of patrons and guardians, the rights of fathers over children, masters over slaves, mothers over orphaned children and their affairs. Other texts dealt with public rights: the right of an official to punish or deal with his subjects in a certain way, the right to delegate power, the right to appoint and supervise officials. Others dealt with procedural rights in criminal and civil cases. Charles Donahue has recently identified 191 texts on subjective rights in the *Digest* alone (one of the four books of Justinian's *Corpus iuris civilis* of 534) and speculates that hundreds if not thousands more such texts can be found in other books of Roman law.

Classical Roman law also referred to subjective rights using the Latin term *libertas,* which roughly translates as "liberty." One's *libertas* at Roman law turned in part on one's status in Roman society: Men had more *libertas* than women, married women more than concubines, adults more than children, free persons more than slaves, and so on. But each person at Roman law had a basic *libertas* inherent in his or her social status. This concept included a basic right to be free from subjection or undue restraint from others who had no rights *(iura)* or claim *(dominium)* over them. Thus the wife had *libertas* from sexual relations with all others besides her husband. The child had *libertas* from the direction of all others save the paterfamilias or his delegates. Even the slave had *libertas* from the discipline of others besides his or her master, and those rights could be vindicated by filing actions before a judge, directly or through a representative.

Some *libertas* interests recognized at Roman law were cast more generally, and not necessarily conditioned on the correlative rights or duties of others. A good example was the freedom of religion guaranteed to Christians and others under the Edict of Milan (313), passed by Emperor Constantine (→ Religious Liberty). This included "the freedom [*libertas*] to follow whatever religion each one wished"; "a public and free liberty to practice their religion or cult"; and a "free permission [*facultas*] to follow their own religion and worship as befits the peacefulness of our times."

Echoes of both *ius* and *libertas* recurred occasionally in later Frankish and Anglo-Saxon texts. In fact, in a few Anglo-Saxon texts from the late ninth and tenth centuries, these terms were variously translated *ryhtes, rihtes,* and *rihta(e)* (*OED*, s.v. "right"). The careful Roman law differentiation of objective and subjective senses of right, however, seems to have been lost in the last centuries of the first millennium after Christ — though a systematic study of the possible rights talk of the Germanic texts of this period is apparently still a desideratum. And what is also apparently still needed is a close study (in a Romance language) of the possible rights talk of Muslim and Jewish scholars in this same period. After all, both of these groups of scholars had access to the ancient Roman law texts that were lost in the West after the sixth century, and both worked out a refined theological jurisprudence in the eighth through the tenth centuries.

3. Medieval Formulations

The rediscovery of the ancient texts of Roman law in the late 11th century helped to trigger a renaissance of subjective rights talk in the West. Brian Tierney has shown that, already in the 12th century, medieval canonists differentiated all manner of rights *(iura)* and liberties *(libertates)*. They grounded these rights and liberties in the law of nature *(lex naturae)* or natural law *(ius naturale)* and associated them variously with a power *(facultas)* inhering in rational human nature and with the property *(dominium)* of a person or the power *(potestas)* of an office of → authority *(officium)*. The early canonists repeated and glossed many of the subjective rights and liberties set out in Roman law — especially the public rights and powers of rulers, the private rights and liberties of property, and what Gratian in about 1140 called the "rights of liberty" *(iura libertatis)* that persons in different stations of life and offices of authority must enjoy. They also began to weave these early Roman law texts into a whole complex latticework of what we now call rights, freedoms, powers, immunities, protections, and capacities for different groups and persons.

Most important to the medieval canonists were the rights needed to protect the freedom of the church *(libertas ecclesiae)*. "Freedom of the church" from civil and feudal control and corruption had been the rallying cry of Pope → Gregory VII (1073-85), which had inaugurated the Papal Revolution of 1075 (→ Law and Legal Theory 3). In defense of this revolution, medieval canonists specified in great detail the rights of the church to make its own laws, to maintain its own courts, to define its own doctrines and liturgies, and to elect and remove its own clergy. They also stipulated the exemptions of church property from civil taxation and takings and the right of the clergy to control and use church property without interference or encumbrance from secular or feudal authorities. They also guaranteed the immunity of the clergy from civil prosecution, military service, and compulsory testimony, and the rights of smaller church entities like parishes, monasteries, charities, and guilds to form and dissolve, to accept and reject members, and to establish order and discipline. In later decrees of the 12th and 13th centuries, the → canon law defined the rights of church → councils and → synods to participate in the election and discipline of → bishops, → abbots, and other clergy. It defined the rights of the lower clergy vis-à-vis their superiors. It defined the rights of the laity to worship, evangelize, maintain religious symbols, participate in the → sacraments, travel on religious → pilgrimages, and educate their children. It defined the rights of the poor, widows, and needy to seek solace, succor, and sanctuary within the church. It even defined the (truncated) rights that Jews, Muslims, and heretics had in Christian society.

These medieval canon law rights were enforced

by a hierarchy of church courts and other administrative offices, each with distinctive rules of litigation, evidence, and judgment, and with ultimate appeal to Rome. These rights formulations were rendered increasingly sophisticated and systematic in the 14th through 16th centuries through the work of such scholars as William of Ockham (ca. 1285-1347), Richard FitzRalph (ca. 1295-1360), John Wycliffe (ca. 1330-84), Jean Gerson (1363-1429), Conrad Summenhart (1465-1511), Francisco Vitoria (ca. 1480-1546), Fernando Vázquez (1512-69), Francisco Suárez (1548-1617), and others. Particularly the formulations of William of Ockham in the 14th century and the Spanish neoscholastic jurists of the 16th century were of monumental importance to the evolution and expansion of Western rights talk. They provided a good deal of the intellectual arsenal for the later rights theories of Johannes Althusius (1557-1638), Hugo Grotius (1583-1645), Samuel von Pufendorf (1632-94), and others.

The medieval canon law formulations of rights and liberties had parallels in medieval secular law. Particularly notable sources were the literally thousands of treaties, concordats, and charters that were issued from the 11th to the 16th centuries by various religious and secular authorities. These were often detailed, and sometimes very flowery, statements of the rights and liberties to be enjoyed by various groups of clergy, nobles, barons, knights, municipal councils, citizens, universities, monasteries, and other corporate entities. A good example was the Magna Carta (1215), the great charter issued by the English Crown at the behest of the church and barons of England. The Magna Carta guaranteed that "the Church of England shall be free [*libera*] and shall have all her whole rights [*iura*] and liberties [*libertates*] inviolable" and that all "free-men [*liberis hominibus*]" were to enjoy their various "liberties" *(libertates)*. These liberties included sundry rights to property, marriage, and inheritance; to freedom from undue military service; and to freedom to pay one's debts and taxes from the property of one's own choosing. The Magna Carta also set out various rights and powers of towns and of local justices and their tribunals, various rights and prerogatives of the king and of the royal courts, and various procedural rights in these courts (including the right to jury trial).

These medieval charters of rights became important prototypes on which 15th- and 16th-century revolutionaries would later call to justify their revolt against arbitrary authorities (→ Revolution). A good example is the Dutch Declaration of Independence of 1581, by which the estates of the Netherlands justified their revolt against Spanish religious and political tyranny on the strength of "the law of nature" and of the "ancient rights, privileges, and liberties" set out in their medieval charters.

4. Protestant Reformation

The 16th-century Protestant → Reformation grounded its revolt not on ancient charters of rights but on biblical calls for freedom. Particularly it found the NT amply peppered with all manner of aphorisms on freedom: "For freedom Christ has set us free. . . . you were called to freedom" (Gal. 5:1, 13). "Where the Spirit of the Lord is, there is freedom" (2 Cor. 3:17). "You will know the truth, and the truth will make you free. . . . you will be free indeed" (John 8:32, 36). You have been given "the freedom of the glory of the children of God" (Rom. 8:21). These and other biblical passages inspired Martin → Luther (1483-1546) to unleash the Reformation in Germany in 1517 in the name of freedom *(libertas, Freiheit)* — freedom of the church from the tyranny of the → pope, freedom of the laity from the hegemony of the → clergy, freedom of the → conscience from the strictures of canon law. "Freedom of the Christian" was thus the rallying cry of the early Protestant Reformation. It drove theologians and jurists, clergy and laity, princes and peasants alike to denounce the medieval church authorities and legal structures with unprecedented alacrity. The church's canon law books were burned. Church courts were closed. Monastic institutions were confiscated. Endowed benefices were dissolved. Church lands were seized. Clerical privileges were stripped. Mendicant begging was banned. Mandatory → celibacy was suspended. Indulgence trafficking was condemned. Annates to Rome were outlawed. Ties to the pope were severed. Each nation, each church, and each Christian was to be free.

Left in such raw and radical form, this early Protestant call for freedom was a recipe for lawlessness and license, as Luther learned the hard way during the Peasants' Revolt of 1525 (→ Peasants' War). Luther and other Protestants soon came to realize that structures of law and authority were essential to protecting order and peace, even as guarantees of liberties and rights were essential to preserving the message and momentum of the Reformation. The challenge for Protestants was to strike new balances between authority and liberty on the strength of cardinal biblical teachings.

One important Protestant contribution to Western rights talk, offered by Philipp → Melanchthon (1497-1560), John → Calvin (1509-64), and others, was to comb through the Bible in order to find passages that could redefine the nature and authority of the → family, the → church, and the → state vis-à-vis each other and their constituents. The → Reformers regarded these three institutions as fundamental orders of creation, equal before God and each other, and vested with certain natural duties and qualities that the other authorities could not trespass. To define these respective offices clearly not only served to check the natural appetite of the *paterfamilias, patertheologicus,* and *paterpoliticus* for tyranny and abuse, it also helped to clarify the liberties of those subject to their authority, and to specify the grounds on which they could protest or disobey.

A second contribution was the Reformers' habit of grounding rights in the duties of the → Decalogue and of other biblical texts. The First Table of the Decalogue prescribes duties of love that each person owes to God — to honor God and God's name, to observe the → Sabbath and to → worship, to avoid false gods and false swearing. The Second Table prescribes duties of → love that each person owes to neighbors — to honor one's parents and other authorities, not to kill, not to commit adultery, not to steal, not to bear false witness, not to covet. The Reformers cast the person's duties toward God as a set of rights that others could not obstruct — the right to religious exercise: the right to honor God and God's name, the right to rest and worship on one's Sabbath, the right to be free from false gods and false oaths. They cast a person's duties toward a neighbor, in turn, as the neighbor's right to have that duty discharged. One person's duties not to kill, to commit adultery, to steal, or to bear false witness thus gives rise to another person's rights to life, property, fidelity, and reputation.

A third contribution was the effort of later Protestants to unpack the political implications of the signature Reformation teaching that a person is at once sinner and saint *(simul iustus et peccator).* On the one hand, Protestants argued, every person is created in the image of God and justified by faith in God. Every person is called to a distinct → vocation, which stands equal in dignity and sanctity to all others. Every person is a prophet, priest, and king and is responsible to exhort, to minister, and to rule in the community. Every person thus stands equal before God and before his or her neighbor. Every person is vested with a natural liberty to live, to believe, to love and serve God and neighbor. Every person is entitled to the vernacular Scripture, to education, to work in a vocation. On the other hand, Protestants argued, every person is sinful and prone to → evil and egoism. Every person needs the restraint of the law to deter him or her from evil and to drive that one to repentance (→ Penitence). Every person needs the association of others to exhort, minister, and rule him or her with law and with love. Every person, therefore, is inherently a communal creature. Every person belongs to a family, a church, and a political community.

By the later 16th century, Protestant groups began to recast these theological doctrines into democratic norms and forms designed to protect rights. Protestant doctrines of the person and society were cast into democratic social forms. Since all persons stand equal before God, they must stand equal before God's political agents in the state. Since God has vested all persons with natural liberties of life and belief, the state must ensure them of similar civil liberties. Since God has called all persons to be prophets, priests, and kings, the state must protect their constitutional freedoms to speak, to preach, and to rule in the community. Since God has created persons as social creatures, the state must promote and protect a plurality of social institutions, particularly the church and the family. Protestant doctrines of sin, in turn, were cast into democratic political forms. The political office must be protected against the sinfulness of the political official. Political power, like ecclesiastical power, must be distributed among self-checking executive, legislative, and judicial branches. Officials must be elected to limited terms of office. Laws must be clearly codified, and discretion closely guarded. If officials abuse their office, they must be disobeyed. If they persist in their abuse, they must be removed, even if by revolutionary force and regicide.

These Protestant teachings were among the driving ideological forces behind the revolts of the French Huguenots, Dutch Pietists, and Scottish Presbyterians against their monarchical oppressors in the later 16th and 17th centuries. They were also critical weapons in the arsenal of the 17th-century English revolutionaries, whose efforts yielded the Petition of Right (1628) and the Bill of Rights (1689). Both these documents set firm limits on royal authority and prescribed rules for royal succession and parliamentary election in England. The Bill of Rights went further in guaranteeing English citizens various "undoubted rights and liberties" — the rights to speech, petition, and election, the right to bear arms, and various criminal procedural protections (right to jury trial, freedom from excessive bail and fines and from cruel and unusual punishment). These were important public law rights that were added to the growing body of private law rights already recognized by the common law and civil law.

Rights

5. **Enlightenment**

While medieval canonists grounded rights in natural law and ancient charters, and while Protestant Reformers grounded them in biblical texts and theological anthropology, → Enlightenment writers in Europe and North America grounded rights in human nature and the social contract. Building in part on ancient Stoic ideas, Thomas Hobbes (1588-1679), John Locke (1632-1704), Jean-Jacques Rousseau (1712-78), Thomas Jefferson (1743-1826), and others argued for a new foundation of rights and political order. Every individual, they argued, was created, or was by nature, equal in virtue and dignity and was vested with inherent and unalienable rights of life, liberty, and property. Each person was naturally capable of choosing his or her own means and measures of → happiness without necessary external reference or commandment. In their natural state, the state of nature, all persons were free to exercise their natural rights fully.

Life in this state of nature, however, was at minimum "inconvenient," as Locke put it — if not "brutish, nasty, and short," as Hobbes put it. For there was no means to balance and broker disputes about one person's rights against those of all others, no incentive to invest or create property or conclude contracts when one's title was not sure, no mechanism for dealing with the needs of children, the weak, the disabled, the vulnerable (→ Persons with Disabilities). As a consequence, rational persons chose to move from the state of nature to a society. They did so by entering into social contracts and ratifying constitutions to govern their newly created societies. By these instruments, persons agreed to sacrifice or limit some of their natural rights for the sake of creating a measure of social order and peace. They also agreed to delegate their natural rights to self-rule to elected officials who would represent and exercise executive, legislative, and judicial authority on their behalf. At the same time, however, these social contracts and political constitutions insisted on the protection of various "unalienable" rights that were to be enjoyed, and the specification of the conditions of "due process of law" under which "alienable" rights could be abridged or taken away. And they also insisted on the right to elect and change their representatives in government, and to be tried in all cases by their peers.

Particularly the American and French constitutions reflected these new Enlightenment views. The Virginia Declaration of Rights (1776), for example, provided in article 1: "That all men are by nature equally free and independent, and have certain inherent rights, of which, when they enter into a state of society, they cannot, by any compact, deprive or divest their posterity; namely, the enjoyment of life and liberty, with the means of acquiring and possessing property, and pursuing and obtaining happiness and safety." The declaration went on to specify the rights of the people to vote and to run for office, their "indubitable, unalienable, and indefeasible right to reform, alter or abolish" their government if necessary, various traditional criminal procedural protections, the right to jury trial in civil and criminal cases, freedom of the press, and various freedoms of religion. But the declaration also reflected traditional Christian sentiments in providing that "no free government, or the blessings of liberty, can be preserved to any people but by a firm adherence to justice, moderation, temperance, frugality, and virtue and by frequent recurrence to fundamental principles," and further by insisting that it was "the mutual duty of all to practice Christian forbearance, love, and charity towards each other." Even stronger such traditional Christian formulations stood alongside the new Enlightenment views in the 1780 Massachusetts Constitution.

The Bill of Rights of 1789, which amended the United States Constitution of 1787, was more forceful in its articulation of basic Enlightenment sentiments on rights. While the Constitution spoke generically of the "blessings of liberty" and specified a few discrete "privileges and immunities," it was left to the Bill of Rights to enumerate the rights of American citizens. The Bill of Rights guaranteed the freedoms of religion, speech, assembly, and press, the right to bear arms, freedom from forced quartering of soldiers, freedom from illegal searches and seizures, various criminal procedural protections (the right to grand jury indictment and trial by jury, the right to a fair and speedy trial, the right to face accusers and have them compelled to appear, freedom from double jeopardy, the privilege against self-incrimination, freedom from excessive bail and cruel and unusual punishment), the right to jury trial in civil cases, the guarantee not to be deprived of life, liberty, or property without due process of law, and the right not to have property taken for public use without just compensation. This original Bill of Rights was later augmented by several other constitutional amendments, the most important of which were the right to be free from → slavery and involuntary servitude, the right to equal protection under the law, and the right for all adults, male and female, to vote.

The French Declaration of the Rights of Man and Citizen (1791) enumerated various "natural, unalienable, and sacred rights," including liberty, property, security, and resistance to oppression, "the freedom to do everything which injures no one else," the right to participate in the foundation and formulation of law, a guarantee that all citizens are equal before the law and equally eligible to all dignities and to all public positions and occupations, according to their abilities. This declaration also included basic criminal procedure protections, freedom of (religious) opinions, freedoms of speech and press, and rights to property. Both the French and American constitutions and declarations were essential prototypes for a substantial number of constitutional and international documents on rights that were forged in the next century.

6. Modern Age

While these Enlightenment foundations and formulations of rights have remained prominent among some theorists, a concept of universal rights predicated on "human dignity" has become increasingly common today. In the mid-20th century, the world stared in horror into Hitler's death camps and Stalin's gulags, where all sense of humanity and dignity had been brutally sacrificed. In response, the world seized anew on the ancient concept of human dignity, claiming this as the "ur-principle" of a new world order. The Universal Declaration of Human Rights set forth by the United Nations in 1948 opened its preamble with what would become classic words: "recognition of the inherent dignity and of the equal and inalienable rights of all members of the human family is the foundation of freedom, justice, and peace in the world."

The United Nations and several nation-states issued a number of landmark documents on human rights thereafter. Foremost among them were the two great international covenants promulgated by the United Nations in 1966. Both these covenants took as their starting point the "inherent dignity" and "the equal and inalienable rights of all members of the human family," and the belief that all such rights "derive from the inherent dignity of the human person." The International Covenant on Economic, Social, and Cultural Rights (1966) posed as essential to human dignity the rights to self-determination, subsistence, work, welfare, security, education, and various other forms of participation in cultural life. The International Covenant on Civil and Political Rights (1966) set out a long catalog of rights to life and to security of person and property, freedom from slavery and cruelty, basic civil and criminal procedural protections, rights to travel and pilgrimage, freedoms of religion, expression, and assembly, rights to marriage and family life, and freedom from discrimination on grounds of race, color, sex, language, and national origin.

A number of other international and domestic instruments took particular aim at racial, religious, and gender discrimination in education, employment, social welfare programs, and other forms and forums of public life, and the protection of children, migrants, workers, and indigenous peoples. Later instruments, like the 1981 U.N. Declaration on the Elimination of All Forms of Intolerance and Discrimination Based on Religion or Belief and the 1989 Vienna Concluding Document, provided important foundations for the protection of religious rights for individuals and groups, though religious rights protections in international law remain surprisingly underdeveloped.

Christian and Jewish communities participated actively as midwives in the birth of this modern rights movement. Individual religious groups issued bold confessional statements and manifestos on human rights shortly after World War II. Several denominations and budding ecumenical bodies joined with Jewish nongovernmental organizations in the cultivation of human rights at the international level. The free-church tradition played a critical role in the civil rights movement in America and beyond (→ Free Church), as did the → liberation theology and Christian Democratic movements in Europe and Latin America.

Various Christian groups also provided an active nursery for the cultivation of new global understandings of human rights predicated on human dignity. In the Declaration on Religious Liberty, *Dignitatis humanae,* and in several other documents produced during and after the Second → Vatican Council (1962-65), the → Roman Catholic Church took some of the decisive first steps, reversing earlier statements like the 1864 → Syllabus of Errors that had stood foursquare against human rights. Every person, the Catholic Church now taught, is created by God with "dignity, intelligence and free will . . . and has rights flowing directly and simultaneously from his very nature." Such rights include the right to life and adequate standards of living, to moral and cultural values, to religious activities, to assembly and association, to marriage and family life, and to various social, political, and economic benefits and opportunities. The church emphasized the religious rights of conscience, worship, assembly, and education, calling them the "first rights" of any civic order. The church also stressed the need to balance individual and associational rights, particularly those involving the church, family, and school. Governments everywhere were encouraged to create conditions conducive to the realization and protection of these inviolable rights and encouraged to root out discrimination, whether social or cultural, whether based on sex, race, color, social distinction, language, or religion. Within a decade, various ecumenical groups, some Protestants, and a few Orthodox Christian groups crafted comparable comprehensive declarations on human rights, albeit with varying emphasis on the concept of human dignity.

Today, the concept of human dignity has become ubiquitous to the point of cliché — a moral trump frayed by heavy use, a general principle harried by constant invocation. We now read regularly of the dignity of luxury, pleasure, and leisure; the dignity of poverty, pain, and imprisonment; the dignity of identity, belonging, and difference; the dignity of ethnic, cultural, and linguistic purity; the dignity of sex, gender, and sexual preference; the dignity of aging, dying, and death. At the same time, the corpus of human rights has become swollen to the point of eruption — with many recent rights claims no longer anchored in universal norms of human dignity but aired as special aspirations of an individual or a group. We now hear regularly of the rights to peace, health, and beauty; the right to rest, holidays, and work breaks; the right to work, development, and economic expansion; the right to abortion, suicide, and death.

On the one hand, the current ubiquity of the principle of human dignity testifies to its universality. Moreover, the constant proliferation of human rights precepts speaks to their power to inspire new hope for many desperate persons and peoples around the world. Additionally, the increased pervasiveness of these norms is partly a function of emerging globalization. Since the first international documents on human dignity and human rights were issued in the mid-20th century, many new voices and values have joined the global dialogue — especially from Africa, Asia, and Latin America, and from various Buddhist, Confucian, Hindu, Islamic, and traditional communities. It is simple ignorance to assume that the first international documents were truly universal statements on human dignity and human rights. The views of Christians, Jews, and Enlightenment exponents dominated them. And it is simple arrogance to assume that the 1940s through 1960s were the golden age of human dignity and human rights. Such theological and legal constructions are in need of constant reformation. The recent challenges of the South and the East to the prevailing Western paradigm of human dignity and human rights might well be salutary.

On the other hand, the very ubiquity of the principle of human dignity today threatens its claims to universality. And the very proliferation of new human rights threatens their long-term effectiveness for doing good. Human dignity needs to be assigned some limits if it is to remain a sturdy foundation for the edifice of human rights. Human rights need to be founded firmly on human dignity and other moral principles, lest they devolve into a gaggle of wishes and wants. Fairness commands as broad a definition of human dignity as possible, so that no legitimate human good is excluded and no legitimate human rights claim is foreclosed. But prudence counsels a narrower definition of human dignity, so that not every good becomes part of human dignity, and not every aspiration becomes subject to human rights vindication.

The task of defining the appropriate ambit of human dignity and human rights today must be a multidisciplinary, multireligious, and multicultural exercise. Many disciplines, religions, and cultures around the globe have unique sources and resources, texts and traditions that speak to human dignity and human rights. Some endorse dignity and rights with alacrity and urge their expansion into new arenas. Others demur and urge their reform and restriction. It is essential that each community be allowed to speak with its own unique accent, to work with its own distinct methods on human dignity and human rights — that the exercise be multi- rather than inter-disciplinary, -religious, and -cultural in character. It is also essential, however, that each of these disciplines, religions, and cultures develops a capacity for bilingualism — an ability to speak with insiders and outsiders alike about their unique understanding of the origin, nature, and purpose of human dignity and human rights.

Bibliography: A. S. Brett, *Liberty, Right, and Nature: Individual Rights in Later Scholastic Thought* (Cambridge, 1997) • I. Brownlie and G. S. Goodwin-Gill, eds., *Basic Documents on Human Rights* (4th ed.; Oxford, 2002) • R. W. Davis, ed., *The Origins of Modern Freedom in the West* (Stanford, Calif., 1995) • C. A. Donahue, "*Ius* in the Subjective Sense in Roman Law: Reflections on Villey and Tierney," *A Ennio Cortese* (ed. D. Maffei; Rome, 2001) 1.506-35 • W. N. Hohfeld, *Fundamental Legal Conceptions* (new ed.; Aldershot, 2001; orig. pub., 1919) • N. Lerner, *Religion, Beliefs, and International Human Rights* (Maryknoll, N.Y., 2000) • O. O'Donovan and J. L. O'Donovan, eds., *From Irenaeus to Grotius: A Sourcebook in Christian Political Thought, 100-1625* (Grand Rapids, 1999) • L. Strauss, *Natural Right and History* (Chicago, 1953) • B. Tierney, *The Idea of Natural Rights: Studies on*

Natural Rights, Natural Law, and Church Law, 1150-1625 (Atlanta, 1997); idem, *Religion, Law, and the Growth of Constitutional Thought, 1150-1650* (Cambridge, 1982) • R. Tuck, *Natural Rights Theories: Their Origins and Development* (Cambridge, 1979) • M. Villey, *La formation de la pensée juridique moderne* (new ed.; Paris, 1975); idem, *Leçons d'histoire de la philosophie du droit* (new ed.; Paris, 1962) • C. Wirszubski, *"Libertas" as a Political Idea at Rome during the Late Republic and Early Principate* (Cambridge, 1960) • J. Witte Jr., *Law and Protestantism: The Legal Teachings of the Lutheran Reformation* (Cambridge, 2002) • J. Witte Jr. and F. S. Alexander, eds., *Modern Christian Teachings on Law, Politics, Society, and Human Nature* (2 vols.; New York, 2005) • J. Witte Jr. and J. D. van der Vyver, eds., *Religious Human Rights in Global Perspective* (The Hague, 1996).

John Witte Jr.

Rig-Veda

The word "Rig-Veda" means literally "sacred knowledge in stanzas." As the sacred text in many strands of → Hinduism, the Rig-Veda is a collection of 1,028 poems, with 10,600 stanzas in all. It is written in ancient Sanskrit and divided into 10 cycles, of which 1 and 8-10 were added later to an older corpus (2-7). In the latter the hymns of a traditional family of poets are collected and arranged according to deities and an ascending number of stanzas. The first part of the first cycle and then the eighth cycle contain poems of a later family, while the second part of the first cycle and the tenth cycle consist of a large appendix to the collection in which later poems, some of a philosophical content, have found a place.

The ninth cycle stands apart inasmuch as it contains only hymns to *soma pavamāna*, the mysterious sacred drink at the moment of its mystically interpreted "purification" in the filter (→ Mysticism 1). This purification, one of the most important components of ancient Indo-Iranian ritual, survives in → Iranian religions as well (ancient Indian *soma* = ancient Iranian *haoma*).

The other deities to which hymns are addressed are, on the one hand, deified natural forces like Agni (Skt. "fire"), which has an important ritual role as mediator between gods and humans, Vayu (wind), or Surya (sun). On the other hand, we have personified ethical and social forces like the solemn truth god Varuṇa, who punishes with dropsy those who lie or break their word; Mitra (ancient Iranian Mithra), who represents harmony, friendship, and integrity; and the hospitality god Aryaman. At the center of the pantheon stands Indra, originally a god of victory who breaks the resistance of enemies but who might now be called the national god of the Vedic Aryans. This god made the world habitable for us, creating water and cows to care for nourishment, smiting → demons that had kept these shut up, and helping those who believe in him and serve him in the ritual (→ Rite), not only in war but also in other critical situations, making their fields fertile, increasing their flocks, and giving them heroic sons. This is the king of the gods, and he is still such in the pantheons of → Buddhism and Hinduism. Here, however, the ancient gods are far less important than Buddha or the supreme Hindu god.

A point worth noting about the → religion of the Rig-Veda is that, unlike later Hinduism, it involves → polytheism without either → temple or images. The gods dwell invisibly in heaven and are present only in the poetic stanzas, which are offered in → sacrifice in a kind of stylized banquet. The sacred word of poetry, which in distinction from what happened in other religions was for many centuries handed down only in oral tradition, contains the truth about the gods and the universe and is thus efficacious in both → prayer and ritual.

The concept of → truth (ancient Indian *ṛta* = ancient Iranian *aša* = classical Skt. *satya*) is of central importance in Indian religion and philosophy. In the Rig-Veda the universe and the gods act in accordance with the truth. In the → Upanishads we attain to immortality by knowledge of the truth. An ideal hero like Rama acts according to the truth in the → Ramayana. Mahatma Gandhi (1869-1948) regarded truth as the center of his worldview.

Bibliography: D. Frawley, *The Rig Veda and the History of India* (New Delhi, 2001) • K. F. Geldner, trans., *Der Rig-Veda. Aus dem Sanskrit ins Deutsche übersetzt und mit einem laufenden Kommentar versehen* (3 vols. in 1; Cambridge, Mass., 2003) • J. Gonda, *The Medium in the Rgveda* (Leiden, 1979); idem, *Die Religionen Indiens*, vol. 1, *Veda und älterer Hinduismus* (Stuttgart, 1960) • B. A. van Nooten and G. B. Holland, eds., *Rig Veda: A Metrically Restored Text, with Introduction and Notes* (Cambridge, Mass., 1994) • H. Oldenberg, *Metrische und textgeschichtliche Prolegomena zu einer kritischen Rigveda-Ausgabe* (Wiesbaden, 1982; orig. pub., 1888); idem, *The Religion of the Veda* (trans. S. B. Shrotri; Delhi, 1988; orig. pub., 1894) • P. Thieme, *Gedichte aus dem Rig-Veda* (Stuttgart, 1964) • W. I. Thompson, *Coming into Being: Artifacts and Texts in the Evolution of Consciousness* (New York, 1996).

Renate Söhnen-Thieme

Rite

1. Religious History
2. Liturgy

1. Religious History

The term "rite" (Lat. *ritus,* orig. "what is correctly reckoned," then "what is appropriate; usage, custom") came into use in → Roman religion for an ordered and solemn ceremony. The adjective *ritualis* thus means "that which relates to religious usage."

1.1. → Theology tends to use "rites," and → religious studies and social anthropology prefer "ritual," for religious ceremonies or for sequences of such ceremonies. Ethnology recognizes that whole groups of human actions and animal modes of behavior have a set and standardized character. Hence that which originally gives a rite its meaning is simply that it takes place.

1.2. For this reason a rite is open to all the meanings that an event may have when it relates to a rite. But the rite then links the meanings more closely to itself than an event does. The form of the rite is bodily action, including speaking and singing, which becomes an elemental mode of secular or sacred celebration. In the sphere of the involved or associated meanings, we first have on the secular side rites of healing fellowship, commemoration (according to a calendar), personal rites (e.g., biological, linked to birth and → death, and biographical, linked to puberty, dedication, or → marriage), and social rites (linked to the building of houses, the founding of cities, the prosecution of war, and the making of peace). Security (apotropaic) rites also call for notice.

Then on the religious side we have rites related to veneration, reconciliation, → sacrifice, and → initiation. The various meanings merge into one another more than they do in the case of ideas or doctrines, but originally secular ceremonies are more general, while the religious are tied more closely to the cult and to → liturgy (→ Sacred and Profane).

1.3. The central point for the development of meanings is the phase, which constitutes a threshold (Lat. *limen*) between differently structured times or localities that affect the persons participating in the rites. This phase may last only less than an hour, or it may go on for several days. It is marked by the putting off the habits, clothes, moral rules, and communications of one stage when those of another have not yet been adopted. The threshold phase is especially productive in → myths, → symbols, rituals, systems of thought, and works of art.

1.4. Threshold conditions often coincide with those of the margins of society or of individual inferiority. Rites here are models or stereotypes that give special help in getting across the critical threshold phase and enable those participating to adjust to what are for them new classifications of reality and new rules governing their relations to → society. Rites that give expression to a permanent threshold state may sometimes take the form of a social drama featuring highly visible rites of a change or enhancement of status.

1.5. Myths may explain what rites mean, with an intermediary step occasionally being a description of the actual course of the ritual. The explanation itself, whether narrative (myth, saga, or legend), enumerative (litany), or representative (stage play or → dance), can change more easily than can the rite itself and can even acquire a measure of independence in entering into a relation of shifting meanings with the rite.

→ Cultic Meal; Passover; Worship 1.1

Bibliography: C. Colpe, "Mysterienkult und Liturgie," *Spätantike und Christentum* (ed. C. Colpe, L. Honnefelder, and M. Lutz-Bachmann; Berlin, 1992) 203-28 • M. Douglas, *Natural Symbols: Explorations in Cosmology* (2d ed.; London, 1973) • A. van Gennep, *The Rites of Passage* (Chicago, 1960; orig. pub., 1908) • C. Humphrey and J. Laidlaw, *The Archetypal Actions of Ritual: A Theory of Ritual Illustrated by the Jain Rite of Worship* (Oxford, 1994) • J. Kreinath, C. Hartung, and A. Deschner, eds., *The Dynamics of Changing Rituals: The Transformation of Religious Rituals within Their Social and Cultural Context* (New York, 2004) • N. Mitchell, *Liturgy and the Social Sciences* (Collegeville, Minn., 1999) • B. G. Myerhoff et al., "Rites of Passages," *EncRel(E)* 12.380-403 • E. G. Parrinder, *Worship in the World's Religions* (New York, 1961) • F. Staal, "The Meaninglessness of Ritual," *Numen* 26 (1979) 2-22 • V. W. Turner, *From Ritual to Theatre: The Human Seriousness of Play* (New York, 1982); idem, *The Ritual Process: Structure and Anti-structure* (Chicago, 1969) • E. M. Zuesse, "Ritual," *EncRel(E)* 12.405-22.

Carsten Colpe

2. Liturgy

2.1. In an ecclesiastical and liturgical context the word "rite" means first the customary way of doing something in → worship (A. Adam and R. Berger). More generally, it occurs also in the areas of → canon law and in the patterns of everyday living. We may thus speak of the rite of a local church or denominational church when what we have in mind is that which distinguishes it liturgically, as well as legally and spiritually.

2.2. We also need to distinguish the use of rites (and of ritual) in → practical theology, which takes into account factors from the history of religion and cultural anthropology, as well as theories from depth psychology, developmental psychology, and → social psychology, which we can refer to only very summarily in this context.

For S. Freud (1856-1939) the rituals of the compulsive neurotic — which include symbolically the averting, as well as the modified fulfillment, of unconscious and repressed impulses — are models of all ritual actions, even in the sphere of → religion, which actions can be defined as a universal compulsive → neurosis. In contrast, value is placed on the ability to develop and carry out rituals in some models in development psychology and interactive theory. Ritual here is the ontogenetic presupposition of the development of social → institutions (E. H. Erikson). It is essential in the development of individual → identity and also in giving equilibrium to society, which must offer its members a part in self-regulation by participation in social gatherings (E. Goffman).

If we see in rituals symbolic substitute actions, especially in situations in which technical control of the circumstances does not yet seem to be possible (A. Hahn), then by means of symbolic expression the ritual action, as in Freud, makes emotional and active relaxation possible, such as we experience in situations in which we are powerless to do anything. This understanding comes close to a functional theory that ascribes to churches the special task of gaining control symbolically, by word or action, over ongoing contingencies in individual and social spheres.

2.3. If we describe worship as an act of human expression (A. R. Sequeira), it shares the ritual dimension of the communicative action (→ Communication) by which we both depict and enact ideas, actions, and emotions (including faith) that are life-determinative. This approach, though, does not decide the question whether Christian worship can simply be defined as ritual from the standpoint of either → anthropology or → theology.

The commonly held theory must be critically tested that regards the disposition for ritual as a basic anthropological category (M. Josuttis) that must be presupposed in all efforts to communicate the → gospel. If there is a positive correlation between the ability to adopt developed symbols (M. Douglas) and therewith the ability for ritual on the one side, and the adhesion of social groups (→ Group and Group Dynamics), the pressure for conformity that governs them (→ Solidarity), and the strength of the ties that bind them on the other, then we can expect a weakening of ritual needs in mobile and permissive societies that have personal rather than positional models of → socialization.

The functioning of (post-)modern "risk societies" (U. Beck) demands that vital life decisions may in principle be revised (→ Postmodernity). Here, then, is a situation that is in striking contrast to the idea of a life firmly linked to a fixed cycle, and it puts a general question to the → occasional services that are popular in the churches but whose point is to depict the irreversibility of transitions and changes of status once they are made, and thus to relieve individuals of the need to constantly validate afresh, either to others or to society, their present position.

In these circumstances the church's rituals are in danger of losing their social reference (their *Sitz im Leben*). Discussions of their theological contents and liturgical reconstructions are not enough, then, to make good the loss. What seems to be needed is a new rooting of these actions in their sociocultural context so that they will again relate to actual life experience.

This need also applies to congregational worship that meets the constitutional needs of a religious group and to the → Eucharist as a ritual of communion or participation. The loss of broader socially significant functions (multifunctionality) has the same effect as the splitting apart of theological and cultural theories of the meaning (→ Culture) of the occasional services and can be made good only by new processes of acculturation. Hence in a culture characterized by frenetic, thoughtless consumption of life resources ("fast-food culture"), the Eucharist might function as a countersymbol and contribute to the emergence of a new "culture of life," albeit with the one presupposition: that the Eucharist itself be clearly articulated and understood as a festive or celebratory meal.

The intended strengthening of social ties in groups and communities naturally cannot disguise the contradiction in principle that exists between (1) the inalienably personal structure of the gospel and faith and (2) ritual modes of representation and communication. Rituals are "necessary but dangerous" (W. Jetter). In this ambivalence they can give community form to the gospel only where the tension is upheld between the self-fulfillment of faith in the medium of symbolic communication and the permeation of life with the forces of faith.

Bibliography: A. Adam and R. Berger, *Pastoralliturgisches Handlexikon* (4th ed.; Freiburg, 1986) • U. Beck, *Risk Society: Towards a New Modernity* (London, 1992) • C. Bell, *Ritual Theory, Ritual Practice*

(Oxford, 1992) • K.-H. Bieritz, "Gegengifte. Kirchliche Kasualpraxis in der Risikogesellschaft," *ZdZ* 46 (1992) 3-10 • R. Bocock, *Ritual in Industrial Society* (London, 1974) • M. Douglas, *Natural Symbols: Explorations in Cosmology* (2d ed.; London, 1973) • É. Durkheim, *The Elementary Forms of Religious Life* (New York, 1995; orig. pub., 1912) • E. H. Erikson, *Identity and the Life Cycle* (New York, 1959); idem, "Ontogeny of Ritualization in Man," *Philosophical Transactions of the Royal Society of London*, ser. B, 251 (1966) 337-49 • S. Freud, *Civilization and Its Discontents* (New York, 1989); idem, "Obsessive Actions and Religious Practices" (1907), *The Standard Edition of the Complete Psychological Works of Sigmund Freud* (24 vols.; ed. J. Strachey; London, 1953-74) 9.117-27 • E. Goffman, *Interaction Ritual: Essays on Face-to-Face Behavior* (New York, 1982); idem, *The Presentation of the Self in Everyday Life* (Garden City, N.Y., 1959); idem, *Stigma: Notes on the Management of Spoiled Identity* (Englewood Cliffs, N.J., 1963) • R. L. Grimes, *Beginnings in Ritual Studies* (rev. ed.; Columbia, S.C., 1995) • I. Gruenwald, *Rituals and Ritual Theory in Ancient Israel* (Leiden, 2003) • A. Hahn, "Kultische und säkulare Riten und Zeremonien in soziologischer Sicht," *Anthropologie des Kults* (Freiburg, 1977) 51-81 • W. Jetter, *Symbol und Ritual. Anthropologische Elemente im Gottesdienst* (2d ed.; Göttingen, 1986) • M. Josuttis, *Praxis des Evangeliums zwischen Politik und Religion. Grundprobleme der praktischen Theologie* (4th ed.; Munich, 1988); idem, *Der Weg in das Leben. Eine Einführung in den Gottesdienst auf verhaltenswissenschaftlicher Grundlage* (3d ed.; Munich, 2000) • T. Luckmann, "Riten als Bewältigung lebensweltlicher Grenzen," *SZS* 3 (1985) 535-51 • H. Maccoby, *Ritual and Morality: The Ritual Purity System and Its Place in Judaism* (Cambridge, 1999) • N. D. Mitchell, *Liturgy and the Social Sciences* (Collegeville, Minn., 1999) • A. R. Sequeira, "Gottesdienst als menschliche Ausdruckshandlung," *GDK* 3.7-39. • V. Turner, *From Ritual to Theatre: The Human Seriousness of Play* (New York, 1982); idem, *The Ritual Process: Structure and Anti-structure* (New York, 1982; orig. pub., 1966).

Karl-Heinrich Bieritz

Roma

Some human rights groups and nongovernmental organizations today have suggested substituting the names "Roma" and "Sinti" for the collective term "Gypsies" (Ger. *Zigeuner*, Gk. *Athinganoi*, Lat. *cingari*, possibly from Pers. *zang* [iron, tin]; Eng. "Gypsy" represents a back-formation of *gipcyan*, var. of "Egyptian," from a belief that Gypsies came originally from Egypt). Since the Middle Ages the traditional designation "Gypsy" has allegedly been perceived as a term of discrimination (→ Prejudice). "Roma" and "Sinti" designate the two largest tribal groups of Gypsies in central Europe, names long familiar only to specialists in Romany scholarship. In fact, however, other tribes are living in the Balkans, which has the largest percentage of Roma in Europe, as well as in Spain, Switzerland, and the British Isles. Moreover, in the Middle East, where some suggest most Roma actually live today, the names "Roma" and "Sinti" are completely unknown.

"Roma" (i.e., "Romans") alludes to → Byzantium in the eastern → Roman Empire as the center from which one can cogently assume that many European Roma (as well as American Roma, following the emanicipation of slaves in Walachia in 1855) dispersed. The name "Sinti" has nothing to do with what earlier scholars in Romany studies assumed was their original home, namely, Sind in the Indus Valley. It derives, rather, from the Yeniche language, one of the languages of central Europe common among Roma groups that do not speak Romany.

The voluntary or enforced marginal status (→ Minorities) of Roma almost always includes a special language that is made up of altered bits of the national language (argot) or that preserves words or even structures from earlier migrations. Thus many Roma families cultivate Romany, which in spite of considerable regional deviations is related to Sanskrit (as shown by August Pott in Halle in 1844/45). This fact suggests an ultimate Indian origin for at least some Roma. Parts of the Bible have been translated into Romany from 1836 onward.

Economically, Roma have engaged in supplementary crafts and trades and services. They often do things that make a nomadic life possible (→ Nomads), but in many parts of Europe they live settled lives. In → industrial societies they often combine a settled life (in communal projects) with a nomadic life during the warmer months. There are economic as well as social reasons for this combination, but nomadic groups face increasing problems (e.g., finding camping sites, complying with hygienic regulations and rules for compulsory schooling).

In their religion Romany groups retain elements from the traditions of peoples with whom they have had prolonged contact, for example, revering the dead (mulo, or spirit of the dead; → Dead, Cult of the), belief in the power of places, a → mother goddess (Bibi), and especially → magic. But Roma also share in the popular religion of the majority population and outwardly make profession of it (→ Islam, Orthodox, or Roman Catholic). Their obvious cultural distinctiveness has exposed them to constant persecution right up to attempted → genocide during World War II (→ Holocaust), though they are now tolerated in modern society.

A variety of Christian missions are at work among Roma in towns, and other missionary societies (→ Mission) try to meet them in their seminomadic and clannish lifestyle with its → taboos. In its pastoral care of nomads the → Roman Catholic Church has special places of pilgrimage for Roma after the model of Saintes Maries de la Mer, on the Rhone delta in southern France. Other missions like the Pentecostals take an international approach, seeking to integrate elements of Romany music, song, and culture (→ Marginalized Groups) or working with the notion of a "lost tribe of Israel."

Bibliography: Z. D. Barany, *The East European Gypsies: Regime Change, Marginality, and Ethnopolitics* (Cambridge, 2002) • D. M. Crowe, *A History of the Gypsies of Eastern Europe and Russia* (New York, 1996) • R. Gronemeyer and G. A. Rakelmann, *Die Zigeuner. Reisende in Europa: Roma, Sinti, Manouches, Gitanos, Gypsies, Kalderasch, Vlach und andere* (Cologne, 1988) • G. Lewy, *The Nazi Persecution of the Gypsies* (New York, 2000) • Y. Matras, *Romani: A Linguistic Introduction* (Cambridge, 2002) • C. Mayerhofer, *Dorfzigeuner. Kultur und Geschichte der Burgenland-Roma von den Ersten Republik bis zur Gegenwart* (Vienna, 1987) • R. C. Moreau, *The Rom: Walking in the Paths of the Gypsies* (Toronto, 2002) • M. Münzel and B. Streck, eds., *Kumpania und Kontrolle. Moderne Behinderungen zigeunerischen Lebens* (Giessen, 1981) • J. Okely, *The Traveller-Gypsies* (Cambridge, 1983) • I. S. Pogany, *The Roma Café: Human Rights and the Plight of the Romani People* (London, 2004) • R. Vossen, *Zigeuner. Roma, Sinti, Gitanos, Gypsies zwischen Verfolgung und Romantisierung* (Frankfurt, 1983) • W. O. Weyrauch, ed., *Gypsy Law: Romani Legal Traditions and Culture* (Berkeley, Calif., 2001).

Bernhard Streck

Roman Catholic Church

The term "Roman Catholic Church" is a specific designation of the church that is in union with the bishop of Rome, known also as the patriarch of the West and the → pope. Since some Eastern churches are also in union with the bishop of Rome but do not worship according to the Latin, or Roman, ritual (e.g., Melchite, Maronite, and Chaldean), the Roman Catholic Church most frequently speaks of itself as the Catholic Church, as can be seen in all 16 documents of the Second → Vatican Council (1962-65), and also throughout the *Catechism of the Catholic Church* (1994; → Catholic, Catholicity, 1.3; Church 3.2).

1. The Church's Developing Self-Understanding

1.1. *Apostles and Early Church*

The Roman Catholic Church traces its local foundation to the witness of → Peter and → Paul to the life, death, and resurrection of Jesus Christ. This witness includes not only their preaching but also their martyrdoms (in 67 or 68). Based on the mission Christ gave the chosen 12 disciples, who were also given a share in his authority, he "sent them out to proclaim the → kingdom of God and to heal" (Luke 9:2; see also 22:29-30). Peter's place of leadership within the college of the → Twelve is grounded in his → confession of faith (Matt. 16:17; cf. 11:25), his leadership in asking questions of Jesus (John 6:68; Matt. 18:21), his testimony at the transfiguration (Matt 17:4), and his preaching after the resurrection (throughout Acts 1–10). As Peter is shown to be *primus inter pares* (first among equals), so the patriarch of the West considers his ministry to be in succession to Peter and of service to the unity among the other patriarchal sees. The slow unfolding of the meaning of this ministry is given in the historical evidence wherein the church was required to address conflicts both within itself and in relation to secular powers — at first the → Roman Empire, and later the regimes beyond it.

At the time of Constantine's founding of Constantinople in the former Byzantium on the Bosporus (326) and of the persistent → Arian attacks on → Athanasius (ca. 297-373), who had sought a review of his position as bishop of Alexandria from Pope Julius I (337-52; DH 132), a significant formulation of primacy arose. Julius agreed to hear the theological and jurisdictional claims of the Arians and Eusebians against Athanasius. In 340, when the Eusebians failed to appear in Rome, Julius held a synod restoring Athanasius and other exiled bishops to their sees (Athanasius, *Contra Arian.* 20-35). The appeal and the judgment testified to Athanasius's faith, its formulation in doctrine, and the jurisdictional ecclesiastical order.

1.2. *Early to Late Middle Ages*

The struggle between the Arian reading of the Scriptures, with its rejection of Christ as divine, and the Athanasian articulation of that mystery in the term *homoousia* was ongoing (→ Nicaea, Councils of, 2.2). In 369 Pope Damasus (366-84) convened a council in Rome that condemned the Arian creed that had been developed at the Synod of Rimini (359), and he did so with the claim that "it never secured the consent of the Roman Bishop, whose opinion should certainly have been sought beforehand" (H. Grisar, 1.330). Damasus's ruling affirmed that Nicaea presents the true teaching of the Gospels, thus testifying to the function of the Petrine office to teach the truth of the Scriptures.

Regarding the relations of the various patriarchal sees to Rome, the First Council of Constantinople (381) prepared a canon asserting that the bishop of Constantinople should have the patriarchy second to Rome, thus seeking to transform the ancient order of Rome, Alexandria, and Antioch (→ Pentarchy).

At the Synod of the Oak (403), John → Chrysostom (ca. 347-407) was condemned and deposed for holding certain teachings of → Origen (ca. 185-ca. 254) that were deemed heretical. In appealing the case to Innocent I (402-17; DH 215-16), Chrysostom assumed the juridical and theological primacy of the bishop of Rome, who overturned the judgment of the synod. In a parallel situation, a theological issue troubling the Eastern and Western church was debated and assessed in 415 at the Synod of Diaspolis in Palestine, which exonerated the Pelagian understanding of the fall and of grace and free will. Informed by the writer Orosius of the confusion, → Augustine (354-430) convened two synods in North Africa, calling upon Innocent I to adjudicate the theological conflict "by the authority of the Apostolic See . . . which has been taken from the authority of the Holy Scriptures" (*Ep.* 71). The papal repudiation of → Pelagianism was developed in relationship to the theological insights presented in Augustine's study (*Ep.* 181).

In addition to the various theological and jurisdictional issues that kept deepening the mystery of the Trinity, Christology, grace, and free will, the church also faced the collapse of the Roman Empire in the West. At the time, → Gregory I, the Great (590-604), was engaged in the pastoral care of souls and in trying to prevent the emperor from exercising any authority within the church. Gregory differentiated the secular civil authority of the emperor from the spiritual authority of the bishop of Rome and condemned the caesaropapism proposed by Emperor Maurice in Constantinople (582-602; → Empire and Papacy 1, 3.1).

An articulation of the relationship of the Petrine office to the political temporal powers was clarified in the politically volatile and tempestuous time that prevailed throughout Europe during the papacy of → Gregory VII (1073-85), who confronted Holy Roman Emperor Henry IV (1056-1106; → Middle Ages 1.3.3). Henry sought to take advantage of the new political-economic feudal structures and the spiritual weakness of the papacy, which was only beginning a process of reform. While agreement within the church upheld the pope's authority in doctrinal and moral matters, his role in relationship to the political, economic, and social shape of the emerging culture was uncertain. How was his authority to be exercised?

Gregory VII made it clear that the pope is not an emperor, monarch, or king; he has no temporal power except in the → Papal States in Italy. However, he is the moral judge over secular rulers by virtue of his power to bind and loose, given that the Petrine office is not that of teacher only but also that of judge, able to condemn and absolve and to assign public or private penance. In the extreme case there was the possibility that a pope could → excommunicate a ruler, which would signify that the Christian subjects of that ruler would have no moral obligation to obey him or her. The pontiff thus asserted that he had the spiritual authority to call everyone to truth and sanctity, including Christian rulers. At the same time, this authority was exercised in a limited way, and only in the areas where secular rulers were in religious relationships with the Holy See.

The Roman Catholic Church, founded on the

word of the Lord (DH 1330), teaches papal primacy in relationship to the universal Catholic Church (see the confession of faith of the Eastern Emperor, Michael VIII Paleologus, at the Second Council of Lyons [1274, DH 861]). The Council of Ferrara-Florence in 1438-45 (→ Reform Councils) confirmed this primacy for the church throughout the world (DH 1307).

1.3. *Nineteenth and Twentieth Centuries*
The Roman Catholic Church understands itself as being both historical and cultural, a way of thinking and reflecting that reached a certain intellectual sophistication in the mid-19th century in the theology of John Henry Cardinal → Newman (1801-90). Especially in his work *Essay on the Development of Christian Doctrine* (1845), Newman presented a coherent integration of the historical trajectories of church teaching. One also finds such a synthesis in the many studies of Christopher Dawson (1889-1970) on religion and → culture. This awareness of the need to listen to "the signs of the times" appears also in the Pastoral Constitution on the Church in the Modern World, *Gaudium et spes* (*GS* 4-10), and in many other documents of Vatican II. Finally, in 1982 John Paul II established a new permanent Pontifical Council for Culture, which is also closely related to the Pontifical Council for Interreligious Dialogue.

Joseph Cardinal Ratzinger (from 2005, Benedict XVI) and Archbishop Tarcisio Bertone have highlighted the role of Vatican I and II in the self-understanding of the church. In "The Primacy of the Successor of Peter in the Mystery of the Church," they cite the constitution *Pastor aeternus* of the First Vatican Council, which discusses the purpose, content, and scope of the primacy. In turn, Vatican II, especially in its Dogmatic Constitution on the Church, *Lumen gentium (LG),* "reaffirmed and completed the teaching of Vatican I [*LG* 18], addressing primarily the theme of its purpose, with particular attention to the mystery of the Church as *Corpus Ecclesiarum* ['corporate body of Churches,' *LG* 23]. This consideration allowed for a clearer exposition of how the primatial office of the Bishop of Rome and the office of the other Bishops are not in opposition but in fundamental and essential harmony" (§5).

Vatican II affirmed both the primacy of the → pope and the relation of this primacy to the college of → bishops, who serve in succession to the → apostles. The Roman Catholic Church finds unity among the bishops, as among the original 12 apostles, to be an essential element for the fullness of the church; this unity is based on the unity of the Logos with the Father and the → Holy Spirit. Vatican II reappropriated the biblical and patristic understandings of the unity among the apostles, or "the Twelve," which was the more ancient designation of those called by Christ to be witnesses together to his life, death, and resurrection and to preach what he had taught them. Only in late Lukan theology were "apostles" and "the Twelve" brought together, being identified as "the 12 apostles." This "new community" centered on Jesus Christ refers back to Israel's hope for a restoration of the 12 tribes, and also forward to the end time, thus symbolizing the eschatological fulfillment of God's promises.

The reappropriation of the patristic tradition also played an important role in the development of the understanding of the bishops collegially gathered together. The language of this bond appears in → Cyprian (d. 258) on the meaning of *fraternitas* (brotherhood, *Ep.* 30; CSEL 3/2.549), in Hilary of Poitiers (d. ca. 367; *Coll. antiar.* B.1.6; CSEL 65.102, 65.105), and in → Leo the Great (440-61; *Ep.* 13.2; *PL* 54.665). The term *collega* (partner) is first found in Cyprian (*Ep.* 22; CSEL 3/2).

Vatican II thus carried forward an understanding of this ancient realization, which John Paul II recalled in his → encyclical on ecumenism, noting that "when the Catholic Church affirms that the office of the Bishop of Rome corresponds to the will of Christ, she does not separate this office from the mission entrusted to the whole body of Bishops, who are also 'vicars and ambassadors of Christ' [*LG* 27]. The Bishop of Rome is a member of the 'College,' and the Bishops are his brothers in the ministry" (*Ut unum sint* 95). Ratzinger and Bertone further noted that "episcopal collegiality does not stand in opposition to the personal exercise of the primacy nor should it relativize it" (§5). The primacy and the collegiality together serve the unity of the church, but in the differing modes that were established by Christ.

Among the new institutions that have been established by the church for signifying and exercising the sense of collegiality of the bishops are the national bishops' conferences. They take their origin from the Synod of Bishops convened by Pope Paul VI (1963-78) in 1965. These national conferences have been brought into closer fraternity since the regional synods of bishops in the 1990s. A more unified mutual self-understanding and support has been developed through these national and regional bishops' conferences and conventions. (See *Ecclesia in Africa* [1995], *Ecclesia in Asia* [1999], *Ecclesia in Oceania* [2001], and *Ecclesia in Europa* [2003], four apostolic exhortations of John Paul II.)

2. Sacramental Character

2.1. *The Church as Sacrament*

Lumen gentium, the Vatican II statement about the nature and mission of the Roman Catholic Church, refers to the *mystērion* (Lat. *sacramentum*) of the visible-invisible nature of the church. It describes this concept as the *sacramentum mundi* (sacrament of the world), understanding the church as a sacrament analogous to the seven sacraments. The church is a "sign and instrument" of God's grace (*LG* 1), given, as testified in Scripture, "as the universal sacrament of salvation" and for "the renewal of the world" (48.2, 3; → Sacrament; Sacramentality). The church is the "people of God" (9-17), called to holiness (39-42), as it engages in an eschatological → pilgrimage to the kingdom of God (48-51).

These statements are oriented to four basic aspects that describe the divine mystery of salvation revealed by the teaching of Christ and continued in the life of the church (*LG* 52):

1. the divine plan of → salvation (§§1, 4), the election of a people of God ordained to proclaim and found the kingdom of God in the world (2, 5, 9, 13);
2. the self-impartation of God in Christ, that is, the saving → incarnation of the Logos in Jesus of Nazareth, with which God's will to save has been disclosed and permanently accomplished;
3. the historical origin of the church, that is, the calling of the disciples of Jesus as apostles with the task of preaching the gospel and spreading abroad God's kingdom (5, 9, 17, 19), along with the sending of the Holy Spirit, who fills the church with life and sanctifies and directs it in order that the wisdom and plan of God may be crowned with success (4, 5, 17); and
4. the self-dedication and faithfulness of the Virgin Mary, whose divine motherhood and perfect appropriation of the grace given to her by God make her a model of faith and a goal for the church (52-69; → Mariology 1.3).

As the fellowship of → faith, → hope, and → love united by the Holy Spirit and endowed with charismatic gifts (*LG* 4; → Charisma), the church is the mystical body of Christ, who is its head and who established it as a visible social structure on earth and furnished it with hierarchical institutions for serving his teaching and mission. In analogy to the human nature that Christ assumed, the church serves as an agency of salvation (8) to make possible the participation of humans in the divine life. At the same time, Christ forms the church as an active subject that represents him (21; → Representation) and invites humans into the gift and work of redemption (3, 26, 28; → Salvation 4). It is especially in the → Eucharist that the unity between Christ and his people is effected. In Christ, then, the church is the sacrament, the sign and instrument, of both inner union with God and the unity of the whole human race (1, 8; see Augustine, *De civ. Dei* 20). This "one, holy, catholic, and apostolic church," which reflects the mystery of the Word made flesh and which manifests itself as one people on the basis of the Trinitarian unity of the Father, Son, and Holy Spirit (*LG* 4), "subsists [*subsistit*] in the Catholic Church" (8.2). This self-understanding governs the church's self-awareness and guides it in all that it says and does, both distinguishing it from, and relating it to, other churches as it sheds light on its constitutive principles, sources, doctrines, motivations, and intentions.

2.2. *The Eucharist*

"The unity of the Church, which the ministry of Peter's Successor serves in a unique way, reaches its highest expression in the Eucharistic Sacrifice, which is the centre and root of ecclesial communion; this communion is also necessarily based on the unity of the Episcopate" (Ratzinger and Bertone, §11). On this subject the Congregation for the Doctrine of the Faith commented earlier in a letter to the bishops, "Every celebration of the Eucharist is performed in union not only with the proper Bishop, but also with the Pope, with the episcopal order, with all the clergy, and with the entire people. Every valid celebration of the Eucharist expresses this universal communion with Peter and with the whole church, or objectively calls for it" (*AAS* 85 [1993] 847).

As the basic ordering of participation in the life of the → Trinity, the sacraments, visible and efficacious signs of invisible grace (DH 1639), both make Christ's presence available to the eyes of faith and effect the participation in the divine life that the Roman Catholic Church claims to be necessary to salvation (*LG* 14). The historical mission of the people of God, which transcends national and ethnic culture and frontiers (9), brings all peoples to union with Christ (13) and into union with each other, thus embracing the world in all its fullness (17). Looking at all the different aspects of the historical and cultural dimensions of the church, one is able to reflect on the elements of mystery that flow from the lives of faith, hope, and charity of the members of the community that make visible and manifest the life of grace.

3. Liturgical Life

The liturgical life of the Roman Catholic Church is the basis and foundation (see 5.1) of its own sacramental nature. It comprises both the public worship of God in liturgical action and the church's liturgical daily prayer. Thus in the corporate and individual exercises and celebrations of liturgical life, the → spirituality of the people of God comes to expression (Vatican II's Constitution on the Sacred Liturgy, *Sacrosanctum Concilium* [*SC*], 5-13).

3.1. *Holy Scripture*

We cannot consider the liturgical reform of the Roman Catholic Church, which has been underway in the thinking of liturgical and historical theologians in both Europe and America from the early part of the 20th century, without also thinking of the clarifications regarding the meaning and place of Holy Scripture in the church that were formulated in Vatican II's Dogmatic Constitution on Divine Revelation, *Dei Verbum (DV)*. The relationship between the Scriptures and the Eucharist is here made clear: "The Church has always venerated the divine Scriptures as she venerated the Body of the Lord, in so far as she never ceases, particularly in the sacred → liturgy, to partake of the bread of life and to offer it to the faithful from the one table of the Word of God and the Body of Christ" (*DV* 21). At the conclusion of the constitution the hope is expressed that the same fervor that fills the church at the celebration of the Eucharist and reception of Holy Communion would flourish so that "the treasure of Revelation entrusted to the Church may more and more fill the hearts of men" (26).

Dei Verbum also underscores the church's responsibility to engage in the broad hermeneutical task of appropriating the mysteries of divine life communicated in the inspired Scriptures. An adequate → hermeneutic is required to incorporate contemporary insights regarding historical and literary forms, as well as other current studies that help uncover the literary dimensions of the human mediation of divine meaning and truth, and also to seek to enter into the interiority of the text, "since sacred Scripture must be read and interpreted with its divine authorship in mind" (*DV* 12.3). This hermeneutic, then, is not grounded in the hubris of a human control of the meaning of the text; rather, it is grounded in a humility that acknowledges "the marvellous 'condescension' of eternal wisdom" that allows God's "ineffable loving-kindness" to be communicated in human words (13). It is clear that the appropriation of this hermeneutic is to be realized by a constant reading of, and meditation on, the Scripture as it forms and nourishes the life of the church. It is to find its most important manifestation in the preaching that is integral to the liturgical eucharistic celebrations that symbolize and effect the unity of every local community and join all the members to Christ, to the local bishop, and through him to the bishop of Rome and to each other (25).

3.2. *Eucharist*

The liturgical life of the church, then, is fed by the divine word that communicates the mystery of God's life. In the person of Christ is found the divine self-communication of the inner life of the Holy Trinity. The liturgy is the praise, gratitude, and thanksgiving (Gk. *eucharistia*) of the people through their High Priest, Jesus Christ, to the Father. This praise and worship has many forms, and it too must find its rightful understanding and expression through an entering into the life of Christ and of the church. The liturgical dimension of the Roman Catholic Church encompasses the entire worship of God and finds its fulfillment in sacramental life and its central expression in the celebration of the Eucharist, the summit of the church's activity, which draws all the people of God into unity and participation in the divine plan of salvation through the sacrificial death of Christ and its completion in his resurrection.

The liturgy, accordingly, is the climax of all that the church does and the source of all its power (*SC* 10). Through it the church shares in Christ's priestly office (7; → Office of Christ) in the sense that Christ, the High Priest, is himself at work here, even as the church continues his priestly work (→ Worship 2.2). The Eucharist, or Mass, is the high point and center of the liturgical action. The observance of eucharistic veneration reflects the rank and dignity of the sacrament of the body of Christ.

The church's life grows through the individual sacraments that are understood to be instituted by Christ, are sources of grace, and are viewed as necessary to salvation (see DH 1601, 1604, 1606, 1608). The basic sacraments of initiation that incorporate the faithful into the church, give fellowship with Christ, and confer the Spirit of adopted sonship include → baptism, → confirmation, and the Eucharist. The four other sacraments, which mark specific situations in human life, are penance (→ Penitence), → anointing of the sick (→ Pastoral Care of the Sick 1), holy orders (→ Ordination), and matrimony (→ Marriage and Divorce 3.2). Overall, "the purpose of the sacraments is to sanctify men, to build up the Body of Christ, and, finally, to give worship to God" (*SC* 59.1).

3.3. *Prayer*

For the Roman Catholic Church, → prayer is a constant way of relating to God. Of primary importance is the Liturgy of the Hours, or the Divine Office (*SC* 83-101), known formerly as the breviary (→ Liturgical Books 1.6). These prayers, principally the Psalms and readings from both the OT and the NT, are understood as the public prayer of the church. It is a source not only of → piety but also of assistance in deepening the heart to Scripture and the Eucharist (90). Private prayers and individual and corporate devotional exercises (→ Devotion, Devotions) prepare believers for conscious and active participation in the liturgy (11-13). Veneration of God is also promoted by many other practices such as grace at meals, evening prayer, prayers to Mary and the → saints, and prayers as a part of → processions and → pilgrimages (→ Popular Religion).

The liturgy involves direct invocation and veneration of God. The Roman Catholic Church, however, also practices prayer directed to God through the invocation and veneration of Mary (→ Mary, Devotion to) and the saints. Because she is "exalted above all angels and men" (*LG* 66), Mary merits a special veneration, not least in light of her having received and accepted — in the "fiat" of Luke 1:38 — the grace that allowed her to be named *theotokos,* "bearer of God" (→ Ephesus, Council of). She is invoked under the titles "advocate," "helper," "benefactress," "mediatrix," and "Our Lady." This honor, however, "is so understood that it neither takes away anything from nor adds anything to the dignity and efficacy of Christ the one Mediator" (*LG* 62.1). By venerating the saints, the church understands itself as being in unity with the communion of saints and thus experiences and participates concretely in eschatological reality, entering into the end time and the eternal character of holiness (50).

3.4. ***Other***

The church also has other rites that denote God's presence in the world, proclaim his sovereignty over persons and things, and seek his aid. The church itself has instituted them after the pattern of the sacraments (*SC* 60), calling them → sacramentals (e.g., → benedictions and → consecrations).

The cycle of the liturgical year (→ Church Year 2.2; Holy Year) presents the work of salvation by means of a fixed sequence of festivals and seasons (*SC* 102-5). → Sunday is always the celebration of the → resurrection of Christ from the dead, the One who establishes the new creation of the people of God and for the salvation of the whole world (106). When the community gathers in a consecrated church, it becomes the church at worship in a holy place (→ Church Architecture; Cathedral). The → tabernacle (§2), where consecrated eucharistic hosts are reserved, is parallel to the holy of holies of the OT. Within the church special places, confessionals, are set aside for penitents. Often there are artistic images of Christ, Mary, the apostles, angels, and the saints, which invite believers to prayer and meditation.

Liturgical books, → liturgical vessels, and → vestments for the celebration of the liturgy are kept in a separate place called the → sacristy. Bibles, prayer books, and → hymnals are often available to assist the faithful in their participation in the celebration of the liturgy (→ Church Music; Mass, Music for the; Hymn; Hymnody; Hymnology).

4. Secular Context and Pastoral Mission

The role of the Roman Catholic Church in secular life is in large measure shaped by its liturgical celebration and its message of modeling one's life according to Christ so that the discipline of Christian virtues can be encouraged, sought, and developed. The church, through the lives of all its members, seeks to do justice to its universal claim by means of its presence and work in the world, especially in conditions of human suffering, which it understands in relation both to the sufferings of Christ on the cross and the healing victory of the resurrection. Thus the church calls especially its laypeople to live Christian → vocations in relation to their places in the world, their gifts, and their many points of connection with worldly activities and institutions.

4.1. ***Engaging the World***

The church understands its relation to the world according to the incarnational dimension of Christ's own life in the world. In *Gaudium et spes* the church is understood as a universal sacrament of salvation, and thus it has the task and goal of renewing and sanctifying earthly reality for God (*GS* 40, 45). Being universal, it is always living and engaging the goods and evils of specific places and times, although "it is not committed to any one culture or to any political, economic or social system" (42.4). The created order itself has gifts that provide human life with the dignity that comes from being in the image of God, but as fallen, humans are called to fellowship with God and are in need of the transformation that allows them a share in the divine economy of salvation (22, 24, 35). While the material creation possesses its own legitimate autonomy and its own truth, goodness, validity, and order (36), human life is that part of God's creation to which his revelation is addressed. Yet it is wounded, weakened, and disfigured by (ungodly) human self-assertion (sin), and it thus needs to be transformed and brought to → perfection (37, 40). There is a formal difference, but no antithesis, between the church and the world (34). The two are related. The world needs the church, and the church finds in the created world that which is to be brought to the saving Word and acts of God's love and redemption (see 23-45, chaps. 2-4).

Some tension within the church in respect to its pastoral activity and response to the world can be found in varying interpretations of *Gaudium et spes.* Some theologians have found the document to be overly optimistic about the human condition in its need for redemption, sensing that it tends toward a semi-Pelagian reading of human reason and freedom in relationship to God's grace (e.g., Joseph Cardinal Ratzinger and Hans Urs von Balthasar). Others seem willing to accept its underlying anthropology as capable of being employed within philosophical, economic, sociological, and political theories that are at odds with the sinful dimension of → human dignity; they see it as seeking human solutions to worldly indignities and use it in adopting secular responses as replacements for God's action in redeeming human life (→ Liberation Theology; Political Theology).

4.2. *Approaches*

Nonetheless, oriented to the saving and sanctification of the world, the ministry of the Roman Catholic Church adopts differing concrete forms of mediating its teaching and mission. The church, knowing the final truth about human beings (*GS* 41), seeks to support individuals in the fuller development of their personalities and in securing the rights and responsibilities that flow from → human dignity. On the basis of its knowledge of revelation, the church can help society to a deeper understanding of the laws of human life (23) and to nurture all that is already present of justice, goodness, and truth (42). Regarding human action in respect to nature, it seeks to shed the light of → revelation on forms of human knowledge that risk turning people into instruments of limited purpose and goals (33-34, 42). To help solve pressing issues of the day, it brings to bear the illuminating principles of Christ (46), and it joins Christ's offer of salvation to its desire for mutual cooperation and a dialogue in which it will also receive insight from the world (40, 44, 92).

The Roman Catholic Church grounds its pastoral mission in eternally revealed principles that arise out of its nature. It teaches that Christ is to be brought to all people, which is to be done with respect for peoples' histories and cultures. Success in this effort requires sagacity and love as the relevant circumstances suggest or demand. Human intelligence, itself being transformed by the gift of faith, is what allows the proper identification of what is needed to develop Christian responses in the world. In the post–Vatican II teachings of the popes and the Holy See, through the pontifical congregations (e.g., Doctrine of the Faith, Catholic Education, Divine Worship and the Discipline of the Sacraments) and the pontifical councils (e.g., Promoting Christian Unity, Justice and Peace, Interreligious Dialogue, the Laity), there has been a development of what the council taught, which has carefully informed the church's pastoral practices (→ Curia 1.2). The pontifical congregations differ from the pontifical councils in that the former are the institutions formed after the Council of → Trent (1545-63), and the latter were formed after Vatican II.

4.3. *Moral Concerns*

One of the more difficult areas of the church's teaching concerns the moral principles of the Roman Catholic Church and their application to human life and social institutions. Many social institutions originally intended to support life and human dignity have come under the control of an instrumental rationality that so interferes with the created order that it places humanly created systems in opposition to divinely created nature. As this tendency increases throughout the world, it can cause states to institute political tyrannies of destruction against their citizens. Thus freedom, once it becomes license, can easily become a lust for power and domination that intrinsically deforms the true nature and proper limits of → freedom (→ Religious Liberty [Foundations]). Still, the church continually tries to translate its teaching, both principles and norms, for contemporary situations. John Paul II offered the insights of Scripture, theology, and anthropology in his encyclical *Veritatis splendor* (1993) in an effort to teach fellow bishops, clergy, religious, and laity the relationship of ancient tradition to contemporary issues. Notable moral concerns are applied by the church to issues of social justice, → sexual ethics, → abortion, → euthanasia, and the → family (→ Birth Control; Economic Ethics; Moral Theology; Social Encyclicals; Social Ethics).

4.4. *Education and Evangelization*

The Roman Catholic Church created monastic schools in Europe in the ninth century and also the great universities at, for example, Bologna, Naples, Padua, Cologne, Paris, Oxford, and Cambridge. It continues to support and create schools and universities all over the world. From local parochial schools to major universities with research and graduate programs, these centers of learning provide a broad contribution to the lives of both the church and world. Also through parishes and educational institutions the church demonstrates a strong commitment to cultural life, including the arts, scholarship, literature, → Christian publishing, and music (*GS* 60).

Within the church's overall pastoral mission lies a renewed sense that the whole church is to be involved in evangelization (→ Evangelism). Indeed, encyclicals and instructions of Paul VI (*Evangelii nuntiandi* [1975], 3-17) and John Paul II (*Veritatis splendor,* 28-34; *Centesimus annus* [1991], 38-54) emphasized the gospel's command to preach and teach about the life, hope, mercy, and forgiveness that are given by Christ to the whole world. In fact, John Paul II advanced the understanding that one of the important elements of what he called "the new evangelization" refers to the need for persons not only to be engaged with the gospel but to seek to transform human cultures, which are constituted by vast systems of meaning that sustain "a way of life." This insight profoundly integrates many of the teachings of Vatican II in a way that calls believers to be attentive within their vocations to how faith in Christ calls for his goodness to inform all human institutions.

4.5. *Recognition of Culture*

This perspective in turn leads to the importance that the Roman Catholic Church places on faith and culture. Already, we have noted John Paul II's establishment of the Pontifical Council for Culture. Attention to culture is of enormous importance in grasping the incarnational reality of the church in the world. Of the 16 documents of Vatican II, 13 refer at some point to the reality of culture, although in no document is there a definition of culture. The Pontifical Council for Culture is regularly engaged in examining the enormous complexity of cultures; it publishes essays on various issues concerning faith and culture in its quarterly journal, *Cultures and Faith.* The articles in this journal frequently address matters such as "dialogues among cultures," religions and culture, the church and → secularization, and the importance of modern means of → communication (→ Culture and Christianity).

5. Organization and Discipline

As the Roman Catholic Church understands itself, its liturgical and secular life and pastoral work demand a social structure (*LG* 8) by means of which to achieve visible and social unity. The church finds one such structure in the legal order (→ Church Law 4.2), expressed by ecclesial discipline (→ Church Government 3; Polity, Ecclesiastical, 2).

5.1. *Basis*

The necessity of social organization does not arise merely from the ordinary social relations essential to human nature, nor from the temporal and spatial conditions of human life. That the church is a corporate social body rests primarily on the theological premise that the church is both the body of Christ and the historically visible presence of the saving will of God. In analogy to the incarnation of Christ, the church assumes the form of this world (*LG* 48, *GS* 40).

By reason of its universal mission (*sacramentum mundi),* the church in principle cannot allow its own order to be arbitrary. Its structure, like its function, rests upon its vocation as an instrument of Christ's salvation. The principle of order that gives the church its social structure corresponds to its Trinitarian origin and to its mediation in salvation history (*LG* 13); it rests, furthermore, on the divine institution of the apostolic office (18; → Apostle, Apostolate). Bishops, as successors of the apostles, are in historic apostolic succession (→ Bishop, Episcopate, 1; Episcopacy). They are leaders of the flock in Christ's stead, being teachers, priests, and rulers (19). The hierarchical organization of the fellowship (→ Hierarchy) means that authority is intrinsic to the office of the bishop. This authority can engage in wide consultation, but it rests ultimately in the bishop's understanding of the needs of the common good of his diocese.

5.2. *Value and Exercise of Discipline*

The Roman Catholic Church claims a special importance for its social structure. It views itself as a "perfect society" because in and by itself it possesses all that is essential to a society, not because it is composed of perfect people, but because it is supernatural in its origin and goal (DH 3167). Representing and communicating God's will to save, it is tied to a discipline established at the very founding of the church and developed in an ecclesiastical code. The regulations are all embraced in → canon law (→ Codex Iuris Canonici [CIC]). Like all laws, they give order and protection to the life of the community; in virtue of their essential relation to the imparting of salvation, however, they go beyond that function. Discipline here has a ministering function. Its aim is to safeguard the ecclesial body, to facilitate its saving work, to give to statements of faith the character of legally binding norms, to protect the purity of teaching (→ Dogma; Dogmatics), and to regulate the church's entire life. Discipline is thus one of the appropriate instruments that Christ has put at the disposal of his church.

When various personal or institutional difficulties arise within the community, there are tribunals, both in the Holy See and in local dioceses, to address them. Similarly, when scandal occurs — and Augustine made it clear in his catechism *(De cat. rud.)* that the faithful should be taught that scandals will arise to injure the community of the church and its God-given mission — there are tribunals that seek to find a way to remove the source and cause of such scandal.

6. Image and Presence

As we examine the teaching and life of the Roman Catholic Church in terms of its order and mission, a mission that it shares with other Christian churches and communions, we note a distinctive historical and sociological form of its presence in the world. This church is distinguished by its autonomous character (→ Autonomy), yet it is also related in many ways to other Christians, other religions, and the cultures of the world (see 7). It has administrative means to address, guide, and encourage the global community.

The Roman Catholic Church is the largest of the Christian churches. With 1.05 billion members in 2000, it constitutes just over half of the Christian world. Churches belonging to the → World Council of Churches have no more than 560 million members. According to the *Annuarium Statisticum Ecclesiae,* 17.3 percent of the world's population belonged to the Roman Catholic Church in the year 2000. Even with a rapid increase recently in its membership (from 757 million in 1978 to 1.05 billion in 2000), its percentage of the world's population has actually declined, from 18.0 percent in 1978.

Continent by continent, the church has grown very unevenly since 1978. The greatest percentage growth has been in Africa (137.4 percent between 1978 and 2000), followed by Asia (69.8), the Americas (54.3), the Pacific countries (46.1), and Europe (5.2). In terms of absolute numbers of the faithful, in 2000 nearly half of all the world's Catholics lived in the Americas (519 million), followed by Europe (280 million), Africa (130 million), Asia (107 million), and the Pacific (8 million).

While → unity is a central theme for the Roman Catholic Church, it nonetheless takes concrete form in many local churches (→ Diocese). These many different churches constitute the one church in unity with the pope (*LG* 23; see 1983 CIC 368). With this double function they have an essential role in the visible development of the Roman Catholic Church, so that even their number is significant.

Another measure of church growth worldwide is the increase in the number of bishops — from 3,714 in 1978 to 4,541 in 2000, an overall growth of 22.3 percent. The various continents all show an increase, though not necessarily in proportion with their respective increase in membership. In terms of percentage growth during this 22-year span, the largest increase in number of bishops was in Africa (39.1 percent), followed by the Pacific (28.7), Asia (20.8), the Americas (19.7), and Europe (19.5). In the year 2000 the largest number of bishops were from the Americas (1,695 bishops), then Europe (1,497), Asia (627), Africa (601), and the Pacific (121).

7. Ecumenical and Interreligious Relations

7.1. *Approach*

The relation of the Roman Catholic Church to churches that are not in communion with the Roman See (see the Decree on Ecumenism of Vatican II, *Unitatis redintegratio* [*UR*] 13) rests on the insight that outside its own structure there may be found many elements of holiness and truth that, along with its own gifts, promote Christian unity (*LG* 8, *UR* 3). The final goal of the ecumenical involvement of the Roman Catholic Church is the full visible unity of the body of Christ (*UR* 4; → Ecumenism, Ecumenical Movement, 1.4.5). Recognizing that separated brethren have "some, though imperfect, communion with the Catholic Church" (3.1), the church increasingly seeks to develop new appreciations of these churches and communions. Actual efforts to achieve visible unity take many forms and are found at every level of church life (→ Dialogue; Ecumenical Theology; Local Ecumenism; National Councils of Churches).

The Roman Secretariat for Christian Unity, which in 1988 became the Pontifical Council for Promoting Christian Unity, was the response of Rome after Vatican II concerning its place in the ecumenical life of the whole church. The principal churches that it is engaged with in ecumenical relations are the Eastern Orthodox (→ Orthodox Christianity; Orthodox Church) and the churches of the Reformation.

The schism that separated the Roman Catholic Church and the Orthodox churches found its most open expression in 1054 in Constantinople with the mutual excommunications of Patriarch Michael Cerularius and the papal legate Cardinal Humbert In 1274 at Lyons and 1438-39 at Florence, serious efforts were undertaken to reestablish unity, but both failed. Patriarch Athenagorus of Constantinople (1948-72) and Paul II met in December 1965 in Jerusalem, where in a common declaration these mutual condemnations were removed. The first official theological dialogue of Orthodox and Catholics took place in 1980 and included six meetings through 1990. Because of political and cultural charges in 1990-91, the dialogue was temporarily suspended. In 2005, with the encouragement of

Benedict XVI, initiatives were established for a resumption of the dialogue.

In order to foster ecumenical relations, early guidelines were established, and in places where there were large communions of either Orthodox or Protestant churches living alongside Roman Catholics, dialogues were undertaken with theologians and scholars from the various traditions. The themes, which were codetermined, led to studies on such issues as baptism, Scripture, justification, the creed, episcopacy and ecclesial oversight, and the Eucharist. Most frequently, these dialogues were bilateral (i.e., constituted with members of one other church and the Roman Catholic Church). As a result of this mode of dialogue, new bilaterals have been established with an increasing number of other churches.

These dialogues have occurred on two levels: national bishops' conferences in dialogue with other churches within the same nation, and internationally, where the Holy See, through its Pontifical Council for Promoting Christian Unity, collaborates with international leaders, bishops, officers, and theologians representing their churches. While the Holy See is not an official member of the World Council of Churches in Geneva, it is an official observer and participates as such regularly. Since Vatican II it has been an official member of the → Faith and Order movement.

In 1993 a new set of guidelines for ecumenism was issued by the Pontifical Council: the *Directory for the Application of Principles and Norms on Ecumenism.* Then in 1995 Pope John Paul II issued his encyclical on ecumenism, *Ut unum sint* (1995), in which he extended a request to other Christian churches and communities to express their understanding of how the Petrine ministry of oversight and of service to the unity of the whole church might be more rightly exercised. The council received approximately 70 responses to this invitation from ecclesial bodies or councils of churches. The work of the council is communicated in its quarterly journal, *Information Service.*

7.2. ***Results***

The growth of the dialogues and of "spiritual ecumenism" has been enormous. As Walter Cardinal Kasper, president of the Pontifical Council for Promoting Christian Unity, has noted, the task that lies before the body of Christ is how we all are to receive (→ Reception, Ecumenical) into our now separated communities unifying ecumenical insights into the mystery of the church. It is clear that the → *Joint Declaration on the Doctrine of Justification,* celebrated by the Holy See and the churches of the → Lutheran World Federation in October 1999, offers one viable model, under the guidance of the Holy Spirit, for this undertaking.

Behind the relation of the Roman Catholic Church to non-Christian religions lies the recognition that God has a universal will to save and that non-Christians relate to the people of God on different levels. The Holy See has a very unique bond with the Jewish community, which was recognized by Vatican II in its Declaration on the Relation of the Church to Non-Christian Religions, *Nostra aetate (NA)* 4. It has established the Commission for Religious Relations with the Jews (→ Jewish-Christian Dialogue). In addition, the Holy See has created the Pontifical Council for Interreligious Dialogue in order to engage in conversation with Muslims, Hindus, and Buddhists (*LG* 16, *NA* 2-5; → Buddhism and Christianity; Islam and Christianity). One of the more interesting documents issued through this pontifical council is *Dialogue and Proclamation* (1991), which acknowledges the close relation between a people's religion and their culture and seeks to detect seeds of good in all religions and cultures in order to bring the world in its fullness into peace and fruitfulness. All peoples have in God the same origin and final goal, and all religious persons and communities seek answers to the mysteries of human existence (*NA* 1-2). Salutary discussion and cooperation with non-Christians is thus needed. The Pontifical Council for Interreligious Dialogue has published a semiannual reflection and report since 1966. Originally called *Bulletin,* in 1995 its title was changed to *Pro Dialogo.*

In an age of globalization the importance of living together in peace and mutual respect is clear. As an acknowledgment of this reality, John Paul II convened two gatherings in Assisi (1986 and 2002) in order to foster a recognition of human dignity, celebrated in a context of prayer, which can assist in building the bonds of peace and fraternity.

Bibliography: Basic sources: AAS (Rome, 1909-) • *Annuario Pontificio* (Rome, 1943-) yearly publication of statistics • *Annuarium Statisticum Ecclesiae* (Rome, 1970-) • *Catechism of the Catholic Church* (2d ed.; Washington, D.C., 1997) • *Compendium of the Social Doctrine of the Church* (Washington, D.C., 2005) • *DEM* (2d ed.; Geneva, 2002) • DH (37th ed.; Freiburg, 1991) • A. Flannery, O.P., ed., *Vatican Council II: The Conciliar and Post Conciliar Documents* (rev. ed.; 2 vols.; Collegeville, Minn., 1992) • F. Gioia, ed., *Interreligious Dialogue* (Boston, 1997) • R. P. McBrien, ed., *Encyclopedia of Catholicism* (San Francisco, 1995) • J. Miller, ed., *Encyclicals of John Paul II* (Huntington,

Ind., 2001) • Pontifical Council for Promoting Christian Unity, *Directory for the Application of Principles and Norms on Ecumenism* (Washington, D.C., 1993) • K. Rahner et al., eds., *SM(E)* (6 vols.; New York, 1968-70) • *Sacrosancto Oecumenicum Concilium Vaticanum II* (Rome, 1966).

Other literature: Benedict XVI, *Mass of Possession of the Chair of the Bishop of Rome* (Homily) (Basilica of St. John Lateran, 2005) • J. Burgess and J. Gros, eds., *Growing Consensus: Church Dialogues in the United States, 1962-1991* (New York, 1995) • A. Grillmeier, *Christ in Christian Tradition,* vol. 1, *From the Apostolic Age to Chalcedon;* vol. 2, *From the Council of Chalcedon to Gregory the Great* (Louisville, Ky., 1975-96) • H. Grisar, *History of Rome and the Popes in the Middle Ages* (3 vols.; London, 1911-12) • J. Gros, H. Meyer, and W. G. Rusch, eds., *Growth in Agreement II: Reports and Agreed Statements of Ecumenical Conversations on a World Level, 1982-1998* (Geneva and Grand Rapids, 2000) • W. Kasper, *Sacrament of Unity: The Eucharist and the Church* (New York, 2004); idem, *That They All May Be One: The Call to Unity Today* (New York, 2004) • R. Latourelle, ed., *Vatican II: Assessment and Perspectives* (vol. 1; New York, 1988) • R. P. McBrien, *Catholicism* (rev. ed.; San Francisco, 1994); idem, *Inside Catholicism: Rituals and Symbols Revealed* (San Francisco, 1995) • H. Meyer and L. Vischer, eds., *Growth in Agreement: Reports and Agreed Statements of Ecumenical Conversations on a World Level* [for the years 1931-82] (New York, 1984) • J. Miller, ed., *Vatican II: An Interfaith Appraisal* (Notre Dame, Ind., 1966) • J. Ratzinger (Benedict XVI), *Pilgrim Fellowship of Faith: The Church as Communion* (San Francisco, 2005) • J. Ratzinger and T. Bertone, "The Primacy of the Successor of Peter in the Mystery of the Church: Reflections of the Congregation for the Doctrine of the Faith," *OR(E),* November 18, 1998, 5-6 • C. Vagaggini, *Theological Dimensions of the Liturgy* (Collegeville, Minn., 1965) • L. Veliko and J. Gros, eds., *Growing Consensus II* (Washington, D.C., 2005) • H. Vorgrimler, ed., *Commentary on the Documents of Vatican II* (vol. 1; New York, 1967) • M. Zöller, *Washington and Rome* (Notre Dame, Ind., 1999).

Arthur L. Kennedy

Roman Empire

1. Age of the Republic

1.1. *Rise of Rome*

The Roman Empire developed out of the city of → Rome. Favorably situated for commerce on the Tiber River and on a road used to transport salt, Rome became an urban center (from 650 B.C. onward) under the influence of an alien aristocracy that spoke another language, the Etruscans of Etruria, Tuscany. Older settlements on the individual Roman hills go back to the 10th/9th and 8th centuries (the legendary date of its founding is 753 B.C.). Most of the people were engaged in agriculture and belonged to the relatively small Latin-Faliscan linguistic group, a branch of Indo-European.

The Etruscans, who provided the king and many patricians, brought water to the Forum valley (which was drained by the Cloaca Maxima, or "greatest sewer") and united various settlements, building a city wall for safety. This ruling class took its religious notions from its Etruscan homeland. A chief temple for the worship of Juno and Minerva, as well as Jupiter, was built on Capitol Hill and became Rome's religious center. Cultic rites were important. To discern the will of the gods study was made of the flight of birds *(auspicium)* and of entrails (*haruspicium;* → Roman Religion 2.1). The symbols of government — especially the *sella curulis* (curule chair) and *fasces* (bundle [of rods], as badge of authority) — were also of Etruscan provenance. Etruscan influence ended with the banishment of the last king around 500 B.C.

The cities of the district of Latium to the south of the Tiber were organized in a union of city-states with a central sanctuary on Alban Hill. Rome gradually assumed leadership of this coalition, triumphing in the Latin War of 340-338 B.C. But since there are hardly any written sources for this early period, reconstruction of the events is very difficult. At the end of the wars, in which there were also reverses, Rome gained control over the Samnite territory by planting colonies in which Roman peasants settled who could also serve as troops.

After the capitulation of the Greek-occupied city of Tarentum (modern Taranto) in 272 B.C., Rome ruled over the whole of what was called Italia, roughly the area south of the Arno and Rubicon Rivers. It did so by means of a system of alliances, using a complex legal structure. It engaged in further wars to extend its scope of action, to ensure its security, to satisfy the need of the aristocracy for glory and recognition, and to answer (very willingly) appeals for help. In this way its sphere of influence expanded across the whole Mediterranean area. It suffered many defeats, but it finally proved victorious in virtue of its superiority in numbers, structures, and technology. The expansion and the possibilities of gain for all strata prevented what might have been internal social conflicts.

The victory over Carthage (near modern Tunis) in the Second Punic War (218-201 B.C.) ensured Rome of supremacy in the Mediterranean. But the enormous efforts needed to defeat the enemy in its own land (culminating in the battle of Zama in 202) brought lasting change to the social structure of Rome.

1.2. *Society and Constitution*

Wealthy nonpatricians (plebeians) who could provide themselves with arms gained an entry into the patrician class. Then after lengthy struggles (the so-called class wars of ca. 494-287 B.C.), the plebeians formed their own organization under the leadership of a people's tribune. Eventually the new aristocracy took over control of the city. The magistrates, who were elected each year, always with at least one colleague, formed the executive. The Senate, with about 300 members, consisted of former officeholders and shaped public opinion. We see traces of this role in its self-description as Senatus Populusque Romanus (SPQR, the Senate and people of Rome), a motto of the Roman Empire. The chief officials, the two consuls, also led the army, which was a self-armed militia up to the time of Marius (ca. 157-86 B.C., consul for the first time in 107 B.C.). The "people," largely coextensive with the militia, chose the officials.

The Roman → family (§2.2) was strictly patriarchal. The wife and children, even adult children, were under the absolute authority of the family head. Families also had slaves (→ Slavery), though at first few in number. The heads of noble families were able to make good their claims to leadership in the state because as patrons they could gather many followers (clients) around them and in this way set up a relationship of mutual loyalty and obligation. Yet this aristocratic model of society could function only as long as the leadership stratum maintained its homogeneity.

The enormous gains in wars against culturally and economically superior powers in the eastern Mediterranean (2nd cent. B.C. onward) gradually corrupted the nobility. Commercial profiteering was thus forbidden to senators, who now invested only in land. As peasants were uprooted by reason of long military service, they could find land only in more and more distant areas. The frequent wars also brought many slaves to Italy, where the wealthy put them to work in profitable, extensive economic ventures (esp. in pastoral farming and on plantations). A new class arose, the knights. Socially they belonged to the senatorial class but were not allowed to make political decisions. They exacted tribute from the provinces in the form of taxes. Many abuses resulted. The reducing of the peasants to poverty threatened the defensive capabilities of Rome, and some aristocrats tried to initiate reforms. The disintegration of the ruling class was now perfectly clear, especially as they began murdering and assassinating one another. At the end came civil wars.

1.3. *Revolutionary Period*

Tiberius Sempronius Gracchus (162-133 B.C.), representing a group of the nobility, wanted to take some state land (in conquered territory) that was being cultivated by senators and give it to landless peasants. He proposed to do so, however, by unconstitutional means, which led to tumult. Under Marius (consul in 107, yearly from 104 to 100 [consecutive terms being admissible at this time], and 86), Germanic tribes were threatening the frontiers. Marius was a "new man" *(homo novus)* who instigated army reforms. Gradually Rome began to use professional soldiers. After their years of service, the soldiers' general would ensure that they received plots of land to cultivate. Soon soldiers became clients of a few generals, and the aristocratic system, which allowed no place for individual greatness, came under stress.

External perils (the Germans; Mithradates the Great, king of Pontus; and pirates) made it necessary to give the generals extraordinary authority, and they soon attained to dangerous positions of power. If the Senate did not fall in with their wishes, they marched their legions in. The aristocracy crumbled. The strongest among the generals fought for supreme power: first Sulla (138-78 B.C.) against Marius, then Caesar (100-44) against Pompey (106-48). After the battle of Pharsalus (near modern Fársala, Greece) in 48 B.C., Caesar became the supreme ruler as dictator for life. When it seemed that no one could stop him, he was assassinated on March 15, 44 B.C., the ides of March. The murderers, among them his former followers Brutus and Cassius, had no solid political concept, and thus the legion would again have to decide who was master.

2. Age of the Principate: Emperors

In the last civil war of the waning republic, Caesar's great-nephew Octavian (63 B.C.–A.D. 14) fought against Mark Antony, his former colleague in the newly created triumvirate (after 43 B.C.), who held power in the eastern Mediterranean with his base in Alexandria (along with Cleopatria). Octavian was victorious at the naval battle of Actium (west-central Greece) in 31 B.C. and then took Alexandria in 30 B.C.

Octavian had at first found support in the legions as Caesar's adopted son, and he also paid them legacies out of Caesar's estate. After the prolonged wars the people now longed for peace, and Octavian, granted the name "Augustus" (exalted, sacred) by the Senate, promised to give it. To be able to ensure peace and to overcome what had thus far been "a crisis without alternatives" (C. Meier), he needed, however, the support of the older senatorial class, which had been decimated by proscriptions but which had indispensable experience in government. Against this background the principate was established (*princeps* = "first [in the Senate]"), which placed power in the hands of the one we now call the emperor. This system preserved the old republican institutions but enhanced the power of the emperor to intervene.

After 27 B.C. Octavian, like his successors, came to be known as Imperator Caesar Augustus. The term "Augustus" belonged to the religious domain and carried a reminder of the founder of Rome, Romulus. The legions were under the emperor alone (*imperium proconsulare maius,* "greater proconsular imperium") and were his true source of power. This arrangement meant that the emperor alone could turn military successes into triumphs. Octavian acquired the actual power of government (initiating laws and assembling the Senate) in 23 B.C. by taking over the office of the people's tribune (*tribunicia potestas,* "tribunician power"), which, since it was reckoned by years, could be used for dating. In this way Octavian avoided conflict with the old republican principles of annual office and collegiality. He made his monarchical claim clear in 2 B.C. by taking the title *pater patriae* (father of the fatherland), which, like the title *pater familias* (father of the [extended] family), carried with it the obligations of care on the one side and obedience on the other.

After his death in A.D. 14 Augustus, like most of his successors, was elevated to deity (apotheosis). Senators had to express their belief in this exaltation, and the emperor cult was added to that of other state gods. Living emperors came closer and closer to divinity, though never actually becoming gods (→ Emperor Worship).

The pseudorepublican character of the principate, that is, the winning of legitimacy by formal appeal to tradition (*mos maiorum,* "ways of the ancestors"), stood in the way of any automatic succession. Chosen successors during the lifetime of their predecessors had to acquire the necessary powers *(imperium proconsulare* and *tribunicia potestas).* A change in rule, especially when unexpected, thus created precarious situations. After the death of blood relatives Augustus unwillingly fixed on his adoptive son Tiberius (14-37). The next emperors came from the old Roman noble family of Augustus. When Nero (54-68) lost the support of senators and the troops, revolts followed in the provinces, Nero committed suicide, and the army had to decide on his successor in the absence of any provision. (The year 69 saw four different emperors.) Fighting ensued, but Vespasian with troops battle-hardened in the Jewish War (66-70) gained the upper hand and set up the Flavian dynasty (69-96). After further crisis men who had achieved greatness in the provinces took power. These men felt under special obligation to their office and people (the so-called humanitarian emperors). Since it chanced that they had no sons, they used adoption to secure the best possible successors (the adoptive emperors). The empire, then, achieved its supreme political and also economic greatness under Trajan (A.D. 98-117), Hadrian (117-38), Antoninus Pius (138-61), and Marcus Aurelius (161-80).

The period of the principate ended with the murder of Commodus (176-92). The rule of one man had gradually given way to that of an institutional empire, for which no alternative was conceivable. The new age was marked by the return of emperors to the Senate. The high social prestige of the latter was confirmed by the handing over to senators of duties and offices. But the army was still the true basis of power. When sudden changes came in leadership with the end of a dynasty, the soldiers had to be given large gifts of money to secure their loyalty. The emperor also had to prove himself as a general.

Amid new conflicts among various contenders, Septimius Severus (193-211) emerged triumphant but had to rely solely on the army. After him came the age of the so-called soldier-emperors (235-84), in which rapid changes took place. To distinguish between legitimate and usurped power became almost impossible. The rapid changes in emperors required massive outlays of money, and economic prosperity quickly declined. Among the 70 or so rulers (some of only local importance), Decius (249-

51) stands out because at a time of domestic and foreign crisis he forcibly imposed consent on the citizens by demanding an act of loyalty (→ Persecution of Christians 2.2-3). We might also mention Aurelian (270-75), who tried to make his personal god, Sol Invictus (invincible sun), the state god.

3. Late Antiquity

The "dominate" (*dominus,* "lord") period of the imperial age came next after 284, which took into account the change in the position of the emperors when the principate came to an end. Because massive intervention into the lives of individual citizens took place in order to secure tax collection, this age has also been called the age of the coercive state of late antiquity. (Late antiquity covers the whole period to the → Middle Ages.)

Diocletian (284-305) achieved a certain consolidation of the empire. Because the tasks of government had grown so much, and to lessen the danger of usurpation, he set up four heads of government (the so-called tetrarchy). By creating an artificial and sacrally validated dynasty according to which emperors were supposedly descendants of Jupiter or his son Hercules, he gave further consecration to the empire and supported it by court ceremony, which increasingly distanced the emperor from his subjects. Everything pertaining to the emperor was sacred. Its artificiality, however, wrecked the tetrarchy. In this regard the dynastic thinking of the soldiers contributed, for they would rather see the son of a successful commander as the new emperor. Diocletian (in the East) and Maximian (in the West) sensationally stepped down in 305, but Constantine, who was not in the system, was elected Augustus by his troops on the sudden death of his father, Constantius, in 306. Attempts at mediation failed, and in the struggle for power Constantine (306-37) finally defeated Maxentius in the West at the battle of the Milvian Bridge (312), not far from Rome, and overthrew Licinius in the East in 324.

Meanwhile the → persecution of Christians (§2) had proved unsuccessful, and Galerius (293-311) recognized them as a legal religious group by an edict of toleration in 311, just before his death. Constantine then tried to restore unity to the empire by confessing Christianity and ensuring its status by the Edict of Milan in 313. The Christian churches were granted civil rights (e.g., that of inheritance), and bishops could be elected as judicial authorities. Church buildings in the form of → basilicas were constructed for the worship of God (→ Church Architecture). Yet ancient rites and cults were not banned. When the unity of faith was threatened by internal disputes, as in the case of the → Donatists or → Arianism and Christology, the emperor intervened personally, even though he had no profound understanding of theological issues and tried to solve the problems by compromises, as at the Council of → Nicaea in 325. His late → baptism on his deathbed, which followed a common practice of the day, is no indication of his actual beliefs (note the legend of Sylvester I baptizing Constantine). The rebuilding of old Byzantium as the new capital of Constantinople (dedicated in 330) was later interpreted as the building of a Christian rival to Rome.

A major task in the fourth century was that of contending for the true faith. In the view of the emperors, such a focus would guarantee the unity of the empire. The attempt of the last member of the family of Constantine, Julian the Apostate (360-63), to reform the old religions was no more than an interlude. With the religious legislation of Theodosius (379-95), Christianity in its Catholic form was the only religion permitted, and it now became the exclusive state religion. Special rights, however, were granted to Jews (→ Judaism). And there were still non-Christians, even in the highest government positions. Christianity itself was absorbing and reinterpreting ancient rites and customs, for example, the celebration of the birth of the sun god on December 25.

The division of the empire into two halves on the death of Theodosius in 395 would prove in hindsight to be final. As the forms of government became fixed, the emperors, often children, became increasingly unimportant. Fluctuating frontiers made it hard for the regents (the army commanders), who in the West were often of Germanic origin, to pursue any firm policies. When the Germanic general Odoacer (ca. 433-93) overthrew the child emperor Romulus Augustus in 476, he was nominally subject to the Eastern emperor, and the West lost its independence. The Ostrogoth Theodoric and his army then occupied Italy, and Theodoric ruled in nominal dependence on Byzantium (493-526). The differences between the Catholic Romans and the Arian Goths, which persisted because of the small number of Ostrogoths, hampered the consolidation of this type of government. In 568 the Lombards invaded Italy. But their style of government bore no relation to that of the empire, and the history of medieval Italy now began.

In Gaul and the Germanic provinces the Frankish kingdom came into being under Clovis (d. 511). Up to the time of the Arab conquests (711) the Visigoths, or western Goths, ruled Spain.

Roman Empire

4. Empire

The Roman Empire reached its greatest extent under Trajan (d. 117), when it was bordered in the west by the Atlantic and included much of Britain (abandoned in 410). In the south the Sahara formed the frontier. To the north it extended to the Rhine and the Danube. The Romans took over what is now Romania for the sake of its ores (101-270). In the east alone did it find worthy foes in the Iranian Parthians or (after 227) Sassanids, based in Mesopotamia. For the most part the Euphrates was the boundary, and any gains beyond that were of short duration. In the third century many emperors lost their lives in wars against these opposing powers. With no lasting success on either side, there was conflict for Armenia to the south of the Caucasus. Armenia had become the first Christian state (traditionally, in 301). Fortifications and camps on the frontiers helped to deter aggression and served as control points. We find works of this kind in England (Hadrian's Wall) and Scotland (Antonine Wall), on the Rhine and the Danube, and in Palestine and North Africa.

Emperors in the second century such as Marcus Aurelius (161-80), by dint of hard conflict, could still hold the Danube frontier against aggressive Germanic tribes, but both northern rivers were repeatedly crossed in the third century, and plundering groups were a scourge to residents well into the interior of the empire. The new city wall at Rome, which Aurelian built, was a sign of the way things were going. Nomadic Mongolian Huns then shattered the Ostrogoth kingdom on the Don in 375, the so-called Völkerwanderung (or great migration of Germanic peoples) began, and the pressure of Germanic tribes on the frontiers became too strong to be kept out of the empire. A sign of the weakness of the empire was the defeat of the emperor Valens (364-78) at Adrianople (modern Edirne in Turkey) in 378 by rebellious Visigoths, who were suffering from lack of supplies.

Some troop units might desert, and domestic unrest was not unknown, but there were no actual revolts within the empire itself, with the exception of the Jewish revolt in Palestine (the Jewish War of 66-70 and the Bar-Kochba revolt in 132-35).

The → cities formed the basis of the Roman Empire. They were of differing legal status. Temples (to Jupiter, Roma, and Augustus), theaters, amphitheaters, and aqueducts characterized them externally. These structures were imposing technical achievements for their time. Fires often afflicted the cities, like the fire in Rome in 64 under Nero. Floods and earthquakes were also a threat. The eruption of Vesuvius in August 79 brought sudden destruction to Pompeii. The uncovered remains of this buried city give us a glimpse into what the daily life was of a city in the empire, though Pompeii was not in fact typical. Urbanization did not take place evenly. Cities were more prominent in the East, less so in the West, where imperial domains figured more largely, especially in North Africa. The division of the empire in 395 also took into account the linguistic division. Greek prevailed in the East, but in the West Latin took over from older languages that had not been reduced to writing.

5. Society

Under Augustus all free residents on the mainland of Italy (ca. 5 million people) had civil → rights. During the first and second centuries A.D. the number of citizens increased greatly as citizenship was granted to foreign nobles who had been won over to Rome, to auxiliary troops after their period of service, to whole cities, and to manumitted slaves. This process was completed by a law of Caracalla (211-17, the Constitutio Antoniniana, in 212), which granted civil rights to almost all free residents, estimated at some 50 to 80 million. Increasing difficulties in defending the frontiers in the fourth century caused the emperor in the East, Valens, to settle within the empire Germanic tribes that had their own laws. It was no longer possible to integrate such groups into the empire, to Romanize them.

Leadership was in the hands of the senators (*ordo senatorius,* "senatorial order"), who had to possess one million sesterces or property worth this amount. One became a senator by inheritance or by imperial nomination. The Senate provided the main government officials and military commanders. After the third century, however, senators became no more than a privileged class living on the land but with no political tasks. Competent military leaders of the equestrian class increasingly replaced them.

To this latter class the emperors entrusted the duties of government. They were dependent on the emperor, and their loyalty was thus assured. They had to have at least 400,000 sesterces. Their main administrative and military duties lay in the provinces, as in the case of Pontius Pilate, procurator of Judaea from A.D. 26 to 36.

Decurions (commanders of ten men), who had to have at least 100,000 sesterces, took the lead in the cities. The decurions had to use some of their income for building and social projects. In prosperous times they did so to enhance their social prestige, but later they were forced by law to take this course, so that appointment to this rank came to be regarded as a punishment.

The army offered the best chance of upward movement for the remaining citizens and residents. It consisted of some 400,000 soldiers. The legion was the most important locus of Romanizing, which was thus most prevalent in provinces near the borders. After 20 years of service in a legion, or 25 years in auxiliary troops, soldiers who were granted an honorable discharge received land grants, on the proceeds of which they could reside in the cities.

Most of the residents of the empire were peasants or manual workers in the cities, which had an average population between 2,000 and 10,000. It should be noted, however, that there were many forms of society with different traditions. Hence we cannot speak of a unified population in the empire.

Slaves formed a large group, but with a varied social status. The major wars of the second century B.C. brought in many slaves, but the numbers declined during the imperial period, which had fewer wars. The humanizing of thought, especially in the second century (→ Stoics), also affected slaves, as did the laws relating to families. The state increasingly had a benevolent social impact. Manumissions became more common. By the first century slaves could hold administrative posts and amass large fortunes, as Pallas did under Claudius.

With the mounting crisis that overtook the empire in the third and fourth centuries, many free citizens became wage earners or tenant farmers who could not leave the land because of the burden of taxation.

Jews formed a special group among residents of the empire, both in Palestine and in several cities. As a largely closed ethnic group, though not unsuccessful in missionary outreach, they had special privileges from the days of Augustus, which they retained under the Christian emperors.

6. Economy

The long period of peace in the first and second centuries allowed the empire to become a unified and very strong economic bloc that could trade with far-distant territories. A stable currency and low rate of inflation were the key. A soldier's pay, for example, increased from 900 sesterces a year in the first century to only 1,200 in the second. With the third-century crisis, however, the emperors needed more and more money, and the debasing of the coinage destroyed confidence in the currency. Diocletian undertook financial reform and tried to impose wage and price controls. Constantine introduced a new and firm gold currency. He used imprints on the coins for propaganda purposes.

The well-built roads were another reason that trading was so prosperous. Soldiers built the roads for military purposes, but they were also essential for trade. The security of the seas from pirates was especially necessary for the grain trade. In the summer grain shipments came to the cities from Egypt and North Africa, for Italy itself could no longer supply Rome. With the swift exchange of skills came a broader cultivation of many plants (grapes, peaches, cherries) and a wider range of production — for example, clay and glass artifacts in the Roman Rhineland, from which they were sent throughout the empire. Italy gradually lost its leading position both economically and administratively.

7. Law

Law was the Romans' greatest cultural achievement. Their legal system is still the basis of many modern European systems (→ Law and Legal Theory). Civil and penal law were first defined or codified in about 450 B.C. in the Twelve Tables, which safeguarded the rights of patricians and plebeians against the caprices of the aristocracy. Greek legal codes might well have had some influence at this point. Those concerned about a point of justice under the law had to see to the enforcement of law.

A feature of Roman law is its orientation to individual cases (→ Casuistry), in contrast to an emphasis on a legal system. The strict formalism of literate → priests that prevailed at first gradually gave way from the third century onward to greater flexibility. Law was further developed by the case-by-case decisions of a magistrate *(praetor)* in the *ius civile*, the law applying to Roman citizens. From A.D. 242 the *praetor peregrinus* saw to cases involving non-Romans (*ius gentium*, the law common to all peoples). Aediles were the officials in charge of trade, and governors were in charge of provincial law (*ius honorarium*, the law developed in praetors' edicts, which supplemented the *ius civile*). Magistrates would publish the principles of decision (i.e., the precedents) at the beginning of their term of office. The Edictum Perpetuum of Hadrian in about A.D. 130 brought this process to a close. Usage and the obligation to consult learned counsel ensured conservative continuity. New laws (*leges*, pl. of *lex*) could also be created by the popular assembly and by the Senate (*senatus consulta*, "senate's advice"). Appeals to the emperors made the emperors themselves the second or final court and therefore a source of law.

From the first century B.C. onward, legal decisions were also discussed in writing. The result was a more precise definition of terms, though without any rigid systematizing. From the days of Augustus jurists, who were always drawn from the senatorial class, were appointed assessors, whose judgments had to be followed. In the second century, the classic age of Roman law, the emperors involved jurists more and more in administration, which now had to be according to legal principles. An official class of jurists thus came into being with some equestrian members, and schools of law provided their training.

The time of creating law ended, and the time of collecting cases and decisions made by the emperors (from Hadrian's time) and jurists began. Since different positions might be taken, a precedence of decision making was established by Constantine in 321 and Theodosius II in 426. A collection was given obligatory force for the first time under Theodosius II (408-50). A final point was reached with the codification by Justinian (527-65), the Corpus Iuris Civilis (Collection of civil law, 533), which consisted of Digests (positions of qualified jurists), Institutions (the official textbook following Gaius), and the Codex (a collection of imperial decisions). To prevent conflict, commentaries were forbidden.

8. Rome as an Idea

From the time of Augustus, according to the view propagated by Virgil (70-19 B.C.) in his epic *Aeneid*, Rome ruled the whole world. Already in the second century B.C. Roma had become an object of cultic worship in the East (fused with emperor worship under Augustus). The idea of Rome was thus sacralized. Increasing Romanizing, symbolized especially by the granting of civil rights to all free residents in 212, brought ongoing identification with Rome. The third-century crisis, however, reawakened local interest.

The sacking of Rome by the Visigoths under Alaric in 410 affected the → symbol more than it did the city itself. → Augustine (354-430) was moved by this event to write his *City of God* (→ Augustine's Theology), in which for the first time the saving work of Christ was seen apart from the Roman Empire, that is, apart from the four empires of Daniel 7. The idea of eternal Rome (Augustine) lived on, however, for the bishop of Rome, in virtue of the prestige of the city as the place of the martyrdom of → Peter and → Paul (→ Martyrs) and the lack of any rival, especially when Carthage faded from the picture with the Arab invasions early in the seventh century, was able to emerge as the → pope, the supreme ecclesiastical leader of the Roman Catholic Christian communion.

Then later Charlemagne (768-814) in 800 took up once again the idea of Rome and its empire in order to secure legitimacy for himself over against Byzantium, and in that way he made the concept a fruitful one for the Middle Ages (*translatio imperii Romani*, "transfer of Roman rule"). This concept compelled German kings also to go to Rome in order to be crowned emperors as well (→ Empire and Papacy). The idea lived on until 1806 in the form of the so-called Holy Roman Empire, and it carried with it a sense of the ongoing presence of the Roman Empire.

The acceptance of Roman law by Bologna jurists in the 11th century had a special influence on the Roman curia (→ Corpus Iuris Canonici) and also on modern European legal codes. Constant efforts were made to link up with the Roman past, as we may see in the Italian → Renaissance, in the French → Revolution (Napoleon as emperor), and finally in 20th-century → fascism.

→ Early Church; New Testament Era, History of

Bibliography: G. ALFÖLDY, *The Social History of Rome* (rev. ed.; London, 1988) • W. AREND, ed., *Altertum. Alter Orient, Hellas, Rom* (4th ed.; Munich, 1989) • H. BENGTSON, *Grundriß der römischen Geschichte, mit Quellenkunde*, vol. 1, *Republik und Kaiserzeit bis 284 n. Chr.* (3d ed.; Munich, 1982) • J. BLEICKEN, *Geschichte der römischen Republik* (5th ed.; Munich, 1999); idem, *Verfassungs- und Sozialgeschichte des römischen Kaiserreiches* (2 vols.; 4th ed.; Paderborn, 1995) • K. CHRIST, *Geschichte der römischen Kaiserzeit. Von Augustus bis zu Konstantin* (4th ed.; Munich, 2002); idem, *Römische Geschichte. Einführung, Quellenkunde, Bibliographie* (5th ed.; Darmstadt, 1994) • W. DAHLHEIM, *Geschichte der römischen Kaiserzeit* (3d ed.; Munich, 2003) • P. GARNSEY and R. SALLER, *The Roman Empire: Economy, Society, and Culture* (Berkeley, Calif., 1987) • A. HEUSS, *Römische Geschichte* (9th ed.; Paderborn, 2003) • H. KÄHLER, *Rom und seine Welt. Bilder zur Geschichte und Kultur* (2 vols.; Munich, 1958-60) • J. MOORHEAD, *The Roman Empire Divided, 400-700* (New York, 2001) • D. S. POTTER, *Literary Texts and the Roman Historian* (London, 1999); idem, *The Roman Empire at Bay, A.D. 180-395* (New York, 2004) • P. SOUTHERN, *The Roman Empire from Severus to Constantine* (London, 2001) • C. G. STARR, *The Roman Empire, 27 B.C.–A.D. 476: A Study in Survival* (New York, 1982) • P. VEYNE, *The Roman Empire* (Cambridge, Mass., 1997) • F. VITTINGHOFF, ed., *Europäische Wirtschafts- und Sozialgeschichte in der römischen Kaiserzeit* (Stuttgart, 1990) • C. WELLS, *The Roman Empire* (Cambridge, Mass., 1992) • H. WOLFRAM, *The Roman Empire and Its Germanic Peoples* (Berkeley, Calif., 1997).

DANKWARD VOLLMER

Roman Religion

1. Definition

1.1. *Distinctions*

In their classic epoch the Romans clearly distinguished their religion — the *cultus deorum* (cult of the gods), *religiones* (pl. religions), but also *religio* (sing.) — from other parts of their → culture. Thus they maintained the difference between *sacer* and *profanus* (→ Sacred and Profane), *ius divinum* and *ius humanum* (divine and human law), and *dies fasti, dies comitiales,* and *dies nefasti* (days for business, for public assemblies, and for neither). The Romans structured religion from different angles:

1. legally, by nature, place, and time, as well as consecrated, taboo, or protected *(res, locus, dies; sacer, religiosus, sanctus);*
2. cultically, by sacred action, observing birds, and the oracle books and observation of sacrifices *(sacra, auspicia, libri Sibyllini* and *haruspicina);*
3. sociologically, by official or private cult; with distinctions of clan, family, and household; for the people vs. on the city level; also according to region and village, gender and status *(sacra publica* and *sacra privata; gentilicia, familiaria, domestica; popularia* vs. *municipalia;* according to *pagi* and *vici);*
4. philosophically, with tractates on religion, → piety, sanctity, faith, and → vows, and then on natural, mythical and political theology *(de religione, pietate, sanctitate, fide, iure iurando; theologia naturalis, fabularis, civilis);* and
5. historically, with distinctions between old and new, traditional and innovative.

A further distinction was made between the Latin and Sabine legacy on the one hand (cult of Jupiter as the god of heaven) and the Greek rite on the other (→ Greek Religion; Hellenistic-Roman Religion), in which the cultic forms and language and at times the → priests were Greek (Apollo; the Aventine triad Ceres, Liber, and Libera; Asclepius). There was also distinction from the Etruscan system *(disciplina),* which up to the very end of the Roman Empire, under Etruscan care, saw to such things as the observing of sacrifices, the interpreting of lightning, rituals for the founding of cities and dedication of temples, and setting up of distinctions between the citizens and the army.

Along with the native and traditional patriarchal religion *(sacra patria, tradita),* there were also foreign cults *(sacra peregrina),* which in war were taken over from enemy cities and in peace were transferred to Rome *(translatio)* by decision of the Senate, being classified as alien, external, and legalized *(aliena, externa, licita).* The Romans were well aware of the heterogeneous and synthetic (not syncretistic) character of their religion. This awareness facilitated reforming efforts to go back to the "pure origin" under the founder of their religion, Pompilius Numa (7th/6th cent. B.C.), the legendary second king of Rome, before the Greeks and Etruscans "flooded" Rome (Varro).

1.2. *Scholarly Definitions*

Early Christianity, with its modified → monotheism, restrained hostility to → images, and spiritualizing of the Jewish sacrificial cult, objected to the → polytheism, nature worship, idolatry, and bloody → sacrifices of paganism. Until well on in the → modern period, this outlook influenced the study of Roman religion, though in the thinking of Roman writers, scholars, and theologians at least, sacrifices, for example, were of no significance.

Comparative → religious studies in the 19th century saw a deeper gulf between mythical and sensuous Hellenic religion — with its original art, with the gods and youthful Homeric heroes, with Dionysus and tragedy, mysteries, and mysticism — and the sober and moral piety of Rome, which was formulated more in legal terms and was poor in mythology and imagination. For newer humanistic students and lovers of antiquity who were trying to escape the modern world, the constitutional state, and Christianity, Roman religion offered a less exotic, archaic, aesthetic, and mystical alternative. Popular research found the primitive features of an original → animism in the supposedly very pronounced Roman → fear of the dead, which involved lemurs, or larvae (the terrifying ghosts of the dead), which needed to be placated yearly, also Parentalia (annual religious festival in honor of the dead), and Feralia (public ceremony placing offerings and gifts at graves).

The shapelessness of the Roman gods — their relatively nonmythical character, the abstract deities (e.g., of chivalry, courage, modesty, and hope — i.e., Honos, Virtus, Pudicitia, and Spes), the so-called gods of the moment, and later ideas of the power and numen of the gods — were taken to be signs of an original "predeism" that the Romans never totally overcame. The scrupulous observance of → rites supposedly indicated externalism and an inner insecurity, Roman religion being finally trapped in ritualism and formalism (J. Kroll). The Romans' belief in their own piety and its obvious success left little room for choice. Their desire to be the most pious of mortals, even more pious than the gods, must be seen as pride and self-righteousness.

Religious typology classifies Roman religion as a national religion to which people belonged by birth as Roman citizens, not by individual conversion. What began as a heterogeneous city religion developed into a universal imperial religion. It was a cultic religion whose center was, not reading from a sacred book or → preaching, but symbolic actions (→ Symbol), among them bloody and nonbloody sacrifices; it was a → nature religion that thematized the forces of nature and of human society, not the historically definable → revelation of a transcendent deity.

As regards at least some individual circles in the classical epoch, we must modify this classification, for with the help also of Pythagorean, Platonic (→ Platonism), Stoic (→ Stoicism), and Epicurean → philosophy, these circles attempted to construct a transnatural and transpersonal concept of God, assumed that Roman religion had been established by the divinely inspired founders Romulus and Numa Pompilius, stressed the historicity of the festivals in the course of the year (Cicero, Livy, Ovid), and in the cult, speculation, and literature made use of many religious writings, especially the Carmen Arvale (chant of the Arval priests, who served Dea Dia, the goddess of growth), Commentarii Augurum (a collection of decrees regarding augury), Cicero's *De natura deorum* (On the nature of the gods), Virgil's *Aeneid,* and Ovid's *Fasti.*

1.3. *Historical Approaches*

A consistent attempt to deal with Roman religion historically tries to find out empirically what the religious attitude was of specific individuals in specific places at specific times (using prosopography, periodizing, regionalizing). Social history studies the function of religion in particular groups, the military being of special significance for Roman religion. In contrast to the frequently preferred religion of the early farmers and nobles, the religion of greater Rome offers rich material and poses new problems. In this regard an account of urban Roman religion must take into consideration all the religions that were to be found in this city of a million people, including the religions of the Syrians and Egyptians (→ Egyptian Religions) and, from the mid-second century B.C., that of the Jews (→ Judaism). The religion of the women has received little attention, but women could hold the priestly office and by the first century A.D. could even preside over mixed societies (→ Priest, Priesthood, 1).

To prevent Roman religion from being considered merely as a cultic religion and to facilitate comparison with Christianity and Judaism, an intellectual account of it must also pay heed to → myth, to philosophy (which might be critical and materialistic, though not to the point of → atheism), to art, to priestly scholarship (in sacral law and cultic history), and even to speculation. A cultural history of Roman religion tries to understand the functions of religion within the culture as a whole. It must take into special account the development of independent spheres that is typical of complex higher cultures and study their relation to religion. The classic themes are morality and religion, eroticism and religion, the family structure, piety shown to parents and the gods, patriarchalism, philosophical skepticism, religious → conservatism (what we could call the Cotta syndrome, from Cicero's discussion in *De nat. deor.*), religious justification of Roman expansionist policies, and the reasons for Rome's greatness. Using the example of other religions, E. → Troeltsch (1865-1923) defined the task as follows: The religious-historical method must above all be cultural-historical, which includes the social-historical (*Augustin, die christliche antike und das Mittelalter* [Munich, 1915]).

2. Epochs

If we take important dates in Rome's social and political history as our guide, we may divide the external history of Roman religion into four epochs.

2.1. *Pre-Republic*

The first is the pre-Republican period, which lasted from the Indo-European Latin and Sabine migration in the Iron Age to Etruscan domination (ca. 1000-500 B.C.). The social structure of the immigrants, their cultural legacy, their myths and rites, and the relation of these factors to those of the existing older Mediterranean traditions are largely unknown, and little light is shed by comparison with unrelated peoples (G. Dumézil). The epoch ended with strong Greek and Greek-Etruscan influence, the building of → temples, large cultic images, and mythological art, which found a firm place in Roman religion.

2.2. *Republic*

Next came the Republican epoch, which lasted from the dedication of the temple of Jupiter Optimus Maximus on the Capitol (traditionally dated September 13, 509/508 or 508/507 B.C.) to the destruction of Republican religion (the middle of the 1st cent. B.C.) and the solid amalgamation of political, military, and intellectual power when Augustus (d. A.D. 14) seized power on March 6 in 12 B.C. This epoch completed the sacral arrangement of time in the Roman calendar and the organization of a hierarchically and functionally structured pantheon and a sacerdotal order with its four main "colleges" of pontiffs *(pontifices)*, augurs *(augures*, responsible for interpreting omens in public life), ten men in charge of the Greek rites *(decemviri sacris faciundis*, "ten men for sacred actions"), and officials in charge of the feast of Jupiter *(epulones)*. A certain central organization of religion came into being that extended beyond the city of Rome itself.

The suppression of the Bacchic mysteries in 186 B.C. gave evidence of the limits of state → tolerance in a classic instance of repressive religious policy. The dying out of many cults, priestly societies, and the augur discipline marked the end of this epoch. Romans no longer understood the prayers and divine names, and only traces of ancient → sanctuaries remained.

2.3. *Empire*

The imperial period followed, which lasted from the supreme pontificate of Augustus (12 B.C.) to the suppression (after A.D. 313) and administrative liquidation of Roman religion by the Christian emperors (379-95). The epoch began with Augustus's attempts at restoration, the development of → emperor worship, the expansion of Roman religion into a universal and cosmopolitan imperial religion *(urbis et orbis*, of the city and of the world), and the reception of Greek and Near Eastern cults (Isis in the 1st to the 4th cent., Mithras in the 2d to the 4th, Sol Invictus in the 3rd to the 4th; → Mystery Religions). The epoch ended with the Latinizing and Romanizing of Western Christianity and the transformation of Roman religion into a cultless religion of the book and art, with a place for education. The end of Roman religion and the development of Roman Catholic religion are parts of the same process in the religious history of late antiquity.

2.4. *After Prohibition*

The last epoch ran from the total prohibition of Roman religion in 395 to the extinguishing of the remaining elements in Rome and other backward areas and the Catholicizing of the Lombards in A.D. 663 (→ Mission 3.2). After some attempts at national restoration and the dying off of the last secret adherents (→ Augustine mentions those who "still worship in secret," *De civ. Dei* 4.1), the disintegrated remnants of Roman religion lingered on in customs and → superstitions, especially among peasants and in parareligious science (→ astrology, hermetics, → alchemy), even in the Roman Catholic Church and the educational sphere (opposition notwithstanding).

3. Theology

3.1. *Subject Matter*

In the second century B.C. Roman priests, philosophers, and scholars began distinguishing between mythical, natural, and civil theology — that is, the mythical theology of the poets, the → natural theology of the philosophers, and the civil theology of the politicians (see 3.2). The term *theologus*, however, had a more restricted meaning. It denoted (1) advocates of the older theology (Orpheus, Musaeus, Linus) and (2) those acquainted with esoteric and secret writings *(interiores et reconditiores litterae:* Cicero *De nat. deor.* 3.42), especially mythographic scholasticism. It was a simple modification of the ancient usage to describe as theologians all those Romans who spoke or wrote about religion(s) argumentatively and methodically, or by way of generalization or rationalization, for scholarly, reforming, edifying, apologetic, or polemical purposes.

The instruments of thought and language that the theologians used derived from the cult, from sacral law, from philology (esp. the etymology of divine names), and from philosophy. M. Tullius Cicero (d. 43 B.C.) wrote classical texts on sacral law, for example, on the constitution of religion(s) in bk. 2 of *De legibus*. He also wrote about the nature of the gods, their (non)being, their form *(figura)*, their location *(locus)*, and their manner of life *(actio vitae)* in the three volumes of his dialogue *De natura deorum*.

Theology might be difficult and obscure, but it was the finest form of intellectual knowledge and a necessary guide to true religion (*De nat. deor.* 1.1). As in Aristotle (384-322 B.C.; → Aristotelianism), it was the last of the three theoretical disciplines, coming after physics and mathematics. Its subject matter was universal, cosmological, anthropological (encompassing the world and humanity), and historical, for by divination and the establishment of religion, Romulus and Numa had laid the foundations of the Roman state, which could not have become so

Roman Religion

great without the gods (*De nat. deor.* 3.2.5). The Roman theology of history found systematic treatment here.

3.2. *Threefold Division*

→ Tertullian (ca. 160-ca. 225), Arnobius (d. ca. 327), Lactantius (d. ca. 325), and Augustine (354-430, *De civ. Dei* 4.27; 6.5; 6.12) passed on the traditional threefold division of theology into mythical, natural, and civil. In so doing, they influenced the systematic theology of Western Christendom. Hellenistic philosophy had developed the concept, and the erudite *pontifex maximus* (high priest) Quintus Mucius Scaevola (d. 82 B.C.) had introduced it into Roman theology. It owed its systematic development there to the most important Roman theologian, Marcus Terentius Varro (116-27 B.C.), in the first book of his *Antiquitates rerum divinarum* (Antiquities of divine things). The 16 books of this work were written 50-45 B.C. and were dedicated to Julius Caesar (100-44) as the then *pontifex maximus*. This fact made the reforming purpose of the book plain to contemporaries.

In bk. 1, frgs. 6-10 of the Cardauns edition, Varro describes the three types of theology: the *mythicon* of poets (dealing with the mythic and fabulous), the *physicon (naturale)* of philosophers, and the *politicon (civile)* of politicians. The first type contains many things that run contrary to the dignity and nature of the immortals. The second teaches what the gods are, where, of what sort, of what nature, whether they had an origin or always existed, whether they consist of → fire, → numbers, or atoms. The third teaches what citizens, especially priests, must know and do in a city. Part of this information is knowing which state gods to venerate and how.

On this basis Varro then treats Roman religion in five parts, with three books to each part. In bks. 2-4 he deals with priests (*de pontificibus, auguribus, quindecimviris sacrorum;* or high priests, diviners, and the 15-member priestly colleges responsible for sacred rites), in 5-7 with sacred places (*de sacellis, aedibus, locis religiosis;* or shrines, temples, and sacred sites), in 8-10 with times (*de feriis, ludis circensibus, ludis scaenicis;* or holidays, circus games, and theatrical games or plays), in 11-13 with events (*de consecrationibus, sacris privatis, sacris publicis;* or dedications, private observances, and public observances), and finally in 14-16 with the gods *(de dis certis, dis incertis, dis praecipuis atque selectis;* or gods who are trustworthy, untrustworthy, and special and select). This summary of Roman theology, which rests on a broad philosophical, priestly, and legal tradition, influenced all the writings that followed.

In his speculations regarding the pure and imageless origins of Roman religion, Varro refers to the pure religion of → Israel and its God (→ Yahweh), whom he equates with Iovis Pater (Father Jove, i.e., Jupiter). The God of the Jews, he said, is Iovis, for it does not matter by what name he is called so long as what is meant is the same (frg. 16).

3.3. *View of History*

The classic Roman view of history divided it into three sections. First came the uncertain period *(spatium incertum)* from the flood at the time of Ogygos, ancient king of Thebes, to the flood suffered by Deucalion, son of Prometheus, at the hand of Zeus, about which nothing is known for sure. The mythical epoch *(spatium fabulosum)* followed, which lasted up to the Trojan War, which we can now firmly date at 1194/1184 B.C. Then came the historical period *(spatium historicum),* from the Trojan War by way of the founding of Rome (753 B.C.) to the then present.

Alongside this model of global epochs were complex generational *(saecula)* doctrines resting on Etruscan traditions. These ideas reckoned the beginning and end of generations and, with a *sacrum saeculare* (secular observance, held at intervals of about 100 years), prayed to the gods for the future of the next Roman generations. The secular games *(ludi saeculares)* of the year 17 B.C. can be reconstructed especially well, since we still have the related Sibylline oracle, also the legal exposition, the cultic song (Horace, "Carmen saeculare"), and the arrangements and reports of the 15 men who were in charge of the festival.

World history was structured according to various models. As regards Jewish and Christian → apocalyptic (the Book of Daniel), we have the four empires that Pompeius Trogus (in *Historiae Philippicae* [ca. 20/0 B.C.]) related to the Assyrians, Medes and Persians, Macedonians and their successors, and Rome. The history of the world and of the human race might be seen in terms of the comprehensive cosmological-astronomical model of the "great year." When all the stars return to their original position, a new global year will begin and all things will be new. The thought here is that of the eternal return (Cicero *De fin.* 2.102).

The Aeneas myth gave rise to many national Roman themes from the seventh century B.C. onward, for example, (1) the dialectic of the destruction of Troy and the founding of Rome; (2) the leading along false paths *(errores)* by the divine plan and destiny *(fatum);* (3) the patriarchal triad Anchises, Aeneas, and Ascanius, loosely surrounded by various female figures (Hecuba, Creusa, Dido, Lavinia), under the protection of Venus, the mother of Aeneas, and pursued by Juno, but with Jupiter having the decisive role; (4) sacral continuity in the "translation" of the Penates (household gods), the fire, and the talismans of the empire *(pignora imperii)*, all kept safe in the Vestal cult; and (5) the looking beyond Greece to Asia, which finally, from the second century B.C. onward, was brought back into the kingdom of the descendants of Aeneas.

The role of Aeneas and his company in the Troy disaster was seen as significant for global history. Depicted in art from the seventh century B.C. and in literature after Naevius in the third century B.C., this tradition was given structured form at the beginning of the imperial age by Virgil (70-19 B.C.), who permeated it with philosophy, poetry, and theology. Virgil's epic thus became the central text in Roman culture and Latin literature. The theology of history in this mythically historical epic was enhanced by Virgil's developing an individual, collective, and cosmological → eschatology in Aeneas's viewing of the underworld (the *katabasis*). This development made of the epic an all-embracing world poem that transcends time and space, proclaims the eternal character of the empire (1.279), and holds out the sincere but futile hope of eternal peace (1.291-96).

4. Evaluation

In an article of this size it is hardly possible to assess and criticize the functions and achievements of Roman religion for individuals, the family, and the state, or for the development of morality, the emotional life, sensitiveness, art, and humanity. But we must at least indicate some lines of approach. The religious consolidation of a socially heterogeneous society and the legitimation of inequality and suppression are marks of the civil religion (*tu regere imperio populos, Romane, memento,* "know, Roman, that it is your business to reign," Virgil, *Aeneid* 6), though → equality of human beings and of the sexes is promoted in the myths and cults of mother earth *(terra mater)* and the goddess Natura and in philosophical theories of the universal nature of → reason and common human relationship. Patriarchal authority *(patria potestas)* is confirmed by sacral law, myths, and ideas of deity, and yet finally, on the basis of the polytheistic principle, women have a certain, if as yet inadequately studied, role in religious actions. Militarism, which had a deep-seated place in Roman culture and which could define → peace only in terms of victory (Augustus, *Res gestae* 13), also made use of religion (martial feasts in the calendar, religion in the army). Discipline and → obedience *(obsequiem)* were also central religious virtues.

Religion did not combat public cruelty, however, and the mild protests of philosophers and poets went unheard. Augustus was proud of having staged eight gladiatorial shows, with 10,000 fighters, for example, at the dedication of the temple of the deified Julius Caesar in 29 B.C. At the dedication of the temple of Mars in 2 B.C., 260 lions and 36 crocodiles served the pleasure of the spectators. The war against nature, the price of the progress of the "second nature" (Cicero's phrase for nature transformed by human activity), was more successful than the extolling of a satisfying rural life with fertility rites and the cults of the goddess of flowers and the spirits of the woods.

In religious policy we must take note of the inability of the elite of Rome to find an appropriate status for the Jews. Despite constructive approaches in the days of the Caesars (see 3.2 on Iao/Iovis), the destruction of Jerusalem and the prevention of its rebuilding precipitated the withdrawal of the Jews from Greco-Roman culture.

Bibliography: L. ADKINS and R. ADKINS, *Dictionary of Roman Religion* (New York, 2000) • F. ALTHEIM, *Griechische götter im alten Rom* (Giessen, 1930); idem, *A History of Roman Religion* (London, 1938) • H. CANCIK, "Libri fatales. Römische Offenbarungsliteratur und Geschichtstheologie," *Apocalypticism in the Mediterranean World and the Near East* (ed. D. Hellholm; Tübingen, 1983) 549-76; idem, "The Reception of Greek Cults in Rome," *ARelG* 1 (1999) 161-73 • H. CANCIK and H. CANCIK-LINDERMAIER, "'The Truth of Images: Cicero and Varro on Image Worship," *Representation in Religion* (ed. J. Assman and A. I. Baumgarten; Leiden, 2001) 43-61 • H. CANCIK and H. SCHNEIDER, eds., *Brill's New Pauly: Encyclopaedia of the Ancient World* (Eng. eds., C. F. Salazar and D. E. Orton; Leiden, 2002ff.) 20 vols. planned • B. CARDAUNS, ed., *M. Terentius Varro, Antiquitates Rerum Divinarum* (Wiesbaden, 1976) • P. CIHOLAS, *The Omphalos and the Cross: Pagans and Christians in Search of a Divine Center* (Mercer, Ga., 2003) • F. COARELLI, *Il Foro Romano* (Rome, 1983) • J. GAGÉ, *Matronalia. Essai sur les dévotions et les organisations culturelles des femmes dans l'ancienne Rome* (Brussels, 1963) • I. GRADEL, *Emperor Worship and Roman Religion* (Oxford, 2002) • C. KOCH, *Der römische Juppiter* (Frankfurt, 1937; repr., Darmstadt, 1968) • D. S. POTTER, *Prophets and Emperors: Human and Divine Authority from Augustus to Theodosius* (Cambridge, Mass., 1994) • G. RADKE, *Die Götter Altitaliens* (2d ed.; Münster, 1979) • D. SABBATUCCI, *La religione di Roma antica dal calendario festivo all'ordine cosmico* (Milan, 1988) • J. SCHEID, *An Introduction to Roman Religion*

(Bloomington, Ind., 2003) • R. Turcan, *The Gods of Ancient Rome: Religion in Everyday Life from Archaic to Imperial Times* (Edinburgh, 2000) • S. Weinstock, *Divius Iulius* (Oxford, 1971) • G. Wissowa, *Religion und Kultus der Römer* (2d ed.; Munich, 1971; orig. pub., 1902).

Hubert Cancik

Romania

	1960	*1980*	*2000*
Population (1,000s):	18,407	22,201	22,505
Annual growth rate (%):	0.67	0.47	–0.23

Area: 237,500 sq. km. (91,699 sq. mi.)

A.D. 2000

Population density: 95/sq. km. (245/sq. mi.)
Births / deaths: 1.09 / 1.22 per 100 population
Fertility rate: 1.40 per woman
Infant mortality rate: 21 per 1,000 live births
Life expectancy: 70.5 years (m: 67.0, f: 74.2)
Religious affiliation (%): Christians 89.1 (Orthodox 84.9, Roman Catholics 15.1, Protestants 11.1, indigenous 1.2, other Christians 1.0), nonreligious 7.1, atheists 2.4, Muslims 1.3, other 0.1.

1. General Features

Romania became a separate state in 1859 as a result of the 1848 revolutions, when Moldavia in the east (between the Eastern Carpathian Mountains and the Prut River) and Walachia in the south (between the Transylvanian Alps and the Danube) elected a common prince, with a united national assembly to follow in 1862. In 1866 the two brought in a foreign ruler, Charles of Hohenzollern-Sigmaringen, who was prince (1866-81) and then king (1881-1914). Independence was consolidated under Charles during the Russo-Turkish War of 1877-78, and Romania became a kingdom in 1881.

In 1916 Romania joined the Allies in World War I, and it enlarged its territory by more than half as much again at the Paris Peace Conference. The expansion changed its character but not its policies. With Transylvania (surrounded by the Carpathians on the north, east, and west) and Bukovina (north of Moldavia), it acquired territories that had been under Hungarian and Austrian influence; it likewise acquired Bessarabia territory (between the Prut and Dniester Rivers) that had been under Russian influence, and also southern Dobruja territory that had belonged to northeastern Bulgaria.

Although ethnic-national criteria were followed in rounding out the country, in 1930, with 28.1 percent of the people belonging to → minorities, tensions were high between the constitutional claim to a "united state" and the political reality of nationalities with their own traditions (esp. Hungarians, Germans, Serbs, and Jews). It was only halfheartedly that Romania observed the provisions of the treaty protecting minorities enacted at the 1919 Paris Peace Conference.

At the beginning of World War II, Romania lost parts of its new lands (Bessarabia, northern Bukovina, a third of Transylvania, and southern Dobruja). Romania at first joined the Axis powers and won back the eastern territories, but then changed to the Allied side and won back northern Transylvania on August 23, 1944. But it then lost eastern territory to the Soviet Union, including Moldavia and a part of Bessarabia.

In 1947 Romania became a people's republic, and in 1965 a socialist republic. Under President Nicolae Ceausescu (1965-89) it increasingly developed into a dictatorship. The bloody end of this regime on December 25, 1989, opened the way to what is as yet an uncertain democratic future (→ Democracy). Of the 21.7 million citizens in 2002, as many as 10.5 percent (2.3 million) were officially members of minority groups. The number of → Roma, however, though difficult to tabulate, is probably much higher than the official figure of 535,000.

2. Churches

2.1. *Romanian Orthodox Church*

The modern *Romanian Orthodox Church* (→ Orthodox Church) was formed by the uniting of the churches of Moldavia and Walachia. The declaration of → autocephaly (1865) followed the political union (1859), which the ecumenical → patriarch ratified in 1881. Already in the 14th century there were bishoprics in Walachia (1359) and Moldavia (1401). The former was also metropolitan for two Bulgarian dioceses (Silistra and Vidin). Romanian came into use in the church with the first translations, which were sponsored by the cities of Transylvanian Saxony and later by the Reformed Hungarian princes of Transylvania in connection with the → Reformation. The first complete translation of the Bible into Romanian appeared in 1688 (→ Bible Versions 4.5).

Up to World War I Transylvania was under the Austro-Hungarian crown. In 1700 the Transylvanian Orthodox Church, with its diocesan seat in Alba Iulia (Karlsburg), formed a → union (§2.2.2) with the → Roman Catholic Church (→ Uniate Churches). This act greatly reduced the number of Orthodox members. In 1765 Maria Theresa (1740-80) placed the Transylvanian Orthodox Church under the → bishop of Buda, but Joseph II (1780-90) gave it its own bishop with a seat in Transylvania, and in 1791 it gained state recognition. After the uniting of Transylvania with the Kingdom of Romania in 1918, the two Orthodox churches formed a patriarchate (1925) with 5 metropolitanates, 13 bishoprics, 14 theological colleges, and 13 seminaries. The Romanian Orthodox Church became the state church (→ Church and State).

The church lost this special position after World War II. It retained its own → monasteries, workshops, factories, presses, and publishing houses, and it promoted itself with the help of many journals and specialized theological works. It still had two theological faculties (Bucharest and Sibiu [Ger. Hermannstadt]) and six seminaries for the training of its clergy. New faculties and seminaries were set up after the 1989 revolution.

In 2003 the Orthodox Church had 21 schools for training cantors, with 900 enrolled students, and 38 theological seminaries (training with secondary-school diploma, or *Abitur*), with 4,700 students. In addition, 15 departments of theology offering several different courses of study were integrated into the various state universities, with approximately 11,000 theology students (→ Theological Education). In 2003 there were 49 diocesan theological periodicals being published, the oldest of which were *Telegraful Roman* (The Romanian telegraph, since 1852) and *Biserica Ortodoxa Romana* (Romanian Orthodox Church, since 1874).

The Holy → Synod is the supreme authority in legal and spiritual matters, and the National Assembly is the representative organ for all administrative issues. The synod and assembly both have an executive arm in the National Church Council. The synod founded and organized two archbishoprics for Romanian Orthodox believers living abroad, one for the United States and Canada at Detroit, Michigan, and one for central and western Europe at Paris. In 1992 the Synod reactivated the Metropolitanate of Bessarabia, with its seat in Chişinău (the capital of Moldova), and in 1993 it reorganized the Metropolitanate of Germany and Central and Northern Europe, with its seat in Berlin. The Orthodox Bishoprics of Gyula (Hungary) and of Vršac (Serbia and Montenegro) both also belong to the Patriarchate of Bucharest.

In 2002 the Orthodox Church had 18.8 million members (86.8 percent of the population). As of 1998 it had 10,068 priests, 161 deacons, 3,382 cantors, 2,482 monks, and 4,246 nuns. It was organized into 6 metropolitanates, 10 archbishoprics, and 13 bishoprics; it had 13,627 church buildings and 451 monasteries. In the same year the church built 145 new church buildings, and another 731 were under construction. It also provided service in hospitals (87 chapels, with 125 priests), prisons (30 chapels, with 37 priests), the military (38 churches and 43 priests), schools (13 chapels, with 46 priests), and children's homes and homes for the aged (7 chapels, with 3 priests).

2.2. *Catholic Churches*

2.2.1. The *Roman Catholic Church* in Romania consists for the most part of Hungarians residing in Romania. In 2002 about 350,000 members were Romanians, and of the rest 36,000 were Germans, 12,000 Slovaks, and others Czechs, Croats, and Bulgarians. The first bishopric was set up in Transylvania at the beginning of the 11th century at Alba Iulia (Karlsburg), and others followed. Membership had dropped to 10 percent of the people at the → Reformation, but the Austrian regime gave strong support. The Diocese of Karlsburg was refounded in 1715. Recatholicizing brought discrimination against Protestants and national tensions.

After World War I the Diocese of Bucharest was founded, and members in Moldavia and Walachia ceased to be under Karlsburg. Under the Communists the church suffered severe repression. Of the four dioceses, only Karlsburg received official sanction, but it was placed under Bucharest, the archdiocese since 1928. The bishop of Karlsburg had to recall Hungarian-speaking priests from Moldavia. Karlsburg had a theological academy for the training of priests. A school for training Romanian priests was established at Iaşi (Ger. Jassy).

After the revolution in 1989 the church restored the dioceses of Timişoara (Hung. Temesvár), Satu Mare (Hung. Szatmár-Németi), and Oradea (Ger. Grosswardein). In 1990 John Paul II (1978-2005) also set up a new diocese of Iaşi. The ending of censorship brought the reorganizing of Roman Catholic publishing and the regular appearance of the weekly *Keresztény szó* (Christian voice). New establishments in the big cities included 16 church secondary schools, 6 medical colleges, 4 departments of theology, and a department for training teachers. Negotiations were started with the government for the return of schools, monasteries, libraries, and museums.

2.2.2. The *Greek Catholic Church* came into being in Transylvania in 1697-1700 when Austrian pressure brought about a union between Rome and the Romanian Orthodox Church. Its diocesan seat was at Făgăraş (Ger. Fogarasch), later Blaj (Ger. Blasendorf). The → pope gave canonical recognition in 1721 and constitutional recognition in 1744.

Under the Communists the church was prohibited. Priests and laity were forced into the Romanian Orthodox Church, church buildings being given to the latter, and the schools were nationalized. Those who wished to remain faithful to the union often joined the Roman Catholic Church. The result was the introduction of the Romanian → Mass after → Vatican II.

The revolution made reorganization possible, and many left the Orthodox Church. In the summer of 1990 two dioceses were established (Cluj and Blaj), and in September 1990 two theological colleges. Negotiations have begun with the Orthodox Church for the return of church buildings.

Although in 1998 the Greek Catholic Church had 638 church communities and 700 official priests, it had only 200 church buildings, 138 of which had been returned by the Orthodox Church. (In 1948 it had approximately 2,500 church buildings.) According to the official census of 2002, the church had 191,500 members, including 161,000 Rumanians, 20,000 Hungarians, and 1,500 Germans. (The church itself, however, puts the figure at 700,000 members.)

2.3. ***Protestant Churches***

2.3.1. The *Reformed Church of Romania* (→ Reformed and Presbyterian Churches) came into existence in Transylvania in the 1550s. In 1559 the Synod of Neumarkt (Rom. Tîrgu Mureş) adopted the Reformed doctrine of the → Eucharist, and the Diet of Turda (June 4-11, 1564) accorded recognition (→ Lutheran Churches). Prince Gábor Bethlen founded a clergy training academy at Karlsburg in 1622. It was moved to Klausenburg (Cluj-Napoca) in 1895, which had become a diocesan seat in the middle of the 19th century.

After World War I came the founding of the bishopric of Grosswardein (Oradea). The two dioceses have formed the one Reformed Church since 1948, but each with its own leadership, bishop, and consistory, and a common synod presided over by one of the two bishops. After 1949 the training of ministers took place at the United Protestant Theological Institute at Cluj-Napoca.

The 1989 revolution freed the church from state regulation. The dioceses have a common retirement program and conduct common courses for clergy education. The Diocese of Transylvania has 461 churches (21 of them mission centers), 138 daughter churches, and 462 diaspora churches. There are 437 ministers, with 60 vacancies. The Diocese of Oradea has 264 churches, and there are 236 ministers, with 44 vacancies. The church lists 701,000 members, of whom 665,300 are Hungarian, 17,500 Romanian, 16,400 Roma, with much smaller numbers of Germans and Ukrainians. The revolution led to the resignation of the two bishops and their helpers. Agreements were made leading to a new administrative division of districts. New officers were elected in 1990. All officers, including bishops, were elected for four-year terms.

On May 12, 1990, the government approved the opening of a church college with seminary rank. The Reformed Church currently has eight secondary schools and one theological institute for training pastors together with the Unitarian Churches, the Evangelical Church of the Augsburg Confession (Saxon), and the Evangelical Lutheran Synodal Presbyterial Church (Hungarian), and one department of theology for training teachers. This particular department offers several courses of study (theology, foreign languages, history, music pedagogy) and functions within the Babes-Bolyai Science University in Cluj-Napoca. The possibility also exists for offering religious instruction at state schools. Additional services performed by the Reformed Church include the necessary development of social welfare institutions and church work in → diaspora communities.

2.3.2. The *Unitarian Churches in Romania* (→ Unitarians) started and received official recognition between 1564 and 1568. It has 67,000 members (most are Hungarian, with a small minority of Romanians and Roma), with an episcopal seat at Cluj-Napoca. After World War II it lost its theological academy, being a Hungarian minority church, but in 1949 it was given its own faculty with three professors in the theological institute set up in that year (see 2.3.1). In the spring of 1990 it began publishing the monthly *Keresztény magvető* (Christian sower) and the church paper *Unitárius közlöny* (Unitarian bulletin). The church has 141 church buildings and 110 pastors.

2.3.3. The *Evangelical Church of the Augsburg Confession* consists almost entirely of German-speaking congregations. It is heir to the 12th-century immigrant church (with special rights) in

Transylvanian Saxony, which went over to → Lutheranism between 1542 and 1550, naming itself *Ecclesia Dei nationalis saxoniae* (Church of God of the Saxon nation); it received official recognition as such in 1554.

In 1940 this church had 250,000 members and its own schools financed by church taxes. But the church was weakened by military service, Russian incursions (1945), and forced resettlement (1952). From the 1960s on there has been migration back to Germany, at an increasing pace after quota negotiations between Bonn and Bucharest in 1978.

After 1989 about two-thirds of the remaining 105,000 church members left; in 2002 only 8,700 members remained (the largest groups were 1,470 Romanians and 1,350 Hungarians). The Saxon congregations, famous for their fortress churches, have become a → diaspora. The five deaneries have 65 ministers, with an episcopal seat at Sibiu. Many foreigners, some today from eastern Europe, study at the German-speaking branch of the Protestant Theological Institute (→ 2.3.1), located since 1955 at Sibiu and, since the fall of 2004, integrated within the national University of Sibiu. The church schools have not yet been restored. The church leadership publishes *Kirchliche Blätter* (Church paper, a monthly) and *Landeskirchliche Informationen* (Regional-church information). In 1991 the church set up a diaconal arm, which, along with traditional forms of neighborly help, established an institutional form of social aid for many others as well as members.

2.3.4. The congregations of the *Evangelical Lutheran Synodal Presbyterial Church of the Augsburg Confession* were under a Hungarian bishop up to World War I. In 1920 they set up their own diocese with a superintendent at the head. They offer training at the Cluj-Napoca Theological Institute (see 2.3.1). The largest groups of this church of 27,000 members are Hungarians (15,200), Germans (6,400), Slavs (3,000), and Romanians (2,200). The Romanian-speaking Lutheran church, deriving from the work of the Norwegian Jewish mission before World War II, has 150 Romanian members. An independent monthly, *Evangélikus harangszó* (Evangelical chime), is published.

2.4. *Other Churches*

The *Old Rite Followers,* or *Lipovenes,* is a group founded in the 18th century. Consisting of Russians living in the Danube delta and using Old Russian in its liturgy, it has 38,000 members. Its metropolitan has his seat at Galați.

The *Armenian-Gregorian Church* (→ Armenian Apostolic Church) has 700 members and is under the care of the Armenian archbishop of Bulgaria.

2.5. *Newer Protestant Churches*

→ *Baptists* found their first members among Germans and Hungarians in Transylvania at the end of the 19th century. In the 20th century they grew rapidly among Romanians. They engage strongly in mission and evangelization. After the revolution they founded a theological institute at Bucharest and a university in Oradea. The Baptists have 126,600 members.

Between the wars the → *Pentecostal Church* (325,000 members) and the → *Adventists* (94,000) gained a footing among Romanians and Hungarians. The two support a seminary for preachers at Bucharest. The Baptists, Pentecostals, and the Christian Gospel Church, which came into being in Walachia, are linked in a common Evangelical Alliance to represent their interests.

3. Other Religions

The *Jewish community* (→ Judaism) has some 6,000 members in Romania. The seat of the chief rabbi is in Bucharest. Jewish immigration started increasing in the 1960s.

→ *Islam,* present since the 14th century, has some 67,000 adherents in Romania. They consist primarily of Turks and Tatars.

4. Church and State

Although the Communist constitution promised → religious liberty, the church was unable to claim this right. The state nationalized church property, took over church schools, and forbade or strictly limited and controlled all diaconal work and public actions, including worship, religious instruction, and training for ministers. Churches of ethnic minorities encountered a policy of ethnic discrimination.

After the 1989 revolution a new law guaranteeing freedom for the churches and their public ministry was then worked out with the input of the churches themselves, although Parliament has yet to ratify it. Various questions such as the right to establish church schools (elementary and high schools) and the return of church property (e.g., buildings seized by the state) are gradually being addressed in a satisfactory fashion. The new constitution of the Romanian state does, however, already guarantee religious freedom for all recognized churches, which are now able to organize and carry out their various activities free of state controls (→ Religious Liberty).

5. Ecumenical Relations

Before the revolution in 1989 ecumenical cooperation between different churches was initiated more by the state than by the churches themselves, enabling the state to exercise control not only over ecumenical activities as such but also over individual churches. The changes that year also brought about a significant change in the ecumenical sphere. Churches were now free to participate and to become engaged in the various world ecumenical associations and organizations. Foreign ecumenical contacts no longer required state authorization, and churches could now also freely develop ecumenical contacts among themselves. Although a more strongly organized ecumenical sensibility is more evident at the level of the various local church communities, it is increasingly emerging in a certain sense at the level of church leadership as well.

This ecumenical movement is still often weak and lacking definite focus, which derives from the fact that during the transitional period after the fall of Communism, churches were more involved in reorganizing their own institutions and activities than in pursuing ecumenical development. The revolution confronted the churches not only with new challenges but also with the necessity of determining their own identity within the new democratic situation.

Bibliography: R. D. Bachman, ed., *Romania: A Country Study* (2d ed.; Washington, D.C., 1991) • D. B. Barrett, G. T. Kurian, and T. M. Johnson, *WCE* (2d ed.) 1.619-23 • N. I. Brânzea, ed., *Religious Life in Romania* (Bucharest, 1999) • A. Du Nay, A. Du Nay, and Á. Kosztin, *Transylvania and the Rumanians* (Hamilton, Ont., 1997) • S. Frunză, *Paşi spre integrare. Religie şi drepturile omului în România* (Steps toward integration. Religion and human rights in Romania) (Cluj-Naoica, 2004) • T. Gilberg, "Religion and Nationality in Romania," *Religion and Nationalism in Soviet and East European Politics* (ed. P. Ramet; Durham, N.C., 1989) 328-51 • D. C. Giurescu and S. Fischer-Galati, eds., *Romania: A Historic Perspective* (New York, 1998) • K. Hitchins, *The Romanians, 1774-1866* (Oxford, 1996); idem, *Rumania, 1866-1947* (Oxford, 1994) • S. Joanta, *Romania: Its Hesychast Tradition and Culture* (Wildwood, Calif., 1992) • I.-V. Leb, ed., *Cultele şi statul în România* (Denominations and the state in Romania) (Cluj-Napoca, 2003) • D. N. Nelson, ed., *Romania after Tyranny* (Boulder, Colo., 1992) • *Die Rumänische Orthodoxe Kirche in der Vergangenheit und heute* (Bucharest, 1979) • E. C. Suttner, "Kirche und Staat," *Südosteuropa-Handbuch,* vol. 2, *Rumänien* (ed. K.-D. Grothusen; Göttingen, 1977) 458-83 • K. W. Treptow, ed., *Tradition and Modernity in Romanian Culture and Civilization, 1600-2000* (Iaşi, 2001).

János Molnár

Romans, Epistle to the

1. General Features
2. Historical Situation
3. Contents
4. Theological Importance

1. General Features

P. → Melanchthon (1497-1560; → Reformers) described the Epistle to the Romans as a compendium of Christian doctrine. In view of the historical circumstances in which Paul wrote it, this judgment has been contested in our day. Paul, it is argued, had a specific historical situation in mind, and his theological argument is thus situational. Paul himself, though, was also in a specific historical situation, which dictated the strategy he used in argument. Attention has also been drawn to the fact that the rhetorical situation (→ Rhetoric 1) influenced his mode of argumentation. G. Bornkamm called Romans Paul's testament. There is truth in all these approaches, although we should not absolutize any of them.

Paul was addressing the church at Rome and clearly dealing with its concrete problems, which would seem to be related to his own. He found controversies within the church (chaps. 14–15) in the context of central theological questions that obviously had a bearing on his theology and strategy of → mission. Thus the epistle, written out of and into a concrete situation, became a theological writing that almost necessarily has the character of a compendium.

If, as some think, Romans is the last of Paul's genuine epistles to have survived, then it is especially important for understanding his intention in the letter that we should see where and to what extent it differs from what he said before. Instructive here are the theological distinctions from Galatians, but we can truly appreciate the profile of these distinctions only when we are aware of the rhetorical means that Paul makes use of in Romans. We must ask whether the differences were necessary because he had to do some substantial theological rethinking, or whether he had to simply look at what he had said before from a different angle for the sake of his audience. One thing that certainly does not change is his thesis that → justification is by → faith and not by works of the → law.

One of the most significant advances in Pauline research occurred when H. D. Betz recognized that we can properly grasp the conception behind Galatians only when we analyze it according to the laws of ancient rhetoric. To be sure, there is keen debate whether Betz was right to classify that letter as apologetic in analogy to a legal defense. In the case of Romans, however, we can show that apologetic elements are dominant, so that it may more accurately be put in the apologetic class. But while the proportions of a defensive address are fairly well observed in Galatians (with *narratio, propositio,* and *argumentatio*), they are not in Romans. Here the *narratio* (1:8[?]-15) is very short, and the *propositio* (1:16-17) is followed at once by a disproportionately long *argumentatio* (1:18–11:36). For that reason we must show how the different parts of the *argumentatio* fit together. What is the inner structure? Surprisingly, the reference to the specific situation at Rome comes only in 14–15, toward the end of the hortatory section (12–15; → Parenesis).

2. Historical Situation

Paul wrote Rome to ask the church there to support him both personally and materially on his mission to Spain (15:24). He also asked the Christians at Rome to wrestle with him in → prayer that his collection for the Jerusalem community would be accepted and that he would be rescued from "the unbelievers in Judea" (vv. 30-31). If this second request seems strange, so is the related circumstance that he wrote as though he was on his way to Jerusalem. These puzzling features become understandable when we take note of the structuring of the *argumentatio* by questions and make a comparison with Galatians in this regard. Paul is dealing with the objections of → Jewish Christians to his theological treatment of the law in Galatians, and he formulates these objections in questions so as to reduce them ad absurdum.

Thus in 3:1 he asks what advantage Jews have and what the value is of → circumcision. Then in 3:5 he asks whether, if our unrighteousness displays God's righteousness, God is unjust. Again in 3:8 he asks whether we should do → evil so that → good may come. The question in 3:31 is whether → faith overthrows the law. Further questions may be found in 6:1, Should we continue in → sin that → grace may abound? 7:7, Is the law sin? 9:14, Is there injustice with God? and 11:11, Have the Jews taken offense in order that they might fall?

R. Bultmann (1884-1976; → Existential Theology) regarded these questions as those of a fictitious opponent that Paul formulated in a provocative way. But if we realize that Galatians with its antinomian theology of the law could be taken in such a way as to force people to ask these questions, then we might regard the positive statements about the law of Moses in Romans as a deliberate softening of the basically critical view of the law in Galatians. Paul had perhaps come to the painful realization that he could not appeal to the agreement of the so-called apostolic council with his more antinomian theological position in the *argumentatio* of Galatians (→ Justification 1.3). He thus faced the possible implications of that position in Rome and rethought what he was trying to say theologically. He was not withdrawing his basic axiom that justification is by faith and not by works of the law (3:20-31), but he was stating this conviction against a new theological background (→ Law and Gospel).

The situation of the Christians in Rome at the time of writing (after 55) had probably been affected by the edict (49?) of Claudius (41-54) that had seemingly expelled all Jews from Rome because of disturbances related to a certain Chrestus (Christ?). In reality, only a few Jews left, among them some Jewish Christians, for example, Aquila and Priscilla (Acts 18:2). When Nero (54-68) revoked the edict, Pauline-minded Jewish Christians no doubt returned and were plunged into debates with other Jewish Christians about the law. This hypothesis fits in well with Paul's arguments in Romans 14–15.

3. Contents

3.1. We have referred above to the basic content of the epistle, namely, justification by faith. Here however, in distinction from Galatians, the key concept is the righteousness of God *(dikaiosynē theou).* It is not just a gift of God to those he pronounces righteous; it is also the power of God. And God's → righteousness (§§1-2) comes historically through the → gospel, which already for its part is the power of God (*dynamis theou,* 1:16-17). The corruption of humanity by the power of sin *(hamartia)* was cosmic in its scope (1:18–3:9), and therefore the opposing power of God also had to be cosmic in its scope.

Where there is faith in the gospel, in which God's righteousness is revealed — faith that is not merely a prerequisite of entry at a single moment (Sanders), for in 1:17 we read, "through faith for faith" *(ek pisteōs eis pistin)* — there the righteousness becomes a power that is at work in history. It has its divine basis in the atoning death of Christ as the act of God (3:25; 5:6-11; → Atonement; Soteriology). Hence faith in the God who justifies implies a renouncing of self-glorying in the light of the divine action (3:27, though see H. Räisänen and E. P. Sanders for a different view). The law itself shows by the example of → Abraham that justification is by faith, that self-justification is not possible (4:1-5). Beginning in 5:12, Paul sets his theology of justification within the schema of → salvation history.

Beginning in 6:1, Paul shows that by → baptism the justified are baptized into *(baptizō eis)* Christ and his death, so that they are no longer under sin as a power but under the righteousness of God as God's power. Sin shall not have dominion over the justified (an imperative deriving from the indicative). Only the justified can know the extent and depth of sin. Those who are still in the sphere of the law do not really understand what they do (7:7-24). But the justified live according to the Spirit and not the flesh (8:1-17). Their freedom, however, is only the beginning of the freedom of all → creation. In 9–11 Paul applies the preaching of justification to → Israel. At the end God will save all Israel (11:26). In this matter Paul offers a different perspective from that of 1 Thess. 2:14-16 or Gal. 4:21-30.

3.2. The exhortations that begin in chap. 12 conclude with a specific admonition to the Christians at Rome. Concretely in 14–15 Paul tells those who are strong in faith, and who eat foods that the law of Moses pronounced unclean, to accept those who are weak; and he tells those who are weak in faith, and who do not understand freedom from the law as the freedom that Christ has won for them, not to despise the strong. This controversy between the strong and the weak mirrors that between those who are faithful to the law and those who are emancipated from it. Paul's counsel is that those who champion freedom from the law should have regard to those who are still living under the control of the Jerusalem way of thinking (see also 1 Corinthians 8). Here again we see clearly that Paul is not taking such a hard line as he did in Galatians.

Only after this admonition does Paul mention his planned visit to Rome. But he will not carry it out as he imagines. His visit to Jerusalem was, as he feared, a personal disaster. When he does come to Rome, it is as a prisoner of the Roman state; ultimately he dies there as a → martyr.

It is debated whether or to what extent chap. 16 is an integral part of Romans.

4. Theological Importance

In its mature form in Romans, Paul's theology of justification, so Protestants are convinced, is basic to evangelical faith. In critical situations in church history the study of Romans has resulted in theological reflection and thus led, at least in part, to success in dealing with the crisis, as we see in the case of → Augustine, M. → Luther, or K. → Barth (→ Augustine's Theology; Luther's Theology; Dialectical Theology).

→ New Testament Era, History of

Bibliography: Commentaries: W. L. Brown and G. W. Brown (New York, 1988) • J. D. G. Dunn (WBC; 2 vols.; Dallas, 1988) • J. A. Fitzmyer (JBC; London, 1990) • K. Haacker (THKNT 6; 2d ed.; Berlin, 2002) • S. Légasse (LeDiv 10; Paris, 2002) • D. J. Moo (NICNT; Grand Rapids, 1996) • L. Morris (PNTC; Grand Rapids, 1988) • A. Pitta (LBibNT 6; Milan, 2001) • T. R. Schreiner (BExC; Grand Rapids, 1998) • M. Theobald (SKK.NT; vol. 1, 2d ed., 1998; vol. 2, 1993) • U. Wilckens (EKKNT 6/1-3; 3 vols.; Neukirchen, 1978-89) • J. Ziesler (TPINTC; London, 1989).

Other works: J. A. Crafton, "Paul's Rhetorical Vision and the Purpose of Romans: Towards a New Understanding," *NovT* 32 (1990) 317-39 • J. D. G. Dunn, *The Theology of Paul the Apostle* (Grand Rapids, 1998) • H. Hübner, *Biblische Theologie des Neuen Testaments,* vol. 2, *Die Theologie des Paulus* (Göttingen, 1993); idem, *Vetus Testamentum in Novo,* vol. 2, *Corpus Paulinum* (Göttingen, 1997) • J. Lambrecht, *Pauline Studies* (Louvain, 1994) • J. D. Moores, *Wrestling with Rationality in Paul: Romans 1–8 in a New Perspective* (Cambridge, 1995) • H. Ponsot, *Une introduction à la Lettre aux Romains* (Paris, 1988) • G. Segalla, *Lettera ai Romani–traduzione strutturata* (Reggio Emilia, 1999) • T. Söding, *Das Liebesgebot bei Paulus. Die Agape im Rahmen der paulinischen Ethik* (Münster, 1995) • M. Theobald, *Der Römerbrief* (Darmstadt, 2000) • A. J. M. Wedderburn, *The Reasons for Romans* (Edinburgh, 1988).

Hans Hübner

Romanticism

Romanticism, an intellectual and artistic movement associated with the fervor of revolutionary change that engaged all of Europe and the United States during the latter third of the 18th and the first third of the 19th century, left no discipline of human endeavor unaltered. There was a Romantic way of playing the violin, as in the spontaneity and virtuosity of Niccolò Paganini (1782-1840), whose left-hand pizzicato, double-stop harmonics, and ricochet bowings made it seem that he played in duet with an invisible devil, a belief he encouraged with his demonic appearance and frenzied style. There was also a Romantic way of engaging a military campaign, as in the ambush tactics and guerrilla warfare first forwarded by Carl von Clausewitz (1780-1831) in his essay "Principles of War" (1812), then developed four years later into a full study of military strategy *Vom Kriege* (On war, 1816; published posthumously in 1832). The sciences witnessed a shift from matter-based physics to energy-based physics, philosophy from → materialism to → idealism, literature and art from mimetic form to subjective expression, politics from monarchical authority to democratic → individualism, religion from ecclesiastical → dogma to intuitive → faith. The religious debates of the Romantic era challenged church authority and explored modes of faith that in previous centuries would have been charged with heresy (→ Religion, Criticism of). Although the scope of Romanticism was pervasive, it by no means swept away all opposition. It instigated and thrived on polemical conflict and ideological faction.

1. Religious Controversy

Nowhere were the inherent antagonisms more assertive or more extreme than in religious controversy, which in Britain aroused the "natural piety" of William Wordsworth (1770-1850), the → skepticism of Lord Byron (1788-1824), and the → atheism of Percy Bysshe Shelley (1792-1822); in Germany, the magic idealism of Novalis (Friedrich von Hardenberg, 1772-1801), the haunted nature of Josef von Eichendorff (1788-1857), and the visionary raptures of Clemens Brentano (1778-1842); in France, the uncertainty of Alfred de Vigny (1797-1863), the anguished → doubt of Alfred de Musset (1810-57), and the "new Christianism" of Claude-Henri de Rouvroy Saint-Simon (1760-1825). Even such attempts to identify an author's religious outlook remain tenuous, because the grappling with ideas was dynamic and often underwent many permutations during a lifetime. Samuel Taylor Coleridge (1772-1834), for example, was the son of an Anglican clergyman, preached as a Unitarian, endeavored to affirm Trinitarian doctrine, and spent the final 15 years of his life as an influential advocate of the Broad Church movement (→ Liberal Theology 2.1). The intense literary probing into every aspect of religious faith prompted John Keble (1792-1866), professor of poetry at Oxford from 1831 to1841, to define literature as secularized religion.

1.1. *Poetic Participation in Divine Creativity*

Among the prominent tenets of Romanticism was the exaltation of the poet and artist as a participant in divine creativity. In his *System des transzendentalen Idealismus* (1800), Friedrich Wilhelm von Schelling (1775-1854) declared that the pervasive energies that constituted all nature had acquired in the human mind a capacity of conscious reflection, the source of → intuition that enabled the individual mind to become attuned to the creative processes of nature. Schelling delivered lectures entitled "Philosophy of Art" at Jena in 1802 and again in 1803. Among his students was Henry Crabb Robinson (1775-1867). Because his parents were → Dissenters, Crabb Robinson was denied admittance to the public schools and universities of England. He therefore enrolled at the University of Jena in 1800. In the course of the next five years he met with Johann Wolfgang von Goethe (1749-1832) and Friedrich Schiller (1759-1805) in nearby Weimar. He also met with Germaine de Staël (1766-1817), who, accompanied by Benjamin Constant (1767-1830), had left France in exile after incurring the disfavor of Napoleon (emp. 1804-15). Both turned to Crabb Robinson for an account of Schelling's philosophy of art, and it was Crabb Robinson's notes that de Staël incorporated into her account in *De l'Allemagne* (Germany, 1810; ET 1814).

The proliferation of Schelling's ideas in England was furthered by their adaptation in Coleridge's *Biographia Literaria* (1815). Coleridge declared that "the primary IMAGINATION" is "the living Power and prime agent of all human perception" and functions "as a repetition in the finite mind of the eternal act of creation in the infinite I AM." The poet thus participates in divine creation and, through "the secondary IMAGINATION," channels a portion of that creativity into poetry. Arthur Schopenhauer (1788-1860), in *Die Welt als Wille und Vorstellung* (The world as will and idea, 1818), provided a further elaboration of the artistic appropriation of divine process. Classical Greek and Roman culture acknowledged the divine rapture of the rhapsode, the *furor divinus* of the inspired poet. Ion, the rhapsode in Plato's dialogue of that name, claims that he surrenders all rational control in the moment of inspiration. The formulations of Schelling, Coleridge, and Schopenhauer differ from that ancient tradition by attributing to the poet and artist a conscious and willful control of their own creativity — not passive submission but active participation.

1.2. *Critique of Christianity*

1.2.1. *Social Criticism*

In addition to the emphasis on individual access to the divine, without the mediation of the church, the authority of the → church (§§2.2.7-8) and the stability of ecclesiastical → hierarchy were further shaken by the same forces of political → revolution and industrial revolution that were reshaping social structure. The parish system throughout Europe had developed under the rural economy of previous generations. The institutional structure of the church was slow in adapting to the massive shift of population from country to city. Mining and manufacturing towns grew rapidly, and a huge increase in urban populations brought about the squalor of overcrowded housing. With no legal constraints, factory owners exercised a ruthless exploitation of their workers. At a time when the church might have served as a moral force for improvement, the clergy was still ensnared in the anachronistic ecclesiastical structures of earlier days. Long hours, poverty-level wages, and crowded slum dwellings without water, heating, or sewers subjected the working class to the menaces of disease. Theft and prostitution were on the rise. Many poets of the period raised an outcry against the church for its failure to remedy the abuses, even accusing the church of complicity in the exploitation (→ Industrial Society).

William Blake (1757-1827), in "Holy Thursday" from the *Songs of Innocence* (1789), described the children from the Charity Schools being ushered by "wise guardians" to St. Paul's Cathedral for Ascension Day services; then, in the corresponding "Holy Thursday" from the *Songs of Experience* (1794), he questioned whether it is "a holy thing to see / . . . Babes reduced to misery, / Fed with cold and usurous hand." He also told of abusive child labor in "The Chimney Sweeper," of poverty and prostitution in "London." The themes of self-righteous oppression emerge again in "The Garden of Love," where "Priests in black gowns were walking their rounds, / And binding with briars my joys and desires." He authored an even more powerful indictment of the slave trade and the repression of women in *The Visons of the Daughters of Albion* (1793). In *The Marriage of Heaven and Hell* (1790) he reverses the corrupt and hypocritical moral codes that condemn the body as evil and exalt the soul as good. In "The Voice of the Devil" he asserts that there is no body distinct from the soul. With the phrase "Eternal Delight" he identifies what arises from the energy of the body. After describing the cannibalistic folly of biblical exegesis, Blake offers a "Bible of hell" based upon this countercredo of salvation though energy. As books in that Bible, Blake produced numerous prophetic works: *America, a Prophecy* (1793), *Europe, a Prophecy* (1794), *The Book of Urizen* (1794), *The Song of Los* (1795), *The Book of Los* (1795), and *The Book of Ahania* (1795). These works were followed by a longer exposition of the means to salvation, *Milton, a Poem* (1804-18), in which Blake endeavored to redeem Milton from the constraints of his Calvinist religion by guiding him, as Virgil guided Dante, on an alternate course to redemption, through the body rather than through spiritual isolation.

1.2.2. *Intellectual Challenge*

In addition to the social criticism of the church, another challenge arose from intellectual quarters, from the scientists and philosophers. The anti-ecclesiastical diatribes of the → Enlightenment were atheistic or agnostic, intellectual arguments against the irrationality of belief in supernatural powers, miracles, and divine intervention. Thus Voltaire (François-Marie Arouet, 1694-1778) denounced Christian faith as superstition, the Gospels and Jesus himself as fictions. In the entry "Atheism" in the *Dictionnaire philosophique* (1764), Voltaire nevertheless supported the argument that an admirable machine, such as this world, required an admirable intelligence as its maker. The purpose of religion, he claimed, was not to establish dogma but to uphold morality. In his chapter "Of Miracles," in *Enquiry concerning Human Understanding* (1748), David Hume (1711-76) declared the inherent contradiction in any attempt to affirm the supernatural or the → miracles of the Bible. George Campbell (1719-96) and William Paley (1743-1805) attempted to refute Hume's argument as *post hoc, propter hoc.* In the Romantic period, Thomas De Quincey (1785-1859) followed Coleridge in pointing out the inadequacy of → experience. Hume himself had declared that, because of the inadequacy of experience, → causality could be demonstrated but never proved. How much more difficult it was to insist on the ability to discern clear boundaries between the natural and the supernatural when human science had yet to fathom the workings of nature. For De Quincey, the essential miracle of Christianity resided in personal faith rather than in biblical history.

Immanuel Kant (1724-1804) had declared that any proof of God's existence entailed its antinomy, the proof of God's nonexistence (→ God, Arguments for the Existence of). In his *Phänomenologie des Geistes* (Phenomenology of mind, 1807), Georg

Wilhelm Friedrich Hegel (1770-1831) answered that Kant's antinomies, by their very necessity, reveal the essential unity of opposition. Faith is inevitably yoked to doubt. Because the human being is compelled by physical and animal nature, so Schopenhauer argued in *The World as Will and Idea* (1818), human actions are instinctively motivated by selfish desire. Influenced by the religions of Vedanta → Hinduism and → Buddhism, Schopenhauer posited an escape through the discipline of the will, redirecting action into → aesthetics, sympathy, and ascetic constraint. Ludwig Feuerbach's (1804-72) first book, *Gedanken über Tod und Unsterblichkeit* (Thoughts on death and immortality, 1830), demonstrated an incompatibility between Christianity and idealism. While he affirmed the Christian tenets that God is love, that God is infinite spirit, he argued that Christianity in itself could not fulfill its promised union between the individual person and the person of Christ. Personhood remained confined by nature and culture. Only a disciplined idealism could lead the person to a more rewarding communal human life.

Distinguished from traditional biblical criticism, which dealt with linguistic aporia and textual minutiae, higher criticism addressed broader aspects of biblical study, including cultural context, authorship and authorial influence, composition, and revision. Its methods were introduced by Johann Gottfried Eichhorn (1752-1827) at Göttingen and developed in his multivolume studies of the Old and New Testaments, study of the Apocrypha, commentary on the Book of Revelation, and three-volume commentary on the Hebrew prophets. A significant influence on the New England → transcendentalists, Eichhorn lectured at Göttingen, where several Americans were sent from Harvard to study higher criticism. This group included George Bancroft (1800-1891), George Ticknor (1791-1871), and Edward Everett (1794-1865), who introduced the methods of higher criticism in their own subsequent work. For New England transcendentalists like Frederic Henry Hedge (1805-90), Theodore Parker (1810-60), Ralph Waldo Emerson (1803-82), Amos Bronson Alcott (1799-1888), and James Freeman Clarke (1810-88), the higher criticism of Eichhorn validated inquiry into established church dogma. Religious authority was removed from its ecclesiastical center and resituated in the intellectual investigation and analysis of the individual. One's own consciousness and intuition became the arbiter.

In Germany, David Friedrich Strauss (1808-74) studied the methods of higher criticism. After completing his doctorate at Tübingen, he attended the lectures of Friedrich → Schleiermacher (1768-1834) at Berlin. Schleiermacher lectured on the Gospel of John and distinguished between the "historical Jesus" and the messianic Christ. The man who lived in Palestine, taught there, and was crucified might not be identical with the risen Christ, as represented in the Gospels or in church dogma. In *Das Leben Jesu kritisch bearbeitet* (1835; translated by Mary Ann Evans [George Eliot] as *The Life of Jesus Critically Examined* [1846]), Strauss explored the cultural proliferation of messianic myths to cast doubt on the supposed virgin birth of Jesus and to challenge the accuracy of the Gospels and the Acts of the Apostles, and consequently of the recorded sayings and deeds of Jesus (→ Jesus Seminar).

The Romantics, even those like Shelley who were caught in a conflicted atheism, were restless in their quest for a tenable religious ground. A fascination with the *Ethics* (1677) of Baruch Spinoza (1632-77) led Goethe, Coleridge, and Wordsworth, among many others, to dwell on the implications of the concept of the essential unity of God and nature, *Deus sive Natura* (God or Nature, Spinoza's Latin formula to express their indistinguishable unity), a reality that admitted no division of mind and matter but was one pervasive entity (→ Monism). Roman Catholics, who had to struggle all the harder to maintain their faith in the face of the betrayals in France, were bereft through most of this period of the intellectual leadership that had been provided by the → Jesuits. The ban against the Jesuits, imposed in 1773, was not lifted until after the fall of Napoleon in 1814, or 41 years later.

2. France

The revolution in France had brought with it even more turmoil in religion and religious thought than elsewhere in Europe. The revolution and the Napoleonic era also made the schism between the first- and second-generation Romantics more profound. France had a history of brutal religious intolerance. The temper of the 1790s was charged with hostility against ecclesiastical, as well as aristocratic, hierarchy.

There was nevertheless a new sympathy for the long-oppressed French Protestants, the → Huguenots. As members of the Reformed Church, established in 1550 by John → Calvin (1509-64), the Huguenots were charged as heretics and executed (→ Persecution of Christians 3.3). Their numbers, however, continued to swell with dissenters from the Catholic Church. When the marriage of Henry of Navarre (1553-1610), a Huguenot, to Marguerite de Valois (1553-1615), daughter of Catherine de Medici, was to be celebrated on St. Bartholomew's Day, August 24, 1572, thousands of Huguenots converged on Paris for the wedding celebrations. Apparently at the instigation of Catherine de Medici, who violently opposed her daughter's marriage to a member of a "heretic" faction, more than 8,000 Huguenots were slaughtered during the night before the wedding. As the persecution continued, 200,000 French Huguenots then fled the country, emigrating to Switzerland, Germany, England, Ireland, and America. The Edict of Toleration (November 28, 1787) partially restored the civil and religious → rights of the Huguenots.

2.1. *First Generation*

Many of the first-generation Romantics in France upheld their religious heritage, but they often distanced themselves from active church affiliation. In his first published work, *Essai sur les révolutions* (1797), François-René Chateaubriand (1768-1848) took the popular stand against → Catholicism yet asked whether any religion could replace Christianity ("Quelle sera la religion qui remplacera le christianisme?"). None of the alternatives seemed satisfactory. The doctrines of the Swedenborgians and the Illuminés, which for a time had attracted William Blake and Percy Bysshe Shelley in England, as well as Pierre-Henri Simon Ballanche (1776-1847) and Victor Hugo (1802-55) in France, remained too marginal. The natural religion promoted by William Paley in England offered no more than material probability. A moral cult, or one based only on virtues, Chateaubriand judged absurd, thus dismissing the convictions subsequently promoted by Victor Cousin (1792-1867) and Alphonse de Lamartine (1790-1869). Confronted with untenable alternatives, Chateaubriand endeavored to resuscitate his Catholic faith in *Le génie du christianisme* (The genius of Christianity, 1802). The occult beliefs of the → Swedenborgians and Illuminés appealed to Ballanche, who sought to confirm a world infused and animated by supernatural presence. His *Du sentiment consideré dans ses rapports avec la littératur et les arts* (Sentiment considered in its relationship to literature and the arts, 1801) emphasized a root principle of his Catholicism: the affirmation in the Nicene Creed "of all things visible and invisible." Like Josef Eichendorff in Germany, Ballanche believed in a nature resonating with the harmonies of divine spirit.

Although her *De l'Allemagne* may seem to suggest otherwise, Germaine de Staël never abandoned her French Huguenot heritage. She was a descendant of a line of Calvinist pastors, and during her years in France she continued to attend the Protestant church in Coppet. Granting in her novel *Delphine* (1802) that religion provided a support for morality among the populace, she also argued in her novel *Corinne* (1807) that morality was more important than religion. She found occasion to criticize the hypocrisy of the clergy, whom she considered as susceptible to temptation and sin as most people. She even has Corinne come to the defense of Catholicism against Oswald's Kantian Protestantism. But in the fourth section of *De l'Allemagne,* on religion and enthusiasm, she observes that the German Protestants have acquired more freedom of thought, even though they have lost some of the mystical faith still retained by the Catholics.

Of Goethe's *Faust,* de Staël observes that it lacks taste, regularity, and conformity to art, but it excels in the chaotic excess of imagination. His devil, Mephistopheles, is not the traditional Prince of Darkness but, rather, a master ironist who finds imperfection and deformity in all humanity, indeed in all creation. He defines himself as "the Spirit who always negates." Faust, for his part, confesses that "two souls dwell in my breast." It is Mephistopheles' business to encourage the depravity of Faust's soul of fleshly passions in order to destroy his soul of lofty ideals. The belief in evil spirits, de Staël notes, is much more at home in German literature than in French. She was, of course, writing before the second generation of French Romanticism, when Gérard de Nerval (1808-55), Théophile Gautier (1811-72), and Charles Nodier (1780-1844) made the demonic seem as if it had always lurked in the French imagination. She concluded that Goethe's *Faust* was a work that undermined morality by dramatizing → reason as subject to the same hunger for gratification as the baser passions. Her translation of *Faust* in French was then translated into English in 1814, when the London publisher John Murray brought out an English version of her work after the original version had been banned in France. Through her liberal selection of passages from Goethe, Schiller, Jean Paul (1763-1825), and other German writers of the period, de Staël became a major mediator of German literature throughout France and England.

In the tradition of Goethe's *Werther,* but also influenced by Jean-Jacques Rousseau's (1712-78) advocacy of a retreat into nature, Étienne Pivert de Sénancour's (1770-1846) *Obermann* (1804) describes the sufferings of its sensitive and tormented semi-autobiographical character in a series of letters written from a lonely valley of the Jura Alps. Coming to terms with his own inability to be and do what he wishes, he resigns himself to an ascetic life, not of religious devotion but of aesthetic contemplation. In his *Observations critiques sur le génie du christianisme* (Critical observations on the genius of Christianity, 1816), Sénancour joins other Romantic contemporaries in advocating a religion free of dogma and priesthood. His *critique* is a nihilistic denial of religion as a force for social or moral improvement. The mystical aspect of Christian faith leads to enthusiasm, not to moral improvement, and the doctrines of original → sin and → atonement lead to guilt, frustration, and self-condemnation. In his *Libres méditations d'un solitaire inconnu* (Books of meditation of an unknown recluse, 1819), Sénancour moved toward a more speculative inquiry into → spiritualism: tolerant not of religion per se, but of one's incapacity to achieve rational conviction; tentative in assessing the possibility of transcendent truth. His *Libres méditations* was subjected to lifelong revision; the final version was published posthumously (ed. by B. Le Gall [1970]).

2.2. *Second Generation*

2.2.1. *Bankruptcy of Traditional Religion*

Many of the second generation of French Romantics moved away from the religious skepticism and opposition to organized religion frequently espoused by the earlier generation. Alfred de Vigny abandoned his Catholic faith at age 18 and reasserted it only at the moment of his deathbed "conversion." Vigny was among those who, witnessing the cruelty and corruption in the world, concluded that God is unjust. He had launched his literary career with adaptations of William Shakespeare (1564-1616) and Lord Byron. In the biblical lyrics for his *Hebrew Melodies* (1815), Byron told the tale "Jephtha's Daughter" (Judges 11). For Byron, the daughter is a bold heroine who, in terms of her father's oath, "has won the great battle" for him and her country. Vigny discerns a very different moral, the command for cruel sacrifice by a jealous God ("Seigneur, vous êtes bien le Dieu de la vengeance: / En échange du crime il vous faut l'innocence"). In other poems on biblical themes, Vigny pronounced a similar indictment of a cruel and unjust God.

Like Sénancour, Vigny objected to the Christian doctrines of original sin and atonement and the threat of eternal torment in hell. In *Eloa* (1824), a narrative poem, he told of the redemption of Satan. And in the "Le Mont des oliviers" (The Mount of Olives), Vigny depicts Christ himself as deserted by God, another version of the theme of the forsaken Christ in a godless universe as introduced by Jean Paul, translated by de Staël, and echoing again and again in the works of the Romantic period. Biblical themes dominated Vigny's first collection, *Poèmes antiques et modernes* (1826). His objections to institutional religion were also developed in *Stello* (1832), a novel presented in case studies, consultations between the poet Stello and Doctor Noir, on the sufferings of writers of unrecognized genius: Nicolas-Joseph Gilbert (1751-80), André de Chénier (1762-94), and Thomas Chatterton (1752-70). Echoing the theme from *Obermann,* Vigny too saw the poet as marginalized and living in isolation. Although one might trace autobiographical relevance in these accounts, Vigny avoided personal feelings. He simply described the condition resulting from a society that recognized nothing of material value in poetry. *Servitude et grandeur militaires* (1835; ET *Servitude and grandeur of arms* [1996]) was a similar tripartite meditation on the condition of the soldier. From his narrative in *Stello,* Vigny went on to write a tragedy, *Chatterton* (1835). Vigny wrote a sequel to *Stello* entitled *Daphné* (1837, not published until 1912), in which he upheld the conviction that morality is more important than religion, but he dismissed the notion that the church could successfully promote moral action or could even satisfy spiritual needs. In *Daphné,* Vigny related the life of Emperor Julian the Apostate (332-63), who provided the model for a stoic persistence of a spiritual philosophy, in spite of the apparent perversion and moral bankruptcy of institutional religion.

Although he shared with Vigny the struggle with the apparent injustice of God for tolerating the torment and pain of innocent people, Alphonse de Lamartine managed to affirm rather than denounce Christianity. In 1817 the death of Julia Charles, the invalid wife of a Paris physician, served as the subject for his collection of poetry *Méditations poétiques* (1820), in which he commenced a spiritual journey caught up in grief and convinced that God ignores his creation and allows it to fall prey to evil. The journey ultimately led him to a trust in God's purpose and a belief that personal misery will be transformed into goodness and salvation. In spite of the lyricism of *Les harmonies poétiques et religieuse* (1830), which attracted the attention of composer Franz Liszt (1811-86), many of the poems are about disharmonies. Vigny's sense of a malignant God and Sénancour's distrust of a corrupt clergy are echoed in Lamartine's themes, but their skepticism and pessimism are radically transformed. He repeated his belief that divine blessings will prevail (→ Optimism and Pessimism). Having celebrated Byron in *Le dernier chant du pèlerinage d'Harold* (The last canto of Harold's pilgrimage, 1825), he imagined Byron, in "L'Homme," recognizing God's presence ("Gloire à toi, dans les temps et dans l'éternité! / Éternelle raison, suprême volonté!"). Based on his tour through Greece, Syria, and Palestine, Lamartine wrote *Voyage en Orient* (1835). What might have been simply a travel account becomes another spiritual journey, for in the course of the trip he lost his only daughter in Beirut during the Christmas holidays just two weeks after visiting the Holy Sepulchre. His Christian faith was shaken. Shortly afterward in Constantinople, he described the Muslim faith as "un christianisme purifé" (a purified Christianity). Having been lauded as foremost among the Catholic poets of the age, Lamartine had three of his works — *Voyage en Orient* (1835), *Jocelyn* (1836), and *La chute d'un ange* (The fall of an angel, 1838) — banned and listed on the Roman Index. In these works he declared that Christianity had fed the populace on superstitions of miracles and legends and that the clergy themselves had lapsed into irrational credulity. Spiritual salvation is a myth of dogmatic theology; mental salvation was to be found only in the discipline of reason.

2.2.2. *Dark Supernaturalism*

In *De l'Allemagne* de Staël commented that the German fascination with → demons, evident in Goethe's *Faust,* was totally at odds with French beliefs. In the works of Nodier, Gautier, and Nerval the demonic asserted its French hegemony. Nodier's *Smarra, ou les démons de la nuit* (Smarra, or the demons of the night, 1821) was among the first of the new tales of vampirism following the popularity of John Polidori's (1795-1821) *The Vampyre* (1819). *Schauerromantik* (Dark romanticism), especially the Gothic novel, typically depicted priests fallen into the worship of Satan. Matthew Gregory Lewis's (1775-1818) *The Monk* (1796) gave the genre its lurid dimension. Ambrosio, abbot of the Capuchin monastery in Madrid, falls from saintliness into utter depravity. Matilda, female agent of evil, disguised herself as the novice Rosario and entered the monastery for the sole purpose of seducing the pious monk, which she manages by having her portrait painted as a nude Madonna. While he worships that image in his cell, Matilda enters, disrobes, revealing herself as the object of his worship. With Ambrosio's sexual desires aroused, Matilda goads him into other conquests: the rape of his sister, the murder of his mother. A corrupt clergy, denounced by Sénancour, is set loose in the Gothic novel, where dissolute priests become sexual predators. The vampire tale added another dimension borrowed from the Black Mass of Satanic worship, for the drinking of Christ's blood is darkly parodied in the vampire's quest for immortality by drinking the blood of his victims. Ruthven, Polodori's vampire, seeks female victims to gratify this thirst. Nodier's Smarra is a female vampire who preys on male victims.

Gautier's *La morte amoureuse* (The amorous dead woman, 1836) describes the double life of the young priest Romuald, a parish priest by day, necrophiliac by night. As lover of the undead courtesan Clarimonde, Romuald becomes the agent as well as the object of her desires. In the tales "Omphale" (1834) and "Arria Marcella" (1852), Gautier further develops the theme of the femmes fatal who draws her energy from the male who succumbs to her attractions.

Nerval frequently turned to German sources. Early in his career he translated *Faust* (1828) and other German works. He recorded his travels to the Near East in *Voyage en Orient* (1851), and to Germany and Austria in *Lorely. Souvenirs d'Allemagne* (1852). His short stories, notably in *Les filles du feu* (Daughters of fire, 1854), develop themes of darker supernaturalism. In *Les chimères* (The chimeras), the 12 sonnets appended to *Les filles du feu,* he adapted scenes from Jean Paul, including "The Speech of the Dead Christ." In his *Aurélia* (1855), written as a patient in an insane asylum, Nerval records his personal struggle with an alter ego who is attempting to escape from his dreams in order to take over his life. Jean Paul's vision of a godless resurrection, from *Siebenkäs* (1797), was also imitated by Ernst August Klingemann in his "Monolog des wahnsinnigen Weltschöpfers" (Monologue of the insane Creator), from *Die Nachtwachen des Bonaventura* (The night watches of Bonaventura, 1804). E. T. A. Hoffmann (1776-1822), in *Die Elixiere des Teufels* (The devil's elixir, 1817), and James Hogg (1770-1835), in *Confessions of a Justified Sinner* (1824), developed the motif of the Doppelgänger, the bifurcated self whose good and evil nature split into separate identities, as in Robert Louis Stevenson's (1850-94) Victorian tale *Dr. Jekyll and Mr. Hyde* (1886). Nerval's tale is more frightening because it derived directly from his asylum nightmares.

3. Germany

3.1. *The Devil and Damnation*

Out of the vague records of a historical Johann Faustus, who lived during the early 16th century, a contemporary of Martin → Luther (1483-1546) and Theophrastus Paracelsus (1493-1541), came the legendary Doctor Faustus, whose exploits with the → devil were recorded in the anonymous *Historia von D. Johann Fausten, dem weit beschreyten Zauberer und Schwartzkünstler* (History of Dr. Johann Faust, the widely decried magician and practitioner of the black arts, 1587), *The Historie of the damnable life and deserved death of Doctor John Faustus* (ET by the unidentified "P. F. Gent," 1592), and Christopher Marlowe's (1564-93) *The Tragicall Historie of Doctor Faustus* (performed in 1597, published in 1604). As de Staël noted, Goethe's interest was aroused by Gotthold Ephraim Lessing's (1729-81) version for puppet theater. In 1772 Susanna Margarethe Brandt was sentenced to death for murdering her own child. Her defense was, literally, that the devil made her do it; the devil, it was discovered, was the man who raped her and subsequently forced her to kill her child. The case provided Goethe the idea for the fate of Margaret in his tragedy. In 1775 he completed a draft of *Faust,* discovered in manuscript late in the 19th century and now known as the *Urfaust.* In 1790 he published *Faust, ein Fragment,* the transition from the *Urfaust* to the completed first part of the drama. *Faust: A Tragedy (Faust I)* was published in 1808. A central text of *Faust II,* entitled *Helena. Klassisch-romantische Phantasmagorie,* was published in 1827. Finally, on July 22, 1831, Goethe announced that he had finished *Faust II.* Goethe died less than a year later (March 22, 1832), and *Faust II* was published posthumously shortly afterward.

In Goethe's conception of the pact with Mephistopheles, the condition of Faust's damnation would be to abandon his engagement in the dynamic process of creation and to surrender to the seduction of the single moment: to say to that moment, "Stay, thou art beautiful" ("Verweile doch, du bist so schön"). The devil, as spirit of negation, cannot engage in God's universe of change; he can only divert the actions of those who do. Paradoxically, as God acknowledges in the "Prologue in Heaven," the devil's interference also may serve as goad to action, which is why, God declares, he has given humans the devil as a companion. Radically different from John Milton's (1608-74) attempt in *Paradise Lost* (1667) to "justify the ways of God to man," Goethe sees the struggle of good versus evil as coincident with the opposition between the dynamic and the static.

3.2. ***Redemption***

Blake in *Milton* (1804-8), Byron in *Manfred* (1817), and Shelley in *Prometheus Unbound* (1820) all addressed damnation, and all three defined the way to → salvation (§8) through self-assertion. Because Satan seduced man into abandoning his own destiny and shackling himself with "mind-forged manacles," Blake asserted a salvation through discovery and liberation of one's own indwelling Christ. With the conviction that guilt and grace are the conditions of the individual mind, Byron's Manfred thrice affirms (I.i.252; III.i.73; III.iv.129-32) Satan's assertion in *Paradise Lost* that "The Mind is its own place, and itself / Can make a Heaven of Hell, a Hell of Heaven" (I.254-55). Shelley observes in his preface, "The only imaginary being resembling in any degree Prometheus, is Satan." At odds with his intention, Milton's Satan gained heroic stature in the popular imagination because "the character of Satan engenders in the mind a pernicious casuistry which leads us to weigh his faults with his wrongs, and to excuse the former because the latter exceed all measure." Shelley inverts the Miltonic myth: Jupiter, the tyrant God of his dramatic poem, has condemned Prometheus to eternal suffering chained to rock. He is freed from his chains by retracting his curse and forgiving his tormentor.

By far the Romantic period's most complex narrative of redemption was Clemens Brentano's *Romanzen von Rosenkranz* (Romances of the Rosary, 1804-12), a vast fragment of 19 romances in 10,604 lines, plus an introduction of 283 lines (*Faust* I and II together total 12,110 lines). Brentano's purpose was to create an apocryphal poem on the origin of the → rosary, which he traces from Salome's erotic dance and the beheading of John the Baptist (Mark 6:14-28 par. Matt. 14:1-11). John was imprisoned for rebuking Herod for taking his half-brother's wife, Herodias. When Herodias's daughter Salome danced for her uncle and stepfather, the drunken Herod promised her anything. On her mother's advice, she asked for John's head. This event is the "old hereditary sin" of the romances, the incestuous lust that is passed on from generation to generation. Brentano drew from the → cabala and mixed in, as well, the legend of Tannhäuser. Recognizing the adversarial role of the → antichrist, Brentano remained opposed to Manichaean → dualism. Evil was not coeternal with God, and it could be thwarted. With the Neoplatonic theologians, Brentano recognized the shadowy nature of the antichrist, the dull shade cast by material being in the divine light. With the light of Marianism, Brentano proposed to dispel the shadowy entity of incestuous darkness. Although incest may have been only a convenient metaphor, it remains nevertheless obvious that sin for Brentano was sexual, as it was, for some people, in the biblical account of the expulsion of Adam and Even from the Garden of Eden.

3.3. ***The Religious Visionary***

The sensuality of religious ecstasy was also an ingredient in Brentano's obsessive fascination for Anna Katharina Emmerick (1774-1824), the nun who experienced → visions and stigmata from 1812 until her death in 1824. In August 1812 a gray cross appeared on her breast. By the end of November she began stigmatic bleeding on her forehead. The wounds of the crown of thorns had encircled her entire head by Christmas, and before the New Year commenced, she had the wounds of the nails in her hands and feet and the spear wound in her side. Brentano spent most of the next five years caring for her, visiting her bedside twice daily and recording her words. By the end of the five years, he had compiled 16,000 manuscript pages. He also kept a comprehensive diary, devoted primarily to her visions. His life became completely absorbed by hers. After her death in 1824 he assembled this material in three volumes, the first of which appeared in 1832. His religious works on the visions of Anna Katharina Emmerick became more popular than his other literary works.

Brentano was not the only Romantic poet to compose an extensive case study of the religious visionary. Other prominent examples were Friedrich Schlegel's *Über die magnetische Behandlung der Gräfin Leśniowska* (On the magnetic treatment of Countess Leśniowska, 1820-26) and Justinus Kerner's (1786-1862) *Die Seherin von Prevorst* (The seer of Prevorst, 1829). Schlegel, foremost literary theorist of German Romanticism, turned late in his career to study the practice of mesmerism, or animal magnetism, together with the artist Ludwig Schnorr (1788-1853). The Countess Franziska Leśniowska (1781/82-1853) sought treatment to ease a nervous condition that had been exacerbated by the suicide of her husband and her sister, both of whom had leaped to their deaths through a window. With the countess under a trance, Schlegel stood at her bedside to record her visions, and Schnorr had his palette and canvas to paint them. Crucial to Schlegel was not simply the healing power of the magnetic treatment or the visions which it induced but primarily the spiritual journey that was opened up to the subject in a trance. The mesmeric trance enabled the mind to perceive the spiritual world.

The poet Justinus Kerner was also a physician who devoted much of his practice to patients suffering mental illness. Friedrich Hölderlin (1770-1843) was one of his patients. Like others who incorporated mesmerism into their medical practice, Kerner believed that in the somnambulant trance the mind found a portal between physical and spiritual being. His own writing on the phenomena was compounded of medical-mystical speculations, and his treatments often bordered on exorcism. Yet he also provided his patients with a sympathetic care that frequently proved successful in treating hysteria, hypochondria, and other neurotic conditions. His best-known case study described his treatment of Friederike Hauffe (1801-29) in *Die Seherin von Prevorst*. In Friedericke's mind a threshold had opened that permitted an invasion of spirit entities. When she was first brought to him in November 1826, he described her as "an image of death, fully wasted, unable to rise or to lie down." His treatment included a daily session of mesmerically induced trances, her response to various metals (with the belief in the "magnetic" nature of their influence), the effect of various herbs (including hallucinogens). During these experiments Friedericke described her hallucinations and spoke in incomprehensible foreign tongues. She accepted Kerner's diagnosis, believed in his treatments, and learned to control her symptoms.

By the time Kerner first attempted to treat him, Hölderlin had already endured 12 years of mental derangement. Hölderlin had been a student together with Schelling and Hegel at Tübingen. Early in his career he completed his lyric novel *Hyperion* (1797-99) and his philosophical tragedy, *Empedokles* (1799). His elegies and hymns were composed in 1801 and 1802. By June of 1802, he was already showing symptoms of confusion and disorientation. After spending a year in his mother's home, he spent two more at the home of a friend where, in 1804, he completed a translation of Sophocles in 1804. In 1806 he was placed in a clinic in Tübingen, and a year later he was transferred to private care, where he occupied a room in a tower until his death in 1843. Kerner, assisted by two other poets, Gustav Schwab (1792-1850) and Ludwig Uhland (1787-1862), brought out an edition of Hölderlin's poetry in 1826. Brentano's sister, Bettina von Arnim (1785-1859), and her husband, Achim von Arnim (1781-1831), visited Hölderlin in his tower. Bettina described his joy in playing the piano and writing spontaneous hexameters for his guests, signing them "Scardanelli" with some fantastic date of the future. Achim von Arnim, who was also Brentano's collaborator on the poems of *Des Knaben Wunderhorn* (The boy's magic horn, 1805-8), wrote a review of the 1826 volume of poems that included a close exposition of the "Hymn of St. John of Patmos." Because visitors found Hölderlin calm and sociable, Arnim was convinced that Hölderlin was merely on a sort of mental journey and that one day he would return and tell what spaces he had explored. In the meantime, all he could do was communicate through the cryptic verses of "Scardanelli."

3.4. *Ecstatic Art-Religion*

Wilhelm Heinrich Wackenroder (1773-98) and Ludwig Tieck (1773-1853) became friends during their school years. Tieck began his studies of theology and philology at Halle; Wackenroder was sent to Erlangen to study law. Both changed universities to study literature at Göttingen. They also attended the art lectures of Johann Dominic Fiorillo (1798-1820), who taught that art was a synthesis of the artist's passion and the stimulus of local character and nature. Wackenroder wrote an essay on Hans Sachs and made plans to travel to Rome with Tieck. But in September 1794 his father called him back to Berlin to begin his law career as court assessor. He continued with a series of essays on art, which Tieck published anonymously as *Herzensergießungen eines kunstliebenden Klosterbruders* (Outpourings of the heart by an art-loving friar, 1797), borrowing the authorial "friar" from Lessing's *Nathan der Weise* (Nathan the wise, 1779) in order to indicate his passionate and devotional sensitivity to art. Tieck wrote a preface to the collection and included a few shorter pieces of his own. Suffering under the burden of the legal career imposed on him by his father, Wackenroder found his love of art stifled. This conflict led to depression, and then to illness. He died of a nervous fever on February 13, 1798, five months before his 25th birthday. "Das Leben des Tonkünstlers Joseph Berglinger" (The life of the composer Joseph Berglinger) may be read as a fictive version of Wackenroder's personal frustration in fulfilling his own artistic longings. "Der nackte Heilige" (The naked saint) is another tale revealing his personally felt religious devotion and martyrdom. A further collection of his essays, *Phantasien über die Kunst* (Phantasies on art, 1799), was published posthumously by Tieck.

The ecstatic art-religion that Wackenroder introduced into German Romanticism was further developed by Tieck in *Franz Sternbalds Wanderungen* (The journey of Franz Sternbald, 1798), the first *Künstlerroman* (artist-novel) of the period, celebrating the art of Albrecht Dürer and the Italian → Renaissance. His play *Leben und Tod der heiligen Genoveva* (Life and death of St. Genevieve, 1800) had its source in the Alsatian *Legenda aurea* (Golden legend), but it transformed the drama of martyrdom through the aesthetics of epiphanic vision. Tieck became well known through his collaboration with August Wilhelm Schlegel (1767-1845) on the translation of Shakepeare's plays. Tieck also gave new dimension to Romantic irony in his comic fairy-tale plays, such as *Der gestiefelte Kater* (Puss-in-Boots, 1797). In *Der Blonde Eckbert* (1797) Tieck tells a tale of incest and → guilt, and in *Der Runenberg* (1804), his protagonist, Christian, is seduced away from family and domestic responsibility by a magical old hag from the forest.

The theme of art-religion and the fascination with the → Middle Ages also informs the work of Novalis. His *Heinrich von Ofterdingen* (1802) transforms the historical character of the medieval bard and minnesinger into a magically inspired poet whose quest for the "blue blossom" of his dreams leads him through the threshold between life and dream. Descending into underground caverns, he finds the book of his own life, which guides him toward the *Erfüllung* (the prophetic fulfillment) partially narrated in the fragmentary novel's incomplete second part. "Our life is no dream," the author declared, "but it can, and perhaps will, become one." In the *Die Lehrlinge zu Sais* (The apprentices at Sais, 1798-99), Novalis tells of the novitiate at the temple of Isis who learns to read the hieroglyphs of nature, a story that recapitulates the Romantic thesis that nature is the coded language through which divinity speaks to humanity.

Among the later Romantics, mystical/magical nature became more pervasively demonized (→ Magic). The seductive powers with which Tieck invested the witch of the forest in *Der Runenberg* are also shared by the marble statue of Venus in Josef von Eichendorff's *Das Marmorbild* (1819). The young Florio encounters the beautiful Bianca and the singer Fortunato at a summer festival. Through them he learns to celebrate the radiant goodness at work in nature, but then he is pulled in the opposite direction by the force of evil that by night and darkness animates the statue of Venus. Donati, a knight who slept by day and served Venus by night, compelled Florio to join them. Although he witnessed her drive Donati into suicidal despair, Florio could not free himself from the same spell. Only the intervention of Fortunato and Bianca succeed into returning him to the world of benevolent light. Eichendorff's strong Catholic faith and his belief in the divine presence in nature inform his lyric poetry and his tales. His novelle, *Aus dem Leben eines Taugenichts* (From the life of a good-for-nothing, 1826), developed a positive morality out of passive receptivity to nature and being attuned to one's own feelings. In his sonnet "The world is too much with us," Wordsworth declared that "getting and spending we lay waste our powers" and that we lose the capacity to see and feel the animate vitality of nature. Eichendorff endorses this same conviction.

4. Britain and the United States

As previously mentioned, members of dissenting churches in Britain were barred from the universites and from many civic posts. Between approximately 1760 and 1825, the Dissenters became a huge segment of the population, and factionalism was undermining the dominance of the Church of England. → Methodism, founded by John (1703-91) and Charles (1707-88) → Wesley, had begun in 1738 as a renewal movement within the Church of England, but its numbers swelled to become the largest of the "Low Churches." Unitarianism actually started in eastern Europe as part of the Protestant Reformation of the 16th century (→ Reformation 4.10-11). In England, Unitarian ideas were introduced in the mid-17th century by John Biddle (1615-62). The first Unitarian congregation was established in London in 1774. Joseph Priestley (1733-1804), scientist and minister, became a vigorous leader of the → Unitarians during the 1780s and 1790s. The → Baptists (or Anabaptists) are more difficult to identify because their doctrines varied among different groups. They were identified as Separatists in the 17th century, not because they departed from the teachings of the church, but because of the ritual prominence they gave to baptism and rebaptism of believers and prodigal sons or daughters who confessed their sins and were thus enabled to reenter the congregation. There was difference of opinion among Baptists on the issues of → predestination (Particular Baptists) versus free will (General Baptists; → Arminianism). Some members advocated independent communities, thus giving rise to the → Mennonites, the Amish, the → Hutterites, the → Moravians, and similar groups who had some impact on the English Baptists, and a much stronger influence among the settlers in the United States.

The literature that flourished in the United States during the first half-century of its existence bore the traces of the many Europeans who had crossed the Atlantic to settle in the New World. Charles Brockden Brown's (1771-1810) novels of the 1790s are peopled with sailors, travelers, first-generation immigrants, and established families. When things go wrong, xenophobic suspicions are aroused. Brown's characters are not devout Christians, but they are nevertheless haunted by a fear of divine wrath. His title character in *Arthur Mervyn* (1800) arrives in Philadelphia during the plague of 1793. He is infected, wanders the abandoned streets with dying victims, and experiences feverish fits that render his perceptions susceptible to hallucinatory visions.

Brown's novels introduced a mode of the psychological Gothic that was later developed by Hoffmann and became prominent in the tales of Nathaniel Hawthorne (1804-64) and Edgar Allan Poe (1809-49). Among the most notable literary trends in America were those that echoed the → Puritan past, that explored the new cities and the new frontier, and that pursued transcendentalist inquiry. The first trend found its finest literary expression in Hawthorne's *Scarlet Letter* (1850), *The House of Seven Gables* (1851), and many of his short stories, such as "Young Goodman Brown" (1835). The second is represented by Charles Brockden Brown and James Fenimore Cooper (1789-1851). The third was taken up by Ralph Waldo Emerson in his many of his essays, especially "The Transcendentalist" (lecture at the Masonic Temple in Boston, January 1842) and "Transcendentalism" (1843, published in the *Dial*).

As defined by Emerson, New England transcendentalism had moved a considerable distance from the philosophy that Kant had promulgated in the 1780s and 1790s. While it utilized many of the tenets of the critical philosophy, it was more concerned with their practical application than their epistemological justification. Kant had described his accomplishment as a Copernican revolution in philosophy, recognizing the individual mind at the center and the essential capacities of that mind as independently intuitive rather than dependent on the external data acquired through the senses. The mind exercised a phenomenological → dialectic as the process of understanding the external world of things, but the mind could also engage a transcendental dialectic as a way of understanding what lies beyond the reach of the senses. The New England transcendentalists emphasized this capacity of knowing truth intuitively, of attaining a rational comprehension of existence beyond sensible experience. Kant's Copernican revolution bolstered the American emphasis on self-reliance. While those who adhered to the Protestant faith of the Methodists, Presbyterians, and Congregationalists saw the movement as an importation of "German atheism," the American Unitarians found themselves persuaded. There was no need to abandon the sound empirical approach to the natural world, for the phenomenological dialectic of experimentation and logical analysis was properly balanced by the transcendental dialectic of intuitive inquiry. According to Emerson, religion not vitalized by intuition was "corpse-cold." Because the transcendental dialectic was an open-ended process, it went far beyond Kant. It welcomed the exploration of the religions of the East. Emerson read Hindu and Buddhist scriptures, not as a challenge to his own religious assumptions, but as a way of extending his understanding of divine revelation. Because God would not have deceived vast populations, there must be truth in these religions.

Poe, too, appropriated themes and techniques from European Romanticism. Brown's attention to the psychological responses and deliberations of his characters, his emphasis on their perceptions and uncertainties, provided a narrative manner also evident in Poe's tales. But Poe was a reader of Gothic Romanticism, and he learned from Hoffmann how to weave hallucinatory distortions into the fabric of detailed realism. In "The Fall of the House of Usher" (1839) Poe transforms the Romantic tale of incest into one of decadence, dissipation, and dissolution. Responding to current experiments with mesmeric somnambulism, believed to open a portal to the spiritual world, Poe wrote "The Facts in the Case of M. Valdemar" (1845), in which a man mesmerized at the very moment of dying is held captive within his body for weeks until the trance is broken, and his body immediately disintegrates in putrid decay. Poe seldom affirms religious beliefs or supernatural presence. For the most part his supernaturalism, like Hoffmann's, is the fevered projection of a delusory protagonist. When Madeline rises from the tomb in "The Fall of the House of Usher," Roderick does not fear that she has risen from the dead: he knows that he had secured his sister in her coffin while she was still alive. The author does not affirm spiritual being, but his characters are obsessively preoccupied with hopes and fears of an afterlife. The haunting resurrection in the tales "Morella" (1835), "Ligeia" (1838), and "Eleanora" (1841) remain fears rather than facts, but they deliberately and effectively tease his reader's own beliefs.

5. Conclusion

In all of its European and American manifestations, Romanticism was shaped by the rationalist impasse of the Enlightenment which preceded it and the fervor of the revolution that ushered it into being. Generally agreed that religious faith could not be grounded on reason alone, some Romantics turned skeptical and dismissed the church as corrupt and religion as a hoax, while others argued that access to divinity could be found through feeling or intuition, immanent in nature or within the self. It was a period that witnessed a virtual epidemic of messiahs, visionaries, and prophets, from Richard Brothers (1757-1824) and Joanna Southcott (1750-1814) in England to Anna Katharina Emmerick and Friederike Hauffe in Germany. It was an age of experiments with mesmerism, with electric and magnetic stimuli, and with drugs, all justified as explorations into spiritual being and the recesses of consciousness. It was an age of inquiry into other religions and revision of traditional dogma. Whether it scorned the pretensions of belief in God or witnessed divine presence in nature and art or warned that powers of darkness had eclipsed the divine light, Romantic literature grappled with the dilemma of the human condition in a vast universe.

Bibliography: J. R. Barth, S.J., *Coleridge and Christian Doctrine* (2d ed.; New York, 1987); idem, *Romanticism and Transcendence: Wordsworth, Coleridge, and the Religious Imagination* (Columbia, Mo., 2003); idem, *The Symbolic Imagination: Coleridge and the Romantic Tradition* (2d ed.; New York, 2001); idem, ed., *The Fountain Light: Studies in Romanticism and Religion* (New York, 2003) • M. Canuel, *Religion, Toleration, and British Writing, 1790-1830* (Cambridge, 2002) • J. M. Chevalier, *Semiotics, Romanticism, and the Scriptures* (Berlin, 1990) • L. C. Delfour, *Catholicisme et Romantisme* (Paris, 1905) • H. Girard, "La penseé religieuse des romantiques," *RHR* 89 (1924) 1-25 • D. Jasper, *The Sacred and Secular Canon in Romanticism: Preserving the Sacred Truths* (New York, 1999) • A. Joussain, *Romantisme et religion* (Paris, 1910) • P. Kluckhohn, *Weltanschauung der Frühromantik* (Leipzig, 1932; repr., Darmstadt, 1966) • J. G. Moseley, *A Cultural History of Religion in America* (Westport, Conn., 1981) • B. Norman, ed., *Religion and French Literature* (Amsterdam, 1998) • R. Petitbon, *L'influence de la pensée religieuse indienne dans le romantisme et le Parnasse* (Paris, 1962) • S. Prickett, *Narrative, Religion, and Science: Fundamentalism versus Irony, 1700-1999* (Cambridge, 1976); idem, *Origins of Narrative: The Romantic Appropriation of the Bible* (Cambridge, 1996); idem, *Romanticism and Religion: The Tradition of Coleridge and Wordsworth in the Victorian Church* (Cambridge, 1976); idem, *Words and the Word: Language, Poetics, and Biblical Interpretation* (Cambridge, 1986) • M. Roston, *Prophet and Poet: The Bible and the Growth of Romanticism* (Evanston, Ill., 1965) • R. M. Ryan, *The Romantic Reformation: Religious Politics in English Literature, 1789-1824* (Cambridge, 1997) • H. Timm, *Die heilige Revolution. Die religiöse Totalitätskonzept der Frühromantik: Schleiermacher, Novalis, Friedrich Schlegel* (Frankfurt, 1978) • A. Viatt, *Le Catholicisme chez les Romantiques* (Paris, 1922).

Frederick Burwick

Rome

1. Concept

Situated on the Tiber, Rome (Lat. and It. Roma) is the capital of Italy and the seat of the papacy. On the basis of its history it is not just the name of a → city but also, like → Jerusalem, a religious concept. It is a holy city, even eschatologically, as the eternal city, *Roma aeterna,* and so forth. This meaning goes back to antiquity, when Rome was the origin and center of the empire that its citizens seized and founded (→ Roman Empire).

2. History

In the following centuries *romanitas,* the culture or aura of the Roman Empire, became a leading concept in movements of church reform (e.g., → Cluny, Order of). This concept was set in opposition to the claims made by secular rulers for the sanctity of their office and their supremacy over the → church. Rome and *romanitas* embodied the church's autonomy, its independence of secular rulers, and its position of spiritual leadership over them (→ Empire and Papacy).

At the time of the → Reformation this order of things was partially reversed. Rome now embodied the secularized, power-made, unspiritual church and could be called the seat of → antichrist. But some ambivalence still persisted. M. → Luther (1483-1546; → Luther's Theology) respected the city of Rome because the tombs of the → apostles Peter and Paul were there, yet he also abhorred its lascivious → Renaissance culture. The ecclesiastical importance of the city promoted its cultural and political importance, and still does.

2.1. *Pre-Christian Period*

Ancient legend has it that Rome was founded in 753 B.C. It brought together settlements on the seven hills (Aventine, Caelian, Capitoline, Esquiline, Palatine, Quirinal, and Viminal). And we read of seven kings. Even before the days of the Republic there were city walls, a first canal system (the Cloaca Maxima), and temples like that of Jupiter Capitolinus (→ Roman Religion). The rise of Rome began with the collapse of the Etruscan kingdom and the establishment of the Republic in 510 B.C.

Little of the architecture of the early Republican age has survived. Greek influence is apparent, as in the temple of Ceres of 493 B.C. The Greek temple was usually a *peripteros,* that is, having a colonnade encircling the cella, or shrine of the god's image. It thus had no specified physical orientation. The Etruscan and Roman style (Jupiter temple) favored the *prostylos* (having pillars in front), that is, a cella with narthex set up on a podium. This style allowed for direction and movement. The two styles were in keeping with the respective religious feelings, and they came together in Rome. They would influence Christian → church architecture.

Engineering (roads and aqueducts) developed strongly in Rome, and the techniques were shared with the conquered provinces. Especially important in the days of the Republic was the Forum Romanum, the marketplace and place of assembly, on which all the important streets converged. Important, too, was the Circus Maximus, the largest of the Roman hippodromes. The public buildings reflected the inner structure of the city-state: the temple, the speaker' platform *(rostra),* the *comitium* for public meetings, the circus for public games. The Republic came to an end with Octavian Augustus (30 B.C.–A.D. 14), and the emperor became sole ruler (27 B.C.).

Among buildings of this new period mention should be made of the baths (of Caracalla and of Diocletian), the triumphal arches, especially that of Titus with its depiction of the Jerusalem temple utensils, the new amphitheater (the Colosseum), and the Pantheon, which prefigured → Renaissance architecture. The population grew at this time to over a million. New roads and bridges were built, and great secular → basilicas like the Basilica Ulpia (A.D. 107-12), the centerpiece of Trajan's Forum, were constructed. In the fourth century basilicas gave large church buildings both their form and their name.

2.2. *Christian Period*

From the third century onward we begin to get evidence of Christian building. First came the → catacombs, underground cemeteries. The paintings here are important witnesses to Christian → piety in about 300. Then after Constantine (306-37) issued the Edict of Milan in 313, the first big churches were built to make room for the growing number of believers. The main form was the basilica, for example, the Lateran Basilica (of St. John), with its three naves and open rafters, built on the imperial grounds. Memorial churches were built over → martyrs' tombs (St. Peter's, St. Paul's outside the Walls, St. Sebastian's, Sts. Marcellinus and Peter). Nearby would often be a mausoleum with a room for burial feasts. Then there were house churches or churches named after landowners (e.g., San Clemente). But in these cases we no longer have the original structures.

Because they were imposing and dignified, Roman churches had a major influence on the architecture and → liturgy of later churches in the → Middle Ages. Constantine gave the bishop of Rome the Lateran Palace, which became the seat of the → pope and later the center of the → Papal States. The papal chapel Sancta Sanctorum in the Lateran, which Nicholas III rebuilt in Gothic style in 1278, held many → relics and thus made Rome a specially holy place for pilgrims. The early Christian period, however, brought few other new features to the city.

2.3. *Middle Ages*

During the Middle Ages Rome underwent many changes with the reconstruction of churches and the putting of ancient basilicas to new uses. Complete reconstruction came, however, only when the popes came back from Avignon in 1417, strengthened their authority, and made Rome the cultural center of Europe.

The Renaissance found its way to Rome under Nicholas V (1447-55). L. B. Alberti (1404-72) and A. Rossellino (1427-79) urged the next pope to continue his efforts. The aesthetic ideas of Renaissance → humanism gave the life of Rome a brilliant, if this-worldly, aspect. Rebuilding St. Peter's was the focal point. The foundation stone was laid in 1506. The reconstruction of Capitol Square embodied Rome's claim to be the *caput mundi* (head of the world). Michelangelo (1475-1564) turned the Capitol toward the city and set it over against St. Peter's. → Catholic reform began under Paul III in 1534.

In 1568 the foundation stone was laid of the Gesù, the mother church of the Jesuit order, and the → baroque era of church building began. This style was in keeping with the liturgical demands of the Council of → Trent. The biggest change in the city came under Sixtus V (1585-90) as churches were translated into the baroque (e.g., St. John Lateran) and St. Peter's Square took on a new look with the obelisk and the double arcades of G. L. Bernini (1598-1680). Rome now bore witness to the new self-consciousness that the Counterreformation and Trent had given the → Roman Catholic Church. The ardor of the baroque style was in keeping with the attempt of the church to inspire and attract and give promise to believers by depicting itself as the church triumphant.

The artist who, along with C. Maderna (1556-1629) and F. Borromini (1599-1667), was able brilliantly to do justice to this task was Giovanni Bernini. Bernini's style was a synthesis of the principles of classical and illusionist form that gave a restrained dramatic force to sculpture and architecture and corresponded to the newly awakened mystical → spirituality (Theresa of Ávila, → Ignatius Loyola; → Mysticism). With contrasting concave and convex forms Bernini gave the churches and palaces their facades, and he offered orientation to pilgrims to Rome by the use of squares as points on which to focus. He played a vital role in finishing St. Peter's, giving plastic shape to the Bridge of Angels, and setting up fountains such as that on the Piazza Navona. The legacy of antiquity, the work of the popes, and the collections and buildings of leading Roman families helped to make Rome a center of secular culture. It is not surprising, then, that artistic Europeans like J. W. von Goethe (1749-1832) experienced such longings for Rome.

3. St. Peter's

St. Peter's in Rome is the central church of Catholic Christendom (→ Catholicism [Roman]) because it was built as a memorial church over the grave of → Peter and because Roman Catholic faith holds that the pope stands in the apostolic succession of Peter (→ Apostle, Apostolate). As such, and as the primary church in Rome, it became one of the most popular pilgrimage goals (→ Pilgrimage). It was built on a hill (Mons Vaticanus) outside the Roman city walls over the course of a two-stage construction history.

3.1. *Old St. Peter's*

The first church of St. Peter was thought to be founded by Emperor Constantine (306-37) during the time of Pope Sylvester I (314-25; → Donation of Constantine).This edifice covered over an ancient circus site and various gravesites. Excavations beneath St. Peter's up to 1951 undertaken by E. Kirschbaum at the behest of → Pius XII (1939-58) revealed not only these sites but also the primitive worship site with the tomb chapel (dating to ca. 150/160) allegedly marking the site of the tomb of Peter. (The tomb itself was not found.)

The appearance of the older church itself is so well documented in drawings from the 16th and 17th centuries that fairly precise information can be gathered. It was a five-aisled basilica with apsed transept. The shrine of St. Peter stood before the intersecting line of the apse beneath a canopy supported by six similar marble columns, four of which are still preserved today. Columnal arcades opened up toward the side aisles, which were divided by four rows of marble columns, 22 in each. The entire interior was covered with frescoes and mosaics, the exterior with plain brickwork.

3.2. *New St. Peter's*

By the second half of the 15th century, St. Peter's was in urgent need of renovation. Influenced by L. B. Alberti (1404-72), Pope Nicolas V (1447-55) decided in 1452 to tear down and rebuild. The new structure was not finished until 1626 with the completion of the facade. The popes of the 15th and 16th centuries viewed this new edifice of St. Peter's from the perspective of the fundamental Renaissance notion of making the ideal of eternity visible in the embodiment of earthly greatness.

First a new choir was built by B. Rossellino (1409-64). In 1506 Pope Julius II (1503-13) engaged the services of D. Bramante (1444-1514), who drafted the daring project of a central edifice of extraordinary dimensions. He envisioned a domed structure over a Greek → cross with secondary domes, galleries, and four corner towers. The construction had progressed as far as the crossing pillars when Bramante died. Raphael (1483-1520) supervised construction until 1520, and then A. da Sangallo the Younger (1483-1546). One unresolved issue was a possible return to the basilican form.

Michelangelo (1475-1564) took over the supervision of construction in 1547. He tightened up the dome and gave it more monumental proportions by strengthening the dome pillars, dividing the supporting wall into parts, and heightening it to 123.4 m. (404.9 ft.). He also divided the exterior facade with colossal pilasters and cornice in order to emphasize through exaggerated dimensions the significance of the tomb of Peter in the style of ancient mausoleums. Influenced by the Counterreformation, a new understanding of the sacred and of → worship emerged, resulting in a new appreciation of the basilica.

From 1605 Maderna completed the construction, expanding the basic form into a Latin cross by means of two inserted bays in the west and enhancing the western facade (by 1626) in the baroque style, thus harmonizing the Renaissance and baroque conceptions.

3.3. *Furnishings*

The furnishings of St. Peter's, which come from virtually every century, similarly serve the ecclesiological program of the papacy. This program is already evident in the entryway, where a representative portal area within Maderna's facade leads into the interior of St. Peter's. Giacomo Manzù created the door to the far left, the "Death Door," in 1964. On the far right is the walled-up Holy Door, which the pope opens only during a → holy year. The portico above the main doorway is dominated by a copy of Giotto's (ca. 1267-1337) mosaic *Navicella* (little ship), depicting the apostles' fishing excursion. Christ is walking on the water and extends his hand to Peter, who is kneeling before him. The ship coursing through the waves symbolizes the → church on the stormy seas of wickedness.

In the central aisle the programmatic axis continues to the dome, the tomb of Peter, and the *Cathedra Petri* (throne of Peter) in the tribune, or raised platform. To the immediate right of the dome stands the statue of the Peter from the old St. Peter's Church. The actual *locus sacer* (sacred place), the grave of Peter and the high, or papal, altar, is crowned by the canopy of G. Bernini (1598-1680), built between 1624 and 1644. Four bronzed spiral pillars (11.4 m. / 37.4 ft. high) support the canopy itself, whose form undulates in baroque curves. In front of this piece, steps in a half circle lead down to the tomb and to the Niche of the Pallium (where, in an ornate silver box, the pallia, or stoles, are held that the pope bestows on newly appointed archbishops). The central dome, on whose inner edge one can read the words to Peter from Matthew 16:18-19, rises above the canopy. Above the words to Peter, mosaics of Cavalier d'Arpino (ca. 1568-1640) illustrate the theme of the office of Peter and ecclesiology: The lower zone depicts the popes and saints whose relics are kept in St. Peter's, then the apostles, then Mary and Christ (→ Jesus), above whom → angels fly. God the Father appears with the gesture of blessing in the dome lantern.

Since 1656 the cathedral → altar has been located in the main axis of the church in the apse and thus behind the canopy as the final element of the liturgical center. Also created by Bernini, it involves a gilt-bronze covering of the ancient bishop's seat under a cluster of angels.

Commensurate with the significance of St. Peter's as the church of the pope and as a pilgrimage center, a great many → devotional images and epitaphs are found in the various chapels, side aisles, and niches. From among the many devotional images, one might mention especially the *Pietà* of Michelangelo.

The epitaphs and tumuli of the popes entombed here naturally constitute a considerable portion of the interior furnishings. Each of the papal tombs reflects the understanding of church and office of the various periods. Sixtus V (1585-90), for example, is venerated by the sciences and by virtue, while Innocent VIII (1484-92) is portrayed both on a throne and, beneath that portrayal, as a dead person. In this way, the office itself is set apart from life and death, the earthly person taken up into the eternal purpose of the church (both works by S. de Pollaiuolo). But one also finds here the equestrian statues of Emperors Constantine and Charlemagne (768-814), as well as the tombs of Emperor Otto II (973-83) and Christina of Sweden (1626-89).

→ Mary, Devotion to

Bibliography: On 1 and 2: L. Bruhns, *Die Kunst der Stadt Rom. Ihre Geschichte von den frühesten Anfängen bis in die Zeit der Romantik* (2 vols.; Vienna, 1951) • W. Buchowiecki, *Handbuch der Kirchen Roms. Der römische Sakralbau in Geschichte und Kunst von der altchristlichen Zeit bis zur Gegenwart* (4 vols.; Vienna, 1967-97) • F. W. Deichmann, *Frühchristliche Kirchen in Rom* (Basel, 1948) • R. Elze, H. Schmidinger, and H. Schulte-Nordholt, eds., *Rom in der Neuzeit. Politische, kirchliche und kulturelle Aspekte* (Vienna, 1976) • H. L. Kessler, *Rome 1300: On the Path of the Pilgrim* (New Haven, 2000) • T. Klauser, *Die römische Petrustradition im Lichte der neuen Ausgrabungen unter der Peterskirche* (Cologne, 1956) • A. La Regina, ed., *Rome, One Thousand Years of Civilization* (Rome, 1992) • P. Lampe, *From Paul to Valentinus: Christians at Rome in the First Two Centuries* (Minneapolis, 2003) • S. McPhee, *Bernini and the Bell Towers: Architecture and Politics at the Vatican* (New Haven, 2002) • D. Redig de Campos, ed., *Art Treasures of the Vatican: Architecture, Painting, Sculpture* (Englewood Cliffs, N.J., 1975) • R. M. San Juan, *Rome: A City out of Print* (Minneapolis, 2001) • H. A. Stützer, *Das antike Rom* (7th ed.; Cologne, 1987).

On 3: W. Buchowiecki, *Handbuch der Kirchen Roms. Der römische Sakralbau in Geschichte und Kunst von der altchristlichen Zeit bis zur Gegenwart* (4 vols.; Vienna, 1967-97) vol. 1 • G. L. Hersey, *High Renaissance Art in St. Peter's and the Vatican* (Chicago, 1993) • H. L. Kessler, *Old St. Peter's and Church Decoration in Medieval Italy* (Spoleto, 2002) • E. Kirschbaum, *The Tombs of St. Peter and St. Paul* (New York, 1959) • R. Krautheimer, *Corpus basilicarum Christianarum Romae = The Early Christian Basilicas of Rome (IV-IX cent.)* (5 vols.; Vatican City, 1937-77) vol. 5 • S. McPhee, *Bernini and the Bell Towers: Architecture and Politics at the Vatican* (New Haven, 2002) • H. A. Millon and C. H. Smyth, *Michelangelo Architect: The Facade of San Lorenzo and the Drum and Dome of St. Peter's* (Milan, 1988) • L. Rice, *The Altars and Altarpieces of New St. Peter's: Outfitting the Basilica, 1621-1666* (Cambridge, 1997) • J. M. C. Toynbee and J. W. Perkins, *The Shrine of St. Peter and the Vatican Excavations* (London, 1956).

Gerlinde Strohmaier-Wiederanders

Rosary

1. Form

"Rosary" (from Lat. *rosarium*, "rose garden") refers to a → meditation on the Christian mysteries of salvation from a Marian standpoint (→ Mary, Devotion to). The name, which derives from the flowers used to adorn statues of Mary, traces back to a Spanish legend (1270) according to which Mary prefers an → Ave Maria to flowers.

The rosary now takes the form of an introduction (→ sign of the cross, reciting of the → Apostles' Creed, Gloria Patri, the → Lord's Prayer, three Ave Marias) and sets of five "mysteries" (each preceded by the Lord's Prayer and followed by ten Ave Marias). In each set, with the help of a string of beads for counting, one mystery from the life of Jesus (→ Christology) or Mary is contemplated. It is customary to divide the mysteries into three groups of five each: the joyful (→ Incarnation), the sorrowful (→ Suffering), and the glorious (see Phil. 2:6-11), but other combinations are possible. In his apostolic letter *Rosarium Virginis Mariae* (October 2002), John Paul II (1978-2005) proposed a fourth set, the "mysteries of light," with a focus on significant moments in Jesus' public ministry.

2. History of Religion

From the standpoint of the history of religion, the origin of the rosary is to be sought in the desire to focus upon a central theme with the help of uniform prayer formulas. The starting point biblically is the exhortation to engage constantly in → prayer (Luke 18:1, 7; 21:36, etc.). In Christian → monasticism this exhortation resulted in an increased use of the prayers in the Psalms and the division of the Psalms into a series of themes. Then came the canonical → hours, which came into play in the 12th century. When the scope, content, and wording proved too much for the laity, the rosary offered a substitute. For a long time its form was variable.

The modern form, fixed from 1483 onward, goes back to the Carthusians Adolf of Essen (d. 1439) and Dominic of Prussia (d. 1427), who for the first time in Trier linked 50 Ave Marias to meditations. The → Benedictines, → Dominicans (Dominic [1172-1221] was for a long time regarded as the author of the rosary), and later the → Jesuits (P. Canisius [1521-97]) popularized the rosary. In 1475 J. Sprenger in Cologne founded the first rosary fraternity (→ Religious Orders and Congregations). The → Reformers (→ Reformation) opposed the rosary as petition, not as praise (W. Beinert and H. Petri, 370, 382).

The → popes of the 19th and 20th centuries up to John XXIII (1958-63) stressed the → Mariological orientation. Paul VI (1963-78), however, in his apostolic exhortation *Marialis cultus* (1974) 42-55, stressed the Christological. In his apostolic letter John Paul II (see 1) declared a "year of the rosary" (October 2002 to October 2003).

3. Prayer

In theological structure the rosary is prayer with a biblical character (featuring the Lord's Prayer and the Ave Maria). It meditates on the mysteries of → salvation history with a Christological focus under a Mariological horizon (i.e., a horizon of unreserved, unconditional faith).

4. Piety

The rosary is of great importance for Roman Catholic → piety (→ Popular Catholicism). Liturgically, the Feast of Our Lady of the Rosary, on October 7, is devoted to it. This date recalls the naval victory over the Ottoman Empire at Lepanto on October 7, 1571, a victory ascribed to the rosary. Leo XIII (1878-1903) appointed October a rosary month, with daily devotions so far as possible. The rosary also governs the → spirituality of many orders, plays a part in the training of priests (→ Religious Educational Theory), and shapes many movements of → popular piety.

Rosary piety also lies behind many important works of art, for example, the triptych in St. Andrew's Church in Cologne (1474) and the interior of the Chapel of the Rosary in Venice, by H. Matisse (1951). In music we find many songs and, especially noteworthy, the 15 "mystery," or "rosary," sonatas for violin by H. Biber at the end of the 17th century. P. Claudel's *La rose et le rosaire* (1946) illustrates the theme in literature.

Bibliography: W. Beinert, ed., *Maria heute ehren* (Freiburg, 1977; 3d ed., 1979) 209-12, 232-38, 249-58 • W. Beinert and H. Petri, eds., *Handbuch der Marienkunde* (Regensburg, 1984) esp. 379-86 • D. B. Bryan, *A Western Way of Meditation: The Rosary Revisited* (Chicago, 1991) • *500 Jahre Rosenkranz, 1475 Köln 1975. Erzbischöfliches Diözesan-Museum Köln, 25. Oktober 1975–15. Januar 1976* (Cologne, 1975) • W. Klein and A. Heinz, "Rosenkranz," *TRE* 29.401-7 • J. D. Miller, *Beads and Prayers: The Rosary in History and Devotion* (London, 2002) • M. B. Pennington, *Praying by Hand: Rediscovering the Rosary as a Way of Prayer* (San Francisco, 1991) • R. Scherschel, *Der Rosenkranz–das Jesusgebet des Westens* (Freiburg, 1979) • H. Schürmann, *Rosenkranz und Jesusgebet. Anleitung zum inneren Beten* (2d ed.; Freiburg, 1989) • A. Winston-Allen, *Stories of the Rose: The Making of the Rosary in the Middle Ages* (University Park, Pa., 1997).

Wolfgang Beinert

Rosicrucians

1. Older Rosicrucians
2. Relations with Freemasonry
3. Modern Descendants

In the course of its history the term "Rosicrucian" has been used for many different movements.

1. Older Rosicrucians

Shortly before the → Thirty Years' War (1618-48), among Tübingen student friends of J. V. Andreae (1586-1654), who later became general superintendent and court preacher, there appeared two anonymous Rosicrucian manifestoes — *Fama Fraternitas* (Account of the brotherhood, 1614) and *Confessio Fraternitatis* (Confession of the fraternity, 1615) — followed by *Chymische Hochzeit Christiani Rosencreutz* (The chemical wedding of Christian Rosenkreutz, 1616), now known to have been written by Andreae. These are the first traces of the report of a secret Rosicrucian fraternity (the "older Rosicrucians"). The aim here was to bring a renewal of the impulses of the Reformation into an ossified Protestant → orthodoxy, with the ultimate goal of a reformation of the whole world and a Christian order of society. The basis would be harmony between (Renaissance) learning and Christian → faith (a goal called pansophia), such as was found, for example, in Paracelsus (1493-1541; → Philosophy of Nature; Science and Theology).

As a model of the renewal of → church, → state, and → society, and in keeping with the → allegorical thinking of the day, use was made of the literary fiction of a brotherhood that was founded by a Christian Rosenkreutz, or "Christian of the rose of the cross" (who supposedly lived 1378-1484), with the aim of reforming the church. In 1604, or 120 years after Rosenkreutz's death, the brotherhood "discovered" the founder's grave.

Various explanations have been given of the symbolism. Both M. → Luther (1483-1546) and Andreae had a rose and a cross in their coat of arms. J. A. Comenius (1592-1670), R. Descartes (1596-1650), and probably also the winter king Frederick V of the Palatinate (1596-1632) were in sympathy with the movement (F. A. Yates). By 1619, however, Andreae himself had drawn apart from it, as we see in the preface to his Christian utopian political novel *Christianopolis.*

2. Relations with Freemasonry

After the end of this first phase, the movement continued in the 17th century in another form through the influence of Elias Ashmole (1617-92) on the developing Freemasons (→ Masons). Ashmole, an English Rosicrucian, was an alchemist and astrologer (→ Alchemy; Astrology).

The Orden der Gold- und Rosenkreuzer (Order of the golden Rosicrucians), which originated in the 18th century, had no continuity with the older form. When it made its way into the Masonic movement in Germany, and until its suppression in Prussia in 1787, it was a powerful force in opposition to the → Enlightenment and Enlightenment trends among Freemasons (seen as a branch of the secret Illuminati). Its members included Frederick William II (1744-97) and J. C. von Wöllner (1732-1800).

3. Modern Descendants

3.1. From the 19th century onward various occult groups (→ Occultism) and neo-Gnostic societies took over the name (→ Gnosis, Gnosticism). The Societas Rosicruciana in Anglia was founded in 1865 with the theosophist F. Hartmann and E. G. Bulwer-Lytton as members. The Hermetic Order of the Golden Dawn (1888) had W. B. Yeats, A. Crowley, and B. Stoker as members. The materials they left behind still influence occult and esoteric writers (→ Esotericism).

The teachings of active groups today are still linked to the occult knowledge of mysteries and to esoteric forms of initiation that we find in Anglo-Indian → theosophy and → anthroposophy, which claim to be true followers of the Rosicrucians. These groups include the Lectorium Rosicrucianum, the Rosicrucian Society (Max Heindel), and the Ancient Mystical Order Rosae Crucis, along with many smaller ones.

3.2. At the heart of modern occult doctrines is the idea of transfiguration. The divine powers (sparks) latent in us must be aroused and set to work until they come to full deity. The process of initiation includes many incarnations (→ Reincarnation). The biblical doctrine of → justification is thus rejected. Modern Rosicrucians emphatically claim to be Christian, but for them → Jesus Christ is only an older brother or initiate, or one religious founder among others (→ Christology). Jan van Rijckenborgh (Lectorium Rosicrucianum) even denies that Christ ever came historically. His sacrificial death on the cross is, van Rijckenborgh thinks, a tragically mistaken teaching.

Because of the neo-Gnostic and occult character of the teaching of these groups, historic Christians cannot possibly belong to them. By its very nature the Lectorium Rosicrucianum forces members out of the church (→ Church Membership 5).

Bibliography: S. Åkerman, *Rose-Cross over the Baltic: The Spread of Rosicrucianism in Northern Europe* (Leiden, 1998) • S. W. Beeler, *The Invisible College: A Study of the Three Original Rosicrucian Texts* (New York, 1991) • H. Lamprecht, *Neue Rosenkreuzer. Ein Handbuch* (Göttingen, 2004) • C. McIntosh, *The Rose-Cross and the Age of Reason: Eighteenth-Century Rosicrucianism in Central Europe and Its Relationship to the Enlightenment* (Leiden, 1992) • E. Philalethes, *The Fame and Confession of the Fraternity of R: C: Commonly, of the Rosie Cross* (London, 1652) • H.-J. Ruppert, *Der Mythos der Rosenkreuzer* (Berlin, 2001) • H. Tilton, *The Quest for the Phoenix: Spiritual Alchemy and Rosicrucianism in the Work of Count Michael Maier (1569-1622)* (Berlin, 2003) • F. A. Yates, *The Rosicrucian Enlightenment* (London, 2002).

Hans-Jürgen Ruppert

Rule of Faith

1. Early Church
2. Reformation

1. Early Church

The phrase "rule of faith" *(regula fidei)*, equivalent to "rule of → truth," is a term and concept that we first find in → Irenaeus (ca. 130-ca. 200). It then occurs in almost all second- and third-century → church fathers but is less common in Constantinian usage. As the defining genitive shows, what is meant is the substance of Christian faith, or → truth as a standard and normative authority.

In the rule of faith the → church has preserved the quintessence of Christian belief, and it has shown its fidelity to the apostolic tradition by maintaining the rule of faith alive and unchanged from the very first. On this view the rule of faith played an important role in the fight against → heresies (§2.2) and schisms. When given in its full form, it contains three main articles, though others might be added. The content is essentially the same, but the formulation may vary, there being room for specific emphasis.

These considerations show unequivocally that the rule of faith is not a fixed formula and should not be viewed as a baptismal symbol or the interpretation of such a symbol. If believers receive the rule of faith in → baptism, it simply means that in the catechism they have been entrusted with the → faith that the church hands down. The rule of faith undoubtedly has helped to shape the baptismal confession, but its own basis is to be sought in the basic content of ceremonial → proclamation as it was influenced by the triadic baptismal formula. We see this understanding, for example, in *1 Clement* 46.6; 58.2 (ca. 96). The actual confession of Christ in the didactic and polemical form that Ignatius (d. before 117?) gave it, a form oriented toward the historical work of salvation (*Eph.* 7.2; 18.2; *Trall.* 9.1-2), was then appended or introduced to these basic proclamations of faith, which in their own turn had attracted various additions.

→ Apostles' Creed; Confession of Faith

Bibliography: H. von Campenhausen, "Das Bekenntnis im Urchristentum," *ZNW* 63 (1972) 210-53 • P. S. Grech, "The Regula Fidei as a Hermeneutical Principle in Patristic Exegesis," *The Interpretation of the Bible* (ed. J. Krasovec; Sheffield, 1998) 589-604 • B. Hägglund, "Die Bedeutung der 'regula fidei' als Grundlage theologischer Aussagen," *StTh* 12 (1958) 1-44 • R. P. C. Hanson, *Tradition in the Early Church* (Philadelphia, 1963) • J. N. D. Kelly, *Early Christian Creeds* (3d ed.; New York, 1972); idem, *Early Christian Doctrines* (5th ed.; London, 1977).

Dietmar Wyrwa

2. Reformation

The term "rule of faith" took on a different connotation at the → Reformation as a result of controversies regarding Scripture, → tradition, and the → teaching office. Scripture itself was now described by the Reformers as the supreme rule of faith (and practice), to which any other rule or rules were secondary and subordinate. This view did not necessarily conflict with that of the → early church, for the Fathers appealed to the rule of faith as both deriving from Scripture and/or faithful to it, in contrast to false heretical interpretations.

The Reformed confessions offer many instances of the equation of the rule of faith with Scripture. Scripture is simply the "rule of faith" and "rule of all truth" in Gallican 4, 5 (1559), "the rule of faith and life" in → Westminster 1.2 (1648), the "only rule of our faith" in J. → Calvin's Confession in the Name of the French Churches (1562), the "infallible rule" in Belgic 7 (1561), and the "rule of faith and all saving truth" in the Irish Articles 1.1 (1615). Westminster 1.9 also affirms that "the infallible rule of interpretation of Scripture is the Scripture itself." Along somewhat different lines the First → Helvetic (1536) and Second Helvetic (1561) confessions (in chap. 2 in each) speak of interpreting Scripture from or out of itself "according to the rule of faith and charity," with "rule" here having much the same sense as analogy of faith in other authors (see H. Heppe, 34-41).

Bibliography: J. Calvin, *Tracts and Treatises* (3 vols.; trans. H. Beveridge; Grand Rapids, 1958) • H. Heppe, *Reformed Dogmatics Set Out and Illustrated from the Sources* (rev. ed.; London, 1950) • P. Schaff, *The Creeds of Christendom, with a History and Critical Notes* (6th ed.; 3 vols.; Grand Rapids, 1983) • F. M. Young, *The Making of the Creeds* (London, 1991).

Geoffrey W. Bromiley

Rules → Household Rules

Rural Missions → Urban Rural Mission

Russia

	1960	*1980*	*2000*
Population (1,000s):	119,906	138,660	146,196
Annual growth rate (%):	1.11	0.66	–0.36

Area: 17,075,400 sq. km. (6,592,800 sq. mi.)

A.D. 2000

Population density: 9/sq. km. (22/sq. mi.)
Births / deaths: 1.02 / 1.51 per 100 population
Fertility rate: 1.35 per woman
Infant mortality rate: 17 per 1,000 live births
Life expectancy: 65.3 years (m: 59.0, f: 72.1)
Religious affiliation (%): Christians 57.1 (Orthodox 52.0, indigenous 4.8, Protestants 1.1, other Christians 1.0), nonreligious 28.3, Muslims 7.7, atheists 4.6, other 2.3.

1. Nineteenth-Century Reforms

1.1. *The Political Background*

Early Russian statehood was based on the Byzantine *symphōnia* principle of a partnership between →

church and state (more often abused than adhered to). That structure came to its final end in Russia with the abolition by Peter the Great (ruled 1682-1725) of the patriarchate and its replacement by the czar as the terrestrial head of the church and a synod ruled by an emperor-appointed bureaucrat. After this point, to use the term "autocrat" for Russian czars would be a misnomer: the post-Petrine era was actually that of western European monarchical absolutism, not autocracy. Nevertheless, the czars, at least beginning with Paul I (1797-1801), quite seriously saw themselves as terrestrial heads of the → Russian Orthodox Church.

Alexander I (1801-25) may have mystically believed in his special mission even beyond Russian frontiers as he initiated the so-called Holy Alliance at the Congress of Vienna (1814-15). Alexander I and Nicholas I (1825-55) took the Holy Alliance seriously. The latter responded positively (as required by the Holy Alliance) to Austria's appeal in 1849 to rescue it from the victorious Hungarian Petőfi rebellion. Austria proved an unreliable ally, however, as it supported Russia's enemies from 1855 to World War I.

Alexander II (1855-81) moved away from the defunct Holy Alliance to Realpolitik, having learned the lesson from Austria's devious behavior in the Crimean War (1853-56). He realized that Russia needed radical internal reform to catch up with the rest of Europe. He began by putting an end to serfdom in 1861, followed by the legal reform of 1864, which introduced open courts and trial by jury. Also in 1864 he established local self-government, using a system of local assemblies, or *zemstva* (sing. *zemstvo*), followed in 1874 by military reforms, which introduced a universal draft system.

Abroad, Alexander II is remembered particularly warmly in the Balkans, where he led a bloody campaign liberating Bulgaria and Serbia from the Turkish yoke. Finland remembers with gratitude his legalization of the Finnish language. Monuments to Alexander are found in the capitals of both countries.

The opening up of frontiers after the closed-door policy of Nicholas I led many Russian students to western European universities shortly after the European revolutionary turmoil of 1830-49, which brought in its train liberal and democratic reforms, including liberalization of the press, formation of political parties, and self-government. The difference between the reforms in Europe and those in Russia was that in Europe the reforms came from below following the → revolutions, while in Russia they were "gifts" of a benevolent czar. By the mid-19th century Russian society thought of itself as being sufficiently mature to have a say in its country's destiny. The paternalistic monarchs, however, refused to recognize this desire, eventually to their own detriment.

Three main political currents dominated Russian society at this time: Slavophiles, Westernizers, and radical socialists or nihilists, as Ivan Turgenev termed them. The split of the educated society into Westernizers and Slavophiles originated from Peter Chaadayev's (1794-1856) *First Philosophical Letter* (1829), in which he castigated Russia for its alleged cultural barrenness. As a deeply religious person, he believed that God created → nations with particular destinies and contributions to the commonweal. Being strictly Eurocentric, as all European thought of the time was, he saw no purpose in Russia's existence. He blamed Russia's problems on → Byzantium, which he quite incorrectly saw as a stagnant society, and believed that Russia's backwardness resulted from its adoption of Christianity from Byzantium. Chaadayev's letter was a challenge to the educated public of Russia regarding Russia's historical purpose and destiny. Those who were offended by his thesis began to dig into Russian history and archaeology, as well as into Byzantinology.

Their research coincided with the Pan-Slavic movement among western and southern Slavs. Russian Slavophiles turned to pre-Petrine Russia for the idea of a paternalistic czar who would rule with a nationally elected consultative land council, which used to be assembled irregularly in Old Russia. Their slogan was "Plenitude of power to the autocrat, plenitude of opinion to the nation" — that is, freedom of oral and written expression. The church was to be an autonomous institution in a symphonic relationship with the monarch (→ Empire and Papacy). Slavophile leaders admired Britain for its absence of a written constitution and for its common law, for they believed that written legislation signified the moral failure of society, mistrust, and lack of fraternal love.

Whereas Slavophiles were trying to develop an ideology based on spiritual values inherited from Byzantium and from the → Orthodox Church, the so-called Westernizers of the Chaadayev generation embraced a Western-leaning nondenominational Christianity. The next generation of Westernizers went on to imitate slavishly the most fashionable political ideas from the West, which after the revolutions of 1830 and 1848-49 happened to be socialism — at first so-called French utopian socialism, and by the late 1870s its Marxist version.

The intellectual patron and inspirer of Russian radicals and populists in the 1850s and early 1860s was Alexander Herzen (1812-70), a wealthy Russian political émigré living in London and publishing there a populist biweekly journal, *The Bell*, the most popular Russian periodical of the time. Even Alexander II was one of its subscribers. When the czar announced his aim of liberating the peasants from serfdom, *The Bell* came out with the following address to the czar: "Thou hast vanquished, O Galilean!" But as soon as the details of the emancipation statute became known, including long-term peasant land-redemption payments, Herzen condemned the emancipation decree as an act of deception, ignoring the fact that the Russian state was practically bankrupt after the Crimean War. Herzen now called on the Russian youth and university students to go to the people (i.e., the peasants) to arouse them politically to revolution. Thousands followed Herzen's appeal, giving up university studies. To their shock they soon discovered that their propaganda of rebellion against the czar not only fell on deaf ears, but most peasants reported them to the police.

Two different conclusions were drawn by radicals from the failure of "going to the people." The majority decided to make use of the reforms by becoming professionals working for *zemstva* as rural doctors, agronomists, nurses, statisticians, or schoolteachers. They were nicknamed "people of small deeds." In contrast, the die-hard radicals, or "great-deeders," considered that the "small-deeders" were perpetuating the hated monarchy by making its reforms work.

The acknowledged leader of the "great-deeders" was Peter Tkachev (1844-85), who claimed to be the first Russian Marxist but, ironically, was also the first revisionist of Marx's revolutionary doctrine (→ Marxism). He replaced the Marxist idea of a spontaneous revolution of masses of industrial workers with a coup d'état — exactly what Lenin would do later. Tkachev argued that in order to achieve a revolutionary situation in Russia, it was necessary to antagonize the people against the → state, and vice versa. This state was to be achieved by unleashing terrorist acts against state officials of all ranks, which would bring about counterterror from the state. This response would destabilize the state and society, whereupon the group of professional revolutionaries totally subordinate to its leader would seize power. He also wrote that the life of a revolutionary movement was merely the youthful span of a single generation. There was therefore no time to be lost.

Reform-minded Russians, having gained self-government on local and provincial levels, called on the czar to "crown the edifice," that is, to establish, if not a legislative body, then at least a consultative parliamentary body in the capital. But the reform process was slowed down after the first attempt on the czar's life, in 1866. At the height of Alexander's reforms a deranged young man fired a pistol at the czar as he was taking an afternoon stroll in St. Petersburg's Summer Gardens. Several other attempts on the czar's life followed.

The political immaturity of Russian liberals was demonstrated by the fact that they saw terrorists as their bedfellows struggling for a liberal or democratic society. Russian society woke up to the fact that the radicals were not liberals, either in ideas or in their aims, when on March 1, 1881, in St. Petersburg Alexander II was assassinated by populists. The paradox is that the czar was on his way to the Senate to announce a manifesto that would lay the foundations for a constitutional government.

1.2. *Foreign Policies*

After the Crimean War Russia became a lonely power. French support for the Polish rebellion of 1863, which began by Polish rebels attacking Russian army barracks at night and slaughtering sleepy and unarmed Russian soldiers, excluded a Russo-French alliance for the time being. Bismarck, who also had problems with suppressing the Polish rebellion on the Prussian side of the partitioned Poland, proposed to Russia the so-called Three Emperors' League, which was most active from 1873 to 1875.

In 1876 there was a particularly bloody Turkish massacre of Bulgarian rebels, which led to an anti-Turkish Serbian rebellion in Bosnia. The tragic fate of the Balkan Slavs raised Pan-Slavist sentiments in Russia. Supplies and volunteer units were sent to the Balkans to help fellow Slavs. There was such an enthusiastic outcry in Russia that in 1877 it declared war on Turkey. This very bloody war ended in 1878 with Russian forces occupying the San Stefano suburb of Constantinople (Yeşilköy, in modern Istanbul). The Treaty of San Stefano created a relatively large self-ruling Bulgarian state and an expanded, independent Serbia.

Such expansion of Russian influence in the Balkans, however, was not to the taste of Austria and other western European powers. Consequently, Bismarck called an international conference in Berlin later in 1878 that deprived the Russian-Balkan alliance of their war gains, returned Bulgaria to diverse degrees of Turkish control (splitting the country into two states), and reducing Serbia in size by granting Bosnia to Austria, which had not participated in the war at all.

Russians were so offended that the public called on the czar to go to war against Germany. But after the exhausting war in the Balkans, Russia could not afford another one; its treasury was empty. This sequence of events ended the Three Emperors' League. Now the only alliance available to Russia was France, which, having lost a war against Germany and seeking ways of revenge and wanting to recover Alsace-Lorraine, was ready to became Russia's ally. Alexander III (1881-94), who hated republics, accepted the proposal, showing his ability to put *raison d'état* above his personal tastes. Thus the knot began to be tied that led eventually to the alliances of World War I.

1.3. ***Internal Policies***

The senseless murder of Alexander II sent shock waves throughout Russia. It so angered the peasants that terrorists circulated false manifestos claiming that the czar was killed by the land-owning gentry in retaliation for giving land to the peasants.

Shocked by the murder, the Russian public was now prepared to tolerate the much tougher regime of Alexander III. Politically, it was a solid reactionary or highly conservative regime. Terrified by the murder of his father, Alexander III expanded the authority of the police and somewhat circumscribed the jurisdiction of the open jury courts.

Somewhat surprisingly, it was under Alexander III that the Russian economy prospered. Its growth was due largely to Sergei Witte, Alexander's ingenious finance minister, who placed the ruble on a solid gold base, making it one of the three major and most stable currencies in the world. Railway construction was booming, and so were mining and industry in general. By the turn of the century Russia was the fifth-leading industrial power in the world. In the two decades before World War I, Russia's economy grew at an annual rate of 6 percent, making it the world's fastest-growing economy. Russia also became one of the major centers for science and education. In the arts, particularly the performing arts, Russia was clearly a world leader.

The ascent to the throne of the young Nicholas II (1894-1917) raised hopes of a return to the reform path of his grandfather Alexander II. These hopes were expressed in several *zemstva* addresses at the czar's coronation. His reply was blunt: "Give up your senseless dreams!" Nicholas declared that the model for his government would be that of his late father, Alexander III.

It was soon realized, however, that the young czar had neither the will nor the stamina of his father. Oppositional activities were renewed; underground political parties, from moderate conservatives and liberals to those on the extreme Left, began to be formed. Inconsistency of state policies and the czar's indecisiveness, as well as the massacre of peaceful labor demonstrators on January 22 (January 9, old style), 1905, so-called Bloody Sunday, resulted in such an uproar that the czar was forced to grant a limited constitution, establishing a parliamentary system in his manifesto of October 17, 1905.

2. Transition to Communism

Reforms after 1905 included religious freedom (esp. the freedom to convert from the Orthodox faith to other religions), abolition of prepublication censorship, and easing of residence limitations for Jews. Also the debts of peasants who had redemption payments remaining were forgiven, and financial support was given to peasants willing to leave their communes to become land-owning farmers.

In 1909 a small group of leading Russian Christian thinkers and philosophers, all former Marxists, published a volume entitled *Signposts,* in which they appealed to the intelligentsia to cease their destructive and subversive work, arguing that however imperfect, the new constitutional regime allowed the system to work toward further reforms and the democratization of society. But the radicalized public ignored those sober voices, believing that there was "no enemy on the Left"; however extreme, all leftists were treated as their allies in a supposedly common struggle against the czarist regime. It was fashionable among wealthy Russians even to donate money to revolutionary parties, including the Bolsheviks, who were soon to "thank" many of the donors by physically liquidating them!

The Provisional Government, which came to power in March 1917 after the abdication of Nicholas II and the collapse of the monarchy, acted on this same principle of "no enemy on the Left," thus taking no effective measures to curb V. I. Lenin's (1870-1924) antigovernment propaganda and preparation for a coup d'état. In fact, as Lenin and his cohorts arrived in Russia by train from territory controlled by Germany, this action in itself was valid ground to arrest and charge them with collaboration with the enemy and with receiving money from the enemy in order to undermine the Russian state. (Although at the time there was no documentation that Lenin had received German money, there was enough evidence to have had him arrested.) But the Provisional Government took no effective measures to prevent a coup d'état, and in little more than a month after coming to power in November 1917, Lenin created the Cheka terror police, which was given practically unlimited punitive powers, including that of executions without trial of "counterrevolutionary elements and black marketeers."

Although before his coup Lenin promised to convene a constituent assembly and to abide by its decisions, when the assembly did meet on January 19 (January 6, old style), 1918, Lenin's Bolsheviks held less than one-quarter of the seats. When Lenin's demand that the assembly recognize the legitimacy of his coup was rejected by an almost 70 percent of the delegates, Lenin had the assembly dissolved by his Red Guard. Arrests of the delegates began immediately after its dissolution.

3. The Soviet Union and Its Collapse

3.1. *Lenin*

Despite Russia's colossal industrial growth mentioned above, almost 80 percent of its population consisted of peasants. Parallel to the "workers and soldiers" soviets (i.e., councils), which were largely controlled by the Bolsheviks, peasants formed their own soviets, which voted by an overwhelming majority in favor of dividing large estates into parcels to be added to the individual peasant plots; collectivization, however, was vetoed by the Provisional Government. In order to break up the peasant opposition, soon after his coup Lenin began to form the so-called committees of the poor, consisting of landless peasants and of all sorts of disreputable elements of the general population. He armed them, appointed them as leaders of villages, and gave them unlimited powers over village life. He described this step as implementation of class war in the countryside.

Lenin then replaced the market economy with a system of armed food requisition detachments, usually made up of, or at least commanded by, Latvian sharpshooters loyal to him or by prisoners of war. These groups went into the villages to forcefully confiscate food from the peasants. Many peasants were killed in these confrontations, while others were left to starve, deprived even of seed for the next year's planting. As Richard Pipes has pointed out, this was a real war between the Bolsheviks and the Russian peasantry, a larger military operation than that of the White Army against the Bolshevik Red Army. The peasants lost this war largely because in most cases each village fought alone, isolated from other villages.

The famine of 1921-22, which carried away the lives of no fewer than 10 million people, was at least as much a product of the peasant-Bolshevik war as it was of a drought in 1920-21. (The drought was also a convenient cover-up for the fact that masses of armed soldiers deserted the battlefields, roamed the country, grabbed power, and emptied out the grain reserves stored in elevators.) The total collapse of the economy forced Lenin to declare his New Economic Policy in 1921, restoring private farming, private trade, and small private enterprises. The revival of agriculture and small private businesses was much speedier than that of the state-controlled heavy industry, although according to Marx heavy industry was supposed to have priority over consumer goods and farm production (→ Economy).

3.2. *Stalin*

To restore the country to "proper" Marxism, private enterprise had to be destroyed once and for all. Thus in 1929 under Joseph Stalin (1879-1953, gen. secy. from 1922), a campaign of "dekulakization" began, that is, the liquidation of well-to-do farmers by mass exile to distant areas in Siberia and the sub-Arctic north. This oppression was followed by the artificially precipitated 1932-33 famine, caused by the decree that not an ear of grain could be picked from the fields — not even from private garden plots — until all the grain requested by the state was delivered. As state-owned machinery was in short supply, snowfalls came to most places before the harvest was completed. Peasants were left to die. This attack was geared at agriculturally rich areas — the Ukraine, the central Russian black-earth region, and the black-earth regions in Siberia and along the Volga River — where the resistance of peasants to collectivization was most active. It is estimated that at least 7 million people starved to death in this campaign, not counting dozens of millions of the Gulag slave laborers and exiles, most of whom died of starvation or from the inhuman living and working conditions.

The 1930s also saw sham trials of Old Bolsheviks, scientists, and Red Army commanders. Up to 80 percent of all senior military commanders were executed on the eve of World War II. The carnage and mass imprisonments were renewed shortly after the end of the war.

3.3. *Khrushchev*

Terror subsided somewhat after the death of Stalin, especially after the speech of Nikita Khrushchev (1894-1971, first secy. 1953-64) at the 20th Communist Party Congress in 1956, in which he presented himself as the savior of the party. Khrushchev claimed that had Stalin lived longer, he would have started another bloody purge of the party. Khrushchev's speech served implicitly as a signal to the Soviet satellite nations to call for more freedom in their countries, which led to the Hungarian revolution in 1956, unrest in Poland, and other stirrings. There was much sympathy for the uprising in Hungary among Soviet youth, but many of them who distributed leaflets in Hungary's support were imprisoned. From this point on, the Russian regime showed ever more signs of senility, while society in general was growing more cynical regarding the regime and Khrushchev's promises of constructing Communism by 1980.

In October 1964 Khrushchev was debunked by the Communist Party Central Committee, the first such case of a party head being censured in Soviet history (and that without bloodshed). The subsequent rule of Leonid Brezhnev (1906-82, first or gen. secy. from 1964) is known as the era of stagnation and gerontology, the latter being personified by the dying Yuri Andropov (1914-84, gen. secy. from 1982) and Konstantin Chernenko (1911-85, gen. secy. from 1984).

3.4. *Gorbachev*

Change came soon after the 54-year-old Mikhail Gorbachev (b. 1931) became the Communist Party general secretary in 1985. Within the next two years he radically redirected the Soviet foreign policy by negotiating a rapprochement with U.S. president Ronald Reagan. At home he proclaimed a period of *glasnost* (openness) and *perestroika* (restructuring), to be expressed in expanded freedoms and a limited democratization of the political process. At the 27th Communist Party Congress (1987), however, there was no way to disguise the deep crisis of the whole Soviet system. Gorbachev nonetheless pressed on with the old clichés, promising to continue the construction of socialism, while in fact the economy had entered a period of negative growth. Gorbachev presented a new Communist Party Program, which was outdated and irrelevant even before it was published.

Somewhat refreshing at the congress was the speech of Boris Yeltsin (b. 1931), who spoke openly about a deep economic and social crisis. Instead of discussing Communist internationalism, Yeltsin dealt with Russia and its problems. Although Yeltsin was soon dismissed from his position as Moscow party boss for criticizing Gorbachev's inept reforms, his alternative position to Gorbachev's and particularly his resignation from the Communist Party in 1990 brought him great popularity as a national leader. In 1991 Yeltsin gained a landslide victory in the first-ever presidential elections in Russia, especially when he mounted a tank in front of the "White House" (the Russian government building at the time).

In the meanwhile the politically insensitive Gorbachev left for summer holidays in the Crimea, having handpicked a government consisting of his most trusted comrades. On August 19, 1991, this trusted government attempted a coup d'état against Gorbachev, falsely declaring to the nation that he was gravely ill in Crimea and unfit to govern. Yeltsin immediately denounced the coup and called for a general strike. Overnight, Yeltsin became the symbol of resistance against the plotters, who lacked national support. Democratically minded Muscovites, as well as most of the armed forces and, most important, the Alpha special security force, put themselves at Yeltsin's disposal, making the White House their base and headquarters.

When by the end of August 20 it became clear that the plotters had failed, a military plane was dispatched to Crimea, and on August 21 Gorbachev arrived in Moscow as a virtual prisoner of Yeltsin, who humiliated Gorbachev by forcing him to read over the electronic media a document of mea culpa and of condemnation of the plotters. Yeltsin continued to be the president of Russia alone, while Gorbachev technically remained the head of the Union of the Soviet Socialist Republics. This dichotomy formally ended on December 26, 1991, when the USSR was abolished at a meeting of the leaders of the three Slavic republics (Russia, Ukraine, and Belarus), replacing the former Soviet Union by the → Commonwealth of Independent States (CIS), a body that has not got off the ground to the present day. For all intents and purposes, the three republics became fully independent states. Within days the non-Slavic republics also declared independence, most of them joining the CIS.

4. The Russian Federation

4.1. *Yeltsin*

Alas, Yeltsin proved to be more of a demagogue than a statesman. Despite promises to the contrary, the Russian economy steadily declined. The Communist Party was a carryover from the Soviet era, when it was the only legal party in the country and was internally highly disciplined; in contrast, the new democratic and liberal parties lacked internal discipline and an authoritative leadership. Yeltsin tried to ban the Communist Party as a terrorist and corrupt institution, but the Constitutional Court ruled that only the Politburo of the Communist Party was guilty of crimes of the Soviet era; consequently, only that body was declared illegal. Yeltsin complained that owing to the party's sabotage of the Parliament, the country was ungovernable.

Consequently on September 21, 1993, Yeltsin appeared on national television to tear up the Soviet-era constitution and dissolve Parliament, which in turn declared Yeltsin deposed. Forces loyal to Yeltsin then barricaded themselves in the Parliament building. A standoff between military forces at Yeltsin's disposal and rebels loyal to his pro-Communist opponents lasted until October 7, when some blood was spilled by both sides. In the last stages of the standoff Patriarch Alexis II (b. 1929), head of the Russian Orthodox Church, tried to mediate between the two sides. The forces loyal to Yeltsin ultimately prevailed, at a cost of 139 lives. The population as a whole was hostile toward the pro-Communist rebels, for the euphoria for democracy had not yet worn off. After seven decades of Communist totalitarianism, people were still willing to believe that the promised reforms would bring prosperity. The leading figures of the resistance were imprisoned, and Yeltsin remained in power.

The new session of Parliament, however, retained a strong presence of Communists and other leftists. Not surprisingly, it granted amnesty to all those who had been imprisoned in connection with the uprising. A new constitution, drafted under Yeltsin's guidance especially to fit the president, was approved in a referendum in December 1993. According to its provisions, the president can dissolve the Parliament, but the latter cannot impeach the president. Whereas with such a populist president as Yeltsin there appeared little danger of the system's degenerating into a dictatorship, the same cannot be said under a president such as Vladimir Putin (b. 1952).

At least in one aspect of his administration, Yeltsin was consistent — in his hatred of Communism, the party that earlier had promoted him to its topmost ranks. It was probably owing to his hatred for the party that Yeltsin consistently defended freedom of speech, including the right to use sharp political satire, even against himself. Several times throughout his tenure the Communist-dominated Parliament tried to reinstall press and other media censorship, yet Yeltsin consistently vetoed all such efforts. In this sense one can call Yeltsin the father of Russian democracy.

During Yeltsin's reign the Communist Party still had a plurality in the Duma, or lower house of Parliament. In 1996, on the eve of the second free presidential election in post-Communist Russia, public opinion polls showed that a clear majority of the population believed that they were materially worse off after perestroika, yet they did not want Communism to return. The outcome of the presidential election was touch-and-go between Yeltsin and the Communist Party boss, Gennady Zyuganov (b. 1944), whom Yeltsin finally defeated in a runoff. The country was by then disillusioned with Yeltsin; the people, though, voted not for Yeltsin but against Zyuganov and all that he stood for. Also in this election citizens were also asked to approve the new constitution, which hardly anyone read. Yet, approved it was.

4.2. *Economic Problems*

The greatest, most persistent problems in post-Communist Russia are pitifully low wages, inability to reduce the rate of inflation to below the rate of growth of wages and salaries, and significant unemployment, especially in the peripheral areas of Russia. Before the collapse of Communism the country was run by a "make-believe economy" subordinate to ideological needs, such as enormous subsidies to quasi-Marxist states from Ghana to Cuba, which the stagnating economy of the Soviet state could ill afford. The downfall of the Communist coup in 1991 brought about a brief interregnum, made use of by the Komsomol (a Communist youth organization), which, along with some sectors of the Communist Party, functioned like a business corporation, its top echelons becoming new capitalists. During the suppression of the coup, the treasuries of both organizations were emptied by officials who had been close to them, which meant that Russia entered the post-Communist era empty-handed.

Yeltsin entrusted the business of restoring the country economically to a group of young, Western-educated Russian economists. The head of that group was Yegor Gaidar (b. 1956) with his program of shock therapy, which amounted to a sudden introduction of market-economy principles in a society that lacked most of the ingredients necessary for such an economy. As an artificial introduction to the market, Gaidar and his group issued vouchers: each Soviet citizen received a voucher without a specific price attached to it, which the (nonexistent) market was to regulate. It was believed that the more enterprising people would buy vouchers from those who did not know what to do with them. In this manner vouchers were expected to gradually acquire value, which the most farsighted speculators would be able to use to buy factories from the state by long-term mortgages at reduced prices. With the collapse of the Soviet centralized economy, most state factories became redundant, available for the picking by those who were willing to do something with them.

Such a "voucherization" program did not succeed in developing a true and free private enterprise. The small minority of new entrepreneurs who succeeded did so by holding on to the skirts of the relevant cabinet ministers. With the advantage of hindsight, many have argued that a better policy for the Russian economic situation would have been a Keynesian system, such as had been successfully applied in the years of the Great Depression, not the shock therapy imposed on the Russian economic reformers by the World Bank.

Nevertheless, during 1992-93 Gaidar managed to fill marketplaces and stores with food and other consumer goods, but at an inhuman price: inflation rose to between 10 and 15 percent per month, with salaries lagging far behind. By 1997 the economy was much more balanced, and there was a real growth in wages. But then in 1998 the Asian and world economic crisis hit the weak Russian economy particularly hard, and Russia defaulted on its foreign debts. The recently somewhat stabilized ruble fell to one-quarter of its predefault value.

4.3. *The War in Chechnya*

The greatest thorn in the side of contemporary Russia has been and remains the Chechen wars. The conflict with the Chechens goes back to the early 19th century. Historically, that mountainous Islamic tribe lived by highway robbery and guerrilla attacks on the neighboring Christian states, predominantly Georgia and Armenia. As far back as the 16th century, the Georgians asked for Russian protection, but only by the end of the 18th century was the Russian Empire capable of responding to this request. Georgia and Armenia had also asked for Russian protection from the onslaughts of Islamic Persia and the Ottoman Empire. The only way the Russian forces could reach those Christian states was via Chechnya, Russian movement through which resulted in 40 years of fighting between Russia and Chechnya and other Islamic areas separating Armenia and Georgia from Russia. That war ended in the defeat of the famed Chechen leader Shāmil (1798?-1871), who, however, was given an estate in central Russia and made a member of Russian nobility.

The Georgians and Armenians, however, remained unsatisfied. Although they wanted to retain their autonomy within the empire, they instead were simply absorbed into Russia. This decision led to some of them participating in the revolutions of 1905 and 1917. During the civil war in Russia the Chechens and their Muslim neighbors mostly supported the Bolshevik cause and fired on the anti-Bolshevik White army, having received assurances from Lenin of freedom of religion and wide autonomy, which was not to be. Consequently, during World War II the Chechens welcomed the German advance forces in the northern Caucasus, eventually fighting on the German side.

Stalin responded by a most brutal deportation of the whole Chechen and Ingush peoples to Kazakhstan and other central Asian republics. Consequently, as the Soviet Union was shedding its border areas, Yeltsin declared the right of all non-Russian ethnic groups to grab as much sovereignty as they wanted. This invitation undoubtedly became an important factor in unleashing local wars in Russia by such groups as the Chechens (M. McCauley, 206-347). The war became extremely brutal on both sides, developing into Chechen terrorist campaigns against innocent civilians like the sacking of the hospital in Budennovsk (1995), the kamikaze attack on the *Nord-Ost* musical at a theater in Moscow (2002), and the revolting mass murder of schoolchildren in Beslan (2004).

4.4. *Putin*

In December 1999 President Yeltsin unexpectedly resigned, naming Vladamir Putin as his interim successor. In March 2000 Putin defeated ten opponents to become president. One of his credentials at the time of his election was his promise to end the Chechen confrontation. Almost 80 percent of the population had voted for him, hoping that he would bring peace and order after Yeltsin's chaotic rule. One would have thought Putin would have renewed negotiations with Aslan Maskhadov (1951-2005), the supreme leader of the Chechen rebellion. Maskhadov had been a highly regarded colonel in the Soviet armed forces, a veteran of the Russian war in Afghanistan (1979-88). He reportedly said that a half hour meeting between him and Putin would end the war.

Putin, however, had chosen a war of attrition as his only course in the Caucasus. After years of fighting, Putin may have been right that no encounter between him and the late colonel would end the war, because by this late stage of the war Maskhadov had become only a titular leader. Although he did not approve the bloody attacks of the Chechen terrorists, he had no control over the guerrillas, as he himself had admitted shortly before his recent violent death. The mountainous terrain and the growing participation of Islamic extremists from the Middle East promise no quick solution.

Eschewing negotiation with the Caucasian rebels, Putin faces a decades-long confrontation, similar to the 19th-century confrontation with Shāmil. Moreover, an internal war fought among citizens of the same state antagonizes the population to a much greater degree than does an international war, which contributes to a climate of mutual hatred and distrust, undermining the very texture of the nation.

Moreover, as the country's president, Putin has demonstrated little patience for opposition and none for critique related to his rule, whether in the form of satire or of political debates critical of him. TV programs unfriendly to Putin have been discontinued, one after the other, though nominally for being financially insolvent.

The arrest in October 2003 of Mikhail Khodorkovsky, the former CEO and coowner of the Russian petroleum company YUKOS, may also have been motivated by political, rather than criminal, causes. Khodorkovsky, after all, has dared to engage in politics, supporting groups that oppose the government's policies. Such developments encourage little optimism regarding the future of democracy in Russia.

Bibliography: General, comprehensive: E. ALLWORTH, ed., *Ethnic Russia in the USSR: The Dilemma of Dominance* (New York, 1979) • J. H. BILLINGTON, *The Icon and the Axe: An Interpretive History of Russian Culture* (New York, 1966) • P. BUSHKOVITCH, *Religion and Society in Russia: The Sixteenth and Seventeenth Centuries* (New York, 1992) • M. CHERNIAVSKY, *Tsar and People: Studies in Russian Myths* (New York, 1969) • J. W. CUNNINGHAM, *The Movement for Church Renewal in Russia, 1905-1906* (Crestwood, N.Y., 1981) • G. FREEZE, *From Supplication to Revolution: A Documentary Social History of Imperial Russia* (New York, 1988) • G. A. HOSKING, *Government and Duma, 1907-1914* (Cambridge, 1973) • F. LIEB, *Sophia und Historie. Aufsätze zur östlichen and westlichen Geistes- und Theologiegeschichte* (ed. M. Rohkrämer; Zurich, 1962) • B. W. LINCOLN, *In the Vanguard of Reform: Russia's Enlightened Bureaucrats, 1825-1861* (DeKalb, Ill., 1982) • M. MALIA, *Alexander Herzen and the Birth of Russian Socialism* (New York, 1965) • R. NICHOLS and T. G. STAVROU, eds., *Russian Orthodoxy under the Old Regime* (Minneapolis, 1978) • M. OLEKSA, *Orthodox Alaska: Theology of Mission* (Crestwood, N.Y., 1992) • R. PIPES, *The Russian Revolution* (2 vols.; New York, 1990) • N. V. RIASANOVSKY and M. D. STEINBERG, *A History of Russia* (7th ed.; New York, 2005) • S. V. RIMSKY, *Rossiyskaia tserkov' v epokhu velikikh reform* (The Russian church in the era of major reform [1860-1970s]) (Moscow, 1999).

After the Soviet collapse: J. ANDERSON, *Religion, State, and Politics in the Soviet Union and Successor States* (Cambridge, 1994) • F. CORLEY, *Religion in the Soviet Union: An Archival Reader* (London, 1996) • N. DAVIS, *A Long Walk to Church: A Contemporary History of Russian Orthodoxy* (Boulder, Colo., 1995) • J. DEVLIN, *Slavophiles and Commissars: Enemies of Democracy in Modern Russia* (London, 1999) • Y. GAIDAR, *State and Evolution: Russia's Search for a Free Market* (Seattle, Wash., 2003) • D. R. HERSPRING, ed., *Putin's Russia: Past Imperfect, Future Uncertain* (2d ed.; Lanham, Md., 2005) • B. KAGARLITSKY, *Russia under Yeltsin and Putin: Neo-liberal Autocracy* (London, 2002) • V. A. KREMENYUK, *Conflicts in and around Russia: Nation-Building in Difficult Times* (Westport, Conn., 1994) • M. MCCAULEY, *Bandits, Gangsters, and the Mafia: Russia, the Baltic States, and the CIS since 1992* (London, 2001) • L. MCDONNELL, *October Revolution: A BBC Correspondent's Eye-Witness Account of the Storming of the Russian Parliament* (Staplehurst, Eng., 1994) • *St. Nikolai Kasatkin and the Orthodox Mission in Japan: A Collection of Writings by an International Group of Scholars* (Point Reyes Station, Calif., 2003).

DIMITRY V. POSPIELOVSKY

Russian Orthodox Church

1. Beginnings

1.1. *The Baptism of Russia*

The historical event known as the baptism of Rus' occurred around 988, when Vladimir I (ruled 980-1015), grand prince of Kiev, ordered the → conversion of all Russians to Byzantine Christianity, beginning in Kiev. There is no evidence of any large-scale resistance to the new faith in the Dnieper River area, since Christianity had been known there for at least a century and a half, and Vladimir's grandmother Princess Olga had been baptized into the Greek church, probably in Constantinople in about 957. Resistance, however, was found in the north and northeast sections of the country, where there was much less familiarity with the new faith.

Literacy came to Russia with → baptism. This conjunction eventually led to an interesting claim by the 19th-century Russian Slavophiles, an intellectual-spiritual movement that extolled Orthodoxy and Slavdom and included such thinkers as Fyodor Dostoyevsky (1821-81) and Vladimir Solovyov (1853-1900). They claimed that Russia was the most Christian of nations, since it had had no pagan civilization in its background; its birth sprang directly from the baptismal font.

Military conquests by the pre-Christian Vladimir had resulted in a state stretching from the Gulf of Finland to the Black Sea, populated by Slavs, Finns, and Lithuanians. To consolidate these ethnic groupings into what might now be called a single → nation, he created, on a hill overlooking Kiev, a pantheon of the country's major tribal deities. To strengthen the authority of these deities he persecuted Christians. Vladimir soon realized, however, that in order to be accepted into the European family of nations, he had to embrace → monotheism.

For Vladimir, the change of religion became more than an act of political calculation. According to the chronicle of Nestor, monk of Kiev (11th-12th cent.), Vladimir's lifestyle changed after his baptism. He adopted a church statute that gave the church broad judicial powers in matters of family law and morals, assigned 10 percent of state income for the church, built churches, and established a welfare system of sorts by ordering horse carts loaded with food and clothes to circulate in urban areas to feed the hungry and clothe the naked. He invited the poor and the hungry to share banquet tables with him. Influenced by Christian ethics, he discontinued the → death penalty until the Byzantine bishops convinced him to restore it. (Because of his largesse, crime was on the rise in the country.)

Anton Kartashev, a leading Russian church historian, has argued that the defect of the Russian baptismal process was that the nation was introduced to the church by emphasizing → rites and rituals, rather than the ethical teaching of Christ. This background played a role in the 17th-century revolt by the → Old Believers (or, as they also called themselves, the Old Ritualists or Old Orthodox).

The effect of Vladimir's conversion was quite striking. Such monks as Theodosius and Anthony of the Kiev Monastery of the Caves became popular spiritual authorities. Yet the first canonized Russians were none of these persons, but two teen-aged sons of Vladimir I, Boris and Gleb, who were murdered by their elder brother, Sviatopolk the Damned. Interestingly, the Greek church was initially opposed to their canonization, arguing that they were victims of internecine struggle, not martyrs for the faith. The Russian argument for their canonization was their remarkable → obedience to their elder brother. Although they had enough loyal troops to fight Sviatopolk, they allegedly stated that after the death of their father, their older brother had full authority over their own life and death. Russians saw their Christlike → humility and readiness to sacrifice themselves as particular virtues. To the present day Boris and Gleb are among the most popular Russian saints.

The conversion of the country to Greek Orthodoxy, instead of to the → Roman Catholic Church, had at least two advantages for the people (→ Orthodox Missions 1). First, Byzantium at the time was the most civilized country in Europe and a very useful trading partner for Russia. Second, Eastern Christians prayed in the vernacular or, in the case of Slavs, in a language based on a Slavic dialect turned into a literary language by the two Macedonian brothers Cyril (ca. 827-69) and Methodius (ca. 815-85). At the time all Slavs could understand this language. Thus, for example, an average parishioner was able to become familiar with the Bible. In fact, the relationship among church, clergy, and laity became much more intimate than in the Western churches, where only the clergy and a tiny minority of the educated upper class knew what was going on. The sermon, in which the → priest at least summarized the service, thus became absolutely indispensable in the West. No such need existed in the Orthodox churches; as a consequence, the Christian East lagged behind the West in developing the art of → preaching.

A disadvantage of the use of the vernacular, however, was that lacking a lingua franca like Latin or Greek, the literate Russian had no direct access to material in classical languages, and translations took time. This factor helps explain the slowness of Russia's overall cultural progress.

1.2. *Domination by Byzantium*

Justinian the Great (527-65) finalized the Byzantine theocratic ideology of *symphōnia,* according to which the empire was ruled by a partnership of the emperor and the chief bishop, who bore the title "patriarch" or "pope." The formula, as it evolved, made the patriarch in charge of ecclesiastical affairs, while the emperor, as anointed by God, was responsible to God rather than to his nation, not only in secular matters but also as the supreme leader of the Christian flock. The *symphōnia* principle has remained utopian, except in cases of very weak kings or in times of governmental crises.

In the sixth century Greek → deacon Agapetus defined the concept of the anointed ruler as follows: "Though an emperor in body be like all other, yet in power of his office he is like God . . . for on earth he has no peer. Therefore as God, be he never chafed or angry; as man, be he never proud. For . . . he is but dust, which thing teaches him to be equal to every man" (M. Cherniavsky, 45 [*PG* 86.1172]). This formula imposed on the ruler only moral limitations and was ineffective when tyrants were in power. Although the concept was spelled out under Justinian, the idea had been there since the time of Constantine (306-37), who declared himself a Christian emperor long before being baptized on his deathbed, in effect placing emperors above the church, in contradiction to the *symphōnia* principle.

By the time of the conversion of Russia, the Western Roman Empire had been replaced by a Frankish Carolingian empire that was essentially hostile to Byzantine Christianity, as demonstrated by the Frankish treatment of the Slavic Christian mission of Cyril and Methodius in Moravia and Pannonia.

At the Great Schism of 1054, Russian princes chose to stay with the Byzantine Empire and its church. However truncated, that church remained the highest spiritual and theological authority for all Eastern Orthodoxy. In the early centuries → bishops and metropolitans, consecrated for Russia in Constantinople by its → patriarch and approved by the emperor, commanded a much higher status than the local barbarian princes. Nevertheless, some of the metropolitans of the Russian church who were consecrated in Constantinople were mere figureheads, since they often lacked familiarity with the local language and region. Moreover, during those early centuries revered monks, especially from the highly respected Monastery of the Caves in Kiev, often had the highest spiritual authority among the populace. Some of these monks even convened clergy assemblies, and on occasion they reprimanded local princes for internecine fighting or for unjust rule, depriving them of Holy Communion and banning them from entering monastery grounds.

Byzantium prevented the election of native Russians to the rank of metropolitan as long as it could. There were only two exceptions: the 11th-century metropolitan Ilarion, famous for his *Sermon on Law and Grace* (ca. 1047-50), and the 12th-century metropolitan Kliment Smoliatich, apparently elected by a local Russian ecclesiastical council. Neither of these leaders served a particularly long time in office.

2. Under the Ruriks (862-1598)

From the alleged foundation of the first Rus' state in 862 until 1598, the Ruriks (or Riurikids) were the ruling dynasty in Russia. Until its centralization in the 15th-16th centuries, Russia was a loose confederation of autonomous appanages with a succession system not from father to oldest son but from father to oldest uncle, then to his nephew, and so forth. Technically at the head of this confederation sat the great prince of Kiev. As the Rurik clan multiplied, a regular succession became virtually impossible.

Since there were many appanage princes but only one metropolitan of Kiev and all Rus', the actual capital of Russia was the city where the metropolitan resided. Moscow became the capital in the 14th century because the metropolitans then chose to support the great princes of Moscow and to make that city their own seat.

2.1. *Relations with the Mongol-Tatars*

Mongol Tatars invaded Russia in the 13th century, beginning a period of 240 years of devastation and subjugation. Once in control of the country, however, the Mongols showed great respect for the Orthodox Church, granting immunities to monasteries and freeing the church and clergy from all taxes, while heavily taxing the state and its population. The russification of the Russian church leadership occurred under the Tatars, for during this period few Byzantines wanted to go to Russia. This new prevalence of native Russian bishops increased cooperation between the high clergy and the Russian princes. Because of the Mongol respect for the church, Russian bishops were in a position to function as intermediaries between the Russian princes and the Mongol khans and in fact often restrained the Tatars from their devastating raids.

With a relative pacification of the country by the late 13th century, an unwritten rule developed that alternated Russian and Greek metropolitans. The Mongols did not interfere with Russian internal affairs except in the form of granting a right of governance to one prince or another, playing them off against each other according to the principle of divide and conquer. In 1204 Byzantium was invaded by Crusaders, who maintained control for roughly 60 years (→ Crusades). In terms of power after this occupation, Byzantium was but a shadow of its past, but theologically it entered a very vibrant period. It was the era of Gregory Palamas (ca. 1296-1359; → Palamism), → Hesychasm (a monastic tradition based on inner, mystical prayer), and brilliant → iconography.

The metropolitan-elect for the whole of Russia in the 1240s was Cyril II. Returning from his → ordination in Nicaea (Constantinople was still in the hands of Crusaders) to his native Galicia, he found Prince Daniel of Volhynia and Galicia negotiating with the → pope to carry out a joint crusade against the Mongols. Having just witnessed what the Crusaders had done in sacking Byzantium, Cyril gave his full support to the submission of Alexander

Nevsky (ca. 1220-63, prince of Novgorod and later grand duke of Kiev and Vladimir) to the Mongols so that they could work together to stop aggression against Russia by the German and Swedish Baltic knights. As both Alexander and the metropolitan realized, this alliance was a threat to the country's very survival. The successors of Cyril II likewise chose to support the grand princes of the principality of Vladimir and its successor, Moscow.

The most revered of the Moscow-oriented metropolitans was Alexis (ca. 1296-1378), a brilliant diplomat and administrator. He ruled the state as regent for the infant prince Dmitry (1350-89), later to be called Donskoi for his success in battle in 1380 on the banks of the Don River against the Tatars, Russia's first major victory over them. This was the beginning of the end of Mongol-Tatar control over Russia, which formally concluded in 1480.

The role of the Orthodox Church and particularly of its bishops during the Tatar rule cannot be overstated. But it was quite a different role from that of the saintly monks of the Kievan Rus'. The church leaders of the Mongol-Tatar era were of necessity diplomats, double-dealers, people who had made moral compromises. This was also the era of warrior-saints. These were mostly princes like Alexander Nevsky, whose canonization was based on a readiness to lay down their lives for others. At this time life was fragile, and a readiness to sacrifice one's life defending one's country and its people was seen as leading to holy martyrdom. In respect to the church leaders who came out from under the Mongol yoke, it is important to note that although they may have been very important partners of the state, their spiritual authority was often lacking.

2.2. *Hesychastic Spirituality*

The Greek recapture of Constantinople from the Latins brought the appearance of such theologians and church fathers as Gregory Palamas and Nicholas Cabasilas (ca. 1322-ca. 1390). Their school of monastic spiritual concentration, emphasizing Hesychasm, was a unique way to self-perfection via ceaseless prayer accompanied by special movements of the body and by breathing marked by inhaling and exhaling the Jesus Prayer, "Lord Jesus Christ, Son of God, have mercy upon me, a sinner." In contrast to the extreme asceticism found, for example, in Western → monasticism, Hesychasts restored the notion of the body as a divinely created vessel of the spirit; human → spirituality was seen as requiring a harmony between the spirit and the body.

Gregory also taught that divine energies can be mediated through → icons, before which so many prayers have been directed to God. In this process of → prayer, humans become cocreators with God in accordance with → *theōsis,* the participation of humans in the divine.

The late 14th to the early 16th centuries saw the height of the Byzantine Hesychastic influence on Russian spirituality. The most influential spiritual leader was Sergius of Radonezh (ca. 1314-92), followed by his many disciples who, emulating their teacher, established scores of monastic communities deep in the woods of Russia, thereby escaping the world of politics and deceptions. Their isolated monasteries soon attracted peasants and other settlers. Inadvertently, therefore, the monks who sought quietude became promoters of the Russian state's expansion eastward and northward. This was also the era of the greatest achievement of Russian iconography, personified in Theophanes (Russ. Feofan) the Greek (ca. 1330/40-1405), Andrey Rublyov (1360 to 1370-ca. 1430), Dionisi (1440-1503), and their schools.

2.3. *Heresies and Disputes*

As post-Mongol Russia was opening up to the world, various → heresies appeared, the most persistent being the so-called Judaizers. This → sect was brought into Russia around 1470 by a Lithuanian Jewish scholar, Zachary (Skhariah) of Kiev, and his associates. Judaizers rejected church rituals and icons, maintained that the OT was superior to the NT, held that the day of rest should be the OT → Sabbath, and believed that → Jesus was merely an OT prophet. They claimed that reverence for the → Trinity was polytheism.

At the very time of these Judaizers, Gennadius (d. after 1504), archbishop of Novgorod, was engaged with a group of learned theologians in preparing the first complete Slavic Bible. One of the translators, a Croatian Dominican monk from Spain named Benjamin, suggested to Gennadius that he emulate the Spanish → Inquisition against the spreading heresy. The idea was supported by Joseph of Volokolamsk (1439/40-1515), abbot of a monastery in Volokolamsk, northwest of Moscow. Joseph and his disciples argued that if people could be executed for killing the body, so much more is the death penalty deserved by heretics who kill the soul; their repentance under duress should not be trusted.

The idea of burning heretics at the stake was rejected by Nil Sorsky (1433-1508), an Athonite Hesychastic monk (→ Athos), who held that repentant heretics should be received like the prodigal son; nonrepentant heretics could be isolated but not deprived of life. Several church councils were devoted to the issue. The ruling grand prince Ivan III the Great (1462-1505) supported Nil, while his son, heir-apparent Vasily III (also called Basil III, 1505-33), sided with Joseph. Eventually the aging Ivan gave in to his son, and shortly before Ivan's death several leading Judaizers were burned at the stake, the first such occurrence in Russian history, while others were sent to various monasteries for atonement and were later pardoned.

To the same period belongs the monastic dispute between the so-called Possessors and Nonpossessors. The Nonpossessors, headed by Nil, preached the imitation of Christ, material → poverty (§5), noninterference into state affairs, and self-support of monks by their own labor, who lived in sketes, or small Hesychastic monastic communities. A searcher after monasticism was free to choose a → starets (or spiritual father) of his liking but then was required to become totally obedient to him. Nil's Rule gave a monk freedom to devise his own worship and prayer discipline.

In contrast, Joseph, the most prominent adherent of Possessionism, formed large monasteries of cenobites, or monks living in larger communities. For them, almost every minute of every day was regulated. Joseph's main monastery at Volokolamsk and others formed on its model engaged in charitable work and had orphanages and old age asylums. In his personal life Joseph was severe on himself, indulging in hard manual work for self-humiliation. He argued, nevertheless, that monasteries must be wealthy in order to accommodate aristocrats who were used to luxury and would not join monasteries with a severe discipline. Without aristocratic monks and their contacts in the government circles, so he maintained, the government would ignore the church, and it would have no influence on state affairs.

Joseph was a strong believer in *symphōnia,* the necessity of sharing power between state and church. But then he argued that since the church may not spill blood, the czar should be responsible for identifying and executing heretics. Thus Joseph, through this "donation" to the czar, was relegating serious theological decisions to the monarch, thus opening a floodgate to interference by the czars in church affairs. This was on the very eve of the era of terror associated with Ivan IV the Terrible (1533-84). After Nil's death his disciples and followers were persecuted for having given asylum to a variety of heretics in their sketes north of the Volga River. The Josephites triumphed.

3. The Time of Troubles (1598-1613)

In 1589 the patriarch of Constantinople granted the Russian church the status of patriarchate equal to that of the Eastern patriarchs. In practice, this decision did not add power to the church, for the head of the Russian church was merely a subject of the czar, who himself possessed the sole right (following Joseph's "donation") to identify and punish heretics. One exception was Patriarch Hermogenus (1606-12), who, although imprisoned in a Kremlin dungeon by Polish occupiers, succeeded in smuggling out appeals to Russian patriots to organize resistance to the Poles.

The Poles ultimately starved Hermogenus to death, but his messages were instrumental in forming the resistance that led to the revival of the Russian state and the election of the first Romanov czar in 1613. The church was the victor in the civil war, the so-called Time of Troubles. Through this time it gained "authority and prestige as the great champion of the interests of the country and the people and the most effective organization . . . [which] survived the collapse of the secular order" (N. V. Riasanovsky, 173).

The Time of Troubles, during which Poland and Sweden invaded Russia, was the first massive encounter of Russians with what they considered to be western Europe. The result of the encounter was a split in society: some wanted to turn their back on Europe, accepting only Western know-how; others wanted to completely imitate Europe and to reject all Russian traditions. The latter were the early Russian Westernizers.

One of the heroes of the Time of Troubles was Archimandrite Dionisi, abbot of the Trinity–St. Sergius Monastery, who succeeded in defending the monastery against an 11-month siege by the Polish army. At the conclusion of the civil war, Dionisi concentrated on the moral revival of Russia. He and many dedicated young priests, calling themselves God-lovers, or zealots, began preaching on a scale never before experienced in Russia. In their sermons, delivered not only in churches but also in other public places, they attacked unfair and corrupt officials and landowners. They also revived the state publishing house for the publication not only of religious literature but also of textbooks and translations of western European books on science, medicine, and other disciplines. Stemming in part from their work, a law was passed in the mid-17th century making poorhouses, orphanages, and homes for the aged the joint responsibility of church and state.

4. Under the Romanovs (1613-1917)

4.1. *Nikon and the Old Believers*

In 1551 a church-state council had agreed on the need for correcting mistakes in religious, primarily liturgical, texts that had been copied by poorly educated scribes. Ancient manuscripts were to be collected in order to establish the most reliable original sources. The council also ruled that primary schools should be established in every parish and higher schools in diocesan centers. Because of the terror of Ivan the Terrible and the subsequent Time of Troubles, next to nothing was done to implement these decisions.

The God-lovers set about to revive this work. Manuscripts were collected from ancient Orthodox sites in the Balkans and the Middle East to serve as models. In the meanwhile, Metropolitan Nikon (1605-81) was elected patriarch in 1652. He was a close friend of the ruling czar, Alexis I (1645-76), who was a very ambitious and energetic member of the God-lovers' circle and likewise a champion of the reform of liturgical texts. Self-taught, Nikon had no patience for time-consuming research and decided, as a shortcut, to adopt Ukrainian and Greek books published in Kiev and Venice as models for Russian publications. The zealots opposed this decision, arguing that the Venetian books were published by Eastern Rite Roman Catholics, who introduced some Roman Catholic concepts, while the Kiev Slavonic-Greek-Latin Academy was modeled on the Jesuit colleges in Poland. They also cited the case of the Kiev Catechism, which a congress of Moldavian Orthodox bishops had condemned as theologically non-Orthodox. But Nikon would not listen to his former friends and began to persecute them for hindering the work, which he had entrusted to learned Greeks of very questionable reputation.

In 1439 at the Council of Florence, the leadership of the Greek church had been effectively forced by Greek emperor John VIII Palaeologus to recognize the papacy on the pope's promise of organizing a pan-European army to relieve Byzantium from the Ottoman offensive. Although the pope's army never materialized and the Greeks severed their relations with the pope by 1453, when Constantinople fell to the Ottoman Turks, the Russians ever since questioned the orthodoxy of the Greeks. For their part, the Greeks were contemptuous of the low educational level of the Russian clergy.

As long as the God-lovers enjoyed the support of the czar, they led a crusade against drunkenness and debauchery and banned the sale of alcohol on Sundays and during fasting periods (which included some 20 weeks of the year). They fought against the practice of abbreviating church services, insisting on full monastic-style liturgies lasting many hours. All this rigorism turned many Russians, particularly the business community, against them. In the meantime, Nikon cited a papal formula that compared the pope's power with sunshine and the monarch's with the moon, which merely reflected the sun — applying this comparison to himself. Having irritated the czar, he abandoned Moscow in 1658, going into self-imposed exile at his favorite monastery, "New Jerusalem," not far from Moscow.

There were minor differences between Greeks and Russians in some external manifestations of church ritual. Believing in the coming liberation of the Balkans and in the prospect of serving in Constantinople with the → ecumenical patriarch, Nikon was eager to streamline the Russian ritual with elements from the Greek → liturgy and brutally forced Russians to adopt changes that many Russians took as insults to their piety. In light of the czar's siding with Nikon and the Greek ritual, some of the God-lovers, such as the archpriest Avvakum (1620/21-82), publicly condemned the czar as a heretic and a servant of the devil. In retribution, Avvakum and close to 20 other leading Old Believers were burned at the stake.

Here we can see the tragic fruit of emphasizing ritual in bringing people into the church in the first centuries of Russian Christianity. Not having been taught to distinguish between relative and absolute values, people left the state church in droves, ready to bear suffering and → persecution. Some 20,000 died by self-immolation for what appear to be mere externalities, although the Old Believers held that deep under the externalities was the essence of their faith. Defending the old Russian ritual unto death, they saw themselves as martyrs.

The Romanov dynasty (1613-1917) paid dearly for its persecution of the Old Believers, who were conservative, deeply patriotic, and traditionalist — the very stuff on which monarchies depend. The persecution and repression of the Old Believers deprived the monarchy of its most reliable base of support, turning a force for national stability into an antagonized destabilizing agent. In the last decades of the Romanov Empire, members of wealthy Old Believer families subsidized revolutionary parties, including the Bolsheviks.

Nikon's retirement to his "New Jerusalem" monastery while refusing to abdicate his patriarchal office led to the ecclesiastical council of 1666-67, in which several Greek bishops participated. The council condemned Nikon's sun-moon doctrine as papist heresy and also the irresponsible abandonment of his office, exiling him to the distant northern Ferapont Monastery. Nikon's fall dealt a double blow to the church. First, the church lost its strongest contingent of believers, as those ready to die for their faith joined the schism; second, the patriarch, in losing his battle for supremacy, lowered the prestige and power of the patriarchal office, even while sending a message to future monarchs to be on their guard against the power ambitions of future patriarchs. While the patriarchal office was vacant, the czar himself ran church affairs. Nikon had been extremely despotic, antagonizing the clergy against himself and his office; his excesses led ultimately to the relatively easy acceptance by parish clergy of the abolition of the patriarchate by Peter the Great (1672-1725, czar 1682-1725).

4.2. *Peter the Great and Feofan*

Peter's childhood and adolescence progressed under the shadows of power intrigues carried on by his half-sister Sophia and also of rebellions of the court guard, mostly made up of Old Believers. The young Peter was fascinated with the technical knowledge of western Europe, and he saw Old Russia as an enemy of → progress. Patriarch Adrian (1627-1700), who had crowned Peter, was an extreme conservative and opposed Westernization.

When Adrian died, Peter decided against electing a new patriarch. Instead, he instructed Feofan Prokopovich (1681-1736), a young Ukrainian professor at the Kiev Academy whom he later made an archbishop and virtual dictator over the Russian church, to produce a statute that would abolish the institution of the patriarchate. Feofan produced *The Spiritual Regulations* in 1720, and the next year all Russian bishops were forced to come to Peter's new capital, St. Petersburg, some in shackles. There Peter forced them, some under torture, to pledge loyalty to the czar as the terrestrial head of the church and the bishops' ultimate judge. They were also required to abide by the new regulations, which replaced the patriarchate with a Holy Synod officially presided over by the most senior bishop, but de facto by an emperor-appointed lay chief procurator. The church became merely a government "department of Orthodox confession," deprived of the right to speak with its own voice, let alone pass judgment on state policies.

The superficially Westernized and poorly educated first Petrine generation of Russian gentry saw the Orthodox Church as irrelevant to the age of reason — until the latter's collapse in the carnage of the French Revolution in France and in the bloody Pugachov Rebellion (1773-74) in Russia. By the end of the 18th century the mood among the gentry changed from self-confident → rationalism to mystical pessimism. A thirst for religion again began to appear in the upper classes. Mentally and emotionally, however, the gentry was too rationalistic and Westernized to be comfortable with a church dominated by the lower classes; instead, a mystical Germanic version of Freemasonry (→ Masons) became the new religion of the upper classes of the fin de siècle.

Essentially, the church survived in villages and on the periphery of the empire. Its survival and even revival was associated with the starets Paissy Velichkovsky (1722-94). He was a student at the Kiev Academy, then a monk in monasteries in Moldavia and Mount Athos, where he engaged in translating works of the Greek fathers into Russian. Eventually he had some 800 disciples, who, fulfilling Paissy's will, returned to Russia and toward the end of the century established the monastic community of Optina, southwest of Moscow, where they revived the Hesychastic traditions of mission to the world.

During the ultrasecular 18th century the Russian bishops endured years of real persecution from the vengefully poisonous Archbishop Feofan. Having a basically Lutheran orientation in his doctrine, he accused Russian bishops of being papist. Then, shortly after Feofan's death, there was a scandalous persecution of Metropolitan Arseni (Matseyevich) of Rostov. He was appointed metropolitan of Rostov in 1741 but refused to pronounce the oath in the wording adopted since Peter the Great, which named the monarch, rather than God, the ultimate judge. Elizabeth (1741-62), the kind empress, allowed him to ignore the oath. The real troubles, however, awaited Arseni under Catherine II (1762-96) after she had confiscated monastic land properties. Arseni wrote letters imploring her to return the properties to the church, since they were used to care for the needy, orphans, and the infirm. But his main request was to restore the patriarchate, arguing that the synodical system was uncanonical. In response, Catherine in 1764 forced the Holy Synod to deprive Arseni of all titles and to confine him in a fortress under an alias until his death. He died in 1772 and was buried in an unmarked grave that has never been identified. The church dared to rehabilitate and canonize him only after the fall of the monarchy, at the church council of 1917-18.

4.3. *Nicholas I and the Uniates*

The Hesychastic monks of the Optina Monastery, with their lay disciples, engaged in a very active publication of theological literature, particularly of the early church fathers and popularizations of Orthodox theology. They thus influenced major reforms in Russian theological schools, bringing them out of their isolation from the secular society. The monks also affected the larger society, for many children of the God-seeking Masonic aristocracy returned to the Orthodox Church through their influence. The monastery served as a center of spiritual renewal throughout the 19th century for most Russian writers and thinkers, particularly the so-called Slavophiles and nativists, both strongly associated with the church renewal that called for independence from state bureaucracy.

Their call did not fit the government of Nicholas I (1825-55), an honest sergeant major by mentality who tried to rule Russia and the church as if they were army regiments. During his reign some improvement was made in the material well-being of rural clergy, particularly in Ukraine and Belorussia.

In these areas, after the 1596 Union of Brest-Litovsk, imposed by force by the Polish government on the local Orthodox population, and until the partitions of Poland in the 18th century, the large Orthodox minority was severely persecuted. In 1839 the so-called Unia, or Eastern Rite Roman Catholicism, was officially discontinued in the empire. Although technically the → Uniates had the right to choose between Latin Rite Roman Catholicism or the Orthodox Church, considerable pressure was applied to make them join the Orthodox Church. Thus the Uniate Church was discontinued in the whole empire except in the ethnic Polish territories. Since most of the land-owning gentry in Ukraine and Belorussia were Roman Catholics, they had given support to the local Uniate parishes and their clergy. Once the Uniate peasants became Orthodox, however, the Polish and Lithuanian gentry discontinued their support.

On the suggestion of a special state investigative commission, a fund was set up distributing half a million rubles a year among the rural clergy of these areas. Later the sum was enlarged, and additional funds were distributed to all rural clergy whose income was below a certain minimum. Yet even on the eve of World War I, according to government calculations, the Russian clergy needed an additional annual distribution of 40 million rubles to assure a decent living standard and to end its material dependence on the peasants. Lacking that sum, the clergy was forced to charge parishioners for all private services, such as weddings, funerals, and memorial services, which tended to sour relations between them and their parishioners.

An important part of clergy income was a piece of farmland attached to each rural parish. The economic duress of the Russian Orthodox Church was largely a consequence of the confiscation of monastic land properties, which cost the church 88 percent of its income. This loss was partly compensated by additional subsidies to the church under Paul I (1796-1801) and Nicholas I and later under Alexander II, yet all of these subsidies were far below the income the church had been accustomed to receiving from its monastery farms and forests before their nationalization.

Even while he was persecuting Old Believers and sectarians, Nicholas ordered local surveys in the 1840s of the religious situation in the empire. Although this approach was a far cry from a systematic census, their findings revealed that millions of Russian peasants belonged to diverse schismatic movements and that close to 70 percent of Russia's merchants and entrepreneurs were Old Believers. This information came as a shock to officials; not until 1905, however, was anything done to legitimize the status of the schismatics. The unreliability of the state surveys was revealed in the discrepancy between its findings and the private work on the subject by such Russian scholars as I. Yuzov (*Starovery i dukhovnye khristiane* [1881]). Whereas the government claimed there were just over a million Old Believers, Doukhobors, and members of various Protestant sects, Yuzov claimed there were well over 10 million. For his part, Aleksandr Prugavin (1850-1920), an expert on sectarians, argued there were up to 15 million non-Orthodox believers in the empire.

4.4. ***Alexander II***

With the accession of the reformist czar Alexander II (1855-81), new hopes arose for greater autonomy for the church. Such hopes were in vain, for the church was run by Count Dmitry Tolstoy (1823-89), who was likely an agnostic or atheist. Wise proposals for reforms to end the ghetto-like status of the church were made by episcopal commissions eager to make the theological schools fully compatible with the secular system in order to end the church's isolation from the rest of society. These proposals, however, were rejected by the chief procurator, although originally he had himself proposed similar reforms. As an aristocrat, he could not bring himself to treat bishops, who were usually of humble social background, as his equals who possessed their own ideas.

The Russian secular intelligentsia of the second half of the 19th century was infatuated with → socialism and → positivism, as demonstrated, for example, in Ivan Turgenev's (1818-83) masterpiece, *Fathers and Sons* (1862). Peasants and workers, however, were still mostly conservative, not responding to the populist-revolutionary propaganda. As the 19th century wore on, the process began to reverse itself: the intelligentsia, particularly those related to the arts and humanities, began to abandon positivism and → Marxism in a quest for

God, as the legacy of Dostoyevsky, Solovyov, the Slavophiles, and the learned monks of the Optina Monastery demonstrated. During this same time, in contrast, the young generation of peasants and workers, graduating from primary and Sunday schools run by the 19th-century populist radicals, were increasingly turning to → atheism and revolutionary radicalism.

4.5. *Nicholas II and Cries for Reform*

In the 20th century the first encounters of the God-seeking intelligentsia with the church leadership began in 1901 in the form of religiophilosophical meetings under the chairmanship of Bishop Sergius (Stragorodsky, 1861-1944), a brilliant young rector of the St. Petersburg Theological Academy, who, after the death of Patriarch Tikhon in 1925, became locum tenens, or patriarchal administrator (1927-43), and finally patriarch (1943-44). The proceedings and debates from these meetings were published in *New Way,* a journal of religion and philosophy. The archreactionary chief procurator, Konstantin Pobedonostsev (1827-1907), terrified by the openness of the discussions and their accessibility to the general public, banned the meetings in 1903. After the revolution of 1905 and the death of Pobedonostsev, however, these religiophilosophical seminars became a regular feature in most cities of the empire.

Before 1906 Protestants in Russia could be only Germans, Estonians, Latvians, or other nationalities that had a historic Protestant identity. Roman Catholicism was legally identified only with Polish, Lithuanian, and other nationalities recognized as historically Roman Catholic. Children born into families where either parent was Orthodox had to be baptized Orthodox, and the parents were required to marry into the Orthodox faith. Much more complicated was the status of Russian converts to such sects as → Baptists or Pentecostals (→ Pentecostalism). As a result of public discontent and the pressure of the first Russian revolution of 1905-6, Nicholas II (1894-1917) was forced to issue his Edict of Religious Tolerance, on October 17, 1906. As early as 1904 the church leadership had pointed out to the czar that granting religious freedom to independent faiths (Protestants, schismatics, Roman Catholics, etc.), while keeping the Orthodox Church on the government's leash, would make the Orthodox Church the only shackled church in the empire.

In 1905 the church leadership petitioned the emperor to allow the convocation of a local ecclesiastical council to elect a patriarch and to free the church from control by the state bureaucracy. (Not since 1700 had the church had a patriarch.) The czar at first agreed but then was dissuaded by Chief Procurator Pobedonostsev, an octogenarian, who feared that freedom of institutions and movements would lead to revolution. Under the pressure of the Holy Synod, however, Pobedonostsev sent questionnaires to all diocesan bishops regarding their views on church reforms. Almost all of the responses, published in three huge folios, called for convocation of a church council and radical reforms, beginning with the freeing of the church from any form of bureaucratic control. A majority of bishops were in favor of some form of participation by the lower clergy and laity in the national ecclesiastical councils. Two preconciliar conferences of the country's leading theologians, in 1906 and 1912, prepared the agenda for the *sobor,* or council, should it be convened.

The first "wake-up call" to the Russian intelligentsia was the 1905-6 revolution, with its ugly mobs and senseless terrorist murders of state employees, from state officials to traffic policemen. The premonition of worse things to come led a group of former Marxist, neo-Christian intellectuals, most of whom had participated in the 1901-3 religiophilosophical meetings, to issue *Landmarks* (1907), a volume appealing to the radical intelligentsia to turn away from radicalism. The book argued that the constitution of October 1905 had opened the way to gradual political and institutional reforms and that the duty now of the intelligentsia was to become a partner with the government, urging it forward in the reforming and gradual democratization of the empire. The message was not heeded at the time, since the intelligentsia's radical majority considered its duty to be constantly in conflict with the government.

To strengthen its position in the Duma (the parliament of czarist Russia), the government used all legal resources to bring priests into the Duma. To the government's disappointment, however, most of the elected rural priests joined leftist factions, while the two bishops allotted seats in the Duma belonged to the right wing. In 1907 the Holy Synod forbade the clergy to join the socialists, on the pain of defrocking. This action was justified, since the radical socialist parties were actively engaged in terrorist actions obviously incompatible with Christian ethics.

Parallel to the 1907 publication by Christian politicians and philosophers — which included such thinkers as Peter Struve (1870-1944), Nicolas Berdyaev (1874-1948), and Sergius Bulgakov (1871-1944) — there was a reform-oriented movement of church renewal consisting of highly educated academic clergy and laity. It fully supported the reform-oriented bishops but feared that the restoration of the patriarchate would lead to despotism by the bishops over the lower clergy. N. P. Aksakov (1848-1909), a lay theologian and an associate of the church renewal movement, wrote in favor of restoring a married episcopate, arguing that the monasticism and contemplation required of a monk were incompatible with the primarily administrative and political functions required of a bishop. The movement also demanded separation of the church from the state and the active participation of the church in public life. With the political reaction of 1907, the renewal movement was silenced by the Holy Synod.

After 1906, however, Nicholas II rejected all petitions for convening a church council. In his view, the time was not ripe for a council as long as the country had not been fully pacified.

4.6. ***Restoration of the Patriarchate***

Since the czar was formally the terrestrial head of the Russian Orthodox Church, his abdication in March 1917 "decapitated" the church, for the synodal system had only a vertical dimension, from top downward. Nevertheless, the collapse of the monarchy caused a general euphoria. The Provisional Government declared religious freedom, recognized the Orthodox Church as first among equals, and enabled it to receive subsidies from the state.

The 564-strong All-Russian Ecclesiastical Council, consisting of bishops, monastics, parish clergy, and laity — the first democratically elected, fully representative Local Council in Russian history since 1700 — convened in August 1917 in Moscow. That May, however, the synod, now consisting of liberal bishops and priests, permitted local diocesan assemblies of priests and laity to depose or reelect bishops. This action led to the forced retirement of bishops who had colluded with the infamous Rasputin (1872?-1916), including the metropolitans of St. Petersburg and Moscow.

The *Sobor* officially represented 117 million Orthodox Christians; over 75,000 churches, 58 chapels, and monasteries; 67 dioceses, with 130 bishops; over 50,000 priests and deacons; and seminaries and 35,000 parochial schools, approximately one-quarter of all primary schools in the empire. Atheism, however, had been spreading rapidly among the lower classes, particularly among young industrial workers educated by radical teachers in the secular state and *zemstva* schools. As one delegate said: "We say we have 110 million Orthodox Christians, but in reality we might have only 10 million." Indeed, according to reports of military chaplains, once the Provisional Government freed Orthodox soldiers from obligatory Communion, the percentage of soldiers taking Communion fell from nearly 100 percent in 1916 to less than 10 percent in 1917. Many of these young men were potential recruits for the Bolshevik antireligious campaigns, persecutions, and murders of clergy and other church activists.

Thanks to all the preparatory work carried out by preconciliar steering committees, numerous major decisions were adopted restoring full canonicity to the church by making it self-governing and independent of the state. The Local Council was divided, however, on the issue of restoring the patriarchate. Only when it became obvious that the Bolsheviks would be victorious did the propatriarchal party prevail, though it was forced to accept several limitations on the patriarch's powers. Local Councils were to meet every three years, when all elected offices would be subject to reelection. Moreover, in addition to the Synod of Bishops, partly elected by the council and partly appointed by the synod, there was now to be a permanent Higher Church Council, consisting mostly of laity and subject to reelection by Local Councils. The patriarch, as chairman of all these bodies, had two votes in case of a tie in elections.

The first patriarch elected by the council was Tikhon (1866-1925), the metropolitan of Moscow and former Russian missionary archbishop of North America. As bishop and pastor, he was loved by ordinary people. The council also authorized the participation by lay parishioners in the choice of parish priests and candidates for episcopate. Another statute adopted by the council recognized the parish as an autonomous property-owning institution and decreed the cooperation of → clergy and laity, a statute modeled on one issued by Tikhon in 1907 in the United States during his tenure there.

Politically, the patriarch and the council tried to maintain neutrality during the civil war, with the right to pass moral judgment on both sides. Patriarch Tikhon and his council repeatedly appealed to both sides in the fighting to stop the bloodshed and to be merciful to prisoners of war. Finally, as news about the Bolshevik mass murders of clergy and laity multiplied, the patriarch issued his famous anathema of February 1, 1918, condemning the perpetrators of terror and calling on Orthodox Christians to form unarmed Christian brotherhoods for the defense of the church, using only the weapons of prayer and unity. He also issued several appeals to the Bolsheviks to discontinue their practice of taking hostages and staging mass executions.

5. The Communist Era (1917-91)

5.1. ***Persecution***

The first bishop to be killed by the Bolsheviks was Metropolitan Vladimir of Kiev, on January 26, 1918.

This was followed ultimately by the execution or death in concentration camps of several hundred bishops, well over 50,000 priests, close to 100,000 monks and nuns, and unaccounted millions of other active servants of the church.

The All-Russian Council was closed by the Bolsheviks in September 1918, when they confiscated the building in which it had been meeting. In October 1919, as the anti-Bolshevik White Russian army was approaching Moscow from the south, Patriarch Tikhon issued an encyclical that forbade his clergy to take sides in the civil war or to publicly greet the Whites. At the same time the patriarch declared his own and the church's civic recognition of, and loyalty to, the Soviet regime, adding that "nobody and nothing can deliver Russia from disorder . . . until the Russian has purified and reborn himself spiritually into a new person."

As early as August 1921, during a time of terrible famine, Patriarch Tikhon appealed to all his flock to share everything they had with those who were starving, and to the clergy to donate for relief all church treasures except the blessed objects used in the Eucharist. He called on world church leaders to send food to the hungry in Russia, yet he and the church were accused by Soviet propaganda of greediness and imprisoned, while thousands of clergy and church activists were murdered, allegedly for resisting the armed teams that were confiscating church treasures.

5.2. ***Lenin, Trotsky, and the Renovationists***
According to Karl Marx (1818-83), religion is a superstructure built on a material base; once this base is removed, religion will disappear. Lenin's decree of February 2, 1918 (January 20, old style), removed the physical base of the church. The government confiscated all church properties, including its places of worship, seminaries, schools, and bank accounts, and deprived the church of any legal status. Overnight the church as an institution ceased to exist. The Soviet state recognized only groups of lay believers (no fewer than 20 persons), who could negotiate with local governments to lease a building for worship. Since the church and believers were the last of society's priorities, they would get the church only if it was not needed for some secular use.

The church survived, owing to its defense groups, who were ready to die for it. Some 70,000 faithful belonged to such groups in Moscow, and roughly as many in St. Petersburg (renamed Leningrad in 1924).

About this time the Soviet press admitted that the church was showing signs of growth. Having seen the inaccuracy of Marx's predictions, Lenin turned to a policy of divide and conquer: tolerance of Protestant sects, but persecution of the Orthodox Church for being a part of the Old Regime. In 1920 Protestant sects and other minority religions began to be favored by the Soviet leadership. They were treated as victims of czarist persecutions and as socialists at heart. Baptists, Pentecostals, and other sects were allowed to form Christian agricultural communes. Aiming at diplomatic recognition by Western powers, the Soviets claimed in their press that the Orthodox Church was being repressed not as a church but as a former czarist partner in the suppression of the sectarians.

In March 1922 the Politburo (the executive committee of the Bolsheviks) accepted a plan of Leon Trotsky (1879-1940) to take advantage of the division in the Orthodox Church between the so-called Renovationists and those loyal to the patriarch. The Renovationists (not to be confused with the church renewal movement of 1905-6 that wanted the independence of the church from the state) were a collection of radical leftist groups of clergy that appeared with the fall of the monarchy. Known also as the "Living Church" movement, they declared themselves socialists, praised Lenin, and attempted to jump on the Soviet bandwagon.

Trotsky urged that the government support the Renovationists financially, on the condition that they break with the patriarch, and also urged them to petition the Soviet government to pardon the imprisoned (propatriarchal) clergy. Some arrested clergy were released, and outsiders were supposed to conclude that the Renovationists' appeals were genuine and that they were not a branch of the Soviet secret police (the GPU). This collaboration, though, simply turned the Renovationist clergy into obedient tools of the GPU. In his memorandum to the Politburo, Trotsky added that the Renovationists were of use only for a short time but then would have to be liquidated, since in the long run their modernism would appeal to the working class more than the conservatism of the patriarchal church.

At first the Renovationist schism appeared to have a future: thousands of priests, monks, and nuns of the patriarchal church were being executed or exiled to the extreme north, and more than two-thirds of all church buildings were handed over by the Soviet government to the Renovationists. Patriarch Tikhon himself was in prison awaiting trial and probable execution. But the Renovationist church buildings stood almost empty, while the patriarchal churches were overflowing.

The patriarch's arrest in 1922 caused an uproar in western Europe, especially in Britain, with whom the Soviet government was negotiating diplomatic recognition. The British government sent an ultimatum to the Soviets demanding the patriarch's release. In June 1923, after being forced to write a letter of apology to the Soviet government blaming himself for having been an opponent of the regime, Tikhon was released. Masses of laity, clergy, and bishops returned to the patriarchal fold. The Renovationist churches emptied. A church without a flock was of no use to the Bolsheviks.

In 1925, at a mere 60 years of age, Patriarch Tikhon died. To this day, some suspect foul play, yet his death did not slow down mass desertions from Renovationism to the patriarchal church.

5.3. ***Stalin and Khrushchev***

Widespread persecution of the church prevented the election of a successor to Tikhon. In contrast to both Renovationists and the sects, the patriarchal Orthodox Church continued to be refused any form of legal status until 1927. In that year Sergius, metropolitan of Moscow, was allowed to be named patriarchal administrator. The Soviets refused to grant any legal recognition to the Patriarchal Synod until Sergius, after four imprisonments, finally acceded to all Soviet demands and issued a mendacious declaration of loyalty in which he denied that the church was being persecuted and even thanked the Soviet government for "its care and concern for the needs of the church." At that very time several scores of thousands of bishops, priests, monks, and nuns were lingering away in the Arctic Solovetski (Solovki) Islands concentration camp. Metropolitan Sergius believed in vain that his actions would gain the release of the imprisoned clergy, allow reopening of a higher theological school in Leningrad, and receive permission to publish a church periodical.

Sergius perhaps thought that he had won some breathing space, but two years later came the bloodiest decade in Soviet history, from 1929 to 1939. The aim was once and for all to liquidate all religions and all clergy. The goal was almost reached: by 1939 only 4 of more than 200 archbishops survived in office; all the others were in hiding, in internal exile, in prisons or concentration camps, or had been executed. And of well over 30,000 parish churches functioning in 1929, fewer than 200 churches survived in 1939.

It was World War II that saved the Russian Orthodox Church. The German attack on the USSR occurred on Sunday, June 22, 1941. Although Joseph Stalin (1879-1953) waited ten days before addressing the nation, and Foreign Minister Vyacheslav Molotov (1890-1986) waited 20 hours to announce the beginning of the war, the patriarchal administrator, Metropolitan Sergius, announced the war to his parishioners that morning during the liturgy, delivering a fiery patriotic sermon calling the nation to its patriotic duty and hinting that the coming trials might blow away "poisonous fumes." He had his sermon mimeographed and distributed to all remaining open churches. The church started a massive campaign of collecting donations for the war needs, with Sergius informing Stalin of all these church activities. Stalin responded with a telegram of thanks but took no further action with the church for the next two years.

Finally, in 1943 Stalin realized that the church could be of use to him. In September he met with three of the four surviving metropolitans. (The fourth, Metropolitan Sergius [Voskresensky, 1898?-1944], remained in Latvia under German occupation, where he was later killed either by the Germans or by Soviet partisans as he tried to steer a line independent of the occupiers while publicly condemning Communism.) The result of the talks was a hurried semblance of a local Church Council at which the septuagenarian Metropolitan Sergius was unanimously elected patriarch. The church was allowed to reopen eight seminaries and two theological academies and to reopen fewer than 2,000 churches, a sharp contrast with the 7,000 churches opened in the German-controlled territories of the USSR.

This turnaround in Stalin's religious policies was motivated by several factors. First, Franklin Roosevelt and Winston Churchill told Stalin that the Western public would be much better disposed toward helping the USSR if it had been assured of religious freedom there. Second, the Church of England petitioned the Soviet government to permit it to visit the USSR to familiarize itself with the religious situation there. Third, with all the Orthodox churches that had been reopened in territories occupied by the Germans, Stalin needed to somewhat match that gesture when the territories would fall to the Soviets in order to placate the population in those areas. Additionally, the Teheran Conference was scheduled shortly after Stalin's encounter with the bishops, and Stalin wanted to appear there as a supporter of democracy.

Although Stalin's religious policies became somewhat tougher after the end of the war, on the whole he held to the 1943 agreement with the church; accordingly, the church had to repay Stalin by praising him in speeches by its hierarchs at all sorts of international peace congresses. The Russian bishops were forced to condemn "capitalist imperialism" and to present the Soviet Union as a supremely peace-loving state, publicly denying that

Russian Orthodox Church

the church encountered any problems in the USSR. In 1961, under Nikita Khrushchev (1953-64), the church was allowed to join the → World Council of Churches, which opened the door for some limited ecumenical contacts.

Although after the end of World War II some churches and monasteries began to be closed, real persecutions with the obvious aim of total annihilation of the church began under Khrushchev. He closed five of the eight seminaries that had been reopened under Stalin. At the 1961 Communist Party Congress he promised to liquidate all traces of religion by 1980, when Communism was to be fully achieved, which, according to Karl Marx, could happen only after all religious belief had withered away. Of the almost 14,000 Orthodox churches surviving at the time of Khrushchev's ascent to power, fewer than 7,000 remained open by the 1980s. A similar fate befell all other religious confessions.

6. End of Repression

The 21 years between Khrushchev's forced retirement in October 1964 (the first bloodless coup in Soviet history) and the ascendancy in 1985 of Mikhail Gorbachev (b. 1931) are known as the era of stagnation and gerontology-in-power. Khrushchev's antireligious assault continued but at a much slower pace.

Things began to change radically in favor of the church in 1987-88 with the approach of the millennium of Russia's conversion to Christianity. The church was allowed to hold international conferences on the history, culture, and theology of Orthodox Christianity. For the first time since the 1920s, Russian scholars in secular fields were allowed to participate, including Boris Rauschenbach (1915-2001), a leader of the Soviet space program, who was not only a believer but a theologian of note.

In 1988 a Local Council of bishops, clergy, and laity met in Moscow. It adopted a statute widening the rights of clergy and parish councils in running their parishes. The statute obligated the patriarch to convene a Local Council at least every five years and a Bishops' Council at least every two years. It was thought at the time that *sobornost* (conciliarity) was at last returning to the church.

The turning point in church-state relations came in April 1990, at a reception by Gorbachev of the leadership of the Russian Orthodox Church. The latter requested civil → rights for all religious believers equal to those of the atheists and the right to open as many churches and theological schools as the church needed. All requests were granted, and later that year a new law declared the Soviet Union a secular state, with equal rights for believers and atheists.

The next Local Council met after the death of Patriarch Pimen (1910-90) and on June 11, 1990, elected Alexis II (Ridiger, b. 1929) as the new patriarch. He at first toyed with the idea of reconvening the council of 1917-18, revising, adopting, and completing its work, but soon that idea was dropped.

On August 19, 1991, a group of Communist diehards attempted a coup against Gorbachev but failed. The anti-Communist forces headed by Boris Yeltsin (b. 1931), president of the Russian Republic, prevailed when the special paramilitary forces went over to his side. When Gorbachev returned to Moscow from an enforced rest in Crimea, power was already in Yeltsin's hands. Shortly thereafter, on December 26, the Soviet Union officially dissolved.

7. Post-Soviet Russia

In contrast to Gorbachev, Yeltsin openly sided with the Orthodox Church and attended services on main feast days. The currently ruling president, Vladimir Putin, has repeatedly stated that he was baptized as an adult and is a practicing Orthodox Christian.

As Russia opened its borders in the early 1990s, thousands of aggressive evangelists of all sorts flocked to Russia, mostly from North America. They typically showed no respect for Russian Christian traditions. The Russian Orthodox Church, coming out of seven decades of suppression, could not compete with these → missionaries and began to pressure President Yeltsin to rewrite the religious law in favor of the Orthodox Church. The new law, passed in 1997, which Yeltsin signed reluctantly under the pressure of Patriarch Alexis and the Russian Parliament, gives full rights to only four so-called historical religions, namely, Russian Orthodoxy, → Islam, → Buddhism, and → Judaism. Of these four, Orthodoxy alone is described as "having played a special role in the history of Russia, in the assertion and development of her spirituality and culture." The other three religions are mentioned as "respected by the State as an inseparable part of the Russian historical legacy." (Ironically, their historical legitimacy is based on their registration 50 years earlier in an antireligious Soviet law!) All other religions would have to prove their existence in Russia for 15 years as private organizations before they could apply for state recognition.

The Bishops' Council of 2000, dedicated to the second millennium of Christianity, revised the 1988 statute giving expanded rights to clergy and parish councils. It mentions Local Councils without stating their periodicity. The main report at that council, delivered by Metropolitan Filaret of Minsk, declared that Local Councils were no longer necessary and could be replaced by bishops' assemblies. In any case, there have been only Bishops' Councils since 1990. According to canon law only a larger council can override a smaller council, while here a small Bishops' Council annulled decisions of the Great Moscow Council of 1917-18, as well as those of 1988.

The 2000 Bishops' Council adopted the first-ever "Foundations of the Russian Orthodox Social Concept," or FROSC. A notable point of FROSC is an affirmation of the right and Christian duty to resist evil and to disregard the state's orders if they contradict Christ's teaching. The document is realistic in admitting that believing Christians are a minority in Russia. In contrast to the Roman Catholic social doctrine based on Leo XIII's self-confident and all-inclusive encyclical *Rerum novarum* (1891), FROSC, although urging the church's involvement in the secular world, is predominantly eschatological. Sadly missing in the document is the eucharistic ecclesiology of such Russian émigré theologians as Georges Florovsky (1893-1979) and Alexander Schmemann (1921-83).

Sobornost is not even mentioned in FROSC. The post-Soviet Orthodox Church does not come close to → conciliarity. It has a pyramidal structure with no feedback and no rights vis-à-vis each echelon of higher authority. While the policies of the Russian state have changed dramatically from Soviet times, the patriarchate and its Holy Synod remain the last bastions of the Soviet era. (The synod is popularly referred to as the "Metropolitburo.") Another lacuna in this document is its complete silence on the seven decades of the church's life under the Communist terror. Christendom has been waiting in vain for disclosures from the Russian Orthodox Church regarding its uniquely tragic experience of survival under an actively and mercilessly cruel theomachistic → totalitarianism. The document mentions the French Revolution but remains suspiciously silent on the Bolshevik tyranny.

The post-Soviet Russian government recognizes its responsibility for the previous destruction of churches and other church-owned buildings. By now most of the church buildings have been returned to the church, and local governments, as well as some wealthy individuals, have been donating generous subsidies for the construction and renovation of churches and monasteries. But most of the secular buildings that used to belong to the church have not been returned — this process is much slower and rather erratic.

Since the collapse of Communism numerous public opinion polls have been taken concerning the beliefs of contemporary Russians. Briefly, the situation at the beginning of the 21st century appears to be the following: among ethnic Russians, about 70 percent describe themselves as religious believers, over 80 percent describe themselves as Orthodox Christians, but only 2-3 percent regularly attend church services. Surprisingly, in some surveys the percentage of people calling themselves Orthodox Christians exceeds those who believe in God.

Since the late 1980s the number of Orthodox churches in the Russian Republic has grown from 4,000 to over 15,000, served by about 13,000 priests. This rate of church openings has forced the church to ordain priests without proper education; in fact, less than half of the priests currently serving have a full → theological education. Most of the others are "ritual performers," as Russians call them, and are unprepared to preach and to teach an increasingly sophisticated flock. This deficiency of the leadership is one of the most acute contemporary church problems, which the present church leadership has so far been unable to solve. Two other critical problems are the need for a respect for legality and the development of a significant horizontal dimension of church life.

→ Orthodox Christianity; Orthodox Church

Bibliography: N. Afanasiev, *Tserkov' Dukha Sviatogo* (Church of the Holy Spirit) (Paris, 1971) • A. Agadjanian, "Breakthrough to Modernity: Apologia for Traditionalism. The Russian Orthodox View of Society and Culture in Comparative Perspective," *RelStSo* 31/4 (2003) 327-46 • P. Bushkovitch, *Religion and Society in Russia: The Sixteenth and Seventeenth Centuries* (Oxford, 1992) • M. Cherniavsky, *Tsar and People: Studies in Russian Myth* (New Haven, 1961) • S. Chetverikov, *Moldavski starets Paisi Velichkovskii* (Moldavian starets Paisi Velichkovskii) (Paris, n.d.) • J. W. Cunningham, *A Vanquished Hope: The Movement for Church Renewal in Russia, 1905-06* (Crestwood, N.Y., 1981) • J. Ellis, *The Russian Orthodox Church: A Contemporary History* (London, 1986) • G. P. Fedotov, *The Russian Religious Mind* (2 vols.; London, 1965-66); idem, *St. Filipp, Metropolitan of Moscow: Encounter with Ivan the Terrible* (Belmont, Mass., 1978); idem, *Sviatye drevnei Rusi* (Saints of ancient Rus) (New York, 1960) • J. Fennell, *The Crisis of Medieval Russia: 1200-1304* (London, 1983); idem, *The Emergence of Moscow: 1304-1359* (London, 1968); idem, *A History of the Russian Church to 1448* (London, 1995) • G. Florovsky, *Aspects of Church History* (Belmont, Mass., 1975); idem, *Bible, Church, Tradition: An Eastern Orthodox View* (Belmont, Mass., 1972); idem, *Christianity and Culture*

(Belmont, Mass., 1974); idem, *Puti russkogo bogoslovia* (Ways of Russian theology) (Paris, 1988) • GRUPPA PETERBURGSKIKH SVIASHCHENNIKOV, *K tserkovnomu soboru* (To the church council) (St. Petersburg, 1906) • A. V. KARTASHEV, *Ocherki po istorii Russkoi tserkvi* (Essays on the history of the Russian church) (vols. 1-2; Paris, 1959); idem, *Tserkov', istoria, Rossia. Statii i vystuplenia* (Church, history, Russia. Articles and speeches) (Moscow, 1996) • A. V. KARTASHEV, I. A. STRATONOV, and METROPOLITAN ELEVFERI, *Iz istorii Khristianskoi tserkvi na rodine i za rubezhom v XX stoletii* (On the history of the Christian church in the homeland and abroad in the 20th cent.) (Moscow, 1995) • S. V. LOBACHEV, *Patriarch Nikon* (St. Petersburg, 2003) • J. MARTIN, *Medieval Russia, 980-1584* (Cambridge, 1995) • J. MEYENDORFF, *The Byzantine Legacy in the Orthodox Church* (Crestwood, N.Y., 1982); idem, *Byzantium and the Rise of Russia* (Crestwood, N.Y., 1989); idem, *Catholicity and the Church* (Crestwood, N.Y., 1983); idem, *Study of Gregory Palamas* (Crestwood, N.Y., 1964) • A. NICHOLS, *Theology in Russian Diaspora: Church, Fathers, Eucharist in Nicolai Afanas'ev* (Cambridge, 1989) • L. NICHOLS and T. G. STAVROU, eds., *Russian Orthodoxy under the Old Regime* (Minneapolis, 1978) • D. OBOLENSKY, *The Byzantine Commonwealth: Eastern Europe, 500-1453* (Crestwood, N.Y., 1974) • N. N. POKROVSKY and S. G. PETROV, eds., *Arkhivy Kremlia. Politburo i tserkov', 1922-1925* (Archives of the Kremlin. The Politburo and the church, 1922-1925) (2 vols.; Novosibirsk, 1997-98) • D. V. POSPIELOVSKY, *A History of Marxist-Leninist Atheism and Soviet Anti-Religion* (3 vols.; Crestwood, N.Y., 1987-88); idem, *The Orthodox Church in the History of Russia* (Crestwood, N.Y., 1998); idem, *The Russian Church under the Soviet Regime* (2 vols.; Crestwood, N.Y., 1984) • N. V. RIASANOVSKY, *A History of Russia* (6th ed.; Oxford, 2000) • S. V. RIMSKY, *Rossiyskaia tserkov' v epokhu velikikh reform* (The Russian church in the era of major reform [1860-1970s]) (Moscow, 1999) • R. R. ROBSON, *Old Believers in Modern Russia* (DeKalb, Ill., 1995) • A. SCHMEMANN, *The Historical Road of Eastern Orthodoxy* (Crestwood, N.Y., 1977) • M. V. SHKAROVSKY, *Natsistskaia Germania i Pravoslavnaia Tserkov'* (Nazi Germany and the Orthodox Church) (Moscow, 2002) • E. N. TRUBETSKOI, *Icons: Theology in Color* (Crestwood, N.Y., 1973) • P. VALLIERE, *Modern Russian Theology: Bukharev, Soloviev, Bulgakov. Orthodox Theology in a New Key* (Grand Rapids, 2000) • S. A. ZENKOVSKY, *Russia's Old-Believers* (Munich, 1970) • N. ZERNOV, *The Russian Religious Renaissance of the Twentieth Century* (London, 1963); idem, *The Russians and Their Church* (3d ed.; London, 1978).

DIMITRY V. POSPIELOVSKY

Ruth, Book of

1. Narrative Elements

The Book of Ruth is a tightly crafted narrative; interpreters consider it a short story or novella. That is, the way it makes sense is as a narrative. And to make sense of it readers need to attend to characterization, setting, and plot.

1.1. *Characterization*

The major characters in the book are Naomi, Ruth, and Boaz. There are also minor characters: Elimelech, Mahlon, Chilion, Orpah, the women of Bethlehem, field hands, the relative nearer than Boaz, and the baby Obed. These characters are known through their own speech and actions; the narrator does not intrude to help us understand them by editorial comment. Readers know the most about Naomi's internal life, and that is because she tells us. Ruth and Boaz have some moving speeches, but they do not disclose what they are feeling or why they behave the way they do.

For Naomi the movement is from a full life through loss of all that she values to restoration. In the structure of ancient Israel, a woman's social place and economic well-being depended on belonging to a male-headed household. At the beginning of the story, even though there is a famine in Judah, Naomi enjoys status because of her marriage, and future security because of her sons. Their deaths in the opening verses of the book leave her with nothing she values. She tries to turn away the two daughters-in-law, who intend to return to Bethlehem with her, but only one of them accepts her urging. On her return to Bethlehem, Naomi describes herself as a bitter and empty woman. Through Ruth, she is restored to a full life.

Ruth, too, loses a husband in the opening verses of the story. We might expect that she, as a Moabite woman without an Israelite man to give her an identity, would disappear from the story. But Ruth claims Israelite identity by pledging herself to Naomi and so becomes the central agent in Naomi's restoration. At pivotal points in the text, other characters point out that Ruth's behavior is not what is expected of a woman in ancient patriarchal culture. Naomi urges her to return to her mother's household and remarry; Boaz praises her for not choosing a younger man. Naomi and Ruth thus work cooperatively to regain social standing through Ruth's marriage to Boaz.

For Boaz, the marriage expands his life, already full by material standards, into one of family and relationship and, as seen from the concluding genealogy, into the ancestry of the Davidic monarchy.

1.2. *Setting*

The temporal setting is in the time of the judges, and the concluding genealogy shows that the story takes place just three generations before King → David. The first chapter contains geographic movement from Bethlehem to Moab and back to Bethlehem, where the rest of the story takes place. The symbolic movement is from famine/death to deepest emptiness and then to restoration.

1.3. *Plot*

The division of the book into four chapters follows the movement of the plot. The first chapter sets the stage, bringing Elimelech, Naomi, and their sons to Moab, then removing the male characters while adding two women before removing one of them. It then links the two remaining women by Ruth's oath, brings them back to Bethlehem, and introduces the Bethlehem women, in the course of which Naomi describes her bitterness.

The second chapter begins the harvest and introduces Boaz and the reaping crew. It establishes cooperative planning between Ruth and Naomi, with Ruth being the principal actor of the two.

The third chapter is the pivotal one in the plot, with Ruth's approach to Boaz at night on the threshing floor, her request for his protection as kinsman, the complication of the nearer kinsman, and Boaz's promise to act as redeeming kinsman if the other will not.

The fourth chapter gives the happy ending: the nearer kinsman demurs; Boaz and Ruth marry and produce a son, to whom Naomi becomes foster mother. The book ends with a genealogy from Perez to David.

2. Historical-Critical Matters

The dating of the text is difficult. Most interpreters date it either quite early, around the time of Solomon, in which case it may function to provide an ancestral story for the Davidic line, or quite late, around the time of Ezra-Nehemiah, in which case it may provide a gentle argument for inclusion of foreigners into the postexilic community.

Authorship is unknown. The story reflects a tradition of levirate marriage in which a dead man's brother was obligated to marry the widow if there were no sons. The story is not otherwise reflected in the Hebrew Bible. There is no external indication that the story reflects historical events, nor any evidence that it could not. The power of the story resides in its narrative force, not in its correspondence to history. Ruth is among the biblical texts for which some interpreters imagine female authorship. The development of women characters, emphasis on women's relationships, and use of "mother's house" (1:8) rather than the usual "father's house" can support this hypothesis, but it is impossible to prove.

In Jewish tradition Ruth is one of the → Megilloth, the five festal scrolls, and is the one read at Shavuot (→ Jewish Practices 2). Ruth enters Christian tradition within the NT, where she appears in Matthew's genealogy of Jesus (1:5), one of four women aside from Mary herself.

3. Central Concepts

3.1. *Redeemer*

The legal background of redemption is in Leviticus 25 for both property and persons. The redeemer (Heb. *gō'ēl*) is a male relative who can come to the rescue of one whose property or person is compromised because of financial exigency. So if one must sell land that belongs to the ancestral allotment, the redeemer buys it back; if a person is sold to a foreigner as a slave, the redeemer is also to buy the person back. The use in Ruth suggests that there is a relationship between the right to buy a field as redeemer and the obligation to enter a levirate marriage.

3.2. *Levirate Marriage*

Deut. 25:5-10 provides for a man whose brother dies childless to marry the widow and produce a son to be considered heir of the deceased. An unusual factor in the way this concept is used in Ruth is that the child born to Ruth and Boaz is described not as the son of Ruth's deceased husband but as the son of Naomi.

4. Theological Implications

God is not a direct character in the book: there is no divine speech and no narrative account of divine activity. References to the deity are all indirect, with the characters presenting a concept of God as the one behind events. Naomi initially sees the presence of God behind the disasters of her life, but the preponderance of references to the deity involve blessing. One might imagine this narrative as the inverse of Job 1:21 — the Lord takes away, and the Lord gives; blessed be the name of the Lord. Because the end of the book includes the ancestry of David, a reader might also be inclined to see the monarchy as a gift of divine → providence.

5. Function

What is the book doing? It is always dangerous to reduce a narrative to a single straightforward message. For all its narrative simplicity, Ruth is a book with multiple possibilities for the interpreter.

It is an understated narrative and does not seem to have a polemical tone — and yet it presents a claim about a Moabite ancestry for the great King David that flies in the face of postexilic xenophobia.

Ruth is also a book about → friendship and → faithfulness. It illustrates care for elders and the maintenance of community standing, even when rebuffed. It also illustrates blessing coming through the one who was rejected.

For the reader who believes in providence, the narrative provides an illustration. Divine blessing is perceived behind the rebuilding of a life for Ruth and Naomi. This is also a story in which even a woman, even a foreign woman, can be of value. Ruth is an instrument of blessing, not only for Naomi but also for the whole people, who are remembering David as the great national identity figure.

Bibliography: Commentaries: A. LACOCQUE (ContCom; Minneapolis, 2004) • A.-J. LEVINE, "Ruth," *The Women's Bible Commentary* (ed. C. A. Newsom and S. H. Ringe; London and Louisville, Ky., 1992) 78-84 • M. MASENYA (NGWANA' MPHAHLELE), "Ruth," *Global Bible Commentary* (ed. D. Patte; Nashville, 2004) 86-91 • K. NIELSEN (OTL; Louisville, Ky., 1997) • K. A. ROBERTSON-FARMER (NIB 2; Nashville, 1998) 889-946 • K. D. SAKENFELD (Interp.; Louisville, Ky., 1999) • J. M. SASSON (BiSe; 2d ed.; Sheffield, 1989) • G. WEST, "Ruth," *Eerdmans Commentary on the Bible* (ed. J. D. G. Dunn and J. W. Rogerson; Grand Rapids, 2003) 208-12.

Other works: J. A. KATES and G. T. REIMER, eds., *Reading Ruth: Contemporary Women Reclaim a Sacred Story* (New York, 1994) • P. TRIBLE, "A Human Comedy," *God and the Rhetoric of Sexuality* (Philadelphia, 1978) 166-99.

ELIZABETH HUWILER

Rwanda

1. General Situation
2. Religious Situation
   2.1. Roman Catholic Church
   2.2. Protestants
   2.3. Church and State

	1960	*1980*	*2000*
Population (1,000s):	2,742	5,163	7,674
Annual growth rate (%):	2.99	3.18	2.37

Area: 26,338 sq. km. (10,169 sq. mi.)

A.D. 2000

Population density: 291/sq. km. (755/sq. mi.)
Births / deaths: 4.11 / 1.74 per 100 population
Fertility rate: 5.45 per woman
Infant mortality rate: 113 per 1,000 live births
Life expectancy: 45.1 years (m: 43.7, f: 46.4)
Religious affiliation (%): Christians 82.0 (Roman Catholics 50.8, Protestants 20.8, Anglicans 7.8, indigenous 1.9, other Christians 0.6), tribal religionists 9.8, Muslims 7.8, other 0.4.

1. General Situation

The Rwandese Republic, in east-central Africa, is bordered by Uganda, Tanzania, Burundi, and the Democratic Republic of the Congo (→ Zaire). The frontiers were fixed during the colonial period (→ Colonialism), during which Rwanda was controlled first by Germany (from 1890), then by Belgium (from 1923).

The official languages of Rwanda are French, English, and Kinyarwanda. The principal people groups are Hutu (85 percent of the population in 2003), Tutsi (14 percent), and Twa (1 percent). Tensions between these groups, in large part fueled by historical grievances, have at times been high, leading to widespread violence (→ Force, Violence, Nonviolence). The minority Tutsi, supported by the colonial powers, for centuries dominated the majority Hutu. In 1959 Hutu discontent sparked a revolt that overthrew the Tutsi monarch and led to the exodus of many Tutsi. A republic was established in 1961, and independence was granted in 1962. Grégoire Kayibanda, a Hutu, became president. In 1963 a Tutsi-led rebel army unsuccessfully attempted to gain control of the country, and a large-scale massacre of Tutsis followed. The government continued under Hutu control, but power changed hands in 1973 when Juvénal Habyarimana, a Hutu and the defense minister, led a bloodless coup and gained control of the country.

Tensions again flared in 1990 when the Rwandan Patriotic Front (RPF), a rebel force consisting primarily of exiled Tutsis, invaded from their base in Uganda. Although a multiparty → democracy was established in 1991, fighting continued until 1992, when a cease-fire and political talks were agreed to. The Rwandan government and the RPF rebels reached a peace accord in 1993.

Massive violence erupted in April 1994, however,

after a plane carrying both Habyarimana and the president of Burundi was shot down, killing both men. Extremist Hutu militias immediately began to massacre large numbers of Tutsis and moderate Hutus. Approximately 800,000 were killed between April and July of that year, and an estimated 2 million Rwandans fled the country, with an additional 1 million internally displaced. The efforts of foreign peacekeeping forces were limited in scope and effectiveness, and the RPF eventually defeated the Hutu-dominated Rwandan army, gaining control over the capital, Kigali, in July 1994. The RPF established a coalition government with Pasteur Bizimungu, a moderate Hutu, as president. There was an outpouring of international humanitarian aid; the peacekeeping operation UNAMIR (U.N. Assistance Mission for Rwanda) remained in Rwanda until April 1996.

The Rwandan government was faced with the difficult tasks of resettling → refugees, alleviating → poverty, and pursuing justice and → reconciliation. By the end of 1996 almost a million of the refugees had returned in successive waves. Earlier, in 1994, the → United Nations established the International Criminal Tribunal for Rwanda. Results were slow, and in order to deal with the large number of cases waiting to be heard, the government began to implement the more traditional village-level system of justice, known as *gacaca.*

In 2000 Bizimungu was succeeded as president by Paul Kagame, former leader of the RPF forces and the first Tutsi president since independence. A new constitution was adopted in 2003, when Kagame was elected to a seven-year term.

Rwanda is one of the most densely populated countries in Africa. Its economy was severely disrupted by the → genocide, and then by the Central African War in neighboring Democratic Republic of Congo. Agriculture (mainly coffee and tea) contributes over 40 percent to its economy, industry only 20 percent. Rwanda is landlocked, which adds significantly to its transportation costs and to the need for maintaining good transport linkages through neighboring countries, especially Kenya, Uganda, and Tanzania.

Rwanda relies heavily on international aid. The government faces additional challenges in rebuilding the education system and in combating AIDS, which in 2000 affected about 10 percent of the population.

2. Religious Situation

Over 80 percent of the people of Rwanda are Christians, with Roman Catholics the largest group. Followers of traditional African religions form the second largest religious group (→ Guinea 2). These religions do not have firmly fixed cultic practices. Many Christians, though, as well as members of other religions, take part secretly in cultic celebrations by night.

→ Islam, the third largest religion in the country, is making serious efforts to expand in Rwanda. Financial incentives support its missionary work, and Muslims have now begun to build schools. A number of former Christians converted to Islam after the genocide, in which the perpetrators were seen as Christians. Some Tutsi were protected by Muslim neighbors, who were largely exempt from the killings.

Many of the older churches are now seeking to regain the trust of their former members. Church buildings were unfortunately the site of some of the massacres, and although some clergy and church workers attempted to stop the slaughter and help its victims, others watched silently or even participated in the killings.

After the 1994 genocide many churches, religious organizations, and other humanitarian groups began providing aid in the form of food, medical and psychological services, and help for orphans and widows. In addition, some groups have been working more directly for justice and reconciliation.

In April 2004 the Protestant Council of Rwanda (founded in 1935, comprising Anglicans, Baptists, Free Methodists, and Presbyterians), the Alliance of Evangelical Churches (a member of the → Worldwide Evangelical Alliance), the → All Africa Conference of Churches, and the → World Council of Churches convened a workshop in Kigali. It issued the Kigali Covenant, an important statement recognizing the failure of local churches and of the larger ecumenical community to address the genocide and urgently calling for the resources needed to complete the task of reconciliation and restoration. Delegates acknowledged the need to be proactive in preventing conflicts and to speak out against any "pronouncements or practices that have the tendency to set one group of people against another."

2.1. ***Roman Catholic Church***

The → Roman Catholic Church initiated Christian mission in 1900 when French → missionaries arrived from Burundi. They sought to secure the conversion of tribal heads and to start schools for their children, a strategy that was very successful, and now the church is the largest Christian community in the country. The first national → priest was ordained in 1917, and the first → bishop consecrated in 1952. The Archdiocese of Kabgayi was formed in

1959. During the violence of 1994, three bishops and about 25 percent of the clergy were killed. In 1997 the Vatican donated $50,000 to help ensure fair trials for religious who were implicated in the violence. In 2003 there were 511 priests serving 3.8 million Catholics.

2.2. *Protestants*

The first Protestants to come to Rwanda were Lutherans of the German Bethel Mission (→ German Missions), who arrived from Tanganyika (modern Tanzania) in 1907. After World War I all German missionaries were expelled, but in the early 1920s the Reformed Société Belge de la Mission Protestante au Congo took up their work and helped form the Église Presbytérienne au Rwanda (→ Reformed and Presbyterian Churches). → Adventists came to Rwanda in 1919, and now are the third largest Christian body in the country. Anglicans, the second-largest church, arrived with the Rwanda Mission of the Church Missionary Society in 1920 (→ Anglican Communion; British Missions).

In 1939 Danish missionaries (→ Scandinavian Missions) from Burundi started the Églises Baptistes au Rwanda (→ Baptists). In 1942 Swedish and Swiss missionaries from the Belgian Congo founded the Église de Pentecôte. Efforts of North American missionaries led to the Église Méthodiste Libre au Rwanda (→ Methodist Churches) in 1943, and to the Association des Églises Baptistes in 1965. Nationals played a big part in missionary work in Rwanda, a fact that histories have largely ignored (→ Mission 3).

In the late 1990s Pentecostal and charismatic renewal movements spread through many of the older churches, and many new → Pentecostal churches have sprung up. The growing membership of the new churches may in part be attributed to a desire to disassociate with the failures of the older churches during the genocide.

2.3. *Church and State*

Relations between → church and state are good. The two work together on developmental issues. There is → religious liberty, with the state expecting respect from the churches. The new constitution (see 1) guarantees freedom of religion and prohibits political organizations that are based on ethnicity or religion.

→ African Theology

Bibliography: D. B. Barrett, G. T. Kurian, and T. M. Johnson, *WCE* (2d ed.) 1.629-32 • R. Dallaire, *Shake Hands with the Devil: The Failure of Humanity in Rwanda* (Toronto, 2003) • A. Destexhe, *Rwanda and Genocide in the Twentieth Century* (New York, 1995) • A. Kagame, *La philosophie bantu comparée* (Paris, 1976) • D. Kamukama, *Rwanda Conflict: Its Roots and Regional Implications* (2d ed.; Kampala, Uganda, 1997) • A. Karamaga, *L'évangile en Afrique. Ruptures et continuité* (Morges, Switz., 1990) • H. McCullum, *The Angels Have Left Us: The Rwanda Tragedy and the Churches* (Geneva, 1995) • L. Melvern, *Conspiracy to Murder: The Rwandan Genocide* (London, 2004) • G. Prunier, *The Rwanda Crisis: History of a Genocide* (New York, 1995) • P. St. John, *Breath of Life: The Story of the Ruanda Mission* (London, 1971) • M. Twagirayesu and J. van Butselaar, *Histoire de l'Église Presbytérienne au Rwanda, 1907-1982* (Kigali, 1982).

Faustin Rwagacuzi† and the Editors

S

Sabbatarians

1. "Sabbatarian" is a term used for Christians who insist that the → Sabbath commandment, like the other nine (→ Decalogue), is still in force, with reference to either the seventh or the first day of the week. Normally agreeing with others that the day should be one of joy, worship, and rest, Sabbatarians also stress the prohibition of work. Sabbatarian trends, often linked to eschatological expectation, existed in many circles in pre-Reformation Europe (e.g., Finland, Hungary, Transylvania, and England), supported in the case of the Lord's Day by legislation dating from Emperors Constantine (306-37) and Justinian (527-65) that forbade work on → Sunday except when necessary in the fields.

During the → Reformation the Augsburg Confession of 1530 (art. 28) opposed Sabbatarians on the ground that the gospel of Christ abrogates the Sabbath day; nonetheless, Martin → Luther also stated in his Large Catechism that the church may designate a particular day for worship. In 1538 Luther argued similarly against the Bohemians in *Wider die Sabbather* (Against the Sabbatarians, *LW* 47.57-98). John → Calvin saw in the commandment a matter of ceremonial, not moral, law, carrying a promise of rest fulfilled in Christ and calling for spiritual observance (*Inst.* 2.8.28-34). Similarly, the Second → Helvetic Confession (1566) commended religious exercises and celebrations on the Lord's Day, but with "free observa-tion" (art. 24).

In contrast, Sabbatarians found a home in the later course of the Reformation in Britain, particularly with the emergence of → Puritanism. Scotland passed Sabbatarian legislation in 1579, and the Irish Articles of 1615 called for rest from common and daily business on Sunday (art. 56). The Westminster Confession of 1647, calling the Lord's day the Sabbath Day, stated the case for Sabbatarians, namely, that rest from "worldly employments and recreations" and devotion to worship and to "duties of necessity and mercy" are a "positive, moral, and perpetual commandment" (art. 21). The American churches in many cases took a similar line, such as the New Hampshire Baptists in their 1833 Confession. The Free Church of Scotland continues to take a strong Sabbatarian stand.

On the basis of ancient legislation Sunday has been a day of general freedom from employment in most Christianized countries, but Sabbatarian groups, such as the Lord's Day Alliance, founded in 1888 in North America, have had to mount campaigns, with much support in both Canada and Britain from labor unions, to prevent secular and commercial interests from hampering freedom of worship and from exploiting workers. The rise of → pluralism has made this effort increasingly difficult.

2. A minority of Sabbatarians have argued that Christians must continue to observe Saturday, rather than Sunday, as the Sabbath as stated in the Ten Commandments. Arising out of Puritanism, the Seventh Day Baptists formed their first congregation in England in 1650 and in the American colonies in 1671; they established the General Conference of Seventh Day Baptists in 1802. By the beginning of the 21st century there were about 4,800 members of the General Conference in the United States and Canada.

The largest Sabbatarian group is Seventh-day Adventism (→ Adventists), which emerged out of the Millerite Adventist revival of the 1840s, also being influenced by the Seventh Day Baptists. The General Conference of Seventh-day Adventists organized in 1863; by the early 21st century the denomination had spread worldwide and had a membership of nearly 14 million. Other, smaller Sabbatarian groups include the Seventh Day Adventist Reform Movement, the International Missionary Society, and several groups that left the → Worldwide Church of God in the 1980s and 1990s as it abandoned Sabbatarianism and other distinctive beliefs. Reflecting their minority position, Saturday Sabbatarians, particularly the Seventh-day Adventists, oppose Sunday legislation and argue for strict separation of → church and state.

3. Doctrinally, the primary issues of Sabbatarianism are two: whether the Sabbath commandment is of a piece with the other commandments or sui generis as a ceremonial and prefigurative injunction, and whether efforts to keep it strictly as part of moral duty to God might not involve legalism or even works righteousness. Biblically and historically, a basic question is whether the substitution of the Lord's Day for the Sabbath has any true justification. Practically, we must ask whether those Sabbatarians who seek or defend legislative protection for the Sunday Sabbath are right and how far they may do so with hope of success in modern secular societies. Conversely, they themselves may ask whether advocates of free observance will not see freedom of worship eroded and their own secularization so advanced that in effect there will soon be little or no observance at all.

Bibliography: A. Balbach, *The History of the Seventh Day Adventist Reform Movement* (Roanoke, Va., 1999) • B. Ball, *The Seventh-day Men: Sabbatarians and Sabbatarianism in England and Wales, 1600-1800* (Oxford, 1994) • D. Carson, ed., *From Sabbath to Lord's Day: A Biblical, Historical, and Theological Investigation* (Grand Rapids, 1982) • *Directory of Sabbath-Observing Groups* (9th ed.; Fairview, Okla., 2001) • T. Eskenazi, D. Harrington, and W. Shea, eds., *The Sabbath in Jewish and Christian Traditions* (New York, 1991) • G. Land, ed., *Adventism in American History* (Grand Rapids, 1986; 2d ed., Berrien Springs, Mich., 1998) • L. Nichols and G. Mather, *Discovering the Plain Truth: How the Worldwide Church of God Encountered the Gospel of Grace* (Downers Grove, Ill., 1998) • D. Sanford, *A Choosing People: The Story of the Seventh Day Baptists* (Nashville, 1992) • R. Schwarz and F. Greenleaf, *Light Bearers: A History of the Seventh-day Adventist Church* (Nampa, Idaho, 2000) • K. Strand, ed., *The Sabbath in Scripture and History* (Washington, D.C., 1982).

Gary Land

Sabbath

The seventh day of the week as a day of rest is one of the basic religious and social institutions of → Judaism and, along with → circumcision, a chief mark of Jewish → identity.

1. Term

In both biblical and postbiblical texts the usual term is *šabbāt*. We also find *šabbātôn* (also meaning "seventh year") and the combination *šabbat šabbātôn,* "Sabbath of complete rest," which can refer to the Sabbath year or to the Day of Atonement.

2. Origin

We have no clear knowledge of the origin of the term, which is etymologically obscure. Some derive it from the Heb. verb *šbt* (cease, celebrate), others from Akkad. *šab/pattu(m)* (the 15th day of the month), others from Heb. *šbʿ* (seven), others from Arab. *šbb* (increase, grow), and still others from Arab. *tbt* (sit).

Theories as to the origin of Sabbath observance include first a Kenite origin (B. D. Eerdmans), which would put the Sabbath before the conquest (→ Israel 1.2). The idea is that the nomadic Kenites, who worked with metals (see Gen. 4:22), kept the day of Saturn (cf. Exod. 32:3; Num. 15:32-36; Amos 5:26). Others look to Babylon (J. Meinhold, G. Robinson). They argue that the similarity in sound between *šabbāt* and the Babylonian *šab/pattu,* points in this direction and indicates an original reference to the day of the full moon. Others support an Ugaritic/Canaanite origin (J. Hehn, H. J. Kraus). Ugaritic texts refer to the division of the calendar into seven-year periods (Danel cycle) and also to cultic seventh-day festivals (Krt legend), which has led to the deduction of a seven-day week. Others again favor an Arabic derivation (D. Nielsen). The ancient Arab worship of the moon focused on four days in the month on which the moon was "sitting" *(tbt)* and thus offered a model for Israel's seven-day-week rhythm. None of these proposals has real cogency. They all suffer from uncertain references and inadequate linguistic and material support.

Theories from → sociology, such as derivation from a special day of rest for farm laborers (H. Webster) or the instituting of market days in an agrarian economy (E. Jenni), are also speculative. Nor can we prove for certain an origin within Israel itself.

The anchoring of the Sabbath commandment in the → Decalogue (Exod. 20:8-11; Deut. 5:12-15, for different reasons) and its place in the so-called → Book of the Covenant in Exod. (34:21) do at least point to early development.

References from the days of the monarchy in Amos 8:5; Hos. 2:11; Isa. 1:13; 2 Kgs. 4:23 mention the Sabbath along with the new moon, though with no closer definition. We may not for certain deduce any connection between the Sabbath and the cycle of the moon (e.g., the Sabbath as originally the day of the full moon). The link with the new moon is customary in later biblical texts (Ezek. 45:17; 46:1; Isa. 66:23; Neh. 10:33; 1 Chr. 23:31), and note also 1QM 2:4 and Col. 2:16. This fact argues for an original distinction between the monthly feast of the new moon and the weekly Sabbath.

The term "Sabbath" used consistently in postexilic texts as a reference to the seven-day week thus probably derives from the preexilic period (→ Israel 1.3-6). Other nonliterary evidence lends support, such as the Yavne Yam ostracon (ca. 625 B.C., *ANET* 568). Scholars debate whether the day was observed cultically (Isa. 1:13; Lev. 23:6) from the outset as one consecrated to God or whether it originally had only a social dimension as a public day of rest (Exod. 23:12; 34:21; Deut. 5:14c-15a).

After the exile (→ Israel 1.7) the Sabbath stood at the heart of the people's religious and social life. Some Priestly or Priestly oriented circles promoted and validated it in the postexilic situation as the main feast day, and in this way they made it an institution that marks the identity of Israel.

3. Biblical Evaluations and Regulations

The biblical texts engage in basic theological reflection on the institution of the Sabbath and also offer extensive rules for its observance. It is considered a sign of God's covenant with his people (Ezek. 20:12, 20; Exod. 31:13, 17a; "perpetual covenant" in v. 16). To observe the Sabbath is to keep the covenant (Isa. 56:6). Observance rests on recollection of the deliverance from Egypt (Deut. 5:15). Yet it is also set in the universal framework of a theology of creation. The seven-day week, with the Sabbath as the climax, corresponds to the order of creation in Gen. 1:1–2:3. Rest on the Sabbath stands related to God's rest when the work of → creation was done (Exod. 20:11; 31:17).

Doing no work defines the character of the Sabbath as a day of rest according to the prohibition in Exod. 20:10 and Deut. 5:14. Economic activity was originally in view (Amos 8:5; Isa. 58:13; Neh. 10:31a; 13:15-22; Jer. 17:21-22, 24, 27; Exod. 34:21). Then domestic duties were included: kindling fires in Exod 35:3, cooking and baking in 16:23, gathering wood in Num. 15:32, leaving home in Exod. 16:29 and Isa. 58:13, though compare 2 Kgs. 4:23. To underline the importance of the Sabbath for the community and its relation to God, the → death penalty was imposed for nonobservance (Exod. 31:14-15; 35:2; Num. 15:32-36). The → priests and Levites were allowed to discharge their cultic duties on the Sabbath. The weekly ministry at the → temple began on the Sabbath (2 Chr. 23:4, 8) with special offerings (Num. 28:9-10; Ezek. 46:4; 1 Chr. 23:31) and the renewing of the shewbread (Lev. 24:5-8; 1 Chr. 9:32).

Another proof of the importance of the Sabbath is the development of the fallow year (Exod. 23:10-11) and the year of release (Deut. 15:1-11) into the sabbatical year (Lev. 25:1-7; Neh. 10:31b), and the (presumably only ideal) establishment of the year of jubilee (Lev. 25:8-55) on the basis of the seven-year cycle. Note also the applying of the sabbatical year to the prophesying of an exile of 70 years (2 Chr. 36:21; Lev. 26:34-35; Jer. 25:11).

4. Developments in Judaism

4.1. These biblical developments found continuation in Judaism, as the Sabbath remained a basic element in Jewish life. Many customs arose that stressed the sanctity of the Sabbath (→ Jewish Practices 2.1). The → synagogue helped to give added strength to the central religious importance of the Sabbath. The people assembled for worship on the Sabbath (→ Worship 1.2), for progressive reading of the → Torah (see Acts 15:21), further readings from the → prophets (§2, i.e., the haftarah, Acts 13:15), and sermonlike addresses (Luke 4:16-27). The family was the main focus of Sabbath observance. Special stress lay on the beginning and the end (the havdala). To give emphasis to the joyful character of the Sabbath, festive clothes were worn and festive meals were served (no fasting), with special rites (including Sabbath lights and songs).

4.2. In ancient times Sabbath piety became very important in struggles against the surrounding world, both at home and in the → diaspora. The Sabbath was a mark of religious confession and ethnic identity. References may be found outside Judaism, for example, in Horace *Sat.* 1.9.69; Juvenal *Sat.* 3.296; Seneca, according to → Augustine *De civ. Dei* 6.11; Suetonius *Tib.* 32; → Tertullian *Ad nat.* 1.13; and reports from Cilician Asia Minor (*OGIS* no. 573) and Egypt (*CPJ* 3.53-56).

To understand the Sabbath we must note especially references to the theology of election. The Sabbath is given to Israel alone and serves to differentiate it from the pagan world (see *Jub.* 2:21-22; *Midr. Gen. Rab.* 11:8). But stress also falls on a universal theology of creation (see *b. Ber.* 29a). The Sabbath is a universal law of the cosmic order. (Note philosophically tinged explanations of the Sabbath in Hellenistic dispersion Judaism: Aristobulus frg. 5, *JSHRZ* 3.2.276-79; Philo *De spec. leg.* 2.59, 70; *De Decal.* 100; *De Abr.* 28–30. Also note the Sabbath structure of the 364-day calendar adopted in priestly circles: *Jub.* 6:30; *1 Enoch* 82:4-6, and Qumran texts; see M. Albani.) We also find interpretations oriented to a theology of history that divides world history according to the seven-day week of creation (see *2 Enoch* 33:1). After six 1,000-year aeons (Ps. 90:4) comes the time of destruction and transition (the fallow year) before the new creation (*b. Sanh.* 97a) or the eschatological age of peace (*Midr. Ps.* 92:2; *Pirqe R. El.* 18). The Sabbath comes to be seen as a symbol of the time of salvation (*m. Tamid* 7:4; *b. Ber.* 57b; *Tg. Yer. II* Exod. 20:2; *Midr. Gen. Rab.* 17:5, also Hippolytus *Comm. in Dan.* 4.23.5). Celebration of the Sabbath is an anticipation of the joyous eschatological age.

Many detailed rules (→ Halakah) protect the sanctity of the Sabbath. Variations exist, usually according to specific groups. The Essenes (CD 10:14–11:18; → Qumran) rigorously prohibited all Sabbath activity, including sexual intercourse (see *Jub.* 50:8). → Rabbis in the tradition of → Pharisaism more pragmatically specify types of work (*m. Šabb.* 7:2; *m. Beṣa* 5:2), and as a result the regulations become increasingly comprehensive and detailed. What motivated the thrust toward precision was essentially a concern to be faithful to the biblical precepts but at the same time to take into account the situations and demands of practical life.

Exceptions figure largely in the → Talmud and → Midrash, but discussion began earlier. In the Maccabean age (→ Israel 1.8) foreign attacks raised the question whether a threat to life takes precedence over Sabbath observance. Some said it did (*Jub.* 50:12-13; 1 Macc. 2:32-38; 2 Macc. 6:11; Josephus *Ant.* 12.274), other said firmly that it did not (1 Macc. 2:39-41; 9:34, 43-44; Josephus *Ant.* 13.12-13 and 18.318-24). The former group argued that a military threat may be actively resisted in spite of the Sabbath. This view prevailed for the most part, and the principle allowed extension to other cases such as that of sickness, on the ground that danger to life overrules the Sabbath. Defining danger to life (*pikuach nefesh* was the technical term) gave rise to much discussion (see *Mek.* on Exod. 31:13 or *t. Šabb.* 15.11-17). Acute threats are primarily in view, but then come broader threats, as in the case of sickness (*m. Yoma* 8:6) or childish anxieties (*t. Šabb.* 15.13). These exceptions lie outside the normal scope of authoritative decisions (*t. Šabb.* 15.12-13.).

4.3. In the Middle Ages Sabbath observance followed the rabbinic tradition, and the normative interpretations in terms of creation and eschatology held sway. New traits entered into Sabbath devotion and theology, however, under the influence of cabalistic ideas (→ Cabala). As something that mediates God's presence, the Sabbath plays a major role in speculations concerning divine powers *(sefirot).* In this context the custom arose of greeting the Sabbath as Israel's bride, from which developed the common Jewish practice of the *kabbalat shabbat,* or receiving of the Sabbath, a centerpiece of which is the song "Lecha Dodi" (Come, my beloved).

In the emancipated, assimilated circles of modern Judaism, change and upheaval have resulted in neglect of Sabbath observance. Reform Judaism (→ Jewish Theology 4) has been concerned to strip away the encrustations of the traditional Sabbath Halakah, even in some cases of adjusting the Sabbath to the Christian → Sunday. Enlightened Orthodox Judaism has tried to support Sabbath observance along stricter traditional lines with a deeper understanding of it. In the State of Israel the Sabbath now ranks as a public holiday.

5. Ramifications for Christianity

The → primitive Christian community largely kept the Sabbath, more strictly in the case of → Jewish Christians, but in that of some Gentile Christians as well (Col. 2:16; → Worship 1). In this regard it was following the practice of Jesus. Jesus observed the Sabbath (Mark 1:21; 6:1-2; Luke 4:16) as an ordinance of God for our good (cf. Mark 2:27 with *Mek.* on Exod. 31:13). He ran up against the Sabbath Halakah with his healings on the Sabbath (Mark 3:1-6 and par.; Luke 13:10-16; 14:1-6; John 5:9-18; 7:15-24) but did not basically question the institution, stressing instead its significance for salvation as a sign of the inbreaking reign of God (→ Kingdom of God; Jesus 4.2).

Christians began to stop keeping the Sabbath in the late first century and increasingly in the second. They celebrated Sunday as the day of the resurrection instead (*Barn.* 15.9; Ign. *Magn.* 9.1). In some cases they attacked both the institution and the practice of the Sabbath (*Diogn.* 4.1; *Barn.* 2.5; the preaching of Peter, according to Clement of Alexandria *Strom.* 6.5.41). Some appealed to Jesus as an example (*Act. Vercell.* 1; *Acts Phil.* 1). Yet Sabbath observance did not cease among Christians. Both → Jewish Christians (*Gos. Thom.* 27) and others observed the Sabbath, sometimes along with Sunday (e.g., the → Ethiopian Orthodox Church, Jacobites, and Thomas Christians; → Oriental Orthodox Churches; also see *Apos. Const.* 2.36.2; 2.59.3; 6.23.3; 7.33.2). Some indeed, on a strict biblical basis, kept the Sabbath instead of Sunday, including groups in Upper Italy, Moravia, Russia, and Transylvania from as early as the 12th century to the 18th, and then, more recently, some among the → Baptists and → Adventists in the 19th century, not to speak of the early Moravians.

All Christians have adopted the seven-day week. In the course of time Sunday as a main feast day took on the character of the Sabbath (the "great Sabbath" in Epiphanius, *Expositio fidei* 24 [*PG* 42.829C]). The biblical commandment was transferred to Sunday, with emphasis on the day of rest, and in this way it made a great impact on social life, first in Christian circles, then in circles outside, and also in the post-Christian secular world.

Bibliography: On 1-4: M. Albani, "Die lunaren Zyklen im 364-Tage-Festkalender," *MuB* 4 (1992) 3-47 • B. D. Eerdmans, *Der Sabbat* (Berlin, 1925) 79-83 • R. Goldenberg, "The Jewish Sabbath in the Roman World up to the Time of Constantine the Great," *ANRW* 2.19.1.414-47 • R. J. Griffith, "The Eschatological Significance of the Sabbath" (Diss., Dallas Theological Seminary, 1990) • I. Grunfeld, *The Sabbath: A Guide to Its Understanding and Observances* (5th ed.; New York, 2003; orig. pub., 1954) • J. Hehn, *Siebenzahl und Sabbat bei den Babyloniern und im Alten Testament* (Leipzig, 1907; repr., 1968) • A. J. Heschel, *The Sabbath: Its Meaning for Modern Man* (New York, 1951; repr., Boston, 2003) • E. Jenni, *Die theologische Begründung des Sabbatgebotes im Alten Testament* (Zurich, 1956) • S. T. Kimbrough, "The Concept of Sabbath at Qumran," *RevQ* 20 (1966) 484-502 • H.-J. Kraus, *Worship in Israel: A Cultic History of the OT* (Richmond, Va., 1966) • E. Lohse, "Σάββατον κτλ.," *TDNT* 7.1-35 • H. A. McKay, *Sabbath and Synagogue: The Question of Sabbath in Ancient Judaism* (Leiden, 1994) • J. Meinhold, *Sabbat und Woche im Alten Testament* (Göttingen, 1905) • D. Nielsen, *Die altarabische Mondreligion und die mosaische Überlieferung* (Strasbourg, 1904) • G. Robinson, *The Origin and Development of the OT Sabbath* (Frankfurt, 1988) • H. Webster, *Rest Days: The Christian Sunday, the Jewish Sabbath, and Their Historical and Anthropological Prototypes* (New York, 1916; repr., Detroit, 1968).

On 5: M. Asiedu-Peprah, *Johannine Sabbath Conflicts as Juridical Controversy* (Tübingen, 2001) • R. T. Beckwith, "The Sabbath and Sunday," *Calendar and Chronology, Jewish and Christian* (Leiden, 1996) 10-50 • E. Haag, *Vom Sabbat zum Sonntag* (Trier, 1991) • E. Lohse, "Jesu Worte über den Sabbat" (1960), *Die Einheit des Neuen Testaments* (2d ed.; Göttingen, 1976) 62-72 • F. Neirynck, "Jesus and the Sabbath: Some Observations on Mk II, 27," *Jésus aux origines de la Christologie* (ed. J. Dupont; Louvain, 1975) 227-70 • W. Rordorf, *Sunday: The History of the Day of Rest and Worship in the Earliest Centuries of the Christian Church* (Philadelphia, 1968) • B. Schaller, *Jesus und der Sabbat* (Münster, 1994) • Y.-E. Yang, *Jesus and the Sabbath in Matthew's Gospel* (Sheffield, 1997).

Berndt Schaller

Sabellianism → Christology 2.1.2; Trinity

Sacrament

1. Problem of Definition
2. Historical Development
    - 2.1. Biblical Aspects
    - 2.2. Early Church
    - 2.3. Early and High Middle Ages
    - 2.4. Reformation Age
        - 2.4.1. Lutheran Tradition
        - 2.4.2. Reformed Tradition
        - 2.4.3. Council of Trent
        - 2.4.4. Eastern Orthodoxy
    - 2.5. Modern Period
3. Systematic and Ecumenical Aspects

1. Problem of Definition

When we try to define the term "sacrament" generally, that is, to grasp conceptually what theological presuppositions are accepted in calling certain things sacraments, whether → baptism and the → Eucharist in the Reformation tradition, or also → confirmation (or chrismation), penance (→ Penitence), matrimony (→ Marriage and Divorce), holy orders, and anointing of the sick (→ Laying on of Hands) in that of Roman Catholics and the Orthodox, we run up against many obstacles. The challenging of the seven sacraments by the → Reformation (see 2.4) may well be due to a lack of clarity and uniformity among the Fathers in defining the term "sacrament" (see 2.2 and 2.3).

Many church ceremonies could be called sacraments, and it is obviously hard to base the use of the term on Scripture (see 2.1). Understandably, then, Roman Catholic theology in the post-Reformation age treats the doctrine of the sacraments, appealing to its own → scholastic tradition, as one of the highly important controversial issues in → ecumenical dialogue. Yet in this area of theological reflection, we now see a good deal of confessional approximation (see 3.2), essentially due to a recognition by all Christian churches in the 21st century that their efforts must focus on addressing the foundations of sacramental thinking (see 3.1; → Sacramentality).

Roman Catholic, Orthodox, and Protestant writers now advocate a distinction between broader and narrower definitions of sacraments, believing that developing agreement along these lines (see 3.3) will help to resolve the controversy about the number of the sacraments. Individual statements in the traditions of the churches may still retain their significance as long as there is openness to the historically conditioned relativity of our possibilities of linguistic expression.

2. Historical Development

The question of the historical origins of the meaning of "sacrament" presupposes a preunderstanding of what we are seeking. Those who do not limit their account of the historical development of the concept to finding the first use of certain ceremonies in the churches but want to probe more deeply into the nature of a sacrament must also take a nuanced view of the roots of the concept in Scripture.

2.1. ***Biblical Aspects***

Understood as the manifesting — the making visible, the revealing in the → Word of God (§3) — of the one divine promise in creaturely reality in its various forms, a sacrament points to the Judeo-Christian experience of → salvation as Scripture bears witness to it. The → revelation (§2) of the transcendent God in historical time can take place only in ways that are accessible to our creaturely human knowledge. If by the sacramental structure of created reality we mean its ability to be of service to God in his self-revelation, then we can speak of the sacramentality of all → creation (§4) and of all → salvation history.

The question of the biblical basis of the narrower and more specific use of the term runs up against the fact that the NT writings have no master concept for the sign-actions (→ Sign 2) found in the Christian communities that later came to be called sacraments. Nevertheless, this fact does not rule out appeal to the biblical testimony, inasmuch as from the time of the Fathers (→ Early Church) the Latin *sacramentum* was used for the Gk. *mystērion* (mystery, secret) relative to certain actions, and *mystērion* itself occurs in some later OT writing influenced by → Hellenism (see Dan. 2:18-19, 27-30, 47; Sir. 27:16-17, 21; Tob. 12:7, 11; Wis. 2:22; 2 Macc. 13:21, etc.), and we find it in the NT epistles as well (1 Cor. 2:7-10; Rom. 16:25-26; Col. 1:26-27; 2:2; Eph. 1:8-10; 3:3-7, 8-12).

Significantly, and obviously in deliberate differentiation from the use in the → mystery religions of antiquity, *mystērion* was not used here for liturgical celebrations but was introduced (in an eschatological and apocalyptic context in Daniel) to denote the salvific counsel of God that we cannot fathom in advance and that we are thus to call the "secret purposes of God" (Wis. 2:22). The term *mystērion* occurs only once in the Gospels, at Mark 4:11 and parallels. And it does so typically in relation to the *basileia tou theou,* the "secret of the → kingdom of God" (§1) being entrusted to the → disciples, to whom it has been given to know God's plans of salvation.

The Christological focus of which we catch an echo here (→ Christology 1), inasmuch as only those who are disciples of Jesus can see the dawning of God's rule, comes out much more clearly in the Pauline and deutero-Pauline literature. "God's wisdom, secret and hidden" (1 Cor. 2:7), has been revealed in Jesus Christ. He is the *mystērion tou theou,* "God's mystery" (Col. 2:2), which was "hidden for ages in God who created all things" (Eph. 3:9). God himself, the mystery of his electing and redeeming → love, is manifested with eschatological definitiveness in the life and destiny of Jesus Christ, who is the sacrament of God. To accept this witness in faith is to be reached first by the word of → proclamation that demonstrates the pneumatic presence of the God-man in the sphere of the church. The task of the community (→ Congregation 1.2-3) is to proclaim the mystery of God, Jesus Christ, to the nations (Col. 1:27-28; → Mission). Thus far the Christological focus of the term "sacrament" in the NT has an ecclesiological component.

As regards specific liturgical celebrations in the church that the postapostolic tradition groups under the term "sacrament," the biblical tradition is not uniform. Especially baptism and the Eucharist, but also other actions that various churches call sacraments, all celebrate God's timelessly efficacious → Easter action in and by Jesus Christ and the sending of the Spirit. But an effort to narrow down historically the term "sacrament" by relating it to a corresponding word of institution by the earthly → Jesus is open to question theologically.

On this basis we may inquire into the significance of sign-acts that later came to be called sacraments in the life of Jesus and the apostolic period. A disputed point exegetically is whether Jesus might have baptized at first (→ Baptism 1) and then later given up the practice. Baptism certainly had a church-constituting function in the first Christian communities. The various meals of Jesus (with sinners, the Last Supper, at the appearances; → Eucharist 2) may be seen as the root of eucharistic practice. His dealings with the sick and with penitent sinners, his call to discipleship, and his high estimation of → marriage (§1.2.2) might help us to situate the sacramental celebrations in their pre-Easter context, even if we cannot draw from this fact any final conclusions regarding the number of the sacraments. We see this approach from the → foot washing and the discussion of its sacramentality in the postapostolic period, for it can appeal to both the precedent and precept of the pre-Easter Jesus (John 13:15), in contrast to baptism, which is commanded only by the risen Christ (Matt. 28:19).

2.2. *Early Church*

In discussing the origins of the use of the term "sacrament" for church ceremonies, we must differentiate the material aspect from the linguistic. The → Apostolic Fathers seldom used the term *mystērion,* which for them denoted God's redeeming mysteries of salvation, as in Ignatius (d. ca. 107), with a focus on the birth, death, and resurrection of Jesus Christ. The word is more common in the second century → apologists, especially in → Justin Martyr (d. ca. 165), in whom we see a growing tendency to use it for ritual presentations of the mysteries of salvation (→ Rite 2). This development is the result of encounter with → Gnosticism and the mystery cults.

Linguistically decisive was the choice of *sacramentum* to render *mystērion* in the Latin translation of the Bible, as used in North Africa and also Italy. → Tertullian (ca. 160-ca. 225) and → Cyprian (ca. 200-258) in particular helped to popularize the Latin term. In Tertullian's works we still find the broader concept defined in terms of salvation history, but we also see in him the clear concern to call specific actions, and more specifically baptism and the Eucharist, sacraments (*Adv. Marc.* 4.34).

The Latin *sacramentum* (etymologically the root *sacr-* suggests the sphere of the numinous, holy, or spiritual) had thus far had two meanings in secular use. In the army it denoted the soldier's oath of loyalty, and in law the money that had to be pledged in case a suit was lost. Self-commitment is the thought in both cases. We might thus infer that the thought of the → covenant (in salvation history) was in the background when *sacramentum* seemed to be a suitable equivalent for *mystērion.* The oath of loyalty made possible a relationship in thought to the church's rite of → initiation. The third-century Latin fathers increasingly used *sacramentum* for baptism and the Eucharist (see Cyprian *Ad Quir.; De eccl.* 15). But the word had other uses. On the one hand, other rites like confirmation, foot washing, and the laying on of hands could be called sacraments; on the other, the broader use in terms of salvation history was not abandoned.

We find the same situation in → Augustine (354-430; → Augustine's Theology), whose theology essentially helped to define the term. More broadly, *sacramentum* denotes a reality that we may grasp historically and palpably but whose meaning escapes direct apprehension and refers us to the transcendent. Augustine accordingly first defined *sacramentum* Christologically and spoke of "the mystery of Christ's divinity and humanity, which was manifested in the flesh" (*De nat. et grat.* 2.2). This salvation-history perspective enabled him, like theologians before him, to speak of the *sacramenta* of Israel (the → Sabbath, → circumcision, the → sacrifices), which are greater in number than those of the Christian church because the Christ-event began the eschatological age of salvation, which demands other and fewer signs.

Augustine was ready to call all church rites *sacramenta* in principle, but among them he obviously regarded baptism and the Eucharist as incomparably more important. Typically, then, he offered his material definition of the term *sacramentum* in the narrower sense when speaking about baptism: "The word is added to the element, and there results the sacrament, as if itself also a kind of visible word" (*In Evang. Iohan.* 80.3). Also at the Eucharist the word of faith *(verbum fidei)* gives the sacrament its efficacy by the powerful presence of the Spirit of God. Linking the term to a material element (water, or bread and → wine) made it more concrete, and this understanding would be a guiding thought in the period that followed.

Also of great theological influence later was the Augustinian definition of the sacrament as a sacred sign *(signum sacrum),* which made possible a distinction between the outward sign *(signum)* and the inner thing signified *(res).* For Augustine the *res sacramenti* (lit. "thing of the sacrament," i.e., that to which the sacrament points) was the redemption accomplished in the Christ-event (→ Soteriology).

2.3. *Early and High Middle Ages*

Up to the end of the first millennium, sacramental theology in the West mainly followed in the steps of Augustine. The result was that the early → Middle Ages saw the Christ-event as the source of the sacramental reality (see Bede [ca. 673-735] and Paschasius Radbertus [ca. 790-ca. 860]). No consensus existed in the first millennium as to the number of the sacraments. Fulbert of Chartes (ca. 970-1028) and Bruno of Würzburg (d. 1045), for example, would allow only baptism and the Eucharist, but Peter Damian (1007-72) listed 12 sacraments.

More profound reflection took place in the St.-Victor school and by Peter Lombard (ca. 1100-1160). Hugh of St.-Victor (1096-1141) pointed the way when he said that a sacrament is a physical or material element that can be perceived by the external senses and that represents a certain invisible and spiritual → grace through a certain similarity, designates that grace through an institution, and contains it through sanctification (*De sacramentis Christianae fidei* 1.9.2). Three basic things — element, grace, and institution — are here said to constitute the sacrament, to which all later views refer. Peter Lombard brought a new dimension into view, with a reference back to Augustine and Hugh, by defining the efficacy of the sacrament as causal: "We have a sacrament in the true sense in that which is a sign of grace and the form of invisible grace in such a way that it gives rise to an image of it and is its cause" (*Sent.* 4.1.4). The *Sentences* also made an impact on the years that followed by numbering and classifying the seven sacraments (4.2.1).

Scholastic speculation soon focused on the sacramental mode of operation ("instrumental causality," see Aquinas *Summa theol.* III, q. 62), the concept of sacrament now being understood from a hylemorphic perspective, which views concrete substance as involving a distinction between matter and form. The theologians of High Scholasticism largely agreed that the determination of the words spoken at the sacramental administration was a matter of the form, but they differed strongly regarding the concrete understanding of the matter in certain cases (esp. penance, orders, and matrimony). As the category of matter replaced the largely object-oriented concept of element, an expansion of meaning took place at the level of the sacramental sign that enabled ritual acts that did not seem to have any element to rate as sacraments. The use of the term "matter" lessened the difficulty in counting them as such by making it possible to regard inner attitudes and outer actions as constitutive parts of a sacrament. Against initial appearances, adoption of the distinction of matter and form thus opened the door to a more personal and dynamic concept of sacramental administration.

In High Scholasticism the tradition also underwent a second modification by adding a third element to Augustine's *signum* or *sacramentum tantum* (sign only) and *res sacramenti* (the effect), namely, *res et sacramentum,* which indicates a first effect related to the sign, for example, the presence of Christ at the Eucharist. Individual theologians offered different definitions of this intermediate, significatory effect.

Using various attempts at classification, Scholasticism supported the increasing agreement about there being seven sacraments. For a material, strongly anthropological orientation in advocacy of the seven, we look to → Thomas Aquinas (ca. 1225-74; → Thomism), who viewed the seven signs as companions on our way to consummation with God but also as means of salvation to prevent or mitigate harm (*Summa theol.* III, q. 65, art. l; → Means of Grace).

The Western fixing on the number seven influenced Eastern theology as well. Thus the union councils of Lyons II (1274) and Florence (1439; → Councils of the Church 3) taught that there are seven sacraments (DH 860 and 1310). The heavily Thomistic Armenian decree of the Council of Florence (1439), in what it says about the matter, dispenser, and effect of each sacrament, might serve as a kind of summary of scholastic speculation. The degree of generalization and formalization of the concept that we see there, however, hardly shows how hard it is across the centuries to bring the various ritual actions of the Christian community under a common concept. In its → reception of the union transactions, Eastern Orthodox theology (→ Orthodox Christianity) remained open in the matter of defining the number of the sacraments.

2.4. *Reformation Age*

In the 16th century confessional influences came to bear on how sacraments were defined. These influences included the teaching of individual → Reformers and the opposition to this teaching in Roman Catholic → polemical theology as it was formulated at the Council of → Trent. To understand the controversy we must have some knowledge of later medieval scholastic theology and the actual administration of the sacraments and sacramental rites (→ Sacramentals). In particular, abuses in → indulgences and in penitential and eucharistic practice provided the occasion for fresh Reformation thinking on the issue of the sacraments.

2.4.1. *Lutheran Tradition*

In the context of his concern about penance and absolution, Martin → Luther (1483-1546; → Luther's Theology) reached the insight that in the pronouncing of the forgiveness of → sins (§3), the promise of God comes to fulfillment and God justifies us by faith alone (→ Justification 2.1; Reformation Principles). This insight had a strong impact on Luther's discussions of the nature of sacraments. Sacraments, too, have a verbal structure. They are saving words from God that are addressed to us, even though we do not deserve them. They are efficacious where there is a trusting → faith.

Luther rarely said anything about the general concept of a sacrament, and what he did say about both the concept and the number of sacraments changed as the years passed and as different situations demanded. Along Augustinian lines the leading criterion in his definition is the presence of an element that becomes a sacrament by means of a word (i.e., a "visible word"). But competing to some extent with this definition is his tracing of sacramental rites to a NT word of institution, which is beyond doubt in the case of penance (→ Penitence 1.4), even though in this case there seems to be no real element.

Luther's concern to be true to the witness of Scripture also brought a rediscovery of the Christological center of the concept in terms of the NT *mystērion* (see 2.1). We find all these aspects in his *Babylonian Captivity of the Church* (1520), in which he first recalls the usage of the Scriptures (*usus Scripturae;* → Typology), according to which Jesus Christ is the "one single sacrament" and there are "three sacramental signs," namely, "baptism, penance, and the bread" (*LW* 36.18). In what follows, though, he allows that strictly we can argue for only two sacraments, baptism and the Eucharist, since penance "lacks the divinely instituted visible sign" (36.124). The Lutheran confessional tradition adopted this stricter usage, which we also find in the Large Catechism (1529, *Book of Concord,* 385.20, 456.1; → Catechism 2), although later Luther was prepared to call penance a sacrament, since it meets the criteria of promise and institution (*LW* 34.356, thesis 34).

The confessional writings also display some openness in the matter. The CA Apol. numbers absolution among the three sacraments in virtue of the divine command and the promise of grace (13.4), thus stating plainly what CA 9-13 had already suggested (→ Augsburg Confession). CA 7 defines the church as "the assembly of all believers among whom the gospel is purely preached and the holy sacraments are administered according to the gospel" (*Book of Concord,* 42.1). Philipp → Melanchthon (1497-1560; → Reformers 2.1.1) added his own emphasis by defining sacraments as rites and ceremonies of the church, an aspect that we find more plainly presented in the Reformed tradition.

2.4.2. *Reformed Tradition*

Ulrich → Zwingli (1484-1531; → Zwingli's Theology) and John → Calvin (1509-64; → Calvin's Theology) agreed that sacraments have ecclesial significance but differed characteristically in their understanding of these sign-actions. Zwingli goes back to the etymological meaning of *sacramentum* (see 2.2) and sees in the sacraments signs of public initiation into the community and of the adoption of a commitment not to fall back into the former way of life. As signs of faith the sacraments are human actions by which the church assures itself of the faith of individuals. Only as his thinking developed did Zwingli see them also as means to confirm faith, as words that come to us by more senses than hearing, and, in the case of the Eucharist, as acts at which Christ is specifically present according to his deity (LCC 24.262-65).

Calvin influenced the Reformed tradition more strongly than Zwingli. In the sacraments he saw gifts of God and outward seals of his promise that we need, in view of the ignorance, sloth, and weakness of our present state. In the broader sense all OT and NT signs that assure us of the truth of the divine promise are sacraments. In the main they confirm rather than awaken faith, which the Holy Spirit has established already by the word of proclamation. In distinction from the Lutheran tradition Calvin did not tie the divine effect too closely to the earthly elements. Decisive for the effects is the opening of trusting hearts by the Spirit to the heavenly gifts. The stress in the Reformed confessions lies on the operation of the Spirit and on faith, with the two sacraments (baptism and the Eucharist) as sensory means of grace that God has instituted in conjunction with the Word. Typical are the Gallican Confession (1559, art. 35), Belgic Confession (1561, art. 33), and Irish Articles (1615, art. 85).

2.4.3. *Council of Trent*

The 1547 Tridentine decree on sacraments deals first with the general doctrine of the sacraments (DH 1601-13). Its theses relate to Reformation teaching. We see here its limitation, for ignorance of Reformation writings and the apologetic stance produced condemnations (→ Teaching Office), the theological reappraisal of which is now a central concern of ecumenical dialogue (see 3.2).

In a foreword to its decree on the sacraments (DH 1600), the council put its statements in the context of the doctrine of justification and thus took up a primary concern of the Reformers. Although the number of seven sacraments was maintained by reference to the institution of all these signs by Jesus Christ (DH 1601), the council recognized the different degrees of importance of the NT sacraments (DH 1603), which in their own turn are to be assessed differently than those of the OT (DH 1602). It contended for their necessity to salvation (DH 1604), rejecting the idea that they simply confirm faith (DH 1605).

Behind the statement in canon 6 (DH 1606) is repudiation of the idea that the sacraments are no more than marks of human confession. Canons 7 and 8 (DH 1607-8) contend for efficacy in all recipients as far as God is concerned and as long as there is performance of the human action (i.e., their value is *ex opere operato,* "by the work performed"). Canon 12 (DH 1612) is also important in this regard, with its assurance that the administration does not depend on the worthiness of the minister. Canon 9 (DH 1609) deals with the indelible character given in baptism, confirmation, and orders, understanding it as a lasting commitment of the recipients to service. Canons 10-12 deal with the minister (DH 1610-12) and stress the special commissioning of individuals to preach the Word and administer the sacraments and the requirement that they must intend to do what the church does in these actions. Canon 13 denounces individual or arbitrary changes in the external administering of sacramental rites by unauthorized pastors (DH 1613).

2.4.4. *Eastern Orthodoxy*

Debates in the Latin West in the 16th and 17th centuries about the traditional doctrine of the sacraments influenced Eastern Orthodox theology by challenging it to confessionally state its own position. After a period of conscious adoption of Reformation thinking (by Metrophanes Critopoulos [1589-1639] in 1624 and Cyril Loucaris [1570-1638] in 1629/31), the confession composed by Peter Mogila (1596-1646) in 1638-40, which was close to Roman Catholicism in its accepting of seven *mystēria* and its use of the categories of matter and form, became normative in the Orthodox doctrinal tradition. The Greek version, as *Orthodoxos homologia* (Orthodox confession), underlay the decisions reached at the Council of Jerusalem in 1672 (→ Modern Church History 3.2.2).

2.5. *Modern Period*

The post-Reformation age saw efforts by both Protestants and Roman Catholics to establish their positions by argument. Lutheran → orthodoxy (§1) for the most part resorted to scholastic terms. The → Enlightenment brought a stronger tendency to deal with the sacraments rationally and to play down the idea that God imparts grace by these acts. Influential along these lines were I. Kant (1724-1804; → Kantianism) and J. G. Fichte (1762-1814; → Idealism 4). Kant accepted the sacraments as church actions, but Fichte was highly skeptical of sacramental thinking and found in the sacraments a threat to the sole necessity of inner conversion of the heart. → Pietism stressed the personal disposition of the recipients, with implications for the discussion of the legitimacy of infant baptism (→ Baptism 2; Baptists 3.4).

In the 20th century Protestants began to make considerable contributions to the understanding of the doctrine of the sacraments (see 3.1). Most important was the → Leuenberg Agreement (1973), which brought pulpit exchanges and intercommunion to the Lutheran, Reformed, and Union signatories. Since on a Reformation view all that is needed for the → unity of the church is agreement on the true doctrine of the gospel and right administration of the sacraments (see §2 of the agreement), what is said about intercommunion presupposes a reworking of the mutual denunciations of the 16th century. The Leuenberg text offers no general definition of a sacrament, but the various ecumenical statements about the → Eucharist (§1.2) are relevant in this regard.

In the Thirty-nine Articles (1571) the → Anglican Communion clearly distinguished the two sacraments of the gospel (art. 25), but many Anglicans also like to speak of additional sacramental rites. The → free churches, especially → Baptists, →

Mennonites, and → Methodists, also insist on only the two sacraments, with an ecclesial and spiritual emphasis; Baptists prefer to speak of ordinances instead of sacraments. The → Salvation Army and the Quakers (→ Friends, Society of) do not administer any sacraments at all.

In the post-Tridentine period debates have arisen among Roman Catholic schools regarding the mode of sacramental efficacy. Thomists argue for a physical operation insofar as God uses the sacraments as his instruments, which means that the sacraments directly impart the grace that they signify. In contrast, Scotists (→ Scotism) advocate an indirect moral mode of operation as the administration of the sacraments moves God to work accordingly. → Neoscholasticism has not been able to overcome the difficulty of this more narrowly focused problem. Only as the sacraments are seen to be appropriate to us as psychosomatic beings and thus to be actions that God has willed does the need vanish to distinguish between physical and moral efficacy.

Early in the 20th century the → liturgical movement and the catechetical revival began to exert a strong influence on Roman Catholic sacramental teaching by bringing a fresh awareness of the communal character of sacramental celebrations and of the dimension of the liturgical events as signs. Most important in this regard was the theology of mysteries of Odo Casel (1886-1948), who brought renewal to the understanding of the Christian sacraments by referring back to the (pagan) mystery cults of antiquity. The assembled congregation is celebrating a cultic, symbolic event and achieves access thereby to the divine sphere.

Rediscovery of the communal dimension finds clear reflection in the texts of → Vatican II (*Sacrosanctum concilium* 26-27 and *Lumen gentium* 11). The dogmatic formulations develop insights that pre-Vatican theology had already addressed broadly (see 3.1). We must put what is said about the sacramentality of the church (*LG* 1, 8, 48) in the context of the social and ecclesial significance of the individual sacramental celebrations and consider the Christological and pneumatological rooting of the concept of the sacrament (→ Holy Spirit 2.5; Church 3.2.3; Roman Catholic Church 2).

Rediscovery of the pneumatological and ecclesiological dimension of sacramental celebrations has given Roman Catholic theology a basis after Vatican II for drawing closer to Eastern Orthodox teaching, which, after a phase of strong Western influence extending into the 19th century, began once again to find nourishment in its own roots. It has emphasized the character of the sacraments as mysteries, the significance of epiclesis, and the symbolism of the number seven.

3. Systematic and Ecumenical Aspects

The age of denominational distinctiveness in the theology of the sacraments has now yielded to a time of nuanced ecumenical cooperation (→ Ecumenical Theology; Ecumenism, Ecumenical Movement; Oikoumene).

3.1. *Theological Concepts*

3.1.1. *Roman Catholic Thought*

Among Roman Catholics up to the middle of the 20th century, one can discern a certain ecclesiological centering of the sacramental concept, of which we see the first beginnings in the 19th-century Tübingen school of J. A. Möhler (1796-1838), J. E. Kuhn (1806-87), P. von Schanz (1841-1905), and M. J. Scheeben (1835-88). O. Semmelroth (1912-79, *Die Kirche als Ursakrament* [1953]) and K. → Rahner (1904-84, *Kirche und Sakramente* [1961; ET *The Church and the Sacraments* (1963)]) consolidated this ecclesiological view. Pioneering Vatican II, these two theologians also helped to give the concept of the sacrament a Christological basis. This corrective relating of the ecclesiological dimension back to the Christ-event as the origin and center of all sacramental reality found linguistic expression in the reserving of the term "primal sacrament" *(Ursakrament)* for Jesus Christ and for the church as simply the basic or root sacrament of all sacramental observances. E. Schillebeeckx contributed to the popularizing of the insight into a Christological anchoring of the concept by his *De Christusontmoeting als sacrament van de Godsontmoeting* (1957; ET *Christ, the Sacrament of the Encounter with God* [1963]).

While the texts of Vatican II received this Christological and ecclesiological aspect of the concept of the sacrament (see 2.5), it was only later that a stress on the anthropological and personal basis of sacramental rites, initiated earlier, became a focus of concern. Rahner in essays in his *Theological Investigations* ("Personal and Sacramental Piety," 2 [1963]; "Considerations on the Active Role of the Person in the Sacramental Event," 14 [1976]) recalled the need for personal involvement in the rites as a prerequisite of their fruitfulness. J. Ratzinger (*Die sakramentale Begründung christlicher Existenz* [1966]) pointed to the relation between sacramental observances and events in human life, finding here a basis for the discussion of the situations behind the observances that has since occupied → pastoral theology (see P. M. Zulehner, *Heirat–Geburt–Tod* [1976]; → Roman Catholic Church 3.2 and 5.4.3).

A place has also been found for ethnological and sociological input (→ Ethnology; Social History), as already in A. von Gennep (1873-1957) in *Les rites de passage* (1909; ET *Rites of Passage* [1960]). Insights from the social sciences and communications theory (→ Communication 5) that we owe to P. Hünermann ("Sakrament–Figur des Lebens," *Anthropologie des Kults* [1977]) and A. Ganoczy (*Einführung in die katholische Sakramentenlehre* [1979; ET *An Introduction to Catholic Sacramental Theology* (1984)]) have also had a decisive influence, as have insights regarding the active dimension of the spoken word contributed in later Roman Catholic thinking by H. J. Weber ("Wort und Sakrament," *MTZ* [1972]; → Action Theory 3.3). We see plainly the fresh evaluation of the → symbol in understanding the sacramentals when we consider the views of L. Boff (*Sacraments of Life* [1987]), T. Schneider (*Zeichen der Nähe Gottes* [1979]), A. Schilson and D. Zadra ("Symbol und Sakrament," *CGG* [1982]), and F. J. Nocke (*Wort und Geste* [1985]).

The relating of communications theory to ecclesial observances means that reference to the sign dimension brings awareness of the underlying liturgical significance of sacramental celebrations, as L. Lies (*Sakramententheologie* [1990]) and K. Richter (*Was die sakramentalen Zeichen bedeuten* [1988; ET *The Meaning of the Sacramental Symbols* (1990)] and [with Schilson] *Den Glauben feiern* [1989]) have proposed in Europe, and F. Taborda (*Sacramentos. Praxis e festa* [1987]) in the context of Latin American → liberation theology. Reference to the concept of symbol also gives an awareness that created reality is claimed for the divine work of salvation. This thought leads to considering how the sacraments and all cosmic sacramentality are tied to this world, inasmuch as they are signs of the Creator that confirm faith, as in the Ignatian tradition of G. Greshake, *Gott in allen Dingen finden* (1986).

3.1.2. *Protestant Thought*
In 20th-century Protestant → systematic theology, we find many discussions of baptism and the Eucharist. In this connection several writers call for a closer defining of the sacramental as the reality that unites the two observances. Only from the 1980s, however, do we find a special treatment of the doctrine of the sacraments as such. U. Kühn (*Sakramente* [1985]) and G. Wenz (*Einführung in die evangelische Sakramentenlehre* [1988]) clearly wrote with ecumenical dialogue in view. R. Hempelmann (*Sakrament als Ort der Vermittlung des Heils* [1992]) was also trying to bring Protestant and Roman Catholic conceptions into conversation.

The skepticism that prevailed earlier in the century regarding a general concept of the sacrament followed in the tradition of F. → Schleiermacher (1768-1834; → Schleiermacher's Theology), who rejected any comprehensive understanding of baptism and the Eucharist as sacraments because there is no biblical basis for it and because it loses sight of the distinctiveness of the two rites. Appeal on behalf of such skepticism might also be made to R. Bultmann (1884-1976; → Existential Theology), who argued that an emphasis on the objective facts of salvation in the sacraments tended to threaten the existential and eschatological dimension of the → kerygma.

K. → Barth (1886-1968; → Dialectical Theology) exerted a great influence on the development of the Protestant position by finding a basis for the sacrament in the history of salvation and the theology of revelation, insofar as God's witness to himself is oriented to our capacity for knowledge and makes use of creaturely realities (*CD* II/1). Barth's biblical use of the term "sacrament" solely when referring to Jesus Christ (ibid.) found a warm reception, but his contesting of the sacramental nature of baptism (*CD* IV/4) was for the most part not adopted. Barth viewed baptism primarily as Spirit baptism, the church's water baptism being simply a human work, so that he saw it as misleading to try to connect the two under the common term "sacrament."

Repudiating Barth, E. Jüngel (*Das Sakrament–was ist das?* [1971]) again stressed the Christological center. In the history and destiny of Jesus, the "humanity of God" as his nature is manifest. The Word, spoken also in baptism and the Eucharist, must be grasped in faith.

3.1.3. *Sacrament as Word-Event*
Along with a Christological defining of the sacrament, a primary Protestant concern is to see the sacrament as a Word-event, as illustrated in the thought of E. Fuchs (1903-83, *Das urchristliche Sakramentsverständnis* [1958]; *Wagnis des Glaubens* [1979]) and G. Ebeling (1912-2001, *Wort Gottes und Tradition* [1964; ET *The Word of God and Tradition* (1968)]; *Dogmatik des christlichen Glaubens* [vol. 3, 1979]). Ebeling contended that in the sacraments the Word links up with basic human situations, which are defined afresh by referring to the stages in Jesus' life. As specific forms of the Word, the sacraments strengthen assurance of faith and hence also our saving relationship with God.

The Barthian focus on the Christological center and Ebeling's concern for the form of the sacrament as word stood against the ecclesial approach to understanding the sacrament. This latter approach was recalled by W. Pannenberg (*Thesen zur Theologie der*

Kirche [1970]), J. Moltmann (*Kirche in der Kraft des Geistes* [1974; ET *The Church in the Power of the Spirit* (1977)]), and U. Kühn (*Sakramente*). Moltmann's pneumatological relating of the Christ-event and the church's action makes it possible to see the sacrament in Trinitarian terms and thus to keep in view God's total saving work in → creation (protological origin) and history (eschatological consummation; → Eschatology 7.1).

P. → Tillich (1886-1965) took a path of his own ("Natur und Sakrament" [1928; ET "Nature and Sacrament," *The Protestant Era* (1948)]; *Systematic Theology*, vol. 3), viewing the things of nature as potential symbols that, as they are taken up into → salvation history, can give presence to the transcendent in the world. Tillich later made this general concept pneumatologically specific and was thus able to relate the "great sacraments" analogically to the potential sacramentality of → nature.

3.2. *Dialogue*

It is possible to develop an agreed general concept of the sacrament that all → denominations can accept only if we pay heed to essential controversial questions. The differences that were formulated in the age of the Reformation and that the denominations have handed down regarding the meaning, number, and mode of operation of the sacraments have been issues in ecumenical dialogue from the start of efforts at Christian reunion (→ Union). Attempts to reach a theologically appropriate definition of the relation between Word and sacrament have been of primary concern since the 1970s. We see this topic in the Catholic-Lutheran Malta report of 1972, the Catholic-Methodist Dublin report of 1976, and the Reformed–Roman Catholic statement *The Presence of Christ in Church and World* of 1977.

A change of emphasis, however, became noticeable from the middle of the 1980s. Along with ecumenical discussions of the basic questions of ecclesiology, the theme of church and sacrament came to occupy more and more place in individual statements (see the report *Perspectives on Koinonia*, issued by Roman Catholics and Pentecostals after their 1985-89 discussions; → Pentecostal Churches). We should also note the Roman Catholic–Methodist *Nairobi Report* of 1986 (→ Methodist Churches) and the Roman Catholic–Orthodox Bari paper "Faith, Sacraments, and the Unity of the Church" (1987).

In Protestant–Roman Catholic conversations some convergence has been achieved regarding the number of sacraments (→ Consensus 4; Dialogue 2.3.1). The same applies to conversations between non–Roman Catholics themselves, for example, between Anglicans and Lutherans, 1970-72, concluding in the Pullach Report (1973), who both differentiate the "scriptural sacraments" of baptism and the Eucharist from the "five commonly so-called sacraments." Note the similar agreement between Roman Catholics and Lutherans in the documents *Ways to Community* (1980) and *Facing Unity* (1984), and in the final statement issued by the Reformed and Roman Catholics after discussions in 1984-90, *Towards a Common Understanding of the Church.* Agreement on the number of sacraments can be presupposed at once when conversations take place among the → Old Catholics, Oriental Orthodox, Orthodox, and Roman Catholics. As regards the → Oriental Orthodox, note the statements issued by Paul VI and Coptic pope Shenouda III in 1973, and by John Paul II and Syrian patriarch Ignatius Zakka I in 1984. For the Old Catholics and Orthodox, see the joint statements issued on each of the sacraments, arising from their meetings in 1985 and 1987.

As regards international multilateral discussion, the official Lima Declaration of 1982 shows that agreement on the understanding of baptism, Eucharist, and ministry can be reached only if there is agreement first on the nature of sacramentality. (See *Churches Respond to BEM: Official Responses to the "Baptism, Eucharist, and Ministry" Text* [6 vols.; WCC, 1986-88].)

3.3. *Ecumenical Perspectives*

Although reflection on the theology of the sacraments has varied greatly in individual churches, one may still trace common features that appear in ecumenical dialogue. One of these is the Christological centrality that biblical usage demands. Another is the focus on the character of the sacraments as Word and proclamation. These agreed features take up concerns that the Protestant tradition preserved and that all the sacramental theology of the later 20th century accepted. Proper to Roman Catholic concepts is recollection of the social and ecclesial dimension of the Christian message and of the personal and situational basis of sacramental actions. Protestant statements in the ecumenical sphere now echo these concerns. Common reception of the concept of the symbol has opened up the anthropological root of the rites. Face to face with urgent pastoral questions in the area of the sacraments, there is now more sensitivity to the common duty of the churches to bring to light the meaning of the observances as a specific form of God's address to us in his saving word of revelation.

There also seems to be consensus that the churches should no longer describe themselves as churches of the Word (Protestant) or of the sacrament (Roman Catholic) but as churches of both

Word and sacrament, for in Word and sacrament they already have fellowship. Yet some skepticism still exists regarding the analogous concept of the sacrament that Roman Catholics favor and that is by no means alien to the Protestant tradition. In this respect one must consider that talking about the sacramentality of the church is secondary. It serves to underline the pneumatologically defined precedence in importance of the Christ-event. It might prove helpful, then, in resolving the problem of the number of the sacraments. The term "sacrament," being analogous, allows of both a broader and a narrower use. In detail, the status of baptism and the Eucharist as major sacraments is beyond dispute. God makes himself known in creaturely reality as the deliverer from the forces of death and sin as by the Spirit he reminds us of his acts in and through Jesus Christ, doing so in constitutive (baptism) and regenerative (Eucharist) acts of the community.

Bibliography: D. M. Baillie, *The Theology of the Sacraments* (London, 1957) 37-124 • C. Barker, *Sacrament* (London, 1996) • *The Book of Concord: The Confessions of the Evangelical Lutheran Church* (ed. R. Kolb and T. J. Wengert; Minneapolis, 2000) • D. Brown and A. Loades, eds., *Christ: The Sacramental Word* (London, 1996) • C. Dooley, ed., *Ecclesial Mediation of Grace: Essays in Sacramental and Liturgical Theology* (Louvain, 1998) • E.-M. Faber, *Einführung in die katholische Sakramentenlehre* (Darmstadt, 2002) • P. Haffner, *The Sacramental Mystery* (Leominster, 1999) • M. G. Lawler, *Symbol and Sacrament: A Contemporary Sacramental Theology* (New York, 1997) • K. Lehmann and W. Pannenberg, eds., *The Condemnations of the Reformation Era: Do They Still Divide?* (Minneapolis, 1990) • D. C. McDougall, *The Cosmos as the Primary Sacrament: The Horizon for an Ecological Sacramental Theology* (New York, 2003) • D. N. Power, *Sacrament: The Language of God's Giving* (New York, 1999) • A. Schmemann, *Introduction to Liturgical Theology* (London, 1966) • T. Schneider, *Zeichen der Nähe Gottes. Grundriß der Sakramententheologie* (7th ed.; rev. with D. Sattler; Mainz, 1998).

Dorothea Sattler

Sacramentality

1. Term
2. Roman Catholic View
3. A Basic Theological Structure
4. View of Liberation Theology
5. Resacralizing of Reality
6. Criticism

1. Term

The term "sacramentality" and the related adjective "sacramental" have no single meaning but are used in different ways in different connections. Formally, "sacramentality" is an abstract term based on "sacrament" and denoting what is essential to a → sacrament as such. It serves, then, to show with what right the church describes various actions as sacraments. In this sense M. J. Scheeben (1835-88) raised the question of the sacramentality of marriage (pp. 593-610).

By its very nature the term "sacramentality" looks beyond the question of the number of sacraments (two or seven) and enables us to identify a larger area of things that the church does not recognize and Christ did not institute as sacraments. Although they are not sacraments in the more precise sense, they seem to have a sacramental structure (see also P. → Tillich, *Systematic Theology*, 3.120-28, and, on this point, U. Reetz).

2. Roman Catholic View

Roman Catholics think first of the sacramentality of the → church (§3.2; → Roman Catholic Church 2; Catholicism [Roman] 3.2). Doctrinally, → Vatican II cautiously received the defining of the church as a sacrament (*veluti sacramentum*, "in the nature of sacrament," *Lumen gentium* [*LG*] 1, cf. §9; H. Döring, 100ff.). It thus accepted the description of the church as a sacrament or "primal sacrament," as given by O. Semmelroth (1912-79), E. H. Schillebeeckx (b. 1914), and others (see M. Bernards). These theologians brought into the concept the vacillating debate about the outer form (special ministry) and the spiritual reality of the church (as Christ's mystical body), which had gone on since J. A. Möhler's (1796-1838) *Die Einheit in der Kirche* (1825, see U. Valeske for bibliography). They laid stress on the relation, suggesting that we can view the outer form of the church and its observances (sacraments) as a sacrament, "a sign and instrument . . . of communion with God" (*LG* 1; → Church 3.2.3).

The structure of a sacrament, or sacramentality, can thus be defined as "a divine bestowal of salvation in an outwardly perceptible form which makes the bestowal manifest; a bestowal of salvation in historical visibility" (Schillebeeckx, *Christ*, 15). The gain in comparison with other views of the church (mystical body, etc.) is that this understanding does not ignore the inalienable character of the church's visible or juridical side, nor does it allow the outer side to compete with the pneumatic reality. Rather, the outer is functionalized as the means of Christ's saving work and thus is integrated into the church's inner reality.

3. A Basic Theological Structure

Among the premises of definitions of this kind, especially from the middle of the 20th century in the Roman Catholic sphere and on the basis of, for example, Möhler, Scheeben, F. Pilgram, and C. Feckes, is the elevating of sacramentality to the status of a basic structure of theology. At the heart of all the contents of → theology are the encounter and mutual self-impartation of ourselves and God, understood in various personalistic ways and effected first through the person and work of Christ and then through the church (as a sacramental extension of the → incarnation) and its sacraments (in the narrower sense; → Theology in the Nineteenth and Twentieth Centuries). The comprehensive approaches adopted by Schillebeeckx, Semmelroth (→ Salvation 4.3), F. Malmberg, and also K. → Rahner (1904-84; → Transcendental Theology) aim for the most part at personalizing an apparently static understanding of objects of faith (→ Grace 3.4). We are not to see these objects as metaphysical entities that work causally but as the sacramental means to mediate the presence of God and the mutual self-imparting of ourselves and God (Schillebeeckx, "Sacraments," 220-21).

Factually, these positions join hands with Protestant criticism of the sacramental thinking or sacramentalism of Roman Catholic theology (F. Gogarten, P. Althaus, G. Ebeling, et al.). Sacramentalism of this type is the opposite of a personal understanding of God's relation to us. Protestant theologians identify as sacramental(ist) the type of thinking that regards the substance of salvation as a reality enclosed in the means, so that appropriation is viewed as independent of conscious reception (faith), a mechanical effect upon a soul that is also thought of in terms of substance (G. Ebeling, *Dogmatik* 3.303ff.).

4. View of Liberation Theology

Advocates of Latin American → liberation theology, in contrast to a supposed ranging of the reality of faith and secular things alongside one another (G. Gutiérrez, 53-61, 201-2), speak of the → neighbor or the oppressed class as a sacrament of the presence of God. Along these lines they understand the class conflict (→ Marxism) and related human action, or the engaged church, as the means by which God actualizes his (ultimately sovereign) kingdom (see Gutiérrez, chap. 12, "The Church: Sacrament of History"). What is sacramental here is the presence of the future → kingdom of God. The term "sacramental" eases the difficulty caused to this theology by its controversial relating of the Marxist view of history to → salvation history (→ Marxism and Christianity). It also reduces the antithesis between divine and human work in the realization of the kingdom of God.

5. Resacralizing of Reality

With its more exact definition of all accessible reality as sacramental reality, the term "sacramentality" implies in every sphere the thesis that we cannot finally or fully grasp this reality by sociological or scientific definition, since it possesses a higher theological dignity. On this basis Schillebeeckx (*Eucharist,* 127-30) interpreted → creation as a means of divine self-communication. Ecologically oriented theologies of creation and → environmental ethics took up this view. Negatively, the concept opposes the supposedly traditional splitting apart of God and → nature or the supposedly → Cartesian objectifying of nonhuman reality. Positively, often following P. Teilhard de Chardin (1881-1955), → process theology, → Buddhism, or the → mysticism of the Eastern church, advocates of sacramentality commend a kind of resacralizing of reality as an escape from the Cartesian worldview (J. Moltmann, H.-R. Müller-Schwefe, P. Gregorios), favoring a description in terms of sacrament or sacramentality (Gregorios, 88-89; Müller-Schwefe, 57-58; cf. S. M. Daecke, *Welt,* 269ff., and "Gott" [1988], 38; C. Link).

By still differentiating God from the world, this concept opens the door to theological reception and to the correction of scientific positions (G. Altner, C. F. von Weizsäcker, K. M. Meyer-Abich; → Philosophy of Nature; Science and Theology) that try to construe the evolutionary process as the self-actualization of the deity (Daecke, "Gott" [1987]; → Pantheism). In this context the term "sacramentality" is meant to uphold the dignity of creation and its penultimate nature by calling it the sphere of the presence and the (in many cases Christocentrically finalized) action of God that lays claim to human action and gives it its norms. It is still an open question whether this kind of functional resacralizing of nature is a tenable solution to the problems of a secular understanding, or whether it will end up merely as the (at best ineffectual) autosuggestion of a religiously affiliated minority.

6. Criticism

Talk of the sacramental structures of reality comes under the criticism of Lutheran theologians who, precisely for the sake of the underived and contingent nature of the divine action, reject the developing of a concept that structures → baptism and the Eucharist a priori (W. Elert, 355-56). The implication here is that we can use the term "sacrament" only for an a posteriori description of signs that have Christ's word of promise. It is not herewith contested that God is present and at work in nature, history (→ Theology of History), and the outer form of the church. What is maintained is that God's presence and work are not *eo ipso* salvific. God is active to save only where he himself, by his word communicated in Christ, has linked his presence and work to specific acts with a view to faith.

What is challenged, then, is the right arbitrarily (i.e., without the permission of the Word) to expand the sacramental sphere. We are not at liberty to universalize the divine action in love in the sacrament. This work goes forward as an address, communicated by the Word and nonderivable → signs, that stands in contrast to the comprehensive reality of experience of the hidden God, who impartially brings about both good and evil, both salvation and judgment.

Bibliography: M. BERNARDS, "Zur Lehre von der Kirche als Sakrament," *MTZ* 20 (1969) 29-54 • B. J. COOKE, *Sacraments and Sacramentality* (Mystic, Conn., 1983) • S. M. DAECKE, "Gott in der Natur," *PTh* 77 (1988) 29-43; idem, "Gott in der Natur?" *EK* 20 (1987) 624-27; idem, "Säkulare Welt–sakrale Schöpfung, geistige Materie," *EvT* 45 (1985) 261-76 • H. DÖRING, *Grundriß der Ekklesiologie. Zentrale Aspekte des katholischen Selbstverständnisses und ihre ökumenische Relevanz* (Darmstadt, 1986) • W. ELERT, *Der christliche Glaube. Grundlinien der lutherischen Dogmatik* (3d ed.; Hamburg, 1956) • C. FECKES, *Das Mysterium der heiligen Kirche* (3d ed.; Paderborn, 1951) • P. GREGORIOS, *The Human Presence: An Orthodox View of Nature* (Geneva, 1978) • G. GUTIÉRREZ, *A Theology of Liberation: History, Politics, and Salvation* (Maryknoll, N.Y., 1973) • E. JÜNGEL, "The Church as Sacrament" (1983), *Theological Essays* (Edinburgh, 1989) 189-213 • C. LINK, *Schöpfung* (2 vols.; Gütersloh, 1991) • J. A. MÖHLER, *Unity in the Church; or, The Principle of Catholicism* (ed. P. C. Erb; Washington, D.C., 1996; orig. pub., 1825) • J. MOLTMANN, *God in Creation* (San Francisco, 1985) • H.-R. MÜLLER-SCHWEFE, *Christus im Zeitalter der Ökumene* (Göttingen, 1986) • K. RAHNER, "The Theology of Symbol," *Theological Investigations* (vol. 4; Baltimore, 1966) 231-52 • U. REETZ, *Das Sakramentale in der Theologie Paul Tillichs* (Stuttgart, 1974) • M. J. SCHEEBEN, *The Mysteries of Christianity* (St. Louis, 1958; orig. pub., 1865) §85, "The Mystery or Sacramentality of Christian Marriage" • E. SCHILLEBEECKX, *Christ, the Sacrament of the Encounter with God* (New York, 1963); idem, *The Eucharist* (London, 1968); idem, "The Sacraments: An Encounter with God," *Theology Today* (ed. J. Feiner, J. Trütsch, and F. Böckle; Milwaukee, Wis., 1965) 194-221 • O. L. SEMMELROTH, *Die Kirche als Ursakrament* (2d ed.; Frankfurt, 1955) • U. VALESKE, *Votum Ecclesiae* (Munich, 1962).

NOTGER SLENCZKA

Sacramentals

Sacramentals are rites in the Roman Catholic Church (→ Rite 2) that are meant to denote God's presence in the world by declaring his sovereignty over persons or things and by seeking his aid. They are "sacred signs which bear a resemblance to the sacraments" but are of less importance than sacraments; they are instituted by the church, not by Christ (*Sacrosanctum concilium* [*SC*] 60; 1983 → CIC 1166-72). They display and promote the church's pastoral task of sanctifying the world for God and permeating all spheres of life (*consecratio mundi;* → Roman Catholic Church 5). They prepare believers to accept the true working of the sacraments and to sanctify life in its various situations (*SC* 60). Their efficacy rests on the → prayer of the church, which shares in the mystery of Christ. (They work *ex opere operantis ecclesiae,* "by the work of the worker [i.e.,] the church," not *ex opere operato,* "by the work performed," as do the sacraments; → Roman Catholic Church 2.)

Distinction is made between consecrations that dedicate persons or things to the service of God or the church, and benedictions that seek God's help for person or things. Among the former are consecrations of monks, nuns, abbots, churches, altars, bells, cemeteries, baptismal water, candles, vestments, and so forth. The Rituale Romanum mentions at least 160 different benedictions, including the → blessing of the pope, bishops, sacraments, → rosaries, rings, bridges, houses, dwellings, and places of work.

We should also mention → exorcisms, for which priests need special and explicit episcopal permission (1983 CIC 1172). As a rule, consecrations are by the bishop, but → priests and, in special cases, qualified laity may dispense benedictions, except for those reserved for bishops or ordinaries (*SC* 79.2; 1983 CIC 1168; → Clergy and Laity 2.1).

Bibliography: J. BAUMGARTNER, ed., *Gläubiger Umgang mit der Welt. Die Segnungen der Kirche* (Zurich, 1976) •

J. M. Champlin, *Special Signs of Grace: The Sacraments and Sacramentals* (Collegeville, Minn., 1986) • A. J. Chupungco, *Liturgical Inculturation: Sacramentals, Religiosity, and Catechesis* (Collegeville, Minn., 1992); idem, ed., *Sacraments and Sacramentals* (Collegeville, Minn., 2000) • M. Collins, editorial, *Blessing and Power* (ed. M. Collins and D. Power; Edinburgh, 1985) ix-xiii • J. Lligadas, "The Doctrine of Blessing in the New Roman Ritual," *Blessing and Power,* ed. Collins and Power, 111-20 • M. Löhrer, "Sakramentalien," *SM* 4.341-47 • D. Power, "On Blessing Things," *Blessing and Power,* ed. Collins and Power, 24-39 • H. J. F. Reinhardt, "Sakramentalien," *HKKR* 836-39 • *Rituale Romanum* (Rome, 1984) "De Benedictionibus" • M. A. Wagner,*The Sacred World of the Christian: Sensed in Faith* (Collegeville, Minn., 1993).

Erwin Fahlbusch

Sacred and Profane

1. Religious and Biblical Aspects
   1.1. Religious, Psychological, and Sociological
   1.2. Biblical
2. Theological Aspects

1. Religious and Biblical Aspects

1.1. ***Religious, Psychological, and Sociological***
The terms "sacred" and "profane" are significant in the vocabulary of comparative religion (→ Religious Studies). When the 19th century found that we do not encounter ideas of → God always and everywhere, but that God "is a late comer in the history of religion" (G. van der Leeuw, *Religion,* 104), a new and universally applicable term for → religion was needed. In 1871 E. B. Tylor (1832-1917) thought that a belief in spiritual beings might be a suitable minimal definition (chap. 11). A little later R. R. Marrett (1866-1943) pointed out that other impersonal notions (e.g., taboo and mana) preceded → animism. Finally, from the 1920s onward "sacred and profane" provided a minimal definition. Important though the idea of God might be for religion, the distinction between sacred and profane offered, so it was thought, an even more significant criterion in defining its nature (N. Söderblom, 162). But scholars who find an original → monotheism in tribal cultures disagree (e.g., W. Schmidt).

1.1.1. Various definitions of sacred are to hand. They fall into two groups. The one sees it as a psychological attitude, the other as a collective commitment. R. Otto (1896-1937) played the most important part in the development of a psychological theory (→ Psychology of Religion). In his 1917 book he defined the sacred as an a priori that underlies all religious → experience. He described it mystically, combined its most significant irrational elements (the *fascinans* and *tremendum*) as the numinous, and detached the numinous from the ethical (see 2).

Later discussion, however, did not agree with this mixing of logical and psychological elements. Under the influence of L. Lévy-Bruhl (1857-1939), who thought that susceptibility to the sacred was the mark of a primitive mentality (pp. 19-36), G. van der Leeuw (1890-1950) understood the sacred psychologically as a phenomenon of the consciousness. M. Eliade (1907-86) reworked the ontological side, arguing that the sacred lives by its antithesis to the profane and manifests itself dialectically in this antithesis; hierophanies thus occur only in (various) modalities and are found in all spheres of human life. Contributions to the Eliade Festschrift written for his 75th birthday brought out the relevance of this insight. Less prominent was a psychology of the sacred, although the ambiguity of the sacred as at once dedicated and unclean invited a new psychoanalytic understanding of the philosophy of consciousness (P. Ricoeur, 524-31).

1.1.2. Psychological explanations of the sacred are a leap in the dark from known social actions and their description to unknown psychological processes. This weakness, generally depicted by E. E. Evans-Pritchard (1902-73, pp. 20-47), was found by W. Baetke (1884-1978) in Otto's account as well. This critique gave rise to an interesting discussion, documented by C. Colpe (1977). In a perceptive article in 1942 Baetke differentiated the sacred from ideas of → power: Power is dependent on the sacred, not vice versa. What is sacred, however, is itself historically determined and obtains only within specific communities. Baetke also pointed out that the sacred has ethical aspects (→ Ethics), since social and legal norms are viewed as sacred. Baetke took a sociological line in his arguments, as did sociological theoreticians (→ Sociology of Religion).

É. Durkheim (1858-1917) took up the thesis of W. Robertson Smith (1846-94) that the religion of the Semites (esp. their sacrifices of fellowship) underlay and represented the social cohesion of the participating groups. Ritual for Durkheim was a means of collective representation, and he understood the distinction between the sacred and the profane as that between the collective and the individual. The sacred points to a collective nexus that it symbolically represents. Something of the relation between the collective and the individual may be seen in the tension be-

Sacred and Profane

tween the two spheres. H. Hubert (1872-1927) and M. Mauss (1872-1950) then carried over the tension to → sacrifice, arguing that individuals can enter into union with the sacred only by the destruction of the animal that represents them. Durkheim's view of the sacred as a ritual act that merely expresses rather than aiming at something found favor among ethnologists (→ Ethnology).

M. → Weber (1864-1920) developed a different sociological theory. He began with the typology of → everyday social actions. In contrast, the sacred is the norm of what is not everyday. The only distinction between the sacred and the profane is that the former is not everyday (*Gesammelte Aufsätze,* 1.250). The distinction from the everyday might manifest itself as magical power (→ Magic) or a → charisma that lays down new ethical rules (*Economy,* 241-45). This view became a fixed part of theories of rule (e.g., G. Balandier).

1.2. *Biblical*

W. Robertson Smith tried to expound the biblical concept of the sacred in terms of the word *ḥērem,* a common Semitic stem that expresses prohibition: "The sacred thing is one which, whether absolutely or in certain relations, is prohibited to human use" (p. 150). It comes close to the Polynesian → taboo (Tongan *tabu*), which combines the various aspects of holiness, prohibition, and uncleanness (F. Steiner, 34-35, 68-77; → Cultic Purity). The more important Hebrew word *qādôš* also has an affinity to rules of purity. Sanctified by God, the Israelites are not to defile themselves by eating unclean animals (Lev. 11:43-45). M. Douglas interpreted these rules for purity, not in terms of preanimistic holiness, but in terms of systems of classification: "If uncleanness is matter out of place, we must approach it through order" (p. 53).

The use of *qādôš* and the Gk. *hagios* in the Bible brings out both the social and the psychological meanings of the sacred. A sacred object is laden with power and demands awe (→ Reverence). Sacred bread *(leḥem qōdeš)* can be eaten without danger only by those who are sacred. → David and his men were at war and, by having refrained from sex, were actually sacred, so that they could eat the bread unharmed (1 Sam. 21:1-6). But when Uzzah, even with good intentions, grasped the → ark of God to prevent it from falling, this action brought down God's wrath upon him. Uzzah died, and David was afraid (2 Sam. 6:1-11). Similarly in 1 Sam. 6:19-20, when the sons of Jeconiah did not welcome the arrival of the ark in Beth-shemesh, God slew 70 of them, and the people of the place asked, "Who is able to stand before the LORD, this holy God?" (v. 20).

The biblical writings also bring out the social side. Holiness extends to the participants in sacred actions. God's appearance on Mount → Sinai (→ Theophany) presupposes the self-sanctifying of the people present there (Exod. 19:10-15). In → holy war the camp must be sacred, and no one who is (sexually) defiled must be there (Deut. 23:9-14). The same applies to sacrifice: "Sanctify yourselves and come with me to the sacrifice [*zebaḥ*]" (1 Sam. 16:5). Holiness establishes a fellowship of its own kind. It demands of individuals the surrender of what they are accustomed to in everyday life.

In the OT, however, the sacred is viewed ethically as well. It demands the observance of definite commands. In the → Holiness Code (Lev. 17–26) Israel's holiness is to live in accordance with the commands of its sacred God (19:2). Prophetic threats (→ Prophet, Prophecy) presuppose Israel's unfaithfulness and therefore its falling under the judgment of the sacred (Isa. 1:4, 16-17). In the → Qumran writings holiness is a quality of the separated community that remained true to the → covenant with the fathers (1QS 8:4-6). The NT follows the same line (1 Cor. 6:1-2).

→ Saints, Veneration of; Sanctification; Sanctuary

Bibliography: W. BAETKE, *Das Heilige im Germanischen* (Tübingen, 1942; first part also in *Die Diskussion um das "Heilige"* [ed. C. Colpe; Darmstadt, 1977] 337-79) • G. BALANDIER, *Political Anthropology* (London, 1970) • C. COLPE, *Die Diskussion um das "Heilige"* (Darmstadt, 1977) • M. DOUGLAS, *Purity and Danger: An Analysis of Concepts of Pollution and Taboo* (Harmondsworth, 1970) • É. DURKHEIM, "Concerning the Definition of Religious Phenomena" (1899), *Durkheim on Religion* (ed. W. S. F. Pickering; Atlanta, 1994) 74-99 • M. ELIADE, *Patterns in Comparative Religion* (London, 1958) • E. E. EVANS-PRITCHARD, *Theories of Primitive Religion* (Oxford, 1965) • H. HUBERT and M. MAUSS, "Essai sur la nature et le fonction du sacrifice" (1899), *Marcel Mauss* (ed. V. Karady; vol. 1; Paris, 1968) 193-307 • G. VAN DER LEEUW, "La structure de la mentalité primitive," *RHPR* 8 (1928) 1-31; idem, *Religion in Essence and Manifestation* (Princeton, 1986; orig. pub., 1933) • L. LÉVY-BRUHL, *Primitives and the Supernatural* (New York, 1935) • R. R. MARETT, "The Conception of Mana," *The Threshold of Religion* (2d ed.; London, 1909; repr., 1979) 99-121 • H.-P. MÜLLER, "קדשׁ *qdš* heilig," *THAT* 2.589-609 • R. OTTO, *The Idea of the Holy: An Inquiry into the Non-rational Factor in the Idea of the Divine and Its Relation to the Rational* (rev. ed.; London, 1924; orig. pub., 1917) • P. RICOEUR, *Freud and Philosophy: An Essay on Interpretation* (New Haven, 1970) • W. SCHMIDT, *Der Ursprung der Gottes-*

idee (12 vols.; Münster, 1912-55) • W. R. SMITH, *Lectures on the Religion of the Semites* (3d ed.; New York, 1927; orig. pub., 1889) • N. SÖDERBLOM, *Das Werden des Gottesglaubens* (2d ed.; Leipzig, 1926) • F. STEINER, *Taboo* (Harmondsworth, 1967) chap. 6 • E. B. TYLOR, *Religion in Primitive Culture* (New York, 1958; orig. pub., 1871) • M. WEBER, *Economy and Society: An Outline of Interpretive Sociology* (3 vols.; New York, 1968; orig. pub., 1922); idem, *Gesammelte Aufsätze zur Religionssoziologie* (vol. 1; Tübingen, 1920).

HANS G. KIPPENBERG

2. Theological Aspects

Systematic theology can separate the sacred and the profane dualistically either by finding the sacred only in cosmic or transcendent developments or by absolutizing the sacred and leaving no place for the profane. The abandonment of → dualism means that "everything secular is potentially sacred" (P. → Tillich, 1.218).

Christianity originated with the experience of the sacred in the revelation of Jesus Christ (J. Splett, 212). In being "in Christ" (2 Cor. 5:17), the sacred has its benchmark (K. Hemmerle, 215) but not its structural plausibility, even in its relation to the profane. In his coincidence of opposites Nicholas of Cusa (1401-64) could thus develop the union of contradictions in the sacred. The late medieval view of the sacred led in M. → Luther (1483-1546; → Luther's Theology) to separation between the sacred and the profane, and in J. → Calvin (1509-64; → Calvin's Theology) to emphasis on purity (→ Sanctification) and the moral aspect of the sacred.

F. → Schleiermacher (1768-1834) linked "God-consciousness," which extends into the sacred, with "self-consciousness," which stays with the profane (*The Christian Faith*, §4). He described human → conscience as being "conjoined with the need of redemption" through an act of "divine causality," which for Schleiermacher is the meaning of the holiness of God (§83). G. W. F. Hegel (1770-1831) stressed the unity of absolute holiness in God to the degree that he is in himself absolutely the universal being (*Elements of the Philosophy of Right*, §§132, 142).

In a structural description that goes beyond É. Durkheim (1858-1917) and N. Söderblom (1866-1931), R. Otto (1869-1937) defined the sacred as a "complex category" that has its original roots in the numinous but is still specifically separated from it (45). It constitutes the link between the irrationally ineffable and the rationally expressible. In extreme cases what is absolutely profane is distinct from it (51; see §1 above). As the fulfillment of an "original feeling-response" (6), the sacred lives by the numinous, the indefinable origin of the "element of awefulness" (13), the psychosomatically stimulating (16), the "strange harmony of contrasts" that dialectically attract and repel (31), a positive "value or worth" (51), the total "energy, or urgency," of being (23). All these factors may be grasped in the "ideogram" (35) of speech, art, and music, of signs and rites in the profane world. The sacred establishes the identity of what is not identical, the coincidence of opposites, whose paradoxical being has sunk into absolute nothing (30). Note the similarities with sunyata (Skt. *śūnyatā*, "emptiness, void") in → Buddhism, the voidness that constitutes ultimate reality.

→ Dialectical theology stressed the existential, personal meaning rather than the structural. Thus for K. → Barth (1886-1968) the sacred God is "not the sacred or numinous of Otto" but "the Holy One of Israel"; the sacred is "separate, that which confronts, arousing awe and the sense of obligation, but . . . fundamentally that which singles out, blesses, helps and restores" (*CD* II/1, 361). The humanities attempted an empirical description. M. Eliade (1907-86), G. van der Leeuw (1890-1950), G. Ebeling (1912-2001), and others sought the manifestation of the sacred in reality, for history too is part of it to the extent that we experience the sacred (Eliade, *Patterns,* 462-65). In view of insoluble empirical tensions and the "ambiguity of the sacred" (Ricoeur, 524-31), to merge the sacred and the profane seems to be just as problematic as a definitive separation of the two (W. Jetter, 127).

P. Tillich's (1886-1965) statement that "everything secular is implicitly related to the holy" means only that the sacred shows itself in the profane and that they are in correlation, as confirmed by "the history of religion and culture" (1.218). The sacred has "'spoken' *to* human existence from beyond it" (1.64).

If for Tillich the sacred leads to "reunion of the separated in all dimensions" (3.243-44), we are close to a dynamic rather than a static view, and a process of moving away and moving together is dialectically possible. The sacred as ongoing origin requires a dynamic, functional structure that can cause movement and bring it to rest in itself. In Christianity this dialectical dynamic has its origin in the cross and → resurrection of Jesus Christ, by which failure in the profane is called into the resurrection of the sacred. The sacred manifests itself when nonbeing is called into being, when the dead are called to life (Rom. 4:17). The → Holy Spirit may thus be viewed functionally as the presence of Jesus Christ in fullness of being (Rom. 8:11).

→ Reverence; Sanctification

Bibliography: S. C. Barton, ed., *Holiness: Past and Present* (London, 2003) • É. Durkheim, *The Elementary Forms of Religious Life* (New York, 1995; orig. pub., 1912) • G. Ebeling, "Profanität und Geheimnis," *Wort und Glaube* (vol. 2; Tübingen, 1969) 184-208 • M. Eliade, *Images and Symbols: Studies in Religious Symbolism* (New York, 1969); idem, *Patterns in Comparative Religion* (London, 1958) • B. Häring, *Das Heilige und das Gute* (Krailling, 1950) • K. Hemmerle, "Das Heilige," *HTTL* 3.213-16 • W. Jetter, *Symbol und Ritual. Anthropologische Elemente im Gottesdienst* (Göttingen, 1978) • G. van der Leeuw *Religion in Essence and Manifestation* (Princeton, 1986; orig. pub., 1933) • R. Ōkōchi and K. Otte, *Tan-ni-sho. Die Gunst des Reinen Landes: Begegnung zwischen Buddhismus und Christentum* (Bern, 1979) • K. Otte, "Rechtfertigung aus Glauben als Religionsgrenzen übersteigende Kraft," *Der Friede unter den Religionen nach Nikolaus von Kues* (ed. R. Haubst; Mainz, 1984) 333-42 • R. Otto, *The Idea of the Holy: An Inquiry into the Nonrational Factor in the Idea of the Divine and Its Relation to the Rational* (rev. ed.; London, 1924; orig. pub., 1917) • P. Ricoeur, *Freud and Philosophy: An Essay on Interpretation* (New Haven, 1970) • N. Söderblom, *Das Werden des Gottesglaubens* (2d ed.; Leipzig, 1926) • J. Splett, "Das Heilige," *HTTL* 3.211-13 • P. Tillich, *Systematic Theology* (3 vols.; Chicago, 1951-63).

Klaus Otte

Sacred Heart of Jesus

1. Development
2. Iconographic Forms
3. Theological Basis
4. Relevance to Piety
5. Devotion to the Heart of Mary

1. Development

Beginning with the work of the Innsbruck patrologist Hugo Rahner (1900-1968), 20th-century research has shown that in the High Middle Ages expressed devotion to the Sacred Heart of Jesus began on the broad basis of Johannine-inspired patristic meditation on the pierced side of the crucified Jesus as the source of sacramental life (John 19:34). The initiators of express devotion to the Sacred Heart belonged to the early Middle Ages (→ Anselm, → Bernard of Clairvaux), and it was further developed in the 13th century by the German Benedictine nuns Mechthild of Hackeborn and Gertrude "the Great" of Helfta. The Carthusians and even more so the → Jesuits made the Sacred Heart a favorite theme of popular devotion, especially after the visions of the Franciscan nun Margareta Mary Alacoque (1647-90).

Although a counterpart to the overstrict Jansenist concept of Christ was welcomed (→ Jansenism), a liturgy of devotion to the Sacred Heart developed only slowly. Only in 1856 did → Pius IX proclaim a universal Feast of the Sacred Heart. Against the sentimentalization that unsuitable artificial forms of expression threatened to bring, Pius XI and → Pius XII issued → encyclicals in 1928 and 1956. Pius XII could build on the findings of theological reflection.

2. Iconographic Forms

One of the great hindrances to devotion to the Sacred Heart was the inability to portray the subject. → Images of Christ with a visible physical heart circulated, but they are obviously tasteless, especially in the form of plaster figures (→ Iconography; Symbol).

3. Theological Basis

Considered from the perspective of Christ's physical heart, it is theologically legitimate to view the person of Christ under the symbol of his heart, especially as the merciful Redeemer. Such a concept is not unfamiliar in Protestant piety (esp. Paul Gerhardt; → Pietism).

4. Relevance to Piety

Despite the iconographic problem, devotion to the Sacred Heart has undoubtedly contributed to an interiorizing of Christ-piety among ordinary Roman Catholics. It still remains to be seen whether greater theological depth can lead it out of the present decline and give it once again a broad impact.

5. Devotion to the Heart of Mary

Having similar roots, devotion to the heart of Mary (→ Mary; Devotion to Mary) crystallized for the first time in 1646 in a Feast of the Heart of Mary established at the Bérullian Oratory in Paris by St. John Eudes (1601-80). This observance became a general Roman Catholic feast on August 22, 1944, under Pius XII. In postconciliar Roman Catholicism it is not a day of obligation and is observed on the Saturday after the Feast of the Sacred Heart, which is on the third Friday after Pentecost.

→ Christology

Bibliography: A. Bea, ed., *Cor Jesu. Commentationes in litteras encyclicas Pii XII "Haurietis aquas"* (Rome, 1959) • J. Le Brun, "Politics and Spirituality: The Devotion to the Sacred Heart," *The Concrete Christian Life* (ed. C. Duquoc; New York, 1971) 29-43 • F. Makower, *Towards Tomorrow: The Society of the Sacred Heart of Jesus* (London, 2000) • H. Rahner, "Flumina de ventre Christi. Die patristische Auslegung von Joh 7,37-38" (1941), *Symbole der Kirche* (Salzburg, 1964) 175-235 • K. Rahner, "'Behold This Heart!' Preliminaries to a Theology of Devotion to the Sacred Heart," *Theological Investigations* (vol. 3; Baltimore, 1967) 321-30; idem, "Some Theses for a Theology of Devotion to the Sacred Heart," ibid., 331-52 • J. Ratzinger, *Behold the Pierced One: An Approach to a Spiritual Christology* (San Francisco, 1986) • L. Scheffczyk, ed., *Faith in Christ and the Worship of Christ: New Approaches to Devotion to Christ* (San Francisco, 1986) • J. Stierli, ed., *Heart of the Saviour: A Symposium on Devotion to the Sacred Heart* (New York, 1957) • W. M. Wright, *Sacred Heart: Gateway to God* (Maryknoll, N.Y., 2001).

Balthasar Fischer†

Sacrifice

1. General

1.1. *Words and Concept*

The English words "sacrifice" and "offering" come from Lat. *sacrificium* and *offero.* Ger. *Opfer* goes back to Lat. *operari,* "be active." The terms suggest an active relation to the reality concerned in the different → religions. The various ways in which the relation is described may thus affect the concept.

Even though a distinction might arise between real and symbolic sacrifice, sacrifice is always at the heart of religion and widely influences human conduct in other spheres as well. In religious history we may understand sacrifice as a separate phenomenon, but only in terms of the combination of its elements, which may change both temporarily and quantitatively.

1.2. *Phenomenology*

1.2.1. Primary elements of sacrifice include (1) a regular action (that might include → magic, but not necessarily), with customary objects (found or brought) and purposeful actions; (2) surprising occurrences (even if only in the mind), special circumstances (either positive or negative), and hoped-for results.

1.2.1.1. The regular action establishes → communication between persons who thus become partners in different ways: eating, giving, taking, exchanging, claiming, or forcing.

Customary objects vary according to what is available (stones, wood) or according to the → culture (animals for hunters and herders, produce for farmers, manufactured goods and money in societies that delegate certain functions to artisans).

Purposeful actions include the offering, dismembering, and eating of animals; the gathering, sharing, or eating of natural things; as well as the presentation of produce, the breeding of livestock, handiwork, and war.

1.2.1.2. Surprising occurrences may be natural or human (physical, moral, or social), or they may relate to time or space.

Special circumstances include good or bad weather, defilement or purification, human conduct (social or antisocial), social unity (orderly or chaotic), inviting or terrifying places, and times of celebration or disaster.

Hoped-for results include recovery from threatening or persistent ills — for example, a return of favorable weather, game, health, or good fortune; socially, the restoration of → peace or prosperity; spatially, the finding of refuge or protection; and temporally, a period of peace and festivity.

1.2.2. Sacrifice arose in virtue of a link between the purposeful action and the desired result by way of cultic → rites. The latter did not derive from sacrifice alone but from the whole system. They have a purpose, as we see in such varied offerings as those of purification, divination, petition, thanksgiving, praise, and expiation. Because of the link there is a relation between the things mentioned in 1.2.1.1 and those mentioned in 1.2.1.2. As a whole the primary elements are all strange and form part of the sacrificial system. The system may be classified according to them, but in its totality it may transcend itself (as in 1.2.2.3). For this reason new and extraordinary realities may be created by the actual actions (as in → myth).

1.2.2.1. Qualitatively, the issue in the burnt offering is no longer to make pleasing, nor in the offering of renunciation conservation, nor in the gift offering payment, nor in the thank offering repayment, nor in the petition offering wooing, even though an action of *do ut des* (i.e., reciprocity) may be involved, whether there be recipients or not.

Offerings of blood, flesh, natural products, manufactured goods, parts of the body, chastity, strength, or virtue are set apart by → consecration and belong henceforth to ancestors (→ Ancestor Worship) or the gods.

A special form of action is the devoting of property, the *pars pro toto* offerings of animal organs, the giving of the first fruits at the start of harvest, the offering on the finishing of a task, the commencement of a journey, or the declaration of war.

1.2.2.2. Special results may also include being delivered from death or rescued from evil. They can occur in nature by offering something like or unlike; socially by a treaty, an → oath, or table fellowship; in physical space by erecting a special building, or in time by observing special points in the agricultural or nomadic year.

Circumstances came to include a greeting offering to bring rain, an offering of hair or clothing for cultic purification, an expiatory offering (→ Sin) to meet some collective crisis or danger, a founding offering on the erection of a → sanctuary in a secular area, an offering of the self (renunciation) on the integration of important times in a myth or cultic tradition into the existing religious calendar.

A result that goes beyond what we find in 1.2.1.2. is the redemption held out in the sacrifice of the → Mass (§2.2.2). As the dedication of celebrant and recipients, this setting is comparable to the special circumstances in the same section above. The event is communion, even with the Savior himself (→ Soteriology). The Host is offered (see customary objects in 1.2.1.1). As Eucharist (thanksgiving), the action transcends the regular actions in 1.2.1.1 (→ Eucharistic Spirituality).

1.2.2.3. In many cases the extraordinary becomes a fact, for example, the creation of the world by a cosmogonic sacrifice that is made to a primal being (→ Creation), with the overcoming of death by the offering up of a hero or a god.

1.3. *History*

A history of sacrifice would have little meaning as such. In history we find no development from predeistic to theistic sacrifice, or from material to spiritual sacrifice. We find only nuances shifting with the reduction of complexity. A classification is possible only with secondary elements, including place (grottoes, stones, trees, → altars, places of → pilgrimage), time (New Year, historical event), function (substitution, representation), celebrant (ruler, priest, herald), or victim (animal, child, maiden, prisoners of war, king). Which elements find a place depends on the culture.

1.4. *Theories of Origin*

Three theories that locate a basic human attitude somewhere between a timeless disposition of soul and a primal historical event have been influential in the interpretation of sacrifice. A (1) psychoanalytic theory presupposes collective murder, a death wish, and substitution (S. Frued; → Psychoanalysis). The (2) cultural-anthropological view sees an origin in the hunt (K. Meuli). The (3) ethological view looks first to → aggression (K. Lorenz). All three theories assume that the shedding of blood and slaughter are primary and lie behind other forms, but in different ways they combine this assumption with a (4) sociological theory that sacrifice is sharing, reclaiming, and dividing (M. Mauss).

With the rituals with which they arranged and shared their meals, early hunters perhaps showed that the killing of animals aroused fear in them at the loss of this possibility of life, and the life lost thus had to be dedicated with the corresponding defensive sacrifice. The cultic offering was thus one of caution, atonement, restoration, and fellowship (W. Burkert). The aggressive instinct produced a chain of violence and counterviolence that could be ended, according to another theory, only by the slaying of a creature that did not participate. Hence arose the idea of substitution, whether animal or human (R. Girard). There is some support for this kind of theory so long as human nature seems to be incapable of living peaceably, but it is going too far to try to find here the one origin of religion and the → sacred.

→ Human Sacrifice

Bibliography: R. Ardrey, *The Hunting Hypothesis* (London, 1976) • A. I. Baumgarten, ed., *Sacrifice in Religious Experience* (Leiden, 2002) • W. Burkert, *Anthropologie des religiösen Opfers. Die Sakralisierung der Gewalt* (2d ed.; Munich, 1987); idem, *Homo Necans: The Anthropology of Ancient Greek Sacrificial Ritual and Myth* (Berkeley, Calif., 1983) • S. Freud, *Beyond the Pleasure Principle* (New York, 1989; orig. pub., 1920); idem, *Totem and Tabu* (London, 1950; orig. pub., 1912-13) • R. Girard, *The Scapegoat* (Baltimore, 1986); idem, *Things Hidden since the Foundation of the World* (London, 1987); idem, *Violence and the Sacred* (Baltimore, 1977) • J. Henninger, "Sacrifice," *EncRel(E)* 12.544-57 • H. Hubert and M. Mauss, *Sacrifice: Its Nature and Function* (Chicago, 1964; orig.

pub., 1898) • K. LORENZ, *On Aggression* (New York, 1966) • P. R. MCKENZIE, *The Christians: Their Practices and Beliefs. An Adaptation of Friedrich Heiler's "Phenomenology of Religion"* (Nashville, 1988) • M. MAUSS, *The Gift: The Form and Reason for Exchange in Archaic Societies* (New York, 1990; orig. pub., 1923-24) • K. MEULI, "Griechische Opferbräuche," *Phyllobolia für Peter von der Mühll zum 60. Geburtstag* (Basel, 1946) • H. MÜLLER-KARPE, *Handbuch der Vorgeschichte* (4 vols.; Munich, 1966-80) 1.224-29, 2.334-71, 3.605-61, 4.584-716 • I. STRENSKI, *Theology and the First Theory of Sacrifice* (Leiden, 2003).

CARSTEN COLPE

2. OT

2.1. *Sources and Theories*

For a systematizing of sacrificial practices in the OT, we turn to late preexilic and exilic-postexilic texts like Deut. 12:6-7, 27, etc.; Ezekiel 40–48; Leviticus 1–5; 6–7 (cf. Exodus 29; Leviticus 8–9; Numbers 8; 28–29, also Lev. 10:12-15; 11–15; 16; 17–26; Numbers 6; 15:1-16, etc.; R. Rendtorff, 6-37). The underlying traditions, the product of a complex cultic and social development, are old. Their origins have been variously sought in pre-Islamic Arabia, Mesopotamia, Syria-Canaan, and the Mediterranean area. Different explanations of their origins have also been suggested (gift, fellowship, divine food, etc.; see L. Sabourin, 1484-88).

A new turn in OT scholarship came with concentration on the history of the tradition, which affected the view of sacrifice as well (A. Alt, V. Maag, L. Rost). The approach might at times be one-sided, as in Rost's relating of the → Passover to the change of pasture. What we still need are not more works on religious history (on Ugarit, see J.-M. de Tarragon, P. D. Miller) but a sociology or a social history of sacrifice in Israel (for a beginning, see G. A. Anderson, 1-25, also W. Burkert) or works on special periods, with an orientation to social anthropology (N. Jay).

2.2. *Historical Development*

It is hardly possible to write a history of sacrifice in Israel without assessing the sources and studying the → history of religion in the Near East (Rendtorff; Rost, *Studien;* Anderson, 27-55). Because the OT books are not simply documenting the age in which they were written and which they recount, one cannot uncritically derive from them a history of sacrifice. (A different view is taken by R. J. Thompson and O. Betz, 1094-96.)

The question of the sacrificial cult in early Israel already raises fundamental issues of research. Hence, although the patriarchal clans that practiced "small cults" doubtless offered sacrifices, which sacrifices were they? We read of sacrifices and fellowship meals (with no → priest or → altar) in Gen. 31:54; 46:1, etc.; of the building of altars (but no offerings) in Gen. 12:7-8; 13:4, 18, etc.; and of an ancient blood rite in connection with the Passover in Exod. 12:21b-23 (on patriarchal religion, see C. Westermann, 105-21, esp. 110-11; also M. Köckert, 150-61, 309-11; on the Passover, E. Otto). The paterfamilias also offered the sacrifices in the case of Gideon and Manoah (Judges 6 and 13; Rost, *Studien,* 17-28, 71-81).

We can see how closely the idea of sacrifice was linked to the development of society and of the concept of God (→ Monotheism) from prophetic criticism of sacrifice and the cult in Amos 4:4-5; 5:21-27; Hos. 4:4-14; 6:6; 14:1-2; Isa. 1:10-13; also Jer. 7:17-20; Isa. 43:23-24, etc. (→ Prophet, Prophecy). Criticism of sacrifice in relation to the message of judgment was a function of prophetic faith in God. Wisdom criticism in Prov. 15:8-9; 21:3, 27; 28:9 (see also Prov. 17:1; 20:25; Ps. 40:6-8; 50:7-14; 51:15-19; 69:30-31) was perhaps part of the same trend (H. J. Boecker).

Though not without parallels, the understanding in Deuteronomy is unique inasmuch as sacrifice is not here an institutionalized cult but a practice of personal → piety, and → Israel is the → people of God rejoicing in a common meal in the presence of → Yahweh (G. Braulik).

2.3. *Terminology and Systematics*

Unlike Latin, with its *sacrificium* (from *sacer facio,* "make holy"), Hebrew had no comprehensive term for a sacrifice apart from *minḥâ* (offering, gift, Gen. 4:3-5, also 1 Sam. 26:19 etc.) and, in Priestly usage, *qorbān* (offering, Lev. 1:2 etc.). Other words denote a specific sacrifice according to type (*zebaḥ* for animals, *ʿōlâ* for the burnt offering), occasion (thanksgiving, free-will, → vow), aim (guilt, sin), time (morning, evening), or material offered (animal, vegetable, cereal, drink, incense, etc.). The oldest was no doubt the animal sacrifice *(zebaḥ;* cf. Ugar. *dbḥ),* which perhaps was originally part of a family meal or larger social gathering (Gen. 31:54; 46:1; 1 Sam. 1:21; 2:13-16; 9:12-13; 15:22, etc.). Yahweh had his share (fat burnt on the altar, spilled blood; see Leviticus 3), but most of the animal was eaten by the participants (→ Cultic Meal).

In the regulations for sacrifices in Leviticus 1–5 and 6–7, animal sacrifices are classified as burnt offerings (chap. 1, also 6:9-13), "sacrifices of well-being" (NRSV; or "peace offerings," RSV; chap. 3, also 7:11-21), and sin and guilt offerings (4–5, also 6:25–7:8). In the first of these types *(ʿōlâ),* the animal was totally burned (Gen. 8:20; Judg. 6:26; 13:15-23; 1 Kgs. 18:23, 32-33; note *kālîl*, "whole burnt offering," in 1 Sam. 7:9). It was common in Canaan (Ugar. *šrp*, Phoenician-Punic *kll*) and in Greece *(holokautōma)*. Rost thus concluded that Israel came to know it only when settled. We see its significance as an offering in → human sacrifice (Genesis 22; 2 Kgs. 3:26-27).

The sacrifice of well-being *(zebaḥ šĕlāmîm*, Ugar. *slmm)*, sometimes called the covenant offering, occurs in the singular only in Amos 5:22 (*šelem;* B. Janowski, "Erwägungen"). A feature of this offering was the sprinkling of blood. It originally came after the burnt offering (Exod. 20:24; Judg. 20:26; 21:4; 2 Sam. 6:17-18, etc.) and only later was associated with the animal sacrifice (Leviticus 3, also 7:11-21).

The sin and guilt offerings *(ḥaṭṭā't* and *'āšām)* gave blood a central expiatory function (Lev. 17:11; → Atonement 1). They formed the climax of the sacrificial system, all other offerings being subsumed under the concept of expiation.

2.4. *Later History*

The spiritualizing of the concepts of sacrifice and the cult began already in the OT, especially in the → Wisdom literature and Wisdom psalms. Thus → fasting, almsgiving, and → prayer might replace the expiatory cult. This tendency later became stronger in Palestinian and Hellenistic → Judaism (note → Qumran, the Targums, Philo; Sabourin, 1503-12). Criticism of the cult made its loss easier to bear after the disaster of A.D. 70.

→ Babylonian and Assyrian Religion; Dietary Laws; Law 1

Bibliography: General and background: G. A. Anderson, *Sacrifices and Offerings in Ancient Israel* (Atlanta, 1987) • G. A. Anderson and S. M. Olyan, *Priesthood and Cult in Ancient Israel* (Sheffield, 1991) • W. Burkert, "Opfertypen und antike Gesellschaftsstruktur," *Der Religionswandel unserer Zeit im Spiegel der Religionswissenschaft* (ed. G. Stephenson; Darmstadt, 1976) 168-87 • W. K. Gilders, "Representation and Interpretation: Blood Manipulation in Ancient Israel and Early Judaism" (2 vols.; diss., Brown University, 2001) • P. Heger, *The Development of Incense Cult in Israel* (Berlin, 1997) • B. Janowski, "Erwägungen zur Vorgeschichte des israelitischen *šᵉlāmîm*-Opfers," *UF* 12 (1980) 231-59 • J. H. Kurtz, *Offerings, Sacrifices, and Worship in the OT* (Peabody, Mass., 1998) • T. A. Marx, "Opfer II/1," *RGG* (4th ed.) 6.572-76 • P. D. Miller, "Prayer and Sacrifice in Ugarit and Israel," *Text and Context* (ed. W. Claassen; Sheffield, 1988) 139-55 • E. Otto, "פָּסַח *pāsaḥ;* פֶּסַח *pesaḥ*," *TDOT* 12.1-24 • L. Sabourin, "Sacrifice," *DBSup* 10.1483-1545 • J.-M. de Tarragon, *Le culte à Ugarit* (Paris, 1980) • R. J. Thompson and O. Betz, "Opfer," *GBL* 2.1092-1101 • R. de Vaux, *Les sacrifices de l'Ancien Testament* (Paris, 1964).

Development: H. J. Boecker, "Überlegungen zur Kultpolemik der vorexilischen Propheten," *Die Botschaft und die Boten* (ed. J. Jeremias and L. Perlitt; Neukirchen, 1981) 169-80 • G. Braulik, "Die Freude des Festes" (1983), *Studien zur Theologie des Deuteronomiums* (Stuttgart, 1988) 161-218 • D. Davies, "An Interpretation of Sacrifice in Leviticus," *ZAW* 89 (1977) 387-98 • C. Eberhart, *Studien zur Bedeutung der Opfer im Alten Testament* (Neukirchen, 2002) • E. Haag, "Opfer und Hingabe im Alten Testament," *Freude am Gottesdienst* (ed. J. Schreiner; Stuttgart, 1983) 333-46 • P. Heger, *The Three Biblical Altar Laws: Developments in the Sacrificial Cult in Practice and Theology* (Berlin, 1999) • B. Janowski, *Sühne als Heilsgeschehen* (2d ed.; Neukirchen, 2000) • B. Janowski and M. Welker, eds., *Opfer. Theologische und kulturelle Kontexte* (Frankfurt, 2000) • N. Jay, "Sacrifice, Descent, and the Patriarchs," *VT* 38 (1988) 52-70 • N. Kiuchi, *The Purification Offering in the Priestly Literature: Its Meaning and Function* (Sheffield, 1987) • M. Köckert, *Vätergott und Väterverheißungen* (Göttingen, 1988) 150-61, 309-11 • B. A. Levine, *In the Presence of the Lord: A Study of Cult and Some Cultic Terms in Ancient Israel* (Leiden, 1974) • S. Lyonnet and L. Sabourin, *Sin, Redemption, and Sacrifice: A Biblical and Patristic Study* (Rome, 1970) • D. McCarthy, "The Symbolism of Blood and Sacrifice," *JBL* 88 (1966) 166-76 • M. H. McEntire, *The Function of Sacrifice in Chronicles, Ezra, and Nehemiah* (Lewiston, N.Y., 1993) • J. Milgrom, *Cult and Conscience: The Asham and the Priestly Doctrine of Repentance* (Leiden, 1976); idem, "Sacrifices and Offerings, OT," *IDBSup* 763-71 • R. Rendtorff, *Studien zur Geschichte des Opfers im alten Israel* (Neukirchen, 1967) • L. Rost, "Erwägungen zum israelitischen Brandopfer" (1958), *Das kleine Credo und andere Studien zum Alten Testament* (Heidelberg, 1965) 112-19; idem, *Studien zum Opfer im alten Israel* (Stuttgart, 1981) • C. Westermann, *Genesis 12–36* (Minneapolis, 1985).

Bernd Janowski

3. NT

3.1. *Jerusalem Cult*

The OT cult continued in the Jerusalem → temple up to A.D. 70 and was briefly restored under Bar Cochba (132-35). We find references to it in the NT, especially in the first chapters of Luke (1:5–2:51) and in Acts (3:1; 8:27b; 21:23-26).

→ Jesus presupposed the practice of sacrifice

(Matt. 5:23-24; Mark 1:44 and par.; Luke 17:14). Yet he also predicted the overthrow of the temple (Mark 13:2 and par.; 14:58; 15:29; Matt. 26:61; John 2:19; Acts 6:14), and in his cleansing of the temple he gave a → sign that there would be no place for the cult when the rule of God was established (Mark 11:15-17 and par.; cf. Rev. 21:22-27).

The → primitive Christian community viewed the temple ambivalently. Though the "house" was the center of worship and the → Eucharist, believers at first took a regular part in temple worship (Acts 3:1, 11; 5:42). To do so was natural for → Jewish Christians, who remained faithful to the law under the leadership of → James, the Lord's brother (Eusebius *Hist. eccl.* 2.23.4-18). But from the very outset the "Hellenists" were critical of the law and the cult in the same way as Jesus had been (Acts 6:13-14; 7:1-53).

3.2. *Sacrifice in Ecclesiology and Parenesis*

Among Christians, reception of OT ideas of sacrifice came first in ecclesiology and → parenesis. The saying of Jesus in Mark 14:58, which is difficult to reconstruct, contrasts a temple "not made with hands" with the earthly temple, which will be destroyed. The community understood itself as this "temple of God" (1 Cor. 3:11, 16; Eph. 2:19-22; 1 Pet. 2:5), and it thus regarded its whole life as sacrificial worship service. The fact that → Paul could use the cultic concept of offering with reference to believers (Rom. 6:12-13, 16, 19) shows that turning to God meant putting one's total self at his disposal as a whole offering (Rom. 15:16; Phil. 2:17, also 2 Tim. 4:6).

The exhortation in Romans offers further elucidation. The church is to offer itself as "a living sacrifice, holy and acceptable to God" (12:1), which is true and proper → worship in the new sense and according to the new thinking (vv. 1c, 2). Similarly, 1 Pet. 2:5 refers to the offering of "spiritual sacrifices" by believers, who are chosen to be God's own people.

3.3. *Christological Reception*

In the early post-Easter period the usual tendency was to see in the death of Jesus not so much a sacrificial death as a vicarious expiation (→ Atonement) along the lines of a noncultic tradition that we see in Isa. 53:10-11 and of which we have a few examples in early Judaism. With no specific reference to sacrifice this tradition finds in → suffering and death a means to expiate guilt and to do away with → sin. In the case of certain chosen people, such suffering might be done vicariously for the sins of others, not simply their own (see Mark 10:45 and par.; 1 Tim. 2:5).

The question how far this noncultic view of atonement was linked to sacrificial ideas arises first in Mark 14:24 par. Matt. 26:28, for here we have a typological reference to Exod. 24:8, so that implicitly the death of Jesus is seen as a covenant sacrifice. Then 1 Cor. 5:7 links the death of Jesus to the Passover, and 1 Pet. 1:18-19 brings in the idea of redemption from "futile ways." We find similar teaching in John 1:29, 36; 19:31-37 and Revelation 4–5, though it should be noted that the slaying of the → Passover lamb had no atoning function as such, and that we thus have here the combination of two separate traditions.

The theme of sacrifice first becomes plainer in Ephesians, which interprets Christ's self-giving as "a fragrant offering and sacrifice to God" (5:2). The allusion to the tradition of the whole offering *(ʿōlâ)* of Exod. 29:18 and Num. 15:24 is evident, since the point is not that *something* is offered but that Jesus offered *himself.* The Christological statement leads on to an ecclesiological statement in Eph. 5:25-27, though it is not developed in detail.

The reference to sacrifice in Rom. 8:32 is subject to debate. Some see a typological allusion to Gen. 22:9, 16, but others disagree. Also contested is Rom. 3:25, where some exegetes, on the basis of the LXX Greek use of *hilastērion* for the Heb. *kappōret* (the cover of the → ark), find a reference to the ritual of the great Day of Atonement (Leviticus 16). Since this allusion is by no means certain, however, others think the Greek simply has the ordinary sense "means of expiation."

Hebrews, in contrast, offers an expressly Christological view of sacrifice. Interpretation of Christ's death as a sacrifice goes hand in hand with the view of Christ as → high priest (→ Christology). Behind this understanding lies a concept of the heavenly → sanctuary that was taken over from Hellenistic → Judaism on the basis of Exod. 25:40, the earthly sanctuary being viewed only as an earthly copy (Heb. 8:5). On this view the Jerusalem cult was only provisional and partial. It pointed ahead to an ultimate fulfillment of salvation (8:1–9:10). As the heavenly high priest (5:10, also 4:14-16; 7:1-28), Jesus Christ with his death offered the definitive sacrifice that effected → life and → salvation for all. In accordance with Leviticus 16 he brought his own blood into the heavenly sanctuary (9:11–10:18). To this once-for-all sacrifice of Jesus Christ corresponds the believers' sacrifice of praise (13:15)

3.4. *Eucharist and Sacrifice*

The NT makes no positive relation between the Eucharist and sacrifice, apart from the Christological motif found in Mark 14:24. Probably replying to a misunderstanding at Corinth, Paul in 1 Cor. 10:18-22 contrasts partaking of the Lord's table with the different forms of participation in sacrificial meals.

The term "sacrifice" is first linked to the Eucharist in *Did.* 14.1 (→ Apostolic Fathers 2.1), but the exact meaning is not clear. The same applies to the use of *thysiastērion* in Ignatius of Antioch (d. ca. 110-17, *Eph.* 5.2-3; *Trall.* 7.2; *Magn.* 7.2; *Phld.* 4). The Christology of *1 Clement* (→ Apostolic Fathers 2.3.1) is close to that of Hebrews when he calls Christ "the high priest of our offerings" (36.1), but these offerings are prayers in the sense of praise offerings (35.12; 52.3). There might be a reference to the Eucharist in *1 Clem.* 44.4, but the theme is not developed.

The thesis is not convincing that the primitive Christian celebration was a new form of the OT thanksgiving offering meal (H. Gese). There might have been a link, however, between the Eucharist and prayer as thanksgiving offering, though such connection is exegetically difficult to establish in detail.

→ Eucharistic Prayers; Justification; Sacrament

Bibliography: P. Billerbeck, "Ein Tempelgottesdienst in Jesu Tagen," *ZNW* 55 (1964) 1-17 • B. Chilton, *The Temple of Jesus: His Sacrificial Program within a Cultural History of Sacrifice* (University Park, Pa., 1992) • J. Dunnill, *Covenant and Sacrifice in the Letter to the Hebrews* (Cambridge, 1992) • J. Fotopoulos, *Food Offered to Idols in Roman Corinth: A Social-Rhetorical Reconsideration of 1 Corinthians 8:1–11:1* (Tübingen, 2003) • H. Gese, "Ps 22 und das Neue Testament," *Vom Sinai zum Zion* (Munich, 1974) 180-201 • F. Hahn, *Theologie des Neuen Testaments,* vol. 2, *Die Einheit des Neuen Testaments* (Tübingen, 2002) esp. §13.4, "Die rettende Kraft des Todes Jesu"; idem, "Das Verständnis des Opfers im Neuen Testament," *Exegetische Beiträge zum ökumenischen Gespräch* (Göttingen, 1986) 262-302 • H.-J. Klauck, *Herrenmahl und hellenistischer Kult* (2d ed.; Münster, 1986) • G. Klinzing, *Die Umdeutung des Kultus in Qumran und im Neuen Testament* (Göttingen, 1971) • W. R. G. Loader, *Sohn und Hoherpriester* (Neukirchen, 1981) • E. Lohse, *Märtyrer und Gottesknecht* (2d ed.; Göttingen, 1963) • H. Moll, *Die Lehre von der Eucharistie als Opfer. Eine dogmengeschichtliche Untersuchung vom Neuen Testament bis Irenäus von Lyon* (Cologne, 1975) • J. Reumann, *The Supper of the Lord* (Philadelphia, 1985) • O. Schmitz, *Die Opferanschauungen des späteren Judentums und die Opferaussagen des Neuen Testamentes* (Tübingen, 1910) • P. Stuhlmacher, "Zur neueren Exegese von Rom 3,24-26," *Jesus und Paulus* (FS W. G. Kümmel; Göttingen, 1975) 315-33 • S. W. Sykes, ed., *Sacrifice and Redemption: Durham Essays in Theology* (Cambridge, 1991) • X. P. B. Viagulamuthu, *Offering Our Bodies as a Living Sacrifice to God: A Study in Pauline Spirituality Based on Romans 12:1* (Rome, 2002).

Ferdinand Hahn

Sacristy

The sacristy, a term derived from Lat. *sacer* (sacred, holy), is a room in a church in which → liturgical vessels, → vestments, and books are kept and in which the clergy make preparations for leading → worship, including robing.

In Roman → basilicas the sacristy is generally near the entrance, where the clergy procession starts. It is often handed over to the → pastor in a liturgical ceremony. As a part of the house of God (*secretarium aedis sacrae,* "sacristy of the sacred building"), it belongs to the total structure of the basilica. In the East it has liturgical significance as part of the sanctuary and as the setting for the service of preparation of the elements for Divine Liturgy. In the West too, it has undergone continuous change in function. In about 820 in Saint Gall, Switzerland, an altar was placed in the sacristy for → relics and the Host. It became especially important for reforming orders (→ Religious Orders and Congregations) as a replacement for the → crypt. In the → baroque period the sacristy was used as a place for private masses.

The sacristy is now usually close to the → altar. In Roman Catholic churches today a small room is normally attached that can be used for public functions, such as for giving notices and reports (e.g., at Santa Maria della Vittoria). In a private chapel next to the sacristy of Santa Maria in Aracoeli is the famous Santo Bambino, a wooden statue of the child Jesus that is featured in a popular Christian ritual.

At the → Reformation the sacristy lost much of its character in Protestant churches because the pastors used fewer vestments. In 1649 J. Furttenbach (1591-1667) proposed putting a small library in the sacristy. Some plans put the sacristy outside the church in an annex close to the altar. It was for the use of the clergy before and after the service and was to be in keeping with the church itself.

Discussion in the 20th century has vehemently attacked the misuse of the sacristy as merely a place of storage. Because of its semisacral character (→ Sacred and Profane), some Protestants now favor using the sacristy as a setting for confessions (→ Confession of Sins) and pastoral → counseling. In Roman Catholic churches it has similarly come to be seen as a spiritual arsenal or armory.

Bibliography: J. A. Abbo, "Sacristy," *NCE* (2d ed.) 12.522 • S. A. Stauffer, *Altar Guild and Sacristy Handbook* (Minneapolis, 2000) • W. Weyres and O. Bartning, eds., *Handbuch für den Kirchenbau* (Munich, 1958).

Gerlinde Strohmaier-Wiederanders

Sadducees

The term "Sadducees" (Gk. *saddoukaioi,* Heb. *ṣaddûqîm,* Aram. *ṣadduqayya,* thought to derive from David's high priest, Zadok [*ṣādôq*], see 2 Sam. 15:24-29) is used for members of a party of priests and nobles in Jerusalem. We have references to them, at times under the name "Boethusians," only occasionally in Josephus and early Christian and rabbinic writings, mostly hostile. Only within limits, then, can we reconstruct their history and character.

Historically important is the question of power in the political and religious life of Palestinian → Judaism from the end of the second century B.C. Under the Romans power lay chiefly with the Sanhedrin majority under the presidency of the Sadducean → high priest, the main concern being to uphold Jewish independence to the greatest extent possible. In the confusion of the revolts of A.D. 66-72/73, the Sadducees as a group suffered ruin with the rest. The destruction of the → temple (§2) robbed them of their ideal and material basis.

Politically as well as religiously conservative, the Sadducees resisted the efforts of the → Pharisees (Acts 23:7), espoused ancient priestly → traditions (→ Priest, Priesthood), stressed the → Pentateuch as the basic sacred text, and rejected orally transmitted laws and later beliefs such as that in the → resurrection (see Mark 12:18; Acts 23:8), clinging to literal exposition and strict legislating. The form of Judaism they represented perished with them, apart from faint echoes in the eighth-century Karaites (→ Judaism 3.2).

→ Jewish Theology 1; New Testament Era, History of; Scribes

Bibliography: P. R. Davies, *Sects and Scrolls: Essays on Qumran and Related Topics* (Atlanta, 1996) • J. Le Moyne, *Les Sadducéens* (Paris, 1972) • E. Main, "Les Sadducéens vus par Flavius Josèphe," *RB* 97 (1990) 161-206 • W. J. Moulder, "Sadducees," *ISBE* 4.278-81 • A. J. Saldarini, *Pharisees, Scribes, and Sadducees in Palestinian Society: A Sociological Approach* (Wilmington, Del., 1988) • E. Schürer, G. Vermes, and F. Millar, *The History of the Jewish People in the Age of Jesus Christ (175 B.C.–A.D. 135)* (3 vols.; rev. ed.; Edinburgh, 1973-87) 2.404-14 • G. Stemberger, *Jewish Contemporaries of Jesus: Pharisees, Sadducees, Essenes* (Minneapolis, 1995) • J. Wellhausen, *The Pharisees and the Sadducees: An Examination of Internal Jewish History* (Macon, Ga., 2001; orig. pub., 1874).

Berndt Schaller

St. Peter's → Rome 3

Saints, Veneration of

1. Religious Roots
2. Biblical Origins
   2.1. OT
   2.2. NT
3. Historical Development
4. Dogmatic Significance
5. Denominational Forms
   5.1. Orthodox Church
   5.2. Roman Catholic Church
   5.3. Reformation Churches
6. Popular Aspects
7. Patron Saints
   7.1. Origin
   7.2. Giving of Personal Names
   7.3. Choice of Saints
8. Auxiliary Saints

1. Religious Roots

A basic human experience is that of viewing certain persons as holy, as manifestations of the divine. This factor has played a determinative role in the development of → religion (→ Sacred and Profane). The transcendent (→ Immanence and Transcendence) is experienced as the wholly other, that which comes to us directly, awakening a feeling of → fear and dread *(mysterium tremendum),* the sacred being something apart *(tabu),* but also of something miraculous and attractive *(mysterium fascinosum)* that kindles awe *(mana).* The basis of such experience is the deity, which is both the ground of being (hence the fascination) and also its limit (hence the feeling of nothingness). There arises in human beings a desire to break through the limit to the ground, and thus religion (Lat. *re-ligare,* "tie back, restrain") develops in the sense of commitment.

"Holiness" becomes the term for human beings as they strive with all their powers to achieve the goal of religion and themselves to become the objects of respect and veneration. Primarily, then, holiness is an objective quality. It denotes the fact that a certain being has become a sign of divine transcendence. In this sense not only persons but also things, places, and times may be called holy. Secondarily, holiness is a subjective characterization. It tells us that certain people have accepted the summons to holiness and are especially seeking union with the deity as the absolutely holy.

Veneration of saints occurs not only in Christianity but also in → Confucianism, → Taoism, → Buddhism, → Jainism, and → Islam.

2. Biblical Origins

There is no veneration of saints in Holy Scripture, for there are no saints in the later ecclesiastical sense. But the basis of a comprehensive theology of saints may be found in it, and indirectly therefore the basis of their veneration.

2.1. *OT*

The OT lays highest stress on the absolute holiness of → Yahweh (Isa. 6:3). This infinitely lofty one manifests himself as the "Holy One of Israel" (so 25 times in Isaiah alone) to the people throughout their history, whom in the → covenant he constitutes "a priestly kingdom and a holy nation" (Exod. 19:6). Hence those who live out the covenant existentially are themselves holy (Lev. 19:2), the basic feature of this holiness being the practice of → love (e.g., Mic. 6:8).

Since human holiness is not individual but has its basis in membership among the holy people, it is a bond of union for those who belong to the covenant. It finds expression in → prayer, especially that of leaders for the people (e.g., Gen. 20:17; 25:21; Exod. 8:8, 12, 28-31; 9:28-29, 33; 10:16-19; 1 Sam. 7:8-9; 12:19-23; 15; Amos 7:2-6, etc.). As ideas about the afterlife became clearer, the dead in heaven also became regarded as members of the covenant, and in one instance we find the idea of their intercession (2 Macc. 15:12-16).

2.2. *NT*

The NT refers to saints in the plural (Matt. 27:52; Acts 9:13, 32, 41; Eph. 5:3, etc.) but, apart from → Jesus, calls only → John the Baptist a "holy man" (Mark 6:20). As in the OT, stress falls on the primary holiness of God, but with the significant modification that, thanks to the gift of the → Holy Spirit (Luke 1:35; 3:22 and par.), Jesus of Nazareth is the Holy One of God in a unique way (Mark 1:24 and par.; Acts 3:14; → Christology). After his exaltation, the bearer of the Spirit becomes the giver of the Spirit, and he continues his divine, saving work as a sanctifying work, constituting a holy people (Rom. 11:7; 1 Cor. 1:2; 1 Pet. 2:9-10; → Sanctification), the holy → church (Eph. 5:26).

In the church, holiness becomes a universal gift that is accepted in → faith, → hope, and → love, and that is freely practiced by the recipients of grace (Rom. 4:5; 1 Thess. 1:3; 1 John 4:16–5:2). As an ontic quality it is given in → baptism and by adoption of the mind of Jesus and is displayed in a morally pure life (Eph. 1:4; 5:1; Phil. 2:5; 4:8; Col. 1:22; 1 Pet. 1:15, etc.). In this way Christians even now are enabled to "share in the inheritance of the saints" (Col. 1:12) that will be fully theirs in the heavenly consummation (Rev. 7:9-11). At the same time, members of the → primitive Christian community understood themselves as "the saints" already here on earth (Rom. 1:7; 15:25-26; 1 Cor. 1:2; 2 Cor. 8:4; 9:1, 12, etc.).

As in the OT, so in the NT we find the idea that in the saved community of the saints one person may represent others. Jesus especially is our advocate (Mark 10:35-45; Luke 13:6-9; 23:34; John 14:13-14), but Stephen (Acts 7:60), → Paul (Rom. 1:9-10; Phil. 1:3-5, etc.), and the church (Acts 12:5) may also serve as advocates. The NT provides no clear example of the intercession of deceased saints.

3. Historical Development

In the early church we find a sense of the holiness of Christians in Christ, attempts to actualize this holiness, and a recognition that Christ is the only Mediator (1 Tim. 2:5: → Soteriology). But it was also thought that pagan mediator-cults express a valid concern. On the basis of Col. 1:24 the idea developed that a secondary mediatorship of Christians, as they are caught up by → grace into the body of Christ, does not compete with the mediatorship of Christ but instead makes the fullness of God's love all the plainer, "for in crowning their merits, you are crowning your own gifts" (Roman Missal, *prefatio* I, *de sanctis*).

The → martyrs were the first in whom this "crowning" found expression, being those who have achieved full → discipleship of Jesus. Veneration of saints may be seen clearly for the first time in *Martyrdom of Polycarp,* where the Christians ask for the martyr's bones, which are "more precious than precious stones" (18.2), bury them, and resolve to celebrate "the birthday of his martyrdom" (18.3, i.e., the day of his "birth" into heaven) with joy and gladness. By the third century the cult of martyrs had spread everywhere.

With the end of → persecution came the view that there is an unbloody martyrdom insofar as believers "put to death the deeds of the body" (Rom. 8:13) and daily take up the cross (Luke 9:23). Thus ascetics such as Anthony (d. 356) in the East and Martin of Tours (d. 397) in the West came to be venerated as saints (→ Asceticism), and later the term "confessors" came into use (first with Pope Sylvester I [314-35]). In accordance with the needs of the time, various types of holy people also came to be venerated, including the → apostles and → disciples who had given the church its start, and → bishops and → church fathers as those who had consolidated the faith.

During the Middle Ages the founders of orders and those who revitalized the church received honor as initiators of Christian → spirituality. Forms of veneration, in addition to the cult of the dead, were remembrance in prayer, the reading of their lives, the valuing of → relics (after the 6th cent., with the interment of relics in the → altar), sermons, → images, adoption as patrons, invocation in emergencies (specific saints being linked to specific needs; see 8), and special feast days marking their death, translation, or canonization.

Since in the early centuries the recognition of dead Christians as saints by way of veneration was a popular decision, though not without the participation of the local bishop, it was hard to limit the number and to avoid abuses. We find the first steps in this direction in the Carolingian period (according to Charlemagne's *Admonitio generalis* [789] and the Council of Frankfurt [794], consent of the diocese is required). In the tenth century Ulrich of Augsburg (d. 973) was the first to be involved in a process of papal canonization. In the 11th and 12th centuries the idea gained ground that papal canonization was necessary if the cult of a saint was to be valid (see 5.2).

In the later Middle Ages the striving for assurance of → salvation and fear of the horrors of war and plague led to a great intensifying and externalizing of the veneration of saints, against which the 16th-century → Reformers (see 5.3) and the Counter-Reformation (see 5.2) contended. In the post-Reformation period, then, the veneration of saints was set within moderate bounds. Today the sense of the solidarity of Christians after death, the longing for models of Christian life, and new reflection on the dogmatic foundation in all Christian denominations have led to a vital interest in the great "cloud of witnesses" (Heb. 12:1).

4. Dogmatic Significance

The term "saint" has come to be used in some circles for the deceased members of the church who by a heroic achievement of Christian love and other Christian → virtues have shown themselves fully open to God's call through Christ in the Holy Spirit. The church, it is thought, must give some recognition to people of this kind. Veneration of saints is meant to honor such people as Christian leaders whom the rest of the church may venerate and invoke as advocates without violating the glorifying of God's holiness or the sole mediatorship of Jesus Christ.

Official teaching has tried to observe these restrictions by distinguishing between adoration *(latria)* and veneration *(dulia)*, the former being reserved for God alone (Second Council of Nicea [787], DH 601). From the days of → Thomas Aquinas (*Summa theol.* III, q. 25, art. 5), the term *hyperdulia* came into use for the veneration of Mary (→ Mariology), though obviously this is no more than a special instance of the veneration of saints.

The basis and possibility of veneration of saints lie solely in the adoration of God as an act of love for God that includes all that he is and all that he does, including the reality of his covenant, which reached its climax in the new and eternal covenant in Christ. → Salvation is always salvation in the communion of saints, love of God is love for redeemed fellow-creatures, and the way to both involves a personal relationship that is grounded in the sole mediatorship of Christ (see 2.2) and that is historically worked out in the church as the fellowship of believers in Christ and of those who live in his grace.

Love of God and love of → neighbor form a distinct but inseparable unity, so that God can be present in the neighbor. The two have always found a place in Christianity, as in the liturgical practice of intercession for the living and the dead (→ Prayer). Saints are nothing apart from God, but God has sanctified them in order to make salvation visible. They are thus a real sign of accomplished redemption. They are a personal confirmation of the facts that our salvation is solely by grace and faith and that the church is eschatologically oriented (→ Eschatology). Encounter with saints, as in veneration, is a spur to encounter with God (see 1 Cor. 4:16; 11:1; Phil. 3:17; 4:9). On this basis, then, it is argued that veneration of saints is Christologically grounded (as Christ meets us in his witnesses and leads us to the Father), ecclesiologically legitimate (as a manifestation of the communion of saints), and soteriologically meaningful (as redemption is always linked to covenant membership).

The interrelation of love of God and love of neighbor also provides a theological justification of intercession and the possibility of its being heard. A presupposition is that there is life after → death and that this life is to be seen as a fulfillment of the love that we have achieved on earth. Hence, love for others still characterizes those who are perfected. Their intercession is simply a continuation of this love, as has been stressed from the time of → Origen (*De orat.* 11.2) by way of Leibniz (*System der Theologie* [3d ed., 1825], 190).

5. Denominational Forms

5.1. *Orthodox Church*

In the → Orthodox Church veneration of saints takes place in church buildings (through → icons), in the liturgy (reading of lives), and in the celebration of saints' days (→ All Saints' Day is observed the Sunday after Pentecost). Since the ninth century there has been a process of canonization that formally resembles the process in Roman Catholicism and that is handled by the autocephalous territorial synod. Local saints may be venerated if the bishop does not object.

5.2. *Roman Catholic Church*

In the → Roman Catholic Church rules for the veneration of saints were laid down by the Council of → Trent (1563, DH 1821-25) and → Vatican II (*Sacrosanctum concilium* [1963], *Lumen gentium* [1964], with a revised calendar in 1969). According to Trent the saints pray for us. It is not obligatory to call upon them and to ask for their intercession, but it is "good and profitable" *(bonum atque utile).* Christ remains the sole Redeemer, and all prayer is heard through him.

Vatican II stresses the significance of the saints as examples actualizing the church's eschatological nature. The core of the veneration of saints is love. The procedure of canonization is regulated by the apostolic constitution *Divinus perfectionis Magister* (January 1983). Here the bishops are given more say. The Roman Congregation for the Causes of Saints makes the final decision, and the → pope makes the pronouncement (→ Promotor fidei).

5.3. *Reformation Churches*

Practice in the Reformation churches has been influenced by the Reformers' criticism of abuses. M. → Bucer, U. → Zwingli (→ Zwingli's Theology), and especially J. → Calvin (→ Calvin's Theology) demanded the cessation of veneration of saints, and M. → Luther rejected invocation of saints as "one of the abuses of the Antichrist" (Schmalk. Art. 2.25) but thought that their faith might serve as a model (WA 38.313-14; → Luther's Theology). According to CA 21, commemoration of saints is valuable, veneration of saints is commended as a strengthening of faith, but invocation of saints is repudiated because it obscures the mediatorship of Christ. Later M. Chemnitz argued that we cannot invoke the dead. Thanks to the → Enlightenment and → rationalism, all forms of veneration of saints were finally abolished.

Protestant calendars (e.g., C. Goltworm 1559, F. Piper, from 1850 to 1870, and the Protestant calendar of 1984, which contains 138 names that are the same as in the Roman Catholic Church) continue to uphold the examples of saints, as also in Protestant histories of the saints (e.g., by G. Tersteegen, W. Löhe, J. Erb, and [for the Reformed] W. Nigg). Since 1987 → ecumenical dialogue has kindled fresh interest in the veneration of saints on the ground that the dead stand in a special relation to God, and their lives, sacrifices, and prayers are for us a model and sign of the working of the Holy Spirit (D. Ritschl). The veneration of saints is no longer a decisive matter in church division.

6. Popular Aspects

Trust in saints, especially by Roman Catholics, finds significant expression in the liturgy and also in practices that have developed independently of it. Thus we may mention the idea of patron saints (for individuals, groups, or churches; see 7), auxiliary saints (see 8), and the customs relating to saints' days and → pilgrimages, which offer a colorful picture of the veneration of saints and which in some cases are taking on new forms or new vitality.

7. Patron Saints

"Patron saints" refers to → saints or → angels whom individuals, groups, or the whole church chooses, invokes, and honors as patrons, defenders, protectors, or advocates for themselves or for certain activities. Underlying the idea of patron saints theologically is the doctrine of the → church as a fellowship in which all the members act on each other's behalf (see 1 Cor. 12:18, 28-30).

7.1. *Origin*

The origin of the concept of a patron lies in Roman → law, according to which the head of a family acted as patron (i.e., guardian, protector) for clients, freedmen, tenant farmers, and others (→ Roman Empire 1.2). The church took up the idea with reference to saints in the second century (*Actus Petri cum Simone,* ca. 150/170). The churches were the first to have patron saints, being named at first after their founders, then from the fourth century onward → apostles and martyrs, whose → relics they preserved. After 545 we find angels also as patron saints (Michael so honored in Ravenna).

In the Middle Ages the patron saints supposedly held the rights to the church and its property. As worship of saints developed, the system expanded further, characterized by subjectivism (saints for each class or profession or for special needs or concerns) and quantitative thinking (i.e., many saints as patrons, like the 14 auxiliary saints in Bavaria and among the Franks).

In the → Orthodox Church, in which patron saints are viewed as brotherly or sisterly helpers within the fellowship of saints, special honor is paid to the saints of house, court, city, or trade. The → Reformers (→ Reformation) rejected the concept as injurious to the divine omnipotence (Luther, *LW* 35.198-99), but even so, many churches retained their patron and held patronal festivals. In Celtic lands many churches and places are named after the otherwise largely unknown saints who founded the churches as the first evangelists.

7.2. *Giving of Personal Names*

From the middle of the third century, Christians also came to be named after → saints. The → Catechismus Romanus and later → canon law made this practice obligatory, though after 1983 the only demand was that the name chosen should not be "foreign to Christian sentiment" (1983 → CIC 855). Puritans, too, made an issue of name-giving, though not with any sense of committal to recognizing patron saints.

7.3. *Choice of Saints*

The choice of patron saints reflects the basic trends and developments of an age. Since the middle of the 19th century, the saints selected have provided us with a useful source in historical research. A distinction may be noted among various groups and types: basic saints (biblical, early church); saints whose relics are possessed; saints chosen by authority (those of the landowner); saints of a class, profession, or people; and specific saints to care for specific needs.

8. Auxiliary Saints

"Auxiliary saints," or "14 holy helpers," refers to a group of 14 → saints who, primarily in Europe, were venerated and invoked by people seeking relief from specific physical problems or concerns. The respective lives, activities, or iconographic attributes (→ Iconography; Symbol) of these saints include parallels to the kind of specific help they were sought to provide.

The cult began in the late → Middle Ages and arose out of an early Christian concept. In precarious situations Christian individuals, classes, guilds, and fraternities looked to these saints for help, comfort, or refuge. The original centers in the 15th century were the → Dioceses of Bamberg and Regensburg, which singled out 14 saints in particular. The cult then spread throughout Germany and also to Italy, Sweden, and Hungary, with the Saturday after the fourth Sunday after Easter as the feast day.

The names of the saints are as follows, with one version of their respective "area of expertise" in parentheses: Acacius (headaches and pain), Barbara (lightning and sudden death), Blaise (throat ailments), Catherine of Alexandria (diseases of the tongue), Christopher (hurricanes and accidents to travelers), Cyriacus (possession by the devil), Denys (headaches and demonic possession), → Erasmus (intestinal diseases), Eustace (dangers of fire), George (skin infections), Giles (insanity, epilepsy, and sterility), Margaret (the needs of pregnant women), Pantaleon (consumption), and Vitus (rabies, snake bites, and Saint Vitus' dance). Sometimes Mary or a local saint took the place of one of these saints or was added as a 15th (→ Mary, Devotion to).

M. → Luther and the other → Reformers (→ Reformation) opposed the idea of certain saints having special powers, since it would infringe upon the sole mediatorship of Christ and denote a lack of trust in God. (See the Large Catechism on the first commandment, also CA Apol. 21.) The → Old Catholic Church also rejects the cult.

Roman Catholic theology now does not accept the idea that specific saints are especially competent to deal with specific needs. It asserts, rather, that the basis of the veneration of saints is the communion of saints (→ Church) and the love of God that holds sway in it, which mediates itself as concrete love by means of concrete relationships.

→ Catholicism (Roman); Church Year; Popular Religion

Bibliography: On 1-6: W. Beinert, "Ekklesiologische Aspekte der Heiligenverehrung," *Cath(M)* 40 (1986) 187-202; idem, ed., *Die Heiligen heute ehren* (Freiburg, 1983) • H. Belting, *Likeness and Presence: A History of the Image before the Era of Art* (Chicago, 1994) • A. H. Bredero, *Christendom and Christianity in the Middle Ages: The Relation between Religion, Church, and Society* (Grand Rapids, 1994) pt. 6, "Saints and Sainthood" • P. Brown, *The Cult of the Saints: Its Rise and Function in Latin Christianity* (Chicago, 1981) • M. Cormack, *The Saints in Iceland: Their Veneration from the Conversion to 1400* (Brussels, 1994) • H. Delehaye, *Les origines du culte des martyrs* (2d ed.; Brussels, 1933); idem, *Sanctus. Essai sur le culte des saints dans l'antiquité* (Brussels, 1967) • J. P. Kirsch, *The Doctrine of the Communion of Saints in the Ancient Church* (Edinburgh, 1910) • F. von Lilienfeld, ed., *Aspekte frühchristlicher Heiligenverehrung* (Erlangen, 1977) • A. B. Mulder-Bakker, *The Invention of Saintliness* (London, 2002) • G. L. Müller, *Gemeinschaft und Verehrung der Heiligen. Geschichtlich-systematische Grundlegung der Hagiologie* (Freiburg, 1986); idem, ed., *Heiligenverehrung. Ihr Sitz im Leben des Glaubens und ihre Aktualität im ökume-*

nischen Gespräch (Munich, 1986) • M. PERHAM, *The Communion of Saints: An Examination of the Place of the Christian Dead in the Belief, Worship, and Calendars of the Church* (London, 1980) • K. M. RINGROSE, *Saints, Holy Men, and Byzantine Society* (New Brunswick, N.J., 1976) • D. RITSCHL, "Überlegungen zur gegenwärtigen Diskussion über Heiligenverehrung," *Konzepte* (Munich, 1986) 60-71 • B. STEIMER, *Lexikon der Heiligen und Heiligenverehrung* (Freiburg, 2003) • S. WILSON, ed., *Saints and Their Cults: Studies in Religious Sociology, Folklore, and History* (Cambridge, 1983).

On 7: H. DELEHAYE, "Loca sanctorum," *AnBoll* 48 (1930) 5-64 • A. M. ORSELLI, *L'idea e il culto del santo patrono cittadino nella litteratura latina cristiana* (Bologna, 1965) • K. I. RABENSTEIN, "Patron Saints," *NCE* (2d ed.) 10.969-76 • H. ROEDER, *Saints and Their Attributes, with a Guide to Localities and Patronage* (Chicago, 1956) • A. SANDOVAL, *The Directory of Saints: A Concise Guide to Patron Saints* (New York, 1996) • R. TERMOLEN and D. LUTZ, *Nothelfer, Patrone in allen Lebenslagen* (Beuron, 2003) • D. WEBB, *Patrons and Defenders: The Saints in the Italian City-States* (London, 1996) • O. WIMMER, H. MELZER, and J. GELMI, *Lexikon der Namen und Heiligen* (6th ed.; Innsbruck, 1988) 951-57.

On 8: W. BEINERT, ed., *Die Heiligen heute ehren* (Freiburg, 1983) • D. H. FARMER, ed., *The Oxford Dictionary of Saints* (2d ed.; Oxford, 1979) • G. L. MÜLLER, *Gemeinschaft und Verehrung der Heiligen. Geschichtlich-systematische Grundlegung der Hagiologie* (Freiburg, 1986) • H. SCHAUERTE, *Die volkstümliche Heiligenverehrung* (Münster, 1948) • G. SCHREIBER, "Nothelfer," *LTK* 7.1050-51; idem, *Die Vierzehn Nothelfer in Volksfrömmigkeit und Sakralkultur. Symbolkraft und Herrschaftsbereich der Wallfahrskapelle, vorab in Franken und Tirol* (Innsbruck, 1959) • G. SCHWAIGER, "Der Heilige in der Welt des frühen Mittelalter," *BGBR* 7 (1973) 27-40 • R. TERMOLEN and D. LUTZ, *Nothelfer, Patrone in allen Lebenslagen* (Beuron, 2003) • M. WALSCH, ed., *Butler's Lives of Patron Saints* (San Francisco, 1987) • M. ZENDER, *Räume und Schichten mittelalterlicher Heiligenverehrung in ihrer Bedeutung für die Volkskunde. Die Heiligen des mittleren Maaslandes und der Rheinlande in Kultgeschichte und Kultverbreitung* (2d ed.; Cologne, 1973).

WOLFGANG BEINERT

Salvation

Overview

What Christianity has to say about salvation (→ Soteriology) is essentially bound up with the name and history of → Jesus Christ (Acts 4:12, "There is salvation in no one else . . ."). This verse expresses a universal claim and distinguishes it from, or even contradicts, what other → religions and → worldviews have to say about salvation. Christianity speaks of salvation as a gift of God's love (→ Grace) for us and our world that transcends → death, bestows → life, and promises eschatological fulfillment (→ Eschatology; Hope). This understanding presupposes that human beings (→ Anthropology) and their world are in need of redemption on account of their imperfection, contingency, and sin. Christian talk of salvation affirms a unique and ongoing saving relationship between → God and the world (→ Word of God) that is revealed in history (→ Revelation; Salvation History). It also includes a summons to be open to this prevenient and abiding reality of God, to enter into the objective salvation-event, and to subjectively appropriate it.

The biblical message of salvation has been developed and shaped in the Christian churches as the basis and sum of their witness in worship, theology, mission, and service. It is the foundation of their existence and commission (→ Church). The relation between God and the world is revealed and communicated under the conditions of time and space, in the context of experience, which is not always the same, and of interpretation, which changes according to experience. This fact explains the variety of Christian churches and their message of salvation (→ Confession of Faith; Pluralism).

Christian churches share the following convictions: (1) the unique historical revelation of God in Jesus Christ (→ Christology) concerns human existence in a comprehensive way, not just individuals, but also the world in which they live (→ Society); (2) the salvation of human beings and their world depends on whether they accept (→ Faith; Penitence) or reject God and the message of his inbreaking kingdom and his word of reconciliation; (3) the conversion of individuals and peoples is not the result of some abstract idea of a saving God as such but, rather, is based on an actual relationship, experienced in faith, between the Holy (God) and human existence. This relationship develops out of a personal encounter and abiding union with Christ (→ Discipleship) in which salvation takes shape and is eschatologically consummated.

Christian churches differ on the following controversial points, sometimes even to the point of contradiction: (1) on setting down the historically unique revelation in creeds and dogmas, as well as interpreting (→ Hermeneutics) it in terms of doctrine (→ Dogma; Dogmatics) and church order, and of theory and practice (→ Ethics; Moral Theology; Social Ethics; Sociology; Norms); (2) on mediating the confessionally defined message of salvation to its recipients by church institutions and means of grace (→ Worship; Preaching; Sacrament; Charity; Mission), as well as its embodiment in daily life and its various stations (→ Work; Vocation; Sexuality; Family; Marriage; Society; State); (3) on the understanding of the relation between God and the world, a relation involving very different realities having to do with structure (→ Incarnation) and process (→ Law and Gospel; Justification; Sanctification; Order of Salvation; Theosis). All of this becomes manifest in symbolic objectifications such as sacraments and church organization (→ Hierarchy; Priest, Priesthood). Also controversial is the description of the relationship between divine omnipotence and human freedom (→ Apocatastasis; Predestination).

The history of Christianity up to recent times shows that the various answers in the debate about the ways and means of salvation, about the locus and reality of the kingdom of God (redemption, the new creation), about the personal and collective praxis in appropriating and actualizing salvation, and about dealing with the world in need of salvation, have always brought about division and given rise to antinomies (→ Heresies and Schisms; Social Movements), all of which have resulted in a plethora of Christian churches and communities. At the same time this multiplicity of churches eventually gave rise to the cause of Christian unity (→ Ecumenism, Ecumenical Movement).

The above references to other articles at least indicate something of the importance and scope of the theme of salvation and provide a rough outline of the theological and ecclesiastical problems and tasks associated with it. The following contributions sketch out the theme within the context of the Bible, the history of the Christian tradition, and the contemporary situation.

Erwin Fahlbusch

1. Biblical Understanding of Salvation

1.1. *General*

Here we will understand salvation as a universal theological concept that according to biblical faith embraces everything that God does to bring humanity and the world to realize their authentic nature. The expectation of salvation is always articulated in light of the experience of its absence. The particular contents of salvation are thus presented in a definite correlation to threat, alienation, and the diminishment of life. Salvation occurs when these negative aspects are overcome by the gift of wholeness, integrity, and health. The appropriation of salvation assumes the form not only of concrete experience but also of hope based on the promise of God.

1.2. *OT*

The two prototypical experiences of salvation in the OT, both constitutive of Israel's faith in → Yahweh, are the exodus, or deliverance of bondage from Egypt (e.g., Exod. 1:8-14; 14–15; 20:2), and the gift of the land as the place of salvation (Gen. 12:1-3; Deut. 26:1-15). They form the background of the institutions that manifest the abiding presence of salvation for Israel: the → covenant, → law, and cult.

This presence, to be sure, rests on God's unbreakable promise, but it is not automatic. By disobedience of God's will the people of Israel can, at least temporarily and partially, fall outside the sphere of salvation. Thus, the preexilic → prophets with their message of doom attack a superficial expectation of salvation (e.g., Amos 5:18-24; Mic. 3:11-12) and call upon people to observe the statutes of God.

The message of salvation acquired a deeper meaning during the time of the exile because of the experience of hardship. As with all of Israel's earlier expectations of salvation, its main themes were inner-worldly: the return of Israel to the land of promise, the renewing of → Jerusalem, and the rebuilding of the → temple. Yet at the same time, their hopes transcended the realm of what can be realized here and now, looking forward to a blessed future to be wrought by the marvelous deeds of God (e.g., Ezekiel 37; 40–48; Isa. 54:9-17; 60; → Eschatology).

Later in → apocalypticism the course of history was viewed as a divinely ordered process leading eschatologically to a new creation (e.g., Isaiah 24–27; Dan. 7:27; 12:1-3). At the same time, the hope of individual salvation grew in importance in postexilic literature, for example, in the Psalms and → Wisdom literature. The basis of this hope was the personal fellowship with God mediated by the law and the cult. Some statements even seem to point to a life beyond the grave (e.g., Ps. 16:9-11; 73:24).

1.3. *NT*

The NT contains a number of concepts of the salvation-event, each expressing a different aspect, such as → kingdom of God in the Synoptic gospels, → life in the Gospel of John, and → justification, → freedom, and → reconciliation in Paul's letters. The NT understanding of salvation is marked chiefly by the following elements.

1.3.1. *Jesus of Nazareth*

Prior to → Easter Jesus announced the nearness of God's kingdom, accepting responsibility for it and demonstrating it in his message and work. In their encounter with Jesus, people acknowledged the God of Israel and thus experienced salvation (Mark 10:52; Luke 7:50).

After Easter salvation was connected with the cross and resurrection of Jesus as the saving events in which God draws near to and justifies humanity. Henceforth we receive salvation exclusively by the proclamation of Jesus as the one in whom God has acted to save and by our participation in this act of God by the word of proclamation. In this sense the name of Jesus is the quintessence of salvation (Matt. 1:21; Acts 4:12).

1.3.2. *Power and Theocentricity*

Salvation is understood as God at work breaking into history. God takes possession of what belongs to him as the Creator by dethroning the powers hostile to him. Thus the work of Jesus is portrayed as a battle against the demonic forces that possess people (Luke 11:20), and submission to the rule of God is presented as liberation (Mark 10:24-26). The Christological → kerygma proclaims the cross of Jesus as the event by which he vicariously triumphed over the alien powers of law, → sin, and → death, thereby freeing those who belong to him (Gal. 2:20; 5:1).

The real upshot of this deliverance is expressed in the statements about reconciliation (Rom. 5:10; 2 Cor. 5:18-20), which means restoration of full fellowship between God and humankind. The theocentric aspect of salvation through Christ is made evident in this explicit coordination of liberation and reconciliation.

1.3.3. *Corporeality*

The NT view of salvation shows its OT roots in the fact that it always has corporeal dimensions. Thus the → healing miracles of Jesus are signs that God wills to save the whole person and the whole of → creation. Future eschatological salvation is pictured in terms of a bodily resurrection and as a new act of creation that surpasses the first (Rev. 21:1). Here we see the essential difference between the NT and the Platonizing tendencies in → Hellenism and → Gnosticism, which could think of salvation only in spiritual terms, that is, as liberation from the realms of creation and matter.

1.3.4. *Tension between the Present and the Future*

The consummation of salvation as fellowship with God and Christ in new bodily form is reserved for the eschatological → future and is now only an object of hope (Rom. 8:24). To be sure, this prospect has its firm basis in the event of salvation already accomplished by the death and resurrection of Jesus Christ. Believers who hear the message of salvation and are united to Christ (→ Faith 2) experience salvation in the present as the reality that determines their existence. They are reconciled to God (Rom. 5:1) and freed from the dominion of antidivine powers, so that already now they are capable of living in a new way in conformity with salvation (Gal. 5:1, 16). John stresses this point with his realized eschatology, wherein salvation is a present reality for those in union with Christ, though here too the fundamental tension between the "already" and the "not yet" is preserved.

1.3.5. *Ecclesiological Aspect*

Just as Israel in the OT, so also the church in the NT is the primary locus of the experience and hope of salvation (→ Church 2.1). This truth comes to expression chiefly in its statements about → baptism and the Lord's Table (→ Eucharist). Baptism is incorporation into the realm subject to Christ and ruled by the → Holy Spirit. Here the saving reality of God's eschatological creation is already symbolically visible in a new human fellowship (Gal. 3:28), and by means of communion at the Lord's Table the church acquires a new form of life shaped by Christ.

→ Christology 1; Gospel 1; Grace 1; Soteriology

Bibliography: J. Becker, *Das Heil Gottes. Heils- und Sündenbegriffe in den Qumrantexten und im Neuen Testament* (Göttingen, 1964) • J. C. Beker, "The Gift and Demand of Salvation," *Paul the Apostle: The Triumph of God in Life and Thought* (Philadelphia, 1980) 255-71 • W. Brueggemann, *Theology of the OT: Testimony, Dispute, Advocacy* (Minneapolis, 1997) • G. W. Bumett, *Paul and the Salvation of the Individual* (Leiden, 2001) • B. S. Childs, "Reconciliation with God," *Biblical Theology of the Old and New Testaments: Theological Reflection on the Christian Bible* (Minneapolis, 1993) 485-531 • O. Cullmann, *Salvation in History* (London, 1967) • W. Foerster and G. Fohrer, "Σῴζω, σωτηρία, κτλ.," *TDNT* 7.965-1024 • J. Jeremias, *Jesus' Promise to the Nations* (Philadelphia, 1982) • E. Käsemann, "The Saving Significance of the Death of Jesus in Paul" and "Justification and Salvation History in the Epistle to the Romans," *Perspectives on Paul* (Philadelphia, 1971) 32-59, 60-78 • N. Lohfink, "Heil als Befreiung in Israel," *Erlösung und Emanzipation* (ed. L. Scheffczyk; Freiburg, 1973) 30-50 • S. Lyonnet, *Sin, Redemption, and Sacrifice: A Biblical and Patristic Study* (Rome, 1970) • G. von Rad, *OT Theology*, vol. 2, *The Theology of Israel's Prophetic Traditions* (Louisville, Ky., 2001) • P. Stuhlmacher, *Reconciliation, Law, and Righteousness* (Philadelphia, 1986).

Jürgen Roloff†

2. Jewish Tradition

2.1. *Types of Jewish Expectation*

The many types of Jewish experience and expectation of salvation are never set forth in systematic or dogmatic terms. Rather, they are expressed in narratives, beseeched in prayers, celebrated in worship, and preserved, learned, and interpreted in traditions. The unity of history is assured by the unity of God. What happens is God's history with his world. The God of Israel has already been at work in history to save and to judge. The remembrance of salvation (e.g., of the exodus, the creation, the election of → Abraham, or in the life of one who prays a psalm or a Kaddish) offers hope for the present and the future.

It makes no difference whether the expectation of salvation is believed to be a *restoration* of creation, paradise, or the kingdom of → David, or whether it is more *utopian-like* (G. Scholem's distinction) as a completely new beginning in the kingdom of heaven. In biblical and postbiblical → Judaism it is always God who acts in his own name to deliver salvation in a historically definite way. God is the only one who brings salvation. Accordingly, salvation is entirely the result of God's works of → love, → righteousness, → truth, liberation, and → peace. The picture of salvation is portrayed in the colors of → salvation history. It presents the role of the Messiah in a variety of images, but not necessarily as the very epitome of salvation. (In Reformed Judaism prayer is for redemption rather than for the Redeemer.)

2.2. *Covenant and Torah*

The → covenant assures the faithfulness of the One who brought, brings, and will bring salvation. Placing all of salvation exclusively in the hands of God makes possible and even demands a variety of ideas and gifts of salvation in dealing with history past and future. The commandments, along with their goal of praising God and of calling for obedience (→ Sanctification), have a constitutive relation to the salvation of the end time (→ Eschatology) because they link past experiences of salvation to eschatological expectations. God comes "even today, if only you will hear his voice" (*b. Sanh.* 98a).

The → Torah was given for the sake of life. In the ritual *Alenu* prayer the Torah is cited, along with → creation and election, as the basis of the hope that God's glory will triumph over all idols and horrors and that all knees will bow before him. "We are to live by the statutes and not die on account of them" (*b. Yoma* 58b; see also Lev. 18:5; Deut. 30:15).

2.3. *Blessings of Salvation*

In the OT and rabbinic writings the blessings of salvation are characterized by verbs like save, liberate, redeem, pardon, guilt, heal, ransom, and others, and by nouns like righteousness, truth, and peace. There is mention of a triad: the land (with the return of the dispersed), the Torah (with the sanctifying of daily life), and the final liberation from every foreign domination. The times, ordering, and events of the future age of salvation are not determined or fixed. Yet this uncertainty does not affect the reality of what is expected. "In that era there will be neither famine nor war, neither jealousy nor strife. Blessings will be abundant, comforts within the reach of all. The one preoccupation of the whole world will be to know the Lord" (Isa. 11:9, Maimonides, *Mishneh Torah* 14.5.12).

2.4. *Public and Material Dimension*

There exists an anti-idealistic modesty in describing the public and material dimension of salvation. The more Christianity became oriented to inward, individualistic, and otherworldly salvation, the more strongly Judaism set its hopes on a real salvation for the whole of reality, while always keeping in mind the present unredeemed state of the world. The hope for a new world and for the end of suffering in this one did not lead to passive resignation, even in times of severe persecution, but to a lively critical attitude that stresses the creative difference of the people of God from the rest of the world and the pursuit of its peoples. The Torah can be understood as the gift whose comprehensive fulfillment brings final salvation, although it was always clear (as in the prayers, for example, on high feast days) that Jews were so to act as if everything depended on them and to pray as if everything depended on God.

2.5. *Experience and Actualization*

The celebrations of the great festivals like the → Passover or Sukkot are reminders of the salvation Israel experienced in history. At the same time, they make salvation really present for those who celebrate. All see themselves as though they were the ones redeemed out of Egypt (→ Haggadah). Learning the Torah actualizes the word of God. Land, Torah, and the coming time of salvation are interrelated as ways and goals (*b. Ber.* 5a).

Israel as the people of God does not understand its election and revelation as its exclusive possession of salvation. The Torah was and is offered to all peoples, and like the wilderness, fire, and water, it is "free for all who come into the world" (*Mek.* on Exod. 20:2). In light of its origin and goal, the particularity of the one people of God and its experiences of salvation are directed to the salvation of all humanity.

2.6. *Salvation History*

The Jewish understanding of salvation history knows no periods totally void of salvation, although Jewish theology after the → Holocaust must take into account that unique experience of the absence of salvation and of the silence of God. Transcending all experiences of salvation will be the hoped-for but still awaited salvation of the coming world.

Bibliography: E. Berkovits, *Faith after the Holocaust* (New York, 1973) • E. Borowitz, *Contemporary Christologies: A Jewish Response* (New York, 1980) • M. Buber, *Kingship of God* (3d ed.; London, 1967) • H. A. Davidson, *Moses Maimonides: The Man and His Works* (New York, 2005) • A. J. Heschel, *God in Search of Man: A Philosophy of Judaism* (Northvale, N.J., 1987) • J. Klausner, *The Messianic Idea in Israel, from Its Beginning to the Completion of the Mishnah* (New York, 1955) • J. J. Petuchowski, *Understanding Jewish Prayer* (New York, 1972) • F. Rosenzweig, *The Star of Redemption* (Notre Dame, Ind., 1985; orig. pub., 1921) • G. G. Scholem, *The Messianic Idea in Judaism, and Other Essays on Jewish Spirituality* (New York, 1974) • E. E. Urbach, *The Sages: Their Concepts and Beliefs* (2d ed.; Jerusalem, 1979).

Martin Stöhr

3. The Orthodox Tradition

3.1. *Biblical Interpretation*

The Eastern Orthodox tradition sees very clearly that the Bible does not define salvation but rather describes it as a many-faceted reality dealing with our relationship to God. In the Bible salvation (Heb. *yĕšûʿâ*, Gk. *sōtēria*) includes → healing of sickness, deliverance from danger, and redemption from enemies, → sin, → death, and eternal damnation. → Jesus (whose name in Hebrew means "Yahweh saves") is the "Savior" or "Redeemer" (Matt. 1:21) and appears as the divine physician of soul and body, the source of perfect health and life, and the liberator from sin and death. Accordingly, salvation in him is liberation and healing, so that we can experience the eternal → love of God and live in fellowship with him and our fellow human beings (Romans 6–8; Colossians 3; Ephesians 2; John 15; Phil. 3:20; Titus 2:13; 2 Tim. 4:18; 1 Cor. 13:12). Christ's salvation involves ontological union with all of humanity without distinction (1 Tim. 2:4; Rom. 5:18; Ephesians 1–3).

3.2. *Church Fathers*

Just as in the Bible, so the → church fathers often illuminate the mystery of salvation achieved in and through Christ by using pictures. Particularly common are the pastoral image of the good shepherd (Matt. 18:12-14), the military image of the victorious strong man (Matt. 12:28), the medical image of the Good Samaritan (Luke 10:29-35), and the legal and cultic image of the → sacrifice, the ransom, or → atonement, which Paul took from the OT (Rom. 3:24; 8:23; 1 Tim. 2:6; Gal. 3:13). Yet, according to the Fathers, none of these images succeeds in fully explaining the mystery of salvation in Christ.

The Orthodox tradition has never given preeminence to the forensic explanation of the salvation-event or accorded it any great significance. Rather, preferring to maintain the ontological and existential character of the event of salvation, it emphasizes the restoration of human nature to its "normal state" — fellowship with God in his love, and participation in his eternal life. Sin, understood as egoism and rejection of fellowship with God and his love, stands in direct opposition to true human nature, created in the image of the triune God of love. Therefore, "salvation is the recovery of that which is in accordance with nature" (John of Damascus, *De fide orth.* 1.30).

The → incarnation of the divine Logos, in whom and by whom all things were created (John 1:3; Col. 1:16), is the beginning of salvation, the healing of our human nature (soul and body), marked by sin and death. For "the unassumed is the unhealed, but what is united with God is also being saved" (Gregory Nazianzus, *Ep.* 101, ad Cledonium, §5 [*PG* 37.181C-184B]). Thus the → incarnation of Christ is viewed as the immortal and eternal hypostatic union of God with human nature (→ Christology 3). The entire life of Christ, and especially his death on the cross, is viewed as redemption and liberation from egoism. His total self-sacrifice, → resurrection, and → ascension are the comprehensive gift of the eternal life of God for the human nature of Christ, thereby granting us liberation from death and transitoriness and eternal participation of body and soul in the divine life (2 Pet. 1:4). All this happens with a view to the assimilation of humanity into God, which is understood as → *theōsis,* or deification, by the grace of the Holy Spirit (2 Cor. 3:18). The Logos took on a human body so that we might receive the → Holy Spirit (see Athanasius, *De incar.* 8).

Salvation and the new life in Christ are bestowed on every person who is ready to receive them. One receives this gift by → conversion (which involves *metanoia,* or repentance), → baptism, the whole sacramental life of the church, and living in accordance with the commandment to love God and neighbor. Salvation in Christ also has a cosmic dimension. The humanity of the risen Christ sets the goal for all creation, namely, its → transfiguration as the new heaven and the new earth (Revelation 21). The church is in the world as its witness and prophet, the conscience and sacrament of this mystery, which embraces the whole earth.

3.3. *Experience of the Saints*

The experience of the saints shows that liberation from sin through cooperation *(synergia)* with the grace of Christ or the Holy Spirit leads to a renewal of spiritual life (Gal. 2:2; Col. 3:10) and growth in love for God and neighbors. Love of neighbor is the indispensable way to salvation (1 John 3:16-17, 23-24).

The social dimension of sin and redemption by Christ is also an essential for the Orthodox Church. It is important to see the active presence of the Spirit of Christ, not only in the sacraments, but also in our striving for righteousness, human dignity, and liberation from every form of oppression.

→ Church 3.1; Eschatology 4; Grace 2; Orthodox Church; Orthodox Christianity

Bibliography: P. Evdokimov, *L'Esprit Saint dans la tradition orthodoxe* (Paris, 1969) • V. Lossky, *In the Image and Likeness of God* (Crestwood, N.Y., 1985); idem, *The Mystical Theology of the Eastern Church* (Crestwood, N.Y., 1976) • G. I. Mantzaridis, *The Deification of Man: St. Gregory Palamas and the Orthodox Tradition* (Crestwood, N.Y., 1984) • P. Nellas, *Deification in Christ: The Nature of the Human Person* (Crestwood, N.Y., 1987) • J. Panagopoulos, "Salvation as Partaking in the Divine Nature," *EkTh* 3 (1982) 176-92 • "Salvation in Orthodox Theology," *IRM* 61 (1972) 401-8 • D. Staniloae, *The Experience of God: Orthodox Dogmatic Theology,* vol. 2, *The World: Creation and Deification* (Brookline, Mass., 2000); idem, "The Orthodox Doctrine of Salvation and Its Implications for Christian Diakonia in the World," *Theology and the Church* (Crestwood, N.Y., 1980) 181-212.

Dan-Ilie Ciobotea

4. Roman Catholic Tradition

4.1. *Patristics*

The Roman Catholic understanding of salvation still includes emphases that derive ultimately from patristic theology (→ Church Fathers; Patristics, Patrology). Since the concept of salvation has from the beginning meant everything that God has done for humanity through → Jesus Christ, it has been necessary to deal with it in connection with → Christology. Athanasius (ca. 297-373) may be regarded as the key figure in patristic Christology (and correspondingly → soteriology). According to Athanasius, salvation was given with the → incarnation. The preexistent Logos assumed a human body in order to redeem sinners. Redemption is nothing less than the deification of humankind (→ Theosis). It includes victory over death (recovery of → immortality) and the restoration of divine sonship. Since the process of deification is based on the incarnation of the Logos and is realized in the → Holy Spirit, salvation not only has a Christological foundation but is related to the doctrine of the → Trinity. These ideas of Athanasius are alive in the Roman Catholic as well as the Orthodox tradition (→ Orthodox Christianity).

The ecclesiological aspect and its mediation so striking in the Roman Catholic understanding of salvation were explicitly developed by Augustine (354-430; → Augustine's theology). The love of God is manifest in the incarnation of the Logos. The death of Jesus means the justification of humanity and is the origin of our righteousness. This righteousness is our salvation because it integrates us into God's design and bestows his love on us. Christ's mediation of salvation is fully realized in the church; he is the head of the church. Christ exerts a steady influence on the faith of its members, and he himself dispenses the means of salvation (→ Sacraments), which the church administers. Clearly it was Augustine who developed the doctrine of salvation into a comprehensive soteriology in terms of → justification and → reconciliation.

4.2. *Middle Ages and the Modern Period*

A fundamental change took place with the transition to the → Middle Ages. Personal and moral ways of thinking became stronger, in contrast to universal and cosmic ideas. With Anselm of Canterbury (1033-1109) soteriology was presented more and more in legal and moral categories. Redemption is satisfaction that Christ vicariously achieved for humanity. Salvation of humanity means deliverance from sin and death and, by God's grace, leads to a life of → faith, → hope, and → love. This life is then no longer under alien control but, rather, is brought to the root and source of its existence in God.

The idea of salvation as satisfaction was taken over and developed with certain modifications by the scholastic theology of the High Middle Ages (esp. Thomas Aquinas and Bonaventure; → Scholasticism). Apart from a few exceptions, this idea of salvation has dominated Roman Catholic academic theology to the present.

4.3. *Twentieth Century*

The 20th century also was to a great extent influenced by → Thomism, although biblical, historical, and personalist elements became more pronounced in contrast to a predominantly moralistic and juridical view. As with Athanasius, many came to conceive of salvation as human participation in the divine nature. Yet this thesis was linked in particular to Jesus' proclamation of the → kingdom of God. The church still had a central role to play, since it conveyed the message of the lordship of God and was even its sign and instrument. We receive salvation when we accept God's lordship. Some theologians understood salvation as a relational event; it is the encounter and dialogue between God and humanity in the church, and it means reconciliation, righteousness, and → freedom.

4.4. *The Present*

The Second → Vatican Council had little to say about soteriology. It nonetheless accelerated a process that overcame the earlier separation of → nature and supernature and closely correlated human self-transcendence and divine action in the idea of salvation (→ Immanence and Transcendence). Salvation today is viewed biblically, historically, and anthropologically. It is present in the self-fulfillment of those who experience it, expressing human integrity, identity, and uniqueness. Christ is the salvation of humankind; this event is personal and Christological. Salvation is given by God *(sola fide)*, but in the power of his grace humans cooperate in the coming of the kingdom, which also involves a transformation of social conditions (→ Liberation Theology).

Bibliography: Catechism of the Catholic Church (Liguori, Mo., 1994) esp. 13-276, "The Profession of Faith" • B. J. Groeschel, *Healing the Original Wound: Reflections on the Full Meaning of Salvation* (Ann Arbor, Mich., 1993) • R. P. McBrien, *Catholicism* (rev. ed.; San Francisco, 1994) • H.-E. Mertens, *Not the Cross, but the Crucified: An Essay in Soteriology* (Louvain, 1992) • P. M. Quay, *The Mystery Hidden for Ages in God* (New York, 1995) • K. Rahner, *Foundations of Christian Faith: An Introduction to the Idea of Christianity* (New York, 1978); idem, "Salvation," *EncTheol* 1499-1530 • J. Ratzinger, *Principles of Christian Theology: Building Stones for a Fundamental Theology* (San Francisco, 1987) • H. Rondet, *The Grace of Christ: A Brief History of the Theology of Grace* (New York, 1967) • E. Schillebeeckx, *Christ: The Experience of Jesus as Lord* (London, 1980) • G. H. Tavard, *The Church, Community of Salvation: An Ecumenical Ecclesiology* (Collegeville, Minn., 1992).

Harald Wagner

5. Reformation Tradition

5.1. *Basic Distinctions in Fundamental Theology*

In its basis and → hope Christian faith has to do with the saving work of Christ, and the → gospel is the proclamation and dawning of salvation. But in defining salvation and distinguishing it from its opposite, some basic distinctions need to be made that involve the total context of theology and the relation of its subject matter to reality. The 19th century attempted to capture these ideas in its theology of → salvation history, but it was not until the 20th century that "salvation" became a basic category and replaced "redemption" in the theological lexicons. Especially German authors have been affected by the wider meaning of salvation in the English tradition and in ecumenical contexts.

This paradigm shift involves a this-worldly, sociopolitical interpretation of the → kingdom of God, using such metaphors as wholeness and healing. It also frees traditional soteriologies from dependence on a metaphysics alien to contemporary thought. Yet, linking salvation so closely to human experience involves dangers that may be classically observed in *The Christian Doctrine of Justification and Reconciliation* (1870-74), by Albrecht Ritschl (1822-89). Here he attempts to free theology from metaphysics and forensic categories, presenting it instead as a "practical intention" of gaining "dominion over the world, especially over the evils arising from it, through trust in God."

The presuppositions of the → Reformation, as well as of the so-called pre-Reformers, were bound up with the many-faceted tension between the longing for salvation and the offer of it, between the individual appropriation of salvation and its sacramental presence. The exclusive claim of salvation in the church *(extra ecclesiam nulla salus)* leads to the question of the true church and to a demand for church reform in keeping with the salvation accomplished by Christ. The mystical experience of salvation, its ethical realization, and its objectification in the → sacraments of the church and doctrine of → grace (→ Means of Grace) were factors that shook the late medieval church. In the → indulgence controversy Luther saw how the inflation of the offers of salvation actually obscured the gospel and how good works overshadowed the reference to Christ, "the true treasure of the church."

5.2. ***Luther***

Martin Luther (1483-1546) integrated the terminology of salvation into the context of → justification. For him, God is "the Justifier and Savior of man the sinner" (*LW* 12.311); justification and salvation are of God (WA 1.111). Justification is defined as God making us righteous, a point of emphasis that became especially clear in Luther's diatribe against Erasmus in *The Bondage of the Will* (1525), a work that not surprisingly was severely criticized by Albrecht Ritschl. For Luther to define salvation by starting with the question of free will is wrong, because salvation is a matter of the reception of grace. Otherwise the work of Christ, whose grace we receive, is superseded (*LW* 33.29, 227). Because salvation is promised to the faithful and enacted by the Word, faith is the basis of salvation. Luther's judgment is that, "since God has taken my salvation out of my hands into his, making it depend on his choice and not mine, and has promised to save me, not by my own work or exertion but by his grace and mercy, I am assured and certain" (*LW* 33.289).

In contrast to the earlier static terminology of salvation, Luther placed a strong emphasis on → Christology, → soteriology, and → eschatology, viewing righteousness not as an attribute we possess, whether as a present or future state, but as a gift from outside of us in the tension of *simul iustus et peccator* (saint and sinner at the same time). Salvation is not a possession or a status beside Jesus Christ, but he himself as the Savior is the salvation. This view creates a basic distinction between *gratia* and *donum* (grace and gift), between God's will unto salvation as grace and the gifts operative in the new life.

In his translation of the NT Luther drew a distinction between Gk. *sōizō* as (1) bringing outward aid and deliverance and (2) making or becoming righteous, and he dissolved the substantive *sōtēria* into a verb or alternately translated it using "salvation" and "eternal blessedness." This distinction between deliverance and salvation is also represented in the → two-kingdoms doctrine. The contemporary problematic of salvation vis-à-vis welfare is contained in Luther's distinction between deliverance and salvation, in line with the distinction of the two kingdoms.

5.3. ***Developments***

In the wake of the Reformation these distinctions were disputed and reinterpreted, for example, in the so-called left wing of the Reformation and in the intra-Lutheran controversies. Philipp Melanchthon (1497-1560) retained the understanding of salvation as a gift of promise and offered this formulation: "You do not believe if you do not believe the salvation promised to you" (CRef 21.169; cf. Heb. 11:1). But this view makes the gospel merely a promise of grace and Christ in his ministry only a guarantee of final salvation. Therefore, by making it necessary to add the grace of the Spirit to that of the Word, Melanchthon's emphasis on the "benefits of Christ" opens the door both to the stress on possessing the Spirit and to the doctrine of the *ordo salutis* (→ way of salvation) in Protestant orthodoxy.

This position changes Luther's "order of the Christian life" involving the simultaneity of faith and → love, → freedom and service, into a process that leads to holiness. The result is that the question of the salvific significance of works and their proof of salvation breaks asunder what Luther joined together, the *pro nobis* (for us) and the *extra nos* (outside of us). The present and future of salvation — that is, justification through faith and eternal salvation — fall apart (cf. Formula of Concord, Ep. 4.7; → Assurance of Salvation).

5.4. ***Calvin and the Seventeenth Century***

With John Calvin (1509-64) the concept of salvation acquires a special meaning (→ Calvin's Theology).

For Calvin, our salvation "rests firmly in" Jesus; "the office of Redeemer was laid upon him that he might be our Savior." But "our redemption would be imperfect if he did not lead us ever onward to the final goal of salvation" (*Inst.* 2.16.1). Nevertheless, because of Calvin's doctrine of → predestination to salvation, the emphasis in Christology is placed on the appropriation of salvation in → sanctification according to the third use of the → law and the means of salvation. The theme of the means and their place in the *ordo salutis* has come to dominate in Reformed as well as in Lutheran orthodoxy (→ Order of Salvation). Objective salvation, by the merits of Christ and his threefold office (→ Office of Christ), had to be mediated to the individual person.

For Stephan Praetorius (1536-1603) "the true majesty for Christians consists of a calm, peaceful, and cheerful conscience, which they possess through knowledge of their salvation in Christ Jesus" (quoted in W. Zeller, 18). Praetorius could in fact agree with Cicero's valuation of a quiet → conscience as the highest good and blessedness. This emphasis made possible the leap from early orthodoxy to the spiritualism of the Quaker movement (→ Friends, Society of). In 1677 William Penn (1644-1718) saw that the point of his admonition was to convert to the Lord in "the promotion of your present and eternal welfare" (p. 379).

5.5. *Pietism and Awakening*

In → Pietism the experience of conversion included the factors of inwardness and otherworldliness, as well as the assurance of salvation in its *praxis pietatis* (practice of → piety). In Pietism becoming aware of the "footprints of God" led to what was supposedly the completion of the Reformation on a worldwide scale, to "betterment on every level" (A. H. Francke). During the awakening movement in Germany the idea of "changing the world by changing individuals" led mostly to an internalization of the legacy of Pietism. But it led also to the diaconate and the → Inner Mission, and in America it brought about social change, especially in the antislavery movement (→ Slavery). Thus Edward Beecher (1803-95) cried in 1868, three years after the end of the Civil War, "Now that God has smitten slavery unto death, he has opened the way for the redemption and sanctification of our whole social system" (C. H. Hopkins, 9). The → Salvation Army, organized by William Booth in 1878, arose out of English Methodism.

5.6. *Enlightenment*

The → Enlightenment with its Erasmian tradition was not merely a countermovement but a continuation of earlier → humanism. J. G. Herder (1744-1803) put its position mildly when he said that whoever might have been the founder of Christianity, Jew or Chinese, son of God or son of Joseph, his work must have contained the rule for the salvation of humanity, or else his would be a forgotten name, for the supreme rule of the religion of humanity and the nations is that sacrificial love brings salvation to humankind as a whole, and you belong to the whole (ed. B. Suphan 20.165.190-91).

5.7. *Twentieth Century*

On the one hand, exegetical and theological work in the 20th century resulted in a critique of the ethicizing and objectifying of salvation and the kingdom of God. Especially for the theology of the Word (→ Dialectical Theology), which depended on Karl Barth's (1886-1968) recovery of Reformation insights, the Christian faith is not a religion of redemption that corresponds to this-worldly or otherworldly expectations of salvation. On the other hand, new movements in America (esp. the → Social Gospel and the work of M. L. → King Jr.) and the churches of the Third World (→ Liberation Theology) revived a social-ethical interpretation of salvation.

The hopes for renewal represented by → vitalism and the youth movement led to → religious socialism, whose total social ideology adopted Marxist elements (→ Marxism) rather than reworking them. After World War II the Christian-Marxist dialogue was taken up (→ Marxism and Christianity), but it was burdened by the experiences people were actually having in socialist countries. The desire to embody salvation in the world often appealed to D. Bonhoeffer (1906-45), but then we also must take seriously his distinction between the ultimate and the penultimate. Is there an → analogy between salvation and welfare (K. Barth)?

5.8. *Continuing Problems*

Although controversies regarding the social question in the 19th century and the ecumenical challenge were sharpened by the → Third World, a historical survey shows that basic decisions and problems are the order of the day in every theological discipline. Should we follow the elder Blumhardt (1805-80) and stress the NT connection between *salvation and healing,* opposing a one-dimensional understanding of salvation (J. M. Lochman)? Or should we affirm a differentiated coordination of *salvation and welfare,* saying that because God has done enough for our salvation, we cannot do enough for the welfare of the world (E. Jüngel)?

If theology follows Rudolf Bultmann and stresses the presence of the salvation-event in the → kerygma, today the theology of the → Word of God seems to many people to be void of the world, offering no salvation at all. Therefore salvation is interpreted in terms of happiness, peace, meaning, or identity, with the danger being that salvation is proclaimed in terms of personal psychological and sociopolitical diagnosis and therapy. If salvation as a universal concept is supposed to constitute the unity of religions, salvation in Christ easily becomes merely a help in fulfilling human expectations and utopias, instead of something that savingly transcends them.

→ Immanence and Transcendence

Bibliography: A. M. Allchin, *Participation in God: A Forgotten Strand in Anglican Tradition* (Wilton, Conn., 1988) • C. E. Braaten and R. W. Jenson, eds., *Union with Christ: The New Finnish Interpretation of Luther* (Grand Rapids, 1998) • G. Ebeling, "Das Verständnis von Heil in säkularisierter Zeit" (1967), *Wort und Glaube* (vol. 3; Tübingen, 1975) 349-61 • D. F. Ford, *Self and Salvation: Being Transformed* (Cambridge, 1999) • G. O. Forde, "The Work of Christ" and "Christian Life," *Christian Dogmatics* (vol. 2; ed. C. E. Braaten and R. W. Jenson; Philadelphia, 1984) 5-99, 391-469 • C. H. Hopkins, *The Rise of the Social Gospel in American Protestantism, 1865-1915* (New Haven, 1961) • V.-M. Kärkkäinen, *One with God: Salvation as Deification and Justification* (Collegeville, Minn., 2004) • M. de Kroon, *The Honour of God and Human Salvation: A Contribution to an Understanding of Calvin's Theology according to His Institutes* (Edinburgh, 2001) • J. M. Lochman, *Reconciliation and Liberation: Challenging a One-Dimensional View of Salvation* (Philadelphia, 1980) • W. Lowe, "Christ and Salvation," *Christian Theology: An Introduction to Its Traditions and Tasks* (2d ed.; ed. P. G. Hodgson and R. H. King; Philadelphia, 1985) 222-48 • K. McConnell, *Salvation: A Comparative Analysis of Differing Theological Traditions* (San Francisco, 1994) • B. L. McCormack, *For Us and Our Salvation: Incarnation and Atonement in the Reformed Tradition* (Princeton, 1993) • W. Pannenberg, "Christology and Soteriology," *Jesus, God and Man* (Philadelphia, 1968) 38-49 • I. D. K. Siggins, *Martin Luther's Doctrine of Christ* (New Haven, 1970) • P. Tillich, *Systematic Theology,* vol. 2, *Existence and the Christ* (Chicago, 1957) • W. Zeller, ed., *Der Protestantismus des 17. Jahrhunderts* (Bremen, 1962).

Gerhard Ringshausen

6. Asia, Africa, and Latin America

6.1. *General*

The theme of salvation intersects many of the concerns of the so-called → contextual theologies. They were made evident at the World Conference on Mission and Evangelism in Bangkok (1972/73; → Missionary Conferences; World Council of Churches). Salvation must be defined in relation to the situation from which it saves: international economic conditions, → racism, ecocatastrophe, and so forth. Stimulated by → black theology in the United States and the quest for identity of African Christians, the Bangkok conference, on the one hand, dealt with the experiences of salvation and their opposite in human existence and modern history and, on the other hand, proposed freeing the → Third World from the Western view of salvation, especially its individualizing and spiritualizing tendencies. The reality of the Christian message in the experience of salvation is central for the life of the churches, in view of both the anthropological presuppositions and the living conditions of its members. → Liberation theology rejects as inadequate a mere theology of the Word or of faith and instead insists on theology as a reflection on the experience of salvation and its realization in practice. What is finally important is that the → church is a community of salvation and a place of healing fellowship.

Since here only a survey of generalizations is possible, we cannot deal with concrete examples, language problems, or methodological differences. Still we must at least note the presence of Western ideas of salvation, still partially dominant also in Asia, Africa, and Latin America.

In general the ideas of salvation appear in various societies as a complex mix of traditional interpretations of Western thought (e.g., the revivalist or doctrinal preaching of salvation, and the ideology of → progress) and of Christianity as it is lived out in a specific geographic and cultural sphere. This subject is thus closely related to the theme of gospel and culture (→ Acculturation). Also, we should not overlook the fact that, beside the more classical theologies of → sin and → grace, redemption through the sacrifice of Christ, and so forth, there prevails a strong emphasis on personal salvation in the churches of the Third World, something that is especially prominent in evangelical and Pentecostal groups.

6.2. *Asia*

Because of industrialization and its consequences, Asia — and especially India — has witnessed a quest for the secular meaning of salvation. The developing nations in Asia are caught up in the struggle for a meaningful life and human welfare. How does this struggle relate to the confession of God as Lord? What does the Christian message have to do with the material, social, and cultural revolutions of our time (M. M. Thomas)? In the context of → poverty, salvation may be experienced as a liberating process, though without losing its otherworldly side. In the Buddhist context (→ Buddhism), even the desire for liberation itself must be overcome, ruling out both hyperactivism and the longing for → heaven.

Also in the new relationship between the religions, which is one of dialogue rather than competition and imperialism, salvation is experienced as something present and real. Salvation is thought of not in traditional terms of → conversion but as a commitment to the living Christ, who is also active in other religions. And instead of being the judge, the church bears witness to the God of Jesus as the source and reconciler of human → spirituality. Along with trends oriented to the "cosmic Christ," there are also — and increasingly so — theologies of the poor, who find salvation in our poor, crucified brother Christ (India, Korea, and the Philippines) or in the destruction of idols in the modern disaster suffered by Japan (K. Koyama).

The two factors of poverty and religion are inseparably connected for Asians and form the context of their life (A. Pieris). Thinking in alternatives (e.g., → immanence and transcendence) is foreign to them. The Asian Christian understanding of salvation is comprehensive and complementary (the Yin-Yang way of thinking). Because salvation for them also transcends all forms of human understanding, it is a mystery, so there can be no absolute theology of salvation (→ Asian Theology).

6.3. *Africa*

Africans feel they have no need to engage in theoretical reflection about salvation. They experience it in the forces and empowerment of life. Salvation is what happens when the forces of sin and → evil that diminish life are warded off and overcome. Salvation has to do with physical and other immediate dangers. Therefore salvation is connected with → healing.

Where Christian salvation is not completely spiritualized, it shows itself in the healing of sickness, infertility, and → death. In African society this healing always has to do with disturbed relations with the invisible world of ancestors, as a disordering of the cosmic whole. Healing restores health and life, and therewith society as well. This understanding is apparent in the position of the medicine man as distinct from that of the witch doctor. And when transposed Christologically, it takes on the significance of *Christus Victor* (→ Christology 5). The message of Jesus Christ transcends a view of salvation tied merely to concrete experience and the social group, but care must be taken to overcome the dichotomy between the spiritual and the physical, a notion alien both to the Christian message itself and to Africans.

In Africa salvation is oriented to the whole person and directed to the welfare of society. It presupposes a vital participation in the power of God, who wills to draw near to humanity. Against this background we can understand the struggle to overcome poverty in South Africa or to confront the evil of the apartheid system with the Christian message of salvation. The divine-human encounter and the triumph over death open up a new future — a revolutionary phenomenon (J. Mbiti; → African Theology).

6.4. *Latin America*

Salvation is one of the themes dealt with in liberation theology, although the traditional Roman Catholic understanding and the individualistic and moralistic views of salvation coming mainly from North America are still dominant in Latin America. In liberation theology salvation is experienced in the liberation of the poor. The poor discover their power in the historical process of liberation from dependence, oppression, and mutilation. They find their encouragement and empowerment in the messianic promise of Jesus (Luke 4), the → Beatitudes, and the identification of the liberating God with the poor (Psalms; Deuteronomy; Matthew 25). The history of their own liberation is staged by the God of the exodus, which is evident to all who read → salvation history with the eyes of the poor. This experience is enabled by means of consciousness-raising on the part of intellectuals, priests, and the → base communities.

Although triumphalistic Christologies are replaced by the image of the poor and persecuted Messiah, the → resurrection is especially important for liberation theology, signaling a new world for the poor, giving them hope and a goal. The battle against such idols as money, power, system, and land does not simply happen without → contemplation. The spirituality of liberation is lived out in the church, born from the people of poverty.

Salvación is thus a matter of earthly existence. So what does it mean in an extreme class society? There is only one history whose finality is Christ, the new man. Its end is the fullness of redemption in the → kingdom of God. The world finds salvation when the kingdom is anticipated and realized in history; the church is the sign and instrument of its coming (L. Boff; → Latin American Theology; Biblical Theology 2; Third World Theology).

7. Ecumenical Aspects

7.1. *Presuppositions*

The theme of salvation is deeply rooted in the missionary tradition that joined the ecumenical movement to the various confessional traditions, with the result that the ecumenical experience of the churches expanded the awareness of their common mission. The mission of the church is anchored in God's Trinitarian work of salvation, and it takes place between the resurrection and the → parousia (→ Eschatology). Its task is to proclaim God's all-embracing *shalom* and to live it out in the struggles of history. The basis of the → World Council of Churches, as revised and strengthened at the New Delhi Assembly (1961), confesses Jesus Christ as God and Savior and affirms the common calling of the churches to "the glory of the one God, Father, Son, and Holy Spirit."

7.2. *Developments*

Historical situations have heightened the tensions surrounding the theme of salvation, keeping the ecumenical movement busy with many questions. For example, how do eschatological salvation and earthly welfare belong together, and how are they to be differentiated? How are we to think of the relation between the kingdom of God and the secular world? In a signal statement the Bangkok World Conference on Mission and Evangelism (1972/73) dealt with the theme "Salvation Today." The context of the Buddhist quest for salvation (→ Buddhism and Christianity), the Vietnam War, and the growing North-South tension led to attempts to articulate the reality of salvation on the level of → experience. Since then the question of salvation has continued to divide evangelicals (→ Evangelicalism) and ecumenicals, "born-again Christians" from the "politicized church." Nevertheless, the strong contextualizing of the Christian message, as well as the linking of salvation to liberation from oppression, has finally found a certain resonance also in circles critical of the ecumenical movement.

Subsequently, there has been success in more closely relating evangelization, spirituality, and advocacy for justice (the fifth WCC assembly, in Nairobi in 1975) and more strongly emphasizing as a central theme the good news for the poor as those who have been sinned against (world mission and evangelism, Melbourne 1980). In 1983 at the sixth WCC assembly, in Vancouver, many attempts were made under the slogan "Jesus Christ, the Life of the World" to bring healing to a world threatened by war, injustice, and catastrophes, issuing in a summons to the churches "to engage in a conciliar process of mutual commitment (covenant) to justice, peace, and the care of creation."

7.3. *Various Accents*

Parallel to such ecumenical developments are the efforts of the confessional world alliances (e.g., the study program of the → World Alliance of Reformed Churches "You Shall Be My Witnesses," against apartheid as sin and → heresy; likewise the → Lutheran World Federation), those of the → Roman Catholic Church (the rights of the poor on the basis of Catholic social teaching) and of the Eastern Orthodox churches (a holistic approach from a Trinitarian perspective, but also the "verticality" of salvation over against social and cultural liberation; → Orthodox Church).

The Orthodox often see themselves as mediators between two prevailing tendencies that cut across confessions and cultures. On the one hand, in liberation theology salvation is realized in the concrete process of liberating people out of poverty, dependence, and bondage, presupposing scientific analysis and critique of ideology. On the other hand, Pentecostal-charismatic movements stress the connection of salvation to spiritual and physical healing from sin and sickness.

7.4. *Ecumenical Discussion*

→ Ecumenical dialogue warns against a narrow one-dimensional preaching of salvation; the two arms of the cross are not to be separated. Yet the conceptual distinction between horizontal and vertical, personal and social, is misleading; it needs to be replaced by identity and relevance (J. Moltmann). The ecumenical encounter of the churches with the Third World fosters a learning process that leads to a comprehensive understanding of salvation that includes both redemption and liberation. Priorities that may be historically necessary in certain circumstances can never represent the totality of salvation; only Christ possesses this totality.

Beside the intensive study on ecclesiology (see the Faith and Order document *Baptism, Eucharist, and Ministry*), efforts are crystallizing to make salvation real for all people, for example, in the matter of human and civil → rights and their implementation in the churches as well. → Dialogue with other religions serves God's plan of salvation insofar as it participates in God's dialogue with the world. But the theological basis and meaning of this plan remain extremely controversial (Acts 4:12!).

The plurality of religions and cultures demands of Christians a dialogic attitude; in certain contexts this attitude can become a matter of life and death. The dialogues do not explicitly claim to solve the basic theoretical problems but aim only to contribute to peace and justice among peoples, and thus to correspond to God's salvation. All our actions and theological reflections are guided by the conviction that we do not build the kingdom of God. Rather, we build up human community in light of the kingdom of God (E. Castro; → Ecumenical Theology).

→ Ecumenism, Ecumenical Movement

Bibliography: On 6: K. C. Abraham and B. Mbuy-Beya, eds., *Spirituality of the Third World* (Maryknoll, N.Y.,

1994) • D. Batstone, ed., *New Visions for the Americas: Religious Engagement and Social Transformation* (Minneapolis, 1993) • L. Boff, *Church, Charism, and Power: Liberation Theology and the Institutional Church* (New York, 1985) • J. Burdick and W. E. Hewitt, eds., *The Church at the Grassroots in Latin America: Perspectives on Thirty Years of Activism* (Westport, Conn., 2000) • R. Elphick and R. Davenport, eds., *Christianity in South Africa* (Berkeley, Calif., 1997) • D. J. Elwood, ed., *What Asian Christians Are Thinking: A Theological Source Book* (Quezon City, 1977) • V. Fabella, ed., *Asia's Struggle for Full Humanity: Towards a Relevant Theology* (Maryknoll, N.Y., 1980) • P. Frostin, *Liberation Theology in Tanzania and South Africa: A First World Interpretation* (Lund, 1988) • K. Gnanakan, ed., *Salvation: Some Asian Perspectives* (Bangalore, 1982) • G. Gutiérrez, *A Theology of Liberation* (new ed.; London, 2001) • J. Míguez Bonino, *Doing Theology in a Revolutionary Situation* (Philadelphia, 1975) • R. Nicolson, *A Black Future? Jesus and Salvation in South Africa* (London, 1990) • M. A. Oduyoye, *Introducing African Women's Theology* (Cleveland, 2001) • C. M. Pemberton, *Circle Thinking: African Women Theologians in Dialogue with the West* (Leiden, 2003) • A. Pieris, "Der Ort der nichtchristlichen Religionen und Kulturen in der Entwicklung einer Theologie der Dritten Welt," *ZMR* 66 (1982) 241-70 • T. Sundermeier, ed., *Christus, der schwarze Befreier. Aufsätze zum schwarzen Bewußtsein und zur schwarzen Theologie in Südafrika* (3d ed.; Erlangen, 1981). See also the bibliography in "Liberation Theology."

On 7: K. Blaser, *Gottes Heil in heutiger Wirklichkeit* (Frankfurt, 1978); idem, *La mission. Dialogues et défis* (Lausanne, 1983) • E. Castro, *Freedom in Mission: The Perspective of the Kingdom of God* (Geneva, 1985) • W. J. Hollenweger, *Interkulturelle Theologie*, vol. 1, *Erfahrungen der Leibhaftigkeit;* vol. 2, *Umgang mit Mythen* (Munich, 1979-82) • R. Lanooy, *For Us and for Our Salvation: Seven Perspectives on Christian Soteriology* (Utrecht, 1994) • J. M. Lochman, *Reconciliation and Liberation: Challenging a One-Dimensional View of Salvation* (Philadelphia, 1980) • J. Moltmann, *The Church in the Power of the Spirit: A Contribution to Messianic Ecclesiology* (Minneapolis, 1993) • A. Pieris, *An Asian Theology of Liberation* (Edinburgh, 1988) • G. Wainwright, *For Our Salvation: Two Approaches to the Work of Christ* (Grand Rapids, 1997) • World Council of Churches, *Bangkok Assembly 1973* (Geneva, 1973).

Klauspeter Blaser†

8. Political and Legal Significance

As distinct from the theological and eschatological understanding of salvation in the sphere of the biblical tradition, Gk. *sōtēria* and especially Lat. *salus* denote the order that is to be upheld even when it is guaranteed by the gods *(theoi sōtēres)*. According to Plato (427-347 B.C.; → Platonism), salvation is the validity of state laws (*Leg.* 4.715D). In the Hellenistic emperor cult, predications of salvation cultically invoke the salvation of the kingdom in that of the ruler (i.e., his health; → Emperor Worship; Hellenism; Roman Empire). This pragmatic political "salutology" (C. Andresen) is to be differentiated from a religiously characterized → soteriology. Only in Christian Latinity were *salus salvare* and *salvator* coined in place of the Roman *(con)servare* and *conservator.*

Because salvation meant order and well-being in the home and the → state, it had for Cicero (106-43 B.C.) the sense of usefulness *(utilitas)*. Directing an oration to Caesar (100-44), Cicero could thus ask who has so little reflected on his own and the common salvation as not to see that your salvation includes his own, and that the life of all depends on your life (*Pro Marcello* 22). Under Augustus (27 B.C.–A.D. 14) the public salvation *(salus publica)* became the world's salvation *(salus mundi)*, the security of the worldwide *orbis Romanus.* The fate of the emperor thus embraced the salvation of the human race. This view justified the overthrow of Nero (54-68).

Within salutology Christians may pray for the salvation of rulers as long as salutology does not become soteriology. But when the *pax Christiana* came to be identified with the *pax Romana* under Constantine, and Augustine (354-430) spoke of the city of God (→ Augustine's Theology), it was easy to expound Christian soteriology as salutology, especially as the Roman ideal of *salus* had made its way into ecclesiology (→ Church 2.2) already by the time of Cyprian (ca. 200-258).

The adoption of Roman law from the time of John of Salisbury (d. 1180) meant a recognition of both common utility and public *salus*, especially in the designation of the community as an organism. For Martin Luther (1483-1546) the salvation of the → state began with the → family (WA 16.543; → Luther's Theology). Baruch Spinoza (1632-77) used the word *salus* as a term for religious and political well-being; both salvation and civic welfare depend upon obedience to established laws.

In the 17th and 18th centuries, according to the Aristotelian and Thomistic common good (→ Scholasticism; Thomism), the *salus publica* as the common welfare was the goal of the state, as distinct from the welfare of the state itself. According to J. S. Pütter (1725-1807), if a police state sought to pro-

Salvation Army

mote the common good, individual police officers, except in certain cases, had no responsibility for the salvation that was to be promoted.

At the end of the 19th century the limitation of the liberal state by human and civil → rights was followed by the adoption of elements of salutology in the welfare state. Under the Third Reich the common good was an indeterminate legal concept enshrining the thesis of Cicero that public salvation is the supreme law (*salus publica suprema lex esto, De leg.* 3.38).

Bibliography: C. Andresen, "Erlösung," *RAC* 6.24-219 • P. J. Bagley, "Religious Salvation and Civil Welfare: 'Salus' in Spinoza's Tractatus theologico-politicus," *StSpin* 12 (1996) 169-84 • H. J. Berman, *Faith and Order: The Reconciliation of Law and Religion* (Atlanta, 1993); idem, *Law and Revolution: The Formation of the Western Legal Tradition* (Cambridge, Mass., 1983) • R. E. Flathman, *The Public Interest* (New York, 1966) • M. Stolleis, *Gemeinwohlformeln im nationalsozialistischen Recht* (Berlin, 1974) • J. Witte Jr., *Law and Protestantism: The Legal Teachings of the Lutheran Reformation* (Cambridge, 2002); idem, *The Reformation of Rights: The Calvinist Tradition of Law, Religion, and Human Rights* (Cambridge, 2005).

Gerhard Ringshausen

Salvation Army

1. Founding and Development
2. Spread and Modern Situation
3. Theological Tradition
4. Life and Practice
5. Self-Understanding
6. Organization
7. Ecumenical Relations

1. Founding and Development

The Salvation Army began in July 1865 in England with the preaching of William Booth (1829-1912, ordained in 1858 in the Methodist New Connexion) at a tent mission arranged by the East London Special Services Committee. Booth had previously done revivalist work in many different places (→ Revivals). In 1865 he organized the East London Christian Mission, a ministry to the working class, with a tent mission at the Quaker cemetery in Whitechapel (London). In 1870 he founded the People's Mission Hall in Whitechapel. He moved out of London to Croydon the same year and changed the name to the Christian Mission. His work focused on areas of the city with the poorest people, whom other churches were not reaching. In 1877 he adopted the so-called hallelujah method, the use of popular gospel songs with the frequent interjection of "Hallelujah!" and → "Amen!"

In 1878, to arouse greater attention and to counter hostile mockery, the first brass band was founded, and at the same time the name "Salvation Army" was adopted in accordance with stricter organization. The language of Christian warfare and a military style of leadership predominated: uniforms, banners, and military titles were introduced, and the members were called "soldiers of salvation." There was no longer any Methodist type of mission conference made up of lay preachers and ordained ministers from different branches of the work. The general superintendent became the general of the new redemptive army. In December 1879 the first edition of the weekly paper *War Cry* appeared. In 1882 → baptism and the → Eucharist were dropped as not necessary to salvation. The sacraments had always been a divisive factor among Christians, and their significance had been obscured. After the model of Catherine Booth (1829-90), wife and cofounder, women were equal from the very first. Today wives of officers and all female officers are ordained.

2. Spread and Modern Situation

Between 1881 and 1885 the Salvation Army won some 250,000 members, all pledged to live biblically. Attempts to forbid their work in Britain lasted up to the 1890s. Their success reduced alcoholism and → prostitution. From Britain the movement spread in 1880 to the United States and Australia, in 1881 to France, in 1882 to Canada, Sweden, Switzerland, and India, in 1883 to South Africa and Sri Lanka, and in 1886 to Germany. By 1890 it had branches in all parts of the world. In 2005 it was working in 109 countries with over one million soldiers.

3. Theological Tradition

The Salvation Army has 11 permanent articles of faith, all in keeping with its derivation from → Methodism. The new name was made official in the Deed of Constitution of August, 7, 1878, and again in the Salvation Army Act of 1980.

Their doctrine of redemption is similar to that of John → Wesley (1703-91). Redemption is universal, applying to all. It is *free,* each person being able either to accept → grace or to reject it. It is *full,* the sanctification of the whole person being the goal of the Christian faith. It is *certain,* direct witness being given to personal → salvation. In individual sanctification the working of the → Holy Spirit receives special stress. The sacraments are not necessary conditions of → salvation. There is no specific theology of the → church or of Christian → ethics. The positions adopted are those of traditional evangelical Protestantism (→ Evangelical Movement).

4. Life and Practice

The Salvation Army has seven ceremonies: commissioning of officers, enrolling of soldiers, handing over of flags, dedication of children, → marriage, → funeral, and a memorial ceremony. There are seven types of gathering, or forms of service. The most important of these are gatherings for sanctification (of believers), for evangelization and revival, and for open-air witness (on streets and squares).

5. Self-Understanding

All Salvationists are soldiers. They all subscribe to a statement of faith and to the "articles of war," which refer to the personal experience of redemption, belief in the triune God, confession of Jesus Christ, and the resolve to be a good soldier. Also included is total abstinence from alcohol, drugs, and tobacco. The soldiers are united in holy love for God and neighbor and want to lead all people to Jesus Christ. The Salvation Army regards itself, according to the witness of the NT, as a Christian church. In ongoing battle with the forces of → evil, it seeks to convey the Word and ordinances of God to all people in all places. Evangelistic preaching and diaconal work go hand in hand and mutually influence one another.

Following the example of their Master, Jesus Christ, the soldiers try to help and comfort and restore their neighbors. Since they view sin as the basic human evil, they never tire of pointing to Jesus Christ as the only Savior. Their over 5,000 social institutions and schools worldwide show that they are not content to offer spiritual help alone. Some 25,000 officers and at least 210,000 voluntary local officers work in these institutions and in the more than 15,000 corps (i.e., local units established for preaching the gospel and for service in the community) and outposts.

6. Organization

The most important units are the corps (the → congregation), the division (regional administration), and the territory (a larger geographic area). The legal position depends on the situation in each territory or the constitution of the country concerned.

7. Ecumenical Relations

In 1948 the Salvation Army was a founding member of the → World Council of Churches (WCC). In 1978 it broke off membership when two Salvationist officers were killed by the Patriotic Front in Rhodesia, to which the WCC had given financial aid through its → Program to Combat Racism. In 1981 it adopted the status of a "befriended organization." This new status clarified the international character of the Salvation Army. Problems also arose out of the strong emphasis that the WCC put on the search for eucharistic unity at its assembly at Nairobi in 1975.

At the special request of the WCC, the Salvation Army responded to the so-called Lima Declaration, *Baptism, Eucharist, and Ministry*, in 1986. It deplored the heavy stress on sacramental unity and feared the isolation of many Christians and churches that continue to regard the preaching of the gospel and personal salvation as the task and goal of their existence. Yet unquestionably the Salvation Army was still ready to cooperate with others, for example, in diaconal work, in → Bible societies, in the World Day of Prayer, and in the → World Evangelical Alliance.

Bibliography: H. Begbie, *The Life of General William Booth* (2 vols.; New York, 1920) • W. Booth, *In Darkest England–and the Way Out* (1890; 6th ed., Chicago, 1970) • R. Collier, *The General next to God* (London, 1965) • S. J. Ervine, *God's Soldier: General William Booth* (2 vols.; London, 1934) • R. Hattersley, *Blood and Fire: William and Catherine Booth and Their Salvation Army* (London, 1999) • E. McKinley, *Marching to Glory: The History of the Salvation Army in the United States, 1880-1992* (2d ed.; Grand Rapids, 1995) • N. Murdoch, *Origins of the Salvation Army* (Knoxville, Tenn., 1994) • R. Sandell, A. Wiggins, and F. Coutts, *The History of the Salvation Army* (3 vols.; London, 1947-55) • C. Spence, *The Salvation Army Farm Colonies* (Tucson, Ariz., 1985) • L. Taiz, *Hallelujah Lads and Lasses: Remaking the Salvation Army in America, 1880-1930* (Chapel Hill, N.C., 2001) • P. Walker, *Pulling the Devil's Kingdom Down: The Salvation Army in Victorian England* (Berkeley, Calif., 2001) • D. Winston, *Red-Hot and Righteous: The Urban Religion of the Salvation Army* (Cambridge, Mass., 1999).

Karl Heinz Gassner

Salvation History

1. Terms and Concept
2. Development and Ascendancy
   2.1. Oscar Cullmann
   2.2. Ecumenical Impact
3. Biblical Data and Theological Reflections after the NT

1. Terms and Concept

A technical term in → biblical theology (§1.2.5), "salvation history" (Ger. *Heilsgeschichte*) arose at a time when, as J. C. Beck put it, history was god (→ Historiography 3.6), not reason (→ Enlightenment) or feeling (→ Experience; Schleiermacher's Theology). Under influences from → covenant theology (§3.1; J. Cocceius [1603-69]) and → Pietism (J. A. Bengel [1687-1752]), the concept developed in the Erlangen school, with its emphases on biblical hermeneutics, confessional ecclesiology, our communion with Christ as a starting point, and Scripture as witness to God's redemptive acts in history.

The word "Heilsgeschichte" seems to have been used first in 1841 by J. C. K. von Hofmann (1810-77; see A. J. Greig, *ExpTim* 87 [1975-76] 118-19). "Salvation history" may be the best Eng. translation, not "holy history" (as if a conduit through "secular history"), not "saving history" or "redemptive history" (as if history redeems), or even "history of salvation" (as if there were an institution dispensing it; C. K. Barrett, 4n.1). Some employ "Heilsgeschichte" in English (*Webster's Unabridged,* 3d ed.: "an interpretation of history emphasizing God's saving acts and viewing Jesus Christ as central in redemption"), not least because it yields the usable adj. *heilsgeschichtlich.* For histories of the concept, see G. Weth, K. G. Steck, D. Wiederkehr, F. Mildenberger.

Because in the NT and patristic material Gk. *oikonomia* has been prominent in discussing Heilsgeschichte, there have often been relationships with "the economy of God," including understandings of the → Trinity, as well as connections with → stewardship, a movement in the 19th and 20th centuries originating in the United States, involving the believer as a steward *(oikonomos)* in the divine economy. Because the Lat. trans. of *oikonomia* was often *dispensatio,* there are links to → dispensation in Orthodox praxis and to → dispensationalism.

2. Development and Ascendancy

Individual theologians like Adolf Schlatter (1852-1938) kept Heilsgeschichte prominent, as in the design of G. Kittel's *TDNT* (vol. 1, 1933, is dedicated to Schlatter; many articles until about 1950 reflect a *heilsgeschichtlich* approach), even in the face of the proliferating → history-of-religions school. But → Culture Protestantism, → liberal theology, and even → dialectical theology had, for different reasons, little interest in salvation history (though eventually it found a place in Karl → Barth's *CD*).

2.1. ***Oscar Cullmann***

Oscar Cullmann (1902-99) brought Heilsgeschichte to its fullest expression and, with pupils and allies, its peak of influence in biblical and ecumenical theology (G. Müller-Fahrenholz, 137-69; E. W. Stegemann and the entire issue of *TZ* 58/3). From his work on the NT and early church, Cullmann developed a Christocentric theology of salvation. There were links with the Erlangen school (e.g., the unity of OT and NT, God's incursions into history, and history as revealed prophecy), but Cullmann insisted that his views arose from the Bible itself. To avoid confusion with Erlangen theology, he once proposed calling his program *Offenbarungsgeschichte,* "revelational history."

Cullmann's work *Christ and Time* (1946) presented a picture of a "continuous redemptive line" running through history from creation to the parousia. This line, designated *oikonomia,* stretches over the entire "present age," which is set between an "age before creation" and a "coming age." Along this timeline one can mark certain *kairoi,* or significant moments in the revealing and executing of God's plan of salvation (e.g., the exodus). In the sweep of past ("formerly"), present ("now"), and future ("then"), the greatest *kairos* is the coming of the Messiah, which for Jewish eschatology is still to happen. For Christians it has already occurred in the "Christ-event," which is *ephapax,* "once for all" (Rom. 6:10; Heb. 7:27, 9:12), giving this "midpoint" in time a unique, absolutely decisive character. The NT understanding of time is thus linear, not cyclical; for believers and the church the "already" (the turning point) has occurred, but there is also a "not yet" (a future age still to come).

This "both-and" eschatology brought Cullmann into debate with supporters of future apocalyptic events as decisive and of "realized eschatology" (e.g., in John's gospel). Paul (and others) are stewards *(oikonomoi)* in the divine economy, and the church is part of an ongoing plan. Cullmann further set forth his views in *Salvation in History* (orig. *Heil als Geschichte;* see K.-H. Schlaudraff for an evaluation of Cullmann's program).

2.2. ***Ecumenical Impact***

Pope John XXIII invited Cullmann to be an observer at the Second Vatican Council. This recognition reflected Cullmann's interest in Protestant-Catholic relationships and his importance in Roman Catholic circles. His Heilsgeschichte, often understood in terms of "the mystery of salvation" *(mysterium salutis),* was influential among Catholic biblical scholars (see J. Frisque) and contributed to the theology of the council (→ Ecumenical Theology 2).

The Cullmann Festschrift edited by F. Christ (1967) and tributes edited by K. Froehlich (*Testimonia oecumenica* [Tübingen, 1982]) suggest the range of Cullmann's impact. Among other treatments reflecting the high-water mark of Heilsgeschichte in theology in the 1960s, see A. Richardson (Anglican), E. C. Rust (Baptist), and I. C. Rottenberg (Presbyterian).

3. Biblical Data and Theological Reflections after the NT

All forms of salvation history appeal to certain biblical passages where "salvation" is the theme (see, e.g., G. O'Collins, *ABD* 5.907-14; J. Reumann, *WThWB* 449-55). In other cases the theme is God's plan or purpose (Gk. *boulē,* Acts 2:23; 4:28; 13:36; Eph. 1:11).

3.1. *OT*

In the OT, where salvation history often fits well, *heilsgeschichtlich* passages cannot be determined by vocabulary like *oikonomia* (rare in the → LXX) but are identified chiefly from content. Obvious choices for *kairoi* in Israel's history include the exodus and the Sinai covenant, plus taking possession of the promised land, as well as highlights in the history of deliverers and kings (K. Koch et al.). In the canonical sequence, stories of the patriarchs preceded; the exile, return, and, amid stark realities, future hopes followed. Creation accounts appear before stories about Abraham and his descendants. From the prophets (ibid., 578-79) can be sketched a line of "earlier Heilsgeschichte," from creation to possession of the land, with David, Zion, and Solomon's temple as the climax; then comes a decline, or "Unheilsgeschichte" (a history of failures, judgment, and woe), leading to the end of Israel, Jerusalem's fall, and captivity in Babylon. Voices were then heard, apocalyptic in nature, projecting a new Heilsgeschichte for the future (Jer. 23:7-8; Isa. 49:23, 26; Ezek. 37:1-14; 39:28).

An account of historical events combining weal and woe is found in the → Deuteronomistic history and its schema on judges and monarchs. Apocalyptic writings developed the idea of "ages" past and to come (→ Apocalypticism 2.2, esp. 2.2.5). In Nehemiah, note the prayer at 9:6-37, covering from creation to the distress of the exile. G. von Rad (*OT Theology* [2 vols.; New York, 1962-65] esp. 2.357-87 on "saving-event," typology, and the two Testaments) and others isolated passages containing what was called Israel's credo (Deut. 26:5-11; 6:20-24; Josh. 24:2-13) and epic accounts from creation or exodus to Sinai or Jerusalem, in the Tetrateuch or Hexateuch or sources like J or P (Koch et al., 573-77). G. E. Wright and others popularized the view of "God who acts" in OT and NT, often together with views on the Testaments as "against their environment."

3.2. *NT*

For the NT, Acts 7 (Stephen's speech) presents an account of Unheilsgeschichte from Abraham to Solomon, and Acts 13 (Paul's sermon) from the exodus to Pentecost. Paul contrasts Adam and Christ (1 Cor. 15:21-22; Rom. 5:12-21, on which see O. Kuss, *Der Römerbrief* [vol. 1; Regensburg, 1957] 275-91) and deals with Israel with great hope in Romans 9–11. Colossians and Ephesians stress God's plan and its being carried out, notably by Paul. One can also put together a sketch of how Paul deals with certain seminal figures: Adam, Abraham, Moses, Christ, and the Adam to come (Barrett). → Luke (§6) and → Acts (§7) are usually regarded as the best NT examples for Heilsgeschichte, in part because, within references to world history (e.g., Luke 3:1-2), it sketches three ages (Israel, the time of Jesus, and the age of the church; H. Conzelmann saw this division as Luke's creation; Cullmann, as a common NT view that Luke developed more fully).

One can break down the Christ-event into a series of *kairoi,* including incarnation, events and aspects of Jesus' ministry, the cross, resurrection, and ascension. Overall, U. Luz (*TRE* 12.600-602) concludes, however, that already in the preaching of Jesus the history of what constitutes Israel ("election," "covenant") recedes, and generally the NT gives Israel's (Un)heilsgeschichte a negative evaluation; Paul seems to evaluate more positively God's past actions to save (e.g., Abraham, Gal. 3:6-18; Romans 4; for "all Israel" "the gifts and the calling of God are irrevocable," Rom. 11:26, 29).

Cullmann's timeline can be read to show a series of OT/NT correspondences, running from the many (or all) at the beginning to the One (Christ), and then from the One to the many (or all); also creation/new creation, Israel/New Israel, the remnant/the 12 balance each other. But others see Paul "paganizing" Israel's Heilsgeschichte (G. Klein, "Römer 4 und die Idee der Heilsgeschichte," *EvT* 23 [1963] 424-47; Gal. 4:3, 8; 3:19 "through angels," not direct from God; the benefits treated as "loss," Phil. 3:5-8) or justification as the key to Heilsgeschichte

(E. Käsemann). Battles have been fought over whether Paul was a "theologian of salvation history" (Cullmann school) or preacher of the kerygma without a framework of Heilsgeschichte. It is noteworthy that many of the patterns of salvation history that have been proposed must be put together by the reader from bits and pieces of biblical data in light of a particular theory.

3.3. *Among Later Theologians*

→ Irenaeus of Lyons, with his sequence of four covenants and Trinitarian roles in the divine economy, can be set forth as a patristic model who, against the Gnostics, reflected a biblical view of salvation. → Origen and → Tertullian make abundant references to *oikonomia* and *dispensatio* and related terms, often in a salvation-historical sense. → Augustine's *City of God,* with its clash of two kingdoms, reflects the economy of God, as do Trinitarian teachings in numerous writers who often distinguished *theologia,* the inner mystery of God, from *oikonomia,* divine actions in history.

The → church year, lectionary readings, and liturgy often reflect the events *(kairoi)* of biblical salvation history, particularly at festivals. Martin → Luther and the → Reformers took over much of this developed and developing view of salvation history and at points revised aspects more biblically. Thus an often unified view of Scripture, church, and world history existed till the Enlightenment. G. W. F. Hegel can be said to have applied salvation-history concepts to "an emancipated secular world history" (Wiederkehr, 463).

4. More Recent Trends

4.1. *Cullmann's Type of Salvation History*

Cullmann's view suffered in the general "decline and fall" of → biblical theology (§1.3.1). It was charged with objectifying "saving facts" *(Heilstatsachen)* in a closed system of history, which must be believed in *(fides quae creditur).* Specifically, there were criticisms of its view of time (J. Barr) and its inability to incorporate Wisdom literature and other parts of the Bible not clearly historical. There were corrections about *oikonomia* ("administration" or "managing" of salvation, not the "plan of salvation," for which the term is *mystērion,* 1 Cor. 4:1; Col. 1:25-27; Eph. 1:9-10; 3:3, 4, 9; Reumann, 1966-67) and debate over whether the view of time and space in Hebrew is linear or spiral. Portrayals of Israel's religion, in contrast to views throughout the ancient Near East, were simplified or, worse, falsified by some supporters of Heilsgeschichte (R. Gnuse). Above all, views of history changed, again (→ Hermeneutics 2.1-3).

The Bultmann school won out in NT studies over the Cullmann school. Subsequently there was a shift away from history of any sort to social and other, often ahistorical, approaches (→ Historiography 3.7).

4.2. *Roman Catholic Acceptance of Heilsgeschichte*

An acceptance of Heilsgeschichte in Roman Catholic theology can be seen, among other places, in K. → Rahner's essays; the survey by K. Berger, A. Darlap, and K. Rahner in *SM(E)* 5.411-25; and in documents of Vatican II (Müller-Fahrenholz, 169-92): *Dei Verbum,* on divine revelation ("economy of revelation" and "history of salvation" at 2; see also 4, 7, 14-15); *Lumen gentium,* on ecclesiology in God's plan (16, 36); *Gaudium et spes,* the church and human history and the modern world (24); and *Nostra aetate,* Heilsgeschichte and Religionsgeschichte (see 2, 3; Müller-Farhrenholz, 183-85). Cullmann himself was received as a *praeceptor* of the church (K. Froehlich, in F. Christ, 214) and "teacher of three popes" (Barth, in Müller-Fahrenholz, 137).

4.3. *Wolfhart Pannenberg*

Pannenberg (b. 1928), the systematician, and a team of scholars in OT, NT, church history, and practical theology carried the approach of G. von Rad and others further in a comprehensive view of *history as revelation.* Events were looked at apocalyptically in light of the expected end. Even the Easter-event of Jesus' resurrection came close to being regarded as something verifiable by historical means, the proleptic anticipation of the end of history.

The universal side of Heilsgeschichte also came to the fore. In *TRE* 12:668-74, reflecting other writings, Pannenberg moves more into a "theology of world history." Wiederkehr sees "universal history" as an outcome of Heilsgeschichte, expressed in → European theology (§2.4), → political and → liberation theology (§2.1), as well as in Asiatic and Eastern systems, yet in continuity with the cross of Christ (pp. 466-67).

4.4. *Modified Revivals*

Gnuse has argued for a view of "Israel's notion of salvation history," free from nature imagery, with history as the arena of divine activity, denoting purpose and reflecting plan, through covenant, word, morality, and "pathos" (from slavery in Egypt, an "ability to 'embrace pain'" [W. Brueggemann]). Such a model from a "peripheral society" could serve biblical theologians well.

M. Hengel supports a chastened version of salvation history: God's hidden actions reflect a will to save, and for the Christian theologian "this history receives its unity and its foundation from the centre and its goal, the person of Jesus Christ" (p. 240), though "a number of lines run side by side" (242) in the OT, for example.

4.5. *Under Other Names*

Though Heilsgeschichte has often disappeared in recent NT and biblical theologies, one finds what Cullmann, von Rad, and others had in mind to be reflected now under emphases on "story," "metastory," and "narrative" (e.g., in Paul: R. B. Hays, *The Faith of Jesus Christ: The Narrative Substructure of Galatians 3:1–4:11* [2d ed.; Grand Rapids, 2002]; B. Witherington III, *Paul's Narrative Thought World: The Tapestry of Tragedy and Triumph* [Louisville, Ky., 1994]).

Bibliography: C. K. Barrett, *From First Adam to Last: A Study in Pauline Theology* (New York, 1962) • F. Christ, ed., *Oikonomia als Thema der Theologie* (Hamburg-Bergstedt, 1967) • O. Cullmann, *Christ and Time: The Primitive Christian Conception of Time and History* (Philadelphia, 1949; rev. ed., 1964); idem, *Salvation in History* (New York, 1967) • J. Frisque, *Oscar Cullmann. Une théologie de l'histoire du salut* (Tournai, 1960) • R. Gnuse, *Heilsgeschichte as a Model for Biblical Theology: The Debate concerning the Uniqueness and Significance of Israel's Worldview* (Lanham, Md., 1989) • M. Hengel, "'Salvation History': The Truth of Scripture and Modern Theology," *Reading Texts, Seeking Wisdom: Scripture and Theology* (ed. D. F. Ford and G. Stanton; Grand Rapids, 2004) 229-44 • E. Käsemann, "Justification and Salvation History in the Epistle to the Romans," *Perspectives on Paul* (Philadelphia, 1971) 60-78 • K. Koch, U. Luz, W. Pannenberg, et al., "Geschichte / Geschichtsschreibung / Geschichtsphilosophie," *TRE* 19.565-698 • F. Mildenberger, "Heilsgeschichte," *RGG* (4th ed.) 3.1584-86 • G. Müller-Fahrenholz, *Heilsgeschichte zwischen Ideologie und Prophetie. Profile und Kritik heilsgeschichtlicher Theorien in der ökumenischen Bewegung zwischen 1948 and 1968* (Freiburg, 1974) • K. Rahner, "History of the World and Salvation-History" (1962), *Theological Investigations* (vol. 5; Baltimore, 1966) 97-114; idem, "Profane History and Salvation History" (1982), ibid., vol. 21 (1988) 3-15 • J. Reumann, "Heilsgeschichte in Luke: Some Remarks on Its Background and Comparison with Paul," *StEv* 4 (1968) 86-115; idem, "OIKONOMIA-Terms in Paul in Comparison with Lucan Heilsgeschichte," *NTS* 13 (1966-67) 147-67 • A. Richardson, *History, Sacred and Profane* (London, 1964) • I. C. Rottenberg, *Redemption and Historical Reality* (Philadelphia, 1964) • E. C. Rust, *Salvation History: A Biblical Interpretation* (Richmond, Va., 1962) • K.-H. Schlaudraff, *Heil als Geschichte? Die Frage nach dem heilsgeschichtlichen Denken, dargestellt anhand der Konzeption Oscar Cullmanns* (Tübingen, 1988) • K. G. Steck, *Die Idee der Heilsgeschichte. Hofmann–Schlatter–Cullmann* (Zollikon, 1959) • E. W. Stegemann, "Cullmanns Konzept der Heilsgeschichte in seiner Zeit," *TZ* 58 (2002) 232-42 • G. Weth, *Die Heilsgeschichte. Ihr universeller und ihr individueller Sinn in der offenbarungsgeschichtlichen Theologie des 19. Jahrhunderts* (Munich, 1931) • D. Wiederkehr, "Heilsgeschichte," *EKL* (3d ed.) 2.460-68 • G. E. Wright, *God Who Acts* (London, 1952) • G. E. Wright and R. H. Fuller, *The Book of the Acts of God: Christian Scholarship Interprets the Bible* (New York, 1957).

John Reumann

Samaritans

Like Jews and Christians, the Samaritans worship the biblical God (→ Judaism). But their Holy Scripture consists only of the → Pentateuch, whose religious laws they observe as the Jews do. Christian interest in them rests not merely in the fact that there is reference to them in the NT (Luke 10:30-37; 17:16-18; John 4:4-42; Acts 8:4-25). Knowledge of their origin and religion helps us also to understand the development of Jewish religion. On the assumption that at central points (esp. → law, → priesthood, and → eschatology) their religion preserves the state of development of Jewish religion in the second century B.C., we may trace more clearly the ways in which rabbinic Judaism developed.

Rabbinic writings (see *Gen. Rab.* 94:7) link the origin of the Samaritans to 2 Kgs. 17:24-41. This passage describes them as semiconverted neighbors, pagan colonists from Cuthah (an ancient city near Babylonia) who settled in Samaria after the destruction of the northern kingdom in 722 B.C. Hence their name "Cuthahites." We first come across this exposition of 2 Kings 17 in Josephus (ca. 37-ca. 100), and we must regard it as anti-Samaritan polemics going back to the days of the Maccabees.

The Samaritans for their part view themselves, not the Jews, as the true → Israel. The Samaritan text of the Pentateuch (cf. the Samaritan version of the → Decalogue in Exodus 20) is the most ancient witness to their religious history. When we compare it with the sections of the Bible found at → Qumran and take into account the characteristic form of Samaritan letters, we see that we have an original form of the text from the second century B.C. In distinction from rabbinic Judaism, the Samaritans have no → Mishnah or → Talmud but in their legal practice refer only to the Pentateuch.

With other hints we may thus conclude that in the

Hasmonean period the Samaritans were a separate religious group made up of Jews living in and around Shechem. The common Jewish inheritance dating from the time of their origin underwent its own development, so that we may not regard all the elements of their religion as ancient. The undoubtedly ancient center of their cult is not → Jerusalem but the holy mountain of Gerizim. There, in distinction from Jewish usage, the passover lambs were slain. In 129 B.C. John Hyrcanus (135-104) destroyed their → altar on Gerizim (there can hardly have been any → temple there), and they no longer had any real sacrificial cult. → Priests (who after 1624 became more like Levites) have maintained a prominent role.

In February 2004 Elazar b. Tsedaka b. Yitzhaq (b. 1927) became the 131st high priest (counting from Moses' brother Aaron). In 2004 there were about 660 adherents in the two centers at Nablus (Shechem) and Holon (Tel Aviv).

Scholarly study of the Samaritans began at the end of the 16th century with J. J. Scaliger (1540-1609) and brought with it fresh insights. The decisive result of research was to make the Samaritan Pentateuch known in Europe with the discovery of a full copy in Damascus by Pietro della Valle (1586-1652). We have Samaritan written sources only from the fourth century A.D. onward. Along with the Samaritan Targum (→ Bible Versions 2), we may mention the Memar Markah (the Samaritan version of the Torah), a work that glorifies → Moses, who occupies a dominant position in Samaritan religion. From the Middle Ages onward, at times in Arabic, we have various independent chronicles, the oldest of which is the Tolidah Chronicle. Many of the Samaritan writings are liturgical texts for feasts and services very much the same as those of the Jews (→ Jewish Practices). We should note a Book of Joshua (in Arabic) that is not at all the same as the biblical book, also Asatir (the Samaritan version of the books Genesis through Joshua), Molad Moshe (a Midrashic-Haggadic work), Kitab al-Mirath (Book of Inheritance), Kitab al-Tabbah (book about the Samaritan Halakah), Kitab al-Kafi (book of Halakah), and Malef (a catechism).

Bibliography: R. T. Anderson and T. Giles, *The Keepers: An Introduction to the History and Culture of the Samaritans* (Peabody, Mass., 2002) • Z. Ben-Hayyim, *The Literary and Oral Tradition* (5 vols.; Jerusalem, 1957-77) • J. Bowman, *Samaritan Documents* (Pittsburgh, 1977) • R. J. Coggins, *Samaritans and Jews: The Origins of Samaritanism Reconsidered* (Atlanta, 1975) • A. D. Crown, *A Bibliography of the Samaritans* (2d ed.; Philadelphia, 1993); idem, ed., *The Samaritans* (Tübingen, 1989) • F. Dexinger, "Reflections on the Relationship between Qumran and Samaritan Messianology," *Qumran-Messianism* (ed. J. H. Charlesworth, H. Lichtenberger, and G. S. Oegema; Tübingen, 1998) 83-99; idem, *Der Taheb* (Salzburg, 1986) • F. Dexinger and R. Pummer, eds., *Die Samaritaner* (Darmstadt, 1992) • J. Macdonald, *The Theology of the Samaritans* (Philadelphia, 1964) • R. Pummer, *The Samaritans* (Leiden, 1987); idem, trans., *Early Christian Authors on Samaritans and Samaritanism: Texts, Translations, and Commentary* (Tübingen, 2002) • J. D. Purvis, *The Samaritan Pentateuch and the Origin of the Samaritan Sect* (Cambridge, Mass., 1968) • *Samaritan Text of the Pentateuch, Compared with the Masoretic Text* (5 vols.; hand-copied by A. Sadaka and R. Sadaka; Tel-Aviv, 1961-65).

Ferdinand Dexinger†

Samuel, Books of

1. Name, Contents, Text
2. Origin
3. Message
4. Influence

1. Name, Contents, Text

The two books of Samuel belong to what are known as the Hebrew canon's "earlier prophets" (Joshua to 2 Kings). They derive their name from Samuel, who in these books variously appears in the role of → prophet, → priest, and judge, and whom, together with Nathan and Gad, rabbinic tradition held to be the author of these books (cf. 1 Chr. 29:29). The Septuagint calls the Books of Samuel and Kings together the Four Books of Kingdoms *(Basileiōn);* the Vg, the Four Books of Kings *(Regum).* The division of Samuel into two books is attested only after 1448 and actually derives from the Septuagint (and the Vg; → Bible Versions).

The content of the Books of Samuel is the description of the transition from the period of the judges to the beginnings and consolidation of the → monarchy in Israel. The primary role players include Samuel in 1 Samuel 1–7 (1–3, his youth; 4–6, the ark's fate; 7, Samuel as judge), → Saul in 1 Samuel 8–15 (8–12, his election to kingship;13–14, his wars; 15, his dismissal), and → David in 1 Samuel 16–2 Samuel 24 (1 Samuel 16–31, David's rise, Saul's fall; 2 Samuel 1–8, David as king of Judah and Israel; 9–20, conflicts in David's family; 21–24, anecdotal material, lists, songs).

The Masoretic text of Samuel is in part only

poorly preserved. The Septuagint and the Hebrew textual fragments found in → Qumran (4QSam[a], 4QSam[b], 4QSam[c], 3rd to 1st cent. B.C.) sometimes provide access to a better text.

2. Origin

Earlier scholarship frequently viewed the numerous repetitions and contradictions in the Books of Samuel (e.g., in the description of the beginnings of the monarchy in 1 Samuel 8–12) as evidence of the presence and continuation in Samuel itself of the sources J and E already familiar from the → Pentateuch. For more recent scholarship these features suggest, rather, that the Books of Samuel are the result of a multilayered redactional process that combined and reinterpreted extremely varied and even mutually contradictory individual traditions. These books acquired their final form during the exile, when the Deuteronomistic redaction turned these traditions and narratives — which to a certain extent had already coalesced — into part of the → Deuteronomistic history, extending from Deuteronomy to 2 Kings.

The Deuteronomistic historian had access not only to numerous smaller individual traditions such as the accounts of David's conquests (2 Sam. 5:17-25; 8:1-5) and of his family (2 Sam. 5:13-16) and officials (2 Sam. 8:16-18; 20:23-26), but also to the following larger traditions: the story of Samuel's youth (1 Samuel 1–3*), the → ark narrative (1 Sam. 4:1b–7:1* and 2 Samuel 6*), the story of Saul's kingship (1 Sam. 9:1–10:16* and 10:17b [LXX]–11:15*, as well as 13:2–14:46*), the story of David's rise (1 Sam. 16:14–2 Sam. 5:10*), and the narrative of David's succession to the throne (2 Samuel 9–20* and 1 Kings 1–2*). The last story has special status among these traditions. Because of its sensitive and realistic portrayal, this work, probably composed in Jerusalem during the time of → Solomon, is generally viewed as one of the early masterpieces of Hebrew narrative.

The task of the Deuteronomistic historian was to combine and fuse together all these extant traditions, a task continued by a prophetic Deuteronomist who added prophetic materials to the overall work commensurate with his own interpretation (e.g., 1 Samuel 15; 28:3-25; 2 Sam. 11:27b–12:15a), and finally by a nomistically oriented circle of Deuteronomistic editors responsible especially for the antimonarchian passages in 1 Samuel 8–12 (i.e., 8:6-22a [with an earlier source text in vv. 11-17*]; 10:18aα²-19a; and chap. 12).

3. Message

The message of the Books of Samuel is multidimensional. Not only do the intentions of the earlier traditions not always coincide with those of the Deuteronomistic editors, even the latter are inclined to accentuate different points. The overriding religious and political question in the Books of Samuel, however, is how to evaluate the institution of the monarchy and the early kings. The early Saul traditions greet Saul's kingship with enthusiasm (cf. 1 Sam. 9:1–10:16* and chap. 11*), and from the very outset the story of David's rise served to demonstrate the divine legitimation of his kingship (e.g., see 1 Sam. 16:18; 17:37; 18:12, 14, 28; 2 Sam. 5:10).

Because the Deuteronomistic historian shared this positive assessment of the monarchy traditions and its initial representatives, he was able to expand even more on the materials before him (e.g., 1 Sam. 10:19b-27a; 11:12-14; 14:47-51; 20:12-17, 42b; 23:16-18; 24:18-22a; 2 Sam. 5:12a) and turn the idea of the divine election of David and the Davidic dynasty into a central theological theme of the Books of Samuel (see 1 Sam. 25:28, 30; 2 Sam. 3:9-10, 17-19; 5:1-2; 6:21a; 7:11b, 16). In contrast, in the name of → theocracy, the nomistically oriented circle condemned the establishment of the monarchy as a rebellion against Yahweh's sole kingship (1 Sam. 8:7; 12:12) and was able to accept the ideal king David (see 1 Sam. 13:13-14; 2 Sam. 22:22-25) only because he could view David as the earthly representative of theocracy, whose merits ultimately benefited Israel, the → people of God (2 Sam. 5:12b; 7:10, 22-24).

The narrative of David's succession to the throne also occupies a special place among the Davidic traditions because of its content. Precisely the earliest, preredactional version of this story betrays a critical view of David and his successor, Solomon, who according to the original wording of 2 Samuel 11–12 (i.e., 11:1-4aα, b, 5-20, 22-27a and 12:24bα², 26-31), was himself the product of David's adulterous relationship with Bathsheba. Chaps. 13–20* do, however, also contain material more sympathetic to David (e.g., see 13:39–14:1, 33; 18:33–19:4), suggesting that these chapters possibly originated independently (perhaps as an earlier source used by the author). The succession narrative acquired its final form as the result of a complex and in part pre-Deuteronomistic redactional process whose result also attests David's magnanimity and piety (see 2 Sam. 9:1; 10:12; 15:25-26; 16:8-12; 19:21-22), as well as the divine legimitation of his kingship (see 2 Sam. 12:24; 14:9; 17:14).

4. Influence

The biblical influence of the Books of Samuel comes to expression in the parallel accounts in Chronicles. As far as the main players are concerned, Chronicles mentions the "seer" and "prophet" Samuel several times (1 Chr. 6:28; 9:22; 11:3; 26:28; 29:29; 2 Chr. 35:18) but then, for Saul, mentions only his death (1 Chronicles 10).

With respect to David, Chronicles mentions especially the accounts from the Books of Samuel dealing with his military successes (1 Chr. 11:10-19; 14:8-17; 18–20), the divine legitimation of his dynasty (chap. 17), and Jerusalem and the cult to be established there (11:4-9; 13; 15:25–16:3; 21). By contrast, Chronicles passes over the entire succession narrative. The dynastic promise in 2 Samuel 7 exerted the greatest influence and was quickly appropriated poetically (Psalm 89), providing the foundation for the Davidic messianology.

→ Israel 1.4

Bibliography: Commentaries: P. K. McCarter (AB 8-9; Garden City, N.Y., 1984) • F. Stolz (ZBK 9; Zurich, 1981).

Other works: C. Conroy, *Absalom Absalom! Narrative and Language in 2 Sam 13–20* (Rome, 1978) • W. Dietrich and T. Naumann, *Die Samuelbücher* (Darmstadt, 1995) • J. P. Fokkelman, *Narrative Art and Poetry in the Books of Samuel* (4 vols.; Assen, 1981-93) • E. Foresti, *The Rejection of Saul in the Perspective of the Deuteronomistic School* (Rome, 1984) • E. Tov, ed., *The Hebrew and Greek Texts of Samuel* (Jerusalem, 1980) • T. Veijola, *David. Gesammelte Studien zu den Davidüberlieferungen des Alten Testaments* (Helsinki, 1990). See also the bibliographies in "David" and "Saul."

Timo Veijola

Sanctification

1. OT
   1.1. Term
   1.2. In Space and Time
   1.3. Expansion and Reinterpretation
2. NT
3. Dogmatics
   3.1. Range and Biblical References
   3.2. Forms
   3.3. Theological Order
   3.4. Historical Development

1. OT

1.1. *Term*

"Sanctification" denotes the transition from the ordinary secular sphere to the sphere of the holy (→ Sacred and Profane), but then also the analogous transition from the sphere of impurity (on the margin) to the normal sphere of purity (e.g., Lev. 11:44). On the OT view God himself is the quintessence of the holy (he is the Holy One, or the Holy One of Israel, and the beings around him are holy ones; see Isa. 6:3; Ps. 89:7; 99:5, 9). Primarily, then, sanctification is movement into proximity to God, though this movement can be understood in different ways.

1.2. *In Space and Time*

First, the movement to the Holy One has spatial aspects. Those who come to the sanctuary must wash and change their clothes (see Gen. 35:2; Exod. 19:10). Objects in the sacral sphere that create contact between God and worshipers are also subject to sanctification (e.g., Exod. 30:22-33). Those who touch what is holy are (dangerously) sanctified (Exod. 29:37).

Then, time also plays a part. The worship of Yahweh was linked to feasts, and sanctification was also related to the → Sabbath (Gen. 2:3, etc.).

Those who served in the institutional sanctuary needed sanctification, namely, → priests and Levites (Exodus 28–30), and also → Nazirites, who were set apart for a period of time (Numbers 6). The same applied finally to objects and people upon whom Yahweh had a special claim (e.g., the firstborn of man and beast, Num. 3:13).

An important area in which God's order marked itself off from what was chaotic and abnormal was the → holy war. Participants had to forgo certain modes of conduct and were thus sanctified (e.g., Isa. 13:3).

1.3. *Expansion and Reinterpretation*

The concept of the holy or of sanctification underwent expansion and reinterpretation in the course of Israel's religious history. In the → Deuteronomistic writings the idea arose that the people of → Israel and its land were all holy (Deut. 7:6-7 etc.). Sanctification thus meant observing the rules that God had given his people. Ethical aspects were added to the ritual aspects (note esp. the Holiness Code, esp. Lev. 20:7-8, 26). People could recognize the claim of Yahweh by their conduct and thus sanctify him (Isa. 29:23). Finally, the thought developed that Yahweh sanctifies himself, asserting himself in the face of a world that is totally different from him (Ezek. 36:23).

Bibliography: S. C. Barton, ed., *Holiness Past and Present* (London, 2003) chaps. 4-7 • J. G. Gammie, *Holiness in Israel* (Minneapolis, 1989) • J. Joosten, *People and Land in the Holiness Code: An Exegetical Study of the Ideational Framework of the Law in Leviticus 17–26* (Leiden, 1996) • W. Kornfeld and H. Ringgren, "קדשׁ *qdš*" etc., *TDOT* 12.521-45.

Fritz Stolz†

2. NT

If what is holy is what God the Holy One claims for himself, sanctification (Gk. *hagiasmos*) is the action, and the result of the action, that conforms to the holy being of God and is outside of the domain of → sin. If the holy God works sanctification, there follows an ethical obligation, which the quotation from Lev. 19:2 in 1 Pet. 1:16 makes clear: "You shall be holy, for I am holy."

The NT calls → Jesus the Holy One of God (Mark 1:24 and par.; John 6:69; see also Luke 1:35 etc.) and recognizes him as the sinless Son of God sent by God (→ Christology 1). In the → Lord's Prayer he taught his disciples to pray for the sanctifying of the name of God, which would finally be accomplished at the coming of the → kingdom of God (Matt. 6:9-10; Luke 11:2).

The → primitive Christian churches knew that, in faith in the saving act of the cross and → resurrection of Jesus Christ, they were sanctified, that is, liberated from the enslaving powers of the world, the → law, sin, and death (Rom. 10:4; Eph. 1:7; → Soteriology). → Baptism as the basis of the Christian life is the cultic rite of the new covenant people (1 Pet. 1:2) by which a new → righteousness and holiness is appropriated to believers (1 Cor. 1:30) and in which sanctification as an ethical action has its basis (Rom. 6:19, 22; 1 Thess. 4:3). The church is the "holy nation" (1 Pet. 2:9), and its members are built up into a "holy temple" (1 Cor. 3:17; Eph. 2:21).

From this position derives the task of doing acts of sanctification, but the relation of received and actualized sanctification, of indicative and imperative, is expounded in various ways. On → Paul's view the indicative of the → salvation-event precedes the imperative of sanctification (Gal. 5:25; Rom. 6:1-11). Sanctification is both freedom and service, for the → new self that is liberated from the powers can choose between only → obedience under the dominion of sin and the obedience of righteousness (Rom. 6:16). As an eschatological goal (1 Thess. 4:3-4), sanctification is anticipated by the "harvest of righteousness" (Phil. 1:11; also Rom. 6:19-22).

The indicative and imperative are related in a slightly different way in 1 Peter with the admonition to achieve sanctification in persecution (3:15).

In the Johannine writings the indicative of the salvation-event can be called holy (John 17:17, 19), but the ideas of the love and knowledge of God are central. The meaning is that we are to keep the commandment and love fellow believers (1 John 2:4; 4:19; John 15:10).

In Hebrews Christ is the heavenly high priest who sanctifies the people (13:12, see also 2:11). Sanctification and the gift of the Spirit to believers are effected by his covenant blood (10:29). The community that is sanctified by him (10:10, 14) is required to "pursue" sanctification (12:14) so as to be able to share in the Father's holiness (12:10).

The NT can interpret the Christ-event as a demand, so that the indicative and imperative coincide: James calls "the law of liberty" the essential content of the Christian message (2:12). This "law" demands concrete acts of mercy (2:13), of → humility (4:6), and of patience (5:10). The prospect of future judgment gives the requirement its special sharpness (4:12; 5:7-11). In debate with an exaggerated Paulinist view that → faith can save without any works at all (2:14-26), the author stresses that faith and works belong together, opposing to works a theoretical understanding of faith as mere belief.

Also in Revelation the indicative and imperative are closely related. The coming Christ is the judge of the world (2:23; 22:12). If Christians overcome, he will give them "the crown of life" (2:7, 10-11; 3:5, etc.).

Matthew calls Jesus the Kyrios, God's Son, who teaches the way of a higher righteousness. In the → Sermon on the Mount he gives directions that are universally binding, both hortatory and admonitory (5:3-12). The eschatological, ethical teaching of Jesus is the basis of the ethical and sacramental life of the community (3:15; 20:27-28; 26:26-29).

→ Ethics 2; Parenesis

Bibliography: H. Balz, "Ἅγιος κτλ.," *EDNT* 1.16-20 • F. W. Horn, *Glaube und Handeln in der Theologie des Lukas* (2d ed.; Göttingen, 1986) • H. H. Schade, *Apokalyptische Christologie bei Paulus* (2d ed.; Göttingen, 1984) • U. Schnelle, *Gerechtigkeit und Christusgegenwart* (2d ed.; Göttingen, 1986).

Georg Strecker†

3. Dogmatics

3.1. *Range and Biblical References*

The word "sanctification" (Heb. *qdš, ṭhr;* Gk. *hagiazō, hagnizō;* Lat. *sanctifico*) denotes separation from the everyday and consecration to God. In the Judeo-Christian tradition the initiative for a life of sanctification comes from God. In the OT (see 1) the term occurs in the context of cult, ethos, and → eschatology. → Jesus Christ comes into this context as the "Holy One of God" (see 2). The "Spirit of holiness" (→ Holy Spirit), who comes on the basis of Jesus' self-offering, sanctifies the new people of God by → baptism and forgiveness to eternal life.

The term "sanctification" lays less stress on world-responsibility in human relations and more on freedom from the schema of this age and on self-purifying in heart and body. Its aim is "deification" (→ Theosis) as the indwelling of Christ by the Holy Spirit and a transformation in love into his image. The imperatives of sanctification rest on the indicative of → salvation. Believers must sanctify themselves, but only as those who have been sanctified by Christ.

Sanctification has its basis in baptism, is fulfilled in the → church by Word and → sacrament, presses on to charismatic fellowship, and comes to its consummation in eschatology. NT → parenesis distinguishes between immature beginners and those who are perfected in the power of the Spirit. It aims at growth into the full stature of Christ.

3.2. *Forms*

From the NT witness there develops, on the one hand, → discipleship of the wandering charismatic Jesus, both in proclamation of the immanent → kingdom of God, even to the point of martyrdom, and in the conflict of → prayer against enslaving → demons, a conflict that was finally institutionalized in → monasticism as a renunciation of avarice, sex, and self-will. On the other hand, the → household rules and other NT ordinances give a sketch of self-sanctifying in the relations of family, society, and church (→ Ethics 2). The two developments come together under the key concept of the family of God.

From the time of Clement of Alexandria (ca. 150-ca. 215) and → Origen (ca. 185-ca. 254), different stages were seen in a movement from bodily → asceticism to a mystical vision of God (→ Mysticism) and spiritual deification. Model → saints were increasingly venerated and invoked.

The schema of beginning, progressing, and perfecting was still influential in → Pietism, → Methodism, and later → Holiness movements. Psychologically, it denotes growth in one's "capacity for an ever more total self-commitment by ever deeper personal acts" (Karl → Rahner, *Theological Investigations,* 3.21), or the movement of transformation from the center of existence to its periphery (E. Brunner, *Dogmatics,* 3.292-93). Paul → Tillich (1886-1965) postulated "four principles determining the New Being as process," namely, "increasing awareness," "increasing freedom," "increasing relatedness," and "increasing transcendence" (*Systematic Theology* 3.231). In regard to forms of sanctification we may also think of daily blessings on rising and retiring, which occur in all traditions. A similar practice occurs in Jewish piety (e.g., in → Hasidism).

3.3. *Theological Order*

On the basis of → Pietism and F. D. E. → Schleiermacher, Tillich schematized the triad → regeneration, justification, and sanctification as being gripped by the new being, paradoxically accepting it, and progressive transformation into it. K. → Barth (1886-1968) saw in justification, sanctification, and vocation the three aspects of Christ's reconciling work.

The → Reformers, however, insisted that sanctification grows out of → justification and is always grounded in it. Yet in expositions of the creed they could expound the whole work of salvation as sanctification, as J. → Calvin (1509-64) did in the Geneva Catechism (qq. 88-91), and Z. Ursinus (1534-83) in the → Heidelberg Catechism (qq. 53-58). So also M. → Luther (1483-1546) in his Large Catechism, which in the third article names the "ways and means" by which the Spirit sanctifies us, on earth by constant forgiveness in the → church, in the eschaton by the resurrection of the dead and eternal life. This sanctifying, or being made holy, is "nothing else than bringing us to the Lord Christ" to receive redemption (§39). Anthropologically, this understanding envisions a form that embraces both growth and crises. We find it earlier in → Augustine (354-430) and then in → Bernard of Clairvaux (1090-1153). Luther thought it through, and Calvin systematized it. According to this form, sanctification is a genuine path leading out of palpable transgressions against the second table of the law (→ Decalogue) and against external worship of God and into abysmal failure both with regard to the first commandment (and thus pride and despair) and with regard to genuinely selfless love of others.

3.4. *Historical Development*

With its "third use of the → law," → Calvinism inaugurated an ethos of this-worldly asceticism. In → Puritanism, though, it threatened to suppress certain vital impulses, especially sexual stirrings. In → Lutheranism the battle cry "at once righteous and a sinner" became the description of a state that led either to → quietism or to vacillation between → ecstasy and → anxiety. The radical reformers wanted full sanctification and separated from the world and the mainline churches.

In → Methodism (→ Methodist Churches) sanctification as a "second blessing" after the first blessing of justification (J. → Wesley) led both to individual sanctification and to a sense of the responsibility of faith for the world. In it, as in the Anglican Church (→ Anglican Communion), Roman Catholic saints (Theresa of Ávila, John of the Cross, and others) were quoted and valued as examples in the practice of sanctification.

→ Grace; New Self; Obedience; Order of Salvation; Penitence; Perfection; Sacred and Profane; Sin; Soteriology

Bibliography: D. Alexander, *The Pursuit of Godliness: Sanctification in Christological Perspective* (Lanham, Md., 1999) • K. Barth, *CD* IV/2, §66; idem, "Rechtfertigung und Heiligung," *ZZ* 5 (1927) 281-309 • S. C. Barton, ed., *Holiness, Past and Present* (Edinburgh, 2003) • P. M. Bassett and W. M. Greathouse, *Exploring Christian Holiness,* vol. 2, *The Historical Development* (Kansas City, Mo., 1985) • *Book of Concord: The Confessions of the Evangelical Lutheran Church* (ed. R. Kolb and T. J. Wengert; Minneapolis, 2000) • C. Colpe, ed., *Die Diskussion um das "Heilige"* (Darmstadt, 1977) • M. E. Dexter et al., *Five Views on Sanctification* (Grand Rapids, 1987) • S. Hauerwas, *Sanctify Them in the Truth: Holiness Exemplified* (Edinburgh, 1998) • O. H. Pesch and A. Peters, *Einführung in die Lehre von Gnade und Rechtfertigung* (3d ed.; Darmstadt, 1994) • D. Peterson, *Possessed by God: A NT Theology of Sanctification and Holiness* (Grand Rapids, 1995) • R. Prenter, *Holiness in the Lutheran Tradition: Man's Concern with Holiness* (London, 1970) • W. T. Purkiser, *Exploring Christian Holiness,* vol. 1, *The Biblical Foundations* (Kansas City, Mo., 1983) • R. S. Taylor, *Exploring Christian Holiness,* vol. 3, *The Theological Formulation* (Kansas City, Mo., 1985) • M. Viller and K. Rahner, *Aszese und Mystik in der Väterzeit* (Freiburg, 1939; 2d ed., 1990).

Albrecht Peters†

Sanctuary

1. In Religion
2. OT
3. Modern Usage
   3.1. In the United States
   3.2. Biblical Background
   3.3. Ecumenical Perspectives

1. In Religion

The sanctuary (Lat. *sanctus,* "sacred, holy"), or holy place, is a central element in → religion and its visible form of expression. Even today one can easily identify a geographic region by its sanctuaries (churches in Christian areas, → mosques in Muslim, stupas in Buddhist, and → temples in Hindu). In this way religion has had an impact on landscape.

The sanctuary may be situated on, in, or by a particular place in nature (a hill, river, fountain, lake, grove, cave, or rock), or it may involve something made by humans (a house, altar, hearth, corner of a room, grave, or meeting place). It may symbolize the center of the world (Gk. *omphalos,* "navel," was a name for the oracle at Delphi), but not universally so. Its origin is often obscure but may often be associated with the manifestation of a deity or a superhuman or sacral power. Such a → revelation, not the place itself, is the basis of its sanctity.

The religious fellowship upholds and protects the sanctity of the place by rules and codes of conduct (involving purity, inviolability, peace, the right of → asylum). If it is important, it will have an altar (of stone or wood) and one or more representations (concrete or abstract) of the powers that are venerated (in pillars, symbols, or statues).

Holy places have often survived, even when the religions that made use of them have changed. Churches have been built on the sites of pagan shrines. Graves of the → saints have replaced ancient sanctuaries. This process continued with the advance of Islam in, for example, Egypt, Lebanon, Asia Minor, and North Africa, where some sites have enjoyed sacral continuity for long periods of time (ancient Egyptian, ancient Semitic, ancient Hittite, Hellenistic, Christian, Islamic).

With the development of solid temples for gods, spirits, or ancestors, great sanctuary complexes were formed that might embrace a whole city. A considerable cultic force was needed to maintain these structures, with great wealth often in landed property. The adytum (Gk. *adyton,* "not to be entered"), or innermost part of the sanctuary, was the dwelling of the god; it might be surrounded by many courts that were reserved for ordinary people. Architects and artists vied with one another in planning and furnishing temples, so that they became important items in the history of art. If the sanctuaries were of higher rank, → pilgrimages began to be made to them (e.g., to → Jerusalem, Mecca, and → Rome, also to sites in China, Japan, and India).

The destruction or profanation (Lat. *profanum* referred to the area in front of the temple, or holy place) of a sanctuary might mean the end of a cult or even a religion (as in the history of Christian and Islamic missions). But the new religion would soon occupy the site, or it would maintain a role in popular belief and → superstition. There might also be a process of spiritualizing and symbolizing, as in → Judaism and Christianity with reference to the Jerusalem temple. In → mysticism the spiritualizing of common, earthly cultic sites is customary (→ Islam; Judaism).

In modern culture some secular buildings have taken on a pseudoreligious significance. Clubhouses, cultural centers, and even high-rise buildings in some sense function as sacral structures in the modern world.

→ Cultic Purity; Sacred and Profane; Sacrifice

Bibliography: S. E. Alcock and R. Osborne, *Placing the Gods: Sanctuaries and Sacred Space in Ancient Greece* (New York, 1994) • E. Bernbaum, *Sacred Mountains of the World* (Berkeley, Calif., 1997) • T. Davidson, "Places, Sacred," *ERE* 10.50-52 • M. V. Fox, ed., *Temple in Society* (Winona Lake, Ind., 1988) • A. Houtman, M. J. H. Poorthuis, and J. Schwartz, eds., *Sanctity of Time and Space in Tradition and Modernity* (Leyden, 1998) • J. A. MacCulloch, "Temples," *ERE* 12.236-46 • J. Z. Smith, *Imagining Religion: From Babylon to Jonestown* (Chicago, 1982) esp. 102-20; idem, *Map Is Not Territory: Studies in the History of Religions* (Leiden, 1978) esp. 104-28 • H. W. Turner, *From Temple to Meeting House: The Phenomenology and Theology of Places of Worship* (The Hague, 1979) • G. Widengren, *Religionsphänomenologie* (Berlin, 1969) chap. 2, "Kultplatz."

Kurt Rudolph

2. OT

Only in the later OT period was it possible to conceive of a regulated relation between → Israel and → Yahweh apart from a special cultic site. In the early days recollection of the mountain sanctuary of → Sinai exerted a big influence (Exodus 19–Numbers 10). Oasis sanctuaries were also important during the nomadic or seminomadic years (→ Nomads), for example, Kadesh (Num. 13:26; 20:1-16) and Beer-lahai-roi (Gen. 16:13-14).

At the time of the conquest the Israelites lived in towns and villages in cultural contact with the original inhabitants, and they had access to the many sanctuaries of these people, which in many cases were marked off as open places ("high places") and furnished in typical fashion (with → altar, holy stone in the form of a pillar [*maṣṣēbâ*], sacred tree, usually stylized as a wooden pillar [*'ăšērâ*]). In some cases there were also urban centers, that is, → temples with rich furnishings and the corresponding cult (e.g., Shechem, Judg. 9:1-6; Shiloh, 1 Samuel 1–4, the → ark being also connected with Shiloh). The stories show that there were at first many sanctuaries. They link their founding or cultic procedures with an early ancestor or hero, such as Bethel (Gen. 28:10-22) and Peniel (32:22-33) with → Jacob. Well-known sanctuaries of the period of the conquest and the monarchy were Gilgal, Bethel, Mizpah, and Shiloh in central Palestine, Tabor and Dan in the north, Hebron and Beer-sheba in the south, and Mahanaim, Peniel, and Mizpah east of the Jordan. There might have been others that are not mentioned in the OT; archaeology, for example, testifies to a sanctuary at Arad in the time of the monarchy.

With the development of the state, a royal cult developed alongside the local cult. → David took over the sanctuary of the Jebusites at → Jerusalem and had the ark brought there (2 Sam. 6:1-19). → Solomon built (or renovated) a temple along with the palace buildings (1 Kings 6). After the partition Jeroboam I set up a similar state cult at Bethel and Dan (1 Kgs. 12:26-33). Under the Omride dynasty this expansion opened the door to conflict between Yahweh and other gods in individual sanctuaries, and → prophets like Hosea and Jeremiah attacked the Canaanite cultic practices at these shrines.

The political destruction of the two kingdoms put an end to the royal cult in both. Many sanctuaries were opened up even more strongly to alien influences. In the Deuteronomic and → Deuteronomistic literature the demand thus arose for restriction to a legitimate sanctuary at Jerusalem (with an attempt at concentration by → Josiah). During the exile forms of → worship (§1) developed that were not tied to a sanctuary (though with orientation to a future sanctuary). In contrast, we find that in the fifth century B.C. at Elephantine in Upper Egypt there was a temple where only Yahweh was worshiped.

Under Persian rule it was possible to rebuild the temple at Jerusalem (dedicated in 515 B.C.). In the Persian and Hellenistic years this sanctuary was the regular cultic center of → Judaism for Palestine and the → diaspora. In about the fourth century the Samaritans set up a rival temple at Gerizim. A crisis came with the desecration of the Jerusalem temple by Antiochus IV Epiphanes in 167 B.C., but a fresh dedication followed under the Maccabees (→ Hasmoneans).

Around 20 B.C. → Herod the Great started to rebuild the Jerusalem temple, following the older plan but on a grander scale and with a Hellenistic coloring (→ Hellenism). The temple became the center of worldwide Judaism, and the cult took on added importance. Both city and temple, however, were destroyed in A.D. 70 at the end of the Jewish War.

→ Priest, Priesthood; Sacred and Profane; Sacrifice; Sanctification

Bibliography: A. Biran, ed., *Temples and High Places in Biblical Times* (Jerusalem, 1981) • A. von Gall, *Alt-israelitische Kultstätten* (Giessen, 1898).

Fritz Stolz†

3. Modern Usage

Sanctuary is traditionally offered by the church as a protective community to → refugees whose basic human → rights are being violated. It is a faith practice that reaches back to the earliest memories of the people of → Israel (§1), and a movement of the ecumenical church in response to the current plight of refugees throughout the world. In January 2000 an estimated 22.3 million persons were listed as of concern to the U.N. High Commissioner for Refugees (11.7 million refugees, 1.2 million asylum-seekers, 2.5 million returned refugees, and 6.9 million internally displaced persons and others of concern). These are people who cross borders without documents to flee → war and → persecution, or they are displaced within their own country. In all cases these are the most vulnerable and suffering people imaginable (→ Marginalized Groups).

3.1. *In the United States*

In the United States the name "sanctuary" has been given to the movement for the protection of refugees from Central America whom the U.S. government has been sanctioning or deporting since 1980, claiming that they were not bona fide political refugees but had crossed the borders for economic reasons. A number of Catholic and Protestant churches have challenged this interpretation of the Refugee Act of 1980, have organized themselves to provide transportation, reception, protection, and relocation of these refugees in what has been called (recovering a term from the times of slavery) the underground railroad, and have declared themselves "sanctuary churches." The U.S. government has arraigned and indicted a number of people involved in these actions. The ethical and legal debate and the processes continue. Churches and individuals engaged in this task have made explicit the theological, biblical, and ethical grounds of their action.

3.2. *Biblical Background*

The Bible is replete with stories and instructions on sanctuary, → asylum, and the treatment of refugees. The Hebrews, displaced from their own land by famine, are enslaved in Egypt. God hears their cry and liberates them from their suffering and bondage. Therefore Israel is to remember that they were once aliens or sojourners and that special care must be taken of the stranger in their midst (Lev. 19:33-34; Deut. 10:18-19). The God who saved Israel from bondage is the protector of the poor and suffering (Psalm 145; Num. 35:9-11).

Within the OT we find both the tradition of cities of refuge and altar sanctuary, both for the purpose of saving human life from blood vengeance until judicial safeguards can be employed. Jesus, who begins life as a refugee child fleeing from Herod, identifies with the poor and persecuted (Matt. 25:43). The early church is instructed to receive the stranger (Heb. 13:2).

3.3. *Ecumenical Perspectives*

The community of faith often affords the only possible protection to people fleeing for their lives. Seeking safe haven from death squads, arbitrary arrest and detention, → torture, or conditions of war, desperate people throughout history — those fleeing internal persecution in their own countries, as well as those who find themselves to be strangers in a strange land — have sought the church as a place of sanctuary. When one has nowhere to turn, the door of the church is a beacon of hope and refuge in a dark and desperate world.

The practice of sanctuary is again emerging as a movement within the ecumenical church, which assumes responsibility for the nonviolent protection of human rights. Sanctuary is more than a matter of individual conscience. It is the church entering into communion with the violated and oppressed and building together a community of solidarity and love. The refugee becomes a gift from God, the presence of Christ to the sanctuary church. The refugee becomes not the object of charity or paternalistic ministry but, rather, the spiritual guide for congregations to help the protective community read the Bible as much of it was written — through the eyes and hearts of refugees.

When the protective community of faith adds a public witness to its practice of sanctuary, then the → state is held accountable for its violations of human rights and the church becomes prophetic. Often the church must practice sanctuary in silence in order to protect those who need refuge. But even in these instances, the church provides documentation of human rights abuses so that the truth can be spoken with authority at a later time. When a church cannot speak publicly of severe repression, it must depend on other communions within the international community to assume the prophetic role.

Refugees who cross international borders without documents and who expose the root causes of their flight into exile can become a part of the witness of the sanctuary church. Refugee rights are directly linked to issues of military intervention, pacification, low-intensity conflict, arms sales, foreign-aid programs, and police training.

As more and more countries adopt highly restrictive policies to prevent the admission of refugees, prophetic witness may risk aiding refugees to cross borders safely. Many nations are trying to deal with the refugee problem by closing borders to applicants for asylum, intercepting boats at sea, and requiring individual proof of refugee status under more restrictive terms. The public resistance of faith communities to these violations of human rights has extended the prophetic role of the church across national borders.

In many instances, refugees become the prophetic voice within the faith community, speaking truth to political powers about the causes of their suffering and exile. In the case of internally displaced people, the church is often the only voice documenting gross violations of human rights, torture, bombing, or starvation of civilian populations in counterinsurgency military strategies. Through this solidarity and communion with the suffering and violated, the sanctuary church becomes one body in Christ.

Bibliography: I. Bau, *This Ground Is Holy: Church Sanctuary and Central American Refugees* (New York, 1985) • H. Cunningham, *God and Caesar at the Rio Grande: Sanctuary and the Politics of Religion* (Minneapolis, 1995) • P. Golden and M. McConnell, *Sanctuary: The New Underground Railroad* (Maryknoll, N.Y., 1986) • J. Schaeffer, ed., *Sanctuary and Asylum: A Handbook for Commitment* (Geneva, 1990).

John Fife

[*Note:* The above section has been adapted, with permission, from the 2d ed. of the *Dictionary of the Ecumenical Movement* (World Council of Churches Publications, 2002).]

Sanctuary Lamp

In Roman Catholic churches the sanctuary light is the hanging light that shines constantly before the → altar, where the reserved sacrament is kept in the → tabernacle (§2). The purpose of the lamp is "to indicate and honor the presence of Christ" (1983 → CIC 940).

Evidence exists of the use of this light in the West from the 11th and 12th centuries. The Rituale Romanum (1614) made it obligatory. Oil or wax is usually burned, but electric light is permitted.

→ Eucharist; Eucharistic Spirituality; Liturgical Books

The Editors

Sanctus → Mass

Santiago Cult

1. James's Life and Burial
2. Political Influence
3. Pilgrimages
4. James as Warrior Saint
5. Current Emphases

1. James's Life and Burial

According to the NT, → James the Elder, son of Zebedee, was a member of the intimate circle of apostles (see Matt. 10:1-4; 17:1-8; 26:36-37; Mark 5:35-42; 13:3). In about the year 44 he was beheaded by → Herod Agrippa I (41-44; Acts 12:2).

Although early witnesses allude to James's mission activity, especially in → Palestine, they provide no concrete information about where he was buried. Only in the seventh century, through the *Breviarum apostolorum,* a Latin version of the Greco-Byzantine apocryphal work *Acts of the Apostles,* was James associated with missionary activity in Spain. Eventually this association, the rumor of which had been spreading since the eighth and ninth centuries, acquired political significance. The "miraculous" discovery of the alleged tomb of James near Compostela during the reign of King Alfonso II of Asturias (791-842) complemented this tradition and also shaped the account of the transfer of James's remains from → Jerusalem to northwestern Spain. (The Spanish form of the apostle's name is "Santo Iago," shortened to "Santiago.")

2. Political Influence

During the 8th and 9th centuries the Spanish Santiago traditions, which were not really fixed until the 12th century, served along with other factors to help legitimize the Christian kings of Asturias as the successors of the ancient empire of the Visigoths. This group had vanished after the Arabic conquest in 711 (note the adoptionist dispute, a → heresy arising in 8th-cent. Spain; → Trinity).

3. Pilgrimages

While the tomb cult in Santiago de Compostela spread out to include virtually all of Europe, prompting an enormous → pilgrimage movement beginning in the 11th and 12th centuries, in Spain itself the apostle acquired the increasingly pronounced contours of a national (warrior) patron, with the two aspects — tomb cult and veneration as a military saint — being variously combined. The development of the great pilgrimages was also part of the increased apostolic devotion in the larger sense that began during the 11th century and that ultimately turned Compostela into the third popular pilgrimage goal in Christendom, after Rome and Jerusalem.

This development was aided by considerable

cult propaganda, which found its clearest expression in the *Liber Sancti Jacobi,* or *Codex Calixtinus,* from the mid-12th century. This book, containing the oldest pilgrimage guide to Compostela, includes also the various routes from France, along with the pilgrimage centers there. The author, hoping thus to promote the pilgrimages themselves, also provided concrete descriptions of the kinds of dangers and practical difficulties facing pilgrims during this period. The thematic link this work similarly establishes between Compostela pilgrimages and Charlemagne (768-814, allegedly the first pilgrim), as well as the accompanying miracle stories, widely circulated in numerous manuscripts, also enhanced Santiago's reputation in central and western Europe.

In the east the cult extended from Scandinavia, the Baltic lands, Poland, down to Hungary, and in isolated instances even to Armenia. An unmistakable high point of the pilgrimages can be found in the 15th century, from which we have several accounts. Only the increasing dangers of such journeys, together with the difficulties inevitably arising within confessionally divided Europe, caused these pilgrimages to recede.

4. James as Warrior Saint

The story of the apostle's aid during the battle of Coimbra (1064) — an account developed further in the forged document *Votos de Santiago* (mid-12th cent.) — is of significance for the development of the Santiago cult in Spain itself. According to this account, the apostle allegedly aided in the battle against the Arabs as early as 844 in Clavijo, the result of which was that all Spaniards were thenceforth to pay an annual thanksgiving tithe *(votos)* to the apostolic seat. The aforementioned *Liber Sancti Jacobi,* the Knights of St. James (established 1170), and later historians beginning in the 13th century all enhanced this understanding of the apostle as a helper in times of war, including in connection with the → Crusades.

In the same connection, the apostle was frequently associated with the unity of the Spanish kingdoms themselves after their loss in 711, though the iconographic portrayal of the saint as a *matamoros,* "Moor-slayer," is attested at the earliest only in the 14th century. Around the same time, the Santiago order of knights, together with the contemporaneously established knightly Order of Calatrava and Order of Alcántara, played an important role in the *reconquista* (→ Spain 1).

This association with aid during battle also made James famous in America as a *mata-indios,* or "Indian-slayer." Although the *conquista* of America had different leaders than the *reconquista* of Spain itself, these warriors did adopt many of the symbols of the latter. It may be noted, however, that the witnesses to St. James as a *mata-indios* actually reflect the broader development of James into a warrior saint, since also in central Europe the Turkish threat beginning in the 15th century (the Ottomans conquered Constantinople in 1453) prompted James to be summoned with increasing frequency as a warrior helper.

In → Latin America one notices the many city names with "Santiago," often associated with a vision of aid during the battle for the locale, as well as the numerous examples of James's patronage of churches. In Central and South America, James developed into a popular saint not only among the conquering class but gradually also among the subjugated Indian population. Popular customs associated with the saint's feast day celebrations occur in many different forms in the various countries, though there is still no comprehensive study of the various representatives of the Santiago cult with respect to locale and history.

5. Current Emphases

Even during the modern period, the Santiago cult remains politicized, especially in Spain. This feature is attested both by competition with → Teresa of Ávila (1515-82; → Contemplation 3; Mysticism 2.6) and by Francisco Franco's (1936-75) more recent attempts to revive the cult's association with pronounced national interests (since 1937). Recently, however, the broader European perspective of the pilgrimages has acquired a greater profile.

→ Saints, Veneration of

Bibliography: T. F. Coffey, L. K. Davidson, and M. Dunn, trans., *The Miracles of Saint James: Translations from the Liber Sancti Jacobi* (New York, 1996) • M. C. Díaz y Díaz et al., *El Códice Calixtino de la Catedral de Santiago. Estudio codicológico y de contenido* (Santiago de Compostela, 1988) • O. Engels, "Die Anfänge des spanischen Jakobusgrabes in kirchenpolitischer Sicht" (1980), *Reconquista und Landesherrschaft. Studien zur Rechts- und Verfassungsgeschichte Spaniens im Mittelalter* (Paderborn, 1989) 301-25; idem, "Die Reconquista," ibid., 279-300 • N. L. Frey, *Pilgrim Stories: On and off the Road to Santiago* (Berkeley, Calif., 1998) • U. Ganz-Blättler, *Andacht und Abenteuer. Berichte europäischer Jerusalem- und Santiago-Pilger (1320-1520)* (3d ed.; Tübingen, 2000) • K. Herbers, *Der Jakobuskult des 12. Jahrhunderts und der "Liber Sancti Jacobi"* (Wiesbaden, 1984); idem,

"Politik und Heiligenverehrung auf der iberischen Halbinsel. Die Entwicklung des 'politischen Jakobus,'" *Politik und Heiligenverehrung im Hochmittelalter* (ed. J. Petersohn; Sigmaringen, 1994) 177-275; idem, ed., *Der Jakobsweg, mit einem mittelalterlichen Pilgerführer unterwegs nach Santiago de Compostela* (7th ed.; Tübingen, 2001) • K. Herbers and R. Plötz, eds., *Der Jakobuskult in "Kunst" und "Literatur"* (Tübingen, 1998) • F. López Alsina, *La ciudad de Santiago de Compostela en la alta Edad Media* (Santiago de Compostela, 1988) • R. Plötz, "Der Apostel Jacobus in Spanien bis zum 9. Jahrhundert," *GAKGS* 30 (1982) 19-145; idem, "Lazo espiritual y cultural entre América y Europa. Santiago de Compostela," *Galicia, Santiago y América* (La Coruña, 1991) 57-74; idem, ed., *Europäische Wege der Santiago-Pilgerfahrt* (2d ed.; Tübingen, 1993) • C. Rudolph, *Pilgrimage to the End of the World: The Road to Santiago de Compostela* (Chicago, 2004) • L. Vázquez de Parga et al., *Las peregrinaciones a Santiago de Compostela* (3 vols.; Madrid, 1948-49) • J. Williams and A. Stones, eds., *The Codex Calixtinus and the Shrine of St. James* (Tübingen, 1992). Also see numberous individual studies in the journal *Compostellanum, Santiago de Compostela* (1956-).

Klaus Herbers

Satan → Devil

SATOR → Word Square

Saudi Arabia

	1960	*1980*	*2000*
Population (1,000s):	4,075	9,604	21,661
Annual growth rate (%):	3.25	5.51	3.07

Area: 2,240,000 sq. km. (865,000 sq. mi.)

A.D. 2000

Population density: 10/sq. km. (25/sq. mi.)
Births / deaths: 3.32 / 0.39 per 100 population
Fertility rate: 5.43 per woman
Infant mortality rate: 18 per 1,000 live births
Life expectancy: 72.9 years (m: 71.4, f: 74.9)
Religious affiliation (%): Muslims 93.3, Christians 4.2 (Roman Catholics 3.4, other Christians 0.9), Hindus 1.2, other 1.3.

1. History and Features
2. Legal Status of Non-Islamic Religions
3. Position of Christians

1. History and Features

From 1745 to 1818, and then from 1824 to 1891, the Saʿūd family controlled two Wahhabi states on the Arabian Peninsula. Then from 1902 onward, with the capture of Riyadh, ʿAbd al-ʿAzīz Ibn Saʿūd (1880-1953) set up what became the modern Kingdom of Saudi Arabia in 1932. The state took on its present-day size with further conquests up to 1934.

Three special features mark Saudi Arabia. First, by means of the conquest of Hejaz in 1924/25, it came to include Mecca and Medina, the two most important → sanctuaries of → Islam, so that the king bears the title "Protector of the Holy Places." Second, the traditional link of the royal house to the puritanical Wahhabi movement in Islam has given this Saudi state a definite religious impress such as we do not commonly find even in premodern Islam and that was almost anachronistic in the first two-thirds of the 20th century. Third, Saudi Arabia is the only Arab state whose core area never suffered under → colonialism. As a result, the various → secularizing European → ideologies have found less of a footing here than in other Islamic states. The linkage of the state in principle to Islamic law is often expressed by the slogan that the country's constitution is the → Qur'an, a position that, until the rise of "reislamization" in the 1970s, was virtually unknown in the Islamic world (→ Islam 4; Shariʿa).

2. Legal Status of Non-Islamic Religions

The factors listed above mean that the position of Christianity and other non-Islamic religions in Saudi Arabia is an especially difficult one. Legally, the situation is determined by the Prophet's tradition *(ḥadīth)*, which as a whole was collected and canonized not before the ninth and tenth centuries, when it became the second material source of Islamic law in addition to the Qur'an. According to one such tradition, of doubtful historicity, Muḥammad (ca. 570-632; →Prophet, Prophecy, 1.5) on his deathbed laid down in his will that Islam should be the only religion on the Arabian Peninsula (*jazīrat al-ʿarab*, "the island of the Arabs"). The second caliph, ʿUmar (634-44), is said to have carried out his wish by expelling Jews and Christians. The wording of the request varies considerably in different traditions, so that variations in principle are possible. There may also be debate as to the exact extent of the *jazīrat al-ʿarab.*

Without question, however, Saudi Arabia holds to the request, and non-Muslims can claim no permanent right of domicile in it and cannot be citizens. Even tighter restrictions apply to the two holy places. Those of other faiths are not allowed entry at all. In the mid-19th century, Ottoman reformers, who were aiming at a general Westernization of the empire (e.g., so that citizenship would no longer be defined in terms of religious affiliation), abolished the prohibition excluding non-Muslims from entering the third holiest place, the → Jerusalem Temple Mount, or Al-Ḥaram al-Sharīf (the noble sanctuary).

3. Position of Christians

After Islam established itself on the peninsula, for over 1,000 years the above rules were hardly more than theoretical. The situation changed when the demand for oil brought the Arabian-American Oil Company (ARAMCO) there in 1936. The conditions of the modern world now led to something of an entry into what had hitherto been an inaccessible land. Yet up to around 1970 there were fewer than 1,000 foreign Christians in Saudi Arabia, mostly Americans living ghetto-style in the ARAMCO compound. Within the compound there was toleration of what was for the most part a very discreet practice of Christianity, but with no official recognition. Any public manifestation of Christianity was strictly forbidden, especially in missionary form.

In the ensuing period the situation has become even more tense, as the building of a modern industrial state has brought in large numbers of foreign workers since the 1970s, but reislamizing trends have increasingly shaped the political climate of the Islamic world. Alongside European and American experts we find, not radicalized Muslims, but Christian workers from the Arab Middle East (Egypt, Palestine, Lebanon, Syria, Iraq) and the → Third World, especially India, Sri Lanka, Korea, and the Philippines. In 2003 there were approximately 4 million foreign workers (esp. in the oil and service sectors), a large number of them Roman Catholics. (There are no official statistics, and estimates vary considerably.) Yet any liberal attitude toward Christians of any denomination is strictly forbidden so as not to give a cause of complaint to radical fundamentalists. Thus, Christian clergy who in the 1980s had worked either underground or with tacit toleration have now been imprisoned or deported.

The dogma that non-Islamic religions are in principle not tolerated in Saudi Arabia has, in combination with the reislamization since the late 1960s, created serious problems when, beginning with the Persian Gulf War (1991) and continuing through the Iraq War (2003), the strategic alliance with the West and especially the United States made the massive presence of non-Islamic troops in Saudi Arabia necessary. Although Islamic law is sufficiently flexible to allow for emergency cases, the legally questionable presence of non-Islamic troops in Saudi Arabia has provoked a constant and increasing anti-Western propaganda, which has brought the Saudi government into a serious and so far unresolved dilemma.

Bibliography: D. B. Barrett, G. T. Kurian, and T. M. Johnson, *WCE* (2d ed.) 1.648-53 • D. Champion, *The Paradoxical Kingdom: Saudi Arabia and the Momentum of Reform* (New York, 2003) • E. A. Doumato, "Saudi Arabia," *OEMIW* 4.4-8 • B. Lewis, *The Crisis of Islam: Holy War and Unholy Terror* (New York, 2003) • S. Pompea, ed., *Saudi Arabia: Issues, Historical Background, and Bibliography* (New York, 2002) • M. al-Rasheed, *A History of Saudi Arabia* (New York, 2002) • S. Schwartz, *The Two Faces of Islam: The House of Sa'ud from Tradition to Terror* (New York, 2002) extensive coverage of Wahhabism • A. al-Yassini, *Religion and State in the Kingdom of Saudi Arabia* (Boulder, Colo., 1985).

Rainer Osswald

Saul

The primary traditions concerning Saul, the first king of → Israel (→ Monarchy in Israel), consist of stories concerning his call (1 Sam. 9:1–10:16), his victory over the Ammonites and elevation to the throne (chap. 11), and his battles against the → Philistines (13:2–14:46). The Deuteronomists later reworked and considerably expanded these traditions (1 Samuel 8; 10:17-27; 12; 15; → Deuteronomistic History). The kingship of Saul, who came from the tribe of Benjamin (9:1-2), represented only a brief episode toward the end of the 11th century (the exact chronology is uncertain).

The introduction of the monarchy itself was an emergency measure prompted by the increasing military pressure of the Philistines, which also attracted other enemies of Israel. After a successful battle against the Ammonites, the people made Saul their king in Benjaminite Gilgal near Jericho (1 Sam. 11:15). He had a modest residence at "Gibeah of Saul" (lit. "Saul's Hill," Tell el-Fûl, 11:4 etc.) and a small standing army (13:2; 14:2; 22:7). Saul's kingship was essentially a national kingship based on his army and one that formally was relatively unsecured and restricted to the area of the later northern kingdom (see 2 Sam. 2:9).

Saul was a charismatic hero who prospered as king only as long as he could successfully resist the Philistines in central Palestine (1 Sam. 13:2–14:46). As soon as he was no longer successful in this regard, he receded in the shadow of → David, whose rise (chaps. 16–31) also represents the story of Saul's demise.

Later biblical tradition views Saul, whom F. L. Ranke called the "first tragic figure of world history," as the failed adversary and predecessor of David (see the titles in Psalms 52; 54; 59; also Acts 13:21-22). According to Chronicles, his only noteworthy accomplishment was that he died by his own hand (1 Chronicles 10).

→ Holy War; Tribes of Israel

Bibliography: W. Dietrich, *Die frühe Königszeit in Israel* (Stuttgart, 1997) • D. Edelman, *King Saul in the Historiography of Judah* (Sheffield, 1991) • J. C. Exum, *Tragedy and Biblical Narrative* (Cambridge, 1992) • V. P. Long, *The Reign and Rejection of King Saul* (Atlanta, 1989) • T. Veijola, *Das Königtum in der Beurteilung der deuteronomistischen Historiographie* (Helsinki, 1977).

Timo Veijola

Scandinavian Missions

1. History
   1.1. Early Missions
   1.2. Nineteenth Century
   1.3. Twentieth Century
2. Cooperation
3. Present and Future

1. History

"Scandinavian" (or "Nordic") is the term for the historically and culturally related northern European countries of Denmark, Finland, Iceland, Norway, and Sweden. In each of these countries, approximately 80 to 90 percent of the people belong, nominally at least, to the Lutheran churches, which since the Reformation have had close relations with the state (→ Lutheran Churches 2; Church and State).

1.1. *Early Missions*

In the Middle Ages missions were occasionally attempted to the Sami (or Lapps), a people with a different language and culture who lived in Finland, Norway, Russia, and Sweden. After the → Reformation (§2.6) Protestants began missionary work to this people. In 1619 an important step was the publication of a Swedish Sami hymnbook. A translation of Martin Luther's (1483-1546; → Luther's Theology) Small → Catechism (§2) followed in 1633. Frederick IV (1699-1730) of Denmark, who had already sent → missionaries to India and set up a missionary college in 1714, then started a Sami mission that brought the gospel to the Samis of Norway. The leading Sami missionary was Thomas von Westen (1682-1727), a Norwegian pastor and zealous Pietist (→ Pietism).

In 1710 the orthodox Norwegian pastor Hans Egede (1686-1758) formulated the first of many proposals for missions to Greenland. Church collections and voluntary gifts provided financial support. The Danish king commissioned Egede for this work but combined the mission with colonial ambitions (→ Colonialism and Mission). After intensive missionary work beginning in 1721, Egede, known as the apostle to Greenland, returned to Copenhagen in 1736 and founded a missionary seminary there. His sons ultimately carried on the work in Greenland. The → Moravian Church (§3) also played a part in this endeavor, and after about a century of work by the Danes and Norwegians, the Eskimos in Greenland were incorporated into the Danish church.

1.2. *Nineteenth Century*

The 19th century was the age of missionary societies. Three factors inspired friends of missions in Scandinavia: Pietism, the Moravian Brethren, and revivals in Britain and America (→ Revivals 2.1-2, 6). Development varied, however, in the different countries. In Denmark the revivals, as regards missions at home and abroad, had more impact on the pastors, especially Vilhelm Beck (1829-1901), than they did in the other countries. There were no mass movements among the laity leading to great missionary activity. Hence the number of Danish missionaries was smaller than elsewhere.

The most important revivalist preacher in Finland was the Pietist Paavo Ruotsalainen (1777-1852), who worked within the Lutheran Church. The Norwegian lay preacher Hans Nielsen Hauge (1771-1824) initiated a large-scale lay awakening that was extremely important for missions abroad. A second movement — the so-called Johnsonian awakening — was named after Gisle Johnson (1822-94).

The largest Lutheran missionary societies in Finland and Sweden bore the imprint of the national churches and clergy. In Sweden in 1856 the Pietist revivalist Carl Olof Rosenius (1816-68) was active in founding a Lutheran → Inner Mission, Evangeliska Fosterlands-Stiftelsen, which also encompasses a large missionary society known today as the Swedish Evangelical Mission. Its first mission was to Ethiopia-Eritrea in 1866, which resulted in the establishment of the Ethiopian Evangelical Church Mekane Yesus and the Evangelical Church of Eritrea. It followed with a mission to India in 1877.

During the course of the 19th century some

Scandinavian missions worked with societies in western Europe such as the Basel Missionary Society (→ German Missions 1). However, large Scandinavian societies were also formed at this time. In 1821 the Danish pastor Bone Falch Rønne (1764-1833) founded Det Danske Missionsselskab (Danish Missionary Fellowship). Originally an auxiliary mission, in 1876 it began work in Manchuria, then in East Jaipur, India, then in Arabia, Tanganyika, and other places. The Danish Brethren Mission was founded in 1843, the Santalmission to northeast India in 1867, and a mission to Israel in 1885.

One of the Swedish missionary pioneers was the linguistically gifted pastor Peter Fjellstedt (1802-81), who translated the Bible and other works into Turkish (→ Bible Versions). In 1874 the mission work in the Church of Sweden was organized as the Svenska Kyrkans Mission (SKM). In 1876, with headquarters at Uppsala, this mission sent its first missionaries to South Africa. The Lunds Missionssällskap was founded in 1845 and later became an auxiliary of the SKM. The largest free church in Sweden is the Congregationalist Svenska Missionsförbundet (1878, known in America as the Mission Covenant Church, later the Evangelical Church). It started work in the Belgian Congo in 1881 and then spread to other fields.

In Finland revival movements first supported the Swedish missions. Beginning in 1870, with the help of Suomen Lähetysseura, the Finnish Evangelical Lutheran Mission, they supported significant work in Namibia. The Finnish pioneer in Africa, Martin Rautanen (1845-1926), wrote a grammar for the Ovambo language and translated the NT and parts of the OT. The Finnish mission society worked together with other → Lutheran churches from many lands. The Finnish Lutheran Gospel Society (1873), which began work in Japan in 1920, and the Finnish Missionary Alliance, which began work in China in 1891, should also be mentioned.

The Norske Misjonsselskap (Norwegian Missionary Fellowship) was founded in 1842 by pastors and lay members influenced both by the Haugean revival and by the Moravians. The pioneer in South Africa was Hans Schreuder (1817-82), who founded a church in Natal/Zululand, became bishop of the mission fields of the Church of Norway in 1867, and started the Lutheran Church in Madagascar in 1867. He wrote a Zulu grammar and translated Luther's Small Catechism and parts of the Bible. An anticlericalist mission to China called Norsk Luthersk Misjonssamband was founded in 1891 and after 1950 worked mainly in Japan and Ethiopia. The Nordiske (Norske) Santalmisjon was founded in 1867, pioneered by the Danish engineer Hans Børresen (1825-1901) and the Norwegian linguistic genius Lars Skrefsrud (1840-1910), who did linguistic and cultural research among the Santal people, work that was completed by Paul Olaf Bodding (1865-1938). The Norske Israelmisjon was founded in 1844.

1.3. *Twentieth Century*

In the 20th century several missionaries from Iceland served in Scandinavian missions. The Iceland Missionary Society was founded in 1929 and by 1992 had sent 29 missionaries to China, Ethiopia, and Kenya.

The most important Scandinavian missions, however, emerged before the beginning of the 20th century. One exception was the free church awakening in connection with the Pentecostal movement (→ Free Church; Pentecostal Churches). The first Scandinavian Pentecostal missionary arrived in Argentina in 1910. Additionally, two Swedes went from Chicago to Belém, Brazil, that same year. They started the Pentecostal movement in that country, a movement that had grown to 30 million persons at the end of the century. By 1980 Scandinavia had approximately 1,350 Pentecostal missionaries. A third of Norwegian missionaries are non-Lutheran; two-thirds from Sweden are free church, mostly Pentecostal; and 20 to 30 percent from Denmark and Finland are free church. The number of Lutheran missionaries has also grown considerably, from 1,200 in 1934 to a peak of 4,000 in 1992. Since then, the missionary role has changed to more short-term assignments. At the beginning of the 21st century, there were about 85 Scandinavian societies at work, with a total of approximately 3,000 missionaries in service.

2. Cooperation

For many years the Scandinavian missions have worked together. Cooperation began with the first Scandinavian → missionary conference, at Malmö, Sweden, in 1863. In 1910 the World Missionary Conference in Edinburgh was instrumental in forming missionary councils with an ecumenical agenda. In 1922 a Nordic missionary council was set up to promote cooperation and to organize conferences.

Scandinavian missionaries have established national churches in Africa, Asia, and Latin America. Missionaries from the Scandinavian lands work together in the Ethiopian Evangelical Mekane Yesus Church. The Northern Evangelical Lutheran Church in India is a product of Danish, Norwegian, Swedish, and American cooperation. There is also joint work in Tanzania, Congo, Hong Kong, Japan, and Taiwan. In 1973, on the initiative of Olav Guttorm Myklebust (1905-2001), the Nordic Institute for Missionary and Ecumenical Research (NIME) was founded (→ Ecumenical Mission). NIME organizes research seminars and promotes the scholarly study of Christian mission and ecumenism worldwide. All Scandinavian theological faculties teach → missiology.

3. Present and Future

As noted, Scandinavian missionaries have established larger and smaller national churches in Africa, Asia, and Latin America, and after World War II they began cooperating with the independent churches of the → Third World. These missions, especially the Norwegian and Finnish, are basically conservative, but in the Third World they are more open ecumenically than at home. They increasingly do diaconal and social work and accept cultural differences, taking the differences into account in practice. Approximately two-thirds of the missionaries have been women. The few ordained ministers mostly engage in social work. Better missionary training is now given in religion and → acculturation.

The societies work in 50 countries and also in Europe among African and Asian Muslims. Isolated during World War II, they received support from the Lutheran churches, the → Lutheran World Federation, and the → International Missionary Council. The position of the societies is stable, even though the number of local branches has declined and the overall economic situation has become more difficult.

Bibliography: General: C. F. Hallencreutz, J. Aagaard, and N. E. Bloch-Hoell, eds., *Missions from the North: Nordic Missionary Council, Fifty Years* (Oslo, 1974) • Nordic Institute for Missionary and Ecumenical Research, *Missio Nordica. Bibliografi över nordisk missionslitteratur = Bibliography of Nordic Mission Literature* (6 vols.; Uppsala, 1991-96) • I. M. Okkenhaug, *Gender, Race, and Religion: Nordic Missions, 1860-1940* (Uppsala, 2003) • K. B. Westman et al., *Nordisk misjonshistorie* (Oslo, 1950)

Journals: Nordisk Missions-Tidsskrift (1891-1998) • *Norsk Tidsskrift for Misjon* (1947-) • *Svensk Missionstidskrift* (1913-96) replaced by *Swedish Missiological Themes* (1997-).

Nils E. Bloch-Hoell†, with Björn Ryman

Schisms → Heresies and Schisms

Schleiermacher, Friedrich Daniel Ernst

Friedrich Schleiermacher (1768-1834), the "church father of the 19th century," was a Protestant theologian, → pastor, and philosopher. Born in Breslau (modern Wrocław) as the eldest son of a Prussian military chaplain, Schleiermacher — who was gifted even as a child — was significantly influenced by the → Moravian Brethren. He attended their school in Niesky beginning in 1783, then their theological seminary in Barby beginning in 1785. Doubts about traditional → dogma, however, aggravated an early alienation from the Moravians so severely that Schleiermacher left the group in 1787 in order to study → theology and especially → philosophy in Halle (1787-89).

The late-Wolffian philosopher and Kant critic J. A. Eberhard strongly influenced Schleiermacher, who independently developed his own relationship with Kant's thinking. After his first theological exam, Schleiermacher worked as a house tutor in Schlobitten, East Prussia (1790-93). After an intermezzo in Berlin (second theological exam, ordination) during which he engaged in significant study of B. Spinoza and F. H. Jacobi, Schleiermacher worked as an assistant pastor in Landsberg an der Warthe (1794-96). In 1796 he accepted the position of Reformed pastor at the Charité, a hospital and home for the aged just outside Berlin. In Berlin itself he found his way to the various salons (esp. H. Herz, Wednesday Society) and in the summer of 1787 began developing closer relationships by way of Friedrich Schlegel with the circle of early → Romantics. The influence of that circle came to expression in Schleiermacher's first (anonymous) publications, *Reden über die Religion* (1799; ET *On Religion: Speeches to Its Cultured Despisers* [1988]) and his ethical *Monologen* (1800; ET *Soliloquies* [1926]), which also reflected his earlier influences (Moravian Brethren, Eberhard, Kant, Spinoza, Jacobi) and interests (religion, sociality, individuality), fusing all these areas into a dense, multifaceted combination of → religion and → modernity.

Schleiermacher's "freethinking" Berlin acquaintances and the allegedly Spinozistic inclinations of his *Speeches* made church leaders suspicious. An unresolved love affair prompted him to accept a pastoral position in Pomeranian Stolp (modern Słupsk) in 1802, where he studied ethical problems and began an epochal translation of Plato. In 1804 he was appointed extraordinary professor of theology in Halle, where he engaged in rather comprehensive lecturing activity. When Napoléon closed the university in Halle in 1806, Schleiermacher, whose disposition was becoming increasingly patriotic on behalf of Prussia, continued his activity as a university chaplain.

Schleiermacher returned to Berlin at the end of 1807. Not until 1809, however, did he once again have stable employment, as Reformed preacher at the Trinity Church, a position he held for the rest of his life. In the same year he married Henriette von Willich, who was 20 years his junior. He was intensively involved in planning for a Prussian reform. His *Gelegentliche Gedanken über Universitäten im deutschen Sinn* (1808; ET *Occasional Thoughts on Universities in the German Sense* [1991]) was determinative for W. von Humboldt's refounding of the Berlin University in 1810, where Schleiermacher was immediately appointed regular professor (and founding dean) of theology; in 1815-16 he also served as rector of the university. From 1810 to 1814 Schleiermacher was part of the Education Section in the Prussian Ministry of the Interior. Schleiermacher made ample use of the right to lecture in philosophy at the university granted to every member of the Philosophical Section of the Academy of Sciences (from 1810), delivering lectures on → ethics, → dialectics, the history of philosophy, → psychology, → politics, → pedagogy, and → aesthetics. His *Kurze Darstellung des theologischen Studiums* (1811; ET *Brief Outline on the Study of Theology* [1966]) integrated in a completely novel fashion the different theological disciplines into a unity viewed from the functional perspective of "church government."

Apart from the OT (which he considered only conditionally canonical), Schleiermacher lectured on virtually every facet of theology; moreover, his lectures were also almost always at the forefront of theological thinking. His *Der christliche Glaube nach den Grundsätzen der evangelischen Kirche im Zusammenhang dargestellt* (1821-22; 2d ed., 1830-31; ET *The Christian Faith* [1963]) built upon the Prussian Lutheran-Reformed Union of 1817, which Schleiermacher himself had long advocated. But Schleiermacher's insistence on the separation of → church and state, already articulated in the *Speeches,* was not received well in the climate of restoration after the Wars of Liberation (1813-14), a climate in which Schleiermacher himself was already considered politically unreliable. Indeed, in the dispute concerning the introduction of a Union agenda, Schleiermacher resolutely opposed state meddling.

Highly respected as a scholar and teacher and famous as a pulpit orator, Schleiermacher died on February 12, 1834, in Berlin.

Bibliography: Primary sources: Dialectic; or, The Art of Doing Philosophy: A Study Edition of the 1811 Notes (trans. T. N. Tice; Atlanta, 1996) • *Kritische Gesamtausgabe* (ed. H.-J. Birkner; Berlin, 1980-) • *Sämmtliche Werke* (30 vols.; Berlin, 1834-64).

Secondary works: J. M. Brandt, *All Things New: Reform of Church and Society in Schleiermacher's Christian Ethics* (Louisville, Ky., 2001) • W. Dilthey, *Leben Schleiermachers* (3d ed.; Göttingen, 1991; orig. pub., 1870) • F. W. Kantzenbach, *Friedrich Daniel Ernst Schleiermacher, mit Selbstzeugnissen und Bilddokumenten* (Hamburg, 1995) • T. M. Kelly, "Schleiermacher and the Turn to the Subject," *Theology at the Void: The Retrieval of Experience* (Notre Dame, Ind., 2002) 11-50 • J. A. Lamm, *The Living God: Schleiermacher's Theological Appropriation of Spinoza* (University Park, Pa., 1996) • M. Redeker, *Schleiermacher: Life and Thought* (Philadelphia, 1973) • R. D. Richardson, ed., *Schleiermacher on Workings of the Knowing Mind: New Translations, Resources, and Understandings* (Lewiston, N.Y., 1998) • S. Sorrentino, ed., *Schleiermacher: Philosophy and the Philosophical Tradition* (Lewiston, N.Y., 1992) • T. N. Tice, *Schleiermacher Bibliography* (Princeton, 1966); idem, *Schleiermacher Bibliography (1784-1984)* (Princeton, 1985).

Bernd Oberdorfer

Schleiermacher's Theology

1. Schleiermacher and the Birth of Modern Protestant Theology

Friedrich Daniel Ernst → Schleiermacher (1768-1834) was a thinker of seminal importance in the history of modern Protestant theology. Although many 18th-century figures addressed the implications of the → Enlightenment for Christian thought, Schleiermacher was the first major post-Enlightenment theologian. He set about rethinking and reconstructing both the method and the content of Christian → theology in response to the various challenges posed by the Enlightenment. Finding rationalistic forms of Christianity (such as → deism) to be religiously inadequate and Protestant → orthodoxy to be unable to meet the Enlightenment's critique of the credibility of supernaturalism and its → skepticism about religion and Christianity, Schleiermacher sought new ways of interpreting the Christian faith and relating it to → modernity. Fully engaged with the live options of his day, he took into account the Kantian critical philosophy, both its critique of the limits of human knowing in the *Critique of Pure Reason* (1787) and its rational reconstruction of → morality in the *Critique of Practical Reason* (1788). Early German → Romanticism, a significant movement beyond and in some senses against the spirit of the Enlightenment, had an enduring impact on his thought.

Additionally, Schleiermacher's religious thought was especially informed by the Reformed theological tradition and Moravian piety. Schleiermacher developed his own distinctive alternative not only to Enlightenment → rationalism and rationalistic versions of Christianity but also to various forms of post-Kantian → idealism. He also differed from the theological conservatives of his day, both supernaturalists and pietists. In light of the pioneering significance of his religious thought and the direction of his solutions to theological problems, Schleiermacher is usually called the father of Protestant → liberal theology.

To speak of Schleiermacher as a "liberal theologian," as is conventional, is to employ an anachronistic term; it was not used to characterize his thought in his own day, and it first gained currency only in the 20th century as a polemical designation. Nevertheless, the term has some utility in suggesting the distinctive features of Schleiermacher's approach to theology. It indicates a willingness to rethink Christian doctrines from the ground up and to revise them if necessary in order to assure both their internal coherence and adequacy to Christian experience and their consistency with contemporary knowledge. As Schleiermacher himself put it in *On the Glaubenslehre,* "Shall the tangle of history so unravel that Christianity becomes identified with barbarism and science with unbelief? . . . Unless the Reformation from which our church first emerged endeavors to establish an eternal covenant between the living Christian faith and completely free, independent scientific enquiry, so that faith does not hinder science and science does not exclude faith, it fails to meet adequately the needs of our time and we need another one. . . . Yet it is my conviction that the basis for such a covenant was already established in the Reformation. It is necessary only that we become more precisely aware of the task at hand so that we can resolve it. . . . Every dogma that truly represents an element of our Christian consciousness can be so formulated that it remains free from entanglements with science" (61, 64).

Schleiermacher's contribution to modern theology hinges on his originality and creativity as a thinker and on his astonishing productivity. He pursued in effect two careers: as university professor (first at the University of Halle, then at the University of Berlin) and as Christian clergyman (having held several pastorates in his youth, and serving as the head pastor at the Trinity Church in Berlin for 25 years). His most influential publications in theology range from an early work of → apologetics *(On Religion: Speeches to Its Cultured Despisers)* to a systematic overview of the theological disciplines *(Brief Outline on the Study of Theology)* and his → dogmatics *(The Christian Faith).* In addition, he published several studies on theological topics (such as the artistically crafted *Christmas Eve: Dialogue on the Incarnation* and essays on the doctrines of the → Trinity and election), as well as historical-critical NT studies (on Timothy, Colossians, and Luke). Engaged in the ecclesiastical controversies of the day such as the proposal to unite the Lutheran and Reformed churches in Prussia into a single Protestant church or the dispute over the king's attempt to impose a national liturgy on the Prussian Protestant church, he addressed them in print as well. Many of Schleiermacher's sermons were printed during his lifetime; Schleiermacher himself published seven volumes of collected sermons, and he had six additional volumes privately printed for his friends. In addition to his publications, Schleiermacher lectured broadly in the theological faculties of the universities of Halle and Berlin: on dogmatic theology, Christian ethics, practical theology, church history, and the NT (including various exegetical courses and innovative lectures on the life of Jesus).

Schleiermacher's creativity and productivity, however, were by no means confined to the theological disciplines and the craft of → preaching. He had serious interests in → philosophy, especially philosophical → ethics; his first major academic book was a critical survey of ethical theories. He published translations of the dialogues of Plato and, as a member of the Berlin Academy of Sciences, presented numerous papers on ancient philosophy and other philosophical and humanistic topics. So serious was Schleiermacher's involvement in philosophy that in addition to his duties in the theology faculty he also lectured in the philosophy faculty of the University of Berlin; his courses included dialectics, philosophical ethics, → hermeneutics, → psychology, the theory of the → state, ancient philosophy (→ Greek Philosophy), and a number of other subjects. Many of his lectures in theology and philosophy have been published in editions that combine Schleiermacher's own outlines, notes, and sketches with student notes.

The impressive breadth of Schleiermacher's involvement in both philosophy and theology has generated an issue that has bedeviled interpreters ever since his lifetime. As Hans-Joachim Birkner has observed, "The question of the relationship of the philosophical and the theological in Schleiermacher's work lies close at hand; indeed, it is unavoidable" (p. 161). He has been suspected of deriving his theology from his philosophy: of allowing substantive philosophical convictions (whether idealist or Spinozist) to infiltrate his theological interpretation of Christian doctrines. Detailed scholarship has attended to the relationship of Schleiermacher's thinking to that of B. Spinoza, I. Kant, J. G. Fichte, and F. Schelling, as well as to the ramifications of his intense study of Plato.

Schleiermacher himself explicitly addressed the question of the relationship of → philosophy and theology in response to critical questions raised by his contemporaries. For example, he wrote to the philosopher F. H. Jacobi in 1818, "My philosophy and my dogmatics are firmly resolved not to contradict each other" (H. Bolli, 118). In another context, he repudiated the charge of illegitimately mixing them: "Although Christianity and speculation must be in harmony, they do not belong together and are not determined by each other" (*On the Glaubenslehre,* 52). Yet Schleiermacher's own statements of his intentions have by no means settled the matter, and the issue remains in dispute among scholars.

2. *On Religion: Speeches to Its Cultured Despisers* (1799)

2.1. *Importance and Setting*

Schleiermacher's *On Religion* is a very useful point of entry to understanding the method and substance of Schleiermacher's religious thought. Despite all the shifts in conceptuality and audience and all the refinements of his thinking that took place subsequent to 1799, there are numerous points of continuity between this early work and Schleiermacher's more mature religious thought. Schleiermacher acknowledged as much himself, for this book remained a constant companion throughout his career; he revised and reissued it three times (1806, 1821, 1831).

The book was written after a decade of important developments in Schleiermacher's life. Having grown up in the household of a Reformed clergyman and having been educated at a Moravian boarding school and seminary, Schleiermacher left these pietistic surroundings to study theology and philosophy at the University of Halle. In the early 1790s he was already trying his hand at writing; recently published manuscripts from the Schleiermacher archives amply document his extended struggle with the philosophical ethics of Kant (Schleiermacher was critical of Kant's notions of the highest good and transcendental freedom) and with the monistic worldview of Spinoza. After passing his theological examinations and being ordained, Schleiermacher was by 1796 the Reformed preacher at the Charité hospital in Berlin.

Entering into the cultural life of Berlin, Schleiermacher became friends with Friedrich Schlegel and the circle of early Romantic poets and thinkers around him. Prompted by his friends to contribute his own book to Romantic literature, Schleiermacher produced *On Religion.* The book addressed a readership skeptical of religion: not only the Romantics but other educated readers shaped by the Enlightenment, for whom religion was a closed book. → Religion, Schleiermacher contended, is not what its critics think it is; it is not to be confused with metaphysics or morals. Rather, religion "has its own province in the mind" as "an astonishing intuition of the infinite" (trans. R. Crouter [so all quotations from *On Religion,* unless noted otherwise], 95, 90). Six themes in this early work characterized Schleiermacher's religious thought throughout his career.

2.2. *Major Themes*

2.2.1. *The Theory of Religion*

Schleiermacher begins his apologetic with a theory of religion that defines the essence of religion: "Religion's essence is neither thinking nor acting, but intuition and feeling" (102). That is, Schleiermacher begins with an abstraction, with what is common to all forms of religion; only later in the book does he turn to the concrete, historical religions. The major task that confronts the interpreter is to unpack the expression "intuition of the universe," which is "the highest and most universal formula of religion." Schleiermacher explains: "The universe exists in uninterrupted activity and reveals itself to us in every moment. Every form that it brings forth, every being to which it gives separate existence according to the fullness of life, every occurrence that spills forth from its ever-fruitful womb, is an action of the same upon us. Thus to accept everything individual as part of the whole, and everything limited as a representation of the infinite is religion" (104, 105). Religion is a way of seeing the whole; just as, to use Schleiermacher's own analogy, people may see in the starry heavens above many different constellations, so too religious people intuit the whole of which they are a part in different ways. Associated with different intuitions are different feelings or subjective responses: → reverence, → humility, gratitude, and so forth.

The second edition of the *Speeches* (1806) substantially revises this theory of religion. Schleiermacher develops a much more complex theory of consciousness and of the religious consciousness, and although he does not eliminate entirely the technical term → "intuition," he shifts the center of gravity to the term "feeling." Feeling no longer denotes a particular subjective response to the universe (such as humility); it has become the embracing term for the fundamental, preconceptual unity of consciousness, prior to its differentiation into perceptions and actions. The formula for the essence of religion has shifted: "the contemplation of the pious is the immediate consciousness of the universal existence of all finite things, in and through the infinite, and of all temporal things in and through the Eternal" (trans. J. Oman, 36).

Schleiermacher's revolutionary move is to specify the defining characteristic of religion and its place in the human consciousness, whether designated "intuition" or "immediate consciousness" or "feeling." Religion is a matter of human consciousness; it is understood in terms of human experience. The theory of consciousness becomes more complex in the course of Schleiermacher's career, and the formula for the essence of religion changes (becoming eventually, in the introduction to *The Christian Faith,* "the feeling of absolute dependence"), but the overall contours of the theory and approach remain constant. The theory of religion in the *Speeches* anticipates the argument of his later philosophical ethics, which plays a crucial and often misunderstood role in the introduction to *The Christian Faith.*

2.2.2. *Doctrines, Ideas as Secondary*

It follows from Schleiermacher's theory of religion that religion is not primarily a matter of holding certain beliefs to be true. Concepts, ideas, and beliefs are secondary; they are derivative from religious experience, not constitutive of it. This is true even of the concept of → God; as Schleiermacher provocatively states in the first edition of the *Speeches,* "whether we have a God as a part of our intuition depends on the direction of our imagination" (138). This theme, announced in the context of an apologetic work aiming to convince "cultured despisers" that their disdain for systems of theology need not alienate them from religion, leads in the different context of Schleiermacher's own doctrinal theology to a distinctive understanding of what Christian doctrines are: "Christian doctrines are accounts of the Christian religious affections set forth in speech" (*The Christian Faith,* §15).

2.2.3. *A Pluralistic Theory*

Schleiermacher's theory of religion is in principle pluralistic. There are many ways of intuiting the universe: as "chaos," as "multiplicity without unity," as "unity in multiplicity" (*On Religion,* 137). Consequently, there are many different forms of religion; all religions, regardless of their particular perspective on the whole, are authentically religious. There is no limit to the diversity of religions: "religion is infinite" (107). This pluralistic theory did not preclude, however, the possibility that some form of religion could be "more sublime" than others (213). Schleiermacher's pluralism is not an affirmation of relativism; it entails that religions are related to each other as the higher is to the lower, not as the true is to the false. This aspect of Schleiermacher's theory anticipates the discipline he later defined as → "philosophy of religion."

2.2.4. *Religion as Social*

"Once there is religion, it must necessarily be social. That not only lies in human nature but also is preeminently the nature of religion" (163). Schleiermacher's theory of religion is in principle a social theory. In the first edition of the *Speeches,* he was primarily concerned to define the characteristics of the "true church" in contrast to the existing churches, of which he was highly critical. But the concern for the social nature of human beings and the social nature of religion persisted throughout his career. Schleiermacher was throughout his life a churchman as well as an academic, and the persistence of the social motif can be tracked not only through the theoretical structures of his philosophical ethics and the ecclesiology of *The Christian Faith* but through his sermons, his lectures on practical theology and Christian ethics, and his involvement in ecclesiastical controversies.

2.2.5. *Supernaturalism*

David Hume in his well-known discussion "Of Miracles" (§10 in his *Enquiry concerning Human Understanding*) argued the case that it was never reasonable to believe that a → miracle, understood as the violation of the laws of nature by supernatural agency, had occurred. To raise the question of the credibility of miracles is ultimately to raise a host of questions about the nature of divine power and its relation to the world of experience and about the nature of Christianity with its stories of the miraculous conception, miracles, and the resurrection of Jesus.

Although it would be too simple to call Schleiermacher an antisupernaturalist, he was clearly not a defender of orthodoxy's insistence on the miraculous, but neither did he jump into the rationalist camp of finding prosaic naturalistic explanations for putatively miraculous events. His revisionist position appears in 1799: "'Miracle' is merely the religious name for events, every one of which, even the most natural and usual, is a miracle as soon as it adapts itself to the fact that the religious view of it can be the dominant one" (133). Although he could call himself a "real supernaturalist" (*On the Glaubenslehre,* 89), his position is a third alternative to rationalistic naturalism and supernaturalism. Schleiermacher works out in greater detail his understanding of the divine causality and its relation to natural causality in his dogmatics.

2.2.6. *Christianity*

To understand a particular religion — what Schleiermacher calls in the *Speeches* a "positive" religion, as distinct from the Enlightenment construction of "natural" religion — it is necessary, he maintains, to locate its "distinctive intuition." What is the distinctive intuition of Christianity? "It is none other than the intuition of the universal straining of everything finite against the unity of the whole and of the way in which the deity handles this striving. . . . Corruption and redemption, enmity and mediation are two sides of this intuition that are inseparably bound to each other" (213).

In this language one can already see what was to become the center of Schleiermacher's analysis of the Christian consciousness in *The Christian Faith:* sin and redemption. How does Christ redeem humanity? In 1787, in the midst of the religious crisis that precipitated his departure from the Moravian Seminary, Schleiermacher had written to his father: "I cannot believe that he who called himself the Son of Man was the true, eternal God; I cannot believe that his death was a vicarious atonement . . . and I cannot believe it to have been necessary, because God, who evidently did not create men for perfection, but for the pursuit of it, cannot possibly intend to punish them eternally, because they have not attained it" (*Life of Schleiermacher,* 1.46-47). Having passed through a period of doubt and of a characteristically Enlightenment appreciation of Christ as teacher and model, Schleiermacher developed an understanding of Christianity centering not on → atonement but on → incarnation: Christ as mediator. In this view the *Speeches* anticipates the → Christology and theory of redemption that he works out in his dogmatics.

3. The Theological System

Schleiermacher's appointment as professor of theology at the University of Halle in 1804 signified a shift in context from the literary and cultural world of Berlin and his full-time pastoral responsibilities in East Prussia (where he had been since 1802) to an academic setting. His duties as professor of theology required him to work out his understanding of all the theological fields and their relations to each other. His *Brief Outline on the Study of Theology* defines the contours of the theological system that he presupposed in all of his subsequent theological writings.

3.1. *The Organization of Theology as a Positive Science*

3.1.1. *Principles of Organization*

"Theology is a positive science, whose parts join into a cohesive whole only through their common relation to a particular mode of faith." The term "positive science" denotes "an assemblage of scientific elements which belong together . . . only insofar as they are requisite for carrying out a practical task" (*Brief Outline,* §1). The other two positive sciences in the German universities were, according to this principle, law and medicine. In the case of Christian theology, the practical task that holds the separate specialties together is the leadership and governance of the Christian → church (§5). For Schleiermacher, the term "theology" does not mean primarily "systematic theology" or "dogmatics"; rather, it is an overarching term that embraces a number of specialties, dogmatics included. In the *Brief Outline* Schleiermacher proposes a threefold understanding of the disciplines of theology: philosophical theology, historical theology, and → practical theology. In each case what constitutes the discipline as theo-

Schleiermacher's Theology

logical is not the subject matter, which could be treated outside of the theological faculty in the relevant philosophical and historical disciplines, but the telos of inquiry: the guidance of the Christian church.

This threefold organization of the theological specialities has, however, a deep background in Schleiermacher's theory of the organization of *all* of human knowing. Such overarching visions were common in Schleiermacher's day; his own system has some points in common with Kant's (see the preface to the latter's *Groundwork for the Metaphysics of Morals* [1785]). Schleiermacher never published this background material, but it is available in the posthumously published lectures on ethics (see *Lectures on Philosophical Ethics*, esp. 147-51, 161-62). His system of the sciences is based on the premise that there are two forms of being, → nature and → reason, and two forms of knowing, → metaphysics (the contemplative or speculative knowledge of the essence of things) and empirical science (the experiential or observational knowledge of the existence of things).

Combining the two schemes generates four sciences: on the one hand, the speculative knowledge of the essence of nature (which Schleiermacher called physics) and empirical knowledge of nature (natural science), and on the other hand the speculative knowledge of the essence of reason (which Schleiermacher called ethics) and the empirical knowledge of the existence of reason (the science of history). Ethics has a broad agenda: to deduce the forms of cultural life (such as the state, the → family, and religious community). In addition, Schleiermacher proposes two further disciplines that fill in the gaps, as it were, between speculative and empirical knowledge: the critical disciplines, which grasp what is historically given and analyze it in terms of the categories deduced speculatively in ethics, and the technical disciplines, which are "rules of art," ways of making a practical connection between the speculative and the empirical.

Once this philosophical background is grasped, Schleiermacher's organization of the theological disciplines falls neatly into place. Ethics and the science of history, and the critical and technical disciplines, are the relevant conceptions. Ethics generates the theory of religion by rationally deducing its essence. Historical theology belongs to the empirical knowledge of history, uncovering what has factually appeared in time. Philosophical theology is a critical discipline that judges the historical in terms of the rational. Practical theology is a technical discipline that guides praxis.

The three disciplines of theology are not simply juxtaposed but are intricately and systematically connected with each other. Philosophical theology, through its subdiscipline apologetic theology, has the normative task of defining the essence of Christianity, but it can do so only on the basis of the knowledge of Christianity as it has appeared in history and as provided by historical theology. Practical theology can carry out its tasks of working out techniques for guiding the church's life only on the basis of the materials provided by historical and philosophical theology. And historical theology, as "the actual corpus of theological study . . . is connected with science, as such [i.e., rational deduction, the discipline of ethics] by means of Philosophical Theology and with the active Christian life by means of Practical Theology" (*Brief Outline*, §28).

3.1.2. *Historical Theology*

Christianity can only be understood, Schleiermacher maintains, on the basis of its past, and for this reason historical theology constitutes the body of theological study. In this fundamental principle can be clearly seen one of the characteristics of post-Enlightenment thinking: its historical consciousness. Christianity is a historical phenomenon that appeared in a particular context and developed over time; thus only a historical understanding of its entire history, not just a knowledge of the Bible alone, is necessary to understand it. To take adequately into account the historicity of the Christian religion, three subdisciplines are required: exegetical theology, which attends to "the original, and therefore for all times normative, representation of Christianity" (*Brief Outline*, §103); church history, conveying "knowledge concerning the total development of Christianity since its establishment as a historical phenomenon" (§149), in which, for the Protestant church, the Reformation is a crucial stage; and finally, as a distinctive third component, "historical knowledge of the present condition of Christianity" (p. 71). This third component of historical theology actually consists of dogmatics and church statistics (a kind of sociology of Christian communities).

The reason for locating dogmatic theology under "historical knowledge of the present condition of Christianity" has to do with Schleiermacher's distinctive understanding of its nature. Dogmatic theology is "the knowledge of doctrine now current in the evangelical Church" (*Brief Outline*, §195; see *Christian Faith*, §19). The object of doctrinal theology is not the Bible but rather Christian religious consciousness or → piety. To locate doctrinal theology within historical theology is to take a bold step in the direction of historicizing the normative theo-

Schleiermacher's Theology

logical task. Schleiermacher's radical reconceptualization of the dogmatic task as a theology of consciousness had already been signaled in the *Speeches,* when he argued that doctrines and ideas are secondary to intuition and feeling. Religious experience itself is primary; Christian doctrines are secondary and properly understood as reflections upon Christian experience, or "accounts of the Christian religious affections set forth in speech" (*Christian Faith,* §15).

With the new conception of dogmatic theology came a new name: Schleiermacher called it *Glaubenslehre,* literally a "doctrine of the faith." Christian ethics is the comparable discipline, parallel to dogmatics, dealing with the Christian life. Schleiermacher published his *Glaubenslehre* (ET *The Christian Faith*) in two editions (1821-22 and 1830-31). While he never published a Christian ethics, he lectured on it a number of times, and his lectures were published posthumously (see *Introduction to Christian Ethics*).

3.1.3. *Philosophical Theology*

As indicated by its placement in the system of the sciences, historical theology (including dogmatics and Christian ethics) belongs to the empirical study of history. But empirical, historical knowledge is not sufficient; "a formula for the distinctive nature of Christianity must be set forth" (*Brief Outline,* §44). That is, a normative statement of the essence of Christianity is needed to guide not only the normative disciplines, dogmatics and Christian ethics, but practical theology as well. This is the task of philosophical theology, which in the first edition of the *Brief Outline* Schleiermacher calls the "root" of theology. Christianity's distinctive nature or essence can be known neither purely rationally (i.e., deduced from reason in ethics) nor empirically (i.e., known through historical studies, whether of the Bible or of church history). It can be known only critically, by working through what is historically given in light of categories known rationally.

While Schleiermacher never produced a philosophical theology per se, he did work out the component that he called apologetic theology in the introduction to *The Christian Faith.* Philosophical theology, as Schleiermacher conceives it, has a second subdiscipline next to apologetics: polemics. Using the organic metaphor of health and disease, Schleiermacher maintains that the church as a historical organism is subject to becoming diseased; polemics functions to perform the diagnosis, critically evaluating historical developments in terms of the categories "heresy" and "schism." In fact, Schleiermacher himself gives considerable scope to heterodoxy as contributing to the further development of Christianity, but he sees the Christian faith as vulnerable to a number of "natural → heresies," which he carefully analyzes in the introduction to *The Christian Faith* (§22).

3.1.4. *Practical Theology*

Practical theology, as a technical discipline, "has only to do with correct procedures for executing all the tasks which are to be included within the notion of 'Church leadership'" (*Brief Outline,* §260). In the first edition he stressed its significance by calling it the "crown" of theological study. Its concerns range from the edifying activities of → worship and → pastoral care to regulative activities relating to morality and to questions of ecclesiastical → polity. Although Schleiermacher is renowned as a dogmatic theologian, he frequently lectured on practical theology; his lectures were published posthumously (see *Christian Caring: Selections from "Practical Theology"*).

3.2. *Schleiermacher's Dogmatics: The Christian Faith*

Schleiermacher's main contribution to the history of Protestant theology is his dogmatics, or *Glaubenslehre.* On the appearance of the first edition in 1821-22, his former student August Twesten claimed that his dogmatics would "begin a new period in the history of our theology" (*KGA* I/7/1, xxxiv), and other friends made similar judgments. The reason for such judgments lies in the revisionist character of the work. *The Christian Faith* is innovative in its method: it no longer followed the scriptural method of orthodox Protestant scholasticism, which developed a system of doctrine based entirely on propositions drawn from Scripture; nor did it follow the path of the rationalistic theologies of the Enlightenment, which based Christian doctrine on reasoning alone. Rather, its method was empirical, as Schleiermacher said, or "phenomenological," as we might say, involving a systematic analysis of the contemporary Protestant religious consciousness.

The *Glaubenslehre* is revisionist in content as well, for Schleiermacher was determined to avoid any collision between Christian doctrine and natural science or historical research and criticism. Consequently, he held that "we must learn to do without what many are still accustomed to regard as inseparably bound to the essence of Christianity," whether it be "the concept of → Creation itself, as it is usually understood," or "the → miracles in the New Testament" (*On the Glaubenslehre,* 60-61, 65). In constant dialogue with the Christian tradition, Schleiermacher revised it wherever he found it to be inadequate.

Schleiermacher's Theology

3.2.1. *Introduction*
Schleiermacher prefaces his exposition of Christian doctrines with an "introduction," whose task it is to define dogmatics and explain the method and structure of the work to follow. A sound grasp of the distinctions between speculative, empirical, and critical disciplines and the characteristic tasks of each is indispensable to understanding the argument of the introduction.

In defining dogmatics, Schleiermacher begins with the claim that "dogmatics is a theological discipline, and thus pertains solely to the Christian Church" (*Christian Faith,* §2). This starting point requires him to explain what a "church" is, and this task in turn leads him to a full-blown theory of religion. As in the second speech in *On Religion,* Schleiermacher in the "propositions borrowed from ethics" (*Christian Faith,* §§3-6) begins with a discussion of the essence of religion. "The self-identical essence of piety is this: the consciousness of being absolutely dependent, or, which is the same thing, of being in relation with God" (§4). In a second step (§§7-10) Schleiermacher borrows propositions from the philosophy of religion (a critical discipline) to lay out the basic differences between types of religions and thus of churches. Again, as in the *Speeches,* the theory of religion is pluralistic. Schleiermacher has set himself the task, not of proving Christianity's superiority, but of locating it within the totality of ways of being religious. In the third step, "Propositions borrowed from Apologetics" (§§11-14), Schleiermacher develops his normative understanding of the essence of Christianity and thus of the Christian church. Only at the end of this intricate argument does the definition of dogmatics appear: "dogmatic theology is the science which systematizes the doctrine prevalent in a Christian church at a given time" (§19).

The definition of the essence of Christianity provided by philosophical theology is the crucial point of entrance into the content of Schleiermacher's dogmatic system: "Christianity is a monotheistic faith, belonging to the teleological type of religion, and is essentially distinguished from other such faiths by the fact that in it everything is related to the redemption accomplished by → Jesus of Nazareth" (§11). The center of Christianity, and the very heart of the *Glaubenslehre,* is the Christian experience of redemption through Christ. The experience of redemption points to the state from which redemption is necessary: sin. The analyses of the consciousness of → sin and of the consciousness of → grace actually form the two halves of part 2 of *The Christian Faith.* In the first half Schleiermacher develops the doctrine of sin; in the second half, he turns to the doctrines of Christ, redemption, and the → church (which includes his → eschatology). Part 2 also analyzes the divine attributes relating to sin (divine holiness and justice) and redemption (divine love and wisdom). The preceding part 1 consists of an analysis of the religious consciousness, "which is always both presupposed by and contained in every Christian Religious Affection" (*Christian Faith,* p. 131). In this part Schleiermacher discusses the doctrines of creation, preservation, and the original perfection of humanity and the world, and the divine attributes of eternity, omnipotence, omniscience, and omnipresence.

Further complicating the architectonic of *The Christian Faith* is Schleiermacher's distinction of the types of dogmatic propositions: "All propositions which the system of Christian doctrine has to establish can be regarded either as descriptions of human states, or as conceptions of divine attributes and modes of action, or as utterances regarding the constitution of the world" (§30). All three forms of proposition are found in the three divisions of the work: in part 1, and in both halves of part 2. The first form of proposition, the description of human states, is, in accordance with Schleiermacher's fundamental method of analyzing the Christian consciousness, the basic form; propositions regarding God and the world have a place in the *Glaubenslehre* only insofar as they can be derived from the first form. This restriction is a way of underscoring the basic methodological point that there can be no independent, philosophical knowledge of God (or of the world) in Christian dogmatics; everything derives from an analysis of Christian experience. This structure means that the doctrine of God is not centralized in a single locus but (much like John → Calvin's distinction between "Knowledge of God the Creator" [*Inst.* 1] and "Knowledge of God the Redeemer" [*Inst.* 2]) is discussed in both part 1 and part 2.

3.2.2. *Part 1: The Relation of God and the World*
An initial analysis of the Christian religious consciousness uncovers the consciousness of being a part of a world. Since the essence of all religion, including Christianity, is the feeling of absolute dependence, it follows that the "original expression of this relationship" between God and the world is that "the world exists only in absolute dependence upon God." In Christian dogmatics, this relationship comes to expression in two claims: "the world was created by God" and "God sustains the world" (§36).

But how should the doctrines of creation and

preservation be understood in the modern world? Schleiermacher makes some bold moves. The doctrine of creation does not say anything about how the world came to be; it would be a mistake to translate the narrative of the first chapters of Genesis into doctrinal claims. There simply is no religious consciousness of origins. Rather, the doctrine serves a purely protective function: the feeling of absolute dependence is contradicted if one were to say that the world emerged through natural processes having nothing to do with God. All that can be said without getting entangled with natural science is that the world arises through divine causality. How, in turn, should the divine causality be understood? Much of part 1 of *The Christian Faith,* whether in analyzing the doctrines of creation and preservation or in discussing the divine attributes, turns on this question. Preservation and eternal omnipotence, it turns out, are the crucial doctrines.

"The religious self-consciousness, by means of which we place all that affects or influences us in absolute dependence on God, coincides entirely with the view that all such things are conditioned and determined by the interdependence of Nature" (§46). Schleiermacher's interpretive move excludes the notion that divine causality operates like finite causality. It follows that he rejects, as he did in the *Speeches,* the idea of miracles as interruptions of the causal nexus: "every absolute miracle would destroy the whole system of nature" (§47.2). Rather, the divine → causality operates in and through the causal order. The divine causality "on the one hand . . . is distinguished from the content of the natural order and thus contrasted with it, and, on the other hand, equated with it in comprehension" (§51). The divine causality does not operate episodically, subject to time; it should be thought of as the preservation of the finite order, or "continuous creativity."

It is hardly surprising that Schleiermacher's understanding of the relationship of God and the world has been judged to be pantheistic. One recent scholar has argued that Schleiermacher's causal → monism is a form of post-Kantian → Spinozism (J. Lamm). If he seems to have sacrificed the divine transcendence to → immanence, Schleiermacher makes a number of denials reminiscent of classical → theism (God is in no respect passive to the world; there is no unactualized potentiality in God). The underlying reason is the principle of absolute dependence: if the world is absolutely dependent on God, God can in no respect be dependent on the world. The result is a revisionist doctrine of God that moves away from classical theism while retaining some of its characteristic features.

3.2.3. *Part 2, First Aspect: The Consciousness of Sin*

To discuss the consciousness of sin is still to deal with an abstraction from the Christian consciousness, for "every Christian is conscious both of sin and of grace as always combined with each other" (§64.1). Schleiermacher's doctrine of sin is revisionist in two respects: its conceptuality and its account of original sin, or the fall. Sin is conceived in terms of the fundamental category, "the feeling of absolute dependence." As an essential feature of human nature, the feeling of absolute dependence cannot fail to exist, but as an abstraction, it can become a reality only in a moment of consciousness in conjunction with the sensible self-consciousness (a term that embraces both perceptions of the world and social and moral feelings, etc.). Sin is defined as "an absence of facility for introducing the God-consciousness into the course of our actual lives and retaining it there"; it is an "obstruction or arrest of the . . . higher self-consciousness" (§11.2). Sin is not defined primarily as concupiscence, misplaced love, pride, or disobedience, but as "God-forgetfulness" or "alienation from God" (§11.2, §§62-63). Schleiermacher's distinctive philosophical conceptuality provides the novel form in which the doctrine is articulated.

Schleiermacher's second innovation is to rethink the doctrine of original sin. There are, he maintains, insuperable internal difficulties with the classic Augustinian doctrine of the fall: a change in human nature because of a historical event is inconceivable; a fall "apart from an already existent sinfulness" is unintelligible; and the problem of divine justice is, on the classical account, insoluble. Still, original sin, as a "complete incapacity for the good" that is "present in an individual prior to any action of his own" (§70), is a meaningful description of Christian experience. So Schleiermacher preserves the doctrine of original sin by reinterpreting it. He explains its universality in developmental and social terms. "We are conscious of sin as the power and work of a time when the God-consciousness had not yet actually emerged in us" (§67).

In human development the consciousness of the world appears before the God-consciousness and thus gets the upper hand, so to speak, a situation that Schleiermacher finds aptly expressed in the Pauline image of the struggle of the flesh with the spirit. Moreover, human beings are social creatures influenced by the deficient God-consciousness of their fellow human beings and of their culture. In this respect, original sinfulness is "transmitted by the voluntary actions of every individual to others," or, in a pithy formula, it is "in each the work of all and in all the work of each" (§71.2). Original sin would not persist were it not ratified, as it were, by the choices of individuals; only by bringing actual sin and original sin together can the problems with the traditional doctrine be resolved. Schleiermacher's doctrine of sin is a clear expression of his critical stance toward tradition: he rethinks and revises classical doctrines, yet he always seeks to remain in continuity with the tradition.

3.2.4. *Part 2, Second Aspect: The Consciousness of Grace*

Schleiermacher's analysis of the consciousness of grace takes up more than half of the entire *Glaubenslehre,* and its agenda is very full; consequently, it has a complex structure. The propositions of the first form, the analysis of the "state of the Christian as conscious of grace" (*Christian Faith,* p. 371), lead into both Christology and the doctrines of → regeneration and → sanctification. The analysis of the "constitution of the world in relation to redemption" is taken up with the doctrine of the church, conceived in a comprehensive fashion: the origin of the church (which is treated in the doctrines of election and the Holy Spirit), the "subsistence of the Church alongside of the World" (p. 582, primarily the doctrines of Scripture and the sacraments), and the "consummation of the Church" (p. 696, eschatology). Finally, the section "the divine attributes which relate to redemption" (p. 723) treats the divine wisdom and love. Only in the conclusion does the doctrine of the Trinity put in a belated appearance, because it is "not an immediate utterance concerning the Christian self-consciousness, but only a combination of several such utterances" (§170).

The key to grasping Schleiermacher's understanding of the consciousness of grace (and thus to organizing this mass of material) is given in §87: "We are conscious of all approximations to the state of blessedness which occur in the Christian life as being grounded in a new divinely effected corporate life, which works in opposition to the corporate life of sin and the misery which develops in it." The experience of redemption does not come to the individual either immediately or in isolation from community; just as sin is a communal matter, so is redemption. Many interpreters have noticed that this principle seems to fit Schleiermacher's definition of the distinctive nature of Roman Catholicism (see §24), an apparent anomaly in a Protestant dogmatics.

Consistent with the whole approach of the *Glaubenslehre,* Schleiermacher charts a revisionist course, taking into account traditional doctrines while recasting them. His Christology may be taken as exemplifying his approach in the second half of part 2; it has attracted more critical comment than other parts of his discussion. The traditional formula for the person of Christ is, "In Jesus Christ divine nature and human nature were combined into one person" (§96). Yet Schleiermacher goes into considerable detail, as he did in the case of the doctrine of original sin, exploring the internal conceptual difficulties with the two-natures doctrine. Yet a purely human Jesus, or an only apparently human Jesus, would fall into two of the "natural heresies" of Christianity, the "Ebionitic" and the "Docetic."

Schleiermacher proposes the way forward in the terms set by his distinctive conceptuality: "The Redeemer . . . is like all men in virtue of the identity of human nature, but distinguished from them all by the constant potency of his God-consciousness, which was a veritable existence of God in him" (§94). If the distinctively human problem is the inhibition of the God-consciousness, Christ is the Redeemer by virtue of his perfect God-consciousness. Redemption, the carrying out of the single divine decree to create and redeem humanity, is made possible through the appearance in history of an archetypal God-consciousness. Such a reformulation, Schleiermacher contends, both expresses in contemporary form the intention of the ancient two-natures doctrine while avoiding its difficulties and is consistent with the biblical portrait of Jesus as found, above all, in the Gospel of John. If in his youth Schleiermacher had found the doctrine of the atonement to be incredible, in his maturity he found a revisionist understanding of the work of Christ that overcame the objections to the traditional formulations: "The Redeemer assumes believers into the power of his God-consciousness, and this is his redemptive activity" (§100); "the Redeemer assumes the believers into the fellowship of his unclouded blessedness [*Seligkeit*], and this is his reconciling activity" (§101).

4. Trajectories in Schleiermacher Scholarship

Schleiermacher's importance for the future of Protestant theology was recognized by his contemporaries. Immediately after his death in 1834, his publisher, Georg Reimer, embarked on the publication of a comprehensive edition of his collected works (including the until then unpublished lectures). Between 1834 and 1864 a total of 31 volumes of the *Sämmtliche Werke* appeared in three major divisions: philosophy, sermons, and theology. Schleiermacher's theological influence was most readily discernible in the so-called mediating theologians (August Twesten, Alexander Schweitzer, and others; → Mediating Theology); remarkably, however, a number of Roman

Catholic theologians (notably Johann Sebastian von Drey) were influenced by him as well. Other currents in German theology (such as the Erlangen experiential theology) took his heritage in a more conservative direction. After the middle of the century the younger generation of theologians shaped by the other great representative of Protestant liberalism, Albrecht Ritschl, found that Schleiermacher's program for theology compensated for deficits in the Ritschlian theology; thus thinkers such as Wilhelm Herrmann and Ernst → Troeltsch sought to reinvigorate it. Because of this shift in theological climate, there was a significant Schleiermacher renaissance at the end of the 19th and beginning of the 20th centuries, with numerous new editions and critical studies.

With the rise of → dialectical theology after World War I, a major shift in the theological perspective on Schleiermacher took place. Karl → Barth proclaimed that theology needed to take an entirely new direction. In 1922 he appealed to the "ancestral line which runs back through → Kierkegaard to → Luther and Calvin, and so to Paul and Jeremiah" — a lineage, he pointedly remarked, that "does not include Schleiermacher" (Barth, *Word of God,* 195). The neoorthodox theology that dominated much of the 20th century repudiated Schleiermacher's theory of religion and his turn to a theology of consciousness. Schleiermacher's entire approach was said to have led Protestant theology into a blind alley; the way ahead was to reverse course and return to a theology of the "Word of God."

The story of the reception of Schleiermacher's theology in the English-speaking world has yet to be researched and told. Although Schleiermacher's important essay on the Trinity appeared in English translation in 1835, a broad influence was hindered by the fact that his major works were not translated for many years (the *Speeches* in 1893, *The Christian Faith* only in 1928). Although Walter → Rauschenbusch, the theologian of the → Social Gospel, appealed with approval to Schleiermacher's corporate understanding of sin, during the period of neoorthodox dominance, North American theologians were not receptive to his influence. Reinhold → Niebuhr, for example, took Schleiermacher to task for an inadequate doctrine of sin, while his brother H. Richard Niebuhr saw in his work the classic exemplification of the "Christ of culture" motif. But with the waning of the power of neoorthodoxy in the new cultural world of the 1960s came a renewed interest in Schleiermacher. His pluralistic theory of religion and his openness to philosophy spoke to the times more than the Barthian critique of "religion." In Germany, Martin Redeker's biography, *Schleiermacher* (1968, ET 1973), and in America Richard R. Niebuhr's *Schleiermacher on Christ and Religion* (1964) were early signals of a second Schleiermacher renaissance.

A new phase in Schleiermacher scholarship began in 1980 with the publication of the first volumes of a new German critical edition of his complete works *(Kritische Gesamtausgabe,* or *KGA).* It has the potential to transform the scholarly assessment of Schleiermacher as previously unknown, inaccessible, or inadequately edited texts (whether monographs, sermons, lectures, or letters) become available. Translations of much of this material into English are under way, both in mainstream presses and in the Schleiermacher Texts and Translations series of Mellen Press. There is a flood of new studies of Schleiermacher's thought, both in Germany and in North America. The *KGA* will not be completed for many years, and the full implications of the new sources and extraordinarily diligent analytic attention to Schleiermacher's thought remain to be seen. As yet unanswered is the question whether the contemporary extensive study of Schleiermacher will in the end constitute an antiquarian study of interest primarily only to specialists, or whether it will contribute to a resolution of the constructive question of whether Protestant liberal theology has a future as well as a past.

Bibliography: Primary sources: Brief Outline on the Study of Theology (Richmond, Va., 1970; rev. ed., Lewiston, N.Y., 1990) • *Christian Caring: Selections from "Practical Theology"* (Philadelphia, 1988) • *The Christian Faith* (Edinburgh, 1928; Philadelphia, 1976) • *Christmas Eve: Dialogue on the Incarnation* (Richmond, Va., 1967; Lewiston, N.Y., 1991) • *Introduction to Christian Ethics* (Nashville, 1989) • *Kritische Gesamtausgabe* [*KGA*] (ed. H.-J. Birkner et al.; Berlin, 1980ff.) • *Lectures on Philosophical Ethics* (Cambridge, 2002) • *The Life of Jesus* (Philadelphia, 1975) • *The Life of Schleiermacher, as Unfolded in His Autobiography and Letters* (2 vols.; London, 1860) • *On Religion: Speeches to Its Cultured Despisers* (1799 ed.) (trans. R. Crouter; Cambridge, 1988); ibid. (1831 ed.) (trans. J. Oman; New York, 1958) • *On the Glaubenslehre: Two Letters to Dr. Lücke* (Atlanta, 1981) • *Servant of the Word: Selected Sermons of Friedrich Schleiermacher* (Philadelphia, 1987).

Secondary works: K. Barth, *The Theology of Schleiermacher: Lectures at Göttingen, Winter Semester 1923/24* (Grand Rapids, 1982); idem, *The Word of God and the Word of Man* (New York, 1957) • H.-J. Birkner, *Schleiermacher-Studien* (Berlin, 1996) • A. Blackwell,

Schleiermacher's Early Philosophy of Life: Determinism, Freedom, and Phantasy (Chico, Calif., 1982) • H. Bolli, ed., *Schleiermacher-Auswahl* (Munich, 1968) • J. M. Brandt, *All Things New: Reform of Church and Society in Schleiermacher's Christian Ethics* (Louisville, Ky., 2001) • R. B. Brandt, *The Philosophy of Schleiermacher: The Development of His Theory of Scientific and Religious Knowledge* (New York, 1941) • J. O. Duke and R. F. Streetman, *Barth and Schleiermacher: Beyond the Impasse?* (Philadelphia, 1988) • B. A. Gerrish, *A Prince of the Church: Schleiermacher and the Beginnings of Modern Theology* (Philadelphia, 1984) • C. L. Kelsey, *Thinking about Christ with Schleiermacher* (Louisville, Ky., 2003) • J. Lamm, *The Living God: Schleiermacher's Theological Appropriation of Spinoza* (University Park, Pa., 1996) • R. R. Niebuhr, *Schleiermacher on Christ and Religion: A New Introduction* (New York, 1964) • M. Redeker, *Schleiermacher: Life and Thought* (Philadelphia, 1973) • G. Spiegler, *The Eternal Covenant: Schleiermacher's Experiment in Cultural Theology* (New York, 1967) • J. Thiel, *God and World in Schleiermacher's Dialektik and Glaubenslehre* (Berne, 1981) • T. N. Tice, *Schleiermacher Bibliography* (Princeton, 1966); idem, *Schleiermacher's Sermons: A Chronological Listing and Account* (Lewiston, N.Y., 1997) • R. R. Williams, *Schleiermacher the Theologian: The Construction of the Doctrine of God* (Philadelphia, 1978).

Walter E. Wyman Jr.

Scholasticism

1. Basic Features
   1.1. Term
   1.2. Authority
   1.3. Reason
2. History
   2.1. Dialectics
   2.2. Faith Seeking Understanding
   2.3. The *quaestio* Method
   2.4. Theology as a Science
   2.5. Conflicts and Shifts
   2.6. William of Ockham
   2.7. Renaissance Critique
   2.8. Post-Renaissance Developments
   2.9. Nineteenth-Century Neoscholasticism

1. Basic Features

1.1. *Term*

The term "Scholasticism" designates a distinctive approach to the whole intellectual endeavor of human beings, an approach that took shape in the urban schools and (later) universities of the West beginning in the 11th century. Scholasticism is thus an original and characteristic product of medieval Western culture. By the time the major universities of the West (esp. Paris, Oxford, and Bologna) were well established in the 13th century, all of university education was undertaken in a scholastic manner. Not only → theology but also → law and medicine (the areas of the three graduate faculties), as well as → philosophy broadly understood (the province of the arts faculty), were taught and learned by scholastic methods.

The term itself was first used in a pejorative sense by 16th-century humanist critics of medieval learning. After the → Renaissance only theology, as well as the forms of philosophy associated with it, continued to be pursued in specifically scholastic ways. In theology and philosophy Scholasticism was, and remains, profoundly influential, especially in its original medieval forms. It is only with scholastic theology and philosophy that this article is concerned.

1.2. *Authority*

Scholasticism depends upon the recognition of authoritative teaching. Some persons are understood to be reliable sources of correct teaching about a given subject matter, and the texts in which their teaching comes down to us have particular → authority. The reasons why a source is viewed as authoritative, as well as the degree of authority that attaches to that source, vary with the subject matter and the source in question. In scholastic theology the highest authority is the Bible, which hands on the teaching of the → prophets and → apostles. They received this teaching by revelation from God, so the Bible supersedes all other authorities, and its teaching cannot be mistaken. Identifying what the Bible actually teaches — interpreting the Bible correctly — is therefore crucial to scholastic theology.

Theology, however, is not alone among the scholastic disciplines in holding that the acceptance of authority is necessary to get at the truth. Respect for those whose teaching has withstood the test of time, and an ongoing critical dialogue with them, is the reasonable way to seek knowledge in any field, as Aristotle (384-322 b.c.) had already shown (see *Meta.* A; → Aristotelianism).

Besides the Bible, scholastic theology recognizes authorities of several other kinds. The consensus of Christian → tradition is, like Scripture itself, beyond correction. The teaching of → councils and → popes (the *canones,* basic to scholastic → church law and theology alike) textually embodies this communal consensus. The Nicene Creed, taken as an authoritative summary of the most important scriptural teachings, is especially central (→ Niceno-Constantinopolitan Creed), but medieval Scholasticism was also shaped by ecclesial events within its own history. Subsequent scholastic theology holds, for example, that the Fourth Lateran Council (1215) settles certain basic questions in Trinitarian and sacramental theology; conversely, the conflicts between pope, emperor, and council in the late 14th and 15th centuries raise questions about how to identify an authoritative consensus of genuine Christian tradition (→ Empire and Papacy).

The → church fathers also carry great weight, though not equal to that of Scripture. Of these Augustine (354-430; → Augustinianism) is clearly preeminent in medieval Scholasticism; Leo the Great (d. 461) and Gregory the Great (ca. 540-604) are also very often cited. Among Eastern Christian writers Pseudo-Dionysius (ca. 500) and John of Damascus (ca. 655-ca. 750) receive particular attention (mainly in Latin translation) from the middle of the 12th century onward. To a lesser degree medieval scholastic theology is engaged with a great many church fathers, both West and East. Their writings were often known from collections of excerpts *(florilegia)* that began to be compiled in the early Middle Ages and, after the mid-12th century, from the *Glossa ordinaria,* a detailed verse-by-verse collection of patristic biblical commentary that served as a standard reference tool in medieval theology. But many texts (e.g., Augustine's *De Trinitate* and some of his anti-Pelagian writings) were evidently known firsthand by various scholastic theologians.

Philosophical texts constitute a further layer of authority, especially, by the mid-13th century, the writings of Aristotle and his Jewish and Muslim interpreters (esp. Maimonides [1135-1204], Avicenna [980-1037], and Averroës [1126-98]). Among scholastic theologians in the Middle Ages the authority of Aristotle was consistently subordinate to that of Scripture and the church fathers, though the same is not always true among philosophers in the arts faculties (most notably Siger de Brabant [ca. 1240-ca. 1284]), at least before the condemnation of 1277 (see below, 2.5). The authority and, even more, the interpretation of Aristotle were in fact subjects of continuing dispute in medieval Scholasticism, and scholastic theologians did not always accord him the level of respect one finds, for example, in Thomas Aquinas (ca. 1225-74).

The highly textual character of scholastic thought naturally makes commentary one of the basic literary genres of Scholasticism. Scholastic theologians regularly composed commentaries on Scripture. Peter Abelard (1079-1142), for example, wrote an extensive commentary on Romans; Bonaventure (ca. 1217-74) produced commentaries on Ecclesiastes and Wisdom, two on John, and a massive one on Luke; Thomas Aquinas wrote line-by-line commentaries on the whole Pauline corpus, the Gospels of Matthew and John, and several OT books. By the 14th century direct commentary on the Bible tended to diminish among scholastic writers. Duns Scotus (ca. 1265-1308; → Scotism) and William of Ockham (ca. 1285-1347) wrote no biblical commentaries, though Peter Auriol (ca. 1280-1322) did.

The church fathers are occasionally the subject of commentary as well. Albert the Great (ca. 1200-1280) and Aquinas, for example, both wrote sizable commentaries on the *Divine Names* of Pseudo-Dionysius. Beginning with Aquinas, Aristotle was often the subject of direct commentary. Aquinas produced detailed commentaries on most of the Aristotelian corpus, others on particular works (e.g., Scotus on the *Metaphysics,* Ockham on the *Physics*). And virtually every scholastic theologian after Alexander of Hales (ca. 1185-1245) produced a substantial "commentary" (sometimes several) on the *Sentences* of Peter Lombard (ca. 1100-1160), although these were not so much genuine commentaries as collections of *quaestiones* (see below, 1.3; 2.3).

1.3. *Reason*

The use of → reason to understand, explain, and defend authoritative teaching is constitutive of Scholasticism. The texts recognized as authorities in the Christian tradition often enough conflict with one another; at least on its face, the testimony of Scripture and the Fathers is not wholly consistent. Where consistency is not a problem, the authoritative claims of the Christian tradition raise basic questions of understanding — questions about what these claims mean, and what their implications are — and also give rise to numerous objections stemming from reason or from the claims of other religions (in the Middle Ages, → Judaism and → Islam). Scholastic theology was committed to resolving these conflicts and answering these questions by the use of reason. Western theologians in the 11th and 12th centuries came to regard such conflicts and questions about what to believe as genuine intellectual problems in the Christian view of the world that needed to be solved by rational means, rather than being regarded simply as the products of human misunderstanding or perversity.

Distinctively scholastic theology can be said to have arisen when this process of rational reflection on authoritative teaching assumed, in the institutional context of the urban schools, a particular practical and literary shape. The attentive reading and retention *(lectio)* of Scripture and the Fathers was an ancient Christian practice, cultivated especially from the early Middle Ages on. The medieval schools developed the practice of isolating focused problems or questions *(quaestiones)* raised by the *lectio* of authoritative texts. While these questions initially took the form of doubts prompted directly by the text, the *quaestio* soon became the standard vehicle for teaching and learning in the schools. It allowed for precise and highly ramified argument, not simply about textual quandaries, but about issues where the fact of the matter was not in doubt, yet the *ratio,* the reasoning by which the fact may be understood, was contested or obscure (such as the existence of → God or the → Trinity).

The formation of a scholastic *quaestio* involves identifying as many arguments as possible on both sides of the issue and reaching a solution that is at once consonant with textual authorities and rationally satisfying (esp. in its ability to offer a cogent response to the arguments or objections on the other side of the question). By this procedure the theological master seeks, as Aquinas puts it, to "instruct his hearers in order that they may be led to an understanding of the truth which they hold. It is necessary that such teaching rely upon reasons which search out the root of this truth, and make it known *how* what is said, is true." Without this argumentative resolution of the *quaestiones,* the hearers "will acquire no knowledge or understanding, and will go away empty" (*Quodlibet* IV, q. 9, art. 3, c).

This move from *lectio* to *quaestio* gave Scholasticism much of its distinctive intellectual flavor and produced the other basic literary genre of Scholasticism: the collection of *quaestiones.* Sometimes these collections of disputed questions arose from the regular teaching activity of the university master in theology (esp., but not only, the "commentaries" on Lombard's *Sentences*), sometimes from public disputations where questions on any matter could be put to the master by others (quodlibetal questions), and sometimes from the independent literary activity of the master (some of the *Summae,* for example).

The appeal to reason in scholastic theology meant, first of all, the use of → logic. The study of logic became basic to the curriculum of the arts faculty and thus served as a foundation for all of the graduate disciplines. Logic itself underwent considerable and sophisticated development in the Middle Ages, especially in the first half of the 12th century (primarily at the hands of Abelard and his school) and in the late 13th and early 14th centuries (esp. in the work of Ockham and Buridan [ca. 1300-1358 or after]). This growth was in part prompted by the reception of the full corpus of Aristotle's logical writings in the West during the 12th century, although medieval logic went well beyond what it had received from Aristotle. Substantial philosophical accounts of → language were also developed in the Middle Ages and used in theology. Of these perhaps the most important were the modistic grammars, which reached their fullest development in the later 13th century and took grammatically detectable "modes of signification" as the key to the meaning of terms and the truth of propositions. Scholastic theologians and philosophers in the Middle Ages (though not necessarily in later types of Scholasticism) were thus practiced at raising and answering semantic or linguistic questions, which they regarded as basic to dealing with the kinds of problems they wanted to solve.

In Scholasticism "reason" also includes the best current knowledge available in all the branches of philosophy. In the Middle Ages this discipline embraced not only → metaphysics and → ethics but the natural → sciences (esp. physics, astronomy, and biology) and what are now thought of as the social sciences (esp. → psychology, including much of scholastic → epistemology, and → politics). None of these subjects was new to the scholastic world when Aristotle's treatises on all of them began to be known in the 13th century. But the introduction of Aristotle on these subjects brought about a crisis and revolution in Western thought and posed for scholastic theology, with renewed and unprecedented intensity, the problem of reconciling the claims of reason with the truths of Christian faith. Scholastic theologians developed a variety of solutions to this problem. Whatever their differences, they held that the teachings of Christianity trump any philosophical claims that may conflict with them, but they ordinarily maintained that Christian theology need not, on the whole, reject Aristotle. These theologians aimed, rather, at a systematic and comprehensive Christian worldview that incorporated Aristotle's novel philosophical claims, rather than rejecting them — though the precise extent to which Aristotle could be reconciled with Christian teaching was contested from the 13th century on (→ Philosophy and Theology).

2. History

2.1. *Dialectics*

Several key developments shaped the history of scholastic theology and philosophy. The restoration of social and economic stability in western Europe in the 11th century allowed for the growth of literacy and the reestablishment of urban cathedral schools, which had originally been set up under Charlemagne (ca. 742-814) for the training of clergy. One fruit of this revitalization of learning was a renewed interest in → dialectics (grammar and logic) and in the application of its tools to the understanding of Christian teaching. The logic in question was what later came to be known as the old logic *(logica vetus):* Aristotle's *Categories* and *On Interpretation,* plus Porphyry's (ca. 232-ca. 303) *Isagoge,* which had long before been rendered into Latin, with commentary, by Boethius (ca. 480-524).

Both sides in the eucharistic controversy of the 11th century made explicit use of grammar and logic to articulate and defend their positions. By a dialectical analysis of the consecration formulas, Berengar of Tours (ca. 1010-88) tried to show that Christ's presence in the Eucharist cannot involve any real alteration of the elements, while Lanfranc of Bec (ca. 1010-89) tried to show dialectically that Christ's presence requires a real, indeed substantial, change in the elements. This dialectical turn marks a clear difference between the 11th-century debates and the argument between Paschasius Radbertus (ca. 790-ca. 860) and Ratramnus (9th cent.) about the same issues two centuries earlier. Similarly, Roscelin (ca. 1050-ca. 1125) applied dialectics to standard Trinitarian formulas; the seemingly tritheistic character of his results soon drew dialectical counterarguments from Anselm (1033-1109), Abelard, and others.

At the same time, these pro-and-con arguments about basic Christian teachings elicited from some Christian writers (such as Peter Damian [1007-72]) a general repudiation of dialectics as a suitable means for approaching the mysteries of the faith. From its emergence scholastic theology thus encountered currents of opposition, which accompanied Scholasticism throughout the Middle Ages and beyond.

2.2. *Faith Seeking Understanding*

Anselm of Canterbury, who, like many early scholastic thinkers, was the product of a monastic rather than an urban intellectual environment, nonetheless articulated the scholastic project of faith seeking understanding *(fides quaerens intellectum)* with great clarity. Following the Vg rendering of Isa. 7:9 ("Unless you believe, you will not understand," a passage that Augustine had stressed), Anselm argues that Christians should not seek a reason for what they believe as a prerequisite for believing it, or in order to make it more certain. This would be laughable, like a mountaineer earnestly trying to shore up Olympus with stakes and ropes (*Epistola de Incarnatione Verbi* 1). Rather, Christians should seek, out of love for the → truth they believe, the deepest reason why it is true (its *ratio veritatis*). The aim is to find "necessary reasons" for the basic truths of Christianity, arguments so compelling that the rational mind cannot help assenting to them, however much this apprehension of the intrinsic rationality of Christian teaching must begin with faith.

Anselm carries out this quest for faith's rational luminosity with great dialectical inventiveness, especially with regard to the existence of God and redemption by Christ as God incarnate. Subsequent scholastic theologians share his basic commitment to the project of finding illuminating and interconnected reasons for what Christians believe, even where they reject the idea (as most theologians did by the 13th century) that the understanding faith seeks requires reasons that rise to the level of strict necessity.

2.3. *The quaestio Method*

In the early 12th century Anselm of Laon (d. 1117), together with his brother Ralph (d. 1133), began compiling the *Glossa ordinaria* in the cathedral school at Laon. In the process they started to identify exegetical *quaestiones,* matters on which the Fathers offered conflicting interpretations of the Bible. This basic element in scholastic method soon underwent considerable development at the hands of Peter Abelard. In his *Sic et non* (Yes and no), a collection of apparently contradictory statements of the Fathers on 150 different theological problems, Abelard argues that we can get at the truth about these matters by resolving the troubling conflicts among our authorities: "By doubting we come to inquiry, and by inquiry we perceive the truth" (p. 103). Abelard is formative of later Scholasticism, not only in his insistence that truth is grasped by the dialectical questioning of received authorities, but in holding that many conflicts in Scripture and tradition can be resolved by close attention to language — in particular, to the different meanings with which different authors often use the same words.

Abelard's own theology was controversial, especially his teaching on the Trinity, which was condemned at the Council of Soissons (1121), and again at the Council of Sens (1140). Abelard's chief adversary in 1140 was Bernard of Clairvaux (1090-1153). Bernard later attacked the Trinitarian views of Gilbert de la Porrée (d. 1154), a leading theologian of the important cathedral school at Chartres and eventually a master at Paris. Bernard was a vigorous and eloquent critic of what he saw as the excesses of reason in emergent scholastic theology and the pride of dialecticians who seek to pry into the mysteries of God. In Bernard's own mystical theology, the central mystery of Christianity — God's descent, in love, into the full reality of our frail and suffering flesh, so that we might ascend, in love, to share in his life — is available only to faith's rapt and obedient apprehension. Its beauty is beyond the scrutiny of dialectical reason, which can only distort it.

In the 14th century another vigorous strain of mystical theology emerged as a counterpoint to Scholasticism, now loosed from the monastic moorings it had in Bernard. For this later tradition too the truths of Christianity are ultimately beyond the grasp of logic (and by now metaphysics), though some of its key figures, such as Meister Eckhart (ca. 1260-ca. 1328), were themselves scholastically trained.

In the mid-12th century Robert of Melun (d. 1167) and Peter Lombard developed their own collections of conflicting patristic *sententiae* (statements or opinions). Unlike Abelard, they organized these patristic views and the questions to which they gave rise around an ordered sequence of topics. The aim was to reach a reasoned understanding of all the essential matters of Christian teaching, using the *quaestio* method to work out a coherent account of what Scripture and the Fathers have delivered to us. Lombard's *Sententiae* became the chief text of the entire *quaestio* literature of medieval Scholasticism (as distinguished from the commentary literature in the narrower sense), especially after Alexander of Hales, the first Franciscan master of theology at Paris, made it his basic text for teaching theology.

Though inevitably overshadowed by the enormous theological research tradition that made its own uses of him, Lombard was no mere compiler. He worked out his own, sometimes innovative solutions to the questions posed to him by Scripture and the Fathers, and later scholastic theologians generally agreed with him as far as he went, with some important exceptions (e.g., whether the *caritas* with which those who are justified love God is the person of the → Holy Spirit himself, as Lombard held, following Augustine, or whether it is a created effect of the Spirit's indwelling, as most subsequent commentators on bk. 1, dist. 17 insisted).

2.4. *Theology as a Science*

The introduction of Aristotle's full corpus of logical writings in the later 12th century (the new logic, or *logica nova*) confronted Scholasticism with a rigorous account of what makes for an organized body of knowledge, or a science. Scholastic theologians gradually responded by trying to show that Christian theology was not merely a piecemeal collection of dialectical exercises but a genuine science, all the parts of which could be traced back to the articles of faith as first principles. This approach required some important modifications in Aristotle's notion of a science, but by the time of Aquinas the scientific character of theology was widely accepted (though argument remained as to exactly how theology counts as a science, and whether it is a speculative or a practical science).

At about the same time, the introduction of the rest of Aristotle's philosophy (see 1.3) confronted scholastic theology with a compelling → worldview at odds, on many points, with the broadly Platonist outlook that had colored Christian thought since ancient times. To this challenge the mendicant theologians of the mid-13th century, especially Albert the Great, Bonaventure, and Thomas Aquinas, responded by developing a comprehensive scientific theology that strives both to unfold the full contents of Christian faith and to take captive the philosophy of Aristotle for Christian purposes (see 2 Cor. 10:4-5). Thus for Aquinas, "Since → grace does not destroy → nature, but perfects it, natural reason must be subservient to faith," in conformity to the apostolic imperative to "take every thought captive in obedience to Christ" (*Summa theol.* I, q. 1, art. 8, ad 2; see also I, q. 1, art. 6, ad 2). Duns Scotus later took a similar view: "Reason is taken captive" by the articles of Christian faith, "yet to Catholics these are more certain [than truths known by natural reason], since they firmly rely on your [God's] supremely solid truth, and not on our blind and often unsteady intellect" (*De primo principio*, 4.86).

2.5. *Conflicts and Shifts*

Between Aquinas and Scotus occurred the Paris and Oxford condemnations of 1277, where church authorities rejected a number of propositions advocated by contemporary philosophers and theologians as incompatible with Christian truth. Although aimed primarily at the seemingly naturalistic and deterministic Aristotelianism of the Paris arts faculty (in part under the influence of Averroës), the condemnations also touched on the views of major scholastic theologians, including Thomas Aquinas (esp. concerning the → soul as the single substantial form of the human being, which seemed incompatible with the Christian doctrine of the soul's → immortality).

In the wake of these condemnations the major → religious orders (§1) defended the orthodoxy of their chief theologians, which for a time (until the early 14th cent.) gave university theology a noticeable school mentality. Thus the → Augustinian Order gathered around Giles of Rome (ca. 1245-1316), and already in the 1280s the → Dominicans mandated the promotion of Aquinas's views by their order, especially against the attacks on Aquinas by Franciscan theologians, which began soon after his death. But soon the authority and interpretation of Aquinas were contested within the Dominican Order itself, especially by Durandus of Saint-Pourçain (ca. 1275-1334), whose views in some respects anticipate Ockham's → nominalism. By the early 14th century Scotus had superseded Bonaventure as the leading theologian among the Franciscans, but Scotus's views were soon sharply attacked (though in different and sometimes opposed ways) by Peter Auriol and William of Ockham, themselves → Franciscans.

At the same time, scholastic theology and philosophy underwent a basic shift in the way questions were treated, and in the kinds of questions that were raised. In the generation of Aquinas and Bonaventure scholastic theologians sought to answer many questions briefly, by succinct arguments that would reconcile ancient authorities, justify their own position, and put relevant objections to rest. Already in the secular master Henry of Ghent (ca. 1217-93), and certainly by the generation of Scotus, the *quaestio* became not so much an argument about what to make of the past as an argument with theological contemporaries. On each question the theologian engaged in detail a broad range of scholastic (esp. recent) views, ranked them according to argumentative merit, and developed his own position in critical dialogue with its most plausible opponents. The length of each question correspondingly tended to increase (sometimes to many dozens of pages in a modern printed edition), and the number of questions treated to decrease.

The text of Lombard, while still the standard framework for the formation of *quaestiones,* rarely any longer received direct comment; the authority of the scriptural and patristic texts behind Lombard, while agreed to by all, was seldom specific enough to settle the technical question at hand. This shift in approach yielded a continuing growth in the precision and complexity of scholastic arguments, but it could also make it hard to see much connection between these arguments and the basic religious and theological questions that originally gave rise to them.

2.6. *William of Ockham*

William of Ockham marks a sea change in scholastic theology and philosophy. His importance extends beyond the introduction of a nominalist philosophy of language and → ontology (i.e., the view that only individuals and their qualities, not common essences or abstract objects, have real or extramental existence; → Language and Theology). Ockham's nominalism is closely tied to his development of a consistently extensional logic, which he applies rigorously against many of the philosophical views of his Franciscan predecessor Duns Scotus and against the tradition of Aristotelian realism more generally. On theological matters Ockham is generally closer to Scotus, especially in Scotus's highly influential structuring of → justification and → salvation around the idea of God's "ordained power" *(potentia ordinata).* Ockham accepts and develops Scotus's view that God's decision to establish the order of salvation that actually obtains, where human freedom and merit play a crucial role, is wholly contingent, so that nothing that happens within this contingent order makes any binding claim on God's freedom and omnipotence.

At the same time, Ockham stringently applies his form of logic to theological questions and finds many of the arguments previously used by scholastic theologians to explain and defend Christian teaching to be unpersuasive, indeed specious. The result is a theology that willingly follows the scholastic tradition in taking reason captive to faith but finds the harmonization of reason with the truths of faith both more difficult and less pertinent than it had seemed before. In theology, philosophical reasoning "should not be introduced unless it manifestly follows from the truths of faith handed on in Holy Scripture or in the decisions of the church. Reason must always be taken captive to their authority." When the teaching of Scripture, the church, and the saints can be "preserved without introducing" them, then there is no use for philosophical arguments in theology (*Scriptum* I, dist. 2, q. 1 [*Opera theologica,* 2.17.18–2.18.3]).

2.7. *Renaissance Critique*

Though initially quite controversial, Ockham became the most influential scholastic theologian of the later 14th and 15th centuries. While many disagreed with him, it was generally acknowledged that he had set the primary agenda for theological and philosophical discussion in the universities. By the 15th century clearly defined schools of thought, each tied to the teaching of a past master, again dominated scholastic theology. To a large extent scholastic discourse took the form of arguments among Ockhamists (of whom Pierre d'Ailly [1350-1420] and Gabriel Biel [ca. 1420-95] are perhaps the most important), Scotists, Albertists, and Thomists (led by John Capreolus [ca. 1380-1444]). Some important scholastically educated figures of the period, however, such as the canonist, philosopher, and mystic Nicholas of Cusa (1401-64), fall outside the boundaries of these rival schools.

In the mid-15th century the Renaissance critique of the scholastic approach to intellectual life began to take shape in Italy. Lorenzo Valla (1407-57) and others argued that the study of Greek and Latin literature ought to be the basis of university education, and that the acquisition of rhetorical skill rather than scholastic logical refinement should be its chief aim. Together with the frontal assault on the teachings of scholastic theology in the Protestant Reformation, this humanist critique of Scholasticism had a sweeping effect on European university life in the 16th century and beyond.

2.8. *Post-Renaissance Developments*
In Catholic countries and their universities, however, scholastic theology and philosophy continued through the → Renaissance and → Reformation. Especially after the Council of → Trent (1545-63), and chiefly in the Spanish universities, Scholasticism underwent a considerable revival, though altered from its medieval form. The characteristically medieval attention to logic and language in the resolution of disputed questions withered, and metaphysics became the predominant area of philosophical concern. The *Summa theologiae* of Thomas Aquinas (upon which Thomas de Vio Cajetan [1469-1534] had already written an article-by-article exposition in the early 16th cent.) generally replaced Lombard's *Sentences* as the primary text for commentary, and the scholastic theologian's *quaestiones* were now mainly Thomas's questions, rather than those generated by a reading of scriptural and patristic sources.

Within this framework theologians like Domingo Báñez (1528-1604), Gabriel Vázquez (1549-1604), and Francisco Suárez (1548-1617) did substantial and sometimes highly original work, and also argued vigorously with one another (e.g., on the relationship between grace and free will). On the Catholic side Scholasticism in this mold continued into the 18th century (thus, e.g., the *Summa Sancti Thomae* of F. C.-R. Billuart [1685-1757]), though by this time a considerable desuetude also set in.

Although the Protestant → Reformers were generally hostile to both the style and content of scholastic theology, a kind of Scholasticism was nonetheless reintroduced into the Protestant universities of central Europe in the late 16th century. Renewed appreciation for logic and metaphysics of a broadly Aristotelian kind marked this Protestant Scholasticism, as well as an extensive use of the disputed question both as a teaching tool and as an organizing principle for the systematic presentation of Protestant theology. Much of the labor of scholastic theologians of the 17th century — Lutheran, Reformed, and Roman Catholic alike — was devoted to the polemical justification of competing denominational positions on disputed doctrines. But the theologians of Protestant → Orthodoxy (§§1-2), as well as their Roman Catholic counterparts, were often extensively engaged with medieval Scholasticism and readily drew on it for support where the doctrine in question was not a matter for confessional dispute (e.g., the Lutheran Johann Gerhard [1582-1637] cites Aquinas and Biel approvingly in Trinitarian theology).

2.9. *Nineteenth-Century Neoscholasticism*
The "neoscholastic" theology and philosophy that emerged in the mid-19th century, initially in Rome, was primarily a revival of Thomism. Its main concern was to recover the mind of Thomas, after a period where the study of Aquinas had been relatively neglected and Catholic theology significantly influenced by rationalist trends in modern philosophy (→ Rationalism). But the main advocates of → neoscholasticism, such as Josef Kleutgen (1811-83) and Johann Baptist Franzelin (1816-86), also drew on other figures from medieval and later Spanish Scholasticism and attempted to apply a scholastic vision to contemporary theological and philosophical problems. *Aeterni Patris* (1879), the encyclical of Leo XIII (1878-1903) that endorsed the "golden wisdom" of Aquinas as the chief guide for the renewal of Catholic theology and philosophy, both reflects and furthers the aims of neoscholasticism.

Up to → Vatican II (1962-65), neoscholastic modes of thought exercised broad influence in Roman Catholic theology. Neoscholasticism is "scholastic," however, primarily in its devotion to some of the great scholastic figures of an earlier age, rather than in its adoption of the dialectical methods of inquiry that characterized medieval Scholasticism.

Bibliography: P. Abelard, *Sic et non: A Critical Edition* (7 pts.; Chicago, 1976-77) • K. G. Appold, *Orthodoxie als Konsensbildung. Das theologische Disputationswesen an der Universität Wittenberg zwischen 1570 und 1710* (Tübingen, 2004) • I. Backus, *The Reception of the Church Fathers in the West: From the Carolingians to the Maurists* (2 vols.; Leiden, 1997) • M.-D. Chenu, *La théologie au douzième siècle* (Paris, 1957; partial ET *Nature, Man, and Society in the Twelfth Century* [2d ed.; Toronto, 1998]); idem, *La théologie comme science au XIIIe siècle* (3d ed.; Paris, 1969) • M. Colish, *Medieval Foundations of the Western Intellectual Tradition* (New Haven, 1997) • W. J. Courtenay, *Schools and Scholars in Fourteenth-Century England* (Princeton, 1987) • G. Dahan, *L'exégèse chrétienne de la Bible en occident médiéval. XIIe-XIVe siècle* (Paris, 1999) • J. Duns Scotus, *Treatise on God as First Principle* (trans. A. B. Wolter; 2d ed.; Chicago, 1982) • G. R. Evans, ed., *Mediaeval Commentaries on the Sentences of Peter Lom-*

bard (Leiden, 2002); idem, ed., *The Medieval Theologians* (Oxford, 2000) • A. Forest, F. van Steenberghen, and M. de Gandillac, *Le mouvement doctrinal du XIe au XIVe siècle* (Paris, 1956) • E. Gilson, *History of Christian Philosophy in the Middle Ages* (New York, 1955) • M. Grabmann, *Geschichte der scholastischen Method* (2 vols., Freiburg, 1909) • J. J. E. Gracia and T. B. Noone, eds., *A Companion to Philosophy in the Middle Ages* (Oxford, 2003) • N. Kretzmann, A. Kenny, and J. Pinborg, eds., *The Cambridge History of Later Medieval Philosophy* (Cambridge, 1982) • U. G. Leinsle, *Einführung in die scholastische Theologie* (Paderborn, 1995) • A. de Libera, *La philosophie médiévale* (5th ed.; Paris, 2001) • L. O. Nielsen, *Theology and Philosophy in the Twelfth Century* (Leiden, 1982) • H. A. Oberman, *The Harvest of Medieval Theology: Gabriel Biel and Late Medieval Nominalism* (4th ed.; Grand Rapids, 2000) • B. Smalley, *The Study of the Bible in the Middle Ages* (3d ed.; Oxford, 1983) • R. W. Southern, *Scholastic Humanism and the Unification of Europe* (2 vols.; Oxford, 1995-2001) • W. Sparn, *Wiederkehr der Metaphysik. Die ontologische Frage in der lutherischen Theologie des frühen 17. Jahrhunderts* (Stuttgart, 1976) • William of Ockham, *Opera theologica* (10 vols.; St. Bonaventure, 1967-86).

Bruce D. Marshall

Scholium

A scholium (Gk. *scholion,* "comment") is a brief explanatory comment on an individual text. With glosses and interpretation scholia early came into use as a hermeneutical tool in literary history (→ Hermeneutics). In the Christian field we find them in → exegesis of the Bible and the Fathers (→ Patristics; Catena), for example, in the *Hypotyposes* of Clement of Alexandria (d. ca. 215) up until the biblical expositions of Martin → Luther (1483-1546; → Luther's Theology).

Bibliography: H. Erbse and D. Fehling, "Scholien," *LAW* 2723-26 • A. Gudemann, "Scholien," *PW* (2d ser.) 3.625-705 • J. Schmid, *LTK* 9.448-49 • C. O. Sloane, "Scholium," *NCE* (2d ed.) 12.779.

Bernd T. Drössler

School and Church

1. History
2. Present Situation
3. Church Views

The relationship between school and church varies a great deal, depending on history, national settings, and religious traditions.

1. History

In the past in Europe, church and school were traditionally closely related. For a long time the church had charge of the school, particularly monastic, cathedral, and parish schools (→ Monastery 4.1; Religious Orders and Congregations 2.3). City and private schools that arose in the later Middle Ages, however, were also still under church control. M. → Luther (1483-1546; → Luther's Theology) encouraged territorial rulers to take responsibility for establishing schools and urged that education become compulsory (which happened by the 17th cent.). Even so, however, there was no questioning the close legal and material link to the church.

During the → Enlightenment an increasingly secular → state developed, which by the 19th century had encouraged a trend toward the separation of school and church. In some places such as the United States, this separation was tied to the explicit opposition to an established church. This view found increasing support among progressive teachers in day schools, who increasingly opposed the spiritual oversight of schools by an established church.

2. Present Situation

In countries like France and the United States, this development brought a complete separation of the public school and church, though for a long time Christian elements found a way into the life of many schools. For example, in the United States, this presence often took the form of a kind of generic → Protestantism. In response, Roman Catholics and many Protestants either denominationally or across denominational lines set up and funded their own schools in which they could not merely retain a few Christian elements but control staff, curriculum, and discipline and offer religious and moral instruction. At the same time, many Christians in the United States continue to wage a battle, successful in part, to prevent the excessive banishing of religion from schools, arguing for a right of prayer, the rights of students to express their convictions and to assemble for religious purposes during out-of-school hours, the need for religiously based ethical instruction, and the place of the Bible among books that may be consulted and quoted.

In other Protestant countries various forms of compromise between school and church have occurred. In England, for example, the churches took

School and Church

the lead in providing schools for popular education, so that when the state took up the challenge in the later 19th century, it established a dual system, making use of the church schools already available and allowing religious instruction at an hour when any with conscientious objections (e.g., on denominational grounds) might withdraw. In the Netherlands, as another example, society was divided along confessional lines into four "pillars" and, as a result, established state-funded Roman Catholic and Calvinist schools in addition to public schools. In some countries, general religious instruction became an integral part of the curriculum in the 1940s.

Germany has tried to set up a form of religious instruction in harmony with both Roman Catholic and Protestant convictions. The various regional states work out this arrangement in the form of Christian community schools, or at least of schools that leave a place for Christian instruction. Other countries that have been under strong Christian influence and that recognize the way in which the church has helped to shape the educational tradition also maintain some form of relationship, but in different and indeed developing ways in detail.

3. Church Views

In their self-understanding, many churches have a sense of responsibility not merely for religious instruction in the strict sense but for education as a whole. This sense does not mean that they think schools and teachers should be under church tutelage. The ethical and academic responsibility of teachers for the curriculum and for school life as a whole will not in any case accept such tutelage.

The church must be ready for free ministry to free schools. This ministry must take the form of critically and constructively accepting the school as the place of education and the sphere in which students, along with necessary and useful knowledge, receive help in orientation to the world, to the tackling of future tasks, and to the ascertaining of their own → identity (→ Pedagogics 2). Involved here are the answers of the Christian tradition to such questions as that of the purpose of life and education. Some churches think they can render their service best by providing their schools under their own control, which compete with state schools or supplement them (→ Education 2). Part of their task may be to provide for children who are handicapped or retarded (→ Persons with Disabilities).

The present age is an age of great variety, experimentation, and transition, especially in the → Third World, where in some cases the state has taken over responsibility for education because of the tardiness of the churches in transferring their schools from the supervision of the mission to that of the national church and the consequent inability to take into account such new goals as national development and cultural independence. Where the transfer has taken place, however, churches have been able not only to retain but to expand their educational work. Thus in many countries in Africa most educational institutions from primary schools to universities are in the hands of the churches.

In addition, even in lands in which the state has become increasingly neutral, often due to the growth of → pluralism, as in the United States, churches have increasingly concluded that they must take up responsibility for providing parents and students who desire it with an education that is still infused with the doctrinal and ethical teaching and spirit of the gospel. Even though it means paying fees in addition to tax support for the public schools, many parents are only too ready to take advantage of the Christian schools that are available. How far this trend may yet become the way of the future in many European lands that have experienced increased minority immigration and the resultant religious pluralism has yet to be determined.

Bibliography: H.-J. Abromeit, *Im Streit um die gute Schule. Der Beitrag der Christen* (Neukirchen, 1991) • H.-C. Berg, ed., *Unterrichtserneuerung mit Wagenschein und Comenius. Versuche evangelischer Schulen, 1985-1989* (Münster, 1990) • J. W. Fraser, *Between Church and State: Religion and Public Education in a Multicultural America* (New York, 1999) • C. L. Glenn, *The Ambiguous Embrace: Government and Faith-Based Schools and Social Agencies* (Princeton, 2000) • M. E. Marty and J. Moore, *Education, Religion, and the Common Good: Advancing a Distinctly American Conversation about Religion's Role in Our Shared Life* (San Francisco, 2000) • K. E. Nipkow, *Bildung als Lebensbegleitung und Erneuerung. Kirchliche Bildungsverantwortung in Gemeinde, Schule und Gesellschaft* (Gütersloh, 1990) • R. R. Parsonage, *Church: Related Higher Education* (Valley Forge, Pa., 1978) • C. T. Scheilke and M. Schreiner, eds., *Handbuch Evangelische Schulen* (Gütersloh, 1999) • P. Schreiner, ed., *Profile ökumenischer Schulen. Beispiele aus Europa* (Münster, 2001) • J. T. Sears, with J. C. Carper, eds., *Curriculum, Religion, and Public Education: Conversations for an Enlarging Public Square* (New York, 1998) • J. L. Seymour, *The Church in the Education of the Public: Refocusing the Task of Religious Education* (Nashville, 1984) • H. Spinder, ed., *Giving Europe a Heart and Soul: A Christian Vision for Education in Europe's Schools* (Münster, 2003) • M. Stallmann, *Christentum und Schule* (Stuttgart, 1958) • J. R. STUMME and R. W. TUTTLE, eds., *Church and State: Lutheran Perspectives* (Minneapolis, 2003).

ULRICH BECKER

Schweitzer, Albert

Albert Schweitzer (1875-1965) was a Protestant theologian, a physician, and an organist. After studying → theology and → philosophy in Strasbourg, Berlin, and Paris, Schweitzer became an assistant pastor in Strasbourg in 1899, a private lecturer in NT in 1902, and also director of the theological seminary in 1903. Theology, philosophy, and music were equally influential in shaping his life and thought.

Schweitzer's revolutionary contribution to theology was his continuation of J. Weiss's understanding of "consistent → eschatology," combined with a comprehensive survey and criticism of life-of-Jesus research *(Von Reimarus zu Wrede)* and a revision of the understanding of → Paul *(Die Mystik des Apostels Paulus)*. Schweitzer's understanding of Jesus' "proleptic messianic consciousness" as the "only possible realization of the messianic idea" also required a total "de-eschatologization" and a retreat to an → ethics whose only possible orientation is the human being → Jesus.

The most characteristic features of Schweitzer's philosophy are his basic, unequivocally humanistic "principle of morality," the "reverence for life" that he considered absolutely necessary for any philosophical thought and thus as universal *(Kulturphilosophie)*. Schweitzer's opposition to nuclear arms and his engagement on behalf of international → peace movements during the final years of his life were logical consequences of his earlier positions, as was also his study of non-Christian religions *(Das Christentum und die Weltreligionen)*.

Over the entire course of Schweitzer's life, spiritual and religious music was anything but merely a secondary hobby. He was a master organ player and composed a large work on J. S. Bach, a treatise on French and German organ construction (1906), and an edition of Bach's organ works (with his teacher, C.-M. Widor, 1912ff.).

In 1913, immediately after finishing medical school (with a dissertation on a psychiatric assessment of Jesus), Schweitzer left academic life and reported to the Paris Missionary Society for service in Africa. Because of the personnel shortage in French Equatorial Africa, the mission director, A. Boegner, immediately appointed him head of the hospital in Lambaréné (on the lower Ogooué River in modern Gabon), which American Presbyterians had founded in 1876 and which the Paris Mission had taken over in 1892 (→ Medical Missions). This time "between water and the primeval forest," which Schweitzer movingly described in constantly reissued writings, was less a time of undisturbed, ongoing development of missionary and medical activity than a series of expansions and defeats, not least as a result of his having been interned during World War I. Not until 1924 were renovations on the hospital able to begin again, though even then they were interrupted by the many lecture and concert trips that Schweitzer undertook in order to secure a measure of financial independence from the mission.

Schweitzer was acknowledged internationally for his work by the Nobel Peace Prize in 1952 and many other honors. The emergence of → dialectical theology called his own theological work into question, though by that time he had long been more interested in a personal understanding of what → discipleship to Jesus means. Although Schweitzer has often been criticized for his patriarchal dealings with Africans, the latter themselves hardly perceived that treatment as such. Critics also point out that Schweitzer apparently never really came to terms with traditional African religions and culture, not least because he never learned an African language.

What ultimately kept Schweitzer at his post to the very end (he died in Lambaréné) was probably the idea of a "fellowship of those marked by pain." Schweitzer viewed service to this idea as fulfilling the highest humanitarian obligation, and it was in this spirit that this European physician wanted to do his part in repaying the debt Europeans owed to the Africans (→ Colonialism and Mission). He had no missionary ambitions in the stricter sense; his greatness is probably still that the innermost impulse and the most profound source of energy for his own life was always Jesus' words that "those who lose their life for my sake, and for the sake of the gospel, will save it" (Mark 8:35).

Bibliography: Primary sources: Das Christentum und die Weltreligionen (1924; ET *Christianity and the Religions of the World* [New York, 1923]) lectures in 1922 • *Gesammelte Werke* (5 vols.; ed. R. Grabs; Berlin, 1971) • *J. S. Bach* (2 vols.; 1905; ET London, 1907) • *Kulturphilosophie* (1923; ET *Philosophy of Civilization* [New York, 1950]) • *Die Mystik des Apostels Paulus* (1930; ET *The Mysticism of Paul the Apostle* [New York, 1931]) • *Out of My Life and Thought: An Autobiography* (rev. ed.; trans. A. B. Lemke; New York, 1990) • *Von Reimarus zu Wrede* (1906; ET *The Quest of the Historical Jesus: A*

Critical Study of Its Progress from Reimarus to Wrede [London, 1910]) • *Werke aus dem Nachlaß* (8 vols.; ed. R. Brüllmann et al.; Munich, 1995-).

Secondary works: J. Bentley, *Albert Schweitzer: The Enigma* (New York, 1992) • J. Brabazon, *Albert Schweitzer: A Biography* (2d ed.; Syracuse, N.Y., 2000) • E. Grässer, *Albert Schweitzer als Theologe* (Tübingen, 1979) • N. S. Griffith and L. Person, *Albert Schweitzer: An International Bibliography* (Boston, 1981) • F. Keppler, "Albert Schweitzer," *CKL* 2.918 • N. Merz, *Reich Gottes im theologischen und philosophischen Denken von Albert Schweitzer* (Basel, 1975) • H. Schützeichel, *Die Orgel im Leben und Denken Albert Schweitzers* (Kleinbittersdorf, 1991).

Hans-Werner Gensichen†

Science and Theology

This article covers the historical and conceptual relationships between Western science and Christian thought, especially → theology. As we shall see, these relationships have moved in both directions, with theology providing foundational assumptions for certain key scientists, and scientific discoveries challenging theology to revisit and revise its conclusions on several matters relating to a Christian understanding of the world, especially the doctrine of → creation.

1. Historical Approaches

Differing theories of the relationship between theology and science have also spawned differing approaches to the history of science and Christianity. Of particular import, in terms of its influence upon recent thought, is the conflict model. The most famous and influential works from this perspective were written in the 19th century by John William Draper (1811-82), *History of the Conflict between Religion and Science* (1874); and Andrew Dickson White (1832-1918), *A History of the Warfare of Science with Theology in Christendom* (1896). Both works are historical overviews of the conflict or warfare between science and theology, and both stress the inevitable victory of science, → reason, and the forces of light over the backwater obscurantism of priests and churches — such was their narrow view of the matter. Despite questionable historical reliability and oversimplifications, this conflict model still has powerful intellectual defenders two centuries later (e.g., Richard Dawkins).

On the other side of the spectrum, historians of science have argued that the Christian worldview (and theology) provided the intellectual milieu in which natural science developed, without which we would not have seen the rise of early modern science as we know it. Important versions of this approach have been put forth by A. N. Whitehead (1861-1947), Michael B. Foster (1903-59), Robert K. Merton (1910-2003), Reijer Hooykaas (1906-94), and Stanley Jaki (b. 1924). The problem with both of these approaches comes from interpreting the complex history of natural science and Christian thought in one-sided, all-or-nothing categories.

The realities and specificities of history have been more complicated, leading historians — notably Herbert Butterfield, David Lindberg, Ronald Numbers, and John Headley Brooke — to put forward a "complexity thesis." On this third view, the relationships between theology and science have been too complex for any overarching generalization of either warfare or support to be plausible. This third approach is becoming the standard view among historians of science.

2. Simplicity, Complexity, Modesty

The theses of conflict and harmony have the value of simplicity, but they do not fit with the historical data. While no doubt an improvement on the simpler theories of the past, the complexity thesis has the problem of not being a proper thesis. It does not add to our fund of historical knowledge and puts forward no positive proposal. It is not really a hypothesis but rather the simple observation that things are complex. While the history of science and Christian thought is indeed complex, and no simple hypothesis will fit all the data, it is possible to propose a modest thesis of support between the creational theology of Western religion and the development of natural science in the early modern period, while at the same time recognizing many areas of conflict and even complete independence. We must first look at various elements of these complex phenomena before we can make any headway with even the most modest of generalizations.

Three areas of interaction are especially important to distinguish. There is the most concrete and specific domain, that of the individual biographies and changing perspectives of particular scientists. Here the complexity thesis is particularly valuable. The second area is that of institutions, both scientific ones and Christian religious institutions (including churches and their governing bodies). Finally, there is the history of ideas, with the interaction between creation theologies that are monotheistic (i.e., Jewish, Christian, and Muslim) and the developing philosophies and paradigms of particular scientific disciplines in Europe.

2.1. First, many working scientists, in their own particular perspectives, found support for their scientific endeavors from their theological faith. In other words, many — but by no means all — of the men and women who were instrumental in the development of specific scientific disciplines were in fact believers, finding in their faith an important impetus to scientific exploration. Nicolaus Copernicus (1473-1543), Galileo Galilei (1564-1642), Johannes Kepler (1571-1630), René Descartes (1596-1650), and Isaac Newton (1642-1727) are all examples of this common pattern.

It is equally true that the scientists often felt it necessary to revise their religious beliefs in the light of their scientific discoveries or based upon their scientific assumptions. Galileo, for example, proposed reading portions of the Bible in ways that did not conflict with the new astronomy he was advocating, while Descartes rejected the possibility of → miracles because of his understanding of God's unchanging character as the author of the laws of → nature.

At the same time it is important to note that individual scientists also found conflict between theology and their growing scientific understanding of the world. Charles Darwin (1809-82) is an example of a scientist who came to believe that a scientific worldview is incompatible with traditional theological belief. Despite such examples, for many if not most of the particular natural philosophers or scientists from the Middle Ages to the middle of the 19th century, religious belief of various types provided a larger philosophy of life within which they pursued their scientific endeavors. As a general rule, the various sciences developed historically in the larger context of a Christian → worldview, which included a particular notion of nature as God's creation, ordered by the divine law. As John H. Brooke correctly notes, "In the past, religious beliefs have served as a presupposition of the scientific enterprise. . . . A doctrine of creation could give coherence to scientific endeavor insofar as it implied a dependable order behind the flux of nature" (p. 19; see also C. Kaiser).

2.2. In a second area of interest, the level of institutional history, the relationships between science and religion are much more mixed. The development of natural science (or natural philosophy, as it was once called) has never been a major goal of the Christian church. However, the church has long valued learning and has established institutions to further teaching and learning of all types — but especially → religious instruction. At best we can say that the church has founded schools, colleges, universities, and hospitals where scientists were able to do their work. But the specific work of natural philosophy and natural science has usually been of little concern to church leaders. Many times the institutional church, along with leaders of popular Christian movements, have opposed scientific discoveries and the views of certain scientists. In a few extreme cases, they oppressed or killed the alleged heretics who were seeking to advance human knowledge. The examples of Copernicus, Galileo, and the Scopes trial (1925) in Dayton, Tennessee, are sober reminders that Christian organizations have sometimes opposed scientific inquiry. Fortunately, these examples are few and far between. If we had to make a modest generalization, we could say that many Christian institutions have provided modest support for scientific inquiry, but just as often a kind of benign neglect has been evident on the part of church leadership, while on occasion the organized church has opposed scientific discovery and the freedom of scientists to publish their ideas openly.

The complex history of interaction between science and theology in the West can thus be seen to support a complex conception of their relationships. For institutions, the story is a mixed one, with the → university in particular being an important Christian contribution to the development of natural philosophy and, later, natural science.

2.3. Finally, at the level of worldviews, the specific paradigms of the various sciences arose in the intellectual context of a theological understanding of the natural world as God's creation, ordered by the will of the Creator into reliable structures that could be discovered and predicted. Christian faith often provided a motive for the scientific efforts of many individual scientists, but this was hardly uniform among them all.

3. Historical Developments

The relationships between Christian theology and natural science in the West have been complex, involving numerous interactions over the millennia.

Science and Theology

3.1. *Classical Period*

The roots of Western science reach back through the Middle Ages to the classical period. All of what we now call science started out as philosophy — specifically, natural philosophy. The greatest of the classical natural philosophers was Aristotle (384-322 B.C.; → Aristotelianism), and much of classical and medieval natural philosophy is a development of the Aristotelian tradition, as modified over time. Important contributions have also come from Neoplatonism and → Stoicism, as these schools were integrated into the larger Aristotelian tradition. This integration took place in a long series of commentaries on the scientific works of Aristotle. Natural philosophers would present their own views in commentaries, which interacted not only with Aristotle but with other commentators before them. The scientific revolution of the 17th century both borrowed from and further developed this tradition in natural philosophy.

During the classical period the church was not particularly interested in natural philosophy. → Greek philosophy was important only as a tool to prepare the way for the gospel, and the theologies of Plato and Aristotle were explicitly rejected by the church. In commenting upon the early chapters of Genesis, however, the best theologians also drew upon natural philosophy to provide an integrated understanding of creation. The *Hexameron* of Basil the Great (ca. 330-79), a commentary on the first six days of creation, was the most influential of these works among the Greeks. In the Latin West *On the Literal Interpretation of Genesis,* by → Augustine (354-430), also drew upon natural philosophy in expounding the meaning of Scripture for his time and culture.

For both Basil and Augustine, the → Word of God took priority over the secular learning of natural → philosophy. Nevertheless, the Bible must be understood as the → truth and must be interpreted in a manner consistent with the truth known from any area of study, including the wisdom of natural philosophy, when that field is relevant. For the church in this period, science rightly understood (and placed within its proper limits) was a servant. This view has come to be called the "handmaiden" metaphor, with theology viewed as the queen of the sciences. The church as institution was not particularly interested in promoting scientific study, but it did sometimes use the results of scientific learning. For the most part, however, the church ignored natural philosophy.

The exception to this rule is John Philoponos (ca. 490-570), who stands head and shoulders above any other early Christian thinker as a natural philosopher. Philoponos, a Christian Neoplatonic scholar of → Alexandria and a natural philosopher in his own right, entered fully into the tradition of commenting upon Aristotle, teaching a kind of natural philosophy influenced by his Christian worldview. He argued against the eternity of the world on philosophical grounds and was critical of Aristotle's views on motion. He was an exception to the general rule of Christian scholarship using, rather than adding to, natural philosophy in this period.

3.2. *Middle Ages*

The Middle Ages was a time of consolidation in learning. The church contributed to the continuation of science in three ways. First, → monasteries, schools, and cathedrals were especially important in the West as repositories of the learning of the Greeks and Romans. Under the handmaiden metaphor the learning of the classical period was important to theological reflection, and monks laboriously copied Greek and Latin books over the centuries. Second, the innovation of the medical hospital, which seems to have arisen in the Byzantine Empire, provided an institutional home for the development of medical knowledge and anatomical research, which flowered in the → Renaissance. Third, the foundation of universities in Europe created centers for learning and research, which aided in the development of medieval and Renaissance natural science. This growth was especially helped in the 12th century by the rediscovery of the Aristotelian tradition in the Latin West just as the new universities were being established.

Both Byzantine and Muslim empires developed important areas of science, medicine, and mathematics from the fall of Rome to the rise of Western universities. These disciplines were for the most part carried out in the Aristotelian tradition. This large literature was then translated into Latin and became the basis for natural philosophy in the arts curriculum of the medieval universities.

Two medieval philosophical movements proved important in adapting this Aristotelian tradition to the philosophical framework of early modern science. First, → voluntarism in natural philosophy insisted that the basic principles of nature are not eternal and necessary but rather the free creation of the first cause (God). Second, → nominalism in metaphysics moved natural philosophy away from metaphysical speculation and toward empirical investigation of the world. In addition, some natural philosophers like Thomas Bradwardine of Oxford (ca. 1295-1349) developed a geometric and mathematical description of the natural world, very much

Science and Theology

in debt to Greek and Arabic mathematics. All of these developments in the arts faculties took place in relative isolation from the theology faculties, except for the foundational presupposition of a first cause who was the lawmaker behind the fundamental principles of nature. The handmaiden metaphor allowed for the development of a semi-independent natural philosophy during the medieval period.

3.3. *Reformation Period*

The scientific revolution of the 16th century borrowed from, and fought against, this earlier medieval tradition. While the Middle Ages made the scientific revolution possible, the new methods provided a real break from the past. What did not disappear during this stage was the larger theistic worldview of the scientists. A good example comes from the work of Copernicus himself. A Polish canon and church administrator, Copernicus pursued his work in the service of the → liturgy of the church. There was a need to revise the church calendar, especially the accurate predication of holy days like Easter. Copernicus organized and defended his proposed model of the solar system as providing a more accurate prediction of things like the winter solstice (→ Church Year).

Galileo, however, not Copernicus, is arguably the first significant modern scientist. The earliest developments in modern science took place in astronomy and physics, and Galileo was in the front rank of the scientific revolution in exactly these subjects. He exemplifies the methods of the new science, which would be experimental, empirical, and mathematical. Galileo, however, was also a lifelong Catholic and believed that his discoveries could and should be brought into harmony with the teachings of Scripture. Here he ran into significant problems with the anti-Protestant forces in the → Roman Catholic Church during the Counter-Reformation. The church, so it taught, alone had the right to establish the meaning of Scripture, not individuals like Galileo. The Copernican "heresy" was condemned in 1616, and Galileo himself was later condemned for promoting it after he had promised not to. In condemning its own sons, Galileo and Copernicus, the institutional Roman Catholic Church was in reality condemning its own assumption of power. Here we find fuel for the false claim that the church has always opposed science.

In Protestant lands science fared a bit better. Kepler, a German Lutheran astronomer, was free to publish his theological, philosophical, and scientific speculations without reproof from his church. Kepler was both a mystic and a mathematician. His defense of Copernicus and the new astronomy drew in equal measure upon Christian truth, geometry, and natural philosophy.

3.4. *Enlightenment*

With the success of the natural sciences, a more mechanistic understanding of the natural world arose in the 17th century. Especially important for this new understanding was the work of the French philosopher and mathematician Descartes, who, however, was profoundly theistic in his understanding of the fundamental principles of nature. For him, God is the ultimate source of the material world and of the laws or principles of the natural world. What Descartes excluded was any appeal to God's special action within the natural sciences. Although this mechanistic worldview is sometimes called Newtonian, we should remember that Newton himself was neither a deist nor a materialist but a Christian theist. Newton wrote as much about the Bible as he did about physics and was deeply influenced by his (non-Trinitarian) religious faith in developing his new natural philosophy on mathematical grounds. This larger theistic framework for the development of natural science would soon be challenged.

In fact, the resulting mechanistic picture of nature challenged the common Christian view that particular, specific acts of nature were the special acts of God; rather, the idea of such acts was often dismissed as a superstition. For scientists and philosophers who embraced both the Christian God and the mechanical philosophy, God acted only through the laws and principles of the natural world, including the basic structures of objects and organisms. The influential scientist Robert Boyle (1627-91) is a good example of one who combined a deep → reverence for the Creator with a strong impulse to study creation according to the methods of the natural sciences, that is, keeping supernatural events out of the explanatory focus of natural philosophy. This division in fact goes back to the distinction between natural philosophy and theology in the Middle Ages, but the 17th and 18th centuries saw a new and powerful revival of it.

The challenge to Christian thought in the 18th century in fact came not from science but rather from antichurch and anticlerical forces in the → Enlightenment. The wars of religion between various factions of Christian Europe made the appeal to → tradition and → authority, an appeal necessary to Christian theology, appear to be absurd. Reason and science were the new substitutes for divine → revelation. It is not science itself but the appeal made to science, nature, and reason by Enlightenment thinkers that resulted in new worldviews that were at odds with historic Christianity.

Science and Theology

The deist movement, which began in England, appealed to reason, science, and nature as superior sources of religious insight. During the 18th century → deism was popular among philosophers, less so among working scientists. Benjamin Franklin (1706-90) is a good example of a scientist who was also a deist. In France it was easy for scientists and philosophers in the Cartesian tradition, such as the Baron d'Holbach (1723-89), to propose a completely materialistic system, which he did in his *System of Nature* (1770), which dispensed with God altogether. By eliminating God from the explanations of science, scientists in this materialist tradition thought they were also eliminating God. In this way the work of the mathematician and astronomer Pierre-Simon de Laplace (1749-1827) was also theologically motivated. He promoted his atheistic materialistic philosophy under the guise of science.

3.5. *Modern Period*

The late 18th and 19th centuries saw a tug-of-war between those who thought both science and reason in general were opposed to Christian faith and those who sought to use science and reason in defense of that same faith. Thomas Huxley (1825-95) and Sigmund Freud (1859-1939) belong to the first group. Huxley was a popular defender of Darwin, who felt that → evolution was incompatible with traditional religion. He coined the term "agnostic" to describe his lack of faith in God. Freud's explanation of religion simply assumed that a scientific worldview makes theology false. God could be nothing more than the psychological projection of our need for a father figure (→ Religion, Criticism of).

The second group included a tradition of British → "natural theology," which sought to demonstrate the wisdom of divine providence in the creation of organisms. William Paley (1743-1805) was the best known, and his book *Natural Theology* (1802) was required reading for those entering Cambridge University. Darwin, the son of a liberal Anglican minister, first encountered biological science in this explicitly Christian context. His theory of biological evolution soon undermined the natural theology he was raised on, since the apparent design of a biological organism could now be subsumed under the larger umbrella of the mechanistic forces of nature. There seemed to be little left for God to do.

Yet specifically Christian opposition to Darwinian evolution (as opposed to its scientific critique) hardly occurred in the 19th century. For the most part, biologists and geologists of faith were able to accommodate long geological ages and some form of organic evolution (often in a version different from Darwin's) in their Christian worldview. Indeed, the most important defender of Darwin in America, Asa Gray (1810-88) of Harvard University, was an explicitly Christian scholar who wrote letters and essays, including to Darwin himself, about the religious implications of evolution. Darwin himself struggled with a continued belief in the providence of God, a struggle brought about by personal suffering in his own family and by the larger problem of death and mutation necessary to the theory of his *Origin of Species* (1859).

God was gradually pushed out of the explanatory scheme of natural science in the modern period. The growing specialization and professionalism of the sciences meant that the theological framework that gave birth to early modern science could now be dispensed with. The sciences were their own justification for the specific mode of rationality and domain of inquiry they perpetuated. God did not enter into the paradigms of the sciences. Particular scientists could be religious or not, depending upon their own larger philosophies of life, but this choice did not affect their discipline. Still, some Christian believers who embraced the new evolutionary theory could welcome this development. In the words of Aubrey Moore of Oxford (1848-90), writing in the celebrated collection of theological essays → *Lux Mundi* (1889), biological evolution forced God to be everywhere, or nowhere, in the natural world. What modern science could not allow was a God who was "an occasional visitor." This mediating position was soon to be tested.

4. Recent Developments

4.1. Following World War I and the end of the era of optimism in Europe, three theological movements arose out of the trenches: two were the old → liberal or modernist theology and the new → fundamentalism that arose against it in the United States. The third theological movement was European in origin and more existentialist: → dialectical theology, or "neoorthodoxy," as it was sometimes called, whose chief proponent was Karl → Barth (1886-1968).

Liberal theologians like Aubrey Moore were willing to accommodate Darwinism and divinity. Even the earliest fundamentalists of the first decades of the 20th century were willing to accept some form of evolution. But as the conflict between → modernism and fundamentalism heated up, the literal interpretation of Genesis (and Revelation) became increasingly important to the popular leaders of fundamentalism. Before the end of the 1920s more than 20 state legislatures in the United States debated anti-Darwinist legislation in respect to public

Science and Theology

school curricula. The fundamentalist-modernist conflict thus moved from the churches to the schools. Once again institutional Christian forces (this time the popular fundamentalist movement) sought to oppose the freedom of scientific inquiry.

To be fair, the fundamentalists did not think of Darwinism as a legitimate science; their primary motivation was clearly biblical rather than scientific. In 1925 in Dayton, Tennessee, at the infamous "Scopes Monkey Trial," the anti-Darwinian legislation was put to the test in a kind of nationwide publicity stunt. Conservative Protestants have continued to oppose organic evolution on religious and scientific grounds ever since. Even those who are young-earth creationists, however, accept other areas of natural science as valid and important sources of knowledge.

Unlike liberals and fundamentalists, the new dialectical theologians were decidedly uninterested in science. Barth's famous rejection of any and all natural theology led to a growing distrust of any attempt to bring science or philosophy into some sort of harmony with the revelation of God in Jesus Christ. Because of its basis in the Word of God, the neoorthodox emphasized the independence of theology from other domains of human knowledge.

4.2. Liberals who sought to bring together theology and science into a larger understanding of the world were often influenced in this period by process metaphysics (→ Process Philosophy). An important figure in this school was the French priest and paleontologist Pierre Teilhard de Chardin (1881-1955), who blended evolution, cosmology, and Christology into an evolutionary theology that brought him into conflict with his → Jesuit superiors. The philosopher Whitehead, the major influence in American process thought, appealed to liberals because he provided a rational way to bring God, philosophy, and science into harmony (→ Process Theology).

The history of the complex interactions between science and theology do not admit of any simple model. In the modern period the institutional support of the church was no longer needed for the development of science. The theological presuppositions that had made science possible in the early modern period were abandoned in favor of a common faith in the sciences as such, propounded by the professional guilds. Individual scientists could continue to find theology important and true, but it was not necessary for their specialization per se. Science and theology became independent intellectual disciplines.

4.3. The single most important work to challenge this status quo at midcentury was neither religious nor scientific. Rather, it was Thomas Kuhn's *Structure of Scientific Revolutions* (1962), a revolutionary work in the → philosophy of science. Drawing on the work of philosophers and historians of science, Kuhn (1922-96) argued that changes in natural science were not based on facts and logic alone. Science was also based on tradition and on "paradigms" of shared values, rationalities, and perspectives that gave shape to each of the scientific disciplines. Science was thus based upon epistemic values and metaphysical presuppositions that it owned but could not justify. Far from being a complete worldview, science depended upon these larger perspectives for the working assumptions by which it did its work. This perspective brought science into closer contact with philosophy and religion. This → postmodern turn in the understanding of science allowed room for a Christian theological worldview once again to enter into dialogue with science.

5. Contemporary Proposals

In the latter decades of the 20th century, one sign of a postmodern turn in the larger Western culture was the desire to bring science, → morality, and → spirituality into closer conversation. Natural science was not seen as a hermetically sealed-off realm of logic and facts but rather as another human, communal, and historical quest for understanding. As such, science could be brought into dialogue with religion. A remarkable resurgence of interest in dialogue between science and religion has been the result. Books, conferences, societies, and even professorial chairs were devoted to this new dialogue.

Prominent among those pressing for greater interaction between science and theology have been scientists who themselves have begun to explore theological issues. The idea of a natural scientist turning to theology for answers captured the popular imagination, as well as the funding dollars of Sir John Templeton (b. 1912). Physicists like Ian Barbour (b. 1923) and John Polkinghorne (b. 1930) and biologists like Arthur Peacocke (b. 1924) and Theodosius Dobzhansky (1900-1975) brought their scientific background and knowledge into the theological conversation, to the enrichment of both.

The current literature contains numerous proposals about how theology and science should interrelate. These views should not be confused with descriptive analyses of how science and theology have in fact related. We can sample only five of these proposals here, in a brief typology of views.

Science falsifies theology. The popular science writer Richard Dawkins, known for his compelling presentation of biological evolution, exemplifies this atheistic position.

Scientific explanation needs theological completion. The recent attempt by "intelligent design" author Michael Behe to insert direct intelligent design into the explanatory scheme of biology is an example of the view that science cannot explain all regularly occurring natural phenomena. The door is open for God to reenter the natural sciences as an explanation of particular events.

Science and theology are independent. The prominence of both linguistic philosophy and neoorthodox theology makes this option a popular one among mainstream theologians. It was recently given a boost by the influential evolutionary biologist Stephen Jay Gould (1941-2002) in his argument for a principle of "nonoverlapping magisteria," (NOMA) regarding religion and science.

Science and theology need to be in dialogue. Theology and science, as intellectual traditions and academic disciplines, do have something to say to each other in this model, but no attempt is made to bring a larger unity or consistent worldview to bear on their differences. Each is allowed to be in conversation, yet remain independent. A good example of this position is the work of psychologist Fraser Watts, a lecturer in theology and science at Cambridge University, who argues for complementarity between theology and science. Also in this general type would be the Scottish theologian Thomas F. Torrance, who brought the theme of natural theology back into the Barthian theological tradition.

Science and theology should move toward integration. This type of proposal suggests that theology and science should be brought into a larger harmony at a philosophical or interdisciplinary level. The notion of integration would bring them both into a harmonious metaphysical synthesis, while the less ambitious models of mutuality or interdisciplinarity allow theology and the special sciences to mutually influence each other in the quest for truth while remaining distinct. A good example of one favoring the integration position is Ian Barbour, while interdisciplinary and postfoundational rationality are being championed by J. Wentzel Van Huyssteen, a professor of theology and science at Princeton Theological Seminary.

Which of these proposals, if any, will influence the coming new century has yet to be seen. What is clear is that a great diversity of views will continue to be proposed by theologians and scientists interested in the interaction of their disciplines. The strong interest and growing literature in science and theology show no sign of abatement in the near future. Such a trend bodes well for those interested in continuing the dialogue between science and theology.

Bibliography: I. Barbour, *Religion and Science* (San Francisco, 1997) • M. J. Behe, W. A. Dembski, and S. C. Meyer, eds., *Science and Evidence for Design in the Universe* (San Francisco, 2000) • J. H. Brooke, *Science and Religion* (Cambridge, 1991) • J. Brooke, M. Osler, and J. van der Meer, eds., *Science in Theistic Contexts* (Chicago, 2001) • H. Butterfield, *The Origins of Modern Science, 1300-1800* (New York, 1965) • R. Dawkins, *River out of Eden* (New York, 1996) • G. Ferngren, ed., *The History of Science and Religion in the Western Tradition: An Encyclopedia* (New York, 2000) • S. Gould, *Rocks of Ages: Science and Religion in the Fullness of Life* (New York, 1999) • E. Grant, *The Foundations of Modern Science in the Middle Ages* (Cambridge, 1996); idem, *God and Reason in the Middle Ages* (Cambridge, 2001) • C. Kaiser, *Creational Theology and the History of Physical Science* (Leiden, 1997) • D. Lindberg, *The Beginnings of Western Science* (Chicago, 1992) • D. Lindberg and R. Numbers, eds., *God and Nature* (Berkeley, Calif., 1986); idem, eds., *When Science and Christianity Meet* (Chicago, 2003) • D. N. Livingstone, *Darwin's Forgotten Defenders* (Grand Rapids, 1987); idem, *Putting Science in Its Place* (Chicago, 2003) • D. N. Livingstone, D. G. Hart, and M. A. Noll, eds., *Evangelicals and Science in Historical Perspective* (New York, 1999) • J. Moore, *Post-Darwinian Controversies* (Cambridge, 1979) • A. Padgett, *Science and the Study of God: A Mutuality Model for Theology and Science* (Grand Rapids, 2003) • A. R. Peacocke, *Theology for a Scientific Age* (Minneapolis, 1993) • A. R. Peacocke, ed., *The Sciences and Theology in the Twentieth Century* (Notre Dame, Ind., 1981) • J. Polkinghorne, *Scientists as Theologians* (London, 1996) • M. Stenmark, *How to Relate Science and Religion* (Grand Rapids, 2004) • T. Torrance, *Theological Science* (Oxford, 1969) • W. Van Huyssteen, *The Shaping of Rationality: Toward Interdisciplinarity in Theology and Science* (Grand Rapids, 1999); idem, ed., *Encyclopedia of Science and Religion* (2 vols.; New York, 2002) • F. Watts, ed., *Science Meets Faith* (London, 1998) • A. N. Whitehead, *Science and the Modern World* (New York, 1925).

Alan G. Padgett

Scientology → Church of Scientology

Scotism

1. Duns Scotus
    1.1. Theology, Metaphysics, and Religious Language
    1.2. God's Existence and Nature
    1.3. Individuation, Universals, and the Trinity

1. Duns Scotus

It is generally thought that the Franciscan John Duns Scotus (ca. 1265-1308) was born either in December 1265 or sometime before March 1266 in the small Scottish village of Duns, just north of the border from England. Scotus was ordained in Northampton in 1291, indicating that he was probably studying in Oxford at this time. He remained in Oxford until perhaps 1301, during which time he began the composition of his questions on various logical and metaphysical works of Aristotle (→ Aristotelianism). As part of their training for the professorship, theology bachelors were required to lecture on the four books of the *Sentences* of Peter Lombard (ca. 1100-1160). We know that Scotus was busy revising the earliest portion of his lectures in or very shortly after 1300, which suggests that he lectured on the *Sentences* during the academic year 1298-99. Two books of this early *Lectura* survive, and the series formed the basis for Scotus's ongoing revision of his lectures for publication — the so-called *Ordinatio.*

Scotus was sent to Paris in about 1301, where he began again to lecture on the *Sentences* in order qualify for a chair in theology at that university. The work survives as a set of examined student notes — the *Reportatio* — and Scotus became regent master in theology at Paris in 1305. From this period date Scotus's *Quodlibetal Questions:* a series of disputed questions originating in the lecture hall on issues raised "on anything by anyone" *(de quolibet a quolibet),* a standard academic exercise held by a regent master during Advent and Lent in the university calendar. In 1307 Scotus was moved to Cologne to teach at the Franciscan house of studies there. He died there the next year, traditionally held to be on November 8, 1308, with most of his works extant only in more or less complete drafts. Scotus was beatified in 1993.

What most distinguishes theology in the 13th and 14th centuries from preceding centuries is the massive and pervasive influence of the newly recovered works of Aristotle. Aristotle's vision of the universe was far less speculative, and philosophically far more sophisticated, than any of the rival theories known at the time. Scotus embraced Aristotle's thought enthusiastically, while feeling free to modify it where necessary, whether for theological or for philosophical reasons. Augustine (→ Augustine's Theology), though, was as important as Aristotle in the formation of Scotus's theological system, and other significant influences include the great Muslim philosopher Avicenna (980-1037; → Islamic Philosophy 4.3) and Anselm of Canterbury (1033-1109). In terms of detailed theological discussion, Scotus's theology engages most deeply with the thought of his immediate predecessors from the 1280s and 1290s, → Franciscans such as Richard of Middleton (ca. 1249-?1302) and William of Ware (fl. 1270-1300), the Augustinian friar Giles of Rome (ca. 1245-1316), and secular theologians such as Godfrey of Fontaines (before 1250–after 1305) and, preeminently, Henry of Ghent (ca. 1217-93). Scotus refers only occasionally to the Dominican Thomas Aquinas (ca. 1225-74), and somewhat more frequently to Aquinas's great Franciscan contemporary Bonaventure (ca. 1217-74).

1.1. *Theology, Metaphysics, and Religious Language*

Scotus holds that → theology is a science in something like the sense proposed by Aristotle, namely, an explanatory deductive system deriving theorems from necessarily true → axioms. The subject of the science is the → God of revealed theology: specifically, God's unique Trinitarian essence. In line with the usual Franciscan position, Scotus holds that theology is a practical science, one whose aim is to issue in praxis — in this case, disposing the theologian to love God.

Theology is complemented by the theoretical, nonrevealed science of → metaphysics. The existence and nature of the one God can be shown by natural → reason and is the object of the science of metaphysics, or the study of being and the other "transcendental" concepts (unity, truth, goodness, all of which are coextensive with being; as well as the pure perfections — attributes that it is simply better to have than not to have; and disjunctive attributes such as "necessary-or-contingent," "cause-or-caused"). Scotus holds that both the coextensive → transcendentals and the disjunctive transcendentals are predicable of everything that there is. He thus attempts to reduce all knowledge to a set of simple, nonoverlapping, nondefinable concepts. In this respect he is the originator of the rationalist tradition of philosophy, exemplified by later thinkers such as G. W. Leibniz.

Each of these concepts, as predicated of different classes of things, is said to be univocal, which is to say that the same concept is predicated in each case. Scotus argues that if this were not so, then it would not be possible for either theology or metaphysics to be scientific, since scientific argument requires unambiguous concepts for its validity, and disambiguation is achieved by securing univocity. Scotus's warrant for this position is traditional: he holds that sound deductive arguments can be found in the → church fathers and that a necessary condition for such argumentation is univocity. Scotus uses his theory of univocity to construct an account of → analogy: analogous concepts are complexes of other concepts, at least one of which must be univocal. These various concepts are derived by abstraction from sense data, thus placing Scotus in the radically empiricist tradition of Aristotelian thinkers in the → Middle Ages.

1.2. *God's Existence and Nature*

Scotus's proof for God's existence aims to satisfy as many of Aristotle's criteria for a scientific proof as possible (→ God, Arguments for the Existence of). The key requirement is that the premises must be necessary. Scotus's premise for his argument is "Some producible nature exists." What Scotus means is that there is a nature ("being producible") that, given the causal constitution of the actual world, can be exemplified (because some things are in fact produced). Scotus considers this premise to be necessary in the sense that, given the causal constitution of the actual world, it cannot fail to be true. The premise immediately implies "Some nature able to produce exists" — that is, the nature *being able to produce* can be exemplified. This statement in turn implies "Some first nature, able to produce, exists" — by which Scotus means that the nature *being a first thing able to produce* can be exemplified. According to Scotus, this conclusion is entailed by the second on the grounds that an infinite regress of causes is impossible (a claim for which Scotus argues on merely conceptual grounds).

The next step in the argument aims to show that this nature is in fact exemplified: thus, "Something first, able to produce, exists." Scotus makes this next step by drawing on the argument's assumption that something is possible if and only if all the causal conditions in the real world for its existence are satisfied. Possibility on this view is tied to causal powers, and if something is possible, then whatever the relevant causal explanation, that explanation must be real (if it were not real, the explanandum would not be possible: its very possibility is tied to the existence of a real explanation). Any first efficient cause is really possible, and its explanation is intrinsic to itself. Some such efficient cause must, then, be real, otherwise there would be no explanation for any causal relations lower down the causal chain (→ Causality). Scotus argues similarly for the existence of a final goal of activity, and for a maximally excellent being.

This argument is located at something of a distance from Aristotelian arguments to an unmoved mover: the argument that, since there is motion, and since both self-motion and an infinite regress of movers are impossible, there must be an unmoved first mover. Scotus, on the contrary, believes there is nothing contradictory about the notion of self-motion: something can certainly have the power to move itself or to change itself in various ways. All it needs is the possession both of the relevant active power and of the relevant passive capacity.

Scotus goes on to derive the intelligence, infinity, simplicity, unicity, and immutability of the first being. Central are infinity and simplicity. Scotus understands God's simplicity in a quasi-mathematical manner: infinity is an intrinsic mode of God's attributes, and it is to be grasped by imagining an infinitely extended magnitude and then removing from this magnitude the imperfection of divisibility (into parts less than the whole). Scotus thus in this context rejects Aristotle's claim that an actual infinity is impossible. Infinity entails simplicity, since the infinite cannot be perfected by features other than itself.

Scotus's understanding of simplicity is at something of a distance from earlier medieval accounts, however. Scotus holds that his univocity theory — coupled with the insight that certain qualitative perfections (such as wisdom and goodness) are real constituents of things in the universe — entails that there is also some sort of distinction between the various divine attributes. This distinction is the so-called formal distinction, different from a real distinction in the sense that real distinction obtains between really separable things, whereas the formal distinction obtains between inseparable constituents of a thing — constituents that Scotus sometimes labels "formalities." Such constituents are typically the essential or necessary attributes of some one thing. Since the constituents are constituents of one thing, they are really identical with each other; this real → identity somehow explains the unity of the thing constituted by the formalities.

Scotus holds that qualitative perfections of creatures are real constituents of these creatures. He also holds the same thing about quantities, such that, when people see a substance, they primarily see its color and shape. Color (quality) and shape (quantity) must therefore be themselves real things. This position makes it relatively easy for Scotus to defend the coherence of the eucharistic doctrine of transubstantiation, maintaining that the thing that is the quantity of the bread can exist as quantity, even if the bread is no longer present. For all this, Scotus would, if strictly philosophical grounds were the only relevant considerations, prefer the doctrine of consubstantiation, since he believes that Christ's presence in the → Eucharist is a case both of that body's bilocation (in heaven and in the Eucharist) and of that body's existence in the same place as some other body (the quantity of the bread). But these conditions could be satisfied just as well if Christ's body were to exist in the same place as another substance (i.e., the substance of the bread). The falsity of consubstantiation, according to Scotus, is thus established not on any philosophical grounds, but rather because transubstantiation was taught by the church at Lateran IV in 1215.

1.3. ***Individuation, Universals, and the Trinity*** Scotus makes use of his formal distinction in a variety of contexts. One of the most important is that of his theories of universals and individuation. Scotus maintains that in order to explain individuation, it is necessary to posit completely nonqualitative "haecceities" (from Lat. *haec,* "this [fem.]"), or "thisnesses." Scotus accepts two different theories about universals, one applicable uniquely in the case of the → Trinity, and one applicable in the case of creatures. What distinguishes the two theories is that the universal divine essence is *indivisible* — numerically singular, and thus numerically identical in each of its exemplifications — whereas all other common essences are *divisible,* and thus identical in each instance of it in some nonnumerical way. (The origins of this teaching are found in Avicenna.)

Scotus accepts that such essences are real on the grounds that relations of similarity between two particulars cannot be self-explanatory; they must have some real explanation in the things that are similar. And this is the (divisible) essence or common nature. Particular substances are not divisible, and this indivisibility requires explanation. The explanation must be something in itself irreducibly indivisible. But anything qualitative ("quidditative" in the technical medieval vocabulary) is shareable and thus divisible in the required sense. Human nature, for example, is divisible into many human beings. So the explanation must lie in something nonquidditative, and the only candidate, according to Scotus, is a thisness, or haecceity. The nature and the haecceity in any given substance are formally distinct: real, but inseparable, and neither is in itself anything like a substance; indeed, each is more like a property of a thing than a thing (each is a formality). In line with this view, Scotus holds that a thing's nature (the common nature in the particular thing) and its haecceity are really identical, and that this relation of real identity is what ties nature and haecceity together.

Scotus makes use of the formal distinction in the theological context of the doctrine of the Trinity. He believes that each divine person's personal property — the property that he does not share with the other persons (paternity, filiation, passive spiration) — is formally distinct from the divine essence, and that each person thus includes two formally distinct constituents: the essence and his personal property. Each person is really distinct from each other person; the unity of essence is in effect understood as the overlap of the persons. Scotus believes that the infinity of the divine essence guarantees its numerical singularity: there cannot be more than one properly infinite thing, and there is a sense in which the persons are infinite only derivatively, as a consequence of the proper infinity of the divine essence.

Scotus's realist understanding of the personal properties has theological consequences. He believes it is true, but not necessary to guarantee unity of the divine essence, that the personal properties are relations of origin (quasi-causal relations between the persons); they could from a philosophical point of view just as well be nonrelational features akin to haecceities. And he believes that each relation is different in kind from each other, such that Son and Spirit are sufficiently distinguished by their relations to the Father irrespective of any relation of origin that exists between Son and Spirit. This means that Scotus rejects the standard Anselmian-Thomist argument in favor of the → *filioque,* namely that the derivation of the Spirit from the Son is necessary for the distinction of Son and Spirit. Scotus argues instead that the Spirit must proceed from the Son on the grounds that the Son possesses, logically prior to the spiration of the Spirit, the power to spirate the Spirit. Since this power is numerically the same in Father and Son, if the Father spirates the Spirit, the Son does too. Underlying this view is an assumption, accepted by Scotus's opponents, that the powers to generate and spirate are possessed by the persons in virtue of their possession of the divine essence, and not of their personal properties.

The divine essence on this view is a numerically singular substance. What prevents it from being a person is the fact that it is possessed by things that are persons: it is exemplified by these persons. Persons are things that are not (and in some sense cannot be) themselves exemplified — the technical term is "communicated." Scotus uses this insight to show why the individual human nature of Christ is not a person: it is communicated to (exemplified by) the second person of the Trinity and thus, like the divine essence, fails to be a person.

1.4. *Freedom and Morality*

Scotus's proof for God's existence relies on an understanding of necessity and possibility that is causal, making these notions parasitic on the constitution of the actual world — something that he inherited from Aristotle. When developing an account of the → freedom of the will, however, Scotus comes up with the modern notion of logical possibility, relying on nothing more than the notion of formal compatibility (thus giving something like the notion of a possible world, doubtless occurring in Leibniz as the result of his reading of later Scotist writers).

One of the places where Scotus makes use of his new "logical" account of modalities is in his attempt to prove that the first cause must have both intellect and will. As he sees it, the existence of contingency in the world requires that the first cause be able to cause contingently — in a nondeterministic way. The reason is that God is the primary cause of every creaturely action; thus if God caused deterministically, no creaturely activity would be contingent.

Scotus offers an introspective proof of creaturely freedom, claiming that we know by experience that we could, in precisely the same circumstances as those in which we acted in one way, have acted instead in a different way. According to Scotus, sustaining this account of freedom requires modalities understood in terms of formal compatibility: several alternative and incompatible states of affairs can be considered with respect to one and the same time, such that the only constraint on the contents of each state of affairs is internal consistency. Scotus uses this synchronic account of modality in his development of a notion of freedom, most clearly found in the (late) final book of the *Metaphysics* questions. According to this account, a free power is "not determined of itself, but can cause this act or the opposite act, and act or not act" in the selfsame circumstances. These features entail, for Scotus, that a free power can "determine itself" in both ways (i.e., both to act rather than not act, and to act in one way rather than another). This account of freedom requires the notion of synchronic contingency, since it requires the notion of real alternatives at the same time. Furthermore, this understanding of alternative possibilities, according to Scotus, entails the notion of freedom. The reason is tied in with Scotus's residual Aristotelianism on the question of modalities. Scotus believes that positing the existence of something both contingent and uncaused would generate a formal contradiction. So *real* contingency — contingency in the real world, as Scotus believed to be observable — requires a real free power.

This account of freedom raises problems for Scotus's account of divine knowledge of free creaturely actions. For according to Scotus, God knows these contingent facts by willing them, and it is hard to see how this willing can guarantee knowledge unless creatures are irresistibly moved by God's will. The account of freedom raises a related problem for Scotus's fundamentally Augustinian view of → predestination. Scotus believes that God gives sufficient → grace to those he predestines for → salvation, and refrains from so doing for those whose own bad actions will damn them. But grace is supposed, among other things, to guarantee morally good actions. And it is hard to see how this position is compatible with the account of freedom Scotus develops. When dealing with the impeccability of the saints in heaven, Scotus in effect allows that God removes any opportunity for (mortal) → sin; perhaps he could argue similarly for the predestined.

This radical account of freedom is applied by Scotus to the case of God too. This position has an interesting consequence for morality when coupled with the general medieval acceptance of the wholly unconditioned nature of God. Nothing external to God can affect God's choices. So while God's own nature is such that it is intrinsically lovable, no other nature is such. This means that while the precepts of the first table of the → Decalogue are natural, and could not be other than they are, the precepts of the second table are the result merely of divine command. If the second table belonged to → natural law, then given God's independence of creatures, he could act morally badly. But God cannot act badly, so the second table cannot belong to natural law but must instead be the result of divine command.

God's freedom does not mean, however, that he is wholly lacking in constraints. His goodness requires that his willing is well ordered: he must choose the goal before the means, and his willing cannot be dependent on things external to him. This means that God's contingent decision to become incarnate must be made prior to his knowledge of the fall of Adam, and prior to his will to save human beings (→ Incarnation). Equally, given that he has decided to save people by Christ's merits, his so doing must involve at least one instance of the most perfect form of so doing. Preserving someone from original sin — paying the debt that would have been incurred had payment not been made — is the most perfect way for someone to be saved by Christ's merits. Such views led Scotus to embrace the doctrine of the immaculate conception of Mary, of which he became one of the earliest, and most influential, defenders (→ Mariology 1.3).

2. Scotus's Followers

2.1. *History*

Roughly speaking, Scotism is a doctrinal trend whose origins are found in the teachings of Duns Scotus. In the century after Scotus's death it would be anachronistic to speak of a Scotist "school." Nevertheless, it is possible to identify thinkers who took their intellectual lead in some way from the teachings of Scotus, and who made use of many of the distinctive philosophical positions developed by him: in particular, who accepted some version of the so-called formal distinction, a distinction between the inseparable properties of some one and the same substance, and who accepted that one substance is distinguished from another by a nonqualitative feature, known as a haecceity, or thisness, proper to the substance (see 1.3).

In the first century following his death, significant Scotists include his pupil and earliest editor, William of Alnwick (ca. 1275-1333), as well as Hugh of Newcastle (fl. ca. 1315), Francis of Meyronnes (d. after 1328), Antonius Andreas (d. ca. 1330), Peter Thomae (d. ca. 1340), Francis of Marchia (d. after 1344), Peter of Navarre (d. 1347), Landulf Carraciolo (d. 1351), Nicolas Bonetus (d. 1343/60), John of Ripa (fl. ca. 1350), and Peter of Aquila (d. 1361). These thinkers defended Scotist theses against the attacks of scholars more influenced by Peter Auriol (ca. 1280-1322) and especially William of Ockham (ca. 1285-1347).

The 15th century saw the beginnings of more formalized philosophical divisions in the arts faculties, especially of German universities, with faculties appointing specialists in the → logic of Albertus Magnus (ca. 1200-1280), Thomas Aquinas (ca. 1225-74), Duns Scotus (the *via antiqua,* divided respectively into the *via Alberti,* the *via Thomae,* and the *via Scoti*), and William of Ockham (the *via moderna*). The logic of the *via Scoti* is notable for allowing the formal distinction to affect the rules of admissible inferences, for example, in accepting the invalidity of certain counterpossible arguments (arguments that have an impossible premise, such as "God is not a Trinity" or "man is not rational").

By the end of the 16th century, there were Scotist chairs outside Germany too, at the universities of Paris, Lyons, Salamanca, Alcalá, Coimbra, Rome, Padua, Budapest, and Cracow. The spread of Scotus's popularity was helped by the printing press, and throughout the period from the 16th to the 18th century there were many printings both of the texts of Scotus and of commentaries on it, beginning with P. Tartaretus (d. 1509/13) and A. Trombetta (1436-1517). The Franciscans named Scotus "doctor of the order" in 1593, and in 1633 the head of the Franciscans set up at Toledo a *cursus philosophicus* compulsory for all observants and conventuals. A flood of writings followed, including especially the *cursus* of the Italians B. Mastrius (1602-73) and B. Bellutus (1600-76), the Irish J. Poncius (1603-72/3), and the French C. Frassen (1620-1711). Frassen, and later Hieronymus de Montefortino (1662-1738), stressed the distinction from → Thomism, in opposition to the Belgian William of Sichem (d. 1691).

Under the direction of L. Wadding (1588-1657), mostly Irish Franciscans from St. Isidore College at Rome edited the *Opera omnia* of Scotus (Lyons, 1639), with excellent commentaries (Mauritius de Portu Fildaeo [Maurice O'Fihely, ca. 1460-1513], F. Lychetus [Lichetto, d. 1520], F. de Pitigianis Aretinus [d. 1616], H. Cavellus [MacCaughwell, 1571-1626], A. Hiquaeus [Hickey, d. 1641], and Poncius) and some inauthentic material. One commentator remarked that in the 17th century the school of Scotus attracted more followers than those of all other schools taken together. Directly or indirectly, Scotism made its impact upon the teaching of philosophy in Germany as well, in C. Scheibler, the "Protestant Suárez" (1589-1653), and G. W. Leibniz (1646-1716). The Iberian Jesuits F. Suárez (1548-1617), P. Fonseca (1528-99), and P. Hurtado de Mendoza (d. 1651) adopted a more eclectic style, fundamentally following the thought of Aquinas but incorporating important elements from Scotus when they felt it philosophically necessary.

With the final eclipse of → Scholasticism during the 18th century, Scotism as a philosophical tendency died, never to be revived — in contrast to Thomism after the official church endorsement in Leo XIII's *Aeterni Patris* (1879). Unlike Aquinas, Scotus has not had the disadvantage of uncritical acceptance and thus has not been the victim of intellectual fashion in the way that his more famous predecessor has. Nevertheless, Scotus's influence on later philosophy was decisive. Like all medieval Aristotelians, he was a convinced empiricist in → epistemology, and one modern commentator has argued that Scotus's theory was the first to allow a purely naturalistic account of cognition, without appeal to any mechanism directly requiring God's existence. This step marks a decisive turn to the → empiricism of the 17th and 18th centuries. Scotus's belief that knowledge can be reduced to a series of nonoverlapping, irreducible simple concepts — though not his belief that such concepts are gained by abstraction — marks him as the direct originator of the rationalist tradition in philosophy.

Evidence of Scotus's influence can be found in C. S. Peirce (1839-1914), though not as was once thought in M. Heidegger (1889-1976), and there has been a lively, if critical, revival in serious Scotus studies over the past half-century. Theologically, Scotus's distinctive positions relate on the whole to very technical questions to which the tradition is unlikely to want to find decisive answers. But his defense of the immaculate conception of Mary was significant in the final declaration of the dogma by Pius IX in 1854. Outside academic circles, Scotus's most insistent and well-known admirer has been the poet G. M. Hopkins (1844-89).

2.2. *Philosophy*

Among the earliest Scotists, one of the key areas of dispute was the precise status of the haecceity. William of Alnwick, the foremost of Scotus's students working through the second decade of the 14th century, held at least two different positions, neither the same as Scotus's. In an early disputed question on individuation, William held that natures are individual of themselves; later, in his *Ordinatio* on the *Sentences,* William accepted something akin to Henry of Ghent's position that individuation is by a negation, though adding the clarification that this negation nevertheless represents a perfection. In both works William objected to Scotus's view that the common nature is somehow prior to its instantiations, on the grounds that this priority entails that the common nature could exist without any of its instantiations. A position not dissimilar to William's earlier nominalist view can be found in another prominent early student of Scotus's, Henry of Harclay (ca. 1270-1317).

A more orthodox Scotist view was taken by Francis of Meyronnes, writing his commentary on the *Sentences* around 1320. Even Francis, however, diverged in key respects from Scotus. He accepted the theory of the nonnumerical unity of common natures, as well as the claim that individuation is by haecceity. But he held that formal distinction obtains only between things that have some sort of quidditative content. Haecceities have no such quidditative content, and thus cannot be formally distinct from their nature. Rather, a haecceity is *modally* distinct from its nature. A haecceity does not affect a thing's kind; it is thus an intrinsic mode of the thing.

Among baroque scholastics, the most notable adherent of haecceities was the Portuguese Jesuit Pedro da Fonseca (1528-99). Against the Italian Thomist Cajetan (1480-1547), Fonseca argued that haecceities can be similar to each other (as individuators) without this requiring that they have anything real in common. Fonseca was convinced of the reality of haecceities because he accepted the view that common natures have in themselves a certain sort of unity prior to instantiation, although — more like Aquinas than Scotus — he did not believe the nature as such to have any sort of real existence other than as instantiated.

A further area of dispute among Scotists of the 16th century onward lay in the scope of the concept of being: whether there is a univocal concept of being that is predicable of concepts as well as of real things (→ Ontology). Most Scotists — for example, Tartaretus, Mastrius, Bellutus, Frassen, the Jesuit G. Vázquez (1549-1604), the Roman Catholic Suárez, and the Protestant Scheibler — have denied this, appealing to the *Reportatio Paris* I, dist. 29, q. 1. But Mastrius and Bellutus tell us that the early Scotist Bonetus favored a univocal concept. Similarly, Fonseca and Hurtado de Mendoza regarded the concept of being in a comprehensive, univocal, and wholly abstract sense as the proper theme of metaphysics, a concept embracing not only everything real (in the sense of the possible) but also objects of thought, not only everything positive but also what is negative. The mainstream of Scotist tradition, then, views being as the first transcendental and pervasive determination that enables an entity to have actual extramental being, so that metaphysics is the limited science of real being *(ens reale).* A smaller group of Scotists, however, views being, to use the term already found in Spanish Scholasticism, as a supratranscendental concept that includes thought-being as well as real being. Historical research in the 20th and present century into Scotus's own thought has opted for the minority view, not that of the main Scotist tradition.

Bibliography: On 1: Primary sources: Contingency and Freedom: Lectura I 39 (trans. A. Vos et al.; Dordrecht, 1994) • *Duns Scotus, Metaphysician* (trans. W. A. Frank and A. B. Wolter; West Lafayette, Ind., 1995) • *Duns Scotus on Divine Love: Texts and Commentary on Goodness and Freedom, God and Humans* (trans. A. Vos et al.; Aldershot, 2003) • *Duns Scotus on the Will and Morality* (trans. A. B. Wolter; Washington, D.C., 1986) • *God and Creatures: The Quodlibetal Questions* (trans. F. Alluntis and A. B. Wolter; Princeton, 1975) • *Opera Omnia* (12 vols.; ed. L. Wadding; Lyons, 1639) • *Opera Omnia* (ed. C. Balič et al.; Rome, 1950-) • *Opera Philosophica* (ed. G. J. Etzkorn et al.; St. Bonaventure, N.Y., 1997-) • *Philosophical Writings: A Selection* (trans. A. B. Wolter; Indianapolis, 1987) • *Treatise on God as First Principle* (trans. A. B. Wolter; 2d ed.; Chicago, 1982).

On 1: Secondary works: R. Cross, *Duns Scotus* (New York, 1999); idem, *Duns Scotus on God* (Aldershot, 2005) • L. Honnefelder, R. Wood, and M. Dreyer, eds., *John Duns Scotus: Metaphysics and Ethics* (Leiden, 1996) • L. Sileo, ed., *Via Scoti. Methodologica ad mentem Joannis Duns Scoti* (2 vols.; Rome, 1995) • T. Williams, ed., *The Cambridge Companion to Duns Scotus* (Cambridge, 2002) • A. B. Wolter, *The Philosophical Theology of John Duns Scotus* (ed. M. M. Adams; Ithaca, N.Y., 1990).

On 2: F. Bak, "Scoti schola numerosior est omnibus aliis simul sumptis," *FrS* 16 (1956) 114-65 • A. Broadie, *The Shadow of Scotus: Faith and Philosophy in Pre-Reformation Scotland* (Edinburgh, 1995) • Commissio Scotistica, *De doctrina Ioannis Duns Scoti,* vol. 4, *Scotismus decursu saeculorum* (Rome, 1968) • R. Cross, "Haecceity, Medieval Theories of," *Stanford Encyclopedia of Philosophy* (ed. E. N. Zalta; Stanford, Calif., 2004) http://plato.stanford.edu/ • T. Hoffmann, *Creatura intellecta. Die Ideen und Possibilien bei Duns Scotus, mit Ausblick auf Franz von Mayronis, Poncius und Mastrius* (Münster, 2002) • L. Honnefelder, *Scientia transcendens. Die formale Bestimmung der Seiendheit und Realität in der Metaphysik des Mittelalters und der Neuzeit* (Hamburg, 1990) • B. Jansen, "Zur Philosophie der Scotisten des 17. Jahrhunderts," *FS* 17 (1936) 25-58, 150-75 • E. Randi, "A Scotist Way of Distinguishing between God's Absolute and Ordained Power," *From Ockham to Wyclif* (ed. A. Hudson and M. Wilks; Oxford, 1987) 43-50.

Richard Cross

Scribes

The principle that → Judaism demanded a life of studying the → Torah and that the Torah must be applied to community life (J. Neusner) found concrete expression among professional scribes. Their prototype was Ezra (ca. 450 B.C.), who was "a scribe skilled in the law of Moses that the Lord the God of Israel had given" (Ezra 7:6). The scribes were expositors who made the directions of the Torah binding in various situations in daily life, teachers who passed on the contents and methods of their exposition to their students, and jurists who played a practical part in administering the law (Sir. 38:24-34). As expositors, they took over a function that had originally been the → priests' (§2; → Law 1), and their influence grew as the temple cult gave way to → synagogue worship (→ Worship 1.2) and the priesthood lost its importance.

For lack of source material it is hard to explain the relation between the scribes and → Pharisees in NT days. They perhaps originally had different concerns — the scribes standing for study of the Torah, the Pharisees for keeping the temple laws of purity in daily life (→ Temple 2) — but a partial overlap apparently quickly came about. Already before A.D. 70 leading scribes were also Pharisees, even though there might be scribes in other Jewish groups as well (e.g., Sadducean scribes, which many have seen implied in Josephus *Ant.* 18.16; → Sadducees). After the disaster of A.D. 70 (→ Israel 1.9), Pharisaic scribes became the normative guardians and teachers of the oral exposition of the law (→ Halakah), which eventually took written form in the → Mishnah and → Talmud. The originally honorary title for teachers, Rabbi (lit. "my teacher," used for Jesus in Mark 9:5; 10:51; 11:21), now became their official title (see Matt. 23:7).

Jesus criticized the scribes for their search for status and their abuse of personal privileges (Mark 12:38-40). We should not fail, however, to note basic agreements (note v. 34). It was the community itself, concerned with the transmission of traditions, that first expressed its rift with the synagogue in a blanket criticism of the scribes (Matthew 23).

Bibliography: G. Baumbach, "Γραμματεύς," *EDNT* 1.259-60 • A. F. J. Klijn, "Scribes, Pharisees, High Priests, and Elders in the NT," *NovT* 2 (1959) 259-67 • J. Neusner, *Das pharisäische und talmudische Judentum* (Tübingen, 1984) • A. J. Saldarini, *Pharisees, Scribes, and Sadducees in Palestinian Society: A Sociological Approach* (new ed.; Grand Rapids, 2001).

Jürgen Roloff†

Scriptural Proof

1. Judaism
2. NT
3. The Fathers and the Middle Ages
4. Reformation
5. Critical Scholarship and Modern Discussion

"Scriptural proof" means a theological procedure by which scriptural passages are adduced or used in order to substantiate, verify, defend, or give authority to dogmatic or ethical assertions.

1. Judaism

The basis for scriptural proof lies within Judaism: neither Greek culture nor the ancient Near East offers parallels. The dominant position of Scripture can be seen in a variety of Jewish traditions. Entire books could be rewritten in a way that brought them "up to date" (so Genesis and Exodus in *Jubilees,* Chronicles within the OT itself), and biblical genres were imitated (Sirach, Wisdom, later psalms). What has been called inner-biblical exegesis, which is a prominent feature in the development of the OT traditions from early times, becomes explicit in late texts like Daniel 9. In the → Qumran scrolls words from difficult texts (Habakkuk, Nahum) were identified with persons or events in the life of the sect. The principle was that everything written is a → symbol for a present-day → experience.

Rabbinic Judaism largely ignored these later works, with the partial exception of Ecclesiasticus (Ben Sira; → Apocrypha; Rabbi, Rabbinism). Scripture, for this tradition, was canonically delimited (→ Canon); it was homogeneous and contained no redundancy. Every part of it, large or small, could be used as proof for the → Halakah. Alongside it, however, ran the parallel current of the "oral" Torah, which was equally authoritative.

2. NT

In the NT it is a hermeneutical principle that the (ancient) Scripture has its meaning in the new era. Quotations are understood to show that events of emergent Christianity, notably the birth and messiahship of Jesus, his → passion, death, → resurrection, and coming in glory (→ Parousia), and the status of the church as the end-time → people of God (→ Apocalyptic) are already prefigured in the OT. A suggestion that long found favor was that a "book of testimonies" was one of the first literary productions of the church. It was thus claimed that scriptural proof formed the basic structure of the theology of the NT. This view seems unlikely, however. Many important elements, such as many parables of Jesus, and likewise terms like *logos* and *sōma pneumatikon* (spiritual body), are scarcely dependent on scriptural proof, and it is never taken as decisive that a doctrine that lacks scriptural proof is thereby invalid.

Another thesis is that the quotations are not isolated oracular units but complexes dependent on their (original) context. This position, however, is also open to question. More likely the view then current in Judaism was followed that, with or without context, the proof is valid. Quotations are taken mainly from the LXX, and the proof sometimes depends on textual variants (cf. *sōma,* "body," in Heb. 10:5 with Ps. 40:6 [LXX 39:7]). Typology, → allegory, and other modes of symbolism are implied. In spite of the importance of scriptural proof, large parts of the OT remain unquoted and uninterpreted in the NT. For example, it is questionable whether Isaiah 53 was used; Hos. 6:1-2, despite its reference to a rising on the third day, is not cited.

In the NT scriptural proof was not indispensable. → Paul considered → homosexuality to be sinful but took → nature as his criterion, although a clear scriptural proof from the OT was available. In the Areopagus speech (Acts 17) he never cited the OT, but he provided a kind of "written proof" from a Greek poet (→ Rhetoric 1). The selection of OT passages for use is very uneven: there is a great predominance of texts from Isaiah, the Psalms, and the → Torah. There are also a few isolated quotations from books outside the Masoretic canon such as *Enoch* (Jude 14-15).

3. The Fathers and the Middle Ages

After the NT period the practice of scriptural proof was rapidly extended to cover the entire OT, notably so in *Barnabas,* and it was commonly accompanied by allegorical → exegesis (§2.1). This development was nourished in controversies such as those against Jews (→ Justin *Dial.,* → Cyprian) and against → Gnostics or Marcionites (→ Tertullian). Cyril of Jerusalem (ca. 315-?386) introduced it into catechetical instruction (→ Catechesis), and Gregory of Nazianzus (329/30-389/90) brought it into homiletical-rhetorical literature (→ Cappadocian Fathers; Literature, Biblical and Early Christian, 3.4.1). On one side, stress lay on OT texts *de Christo,* which were taken to attest the preexistence of Christ, his incarnation and work of redemption (→ Soteriology), his passion, crucifixion, resurrection on the third day, and ascension. On another side, texts witnessed to the superiority of the eternal law of Christ over the Jewish ceremonial → law (§1), the church's appropriation of the inheritance of → Israel (§1), and the universality of Christianity. In this regard the spiritual sense is particularly important (→ Augustine's Theology 8; Exegesis, Biblical, 2.1.2). Books that lie outside the MT canon could count as valid sources for scriptural proof (e.g., Wisdom and Tobit for → Augustine). → *Catenae,* or "chains," formed a mode by which texts with a similar reference were grouped together.

Scripture had unrestricted authority. Alongside it, however, there stood the twofold authority of church tradition and "rational grounds." If Scripture is, on one side, the inexhaustible source of "proof texts" (*dicta probantia,* "statements that prove"), on the other side, it provides the subject matter in which → reason enlightened by → faith immerses itself in order to attain to *intellectus fidei* (understanding of/in faith) and thus to achieve the true verification of dogmas (→ Dogma). In the later

Middle Ages voices calling for reform (Marsilius of Padua, William of Ockham, John → Wycliffe) used scriptural proof as a decisive argument (e.g., against papal claims) and thus came close to the principle of *sola Scriptura.*

4. Reformation

In spite of all continuity with his inheritance from the Middle Ages, the position of Martin → Luther (1483-1546; → Luther's Theology) is entirely different. In him the rational element in scriptural proof becomes less. Scripture does not really "prove"; rather, it demands faith. *Sola Scriptura* thus correlates with *sola gratia* and *sola fide* (→ Reformation Principles). The authority of the church, of tradition, and of reason is under that of Scripture, not alongside it.

Furthermore, Luther argued strongly against the allegorization that was involved in the traditional use of scriptural proof. He stressed the plain or literal sense, which for him was also the sense of the → gospel. At this point he introduced in addition a certain historical element: the emphasis lies on those passages that seem to be theologically explicit, especially texts from Romans and Galatians. For Luther the gospel also is itself a criterion that has an effect on scriptural proof. Books that are not aware of the true gospel, that do not "push" Christ, lose their full authority. Ceremonial laws in the OT, now taken in a more literal way, are of uncertain value. Exod. 20:2 identified the deity as the one who "brought you out of the land of Egypt," but this statement is true only for Israelites. Gentile Christians, Luther maintains, identify their God in a different way. This scriptural proof shows that the laws of Moses are not binding on non-Israelites. For them, only those laws that reflect natural law (→ Law 2; Law and Gospel) are obligatory. Thus → biblicism of any kind is absent from Luther's thought.

John → Calvin (1509-64; → Calvin's Theology) holds strictly to the canon. The OT, understood analogically, has the same revelatory value as the NT (→ Revelation). The humanistic (→ Humanism), critical element, however, is more important than with Luther. The OT is itself valid as authority, without having to be interpreted "Christologically." The obligation to prove everything in the Bible to be valid is greater, and likewise also the obligation to use scriptural proof in order to prove all doctrine (and → ethics) to be in accord with Scripture. We see here the root of Puritanism (→ Puritans) and later, mixed in with elements of a historical → positivism, of → fundamentalism.

Scriptural proof plays a very important part in the post-Reformational confessions. Biblical quotations are introduced, however, in very different modes and degrees. Sometimes entire sentences are integrated into the confession, but sometimes only chapter-and-verse references are given. Later, as in the → Westminster Confession, scriptural proof is rather regularly provided, but only in the form of footnotes, which often leave it unclear what relation the biblical passage has to the doctrinal element being proved. The procedure presupposes that everything in the Scripture has perspicuity.

5. Critical Scholarship and Modern Discussion

In Protestant → orthodoxy (§§1-2) scriptural proof lost something of its importance, in that no unity in theological interpretation was achieved. Lutherans and Reformed could not agree. Moreover, scriptural proof was used also by Socinians (→ Unitarians) and → Anabaptists for the support of their own views. In addition, it had become clear to many educated laypeople (→ Clergy and Laity) that the texts on which the proof was supposed to rest often did not have the meaning that the proof was supposed to demonstrate. This perception was fully confirmed by the rising tide of historical-critical → exegesis (§2.1.5). Many texts did not have in their original context the meaning that was assigned to them in the later scriptural proof. For example, some texts that were taken to be messianic (→ Messianism) were not originally messianic at all, while texts that had been perceived as predictive were in fact concerned with the past; and → Adam did not introduce death into the world.

Ideas like → salvation history may be regarded as an attempt to place scriptural proof on a new basis. In it the proof is not carried out through individual biblical texts but through a history that runs through the entire Bible and that itself represents a kind of prophecy. In modern times less is said about "proof." Rather, one asks whether a doctrine is "in accord with Scripture." Even within fundamentalism there is an aversion to "proof-texting" — at least theoretically so — although fundamentalist praxis still remains very much dependent on exactly that approach. → Biblical theology also can perhaps be regarded as an attempt to deploy scriptural proof on a scholarly level and in the context of the entire Bible.

The trend in modern discussion, then, is to view scriptural proof as something that is valid only when there is reference to a broader context. → Feminism, → liberation theology, and various approaches through social history all emphasize the importance of the context, without which any scripture proof would remain insignificant (→ Contextual Theology). Special emphasis is attached to the history of interpretation; it was often not originally, but only on the basis of later exegesis, that biblical passages were understood in the sense necessary for scriptural proof. The conviction, traditional within → Protestantism, that scriptural proof is to be valued as a constitutive mark of difference between Protestantism and → Catholicism, has become problematic. Yet scriptural proof remains an indisputable constituent of the biblical witness, and every → theology must take it seriously as a link in the interpretation of the various stages of revelation.

→ Promise and Fulfillment

Bibliography: J. Barr, *Old and New in Interpretation* (London, 1966) • K. Barth, *CD* • J. Barton, *Oracles of God* (London, 1986) • H. Bornkamm, *Luther and the OT* (Philadelphia, 1969) • D. A. Carson and H. G. M. Williamson, eds., *It Is Written: Scripture Citing Scripture* (Cambridge, 1988) • C H. Cosgrove, *Appealing to Scripture in Moral Debate: Five Hermeneutical Rules* (Grand Rapids, 2002) • H. Diem, *Was heißt Schriftgemäß?* (Neukirchen, 1958) • C. H. Dodd, *According to the Scriptures* (London, 1952) • M. Fishbane, *Biblical Interpretation in Ancient Israel* (Oxford, 1985) • D. H. Kelsey, *The Uses of Scripture in Recent Theology* (Philadelphia, 1975) • M. J. Mulder, ed., *Mikra: Text, Translation, Reading, and Interpretation of the Hebrew Bible in Ancient Judaism and Early Christianity* (Assen, 1988) • M. Sæbø, ed., *Hebrew Bible, OT: The History of Its Interpretation* (vol. 1; Göttingen, 1996) • J. Wirsching, *Was ist schriftgemäß?* (Gütersloh, 1971).

James Barr

Seafarers' Mission

1. Settings

Seafarers' mission is a workplace ministry with people of the sea and their families, including commercial fishers, seafarers, port and oil-rig workers, harbor officials, dock workers, truckers, and shipboard vendors, including prostitutes. The 1,900 seafarers' missions throughout the world, both professional and voluntary, occur in three kinds of locales: *on shore,* with chapel, social center, and transportation services to local parishes to aid spiritual development, as well as resources for meeting physical fitness and cultural needs for crews on leave far from home; *on shipboard while at dock,* permitting ministers to bring worship, Bible study, → counseling, problem-solving, and justice-seeking skills to crews and captains who cannot leave a ship; and *at sea,* with chaplains sailing on cruise ships and in the merchant marine (i.e., the commercial ships of a nation).

The chaplains in all three locales are men and women from many different backgrounds, laity and clergy, with many trained as → missionaries. Seafarers' center hospitality staff and trained ship's visitors are often local port society members, retired seafarers, and members recruited from mission-minded churches near port. Some crew members choose to be ministering seafarers, trained to provide for the spiritual needs of the crew throughout the voyage. On shore, ministering seafarers organize Sunday → worship transportation and may help crew members changing ships to find port housing. On shipboard at dock, they tell the chaplain which seafarers need a visit, and they assist at worship. At sea, they organize prayer groups and Bible studies and maintain worship and Scripture resources for the crew.

Seafarers' missions work with three types of crews: (1) tugs, ferries, barges, and fishing vessels with indigenous crews staying in national waters (these crews mostly go home at night, although some are away as long as two weeks); (2) freighters and tankers with small international crews averaging 20 persons, who may be away from home for up to a year; and (3) passenger and cruise vessels with large international crews averaging 600, where a tour of duty might be a renewable six months. For the last two types of crews, seafarers' workplaces are also their homes.

2. Approaches

The missions need to attend to the body, mind, and spirit of seafarers, and thus the activities are varied. They include providing the → sacraments, → preaching, teaching with bilingual Bibles, showing

Christian seafarers how to carry the gospel with them around the world, distributing free copies of videos suitable for Christian witness, developing a seafarers' correspondence course for → catechesis, keeping crew members connected to their home faith traditions, training ministering seafarers and ship's visitors, connecting seafarers with supportive → congregations, arranging soccer matches between ships' crews in port, gathering clothing and gifts for Christmas-at-sea, finding interpreters, providing spaces and meals for Muslim crews fasting during Ramadan, negotiating shore-leave confusions brought on by 9/11, referring seafarers in salary disputes to the International Transport Workers' Federation, pursuing legal remedies to human → rights abuses, and taking seafarers to doctors, shopping centers, or airports to fly home at tour's end. Other activities are counseling and praying with the grieving, tempted, depressed, and lonely and making Internet, phones, and phone cards available.

Each Christian seafarers' mission is committed to communicate the Christian message by an approach consistent with its own tradition's view of Scripture and with its perception of the seafarers' needs. The three approaches described here are all evangelical (→ Evangelism) but differ as to the particular central values that undergird them. All traditions value all three of the following, although each has a particular focus. These approaches are *ecclesial evangelism,* in which the chaplains and ship's visitors view the seafarers primarily as actual and potential members of the body of Christ who need the sacraments and teachings of the church so as to be joined to the community of believers. This ministry focuses on group activities, like corporate worship and biblical and confessional study. Seafarers and congregations will be aided to connect with one another, for the benefit of both. Roman Catholics and Lutherans prefer this approach. The Nordic nations and Germany, with tax-supported national churches (→ Volkskirche), have long used this approach to develop national parishes abroad, whereby the national ethnic identity, as well as the religious identity of their own seafarers traveling on their own ships, can be strengthened when in a foreign port.

In *individual evangelism* the chaplain and ship's visitor view the seafarer as primarily an *individual* who is long isolated from family and who needs → pastoral care and support to avoid despair or temptation. For someone who is not yet a believer, the minister will focus on developing his or her personal decision for Christ and for salvation, providing → baptism, strengthening personal morality and piety, and providing individual counsel through prayer. Baptist traditions worldwide, nondenominational seafarers' missions, and Campus Crusade for Christ prefer this approach. Visitors trained in → Clinical Pastoral Education (CPE) also prefer this approach for its nondenominational presuppositions. They too view the seafarer as an individual in a difficult setting of loneliness and high group stress. CPE-trained chaplains view the important decisions to be made by the seafarer as "for self" and for emotional health. The chaplain might not discuss spiritual health as separate from mental health unless the seafarer raises the issue, despite the chaplain's own belief.

Finally, in *worker-welfare evangelism* the chaplain and ship's visitors view the seafarers primarily as *employees* in very dangerous jobs. Chaplains assist seafarers with basic needs such as weather-worthy clothing as well as with vocational counseling. Centers for seafarers' rights aid seafarers who are caught in situations of impaired justice by means of negotiation, repatriation, and lawsuits in the case of ships abandoned with unpaid crews aboard. They work to put into effect biblical models of social justice for seafarers in the dangerous shipping industry with the aid of such bodies as the International Committee on Seafarers' Welfare, the International Labor Organization (ILO), and the International Marine Organization (IMO). Reformed missions know this approach as the "Christ and culture," or transformational, approach (→ Culture and Christianity 3.1). Episcopalians in the United States prefer this method and have supported these commitments to the gospel with three Centers for Maritime Education and a Center for Seafarers' Rights to elevate the standards of professionalism and safety for merchant mariners. Some seafarers' centers sponsored by the Christian Reformed Church in North America have adopted this model, while others continue the approach of ecclesial evangelism.

3. History

3.1. *NT*

The origin of seafarers' missions on the open seas could be traced back to → Paul, the maker of tents and sails (Acts 18:3). His three shipwrecks and day-and-a-half adrift at sea made clear to converted Gentiles that neither the chaos of the sea nor the suspect life of an audience of seafarers would stop his witness (2 Cor. 11:25-33). In Rom. 15:22-29 Paul wrote of his desire to continue his mission after Rome by sailing to Spain. Paul's seafaring commitments were fleshed out by the account in Acts of one of these voyages on a grain ship and its shipwreck on Malta. On that voyage Paul functioned as chaplain to the crew for their protection, despite the shipowner's refusal to listen to the ship-saving word of God that rested on Paul (chap. 27). Acts 20:13–28:15 names more than two dozen shore towns and islands that Paul reached by sailing routes. Once Christianity became the religion of the → Roman Empire in 324, Paul's concern for those at sea could become a choice for mission.

3.2. *Early Ministries*

After Constantine (306-37) made Christianity the empire's religion, its commitment to sailing missions increased. The earliest organized Christian maritime mission after Constantine was to seafarers serving a nation's goals of exploration, military expansion, or defense. Western nations soon believed that when soldiers went to sea, the comfort and strength of their God and the perspective of their nation's faith needed to go with them. Thus, a priest accompanied Leif Eriksson on his voyage of discovery to the New World (ca. 1000), and Franciscan friars followed the navy of the → Crusades. They held daily mass (weather permitting), heard confessions, and offered prayers for the care of souls. When priests sailed as passengers, they would offer the same to passengers and crew.

3.3. *Roman Catholic Apostolate of the Sea*

A coordinated land-based mission to commercial seafarers was a comparatively late development among Roman Catholics. Catholic laity began the first mission in Glasgow, Scotland, to meet the religious needs of Roman Catholic commercial seafarers working in a Protestant environment. There in 1920 the three laypersons Peter Anson, Arthur Gannon, and Brother Daniel Shields founded *Apostolatus Maris,* or Apostolate of the Sea (AOS). In 1922 Pius XI approved it, encouraging its development around the world. In 1970 AOS became the responsibility of the Pontifical Commission (since 1988, Pontifical Council) for the Pastoral Care of Migrants and Itinerant Peoples (→ Curia 1.2.4). In 1997 John Paul II in his apostolic letter *Stella maris* (Star of the sea) updated the previous norms and defined the mission of AOS as the pastoral accompaniment and care of those who live and work in the maritime world of commercial shipping and fishing, as well as their families, port personnel, and those who travel at sea.

The AOS today is a worldwide network with more than 100 seafarer centers, all known as Stella Maris. Each local or national branch of the AOS is under the responsibility of the local → bishop or bishops' conference. An outstanding example of this care is the AOS in the Philippines, where the diocese provides extensive education and support systems for the families of those long at sea. Through its "maritime sector" the pontifical council does international coordination. The AOS is a founding member of the International Christian Maritime Association (see 5) and is fully committed to working ecumenically in the framework of the policy of the → Roman Catholic Church. To that end, blessings of the fishing and commercial fleets and celebrations of National Maritime Day on May 22 have become ecumenical in the United States.

3.4. *Protestant Efforts*

The commitment of the Protestant Reformation to the priesthood of all believers (→ Priest, Priesthood, 4) led to a decision by Protestant nations (e.g., Great Britain) to make naval captains responsible for holding morning and evening services in the absence of clergy. Some believing captains within the merchant marine, like Paul Cuffee (1759-1817), a black Quaker from Massachusetts, voluntarily attended to the spiritual and social welfare of their crews. The Englishman John Newton (1725-1807, author of "Amazing Grace"), as a converted slave ship captain, eventually repudiated the slave trade and supported the movement for its abolition, led by William → Wilberforce (1759-1833). The Naval and Military Bible Society (founded 1779 and still in existence) was the first British association to purchase and distribute Bibles among Protestant naval and military crews.

Despite such enlightened principles, there was little support for the offering of divine worship, the development of Christian piety within the crew, and the promotion of a safe, dignified Christian life on board navy ships. The British military practice in the 18th and 19th centuries of abducting untrained youth for a naval ship's crew (impressment) worked against a safe and spiritual life at sea. Merchant mariners' concerns were not yet addressed, although the terrors of life on commercial ships and of the sea were substantially the same as for naval personnel.

3.4.1. *British*

The development of British commercial seafarers' missions exemplifies the formation of all modern Protestant missions to the merchant marine. The common practices of these often lay-led missions were visiting aboard ship; providing preaching, baptism, Holy Communion, and Bible study; developing seafarers into lay ministers to the crew; corresponding with seafarers; provisioning seafarers and their families on land; and fund-raising and recruiting volunteers to spread the mission to ever more ports (→ Lay Movements).

At the beginning of the 19th century, the merchant fleet grew with the age of steam and became separated from naval oversight. Merchant seafarers often found themselves living a life of voluntary serfdom and draconian discipline, ending only when the ship docked again at home port. Ultimately, converted seafarers took up the proclamation of the gospel to the merchant marine. G. C. Smith (1782-1863), converting to Christianity after an infamous life at sea, began his public ministry in the ports of southwestern England in 1804. When seafarers invited him on board to preach, his witness as a converted seafarer was persuasive to both seafarers and believers on shore, because he spoke from knowledge of the seafarer's courage in a dangerous occupation, social isolation, and oppression, as well as from knowledge of their dissolute lives. Smith is credited with starting the first mission solely focused on seafarers and fishers worldwide, the Port of London Society, in 1818 (→ British Missions).

Smith credited the Wesleyan Methodists as his inspiration in their evangelical zeal in designing a ministry for the forgotten merchant marine. Zebedee Rogers, a Wesleyan Methodist shoemaker, designed the Bethel Flag (1817), a blue flag with the white lettering "Bethel" (meaning "house of God"), with a star of Bethlehem and Noah's dove of peace. This flag was raised over a ship in port where Divine Services were being held for seafarers from all vessels. Some 42 nations still allow the Bethel Flag to be flown over a shipboard national ensign an hour before Divine Services. Out of the development of the Bethel Flag came the Bethel movement, which promotes seafarer-initiated, on-board cell groups that support spiritual development. In 1819 converted seafarers formed the British and Foreign Seamen's Friend Society and Bethel Union. The words "Bethel Union" referred to the goal of encouraging seafarers to join in a "union" of Christian fellowship and mission on board ship and in port.

Beginning in 1822, the Church of England started its own mission with the Port of Dublin Society, complete with a floating chapel — a ship dedicated solely to worship, teaching, and the care of souls. By 1840 the Anglicans had settled on the pattern of caring for souls aboard ship and worshiping ashore in seafarers' chapels, which continues to this day. In 1856 these efforts were consolidated in the Church of England's global Missions to Seamen. Seafarers soon knew its ensign, a flying angel, as a sign of help at hand.

Methodists who had formerly worked with the nondenominational British Sailors' Society formed their own society in 1843, the Wesleyan Seamen's Mission. Two innovations of this mission have continued until today: women being recruited for direct evangelical ministry to seafarers, and crew members being formally recruited on ship to be ministering seafarers.

3.4.2. *North American*

The Unitarians, led by Joseph Tuckerman (1778-1840), made the first organized efforts at seafarers' mission in 1812 through the Boston Society for the Religious and Moral Improvement of Seamen. The Congregationalists developed the Boston Seaman's Friend Society in 1818, a ministry continued today by the United Church of Christ. In 1828 the Methodist-Episcopal Boston Port Society called Edward Thompson Taylor (1793-1871), a former seafarer. His Mariner's House still serves seafarers today, although now as a seafarers' inn. The Congregational and Presbyterian maritime missions are particularly noteworthy for involving seminarians from Andover Theological Seminary and from Yale's Divinity School since 1831, a practice that continues today through seminarians involved in maritime ministry as part of their CPE. The New England Seafarers' Mission now attends to seafarers' needs for the Evangelical Covenant Church.

The War of 1812 brought the attention of eastern U.S. Bible societies to the need for Bibles at sea. By 1816 they had joined together to form the American Bible Society, the forefront of ecumenical Bible distribution to seafarers in America's age of revivals. From 1816 to 1821 Ward Stafford led the (Calvinist) Female Missionary Society for the Poor of the City of New York and Its Vicinity into a maritime ministry with the first shore-based Mariners' Church, a kind of church existing today worldwide.

Meanwhile, the Bethel movement spread from England to the North American mainland at St. John, New Brunswick, in 1820. The New York Bethel Union began in 1821, followed by unions in Philadelphia, Baltimore, Savannah (Georgia), Portland (Maine), and New Orleans. Today, following the Bethel Union's lead, many seafarers' missions are incorporated as nonsectarian. Even among denominationally identified seafarers' missions, most have board members and volunteers from other traditions.

In 1834 a group of young Episcopalians began a mission that also focused on seafarers' welfare. Its unique approach was to develop a floating church in New York harbor for seafarers, the *Floating Church of Our Savior* (1844). This was a church with a steeple built on a converted ferry and tied up at a dock. Soon Philadelphia had its own floating church, the *Floating Church of the Redeemer* (1849). These two undertakings were the first endeavors of what would become the Seamen's Church Institute of

New York and New Jersey and the Seamen's Church Institute of Philadelphia. In 1982 Episcopalians started the Center for Seafarers' Rights to provide legal research, education, advocacy, and assistance on seafarers' rights issues. In 2003 a new phase of cooperative work began as 19 port chaplaincies in the United States formed the Alliance of Episcopal Maritime Ministries.

American Lutheran maritime missions had an early start in Savannah in 1821. Outside of Georgia, the variety of languages and the number of different American Lutheran church bodies made it difficult to initiate a cooperative port ministry, even though Lutherans came from great seafaring nations. Lutheran congregations, however, readily welcomed seafarers of their own nationality. Such formative hospitality has ensured that Lutheran maritime mission today still stresses building congregational connections with seafarers. In 1873 in response to a revival in the Church of Sweden, the Swedish Evangelical Missionary Society sent Per Johan Svärd (1845-1901) to begin a seafarers' church and sailors' home in New York, with the strong support of the Augustana Synod, an American denomination of Swedish Lutherans. The sailors' home continues today in New York as the Seafarers and International House. Finally, in 1981, Lutheran maritime ministries formed an association through the Lutheran Association for Maritime Ministry, an interdenominational and international Lutheran association for port chaplains, ship's visitors, and supporting congregations. Since 1981 they have focused on developing scriptural and catechetical resources to seafarers.

In 1932 North American seafarers' missions formed the International Council of Seamen's Agencies to coordinate work between ports and missions. In 1991 it became the North American Maritime Ministry Association (NAMMA), which functions today as an ecumenical Christian association of seafarers' missions and other organizations and individuals working with similar organizations for the betterment of the lot of seafarers. NAMMA has provided an important venue for the discussion of various ecumenical approaches, interreligious concerns, and cooperative work between labor and management in the maritime industry.

3.4.3. *German and Scandinavian*

German, Swedish, Norwegian, Danish, and Finnish Lutheran seafarers' missions were developed in national and foreign ports to assure the continuing national culture and religious identity of the seafarers of each of these nations. J. H. Wichern (1808-81), who had bemoaned the lack of Lutheran church work among German seafarers in Hamburg after noting what was being done for seafarers by the American Seamen's Friend Society and the Destitute Sailors' Asylum in London, started planning for a German foreign port mission. As a result, the → Inner Mission began in 1850 among German seafarers in Antwerp and later in Cardiff and Hamburg. Eventually, a nationally supported system of 200 German seamen's missions was at work (→ German Missions). The national and religious disruptions of World War II reduced the national German seafarers' missions to 27 centers abroad and 17 at home. Today, these German seamen's missions employ the worker-welfare approach to evangelism and have been in the forefront of developing sailing chaplains' programs, while retaining their focus on German seafarers.

In the Scandinavian and Finnish Lutheran churches, each national church developed seafarers' centers with goals of providing worship, attending to straying souls from their own country, and supporting national ideals of decency and good citizenship. Retired Scandinavian and Finnish seafarers, as well as nationally oriented societies like the Sons of Norway, formed the bulk of ship's visitors for these foreign missions. In all these national Lutheran churches, the focus is on reaching out to isolated nationals on foreign soil. There is presently much discussion of how such concentration on individual nationals will be effective, given the prevalence of multinational crews.

3.4.4. *Indigenous Ministries*

The worldwide nature of the early Western church allowed for an indigenous priesthood from its origins, including indigenous port chaplains. Since the work of the Apostolate of the Sea was assigned to the care of indigenous dioceses, local → priests were its initial mentors. Among Protestants, the situation has been different. By the mid-19th century the port societies associated with the Bethel movement had contacted missionaries in ports visited by whalers to establish the movement in such places as Australia, Tahiti, Baffin Bay, Rio de Janeiro, and Hawaii. These ministers were northern European men who knew the indigenous languages. The chaplains of the German and Scandinavian Lutheran churches were also northern European, since they aimed to support the national identity of seafarers from those countries.

Only with the collapse of the colonial era and the development of indigenous Protestant churches did already established Protestant port chaplaincies develop indigenous leadership. Today, for example, an Indian Anglican is port chaplain at Mangalore, India, on behalf of the Church of South India. A Madagascan Lutheran woman ministers to portside prostitutes in Toamasina, Madagascar. Indigenous port chaplains also serve in many seafarers' centers throughout South America. Completely new indigenous ministries have also developed, such as the Korea Harbor Evangelism (1974) and Korea International Maritime Mission (1982). In the United States the goal of maritime ministries, except those of the German and Scandinavian national churches, has been to increase the number of male and female chaplains and ship's visitors of different nationalities, since ships' crews are no longer of one race, nation, language, or gender.

4. Contemporary Issues Facing Seafarers

Still today, some run away to sea, drawn by its beauty, its promise of adventure, and a life far from social convention. Many others, especially in developing countries, work their way to sea. Wages on land may not be enough to support a family, so that anxiety about the risks of seafaring and its loneliness are set aside for the sake of a better-paying job. The sea, however, is no tamer now than it ever has been. Besides violent storms, rogue waves, and a lack of an international alert system for tsunamis, pirates hired by criminal bosses or → terrorists still pose a danger. Cruise ships are also vulnerable, as the passengers of the Greek ship *Achille Lauro* experienced to their horror in 1985 during the hijacking of their vessel.

4.1. *Unregulated Shipping*

According to the International Labor Organization (ILO), the basic rights of seafarers are the right to life, the right to a written seafaring contract, the right to wages, the right to shore leave, the right to free association (collective bargaining), the right to free medical care if injured at sea, the right to be repatriated at the end of the voyage, and the right to respect, regardless of age, religion, ethnic background, or gender. The U.N. Declaration of Human Rights, the National Interfaith Committee on Worker Justice, and the Lord's Day Alliance also support the right of all seafarers to have a holy day to worship, free of labor. Recent changes in the shipping industry, however, have made it difficult for seafarers to know whether these rights will be honored when they sign a contract.

Before World War II a ship was assumed to be based at the home port noted on its stern, and its well-paid crew was assumed to come from that nation. Since then, many of the 40,000 large merchant ship owners, including American oil companies, have registered their ships in nations with the lowest registration costs and fewest requirements. Such nations as Panama, Liberia, and land-locked Bolivia, which have often had poor human rights records, have became the guarantors of the safety of ships and their crews. To seafarers' missions who support the conventions of the ILO, these "open registry vessels" are known as "flags of convenience" (FOC) ships. Most cruise lines also operate as FOC vessels, often to the endangerment of passengers and crew. Offenses that have been documented on FOC ships include denial of wages, abandonment of the ship and crew when the owner goes bankrupt, overworked and sleep-deprived crews running ships aground, crews obliged to clean tankers' holds of toxic substances and to dump the residue at sea, unrepaired ships, unsanitary conditions, and poor or inappropriate diets (e.g., pork for Muslims). While any of these offenses might occur on a ship with a standard registry, they are far more common on FOC ships.

4.2. *Port Security and Shore Leave*

Since the terrorist attacks of September 11, 2001, the United States and other nations have tightened port security to an extent that seafarers of certain nations may be refused shore leave, despite their rights as guaranteed by the → United Nations. At the same time, ships' visitors have found their access to ships curtailed as some authorities have denied passes to volunteers in the interests of working with "traceable" staff. For many ministries, loss of volunteers is akin to the loss of the ministry itself.

4.3. *Fishing a Vulnerable Ocean*

An underregulated worldwide fishing industry in the 19th and 20th centuries has led to an overfished ocean today. Fishing banks are depleted, shellfish are below size, and oil spills, toxic waste, and nonbiodegradable trash harm sea and shore creatures. Large commercial fishing enterprises drag-net fish, catching porpoises and turtles as collateral damage, or they long-line fish with hundreds of hooks and catch enormous numbers of seabirds, like the albatross. Today, commercial fishers have begun to view themselves as dangerous to the oceans and are working for change in the industry (→ Environment; Environmental Ethics). However, reductions in the length of seasons and of the amount of permitted catch have sent fishing fleets farther and farther off shore, have increased competition, and have contributed to a greater loss of fishers and their ships.

5. International Christian Maritime Association.

The International Christian Maritime Association (ICMA) was founded in 1969 as an association of Christian organizations, including NAMMA, engaged in welfare work for seafarers' and their families. In 2005 it comprised 27 Christian nonprofit organizations. As it developed, ICMA has provided a concerted response to unregulated global shipping and commercial fishing. In an unprecedented way, these missions, which employ three different approaches to evangelism (see 2), have been able to speak together on behalf of seafarers and commercial fishers within and without the shipping industry. Since ships travel between continents with multinational crews, interagency and interdenominational cooperation offers greater opportunity for the relief of seafarers and ships in distress. The ICMA has been instrumental in improving the standards for port chaplaincy by providing training schools in Rotterdam and Hong Kong. The NAMMA-affiliated Houston Maritime Chaplaincy Training Program has focused on relevant biblical/theological issues, CPE, administration, seafarers' rights, and ship visitation. The U.S. Roman Catholic Church has made this training mandatory for its chaplains, and other churches are following suit.

Closely related to these training programs is the specialized research required for effective training and resource development. Roald Kverndel's *Seamen's Missions: Their Origin and Early Growth* (1986) was the first documented history of the seafarers' mission movement. The International Association for the Study of Maritime Mission was founded in Leeds, England, in 1990. Besides the issue of relating to other faiths in today's context of religious pluralism at sea, an impending concern for ICMA is the matter of the natural rights of the oceans themselves to life and respect. "Work with me, not against me" would seem to be the cry of the oceans to the shipping industry, seafarers, commercial fishers, and the maritime missions for the next century.

Bibliography: P. F. Anson, *The Church and the Sailor: A Survey of the Sea-Apostolate Past and Present* (London, 1948) • P. K. Chapman, *Trouble Abroad: The Plight of International Seafarers* (Ithaca, N.Y., 1992) • A. D. Couper, *Voyages of Abuse: Seafarers, Human Rights, and International Shipping* (London, 1999) • W. Down, *On Course Together: The Churches' Ministry in the Maritime World Today* (Norwich, 1989) • K. Kalliala, *Strangership: A Theological Étude on Strangers Aboard and Abroad* (Helsinki, 1997) on the Finnish Seamen's Mission • R. Kverndal, *Seamen's Missions: Their Origin and Early Growth* (Pasadena, Calif., 1986); idem, *The Way of the Sea: The Shape of Mission in the Seafaring World* (Pasadena, Calif., 2006) • K. M. Lai, *An Unconditional Love Story: Meeting the People of the Sea* (Beach Park, Ill., 2002) • W. Langewiesche, *The Outlaw Sea: A World of Freedom, Chaos, and Crime* (New York, 2004) • T. Mall, *Developing Ministries to Seafarers* (Beach Park, Ill., 2002) • R. D. Mattison, *True North: Steering by Scripture at Sea; A Companion Journal to Water Words* (Beach Park, Ill., 2003); idem, *Water Words: Sea Readings for the People of the Sea* (Beach Park, Ill., 2002) • P. G. Mooney, *Maritime Mission: History, Developments, a New Perspective* (Zoetermeer, 2005) • M. Nun, *The Sea of Galilee and Its Fishermen in the NT* (Kibbutz Ein Gev, Israel, 1989) • R. Pedersen, "Theology of Controversy: Reflections of a Lutheran Seamen's Chaplain" (ICMA World Conference, New Orleans, July 30, 2004) • C. Safina, *Eye of the Albatross: Visions of Hope and Survival* (New York, 2002) • Seamen's Church Institute, *The Nicos V. Vardinoyannis Seafarers' Handbook* (New York, 1999) • J. M. Seymour, *Ships, Sailors, and Samaritans* (New Haven, 1976) • M. G. Sherar, *Shipping Out: A Sociological Study of American Merchant Seamen* (Cambridge, Md., 1973) • R. Tiangco and R. Jackson, *Handbook of Rights and Concerns for Mariners* (Centreville, Md., 2002) • V. A. Yzermans, *American Catholic Seafarers' Church* (Washington, D.C., 1995).

Robin Dale Mattison

Seal of the Confessional

The "seal of the confessional" is the guarantee that whatever a penitent shares in the rite of penance (→ Penitence) will not be disclosed by any who hear it. The duty of silence that members of the clergy accept at → ordination corresponds to the right of silence that the state extends to the clergy in court. The church's basis for it is the Christian → love that does not expose a neighbor except in emergency (Matt. 18:15) and that accepts responsibility for penitents, and also the confidence it has in its own → pastoral care.

Roman Catholic → canon law (1983 → CIC 983-84, 1917 CIC 889-90) strictly forbids any revealing of what is learned in confession or any use of it to the disadvantage of the penitent. The best-known → martyr of the seal of the confessional (whose death, however, as officially declared only in the 20th cent., was actually due to other causes) was John of Nepomuk (ca. 1345-93). The → Anglican Communion, the → Orthodox Church, and the → Old Catholic churches all recognize the seal as well.

The Protestant church regards the seal of the confessional as a special instance of pastoral secrecy. Following M. → Luther (1483-1546), the → Lutheran churches have made it inviolable. Reformed → church orders demand confidential administration of → church discipline for offenses that are not publicly known. Many orders and rules for pastors make the seal an official pastoral duty, which means in practice that they must not use what they learn in either → preaching or teaching. The rule of confidentiality applies also to other workers, helpers, and spouses, and also in → supervision. Ministers must not even speak to the penitent about what is learned unless by request. The penitent must give agreement that expert help be sought, and in their own confession pastors must not say who has confessed to them. Only when it is to prevent the → death of an innocent person or to prevent a → suicide do most Protestant churches consider that what has been learned in the confessional may be used in neighborly love without any betrayal of the penitent.

The seal of the confessional creates problems for witnesses in court proceedings. In Roman Catholic canon law the → priest cannot be asked to tell what he has learned from confession in a church case. The seal enjoys similar protection in Protestant disciplinary proceedings against holders of church offices (→ Ministry, Ministerial Offices). Concordats and state laws give many ministers similar protection as witnesses and even the right to refuse to testify if their knowledge comes from the confessional or from the general cure of souls. They must claim the right to be silent, however; untruthful evasion or denial is punishable. They are not bound by any desire of those who have been put under pastoral care that they should speak, for the duty of silence protects church work absolutely. Many states protect the helpers and also the personal papers of ministers. In English law the question is debated how far the privilege of silence extends in the case of the confession of serious crimes (see can. 113 [1603]). In most of the states in the United States, conversations between priests and penitents are privileged communications and are not required to be disclosed on the witness stand (→ Law and Legal Theory).

Bibliography: W. W. Blume, *American Civil Procedure* (Englewood Cliffs, N.J., 1955) 116-17 • A. von Campenhausen, ed., *JusEcc* 30 (1983) esp. 133-54 • J. T. Cox and D. F. M. Macdonald, *Practice and Procedure in the Church of Scotland* (6th ed.; Edinburgh, 1976) 76-77, 328-29 • H. Halsbury, *Laws of England* (4th ed.; London, 1975) 14.143, 566 • J. L. McCarthy, "Confession, Seal of," *NCE* (1st ed.) 4.133-35 • E. G. Moore, *English Canon Law* (Oxford, 1967) 95-96 • A. Stein, *Evangelisches Kirchenrecht* (Neuwied, 1980) 70-74 • R. Weigand, "Bußsakrament," *HKKR* (2d ed.) 841-56.

Albert Stein†

Sect

1. Term
2. Typology
3. Evaluation

1. Term

The term "sect" is a loanword from Lat. *secta, sequor,* and in the first instance it has the neutral sense of a school, following, party, or teaching, like the Lat. *haeresis,* a cognate of Gk. *hairesis.* Derivation from *seco* (cut, separate, break away) is etymologically incorrect but has led to popular disparagement.

In the NT *hairesis* is used negatively (1 Cor. 11:18-19; Gal. 5:20; 2 Pet. 2:1) to speak of factions that produce *schismata* (divisions, schisms) in the church (→ Heresies and Schisms). As a result, the church throughout its history has used the term "sect" for heterodox opinions and parties, just as Paul said the Jews used it to denote the followers of "the Way" (Acts 24:14). In classical Greek *hairetikos* could denote "one who can choose [aright]," but in Christianity it has always designated one who has chosen wrongly. After the → Reformation of the 16th century, "sect" commonly denoted Christian churches or congregations that did not have national recognition. "Sect" and "heretic" grew to be synonymous terms, heartily applied by historic churches and deeply resented by minority and socially marginal communions.

It was left to → sociology and the academic study of religion (→ Religious Studies) to restore the neutral sense by seeing in the phenomenon a normal historical process of separating from a parent church that is implicit already in the gospel, and therefore as the legitimate formation of groups. Max → Weber's (1864-1920) now century-old study translated into English as *The Protestant Ethic and the Spirit of Capitalism* (1904-5; first ET 1930) saw churches as Christian religious institutions exhibiting and tolerating a broad spectrum of commitment and conduct, and sects as voluntary associations of adherents to agreed-upon doctrine and discipline.

While Weber recognized the church-sect dichotomy, his contemporary Ernst → Troeltsch (1865-1923) gave this concept its classic treatment in *The Social Teaching of the Christian Churches* (1911; ET 1931). He saw these different ways of being Christian anticipated in the NT itself. Churches make peace with the world (Romans 13); sects are self-conscious resident aliens (1 Pet. 2:11). Indeed, Troeltsch believed churches could comprehend sects, as shown by the → Roman Catholic Church's

Sect

hundreds of → religious orders, sodalities, and confraternities. Troeltsch added a third category, → mysticism, to his typology. The → individualism of mysticism in his definition caused Howard Becker and others to replace the term "mysticism" with "cult," a word that came to have an almost totally negative connotation in the late 20th century.

About the time these works by Weber and Troeltsch appeared in English, the Yale theologian and sociologist of religion H. Richard Niebuhr (1894-1962) applied the church-sect typology to Christian religious movements in the United States in *The Social Sources of Denominationalism* (1929). For Niebuhr, American denominationalism reflected class differences more than theology. He also believed that after a generation or so, the new sect lost its taste for alien residency and evolved toward a church form known as a → denomination.

Joachim Wach (1898-1955) in *Sociology of Religion* (1944) developed the Weber-Troeltsch recognition that sects may subsist within their churches of origin. Some sects withdraw or are expelled and form freestanding ecclesial entities. Others become what he termed *ecclesiolae in ecclesia,* or "little churches within the church," with varying degrees of organization and voluntary commitment to membership.

2. Typology

From Howard Becker's 1932 *Systematic Sociology* until the present, no universal consensus on the definition and typology of sects and cults has been established. Thus no designation of specific religious movements as sects or cults is given here. The work of scholars such as H.-D. Reimer, Roy Wallis, Bryan Wilson, and J. M. Yinger shows efforts from the 1950s to the 1970s to identify the characteristics and define a gestalt of types and subtypes of sects. Readers are directed to their work to learn how they classify various movements. Their research will also guide one to monographs about specific denominations studied through the lens of church-sect typology. Generally, a sect is seen as a movement related to a parent tradition, often seeking to remain within its home church, while a cult is viewed as promoting novel beliefs and practices independent of either churches or sects.

In the 1970s many social scientists began to replace "cult" with "new religious movement" (NRM), which was advanced as a value-neutral term for fair-minded scholarly application. Though electing not to accept this new vocabulary, sociologist Jeffrey Hadden (1936-2003) established the Religious Movements Homepage Project (RMHP) on the Internet in 1996 to promote dialogue and publication on conceptualizing "sect" and "cult." Sociologist Douglas E. Cowan is the project's current editor-in-chief. RMHP is concerned primarily with how to recognize and study so-called cults or new religious movements, but inevitably this goal involves sect-cult differentiation and definition.

Several characteristics appear on most lists of sectarian movements: (1) rooted in an impulse to reform or renew the parent church; (2) powerful charismatic leadership, especially in the first generation; (3) distinctive teaching well articulated by the leader(s); (4) voluntary association demanding a high level of personal commitment to doctrine, lifestyle, and the group; (5) strong group discipline; (6) a sense of being superior to those less committed to what the group sees as core values of the church; (7) a tendency to develop freestanding, even separatist, structures to ensure the continuation of the message and ministry; (8) little appeal to persons with economic, social, or political power; and (9) often indifferent or hostile to secular society and the state.

3. Evaluation

Hadden observed that the evidence suggests something quite different from the two-centuries-old belief by scholars in many disciplines that → secularization is the inevitable result of science and → reason, and that → religion is dying as "a viable institution and belief system." Instead of "withering in the face of science, with its capacity for seemingly endless new discoveries and alternative perspectives for understanding our world, religion has proved itself to be quite robust — capable of renewal, reinvigoration, and even reinvention in ways that most scholars could never have imagined. Indeed, as we begin the 21st century, religion appears to be one of the principal means by which human cultures are being renewed" (http://religiousmovements.lib.virginia.edu/welcome/mission.htm).

Thus far no definition exists that convincingly covers the variety of expressions of religious life. A static study is not possible in an age of → tolerance, religious → pluralism, and rapid change in both churches and societies. Sects and cults are forms of the renewal, reinvigoration, and reinvention of religion, constantly demanding from the churches careful information, the kindling of a gospel-sharpened understanding for the discernment of spirits, self-criticism, and ongoing reformation. Researching and conceptualizing the associated phenomena and the dynamics between church and sect, church and cult, and sect and cult is a creditable element of the social-scientific study of religion.

Bibliography: H. Becker, *Systematic Sociology on the Basis of the Beziehungslehre and Gebildelehre of Leopold von Wiese* (New York, 1932) • J. Beckford, *Cult Controversies: The Societal Response to the New Religious Movements* (New York, 1985) • D. Bromley and J. Hadden, eds., *The Handbook of Cults and Sects in America* (2 vols.; Greenwich, Conn., 1993) • M. Hill, "Sects," *EncRel(E)* 13.154-59; idem, *A Sociology of Religion* (New York, 1973) esp. chap. 3, "Church and Sect" • *JSSR* • J. Melton, *The Encyclopedic Handbook of Cults in America* (New York, 1986) • H. R. Niebuhr, *The Social Sources of Denominationalism* (New York, 1957; orig. pub., 1929) • H.-D. Reimer, ed., *Stichwork "Sekten." Glaubensgemeinschaften ausserhalb der Kirchen* (6th ed.; Stuttgart, 1988) • Religious Movements Homepage Project, http://www.religiousmovements.org • *SocAn* • R. Stark, *The Future of Religion: Secularization, Revival, and Cult Formation* (Berkeley, Calif., 1985); idem, *A Theory of Religion* (New York, 1987) • E. Troeltsch, *The Social Teaching of the Christian Churches* (2 vols.; New York, 1931; orig. pub., 1911) • J. Wach, *Sociology of Religion* (Chicago, 1944) • R. Wallis, ed., *Sectarianism: Analyses of Religious and Non-religious Sects* (New York, 1975) • M. Weber, *The Protestant Ethic and the Spirit of Capitalism* (Los Angeles, 2002; orig. pub., 1904-5; first ET, 1930) • B. Wilson, *Religious Sects: A Sociological Study* (New York, 1970); idem, *The Social Dimensions of Sectarianism: Sects and New Religious Movements in Contemporary Society* (Oxford, 1990) • B. Wilson and J. Cresswell, eds., *New Religious Movements: Challenge and Response* (New York, 1999) • J. M. Yinger, *Religion, Society, and the Individual* (New York, 1957) esp. chap. 6, "Religion and Variation among Societies."

Charles W. Brockwell Jr.

Secular Institutes

In Christian history two motives have led to the founding of religious societies. The first has been a resolve to shun and flee the world *(fuga mundi)*, the second a resolve to work in the world as it is by word and action *(professio in hoc mundo)*. Many orders in Latin Christianity and congregations in the → Roman Catholic Church resembled at first the modern secular institutes. We might think of the original efforts made by Angela Merici (1474-1540), Mary Ward (1585-1645), Vincent de Paul (1581-1660), and Pierre-Joseph Picot de Clorivière (1735-1820) in this way. At the time, hierarchical tests and prescripts and instructions reduced their secular character and pushed them into more cloistered paths.

The social needs and the areligious relations of the 19th and 20th centuries, however, brought many spontaneous new beginnings (→ Modern Church History 1.3; Monasticism 5.4; Religious Orders and Congregations 2.5). The 1947 apostolic → constitution *Provida Mater Ecclesia* grouped together these various societies, all laboring quietly, under the title *instituta saecularis* (secular institutes). It defined them as "societies, clerical or lay, whose members make profession of the evangelical counsels, living in a secular condition for the purpose of Christian perfection and full apostolate" (art. 1) and accorded them papal recognition as such (→ Pope, Papacy). → Vatican II stressed that they had to work "in the world and, as it were, from the world" *(in saeculo ac veluti ex saeculo)*. Profession conferred consecration on those concerned but without making the related societies into "religious institutes" (*Perfectae caritatis* 11).

The 1983 → CIC systematized the legal norms. The task is to "contribute to the sanctification of the world, especially from within" (can. 710). Members accept → celibacy, → poverty, and → obedience in different forms but live "in the ordinary conditions of the world" (714). All members play an active part in the work of the institutes (716). They have a right to spiritual care and religious training (719 and 724) and a duty to cooperate in general pastoral work (713 and 715). They might even be called monks and nuns without cloister or special garb. Their place is within Roman Catholic theology and practice. According to 725, "other members of Christ's faithful who seek evangelical perfection according to the spirit of the institute and who share in its mission" may become associates.

In 1976 a Vatican study document considered a wider membership of married persons. But leaders of → base communities, for example, were not included.

For further clarification and mutual learning, national and international associations have remained open to secular → priests and have catered to them. Second, a dedicated fellowship of this kind that has no home of its own can also give otherwise isolated laypeople the strength to witness and serve in their daily jobs (→ Lay Apostolate). A third type of secular institute devotes itself to specific tasks as defined by the particular institution but is open to secular or lay members.

→ Opus Dei is often called a secular institute, but after 1982 it was constituted a personal → prelature. Certain orders and societies of apostolic life are also close to secular institutes in type and task but are not secular institutes as such.

In 2002 there were 160 secular institutes world-

Secularism

wide, with a total of 60,000 members. In the United States in 2004 most secular institutes were for women (18), others for priests (4), men (3), women, men, and priests (3), priests and deacons (1), and priests, men, and married couples (1). The diocesan role of secular institutes is hard to estimate, since full statistics are not available.

Bibliography: H. U. von Balthasar, *Our Task: A Report and a Plan* (San Francisco, 1994) on the Community of St. John • Congregation for Institutes of Consecrated Life and Societies of Apostolic Life, *Starting Afresh from Christ: A Renewed Commitment to Consecrated Life in the Third Millennium* (Vatican City, 2002) • S. Holland, "Secular Institutes," *NCE* (1st ed.) 12.861-63 • John Paul II, "Bearing Witness to Christ in Secular Life," *OR(E)*, February 12, 1997, 5; idem, *The Consecrated Life (Vita Consecrata)* (Washington, D.C., 1996) • United States Conference of Secular Institutes, *Adjusting to a Secular Institute Lifestyle* (Washington, D.C., 1994).

Heiner Grote†

Secularism

1. Definition
2. History
3. Culture
4. Christian Reception and Criticism
5. Modern Discussion

1. Definition

"Secularism" denotes the many-faceted process of the disintegrating of the medieval European world, which stood under Christian influence, by the modern world (→ Modern Period; Modernity 4.3). In a transferred sense it denotes analogous processes in other cultures. As a category in the history of culture, it differs from → secularization. It indicates a turning against God and the Christian faith that some evaluate positively, others negatively.

In the history of Western culture secularism goes back fundamentally to the → Middle Ages. It assumed a new quality in the reconstruction of life and learning in the 16th and 17th centuries, was pushed forward in the 18th and 19th centuries, and largely came to completion in the 20th century (→ Enlightenment; Modern Church History).

To denote the process that embraces such varied spheres as the history of ideas, art, morality, law, politics, and economics (→ Culture and Christianity 3), the term "secularism" is irreplaceable, even though great differences exist in describing and evaluating it. A debated issue is whether the process is specifically alien to the substance of Christianity, which survives in the mode of a pseudomorphosis, or whether the spiritual is replaced by originally secular contents and structures, in which case the question then arises how far the form of what is replaced influences that which replaces it.

2. History

As analyses of the term show (H. Lübbe, H. Strätz and H. Zabel), a conceptualizing of the process as secularism took place only in the 19th century as studies of it developed. It was originally seen as a corrective both of the current fear of rationalistic destruction (→ Rationalism) and of the romantic conjuring up of a return of Christianity (→ Romanticism). G. W. F. Hegel (1770-1831; → Hegelianism) did not view the overcoming of the antithesis between the spiritual and the secular as a replacing of the one by the other but as a bringing of the Christian principle into the secular sphere. In this sense his disciple K. L. Michelet (1801-93) saw secularizing as a category in church history denoting, not decay, but the fulfillment of the Christian principle. R. Rothe (1799-1867) called this process secularizing and viewed the secularizing of the church as complementary to the development of the state (→ Church and State 2).

In opposition to the contemporary effort of → restoration (§4) to Christianize all spheres of life, radical left-wing Hegelianism (esp. L. Feuerbach) saw secularizing as a simple replacing of Christian ideas and forms of life by those that were secular. It saw this process as valid, since there is an original worldly right of possession of treasures that religion has located in heaven. The primary aim in putting humanity and nature in place of God is not to deify them. Dechristianizing is meant to result in sacralizing the secular, though this thought is implicitly retracted in later texts. Some of the same quasi-religious fervor lives on in the promotion of secularism in → positivism and the Deutsche Gesellschaft für ethische Kultur (German society of ethical culture, F. Jodl); note also the eclectic school of V. Cousin (1792-1867) and the secularism of Anglo-American → freethinkers (G. J. Holyoake).

3. Culture

As a cultural rather than a political term (→ Culture 4), "secularism" appears marginally in W. Dilthey (1833-1911), E. → Troeltsch (1865-1923), and M. → Weber (1864-1920). Referring to the legal term "secularization," Dilthey used "secularism" for processes in the history of art and ideas (e.g., the replacing of a theology of history with a philosophy, or of a literature of meditation with one of psychology). Troeltsch had social secularism in view as well as that of ideas (religious individualism), and at times Weber could use the term for the withering of religious roots and the eliminating of transcendental explanations of thoughts and institutions (→ Sociology of Religion).

4. Christian Reception and Criticism

The meeting of the → International Missionary Council at Jerusalem in 1928 tried to reverse the disintegration of Christianity by fighting secularism (→ Missionary Conferences 2; Mission 2). "Secularism" had first appeared around 1850 as a term used by British secularists to denote the substituting of secular contents and reasonings for Christian, and a little later it came to be linked with an atheistic program (→ Atheism). The actual term came into the German sphere around 1930 in the form of a reaction to the social process of the segmentation of religion, a process that had entered a new phase when neutral → states replaced kingdoms that had seen themselves as Christian. At this time the fight became also a fight against → liberalism and → pluralism (§1; K. Nowak). Secularism now came to be seen as a reprehensible category, and conservative criticism of the culture took on shrill theological notes as it stylized the present age chiliastically as the age of the decisive conflict against a secularization that is estranged from God.

In the face of this rejection of secularism, which at first he shared, D. → Bonhoeffer (1906-45) later avoided the term and in his later letters from prison conceived instead of the "world come of age" (→ Religionless Christianity). F. Gogarten (1887-1967; → Dialectical Theology) overlapped Bonhoeffer with his influential and supposedly neutral distinction between secularism that is hostile to God and a valid secularization. Appealing to a specific interpretation of NT texts, he found in the latter a fruit of Christian faith, making it dependent on responsibility before God. As he saw it, the idea of a secularism that is not subject to the office of faith as a guardian bears witness to the perversion of modern thinking.

5. Modern Discussion

H. Blumenberg doubts the suitability of secularism as a category in the history of culture, since it gives an impression of culpability (F. Delekat) and is hard to use in a way that is descriptively neutral. For him the disintegration of the Christian world is not a putting of the substance of Christianity into secular forms but a replacing of ancient answers within a relatively constant explanation of the world. Yet even in his criticism he cannot avoid using the term or offering a functional interpretation of the processes that it denotes. The themes that it most commonly embraces, whether → eschatology and the philosophy of history (K. Löwith) or theological and legal concepts (C. Schmitt), have not thus far been described so precisely that a true conceptualizing of secularism is possible. We have instead a description of the literary phenomena (A Schöne, G. Kaiser, M. Kaempfert). What we find, as in Feuerbach, is often a direct transforming of secularizing into sacralizing, though this tendency weakens as the process continues.

As the process came to completion in what had hitherto been cultures under Christian influence (see 1.1), the question arose for the → philosophy of religion of relating definitely nonreligious answers and forms of life to new religious answers and forms of life (→ Civil Religion; Esotericism; New Age; Sociology of Religion 3.3). A special question is how far transitional forms appear in these new formulations. Another debatable issue is how far similar processes affect other cultures that are now undergoing new developments (e.g., → Islam).

Bibliography: Western discussions: K. Bartl, *Theologie und Säkularität. Die theologischen Ansätze Friedrich Gogartens und Dietrich Bonhoeffers zur Analyse und Reflexion der säkularisierten Welt* (Frankfurt, 1990) • H. Blumenberg, *The Legitimacy of the Modern Age* (Cambridge, Mass., 1983; orig. pub., 1966) • D. Bonhoeffer, *Letters and Papers from Prison* (ed. E. Bethge; New York, 1972) • C. G. Brown, *The Death of Christian Britain: Understanding Secularisation, 1800-2000* (London, 2001) • S. Bruce, *God Is Dead: Secularization in the West* (Oxford, 2002) • F. Delekat, *Über den Begriff der Säkularisation* (Heidelberg, 1958) • R. K. Fenn, *Beyond Idols: The Shape of a Secular Society* (Oxford, 2001) • F. Gogarten, *Despair and Hope for Our Time* (Phildelphia, 1970; orig. pub., 1953) • G. J. Holyoake, *Secularism, the Practical Philosophy of the People* (London, 1854) • W. Jaeschke, *Die Suche nach den eschatologischen Wurzeln der Geschichtsphilosophie. Eine historische Kritik der Säkularisierungsthese* (Munich, 1976) • M. Kaempfert, *Säkularisation und neue Heiligkeit. Religiöse und religionsbezogene Sprache bei Friedrich Nietzsche* (Berlin, 1971) • G. Kaiser, *Pietismus und Patriotismus im literarischen Deutschland. Ein Beitrag zum Problem der Säkularisation* (2d ed.; Wiesbaden, 1973) • K. Löwith, *Meaning in History: The Theological Implications of the Philosophy of History* (Chicago, 1949) • H. Lübbe, *Säkularisierung. Geschichte eines ideenpolitischen Begriffs* (Freiburg, 1965) • H. McLeod, *Secularisation in Western Europe, 1848-1914* (New York, 2000) • J. B. Metz, *Theology of the World* (London, 1969) • K. Nowak, "Zur protestantischen Säkularismus-Debatte um 1930. Ein begriffsgeschichtliche Rückblick in der Prägephase einer Verdammungskategorie," *WPKG* 69 (1980) 37-51 • C. Schmitt, *Political Theology: Four Chapters on the Concept of Sovereignty* (Cambridge, Mass., 1985) • A. Schöne, *Säkularisation als sprachbildende Kraft* (Göttingen, 1958) • H. W. Strätz and H. Zabel, "Säkularisation, Säkularisierung," *GGB* 5.789-829.

Non-Western settings: N. S. Al-Ali, *Secularism, Gender, and the State in the Middle East* (Cambridge, 2000) • T. Asad, *Formations of the Secular: Christianity, Islam, Modernity* (Stanford, Calif., 2003) • A. Davison, *Secularism and Revivalism in Turkey: A Hermeneutic Reconsideration* (New Haven, 1998) • K. Gahrana, *Right to Freedom of Religion: A Study in Indian Secularism* (Denver, 2001) • A. Nandy, *Time Warps: Silent and Evasive Pasts in Indian Politics and Religion* (New Brunswick, N.J., 2002) • A. Sharma, ed., *Hinduism and Secularism: After Ayodhrya* (New York, 2001) • A. Tamimi and J. L. Esposito, eds., *Islam and Secularism in the Middle East* (New York, 2000) • N. S. Yāred, *Secularism and the Arab World, 1850-1939* (London, 2002).

Walter Jaeschke

Secularization

1. Church History
   1.1. Background
   1.2. Reformation Period
   1.3. Jesuit Suppression, Josephinism
   1.4. France and Germany
   1.5. Twentieth Century
2. Sociological Aspects
   2.1. Definition
   2.2. Causes
   2.3. Universality and Irreversibility

1. Church History

1.1. *Background*

According to Roman Catholic → canon law, "secularization" means the transfer of persons and things from the sacral sphere to the temporal. While the secularization of individuals (e.g., from those in monastic orders to the status of secular clergy or laymen; → Church Law) is known only where Catholic canon law is accepted, "secularization" in the sense of the desacralizing of material goods is widely used for the change from church to lay property. (German distinguishes *Säkularisierung,* "mental detachment with regard to religion," from *Säkularisation,* "transfer of ecclesiastical persons and material goods, real estate, and rights of government to civil possession.")

In the Middle Ages and early modern times, sovereign rights were regarded as property. German historiography thus distinguishes between the secularization of sovereignty and that of material goods. A common view, found not merely in Christianity, is that material goods donated to spiritual institutions are dedicated irrevocably, since the dedication is to the deity (see Liber Sextus 5.13.51; → Corpus Iuris Canonici 1.3). Canon law limits the use of church property to narrowly prescribed purposes, for example, worship, the building and maintenance of cultic structures, the support of the clergy, and educational and welfare institutions. There are strong sanctions against desacralization (see Daniel 5; Matt. 21:12).

Like the institutions of other religions, the Christian church received material goods from the very first (Acts 4:35-36), though they might often be used for nonreligious ends. Canon law lays down precise conditions under which this transfer might take place and, with institutionalizing and centralizing, related the legality of such transactions to the consent of church authorities — in the last resort, the → pope. In the → Roman Catholic Church papal consent also became necessary for any changing of purposes, for example, to use for schools or charities instead of for worship. The power of → dispensation claimed by the papacy has even permitted alienation for the defense of Christianity against unbelievers, such as was invoked during warfare against Islam from the 8th century, for the → Crusades and the Reconquista, and during wars against the Ottomans from the 14th to the 18th century.

1.2. *Reformation Period*

Despite all secularization, church possessions steadily increased and aroused the greed of secular powers. Various methods of secularization arose, ranging from the use of raw → force to dispensation under more or less political pressure, then to the quiet secularization by alienation of church funds to provide for members of ruling dynasties or aristocratic and bourgeois families. Amortization laws limited or prevented the accumulation of property of the so-called dead hand *(manus mortua),* that is, property left in perpetuity to an ecclesiastical corporation.

In → Protestantism release from the Roman → curia made reassignment to other purposes easier. Yet, unlike Henry VIII of England (1509-47) and

Edward's regents, the German princes and Swiss cities stayed closer to the original intentions when disposing of monastic and other ecclesiastical buildings, properties, and endowments. At the same time, all of them to varying degrees took fiscal advantage of the schisms. Protestant princes and magistrates took over some church property, and in Germany both Protestant and Roman Catholic princes wrested control of many states from episcopal government. The → Thirty Years' War (1618-48) set off another round of secularization. The Roman curia never ratified these developments and protested solemnly but in vain against the 1648 Peace of Westphalia. In 1681 Louis XIV of France then seized control of Strasbourg.

1.3. *Jesuit Suppression, Josephinism*

If 17th-century secularization was mostly by force, critical discussion of church possessions followed in the 18th century (→ Enlightenment; Natural Law; Revolution 2). From the standpoint of dependence on an external power like the papacy, the right to individual property, and secular utility, Roman Catholics as well as Protestants began to question the way in which the amount of church property exceeded essential needs. A new wave of secularization followed with the expropriation of the → Jesuits in Portugal (1759), then France (1764) and Naples (1767). In 1773 Clement XIV (1769-74), under political pressure from the Bourbons, finally dissolved the order completely. Its possessions did not go to the curia, as planned, but to all the various states, apart from Protestant Prussia and Orthodox Russia, which did not recognize the suppression. The dismissal of the Jesuits from the South American → reductions as early as 1750 and 1768 had a particularly devastating effect on the Indians who lived in them. The German Roman Catholic state put Jesuit property to different uses, ranging from the founding of a university in Münster to providing for relatives in Bavaria.

In Austria in terms of the same rational criticism, → Josephinism — especially under Holy Roman Emperor Joseph II (1765-90) — took over church property and endowments to fund state enterprises and also took steps to restrict the church's influence to the cultic and pastoral sphere. Along the lines of older trends in church-state relations, educational and welfare institutions, with the help of church endowments, were now to be state functions, and the legal sway of Rome was to be controlled. As a consequence over 700 monasteries were dissolved, and their possessions were taken over.

1.4. *France and Germany*

In 1789 the French → Revolution (§2.4) seized church property root and branch. Recognition of the Rhine frontier by the Peace of Lunéville (1801), acceptance of the principle of compensation for dispossessed German princes on the left bank, and the acceptance of the French state by Pius VI (1775-99) in the 1801 → concordat did more than French and Russian pressure to trigger in Germany the processes known as the secularization, or the Great Secularization. A resolution in 1803 handed over the episcopal states that remained after 1648 to the neighboring secular princes, and the Congress of Vienna added its ratification in 1815. The congress restored the → Papal States, which had been taken over in the revolutionary wars, but they fell victim to Italian unification in 1870. The papacy finally accepted the status quo by signing the Lateran treaties in 1929.

The appropriating of church possessions sanctioned in 1803 made an even bigger impact on the church than what was for the most part the quiet dispossessing of the church politically. Apart from funding cathedrals and providing pensions for former church officials, the state took over all church properties, including those of churches of the Augsburg Confession, using some for purposes of worship and the common good but the rest to ease the general financial situation. The loss of cultural goods (sacred implements, libraries, musical instruments, prints and manuscripts, archives, sculptures, and buildings), and in particular the decline of ecclesiastical institutions concerned with welfare and education (18 universities), had consequences right up to the 20th century. Clergy might still receive help with their education, but lay Roman Catholics lost most of the church's institutions of higher learning (→ Clergy and Laity). New charitable orders tried to meet the increased social needs that resulted from secularization and were made even worse by industrialization (→ Industrial Society).

1.5. *Twentieth Century*

The 20th century saw secularization in France (esp. in 1901-5 during the → Kulturkampf) and Portugal (in connection with the revolution of 1910), in Germany under National Socialism, and in socialist countries, most radically in the → Soviet Union and Czechoslovakia. With new definitions of the relation between → church and state, former Communist states have sought tenable regulations for the holding of property by the churches.

In Germany the Weimar Constitution (1919-33) recognized the special position of the church, and the modern German state has followed suit. In a country like England a measure of control is exercised over what are still extensive church endowments by the church commissioners. Local congregations, church societies, and individual institutions may have extensive holdings in most countries, regulated in various ways by law but not subject to secularization.

→ Law and Legal Theory; Modern Church History 1; Sacred and Profane

Bibliography: General: G. B. CLEMENS, *Immobilienhändler und Spekulanten* (Boppard, 1995) • I. CRUSIUS, ed., *Zur Säkularisation geistlicher Institutionen im 16. und im 18./19. Jahrhundert* (Göttingen, 1996) • P. E. GLASNER, *The Sociology of Secularization* (London, 1977) • R. H. HELMHOLZ, ed., *Canon Law in Protestant Lands* (Berlin, 1992) • H. KIER and F. G. ZEHNDER, eds., *Lust und Verlust* (Cologne, 1995) • J. KIRMEIER and M. TREML, eds., *Glanz und Ende der alten Klöster. Säkularisation im bayerischen Oberland, 1803* (Munich, 1991) • A. LANGNER, ed., *Säkularisation und Säkularisierung im 19. Jahrhundert* (Paderborn, 1976) • A. LATREILLE, *L'Église catholique et la Révolution française* (2 vols.; Paris, 1946; 2d ed., 1970-71) • D. MARTIN, *A General Theory of Secularization* (Oxford, 1978) • H. C. MEMPEL, *Die Vermögenssäkularisation, 1803-10* (2 vols.; Munich, 1979) • R. FREIIN VON OER, "Der Eigentumsbegriff in der Säkularisationdiskussion am Ende des Alten Reiches," *Eigentum und Verfassung* (ed. R. Vierhaus; Göttingen, 1972) 193-228 • A. RAUSCHER, ed., *Säkularisierung und Säkularisation vor 1800* (Paderborn, 1976) • W. SCHIEDER and A. KUBE, *Säkularisation und Mediatisierung* (Boppard, 1987) • P. SCHMIDT, *Die Privatisierung des Besitzes der Toten Hand in Spanien* (Stuttgart, 1990) • D. STUTZER, *Klöster als Arbeitgeber um 1800* (Göttingen, 1986) • T. TACKETT, *Religion, Revolution, and Regional Culture in Eighteenth-Century France* (Princeton, 1986) • E. WEIS, *Die Säkularisation der bayerischen Klöster, 1802/03* (Munich, 1983) • B. WILSON, "Secularization: The Inherited Model," *The Sacred in a Secular Age* (ed. P. E. Hammond; Berkeley, Calif., 1985) 9-20.

Works occasioned by the bicentennial in 2003 of the "great secularization" in Germany: G. CHRIST, "Die Fürstbischöfe in der letzten Phase des alten Reiches," *ZBLG* 66 (2003) 461-93 • W. FRESE, ed., *Zwischen Revolution und Reform* (Münster, 2004) • V. HIMMELEIN and H. U. RUDOLF, eds., *Alte Klöster–neue Herren. Die Säkularisation im deutschen Südwesten, 1803* (3 vols.; Ostfildern, 2003) • H. KLUETING, ed., *200 Jahre Reichsdeputationshauptschluss* (Münster, 2005) • G. MÖLICH, J. OEPEN, and W. ROSEN, eds., *Klosterkultur und Säkularisation im Rheinland* (Essen, 2002) • *RoJKG* 23 (2004) • A. SCHMID, ed., *Die Säkularisation in Bayern, 1803. Kulturbruch oder Modernisierung?* (Munich, 2003) • E. WEICK and W. REININGHAUS, eds., *Klostersturm und Fürstenrevolution* (Dortmund, 2003) • G. WEISS and G. DETHLEFS, eds., *Zerbrochen sind die Fesseln des Schlendrians* (Münster, 2002).

RUDOLFINE FREIIN VON OER

2. Sociological Aspects

2.1. *Definition*

2.1.1. Sociologically, "secularization" is a multifaceted term, referring to (1) the changing position of → religion in → society, (2) the fluctuating degree of religiosity in people, or (3) changes that manifest themselves in a religion itself. The various changes are relatively independent of one another.

On the first level of meaning premodern European society as a whole was more or less permeated by religion in its Christian form. A structure of religious values, norms, symbols, and convictions overarched the nexus of society almost like a "sacred canopy" (P. Berger). This unifying factor broke apart in the process of social differentiation (→ Modern Period; Modernity). Relatively autonomous spheres developed, such as → politics, → economics, → law, and → science, which increasingly functioned on the basis of independent principles (e.g., power, profit, or knowledge). Religious connections became increasingly less important in such spheres. Within society religion was increasingly marginalized, with its sphere of competence becoming limited to only the church. Thus a process of demystification took place (M. → Weber). In the autonomous subsystems appeal came to be made less and less to nonnatural causes and sources of knowledge.

This development had no direct consequences for the second area of meaning: one's personal sense of religion. Religion and the church could still be of influence for the → family, the neighborhood, and the school (→ School and Church). In the → Reformation and Counter-Reformation (→ Catholic Reform and Counterreformation), the churches thought they should even increase this influence, leading, in some countries during the 20th century, to societies that are organized along denominational lines. In such cases schools, political parties, broadcasting companies, hospitals, and various other organizations of the society have a denominational basis, a social form that has been called pillarization (R. Steininger; → Modern Church History 1.3). Pillarization functions within a secularizing society as a protective wall enclosing certain parts of the private sphere rather than restoring the premodern situation. But at least in the West the Christian religion has gradually been losing its influence, even in the private sphere. This process is accelerating. It finds expression in some countries in official disaffiliation from the church or in reduced membership in the church or a decline of members actually participating in church activities. Some writers refer to this reduced participation as secularization, though such reference is problematic (see 2.1.2).

At the same time, there have been changes in religion itself (the third area of meaning). In the history of religion a dualistic schema of nature and the supernatural long ago ousted a monistic view of the world (→ Monism); → Judaism stressed divine transcendence, and Christianity followed suit. But this → dualism is now weakening. Belief (→ Faith 3.4.7) in a "supernature" has lost its contours, and the concept of → God (§7.2) is not so marked by personal features. One might say that demystifying has now come into the religious sphere. This process goes along with many nonreligious factors (see 2.2) and confronts the churches with the question of whether and how far they must adapt their teaching to these developments. → Pluralism (§2) has come into the churches themselves, which manifest a broad spectrum of opinions ranging from → fundamentalism to → liberalism.

2.1.2. In using the term "secularization," we must consider that it was coined in the sphere of Christian discourse and in a society in which Christianity was the dominant form of religion. Even if Christianity is losing its social significance, we cannot say that religion as a whole is disappearing. Several rivals to Christianity are on the scene, so that we must ask whether the term "secularization" does true justice to the modern situation (→ Sociology of Religion 3). The answer depends especially on the definition of religion, whether considered in terms of its content or in terms of its function. In the former case some reference to a superempirical reality goes hand in hand with religion. In the second we define as religion that which takes over the former functions of (the Christian) religion, for example, giving meaning to life. We might call belief in science or → Marxism, for example, religion in this sense.

If, as is to be recommended, we maintain a definition in terms of content, then we may still speak of secularization in the first and third senses mentioned at the outset. The social nexus is more or less autonomous relative to religion, and a trend toward a new monism may be detected in religions. As regards the second level of meaning, the meaning of secularization is less clear. The number of adherents of new religions is much smaller than that of those who have abandoned Christianity, but it is too early to make a general judgment about nonreligious moderns (→ Religionless Christianity).

2.2. *Causes*

Historical movements are too complex and the phenomena too multifaceted for us to trace back secularization to a single cause. Secularization is an important factor in larger sociocultural changes that we might bring under the common denominator of modernization (→ Modernity). We may note here only three specific aspects of this process. First are the things that favor differentiation, for example, increase in population, technological progress (→ Technology), political centralization (→ Modern Period 2; State), scientific discoveries, and the influence of capital in the age of exploration (→ Colonialism). Then there is the secularizing function of some Judeo-Christian ideas such as God's absolute transcendence. These ideas demystified the world, less so in Roman Catholicism than, for example, in → Calvinism. Secularization found here unintended theological legitimation. Finally, we may note the role of the elite in the autonomous spheres, those who as the "professional vanguard" knew how to systematically eliminate religious and, in part, ethical factors when defining economic, political, legal, and academic problems. In this regard mention must also be made of certain theologians who encouraged a process of adjustment in the church and to this end propagated among other things a nondualistic worldview (→ Process Theology).

The function of the elite shows that we may also view secularization as a battle slogan, a tool in the struggle for the right to have a say in interpreting the world (→ Worldview). It is very hard to separate ideology from the descriptive use of the term, which limits its academic usefulness.

2.3. *Universality and Irreversibility*

Two questions are particularly important. Is secularization a universal process? and Is it an irreversible process? In reply, it is important that we differentiate the levels of meaning. Structural differentiation is taking place everywhere. But it is difficult to say at the moment whether and when this process in the Islamic world, for example, will have the same effects as it has had in the Western world. It is possible that the relations between religion and other sectors of society, especially the political, will in the long term show up a different pattern. Even if a long-term process is not necessarily irreversible, it is hard to think that reversal will take place in the foreseeable future.

Differentiation, however, does not necessarily bring with it the end of the church or religion. As noted, religion is strong in many countries like the United States and those of the Third World, and → Islam is on the march, while even in western Europe new forms of religion may be seen. As regards individual religion, much depends on how powerfully a modern scientific worldview spreads across the globe and on how far it too comes under radical criticism.

Bibliography: R. N. Bellah, "Religious Evolution," *ASR* 29 (1964) 358-74 • P. L. Berger, *The Sacred Canopy: Elements of a Sociological Theory of Religion* (New York, 1990; orig. pub., 1967) • K. W. Dahm, V. Drehsen, and G. Kehrer, *Das Jenseits der Gesellschaft. Religion im Prozeß sozialwissenschaftlicher Kritik* (Munich, 1975) • K. Dobbelaere, *Secularization: An Analysis at Three Levels* (Brussels, 2002) • G. Dux, *Die Logik der Weltbilder. Sinnstrukturen im Wandel der Geschichte* (3d ed.; Frankfurt, 1990) • R. K. Fenn, *The Secularization of Sin: An Investigation of the Daedalus Complex* (Louisville, Ky., 1991); idem, *Toward a Theory of Secularization* (Storrs, Conn., 1978) • K. Gabriel, *Christentum zwischen Tradition und Moderne* (7th ed.; Freiburg, 2000) • A. M. Greeley, *Unsecular Man: The Persistence of Religion* (New York, 1972) • J. K. Hadden and A. Shupe, eds., *Secularization and Fundamentalism Reconsidered* (New York, 1989) • F. X. Kaufmann, *Religion und Modernität. Sozialwissenschaftliche Perspektiven* (Tübingen, 1988) • N. Luhmann, *Funktion der Religion* (5th ed.; Frankfurt, 1999; orig. pub., 1977) • D. Martin, *A General Theory of Secularization* (Aldershot, 1993; orig. pub., 1978) • R. Steininger, *Polarisierung und Integration. Eine vergleichende Untersuchung der strukturellen Versäulung der Gesellschaft in den Niederlanden und in Österreich* (Meisenheim, 1975) • W. H. Swatos Jr. and D. V. A. Olson, eds., *The Secularization Debate* (Lanham, Md., 2000).

Leo Laeyendecker

Self

1. Term

The term "self" commonly refers to the aspect of a person that is considered "inner"; it is often used interchangeably with "subject," "person," "identity," "soul," and "mind." As a term of identification, self is opposed to that which is nonself. It is usually used in specific reference to the individual or item as bounded and distinct from others or from external entities and events. For persons, it is that which can be identified as one's experience of continuity over time and place. The self is the subject and object of human consciousness. To say "I am (*or* I am not) myself" implies a reference point that is the "I" and is not the "I," subject and object, the one knowing and the one known.

Key questions in theorizing the self include: Is the self substance or event, an unchanging given or a developing emergent? To what extent is "self" thought of and practiced in normative terms? How does the self relate to the body and other aspects of personhood? Is there a self in actuality, or is it simply a pragmatically useful hypothetical construct? Is there a self that can be postulated across time and place, or do differing theories really represent differing selves?

2. Historical Development

The Hebrew Bible does not have a term that translates easily into the modern sense of the word "self." *Rûaḥ* (breath/spirit), *nepeš* (soul), and *lēb* (heart) provide the closest parallels, and their usage suggests a monistic Hebraic concept of self in which body, in terms of both bodily organs and breath, is an expression of the whole.

Ancient Greek philosophers also did not use the term "self," but their ruminations on mind, → soul, and person form the basis in Western thought for modern conceptions of self. The system of thought of Socrates (ca. 470-399 B.C.) indicates a shift from investigation of the cosmos and attention to the gods of the universe to reflection on the inner life of human beings. Socrates postulated an internal conflict between, on the one hand, the inner force that compelled, guided, and reasoned and, on the other, the desires of the body. This inner invisible force, as opposed to the visible body, is constant, unchanging, and closest to God and therefore a most suitable object of one's examination. Plato (427-347; → Platonism) continued in this vein, stressing the soul or mind as the internal seat of higher good in conflict with feelings and desires for sensual pleasure. Aristotle (384-322; → Aristotelianism), however, proposed that the soul must be dependent on the body, not a thing that is placed in or trapped in a body. The self, for Aristotle, is equated with the total functioning of a being.

Ancient Eastern texts on the meaning of persons and soul examine tensions similar to those explored by the Greeks, but they follow somewhat different emphases in their attempts to resolve those tensions. → Confucianism was more interested in the moral goodness or evil of a self than in the metaphysical explanations for that good or evil in human nature. In the Hindu → Upanishads the self is portrayed as an inward substance that is more or less bodiless and timeless. While the relation of the physical body to the inner self is nuanced differently in different strands of Hindu thought, the *Ātman,* or Universal Self, is generally thought to be the divine within what in its purist sense is Brahman, or Totality. Buddhists take this idea further with the concept of *anātman,* the absence of a permanent self. The point of the spiritual journey through many → reincarnations is to seek nirvana and the realization of the self as illusion.

Platonic thought had the most influence on early Christians, which can be seen in the Pauline writings of the NT, where *sōma* (body) and *psychē* (soul) are set in more dualistic relationship than was the case for Hebraic thought. This kind of qualified dualism, however, also seeks to maintain the value of the material and the importance of embodied identity. Nevertheless, the tensions in Christian thought between monistic and dualistic approaches to soul, or what in some strands of the tradition is understood as mind (or reason) and body, point to the difficulties in interpreting the meaning of self in Christian thought.

Augustine's (354-430; → Augustine's Theology) self-reflection in his *Confessions* has perhaps had the most enduring effect on the concept of the self in Western Christianity. Augustine encouraged self-reflection as a means to remove the obstacles to God in the self, understood as body and human will, in order to reach greater union with God in the innermost regions of the soul. → Sin, defined as self-indulgence, self-satisfaction, and self-pride, implied that the self was a problem to be overcome; the path to → salvation, though, included a turn within to find one's innermost need for relationship with God. Self-knowledge through introspection as necessary for God-knowledge is a common theme in Christian thought, although the meaning of this concept in pre-20th-century terms should not be construed through later psychological theories. In Augustine and other early theologians this kind of introspection was more focused on the self in relation to God and others than on the self in relation to itself.

While Augustine was setting the path for Western Christianity, Eastern Christianity was developing a slightly different emphasis. Although not denying the significance of guilt and sin, the → Cappadocians emphasized the *imago Dei* and the potential for → perfection of human nature through communion with God (→ Theosis).

The Middle Ages, with an emphasis on religious authority and identity based on socioeconomic class, was relatively silent on issues related to self and the individual. During this time, however, Thomas Aquinas (ca. 1225-74; → Thomism) influenced Christian ideas by adopting a more Aristotelian view of self, along with emphasis on the natural goodness of the body.

As Western thought shifted into the era of the → Enlightenment, René Descartes (1596-1650; → Cartesianism) arguably provided the basis for modern Western conceptions of self. His famous axiom *Cogito, ergo sum* (I think, therefore I am) exemplified emphasis on the self as thinker and knower. With human reason as the center of knowledge, interest again arose in what made human beings who they are — who was it that reasoned, thought, spoke, and knew? The self as rational entity, as opposed to body, was the one thing of which Descartes could be certain.

Enlightenment thinkers continued to develop the debates of the early Greeks, and they remain recognizable as key issues to this day. British empiricist John Locke (1632-1704; → Empiricism) suggested that no innate self existed; rather, the self started as a blank slate, a *tabula rasa,* that through the sense experience of the body developed into an enduring pattern and structure. Later David Hume (1711-76) argued that the self was actually no more than an illusion, a "bundle of perceptions," an accumulation of experience through sense perception that gave the impression of something actual.

In response to empiricist approaches Immanuel Kant (1724-1804; → Kantianism) proposed that a thing or a person had value in and of itself but that no thing can be known in and of itself. It can be known only through our experience of it, through appearances. Kant posited a self that can be known and a self that cannot be known, even by oneself. Selfhood as we know it, then, is something that is realized, a phenomenon, an object of knowledge, but about self as metaphysical principle, or knower, we can say nothing. Kant saw each person as an end in himself or herself, and as the bearer of an absolute moral law.

Idealists responded with a focus on the conflict between self and other (→ Idealism). G. W. F. Hegel (1770-1831) suggested that the self develops in a continual cycle of conflictual interactions with others in the world. The self discovers and knows itself through positing and encountering the opposite, or no-self. I become myself through interactions with what is not me. Later Karl Marx (1818-83) put these conflicts in a social context in which one can be alienated from self through material, socioeconomic conditions (→ Marxism).

Existentialists revised this notion of alienation and conflict, presenting it as an internal struggle. Søren Kierkegaard (1813-55; → Existentialism) argued that the dread of not being is essential to being human. The resultant → anxiety propels persons into actions and choices, which can enhance or diminish self. Anxiety is inescapable; one should therefore cultivate an awareness of how that anxiety operates and impacts the choices one makes in life. Using self in the normative sense, Kierkegaard equated more consciousness of self with more self.

3. Modern Psychology

From these philosophical underpinnings emerged theories of the self in modern → psychology. In modern times "self" usually means the inner psychological aspect of personhood. William James (1842-1910), often cited as the founder of modern psychology, or at least of American psychology, developed an explicit theory of the self as having two aspects: the self as known, or the empirical self, and the self as knower, or the pure ego. In the former the self is "me" and all that I can claim as me — material, social, and spiritual; this is the realm of psychological concern. This self is dynamic and in constant change. The latter aspect, pure ego, is the "I," the abstract one who knows and seems to appear constant over time, beyond consciousness.

Though he did not develop an explicit theory of the self, Sigmund Freud (1856-1939) has probably had the most influence on modern psychological conceptions of self. According to Freud's psychoanalytic theory, the unconscious has the most influence on human personality and behavior; the conscious self is but the "tip of the iceberg" (→ Psychoanalysis). The psyche develops over time, built up through internalized objects born out of libidinal conflicts tied to somatic functions, and prone to fragmentation. Freud's ego, one part of the tripartite structure of Freud's psyche (consisting of id, ego, and superego), should not be equated with the self of James and later psychologists or with the pure ego or self of earlier philosophers. His theory indicates that the conscious and unconscious, the known and the knower, are more ambiguous than such an equation would suggest.

Object-relations theorists developed and revised Freud's theories, with emphasis on the infant/parent relationship, although in various ways they have maintained a theory of the primacy of the unconscious in psychic development and experience of a self. D. W. Winnicott introduced the "true self," innate spontaneous needs and feelings in need of expression, and the "false self," conditioned responses based on external expectation. Heinz Kohut developed a psychoanalytically based "self psychology" that emphasizes the development of a nuclear self through empathic attachments to others and the need to love oneself.

Carl Jung (1875-1961), an early Freud revisionist, took the psychoanalytic theory of self in a radically different direction, using self in a normative sense as something to be sought after and achieved. Jung's self is the hidden personality constituent one finds on the road to integration, wholeness, and balance. Jung's stress on self-realization or self-actualization was a precursor to contemporary humanistic theories such as those of Abraham Maslow (1908-70) and Carl Rogers (1902-87).

Throughout the 20th century, in contrast to the psychoanalytically based personality theorists, logical positivists in psychology denied any notion of an "internal" self (→ Positivism). The self is an unneeded hypothetical construct, according to behaviorists, since human behavior can be understood completely through observable and measurable patterns, not through introspection and self-reflection.

4. Postmodern Concerns

The postmodern emphasis on particularity and questions about universal → truth raise concerns about the appropriateness of any one theory of the self or any notion that the self might be the same across difference. Some proclaim → postmodernism as an era marking the "death of the subject." Critiques of objectivity and universal truth lead to critiques of the autonomous and stable self in favor of a self that is fluid, multiple, contingent, decentered, and deconstructed. Theorists in African American and non-Western cultures suggest that the selves of Asian peoples, African peoples, and others are in fact different from those described by Western philosophy and psychology.

Feminist psychology, anthropology, and sociology explore the differences between the male self and the female self and debate the extent to which these differences are innate or socially constructed (→ Feminism). These theorists argue that "natural" is actually a construction of culture read back into history as that which is unchanging and has always been. Nancy Chodorow has proposed, in an alternative psychoanalytic theory of self, that gendered differences in personality are based on processes of internalization carried out in particular → family structures that make women develop more emphasis on nurturing and relationship. If the family structure were different, then women's self would be different. What is deemed "natural" to women may in fact be an effect of a patriarchal family structure.

The use of self as a normative concept is thus also called into question. Feminists and postmodern theorists have argued that a particular vision for what is valuable and good undergirds any theory of the self. Carol Gilligan's research shows that Erik Erikson's (1902-94) psychoanalytic developmental theory of the self is in fact a theory of male development tied to the Western ideology of → autonomy, self-sufficiency, and the → rights of the individual. When examined, women's lives suggested that the self developed out of relationships and intimacy, rather than independence.

Poststructuralists posit that the self is actually a discursive effect, inseparable from → ideology. In this view we are compelled to consider to what extent a theory or science is prescriptive rather than descriptive and to question who profits from any particular position on what is real and actual. Theories of the self must address not only the sense of continuity over time and place experienced by most people but also change, difference, and multiplicity. Is there an essential self that exists untouched by and under layers of culture? If so, can we know it?

Advances in science and technology have also impacted theories of the self. Brain studies call for more thorough consideration of the ties between mind and body. Genetic therapies, psychopharmacology, and new surgical techniques raise questions about what it means to speak of a "true" or "authentic" self. Once again the relationship of self to body is in the center of debate. In day-to-day conversation persons do not make distinctions between body and self. We say, "I am running," not "My body is running"; we say, "I think," not "My mind thinks." In times of illness or in discussions of appearance, however, we often try to make a distinction between one's body and the "real" me.

5. Implications for Christian Theology

Philosophies and psychologies of the self have clear implications for theological → anthropology. There are underlying ontological assumptions in any of the above theoretical constructions that may or may not resonate with any particular theological conviction related to who persons are in relation to God. Since the appearance of modern psychology, some scholars have attempted to clarify the difference between self and soul, and yet in common usage references to the soul often sound like references to an internal emotional or rational center that could also be called the self.

In the mid-20th century Paul Tillich (1886-1966) argued that self-reflection and self-acceptance are crucial to salvation, understood as healing. He suggested that theologians should take seriously the questions raised by psychology and psychoanalytic theories. Seward Hiltner (1909-84), a pastoral theologian, influenced many in the field of → pastoral care to consider a two-way critical conversation between theologians and psychological theorists so that theological responses to questions of what it means to be human would be informed by and critical of the knowledge developed in each of the fields. Since the inception of the field known as pastoral care, pastoral theologians have debated the extent to which particular psychological theories of the self are compatible with particular theological anthropologies.

Theological accounts of salvation, → healing, and → resurrection run directly into issues of (1) how one speaks of the healing of the soul/spirit without denying the resurrection of the body, (2) whether a vital self or spirit requires a vital body, and (3) the self as body/mind/spirit created in the image of God and yet also that which seems to urge persons toward sin. A theological anthropology informed by the theory of self as a seat of conflict between bodily desires and rational thought says something quite different about the human condition than one that poses the self as primarily constituted by relationships to others. Postmodern critiques of nature and essence raise serious questions about what it means to say that human beings are created in the image of God. Theologies of the image of God, body and soul, and the human condition must take into account current theories of self in other fields without reducing theology to psychology.

It is clear from the historical development of the concept "self" that the word is used in a multitude of ways, indicating everything from an internal entity to the whole of the person. A current challenge is to consider in what ways "soul," "body," "person," "identity," "subject," "mind," and "self" are used interchangeably or distinctively as a means to support and perpetuate certain ideologies and in what ways those ideologies are tied to particular theological positions.

Bibliography: W. T. Anderson, *The Future of the Self: Inventing the Postmodern Person* (New York, 1997) • N. Chodorow, *The Reproduction of Mothering: Psychoanalysis and the Sociology of Gender* (2d ed.; Berkeley, Calif., 1999; orig. pub., 1978) • J. Flax, *Disputed Subjects: Essays on Psychoanalysis, Politics, and Philosophy* (New York, 1993) • K. Gergen, *The Saturated Self: Dilemmas of Identity in Contemporary Life* (New York, 1991) • C. Gilligan, "Woman's Place in Man's Life Cycle," *In a Different Voice* (Cambridge, Mass., 1993) 5-23 • E. Keen, *A History of Ideas in American Psychology* (Westport, Conn. 2001) • J. Lapsley, "The 'Self,' Its Vicissitudes and Possibilities: An Essay in Theological Anthropology," *PastPsy* 35/1 (1986) 23-45 • J. D. Levin, *Theories of the Self* (Washington, D.C., 1992) • R. W. Lundin, *Theories and Systems of Psychology* (5th ed.;

Lexington, Mass., 1996) • T. W. ORGAN, *Philosophy and the Self: East and West* (Cranbury, N.J., 1987) • R. PORTER, ed., *Rewriting the Self: Histories from the Middle Ages to the Present* (London, 1997) • W. PROUDFOOT, *God and the Self: Three Types of Philosophy of Religion* (Cranbury, N.J., 1976) • W. S. SAHAKIAN, *History and Systems of Psychology* (New York, 1975) • R. C. SOLOMON, *Continental Philosophy since 1750: The Rise and Fall of the Self* (Oxford, 1988) • J. STRAUSS and G. R. GOETHALS, eds., *The Self: Interdisciplinary Approaches* (New York, 1991).

JEANNE HOEFT

Semi-Pelagianism → Pelagianism 4

Semites

In 1781 A. L. Schlözer (1735-1809) used the term "Semitic" for the first time for the supposed original language of the Syrians, Babylonians, Hebrews, and Arabs, and J. G. Eichhorn (1752-1827) then popularized it for languages related to Hebrew (→ Hebrew Language). The term "Semites" goes back to Shem, the son of Noah. According to the table in Genesis 10, Shem and his brothers, Ham and Japheth, were the ancestors of all nations after the flood (v. 32). Though interpretation of the table is complex, ethnic considerations obviously played no great part in it. The dominant interest is in → Abraham, who, as the ancestral head of the people of → Israel (§1), is traced back genealogically to Shem (Gen. 11:10-32), thus giving Shem early preeminence (9:26-27).

For various reasons, political, religious, and ethnic, Ham is the rival and can take many different forms, for example, "Canaan" (Gen. 9:18-27) and "Egypt" (Ps. 78:51; 105:23, 27; 106:22). Also note that Egypt, Canaan, and others are the children of Ham in Gen. 10:6 and 1 Chr. 1:8.

Neither the text nor what we know of the ancient history of the Near East supports the idea of a Semitic people group. Back as far as the third millennium, the documentary evidence rules out any ethnic identification or racial characterization of the many known peoples and immigrants in these areas, along with their social structures (→ Anti-Semitism, Anti-Judaism; Racism 1.3; Hebrews). For this reason reconstruction of an ancient Semitic religion raises serious problems.

At the same time, we can distinguish a Semitic language group from a Hamitic or Indo-European. As inflected language systems, the Semitic languages all probably developed in prehistoric times in northwest Africa and western Europe and had a common (ethnic?) origin. Original linguistic links are clearest in ancient Egyptian, in which we find both Semitic and Hamitic elements.

The oldest Semitic languages (Eblaite, Akkadian) date from the middle of the third millennium. We find North Semitic (Eblaite, known from the clay-tablet archives found in 1975 in Ebla, or modern Tall Mardīkh, near Aleppo), Northeast Semitic (Akkadian, plus the Babylonian and Assyrian dialects), Northwest Semitic (Ugaritic, perhaps originally a North Semitic language), with its Canaanite branches (Phoenician-Punic and Hebrew), and Aramaic and South Semitic (Old South Arabic, Ethiopic, North Arabic).

The alphabet, a model for others, developed in Northwest Semitic. For the first time it made reading and writing possible for many classes.

Bibliography: P. R. BENNETT, *Comparative Semitic Linguistics: A Manual* (Winona Lake, Ind., 1998) • D. COHEN, *Les langues chamito-sémitiques* (Paris, 1988) • W. DAUM, *Ursemitische Religion* (Stuttgart, 1985) • A. DOLGOPOLSKII, *From Proto-Semitic to Hebrew: Phonology. Etymological Approach in a Hamito-Semitic Perspective* (Milan, 1999) • G. B. GRAGG, "Semites," *OEANE* 4.516-27 • J. HUEHNERGARD et al., "Languages," *ABD* 4.155-229; idem, "New Directions in the Study of Semitic Languages," *The Study of the Ancient Near East in the Twenty-first Century* (ed. J. S. Cooper and G. M. Schwartz; Winona Lake, Ind., 1996) 251-72 • S. MOSCATI, *The Semites in Ancient History* (Cardiff, 1959) • W. VON SODEN, *The Ancient Orient: An Introduction to the Study of the Ancient Near East* (Grand Rapids, 1994).

HERMANN SPIECKERMANN

Senegal

	1960	*1980*	*2000*
Population (1,000s):	3,187	5,538	9,495
Annual growth rate (%):	2.58	2.81	2.59

Area: 196,712 sq. km. (75,951 sq. mi.)

A.D. 2000

Population density: 48/sq. km. (125/sq. mi.)
Births / deaths: 3.90 / 1.31 per 100 population
Fertility rate: 5.18 per woman
Infant mortality rate: 56 per 1,000 live births
Life expectancy: 53.3 years (m: 52.3, f: 54.3)
Religious affiliation (%): Muslims 87.5, tribal religionists 6.3, Christians 5.7 (Roman Catholics 5.5, other Christians 0.3), other 0.5.

1. General Situation
2. Religious Situation

1. General Situation

The Republic of Senegal is the westernmost country on the African continent. It is home to over 50 ethnic groups in three main linguistic families. Two-thirds of the population live in coastal areas, with more than one-quarter of the population in the capital, Dakar. The major ethnic groups are the Wolof (43 percent of the total population), Pular (24 percent), Serer (15 percent), and Jola (4 percent). The seminomadic Soninke and the Tukulor live in the Senegal valley. The Fulbe and Mandinka are mainly herding nomads on the arid savanna of the central and eastern parts of Senegal. Other ethnic and national groups (e.g., Cape Verdeans, Lebanese, and French) form only a small minority. The official language is French, but Wolof, Pulaar, Jola, and Mandinka are important popular languages.

1.1. Senegal's economy has suffered from a lack of diversification (an overreliance on peanuts and → tourism), the dominance of the public sector, and relative investment inefficiency. Attempts are being made to diversify agriculture, and in 1994 economic reforms were initiated. The Senegalese currency, which had been linked at a fixed rate to the French franc, was devaluated by 50 percent. Government control and subsidies have decreased, and private activity now accounts for 82 percent of the gross domestic product (GDP). During the years 1995-2003, the GDP grew at an average of 5 percent annually, and inflation is now in the low single digits.

All industrial production centers on Dakar and its suburbs (2.2 million inhabitants in 2003). Almost 50 percent of the people live in cities, and urban → poverty and misery are Senegal's worst social problems. Though the majority of the labor force works on the land, agriculture contributes less than 20 percent of the GDP.

1.2. In the Senegambia region the savanna meets the Atlantic coast, and the history of the local people has a dynamic quality. From at least the tenth century there has been considerable north-south trading through the Sahara, which has influenced several aspects of regional life. Thus for centuries great numbers of horses have been traded from the north.

Brought by traders and having taken root early on, → Islam has had a mobilizing effect on political life. For a time the region fell under the influence of the great medieval savanna states of Mali and Songhai. After their collapse by the end of the 16th century, rival smaller states governed political life.

The Portuguese landed in the 15th century between the mouths of the Senegal and the Gambia rivers, followed by the Dutch, French, and English in the 16th century. The coastal strip and the nearby Île de Gorée became centers of the transatlantic slave trade (→ Slavery). The trans-Sahara trade lost its determinative significance later as a result of the strength of the transatlantic trade.

In the second half of the 19th century the French broke the last resistance of local rulers and made Senegal a base for their colonial penetration of West Africa (→ Colonialism). The variously named Social Democratic Party, founded by the poet and philosopher Léopold Sédar Senghor (1906-2001), developed into the main nationalistic force in the country (→ Nation, Nationalism). The concept of *négritude,* with its stress on African values and history, linked Senghor to the political philosophy of African → socialism, which rejected → class conflict and → atheism.

Senegal gained its independence from France in 1960, and until Senghor stepped down voluntarily from the presidency at the turn of the year 1980/81, he was in undisputed control of Senegal's power structure. In spite of a confessed socialism on the basis of African community values, a small, largely technocratic, and Western-oriented political elite took over most of Senegal's economic wealth. Senghor's successor, Abdou Diouf (president 1980-2000), adopted from the outset a concept of democratic openness (esp. freedom for political parties), remitted the debts of farmers, reformed unions, and took measures against corruption.

Abdoulaye Wade, of the Senegalese Democratic Party, was elected president in April 2000, defeating Diouf in a runoff election. In January 2001 a new constitution was adopted that established a unicameral parliament and reduced future presidential terms to five years (after the completion of Wade's present seven-year term in 2007).

An armed separatist movement was active in the Casamance region, with whom the government signed a peace pact in March 2001. In September 2002 more than 1,000 passengers perished when a state-owned ferry sank off the coast of Gambia.

2. Religious Situation

2.1. Close to 90 percent of the people of Senegal adhere to Islam, which has been rooted in all parts of the land for a thousand years. Senegal has nevertheless retained its national languages, cultural features, religions, and forms of social organization. Worth noting in this regard is the great epic of Sundiata (also called Sun-Jata or Son-Jara), which is still sung by *griots* (bards). Many uncodified oral versions exist that show traces of Islam — for example, the linking of the genealogies of local ruling families with figures in the → Qur'an — but they are nonetheless clearly pre-Islamic. The main theme of the story is the way in which the hero Sundiata overcame magical threats by the use of stronger → magic.

Islam in this region has long been familiar with the jihad (→ War 2). A typical feature of Islam in Senegal is the three Sufi brotherhoods Qādirīyah, Tijānīyah, and Muridīyah, to one of which 80 to 90 percent of all Muslims in Senegal belong. The largest and most influential is the Muridīyah, which is thought to control half the Senegalese peanut production. Thus far brotherhood representatives have supported government policies in return for privileges.

2.2. Christians represent a small minority in Senegal. Christianity is strongest among the Serer and Diola people in the southwest. The largest group is the → Roman Catholic Church. Dakar is an archdiocese; the first native bishop was consecrated in 1962.

Protestants form only an insignificant minority. An important Protestant church is the Église Protestante de Sénégal, founded by the Paris Mission (→ French Missions) in 1863. Two-thirds of its members, however, are Europeans. The Lutheran Church, started in 1974 by the Finnish Lutheran Mission, is the largest Protestant denomination, with 3,300 members in 2000. After World War II the → Pentecostal churches began work in Senegal. The → Assemblies of God have done intensive radio → evangelism in various native languages.

→ African Theology

Bibliography: D. B. Barrett, G. T. Kurian, and T. M. Johnson, *WCE* (2d ed.) 1.653-56 • R. M. Baum, *Shrines of the Slave Trade: Diola Religion and Society in Precolonial Senegambia* (New York, 1999) • L. C. Behrman, *Muslim Brotherhoods and Politics in Senegal* (Cambridge, Mass., 1970) • R. Bertol, *Sundiata: The Epic of the Lion King, Retold* (New York, 1970) • S. Gellar, *Senegal: An African Nation between Islam and the West* (2d ed.; Westview, Colo., 1995) • J. W. Johnson and F.-D. Sisòkò, *The Epic of Son-Jara* (Bloomington, Ind., 1986) • D. E. Maranz, *Peace Is Everything: World View of Muslims in the Senegambia* (Dallas, 1993) • L. O. Sanneh, *Piety and Power: Muslims and Christians in West Africa* (Maryknoll, N.Y., 1996) • L. S. Senghor, "Negritude: A Humanism of the Twentieth Century," *I Am because We Are: Readings in Black Philosophy* (ed. F. L. Hord and J. S. Lee; Amherst, Mass., 1995) 45-54 • G. T. Stride and C. Ifeka, *Peoples and Empires of West Africa: West Africa in History, 1000-1800* (New York, 1971) • L. A. Villalón, *Islamic Society and State Power in Senegal* (Cambridge, 1995).

Paul Jenkins and Peter Haenger

Separatism

1. Political
2. Ecclesiastical

1. Political

Separatism is a breakaway movement either politically or ecclesiastically. In French *séparatisme* also denotes the separation of → church and state. Politically, separatism involves the efforts to detach a state or a federation of states and either to make them independent or to incorporate them into a neighboring state. Germany after World War I saw a movement between 1919 and 1924 for a free Rhenish state. The term "separatism" replaced older ones such as *Sonderbündelei* ("special clustering," after *Sonderbund,* "special federation," used in the 19th century by Roman Catholic Swiss cantons in their attempt to join together) or "secession" (for the attempt of U.S. Southern states in 1861-65 to break free from the Union).

Political separatism is primarily an expression of ethnic, cultural, or religious → minorities who feel discriminated against politically and legally (e.g., the Basques, Catalans, → Kurds, Tamils, or French Canadians). When Communism collapsed in Eastern Europe, separatist movements in many regions resulted in the formation of many new states, for example, the Baltic states in the former → Soviet Union, Slovakia out of Czechoslovakia, and Croatia out of Yugoslavia. Smaller separatist movements exist in Britain (Scots) and France (Bretons), while separatism in Bosnia and Herzegovina has plunged the region into civil war.

2. Ecclesiastical

Ecclesiastical separatism is essentially older than political separatism. The term in this context denotes the separation of individuals or groups from a → church. The → early church used the term "schism" (→ Heresies and Schisms 3), and this word is still current today but is heavily freighted ecclesiologically and legally.

Separatism is a Protestant variation and strictly applies only in the Protestant sphere. We find it used technically already in Anabaptism (→ Baptists) during the Reformation period. At the end of the

16th century the English Separatists were radical → Puritans who wished to speed up reform by forming their own congregations apart from the national church (e.g., the Brownists and Barrowists), thus earning for themselves the title "schismatic persons." In Holland and Germany the term gained a footing only in the days of → Pietism.

2.1. For all the differences in conditions and causes, the many Protestant manifestations of separatism always have their roots in criticism of the doctrine or practice of the church, which then leads to separation. (F. → Schleiermacher's interpretation of separatism in his *Kurze Darstellung* [Brief outline] as "those conditions which especially indicate a weakening of the impetus to community" [§57] is historically questionable.)

2.2. The left wing of the → Reformation was already a protest against Reformation ecclesiology and the implied practice. It was also an expression of the desire to achieve Christian perfection as opposed to the mainline churches, with their institutional structures and readiness to compromise with the world. The efforts to solve the dialectical tensions in the concept of the → church (§3.4.1) are evidenced by two alternative models. The Anabaptists wanted the church to be a people visibly separated from the world, the communion of saints that by Bible-centered renewal would represent primitive Christianity, for example, by adult baptism, strict church discipline, the refusal to take oaths, and → pacifism. Separatism involved a withdrawal from every ungodly "abomination," including "all popish and antipopish [i.e., Reformation] works and church services, meetings, and church attendance" (Schleitheim Articles 4 [1527]).

The other model is that of the mystical spiritualists (→ Mysticism 2.5.2; Spiritualism), who regarded all external things — the outward word of Scripture, the sacraments, ordinances, ministries, and forms of worship — as of little worth. For them the true church was the invisible, spiritual church. They stood indifferently aloof from the institutional church of sects both old and new (the traditional churches and the Anabaptist groups), or else they denounced them as signs of end-time anti-Christian Babylon (see Revelation 18). Some (e.g., the Schwenckfeldians) separated from the churches, but many more remained in the external fellowship of their religious party, avoiding a sectarian spirit, and adopted a nonparty stance.

2.3. In England, apart from the "privy churches" of Mary's reign, separatism took hold only as a result of the settlement under Elizabeth I (1558-1603). A radical Puritan minority found their hopes dashed of a more consistently biblical reformation and did not think the → Anglican Church capable of being reformed because of its episcopal constitution and its ties to the state. Congregations of Separatists began to form, first of all the Brownists under R. Browne (ca. 1550-1633; see his *Treatise of Reformation* [1582]) and then the Congregationalists (see John Robinson's *Justification of Separation from the Church* [1610]) and Baptists. Later, → "Dissenters" became the common term for these and other groups, for example, Presbyterians, Quakers, and, after the 18th century, Methodists and Unitarians.

2.4. → Pietism had separatist potentiality from the very first. Analysis of faults in the national churches commonly led to abandonment of all hopes of reform and the separating of the devout into their own church, along with renunciation of the world in disjunction from a church that was thought to be too worldly. The rise of separatism depended on various factors in theology, ecclesiastical politics, and group dynamics. In radical Pietism we find both individual separatism and the formation of separate fellowships. The neo-Baptists (in U.S. → Brethren churches [§1]) with their strict → biblicism laid claim to the older Anabaptist legacy, but most Pietist separatists were in the tradition of mystical spiritualism and rejected the building of new external fellowships as sectarianism.

2.5. In the 19th century → revivals and their impact formed the background for separation in many countries and for the formation of → free churches — for example, the Free Church of Scotland, the *Églises libres* in French Switzerland, and the Old Reformed Church in Lower Saxony. With various emphases and in different combinations, such factors were at work as opposition to the → Enlightenment, which had penetrated theology and the church; the renewal and strengthening of a confessional sense (→ Confession of Faith 4); and the revitalizing of efforts to secure spiritual independence of state influence. In Germany the → unions and the associated politics brought about the separation of Old Lutheran congregations from the various territorial churches.

2.6. In different manifestations and groupings neopietism (→ Charismatic Movement; Evangelical Movement; Holiness Movement) has involved great differences in the understanding of the community, with tensions between conceptions favoring a free church on the one hand and a national church (→ Volkskirche) on the other. The development of alternative institutions promotes a tendency toward separatism.

Bibliography: M. Brecht et al., eds., *Geschichte des Pietismus* (4 vols.; Göttingen, 1993-2004) esp. vol. 1 • M. R. Greenshields and T. A. Robinson, eds., *Orthodoxy and Heresy in Religious Movements: Discipline and Dissent* (Lewiston, N.Y., 1992) • F. Jung, *Die deutsche evangelikale Bewegung* (3d ed.; Bonn, 2001) • B. M. Roehner, *Separatism and Integration: A Study in Analytical History* (Lanham, Md., 2002) • M. Spencer, ed., *Separatism: Democracy and Disintegration* (Lanham, Md., 1998) • J. Wallmann, *Der Pietismus* (Göttingen, 1990) • M. R. Watts, *The Dissenters* (vol. 1; Oxford, 1978) • B. R. White, *The English Separatist Tradition: From the Marian Martyrs to the Pilgrim Fathers* (Oxford, 1971).

Hans Schneider

Septuagint

Overview

As the first written biblical translation, as a document of Hellenistic Judaism, and as an important source and resource for the authors of the NT and other early Christians, the Septuagint was enormously influential in antiquity and is eminently worthy of continued research today. Its full integration into biblical scholarship will enrich our understanding of and appreciation for those responsible for this remarkable document (or series of documents; → Bible Versions 2.1).

When the writers of the NT wished to cite what was for them and their audience authoritative writ, they typically introduced their citations with expressions like "as it was written," with or without a specific attribution. These citations often vary considerably from the traditional Hebrew text (the Masoretic Text, MT), which was surely known, in at least its consonantal form, by the first century A.D. Taken as a whole, these scriptural citations approximate, when they do not equal, what we today refer to as the Septuagint. Given that the Septuagint was in Greek and that this was also the language of the NT writers, such a coincidence may not occasion much surprise. In fact, however, there are a number of surprising, as well as illuminating, factors in this relationship.

1. Translation Process

The Septuagint, or in the first instance the Old Greek translation of the Pentateuch, or → Torah, is a product of Alexandrian Jewry in the first half of the third century B.C. As narrated in such sources as the *Letter of Aristeas* (probably composed a century or so after the fact; → Pseudepigrapha 1.3), 72 translators were responsible for this version. (The number 72 was later rounded off to 70, Lat. *septuaginta,* the number thus giving the name "Septuagint" to the translation and serving as the source of the commonly used abbreviation "LXX.")

The impetus for this novel enterprise, we are told, lay with King Ptolemy II Philadelphus (285-246 B.C.), who desired this sacred text, in nonbarbarian Greek, for his growing library. Although many scholars cast doubt on this royal connection, it fits in well with what is known of the era and forms a fitting complement to the other need this translation would fulfill, namely, that of understanding the Scriptures. The Jews in Alexandria recognized that few of them were fluent any longer in Hebrew, for most had adopted the Greek lingua franca.

There were no precedents for the work of these translators, so they wisely adopted a fairly literal approach to the Hebrew text, sometimes bending the Greek too far in their efforts to reflect the sacred words. But on the whole, their literalism is sensible and can be comprehended in both narrative and legal sections. Although the *Letter of Aristeas* portrays the LXX Pentateuch as the work of one committee, modern scholars have detected five and perhaps six separate translators, whose identifying characteristics can be recognized, even as they share a common overall approach.

Initially, the term "Septuagint" referred specifically to the translators responsible for the LXX Pentateuch. The term later expanded to include the Greek version of any of the books of the OT, whether such material was a translation from a Semitic (Hebrew or Aramaic) text or an original Greek composition, as is the case for much of what we today call the → Apocrypha, or the deuterocanonical literature. Ultimately, the term "Septuagint" came to encompass almost anything in Greek that was regarded by a community as Scripture. We cannot be certain how inclusively or expansively this term was applied in the first-century Jewish communities in Palestine, when and where the NT was being composed, but it is likely that the designation was understood rather broadly.

It is also likely that the writers of the NT understood the Scripture they cited to be the result of divine → inspiration. The author of the *Letter of Aristeas,* however, did not share this view, or at least did not articulate it. Rather, he describes a procedure whereby the translators divided themselves into subcommittees, prepared drafts, debated them, and arrived at a final version on the basis of compromise and consensus. Apart from the fact that these translators appear to have enjoyed royal patronage and palatial surroundings, their deliberations did not differ markedly from those of today's Bible translation enterprises.

2. Reception

The author of the *Letter of Aristeas* asserts that the third-century Jewish community in → Alexandria received this translation of the Pentateuch as a document equal in value and validity to the Hebrew original. This report would support the view that the translators were somehow inspired in their task, although the only miraculous aspect that the letter's author allows for is that the 72 translators completed their work in exactly 72 days, and he seems almost apologetic for this "coincidence." A curse was placed on any who would change even one iota of this now-sacred Greek version. Although subsequent revisers readily ignored this anathema (if they knew of it), at least some within the Jewish community accepted the special nature of the Septuagint.

The *Letter of Aristeas* describes what some believed within a Jewish community in the mid-second century B.C. Perhaps the fullest statement of this belief is found in the work of the philosopher Philo (ca. 15-10 B.C.–A.D. 45-50), himself an Alexandrian. He speaks of those responsible for the Septuagint not as translators but as prophets. In this way he is able to account for differences between the MT and the LXX. He also recounts that the date of the Septuagint's ratification by the Alexandrian Jewish community was celebrated as a holiday and that tours could be taken to the island of Pharos, where the translators/prophets are said to have labored. Later Jewish sources, as transmitted in the → Talmud, were divided as to whether the Greek translation was, on the whole, a positive (*b. Meg.* 9a-b) or a negative (*Sop.* 1.8) development, but they dismissed any notion that the Greek text, whatever its value, was the result of divine inspiration.

We do not know exactly which account of Septuagint origins was prevalent among those responsible for the NT. We do know that the rather rational account of Aristeas was greatly expanded among early Christians, admittedly in the centuries following the NT's composition. For the most part, this development took the form of heightening the instances of → miracles in the entire process, thus providing increasingly explicit indications of divine inspiration. Thus, in its fullest formulation, as found for example in the work of the bishop Epiphanius (ca. 315-403), each of the 72 translators was placed in a separate cell and worked in complete isolation from the others (*De mens. et pond.* 3.6). When they compared their results, they found that the translations were identical in every respect. Only God, it was believed, could bring about such absolute accord. It would be surprising if some such legends were not also circulating in first-century Palestine.

3. Composition

The Greek translators of many of the later books of the Hebrew Bible consciously modeled their efforts on the translation of the Pentateuch, a decision that was not surprising, given the extra reverence in which the Torah has traditionally been held by the Jewish community. In contrast, many other books seem to have been handled in a far freer fashion, occasionally bordering on what we would term paraphrase. Outside of the Pentateuch, though, there is no obvious pattern in how literally or freely a given book or block of material was handled.

The search for a pattern is further complicated by the fact that what we call the Septuagint is not in any way a unified document. In some cases, such as the Book of Daniel, the earliest translation was almost universally supplanted by a later version attributed to Theodotion (2d cent. A.D.). In addition, the LXX Book of Ecclesiastes, extremely literal in terms of both word choice and grammar, seems to derive from Aquila (2d cent. A.D.), another early Jewish translator or reviser. And still other blocks of Septuagint material, such as Kingdoms (i.e., 1-2 Samuel and 1-2 Kings), combine original wording with revision. Because our earliest complete Septuagint texts are uncials from the third and fourth centuries A.D., it is not possible to know whether this uneven text goes back to the first century, but there are some indications that it does. It is also possible, even likely, that NT writers had access to forms of the Septuagint (using that term broadly here to refer to any Greek version of the Hebrew Bible) that are no longer extant. Furthermore, we must reckon with the fact that some writers may have relied on their own memory, that others probably adapted the Greek before them to suit the NT context they were developing, and that still others translated the Hebrew on their own, now and then inadvertently using the same wording as a Septuagint text.

Although we can say generally that NT citations of Scripture do not regularly follow the MT, conclusive demonstration in particular cases may be difficult. Quite simply, the process of retroversion — in this case, establishing the likely Hebrew that lies behind a Greek text — is far from an exact science. Even when the difficulties of retroversion are taken into account, Hebrew and Greek versions are not identical in their wording and, on occasion, in their order. For some books, such as Jeremiah, the text is almost 15 percent shorter in the LXX than in the MT. The LXX Book of Proverbs does not exhibit quantitative differences of such a degree, but qualitatively it is at wide variance from the MT in its wording of certain passages.

To account for these differences, scholars have devised two differing explanations. In one view the translators faithfully reflected what was in their Hebrew; differences between their Greek and our Hebrew arise from the fact that their Hebrew differed, to a greater or lesser extent, from the MT. According to the other explanation, the translators had before them a Hebrew text virtually identical to the consonantal MT, but they felt themselves empowered to make all sorts of changes for a variety of reasons, including the need to explain what they saw as obscure and the desire to update or accommodate the Semitic Hebrew to the Hellenistic world they inhabited. Surely there is validity to both views and to permutations that combine them. It cannot be proved that the writers of the NT were aware of these textual variations, but they may well have been. If so, they may have consciously chosen the rendering that best reflected their understanding and application of Scripture.

Variations, often substantial, can also occur as a result of the process of revision and retranslation, referred to above. In the case of revision, the older Greek text is judged on the whole to be a satisfactory representation of the Hebrew for a given community; changes, generally sporadic, are introduced for the purpose of clarification, updating, and especially to bring the Greek into line with the Hebrew text then in use by the community. So far as we can tell, this last effort consistently served to produce a Greek that reflected more closely the MT (sometimes its vocalization, in addition to its consonants). Translators, if they are not the creators of the first version in their language, are either unaware of earlier efforts or are in rather thoroughgoing disagreement with the procedures used for the earlier rendering of the foreign-language text.

It is not easy, and in some cases not possible, to discern whether a given Greek version is a revision or a translation. In addition to Theodotion and Aquila, mentioned above, another ancient Greek version is attributed to Symmachus (late 2d cent. A.D.). In all probability, each of these three individuals (and the schools or movements of which they were a part) was Jewish, although from antiquity on there is considerable disagreement on biographical particulars. Aquila is generally described as hyperliteral, and Symmachus's text is marked by the type of freedom that privileges the Greek over the Hebrew. Theodotion tended to adopt a middle road.

None of these three versions, to say nothing of others that were transmitted anonymously, has been preserved, except in fragments, mostly in the margins of manuscripts that reflect some knowledge of the *Hexapla* of Origen (ca. 185-ca. 254). There is often doubt as to the correct attribution of such marginal readings, and in any case their accuracy is difficult to validate beyond noting whether or not a given phrase coincides with the generally acknowledged characteristics of a specific translator/reviser.

Although nothing even approaching certitude is possible when speaking of the "lives" of these individuals, ancient evidence would place them after the composition of most, if not all, of the NT. Hence, it is surprising and puzzling when readings associated with Theodotion show up, with some frequency, in the NT. This observation has led to the positing of a proto-Theodotion, who apparently lived and worked in the late first century B.C. and possibly into the first century A.D.

4. Example

It is appropriate to conclude with a specific example, in this instance from Acts 15, which is an account of a crucial meeting in Jerusalem that defined the nature and extent of Christian missionary activity. As recorded in the NT:

> After this I will return, and I will rebuild the dwelling of David that has fallen. I will rebuild its ruins and will set it up, *in order that the rest of the peoples may seek the Lord* — even all the nations over whom my name has been called, says the Lord, who has been making these things known from the beginning. (Acts 15:16-18)

In several smaller ways and in some crucial ones, this passage from Acts differs from the MT of Amos 9:11-12, while at the same time clearly referring to it:

> On that day I will raise up the booth of David that is fallen and repair their breaches and raise up its ruins and rebuild it as in the days of old, *in order that they may possess the remnant of Edom* and all the nations who are called by my name, says the Lord, who does these things. (MT)

From the perspective of the NT, the most important difference lies in the NT's wording in v. 17, "in order that the rest of the peoples may seek the Lord," where the MT of Amos has "in order that they may possess the remnant of Edom." We must turn to the LXX translation of this same Amos passage, as did the author of Acts, to understand at least in part what has happened:

> On that day I will raise up the dwelling of David that has fallen and rebuild its fallen parts, and raise up its ruins and rebuild it as in the days of old, *in order that the rest of the peoples* and all the nations over whom my name has been called *may seek me*, says the Lord, who does these things. (LXX)

The author of Acts did not simply duplicate what he found in his Scripture, unless we wish to posit (as few would) that there existed an earlier Greek text identical to his. Rather, he adopted and adapted to his context the LXX of Amos in order to prove the divine sanction for the Gentile ministry being supported by Paul and his allies. This point was crucial for determining the direction early Christianity took. We cannot know whether this author consciously chose from among different Hebrew and Greek versions. All we know is that this is the text he composed. (For more on this and related issues, see the monograph of T. McLay cited below, from which the above English translations are taken.)

→ Masorah, Masoretes

Bibliography: K. De Troyer, *Rewriting the Sacred Text: What the Old Greek Texts Tell Us about the Literary Growth of the Bible* (Leiden, 2003) • C. Dogniez, *Bibliography of the Septuagint = Bibliographie de la Septante (1970-1993)* (Leiden, 1995) • N. Fernández Marcos, *The Septuagint in Context: Introduction to the Greek Version of the Bible* (Leiden, 2000) • L. J. Greenspoon, "Hebrew into Greek: Interpretation In, By, and Of the Septuagint," *A History of Biblical Interpretation,* vol. 1, *The Ancient Period* (ed. A. J. Hauser and D. F. Watson; Grand Rapids, 2003) 80-113; idem, "It's All Greek to Me: Septuagint Studies since 1968," *CR.BS* 5 (1997) 147-74; idem, "Jewish Translations of the Bible," *The Jewish Study Bible* (ed. A. Berlin and M. Z. Brettler; New York, 2004) 2005-20 • S. Jellicoe, *The Septuagint and Modern Study* (Oxford, 1968) • K. H. Jobes and M. Silva, *Introduction to the Septuagint* (Grand Rapids, 2000) • R. T. McLay, *The Use of the Septuagint in NT Research* (Grand Rapids, 2003) • H. M. Orlinsky, "The Septuagint as Holy Writ and the Philosophy of the Translators," *HUCA* 46 (1975) 89-114 • E. Tov, *The Text-Critical Use of the Septuagint in Biblical Research* (2d ed.; Jerusalem, 1997) • J. W. Wevers, "The Interpretative Character and Significance of the Septuagint Version," *Hebrew Bible, OT: The History of Its Interpretation* (ed. M. Sæbø; Göttingen, 1996) 1.84-107.

Leonard J. Greenspoon

Serbia and Montenegro → Yugoslavia

Sermon on the Mount

1. Title
2. Contents
   2.1. Beatitudes
   2.2. OT Ethical Commands
   2.3. Blessing and Curse
   2.4. Basic Focus
3. Origin
4. Influence
5. Modern Approach

1. Title

The title "Sermon on the Mount," which goes back to → Augustine (354-430), became established by the 16th century. It is used for the long address by Jesus at the beginning of Matthew (chaps. 5–7) and hence at the beginning of the NT. It has often been regarded as a summary of the preaching or ethics of Jesus. Sometimes the term is used, then, for all that → Jesus proclaimed and not just for these three chapters. In the → modern period, in which the sermon is valued as a secularized legacy of the church, the reference to Jesus and the Bible is often slight.

2. Contents

In Matthew Jesus is speaking to the → disciples, though openly. The Sermon on the Mount applies to those who have received the → gospel of the nearness of the → kingdom of God (4:17) and have seen the → miracles of Jesus (4:23-25; 9:35).

Like all the addresses of Jesus in Matthew, Mark, and Luke, it consists of a series of sections complete in themselves. Sometimes their connection with one another is not made explicit. It could be organized as follows.

2.1. *Beatitudes*

The → Beatitudes are a comforting reminder of the nearness of the kingdom (Matt. 5:3-12). The disciples — living in reference to God alone, hungering for → righteousness, persecuted on account of it — are the light of the world until the kingdom comes. Their good deeds are to cause people to praise God (5:13-16). This task is the theme of the Sermon on the Mount.

2.2. *OT Ethical Commands*

How to perform this task we learn from the ethical commandments of the OT (5:17–7:12).

Basis, 5:17-20. Jesus himself came to fulfill the → law and the → prophets, that is, to do and teach them with neither subtraction nor addition (not to perfect or transcend them). The disciples should live according to this righteousness, which exceeds that of the → scribes and → Pharisees, who attentuate it.

Six antitheses as examples, 5:21-48. These examples culminate in love of enemies (→ Enemy), in which God's children act after the example of their Father (v. 45). One might also refer in this regard to the → Decalogue (19:16-22) or the twofold command of → love (22:34-40).

Guidelines for implementation, 6:1–7:12. Some righteous deeds like almsgiving, → prayer, and → fasting must not be done publicly; otherwise the doer will be praised instead of God (6:1-18). Righteousness is life's task, and it demands an ethic of work that focuses on the day at hand (6:19-34). One should not provoke non-Christians by judging or currying favor with them; one should pray for them (7:1-11). The → Golden Rule is equated with "the law and the prophets" (v. 12), and in content Matthew thinks it is the same as the command to love one's → neighbor as oneself. It forms the conclusion to the whole section (5:17–7:12).

2.3. *Blessing and Curse*

The final section of the sermon is a sort of blessing and curse (7:13-27). The disciples must take the narrow way of the minority, which leads to eternal → life (vv. 13-14). They must reject messengers who may prophesy or work miracles but forget the Sermon on the Mount (vv. 15-23). The only house (i.e., a life's work, 1 Cor. 3:10-15?) that will stand in the judgment is that of those who keep the sermon (7:24-27).

2.4. *Basic Focus*

The Sermon on the Mount is thus ethics, and its theme is narrower than is often thought. We must look elsewhere for what Jesus says about mission (chap. 10; 28:16-20) or the life of the community (chap. 18). The Sermon on the Mount is one set of commands, albeit the basic one, that it was the task of Jesus to teach after preaching about the kingdom.

They do not demand a righteousness of works (as Luther would put it), nor are they delineating a given righteousness of faith. They are posing a life task. Jesus himself helps us to keep them by example (11:28-30), by his atoning death (1:21; 26:26-29), and by his support (18:20; 28:20). All power is given to him (11:25-27; 28:16-20) as the Messiah promised in the OT (→ Christological Titles). Sent personally only to → Israel, after → Easter his disciples were sent to the Gentiles (10:5-6; 28:19-20). Those who follow the Sermon on the Mount are not only his disciples but are also his representatives. The kingdom is still near.

3. Origin

Today the Sermon on the Mount is usually thought to have grown out of isolated texts. There is a shorter parallel in the Sermon on the Plain in Luke 6:20-49. Roughly the sections missing here are Matt. 5:13-37 and 6:1-34. Luke has some of this material separately (e.g., the Lord's Prayer, 11:2-4) and in a different sequence, but some is peculiar to Matthew (e.g., 6:1-18). Luke's sermon seems to be a preparatory version. Matthew and Luke found it in the same source or in a common oral tradition, and then Matthew built it up. But even before Matthew some or all of it might have taken shape as the Sermon on the Mount. Less likely, it is an epitome of Jesus' preaching assembled in the middle of the first century in Jerusalem and incorporated integrally by Matthew into his gospel (H. D. Betz).

The material and the main thoughts are Jewish, as is the attack on the supposed laxity of related groups (e.g., → Qumran). The reference to hating one's enemy (Matt. 5:43) corresponds to a theme of the → anti-Semitism of antiquity (Tacitus *Hist.* 5.5). Many things we also find in other parts of the NT (e.g., 1 Pet. 2:12), some in sharper form (e.g., 1 Cor. 7:10-11; Jas. 5:12). Jesus may be the author or mediator of passages for which there are no parallels, such as the prohibition of divorce and swearing, love of enemies, and the → Lord's Prayer. How much else comes from him depends on our assessment of the Jesus tradition as a whole.

The distinctive feature of the Sermon on the Mount is the focus especially on social commandments with the aim of applying Jesus' witness to the kingdom to Christians with the help of good Jewish (Jewish-Hellenistic?) thinking about faithfulness to the law as a missionary lifestyle (cf. Rom. 2:17-24). In content it reaches a hopeful climax with the demand that, like God, we should do even to personal enemies or enemies of the faith the → good that we would like them to do to us.

The situation of Matthew's community is relevant in this regard. After the disaster of the Jewish revolt against Rome in A.D. 70, it was under pressure from → Judaism. It shared the ill repute that fell on Judaism. Faced with the social and material devastation caused by the war, it lacked any influence. Not by accident, then, it found in love of enemies the strongest expression of the nearness of the kingdom.

4. Influence

The Sermon on the Mount has had an influence extending even to contemporary everyday speech. Its history has not yet been explored in full. As regards the history of exposition in particular, it is usually sketched as a series of types. Older types still live on, in and alongside newer ones. Expositors often combine several. Along with professional exposition we find an unusual amount of nonprofessional and wild exegesis. The types may be distinguished by leading themes, such as practicability, law/gospel, rationality (→ Natural Law), and political significance.

If we take, for example, the question whether we can or should follow the Sermon on the Mount, we find the following answers. The → early church regarded it as "a perfect standard of the Christian life" (Augustine). This view lived on (often sharpened legally) in reforming movements and minority churches (e.g., the → Waldensians, → Francis of Assisi, → Bohemian Brethren, Baptists, → peace churches, L. Tolstoy). The mainline Catholic Church of the Middle Ages did not regard the specific commands of the Sermon on the Mount as necessary to salvation but, in distinction from the Decalogue and the commandment to love, applied them only to those who are perfect as "evangelical counsels" (*consilia evangelica;* → Monasticism). But this idea is hardly advocated today.

M. → Luther (1483-1546) went back to Augustine, but he thought that although the Christian as a private person must observe the Sermon on the Mount, as a secular person, in → responsibility for others, he or she would come into conflict with it precisely out of love of neighbor. The age that followed appealed to Luther's → dialectic but did not keep to it strictly (→ Two Kingdoms Doctrine). In Protestant Europe the view that one cannot fulfill the demands of the Sermon on the Mount became stronger. Lutheran → orthodoxy (§1) found in the Sermon on the Mount a mirror held up to sin.

Under the impact of I. Kant's (1724-1804) → emancipation of the ethical subject, → liberal theology taught a love that in the spirit of the Sermon on the Mount will also have an influence in the → state and the economy, where other laws obtain. Recognition of the historical distance led to a view that the Sermon on the Mount is obsolete, either except for giving a mere ethical impulse (A. → Schweitzer [1875-1965]) or altogether. In contrast, → religious socialism found in it the norms of a new → society (R. → Niebuhr [1892-1971]).

→ Dialectical theology argued that Jesus alone fulfilled the Sermon on the Mount, and that only in this way, and as an example, it is also command (E. Thurneysen [1888-1974], K. → Barth [1886-1968]). Under the Führer (→ Fascism) obedience to the Preacher of the Sermon on the Mount offered an alternative that did not finally rule out resistance (D. → Bonhoeffer [1906-45]). Outside Christianity various people have used the Sermon on the Mount since the 19th century, mostly selectively (e.g., R. M. Roy, M. K. Gandhi, E. Fromm).

We can see what is right and wrong in exposition of the sermon only in the course of a history of its influence, but as yet we have only the beginnings of such a history.

5. Modern Approach

The empirical turn of the last decades of the 20th century made the Sermon on the Mount a center of discussion once again, especially as the theme of → political theology (which in the matter of peace extends far beyond the churches), less in such matters as church reform, the basis of → mission, and human → rights (Martin Luther → King Jr.). Exegesis has made a fresh start. Almost all types of interpretation are still present and are in conflict with one another.

Provisionally, one might make the following points:

- The Sermon on the Mount posed a life's task in a particular situation of primitive Christianity (bearing witness by righteousness to the nearness of the kingdom of God experienced in Jesus). It gives this task concreteness with the help of the OT commandments.
- The Sermon on the Mount has become part of the biblical → canon, which is the starting point of → theology and → ethics, even though they may go off in different directions.
- To let ourselves be simply moved by the Sermon on the Mount is not unchristian and may be commanded in many situations. To impose it responsibly on others, a → hermeneutics of the ethical is needed that will relate the basic text to the real world today. This hermeneutics will be learned from the history of the influence of the Sermon on the Mount and from modern ethical reflection. It does not rule out the working of the Sermon on the Mount as a promise of salvation, a call to repentance (even in respect of the results of its own anti-Judaism), and a course of instruction.
- The Sermon on the Mount applies especially to the Christian community. But it expects its observance to have a missionary impact. Its commands, because they are rational, might also become rules of life outside the → congregation.

• The Sermon on the Mount does not offer any political program, nor is it a political instrument, but it accompanies Christians and the churches into politics and influences both goals and style. Christians cannot rule the world or revolutionize it by means of the Sermon on the Mount; without it, however, they ought not even to try.

Bibliography: G. Barth, "Bergpredigt," *TRE* 5.603-18 • U. Berner, *Die Bergpredigt. Rezeption und Auslegung im 20. Jahrhundert* (2d ed.; Göttingen, 1983) • H. D. Betz, *The Sermon on the Mount* (Minneapolis, 1995) • D. Bonhoeffer, *Dietrich Bonhoeffer Works,* vol. 4, *Discipleship* (Minneapolis, 2000; orig pub., 1937) • W. D. Davies, *The Sermon on the Mount* (Cambridge, 1966); idem, *The Setting of the Sermon on the Mount* (Cambridge, 1963) • W. D. Davies and D. C. Allison, *The Gospel according to Saint Matthew* (vol. 1; Edinburgh, 1988) • U. Duchrow, *Christenheit und Weltverantwortung* (Stuttgart, 1970) • M. Dumais, *Le Sermon sur la Montagne* (Paris, 1995) • R. A. Guelich, *The Sermon on the Mount: A Foundation for Understanding* (Waco, Tex., 1982) • J. D. Kingsbury, *Matthew: Structure, Christology, and Kingdom* (Philadelphia, 1975) • W. S. Kissinger, *The Sermon on the Mount: A History of Interpretation and Bibliography* (Metuchen, N.J., 1975) • U. Luz, *Matthew 1–7* (Minneapolis, 1990); idem, *The Theology of the Gospel of Matthew* (Cambridge, 1995) • D. Patte, *The Gospel according to Matthew: A Structural Commentary on Matthew's Faith* (Philadelphia, 1986) • R. Schnackenburg, *The Gospel of Matthew* (Grand Rapids, 2002) • G. Strecker, *The Sermon on the Mount: An Exegetical Commentary* (Nashville, 1988).

Christoph Burchard

Serpent

In both space and time the serpent has been a widely distributed symbol and even today figures as such in dreams and movies. The serpent is both sinister and dangerous yet also beautiful and mysterious. We find this ambivalence in all → religions. The serpent is a → symbol (§1) of the world of the dead, the underworld, and chaos, yet on account of its regular marking it also represents new → life and → immortality. It is also a phallic symbol. It often lives in water. Related to it is the dragon that lives in water or that breathes out fire. It gives wisdom and power but also is cunning and malicious.

Especially its cunning gave the serpent a place in Judaism and Christianity (Gen. 49:17; Ps. 140:3, etc.). Genesis 3:1 made a decisive impact. There it entices to → sin (§1) against the will of God and brings sin, → death, and corruption into the world. Even so, it is still a creature of God. The demonic power that entices to sin is not independent of the Creator, to whose will everything is subject. Hence the cunning of the serpent can even be an example for us in Matt. 10:16.

The bronze (or copper) serpent of Num. 21:4-9 was a sign of healing set on a pole by → Moses in order that those who looked at it, even though bitten by snakes, might be kept alive by the kindness of → Yahweh. Here again we see the ambivalence of the symbol. In John 3:14 this → sign (§2) points us to God's healing power by means of the lifting up of the Son of Man on the cross.

→ Animals

Bibliography: W. Foerster et al., "Ὄφις," *TDNT* 5.566-82 • K. R. Joines, *Serpent Symbolism in the OT* (Haddonfield, N.J., 1974) • M. Lurker, "Snakes," *EncRel(E)* 13.370-74 • E. Wiesel, "Supporting Roles: The Serpent," *BibRev* 13, no. 6 (1997) 18-19 • L. S. Wilson, *The Serpent Symbol in the Ancient Near East* (Lanham, Md., 2001).

Thaddeus A. Schnitker

Servant of the Lord

1. OT Usage
2. Deutero-Isaiah
3. NT

1. OT Usage

The Hebrew word *'ebed* means one who stands in service, whether as slave or royal minister. The *'ebed* enjoys his master's protection. Thus the author of a psalm of complaint can appeal to God as "your servant" (Ps. 86:2, and many other references). The phrase "Servant of the Lord" almost always has in view the special relation of an individual to God. From the time of the exile it became an honorary title for such model figures as → Moses, → David, and the → prophets.

2. Deutero-Isaiah

In Deutero-Isaiah four texts that have been traditionally understood Christologically (42:1-4 [5-7]; 49:1-6 [7-9]; 50:4-9 [10-11]; 52:13–53:12) refer to an unnamed Servant of the Lord. From B. Duhm's day (1892) they have been regarded as a related group. Debate centers on whether the Servant is individual or collective, present or future, a prophet or a king.

2.1. In Deutero-Isaiah → Israel is addressed as the Servant of the Lord only in salvation oracles

(41:8-9; 44:1-2; 44:21; passages independent of these oracles include Jer. 30:10-11 = 46:27-28) and in the responsive song of praise (Isa. 48:20; cf. Ps. 136:22). Such is the case nowhere else in the OT. Since even in the exile people viewed deliverance from personal need as a hearing of their complaints, the chapters take up this individual experience of God as Deliverer and make use of the form of a promise of divine hearing (salvation oracle) in their proclaiming of → salvation. The address "my servant" is thus conditioned on adoption of the genre. The addition of the words "Jacob" or "Israel" denotes transferred use. Outside salvation oracles the reference in 44:26 is to the prophet; in 43:10 it is either to the prophet (MT) or, better, to the Israelites in the plural (1QIsa). This, then, is the normal usage.

Advocates of a collective sense presuppose that for the author the term has a fixed sense and therefore must always mean Israel. The difficulty here is that in 49:4-5 the Servant of the Lord has a ministry to Israel. A contrast is also made between the perfect Servant and obdurate Israel. Champions of the collective view have thus to find in the Servant of the songs the ideal Israel represented by past prophets, the author himself, and most fully the future Messiah (→ Messianism). This line of interpretation has persisted in the 20th century almost solely in the English-speaking world. German-speaking scholarship since Duhm favors an individual understanding.

2.2. In 42:1-4 the Servant of the Lord has the task of proclaiming to the nations the settling of a legal dispute *(mišpāṭ)*. In context this proclamation is the judgment that their gods are nonexistent and that → Yahweh alone saves (41:1-5, 21-29; 43:8-15; 44:6-8, 21-22; 45:20-25). We see from 49:1-6 that this work is an extension of the original task of gathering Israel. It is fulfilled by the proclaiming of salvation and a summoning to universal praise of Yahweh. The fact that this task is discharged by the author suggests his equation with the Servant.

2.3. In keeping with his twofold task, the Servant has both prophetic and royal features. The prophet is the mediator of the divine message in Israel, while the king is the central mediator between gods and human beings among the nations, he alone announcing judgment on alien peoples and giving himself the title "Servant of Marduk" and of other gods.

2.4. On the view that the author of Deutero-Isaiah is the Servant of the Lord — a thesis that has been increasingly favored since S. Mowinckel (1921) — the first three songs come from his own pen, and the fourth, after his death, from his disciples. His → suffering and death for the sake of his mission are seen as having vicarious significance for all.

3. NT

Isaiah 53 finds an echo in the eucharistic saying "for many" in Mark 14:24 (→ Eucharist 2). Apart from this one reference, the passion narratives and → Paul do not specifically understand the crucifixion of → Jesus in these terms. In 1 Pet. 2:21-25 (cf. 1 John 3:5) and John 1:29, however, as also in the Lamb of Revelation (5:6 etc.), there is clear allusion to the Servant.

Philip in Acts 8:34-35, in answer to the eunuch's question regarding who the prophet is speaking about in the final song, refers expressly to Jesus, whom the infant church also entitles God's "holy servant" in Acts 4:30.

→ Christological Titles 3.7; Jeremiah, Book of, 3.2

Bibliography: B. Duhm, *Das Buch Jesaia* (HKAT; Göttingen, 1892; 5th ed., 1968) • E. R. Ekblad, *Isaiah's Servant Poems according to the Septuagint* (Louvain, 1999) • H. Haag, *Der Gottesknecht bei Deuterojesaja* (2d ed.; Darmstadt, 1993) • I. Knohl, *The Messiah before Jesus: The Suffering Servant of the Dead Sea Scrolls* (Berkeley, Calif., 2000) • S. Mowinckel, *Der Knecht Jahwäs* (Giessen, 1921) • H. H. Rowley, *The Servant of the Lord, and Other Essays on the OT* (2d ed.; Oxford, 1965) 1-60 • C. Westermann, *Sprache und Struktur der Prophetie Deuterojesajas* (Stuttgart, 1981). See also the bibliography in "Isaiah, Book of."

Eberhard Ruprecht

Service Society

1. Term

Descriptively, the term "service society" refers to a national → economy in which a majority of workers are engaged in the vocations and various branches of the service sector (i.e., the sector producing services, not goods). According to this criterion, the United States, Canada, the wealthier European countries, and Australia passed the threshold from an → industrial society to a service society as early as the 1960s and 1970s. In the meantime, the predominant vocational activity in many other countries, especially in Europe and Asia, has shifted in the same direction.

A more theoretically oriented understanding of the term "service society" involves the socioeconomic theory of modernization, which holds that all societies pass through three stages of economic development. The primiary stage generally encompasses a relatively long historical period as an agricultural society, with a lower material standard of living. Under the dynamic influence of technological → progress, societies then enter a *secondary* stage and become industrial societies.

At this stage, higher economic productivity also raises the living standard of an increasingly larger part of the population. This transformation, however, is accompanied by many negative developments. Migration into the big cities radically alters the traditional lifestyle of workers and generates a whole array of social, medical, and technological problems. Work in factories associated with heavy industry becomes more dangerous and inhumane. Class-related and other social conflicts increase. The → environment is increasingly exploited and in part permanently destroyed.

Against this negative background of industrialization, some theoreticians have interpreted the transition — evident in the most advanced societies — of production and consumption more in the direction of service industries as the transition into a tertiary stage of economic development in which the positive aspects of socioeconomic progress predominate. These theories generally interpret the growth of the service sector as indicating that → consumption itself has reached a qualitatively higher level insofar as the demand for the products such as → education, entertainment, culture, health care, → tourism, and financial services arises only after elementary needs have already been met and only after large portions of the population already enjoy a high standard of living.

Unlike the situation involving foodstuffs and material goods, one need not necessarily expect that the demand for such products will quickly reach a saturation level, and some thus hope that expanding services might guarantee full employment in stable, growing economies. The sphere of → work in service societies would then tend to change positively, with work itself becoming more involved with personal interaction with customers, clients, patients, pupils, and so on, and with activities that are more intensively knowledge-based. Some advocates of postindustrialism consider this type of work as more resistant to the mechanization and automation familiar from factory work.

This allegedly limitless demand for services in connection with the allegedly limited possibility of replacing the human labor element with technology has led some to maintain that the service society represents a new stage of potential economic and social stability and balance. From this perspective, industrial society — one plagued by so many crises, conflicts, and creative destruction — might represent a historically brief but painful stage between the impoverished epoch of the agricultural society and the epoch of the service society, the prosperity of the latter based on the firm foundation of a highly productive economy that in its own turn has been revolutionized by technological progress.

2. Critical Discussion

This optimistic understanding of the service society derives from a period in which national economies in many countries showed extraordinary rates of growth, welfare-state services were greatly expanded, and many believed that both economic and social progress could be attained by careful planning (→ Social Services). The disappearance of these conditions generated increasingly heated discussions concerning this optimistic prognosis. Three aspects were especially subject to critical examination: the thesis that service industries would continually expand, the thesis of societal amelioration, and the thesis of an epochal transition to postindustrialism.

2.1. *Expansionist Thesis*

In economic terms, the expansion of the service industries is generally explained by adducing the growing needs of businesses and those of private households. Accordingly, the sphere of production and distributive services can be distinguished from that of social and personal services. In each of the two spheres the increase in demand for services derives from two completely different sources. Although such increase can attest the emergence of completely new needs or functional demands, it can also involve merely a different form of work organization. On an empirical level, the production and distributive services have proved to be the most important cause of expansion, since over the course of the development of capitalist industrial societies, numerous new functional demands invariably arise. That is, the emergence of multifarious production organizations, the increasingly specialized and dispersed division of labor, and the emergence of increasingly research-intensive developmental processes and increasingly complex marketing tasks — all these factors also prompted the emergence of increasingly specialized service industries in trade,

Service Society

transportation, management, financial services, advertising, education, and science.

Critics do point out that, at least to a certain extent, this growth represents merely a statistical artifact insofar as it is based merely on a reorganization of labor processes and entrepreneurial structures. In the United States, for example, the complex division and outsourcing of many services are much more pronounced than, for example, in Japan and Germany, where such functions are more frequently addressed in-house. Factors militating against the expectation that such services will continue to expand include the fact that the revolution of information and communication technology has provided enormous opportunities for the rationalization and conservation of work.

New kinds of service industries have also emerged in connection with consumption and household demands. Higher incomes, longer life expectancy, urban living, altered value structures and expectations, as well as many other influences have contributed to the growth of health services, educational services, tourism, gastronomy, culture, and new "fun services." In precisely this context, however, and much more pronounced than in the case of production-oriented services, critics object that this alleged growth does not really represent genuine growth at all, but merely an altered form of social labor. That is, in earlier times personal care (for the elderly, children, etc.), education, food services, and many other activities were carried out as informal and unpaid family and household labor (esp. by women) or perhaps as mutual help in community networks. Increasingly, however, these same services are now offered commercially as paid labor or as part of welfare-state services. Internationally, both the type and the extent of this change in form vary widely. Moreover, since many of the ascertainable differences often derive from deeply rooted cultural peculiarities, one cannot really expect that all societies will develop similarly in this regard.

For example, in the Protestant and socially democratic Scandinavian countries, social services have had a much stronger tendency to migrate from the sphere of informal labor and come under state purview than has been the case in the countries of southern Europe, which have a conservative Catholic tradition. Against this background, one can easily imagine how the service sector might well shrink and be displaced once more to the private domestic sphere, for example, if the services offered either commercially or by the welfare state become too expensive. Jonathan Gershuny has been especially intent on maintaining that societies are moving less toward a "service society" than toward a "self-service society," meaning that service offerings will be increasingly replaced by a combination of industrially produced household gadgets and informal labor. (For example, the private car replaces the railway, TV replaces the movie theater, ready-to-serve meals replace restaurant and other gastronomical services, and the Internet replaces the need to go personally to stores, banks, or administrative offices.)

2.2. *Social Amelioration Thesis*

From the very outset, the → optimism associated with the theory of the service society has encountered a great deal of skepticism. One objection has been that the growth of service industries is merely an indicator of faulty social development and the unwelcome costs of modernization. Such applies, for example, to services that compensate for the functional loss of families and neighborhoods or for the increased output required for security, medical care, and repair of the damaged environment. Moreover, the growth of certain services has also provoked cultural concerns from virtually every ideological quarter. Such concern involves the unchecked growth of tourism, inflated → bureaucracies, superfluous advertising, excessive social services, the proliferation of fast-food restaurants, and excessive offerings from the media and from the entertainment industry (→ Mass Media). Even the growth of scientific specialization and of professional vocations, though usually viewed quite positively, has been criticized for allegedly subjecting the general population to increased control and for usurping its capacity to make its own decisions.

Similarly substantive arguments are leveled against the hope in an amelioration of the work sphere. Critics point out that, for example, many jobs in the service industries are low paid, the work hours and conditions are often unattractive, and many such jobs are clearly located at the lower end of the social scale as far as prestige is concerned. Nor can we really ascertain yet the potential negative consequences of a future rationalization and automation of the service industries.

2.3. *Social Transition Thesis*

Most scholars reject the notion that an expansion of the service industries will advance us to a new stage of societal development. On this view, modern service societies are nothing more than the most highly developed → capitalist *industrial* societies, in which market relationships and commodification have expanded into virtually every corner of society and in which the development, production, and turnover of industrial goods requires ever more complex services.

→ Economic Ethics

Bibliography: D. Bell, *The Coming of Post-industrial Society: A Venture in Social Forecasting* (New York, 1973) • J. Fourastié, *Le grand espoir du XXe siècle; progrès technique, progrès économique, progrès social* (rev. ed.; Paris, 1989) • J. Gershuny, *Changing Times: Work and Leisure in Postindustrial Society* (Oxford, 2000) • J. Gershuny and I. D. Miles, *The New Service Economy: The Transformation of Employment in Industrial Societies* (New York, 1983) • P. Gross, *Die Verheißungen der Dienstleistungsgesellschaft. Soziale Befreiung oder Sozialherrschaft?* (Opladen, 1983) • S. Illeris, *The Service Economy: A Geographical Approach* (Chicester, Eng., 1996) • I. Illich et al., *Disabling Professions* (new ed.; London, 1987).

Uwe Engfer

Seventh-day Adventists → Adventists

Sex Education

1. Basic Issues
2. History
3. Contemporary Debate
   3.1. Goals
   3.2. Institutional Responsibility
   3.3. Effectiveness
   3.4. Values
4. Risk Factors
5. Christian Perspective

1. Basic Issues

Sex education is an intensely debated issue in contemporary Western society. Sex education takes a variety of forms based on (1) the background cultural metanarrative framing the understood meaning of → sexuality; (2) the ethical framework for the valuation of sexual action embedded in or shaping the educational approach; (3) the understanding of "audience" characteristics, including age and developmental readiness for different types of information and intervention; (4) the goals of the educational intervention (e.g., to decrease adolescent pregnancy rates, to shape moral character); (5) the agents structuring and providing the education (e.g., families, churches, schools); and (6) the range of intervention methods utilized, from communicating biological information to shaping a child's environment.

Statistics on adolescent sexual activity fuel the perceived need of the general populace for more, and more effective, sex education and research into the determinants of sexual activity. Adolescent sexual activity in the United States seems to have peaked in the late 1980s and to be slightly declining. In the early 1990s, 54 percent of all high school students reported having had sexual intercourse, and 39 percent were sexually active. By 1997 these percentages had declined to 48 percent and 35 percent respectively, with higher rates for African American and Hispanic students, and for urban males. Approximately one million American teenagers become pregnant annually, with one-third of these pregnancies ending in elective → abortion. The growing spread of some sexually transmitted infections (STIs) such as HIV/AIDS is broadly recognized, but an alarming spread of other serious diseases is less recognized. Two of the most common are chlamydia, a mostly curable bacterial infection associated with adult infertility, and the incurable human papilloma virus, estimated to now infect almost 50 percent of sexually active adolescents and associated with cervical cancer.

International comparisons of sexual behavior patterns are difficult because of differing reporting standards. Research suggests that teenage sexual activity rates are not radically different between the United States, Canada, France, Great Britain, and Sweden (J. E. Darroch et al.). The proportion of women who have first intercourse before age 20 ranges from 75 percent in Canada to 86 percent in Sweden, and median age of first intercourse ranges only from 17.1 to 17.5. Young women in the United States and in Sweden, though, are more likely to have sex early (before age 15: 14 percent in the U.S., 12 percent in Sweden, but 4-9 percent in the other three countries), and more likely to have two or more partners in a year if they are sexually active.

More striking differences emerged in the consequences of sexual behavior, however: U.S. women were roughly two times (compared to Canada and the U.K.) or four times (compared to Sweden and France) more likely to get pregnant, with this difference possibly related to the more frequent use of the contraceptive pill in other countries by young women. U.S. women are less likely to end a pregnancy by abortion and hence more likely to give birth; abortions per pregnancy are much higher for the Europeans. In terms of raw numbers, though, U.S. women are more likely to have an abortion than these European women because they are substantially more likely to get pregnant, though even these statistics are questionable, since in some countries "missed periods" might be treated by gynecological procedures that would abort a pregnancy without either the pregnancy or the abortion being reported as such.

2. History

Anthropological studies across many cultures have clearly established that sexuality is everywhere seen as a human characteristic and activity with special meaning and significance. Hence, it is regulated by moral systems and guarded by cultural institutions — most obviously, → marriage. All cultures have methods to educate their young in shared understandings of sexuality. The Hebrews saw the socialization of children by parents into obedience to God's revealed law, including its regulation of sexual action, to be central to their religious identity (Deut. 6:1-9). Within the Christian tradition, proclamation of the need for sexual purity and the complementary defense of the blessedness of marital sexual expression (Heb. 13:4; 1 Tim. 4:1-5) constitute a type of sex education. But modern sex education, dating from the late 19th century, stresses the inclusion of biological, hygienic, and contraceptive information.

Urbanization, industrialization, family breakdown, and weakening consensus on Christian sexual morality have contributed to cyclic fluctuations in sexual behavior in the United States and Europe (J. W. Maddock). Rates of illegitimacy and → prostitution in urban settings during periods in the 18th and 19th centuries, for instance, were as high or higher than present-day rates. Early sex education programs in the late 1800s were organized under the rubric "social hygiene." These programs aimed at suppressing immoral sexual expression using the current medical knowledge to warn of the consequences of disease and pregnancy. Such programs have been described as "authoritarian and moralistic" (Maddock, 6). In the early 20th century the development of feminist concern for the empowerment of women to control their reproductive destinies led Margaret Sanger and others to link information about → birth control to sex education.

A variety of developments influenced the evolution of sex education throughout the 20th century. A reduction of sexuality to a purely natural impulse was motivated by ideological movements, including the popular spread of a Darwinian ideology emphasizing the fundamental identity of humans as biological creatures driven to reproduce and, in the 1940s, Sigmund Freud's argument for the centrality of sexual motivation in life. Unprecedented public discussion of sexuality was fueled in the 1950s by Alfred Kinsey's highly publicized research on a range of sexual practices, furthered in the 1970s by subsequent research on sexual response and sexual functioning by William Masters and Virginia Johnson, and by the escalating media influence of radio, television, motion pictures, and eventually the Internet. These advances colluded with various other cultural dynamics to challenge fundamentally the traditional family structure and role in sex education. The spike in divorce following World War II led to an impetus for "family life education." The legalization of elective abortion and the development of multiple effective methods of contraception have served to break the previously firm link between sexual intercourse and reproduction and thus to allow for the idea of recreational sex. Finally, the "sexual revolution" of the 1960s and 1970s transferred the → Enlightenment emphasis on the overthrow of traditional authority from the epistemological into the moral realm and dramatically expanded options for sexual behavior.

During this period support for sex education in the public schools grew, due in large part to the perceived irrelevance of the Christian church as a moral guide for sexual behavior and because of Enlightenment confidence in science as a trustworthy guide for human progress. In this context, major professional organizations advancing the cause of "scientific" sex education were formed — including the Sex Information and Education Council of the United States, and the American Association of Sex Educators and Counselors — and curricula multiplied. The "biologicalization" of contemporary sex education is in part an expression of a conviction regarding the types of (biological) knowledge needed by young people, but it also is an effective justification for moving the locus of sexuality education from those societal institutions that have traditionally taken responsibility for it, especially → family and → church, in favor of scientifically informed instruction in the schools.

3. Contemporary Debate

Bitter controversy has surrounded the development and implementation of sex education curricula throughout the United States, since it has inevitably exposed deep differences concerning values in the population. Entering the 21st century, controversy concerning sex education continues over issues including (1) the goals of sex education, (2) institutional responsibility for sex education, (3) the effectiveness of sex education, and (4) the possibility of value neutrality in sex education.

3.1. *Goals*

Divergent goals define the two major approaches to sex education today: abstinence programs and comprehensive programs. The former emphasize, to varying degrees of exclusivity, abstinence as the only safe way to prevent disease and pregnancy; the latter emphasize the provision of accurate information to

Sex Education

ground future decision-making concerning responsible sexual behavior. As of this writing, abstinence programs are the preferred option of school sex education, accounting for 70 percent of sex education programs chosen by school districts, with the shift away from comprehensive programs beginning in the late 1980s.

3.2. *Institutional Responsibility*

Debates continue about the responsibility of schools in sexually educating youth in relation to that of parents and churches. Proponents of public school sex education argue that their involvement is necessitated by the failure of many parents, and of churches and other institutions, to provide meaningful information to their children.

3.3. *Effectiveness*

With sexual activity rates among youth high and STIs at record levels, a good argument can be made for the ineffectiveness of public comprehensive sex education. For instance, the major outcome variable cited in support of public sex education, the decline in live births to teenage mothers, may be as much a function of increased utilization of elective abortion as increased contraceptive utilization. Despite the shift in recent years toward abstinence education, significant confusion exists as to how effective this alternative approach is.

3.4. *Values*

Comprehensive programs generally value freedom of choice and strike a stance of value-neutrality. The reigning ideology has been to provide students with supposedly objective information that empowers them to make their choices within the context of their subjective values. → Postmodern perspectives, however, challenge the possibility of objectivity, and certainly many Christians feel that the messages of public sex education are anything but value-neutral. Developmental research suggests, furthermore, that in a morally weighted area like sexuality, adult acceptance and nonjudgmentalism when "deviant" opinions are expressed (i.e., value-neutrality) is understood as approval rather than neutrality. Thus, "neutral" responses may convey adult approval of destructive values leading to risky sexual activity. Youth are more likely to internalize morals when educators strongly believe in the values they teach.

4. Risk Factors

Empirically documented risk factors associated with sexual experimentation include *individual* factors such as low intellectual ability, poor performance in school, history of sexual abuse, and lack of religious faith; *familial* factors such as single-parent households, lack of perceived closeness to a parent, and low socioeconomic status; *extrafamilial* factors such as sexually active peers and lack of positive experiences in school; and *macrosystem* factors such as permissive cultural and community standards, lack of church attendance, and media messages approving sexual experimentation (D. F. Perkins et al.).

Notably lacking among the demonstrated predictors of sexual activity is intellectual knowledge about human sexuality. If the goal of sex education is to change behavior, intervention with these risk factors clearly must involve something broader than intellectual instruction. Instilling religious faith, preventing the breakup of families, and intervention in the messages of popular culture are all "broader" than merely teaching the biological facts of sexual reproduction. Despite evidence that programs integrating interventions at multiple levels are more effective, research demonstrates that active providers of sex education have tended to retreat into their respective professional communities. Collaboration could enhance educational effectiveness while allowing families to retain primary influence and responsibility for instilling values and shaping the sexual character of their youth.

5. Christian Perspective

As Maddock has observed, "The family is inevitably the primary source of sexuality education for children . . . sexuality education occurs in close relationships even if adults are not aware of providing it" (p. 17). The ability of churches to support families in providing sex education is compromised by ignorance, conflict among the churches themselves regarding core sexual morality, the temptation to avoid controversial topics, and the tendency for some to overutilize negative messages about sexuality to "scare kids chaste." The explosion of sexual images and information in the media further challenge Christian efforts to direct sex education.

Despite these obstacles, biblically based Christianity offers a fundamentally positive perspective on sexuality. Humans are physical beings formed from the dust of the ground and made "living *souls*" (Gen. 2:7 lit.) created in God's image and hence more than their bodies. The goodness of bodily existence is supported by the doctrines of → creation, the → incarnation of Christ, and the ultimate → resurrection of the body. Reproduction is given as a gift by God at creation, and sexual intercourse is given as an act that creates union — "one flesh" — between a man and a woman. Sexuality, however, was twisted and broken by the fall, tainted by evil motives and desires. It is a sacred gift but one easily exploited through human selfishness. Moral boundaries protect sexuality and hence individuals and relationships from harm and provide a context for the full experiencing and celebration of sexuality.

To contribute to the formation of church-based sex education efforts, a five-factor heuristic model for conceptualizing the individual and interpersonal processes that shape the sexuality choices made by youth and from which broad-based familial and church sex education interventions can be conceptualized has been proposed (S. L. Jones and B. B. Jones, S. L. Jones and J. G. Laskowski). The five factors are:

Needs. Youth are more likely to act maladaptively when their most basic human needs are inadequately met. The two basic human needs are construed as *relatedness* (a need to love and be loved by others; Gen. 2:18) and *significance* (a need to define or establish one's sense of personal worth; Gen. 2:15). Youth who are close to one or both parents (relatedness) and who perform better or are more involved in school (significance) are less likely to experiment sexually; effective sex education will address these needs.

Values. Parents, peers, church, and culture shape children's attitudes and values toward sex. Attitudes toward the physical body, sexual intercourse inside and outside of marriage, moral norms themselves and their transgression, and other aspects of sexual life form the context of all sexual decision-making.

Beliefs. Decisions about sexual action are made in the context of beliefs, such as one's perception of the biological realities of sexual action, the behavioral realities of what people do and moral perspectives on such behavior, and the meaning and role of sexuality in human life.

Skills. Research indicates that the sexual debut of many women is unwanted or involuntary at some level, and that the women often lack the knowledge and necessary skills to extricate themselves from situations that result in loss of virginity. Assertiveness skills to resist pressure and even repulse unwanted advances should be cultivated to diminish such experiences. Other relevant skills include anticipating consequences of actions, self-control, empathy, and decision-making skills.

Supports. Major determinants of youth and adult sexual action are "external" to the person but can nonetheless be targets for intervention. Because participation in church or youth group predicts a delay of sexual experimentation, and since the behavior of an adolescent's peer group is frequently predictive of sexual behavior, parents and churches can seek to create potent and appealing interpersonal environments where sexual chastity is valued. Because youth who are close to a parent are unlikely to be engaged in sexual behavior, parents can seek to foster the needed closeness with themselves or facilitate relationships with other caring and mature adults who can serve as parental surrogates.

Bibliography: J. E. Darroch, S. Singh, J. J. Frost, et al., "Differences in Teenage Pregnancy Rates among Five Developed Countries: The Roles of Sexual Activity and Contraceptive Use," *FPP* 33 (2001) 244-50, 281 • S. Grenz, *Sexual Ethics: A Biblical Perspective* (Dallas, 1990) • John Paul II, *The Theology of the Body: Human Love in the Divine Plan* (Boston, 1997) • S. L. Jones and B. B. Jones, *How and When to Tell Your Kids about Sex: A Lifelong Approach to Shaping Your Child's Sexual Character* (Colorado Springs, 1993) • S. L. Jones and J. G. Laskowski, "An Eclectic Theoretical Model to Guide Sex Education," *MF.CJ* 4 (2001) 213-26 • J. W. Maddock, "Sexuality Education: A History Lesson," *JPsHS* 9/3-4 (1997) 1-22 • R. T. Michael, J. H. Gagnon, E. O. Laumann, and G. Kolata, *Sex in America: A Definitive Survey* (Boston, 1997) • D. F. Perkins, T. Luster, F. A. Villarruel, and S. Small, "An Ecological, Risk-Factor Examination of Adolescents' Sexual Activity in Three Ethnic Groups," *JMF* 60 (1998) 660-73 • L. B. Smedes, *Sex for Christians: The Limits and Liberties of Sexual Living* (rev. ed.; Grand Rapids, 1994).

Stanton L. Jones and Jennifer N. Gorham

Sexism

1. Sexism and Gender Stereotyping
2. Religion and Sexism
3. Contributions of the Ecumenical Movement
4. Issues
   - 4.1. Violence against Women
   - 4.2. Increasing Racism and Xenophobia
   - 4.3. Economic Obstacles

1. Sexism and Gender Stereotyping

Sexism is the ideology of male superiority and the practice, sometimes conscious and sometimes unconscious, of male supremacy over women. Sexism is integrally related to patriarchy, referring to structures and systems in which male heads of households hold sovereignty over all others — women, children, slaves of both sexes, and other property. Within this hierarchical order of things, women are seen to be weaker than men, in need of male protection and guidance. Even where the equality of women and men has been established legally and where the rights of women are said to be guaranteed and protected, men's presumption of privilege and place as the head of the orders of things often persists in familial, sociocultural, economic, political, and religious settings. Like ineffectual → civil rights legislation in the face of still-present → racism, so long as the ideology of male superiority remains intact or lingers, sexism is a reality (→ Feminism; Feminist Theology).

Sexism as discrimination on the basis of sex is analogous to racism as discrimination on the basis of race or classism on the basis of class. Although there has been much discussion of the ways in which sexism and racism and classism interact, this interaction clearly puts women at risk of double or triple oppression. It also means that women themselves are agents of the oppression of other women.

Sexism is predicated on gender stereotyping. As above, women are seen to be weaker than men. Women are assigned roles on the basis of a centuries-long assumption that they are more caring and more emotional than men. Given their capacity for biological, as well as social, mothering, women have been thought to be best suited primarily, if not exclusively, to be wives and mothers. Already in the Greek Enlightenment of the 5th and 6th centuries B.C., Aristotle argued that women had limited psychological and cognitive powers, thereby justifying women's exclusion from political life and their social subjugation to men. Men's superior rationality was asserted by the 18th-century European → Enlightenment, which subsequently gave rise to the 19th-century notion of "the feminine soul," including notions of women's moral and spiritual superiority. While affirmation of these qualities in women influenced some women's social and religious initiatives of reform, these ideas also reinforced women's economic, political, and social disenfranchisement. Women were shut out of public spheres of life and production and confined to the domestic sphere of private life. They were to be "angels of the house," there safe from the wild and competitive sea of rising industrial → capitalism.

These gender stereotypes have been harmful for men as well as for women. While women who "get out of their place" or are "uppity" may be verbally or physically assaulted or suffer other subtle or not so subtle (often economic or professional) sanctions, men who do not fulfill expected roles are said to be "effeminate." Gender stereotypes continue to be expressed in popular culture, the → mass media, advertising, literature, and religious symbols and are endemic to the socialization of men and women in families, schools, and religious and other sociocultural institutions. The seeming unchangeability of these stereotypes has made them appear to be natural.

2. Religion and Sexism

Religious symbols and structures have played a crucial role in justifying and sanctifying the status quo of gender stereotyping, of which sexism is a consequence. From the early Fathers of the Christian church onward through the centuries, theology has blamed a woman, and therefore all women, for → sin and → death. The → church fathers taught that women possess the image of God only through the headship of men, since women were created from men. Women are the realm of flesh (the body, sexuality, menstruation, and childbirth are all considered impure), in relation to the realm of the spirit, occupied by men. Moreover, women's derivative, impure, and subordinate status in relation to men has been justified as God-given punishment.

Traditionally, women were presented with two options: Eve or Mary, that is, the sexual temptress or the self-effacing, submissive mother. Accordingly, women have been excluded from traditional representations of the divine and of Christ. In churches of the reformations, women have been absent from the imagery and language of hymns, liturgies, confessions, and prayers, all of which refer to "men," "fathers," and "brothers." Women have been told to be "silent in the churches" (1 Cor. 14:34); women must redeem Eve by bearing children in pain (1 Tim. 2:11-15). Women in Eastern Orthodox and Roman Catholic churches have been able to identify with the image of Mary the Mother of God.

From the 2d-century theologian → Tertullian (ca. 160-ca. 225), who called women the "devil's gateway," to the 20th-century theologian Karl → Barth (1886-1968), who cast women as receptive and passive, the Christian tradition has lent imagery and language that has served as religious sanctification for the subordination of women in wider sociocultural contexts.

Another trajectory within the Christian tradition, however, may be retrieved for the sake of thoroughgoing reform. NT texts include names of women apostles (Mary Magdalene, Junia) and of women community leaders or heads of household (Martha, Lydia). And from the second century onward, there have been Christian groups whose expectation of the kingdom of God and whose sense of the Spirit's power have encouraged equality and mutuality among women and men (→ Cathari; Friends, Society of; Montanism; Waldenses).

3. Contributions of the Ecumenical Movement

In the 20th century the ecumenical movement was ahead of most churches in giving serious and sustained attention to the question of the image, role, and status of women in church and society (→ Ecumenism, Ecumenical Movement). Already in 1927, at the First World Conference on → Faith and Order, held in Lausanne, the seven women delegates presented a statement asking that the issue of women's place in the church be addressed at the meeting. Before the founding assembly of the → World Council of Churches (WCC), in Amsterdam in 1948, a questionnaire was sent out to survey the status of women. But the deep-seated structures of male privilege and men's place of headship in church and society were taken for granted.

The patriarchal structures that engender sexism were challenged in 1974, when the word "sexism" was introduced into the ecumenical lexicon. Pauline Webb, speaking at a women's consultation sponsored by the WCC in Berlin, "Sexism in the 1970s," described sexism as heresy and declared it to be a Christian duty to expose and erase it from church and social attitudes, behaviors, and structures. The theological basis for Webb's description and declaration was her affirmation that women and men alike are created in the image of God.

During the consultation women from countries in the Southern Hemisphere spoke about the problem of sexual oppression in relation to imperial oppression also experienced by men, who, resigned to their inability to alter their structural situation under *imperium,* react by adopting sexist attitudes and behaviors. Viewed from this perspective, sexism is not only a struggle between men and women on the basis of sexual and gender stereotypes; it is a common struggle within the wider struggle for liberation of the oppressed classes, races, and peoples of the world. Accordingly, there was resistance at the Berlin consultation to using the word "sexism" in what was perceived to be a white, middle-class sense.

Among the recommendations made by the 1974 consultation on sexism to the Fifth WCC Assembly, in Nairobi in 1975, was that there be sustained study of the challenge identified in Berlin. The result was the study "The Community of Women and Men in the Church" (1978-81), which engaged women and men in local study groups and held seven regional and three study consultations to address the ordination of women (→ Ordination 7.4), theological anthropology, and the authority of Scripture as related to the image and role of women in the church. At the heart of the study's findings was the urgent concern that sexism, discrimination against women, is a barrier to the unity of the church.

The ecumenical decade "The Churches in Solidarity with Women" (1988-98) was a further WCC initiative to take this concern seriously. The decade was inaugurated during the Easter season with the question: "Who will roll the stone away?" The stone was understood to be sexism in church and society, and the decade was designed to be for the entire church, not only a women's decade. Given the centuries of oppression experienced by women on the basis of sexuality, gender, race, ethnic origin, and class, the decade called the churches to conversion, to a reinterpretation and a reordering of Christian faith, life, and witness.

At the midpoint of the decade, in 1992, using the Pauline image of "living letters," over 70 visiting teams composed of two men and two women each from WCC member churches went to more than 330 churches, 68 national councils of churches, and 650 women's groups worldwide. The summary report of the teams both affirmed women's deep love for and dedication to the church and exposed serious obstacles, stones still in the way, of women's full participation in the church: "As 'living letters' we encountered three issues of deep concern to women in all regions: violence against women, even within the 'safe womb' of family and church; the impact of increasing racism and → xenophobia; and the effect of the global economic crisis on women's lives."

4. Issues

The issues of deep concern to women identified by the visiting teams after conversations worldwide confirm numerous other estimations of the practical consequences of sexism.

4.1. *Violence against Women*

Violence against women may be considered the practice of sexism in its extremity (→ Force, Violence, Nonviolence). But the violence that is endemic worldwide is more pervasive and more pernicious than simply physical assault. Physical assault or violation is rampant, taking place also in marriage and in the church. Violence is also an assault on personal freedom of choice, of movement, and of self-determination. When women speak of and suffer violence, therefore, it relates to their most basic sense of safety, not only bodily but emotionally and spiritually.

One sociocultural form of violence is pornography. Women are bombarded daily in all spheres of life by pornographic depictions of women. Pornography is the practice of representation that violates the personal or corporate integrity of that which is presented. Women are reduced to sex objects to sell products or to encourage a disrespectful view of women. Pornographic representation, furthermore, is not unrelated to the alarming global rise in sex-related violence against women by torture, kidnapping, murder, and attacks by soldiers, police, and paramilitary groups.

Another sociocultural form of violence against women occurs in educational settings. This violence includes not only escalating date rape but the tendency for girls and young women to be academically "tracked" in their education in ways that are patterned on centuries-old stereotypes. Not only are women still left out of history; it is still assumed that women are not fitted for "the hard sciences."

4.2. *Increasing Racism and Xenophobia*
Racism and xenophobia compound the oppression of women already oppressed. Here white women, in particular, are culpable. White women may choose to benefit from the white male patriarchal structures and system, either by becoming wives and mothers or by pursuing professions according to prescribed patterns. This is infinitely more difficult for women of color in countries of the Northern Hemisphere, and nearly impossible for women in countries of the Southern Hemisphere. Moreover, as noted above, men in countries of the Southern Hemisphere, living in imperialist or postcolonial contexts, often assert some sense of power by taking on sexist attitudes and behaviors.

4.3. *Economic Obstacles*
The "feminization of poverty" has been an alarming global trend in the last decades. This trend is driven in many countries by women's lack of property or inheritance rights. In countries where these rights are legally guaranteed, the rights may nonetheless not be honored. Even for women who are educated and have pursued professional careers, there are obstacles: the gender-specific division of work; glass ceilings, including stained-glass ceilings; lower pay for the same work. Moreover, as alluded to above, there is structural injustice in the workplace: sexual harassment ranging from verbal assault to physical touching and threats of recrimination in case of refusal. In countries of the Southern Hemisphere, women carry the double and triple burden of work related to keeping the household together and maintaining sufficient income.

The impoverishment of women is also manifest in the disadvantage of women in the realm of health care, whether prenatal or in old age or anywhere in between. Women worldwide suffer neglect in nourishment and medical care and health care education.

The discussion about sexism in church and society is still one of the most volatile contemporary issues. Sexism, tangled as it is in male privilege and power, rooted in gender stereotypes, impacts every arena of life and thought. Religion, including Christianity, has so far helped ensure that extant attitudes, behaviors, and structures are sanctified as unchanging and unchangeable. Yet religion, including Christianity, also has the rich resources to encourage change toward ideologies and practices that affirm the full humanity of women worldwide.

Bibliography: P. Allen, *The Concept of Woman* (2 vols.; Grand Rapids, 1997-2002) • S. Cunningham, ed., *We Belong Together: Churches in Solidarity with Women* (New York, 1992) • E. L. Graham, *Making the Difference: Gender, Personhood, and Theology* (Minneapolis, 1995) • G. Lerner, *The Creation of Patriarchy* (New York, 1986) • M. A. May, *Bonds of Unity: Women, Theology, and the Worldwide Church* (Atlanta, 1989) • M. E. Nussbaum, *Sex and Social Justice* (Oxford, 1999) • M. A. Oduyoye, *Who Will Roll the Stone Away? The Ecumenical Decade of the Churches in Solidarity with Women* (Geneva, 1990) • E. Raiser, "Inclusive Community," *History of the Ecumenical Movement,* vol. 3, *1968-2000* (ed. J. Briggs, M. A. Oduyoye, and G. Tsetsis; Geneva, 2004) 243-77.

Melanie A. May

Sexual Ethics

1. Concept and Concerns
2. Roman Catholic
3. Reformation
4. Modern Protestant
5. Issues

1. Concept and Concerns
Sexual ethics involves the search not only for ethical orientation for personal → behavior in the intimate sphere of auto-, homo-, and heterosexuality (→ Sexuality) but also for the social structuring of the political, economic, legal, and individual conditions affecting the emergence and development both of communities in the private sphere and of relationships between the sexes in both the private and the public spheres. It has, then, a key role as regards the understanding and acceptance of the basic ethical and anthropological conceptions of a specific epoch or social group and also of the changing or further development of these conceptions.

Thus in the Middle Ages the distinction between → celibacy and the married state was the most visible expression of the differentiating of a higher morality (one committed to the evangelical counsels) from ordinary lay morality (based on the → Decalogue). The marriages of former nuns and monks (→ Monasticism) were the final element in signaling the overcoming of this distinction (→

Clergy and Laity 2; Reformation 4), a process that was repeated in the 1960s. When traditional normative → ethics, which was based either on the orders of creation (Lutheranism) or on → natural law (Roman Catholicism) and which found everyday manifestation especially in the institutions of → marriage and the → family, was challenged by situation ethics, it was again sexual ethics as a "morality without norms" (J. Fletcher) that promoted the paradigm shift, at least in the public arena.

2. Roman Catholic

The basic sexual ethics for the → Roman Catholic Church, which was developed by → Augustine (354-430; → Augustine's Theology) and Thomas → Aquinas (ca. 1225-74; → Thomism) and which is still valid today, rests on the Greek-Stoic conceptual schema of essence and phenomenon (→ Greek Philosophy; Stoicism). On this view we attain to perfection only when we overcome that which is sensually individual and seek to actualize that which is rationally universal. In keeping with this → anthropology, "the faithful of the present time, and indeed today more than ever, must use the means which have always been recommended by the Church for living a chaste life. These means are discipline of the senses and the mind, watchfulness and prudence in avoiding occasions of sin, the observance of modesty, moderation in recreation, wholesome pursuits, assiduous prayer, and frequent reception of the Sacraments of Penance and the Eucharist" (*Persona humana* [1975] §12).

After → Vatican II there developed a general atmosphere of openness vis-à-vis the two cornerstones of Roman Catholic sexual ethics: the forbidding of contraception, and sex only for purposes of procreation in marriage. Nevertheless, moral theologians who developed positions in sexual ethics affirming corporeality and sensuality in accordance with one's own → conscience (e.g., A. Gross and S. H. Pfürtner, Pfürtner, W. Bartholomäus, and in the United States esp. C. E. Curran and J. J. McNeill) were quickly reined in by the → teaching office (§1), which has refused to let itself be swayed by the broad discussion of sexual ethics that has taken place within the → moral theology of the Catholic Church (F. Böckle).

3. Reformation

Reformation sexual ethics, which was oriented to biblical anthropology and influenced by Martin → Luther (1483-1546; → Luther's Theology), broke free from the classical → dualism of essence and phenomenon. It focused instead on the total person. Calling by God entails the fulfillment of what is individual, not its stripping away. We do not stand before God as nonsexual beings but as man and woman, and it is as such that we must prove ourselves. Marriage and the family, as the setting favored by the order of creation for the encounter of male and female, took on higher ranking in Reformation theology, far above secular or religious → asceticism. At the same time, this higher estimation of sexuality was restricted to marital sexuality. The innerworldly asceticism of → Calvinism made the restriction even sharper, and the sexual-ethical praxis of the various Christian churches became increasingly indistinguishable for their members.

4. Modern Protestant

Only after World War II did reaction to progressive processes of social → emancipation bring a return in → Protestantism to the biblical and Reformation concept of totality that stresses sexuality as a good gift of God. While the first pioneers in sexual ethics after the war (K. → Barth, H. Thielicke) still treated emancipatory processes with caution, the next generation pointed to the interdependence of the structures of society and sexual conduct (S. Keil, H. Ringeling). The upshot of this discussion was a 1971 memorandum on sexual ethics by the German Evangelical Church (EKD).

The new focus on what is individual and the bodily made possible an understanding of the variety of forms in which we can meet the ethical demand to respect the life of the → neighbor (K. E. Løgstrup). The point was not made, however, that the justifying → love of God that makes human life possible applies to all people, irrespective of their sexual orientation as gays, lesbians, or heterosexuals, and thus encompasses varying forms of lifestyle and companionship, including singles, couples, and family groupings.

All the more clearly, however, a distinction was made even at that time between generative activity and sexuality in accordance with the sociological distinction between procreative functions and social functions (H. Kentler). Sexual intimacy was accorded its own value apart from the act of conception.

Steps were also taken to break the marital monopoly on sexuality by viewing marriage and divorce as processes that might responsibly include sexual experience before and after marriage.

→ Abortion; Identity; Libido; Prostitution; Sex Education; Sexism; Shame; Tolerance

Bibliography: K. Barth, "Freedom in Fellowship," *CD* III/4, §54, 116-323 • W. Bartholomäus, *Glut der*

Begierde–Sprache der Liebe. Unterwegs zur ganzen Sexualität (Munich, 1987) • F. Böckle, ed., *Menschliche Sexualität und kirchliche Sexualmoral* (Düsseldorf, 1977) • Congregation for the Doctrine of the Faith, *Persona humana: Declaration on Certain Questions concerning Sexual Ethics* (Rome, 1975) • C. E. Curran, *Issues in Sexual and Medical Ethics* (Notre Dame, Ind., 1978) • J. Fletcher, *Situation Ethics: The New Morality* (Philadelphia, 1966) • A. Gross and S. H. Pfürtner, eds., *Sexualität und Gewissen* (Mainz, 1973) • C. E. Gudorf, *Body, Sex, and Pleasure: Reconstructing Christian Sexual Ethics* (Cleveland, 1994) • I. P. Hanigen, *Homosexuality: The Test Case for Christian Sexual Ethics* (New York, 1988) • S. Keil, *Protestantische Positionen. Beiträge zur Sexualethik und Familienpolitik* (Grafschaft, 2004); idem, *Sexualität. Erkenntnisse und Maßstäbe* (Stuttgart, 1966) • S. Keil and M. Haspel, eds., *Gleichgeschlechtliche Lebensgemeinschaften in sozialethischer Perspektive* (Neukirchen, 2000) • H. Kentler, ed., *Texte zur Sozio-Sexualität* (Opladen, 1973) • R. D. Lawler, *Catholic Sexual Ethics: A Summary, Explanation, and Defense* (Huntington, Ind., 1998) • K. E. Løgstrup, *The Ethical Demand* (Philadelphia, 1971; orig. pub., 1956) • J. J. McNeill, *The Church and the Homosexual* (exp. ed.; Boston, 1988) • S. H. Pfürtner, *Kirche und Sexualität* (Reinbek, 1972) • Rat der EKD, *Denkschrift zu Fragen der Sexualität* (Gütersloh, 1971) • H. Ringeling, *Theologie und Sexualität* (Gütersloh, 1968) • H. Thielicke, *Theological Ethics* (2d ed.; 3 vols.; Grand Rapids, 1979; orig. pub., 1951-64).

Siegfried Keil

5. Issues

In many churches today affirmation of traditional Christian ideals of → marriage and → family exists side by side with the relaxing of strictures on divorce and remarriage and on sexual intimacy outside marriage. The tension caused by these contrasting ethical perspectives is heightened by actual practices. In the United States some surveys indicate that as many as 72 percent of high school seniors have engaged in sexual intercourse. Half or more of the persons coming to priests or pastors for marriage have been cohabiting. In Norway unmarried couples that live together have increased in numbers by 64 percent in the most recent census. A growing phenomenon in the Christian West is cohabitation among older widows and widowers. They desire intimacy and companionship but for a variety of personal and financial reasons see marriage as impractical. Many would still like the blessing of the church on their relationship. Meanwhile, the facts that one in three marriages ends in divorce and that one in three marriages is a remarriage have become familiar statistics. Do the churches reframe their moral teachings, as some have begun to do, in order to deal realistically with these developments, or do they retrench and vigorously reiterate traditional precepts of sexual morality?

Those advocating the blessing of gay unions or gay marriages have made the erosion of traditional marriage and sexual norms the occasion for calling an end to the idealization and exclusive prerogatives of heterosexual marriage. It is time, they maintain, for a renewal of commitment to fidelity, caring, and justice that includes all partnerships. A number of countries in Europe have registered partnership laws for gay and lesbian couples. In Denmark and Canada, for example, the church has recognized such partnerships as well. Advocates for the protection of traditional marriage have fought the blessing of same-sex unions in the church and gay marriage in the civil realm. Some of these conservatives would agree to some form of legal recognition for homosexual couples to protect their civil → rights. Yet other conservative voices fear that such halfway measures would soon be extended to heterosexual couples who want to avoid the greater commitments of marriage. Indeed, in France heterosexual couples can now sign a "civil solidarity pact" providing the same legal privileges as marriage but without the lifetime commitment entailed.

In almost all the Protestant churches of Europe and North America, the debate rages over the blessing of same-sex unions and the → ordination of persons in committed homosexual unions. While welcoming gay, lesbian, bisexual, and transgendered (GLBT) persons, churches have not affirmed their sexuality. The Evangelical Church in Germany is typical in its 1988 position statement, which mentions → homosexuality largely in terms of "understanding" and "caring" for homosexual persons as objects of → pastoral care. However, there are also strong movements seeking full acceptance of GLBT persons. Lutheran and Anglican church bodies, as well as others, have seen these internal debates about homosexuality in the church reflected in divisions within their respective worldwide, multicultural communions (→ Lutheran Churches; Anglican Communion).

The divide in sexual ethics is also plain when we observe how different Christian traditions respond to the AIDS epidemic. At the one extreme, some continue to regard AIDS as God's judgment on sexual sin, or at least as the sad consequence of immoral sexual conduct. At the other end are those whose first concern is not judgment on the behavior of persons who contract the disease through sexual activity but prevention and cure. For many of the former in the churches of both the North and the South, the idea of promoting safe sex through the use of condoms is simply a way of promoting sexual immorality; only abstinence will do. For the latter, there is no desire to promote promiscuity, but realistically there is an urgent and immediate need to prevent the disease through safe sex.

Feminist theologians and ethicists have challenged sexism in all aspects of our common life. They advocate full sexual equality for women; they are sexual beings in their own right, with rights to sexual pleasure and autonomy, not simply reproducers or sexual property. Feminists point out that gender roles are socially constructed, not simply given, a view that opens the door to reconstructing basic relationships of men and women in society. For many, these developments have been liberating. Feminists have uncovered the exploitation and injustices done to women. For some traditionalists, women and men alike, it has been confusing and disconcerting, despite decades of development and social reconstruction.

Bibliography: W. Countryman, *Dirt, Greed, and Sex: Sexual Ethics in the NT and Their Implications for Today* (Minneapolis, 1990) • M. M. Ellison, *Same-Sex Marriage?* (Cleveland, 2004) • R. Gagnon, *The Bible and Homosexual Practice: Texts and Hermeneutics* (Nashville, 2001) • C. Gudorf, *Body, Sex, and Pleasure: Reconstructing Christian Sexual Ethics* (Cleveland, 1994) • P. B. Jung and R. F. Smith, *Heterosexism: An Ethical Challenge* (New York, 1994) • J. Nelson, *Embodiment: An Approach to Sexuality and Christian Theology* (Minneapolis, 1978) • M. Nissinen, *Homoeroticism in the Biblical World* (Minneapolis, 1998) • *Some Issues in Human Sexuality: A Guide to the Debate* (London, 2003) published for the House of Bishops of the General Synod of the Church of England.

James M. Childs Jr.

Sexuality

1. Definitions

Sexuality refers to a dimension of human nature and experience that is intimately related to, but not identical with, sex and gender. *Sex* refers to a distinction based on reproductive function: individuals in a species who produce large, nutrient-rich gametes (eggs) are called female, while those who produce small, mobile gametes (sperm) are called male. *Gender* refers to psychological and behavioral differences associated with females and males. *Gender identity* reflects one's internal sense of being male or female, while *gender role* refers to cultural expectations about how females and males should behave.

Sexuality is a complex, multilayered concept that refers to erotic desire and behaviors associated with sexual arousal, pleasure, and reproduction (genital sexuality), but it extends to embrace "our ways of being in the world as persons embodied with biological femaleness or maleness and with internalized understandings of what these genders mean" (J. B. Nelson and S. P. Longfellow, xiv). Our sexuality reflects a fundamental human incompleteness that finds its fulfillment in physically, emotionally, and spiritually intimate relationships with others.

2. Historical and Cultural Perspectives

Every human culture expresses, responds to, and controls sexuality through normative frameworks and social institutions. These frameworks reflect broad cultural values, as well as more specific beliefs about the purposes, functions, and nature of sexuality. The various aspects of sexuality — including pleasure, intimacy, reproduction, parenthood, kinship systems, economics, and social status — may be emphasized or minimized. For example, in North America and Europe attitudes toward sexuality reflect the post-Enlightenment prioritizing of individual → freedom, egalitarianism, and personal fulfillment; in some Middle Eastern and Asian contexts, precedence is given to hierarchy, community identity, social responsibility, and interdependence. Western sexual expression thus generally finds approval in any form that involves the free consent of participating adults. In the East, sex outside of marriage, particularly by women, is often seen as a threat to the status of the → family and makes a socially desirable → marriage unlikely.

Despite considerable diversity in particular forms

and emphases, there are some common themes across cultures. For example, all cultures distinguish two main sex/gender categories (female and male), create social structures that regulate sexual relationships between them, and create a space for the rearing of children. In all well-documented cultures historically and currently, being female has been associated with lower status and domination by males. Female sexuality is frequently controlled by males for reproductive or economic purposes and for social status. The extent of this control varies but remains true even in modern Western culture. Social role and status (e.g., of slaves, members of particular racial or ethnic groups, the aristocracy) are also associated with varying degrees of control over, and different sets of rules regarding, sexual expression.

Cultures also vary in their awareness and tolerance of individuals who are not obviously female or male. They include intersexed people (pseudohermaphrodites), those who take on the identity and roles of the other sex, and people who are erotically attracted to members of their own, or both, sexes. Such individuals may be socially invisible or become the subject of moral censure, fear, or hostility; they may be tolerated or may be given a unique social role (G. Herdt).

3. In the History of Christianity

The Christian church has been a dominant shaping force in Western culture, and its attitudes toward sexuality have become embedded in the cultural landscape. These attitudes are varied and sometimes internally contradictory.

In the → early church, thinking about sexuality was influenced by the values and structures of the Greco-Roman world, which included strong social hierarchies and patriarchal families. The elite few had considerable power over the many, and men had almost absolute power over their wives, children, other dependents, servants, and slaves. Philosophical and religious views of the time (e.g., → Platonism) taught the duality of human nature, consisting of material body and immaterial, immortal → soul. The material was viewed as distorted or evil, while knowledge and the spiritual were elevated as pure or ideal (→ Gnosis, Gnosticism). A number of influential pagan thinkers, including the → Stoics, promoted the avoidance of pleasure and sexual abstinence. These ideas influenced the worldviews and thoughts of early Christians. One sees both integration and rejection of these values and perspectives among the shapers of the early church.

The early → church fathers, including Origen, Jerome, Tertullian, and, most significantly, Augustine, affirmed the goodness of marriage and procreation, while simultaneously expressing great unease with the power, intensity, and pleasure of sexual desire and expression. They argued that "lust (hence sin) taints all sexual activity. Hence, it should be as restrained and infrequent as possible, even in marriage" (D. Doriani, 35). Virginity, celibacy, and chastity within marriage were approved of and encouraged. Thus a Gnostic → dualism, which valued the rational and spiritual dimensions of marriage but denigrated its bodily pleasures, entered into the church's understandings of sexuality.

While sexual pleasure was viewed with suspicion, genital sexuality was approved for the purposes of procreation. Even this dimension was considered tainted, however, for many believed that original sin was transmitted through procreation. Over the centuries theologians developed the doctrine of the immaculate conception of Mary to resolve the problem of how Christ could avoid the taint of original sin. This doctrine states that through God's miraculous dispensation, Mary was conceived without sin and thus made fit to later produce a sinless Christ (→ Mariology 1.3).

Leaders of the → Reformation rejected a number of traditional Roman Catholic doctrines, including many relating to sexuality. They disapproved of mandatory → celibacy for the clergy and viewed marriage and sexual expression within marriage as healthy gifts of God to be enjoyed. They recognized the dangers associated with powerful sexual passions but did not view sexual pleasure as inherently suspect. Although some Protestant traditions incorporate an unease and → asceticism with regard to sexuality, in general the Protestant churches have, at least officially, held a high view of human sexuality.

Gnostic, ascetic, and Christian traditions that are negative or ambivalent toward sexuality are deeply embedded in Western culture. Equally interwoven, however, are other Christian traditions that affirm the goodness of the physical creation, human relationality and intimacy, and → Enlightenment ideals of individual freedom and equality, tolerance, and personal fulfillment. Inevitably, contradictions and conflicts regarding sexuality emerge from the coexistence of these views. For example, Enlightenment thinkers failed to extend their ideals to women (and other relatively powerless groups), while, conversely, Enlightenment values were sometimes quietly and uncritically embraced by mainline Protestants.

Protestant theologians today tend to emphasize the intimately relational and personally fulfilling aspects of sexuality and its expression (e.g., J. B. Nelson, L. B. Smedes), and there is generally a more accepting and flexible attitude toward premarital sex, divorce, remarriage, and contraception (→ Birth Control). The → Roman Catholic Church has consistently reconfirmed traditional views of sexuality and its expression but emphasizes both the procreative and the unitive aspects of sexuality and encourages married couples to enjoy sexual pleasure as a gift of God, even when procreation is unlikely or impossible (e.g., for infertile couples or postmenopausal women). Overall, both Protestants and Catholics have a wide range of attitudes toward sexuality, which the diversity of official church positions on the subject reflects.

4. In the Bible and Its Interpretation

Foundational biblical texts for understanding human sexuality are found in the original creation narratives. Gen. 1:26-31, in which humankind is created in God's image as male and female, is usually understood to reveal God's internal relationality (i.e., the persons of the → Trinity). Humankind images God as both female and male persons in relationship. Gen. 2:18-23, in which the man is given the woman as a suitable partner, underscores this inherent need for relationship and suggests a sexual dimension to the deepest and most intimate relationships. Images of God as a bridegroom and God's people as a bride (sometimes an unfaithful spouse) also occur throughout the Bible, reinforcing the message of the fundamental relationality of God and of humankind. Procreation is also recognized as a human calling in Gen. 1:28.

The Bible endorses sexual passion in the Song of Solomon and also in Prov. 5:18-19. Other passages (Luke 20:34-36; Gal. 3:28; Rev. 14:4), however, suggest an eschatological vision of transformation or transcendence of sexual relationality and marriage.

Scripture also contains various comments and prescriptions regarding sexual expression. Levitical laws address sexuality in the context of purity, outlining acceptable sexual practices and prescribing cleansing rituals and punishments for violations. → Jesus comments on marriage, divorce, and sexual faithfulness, in the context of the family and legal structures of his day. Paul addresses sexual purity and practice, both within and outside of marriage, as the early church attempted to apply the gospel to its cultural context.

While the Bible does not speak with a singular voice on sexuality, Christians recognize that there is an overarching coherence to Scripture. The challenge is how to faithfully interpret the message. Some argue that scriptural comments on sexuality are absolute, universal prescriptions. Others believe that the Bible is irrelevant to modern issues and understandings. And many suggest that the Bible reveals faithful but culturally specific responses to God's gift of sexuality, models we need to flexibly apply to our present contexts. These diverse perspectives underlie many disagreements among Christians about God's will for sexuality.

Stephen Barton and William Countryman suggest that we should develop our theologies of sexuality through a combination of rational understanding and radical personal transformation through the work of the Spirit, yielding the self completely to God's reign. Countryman shows how the early church struggled to live out this transforming power of the gospel in the context of first-century Middle Eastern culture. The church challenged prevailing views of the structure of family and society, the inequality of men and women, legal understandings of property, and the purity rules that governed "righteous" living. He argues that today we are called to emulate the early church by radically surrendering to God our cherished ideals, familiar social structures, and laws of moral purity.

Principles of sexual equality, the freedom to yield oneself to God (not to social rules or the household patriarch), and the radical inclusiveness of God's grace should guide all outworkings of sexual expression and relationship. The Scriptures relativize our own ways of understanding sexuality and remind us that our calling is to "seek, with the help of the past, to understand the present in its own terms and proclaim the gospel in ways pertinent to it" (Countryman, 238). Countryman represents a theological perspective on sexuality that does not turn relevant biblical texts into absolute prescriptions yet views the Bible as a source of relevant and challenging guidance for the sexual issues that currently face us.

5. In Science

Scientific studies of human sexuality have contributed to a diversity of perspectives on its nature. Interpretations of this research continue to shape attitudes and beliefs about the range of possible experiences and expressions of sexuality. These interpretations sometimes contrast with, and other times complement or confirm, traditional Christian perspectives. Overall, there is considerable debate about the ways in which Christians can and should engage scientific and theological perspectives on sexuality.

5.1. *Evolutionary Perspectives*

Evolutionary psychologists remind us that humankind is part of the physical world, that we are fully embodied, and that all human beings share a basic nature. Because women and men have different roles in the reproductive process, however, a number of psychological and behavioral differences between the sexes may have evolved. These include, for example, differences in the conditions under which men and women are willing to engage in sexual intercourse and the qualities desired in a mate (for an extensive overview, see L. Mealey, *Sex Differences*). This approach to human sexuality has the power to account for certain universal patterns but focuses primarily on genetic self-interest and reproductive goals.

Evolutionary theory describes human sexuality in terms that often conflict with Christian perspectives (→ Evolution). Christian beliefs in the innate human need for relationship, however, and the call to "be fruitful and multiply" can harmonize with the evolutionary view that we are formed to seek out a mate with whom we cooperate to produce and raise children.

5.2. *Biological Perspectives*

The physical differentiation of humans into female and male sexes is not simply determined at conception by the nature of the sex chromosomes (XX for female, XY for male). It is a complex process involving multiple genes and physiological structures and processes. The human fetus has the potential to develop fully as female or male until roughly seven weeks after conception, and even beyond this time, exposure to certain hormones can redirect this process. Many aspects of biological sex emerge during fetal development, while others do not emerge until adolescence or later.

In most cases this complex process results in an individual who is consistently female or male at the genetic, gonadal (ovaries and testes), external genital, hormonal, and neural levels. On occasion, however, a newborn will be "intersexed," that is, inconsistently female and male in one or more of these dimensions. For example, an XY fetus with complete androgen insensitivity syndrome has undescended testes, no other internal reproductive organs, and female external genitalia, including a partial vagina. Such infants are identified and raised as female and usually have a consistent female gender identity but are genetically and gonadally male.

Females and males are remarkably similar, but there are some small average differences in physiological, neural, and cognitive functions directly and indirectly related to sexuality (see D. Kimura, *Sex and Cognition*).

Certain basic physiological (hormonal and neural) conditions must be present for the experience and expression of sexual desire, arousal, and orgasm. These physiological aspects of sexuality function to some degree throughout the life span. Infants and young children can experience pleasure and some arousal through genital stimulation. Erection and vaginal lubrication occur from shortly after birth. At puberty a fairly sudden increase in circulating hormones is associated with enhanced interest in sexual activity and stronger responses to sexual stimulation. Sexual desire in males seems to peak around the early 20s, while in females the peak may occur in the 30s and 40s. After this peak, desire gradually declines, although there is considerable variation among individuals.

5.3. *Psychosocial Perspectives*

Sexual desire and arousal are enhanced or inhibited to varying degrees as a result of psychological factors, including sensory stimulation (e.g., the sight of the loved one), certain environmental conditions (e.g., privacy or lack thereof), internal emotional longings (e.g., desire for closeness, desire for children), and social expectations. For example, although women are slightly more easily aroused near ovulation, they can and do enjoy sexual activities throughout their menstrual cycle. As well, sexually active adult males who experience major reductions in testosterone (e.g., through physical or chemical castration) can often continue to engage in sexual intercourse, even with reduced sexual desire.

Virtually the first question asked when an infant is born is whether it is a boy or a girl. The answer shapes the way people treat and perceive the infant. Female and male infants are also born with somewhat distinct (though overlapping) response tendencies and orientations to the world. The dynamic between these innate tendencies and particular sociocultural contexts shapes the child's sexuality and gender identity and role. Systematic differential socialization of girls and boys influences brain organization, psychological states, behaviors, and even bodies. For example, in North America boys are encouraged to be more physically active than girls, and they are dressed in ways that facilitate this activity. Differences in degree and type of activity have an effect on the developing skeletal and muscular aspects of the body and on the neural circuits that underlie complex patterns of behavior (see esp. J. Lorber, "Believing Is Seeing").

Cultural values and expectations interact with biological aspects of sexuality to shape the ways in which people experience themselves as gendered and sexual beings. They also teach us how to express our sexuality as we learn what is considered appropriate and inappropriate in our context.

6. Interactions of Science and Theology

Scientific approaches can describe sexuality, explain proximate causes, and report on the consequences of various forms of sexual expression. The interpretation of those observations, however, involves philosophical and theological presuppositions, commitments, and insights. What is the relative contribution of innate, biological factors and of sociocultural/experiential elements? How do we evaluate "healthy" sexuality? On what grounds do we draw conclusions about the morality of certain expressions of sexuality?

One common distinction in debates about human sexuality is between *essentialism* and *constructionism*. Essentialists argue that there are female and male natures, or "essences," that are universal and constant across cultures. This sexual nature can be understood as a product of our evolutionary history and current biology (esp. our neurophysiology), as a distinction designed by God in the creation of humankind, or as both. Essentialists vary in the specific characteristics they attribute to female and male natures and in the degree of overlap and flexibility, but all share the view that there is a core sexual identity that is expressed in cultural contexts but is not itself altered by them.

Constructionists take the view that sexuality cannot be understood apart from the historical, social, and cultural contexts in which it is defined and observed. Its meaning changes over history and across cultures, and culture informs individuals about the relevant gender categories and the sexual expressions expected, permitted, and prohibited for that individual. Strong constructionists argue that culture shapes our embodied sexuality, such that even biological sexual distinctions are culturally relative. While constructionists vary in the degree to which they believe culture shapes sexuality, they all focus on socially given meanings, flexibility, and the potential for change, and they minimize universal, stable, and innate realities.

Christians tend to understand human sexuality in somewhat essentialist terms. Gen. 1:27 suggests that God created humankind male and female. While Scripture is not very explicit about the physical, psychological, behavioral, and possibly spiritual characteristics associated with each of the sexes (although see M. S. Van Leeuwen, *Gender and Grace*), most Christians believe that there is some kind of sexual nature embedded within each person. The form and expression of this sexual nature has been distorted by the effects of sin, but our calling is to redeem that nature and cultivate its God-given potentials.

Some Christians, however, take a more constructionist stance when they question the clarity with which we can know what it is to be female or male, and what God's "ideal" for maleness and femaleness might look like. They remind us that we "see through a glass darkly" and draw our attention to the sociocultural contexts within which biblical passages on sexuality were written and the very different audiences they address. They also point out that the Bible suggests that sexual distinctions may be transformed or transcended in the → kingdom of God.

Some Christian and post-Christian feminists integrate Enlightenment ideas of personal fulfillment and liberation with science-based understandings of sexual variation and a broad definition of sexuality (→ Feminism). They reinterpret Scripture and Christian tradition as encouraging the celebration of sexuality and sexual expression in a variety of relationships. They reject dichotomous notions of sexuality as socially constructed and embrace sexual diversity as an expression of the abundance of God's good → creation. They also recognize an erotic dimension to God's relationship with humankind (e.g., C. Heyward, *Touching Our Strength*).

Controversies about human sexuality that appeal to science often fail to recognize that purposive, moral, and normative dimensions can be influenced, but not determined, by scientific data. Regardless of our worldview — Christian, → materialist, or → humanist — we select and interpret scientific data in light of our presuppositions. When done without awareness or acknowledgment, the result can involve distortions of science, theology, and practice.

Christians are called to consider whether the consequences of their sometimes oversimplified essentialist views of human sexuality in fact lead to the kinds of loving response to God and → love for one's neighbor that are the greatest of the commandments. Scholars such as Lisa Sowle Cahill and Mary Stewart Van Leeuwen have shown that it is possible to take seriously modern scientific insights into human sexuality, a critical engagement with Enlightenment ideas, cross-cultural sensitivity, and challenges from postmodern and feminist perspectives and to meaningfully integrate them all with traditional Christian understandings that reflect the spirit of the gospel.

7. Current Issues

Few issues generate as much controversy, emotional heat, and divisive conflict among Christians as those related to sexuality. During the late 20th and early 21st centuries, battles have continually been waged over the → ordination of women, headship in marriage, divorce and remarriage, premarital sex, celibacy of the priesthood, abortion, sexual orientation, and same-sex marriage. Other issues with a sexual dimension, such as single parenthood, the feminization of poverty, the political powerlessness of women in many countries, the cult of machismo in Latin America, and female genital circumcision, are rarely addressed by Christians.

Although several other items on the above list affect far more people within and outside the church, the issues that are currently the most debated and divisive are → homosexuality, same-sex marriage, and → abortion. Positions on these issues are influenced by beliefs about human sexuality in general, which are based on both theological commitments and scientific/experiential understandings. Relatively few Christians seem to recognize that the biblical witness, theological conclusions, and scientific insights are often ambiguous, complex, or tentative. As noted above, oversimplified approaches to Scripture and to science, coupled with a lack of historical awareness, can polarize people's positions and prevent meaningful and loving dialogue.

7.1. *Homosexuality*

Several aspects of homosexuality receive attention from Christians: what it means to have a homosexual orientation, whether this orientation can be "healed," and whether it can be legitimately expressed in intimate relationships. While some still believe that a homosexual orientation is a chosen perversion of human sexuality, others see homosexuality as a relatively stable characteristic that emerges through processes over which a person has no control. The question of whether a homosexual orientation is a symptom of abnormal development or whether it represents a natural and potentially healthy variation in human sexuality remains controversial.

Of more concern among Christians is whether a homosexual orientation can be "healed," or changed. If human sexuality is intended to be expressed in exclusively female and male forms and to draw us into relationships that have the potential for procreation, then sexual attraction to members of one's own sex appears to be an abnormal condition in need, if possible, of healing. However, if we understand sexuality primarily as that aspect of human nature that draws us into relationship, with procreation a valued but secondary and nonessential dimension, then it becomes more difficult to call homosexuality pathological. Having a homosexual orientation is not reliably associated with any signs of physical, psychological, or spiritual illness, although some evidence suggests increased risks for mental illness. Furthermore, while anecdotal and testimonial evidence suggests that change is possible, numerous scientific studies on the efficacy of therapeutic interventions intended to alter orientation show that genuine, stable changes of orientation appear to be relatively infrequent and poorly understood. Since people come to identify themselves as homosexual for a variety of reasons, some of those reasons may reflect conditions in a person's life that, if healed or altered, may lead to a change of orientation, while other paths to homosexuality may be irreversible.

7.2. *Same-Sex Marriage*

Whether a reversal of sexual orientation is desirable or even possible, an even more difficult question is whether (and if so, how) a homosexual orientation should be expressed in relationship. Same-sex marriage is one answer to this question. For some Christians any expression of genital sexuality outside of a heterosexual marriage is morally wrong, and therefore persons with a homosexual orientation must accept a life of celibacy. The immorality of homosexual erotic activity is, for these persons, further supported by the structure and function of the reproductive organs themselves, leading to the conclusion that such activity is unnatural.

For other Christians, celibacy is a calling, not something to be imposed upon an entire set of people. Erotic sexuality can be legitimately expressed through means other than genital sexual intercourse. They argue that faithfulness, commitment, and intimacy are the criteria for marriage, standards to which persons of all orientations are called. Some go further to suggest that marriage itself is a patriarchal institution that can no longer legitimately express the gospel and therefore ought to be abandoned for a new, more egalitarian mode of intimacy and connection. (Few of those now favoring this latter position, however, are Christian.)

A question that lies at the heart of this heated debate is whether God has ordained only monogamous, heterosexual marriage as part of the good structure of creation. Many fear that legitimation of any intimate, committed relationship outside this ideal will lead to serious negative consequences for society as a whole. This fear, however, is partly based on an ahistorical and ethnocentric view of marriage, a social structure that takes many forms and plays different roles in various cultures, not necessarily to the detriment of those cultures. For example, the ancient Hebrews thrived and received God's covenant blessings, even as their leaders engaged in polygamous marriages and fathered children with concubines.

Do gospel principles of → faithfulness, human → equality, inclusive → grace, and obedient surrender to the Spirit transcend and transform our understanding of human sexuality and its appropriate expression? Or do these principles require an absolute commitment to heterosexual, monogamous, faithful marriage and to sexual abstinence outside of this context? A growing number of Christians, including scientists and theologians, answer no to the latter question. They challenge the absolutizing and idealizing of particular understandings of sexuality and marriage (see works listed below by Countryman, Nelson, and Nelson and Longfellow). Still others have a high view of marriage and family, believe that sexuality is best expressed within this context, yet believe it appropriate to extend this opportunity to homosexual as well as heterosexual couples (D. G. Myers and L. D. Scanzoni). Other thoughtful theologians and Christian leaders, however, disagree.

In the midst of this struggle, people with very different positions on this difficult issue are beginning to sit down together to share and to listen to one another (see T. Bradshaw, *The Way Forward*).

7.3. *Abortion*

Abortion is another difficult issue that has become heated and divisive for Christians. While no Christian denomination views abortion as desirable, North American and European churches vary on whether, under certain circumstances, it can ever be acceptable. → Roman Catholic, Southern Baptist, → Orthodox, and Missouri Synod Lutheran churches are all strongly opposed to abortion, except in cases when the life of the mother is at risk. Presbyterian, United Methodist, Episcopal/Anglican, and United Church of Canada churches take the position that abortion can be a morally acceptable choice in situations varying (depending on the denomination) from risk to the mother, abnormalities in the fetus, rape, and physical or emotional inability to care for a child.

While there are many dimensions to the issue of abortion, here we focus on those aspects more directly related to sexuality and its appropriate expressions. While there are various theological perspectives on sexuality, the church today agrees that sexuality is a good gift of God to draw us into joyful, pleasurable relationship with one another, and that we are called to faithfulness in those relationships. These views suggest that healthy expressions of sexuality should involve responsibility, self-control, enjoyment, and a profound commitment to and respect for the other. One of the gifts of sexual intimacy is children. Even if we accept contraception as part of a responsible expression of our sexuality, there always remains, for fertile heterosexual couples, the possibility of conception. Under ideal circumstances, all children conceived would be healthfully nourished in the womb and welcomed and nurtured once born.

Broken and sinful realities, however, include social structures and practices where women often have little power or freedom to choose when and with whom they engage in sexual intimacy, or where there is limited or no access to contraception. Both women and men may also have distorted ideas about sexual freedom or the proper role of sexual intimacy in relationships, often as a result of media portrayals. These portrayals are not often challenged by families and communities (including church communities), who may be unwilling to speak, or are simply uncomfortable in speaking, about sexual intimacy and therefore offer little guidance. When an undesired conception occurs under these circumstances, there is a tendency to hold the couple, and especially the woman, individually responsible, when in fact the community played a significant role. Some churches have recognized the role and responsibility of the community and offer counseling to these women to help them explore their options (although churches with strong positions against abortion will emphasize the negative emotional consequences of having an abortion and direct these women toward adoption), and some offer private adoption services (→ Abortion Counseling). Prevention of unwanted conceptions through healthy, frank education about human sexuality and its expression, action to change social practices and cultural values that lead to such conceptions, and effective long-term support for women who bear children under difficult circumstances receive considerably less energy and attention than attempts to make abortion generally illegal.

At the same time, the belief that we have the freedom and the right to enjoy pleasure and fulfillment from genital sexual expression without bearing any long-term consequences is a manifestation of individualist Enlightenment, not Christian, ideals. While sexual expression has a legitimate unitive aspect distinct from its procreative aspect, conception is always a possibility for fertile heterosexual couples. Thus the choice to engage in sexual intercourse is far more serious than the promoters of sexual freedom suggest. Abortion as a means of birth control is not only unhealthy, it raises difficult questions about the status of the fetus as a full or potential human being.

Abortion is therefore a complex issue, even when we consider only those aspects related to sexuality. Considerations of freedom, power, communal and individual responsibility, all of which are addressed in the Gospels, are relevant in considering how Christians should respond to abortion and its causes and consequences.

→ Ethics; Sexual Ethics

Bibliography: S. C. BARTON, "Is the Bible Good News for Human Sexuality? Reflections on Method in Biblical Interpretation," *ThSex* 1 (1994) 42-54 • T. BRADSHAW, ed., *The Way Forward? Christian Voices on Homosexuality and the Church* (2d ed.; Grand Rapids, 2003) • J. BUTLER, *Bodies That Matter: On the Discursive Limits of "Sex"* (New York, 1993) • L. S. CAHILL, *Sex, Gender, and Christian Ethics* (Cambridge, 1996) • L. W. COUNTRYMAN, *Dirt, Greed, and Sex: Sexual Ethics in the NT and Their Implications for Today* (Philadelphia, 1988) • D. DORIANI, "The Puritans, Sex, and Pleasure," *Christian Perspectives on Sexuality and Gender* (ed. A. Thatcher and E. Stuart; Grand Rapids, 1996) 33-51 • S. GOLDBERG, "Reaffirming the Obvious," *Society* 23/6 (1986) 4-7 • S. J. GRENZ, "Theological Foundations for Male-Female Relationships," *JETS* 41 (1998) 615-30 • G. HERDT, ed., *Third Sex, Third Gender: Beyond Sexual Dimorphism in Culture and History* (New York, 1994) • C. HEYWARD, *Touching Our Strength: The Erotic as Power and the Love of God* (San Francisco, 1989) • D. KIMURA, *Sex and Cognition* (Cambridge, Mass., 1999) • H. LOOY, "Male and Female God Created Them: The Challenge of Intersexuality," *JPsC* 21 (2002) 10-20; idem, "Sex Differences: Evolved, Constructed, and Designed," *JPsT* 29 (2001) 301-13 • J. LORBER, "Believing Is Seeing: Biology as Ideology," *GenSoc* 7 (1993) 568-81 • L. MEALEY, *Sex Differences: Developmental and Evolutionary Strategies* (San Diego, Calif., 2000) • D. G. MYERS and L. D. SCANZONI, *What God Has Joined Together? A Christian Case for Gay Marriage* (San Francisco, 2005) • J. B. NELSON, *Embodiment: An Approach to Sexuality and Christian Theology* (Minneapolis, 1978) • J. B. NELSON and S. P. LONGFELLOW, eds., *Sexuality and the Sacred: Sources for Theological Reflection* (Louisville, Ky., 1994) • U. RANKE-HEINEMANN, *Eunuchs for the Kingdom of Heaven: Women, Sexuality, and the Catholic Church* (trans. P. Heinegg; New York, 1990) • L. B. SMEDES, *Sex for Christians: The Limits and Liberties of Sexual Living* (rev. ed.; Grand Rapids, 1994) • M. S. VAN LEEUWEN, *Gender and Grace: Love, Work, and Parenting in a Changing World* (Downers Grove, Ill., 1990); idem, "Of Hoggamus and Hogwash: Evolutionary Psychology and Gender Relations," *JPsT* 30 (2001) 101-11.

HEATHER LOOY

Shamanism

The term "shamanism" is used for anything that has to do with shamans. It comes from Evenki, a Tungusic language of Siberia, and denotes beating around oneself. Scholars have for many years disputed the definition, origin, extent, and exact scope of shamanism. Their uncertainty bears witness to the gap between the West and the intercultural and religious phenomenon known as shamanism. Women as well as men are shamans. They may be found in the north of Asia, America, and Europe, among Inuits, Indians, Siberians, Mongols, Koreans, Lapps, and others. Despite what they have in common, their belief systems differ, so that we cannot call shamanism their → religion.

These peoples live hard lives in harsh areas. They depend on hunting and, wherever possible, raise reindeer. Their settlements are necessarily small and scattered over wide territories. → Animals are close to them and are important in their religion. Siberians are said to think of the animal world as the final reality to which we return at death. We humans differ from them in body but not in → soul.

For shamanism there is an unseen world of spirits alongside or behind the world we see. Believers see or detect spirits, to which shamans are especially close. At consecration they are conducted to the upper- and underworlds and are associated with the spirits as permanent helpers. A spirit becomes their alter ego and combats the escorts, or "soul-bearers," of other shamans. Helping spirits are animal-like but have a human appearance and can often be the marriage partners of shamans.

The shamans, as religious specialists, have the features of → prophets, → priests, counselors, and charismatics. Their calling gives them more than earthly authority, as in the case of prophets. Most of them resist this calling at first, then fall sick, and are healed only when they accept their election. Then follows the painful experience of dying and being born again. Spirits tear the flesh from their bones and give them new flesh. They serve their communities like priests. They hazard their lives in mutual conflicts in which they represent their clans or themselves. The one whose alter ego is defeated dies. Those called by spirits are also like priests in that they must be taught by experienced shamans. As counselors they devote themselves mostly to individuals (e.g., the sick). For this purpose, like charismatics, they have extraordinary gifts.

Shamans work ecstatically (→ Ecstasy). Either they give up all sense of their bodies so as to lead the souls of the sick out of the upper- or underworld, and their bodily functions then become weaker (→

Health and Illness), or self-awareness leaves them in order to give place to a different awareness, in which case their body can do things of extraordinary power. Shamans control the coming and going of their consciousness, which is a distinguishing feature. They do it ritually, mostly with the help of drums (→ Dance; Rite).

Bibliography: L. J. Bean, *California Indian Shamanism* (Menlo Park, Calif., 1992) • S. O. Glosecki, *Shamanism and Old English Poetry* (Garland, N.Y., 1989) • G. Harvey, *Shamanism: A Reader* (London, 2003) • A. Hultkranz, *Shamanic Healing and Ritual Drama: Health and Medicine in Native North American Religious Traditions* (New York, 1992) • M. D. Jakobsen, *Shamanism: Traditional and Contemporary Approaches to the Mastery of Spirits and Healing* (New York, 1999) • B. Kapferer, *The Feast of the Sorcerer: Practices of Consciousness and Power* (Chicago, 1997) • V. V. Khagdev, *Shamanizm i miroviye religii* (Shamanism and world religions) (Irkutsk, 1998) diss. by a Siberian shaman • C. Laderman, *Taming the Wind of Desire: Psychology, Medicine, and Aesthetics in Malay Shamanistic Performance* (Berkeley, Calif., 1991) • E. J. Langdon, *Portals of Power: Shamanism in South America* (Albuquerque, N.M., 1992) • C. S. MacClain, ed., *Women as Healers: Cross-Cultural Perspectives* (New Brunswick, N.J., 1989) • S. A. Osterreich, *Native North American Shamanism: An Annotated Bibliography* (Westport, Conn., 1998).

Hans-Jürgen Greschat

Shame

1. Term, Forms
2. Functions
3. Shame and Sin

1. Term, Forms

The word "shame" refers both to an emotion and to a basic disposition.

1.1. Shame appears as a type of → anxiety, the anxiety of shame ("I am afraid of being exposed and thus humiliated"). Such anxiety can manifest itself as a subtle warning (signal form) or as overwhelming panic.

1.2. Shame also occurs as a complex emotion in reference to a depressive core feeling ("I have exposed myself and feel humiliated; I want to disappear; I don't want to exist any longer as such a being that has thus exposed itself; I can extirpate this perceived contempt only by eliminating that which is exposed, either by hiding or disappearing myself or, if necessary, by my own elimination"; → Depression; Suicide). The elements of seeing and disappearing — that is, of the eye — play particularly important roles in the feeling of contempt and its appropriate → atonement.

1.3. Whereas the first two forms view emotional shame as negative, the third exhibits an opposite, positive side (G. H. Seidler). Here the feeling of shame constitutes a kind of feeling of honor or dignity, functioning as a way to protect oneself socially and personally; it represents a character trait running counter to self-exposure, that is, to revealing oneself ("I have to hide behind a mask to shield my inner disposition from the intrusive gaze of others; I also have to conceal my own gaze, check my own curiosity, and rein in my own pushiness"). In the words of F. Hebbel (1813-63): "Shame refers to that inner boundary of sin in human beings; there where a person begins to blush, the more noble self begins."

As a mode of protection or as preventive self-concealment (Gk. *aidōs*, Lat. *pudor*), shame is the antithesis of the emotion of feeling exposed and represents a disposition of respect for others and for oneself (J. W. Goethe's "reverence for oneself"). → Psychoanalysis understands this situation as the formation of a reaction. Such feelings of shame manifest themselves as tact, discretion, and modesty and also come to expression as sexual shame (→ Sexuality). In this sense, shame keeps watch over the private, inward sphere, guarding the heart of the personality itself — our most intensive feelings, our → identity and integrity, and especially our sexual desires, experiences, and body parts. Without this outer covering of shame, individuals feel robbed of their dignity — unless they voluntarily forgo it for the larger and more comprehensive dignity of → love. This third form of shame protects the independent → self with its attendant boundaries and prevents others from intruding into the private sphere, and prevents also the fulfillment of one's wish to merge with the other, or self-dissolution from the inside, as it were.

2. Functions

2.1. Shame keeps watch over the boundaries of privacy and intimacy; → guilt limits the expansion of → power. Shame covers and conceals weakness, whereas feelings of guilt impose restrictions on strength. Shame protects an integrated understanding of self, guilt the integrity of the other. Because the mutual relationship between perception and expression shapes the core of the self, shame can be viewed as the basic form of protection within interpersonal relationships to the extent that the latter are themselves shaped by expression and communication as well as by perception and awareness. Within the motor-active and motor-aggressive sphere (→ Aggression), guilt has the same function of protecting physical integrity from violation.

2.2. This model of internal and external boundaries can be understood in a horizontal fashion. The vertical dimension, however, is also indispensable insofar as the phenomena of shame are inconceivable without the inclusion of ideal constructions and a participation of these ideals in a broader community (→ Society; Group and Group Dynamics). The "inner boundary" of privacy articulated by the horizontal model circumscribes a core of identity and integrity, a core that in its own turn is subject to the primacy of certain ideals and values (→ Norms).

The ideal self corresponds inwardly to the image of the ideal other, before whose eye a person must pass review and by whom we want to be accepted and respected. In this sense the other is viewed as an → authority *(auctoritas),* as a power granting inner growth to a person — originally probably an enhanced parental figure but in reality a hierarchical principle appearing inwardly as the ego-ideal and externally as the "spirit of the community" or as "God." In this sense, this inner authority — as both "eye" and "image" — represents both that which is most intimate to a person's self and the best elements of the community in which that person wants to participate, whether the latter be understood concretely, atemporally, or abstractly.

2.3. Shame thus has a double function. It protects the integrity of the self by checking excessive exposure or revelation and excessive curiosity. At the same time, it serves the community's guiding ideals and forms of preservation through its inherent element of → reverence and through the sanctions of ridicule and disgrace. Although the values articulated by shame and honor vary from → culture to culture, they invariably serve to secure social structures of the hierarchy and its defining boundaries.

In every cultural sphere, manifestations of a loss of control are generally subjected to social shame, that is, to ridicule. Such cases involve repeatedly postulated forms of control over one's emotions, corporeality, and movement in the larger sense; over forms of expression and gestures in particular; and over impulsive desires. Social hierarchies are based on obligations requiring specific checks and controls on the part of the individual, and an individual's failure to abide by them leads to a forfeiture of the respect of others. In this context, especially a sudden loss of control leads to social shame.

3. Shame and Sin

According to the interpretations of → Midrash and Rashi (= Rabbi Shlomo Yitzḥaqi, 1040-1105), the story of Adam and Eve (Genesis 3) focuses on the danger of seeing, of knowing, and of more profound insight leading to the terrible anxiety of being exposed and punished for having seen. In that sense, the story is alluding to the introduction of shame: curiosity and self-exposure are suddenly seen to be extremely dangerous and are thus accompanied by constant references to shame.

→ Augustine (354-430; → Augustine's Theology 5) views the feeling of shame as a consequence of the fall (→ Sin 1) Before the fall, human beings had complete control of their bodies; without the concurrence of the will, desire was unable to excite the sexual members. Afterward Adam and Eve noticed the movement of their members, which made their nakedness seem indecent; this shameless novelty opened their eyes and awakened shame: "Human nature, then, is without doubt ashamed of this lust; and justly so, for the insubordination of these [sexual] members, and their defiance of the will, are the clear testimony of the punishment of man's first sin" (*De civ. Dei* 14.20).

The → Talmud emphasizes the central ethical role of honor and dignity and thus understands making someone else feel shame as constituting a preeminent sin ("making another person's face pale before the many"). This theme is addressed in part of the *Gemara,* which in its own turn refers to *m. B. Meṣ.* 58b-59b under the approximate heading "hurting through words, offense, wounding feelings, shaming." Propositions maintain that those who shame others are in effect shedding blood and will have no part in the coming world; indeed, it would be better for such persons to throw themselves into an oven than to shame their → neighbor publicly. The Talmud views such shaming of others as worse than adultery, as something that leads to a surrender of personhood and of a person's internal and external identity; without honor and respect, life is not possible. Indeed, shaming another person constitutes such a profound injury that it is comparable to shedding blood and similarly leads to ressentiment and revenge.

Bibliography: D. Bonhoeffer, *Ethics* (ed. E. Bethge; New York, 1955) • N. Bowen, "Damage and Healing: Shame and Honor in the OT," *Koinonia* 3 (1991) 29-36 • H. P. Duerr, *Nacktheit und Scham* (4th ed.; Frankfurt, 1994) • N. Elias, *The Civilizing Process: Sociogenetic and Psychogenetic Investigations* (rev. ed.; Oxford, 2000; orig. pub., 1976) • E. H. Erikson, *Childhood and Society* (rev.

ed.; London, 1995; orig. pub., 1950) • M. Fossum and M. Mason, *Facing Shame* (New York, 1985) • J. Fowler, "Shame: Towards a Practical Theological Understanding," *CCen* 93 (1993) 816-19 • S. Kierkegaard, *The Concept of Anxiety: A Simple Psychologically Orienting Deliberation on the Dogmatic Issue of Hereditary Sin* (Princeton, 1980; orig. pub., 1844) • H. Kohut, *The Restoration of the Self* (New York, 1977) • J. L. McNish, *Transforming Shame: A Pastoral Response* (Binghamton, N.Y., 2004) • S. Neckel, *Status und Scham* (Frankfurt, 1991) • M. C. Nussbaum, *Hiding from Humanity: Disgust, Shame, and the Law* (Princeton, 2004) • C. D. Schneider, "Shame," *DPC* 1160-63 • G. H. Seidler, *In Others' Eyes: An Analysis of Shame* (Madison, Conn., 2000) • R. Sterba, "The Fate of the Ego in Analytic Theory," *IJPsa* 15 (1934) 117-26 • L. Wurmser, *Flight from Conscience: Psychodynamic Treatment of Character Perversion, Obsessive-Compulsive Disorder, and Addiction* (Northvale, N.J., 2001); idem, *The Mask of Shame* (Baltimore, 1981); idem, *Das Rätsel des Masochismus* (2d ed.; Berlin, 1998); idem, "The Shame about Existing: A Comment about the Analysis of 'Moral' Masochism," *The Widening Scope of Shame* (ed. M. R. Lansky and A. P. Morrison; Hillsdale, N.J., 1997) 367-82; idem, *Die zerbrochene Wirklichkeit. Psychoanalyse als das Studium von Konflikt und Komplementarität* (3d ed.; 2 vols.; Göttingen, 2001-2).

Léon Wurmser

Shari'a

1. Term

The word "Shari'a" (Arab. *sharī'ah,* etymologically "a path to water"; pl. *sharā'i'*) appears once in the → Qur'ān (45:18) in the sense of a religious path to be followed, as does the synonymous *shir'ah* (5:48). In Islamic usage *sharī'ah* (also *shar'*) refers to the successive religions revealed by God to his messengers *(rusul,* sing. *rasūl),* culminating in the final messenger, Muḥammad (ca. 570-632), as well as more narrowly to their practical ordinances, both taken as a whole and individually. It is Shari'a in the latter sense of a revealed religious law, especially Islamic law, that concerns us here.

For most Muslims → Islam is a legalistic religion, and Muslims understand the earlier revealed religions of → Judaism and Christianity as similarly legalistic. Whereas the theological doctrines of Islam corroborate and clarify the theological truths of the earlier revelations, the religious law of Islam abrogates the divinely ordained laws that preceded it. It is disputed among Muslim scholars whether this abrogation *(naskh)* is total or whether some elements of the earlier laws continue to bind Muslims *(shar' man qablana shar' lanā,* "the law of those before us is law for us"). Muslims commonly view the changes in law introduced by Islam as tending in the direction of freedom from burdensome restrictions (see Qur'ān 7:157) and accordingly speak of Islam as *dīn al-yusr,* "the religion of ease." The account of the Shari'a given here focuses almost exclusively on developments within → Sunni Islam, the tradition of the great majority of Muslims.

2. The Sources of Law

There is widespread agreement among Sunni jurists that there are four primary sources of Islamic law. The first in prominence is the Qur'ān, the word of God revealed to Muḥammad. Only a relatively small proportion, traditionally 500 verses, of the more than 6,000 verses of the Qur'ān deal with legal topics, but these 500 include the fundamental rituals of → prayer *(ṣalāt),* the fast of Ramadan, the *zakāt* alms-tax on property, the → pilgrimage *(ḥajj),* and basic elements of contract, marriage, divorce, inheritance, the law of war *(jihād),* and criminal law. The authenticity of the Qur'ānic text is regarded as beyond question, based as it is upon widespread unbroken transmission from generation to generation (= the doctrine of *tawātur,* "concurrence"). There is, in fact, very substantial uniformity in the received Qur'ānic text, uniformity that is generally attributed to the promulgation by Caliph 'Uthmān (d. 656) of an official text of the Qur'ān, the most significant governmental act by far in the entire history of Islamic law. Agreement on the text of the Qur'ān does not, however, preclude widespread disagreement on its interpretation.

The second revealed source of Islamic law is the → Sunna, or precedent of Muḥammad, which encompasses his statements, actions, and tacit approval of the statements and actions of others. The great majority of jurists regard the Sunna as of fully equal authority with the Qur'ān on all matters. Thus the Sunna can govern the interpretation of the Qur'ān or even abrogate a prior inconsistent Qur'ānic provision. In most cases, however, the Sunna is known by hadith (*ḥadīth,* reports) that, unlike the Qur'ān, were never promulgated in an official collection, and the reliability of many of these reports has long been a topic of dispute. The developments in the specialist study of such reports, culminating among Sunnis in the highly regarded collections of al-Bukhārī (d. 870) and Muslim ibn al-Ḥajjāj (d. 875), came after the formative period of Sunni law, and in any case these and similar collections did not definitively resolve the question of authenticity.

The third source of law is the → consensus *(ijmā')* of the expert jurists (*mujtahids,* see 3). The theory of consensus holds that if the expert jurists alive at a particular time agree on the answer to a legal question, their agreement serves to identify the one correct opinion and binds all subsequent Muslims. The theory of consensus does not, however, guarantee that any such agreement will take place, and in fact the instances of consensus are few in relation to the many issues that remain disputed.

The fourth source is → analogy *(qiyās),* which provides for the generalization of a specific provision of the revealed law to encompass cases not expressly within its terms. The theory of analogy was extensively developed by the medieval Muslim jurists, and several varieties of analogy were distinguished. The form of analogy most widely accepted does not proceed directly from case to case but seeks to identify the element, the so-called cause *('illah),* in the case addressed by revelation that accounts for how it has been regulated. Once this element is identified, the same regulation can be extended to any and all cases in which the same causal element is found. For example, on the assumption that grape wine is *khamr,* the drinking of which is prohibited by the Qur'ān (5:90), jurists who determine that grape wine was prohibited because of its power to intoxicate can appeal to analogy in extending this prohibition to all other intoxicants.

3. *Ijtihād* and the Schools of Law

Islamic tradition traces the main institutions of Islamic law back to the time of Muḥammad and his immediate followers (his *ṣaḥābah,* "companions") and portrays Muḥammad as appointing judges and other officials to administer the law of the Qur'ān and Sunna. Most important, Muḥammad ordained recourse to *ijtihād* (lit. "exertion," here legal reasoning in the broadest sense) in the absence of clear guidance in the Qur'ān and Sunna, and it is *ijtihād* that gave rise to the enormous development of Islamic law. Because the legal opinions arrived at by *ijtihād* are generally admitted to be no more than probably correct, Islamic law tolerates an enormous range of disagreement *(ikhtilāf).* There is equally diversity of opinion on what to make of this ubiquitous disagreement. Many regard it as a mercy of God, in that it offers Muslims a range of valid solutions to their everyday legal problems. At the same time, many continue to believe that only one of the various discordant opinions correctly reflects God's law, although precisely which one may be unknowable. A distinction is sometimes made between the Shari'a, the law actually ordained by God, and the *fiqh* (understanding) of that law on the part of the legal scholars *(fuqahā',* sing. *faqīh).* Accordingly, *fiqh* is the common term for the law developed by the jurists.

Qualifying as a *mujtahid* (i.e., one capable of engaging in *ijtihād*) is essentially a question of learning and ability and thus potentially open to all Muslims. Until recently, however, most Sunni Muslims have held that the "gate of *ijtihād* was closed," that is, that *mujtahids* of the highest rank were not to be found after the early centuries of Islam. These Muslims were content with following (*taqlīd,* "investing with authority") the legal opinions of one or another of four early *mujtahids* whose teachings were continuously studied and elaborated by successive generations of jurists in scholarly traditions known as legal schools *(madhāhib,* sing. *madhhab).* The four extant Sunni schools — the Hanafis, Malikis, Shafi'is, and Hanbalis — follow Abū Ḥanīfah (d. 767), Mālik ibn Anas (d. 795), al-Shāfi'ī (d. 820), and Aḥmad ibn Ḥanbal (d. 855) respectively. The present situation among Twelver Shiites is significantly different, in that ordinarily adherence to the teachings of a living *mujtahid* is required, a principle that accounts for the emergence at any given time of a small number of prominent grand ayatollahs (Arab., lit. "signs of God"), who serve as loci *(marāji',* sing. *marja')* of *taqlīd* for their followers (→ Shia, Shiites).

In the premodern period training in the law developed by the schools was an integral part of a comprehensive Islamic education and served as preparation for a variety of careers but not typically that of professional advocate, a figure rare in traditional Muslim courts. The influence of the different legal schools waxed and waned for a variety of personal and political reasons, and change of affiliation by individuals from one school to another was possible. In some regions and for relatively long periods of time, a single school could come to enjoy a virtual monopoly of influence, for example, the Maliki school in Islamic Spain and North Africa, the Hanafi school in Mogul India and the Ottoman Empire, the Shafi'i school in Indonesia, and the Twelver Shiite school in Iran from the time of the Safavids.

Most of the legal writing produced by the jurists

of the various schools over the centuries, much still in manuscript, can be classified as either legal theory (*uṣūl al-fiqh*, "the roots of understanding") or substantive law (*furū' al-fiqh*, "the branches of understanding"). Legal theory identifies the sources of the law, guides the interpretation of the textual sources, and defines the authority of the opinions arrived at by *ijtihād*. The substantive law represents the rules of law that result from the application of *ijtihād* to the sources. These are typically presented in more or less comprehensive treatises, but also in collections of responsa *(fatāwā*, sing. *fatwā)* on the part of respondents (the muftis), both official and unofficial, to inquiries on a wide range of questions.

4. The Substantive Law

The substantive law of Islam propounded in the books of *furū' al-fiqh* and *fatāwā* operates with a number of general classifications. The most basic of these is the classification of all human → acts under one of five categories *(aḥkām*, sing. *ḥukm)*. Acts are (1) obligatory *(wājib)*, (2) recommended *(mandūb)*, (3) disapproved *(makrūh)*, (4) permitted *(mubāḥ)*, or (5) prohibited *(ḥarām)*, with the first four collectively constituting the domain of the licit *(ḥalāl)*. Marriage under normal circumstances, for example, is commonly categorized as recommended.

A second broad classification is between the claims of God *(ḥuqūq Allāh)* and those of humans *(ḥuqūq al-ādamiyīn)*. As distinguished from the claims of humans, such as a monetary debt, the claims of God, such as the obligatory rituals and certain criminal penalties, are not subject to waiver *(isqāṭ)*, but they may be subject to special excuses: for example, menstruating women are exempted from prayer by a dispensation *(rukhṣah*, pl. *rukhaṣ)*. There is disagreement whether stratagems *(ḥiyal*, sing. *ḥīlah)* may be employed to escape claims of either sort.

A third classification serves to organize the subject matter of the substantive law under such headings as ritual law *('ibādāt)*, family law (*munākaḥāt*, "matrimonial matters"), commercial law *(mu'āmalāt)*, and criminal law (*'uqūbāt*, → "punishments"). The ritual law is distinguished from the other areas of the law in the extent to which it rests on detailed provisions of the Qur'ān and Sunna to the exclusion of analogy, which by its nature is inapplicable to matters resisting rational analysis.

The scope of classic Islamic law is extremely broad, ranging from details of ablutions required for prayer to the structure of the Islamic state. Not all areas of law, however, were equally developed. Greatest attention was devoted to the elaboration of the private law, including the ritual law, in its most minute details. By contrast, Islamic public law *(al-aḥkām al-sulṭānīyah)* was little cultivated, perhaps because the jurists had a very limited influence in shaping the institutions of the state, which early on fell into the hands of temporal rulers who were often brutal tyrants. Public-law doctrines tend to present an idealized account of the caliphate and other governmental offices, and only belatedly and grudgingly did many jurists come to acknowledge how far the reality had departed from the ideal.

Even a cursory review of the substantive law is not possible here, but several common misapprehensions should be addressed. Islamic law, at least as far as the doctrine is concerned, accords women property rights far more extensive than did Western law until quite recently. Even married women, for example, retain full control over the → property they bring into the marriage. In contrast, women are disadvantaged vis-à-vis men in the share of the estate they receive as heirs and are under various disabilities with respect to engaging fully in public life. The situation of non-Muslims following other revealed faiths, such as Jews and Christians, is broadly comparable. As subjects of the Islamic state, they fall under its protection *(dhimmah)* and are granted extensive rights to practice their religion and live their lives in accordance with its teachings, even to the point of retaining their own religious courts. Yet, like women, they are barred from filling various state offices and participating fully in public life. Islamic criminal law has a reputation for cruelty, undoubtedly stemming from such harsh punishments as stoning for certain cases of fornication and amputation for theft, both among the *ḥudūd* (sing. *ḥadd*), that is, crimes with defined penalties. In the absence of a confession, however, the standard of proof for these *ḥudūd* is high: four male eyewitnesses in the case of fornication, two in the case of theft.

5. Islamic Law in Practice

As a religious law, Islamic law binds individual Muslims, including the ruler and other governmental officials, and threatens those who violate its prescriptions with punishment in the hereafter (→ Hell). Islamic law itself also provides for the exercise of coercion in this world, above all in the resolution of disputes. The → power that can apply such coercion flows, according to juristic theory, from the single figure at the head of the state, ideally an elected caliph, but in practice far more often a self-imposed temporal ruler *(sulṭān)*. In keeping with this theory, the authority of the qadi (*qāḍī*, "judge") and other state officials has its source in a delegation *(tafwīḍ)* from the ruler. Islamic law recognizes the authority of the ruler to supplement the law of the jurists with such administrative measures as are necessary for the welfare of his subjects and are not in conflict with the clear prescriptions of the revealed texts (*siyāsah shar'īyah,* "administration within the scope of the Shari'a"). But state regulations did not always remain within the boundaries of the Shari'a, and complaints about crimes and punishments not sanctioned by Islam and un-Islamic taxes *(mukūs,* sing. *maks)* are common.

Given the geographic and temporal scope of Islamic civilization, the question of how fully Islamic law was actually implemented at any given time and place cannot be given a simple answer. The traditional qadi's court *(maḥkamah)* has jurisdiction over cases of all kinds, and since such courts were a regular feature of premodern Muslim societies, we may assume that Islamic law enjoyed a considerable measure of respect. The recurrent appearance throughout Islamic history of revivalist movements and regimes testifies to a continuing concern for the full implementation of the Shari'a. Further generalizations are hazardous. It is safe to say that there was widespread compliance with the ritual law, except for the *zakāt* tax, and with family law, although Islamic law was sometimes in competition with local customary law in such matters as inheritance.

6. The Shari'a in Modern Times

The ascendancy of the Western powers vis-à-vis the leading Muslim states, which became increasingly evident in the 19th century, led to a marked diminution in the role of the Shari'a in Muslim societies. In some cases the authority of the Shari'a was curtailed directly by colonial powers, such as the British in India or the French in Algeria, who introduced radical changes in the legal systems over which they assumed control (→ Colonialism). In other cases, such as that of the Ottomans, Muslim governments set about reforming their judicial systems along Western lines. In both cases, the formerly general jurisdiction of the Shari'a courts shrank and, along with it, the standing of the traditionally trained qadis. Characteristic of these developments is the appearance of law codes modeled after those of Europe, even when the content was Islamic, as in the Ottoman Civil Code *(Mecelle)* of 1877, and the rise of new legal personnel, including judges and lawyers whose legal education no longer emphasized mastery of the *fiqh* texts.

Among those devoted to Islamic law, one response to the crisis of Western domination was a call for a renewal of Islamic law to render it suitable for the novel circumstances into which Muslims had been thrust. The reformers, led by the Egyptian Muḥammad 'Abduh (d. 1905) and his Syrian disciple Muḥammad Rashīd Riḍā (d. 1935), regarded the aura of sanctity that had come to surround the law of the schools as a major obstacle to their goals. Drawing upon a distinguished line of premodern critics of *taqlīd,* whose writings they were instrumental in disseminating, they called for a revival of *ijtihād.* The modern reformers had in mind a radical revision of the classic law. This revision they undertook in part by championing long-abandoned minority opinions preserved in the vast *fiqh* literature and by elevating to prominence doctrines that had hitherto been relegated to marginal status in legal theory. Thus they made frequent appeal to the welfare *(maṣlaḥah)* of the Muslims as the basis for doing away with old institutions and establishing new ones, as well as to "dire necessity" *(ḍarūrah)* as grounds for temporarily suspending the application of prohibitions such as that against usury *(ribā).*

The upshot of these developments was that with few exceptions the many Muslim nation-states that emerged in the 20th century had legal systems that limited the sphere of the application of the Shari'a to family law, often in the form of a code incorporating restrictions on polygamy and the unilateral repudiation of wives *(ṭalāq),* justified as instances of the modern *ijtihād* called for by the reformers. While this situation may have had the support of the ruling Westernized elites, it was profoundly unsatisfactory to Shari'a scholars, traditional and reformist, and to the common people. Calls for a return to a full implementation of Islamic law *(taṭbīq al-sharī'ah)* became increasingly widespread in the 1970s, and in response to such pressures constitutions were in some cases amended to provide for the Shari'a (alternatively, the principles of the Shari'a) as a principal source of national legislation (e.g., Syria in 1973).

Concurrently, the reformist agenda of undermining the authority of the traditional schools of law proved to be extraordinarily successful, particularly in the Arab Middle East, where it often went hand-in-hand with the adoption of a *salafī* (lit. "early Muslim," i.e., fundamentalist) theology. Very few traditional jurists have been able to escape contact with reformist thought, and reformist and more traditional jurists now commonly collaborate in the various international academies for the study of Islamic law, such as those attached to the Rābiṭat al-'Ālam al-Islāmī (Muslim World League, 1978) and the Munaẓẓamat al-Mu'tamar al-Islāmī (Organization of the Islamic Conference, 1981). These academies are engaged in addressing a host of modern problems, including those stemming from recent efforts to create banks and other financial institutions that operate in accordance with Islamic law. In addition, individual reformist jurists have been able to achieve considerable influence, and their *fatāwā* are widely disseminated in print and through radio, television, and, more recently, videos and the Internet. Those participating in this revival of legal thought commonly regard their work as marking an indispensable preparatory stage toward the integral application of the Shari'a.

Steps toward a fuller implementation of the Shari'a, often by the introduction of Islamic criminal law, have already been taken in a number of countries (e.g., Libya, Pakistan, Sudan, and northern Nigeria), most dramatically and successfully in the Islamic Republic of Iran (1979). The return to the Shari'a, however, has not generally led to the abolition of such borrowed institutions as constitutions, codes of law, or the bar, which far from being regarded as alien to the Shari'a, are now seen as essential to its successful reintroduction. The worldwide resurgence of Islam and the efforts to implement the Shari'a, often vaguely defined, raise justified concerns both inside and outside the Muslim world that, unless drastically reinterpreted, Islamic law will adversely affect the rights of such classes as women, homosexuals and other Muslim minorities, and non-Muslims. The efforts by liberal Muslims to reformulate Islamic law on such sensitive areas have so far failed to gain popular support.

→ Law and Legal Theory

Bibliography: F. ABDUL RAUF, *Islam, a Sacred Law: What Every Muslim Should Know about the Sharī'ah* (Brattleboro, Vt., 1999) • J. N. D. ANDERSON, *Law Reform in the Muslim World* (London, 1976) • AVERROËS, *The Distinguished Jurist's Primer: A Translation of Bidāyat al-Mujtahid* (trans. I. A. K. Nyazee; 2 vols.; Reading, 1997) • N. J. COULSON, *A History of Islamic Law* (Edinburgh, 1964) • W. B. HALLAQ, *A History of Islamic Legal Theories: An Introduction to Sunnī Uṣūl al-fiqh* (Cambridge, 1997) • IBN AL-NAQĪB, *Reliance of the Traveller: A Classic Manual of Islamic Sacred Law* (trans. N. H. M. Keller; Evanston, Ill., 1994) • M. H. KAMALI, *Principles of Islamic Jurisprudence* (Cambridge, 2003) • M. K. MASUD, B. MESSICK, and D. S. POWERS, eds., *Islamic Legal Interpretation: Muftis and Their Fatwas* (Cambridge, Mass., 1996) • AL-MĀWARDĪ, *The Ordinances of Government* (trans. W. H. Wahba; Reading, 1996) • A. E. MAYER, *Islam and Human Rights: Tradition and Politics* (Boulder, Colo., 1999) • C. MELCHERT, *The Formation of the Sunni Schools of Law, 9th-10th Centuries* C.E. (Leiden, 1997) • H. MODARRESSI TABĀTABĀ'I, *An Introduction to Shī'ī Law: A Bibliographical Study* (London, 1984) • J. SCHACHT, *An Introduction to Islamic Law* (Oxford, 1964) • AL-SHĀFI'Ī, *Treatise on the Foundations of Jurisprudence* (trans. M. Khadduri; Cambridge, 1987) • F. E. VOGEL, *Islamic Law and Legal System: Studies of Saudi Arabia* (Leiden, 2000) • B. G. WEISS, *The Spirit of Islamic Law* (Athens, Ga., 1998).

ARON ZYSOW

Shia, Shiites

1. Term
2. Origins
3. Shiite Ideology
4. Religious Ramifications of Shiite Opposition
5. Other Shiite Factions
6. Suffering, Martyrdom, and Shrine Culture
7. Shiite Theology and Jurisprudence

1. Term

The word "Shia" (Arab. *shī'ah,* "a separate or distinct party of people who follow or conform with one another" [though perhaps without full agreement]) applies to one person or many, male or female. Broadly, it refers to Muslims who hold that the family of the Prophet Muḥammad (ca. 570-632), the *ahl al-bayt* (lit. "people of the house"), has a privileged position in the political and religious leadership *(imāma)* of the Muslim community.

When used in the specific sense of partisans, it designates all those who believe that 'Alī ibn Abī Ṭālib (d. 661), cousin and son-in-law of Muḥammad, was the legitimate head *(imām)* of Muslim polity and ultimate authority on questions of law and doctrine in → Islam, having inherited the Prophet's political and religious authority immediately following the latter's death. This belief in 'Alī's leadership also led the Shia to refuse to acknowledge the first three caliphs recognized by the majority Sunni community — Abū Bakr (632-34), 'Umar (634-44), and 'Uthmān (644-56) — whom they considered usurpers of the leadership that rightfully belonged to 'Alī and his descendants.

2. Origins

The historical origins of the Shiite movement are difficult to reconstruct with certainty because of the biased presentation of its beginnings by → Sunni historians. Modern Western scholars, depending solely on Sunni sources, have generally dismissed

Shia, Shiites

Shiism as a heterodoxy that deviated from the majority Sunni orthodoxy. Accordingly, Shiites appear as followers of a political claimant who, having failed to establish an ideal Muslim rule, was gradually transformed into a religious figurehead. An objective reading of these tendentious sources, in light of the Shiite accounts of their own history, provides a different estimation of the Shiite minority movement.

Muḥammad's message, as embodied in the → Qur'ān, provided immense spiritual as well as sociopolitical impetus for the establishment of the ideal community of Islam. Muḥammad himself was not only the founder of a new religion but also the custodian of a new social order. Consequently, the question of leadership was the crucial issue that divided Muslims into various factions in the years following his death. The early years of Islamic history were characterized by a steady string of military victories under the first three caliphs. But as this period reached its end and civil wars broke out under 'Uthmān, the third caliph, contention arose over the necessity of a qualified leadership to assume the office of imam.

Most of these early discussions about leadership took political form, but eventually the debates addressed the religious connection between divine guidance and the creation of the Islamic world order. These debates also highlighted the inevitable interdependence between the religious and the political in Islam. The rise of some prominent descendants of 'Alī as messianic savior *(al-mahdī)* and the sympathetic, even enthusiastic, following they attracted reveal the tension that was felt in the awareness that the Islamic ideal lacked actualization in the real world, as well as the belief that it was the divinely guided Mahdi who could and would establish an ideal, just society. Such expectations put the legitimacy of the Sunni caliphate in question, and the conflict between the 'Alids and their opponents assumed a religious-theological, not simply a political, dimension.

3. Shiite Ideology

From the early days of Islam, some Muslims regarded the legitimate head of state not merely in political but also in religious terms. They maintained that Muḥammad himself held authority in all realms — spiritual and temporal, moral and civil. His spiritual authority included the power to interpret the message in the Qur'ān without corrupting the revelation. Islam, in order to continue its function of directing the faithful toward the creation of a just and equitable order, needed a leader who could perform the Prophet's comprehensive role authoritatively. The exaltation of the Prophet and his rightful successor gave rise to the concept of a messianic imam, the Mahdi, from among the descendants of the Prophet who could create an ideal Islamic community (→ Messianism). The thrust of the Shiite ideology was the concept of the *wilāya* (authority) of 'Alī, who was the first to assert that the family of the Prophet had a special entitlement to lead the community. In fact, acknowledgment of 'Alī's *wilāya* became the sole criterion among Shiites for judging true faith.

The Shiite concept of imam — which identified the legitimate head of state as God's caliph *(khalīfa)*, or deputy, on earth — was bound to meet with much resistance, since it demanded the recognition of 'Alī and his descendants as the imams with the real control of Muslim polity. Furthermore, it also was a challenge to the Umayyad rulers (661-750) and a rallying point for all who felt discriminated against or mistreated by the ruling house. Consequently, from its inception Shiism functioned as an opposition party, challenging the performance of the government.

4. Religious Ramifications of Shiite Opposition

Several protest movements arose under a wide range of leaders from among 'Alī's descendants who were able to arouse in their followers a genuine religious urge to achieve sociopolitical goals. Shiite attempts at direct political action, however, were met with brutal resistance from the ruling dynasty, and their efforts quickly met with failure. The resultant frustration produced further Shiite factions. The radical factions insisted on armed resistance to the oppressive rule of the caliphate. These were also labeled as *ghulāt* (zealots) by mainstream Shiites because of the extravagant claims they made for their imams. The moderate factions, having experienced the futility of direct political action, were prepared to postpone indefinitely the establishment of true Islamic rule under their messianic leader, the Mahdi. More than any other factor, the murder of the third Shiite imam, Ḥusayn, the younger son of 'Alī and Fāṭima, the Prophet's daughter, and his followers by Umayyad troops at Karbala, Iraq, in 680, followed in 739 by the failure of the revolt of Zayd, Ḥusayn's grandson, marked the turn toward a quietist attitude by these factions, who previously had been willing to fight for their ideals.

Shiite efforts until the time of Abbasid victory in 750 were still lacking a well-formulated doctrine of the imamate. At that time the great imam Ja'far al-Ṣādiq (d. 765), who had been largely responsible for the moderation and discipline of the radical elements, provided Shiism with a sectarian credo. In the political turmoil of the eighth century, the 'Alid imams had the opportunity to propagate Shiite viewpoints without inhibition and to modify the revolutionary tone of early Shiism to become a more sober and tolerant school of Islamic thought. The Shiite leaders encouraged, and even required, the use of prudent concealment *(taqiyya)* in the propagation of their faith so as to avoid pressing for the establishment of the 'Alid rule and the overthrow of the illegitimate caliphate. *Taqiyya*-oriented life also signified the will of the Shiite minority to continue to strive for the realization of the ideal by preparing the way for such an insurrection in the future.

Al-Ṣādiq's contribution in shaping the religious and juridical direction of Shiism was central. He was acknowledged by all the Shiite factions as their imam, including those of radical leaning who led the revolts to establish 'Alids as the legitimate head of state. He was also recognized as an authentic transmitter of the traditions in the Sunnite compilations. Under his leadership moderate Shiism, with its veneration of the Prophet's family, came to be sanctioned by the Sunnite majority as a valid expression of personal piety. For the majority of Shiites his attitude toward politics became the cornerstone of their political theory, which, in the absence of the imam's political authority, did not teach its followers to overthrow tyrannical rulers and replace them by their imam. They had to wait for the messianic descendant from the "seed of the Prophet through his daughter Fāṭima and grandson Ḥusayn" to emerge as the Mahdi of the community. The doctrine of the imamate clarified the dilemma that although the imam was entitled to exercise comprehensive political authority as the head of the state, his imamate was not contingent upon his being invested as the political head. The imamate was seen more realistically as a spiritual-moral, rather than a political, office.

The mainstream Shiites continued to uphold the leadership of the descendants of 'Ali and Fāṭima through Ja'far al-Ṣādiq until the line reached the 12th imam, who was believed to be in concealment until the end of time. He is regarded as the promised messianic Mahdi, whose return to launch the final revolution that will establish the kingdom of God on earth is awaited by his followers. Muslim eschatology describes in great detail the return of the Mahdi with Jesus to usher in the battle of Armageddon and the ultimate defeat of the → antichrist *(al-Dajjāl)* and the victory of God's justice on earth. This school of Shiism is known as the Ithna 'Ashariyya, or "Twelvers." In the absence of the Hidden Imam, their religious scholars, the ayatollahs, fulfill the role of functional imams and, like the Roman Catholic → pope, lead the community in all its religious affairs. They form the majority of the Shiites in many parts of the world, mainly in Iran, Iraq, and Lebanon.

5. Other Shiite Factions

The Shiite movement was represented by various leaders, all members of the Hashimite clan, who represented different trends of thought. Whereas the mainstream followed the line of the 12 imams, others adhered to the imam who called for political action and an activist response to the unjust governments in power. The latter included an extremist trend in Shiism calling for the overthrow of Sunni dynasties. Mainstream Shiites condemned this trend, and over the course of history such minority factions have died out. Besides the Twelvers, the two factions that were once politically activist and that have survived the vicissitudes of history are the Zaydiyya and the Ismailis. Their survival strategy, not unlike that in Iraq or in Lebanon today, has been to abandon political idealism, concentrating their opposition instead on spiritual and mystical paths. Until recently, however, Zaydiyya, who are mainly in Yemen and also in small numbers in Iraq and East Africa, believed that the imam ought to be a ruler of the → state and therefore must fight for his rights.

The Ismailis, so named after Ismā'īl, the eldest son of al-Ṣādiq, who predeceased his father, believed that Ismā'īl's son Muḥammad was their seventh imam. The → number seven derives its symbolic religious significance in Ismaili theology from this seventh imam, who was also believed to be a messianic leader. The esoteric interpretation of the Qur'ān, which was an overall heritage of all Shiites, found its sustained connection with this faction, earning them the title of Baṭiniyya (i.e., those who believe in the *bāṭin* [hidden, inner] meanings of the Qur'ān). After an initial dormant period in the movement's history, with almost three descendants of the seventh imam believed to be "concealed imams," Ismailis attained political and religious prominence under the Fatimid dynasty (909-1171), which challenged the supremacy of the vast Sunni Abbasid caliphate.

The Ismailis are divided today into two main branches: the Musta'lī (known as Bohoras) and the Nizārī (known as Aga Khanis). The Bohoras today trace their origins to the religious teachers in Yemen and continue much of the Fatimid religious heritage under their present religious guide (the *dā'ī*), who resides in India and represents the 21st hidden Fatimid imam. Outside India they are to be found in the Persian Gulf, southern Arabia, and Syria. The Aga Khanis trace their origins to Iran, where their leaders had established the religious order. Since then, under the leadership of an aga khan (lit. "chief commander"), they have mainly pursued a mystical path. They are concentrated in central Asia, Iran, Pakistan, and India (→ Iranian Religious 11).

6. Suffering, Martyrdom, and Shrine Culture

As a minority community, Shiites suffered oppression under the majority Sunni dynasties throughout much of their history until the 16th century, when Iran adopted Shiism as the official state religion. Martyrdom *(shahāda)* became a religious factor in Shiite political history, sustained by a doctrine that God is just and commands human society to replace an unjust rule by a just and legitimate one. The ensuing struggle to install a legitimate political authority resulted in the murder of several Shiite leaders. These violent deaths were regarded by succeeding generations as martyrdom suffered in order to defeat the forces of oppression and falsehood.

The most powerful symbol of martyrdom is the third Shiite imam, Ḥusayn ibn ʿAlī (d. 680), Muḥammad's grandson, whose martyrdom is annually commemorated with solemnity throughout the Shiite world in the festival of Ashura (*ʿashūrā,* from *ʿasharah,* "ten"). In Karbala on the tenth day of Muharram, Ḥusayn and his family and friends were mercilessly killed by Umayyad troops. The Shiites have preserved this moment in their religious history as a tragic event reminding them of the corrupt nature of power and the way righteous ones suffer. For the greater part of Shiite history, the memory of the tragedy of Karbala has been tempered by the tradition of political quietism; at times, however, the episode has encouraged activism to counter injustice in society.

The commemoration of the tragedy has served as a principal platform of communication with the Shiite public through which sociopolitical and religious ideas have been disseminated by their leaders, like Ayatollahs Khomeini (d. 1989) and Muḥammad Bāqir Ṣadr (d. 1980). It has also become, for instance in Lebanon and Iraq, a model in the struggle to improve the standing and increase the influence of the Shiite population in those countries. In contrast to Sunnism, in Shiism special buildings constructed for the purpose of such commemoration, the *ḥusayniyya,* have served as crucial centers for public religious education and mourning rituals. Besides the *madrasas* (seminaries), the *ḥusayniyya* were used by the religious leaders to disseminate either an activist or quietist ideology for their followers. The Iranian revolution in 1978-79 used the Karbala paradigm to mobilize the people against the corrupt rule of the shah.

Closely related to martyrdom in Shiism was the shrine culture encouraged by the religious practice of visitation *(ziyāra)* of *mashhad* (a place where a martyr died and is buried). In Shiite piety all imams are revered as martyrs, and their tombs are visited in the belief that such a devotional act will win forgiveness of sins and a share in the final victory of the messianic Imam al-Mahdi. The tombs visited include those of both male and female members of the Prophet's family. In the Muslim world, for instance in Iraq and Iran, it is common for both the Shiites and the Sunnis to undertake these → pilgrimages. The shrines are richly endowed, and lavish gifts are bestowed by various Muslim rulers, especially those of Shiite dynasties. Towns have grown up around them, and important centers of Shiite learning exist in and around the shrines in Najaf, Iraq, and in Qom and Mashhad, Iran.

7. Shiite Theology and Jurisprudence

Shiism holds five fundamental principles or beliefs: (1) the unity of God, (2) the justice of God, (3) prophecy, (4) the imamate, and (5) the day of judgment. On every tenet but the fourth, Shiites in general share common ground with Sunnis, although there are differences on points of detail. The belief in the justice of God, for example, is similar to that of the Sunni Muʿtazilites, rationalist theologians who were active from the eighth to the tenth century, when they were eclipsed by the traditionalist Sunni theologians known as the Ashʿarites. In the ninth and tenth centuries, when the theological exposition of the Shiite school was being worked out, its theologians adopted an essentially rational theology in which → reason was prior to both sources of revelation, the Qur'ān and the → Sunna (the body of Islamic custom based on Muḥammad's words and deeds). Reason is God's endowment for humanity. It guides a person to ethical knowledge and asserts that → good and → evil are rational categories, independent of whether revelation declares them as such. While belief (4), the imamate, is not a fundamental principle of religion for Sunnis, for Shiites it is the central and cardinal principle.

Shiite jurisprudence confers on reason the priority, in accord with its rational theology. The comprehensiveness of Islamic revelation must be discovered, interpreted, and applied by use of reason. Accordingly, in their legal theory Shiites include reason as a fourth source of authority in deducing rulings of the → Shari'a, in addition to the Qur'ān, the Sunna, and the consensus *(ijmā')* of jurists, which Sunni legal scholars accept. Not just anyone, however, can undertake the interpretation of the scriptural sources rationally. Only a religiously qualified person can assume the authority that accrues to the imam as the rightful successor of the Prophet. This authority in Shiism is invested in a jurist *(mujtahid)* who applies his independent reasoning in issuing a judicial decision *(fatwā)*. Moreover, Shiites include the communications of their imams as part of the Sunna. Although the Shiite Sunna differs only in minor ways from the Sunna accepted by Sunnis, Shiites have their own compilations of prophetic traditions. Although Shiites have been developing their religious-legal practice ever since the Middle Ages, only recently have Sunni scholars in Egypt formally acknowledged the validity of this practice.

Bibliography: M. Ayoub, *Redemptive Suffering in Islam: A Study of the Devotional Aspects of 'Āshūrā' in Twelver Shī'ism* (The Hague, 1978) • J. A. Bill and J. A. Williams, *Roman Catholics and Shi'i Muslims: Prayer, Passion, and Politics* (Chapel Hill, N.C., 2002) • D. M. Donaldson, *The Shī'ite Religion: A History of Islam in Persia and Irak* (London, 1933) • ibn al-Muṭahhar al-Ḥillī, *Al-Bābu 'l-Ḥādi 'Ashar: A Treatise on the Principles of Shī'ite Theology, with Commentary by Miqdād Fāḍil al-Ḥillī* (trans. W. M. Miller; London, 1958) • Ibn Bābawayhi, *A Shi'ite Creed* (trans. A. A. A. Fyzee; London, 1942) trans. of "Risālat al-I'tiqādāt" • S. H. M. Jafri, *The Origins and Early Development of Shi'a Islam* (Karachi, 2000) • W. Madelung, "Imāma"; "'Iṣma"; "Ismā'īliyya"; "Zaydiyya," *EI²* 3.1163-69; 4.182-84, 198-206; 11.477-81; idem, *The Succession to Muhammad: A Study of the Early Caliphate* (Cambridge, 1997) • S. al-Mufīd, *Kitāb al-Irshād: The Book of Guidance into the Lives of the Twelve Imams* (trans. I. K. A. Howard; Horsham, 1981) • A. A. Sachedina, *Islamic Messianism: The Idea of Mahdī in Twelver Shī'ism* (Albany, N.Y., 1981); idem, *The Just Ruler in Shī'ite Islam: The Comprehensive Authority of the Jurist in Imamite Jurisprudence* (New York, 1988).

Abdulaziz Sachedina

Shinto

1. Term

Shinto is Japan's native, national → religion. The word means "way [*tō;* cf. Chin. *tao*] of the gods [*shin*]," though the sign for *shin,* when alone, reads *kami.* Kami are the many mythological or legendary figures that occur in the oldest Japanese written sources (i.e., *Kojiki* [Records of ancient matters] and *Nihon shoki,* or *Nihon-gi* [Chronicles of Japan]). Prominent kami are Izanagi and Izanami, who created the islands of Japan, the sun goddess Amaterasu, and the storm god Susanoo, who destroyed the rice fields and thus had to be banished. Kami may also be historical personages such as Sugawara Michizane (845-903), patron of calligraphy and learning. Natural phenomena like mountains and trees may also be honored as kami.

Shinto is expressly → polytheistic. The unity of the world of experience is secured partly by the mythological relationship of many kami, partly by the worshiping of the same kami in many separate regions (e.g., the kami Inari in the Fushimi shrine near Kyōto, and also in the Kasama shrine north of Tokyo), and partly by the multiple organizational interconnections of the shrines.

2. History

Historically, Shinto developed clearly only in the age of the adoption of Chinese culture (writing and → Confucianist thinking) and Taoist thought (→ Taoism; Buddhism) — that is, in the sixth to eighth centuries A.D. While Buddhist deities were also introduced to protect the state, which was organizing itself on the Chinese pattern, the → myths and rites that varied from place to place needed to be brought under a single common denominator. The way of the kami was thus integrated under the ruling Yamato clan, so that the sun goddess Amaterasu, who was regarded as the imperial matriarch, became a central figure among the kami. Fluctuating relations between Buddhism and Shinto resulted in a syncretistic symbiosis known as Ryobu Shinto (two-aspects Shinto; → Syncretism), which expounded the kami as manifestations of the Buddhist bodhisattva (esp. 12th to 15th cents.). But then the exposition was reversed to give priority to the kami, a reaction that was promoted as Yoshida Shinto, or Yuiitsu Shinto (the only Shinto), by Yoshida Kanetomo (1435-1511), among others.

The 18th century brought increasingly intellectual concentration on the sources of Shinto, now regarded as an emphatically Japanese cultural legacy. Especially important was the Kokugaku (national learning) movement, whose leaders were Motoori Norinaga (1730-1801) and Hirata Atsutane (1776-1843).

After the Meiji restoration in 1868 religion occupied a key position in political ideology. In the meantime the first religious communities had been founded, which the controlling state authorities would later defame as sects. Among them were the Kurozumikyo (from 1814), Tenrikyo (from 1837, first revelation), and Konkokyo (from 1859). Although they carry important Shintoist features, these organizations are now included among the → new religions.

3. Cult

A typical Shinto shrine consists of a place of prayer *(haiden)* at the front and an elevated but smaller chamber *(honden)* at the back that is honored as the abode of the kami and that only the → priests may enter. In front of the *haiden* hangs a stout rope with which worshipers may strike a gong to arouse the attention of the kami. A fence usually separates the precincts from the secular world outside (→ Sacred and Profane). The fence has a closed gate but also one or more open gates that point the way into the shrine. These gates, called *torii,* have a purely symbolic value (→ Symbol) and lead visitors away from the spheres of normal habitation and work, where the first gates usually stand, increasingly along the path to the holy place.

In the precincts of the shrine, worshipers wash their mouths and hands from a covered cup (→ Cultic Purity), proceed to the prayer chamber, sound the gong, and place a coin in the wooden chest in front of it. They then make their → prayer, clap twice, quietly bow with their hands together, and then clap a third time. They next buy a *mikuji,* a reading of their fortune in folded white paper that is then wrapped around a branch or shrub in the precincts, or pay for a votive tablet on which a personal concern is written. Larger groups representing families or firms are purified by a Shinto priest in the prayer chamber with a fan hung with white paper. The priest then recites prayers *(norito)* that are written on ancient models for each specific situation. Finally, each takes a drink of rice wine out of a small shallow bowl.

Millions visit Shinto shrines at New Year. Various festivals *(matsuri)* are occasions for other visits. Often the shrine kami will then be carried in a portable shrine *(mikoshi)* through the protected precincts, and a colorful procession will follow. A symbol of unity is offered in this way as various groups make their contributions to the procession. Demographic changes mean that participants are no longer restricted to clan members *(ujiko)* of the clan god *(ujigami).* The sense of solidarity thus covers a broader segment of the people and ultimately the total population of Japan.

4. Shinto and the State

Shinto is a national religion that enjoys wide acceptance and meets with little resistance, though it is not now a state religion. Postwar history differs in this regard from that of the nationalism fed by the Shintoist *tenno* (emperor) cult. In 1945 the occupying Americans put an end to the status of Shinto as a state religion while allowing *tennoism* to remain in secularized form as a symbol of national unity.

Since that time there have been efforts to reverse the situation. Thus the Yasukuni shrine has become a state shrine, not just a secular but a religious institution honoring the war dead and war criminals executed after the war. The main opponents of this trend are strict Buddhist groups and the Christian churches (→ Japan 4).

Less in the center of national discussion, but not without subtle implications, is the question of the financing of the reconstruction of the Shinto shrine at Ise, which takes place every 20 years (1973, 1993, etc.). If the state ever bears the costs, it will be an important step toward fresh state recognition of the religious aspects of *tennoism,* for this shrine is the main cultic site of the sun goddess (Amaterasu Omikami), who is revered as the ancestress of the emperors (→ Ancestor Worship). As yet, however, the project is privately financed (e.g., by large corporations).

5. Shinto and Christianity

Little → dialogue takes place between Shinto and Christianity. Since Christians form such a tiny minority in Japan, leading Shinto priests see hardly any reason for dialogue with them. The priests take the view that other countries have their own gods and festivals, and at most only curiosity would lead one to discuss these. And indeed, we have in Shinto a locally and nationally restricted religion that over the years has been able to accommodate itself and develop to an ever greater degree, and in Christianity a faith that makes a universal claim but that through adjustments to time and place threatens to lose its universal character. These are the two religions that now stand juxtaposed to one another.

Christians should be aware, on the one hand, of the political dangers and, on the other, of the positive aspects of Shinto's respect for → nature and for others (in the sense of a naturally restricted society). The best representatives of the Shintoist view, whether humble villagers or high-ranking priests, may well avoid the misuse (for centralized political ends) of the external, ritualized purity and inward loyalty and sincerity that rate as the essential values of Shinto.

Bibliography: J. Herbert, *Bibliographie du shintō et des sectes shintōïstes* (Leiden, 1968); idem, *Shintō: At the Fountain-Head of Japan* (London, 1967) • D. C. Holtom, *Modern Japan and Shinto Nationalism* (rev. ed.; New York, 1963); idem, *The Political Philosophy of Modern Shintō* (Chicago, 1922; repr., New York, 1984) • E. Lokowandt, *Die rechtliche Entwicklung des Staats-Shintō in der ersten Hälfte der Meiji-Zeit (1868-1890)* (Wiesbaden, 1978); idem, *Zum Verhältnis von Staat und Shintō im heutigen Japan. Eine Materialsammlung* (Weisbaden, 1981) • N. Naumann, *Die einheimische Religion Japans,* vol. 1, *Bis zum Ende der Heian-Zeit* (Leiden, 1988) • J. K. Nelson, *Enduring Identities: The Guise of Shinto in Contemporary Japan* (Honolulu, 2000); idem, *A Year in the Life of a Shinto Shrine* (Seattle, Wash., 1996) • S. Ono, *Shinto, the Kami Way* (Rutland, Vt., 1962) • S. D. B. Picken, *Historical Dictionary of Shinto* (Lanham, Md., 2002) • H. Yamashita, *Competitiveness and the Kami Way* (Aldershot, 1996).

Michael Pye